# The Oxford
# Paperback

*Carole Laing*

**Fourth Edition**

Editor **Elaine Pollard**

Senior Editor **Helen Liebeck**

OXFORD UNIVERSITY PRESS

1994

Oxford University Press, Walton Street, Oxford OX2 6DP

Oxford New York
Athens Auckland Bangkok Bombay
Calcutta Cape Town Dar es Salaam Delhi
Florence Hong Kong Istanbul Karachi
Kuala Lumpur Madras Madrid Melbourne
Mexico City Nairobi Paris Singapore
Taipei Tokyo Toronto
and associated companies in
Berlin Ibadan

Oxford is a trade mark of Oxford University Press

British Library Cataloguing in Publication Data
Data available

Library of Congress Cataloging in Publication Data
The Oxford paperback dictionary / editor, Elaine Pollard ; senior
editor, Helen Liebeck.—4th ed.
p. cm.
1. English language—Dictionaries. I. Pollard, Elaine.
II. Liebeck, Helen.
423—dc20 PE1628.O94 1994 93–43215
ISBN 0-19-280012-4

Typeset by Barbers Ltd.
Printed in Great Britain by
Clays Ltd.
Bungay, Suffolk

# Preface

*The Oxford Paperback Dictionary* was first published in 1979 as an entirely new member of the Oxford family of dictionaries, specially prepared as a compact, up-to-date guide to current English words and phrases, with the emphasis on a clear expansive style and straightforward definitions.

This new edition preserves the aims of previous editions in making information easy to find and to understand, retaining popular features such as the use of examples to illustrate meanings and easy-to-read guidance on the pronunciation of difficult words. More prominence has been given in this edition to controversial aspects of the language, with an increased number of notes on points of correct usage and etymological details.

The overall layout of the entries has been improved, using successful techniques adopted by other Oxford dictionaries and making all the information provided clearer and more accessible. In addition, the dictionary now uses very few abbreviations, in particular giving grammatical labels in full. This change seemed particularly appropriate in the light of the new emphasis on English grammar in the national curriculum for schools.

Dictionaries are frequently used to settle questions of spelling, and consequently for this edition we have included many alternative spellings and guidance on American English variants.

An important feature of the previous edition was the inclusion of entries for the names of famous people, places, and institutions. This proved to be tremendously popular, and has been retained. Of course, since the publication of the last edition, the world has changed in many ways, and for this new edition the coverage has been brought up to date and expanded to reflect changes in the world political situation, advances in technology, etc., which have introduced new names and terms into everyday language whilst making others redundant.

No selection, or its principles, can satisfy everyone. Our general aim for this new edition has been to include items of relevance to the modern world that have a permanent place in their own field and are known to a wider public—information that will be useful and interesting to the wide variety of users of the kind that the dictionary has already attracted in homes, offices, and schools throughout the English-speaking world.

HELEN LIEBECK
ELAINE POLLARD

# Editorial team

**Editor**          Elaine Pollard

**Senior Editor**   Helen Liebeck

**Contributors**    Rosamund Ions
                    Duncan Marshall

## Acknowledgements

The editors would particularly like to thank Judith Pearsall for help and guidance during the planning stages and preliminary editing of this edition. Special tribute is due to the work of Joyce Hawkins, who created the first edition and edited the second and third editions, with the express aim of creating a dictionary that would be less formal than traditional dictionaries, while upholding traditional standards of correctness. When it first appeared, *The Oxford Paperback Dictionary* was declared by reviewers to 'set new standards of clarity'. We hope that this new edition remains true to the aims and achievements of its predecessor.

# How to use this dictionary

These notes are intended as a brief guide to the conventions adopted in this dictionary. We have followed throughout a flexible policy of presenting the information in the clearest, most helpful form for the user.

## 1 Headword

The headword is printed in bold type. If the word is not naturalized in English, it is printed in bold italic type.

Alternative spellings are given before the definition. The form given as the headword is the preferred form.

Words that are normally spelt with a capital initial letter are given in this form as the headword. When they are in some senses spelt with a small initial letter and in others with a capital this is indicated by repetition of the full word in the appropriate form within the entry (as at **dame**).

If a sense of a word is always used in the plural form, this is indicated by repetition of the headword in plural form at the beginning of the appropriate sense (as at **arm**$^2$).

Alternative American spellings are indicated by the label *Amer.* e.g. **colour** (*Amer.* **color**).

## 2 Inflections

Plurals of nouns, comparatives in -*er* and superlatives in -*est* of adjectives and adverbs, and verb forms are given only if they are irregular or if there might be doubt about the spelling.

When only two verb forms are given:

> **admit** *verb* (**admitted, admitting**)

the first form is both the past tense (*he admitted it*) and the past participle (*it was admitted*), while the second form is the present participle.

When three forms are given:

> **come** *verb* (**came, come, coming**)
> **freeze** *verb* (**froze, frozen, freezing**)

the first is the past tense (*he came; it froze*) and the second is the past participle (*he had come; it was frozen*), and the third is the present participle.

## 3 Subject and usage labels

Subject labels are used to help clarify the subject field to which a particular sense applies. They are not used when this is clear from the definition itself.

Words and phrases more common in informal spoken English than formal written English are labelled (*informal*) or (*slang*).

Usage notes found at the end of entries give guidance on the current norms of standard English, i.e. the form of written and spoken English most generally accepted as a normal basis of communication in everyday life in the United Kingdom. Some of the rules given may legitimately be broken in less formal English, and especially in conversation.

## 4 Phrases and compounds

Phrases and multi-word compounds are grouped together in alphabetical order at the end of the main word. This section is introduced by the symbol □.

If a compound has become so fixed that the preferred form is now as a single word with no space or hyphen (e.g. bathroom), it is treated as a main entry with its own headword.

Multi-word compounds (i.e. those consisting of two or more separate or hyphenated words) are covered under the headword for the first of the words that make up the compound (e.g. **rat race** will be found at the entry for **rat**).

Compounds consisting of words separated by a space (not hyphenated) are assumed to be nouns and are only given a part of speech label if this is not the case. Hyphenated compounds are given a part of speech label.

## 5 Derivatives

Words formed by adding an easily understood ending to another word are in many cases listed at the very end of the entry for the main word (e.g. **randomly** is listed at **random**), after any compounds and phrases. In this position they are not defined since they can be understood from the sense of the main word. When further explanation is needed, they are treated as main entries in their own right (e.g. **changeable**).

## 6 Cross-references

A cross-reference to a main entry is indicated by small capitals e.g.:

> **mice** *see* MOUSE.
> **color** Amer. spelling of COLOUR.

## 7  Proprietary terms (trade marks)

This book includes some words which are or are asserted to be proprietary names or trade marks. Their inclusion does not imply that they have acquired for legal purposes a non-proprietary or general significance, nor is any other judgement implied concerning their legal status. In cases where the editor has some evidence that a word is used as a proprietary name or trade mark this is indicated by the label (*trade mark*), but no judgement concerning the legal status of such words is made or implied thereby.

# Pronunciation

A guide to pronunciation is given for any word that is difficult to pronounce, or difficult to recognize when read, or spelt the same as another word but pronounced differently. The pronunciation given represents the standard speech of southern England. It is shown in brackets, usually just after the word itself.

Words are broken up into small units, usually of one syllable. The syllable that is spoken with most stress in a word of two or more syllables is shown in heavy letters, like **this**.

The sound represented are as follows:

a *as in* cat
ă *as in* ago
ah *as in* calm
air *as in* hair
ar *as in* bar
aw *as in* law
ay *as in* say
b *as in* bat
ch *as in* chin
d *as in* day
e *as in* bed
ĕ *as in* taken
ee *as in* meet
eer *as in* beer
er *as in* her
ew *as in* few
ewr *as in* pure
f *as in* fat
g *as in* get
h *as in* hat

i *as in* pin
ĭ *as in* pencil
I *as in* eye
j *as in* jam
k *as in* king
l *as in* leg
m *as in* man
n *as in* not
ng *as in* sing, finger
nk *as in* thank
o *as in* top
ŏ *as in* lemon
oh *as in* most
oi *as in* join
oo *as in* soon
oor *as in* poor
or *as in* corn
ow *as in* cow
p *as in* pen
r *as in* red

s *as in* sit
sh *as in* shop
t *as in* top
th *as in* thin
*th as in* this
u *as in* cup
ŭ *as in* circus
uu *as in* book
v *as in* van
w *as in* will
y *as in* yes
   or when preceded
   by a consonant = I
   *as in* cry, realize
yoo *as in* unit
yoor *as in* Europe
yr *as in* fire
z *as in* zebra
*zh as in* vision

A consonant is sometimes doubled to show that the vowel just before it is short (like the vowels in *cat, bed, pin, top, cup*). The pronunciation of a word (or part of a word) is sometimes indicated by giving a well-known word that rhymes with it.

# Abbreviations

| | | | |
|---|---|---|---|
| *Amer.* | American | *Geol.* | Geology |
| *Archaeol.* | Archaeology | *Gk.* | Greek |
| *Archit.* | Architecture | *hist.* | historical |
| *Austral.* | Australian | *Med.* | Medicine |
| *Brit.* | British | *myth.* | Mythology |
| *c.* | circa, about | *Psychol.* | Psychology |
| *Chem.* | Chemistry | *Rom.* | Roman |
| foll. | followed | *Scand.* | Scandinavian |

Abbreviations that are in general use (such as ft, RC, and UK) appear in the dictionary itself.

# Aa

**A** *noun* (*plural* **As** *or* **A's**) **1** the first letter of the alphabet. **2** the first of a series of things; the highest or best grade (of marks, roads, etc.). **3** *Music* the sixth note of the scale of C major. ●*abbreviation* **1** ampere(s). **2** answer. □ **A1** (*informal*) in perfect condition; first-rate. **A1, A2,** etc. the standard paper size, each half the previous one, e.g. A4 = 297 × 210mm, A5 = 210 × 148mm. **from A to Z** from beginning to end.

**a** *adjective* (called the *indefinite article*) **1** one person or thing but not any specific one; *I need a knife.* **2** per; *we pay £40 a year.*

**Å** *abbreviation* ångström(s).

**AA** *abbreviation* **1** Automobile Association. **2** Alcoholics Anonymous.

**AAA** *abbreviation* **1** (in Britain) Amateur Athletic Association. **2** American *or* Australian Automobile Association.

**aardvark** (ard-vark) *noun* an African animal with a bulky pig-like body and a thick tail, feeding on termites.

**aardwolf** (ard-wuulf) *noun* (*plural* **aardwolves**) an animal of south and eastern Africa, resembling a small striped hyena, that feeds on insect larvae and termites.

**Aaron** (air-ŏn) brother of Moses and traditional founder of the Jewish priesthood. □ **Aaron's rod** any of several tall flowering plants, especially mullein. (¶ In the Bible, Aaron's rod sprouted and blossomed as a sign that he was designated by God as high priest of the Hebrews.)

**aback** *adverb* □ **taken aback** surprised, shocked.

**abacus** (ab-ă-kŭs) *noun* (*plural* **abacuses**) **1** a frame containing parallel rods with beads that slide up and down, used for counting. **2** *Archit.* a flat slab on top of a column or pillar.

**abaft** *adverb* in the stern half of a ship. ●*preposition* nearer to the stern than.

**abalone** (ab-ă-loh-ni) *noun* an edible mollusc with an ear-shaped shell lined with mother-of-pearl.

**abandon** *verb* **1** go away from (a person or thing or place) without intending to return; *abandon ship.* **2** give up, cease work on; *abandon the attempt.* **3** yield completely to an emotion or impulse; *abandoned himself to despair.* ●*noun* careless freedom of manner. □ **abandonment** *noun*

**abandoned** *adjective* **1** deserted, forsaken. **2** (of behaviour) lacking restraint, depraved.

**abase** *verb* humiliate, degrade. □ **abasement** *noun*

**abashed** *adjective* embarrassed, ashamed.

**abate** *verb* make or become less strong or intense; *the storm abated.*

**abattoir** (ab-ă-twar) *noun* a slaughterhouse.

**abbacy** *noun* the office of abbot or abbess.

**abbé** (ab-ay) *noun* a Frenchman who is entitled to wear ecclesiastical dress.

**abbess** (ab-ess) *noun* a woman who is head of a community of nuns.

**abbey** *noun* **1** a building occupied by monks or nuns living as a community. **2** the community itself.

**abbot** *noun* a man who is head of a community of monks.

**abbreviate** *verb* shorten (especially a word or title).

**abbreviation** *noun* **1** abbreviating, being abbreviated. **2** a shortened form of a word or title.

**ABC** *noun* **1** the alphabet. **2** the elementary facts of a subject; *the ABC of carpentry.* **3** an alphabetically arranged guide. ●*abbreviation* Australian Broadcasting Corporation.

**abdicate** *verb* resign from the throne; give up (office, responsibility, etc.). □ **abdication** *noun*

**abdomen** (ab-dŏm-ĕn) *noun* **1** the part of the body below the chest and diaphragm, containing most of the digestive organs; the belly. **2** the hindmost section of the body of an insect, spider, or crustacean; *head, thorax, and abdomen.* □ **abdominal** (ăb-dom-inăl) *adjective*, **abdominally** *adverb*

**abduct** *verb* carry off (a person) illegally by force or fraud. □ **abduction** *noun*, **abductor** *noun*

**abeam** *adverb* at right angles to a ship's or an aircraft's length.

**abed** *adverb* (*old use*) in bed.

**Aberdeen** a city in NE Scotland. □ **Aberdeen Angus** a Scottish breed of black hornless cattle.

**Aberdonian** *adjective* of Aberdeen. ●*noun* a person from Aberdeen.

**Aberfan** (ab-er-van) a village in South Wales where, in 1966, a slag-heap collapsed, killing 28 adults and 116 children.

**aberrant** (ab-e-rănt) *adjective* deviating from what is normal or accepted.

**aberration** (ab-er-ay-shŏn) *noun* **1** a deviation from what is normal. **2** a mental or moral lapse. **3** distortion of an image because of a defect in a lens or mirror. **4** the apparent change in the position of a celestial body caused by the observer's motion and the finite speed of light.

**abet** *verb* (**abetted, abetting**) (usually **aid and abet**) encourage or assist (an offender or offence). □ **abetter** (*or*, in legal use) **abettor** *noun*, **abetment** *noun*

**abeyance** (ă-bay-ăns) *noun* □ **in abeyance** (of a right, rule, or problem etc.) suspended for a time.

**abhor** (ăb-hor) *verb* (**abhorred, abhorring**) detest.

**abhorrent** (*rhymes with* torrent) *adjective* detestable. □ **abhorrence** *noun*

**abide** *verb* (**abided** (in sense 1 **abode**), **abiding**) **1** (*old use*) remain; dwell. **2** bear, endure; *I can't abide wasps.* □ **abide by** act in accordance with (a rule, decision, etc.); keep (a promise).

**abiding** *adjective* long-lasting, permanent.

**Abidjan** (ab-i-jahn) the chief port and former capital of the Ivory Coast.

**ability** *noun* **1** the capacity or power to do something. **2** cleverness, talent.

**ab initio** (ab in-ish-i-oh) *adverb* from the beginning. (¶ Latin.)

**abject** (ab-jekt) *adjective* **1** wretched, without resources; *abject poverty.* **2** lacking all pride; *an abject coward; an abject apology.* □ **abjectly** *adverb*, **abjection** *noun*

**abjure** (ăb-joor) *verb* renounce; repudiate. □ **abjuration** *noun*

**ablative** (ab-lă-tiv) *noun* the grammatical case (especially in Latin) that indicates the agent, instrument, or location of an action.

**ablaut** (ab-lowt) *noun* a change of vowel in related words (e.g. *sing, sang, sung*).

**ablaze** *adjective* blazing.

**able** *adjective* **1** having the ability to do something. **2** having great ability; competent. □ **able-bodied** *adjective* fit, healthy. **able-bodied seaman** an ordinary trained seaman. □ **ably** *adverb*

**abled** *adjective* able-bodied.

**ablution** (ă-bloo-shŏn) *noun* **1** (**ablutions**) (*informal*) ordinary washing of the body; *perform one's ablutions;* a place for doing this. **2** ceremonial washing of hands, vessels, etc.

**ABM** *abbreviation* anti-ballistic missile.

**abnegate** (ab-ni-gayt) *verb* give up or renounce (a pleasure, right, etc.). □ **abnegation** *noun*

**abnormal** *adjective* different from what is normal. □ **abnormally** *adverb*, **abnormality** (ab-nor-mal-iti) *noun*

**aboard** *adverb & preposition* on or into a ship, aircraft, or train.

**abode**[1] *noun* (*old use*) a dwelling-place.

**abode**[2] *see* ABIDE.

**abolish** *verb* put an end to. □ **abolition** (abŏ-lish-ŏn) *noun*

**abolitionist** *noun* a person who favours abolishing capital punishment.

**A-bomb** *noun* an atomic bomb.

**abominable** *adjective* **1** detestable, loathsome. **2** very bad or unpleasant; *abominable weather.* □ **Abominable Snowman** a large man-like or bear-like animal said to exist in the Himalayas; a yeti. □ **abominably** *adverb*

**abominate** *verb* detest, loathe.

**abomination** *noun* **1** loathing. **2** something loathed.

**aboriginal** *adjective* existing in a land from earliest times or from before the arrival of colonists. ● *noun* an aboriginal inhabitant.

**aborigine** (ab-er-ij-in-ee) *noun* **1** an aboriginal inhabitant of a country. **2** (**Aborigines**) those of Australia.

■**Usage** *Aboriginal* is the preferred singular form, *Aborigines* the plural.

**abort** (ă-bort) *verb* **1** cause an abortion of or to; suffer abortion. **2** end or cause to end prematurely and unsuccessfully.

**abortion** *noun* **1** the expulsion (either spontaneous or induced) of a foetus from the womb before it is able to survive independently. **2** a misshapen creature or thing.

**abortionist** *noun* a person who practises abortion, especially illegally.

**abortive** *adjective* **1** producing abortion. **2** unsuccessful; *an abortive attempt.*

**abound** *verb* **1** be plentiful; *fish abound in the river.* **2** (foll. by *in* or *with*) have in great quantities; *the river abounds in fish.*

**about** *preposition & adverb* **1** approximately; *about £10.* **2** in connection with; on the subject of; *what is he talking about?* **3** all around; *look about you.* **4** somewhere near, not far off; *he's somewhere about.* **5** here and there in (a place); *papers were lying about the room.* **6** on the move, in circulation; *will soon be about again.* **7** so as to face in the opposite direction; *put the ship about.* **8** in rotation; *on duty week and week about.* □ **about-face, about-turn** *noun* a reversal of previous actions or opinions. **be about to** be on the point of doing something.

**above** *adverb* **1** at or to a higher point; overhead; in heaven. **2** in addition. **3** earlier in a book or article; *mentioned above.* ● *preposition* **1** over; higher than; more than. **2** upstream from. **3** beyond the level or reach of; *she is above suspicion.* **4** more important than; *this above all.* □ **above board** without deception or concealment, done honourably. **above oneself** conceited, arrogant.

**abracadabra** (abră-kă-dab-ră) *noun* **1** a supposedly magic formula or spell. **2** gibberish.

**abrade** (ă-**brayd**) *verb* scrape or wear away by rubbing.

**Abraham** the Hebrew patriarch from whom all Jews trace their descent.

**abrasion** (ă-**bray**-zhŏn) *noun* abrading; an abraded place.

**abrasive** (ă-**bray**-siv) *adjective* **1** causing abrasion. **2** capable of polishing surfaces by rubbing or grinding. **3** harsh, causing angry feelings; *an abrasive personality.* ●*noun* an abrasive substance.

**abreast** *adverb* **1** side by side and facing the same way. **2** (foll. by *of*) keeping up with; up to date with; *keep abreast of modern developments.*

**abridge** *verb* shorten by using fewer words. □ **abridgement** *noun*

**abroad** *adverb* **1** away from one's own country. **2** far and wide, everywhere; *scattered the seeds abroad.* **3** out and about; *nothing was abroad.*

**abrogate** (**ab**-rŏ-gayt) *verb* cancel, repeal; *abrogate a law.* □ **abrogation** *noun*

**abrupt** *adjective* **1** sudden; *came to an abrupt stop.* **2** disconnected, not smooth; *short abrupt sentences.* **3** curt. **4** (of a slope) very steep. □ **abruptly** *adverb*, **abruptness** *noun*

**abscess** (**ab**-sis) *noun* a collection of pus formed in the body.

**abscissa** (ab-**sis**-ă) *noun* (*plural* **abscissae** or **abscissas**) *Maths* a coordinate measured parallel to a horizontal axis.

**abscond** (ăb-**skond**) *verb* go away secretly, especially after wrongdoing. □ **absconder** *noun*

**abseil** (**ab**-sayl) *verb* descend a rock-face using a doubled rope fixed at a higher point. ●*noun* this process.

**absence** *noun* **1** being away; the period of this. **2** lack, non-existence; *in the absence of proof.* □ **absence of mind** inattention.

**absent** *adjective* (**ab**-sĕnt) **1** not present; *absent from school.* **2** non-existent. **3** with one's mind on other things; *stared in an absent way.* □ **absent-minded** *adjective* with one's mind on other things; forgetful. **absent oneself** (*pronounced* ăb-**sent**) stay away. □ **absently** *adverb*, **absent-mindedly** *adverb*

**absentee** *noun* a person who is absent from work etc. □ **absentee landlord** one who seldom visits the premises he or she lets.

**absenteeism** *noun* frequent absence from work or school.

**absinth** (**ab**-sinth) *noun* **1** wormwood. **2** (usually **absinthe**) a green aniseed-flavoured liqueur based on this.

**absolute** *adjective* **1** complete; *absolute silence.* **2** unrestricted; *absolute power.* **3** independent, not relative; *there is no absolute standard for beauty.* **4** (*informal*) utter, out-and-out; *it's an absolute miracle.* □ **absolute**

**majority** a majority over all rivals combined. **absolute pitch** the ability to recognize or sing any given note. **absolute temperature** one measured from absolute zero. **absolute zero** the lowest possible temperature ($-273.15$°C or 0 K).

**absolutely** *adverb* **1** completely. **2** without restrictions, unconditionally. **3** actually; *it absolutely exploded.* **4** (*informal, pronounced* ab-sŏ-**loot**-li) quite so, yes.

**absolution** (absŏ-**loo**-shŏn) *noun* a priest's formal forgiveness of penitents' sins.

**absolutism** *noun* **1** the principle of a ruler having complete and unrestricted power. **2** the principle of having a rule etc. that must apply in all cases.

**absolve** *verb* **1** clear of blame or guilt. **2** give absolution to (a person). **3** free from an obligation.

**absorb** *verb* **1** take in, combine or merge into itself or oneself; *absorb fluid*; *absorb knowledge*; *the large firm absorbed the smaller ones.* **2** reduce the effect of; *buffers absorbed most of the shock.* **3** occupy the attention or interest of; *an absorbing book.* □ **absorber** *noun*

**absorbent** *adjective* able to absorb moisture etc. □ **absorbency** *noun*

**absorption** *noun* **1** absorbing or being absorbed. **2** being engrossed or mentally occupied. □ **absorptive** *adjective*

**abstain** *verb* **1** keep oneself from some action or indulgence, especially from drinking alcohol. **2** refrain from using one's vote. □ **abstainer** *noun*

**abstemious** (ăb-**steem**-iŭs) *adjective* sparing in one's taking of food and drink. □ **abstemiously** *adverb*, **abstemiousness** *noun*

**abstention** *noun* abstaining, especially from voting.

**abstinence** (**ab**-stin-ĕns) *noun* abstaining, especially from food or alcohol. □ **abstinent** *adjective*

**abstract** *adjective* (*pronounced* **ab**-strakt) **1** having no material existence; *beauty is an abstract quality.* **2** theoretical rather than practical. ●*noun* (*pronounced* **ab**-strakt) **1** an abstract quality or idea. **2** a summary. **3** an example of abstract art. ●*verb* (*pronounced* ăb-**strakt**) **1** take out; separate; remove. **2** make a written summary. □ **abstract art** art which does not represent things pictorially but expresses the artist's ideas or sensations. **abstract noun** a noun denoting a quality or state. **in the abstract** regarded theoretically; *he favours economy in the abstract but refuses to economize.* □ **abstractly** *adverb*, **abstractness** *noun*, **abstractor** *noun*

**abstracted** *adjective* with one's mind on other things, not paying attention. □ **abstractedly** *adverb*

**abstraction** *noun* **1** abstracting, removing. **2** an abstract idea. **3** abstractedness.

**abstruse** (ăb-**strooss**) *adjective* hard to understand; profound. □ **abstrusely** *adverb*, **abstruseness** *noun*

**absurd** *adjective* **1** not in accordance with common sense, very unsuitable. **2** ridiculous, foolish. □ **absurdly** *adverb*, **absurdity** *noun*

**ABTA** *abbreviation* Association of British Travel Agents.

**Abu Dhabi** (ab-oo **dah**-bi) an emirate belonging to the federation of United Arab Emirates; its capital city, also the capital of the UAE.

**Abuja** the capital of Nigeria.

**abundance** *noun* a quantity that is more than enough; plenty.

**abundant** *adjective* **1** more than enough, plentiful. **2** (foll. by *in*) having plenty of something; rich; *a land abundant in minerals.* □ **abundantly** *adverb*

**abuse** *noun* (*pronounced* ă-**bewss**) **1** a misuse. **2** an unjust or corrupt practice. **3** improper or bad treatment; *child abuse.* **4** abusive words, insults. ●*verb* (*pronounced* ă-**bewz**) **1** make a bad or wrong use of; *abuse one's authority.* **2** ill-treat. **3** attack in words, utter insults to or about.

**abusive** (ă-**bew**-siv) *adjective* insulting; criticizing harshly or angrily. □ **abusively** *adverb*

**abut** (ă-**but**) *verb* (**abutted**, **abutting**) have a common boundary, end or lean against; *their land abuts on ours; the garage abuts against the house.*

**abutment** *noun* a structure supporting the end of a bridge, arch, etc.

**abysmal** (ă-**biz**-măl) *adjective* **1** extreme and deplorable; *abysmal ignorance.* **2** (*informal*) extremely bad; *their taste is abysmal.* □ **abysmally** *adverb*

**abyss** (ă-**biss**) *noun* a hole so deep that it appears bottomless.

**abyssal** (ă-**bis**-ăl) *adjective* at or of the ocean depths or floor.

**Abyssinia** a former name of Ethiopia. □ **Abyssinian** *adjective & noun*

**AC** *or* **a.c.** *abbreviation* alternating current.

**Ac** *symbol* actinium.

**a/c** *abbreviation* account.

**acacia** (ă-**kay**-shă) *noun* **1** a tree or shrub from which gum arabic is obtained. **2** a related tree (the false acacia or locust tree) grown for ornament.

**academe** (ak-ă-**deem**) *noun* (*literary*) a university environment.

**academia** *noun* the academic world; scholarly life.

**academic** (akă-**dem**-ik) *adjective* **1** of a school, college, or university. **2** scholarly as opposed to technical or practical; *academic subjects.* **3** of theoretical interest only, with no practical application. ●*noun* an academic person. □ **academically** *adverb*

**academician** (ă-kad-ĕ-**mish**-ăn) *noun* a member of an Academy.

**Académie française** (a-kad-em-ee frahn-**sez**) the French Academy, a literary association of 40 French scholars and writers.

**Academy** *noun* a society of distinguished scholars or artists. □ **Academy award** any of the awards of the Academy of Motion Picture Arts and Sciences (Hollywood, USA) given annually for success in the film industry.

**academy** *noun* **1** a school, especially for specialized training. **2** (in Scotland) a secondary school.

**Acadian** (ă-**kay**-diăn) *adjective* of Acadia, a former French colony (Acadie; now Nova Scotia) on the east coast of North America; of Acadians. ●*noun* a native or inhabitant of Acadia; a descendant of Acadian immigrants in Louisiana.

**acanthus** *noun* a Mediterranean plant with large thistle-like leaves.

**a cappella** *adjective & adverb* (of choral music) unaccompanied.

**ACAS** (ay-**kass**) *abbreviation* Advisory, Conciliation, and Arbitration Service.

**acc** *abbreviation Grammar* accusative.

**accede** (ăk-**seed**) *verb* **1** take office; become monarch. **2** agree to what is proposed.

**accelerate** *verb* **1** move faster or happen earlier or more quickly. **2** cause to do this. **3** increase the speed of a motor vehicle. □ **acceleration** *noun*

**accelerator** *noun* **1** a device for increasing speed. **2** the pedal operating this. **3** *Physics* an apparatus which can make charged particles move at very high speeds.

**accelerometer** *noun* an instrument for measuring acceleration or vibrations.

**accent** *noun* (*pronounced* ak-**sĕnt**) **1** emphasis on a syllable or word. **2** a mark indicating such emphasis or the quality of a vowel-sound. **3** a national, local, or individual way of pronouncing words. **4** the emphasis given to something; *the accent is on quality.* ●*verb* (*pronounced* ăk-**sent**) **1** pronounce with an accent. **2** emphasize. **3** write accents on. □ **accentual** (ak-sen-tew-ăl) *adjective*

**accentor** *noun* a small songbird of a kind that includes the hedge-sparrow.

**accentuate** (ăk-sen-tew-ayt) *verb* emphasize. □ **accentuation** *noun*

**accept** *verb* **1** take (a thing offered) willingly; say yes to an offer or invitation. **2** undertake (a responsibility); *we accept* *liability for the accident.* **3** treat as welcome; *they were never really accepted by their neighbours.* **4** agree to; *we accept the proposed changes.* **5** take as true; *we do not accept your conclusions.* □ **acceptance** *noun*, **acceptor** *noun*

**acceptable** *adjective* **1** worth accepting, welcome. **2** tolerable; *an acceptable risk.* □ **acceptably** *adjective*, **acceptability** *noun*

**access** (**ak**-sess) *noun* **1** a way in, a means of approaching or entering. **2** the right or opportunity of reaching or using; *students need access to books.* **3** (*old use*) an attack of emotion; *a sudden access of rage.* ●*verb* retrieve (information stored in a computer). □ **access course** a course that gives entry to a higher education course for people who do not have formal qualifications. **access road** a road giving access only to the properties along it. **access time** *Computing* the time taken to retrieve data from storage. **direct** *or* **random access** the process of storing or retrieving information in a computer without having to read through items stored previously.

**accessible** *adjective* able to be reached or used. □ **accessibly** *adverb*, **accessibility** *noun*

**accession** (ăk-**sesh**-ŏn) *noun* **1** reaching a rank or position; *the Queen's accession to the throne.* **2** an addition; being added; *recent accessions to the library.* ●*verb* record the addition of (a new item) to a library or museum.

**accessory** (ăk-**sess**-er-i) *adjective* additional, extra. ●*noun* **1** a thing that is extra, useful, or decorative but not essential; a minor fitting or attachment. **2** a person who helps another in a crime.

**accident** *noun* **1** an unexpected or undesirable event, especially one causing injury or damage. **2** chance, fortune; *we met by accident.*

**accidental** *adjective* happening or done by accident. ●*noun* a sharp, flat, or natural sign attached to a note in music, showing temporary departure from the key signature. □ **accidentally** *adverb*

**acclaim** (ă-**klaym**) *verb* welcome with shouts of approval; applaud enthusiastically. ●*noun* a shout of welcome; applause. □ **acclamation** (aklă-**may**-shŏn) *noun*

**acclimatize** *verb* (also **acclimatise**) make or become used to a new climate or new conditions. □ **acclimatization** *noun*

**accolade** (ak-ŏ-**layd**) *noun* **1** praise, approval. **2** a touch on the shoulder with a sword, given when a knighthood is conferred.

**accommodate** *verb* **1** provide lodging or room for. **2** provide or supply; *the bank will accommodate you with a loan.* **3** adapt;

harmonize; *I will accommodate my plans to yours.*

**accommodating** *adjective* willing to do as one is asked; obliging.

**accommodation** *noun* **1** lodgings, living-premises. **2** the process of accommodating or adapting. **3** provision. □ **accommodation address** a postal address used by a person who is unable or unwilling to give a permanent address.

**accompaniment** *noun* **1** an instrumental part supporting a solo instrument or voice. **2** an accompanying thing.

**accompanist** *noun* a person who plays a musical accompaniment.

**accompany** *verb* (**accompanied**, **accompanying**) **1** go with, travel with as a companion or helper. **2** be present with. **3** provide in addition. **4** play a musical accompaniment to.

**accomplice** (ă-**kum**-plis) *noun* a partner in wrongdoing.

**accomplish** (ă-**kum**-plish) *verb* succeed in doing, fulfil.

**accomplished** *adjective* skilled, having many accomplishments.

**accomplishment** *noun* **1** a skill. **2** accomplishing, completion. **3** a thing accomplished.

**accord** *noun* consent, agreement. ●*verb* **1** be in harmony or consistent. **2** (*formal*) give or grant; *he was accorded this privilege.* □ **of one's own accord** without being asked or compelled. **with one accord** all agreeing; all together.

**accordance** *noun* agreement, conformity. □ **accordant** *adjective*

**according** *adverb* □ **according as** in proportion as; in a manner depending on whether; *he was praised or blamed according as his work was good or bad.* **according to** **1** as stated by or in; *according to the Bible.* **2** in a manner consistent with or in proportion to; *grouped according to size.*

**accordingly** *adverb* **1** according to what is known or stated; *ask what they want and act accordingly.* **2** therefore.

**accordion** *noun* a portable box-shaped musical instrument with bellows, metal reeds, and keys or buttons. □ **accordionist** *noun*

**accost** (ă-**kost**) *verb* **1** approach and speak to. **2** (of a prostitute) solicit.

**account** *noun* **1** a statement of money paid or owed. **2** a credit arrangement with a bank or firm. **3** importance; *that is of no account.* **4** a description, a report. ●*verb* regard as; *a person is accounted innocent until proved guilty.* □ **account for 1** give a reckoning of (money received). **2** explain the cause of; be the explanation of. **3** bring about the death or destruction etc. of. **4** supply or constitute (an amount). **give a**

**good account of oneself** perform well. **keep accounts** keep a systematic record of money spent and received. **on account 1** as an interim payment; *here is £10 on account.* **2** debited to be paid for later; *bought it on account.* **on account of** because of. **on no account** under no circumstances, never. **on one's own account** for one's own purposes and at one's own risk. **take into account** make allowances for. **turn to account** use profitably, make good use of.

**accountable** *adjective* **1** obliged to give a reckoning or explanation for one's actions etc.; responsible. **2** able to be explained. □ **accountability** *noun*

**accountant** *noun* one whose profession is to keep and examine business accounts. □ **accountancy** *noun*

**accounting** *noun* keeping or examining accounts; accountancy.

**accoutrements** (ă-koo-trĕ-mĕnts) *plural noun* (*Amer.* **accouterments**) equipment; a soldier's outfit other than weapons and clothes.

**Accra** (ă-**krah**) the capital of Ghana.

**accredited** (ă-**kred**-itid) *adjective* **1** officially recognized; *our accredited representative.* **2** generally accepted or believed. **3** certified as being of a prescribed quality.

**accretion** (ă-**kree**-shŏn) *noun* **1** a growth or increase by means of gradual additions. **2** the growing of separate things into one.

**accrue** (ă-**kroo**) *verb* come as a natural increase or advantage; accumulate; *interest accrues on investments.* □ **accrual** *noun*

**accumulate** *verb* **1** acquire an increasing quantity of. **2** increase in quantity or amount. □ **accumulation** *noun*, **accumulative** *adjective*

**accumulator** *noun* **1** a rechargeable battery. **2** a bet placed on a series of events, winnings from each being staked on the next. **3** a storage register in a computer.

**accurate** *adjective* free from error, conforming exactly to a standard or to truth; careful and exact. □ **accurately** *adverb*, **accuracy** *noun*

**accursed** (ă-**ker**-sid) *adjective* **1** under a curse. **2** (*informal*) detestable, hateful.

**accusation** *noun* **1** accusing; being accused. **2** a statement accusing a person of a wrongdoing.

**accusative** (ă-**kew**-ză-tiv) *noun Grammar* the objective form of a word, e.g. *him* in '*we saw him*'.

**accuse** *verb* state that one lays blame for a fault or wrongdoing on (a named person). □ **accuser** *noun*, **accusingly** *adverb*

**accustom** *verb* make used (to something).

**accustomed** *adjective* **1** (usually foll. by *to*) used to a thing. **2** usual, customary; *in his accustomed seat.*

**ace** *noun* **1** a playing-card with one spot. **2** a person who excels at something. **3** (in tennis) a serve that one's opponent cannot return. □ **have an ace up one's sleeve** have something effective kept secretly in reserve. **play one's ace** use one's best resource. **within an ace of** on the verge of; *was within an ace of collapse.*

**acellular** *adjective* having no cells; not consisting of cells.

**acerbic** (ă-**ser**-bik) *adjective* harsh and sharp, especially in speech or manner. □ **acerbity** *noun*

**acetaldehyde** *noun* a colourless volatile liquid aldehyde.

**acetate** (**ass**-it-ayt) *noun* **1** a compound derived from acetic acid. **2** a fabric made from cellulose acetate.

**acetic** (ă-**see**-tik) *adjective* of vinegar. □ **acetic acid** the acid that gives vinegar its characteristic taste and smell.

**acetone** (**ass**-i-tohn) *noun* a colourless liquid used as a solvent.

**acetylene** (ă-**set**-i-leen) *noun* a gas that burns with a bright flame, used in cutting and welding metal.

**ache** *verb* **1** suffer a dull continuous physical or mental pain. **2** yearn. ●*noun* a dull continuous pain. □ **achy** *adjective*

**Achebe** (ă-**chay**-bi), Chinua (Albert Chinualungu) (born 1930), Nigerian novelist, poet, and writer of short stories.

**achieve** *verb* accomplish, gain or reach by effort. □ **achievable** *adjective*, **achievement** *noun*

**Achilles** (ă-**kil**-eez) (*Gk. legend*) a Greek hero of the Trojan War, whose mother had plunged him in the river Styx during his infancy, making his body invulnerable except for the heel by which she held him. □ **Achilles heel** a weak or vulnerable point. **Achilles tendon** the tendon connecting the heel with the calf muscles.

**achromatic** (ak-rŏ-**mat**-ik) *adjective* (in optics) **1** free from colour. **2** transmitting light without decomposing it into constituent colours.

**acid** *adjective* **1** sharp-tasting, sour. **2** looking or sounding bitter; *acid remarks.* ●*noun* **1** any of a class of substances containing hydrogen that can be replaced by a metal to form a salt. **2** a sour substance. **3** (*slang*) the drug LSD. □ **acid house** synthesized rock music with a repetitive beat, often associated with the taking of illegal drugs. **acid rain** rain made acid by contamination from power-stations, factories, etc. **acid test** a severe or conclusive test. (¶ Acid is applied to a metal to test whether it is gold or not.) □ **acidly** adverb

**acidic** (ă-sid-ik) adjective of or like an acid.

**acidify** (ă-sid-i-fy) verb (**acidified, acidifying**) make or become acid.

**acidity** (ă-sid-iti) noun **1** being acid. **2** an over-acid condition of the stomach.

**acidosis** (asid-oh-sis) noun an over-acid condition of the blood or body tissues.

**acidulated** (ă-sid-yoo-layt-id) adjective made slightly acid.

**acidulous** adjective somewhat acid.

**ack-ack** (informal) adjective anti-aircraft. ●noun an anti-aircraft gun.

**acknowledge** verb **1** admit that something is true or valid. **2** confirm the receipt of (a letter etc.). **3** express thanks for; acknowledge his services to the town. **4** indicate that one has noticed or recognized; he acknowledged my presence with a sniff. □ **acknowledgement** noun

**acme** (ak-mi) noun the highest point, the peak of perfection.

**acne** (ak-ni) noun inflammation of the oil-glands of the skin, producing red pimples.

**acolyte** (ak-ŏ-lyt) noun **1** a person who assists a priest in certain church services. **2** an attendant.

**Aconcagua** (ak-on-kag-wă) the highest mountain in South America, an extinct volcano in the Andes.

**aconite** noun a perennial plant of the buttercup family, with a poisonous root. □ **winter aconite** a yellow-flowered plant that blooms in winter.

**acorn** noun the fruit of the oak-tree, with a cup-like base.

**acoustic** (ă-koo-stik) adjective **1** of sound or the sense of hearing; of acoustics. **2** (of a musical instrument etc.) without electrical amplification. ●noun (**acoustics**) the properties of sound; the qualities of a room that make it good or bad for carrying sound. □ **acoustically** adverb

**acquaint** verb make aware or familiar; acquaint him with the facts. □ **be acquainted with** know slightly.

**acquaintance** noun **1** being acquainted. **2** a person one knows slightly.

**acquiesce** (akwi-ess) verb **1** agree without protest, assent. **2** (foll. by in) accept as an arrangement.

**acquiescent** (akwi-ess-ĕnt) adjective acquiescing. □ **acquiescence** noun

**acquire** verb gain possession of. □ **acquired immune deficiency syndrome** = AIDS. **acquired taste** a liking gained gradually.

**acquisition** (akwi-zish-ŏn) noun **1** acquiring. **2** something acquired.

**acquisitive** (ă-kwiz-itiv) adjective keen to acquire things.

**acquit** verb (**acquitted, acquitting**) declare (a person) to be not guilty of the crime with which he or she was charged. □ **acquit oneself** conduct oneself, perform; he acquitted himself well in the test.

**acquittal** (ă-kwi-t'l) noun acquitting; a verdict acquitting a person.

**acre** (ay-ker) noun a measure of land, 4840 sq. yds, 0.405 ha.

**acreage** (ay-ker-ij) noun a number of acres; the extent of a piece of land.

**acrid** (ak-rid) adjective **1** having a bitter smell or taste. **2** bitter in temper or manner. □ **acridity** (ă-krid-iti) noun

**acrimony** (ak-ri-mŏni) noun bitterness of manner or words. □ **acrimonious** (akri-moh-niŭs) adjective, **acrimoniously** adverb

**acrobat** noun a performer of spectacular gymnastic feats. □ **acrobatic** adjective, **acrobatically** adverb

**acrobatics** noun (as plural) acrobatic feats; (as singular) the art of performing these.

**acronym** (ak-rŏ-nim) noun a word formed from the initial letters of other words, e.g. NATO.

**acrophobia** noun an abnormal fear of heights.

**acropolis** (ă-krop-ŏ-lis) noun **1** the citadel or upper fortified part of an ancient Greek city. **2** (**the Acropolis**) that of Athens.

**across** preposition & adverb **1** from one side of a thing to the other. **2** to or on the other side of. **3** so as to be understood or accepted; got his points across to the audience. **4** so as to form a cross or intersect; laid across each other. □ **across the board** applying to all.

**acrostic** (ă-kros-tik) noun a word-puzzle or poem in which the first or last letters of each line form a word or words.

**acrylic** (ă-kril-ik) adjective of a synthetic material made from an organic acid (**acrylic acid**). ●noun an acrylic fibre, plastic, or resin. □ **acrylic paint** artists' paint made from a plastic solution.

**ACT** abbreviation Australian Capital Territory.

**act** noun **1** something done. **2** the process of doing something; caught in the act. **3** a decree or law made by a parliament. **4** each of the main divisions of a play. **5** each of a series of short performances in a programme; a circus act. **6** (informal) a pose or pretence; put on an act. ●verb **1** perform actions, behave; you acted wisely. **2** function; the brakes did not act. **3** have an effect; acid acts on metal. **4** portray by actions; perform a part in a play etc. □ **act of God** an uncontrollable natural event, e.g. an earthquake. **Acts (of the Apostles)** the fifth book of the New Testament, relating the early history of the Church in the time of St Peter and St Paul. **act up** (informal) behave badly; give trouble. **get one's act**

**together** (*slang*) become organized; prepare.

**acting** *adjective* serving temporarily, especially as a substitute; *the acting headmaster.*

**actinic** (ak-**tin**-ik) *adjective* having photochemical properties, as of short-length radiation.

**actinide** *noun* any of the series of 15 radioactive elements with atomic numbers between 89 (actinium) and 103 (lawrencium).

**actinium** (ak-**tin**-iŭm) *noun* a radioactive metallic element (symbol Ac) that occurs in pitchblende.

**action** *noun* **1** the process of doing something, the exertion of energy or influence; *go into action; the action of acid on metal.* **2** a thing done; *generous actions.* **3** a series of events in a story or play; *the action is set in Spain.* **4** a way or manner of moving or functioning; the mechanism of an instrument. **5** a lawsuit. **6** a battle; *he was killed in action.* □ **action replay** a playback (at normal or reduced speed) of a televised incident in a sports event. **action stations** positions taken up by troops etc. ready for battle. **out of action** not working. **take action** do something.

**actionable** *adjective* giving cause for a lawsuit.

**Action Directe** (ak-si-awn dee-**rekt**) a group of extreme left-wing French terrorists. (¶ French, = immediate action.)

**activate** *verb* make active; cause a chemical reaction in; make radioactive. □ **activation** *noun*, **activator** *noun*

**active** *adjective* **1** moving about, characterized by energetic action. **2** taking part in activities. **3** functioning, in operation. **4** having an effect; *the active ingredients.* **5** radioactive. ● *noun* the form of a verb used when the subject of the sentence is the doer of the action, e.g. *saw* in '*we saw him*'. □ **active service** military service in wartime. □ **actively** *adverb*

**activist** *noun* one who follows a policy of vigorous action, especially in politics. □ **activism** *noun*

**activity** *noun* **1** being active; busy or energetic action. **2** (often as **activities**) a particular pursuit, action, etc.; *outdoor activities.*

**actor** *noun* a performer in a play or a film.

**actress** *noun* a woman who acts in a play or film.

**actual** *adjective* existing in fact, real; current. □ **actually** *adverb*

**actuality** (ak-tew-**al**-iti) *noun* **1** reality. **2** (**actualities**) existing conditions.

**actuary** (**ak**-tew-er-i) *noun* an expert in statistics who calculates insurance risks and premiums. □ **actuarial** (ak-tew-**air**-iăl) *adjective*

**actuate** *verb* **1** activate (a movement or process). **2** be a motive for (a person's actions).

**acuity** (ă-**kew**-iti) *noun* sharpness, acuteness.

**acumen** (**ak**-yoo-men) *noun* sharpness of mind; shrewdness.

**acupressure** *noun* applying pressure with the thumbs or fingers to specific points on the body as therapy.

**acupuncture** (**ak**-yoo-punk-cher) *noun* pricking the tissues of the body with fine needles as medical treatment or to relieve pain. □ **acupuncturist** *noun*

**acute** *adjective* **1** very perceptive, having a sharp mind. **2** sharp or severe in its effect; *acute pain; an acute shortage.* **3** (of an illness) coming sharply to a crisis of severity; *acute appendicitis.* □ **acute accent** a mark (´) over a vowel, as over *e* in *café.* **acute angle** an angle of less than 90°. □ **acutely** *adverb*, **acuteness** *noun*

**AD** *abbreviation* (in dates) after the supposed date of Christ's birth. (¶ From the Latin *anno domini* = in the year of Our Lord.)

**ad** *noun* (*informal*) an advertisement.

**adage** (**ad**-ij) *noun* a proverb, a saying.

**adagio** (ă-**dahj**-yoh) *adverb* (in music) in slow time. ● *noun* (*plural* **adagios**) a movement to be played in this way.

**Adam**[1] (in Hebrew tradition) the first man. □ **Adam's apple** the lump of cartilage at the front of the neck. **not know a person from Adam** be unable to recognise him or her.

**Adam**[2], Robert (1728–92) and his brother James (1730–94), Scottish architects and interior designers.

**adamant** (**ad**-ă-mănt) *adjective* unyielding to requests; determined.

**adapt** *verb* make or become suitable for a new use or situation. □ **adaptation** *noun*

**adaptable** *adjective* **1** able to be adapted. **2** able to adapt oneself. □ **adaptability** *noun*

**adaptor** *noun* **1** a device that connects pieces of equipment that were not originally designed to be connected. **2** a device for connecting several plugs to one socket.

**ADC** *abbreviation* aide-de-camp.

**add** *verb* **1** join (one thing to another) as an increase or supplement. **2** put numbers or amounts together to get a total. **3** make a further remark. □ **add up 1** find the total of. **2** (*informal*) seem consistent or reasonable; *his story doesn't add up.* **add up to 1** yield as a total. **2** (*informal*) result in, be equivalent to.

**addendum** *noun* (*plural* **addenda**) something added at the end of a book etc.

**adder** *noun* **1** a small poisonous snake, a viper. **2** any of various harmless snakes of

North America. **3** (also **death adder**) a poisonous snake of the cobra family, found in Australia and nearby islands.

**addict** (ad-ikt) *noun* a person who is addicted to something, especially to drugs.

**addicted** (ă-**dik**-tid) *adjective* **1** doing or using something as a habit or compulsively. **2** devoted to something as a hobby or interest. □ **addiction** *noun*

**addictive** (ă-**dik**-tiv) *adjective* causing addiction.

**Addis Ababa** the capital of Ethiopia.

**Addison's disease** a condition caused by malfunction of the adrenal glands, producing great weakness and often a bronze colouring of the skin. (¶ First described by the English physician Thomas Addison (1793-1860).)

**addition** *noun* **1** adding, being added. **2** a thing added to something else. □ **in addition** as an extra thing or circumstance.

**additional** *adjective* added, extra. □ **additionally** *adverb*

**additive** (**ad**-it-iv) *noun* a substance added in small amounts, especially to colour, flavour, or preserve food.

**addle** *verb* muddle or confuse; *addle one's brains*.

**addled** *adjective* (of an egg) rotten, producing no chick.

**address** *noun* **1** the place where a person lives; particulars of where mail should be delivered. **2** a speech delivered to an audience. **3** the part of a computer instruction that specifies the location of a piece of stored information. ● *verb* **1** write directions for delivery on (an envelope or parcel). **2** speak or write to (a person, audience, etc.); direct (one's remarks) to a person. **3** apply (oneself) to a task or problem, direct one's attention to (a problem). **4** take aim at (the ball) in golf. **5** store or retrieve (a piece of information) by using an address (see *noun* sense 3). □ **forms of address** words (such as *Mr, Sir, Your Majesty*) used in addressing a person.

**addressee** (ad-ress-**ee**) *noun* a person to whom a letter etc. is addressed.

**adduce** (ă-**dewss**) *verb* cite as an example or proof. □ **adducible** (ă-**dewss**-ibŭl) *adjective*

**Adelaide** the capital of South Australia.

**Adélie Land** (ă-**day**-li) (also **Adélie Coast**) French territory in the coastal region of Antarctica, south of Australia.

**Aden** (**ay**-d'n) a seaport and capital of South Yemen (1967-90) prior to unification of North and South Yemen. □ **Gulf of Aden** an arm of the Indian Ocean at the entrance to the Red Sea.

**Adenauer** (**ah**-děn-ow-er), Konrad (1876-1967), German statesman, Chancellor of West Germany (1949-63).

**adenoids** (**ad**-in-oidz) *plural noun* enlarged spongy tissue between the back of the nose and the throat, often hindering breathing. □ **adenoidal** *adjective*

**adenoma** (ad-in-**oh**-mă) *noun* a benign gland-like tumour.

**adept** (**ad**-ept) *adjective* very skilful. ● *noun* one who is very skilful; *an adept at carpentry*.

**adequate** *adjective* **1** sufficient, satisfactory. **2** passable but not outstandingly good. □ **adequately** *adverb*, **adequacy** *noun*

**à deux** (a dœ) *adverb & adjective* for or between two. (¶ French.)

**adhere** (ăd-**heer**) *verb* **1** stick when glued or by suction, or as if by these. **2** remain faithful, continue to give one's support (to a person or cause). **3** (foll. by *to*) keep to and not alter; *we adhered to our plan*.

**adherent** *adjective* sticking, adhering. ● *noun* a supporter of a party or doctrine. □ **adherence** *noun*

**adhesion** (ăd-**hee**-zhŏn) *noun* **1** adhering. **2** tissue formed when normally separate tissues of the body grow together as a result of inflammation or injury.

**adhesive** *adjective* causing things to adhere, sticky; *adhesive tape*. ● *noun* an adhesive substance. □ **adhesiveness** *noun*

**ad hoc** for a specific purpose; *an ad hoc arrangement*. (¶ Latin, = for this.)

**adieu** (ă-**dew**) *interjection & noun* (*plural* **adieus**) goodbye.

**Adi Granth** (ah-di **grunt**) the sacred scripture of Sikhism.

**ad infinitum** (in-fin-**I**-tŭm) without limit, for ever. (¶ Latin, = to infinity.)

**adipose** (**ad**-i-pohs) *adjective* of animal fat; fatty. □ **adiposity** (ad-i-**poss**-iti) *noun*

**Adirondack Mountains** (ad-i-**ron**-dak) (also **Adirondacks**) a range of mountains in New York State.

**adj.** *abbreviation* adjective.

**adjacent** *adjective* lying near, adjoining.

**adjective** (**aj**-ik-tiv) *noun* a word added to a noun to describe a quality or modify a meaning, e.g. *old, tall, Swedish, my, this*. □ **adjectival** (aj-ik-**ty**-văl) *adjective*, **adjectivally** *adverb*

**adjoin** *verb* be next or nearest to.

**adjourn** (ă-**jern**) *verb* **1** postpone, break off temporarily. **2** break off and go elsewhere; *let's adjourn to the bar*. □ **adjournment** *noun*

**adjudge** *verb* decide or award judicially; *he was adjudged to be guilty*.

**adjudicate** (ă-**joo**-dik-ayt) *verb* **1** act as judge in a court, tribunal, or competition. **2** judge and pronounce a decision upon. □ **adjudication** *noun*, **adjudicator** *noun*

**adjunct** (**ad**-junkt) *noun* something added or attached but subordinate.

**adjure** (ă-joor) *verb* command or urge solemnly; *I adjure you to tell the truth.* □ **adjuration** *noun*

**adjust** *verb* **1** arrange, put into the proper position. **2** alter by a small amount so as to fit or be right for use; *the brakes need adjusting.* **3** adapt or adapt oneself to new circumstances; *he had difficulty in adjusting to civilian life.* **4** assess (loss or damage) in settlement of an insurance claim. □ **adjuster** *noun*, **adjustment** *noun*, **adjustable** *adjective*

**adjutant** (aj-oo-tănt) *noun* an army officer assisting a superior officer with administrative work. □ **adjutant bird** a large Indian stork.

**Adler**[1], Alfred (1870–1937), Austrian psychologist and psychiatrist, who introduced the concept of the 'inferiority complex'.

**Adler**[2], Larry (Lawrence Cecil) (born 1914), American harmonica player.

**ad lib** *adverb* as one pleases, without restraint. (¶ From the Latin *ad libitum*, according to pleasure.) ●*adjective* said or done impromptu; improvised. ●*verb* (**ad libbed**, **ad libbing**) (*informal*) speak impromptu, improvise (remarks or actions).

**adman** (ad-man) *noun* (*plural* **admen**) (*informal*) a person who composes commercial advertisements.

**admin** (ad-min) *noun* (*informal*) administration.

**administer** *verb* **1** manage (business affairs), be an administrator; *administer a person's estate.* **2** give or hand out formally, provide; *administer the sacrament; administer punishment.*

**administrate** *verb* act as administrator (of).

**administration** *noun* **1** administering. **2** the management of public or business affairs. **3** the people who administer an organization etc.; the government.

**administrative** *adjective* of or involving administration.

**administrator** *noun* **1** a person responsible for administration; one who has a talent for this. **2** a person appointed to administer an estate.

**admirable** *adjective* worthy of admiration, excellent. □ **admirably** *adverb*

**admiral** *noun* a naval officer of high rank, commander of a fleet or squadron. □ **Admiral of the Fleet, Admiral, Vice Admiral, Rear Admiral** the four grades of such officers. **red admiral, white admiral** European species of butterfly.

**Admiralty** *noun* (in full **Admiralty Board**) the former name for the department of State superintending the Royal Navy.

**admire** *verb* **1** regard with pleasure or satisfaction; think highly of. **2** express admiration of. □ **admiration** *noun*, **admirer** *noun*

**admissible** *adjective* capable of being admitted or allowed.

**admission** *noun* **1** admitting; being admitted. **2** the charge for this. **3** a statement admitting something, a confession.

**admit** *verb* (**admitted, admitting**) **1** allow to enter. **2** accept into a school etc. as a pupil or into a hospital as a patient. **3** accept as true or valid. **4** state reluctantly; *we admit that the task is difficult.* □ **admit of** leave room for; *the plan does not admit of improvement.*

**admittance** *noun* being allowed to enter, especially into a private place.

**admittedly** *adverb* as must be admitted.

**admixture** *noun* something added as an ingredient.

**admonish** (ăd-mon-ish) *verb* **1** advise or urge seriously. **2** reprove mildly but firmly. □ **admonishment** *noun*, **admonition** (admŏn-ish-ŏn) *noun*, **admonitory** (ădmon-it-er-i) *adjective*

**ad nauseam** (naw-si-am) to a sickening extent; excessively. (¶ Latin.)

**ado** (ă-doo) *noun* fuss, trouble, excitement.

**adobe** (ă-doh-bi) *noun* **1** sun-dried clay brick. **2** clay for making this.

**adolescent** (ad-ŏ-less-ĕnt) *adjective* between childhood and maturity. ●*noun* an adolescent person. □ **adolescence** *noun*

**Adonis** (ă-doh-nis) (*Gk. myth.*) a handsome young man, loved by Aphrodite.

**adopt** *verb* **1** take into one's family as a relation, especially as one's child with legal guardianship. **2** take (a person) as one's heir or representative; *adopt a candidate.* **3** take and use as one's own; *adopted this name or custom.* **4** accept responsibility for maintenance of (a road etc.). **5** approve or accept (a report or financial accounts). □ **adoption** *noun*

**adoptive** *adjective* related by adoption; *his adoptive parents.*

**adorable** *adjective* **1** very lovable. **2** (*informal*) delightful. □ **adorably** *adverb*

**adore** *verb* **1** love deeply. **2** worship as divine. **3** (*informal*) like very much. □ **adoration** *noun*, **adorer** *noun*

**adorn** *noun* **1** to decorate with ornaments. **2** to be an ornament to. □ **adornment** *noun*

**ADP** *abbreviation* automatic data processing.

**adrenal** (ă-dree-năl) *noun* (in full **adrenal gland**) either of two ductless glands on top of the kidneys, secreting adrenalin.

**adrenalin** (ă-dren-ă-lin) *noun* (also **adrenaline**) a hormone that stimulates the nervous system, secreted by a part of the adrenal glands or prepared synthetically.

**Adriatic** (ay-dri-at-ik) *adjective* of the Adriatic Sea, between Italy and the former Yugoslavia. ●*noun* the Adriatic Sea.

**adrift** *adverb & adjective* **1** drifting. **2** (*informal*) unfastened, loose. **3** (*informal*) wrong; not as planned; *our plans went adrift.*

**adroit** (ă-droit) *adjective* skilful; ingenious. □ **adroitly** *adverb*, **adroitness** *noun*

**adsorb** *verb* (of a solid) hold (particles of a gas or liquid) to its surface. □ **adsorption** *noun*

**adulation** (ad-yoo-lay-shŏn) *noun* excessive flattery. □ **adulatory** (ad-yoo-layt-er-i) *adjective*

**adult** (ad-ult) *adjective* grown to full size or strength, mature. ●*noun* an adult person. □ **adulthood** *noun*

**adulterant** *noun* a substance added in adulterating something.

**adulterate** *verb* make impure or poorer in quality by adding another substance. □ **adulteration** *noun*

**adulterer** *noun* a person who commits adultery.

**adulteress** *noun* a woman who commits adultery.

**adultery** *noun* the act of being unfaithful to one's wife or husband by voluntarily having sexual intercourse with someone else. □ **adulterous** *adjective*

**adumbrate** *verb* foreshadow. □ **adumbration** *noun*

**adv.** *abbreviation* adverb.

**ad valorem** (ad vă-law-rem) *adverb & adjective* (of taxes) in proportion to the estimated value of the goods concerned. (¶ Latin.)

**advance** *verb* **1** move or put forward; make progress. **2** help the progress of; *advance someone's interests.* **3** bring forward or make; *advance a suggestion.* **4** bring (an event) to an earlier date. **5** lend (money), pay before a due date; *advance her a month's salary.* ●*noun* **1** a forward movement, progress. **2** an increase in price or amount. **3** a loan, payment beforehand. **4** (**advances**) attempts to establish an amorous relationship or a business agreement. ●*adjective* going before others; done or provided in advance; *the advance party; advance bookings.* □ **in advance** ahead in place or time. □ **advancement** *noun*

**advanced** *adjective* **1** far on in progress or in life; *an advanced age.* **2** not elementary; *advanced studies.* **3** (of ideas etc.) new and not yet generally accepted. □ **Advanced level** (also **A level**) an examination of a standard higher than Ordinary level and GCSE.

**advantage** *noun* **1** a favourable condition or circumstance. **2** benefit, profit; *the treaty is to their advantage; turn it to your advantage.* **3** the next point won after deuce in tennis. □ **take advantage of** make use of; exploit.

**advantageous** (ad-van-tay-jŭs) *adjective* profitable, beneficial. □ **advantageously** *adverb*

**Advent** *noun* **1** the coming of Christ. **2** the season (with four Sundays) before Christmas Day. **3** (**advent**) the arrival of an important person, event, or development.

**Adventist** *noun* a member of a sect believing that Christ's second coming is very near.

**adventitious** (ad-ven-tish-ŭs) *adjective* **1** accidental, casual. **2** (of roots etc.) occurring in an unusual place.

**adventure** *noun* **1** an exciting or dangerous experience. **2** willingness to take risks; *the spirit of adventure.* □ **adventure playground** a playground with climbing-frames, building blocks, etc. □ **adventurous** *adjective*, **adventurously** *adverb*

**adventurer** *noun* **1** a person who seeks adventures. **2** a person who is ready to make gains by risky or unscrupulous methods.

**adverb** *noun* a word that qualifies a verb, adjective, or other adverb and indicates how, when, or where, e.g. *gently, fully, soon.* □ **adverbial** *adjective*, **adverbially** *adverb*

**adversary** (ad-ver-ser-i) *noun* an opponent, an enemy.

**adverse** (ad-vers) *adjective* unfavourable; harmful; *an adverse report; the drug has no adverse effects.* □ **adversely** *adverb*

**adversity** (ăd-vers-iti) *noun* misfortune, trouble.

**advert** *noun* (*informal*) an advertisement.

**advertise** *verb* **1** make generally known; *advertise a meeting.* **2** promote (goods or services) publicly to encourage people to buy or use them. **3** ask or offer by public notice; *advertise for a secretary.* □ **advertiser** *noun*

**advertisement** *noun* **1** advertising. **2** a public notice advertising something.

**advice** *noun* **1** an opinion given about what to do or how to behave. **2** a piece of information; *we received advice that the goods had been dispatched.* □ **advice note** a document sent by supplier to customer stating that specified goods have been dispatched.

**advisable** *adjective* worth recommending as a course of action. □ **advisability** *noun*

**advise** *verb* **1** give advice to, recommend. **2** inform, notify.

**advisedly** (ad-vyz-id-li) *adverb* after careful thought; deliberately.

**adviser** *noun* (also **advisor**) a person who advises a politician, ruler, etc.

**advisory** *adjective* giving advice, having the power to advise; *an advisory committee.*

**advocaat** (ad-vŏ-kaht) *noun* a liqueur of eggs, sugar, and brandy.

**advocacy** (ad-vŏk-ăsi) *noun* **1** the advocating of a policy etc. **2** the function of an advocate.

**advocate** *verb* (*pronounced* ad-vŏ-kayt) recommend; *I advocate caution.* ●*noun* (*pronounced* ad-vŏ-kăt) **1** a person who advocates a policy; *an advocate of reform.* **2** a person who pleads on behalf of another; a lawyer presenting a client's case in a lawcourt.

**adze** (*rhymes with* lads) *noun* (*Amer.* **adz**) an axe with a blade at right angles to the handle, used for trimming large pieces of wood.

**Aegean** (i-jee-ăn) *adjective* of the Aegean Sea, between Greece and Turkey. ●*noun* the Aegean Sea.

**aegis** (ee-jis) *noun* protection, sponsorship; *under the aegis of the Law Society.*

**Aeneas** (i-nee-ăs) (*Gk.* & *Rom. legend*) a Trojan leader, regarded by the Romans as the founder of their State.

**Aeneid** (ee-nee-id) a Latin epic poem by Virgil, which relates the wanderings of Aeneas after the fall of Troy.

**aeolian** (ee-oh-li-ăn) *adjective* wind-borne. □ **aeolian harp** a stringed instrument giving musical sounds when exposed to wind. (¶ Named after Aeolus, god of the winds in Greek mythology.)

**aeon** (ee-ŏn) *noun* (also **eon**) an immense time.

**aerate** (air-ayt) *verb* **1** expose to the chemical action of air; *aerate the soil by forking it.* **2** add carbon dioxide to (a liquid) under pressure; *aerated water.* □ **aeration** *noun*

**aerial** (air-iăl) *adjective* **1** of or like air. **2** existing in the air; suspended overhead; *an aerial railway.* **3** by or from aircraft; *aerial bombardment.* ●*noun* a wire or rod for transmitting or receiving radio waves.

**aero-** *combining form* air; aircraft; *aero-engine.*

**aerobatics** *plural noun* spectacular feats of flying aircraft. □ **aerobatic** *adjective*

**aerobic** (air-oh-bik) *adjective* **1** using oxygen from the air. **2** (of exercises) designed to increase the intake of oxygen and strengthen the heart and lungs. ●*noun* (**aerobics**) exercises of this kind.

**aerodrome** *noun* an airfield.

**aerodynamics** *noun* interaction between airflow and the movement of solid bodies (e.g. aircraft, bullets) through air. □ **aerodynamic** *adjective*

**aerofoil** *noun* an aircraft wing, fin, or tailplane.

**aerogramme** *noun* (also **aerogram**) an airmail letter in the form of a single sheet folded and sealed.

**aeronautics** *noun* the scientific study of the flight of aircraft. □ **aeronautic** *adjective*, **aeronautical** *adjective*

**aeroplane** *noun* a power-driven aircraft with wings.

**aerosol** *noun* **1** a substance sealed in a container under pressure, with a device for releasing it as a fine spray. **2** the container itself.

**aerospace** *noun* **1** earth's atmosphere and space beyond it. **2** the technology of aviation in this region.

**Aeschylus** (ees-ki-lŭs) (525–456 BC) Greek dramatist.

**Aesop** (ee-sop) (6th century BC) Greek teller of animal fables with a moral.

**aesthete** (ees-theet) *noun* (*Amer.* **esthete**) a person who claims to have great understanding and appreciation of what is beautiful.

**aesthetic** (iss-thet-ik) *adjective* (*Amer.* **esthetic**) **1** relating to the appreciation of beauty; *the aesthetic standards of the times.* **2** having or showing such appreciation. **3** artistic, tasteful. ●*noun* (**aesthetics**) a branch of philosophy dealing with the principles of beauty and tastefulness. □ **aesthetically** *adverb*

**aetiology** (ee-ti-ol-ŏji) *noun* (*Amer.* **etiology**) **1** the study of causes or reasons. **2** a scientific account of the causes of a disease. □ **aetiological** *adjective*, **aetiologically** *adverb*

**AF** *abbreviation* audio frequency.

**afar** *adverb* far off, far away.

**affable** *adjective* polite and friendly. □ **affably** *adverb*, **affability** *noun*

**affair** *noun* **1** a thing done or to be done; a matter, a concern. **2** (*informal*) an event; a thing; *this camera is a complicated affair.* **3** a temporary sexual relationship between two people who are not married to each other. **4** (**affairs**) public or private business; *current affairs; put your affairs in order.*

**affect** *verb* **1** have an effect on; *the new tax laws affect us all.* **2** arouse sadness or sympathy in; *the news of his death affected us deeply.* **3** (of a disease) attack or infect; *tuberculosis affected his lungs.* **4** pretend to have or feel; *she affected ignorance.* **5** like and make a display of using or wearing; *he affects velvet jackets.*

▪**Usage** The words *affect* and *effect* have totally different meanings and should not be confused.

**affectation** *noun* behaviour that is put on for display and is not natural or genuine.

**affected** *adjective* **1** full of affectation. **2** pretended.

**affection** *noun* **1** love, a liking. **2** a disease or diseased condition.

**affectionate** *adjective* showing affection, loving. □ **affectionately** *adverb*

**affiance** (ă-fy-ăns) *verb* (*literary*) betroth.

**affidavit** (af-i-**day**-vit) *noun* a written statement for use as legal evidence, sworn on oath to be true. (¶ Latin.)

**affiliate** (ă-**fil**-i-ayt) *verb* connect as a subordinate member or branch; *the club is affiliated to a national society.* ●*noun* an affiliated person or organization. □ **affiliation order** an order compelling the father of an illegitimate child to help support it. □ **affiliation** *noun*

**affinity** (ă-**fin**-iti) *noun* **1** a strong natural liking or attraction. **2** relationship (especially by marriage) other than blood-relationship. **3** similarity; close resemblance or connection; *affinities between different languages.* **4** *Chemistry* the tendency of certain substances to combine with others.

**affirm** *verb* **1** assert, state as a fact. **2** make an affirmation instead of an oath.

**affirmation** (af-er-**may**-shŏn) *noun* **1** affirming. **2** a solemn declaration made instead of an oath by a person who has conscientious objections to swearing an oath or who has no religion.

**affirmative** (ă-**ferm**-ătiv) *adjective* affirming, agreeing; *an affirmative reply.* ●*noun* an affirmative word or statement; *the answer is in the affirmative.* □ **affirmatively** *adverb*

**affirmatory** (ă-**fer**-mă-ter-i) *adjective* affirming.

**affix** *verb* (*pronounced* ă-**fiks**) **1** stick on, attach. **2** add in writing; *affix your signature.* ●*noun* (*pronounced* **af**-iks) a prefix or suffix.

**afflict** *verb* distress physically or mentally; be the cause of suffering; *he is afflicted with rheumatism.*

**affliction** *noun* **1** pain, distress, misery. **2** something that causes this.

**affluent** (**af**-loo-ĕnt) *adjective* rich; *the affluent society.* □ **affluently** *adverb*, **affluence** *noun*

**afford** *verb* **1** have enough money, means, or time for a specified purpose; *we can afford to pay £50.* **2** be in a position to do something; *we can't afford to be critical.* **3** (*formal*) provide; *her diary affords no information.*

**afforest** *verb* plant with trees to form a forest. □ **afforestation** *noun*

**affray** (ă-**fray**) *noun* a breach of the peace by fighting or rioting in public.

**affront** (ă-**frunt**) *verb* **1** insult deliberately; offend or embarrass. **2** face, confront. ●*noun* a deliberate insult or show of disrespect.

**Afghan** (**af**-gan) *noun* **1** a native of Afghanistan. **2** the language spoken there, Pashto. **3** (**afghan**) a loose sheepskin coat with shaggy fleece lining. □ **Afghan hound** a tall breed of dog with long silky hair.

**Afghanistan** (af-gan-i-stan) a country in central Asia.

**aficionado** (ă-fis-yon-**ah**-doh) *noun* (*plural* **aficionados**) a devotee of a particular sport or pastime. (¶ Spanish.)

**afield** *adverb* far away from home; to or at a distance.

**aflame** *adverb* & *adjective* in flames, burning.

**afloat** *adverb* & *adjective* **1** floating. **2** at sea, on board ship; *enjoying life afloat.* **3** flooded.

**afoot** *adverb* & *adjective* progressing, in operation; *there's a scheme afoot to improve the roads.*

**aforementioned** *adjective* referred to previously.

**aforesaid** *adjective* mentioned previously.

**aforethought** *adjective* premeditated, planned in advance; *with malice aforethought.*

**a fortiori** (ay-for-ti-**or**-I) *adverb* & *adjective* with yet stronger reason than a conclusion already accepted. (¶ Latin.)

**afraid** *adjective* **1** alarmed, frightened, anxious about consequences. **2** politely regretful; *I'm afraid there's none left.*

**afresh** *adverb* anew, beginning again.

**Africa** a continent south of the Mediterranean Sea between the Atlantic and Indian Oceans.

**African** *adjective* of Africa or its people or languages. ●*noun* a native of Africa, especially a Black person. □ **African violet** an East African plant with purple, pink, or white flowers.

**African National Congress** a South African political party and Black nationalist organization, campaigning for racial equality.

**Afrikaans** (af-ri-**kahns**) *noun* a language developed from Dutch, used in South Africa.

**Afrikaner** (af-ri-**kah**-ner) *noun* a White person in South Africa whose native language is Afrikaans.

**Afro** (**af**-roh) *adjective* (of hair) tightly curled and bushy. ●*noun* (*plural* **Afros**) an Afro hairstyle.

**Afro-** *combining form* African.

**Afro-American** *adjective* of American Blacks or their culture. ●*noun* an American Black.

**Afro-Caribbean** *noun* a Caribbean person of African descent. ●*adjective* of Afro-Caribbeans.

**aft** *adverb* in or near or towards the stern of a ship or the tail of an aircraft.

**after** *preposition* **1** behind in place or order. **2** at a later time than. **3** in spite of; *after all I did for him he still ignored me.* **4** as a result of; *after what he did to my family, I hate him.* **5** in pursuit or search of; *run after him.* **6** about, concerning; *he asked after you.* **7** in imitation of; *painted after the manner of Picasso; named after a person.* ●*adverb* **1** behind; *Jill came tumbling after.* **2** later; *twenty* *years after.* ●*conjunction* at or in a time later than; *they came after I left.* ●*adjective* **1** later, following; *in after years.* **2** nearer the stern in a boat; *the after cabins.* ●*noun* (**afters**) (*informal*) dessert, pudding. □ **after-care** *noun* further care or treatment of a patient who has left hospital; rehabilitation of a discharged prisoner. **after-effect** *noun* an effect that arises or persists after its cause has gone.

**afterbirth** *noun* the placenta and foetal membrane discharged from the womb after childbirth.

**afterlife** *noun* life in a later part of a person's lifetime or after death.

**aftermath** *noun* **1** events or circumstances that follow and are a consequence of an event; *the aftermath of war.* **2** new grass growing after mowing.

**afternoon** *noun* the time from noon to evening.

**afterpains** *plural noun* pains caused by contraction of the womb after childbirth.

**aftershave** *noun* a lotion for use after shaving.

**aftertaste** *noun* a taste that remains after something has been swallowed.

**afterthought** *noun* something thought of or added later.

**afterwards** *adverb* (*Amer.* **afterward**) at a later time.

**Ag** *symbol* silver.

**Aga** (**ah-gă**) *noun* (*trade mark*) a large cooking stove that can also run a heating system.

**again** *adverb* **1** another time, once more; *try again.* **2** as before, to or in the original place or condition; *you'll soon be well again.* **3** furthermore, besides. **4** on the other hand; *I might, and again I might not.*

**against** *preposition* **1** in opposition to. **2** in contrast to; *against a dark background.* **3** in preparation for, in anticipation of; *saved against a rainy day.* **4** opposite, so as to cancel or lessen; *allowances to be set against income.* **5** into collision or contact with; *lean against the wall.*

**Aga Khan** (ah-gă **kahn**) the spiritual leader of Ismaili Muslims.

**Agamemnon** (ag-ă-**mem**-nŏn) (*Gk. legend*) king of Mycenae and leader of the Greek expedition against Troy.

**agape** *adjective* gaping, open-mouthed.

**agar** (ay-gar) *noun* (also **agar-agar**) a substance obtained from seaweed, added to food to thicken it or make it set like jelly.

**agaric** (ag-er-ik) *noun* a fungus with a cap and stalk, e.g. the common mushroom.

**agate** (ag-ăt) *noun* a very hard stone with patches or concentric bands of colour.

**agave** (ă-gah-vi) *noun* a plant with spiny leaves and a tall stem, some kinds of which

are a source of fibre (especially sisal), others of alcoholic drinks, and a few are ornamental.

**age** *noun* **1** the length of time a person has lived or a thing has existed. **2** the later part of life, old age. **3** a historical period, a time with special characteristics or events; *the Elizabethan Age; the atomic age.* **4** (*informal*) a very long time; *it took ages; it seemed an age before he came.* ●*verb* (**aged, ageing**) **1** grow old, show signs of age. **2** become mature; *heavy wines age slowly.* **3** cause to become old; *worry aged him rapidly.* **4** allow to mature. □ **age group** *noun* people who are all of a similar age. **age of consent** the age at which consent to sexual intercourse is valid in law. **age-old** *adjective* having existed for a very long time. **be your age!** (*informal*) behave more sensibly. **of age** having reached the age at which one has an adult's legal rights and obligations. **under age** not yet of age.

**aged** *adjective* **1** (*pronounced* ayjd) of the age of; *aged 10.* **2** (*pronounced* ay-jid) very old; *an aged man.*

**ageism** (**ayj**-izm) *noun* prejudice or discrimination on the grounds of age. □ **ageist** *adjective* & *noun*

**ageless** *adjective* not growing or appearing old.

**agelong** *adjective* existing for a very long time.

**agency** *noun* **1** the business or place of business of an agent; *a travel agency.* **2** the means through which something is done; *fertilized by the agency of bees.*

**agenda** (ă-**jen**-dă) *noun* (*plural* **agendas**) a programme of items of business to be dealt with at a meeting.

**agent** *noun* **1** a person who does something or instigates some activity; *he is a mere instrument, not an agent.* **2** one who acts on behalf of another; *write to our agents in Rome.* **3** something that produces an effect or change; *soda is the active agent.* **4** a spy; a secret agent.

**agent provocateur** (azh-ahn prŏ-vok-ă-ter) (*plural* **agents provocateurs** *pronounced* same) a person employed to detect suspected offenders by tempting them to do something illegal.

**agglomerate** *verb* (*pronounced* ă-glom-er-ayt) collect or become collected into a mass. ●*noun* (*pronounced* ă-**glom**-er-ăt) something composed of clustered fragments. □ **agglomeration** *noun*

**agglutinate** (ă-**gloo**-tin-ayt) *verb* stick or fuse together. □ **agglutination** *noun*, **agglutinative** *adjective*

**aggrandize** (ă-**gran**-dyz) *verb* (also **aggrandise**) increase the power, wealth, or importance of. □ **aggrandizement** *noun*

**aggravate** *verb* **1** make worse or more serious. **2** (*informal*) annoy. □ **aggravation** *noun*

**aggregate** *adjective* (*pronounced* ag-ri-găt) combined, total; *the aggregate amount.* ●*noun* (*pronounced* ag-ri-găt) **1** a total; a mass or amount brought together. **2** hard substances (sand, gravel, broken stone, etc.) mixed with cement to make concrete. ●*verb* (*pronounced* ag-ri-gayt) **1** collect or form into an aggregate, unite. **2** (*informal*) amount to (a total). □ **in the aggregate** as a whole, collectively. □ **aggregation** *noun*

**aggression** *noun* **1** unprovoked attacking. **2** a hostile action, hostile behaviour.

**aggressive** *adjective* **1** apt to make attacks; showing hostility or aggression. **2** self-assertive, forceful; *an aggressive salesman.* □ **aggressively** *adverb*, **aggressiveness** *noun*

**aggressor** *noun* a person or country that attacks first or begins hostilities.

**aggrieved** (ă-greevd) *adjective* made resentful by unfair treatment.

**aggro** *noun* (*slang*) deliberate trouble-making.

**aghast** (ă-gahst) *adjective* filled with consternation.

**agile** *adjective* nimble, quick-moving. □ **agilely** *adverb*, **agility** (ă-jil-iti) *noun*

**Agincourt** (aj-in-kor) a village in northern France, scene of an English victory (1415) under Henry V in the Hundred Years War.

**agitate** *verb* **1** shake or move briskly. **2** disturb, cause anxiety to. **3** stir up public interest or concern. □ **agitation** *noun*, **agitator** *noun*

**agitprop** *noun* the spreading of political propaganda.

**agley** (ă-glay) *adverb* (*Scottish*) askew, awry.

**aglow** *adjective* glowing. ●*adverb* glowingly.

**AGM** *abbreviation* annual general meeting.

**agnail** (ag-nail) *noun* = HANGNAIL.

**Agnes**, St, Christian martyr, whose emblem is a lamb. Feast day, 21 January.

**Agni** (in Hinduism) the Vedic god of fire, who takes offerings to the gods in the smoke of sacrifice and returns to the earth as lightning.

**agnostic** (ag-nos-tik) *noun* a person who believes that nothing can be known about the existence of God or of anything except material things. □ **agnosticism** *noun*

**ago** *adverb* in the past.

**agog** (ă-gog) *adjective* eager, expectant.

**agonize** *verb* (also **agonise**) suffer or cause to suffer mental or physical agony; *he agonized over the decision for weeks.* □ **agonized** *adjective* expressing agony; *an agonized look.* □ **agonizingly** *adverb*

**agony** *noun* extreme mental or physical suffering. □ **agony aunt** (*informal*) the

(female) editor of an agony column. **agony column** the personal column of a newspaper; a regular newspaper or magazine feature offering advice on readers' personal difficulties.

**agoraphobia** (ag-er-ă-foh-biă) *noun* abnormal fear of open spaces or public places. □ **agoraphobic** *noun & adjective*

**AGR** *abbreviation* advanced gas-cooled (nuclear) reactor.

**Agra** (ah-gră) a city on the River Jumna in northern India, site of the Taj Mahal.

**agrarian** (ă-grair-iăn) *adjective* of agricultural land or its cultivation; of landed property.

**agree** *verb* (**agreed, agreeing**) **1** hold a similar opinion. **2** consent, say that one is willing. **3** get on well together. **4** be consistent, harmonize; *your story agrees with what I've heard already.* **5** suit a person's health or digestion; *curry doesn't agree with me.* **6** correspond in grammatical case, number, gender, or person; *the pronoun 'she' agrees with the noun 'woman'; 'he' agrees with 'man'.*

**agreeable** *adjective* **1** pleasing, pleasant; *an agreeable voice.* **2** willing to agree; *we'll go if you are agreeable.* □ **agreeably** *adverb*

**agreement** *noun* **1** agreeing. **2** harmony in opinion or feeling. **3** an arrangement agreed between people.

**agribusiness** *noun* the industries concerned with the manufacture and distribution of agricultural produce or machinery.

**Agricola** (ă-grik-ŏ-lă) (40–93), Roman senator and general, governor of Britain from AD 78.

**agriculture** *noun* the process of cultivating land on a large scale and rearing livestock. □ **agricultural** *adjective*, **agriculturally** *adverb*

**agrimony** (ag-ri-mŏn-i) *noun* a perennial plant with small yellow flowers.

**Agrippa** (ă-grip-ă) (64–12 BC), the right-hand man of Augustus.

**agronomy** (ă-gron-ŏmi) *noun* the science of soil management and crop production.

**aground** *adverb & adjective* on or touching the bottom in shallow water; *the ship ran aground.*

**ague** (ay-gew) *noun* malarial fever; a fit of shivering.

**AH** *abbreviation* (in dates) of the Muslim era. (¶ Short for Latin *anno Hegirae*, in the year of the Hegira.)

**ah** *interjection* an exclamation of surprise, pity, admiration, etc.

**aha** *interjection* an exclamation of surprise, triumph, or mockery.

**ahead** *adverb* further forward in space, time, or progress; *try to plan ahead; full speed ahead!*

**ahem** *interjection* the noise made when clearing one's throat.

**ahimsa** (ă-**him**-să) *noun* (in Hinduism, Buddhism, Jainism) the doctrine of non-violence or non-killing.

**ahoy** *interjection* a cry used by seamen to call attention.

**Ahriman** (ah-ri-măn) the evil spirit in Zoroastrianism.

**Ahura Mazda** (ă-**hoor**-ă maz-dă) (later called *Ormuzd*) the creator god in Zoroastrianism, the force for good.

**AI** *abbreviation* **1** artificial intelligence. **2** artificial insemination.

**AID** *abbreviation* artificial insemination by donor.

**aid** *verb* help. ●*noun* **1** help. **2** something that helps; *a hearing aid*. **3** food, money, etc., sent to a country to help it; *overseas aid*.

**aide** *noun* **1** an aide-de-camp. **2** an assistant.

**aide-de-camp** (ayd-dĕ-**kahng**) *noun* (*plural* **aides-de-camp**, *pronounced* aydz-) a naval or military officer acting as assistant to a senior officer.

**Aids** *abbreviation* (also **AIDS**) acquired immune deficiency syndrome, an often fatal condition that develops after infection with the HIV virus, breaking down a person's natural defences against illness.

**AIH** *abbreviation* artificial insemination by husband.

**aikido** (I-ki-doh) *noun* a Japanese form of self-defence.

**ail** *verb* (*old use*) make ill or uneasy; *what ails him?*

**aileron** (**ail**-er-ŏn) *noun* a hinged flap on an aeroplane wing, used to control balance.

**ailing** *adjective* unwell; in poor condition.

**ailment** *noun* a slight illness.

**aim** *verb* **1** point or send towards a target; direct (a blow, missile, remark, etc.) towards a specified object or goal. **2** attempt, try; *we aim to please the customers*. ●*noun* **1** the act of aiming; *take aim*. **2** purpose, intention; *what is his aim?*

**aimless** *adjective* without a purpose. □ **aimlessly** *adverb*, **aimlessness** *noun*

**ain't** = am not, is not, are not, has not, have not.

▪**Usage** This word is avoided in standard speech except in humorous use, e.g. *she ain't what she used to be*.

**Ainu** (ay-noo) *noun* (*plural* **Ainu** or **Ainus**) a member of the non-Mongoloid aboriginal inhabitants of Japan, with very thick wavy hair.

**air** *noun* **1** the mixture of gases surrounding the earth. **2** the earth's atmosphere; open space in this; this as the place where aircraft operate. **3** an impression given; *an air of mystery*. **4** an impressive manner; *he does*

things with such an air. **5** a melody, a tune. ●*verb* **1** expose to the air, ventilate (a room etc.) so as to freshen it. **2** put (clothes etc.) into a warm place to finish drying. **3** express publicly; *air one's opinions*. □ **air bag** a safety device in a car that fills with air on impact to protect the driver in a collision. **air-bed** *noun* an inflatable mattress. **air brake** a brake worked by compressed air. **air-brick** *noun* a brick with holes in it, used for ventilation. **air-conditioned** *adjective* supplied with **air-conditioning** *noun*, a system controlling the humidity and temperature of the air in a room or building. **air force** a branch of the armed forces that uses aircraft for fighting. **air hostess** a stewardess in a passenger aircraft. **air letter** a folding sheet of light paper that may be sent cheaply by airmail. **air pocket** a partial vacuum in the air causing aircraft in flight to drop suddenly. **air raid** an attack by aircraft dropping bombs. **air rifle** a rifle using compressed air to fire pellets. **air speed** an aircraft's speed relative to the air. **air terminal** a building in a city to which passengers report to be transported to an airport. **air traffic control** airport officials who are responsible for the safe movement of aircraft and who give radio instructions to pilots. **air traffic controller** an official who controls air traffic by radio. **by air** in or by aircraft. **in the air 1** current, exerting an influence; *dissatisfaction is in the air*. **2** (of plans etc.) undecided; uncertain; *these plans are still in the air*. **on the air** broadcast or broadcasting by radio or television. **put on airs** behave in an affected haughty manner.

**airbase** *noun* a base for military aircraft.

**airborne** *adjective* **1** transported by the air; *airborne pollen*. **2** in flight after taking off; *no smoking until the plane is airborne*. **3** transported by aircraft; *airborne troops*.

**airbrush** *noun* a device for spraying paint by means of compressed air.

**Airbus** *noun* (*trade mark*) a short-distance passenger aircraft.

**aircraft** *noun* (*plural* **aircraft**) **1** a machine capable of flight. **2** such craft collectively, including aeroplanes, gliders, and helicopters. □ **aircraft carrier** *noun* a ship that carries and acts as a base for aircraft.

**aircraftman** *noun* the lowest rank in the RAF.

**aircraftwoman** *noun* the lowest rank in the WRAF.

**aircrew** *noun* the crew of an aircraft.

**Airedale** (**air**-dayl) *noun* a large rough-coated terrier.

**airer** *noun* a structure on which clothes are aired.

**airfield** *noun* an area of open level ground equipped with hangars and runways for aircraft.

**airflow** *noun* a flow of air.

**airgun** *noun* a gun in which compressed air propels the missile.

**airless** *adjective* **1** stuffy. **2** without a breeze, calm and still. □ **airlessness** *noun*

**airlift** *noun* large-scale transport of troops or supplies by aircraft, especially in an emergency. ●*verb* transport in this way.

**airline** *noun* a regular service of air transport for public use; a company providing this.

**airliner** *noun* a large passenger aircraft.

**airlock** *noun* **1** a stoppage of the flow in a pump or pipe, caused by an air bubble. **2** a compartment with an airtight door at each end, providing access to a pressurized chamber.

**airmail** *noun* mail carried by air. ●*verb* send by airmail.

**airman** *noun* (*plural* **airmen**) a male member of an air force.

**airplane** *noun* (*Amer.*) = AEROPLANE.

**airplay** *noun* the playing of a record, CD, etc. on radio; *it's had a lot of airplay.*

**airport** *noun* an airfield with facilities for passengers and goods.

**airscrew** *noun* a propeller.

**airship** *noun* a power-driven aircraft that is lighter than air.

**airsick** *adjective* made sick or queasy by the motion of an aircraft. □ **airsickness** *noun*

**airspace** *noun* the atmosphere above a country and subject to its control.

**airstrip** *noun* a strip of ground prepared for aircraft to land and take off.

**airtight** *adjective* not allowing air to enter or escape.

**airwaves** *plural noun* (*informal*) radio waves used in broadcasting.

**airway** *noun* **1** a regular route of aircraft. **2** a ventilating passage in a mine. **3** a passage for air into the lungs; a device to secure this.

**airworthy** *adjective* (of an aircraft) fit to fly. □ **airworthiness** *noun*

**airy** *adjective* (**airier**, **airiest**) **1** well-ventilated. **2** light as air. **3** careless and light-hearted; *an airy manner.* □ **airy-fairy** *adjective* fanciful, impractical. □ **airily** *adverb*, **airiness** *noun*

**aisle** (*rhymes with* mile) *noun* **1** a side part of a church. **2** a gangway between rows of pews or seats.

**aitch** (aych) *noun* the letter H.

**aitchbone** *noun* the rump bone of an animal; a cut of beef lying over this.

**Ajantha** (ă-jun-tă) a village in south central India, with caves containing fine examples of Buddhist frescoes and sculptures.

**ajar** *adverb & adjective* slightly open.

**Ajax** (*Gk. legend*) a Greek hero of the Trojan War.

**Ajman** the smallest emirate of the United Arab Emirates.

**AK** *abbreviation* Alaska.

**aka** *abbreviation* also known as.

**Akela** (ah-kay-lä) *noun* an adult leader of a group of Cub Scouts.

**Akihito** (born 1933), emperor of Japan from 1989.

**akimbo** (ă-kim-boh) *adverb* with hands on hips and elbows pointed outwards.

**akin** *adjective* (usually foll. by *to*) related, similar; *a feeling akin to envy.*

**AL** *abbreviation* Alabama.

**Al** *symbol* aluminium.

**Ala.** *abbreviation* Alabama.

**à la** *preposition* in the style of. (¶ French.)

**Alabama** (al-ă-bam-ă) a State of the south-eastern USA, on the Gulf of Mexico.

**alabaster** (al-ă-bah-ster) *noun* a translucent usually white form of gypsum, often carved into ornaments.

**à la carte** (a lah **kart**) (of a restaurant meal) ordered as separate items from a menu. (¶ French.)

**alacrity** (ă-lak-riti) *noun* prompt and eager readiness.

**Aladdin's cave** a room or box etc. filled with wonderful things. (¶ Named after the hero of an Oriental tale.)

**Alamein** *see* EL ALAMEIN.

**Alamo, the** (al-ă-moh) a mission building in San Antonio, Texas, site of a siege in 1836 during the Texan struggle for independence.

**à la mode** (a lah **mohd**) in fashion, fashionable. (¶ French.)

**alarm** *noun* **1** a warning sound or signal, an apparatus giving this. **2** an alarm clock. **3** fear caused by expectation of danger. ●*verb* arouse to a sense of danger, to frighten. □ **alarm clock** a clock with a device that sounds at a set time.

**alarmist** *noun* a person who raises unnecessary or excessive alarm.

**alas** *interjection* an exclamation of sorrow.

**Alaska** (ă-las-kă) a State of the USA, extending into the Arctic Circle. □ **Alaskan** *adjective & noun*

**alb** *noun* a long white robe worn by some Christian priests.

**albacore** *noun* an edible sea fish with very long fins, a type of tuna.

**Alban** (**awl**-băn), St (3rd century), the first British martyr. Feast day, 20 June.

**Albania** a country between Greece and the former Yugoslavia. □ **Albanian** *adjective & noun*

**albatross** *noun* **1** a long-winged sea bird related to the petrel. **2** a constant burden or encumbrance. **3** (in golf) a score of 3 under par at a hole.

**albeit** (awl-**bee**-it) *conjunction* although.

**Albert**, Prince (1819–61), prince of Saxe-Coburg-Gotha, consort of his cousin Queen Victoria, whom he married in 1840.

**Alberta** (al-**ber**-tă) a province of western Canada.

**albino** (al-**bee**-noh) *noun* (*plural* **albinos**) a person or animal with no colouring pigment in the skin and hair (which are white) and the eyes (which are pink).

**Albinoni** (al-bi-**noh**-ni) Tomaso (1671–1750), Italian composer.

**Albion** (**al**-bi-ŏn) (*poetic*) Britain.

**album** *noun* **1** a book for autographs, photographs, postage stamps, etc. **2** a long-playing record.

**albumen** (**al**-bew-min) *noun* white of egg.

**albumin** *noun* water-soluble protein found in egg white, milk, blood, etc.

**Alcatraz** (al-kă-**traz**) a rocky island in San Francisco Bay, California, formerly (1934–62) the site of a top-security Federal prison.

**alchemy** (**al**-kĕmi) *noun* a medieval form of chemistry, the chief aim of which was to discover how to turn ordinary metals into gold. □ **alchemist** *noun*

**Alcock** (**awl**-kok), Sir John William (1892–1919), English aviator, who with Sir A. W. Brown made the first direct non-stop transatlantic flight (14–15 June 1919).

**alcohol** *noun* **1** a colourless inflammable liquid, the intoxicant present in wine, beer, whisky, etc. **2** any liquor containing this. **3** a chemical compound of this type.

**alcoholic** *adjective* **1** of or containing alcohol. **2** caused by drinking alcohol. ●*noun* a person suffering from alcoholism.

**alcoholism** *noun* a diseased condition caused by continual heavy drinking of alcohol.

**Alcott** (**awl**-kot), Louisa May (1832–88), American novelist, author of *Little Women*.

**alcove** *noun* a recess in a wall.

**Aldebaran** (al-**deb**-er-ăn) the brightest star in the constellation Taurus.

**aldehyde** (**al**-di-hyd) *noun* **1** a fluid with a suffocating smell, obtained from alcohol. **2** a compound with the same structure.

**al dente** (al **den**-tay) (of pasta or vegetables) cooked so as to be still firm when bitten. (¶ Italian, = 'to the tooth'.)

**alder** (**awl**-der) *noun* a tree of the birch family.

**alderman** (**awl**-der-măn) *noun* (*plural* **aldermen**) **1** (mainly *hist.*) a co-opted member of an English county or borough council, next in dignity to the mayor. **2** an elected member of the municipal governing

body in Australian and some American cities.

**Alderney** (**awl**-der-ni) one of the Channel Islands. ●*noun* a breed of small dairy cattle that originated in Alderney.

**ale** *noun* beer. □ **real ale** beer regarded as brewed and stored in the traditional way, with secondary fermentation in the container from which it is dispensed.

**aleatory** (**ay**-li-ă-ter-i) *adjective* depending on random choice.

**Alekhine** (**al**-i-keen *or* **al**-yĕ-kin), Alexander (1892–1946), Russian chess-player, world champion 1927–35 and 1937–46.

**alembic** (ă-**lem**-bik) *noun* an apparatus formerly used in distilling.

**alert** *adjective* watchful, observant. ●*noun* **1** a state of watchfulness or readiness. **2** a warning of danger; notice to stand ready. ●*verb* warn of danger, make alert. □ **on the alert** on the lookout, watchful. □ **alertness** *noun*

**Aleut** (ă-**lewt**) *noun* a native or the language of the Aleutian Islands.

**Aleutian Islands** (ă-**lew**-shăn) (also **Aleutians**) a group of islands in US possession, extending south-west from Alaska.

**A level** = ADVANCED LEVEL.

**Alexander** 'the Great' (356–323 BC), king of Macedon from 336 BC.

**Alexander Nevski** (**nef**-ski) (1220–63), Russian saint and national hero, called 'Nevski' from the River Neva, on the banks of which he defeated the Swedes.

**Alexander technique** a method of controlling posture as an aid to well-being.

**Alexandria** the chief port of Egypt, named after its founder Alexander the Great.

**alexandrine** (al-ig-**zan**-dryn) *noun* a verse of six iambic feet. ●*adjective* of or in this metre.

**alfalfa** (al-**fal**-fă) *noun* lucerne.

**Alfonso** the name of 13 kings of parts of Spain, of whom the last, Alfonso XIII (1886–1941), was forced to abdicate when a republic was established in 1931.

**Alfred** 'the Great' (849–99), king of Wessex from 871.

**alfresco** (al-**fres**-koh) *adjective & adverb* in the open air; *eating alfresco*. (¶ Italian.)

**algae** (**al**-jee) *noun* (*singular* **alga**, *pronounced* **al**-gă) water plants with no true stems or leaves.

**Algarve** (al-**garv**) the southernmost province of Portugal, on the Atlantic coast.

**algebra** (**al**-jib-ră) *noun* a branch of mathematics in which letters and symbols are used to represent quantities. □ **algebraic** (alji-**bray**-ik) *adjective*, **algebraically** *adverb*

**Algeria** a country in North Africa on the Mediterranean coast. □ **Algerian** *adjective & noun*

**Algiers** (al-**jeerz**) the capital of Algeria.

**Algonquian** (al-**gon**-kwi-ăn) *noun* (also **Algonkian**) **1** a member of a large group of North American Indian tribes speaking related languages. **2** any of their languages or dialects. ● *adjective* of this people or their languages.

**Algonquin** (al-gon-**kwin**) *noun* **1** an American Indian of a people in the districts of Ottawa and Quebec. **2** their language. ● *adjective* of this people or their language.

**algorithm** (al-ger-*ith*ĕm) *noun* a procedure or set of rules for solving a problem, especially by computer. □ **algorithmic** (al-ger-ith-mik) *adjective*

**Alhambra** a fortified Moorish palace built in 1248–1354 near Granada in Spain.

**Ali** (ah-li), Muhammad (original name; Cassius Clay) (born 1942), American world champion heavyweight boxer.

**alias** (ay-li-ăs) *noun* (*plural* **aliases**) a false name, an assumed name; *Brown had several aliases.* ● *adverb* known as; also called; *John Brown, alias Peter Harrison.*

**Ali Baba** (al-i **bah**-bă) the hero of a story from the *Arabian Nights*, who discovered the magic formula ('Open, Sesame!') which opened the cave in which forty robbers kept their stolen treasure.

**alibi** (al-i-by) *noun* (*plural* **alibis**) **1** evidence that an accused person was elsewhere when a crime was committed. **2** (*informal*) an excuse, an answer to an accusation.

▪**Usage** The use in sense 2 is considered incorrect by some people.

**alien** (ay-li-ĕn) *noun* **1** a person who is not a subject of the country in which he or she is living. **2** a being from another world. ● *adjective* **1** foreign, not one's own, unfamiliar; *alien customs.* **2** of a different nature; contrary; *cruelty is alien to her character.*

**alienable** *adjective Law* able to be transferred to new ownership.

**alienate** (ay-li-ĕn-ayt) *verb* cause to become unfriendly or hostile. □ **alienation** *noun*

**alight**¹ *verb* **1** get down from a horse or a vehicle. **2** descend and settle; *the bird alighted on a branch.*

**alight**² *adjective* on fire, lit up.

**align** (ă-lyn) *verb* **1** place in line, bring into line. **2** join as an ally; *they aligned themselves with the Liberals.* □ **alignment** *noun*

**alike** *adjective & adverb* like one another; in the same way.

**alimentary** (ali-ment-er-i) *adjective* of food or nutrition; nourishing. □ **alimentary canal** the tubular passage through which food passes from mouth to anus in the process of being digested.

**alimony** (al-i-mŏni) *noun* an allowance payable to a spouse or former spouse after a legal separation or divorce.

▪**Usage** In UK usage this is now called *maintenance.*

**A-line** *adjective* (of a skirt) not gathered at the waist and only very slightly flared.

**aliphatic** (al-i-fat-ik) *adjective* (of chemical compounds) related to fats; in which carbon atoms form open chains.

**aliquot** (al-i-kwot) *Maths* ● *adjective* that produces a quotient without a fraction when a given larger number is divided by it. ● *noun* **1** an aliquot part. **2** a representative portion of a substance.

**alive** *adjective* **1** living. **2** (foll. by *to*) alert; *he is alive to the possible dangers.* **3** active, lively. **4** (foll. by *with*) swarming with; full of; *the place was alive with policemen.*

**alkali** (al-kă-ly) *noun* (*plural* **alkalis**) any of a class of substances (such as caustic soda, potash, and ammonia) that neutralize and are neutralized by acids, have a pH of more than 7, and form caustic or corrosive solutions in water. □ **alkaline** (al-kă-lyn) *adjective*, **alkalinity** (alkă-lin-iti) *noun*

**alkaloid** (al-kă-loid) *noun* any of a large group of nitrogen-containing substances derived from plants, many of which are used in medicine, e.g. morphine, quinine.

**alkane** *noun* any of a series of saturated aliphatic hydrocarbons, including methane, ethane, and propane.

**alkene** *noun* any of a series of unsaturated aliphatic hydrocarbons, including ethylene and propene.

**alkyl** (al-kil) *adjective* from or related to a hydrocarbon of the paraffin series.

**alkyne** *noun* any of a series of unsaturated aliphatic hydrocarbons containing a triple bond, including acetylene.

**all** *adjective* the whole amount, number, or extent of; *waited all day; beyond all doubt.* ● *noun* all persons concerned, everything; *all are agreed; all is lost; the score is four all.* ● *adverb* entirely, quite; *dressed all in white; an all-powerful dictator.* □ **all along** from the beginning; *I knew all along.* **All Blacks** the New Zealand international Rugby football team, so called from the colour of their uniforms. **all but** very little short of; very nearly; *it is all but impossible.* **all-clear** *noun* a signal that a danger is over. **all comers** *plural noun* anyone who applies, accepts a challenge, etc. **All Fools' Day** = APRIL FOOL'S DAY, 1 April. **all for** (*informal*) much in favour of. **all found** with board and lodging provided free. **all in** (*informal*) exhausted. **all-in** *adjective* including everything; *the all-in price.* **all-in wrestling** freestyle wrestling. **all in all** everything considered. **all one to** a matter of indifference to. **all out** using all possible strength, energy, or speed. **all right 1** as desired, satisfactorily. **2** in good condition; safe and sound. **3** yes, I consent. **all-round** *adjective* general, not specialized; *a good all-round education; an all-round athlete.* **All Saints' Day** 1 November. **all set** (*informal*) ready to start. **All Souls' Day** 2 November. **all there** (*informal*) mentally alert; *not quite all there.* **all the same 1** in spite of this. **2** making no difference. **all-time** *adjective* unsurpassed; *an all-time record.* **be all eyes** *or* **ears** be watching or listening intently. **on all fours** crawling on hands and knees.

**Allah** (**al-ă**) the Muslim and Arab name of God.

**Allahabad** (al-ă-hă-**bahd**) an Indian city at the confluence of the River Jumna with the Ganges. It is a place of Hindu pilgrimage.

**allay** (ă-**lay**) *verb* (**allayed, allaying**) calm, put at rest; *to allay suspicion.*

**allegation** (ali-**gay**-shŏn) *noun* a statement or accusation, especially one made without proof.

**allege** (ă-**lej**) *verb* declare (especially to those doubting one's truthfulness) without proof; *alleging that he was innocent; the alleged culprit.*

**allegedly** (ă-**lej**-idli) *adverb* according to allegation.

**Allegheny Mountains** (al-i-**gay**-ni) (also **Alleghenies**) a mountain range forming part of the Appalachians in the eastern USA.

**allegiance** (ă-**lee**-jăns) *noun* support of a government, sovereign, cause, etc.

**allegorize** (al-ig-er-ryz) *verb* (also **allegorise**) treat as an allegory or by means of an allegory.

**allegory** (al-ig-er-i) *noun* a story or description in which the characters and events symbolize some deeper underlying meaning. □ **allegorical** (alig-o-ri-kăl) *noun,* **allegorically** *adverb*

**allegretto** (ali-**gret**-oh) *adverb* (in music) in fairly brisk time. ● *noun* (*plural* **allegrettos**) a movement to be played in this way.

**allegro** (ă-**lay**-groh) *adverb* (in music) fast and lively. ● *noun* (*plural* **allegros**) a movement to be played in this way.

**alleluia** *interjection & noun* (also **hallelujah**) praise to God.

**Allen**[1] (*trade mark*) □ **Allen key** a kind of spanner designed to fit and turn an **Allen screw**, a screw with a hexagonal socket in the head.

**Allen**[2], Woody (original name: Allen Stewart Konigsberg) (born 1935), American film comedian, director, and scriptwriter.

**Allende** (a-**yen**-di), Salvador (1908–73), President of Chile 1970–3.

**allergen** (**al**-er-jin) *noun* an allergenic substance.

**allergenic** (al-er-**jen**-ik) *adjective* causing an allergic reaction.

**allergic** (ă-**ler**-jik) *adjective* **1** (foll. by *to*) having an allergy to something. **2** caused by an allergy; *an allergic reaction.* **3** (*informal*) (foll. by *to*) having a strong dislike of something; *allergic to hard work.*

**allergy** (**al**-er-ji) *noun* a condition producing an unfavourable reaction to certain foods, pollens, etc.

**alleviate** (ă-**lee**-vi-ayt) *verb* lessen, make less severe; *to alleviate pain.* □ **alleviation** *noun*

**alley** *noun* (*plural* **alleys**) **1** (also **alleyway**) a narrow passage or street between buildings. **2** a path bordered by hedges or shrubbery. **3** a long channel for balls in games such as tenpin bowling and skittles.

**alliance** *noun* a union or association formed for mutual benefit, especially of countries by treaty or families by marriage.

**allied** *see* ALLY. ● *adjective* of the same general kind, similar.

**alligator** *noun* a reptile of the crocodile family, found especially in the rivers of tropical America and China.

**alliteration** (ă-lit-er-ay-shŏn) *noun* the occurrence of the same letter or sound at the beginning of several words in succession, e.g. *sing a song of sixpence.* □ **alliterative** (ă-**lit**-er-ătiv) *adjective*

**allocate** (**al**-ŏ-kayt) *verb* (usually foll. by *to*) allot or assign to (a person, place, etc.). □ **allocation** *noun,* **allocator** *noun*

**allot** (ă-**lot**) *verb* (**allotted, allotting**) distribute officially, give as a share of things available or tasks to be done.

**allotment** *noun* **1** allotting. **2** a share allotted. **3** a small area of public land let out for cultivation.

**allotrope** (**al**-ŏ-trohp) *noun* one of the forms of an element that exists in different physical forms; *diamond and graphite are allotropes of carbon.*

**allotropy** (ă-**lot**-rŏ-pi) *noun* the existence of several forms of a chemical element in the same state (gas, liquid, or solid) but with different physical or chemical properties. □ **allotropic** (al-ŏ-**trop**-ik) *adjective*

**allow** *verb* **1** permit; *dogs are not allowed in the park.* **2** permit to have, give a limited quantity or sum; *allow him £200 a year.* **3** add or deduct in estimating; *allow 10% for inflation; allow for shrinkage.* **4** agree that something is true or acceptable; *I allow that you have been patient.*

**allowable** *adjective* able to be allowed. □ **allowably** *adverb*

**allowance** noun **1** allowing. **2** an amount or sum allowed. □ **make allowances for** to be lenient towards or because of; *make allowances for his youth.*

**allowedly** adverb as is generally admitted or agreed.

**alloy** noun (*pronounced* al-oi) **1** a metal formed of a mixture of metals or of metal and another substance. **2** an inferior metal mixed with one of greater value. ●verb (*pronounced* ă-**loi**) (**alloyed, alloying**) **1** mix with metal(s) of lower value. **2** weaken or spoil by something that reduces value or pleasure.

**allspice** noun **1** spice made from the dried and ground berries of the pimento. **2** this berry.

**allude** (ă-**lewd**) verb refer briefly or indirectly in speaking; *he alluded to the troubles in Ireland.*

**allure** (ăl-**yoor**) verb entice, attract. ●noun attractiveness. □ **allurement** noun

**alluring** adjective attractive, charming.

**allusion** noun (often foll. by *to*) a brief or indirect reference to something.

**allusive** (ă-**loo**-siv) adjective containing allusions. □ **allusively** adverb

**alluvial** (ă-**loo**-viăl) adjective made of soil and sand left by rivers or floods.

**alluvium** (ă-**loo**-viŭm) noun an alluvial deposit.

**ally** noun (*pronounced* al-**I**) **1** a country in alliance with another. **2** a person who cooperates with another. ●verb (*pronounced* ăl-**I**) (**allied, allying**) form an alliance. □ **the Allies** the nations allied in opposition to Germany and her supporters in each of the two World Wars.

**Alma Mater** (al-mă **mah**-ter) noun one's university, college, or school.

**almanac** (**awl**-măn-ak) noun (also **almanack**) **1** an annual publication containing a calendar with times of sunrise and sunset, astronomical data, dates of anniversaries, and sometimes other information. **2** a yearbook of sport, theatre, etc.

**Alma-Tadema** (al-mă-**tad**-imă), Sir Lawrence (1836–1912), Dutch-born painter who settled in England.

**almighty** adjective **1** all-powerful. **2** (*informal*) very great; *an almighty nuisance.* ●adverb (*slang*) very; *almighty glad.* □ **the Almighty** God.

**almond** (**ah**-mŏnd) noun **1** the kernel of the fruit of a tree related to the peach. **2** this tree. □ **almond-eyed** adjective having eyes that appear to narrow and slant upwards at the outer corners.

**almoner** (**ah**-mŏn-er) noun **1** an official distributor of alms. **2** (*hist.*) a social worker attached to a hospital, seeing to the aftercare of patients.

■**Usage** The usual term now for sense 2 is *medical social worker.*

**almonry** (**ah**-mŏn-ri) noun a place for the distribution of alms.

**almost** adverb all but, nearly.

**alms** (*pronounced* ahmz) noun (*old use*) money and gifts given to the poor.

**almshouse** noun (*hist.*) a house founded by charity for poor people.

**aloe** noun **1** a plant with thick sharp-pointed leaves and bitter juice. **2** (**aloes;** in full **bitter aloes**) a strong laxative made from aloe juice.

**aloft** adverb high up; up in the air.

**alone** adjective not with others; without the company or help of others or other things. ●adverb only, exclusively; *you alone can help.*

**along** adverb **1** onward; *push it along.* **2** through part or the whole of a thing's length; *along by the hedge.* **3** with oneself, or others; *I brought my sister along; I'll be along soon.* ●preposition close to or parallel with the length of something; *along the wall.* □ **along with** together with; in addition to.

**alongside** adverb close to the side of a ship or pier. ●preposition beside.

**aloof** adverb apart; *he kept aloof.* ●adjective unconcerned, cool and remote in character, not friendly. □ **aloofly** adverb, **aloofness** noun

**alopecia** (alŏ-**pee**-shă) noun *Med.* loss or absence of hair; baldness.

**aloud** adverb in a voice loud enough to be heard, not silently or in a whisper.

**alp** noun **1** a high mountain. **2** (**the Alps**) a high range of mountains in Switzerland and adjoining countries. **3** pasture land on mountains in Switzerland.

**alpaca** (al-**pak**-ă) noun **1** a llama of South America, with long wool. **2** its wool; fabric made from this.

**alpenhorn** noun a long wooden horn formerly used by herdsmen in the Alps.

**alpenstock** noun a long iron-tipped stick used in mountain-climbing.

**alpha** (al-fă) noun **1** the first letter of the Greek alphabet (A, α); a first-class mark for a piece of work. **2** (in names of stars) the chief star in a constellation. □ **alpha and omega** the beginning and the end. **alpha particles** (*or* **rays**) helium nuclei emitted by radioactive substances (originally regarded as rays).

**alphabet** noun **1** the letters used in writing a language. **2** a list of these in a set order.

**alphabetical** adjective in the order of the letters of the alphabet. □ **alphabetically** adverb

**alphabetize** *verb* (also **alphabetise**) put into alphabetical order. □ **alphabetization** *noun*

**alphanumeric** (al-fă-new-merrik) *adjective* containing both letters and numbers.

**alpine** *adjective* **1** of high mountains; growing on these. **2** (**Alpine**) of the Alps. ●*noun* a plant suited to mountain regions or grown in rock-gardens.

**already** *adverb* **1** before this time; *had already gone.* **2** as early as this; *is he back already?*

**alright** *adverb* = ALL RIGHT.

■**Usage** This spelling is considered incorrect by many people.

**Alsace** (al-sas) a province of northern France, west of the Rhine.

**Alsatian** (al-say-shăn) *noun* (also **German shepherd**) a dog of a large strong breed, often trained as police dogs. ●*adjective* of Alsace.

**also** *adverb* in addition, besides. □ **also-ran** *noun* **1** a horse or dog not among the first three to finish in a race. **2** a person who fails to win distinction.

**Alta.** *abbreviation* Alberta.

**Altai Mountains** (al-ty) a range of mountains in Central Asia.

**Altamira** (altă-meer-ă) the site of a cave in northern Spain with palaeolithic paintings.

**altar** *noun* **1** the table on which bread and wine are consecrated in the Communion service. **2** any structure on which offerings are made to a god.

**altarpiece** *noun* a painting behind an altar.

**Altdorfer** (alt-dor-fer), Albrecht (*c.*1485–1538), German painter.

**alter** *verb* make or become different, change in character, position, etc.; *alter a garment; alter the clock.* □ **alteration** *noun*

**altercation** (ol-ter-kay-shŏn) *noun* a noisy dispute or quarrel.

**alter ego** (awl-ter ee-goh) **1** one's hidden or second self. **2** a close friend.

**alternate** *adjective* (*pronounced* ol-ter-năt) happening or following in turns, first the one and then the other; *on alternate days.* ●*verb* (*pronounced* ol-ter-nayt) **1** arrange, perform, or occur alternately. **2** consist of alternate things. □ **alternate angles** two angles, not adjoining one another, formed on opposite sides of a line that intersects two other lines. **alternating current** electric current that reverses its direction at regular intervals. □ **alternately** *adverb*, **alternation** *noun*

■**Usage** See the note on **alternative**.

**alternative** (ol-ter-nă-tiv) *adjective* **1** available in place of something else. **2** unconventional; not traditional; *alternative medi-*cine; *alternative comedy.* ●*noun* one of two or more possibilities. □ **alternatively** *adverb*

■**Usage** Do not confuse *alternative* with *alternate*; *alternative colours* means that one colour can be chosen instead of another or others, *alternate colours* means that there is first one colour then another.

**Alternative Service Book** a book containing the public liturgy of the Church of England published in 1980 as the alternative to the Book of Common Prayer.

**alternator** (ol-ter-nay-ter) *noun* a dynamo giving alternating current.

**although** *conjunction* though.

**altimeter** (al-ti-meet-er) *noun* an instrument used in aircraft showing the height above sea level.

**altitude** *noun* **1** the height above sea level. **2** the distance of a star etc. above the horizon, measured as an angle.

**alto** (al-toh) *noun* (*plural* **altos**) **1** the highest adult male singing-voice. **2** a contralto. **3** a singer with such a voice; a part written for it. **4** a musical instrument with the second or third highest pitch in its group; *alto-saxophone.*

**altogether** *adverb* **1** entirely, totally. **2** on the whole. □ **in the altogether** nude.

■**Usage** Do not confuse with *all together* meaning 'all at once' or 'all in one place'.

**altruism** (al-troo-izm) *noun* unselfishness. □ **altruist** *noun*, **altruistic** *adjective*, **altruistically** *adverb*

**alum** (al-ŭm) *noun* a white mineral salt used in medicine and in dyeing.

**alumina** (ă-loo-min-ă) *noun* an oxide of aluminium, e.g. corundum.

**aluminium** *noun* a chemical element (symbol Al), a lightweight silvery metal.

**aluminize** (ă-lew-mi-nyz) *verb* (also **aluminise**) coat with aluminium.

**alumna** (ă-lum-nă) *noun* (*plural* **alumnae**) a female former pupil or student.

**alumnus** (ă-lum-nŭs) *noun* (*plural* **alumni**, *pronounced* ă-lum-ny) a former pupil or student.

**always** *adverb* **1** at all times, on all occasions. **2** whatever the circumstances; *you can always sleep on the floor.* **3** repeatedly; *he is always complaining.*

**alyssum** (al-iss-ŭm) *noun* a plant with small usually yellow or white flowers.

**Alzheimer's disease** (alts-hy-měrz) a brain disorder causing senility.

**AM** *abbreviation* amplitude modulation.

**Am** *symbol* americium.

**am** *see* BE.

**a.m.** *abbreviation* before noon. (¶ From the Latin *ante meridiem*.)

**amah** (ah-mă) *noun* (formerly in the Far East and India) a nursemaid or maid.

**amalgam** *noun* **1** an alloy of mercury and another metal, used especially in dental fillings. **2** any soft pliable mixture.

**amalgamate** *verb* mix; combine. □ **amalgamation** *noun*

**amanuensis** (ă-man-yoo-en-sis) *noun* (*plural* **amanuenses**) a literary assistant, especially one who writes from dictation.

**amaryllis** (amă-ril-iss) *noun* a lily-like plant growing from a bulb.

**amass** (ă-mass) *verb* heap up; collect; *amassed a large fortune.*

**amateur** (am-ă-ter) *noun* a person who does something as a pastime rather than as a profession.

**amateurish** (am-ă-ter-ish) *adjective* inexpert, lacking professional skill. □ **amateurishly** *adverb*, **amateurishness** *noun*

**Amati** (ă-mah-ti) the name of an Italian family of violin-makers, working in the 16th and 17th centuries.

**amatory** (am-ă-ter-i) *adjective* showing sexual love.

**amaze** *verb* overwhelm with wonder. □ **amazement** *noun*

**Amazon 1** (*Gk. myth.*) a woman of a race of female warriors. **2** a great river in South America flowing into the Atlantic Ocean on the north coast of Brazil. (¶ So named because of a legend that a race of female warriors lived somewhere on its banks.) ●*noun* (**amazon**) a tall and strong or athletic woman. □ **Amazonian** (am-ă-zoh-niăn) *adjective*

**ambassador** *noun* **1** a diplomat sent by one country as a permanent representative or on a special mission to another. **2** an official messenger. □ **ambassadorial** (am-bas-ă-dor-iăl) *adjective*

**amber** *noun* **1** a hardened clear yellowish-brown resin used for making ornaments. **2** a yellow traffic-light shown as a cautionary signal between red and green. ●*adjective* **1** made of amber. **2** coloured like amber.

**ambergris** (am-ber-grees) *noun* a wax-like substance found floating in tropical seas and present in the intestines of sperm whales, used as a fixative in perfumes.

**ambidextrous** (ambi-deks-trŭs) *adjective* able to use either hand equally well.

**ambience** (am-bi-ĕns) *noun* environment, surroundings.

**ambient** *adjective* surrounding; *ambient temperature.*

**ambiguous** (am-big-yoo-ŭs) *adjective* **1** having two or more possible meanings. **2** doubtful, uncertain; *the outcome is ambiguous.* □ **ambiguously** *adverb*, **ambiguity** (ambig-yoo-iti) *noun*

**ambit** *noun* the bounds, scope, or extent of something.

**ambition** *noun* **1** a strong desire to achieve something. **2** the object of this.

**ambitious** (am-bish-ŭs) *adjective* full of ambition. □ **ambitiously** *adverb*

**ambivalent** (am-biv-ălĕnt) *adjective* with mixed feelings towards a certain object or situation. □ **ambivalently** *adverb*, **ambivalence** *noun*

**amble** *verb* walk at a slow easy pace. ●*noun* a slow easy pace.

**Ambrose**, St (*c.*339–97), bishop of Milan. Feast day, 7 December.

**ambrosia** (am-broh-ziă) *noun* **1** (*Gk. & Rom. myth.*) the food of the gods. **2** something delicious.

**ambulance** *noun* a vehicle equipped to carry sick or injured people.

**ambulatory** (am-bew-lă-ter-i) *adjective* **1** of or for walking. **2** movable. ●*noun* a place for walking, as in a cloister.

**ambuscade** (am-bŭs-kayd) *noun* an ambush. ●*verb* ambush.

**ambush** *noun* **1** the placing of troops etc. in a concealed position to make a surprise attack. **2** such an attack. ●*verb* lie in wait for, attack from an ambush.

**ameba** Amer. spelling of AMOEBA.

**ameliorate** (ă-mee-li-er-ayt) *verb* make or become better. □ **amelioration** *noun*

**amen** (ah-men *or* ay-men) *interjection* (in prayers) so be it.

**amenable** (ă-meen-ăbŭl) *adjective* **1** willing to be guided or controlled by some influence; *he is not amenable to discipline.* **2** subject to a legal authority; *we are all amenable to the law.* □ **amenably** *adverb*, **amenability** *noun*

**amend** *verb* correct an error in; make minor alterations in; *they amended the agreement.* □ **make amends** compensate or make up for something.

▪**Usage** *Amend* is often confused with *emend*, a more technical word used for the correction of text.

**amendment** *noun* a minor alteration or addition in a document, statement, etc.

**amenity** (ă-meen-iti) *noun* **1** pleasantness of a place or circumstance. **2** a feature of a place etc. that makes life there easy or pleasant.

**America 1** (also **the Americas**) a continent of the western hemisphere consisting of the two great land masses, North America and South America, joined by the narrow isthmus of Central America. **2** the USA.

**American** *adjective* **1** of the continent of America. **2** of the USA. ●*noun* **1** a native of America. **2** a citizen of the USA. **3** the English language as spoken in the USA.

□ **American dream** the ideals of democracy, equality, and prosperity. **American football** a form of football played in the USA between two teams of 11 players with an oval ball and an H-shaped goal, on a field marked out as a gridiron. **American Indian** *see* INDIAN. **American tournament** one in which each competitor plays each of the others in turn. **American Legion** *see* LEGION.

**Americanism** *noun* a word or phrase used in American English but not in standard English in Britain.

**Americanize** *verb* (also **Americanise**) make American in form or character. □ **Americanization** *noun*

**America's Cup** an international yachting trophy named after the yacht *America*, which won it in 1851.

**americium** (am-er-iss-iŭm) *noun* an artificially made radioactive metallic element (symbol Am), which emits gamma radiation.

**Amerindian** *adjective & noun* (also **Amerind**) = AMERICAN INDIAN (*see* INDIAN).

**amethyst** (am-i-thist) *noun* a semiprecious stone, purple or violet quartz.

**Amharic** (am-ha-rik) *noun* the official and trade language of Ethiopia. ● *adjective* of this language.

**amiable** (aym-i-ăbŭl) *adjective* feeling and inspiring friendliness; good-tempered. □ **amiably** *adverb*, **amiability** *noun*

**amicable** (am-ik-ăbŭl) *adjective* friendly. □ **amicably** *adverb*, **amicability** *noun*

**amid**, **amidst** *preposition* in the middle of, during; *amid shouts of dismay.*

**amide** (a-myd) *noun* a compound in which an acid radical or metal atom replaces a hydrogen atom of ammonia.

**amidships** *adverb* in the middle of a ship.

**amine** (ay-meen) *noun* a compound in which an alkyl or other non-acidic radical replaces a hydrogen atom of ammonia.

**amino acid** (ă-mee-noh) an organic acid found in proteins.

**amir** alternative spelling of EMIR.

**Amis** (ay-miss), Sir Kingsley (born 1922), English novelist and poet, author of *Lucky Jim*, and son Martin Louis (born 1949), English novelist.

**amiss** *adjective* wrong, out of order; *something is amiss.* ● *adverb* wrongly; faultily; *don't take this amiss.*

**amity** *noun* friendly feeling.

**Amman** (ă-mahn) the capital of Jordan.

**ammeter** (am-it-er) *noun* an instrument that measures electric current, usually in amperes.

**ammo** *noun* (*informal*) ammunition.

**ammonia** *noun* **1** a colourless gas with a strong smell. **2** a solution of this in water.

**ammonite** (am-ŏ-nyt) *noun* the fossil of a coil-shaped shell.

**ammunition** *noun* **1** a supply of bullets, shells, grenades, etc. **2** facts and reasoning used to prove a point.

**amnesia** (am-nee-ziă) *noun* loss of memory. □ **amnesiac** *adjective & noun*

**amnesty** (am-nis-ti) *noun* a general pardon, especially for offences against the State.

**Amnesty International** an international organization whose aim is to publicize violations of human rights and obtain the release of political prisoners.

**amniocentesis** (amni-ŏ-sen-tee-sis) *noun* a prenatal test for foetal abnormality in which a hollow needle is inserted into the womb to withdraw a sample of the fluid there for analysis.

**amnion** *noun* (*plural* **amnia**) the innermost membrane enclosing an embryo.

**amniotic fluid** the fluid that surrounds a foetus in the womb.

**amoeba** (ă-mee-bă) *noun* (*Amer.* **ameba**) (*plural* **amoebae** (*pronounced* ă-mee-bee) or **amoebas**) a microscopic organism consisting of a single cell which changes shape constantly.

**amok** *adverb* (also **amuck**) □ **run amok** run wild.

**among** *preposition* (also **amongst**) **1** surrounded by; in with; *poppies amongst the corn.* **2** in the number of; *this is reckoned among his best works.* **3** within the limits of, between; *have only £5 amongst us; quarrelled among themselves.*

**Amontillado** (ă-mon-til-ah-doh) *noun* a medium dry sherry of a matured type.

**amoral** (ay-mo-răl) *adjective* not based on moral standards, neither moral nor immoral.

**amorous** (am-er-ŭs) *adjective* of, showing, or readily feeling sexual love. □ **amorously** *adverb*

**amorphous** (ă-mor-fŭs) *adjective* having no definite shape or form.

**amortize** (ă-mor-tyz) *verb* (also **amortise**) pay off (a debt) gradually by money regularly put aside.

**Amos** (ay-moss) **1** a Hebrew minor prophet (*c.*760 BC). **2** the book of the Old Testament containing his prophecies.

**amount** *noun* **1** the total of anything. **2** a quantity; *a small amount of salt.* ● *verb* (foll. by *to*) **1** add up to. **2** be equivalent to.

**amour** (a-moor) *noun* a love affair, especially a secret one.

**amour propre** (a-moor propr) *noun* self-respect. (¶ French.)

**amp** *noun* **1** an ampere. **2** (*informal*) an amplifier.

**amperage** (am-per-ij) *noun* the strength of electric current, measured in amperes.

**ampere** (am-pair) *noun* a unit for measuring electric current (symbol A). (¶ Named after the French physicist A. M. Ampère (1775–1836).)

**ampersand** *noun* the sign '&' (= and).

**amphetamine** (am-fet-ă-meen) *noun* a drug used as a stimulant or to relieve congestion.

**amphibian** (am-fib-iăn) *noun* **1** an animal able to live both on land and in water; one (e.g. a frog) that develops through a stage in which it lives in water, to an adult state in which it breathes air. **2** an aircraft that can take off from and alight on both land and water. **3** a vehicle that can move on both land and water.

**amphibious** (am-fib-iŭs) *adjective* **1** living or operating both on land and in water. **2** involving both sea and land forces; *amphibious operations*.

**amphitheatre** *noun* (*Amer.* **amphitheater**) an oval or circular unroofed building with tiers of seats surrounding a central arena.

**amphora** (am-fer-ă) *noun* (*plural* **amphorae**, *pronounced* -ee) an ancient Greek or Roman jar with two handles and a narrow neck.

**ample** *adjective* **1** plentiful, quite enough; *ample evidence*. **2** large, of generous proportions. □ **amply** *adverb*

**amplifier** *noun* a device that increases the loudness of sounds or the strength of radio signals.

**amplify** *verb* (**amplified**, **amplifying**) **1** increase the strength of; *to amplify sound*. **2** make fuller, add details to; *please amplify your story*. □ **amplification** *noun*

**amplitude** *noun* **1** breadth. **2** largeness, abundance. **3** the maximum departure from average of oscillation, alternating current, etc. □ **amplitude modulation** the systematic variation of wave amplitude, leaving the frequency unaltered; used especially in broadcasting.

**ampoule** (am-pool) *noun* a small sealed container holding a liquid, especially for injection.

**amputate** *verb* cut off by surgical operation. □ **amputation** *noun*

**amputee** *noun* a person who has had a limb amputated.

**Amritsar** (am-rit-ser) a city in Punjab in NW India, the centre of the Sikh faith.

**Amsterdam** the capital of the Netherlands.

**amuck** *adverb* = AMOK.

**Amu Darya** (ah-moo dah-riă) a great river of central Asia (formerly known as the Oxus) rising in the Pamirs and flowing into the Aral Sea.

**amulet** (am-yoo-lit) *noun* a thing worn as a charm against evil.

**Amundsen** (ah-mund-sĕn), Roald (1872–1928), Norwegian polar explorer, the first to reach the South Pole (December 1911).

**amuse** *verb* **1** cause to laugh or smile. **2** make time pass pleasantly for. □ **amusing** *adjective*

**amusement** *noun* **1** something that amuses. **2** being amused. **3** a machine for entertainment at a fairground etc. □ **amusement arcade** an indoor area with slot-machines, electronic games, etc.

**an** *adjective* the form of *a* used before vowel sounds other than 'u' (*pronounced* yoo); *an egg, an hour* (but *a unit*).

**Anabaptist** *noun* a member of a Protestant religious group (especially in the 16th century) practising adult baptism.

**anabolic steroid** (an-ă-bol-ik) a steroid hormone used to build up bone and muscle tissue.

**anabolism** (ă-nab-ŏ-lizm) *noun* a biochemical process in which complex molecules are formed from simple ones using energy.

**anachronism** (ăn-ak-rŏn-izm) *noun* **1** a mistake in placing something into a particular historical period. **2** the thing wrongly placed. **3** a person, custom, or idea regarded as out of date. □ **anachronistic** (ă-nak-rŏn-ist-ik) *adjective*

**anaconda** (ană-kon-dă) *noun* a large snake of tropical South America.

**anaemia** (ă-nee-miă) *noun* (*Amer.* **anemia**) lack of red corpuscles, or of their haemoglobin in blood, resulting in paleness and weariness.

**anaemic** (ă-nee-mik) *adjective* (*Amer.* **anemic**) **1** suffering from anaemia. **2** pale, weak in colour. **3** lacking vigour or positive characteristics. □ **anaemically** *adverb*

**anaerobic** *adjective* not requiring air or oxygen.

**anaesthesia** (anis-theez-iă) *noun* (*Amer.* **anesthesia**) loss of sensation, especially that induced by anaesthetics.

**anaesthetic** (anis-thet-ik) *noun* (*Amer.* **anesthetic**) a substance that produces loss of sensation and of ability to feel pain. ● *adjective* having this effect.

**anaesthetist** (ăn-ees-thĕt-ist) *noun* (*Amer.* **anesthetist**) a person trained to administer anaesthetics.

**anaesthetize** (ăn-ees-thĕt-yz) *verb* (also **anaesthetise**; *Amer.* **anesthetize**) administer an anaesthetic to (a person etc.). □ **anaesthetization** *noun*

**anaglypta** *noun* thick wallpaper with a raised pattern, usually for painting over.

**anagram** (an-ă-gram) *noun* a word or phrase formed from the rearranged letters of another (e.g. *cart-horse* is an anagram of *orchestra*).

**anal** *adjective* of the anus.

**analgesia** (an-ăl-**jees**-iă) *noun* loss of ability to feel pain while still conscious.

**analgesic** (an-ăl-**jee**-sik) *adjective* relieving pain. ●*noun* a drug that relieves pain.

**analog** Amer. spelling of ANALOGUE.

**analogous** (ă-**nal**-ŏgŭs) *adjective* similar in certain respects. □ **analogously** *adverb*

**analogue** (an-ă-log) *noun* (*Amer.* **analog**) something that is analogous to something else. □ **analogue computer** one that makes calculations with data represented by physical quantities such as length, weight, or voltage; *a slide rule is a simple analogue computer* (compare *digital computer*).

**analogy** (ă-**nal**-ŏji) *noun* partial likeness between two things which are compared; *the analogy between the human heart and a pump.*

**analyse** *verb* (*Amer.* **analyze**) **1** separate (a substance etc.) into its parts to identify it or study its structure. **2** examine and interpret; *tried to analyse the causes of their failure.* **3** psychoanalyse.

**analysis** *noun* (*plural* **analyses**, *pronounced* ă-**nal**-i-seez) **1** analysing. **2** a statement of the result of this. **3** psychoanalysis.

**analyst** (an-ă-list) *noun* **1** a person who is skilled in analysis of chemical substances etc. **2** a psychoanalyst.

**analytical** (ană-**lit**-ik-ăl) *adjective* (also **analytic**) of or using analysis. □ **analytically** *adverb*

**analyze** Amer. spelling of ANALYSE.

**anapaest** (**an**-ă-peest) *noun* (*Amer.* **anapest**) *Poetry* a metrical foot with two short or unstressed syllables followed by one long or stressed syllable (as in the word *cigarette*).

**anarchist** (**an**-er-kist) *noun* a person who believes that government is undesirable and should be abolished. □ **anarchism** *noun*, **anarchistic** (an-er-**kist**-ik) *adjective*

**anarchy** (**an**-er-ki) *noun* **1** absence of government or control, resulting in lawlessness. **2** disorder, confusion. □ **anarchic** (ăn-**ar**-kik) *adjective*, **anarchical** *adjective*

**anathema** (ăn-**ath**-imă) *noun* **1** a detested person or thing; *blood sports are anathema to him.* **2** a formal curse of the Church, excommunicating someone or condemning something as evil.

**anathematize** (ăn-**ath**-im-ă-tyz) *verb* (also **anathematise**) curse.

**Anatolia** (an-ă-**toh**-liă) Asia Minor; the western peninsula of Asia that now forms the greater part of Turkey. □ **Anatolian** *adjective*

**anatomy** *noun* **1** the scientific study of bodily structures. **2** the bodily structure of an animal or plant. □ **anatomical** (ană-**tom**-ikăl) *adjective*, **anatomically** *adverb*

**anatto** alternative spelling of ANNATTO.

**ANC** *abbreviation* African National Congress.

**ancestor** *noun* **1** any of the persons from whom a person is descended, especially those more remote than grandparents. **2** an early type of animal, plant, or machine etc. from which later ones have evolved. □ **ancestral** *adjective*

**ancestry** *noun* a line of ancestors.

**anchor** *noun* **1** a heavy metal structure used to moor a ship to the sea-bottom or a balloon etc. to the ground. **2** anything that gives stability or security. ●*verb* **1** lower an anchor, make secure with an anchor. **2** fix firmly.

**anchorage** *noun* **1** a place where ships may anchor safely. **2** the charge for this.

**anchorite** (ank-er-ryt) *noun* a hermit, a religious recluse.

**anchorman** *noun* (*plural* **anchormen**) **1** a strong member of a sports team who plays a vital part (e.g. at the back of a tug-of-war team or as last runner in a relay race). **2** one who co-ordinates activities. **3** the compère in a broadcast TV or radio programme.

**anchovy** (an-chŏvi) *noun* a small strong-flavoured fish of the herring family.

**ancien régime** (ahn-sian re-*zh*eem) (*plural* **anciens régimes**, *pronounced* same) a former political system, especially that of pre-Revolutionary France (before 1787). (¶ French, = old rule.)

**ancient** *adjective* **1** belonging to times long past. **2** having lived or existed for a long time. □ **ancient history** history of the period before the end of the Western Roman Empire in AD 476.

**ancillary** (an-**sil**-er-i) *adjective* helping in a subsidiary way; *ancillary services.*

**and** *conjunction* **1** together with; *cakes and buns.* **2** then again repeatedly or increasingly; *gets better and better, miles and miles.* **3** added to; *two and two make four.* **4** to; *go and buy one.* **5** with this consequence; *move and I shoot.*

**Andalusia** (an-dă-**loo**-siă) (also **Andalucia**) the southernmost region of Spain, bordering on the Atlantic Ocean and the Mediterranean Sea. □ **Andalusian** *adjective*

**Andaman and Nicobar Islands** (an-dă-măn, nik-ŏ-bar) a Union Territory of India, consisting of two groups of islands in the Bay of Bengal.

**andante** (an-**dan**-ti) *adverb & adjective* (of music) in moderately slow time. ●*noun* a movement to be played in this way.

**andantino** (an-dan-**tee**-noh) *adverb & adjective* (of music) rather quicker than andante. ● *noun* a movement to be played in this way.

**Andersen**, Hans Christian (1805–75), Danish writer of fairy tales, including 'The Snow Queen' and 'The Ugly Duckling'.

**Anderson**[1], Elizabeth Garrett (1836–1917), pioneer of medical training for women.

**Anderson**[2], Marian (1902–93), Black American contralto.

**Andes** a range of mountains in western South America. □ **Andean** (an-**dee**-ăn) *adjective*

**Andhra Pradesh** (**ahn**-dră pră-**desh**) a State in SE India.

**andiron** (**and**-I-ern) *noun* a firedog.

**and/or** *conjunction* together with or as an alternative.

■**Usage** This use is usually restricted to official, legal, and business documents.

**Andorra** (and-o-ră) a self-governing principality in the Pyrenees under the joint sovereignty of France and Spain. □ **Andorran** *adjective & noun*

**Andrea del Sarto** (1486–1531), Italian Renaissance painter.

**Andrew**[1], Prince (other names: Albert Christian Edward), Duke of York (born 1960), second son of Queen Elizabeth II and Prince Philip.

**Andrew**[2], St (1st century) one of the twelve Apostles, the patron saint of Scotland. Feast day, 30 November.

**Andrews**, Julie (original name: Julia Elizabeth Wells) (born 1935), British singer and actress.

**Androcles** (an-drŏ-kleez) a runaway slave in a Roman legend, who extracted a thorn from the paw of a lion, which later refrained from attacking him when he faced it in the arena.

**androgynous** (an-**droj**-inŭs) *adjective* (of a plant, animal, or person) having both male and female reproductive organs.

**android** *noun* (in science fiction) a robot in human form.

**Andromeda** (an-**drom**-id-ă) **1** (*Gk. legend*) a king's daughter who was fastened to a rock as a sacrifice to a sea monster, and was rescued by Perseus. **2** a constellation conspicuous for its great spiral nebula.

**Andropov**, Yuri Vladimirovich (1914–84), President of the former USSR 1983–4.

**anecdote** (**an**-ik-doht) *noun* a short amusing or interesting story, especially one that is true.

**anemia** Amer. spelling of ANAEMIA.

**anemic** Amer. spelling of ANAEMIC.

**anemometer** (anim-**om**-it-er) *noun* an instrument for measuring the force of wind.

**anemone** (ă-**nem**-ŏni) *noun* a plant related to the buttercup, with white or brightly coloured flowers.

**aneroid barometer** (**an**-er-oid) a barometer that measures air-pressure by the action of air on the lid of a box containing a vacuum, not by the height of a fluid column.

**anesthesia** etc. Amer. spelling of ANAESTHESIA etc.

**aneurysm** (**an**-yoor-izm) *noun* (also **aneurism**) permanent abnormal enlargement of an artery.

**anew** *adverb* again; in a new or different way.

**angel** *noun* **1** an attendant or messenger of God. **2** a very beautiful or kind person. □ **angel cake** very light sponge cake.

**angelfish** *noun* a fish with wing-like fins.

**angelic** *adjective* of or like an angel. □ **angelically** *adverb*

**angelica** (an-**jel**-ikă) *noun* **1** a fragrant plant used in cookery and medicine. **2** its candied stalks.

**Angelou**, Maya (born 1928), Black American novelist and poet.

**angelus** (**an**-jil-ŭs) *noun* (in the RC Church) **1** a prayer to the Virgin Mary commemorating the Incarnation, said at morning, noon, and sunset. **2** a bell rung as a signal for this.

**anger** *noun* the strong feeling caused by extreme displeasure. ● *verb* make angry.

**Angevin** (an-ji-vin) *adjective* **1** of Anjou, a former province of France. **2** of the Plantagenet kings of England from Henry II (son of Geoffrey, Count of Anjou) to Richard II (deposed 1399). ● *noun* an Angevin person or ruler.

**angina** (an-**jy**-nă) *noun* (in full **angina pectoris**) (**pek**-tŏ-ris) sharp pain in the chest caused by overexertion when the heart is diseased.

**angiosperm** (**an**-ji-ŏ-sperm) *noun* a member of the group of flowering plants that have seeds enclosed in an ovary.

**Angkor** (**ang**-kor) the capital of the ancient kingdom of Khmer, in NW Cambodia, famous for its temples.

**Angle** *noun* a member of a North German tribe who settled in England in the 5th century. □ **Anglian** *adjective*

**angle**[1] *noun* **1** the space between two lines or surfaces that meet. **2** a point of view; *written from the woman's angle*. ● *verb* **1** move or place in a slanting position. **2** present (news etc.) from a particular point of view.

**angle**[2] *verb* **1** fish with hook and bait. **2** try to obtain by hinting; *angling for an invitation*. □ **angler** *noun*

**Anglesey** (**ang**-ĕl-see) an island off the north-west tip of Wales.

**Anglican** *adjective* of the Church of England or other Church in communion with it. ●*noun* a member of the Anglican Church. □ **Anglicanism** *noun*

**Anglicism** (ang-li-sizm) *noun* a peculiarly English word or custom.

**anglicize** (ang-li-syz) *verb* (also **anglicise**) make English in form or character.

**angling** *noun* the sport of fishing.

**Anglo-** *combining form* English, British.

**Anglo-Catholic** *adjective* of the section of the Church of England that stresses its unbroken connection with the early Christian Church and objects to being called Protestant. ●*noun* a member of this section of the Church.

**Anglo-French** *adjective* English (or British) and French. ●*noun* the French language as developed in England after the Norman Conquest.

**Anglo-Indian** *adjective* **1** of England and India. **2** of British descent but having lived for a long time in India. **3** of mixed British and Indian parentage. ●*noun* an Anglo-Indian person.

**Anglo-Norman** *adjective* English and Norman. ●*noun* Norman dialect used in England after the Norman conquest.

**Anglophile** (ang-loh-fyl) *noun* a person who loves England or English things.

**Anglo-Saxon** *noun* **1** an English person of the period before the Norman Conquest. **2** the English language of this period, also called *Old English*. **3** a person of English descent. ●*adjective* of the Anglo-Saxons or their language.

**Angola** (an-goh-lă) a country on the west coast of Africa. □ **Angolan** *adjective & noun*

**angora** *noun* **1** yarn or fabric made from the hair of angora goats or rabbits. **2** a long-haired variety of cat, goat, or rabbit.

**angostura** (ang-öss-tewr-ă) *noun* the bitter bark of a South American tree, used as a flavouring.

**angry** *adjective* (**angrier, angriest**) **1** feeling or showing anger. **2** inflamed; *an angry sore*. □ **angrily** *adverb*

**angst** *noun* anxiety; a feeling of guilt or remorse.

**angstrom** (ang-ström) *noun* a unit of length used in measuring wavelengths. (¶ Named after A. J. Ångström (1814–74), Swedish physicist.)

**Anguilla** (ang-wil-ă) one of the Leeward Islands in the West Indies, a British dependency with full self-government.

**anguish** *noun* severe physical or mental pain.

**anguished** *adjective* feeling anguish.

**angular** *adjective* **1** having angles or sharp corners. **2** lacking plumpness or smoothness. **3** measured by angle; *the an-*

*gular distance*. □ **angularity** (ang-yoo-la-riti) *noun*

**Angus** *noun* = ABERDEEN ANGUS.

**anhydrous** *adjective* *Chem.* without water.

**aniline** (an-il-een) *noun* an oily liquid obtained from nitrobenzene, used in the manufacture of dyes and plastics.

**animadvert** (anim-ad-vert) *verb* (*literary*) make hostile criticisms. □ **animadversion** *noun*

**animal** *noun* **1** a living thing that can feel and move voluntarily. **2** such a being other than a human being. **3** a four-footed animal distinguished from a bird, fish, reptile, or insect. **4** a brutish or uncivilized person. ●*adjective* of, from, or relating to animal life. □ **animal husbandry** the science of breeding and caring for farm animals. **animal magnetism** sex appeal; sexual attractiveness. **animal rights** the natural right of animals to live free from human exploitation.

**animalism** *noun* **1** the nature and activity of animals; concern with physical matters; sensuality. **2** the belief that humans are simply animals.

**animate** *adjective* (*pronounced* an-im-ăt) living. ●*verb* (*pronounced* an-im-ayt) **1** give life or movement to; make lively; *an animated discussion*. **2** motivate; *he was animated by loyalty*. **3** produce as an animated cartoon. □ **animated cartoon** a film made by photographing a series of drawings, giving an illusion of movement. □ **animator** *noun*

**animation** *noun* **1** animating. **2** liveliness.

**animism** *noun* belief that all beings and natural things such as rocks, streams, and winds have a living soul. □ **animistic** *adjective*

**animosity** (anim-os-iti) *noun* a spirit of hostility.

**animus** (an-imŭs) *noun* animosity shown in speech or action.

**anion** (an-I-ŏn) *noun* an ion with a negative charge. □ **anionic** (an-I-on-ik) *adjective*

**anise** *noun* a plant with aromatic seeds.

**aniseed** *noun* the sweet-smelling seed of the plant anise, used for flavouring.

**Anjou** (ahn-zhoo) a former province of western France, on the Loire.

**Ankara** (ank-er-ă) the capital of Turkey.

**ankle** *noun* **1** the joint connecting the foot with the leg. **2** the slender part between this and the calf.

**anklet** *noun* an ornamental chain or band worn around the ankle.

**ankylosis** (ang-ki-loh-sis) *noun* stiffening of a joint by fusion of the bones.

**annals** (an-ălz) *plural noun* a history of events year by year; historical records. □ **annalist** *noun*

**Annapurna** (an-ă-per-nă) a ridge of the Himalayas, in north central Nepal.

**annatto** noun (also **anatto**) an orange-red dye from the pulp of a tropical fruit, used for colouring foods.

**Anne**[1] (1665-1714) queen of Great Britain and Ireland 1702-14.

**Anne**[2], Princess (other names: Elizabeth Alice Louise), the Princess Royal (born 1950), daughter of Queen Elizabeth II and Prince Philip.

**Anne**[3], St (in Christian tradition) the mother of the Virgin Mary. Feast day, 26 July.

**anneal** verb heat (metal or glass) and cool it slowly, especially to toughen it.

**Anne Boleyn** see BOLEYN.

**Anne of Cleves** (1515-57) the fourth wife of Henry VIII.

**annex** (ăn-eks) verb **1** add or join to a larger thing. **2** take possession of; to annex territory. □ **annexation** noun

**annexe** (an-eks) noun a building attached to a larger one or forming a subordinate part of a main building.

**Annigoni** (an-i-goh-ni), Pietro (1910-88), Italian artist noted for his portraits.

**annihilate** (ă-ny-hil-ayt) verb destroy completely. □ **annihilation** noun, **annihilator** noun

**anniversary** noun the yearly return of the date of an event; a celebration of this.

**Anno Domini** (an-oh dom-in-I) in the year of Our Lord; indicating a date after Christ's birth (usually shortened to AD).

**annotate** (an-oh-tayt) verb add notes of explanation to; an annotated edition. □ **annotation** noun

**announce** verb **1** make known publicly or to an audience. **2** make known the presence or arrival of. □ **announcement** noun

**announcer** noun a person who announces items in a broadcast.

**annoy** verb **1** cause slight anger to. **2** be troublesome to, harass. □ **annoyance** noun

**annoyed** adjective slightly angry.

**annual** adjective **1** coming or happening once every year; her annual visit. **2** of one year, reckoned by the year; her annual income. **3** lasting only one year or season; annual plants. ● noun **1** a plant that lives for one year or one season. **2** a book or periodical published in yearly issues. □ **annually** adverb

**annualized** adjective (of rates of interest, inflation, etc.) calculated on an annual basis from information about figures given for a shorter period.

**annuity** (ă-new-iti) noun a fixed annual allowance, especially one provided by a form of investment.

**annul** (ă-nul) verb (**annulled, annulling**) make null and void, to destroy the validity of; the marriage was annulled. □ **annulment** noun

**annular** (an-yoo-ler) adjective ring-like. □ **annular eclipse** a solar eclipse in which a ring of light remains visible.

**annulate** adjective marked with or formed of rings.

**Annunciation** noun **1** the announcement by the angel Gabriel to the Virgin Mary that she was to be the mother of Christ. **2** the festival commemorating this (25 March; also called Lady Day).

**anode** (an-ohd) noun the electrode by which current enters a device.

**anodize** (an-ŏ-dyz) verb (also **anodise**) coat (metal) with a protective layer by electrolysis.

**anodyne** (an-ŏ-dyn) noun **1** a drug that relieves pain. **2** anything that relieves pain or distress. ● adjective relieving pain or distress.

**anoint** verb **1** apply ointment or oil to, especially as a sign of consecration. **2** smear or rub with grease.

**anomaly** (ă-nom-ăli) noun something that deviates from the general rule or the usual type, an irregularity or inconsistency; the many anomalies in our tax system. □ **anomalous** adjective

**anon** (ă-non) adverb (old use) soon, presently; I will say more of this anon.

**anon.** abbreviation anonymous (author).

**anonymity** (an-ŏn-im-iti) noun being anonymous.

**anonymous** (ă-non-im-ŭs) adjective **1** with a name that is not known or not made public; an anonymous donor. **2** written or given by such a person; an anonymous gift; an anonymous letter. □ **anonymously** adverb

**anorak** (an-er-ak) noun a waterproof jacket, usually with a hood attached.

**anorexia** (an-er-eks-iă) noun lack of appetite, especially (in full **anorexia nervosa**) a medical condition characterized by an obsessive desire to lose weight and refusal to eat normally. □ **anorexic** adjective & noun

**A. N. Other** a player or person not named or not yet selected. (¶ From another.)

**another** adjective **1** additional, one more. **2** different; fit another pipe, this one leaks. **3** some or any other; will not do another man's work. ● pronoun another person or thing.

**Anouilh** (an-oo-ee), Jean (1910-87), French playwright.

**Ansaphone** noun (trade mark) an answering machine.

**answer** noun something said, needed, or done to deal with a question, accusation, or problem. ● verb **1** make an answer to;

say, write, or do something in return.
**2** suffice or be suitable for; *this will answer the purpose.* **3** (foll. by *to, for*) take responsibility; vouch; *I will answer for his honesty; they must answer for their crimes.* **4** (foll. by *to*) correspond; *this bag answers to the description of the stolen one.* □ **answer back** answer a rebuke cheekily. **answering machine** a machine that answers telephone calls and records messages.

**answerable** *adjective* **1** able to be answered. **2** having to account for something.

**ant** *noun* a very small insect of which there are many species, all of which form and live in highly organized groups.

**antacid** (ant-**ass**-id) *noun* a substance that prevents or corrects acidity.

**antagonism** (an-**tag**-ŏn-izm) *noun* active opposition, hostility.

**antagonist** (an-**tag**-ŏn-ist) *noun* an opponent; one who is hostile to something. □ **antagonistic** (an-tag-ŏn-**ist**-ik) *adjective,* **antagonistically** *adverb*

**antagonize** *verb* (also **antagonise**) arouse antagonism in.

**Antananarivo** (ant-ă-nan-ă-**ree**-voh) the capital of Madagascar.

**Antarctic** *adjective* of the regions round the South Pole. ●*noun* **1** these regions. **2** the Antarctic Ocean, the sea surrounding Antarctica. □ **Antarctic Circle** an imaginary line round the Antarctic region, the line of latitude 60° 30' S.

**Antarctica** the continent mainly within the Antarctic Circle.

**ante** (**an**-ti) *noun* **1** a stake put up by a poker-player before drawing new cards. **2** an amount payable in advance. ●*verb* put up an ante; pay up.

**ante-** (**an**-ti) *combining form* before.

**anteater** *noun* an animal that feeds on ants and termites.

**antecedent** (ant-i-**seedn't**) *noun* **1** a preceding thing or circumstance; *the war and its antecedents; I know nothing of his antecedents.* **2** a noun, clause, or sentence to which a following pronoun refers (in *the book which I have,* 'book' is the antecedent of 'which'). ●*adjective* previous.

**antechamber** *noun* an ante-room.

**antedate** *verb* **1** precede in time. **2** put an earlier date on (a document) than that on which it was issued.

**antediluvian** (anti-di-**loo**-viăn) *adjective* **1** of the time before Noah's Flood. **2** (*informal*) completely out of date.

**antelope** *noun* a swift-running animal (e.g. chamois, gazelle) resembling a deer, found especially in Africa.

**antenatal** *adjective* **1** before birth. **2** during pregnancy; *antenatal care.*

**antenna** *noun* **1** (*plural* **antennae,** *pronounced* an-**ten**-ee) each of a pair of flexible sensitive projections on the heads of insects, crustaceans, etc.; a feeler. **2** (*plural* **antennas**) an aerial.

**antepenultimate** (anti-pin-**ult**-imăt) *adjective* last but two.

**ante-post** *adjective* (of bets) made before the runners' numbers are made known.

**anterior** *adjective* coming before in position or time.

**ante-room** *noun* a small room leading to a main one.

**anthem** *noun* **1** a short musical composition to be sung in religious services, often with words taken from the Bible. **2** a solemn hymn of praise or loyalty.

**anther** *noun* the part of a flower's stamen that contains pollen.

**anthill** *noun* a mound over an ants' nest.

**anthologist** *noun* a person who compiles an anthology.

**anthology** (an-**thol**-ŏji) *noun* a collection of passages from literature, especially poems.

**Anthony**[1], St (of Egypt, *c.*251–356), the founder of monasticism. Feast day, 17 January.

**Anthony**[2], St (of Padua, 1195–1231), Franciscan friar, invoked as the finder of lost objects.

**anthracite** *noun* a hard form of coal that burns with little flame or smoke.

**anthrax** *noun* a disease of sheep and cattle that can be transmitted to people.

**anthropocentric** *adjective* regarding human beings as the centre of existence.

**anthropoid** (an-**thrŏp**-oid) *adjective* human in form. ●*noun* an anthropoid ape such as a gorilla or chimpanzee.

**anthropologist** *noun* an expert in anthropology.

**anthropology** (anthrŏ-**pol**-ŏji) *noun* the scientific study of mankind, especially of human origins, development, customs, and beliefs. □ **anthropological** (an-thrŏp-ŏ-loj-ikăl) *adjective,* **anthropologically** *adverb*

**anthropomorphic** (an-thrŏp-ŏ-**mor**-fik) *adjective* attributing human form or personality to a god, animal, or object. □ **anthropomorphism** *noun*

**anthropomorphous** (an-thrŏp-ŏ-**mor**-fŭs) *adjective* in human form.

**anti** *noun* (*plural* **antis**) a person who opposes a particular policy, cause, group, etc. ●*preposition* opposed to.

**anti-** *combining form* **1** against, opposed to; *anti-slavery.* **2** preventing, counteracting; *anti-perspirant.*

**anti-abortion** *adjective* opposing abortion. □ **anti-abortionist** *noun*

**anti-aircraft** *adjective* used against enemy aircraft.

**anti-ballistic missile** a missile that can destroy ballistic missiles in the air.

**antibiotic** (anti-by-ot-ik) *noun* a substance capable of destroying or preventing the growth of bacteria. ● *adjective* functioning in this way.

**antibody** (**an**-ti-bodi) *noun* a protein formed in the blood in reaction to certain substances which it then attacks and destroys.

**antic** *noun* (usually as **antics**) absurd or foolish behaviour, especially movements intended to cause amusement.

**Antichrist** *noun* an enemy of Christ.

**anticipate** *verb* **1** deal with or use before the proper time; *anticipate one's income.* **2** take action before someone else has had time to do so; *others may have anticipated Columbus in the discovery of America.* **3** notice what needs doing and take action in advance; *anticipate someone's needs; the boxer anticipated the blow.* **4** expect; *we anticipate that it will rain.* □ **anticipation** *noun*, **anticipatory** (an-tiss-i-**payt**-er-i) *adjective*

■ **Usage** Many people regard the use in sense 4 as unacceptable, but it is very common in informal use.

**anticlerical** *adjective* opposed to clerical influence, especially in politics.

**anticlimax** *noun* a disappointing ending or outcome of events where a climax was expected.

**anticlockwise** *adverb & adjective* moving in a curve from right to left, in the opposite direction to the hands of a clock.

**anticoagulant** *noun* a substance that prevents or slows down the clotting of blood.

**anticyclone** *noun* an area in which atmospheric pressure is high, producing fine settled weather, with an outward flow of air.

**antidepressant** *noun* a drug that counteracts mental depression.

**antidote** (**an**-ti-doht) *noun* **1** a substance that counteracts the effects of a poison or a disease. **2** anything that counteracts unpleasant effects.

**antifreeze** *noun* a substance added to water to lower its freezing-point, used especially in a vehicle's radiator to prevent freezing.

**antigen** (**an**-ti-jĕn) *noun* a substance (e.g. a toxin) that causes the body to produce antibodies.

**Antigua and Barbuda** (an-**teeg**-ă, bar-**boo**-dă) a country consisting of two islands in the Caribbean Sea. □ **Antiguan** *adjective & noun*, **Barbudan** *adjective & noun*

**anti-hero** *noun* a central character in a story or drama who lacks conventional heroic attitudes.

**antihistamine** (anti-**hist**-ă-meen) *noun* a substance that counteracts the effects of histamine, used in treating allergies.

**antiknock** *noun* a substance added to motor fuel to prevent or reduce knocking.

**Antilles** (an-**til**-eez) a group of islands forming the greater part of the West Indies.

**anti-lock** *adjective* (of brakes) designed to prevent locking and skidding when applied suddenly.

**antilog** *noun* (*informal*) an antilogarithm.

**antilogarithm** *noun* the number to which a given logarithm belongs.

**antimacassar** (anti-mă-**kas**-er) *noun* a small protective cover for the backs or arms of chairs etc. (¶ Originally a protection against the Macassar oil that was used on hair.)

**antimatter** *noun* matter composed solely of antiparticles.

**antimony** (**an**-ti-mŏni) *noun* a chemical element (symbol Sb), a brittle silvery metal used in alloys.

**antinomy** (an-**tin**-ŏmi) *noun* contradiction between two reasonable beliefs or conclusions.

**antinovel** *noun* a work of fiction that deliberately avoids the normal patterns and conventions of most novels.

**anti-nuclear** *adjective* opposed to the development and use of nuclear weapons or power.

**antiparticle** *noun* an elementary particle with the same mass as another particle but opposite electrical charge and magnetic properties.

**antipasto** *noun* (*plural* **antipastos** *or* **antipasti**) a starter or appetizer, especially as part of an Italian meal.

**antipathy** (an-**tip**-ă-thi) *noun* **1** a strong and settled dislike. **2** the object of this.

**antiperspirant** (anti-**per**-spi-rănt) *noun* a substance that prevents or reduces sweating.

**antiphon** (**an**-ti-fŏn) *noun* a verse of a psalm etc. sung by part of a choir in response to one sung by the other part. □ **antiphonal** (an-**tif**-ŏn-ăl) *adjective*

**antipodes** (an-**tip**-ŏ-deez) *plural noun* **1** places on opposite sides of the earth. **2** (**the Antipodes**) the Australasian regions, almost diametrically opposite Europe. □ **antipodean** (antip-ŏ-**dee**-ăn) *adjective*

**antipope** *noun* a person set up as pope in opposition to one chosen by church law.

**antipyretic** *adjective* (of a drug) preventing or reducing fever.

**antiquary** (an-tik-wer-i) *noun* one who studies or collects antiques or antiquities. □ **antiquarian** (anti-**kwair**-iăn) *adjective & noun*

**antiquated** (an-ti-kway-tid) *adjective* old-fashioned, out of date.

**antique** (an-**teek**) *adjective* belonging to the distant past, in the style of past times. ●*noun* an antique object, especially furniture or a decorative object of a kind sought by collectors.

**antiquity** (an-**tik**-witi) *noun* **1** ancient times, especially before the Middle Ages. **2** (**antiquities**) objects dating from ancient times. **3** great age.

**antirrhinum** (anti-**ry**-nŭm) *noun* a garden flower commonly called snapdragon.

**antiscorbutic** (anti-skor-**bew**-tik) *adjective* preventing or curing scurvy.

**anti-Semitic** (anti-sim-**it**-ik) *adjective* hostile to Jews. □ **anti-Semitism** (anti-**sem**-it-izm) *noun*

**antiseptic** *adjective* **1** preventing the growth of bacteria etc. that cause things to become septic. **2** thoroughly clean and free from germs. ●*noun* a substance with an antiseptic effect.

**antiserum** *noun* serum containing a large number of antibodies.

**antisocial** *adjective* **1** opposed to the social institutions and laws of an organized community. **2** interfering with amenities enjoyed by others; *it's antisocial to leave litter*. **3** unsociable, withdrawing oneself from others. □ **antisocially** *adverb*

**antistatic** *adjective* counteracting the effects of static electricity.

**antitetanus** *adjective* effective against tetanus.

**antithesis** (an-**tith**-i-sis) *noun* (*plural* **antitheses**) **1** the direct opposite of something, opposition or contrast; *slavery is the antithesis of freedom*. **2** contrast of ideas emphasized by choice of words or by their arrangement. □ **antithetical** *adjective*, **antithetically** *adverb*

**antitoxin** *noun* a substance that neutralizes a toxin and prevents it from having a harmful effect. □ **antitoxic** *adjective*

**antitrades** *plural noun* winds blowing in the opposite direction to trade winds.

**antitrust** *adjective* (especially *Amer.*) (of a law) opposed to or controlling trusts or monopolies.

**antler** *noun* a branched horn; one of a pair of these on a stag or other deer. □ **antlered** *adjective*

**Antony**[1] alternative spelling of ANTHONY.

**Antony**[2], Mark (*c.*83–30 BC), Roman general and politician.

**antonym** (**ant**-ŏn-im) *noun* a word that is opposite in meaning to another.

**Antrim** a district and former county of Northern Ireland.

**Antwerp** a city and seaport of Belgium.

**Anuradhapura** (ă-noor-ă-dă-**poor**-ă) the ancient capital of Sri Lanka (4th century BC–AD 760), site of numerous Buddhist foundations.

**anus** (ay-nŭs) *noun* the opening at the end of the alimentary canal, through which solid waste matter passes out of the body.

**anvil** *noun* a block of iron on which a smith hammers metal into shape.

**anxiety** *noun* **1** the state of being anxious. **2** something causing this.

**anxious** *adjective* **1** troubled and uneasy in mind. **2** causing worry, filled with such feeling; *an anxious moment*. **3** eager; *anxious to please*. □ **anxiously** *adverb*

**any** *adjective* **1** one or some (but no matter which) from several. **2** every, whichever you choose; *any fool knows that*. **3** in a significant amount; *did not stay any length of time*. ●*pronoun* any person, thing, or amount; *I can't find any of them; we haven't any*. ●*adverb* at all, in some degree; *he isn't any better*. □ **any more** to any further extent.

**anybody** *noun & pronoun* **1** any person. **2** a person of importance; *is he anybody?*

**anyhow** *adverb* **1** anyway. **2** not in an orderly manner; *work was done all anyhow*.

**anyone** *noun & pronoun* anybody.

**anything** *noun & pronoun* any thing; *anything will do*. □ **anything but** not at all; far from being; *it's anything but cheap*. **like anything** with great intensity.

**anyway** *adverb* **1** in any manner. **2** at any rate. **3** to resume; *anyway, as I was saying*.

**anywhere** *adverb* in or to any place. ●*pronoun* any place.

**Anzac** *noun* **1** a member of the Australian and New Zealand Army Corps (1914–18). (¶ Named from the initial letters of the Corps.) **2** an Australian or a New Zealander.

**Anzus** the combination of Australia, New Zealand, and the USA for the security of the Pacific Ocean. (¶ Named from the initials of these countries.)

**AOB** *abbreviation* any other business.

**aorta** (ay-**or**-tă) *noun* the major artery through which blood is carried from the left side of the heart. □ **aortic** *adjective*

**apace** *adverb* (*literary*) swiftly; *work proceeded apace*.

**Apache** (ă-**pach**-i) *noun* a member of a tribe of North American Indians inhabiting the south-western part of the USA.

**apache** (ă-**pash**) *noun* a violent street ruffian, originally in Paris *c.*1900.

**apart** *adverb* **1** aside, separately, to or at a distance. **2** into pieces; *it came apart*. □ **apart from** independently of, other than; *has no books apart from these*. **joking apart** speaking seriously, without joking.

**apartheid** (ă-**part**-ayt) *noun* a policy (especially formerly in South Africa) of racial segregation, separating Europeans and non-Europeans.

**apartment** *noun* **1** a set of rooms. **2** (*Amer.*) a flat.

**apathy** (**ap**-ă-thi) *noun* lack of interest or concern. □ **apathetic** (apă-**thet**-ik) *adjective*, **apathetically** *adverb*

**ape** *noun* any of the four primates (gorilla, chimpanzee, orang-utan, gibbon) most closely related to man. ●*verb* to imitate, to mimic.

**apeman** *noun* an extinct primate thought to have been the forerunner of humans.

**Apennines** (**ap**-i-nynz) *plural noun* a mountain range in Italy.

**aperient** (ă-**peer**-iĕnt) *adjective* laxative. ●*noun* a laxative medicine.

**aperitif** (ă-pe-ri-**teef**) *noun* an alcoholic drink taken before a meal.

**aperture** *noun* an opening, especially one that admits light.

**Apex** *noun* (also **APEX**) a system of reduced fares for scheduled flights when paid for in advance. (¶ From *A*dvance *P*urchase *Ex*cursion.)

**apex** (**ay**-peks) *noun* (*plural* **apexes**) the tip or highest point, the pointed end; *the apex of a triangle.*

**aphasia** (ă-**fay**-ziă) *noun* loss of the ability to speak or understand language as a result of brain damage.

**aphelion** (ă-**fee**-li-ŏn) *noun* (*plural* **aphelia**) the point in a planet's or comet's orbit when it is furthest from the sun.

**aphid** (**ay**-fid) *noun* a small insect such as a greenfly or blackfly feeding in large numbers on plants.

**aphis** (**ay**-fiss) *noun* (*plural* **aphides**, *pronounced* **ay**-fid-eez) an aphid.

**aphorism** (**af**-er-izm) *noun* a short wise saying, a maxim.

**aphrodisiac** (afrŏ-**diz**-iak) *adjective* arousing sexual desire. ●*noun* an aphrodisiac substance.

**Aphrodite** (af-rŏ-**dy**-ti) (*Gk. myth.*) the goddess of beauty, fertility, and sexual love, identified by the Romans with Venus.

**Apia** (a-**pee**-ă) the capital of Western Samoa.

**apiary** (**ay**-pi-er-i) *noun* a place with a number of hives where bees are kept.

**apiculture** *noun* bee-keeping.

**apiece** *adverb* to each, for or by each one of a group; *cost a penny apiece.*

**aplomb** (ă-**plom**) *noun* dignity and confidence.

**apocalypse** (ă-**pok**-ă-lips) *noun* **1** (**the Apocalypse**) Revelation, the last book in the New Testament, containing a proph-

etic description of the end of the world. **2** a violent and destructive event.

**apocalyptic** (ă-pok-ă-**lip**-tik) *adjective* of or like an apocalypse; prophesying events of this kind.

**Apocrypha** (ă-**pok**-rif-ă) *plural noun* those books of the Old Testament that were not accepted by Jews as part of the Hebrew Scriptures and were excluded from the Protestant Bible at the Reformation.

**apocryphal** (ă-**pok**-rif-ăl) *adjective* unlikely to be true; *an apocryphal account of his travels.*

**apogee** (**ap**-ŏ-jee) *noun* **1** the point in the orbit of the moon or any planet when it is at its furthest point from earth. **2** the highest or most distant point; a climax.

**apolitical** (ay-pŏ-**lit**-ikăl) *adjective* not political, not concerned with politics.

**Apollo 1** (*Gk. myth.*) a god associated with the sun, music, and prophecy, represented in art as the ideal type of manly beauty. **2** the American space programme for landing men on the moon, which achieved its object on 20 July 1969.

**Apollyon** (a-**pol**-yŏn) the Devil.

**apologetic** *adjective* making an apology. ●*noun* (**apologetics**) a reasoned defence, especially of Christianity. □ **apologetically** *adverb*

**apologia** (ap-ŏ-**loh**-jiă) *noun* a formal defence of belief or conduct.

**apologist** *noun* a person who explains or defends a doctrine by reasoned argument.

**apologize** *verb* (also **apologise**) make an apology.

**apology** *noun* **1** a statement of regret for having done wrong. **2** an explanation or defence of one's beliefs. **3** a poor or scanty specimen; *this feeble apology for a meal.*

**apophthegm** (**ap**-ŏth-em) *noun* a terse or pithy saying.

**apoplectic** (apŏ-**plek**-tik) *adjective* **1** of apoplexy. **2** suffering from apoplexy. **3** (*informal*) furious, enraged.

**apoplexy** (**ap**-ŏ-plek-si) *noun* sudden inability to feel and move, caused by blockage or rupture of an artery in the brain; a stroke.

**apostasy** (ă-**poss**-tă-si) *noun* renunciation of one's beliefs, principles, or party.

**apostate** (ă-**poss**-tayt) *noun* a person who renounces a former belief, principle, etc.

**a posteriori** *adjective* (of reasoning in logic) proceeding from effect to cause; inductive. (¶ Latin, = from what comes after.)

**Apostle** *noun* **1** any of the twelve men sent out by Christ to preach the Gospel. **2** (**apostle**) a leader or teacher of a new faith or movement.

**apostolic** (apŏ-**stol**-ik) *adjective* **1** of or relating to the Apostles or their teaching. **2** of or relating to the pope. □ **apostolic**

**succession** transmission of spiritual authority from the Apostles through successive popes and bishops.

**apostrophe** (ă-pos-trŏ-fi) *noun* **1** a punctuation mark (') used to show that letters or numbers have been omitted (as in *can't* = cannot; '65 = 1965), or showing the possessive case (*the boy's book, the boys' books*), or the plurals of letters (*there are two l's in 'Bell'*). **2** a passage in a speech or poem etc. addressing an absent person or an abstract idea.

**apostrophize** (ă-pos-trŏ-fyz) *verb* (also **apostrophise**) to address in an apostrophe.

**apothecary** (ă-poth-ik-eri) *noun* (*old use*) a pharmaceutical chemist. □ **apothecaries' weight, apothecaries' measure** a system of units formerly used in weighing drugs.

**apotheosis** (ă-poth-ee-oh-sis) *noun* (*plural* **apotheoses**, *pronounced* -oh-seez) **1** elevation to the status of a god, deification. **2** a thing's highest development; an ideal, a perfect example.

**appal** (ă-pawl) *verb* (*Amer.* **appall**) (**appalled, appalling**) fill with horror or dismay, shock deeply.

**Appalachian Mountains** (apă-lay-chi-ăn) (also **Appalachians**) a system of mountains in eastern North America.

**appalling** *adjective* (*informal*) shocking, unpleasant.

**apparatus** *noun* **1** the equipment used for doing something; the instruments etc. used in scientific experiments. **2** a complex organization or system.

**apparel** *noun* (*formal* or *old use*) clothing.

**apparent** (ă-pa-rěnt) *adjective* **1** clearly seen or understood; obvious; *it became apparent.* **2** seeming but not real; *his reluctance was only apparent.* □ **heir apparent** *see* HEIR. □ **apparently** *adverb*

**apparition** (apă-rish-ŏn) *noun* **1** something that appears, especially something remarkable or unexpected. **2** a ghost.

**appeal** *verb* (**appealed, appealing**) **1** make an earnest or formal request; *appealed for contributions.* **2** ask a person or go to a recognized authority for an opinion; *appealed to the chairman.* **3** take a case to a higher court for judicial review of a lower court's decision. **4** be of interest, attract; *cruises don't appeal to me.* ● *noun* **1** the act of appealing. **2** a judicial review of a case by a higher court; a request for this. **3** attraction, interest, pleasantness. **4** a request for public donations to a cause.

**appealing** *adjective* attractive, likeable.

**appear** *verb* **1** become or be visible. **2** present oneself, especially formally or publicly; *the Minstrels are appearing at the Victoria Theatre.* **3** act as counsel in a lawcourt; *I*

*appear for the defendant.* **4** be published; *the story appeared in the newspapers.* **5** give a certain impression; *you appear to have forgotten.*

**appearance** *noun* **1** appearing. **2** an outward sign, form, or impression; *has an appearance of prosperity.* □ **keep up appearances** keep an outward show of prosperity or good behaviour. **put in an appearance** be present, especially for only a short time. **to all appearances** so far as can be seen; *he was to all appearances dead.*

**appease** *verb* make calm or quiet by making concessions or by satisfying demands. □ **appeasement** *noun*

**appellant** (ă-pel-ănt) *noun* a person making an appeal to a higher court.

**appellate** (ă-pel-ăt) *adjective* (especially of a court) concerned with appeals.

**appellation** (ap-ěl-ay-shŏn) *noun* (*formal*) **1** naming. **2** a name or title.

**append** *verb* **1** attach. **2** add at the end; *append one's signature.*

**appendage** (ă-pen-dij) *noun* a thing added to or forming a natural part of something larger or more important.

**appendectomy** *noun* (also **appendicectomy**) the surgical removal of the appendix.

**appendicitis** *noun* inflammation of the appendix of the intestine.

**appendix** *noun* **1** (*plural* **appendices**, *pronounced* ă-pen-di-seez) a section with supplementary information at the end of a book or document. **2** (*plural* **appendixes**) a small tube of tissue closed at one end, forming an outgrowth of the intestine.

**appertain** (ap-er-tayn) *verb* (foll. by *to*) relate, belong, or be appropriate to.

**appetite** *noun* **1** physical desire, especially for food. **2** a desire or liking; *an appetite for power.*

**appetizer** *noun* (also **appetiser**) something eaten or drunk to stimulate the appetite.

**appetizing** *adjective* (also **appetising**) stimulating the appetite; *an appetizing smell.* □ **appetizingly** *adverb*

**applaud** *verb* **1** show approval of (a thing) by clapping one's hands. **2** praise; *we applaud your decision.*

**applause** *noun* **1** hand-clapping by people applauding. **2** warm approval.

**apple** *noun* **1** a round firm fruit with crisp juicy flesh. **2** the tree that bears this. □ **apple of one's eye** a cherished person or thing. **apple-pie order** extreme neatness. **upset the apple cart** spoil carefully laid plans.

**Appleton** (ap-ěl-tŏn), Sir Edward Victor (1892–1965), English physicist.

**appliance** *noun* a device, an instrument; a machine or piece of equipment.

**applicable** (ap-lik-ăbŭl) *adjective* able to be applied; appropriate. □ **applicability** (ăplik-ă-**bil**-iti) *noun*

**applicant** (ap-lik-ănt) *noun* a person who applies for something, especially a job.

**application** *noun* **1** applying something, putting one thing on another; *ointment for external application only.* **2** the thing applied. **3** making a formal request; the request itself; *his application was refused.* **4** bringing a rule into use; putting something to practical use; relevance. **5** the ability to apply oneself.

**applicator** *noun* a device for applying something.

**applied** *see* APPLY. ●*adjective* put to practical use; not merely theoretical; *applied science*; *applied mathematics.*

**appliqué** (ă-**plee**-kay) *noun* **1** a piece of cut-out material sewn or fixed ornamentally to another. **2** needlework of this kind. ●*verb* (**appliquéd, appliquéing**) ornament with appliqué.

**apply** *verb* (**applied, applying**) **1** put (a thing) into contact with another; spread on a surface. **2** bring into use or action; put into effect; *apply economic sanctions.* **3** be relevant; *what I said does not apply to you.* **4** make a formal request; *to apply for a job.* □ **apply oneself** give one's attention and energy to a task.

**appoint** *verb* **1** choose (a person) for a job; set up by choosing members; *appoint a committee.* **2** fix or decide by authority; *they appointed a time for the next meeting.* □ **well-appointed** *adjective* well equipped or furnished.

**appointee** *noun* the person appointed.

**appointment** *noun* **1** an arrangement to meet or visit at a particular time. **2** appointing a person to a job. **3** the job or position itself. **4** (**appointments**) equipment, furniture.

**apportion** (ă-**por**-shŏn) *verb* divide into shares, allot. □ **apportionment** *noun*

**apposite** (ap-ŏ-zit) *adjective* (of a remark) appropriate for a purpose or occasion. □ **appositely** *adverb*, **appositeness** *noun*

**apposition** (apŏ-**zish**-ŏn) *noun* **1** placing side by side. **2** a grammatical relationship in which a word or phrase is placed with another which it describes, e.g. in 'the reign of Elizabeth, our Queen', *our Queen* is in apposition to *Elizabeth.*

**appraise** *verb* estimate or assess the value or quality of. □ **appraisal** *noun*

**appreciable** (ă-**pree**-shă-bŭl) *adjective* able to be seen or felt; considerable; *an appreciable change in temperature.* □ **appreciably** *adverb*

**appreciate** *verb* **1** value greatly, be grateful for. **2** enjoy intelligently; *to appreciate Eng-*lish poetry. **3** understand; *we appreciate their reluctance to give details.* **4** rise or raise in value; *the investments have appreciated greatly.* □ **appreciation** *noun*

**appreciative** (ă-**pree**-shă-tiv) *adjective* feeling or showing grateful recognition or enjoyment. □ **appreciatively** *adverb*

**appreciatory** (ă-**pree**-shă-ter-i) *adjective* showing appreciation.

**apprehend** (apri-hend) *verb* **1** seize, arrest. **2** grasp the meaning of, understand.

**apprehension** (apri-hen-shŏn) *noun* **1** a feeling of fear about a possible danger or difficulty. **2** understanding. **3** arrest.

**apprehensive** (apri-hen-siv) *adjective* feeling apprehension, anxious. □ **apprehensively** *adverb*, **apprehensiveness** *noun*

**apprentice** *noun* **1** one who is learning a craft and is bound to an employer by legal agreement. **2** a novice. ●*verb* (usually as **apprenticed to**) working as an apprentice for an employer; *he was apprenticed to a blacksmith.* □ **apprenticeship** *noun*

**apprise** (ă-**pryz**) *verb* (*formal*) inform.

**appro** (ap-roh) *noun* (*informal*) □ **on appro** on approval.

**approach** *verb* **1** come near or nearer in space or time. **2** set about doing or tackling; *approach the problem in a practical way.* **3** go to with a request or offer; *approach your bank for a loan.* **4** be similar to; *a dislike that approaches hatred.* ●*noun* **1** approaching; *watched their approach.* **2** a way of reaching a place. **3** the final part of an aircraft's flight before landing. **4** a method of doing or tackling something. **5** an effort to establish an agreement or friendly relations. **6** an approximation; *his nearest approach to a smile.*

**approachable** *adjective* able to be approached; friendly and easy to talk to. □ **approachability** *noun*

**approbation** (aprŏ-**bay**-shŏn) *noun* approval.

**appropriate**[1] (ă-**proh**-pri-ăt) *adjective* suitable, proper. □ **appropriately** *adverb*, **appropriateness** *noun*

**appropriate**[2] (ă-**proh**-pri-ayt) *verb* **1** take and use as one's own. **2** set aside for a special purpose; *£500 was appropriated to the sports fund.* □ **appropriation** *noun*, **appropriator** *noun*

**approval** *noun* feeling, showing, or saying that one considers something to be good or acceptable. □ **on approval** (of goods) taken by a customer for examination without obligation to buy unless satisfied.

**approve** *verb* **1** say or feel that something is good or suitable. **2** sanction, agree to; *the committee approved the expenditure.*

**approx.** *abbreviation* approximate; approximately.

**approximate** *adjective* (*pronounced* ă-prok-sim-ăt) almost exact or correct but not completely so. ● *verb* (*pronounced* ă-prok-sim-ayt) **1** be almost the same; *a story that approximated to the truth.* **2** make approximately the same. □ **approximately** *adverb*, **approximation** *noun*

**appurtenance** (ă-per-tin-ăns) *noun* (usually as **appurtenances**) a minor piece of property, or a right or privilege, that goes with a more important one.

**APR** *abbreviation* annualized (or annual) percentage rate (of interest on a credit arrangement).

**Apr.** *abbreviation* April.

**après-ski** (ap-ray-skee) *noun* social activities following a day's skiing. (¶ French.)

**apricot** *noun* **1** a juicy stone-fruit related to the plum and peach, orange-pink when ripe. **2** this colour.

**April** the fourth month of the year. □ **April fool** a person who is hoaxed on **April Fool's Day** (1 April).

**a priori** (ay pry-or-I) *adjective* **1** (of reasoning in logic) from cause to effect; deductive. **2** (of concepts) not derived from experience. **3** assumed without investigation. ● *adverb* **1** deductively; logically. **2** as far as one knows. (¶ Latin, = from what is before.)

**apron** *noun* **1** a garment worn over the front part of the body to protect the wearer's clothes. **2** an extension of a theatre stage in front of the curtain. **3** a hard-surfaced area on an airfield, where aircraft are manoeuvred or loaded and unloaded. □ **tied to mother's apron strings** excessively dependent on or dominated by her.

**apropos** (aprŏ-**poh**) *adverb* appropriately, to the point. ● *adjective* suitable or relevant to what is being said or done. □ **apropos of** concerning, with reference to; *apropos of elections, who is to be our new candidate?*

**apse** *noun* a recess with an arched or domed roof, especially in a church.

**apsis** *noun* (*plural* **apsides**, *pronounced* ap-sid-eez) each of the points on the orbit of a planet or satellite etc. that are nearest to or furthest from the body round which it moves.

**apt** *adjective* **1** suitable, appropriate; *an apt quotation.* **2** having a certain tendency; likely; *he is apt to be careless.* **3** quick at learning. □ **aptly** *adverb*, **aptness** *noun*

**aptitude** *noun* a natural ability or skill.

**Aqaba** (ak-ă-bă) the only port in Jordan, on the Gulf of Aqaba, the north-east arm of the Red Sea.

**aqua** *noun* the colour aquamarine.

**aqualung** *noun* a diver's portable breathing-apparatus consisting of cylinders of compressed air connected to a face-mask.

**aquamarine** (akwă-mă-**reen**) *noun* **1** a bluish-green gemstone. **2** its colour.

**aquaplane** *noun* a board on which a person stands to be towed by a speedboat. ● *verb* **1** ride on such a board. **2** glide uncontrollably on a wet road surface.

**aqua regia** (ree-jiă) a highly corrosive mixture of acids.

**aquarium** (ă-kwair-iŭm) *noun* (*plural* **aquariums**) a tank in which fish are kept for display; a building containing a lot of these.

**Aquarius** (ă-kwair-iŭs) the eleventh sign of the zodiac, the Water-carrier. □ **Aquarian** *adjective & noun*

**aquatic** (ă-kwat-ik) *adjective* **1** growing or living in or near water; *aquatic plants.* **2** taking place in or on water; *aquatic sports.*

**aquatint** *noun* an etching made on copper by using nitric acid.

**aqua vitae** strong alcoholic spirit, especially brandy.

**aqueduct** (ak-wi-dukt) *noun* an artificial channel carrying water across country, especially one like a bridge over a valley or road.

**aqueous** (ay-kwi-ŭs) *adjective* **1** of or like water. **2** produced by water. □ **aqueous humour** clear fluid in the eye between the lens and the cornea.

**aquiline** (ak-wi-lyn) *adjective* hooked like an eagle's beak; *an aquiline nose.*

**Aquinas** (ă-kwy-năs), St Thomas (1225–74), Italian theologian, a Dominican friar. Feast day, 7 March.

**Aquitaine** (ak-wi-**tayn**) an ancient province of SW France.

**AR** *abbreviation* Arkansas.

**Ar** *symbol* argon.

**Arab** *noun* **1** a member of a Semitic people originating in Saudi Arabia and neighbouring countries, now widespread throughout the Middle East and North Africa. **2** a horse of a breed native to Arabia. ● *adjective* of Arabs.

**arabesque** (a-ră-besk) *noun* **1** an elaborate design with intertwined leaves, branches, and scrolls. **2** a ballet dancer's posture poised on one leg with the other stretched backwards horizontally. **3** a short elaborate piece of music.

**Arabia** a peninsula in the Middle East between the Red Sea and the Persian Gulf.

**Arabian** *adjective* of Arabia. □ **Arabian Nights** the popular title of a collection of Oriental folk tales mostly dating from the 9th century. **Arabian Sea** the north-western part of the Indian Ocean, between Arabia and India.

**Arabic** adjective of the Arabs or their language. ●noun the language of the Arabs. □ **arabic figures** the symbols 1, 2, 3, 4, 5, etc.

**arable** (a-ră-bŭl) adjective (of land) suitable for growing crops. ●noun arable land.

**arachnid** (ă-**rak**-nid) noun a member of the class of animals including spiders, scorpions, and mites.

**arachnophobia** noun an abnormal fear of spiders.

**Arafat** (a-ră-fat), Yasser (born 1929), leader of the Palestine Liberation Organization from 1968.

**Aragon** (a-ră-gŏn) a region of NE Spain, bounded by the Pyrenees.

**arak** alternative spelling of ARRACK.

**Aral Sea** an inland sea in central Asia, east of the Caspian Sea.

**Aramaic** (a-ră-**may**-ik) noun a Semitic language spoken in Syria and Palestine in New Testament times.

**Aran** adjective made in the knitted patterns traditional to the **Aran Islands**, off the west coast of Ireland.

**Aranda** (ă-**ran**-dă) noun **1** a member of an Aboriginal people of central Australia. **2** their language.

**Ararat** (a-ră-rat) either of two mountain peaks in eastern Turkey, where Noah's ark is said to have rested after the Flood.

**arbiter** (**ar**-bit-er) noun **1** a person who has the power to decide what shall be done or accepted, one with entire control; designers who are the arbiters of fashion. **2** an arbitrator.

**arbitrary** (**ar**-bit-rer-i) adjective **1** based on random choice or impulse, not on reason; an arbitrary selection. **2** despotic, unrestrained; arbitrary powers. □ **arbitrarily** adverb, **arbitrariness** noun

**arbitrate** verb act as an arbitrator.

**arbitration** noun settlement of a dispute by a person or persons acting as arbitrators.

**arbitrator** noun an impartial person chosen to settle a dispute between two parties.

**arbor**¹ noun an axle or spindle on which a wheel etc. revolves in mechanism.

**arbor**² Amer. spelling of ARBOUR.

**Arbor Day** a day set apart in the USA and other countries for the public planting of trees.

**arboreal** (ar-**bor**-iăl) adjective **1** of trees. **2** living in trees.

**arboretum** (ar-bor-**ee**-tŭm) noun (plural **arboreta**) a place where rare trees are grown for study and display.

**arboriculture** noun cultivation of trees and shrubs.

**arbour** (**ar**-ber) noun (Amer. **arbor**) a shady place among trees, especially in a garden

with climbing plants growing over a framework.

**arbutus** (ar-**bew**-tŭs) noun an evergreen tree or shrub with strawberry-like fruits.

**ARC** abbreviation Aids-related complex; early symptoms suffered by a person infected with the HIV virus.

**arc** noun **1** part of the circumference of a circle or other curve. **2** anything shaped like this. **3** a luminous electric current passing across a gap between two terminals. ●verb (**arced**, **arcing**) **1** form an arc; move in a curve. **2** form an electric arc. □ **arc lamp**, **arc light** lighting using an electric arc. **arc welding** welding by means of an electric arc.

**arcade** noun **1** a covered passage or area, usually with shops on both sides. **2** a series of arches supporting or along a wall.

**Arcadia** (ar-**kay**-diă) a mountainous area in the central Peloponnese in Greece, in poetic fantasy the idyllic home of song-loving shepherds.

**Arcadian** noun a country dweller with a peaceful life. ●adjective poetically rural.

**arcane** (ar-**kayn**) adjective mysterious, secret.

**arch**¹ noun **1** a curved structure supporting the weight of what is above it or used ornamentally. **2** something shaped like this. **3** the curved under-part of the foot. ●verb form into an arch.

**arch**² adjective consciously or affectedly playful; an arch smile. □ **archly** adverb

**arch-** combining form **1** chief. **2** extreme.

**Archaean** (ah-kee-ăn) (Amer. **Archean**) adjective of the earliest geological era.

**archaeologist** noun (Amer. **archeologist**) an expert in archaeology.

**archaeology** (ar-ki-**ol**-ŏji) noun (Amer. **archeology**) the scientific study of civilizations through their material remains. □ **archaeological** adjective

**archaeopteryx** (ar-kee-**op**-tĕ-riks) noun a fossil bird with teeth, feathers, and a long bony tail.

**archaic** (ar-**kay**-ik) adjective belonging to former or ancient times.

**archaism** (**ar**-kay-izm) noun an archaic word or expression.

**Archangel** a port in northern Russia.

**archangel** noun an angel of the highest rank.

**archbishop** noun a bishop ranking above other bishops in a province of the Church.

**archbishopric** noun the office or diocese of an archbishop.

**archdeacon** noun a priest ranking next below a bishop. □ **archdeaconry** noun

**archdiocese** (arch-**dy**-ŏ-sis) noun the diocese of an archbishop.

**archduke** noun (hist.) chief duke, especially as the title of a son of an Austrian Emperor.

**Archean** Amer. spelling of ARCHAEAN.

**arch-enemy** noun the chief enemy.

**archeologist** Amer. spelling of ARCHAE-OLOGIST.

**archeology** Amer. spelling of ARCHAE-OLOGY.

**archer** noun **1** a person who shoots with bow and arrows. **2** (**the Archer**) a sign of the zodiac, Sagittarius.

**archery** noun the sport of shooting with bows and arrows.

**archetype** (ar-ki-typ) noun an original model from which others are copied. □ **archetypal** adjective

**archidiaconal** (arki-dy-**ak**-ŏnăl) adjective of an archdeacon.

**archiepiscopal** (arki-i-**pisk**-ŏpăl) adjective of an archbishop or archbishopric.

**archimandrite** (arki-**man**-dryt) noun the head of a large monastery in the Orthodox Church.

**Archimedes** (arki-**mee**-deez) (3rd century BC) Greek mathematician and inventor.

**archipelago** (arki-**pel**-ă-goh) noun (plural **archipelagos**) **1** a group of many islands. **2** a sea containing such a group.

**architect** noun **1** a designer of buildings. **2** (foll. by of) a person who brings about a specified thing; architect of peace.

**architecture** noun **1** the art or science of designing buildings. **2** the design or style of a building or buildings. □ **architectural** adjective, **architecturally** adverb

**architrave** (ar-ki-trayv) noun **1** the horizontal piece resting on the columns of a building. **2** the surround of a doorway or window.

**archive** (ar-kyv) noun (often **archives**) the records or historical documents of an institution or community.

**archivist** (ar-kiv-ist) noun a person trained to deal with archives.

**archway** noun a passageway under an arch.

**Arctic** adjective **1** of the regions round the North Pole. **2** (**arctic**) very cold; the weather was arctic. ●noun **1** the Arctic regions. **2** the Arctic Ocean, the ocean surrounding the North Pole, lying within the Arctic Circle. □ **Arctic Circle** an imaginary line round the Arctic region, the line of latitude 66° 30' N.

**Arcturus** (ark-tewr-ŭs) the brightest star in the northern sky, in the constellation Boötes.

**Ardennes** (ar-den), **the** a forested upland region including parts of Belgium, Luxemburg, and northern France.

**ardent** (ar-dĕnt) adjective full of ardour; enthusiastic. □ **ardently** adverb

**ardour** (ar-der) noun great warmth of feeling.

**arduous** (ar-dew-ŭs) adjective needing much effort; laborious. □ **arduously** adverb

**are**[1] see BE.

**are**[2] (pronounced ar) noun an area of 100 square metres.

**area** noun **1** the extent or measurement of a surface. **2** a region; a space for a specific purpose; picnic area. **3** the field of an activity or subject; in the area of finance. **4** a small sunken courtyard in front of the basement of a house.

**arena** (ă-ree-nă) noun the level area in the centre of a sports stadium or an amphitheatre.

**aren't** (informal) = ARE NOT.

∎**Usage** The phrase aren't I? is a recognized colloquialism for am I not?

**areola** (ă-ree-ŏlă) noun (plural **areolae**) a circular coloured area, especially around a nipple.

**Areopagus** (a-ri-op-ăgŭs) **1** a hill at Athens. **2** a council or judicial court of ancient Athens meeting on this hill.

**Ares** (air-eez) (Gk. myth.) the god of war, identified by the Romans with Mars.

**arête** (a-ret) noun a sharp ridge on a mountain.

**Argentina** (ar-jĕn-teen-ă) a country in the southern part of South America. □ **Argentine** (ar-jĕn-tyn) adjective & noun, **Argentinian** (ar-jĕn-tin-iăn) adjective & noun

**argon** noun a chemical element (symbol Ar), an inert gas used e.g. in electric-light bulbs and in arc welding.

**Argonauts** (ar-gŏ-nawts) plural noun (Gk. legend) the heroes who accompanied Jason on the ship Argo in quest of the Golden Fleece.

**argosy** (ar-gŏsi) noun (poetic) a large merchant ship.

**argot** (ar-goh) noun the special jargon of a group.

**arguable** adjective **1** able to be asserted. **2** open to doubt or dispute, not certain. □ **arguably** adverb

**argue** verb **1** express disagreement, exchange angry words. **2** give reasons for or against something, debate. **3** (foll. by into, out of) persuade by talking; argued him into going. **4** indicate; their lifestyle argues that they are well off. □ **argue the toss** (informal) to dispute about a choice.

**argument** noun **1** a discussion involving disagreement; a quarrel. **2** a reason put forward. **3** a theme or chain of reasoning.

**argumentation** noun arguing.

**argumentative** (arg-yoo-**ment**-ătiv) adjective fond of arguing. □ **argumentatively** adverb

**Argus** (Gk. myth.) a monster with many eyes, slain by Hermes.

**aria** (ah-riă) *noun* an operatic song for one voice.

**Arianism** (air-i-an-izm) *noun* the principal heresy denying the divinity of Christ, named after its author Arius (*c*.250–*c*.336), priest of Alexandria. □ **Arian** *adjective & noun*

**arid** (a-rid) *adjective* **1** dry, parched; *arid regions.* **2** uninteresting; *an arid discussion.* □ **aridly** *adverb,* **aridness** *noun,* **aridity** (ă-**rid**-iti) *noun*

**Aries** (air-eez) the first sign of the zodiac, the Ram. □ **Arian** (air-iăn) *adjective & noun*

**aright** *adverb* rightly.

**arise** *verb* (**arose, arisen**) **1** come into existence, come to people's notice; *problems arose.* **2** (*old use*) get up, stand up; rise from the dead.

**aristocracy** (a-ri-stok-răsi) *noun* **1** the hereditary upper classes; the nobility. **2** a country ruled by these. **3** the best of a category.

**aristocrat** (a-ris-tŏ-krat) *noun* a member of the aristocracy, a noble.

**aristocratic** (a-ris-tŏ-**krat**-ik) *adjective* **1** of the aristocracy. **2** noble in style. □ **aristocratically** *adverb*

**Aristophanes** (a-ris-tof-ă-neez) (*c*.450–*c*.385 BC), Greek comic playwright.

**Aristotle** (384–322 BC), Greek philosopher. □ **Aristotelian** *adjective & noun*

**arithmetic** ● *noun* (*pronounced* ă-**rith**-mě-tik) the science of numbers; calculating by means of numbers. ● *adjective* (*pronounced* ă-rith-met-ik) (also **arithmetical**) of arithmetic. □ **arithmetic mean** = AVERAGE (SENSE 1). **arithmetic progression** a sequence of numbers with constant intervals (e.g. 9, 7, 5, 3, etc.). □ **arithmetically** *adverb*

**Ariz.** *abbreviation* Arizona.

**Arizona** (a-ri-**zoh**-nă) a State of the southwestern USA.

**ark** *noun* Noah's boat or a model of this. □ **Ark of the Covenant** a wooden chest in which the writings of Jewish Law were kept.

**Ark.** *abbreviation* Arkansas.

**Arkansas** (ar-kăn-saw) a State of the southern central USA.

**arm¹** *noun* **1** either of the two upper limbs of the human body. **2** a sleeve of a garment. **3** something shaped like an arm or projecting from a main part; *an arm of a sea; the arms of a chair.* □ **arm in arm** (of people) with the arm of one linked in the arm of another. **arm of the law** the authority or power of the law. **arm-wrestling** *noun* a trial of strength in which contestants grasp hands with elbows resting on a surface and each tries to force the other's arm down. **at arm's length** at a distance. **with open arms** cordially.

**arm²** *verb* **1** supply or fit with weapons. **2** make (a bomb etc.) ready to explode; *the device was not yet armed.* ● *noun* **1** each of the kind of troops of which an army etc. is composed; *the Fleet Air Arm.* **2** (**arms**) weapons. **3** (**arms**) = *coat of arms.* □ **armed forces** *or* **services** military forces. **arms race** competition among nations in accumulating weapons. **under arms** equipped for war. **up in arms** protesting vigorously.

**armada** (ar-**mah**-dă) *noun* a fleet of warships. □ **the (Spanish) Armada** a naval invasion force sent by Spain against England in 1588.

**armadillo** (ar-mă-**dil**-oh) *noun* (*plural* **armadillos**) a small burrowing animal of South America with a body covered with a shell of bony plates.

**Armageddon 1** (in the Bible) the scene of the final conflict between the forces of good and evil at the end of the world. **2** any decisive conflict.

**Armagh** (ar-**mah**) a district and former county of Northern Ireland.

**armament** *noun* **1** the weapons with which an army or a ship, aircraft, or fighting vehicle is equipped. **2** the process of equipping for war.

**armature** (ar-mă-choor) *noun* **1** the wire-wound core of a dynamo or electric motor. **2** a bar placed in contact with the poles of a magnet to preserve its power or transmit force to support a load. **3** a framework round which a clay or plaster sculpture is modelled.

**armband** *noun* a band worn round the arm or sleeve.

**armchair** *noun* **1** a chair with arms or raised sides. **2** (used as *adjective*) theoretical rather than active; reading about something rather than doing it; *armchair gardeners; an armchair traveller.*

**Armenia** a republic to the east of the Black Sea, bordering on Turkey. □ **Armenian** *adjective & noun*

**armful** (*plural* **armfuls**) *noun* as much as the arms can hold.

**armhole** *noun* an opening in a garment through which the arm is inserted.

**armistice** *noun* an agreement during a war or battle to stop fighting for a time. □ **Armistice Day** 11 November, the anniversary of the armistice that in 1918 ended the First World War, now replaced (in the UK) by Remembrance Sunday and (in the USA) by Veterans Day.

**armlet** *noun* an armband.

**armor** etc. Amer. spelling of ARMOUR etc.

**armorial** *adjective* of heraldry or coats of arms.

**armour** *noun* (*Amer.* **armor**) **1** a protective covering for the body, formerly worn in fighting. **2** metal plates covering a warship, car, or tank to protect it from missiles. **3** armoured fighting vehicles collectively.

**armoured** *adjective* (*Amer.* **armored**) **1** covered or protected with armour; *an armoured car.* **2** equipped with armoured vehicles; *armoured divisions.*

**armoury** (ar-mer-i) *noun* (*Amer.* **armory**) a place where weapons and ammunition are stored.

**armpit** *noun* the hollow under the arm below the shoulder.

**Armstrong¹**, Louis (1900–71), known as 'Satchmo' (short for 'Satchelmouth'), American jazz trumpeter and singer.

**Armstrong²**, Neil Alden (born 1930), American astronaut, the first man to set foot on the moon (July 1969).

**army** *noun* **1** an organized force equipped for fighting on land. **2** a vast group; *an army of locusts.* **3** a body of people organized for a particular purpose; *an army of helpers.*

**Arne**, Thomas (1710–78), English composer whose most famous song is 'Rule, Britannia'.

**arnica** *noun* **1** a plant with yellow flowers. **2** a substance prepared from this, used to treat bruises.

**Arno** a river of northern Italy, flowing through Florence and Pisa.

**Arnold¹**, Malcolm (born 1921), British composer.

**Arnold²**, Matthew (1822–88), English poet.

**aroma** (ă-roh-mă) *noun* a smell, especially a pleasant one.

**aromatherapy** *noun* the use of essential plant oils in massage.

**aromatic** *adjective* **1** fragrant, spicy. **2** (of organic compounds) having an unsaturated ring of atoms, especially containing a benzene ring. ●*noun* an aromatic substance or plant.

**arose** *see* ARISE.

**around** *adverb & preposition* **1** all round, on every side, in every direction. **2** about, here and there; *he's somewhere around.* **3** about, approximately at; *be here around five o'clock.*

**arouse** *verb* rouse; stimulate.

**Arp**, Jean (*or* Hans) (1887–1966), French sculptor, painter, and poet, a founder of the Dada movement.

**arpeggio** (ar-pej-i-oh) *noun* (*plural* **arpeggios**) the notes of a musical chord played in succession instead of simultaneously.

**arrack** *noun* (also **arak**) alcoholic spirit, especially made from coco sap or rice.

**arraign** *verb* accuse; find fault with. □ **arraignment** *noun*

**arrange** *verb* **1** put into a certain order, adjust; place attractively. **2** form plans; settle the details of; prepare; *arrange to be there*; *arrange a meeting.* **3** adapt (a musical composition) for voices or instruments other than those for which it was written. □ **arrangement** *noun*, **arranger** *noun*

**arrant** (a-rănt) *adjective* downright, out-and-out; *this is arrant nonsense!*

**arras** (a-răs) *noun* a richly decorated tapestry or wall-hanging.

**array** *verb* **1** arrange in order; *arrayed his forces along the river.* **2** dress; *arrayed in her coronation dress.* ●*noun* **1** an imposing series; a display; *a fine array of tools.* **2** an ordered arrangement. **3** an arrangement of data in a computer, so constructed that a program can extract the items by means of a key.

**arrears** *plural noun* **1** money that is owing and ought to have been paid earlier; *arrears of rent.* **2** work that should have been finished but is still waiting to be dealt with; *arrears of correspondence.* □ **in arrears** behind with payment or work; *he is in arrears with his rent*; *the rent is in arrears.*

**arrest** *verb* **1** stop or check (a process or movement). **2** attract (a person's attention). **3** seize by authority of the law. ●*noun* **1** stoppage. **2** seizure, legal arresting of an offender; *he is under arrest.*

**arrestable** *adjective* such that the offender may be arrested without a warrant; *an arrestable offence.*

**arrester** *noun* (also **arrestor**) a device for slowing an aircraft after landing.

**Arrhenius** (ă-ray-niŭs *or* ă-ree-niŭs), Svante August (1859–1927), Swedish scientist, one of the founders of modern physical chemistry.

**arris** (a-ris) *noun* the sharp edge formed where two surfaces meet to form an angle, especially in architecture.

**arrival** *noun* **1** arriving. **2** a person or thing that has arrived.

**arrive** *verb* **1** reach one's destination or a point on a journey. **2** come at last, make an appearance; *the great day arrived*; *the baby arrived on Tuesday.* **3** (foll. by *at*) reach (a conclusion, decision, etc.). **4** be recognized as having achieved success in the world.

**arrogant** (a-rŏ-gănt) *adjective* proud and overbearing through an exaggerated feeling of one's superiority. □ **arrogantly** *adverb*, **arrogance** *noun*

**arrogate** (a-rŏ-gayt) *verb* **1** claim or seize without having the right to do so. **2** attribute or assign to another person unjustly. □ **arrogation** *noun*

**arrow** *noun* **1** a straight thin pointed shaft to be shot from a bow. **2** a line with an outward-pointing V at the end, used to show direction or position.

**arrowhead** *noun* the head of an arrow.

**arrowroot** *noun* an edible starch prepared from the root of a plant.

**arse** *noun* (*Amer.* **ass**) (*vulgar*) the buttocks or rump.

**arsehole** *noun* (*Amer.* **asshole**) (*vulgar slang*) **1** the anus. **2** (*offensive*) a stupid person; an idiot.

**arsenal** *noun* a place where weapons and ammunition are stored or manufactured.

**arsenic** (ar-sĕn-ik) *noun* **1** a chemical element (symbol As), a brittle steel-grey substance. **2** a highly poisonous white compound of this. □ **arsenical** (ar-sen-ikăl) *adjective*

**arson** *noun* the act of setting fire to a house or other property intentionally and unlawfully. □ **arsonist** *noun*

**art¹** *noun* **1** the production of something beautiful; skill or ability in such work. **2** works such as paintings or sculptures. **3** (**the arts**) creative activities such as painting, music, theatre, writing. **4** (**arts**) subjects (e.g. languages, literature, history) associated with creative skill as opposed to sciences where exact measurements and calculations are used. **5** any practical skill; a knack; *the art of sailing*. **6** cunning, artfulness. □ **art deco** a style of decorative art and architecture popular in the 1920s and 1930s, characterized by geometric patterns, sharp edges, and bright colours. **art gallery** a gallery where paintings or pieces of sculpture are displayed. **art nouveau** (ah noo-**voh**) an art style of the late 19th century characterized by flowing lines and natural forms. **arts and crafts** decorative design and handicraft.

**art²** (*old use*) the present tense of **be**, used with *thou*.

**artefact** (ar-ti-fakt) *noun* (also **artifact**) a man-made object; a simple prehistoric tool or weapon.

**arterial** (ar-teer-iăl) *adjective* of an artery. □ **arterial road** an important main road.

**arteriosclerosis** (ar-teer-i-oh-skleer-oh-sis) *noun* a condition in which the walls of arteries become thicker and less elastic so that blood circulation is hindered.

**artery** *noun* **1** any of the tubes carrying blood away from the heart to all parts of the body. **2** an important transport route.

**artesian well** (ar-tee-ziăn) a well bored vertically into a place where a constant supply of water will rise to the earth's surface with little or no pumping.

**artful** *adjective* crafty; cunningly clever at getting what one wants. □ **artfully** *adverb*, **artfulness** *noun*

**arthritis** (arth-ry-tiss) *noun* a condition in which there is pain and stiffness in the joints. □ **arthritic** (arth-**rit**-ik) *adjective & noun*

**arthropod** (arth-rŏ-pod) *noun* an animal of the group that includes insects, spiders, crustaceans, and centipedes.

**Arthur** reputed king of the Britons (perhaps 5th or 6th century), legendary leader of the Knights of the Round Table at his court at Camelot. □ **Arthurian** (ar-thewr-iăn) *adjective & noun*

**artic** (ar-tik) *noun* (*informal*) an articulated vehicle.

**artichoke** *noun* a plant related to the thistle, with a flower consisting of thick leaf-like scales used as a vegetable (also called **globe artichoke**). *See also* JERUSALEM ARTICHOKE.

**article** *noun* **1** a particular or separate thing; *articles of clothing*; *toilet articles*. **2** a piece of writing, complete in itself, in a newspaper or periodical; *an article on immigration*. **3** a separate clause or item in an agreement; *articles of apprenticeship*. **4** *Grammar* a word used before a noun to identify what it refers to (e.g. *a*, *the*). ● *verb* bind by articles of apprenticeship. □ **definite article** the word 'the'. **indefinite article** 'a' or 'an' (or their equivalents in another language).

**articled clerk** a trainee solicitor.

**articular** (ar-tik-yoo-ler) *adjective* of a joint or joints of the body.

**articulate** *adjective* (*pronounced* ar-tik-yoo-lăt) **1** spoken clearly, in words. **2** able to express ideas clearly. ● *verb* (*pronounced* ar-tik-yoo-layt) **1** say or speak distinctly; *articulating each word with care*. **2** form a joint, connect by joints; *this bone is articulated with another*. □ **articulated vehicle** one that has sections connected by a flexible joint or joints. □ **articulately** *adverb* **articulation** *noun*

**artifact** alternative spelling of ARTEFACT.

**artifice** (ar-ti-fiss) *noun* trickery; a clever trick intended to mislead someone.

**artificer** (ar-tif-i-ser) *noun* a skilled craftsman or mechanic.

**artificial** *adjective* not originating naturally; made by human skill in imitation of something natural. □ **artificial insemination** injection of semen into the womb artificially so that conception may take place without sexual intercourse. **artificial intelligence** the development of computers to do things that normally need human intelligence, such as using language. **artificial respiration** the process of forcing air into and out of the lungs to start natural breathing or stimulate it when it has failed. □ **artificially** *adverb*, **artificiality** (arti-fishi-al-iti) *noun*

**artillery** *noun* **1** large guns used in fighting on land. **2** a branch of an army that uses these. □ **artilleryman** *noun*

**artisan** (ar-ti-zan) *noun* a skilled manual worker, craftsman, or craftswoman.

**artist** noun **1** a person who produces works of art, especially paintings. **2** a person who does something with exceptional skill. **3** a professional entertainer.

**artiste** (ar-**teest**) noun a professional entertainer.

**artistic** adjective **1** showing or done with skill and good taste. **2** of art or artists. □ **artistically** adverb

**artistry** noun artistic skill.

**artless** adjective free from artfulness; simple and natural. □ **artlessly** adverb, **artlessness** noun

**artwork** noun **1** pictures and diagrams in books, advertisements etc. **2** paintings, sculptures, etc.; an exhibition of children's artwork.

**arty** adjective (informal) with an exaggerated and often affected display of artistic style or interests. □ **artiness** noun

**arty-crafty** adjective (informal) of arts and crafts.

**arum** (**air**-ŭm) noun a plant with a flower consisting of a single petal-like part surrounding a central spike. □ **arum lily** a cultivated white arum.

**Arunachal Pradesh** (ah-rŭn-ah-chăl prǎ-**desh**) a State of NE India.

**Aryan** (**air**-iǎn) adjective **1** of the original Indo-European language; of its speakers or their descendants. **2** (in Nazi ideology) of non-Jewish extraction. ●noun an Aryan person.

**As** symbol arsenic.

**as** adverb **1** in the same degree, equally. **2** similarly, like. **3** in the character of; Olivier as Hamlet. ●conjunction **1** at the same time that; they came as I left. **2** because, for the reason that; as he refuses, we can do nothing. **3** in the way in which; do as I do. ●relative pronoun that, who, which; I had the same trouble as you; he was a foreigner, as I knew from his accent. □ **as for** with regard to; as for you, you're hopeless! **as from** from the date stated; your salary will be increased as from 1 April. **as if** as it would be if; he said it as if he meant it. **as it was** in the actual circumstances. **as it were** as if it was actually so; he became, as it were, a man without a country. **as of** at the date mentioned; that was the position as of last Monday. **as though** as if. **as to** with regard to; said nothing as to holidays. **as well 1** in addition, too. **2** desirable; it might be as well to go. **as well as** in addition to. **as yet** up to this time.

**asafoetida** (ass-ǎ-**feet**-idǎ) noun (Amer. **asafetida**) a strong-smelling plant gum, used as a cooking spice and formerly in medicine.

**a.s.a.p.** abbreviation as soon as possible.

**asbestos** noun a soft fibrous mineral substance, made into fireproof material or used for heat insulation.

**asbestosis** (ass-best-**oh**-sis) noun a lung disease caused by inhaling asbestos particles.

**ascend** verb go or come up. □ **ascend the throne** become king or queen.

**ascendancy** (ǎ-**sen**-dǎn-si) noun the state of being dominant.

**ascendant** adjective **1** ascending, rising. **2** Astronomy rising towards a point above the observer. **3** Astrology just above the eastern horizon. □ **in the ascendant** rising in power or influence.

**ascension** (ǎ-**sen**-shŏn) noun **1** ascent. **2** (**the Ascension**) the taking up of Christ into heaven, witnessed by the Apostles. □ **Ascension Day** the Thursday on which this is commemorated, the 40th day after Easter.

**Ascension Island** a small island in the South Atlantic, incorporated with St Helena.

**ascent** noun **1** ascending. **2** a way up, an upward slope or path.

**ascertain** (ass-er-**tayn**) verb find out by making enquiries. □ **ascertainment** noun

**ascetic** (ǎ-**set**-ik) adjective self-denying, not allowing oneself pleasures and luxuries. ●noun a person who leads a severely simple life without ordinary pleasures, often for religious reasons. □ **asceticism** (ǎ-**set**-i-sizm) noun

**ASCII** (**ass**-kee) abbreviation (also **ASCII code**) Computing American Standard Code for Information Interchange: a code assigning a different number to each letter and character for computing purposes.

**ascorbic acid** (ǎ-**skor**-bik) vitamin C, found especially in citrus fruits and in vegetables.

**Ascot** a racecourse near Windsor, Berks., scene of an annual race meeting in June.

**ascribe** (ǎ-**skryb**) verb attribute. □ **ascription** (ǎ-**skrip**-shŏn) noun

**asepsis** (ay-**sep**-sis) noun aseptic methods or conditions.

**aseptic** (ay-**sep**-tik) adjective free from bacteria that cause something to become septic; surgically clean. □ **aseptically** adverb

**asexual** (ay-**seks**-yoo-ăl) adjective without sex or sex organs. □ **asexually** adverb

**ASH** abbreviation Action on Smoking and Health.

**ash** noun **1** a tree with silver-grey bark and close-grained wood. **2** this wood. **3** the powder that remains after something has burnt. **4** (**the Ashes**) a trophy awarded as the symbol of victory in a set of Anglo-Australian cricket matches. □ **Ash Wednesday** the first day of Lent.

**ashamed** *adjective* feeling shame.

**ashcan** *noun* (*Amer.*) a dustbin.

**Ashcroft**, Dame Peggy (Edith Margaret Emily) (1907–91), English stage and film actress.

**Ashdown**, Paddy (Jeremy John Durham) (born 1941), British politician, leader of the Liberal Democratic Party from 1988.

**Ashe**, Arthur Robert (1943–93), American tennis player.

**ashen** *adjective* pale as ashes.

**Ashkenazi** (ash-ki-**nah**-zi) *noun* (*plural* **Ashkenazim**) a Jew of northern or eastern Europe, as distinct from a Sephardi. □ **Ashkenazic** *adjective*

**Ashkenazy**, Vladimir Davidovich (born 1937), Russian-born Icelandic pianist.

**ashlar** *noun* square-cut stones; masonry made of these.

**Ashley**, Laura (1925–85), English designer of textiles and fashion in traditional patterns.

**Ashmolean Museum** (ash-**moh**-liăn) a museum of art and antiquities in Oxford.

**ashore** *adverb* to or on shore.

**ashram** *noun* a place of religious learning or retreat for Hindus.

**Ashton**, Sir Frederick (1904–88), British choreographer and ballet director.

**ashtray** *noun* a receptacle for tobacco ash and stubs.

**ashy** *adjective* **1** ashen. **2** covered with ash.

**Asia** (**ay**-shă) the largest of the continents, extending from Europe to the Pacific Ocean. □ **Asian** *adjective & noun*

**Asia Minor** a peninsula of western Asia between the Mediterranean and the Black Sea, including most of Turkey.

**Asiatic** (ay-si-**at**-ik) *adjective* of Asia. ● *noun* an Asian.

---

■ **Usage** *Asian* is the preferred word when used of people.

---

**aside** *adverb* **1** to or on one side, away from the main part or group; *pull it aside*; *step aside*. **2** away from one's thoughts or from consideration. **3** in reserve; *put money aside for a holiday*. ● *noun* words spoken so that only certain people will hear.

**Asimov** (**a**-sim-of), Isaac (born 1920), Russian-born American writer of science fiction.

**asinine** (**ass**-i-nyn) *adjective* silly, stupid.

**ask** *verb* **1** call for an answer to or about, address a question to (a person). **2** seek to obtain from another person; *ask a favour of him*; *asked £5 for the book*. **3** invite; *ask him to dinner*. □ **ask after** inquire about (a person). **ask for it** (*informal*) behave in such a way that trouble is likely. **asking price** the price at which something is offered for sale. **I ask you!** an exclamation of disgust.

**askance** (ă-**skanss**) *adverb* sideways. □ **look askance at** regard with distrust or disapproval.

**askew** *adverb & adjective* not straight or level.

**aslant** *adverb* on a slant, obliquely. ● *preposition* obliquely across.

**asleep** *adverb & adjective* **1** in or into a state of sleep. **2** numbed; *my foot is asleep*.

**ASLEF** *abbreviation* Associated Society of Locomotive Engineers and Firemen.

**asocial** (ay-**soh**-shăl) *adjective* **1** not social, not sociable. **2** (*informal*) inconsiderate.

**asp** *noun* a small poisonous snake.

**asparagus** (ă-**spa**-ră-gŭs) *noun* a plant whose young shoots are cooked and eaten as a vegetable.

**aspartame** (ă-**spar**-taym) *noun* a very sweet low-calorie substance used as a sweetener.

**aspect** *noun* **1** a viewpoint; a feature to be considered; *this aspect of the problem*. **2** the look or appearance of a person or thing; *the forest had a sinister aspect*. **3** the direction a thing faces, a side facing this way; *the house has a southern aspect*. **4** (in astrology) the relative position of a star or group of stars, regarded as having influence on events.

**aspen** *noun* a poplar with leaves that move in the slightest wind.

**asperity** (ă-**spe**-riti) *noun* harshness or severity, especially of manner.

**aspersions** (ă-**sper**-shŏnz) *plural noun* □ **cast aspersions on** attack the reputation of.

**asphalt** (**ass**-falt) *noun* **1** a black sticky substance like coal tar. **2** a mixture of this with gravel etc. used for paving. ● *verb* surface with asphalt.

**asphodel** (**ass**-fŏ-del) *noun* a plant of the lily family.

**asphyxia** (ă-**sfiks**-iă) *noun* a condition caused by lack of air in the lungs; suffocation.

**asphyxiate** (ă-**sfiks**-i-ayt) *verb* suffocate. □ **asphyxiation** *noun*

**aspic** *noun* a savoury jelly used for coating meats, eggs, etc.

**aspidistra** *noun* a house-plant with broad tapering leaves.

**aspirant** (**ass**-per-ănt) *noun* a person who aspires to something.

**aspirate** *noun* (*pronounced* **ass**-per-ăt) the sound of *h*. ● *verb* (*pronounced* **ass**-per-ayt) **1** pronounce with an *h*. **2** draw out with an aspirator.

**aspiration** (ass-per-**ay**-shŏn) *noun* **1** ambition, strong desire. **2** aspirating. **3** the drawing of breath.

**aspirator** *noun* a device used to suck fluid from a cavity.

**aspire** *verb* have a high ambition; *he aspires to become president*; *aspires to the presidency*.

**aspirin** *noun* a medicinal drug used to relieve pain and reduce fever; a tablet of this.

**Asquith**, Herbert Henry, 1st Earl of Oxford and Asquith (1852–1928), British statesman, Prime Minister 1908–16.

**ass¹** noun **1** a donkey. **2** (informal) a stupid person.

**ass²** noun (Amer.) = ARSE.

**assagai** alternative sp. of ASSEGAI.

**assail** (ă-sayl) verb **1** attack violently and persistently. **2** begin (a task) resolutely.

**assailant** noun an attacker.

**Assam** (a-sam) a State in NE India.

**assassin** noun a killer, especially of a political or religious leader.

**assassinate** verb kill (an important person) by violent means, usually from political or religious motives. □ **assassination** noun

**assault** noun **1** a violent attack. **2** an unlawful personal attack on another person, even if only with menacing words. ● verb make an assault on. □ **assault and battery** Law a threatening act resulting in physical harm to someone. **assault course** an obstacle course used e.g. for training soldiers.

**assay** (ă-say) noun a test of metal or ore for quality. ● verb make an assay of.

**assegai** (ass-ig-I) noun (also **assagai**) a light iron-tipped spear of South African peoples.

**assemblage** noun **1** assembling. **2** an assembled group.

**assemble** verb **1** bring or come together. **2** fit or put together.

**assembler** noun **1** a worker who assembles a machine, garment, etc. **2** a computer program that translates instructions from a low-level language into a form that can be understood and executed by the computer. **3** the low-level language itself; assembly language.

**assembly** noun **1** assembling. **2** an assembled group, especially of people meeting for a specific purpose. □ **assembly language** Computing a low-level symbolic code converted by an assembler. **assembly line** a sequence of machines and workers through which parts of a product move to be assembled in successive stages.

**assent** verb consent, express agreement. ● noun (official) consent or approval.

**assert** verb **1** declare as true, state; asserted his innocence. **2** enforce a claim to (rights etc.); asserted his authority. □ **assert oneself** take effective action; use one's authority; insist on one's rights.

**assertion** noun **1** asserting. **2** a statement that something is a fact.

**assertive** adjective asserting oneself, self-assertive; positive, confident. □ **assertively** adverb, **assertiveness** noun

**assess** verb **1** decide or fix the amount or value of. **2** estimate the worth, quality, or likelihood of. □ **assessment** noun

**assessor** noun **1** a person who assesses, especially for tax and insurance. **2** one who advises a judge in court on technical matters.

**asset** (ass-et) noun **1** any property that has money value. **2** a useful or valuable quality or skill; a person or thing regarded as useful. □ **asset-stripping** noun the practice of taking over a company and selling off its assets to make a profit.

**asseverate** (ă-sev-er-ayt) verb (formal) assert solemnly. □ **asseveration** noun

**asshole** noun (Amer.) = ARSEHOLE.

**assiduous** (ă-sid-yoo-ŭs) adjective diligent and persevering. □ **assiduously** adverb, **assiduity** (ass-id-yoo-iti) noun

**assign** verb **1** allot; rooms were assigned to us. **2** appoint or designate to perform a task etc.; assign your best investigator to the job. **3** ascribe, regard as belonging to; we cannot assign an exact date to Stonehenge.

**assignation** (ass-ig-nay-shŏn) noun **1** assigning; being assigned. **2** an arrangement to meet; an appointment.

**assignment** noun **1** assigning; being assigned. **2** a thing or task that is assigned to a person; a share.

**assimilate** verb **1** absorb into the body or into a group or system; become absorbed into something. **2** absorb into the mind as knowledge. □ **assimilable** adjective, **assimilation** noun

**Assisi** (ă-see-see) a town in central Italy, famous as the birthplace of St Francis.

**assist** verb help. □ **assistance** noun

**assistant** noun **1** a person who assists, a helper. **2** a person who serves customers in a shop. ● adjective assisting, helping, and ranking next below a senior person; the assistant manager.

**assizes** plural noun until 1972, a court sitting periodically in each county in England and Wales to deal with civil and criminal cases.

**associate** verb (pronounced ă-soh-shi-ayt) **1** join or cause to join as a companion, colleague, or supporter. **2** (usually foll. by with) have frequent dealings; spend a lot of time with; he associates with dishonest dealers. **3** connect in one's mind; we associate pyramids with Egypt. ● noun (pronounced ă-soh-shi-ăt) **1** a partner, colleague, or companion. **2** one who has been admitted to a lower level of membership of an association without the status of a full member. ● adjective (pronounced ă-soh-shi-ăt) **1** associated. **2** having subordinate membership. □ **associative** adjective

**association** noun **1** associating; being associated; companionship. **2** a group of people organized for some common purpose; *the Automobile Association.* **3** a mental connection between ideas. □ **Association football** a form of football played with a spherical ball that may not be handled except by the goalkeeper.

**assonance** (ass-ŏn-ăns) *noun* resemblance of sound between two syllables; a rhyme depending on similarity of vowel sounds in syllables that do not form a complete rhyme (as in *vermin/furnish*) or in consonants only (as in *killed/cold*).

**assort** *verb* **1** arrange in sorts, classify. **2** suit or harmonize (with another person or thing).

**assorted** *adjective* of different sorts put together; *assorted chocolates.*

**assortment** *noun* **1** a collection composed of several sorts. **2** classification.

**assuage** (ă-swayj) *verb* soothe, make less severe; *to assuage one's thirst.* □ **assuagement** *noun*

**assume** *verb* **1** take as true or sure to happen before there is proof; *we assume that we shall win.* **2** take on, undertake; *he assumed the extra responsibility.* **3** put on; *assumed a serious expression.*

**assuming** *adjective* presumptuous. ●*conjunction* (often foll. by *that*) if we assume that something is the case or will happen; *assuming that we finish it today, we can deliver it tomorrow.*

**assumption** *noun* **1** assuming. **2** something taken for granted, something assumed but not proved. **3** (**the Assumption**) the reception of the Virgin Mary into heaven; the festival commemorating this (15 August).

**assurance** *noun* **1** a formal declaration or promise given to inspire confidence. **2** life insurance. **3** self-confidence.

■**Usage** Insurance companies use the term *assurance* of policies where a sum is payable after a fixed number of years or on the death of the insured person, and *insurance* of policies relating to events such as fire, accident, or death within a limited period. In popular usage the word *insurance* is used in both cases.

**assure** (ă-shoor) *verb* **1** declare confidently, promise; *I assure you there is no danger.* **2** cause to know for certain; *tried the door to assure himself that it was locked.* **3** make certain, ensure; *this will assure your success.* **4** insure by means of an assurance policy.

**assured** (ă-shoord) *adjective* **1** sure. **2** confident; *has an assured manner.* **3** payable under an assurance policy; *the sum assured.*

**assuredly** (ă-shoor-idli) *adverb* certainly.

**Assyria** an ancient country in what is now northern Iraq. □ **Assyrian** *adjective & noun*

**AST** *abbreviation* Atlantic Standard Time.

**Astaire** (ă-stair), Fred (Frederick Austerlitz) (1899–1987), American dancer and film actor.

**astatine** (ass-tă-teen) *noun* a radioactive element (symbol At).

**aster** *noun* a garden plant with daisy-like flowers of various colours.

**asterisk** *noun* a star-shaped symbol (*) used to draw attention to something or as a reference mark. ●*verb* mark with an asterisk.

**astern** *adverb* **1** in, at, or towards the stern of a ship or the tail of an aircraft; behind. **2** backwards; *full speed astern!*

**asteroid** (ass-ter-oid) *noun* **1** any of the small planets revolving round the sun, especially between the orbits of Mars and Jupiter. **2** a starfish.

**asthma** (ass-mă) *noun* a chronic condition causing difficulty in breathing.

**asthmatic** (ass-mat-ik) *adjective* **1** of asthma. **2** suffering from asthma. ●*noun* an asthmatic person.

**astigmatism** (ă-stig-mă-tizm) *noun* a defect in an eye or lens, preventing proper focusing. □ **astigmatic** (ass-tig-mat-ik) *adjective*

**astir** *adverb & adjective* in motion, moving.

**astonish** *verb* surprise very greatly. □ **astonishment** *noun*

**astound** *verb* shock with surprise.

**astraddle** *adverb* astride.

**astrakhan** (astră-kan) *noun* the dark tightly-curled fleece of lambs from Astrakhan in Russia; fabric imitating this.

**astral** (ass-trăl) *adjective* of or from the stars.

**astray** *adverb & adjective* away from the right path. □ **go astray** (of things) be mislaid. **lead astray** lead into error or wrongdoing.

**astride** *adverb* **1** with legs wide apart. **2** with one leg on either side of something. ●*preposition* astride of; extending across.

**astringent** (ă-strin-jĕnt) *adjective* **1** causing skin or body tissue to contract, stopping bleeding. **2** harsh, severe. ●*noun* an astringent substance, used medically or in cosmetics. □ **astringency** *noun*

**astro-** *combining form* of the stars; relating to outer space.

**astrolabe** (ass-trŏ-layb) *noun* an instrument formerly used for measuring the altitudes of stars.

**astrology** (ă-strol-ŏji) *noun* study of the supposed influence of stars on human affairs. □ **astrologer, astrologist** *noun*, **astrological** *adjective*

**astronaut** *noun* a crew member of a spacecraft.

**astronautics** *noun* the scientific study of space travel and its technology.

**astronomical** *adjective* **1** of astronomy. **2** enormous in amount; *an astronomical sum of money.* □ **astronomically** *adverb*

**astronomy** (ă-stron-ŏmi) *noun* the scientific study of the stars and planets and their movements. □ **astronomer** *noun*

**astrophysics** (ass-troh-**fiz**-iks) *noun* the branch of astronomy concerned with the physics and chemistry of the heavenly bodies. □ **astrophysical** *adjective*, **astrophysicist** *noun*

**Astroturf** *noun* (*trade mark*) an artificial grass surface for sports fields.

**Asturias** (ă-stewr-iăs) a region of NW Spain.

**astute** (ă-**stewt**) *adjective* shrewd, quick at seeing how to gain an⁻ advantage. □ **astutely** *adverb*, **astuteness** *noun*

**Asunción** (ă-sŭn-si-**ohn**) the capital of Paraguay.

**asunder** (ă-**sun**-der) *adverb* (*literary*) apart, into pieces; *torn asunder*.

**Aswan** (a-**swahn**) a city in southern Egypt near which are two dams across the Nile.

**asylum** *noun* **1** refuge and safety; a place of refuge. **2** (*old use*) a mental home or institution. □ **political asylum** protection given by a State to a person who has fled from political persecution in another country.

**asymmetry** (a-**sim**-it-ri) *noun* lack of symmetry. □ **asymmetric** *adjective*, **asymmetrical** *adjective*

**At** *symbol* astatine.

**at** *preposition* expressing position or state: **1** of place, order, or time of day; *at the top*; *came at midnight*. **2** of condition or occupation; *at ease*; *they are at dinner*. **3** of price, amount, or age, etc.; *sold at £1 each*; *left school at 15*. **4** of cause; *was annoyed at his failure*. **5** of direction towards; *aimed at the target*. □ **at all** in any way, to any extent, of any kind. **at-home** *noun* a reception for visitors between certain hours. **at it** engaged in some activity; working. **at that 1** at that point. **2** moreover.

**Atatürk** (at-ă-terk), Kemal (1881–1938), Turkish general and statesman, the founder of Turkey as a modern secular State.

**atavism** (at-ă-vizm) *noun* likeness to remote ancestors rather than to parents; reversion to an earlier type.

**atavistic** (at-ă-**vis**-tik) *adjective* like a remote ancestor.

**ataxia** *noun* *Med.* difficulty in controlling bodily movements.

**ate** *see* EAT.

**atheist** (**ayth**-ee-ist) *noun* a person who believes that there is no God. □ **atheism** *noun*, **atheistic** (ayth-ee-**ist**-ik) *adjective*

**Athene** (ăth-ee-ni) (*Gk. myth.*) the goddess of wisdom, identified by the Romans with Minerva.

**Athens** the capital of Greece.

**atherosclerosis** (ath-ĕ-roh-sklĕ-**roh**-sis) *noun* damage to the arteries caused by a build-up of fatty deposits.

**athlete** *noun* a person who is good at athletics. □ **athlete's foot** an infectious fungal condition affecting the feet.

**athletic** *adjective* **1** of athletes. **2** physically strong and active, muscular in build. **3** (**athletics**) (treated as *pl.* or *singular*) physical exercises and sports, especially competitions in running, jumping, etc. □ **athletically** *adverb*, **athleticism** *noun*

**Athos** (ath-oss) *or* (ay-thoss) a mountainous peninsula on the coast of Macedonia, an autonomous district of Greece inhabited by monks of the Eastern Orthodox Church. □ **Athonite** *adjective & noun*

**Atlantic** *adjective* of the Atlantic Ocean. ●*noun* (in full **Atlantic Ocean**) the ocean lying between the Americas and Europe/Africa.

**Atlantis** (*Gk. legend*) a beautiful and prosperous island in the Atlantic Ocean, overwhelmed by the sea.

**Atlas** (*Gk. myth.*) one of the Titans, who was punished for his part in their revolt against Zeus by being made to support the heavens.

**atlas** *noun* a book of maps.

**Atlas Mountains** a range of mountains in North Africa extending from Morocco to Tunis.

**atmosphere** *noun* **1** the mixture of gases surrounding the earth or any star or planet. **2** the air in any place. **3** a psychological environment; a feeling or tone conveyed by something; *an atmosphere of peace and calm*. **4** a unit of pressure, equal to the pressure of the atmosphere at sea level. □ **atmospheric** *adjective*

**atmospherics** *plural noun* electrical disturbances in the atmosphere; crackling sounds or other interference in telecommunications caused by these.

**atoll** (at-ol) *noun* a ring-shaped coral reef enclosing a lagoon.

**atom** *noun* **1** the smallest particle of a chemical element. **2** this as a source of atomic energy. **3** a very small quantity or thing; *there's not an atom of truth in it*. □ **atom bomb** = *atomic bomb*.

**atomic** *adjective* of an atom or atoms. □ **atomic bomb** a bomb that derives its destructive power from atomic energy. **atomic energy** energy obtained as the result of nuclear fission. **atomic mass** the mass of an atom measured in *atomic mass units*. **atomic mass unit** a unit of mass used to express atomic and molecular weights, equal to one-twelfth of the mass of an atom of carbon-12. **atomic number** the number of protons in the nucleus of an atom. **atomic theory** the theory that all matter consists of atoms. **atomic weight** = RELATIVE ATOMIC MASS.

**atomize** (also **atomise**) *verb* reduce to atoms or fine particles.

**atomizer** (also **atomiser**) *noun* a device for reducing liquids to a fine spray.

**atonal** (ay-toh-năl) *adjective* (of music) not written in any particular key or scale-system. □ **atonality** (ay-toh-**nal**-ĭti) *noun*

**atone** *verb* make amends; make up for some error or deficiency.

**atonement** *noun* **1** atoning. **2** (**the Atonement**) the expiation of man's sin by Christ. □ **Day of Atonement** the most solemn religious fast of the Jewish year, eight days after the Jewish New Year.

**atrium** (ay-tri-ŭm) *noun* (*plural* **atria** or **atriums**) **1** the central court of an ancient Roman house. **2** either of the two upper cavities in the heart.

**atrocious** (ă-**troh**-shŭs) *adjective* **1** extremely wicked; brutal. **2** (*informal*) very bad or unpleasant. □ **atrociously** *adverb*

**atrocity** (ă-**tross**-iti) *noun* wickedness; a wicked or cruel act.

**atrophy** (at-rŏ-fi) *noun* wasting away through undernourishment or lack of use. ●*verb* (**atrophied**, **atrophying**) **1** cause atrophy in. **2** suffer atrophy.

**atropine** (at-rŏ-peen) *noun* a poisonous alkaloid in deadly nightshade.

**attaboy** *interjection* (*Amer. slang*) an exclamation of admiration or encouragement.

**attach** *verb* (often foll. by *to*) **1** fix to something else. **2** join as a companion or member; assign (a person) to a particular group. **3** attribute; *we attach no importance to the matter.* **4** be ascribed, be attributable; *no blame attaches to the company.* **5** make a legal attachment of (money or goods).

**attaché** (ă-tash-ay) *noun* a person who is attached to the staff of an ambassador in some specific field of activity; *the military attaché.* □ **attaché case** a small rectangular case for carrying documents etc.

**attached** *adjective* **1** fastened on. **2** bound by affection or loyalty; *she is very attached to her cousin.*

**attachment** *noun* **1** attaching; being attached. **2** something attached; an extra part that fixes on. **3** affection, devotion. **4** legal seizure of property.

**attack** *verb* **1** act violently against; start a fight. **2** criticize strongly. **3** act harmfully on; *rust attacks metals.* **4** begin vigorous work on. ●*noun* **1** a violent attempt to hurt, overcome, or defeat. **2** strong criticism. **3** a sudden onset of illness; *an attack of flu.* □ **attacker** *noun*

**attain** *verb* succeed in doing or getting. □ **attainable** *adjective*

**attainment** *noun* **1** attaining. **2** something attained; a personal achievement.

**attar** (at-er) *noun* fragrant oil obtained from flowers; *attar of roses.*

**attempt** *verb* make an effort to accomplish; *that's attempting the impossible.* ●*noun* **1** an effort to accomplish something. **2** an attack; an effort to overcome or surpass something.

**Attenborough**[1], Sir David Frederick (born 1926), British naturalist and broadcaster.

**Attenborough**[2], Lord Richard Samuel (born 1923), British film actor and director.

**attend** *verb* **1** be present at; go regularly to; *attend school.* **2** (usually foll. by *to*) apply one's mind to, give care and thought to; deal with; *attend to the matter.* **3** look after; *which doctor is attending you?* **4** accompany as an attendant.

**attendance** *noun* **1** attending. **2** the number of people present.

**attendant** *noun* a person who is present as a companion or whose function is to provide service. ●*adjective* accompanying; being in attendance (on a person).

**attention** *noun* **1** applying one's mind to something, mental concentration. **2** awareness; *it attracts attention.* **3** consideration, care; *she shall have every attention.* **4** action to repair or improve something; *this chair needs some attention.* **5** a soldier's erect attitude of readiness with feet together and arms stretched downwards; *stand at attention.* **6** (**attentions**) small acts of kindness or courtesy. ●*interjection* an exclamation used to call people to take notice or to assume an attitude of attention.

**attentive** *adjective* **1** paying attention, watchful. **2** devotedly showing consideration or courtesy to another person. □ **attentively** *adverb*, **attentiveness** *noun*

**attenuate** (ă-ten-yoo-ayt) *verb* **1** make slender or thin. **2** make weaker, reduce the force or value of. □ **attenuation** *noun*

**attest** (ă-test) *verb* **1** provide clear proof of. **2** declare to be true or genuine. □ **attested cattle** cattle certified free from tuberculosis. □ **attestation** (at-ess-tay-shŏn) *noun*

**Attic** *adjective* of ancient Athens or Attica, or the form of Greek used there.

**attic** *noun* a room in the top storey of a house, immediately below the roof.

**Attica** the easternmost part of central Greece, in ancient times the territory of Athens (its chief city).

**Attila** (at-il-ă) *or* (ă-til-ă) king of the Huns 434–53, who inflicted great devastation on much of the Roman Empire.

**attire** *noun* (*formal*) clothes. ●*verb* (*formal*) clothe.

**attitude** *noun* **1** a way of thinking or behaving. **2** a position of the body or its parts. **3** the position of an aircraft etc. in relation to given points. □ **attitude problem** an unhelpful attitude or approach.

**attitudinize** *verb* (also **attitudinise**) behave in an artificial, affected way; pose.

**Attlee**, Clement Richard, 1st Earl (1883–1967), British statesman, Prime Minister 1945–51, whose government set up the Welfare State.

**attorney** (ă-ter-ni) *noun* (*plural* **attorneys**) **1** a person who is appointed to act on behalf of another in business or legal matters. **2** (*Amer.*) a lawyer, especially one qualified to act for clients in legal proceedings. □ **Attorney-General** *noun* the chief legal officer in some countries, appointed by the Government.

**attract** *verb* **1** draw towards itself by unseen force; *a magnet attracts iron.* **2** get the attention of. **3** arouse the interest or pleasure of.

**attraction** *noun* **1** attracting. **2** the ability to attract. **3** something that attracts by arousing interest or pleasure.

**attractive** *adjective* **1** able to attract, pleasing in appearance or effect. **2** having the ability to draw towards itself by unseen force; *the attractive force of a magnet.* □ **attractively** *adverb*, **attractiveness** *noun*

**attribute** *verb* (*pronounced* ă-**trib**-yoot) regard as belonging to, originated by, or written or said by; *this play is attributed to Shakespeare.* ●*noun* (*pronounced* **at**-rib-yoot) **1** a quality that is characteristic of a person or thing; *kindness is one of his attributes.* **2** an object regularly associated with a person or thing; *a pair of scales is an attribute of Justice.* □ **attributable** (ă-**trib**-yoo-tăbl) *adjective*, **attribution** (at-rib-**yoo**-shŏn) *noun*

**attributive** (ă-**trib**-yoo-tiv) *adjective* *Grammar* expressing an attribute and placed before the word it describes, e.g. 'old' in *the old dog* (but not in *the dog is old*). □ **attributively** *adverb*

**attrition** (ă-**trish**-ŏn) *noun* **1** wearing something away by rubbing. **2** a gradual wearing down of strength and morale by continuous harassment; *a war of attrition.*

**attune** *verb* harmonize or adapt (one's mind etc.) to a matter or idea.

**Atwood**, Margaret Eleanor (born 1939), Canadian poet and novelist.

**atypical** (ay-**tip**-ikăl) *adjective* not typical; not conforming to a type. □ **atypically** *adverb*

**Au** *symbol* gold.

**aubergine** (**oh**-ber-*zh*een) *noun* the deep purple fruit of the eggplant, used as a vegetable.

**Aubrey**, John (1626–97), English antiquarian, a pioneer of field archaeology.

**aubrietia** (aw-**bree**-shă) *noun* (also **aubretia**) a low-growing perennial rockplant, flowering in spring.

**auburn** (**aw**-bern) *adjective* (of hair) reddish-brown.

**auc** *abbreviation* (in dates) ab urbe condita (¶ Latin, = from the founding of the city, i.e. Rome, taken as 753 BC.)

**Auckland 1** the largest city and chief seaport of New Zealand. **2** the province of New Zealand comprising the northern part of North Island.

**auction** *noun* a public sale in which articles are sold to the highest bidder. ●*verb* sell by auction. □ **auction bridge** a form of the card-game bridge in which players bid for the right to name trumps.

**auctioneer** *noun* a person who conducts an auction.

**audacious** (aw-**day**-shŭs) *adjective* bold, daring. □ **audaciously** *adverb*, **audacity** (aw-**dass**-iti) *noun*

**Auden**, W(ystan) H(ugh) (1907–73), English poet and dramatist.

**audible** *adjective* loud enough to be heard. □ **audibly** *adverb*, **audibility** *noun*

**audience** *noun* **1** people who have gathered to hear or watch something. **2** people within hearing. **3** a formal interview with a ruler or other important person.

**audio** *noun* (*plural* **audios**) sound or its reproduction. □ **audio frequency** a frequency comparable to that of ordinary sound. **audio typist** one who types from a recording.

**audio-** *combining form* hearing or sound.

**audiotape** *noun* (also **audio tape**) magnetic tape for recording sound; a recording on this.

**audio-visual** *adjective* (of teaching aids etc.) using both sight and sound.

**audit** *noun* an official examination of accounts to see that they are in order. ●*verb* (**audited**, **auditing**) make an audit of.

**audition** *noun* a trial to test the ability of a prospective performer. ●*verb* **1** hold an audition. **2** be tested in an audition.

**auditor** *noun* a person who makes an audit.

**auditorium** (awdit-or-iŭm) *noun* (*plural* **auditoriums** or **auditoria**) the part of a theatre etc. in which an audience sits.

**auditory** (aw-**dit**-er-i) *adjective* of or concerned with hearing.

**Audubon** (**aw**-dŭb-ŏn), John James (1785–1851), American naturalist and artist.

**au fait** (oh **fay**) (usually foll. by *with*) well acquainted with (a subject). (¶ French.)

**Aug.** *abbreviation* August.

**Augean** (aw-jee-ăn) *adjective* **1** of the legendary king Augeus or his filthy stables, which Hercules cleaned in a day by diverting a river through them. **2** filthy.

**auger** (awg-er) *noun* a tool with a spiral point for boring holes in wood.

**aught** (*pronounced* awt) *noun* (*old use*) anything; *for aught I know*.

**augment** (awg-ment) *verb* add to; increase. □ **augmentation** *noun*

**au gratin** (oh grat-an) cooked with a crust of breadcrumbs or melted cheese. (¶ French.)

**augur** (awg-er) *verb* foretell, be a sign of; *this augurs well for your future*.

**augury** *noun* **1** an omen. **2** interpretation of omens.

**August** *noun* the eighth month of the year.

**august** (aw-gust) *adjective* majestic, imposing.

**Augustan** (aw-gus-tăn) *adjective* **1** of the reign of Augustus. **2** (of any national literature) classical, stylish (in English literature, of the 17th–18th centuries). ●*noun* a writer of an Augustan period.

**Augustine¹** (aw-gus-tin), St (of Canterbury, died *c.*604), the first archbishop of Canterbury. Feast day, 26 May.

**Augustine²** (aw-gus-tin), St (of Hippo in North Africa, 354–430), bishop and theologian, who profoundly influenced all later Western theology. Feast day, 28 August.

**Augustinian** (aw-gŭs-tin-ian) *adjective* of St Augustine of Hippo. ●*noun* a member of any of the RC religious orders that observe a rule based on his writings.

**Augustus** (aw-gus-tŭs) (63 BC–AD 14), the first Roman emperor.

**auk** *noun* a northern sea bird with small narrow wings.

**auld lang syne** (*Scottish*) days of long ago.

**aunt** *noun* **1** a sister or sister-in-law of one's father or mother. **2** (*children's informal*) an unrelated woman friend; *Aunt Jane*. □ **Aunt Sally 1** a figure used as a target in a throwing-game. **2** a target of general abuse or criticism.

**auntie** *noun* (also **aunty**) (*informal*) an aunt.

**au pair** (oh **pair**) a young person from overseas helping with housework and receiving board and lodging in return.

**aura** (or-ă) *noun* a distinctive atmosphere surrounding a person or thing; *an aura of happiness*.

**aural** (or-ăl) *adjective* of the ear or hearing. □ **aurally** *adverb*

**aureate** (or-iăt) *adjective* (*poetic*) **1** golden; brilliant. **2** (of language) flowery, elaborate.

**Aurelius** (aw-ree-liŭs), Marcus (AD 121–80), Roman emperor AD 161–80.

**aureole** (or-iohl) *noun* (also **aureola**, *pronounced* aw-ree-ŏlă) **1** a celestial crown or halo, especially on a painting etc. of a divine figure. **2** a corona round the sun or moon.

**au revoir** (oh rĕ-vwar) goodbye for the moment. (¶ French.)

**auricle** (or-i-kŭl) *noun* **1** the external part of the ear. **2** an atrium of the heart. □ **auricular** (aw-rik-yoo-ler) *adjective*

**auricula** *noun* a primula which has clusters of flowers, often with white centres.

**auriferous** (aw-rif-er-ŭs) *adjective* yielding gold.

**aurochs** (or-ŏks) *noun* an extinct European wild ox.

**Aurora** (aw-ror-ă) (*Rom. myth.*) the goddess of the dawn, corresponding to the Greek Eos.

**aurora** (aw-ror-ă) *noun* bands of coloured light appearing in the sky at night and probably caused by electrical radiation from the north and south magnetic poles. □ **aurora australis** (also called the **southern lights**) these lights in the Southern hemisphere. **aurora borealis** (bor-i-ay-lis), (also called the **northern lights**) these lights in the Northern hemisphere.

**Auschwitz** (owsh-vits) a town in Poland, site of a Nazi concentration camp in the Second World War.

**auscultation** (aw-skŭl-tay-shŏn) *noun* listening to the sounds of the heart, lungs, etc., for medical diagnosis.

**auspice** (aw-spis) *noun* **1** an omen. **2** (**auspices**) (usually **under the auspices of**) patronage; *under the auspices of the Red Cross*.

**auspicious** (aw-spish-ŭs) *adjective* showing signs that promise success. □ **auspiciously** *adverb*

**Aussie** (oz-i) (*informal*) *noun* an Australian. ●*adjective* Australian.

**Austen**, Jane (1775–1817), English novelist.

**austere** (aw-steer) *adjective* severely simple and plain without ornament or comfort. □ **austerely** *adverb*

**austerity** (aw-ste-riti) *noun* being austere, an austere condition; *the austerities of life in wartime*.

**Austerlitz** (aw-ster-lits) a town in the Czech Republic, scene in 1805 of Napoleon's defeat of the Austrians and Russians.

**Austin**, Herbert, 1st Baron (1866–1941), English motor manufacturer.

**Austin Friars** Augustinian Friars.

**austral** (aw-străl) *or* (oss-trăl) *adjective* **1** southern. **2** (**Austral**) Australian; Australasian.

**Australasia** (oss-trăl-ay-zhă) Australia, New Zealand, and neighbouring islands in the South Pacific. □ **Australasian** *adjective & noun*

**Australia** (oss-**tray**-liă) a continent between the Pacific and Indian Oceans. □ **Australia Day** an annual public holiday in Australia, held on the first Monday after 25 January to commemorate the first settlement (1788).

**Australian** *noun* a person from Australia. ●*adjective* of Australia. □ **Australian (National) Rules football** a form of football played in Australia by teams of 18 players with an oval ball.

**Australian Capital Territory** the area of Australia containing Canberra.

**Austria** (oss-stri-ă) a country in central Europe. □ **Austrian** *adjective & noun*

**autarchy** (**aw**-tar-ki) *noun* a system of government with unrestricted powers; autocracy.

**autarky** (**aw**-tar-ki) *noun* self-sufficiency, especially in economic affairs.

**authentic** *adjective* genuine, known to be true. □ **authentically** *adverb*, **authenticity** *noun*

**authenticate** *verb* prove the truth or authenticity of. □ **authentication** *noun*

**author** *noun* **1** the writer of a book or books etc. **2** the originator of a plan or policy. □ **authorship** *noun*

**authoress** *noun* **1** a woman who writes books. **2** a woman who originates a plan or policy.

**authorise** alternative sp. of AUTHORIZE.

**authoritarian** (awth-o-ri-**tair**-iăn) *adjective* favouring or enforcing complete obedience to authority. ●*noun* a supporter of such principles.

**authoritative** (awth-**o**-ri-tă-tiv) *adjective* having or using authority. □ **authoritatively** *adverb*

**authority** *noun* **1** the power or right to give orders and make others obey, or to take specific action. **2** a person or group with such power. **3** a person with specialized knowledge; a book etc. that can supply reliable information; *he is an authority on spiders.*

**authorize** *verb* (also **authorise**) **1** give authority to. **2** give authority for, sanction; *I authorized this payment.* □ **Authorized Version** the English translation of the Bible (1611) made by order of King James I. □ **authorization** *noun*

**autistic** (aw-**tiss**-tik) *adjective* having a form of mental illness that causes a person to withdraw into a private world and be unable to communicate with others or respond to the real environment; *autistic children.* □ **autism** (**aw**-tizm) *noun*

**auto** *noun* (plural **autos**) (*Amer. informal*) a motor car.

**auto-** *combining form* **1** self; own. **2** of or by oneself or itself, automatic.

**autobahn** (**aw**-tŏ-bahn) *noun* a German, Austrian, or Swiss motorway.

**autobiography** *noun* the story of a person's life written by himself or herself. □ **autobiographical** *adjective*

**autoclave** (**aw**-tŏ-klayv) *noun* a sterilizer using high-pressure steam.

**autocracy** (aw-**tok**-răsi) *noun* rule by an autocrat; dictatorship.

**autocrat** (**aw**-tŏ-krat) *noun* a person with unlimited power; a dictatorial person. □ **autocratic** (aw-tŏ-**krat**-ik) *adjective*, **autocratically** *adverb*

**autocross** *noun* motor racing across country.

**Autocue** *noun* (*trade mark*) a device showing a television speaker the script as an aid to memory.

**auto-da-fé** (aw-toh-da-**fay**) *noun* (plural **autos-da-fé**) **1** (*hist.*) the ceremonial judgement of heretics by the Spanish Inquisition. **2** the execution of heretics by public burning. (¶ Portuguese, = act of the faith.)

**autogiro** (aw-tŏ-**jy**-roh) *noun* (also **autogyro**) (plural **autogiros**) an aircraft resembling a helicopter but with wings that are not powered and rotate in the slipstream.

**autograph** *noun* a person's signature, especially that of a celebrity. ●*verb* sign one's name on or in; *the author will autograph copies of his book tomorrow.*

**autoimmune** *adjective* (of a disease) caused by the action of antibodies produced against substances naturally present in the body. □ **autoimmunity** *noun*

**automat** *noun* (*Amer.*) **1** a slot-machine. **2** a cafeteria selling food and drink from slot-machines.

**automate** *verb* control or operate by automation; *the process is fully automated.*

**automatic** *adjective* **1** working of itself without direct human control, self-regulating. **2** firing repeatedly until pressure on the trigger is released; *an automatic pistol.* **3** done without thought, done from habit or routine; *made an automatic gesture of apology.* ●*noun* **1** an automatic machine, tool, or firearm. **2** a vehicle with a system for automatic gear-change. □ **automatic pilot** a device in an aircraft or ship to keep it on a set course. **automatic transmission** a system in a vehicle for changing gear automatically. □ **automatically** *adverb*

**automation** *noun* the use of automatic methods or equipment to save labour.

**automatism** (aw-**tom**-ă-tizm) *noun* **1** involuntary action. **2** unthinking routine.

**automaton** (aw-tom-ă-tŏn) *noun* (*plural* **automata** *or* **automatons**) a robot; a person who seems to act like one, mechanically and without thinking.

**automobile** (aw-tŏm-ŏ-beel) *noun* (*Amer.*) a motor car.

**automotive** (aw-tŏm-**oh**-tiv) *adjective* concerned with motor vehicles.

**autonomous** (aw-**tonn**-ŏ-mŭs) *adjective* self-governing. □ **autonomy** *noun* self-government, independence.

**autopilot** *noun* = AUTOMATIC PILOT.

**autopsy** (aw-top-si) *noun* a post-mortem.

**autoroute** *noun* a French motorway.

*autostrada* (aw-tŏ-strah-dă) *noun* (*plural* **autostradas** *or* **autostrade**) an Italian motorway.

**auto-suggestion** *noun* the process of unconsciously influencing one's own attitudes, behaviour, etc. oneself.

**autumn** *noun* the season between summer and winter. □ **autumnal** (aw-**tum**-năl) *adjective*

**Auvergne** (oh-**vern**) a region of south central France.

**auxiliary** (awg-**zil**-yer-i) *adjective* giving help or support; *auxiliary services*. ●*noun* **1** a helper. **2** (**auxiliaries**) foreign or allied troops employed by a country at war. □ **auxiliary verb** one used in forming parts of other verbs, e.g. *have* in *I have finished*.

**AV** *abbreviation* Authorized Version.

**avail** *verb* be of help or advantage; *nothing availed against the storm*. ●*noun* effectiveness, advantage; *it was of no avail*. □ **avail oneself of** make use of.

**available** *adjective* ready or able to be used; obtainable. □ **availability** *noun*

**avalanche** (av-ă-lahnsh) *noun* **1** a mass of snow or rock pouring down a mountainside. **2** a great onrush; *an avalanche of letters*.

**Avalon** (av-ă-lŏn) **1** (in Arthurian legend) the place to which King Arthur was conveyed after death. **2** (*Welsh myth.*) an island paradise of the blessed dead.

**avant-garde** (av-ahn **gard**) *adjective* using or favouring an ultra-modern style, especially in art or literature; new, innovative. ●*noun* an avant-garde group.

**avarice** (av-er-iss) *noun* greed for gain. □ **avaricious** (av-er-**ish**-ŭs) *adjective*

**avatar** (av-ă-tar) *noun* (in Hinduism) the descent to earth of a deity in human, animal, or superhuman form.

**Ave** (**ah**-vay) *noun* (in full **Ave Maria**, *pronounced* mă-**ree**-ă) Hail Mary. (¶ Latin.)

**Ave.** *abbreviation* Avenue.

**avenge** *verb* take vengeance for (a wrongdoing); *resolved to avenge their mother's murder*; *avenging himself for these injustices*. □ **avenger** *noun*

**avenue** *noun* **1** a wide street or road, especially one lined with trees. **2** a way of approaching or making progress; *other avenues to fame*.

**aver** (ă-**ver**) *verb* (**averred, averring**) assert, state as true. □ **averment** *noun*

**average** *noun* **1** the value arrived at by adding several quantities together and dividing the total by the number of quantities. **2** the standard or level regarded as usual. **3** *Law* damage to or loss of a ship or cargo. ●*adjective* **1** found by making an average; *the average age of the pupils is fifteen*. **2** of the ordinary or usual standard; *people of average intelligence*. ●*verb* **1** amount to or produce as an average; *the car averaged 40 miles to the gallon*. **2** calculate the average of. □ **on average, on an average** as an estimated average rate; normally.

**averse** (ă-**verss**) *adjective* (usually foll. by *to*) unwilling, disinclined; *he is averse to hard work*.

**aversion** (ă-**ver**-shŏn) *noun* **1** (usually foll. by *to* or *for*) a strong dislike. **2** something disliked.

**avert** (ă-**vert**) *verb* **1** turn away; *people averted their eyes*. **2** prevent, ward off; *managed to avert disaster*.

**Avesta** (ă-**vest**-ă) *noun* the sacred writings of Zoroastrianism.

**Avestan** (ă-**vest**-ăn) *noun* the ancient east-Iranian language in which the Avesta is written. ●*adjective* of Avestan or the Avesta.

**aviary** (**ay**-vi-er-i) *noun* a large cage or building for keeping birds.

**aviation** (ay-vi-**ay**-shŏn) *noun* the practice or science of flying aircraft.

**aviator** (**ay**-vi-ay-ter) *noun* a pilot or member of an aircraft crew in the early days of aviation.

**avid** (av-id) *adjective* eager, greedy; keen; *an avid photographer*; *avid for more news*. □ **avidly** *adverb*, **avidity** (ă-**vid**-iti) *noun*

**Avignon** (a-**veen**-yawn) a city on the Rhône in southern France, residence of the popes during their exile from Rome in the 14th century.

**avionics** (ay-vi-**on**-iks) *noun* the application of electronics in aviation.

**avocado** (av-ŏ-**kah**-doh) *noun* (*plural* **avocados**) (in full **avocado pear**) a dark green pear-shaped fruit with creamy edible flesh.

**avocation** (av-ŏ-**kay**-shŏn) *noun* **1** a secondary activity done in addition to one's main work. **2** (*informal*) one's occupation.

**avocet** (av-ŏ-set) *noun* a wading bird with long legs and an upturned bill.

**Avogadro** (av-ŏ-**gad**-roh), Amadeo (1776–1856), Italian physicist, noted for his work on gases.

**avoid** verb 1 keep oneself away from (something dangerous or undesirable). 2 refrain from; avoid making rash promises. □ **avoidable** adjective, **avoidance** noun

**avoirdupois** (av-er-dew-**poiz**) noun (in full **avoirdupois weight**) a system of weights based on a pound of 16 ounces or 7000 grains.

**Avon** a county of SW England.

**avow** verb (formal) admit, declare openly. □ **avowal** noun, **avowedly** (ă-**vow**-idli) adverb

**avuncular** (ă-**vunk**-yoo-ler) adjective of or like a kindly uncle; friendly, caring.

**AWACS** (**ay**-waks) abbreviation airborne warning and control system: an airborne long-range radar system.

**await** verb 1 wait for; I await your reply. 2 be waiting for; a surprise awaits you.

**awake** verb (**awoke**, **awoken**) 1 wake, cease to sleep. 2 become active. 3 rouse from sleep. ● adjective 1 not yet asleep, no longer asleep. 2 alert, aware; he is awake to the possible danger.

**awaken** verb awake. □ **awakening** noun

**award** verb give by official decision as a payment or prize. ● noun 1 a decision of this kind. 2 a thing awarded.

**aware** adjective 1 having knowledge or realization; I am aware of this possibility. 2 well-informed. □ **awareness** noun

**awash** adjective 1 covered by water; flooded. 2 (foll. by with) overflowing, full; the place was awash with journalists.

**away** adverb 1 to or at a distance. 2 out of existence; the water has boiled away. 3 constantly, persistently; we worked away at it. ● adjective played or playing on an opponent's ground; an away match. ● noun an away match win.

**awe** noun respect combined with fear or wonder. ● verb fill with awe. □ **awe-inspiring** adjective magnificent; causing awe.

**aweigh** (ă-**way**) adverb (of an anchor) hanging just clear of the sea-bottom.

**awesome** adjective 1 inspiring awe; dreaded. 2 (slang) excellent.

**awestricken**, **awestruck** adjective suddenly filled with awe.

**awful** adjective 1 extremely bad or unpleasant; an awful accident. 2 (informal) extreme, very great; that's an awful lot of money.

**awfully** adverb 1 badly; unpleasantly. 2 (informal) very; very much.

**awhile** adverb for a short time.

**awkward** adjective 1 difficult to use or deal with. 2 clumsy, having little skill. 3 inconvenient; came at an awkward time. 4 embarrassed; I feel awkward about it. □ **awkwardly** adverb, **awkwardness** noun

**awl** noun a small pointed tool for making holes, especially in leather or wood.

**awn** noun the bristly head of the sheath of barley and other grasses.

**awning** noun a roof of canvas etc. stretched on a frame as a shelter against sun or rain.

**awoke**, **awoken** see AWAKE.

**AWOL** (**ay**-wol) abbreviation absent without leave; gone AWOL.

**awry** (ă-**ry**) adverb 1 twisted towards one side. 2 amiss; plans went awry. ● adjective crooked; wrong.

**axe** noun (Amer. **ax**) 1 a chopping-tool with a heavy blade. 2 (**the axe**) dismissal (of employees); abandonment of a project etc. ● verb cut (costs or staff) drastically; dismiss; abandon; the project was axed. □ **have an axe to grind** have some personal interest involved and be anxious to take care of it.

**axes** see AXIS.

**axial** adjective 1 of or forming an axis. 2 round an axis. □ **axially** adverb

**axil** noun the angle where a leaf joins a stem.

**axiom** (**aks**-i-ŏm) noun an accepted general truth or principle.

**axiomatic** (aks-i-ŏm-**at**-ik) adjective 1 of or like an axiom. 2 self-evident.

**axis** noun (plural **axes**) 1 an imaginary line through the centre of an object, round which it rotates when spinning. 2 a line about which a regular figure is symmetrically arranged. 3 a reference line for the measurement of coordinates etc. 4 the relation between countries, regarded as a common pivot on which they move; (**the Axis**) the alliance between Germany and Italy (and later Japan) in the Second World War.

**axle** noun the bar or rod on which a wheel or wheels turn.

**axolotl** (ax-ŏ-**lot**-ĕl) noun a newt-like amphibian found in Mexican lakes.

**ayah** noun a native nurse or maidservant, especially formerly in India.

**ayatollah** (I-ă-**tol**-ă) noun a Shiite Muslim religious leader in Iran.

**Ayckbourn**, Alan (born 1939), English playwright, noted for his domestic comedies.

**aye**[1] (pronounced I) (also **ay**) adverb (old or dialect use) yes. ● noun a vote in favour of a proposal; the ayes have it.

**aye**[2] (pronounced ay) adverb (old use) always.

**Ayers Rock** (pronounced airz) a red rock-mass in Northern Territory, Australia.

**Ayrshire** noun an animal of a breed of mainly white dairy cattle.

**AZ** abbreviation Arizona.

**azalea** (ă-**zay**-liă) noun a shrub-like flowering plant of the rhododendron family.

**Azerbaijan** (az-er-by-**jahn**) a republic of Eastern Europe between the Black Sea and the Caspian Sea.

**Azikiwe** (az-i-**kee**-way), (Benjamin) Nnamdi (born 1904), Nigerian statesman, first President of the Republic of Nigeria 1963–6.

**azimuth** (**az**-i-mŭth) *noun* **1** an arc of the sky from the zenith to the horizon. **2** the angle between this arc and the meridian. **3** a directional bearing. □ **azimuthal** *adjective*

**Azores** (ă-**zorz**), **the** a group of volcanic islands in the North Atlantic, in Portuguese possession.

**Azov** (**az**-of), **Sea of** an inland sea of Eastern Europe, connected to the Black Sea by a narrow strait.

**Azrael** (**az**-rayl) (*Jewish* & *Muslim myth.*) the angel who severs the soul from the body at death.

**AZT** *abbreviation* a drug developed for use in the treatment of Aids.

**Aztec** *noun* **1** a member of an Indian people of Mexico before the Spanish conquest (1521). **2** the language of this people. ● *adjective* of the Aztecs or their language.

**azure** (**a**-*zh*er, **az**-yoor) *adjective* & *noun* sky-blue.

# Bb

**B** *noun (plural* **Bs** *or* **B's)** **1** the second letter of the alphabet. **2** *Music* the seventh note of the scale of C major. **3** the second point, example, etc.; the second highest category (of roads, marks, etc.). **4** (B, 2B, 3B, etc.) (of a pencil lead) soft; softer than H and HB (the higher the number, the softer and blacker the lead). ● *symbol* boron.

**b.** *abbreviation* born.

**BA** *abbreviation* **1** Bachelor of Arts. **2** British Airways.

**Ba** *symbol* barium.

**baa** *noun* the cry of a sheep or lamb.

**Baader-Meinhof Group** (bah-der **myn**-hof) *see* RED ARMY FACTION.

**Baalbek** (**bahl**-bek) a town in eastern Lebanon with many temples, houses, and mosaics from the Roman period.

**baas** *noun (South African)* boss, master.

**baasskap** *noun* (in South Africa) domination of non-Whites by Whites.

**Babbage**, Charles (1791–1871), English mathematician and inventor, pioneer of machine computing.

**babble** *verb* **1** chatter in a thoughtless or confused way. **2** make a continuous murmuring sound; *a babbling brook.* ● *noun* babbling talk or sound.

**babe** *noun* **1** *(literary)* a baby. **2** *(Amer. slang)* a man's girlfriend.

**babel** (**bay**-bĕl) *noun* a confused noise or scene. □ **Tower of Babel** (in the Old Testament) a high tower built in an attempt to reach heaven, which God frustrated by confusing the languages of its builders so that they could not understand one another.

**baboon** *noun* a large long-nosed African or Arabian monkey.

**Babur** (**bah**-boor) (1483–1530), the first Mogul emperor, who invaded India *c.*1525.

**baby** *noun* **1** a very young child or animal. **2** a babyish or timid person. **3** *(Amer. slang)* a man's girlfriend. **4** something small of its kind. **5** something that is one's personal concern or creation. ● *verb* **(babied, babying)** treat like a baby, pamper. □ **baby boom** *(informal)* a temporary marked increase in the birth rate. **Baby Buggy** *(trade mark)* a light collapsible pushchair. **baby carriage** *(Amer.)* a pram. **baby grand** the smallest kind of grand piano. **be left holding the baby** *(informal)* be left with an unwelcome responsibility. □ **babyhood** *noun*

**Babygro** *noun (plural* **Babygros)** *(trade mark)* a stretchy all-in-one baby suit.

**babyish** *adjective* like a baby.

**Babylon** **1** the capital of Babylonia. **2** *(scornful)* (among Blacks, especially Rastafarians) White society or its representatives, especially the police.

**Babylonia** the ancient name for southern Mesopotamia, a powerful kingdom until 538 BC. □ **Babylonian** *adjective & noun*

**babysit** *verb* look after a child in its home while its parents are out. □ **babysitter** *noun*

**Bacall**, Lauren (original name: Betty Perske) (born 1924), American actress.

**baccalaureate** (bak-ă-**lor**-iăt) *noun* the final secondary school examination in France and many international schools.

**baccarat** (**bak**-er-ah) *noun* a gambling cardgame.

**Bacchanalia** *plural noun* **1** the Roman festival of Bacchus, the god of wine. **2** (**bacchanalia**) drunken revelry.

**Bacchus** (**bak**-ŭs) *(Gk. myth.)* another name for Dionysus.

**baccy** *noun (informal)* tobacco.

**Bach** *(pronounced* bahk), Johann Sebastian (1685–1750), and his sons Carl Philipp Emanuel (1714–88), and Johann Christian (1735–82), German composers.

**bachelor** *noun* **1** an unmarried man. **2** a person who holds a university first degree; *Bachelor of Arts.* □ **bachelor girl** an independent young single woman. □ **bachelorhood** *noun*

**bacillus** (bă-**sil**-ŭs) *noun (plural* **bacilli**, *pronounced* bă-**sil**-I) a rod-like bacterium.

**back** *noun* **1** the rear surface of the human body from neck to hip; the corresponding part of an animal's body. **2** that part of a chair etc. against which a seated person's back rests. **3** the part or surface of an object that is less used or less important; the part furthest from the front. **4** the part of a garment covering the back. **5** a defensive player near the goal in football etc.; this position. ● *adjective* **1** situated behind; *the back teeth*; *back streets.* **2** of or for a past time; *back pay.* ● *adverb* **1** at or towards the rear, away from the front or centre. **2** in check; *hold it back.* **3** in or into a previous time or position or condition; *I'll be back at six.* **4** in return; *pay it back.* ● *verb* **1** go or cause to go backwards. **2** (of wind) change gradually in an anticlockwise direction. **3** give one's support to, assist. **4** give financial support to; *he is backing the play.*

**5** lay a bet on. **6** cover the back of; *the rug is backed with canvas.* □ **at the back of** being the underlying cause or motive of (a thing). **back and forth** to and fro. **back boiler** a boiler behind a domestic fire or cooking range. **back-crawl** *noun* = BACK-STROKE. **back door** secret, unusual, or underhand methods; *becoming a member by the back door; back-door methods.* **back down** give up a claim; withdraw one's argument. **back number 1** an old issue of a periodical. **2** an out-of-date person or idea. **back of beyond** a very remote place. **back out** withdraw from an agreement. **back-pedal** *verb* change one's mind; try to reverse one's previous decision or commitment. **back seat 1** a seat at the back. **2** a less prominent position. **back-seat driver** a person who has no responsibility but is eager to give orders to one who has. **back to front** with the back placed where the front should be. **back up 1** give one's support to; confirm (a statement). **2** *Computing* make a backup copy of (a file, disk, etc.). **have one's back to the wall** be fighting for survival in a desperate situation. **on the back-burner** left aside for consideration at a later date; postponed. **put** (or **get**) **a person's back up** offend or antagonize him or her.

**backache** *noun* pain in one's back.

**backbencher** *noun* an ordinary MP who does not hold a senior office (compare *front-bencher*).

**backbiting** *noun* spiteful talk, especially about a person who is not present.

**backbone** *noun* **1** the column of small bones down the centre of the back, the spine. **2** strength of character.

**backchat** *noun* (*informal*) cheeky words in response to a rebuke.

**backcloth** *noun* = BACKDROP.

**backcomb** *verb* comb (a section of hair) towards the roots while holding the ends, in order to make it bushy.

**backdate** *verb* declare that (a thing) is to be regarded as valid from some date in the past.

**backdrop** *noun* **1** a flat painted curtain at the back of a stage set. **2** the background to a scene or situation.

**backer** *noun* a person who supports another, especially financially.

**backfire** *verb* **1** ignite or explode prematurely, especially in an internal combustion engine. **2** produce an undesired effect, especially upon the originators; *their plan backfired.* ●*noun* an instance of backfiring.

**backgammon** *noun* a game played on a double board with draughts and dice.

**background** *noun* **1** the back part of a scene or picture; the setting for the chief objects or people. **2** an inconspicuous position; *he was kept in the background; background music.* **3** the conditions and events surrounding and influencing something; a person's family life, education, experience, etc.

**backhand** *adjective* (of a stroke or blow) made with the back of the hand turned outwards. ●*noun* a backhand stroke or blow.

**backhanded** *adjective* **1** backhand. **2** indirect; ambiguous; *a backhanded compliment.*

**backhander** *noun* **1** a backhanded stroke, blow, or remark. **2** (*slang*) a bribe, a reward for services rendered.

**backing** *noun* **1** help, support. **2** material used to support or line a thing's back. **3** a musical accompaniment to a pop singer.

**backlash** *noun* **1** a violent and usually hostile reaction to some event or development. **2** a recoil in machinery; excessive play between parts.

**backless** *adjective* **1** without a back. **2** (of a dress) cut low at the back.

**backlist** *noun* a publisher's list of books still available.

**backlog** *noun* arrears of work.

**backpack** *noun* **1** a rucksack. **2** a package of equipment carried similarly.

**backside** *noun* (*informal*) the buttocks.

**backslide** *verb* slip back from good behaviour into bad.

**backspace** *verb* cause a typewriter carriage, computer cursor, etc. to move one space back.

**backspin** *noun* a backward spinning movement of a ball, reducing its speed as it bounces.

**backstage** *adjective & adverb* behind the stage of a theatre, in the wings or dressing-rooms.

**backstitch** *verb* sew by inserting the needle each time behind the place where it has just been brought out. ●*noun* a stitch made in this way.

**backstreet** *noun* a side-street, an alley. ●*adjective* illegal, illicit; *backstreet abortions.*

**backstroke** *noun* a swimming stroke done lying on the back.

**backtrack** *verb* **1** go back the same way that one came. **2** back down from an argument or policy, reverse one's previous action.

**backup** *noun* (often used as *adjective*) **1** support; reserve; *a backup team.* **2** *Computing* the copying of data, files, disks, etc. for safety; the copy itself.

**backward** *adjective* **1** directed towards the back or the starting-point. **2** having made less than normal progress. **3** diffident, not putting oneself forward. ●*adverb* backwards. □ **backwardness** *noun*

**backwards** *adverb* **1** away from one's front, towards the back. **2** with the back foremost; in a reverse direction or order. □ **backwards and forwards** to and fro.

**bend over backwards** (*informal*) to do one's utmost.

**backwash** *noun* **1** a backward flow of water. **2** the after-effects of an action or event.

**backwater** *noun* **1** a stretch of stagnant water joining a stream. **2** a place unaffected by progress or new ideas.

**backwoods** *noun* **1** remote uncleared forest. **2** a remote or backward area. □ **backwoodsman** *noun*

**backyard** *noun* a yard at the back of a house.

**Bacon**[1], Francis, Baron Verulam, Viscount St Albans (1561–1626), English lawyer and philosopher, pre-eminent in the late Elizabethan and early Stuart periods.

**Bacon**[2], Francis (1909–92), British painter, whose work is characterized by lurid colours and distorted creatures.

**bacon** *noun* salted or smoked meat from the back or sides of a pig. □ **bring home the bacon** (*informal*) **1** achieve success. **2** provide financial support for one's family.

**bacteriology** *noun* the scientific study of bacteria. □ **bacteriological** *adjective*, **bacteriologist** *noun*

**bacterium** (bak-**teer**-iŭm) *noun* (*plural* **bacteria**) a microscopic organism. □ **bacterial** *adjective*

**Bactrian camel** the two-humped camel of central Asia.

**bad** *adjective* (**worse, worst**) **1** wicked, evil. **2** unpleasant. **3** serious, severe. **4** inferior, of poor quality; worthless; decayed. **5** harmful; unsuitable; *sweets are bad for the teeth.* **6** in ill health, diseased. **7** (**badder, baddest**) (*slang*) excellent. ● *adverb* (*Amer. informal*) badly; *is he hurt bad?* ● *noun* that which is bad or unfortunate. □ **bad blood** ill feeling, enmity. **bad debt** one that will not be repaid. **bad-mouth** *verb* (especially *Amer. slang*) insult, put down. **bad news** (*informal*) an unpleasant or troublesome person or thing; *that boyfriend of hers is bad news.* **bad-tempered** *adjective* irritable. **be in a bad way** be ill or in trouble. **feel bad about** (*informal*) feel upset or guilty about. **not bad** (*informal*) quite good. **too bad** (*informal*) regrettable. □ **badness** *noun*

**baddy** *noun* (*informal*) a villain.

**bade** *see* BID[2].

**Baden-Powell** (bay-děn-**pohl**), Robert Stephenson Smyth, 1st Baron (1857–1941), English soldier, founder of the Boy Scouts (1908) and Girl Guides (1910).

**badge** *noun* a thing worn to show one's rank, membership of an organization, support for a cause, etc.

**badger** *noun* a nocturnal animal that has a black and white striped head and lives in a burrow (or set). ● *verb* pester.

**badinage** (bad-in-ah*z*h) *noun* banter. (¶ French.)

**badlands** *plural noun* **1** a barren eroded region. **2** (**the Badlands**) a section of SW South Dakota and NW Nebraska.

**badly** *adverb* (**worse, worst**) **1** in an inferior, unsuitable, or defective way. **2** so as to inflict much injury; severely. **3** (*informal*) very much.

**badminton** *noun* a game played with rackets and shuttlecocks across a high net.

**Baez**, Joan (born 1941), American singer.

**Baffin Bay** the strait between **Baffin Island** (the largest island in the Canadian Arctic) and Greenland, named after the English explorer William Baffin (*c.*1584–1622), who discovered the island in 1616.

**baffle** *verb* **1** puzzle, perplex. **2** frustrate; *baffled their attempts.* ● *noun* a screen placed so as to hinder or control the passage of sound, light, or fluid. □ **bafflement** *noun*

**BAFTA** *abbreviation* British Association of Film and Television Arts.

**bag** *noun* **1** a container made of flexible material, used for holding or carrying things. **2** something resembling a bag; *bags under the eyes.* **3** (*offensive slang*) a woman. **4** the amount of game short by a sportsman. **5** (**bags**) (*informal*) plenty; *bags of room.* ● *verb* (**bagged, bagging**) **1** put into a bag or bags. **2** kill or capture; *bagged a pheasant.* **3** (*informal*) take possession of, stake a claim to. **4** hang loosely. □ **bag lady** a homeless woman who carries her possessions in shopping bags. **in the bag** (*informal*) secured as one wished.

**bagatelle** (bag-ă-**tel**) *noun* **1** a board game in which small balls are struck into holes. **2** something small and unimportant. **3** a short piece of music.

**bagel** (**bay**-gěl) *noun* a hard bread roll in the shape of a ring.

**bagful** *noun* (*plural* **bagfuls**) as much as a bag will hold.

**baggage** *noun* **1** luggage. **2** portable equipment.

**baggy** *adjective* (**baggier, baggiest**) hanging in loose folds. □ **baggily** *adverb*, **bagginess** *noun*

**Baghdad** (bag-**dad**) the capital of Iraq.

**bagpipe** *noun* (also **bagpipes**) a musical instrument with air stored in a bag and pressed out through pipes.

**baguette** (ba-**get**) *noun* a long thin French loaf.

**bah** *interjection* an exclamation of contempt or disgust.

**Baha'i** (bah-**hah**-i) *noun* **1** a religion founded in Persia in the 19th century by Baha'ullah

(1817–92) and his son, whose quest is for world peace and unity. **2** a follower of this religion.

**Bahamas** (bă-**hah**-măz) a group of islands in the West Indies. □ **Bahamian** adjective & noun

**Bahrain** (bah-**rayn**) a sheikhdom consisting of a group of islands in the Persian Gulf. □ **Bahraini** adjective & noun

**Baikal** (by-**kahl**), **Lake** a large lake in southern Siberia.

**bail**¹ noun **1** money or property pledged as security that a person accused of a crime will return to stand trial. **2** permission for a person's release on such security. ● verb **1** obtain or allow (a person's) release on bail. **2** (usually foll. by out) relieve by financial help in an emergency; bail the firm out. □ **bail bandit** a person who commits a crime while on bail awaiting trial. **stand** (or **go**) **bail for** pledge money as bail for (a person). **on bail** released after payment of bail.

**bail**² noun **1** either of the two cross-pieces resting on the three stumps in cricket. **2** a bar separating horses in an open stable. **3** a bar holding paper against the platen of a typewriter.

**bail**³ verb (also **bale**) scoop out (water that has entered a boat); clear (a boat) in this way.

**bailey** noun the outer wall of a castle; a courtyard enclosed by this.

**Bailey bridge** a bridge made in prefabricated sections designed for rapid assembly. (¶ Named after its designer Sir Donald Bailey (1901–85).)

**bailiff** noun **1** a law officer who helps a sheriff, serving writs and performing arrests. **2** a landlord's agent or steward. **3** the leading civil officer in each of the Channel Islands.

**bailiwick** noun **1** the authority or territory of a bailiff. **2** a person's particular interest.

**bain-marie** (ban-ma-**ree**) noun (plural **bains-marie**, pronounced same) a vessel of hot water in which a dish of food is placed for slow cooking. (¶ French.)

**Baird**, John Logie (1888–1946), Scottish pioneer of television.

**bairn** noun (especially Scottish) a child.

**bait** noun **1** food placed to attract prey. **2** an enticement. ● verb **1** place bait on or in; bait the trap. **2** torment by jeering.

**baize** noun thick woollen green cloth, used for covering tables.

**bake** verb **1** cook or be cooked by dry heat, especially in an oven. **2** expose to great heat; harden or be hardened by heat. □ **baked beans** cooked haricot beans, usually tinned in tomato sauce.

**Bakelite** (**bay**-kĕ-lyt) noun (trade mark) a hard plastic. (¶ Named after its Belgian-American inventor L. H. Baekeland (died 1944).)

**Baker**, Dame Janet Abbott (born 1933), English mezzo-soprano singer.

**baker** noun one who bakes and sells bread. □ **baker's dozen** thirteen. (¶ From the former custom of allowing the retailer to receive thirteen loaves for each twelve paid for.)

**Baker day** (British informal) a day set aside for in-service training of teachers. (¶ Named after Kenneth Baker, Education Secretary who introduced them.)

**bakery** noun a place where bread and cakes are baked or sold.

**Bakewell tart** a tart containing almond-flavoured sponge-cake over a layer of jam. (¶ Named after a town in Derbyshire.)

**baking** adjective (informal) (of weather etc.) very hot.

**baking powder** a mixture of powders used as a raising agent for cakes etc.

**baking soda** sodium bicarbonate, used in baking.

**baklava** (bak-lă-vă) noun a rich cake of flaky pastry, honey, and nuts. (¶ Turkish.)

**baksheesh** noun (in the Middle East) a gratuity, a tip.

**Baku** (ba-**koo**) the capital of Azerbaijan on the shore of the Caspian Sea.

**Balaclava** (bal-ă-**klah**-vă) a Crimean village, scene of a battle (1854) in the Crimean War. ● noun (in full **Balaclava helmet**) a woollen helmet covering the head and neck.

**balalaika** (bal-ă-**ly**-kă) noun a guitar-like instrument with a triangular body. (¶ Russian.)

**balance** noun **1** a weighing-apparatus with two pans hanging from a crossbar. **2** a balance wheel. **3** an even distribution of weight or amount, a steady position. **4** the difference between credits and debits. **5** money remaining after payment of a debt. ● verb **1** consider by comparing; balance one argument against another. **2** be or put or keep (a thing) in a state of balance. **3** compare the debits and credits of an account and make the entry needed to equalize these; have these equal. □ **balance of payments** the difference between the amount paid to foreign countries for imports and services and the amount received from them for exports etc. in a given period. **balance of power 1** a situation in which the chief States have roughly equal power. **2** the power to decide events, held by a small group when the larger groups are of equal strength to each other. **balance of trade** the difference in value between imports and exports. **balance sheet** a written statement of assets and liabilities. **balance wheel** a wheel regulating the speed of a clock or watch. **in the balance** with the outcome still uncertain. **off balance** in danger of falling. **on balance** taking everything into consideration.

**Balanchine** (bal-ahn-sheen), George (real name Balanchivadze) (1904–83), Russian-American dancer, choreographer, and ballet director.

**balcony** (bal-kŏni) *noun* **1** a platform with a rail or parapet, projecting outside an upper storey of a building. **2** an upper floor of seats in a cinema or above the dress circle in a theatre. □ **balconied** *adjective*

**bald** *adjective* **1** with the scalp wholly or partly hairless. **2** (of animals) lacking the usual hair or feathers. **3** (of tyres) with the tread worn away. **4** bare, without details; *bald facts*. □ **bald eagle** an eagle with white feathers on its head and neck, the emblem of the USA. □ **baldly** *adverb*, **baldness** *noun*

**balderdash** *noun* nonsense.

**balding** *adjective* becoming bald.

**Baldwin**, Stanley, 1st Earl (1867–1947), British Conservative statesman, Prime Minister 1923–9, 1935–7.

**bale**[1] *noun* **1** a large bundle of straw etc. bound with cord or wire. **2** a large package of goods. ●*verb* make into a bale. □ **bale out** make a parachute descent from an aircraft in an emergency.

**bale**[2] alternative spelling of BAIL[3].

**Balearic Islands** (bal-i-a-rik) (also **Balearics**) a group of Mediterranean islands off the east coast of Spain, of which Majorca is the largest.

**baleen** (bă-leen) *noun* whalebone.

**baleful** *adjective* menacing; destructive; *a baleful look*. □ **balefully** *adverb*

**Balfour** (bal-foor), Arthur James, 1st Earl (1848–1930), British Conservative statesman, Prime Minister 1902–5.

**Bali** (bah-li) an island of Indonesia. □ **Balinese** *adjective & noun*

**balk** alternative spelling of BAULK.

**Balkan** (bawl-kăn) *adjective* of the peninsula in SE Europe bounded by the Adriatic, Aegean, and Black Seas, or of its people or countries. ●*noun* (**the Balkans**) the Balkan countries.

**ball**[1] *noun* **1** a solid or hollow sphere. **2** a single delivery of the ball by the bowler in cricket or by the pitcher in baseball. **3** a rounded part; *the ball of the foot*. **4** (**balls**) (*vulgar*) the testicles. **5** (**balls**) (usually as *interjection*) (*vulgar*) nonsense. ●*verb* form into a ball. □ **ball-and-socket joint** a joint in which a rounded end lies in a concave socket, allowing wide movement. **ball-**

**bearing** *noun* a bearing using small steel balls; one of these balls. **ball game 1** a game played with a ball. **2** (*informal*) a situation; a matter; *a whole new ball game*. **balls-up** *noun* (*vulgar*) something done badly; a mess. **on the ball** (*informal*) alert, competent. **start the ball rolling** start a discussion or activity.

**ball**[2] *noun* a formal social gathering for dancing. □ **have a ball** (*informal*) enjoy oneself.

**ballad** *noun* **1** a simple song or poem; one telling a story. **2** a slow sentimental song.

**ballade** (ba-lahd) *noun* a poem with sets of three verses each ending with the same refrain line.

**Ballard**, J(ames) G(raham) (born 1930), English novelist, noted for science fiction.

**ballast** (bal-ăst) *noun* **1** heavy material placed in a ship's hold to improve its stability. **2** coarse stones etc. forming the bed of a railway or road. **3** a device to stabilize current in an electric circuit.

**ballboy** *noun* a boy who fetches balls that go out of play during a tennis match.

**ballcock** *noun* a device with a floating ball controlling the water level in a cistern.

**ballerina** (ba-ler-ee-nă) *noun* a female ballet dancer.

**ballet** (bal-ay) *noun* a form of dancing and mime to music; a performance of this. □ **balletic** (bă-let-ik) *adjective*

**ballgirl** *noun* a girl who fetches balls that go out of play during a tennis match.

**ballistic** (bă-lis-tik) *adjective* of projectiles such as bullets and missiles. ●*noun* (**ballistics**) (usually treated as *singular*) the scientific study of projectiles and firearms. □ **ballistic missile** a missile that is powered and directed at its launch stage and falls by gravity onto its target.

**ballocking** alternative spelling of BOLLOCKING.

**ballocks** alternative spelling of BOLLOCKS.

**balloon** *noun* **1** a small inflatable rubber bag, used as a child's toy or a decoration. **2** a large inflatable sphere often carrying a basket in which passengers may ride. **3** a balloon-shaped line enclosing the words or thoughts of a character in a comic strip or cartoon. ●*verb* swell like a balloon.

**balloonist** *noun* a person who travels by balloon.

**ballot** *noun* **1** the process of (usually secret) voting by means of papers or tokens. **2** a paper or token used in this. **3** the number of such votes recorded. ●*verb* (**balloted**, **balloting**) **1** vote by ballot. **2** take a ballot of; *balloting their members*. □ **ballot box** a container for ballot-papers. **ballot paper** a paper used in voting by ballot.

**ballpark** noun (*Amer.*) **1** a baseball ground. **2** (*informal*) an area of activity, responsibility, etc. **3** (often used as *adjective*) approximate; *a ballpark figure*.

**ballpoint** noun (in full **ballpoint pen**) a pen with a tiny ball as its writing point.

**ballroom** noun a large room where dances are held. □ **ballroom dancing** formal social dancing for couples; e.g. the waltz, foxtrot, etc.

**bally** adjective & adverb (*slang*) a mild swearword; a milder form of 'bloody'.

**ballyhoo** noun **1** loud noise; fuss. **2** extravagant publicity.

**balm** (*pronounced* bahm) noun **1** = BALSAM (sense 1). **2** a fragrant ointment. **3** a healing or soothing influence. **4** (also **lemon balm**) a herb with lemon-scented leaves.

**Balmoral Castle** a holiday residence of the British royal family, near Braemar in Scotland.

**balmy** (bah-mi) adjective (**balmier, balmiest**) **1** like balm, fragrant. **2** soft and warm; *balmy air*. **3** (*slang*) barmy.

**baloney** alternative spelling of BOLONEY.

**balsa** (bawl-să) noun (also **balsa wood**) very lightweight wood from a tropical American tree.

**balsam** (bawl-săm) noun **1** a fragrant medicinal gum exuded by certain trees. **2** a tree producing this. **3** a kind of flowering plant. □ **balsamic** (bawl-sam-ik) adjective

**Baltic** (bawl-tik) adjective of the **Baltic Sea**, an almost land-locked sea of NE Europe. ●noun the Baltic Sea. □ **Baltic Exchange** the world market, in London, for the chartering of cargo ships.

**Baltimore** (bawlt-i-mor) a seaport in north Maryland, USA.

**baluster** (bal-ŭster) noun a short post or pillar supporting a rail.

**balustrade** (bal-ŭs-trayd) noun a row of short posts or pillars supporting a rail or stone coping round a balcony or terrace.

**Balzac** (bal-zak), Honoré de (1799–1850), French novelist.

**Bamako** (bam-ă-koh) the capital of Mali.

**bamboo** (bam-boo) noun a giant tropical woody grass with hollow stems. □ **bamboo shoot** the young shoot of a bamboo, eaten as a vegetable.

**bamboozle** verb (*informal*) **1** hoax, cheat. **2** mystify. □ **bamboozlement** noun

**ban** verb (**banned, banning**) forbid officially. ●noun an order that bans something.

**banal** (bă-nahl) adjective commonplace, uninteresting. □ **banality** noun

**banana** noun the finger-shaped fruit of a tropical tree. □ **banana republic** (*scornful*) a small country dependent on foreign capital and regarded as economically unstable. **go bananas** (*slang*) go crazy.

**band** noun **1** a narrow strip, hoop, or loop. **2** a range of values, wavelengths, etc. within a series. **3** an organized group of people with a common purpose. **4** a set of people playing music together. ●verb **1** put a band of metal, paper, etc. on or round. **2** unite in an organized group; *they banded together*.

**Banda**, Hastings (Kamuzu) (born 1906), Malawi statesman, first Prime Minister (1964) and President (1966) of an independent Malawi.

**bandage** noun a strip of material for binding up a wound. ●verb bind up with this.

**bandanna** (ban-dan-ă) noun a large coloured handkerchief or neckerchief.

**Bandaranaike** (banda-ră-ny-kĕ), Sirimavo Ratwatte Dias (born 1916), Sinhalese stateswoman, Prime Minister of Sri Lanka 1960–5 and 1970–7, the world's first woman prime minister.

**Bandar Seri Begawan** (ban-dar se-ri bĕ-gah-wăn) the capital of Brunei.

**b. & b.** abbreviation bed and breakfast.

**bandeau** (ban-doh) noun (*plural* **bandeaux**, (*pronounced* ban-dohz) a strip of material worn round the head.

**bandicoot** noun **1** a large rat found in India. **2** a rat-like Australian marsupial.

**bandit** noun a member of a band of robbers. □ **banditry** noun

**bandmaster** noun the conductor of a musical band.

**bandolier** (band-ŏ-leer) noun (also **bandoleer**) a shoulder belt with loops for ammunition.

**bandsaw** noun a power saw consisting of a toothed steel belt running over wheels.

**bandsman** noun (*plural* **bandsmen**) a member of a jazz band, brass band, etc.

**bandstand** noun a covered outdoor platform for a musical band.

**bandwagon** noun □ **climb** or **jump on the bandwagon** join a successful enterprise or follow its example.

**bandwidth** noun a range of frequencies in telecommunications etc.

**bandy** verb (**bandied, bandying**) **1** pass to and fro; *the story was bandied about*. **2** exchange (words) in quarrelling. ●adjective (**bandier, bandiest**) (of legs) curving apart at the knees. □ **bandy-legged** adjective having bandy legs. □ **bandiness** noun

**bane** noun a cause of trouble, misery, or anxiety. □ **baneful** adjective

**bang** verb **1** make a sudden loud noise like an explosion. **2** strike or shut noisily. **3** (foll. by *into*, *against*, etc.) collide with, bump into. **4** (*vulgar slang*) have sexual intercourse (with). ●noun **1** a sudden loud noise of or like an explosion. **2** a sharp blow. ●*adverb* **1** with a bang, abruptly; *bang go my chances.* **2** (*informal*) exactly; *bang in the middle.* □ **go with a bang** be very successful or impressive.

**banger** *noun* **1** a firework made to explode noisily. **2** (*slang*) a noisy old car. **3** (*slang*) a sausage.

**Bangkok** (bang-**kok**) the capital of Thailand.

**Bangladesh** (bang-lă-**desh**) a country in SE Asia bordering on northern India. □ **Bangladeshi** *adjective & noun*

**bangle** *noun* a rigid bracelet or anklet.

**Bangui** (bang-**i**) the capital of the Central African Republic.

**banian** alternative spelling of BANYAN.

**banish** *verb* **1** condemn to exile. **2** dismiss from one's presence or one's mind; *banish care.* □ **banishment** *noun*

**banister** *noun* (also **bannister**) **1** each of the uprights supporting the handrail of a stair. **2** (**banisters**) these uprights and the rail together.

**banjo** (**ban**-joh) *noun* (*plural* **banjos**) a stringed instrument like a guitar with a circular body.

**Banjul** (ban-**jool**) the capital of the Gambia.

**bank¹** *noun* **1** a slope, especially at the side of a river. **2** a raised mass of sand etc. in a river bed. **3** a long mass of cloud, snow, or other soft substance. **4** a row or series of lights, switches, etc. ●*verb* **1** (often foll. by *up*) build or form a bank; *bank up the fire.* **2** (of a motorcycle, aircraft, etc.) tilt or be tilted sideways in rounding a curve.

**bank²** *noun* **1** an establishment for depositing, withdrawing, and borrowing money. **2** the money held by the banker in some gambling games. **3** a place for storing a reserve supply; *a blood bank.* ●*verb* **1** place or keep money in a bank. **2** (foll. by *on*) base one's hopes on; *we are banking on your success.* □ **bank card** = CHEQUE CARD. **bank holiday** a day (other than Sunday) on which banks are officially closed, usually kept as a public holiday.

**banker** *noun* **1** a person who runs a bank. **2** the keeper of a bank in some gambling games. □ **banker's card** = CHEQUE CARD. **banker's order** = STANDING ORDER.

**banking** *noun* the business of running a bank.

**banknote** *noun* a piece of paper money.

**bankrupt** *noun* a person who is unable to pay his or her debts in full and whose estate is administered and distributed for the benefit of his creditors. ●*adjective* **1** declared by a lawcourt to be a bankrupt. **2** (often foll. by *of*) exhausted; drained (of emotion etc.). ●*verb* make bankrupt. □ **bankruptcy** *noun*

**banksia** *noun* an evergreen flowering shrub native to Australia.

**banner** *noun* **1** a flag. **2** a strip of cloth bearing an emblem or slogan, hung up or carried in a procession etc. □ **banner headline** a large front-page newspaper headline.

**Bannister**, Sir Roger Gilbert (born 1929), British runner, the first to run the mile in under 4 minutes (6 May 1954).

**bannister** alternative spelling of BANISTER.

**bannock** *noun* (*Scottish & N. England*) a round flat loaf, usually unleavened.

**Bannockburn** a village in central Scotland, scene of a decisive victory of the Scots under Robert the Bruce over the English army of Edward II in 1314.

**banns** *plural noun* a public announcement in church of a forthcoming marriage between two named people.

**banquet** *noun* an elaborate ceremonial meal. ●*verb* (**banqueted, banqueting**) take part in a banquet.

**banshee** (**ban**-shee) *noun* (*Irish & Scottish*) a female spirit whose wail is superstitiously believed to foretell a death in a house.

**bantam** *noun* a small domestic fowl.

**bantamweight** *noun* a weight in certain sports between featherweight and flyweight, in boxing 51–4 kg.

**banter** *noun* good-humoured teasing. ●*verb* joke in a good-humoured way.

**Banting**, Sir Frederick Grant (1891–1941), Canadian surgeon, whose isolation of insulin (1921) revolutionized the treatment of diabetes.

**Bantu** (ban-**too**) *noun* (*plural* **Bantu** or **Bantus**) (often *offensive*) one of a group of Black African peoples or their languages.

**Bantustan** (ban-too-**stahn**) *noun* formerly, under the apartheid system, one of the territories (officially called homelands) reserved for Black South Africans.

**banyan** *noun* (also **banian**) an Indian fig tree with self-rooting branches.

**baobab** (**bay**-oh-bab) *noun* an African tree with a massive trunk and large edible pulpy fruit.

**bap** *noun* a soft flat bread roll.

**baptise** alternative spelling of BAPTIZE.

**baptism** *noun* the religious rite of sprinkling a person with water or immersing him or her in it to symbolize purification and (with Christians) admission to the Church. □ **baptism of fire 1** a soldier's experience of fighting for the first time. **2** a painful first experience. □ **baptismal** *adjective*

**Baptist** *noun* **1** a member of a Protestant religious denomination believing that baptism should be by immersion and performed at an age when the person is old enough to understand its meaning. **2 (the Baptist)** St John, who baptized Christ.

**baptistery** (bap-tist-eri) *noun* **1** a building or part of a church used for baptism. **2** a tank used in a Baptist chapel for baptism by immersion.

**baptize** *verb* (also **baptise**) **1** perform baptism on. **2** name or nickname.

**bar** *noun* **1** a long piece of solid material. **2** a narrow strip; *bars of colour.* **3** any barrier or obstacle; a sandbank. **4** each of the vertical lines dividing a piece of music into equal units; a unit contained by these. **5** a partition (real or imaginary) across a court of justice separating the judge, jury, and certain lawyers from the public. **6 (the Bar)** barristers. **7** a counter or room where alcohol is served. **8** a place where refreshments are served across a counter; *a coffee bar.* **9** a shop counter selling a single type of commodity or service. **10** a unit of pressure used in meteorology. ● *verb* (**barred, barring**) **1** fasten with a bar or bars. **2** keep in or out by this. **3** obstruct; *barred the way.* **4** prevent or prohibit. ● *preposition* except; *it's all over bar the shouting.* □ **bar billiards** a form of billiards with holes in the table. **bar code** a pattern of stripes (on packaging etc.) containing information for processing by a computer. **bar-coded** *adjective* marked with a bar code. **bar sinister** = BEND SINISTER. **be called to the Bar** become a barrister. **behind bars** in prison.

**Barabbas** (ba-rab-as) the robber whom Pontius Pilate released from prison to the Jews instead of Jesus Christ.

**barathea** (ba-rath-ee-a) *noun* a fine woollen cloth.

**barb** *noun* **1** the backward-pointing part of an arrowhead, fish-hook, etc. that makes it difficult to withdraw. **2** a wounding remark. **3** a small pointed projecting part or filament.

**Barbados** (bar-bay-dŏs) an island in the West Indies. □ **Barbadian** *adjective & noun*

**barbarian** *noun* an uncivilized person. ● *adjective* of barbarians.

**barbaric** (bar-ba-rik) *adjective* suitable for barbarians, rough and wild. □ **barbarically** *adverb*

**barbarism** (bar-bă-rizm) *noun* **1** an uncivilized condition or practice. **2** an unacceptable use of words.

**barbarity** (bar-ba-riti) *noun* savage cruelty; a savagely cruel act.

**barbarous** (bar-ber-ŭs) *adjective* uncivilized, cruel. □ **barbarously** *adverb*

**Barbary** an old name for the western part of North Africa. □ **Barbary ape** a macaque of North Africa and Gibraltar.

**barbecue** (bar-bi-kew) *noun* **1** a device for cooking food outdoors consisting of a grid suspended over a container for burning charcoal. **2** an open-air party at which food is cooked on this. **3** the food itself. ● *verb* cook on a barbecue.

**barbed** *adjective* having a barb or barbs. □ **barbed wire** wire with short sharp points at intervals.

**barbel** *noun* **1** a beard-like filament at the mouth of certain fishes. **2** a large European freshwater fish with such filaments.

**barbell** *noun* a metal rod used in weightlifting, with adjustable weighted discs at each end.

**barber** *noun* a men's hairdresser. □ **barber-shop (quartet)** *noun* (*informal*) close harmony singing for four male voices.

**barbican** *noun* an outer defence of a castle or city, especially a double tower over a gate or bridge.

**barbie** *noun* (*Australian slang*) a barbecue.

**Barbirolli** (bar-bi-rol-i), Sir John (1899–1970), English conductor.

**barbiturate** (bar-bit-yoor-ăt) *noun* a sedative drug.

**barbituric acid** (bar-bi-tewr-ik) an acid from which barbiturates are obtained.

**Barbuda** *see* ANTIGUA AND BARBUDA.

**barcarole** (bar-kă-rohl) *noun* (also **barcarolle**) **1** a gondolier's song. **2** a piece of music with a steady lilting rhythm.

**Barcelona** (bar-si-loh-nă) a city and province of Catalonia in NE Spain.

**bard** *noun* **1** (*hist.*) a Celtic minstrel. **2** (*formal*) a poet. **3** a prizewinner at an Eisteddfod. □ **the Bard of Avon** Shakespeare. □ **bardic** *adjective*

**Bardot** (bar-doh), Brigitte (born 1934), French film actress.

**bare** *adjective* **1** without clothing or covering; *the trees were bare; with one's bare hands.* **2** plain, without detail; undisguised; *the bare facts.* **3** empty; *the cupboard was bare.* **4** only just sufficient; *the bare necessities of life.* ● *verb* uncover; reveal; *bared its teeth in a snarl.* □ **bareness** *noun*

**bareback** *adjective & adverb* on a horse without a saddle.

**barefaced** *adjective* shameless, undisguised.

**barefoot** *adjective & adverb* wearing nothing on the feet.

**bareheaded** *adjective* not wearing a hat.

**barely** *adverb* **1** scarcely, only just. **2** scantily; *barely furnished.*

**Barenboim**, Daniel (born 1942), Israeli conductor and pianist.

**Barents Sea** (ba-rĕnts) a part of the Arctic Ocean, north of Russia. (¶ Named after the Dutch explorer Willem Barents (died 1597).)

**bargain** noun **1** an agreement. **2** something obtained as a result of this; a thing got cheaply. ●verb discuss the terms of an agreement. □ **bargain for** or **on** to be prepared for, to expect; *didn't bargain on his arriving so early*; *got more than he bargained for*. **into the bargain** in addition to other things.

**barge** noun a large flat-bottomed boat for use on canals or rivers, especially for carrying goods. ●verb move clumsily or heavily. □ **barge in** intrude.

**bargee** (bar-**jee**) noun a person in charge of a barge.

**bargepole** noun a long pole for pushing from a barge. □ **would not touch with a bargepole** (*informal*) refuse to have anything to do with.

**baritone** noun **1** a male voice between tenor and bass. **2** a singer with such a voice; a part written for this.

**barium** (**bair**-ium) noun a chemical element (symbol Ba), a soft silvery-white metal. □ **barium meal** a mixture of barium sulphate and water swallowed to reveal the stomach and intestines in X-rays.

**bark¹** noun the outer layer of tree-trunks and branches. ●verb **1** peel bark from. **2** scrape the skin off accidentally; *barked my knuckles*.

**bark²** noun the sharp harsh sound made by a dog or fox. ●verb **1** make this sound. **2** speak in a sharp commanding voice; *barked out orders*. □ **bark up the wrong tree** direct one's effort or complaint in the wrong direction.

**barker** noun a tout at an auction or sideshow.

**barley** noun a cereal plant; its grain. □ **barley sugar** a sweet made of boiled sugar. **barley water** a drink made from barley.

**barleycorn** noun a grain of barley.

**barm** noun froth on fermenting malt liquor.

**barmaid** noun a woman serving in a pub, wine bar, etc.

**barman** noun (*plural* **barmen**) a man serving in a pub, wine bar, etc.

**bar mitzvah** (**mits**-vă) **1** a Jewish boy aged 13, when he takes on the responsibilities of an adult under Jewish law. **2** the solemnization of this event by calling upon the boy to read from the Scriptures in a synagogue service. (¶ Hebrew, = son of commandment.)

**barmy** adverb (*slang*) crazy.

**barn** noun a simple roofed building for storing grain or hay etc. on a farm. □ **barn dance** a social gathering for country dancing. **barn owl** an owl that often breeds and roosts in barns and other buildings.

**Barnabas**, St (1st century), a Cypriot Levite, who accompanied St Paul on missionary journeys. Feast day, 11 June.

**barnacle** noun a shellfish that attaches itself to objects under water. □ **barnacle goose** an Arctic goose visiting Britain in winter.

**Barnard**, Christiaan (Neethling) (born 1922), South African surgeon, pioneer of human heart transplantation (1967).

**Barnardo**, Thomas John (1845–1905), British philanthropist, founder of a chain of homes for destitute children.

**barney** noun (*slang*) a noisy quarrel.

**barnstorm** verb tour rural districts as an actor or political campaigner. □ **barnstormer** noun

**barnyard** noun a yard beside a barn.

**barograph** (**ba**-rŏ-grahf) noun a barometer that produces a graph showing the atmospheric pressure.

**barometer** (bă-**rom**-it-er) noun an instrument measuring atmospheric pressure, used for forecasting the weather. □ **barometric** (ba-rŏ-**met**-rik) adjective

**baron** noun **1** a member of the lowest rank of the British peerage (called *Lord* —), or of foreign nobility (called *Baron* —). **2** a man who held lands etc. from the king in the Middle Ages. **3** a magnate; *a newspaper baron*. □ **baron of beef** a double sirloin. □ **baronial** (bă-**roh**-niăl) adjective

**baroness** noun **1** a woman holding the rank of baron. **2** a baron's wife or widow.

**baronet** noun a holder of a British hereditary title ranking below a baron but above a knight, having the title 'Sir' (*abbreviation* **Bart.** or **Bt.**) □ **baronetcy** noun

**barony** noun the rank or lands of a baron.

**baroque** (bă-**rok**) adjective of the ornate architectural style of the 17th and 18th centuries, or of comparable musical developments *c.*1600–1750. ●noun this style of ornamentation.

**barouche** (ba-**roosh**) noun a four-wheeled horse-drawn carriage with seats for two couples facing each other.

**barque** (*pronounced* bark) noun a sailing-ship with the rear mast fore-and-aft rigged and other masts square-rigged.

**barrack** verb **1** shout protests or jeer at. **2** lodge (soldiers) in barracks.

**barracks** noun **1** a large building or group of buildings for soldiers to live in. **2** a large, plain, and ugly building.

**barracuda** (ba-ră-**koo**-dă) noun (*plural* **barracuda** or **barracudas**) a large tropical marine fish of the West Indies.

**barrage** (ba-rah*zh*) noun **1** an artificial barrier, especially one damming a river. **2** a heavy continuous bombardment by artillery. **3** a rapid fire of questions or comments. □ **barrage balloon** a large balloon anchored to the ground as part of a barrier against aircraft.

**barratry** (ba-ră-tri) *noun* fraud or gross negligence by a ship's master or crew at the expense of the owner or user.

**barre** *noun* a horizontal bar used by dancers while exercising.

**barrel** *noun* **1** a large round container with flat ends. **2** the amount this contains, (as a measure of mineral oil) 35 gallons (42 US gallons). **3** a tube-like part, especially of a gun. ●*verb* (**barrelled, barrelling**; *Amer.* **barreled, barreling**) put into barrels. □ **barrel organ** a mechanical musical instrument, played by turning a handle to rotate a pin-studded cylinder which acts on keys, pipes, or strings to sound notes. **over a barrel** (*informal*) in a helpless position.

**barren** *adjective* **1** not fertile enough to produce crops; *barren land.* **2** not producing fruit or seeds; *a barren tree.* **3** unable to have young ones. **4** unproductive; unstimulating. □ **barrenness** *noun*

**Barrett**, Elizabeth, *see* BROWNING.

**barricade** *noun* a barrier, especially one hastily erected as a defence. ●*verb* block or defend with a barricade.

**Barrie**, Sir J(ames) M(atthew) (1860–1937), Scottish dramatist and novelist, author of *Peter Pan.*

**barrier** *noun* something that prevents or controls advance, access, or progress. □ **barrier cream** a cream used to protect the skin from damage or infection. **barrier reef** a coral reef with a channel between it and the land.

**barring** *preposition* except, not including.

**barrister** (ba-ris-ter) *noun* a lawyer qualified to represent clients in the higher lawcourts.

**barrow** *noun* **1** a wheelbarrow. **2** a small cart with two wheels, pulled or pushed by hand. **3** a prehistoric burial mound.

**Bart.** *abbreviation* Baronet.

**bartender** *noun* a barman or barmaid.

**barter** *verb* trade by exchanging goods etc. for other goods, not for money. ●*noun* trading by exchange.

**Bartholomew**, St (1st century), one of the twelve Apostles. Feast day, 12 August.

**Bartók** (**bar-tok**), Béla (1881–1945), Hungarian composer.

**baryon** (ba-ri-on) *noun* a heavy elementary particle of mass equal to or greater than a proton.

**Baryshnikov**, Mikhail Nikolayevich (born 1948), Latvian-born American ballet dancer.

**baryta** (bă-ry-tă) *noun* barium oxide or hydroxide.

**barytes** (bă-ry-teez) *noun* barium sulphate, used in some white paints.

**basal** (bay-săl) *adjective* of, at, or forming the base of something.

**basalt** (ba-sawlt) *noun* a dark rock of volcanic origin. □ **basaltic** (bă-sawl-tik) *adjective*

**base** *noun* **1** the lowest part of anything; the part on which it rests or is supported. **2** a starting-point. **3** the headquarters of an expedition or other enterprise. **4** a substance into which other things are mixed; *some paints have an oil base.* **5** a cream or liquid applied to the skin as a foundation for make-up. **6** a substance (e.g. an alkali) capable of combining with an acid to form a salt. **7** each of the four stations to be reached by a runner in baseball. **8** the number on which a system of counting is based (e.g. 10 in decimal counting). ●*verb* use as a base or foundation or as evidence for a forecast. ●*adjective* **1** dishonourable; *base motives.* **2** of inferior value; *base metals.* **3** debased, not of acceptable quality; *base coins.* □ **base rate** an interest rate set by the Bank of England, used as the basis for other interest rates. □ **baseness** *noun*

**baseball** *noun* a team game in which runs are scored by hitting a ball and running round a series of four bases.

**baseless** *adjective* without foundation; *baseless rumours.*

**baseline** *noun* **1** a line used as a base or starting-point. **2** the line at each end of a tennis court.

**basement** *noun* the lowest storey of a building, below ground level.

**bases** *see* BASIS.

**bash** *verb* **1** strike violently. **2** attack with blows, words, or hostile actions. ●*noun* a violent blow or knock. □ **have a bash** (*informal*) have a try.

**bashful** *adjective* shy and self-conscious. □ **bashfully** *adverb*, **bashfulness** *noun*

**BASIC** *noun* a computer programming language using familiar English words. (¶ From the initials of Beginners' All-purpose Symbolic Instruction Code.)

**basic** *adjective* forming a base or starting-point, fundamental; *basic principles*; *basic rates of pay* ●*plural noun* (**basics**) basic facts or principles etc. □ **basic slag** a by-product formed in steel manufacture, containing phosphates and used as a fertilizer. □ **basically** *adverb*

**Basie** (**bay-see**), 'Count' (William) (1904–84), American jazz band-leader.

**Basil**, St, 'the Great' (c. 330–79), Greek bishop, whose monastic rule is the basis of that followed in the Orthodox Church. Feast day, 14 June.

**basil** *noun* a sweet-smelling herb.

**basilica** (bă-**zil**-ikă) *noun* a large Roman hall or Christian church with two rows of columns and an apse at one end.

**basilisk** (**baz**-il-isk) *noun* **1** a small tropical American lizard. **2** a mythical reptile said to cause death by its glance or breath.

**basin** *noun* **1** a round open dish. **2** the amount a basin contains. **3** a washbasin. **4** a sunken place where water collects; the area drained by a river. **5** an almost landlocked harbour; *a yacht basin*. □ **basinful** *noun* (*plural* **basinfuls**).

**basis** *noun* (*plural* **bases**, *pronounced* bay-seez) a foundation or support; a main principle.

**bask** *verb* **1** expose oneself comfortably to a pleasant warmth. **2** (foll. by *in*) enjoy (approval, success, etc.); *basking in glory*.

**basket** *noun* **1** a container made of interwoven cane, wire, etc. **2** this with its contents. **3** the hoop through which players try to throw the ball in basketball; a point scored in this way. **4** an assorted set; *a basket of currencies*. □ **basket weave** a weave resembling basketwork.

**basketball** *noun* a team game in which points are scored by putting the ball through a high hoop.

**basketful** *noun* (*plural* **basketfuls**) the amount a basket will hold.

**basketry** *noun* basketwork.

**basketwork** *noun* the craft of weaving baskets; the work produced.

**basking shark** *noun* a large shark that lies near the surface of the water.

**Basque** (*pronounced* bahsk) *noun* **1** a member of a people living in the western Pyrenees. **2** their language.

**bas-relief** (**bas**-ri-leef) *noun* sculpture or carving with figures projecting slightly from the background.

**bass**¹ (*pronounced* bas) *noun* (*plural* **bass**) a fish of the perch family.

**bass**² (*pronounced* bayss) *adjective* deep-sounding; of the lowest pitch in music. ●*noun* **1** the lowest male voice; a singer with such a voice; a part written for this. **2** the lowest-pitched member of a group of similar musical instruments. **3** (*informal*) a double bass; a bass guitar. □ **bass clef** *Music* a clef placing F below middle C on the second highest line of the stave.

**basset** (**bas**-it) *noun* (also **basset-hound**) a short-legged hound used for hunting hares etc.

**bassinet** *noun* a hooded wicker cradle or pram for a baby.

**basso** *noun* (*plural* **bassos** or **bassi**) a singer with a bass voice.

**bassoon** (bă-**soon**) *noun* a deep-toned woodwind instrument. □ **bassoonist** *noun*

**Bass Strait** (*pronounced* bas) a strait between Australia and Tasmania.

**bast** *noun* fibrous material obtained from the inner bark of the lime-tree or other sources, used for matting etc.

**bastard** *noun* (often *offensive*) **1** an illegitimate child. **2** (*slang*) an unpleasant or difficult person or thing. **3** (*slang*) a person. ●*adjective* **1** of illegitimate birth. **2** hybrid. **3** (of plants and animals) resembling the species whose name is taken. □ **bastardy** *noun*

**bastardize** *verb* (also **bastardise**) **1** declare (a person) illegitimate. **2** corrupt; spoil.

**baste** (*pronounced* bayst) *verb* **1** sew together temporarily with long loose stitches. **2** moisten with fat during cooking. **3** thrash.

**Bastille** (bas-**teel**) (*hist.*) a prison in Paris; its storming on 14 July 1789 marked the start of the French Revolution. □ **Bastille Day** the anniversary of this event, kept as a national holiday in France.

**bastinado** (bas-tin-ay-doh) *noun* torture by caning on the soles of the feet.

**bastion** (**bas**-ti-ŏn) *noun* **1** a projecting part of a fortification. **2** a fortified place near hostile territory. **3** something serving as a stronghold; *a bastion of democracy*.

**bat**¹ *noun* **1** a shaped wooden implement for striking the ball in games. **2** a batsman. ●*verb* (**batted**, **batting**) **1** use a bat. **2** strike with a bat; hit. **3** flutter; *it batted its wings*. □ **not bat an eyelid** show no reaction. **off one's own bat** without prompting or help from another person.

**bat**² *noun* a small flying mammal with a mouselike body.

**batch** *noun* **1** a number of things produced at the same time. **2** a number of people or things dealt with as a group. ●*verb* group (items) for batch processing. □ **batch processing** the processing by a computer etc. of similar transactions in batches in order to make economical use of time.

**bated** (**bay**-tid) *adjective* □ **with bated breath** very anxiously.

**Bates**, H(erbert) E(rnest) (1905–74), English novelist and writer of short stories.

**bath** *noun* **1** a large container for water, in which one sits to wash all over; the washing of the body in this. **2** a liquid in which something is immersed; its container. **3** (**baths**) a public building with baths or a swimming pool. ●*verb* wash in a bath.

**Bath chair** an old-fashioned type of wheelchair.

**bathe** *verb* **1** apply liquid to; immerse in liquid. **2** make wet or bright all over; *fields were bathed in sunlight*. **3** swim for pleasure. ●*noun* a swim. □ **bathing costume**, **bathing suit** a garment worn for swimming.

**bathos** (**bay**-thoss) *noun* an anticlimax; descent from something important to something trivial. □ **bathetic** *adjective*

**bathrobe** *noun* (especially *Amer.*) a dressing gown, especially one made of towelling.

**bathroom** *noun* **1** a room containing a bath. **2** (*Amer.*) a room with a toilet.

**bathyscaphe** (**ba**-thi-skaf) *noun* a manned vessel for deep-sea diving, with special buoyancy gear.

**bathysphere** (**ba**-thi-sfeer) *noun* a spherical diving-vessel for deep-sea observation.

**batik** (ba-**teek**) *noun* **1** a method (originating in Java) of printing coloured designs on textiles by waxing the parts not to be dyed. **2** fabric treated in this way.

**Batista** (ba-**teest**-ă), Fulgencio (1901–73), Cuban military leader, President of Cuba 1940–4 and 1952–9.

**batiste** (bat-**eest**) *noun* a very soft fine woven fabric.

**batman** *noun* (*plural* **batmen**) a soldier acting as an officer's personal servant.

**baton** (**bat**-ŏn) *noun* **1** a short thick stick, especially one serving as a symbol of authority; a truncheon. **2** a thin stick used by the conductor of an orchestra for beating time. **3** a short stick or tube carried in relay races. □ **baton round** a rubber or plastic bullet.

**batrachian** (bă-**tray**-kiăn) *noun* an amphibian (such as a frog or toad) that discards its gills and tail when adult.

**bats** *adjective* (*slang*) crazy.

**batsman** *noun* (*plural* **batsmen**) a player who is batting in cricket or baseball; one who specializes in batting.

**battalion** *noun* an army unit made up of several companies and forming part of a regiment.

**batten** *noun* a strip of wood or metal fastening or holding something in place. ●*verb* **1** fasten with battens; close securely; *batten down the hatches*. **2** feed greedily; thrive or prosper at the expense of others or so as to injure them; *pigeons battening on the crops*.

**Battenberg (cake)** a cake made in a rectangular shape to show alternating pink and yellow squares when cut, covered with marzipan.

**batter** *verb* hit hard and often; subject to repeated violence; *battered babies*; *battered wives*. ●*noun* **1** a beaten mixture of flour, eggs, and milk, for cooking. **2** a batsman in baseball. □ **batterer**

**battering ram** an iron-headed beam formerly used in war to breach walls or gates.

**battery** *noun* **1** a group of big guns on land or on a warship. **2** an artillery unit of guns, men, and vehicles. **3** a set of similar or connected units of equipment, or of cages for poultry etc. **4** an electric cell or group of cells supplying current. **5** *Law* unlawful physical violence against a person.

**battle** *noun* **1** a fight between large organized forces. **2** any struggle or contest; *a battle of wits*. ●*verb* engage in battle, struggle. □ **battle-cry** *noun* a war-cry; a slogan.

**battle royal** **1** a fight involving a lot of people. **2** a heated and prolonged argument.

**battleaxe** *noun* **1** a heavy axe used as a weapon in ancient times. **2** (*informal*) a formidable aggressive woman.

**battlebus** *noun* a bus equipped for use in a political campaign.

**battledore** *noun* a small racket used with a shuttlecock in the ancient volleying game **battledore and shuttlecock**

**battledress** *noun* the everyday uniform of a soldier.

**battlefield** *noun* a place where a battle is fought.

**battleground** *noun* a battlefield.

**battlements** *plural noun* a parapet with gaps at intervals, originally for firing from.

**battleship** *noun* the most heavily armed kind of warship.

**batty** *adjective* (*slang*) crazy.

**batwing** *adjective* (of a sleeve) triangular in shape, narrow at the wrist and wide at the top.

**bauble** *noun* a showy but valueless ornament or fancy article.

**Baudelaire** (**boh**-dĕ-lair), Charles (1821–67), French poet and critic.

**Bauhaus** (*rhymes with* cow-house) a German school of architecture and design established by Gropius in 1919.

**baulk** (*pronounced* bawlk) (also **balk**) *verb* **1** shirk, jib at; *baulked the problem*. **2** frustrate; *it baulked him of his prey*. ●*noun* **1** a stumbling-block, a hindrance. **2** a roughly squared timber beam. **3** the area of a billiard table within which the cue-balls are placed at the start of a game.

**bauxite** (**bawk**-syt) *noun* the clay-like substance from which aluminium is obtained.

**Bavaria** a region of southern Germany. □ **Bavarian** *adjective & noun*

**bawdy** *adjective* (**bawdier**, **bawdiest**) humorous in a coarse or indecent way. □ **bawdily** *adverb*, **bawdiness** *noun*

**bawl** *verb* **1** shout or cry loudly. **2** weep noisily, howl. □ **bawl out** (*informal*) scold severely.

**Bax**, Sir Arnold Edward Trevor (1883–1953), English composer.

**Baxter**, James Keir (1926–72), New Zealand poet.

**bay**[1] *noun* a laurel with dark green leaves that are dried and used for flavouring food.

**bay**[2] *noun* part of the sea or of a large lake within a wide curve of the shore.

**bay³** *noun* **1** each of a series of compartments in a building, structure, or area. **2** a recess in a room or building. **3** an area off a road for parking or unloading. □ **bay window** a window projecting from the outside wall of a house.

**bay⁴** *noun* the deep drawn-out cry of a large dog or of hounds in pursuit of a hunted animal. ●*verb* make this sound. □ **at bay** forced to face attackers in a desperate situation. **keep at bay** hold off.

**bay⁵** *adjective* reddish-brown. ●*noun* a bay horse.

**bayberry** *noun* a fragrant North American tree.

**Bayeux Tapestry** (by-er) a long strip of Anglo-Saxon embroidery depicting the Norman Conquest, kept at Bayeux in Normandy.

**Bay of Bengal** the part of the Indian Ocean lying between India and Burma.

**bayonet** (bay-ŏn-et) *noun* a dagger-like blade that can be fixed to the muzzle of a rifle and used in hand-to-hand fighting. ●*verb* (**bayoneted, bayoneting**) stab with a bayonet. □ **bayonet fitting** an electrical fitting pushed into a socket and twisted.

**Bayreuth** (by-roit) a town in Bavaria associated with Wagner.

**bazaar** *noun* **1** a group of shops or stalls in an Oriental country. **2** a sale of goods to raise funds.

**bazooka** (bă-zoo-kă) *noun* a portable weapon for firing anti-tank rockets.

**BBC** *abbreviation* British Broadcasting Corporation.

**BC** *abbreviation* British Columbia.

**BC** *abbreviation* (in dates) before Christ.

**BCG** *abbreviation* Bacillus Calmette-Guérin, an anti-tuberculosis vaccine.

**BD** *abbreviation* Bachelor of Divinity.

**bdellium** (del-i-ŭm) *noun* **1** a resin used as a perfume. **2** the tree producing this.

**Be** *symbol* beryllium.

**be** *verb* (**am, are, is; was, were; been, being**) **1** exist, occur, live; occupy a position. **2** have a certain identity, quality, or condition. **3** become. ●*auxiliary verb*, used to form parts of other verbs; *it is rising*; *he was killed*. □ **be-all and end-all** the supreme purpose or essence. **be that as it may** no matter what the facts about it may be. **let it be** do not disturb it.

**beach** *noun* the shore between high- and low-water mark, covered with sand or pebbles. ●*verb* bring on shore from out of the water.

**beachcomber** (beech-koh-mer) *noun* a person who searches beaches for useful or valuable things.

**beachhead** *noun* a fortified position set up on a beach by landing forces.

**Beach-la-Mar** (beech-lă-**mar**) *noun* an English-based creole language used in islands of the West Pacific.

**beacon** *noun* **1** a fire or light on a hill or tower, used as a signal or warning. **2** a signal station such as a lighthouse. □ **Belisha beacon** an amber globe on a pole, marking certain pedestrian crossings.

**bead** *noun* **1** a small shaped piece of hard material pierced for threading with others on a string, or for sewing on to fabric. **2** a drop of liquid on a surface. **3** a small knob forming the sight of a gun. **4** a strip on the inner edge of a pneumatic tyre, for gripping the wheel. **5** a small round moulding, often applied in moulds like a series of beads. **6** (**beads**) a necklace of beads; a rosary. □ **draw a bead on** take aim at.

**beaded** *adjective* **1** decorated with beads. **2** forming or covered with beads of moisture.

**beading** *noun* **1** a decoration of beads. **2** a moulding or carving like a series of beads. **3** a strip of wood or plastic with one side rounded, used as a trimming. **4** the bead of a tyre.

**beadle** *noun* **1** a ceremonial officer of a church, college, etc. **2** (*Scottish*) a church officer serving the minister. **3** (*old use*) a minor officer of a parish.

**beady** *adjective* like beads; (of eyes) small and bright. □ **beadily** *adverb*

**beagle** *noun* a small hound used for hunting hares.

**beak** *noun* **1** a bird's horny projecting jaws. **2** any similar projection such as a spout. **3** (*slang*) a person's nose. **4** (*slang*) a magistrate.

**beaker** *noun* **1** a small open glass vessel with straight sides and a lip for pouring liquids, used in laboratories. **2** a tall cup or tumbler.

**beam** *noun* **1** a long piece of squared timber or other solid material, supported at both ends and carrying the weight of part of a building or other structure. **2** a ship's breadth at its widest part. **3** the crosspiece of a balance, from which the scales hang. **4** a ray or stream of light or other radiation; a radio signal used to direct the course of an aircraft. **5** a radiant smile. ●*verb* **1** send out (light or other radiation). **2** smile radiantly. □ **broad in the beam** (*informal*) wide at the hips. **off (the) beam** (*informal*) mistaken. **on the beam** (*informal*) correct or appropriate.

**bean** *noun* **1** a plant bearing kidney-shaped seeds in long pods. **2** its seed used as a vegetable. **3** a similar seed of coffee and other plants. □ **bean sprouts** sprouts of bean seeds used in salads and as a vegetable. **full of beans** (*informal*) in high spirits. **not a bean** (*slang*) no money.

**beanbag** *noun* **1** a small bag filled with dried beans and used for throwing or carrying in games. **2** a large bag filled with plastic granules and used as a seat.

**beanfeast** *noun* **1** (*informal*) a celebration. **2** a workers' annual dinner.

**beano** *noun* (*plural* **beanos**) (*slang*) a lively party.

**beanpole** *noun* (*informal*) a tall thin person.

**bear**[1] *noun* **1** a large heavy animal with thick fur. **2** a child's toy like this animal. **3** a rough ill-mannered person. **4** (*Stock Exchange*) a person who sells shares, hoping to buy them back more cheaply (compare BULL sense 4). □ **Great Bear, Little Bear** constellations near the North Pole. **bearhug** *noun* a big hug; a tight embrace. **bear market** a situation where share prices are falling rapidly.

**bear**[2] *verb* (**bore, borne, bearing**; see the note under BORNE) **1** carry, support. **2** have or show a certain mark or characteristic; *he still bears the scar.* **3** have in one's heart or mind; *bear a grudge; I will bear it in mind.* **4** bring, provide. **5** endure, tolerate; *grin and bear it.* **6** be fit for; *his language won't bear repeating.* **7** produce, give birth to; *land bears crops; she had borne him two sons.* **8** turn, diverge; *bear right when the road forks.* □ **bear down** press downwards. **bear down on** move rapidly or purposefully towards. **bear on** be relevant to; *matters bearing on public health.* **bear out** confirm. **bear up** be strong enough not to give way or despair. **bear with** tolerate patiently. **bear witness to** provide evidence of the truth of.

**bearable** *adjective* able to be borne, endurable. □ **bearably** *adverb*

**beard** *noun* **1** hair on and round a man's chin. **2** a similar hairy or bristly growth of hair on an animal or plant. ● *verb* confront boldly; *beard the lion in his den.* □ **bearded** *adjective*

**Beardsley**, Aubrey Vincent (1872–98), English artist and illustrator.

**bearer** *noun* **1** one who carries or bears something; *cheque is payable to bearer.* **2** one who helps to carry something (e.g. a coffin to the grave, a stretcher).

**beargarden** *noun* a scene of uproar.

**bearing** *noun* **1** deportment, behaviour; *soldierly bearing.* **2** relationship, relevance; *it has no bearing on this problem.* **3** a compass direction. **4** a device reducing friction in a part of a machine where another part turns. **5** a heraldic emblem. □ **get one's bearings** find out where one is by recognizing landmarks etc.

**Béarnaise sauce** (bay-ă-nayz) a rich sauce thickened with egg yolks.

**bearskin** *noun* a tall black fur headdress worn by some regiments on ceremonial occasions.

**beast** *noun* **1** a large four-footed animal. **2** a cruel or disgusting person. **3** (*informal*) a disliked person or thing; something difficult. **4** (**the beast**) the animal nature in humans.

**beastly** *adjective* (**beastlier, beastliest**) **1** like a beast or its ways. **2** (*informal*) abominable, very unpleasant. ● *adverb* (*informal*) very, unpleasantly; *it was beastly cold.*

**beat** *verb* (**beat, beaten, beating**) **1** hit repeatedly, especially with a stick. **2** shape or flatten by blows; *beat a path.* **3** mix vigorously to a frothy or smooth consistency; *beat the eggs.* **4** (of the heart) expand and contract rhythmically. **5** overcome, do better than. **6** sail towards the direction from which the wind is blowing, by tacking in alternate directions. ● *noun* **1** a regular repeated stroke; a sound of this; recurring emphasis marking rhythm in music or poetry. **2** a police officer's route or area; a person's habitual round. □ **beat about the bush** discuss a subject without coming to the point. **beat down 1** cause (a seller) to lower the price by bargaining. **2** (of the sun, rain, etc.) shine or fall fiercely, heavily, etc. **beat a retreat** go away defeated. **beaten track** a well-worn path; *off the beaten track.* **beat it** (*slang*) go away. **beat off** drive off by fighting. **beat up** assault violently.

**beater** *noun* **1** an implement for beating things. **2** a person employed to drive game out of cover towards those waiting with guns to shoot it.

**beatific** (bee-ă-**tif**-ik) *adjective* showing great happiness; *a beatific smile.*

**beatification** *noun* the pope's official statement that a dead person is among the Blessed, the first step towards canonization.

**beatify** (bee-at-i-fy) *verb* (**beatified, beatifying**) honour by beatification.

**beatitude** (bee-at-i-tewd) *noun* **1** blessedness. **2** (**the Beatitudes**) the declarations made by Christ in the Sermon on the Mount, beginning 'Blessed are ...'.

**Beatles** an English rock group consisting of George Harrison (born 1943), John Lennon (1940–80), Paul McCartney (born 1942), and Ringo Starr (Richard Starkey, born 1940), whose music and ideas became popular with their generation throughout the world in the 1960s.

**beatnik** *noun* a member of a movement of socially unconventional young people in the 1950s.

**Beaton**, Sir Cecil Walter Hardy (1904–80), English photographer.

**beau** (*pronounced* boh) *noun* (*plural* **beaux**, *pronounced* bohz) **1** a boyfriend. **2** a fop, a dandy.

**Beaufort scale** (**boh**-fert) a scale and description of wind velocity ranging from 0 (calm) to 12 (hurricane). (¶ Named after its inventor Sir F. Beaufort, English admiral (died 1857).)

**Beaujolais** (**boh**-zhŏ-lay) *noun* a red or white burgundy wine from Beaujolais, France. □ **Beaujolais Nouveau** (noo-**voh**) Beaujolais wine sold in the first year of a vintage.

**beaut** *noun* (*slang*) a beauty.

**beauteous** *adjective* (*poetic*) beautiful.

**beautician** (bew-**tish**-ăn) *noun* a person who gives beauty treatment.

**beautiful** *adjective* **1** having beauty, giving pleasure to the senses or the mind. **2** very satisfactory. □ **beautifully** *adverb*

**beautify** *verb* (**beautified, beautifying**) make beautiful. □ **beautification** *noun*

**beauty** *noun* **1** a combination of qualities that give pleasure to the sight or other senses or to the mind. **2** a person or thing having this; a beautiful woman. **3** a fine specimen; *here's a beauty*. **4** a beautiful feature; *that's the beauty of it.* □ **beauty parlour** a beauty salon. **beauty queen** a woman judged to be the most beautiful in a competition. **beauty salon** an establishment for giving cosmetic treatments to the face, body, etc. **beauty spot 1** a place with beautiful scenery. **2** a birthmark or artificial patch on the face, said to heighten beauty.

**Beauvoir** (boh-**vwar**), Simone de (1908–86), French existentialist novelist and feminist.

**beaux** *see* BEAU.

**beaver** *noun* **1** an animal with soft fur and strong teeth that lives both on land and in water. **2** its brown fur. **3** a hat made of this. **4** (**Beaver**) a member of a junior branch of the Scout Association. **5** (*old use*) the lower part of the face-guard of a helmet. ● *verb* (usually foll. by *away*) work hard.

**Beaverbrook**, William Maxwell Aitken, 1st Baron (1879–1964), Canadian-born British Conservative politician and newspaper proprietor.

**bebop** *noun* a type of 1940s jazz music.

**becalmed** (bi-**kahmd**) *adjective* (of a sailing boat) unable to move because there is no wind.

**became** *see* BECOME.

**because** *conjunction* for the reason that; *did it because I was asked.* □ **because of** by reason of, on account of; *because of his age.*

**béchamel sauce** (besh-ă-mel) a thick white sauce.

**beck** *noun* **1** (*N. England*) a brook, a mountain stream. **2** (*old use*) a gesture. □ **at someone's beck and call** always ready and waiting to obey his or her orders.

**Becket**, St Thomas à (*c.*1118–70), Archbishop of Canterbury and Chancellor under Henry II, murdered in Canterbury Cathedral. Feast day, 29 December.

**Beckett**, Samuel Barclay (1906–89), Irish dramatist, novelist, and poet, author of the play *Waiting for Godot*.

**beckon** *verb* (**beckoned, beckoning**) signal or summon by a gesture.

**become** *verb* (**became, become, becoming**) **1** come or grow to be; begin to be. **2** suit, be becoming to.

**becoming** *adjective* giving a pleasing appearance or effect, suitable. □ **becomingly** *adverb*

**becquerel** (bek-er-ĕl) *noun* a unit of radioactivity. (¶ Named after A. H. Becquerel (1852–1908), French physicist.)

**bed** *noun* **1** a thing to sleep or rest on, a piece of furniture with a mattress and coverings. **2** the use of a bed; being in bed; *it's time for bed!* **3** a flat base on which something rests, a foundation. **4** the bottom of the sea or a river etc. **5** a layer; *a bed of clay.* **6** a garden plot for plants. ● *verb* (**bedded, bedding**) **1** provide with a place to sleep; put or go to bed. **2** place or fix in a foundation; *the bricks are bedded in concrete.* **3** plant in a garden bed; *he was bedding out seedlings.* □ **bed and breakfast** a room and breakfast in a guest house, hotel etc.; an establishment providing this. **go to bed with** have sexual intercourse with. **no bed of roses** not a pleasant or easy situation.

**B.Ed.** *abbreviation* Bachelor of Education.

**bedaub** *verb* smear all over.

**bedbug** *noun* a bug infesting beds.

**bedclothes** *plural noun* sheets and quilts etc.

**bedding** *noun* mattresses and bedclothes. □ **bedding plant** a plant suitable for planting when it is in flower as part of a display, discarded at the end of the season.

**Bede**, 'the Venerable' (*c.*673–735), English monk and historian.

**bedevil** *verb* (**bedevilled, bedevilling**; *Amer.* **bedeviled, bedeviling**) **1** cause trouble or difficulties for; *the show has been bedevilled with problems.* **2** confound, confuse. □ **bedevilment** *noun*

**bedfellow** *noun* **1** a person who shares one's bed. **2** an associate.

**Bedfordshire** a county of England.

**bedlam** (bed-lăm) *noun* uproar.

**Bedouin** (bed-oo-in) *noun* (also **Beduin**) (*plural* **Bedouin**) a member of an Arab people living in tents in the desert.

**bedpan** *noun* a pan for use as a lavatory by a person confined to bed.

**bedpost** *noun* one of the upright supports of a bedstead.

**bedraggled** (bi-**drag**-ŭld) *adjective* hanging in a limp untidy way, especially when wet.

**bedrest** *noun* rest in bed to recover from an illness.

**bedridden** *adjective* confined to bed through illness or weakness.

**bedrock** *noun* **1** solid rock beneath loose soil. **2** basic facts or principles.

**bedroom** *noun* a room for sleeping in.

**Beds.** *abbreviation* Bedfordshire.

**bedside** *noun* a position by a bed.

**bedsit** *noun* (also **bedsitter, bedsitting room**) a room used for both living and sleeping in.

**bedsore** *noun* a sore caused by pressure, developed by lying in bed for a long time.

**bedspread** *noun* a covering spread over a bed.

**bedstead** *noun* a framework supporting the springs and mattress of a bed.

**bedstraw** *noun* a small herbaceous plant.

**Beduin** alternative spelling of BEDOUIN.

**bedwetting** *noun* involuntary urination when asleep in bed.

**bee** *noun* **1** a four-winged stinging insect that produces wax and honey after gathering nectar and pollen from flowers. **2** (especially *Amer.*) a meeting for work or amusement. □ **have a bee in one's bonnet** have a particular idea that occupies one's thoughts continually. **bee-keeper** *noun* a person who keeps bees in hives.

**Beeb** *noun* (*informal*) (usually **the Beeb**) the BBC.

**beech** *noun* **1** a tree with smooth bark and glossy leaves. **2** its hard wood.

**Beecham**, Sir Thomas (1879–1961), English conductor and impresario.

**beef** *noun* **1** the flesh of an ox, bull, or cow used as meat. **2** (*informal*) muscular strength, brawn. **3** (*slang*) a grumble. ● *verb* (*slang*) grumble. □ **beef tea** the juice from stewed beef, for invalids. **beef tomato** a very large tomato. **beef up** (*slang*) strengthen.

**beefburger** *noun* a flat round cake of minced beef, served fried.

**beefeater** *noun* a warder in the Tower of London, or a member of the Yeomen of the Guard, wearing Tudor dress as uniform.

**beefy** *adjective* (**beefier, beefiest**) having a solid muscular body. □ **beefiness** *noun*

**beehive** *noun* **1** an artificial shelter for a colony of bees. **2** a busy place.

**beeline** *noun* □ **make a beeline for** go straight or rapidly towards.

**Beelzebub** (bi-el-zi-bub) (in the New Testament) the Devil; (in the Old Testament) a Philistine god.

**been** *see* BE.

**beep** *noun* a short light sound; *a beep on the horn.* ● *verb* emit a beep.

**beer** *noun* an alcoholic drink made from malt and flavoured with hops.

**beeswax** *noun* a yellowish substance secreted by bees, used for polishing wood.

**beet** *noun* a plant with a fleshy root used as a vegetable or for making sugar.

**Beethoven** (bayt-hoh-věn), Ludwig van (1770–1827), German composer.

**beetle** *noun* **1** an insect with hard wing-covers. **2** a heavy-headed tool for crushing or ramming things.

**beetle-browed** *adjective* with eyebrows projecting.

**beetling** *adjective* overhanging, projecting; *beetling brows.*

**Beeton**, Mrs (Isabella Mary) (1836–65), English author of a book on cookery and household management.

**beetroot** *noun* the fleshy dark red root of a beet, used as a vegetable.

**befall** (bi-**fawl**) *verb* (**befell, befallen, befalling**) (*formal*) happen, happen to.

**befit** (bi-**fit**) *verb* (**befitted, befitting**) be right and suitable for.

**before** *adverb, preposition, & conjunction* **1** at an earlier time; earlier than. **2** ahead; ahead of; in front of; *they sailed before the wind.* **3** rather than, in preference to; *death before dishonour!* □ **Before Christ** (of dates) reckoned backwards from the year of the birth of Christ.

**beforehand** *adverb* in advance, in readiness.

**befriend** *verb* act as a friend to; help.

**befuddle** *verb* stupefy, make confused.

**beg** *verb* (**begged, begging**) **1** ask for as charity or as a gift, obtain a living in this way. **2** request earnestly, humbly, or formally; *I beg your pardon; beg to differ.* **3** (of a dog) sit up expectantly with forepaws off the ground. □ **beg off 1** ask to be excused from doing something. **2** get (a person) excused from a punishment. **beg the question** use circular reasoning; assume the truth of something needing proof. **go begging** (of things) be available but unwanted.

**began** *see* BEGIN.

**beget** (bi-get) *verb* (**begot, begotten, begetting**) (*literary*) **1** be the father of. **2** give rise to; *war begets misery and ruin.*

**beggar** *noun* **1** a person who lives by begging. **2** (*informal*) a person; *you lucky beggar!*

●verb **1** reduce to poverty. **2** make poor or inadequate; *the scenery beggars description.*

**beggarly** *adjective* mean and insufficient.

**Begin**, Menachem (1913–92), Israeli statesman, Prime Minister 1977–84.

**begin** *verb* (**began**, **begun**, **beginning**) **1** perform the earliest or first part of (some activity); start speaking; be the first to do something. **2** come into existence. **3** have as its first element or starting-point. □ **not begin to** not in any way; be totally unable to; *I can't begin to thank you enough*; *this doesn't begin to explain why.* **to begin with** as the first thing.

**beginner** *noun* a person who is just beginning to learn a skill.

**beginning** *noun* **1** the first part. **2** the starting-point, the source or origin.

**begone** (bi-**gon**) *interjection* (*poetic*) go away immediately; *begone dull care!*

**begonia** (bi-**goh**-niă) *noun* a plant with colourful flowers and often ornamental leaves.

**begot**, **begotten** *see* BEGET.

**begrudge** *verb* grudge.

**beguile** (bi-**gyl**) *verb* **1** win the attention or interest of, charm. **2** deceive. □ **beguiling** *adjective*

**beguine** (bi-**geen**) *noun* a West Indian dance.

**begum** (**bay**-gŭm) *noun* (in Pakistan and India) **1** the title of a Muslim married woman. **2** a Muslim woman of high rank.

**begun** *see* BEGIN.

**behalf** *noun* □ **on behalf of** (*Amer.* **in behalf of**), **on a person's behalf** in aid of; as the representative of; *speaking on behalf of his client.*

**behave** *verb* **1** act or react in some specified way; function. **2** show good manners; *the child must learn to behave.*

**behaviour** *noun* (*Amer.* **behavior**) a way of behaving; treatment of others; manners. □ **behavioural** *adjective*

**behaviourism** *noun* (*Amer.* **behaviorism**) the psychological theory that the analysis of behaviour is the most important method of study, and that behaviour is simply a learned response to external stimuli.

**behead** *verb* cut the head from; execute (a person) in this way.

**beheld** *see* BEHOLD.

**behest** *noun* (*formal*) a command; a request; *at the behest of the Queen.*

**behind** *adverb* **1** in or to the rear. **2** remaining after others have gone. **3** behindhand. ●*preposition* **1** in the rear of, on the further side of. **2** causing. **3** supporting. **4** having made less progress than; *some countries are behind others in development.* **5** later than; *we are behind schedule.* ●*noun* (*informal*) the buttocks.

□ **behind the scenes** backstage; hidden from public view or knowledge. **behind time** late. **behind the times** old-fashioned, out of date.

**behindhand** *adverb* & *adjective* **1** in arrears. **2** late, behind time; out of date.

**behold** *verb* (**beheld**, **beholding**) (*old use*) see, observe. □ **beholder** *noun*

**beholden** *adjective* owing thanks; *we don't want to be beholden to anybody.*

**behove** *verb* (*formal*) be incumbent on; befit; *it ill behoves him to protest.*

**beige** (*pronounced* bayzh) *noun* a light fawn colour. ●*adjective* of this colour.

**Beijing** (bay-**jing**) the official Chinese form of **Peking**.

**being** *noun* **1** existence. **2** essence or nature. **3** something that exists and has life, especially a person.

**Beirut** (bay-**root**) the capital of Lebanon.

**bejewelled** *adjective* (*Amer.* **bejeweled**) adorned with jewels.

**bel** *noun* a unit (= 10 decibels) used in comparing power levels in electrical communication.

**belabour** *verb* (*Amer.* **belabor**) **1** attack with blows or words. **2** labour (a subject).

**Belarus** (also **Belorussia**) a republic in Eastern Europe. □ **Belarussian** *adjective*

**belated** (bi-**lay**-tid) *adjective* coming very late or too late. □ **belatedly** *adverb*

**belay** *verb* secure (a rope) by winding it round a peg or spike. ●*noun* the securing of a rope in this way.

**belch** *verb* **1** send out wind from the stomach noisily through the mouth. **2** send out from an opening or funnel; gush; *a chimney belching smoke.* ●*noun* an act or sound of belching.

**beleaguer** (bi-**leeg**-er) *verb* **1** besiege. **2** harass, oppress.

**Belfast** (bel-**fahst**) the capital of Northern Ireland.

**belfry** *noun* a bell tower, a space for bells in a tower.

**Belgium** a country in western Europe. □ **Belgian** *adjective* & *noun*

**Belgrade** the chief city of Serbia and capital of the former Yugoslavia.

**belie** *verb* (**belied**, **belying**) **1** fail to confirm, show to be untrue. **2** give a false idea of.

**belief** *noun* **1** the feeling that something is real and true; trust, confidence. **2** something accepted as true; what one believes. **3** acceptance of the teachings of a religion etc.; these teachings.

**believe** *verb* **1** accept as true or as speaking or conveying truth. **2** think, suppose; *I believe it's raining.* **3** have religious faith. □ **believe in** have faith in the existence of;

feel sure of the value or worth of. □ **believable** adjective, **believer** noun

**Belisha beacon** (bi-lee-shă) a flashing amber globe on a pole marking a pedestrian crossing.

**belittle** verb imply that (a thing) is unimportant or of little value. □ **belittlement** noun

**Belize** (bĕl-eez) a country in Central America, on the Caribbean coast. □ **Belizean** (bĕl-ee-zhăn) adjective & noun

**Bell**, Alexander Graham (1847–1922), Scottish-American inventor of the telephone.

**bell** noun **1** a cup-shaped metal instrument that makes a ringing sound when struck; a device making a ringing or buzzing sound to attract attention in a house etc. **2** the sound of this, especially as a signal. **3** a bell-shaped thing. **4** (informal) a telephone call. □ **give a person a bell** (informal) telephone him or her. **bell-bottomed** adjective (of trousers) widening from knee to ankle. **bell jar** a bell-shaped glass cover or container. **bell pull** a handle or cord operating a bell when pulled. **bell push** a button pressed to operate an electric bell.

**belladonna** noun **1** deadly nightshade. **2** a medicinal drug prepared from this.

**belle** (pronounced bel) noun a beautiful woman.

**belles-lettres** (bel-letr) plural noun literary writings or studies.

**bellicose** (bel-i-kohs) adjective eager to fight; warlike.

**belligerent** (bi-lij-er-ĕnt) adjective **1** waging a war; the belligerent nations. **2** aggressive, showing eagerness to fight; a belligerent reply. □ **belligerently** adverb, **belligerence** noun

**Bellini**[1] (bel-ee-ni), Jacopo, Gentile, and Giovanni, a family of 16th-century Venetian painters.

**Bellini**[2] (bel-ee-ni), Vincenzo (1801–35), Italian composer of operas.

**Belloc**, Hilaire (1870–1953), English poet and author.

**Bellow**, Saul (born 1915), American novelist.

**bellow** noun **1** the loud deep sound made by a bull. **2** a deep shout. ● verb utter a bellow.

**bellows** plural noun **1** an apparatus for driving air into or through something. **2** a device or part that can be expanded or flattened in a series of folds.

**belly** noun **1** the abdomen. **2** the stomach. **3** a bulging or rounded part of something. ● verb (**bellied**, **bellying**) swell, bulge; the sails bellied out. □ **belly button** (informal) the navel. **belly dance** an oriental dance by a woman, with erotic movement of the belly. **belly laugh** a deep loud laugh.

**bellyache** noun (informal) pain in the belly. ● verb (slang) grumble.

**bellyflop** noun an awkward dive in which the body hits the water almost horizontally.

**bellyful** noun **1** as much as one wants or can eat. **2** (informal) more than one can tolerate.

**Belmopan** (bel-moh-pan) the capital of Belize.

**belong** verb **1** (foll. by to) be rightly assigned as property or as a part or inhabitant etc.; the house belongs to me; that lid belongs to this jar. **2** be a member; we belong to the club. **3** have a rightful or usual place; the pans belong in the kitchen.

**belongings** plural noun personal possessions.

**Belorussia** see BELARUS.

**beloved** adjective (pronounced bi-luvd) dearly loved; she was beloved by all. ● adjective & noun (pronounced bi-luv-id) darling; my beloved wife.

**below** adverb **1** at or to a lower position; downstream. **2** at the foot of a page; further on in a book or article; see chapter 6 below. ● preposition **1** lower in position, amount, or rank etc. than. **2** downstream from; the bridge is below the ford.

**Belsen** a village in Germany, site of a Nazi concentration camp in the Second World War.

**belt** noun **1** a strip of leather or other material worn round the waist. **2** a continuous moving strap passing over pulleys and so driving machinery; a fan belt. **3** a long narrow region or strip; a belt of rain will move eastwards. **4** (slang) a heavy blow. ● verb **1** put a belt round. **2** attach with a belt. **3** thrash with a belt; (slang) hit. **4** (slang) hurry, rush. □ **below the belt** unfair, unfairly. **belt out** (slang) sing or play loudly; belting out pop songs. **belt up** (informal) **1** wear a seat-belt. **2** (slang) be quiet. **tighten one's belt** live more frugally. **under one's belt** (informal) obtained or achieved.

**beluga** (bi-loo-gă) noun **1** a large sturgeon. **2** caviare from this. **3** a white whale.

**belvedere** (bel-vi-deer) noun a raised turret or summer-house from which to view scenery.

**bemoan** verb lament, complain of.

**bemused** (bi-mewzd) adjective **1** bewildered. **2** lost in thought.

**ben** noun (Scottish) a high mountain; Ben Nevis.

**Ben Bella**, Ahmed (born 1916), Algerian leader, the country's first Prime Minister (1962–65) and President (1963–65).

**bench** noun **1** a long seat of wood or stone. **2** a long working-table in certain trades or in a laboratory. **3** a lawcourt. **4** the judges or magistrates hearing a case.

**bencher** *noun* a senior member of an Inn of Court.

**benchmark** *noun* **1** a surveyor's mark used as a reference point in measuring altitudes. **2** a standard or point of reference.

**bend**¹ *verb* (**bent, bending**) **1** force out of straightness, make curved or angular. **2** become curved or angular. **3** turn downwards, stoop. **4** turn in a new direction; *they bent their steps homeward.* **5** (*slang*) corrupt. ●*noun* **1** a curve or turn. **2** (**the bends**) sickness due to too rapid decompression, e.g. after diving. □ **bend the rules** interpret them loosely to suit oneself. **round the bend** (*slang*) crazy. □ **bendy** *adjective*

**bend**² *noun* **1** any of various knots. **2** (in heraldry) a stripe from the dexter chief to the sinister base. ●*verb* (**bent, bending**) attach (a rope or sail etc.) with a knot. □ **bend sinister** (in heraldry) a diagonal stripe from top left to bottom right of a shield, sometimes used as a sign of bastardy.

**bender** *noun* (*slang*) a wild drinking-session.

**beneath** *adverb & preposition* **1** below, under, underneath. **2** not worthy of, not befitting.

**Benedict**, St (*c.*480–*c.*550), a hermit, living in Italy. Feast day, 21 March.

**Benedictine** *noun* **1** (*pronounced* ben-i-**dik**-tin) a monk or nun following the monastic rule of St Benedict. **2** (*pronounced* ben-i-**dik**-teen) (*trade mark*) a liqueur originally made by monks of this order. ●*adjective* of St Benedict or the Benedictines.

**benediction** (ben-i-**dik**-shŏn) *noun* a spoken blessing. □ **benedictory** *adjective*

**benefaction** *noun* **1** a donation; a gift. **2** giving; doing good.

**benefactor** *noun* a person who gives financial or other help.

**benefactress** *noun* a female benefactor.

**benefice** (**ben**-i-fiss) *noun* a position that provides a clergyman with a livelihood; charge of a parish.

**beneficent** (bin-**ef**-i-sĕnt) *adjective* conferring blessings or favours. □ **beneficence** *noun*

**beneficial** *adjective* having a helpful or useful effect. □ **beneficially** *adverb*

**beneficiary** (ben-i-**fish**-er-i) *noun* a person who receives a benefit; one who is left a legacy under someone's will.

**benefit** *noun* **1** something helpful, favourable, or profitable. **2** an allowance of money etc. to which a person is entitled from an insurance policy or government funds. **3** a performance or game held to raise money for a charitable cause. ●*verb* (**benefited, benefiting**) **1** do good to. **2** receive benefit. □ **benefit of the doubt** the assumption that a person is innocent

(or right) rather than guilty (or wrong) when nothing can be fully proved either way.

**Benelux** (**ben**-i-luks) a collective name for Belgium, the Netherlands, and Luxemburg.

**benevolent** *adjective* **1** wishing to do good to others; kindly and helpful. **2** charitable; *a benevolent fund.* □ **benevolently** *adverb*, **benevolence** *noun*

**Bengal** (ben-**gawl**) a former province of NE India, now divided into West Bengal (a State of India) and Bangladesh. □ **Bengali** *adjective & noun* (*plural* **Bengalis**).

**Ben Gurion** (goor-i-ŏn), David (1886–1973), Polish-born Zionist, the first Prime Minister of Israel (1948–53, 1955–63).

**benighted** *adjective* **1** overtaken by night. **2** intellectually or morally ignorant.

**benign** (bi-**nyn**) *adjective* **1** kindly. **2** mild and gentle in its effect; (of a tumour) not malignant. □ **benignly** *adverb*

**benignant** (bi-**nig**-nănt) *adjective* kindly.

**benignity** (bi-**nig**-niti) *noun* kindliness.

**Benin** (ben-**een**) a country in West Africa. □ **Beninese** *adjective & noun*

**Bennett**¹ Alan (born 1934), English playwright.

**Bennett**² (Enoch) Arnold (1867–1931), English novelist.

**Ben Nevis** (**nev**-iss) the highest mountain in the British Isles, in western Scotland.

**bent** *see* BEND¹. ●*noun* a natural skill or liking; *she has a bent for music.* ●*adjective* (*slang*) dishonest. □ **bent on** determined or seeking to do something; *bent on mischief.*

**Bentham** (**ben**-tăm) *or* (**ben**-thăm), Jeremy (1748–1832), English philosopher, who upheld the theory of utilitarianism.

**bentwood** *noun* wood that has been artificially bent into a permanent curve, used for making chairs etc.

**benumb** *verb* make numb.

**Benz**, Karl Friedrich (1844–1929), German engineer, a pioneer of the motor car.

**benzene** (**ben**-zeen) *noun* a colourless liquid obtained from petroleum and coal tar, used as a solvent, as fuel, and in the manufacture of plastics.

**benzine** (**ben**-zeen) *noun* a colourless liquid mixture of hydrocarbons obtained from petroleum and used as a solvent in dry-cleaning.

**benzoin** *noun* a strong-smelling resin from a tropical tree. □ **benzoic** (ben-**zoh**-ik) *adjective*

**benzol** *noun* benzene, especially in the unrefined state.

**Beowulf** (**bay**-ŏ-wuulf) a legendary Swedish hero (6th century) celebrated in the Old English poem 'Beowulf'.

**bequeath** (bi-kwee*th*) verb leave as a legacy.

**bequest** (bi-**kwest**) noun a legacy.

**berate** (bi-**rayt**) verb scold.

**Berber** noun **1** a member of a group of North African peoples. **2** their language.

**berberis** (**ber**-ber-iss) noun a prickly shrub with yellow flowers.

*berceuse* (bair-**serz**) noun a piece of music in the style of a lullaby.

**bereave** verb deprive, especially of a relative, by death; *the bereaved husband*. □ **bereavement** noun

**bereft** adjective (foll. by *of*) deprived; *bereft of reason*.

**beret** (**bair**-ay) noun a soft round flat cap with no peak.

**Berg** (*pronounced* bairg), Alban (1885–1935), Austrian composer, a pupil of Schoenberg.

**berg** noun an iceberg.

**bergamot** (**ber**-gă-mot) noun **1** a perfume from the rind of a citrus fruit. **2** the tree bearing this. **3** a fragrant herb.

**Bergman**[1], Ingmar (born 1918), Swedish film and theatre director.

**Bergman**[2], Ingrid (1915–82), Swedish film and stage actress.

**beriberi** (*pronounced as* berry-berry) noun a disease affecting the nervous system, caused by lack of vitamin B₁.

**Bering Sea** (**bair**-ing) the northernmost part of the Pacific Ocean, between Alaska and Siberia. (¶ Named after the Danish explorer V. J. Bering (1681–1741).)

**Berio**, Luciano (born 1925), Italian composer.

**berk** noun (also **burk**) (*slang*) a stupid person.

**berkelium** (ber-**kee**-liŭm) noun an artificially made radioactive metallic element (symbol Bk).

**Berks.** abbreviation Berkshire.

**Berkshire** (**bark**-sher) a southern county of England.

**Berlin**[1] the capital of Germany.

**Berlin**[2], Irving (1888–1989), Russian-born American song-writer.

**Berlioz** (**bair**-li-ohz), Hector (1803–69), French composer.

**Bermuda** a group of islands in the West Atlantic. □ **Bermuda shorts** (also **Bermudas**) knee-length shorts. □ **Bermudian** adjective

**Bern** alternative sp. of BERNE.

**Bernard**, St (*c.*996–*c.*1081), priest who founded two hospices in the Alps to aid travellers. St Bernard dogs are named after him.

**Berne** (*pronounced* bern) (also **Bern**) the capital of Switzerland.

**Bernhardt** (**bairn**-hart), Sarah (real name; Rosine Bernard), (1844–1923), French actress, known as 'the divine Sarah'.

**Bernini** (bair-**nee**-ni), Gianlorenzo (1598–1680), Italian sculptor, painter, and architect.

**Bernstein** (**bern**-styn, -steen), Leonard (1918–90), American conductor and composer.

**Berry**, Chuck (Charles Edward) (born 1931), American rock-and-roll singer and songwriter.

**berry** noun a small round juicy stoneless fruit.

**berserk** (ber-**zerk**) adjective frenzied. □ **go berserk** go into an uncontrollable and destructive rage.

**berth** noun **1** a bunk or sleeping-place in a ship or train. **2** a place for a boat to moor. **3** (*slang*) a job, employment. ● verb moor at a berth. □ **give a wide berth to** keep at a safe distance from.

**beryl** noun a transparent usually green precious stone.

**beryllium** (bĕ-**ril**-iŭm) noun a very light hard greyish-white metallic element (symbol Be), used in alloys where lightness and a high melting-point are important.

**beseech** verb (**besought**, **beseeching**) implore; beg earnestly.

**beset** verb (**beset**, **besetting**) hem in, surround; afflict (a person) persistently; *the temptations that beset people*.

**beside** preposition **1** at the side of, close to. **2** compared with; *his work looks poor beside yours*. □ **beside oneself** frantic with worry; overwhelmed. **beside the point** having nothing to do with it, irrelevant.

**besides** preposition in addition to; other than; *he has no income besides his pension*. ● adverb also.

**besiege** verb **1** lay siege to. **2** crowd round with requests or questions.

**besmirch** verb **1** dirty, discolour. **2** dishonour; damage (a person's reputation).

**besom** (**bee**-zŏm) noun a broom made by tying a bundle of twigs to a long handle.

**besotted** (bi-**sot**-id) adjective infatuated.

**besought** see BESEECH.

**bespeak** verb (**bespoke**, **bespoken**, **bespeaking**) **1** engage beforehand. **2** order (goods). **3** be evidence of.

**bespectacled** adjective wearing spectacles.

**bespoke** see BESPEAK. ● adjective (of clothes) made to order; (of a tailor etc.) making such clothes.

**Best**, George (born 1946), Irish footballer.

**best** adjective of the most excellent kind; most satisfactory. ● adverb in the best manner, to the greatest degree. ● noun **1** that which is best; the chief merit or advantage. **2** (foll. by *of*) the winning majority of (games played etc.); *the best of three games.* **3** one's best clothes. ●*verb* (*informal*) defeat, outdo, outwit. □ **at best** taking the most hopeful view. **best man** the bridegroom's chief attendant at a wedding. **best part of** most of. **best-seller** *noun* a book that sells in very large numbers. **do one's best** do all one can. **he had best...**, **it is best...**, etc. the most sensible thing to do is...; *we had best go*; *it is best ignored.* **make the best of** be as contented as possible with; do what one can with. **put one's best foot forward** walk or work as fast as one can.

**bestial** (best-iăl) *adjective* **1** brutish, cruel. **2** of or like a beast.

**bestiality** *noun* **1** bestial behaviour. **2** sexual intercourse between a person and an animal.

**bestiary** (best-i-er-i) *noun* a medieval collection of descriptions of animals.

**bestir** *verb* (**bestirred, bestirring**) □ **bestir oneself** rouse or exert oneself.

**bestow** *verb* present as a gift. □ **bestowal** *noun*

**bestrew** *verb* **1** strew. **2** lie scattered over. □ **bestrewn** *adjective*

**bestride** *verb* (**bestrode, bestridden, bestriding**) sit or stand astride over.

**bet** *noun* **1** an agreement pledging something that will be forfeited if one's forecast of some event proves wrong. **2** the money etc. pledged. **3** (*informal*) a choice, possibility, or course of action; *your best bet is to call tomorrow.* **4** (*informal*) a prediction, an opinion; *my bet is that he won't come.* ●*verb* (**bet** *or* **betted, betting**) **1** make a bet; pledge in a bet. **2** (*informal*) predict, think most likely. □ **you bet** (*slang*) you may be sure.

**beta** (bee-tă) *noun* **1** the second letter of the Greek alphabet (B, β). **2** a second-class mark in an examination. **3** (in names of stars) the second-brightest in a constellation. □ **beta blocker** a drug used to prevent increased cardiac activity. **beta particles** fast-moving electrons emitted by radioactive substances.

**betake** *verb* (**betook, betaken, betaking**) □ **betake oneself** go.

**betatron** *noun* an apparatus for accelerating electrons in a circular path.

**betel** (bee-těl) *noun* a leaf chewed in eastern countries with **betel-nut** (the areca nut).

**Betelgeuse** (bee-těl-jerz) a large variable star in the constellation Orion.

**bête noire** (bayt nwar) (*plural* **bêtes noires**, *pronounced* same) a thing or person that one dislikes or fears very much. (¶ French, = black beast.)

**bethink** *verb* (**bethought, bethinking**) □ **bethink oneself** (*literary*) remind oneself, remember.

**Bethlehem** a small town near Jerusalem, the reputed birthplace of Jesus Christ.

**betide** *verb* happen to; *see* WOE BETIDE.

**betimes** *adverb* (*formal*) in good time, early.

**Betjeman** (bech-ĕ-măn), Sir John (1906–84), English poet and writer, Poet Laureate from 1972.

**betoken** *verb* be a sign of.

**betook** *see* BETAKE.

**betray** *verb* **1** give up or reveal disloyally to an enemy. **2** be disloyal to. **3** show unintentionally; *betray one's feelings.* □ **betrayal** *noun*, **betrayer** *noun*

**betroth** (bi-troh*th*) *verb* (*formal*) engage with a promise to marry. □ **betrothal** *noun*

**better**[1] *adjective* **1** of a more excellent kind; more satisfactory. **2** partly or fully recovered from an illness. ●*adverb* in a better manner, to a better degree; more usefully. ●*noun* **1** that which is better. **2** (**betters**) people who are of higher status than oneself. ●*verb* improve, do better than. □ **better half** (*humorous*) one's husband, wife, or partner. **better oneself** get a better social position or status. **better part of** most of. **get the better of** overcome. **go one better** do better than someone else's effort. **had better** would find it wiser or more sensible to.

**better**[2] *noun* a person who bets.

**betterment** *noun* making or becoming better, improvement.

**betting-shop** *noun* a bookmaker's office.

**between** *preposition & adverb* **1** in the space bounded by two or more points, lines, or objects. **2** intermediate to, especially in time, quantity, or quality. **3** separating; *the difference between right and wrong.* **4** to and from; *the liner sails between Naples and Haifa.* **5** connecting; *the great love between them.* **6** shared by; *divide the money between you.* **7** taking one and rejecting the other; *choose between them.* □ **between ourselves**, **between you and me** in confidence; to be kept secret.

---

■**Usage** The phrase *between you and I* is incorrect.

---

**betwixt** *preposition & adverb* (*old use*) between. □ **betwixt and between** midway.

**Bevan**, Aneurin (1897–1960), British Labour politician, creator of the National Health Service.

**bevel** (bev-ĕl) *noun* **1** a sloping edge or surface. **2** a tool for making such slopes. ●*verb* (**bevelled, bevelling**; *Amer.* **beveled, beveling**) give a sloping edge to.

**beverage** (bev-er-ij) *noun* any drink.

**Beveridge**, William Henry, 1st Baron (1879–1963), British economist whose report (completed in 1942) led to the establishment of a national insurance scheme.

**bevvy** *noun* (*plural* **bevvies**) (*slang*) an alcoholic drink; *have a few bevvies.*

**bevy** (bev-i) *noun* a company, a large group.

**bewail** *verb* wail over; mourn for.

**beware** *verb* be on one's guard.

**bewilder** *verb* puzzle, confuse. □ **bewilderment** *noun*

**bewitch** *verb* **1** put under a magic spell. **2** delight very much.

**beyond** *adverb & preposition* **1** at or to the further side of; further on. **2** outside; outside the scope or understanding of; *this is beyond repair; it is beyond me; he lives beyond his income.* **3** besides, except. □ **beyond doubt** quite certain; unquestionably.

**bezel** (bez-ĕl) *noun* **1** the sloping edge of a chisel; an oblique face of a cut gem. **2** a rim holding a gem in position.

**bezique** (bi-zeek) *noun* a card-game for two players.

**b.f.** *abbreviation* **1** bloody fool. **2** (also **b/f**) brought forward.

**BFPO** *abbreviation* British Forces Post Office.

**Bhagavadgita** (bah-gĕ-vahd-**gee**-tă) *noun* the 'Song of the Lord' (i.e. Krishna), the most famous religious text of Hinduism.

**bhakti** (**bahk**-ti) *noun* (in Hinduism) worship directed to one supreme deity, usually Vishnu or Siva.

**bhang** (*pronounced* bang) *noun* the dried leaves and flower-tops of Indian hemp smoked or chewed as a narcotic and intoxicant.

**bhangra** *noun* rock music combining traditional Punjabi music with Western popular music.

**Bhopal** (boh-**pahl**) a city in central India, the capital of Madhya Pradesh, where in 1984 leakage of poisonous gas from an American-owned pesticide factory caused thousands of deaths and injuries.

**b.h.p.** *abbreviation* brake horse power.

**Bhutan** (boo-**tahn**) a country between India and Tibet. □ **Bhutanese** *adjective & noun* (*plural* **Bhutanese**).

**Bhutto¹** (**boo**-toh), Benazir (born 1953), Pakistani stateswoman, Prime Minister 1988–90 and from 1993.

**Bhutto²** (**boo**-toh), Zulfikar Ali (1928–79), the first civilian President (1971–3) and later Prime Minister (1973–7) of Pakistan.

**Bi** *symbol* bismuth.

**bi-** *combining form* two; twice.

**biannual** *adjective* appearing or happening twice a year. □ **biannually** *adverb*

**bias** *noun* **1** (often foll. by *towards, against*) an opinion or influence that strongly favours one side in an argument or one item in a group or series. **2** the slanting direction across threads of woven material.

**3** the tendency of a ball in the game of bowls to swerve because of the way it is weighted. ●*verb* (**biased, biasing**) give a bias to, influence. □ **cut on the bias** (of fabric) cut with the threads running slantwise across the up-and-down line of a garment. **bias binding** a strip of fabric cut on the bias and used to bind edges.

**biathlon** *noun* a contest in skiing and shooting or cycling and running.

**bib** *noun* **1** a cloth or plastic covering put under a young child's chin to protect the front of its clothes while it is eating; any similar covering. **2** the front part of an apron, above the waist.

**Bible** *noun* **1** (**the Bible**) the Christian scriptures; the Jewish scriptures. **2** (**bible**) a copy of either of these. **3** a book regarded as authoritative. □ **Bible-bashing, Bible-thumping** (*slang*) aggressive fundamentalist preaching.

**biblical** *adjective* of or in the Bible.

**bibliography** (bibli-**og**-răfi) *noun* **1** a list of books or articles about a particular subject or by a particular author. **2** the study of the history of books and their production. □ **bibliographer** *noun*, **bibliographical** (bib-li-ŏ-**graf**-ikăl) *adjective*

**bibliophile** (**bib**-li-ŏ-fyl) *noun* a lover of books.

**bibulous** (**bib**-yoo-lŭs) *adjective* addicted to alcoholic drink.

**bicameral** (by-**kam**-er-ăl) *adjective* (of a parliament, senate, etc.) having two chambers.

**bicarb** *noun* (*informal*) = *bicarbonate of soda.*

**bicarbonate** *noun* any acid salt of carbonic acid. □ **bicarbonate of soda** sodium bicarbonate, used in baking powder or to correct acidity.

**bicentenary** (by-sen-**teen**-er-i) *noun* a 200th anniversary.

**bicentennial** (by-sen-**ten**-iăl) *adjective* of a bicentenary. ●*noun* a bicentenary.

**biceps** (**by**-seps) *noun* the large muscle at the front of the upper arm, which bends the elbow.

**bicker** *verb* quarrel constantly about unimportant things.

**bicuspid** (by-**kusp**-id) *adjective* having two cusps. ●*noun* a bicuspid tooth; a premolar.

**bicycle** *noun* a two-wheeled vehicle driven by pedals. ●*verb* ride on a bicycle.

**bicyclist** *noun* a person who rides a bicycle.

**bid¹** *noun* **1** an offer of a price to buy something, especially at an auction. **2** a statement of the number of tricks a player proposes to win in a card-game. **3** an effort to obtain something; *made a bid for popular support.* ●*verb* (**bid, bidding**) make a bid. □ **bidder** *noun*

**bid²** *verb* (**bid**, *old use* **bade** (*pronounced* bad); **bid** *or* **bidden, bidding**) **1** command; *do as* *you are bid.* **2** say as a greeting or farewell; *bidding them good night.*

**biddable** *adjective* willing to obey.

**bidding** *noun* **1** a command or request. **2** bids in an auction or card-game.

**biddy** *noun* □ **old biddy** (*slang*) an elderly woman.

**bide** *verb* □ **bide one's time** wait for a good opportunity.

**bidet** (**bee**-day) *noun* a low narrow basin that one can sit on to wash the genital area.

**biennial** (by-**en**-iăl) *adjective* **1** lasting or living for two years. **2** happening every second year. ● *noun* a plant that lives for two years, flowering and dying in the second. □ **biennially** *adverb*

**bier** *noun* a movable stand on which a coffin or a dead body is placed before burial.

**biff** (*slang*) *verb* hit. ● *noun* a blow.

**bifid** (**by**-fid) *adjective* divided by a deep cleft into two parts.

**bifocal** (by-**foh**-kăl) *adjective* having two foci. ● *noun* (**bifocals**) spectacles with each lens made in two sections, the upper part for looking at distant objects and the lower part for reading and other close work.

**bifurcate** (**by**-fer-kayt) *verb* divide into two branches. □ **bifurcation** *noun*

**big** *adjective* (**bigger**, **biggest**) **1** large in size, amount, or intensity. **2** more grown up, elder; *my big sister.* **3** important; *the big match.* **4** boastful, pretentious; *big talk.* **5** (*informal*) generous; *that's big of you.* ● *adverb* (*informal*) on a large scale; *think big.* □ **Big Apple** (*slang*) New York city. **Big Bang** (*informal*) the overnight introduction of important changes on the Stock Exchange (27 October 1986), including abolition of the distinction between brokers and jobbers. **big bang theory** the theory that the universe began with a massive explosion of dense matter. **Big Ben** the great bell, clock, and tower of the Houses of Parliament. **Big Brother** a dictator who exercises close control of everything while pretending to be kindly. **big business** commerce on a large financial scale. **big deal!** (*slang*) I am not impressed. **big end** the end of a connecting-rod that encircles the crankshaft in an engine. **big game** the larger animals hunted for sport. **big-head** *noun* (*informal*) a conceited person. **big-hearted** *adjective* generous. **big noise**, **big shot** (*informal*) an important person. **big stick** (*informal*) threat of force. **big time** (*slang*) the highest or most important level among entertainers. **big top** the main tent at a circus. **big wheel** a Ferris wheel. **too big for one's boots** (*slang*) conceited. □ **biggish** *adjective*

**bigamist** *noun* a person guilty of bigamy.

**bigamy** *noun* the crime of marrying while still married to another person. □ **bigamous** *adjective*, **bigamously** *adverb*

**bight** (*rhymes with* kite) *noun* **1** a long inward curve in a coast; *the Great Australian Bight.* **2** a loop of rope.

**bigot** (**big**-ŏt) *noun* a person who holds an opinion obstinately and is intolerant towards those who do not. □ **bigoted** *adjective*, **bigotry** *noun*

**bigwig** *noun* (*informal*) an important person.

**Bihar** (bi-**har**) a State in NE India. □ **Bihari** *noun*, *adjective*

**bijou** (**bee**-zhoo) *adjective* small and elegant.

**bike** (*informal*) *noun* a bicycle or motor cycle. ● *verb* travel on a bike.

**bikini** *noun* a woman's two-piece swimming costume consisting of a bra and briefs.

**Biko** (**bee**-koh), Steve (Stephan Bantu) (1946–77), Black radical leader in South Africa, who was arrested in 1977 and died in custody before he could be brought to trial.

**bilateral** (by-**lat**-erăl) *adjective* of or on two sides; having two sides; *a bilateral agreement.* □ **bilaterally** *adverb*

**bilberry** *noun* **1** the small round dark-blue fruit of a wild shrub. **2** this shrub.

**bile** *noun* a bitter yellowish liquid produced by the liver and stored in the gall bladder, aiding digestion of fats.

**bilge** (*pronounced* bilj) *noun* **1** a ship's bottom, inside and outside. **2** the water that collects there. **3** (*slang*) worthless ideas or talk.

**bilharzia** (bil-**har**-ziă) *noun* a tropical disease caused by a parasitic flatworm.

**bilingual** (by-**ling**-wăl) *adjective* **1** written in two languages. **2** able to speak two languages.

**bilious** (**bil**-yŭs) *adjective* **1** affected by sickness assumed to be caused by too much bile. **2** of a sickly yellowish colour or shade; *a bilious green.* **3** (*informal*) bad-tempered. □ **biliousness** *noun*

**bilk** *verb* (*slang*) escape paying one's debts to; defraud.

**bill¹** *noun* **1** a written statement of charges for goods supplied or services rendered. **2** a poster or placard. **3** a programme of entertainment. **4** the draft of a proposed law, to be discussed by a parliament (and called an Act when passed). **5** (*Amer.*) a banknote; *a ten-dollar bill.* **6** a certificate. ● *verb* **1** announce in a bill or poster; *Olivier was billed to appear as Hamlet.* **2** send a note of charges to. □ **bill of exchange** a written order to pay a specified sum of money on a particular date to a named person or to the bearer. **bill of fare** a menu. **bill of lading** a list giving details of a ship's cargo. **fill the bill** be or do what is required.

**bill²** *noun* a bird's beak. ● *verb* (of doves) stroke each other with their bills.

**billabong** *noun* (*Austral.*) a river branch forming a backwater or stagnant pool.

**billboard** *noun* a hoarding for advertisements.

**billet** *noun* **1** a lodging for troops or evacuees, especially in a private house. **2** (*informal*) a position, a job. **3** a thick piece of firewood. ● *verb* (**billeted, billeting**) lodge (a soldier etc.) in a billet.

**billet-doux** (bil-ay-doo) *noun* (*plural* **billets-doux**, *pronounced* same) (*old use*, often *humorous*) a love-letter.

**billhook** *noun* a long-handled tool with a curved blade for lopping trees.

**billiards** *noun* a game played with cues and three balls on a cloth-covered table.

**billion** *noun* **1** a million million. **2** a thousand million. □ **billionth** *adjective & noun*

■**Usage** The sense 'a thousand million' was originally used in the USA but is now common in Britain and elsewhere.

**billionaire** *noun* a person who has over a billion pounds, dollars, etc.

**billow** *noun* a great wave. ● *verb* rise or roll like waves; *smoke billowed forth*. □ **billowy** *adjective*

**billposter** *noun* (also **billsticker**) a person who sticks advertisements or notices onto walls, shop windows, or hoardings.

**billy** *noun* (also **billycan**) a tin can or enamelled container with a lid, used as an outdoor cooking-pot.

**billy-goat** *noun* a male goat.

**billy-o** *noun* □ **like billy-o** (*informal*) vigorously.

**bimbo** *noun* (*plural* **bimbos** or **bimboes**) (*slang*, usually *scornful*) an attractive but unintelligent young woman.

**bimedia** *adjective* involved in or working in two of the mass communication media, especially radio and television.

**bimetallic** *adjective* using or made of two metals.

**bimonthly** *adjective* **1** happening every second month. **2** happening twice a month.

**bin** *noun* **1** a large rigid container or enclosed space, usually with a lid, used for storing coal, grain, flour, etc. **2** a receptacle for rubbish or litter. □ **bin-liner** *noun* a plastic bag for lining a rubbish bin.

**binary** (by-ner-i) *adjective* **1** of a pair or pairs. **2** of the binary system. ● *noun* something having two parts. □ **binary digit** *or* **number** either of the two digits, 0 and 1, used in the binary system. **binary star** two stars that revolve round each other. **binary system** a system using the numbers 0 and 1 to code information, especially in computing.

**bind** *verb* (**bound, binding**) **1** tie or fasten; tie up. **2** hold together; unite; *bound by ties of friendship*. **3** encircle with a strip or band of material; *bind up the wound*. **4** cover the edge of (a thing) in order to strengthen it or as a decoration. **5** fasten the pages of (a book) into a cover. **6** stick together in a solid mass; *bind the mixture with egg yolk*. **7** place under an obligation or a legal agreement. ● *noun* (*slang*) a bore, a nuisance. □ **bind over** *Law* order to keep the peace.

**binder** *noun* **1** a person or thing that binds. **2** a loose cover for papers. **3** a bookbinder. **4** (*hist.*) a machine for binding harvested grain into sheaves.

**bindery** *noun* a workshop where books are bound.

**binding** *noun* **1** fabric used for binding edges. **2** the strong covering holding the leaves of a book together. ● *adjective* making a legal obligation; *the agreement is binding on both parties*.

**bindweed** *noun* a wild convolvulus.

**Binet** (bee-nay), Alfred (1857–1911), French psychologist, the originator of a modern system of intelligence testing.

**binge** (*pronounced* binj) (*slang*) *noun* a bout of excessive eating, drinking, etc. ● *verb* indulge in a binge.

**bingo** *noun* a gambling game played with cards on which numbered squares are covered as the numbers are called at random. ● *interjection* an exclamation at a sudden action or event.

**binman** *noun* (*informal*) a dustman.

**binnacle** (bin-ă-kŭl) *noun* a non-magnetic stand for a ship's compass.

**binocular** (bin-ok-yoo-ler) *adjective* for or using both eyes. ● *noun* (**binoculars**) an instrument with lenses for both eyes, making distant objects seem nearer.

**binomial** (by-noh-mi-ăl) *noun* an algebraic expression consisting of two terms linked by a plus or minus sign. ● *adjective* consisting of two terms or names. □ **binomial theorem** a formula for finding any power of a binomial.

**bio-** *combining form* **1** life. **2** of living things.

**biochemistry** *noun* chemistry of living organisms. □ **biochemical** *adjective*, **biochemist** *noun*

**biodegradable** (by-oh-di-gray-dă-bŭl) *adjective* able to be broken down by bacteria in the environment.

**bioengineering** *noun* the application of engineering techniques to biological processes.

**biogenesis** *noun* **1** the hypothesis that a living thing originates only from a similar living thing. **2** the production of substances by living things.

**biographer** *noun* a person who writes a biography.

**biography** *noun* the story of a person's life written by another. □ **biographical** *adjective*

**biological** *adjective* of biology or living organisms. □ **biological clock** an internal mechanism controlling the rhythmic pattern of activities of a living thing. **biological control** control of plant pests by introducing natural predators. **biological warfare** the use of organisms to spread disease against an enemy. □ **biologically** *adverb*

**biology** *noun* the scientific study of the life and structure of living things. □ **biologist** *noun*

**biomass** *noun* the total quantity or weight of organisms in a given area or volume.

**bionic** (by-**on**-ik) *adjective* **1** of bionics. **2** (of a person or faculties) operated by electronic means, not naturally. ●*noun* (**bionics**) the study of mechanical systems that function like parts of living beings.

**biophysics** *noun* the scientific study of the properties of physics in living organisms, and investigation of biological matters by means of modern physics. □ **biophysical** *adjective*, **biophysicist** *noun*

**biopsy** (by-op-si) *noun* examination of tissue cut from a living body.

**biorhythm** (by-ŏ-ri*th*m) *noun* any of the recurring cycles of physical, emotional, and intellectual activity said to occur in people's lives.

**bioscope** *noun* (*South African*) a cinema.

**biosphere** (by-ŏ-sfeer) *noun* the regions of the earth's crust and atmosphere occupied by living things.

**biosynthesis** *noun* the production of organic molecules by living things. □ **biosynthetic** *adjective*

**biotechnology** *noun* the use of living micro-organisms and biological processes in industrial and commercial production.

**biotin** *noun* a vitamin of the B complex, found in egg yolk, liver, and yeast.

**bipartisan** (by-parti-**zan**) *adjective* of or involving two political or other parties.

**bipartite** (by-**par**-tyt) *adjective* having two parts, shared by or involving two groups.

**biped** (by-ped) *noun* a two-footed animal.

**biplane** (by-playn) *noun* an aeroplane with two sets of wings, one above the other.

**birch** *noun* **1** a deciduous tree with smooth bark and slender branches. **2** a bundle of birch twigs used for flogging. ●*verb* flog with a birch.

**bird** *noun* **1** a feathered animal with two wings and two legs. **2** (*slang*) a person; *he's a cunning old bird.* **3** (*slang*) a young woman. **4** (*slang*) a prison sentence. □ **a bird in the hand** something secured or certain.

**bird of paradise** a New Guinea bird, the male of which has brightly coloured plumage. **bird of passage 1** a migrant bird. **2** a person who travels constantly. **bird of prey** a bird which hunts animals for food. **bird's-eye view** a general view from above. **birds of a feather** similar people. **bird-watcher** *noun* one who studies the habits of birds in their natural surroundings. **get the bird** (*slang*) be hissed and booed; be rejected. **strictly for the birds** (*informal*) trivial, unimportant.

**birdie** *noun* **1** (*informal*) a little bird. **2** a score of one stroke under par for a hole at golf.

**birdlime** *noun* a sticky substance spread to trap birds.

**birdseed** *noun* a blend of seeds for caged birds.

**biretta** (bir-et-ă) *noun* a square cap worn by Roman Catholic priests.

**Biro** *noun* (*trade mark*) a ball-point pen.

**birth** *noun* **1** the emergence of young from the mother's body. **2** origin, parentage; *he is of noble birth.* □ **birth certificate** an official document giving the date and place of a person's birth. **birth control** prevention of unwanted pregnancy; contraception. **birth rate** the number of births in one year for every 1000 persons. **give birth to 1** produce (young). **2** be the cause of, originate.

**birthday** *noun* an anniversary of the day of one's birth. □ **in one's birthday suit** (*humorous*) naked.

**birthmark** *noun* an unusual coloured mark on a person's skin at birth.

**birthplace** *noun* the house or district where one was born.

**birthright** *noun* a privilege or property to which a person has a right through being born into a particular family or country.

**birthstone** *noun* a gem associated with a particular month or sign of the zodiac.

**Biscay** (bis-kay), **Bay of** part of the North Atlantic between the north coast of Spain and the west coast of France, notorious for storms.

**biscuit** (**bis**-kit) *noun* **1** a small flat thin piece of a pastry or cake-like substance baked crisp. **2** fired unglazed pottery. **3** light-brown colour.

**bisect** (by-**sekt**) *verb* divide into two equal parts. □ **bisection** *noun*, **bisector** *noun*

**bisexual** (by-seks-yoo-ăl) *adjective* **1** of two sexes. **2** having both male and female sexual organs in one individual. **3** sexually attracted to people of both sexes. ●*noun* a bisexual person. □ **bisexuality** *noun*

**bishop** *noun* **1** a clergyman of high rank with authority over the work of the Church in a city or district (his *diocese*). **2** a chess piece shaped like a mitre.

**bishopric** *noun* the office or diocese of a bishop.

**Bismarck** (biz-mark), Otto Eduard Leopold, Prince von (1815–98), German statesman.

**Bismarck Archipelago** a group of over 200 islands off NE Papua New Guinea.

**bismuth** (biz-mŭth) *noun* **1** a chemical element (symbol Bi), a greyish-white metal used in alloys. **2** a compound of this used in medicines.

**bison** (by-sŏn) *noun* (*plural* **bison**) a wild hump-backed ox of Europe or North America.

**bisque** (*pronounced* bisk) *noun* **1** an extra turn, stroke, etc., allowed to an inferior player in some games. **2** unglazed white porcelain. **3** a rich soup made from shellfish.

**bistre** (bis-ter) *noun* (*Amer.* **bister**) **1** a brown pigment prepared from soot. **2** its colour.

**bistro** (bee-stroh) *noun* (*plural* **bistros**) a small informal restaurant.

**bit¹** *noun* **1** a small piece or amount. **2** a short time or distance; *wait a bit*. **3** a small coin. □ **bit by bit** gradually. **a bit on the side** (*slang*) a sexual relationship involving infidelity. **bit part** a small part in a play or film. **bits and pieces** odds and ends. **do one's bit** (*informal*) do one's share.

**bit²** *noun* **1** a metal bar forming the mouthpiece of a bridle. **2** the part of a tool that cuts or grips when twisted; the boring-piece of a drill. □ **take the bit between one's teeth** take decisive action.

**bit³** *noun Computing* a unit of information expressed as a choice between two possibilities. (¶ From *bi*nary dig*it*).

**bit⁴** *see* BITE.

**bitch** *noun* **1** a female dog; a female fox, wolf, otter, etc. **2** (*scornful*) a spiteful woman. **3** (*informal*) an unpleasant or difficult thing. ●*verb* (*informal*) speak spitefully; grumble sourly. □ **bitchy** *adjective*, **bitchiness** *noun*

**bite** *verb* (**bit, bitten, biting**) **1** cut into or nip with the teeth. **2** (of an insect) sting; (of a snake) pierce with its fangs. **3** accept bait; *the fish are biting*. **4** grip or act effectively; *wheels can't bite on a slippery surface*. ●*noun* **1** an act of biting. **2** a wound made by this. **3** a mouthful cut off by biting. **4** food to eat, a small meal. **5** the taking of bait by a fish. **6** a firm grip or hold; *this drill has no bite*. **7** the way the teeth close in biting. **8** sharpness, effectiveness. □ **bite a person's head off** reply angrily. **bite the dust** (*slang*) die; fail; break down.

**biting** *adjective* **1** causing a smarting pain; *a biting wind*. **2** (of remarks) sharp and critical.

**bitten** *see* BITE.

**bitter** *adjective* **1** tasting sharp; not sweet. **2** showing, feeling, causing, or caused by mental pain or resentment; *bitter remarks*. **3** piercingly cold; *a bitter wind*. ●*noun* **1** beer flavoured with hops and tasting slightly bitter. **2** (**bitters**) liquor flavoured with bitter herbs to give a stimulating taste. □ **bitter-sweet** *adjective* sweet but with a bitter taste at the end; pleasant but with a mixture of something unpleasant. □ **bitterly** *adverb*, **bitterness** *noun*

**bittern** *noun* a marsh bird related to the heron, especially the kind known for the male's booming note.

**bitty** *adverb* made up of unrelated bits.

**bitumen** (bit-yoo-měn) *noun* a black sticky substance obtained from petroleum, used for covering roads etc. □ **bituminous** (bit-yoo-min-ŭs) *adjective*

**bivalve** (by-valv) *noun* a shellfish with a hinged double shell.

**bivouac** (biv-oo-ak) *noun* a temporary camp without tents or other cover. ●*verb* (**bivouacked, bivouacking**) camp in a bivouac.

**bi-weekly** *adjective* **1** happening every second week. **2** happening twice a week.

**biz** *noun* (*informal*) business.

**bizarre** (biz-ar) *adjective* strikingly odd.

**Bizet** (bee-zay), Georges (originally Alexandre Césare Léopold) (1838–75), French composer.

**Bk** *symbol* berkelium.

**blab** *verb* (**blabbed, blabbing**) talk indiscreetly, let out a secret.

**blabber** *noun* (also **blabbermouth**) a person who blabs. ●*verb* (often foll. by *on*) talk at length about trivial things.

**black** *adjective* **1** of the very darkest colour, like coal or soot. **2** having a black skin. **3** (**Black**) of the human group with dark-coloured skin, especially Africans. **4** soiled with dirt. **5** dismal; hostile; not hopeful; disastrous. **6** evil, wicked. **7** not to be handled by trade-unionists while others are on strike; *declared the cargo black*. ●*noun* **1** black colour. **2** a black substance or material; black clothes. **3** the black ball in snooker etc. **4** the black pieces in chess etc.; the player using these. **5** the credit side of an account. **6** (**Black**) a member of a dark-skinned race, especially an African. ●*verb* **1** make black. **2** polish with blacking. **3** declare goods or work to be 'black'. □ **black beetle** a cockroach. **black belt** the highest grade of proficiency in judo, karate, etc.; the holder of this. **black box** an electronic device in an aircraft recording information about its flight. **black comedy** comedy presenting a tragic theme or situation in comic terms. **black economy**

an unofficial system of employing and paying people without observing legal requirements such as payment of income tax and National Insurance contributions. **black eye** an eye with the skin round it darkened by a bruise. **black hole** a region in outer space with a gravitational field so intense that no matter or radiation can escape from it. **black ice** hard thin transparent ice on roads. **black magic** magic involving the invocation of evil spirits. **black mark** a mark of disapproval. **black market** the illegal buying and selling of goods or currencies. **black marketeer** one who trades in the black market. **black out 1** cover windows etc. so that no light can penetrate. **2** suffer temporary loss of consciousness or sight or memory. **black pepper** pepper from the whole of the pepper berry including the outer husk. **black pudding** a large dark sausage containing blood, suet, etc. **black sheep** a member of a family or other group regarded as a disgrace or failure. **black spot 1** a place where conditions are dangerous or difficult. **2** a plant disease producing black spots. **black tea** tea that is fully fermented before drying (compare *green tea*). **black tie** a man's black bow-tie worn with a dinner jacket. **black velvet** a mixture of stout and champagne. **black widow** a poisonous spider found in tropical and subtropical regions. (The female of a North American species devours its mate.) **in a person's black books** having earned his or her disapproval. **in black and white** recorded in writing or print. **in the black** having a credit balance. □ **blackly** *adverb*, **blackness** *noun*

**blackball** *verb* prevent (a person) from being elected as a member of a club by voting against him or her at a secret ballot.

**blackberry** *noun* **1** the bramble. **2** its small dark berry.

**blackbird** *noun* a European songbird, the male of which is black.

**blackboard** *noun* a board with a smooth dark surface for writing on with chalk.

**blackcock** *noun* a male black grouse.

**Black Country** the industrial area in the English Midlands.

**Black Death** an epidemic of plague in Europe during the 14th century.

**blacken** *verb* **1** make or become black. **2** say unpleasant things about; *blackened his character*.

**blackfly** *noun* a kind of insect infesting plants.

**Black Forest** a hilly wooded region in SW Germany, east of the Rhine valley. □ **Black Forest gateau** chocolate cake with cherries and cream.

**Black Friars** Dominicans, so called from their black cloaks.

**blackguard** (blag-erd) *noun* a scoundrel. □ **blackguardly** *adverb*

**blackhead** *noun* a small black-topped lump blocking a pore in the skin.

**blacking** *noun* black polish for shoes.

**blackjack** *noun* = PONTOON.

**blacklead** *noun* graphite.

**blackleg** *noun* a person who works while fellow workers are on strike. ● *verb* (**blacklegged, blacklegging**) act as a blackleg.

**blacklist** *noun* a list of people who are disapproved of. ● *verb* put on a blacklist.

**blackmail** *verb* demand payment or action from (a person) by threats especially of revealing a discreditable secret. ● *noun* the crime of demanding payment in this way; the money itself. □ **blackmailer** *noun*

**Black Maria** a secure van for taking prisoners to and from prison or into custody.

**Black Mass** a blasphemous misrepresentation of the Mass, in worship of Satan.

**blackout** *noun* **1** temporary loss of consciousness or memory. **2** loss of electric power, radio reception, etc. **3** temporary suppression of news. **4** compulsory darkness at night during wartime.

**Black Power** a militant movement supporting civil rights, political power, etc., for Blacks.

**Black Prince** the name given in the 16th century to Edward Plantagenet (1330–76), eldest son of Edward III of England.

**Black Rod** the chief gentleman usher of the Lord Chamberlain's department, who is also usher to the House of Lords, so called from his ebony rod of office.

**Black Sea** a tideless sea between Russia, Ukraine, Turkey, Bulgaria, and Romania.

**blackshirt** *noun* (*hist.*) a member of a Fascist organization.

**blacksmith** *noun* a smith who works in iron.

**blackthorn** *noun* a thorny shrub bearing white flowers and sloes.

**Black Watch** the Royal Highland Regiment whose uniform includes a dark-coloured tartan.

**bladder** *noun* **1** a sac in which urine collects in human and animal bodies. **2** an inflatable bag, e.g. in a football.

**bladderwrack** *noun* brown seaweed with air sacs among its fronds.

**blade** *noun* **1** the flattened cutting part of a knife, sword, chisel, etc. **2** the flat wide part of an oar, spade, propeller, etc. **3** a flat narrow leaf, especially of grass and cereals. **4** a broad flattish bone; *shoulder-blade*.

**Blake**, William (1757–1827), English artist and poet.

**blame** verb hold responsible and criticize for a fault. ●noun responsibility for a fault; criticism for doing wrong.

**blameless** adjective deserving no blame, innocent.

**blanch** verb **1** make or become white or pale. **2** whiten (a plant) by depriving it of light. **3** immerse (vegetables) briefly in boiling water. **4** peel (almonds etc.) by scalding.

**blancmange** (blă-**monj**) noun a flavoured jelly-like pudding made with milk.

**bland** adjective **1** mild in flavour; tasteless and dull; bland foods. **2** gentle and casual in manner, not irritating or stimulating. □ **blandly** adverb, **blandness** noun

**blandish** verb flatter, coax. □ **blandishment** noun

**blank** adjective **1** not written or printed on, unmarked; (of a wall) without ornament or opening. **2** without interest or expression; without result. ●noun **1** a blank space or paper; an empty surface; his mind was a blank. **2** a blank cartridge. □ **blank cartridge** one that contains no bullet. **blank cheque 1** a cheque with the amount left blank, to be filled in by the payee. **2** (informal) unlimited freedom of action. **blank off** seal (an opening). **blank out** cross out; obscure. **blank verse** verse written in lines of usually ten syllables, without rhyme. □ **blankly** adverb, **blankness** noun

**blanket** noun **1** a thick covering made of woollen or other fabric. **2** a thick covering mass; a blanket of fog. ●adjective covering everything; inclusive; a blanket agreement. ●verb (**blanketed, blanketing**) cover with a blanket. □ **blanket stitch** an embroidery stitch suitable for finishing a raw edge.

**blare** noun a harsh loud sound like that of a trumpet. ●verb make such a sound.

**blarney** noun smooth talk that flatters and deceives people. ●verb flatter, cajole.

**blasé** (blah-zay) adjective bored or unimpressed by things because one has experienced or seen them so often.

**blaspheme** verb utter blasphemies. □ **blasphemer** noun

**blasphemy** (blas-fĕmi) noun contemptuous or irreverent talk about God and sacred things. □ **blasphemous** adjective, **blasphemously** adverb

**blast** noun **1** a sudden strong rush of wind or air, a wave of air from an explosion. **2** a single emission of sound by a wind instrument, whistle, car horn, etc. **3** (informal) a severe reprimand. ●verb **1** blow up with explosives. **2** cause to wither, blight, destroy. ●interjection damn. □ **at full blast** at maximum power or speed. **blast-furnace** noun a furnace for smelting ore, with compressed hot air driven in. **blast off** (of

a spacecraft) take off from a launching site. **blast-off** noun the launching of a spacecraft.

**blasted** adjective (informal) damned.

**blatant** (blay-tănt) adjective **1** attracting attention in a loud, obtrusive way. **2** obvious and unashamed; a blatant lie. □ **blatantly** adverb

**blather** (also **blether**) (informal) verb chatter foolishly. ●noun foolish chatter.

**blaze**¹ noun **1** a bright flame or fire. **2** a bright light, a brightly coloured display. **3** an outburst; a blaze of anger. **4** (**blazes**) (slang) hell; what the blazes is that?; go to blazes. ●verb **1** burn or shine brightly. **2** have an outburst of intense feeling or anger. □ **blaze away** fire a gun continuously. **like blazes** very quickly, exceedingly.

**blaze**² noun **1** a white mark on an animal's face. **2** a mark chipped in the bark of a tree to mark a route. ●verb mark (a tree or route) with blazes. □ **blaze a trail** make such marks; pioneer and show the way for others to follow. **blaze something abroad** make it widely known.

**blazer** noun a loose-fitting jacket, often in the colours of a school, club, or team.

**blazon** (blay-zŏn) noun a heraldic shield, a coat of arms. ●verb **1** proclaim. **2** describe or paint (a coat of arms); inscribe with arms, names, etc., in colours.

**bleach** verb whiten by sunlight or chemicals. ●noun a bleaching substance.

**bleak** adjective cold and cheerless; the future looks bleak. □ **bleakly** adverb, **bleakness** noun

**bleary** adjective watery and seeing indistinctly; bleary eyes. □ **blearily** adverb, **bleariness** noun

**bleat** noun the cry of a sheep, goat, or calf. ●verb **1** make this cry. **2** speak or say plaintively.

**bleed** verb (**bled, bleeding**) **1** leak blood or other fluid. **2** draw blood or fluid from. **3** (of dye) come out in water; run. **4** extort money from.

**bleeding** adjective & adverb (vulgar) bloody, damned.

**bleep** noun a short high-pitched sound used as a signal. ●verb make this sound.

**bleeper** noun a small electronic device that bleeps to contact the person carrying it.

**blemish** noun a flaw that spoils a thing's perfection. ●verb spoil with a blemish.

**blench** verb flinch.

**blend** verb **1** mix in order to get a certain quality. **2** mingle, become a mixture. **3** have no sharp or unpleasant contrast; the colours blend well. ●noun a mixture of different sorts; a blend of tea.

**blender** noun **1** something that blends things. **2** a kitchen appliance for liquidizing or puréeing food.

**blenny** noun a small marine fish with spiny fins.

**Blériot** (ble-ri-oh), Louis (1872–1936), French pioneer in aviation, the first to cross the English Channel in a monoplane (25 July 1909).

**bless** verb **1** make sacred or holy with the sign of the Cross. **2** call holy, praise; to bless God. **3** call God's favour upon; Christ blessed the children. □ **be blessed with** be fortunate in having; be blessed with good health. **bless my soul!** an exclamation of surprise. **bless you!** an exclamation of gratitude, or to a person who has just sneezed.

**blessed** (bles-id) adjective **1** holy, sacred; the Blessed Virgin. **2** in paradise. **3** (old use) fortunate; blessed are the meek. **4** (slang) damned; the blessed thing slipped. □ **blessedness** noun

**blessing** noun **1** God's favour; a prayer for this. **2** a short prayer of thanks to God before or after a meal. **3** something one is glad of; a blessing in disguise.

**blest** adjective (old use) blessed; our blest Redeemer.

**blether** verb & noun = BLATHER.

**blew** see BLOW¹.

**Bligh**, William (1754–1817), British naval officer, commander of HMS Bounty whose crew mutinied in 1789.

**blight** noun **1** a disease that withers plants. **2** a fungus or insect causing this disease. **3** a malignant influence. **4** an unsightly area. ●verb **1** affect with blight. **2** spoil.

**blighter** noun (informal) a person or thing, especially an annoying one.

**Blighty** noun (slang) Britain; home (especially after military service abroad).

**blimey** (bly-mi) interjection (slang) an exclamation of surprise.

**blimp** noun **1** a small non-rigid airship. **2** a soundproof cover for a cine-camera. □ **(Colonel) Blimp** a person firmly opposed to reform (¶ named after a cartoon character representing a fat pompous elderly man).

**blind** adjective **1** without sight. **2** without foresight or understanding; without adequate information; blind obedience. **3** concealed; blind hemming. **4** (of a plant) failing to produce a flower. **5** (in cookery) without filling; bake it blind. **6** (of a tube) closed at one end. ●adverb blindly. ●verb **1** make blind; dazzle with bright light. **2** take away the power of judgement; overawe; blinded with science. **3** (slang) go along recklessly. ●noun **1** a screen, especially on a roller, for a window. **2** a pretext.

□ **blind alley 1** an alley that is closed at one end. **2** a situation with no prospects of improvement or success. **blind bend** a road bend where it is impossible to see what is coming. **blind date** a date between people who have not met before. **blind drunk** (informal) very drunk indeed. **blind man's buff** a game in which a blindfolded player tries to catch others. **blind spot 1** a point on the eye that is insensitive to light. **2** an area where understanding is lacking. **3** an area cut off from a motorist's vision. **not a blind bit of** (slang) not the slightest. **turn a blind eye** pretend not to notice. □ **blindly** adverb, **blindness** noun

**blindfold** adjective & adverb with the eyes covered with a cloth to block one's sight. ●noun a cloth used for this. ●verb cover the eyes with a cloth.

**blindworm** noun a slow-worm (so called from its small eyes).

**blink** verb **1** open and shut the eyes rapidly. **2** shine unsteadily; flicker. ●noun **1** an act of blinking. **2** a quick gleam. □ **on the blink** (slang) not working properly; out of order.

**blinker** verb obstruct the sight or understanding of. ●plural noun (**blinkers**) leather pieces fixed on a bridle to prevent a horse from seeing sideways.

**blinking** adjective & adverb (slang) damned.

**blip** noun **1** a spot of light on a radar screen. **2** a quick electronic popping sound. **3** a minor problem, mistake, or change. ●verb (**blipped, blipping**) make a blip.

**bliss** noun perfect happiness. □ **blissful** adjective, **blissfully** adverb

**blister** noun **1** a bubble-like swelling on the skin, filled with watery liquid. **2** a raised swelling, e.g. on a painted surface. ●verb **1** cause a blister on; be affected with blisters. **2** criticize severely.

**blithe** (rhymes with scythe) adjective casual and carefree. □ **blithely** adverb

**blithering** adjective (informal) hopeless, contemptible; blithering idiot.

**B.Litt.** abbreviation Bachelor of Letters.

**blitz** noun **1** a violent attack, especially from aircraft. **2** an intensive period of work; have a blitz on this room. **3** (**the Blitz**) German air raids on London in 1940. ●verb attack or damage in a blitz.

**blitzkrieg** (blits-kreeg) noun an intense military campaign intended to bring about a swift victory.

**blizzard** noun a severe snowstorm.

**bloat** verb cause to swell out with fat, gas, or liquid.

**bloated** adjective **1** swollen with fat, gas, or liquid. **2** puffed up with pride or self-indulgence.

**bloater** noun a salted smoked herring.

**blob** *noun* a drop of liquid; a round mass or spot.

**bloc** *noun* a group of parties or countries who unite to support a particular interest.

**block** *noun* **1** a solid piece of wood, stone, or other hard substance. **2** a large piece of wood for chopping or hammering on; that on which condemned people were beheaded. **3** the main part of a petrol engine, consisting of the cylinders and valves. **4** a compact mass of buildings bounded by streets; *drive round the block*. **5** a large building divided into separate flats or offices. **6** a large section of shares, seats, etc. as a unit. **7** a pad of paper for drawing or writing on. **8** an obstruction. **9** (*slang*) the head. ●*verb* **1** obstruct, prevent the movement or use of. **2** stop (a bowled ball) with the bat. □ **block and tackle** a system of pulleys and ropes used for lifting things. **block capitals** = *block letters*. **block diagram** a diagram showing the general arrangement of parts in an apparatus. **block in** sketch in roughly. **block letters** plain capital letters. **block vote** a voting system in which each voter has influence according to the number of people he or she represents.

**blockade** *noun* the blocking of access to a place in order to prevent the entry of goods etc. ●*verb* set up a blockade of.

**blockage** *noun* **1** something that blocks. **2** the state of being blocked.

**blockbuster** *noun* **1** something very powerful or successful. **2** a huge bomb.

**blockhead** *noun* a stupid person.

**blockhouse** *noun* **1** a reinforced concrete military shelter. **2** (*hist.*) a timber building used as a fort.

**bloke** *noun* (*slang*) a man.

**blond** (of a woman or her hair **blonde**) *adjective* fair-haired; (of hair) fair. ●*noun* a fair-haired person.

**blood** *noun* **1** the red oxygen-bearing liquid circulating in the bodies of animals. **2** bloodshed; the guilt for this. **3** temper; courage; *his blood is up*. **4** race, descent, parentage; *they are my own blood*. ●*verb* give a first taste of blood to (a hound); initiate. □ **blood bath** a massacre. **blood brother 1** a brother by birth. **2** a close friend to whom one has sworn loyalty by the ceremonial mingling of blood. **blood count** the number of corpuscles in a specific amount of blood. **blood-curdling** *adjective* horrifying. **blood donor** a person who gives blood for transfusion. **blood group** any of the classes or types of human blood. **blood-heat** *noun* normal human temperature, about 37°C or 98.4 F. **blood-letting** *noun* **1** removal of some of a patient's blood. **2** bloodshed; killing. **blood-money** *noun*

**1** money paid as compensation for a death. **2** money paid to a killer. **blood orange** an orange with red-streaked pulp. **blood-poisoning** *noun* the condition that results when the bloodstream is infected with harmful micro-organisms. **blood pressure** the pressure of blood within the arteries and veins; abnormally high pressure of this kind. **blood-red** *adjective* as red as blood. **blood sports** sports involving killing or wounding animals. **blood sugar** the amount of glucose in the blood. **blood test** an examination of a specimen of blood in medical diagnosis. **blood vessel** a vein, artery, or capillary tube carrying blood.

**bloodhound** *noun* a large keen-scented dog formerly used in tracking.

**bloodless** *adjective* **1** having no blood; looking pale, drained of blood. **2** without bloodshed. **3** without vitality.

**bloodshed** *noun* the killing or wounding of people.

**bloodshot** *adjective* (of eyes) red from dilated veins.

**bloodstain** *noun* a stain made by blood.

**bloodstained** *adjective* **1** stained with blood. **2** disgraced by bloodshed.

**bloodstock** *noun* thoroughbred horses.

**bloodstream** *noun* the blood circulating in the body.

**bloodsucker** *noun* **1** a creature that sucks blood. **2** a person who extorts money.

**bloodthirsty** *adjective* eager for bloodshed.

**bloody** *adjective* **1** bloodstained. **2** with much bloodshed; *a bloody battle*. **3** (*vulgar slang*) damned, very great. ●*adverb* (*vulgar slang*) very; *bloody awful*. ●*verb* (**bloodied**, **bloodying**) stain with blood. □ **Bloody Mary** a drink of mixed vodka and tomato juice (¶ the nickname of Mary Tudor, in whose reign many Protestants were executed). **bloody-minded** *adjective* deliberately uncooperative. □ **bloodily** *adverb*, **bloodiness** *noun*

**bloom** *noun* **1** a flower. **2** beauty, perfection; *in the bloom of youth*. **3** fine powder on fresh ripe grapes etc. ●*verb* **1** bear flowers, be in bloom. **2** be in full beauty. □ **in bloom** in flower, flowering.

**bloomer** *noun* (*slang*) **1** a blunder. **2** a long loaf with diagonal marks. **3** (**bloomers**) (*informal*) knickers with legs.

**blooming** *adjective* & *adverb* (*slang*) damned; really.

**blossom** *noun* **1** a flower, especially of a fruit tree. **2** a mass of such flowers. ●*verb* **1** open into flowers. **2** develop and flourish.

**blot** *noun* **1** a spot of ink etc. **2** something ugly; *a blot on the landscape*. **3** a fault, a disgraceful act or quality. ●*verb* (**blotted**, **blotting**) **1** make a blot or blots on. **2** dry with blotting-paper, soak up. □ **blot one's copybook** spoil one's good record. **blot out 1** destroy, obliterate; *blot out the memory.* **2** obscure; *mist blotted out the view.* **blotting-paper** *noun* absorbent paper for drying ink writing.

**blotch** *noun* a large irregular mark. □ **blotched** *adjective*, **blotchy** *adjective*

**blotter** *noun* a pad of blotting-paper.

**blotto** *adjective* (*slang*) very drunk.

**blouse** *noun* **1** a shirt-like garment worn by women. **2** a waist-length coat forming part of a military uniform.

**blouson** (bloo-zon) *noun* a short full jacket gathered in at the waist.

**blow¹** *verb* (**blew, blown, blowing**) **1** send out a current of air or breath; move or be moved by this. **2** move or flow as a current of air does. **3** shape (molten glass) by blowing into it. **4** puff and pant. **5** swell. **6** melt with too strong an electric current; *blow the fuse; a fuse has blown.* **7** break with explosives. **8** (*slang*) reveal; *the spy's cover was blown.* **9** (*slang*) spend recklessly. ● *interjection* (*slang*) damn; *blow you Jack, I'm all right.* ● *noun* **1** an act of blowing. **2** exposure to fresh air. □ **blow-dry** *verb* use a hand-held drier to style (washed hair) while drying it. **blow one's own trumpet** praise oneself. **blow one's top** (*informal*) show great anger. **blow-out** *noun* **1** a burst tyre. **2** a melted fuse. **3** a rapid uncontrolled upward rush of oil or gas from a well. **4** (*slang*) a large meal. **blow over** die down without serious consequences. **blow the mind** produce hallucinations; astound. **blow up 1** inflate. **2** exaggerate; *you've blown this problem up out of all proportion.* **3** make an enlargement of (a photograph). **4** explode; shatter by an explosion. **5** lose one's temper; reprimand severely. **6** become a crisis; *this problem has blown up recently.* **blow-up** *noun* **1** (*informal*) an enlargement of a photograph. **2** an explosion.

**blow²** *noun* **1** a stroke with a hand or weapon. **2** a shock, a disaster. □ **blow-by-blow** *adjective* telling all the details of an event in their order of occurrence.

**blower** *noun* **1** a person or thing that blows. **2** (*informal*) a telephone.

**blowfly** *noun* a fly that lays its eggs on meat.

**blowhole** *noun* **1** the nostril of a whale. **2** a hole (especially in ice) for breathing or fishing through.

**blowlamp** *noun* a portable burner producing a very hot flame that can be directed on to a selected spot.

**blown** *see* BLOW¹.

**blowpipe** *noun* **1** a tube through which air is blown. **2** a tube for sending out darts or pellets by blowing.

**blowtorch** *noun* = BLOWLAMP.

**blowy** *adjective* windy.

**blowzy** (*rhymes with* drowsy) *adjective* **1** red-faced and coarse-looking. **2** slovenly.

**blubber** *noun* whale fat. ● *verb* weep noisily. ● *adjective* (of lips) thick, swollen.

**bludgeon** (bluj-ĕn) *noun* a short stick with a thickened end, used as a weapon. ● *verb* **1** strike with a bludgeon. **2** compel forcefully; bully.

**blue** *adjective* **1** of the colour of the sky on a cloudless day. **2** unhappy, depressed. **3** indecent, obscene; *blue jokes.* ● *noun* **1** blue colour. **2** a blue substance or material; blue clothes. **3** the distinction awarded to a member of Oxford or Cambridge University chosen to represent either of these against the other in a sport; a holder of this. **4** (**the blues**) a state of depression. **5** (**blues**) (treated as *singular* or *plural*) melancholy music of Black American origin. ● *verb* (**blued, blueing**) **1** make blue. **2** (*informal*) spend recklessly. □ **blue baby** one with blueness of the skin from a heart defect. **blue blood** aristocratic descent. **Blue Book** a parliamentary or Privy Council report. **blue cheese** cheese with veins of blue mould. **blue-chip** *adjective* (of shares) fairly reliable as an investment though less secure than gilt-edged. (¶ So called from the high-valued blue chips in the game of poker.) **blue-collar worker** a manual or industrial worker. **blue-eyed boy** (*informal*) a favourite. **blue funk** (*slang*) a state of terror. **blue-pencil** *verb* censor or cut (a book, film, etc.). **Blue Peter** a blue flag with a white square, hoisted by a ship about to sail. **Blue Riband** (*or* **Ribbon**) **of the Atlantic** a trophy for the ship making the fastest sea-crossing of the Atlantic. **blue tit** a tit with blue wings, tail, and top of head. **blue whale** a rorqual, the largest known living animal. **once in a blue moon** very rarely. **out of the blue** unexpectedly. **true blue** faithful, loyal. □ **blueness** *noun*

**bluebell** *noun* a plant with blue bell-shaped flowers.

**blueberry** *noun* **1** a shrub with edible blue berries. **2** its fruit.

**bluebottle** *noun* a large fly with a bluish body.

**bluegrass** *noun* instrumental music influenced by American folk and country music.

**blueprint** *noun* **1** a blue photographic print of building plans. **2** a detailed plan or scheme.

**bluestocking** *noun* a learned woman. (¶ Named after the 'Blue Stocking Club', an 18th-century London literary group, many of whose male members wore grey or 'blue' worsted stockings instead of the black silk of formal dress.)

**bluey** *adjective* rather blue; *bluey-green*.

**bluff**[1] *adjective* **1** with a broad steep front; *a bluff headland*. **2** abrupt, frank, and hearty in manner. ●*noun* a bluff headland or cliff. □ **bluffness** *noun*

**bluff**[2] *verb* deceive someone by making a pretence, especially of strength. ●*noun* bluffing, a threat intended to get results without being carried out.

**bluish** *adjective* rather blue.

**Blunden**, Edmund Charles (1896–1974), English poet.

**blunder** *verb* **1** move clumsily and uncertainly. **2** make a blunder. ●*noun* a mistake made especially through ignorance or carelessness. □ **blunderer** *noun*

**blunderbuss** *noun* an old type of gun firing many balls at one shot.

**Blunt**, Anthony Frederick (1907–83), British art historian who worked as a spy for the former Soviet Union.

**blunt** *adjective* **1** not sharp or pointed. **2** speaking or expressed in plain terms; *a blunt refusal*. ●*verb* make or become blunt. □ **bluntly** *adverb*, **bluntness** *noun*

**blur** *noun* **1** a confused or indistinct appearance. **2** a smear. ●*verb* (**blurred, blurring**) **1** make or become indistinct. **2** smear.

**blurb** *noun* a description of something praising it, e.g. in advertising matter.

**blurt** *verb* (usually foll. by *out*) utter abruptly or tactlessly; *blurted it out*.

**blush** *verb* become red in the face from shame or embarrassment. ●*noun* such reddening of the face.

**blusher** *noun* a cosmetic used to give a rosy colour to the cheeks.

**bluster** *verb* **1** be windy, blow in gusts. **2** talk aggressively, especially with empty threats. ●*noun* such talk. □ **blustery** *adjective*

**Blyton**, Enid (1897–1968), English writer of books for children.

**BMA** *abbreviation* British Medical Association.

**B. Mus.** *abbreviation* Bachelor of Music.

**BMX** *noun* **1** organized bicycle racing on a dirt track. **2** a kind of bicycle for use in this.

**BO** *abbreviation* (*informal*) body odour.

**boa** (boh-ă) *noun* a large non-poisonous South American snake that squeezes its prey to suffocate it. □ **boa constrictor** a Brazilian species of boa.

**Boadicea** = BOUDICCA.

**boar** *noun* **1** a wild pig. **2** an uncastrated domestic male pig.

**board** *noun* **1** a thin flat piece of sawn timber. **2** a flat piece of wood or stiff material for a special purpose, e.g. a notice-board, a diving board, a chessboard. **3** thick stiff paper used for book covers. **4** daily meals obtained in return for payment or services; *board and lodging*. **5** a committee, e.g. the directors of a company or the members of a regional authority. ●*verb* **1** cover with boards. **2** go on board (a ship, aircraft, etc.). **3** receive or provide with meals and accommodation for payment. □ **board game** a game played on a specially marked board. **board up** block with fixed boards. **go by the board** be ignored or rejected. **on board** on or in a ship, aircraft, etc. **take on board** accept (a new idea etc.) and consider or act upon it.

**boarder** *noun* **1** a person who boards with someone. **2** a resident pupil at a boarding-school.

**boarding** *noun* **1** boards. **2** material from which these are cut; a structure or covering made of this.

**boarding house** a house at which board and lodging may be obtained for payment.

**boarding-school** *noun* a school in which pupils receive board and lodging.

**boardroom** *noun* a room where the meetings of the board of a company etc. are held.

**boast** *verb* **1** speak with great pride and try to impress people, especially about oneself. **2** possess as something to be proud of; *the town boasts a fine park*. ●*noun* **1** a boastful statement. **2** something one is proud of. □ **boaster** *noun*

**boastful** *adjective* boasting frequently, full of boasting. □ **boastfully** *adverb*, **boastfulness** *noun*

**boat** *noun* **1** a small vessel for travelling on water; (*loosely*) a ship. **2** a boat-shaped serving dish for sauce or gravy. □ **boathook** *noun* a long pole with a hook and spike at the end for moving boats. **boat people** refugees leaving a country by sea. **Boat Race** an annual rowing competition on the Thames between Oxford and Cambridge Universities. **boat-train** a train timed to carry passengers to or from a ship's docking-place. **in the same boat** suffering the same troubles.

**boater** *noun* a hard flat straw hat.

**boathouse** *noun* a shed at the water's edge for housing boats.

**boating** *noun* rowing or sailing for pleasure.

**boatman** *noun* (*plural* **boatmen**) a person who rents out boats or provides transport by boat.

**boatswain** (boh-sŭn) *noun* (also **bosun**, **bo'sun**) a ship's officer in charge of rigging, boats, anchors, etc.

**bob** *verb* (**bobbed, bobbing**) **1** make a jerky movement, move quickly up and down. **2** cut (hair) in a bob. ●*noun* **1** a bobbing movement. **2** a straight hairstyle with the hair cut at the same length just above the shoulders. **3** (*plural* **bob**) (*slang, old use*) a shilling, 5p. □ **bob's your uncle** (*slang*) success has been achieved.

**bobbin** *noun* a small spool holding thread or wire in a machine.

**bobble** *noun* a small ornamental woolly ball.

**bobby** *noun* (*informal*) a policeman. □ **bobby pin** (*Amer.* & *Austral.*) a flat hairpin; a hairgrip.

**bobsleigh** (bob-slay), **bobsled** *noun* a sledge with two sets of runners, especially with mechanical steering, used for tobogganing. □ **bobsleighing** *noun*

**bobtail** *noun* a docked tail; a horse or dog having this.

**Boccaccio** (bok-**ah**-chi-oh), Luigi (1313–75), Italian novelist, poet, and humanist.

**Boccherini** (bok-er-**ee**-ni), Luigi (1743–1805), Italian composer and cellist.

**Boche** (*pronounced* bosh) *noun* (*offensive slang*) a German, especially a soldier.

**bod** *noun* (*informal*) a person.

**bode** *verb* (*literary*) be a sign of, promise; *it boded well for their future.*

**bodega** (boh-**dee**-gǎ) *noun* a cellar or shop selling wine, especially in Spanish-speaking countries.

**bodge** = BOTCH.

**Bodhisattva** (bod-i-**saht**-vǎ) *noun* (in Buddhism) one who is destined to become enlightened.

**bodice** (bod-iss) *noun* **1** the upper part of a woman's dress, down to the waist. **2** a woman's vest-like undergarment.

**bodily** *adjective* of the human body or physical nature. ● *adverb* **1** in person, physically. **2** as a whole; *the bridge was moved bodily 50 yards downstream.*

**bodkin** *noun* a blunt thick needle with a large eye, for drawing tape etc. through a hem.

**Bodleian Library** (bod-li-ǎn) the library of Oxford University.

**body** *noun* **1** the structure of bones, flesh, etc., of a human being or animal, living or dead. **2** a corpse, a carcass. **3** the trunk, the main part of a body apart from the head and limbs. **4** the main part of anything; *the body of a concert hall.* **5** (*informal*) a person; *she's a cheerful old body.* **6** a group or quantity of people, things, or matter, regarded as a unit. **7** a distinct piece of matter; an object in space. **8** thick texture, strong quality; *this fabric has more body*; *this wine has no body.* □ **body-blow** *noun* a severe setback. **body-building** *noun* strengthening of the body by exercises. **body-check** *Sport* ● *noun* a deliberate obstruction of one player by another. ● *verb* obstruct another player in this way. **body double** a stand-in for a film actor in physical or nude scenes. **body language** involuntary movements or attitudes by which a person communicates

his or her feelings or moods etc. **body odour** the smell of the human body, especially when unpleasant. **body politic** *noun* the nation or State regarded as a political unit. **body stocking** a woman's undergarment which covers the torso. **body warmer** a sleeveless padded jacket. **in a body** all together. **keep body and soul together** have just enough food etc. to remain alive.

**bodyguard** *noun* an escort or personal guard to protect a person's life.

**bodysuit** *noun* a close-fitting one-piece stretch garment used mainly for sport.

**bodywork** *noun* the shell of a motor vehicle.

**Boer** (boh-er) *noun* **1** an Afrikaner. **2** (*old use*) an early Dutch inhabitant of the Cape. ● *adjective* of Boers. □ **Boer War** either of two wars fought by Britain in South Africa, 1880–1 and 1899–1902.

**boffin** *noun* (*informal*) a person engaged in technical research.

**bog** *noun* **1** an area of ground that is permanently wet and spongy, formed of decayed plants etc. **2** (*slang*) a lavatory. □ **bog down** (**bogged**, **bogging**) cause to be stuck and unable to make progress. □ **boggy** *adjective*

**Bogarde**, Dirk (real name; Derek Niven van den Bogaerde) (born 1921), British actor.

**Bogart** (boh-gart), Humphrey (1899–1957), American film actor.

**bogey** *noun* (*plural* **bogeys**) **1** (in golf) a score of one stroke over par at a hole. **2** (also **bogy**) an evil or mischievous spirit; something that causes fear or trouble. **3** (also **bogy**) (*slang*) a piece of dried mucus from the nose.

**bogeyman** *noun* (also **bogyman**) an imaginary person feared by children.

**boggle** *verb* be surprised or baffled; *the mind boggles at the idea.*

**bogie** (boh-gi) *noun* an undercarriage fitted below a railway vehicle, pivoted at the end for going round curves.

**Bogotá** (bog-ŏ-**tah**) the capital of Colombia.

**bogus** *adjective* sham, counterfeit.

**bogy** alternative spelling of BOGEY (senses 2, 3).

**bogyman** alternative spelling of BOGEYMAN.

**Bohemia** an area of the Czech Republic.

**Bohemian** *adjective* **1** of Bohemia. **2** (also **bohemian**) unconventional in one's way of living. ● *noun* **1** a native or inhabitant of Bohemia. **2** (also **bohemian**) a person of bohemian habits.

**Bohr** (*pronounced* bor), Niels Hendrik David (1885–1962), Danish physicist, a major figure in the development of quantum physics.

**boil** *verb* **1** bubble up and change into vapour through being heated. **2** heat (a liquid or its container) so that the liquid boils; cook, wash, or process in this way; be heated or cooked etc. in this way. **3** seethe like boiling liquid; be hot with anger. ●*noun* **1** boiling point; *on the boil*; *off the boil*. **2** an inflamed swelling under the skin, producing pus. □ **boil down 1** reduce or be reduced in quantity by boiling. **2** (*informal*) express or be expressed in fewer words. **boiled sweet** a sweet made of boiled sugar. **boiling hot** (also **boiling**) (*informal*) very hot. **boiling point** *noun* **1** the temperature at which a liquid boils. **2** a state of great anger or excitement. **boil over** overflow when boiling.

**boiler** *noun* **1** a container in which water is heated. **2** a water-tank in which a hot-water supply is stored. **3** a closed metal tub for boiling laundry. **4** a fowl too tough to roast but suitable for boiling. □ **boiler suit** a one-piece garment combining overalls and shirt, worn for rough work.

**boisterous** *adjective* **1** noisy and cheerful; *boisterous children*. **2** stormy; windy. □ **boisterously** *adverb*

**bold** *adjective* **1** confident and courageous. **2** without feelings of shame, impudent. **3** (of colours) strong and vivid. ●*noun* boldface type. □ **boldly** *adverb*, **boldness** *noun*

**boldface** *noun* type with thick heavy lines.

**bole** *noun* the trunk of a tree.

**bolero** *noun* (*plural* **boleros**) **1** (*pronounced* bŏ-**lair**-oh) a Spanish dance; the music for this. **2** (*pronounced* **bol**-er-oh) a woman's short jacket with no front fastening.

**Boleyn** (bŏ-**lin**), Anne (1507–36), the second wife of Henry VIII, and mother of Elizabeth I.

**Bolivia** (bŏ-**liv**-iă) a landlocked country in South America. □ **Bolivian** *adjective & noun* (¶ Named after the Venezuelan statesman Simon Bolivar (1783–1830), who did much to free South America from Spanish rule.)

**boll** *noun* the round seed-vessel of the cotton or flax plant etc.

**bollard** (**bol**-ard) *noun* **1** a short thick post to which a ship's mooring-rope may be tied. **2** a short post for keeping traffic off a path, traffic island, etc.

**bollocking** *noun* (also **ballocking**) (*vulgar slang*) a severe reprimand.

**bollocks** *plural noun* (also **ballocks**) (*vulgar slang*) **1** (usually as *interjection*) rubbish, nonsense. **2** testicles.

**boloney** (bŏ-**loh**-ni) *noun* (also **baloney**) (*slang*) nonsense.

**Bolshevik** *noun* **1** a member of the extremist faction of the Russian socialist party which was renamed the (Russian) Communist Party in 1918. **2** any socialist extremist. □ **Bolshevism** *noun*, **Bolshevist** *noun*

**Bolshie** *adjective* (also **Bolshy**) (*slang*) **1** Bolshevik, left-wing. **2** (also **bolshie**) rebellious, uncooperative. □ **bolshiness** *noun*

**Bolshoi Ballet** (bol-shoi) a Moscow ballet company dating from 1776. (¶ Russian, = great.)

**bolster** *noun* a long under-pillow for the head of a bed. ●*verb* support, prop; *bolster up confidence*.

**bolt¹** *noun* **1** a sliding bar for fastening a door. **2** the sliding part of a rifle-breech. **3** a strong metal pin for fastening things together. **4** a shaft of lightning. **5** a roll of fabric. **6** an arrow shot from a crossbow. **7** the act of bolting. ●*verb* **1** fasten with a bolt or bolts. **2** run away, (of a horse) run off out of control. **3** (of plants) run to seed. **4** gulp down (food) hastily. □ **a bolt from the blue** a complete (usually unwelcome) surprise. **bolt-hole** *noun* a place into which one can escape. **bolt upright** quite upright.

**bolt²** *verb* (also **boult**) sift (flour etc.).

**Boltzmann** (**bolts**-măn), Ludwig (1844–1906), Austrian physicist.

**bomb** *noun* **1** a container filled with explosive or incendiary material to be set off by impact or by a timing device. **2** (**the bomb**) an atomic or hydrogen bomb. **3** (*slang*) a large sum of money. ●*verb* attack with bombs. □ **go like a bomb** (*slang*) **1** be very successful. **2** go or move very fast.

**bombard** *verb* **1** attack with many missiles, especially from big guns. **2** send a stream of high-speed particles against. **3** attack with questions or complaints. □ **bombardment** *noun*

**bombardier** *noun* **1** a non-commissioned officer in the artillery. **2** (*Amer.*) a person who releases bombs from an aircraft.

**bombast** (**bom**-bast) *noun* pompous words or speech. □ **bombastic** (bom-**bas**-tik) *adjective*

**Bombay** a city and port on the west coast of India.

**Bombay duck** (also **bummalo**) a kind of dried fish eaten as a relish, especially with curry.

**bombazine** (bom-bă-**zeen**) *noun* a twilled worsted dress-material, especially the black kind formerly much used for mourning.

**bomber** *noun* **1** an aircraft that carries and drops bombs. **2** a person who throws or plants bombs. □ **bomber jacket** a jacket gathered into a band at waist and cuffs.

**bombshell** *noun* something that comes as a great surprise and shock.

**bona fide** (boh-nă fy-di) genuine, without fraud; *bona fide customers*.

**bonanza** (bŏ-**nan**-ză) *noun* a source of sudden great wealth or luck; a windfall.

**Bonaparte** (**bohn**-ă-part) the name of a Corsican family including the three French rulers named Napoleon.

**bon-bon** *noun* a sweet.

**Bond**, James, a secret agent in the spy novels of Ian Fleming.

**bond** *noun* **1** something that binds, attaches, or restrains, e.g. a rope. **2** something that unites people. **3** a binding agreement; a document containing this. **4** money deposited as a guarantee. **5** a document issued by a government or public company acknowledging that money has been lent to it and will be repaid usually with interest. **6** writing-paper of high quality. ●*verb* **1** connect or unite with a bond, link with an emotional bond. **2** put into a Customs warehouse. **3** insure a contract etc. by means of a financial bond. □ **in bond** stored in a Customs warehouse until duties are paid.

**bondage** *noun* slavery, captivity.

**bonded** *adjective* **1** stored in bond; *bonded whisky*. **2** storing in bond; *a bonded warehouse*.

**bone** *noun* **1** any of the hard parts (other than teeth, nails, horns, and cartilage) of an animal's body, making up the skeleton in vertebrates. **2** a piece of bone with meat on it, as food. **3** the substance from which such parts are made; a similar hard substance. ●*verb* remove the bones from. □ **bone china** fine china made of clay mixed with bone ash. **bone-dry** *adjective* quite dry. **bone-idle** *adjective* very lazy. **bone of contention** the subject of a dispute. **bone marrow** = MARROW (sense 1). **bone-meal** *noun* crushed powdered bones used as a fertilizer. **feel in one's bones** feel sure by intuition. **have a bone to pick** (usually foll. by *with*) have something to argue or complain about. **make no bones about 1** raise no objection to. **2** speak frankly about. **to the bone** thoroughly, completely; to the bare minimum. **bone up on** (*informal*) research (a subject) quickly to get a brief understanding of it or as revision. □ **boneless** *adjective*

**boneshaker** *noun* a decrepit or uncomfortable old vehicle.

**bonfire** *noun* a large fire built in the open air. □ **Bonfire Night** 5 November, when bonfires are lit in memory of the Gunpowder Plot.

**bongo** *noun* (*plural* **bongos** or **bongoes**) each of a pair of small drums played with the fingers.

**bonhomie** (**bon**-ŏmi) *noun* a genial manner. (¶ French.)

**Boniface**, St (680–754), the English-born apostle of Germany. Feast day, 5 June.

**bonk** *verb* (*informal*) **1** make an abrupt thudding sound; bump. **2** have sexual intercourse with; copulate. ●*noun* (*informal*) **1** a bump. **2** sexual intercourse.

**bonkers** *adjective* (*slang*) crazy.

**Bonn** a city in Germany, the former capital of West Germany.

**Bonnard** (bon-**ar**), Pierre (1867–1947), French painter.

**bonnet** *noun* **1** a hat with strings that tie under the chin. **2** a Scotch cap. **3** (*British*) a hinged cover over the engine etc. of a motor vehicle (= *Amer.* HOOD).

**bonny** *adjective* (**bonnier**, **bonniest**) **1** healthy-looking. **2** (*Scottish & N. England*) good-looking.

**bonsai** (**bon**-sy) *noun* **1** a plant or tree grown in miniature form in a pot by artificially restricting its growth. **2** the method of cultivating this. (¶ Japanese.)

**bonus** *noun* (*plural* **bonuses**) a payment or benefit in addition to what is usual or expected.

**bon vivant** (bawn vee-**vahn**) (*plural* **bons vivants**, *pronounced* same) a person fond of good food and drink. (¶ French, = one who lives well.)

**bon voyage** (bawn vwah-**yah**zh) an expression of good wishes to someone starting a journey. (¶ French.)

**bony** *adjective* (**bonier**, **boniest**) **1** like bones. **2** having large or prominent bones, having bones with little flesh. **3** full of bones. □ **boniness** *noun*

**bonze** *noun* a Buddhist priest in Japan or China.

**boo** *interjection* **1** a sound made to show disapproval or contempt. **2** an exclamation used to startle someone. ●*verb* show disapproval by shouting 'boo'.

**boob** (*slang*) **1** a foolish person. **2** a stupid mistake. **3** (*slang*) a woman's breast. ●*verb* (*slang*) make a stupid mistake.

**booby** *noun* a foolish person. □ **booby prize** a prize given as a joke to the competitor with the lowest score. **booby trap 1** a hidden trap rigged up for a practical joke. **2** a hidden bomb placed so that it will explode when some apparently harmless object is touched or moved.

**boogie** *verb* (*slang*) dance to pop music. □ **boogie-woogie** *noun* a style of playing blues or jazz on the piano, marked by a persistent bass rhythm.

**book** *noun* **1** a series of written or printed or plain sheets of paper fastened together at one edge and enclosed in a cover. **2** a literary work that would fill such a book or books if printed; *he is working on his book*. **3** a number of cheques, stamps, tickets, matches, etc. fastened together in the shape of a book. **4** each of the main divisions of a written work. **5** a libretto; the script of a play. **6** a record of bets made. ●*verb* **1** reserve (a seat or accommodation etc.); buy (tickets) in advance; make a reservation. **2** engage a performer. **3** take the personal details of (an offender or rule-breaker). **4** enter in a book or list. □ **book club** a society whose members can buy certain books at a reduced price. **book-ends** a pair of supports for keeping a row of books upright. **book in** register at a hotel etc. **book-plate** *noun* a decorative label in a book bearing the owner's name. **book token** a voucher that can be exchanged for books of a given value. **bring to book** make (a person) answer for his or her conduct. **by the book** in accordance with the correct procedure. **in a person's good** (*or* **bad**) **books** in (or out of) favour with him or her.

**bookbinding** *noun* binding books professionally. □ **bookbinder** *noun*

**bookcase** *noun* a piece of furniture with shelves for books.

**bookie** *noun* (*informal*) a bookmaker.

**booking** *noun* a reservation; an engagement to perform somewhere. □ **booking-office** *noun* an office where tickets are sold.

**bookish** *adjective* fond of reading.

**bookkeeping** *noun* the systematic recording of business transactions. □ **bookkeeper** *noun*

**booklet** *noun* a small thin usually paper-covered book.

**bookmaker** *noun* a person whose business is taking bets. □ **bookmaking** *noun*

**bookmark** *noun* a strip of paper or other material placed between the pages of a book to mark a place.

**Book of Common Prayer** the official service book of the Church of England.

**bookstall** *noun* a stall or kiosk at which books and newspapers are sold.

**bookworm** *noun* **1** a grub that eats holes in books. **2** a person who is very fond of reading.

**Boole**, George (1815–64), English mathematician, who developed an algebraic system of reasoning, known as **Boolean algebra**.

**boom**[1] *verb* **1** make a hollow deep resonant sound. **2** have a period of prosperity or rapid economic growth. ●*noun* **1** a booming sound. **2** a period of increased growth, prosperity, or value.

**boom**[2] *noun* **1** a long pole used to keep the bottom of a sail stretched. **2** a floating barrier or a heavy chain across a river or a harbour entrance. **3** a long pole carrying a microphone.

**boomerang** *noun* **1** a curved wooden missile that can be thrown so that it returns to the thrower if it fails to hit anything. **2** something that causes unexpected harm to its originator. ●*verb* act as a boomerang.

**boon** *noun* a benefit. □ **boon companion** a favourite social companion.

**boor** *noun* an ill-mannered person. □ **boorish** *adjective*, **boorishly** *adverb*, **boorishness** *noun*

**boost** *verb* **1** push upwards. **2** increase the strength, value, or good reputation of; promote. ●*noun* **1** an upward thrust. **2** an increase.

**booster** *noun* **1** a device for increasing power or voltage. **2** an auxiliary engine or rocket for extra initial speed. **3** a second injection renewing the effect of the first one.

**boot** *noun* **1** a shoe or outer covering for the foot and ankle or leg. **2** (*British*) a compartment for luggage in a car. **3** (**the boot**) (*slang*) dismissal. ●*verb* kick. □ **put the boot in 1** kick brutally. **2** criticize fiercely; harm a person.

**bootblack** *noun* (*Amer.*) a person who polishes boots and shoes.

**bootee** *noun* a baby's knitted or crocheted boot.

**Booth**, William (1829–1912), founder of the Salvation Army.

**booth** *noun* **1** a small temporary shelter at a market or fair. **2** an enclosure for a public telephone. **3** a compartment in a large room, e.g. for voting at elections.

**bootleg** *verb* (**bootlegged**, **bootlegging**) **1** smuggle (alcohol). **2** make and sell illicitly. ●*adjective* smuggled or sold illicitly. □ **bootlegger** *noun*

**booty** *noun* loot.

**booze** (*informal*) *verb* drink alcohol, especially in large quantities. ●*noun* alcoholic drink. □ **boozy** *adjective*

**boozer** *noun* **1** (*informal*) a person who boozes. **2** (*slang*) a public house.

**bop** *noun* **1** (*informal*) a dance. **2** = BEBOP. ●*verb* (*informal*) dance, especially to pop music.

**boracic** *adjective* = BORIC.

**borage** (*rhymes with* porridge) *noun* a plant with blue flowers and hairy leaves, used in salads.

**borax** *noun* a soluble white powder that is a compound of boron, used in making glass, enamels, and detergents.

**Bordeaux** (bor-**doh**) *noun* a red or white wine from Bordeaux in SW France.

**border** *noun* **1** an edge or boundary, the part near this. **2** the line dividing two countries, the area near this. **3** an edging. **4** a strip of ground round a garden or a part of it. **5** (**the Border**) that between England and Scotland or (*Amer.*) between the USA and Mexico. **6** (**the Borders**) a local government region of southern Scotland. ●*verb* put or be a border to. □ **border on 1** be next to. **2** come close to; *it borders on the absurd*.

**borderland** *noun* the district near a boundary.

**borderline** *noun* the line that marks a boundary. ●*adjective* on the boundary between different groups or categories.

**bore**¹ *verb* **1** make (a hole or well etc.) with a revolving tool or by digging out soil. **2** pierce or penetrate in this way. ●*noun* **1** the hollow inside of a gun barrel or engine cylinder; its diameter. **2** a hole made by boring.

**bore**² *verb* make (a person) feel tired or uninterested by being dull or tedious. ●*noun* a boring person or thing. □ **boredom** *noun*, **boring** *adjective*

**bore**³ *noun* a tidal wave with a steep front that moves up some estuaries; *the Severn bore*.

**bore**⁴ *see* BEAR².

**Borg**, Björn Runę (born 1956), Swedish tennis player.

**Borges** (**bor**-hez), Jorge Luis (1899–1986), Argentinian writer of short stories, poems, and essays.

**boric** (**bor**-ik) *adjective* of boron. □ **boric acid** a substance derived from boron, used as a mild antiseptic.

**Boris Godunov** *see* GODUNOV.

**Born**, Max (1882–1970), German theoretical physicist, one of the founders of quantum mechanics.

**born** (See the note under BORNE.) ●*adjective* **1** destined by birth; *born to suffer*; *born to be king*. **2** having a certain order, status, or place of birth; *first-born*; *well-born*; *French-born*. **3** having a natural quality or ability; *a born leader*. □ **be born** be brought forth by birth. **born-again** *adjective* having experienced a revival of faith etc. **in all one's born days** (*informal*) in all one's lifetime. **born of** originating from; *their courage was born of despair*. **not born yesterday** experienced in people's ways and not easy to deceive.

**borne** *see* BEAR².

∎**Usage** The word *borne* is used as part of the verb *to bear* when it comes before *by* or after *have*, *has*, or *had*, e.g. *children (who were) borne by Eve; she had borne him a son*. The word *born* is used in *a son was born*.

**Borneo** a large island of the Malay Archipelago.

**Borodin** (bo-rŏ-din), Alexander (1833–87), Russian composer.

**boron** (**bor**-on) *noun* a chemical element (symbol B) that is very resistant to high temperatures.

**borough** (**bu**-ră) *noun* **1** (*old use*) a town with a corporation and with privileges (e.g. rights of self-government) conferred by royal charter. **2** a town represented by an MP; a town or district granted the status of a borough. **3** an administrative area of Greater London or of New York City. **4** a territorial division in Alaska, corresponding to a county.

**Borrow**, George (1803–81), English traveller and writer.

**borrow** *verb* **1** get the temporary use of, on the understanding that the thing received is to be returned. **2** use without being the inventor; copy; *borrow their methods*. □ **borrowed time** an extension of one's life beyond an illness or crisis which could have ended it. □ **borrower** *noun*

**borsch** alternative spelling of BORTSCH.

**Borstal** *noun* (*Brit.*) a former name for an institution to which young offenders were sent for reformative training. (= *Amer.* reformatory.)

∎**Usage** Now called *detention centre* and *youth custody centre*.

**bortsch** (*pronounced* borch) *noun* (also **borsch**) a highly seasoned Russian or Polish soup of beetroot, cabbage, and other ingredients.

**borzoi** (**bor**-zoi) *noun* a large dog with a narrow head and silky coat.

**Bosch** (*pronounced* bosh), Hieronymus (*c*.1450–1516), Dutch painter.

**bosh** *noun & interjection* (*slang*) nonsense.

**Bosnia and Hercegovina** (**boz**-niă, herts-i-gŏv-**een**-ă) a republic of Eastern Europe, formerly part of Yugoslavia. □ **Bosnian** *adjective & noun*

**bosom** *noun* **1** a person's breast. **2** the part of a garment covering this. **3** the centre or inmost part; *returned to the bosom of his family*. □ **bosom friend** one who is dear and close.

**Bosporus** (also **Bosphorus**) a strait connecting the Black Sea and the Sea of Marmara, with Istanbul at its south end.

**boss**¹ (*informal*) *noun* a person who controls or gives orders to workers. ●*verb* be the boss of; give orders to; *boss someone about*.

**boss**² *noun* a round projecting knob or stud.

**bossa nova** *noun* a dance similar to the samba; the music for this.

**boss-eyed** *adjective* (*slang*) **1** blind in one eye; cross-eyed. **2** crooked.

**bossy** *adjective* (**bossier**, **bossiest**) (*informal*) fond of ordering people about; doing this continually. □ **bossily** *adverb*, **bossiness** *noun*

**Boston** the capital and a seaport of Massachusetts. □ **Boston tea-party** a violent demonstration by American colonists who in 1773 threw cargoes of tea into Boston harbour in protest against the imposition of a tax on tea by the British government.

**bosun**, **bo'sun** alternative spellings of BOATSWAIN.

**Boswell**, James (1740–95), Scottish author, biographer of Samuel Johnson.

**botanical** (bŏ-tan-ikăl) *adjective* of botany. □ **botanical gardens** gardens where plants and trees are grown for scientific study.

**botanist** *noun* an expert in botany.

**botany** *noun* the scientific study of plants.

**Botany Bay** a bay near Sydney, New South Wales, Australia (originally so called from the variety of plants found there).

**Botany wool** wool from merino sheep, especially from Australia.

**botch** *verb* (also **bodge**) spoil by poor or clumsy work. ●*noun* a clumsy piece of work.

**both** *adjective, pronoun,* & *adverb* the two, not only the one.

**Botha**[1] (**boh**-tă), Louis (1862–1919), South African soldier and statesman, first President of the Union of South Africa (1910–19).

**Botha**[2], P(ieter) W(illem) (born 1916), President of South Africa 1984–89.

**Botham** (**boh**-thăm), Ian Terence (born 1955), English cricketer.

**bother** *verb* **1** cause trouble, worry, or annoyance to; pester. **2** take trouble, feel concern. ●*interjection* an exclamation of annoyance. ●*noun* **1** worry; minor trouble. **2** a person or thing causing this.

**botheration** *interjection & noun* (*informal*) bother.

**bothersome** *adjective* causing bother.

**Botswana** (bot-**swah**-nă) an inland country of southern Africa.

**Botticelli** (bot-i-**chel**-i), Sandro (Alessandro) (1445–1510), Florentine painter.

**bottle** *noun* **1** a narrow-necked container for storing liquid. **2** the amount contained in this. **3** a baby's feeding-bottle; milk from this. **4** a hot-water bottle. **5** (**the bottle**) drinking alcoholic drinks; *too fond of the bottle.* **6** (*slang*) courage. ●*verb* **1** store in bottles. **2** preserve in glass jars; *bottled fruit.* □ **bottle bank** a place where bottles can be left for recycling. **bottle-fed** *adjective* fed with milk from a feeding-bottle. **bottle green** dark green. **bottle party** a party to which guests bring bottles of wine etc.

**bottleneck** *noun* **1** a narrow stretch of road where traffic cannot flow freely. **2** anything similarly obstructing progress.

**bottlenose dolphin** a dolphin with a bottle-shaped snout.

**bottom** *noun* **1** the lowest part of anything, the part on which it rests; the lowest place; the end furthest away; *the bottom of the garden.* **2** the buttocks, the part of the body on which one sits. **3** the ground under a stretch of water. **4** bottom gear. **5** a ship's keel or hull. ●*adjective* lowest in position, rank, or degree. ●*verb* **1** provide with a bottom. **2** reach or touch bottom. □ **at bottom** basically, really. **be at the bottom of** be the underlying cause or originator of. **bottom drawer** a woman's store of clothes and linen etc. collected in preparation for marriage. **bottom line 1** the amount of total assets after profit and loss etc. have been calculated. **2** the basic essential requirement. **from the bottom of one's heart** with deep feeling, sincerely. **get to the bottom of** find out the cause or origin of. **bottom out** reach the lowest level; *the recession has bottomed out.*

**bottomless** *adjective* **1** extremely deep. **2** inexhaustible; *a bottomless purse.*

**bottommost** *adjective* lowest.

**botulism** (**bot**-yoo-lizm) *noun* a kind of food poisoning.

**Boucher** (boo-**shay**), François (1703–70), French painter and decorative artist.

**bouclé** (**boo**-klay) *noun* **1** yarn with one of its strands looped at intervals. **2** fabric made from this.

**Boudicca** (boo-**dik**-ă) (popularly known as Boadicea, died AD 62), a queen of the ancient Britons in eastern England who led her forces against the Romans.

**boudoir** (**boo**-dwar) *noun* a woman's private room.

**bouffant** (**boo**-fawn) *adjective* (of hair) puffed out, backcombed.

**bougainvillea** (boo-găn-**vil**-iă) *noun* a tropical shrub with red or purple bracts.

**bough** *noun* a large branch coming from the trunk of a tree.

**bought** *see* BUY.

**bouillon** (**boo**-yawn) *noun* thin clear soup, broth.

**boulder** (**bohl**-der) *noun* a large smooth rounded rock.

**boule** (*pronounced* bool) *noun* (also **boules**, *pronounced* same) a French game similar to bowls played on rough ground with heavy metal balls.

**boulevard** (**boo**-lĕ-vard) *noun* a wide street, often with trees on each side.

**Boulez** (**boo**-lez), Pierre (born 1925), French composer and conductor, who developed a technique of total serialism.

**Boult** (*pronounced* bohlt), Sir Adrian Cedric (1889–1983), English conductor.

**boult** alternative spelling of BOLT[2].

**bounce** *verb* **1** spring back when sent against something hard; cause to do this. **2** (*slang*) (of a cheque) be sent back by the bank because there is not enough money in the account to pay it. **3** jump suddenly; move in a lively manner. **4** (*informal*) force into hasty action. ●*noun* **1** bouncing; the power of bouncing. **2** a strongly self-confident manner. □ **bounce back** recover well after a setback. □ **bouncy** *adjective*

**bouncer** *noun* **1** a bowled ball that bounces forcefully. **2** (*slang*) a person employed to expel troublesome people from a club etc.

**bouncing** *adjective* big and healthy, boisterous.

**bound**¹ *verb* limit, be the boundary of. ●*plural noun* (**bounds**) limits. □ **out of bounds** outside the areas one is allowed to enter.

**bound**² *verb* jump or spring; run with jumping movements. ●*noun* a bounding movement.

**bound**³ *adjective* going or heading towards; *bound for Spain*; *northbound traffic*.

**bound**⁴ *see* BIND. ●*adjective* obstructed or hindered by; *fog-bound*. □ **bound to** certain to. **bound up with** closely associated with. **I'll be bound** I feel certain.

**boundary** *noun* **1** a line that marks a limit. **2** a hit to or over the boundary of the field in cricket.

**bounden** *adjective* obligatory. □ **one's bounden duty** a duty dictated by one's conscience.

**bounder** *noun* (*old use*, *slang*) a cad.

**boundless** *adjective* without limits.

**bountiful** *adjective* **1** giving generously. **2** abundant.

**bounty** *noun* **1** generosity in giving. **2** a generous gift. **3** a reward or payment given as an inducement.

**bouquet** (boo-**kay**) *noun* **1** a bunch of flowers, especially professionally arranged. **2** a compliment, praise. **3** the scent of wine. □ **bouquet garni** (gar-ni) (*plural* **bouquets garnis**) a bunch of herbs used for flavouring.

**Bourbon** (boor-bŏn) the name of a branch of the French royal family whose members ruled in France from 1589 (Henry IV) until 1848 (Louis Philippe), Spain (1700-1931), and Naples (1734-1806, 1815-60).

**bourbon** (ber-bŏn) *noun* **1** whisky made mainly from maize. **2** a chocolate-flavoured biscuit.

**bourgeois** (boor-*zh*wah) *adjective* (*scornful*) of the middle class; having conventional ideas and tastes. ●*noun* a bourgeois person.

**bourgeoisie** (boor-*zh*wah-zi) *noun* (*scornful*) the bourgeois class.

**bourn** (*pronounced* boorn) *noun* a small stream.

**bourrée** *noun* a lively French dance; the music for this.

**bourse** (*pronounced* boorss) *noun* **1** a money-market. **2** (**Bourse**) the Paris Stock Exchange.

**bout** *noun* **1** a period of activity, work, or illness. **2** a boxing contest.

**boutique** (boo-**teek**) *noun* a small shop selling clothes etc. of the latest fashion.

**bouzouki** (boo-**zoo**-ki) *noun* (*plural* **bouzoukis**) a Greek stringed instrument of the lute family.

**bovine** (**boh**-vyn) *adjective* **1** of or like cattle. **2** dull and stupid. □ **bovine spongiform encephalopathy** *see* BSE.

**bow**¹ (*rhymes with* go) *noun* **1** a piece of wood, plastic, etc., curved by a tight string joining its ends, used for shooting arrows. **2** a rod with horsehair stretched between its ends, used for playing the violin etc. **3** a knot made with a loop or loops; ribbon etc. tied in this way. □ **bow-legged** *adjective* having bandy legs. **bow-tie** *noun* a man's necktie tied into a bow. **bow-window** *noun* a curved bay window.

**bow**² (*rhymes with* cow) *noun* bending of the head or body in greeting, respect, agreement, etc. ●*verb* **1** make a bow; bend in greeting etc. **2** bend downwards under a weight. **3** submit or give in; *must bow to the inevitable*. □ **bow and scrape** be obsequiously polite; grovel.

**bow**³ (*rhymes with* cow) *noun* **1** the front or forward end of a boat or ship. **2** the oarsman nearest the bow.

**bowdlerize** (**bowd**-ler-ryz) *verb* (also **bowdlerise**) remove words or scenes considered improper from (a book etc.); censor. (¶ Named after T. Bowdler who in 1818 produced a censored version of Shakespeare's plays.)

**bowel** *noun* **1** the intestine. **2** (**bowels**) the innermost parts.

**Bowen** (**boh**-in), Elizabeth Dorothea Cole (1899-1973), Anglo-Irish novelist and writer of short stories.

**bower** (*rhymes with* flower) *noun* a leafy shelter.

**bowerbird** *noun* a bird of Australia and New Guinea, the male of which builds decorated 'bowers' during courtship.

**Bowie** (**boh**-i), David (real name, David Robert Jones) (born 1947), British rock singer, composer, and actor.

**bowie knife** (**boh**-i) a long hunting-knife with a double-edged point.

**bowl**¹ *noun* **1** a basin for holding food or liquid. **2** this with its contents; the amount it contains. **3** the hollow rounded part of a spoon, tobacco-pipe, etc. **4** (*Amer.*) an outdoor stadium for football.

**bowl**² *noun* **1** a heavy ball that is slightly asymmetrical, so that it rolls in a curve, used in the game of bowls. **2** a large, heavy ball with indents for gripping, used in tenpin bowling. **3** a ball used in skittles. ● *verb* **1** send rolling along the ground. **2** be carried fast and smoothly by car etc.; *bowling along the M4*. **3** send a ball to be played by a batsman; dismiss by knocking down a wicket with this. **4** (**bowls**) a game played by rolling asymmetrical bowls towards a jack. □ **bowl over 1** knock down. **2** overwhelm with surprise or emotion.

**bowler** *noun* **1** a person who plays bowls. **2** a person who bowls in cricket. **3** (in full **bowler hat**) a stiff felt hat with a rounded top.

**bowline** (boh-lin) *noun* a simple knot for forming a non-slipping loop at the end of a rope.

**bowling** *noun* playing bowls or skittles or a similar game. □ **bowling alley** a long enclosure for playing skittles etc. **bowling green** a lawn for playing bowls.

**bowsprit** (boh-sprit) *noun* a long pole projecting from the stem of a ship, to which ropes from the front mast and sails are fastened.

**bow-wow** *interjection* an imitation of a dog's bark. ● *noun* a child's word for a dog.

**box**[1] *noun* **1** a container with a flat base and usually a lid. **2** the amount it contains. **3** a box-like receptacle, a money box, pillar-box, etc. **4** a compartment, e.g. with seats for several persons in a theatre, for a horse in a stable or vehicle, for the jury or witnesses in a lawcourt. **5** a small hut or shelter; *sentry-box*. **6** a receptacle at a newspaper office for replies to an advertisement. **7** a coachman's seat. **8** (**the box**) (*slang*) television. ● *verb* put into a box. □ **box girder** a girder made of metal plates fastened in a box shape. **box in** *or* **up** shut into a small space, preventing free movement. **box junction** a road intersection marked with crossing yellow stripes which vehicles may not enter (except when turning right) unless the exit is clear. **box number** a number used to identify a box in a newspaper office or post office to which letters to an advertiser may be sent. **box office** an office for booking seats at a theatre etc. **box pleat** an arrangement of parallel pleats folding in alternate directions, forming a raised strip. **box spring** each of a set of vertical springs in a mattress.

**box**[2] *verb* fight with the fists; engage in boxing. ● *noun* a slap with the open hand. □ **box a person's ears** slap him or her.

**box**[3] *noun* **1** a small evergreen shrub. **2** its wood.

**Box and Cox** two people who take turns at doing the same thing. (¶ Named after two characters in a play to whom a landlady let

the same room, one being at work all day and the other all night.)

**Boxer** *noun* (*hist.*) a member of a fanatical Chinese secret organization in the late 19th century.

**boxer** *noun* **1** a person who boxes, especially as a sport. **2** a dog of a breed resembling the bulldog. □ **boxer shorts** men's loose underparts like shorts.

**boxing** *noun* the sport of fighting with the fists. □ **boxing gloves** padded leather mittens worn in boxing.

**Boxing Day** the first weekday after Christmas Day, when Christmas-boxes used to be presented.

**boxroom** *noun* a small spare room often used for storage.

**boy** *noun* **1** a male child. **2** a young man. **3** a young male employee; *a van boy*. **4** (in some countries) a male servant. ● *interjection* an exclamation of surprise or joy. □ **boy scout** = SCOUT (sense 3). □ **boyhood** *noun*

**Boycott**, Geoffrey (born 1940), English cricketer.

**boycott** (boy-kot) *verb* refuse to have anything to do with; *boycotted the goods*. ● *noun* boycotting, treatment of this kind.

**boyfriend** *noun* a person's regular male companion or lover.

**boyish** *adjective* like a boy. □ **boyishly** *adverb*, **boyishness** *noun*

**Boyle**, Robert (1627–91), English scientist, a founder of the Royal Society. □ **Boyle's law** the volume of a fixed quantity of gas at constant temperature is inversely proportional to its pressure.

**Boyne** a river in the Republic of Ireland, scene of the victory of a Protestant army under William III over the Catholic forces of the deposed James II in 1690.

**BP** *abbreviation* **1** British Petroleum. **2** British Pharmacopoeia. **3** blood pressure.

**BP** *abbreviation* (in geological dating) before the present.

**Bq** *abbreviation* becquerel.

**BR** *abbreviation* British Rail.

**Br** *symbol* bromine.

**bra** *noun* a woman's undergarment worn to cover and support the breasts.

**Brabham**, Jack (Sir John Arthur) (born 1926), Australian motor-racing driver, three times world champion.

**brace** *noun* **1** a device that clamps things together or holds and supports them in position. **2** (*plural* **brace**) a pair; *five brace of partridge*. **3** a connecting mark used in printing ({ or }). **4** (**braces**) straps used to keep trousers up, fastened to the waistband and passing over the shoulders. ● *verb* support, give firmness to. □ **brace and bit** a revolving tool for boring holes, with a D-shaped central handle. **brace oneself**,

**brace up** steady oneself in order to meet a blow or shock.

**bracelet** *noun* an ornamental band or chain worn on the arm.

**brachiosaurus** (brak-i-ŏ-**sor**-ŭs) *noun* (*plural* **brachiosauruses**) a huge dinosaur with forelegs shorter than its hind legs.

**bracing** *adverb* invigorating, stimulating.

**bracken** *noun* a large fern that grows on waste land; a mass of such ferns.

**bracket** *noun* **1** a support projecting from an upright surface. **2** any of the marks used in pairs for enclosing words or figures, ( ), [ ], { }. **3** a group bracketed together as similar or falling between certain limits; *an income bracket.* ●*verb* (**bracketed, bracketing**) **1** enclose or join by brackets. **2** put together to imply connection or equality. **3** place shots both short of a target and beyond it in order to find the range.

**brackish** *adjective* slightly salty; *brackish water.*

**bract** *noun* a leaf-like part of a plant, often highly coloured, e.g. in bougainvillea and poinsettia.

**brad** *noun* a thin flat nail with the head formed by a slight enlargement at the top.

**bradawl** *noun* a small tool for boring holes by hand.

**Bradbury**[1], Malcolm Stanley (born 1932), English satirical novelist and critic.

**Bradbury**[2], Ray Douglas (born 1920), American writer of science fiction.

**Bradman**, Sir Donald George (born 1908), Australian cricketer.

**brae** (*pronounced* bray) *noun* (*Scottish*) a hillside.

**brag** *verb* (**bragged, bragging**) boast. ●*noun* a boast.

**Bragg**, Sir William Henry (1862–1942), English physicist, a founder of solid-state physics.

**braggart** *noun* a person who brags.

**Brahma** *noun* **1** the Hindu creator. **2** = BRAHMAN (sense 2).

**Brahman** (brah-măn) *noun* **1** (also **brahman, Brahmin**) a member of the highest or priestly Hindu caste. **2** the supreme divine Hindu reality. □ **Brahmanic** *adjective*, **Brahmanism** *noun*

**Brahmaputra** (brah-mă-**poo**-tră) a river that flows from Tibet through the Himalayas and NE India to join the Ganges at its delta (in Bangladesh) on the Bay of Bengal.

**Brahms**, Johannes (1833–97), German composer and pianist.

**braid** *noun* **1** a woven ornamental trimming. **2** a plait of hair. ●*verb* **1** plait. **2** trim with braid.

**Braille** (*pronounced* brayl) *noun* a system of representing letters etc. by raised dots which blind people can read by touch. (¶ Named after its inventor, Louis Braille, who perfected it in 1834.)

**brain** *noun* **1** the organ that is the centre of the nervous system in animals, a mass of soft grey matter in the skull. **2** (often **brains**) the mind or intellect, intelligence. **3** an intelligent person; (also **brains**) one who originates a complex plan or idea. ●*verb* kill by a heavy blow on the head. □ **brain death** incurable brain damage resulting in the person being unable to breathe independently. **brain drain** the loss of clever and skilled people by emigration. **brains trust** a group of people giving impromptu answers to questions as a form of entertainment. **brain-teaser** *noun* a puzzle or problem. **on the brain** obsessively in one's thoughts.

**brainchild** *noun* a person's clever idea or invention.

**Braine**, John Gerard (1922–86), English novelist.

**brainless** *adjective* stupid.

**brainpower** *noun* mental ability, intelligence.

**brainstorm** *noun* **1** a sudden violent mental disturbance. **2** (*Amer.*) a sudden bright idea. **3** a mental lapse; a sudden inability to remember. **4** (also **brainstorming**) (*Amer.*) a spontaneous discussion in search of new ideas.

**brainwash** *verb* force (a person) to reject old beliefs and accept new ones by subjecting him or her to great mental pressure.

**brainwave** *noun* **1** an electrical impulse in the brain. **2** (*informal*) a sudden bright idea.

**brainy** *adjective* (**brainier, brainiest**) (*informal*) clever, intelligent.

**braise** *verb* cook slowly with very little liquid in a closed container.

**brake** *noun* **1** a device for reducing the speed of something or stopping its motion. **2** the pedal etc. operating this. **3** a thicket. **4** an estate car. ●*verb* slow down by means of a brake. □ **brake drum** a cylinder attached to a wheel, on which the brake shoe presses. **brake horsepower** the power of an engine measured by the force needed to brake it. **brake lining** a strip of fabric attached to a brake shoe to increase the friction. **brake shoe** a long curved block acting on a wheel to brake it.

**bramble** *noun* **1** a rough shrub with long prickly shoots, a blackberry-bush. **2** (*Scottish & N. England*) a blackberry.

**brambling** *noun* a small brightly coloured finch.

**bran** *noun* coarse meal consisting of the ground inner husks of grain, sifted out from flour. □ **bran tub** a tub filled with bran into which children dip for concealed toys etc.

**Branagh** (bran-ă), Kenneth Charles (born 1960), English actor, producer, and director.

**branch** noun 1 an arm-like part of a tree. 2 a similar part of anything; a lateral extension of a river, road, railway, etc. 3 a subdivision of a family, group of languages, or subject. 4 a local shop or office etc. belonging to a larger organization. ● verb send out branches; divide into branches. □ **branch off** leave a main route and take a minor one. **branch out** begin a new line of activity.

**brand** noun 1 a trade mark; a particular make of goods. 2 a mark of identification made with a hot iron; the iron used for this. 3 a piece of burning or charred wood. ● verb 1 mark with a hot iron; label with a trade mark. 2 give a bad name to; *he was branded as a troublemaker.* 3 impress on the memory. □ **brand-new** adjective completely new.

**brandish** verb wave (a thing) in display or threateningly.

**Brando**, Marlon (born 1924), American film actor.

**Brandt**, Willy (Herbert Ernst Karl Frahm) (1913–92), German statesman, Chancellor of West Germany 1969–74.

**brandy** noun a strong alcoholic spirit distilled from wine or fermented fruit juice. □ **brandy snap** a thin crisp curled wafer of gingerbread.

**brant** Amer. spelling of BRENT.

**Braque** (*pronounced* brahk), Georges (1882–1963), French painter who, with Picasso, inaugurated cubism.

**brash**[1] adjective vulgarly self-assertive; impudent. □ **brashly** adverb, **brashness** noun

**brash**[2] noun loose broken rock or ice.

**Brasilia** the capital of Brazil.

**brass** noun 1 a yellow alloy of copper and zinc. 2 a thing or things made of this. 3 the brass wind instruments of an orchestra. 4 a brass memorial tablet in a church. 5 (*informal*) money. 6 (*slang*) impudence. 7 (*slang*) high-ranking officers or officials; *the top brass.* ● adjective made of brass. □ **brass band** a band playing brass and percussion instruments only. **brass-rubbing** noun taking an impression of brass memorial tablets by rubbing heelball over paper; an impression produced from one of these. **get down to brass tacks** (*slang*) consider the basic facts or practical details.

**brasserie** (bras-er-i) noun a bar where food can be obtained as well as drinks; an informal licensed restaurant.

**brassica** noun a plant of the family that includes cabbage and turnip.

**brassière** (bras-i-air) noun a bra.

**brassy** adjective (**brassier, brassiest**) 1 like brass in appearance or sound. 2 bold and vulgar. □ **brassiness** noun

**brat** noun (*scornful*) a child, especially a badly-behaved one.

**Bratislava** the capital of Slovakia.

**Braun**[1] (*pronounced* brown), Karl Ferdinand (1850–1918), German physicist.

**Braun**[2] (*pronounced* brown), Werner von (1912–77), German rocket engineer.

**bravado** (bră-**vah**-doh) noun a show of boldness.

**brave** adjective 1 able to face and endure danger or pain. 2 spectacular; *a brave show of peonies.* ● noun a North American Indian warrior. ● verb face and endure with bravery. □ **bravely** adverb, **bravery** noun

**bravo**[1] interjection & noun (plural **bravos**) a cry of 'well done!'

**bravo**[2] noun (plural **bravoes** or **bravos**) a hired ruffian or killer.

**bravura** (bră-**voor**-ă) noun 1 a brilliant or ambitious performance. 2 a style of music requiring brilliant technique, especially in singing. 3 bravado.

**brawl** noun a noisy quarrel or fight. ● verb take part in a brawl.

**brawn** noun 1 muscular strength. 2 jellied chopped meat from a pig's head pressed in a mould.

**brawny** adjective (**brawnier, brawniest**) strong and muscular.

**bray** noun the cry of a donkey; a sound like this. ● verb make this cry or sound.

**braze** verb solder with an alloy of brass and zinc.

**brazen** (bray-zĕn) adjective 1 made of brass, like brass. 2 shameless, impudent. □ **brazen it out** behave, after doing wrong, as if one has nothing to be ashamed of.

**brazier** (bray-zi-er) noun a basket-like stand for holding burning coals.

**Brazil** a country in NE South America. ● noun a Brazil nut. □ **Brazil nut** a large three-sided nut. □ **Brazilian** adjective & noun

**Brazzaville** the capital of the Republic of the Congo.

**breach** noun 1 the breaking or neglect of a rule or agreement etc. 2 an estrangement. 3 a broken place, a gap. ● verb break through, make a gap in. □ **breach of the peace** the crime of causing a public disturbance. **step into the breach** give help in a crisis.

**bread** noun 1 a food made of flour and liquid, usually leavened by yeast, and baked. 2 (*slang*) money. □ **bread and butter** one's livelihood; a basic income.

**breadboard** noun 1 a board for cutting bread on. 2 a board for making experimental models of an electric circuit etc.

**breadcrumbs** *plural noun* bread crumbled for use in cooking.

**breaded** *adjective* coated with breadcrumbs.

**breadfruit** *noun* the fruit of a tropical tree, with white pulp like new bread.

**breadline** *noun* □ **on the breadline** living in extreme poverty.

**breadth** *noun* width, broadness.

**breadwinner** *noun* the member of a family who earns the money to support the others.

**break** *verb* (**broke**, **broken**, **breaking**) **1** fall into pieces; cause to do this. **2** damage, make or become unusable. **3** fail to keep (a promise). **4** stop for a time, make or become discontinuous; *broke the silence*; *we broke for coffee*; *broke the strike*. **5** make a way suddenly or violently. **6** emerge or appear suddenly. **7** reveal (news etc.); become known; *the story broke*. **8** surpass; *broke the world record*. **9** make or become weak; overwhelm with grief etc.; destroy; *the scandal broke him*. **10** (of a voice) change its even tone, either with emotion or (of a boy's voice) by becoming suddenly deeper at puberty. **11** (of a ball) change direction after touching the ground. **12** (of waves) fall in foam. **13** (of boxers) come out of a clinch. ●*noun* **1** act or process of breaking. **2** an escape; a sudden dash. **3** a gap, a broken place. **4** an interval, e.g. between periods of work or exercise. **5** points scored continuously in billiards, snooker, etc. **6** (*informal*) a piece of luck. **7** a fair chance; *give him a break.* □ **break down 1** demolish. **2** cease to function; (of a person's health) collapse. **3** give way to emotion. **4** act upon chemically and reduce to constituent parts. **5** analyse; *break down the expenditure.* **break-dancing** *noun* an acrobatic style of dancing to rock music. **break even** make gains and losses that balance exactly. **break in 1** force one's way into a building. **2** interrupt. **3** accustom to a new routine. **break-in** *noun* a forcible entry, especially by a thief. **breaking-point** *noun* the point at which a person or thing gives way under stress. **break in on** disturb, interrupt. **break into 1** enter forcibly. **2** burst into (song, laughter, etc.). **3** change pace for (a faster one); *broke into a run.* **break of day** dawn. **break off 1** detach by breaking. **2** bring to an end. **3** stop speaking. **break out 1** begin suddenly. **2** exclaim. **3** force one's way out. **4** develop (a rash etc.). **break service** win a game at tennis when one's opponent is serving. **break the ice** overcome formality. **break up 1** break into small pieces. **2** bring or come to an end. **3** separate. **4** (of schoolchildren) begin holidays when school closes at the end of term. **break**

**wind** expel wind from the anus; to belch. □ **breakable** *adjective*

**breakage** *noun* **1** breaking. **2** something broken.

**breakaway** *noun* **1** becoming separate or free. **2** an outside second-row forward in Rugby football. ●*adjective* that breaks or has broken away; *a breakaway group*.

**breakdown** *noun* **1** mechanical failure. **2** weakening. **3** a collapse of health or mental stability. **4** an analysis of statistics.

**breaker** *noun* a heavy ocean-wave that breaks on the coast or over a reef.

**breakfast** *noun* the first meal of the day. ●*verb* eat breakfast.

**breakneck** *adjective* (of speed) dangerously fast.

**breakthrough** *noun* **1** breaking through an obstacle etc. **2** a major advance in knowledge.

**breakup** *noun* breaking up; collapse; dispersal.

**breakwater** *noun* a wall built out into the sea to protect a harbour or coast against heavy waves.

**Bream**, Julian Alexander (born 1933), British guitarist.

**bream** *noun* **1** a yellowish freshwater fish with an arched back. **2** (also **sea bream**) a similarly shaped marine fish.

**breast** *noun* **1** either of the two milk-producing organs on the upper front of a woman's body; the corresponding part of a man's body. **2** the upper front part of the human body or of a garment covering this. **3** the corresponding part in animals. **4** something shaped like this; *the chimney-breast.* ●*verb* face and advance against; *breasted the waves.* □ **breast-feed** *verb* feed (a baby) by allowing it to suck at the mother's breast. **breast-fed** *adjective* fed in this way. **breast-stroke** *noun* a swimming stroke performed face downwards, with horizontal sweeping movements of the arms.

**breastbone** *noun* the flat vertical bone in the chest or breast, joined to the ribs.

**breastplate** *noun* a piece of armour covering the breast.

**breastwork** *noun* a low temporary defensive wall or parapet.

**breath** (*pronounced* breth) *noun* **1** air drawn into and sent out of the lungs. **2** breathing in; *take six deep breaths.* **3** a gentle blowing; *a breath of wind.* **4** a hint or slight rumour; *not a breath of scandal.* □ **breath test** a test for alcohol on the breath, using a Breathalyser. **in the same breath** immediately after saying something else. **out of breath** panting after exercise. **save one's breath** refrain from useless discussion. **take one's**

**breath away** surprise or delight. **under one's breath** in a whisper.

**breathalyse** verb (also **breathalyze**) test with a Breathalyser.

**Breathalyser** noun (also **Breathalyzer**) (trade mark) a device that measures the amount of alcohol in a person's breath as he or she breathes out.

**breathe** (pronounced breeth) verb **1** draw air into the lungs and send it out again; (of plants) respire. **2** take into or send out of the lungs; breathing cigar smoke. **3** utter; don't breathe a word of it. □ **breathe again** feel relieved of fear or anxiety. **breathing-space** noun room to breathe; a pause to recover from effort.

**breather** noun **1** a pause for rest. **2** a short period in the fresh air.

**breathless** adjective **1** out of breath, panting. **2** holding one's breath with excitement. □ **breathlessly** adverb, **breathlessness** noun

**breathtaking** adjective very exciting, spectacular.

**breathy** (breth-i) adjective with a noticeable sound of breathing.

**Brecht** (pronounced brekt), Bertolt (1898–1956), German dramatist, producer, and poet.

**bred** see BREED.

**breech** noun **1** the back part of a gun barrel. **2** (old use) the buttocks. □ **breech birth** (also **breech delivery**) a birth in which the baby's buttocks or feet appear first.

**breeches** (brich-iz) plural noun trousers reaching to just below the knee. □ **breeches buoy** a lifebuoy with canvas breeches for the user's legs.

**breed** verb (**bred**, **breeding**) **1** produce offspring. **2** keep (animals) for the purpose of producing young. **3** train, bring up. **4** give rise to. **5** create (fissile material) by nuclear reaction. ● noun a variety of animals etc. within a species, having similar appearance.

**breeder** noun a person who breeds animals. □ **breeder reactor** a nuclear reactor that produces more fissile material than it uses in operating.

**breeding** noun **1** the production of young from animals, propagation. **2** good manners resulting from training or background.

**breeze¹** noun **1** a light wind. **2** (Amer., informal) an easy task. ● verb (informal) move in a lively or casual manner; they breezed in.

**breeze²** noun small cinders. □ **breeze-block** noun a lightweight building block made of breeze with sand and cement.

**breezy** adjective (**breezier, breeziest**) **1** exposed to wind. **2** pleasantly windy.

**3** lively, jovial. □ **breezily** adverb, **breeziness** noun

**Bren gun** a lightweight machine-gun.

**brent** noun (Amer. **brant**) (in full **brent-goose**) a small wild goose.

**brethren** plural noun (old use) brothers.

**Breton¹** (bret-ŏn) adjective of Brittany or its people or language. ● noun **1** a native of Brittany. **2** the Celtic language of Brittany.

**Breton²** (bret-awn), André (1896–1966), French surrealist poet.

**breve** (pronounced breev) noun **1** a mark placed over a short or unstressed vowel (e.g. ŏ). **2** a note in music, equal to two semibreves.

**breviary** (breev-i-er-i) noun a book of prayers to be said daily by Roman Catholic priests.

**brevity** (brev-iti) noun shortness, briefness.

**brew** verb **1** make (beer) by boiling and fermentation; make (tea) by infusion. **2** be being prepared in this way; the tea is brewing. **3** bring about; develop; trouble is brewing. ● noun **1** liquid made by brewing. **2** an amount brewed. □ **brew-up** noun (informal) an instance of making tea.

**brewer** noun a person whose trade is brewing beer.

**brewery** noun a building in which beer is brewed.

**Brezhnev** (brezh-nef), Leonid Ilyich (1906–83), Soviet statesman, President of the former USSR 1977–82.

**briar** alternative spelling of BRIER.

**bribe** noun something offered in order to influence a person to act in favour of the giver. ● verb persuade by a bribe. □ **bribery** noun

**bric-à-brac** (brik-ă-brak) noun odd items of furniture, ornaments, etc., of no great value.

**brick** noun **1** a block of baked or dried clay or other substance used to build walls; building work consisting of such blocks. **2** a child's toy building block. **3** a rectangular block of something. **4** (slang) a kind-hearted, helpful person. ● adjective **1** built of brick. **2** brick-red. ● verb block with brickwork. □ **brick-red** adjective of the red colour of bricks. **drop a brick** (slang) say something tactless or indiscreet.

**brickbat** noun **1** a piece of brick, especially one used as a missile. **2** an uncomplimentary remark; a criticism.

**brickie** noun (informal) a bricklayer.

**bricklayer** noun a worker who builds with bricks.

**brickwork** noun a structure made of bricks.

**bridal** adjective of a bride or wedding.

**Bride**, St see BRIDGET¹.

**bride** noun a woman on her wedding day; a newly married woman.

**bridegroom** *noun* a man on his wedding day; a newly married man.

**bridesmaid** *noun* an unmarried woman or girl attending the bride at a wedding.

**bridge** *noun* **1** a structure providing a way across a river, railway, etc. **2** the raised platform on a ship from which the captain and officers direct its course. **3** the bony upper part of the nose. **4** something that joins, connects, or supports other parts. **5** a card-game developed from whist. ● *verb* make or form a bridge over. □ **bridge roll** an oval soft bread roll. **bridging loan** a loan given for the period between two transactions, e.g. between buying a new house and selling one's own.

**bridgehead** *noun* a fortified area established in enemy territory, especially on the far side of a river.

**Bridges**, Robert Seymour (1844–1930), English poet, Poet Laureate 1913–30.

**Bridget¹**, St (early 6th century), Irish abbess. Feast day, 1 February.

**Bridget²**, St (*c.*1303–73), Swedish nun and visionary, who founded a religious order (Brigittines). Feast day, 8 October.

**bridgework** *noun* a dental structure made to cover a gap, joined to the teeth on either side.

**bridle** *noun* the part of a horse's harness that goes on its head. ● *verb* **1** put a bridle on. **2** restrain, keep under control. **3** draw one's head up in pride or scorn. □ **bridlepath** *noun* a path for horse-riding and walking but not for vehicles.

**Brie** (*pronounced* bree) *noun* a soft white cheese.

**brief** *adjective* **1** lasting only for a short time. **2** concise. **3** short in length. ● *noun* **1** a summary of the facts of a case, drawn up for a barrister. **2** a case given to a barrister. **3** instructions and information given in advance. **4** (**briefs**) very short close-fitting pants or knickers. ● *verb* **1** give a legal brief to. **2** instruct or inform concisely in advance. □ **hold no brief for** not be obliged to support. **in brief** in a few words. □ **briefly** *adverb*, **briefness** *noun*

**briefcase** *noun* a flat case for carrying documents.

**brier** *noun* (also **briar**) **1** a thorny bush, the wild rose. **2** a shrub with a hard woody root used for making tobacco pipes; a pipe made of this.

**Brig.** *abbreviation* Brigadier.

**brig¹** *noun* (*Scottish* & *N. England*) a bridge.

**brig²** *noun* a square-rigged sailing-vessel with two masts.

**brigade** *noun* **1** an army unit forming part of a division. **2** a group of people organized for a particular purpose.

**brigadier** *noun* an officer commanding a brigade; a staff officer of similar status.

**brigand** (**brig**-ănd) *noun* a member of a band of robbers. □ **brigandage** *noun*

**brigantine** *noun* a two-masted ship with a square-rigged foremast and a fore-and-aft rigged mainmast.

**bright** *adjective* **1** giving out or reflecting much light; shining. **2** intense, vivid. **3** cheerful. **4** quick-witted, clever. ● *adverb* brightly. □ **brightly** *adverb*, **brightness** *noun*

**brighten** *verb* make or become brighter.

**Bright's disease** a kidney disease.

**brill** *noun* a flatfish like a turbot. ● *adjective* (*slang*) brilliant, very good.

**brilliant** *adjective* **1** very bright or sparkling. **2** very clever. ● *noun* a cut diamond with many facets. □ **brilliantly** *adverb*, **brilliance** *noun*, **brilliancy** *noun*

**brilliantine** *noun* a substance used to make the hair glossy.

**brim** *noun* **1** the edge of a cup, hollow, or channel. **2** the projecting edge of a hat. ● *verb* (**brimmed**, **brimming**) fill or be full to the brim. □ **brim-full** *adjective* (also **brimful**) full to the brim. **brim over** overflow.

**brimstone** *noun* (*old use*) sulphur.

**brindled** (**brin**-d'ld) *adjective* brown with streaks of other colour; *the brindled cow.*

**Brindley**, James (1716–72), pioneer British canal builder.

**brine** *noun* salt water.

**bring** *verb* (**brought**, **bringing**) **1** cause to come, especially with oneself by carrying, leading, or attracting. **2** produce as profit or income. **3** result in, cause; *war brought famine.* **4** put forward (charges etc.) in a lawcourt; *they brought an action for libel.* **5** cause to arrive at a particular state; *bring it to the boil.* **6** adduce (evidence, an argument, etc.). □ **bring about** cause to happen. **bring-and-buy sale** a sale at which people contribute goods and buy things contributed by others. **bring back** restore; make one remember. **bring down** cause to fall. **bring forth** give birth to; cause; (*old use*) produce. **bring forward** **1** arrange for (a thing) to happen earlier than was intended. **2** call attention to (a matter). **3** transfer from a previous page or account. **bring in 1** initiate, introduce. **2** produce as profit or income. **3** pronounce as a verdict in court. **bring into being** cause to exist. **bring off** do successfully. **bring on** cause to develop rapidly. **bring out 1** cause to appear, show clearly. **2** publish. **bring the house down** get loud applause in a theatre etc. **bring to bear** concentrate as an influence; *pressure was brought to bear on the dissenters.* **bring up 1** look after and train (growing chil-

dren). **2** vomit. **3** mention for discussion.
**bring up the rear** come last in a line.

**brinjal** *noun* (in India and Africa) an aubergine.

**brink** *noun* **1** the edge of a steep place or of a stretch of water. **2** the verge, the edge of something unknown, dangerous, or exciting.

**brinkmanship** *noun* the art of pursuing a dangerous policy to the brink of disaster.

**briny** *adjective* salty. ●*noun* (*humorous*) the sea.

**brio** (**bree**-oh) *noun* dash, verve, vivacity. (¶ Italian.)

**brioche** (**bree**-osh) *noun* a small round sweet bread roll.

**briquette** (brik-et) *noun* a block of compressed coal-dust.

**Brisbane** an Australian seaport, the capital of Queensland.

**brisk** *adjective* active, lively, moving quickly. □ **briskly** *adverb*, **briskness** *noun*

**brisket** (**brisk**-it) *noun* a joint of beef cut from the breast.

**brisling** (**briz**-ling) *noun* a small herring or sprat, processed like sardines.

**bristle** *noun* **1** a short stiff hair. **2** any of the stiff pieces of hair or wire etc. in a brush. ●*verb* **1** (of an animal) raise the bristles in anger or fear. **2** show indignation. **3** be thickly set with bristles. □ **bristle with** be full of; *the place was bristling with security guards.* □ **bristly** *adjective*

**Bristol fashion** *Naut.* in good order.

**Brit** *noun* (*informal*) a British person.

**Brit.** *abbreviation* **1** British. **2** Britain.

**Britain** (in full **Great Britain**) England, Wales, and Scotland.

**Britannia** the personification of Britain, shown as a woman with a shield, helmet, and trident. □ **Britannia metal** a silvery alloy of tin, antimony, and copper.

**Britannic** *adjective* of Britain; *Her Britannic Majesty.*

**Briticism** (**brit**-i-sizm) *noun* an English word or idiom used only in Britain.

**British** *adjective* of Great Britain or its inhabitants. ●*noun* (**the British**) British people.

**British Academy** an institution founded in 1901 for the promotion of historical, philosophical, and philological studies.

**British Columbia** a province of Canada, on the west coast.

**British Council** an organization (established in 1934) whose aim is the promotion of Britain and English abroad and of cultural relations with other countries.

**British Isles** Britain and Ireland with the islands near their coasts.

**British Legion** = ROYAL BRITISH LEGION.

**British Library** the national library of Britain, in London (formerly part of the British Museum).

**British Museum** a national museum of antiquities etc. in London, dating from 1753.

**British thermal unit** the amount of heat needed to raise 1lb of water through 1°F, equivalent to $1.055 \times 10^3$ joules.

**Briton** *noun* **1** a native or inhabitant of southern Britain before the Roman conquest. **2** a British person.

**Brittany** a district of NW France.

**Britten**, (Edward) Benjamin, Lord (1913–76), English composer, conductor, and pianist.

**brittle** *adjective* hard but easily broken. ●*noun* a brittle sweet made of nuts and melted sugar. □ **brittle-bone disease** = OSTEOPOROSIS. □ **brittleness** *noun*

**broach** *verb* **1** make a hole in and draw out liquid. **2** begin a discussion of; *broached the topic.* **3** veer or cause (a ship) to veer and present its side to the wind and waves.

**broad** *adjective* **1** large across, wide. **2** measuring from side to side; *50 ft. broad.* **3** full and complete; strong; *broad daylight*; *a broad hint*; *a broad Yorkshire accent.* **4** in general terms, not detailed; *in broad outline.* **5** rather coarse; *broad humour.* **6** tolerant, liberal; *a broad view.* ●*noun* **1** the broad part. **2** (*Amer. slang*) a prostitute; a woman. **3** (**the Broads**) large areas of water in East Anglia, formed where rivers widen. □ **broad bean** an edible bean with large flat seeds. **broad-leaved** *adjective* (of trees) deciduous and of a hard-timbered variety. **broad-minded** *adjective* having tolerant views. □ **broadness** *noun*

**broadcast** *verb* (**broadcast**, **broadcasting**) **1** send out by radio or television. **2** speak or appear in a radio or television programme. **3** make generally known. **4** sow (seed) by scattering, not in drills. ●*noun* a broadcast programme. ●*adverb* scattered freely. □ **broadcaster** *noun*

**broadcloth** *noun* fine woollen or worsted cloth used in tailoring (originally woven on a wide loom).

**broaden** *verb* make or become broad.

**broadloom** *adjective* (especially of carpets) woven in broad widths.

**broadly** *adverb* **1** in a broad way. **2** in a general way; *broadly speaking.*

**broadsheet** *noun* **1** a large-sized newspaper. **2** a large sheet of paper printed on one side only, especially with information.

**broadside** *noun* **1** the firing of all guns on one side of a ship. **2** a strong attack in words. **3** the side of a ship above the water. □ **broadside on** sideways on.

**broadsword** *noun* a sword with a broad blade, used for cutting rather than thrusting.

**Broadway** a long street in New York City, famous for its theatres.

**brocade** (brŏ-**kayd**) *noun* fabric woven with raised patterns. □ **brocaded** *adjective*

**broccoli** (**brok**-ŏli) *noun* a vegetable with tightly packed green or purple flower heads.

**brochette** (bro-**shet**) *noun* a skewer on which chunks of meat or vegetable are grilled or barbecued.

**brochure** (**broh**-shoor) *noun* a booklet or pamphlet containing information.

**broderie anglaise** (broh-dri ahn-**glayz**) open embroidery on white linen or other fabric.

**brogue** (*rhymes with* rogue) *noun* **1** a strong shoe with pattens of little holes. **2** a dialectal accent, especially Irish.

**broil** *verb* **1** (*Amer.*) grill (meat). **2** make or be very hot.

**broiler** *noun* a young chicken suitable for broiling or roasting.

**broke** *see* BREAK. ●*adjective* (*informal*) having no money.

**broken** *see* BREAK. ●*adjective* **1** having been broken. **2** beaten; exhausted. **3** (of language) badly spoken by a foreigner; *broken English.* **4** interrupted; *broken sleep.* □ **broken-down** *adjective* worn out; not functioning. **broken-hearted** *adjective* overwhelmed with grief. **broken home** a family lacking one parent through divorce or separation. □ **brokenly** *adverb*

**broker** *noun* **1** an agent who buys and sells things on behalf of others. **2** a member of the Stock Exchange dealing in stocks and shares. **3** an official licensed to sell the goods of someone unable to pay his or her debts.

■**Usage** In Britain from October 1986 officially called **broker-dealer** and entitled to act as agent and principal in share dealings.

**brokerage** *noun* a broker's fee or commission.

**brolly** *noun* (*informal*) an umbrella.

**bromide** (**broh**-myd) *noun* **1** a compound of bromine, used in medicine to calm the nerves. **2** a boring or obvious remark. **3** a reproduction on paper coated with silver bromide emulsion.

**bromine** (**broh**-meen) *noun* a dark-red liquid chemical element (symbol Br), compounds of which are used in medicine and photography.

**bronchial** (**bronk**-iăl) *adjective* of the branched tubes into which the windpipe divides, leading into the lungs.

**bronchitis** (brong-ky-tiss) *noun* inflammation of the mucous membrane inside the bronchial tubes.

**bronchus** *noun* (*plural* **bronchi**) either of the two major branches of the windpipe.

**bronco** (**brong**-koh) *noun* (*plural* **broncos**) a wild or half-tamed horse of western North America.

**Brontë** (**bron**-tay), Charlotte (1816–55), Emily (1818–48), and Anne (1820–49), English novelists.

**brontosaurus** (bront-ŏ-**sor**-ŭs) *noun* (*plural* **brontosauruses**) a large dinosaur that fed on plants.

**bronze** *noun* **1** a brown alloy of copper and tin. **2** a thing made of this; a bronze sculpture; a bronze medal (awarded as third prize). **3** its colour. ●*adjective* made of bronze; bronze-coloured. ●*verb* make or become tanned by sun. □ **Bronze Age** the period when weapons and tools were made of bronze.

**brooch** (*rhymes with* coach) *noun* an ornamental hinged pin fastened with a clasp.

**brood** *noun* **1** the young birds or other animals produced at one hatching or birth. **2** a family of children. ●*verb* **1** sit on eggs to hatch them. **2** think long and deeply or resentfully.

**broody** *adjective* **1** (of a hen) wanting to brood. **2** thoughtful and depressed. **3** (*informal*) wanting to have a baby.

**brook** *noun* a small stream. ●*verb* tolerate; *he would brook no interference.*

**Brooke**, Rupert Chauner (1887–1915), British poet.

**broom** *noun* **1** any of several shrubs, often with yellow flowers. **2** a long-handled brush for sweeping floors. □ **new broom** a newly appointed official who gets rid of old methods etc.; *a new broom sweeps clean* (proverb).

**broomstick** *noun* a broom-handle.

**Bros.** (*pronounced* bross) *abbreviation* Brothers.

**broth** *noun* the water in which meat or fish has been boiled; soup made with this.

**brothel** (**broth**-ĕl) *noun* a house where prostitutes work.

**brother** *noun* **1** a son of the same parents as another person. **2** a man who is a fellow member of a Church, trade union, or other association. **3** a monk who is not a priest; (**Brother**) his title. □ **brother-in-law** *noun* (*plural* **brothers-in-law**) the brother of one's husband or wife; the husband of one's sister. □ **brotherly** *adjective*

**brotherhood** *noun* **1** the relationship of brothers. **2** brotherliness, comradeship. **3** an association of men; its members.

**brought** *see* BRING.

**brougham** (broo-ăm) *noun* a horse-drawn closed carriage with a driver perched outside in front.

**brouhaha** (broo-hah-hah) *noun* a commotion.

**brow** *noun* **1** an eyebrow. **2** the forehead. **3** a projecting or overhanging part; the summit of a hill.

**browbeat** *verb* (**browbeat**, **browbeaten**, **browbeating**) intimidate.

**Brown¹**, Sir Arthur Whitten (1886–1948), aviator, born in Scotland of American parents, who in 1919 made a pioneer transatlantic flight with J. W. Alcock.

**Brown²**, John (1800–59), American abolitionist, commemorated in the popular marching-song 'John Brown's Body'.

**Brown³**, 'Capability' (Lancelot) (1716–83), English landscape gardener, known as 'Capability' because he would tell his patrons that their estates had 'great capabilities'.

**brown** *adjective* **1** of a colour between orange and black. **2** having skin of this colour; sun-tanned. **3** (of bread) made with wholemeal or wheatmeal flour. ● *noun* **1** brown colour. **2** a brown substance, material, or thing; brown clothes. **3** the brown ball in snooker etc. ● *verb* make or become brown. □ **browned off** (*slang*) bored, fed up. **Brown Owl** an adult leader of a Brownie pack. **brown paper** strong coarse paper for wrapping parcels etc. **brown rice** unprocessed rice with only the outer husk of the grain removed. **brown sugar** sugar that is only partly refined. □ **brownish** *adjective*

**brownie** *noun* **1** a benevolent elf. **2** a small square chocolate cake. **3** (**Brownie**, in full **Brownie Guide**) a member of a junior branch of the Guides. □ **earn Brownie points** (*informal*) do good deeds in order to earn recognition.

**Browning**, Elizabeth Barrett (1806–61), and husband Robert (1812–89), English poets.

**browning** *noun* a substance for colouring gravy.

**browse** (*rhymes with* cows) *verb* **1** feed as animals do, on leaves or grass etc. **2** look through a book, or examine items for sale, in a casual leisurely way.

**brucellosis** (broo-sel-oh-sis) *noun* a disease caused by bacteria, affecting cattle and some other farm animals.

**Bruch** (*pronounced* bruuk), Max (1838–1920), German composer.

**Bruckner** (bruuk-ner), Anton (1824–96), Austrian composer and organist.

**Bruegel** (brer-gĕl), Pieter (*c.*1525–69), Flemish artist.

**bruise** (*pronounced* brooz) *noun* an injury caused by a knock or by pressure that discolours the skin without breaking it. ● *verb* **1** cause a bruise or bruises on. **2** show the effects of a knock etc.; be susceptible to bruises.

**bruiser** *noun* (*informal*) **1** a large tough-looking person. **2** a boxer.

**bruit** (*pronounced* broot) *verb* (*old use*) spread (a report).

**Brummell** (brum-ĕl), 'Beau' (George Bryan) (1778–1840), Regency dandy and arbiter of fashion, a close friend of the Prince Regent.

**brunch** *noun* a meal combining breakfast and lunch.

**Brunei** (broo-ny) a country on the island of Borneo. □ **Bruneian** *adjective*

**Brunel** (bruu-nel), Sir Marc Isambard (1769–1849), French-born engineer who worked in the USA and in England. His son Isambard Kingdom Brunel (1806–59) designed the Clifton suspension bridge at Bristol, the Great Western Railway and other railways, and the first successful transatlantic steamship.

**Brunelleschi** (broo-nel-esk-i) (1377–1446), Florentine architect, who is often credited with the 'discovery' of perspective.

**brunette** (broo-net) *noun* a woman with dark-brown hair.

**Bruno** (broo-noh), St (*c.*1032–1101), German founder of the Carthusian order.

**Brunswick** a city and ancient duchy of northern Germany. □ **Brunswicker** *noun*

**brunt** *noun* the chief stress or strain; *bore the brunt of the attack.*

**brush** *noun* **1** an implement with bristles of hair, wire, or nylon, etc., set in a solid base, used for cleaning or painting, grooming the hair, etc. **2** a brush-like piece of carbon or metal for making a good electrical connection. **3** a fox's bushy tail. **4** each of a pair of thin sticks with long wire bristles for striking a drum, cymbal, etc. **5** a short sharp encounter. ● *verb* **1** use a brush on, remove with a brush or by passing something lightly over the surface of. **2** touch lightly in passing. □ **brush aside** reject casually or curtly. **brush off** reject curtly, snub. **brush-off** *noun* a curt rejection, a snub. **brush up 1** smarten. **2** study and revive one's former knowledge of.

**brushed** *adjective* with raised nap; *brushed nylon.*

**brushwood** *noun* **1** undergrowth. **2** cut or broken twigs.

**brushwork** *noun* the style of the strokes made with a painter's brush.

**brusque** (*pronounced* bruusk) *adjective* curt and offhand in manner. □ **brusquely** *adverb*, **brusqueness** *noun*

**Brussels** the capital of Belgium; headquarters of the European Commission. □ **Brussels sprouts** a vegetable consisting of small cabbage-like buds growing close to the stem of the plant.

**brutal** *adjective* very cruel, merciless. □ **brutally** *adverb*, **brutality** *noun*

**brutalize** *verb* (also **brutalise**) **1** make or become brutal. **2** treat brutally. □ **brutalization** *noun*

**brute** *noun* **1** an animal other than a human. **2** a brutal person. **3** (*informal*) an unpleasant or difficult person or thing. □ **brute force** cruel and unthinking force. □ **brutish** *adjective*

**Brutus** (**broo**-tŭs), Marcus Junius (85–42 BC), Roman senator, who with Cassius led the conspirators who assassinated Julius Caesar in 44 BC.

**bryony** (**bry**-ŏni) *noun* a climbing plant with black or white berries.

**Brythonic** (bri-**thon**-ik) *adjective* of the Celts of southern Britain or their languages. ● *noun* the southern group of the Celtic languages, including Welsh, Cornish, and Breton.

**BS** *abbreviation* **1** Bachelor of Surgery. **2** British Standard(s).

**B.Sc.** *abbreviation* Bachelor of Science.

**BSE** *abbreviation* bovine spongiform encephalopathy; a usually fatal cattle disease, popularly known as 'mad cow disease'.

**BST** *abbreviation* British Summer Time.

**BT** *abbreviation* British Telecom.

**Bt.** *abbreviation* Baronet; *Sir John Davis, Bt.*

**BTU** *abbreviation* (also **B.th.u.**) British Thermal Unit.

**bubble** *noun* **1** a thin ball of liquid enclosing air or gas. **2** a small ball of air in a liquid or in a solidified liquid, such as glass. **3** a transparent domed cover. ● *verb* **1** send up bubbles; rise in bubbles; make the sound of these. **2** show great liveliness. □ **bubble and squeak** cooked cabbage and potato chopped, mixed, and fried. **bubble bath** a substance added to bath water to make it foam. **bubble car** a small domed car. **bubble gum** chewing gum that can be blown into large bubbles. **bubble plastic**, **bubble wrap** sheets of transparent, flexible plastic containing bubbles of air, used for packaging, insulation, etc.

**bubbly** *adjective* full of bubbles.

**bubo** *noun* (*plural* **buboes**) an inflamed swelling in the groin or armpit.

**bubonic plague** (bew-**bon**-ik) a contagious disease with buboes.

**buccaneer** *noun* a pirate, an unscrupulous adventurer. □ **buccaneering** *adjective & noun*

**Buchan** (**buk**-ăn), John, 1st Baron Tweedsmuir (1875–1940), Scottish writer, Governor-General of Canada 1935–40.

**Bucharest** (bew-kă-**rest**) the capital of Romania.

**Buchenwald** (**buuk**-ĕn-vahlt) a village in eastern Germany, site of a Nazi concentration camp in the Second World War.

**buck** *noun* **1** the male of a deer, hare, or rabbit. **2** (*Amer. & Austral. slang*) a dollar. ● *verb* **1** (of a horse) jump with the back arched. **2** (*slang*) resist or oppose; *bucking the system.* □ **a fast buck** (*informal*) easy money. **buck-teeth** *noun* front upper teeth that stick out. **buck up** (*informal*) **1** make haste. **2** make or become more cheerful. **pass the buck** (*slang*) shift responsibility (and possible blame) to someone else.

**bucked** *adjective* cheered and encouraged.

**bucket** *noun* **1** a round open container with a handle. **2** this with its contents; the amount it contains. ● *verb* **1** move along fast and bumpily. **2** pour heavily; *rain was bucketing down.* □ **bucket seat** a seat with a rounded back, for one person. **bucket shop 1** (*informal*) a travel agency specializing in cheap air tickets. **2** an unregistered agency dealing in speculation on the stock market. □ **bucketful** *noun* (*plural* **bucketfuls**).

**Buckingham Palace** the London residence of the British sovereign since 1837.

**Buckinghamshire** a southern county of England.

**buckle** *noun* a device usually with a hinged pin, through which a belt or strap is threaded to secure it. ● *verb* **1** fasten with a buckle. **2** crumple under pressure; cause to do this. □ **buckle down to** set about doing; get on with.

**buckler** *noun* a small round shield with a handle.

**buckram** (**buk**-răm) *noun* stiffened cloth, especially that used for binding books.

**Buck's Fizz** a cocktail of champagne and orange juice.

**Bucks.** *abbreviation* Buckinghamshire.

**buckshee** *adjective & adverb* (*slang*) free of charge.

**buckshot** *noun* coarse lead shot.

**buckskin** *noun* **1** leather from a buck's skin. **2** a thick smooth cotton or woollen fabric.

**buckthorn** *noun* a kind of thorny shrub.

**buckwheat** *noun* the seed of a cereal plant used to make flour or cooked as a grain.

**bucolic** (bew-**kol**-ik) *adjective* characteristic of country life.

**bud** *noun* **1** a small knob that will develop into a branch, leaf-cluster, or flower. **2** a flower or leaf not fully open. ● *verb* (**bud-**

**ded, budding**) **1** form buds. **2** graft a bud of (a plant) on to another.

**Budapest** (bew-dă-**pest**) the capital of Hungary.

**Buddha** (**buud**-ă) noun **1** the title (often treated as a name) of the Indian philosopher Gautama (5th century BC), and of a series of teachers of Buddhism. **2** a statue or carving representing Gautama Buddha.

**Buddhism** (**buud**-izm) noun an Asian religion based on the teachings of Buddha. □ **Buddhist** adjective & noun

**budding** adjective beginning to develop; a budding poet.

**buddleia** (**bud**-liă) noun a shrub or tree with fragrant lilac or yellow flowers.

**buddy** noun (informal) a friend.

**budge** verb **1** move slightly. **2** cause to alter a position or opinion.

**budgerigar** (**buj**-er-i-gar) noun an Australian parakeet, often kept as a cage-bird.

**budget** noun **1** an estimate or plan of income and expenditure. **2** (**the Budget**) that made annually by the Chancellor of the Exchequer. **3** the amount allotted for a particular purpose. ● verb (**budgeted, budgeting**) plan or allot in a budget. □ **budgetary** adjective

**budgie** noun (informal) a budgerigar.

**Buenos Aires** (bwayn-ŏs I-reez) the capital of Argentina.

**buff** noun **1** strong velvety dull-yellow leather. **2** a yellowish beige colour. **3** the bare skin; stripped to the buff. **4** (informal) an enthusiast; film buffs. (¶ Originally, an enthusiast for going to fires, from the buff-coloured uniforms once worn by New York volunteer firemen.) ● adjective yellowish beige. ● verb polish with soft material.

**buffalo** noun (plural **buffaloes** or **buffalo**) **1** a wild ox found in Asia and Africa. **2** a North American bison.

**Buffalo Bill** (real name; William Frederick Cody) (1846–1917), American showman who toured with his 'Wild West' show.

**buffer** noun **1** something that lessens the effect of an impact; a device for this purpose on a railway engine or at the end of a track. **2** (slang) a fellow. ● verb act as a buffer to. □ **buffer State** a small country between two powerful ones, thought to reduce the chance of war between them.

**buffet**[1] (**buu**-fay) noun **1** a counter where food and drink may be bought and consumed. **2** provision of food where guests serve themselves; buffet lunch. **3** (also pronounced buf-it) a sideboard or a cupboard in a recess, for dishes etc. □ **buffet car** a railway coach serving refreshments.

**buffet**[2] (**buf**-it) noun a blow, especially with the hand. ● verb (**buffeted, buffeting**) strike or jolt repeatedly.

**buffoon** (buf-**oon**) noun a person who plays the fool. □ **buffoonery** noun

**bug** noun **1** an insect with mouthparts adapted for piercing and sucking; any small insect. **2** (informal) a micro-organism, especially one causing disease. **3** (informal) a great enthusiasm. **4** (slang) a small hidden microphone installed secretly. **5** (slang) a defect in a machine etc. ● verb (**bugged, bugging**) (slang) **1** fit with a hidden microphone secretly so that conversations etc. can be overheard. **2** annoy.

**bugbear** noun something feared or disliked.

**bugger** noun **1** a person who practises buggery. **2** (vulgar) an unpleasant or difficult person or thing. ● verb (vulgar) (often foll. by up) spoil, ruin. ● interjection (vulgar) damn. □ **bugger-all** noun (vulgar) nothing. **bugger off** go away.

**buggery** noun sodomy.

**buggy** noun **1** (old use) a light horse-drawn carriage. **2** a small sturdy vehicle; beach buggy. **3** a lightweight folding pushchair.

**bugle** noun a brass instrument like a small trumpet, used for sounding military signals. □ **bugler** noun

**bugloss** (bew-gloss) noun a wild plant with bristly leaves and blue flowers.

**build** verb (**built, building**) construct by putting parts or material together. ● noun bodily shape; of slender build. □ **build on** rely on. **build up 1** accumulate; establish gradually. **2** fill in with buildings. **3** boost with praise or flattering publicity. **build-up** noun **1** advance publicity. **2** a gradual approach to a climax. **3** an increase.

**builder** noun a person who builds; one whose trade is building houses etc.

**building** noun **1** the constructing of houses etc. **2** a permanent built structure that can be entered. □ **building society** an organization that accepts deposits and lends out money, especially to people wishing to buy a house.

**built** see BUILD. ● adjective having a specified build; sturdily built. □ **built-in** adjective incorporated as part of a structure. **built-up** adjective filled in with buildings; densely developed; a built-up area.

**Bujumbura** (boo-jŭm-**boor**-ă) the capital of Burundi.

**bulb** noun **1** a thick rounded mass of scale-like leaves from which a stem grows up and roots grow down. **2** a plant grown from this. **3** a bulb-shaped object. **4** an electric lamp; the glass part of this.

**bulbous** (**bul**-bŭs) adjective shaped like a bulb; fat and bulging.

**Bulgar** (**bul**-gar) adjective & noun = BULGARIAN.

**bulgar** alternative spelling of BULGUR.

**Bulgaria** a country in SE Europe, on the Black Sea. □ **Bulgarian** *adjective & noun*

**bulge** *noun* a rounded swelling, an outward curve. ● *verb* form a bulge, cause to swell out.

**bulgur** *noun* (also **bulgar**, **bulghur**) (in full **bulgur wheat**) wheat grains that have been partly boiled and dried, so that they only need to be soaked before being eaten.

**bulimia** (bew-**lim**-iă) *noun* (in full **bulimia nervosa**) a psychological condition causing bouts of compulsive overeating followed by self-induced vomiting, purging, or fasting.

**bulk** *noun* **1** size or magnitude, especially when great. **2** the greater part, the majority. **3** a large shape or body or person. ● *verb* increase the size or thickness of; *bulk it out*. □ **bulk buying** buying a large quantity at one time, often at a discount. **in bulk** in large amounts; in a mass, not packaged.

**bulkhead** *noun* an upright partition in a ship, aircraft, or vehicle.

**bulky** *adjective* (**bulkier**, **bulkiest**) taking up much space. □ **bulkiness** *noun*

**bull** *noun* **1** an uncastrated male of any animal of the ox family. **2** the male of the whale, elephant, and other large animals. **3** (**the Bull**) a sign of the zodiac, Taurus. **4** (*Stock Exchange*) a person who buys shares hoping to sell them at a higher price (compare BEAR¹ sense 4). **5** the bull's-eye of a target. **6** an official edict issued by the pope. **7** (*slang*) an obviously absurd statement; lies, nonsense. **8** (*slang*) routine tasks regarded as unnecessary. □ **bull-headed** *adjective* obstinate, blundering. **bull market** a situation where share prices are rising rapidly. **bull-terrier** *noun* a dog of a breed originally produced by crossing a bulldog and a terrier.

**bulldog** *noun* a dog of a powerful breed with a short muzzle and a short thick neck. □ **bulldog clip** a spring clip that closes very strongly.

**bulldoze** *verb* **1** clear with a bulldozer. **2** (*informal*) force or intimidate; *he bulldozed them into accepting it.*

**bulldozer** *noun* a powerful tractor with a broad steel sheet mounted in front, used for shifting earth or clearing ground.

**bullet** *noun* a small round or conical missile used in a rifle or revolver.

**bulletin** *noun* **1** a short official statement of news. **2** a society's regular list of information and news.

**bulletproof** *adjective* designed to protect people from bullets.

**bullfight** *noun* the sport of baiting and killing bulls for public entertainment, as in Spain. □ **bullfighter** *noun*, **bullfighting** *noun*

**bullfinch** *noun* a songbird with a black head and (in the male) a pinkish breast.

**bullfrog** *noun* a large American frog with a bellowing cry.

**bullion** *noun* gold or silver in bulk or bars, before coining or manufacture.

**bullock** *noun* a bull after castration.

**bullring** *noun* an arena for bullfights.

**bull's-eye** *noun* **1** the centre of a target. **2** a large hard round peppermint sweet. **3** a hemisphere or thick disc of glass as a window.

**bullshit** (*vulgar slang*) *noun* (often as *interjection*) rubbish, nonsense. ● *verb* (**bullshitted**, **bullshitting**) talk rubbish; try to convince (a person) of something when one knows nothing about it.

**bully** *noun* a person who uses strength or power to hurt or frighten others. ● *verb* (**bullied**, **bullying**) behave as a bully towards, intimidate. □ **bully for you!** (*informal*) bravo! **bully off** start play in hockey, where two opposing players tap the ground and each other's stick alternately three times before hitting the ball. **bully-off** *noun* this procedure.

**bully beef** corned beef.

**bulrush** *noun* a tall rush with a thick velvety head.

**bulwark** (**buul**-werk) *noun* **1** a wall of earth built as a defence. **2** something that acts as a protection or defence. **3** (**bulwarks**) a ship's side above the level of the deck.

**bum** (*slang*) *noun* **1** the buttocks. **2** a beggar, a loafer.

**bumbag** *noun* (*slang*) a small pouch strapped around the waist or hips.

**bumble** *verb* **1** move or act in a blundering way. **2** ramble in speaking.

**bumble-bee** *noun* a large bee with a loud hum.

**bumf** *noun* (also **bumph**) (*slang*, *humorous*) documents, papers.

**bummalo** *noun* a small fish of the Indian Ocean, dried and eaten as a relish with curry. *See* BOMBAY DUCK.

**bump** *verb* **1** knock with a dull-sounding blow; hurt by this. **2** travel with a jolting movement. ● *noun* **1** a bumping sound, knock, or movement. **2** a raised mark left by a blow. **3** a swelling or lump on a surface. □ **bump into** (*informal*) meet by chance. **bump off** (*slang*) kill. **bump up** (*informal*) raise; *bumped up the price.*

**bumper** *noun* **1** (usually used as *adjective*) unusually large or plentiful; *a bumper crop.* **2** a horizontal bar attached to the front or back of a motor vehicle to lessen the effect of a collision. **3** a ball in cricket that rises high after pitching. □ **bumper car** = DODGEM.

**bumph** alternative spelling of BUMF.

**bumpkin** *noun* a country person with awkward manners.

**bumptious** (**bump**-shŭs) *noun* conceited.

**bumpy** *adjective* (**bumpier, bumpiest**) full of bumps; causing jolts.

**bun** *noun* **1** a small round sweet cake. **2** hair twisted into a bun shape at the back of the head.

**bunch** *noun* **1** a cluster; *a bunch of grapes*. **2** a number of small similar things held or fastened together; *a bunch of keys*. **3** (*slang*) a mob, a gang. ●*verb* come or bring together into a bunch or in folds.

**bunchy** *adjective* gathered in clumsy folds.

**bundle** *noun* **1** a collection of things loosely fastened or wrapped together. **2** (*slang*) a large amount of money. ●*verb* **1** make into a bundle. **2** put away hastily and untidily, push hurriedly; *bundled him into a taxi*. □ **go a bundle on** (*slang*) like immensely.

**bung** *noun* a stopper for closing a hole in a barrel or jar. ●*verb* **1** close with a bung. **2** (*slang*) throw or toss; *bung it over here*. □ **bunged up** blocked.

**bungalow** *noun* a one-storeyed house.

**bungee** (**bun**-jee) *noun* an elasticated rope used for securing baggage or in bungee jumping. □ **bungee jumping** the sport of jumping from a height attached to a bungee.

**bungle** *verb* spoil by lack of skill; tackle clumsily and without success. ●*noun* a bungled attempt. □ **bungler** *noun*

**bunion** *noun* a swelling at the base of the big toe, with thickened skin.

**bunk** *noun* **1** a built-in shelf-like bed, e.g. on a ship. **2** (*slang*) nonsense, rubbish. □ **bunk beds** a pair of small single beds mounted one above the other as a unit. **bunk off** (*slang*) run away; play truant. **do a bunk** (*slang*) run away.

**bunker** *noun* **1** a container for fuel. **2** a sandy hollow forming a hazard on a golf course. **3** a reinforced underground shelter. ●*verb* put fuel into the bunkers of (a ship).

**bunkered** *adjective* trapped in a bunker at golf.

**bunkum** *noun* nonsense, rubbish.

**bunny** *noun* a child's word for a rabbit.

**Bunsen**, Robert Wilhelm Eberhard (1811–99), German chemist, a pioneer of spectral analysis. □ **Bunsen burner** a laboratory instrument devised by Bunsen, with a vertical tube burning a mixture of air and gas.

**bunting** *noun* **1** flags and streamers for decorating streets and buildings. **2** a loosely-woven fabric used for making these. **3** a bird related to the finches.

**Buñuel** (boon-**wel**), Luis (1900–83), Spanish surrealist film director.

**Bunyan**, John (1628–88), English writer, author of *The Pilgrim's Progress*.

**buoy** (*pronounced* boi) *noun* an anchored floating object marking a navigable channel, showing the position of submerged rocks etc. ●*verb* **1** mark with a buoy or buoys. **2** (usually foll. by *up*) keep (a thing) afloat. **3** encourage, uplift; *buoyed up with new hope*.

**buoyant** (**boy**-ănt) *adjective* **1** able to float. **2** light-hearted, cheerful. □ **buoyantly** *adverb*, **buoyancy** *noun*

**BUPA** *abbreviation* British United Provident Association, a private health insurance organization.

**bur** *noun* (also **burr**) a plant's seed-case or flower that clings to hair or clothing; the plant itself.

**Burbage**, Richard (*c.*1567–1619), English actor, the original performer of most of Shakespeare's great tragic roles.

**burble** *verb* **1** make a gentle murmuring sound. **2** speak lengthily.

**burbot** *noun* (*plural* **burbot**) an eel-like freshwater fish.

**burden** *noun* **1** something carried, a heavy load. **2** something difficult to bear; *the heavy burden of taxation*. **3** the chief theme of a speech etc. ●*verb* **1** load, put a burden on. **2** oppress. □ **beast of burden** an animal that carries packs on its back. **the burden of proof** the obligation to prove what one says.

**burdensome** *adjective* troublesome, tiring.

**burdock** *noun* a plant with prickly flowers and docklike leaves.

**bureau** (**bewr**-oh) *noun* (*plural* **bureaux** *or* **bureaus**) **1** a piece of furniture with drawers and a hinged flap for use as a desk. **2** an office or department; *a travel bureau*; *the Information Bureau*.

**bureaucracy** (bewr-**ok**-răsi) *noun* **1** government by State officials not by elected representatives. **2** these officials. **3** excessive official routine, especially because there are too many offices or departments.

**bureaucrat** (**bewr**-ŏ-krat) *noun* **1** an official who works in a government office. **2** one who applies the rules of a department without exercising much judgement.

**bureaucratic** (bewr-ŏ-**krat**-ik) *adjective* **1** of bureaucracy. **2** of or like bureaucrats.

**burette** (bewr-**et**) *noun* (*Amer.* **buret**) a graduated glass tube with a tap, used for measuring small quantities of liquid.

**burgeon** (**ber**-jŏn) *verb* begin to grow rapidly.

**burger** *noun* (*informal*) a hamburger.

**Burgess**¹ (**ber**-jis), Anthony (John Burgess Wilson) (1917–93), English novelist, critic, and composer.

# Burgess | bury

**Burgess²**, Guy Francis de Moncy (1911–63), British Foreign Office official who, with Donald MacLean, became a spy for the former Soviet Union.

**burgess** (ber-jis) noun **1** a citizen of a town or borough. **2** (old use) an MP for a borough or university.

**burgh** (bu-ră) noun (hist.) a borough in Scotland.

**burgher** noun a citizen of a Continental town.

**burglar** noun a person who enters a building illegally, especially in order to steal. □ **burglary** noun

**burgle** verb rob as a burglar.

**burgomaster** (berg-ŏ-mah-ster) noun the mayor of a Dutch or Flemish town.

**burgundy** noun **1** (also **Burgundy**) a red or white wine from Burgundy in France; a similar wine from elsewhere. **2** a dark purplish red colour.

**burial** noun **1** burying; being buried; a funeral. **2** a grave or its remains.

**burin** (bewr-in) noun an engraving-tool.

**burk** alternative spelling of BERK.

**Burke¹**, Edmund (1729–97), British man of letters and politician.

**Burke²**, John (1787–1848), Irish-born compiler of a 'Peerage and Baronetage' (1826), issued periodically since 1847.

**Burkina** (ber-keen-ă) an inland country of western Africa. □ **Burkinan** adjective & noun

**burlesque** (ber-lesk) noun a mocking imitation.

**burly** adjective (**burlier, burliest**) with a strong heavy body, sturdy.

**Burma** (from 1989 officially called **Myanmar**) a country of SE Asia, on the Bay of Bengal.

**Burmese** noun (plural **Burmese**) **1** a person from Burma. **2** the language of Burma. ● adjective of Burma or its people or language.

**burn¹** verb (**burned** or **burnt** (see note at end of entry), **burning**) **1** blaze or glow with fire. **2** produce heat or light; be alight. **3** damage, hurt, or destroy by fire, heat, or the action of chemicals; be injured or damaged in this way. **4** use as fuel. **5** be able to be set on fire. **6** feel or cause to feel hot. **7** make or become brown from heat or light. ● noun a mark or sore made by burning. □ **burn one's boats** or **bridges** do something deliberately that makes retreat impossible. **burn the midnight oil** study far into the night. **burn-out** noun exhaustion.

■**Usage** The form burnt (not burned) is always used for adjectival uses of the past participle, e.g. in a burnt offering. For the verb, either burned or burnt may be used.

**burn²** noun (Scottish) a brook.

**Burne-Jones**, Sir Edward Coley (1833–98), English painter and designer of tapestry and stained glass.

**burner** noun the part of a lamp or cooker that emits and shapes the flame.

**Burney**, 'Fanny' (Frances) (1752–1840), English novelist and diarist.

**burning** see BURN¹. ● adjective **1** intense; a burning desire. **2** hotly discussed, vital; a burning question.

**burnish** verb polish by rubbing.

**burnous** (ber-noos) noun an Arab or Moorish hooded cloak.

**Burns**, Robert (1759–96), Scottish poet and songwriter, whose birthday (25 January) is celebrated annually with feasting and drinking.

**burnt** see BURN¹. ● adjective of a deep shade; burnt sienna, burnt umber.

**burp** noun (informal) a belch, a belching sound. ● verb **1** (informal) belch. **2** cause (a baby) to bring up wind from the stomach.

**burr¹** noun **1** a whirring sound. **2** the strong pronunciation of 'r'; a soft country accent, especially one using this. **3** a small drill. ● verb make a whirring sound.

**burr²** alternative spelling of BUR.

**Burroughs** (bu-rohz), William Seward (born 1914), American novelist.

**burrow** noun a hole or tunnel dug by a fox or rabbit etc. as a dwelling. ● verb **1** dig a burrow, tunnel. **2** form by tunnelling. **3** search deeply, delve.

**bursar** (ber-ser) noun **1** a person who manages the finances and other business of a school or college. **2** a student who holds a bursary.

**bursary** (ber-ser-i) noun a grant given to a student.

**burst** verb (**burst, bursting**) **1** force or be forced open; fly violently apart because of pressure inside; buds are bursting. **2** appear or come suddenly and forcefully; burst into flame. **3** let out a violent expression of feeling; burst into tears; burst out laughing. ● noun **1** a bursting, a split. **2** an explosion or outbreak; a series of shots; a burst of gunfire. **3** a brief violent effort; a spurt.

**bursting** adjective full to breaking-point; sacks bursting with grain; bursting with energy.

**Burton**, Richard (original name: Richard Jenkins) (1925–84), Welsh stage and film actor.

**burton** noun □ **go for a burton** (slang) be lost, destroyed, or killed.

**Burundi** (bu-run-di) a country in East Africa. □ **Burundian** adjective & noun

**bury** verb (**buried, burying**) **1** place (a dead body) in the earth, a tomb, or the sea. **2** put underground, hide in earth etc. **3** cover up; put in an obscure place to be forgotten; *buried himself in the country*. **4** put (a feeling, idea, etc.) out of one's mind. **5** involve oneself deeply; *buried in a book*; *buried herself in her work*. □ **bury the hatchet** cease quarrelling.

**bus** *noun* (*plural* **buses** *or Amer.* **busses**) **1** a long-bodied passenger vehicle. **2** *Computing* a defined set of conductors carrying data and control signals within a computer. ● *verb* (**bused**, **busing** or **bussed**, **bussing**) **1** travel by bus. **2** transport by bus; (*Amer.*) take (children) to a distant school by bus in order to counteract racial segregation. □ **bus lane** a strip of road for use by buses only. **bus station** an area where a number of buses stop, with facilities for passengers. **bus stop** the regular stopping-place of a bus.

**busbar** *noun* an electrical conductor or set of conductors for collecting and distributing electric current.

**busby** (**buz**-bi) *noun* a tall fur cap worn by hussars on ceremonial occasions.

**Bush**, George Herbert Walter (born 1924), 41st President of the USA 1989–92.

**bush¹** *noun* **1** a shrub. **2** a thick growth or clump; *a bush of hair*. **3** wild uncultivated land, especially in Africa and Australia. □ **bush-baby** *noun* a small African tree-climbing lemur. **bush telegraph** a way in which news is passed on unofficially.

**bush²** *noun* **1** a metal lining for a round hole in which something fits or revolves. **2** an electrically insulating sleeve. ● *verb* fit with a bush.

**bushed** *adjective* (*informal*) tired out.

**bushel** *noun* a measure for grain and fruit (8 gallons). □ **hide one's light under a bushel** conceal one's abilities.

**bushido** (boo-**shee**-doh) *noun* the strict ethical code of the Japanese samurai, involving military skill, fearlessness, and obedience to authority.

**bushman** *noun* (*plural* **bushmen**) **1** a person who lives or travels in the Australian bush. **2** (**Bushman**) a member or the language of an aboriginal people in South Africa.

**bushy** *adjective* (**bushier**, **bushiest**) **1** growing thickly. **2** covered with bushes.

**business** *noun* **1** a trade, a profession; a person's usual occupation. **2** buying and selling, trade. **3** a commercial firm; a shop; *they own a grocery business*. **4** a thing needing to be dealt with; the agenda. **5** a difficult matter; *what a business it is!*. **6** an affair, subject, or device. □ **business park** an area designed for commerce and light industry. **have no business to** have no right to (do something).

**businesslike** *adjective* practical, systematic, rational.

**businessman** *noun* (*plural* **businessmen**) a man engaged in trade or commerce, especially at a senior level.

**businesswoman** *noun* (*plural* **businesswomen**) a woman engaged in trade or commerce, especially at a senior level.

**busk** *verb* perform in the street to entertain passers-by and collect money. □ **busker** *noun*

**busman** *noun* (*plural* **busmen**) the driver of a bus. □ **busman's holiday** leisure time spent doing something similar to one's usual work.

**bust** *noun* **1** a sculpture of the head, shoulders, and chest. **2** the bosom. **3** the measurement round a woman's body at the bosom. ● *verb* (**busted** *or* **bust**, **busting**) (*informal*) **1** break; burst. **2** raid, search. **3** arrest. ● *adjective* (*informal*) **1** burst, broken. **2** bankrupt. □ **bust-up** *noun* (*slang*) a quarrel.

**bustard** *noun* a large swift-running bird.

**bustle** *verb* **1** make a show of hurrying. **2** cause to hurry. ● *noun* **1** excited activity. **2** padding formerly used to puff out the top of a woman's skirt at the back.

**busty** *adjective* (**bustier**, **bustiest**) having a large bust.

**busy** *adjective* (**busier**, **busiest**) **1** working, occupied; having much to do. **2** full of activity; *a busy day*. **3** (of a telephone line) engaged. **4** (of a picture or design) too full of detail. ● *verb* (**busied**, **busying**) keep busy; *busy oneself*. □ **busily** *adverb*

**busybody** *noun* a meddlesome person.

**but** *conjunction* however; on the other hand. ● *preposition* except; *there's no one here but me*. ● *adverb* only, no more than; *we can but try*. ● *noun* an objection; *ifs and buts*. □ **but for** were it not for; *I'd have drowned but for you.*

**butane** (**bew**-tayn) *noun* an inflammable gas produced from petroleum, used in liquid form as a fuel.

**butch** *adjective* (*slang*) tough-looking; masculine, mannish.

**butcher** *noun* **1** a person whose trade is to slaughter animals for food; one who cuts up and sells animal flesh. **2** a person who has people killed needlessly or brutally. ● *verb* **1** slaughter or cut up (an animal) for meat. **2** kill needlessly or brutally. **3** (*informal*) ruin, make a mess of. □ **butcher's** *noun* (*rhyming slang*, short for 'butcher's hook') a look.

**butchery** *noun* **1** a butcher's trade. **2** needless or brutal killing.

**butler** *noun* the chief manservant of a household.

**butt¹** *noun* **1** the thicker end of a tool or weapon. **2** a short remnant, a stub. **3** a large cask or barrel. **4** the mound of earth behind the targets on a shooting-range. **5** a person or thing that is a target for ridicule or teasing. **6** (**butts**) a shooting-range. **7** (*Amer. slang*) the buttocks.

**butt²** *verb* **1** push with the head like a ram or goat. **2** meet or place edge to edge; *the strips should be butted against each other, not overlapping.* ●*noun* **1** an act of butting. **2** a butted join. □ **butt in** interrupt; meddle.

**butte** (*pronounced* byoot) *noun* (*Amer.*) an isolated, steep-sided hill.

**butter** *noun* **1** a fatty food substance made from cream by churning. **2** a similar substance made from other materials; *peanut butter.* ●*verb* spread, cook, or serve with butter. □ **butter-bean** *noun* a large pale flat bean. **butter-cream, butter-icing** *noun* a mixture of butter, sugar, and flavourings for filling or coating cakes. **butter-fingers** *noun* (*informal*) a person likely to drop things. **butter muslin** a thin loosely-woven fabric. **butter up** (*informal*) flatter.

**buttercup** *noun* a wild plant with bright yellow cup-shaped flowers.

**butterfly** *noun* **1** an insect with four often brightly coloured wings and knobbed feelers. **2** (in full **butterfly stroke**) a swimming stroke in which both arms are lifted at the same time. □ **butterfly nut** a kind of wing-nut. **have butterflies in the stomach** feel nervous tremors.

**buttermilk** *noun* the liquid left after butter has been churned from milk.

**butterscotch** *noun* a hard toffee.

**buttery** *adjective* like or containing butter. ●*noun* a snack bar; a food store, especially in a college.

**buttock** *noun* either of the two fleshy rounded parts at the lower or rear end of the back of the human or an animal body.

**button** *noun* **1** a knob or disc sewn on a garment as a fastener or ornament. **2** a small rounded object; a knob pressed to operate an electric bell etc. ●*verb* (**buttoned, buttoning**) fasten with a button or buttons. □ **button mushroom** a small unopened mushroom.

**buttonhole** *noun* **1** a slit through which a button is passed to fasten clothing. **2** a flower worn in the buttonhole of a lapel. ●*verb* accost and detain with conversation.

**buttress** *noun* **1** a support built against a wall. **2** a thing that supports or reinforces something. ●*verb* prop up.

**butty** *noun* (*N. England*) a sandwich.

**butyl** (byoo-tyl) *noun* the univalent alkyl radical $C_4H_9$. □ **butyl rubber** synthetic rubber used to make tyre inner tubes.

**buxom** *adjective* plump and healthy-looking; busty.

**buy** *verb* (**bought, buying**) **1** obtain in exchange for money or by some sacrifice.

**2** win over by bribery. **3** (*slang*) believe, accept the truth of; *no one would buy that excuse.* **4** (*slang*) receive as a punishment. ●*noun* a purchase; *a good buy.* □ **buy off** get rid of by payment. **buy out** obtain full ownership by paying (another person) to give up his or her share. **buy up** buy all or as much as possible of.

**buyer** *noun* **1** a person who buys something. **2** an agent choosing and buying stock for a large shop. □ **buyers' market** a state of affairs when goods are plentiful and prices are low.

**buyout** *noun* the purchase of a controlling share in a company; the buying of a company by people who work there; *a management buyout.*

**buzz** *noun* **1** a vibrating humming sound. **2** a rumour. **3** (*slang*) a telephone call; *give me a buzz.* **4** (*slang*) a thrill. ●*verb* **1** make a buzz. **2** be filled with a buzzing noise. **3** go about quickly and busily. **4** threaten (an aircraft) by flying close to it. □ **buzz off** (*slang*) go away.

**buzzard** *noun* a large bird of the hawk family.

**buzzer** *noun* a device that produces a buzzing note as a signal.

**buzzword** *noun* (*informal*) a piece of fashionable jargon.

**by** *preposition* **1** near, beside. **2** via; past. **3** during; *came by night.* **4** through the agency or means of; (of an animal) having as its sire. **5** (of members or measurements) taking it together with; *multiply six by four*; (expressing dimensions) *it measures ten feet by eight.* **6** not later than. **7** according to; *judging by appearances*; *sold by the dozen.* **8** after, succeeding; *bit by bit.* **9** to the extent of; *missed it by inches.* **10** in respect of; *a tailor, Jones by name*; *pull it up by the roots.* **11** in the belief of; *swear by God.* **12** between the compass points indicated; *north by north-west.* ●*adverb* **1** near; *sat by.* **2** aside; in reserve; *put £5 by.* **3** past; *walked by.* □ **by and by** before long. **by and large** on the whole, considering everything. **by oneself** alone; without help.

**bye** *noun* **1** a run scored in cricket from a ball that passes the batsman without being hit. **2** a hole or holes remaining unplayed when a golf match is ended. **3** the status of having no opponent for one round in a tournament and so advancing to the next as if having won. ●*interjection* = BYE-BYE.

**bye-bye** *interjection* (*informal*) goodbye.

**by-election** *noun* an election to fill a vacancy caused by the death or resignation of an MP.

**Byelorussia** alternative name for BELARUS. □ **Byelorussian** *adjective & noun*

**bygone** *adjective* belonging to the past. ● *plural noun* (**bygones**) things belonging to the past; *let bygones be bygones*.

**by-law** *noun* a law or regulation made by a local authority or by a company.

**byline** *noun* **1** a line in a newspaper etc. naming the writer of an article. **2** a secondary line of work. **3** the goal-line or touch-line of a football pitch.

**bypass** *noun* **1** a road taking traffic round a congested area. **2** a secondary channel allowing something to flow when the main route is blocked. **3** a surgical operation to redirect the flow of blood away from a damaged part of the heart. ● *verb* **1** avoid by means of a bypass. **2** omit or ignore (procedures, regulations, etc.) in order to act quickly.

**byplay** *noun* action, usually without speech, of minor characters in a play etc.

**by-product** *noun* **1** a substance produced during the making of something else. **2** a secondary result.

**Byrd**[1] (*pronounced* berd), Richard Evelyn (1888–1957), American polar explorer.

**Byrd**[2] (*pronounced* berd), William (1543–1623), English composer.

**byre** *noun* a cowshed.

**byroad** *noun* a minor road.

**Byron**, George Gordon, 6th Baron (1788–1824), English Romantic and satirical poet.

**byssinosis** (bis-in-**oh**-sis) *noun* a lung disease caused by much breathing in of textile fibre dust.

**bystander** *noun* a person standing near but taking no part when something happens; an onlooker.

**byte** (*rhymes with* kite) *noun* a fixed number of bits (= binary digits) in a computer, often representing a single character.

**byway** *noun* a byroad.

**byword** *noun* **1** a person or thing spoken of as a notable example; *the firm became a byword for mismanagement*. **2** a familiar saying.

**Byzantine** (bi-**zan**-tyn) *adjective* **1** of Byzantium or the Eastern Roman Empire. **2** (of a situation, attitude, etc.) complicated, inflexible, underhand.

**Byzantium** (bi-**zan**-tiŭm *or* by-**zan**-tiŭm) an ancient Greek city on the Bosporus, refounded by Constantine the Great as Constantinople (modern Istanbul).

# Cc

**C** noun (plural **Cs** or **C's**) **1** *Music* the first note of the scale of C major. **2** the third highest category, mark, etc.; the third example, item in a list, etc. **3** (as a Roman numeral) 100. ● *abbreviation* **1** Celsius, centigrade. **2** coulomb(s). **3** capacitance. ● *symbol* carbon.

© *symbol* copyright.

**c.** *abbreviation* **1** century. **2** cent(s).

**c.** *abbreviation circa*, about.

**CA** *abbreviation* California.

**Ca** *symbol* calcium.

**CAA** *abbreviation* Civil Aviation Authority.

**cab** noun **1** a taxi. **2** a compartment for the driver of a train, lorry, or crane.

**cabal** (kă-**bal**) noun a secret plot; the people engaged in it.

**cabaret** (kab-ă-ray) noun an entertainment provided in a restaurant or nightclub.

**cabbage** noun **1** a vegetable with green or purple leaves usually forming a round head. **2** (*informal*) a person who lives without interests or ambition. □ **cabbage white** a butterfly whose caterpillars feed on cabbage leaves.

**cabbalistic** (kab-ă-**list**-ik) *adjective* having a mystical sense, occult.

**cabby** noun (also **cabbie**) (*informal*) a taxi driver.

**caber** (**kay**-ber) noun a roughly-trimmed tree-trunk used in the Scottish sport of tossing the caber.

**cabin** noun **1** a small dwelling or shelter, especially of wood. **2** a compartment in a ship or aircraft or spacecraft. **3** a driver's cab. □ **cabin cruiser** a large motor boat with a cabin or cabins.

**Cabinda** (kă-**bin**-dă) a small region on the west coast of Africa, part of Angola but separated from it by Zaire.

**cabinet** noun **1** a cupboard or container for storing or displaying things. **2** (**Cabinet**) the group of ministers chosen by the Prime Minister to be responsible for government policy. □ **cabinet-maker** noun a skilled joiner; a maker of high-quality furniture.

**cable** noun **1** a thick rope of fibre or wire. **2** an anchor-chain. **3** a set of insulated wires for carrying electricity or electronic signals. **4** a telegram sent abroad. **5** (in full **cable stitch**) a knitted pattern looking like twisted rope. ● *verb* send a telegram to (a person) abroad; transmit (money or information) in this way. □ **cable-car** noun any of the cars in a **cable railway**, a railway with cars drawn by an endless cable by

means of a stationary engine. **cable television** transmission of television programmes by cable to subscribers.

**caboodle** (kă-boo-d'l) noun □ **the whole caboodle** (*slang*) the whole lot.

**caboose** (kă-**booss**) noun **1** (*Amer.*) a guard's van, especially on a goods train. **2** a kitchen on a ship's deck.

**Cabot** (**kab**-ŏt), John (died *c*.1498), Venetian explorer and navigator who discovered the mainland of North America a year before Columbus.

**cabriole** (kab-ri-ohl) noun a curved leg on furniture.

**cabriolet** (kab-ri-oh-lay) noun **1** a car with a folding top. **2** a light two-wheeled one-horse carriage with a hood.

**cacao** (kă-**kay**-oh) noun (plural **cacaos**) **1** a tropical tree producing a seed from which cocoa and chocolate are made. **2** its seed.

**cachalot** (kash-ă-lot) noun a sperm whale.

**cache** (*pronounced* kash) noun **1** a hiding-place for treasure or stores; the hidden items. **2** *Computing* an area of memory which improves the speed of a computer system by anticipating what the computer will be requested to do. ● *verb* place in a cache.

**cachet** (kash-ay) noun **1** a distinguishing mark or seal. **2** prestige. **3** a flat capsule enclosing an unpleasant medicine.

**cachou** (kash-oo) noun a lozenge to sweeten the breath.

**cack-handed** *adjective* (*informal*) clumsy.

**cackle** noun **1** the loud clucking noise a hen makes after laying. **2** a loud silly laugh. **3** noisy chatter. ● *verb* **1** give a cackle. **2** chatter noisily.

**cacophony** (kă-**kof**-ŏni) noun a harsh discordant sound. □ **cacophonous** *adjective*

**cactus** noun (plural **cactuses** or **cacti**, *pronounced* **kak**-ty) a plant from a hot dry climate, with a fleshy stem and usually prickles but no leaves.

**CAD** *abbreviation* computer aided design.

**cad** noun (*old use*) a man who behaves dishonourably. □ **caddish** *adjective*

**cadaver** noun a corpse.

**cadaverous** (kă-**dav**-er-ŭs) *adjective* gaunt and pale, like a corpse.

**Cadbury**, George (1839–1922), English cocoa and chocolate manufacturer.

**caddie** (also **caddy**) noun a person who carries a golfer's clubs during a game. ● *verb* (**caddied**, **caddying**) act as caddie.

□ **caddie car**, **caddie cart** a light trolley to carry golf-clubs during a game.

**caddis-fly** *noun* a four-winged insect living near water.

**caddis-worm** *noun* (also **caddis**) the larva of the caddis-fly.

**caddy**[1] *noun* a small container for tea.

**caddy**[2] *see* CADDIE.

**cadence** (**kay**-děns) *noun* **1** rhythm in sound. **2** the rise and fall of the voice in speaking. **3** the end of a musical phrase.

**cadenza** (kǎ-**den**-zǎ) *noun* an elaborate passage for a solo instrument or voice, showing off the performer's skill.

**cadet** (kǎ-**det**) *noun* a young person receiving elementary training for service in the armed forces or the police force.

**cadge** *verb* ask for as a gift; go about begging.

**cadi** *noun* a judge in a Muslim country.

**Cadiz** (kǎ-**diz**) a port in SW Spain.

**cadmium** (**kad**-miŭm) *noun* a chemical element (symbol Cd) that looks like tin.

**cadre** (**kah**-der) *noun* **1** a basic unit, especially of servicemen. **2** a group of political activists.

**caecum** (**see**-kŭm) *noun* (*Amer.* **cecum**) (*plural* **caeca**) a tubular pouch forming the first part of the large intestine.

**Caenozoic** alternative spelling of CENOZOIC.

**Caerphilly** (kair-**fil**-i) *noun* a mild crumbly white cheese, named after the town in Wales where it was originally made.

**Caesar** = JULIUS CAESAR. ● *noun* a title of the Roman emperors.

**Caesarean** (siz-**air**-iǎn) (*Amer.* **Cesarean**, **Cesarian**) *noun* (in full **Caesarean section**) a surgical operation by which a child is taken from the womb by cutting through the wall of the abdomen and into the womb (¶ so called from the story that Julius Caesar was born in this way.)

**caesium** (**see**-zi-ŭm) *noun* (*Amer.* **cesium**) a soft silver-white metallic element (symbol Cs).

**caesura** (siz-**yoor**-ǎ) *noun* a short pause in a line of verse.

**café** (**kaf**-ay) *noun* a small tea shop or restaurant.

**cafeteria** (kaf-i-**teer**-iǎ) *noun* a café where customers serve themselves from a counter.

**cafetière** (ka-fě-**tyair**) *noun* a coffee-pot with a plunger to keep the ground coffee separate from the liquid.

**caffeine** (**kaf**-een) *noun* a stimulant found in tea and coffee.

**caftan** (**kaf**-tǎn) *noun* (also **kaftan**) **1** a long coat-like garment worn by men in the Middle East. **2** a woman's long loose dress.

**Cage**, John (1912–92), American composer, often using experimental techniques.

**cage** *noun* **1** a framework with wires or bars in which birds or animals are kept. **2** any similar structure; the enclosed platform in which people travel in a lift or the shaft of a mine. ● *verb* put or keep in a cage. □ **cagebird** *noun* a bird of a kind usually kept in a cage.

**cagey** *adjective* (**cagier**, **cagiest**) (also **cagy**) (*informal*) cautious about giving information, secretive. □ **cagily** *adverb*, **caginess** *noun*

**Cagney**, James (1904–86), American film actor.

**cagoule** (kǎ-**gool**) *noun* a thin waterproof jacket with a hood.

**cahoots** (kǎ-**hoots**) *plural noun* (*slang*) □ **in cahoots with** in league with.

**caiman** alternative spelling of CAYMAN.

**Cain** the eldest son of Adam, and murderer of his brother Abel. □ **raise Cain** *see* RAISE.

**Caine**, Michael (original name; Maurice Micklewhite) (born 1933), English film actor.

**Cainozoic** (kain-ŏ-**zoh**-ik) = CENOZOIC.

**cairn** *noun* **1** a pyramid of rough stones set up as a landmark or a monument. **2** (in full **cairn terrier**) a small shaggy short-legged terrier.

**cairngorm** *noun* a yellow or wine-coloured semiprecious form of quartz from the Cairngorm mountains in Scotland.

**Cairo** the capital of Egypt.

**caisson** (**kay**-sŏn) *noun* a watertight chamber inside which work can be carried out on underwater structures.

**cajole** (kǎ-**johl**) *verb* coax. □ **cajolery** *noun*

**Cajun** (**kay**-jŭn) *adjective* (of music, food, culture, etc.) in the style of French Louisiana.

**cake** *noun* **1** a baked sweet bread-like food made from a mixture of flour, fats, sugar, eggs, etc. **2** a mixture cooked in a round flat shape; *fish cakes*. **3** a shaped or hardened mass; *a cake of soap*. ● *verb* **1** harden into a compact mass. **2** encrust with a hardened mass. □ **a piece of cake** (*informal*) something easily achieved. **sell** (or **go**) **like hot cakes** (*informal*) sell very quickly.

**calabash** (**kal**-ǎ-bash) *noun* **1** a tropical American tree with fruit in the form of large gourds. **2** this or a similar gourd whose shell serves for holding liquid etc. **3** a bowl or pipe made from a gourd.

**calabrese** (kal-ǎ-**breez**) *noun* a variety of broccoli.

**Calabria** (kǎ-**lab**-riǎ) the SW promontory of Italy.

**calamine** *noun* a pink powder, chiefly zinc carbonate or oxide, used in skin lotions.

**calamity** *noun* a disaster. □ **calamitous** *adjective*

**calcareous** (kal-**kair**-ius) *adjective* of or containing calcium carbonate.

**calceolaria** (kalsi-ŏ-**lair**-iă) *noun* a garden plant with slipper-shaped flowers.

**calces** *see* CALX.

**calciferol** *noun* vitamin D₂, essential for the depositing of calcium in the bones.

**calciferous** *adjective* yielding calcium salts, especially calcium carbonate.

**calcify** (**kal**-si-fy) *verb* (**calcified, calcifying**) harden by a deposit of calcium salts. □ **calcification** *noun*

**calcine** (**kal**-syn) *verb* reduce (a substance) or be reduced to quicklime or powder by heating to a high temperature without melting it. □ **calcination** *noun*

**calcium** *noun* a greyish-white chemical element (symbol Ca), present in bones and teeth and forming the basis of lime. □ **calcium carbonate** a white insoluble solid occurring as chalk, marble, etc.

**calcite** *noun* natural crystalline calcium carbonate.

**calculable** *adjective* able to be calculated.

**calculate** *verb* **1** find out by using mathematics, count. **2** plan deliberately; intend. **3** (*Amer. informal*) suppose, believe. □ **calculation** *noun*

**calculated** *adjective* **1** (of an action) done deliberately or with foreknowledge. **2** intended or designed to have a particular effect; *a speech calculated to cause trouble for the government.*

**calculating** *adjective* (of people) shrewd, scheming.

**calculator** *noun* **1** a device used in making calculations, especially a small electronic one. **2** one who calculates.

**calculus** (**kal**-kew-lŭs) *noun* (*plural* **calculi** or **calculuses**) **1** a branch of mathematics that deals with problems involving rates of variation. **2** a stone formed in the body.

**Calcutta** a port on the east coast of India, capital of West Bengal.

**Calder** (**kawl**-der), Alexander (1898–1976), American sculptor and painter, the originator of mobiles.

**caldron** alternative spelling of CAULDRON.

**Caledonian** (kali-**doh**-niăn) *adjective* of Scotland. ●*noun* (*literary*) a person from Scotland.

**Caledonian Canal** a canal in northern Scotland linking the North Sea with the Atlantic Ocean.

**calendar** *noun* **1** a chart showing the days, weeks, and months of a particular year. **2** a device displaying the date. **3** a list of dates or events of a particular kind; *the Racing Calendar.* **4** the system by which time is divided into fixed periods; *the Gregorian*

*calendar.* □ **calendar year** the period from 1 January to 31 December inclusive.

**calender** *noun* a machine in which cloth or paper is pressed by rollers to glaze or smooth it. ●*verb* press in a calender.

**calends** *plural noun* (also **kalends**) the first day of the month in the ancient Roman calendar.

**calendula** *noun* a plant with orange or yellow flowers; the marigold.

**calf** *noun* (*plural* **calves**) **1** the young of cattle, also of the elephant, whale, and certain other animals. **2** calfskin. **3** the fleshy back part of the leg below the knee. □ **calf-love** *noun* childish romantic love.

**calfskin** *noun* leather made from the skin of a calf.

**calibrate** (**kal**-i-brayt) *verb* **1** mark or correct units of measurement on a gauge. **2** measure the calibre of. □ **calibration** *noun*, **calibrator** *noun*

**calibre** (**kal**-i-ber) *noun* (*Amer.* **caliber**) **1** the diameter of the inside of a tube or gun barrel. **2** the diameter of a bullet or shell. **3** ability, importance; *we need a man of your calibre.*

**calices** *see* CALIX.

**calico** *noun* (*plural* **calicoes** or *Amer.* **calicos**) **1** cotton cloth, especially plain white or unbleached. **2** (*Amer.*) printed cotton fabric. ●*adjective* **1** made of calico. **2** (*Amer.*) multicoloured.

**Calif.** *abbreviation* California.

**California** a state of the USA, on the Pacific coast. □ **Californian poppy** a small cultivated poppy. □ **Californian** *adjective & noun*

**californium** *noun* an artificially made radioactive metallic element (symbol Cf), used in industry and medicine as a source of neutrons.

**Caligula** (kă-**lig**-yoo-lă) the nickname of Gaius, Roman emperor 37–41.

**caliper** alternative spelling of CALLIPER.

**caliph** (**kay**-lif) *noun* the former title of certain Muslim leaders.

**calisthenics** alternative spelling of CALLISTHENICS.

**calix** (**kay**-liks) *noun* (*plural* **calices**, *pronounced* **kay**-li-seez) a cup-like cavity or organ.

**calk** alternative spelling of CAULK.

**call** *noun* **1** a shout or cry. **2** the characteristic cry of a bird. **3** a signal on a bugle etc. **4** a short visit. **5** a summons; an invitation. **6** a demand, a claim; *I have many calls on my time.* **7** a need, occasion; reason; *there's no call for you to worry.* **8** a declaration of trumps etc. in card-games; a player's right or turn to make this. **9** an act of telephoning, a conversation on the telephone. ●*verb* **1** shout or speak loudly. **2** utter a call.

**3** pay a short visit. **4** name; describe or address as; *I call that cheating.* **5** declare (a trump suit etc.) in card-games. **6** rouse deliberately; summon to get up. **7** summon; *call the fire brigade.* **8** command or invite, urge as if by commanding; *call a strike; duty calls.* **9** communicate with by telephone or radio. □ **call a person's bluff** challenge him or her to carry out a threat. **call-box** *noun* a telephone box. **call for** **1** demand, require. **2** come and collect. **call-girl** *noun* a prostitute who accepts appointments by telephone. **call in 1** pay a casual visit. **2** seek advice or help from. **3** order the return of, take out of circulation. **call it a day** stop working. **call off** **1** call away. **2** cancel; *the strike was called off.* **call of nature** a need to go to the lavatory. **call on 1** make a short visit to (a person). **2** appeal to; request. **call out** summon to action; order to come out on strike. **call the tune** (*or* **the shots**) control the proceedings. **call to mind** **1** remember; cause to remember. **call up 1** (*Amer.*) telephone. **2** bring back to one's mind. **3** summon for military service. **call-up** *noun* a summons for military service. **on call** available to be called out on duty. **within call** near enough to be summoned by calling. □ **caller** *noun*

**Callaghan**, (Leonard) James, Baron (born 1912), British Labour statesman, Prime Minister 1976–79.

**Callas**, Maria (real name; Kallageropoulos) (1923–77), operatic coloratura soprano, born in America of Greek parents.

**calligraphy** (kă-**lig**-răfi) *noun* **1** beautiful handwriting; the art of producing this. **2** handwriting. □ **calligrapher** *noun*

**calling** *noun* an occupation, a profession or trade; a vocation.

**calliper** (**kal**-i-per) *noun* (also **caliper**) **1** a metal support for a weak or injured leg. **2** (**callipers**) compasses for measuring the diameter of tubes or of round objects.

**callisthenics** *plural noun* (also **calisthenics**) exercises to develop elegance and grace of movement.

**callosity** (kă-**loss**-iti) *noun* a callus.

**callous** (**kal**-ŏs) *adjective* **1** unsympathetic. **2** (also **calloused**) hardened, having calluses. □ **callously** *adverb*, **callousness** *noun*

**callow** (*rhymes with* shallow) *adjective* immature and inexperienced. □ **callowness** *noun*

**callus** (**kal**-ŭs) *noun* (*plural* **calluses**) an area of thick hardened skin or tissue.

**calm** *adjective* **1** quiet and still, not windy. **2** not excited or agitated. **3** casual and confident. ●*noun* a calm condition or period, lack of strong winds. ●*verb* make or

become calm. □ **calmly** *adverb*, **calmness** *noun*

**calomel** (**kal**-ŏ-mel) *noun* a compound of mercury, used as a laxative.

**Calor gas** (*trade mark*) liquefied butane stored under pressure in containers for domestic use.

**calorie** *noun* **1** a unit for measuring a quantity of heat. **2** a unit for measuring the energy value of food. □ **caloric** *adjective*

**calorific** *adjective* producing heat.

**calorimeter** (kal-ŏ-**rim**-it-er) *noun* an instrument for measuring heat.

**calumniate** (kă-**lum**-ni-ayt) *verb* slander. □ **calumniation** *noun*

**calumny** (**kal**-ŭm-ni) *noun* **1** slander. **2** a slanderous statement.

**Calvary** the place (just outside ancient Jerusalem) where Christ was crucified.

**calve** *verb* give birth to a calf.

**Calvin**, John (1509–64), French Protestant religious reformer, living in Switzerland.

**Calvinism** *noun* the teachings of John Calvin and of his followers. □ **Calvinist** *noun*, **Calvinistic** *adjective*

**calx** *noun* (*plural* **calces**, *pronounced* **kal**-seez) the powdery or crumbling substance left after the burning of a metal or mineral.

**calypso** *noun* (*plural* **calypsos**) a West Indian song with a variable rhythm and topical usually improvised lyrics.

**calyx** (**kay**-liks) *noun* (*plural* **calyxes** *or* **calyces**, *pronounced* **kay**-li-seez) a ring of leaves (sepals) enclosing an unopened flower bud.

**cam** *noun* a projecting part on a wheel or shaft, shaped or mounted so that its circular motion, as it turns, transmits an up-and-down or back-and-forth motion to another part.

**camaraderie** (kamă-**rah**-der-i) *noun* comradeship, friendship.

**Camargue** (ka-**marg**), **the** a region of the Rhône delta in SE France, characterized by numerous shallow salt lagoons and noted for its white horses.

**camber** *noun* a slight arch or upward curve given to a surface, especially of a road. □ **cambered** *adjective*

**Cambodia** (kam-**boh**-diă) a country in SE Asia between Thailand and the south of Vietnam; formerly called Kampuchea. □ **Cambodian** *adjective & noun*

**Cambrian** *adjective* **1** Welsh. **2** *Geol.* of the first period of the Palaeozoic era. ●*noun* this period.

**cambric** *noun* thin linen or cotton cloth.

**Cambridge** a city in Cambridgeshire on the River Cam, seat of a major English university. □ **Cambridge blue** light blue.

**Cambridgeshire** an east midland county of England.

**Cambs.** *abbreviation* Cambridgeshire.

**camcorder** *noun* a combined video camera and sound recorder.

**came** *see* COME.

**camel** *noun* 1 a long-necked animal with either one or two humps on its back, used in desert countries for riding and for carrying goods. 2 a fawn colour. □ **camel-hair** *noun* fine soft hair used in artists' brushes; fabric made of this.

**camellia** (ka-**meel**-iă) *noun* an evergreen shrub from China and Japan with shiny leaves and showy flowers.

**Camelot** (**kam**-i-lot) (in legend) the place where King Arthur held his court.

**Camembert** (**kam**-ĕm-bair) *noun* a soft rich cheese of the kind made in Normandy, France.

**cameo** (**kam**-i-oh) *noun* (*plural* **cameos**) 1 a small piece of hard stone carved with a raised design. 2 something small but well executed, e.g. a short description or a part in a play.

**camera** *noun* an apparatus for taking photographs, moving pictures, or television pictures. □ **in camera** (of the hearing of evidence or lawsuits) in the judge's private room; in private, in secret. **camera obscura** a darkened room or box with a hole through which the image of an external object can be projected to form a picture on the opposite wall.

**cameraman** *noun* (*plural* **cameramen**) a person whose job is to operate a film camera or television camera.

**Cameroon** (kam-er-**oon**) a country on the west coast of Africa. □ **Cameroonian** *adjective & noun*

**camiknickers** *plural noun* a woman's undergarment combining camisole and knickers.

**camisole** (**kam**-i-sohl) *noun* a woman's bodice-like garment or undergarment with shoulder straps.

**camomile** (**kam**-ŏ-myl) *noun* (also **chamomile**) a sweet-smelling plant with daisy-like flowers which are dried for use in medicine as a tonic.

**camouflage** (**kam**-ŏ-flah*zh*) *noun* a method of disguising or concealing objects by colouring or covering them so that they look like part of their surroundings. ● *verb* conceal in this way.

**camp¹** *noun* 1 a place where people live temporarily in tents, huts, or similar shelters; a place where troops are lodged or trained. 2 the occupants. 3 a group of people with the same ideals. ● *verb* 1 sleep in a tent; live in a camp. 2 live temporarily as if in a camp. □ **camp-bed** *noun* a folding portable bed. **camp-follower** *noun* 1 a hanger-on providing services to a military camp etc. 2 a person who is sympathetic to a group without officially being a member. **camp out** sleep in a tent or in the open.

**camp²** *adjective* 1 effeminate; homosexual. 2 exaggerated in style, especially for humorous effect. ● *noun* such a style or manner.

**campaign** *noun* 1 a series of military operations with a set purpose, usually in one area. 2 a similar series of planned activities; *an advertising campaign.* ● *verb* take part in a campaign. □ **campaigner** *noun*

**campanile** (kam-pă-**nee**-li) *noun* a bell-tower, especially a free-standing one in Italy.

**campanology** (kamp-ăn-**ol**-ŏji) *noun* 1 the study of bells (their ringing, founding, etc.). 2 bell-ringing. □ **campanologist** *noun*

**campanula** (kăm-**pan**-yoo-lă) *noun* a plant with bell-shaped usually blue or white flowers.

**Campbell¹** (**kam**-bĕl), Sir Malcolm (1885–1948), English racing-driver and holder of the world land-speed record until 1950, and son Donald Malcolm (1921–67), holder of the world water-speed record.

**Campbell²** (**kam**-bĕl), Roy (1901–57), South African poet.

**Camp David** the retreat in the Appalachian Mountains, Maryland, of the President of the USA.

**camper** *noun* 1 a person who is camping. 2 a large motor vehicle with beds, cooking stove, etc.

**camphor** *noun* a strong-smelling white substance used in medicine and mothballs and in making plastics.

**camphorated** *adjective* containing camphor.

**campion** *noun* a wild plant with pink or white flowers.

**campsite** *noun* a place for camping, especially one equipped for holiday-makers.

**campus** *noun* (*plural* **campuses**) the grounds of a university or college.

**CAMRA** (**kam**-ră) *abbreviation* Campaign for Real Ale.

**camshaft** *noun* a shaft carrying cams.

**Camus** (ka-**moo**), Albert (1913–60), French writer of novels, plays, and essays.

**can¹** *noun* 1 a metal or plastic container for liquids. 2 a sealed tin in which food or drink is preserved. 3 either of these with its contents; the amount it contains. ● *verb* (**canned, canning**) preserve in a sealed can. □ **carry the can** (*slang*) bear the responsibility or blame. **in the can** (*informal*) finished, ready.

**can²** *auxiliary verb* (*past* **could**) expressing ability or knowledge of how to do something (*he can play the violin*), or permission (*you can go*), or desire or liberty to act (*we cannot allow this*).

**■Usage** When expressing permission, *may* is a more formal alternative to *can*.

**Canaan** the land (later known as Palestine) which the Israelites gradually conquered and occupied; the Promised Land.

**Canada** a country in North America. □ **Canada goose** a wild North American goose with a brownish-grey body and white neck and breast. □ **Canadian** *adjective & noun*

**canal** *noun* **1** a channel cut through land for navigation or irrigation. **2** a tubular passage through which food or air passes in a plant or animal body; *the alimentary canal.*

**Canaletto** (kan-ă-let-oh) Giovanni Antonio Canale (1697–1768), Italian painter.

**canalize** (kan-ă-lyz) *verb* (also **canalise**) channel. □ **canalization** *noun*

**canapé** (kan-ăpay) *noun* a small piece of bread or pastry spread with savoury food.

**canard** *noun* a false rumour or story.

**canary** *noun* a small yellow songbird.

**Canary Islands** (also **Canaries**) a group of islands, provinces of Spain, off the NW coast of Africa.

**canasta** (kă-nas-tă) *noun* a card-game played with two packs of cards including the jokers.

**Canberra** (kan-ber-ă) the capital of Australia.

**cancan** *noun* a lively stage dance involving high kicking.

**cancel** *verb* (**cancelled, cancelling**; *Amer.* **canceled, canceling**) **1** say that (something already decided on or arranged) will not be done or take place. **2** order (a thing) to be discontinued. **3** neutralize; *forgot to cancel my indicator.* **4** cross out. **5** mark (a stamp or ticket) in order to prevent further use. □ **cancel out** counterbalance, neutralize (each other). □ **cancellation** *noun*

**cancer** *noun* **1** a tumour, especially a malignant one. **2** a disease in which malignant growths form. **3** something evil that spreads destructively. **4** (**Cancer**) the fourth sign of the zodiac, the Crab. □ **tropic of Cancer** *see* TROPIC. □ **cancerous** *adjective*

**candela** (kan-deel-ă) *noun* a unit for measuring the brightness of a source of light.

**candelabrum** (kandi-lab-rŭm) *noun* (also **candelabra**; *plural* **candelabra**; *Amer.* **candelabrums** *or* **candelabras**) a large branched candlestick or holder for lights.

**candid** *adjective* **1** frank, not hiding one's thoughts. **2** (of a photograph) taken informally, usually without the subject's knowledge. □ **candidly** *adverb*, **candidness** *noun*

**candida** *noun* a fungus causing thrush.

**candidate** *noun* **1** a person who seeks or is nominated for appointment to an office or position. **2** a person taking an examination. □ **candidacy** (kan-did-ă-si) *noun*, **candidature** (kan-did-ă-cher) *noun*

**candied** (kan-did) *adjective* encrusted with sugar, preserved in sugar. □ **candied peel** peel of citrus fruits candied for use in cooking.

**candle** *noun* a stick of wax with a wick through it, giving light when burning. □ **cannot hold a candle to** is very inferior to. **not worth the candle** not justifying the trouble or cost.

**candlelight** *noun* light from candles. □ **candlelit** *adjective*

**Candlemas** *noun* the feast of the Purification of the Virgin Mary, when candles are blessed (2 February).

**candlepower** *noun* a unit of measurement of light, expressed in candelas.

**candlestick** *noun* a holder for one or more candles.

**candlewick** *noun* **1** a fabric with a raised tufted pattern worked in soft cotton yarn. **2** this yarn.

**candour** (kan-der) *noun* (*Amer.* **candor**) frankness; openness.

**candy** *noun* (*Amer.*) sweets; a sweet.

**candyfloss** *noun* a fluffy mass of spun sugar round a stick.

**candystripe** *noun* alternate stripes of white and a colour. □ **candystriped** *adjective*

**candytuft** *noun* a plant growing in tufts with white, pink, or purple flowers.

**cane** *noun* **1** the hollow jointed stem of tall reeds and grasses (e.g. bamboo, sugar cane), the solid stem of slender palms. **2** the material of these used for making furniture etc. **3** a stem or a length of it; a slender rod; a walking stick. **4** a raspberry plant. ●*verb* **1** punish by beating with a cane. **2** weave cane into (a chair etc.). □ **cane sugar** sugar obtained from the juice of sugar cane.

**canine** (kay-nyn) *adjective* of dogs. ●*noun* **1** a dog. **2** (in full **canine tooth**) a strong pointed tooth next to the incisors.

**canister** *noun* **1** a metal box or other container. **2** a cylinder, filled with shot or tear-gas, that bursts and releases its contents when fired from a gun or thrown.

**canker** *noun* **1** a disease that destroys the wood of plants and trees. **2** a disease that causes ulcerous sores in animals. **3** a corrupting influence.

**cannabis** (kan-ă-bis) *noun* **1** a hemp plant. **2** a preparation of this for smoking or chewing as an intoxicant drug.

**canned** *see* CAN¹. ●*adjective* **1** recorded for reproduction; *canned music*. **2** tinned; *canned fruit*. **3** (*slang*) drunk.

**cannelloni** (kan-ĕ-**loh**-ni) *plural noun* rolls of pasta with a savoury filling.

**cannery** *noun* a canning-factory.

**cannibal** *noun* a person who eats human flesh; an animal that eats its own kind. □ **cannibalism** *noun*, **cannibalistic** *adjective*

**cannibalize** *verb* (also **cannibalise**) dismantle (a machine etc.) in order to provide spare parts for others. □ **cannibalization** *noun*

**cannon** *noun* **1** (*plural* **cannon**) an old type of large heavy gun firing solid metal balls. **2** an automatic shell-firing gun used in aircraft. **3** a shot in billiards in which the player's ball hits the two other balls in succession. ●*verb* (**cannoned, cannoning**) **1** collide heavily. **2** make a cannon at billiards. □ **cannon-ball** *noun* a large ball fired from a cannon. **cannon-fodder** *noun* soldiers regarded merely as material to be expended in war.

**cannonade** *noun* continuous heavy gunfire. ●*verb* bombard with a cannonade.

**cannot** = can not.

**canny** *adjective* (**cannier, canniest**) **1** shrewd. **2** (*Scottish & N. England*) good, pleasant; clever, neat. □ **cannily** *adverb*, **canniness** *noun*

**canoe** *noun* a light narrow boat propelled by paddles. ●*verb* (**canoed, canoeing**) paddle or travel in a canoe. □ **canoeist** *noun*

**canon** *noun* **1** a general principle. **2** a set of writings accepted as genuinely by a particular author; sacred writings included in the Bible. **3** a clergyman who is one of a group with duties in a cathedral. **4** the central unchanging part of the Roman Catholic mass. **5** a passage or piece of music in which a theme is taken up by several parts in succession. □ **canon law** Church law.

**cañon** alternative spelling of CANYON.

**canonical** (kă-**non**-ikăl) *adjective* **1** ordered by canon law. **2** included in the canon of Scripture. **3** standard, accepted. ●*plural noun* (**Canonicals**) the canonical dress of clergy. □ **canonically** *adverb*

**canonize** *verb* (also **canonise**) declare officially to be a saint. □ **canonization** *noun*

**canoodle** *verb* (*informal*) kiss and cuddle.

**canopied** *adjective* having a canopy.

**canopy** *noun* **1** a hanging cover forming a shelter above a throne, bed, or person etc. **2** any similar covering. **3** the part of a parachute that spreads in the air.

**cant** *verb* slope, tilt. ●*noun* **1** a tilted or sloping position. **2** insincere talk. **3** jargon.

**can't** (*informal*) = can not.

**Cantab.** *abbreviation* Cantabrigian; of Cambridge University.

**cantabile** (kan-**tah**-bi-lay) *adverb & adjective Music* in smooth flowing style.

**cantaloup** (**kan**-tă-loop) *noun* (also **cantaloupe**) a small round melon with orange-coloured flesh.

**cantankerous** (kan-**tank**-er-ŭs) *adjective* bad-tempered. □ **cantankerously** *adverb*, **cantankerousness** *noun*

**cantata** (kan-**tah**-tă) *noun* a musical composition for singers, like an oratorio but shorter.

**canteen** *noun* **1** a restaurant for the employees of a factory, office, etc. **2** a case or box containing a set of cutlery. **3** a soldier's or camper's water-flask.

**canter** *noun* a slow easy gallop. ●*verb* ride at a canter, gallop gently.

**Canterbury** a city in Kent, seat of the archbishop who is Primate of All England.

**canticle** (**kan**-ti-kŭl) *noun* a song or chant with words taken from the Bible.

**cantilever** (**kan**-ti-lee-ver) *noun* a projecting beam or girder fixed at one end only, supporting a balcony or similar structure. □ **cantilever bridge** a bridge made of cantilevers projecting from piers and connected by girders.

**canto** *noun* (*plural* **cantos**) each of the sections into which a long poem is divided.

**canton** *noun* a division of a country, especially of Switzerland.

**Cantonese** *noun* **1** (*plural* **Cantonese**) a native or inhabitant of the city of Canton in China. **2** a Chinese language spoken in southern China and in Hong Kong. ●*adjective* of Canton or its people or language.

**cantor** *noun* **1** the leader of the singing of a church choir in a religious service. **2** the leader of the prayers of a congregation in a synagogue.

**Canute** alternative spelling of CNUT.

**canvas** *noun* **1** strong coarse cloth used for making tents and sails etc. and by artists for painting on. **2** a piece of canvas for painting on; an oil-painting. □ **under canvas 1** in tents. **2** with sails spread.

**canvass** *verb* **1** visit in order to ask for votes, orders for goods, or opinions. **2** propose (a plan). ●*noun* canvassing. □ **canvasser** *noun*

**canyon** (**kan**-yŏn) *noun* (also **cañon**) a deep gorge, usually with a river flowing through it.

**CAP** *abbreviation* Common Agricultural Policy (of the EC).

**cap** *noun* **1** a soft head-covering without a brim but often with a peak. **2** an academic headdress, a mortar-board. **3** a cap-like cover; a top for a bottle, pen, etc. **4** = PERCUSSION CAP. **5** a dental crown. ●*verb* (**capped**, **capping**) **1** put a cap on; cover the top or end of. **2** award a sports cap to. **3** excel, outdo.

**capability** noun **1** ability, power. **2** an undeveloped or unused faculty or ability.

**capable** adjective **1** competent. **2** (foll. by of) having a certain ability or capacity; quite capable of lying. □ **capably** adverb

**capacious** (kǎ-pay-shŭs) adjective roomy, able to hold much. □ **capaciously** adverb, **capaciousness** noun

**capacitance** noun **1** ability to store an electric charge. **2** the measure of this; the ratio of the change in the electric charge of a body to a corresponding change in its potential (symbol C).

**capacitor** (kǎ-pas-it-er) noun a device storing a charge of electricity.

**capacity** noun **1** the ability to contain or accommodate, the amount that can be contained. **2** ability, capability; working at full capacity. **3** a position or function; signed it in his capacity as chairman. □ **to capacity** fully; the hall was filled to capacity.

**caparison** (kǎ-pa-ri-sǒn) (literary) verb deck out. ●noun **1** a horse's trappings. **2** equipment, finery.

**cape¹** noun **1** a cloak. **2** a very short similarly shaped part of a coat etc., covering the shoulders.

**cape²** noun a coastal promontory. □ **the Cape 1** = CAPE OF GOOD HOPE. **2** = CAPE PROVINCE.

**Cape Horn** the southernmost point of South America, on an island south of Tierra del Fuego, belonging to Chile.

**Cape of Good Hope** a mountainous promontory near the southern extremity of South Africa, south of Cape Town.

**Cape Province** the southern province of the Republic of South Africa.

**caper¹** verb jump or run about playfully. ●noun **1** capering. **2** (slang) an activity, an occupation, an escapade.

**caper²** noun **1** a bramble-like shrub. **2** one of its buds pickled for use as a flavouring.

**capercaillie** (kap-er-**kayl**-i) noun a bird, the largest European grouse.

**Cape Town** one of the two capital cities of South Africa; the legislative capital.

**Cape Verde** (kayp **verd**) a group of islands off the west coast of Africa. □ **Cape Verdean** adjective & noun

**capillarity** noun the rise or depression of a liquid in a narrow tube.

**capillary** (kǎ-**pil**-er-i) noun any of the very fine branching blood vessels that connect veins and arteries. ●adjective of or like a capillary. □ **capillary action** = CAPILLARITY.

**capital** adjective **1** principal, most important. **2** (informal) excellent. **3** involving the death penalty; a capital offence; capital punishment.

**4** very serious; fatal; a capital error. **5** (of letters) of the form and size used to begin a name or a sentence. ●noun **1** the chief town or city of a country. **2** a capital letter. **3** the head or top part of a pillar. **4** wealth or property that is used or invested to produce more wealth; the money with which a business etc. is started. □ **capital gain** profit from the sale of investments or property. **capital goods** goods such as ships, railways, machinery, etc., used in producing consumer goods. **capital levy** a tax on wealth or property as opposed to income. **capital sum** a lump sum of money, especially that payable to an insured person. **capital transfer tax** (hist.) a tax on capital that is transferred from one person to another, e.g. by inheritance (replaced in 1986 by inheritance tax). **make capital out of** use (a situation etc.) to one's own advantage.

**capitalism** (kap-it-ǎl-izm) noun an economic system in which trade and industry are controlled by private owners for profit.

**capitalist** (kap-it-ǎ-list) noun **1** one who has much capital invested, a rich person. **2** a person who favours capitalism. ●adjective of or favouring capitalism. □ **capitalistic** adjective

**capitalize** (kap-it-ǎ-lyz) verb (also **capitalise**) **1** write or print as a capital letter. **2** convert into capital; provide with capital. □ **capitalize on** profit by, use (a thing) to one's advantage. □ **capitalization** noun

**capitation** noun a tax or fee paid per person.

**Capitol 1** the building in Washington DC in which the Congress of the USA meets. **2** the temple of Jupiter in ancient Rome.

**capitulate** verb surrender. □ **capitulation** noun

**capo** (kap-oh) noun (plural **capos**) a device fitted across the strings of a guitar, banjo, etc. to raise their pitch equally.

**capon** (kay-pǒn) noun a domestic cock castrated and fattened for eating.

**Capone** (kǎ-**pohn**), Al (Alphonse) (1889–1947), American gangster who dominated organized crime in Chicago in the 1920s.

**Cappadocia** (kap-ǎ-**doh**-shǎ) the ancient name for the central region of Asia Minor (modern Turkey).

**cappuccino** (kah-poo-**chee**-noh) noun (plural **cappuccinos**) coffee made with frothy steamed milk. (¶ Italian.)

**Capri** (kap-ree or kǎ-**pree**) an island off the west coast of Italy, in the Bay of Naples.

**caprice** (kǎ-**prees**) noun **1** a whim. **2** a piece of music in a lively fanciful style.

**capricious** (kǎ-**prish**-ŭs) adjective **1** guided by caprice, impulsive. **2** changeable; a *capricious breeze.* □ **capriciously** *adverb*, **capriciousness** *noun*

**Capricorn** *noun* the tenth sign of the zodiac, the Goat. □ **tropic of Capricorn** *see* TROPIC. □ **Capricornian** *adjective & noun*

**capsicum** (kap-si-kŭm) *noun* **1** a plant with hollow edible fruits, especially varieties of sweet pepper. **2** the fruits themselves, often red or green, used as a vegetable.

**capsize** *verb* overturn; *a wave capsized the boat; the boat capsized.*

**capstan** (kap-stǎn) *noun* **1** a thick revolving post used to pull in a rope or cable that winds round it as it turns, e.g. for raising a ship's anchor. **2** a revolving spindle on a tape recorder. □ **capstan lathe** a lathe with a revolving tool-holder.

**capsule** *noun* **1** a small soluble case in which a dose of medicine is enclosed for swallowing. **2** a plant's seed-case that splits open when ripe. **3** a detachable compartment of a spacecraft, containing instruments or crew.

**capsulize** *verb* (also **capsulise**) put (information etc.) into a compact form.

**Capt.** *abbreviation* Captain.

**captain** *noun* **1** a person given authority over a group or team. **2** an army officer ranking below a major and above a lieutenant. **3** a naval officer ranking below a rear admiral and above a commander. **4** the person commanding a ship. **5** the pilot of a civil aircraft. ●*verb* act as captain of. □ **captaincy** *noun*

**caption** (kap-shŏn) *noun* **1** a short title or heading. **2** a description or explanation printed with an illustration etc. **3** words shown on a cinema or television screen. ●*verb* provide with a caption.

**captious** (kap-shŭs) *adjective* fond of finding fault or raising objections about trivial matters. □ **captiously** *adverb*, **captiousness** *noun*

**captivate** *verb* fascinate, charm. □ **captivation** *noun*

**captive** *adjective* **1** taken prisoner. **2** kept as a prisoner, unable to escape. ●*noun* a captive person or animal. □ **captive audience** people who cannot get away easily and therefore cannot avoid being addressed.

**captivity** *noun* the state of being held captive.

**captor** *noun* one who captures a person or animal.

**capture** *verb* **1** make a prisoner of. **2** take or obtain by force, trickery, attraction, or skill. **3** portray; record on film etc. **4** put (data) into a form accessible by computer. ●*noun* **1** capturing. **2** a person or thing captured.

**Capuchin** (kap-yoo-chin) *noun* **1** a friar of a branch of the Franciscan order. **2** (capu-

chin) a monkey or pigeon with a hood-like crown.

**capybara** (kap-i-bar-ǎ) *noun* a large South American rodent related to the guinea pig.

**car** *noun* **1** a motor car. **2** a carriage of a specified type; *dining-car.* **3** the passenger compartment of an airship, balloon, cable railway, or lift. □ **car-boot sale** an outdoor sale at which people sell unwanted possessions etc. from the boots of their cars. **car-ferry** *noun* a ferry that can carry cars. **car park** an area for parking cars. **car phone** a radio-telephone for use in a car.

**Caracas** (kǎ-rak-ǎs) the capital of Venezuela.

**carafe** (kǎ-raf) *noun* a glass bottle in which wine or water is served at the table.

**caramel** *noun* **1** burnt sugar used for colouring and flavouring food. **2** a kind of toffee tasting like this.

**caramelize** *verb* (also **caramelise**) turn or be turned into caramel. □ **caramelization** *noun*

**carapace** (ka-rǎ-payss) *noun* the shell on the back of a tortoise or crustacean.

**carat** (ka-rǎt) *noun* **1** a unit of weight for precious stones, 200 milligrams. **2** a measure of the purity of gold, pure gold being 24 carat.

**Caravaggio** (ka-rǎ-vaj-i-oh), Michelangelo Merisi da (1571–1610), Italian painter, noted for his realistic depiction of traditional religious subjects.

**caravan** *noun* **1** a vehicle equipped for living in and usually towed by a car. **2** a company of people (e.g. merchants) travelling together across desert country.

**caravanning** *noun* travelling by caravan, especially on holiday.

**caravanserai** (ka-rǎ-van-ser-i) *noun* (in eastern countries) an inn with a large central courtyard for accommodation of travelling caravans.

**caraway** *noun* a plant with spicy seeds that are used for flavouring cakes etc.

**carbide** (kar-byd) *noun* a compound of carbon, the compound used in making acetylene gas.

**carbine** (kar-byn) *noun* a short light automatic rifle.

**carbohydrate** *noun* **1** an organic compound, such as the sugars and starches, composed of carbon, oxygen, and hydrogen. **2** (**carbohydrates**) starchy foods, considered to be fattening.

**carbolic** *noun* (in full **carbolic acid**) phenol, especially when used as a disinfectant.

**carbon** *noun* **1** a chemical element (symbol C) that is present in all living matter and occurs in its pure form as diamond and graphite. **2** a rod of carbon in an arc lamp. **3** carbon paper; a copy made with this. □ **carbon copy 1** a copy made with carbon paper. **2** an exact copy. **carbon dating** a method of deciding the age of prehistoric objects by measuring the decay of radiocarbon in them. **carbon dioxide** a colourless odourless gas formed by the burning of carbon or breathed out by animals in respiration. **carbon fibre** a thin strong filament of carbon, used as a strengthening material and in protective clothing. **carbon-14** noun a radioisotope used in carbon dating. **carbon monoxide** a very poisonous gas formed when carbon burns incompletely, occurring e.g. in the exhaust of motor engines. **carbon paper** thin paper coated with pigment, placed between sheets of writing paper for making copies of what is written or typed on the top sheet. **carbon tax** a tax on carbon emissions that result from burning fossil fuels because of their damage to the environment. **carbon tetrachloride** a colourless liquid used as a solvent in dry cleaning etc. **carbon-12** noun a stable isotope of carbon, used as a standard in calculating atomic mass.

**carbonaceous** (kar-bŏn-**ay**-shŭs) adjective **1** consisting of or containing carbon. **2** of or like coal or charcoal.

**carbonate** noun a compound that releases carbon dioxide when mixed with acid.

**carbonated** adjective charged with carbon dioxide; (of drinks) made fizzy with this.

**carbonic** adjective of carbon. □ **carbonic acid** a weak acid formed from carbon dioxide and water.

**carboniferous** (kar-bŏn-**if**-er-ŭs) adjective **1** producing coal. **2** (**Carboniferous**) of the geological period in the Palaeozoic era when many coal deposits were created. ● noun (**Carboniferous**) this period.

**carbonize** verb (also **carbonise**) **1** convert (a substance that contains carbon) into carbon alone, e.g. by heating or burning it. **2** coat with carbon. □ **carbonization** noun

**carborundum** (kar-ber-**un**-dŭm) noun a hard compound of carbon and silicon used for polishing and grinding things.

**carboy** (**kar**-boi) noun a large round bottle surrounded by a protecting framework, used for transporting liquids safely.

**carbuncle** noun **1** a severe abscess in the skin. **2** a bright red gem cut in a knob-like shape.

**carburettor** noun (Amer. **carburetor**) an apparatus for mixing fuel and air in an internal-combustion engine.

**carcass** noun (also **carcase**) **1** the dead body of an animal, especially one prepared for cutting up as meat. **2** the bony part of

the body of a bird before or after cooking. **3** a framework; the foundation structure of a tyre. **4** (informal) a person's body. **5** the worthless remains of something.

**carcinogen** (kar-**sin**-ŏ-jin) noun a cancer-producing substance.

**carcinogenic** (kar-sin-ŏ-**jen**-ik) adjective producing cancer.

**carcinoma** (kar-sin-**oh**-mă) noun (plural **carcinomata** or **carcinomas**) a cancerous growth.

**card**[1] noun **1** thick stiff paper or thin cardboard; a small piece of this used e.g. to send messages or greetings, or to record information such as a person's name or the title of a book and used for identification or in a card index. **2** a small flat usually rectangular piece of thin pasteboard, plastic, etc., recording membership or identifying the bearer. **3** a programme of events at a race meeting. **4** a playing card. **5** (informal) an odd or amusing person. **6** (**cards**) card-playing, card-games. **7** (**cards**) (informal) an employee's official documents held by the employer. □ **be on the cards** be likely or probable. **card-carrying member** a registered member of a political party, trade union, etc. **card index** an index in which each item is entered on a separate card. **card-sharp**, **card-sharper** noun a person who makes a living by cheating at card-games. **card vote** a block vote in trade-union meetings. **have a card up one's sleeve** have something held in reserve secretly. **play one's cards right** behave with good judgement. **put one's cards on the table** be frank about one's resources and intentions.

**card**[2] noun a wire brush or toothed instrument for cleaning or combing wool. ● verb clean or comb with this.

**cardamom** (**kar**-dă-mŏm) noun spice from the seed-capsules of a plant of the ginger family.

**cardboard** noun pasteboard or stiff paper, especially for making into boxes. □ **cardboard city** an area where many homeless people sleep using cardboard boxes for shelter.

**cardiac** (**kar**-di-ak) adjective of the heart.

**Cardiff** the capital of Wales.

**cardigan** noun a knitted jacket. (¶ Named after the 7th Earl of Cardigan (died 1868), who led the disastrous Charge of the Light Brigade in the Crimean War.)

**Cardin** (**kar**-dan), Pierre (born 1922), French fashion designer.

**cardinal** adjective **1** chief, most important; the cardinal virtues. **2** deep scarlet. ● noun a member of the Sacred College of the Roman Catholic Church, which elects the pope. □ **cardinal numbers** the whole numbers, 1, 2, 3, etc. **cardinal points** the four main points of the compass, North, South, East, and West.

**cardiogram** noun an electrocardiogram.

**cardiograph** noun a device recording heart movements; an electrocardiograph.

**cardiology** (kar-di-**ol**-ŏji) noun the branch of medicine dealing with diseases and abnormalities of the heart. □ **cardiological** adjective, **cardiologist** noun

**cardiovascular** adjective of the heart and blood vessels.

**cardphone** noun a public telephone operated by a machine-readable card instead of money.

**care** noun **1** serious attention and thought; planned with care. **2** caution to avoid damage or loss; handle with care. **3** protection, charge, supervision; left the child in her sister's care. **4** worry, anxiety; freedom from care. ●verb **1** feel concern or interest. **2** feel affection or liking. **3** feel willing; like; would you care to try one? □ **care for** have in one's care; take care of. **care of** (abbreviation **c/o**) to the address of (someone who will deliver or forward things); write to him care of his bank. **in care** taken into the care of a local authority. **take care** be cautious. **take care of 1** take charge of; see to the safety or well-being of. **2** deal with.

**careen** (kă-**reen**) verb **1** tilt or keel over to one side. **2** swerve about.

**career** noun **1** progress through life, especially in a profession. **2** an occupation, a way of making a living, especially one with opportunities for advancement or promotion. **3** (used as adjective) following a career; working permanently in a profession; a career woman. **4** quick or violent forward movement. ●verb move swiftly or wildly.

**careerist** noun a person who is keen to advance in a career.

**carefree** adjective light-hearted through being free from anxiety or responsibility.

**careful** adjective **1** giving serious attention and thought, painstaking; a careful worker. **2** done with care; careful work. **3** cautious, avoiding damage or loss. □ **carefully** adverb

**careless** adjective **1** not careful. **2** unthinking, insensitive. **3** casual and light-hearted. □ **carelessly** adverb, **carelessness** noun

**carer** noun a person who looks after a sick or disabled person at home.

**caress** (kă-**ress**) noun a loving touch. ●verb touch lovingly.

**caret** (**ka**-rit) noun a mark (^) indicating a proposed insertion in printing or writing.

**caretaker** noun **1** a person employed to look after a house or building. **2** (usually used as adjective) having temporary authority or power; a caretaker government.

**careworn** adjective showing signs of prolonged worry.

**Carey**, George Leonard (born 1935), Archbishop of Canterbury from 1991.

**cargo** noun (plural **cargoes** or **cargos**) goods carried on a ship or aircraft.

**Carib** (**ka**-rib) noun **1** a member of a group of American Indian inhabitants of the Lesser Antilles and parts of the neighbouring South American coast, or their descendants. **2** their language.

**Caribbean** (ka-ri-**bee**-ăn) adjective of the **Caribbean Sea**, a part of the Atlantic off Central America. ●noun the Caribbean Sea.

**caribou** (**ka**-ri-boo) noun (plural **caribou**) a North American reindeer.

**caricature** (**ka**-rik-ă-choor) noun a picture, description, or imitation of a person or thing that exaggerates certain characteristics, especially for comic effect. ●verb make a caricature of.

**caricaturist** noun a person who makes caricatures.

**caries** (**kair**-eez) noun (plural **caries**) decay in bones or teeth; dental caries.

**carillon** (kă-**ril**-yŏn) noun a set of bells sounded either from a keyboard or mechanically.

**carioca** (ka-ri-**oh**-kă) noun a Brazilian dance resembling the samba.

**carjack** verb steal (an occupied car) by threatening the driver with violence. □ **carjacking** noun

**Carlovingian** adjective & noun = CAROLINGIAN.

**Carlyle**, Thomas (1795–1881), Scottish historian and political philosopher.

**Carmelite** (**kar**-měl-lyt) noun a member of an order of friars (also called White Friars) or of a corresponding order of nuns. ●adjective of this order.

**carminative** (**kar**-min-ătiv) adjective curing flatulence. ●noun a carminative drug.

**carmine** (**kar**-min) adjective deep red. ●noun **1** this colour. **2** carmine pigment made from cochineal.

**carnage** (**kar**-nij) noun the killing of many people.

**carnal** (**kar**-năl) adjective of the body or flesh, not spiritual; carnal desires. □ **carnally** adverb

**carnation** noun a cultivated clove-scented pink.

**carnelian** noun = CORNELIAN.

**carnet** (**kar**-nay) noun a permit to drive across a frontier or use a camping-site.

**carnival** noun festivities and public merry-making, usually with a procession.

**carnivore** (**kar**-niv-or) noun a carnivorous animal or plant.

**carnivorous** (kar-**niv**-er-ŭs) adjective feeding on flesh or other animal matter.

**carob** (ka-rŏb) *noun* the horn-shaped edible pod of a Mediterranean evergreen tree, similar in taste to chocolate.

**carol** *noun* a joyful song, especially a Christmas hymn. ●*verb* (**carolled, carolling**; *Amer.* **caroled, caroling**) **1** sing carols. **2** sing joyfully.

**Carolean** (ka-rŏ-lee-ăn) *adjective* (also **Caroline**) of the time of Charles I or Charles II of England.

**Carolina** *see* NORTH CAROLINA, SOUTH CAROLINA.

**Carolingian** *adjective* of the Frankish dynasty founded by Charlemagne. ●*noun* a member of this dynasty.

**carotene** *noun* an orange-coloured pigment found in carrots, tomatoes, etc., a source of vitamin A.

**Carothers** (kă-ru*th*-erz), Wallace Hume (1896–1937), American industrial chemist, who developed the synthetic fibre nylon.

**carotid** (kă-rot-id) *noun* either of the two great arteries (one on either side of the neck) carrying blood to the head. ●*adjective* of these arteries.

**carouse** (kă-rowz, (*rhymes with* cows)) *verb* drink and be merry. ☐ **carousal** *noun*

**carousel** (ka-rŏ-sel) *noun* **1** (*Amer.*) a merry-go-round. **2** a rotating conveyor or delivery system for luggage at an airport etc.

**carp** *noun* (*plural* **carp**) an edible freshwater fish that lives in lakes and ponds. ●*verb* keep finding fault, raise petty objections.

**carpal** (kar-păl) *adjective* of the wrist joint. ●*noun* a wrist-bone.

**Carpathian Mountains** (kar-pay-thi-ăn) (also **Carpathians**) a system of mountains extending south-east from Poland, through Ukraine into Romania.

**carpel** (kar-pĕl) *noun* the pistil of a flower, the part in which the seeds develop.

**carpenter** *noun* a person who makes or repairs wooden objects and structures. ●*verb* do or make by carpenter's work. ☐ **carpentry** *noun*

**carpet** *noun* **1** a thick textile covering for floors. **2** a thick layer underfoot; *a carpet of leaves.* ●*verb* (**carpeted, carpeting**) **1** cover with a carpet. **2** (*informal*) reprimand. ☐ **carpetbag** *noun* a travelling-bag of the kind formerly made of carpet-like material. **carpet-bagger** *noun* **1** a political candidate etc. without local connections. **2** (*hist.*) an adventurer from the northern States after the American Civil War who went into the southern States to profit from their reorganization. **on the carpet** (*informal*) being reprimanded.

**carpeting** *noun* material for carpets.

**carport** *noun* an open-sided shelter for a car.

**carpus** *noun* (*plural* **carpi**) the set of small bones forming the wrist.

**carrageen** *noun* (also **carragheen**) edible red seaweed.

**carrel** *noun* a small reading cubicle in a library.

**Carreras**, José (born 1946), Spanish operatic tenor.

**carriage** *noun* **1** a wheeled vehicle, usually horse-drawn, for carrying passengers. **2** a railway vehicle for passengers. **3** the carrying of goods from place to place; the cost of this. **4** a gun-carriage. **5** a moving part carrying or holding something in a machine; the roller of a typewriter. **6** the posture of the body when walking. ☐ **carriage clock** a small portable clock with a rectangular case and a handle on top.

**carriageway** *noun* the part of the road on which vehicles travel.

**carrier** *noun* **1** a person or thing that carries something. **2** a person or company that transports goods or people. **3** a support for luggage or a seat for a passenger on a bicycle etc. **4** a person or animal that transmits a disease to others without being affected by it. **5** an aircraft-carrier. **6** a carrier bag. ☐ **carrier bag** a paper or plastic bag with handles, for holding shopping etc. **carrier pigeon** a pigeon trained to carry messages. **carrier wave** *Radio* a high-frequency wave that is modulated either in amplitude or frequency to convey a signal.

**carrion** (ka-ri-ŏn) *noun* dead and decaying flesh. ☐ **carrion crow** a black crow that lives on carrion and small animals.

**Carroll**, Lewis (pseudonym of Charles Lutwidge Dodgson) (1832–98), English writer, author of *Alice's Adventures in Wonderland* and *Through the Looking-Glass.*

**carrot** *noun* **1** a plant with a tapering orange-coloured root. **2** this root, used as a vegetable. **3** a means of enticing someone to do something.

**carroty** *adjective* orange-red.

**carry** *verb* (**carried, carrying**) **1** take from one place to another. **2** have on one's person; *he is carrying a gun.* **3** conduct; take; *wires carry electric current.* **4** support the weight of, bear. **5** involve, entail; *the crime carries a life sentence.* **6** extend; *don't carry modesty too far.* **7** reckon in the next column when adding figures. **8** win, capture; approve (a motion); *the motion was carried.* **9** (of a newspaper or broadcast) contain; *all the tabloids carried the story.* **10** hold and move (the body) in a certain way. **11** be transmitted clearly; *sound carries across water.* **12** be the driving force behind or mainstay of; *she carries the department.* ●*noun* **1** carrying. **2** (in golf) the flight of a ball before it pitches. ☐ **carry-cot** *noun* a baby's portable cot. **carry forward** transfer to a new page of accounts in bookkeeping. **carry off 1** cause the death of; *plague carried off most of the village.* **2** win (a prize). **3** deal with (a situation) successfully. **carry on 1** continue; take part in (a conversation); manage or conduct (a business etc.). **2** (*informal*) behave excitedly; complain lengthily. **carry-on** *noun* (*informal*) a fuss; excitement. **carry on with** (*informal*) have an affair with; flirt with. **carry out** put into practice, accomplish. **carry-out** *noun* **1** = TAKE-AWAY. **2** alcohol bought to be drunk somewhere else. **carry over 1** carry forward in bookkeeping. **2** postpone. **get carried away** get very excited.

**carsick** *adjective* made sick or queasy by the motion of a car. □ **carsickness** *noun*

**cart** *noun* **1** a two-wheeled vehicle used for carrying loads, pulled by a horse etc. **2** a light vehicle with a shaft, pushed or drawn by hand. ●*verb* **1** carry in a cart, transport. **2** (*slang*) carry laboriously, lug. □ **put the cart before the horse** put a thing first when it should logically come second.

**carte blanche** (kart **blahnsh**) full power to act as one thinks best. (¶ French, = blank paper.)

**cartel** (kar-**tel**) *noun* a combination of business firms to control production, marketing, etc., and avoid competing with one another.

**Carter**, Jimmy (James Earl) (born 1924), 39th President of the USA 1977–81.

**Cartesian** (kar-**tee**-ziăn) *adjective* of the philosopher Descartes (17th century) or his theories. ●*noun* a follower of Descartes. □ **Cartesian coordinates** a system for locating a point by reference to its distance from axes intersecting at right angles.

**Carthage** an ancient Phoenician city on the north coast of Africa, near Tunis.

**carthorse** *noun* a strong horse fit for heavy work.

**Carthusian** (kar-**thew**-ziăn) *noun* a member of an order of monks founded at La Grande Chartreuse near Grenoble, France. ●*adjective* of this order.

**cartilage** *noun* tough white flexible tissue attached to the bones of animals. □ **cartilaginous** (karti-**laj**-inŭs) *adjective*

**Cartland**, Dame Barbara Hamilton (born 1901), English writer of romantic fiction.

**cartography** (kar-**tog**-răfi) *noun* map-drawing. □ **cartographer** *noun*, **cartographic** (kartŏ-**graf**-ik) *adjective*

**carton** *noun* a cardboard or plastic container.

**cartoon** *noun* **1** an amusing drawing in a newspaper etc., especially as a comment on public matters. **2** a sequence of these telling a comic or serial story. **3** an animated cartoon. **4** a drawing made by an artist as a preliminary sketch for a painting etc. ●*verb* draw cartoons; represent in a cartoon.

**cartoonist** *noun* a person who draws cartoons.

**cartouche** (kar-**toosh**) *noun* **1** a scroll-like ornamentation in architecture etc. **2** an oval emblem of an ancient Egyptian king.

**cartridge** *noun* **1** a tube or case containing explosive for firearms or blasting, with bullet or shot if for a rifle etc. **2** a sealed case holding film, recording-tape, etc., put into apparatus and removed from it as a unit. **3** the detachable head of a pick-up on a record player, holding the stylus. □ **cartridge paper** thick strong paper for drawing.

**cartwheel** *noun* **1** the wheel of a cart. **2** a circular sideways handspring with arms and legs extended.

**Caruso** (kă-**roo**-soh), Enrico (1873–1921), Italian operatic tenor.

**carve** *verb* **1** form or inscribe by cutting solid material. **2** cut (cooked meat) into slices for eating. □ **carve out** make by great effort; *carved out a career for himself.* **carve up** divide into parts or shares.

**carvel-built** *adjective* (of a boat) made with planks joined smoothly and not overlapping.

**carver** *noun* **1** a person who carves. **2** a knife for carving meat. **3** an armchair in a set of dining chairs.

**carvery** *noun* a buffet or restaurant where meat is carved from a joint as required.

**carving** *noun* a carved object or design.

**Cary** (**kair**-i), (Arthur) Joyce (Lunel) (1888–1957), British novelist.

**caryatid** (ka-ri-**at**-id) *noun* (*plural* **caryatides**, *pronounced* ka-ri-**at**-i-deez, *or* **caryatids**) a sculptured female figure used as a supporting pillar.

**Casanova** (kas-ă-**noh**-vă) *noun* a man with a reputation for having many love affairs. (¶ Named after an 18th-century Italian adventurer.)

**casbah** alternative spelling of KASBAH.

**cascade** (kas-**kayd**) *noun* **1** a waterfall. **2** something falling or hanging like this. ●*verb* fall as or like a cascade.

**cascara** (kas-**kar**-ă) *noun* the bark of a North American buckthorn, used as a laxative.

**case**[1] **1** an instance or example of the occurrence of something; an actual state of affairs. **2** a condition of disease or injury; a person suffering from this; *two cases of measles.* **3** something being investigated by police etc.; *a murder case.* **4** a lawsuit. **5** a set of facts or arguments supporting something. **6** *Grammar* the form of a noun or pronoun that shows its relationship to another word, e.g. in *Mary's hat*, *'s* shows the possessive case. □ **case history** a record of the past history of a patient etc. **case-law** noun law as established by cases decided. **in any case** whatever the facts are; whatever may happen. **in case** lest something should happen. **in case of fire** etc., if there should be a fire etc.

**case²** noun **1** a container or protective covering. **2** this with its contents, the amount it contains. **3** a suitcase. ●verb enclose in a case. □ **case-harden** verb **1** harden the surface of (metal). **2** make unfeeling or unsympathetic.

**casein** (**kay**-seen) noun a protein found in milk, the basis of cheese.

**casement** noun a window that opens on hinges at the side, like a door.

**casework** noun social work that involves studying a person's family and background. □ **caseworker** noun

**cash** noun **1** money in coin or notes. **2** immediate payment for goods, as opposed to hire purchase etc. **3** (informal) money, wealth; they're short of cash. ●verb give or get cash for; cashed a cheque. □ **cash and carry** a method of trading (especially wholesale) where goods are paid for in cash and taken away by the buyer; a store where this operates. **cash crop** a crop grown for selling. **cash desk** a counter where payment is made in a shop etc. **cash dispenser** (also **cashpoint**, **cash machine**) a machine for withdrawing money from one's bank or building society account using a cashcard. **cash flow** the movement of money out of and into a business as goods are bought and sold. **cash in on** make a large profit from; turn to one's advantage. **cash on delivery** payment to be made when goods are delivered, not at the time of purchase. **cash register** a machine in a shop etc. for recording the amount of each sale.

**cashable** adjective able to be cashed.

**cashcard** noun a plastic card for withdrawing money from a cash dispenser.

**cashew** (**kash**-oo) noun the small edible kidney-shaped nut of a tropical tree.

**cashier** noun a person employed to receive and pay out money in a bank, shop etc. ●verb dismiss from service, especially with disgrace.

**cashmere** noun **1** a very fine soft wool, especially that from the Kashmir goat. **2** fabric made from this.

**cashpoint** = CASH DISPENSER.

**casing** noun **1** a protective covering or wrapping. **2** the material from which this is made.

**casino** noun (plural **casinos**) a public building or room for gambling and other amusements.

**cask** noun **1** a barrel, especially for alcoholic drinks. **2** its contents.

**casket** noun **1** a small usually ornamental box for holding valuables etc. **2** (Amer.) a coffin.

**Caspian Sea** a landlocked sea to the north of Iran.

**Cassandra** (kă-**san**-dră) noun a person who prophesies disaster. (¶ Named after a prophetess in Greek legend who foretold evil events but was doomed never to be believed.)

**cassata** (kă-**sah**-tă) noun ice cream containing fruit and nuts.

**cassava** (kă-**sah**-vă) noun a tropical plant with starchy roots from which tapioca is obtained.

**casserole** noun **1** a covered dish for cooking food in the oven. **2** food cooked in this. ●verb cook (food) in a casserole.

**cassette** (kă-**set**) noun a small sealed case containing a reel of film or magnetic tape.

**cassia** noun **1** a kind of cinnamon. **2** a plant producing senna leaves.

**Cassiopeia** (kas-i-ŏ-**pay**-ă) a W-shaped northern constellation, named after the mother of Andromeda in Greek mythology.

**cassis** (ka-**sees**) noun blackcurrant-flavoured syrup, often alcoholic as a drink. (¶ French.)

**cassock** noun a long garment worn by certain clergy and members of a church choir.

**cassoulet** (**ka**-soo-lay) noun a stew of meat and beans.

**cassowary** (kas-ŏ-**wer**-i) noun a large flightless Australasian bird.

**cast** verb (**cast**, **casting**) **1** throw, emit; cast a net; cast a shadow. **2** shed. **3** turn or send in a particular direction; cast your eye over this. **4** record or register (one's vote). **5** make (an object) by pouring metal etc. into a mould and letting it harden. **6** calculate; cast a horoscope. **7** select actors for a play etc.; assign a role to. ●noun **1** an act of casting; the throwing of a missile, dice, fishing-line or net, etc. **2** something made by putting soft material into a mould to harden; a plaster cast (see PLASTER). **3** a set of actors cast for parts in a play. **4** the form, type, or quality (of features, the mind, etc.). **5** a tinge of colour. **6** a slight squint. □ **cast about for** search or look for. **cast down** depress, cause dejection in. **cast iron** a hard alloy of iron made by casting in a mould. **cast-iron** adjective **1** made of cast iron. **2** very strong. **cast off 1** release a ship from its moorings. **2** (in knitting) loop stitches off a needle to finish off a piece of knitting. **cast-offs** plural noun clothes that the owner will not wear again.

**cast on** (in knitting) create stitches, looping them on to a needle.

**castanets** (kahst-ă-**nets**) *plural noun* a pair of shell-shaped pieces of wood etc., struck together with the fingers, especially as an accompaniment to a Spanish dance.

**castaway** *noun* a shipwrecked person.

**caste** (*pronounced* kahst) *noun* **1** each of the hereditary Hindu social divisions or classes. **2** any exclusive social class.

**castellated** (kas-**těl**-ayt-id) *adjective* having turrets or battlements like a castle. □ **castellation** *noun*

**caster** alternative spelling of CASTOR.

**castigate** (**kas**-ti-gayt) *verb* punish or criticize severely. □ **castigation** *noun*, **castigator** *noun*

**Castile** (kas-**teel**) the central plateau of the Iberian peninsula, a former Spanish kingdom.

**Castilian** (kas-**til**-iăn) *noun* **1** a native or inhabitant of Castile. **2** the language of Castile; standard literary Spanish. ●*adjective* of Castile or its people or language.

**casting** *noun* a metal object that has been cast in a mould.

**casting vote** a vote that decides the issue when votes on each side are equal.

**castle** *noun* **1** a large fortified building or group of buildings. **2** a chess-piece also called a rook. ●*verb* (in chess) move the king two squares towards a rook and the rook to the square the king has crossed. □ **castles in the air** day-dreams.

**Castor 1** (*Gk. myth.*) the twin brother of **Pollux. 2** a bright star in the constellation Gemini.

**castor** *noun* (also **caster**) **1** a small container for sugar or salt, with a perforated top for sprinkling from. **2** a small swivelled wheel fixed to each leg of a piece of furniture so that it can be moved easily. □ **castor oil** from the seeds of a tropical plant, used as a purgative and as a lubricant. **castor sugar** finely granulated white sugar.

**castrate** (kas-**trayt**) *verb* remove the testicles of; geld. □ **castration** *noun*

**castrato** *noun* (*plural* **castrati**) (*hist.*) a castrated male soprano or alto singer.

**Castries** (kas-**treess**) the capital of St Lucia.

**Castro**, Fidel (born 1927), Cuban statesman, leader of the Communist regime in Cuba since 1959.

**casual** *adjective* **1** happening by chance; *a casual encounter*. **2** made or done without forethought; not serious; not methodical; *a casual remark*; *a casual inspection*. **3** informal, for informal occasions; *casual clothes*. **4** irregular, not permanent; *found some casual work*; *casual labourers*. ●*noun*

(**casuals**) casual clothes; casual shoes. □ **casually** *adverb*, **casualness** *noun*

**casualty** *noun* **1** a person who is killed or injured in a war or accident. **2** a thing lost or destroyed. **3** (in full **casualty department**) the part of a hospital where victims of accidents are treated.

**casuist** *noun* a person who uses clever but false reasoning, especially on moral issues. □ **casuistic** *adjective*, **casuistry** *noun*

**CAT** *abbreviation* **1** computer-assisted testing. **2** computerized axial tomography.

**cat** *noun* **1** a small furry domesticated animal often kept as a pet. **2** a wild animal related to this, e.g. lion, tiger. **3** (*informal*) a spiteful or malicious woman. **4** the cat-o'-nine-tails. □ **cat-and-dog life** a life with perpetual quarrels. **cat burglar** a burglar who enters by climbing to an upper floor. **cat-o'-nine-tails** *noun* a whip with nine knotted lashes, formerly used for flogging people. **cat's-cradle** *noun* a game with string forming looped patterns between the fingers. **cat's-paw** *noun* a person who is used by another to do something risky. (¶ From the fable of the monkey who used the paw of his friend the cat to rake hot chestnuts out of the fire.) **let the cat out of the bag** give away a secret. **put the cat among the pigeons** cause trouble. **the cat's whiskers** (*informal*) an excellent person or thing.

**catabolism** (kă-**tab**-ŏ-lizm) *noun* destructive metabolism, the breaking down of complex substances in the body. □ **catabolic** (kat-ă-**bol**-ik) *adjective*

**catachresis** (kat-ă-**kree**-sis) *noun* incorrect use of words. □ **catachrestic** *adjective*

**cataclysm** (**kat**-ă-klizm) *noun* a violent upheaval or disaster. □ **cataclysmic** (kată-**kliz**-mik) *adjective*

**catacombs** (**kat**-ă-koomz) *plural noun* a series of underground galleries with side recesses for tombs.

**catafalque** (**kat**-ă-falk) *noun* a decorated platform on which the coffin of a distinguished person stands during the funeral or lying in state, or on which it is drawn in procession.

**Catalan** *adjective* of Catalonia or its people or language. ●*noun* **1** a native or inhabitant of Catalonia. **2** a language (closely related to Provençal) used in Catalonia, Andorra, the Balearic Islands, and some parts of southern France.

**catalepsy** (**kat**-ă-lepsi) *noun* a condition in which a person becomes rigid and unconscious. □ **cataleptic** (kată-**lep**-tik) *adjective*

**catalogue** *noun* (*Amer.* **catalog**) a list of items, usually in systematic order and with a description of each. ●*verb* (**catalogued**,

**cataloguing**) list in a catalogue. □ **cataloguer** noun

**Catalonia** a district of NE Spain.

**catalyse** (**kat-ă-lyz**) verb (Amer. **catalyze**) accelerate or produce by catalysis.

**catalysis** (**kă-tal-i-sis**) noun (plural **catalyses**) the action of a catalyst.

**catalyst** (**kat-ă-list**) noun 1 a substance that aids or speeds up a chemical reaction while remaining unchanged itself. 2 a person or thing that precipitates a change.

**catalytic** adjective of or involving catalysis. □ **catalytic converter** part of an exhaust system that converts pollutant gases into harmless products.

**catamaran** (**kat-ă-mă-ran**) noun 1 a boat with parallel twin hulls. 2 a raft of yoked logs or boats.

**catapult** noun 1 a device with elastic for shooting small stones. 2 a device for launching a glider, or an aircraft from the deck of a carrier. ●verb 1 hurl from a catapult; fling forcibly. 2 rush violently.

**cataract** noun 1 a large waterfall; a rush of water. 2 a condition in which the lens of the eye becomes cloudy and obscures sight; this opaque area.

**catarrh** (**kă-tar**) noun inflammation of mucous membrane, especially of the nose and throat, accompanied by a watery discharge. □ **catarrhal** adjective

**catastrophe** (**kă-tas-trŏfi**) noun a sudden great disaster. □ **catastrophic** (**kată-strof-ik**) adjective, **catastrophically** adverb

**catatonia** noun 1 schizophrenia with intervals of catalepsy and sometimes violence. 2 catalepsy. □ **catatonic** adjective

**catcall** noun a shrill whistle of disapproval.

**catch** verb (**caught, catching**) 1 capture in a net or snare or after a chase. 2 overtake. 3 grasp and hold (something moving). 4 come unexpectedly upon; take by surprise; detect; trap into a mistake or contradiction etc. 5 be in time for and get on (a train etc.). 6 (informal) hear (a broadcast); watch (a film). 7 get briefly; caught a glimpse of it. 8 become or cause to become fixed or prevented from moving. 9 hit; the blow caught him on the nose. 10 begin to burn. 11 become infected with; caught a cold. ●noun 1 the act of catching. 2 something caught or worth catching; he's a good catch. 3 a concealed difficulty or disadvantage. 4 a device for fastening something. 5 a round for singing by three or more voices. □ **catch-all** noun a thing for including many items. **catch-as-catch-can** noun wrestling in which few holds are barred. **catch it** (informal) be scolded or punished. **catch on** (informal) 1 become popular. 2 understand what is meant. **catch out** detect in a mistake. **catch-**

**phrase** noun a phrase in frequent current use, a catchword or slogan. **catch up** 1 reach (someone ahead). 2 do or complete arrears of work.

**catcher** noun 1 one who catches. 2 a baseball fielder who stands behind the batter.

**catching** adjective infectious.

**catchline** noun a short line of type, especially as a heading.

**catchment area** 1 an area from which rainfall drains into a river or reservoir. 2 an area from which a hospital draws its patients or a school its pupils.

**catchpenny** adjective intended to sell quickly.

**catch-22** noun (informal) a dilemma where the victim is bound to suffer, no matter which course of action is chosen. (¶ From the title of a comic novel by J. Heller (1961), set in the Second World War, in which the hero wishes to avoid flying any more missions and decides to go crazy, only to be told that anyone who wants to get out of combat duty is not really crazy.)

**catchweight** adjective & noun (in sports) accepting a contestant at the weight he or she happens to be, not at one fixed for that sport.

**catchword** noun a memorable word or phrase that is often used, a slogan.

**catchy** adjective (informal) (**catchier, catchiest**) pleasant and easy to remember; a catchy tune.

**catechism** (**kat-i-kizm**) noun 1 a summary of the principles of a religion in the form of questions and answers. 2 a series of questions.

**catechize** (**kat-i-kyz**) verb (also **catechise**) put a series of questions to (a person). □ **catechist** noun

**catechumen** (**kat-i-kew-min**) noun a convert to Christianity who is being instructed before baptism.

**categorical** (**kat-ig-o-ri-kăl**) adjective absolute, unconditional; a categorical refusal. □ **categorically** adverb

**categorize** (**kat-ig-eryz**) verb (also **categorise**) place in a particular category. □ **categorization** noun

**category** (**kat-ig-eri**) noun a class of things.

**cater** (**kay-ter**) verb provide what is needed or wanted, especially food or entertainment; cater for 50 people. □ **cater to** pander to (people's bad inclinations).

**caterer** noun one whose trade is to supply food for social events.

**caterpillar** noun 1 the larva of a butterfly or moth. 2 (**Caterpillar**, in full **Caterpillar track** or **tread**) (trade mark) a steel band passing round two wheels of a tractor or tank, enabling it to travel over very rough ground.

**caterwaul** verb make a cat's howling cry.

**catfish** noun a large usually freshwater fish with whisker-like feelers round the mouth.

**catgut** noun a fine strong cord made from the dried intestines of animals, used for the strings of musical instruments and for sewing up surgical incisions.

**catharsis** (kă-**thar**-sis) noun relief of strong feelings or tension, e.g. by giving vent to them in drama or art etc.

**cathartic** adjective **1** producing or causing catharsis. **2** laxative. ●noun a laxative.

**Cathay** (kă-**thay**) (poetic) the name by which China was known in medieval Europe.

**cathedral** noun the principal church of a diocese.

**Cather,** Willa Sibert (1876–1974), American novelist.

**Catherine II** 'the Great' (1729–96), Russian empress, reigned 1762–96.

**Catherine de Medici** (med-i-chi or med-ee-chi) (1519–89), Queen of France, who instigated the massacre of the Huguenots in 1572.

**Catherine of Aragon** (1485–1536), Spanish princess, first wife of Henry VIII and mother of Mary I.

**Catherine wheel** a rotating firework. (¶ Named after a saint who was tortured on a spiked wheel.)

**catheter** (**kath**-it-er) noun a tube inserted into a body cavity to drain fluid, especially into the bladder to extract urine.

**cathode** (**kath**-ohd) noun the electrode by which current leaves a device. □ **cathode-ray tube** a vacuum tube in which beams of electrons are directed against a fluorescent screen where they produce a luminous image, e.g. the picture tube of a television set.

**Catholic** adjective **1** of all Churches or Christians. **2** Roman Catholic. **3** (**catholic**) universal, including many or most things; his tastes are catholic. ●noun a Roman Catholic. □ **Catholicism** (kă-**thol**-i-sizm) noun, **catholicity** (kath-ŏ-**liss**-iti) noun

**cation** (**kat**-I-ŏn) noun an ion with a positive charge. □ **cationic** (kat-I-**on**-ik) adjective

**catkin** noun a spike of small soft flowers hanging from trees such as willow and hazel.

**catmint** noun a plant with a strong smell that is attractive to cats.

**catnap** noun a short nap. ●verb (**catnapped, catnapping**) have a catnap.

**catnip** noun catmint.

**Cat's-eye** noun (trade mark) each of a line of reflector studs marking the centre or edge of a road.

**catsuit** noun a one-piece garment covering the whole body, with sleeves and trouser legs.

**catsup** (Amer.) = KETCHUP.

**cattery** noun a place where cats are bred or boarded.

**cattle** plural noun large ruminant animals with horns and cloven hoofs, bred for their milk or meat. □ **cattle-cake** noun concentrated food for cattle, in cake form. **cattle-grid** noun a grid covering a ditch so that vehicles can pass but not cattle or sheep etc.

**catty** adjective (**cattier, cattiest**) spiteful, speaking spitefully. □ **cattily** adverb, **cattiness** noun

**Catullus** (kă-**tul**-ŭs), Gaius Valerius (c.84–c.54 BC), Roman poet.

**catwalk** noun a raised narrow pathway.

**Caucasian** (kaw-**kay**-ziăn) adjective **1** of the Caucasus. **2** of the White or light-skinned race. ●noun a Caucasian person.

**Caucasoid** (**kaw**-kă-soid) adjective of the Caucasian race.

**Caucasus** (**kaw**-kă-sŭs) a mountain range following the boundary between Georgia and Russia, between the Black Sea and the Caspian Sea.

**caucus** (**kaw**-kŭs) noun **1** (often scornful) a small group in a local branch of a political party, making plans, decisions, etc. **2** (Amer.) a meeting of party leaders to decide policy etc. **3** (Austral.) the parliamentary members of a political party who decide policy etc.; a meeting of these.

**caudal** (**kaw**-dăl) adjective of or at the tail.

**caudate** adjective having a tail.

**caught** see CATCH.

**caul** (pronounced kawl) noun **1** a membrane enclosing a foetus in the womb. **2** part of this found on a child's head at birth.

**cauldron** noun (also **caldron**) a large deep pot for boiling things in.

**cauliflower** noun a cabbage with a large white flower-head. □ **cauliflower ear** an ear thickened by repeated blows, e.g. in boxing.

**caulk** (pronounced kawk) verb (also **calk**) make (a boat) watertight by filling seams or joints with waterproof material, or by driving edges of plating together.

**causal** adjective **1** of or forming a cause. **2** relating to cause and effect. □ **causally** adverb

**causality** (kaw-**zal**-iti) noun the relationship between cause and effect.

**causation** noun **1** the act of causing. **2** causality.

**causative** (**kaw**-ză-tiv) adjective acting as or expressing a cause.

**cause** noun **1** a person or thing that makes something happen or produces an effect. **2** a reason; there is no cause for anxiety. **3** a purpose or aim for which efforts are made; a movement or charity; *a good cause.* **4** a lawsuit; a case. ●*verb* be the cause of, produce, make happen.

**cause célèbre** (kohz say-**lebr**) (*plural* **causes célèbres**, *pronounced* same) a lawsuit or other issue that rouses great interest. (¶ French.)

**causeway** *noun* a raised road across low or wet ground.

**caustic** *adjective* **1** able to burn or corrode things by chemical action. **2** sarcastic. ●*noun* a caustic substance. □ **caustic soda** sodium hydroxide. □ **caustically** *adverb*, **causticity** (kaws-**tiss**-iti) *noun*

**cauterize** *verb* (also **cauterise**) burn the surface of (living tissue) with a caustic substance or a hot iron in order to destroy infection or stop bleeding. □ **cauterization** *noun*

**caution** *noun* **1** avoidance of rashness, attention to safety. **2** a warning against danger etc. **3** a warning and reprimand; *let him off with a caution.* **4** (*informal*) an amusing person or thing. ●*verb* **1** warn. **2** warn and reprimand.

**cautionary** *adjective* conveying a warning; *a cautionary tale.*

**cautious** *adjective* having or showing caution. □ **cautiously** *adverb*, **cautiousness** *noun*

**cavalcade** (kav-ăl-**kayd**) *noun* a procession, especially of people on horseback or in cars.

**cavalier** *noun* **1** (**Cavalier**) a supporter of Charles I in the English Civil War. **2** a courtly gentleman. ●*adjective* arrogant, offhand; *a cavalier attitude.*

**cavalry** *noun* troops who fight on horseback or in armoured vehicles.

**cave** *noun* a natural hollow in the side of a hill or cliff, or underground. □ **cave in** **1** fall inwards, collapse. **2** cause to do this. **3** withdraw one's opposition; give up.

**caveat** (**kav**-i-at) *noun* a warning. (¶ Latin, = let him beware.)

**caveat emptor** the principle that the buyer alone is responsible if dissatisfied.

**Cavell** (kă-**vel**), Edith (1865–1915), English nurse, executed by the Germans as a spy.

**caveman** *noun* (*plural* **cavemen**) **1** a person of prehistoric times living in caves. **2** a man with a rough primitive manner.

**Cavendish**, Henry (1731–1810), English scientist.

**cavern** *noun* a large cave.

**cavernous** *adjective* like a cavern; large and dark or hollow.

**caviare** (kav-i-**ar**) *noun* (*Amer.* **caviar**) the pickled roe of sturgeon or other large fish.

**cavil** *verb* (**cavilled**, **cavilling**; *Amer.* **caviled**, **caviling**) raise petty objections. ●*noun* a petty objection.

**caving** *noun* the sport of exploring caves.

**cavity** *noun* **1** a hollow within a solid body. **2** a decayed part of a tooth. □ **cavity wall** a double wall with a space between.

**cavort** (kă-**vort**) *verb* caper about excitedly.

**caw** *noun* the harsh cry of a rook, raven, or crow. ●*verb* make this sound.

**Caxton**, William (*c.*1422–91), the first English printer.

**Cayenne** the capital of French Guiana.

**cayenne pepper** (kay-**en**) a hot red powdered pepper.

**cayman** *noun* (*plural* **caymans**) (also **caiman**) a reptile similar to an alligator, found in South America.

**Cayman Islands** (also **Caymans**) three islands in the Caribbean Sea, a British dependency.

**CB** *abbreviation* citizens' band.

**CBE** *abbreviation* Commander of the Order of the British Empire.

**CBI** *abbreviation* Confederation of British Industry.

**cc** *abbreviation* (also **c.c.**) **1** carbon copy or copies. **2** cubic centimetre(s).

**CD** *abbreviation* compact disc. □ **CD-ROM** *noun* a compact disc storing data for use as a read-only memory (for display on a computer screen).

**Cd** *symbol* cadmium.

**cd** *abbreviation* candela.

**CDT** *abbreviation* craft, design, and technology.

**Ce** *symbol* cerium.

**cease** *verb* come or bring to an end, stop. ●*noun* ceasing. □ **cease-fire** *noun* a signal to stop firing guns in war, a truce.

**ceaseless** *adjective* not ceasing, going on continually. □ **ceaselessly** *adverb*

**Ceauçescu** (chow-**shess**-koo), Nicolae (1918–89), Romanian statesman, first president of the republic of Romania 1974–89.

**Cecilia** (si-**see**-liă), St (2nd or 3rd century), a martyr in the early Roman Church, patron saint of church music. Feast day, 22 November.

**cecum** *Amer.* spelling of CAECUM.

**cedar** (**see**-der) *noun* **1** an evergreen tree with hard sweet-smelling wood. **2** its wood.

**cede** (*pronounced* seed) *verb* give up one's rights to or possession of; *they were compelled to cede certain territories.*

**cedilla** (si-**dil**-ă) *noun* a mark written under *c* in certain languages to show that it is pronounced as *s* (as in *façade*).

**Ceefax** *noun* (*trade mark*) a teletext service produced by the BBC.

**ceilidh** (**kay**-li) *noun* (*Scottish & Irish*) an informal gathering for traditional music and dancing etc.

**ceiling** *noun* **1** the under-surface of the top of a room. **2** the maximum altitude at which a particular aircraft can fly. **3** an upper limit or level; *wage ceilings*.

**celandine** (**sel**-ăn-dyn) *noun* a small wild plant with yellow flowers.

**Celebes** (se-**lee**-biz) the former name of Sulawesi.

**celebrant** *noun* an officiating priest, especially at the Eucharist.

**celebrate** *verb* **1** mark (a special day or event) in some way, especially with festivities; make merry on such an occasion. **2** officiate at (a religious ceremony). **3** praise publicly. □ **celebration** *noun*, **celebratory** (sel-e-**bray**-tŏ-ri) *adjective*

**celebrated** *adjective* famous.

**celebrity** (si-**leb**-riti) *noun* **1** a well-known person. **2** fame, being famous.

**celeriac** (si-**le**-ri-ak) *noun* a kind of celery with an edible turnip-like root.

**celerity** (si-**le**-riti) *noun* (*literary*) swiftness.

**celery** *noun* a garden plant with crisp juicy stems used in salads or as a vegetable.

**celesta** (si-**lest**-ă) *noun* a small keyboard instrument with hammers striking metal plates to produce a bell-like sound.

**celestial** *adjective* **1** of the sky. **2** of heaven, divine. □ **celestial equator** the circle of the sky in the plane perpendicular to the earth's axis.

**celiac** Amer. spelling of COELIAC.

**celibate** (**sel**-ib-ăt) *adjective* remaining unmarried or abstaining from sexual relations, especially for religious reasons. ●*noun* a celibate person. □ **celibacy** (**sel**-ib-ăsi) *noun*

**cell** *noun* **1** a very small room, e.g. for a monk in a monastery or for confining a prisoner. **2** a compartment in a honeycomb. **3** a device for producing electric current by chemical action. **4** a microscopic unit of living matter. **5** a small group of people forming a centre or nucleus of political activities.

**cellar** *noun* **1** an underground room used for storing things. **2** a room in which wine is stored, a stock of wine.

**Cellini** (chel-**ee**-ni), Benvenuto (1500–71), Italian Renaissance goldsmith, metalworker, and sculptor.

**cellist** (**chel**-ist) *noun* a person who plays the cello.

**cello** (**chel**-oh) *noun* (*plural* **cellos**) an instrument like a large violin, played held upright between the knees of the seated player.

**Cellophane** (**sel**-ŏ-fayn) *noun* (*trade mark*) thin moisture-proof transparent material used for wrapping things.

**cellphone** *noun* a small portable telephone having access to a cellular radio system.

**cellular** (**sel**-yoo-ler) *adjective* **1** of cells, composed of cells. **2** woven with an open mesh; *cellular blankets*. □ **cellular radio** or **telephone** a system of mobile telephone transmission with an area divided into cells, each served by a small transmitter.

**cellule** *noun* a small cell or cavity.

**cellulite** (**sel**-yoo-lyt) *noun* a lumpy form of fat, especially on the hips and thighs of women, producing puckering of the skin.

**celluloid** (**sel**-yoo-loid) *noun* **1** a plastic made from cellulose nitrate and camphor. **2** cinema film.

**cellulose** (**sel**-yoo-lohz) *noun* **1** an organic substance found in all plant tissues and in textile fibres derived from these; this used in making plastics. **2** paint or lacquer made from this.

**Celsius** (**sel**-si-ŭs) *adjective* of a scale of temperature on which water freezes at 0° and boils at 100°. (¶ Named after A. Celsius, Swedish astronomer (1701–44), who devised the scale.)

---

■**Usage** See note at CENTIGRADE.

---

**Celt** (*pronounced* kelt) *noun* a member of an ancient European people who settled in Britain before the coming of the Romans, or their descendants especially in Ireland, Wales, Cornwall, and Scotland.

**Celtic** (**kelt**-ik) *adjective* of the Celts. ●*noun* a group of languages spoken by these, now with two main divisions, (i) Irish, Scots Gaelic, and Manx, (ii) Welsh, Cornish, and Breton. □ **Celtic Sea** the sea between South Ireland and Cornwall.

**cement** *noun* **1** a grey powder, made by burning lime and clay, that sets to a stonelike mass when mixed with water and is used for building. **2** any similar soft substance that sets firm. ●*verb* **1** put cement on or in, join with cement. **2** unite firmly.

**cemetery** *noun* a burial ground other than a churchyard.

**cenobite** Amer. spelling of COENOBITE.

**cenotaph** (**sen**-ŏ-tahf) *noun* **1** a tomb-like monument to a person buried elsewhere. **2** (**the Cenotaph**) a monument in Whitehall, London, commemorating the dead of both World Wars.

**Cenozoic** (see-nŏ-**zoh**-ik) *adjective* (also **Caenozoic, Cainozoic**) of the third and most recent geological era, lasting from about 65 million years ago to the present day. ●*noun* this era.

**censer** (sen-ser) *noun* a container in which incense is burnt, swung on chains in a religious ceremony to disperse its fragrance.

**censor** (sen-ser) *noun* a person authorized to examine letters, books, films, etc. and remove or ban anything regarded as harmful. ● *verb* subject to such examination or removal. □ **censorship** *noun*

**censorious** (sen-sor-iŭs) *adjective* severely critical. □ **censoriously** *adverb*

**censure** (sen-sher) *noun* strong criticism or condemnation. ● *verb* blame or rebuke.

■**Usage** Do not confuse with CENSOR.

**census** (sen-sŭs) *noun* an official count of the population or of things (e.g. traffic).

**cent** *noun* **1** one 100th of a dollar or of certain other metric units of currency; a coin of this value. **2** (*informal*) a very small amount of money; *I haven't a cent.*

**centaur** (sen-tor) *noun* **1** a creature in Greek mythology with the upper half of a man and the lower half of a horse. **2** (**the Centaur**) the southern constellation Centaurus.

**centenarian** (sen-tin-air-iăn) *noun* a person who is 100 years old or more.

**centenary** (sen-teen-eri) *noun* a 100th anniversary.

**centennial** (sen-ten-iăl) *adjective* of a centenary. ● *noun* (*Amer.*) a centenary.

**center** Amer. spelling of CENTRE.

**centerboard** Amer. spelling of CENTRE-BOARD.

**centerfold** Amer. spelling of CENTREFOLD.

**centesimal** (sen-tes-imăl) *adjective* reckoning or reckoned by hundreds.

**centi-** (sent-i) *combining form* one 100th; a hundred.

**centigrade** (sent-i-grayd) *adjective* **1** = CELSIUS. **2** of or using a scale divided into 100 degrees.

■**Usage** In sense 1, *Celsius* is preferred in technical contexts.

**centigram** *noun* (also **centigramme**) one 100th of a gram.

**centilitre** *noun* (*Amer.* **centiliter**) one 100th of a litre.

**centime** (sahn-teem) *noun* one 100th of a franc; a coin of this value.

**centimetre** *noun* (*Amer.* **centimeter**) one 100th of a metre, about 0.4 inch.

**centipede** *noun* a small crawling creature with a long thin segmented body and many legs, one pair on each segment.

**Central** a local government region of Scotland.

**central** *adjective* **1** of or at or forming the centre. **2** chief, most important; *the central character in this novel.* □ **central bank** a national (not commercial) bank, issuing currency. **central heating** a system of heating a building from one source by circulating hot water, air, or steam in pipes. **central nervous system** the brain and spinal cord. **central processor** (also **central processing unit**) the part of a computer that controls and coordinates the activities of other units and performs the actions specified in the program. □ **centrally** *adverb*, **centrality** (sen-tral-iti) *noun*

**Central African Republic** a country in central Africa.

**Central America** the narrow southern part of North America, south of Mexico.

**Central Intelligence Agency** a federal agency of the USA responsible for coordinating government intelligence activities (*abbreviation* **CIA**).

**centralism** *noun* a centralizing policy, especially in administration. □ **centralist** *noun*

**centralize** *verb* (also **centralise**) bring under the control of one central authority. □ **centralization** *noun*

**centre** *noun* (*Amer.* **center**) **1** the middle point or part. **2** a point towards which interest is directed or from which administration etc. is organized. **3** a place where certain activities or facilities are concentrated; *a shopping centre.* **4** a political party or group holding moderate opinions between two extremes. **5** a centre forward. ● *adjective* of or at the centre. ● *verb* (**centred**, **centring**) **1** place in or at the centre. **2** concentrate or be concentrated at one point; *the debate centred on the new proposals.* **3** kick or hit from the wing towards the middle of the pitch in football or hockey. □ **centre back** *Sport* the middle player or position in a half-back line. **centre forward** the player in the middle of the forward line in football or hockey; this position. **centre half** = CENTRE BACK. **centre of gravity** (also **centre of mass**) the central point in an object about which its mass is evenly balanced. **centre-piece** *noun* an ornament for the middle of a table etc.; a central item. **centre spread** two facing middle pages of a magazine, newspaper, etc.

**centreboard** *noun* (*Amer.* **centerboard**) a retractable keel in a sailing boat or sailboard.

**centrefold** *noun* (*Amer.* **centerfold**) a centre spread of a magazine, newspaper, etc., especially with nude photographs.

**centric** *adjective* (also **centrical**) **1** at or near the centre. **2** from a centre.

**centricity** (sen-tris-iti) *noun* being central or a centre.

**centrifugal** (sen-tri-few-găl) *adjective* moving away from the centre or axis. □ **centrifugal force** a force that appears to cause a body that is travelling round a centre to fly outwards and off its circular path. □ **centrifugally** adverb

**centrifuge** (**sen**-tri-fewj) noun a machine using centrifugal force to separate substances, e.g. milk and cream.

**centripetal** (sen-**trip**-it'l or sen-tri-**pee**-tăl) adjective moving towards the centre or axis. □ **centripetal force** a force acting on a body causing it to move towards a centre.

**centrist** noun a person who adopts a central position in politics etc. □ **centrism** noun

**centurion** (sen-**tewr**-iŏn) noun an officer in the ancient Roman army, originally one commanding 100 infantrymen.

**century** noun 1 a period of 100 years; one of these periods reckoned from the birth of Christ. 2 100 runs made by a batsman in one innings at cricket.

**cephalic** (si-**fal**-ik) adjective of or in the head.

**cephalopod** (**sef**-ăl-ŏ-pod) noun a mollusc (such as the octopus) which has a distinct head with a ring of tentacles round the mouth.

**ceramic** (si-**ram**-ik) adjective of pottery or similar substances. ●noun 1 a ceramic substance. 2 (**ceramics**) the art of making pottery.

**Cerberus** (**ser**-ber-ŭs) (Gk. myth.) the monstrous three-headed watchdog guarding the entrance to Hades.

**cereal** noun 1 a grass, such as wheat, rye, oats, or rice, producing an edible grain. 2 its seed. 3 a breakfast food made from such grain.

**cerebellum** (se-ri-**bel**-ŭm) noun (plural **cerebellums** or **cerebella**) a small part of the brain, located in the back of the skull.

**cerebral** (**se**-ri-brăl) adjective 1 of the brain. 2 intellectual. □ **cerebral palsy** paralysis resulting from brain damage before or at birth, involving muscle spasms and involuntary movements.

**cerebration** (se-ri-**bray**-shŏn) noun activity of the brain, thought.

**cerebrospinal** (se-ri-broh-**spy**-năl) adjective of the brain and spinal cord.

**cerebrum** (**se**-ri-brŭm) noun (plural **cerebra**) the principal part of the brain, located in the front of the skull.

**ceremonial** adjective of a ceremony; used in ceremonies; formal. ●noun 1 ceremony. 2 a system of rules for ceremonies. □ **ceremonially** adverb

**ceremonious** adjective full of ceremony, elaborately performed. □ **ceremoniously** adverb

**ceremony** noun 1 a set of formal acts, especially those used on religious or public occasions. 2 formal politeness.

**Ceres** (**seer**-eez) 1 (Rom. myth.) a corn-goddess. 2 the largest of the asteroids.

**cerise** (sĕr-**eez**) adjective & noun light clear red.

**cerium** (**seer**-i-ŭm) noun a chemical element (symbol Ce), a soft grey metal used in cigarette lighter flints and as a polishing agent.

**CERN** (pronounced sern) abbreviation European Organization for Nuclear Research. (¶ From the initials of its former French title.)

**cert** noun (slang) a certainty, something sure to happen or to be successful; a dead cert.

**certain** adjective 1 feeling sure, convinced. 2 known without doubt. 3 able to be relied on to come or happen or be effective. 4 specific but not named or stated for various reasons. 5 small in amount but definitely there; I feel a certain reluctance. 6 existing but not well known; a certain John Smith. □ **for certain** without doubt, as a certainty.

**certainly** adverb 1 without doubt. 2 yes.

**certainty** noun 1 being certain. 2 something that is certain.

**Cert. Ed.** abbreviation Certificate in Education.

**certifiable** adjective able to be certified; deserving to be certified as insane. □ **certifiably** adverb

**certificate** noun an official written or printed statement giving certain facts. □ **Certificate of Secondary Education** (Brit.) see CSE. □ **certificated** adjective

**certify** verb (**certified**, **certifying**) declare formally; show on a certificate or other document. □ **certification** noun

**certitude** (**ser**-ti-tewd) noun a feeling of certainty.

**cerulean** (si-**roo**-li-ăn) adjective (literary) sky-blue.

**Cervantes** (ser-**van**-teez), Miguel de (1547-1616), Spanish novelist and dramatist, author of Don Quixote.

**cervical** (ser-**vy**-kăl or **ser**-vik-ăl) adjective 1 of the neck; cervical vertebrae. 2 of a cervix, of the cervix of the womb. □ **cervical smear** a smear taken from the neck of the womb as a routine examination for cervical cancer.

**cervix** (**ser**-viks) noun (plural **cervices**, pronounced **ser**-vi-seez) 1 the neck. 2 a neck-like structure; the neck of the womb.

**Cesarean**, **Cesarian** Amer. spelling of CAESAREAN.

**cesium** Amer. spelling of CAESIUM.

**cessation** (sess-**ay**-shŏn) noun ceasing.

**cession** (**sesh**-ŏn) noun ceding, giving up.

**cesspit** noun (also **cesspool**) a covered pit where liquid waste or sewage is stored temporarily.

**cetacean** (si-tay-shăn) *noun* a member of the order of animals that contains whales, dolphins, and porpoises. ● *adjective* of this order.

**cetane** *noun* a liquid hydrocarbon used in standardizing ratings of diesel fuel.

**Ceylon** the former name of Sri Lanka.

**Cézanne** (say-zan), Paul (1839–1906), French painter, a forerunner of cubism.

**Cf** *symbol* californium.

**cf.** *abbreviation* compare (¶ short for the Latin *confer*.)

**CFC** *abbreviation* chlorofluorocarbon, a usually gaseous compound of carbon, hydrogen, and fluorine, used in refrigerants, aerosols, etc., and thought to harm the ozone layer.

**CFE** *abbreviation* College of Further Education.

**cg** *abbreviation* centigram(s).

**Chablis** (shab-lee) *noun* a dry white burgundy wine.

**cha-cha** *noun* (also **cha-cha-cha**) a Latin American dance.

**chaconne** *noun* a set of musical variations over a ground bass.

**Chad** a country in North Africa. □ **Chadian** *adjective & noun*

**Chadwick**, Sir James (1891–1974), English physicist, who discovered the neutron.

**chafe** (*pronounced* chayf) *verb* **1** warm by rubbing. **2** make or become sore from rubbing. **3** become irritated or impatient.

**chafer** (chay-fer) *noun* a large slow-moving beetle, especially a cockchafer.

**chaff** *noun* **1** corn-husks separated from the seed by threshing or winnowing. **2** hay or straw cut up as food for cattle. **3** good-humoured teasing or joking. ● *verb* tease or joke in a good-humoured way.

**chaffinch** *noun* a common European finch.

**chafing-dish** (chay-fing-dish) *noun* a pan with a heater under it for cooking food or keeping it warm at the table.

**Chagall** (shă-gal), Marc (1887–1985), French painter, born in Russia.

**chagrin** (shag-rin) *noun* a feeling of annoyance and embarrassment or disappointment.

**chain** *noun* **1** a series of connected metal links. **2** a connected series or sequence; *a chain of mountains; a chain of events.* **3** a number of shops or hotels etc. owned by the same company. **4** a unit of length for measuring land, 66 ft. ● *verb* make fast with a chain or chains. □ **chain-gang** *noun* (*hist.*) a team of convicts chained together to work out of doors. **chain letter** a letter of which the recipient is asked to make copies and send these to other people, who will do the same. **chain mail** armour made of interlaced rings. **chain reaction** a chemical or other change forming products that themselves cause more changes; a series of

events each of which causes or influences the next. **chain-saw** *noun* a saw with teeth set on an endless chain. **chain-smoke** *verb* smoke many cigarettes in a continuous succession. **chain-smoker** *noun* a person who chain-smokes. **chain stitch** a looped stitch that looks like a chain, in crochet or embroidery. **chain store** one of a series of similar shops owned by one firm.

**chair** *noun* **1** a movable seat, with a back, for one person. **2** a position of authority at a meeting; a chairperson. **3** a professorship. **4** (*Amer.*) the electric chair. ● *verb* **1** seat in a chair of honour. **2** carry in triumph on the shoulders of a group. **3** act as chairperson of. □ **chair-lift** *noun* a series of chairs suspended from an endless cable, for carrying people up a mountain.

**chairman** *noun* (*plural* **chairmen**) **1** a person who presides over a meeting or a committee. **2** the president of a board of directors. □ **chairmanship** *noun*

**chairperson** *noun* a chairman or chairwoman.

**chairwoman** *noun* (*plural* **chairwomen**) **1** a woman who presides over a meeting. **2** a woman who is president of a board of directors.

**chaise longue** (shayz lawng) (*plural* **chaise longues** or **chaises longues**, *pronounced* same) a chair with a very long seat on which one can lie back and stretch out one's legs.

**chalcedony** (kal-sed-ŏni) *noun* a type of quartz including many varieties regarded as precious stones, e.g. onyx and jasper.

**chalet** (shal-ay) *noun* **1** a Swiss hut or cottage. **2** a small villa. **3** a small hut in a holiday camp etc.

**chalice** (chal-iss) *noun* a large goblet for holding wine; one from which consecrated wine is drunk at the Eucharist.

**chalk** *noun* **1** a soft white limestone. **2** a piece of this or of similar substance, white or coloured, used in crayons for drawing. ● *verb* write, draw, or mark with chalk, rub with chalk. □ **by a long chalk** by far. **chalk up 1** make a note of something. **2** achieve; *chalked up another victory.* □ **chalky** *adjective*

**challenge** *noun* **1** a call to demonstrate one's ability or strength. **2** a call or demand to respond; a sentry's call for a person to identify himself or herself. **3** a formal objection, e.g. to a jury member. **4** a difficult or demanding task. ● *verb* **1** issue a challenge to. **2** raise a formal objection to. **3** question the truth or rightness of. □ **challenger** *noun*

**challenging** *adjective* offering problems that test one's ability; stimulating.

**chamber** *noun* **1** an assembly hall; the hall used for meetings of a parliament etc.; the members of the group using it. **2** a cavity or compartment in the body of an animal or plant, or in machinery. **3** (*old use*) a room, a bedroom. **4** (**chambers**) a set of rooms; a judge's room for hearing cases that do not need to be taken in court. □ **chamber music** music written for a small group of players. **Chamber of Commerce** an association to promote local commercial interests. **chamber-pot** *noun* a receptacle for urine etc., used in the bedroom.

**Chamberlain**, Arthur Neville (1869–1940), British statesman, Prime Minister 1937–40.

**chamberlain** (**chaym-ber-lin**) *noun* an official who manages the household of the sovereign or a great noble.

**chambermaid** *noun* a woman employed to clean bedrooms in a hotel.

**chameleon** (kă-**mee**-li-ŏn) *noun* a small lizard that can change colour according to its surroundings.

**chamfer** (**cham**-fer) *verb* bevel the edge or corner of. ●*noun* a bevelled surface at an edge.

**chamois** *noun* (*plural* **chamois**) **1** (*pronounced* **sham**-wah) a small wild antelope found in the mountains of Europe and Asia. **2** (*pronounced* **sham**-i) (in full **chamois leather**) a piece of soft yellowish leather made from the skin of sheep, goats, and deer and used for washing and polishing things.

**chamomile** alternative spelling of CAMO-MILE.

**champ** *verb* munch noisily, make a chewing action or noise. ●*noun* (*slang*) a champion. □ **champ at the bit** show impatience.

**champagne** *noun* **1** a sparkling white wine from Champagne in France or elsewhere. **2** its pale straw colour.

**champion** *noun* **1** a person or thing that has defeated all others in a competition. **2** a person who fights, argues, or speaks in support of another or of a cause. ●*adjective & adverb* (*informal*) splendid, splendidly. ●*verb* support as a champion.

**championship** *noun* **1** (often as **championships**) a contest to decide the champion in a sport etc. **2** the position of champion.

**chance** *noun* **1** the way things happen through no known cause or agency; luck, fate. **2** a possibility, likelihood. **3** an opportunity, an occasion when success seems very probable. ●*verb* **1** happen without plan or intention. **2** (*informal*) risk; *let's chance it.* ●*adjective* coming or happening by chance; *a chance meeting.* □ **by chance** as it happens or happened, without being planned. **chance on** come upon or find by chance. **chance one's arm** (*informal*) take a chance although failure is probable. **take a chance** take a risk, act in the hope that a particular thing will (or will not) happen.

**chancel** (**chahn**-sĕl) *noun* the part of a church near the altar, used by the clergy and choir.

**chancellery** (**chahn**-sĕl-er-i) *noun* **1** a chancellor's position, department, or official residence. **2** (*Amer.*) an office attached to an embassy or consulate.

**chancellor** *noun* **1** a State or law official of various kinds. **2** the chief minister of State in some European countries. **3** the non-resident head of a university. □ **Chancellor of the Exchequer** the finance minister of the UK, who prepares the budget. **Lord Chancellor** the highest officer of the Crown, presiding over the House of Lords. □ **chancellorship** *noun*

**Chancery** (**chahn**-ser-i) *noun* the Lord Chancellor's division of the High Court of Justice.

**chancy** *adjective* (**chancier**, **chanciest**) risky, uncertain.

**chandelier** (shan-dĕ-**leer**) *noun* an ornamental hanging fixture with supports for several lights.

**Chandigarh** (chun-di-**gar**) **1** a Union Territory in India. **2** a city in this Territory, capital of Punjab and Haryana.

**Chandler**, Raymond (1888–1959), American writer of detective novels.

**chandler** *noun* a dealer in ropes, canvas, and other supplies for ships.

**Chanel** (shă-**nel**), 'Coco' (Gabrielle Bonheur) (1883–1971), French fashion designer and perfume manufacturer.

**change** *verb* **1** make or become different. **2** pass from one form or phase into another. **3** take or use another instead of. **4** put fresh clothes or coverings etc. on. **5** go from one to another; *change trains.* **6** exchange; give small money in change for notes or larger coins. ●*noun* **1** changing, alteration. **2** a substitution of one thing for another; variety. **3** a fresh occupation or surroundings. **4** money in small units. **5** money returned as the balance when the price is less than the amount offered in payment. **6** (**changes**) the different orders in which a peal of bells can be rung. □ **change down** change to a lower gear. **change hands** pass into another person's possession. **change of heart** an alteration in one's attitude or feelings. **the change (of life)** the menopause. **change over** change from one system or position to another. **change-over** *noun* a change of this kind. **change-ringing** *noun* ringing a peal of

bells in a series of different sequences.
**change up** change to a higher gear. **for a change** for the sake of variety, to vary one's routine. **get no change out of** (*slang*) **1** fail to get the better of. **2** fail to get information from.

**changeable** *adjective* **1** able to be changed. **2** altering frequently; *changeable weather*.

**changeling** (**chaynj**-ling) *noun* a child or thing believed to have been substituted secretly for another.

**channel** *noun* **1** the sunken bed of a stream of water. **2** the navigable part of a waterway, deeper than the parts on either side. **3** a stretch of water, wider than a strait, connecting two seas. **4** a passage along which a liquid may flow, a sunken course or line along which something may move. **5** any course by which news or information etc. may travel. **6** a band of broadcasting frequencies reserved for a particular set of programmes. **7** a circuit for transmitting electrical signals. **8** a lengthwise section of recording tape. ●*verb* (**channelled, channelling**; *Amer.* **channeled, channeling**) **1** form a channel or channels in. **2** direct through a channel or desired route. □ **the Channel** the English Channel. **Channel Tunnel** a tunnel built under the English Channel, linking Britain and France.

**Channel Islands** a group of islands in the English Channel off the NW coast of France, of which the largest are Jersey, Guernsey, and Alderney.

**chant** *noun* **1** a tune to which the words of psalms or other works with irregular rhythm are fitted by singing several syllables or words to the same note. **2** a monotonous song. **3** a rhythmic call or shout. ●*verb* **1** sing, especially a chant. **2** call or shout rhythmically.

**chanter** *noun* **1** a person who chants. **2** the melody-pipe of bagpipes.

**chanterelle** (shahn-ter-**el**) *noun* a yellow edible funnel-shaped fungus.

**chantry** *noun* a chapel founded for priests to sing masses for the founder's soul.

**chaos** (**kay**-oss) *noun* great disorder.

**chaotic** (kay-**ot**-ik) *adjective* confused; disordered. □ **chaotically** *adverb*

**chap** *verb* (**chapped, chapping**) (of skin) split or crack, become cracked. ●*noun* **1** a crack in the skin. **2** (*informal*) a man or boy. **3** (**chaps**) long leather leggings worn by cowboys.

**chaparral** (chap-er-**al**) *noun* (*Amer.*) dense tangled brushwood, especially in the southwestern USA and Mexico.

**chapati** *noun* (also **chapati, chupatty**) a thin flat circle of unleavened bread, usually eaten with an Indian meal.

**chapel** *noun* **1** a place used for Christian worship, other than a cathedral or parish church. **2** a service in this. **3** a place with a separate altar within a church or cathedral. **4** a section of a trade union in a printing works.

**chaperon** (**shap**-er-ohn) *noun* an older woman in charge of a girl or young unmarried woman on social occasions. ●*verb* act as chaperon to. □ **chaperonage** *noun*

**chaplain** (**chap**-lin) *noun* a member of the clergy attached to a chapel in a private house or institution, or to a military unit.

**chaplet** (**chap**-lit) *noun* **1** a wreath for the head. **2** a short rosary.

**Chaplin**, Charlie (Sir Charles Spencer) (1889–1977), English comic film actor and director.

**chappie** *noun* (*informal*) a chap, a man.

**chapter** *noun* **1** a division of a book, usually numbered. **2** the canons of a cathedral or members of a monastic order; a meeting of these. □ **chapter and verse** an exact reference to a passage or authority. **chapter of accidents** a series of misfortunes.

**char** *noun* **1** a charwoman. **2** (*plural* **char**) a kind of small trout. **3** (*slang*) tea. ●*verb* (**charred, charring**) **1** work as a charwoman. **2** make or become black by burning.

**charabanc** (**sha**-ră-bank) *noun* an early form of bus with bench seats, used for outings.

**character** *noun* **1** all those qualities that make a person, group, or thing what he, she, or it is and different from others. **2** a person's moral nature. **3** moral strength. **4** a person, especially a noticeable or eccentric one. **5** a person in a novel or play etc. **6** a description of a person's qualities, a testimonial. **7** a letter, sign, or mark used in a system of writing or printing etc. **8** a physical characteristic of a plant or animal. □ **in character** appropriate to a person's general character. **out of character** not consistent with a person's character.

**characteristic** *adjective* forming part of the character of a person or thing, showing a distinctive feature. ●*noun* a characteristic feature. □ **characteristically** *adverb*

**characterize** *verb* (also **characterise**) **1** describe the character of. **2** be a characteristic of. □ **characterization** *noun*

**characterless** *adjective* lacking any positive character.

**charade** (shă-**rahd**) *noun* **1** (usually as **charades**, treated as *singular*) a game which involves guessing a word from acted clues. **2** an absurd pretence.

**charcoal** *noun* a black substance made by burning wood slowly in an oven with little air, used as a filtering material, as fuel, or for drawing. □ **charcoal grey** very dark grey.

**chard** *noun* a kind of beet with edible leaves and stalks.

**charge** *noun* **1** the price asked for goods or services. **2** the quantity of material that an apparatus holds at one time; the amount of explosive needed for one explosion. **3** the electricity contained in a substance; energy stored chemically for conversion into electricity. **4** a task or duty; custody. **5** a person or thing entrusted. **6** formal instructions about one's duty or responsibility. **7** an accusation, especially of having committed a crime. **8** a rushing attack. ●*verb* **1** ask as a price. **2** record as a debt; *charge it to my account.* **3** load or fill; put a charge into. **4** give an electric charge to; store energy in. **5** give as a task or duty; entrust. **6** accuse formally. **7** move wildly and rapidly; rush; *children charging about all over the place.* **8** rush forward in attack. □ **charge card** a credit card. **charge-hand** *noun* a worker ranking just below a foreman. **charge-nurse** *noun* a nurse in charge of a ward. **in charge** in command. **take charge** take control.

**chargeable** *adjective* able to be charged.

**chargé d'affaires** (shar-*zh*ay da-**fair**) *noun* (*plural* **chargés d'affaires**, *pronounced* same) **1** an ambassador's deputy. **2** an envoy to a minor country.

**charger** *noun* **1** a cavalry horse. **2** an apparatus for charging a battery.

**chariot** *noun* a two-wheeled horse-drawn carriage used in ancient times in battle and in racing.

**charioteer** *noun* the driver of a chariot.

**charisma** (kă-**riz**-mă) *noun* the power to inspire devotion and enthusiasm; great charm.

**charismatic** (ka-riz-**mat**-ik) *adjective* **1** having charisma. **2** (of Christian worship) characterized by spontaneity and utterances made while in religious ecstasy.

**charitable** *adjective* **1** generous in giving to the needy. **2** of or belonging to charities; *charitable institutions.* **3** unwilling to think badly of people or acts. □ **charitably** *adverb*

**charity** *noun* **1** leniency or tolerance in judging others; unwillingness to think badly of people or acts. **2** generosity in giving to the needy. **3** an institution or fund for helping the needy. **4** loving kindness towards others.

**charlady** *noun* a charwoman.

**charlatan** (**shar**-lă-tăn) *noun* a person who falsely claims to be an expert.

**Charlemagne** (**shar**-lĕ-mayn) (742–814), ruler of the Franks in northern Europe from 768, and emperor from 800.

**Charles**[1] the name of two kings of Britain: Charles I (reigned 1625–49), Charles II (reigned 1660–85).

**Charles**[2] the name of ten kings of France.

**Charles**[3] the name of four kings of Spain.

**Charles**[4], Prince, (other names; Philip Arthur George), Prince of Wales (born 1948), eldest son of Queen Elizabeth II and Prince Philip.

**charleston** *noun* (also **Charleston**) a lively dance of the 1920s, with side-kicks from the knee.

**charlie** *noun* (*informal*) a fool.

**charlock** *noun* wild mustard, a weed with yellow flowers.

**charlotte** (**shar**-lŏt) *noun* a pudding of stewed fruit with a covering of breadcrumbs, biscuits, etc.

**Charlton**, Bobby (Robert) (born 1937), English footballer.

**charm** *noun* **1** attractiveness; the power of arousing admiration. **2** an act or object or words believed to have magic power. **3** a small ornament worn on a chain or bracelet. ●*verb* **1** give pleasure to. **2** influence by personal charm. **3** influence as if by magic. □ **charmer** *noun*

**charming** *adjective* delightful.

**charnel house** (**char**-nĕl) a place in which the bodies or bones of the dead are kept.

**Charon** (**kair**-ŏn) (*Gk. myth.*) the aged ferryman who conveyed the souls of the dead across the river to Hades.

**chart** *noun* **1** a map designed for navigators on water or in the air. **2** an outline map showing special information; *a weather chart.* **3** a diagram, graph, or table giving information in an orderly form; *a temperature chart.* **4** (**the charts**) a listing of the recordings that are currently most popular. ●*verb* make a chart of, map.

**charter** *noun* **1** a document from a ruler or government granting certain rights or defining the form of an institution. **2** the chartering of a ship, aircraft, or vehicle. ●*verb* **1** grant a charter to, found by charter. **2** let or hire a ship, aircraft, or vehicle. □ **charter flight** a flight by chartered aircraft as opposed to a regular scheduled flight.

**chartered** *adjective* (of an accountant, engineer, librarian, etc.) qualified according to the rules of a professional association which has a royal charter.

**Chartism** (*hist.*) a popular movement in Britain for electoral and social reform in 1837–48. □ **Chartist** *noun*

**chartreuse** (shar-**trerz**) *noun* a fragrant green or yellow liqueur.

**charwoman** *noun* (*plural* **charwomen**) a woman employed to clean a house.

**chary** (**chair**-i) *adjective* **1** cautious, wary. **2** sparing; *chary of giving praise.*

**Charybdis** (kă-**rib**-dis) (*Gk. legend*) a dangerous whirlpool in a narrow channel, opposite the cave of Scylla.

**chase** *verb* **1** go quickly after in order to capture, overtake, or drive away. **2** hurry; *chasing round the shops.* **3** (*informal*) try to attain. **4** engrave or emboss (metal). ●*noun* **1** chasing, pursuit. **2** hunting, especially as a sport. **3** a steeplechase. **4** unenclosed parkland, originally for hunting. □ **chase up** (*informal*) investigate and find; try to hasten (suppliers or supplies). **give chase** begin to pursue.

**chaser** *noun* **1** a horse for steeplechasing. **2** (*informal*) a drink taken after a drink of another kind, e.g. beer after spirits.

**chasm** (**kaz**-ŭm) *noun* a deep opening or gap, especially in earth or rock.

**chassis** (**sha**-see) *noun* (*plural* **chassis**, pronounced **sha**-seez) a base-frame, especially of a vehicle, on which other parts are mounted.

**chaste** (pronounced chayst) *adjective* **1** virgin, celibate. **2** not having sexual intercourse except with the person to whom one is married. **3** simple in style, not ornate. □ **chastely** *adverb*

**chasten** (**chay**-sĕn) *verb* **1** discipline, punish by inflicting suffering. **2** subdue the pride of.

**chastise** (chas-**tyz**) *verb* **1** scold severely. **2** punish, especially by beating. □ **chastisement** *noun*

**chastity** *noun* **1** being chaste; virginity, celibacy. **2** simplicity of style.

**chasuble** (**chaz**-yoo-bŭl) *noun* a loose garment worn over all other vestments by a priest celebrating Mass or the Eucharist.

**chat** *noun* **1** a friendly informal conversation. **2** a small bird with a harsh-sounding call. ●*verb* (**chatted, chatting**) have a chat; converse informally. □ **chat show** a broadcast programme in which celebrities are interviewed informally. **chat up** (*Brit. informal*) chat to (a person) flirtatiously or with a particular motive.

**château** (shat-**oh**) *noun* (*plural* **châteaux**, pronounced shat-**ohz**) a castle or large country house in France.

**chatelaine** (shat-ĕ-layn) *noun* the mistress of a large house.

**chattel** *noun* (usually as **chattels**) a movable possession (as opposed to a house or land).

**chatter** *verb* **1** talk quickly and continuously about unimportant matters. **2** make sounds like this, as some birds and animals do. **3** make a repeated clicking or rattling sound. ●*noun* **1** chattering talk. **2** a chattering sound. □ **chatterer** *noun*

**chatterbox** *noun* a talkative person.

**chatty** *adjective* (**chattier, chattiest**) **1** fond of chatting. **2** resembling chat; informal; *a chatty description.* □ **chattily** *adverb*, **chattiness** *noun*

**Chaucer**, Geoffrey (*c.*1342–1400), English poet, author of *The Canterbury Tales.*

**chauffeur** (**shoh**-fer) *noun* a person employed to drive a car. ●*verb* drive as chauffeur.

**chauffeuse** (**shoh**-ferz) *noun* a woman employed to drive a car.

**chauvinism** (**shoh**-vin-izm) *noun* **1** exaggerated patriotism. **2** a pompous, self-satisfied belief that one's own sex or group is superior. □ **chauvinist** *noun*, **chauvinistic** *adjective*

**cheap** *adjective* **1** low in price, worth more than it cost. **2** charging low prices, offering good value. **3** poor in quality, of low value. **4** showy but worthless, silly. ●*adverb* cheaply; *we got it cheap.* □ **cheaply** *adverb*, **cheapness** *noun*

**cheapen** *verb* make or become cheap.

**cheapish** *adjective* rather cheap.

**cheapjack** *noun* a seller of shoddy goods at low prices. ●*adjective* of poor quality, shoddy.

**cheapskate** *noun* (*informal*) a mean stingy person.

**cheat** *verb* **1** act dishonestly or unfairly in order to win some profit or advantage. **2** trick, deceive; deprive by deceit. ●*noun* **1** a person who cheats, an unfair player. **2** a deception.

**check¹** *verb* **1** stop or slow the motion of suddenly; restrain. **2** make a sudden stop. **3** threaten (an opponent's king) at chess. **4** test or examine to make sure that something is correct or in good condition. **5** (*Amer.*) correspond when compared. ●*noun* **1** a stopping or slowing of motion, a pause; a loss of the scent in hunting. **2** a restraint. **3** a control to secure accuracy; a test or examination to see whether something is correct or in good working order. **4** (*Amer.*) a receipt for something handed over; a bill in a restaurant. **5** (*Amer.*) a cheque. **6** (in chess) exposure of a king to possible capture. □ **check in** register on arrival, e.g. as a passenger at an airport. **check-in** *noun* the act of checking in; the place where this is done. **check-list** *noun* a complete list of items, used for reference. **check off** mark (items) on a list as correct, dealt with, etc. **check on** or **up** or **up on** examine or investigate the correctness of. **check out** **1** register on departure or dispatch. **2** check on. **check-up** *noun* a thorough examination, especially a medical one. **keep in check** keep under control.

**check²** *noun* a pattern of squares like a chessboard, or of crossing lines.

**checked** *adjective* having a check pattern.

**checker** *noun* **1** alternative spelling of CHEQUER. **2** (**checkers**) (*Amer.*) the game of draughts. **3** a person who examines and checks work.

**checkmate** *noun* **1** (in chess) = MATE². **2** a complete defeat. ●*verb* **1** put into checkmate in chess. **2** defeat finally, foil.

**checkout** *noun* **1** the act of checking out. **2** a place where goods are paid for by customers in a supermarket.

**checkpoint** *noun* a place or barrier where documents, vehicles, etc. are checked or inspected.

**Cheddar** *noun* a firm cheese of a kind originally made at Cheddar in Somerset.

**cheek** *noun* **1** either side of the face below the eye. **2** (*slang*) a buttock. **3** impudent speech, quiet arrogance. ●*verb* address cheekily. □ **cheek by jowl** close together, in close association.

**cheeky** *adjective* (**cheekier, cheekiest**) showing bold or cheerful lack of respect. □ **cheekily** *adverb*, **cheekiness** *noun*

**cheep** *noun* a weak shrill cry like that made by a young bird. ●*verb* make such a cry.

**cheer** *noun* **1** a shout of encouragement or applause. **2** cheerfulness. ●*verb* **1** utter a cheer; encourage or applaud with cheers. **2** comfort, gladden. □ **cheer-leader** *noun* a person who encourages an audience to cheer and applaud. **cheer up** make or become more cheerful.

**cheerful** *adjective* **1** visibly happy, contented, in good spirits. **2** pleasantly bright; *cheerful colours*. □ **cheerfully** *adverb*, **cheerfulness** *noun*

**cheerio** *interjection* (*informal*) goodbye.

**cheerless** *adjective* gloomy, dreary.

**cheery** *adjective* exuberantly happy. □ **cheerily** *adverb*

**cheese** *noun* **1** a food made from milk curds. **2** a shaped mass of this. **3** thick stiff jam; *damson cheese*. □ **cheese-paring** *adjective* stingy. **cheese plant** a plant with large glossy leaves with holes in them. □ **cheesy** *adjective* ill-smelling.

**cheeseburger** *noun* a hamburger with cheese in or on it.

**cheesecake** *noun* **1** a tart with a filling of cream cheese or curd cheese, often flavoured with fruit. **2** (*slang*) the portrayal of women in a sexually attractive manner.

**cheesecloth** *noun* a thin loosely-woven cotton fabric.

**cheesed** *adjective* (*slang*) (often foll. by *off*) bored, exasperated; *cheesed off with work*.

**cheetah** (**chee-tă**) *noun* a swift, large animal of the cat family with a spotted coat.

**chef** (*pronounced* shef) *noun* a professional cook; the chief male cook in a restaurant etc.

**chef-d'œuvre** (shay-**dervr**) *noun* (*plural* **chefs-d'œuvre**, *pronounced* same) a masterpiece. (¶ French.)

**Chekhov** (**chek**-off), Anton Pavlovich (1860–1904), Russian dramatist and short-story writer, whose plays include *Uncle Vanya* and *The Cherry Orchard*.

**Chelsea pensioner** an inmate of the Chelsea Royal Hospital in London for old or disabled soldiers.

**chemical** *adjective* of, using, or produced by chemistry. ●*noun* a substance obtained by or used in a chemical process. □ **chemical engineering** engineering concerned with processes that involve chemical change and with the equipment needed for these. **chemical warfare** warfare using poison gas and other chemicals. □ **chemically** *adverb*

**chemise** (shĕm-**eez**) *noun* a loose-fitting undergarment or dress formerly worn by women, hanging straight from the shoulders.

**chemist** *noun* **1** a person or firm dealing in medicinal drugs. **2** a scientist skilled in chemistry.

**chemistry** *noun* **1** the scientific study of substances and their elements and of how they react when combined or in contact with one another. **2** chemical structure, properties, and reactions. **3** (*informal*) the relationship between people; sexual attraction.

**chemotherapy** (kem-ŏ-th'e-ră-pi) *noun* treatment of disease by medicinal drugs and other chemical substances.

**chenille** (shĕn-**eel**) *noun* a fabric with a long velvety pile, used for furnishings.

**Cheops** (**ki**-ops) = KHUFU.

**cheque** *noun* (*Amer.* **check**) **1** a written order to a bank to pay out money from an account. **2** the printed form on which this is written. □ **cheque-book** *noun* a book of printed cheques. **cheque card** a card guaranteeing payment of a bank customer's cheques.

**chequer** (**chek**-er) *noun* (also **checker**) a pattern of squares, especially of alternate squares of colour.

**chequered** *adjective* (also **checkered**) **1** marked with a pattern of squares. **2** with varied fortunes; *a chequered career*.

**Chequers** (**chek**-erz) a Tudor mansion in Buckinghamshire, country seat of the Prime Minister in office.

**Cherenkov** (chi-**reng**-kof), Pavel Alekseyevich (1904–90), Russian physicist, who discovered the type of radiation now named after him.

**cherish** *verb* **1** look after lovingly. **2** be fond of. **3** keep in one's heart; *we cherish hopes of his return.*

**Chernobyl** (cher-**nob**-il) a city near Kiev in Ukraine, where in 1986 explosions at a nuclear power station resulted in a serious escape of radioactivity which spread to a number of countries of Europe.

**Cherokee** *noun* a member of an American Indian tribe of the southern USA.

**cheroot** (shĕ-**root**) *noun* a cigar with both ends open.

**cherry** *noun* **1** a small soft round fruit with a stone. **2** a tree producing this or grown for its ornamental flowers. **3** the wood of this tree. **4** deep red. ● *adjective* deep red.

**cherub** *noun* **1** (*plural* **cherubim**) any of the angelic beings usually grouped with the seraphim. **2** a representation (in art) of a chubby infant with wings. **3** an angelic child.

**cherubic** (chĕ-**roo**-bik) *adjective* like a cherub, with a plump innocent face.

**chervil** *noun* a herb used for flavouring.

**Ches.** *abbreviation* Cheshire.

**Cheshire** a north midland county of England. ● *noun* a mild crumbly cheese originally made in Cheshire. □ **like a Cheshire cat** with a broad fixed grin.

**chess** *noun* a game of skill for two players with 16 pieces each, played on a chessboard.

**chessboard** *noun* a chequered board of 64 squares on which chess is played.

**chessman** *noun* any of the pieces with which chess is played.

**chest** *noun* **1** a large strong box for storing or shipping things in. **2** the upper front surface of the body; the part containing the heart and lungs. □ **chest of drawers** a piece of furniture with drawers for storing clothes etc. **get it off one's chest** (*informal*) reveal what one is anxious about. **play it close to one's chest** be secretive.

**chesterfield** *noun* a sofa with arms and back of the same height.

**Chesterton**, G(ilbert) K(eith) (1874–1936), English essayist, novelist, and poet.

**chestnut** *noun* **1** a tree with hard brown edible nuts. **2** the wood of this tree. **3** its nut. **4** deep reddish brown. **5** a horse of a reddish-brown colour. **6** an old joke or story. ● *adjective* deep reddish-brown.

**chesty** *adjective* (*informal*) inclined to suffer from bronchial diseases; showing symptoms of these. □ **chestiness** *noun*

**cheval-glass** (shĕv-**al**-glahs) *noun* a tall mirror mounted in a frame so that it can be tilted.

**chevalier** (shev-ă-**leer**) *noun* a member of certain orders of knighthood or other groups.

**Cheviot Hills** (**chev**-i-ŏt *or* **chee**-vi-ŏt) (also **Cheviots**) a range of hills on the border between England and Scotland.

**chevron** (**shev**-rŏn) *noun* a V-shaped stripe or bar.

**chew** *verb* work or grind between the teeth; make this movement. ● *noun* **1** the act of chewing. **2** something for chewing. □ **chewing gum** a sticky substance flavoured for prolonged chewing. **chew over** (*informal*) think over. **chew the fat** (*slang*) chat.

**chewy** *adjective* **1** suitable for chewing. **2** needing to be chewed, not soft.

**chez** (*pronounced* shay) *preposition* at the home of. (¶ French.)

**Chiang Kai-shek** (1887–1975), Chinese leader who opposed the Communists.

**Chianti** (ki-**an**-ti) *noun* a dry red Italian wine.

**chiaroscuro** (ki-ar-ŏ-**skoor**-oh) *noun* **1** treatment of the light and dark parts in a painting. **2** light and shade effects in nature. **3** use of contrast in literature etc.

**chic** (*pronounced* sheek) *adjective* stylish and elegant. ● *noun* stylishness and elegance.

**Chicago** (shi-**kah**-goh) a city in Illinois, on Lake Michigan.

**chicane** (shi-**kayn**) *noun* **1** chicanery. **2** an artificial barrier or obstacle on a motor-racing course. ● *verb* use chicanery, cheat.

**chicanery** (shi-**kayn**-er-i) *noun* trickery used to gain an advantage.

**Chichester**, Sir Francis Charles (1901–72), English yachtsman, who sailed alone round the world in 1966–7.

**chick** *noun* **1** a young bird before or after hatching. **2** (*slang*) a young woman. □ **chick pea** a dwarf pea with yellow seeds used as a vegetable.

**chicken** *noun* **1** a young bird, especially of the domestic fowl. **2** the flesh of domestic fowl as food. **3** (*informal*) a coward. ● *adjective* (*informal*) afraid to do something, cowardly. □ **be no chicken** (*slang*) be no longer young. **chicken-feed** *noun* **1** food for poultry. **2** (*informal*) something that is small in amount. **chicken-hearted** *adjective* cowardly. **chicken out** (*informal*) withdraw through cowardice. **chicken-wire** *noun* lightweight wire netting.

**chickenpox** *noun* an infectious disease, especially of children, with red spots on the skin.

**chickweed** *noun* a weed with small white flowers.

**chicle** (**chik**-ŭl) *noun* the milky juice of a tropical American tree, used chiefly in chewing gum.

**chicory** *noun* a blue-flowered plant, cultivated for its salad leaves and for its root, which is roasted, ground, and used with or instead of coffee.

**chide** *verb* (**chided** *or* **chid, chided** *or* **chidden, chiding**) (*old use*) scold.

**chief** *noun* **1** a leader or ruler. **2** a person with the highest authority. ●*adjective* **1** highest in rank or authority. **2** most important. □ **Chief Constable** the head of the police force of an area. □ **chiefly** *adverb*

**chieftain** (**cheef**-tăn) *noun* the chief of a tribe, clan, or other group.

**chiffchaff** *noun* a small European warbler.

**chiffon** (**shif**-on) *noun* a thin almost transparent fabric of silk or nylon etc.

**chiffonier** (shif-ŏn-**eer**) *noun* a movable low cupboard with a top used as a sideboard.

**chignon** (**sheen**-yawn) *noun* a knot or roll of long hair, worn at the back of the head by women.

**chigoe** *noun* a tropical flea that burrows into the skin.

**chihuahua** (chi-**wah**-wă) *noun* a very small smooth-haired dog of a breed that originated in Mexico.

**chilblain** *noun* a painful swelling on the hand, foot, or ear, caused by exposure to cold and by poor circulation.

**child** *noun* (*plural* **children**) **1** a young human being below the age of puberty; a boy or girl. **2** a son or daughter. □ **child abuse** maltreatment of a child, especially by violence or sexual interference. **child-bearing** *noun* pregnancy and childbirth. **child benefit** a regular payment made by the state to the parents of a child up to a certain age. **child-minder** *noun* a person who looks after children for payment. **child's play** something very easy to do.

**childbirth** *noun* the process of giving birth to a child.

**childhood** *noun* the condition or period of being a child.

**childish** *adjective* like a child; unsuitable for a grown person. □ **childishly** *adverb*, **childishness** *noun*

**childless** *adjective* having no children.

**childlike** *adjective* having the good qualities of a child, simple and innocent.

**children** *see* CHILD.

**Chile** (**chil**-i) a country in South America, on the Pacific coast. □ **Chilean** *adjective & noun*

**chili** alternative spelling of CHILLI.

**chill** *noun* **1** unpleasant coldness. **2** an illness with feverish shivering. **3** a feeling of discouragement. ●*adjective* chilly. ●*verb* preserve at a low temperature without freezing; *chilled beef.*

**chiller** *noun* a cold cabinet; a refrigerator.

**chilli** *noun* (*plural* **chillies**) (also **chili**) a hot-tasting dried pod of red pepper used as a relish or seasoning. □ **chilli con carne** (*pronounced* **kar**-ni) a stew of minced beef and beans flavoured with chillies.

**chilly** *adjective* (**chillier, chilliest**) **1** rather cold, unpleasantly cold. **2** cold and unfriendly in manner. □ **chilliness** *noun*

**Chiltern Hills** (also **Chilterns**) a range of hills in southern England.

**Chiltern Hundreds** □ **apply for the Chiltern Hundreds** (of an MP) apply for stewardship of a district (formerly called a *hundred*) which includes part of the Chiltern Hills and is Crown property, and hence be allowed to resign one's seat, since the holding of an office of profit under the Crown disqualifies a person from being an MP.

**chime** *noun* a tuned set of bells; a series of notes sounded by these. ●*verb* **1** (of bells) ring. **2** (of a clock) show the hour by chiming. □ **chime in** insert an unexpected remark when others are talking. **chime with** *or* **chime in with** agree or correspond with.

**chimera** (ky-**meer**-ă) *noun* **1** (*Gk. myth.*) a monster with a lion's head, goat's body, and serpent's tail. **2** a wild or fantastic creation of the mind.

**chimney** *noun* (*plural* **chimneys**) a structure carrying off smoke or gases from a fire. □ **chimney-breast** *noun* a projecting wall surrounding a chimney. **chimney pot** a pipe fitted to the top of a chimney. **chimney-stack** *noun* a number of chimneys standing together. **chimney-sweep** *noun* a person whose trade is to remove soot from inside chimneys.

**chimp** *noun* (*informal*) a chimpanzee.

**chimpanzee** *noun* an African ape, smaller than a gorilla.

**chin** *noun* the front of the lower jaw. □ **chin-wag** *noun* (*informal*) a chat. **keep one's chin up** (*informal*) remain cheerful.

**China** a country in eastern Asia.

**china** *noun* **1** fine earthenware porcelain. **2** articles made of this; *household china.* □ **china clay** Kaolin.

**chinagraph** *noun* a pencil that can write on china and glass.

**Chinaman** *noun* (*plural* **Chinamen**) (*old use*, now usually *offensive*) a Chinese man.

**China Sea** a part of the Pacific Ocean off the coast of China, divided by the island of Taiwan into the **East China Sea** in the north and the **South China Sea** in the south.

**Chinatown** a section of a town in which the Chinese live as a group.

**chinchilla** (chin-**chil**-ă) *noun* **1** a small squirrel-like South American rodent. **2** its soft grey fur. **3** a breed of cat or rabbit.

**chine** *noun* **1** an animal's backbone; a joint of meat containing part of this. **2** a mountain ridge. ●*verb* cut along and separate the backbone in (a joint of meat).

**Chinese** *adjective* of China or its people or language. ●*noun* **1** (*plural* **Chinese**) a native of China, a person of Chinese descent. **2** the language of China. □ **Chinese lantern** a collapsible paper lantern; a plant with an orange-coloured calyx resembling this. **Chinese leaves** a vegetable with long pale cabbage-like leaves that can be cooked or eaten raw in salads.

**Ch'ing** the name of the Manchu dynasty of China, 1644–1912.

**Chink** *noun* (*offensive*) a Chinese person.

**chink** *noun* **1** a narrow opening or slit. **2** a sound like glasses or coins being struck together. ●*verb* make or cause to make this sound.

**chinless** *adjective* (*informal*) weak or feeble in character.

**chinoiserie** (shin-**wah**-zer-i) *noun* imitation Chinese motifs in furniture or decoration.

**Chinook** (chi-**nuuk**) *noun* (*plural* **Chinook**) a member of a North American Indian people of the Pacific coast.

**chintz** *noun* a cotton cloth with a printed pattern, usually glazed, used for furnishings.

**chintzy** *adjective* **1** like chintz; characteristic of a decorating style associated with chintz. **2** cheap, gaudy.

**chip** *noun* **1** a thin piece cut or broken off something hard. **2** a fried oblong strip of potato. **3** (*Amer.*) a potato crisp. **4** wood split into strips for making baskets. **5** a place from which a chip has been broken. **6** a counter used to represent money, especially in gambling. **7** a microchip. ●*verb* (**chipped, chipping**) **1** cut or break at the surface or edge; shape or carve by doing this. **2** make (potatoes) into chips. □ **a chip off the old block** a child who is very like its parent. **a chip on one's shoulder** (*informal*) something about which one feels bitter or resentful. **chip in** (*informal*) **1** interrupt with a remark when someone is speaking. **2** contribute money. **have had one's chips** (*slang*) be defeated; die. **when the chips are down** (*informal*) when it comes to the point.

**chipboard** *noun* thin material made of compressed wood chips and resin.

**chipmunk** *noun* a small striped squirrel-like animal of North America.

**chipolata** (chipŏ-**lah**-tă) *noun* a small sausage.

**Chippendale** *noun* an 18th-century style of English furniture, named after its designer Thomas Chippendale (died 1779).

**chippings** *plural noun* chips of stone etc., used for making a road-surface.

**chiromancy** (**ky**-rŏ-man-si) *noun* palmistry. □ **chiromancer** *noun*

**chiropody** (ki-**rop**-ŏdi) *noun* the treatment of ailments of the feet. □ **chiropodist** *noun*

**chiropractic** (ky-rŏ-**prak**-tik) *noun* treatment of certain disorders by manipulation of the joints, especially those of the spine, not by medicinal drugs or surgery. □ **chiropractor** *noun*

**chirp** *noun* the short sharp note made by a small bird or a grasshopper. ●*verb* make this sound.

**chirpy** *adjective* lively and cheerful.

**chirrup** *noun* a series of chirps. ●*verb* make this sound.

**chisel** *noun* a tool with a bevelled edge for shaping wood, stone, or metal. ●*verb* (**chiselled, chiselling**; *Amer.* **chiseled, chiseling**) **1** cut or shape with a chisel. **2** (*slang*) treat unfairly, swindle.

**chit** *noun* **1** (often *scornful*) a young child, a small young woman; *only a chit of a girl*. **2** a short written note. **3** a note containing an order or statement of money owed.

**chit-chat** *noun* chat, gossip.

**chitin** (**ky**-tin) *noun* a substance forming the horny constituent in the hard outer covering of certain insects, spiders, and crustaceans.

**chitterlings** *plural noun* the small intestines of a pig, cooked as food.

**chivalry** (**shiv**-ăl-ri) *noun* courtesy and considerate behaviour, especially towards weaker people. □ **chivalrous** *adjective*

**chive** (*rhymes with* hive) *noun* a herb with long tubular onion-flavoured leaves.

**chivvy** *verb* (**chivvied, chivvying**) (*informal*) keep urging (a person) to hurry; harass, nag.

**chloral** (**klor**-ăl) *noun* **1** a colourless liquid used in making DDT. **2** (also **chloral hydrate**) a white crystalline compound made from this liquid and used as a sedative or anaesthetic.

**chloride** (**klor**-ryd) *noun* a compound of chlorine and one other element.

**chlorinate** (**klor**-in-ayt) *verb* treat or sterilize with chlorine. □ **chlorination** *noun*

**chlorine** (**klor**-een) *noun* a chemical element (symbol Cl), a poisonous gas used in sterilizing water and in industry.

**chlorofluorocarbon** *see* CFC.

**chloroform** (**klo**-rŏ-form) *noun* a liquid that gives off vapour which causes unconsciousness when breathed. ●*verb* make unconscious by this.

**chlorophyll** (klo-rŏ-fil) *noun* the green colouring-matter in plants.

**choc-ice** *noun* a small bar of ice cream coated with chocolate.

**chock** *noun* a block or wedge used to prevent something from moving. ●*verb* wedge with a chock or chocks. □ **chock-a-block** *adverb & adjective* crammed or crowded together. **chock-full** *adjective* crammed full.

**chocolate** *noun* **1** a powdered or solid food made from roasted ground cacao seeds. **2** a drink made with this. **3** a sweet made of or covered with this. **4** dark brown colour. ●*adjective* **1** flavoured or coated with chocolate. **2** dark brown.

**choice** *noun* **1** choosing; the right of choosing. **2** a variety from which to choose; *a wide choice of holidays.* **3** a person or thing chosen; *this is my choice.* ●*adjective* of the best quality.

**choir** *noun* **1** an organized band of singers, especially leading the singing in church. **2** the part of the church where these sit.

**choirboy** *noun* a boy who sings in a church choir, a chorister.

**choke** *verb* **1** cause to stop breathing by squeezing or blocking the windpipe or (of smoke etc.) by being unfit to breathe. **2** be unable to breathe from such causes. **3** make or become speechless from emotion. **4** clog, smother; *the garden is choked with weeds.* ●*noun* **1** a valve controlling the flow of air into a petrol engine. **2** *Electronics* a device for smoothing the variations of an alternating current. □ **choke back** suppress (feelings) with difficulty. **choke up** block completely.

**choker** *noun* **1** a high stiff collar. **2** a close-fitting necklace.

**choler** (kol-er) *noun* (*old use*) **1** one of the four humours, bile. **2** anger, bad temper.

**cholera** (kol-er-ă) *noun* an infectious and often fatal disease causing severe diarrhoea.

**choleric** (kol-er-ik) *adjective* easily angered, often angry.

**cholesterol** (kŏl-est-er-ŏl) *noun* a fatty substance found in animal tissues, thought to cause hardening of the arteries in high concentration.

**chomp** *verb* munch noisily.

**Chomsky** (chom-ski), (Avram) Noam (born 1928), American linguistics scholar and political commentator.

**choose** *verb* (**chose, chosen, choosing**) **1** select out of a greater number of things. **2** decide; prefer; desire. □ **there is nothing to choose between them** they are about equal.

**choosy** *adjective* (*informal*) careful and cautious in choosing; hard to please, fussy.

**chop** *verb* (**chopped, chopping**) **1** cut by a blow with an axe or knife. **2** hit with a short downward stroke or blow. ●*noun* **1** a cutting stroke, especially with an axe. **2** a chopping blow. **3** a thick slice of meat, usually including a rib. **4** (**chops**) the jaws of an animal. □ **chop and change** keep changing. **chop up** chop into small pieces. **get the chop** (*slang*) **1** be axed; be dismissed. **2** be murdered.

**Chopin** (shoh-pan), Fryderyk (Frédéric) (1810–49), Polish composer, whose works are chiefly for the piano.

**chopper** *noun* **1** a chopping tool; a short axe. **2** (*informal*) a helicopter. **3** a type of bicycle or motor cycle with high handlebars.

**choppy** *adjective* **1** full of short broken waves. **2** jerky, not smooth. □ **choppiness** *noun*

**chopstick** *noun* each of a pair of sticks used by the Chinese and Japanese to lift food to the mouth.

**chopsuey** (chop-soo-i) *noun* a Chinese dish made with small pieces of meat fried with rice and vegetables.

**choral** (kor-ăl) *adjective* written for a choir or chorus; sung or spoken by these. □ **chorally** *adverb*

**chorale** (kor-ahl) *noun* **1** a choral composition, using the words of a hymn. **2** (*especially Amer.*) a choir.

**chord** (*pronounced* kord) *noun* **1** a combination of notes sounded together in harmony. **2** a straight line joining two points on a curve.

**chore** (*pronounced* chor) *noun* a routine or tedious task.

**choreograph** (ko-ri-ŏ-grahf) *verb* provide choreography for.

**choreography** (ko-ri-og-răfi) *noun* the design of ballets or stage dances; the sequence of steps involved in this. □ **choreographer** *noun*, **choreographic** *adjective*

**chorister** (ko-ris-ter) *noun* a member of a choir.

**chortle** *noun* a loud gleeful chuckle. ●*verb* utter a chortle.

**chorus** *noun* **1** a group of singers. **2** a piece of music for these. **3** something spoken or sung by many people together; *a chorus of approval.* **4** the refrain or main part of a song. **5** a group of singing dancers in a musical comedy. ●*verb* (**chorused, chorusing**) sing, speak, or say in chorus. □ **in chorus** speaking or singing all together.

**chose, chosen** *see* CHOOSE.

**Chou En-lai** (choh en-ly) (1898–1976), Chinese statesman, one of the founders of the Chinese Communist party, Premier 1949–76.

**chough** (*pronounced* chuf) *noun* a red-legged crow.

**choux pastry** (*pronounced* shoo) very light pastry enriched with eggs.

**chow** (*rhymes with* cow) *noun* **1** a long-haired dog of a Chinese breed. **2** (*slang*) food.

**chowder** *noun* (*Amer.*) a thick soup containing clams or fish.

**chow mein** (*pronounced* mayn) a Chinese dish of fried noodles with shredded meat and vegetables.

**chrism** *noun* consecrated oil.

**Christ** *noun* **1** the title of Jesus (= 'the anointed one'), now treated as a name. **2** the Messiah as prophesied in the Old Testament. ●*interjection* (*slang*) expressing surprise or anger.

**Christadelphian** (kristă-**del**-fiăn) *noun* a member of a religious sect rejecting the doctrine of the Trinity and expecting the second coming of Christ.

**christen** *verb* **1** admit to the Christian Church by baptism. **2** give a name or nickname to.

**Christendom** (**kris**-ĕn-dŏm) *noun* all Christians, all Christian countries.

**christening** *noun* the ceremony of baptizing or naming.

**Christian** *adjective* **1** of the doctrines of Christianity; believing in or based on these. **2** of Christians. **3** showing the qualities of a Christian; kindly, humane. ●*noun* **1** a person who believes in Christianity. **2** a kindly or humane person. □ **Christian era** the period from the birth of Christ onwards. **Christian name** a name given at a christening, a person's given name. **Christian Science** a religious system claiming that health and healing can be achieved through the mental effect of the Christian faith, without medical treatment. **Christian Scientist** one who believes in this system.

**Christianity** *noun* **1** the religion based on the belief that Christ was the incarnate Son of God, and on his teachings. **2** being a Christian.

**Christie¹**, Dame Agatha (1890–1976), English author of detective fiction.

**Christie²**, Linford (born 1960), English sprinter.

**Christie's** a London firm of auctioneers of works of art.

**Christmas** *noun* (*plural* **Christmases**) the Christian festival (celebrated on 25 December) commemorating Christ's birth; the period about this time. □ **Christmas box** a small present or gratuity given at Christmas, especially to employees. **Christmas Day** 25 December. **Christmas Eve** 24 December. **Christmas pudding** a rich dark steamed pudding with dried fruit, eaten at Christmas. **Christmas rose** white-flowered hellebore, blooming in winter. **Christmas tree** an evergreen (or artificial) tree decorated at Christmas.

**Christmassy** *adjective* looking festive, typical of Christmas.

**Christopher**, St, legendary martyr, adopted as the patron saint of travellers.

**chromatic** (krŏ-**mat**-ik) *adjective* of colour, in colours. □ **chromatic scale** (in music) a scale that ascends or descends by semitones.

**chromatin** *noun* chromosome material in a cell nucleus that takes up stain easily, making it visible under a microscope.

**chromatography** (kroh-mă-**tog**-ră-fi) *noun* separation of a mixture into its component substances by passing it over material which absorbs these at different rates so that they appear as layers, often of different colours.

**chrome** (*pronounced* krohm) *noun* **1** chromium. **2** (in full **chrome yellow**) yellow colouring-matter obtained from a compound of chromium.

**chromite** *noun* a mineral of chromium and iron oxides.

**chromium** (**kroh**-mi-ŭm) *noun* a chemical element (symbol Cr), a hard metal used in making stainless steel and for coating other metals; *chromium-plated*.

**chromosome** (**kroh**-mŏ-sohm) *noun* one of the tiny thread-like structures in animal and plant cells, carrying genes.

**chronic** *adjective* **1** (of a disease etc.) affecting a person for a long time, constantly recurring. **2** having had an illness or a habit for a long time; *a chronic invalid*. **3** (*informal*) very unpleasant; *this weather is chronic*. **4** (*informal*) habitual; *a chronic liar*. □ **chronically** *adverb*

**chronicle** (**kron**-ikŭl) *noun* **1** a record of events in the order of their happening. **2** (**Chronicles**) either of two books of the Old Testament recording the history of Israel and Judah. ●*verb* record in a chronicle. □ **chronicler** *noun*

**chronological** (kron-ŏ-**loj**-ikăl) *adjective* arranged in the order in which things occurred. □ **chronologically** *adverb*

**chronology** (krŏn-**ol**-ŏji) *noun* the arrangement of events in the order in which they occurred.

**chronometer** (krŏn-**om**-it-er) *noun* a time-measuring instrument, especially one used in navigation.

**chrysalis** (**kris**-ă-lis) *noun* (*plural* **chrysalises**) the stage in an insect's life when it forms a sheath inside which it changes from a grub to an adult insect, especially a butterfly or moth.

**chrysanthemum** *noun* a garden plant with bright flowers, blooming in autumn.

**chrysoberyl** (kris-ŏ-**berril**) *noun* a yellowish-green gem.

**chrysolite** (kris-ŏ-lyt) *noun* a precious stone, a variety of olivine.

**chrysoprase** (kris-ŏ-prayz) *noun* an apple-green variety of chalcedony.

**Chrysostom** (kris-ŏ-stŏm), St John (*c.*347–407), Greek patriarch of Constantinople.

**chub** *noun* (*plural* **chub**) a thick-bodied river fish.

**Chubb** *noun* (in full **Chubb lock**) (*trade mark*) a lock with a device for fixing the bolt immovably should someone try to pick it.

**chubby** *adjective* (**chubbier**, **chubbiest**) round and plump. □ **chubbiness** *noun*

**chuck** *verb* **1** (*informal*) throw carelessly or casually. **2** (*informal*) give up, resign. **3** touch playfully under the chin. ●*noun* **1** a playful touch. **2** the part of a lathe that grips the drill; the part of a drill that holds the bit. **3** a cut of beef from the neck to the ribs; chuck steak. □ **chuck out** (*informal*) **1** throw away. **2** expel (a troublesome person).

**chuckle** *noun* a quiet or half-suppressed laugh. ●*verb* give a chuckle.

**chuff** *verb* (of an engine) work with a regular sharp puffing sound.

**chuffed** *adjective* (*slang*) pleased.

**chug** *verb* (**chugged, chugging**) make a dull short repeated sound, like an engine running slowly. ●*noun* this sound.

**chukka boot** an ankle-high leather boot.

**chukker** *noun* (also **chukka**) a period of play in polo.

**chum** *noun* (*informal*) a close friend. □ **chum up** (**chummed, chumming**) (*informal*) form a close friendship.

**chummy** *adjective* very friendly.

**chump** *noun* **1** (*informal*) a foolish person. **2** a short thick block of wood. □ **chump chop** a chop from the thick end of a loin of mutton.

**chunk** *noun* **1** a thick piece of something. **2** a substantial amount.

**chunky** *adjective* **1** short and thick. **2** in chunks; containing chunks.

**Chunnel** *noun* (*informal*) the Channel Tunnel.

**chunter** *verb* (*informal*) mutter, grumble.

**chupatty** alternative spelling of CHAPATTI.

**church** *noun* **1** a building for public Christian worship. **2** a religious service in this; *see you after church.* **3** (**the Church**) the whole body of Christian believers; a particular group of these; the clergy. □ **Church of England** the English branch of the Western Church, rejecting the pope's supremacy. **Church of Scotland** the national (Presbyterian) Church of Scotland.

**churchgoer** *noun* a person who attends church regularly.

**Churchill**, Sir Winston Leonard Spencer (1874–1965), British statesman, Prime Minister 1940–5.

**churchman** *noun* (*plural* **churchmen**) **1** a clergyman. **2** a member of a Church.

**churchwarden** *noun* a representative of a parish who helps with the business of the church.

**churchyard** *noun* the enclosed land round a church, often used for burials.

**churlish** *adjective* ill-mannered, surly. □ **churlishly** *adverb*, **churlishness** *noun*

**churn** *noun* **1** a machine in which milk is beaten to make butter. **2** a large can in which milk is carried from a farm. ●*verb* **1** beat (milk) or make (butter) in a churn. **2** stir or swirl violently. □ **churn out** produce in quantity. **churn up** break up the surface of.

**chute** (*pronounced* shoot) *noun* **1** a sloping or vertical channel down which things can slide or be dropped. **2** (*informal*) a parachute.

**chutney** *noun* a highly seasoned mixture of fruit, vinegar, sugar, spices, etc.

**chutzpah** (khuuts-pă) *noun* (*slang*) shameless cheek; impudence.

**CI** *abbreviation* Channel Islands.

**Ci** *abbreviation* curie.

**CIA** *abbreviation* (in the USA) Central Intelligence Agency.

**ciao** (*pronounced* chow) *interjection* (*informal*) **1** goodbye. **2** hello.

**cicada** (sik-ah-dă) *noun* a grasshopper-like insect that makes a shrill chirping sound.

**cicatrice** (sik-ă-triss) *noun* the scar left by a healed wound.

**Cicero** (sis-er-oh), Marcus Tullius (106–43 BC), Roman statesman, orator, and writer.

**cicerone** (chich-er-**oh**-ni) *noun* (*plural* **ciceroni**) a guide who shows antiquities to visitors.

**CID** *abbreviation* Criminal Investigation Department.

**Cid** (*pronounced* sid), **el** *or* **the** the title in Spanish literature of Ruy Diaz, 11th-century champion of Christianity against the Moors.

**cider** *noun* a alcoholic drink made from fermented apples.

**c.i.f.** *abbreviation* cost, insurance, freight.

**cigar** *noun* a roll of tobacco leaves for smoking.

**cigarette** *noun* a roll of shredded tobacco enclosed in thin paper for smoking.

**ciliate** (sil-i-ăt) *adjective* having cilia.

**cilium** (sil-i-ŭm) *noun* (*plural* **cilia**) **1** each of the minute hairs fringing a leaf, an insect's wing, etc. **2** a hairlike vibrating organ on animal or vegetable tissue.

**cinch** (*pronounced* sinch) *noun* (*slang*) **1** a certainty. **2** an easy task.

**cinchona** (sink-**oh**-nă) *noun* **1** a South American evergreen tree or shrub whose bark is the source of quinine. **2** this bark.

**cincture** (sink-tewr) *noun* (*literary*) a girdle, belt, or border.

**cinder** *noun* **1** a small piece of partly burnt coal or wood. **2** (**cinders**) ashes.

**Cinderella** *noun* a person or thing that is persistently neglected in favour of others. (¶ Named after a girl in a fairy tale.)

**cine-** (sin-i) *combining form* cinematographic; *cine-camera*; *cine-film*; *cine-projector*.

**cinema** *noun* **1** a theatre where motion pictures are shown. **2** films as an art form or an industry. □ **cinematic** *adjective*

**cinematographic** (sini-matŏ-**graf**-ik) *adjective* for taking or projecting motion pictures.

**cinematography** (sini-mă-**tog**-răfi) *noun* the art of making motion-picture films.

**cineraria** (sin-er-**air**-iă) *noun* a plant with brightly coloured daisy-like flowers.

**cinerary urn** (sin-er-er-i) an urn for holding a person's ashes after cremation.

**cinnabar** (sin-ă-bar) *noun* **1** red mercuric sulphide; the pigment obtained from this, vermilion. **2** a moth with reddish-marked wings.

**cinnamon** (sin-a-mŏn) *noun* **1** spice made from the inner bark of a south-east Asian tree. **2** its colour, yellowish-brown.

**cinque** (*pronounced* sink) *noun* the five on dice.

**cinquefoil** (sink-foil) *noun* **1** a plant with a compound leaf of five leaflets, potentilla. **2** an ornament with five cusps.

**Cinque Ports** (*pronounced* sink) a group of medieval ports in south-east England (originally five; Dover, Hastings, Hythe, Romney, and Sandwich; Rye and Winchelsea were added later) formerly allowed various trading privileges in return for providing the bulk of England's navy.

**cipher** (sy-fer) *noun* (also **cypher**) **1** a symbol (0), representing nought or zero. **2** any Arabic numeral. **3** a person or thing of no importance. **4** a set of letters or symbols representing others, used to conceal the meaning of a message etc. ●*verb* write in cipher.

**circa** (ser-kă) *preposition* (preceding a date) about; *china from circa 1850*.

**circadian** (ser-**kay**-diăn) *adjective* (of biological processes) occurring about once a day.

**Circassian** (ser-kas-iăn) *adjective* of a group of people from the north Caucasus on the border between Georgia and Russia. ●*noun* a member of this group.

**Circe** (ser-si) (*Gk. legend*) an enchantress who detained Odysseus on her island and changed his companions into pigs.

**circle** *noun* **1** a perfectly round plane figure. **2** the line enclosing it, every point on which is the same distance from the centre. **3** something shaped like this, a ring. **4** curved rows of seats rising in tiers at a theatre etc. above the lowest level. **5** a number of people bound together by similar interests; *in business circles*. ●*verb* move in a circle, form a circle round. □ **come full circle** pass through a series of events etc. and return to the starting-point. **go round in circles** be busy but making no progress.

**circlet** (ser-klit) *noun* a circular band worn as an ornament, especially round the head.

**circuit** (ser-kit) *noun* **1** a line, route, or distance round a place; a motor-racing track. **2** a closed path for an electric current; an apparatus with conductors, valves, etc., through which electric current passes. **3** the journey of a judge round a particular district to hold courts; the district itself. **4** a group of Methodist churches in a district. **5** a sequence of sporting events; *the American golf circuit*. **6** a chain of theatres or cinemas. □ **circuit-breaker** *noun* a device for interrupting an electric current.

**circuitous** (ser-**kew**-it-ŭs) *adjective* roundabout, indirect. □ **circuitously** *adverb*

**circuitry** (ser-kit-ri) *noun* electric circuits; the equipment forming these.

**circular** *adjective* **1** shaped like a circle. **2** moving round a circle; following a route that brings travellers back to the starting-point. **3** (of reasoning) using as evidence for its conclusion the very thing that it is trying to prove. **4** addressed to a number of people; *a circular letter*. ●*noun* a circular letter or advertising leaflet. □ **circular saw** a power saw with a rotating toothed disc. □ **circularity** (ser-kew-**la**-riti) *noun*

**circularize** *verb* (also **circularise**) send a circular to.

**circulate** *verb* **1** go round continuously. **2** pass from place to place. **3** cause to move round; send round; *we will circulate this letter*. **4** circularize; *we will circulate these people*.

**circulation** *noun* **1** circulating, being circulated. **2** the movement of blood round the body, pumped by the heart. **3** the number of copies sold or distributed, especially of a newspaper.

**circulatory** (ser-kew-**layt**-er-i) *adjective* of the circulation of blood.

**circum-** *combining form* around, about.

**circumcise** *verb* cut off the foreskin of (a male person) or the clitoris of (a female) as a religious rite or surgically. □ **circumcision** *noun*

**circumference** (ser-**kum**-fer-ĕns) *noun* the boundary of a circle, the distance round this.

**circumflex** (ser-**kŭm**-fleks) *noun* (in full **circumflex accent**) a mark (ˆ) over a vowel, as over *e* in *fête*.

**circumlocution** (ser-kŭm-lŏ-**kew**-shŏn) *noun* **1** use of many words where a few would do. **2** evasive talk.

**circumnavigate** *verb* sail completely round. □ **circumnavigation** *noun*

**circumscribe** *verb* **1** draw a line round. **2** mark the limits of, restrict.

**circumscription** *noun* circumscribing.

**circumspect** (ser-**kŭm**-spekt) *adjective* cautious and watchful, wary. □ **circumspection** *noun*

**circumstance** *noun* **1** any of the conditions or facts connected with an event, person, or action; *he was a victim of circumstances*. **2** (**circumstances**) one's financial situation; *what are his circumstances?* **3** ceremony; *pomp and circumstance*. □ **in** or **under the circumstances** owing to or making allowances for the situation. **under no circumstances** not (do something) whatever happens; never.

**circumstantial** (ser-kŭm-**stan**-shăl) *adjective* **1** giving full details. **2** consisting of facts that strongly suggest something but do not provide direct proof; *circumstantial evidence*. □ **circumstantially** *adverb*, **circumstantiality** *noun*

**circumvent** (ser-kŭm-**vent**) *verb* evade, find a way round; *managed to circumvent the rules*. □ **circumvention** *noun*

**circus** *noun* **1** a travelling show with performing acrobats, clowns, and often animals. **2** (*informal*) a scene of lively action. **3** (*informal*) a group of people performing in sports or a series of lectures etc. either together or in succession. **4** (*in place-names*) an open space in a town, where streets converge; *Piccadilly Circus*. **5** (in ancient Rome) an arena for sports and games.

**cirque** (*pronounced* serk) *noun* a bowl-shaped hollow on a mountain.

**cirrhosis** (si-**roh**-sis) *noun* a chronic disease, especially of alcoholics, in which the liver hardens into many small projections.

**cirrus** (**si**-rus) *noun* (*plural* **cirri**) light wispy clouds.

**CIS** *abbrev.* Commonwealth of Independent States, a loose confederation of former constituent republics of the USSR.

**cissy** *noun* alternative spelling of SISSY.

**Cistercian** (sis-**ter**-shăn) *noun* a member of a religious order that was founded as a branch of the Benedictines. ●*adjective* of this order.

**cistern** (**sis**-tern) *noun* **1** a tank or other vessel for storing water; the tank above a lavatory. **2** an underground reservoir.

**citadel** (**sit**-ă-děl) *noun* a fortress overlooking a city.

**citation** *noun* **1** citing; a passage cited. **2** *Military* an official mention or award for bravery etc.

**cite** (*pronounced as* sight) *verb* **1** quote or mention as an example or to support an argument. **2** mention in a official dispatch. **3** summon to appear in court.

**citizen** *noun* **1** an inhabitant of a city. **2** a person who has full rights in a country or commonwealth by birth or by naturalization. □ **Citizens' Advice Bureau** (in the UK) an office where the public can receive free advice on civil matters. **citizen's band** radio frequencies to be used by private individuals for local communication. **Citizens' Charter** a British government document produced in 1991, designed to guarantee that public services meet certain standards of performance. □ **citizenship** *noun*

**citizenry** *noun* citizens collectively.

**citrate** *noun* a salt of citric acid.

**citric acid** (**sit**-rik) the acid in the juice of lemons, limes, etc.

**citronella** *noun* a lemon-scented grass from S. Asia which yields an oil used as an insect repellent and a fragrance.

**citrus** (**sit**-rŭs) *noun* any of a group of related trees including lemon, orange, and grapefruit. □ **citrus fruit** fruit from such a tree.

**city** *noun* **1** a large and important town, a town with special rights given by charter and containing a cathedral. **2** (**the City**) the oldest part of London, governed by the Lord Mayor and Corporation, now a centre of commerce and finance.

**civet** (**siv**-it) *noun* **1** (also **civet-cat**) a cat-like animal of Central Africa. **2** a musky-smelling substance obtained from its glands, used in making perfumes.

**civic** (**siv**-ik) *adjective* of or proper to a city or town; of citizens or citizenship. ●*noun* (**civics**) the study of municipal government and the rights and duties of citizens. □ **civic centre** an area containing municipal offices and other public buildings.

**civil** *adjective* **1** belonging to citizens. **2** of the general public, not the armed forces or the Church; *civil aviation*; *civil marriage*. **3** involving civil law not criminal law; *a civil dispute*. **4** polite and obliging. □ **civil defence** an organization for protecting and assisting civilians in an air raid or other enemy action or in a natural disaster. **civil disobedience** a form of peaceful protest involving refusal to comply with certain laws. **civil engineering** the designing and construction of roads, bridges, canals, etc. **civil law** law dealing with the private rights of citizens, not with crime. **civil liberties** freedom of action and speech; basic rights of the individual. **civil list** the allowance of money made by Parliament for the sovereign's household expenses. **civil rights** the rights of a citizen. **civil servant** an employee of the **civil service**, all government departments other than the armed forces. **civil war** war between groups of citizens of the same country. □ **civilly** *adverb*

**civilian** *noun* a person not serving in the armed forces.

**civility** *noun* politeness; an act of politeness.

**civilization** *noun* (also **civilisation**) **1** making or becoming civilized. **2** a stage in the evolution of organized society; a particular type of this; *ancient civilizations.* **3** civilized conditions or society; *far from civilization.*

**civilize** *verb* (also **civilise**) **1** cause to improve from a savage or primitive stage of human society to a more developed one. **2** improve the behaviour of.

**civvies** (**siv-iz**) *plural noun* (*slang*) civilian clothes.

**Civvy Street** (*slang*) civilian life.

**Cl** *symbol* chlorine.

**cl** *abbreviation* centilitre(s).

**clack** *noun* **1** a short sharp sound like that made by plates struck together. **2** the noise of chatter. ●*verb* make such a sound or noise.

**clad** *adjective* **1** clothed; *warmly clad.* **2** covered with cladding; *iron-clad.*

**cladding** *noun* material applied to the surface of another as a protective covering.

**cladistics** (**klă-dist-iks**) *noun* a method of studying the relationship of groups of living things by tracing the course of their development from a common ancestor, by analysis of shared features.

**claim** *verb* **1** request as one's right or due. **2** declare that something is true or has been achieved; state without being able to prove. **3** have as an achievement or consequence; *the floods claimed many lives.* ●*noun* **1** a request for something as one's right; *lay claim to.* **2** the right to something; *a widow has a claim on her deceased husband's estate.* **3** a statement claiming that something is true, an assertion. **4** a thing (especially land) claimed.

**claimant** *noun* a person who makes a claim, especially in law.

**clairvoyance** (**klair-voy-ăns**) *noun* the supposed power of seeing in the mind either future events or things that are hap-

pening or existing out of sight. □ **clairvoyant** *noun & adjective*

**clam** *noun* a large shellfish with a hinged shell. □ **clam up** (**clammed, clamming**) (*informal*) refuse to talk.

**clamber** *verb* climb with some difficulty using the hands and feet. ●*noun* a difficult climb.

**clammy** *adjective* unpleasantly moist and sticky. □ **clammily** *adverb*, **clamminess** *noun*

**clamour** *noun* (*Amer.* **clamor**) **1** a loud confused noise, especially of shouting. **2** a loud protest or demand. ●*verb* make a loud protest or demand. □ **clamorous** *adjective*

**clamp** *noun* **1** a device for holding things tightly, often with a screw. **2** a mound of potatoes etc. stored under straw and earth. ●*verb* grip with a clamp; fix firmly. □ **clamp down on** become stricter about; put a stop to.

**clan** *noun* **1** a group with a common ancestor; *the Scottish clans.* **2** a large family forming a close group.

**clandestine** (**klan-dest-in**) *adjective* kept secret, done secretly. □ **clandestinely** *adverb*

**clang** *noun* a loud ringing sound. ●*verb* make a clang.

**clanger** *noun* (*slang*) a blunder; *drop a clanger.*

**clangour** (**klang-er**) *noun* (*Amer.* **clangor**) a clanging noise. □ **clangorous** *adjective*

**clank** *noun* a metallic sound like that of metal striking metal. ●*verb* make a clank.

**clannish** *adjective* showing clan feeling, clinging together and excluding others.

**clansman** *noun* (*plural* **clansmen**) a member of a clan.

**clap**[1] *noun* **1** the sharp noise of thunder. **2** the sound of the palms of the hands being struck together, especially in applause. **3** a friendly slap; *gave him a clap on the shoulder.* ●*verb* (**clapped, clapping**) **1** strike the palms loudly together, especially in applause. **2** flap (wings) audibly. **3** put or place quickly; *clapped him into gaol.* □ **clap eyes on** (*informal*) catch sight of. **clapped out** (*slang*) worn out; exhausted.

**clap**[2] *noun* (*vulgar*) venereal disease, gonorrhoea.

**clapper** *noun* the tongue or striker of a bell. □ **going like the clappers** (*slang*) going very fast.

**clapperboard** *noun* a device in film-making of hinged boards struck together to synchronize the starting of the picture and sound.

**claptrap** *noun* pretentious talk or ideas; nonsense.

**claque** (*pronounced* klak) *noun* a group of people hired to applaud something.

**Clare**, St (1194-1253), foundress of the 'Poor Clares', an order of Franciscan nuns.

**claret** (kla-rĕt) *noun* a dry red wine, especially from Bordeaux.

**clarify** *verb* (**clarified, clarifying**) **1** make or become clear or easier to understand. **2** remove impurities from (fats), e.g. by heating. □ **clarification** *noun*

**clarinet** (kla-rin-et) *noun* a woodwind instrument with finger-holes and keys.

**clarinettist** *noun* (*Amer.* **clarinetist**) a person who plays the clarinet.

**clarion** (kla-ri-ŏn) *noun* **1** a loud clear rousing sound. **2** (*old use*) a shrill war-trumpet.

**clarity** *noun* clearness.

**Clarke**, Arthur Charles (born 1917), English writer of science-fiction stories and novels.

**clash** *verb* **1** strike making a loud harsh sound like that of cymbals. **2** conflict; disagree. **3** take place inconveniently at the same time as something else. **4** (of colours) produce an unpleasant visual effect by not being harmonious. ●*noun* **1** a sound of clashing. **2** a conflict; a disagreement. **3** a clashing of colours.

**clasp** *noun* **1** a device for fastening things, with interlocking parts. **2** a grasp, a handshake. ●*verb* **1** fasten; join with a clasp. **2** grasp; hold or embrace closely. □ **clasp-knife** *noun* a folding knife with a catch to hold the blade open.

**class** *noun* **1** people, animals, or things with some characteristics in common. **2** people of the same social or economic level; *the working class; the upper class*. **3** a set of students taught together; a session when these are taught. **4** a division according to quality; *first class; tourist class*. **5** distinction, high quality; *a tennis player with class*. ●*verb* place in a class, classify. □ **in a class of its own** much superior to everything else of its kind.

**classic** *adjective* **1** having a high quality that is recognized and unquestioned; *Hardy's classic novel*. **2** very typical; *a classic case of malnutrition*. **3** having qualities like those of classical art, simple and harmonious; *classic clothes*. **4** famous through being long established; *the classic races*. ●*noun* **1** a classic author or work etc.; *'David Copperfield' is a classic*. **2** a garment in classic style. **3** a classic race. **4** (**classics**) the study of ancient Greek and Roman literature, culture, etc.

**classical** *adjective* **1** model or first-class, especially in literature. **2** of ancient Greek and Roman art, literature, and culture; *a classical scholar*. **3** restrained, traditional, or standard in style. **4** (of music) serious or conventional, or of the period *c*.1750-1800. **5** (of a language) of the form used by ancient standard authors. □ **classically** *adverb*

**classicism** *noun* following of the classic style.

**classicist** *noun* a classical scholar.

**classificatory** *adjective* of or involving classification.

**classified** *adjective* **1** (of advertisements) arranged according to subject-matter. **2** (of information) designated as officially secret.

**classify** *verb* (**classified, classifying**) arrange systematically in classes or groups, put into a particular class. □ **classification** *noun*, **classifiable** *adjective*

**classless** *adjective* without distinctions of social class.

**classroom** *noun* a room where a class of students is taught.

**classy** *adjective* (*slang*) stylish, superior. □ **classily** *adverb*, **classiness** *noun*

**clatter** *noun* **1** a sound like that of plates rattled together. **2** noisy talk. ●*verb* make or cause to make a clatter.

**Claudius** (10 BC-AD 54), Tiberius Claudius Nero Germanicus, Roman emperor 41-54.

**clause** *noun* **1** a single part in a treaty, law, or contract. **2** *Grammar* a part of a sentence, with its own finite verb. □ **clausal** *adjective*

**claustrophobia** (klaw-strŏ-**foh**-biă) *noun* abnormal fear of being in an enclosed space. □ **claustrophobic** *adjective*

**clavichord** (**klav**-i-kord) *noun* an early small stringed keyboard instrument with a very soft tone.

**clavicle** (**klav**-ikŭl) *noun* the collar-bone.

**claw** *noun* **1** the pointed nail on an animal's or bird's foot; a foot with such nails. **2** the pincers of a shellfish; *a lobster's claw*. **3** a device like a claw, used for grappling and holding things. ●*verb* grasp, scratch, or pull with a claw or the hands. □ **claw back** regain laboriously or gradually. **claw-hammer** *noun* a hammer with a head divided at one end for pulling out nails.

**Clay**, Cassius, *see* ALI.

**clay** *noun* stiff sticky earth that becomes hard when baked, used for making bricks and pottery. □ **clay pigeon** a breakable disc thrown up as a target for shooting. □ **clayey** *adjective*

**claymore** *noun* (*hist.*) a Scottish two-edged broadsword.

**clean** *adjective* **1** free from dirt or impurities, not soiled. **2** not yet used; *a clean page*. **3** (of a nuclear bomb) producing relatively little fallout. **4** containing or involving nothing dishonourable; (of a licence) with no endorsements. **5** attentive to cleanliness, with clean habits. **6** without projections or roughness, smooth and even. **7** keeping to the rules; not unfair; *a clean fighter*. **8** free from indecency; *clean jokes*. ●*adverb* completely, entirely; *I clean forgot*. ●*verb* make or become clean. ●*noun* an act of cleaning. □ **clean-cut** *adjective* sharply outlined; *clean-cut features*. **clean out 1** clean the inside of. **2** (*slang*) use up all the supplies or money of. **clean-shaven** *adjective* without beard, moustache, or whiskers. **clean up 1** make clean and tidy. **2** rid of crime and corruption. **3** (*informal*) make a gain or profit. **make a clean breast of** confess fully about. □ **cleanness** *noun*

**cleaner** *noun* **1** a device or substance used for cleaning things. **2** a person employed to clean rooms. **3** (**cleaners**) a dry-cleaning establishment. □ **take to the cleaners** (*slang*) **1** rob or defraud. **2** criticize strongly.

**cleanly**[1] *adverb* in a clean way.

**cleanly**[2] (**klen**-li) *adjective* attentive to cleanness, with clean habits. □ **cleanliness** *noun*

**cleanse** (*pronounced* klenz) *verb* make thoroughly clean. □ **cleanser** *noun*

**clear** *adjective* **1** transparent; not cloudy; *clear glass*; *clear water*; *clear soup*. **2** free from blemishes. **3** free from guilt; *a clear conscience*. **4** easily seen, heard, or understood; distinct. **5** evident; *a clear case of cheating*. **6** free from doubt, not confused. **7** free from obstruction or from something undesirable. **8** net, without deductions, complete; *a clear £1000*; *give 3 clear days' notice*. ●*adverb* **1** clearly. **2** completely. **3** apart, not in contact; *stand clear!* ●*verb* **1** make or become clear. **2** free (one's throat) of phlegm or huskiness by a slight cough. **3** get past or over, especially without touching. **4** get approval or authorization for; *clear goods through customs*. **5** pass (a cheque) through a clearing house. **6** make as net gain or profit. □ **clear away** remove; remove used crockery etc. after a meal. **clear-cut** *adjective* very distinct; not open to doubt. **clear off** (*slang*) go away. **clear the decks** clear away hindrances and prepare for action. **clear up 1** tidy up. **2** become better or brighter. **3** solve (a mystery, problem, etc.). **in the clear** free of suspicion or difficulty. □ **clearly** *adverb*, **clearness** *noun*

**clearance** *noun* **1** clearing. **2** authorization, permission. **3** the space left clear when one object moves within or past another. □ **clearance order** an order for the demolition of buildings.

**clearing** *noun* an open space from which trees have been cleared in a forest.

**clearing bank** a large bank which is a member of a clearing house.

**clearing house 1** an office at which banks exchange cheques and settle the balances. **2** an agency that collects and distributes information etc.

**clearway** *noun* a main road (other than a motorway) on which vehicles must not stop.

**cleat** *noun* **1** a short piece of wood or metal with projecting ends round which a rope may be fastened. **2** a strip or other projecting piece fixed to a gangway etc. or to footwear, to prevent slipping. **3** a wedge. ●*verb* fasten to a cleat.

**cleavage** *noun* **1** a split, a division made by cleaving. **2** the hollow between a woman's breasts.

**cleave**[1] *verb* **1** divide by chopping; split or become split. **2** make a way through.

■**Usage** The past tense may be either *cleaved* or *clove* or *cleft*, *has cloven* or *has cleft*; *he cleaved it in two*, *he clove it in two*, *he cleft in two*. *Clove* and *cleft* are rather old-fashioned. In the past perfect, both are used. The adjectives *cloven* and *cleft* are used of different objects (*see* CLEFT *and* CLOVEN).

**cleave**[2] *verb* (*literary*) adhere, cling.

**cleaver** *noun* a butcher's chopper.

**clef** *noun* a symbol on a stave in a musical score, showing the pitch of the notes (e.g. treble, bass).

**cleft** *see* CLEAVE[1]. ●*adjective* split, partly divided; with a V-shaped hollow; *a cleft stick*. ●*noun* a split, a cleavage. □ **cleft palate** a defect in the roof of the mouth where two sides of the palate failed to join before birth. **in a cleft stick** in a difficult dilemma.

**clematis** (**klem**-ă-tiss *or* klim-**ay**-tiss) *noun* a flowering climbing plant.

**clemency** (**klem**-ĕn-si) *noun* **1** mildness, especially of weather. **2** mercy.

**clement** *adjective* **1** (of weather) mild, pleasant. **2** merciful.

**clementine** (**klem**-ĕn-tyn) *noun* a citrus fruit resembling a small orange.

**clench** *verb* **1** close (the teeth or fingers) tightly. **2** grasp tightly. **3** fasten (a nail or rivet) by hammering the point sideways after it is driven through. ●*noun* a clenching action; a clenched state.

**Cleopatra** (69–30 BC), ruler of Egypt from 51 BC.

**clerestory** (**kleer**-stor-i) *noun* an upper row of windows in a large church, above the level of the roofs of the aisles.

**clergy** *noun* the people who have been ordained as priests or ministers of the Christian Church.

**clergyman** *noun* (*plural* **clergymen**) a member of the clergy.

**cleric** (kle-rik) *noun* a member of the clergy.

**clerical** *adjective* **1** of clerks. **2** of the clergy. □ **clerical collar** an upright white collar fastening at the back, worn by clergy.

**clerihew** (kle-ri-hew) *noun* a short witty verse in 4 lines of unequal length, rhyming in couplets and referring to a famous person.

**clerk** (*pronounced* klark) *noun* **1** a person employed to keep records or accounts etc. in an office. **2** an official who keeps the records of a court or council etc. □ **clerk of (the) works** the overseer of building works.

**Cleveland** a county of north-east England (1974–94).

**clever** *adjective* **1** quick at learning and understanding things, talented. **2** showing skill; *a clever plan.* □ **cleverly** *adverb*, **cleverness** *noun*

**cliché** (klee-shay) *noun* a hackneyed phrase or idea. □ **clichéd** *adjective* (also **cliché'd**).

**click** *noun* a short sharp sound like that of billiard balls colliding. ●*verb* **1** make or cause to make a click; fasten with a click. **2** (*informal*) be a success. **3** (*informal*) become understood. **4** (*informal*) get on well; *we just clicked.*

**client** *noun* **1** a person using the services of a lawyer, architect, or other professional person. **2** a customer.

**clientele** (klee-on-tel) *noun* clients, customers.

**cliff** *noun* a steep rock-face, especially on a coast. □ **cliff-hanger** *noun* a story or contest full of suspense.

**climacteric** (kly-mak-ter-ik) *noun* the period of life when fertility and sexual activity begin to decline.

**climactic** (kly-mak-tik) *adjective* of a climax.

**climate** *noun* **1** the regular weather conditions of an area. **2** an area with certain weather conditions; *living in a hot climate.* **3** a general attitude or feeling; an atmosphere; *a climate of hostility.* □ **climatic** (kly-mat-ik) *adjective*, **climatically** *adverb*

**climax** *noun* **1** the event or point of greatest interest or intensity. **2** an orgasm. ●*verb* reach or bring to a climax.

**climb** *verb* **1** go up or over; move upwards. **2** grow up a support; *a climbing rose.* ●*noun* an ascent made by climbing. □ **climb down 1** go downwards by effort. **2** retreat from a position taken up in argument. **climb-down** *noun* a retreat of this kind. **climbing frame** a structure of joined pipes and bars for children to climb on.

**climber** *noun* **1** one who climbs, a mountaineer. **2** a climbing plant.

**clime** *noun* (*literary*) **1** a region. **2** a climate.

**clinch** *verb* **1** fasten securely; clench (a nail or rivet). **2** (in boxing) be too close together for a full-arm blow. **3** settle conclusively; *clinched the deal.* ●*noun* **1** a clinching position in boxing. **2** (*informal*) an embrace.

**clincher** *noun* a decisive point that settles an argument, proposition, etc.

**cling** *verb* (**clung**, **clinging**) **1** hold on tightly. **2** become attached, stick. **3** remain close or in contact; be emotionally attached or dependent. **4** refuse to abandon; *clinging to hopes of rescue.* □ **cling film** thin clinging polythene used as a wrapping for food.

**clinic** *noun* **1** a private or specialized hospital. **2** a place or session at which specialized treatment or advice is given to visiting persons; *antenatal clinic.*

**clinical** *adjective* **1** of a clinic. **2** of or used in the treatment of patients. **3** of or based on observed signs and symptoms; *clinical medicine; clinical death.* **4** looking bare and hygienic. **5** unemotional, cool and detached. □ **clinically** *adverb*

**clink**[1] *noun* a thin sharp sound like glasses striking together. ●*verb* make or cause to make this sound.

**clink**[2] *noun* (*slang*) prison; *in clink.*

**clinker** *noun* a mass of slag or lava; rough stony material left after coal has burnt.

**clinker-built** *adjective* (of a boat) made with the outside planks overlapping downwards.

**Clinton,** Bill (William Jefferson) (born 1946), American Democratic statesman, 42nd President of the USA from 1993.

**clip**[1] *noun* **1** a device for holding things tightly or together; a paper-clip. **2** a magazine for a firearm. **3** an ornament fastened by a clip. ●*verb* (**clipped**, **clipping**) fix or fasten with a clip. □ **clip-on** *adjective* attached by a clip.

**clip**[2] *verb* (**clipped**, **clipping**) **1** cut or trim with shears or scissors. **2** punch a small piece from (a ticket) to show that it has been used. **3** (*informal*) hit sharply; *clipped his ear.* ●*noun* **1** the act or process of clipping; a piece clipped off or out. **2** the wool cut from a sheep or flock at one shearing. **3** an extract from a film. **4** (*informal*) a sharp blow. **5** a rapid pace; *going at quite a clip.* □ **clip-joint** *noun* (*slang*) a club charging high prices.

**clipboard** *noun* a portable board with a spring clip at the top for holding papers.

**clipper** *noun* **1** a fast sailing-ship. **2** (**clippers**) an instrument for clipping hair etc.

**clipping** *noun* a piece clipped off or out, especially from a newspaper.

**clique** (*pronounced* kleek) *noun* a small exclusive group. □ **cliquey** *adjective*, **cliquish** *adjective*

**clitoris** (klit-er-iss) *noun* a small sensitive erectile part of the female genitals, at the upper end of the vulva. □ **clitoral** *adjective*

**Cllr.** *abbreviation* Councillor.

**cloaca** (kloh-ay-kă) *noun* the excretory opening at the end of the intestinal canal in birds, reptiles, etc.

**cloak** *noun* **1** a loose sleeveless outdoor garment. **2** something that conceals; *under the cloak of darkness.* ● *verb* cover or conceal. □ **cloak-and-dagger** *adjective* involving intrigue and espionage.

**cloakroom** *noun* **1** a room where outdoor clothes and packages etc. may be left temporarily. **2** a lavatory.

**clobber** *noun* (*slang*) clothing and equipment. ● *verb* (*slang*) **1** hit repeatedly. **2** defeat. **3** criticize severely.

**cloche** (*pronounced* klosh) *noun* **1** a portable glass or plastic cover for outdoor plants. **2** a woman's close-fitting bell-shaped hat.

**clock** *noun* **1** an instrument (other than a watch) for measuring and showing the time. **2** a measuring device resembling this, e.g. a speedometer. **3** time considered as something to be beaten; *run against the clock.* **4** the seed-head of a dandelion. ● *verb* **1** time (a race or competitor). **2** (*informal*) (often foll. by *up*) achieve as a speed; *he clocked up 10 seconds for the 100 metres.* **3** (*slang*) hit. □ **clock golf** a game in which a golf-ball is putted into a hole from points marked round this. **clock in** *or* **on** register one's arrival at work. **clock out** *or* **off** register one's departure from work. **round the clock** all day and night.

**clockwise** *adverb & adjective* moving in a curve from left to right, in the same direction as the hands of a clock.

**clockwork** *noun* a mechanism with wheels and springs; *clockwork toys.* □ **like clockwork** with perfect regularity and precision; smoothly.

**clod** *noun* a lump of earth or clay.

**clodhoppers** *plural noun* (*informal*) large heavy shoes.

**clog** *noun* a wooden-soled shoe. ● *verb* (**clogged**, **clogging**) **1** cause an obstruction in. **2** become blocked.

**cloister** *noun* **1** a covered walk along the side of a church or other building, looking on a courtyard. **2** a monastery or convent; life in this. □ **cloistral** *adjective*

**cloistered** *adjective* sheltered, secluded.

**clomp** *verb* walk with a heavy tread; clump.

**clone** *noun* a group of plants or organisms produced asexually from one ancestor; a member of this group. ● *verb* propagate or become propagated as a clone. □ **clonal** *adjective*

**clonk** *noun* an abrupt heavy sound of impact. ● *verb* **1** make this sound. **2** (*informal*) hit.

**close**[1] (*pronounced* klohs) *adjective* **1** near in space or time. **2** near in relationship; *a close relative.* **3** nearly alike; *a close resemblance.* **4** in which the competitors are nearly equal; *a close contest.* **5** dense, compact; detailed; concentrated. **6** secretive. **7** stingy, mean. **8** humid; without fresh air. ● *adverb* closely, in a near position; *they live close by.* ● *noun* **1** a cul-de-sac. **2** the grounds round a cathedral or abbey etc., usually with its buildings (houses etc.). □ **at close quarters** very close together. **close harmony** harmony in which the notes are close together. **close season** the season when killing of game etc. is forbidden by law. **close shave** (*informal*) a narrow escape. **close-up** *noun* a photograph giving a detailed view of something. □ **closely** *adverb*, **closeness** *noun*

**close**[2] (*pronounced* klohz) *verb* **1** shut, block up. **2** be or declare to be not open to the public. **3** bring or come to an end. **4** bring or come closer or into contact; *close the ranks.* **5** make (an electric circuit) continuous. ● *noun* a conclusion, an end. □ **closed book** a subject one does not understand. **closed-circuit television** that transmitted by wires, not waves, to a restricted number of screens. **close down** shut completely; cease working. **closed shop** the system whereby membership of a trade union is a condition of employment. **close in (on)** approach from all sides. **close with** accept (an offer); accept the offer made by (a person).

**closet** *noun* **1** a cupboard. **2** a small room. **3** = WATER-CLOSET. **4** (used as *adjective*) secret; *a closet homosexual.* ● *verb* (**closeted**, **closeting**) shut away in private conference or study.

**closure** (kloh-zher) *noun* **1** closing; a closed condition. **2** a decision in Parliament to take a vote without further debate.

**clot** *noun* **1** a small thickened mass of blood or other liquid. **2** (*informal*) a stupid person. ● *verb* (**clotted**, **clotting**) form clots. □ **clotted cream** cream thickened by being scalded.

**cloth** *noun* **1** woven or felted material. **2** a piece of this for a special purpose; a dishcloth, tablecloth, etc. **3** clerical clothes; the clergy; *respect for his cloth.*

**clothe** *verb* (**clothed** *or* **clad**, **clothing**) put clothes upon; provide with clothes.

**clothes** *plural noun* **1** things worn to cover the body and limbs. **2** bedclothes. □ **clotheshorse** *noun* a frame with bars for drying wet clothes. **clothes-line** *noun* a rope or wire on which washed clothes are hung to dry. **clothes-peg** *noun* a clip for securing clothes to a clothes-line.

**clothier** (kloh-thi-er) *noun* a seller of men's clothes.

**clothing** *noun* clothes, garments.

**cloud** *noun* **1** a visible mass of condensed watery vapour, floating in the sky. **2** a mass of smoke or mist etc. **3** a mass of things moving in the air; *a cloud of insects.* **4** a state of gloom, trouble, or suspicion; *casting a cloud over the festivities.* ● *verb* **1** cover or darken with clouds or gloom or trouble. **2** (often foll. by *over*) become overcast, indistinct, or gloomy. □ **cloud chamber** a device containing vapour for tracking the paths of charged particles, X-rays, and gamma rays. **cloud-cuckoo-land** *noun* a fanciful or ideal place. **on cloud nine** (*informal*) extremely happy. **under a cloud** out of favour; under suspicion. **with one's head in the clouds** day-dreaming.

**cloudburst** *noun* a sudden violent rainstorm.

**cloudless** *adjective* free from clouds.

**cloudy** *adjective* (**cloudier**, **cloudiest**) **1** covered with clouds. **2** not transparent; *a cloudy liquid.* □ **cloudily** *adverb,* **cloudiness** *noun*

**clout** *noun* (*informal*) **1** a blow. **2** power of effective action; *trade unions with clout.* ● *verb* (*informal*) hit.

**clove** *see* CLEAVE¹. ● *noun* **1** one of the small bulbs making up a compound bulb; *a clove of garlic.* **2** the dried unopened flower bud of tropical myrtle, used as a spice. □ **clove hitch** a knot used to secure a rope round a spar or pole.

**cloven** *see* CLEAVE¹. □ **cloven hoof** one that is divided, like those of oxen or sheep.

**clover** *noun* a plant with three-lobed leaves, used for fodder. □ **in clover** in ease and luxury.

**clown** *noun* **1** a performer who does comical tricks and actions. **2** a person who is always behaving comically. ● *verb* behave as a clown. □ **clownish** *adjective*

**cloy** *verb* sicken by glutting with sweetness or pleasure; *cloy the appetite.*

**cloying** *adjective* sickeningly sweet.

**club** *noun* **1** a heavy stick with one end thicker than the other, used as a weapon. **2** a stick with a shaped head used to hit the ball in golf. **3** a playing card of the suit (**clubs**) marked with black clover-leaves. **4** an organization offering members sporting facilities, entertainment, etc.; their premises. ● *verb* (**clubbed**, **clubbing**) **1** strike with a club. **2** join in subscribing; *we clubbed together to buy a boat.* □ **club class** a class of aircraft fare designed for business travellers. **club-foot** *noun* a deformed foot. **club-root** a disease causing distortion of the root of cabbage and similar plants. **club sandwich** a three-decker sandwich.

**clubbable** *adjective* sociable, likely to be a good member of a social club.

**clubhouse** *noun* the premises used by a club.

**cluck** *noun* the throaty cry of a hen. ● *verb* utter a cluck.

**clue** *noun* **1** a fact or idea that gives a guide to the solution of a problem. **2** a word or words indicating what is to be inserted in a crossword puzzle. ● *verb* provide with a clue. □ **clue up** (or **in**) (*slang*) inform. **not have a clue** (*informal*) be ignorant or incompetent.

**clueless** *adjective* **1** without a clue. **2** (*informal*) stupid or incompetent.

**clump** *noun* **1** a cluster or mass. **2** a clumping sound. ● *verb* **1** form a clump; arrange in a clump. **2** walk with a heavy tread; clomp.

**clumsy** *adjective* (**clumsier**, **clumsiest**) **1** heavy and ungraceful. **2** large and difficult to handle or use. **3** done without tact or skill; *a clumsy apology.* □ **clumsily** *adverb,* **clumsiness** *noun*

**clung** *see* CLING.

**clunk** *noun* a dull sound like thick metal objects striking together. ● *verb* make this sound.

**cluster** *noun* a small close group or bunch. ● *verb* bring or come together in a cluster.

**clutch¹** *verb* grasp tightly; seize eagerly. ● *noun* **1** a tight grasp; a clutching movement. **2** a device for connecting and disconnecting certain working parts in machinery, especially the engine and the transmission in a vehicle; the pedal or other device operating this. □ **clutch bag** a slim handbag without handles.

**clutch²** *noun* **1** a set of eggs for hatching. **2** the chickens hatched from these.

**clutter** *noun* **1** things lying about untidily. **2** a crowded untidy state. ● *verb* fill with clutter, crowd untidily.

**Clwyd** (kloo-id) a county in NE Wales.

**Clyde** a river in SW Scotland, formerly famous for shipbuilding.

**Clydesdale** *noun* a horse of a heavily-built breed used for pulling things.

**Cm** *symbol* curium.

**cm** *abbreviation* centimetre.

**CND** *abbreviation* Campaign for Nuclear Disarmament.

**Cnut** (kă-newt) (also **Canute**) (c.994–1035), Danish king of England 1017–35, remembered for his demonstration of his inability to stop the rising tide to fawning courtiers who had told him he was all-powerful.

**CO** *abbreviation* **1** Colorado. **2** Commanding Officer.

**Co** *symbol* cobalt.

**Co.** abbreviation **1** Company; *Briggs & Co.* **2** County; *Co. Durham*.

**c/o** abbreviation care of (*see* CARE).

**co-** combining form together with, jointly; *co-author; coexistence*.

**coach** noun **1** a single-decker bus. **2** a large four-wheeled horse-drawn carriage. **3** a railway carriage. **4** an instructor in sports. **5** a teacher giving private specialized tuition. ●*verb* train or teach.

**coachwork** noun the bodywork of a vehicle.

**coagulant** (koh-ag-yoo-lănt) noun a substance that causes coagulation.

**coagulate** (koh-ag-yoo-layt) verb change from liquid to semisolid, clot. □ **coagulation** noun

**coal** noun **1** a hard black mineral used for burning to supply heat. **2** a piece of this. □ **carry coals to Newcastle** take a thing to a place where it is already plentiful. **coal gas** mixed gases extracted from coal, used for lighting and heating. **coal-scuttle** noun a container for coal to supply a domestic fire. **coal tar** tar produced when gas is made from coal. **coal-tit** noun a small greyish bird with a black head.

**coalesce** (koh-ă-less) verb combine and form one whole. □ **coalescence** noun, **coalescent** adjective

**coalface** noun the exposed working surface of coal in a mine.

**coalfield** noun an area where coal occurs naturally.

**coalition** (koh-ă-lish-ŏn) noun **1** union. **2** a temporary union between political parties.

**coalmine** noun a mine where coal is dug. □ **coalminer** noun

**coarse** adjective **1** composed of large particles, rough or loose in texture. **2** rough or crude in manner or behaviour, not refined; vulgar; *coarse language*. **3** inferior, common. □ **coarse fish** freshwater fish other than salmon and trout. □ **coarsely** adverb, **coarseness** noun

**coarsen** verb make or become coarse.

**coast** noun the seashore and the land near it; its outline. ●*verb* **1** sail along a coast. **2** ride down a hill without using power. □ **the coast is clear** there is no chance of being seen or hindered.

**coastal** adjective of or near the coast.

**coaster** noun **1** a ship that trades between ports on the same coast. **2** a tray for a decanter; a small mat for a glass.

**coastguard** noun **1** a public organization that keeps watch on the coast to report passing ships, save lives at sea, prevent smuggling, etc. **2** any of its members.

**coastline** noun the shape or outline of a coast; *a rugged coastline*.

**coat** noun **1** an outdoor garment with sleeves. **2** an animal's hair or fur. **3** a covering layer; *a coat of paint*. ●*verb* cover with a layer; form a covering to. □ **coat-hanger** see HANGER (sense 3). **coat of arms** a design on a shield, used as an emblem by a family, city, or institution. **coat of mail** a jacket made of chain mail.

**coating** noun **1** a covering layer. **2** material for coats.

**coax** verb **1** persuade gently or gradually. **2** obtain in this way; *coaxed a smile out of her.*

**coaxial** (koh-aks-iăl) adjective having an axis in common. □ **coaxial cable** an electric cable in which there are two conductors, one inside the other with a layer of insulating material between.

**cob** noun **1** a male swan. **2** a sturdy short-legged horse for riding. **3** a large kind of hazelnut. **4** a round-headed loaf. **5** the central part of an ear of maize, on which the corn grows.

**cobalt** (koh-bollt) noun **1** a chemical element (symbol Co), a hard white metal used in many alloys and with radioactive forms used in medicine and industry. **2** colouring-matter made from this; its deep-blue colour.

**cobber** noun (*Austral. & NZ, informal*) a friend, a mate.

**cobble** noun (in full **cobblestone**) a rounded stone used for paving. ●*verb* **1** pave with cobblestones. **2** put together or mend roughly.

**cobbler** noun **1** a shoe-repairer. **2** stewed fruit or meat topped with scones. **3** (**cobblers**) (*slang*) nonsense.

**COBOL** (koh-bol) noun a high-level computer language designed for use in business. (¶ From the initials of Common Business Oriented Language.)

**cobra** (koh-bră) noun a poisonous snake of India or Africa which rears up and spreads its neck like a hood when excited.

**cobweb** noun the fine network spun by a spider; a strand of this. □ **cobwebby** adjective

**coca** (koh-kă) noun a South American shrub with leaves that are chewed as a stimulant.

**cocaine** (kŏ-kayn) noun a drug made from coca, used as a local anaesthetic or as a stimulant.

**coccyx** (kok-siks) noun (*plural* **coccyges**, *pronounced* kok-si-jeez) a small triangular bone at the base of the spine.

**cochineal** (koch-in-eel) noun bright red colouring-matter made from the dried bodies of certain insects.

**cochlea** (kok-liă) noun (*plural* **cochleae**) the spiral cavity of the inner ear.

**cock** noun **1** a male bird, especially of the domestic fowl. **2** a tap or valve for controlling the flow of a liquid. **3** (*vulgar*) the penis. **4** a lever in a gun, raised ready to be released by the trigger. **5** (*slang*) (as a form of address) friend; fellow. ●*verb* **1** tilt or turn upwards; *the dog cocked his ears.* **2** raise the cock of (a gun) ready for firing; set (the shutter of a camera) ready for release. □ **at half cock** only half ready. **cock-a-doodle-doo** *interjection* the sound of a cock crowing. **cock-a-hoop** *adjective* pleased and triumphant. **cock-a-leekie** *noun* soup of chicken boiled with leeks. **cock-and-bull story** a foolish story that one should not believe. **cock crow** dawn. **cock-eyed** *adjective* (*informal*) **1** crooked, askew. **2** absurd, not practical. **cock-fighting** *noun* setting cocks to fight as a sport.

**cockade** (kok-**ayd**) *noun* a rosette of ribbon worn on a hat as a badge.

**cockatiel** *noun* (also **cockateel**) a small Australian parrot with a long tapering crest.

**cockatoo** *noun* (*plural* **cockatoos**) a crested parrot.

**cockchafer** (kok-**chay**-fer) *noun* a large flying beetle.

**Cockcroft**, Sir John Douglas (1897–1967), English physicist who, with E. T. S. Walton, in 1932 succeeded in 'splitting the atom'.

**cocked hat** a triangular hat worn with some uniforms.

**cockerel** *noun* a young domestic cock.

**Cockerell**, Sir Christopher Sydney (born 1910), English engineer, inventor of the hovercraft.

**cocker spaniel** a small spaniel with a silky coat.

**cockle** *noun* **1** an edible shellfish. **2** a small shallow boat. **3** a pucker or bulge. ●*verb* pucker (a stiff substance); become puckered. □ **warm the cockles of one's heart** make one contented.

**cockney** *noun* (*plural* **cockneys**) **1** a native of the East End of London. **2** the dialect or accent of this area. ●*adjective* of cockneys or cockney.

**cockpit** *noun* **1** the compartment for the pilot and crew of an aircraft. **2** the well where the wheel is situated in certain small yachts etc. **3** the driver's seat in a racing-car. **4** a place made for cock-fighting.

**cockroach** *noun* a flat brown beetle-like insect that infests kitchens etc.

**cockscomb** *noun* the crest of a cock.

**cocksure** *adjective* over-confident; arrogant.

**cocktail** *noun* **1** a mixed alcoholic drink. **2** an appetizer containing shellfish or fruit; *prawn cocktail.* **3** any mixture of diverse elements. □ **cocktail dress** a short evening dress. **cocktail stick** a small pointed stick for serving an olive, cherry, etc.

**cocky** *adjective* (**cockier, cockiest**) conceited and arrogant. □ **cockily** *adverb*, **cockiness** *noun*

**coco** *noun* (*plural* **cocos**) a tropical palm tree producing coconuts.

**cocoa** *noun* **1** powder made from crushed cacao seeds. **2** a drink made from this. □ **cocoa bean** a cacao seed. **cocoa butter** a fatty substance obtained from cacao seeds.

**coconut** *noun* **1** the hard-shelled nut of the coco palm, containing a sweet juice. **2** its edible white lining. □ **coconut matting** matting made from the tough fibre of the coconut's outer husk. **coconut shy** a fairground amusement where balls are thrown to dislodge coconuts from a stand.

**cocoon** (kŏ-**koon**) *noun* **1** the silky sheath round a chrysalis. **2** a protective wrapping. ●*verb* protect by wrapping completely.

**Cocos Islands** (koh-koss) (also **Keeling Islands**) a group of about twenty small islands in the Indian Ocean, administered by Australia.

**cocotte** (kŏ-**kot**) *noun* a small fireproof dish for cooking and serving food.

**Cocteau** (kok-toh), Jean Maurice (1889–1963), French dramatist and film director.

**COD** *abbreviation* cash or (*Amer.*) collect on delivery.

**cod** *noun* (*plural* **cod**) a large sea fish used as food. □ **cod-liver oil** oil obtained from cod livers, rich in vitamins A and D.

**coda** (koh-dă) *noun* the concluding passage of a piece of music.

**coddle** *verb* **1** cherish and protect carefully; pamper. **2** cook (eggs) in water just below boiling point.

**code** *noun* **1** a prearranged word or phrase representing a message, for secrecy. **2** a system of words, letters, or symbols used to represent others, especially in order to send messages by machine (e.g. the *Morse code*). **3** a set of laws or rules; *a code of practice for advertisers.* **4** a set of program instructions for use in a computer. ●*verb* put into code.

**codeine** (koh-deen) *noun* a white substance made from opium, used to relieve pain or induce sleep.

**codependency** *noun* addiction to a supportive role in a relationship.

**codex** (koh-deks) *noun* (*plural* **codices**, *pronounced* koh-di-seez) **1** an ancient manuscript text in book form, not a continuous roll. **2** a collection of pharmaceutical descriptions of drugs etc.

**codfish** *noun* a cod.

**codger** *noun* (*informal*) a person, especially a strange one.

**codicil** (koh-di-sil) *noun* an addition to a will.

**codify** (koh-di-fy) *verb* (**codified, codifying**) arrange (laws or rules) systematically into a code. □ **codification** *noun*, **codifier** *noun*

**codling** *noun* **1** (also **codlin**) a kind of cooking apple. **2** a moth whose larva feeds on apples. **3** a small codfish.

**codpiece** *noun* a bag or flap at the front of men's breeches in 15th- and 16th-century dress.

**codswallop** *noun* (*slang*) nonsense, rubbish.

**Cody**, William Frederick, *see* BUFFALO BILL.

**Coe**, Sebastian (born 1956), English middle-distance runner.

**coed** *adjective* (*informal*) coeducational. ●*noun* (especially *Amer.*) a girl at a coeducational school or college.

**coeducation** *noun* education of boys and girls in the same classes. □ **coeducational** *adjective*

**coefficient** (koh-i-fish-ĕnt) *noun* **1** *Maths* a quantity placed before and multiplying an algebraic expression. **2** *Physics* a multiplier or factor by which a property is measured; *coefficient of expansion*.

**coelacanth** (seel-ă-kanth) *noun* a large sea fish formerly thought to be extinct.

**coelenterate** (si-len-ter-ayt) *noun* a sea animal with a simple tube-shaped or cup-shaped body (including sea anemones, jellyfish, and corals).

**coeliac disease** (seel-i-ak) (*Amer.* **celiac**) a disease causing inability to digest gluten.

**coenobite** (seen-ŏ-byt) *noun* (*Amer.* **cenobite**) a monk who lives as a member of a monastic community.

**coequal** *adjective* equal to one another.

**coerce** (koh-erss) *verb* compel by threats or force. □ **coercion** (koh-er-shŏn) *noun*

**coercive** (koh-er-siv) *adjective* using coercion.

**coeval** (koh-ee-văl) *adjective* having the same age; existing at the same epoch. ●*noun* a coeval person, a contemporary.

**coexist** *verb* exist together, especially in peace despite different views. □ **coexistence** *noun*, **coexistent** *adjective*

**coextensive** *adjective* extending over the same space or time.

**C. of E.** *abbreviation* Church of England.

**coffee** *noun* **1** the bean-like seeds of a tropical shrub, roasted and ground for making a drink. **2** this drink. **3** light brown colour. □ **coffee bar**, **coffee shop** a place serving coffee and light refreshments. **coffee-table** *noun* a small low table. **coffee-table book** a large attractive book with a lot of pictures.

**coffer** *noun* **1** a large strong box for valuables. **2** (**coffers**) funds, financial resources. □ **coffer-dam** *noun* a temporary watertight structure placed round an area of water which can then be pumped dry to allow work to be done within.

**coffin** *noun* a box in which a dead body is placed for burial or cremation.

**cog** *noun* each of a series of teeth on the edge of a wheel, fitting into and pushing those on another wheel.

**cogent** (koh-jĕnt) *adjective* convincing, compelling belief; *a cogent argument*. □ **cogently** *adverb*, **cogency** *noun*

**cogitate** (koj-i-tayt) *verb* think deeply. □ **cogitation** *noun*

**cognac** (kon-yak) *noun* high-quality brandy; that made in Cognac in western France.

**cognate** (kog-nayt) *adjective* having the same source or origin; (of things) related. ●*noun* **1** a relative. **2** a cognate word.

**cognition** (kog-ni-shŏn) *noun* the faculty of knowing or perceiving things.

**cognitive** (kog-ni-tiv) *adjective* of cognition.

**cognizant** (kog-ni-zănt) *adjective* aware, having knowledge. □ **cognizance** *noun*

**cognomen** (kog-noh-men) *noun* **1** a nickname. **2** an ancient Roman's personal name or epithet.

**cognoscente** (kon-yosh-en-ti) *noun* (plural **cognoscenti**) a connoisseur. (¶ Italian.)

**cogwheel** *noun* a wheel with cogs.

**cohabit** *verb* live together as husband and wife (especially of a couple who are not married to each other). □ **cohabitation** *noun*

**cohere** (koh-heer) *verb* **1** stick together, remain united in a mass; *the particles cohere*. **2** be logical or consistent.

**coherent** (koh-heer-ĕnt) *adjective* **1** cohering. **2** connected logically, not rambling in speech or in reasoning. □ **coherently** *adverb*, **coherence** *noun*

**cohesion** (koh-hee-zhŏn) *noun* cohering, a tendency to stick together. □ **cohesive** *adjective*

**cohort** *noun* **1** a division of the ancient Roman army, one-tenth of a legion. **2** persons grouped together; a group having a common statistical characteristic.

**coif** *noun* (*old use*) a close-fitting cap.

**coiffed** (*pronounced* kwahft) *adjective* (of the hair) arranged, done.

**coiffeur** (kwah-fer) *noun* a hairdresser. (¶ French.)

**coiffeuse** (kwah-ferz) *noun* a female hairdresser.

**coiffure** (kwahf-yoor) *noun* a hairstyle.

**coil** *verb* wind into rings or a spiral. ●*noun* **1** something coiled. **2** one ring or turn in this. **3** a length of wire wound in a spiral to conduct electric current. **4** a contraceptive device for insertion into the womb.

**coin** *noun* a small stamped piece of metal as official money; coins collectively. ●*verb*

**1** make (coins) by stamping metal. **2** (*informal*) make (money) in large quantities. **3** invent (a word or phrase). □ **coin-box** *noun* a telephone operated by inserting coins.

**coinage** *noun* **1** coining. **2** coins; the system of coins in use. **3** a coined word or phrase.

**coincide** (koh-in-**syd**) *verb* **1** occur at the same time; *his holidays don't coincide with hers.* **2** occupy the same portion of space. **3** agree; *our tastes coincide.*

**coincidence** (koh-**in**-si-děnss) *noun* **1** coinciding. **2** occurrence of similar events at the same time by chance.

**coincident** (koh-**in**-si-děnt) *adjective* coinciding.

**coincidental** (koh-in-si-**den**-t'l) *adjective* happening by coincidence. □ **coincidentally** *adverb*

**coir** (**koi**-er) *noun* fibre from the outer husk of the coconut, used for ropes, matting, etc.

**coition** (koh-**ish**-ŏn) *noun* sexual intercourse.

**coitus** (koh-it-ŭs) *noun* coition. □ **coitus interruptus** sexual intercourse with withdrawal of the penis before ejaculation. □ **coital** *adjective*

**coke** *noun* **1** the solid substance left after coal gas and coal tar have been extracted from coal, used as fuel. **2** (*slang*) cocaine.

**Col.** *abbreviation* Colonel.

**col** *noun* a depression in a range of mountains.

**cola** (**koh**-lă) *noun* (also **Kola**) **1** a West African tree with seed producing an extract used as a tonic etc. **2** a carbonated drink flavoured with this.

**colander** (**kul**-ăn-der) *noun* a container with holes for straining water from foods.

**cold** *adjective* **1** at or having a low temperature. **2** not heated, having cooled after being heated or cooked; *cold meat.* **3** (*slang*) unconscious; *knocked him cold.* **4** without friendliness, affection, or enthusiasm; *got a cold reception.* **5** (of colours) suggesting coldness. **6** (of the scent in hunting) faint because no longer fresh. **7** (in children's games) far from finding or guessing what is sought. ● *adverb* in a cold state. ● *noun* **1** lack of heat or warmth; low temperature. **2** an infectious illness causing catarrh and sneezing. □ **cold-blooded** *adjective* **1** having a body temperature that varies with the temperature of surroundings. **2** unfeeling, deliberately ruthless; *a cold-blooded killer.* **cold call** use the method of cold calling to sell goods or services. **cold calling** a sales method using a telephone directory, mailing list, etc. to contact people who have not previously shown interest. **cold chisel** a chisel for cutting metal, stone, or brick.

**cold comfort** poor consolation. **cold cream** ointment for cleansing and softening the skin. **cold frame** an unheated frame for growing plants. **cold fusion** nuclear fusion at room temperature. **cold shoulder** deliberate unfriendliness. **cold-shoulder** *verb* treat with deliberate unfriendliness. **cold sore** inflammation and blistering around the mouth, caused by a virus infection. **cold storage 1** storage in a refrigerated place. **2** postponement (of plans etc.). **cold turkey** (*slang*) sudden withdrawal of narcotic drugs from an addict. **cold war** intense hostility between nations without actual fighting. **get cold feet** feel afraid or reluctant. **in cold blood** without passion, deliberately and ruthlessly. **leave out in the cold** ignore or neglect. **throw** *or* **pour cold water on** make discouraging remarks about. □ **coldly** *adverb*, **coldness** *noun*

**Colditz** a town in eastern Germany, noted for its castle which was used as a top-security camp for Allied prisoners in the Second World War.

**cole** *noun* any of various plants of the cabbage family, especially (**cole-seed**) rape.

**Coleridge**, Samuel Taylor (1772–1834), English poet.

**coleslaw** *noun* finely shredded raw cabbage with carrots etc. coated in dressing, as a salad.

**Colette** the pen-name of Sidonie Gabrielle (1873–1954), French novelist.

**coleus** (**koh**-li-ŭs) *noun* a plant with coloured leaves.

**coley** *noun* any of several edible fish, e.g. the rock-salmon.

**colic** *noun* severe abdominal pain. □ **colicky** *adjective*

**colitis** (kŏ-**ly**-tiss) *noun* inflammation of the lining of the colon.

**collaborate** *verb* work in partnership. □ **collaboration** *noun*, **collaborator** *noun*

**collage** (kol-**ah***zh*), *noun* an artistic composition made by fixing bits of paper, cloth, string, etc. to a surface.

**collagen** (**kol**-ă-jin) *noun* a protein substance found in bone and tissue, yielding gelatin on boiling.

**collapse** *verb* **1** fall down or in suddenly. **2** lose strength, force, or value suddenly; *enemy resistance collapsed.* **3** fold or be foldable. **4** cause to collapse. ● *noun* collapsing; a breakdown.

**collapsible** *adjective* made so as to fold together compactly; *a collapsible canoe.*

**collar** *noun* **1** band round the neck of a garment. **2** a band of leather etc. put round the neck of an animal. **3** a band, ring, or pipe holding part of a machine. **4** a cut of bacon from near the head. ● *verb* (*informal*) seize, take for oneself. □ **collar-bone** *noun* the bone joining the breastbone and shoulder-blade; the clavicle.

**collate** (kŏ-**layt**) *verb* **1** compare in detail. **2** collect and arrange systematically; *collate information*. □ **collator** *noun*

**collateral** (kŏ-**lat**-er-ăl) *adjective* **1** side by side, parallel. **2** additional but subordinate; *collateral evidence*. **3** descended from the same ancestor but by a different line; *a collateral branch of the family.* ●*noun* a collateral person or security. □ **collateral damage** destruction or injury beyond that intended or expected, especially around a military target. **collateral security** an additional security pledged; security lodged by a third party, or consisting of stocks, shares, property, etc. as opposed to a personal guarantee. □ **collaterally** *adverb*

**collation** *noun* **1** collating; something collated. **2** a light meal.

**colleague** *noun* a fellow official or worker, especially in a business or profession.

**collect**[1] (**kol**-ekt) *noun* a short prayer of the Church of England or the Roman Catholic Church.

**collect**[2] (kŏ-**lekt**) *verb* **1** bring or come together. **2** get from a number of people; ask for (payment or contributions) from people. **3** seek and obtain specimens of, especially as a hobby or for study. **4** fetch; *collect the children from school.* **5** gather (one's thoughts) into systematic order or control. ●*adjective & adverb* (*Amer.*) (of a parcel, telephone call, etc.) to be paid for by the recipient.

**collectable** *adjective* (also **collectible**) suitable for being collected as a hobby etc. ●*noun* an object of this kind.

**collected** *adjective* **1** grouped or gathered together. **2** calm and self-controlled. □ **collectedly** *adverb*

**collection** *noun* **1** collecting. **2** money collected for a charity etc. **3** objects collected or placed together.

**collective** *adjective* of a group taken as a whole; *our collective impression of the new plan.* ●*noun* a collective farm. □ **collective bargaining** bargaining by an organized group of employees. **collective farm** a farm or group of smallholdings organized and run by its workers, usually under State control. **collective noun** a noun that is singular in form but denotes many individuals, e.g. *army, cattle, committee, herd.* **collective ownership** ownership of land etc. by all and for the benefit of all. □ **collectively** *adverb*

**collectivism** *noun* the theory or practice of collective ownership. □ **collectivist** *noun*

**collectivize** *verb* (also **collectivise**) bring from private into collective ownership. □ **collectivization** *noun*

**collector** *noun* a person who collects things. □ **collector's piece** *or* **item** a thing worth placing in a collection because of its beauty or variety.

**colleen** (kol-**een**) *noun* (*Irish*) a girl.

**college** *noun* **1** an educational establishment for higher or professional education. **2** an independent part of a university with its own teachers and students. **3** (in names) a school; *Eton College.* **4** the buildings of any of these. **5** an organized body of professional people with common purposes and privileges; *the Royal College of Surgeons.*

**collegiate** (kŏ-**lee**-ji-ăt) *adjective* of or belonging to a college or college student. □ **collegiate church** a church (other than a cathedral) with a chapter of canons but without bishops, or (*Scottish & Amer.*) associated jointly with others under a group of pastors.

**collide** *verb* **1** (of a moving object) strike violently against something; meet and strike. **2** (of interests or opinions) conflict; (of persons etc.) have such a conflict.

**collie** *noun* a sheepdog with a long pointed muzzle and shaggy hair.

**collier** *noun* **1** a coalminer. **2** a ship that carries coal as its cargo.

**colliery** *noun* a coalmine and its buildings.

**Collins,** (William) Wilkie (1824–89), English novelist.

**collision** *noun* colliding, the striking of one body against another.

**collocate** *verb* **1** place together or side by side. **2** bring together for purposes of comparison. □ **collocation** *noun*, **collocator** *noun*

**colloid** *noun* a gluey substance. □ **colloidal** *adjective*

**colloquial** (kŏ-**loh**-kwee-ăl) *adjective* suitable for ordinary conversation but not for formal speech or writing. □ **colloquially** *adverb*

**colloquialism** *noun* a colloquial word or phrase.

**colloquy** (**kol**-ŏ-kwi) *noun* (*formal*) a conversation.

**collude** *verb* conspire together.

**collusion** (kŏ-**loo**-*zh*ŏn) *noun* an agreement between two or more people for a deceitful or fraudulent purpose. □ **collusive** *adjective*

**collywobbles** *plural noun* (*informal*) **1** stomach-ache. **2** nervousness.

**Cologne** (kŏ-**lohn**) a city in Germany, on the Rhine.

**cologne** (kŏ-**lohn**) *noun* eau-de-Cologne or other lightly scented liquid, used to cool and scent the skin.

**Colombia** a country in South America. □ **Colombian** adjective & noun

**Colombo** the capital of Sri Lanka.

**colon** (koh-lŏn) noun **1** the lower and greater part of the large intestine. **2** a punctuation mark (:) used (1) to show that what follows is an example or list or summary of what precedes it, or a contrasting idea, (2) between numbers that are in proportion, e.g. 1 : 2 = 2 : 4.

**colonel** (ker-nĕl) noun **1** an army officer commanding a regiment, ranking next below a brigadier. **2** a lieutenant-colonel. □ **colonelcy** noun

**colonial** adjective of a colony or colonies. ● noun an inhabitant of a colony.

**colonialism** noun the policy of acquiring or maintaining colonies.

**colonic** (koh-lon-ik) adjective of the intestinal colon.

**colonist** noun a pioneer settler in a colony.

**colonize** verb (also **colonise**) establish a colony in. □ **colonization** noun

**colonnade** noun a row of columns.

**colony** noun **1** an area of land settled or conquered by a distant State and controlled by it. **2** its inhabitants. **3** people of one nationality or occupation etc. living in a particular area; the area itself; the artists' colony. **4** a group of animals or organisms living close together.

**colophon** (kol-ŏ-fŏn) noun **1** a decoration at the end of a chapter or book etc., giving the writer's or printer's name. **2** a publisher's or printer's imprint, especially on a title-page.

**color** Amer. spelling of COLOUR.

**Colorado** (kolŏ-rah-doh) a State of the central USA. □ **Colorado beetle** a black and yellow beetle that is very destructive to the potato plant.

**colorant** Amer. spelling of COLOURANT.

**coloration** noun (also **colouration**) colouring.

**coloratura** (kol-er-ă-toor-ă) noun **1** elaborate ornamentation of a vocal melody. **2** a soprano skilled in singing this.

**colorful** Amer. spelling of COLOURFUL.

**colossal** adjective **1** immense. **2** (informal) remarkable, splendid. □ **colossally** adverb

**Colosseum** (kol-ŏ-see-ŭm) a vast amphitheatre in Rome, begun c.AD 75.

**Colossians** (kŏ-losh-ănz) □ **Epistle to the Colossians** a book of the New Testament, an epistle of St Paul to the Church at Colossae in Asia Minor.

**colossus** (ko-los-ŭs) noun (plural **colossi**, pronounced kŏ-los-I, or **colossuses**) **1** an immense statue. **2** a person of immense importance and influence.

**colostomy** (kŏ-lost-ŏmi) noun an operation to make an opening in the abdominal wall through which the bowel can empty.

**colour** (Amer. **color**) noun **1** the sensation produced by rays of light of different wavelengths; a particular variety of this. **2** the use of all colours, not only black and white; a colour film. **3** ruddiness of complexion. **4** the pigmentation of the skin, especially if dark. **5** pigment, paint, or dye. **6** the flag of a ship or regiment. **7** (**colours**) an award given to regular or leading members of a sports team. ● verb **1** put colour on; paint, stain, or dye. **2** change colour; blush. **3** give a special character or bias to; his political opinions colour his writings. □ **colour bar** racial discrimination against non-White people. **colour-blind** adjective unable to see the difference between certain colours. **colour-sergeant** noun a senior sergeant of an infantry company. **give** or **lend colour to** give an appearance of truth to. **in its true colours** with its real characteristics revealed.

**colourant** noun (Amer. **colorant**) colouring matter.

**colouration** alternative spelling of COLORATION.

**coloured** (Amer. **colored**) adjective **1** having colour. **2** wholly or partly of non-White descent. **3** (**Coloured**) (in South Africa) of mixed White and non-White descent. ● noun **1** a coloured person. **2** (**Coloured**) (in South Africa) a person of mixed White and non-White descent.

**colourful** adjective (Amer. **colorful**) **1** full of colour. **2** with vivid details; a colourful account of his journey. □ **colourfully** adverb

**colouring** noun (Amer. **coloring**) **1** the way in which something is coloured. **2** a substance used to colour things.

**colourless** adjective (Amer. **colorless**) without colour.

**colposcopy** noun examination of the vagina and neck of the womb.

**colt** (rhymes with bolt) noun a young male horse.

**colter** Amer. spelling of COULTER.

**Coltrane** (kol-trayn), John William (1926–67), American jazz saxophonist.

**coltsfoot** noun a weed with yellow flowers.

**Columba**, St (c.521–97), Irish missionary, who established a monastery on the island of Iona. Feast day, 9 June.

**Columbia, District of** a district of the USA coextensive with the city of Washington.

**columbine** noun a plant bearing purple-blue flowers with pointed spurs at the back of each one.

**Columbus**, Christopher (1451–1506), Italian explorer in the service of Spain, who in 1492 discovered the New World.

**column** *noun* **1** a round pillar. **2** something shaped like this; *a column of smoke*. **3** a vertical section of a printed page; *there are two columns on this page.* **4** a regular feature in a newspaper. **5** a long narrow formation of troops or vehicles etc. □ **columnar** (kŏ-**lum**-ner) *adjective*

**columnist** (**kol**-ŭm-ist) *noun* a journalist who regularly writes a column.

**coma** (**koh**-mă) *noun* a state of deep unconsciousness.

**Comanche** (kŏ-**man**-chi) *noun* **1** a North American Indian people of Texas and Oklahoma. **2** their language.

**comatose** (**koh**-mă-tohs) *adjective* **1** in a coma. **2** drowsy.

**comb** *noun* **1** a strip of plastic etc. with teeth, used for tidying the hair or holding it in place. **2** something shaped or used like this, e.g. for separating strands of wool or cotton. **3** the fleshy crest of a fowl. **4** a honeycomb. ● *verb* **1** tidy or untangle with a comb. **2** search thoroughly. □ **comb out** get rid of (unwanted people or things) from a group.

**combat** *noun* a fight or contest. ● *verb* (**combated, combating**) fight, counter; *to combat the effects of alcohol.*

**combatant** (**kom**-bă-tănt) *adjective* fighting. ● *noun* one who is engaged in fighting.

**combative** (**kom**-bă-tiv) *adjective* eager to fight, aggressive.

**combe** alternative spelling of COOMB.

**combination** *noun* **1** combining, being combined. **2** a number of people or things that are combined. **3** a sequence of numbers or letters used in opening a combination lock. **4** (**combinations**) a one-piece undergarment covering the body and legs. □ **combination lock** a lock that can be opened only by turning one or more dials into a particular series of positions.

**combine** *verb* (*pronounced* kŏm-**byn**) join or be joined into a group, set, or mixture. ● *noun* (*pronounced* **kom**-byn) **1** a combination of people or firms acting together in business. **2** (in full **combine harvester**) a combined reaping and threshing machine.

**combings** *plural noun* loose hair removed by a comb or brush.

**combining form** *noun* a word or partial word used in combination with another to form a different word (e.g. *Anglo-* = English).

**combo** *noun* (*plural* **combos**) (*slang*) a small jazz or dance band.

**combustible** (kŏm-**bust**-ibŭl) *adjective* capable of catching fire and burning, used for burning. ● *noun* a combustible substance. □ **combustibility** *noun*

**combustion** (kŏm-**bus**-chŏn) *noun* **1** the process of burning. **2** a chemical process (accompanied by heat) in which substances combine with oxygen in air.

**come** *verb* (**came, come, coming**) **1** move or be brought towards the speaker or a place or point. **2** (of an illness) begin to develop. **3** arrive, reach a point, condition, or result; happen; *when winter comes; we came to a decision.* **4** be available; *the dress comes in 3 sizes.* **5** occur as a result; *that's what comes of being too confident.* **6** (foll. by *from*) be descended; *she comes from a rich family.* **7** (*slang*) have a sexual orgasm. ● *interjection* think again, don't be hasty; *oh come, it's not that bad!* □ **come about** happen. **come across** find or meet unexpectedly. **come again?** (*informal*) what did you say? **come along** make progress, thrive; *coming along nicely; come along!* **come by** obtain (a thing). **come clean** (*informal*) confess fully. **come down 1** collapse; fall, become lower. **2** decide. **come down on** rebuke. **come from** have as one's birthplace or as a place of origin. **come-hither** *adjective* enticing, flirtatious. **come in 1** take a specified position in a race or competition; *he came in third.* **2** be received as income. **3** have a part to play, serve a purpose; *it will come in useful; where do I come in?* **come in for** receive a share of. **come into** inherit. **come of age** reach adult status. **come off 1** become detached or separated, be detachable; fall from. **2** fare, acquit oneself; *they came off well.* **come off it!** (*informal*) stop talking or behaving like that. **come on 1** make progress, thrive. **2** begin; *it's coming on to rain.* **3** find or meet unexpectedly. **come on!** hurry up. **come-on** *noun* (*slang*) an enticement. **come out 1** go on strike. **2** emerge with a specified result. **3** (of the sun, moon, etc.) emerge from behind clouds. **4** become known; be published; be solved. **5** erupt; become covered (in a rash). **6** declare one's opinions or feelings publicly; *came out in favour of the plan; came out as a homosexual.* **come out with** utter. **come over 1** affect; *what has come over you?* **2** (*informal*) be affected with a feeling; *she came over faint.* **come round 1** make a casual or informal visit. **2** recover from faintness or bad temper. **3** be converted to another person's opinion. **4** recur. **come to 1** amount to, be equivalent to. **2** regain consciousness. **come to pass** (*old use*) happen. **come true** happen in the way that was prophesied or hoped. **come up** arise for discussion etc., occur; *a problem has come up.* **come upon** find or meet unexpectedly. **come up to** equal; *it doesn't come up to our expectations.* **come up with**

contribute (a suggestion etc.). **come what may** whatever may happen.

**comeback** noun **1** a return to one's former successful position. **2** (informal) a reply or retort.

**Comecon** (kom-i-kon) an economic organization of eastern European countries, founded in 1949 and dissolved in 1991. (¶ The name is formed from the initial letters of Council for Mutual Economic Assistance.)

**comedian** noun **1** an actor who plays comic parts. **2** a humorous entertainer. **3** a person who behaves humorously.

**comedienne** (kŏ-mee-di-en) noun a female comedian.

**comedown** noun **1** a loss of status. **2** a disappointment.

**comedy** noun **1** a light amusing play or film. **2** the branch of drama that consists of such plays. **3** humour.

**comely** (**kum**-li) adjective (old use) good-looking. □ **comeliness** noun

**comer** (**kum**-er) noun one who comes, especially as an applicant; the first comers; all comers.

**comestibles** (kŏm-est-i-bŭlz) plural noun (formal) things to eat.

**comet** (**kom**-it) noun an object in space that orbits the sun, usually with a bright, burning centre and a long, hazy tail pointing away from the sun.

**comeuppance** noun (informal) deserved punishment.

**comfit** noun (old use) a sweet consisting of a nut etc. in sugar.

**comfort** noun **1** a state of ease and contentment. **2** relief of suffering or grief. **3** a person or thing that gives this. ●verb give comfort to. □ **comfort station** (Amer.) a public lavatory.

**comfortable** adjective **1** giving ease and contentment. **2** not close or restricted; won by a comfortable margin. **3** feeling at ease, in a state of comfort. □ **comfortably** adverb

**comforter** noun **1** a person who comforts. **2** a baby's dummy. **3** (Amer.) a duvet, a quilt. **4** (old use) a woollen scarf.

**comfrey** (**kum**-fri) noun a tall plant with bell-shaped purple or white flowers.

**comfy** adjective (informal) comfortable.

**comic** adjective **1** causing amusement or laughter. **2** of comedy. ●noun **1** a comedian. **2** a paper (usually for children) with series of strip cartoons. □ **comic strip** a sequence of drawings telling a story. □ **comical** adjective, **comically** adverb

**coming** see COME. ●adjective **1** approaching, next; the coming week. **2** likely to be important in the near future; a coming man. ●noun arriving; comings and goings.

**comity** noun (formal) **1** courtesy, friendship. **2** an association of nations etc. for their mutual benefit. □ **comity of nations** nations' friendly recognition of each other's laws and customs.

**comma** noun a punctuation mark (,) indicating a slight pause or break between parts of a sentence, or separating words or figures in a list.

**command** noun **1** an order, an instruction. **2** an instruction to a computer. **3** the right to control others, authority; she is in command. **4** ability to use something, mastery; he has a great command of languages. **5** a body of troops or staff; Bomber Command. ●verb **1** give a command or order to. **2** have authority over. **3** have at one's disposal; the firm commands great resources. **4** deserve and get; they command our respect. **5** look down over or dominate from a strategic position; the tower commands the harbour. □ **command module** the control compartment in a spacecraft.

**commandant** (kom-ăn-dant) noun the officer in command of a military establishment.

**commandeer** verb **1** seize for military purposes. **2** seize for one's own purposes.

**commander** noun **1** the person in command. **2** a naval officer ranking next below a captain. **3** (in full **knight commander**) a member of a higher class in some orders of knighthood. □ **commander-in-chief** noun the supreme commander, especially of a nation's forces.

**commandment** noun **1** a divine command. **2** (**Commandment**) (in Christian belief) any of the ten laws given by God to Moses.

**commando** noun (plural **commandos**) **1** a military unit specially trained for making raids and assaults. **2** a member of such a unit.

**commemorate** verb **1** keep in the memory by means of a celebration or ceremony. **2** be a memorial to; a plaque commemorates the victory. □ **commemoration** noun, **commemorative** adjective

**commence** verb begin. □ **commencement** noun

**commend** verb **1** praise. **2** recommend. **3** entrust, commit; commending his soul to God. □ **commendation** noun

**commendable** adjective worthy of praise. □ **commendably** adverb

**commensurable** (kŏ-men-sher-ăbŭl) adjective able to be measured by the same standard.

**commensurate** (kŏ-men-sher-ăt) adjective **1** of the same size or extent. **2** proportionate; the salary is commensurate with the responsibilities.

**comment** *noun* an opinion given briefly about an event or in explanation or criticism. ●*verb* utter or write comments.

**commentary** *noun* **1** a descriptive spoken account of an event or performance as it happens. **2** a collection of explanatory comments; *a new commentary on the Bible.*

**commentate** *verb* act as commentator.

**commentator** *noun* **1** a person who broadcasts a commentary. **2** a person who comments on current events.

**commerce** (**kom**-erss) *noun* all forms of trade and the services that assist trading, e.g. banking and insurance.

**commercial** *adjective* **1** of or engaged in commerce. **2** (of broadcasting) financed by firms etc. whose advertisements are included; *commercial radio.* **3** intended to produce profits. ●*noun* a broadcast advertisement. □ **commercial traveller** a firm's representative who visits shops etc. to show samples and get orders. □ **commercially** *adverb*

**commercialism** *noun* commercial practices and attitudes.

**commercialize** *verb* (also **commercialise**) make commercial, alter in order to make profitable; *a commercialized resort.* □ **commercialization** *noun*

**Commie** *noun* (*slang, scornful*) a Communist.

**commination** *noun* (*literary*) threatening of divine vengeance. □ **comminatory** (**kom**-in-ă-ter-i) *adjective*

**commingle** *verb* (*literary*) mingle.

**comminute** *verb* reduce to small portions or fragments. □ **comminution** *noun*

**commiserate** (kŏ-**miz**-er-ayt) *verb* express pity for, sympathize. □ **commiseration** *noun*

**commissar** (kom-i-**sar**) *noun* (*hist.*) head of a Soviet government department.

**commissariat** (kom-i-**sair**-iăt) *noun* **1** a stock of food. **2** a military department supplying this.

**commissary** (kom-**iss**-er-i) *noun* **1** a deputy; a delegate. **2** (*Amer.*) a store where food and other supplies are sold at a military base. **3** (*Amer.*) a restaurant in a film studio or factory etc.

**commission** *noun* **1** the authority to perform a certain task or duty. **2** the task etc. given; *a commission to paint a portrait.* **3** the body of people to whom such authority is given. **4** a warrant conferring authority especially on officers above a certain rank in the armed forces. **5** performance, committing; *the commission of a crime.* **6** payment to an agent for selling goods or services etc. often calculated in proportion to the amount sold. ●*verb* **1** give a commission to. **2** place an order for; *commissioned a portrait.* □ **commission-agent** *noun* a

bookmaker. **commissioned officer** an officer in the armed forces who holds a commission. **in commission** ready for service. **out of commission** not in commission; not in working order.

**commissionaire** (kŏ-mish-ŏn-**air**) *noun* a uniformed attendant at the entrance to a theatre, hotel, etc.

**commissioner** *noun* **1** a person appointed by commission (e.g. the head of Scotland Yard). **2** a member of a commission. **3** a government official in charge of a district abroad. □ **Commissioner for Oaths** a solicitor before whom oaths may be sworn by people making affidavits.

**commit** *verb* (**committed, committing**) **1** do, perform; *commit a crime.* **2** entrust for safe keeping or treatment; send to prison. **3** pledge, bind with an obligation; (**commit oneself**) give a definite statement or opinion. □ **commit to memory** memorize.

**committed** *adjective* dedicated or pledged, especially to support a doctrine or cause.

**commitment** *noun* **1** committing. **2** the state of being involved in an obligation. **3** an obligation or pledge.

**committal** *noun* committing to prison or some other place of confinement.

**committee** *noun* a group of people appointed to attend to special business or to manage the business of a club etc. □ **committee stage** the third of five stages of a bill's progress through Parliament.

**commode** (kŏ-**mohd**) *noun* **1** a chamber-pot mounted in a chair with a cover. **2** a chest of drawers.

**commodious** (kŏ-**moh**-di-ŭs) *adjective* roomy.

**commodity** *noun* an article of trade, a product.

**commodore** (**kom**-ŏ-dor) *noun* **1** a naval officer ranking above a captain and below a rear admiral. **2** the commander of a squadron or other division of a fleet. **3** the president of a yacht club.

**common** *adjective* **1** of or affecting the whole community. **2** belonging to or shared by two or more people or things. **3** occurring frequently, familiar; *a common weed.* **4** without special distinction, ordinary; *the common house-spider.* **5** ill-bred, not refined in behaviour or style. ●*noun* **1** an area of unfenced grassland for all to use. **2** (**the Commons**) = HOUSE OF COMMONS. □ **Common Agricultural Policy** a system in the EC controlling the price of agricultural products and providing subsidies for some farmers. **common denominator** **1** *Maths* a common multiple of the numbers below the line of several fractions. **2** a common feature of several situations, members of a group, etc. **Common Era**

the Christian era. **common law** unwritten law based on custom and former court decisions. **common-law husband** or **wife** one recognized by common law without an official ceremony, usually after a period of cohabitation. **Common Market** the European Community. **common noun** Grammar a name denoting a class of objects or a concept, not a particular individual. **common or garden** (informal) ordinary. **common room** a room for social purposes at a school, college, or workplace. **common sense** normal good sense in practical matters, gained by experience. **common-sense** adjective showing common sense. **common time** (in music) four crotchet beats in a bar. **in common** in joint use; shared as a possession, characteristic, or interest. □ **commonly** adverb, **commonness** noun

**commonality** noun **1** the sharing of a characteristic. **2** the common people.

**commonalty** (kom-ŏn-ăl-ti) noun **1** the common people. **2** a corporate body.

**commoner** noun one of the common people, not a member of the nobility.

**commonplace** adjective ordinary, usual; lacking originality. ●noun something commonplace.

**commonwealth** noun **1** an independent State or community. **2** a republic. **3** a federation of States; the Commonwealth of Australia. **4** (**the Commonwealth**) an association of the UK and various independent States (formerly subject to Britain) and dependencies; (in history) the republican government of Britain between the execution of Charles I (1649) and the Restoration (1660). □ **Commonwealth Day** the name since 1959 of what was formerly called Empire Day, celebrated until 1965 on 24 May (Queen Victoria's birthday), now celebrated on the second Monday in March. **New Commonwealth** those countries which have achieved self-government within the Commonwealth since 1945.

**commotion** noun uproar, fuss and disturbance.

**communal** (kom-yoo-năl) adjective shared between members of a group or community; a communal kitchen. □ **communally** adverb

**commune** noun (pronounced kom-yoon) **1** a group of people, not all of one family, sharing accommodation and goods. **2** a small district of local government in France and certain other European countries. ●verb (pronounced kŏ-mewn) communicate mentally or spiritually; communing with nature.

**communicable** adjective able to be communicated or passed on.

**communicant** noun **1** a person who receives Holy Communion, especially regularly. **2** a person who communicates information.

**communicate** verb **1** make known. **2** transfer, transmit; communicated the disease to others. **3** (often foll. by with) pass news and information to and fro; have social dealings; have a meaningful relationship; young people cannot always communicate with older ones. **4** be connected; the passage communicates with the hall and stairs.

**communication** noun **1** communicating. **2** something that communicates information, a letter or message. **3** a means of communicating, e.g. a road, railway, telegraph line, radio, or other link between places. □ **communication cord** a cord or chain inside a train, to be pulled to stop the train in an emergency. **communication(s) satellite** a satellite used to relay telephone circuits or broadcast programmes.

**communicative** (kŏ-mew-nik-ătiv) adjective ready and willing to talk and give information.

**communion** noun **1** fellowship, having ideas or beliefs in common; Churches in communion with each other. **2** social dealings between people. **3** a body of Christians belonging to the same denomination; the Anglican communion. **4** (**Communion** or **Holy Communion**) the Christian sacrament in which bread and wine are consecrated and consumed; the Eucharist.

**communiqué** (kŏ-mew-ni-kay) noun an official communication giving a report.

**communism** noun **1** a social system in which property is owned by the community and each member works for the common benefit. **2** (**Communism**) the form of socialist society established in Cuba, China, and previously in the former Soviet Union.

**communist** noun **1** a supporter of communism. **2** (**Communist**) a member of the **Communist Party**, a political party supporting Communism. □ **communistic** adjective

**community** noun **1** a body of people living in one place or country and considered as a whole. **2** a group with common interests or origins; the immigrant community. **3** fellowship, being alike in some way; community of interests. □ **community centre** a place providing social, recreational, and educational facilities for a neighbourhood. **community charge** (also **poll tax**) a UK tax formerly levied locally on every adult (now replaced by council tax). **community service** performance of specified unpaid services to the community, especially as an

alternative to serving a prison sentence.
**community singing** organized singing by
a large gathering of people.

**commutable** *adjective* exchangeable, able to
be exchanged for money.

**commute** *verb* **1** travel some distance to and
from one's daily work. **2** exchange for
something else; *commuted part of his pension
for a lump sum.* **3** change (a punishment)
into something less severe. □ **commuta-
tion** *noun*

**commuter** *noun* a person who commutes to
and from work.

**Comoros** (kŏm-or-ohz) a group of islands
off the east coast of Africa. □ **Comoran** *adjective & noun*

**compact** *noun* (*pronounced* **kom**-pakt) **1** an
agreement, a contract. **2** a small flat container for face powder. ● *adjective* (*pronounced* kŏm-**pakt**) **1** closely or neatly
packed together. **2** concise. ● *verb*
(*pronounced* kŏm-**pakt**) make compact;
join or press firmly together or into a small
space. □ **compact disc** a disc without
grooves, on which sound or information is
recorded digitally for reproduction by
means of a laser beam directed on to it.
□ **compactly** *adverb*, **compactness** *noun*

**companion** *noun* **1** a person who accom-
panies another or who shares in his or her
work, pleasures, or misfortunes etc. **2** the
title of a member of certain orders; *Companion of Honour.* **3** a woman employed to
live with and accompany another. **4** each
of two things that match or go together; *the
companion volume will be published later.*
□ **companion-way** *noun* a staircase from a
ship's deck to the saloon or cabins.

**companionable** *adjective* friendly, sociable.
□ **companionably** *adverb*

**companionship** *noun* the state of being
companions, the friendly feeling of being
with another or others.

**company** *noun* **1** companionship; *travel with
us for company.* **2** a number of people
assembled; guests. **3** the people with whom
one spends one's time; *got into bad company.* **4** people working together or united
for business purposes, a firm; *the ship's
company.* **5** a subdivision of an infantry
battalion. □ **keep a person company**
accompany him or her, especially for
companionship. **part company** go
different ways after being together; cease
associating.

**comparable** (kom-per-ăbŭl) *adjective* (often
foll. by *to, with*) able or suitable to be
compared, similar. □ **comparably** *adverb*,
**comparability** *noun*

**comparative** *adjective* **1** involving comparison; *a comparative study of the output of two
firms.* **2** estimated by comparison; relative;
*their comparative merits; living in comparative
comfort.* **3** of a grammatical form used in
comparing, expressing 'more', e.g. *bigger,
greater, worse.* ● *noun* a comparative form of
a word. □ **comparatively** *adverb*

**compare** *verb* judge the similarity between
(one thing and another). □ **beyond compare** without equal. **compare notes** exchange ideas or conclusions. **compare to**
liken, declare to be similar; *he compared the
human body to a machine.* **compare with**
**1** consider (things or people) together so as
to judge their similarities and differences.
**2** be worthy of comparison; *he cannot
compare with Dickens as a novelist.*

**comparison** *noun* comparing. □ **beyond
comparison** not comparable because one
is so much better than the other(s).

**compartment** *noun* **1** one of the spaces into
which a structure or other object is
divided, separated by partitions. **2** such a
division of a railway carriage.

**compartmental** (kom-part-**men**-t'l) *adjective* of or divided into compartments or
categories.

**compartmentalize** (kom-part-**ment**-ă-
lyz) *verb* (also **compartmentalise**) divide
into compartments or categories.

**compass** *noun* **1** a device for determining
direction, with a needle that points to the
magnetic north. **2** circumference, boundary; range, scope. **3** (**compasses**) an instrument used for drawing circles, usually
with two legs joined at one end. ● *verb* encompass.

**compassion** *noun* a feeling of pity that
makes one want to help or show mercy.
□ **compassionate** *adjective*, **compas-
sionately** *adverb*

**compatible** (kŏm-**pat**-ibŭl) *adjective* **1** capable of living together harmoniously. **2** able
to exist or be used together; *at a speed
compatible with safety.* □ **compatibly** *adverb*,
**compatibility** *noun*

**compatriot** (kŏm-**pat**-ri-ŏt) *noun* a person
from the same country as another.

**compel** *verb* (**compelled, compelling**)
**1** use force or influence to cause (a person)
to do something; allow no choice of action.
**2** arouse irresistibly; *his courage compels
admiration.*

**compendious** (kŏm-**pen**-di-ŭs) *adjective*
giving much information concisely.

**compendium** (kŏm-**pen**-di-ŭm) *noun* (*plural*
**compendiums** *or* **compendia**) **1** a concise
and comprehensive summary. **2** a collection of table-games.

**compensate** *verb* **1** make a suitable payment in return for (loss or damage).
**2** serve as a counterbalance; *our present
success compensates for earlier failures.*

**compensation** *noun* **1** compensating or being compensated. **2** money etc. given to compensate for loss or damage.

**compensatory** (kom-pĕn-say-ter-i) *adjective* compensating.

**compère** (kom-pair) *noun* a person who introduces the performers in a variety show etc. ● *verb* act as compère (to).

**compete** *verb* take part in a competition or other contest.

**competence** (kom-pi-tĕns) *noun* (also **competency**) **1** being competent, ability; legal capacity. **2** a comfortably adequate income.

**competent** (kom-pit-ĕnt) *adjective* **1** having the ability or authority to do what is required. **2** adequate, satisfactory; *a competent knowledge of French*. □ **competently** *adverb*

**competition** *noun* **1** a contest in which people try to do better than their rivals. **2** competing; *competition for export markets*. **3** those competing with oneself; *we have strong foreign competition*.

**competitive** *adjective* **1** of or involving competition; *competitive sports*; *the competitive spirit*. **2** (of a price) one which compares favourably with those of rivals. □ **competitively** *adverb*, **competitiveness** *noun*

**competitor** *noun* one who competes; a rival.

**compile** *verb* **1** collect and arrange (information) into a list or book. **2** make up (a book etc.) in this way. **3** *Computing* translate (a programming language) into machine code. □ **compilation** (kom-pil-ay-shŏn) *noun*

**compiler** *noun* **1** a person who compiles information into a list or book. **2** *Computing* a program that translates instructions from a high-level language into a form which can be understood by the computer.

**complacent** (kŏm-play-sĕnt) *adjective* self-satisfied. □ **complacently** *adverb*, **complacency** *noun*

■**Usage** Do not confuse with **complaisant**.

**complain** *verb* **1** say that one is dissatisfied, protest that something is wrong. **2** (foll. by *of*) state that one is suffering from (a pain etc.); state a grievance concerning.

**complainant** *noun* the plaintiff (in certain lawsuits).

**complaint** *noun* **1** a statement saying that one is dissatisfied, a protest. **2** a cause of dissatisfaction; *a list of complaints*. **3** an illness.

**complaisant** (kŏm-play-zĕnt) *adjective* willing to do what pleases others. □ **complaisance** *noun*

■**Usage** Do not confuse with **complacent**.

**complement** (kom-pli-mĕnt) *noun* **1** that which makes a thing complete. **2** the number or quantity needed to fill something; *the bus had its full complement of passengers*. **3** *Grammar* the word(s) added to a verb to complete the predicate. **4** the number of degrees needed to make up an angle to 90°. ● *verb* make complete; form a complement to; *the hat complements the outfit*.

■**Usage** Do not confuse with **compliment**.

**complementary** *adjective* completing, forming a complement. □ **complementary colours** two colours of light which when mixed have the appearance of white light (e.g. blue and yellow). **complementary medicine** medical methods not officially recognized or not based on modern scientific knowledge, offered as an alternative to conventional medicine.

■**Usage** Do not confuse with **complimentary**.

**complete** *adjective* **1** having all its parts, not lacking anything. **2** finished; *the work is now complete*. **3** thorough, in every way; *a complete stranger*. ● *verb* **1** add what is lacking to (a thing) and make it complete. **2** finish (a piece of work etc.). **3** add what is required to (a thing); *complete the questionnaire*. □ **completely** *adverb*, **completeness** *noun*

**completion** (kŏm-plee-shŏn) *noun* completing, being completed.

**complex** (kom-pleks) *adjective* **1** made up of parts. **2** complicated. ● *noun* **1** a complex whole. **2** a connected group of feelings or ideas that influence a person's behaviour or mental attitude; *a persecution complex*. **3** a set of buildings. □ **complexity** (kŏm-pleks-iti) *noun*

**complexion** *noun* **1** the colour, texture, and appearance of the skin of the face. **2** the general character or nature of things; *that puts a different complexion on the matter*.

**compliance** *noun* **1** obedience to a request or command. **2** a tendency or willingness to yield.

**compliant** (kŏm-ply-ănt) *adjective* complying, obedient.

**complicate** *verb* make complex or complicated.

**complicated** *adjective* made up of many parts; difficult to understand or use because of this.

**complication** *noun* **1** complicating; being made complicated. **2** a complex combination of things. **3** something that complicates or adds difficulties. **4** an illness or condition that arises during the course of another and makes it worse.

**complicity** (kŏm-**plis**-iti) *noun* partnership or involvement in wrongdoing.

**compliment** *noun* **1** an expression of praise or admiration. **2** (**compliments**) formal greetings. ●*verb* pay a compliment to, congratulate.

■**Usage** Do not confuse with **complement**.

**complimentary** *adjective* **1** expressing a compliment. **2** given free of charge.

■**Usage** Do not confuse with **complementary**.

**compline** (kom-plin) *noun* the last service of the day in the Roman Catholic and High Anglican Church.

**comply** (kŏm-**ply**) *verb* (**complied, complying**) (often foll. by *with*) do as one is asked or ordered; *comply with the rules.*

**component** (kŏm-**poh**-nĕnt) *noun* each of the parts of which a thing is composed. ●*adjective* being a component.

**comport** *verb* □ **comport oneself** (*literary*) behave; conduct oneself. **comport with** suit, befit. □ **comportment** *noun*

**compose** *verb* **1** form, make up; *the group was composed of 20 students.* **2** create in music or literature. **3** arrange into good order. **4** make calm; *to compose oneself.* **5** *Printing* set up (type).

**composed** *adjective* calm, with one's feelings under control. □ **composedly** (kŏm-**pohz**-id-li) *adverb*

**composer** *noun* a person who composes music etc.

**composite** (kom-pŏ-zit) *adjective* **1** made up of a number of parts or styles. **2** (of a plant) having a head of many flowers forming one bloom. ●*noun* **1** something made up of a number of parts. **2** a composite plant.

**composition** *noun* **1** putting together into a whole, composing. **2** something composed; a piece of music or writing; a short essay written as a school exercise. **3** the parts of which something is made up; *the composition of the soil.* **4** the arrangement of parts of a picture. **5** a compound artificial substance. □ **compositional** *adjective*

**compositor** *noun* a person who sets up type for printing.

**compos mentis** in one's right mind, sane. (¶ *Latin.*)

**compost** *noun* **1** a mixture of decaying substances added to soil to improve it. **2** a mixture usually of soil and other ingredients for growing seedlings, cuttings, etc. ●*verb* treat with compost; make into compost.

**composure** *noun* calmness of mind or manner.

**compote** (kom-poht) *noun* fruit preserved or cooked in syrup.

**compound**[1] (kom-pownd) *adjective* made up of several parts or ingredients. ●*noun* a compound thing or substance. □ **compound fracture** one where the fractured bone has pierced the skin. **compound interest** interest paid on the original capital and on the interest that has been added to it. **compound time** (in music) that with a subdivision of the unit into three, six, or nine.

**compound**[2] (kŏm-**pownd**) *verb* **1** put together to form a whole, combine. **2** add to or increase. **3** come to an agreement, settle; *he compounded with his creditors.* **4** agree to refrain from revealing (a crime); *compounding a felony.*

**compound**[3] (kom-pownd) *noun* a fenced-in enclosure; (in India, China, etc.) an enclosure in which a house or factory stands.

**comprehend** *verb* **1** grasp mentally, understand. **2** include.

**comprehensible** *adjective* able to be understood. □ **comprehensibly** *adverb*, **comprehensibility** *noun*

**comprehension** *noun* **1** understanding. **2** a text set as a test of understanding. **3** inclusion.

**comprehensive** *adjective* **1** inclusive; including much or all. **2** (of motor insurance) providing protection against most risks. ●*noun* (in full **comprehensive school**) a large secondary school for children of all abilities. □ **comprehensively** *adverb*, **comprehensiveness** *noun*

**compress** *verb* (*pronounced* kŏm-**press**) squeeze together to force into less space. ●*noun* (*pronounced* **kom**-press) a pad or cloth pressed on the body to stop bleeding or to cool inflammation etc.

**compressible** *adjective* able to be compressed.

**compression** *noun* **1** compressing. **2** reduction in volume of the fuel mixture in an internal-combustion engine before ignition.

**compressor** *noun* a machine for compressing air or other gases.

**comprise** (kŏm-**pryz**) *verb* **1** include; consist of. **2** form, make up; *these three rooms comprise the apartment.*

■**Usage** In sense 2 it is better to use *compose* or *constitute*. Note that it is incorrect to use *comprise* with *of*, as in *the group was comprised of twenty students*; correct usage here is *was composed of*.

**compromise** (kom-prŏ-myz) *noun* **1** making a settlement by each side giving up part of its demands. **2** a settlement made in this way. **3** something that is half-way between opposite opinions or courses of action etc. ●*verb* **1** settle a dispute by a compromise. **2** expose to danger, suspicion, or scandal by unwise action.

**Compton**, Arthur Holly (1892–1962), American physicist, noted for his research on X-rays and nuclear energy.

**Compton-Burnett**, Dame Ivy (1884–1969), English novelist.

**comptroller** (*pronounced as* controller) *noun* (in titles of some financial officers) controller.

**compulsion** *noun* **1** compelling, being compelled. **2** an irresistible urge.

**compulsive** *adjective* **1** compelling; irresistible. **2** acting as if from compulsion; *a compulsive gambler.* □ **compulsively** *adverb*

**compulsory** *adjective* that must be done, required by the rules etc. □ **compulsorily** *adverb*

**compunction** *noun* the pricking of conscience; a slight regret or scruple.

**computable** *adjective* able to be computed.

**compute** *verb* reckon mathematically, calculate. □ **computation** *noun*, **computational** *adjective*

**computer** *noun* an electronic machine for making calculations, storing and analysing information fed into it, or controlling machinery automatically. □ **computer-literate** *adjective* able to use computers. **computer science** the study of the principles and use of computers. **computer virus** a computer code, introduced maliciously, which reproduces itself and corrupts the system or destroys data.

**computerize** *verb* (also **computerise**) equip with, perform, or produce by computer. □ **computerization** *noun*

**comrade** *noun* **1** a companion who shares one's activities. **2** a fellow socialist or Communist. □ **comradely** *adverb*, **comradeship** *noun*

**con**[1] *verb* (**conned, conning**) (*informal*) persuade or swindle after winning a person's confidence. ●*noun* (*slang*) **1** a confidence trick. **2** a convict. □ **con man** a confidence trickster.

**con**[2] *noun* (usually as **cons**) reasons against; *consider the pros and cons.*

**con**[3] *verb* (*Amer.* **conn**) (**conned, conning**) direct the steering of (a ship or helicopter).

**Conakry** (kon-ă-kri) the capital of Guinea.

**concatenate** (kŏn-kat-in-ayt) *verb* link together, form a sequence or combination of. □ **concatenation** *noun*

**concave** *adjective* curving like the surface of a ball as seen from the inside. □ **concavity** (kŏn-**kav**-iti) *noun*

**conceal** *verb* keep secret or hidden. □ **concealment** *noun*

**concede** (kŏn-**seed**) *verb* **1** admit to be true. **2** grant, allow; yield; *they conceded us the right to cross their land.* **3** admit defeat in, especially before the official end of the contest.

**conceit** *noun* too much pride in oneself.

**conceited** *adjective* being too proud of oneself. □ **conceitedly** *adverb*

**conceivable** *adjective* able to be imagined or believed. □ **conceivably** *adverb*

**conceive** *verb* **1** become pregnant. **2** form (an idea or plan etc.) in the mind; think, imagine.

**concentrate** *verb* **1** employ all one's thought, attention, or effort on something. **2** bring or come together to one place. **3** make less dilute. ●*noun* a concentrated substance or solution.

**concentrated** *adjective* **1** (of a solution etc.) having a large proportion of effective elements, not dilute. **2** intense; *concentrated hatred.*

**concentration** *noun* **1** concentrating or being concentrated. **2** mental attention. **3** a concentrate. **4** the amount of a substance contained in another substance. □ **concentration camp** a place where civilian political prisoners are brought together and confined.

**concentric** (kŏn-**sen**-trik) *adjective* having the same centre; *concentric circles.* □ **concentrically** *adverb*

**concept** (**kon**-sept) *noun* an idea, a general notion; *the concept of freedom.*

**conception** *noun* **1** conceiving; being conceived. **2** an idea.

**conceptual** *adjective* of mental concepts. □ **conceptually** *adverb*

**conceptualize** *verb* (also **conceptualise**) form a mental concept of. □ **conceptualization** *noun*

**concern** *verb* **1** be about, have as its subject; *the story concerns a group of rabbits.* **2** be of importance to, affect. **3** take up the time or attention of. ●*noun* **1** something of interest or importance, a responsibility; *it's no concern of mine.* **2** a connection, a share; *he has a concern in industry.* **3** worry, anxiety. **4** a business, a firm; *a going concern.*

**concerned** *adjective* **1** worried, anxious. **2** involved, interested. □ **concernedly** *adverb*, **concernedness** *noun*

**concerning** *preposition* about, in regard to.

**concert** *noun* a musical performance of usually several separate compositions. □ **concert pitch** *Music* the pitch internationally agreed whereby A above middle C

= 440 Hz. **in concert** in combination, together.

**concerted** (kŏn-**sert**-id) *adjective* **1** jointly arranged; done in cooperation. **2** (of music) arranged in parts for voices or instruments.

**concertina** *noun* a portable musical instrument with hexagonal ends and bellows, played by squeezing while pressing studs at each end. ● *verb* (**concertinaed, concertinaing**) fold or collapse like the bellows of a concertina.

**concerto** (kŏn-**cher**-toh) *noun* (*plural* **concertos** *or* **concerti**) a musical composition for one or more solo instruments and an orchestra.

**concession** *noun* **1** conceding. **2** something conceded. **3** a right given by the owners of land to extract minerals etc. from it or to sell goods there; *an oil concession.* **4** a reduction in price for certain categories of person. □ **concessionary** *adjective*

**concessionaire** *noun* the holder of a concession.

**conch** *noun* the spiral shell of a kind of shellfish, sometimes used as a horn.

**conchology** (konk-**ol**-ŏji) *noun* the study of shells and shellfish. □ **conchologist** *noun*

**concierge** (kon-si-**erzh**) *noun* (in France and French-speaking countries) a doorkeeper or porter, especially in a block of flats.

**conciliate** *verb* **1** overcome the anger or hostility of, win the goodwill of. **2** reconcile (people who disagree). □ **conciliation** *noun*, **conciliator** *noun*, **conciliatory** (kŏn-**sil**-i-ătri) *adjective*

**concise** (kŏn-**syss**) *adjective* brief, giving much information in few words. □ **concisely** *adverb*, **conciseness** *noun*

**conclave** (**kon**-klayv) *noun* **1** a private meeting. **2** *RC Church* an assembly of cardinals for the election of a pope.

**conclude** *verb* **1** bring or come to an end. **2** arrange, settle finally; *they concluded a treaty.* **3** arrive at a belief or opinion by reasoning.

**conclusion** *noun* **1** ending, an end; *at the conclusion of his speech.* **2** arrangement, settling; *conclusion of the treaty.* **3** a belief or opinion based on reasoning. □ **in conclusion** lastly, to conclude.

**conclusive** *adjective* ending doubt, completely convincing; *conclusive evidence of his guilt.* □ **conclusively** *adverb*

**concoct** (kŏn-**kokt**) *verb* **1** prepare by putting ingredients together. **2** invent; *concocted an excuse.* □ **concoction** *noun*

**concomitant** (kŏn-**kom**-i-tănt) *adjective* accompanying. ● *noun* an accompanying thing. □ **concomitance** *noun*

**concord** *noun* agreement or harmony between people or things. □ **concordant** (kŏn-**kor**-dănt) *adjective*

**concordance** (kŏn-**kor**-dănss) *noun* **1** agreement. **2** an index of the words used in a book or an author's writings; *a concordance to the Bible.*

**concordat** (kon-**kor**-dat) *noun* an agreement made, especially between Church and State.

**Concorde** a supersonic airliner, built jointly by Britain and France.

**concourse** (kon-**korss**) *noun* **1** a crowd, a gathering. **2** an open area through which people pass e.g. at a railway terminus.

**concrete** (**kon**-kreet) *noun* a mixture of cement with sand and gravel, used for building and paving. ● *adjective* **1** existing in material form, able to be touched and felt. **2** definite, positive; *concrete evidence.* ● *verb* cover with or embed in concrete. □ **concrete jungle** an unattractive city area considered as a place where people have to struggle for survival.

**concretion** (kŏn-**kree**-shŏn) *noun* a hard solid mass.

**concubine** (**konk**-yoo-byn) *noun* **1** a secondary wife in countries where polygamy is customary. **2** a woman who lives with a man as his wife. □ **concubinage** (kŏn-**kew**-bin-ij) *noun*

**concupiscence** *noun* (*formal*) lust; sexual desire. □ **concupiscent** *adjective*

**concur** (kŏn-**ker**) *verb* (**concurred, concurring**) **1** agree in opinion. **2** happen together, coincide.

**concurrence** (kŏn-**ku**-rĕns) *noun* **1** agreement; *concurrence of opinion.* **2** simultaneous occurrence of events.

**concurrent** (kŏn-**ku**-rĕnt) *adjective* existing or occurring at the same time. □ **concurrently** *adverb*

**concuss** (kŏn-**kus**) *verb* affect with concussion.

**concussion** (kŏn-**kush**-ŏn) *noun* **1** injury to the brain caused by a hard blow. **2** violent shaking.

**condemn** *verb* **1** express strong disapproval of. **2** pronounce guilty, convict. **3** sentence; *was condemned to death.* **4** destine to an unhappy fate. **5** declare unfit for use or uninhabitable; *condemned houses.* □ **condemned cell** a cell for a prisoner condemned to death. □ **condemnation** (kon-dem-**nay**-shŏn) *noun*

**condemnatory** (kŏn-**dem**-nă-ter-i) *adjective* expressing condemnation.

**condensation** *noun* **1** condensing or being condensed. **2** condensed liquid (especially tiny droplets of water on a cold surface).

**condense** *verb* **1** make denser or more concentrated. **2** change or be changed from gas or vapour into liquid. **3** express in fewer words; *a condensed report on the meeting.* □ **condensed milk** milk made thick by evaporation and sweetened.

**condenser** *noun* **1** an apparatus for condensing vapour. **2** *Electricity* = CAPACITOR. **3** a lens for concentrating light.

**condescend** *verb* behave in a way that shows one's feeling of dignity or superiority. □ **condescension** *noun*

**condiment** (kon-di-mĕnt) *noun* a seasoning (such as salt or pepper) for food.

**condition** *noun* **1** the state in which a person or thing is with regard to characteristics and circumstances. **2** a state of physical fitness or (of things) fitness for use; *get into condition*; *out of condition.* **3** an illness or abnormality; *she has a heart condition.* **4** something required as part of an agreement. **5** (**conditions**) the facts, situations, or surroundings that affect something; *working conditions are good.* ●*verb* **1** bring into a desired condition; make physically fit; put into a proper state for work or use. **2** have a strong effect on. **3** train, accustom. □ **conditioned reflex** *or* **response** a reaction produced by training, not a natural one. **on condition that** provided that (a thing will be done).

**conditional** *adjective* containing a condition or stipulation; *a conditional agreement.* □ **conditionally** *adverb*

**conditioner** *noun* a substance that conditions hair, fabric, etc.

**condole** (kŏn-**dohl**) *verb* (foll. by *with*) express sympathy.

**condolence** *noun* (often as **condolences**) expression of sympathy.

**condom** (**kon**-dŏm) *noun* a contraceptive sheath worn by men.

**condominium** (kon-dŏ-**min**-iŭm) *noun* **1** joint control of a State's affairs by two or more other States. **2** (*Amer.*) a building in which flats are owned individually.

**condone** (kŏn-**dohn**) *verb* forgive or overlook (wrongdoing) without punishment.

**condor** *noun* **1** a large vulture of South America. **2** a smaller vulture (the **California condor**) of North America.

**conducive** (kŏn-**dew**-siv) *adjective* (often foll. by *to*) helping to cause or produce; *an atmosphere that is conducive to work.*

**conduct** *verb* (*pronounced* kŏn-**dukt**) **1** lead or guide. **2** be the conductor of (a choir, orchestra, etc.). **3** manage or direct (business, negotiations, or an experiment). **4** have the property of allowing heat, light, sound, or electricity to pass along or through. ●*noun* (*pronounced* **kon**-dukt) **1** a person's behaviour. **2** managing or directing affairs; *the conduct of the war.* □ **conduct oneself** behave.

**conductance** *noun* the power of a specified body to conduct electricity.

**conduction** *noun* the transmission or conducting of heat or electricity etc.

**conductive** *adjective* able to conduct heat or electricity. □ **conductivity** *noun*

**conductor** *noun* **1** a person who directs the performance of an orchestra or choir etc. by gestures. **2** one who collects the fares in a bus. **3** a substance that conducts heat or electricity etc.

**conductress** *noun* a woman bus-conductor.

**conduit** (**kon**-dit *or* **kon**-dwit) *noun* **1** a pipe or channel for conveying liquids. **2** a tube or trough protecting insulated electric wires.

**cone** *noun* **1** a solid body that narrows to a point from a round flat base. **2** something shaped like this. **3** the dry fruit of certain evergreen trees, consisting of woody scales arranged in a shape suggesting a cone.

**coney** alternative spelling of CONY.

**confab** (**kon**-fab) *noun* (*informal*) a chat.

**confabulate** *verb* converse, chat. □ **confabulation** *noun*

**confection** *noun* a sweet dish or delicacy.

**confectioner** *noun* a maker or retailer of confectionery.

**confectionery** *noun* sweets, cakes, and pastries.

**confederacy** *noun* a union of States, a confederation.

**confederate** *adjective* allied, joined by agreement or treaty. ●*noun* **1** a member of a confederacy. **2** an ally, an accomplice. □ **Confederate States** the 11 southern States which seceded from the United States in 1860–1 and formed a confederacy of their own (thus precipitating the American Civil War), which was overthrown in 1865.

**confederated** *adjective* united by agreement or treaty.

**confederation** *noun* **1** joining in an alliance. **2** a confederated group of people, organizations, or States.

**confer** *verb* (**conferred**, **conferring**) **1** grant, bestow. **2** hold a conference or discussion. □ **conferrable** (kŏn-**fer**-ăbŭl) *adjective*

**conference** *noun* a meeting for discussion.

**conferment** (kŏn-**fer**-mĕnt) *noun* granting, bestowing.

**confess** *verb* **1** (often foll. by *to*) state formally that one has done wrong or has a weakness; *confessed to the crime.* **2** state one's attitude or reaction reluctantly; *I must confess that I am puzzled.* **3** declare one's sins formally, especially to a priest. **4** (of a priest) hear the confession of.

**confessedly** (kŏn-**fess**-idli) *adverb* admittedly; by one's own confession.

**confession** noun **1** confessing. **2** a thing confessed, a statement of one's wrongdoing. **3** a declaration of one's beliefs; *a confession of faith*.

**confessional** noun an enclosed stall in a church, where a priest sits to hear confessions.

**confessor** noun **1** a priest who hears confessions and gives spiritual counsel. **2** (*hist.*) a person who keeps to the Christian faith in the face of danger; *King Edward the Confessor*.

**confetti** noun bits of coloured paper thrown by wedding guests at the bride and groom.

**confidant** (**kon**-fid-ant) noun a person in whom one confides.

**confidante** noun a woman in whom one confides.

**confide** verb **1** (foll. by *in*) talk confidentially to; *confided in his friend*. **2** (usually foll. by *to*) tell (a secret) in confidence. **3** (foll. by *to*) entrust (an object, task, etc.) to.

**confidence** noun **1** firm trust. **2** a feeling of certainty, self-reliance, boldness; *he lacks confidence*. **3** something told confidentially; *has listened to many confidences*. □ **confidence trick** (*Amer.* **confidence game**) a trick in which a victim is persuaded to trust a swindler. **confidence trickster** a person who defrauds or tricks people, a swindler. **in confidence** as a secret. **in a person's confidence** trusted with his or her secrets.

**confident** adjective feeling confidence, bold. □ **confidently** adverb

**confidential** adjective **1** spoken or written in confidence, to be kept secret. **2** entrusted with secrets; *a confidential secretary*. **3** confiding; *spoke in a confidential tone*. □ **confidentially** adverb, **confidentiality** noun

**configuration** noun **1** a method of arrangement (e.g. of apparatus or parts of a computer system). **2** a shape or outline.

**configure** verb set up (a computer system, apparatus, etc.) for a particular purpose.

**confine** (kŏn-**fyn**) verb **1** keep or restrict within certain limits. **2** keep shut up. ● noun (**confines**) (*pronounced* **kon**-fynz) the limits or boundaries of an area.

**confined** adjective narrow, restricted; *a confined space*.

**confinement** noun **1** confining; being confined. **2** the time during which a woman is giving birth to a baby.

**confirm** verb **1** provide supporting evidence for the truth or correctness of; prove. **2** establish more firmly; *it confirmed him in his dislike of animals*. **3** make definite or valid formally; *bookings made by telephone must be confirmed in writing*. **4** administer the rite of Christian confirmation to.

**confirmation** noun **1** confirming. **2** something that confirms. **3** a religious rite confirming a baptized person as a member of the Christian Church. **4** a ceremony confirming a person in the Jewish faith.

**confirmed** adjective firmly settled in some habit or condition; *a confirmed bachelor*.

**confiscate** (**kon**-fis-kayt) verb take or seize by authority. □ **confiscation** noun

**conflagration** (kon-flă-**gray**-shŏn) noun a great and destructive fire.

**conflate** verb combine or blend together (especially two texts into one). □ **conflation** noun

**conflict** noun (*pronounced* **kon**-flikt) **1** a fight, a struggle. **2** disagreement between people with different ideas or beliefs. ● verb (*pronounced* kŏn-**flikt**) **1** fight, struggle. **2** be in opposition or disagreement.

**confluence** (**kon**-floo-ĕns) noun a place where two rivers join.

**confluent** (**kon**-floo-ĕnt) adjective flowing together, uniting.

**conform** verb **1** keep to rules or general custom; *she refuses to conform*. **2** (foll. by *to*, *with*) comply with; be in accordance with; *it doesn't conform to my idea of art*.

**conformable** adjective **1** similar. **2** consistent; adaptable.

**conformation** noun the way a thing is formed, its structure.

**conformist** (kŏn-**form**-ist) noun a person who readily conforms to established rules or standards etc. □ **conformism** noun

**conformity** noun conforming to established rules or standards etc.

**confound** verb **1** astonish and perplex. **2** confuse. **3** (*old use*) defeat, overthrow. ● interjection an exclamation of annoyance; *confound it!*

**confounded** adjective (*informal*) damned; *a confounded nuisance*.

**confront** (kŏn-**frunt**) verb **1** be or come face to face with; *the problems confronting us*. **2** face boldly as an enemy or in defiance. **3** bring face to face; *we confronted him with his accusers*. □ **confrontation** (kon-frun-tay-shŏn) noun

**Confucianism** (kŏn-**few**-shăn-izm) noun the moral and religious system founded by Confucius. □ **Confucian** adjective & noun

**Confucius** (kŏn-**few**-shŭs) (551–479 BC), the most influential Chinese philosopher.

**confuse** verb **1** throw into disorder, mix up. **2** throw the mind or feelings of (a person) into disorder; destroy the composure of. **3** fail to distinguish between. **4** make unclear; *confuse the issue*. □ **confusable** adjective

**confused** adjective (of a person) not mentally sound.

**confusedly** (kŏn-few-zid-li) *adverb* in a confused way.

**confusion** *noun* **1** confusing. **2** a confused state.

**confute** (kŏn-fewt) *verb* prove (a person or argument) to be wrong. □ **confutation** (kon-few-**tay**-shŏn) *noun*

**conga** *noun* **1** a dance in which people form a long winding line. **2** a tall narrow drum beaten with the hands.

**congeal** (kŏn-jeel) *verb* make or become semi-solid instead of liquid.

**congenial** (kŏn-jeen-iăl) *adjective* **1** pleasant because similar to oneself; *a congenial companion*. **2** suited or agreeable to oneself; *a congenial climate*. □ **congenially** *adverb*, **congeniality** *noun*

**congenital** (kŏn-jen-it'l) *adjective* **1** existing since a person's birth; *a congenital deformity*. **2** born in a certain condition; *a congenital idiot*. □ **congenitally** *adverb*

**conger** (kong-er) *noun* (in full **conger eel**) a large sea eel.

**congested** *adjective* **1** too full, overcrowded. **2** (of an organ or tissue of the body) abnormally full of blood or mucus.

**congestion** (kŏn-jes-chŏn) *noun* a congested condition.

**conglomerate** *adjective* (*pronounced* kŏn-**glom**-er-ăt) gathered into a mass. ● *noun* **1** a conglomerate mass. **2** a group formed by merging several different firms. ● *verb* (*pronounced* kŏn-**glom**-er-ayt) gather into a mass.

**conglomeration** *noun* a mass of different things put together.

**Congo** a country in West Africa. □ **Congolese** *adjective & noun*

**congratulate** *verb* express pleasure to (a person) about his or her achievement or good fortune.

**congratulation** *noun* **1** congratulating. **2** an expression of this.

**congratulatory** (kŏn-**grat**-yoo-lă-ter-i) *adjective* expressing congratulations.

**congregate** *verb* flock together.

**congregation** *noun* a group of people gathered for religious worship. □ **congregational** *adjective*

**Congregationalism** *noun* a form of church organization in which each local church is independent. □ **Congregationalist** *noun*

**congress** *noun* **1** a formal meeting of representatives, for discussion. **2** (**Congress**) the law-making body of a country, especially of the USA. □ **Library of Congress** the US national library, in Washington, DC.

**congressional** (kŏn-gresh-ŏn-ăl) *adjective* of a congress.

**congressman** *noun* (*plural* **congressmen**) a male member of the US Congress.

**congresswoman** *noun* (*plural* **congresswomen**) a female member of the US Congress.

**Congreve** (kon-greev), William (1670–1729), English playwright.

**congruent** (kong-roo-ĕnt) *adjective* **1** suitable, consistent. **2** (of geometrical figures) having exactly the same shape and size. □ **congruence** *noun*, **congruency** *noun*

**conic** (kon-ik) *adjective* of a cone.

**conical** *adjective* cone-shaped. □ **conically** *adverb*

**conifer** (kon-i-fer) *noun* a coniferous tree.

**coniferous** (kŏ-nif-er-ŭs) *adjective* bearing cones.

**conjectural** *adjective* based on conjecture.

**conjecture** *verb* guess. ● *noun* a guess.

**conjoin** *verb* (*formal*) join together.

**conjugal** (kon-jŭg-ăl) *adjective* of marriage, of the relationship between husband and wife. □ **conjugally** *adverb*

**conjugate** *verb* (*pronounced* **kon**-jŭg-ayt) **1** give the different forms of (a verb). **2** unite, become fused. ● *adjective* (*pronounced* **kon**-jŭg-ăt) joined together, fused. □ **conjugation** *noun*

**conjunction** *noun* **1** a word that joins words, phrases, or sentences, e.g. *and, but*. **2** combination, union; *the four countries acted in conjunction*. **3** the occurrence of events etc. at the same time. **4** the apparent nearness of two or more heavenly bodies to each other.

**conjunctiva** (kon-junk-tyv-ă) *noun* the mucous membrane covering the eyeball and inner eyelid.

**conjunctive** *adjective* joining.

**conjunctivitis** *noun* inflammation of the surface of the conjunctiva.

**conjure** (kun-jer) *verb* **1** perform tricks which appear to be magical; *conjuring tricks*. **2** summon (a spirit) to appear. □ **conjure up 1** produce as if from nothing; *they managed to conjure up a meal*. **2** produce in the mind; *mention of the Arctic conjures up visions of snow and ice*.

**conjuror** *noun* (also **conjurer**) a person who performs conjuring tricks.

**conk** (*slang*) *noun* the nose; the head. ● *verb* hit on the head. □ **conk out** (*slang*) **1** (of a machine) break down, fail. **2** (of a person) become exhausted and give up; faint; die.

**conker** *noun* (*informal*) the fruit of the horse chestnut tree.

**conn** Amer. spelling of CON[3].

**Conn.** *abbreviation* Connecticut.

**connect** *verb* **1** join or be joined. **2** (of a train etc.) be timed to arrive so that passengers from one train etc. can catch another to continue their journey. **3** put into communication by telephone. **4** think of (things or persons) as being associated with each other.

**Connecticut** (kŏn-et-i-kŭt) a State on the east coast of the USA.

**connection** *noun* **1** connecting, being connected. **2** a place where things connect; a connecting part. **3** a train etc. timed to connect with another. **4** a link, especially by telephone. **5** (often as **connections**) a relative or associate, especially with influence. **6** a link or relationship between ideas. □ **in connection with** with reference to, concerning.

**connective** *adjective* connecting; *connective tissue*.

**connector** *noun* a thing that connects others.

**Connery**, Sean (originally Thomas) (born 1930), Scottish-born film actor, best known for his portrayal of James Bond.

**conning tower** **1** a raised structure on a submarine, containing the periscope. **2** an armoured pilot-house on a warship.

**connive** (kŏ-nyv) *verb* **1** (foll. by *at*) take no notice of (wrongdoing), thus seeming to consent to it. **2** (foll. by *with*) conspire. □ **connivance** *noun*

**connoisseur** (kon-ă-ser) *noun* a person with great experience and appreciation of artistic and similar subjects.

**Connors**, Jimmy (James Scott) (born 1952), American tennis player.

**connote** (kŏ-noht) *verb* imply in addition to the literal meaning. □ **connotation** *noun*, **connotative** (kon-ŏ-tay-tiv) *adjective*

**connubial** (kŏ-new-biăl) *adjective* of marriage, of the relationship between husband and wife.

**conquer** *verb* **1** overcome in war, win. **2** overcome by effort; *conquer one's fear*. □ **conqueror** *noun*

**conquest** *noun* **1** conquering. **2** (**the Conquest** *or* **Norman Conquest**) conquest of England by the Normans in 1066. **3** something got by conquering.

**conquistador** (kon-kwist-ă-dor) *noun* (*plural* **conquistadores**, *pronounced* kon-kwist-ă-dor-ez, *or* **conquistadors**) a conqueror, especially a member of the Spanish soldiers and adventurers who conquered South America in the 16th c.

**Conrad**, Joseph (1857–1924), Polish-born British novelist.

**Conran**, Sir Terence Orby (born 1931), English entrepreneur and designer of furniture.

**consanguineous** (kon-sang-win-iŭs) *adjective* descended from the same ancestor. □ **consanguinity** *noun*

**conscience** *noun* **1** a person's sense of what is right and wrong, especially in his or her own behaviour. **2** a feeling of remorse.

□ **conscience clause** a clause (in a rule etc.) exempting a person from complying with this rule if he or she feels it is morally wrong. **conscience money** money paid by a person who feels guilty, especially about having evaded payment previously. **on one's conscience** causing one to feel guilty or remorseful.

**conscientious** (kon-shi-en-shŭs) *adjective* showing or done with careful attention. □ **conscientious objector** one who refuses to do something (especially to serve in the armed forces in a war) because he or she believes it is morally wrong. □ **conscientiously** *adverb*, **conscientiousness** *noun*

**conscious** *adjective* **1** with one's mental faculties awake, aware of one's surroundings. **2** aware; *he was conscious of his guilt*. **3** realized by oneself, intentional; *a conscious insult*. □ **consciously** *adverb*, **consciousness** *noun*

**conscript** *verb* (*pronounced* kŏn-skript) summon for compulsory military service. ●*noun* (*pronounced* kon-skript) a conscripted recruit. □ **conscription** *noun*

**consecrate** *verb* make or declare sacred; dedicate formally to the service or worship of God. □ **consecration** *noun*

**consecutive** (kŏn-sek-yoo-tiv) *adjective* following continuously, in unbroken order. □ **consecutively** *adverb*

**consensus** (kŏn-sen-sŭs) *noun* general agreement in opinion.

**consent** *verb* say that one is willing to do or allow what someone wishes. ●*noun* agreement, permission.

**consequence** *noun* **1** a result produced by some action or condition. **2** importance; *a person of consequence; the matter is of no consequence*. □ **in consequence** as a result. **take the consequences** accept whatever results from one's choice or action.

**consequent** *adjective* following as a result.

**consequential** (kon-si-kwen-shăl) *adjective* **1** following as a result. **2** important. □ **consequentially** *adverb*

**consequently** *adverb* as a result, therefore.

**conservancy** *noun* **1** a committee with authority to control a port or river etc.; *the Thames Conservancy*. **2** official conservation (of forests etc.).

**conservation** *noun* **1** conserving, being conserved. **2** preservation, especially of the natural environment.

**conservationist** *noun* a person who supports environmental conservation.

**conservatism** *noun* a conservative attitude; conservative principles (general or political).

**conservative** *adjective* **1** disliking or opposed to great or sudden change.

**2** moderate, avoiding extremes; *a conservative estimate.* **3** (**Conservative**) of the Conservative Party. ●*noun* **1** a conservative person. **2** (**Conservative**) a member or supporter of the Conservative Party. □ **Conservative Party** a political party favouring private enterprise and freedom from State control. □ **conservatively** *adverb*

**conservatoire** (kon-**ser**-vă-twar) *noun* a school of music or other arts.

**conservator** (**kon**-ser-vay-ter *or* kŏn-**serv**-ă-ter) *noun* a person who conserves or keeps something safe; one who preserves and restores articles in a museum etc.

**conservatory** *noun* **1** a greenhouse, especially one attached to a house. **2** (especially *Amer.*) = CONSERVATOIRE.

**conserve** *verb* (*pronounced* kŏn-**serv**) keep from harm, decay, or loss, for future use. ●*noun* (*pronounced* **kon**-serv) jam made from fresh fruit and sugar.

**consider** *verb* **1** think about, especially in order to make a decision; weigh the merits of. **2** make allowances for; *consider people's feelings.* **3** think to be, suppose; *consider yourself lucky.*

**considerable** *adjective* fairly great in amount or extent; *of considerable importance.* □ **considerably** *adverb*

**considerate** *adjective* taking care not to inconvenience or hurt others. □ **considerately** *adverb*

**consideration** *noun* **1** careful thought. **2** being considerate, kindness. **3** a fact that must be kept in mind; *time is now an important consideration.* **4** payment given as a reward; *he will do it for a consideration.* □ **in consideration of** in return for; on account of. **take into consideration** allow for. **under consideration** being considered.

**considering** *preposition* taking into consideration; *she is very active, considering her age.* ●*adverb* (*informal*) taking everything into account; *you've done very well, considering.*

**consign** *verb* **1** hand over or deliver formally. **2** give into someone's care.

**consignee** (kon-sy-**nee**) *noun* the person to whom goods etc. are consigned.

**consignment** *noun* **1** consigning. **2** a batch of goods etc. consigned.

**consignor** *noun* one who consigns goods etc. to another.

**consist** *verb* **1** (foll. by *of*) be made up of; *the flat consists of 3 rooms.* **2** (foll. by *in*) have as its basis or essential feature; *their happiness consists in hoping.*

**consistency** *noun* **1** the degree of thickness, firmness, or solidity; *mix it to the consistency of thick cream.* **2** being consistent.

**consistent** *adjective* **1** conforming to a regular pattern or style, unchanging; *they have*

*no consistent policy.* **2** not contradictory; *their reforms are consistent with their general policies.* □ **consistently** *adverb*

**consistory** *noun* a council of cardinals, or of the pope and cardinals.

**consolable** *adjective* able to be consoled.

**consolation** *noun* consoling; being consoled. □ **consolation prize** a prize given to a competitor who has just missed winning one of the main prizes.

**console¹** (kŏn-**sohl**) *verb* comfort in time of sorrow or disappointment.

**console²** (**kon**-sohl) *noun* **1** a bracket to support a shelf. **2** a frame containing the keyboards and stops etc. of an organ. **3** a panel holding the controls of electrical or other equipment. **4** a cabinet containing a radio or television set, designed to stand on the floor.

**consolidate** *verb* **1** make or become secure and strong; *consolidating his position as leader.* **2** combine or become combined, merge. □ **consolidation** *noun*

**consommé** (kŏn-**som**-ay) *noun* clear meat soup.

**consonance** (**kon**-sŏ-năns) *noun* agreement, harmony.

**consonant** *noun* **1** a letter of the alphabet other than a vowel. **2** the speech sound it represents. ●*adjective* consistent, harmonious; *actions that are consonant with his beliefs.* □ **consonantal** *adjective*

**consort** *noun* (*pronounced* **kon**-sort) **1** a husband or wife, especially of a monarch. **2** (usually *hist.*) a small group of players, singers, or instruments. ●*verb* (*pronounced* kŏn-**sort**) associate, keep company; *consorting with criminals.*

**consortium** (kŏn-**sort**-iŭm) *noun* (*plural* **consortia** *or* **consortiums**) a combination of countries, companies, or other groups acting together.

**conspicuous** *adjective* **1** easily seen, attracting attention. **2** worthy of notice. □ **conspicuously** *adverb*, **conspicuousness** *noun*

**conspiracy** *noun* **1** conspiring. **2** a plan made by conspiring.

**conspirator** *noun* a person who conspires. □ **conspiratorial** *adjective*, **conspiratorially** *adverb*

**conspire** *verb* **1** plan secretly with others, especially for some unlawful purpose. **2** (of events) seem to combine; *events conspired to bring about his downfall.*

**Constable** (**kun**-stă-bŭl), John (1776–1837), English painter of landscapes.

**constable** *noun* **1** a police officer of the lowest rank. **2** the governor of a royal castle.

**constabulary** (kŏn-**stab**-yoo-ler-i) *noun* a police force.

**constancy** *noun* **1** the quality of being constant and unchanging. **2** faithfulness.

**constant** *adjective* **1** happening or continuing all the time; happening repeatedly. **2** unchanging, faithful; *remained constant to his principles.* ●*noun* something that is constant and does not vary. □ **constantly** *adverb*

**Constantine** (died 337), Roman emperor from 306, who encouraged toleration of the Christian faith.

**Constantinople** the former name of Istanbul.

**constellation** *noun* a group of fixed stars.

**consternation** *noun* anxiety or dismay.

**constipate** *verb* (usually as **constipated** *adjective*) affected with constipation.

**constipation** *noun* difficulty in emptying the bowels.

**constituency** *noun* **1** a body of voters who elect a representative. **2** the district and its residents so represented.

**constituent** *adjective* forming part of a whole; *its constituent parts.* ●*noun* **1** a constituent part. **2** a member of a constituency.

**constitute** *verb* **1** make up, form; *12 months constitute a year.* **2** appoint; *they constituted him chief adviser.* **3** establish or be; *this does not constitute a precedent.*

**constitution** *noun* **1** constituting. **2** composition. **3** the principles according to which a country is organized. **4** general condition and character, especially of a person's body; *she has a strong constitution.*

**constitutional** *adjective* **1** of a country's constitution; established, permitted, or limited by this; *a constitutional crisis; constitutional government.* **2** of or produced by a person's physical or mental constitution; *a constitutional weakness.* ●*noun* a regular walk taken for the sake of one's health. □ **constitutionally** *adverb*, **constitutionality** *noun*

**constitutive** *adjective* **1** able to form or appoint; constituent. **2** essential.

**constrain** *verb* **1** compel; oblige. **2** confine; restrict.

**constrained** *adjective* (of the voice, manner, etc.) strained; showing constraint.

**constraint** *noun* **1** constraining, being constrained; compulsion. **2** a strained manner caused by holding back one's natural feelings.

**constrict** *verb* tighten by making narrower, squeeze. □ **constriction** *noun*, **constrictive** *adjective*

**constrictor** *noun* **1** a snake that kills by squeezing its prey to prevent it breathing. **2** a muscle that contracts an organ or part of the body.

**construct** *verb* (*pronounced* kŏn-**strukt**) make by placing parts together. ●*noun* (*pronounced* **kon**-strukt) something constructed, especially by the mind. □ **constructor** *noun*

**construction** *noun* **1** constructing; being constructed. **2** something constructed. **3** two or more words put together to form a phrase, clause, or sentence. **4** an interpretation; *put a bad construction on their refusal.* □ **constructional** *adjective*

**constructive** *adjective* offering helpful suggestions; *they made constructive criticisms.* □ **constructively** *adverb*

**constructivism** *noun* an artistic movement, originating in the 1920s, concerned with producing sculptures composed from a number of pieces, often of different materials, and usually non-representational. □ **constructivist** *noun*

**construe** (kŏn-**stroo**) *verb* **1** interpret, explain; *her words were construed as a refusal.* **2** combine (words with others) grammatically. **3** analyse the syntax of. **4** translate word for word.

**consubstantiation** *noun* the doctrine, associated especially with Luther, that in the Eucharist, after the consecration of the elements, the body and blood of Christ are present along with the bread and wine.

**consul** *noun* **1** either of the two chief magistrates in ancient Rome. **2** an official appointed to live in a foreign city to assist and protect his or her countrymen who live or visit there and to help commercial relations between the two countries. □ **consular** (**kons**-yoo-ler) *adjective*

**consulate** *noun* **1** the official premises of a consul. **2** a consul's position.

**consult** *verb* **1** seek information or advice from. **2** confer; *they consulted with their fellow-workers.* □ **consultation** *noun*

**consultancy** *noun* the position or business of a consultant.

**consultant** *noun* a person qualified to give expert professional advice.

**consultative** (kŏn-**sult**-ă-tiv) *adjective* for consultation; *a consultative committee.*

**consulting** *adjective* giving professional advice; *a consulting physician.* □ **consulting-room** *noun* a room in which a doctor interviews patients.

**consume** *verb* **1** use up; *much time was consumed in waiting.* **2** eat or drink up. **3** destroy completely; overwhelm; *fire consumed the buildings.* □ **consumable** *adjective & noun*

**consumer** *noun* a person who buys or uses goods or services. □ **consumer goods** those bought and used by individual consumers rather than used for producing other goods.

**consumerism** *noun* **1** the protection of consumers' interests. **2** high consumption of goods etc.

**consuming** *adjective* overwhelming, dominating; *a consuming ambition*.

**consummate** *verb* (*pronounced* **kon-sŭm-ayt**) **1** accomplish, make complete. **2** complete (a marriage) by sexual intercourse between the partners. ● *adjective* (*pronounced* kŏn-**sum**-ăt) supremely skilled; *a consummate artist*. □ **consummation** *noun*

**consumption** *noun* **1** consuming, using up, destruction. **2** the amount consumed. **3** (*old use*) tuberculosis of the lungs.

**consumptive** *adjective* (*old use*) suffering from tuberculosis of the lungs. ● *noun* a person with tuberculosis.

**cont.** *abbreviation* **1** continued. **2** contents.

**contact** (**kon**-takt) *noun* **1** touching, coming together. **2** being in touch, communication. **3** a connection for the passage of electric current. **4** a person who has recently been near someone with a contagious disease and may carry infection. **5** an acquaintance who may be contacted when one needs information or help. ● *verb* get in touch with (a person). □ **contact lens** a small lens worn directly on the eyeball to correct vision.

**contagion** (kŏn-**tay**-jŏn) *noun* **1** the spreading of disease by contact or close association. **2** a disease spread in this way. **3** a corrupting influence.

**contagious** (kŏn-**tay**-jŭs) *adjective* **1** able to be spread by contact or close association; *a contagious disease*. **2** capable of spreading disease in this way; *all these children are now contagious*.

**contain** *verb* **1** have within itself; *the atlas contains 40 maps*. **2** consist of, be equal to; *a gallon contains 8 pints*. **3** restrain; *try to contain your laughter*. **4** keep within limits; *enemy troops were contained in the valley*.

**container** *noun* **1** a box or bottle etc. designed to contain a substance or goods. **2** a large metal box for transporting goods.

**containerize** *verb* (also **containerise**) transport by container; convert to this method of transporting goods. □ **containerization** *noun*

**containment** *noun* the policy of preventing the expansion of a hostile country or influence.

**contaminant** *noun* a substance that contaminates or pollutes.

**contaminate** *verb* pollute. □ **contamination** *noun*, **contaminator** *noun*

**contemplate** (**kon**-tĕm-playt) *verb* **1** gaze at thoughtfully. **2** consider. **3** intend. **4** meditate. □ **contemplation** *noun*

**contemplative** (kŏn-**tem**-plă-tiv) *adjective* thoughtful; devoted to religious contemplation. ● *noun* a contemplative person.

**contemporaneous** *adjective* existing or occurring at the same time. □ **contemporaneously** *adverb*, **contemporaneity** *noun*

**contemporary** (kŏn-**tem**-per-er-i) *adjective* **1** living or occurring at the same time; of roughly the same age. **2** modern in style or design. ● *noun* a person contemporary with another; *Dickens and his contemporaries*.

**contempt** *noun* **1** the process or feeling of despising a person or thing. **2** the condition of being despised; *fell into contempt*. **3** disrespect. □ **contempt of court** disobedience or disrespect towards a court of law or its processes.

**contemptible** *adjective* deserving contempt. □ **contemptibly** *adverb*, **contemptibility** *noun*

**contemptuous** *adjective* feeling or showing contempt. □ **contemptuously** *adverb*

**contend** *verb* **1** strive or fight in competition or against difficulties. **2** assert, argue; *the defendant contends that he is innocent*. □ **contender** *noun*

**content¹** (kŏn-**tent**) *adjective* contented, satisfied with what one has. ● *noun* being contented, satisfaction. ● *verb* make content, satisfy. □ **to one's heart's content** as much as one desires.

**content²** (**kon**-tent) *noun* what is contained in something; *the contents of the barrel*; *butter has a high fat content*.

**contented** *adjective* happy with what one has; satisfied. □ **contentedly** *adverb*

**contention** *noun* **1** contending; quarrelling, arguing. **2** an assertion made in arguing.

**contentious** (kŏn-**ten**-shŭs) *adjective* **1** quarrelsome. **2** likely to cause contention. □ **contentiously** *adverb*

**contentment** *noun* a contented state; tranquil happiness.

**contest** *noun* (*pronounced* **kon**-test) **1** a struggle for superiority or victory. **2** a competition, a test of skill or ability etc. between rivals. ● *verb* (*pronounced* kŏn-**test**) **1** compete for or in; *contest a seat at an election*; *contest an election*. **2** dispute, challenge; *contest a statement*; *contest a will*.

**contestant** *noun* one who takes part in a contest, a competitor.

**context** *noun* **1** the words that come before and after a particular word or phrase and help to fix its meaning. **2** the circumstances in which an event occurs; *shortages were tolerated in the context of war*. □ **out of context** without the surrounding words and therefore giving a false impression of the meaning.

**contiguous** (kŏn-**tig**-yoo-ŭs) *adjective* (usually foll. by *to*, *with*) adjoining, in contact; *Kent is contiguous to Surrey.* ☐ **contiguously** *adverb*, **contiguity** (kon-tig-yoo-iti) *noun*

**continent**[1] *noun* **1** any of the main land masses of the earth (Europe, Asia, Africa, North and South America, Australia, Antarctica). **2** (**the Continent**) the mainland of Europe as distinct from the British Isles.

**continent**[2] *adjective* able to control the excretion of one's urine and faeces. ☐ **continence** *noun*

**continental** *adjective* **1** of a continent. **2** (**Continental**) of the Continent. ☐ **continental breakfast** a light breakfast of coffee and rolls etc. **continental climate** a climate with wide variations in temperature. **continental quilt** a duvet. **continental shelf** the shallow seabed bordering a continent.

**contingency** (kŏn-**tin**-jĕn-si) *noun* **1** something unforeseen. **2** a possibility, something that may occur at a future date.

**contingent** (kŏn-**tin**-jĕnt) *adjective* **1** happening by chance. **2** possible, liable to occur but not certain. **3** (usually foll. by *on*, *upon*) depending on something that may or may not happen; *an advantage that is contingent on the success of the expedition.* ●*noun* **1** a body of troops or ships etc. contributed to form part of a force. **2** a group of people forming part of a gathering.

**continual** *adjective* constantly or frequently recurring; always happening. ☐ **continually** *adverb*

**continuance** *noun* **1** continuing. **2** duration.

**continuation** *noun* **1** continuing, starting again after ceasing. **2** a thing that continues something else.

**continue** *verb* **1** keep up (an action etc.); do something without ceasing; *continue to eat*; *continue the struggle.* **2** remain in a certain place or condition; *he will continue as manager.* **3** go further; *the road continues beyond the bridge.* **4** begin again after stopping; *the discussion will continue next week.*

**continuity** (kon-tin-**yoo**-iti) *noun* **1** being continuous. **2** the uninterrupted succession of things. **3** linkage between broadcast items.

**continuo** *noun* (*plural* **continuos**) *Music* an accompaniment providing a bass line, usually played on a keyboard instrument.

**continuous** *adjective* continuing, without a break; uninterrupted, unbroken. ☐ **continuous assessment** regular assessment of work produced throughout a course of study, the marks contributing to the final grade awarded. ☐ **continuously** *adverb*

**continuum** (kŏn-**tin**-yoo-ŭm) *noun* (*plural* **continua**) something that extends continuously.

**contort** (kŏn-**tort**) *verb* force or twist out of the usual shape. ☐ **contortion** (kŏn-**tor**-shŏn) *noun*

**contortionist** (kon-**tor**-shŏn-ist) *noun* a performer who twists his or her body into unusual postures.

**contour** (**kon**-toor) *noun* **1** a line (on a map) joining the points that are the same height above sea-level. **2** an outline.

**contra** *noun* (in Nicaragua) a counter-revolutionary, a member of the forces opposing the Sandinista government.

**contra-** *combining form* against.

**contraband** *noun* **1** smuggled goods. **2** smuggling.

**contraception** (kon-tră-**sep**-shŏn) *noun* the prevention of pregnancy; the use of contraceptives.

**contraceptive** (kon-tră-**sep**-tiv) *adjective* preventing pregnancy. ●*noun* a contraceptive drug or device.

**contract** *noun* (*pronounced* **kon**-trakt) **1** a formal agreement between people or groups or countries. **2** a document setting out the terms of such an agreement. ●*verb* (*pronounced* kŏn-**trakt**) **1** make or become smaller or shorter. **2** arrange or undertake by contract; *they contracted to supply oil to the factory.* **3** catch (an illness); form or acquire (a habit, a debt, etc.). ☐ **contract bridge** a form of bridge in which only tricks bid and won count towards the game. **contract in** (*or* **out**) choose to enter (or not enter) a scheme or commitment.

**contractable** *adjective* (of a disease) able to be contracted.

**contractible** *adjective* able to be shrunk or drawn together.

**contractile** *adjective* able to contract or to produce contraction. ☐ **contractility** *noun*

**contraction** *noun* **1** contracting. **2** a shortened form of a word or words (e.g. *he's*). **3** shortening of the uterine muscles during childbirth.

**contractor** *noun* one who makes a contract, especially for constructing a building.

**contractual** (kŏn-**trakt**-yoo-ăl) *adjective* of a contract. ☐ **contractually** *adverb*

**contradict** *verb* **1** state that (what is said) is untrue or that (a person) is wrong. **2** state the opposite of, be contrary to; *these rumours contradict previous ones.* ☐ **contradiction** *noun*, **contradictory** *adjective*

**contradistinction** *noun* a distinction made by contrasting.

**contraflow** *noun* transfer of traffic from its usual half of the road to the other half by borrowing one or more lanes.

**contralto** (kŏn-**tral**-toh) *noun* (*plural* **contraltos**) **1** the lowest female singing-voice. **2** a singer with such a voice; a part written for it.

**contraption** *noun* (*informal*) an odd-looking gadget or machine.

**contrapuntal** *adjective* of or in counterpoint. □ **contrapuntally** *adverb*

**contrariwise** (kŏn-**trair**-i-wyz) *adverb* on the other hand; in the opposite way.

**contrary** (**kon**-tră-ri) *adjective* **1** opposite in nature; opposed; *the result was contrary to expectation.* **2** opposite in direction; *delayed by contrary winds.* **3** (*pronounced* kon-**trair**-i) doing the opposite of what is expected or advised, wilful. ●*noun* the opposite. ●*adverb* in opposition, against; *acting contrary to instructions.* □ **on the contrary** in denial of what has just been said or implied and stating that the opposite is true. **to the contrary** proving or indicating the opposite; *there is no evidence to the contrary.* □ **contrariness** *noun*

**contrast** *noun* (*pronounced* **kon**-trahst) **1** the act of contrasting. **2** a difference clearly seen when things are put together. **3** something showing such a difference. **4** the degree of difference between tones or colours. ●*verb* (*pronounced* kon-**trahst**) **1** compare or oppose two things so as to show their differences. **2** show a striking difference when compared.

**contravene** (kon-tră-**veen**) *verb* act in opposition to, conflict with; *contravening the law.* □ **contravention** (kontră-ven-shŏn) *noun*

**contretemps** (**kon**-trĕ-tahn) *noun* an unfortunate happening; a mishap.

**contribute** (kŏn-**trib**-yoot) *verb* **1** give jointly with others, especially to a common fund. **2** supply for publication in a newspaper or magazine or book. **3** help to bring about; *drink contributed to his ruin.* □ **contribution** *noun*, **contributor** *noun*

**contributory** (kŏn-**trib**-yoo-ter-i) *adjective* **1** contributing to a result. **2** involving contributions to a fund; *a contributory pension scheme.*

**contrite** (**kon**-tryt) *adjective* penitent, feeling guilty. □ **contritely** *adverb*, **contrition** (kŏn-**trish**-ŏn) *noun*

**contrivance** (kŏn-**try**-văns) *noun* **1** contriving. **2** something contrived, a plan. **3** a mechanical device.

**contrive** *verb* plan cleverly; achieve in a clever or resourceful way; manage. □ **contriver** *noun*

**contrived** *adjective* artificial, forced.

**control** *noun* **1** the power to give orders or to restrain something. **2** a means of restraining or regulating; a device by which a machine is operated. **3** restraint, self-restraint. **4** a standard of comparison for checking the results of an experiment. **5** a place where cars taking part in a race must stop for inspection etc. ●*verb* (**controlled**, **controlling**) **1** have control of, regulate. **2** restrain. □ **controlling interest** ownership of so many shares etc. in a business that the holder can control its policies. **control tower** a tall building from which air traffic is controlled at an airport. **in control** controlling, in charge. **out of control** no longer able to be controlled. **under control** controlled, in proper order.

**controllable** *adjective* able to be controlled.

**controller** *noun* **1** a person or thing that controls. **2** a person in charge of expenditure.

**controversial** (kontrŏ-**ver**-shăl) *adjective* causing controversy.

**controversy** (**kon**-trŏ-ver-si *or* kŏn-**trov**-er-si) *noun* a prolonged argument or dispute.

**controvert** (**kon**-trŏ-vert) *verb* deny the truth of; contradict. □ **controvertible** *adjective*

**contumacy** (**kon**-tew-mă-si) *noun* stubborn refusal to obey or comply. □ **contumacious** (kon-tew-**may**-shŭs) *adjective*

**contumely** (**kon**-tewm-li) *noun* **1** an insult. **2** a disgrace.

**contuse** (kŏn-**tewz**) *verb* bruise.

**contusion** (kŏn-**tew**-*zh*ŏn) *noun* a bruise.

**conundrum** (kŏ-**nun**-drŭm) *noun* a hard question; a riddle.

**conurbation** (kon-er-**bay**-shŏn) *noun* a large urban area.

**convalesce** *verb* regain health after illness. □ **convalescence** *noun*, **convalescent** *adjective & noun*

**convection** *noun* the transmission of heat within a liquid or gas by movement of the heated parts. □ **convective** *adjective*

**convector** *noun* a heating appliance that circulates warmed air by convection.

**convene** *verb* assemble, cause to assemble.

**convener** *noun* (also **convenor**) **1** a person who convenes a meeting. **2** a senior trade union official at a workplace.

**convenience** *noun* **1** the quality of being convenient. **2** something that is convenient. **3** a lavatory; *public conveniences.* □ **at your convenience** whenever or however you find convenient. **convenience foods** those needing little preparation.

**convenient** *adjective* **1** easy to use or deal with, not troublesome. **2** available or occurring at a suitable time or place; with easy access; *convenient for station and shops.* □ **conveniently** *adverb*

**convenor** alternative spelling of CONVENER.

**convent** *noun* **1** a religious community of nuns. **2** a building in which they live. **3** (in full **convent school**) a school run by members of a convent.

**convention** noun 1 a formal assembly. 2 a formal agreement, especially between countries; *the Geneva Convention*. 3 an accepted custom.

**conventional** adjective done or doing things according to conventions; traditional. □ **conventional weapons** non-nuclear weapons. □ **conventionally** adverb, **conventionalism** noun, **conventionality** noun

**converge** verb come to or towards the same point. □ **convergence** noun, **convergent** adjective

**conversant** (kŏn-ver-sănt) adjective (foll. by *with*) having a knowledge of.

**conversation** noun informal talk between people. □ **conversation piece** something unusual that becomes the subject of conversation. □ **conversational** adjective, **conversationally** adverb

**conversationalist** noun a person who is good at conversation.

**converse¹** (kŏn-**verss**) verb hold a conversation.

**converse²** (**kon**-verss) adjective opposite, contrary. ●noun an idea or statement that is the opposite of another. □ **conversely** adverb

**conversion** noun 1 converting or being converted. 2 a converted building.

**convert** verb (*pronounced* kŏn-**vert**) 1 change from one form, use, or character to another. 2 be able to be changed; *the sofa converts into a bed*. 3 cause (a person) to change his or her attitude or beliefs; *he was converted to Christianity*. 4 score a goal from (a try in Rugby football). ●noun (*pronounced* **kon**-vert) a person who is converted, especially to a religious faith.

**converter** noun (also **convertor**) 1 a person or thing that converts. 2 an electrical apparatus that converts alternating current to direct current and vice versa.

**convertible** adjective able to be converted. ●noun a car with a roof that can be folded down or removed. □ **convertibility** noun

**convex** (**kon**-veks) adjective curving like the surface of a ball as seen from the outside. □ **convexity** (kŏn-**veks**-iti) noun

**convey** verb 1 carry, transport, or transmit. 2 communicate as an idea or meaning. □ **conveyable** adjective

**conveyance** noun 1 conveying. 2 a means of transport; a vehicle. 3 transfer of the legal ownership of land etc.; a document effecting this.

**conveyancing** noun the business of transferring the legal ownership of property. □ **conveyancer** noun

**conveyor** noun a person or thing that conveys. □ **conveyor belt** a continuous

moving belt for conveying objects in a factory etc.

**convict** verb (*pronounced* kŏn-**vikt**) prove or declare (a person) to be guilty of a crime. ●noun (*pronounced* **kon**-vikt) a person serving a prison sentence.

**conviction** noun 1 convicting; being convicted. 2 being convinced. 3 a firm opinion or belief. □ **carry conviction** be convincing.

**convince** verb make (a person) feel certain that something is true; *I am convinced of his honesty*.

**convivial** (kŏn-**viv**-iăl) adjective sociable and lively. □ **convivially** adverb, **conviviality** (kŏn-vivi-**al**-iti) noun

**convocation** noun 1 convoking. 2 an assembly convoked.

**convoke** verb (*formal*) summon (people) to assemble.

**convoluted** (kon-vŏ-**loo**-tid) adjective 1 coiled, twisted. 2 complicated, involved.

**convolution** (kon-vŏ-**loo**-shŏn) noun 1 a coil, a twist. 2 complexity.

**convolvulus** noun a twining plant with trumpet-shaped flowers.

**convoy** (**kon**-voi) verb escort and protect, especially with an armed force or warships. ●noun a group of ships or vehicles travelling under escort or together.

**convulse** verb 1 cause violent movement in. 2 cause to double up with laughter.

**convulsion** noun 1 a violent movement of the body, especially caused by muscles contracting involuntarily. 2 a violent upheaval. 3 (**convulsions**) a violent fit of laughter.

**convulsive** adjective like a convulsion; producing upheaval. □ **convulsively** adverb

**cony** noun (also **coney**) rabbit fur used in making clothes.

**coo** verb make a soft murmuring sound. ●noun a cooing sound. ●interjection (*slang*) an exclamation of surprise.

**cooee** interjection a cry to attract attention.

**Cook¹**, James (1728–79), English naval explorer of New Zealand, Australia, and North America.

**Cook²**, Thomas (1808–92), the first English travel agent.

**cook** verb 1 prepare (food) for eating, by using heat. 2 undergo this preparation; *lunch is cooking*. 3 (*informal*) alter or falsify in order to produce a desired result; *cook the books*. ●noun a person who cooks, especially as a job. □ **cook-chill** adjective (of food) sold in pre-cooked refrigerated form. **cook up** (*informal*) concoct; invent; *cook up an excuse*. **what's cooking?** (*informal*) what is happening or being planned?

**cookbook** noun a cookery book.

**cooker** *noun* **1** a container or stove for cooking food. **2** a cooking apple.

**cookery** *noun* the art and practice of cooking.

**cookie** *noun* **1** (*Amer.*) a sweet biscuit. **2** (*Scottish*) a plain bun.

**Cookson**, Catherine Anne (born 1906), English writer of romantic fiction.

**cool** *adjective* **1** moderately cold, not hot or warm. **2** (of colours) suggesting coolness. **3** calm and unexcited. **4** not enthusiastic; *got a cool reception.* **5** casual and confident; calmly audacious; *a cool request for a loan.* ●*noun* **1** coolness; cool air, a cool place; *the cool of the evening.* **2** (*slang*) calmness, composure; *keep your cool.* ●*verb* make or become cool. □ **cool-bag**, **cool-box** *noun* an insulated container for keeping food cool. **cooling-off period** an interval to allow for a change of mind before action. **cooling tower** a tower for cooling hot water in an industrial process so that it can be reused. **cool it** (*slang*) calm down. □ **coolly** *adverb*, **coolness** *noun*

**coolant** *noun* a fluid used for cooling machinery etc.

**cooler** *noun* **1** a piece of equipment in which things are cooled. **2** (*Amer.*) a refrigerator. **3** (*slang*) a prison cell.

**coolie** *noun* an unskilled native labourer in Eastern countries.

**coomb** *noun* (also **combe**) a valley on the side of a hill; a short valley running up from the coast.

**coop** *noun* a cage for poultry. ●*verb* (usually foll. by *up*) confine or shut in; *he is cooped up in his room.*

**co-op** *noun* (*informal*) a cooperative society or shop.

**Cooper**[1], Gary (original name: Frank James) (1901–61), American film actor.

**Cooper**[2], James Fenimore (1789–1851), American novelist.

**cooper** *noun* a person whose job is making and repairing barrels and tubs.

**cooperate** *verb* (also **co-operate**) work with another or others. □ **cooperation** *noun*, **cooperator** *noun*

**cooperative** (also **co-operative**) *adjective* **1** of or providing cooperation. **2** willing to cooperate. **3** owned and run jointly by its members with profits shared between them. ●*noun* a farm or society organized on a cooperative basis. □ **cooperatively** *adverb*

**co-opt** *verb* appoint to become a member of a group by the invitation of its existing members. □ **co-option** *noun*, **co-optive** *adjective*

**coordinate** (also **co-ordinate**) *adjective* (*pronounced* koh-**ord**-in-ăt) equal in importance. ●*noun* (*pronounced* koh-**ord**-in-ăt) **1** a coordinate thing. **2** any of the

magnitudes used to give the position of a point etc., e.g. latitude and longitude. **3** (**coordinates**) matching items of clothing designed to be worn together. ●*verb* (*pronounced* koh-**ord**-in-ayt) bring (parts etc.) into a proper relationship; work or cause to work together efficiently. □ **coordination** *noun*, **coordinator** *noun*

**coot** *noun* a black aquatic bird with a horny white plate on the forehead.

**cop** (*slang*) *verb* (**copped**, **copping**) catch; *you'll cop it!* ●*noun* **1** capture; *it's a fair cop.* **2** a police officer. □ **cop it** get into trouble, be punished. **cop out** back out; fail to do what one promised. **cop-out** *noun* an evasion or failure of this kind. **not much cop** not very good.

**copal** (**koh**-păl) *noun* the resin of various tropical trees, used for varnish.

**copartner** *noun* a partner; an associate. □ **copartnership** *noun*

**cope**[1] *verb* (often foll. by *with*) deal effectively with; manage successfully.

**cope**[2] *noun* a long loose cloak worn by clergy.

**copeck** (**koh**-pek) *noun* (also **Kopek**, **Kopeck**) a Russian coin, one hundredth of a rouble.

**Copenhagen** (koh-pĕn-**hay**-gĕn) the capital of Denmark.

**Copernicus** (kŏ-**per**-nik-ŭs), Nicolaus (1473–1543), Polish astronomer, who rejected the orthodox view that the Earth was the centre of the universe and suggested that planets orbit the sun.

**copier** *noun* a copying machine, a photo-copier.

**copilot** *noun* a second pilot in an aircraft.

**coping** (**koh**-ping) *noun* the top row of masonry (usually sloping) in a wall. □ **coping saw** a D-shaped saw for cutting curves in wood. **coping-stone** *noun* one of the stones forming the top of a wall.

**copious** *adjective* existing in large amounts; plentiful. □ **copiously** *adverb*

**Copland** (**kohp**-lănd), Aaron (1900–90), American composer.

**copper**[1] *noun* **1** a chemical element (symbol Cu), a reddish-brown metal. **2** a coin made of copper or a copper alloy. **3** a reddish-brown colour. **4** a large metal vessel for boiling things, especially laundry. ●*adjective* **1** made of copper. **2** reddish-brown. □ **copper beech** a beech tree with copper-coloured leaves. **copper-bottomed** *adjective* **1** having the bottom sheathed with copper. **2** reliable; genuine. **copper sulphate** a blue crystalline solid used in electroplating, dyeing, and plant sprays.

**copper**[2] *noun* (*Brit. slang*) a police officer.

**copperplate** *noun* a type of elaborate, clear handwriting.

**coppice** *noun* a wood of small trees and undergrowth, grown for periodic cutting.

**Coppola**, Francis Ford (born 1939), American film director, writer, and producer.

**copra** *noun* dried coconut-kernels.

**copse** *noun* a coppice.

**Copt** *noun* **1** an Egyptian of the period from the mid 4th century BC onwards. **2** a member of the Coptic Church.

**Coptic** *adjective* **1** of the Copts. **2** of Coptic. ●*noun* the language of the Copts, now used only as the liturgical language of the Coptic Church.

**copula** *noun Grammar* a connecting word, especially a part of the verb *to be* connecting the predicate with the subject.

**copulate** (**kop**-yoo-layt) *verb* have sexual intercourse; (of animals) mate. □ **copulation** *noun*

**copy** *noun* **1** a thing made to look like another. **2** one specimen of a book or document or newspaper. **3** material for printing; material for newspaper reporting. **4** the text of an advertisement. ●*verb* (**copied, copying**) **1** make a copy of. **2** try to do the same as, imitate. □ **copy-typist** *noun* a typist who types from documents rather than from dictation.

**copybook** *noun* a book containing models of handwriting for learners to imitate. ●*adjective* **1** very good, model. **2** boringly conventional.

**copycat** *noun* (*informal*) a person who copies another.

**copyist** *noun* a person who makes copies of documents etc.

**copyright** *noun* the sole legal right to print, publish, perform, film, or record a literary or artistic or musical work. ●*adjective* (of material) protected by copyright.

**copywriter** *noun* a person who writes or prepares advertising copy for publication.

**coq au vin** (kok oh **van**) a casserole of chicken pieces in wine. (¶ French.)

**coquette** (kŏ-**ket**) *noun* a woman who flirts. □ **coquettish** *adjective*

**cor** *interjection* (*slang*) an exclamation of surprise.

**coracle** (**ko**-ră-kŭl) *noun* a small wickerwork boat covered with watertight material.

**coral** *noun* **1** a hard red, pink, or white substance formed by the skeletons of tiny sea creatures. **2** yellowish- or reddish-pink colour. ●*adjective* yellowish- or reddish-pink.

**coralline** *adjective* of or like coral. ●*noun* a seaweed with a hard jointed stem.

**Coral Sea** a part of the Pacific lying between Australia, New Guinea, and Vanuatu.

**cor anglais** (kor **ahng**-lay) (*plural* **cors anglais**, *pronounced* korz **ahng**-lay) an alto woodwind instrument of the oboe family.

**corbel** (**kor**-bĕl) *noun* a stone or timber projection from a wall, to support something. □ **corbelled** *adjective*

**corbie** *noun* (*Scottish*) a raven, a black crow.

**Corcyra** the former name of Corfu.

**cord** *noun* **1** long thin flexible material made from twisted strands; a piece of this; electric flex. **2** a similar structure in the body. **3** corduroy material. **4** (**cords**) corduroy trousers. **5** a measure of cut wood (usually 128 cubic feet, 3.6 cubic metres). ●*verb* fasten or bind with cord.

**corded** *adjective* (of fabric) with raised ridges.

**cordial** *noun* an essence flavoured with fruit etc., diluted to make a drink. ●*adjective* warm and friendly. □ **cordially** *adverb*, **cordiality** (kor-di-**al**-iti) *noun*

**cordite** (**kor**-dyt) *noun* a smokeless explosive used in bullets and shells.

**cordless** *adjective* powered by a charging unit rather than an electric cable; *cordless phone.*

**Cordoba** (**kor**-dŏ-bă) a city in southern Spain.

**cordon** *noun* **1** a ring of people or military posts etc. enclosing or guarding something. **2** an ornamental cord or braid worn as a badge of honour. **3** a fruit tree with its branches pruned so that it grows as a single stem. ●*verb* enclose with a cordon.

**cordon bleu** (kor-don **bler**) of the highest degree of excellence in cookery. (¶ French, = blue ribbon.)

**corduroy** *noun* **1** cotton cloth with velvety ridges. **2** (**corduroys**) trousers made of corduroy fabric.

**core** *noun* **1** the horny central part of certain fruits, containing the seeds. **2** the central or most important part of something. **3** a unit in the structure of a computer memory storing one bit of data. **4** the part of a nuclear reactor that contains the fissile material. ●*verb* remove the core from. □ **to the core** thoroughly, entirely. □ **corer** *noun*

**co-respondent** (koh-ri-**spon**-dĕnt) *noun* the person with whom the person proceeded against in a divorce suit (the *respondent*) is said to have committed adultery.

**Corfu** an island off the west coast of Greece.

**corgi** *noun* (*plural* **corgis**) a dog of a small Welsh breed with a foxlike head.

**coriander** (ko-ri-**and**-er) *noun* an aromatic plant, the seeds and leaves of which are used for flavouring.

**Corinthian** (kŏ-**rinth**-iăn) *adjective* **1** of Corinth, a city of Ancient Greece. **2** of the most ornate of the five classical orders of architecture. □ **Epistle to the Corinthians** either of two books of the New Testament.

**Coriolanus** (ko-ri-ŏ-**lay**-nŭs), Gnaeus Marcius (5th cent. BC), Roman general.

**Coriolis** (ko-ri-**oh**-lis), Gaspard Gustave de (1792–1843), French engineer, whose name is applied to an effect which helps to explain the movement of an air mass or the rotation of a rocket over the earth's surface.

**cork** *noun* **1** a light tough substance, the thick outer bark of a South European oak. **2** a piece of this used as a float. **3** a bottle-stopper made of this or similar material. ●*verb* stop up with a cork.

**corkage** *noun* a charge made by a restaurant for serving wine brought from elsewhere.

**corked** *adjective* (of wine) contaminated by a decayed cork.

**corker** *noun* (*slang*) an excellent person or thing.

**corkscrew** *noun* **1** a tool for extracting corks from bottles. **2** a spiral thing.

**corm** *noun* a rounded underground base of a stem, from the top of which buds sprout.

**cormorant** *noun* a large black sea bird.

**corn** *noun* **1** grain or seed, especially of cereal. **2** plants that produce grain. **3** (*Amer.*) maize. **4** a single grain of wheat or pepper etc. **5** (*slang*) something corny. **6** a small tender area of horny hardened skin on the foot. □ **corn dolly** a figure made from twisted straw. **corn on the cob** maize cooked and eaten from the cob.

**corncrake** *noun* a bird with a harsh cry.

**cornea** (**korn**-iă) *noun* the tough transparent outer covering of the eyeball. □ **corneal** *adjective*

**corned** *adjective* preserved in salt; *corned beef*.

**cornelian** *noun* (also **carnelian**) a reddish or white semi-precious stone.

**corner** *noun* **1** the angle or area where two lines or sides meet. **2** a difficult position, one with no escape. **3** a hidden or remote place. **4** a free hit or kick from the corner of the field in hockey or Association football. **5** a virtual monopoly of a certain type of goods or services, enabling the holder to control the price. ●*verb* **1** drive into a corner; force into a position from which there is no escape. **2** obtain (all or most of something) for oneself; establish a monopoly of. **3** move round a corner; *the car had cornered too fast.*

**cornerstone** *noun* **1** a stone in the projecting angle of a wall. **2** a basis, a vital foundation.

**cornet** *noun* **1** a brass musical instrument like a small trumpet. **2** a cone-shaped wafer holding ice cream.

**cornfield** *noun* a field where corn grows.

**cornflakes** *plural noun* a breakfast cereal of toasted maize flakes.

**cornflour** *noun* flour made from maize or rice, used to thicken sauces.

**cornflower** *noun* a plant with deep blue flowers, originally growing wild in cornfields.

**cornice** (**korn**-iss) *noun* a band of ornamental moulding round the wall of a room just below the ceiling or crowning a building.

**Cornish** *adjective* of Cornwall or its people or language. ●*noun* the ancient language of Cornwall. □ **Cornish pasty** a mixture of meat and vegetables wrapped in pastry.

**cornucopia** (kor-new-koh-piă) *noun* **1** a horn of plenty, a horn-shaped container overflowing with fruit and flowers. **2** an abundant supply.

**Cornwall** a county of south-west England.

**corny** *adjective* (**cornier, corniest**) (*informal*) repeated so often that people are tired of it; over-sentimental. □ **cornily** *adverb*, **corniness** *noun*

**corolla** (kŏ-**rol**-ă) *noun* the petals of a flower.

**corollary** (kŏ-**rol**-er-i) *noun* a natural consequence or result, something that follows logically after something else is proved.

**corona** (kŏ-**roh**-nă) *noun* a small circle or glow of light round something.

**coronary** (**ko**-rŏn-er-i) *adjective* of the arteries supplying blood to the heart. ●*noun* **1** a coronary artery. **2** (in full **coronary thrombosis**) blockage of a coronary artery by a clot of blood.

**coronation** *noun* the ceremony of crowning a king, queen, or consort.

**coroner** (**ko**-rŏn-er) *noun* an officer who holds an inquest into the cause of a death thought to be from violence or unnatural causes, or an inquiry in cases of treasure trove.

**coronet** *noun* **1** a small crown. **2** a band of gold or jewels etc. for the head.

**corpora** see CORPUS.

**corporal**[1] *adjective* of the body. □ **corporal punishment** punishment by whipping or beating. □ **corporality** *noun*

**corporal**[2] *noun* a non-commissioned officer ranking just below sergeant.

**corporate** (**kor**-per-ăt) *adjective* **1** shared by members of a group; *corporate responsibility*. **2** united in one group; *a corporate body*. □ **corporate raider** (*Amer.*) a person who makes an unwelcome takeover bid by buying up a company's shares on the stock market.

**corporation** *noun* **1** a group of people authorized to act as an individual, especially in business. **2** a group of people elected to govern a town. **3** (*informal*) a large stomach.

**corporative** *adjective* **1** of a corporation. **2** governed by or organized in corporations.

**corporeal** (kor-**por**-iăl) *adjective* bodily, physical; material. □ **corporeally** *adverb*, **corporeality** *noun*

**corps** (*pronounced* kor) *noun* (*plural* **corps**, *pronounced* korz) **1** a military force, an army unit; *the Royal Army Medical Corps*. **2** a body of people engaged in a special activity; *the diplomatic corps*.

**corpse** *noun* a dead body.

**corpulent** (**kor**-pew-lĕnt) *adjective* having a bulky body; fat. □ **corpulence** *noun*

**corpus** *noun* (*plural* **corpora**) a large collection of writings etc.

**Corpus Christi** a Christian festival in honour of the Eucharist, celebrated on the Thursday after Trinity Sunday.

**corpuscle** (**kor**-pŭs-ŭl) *noun* any of the red or white cells in the blood. □ **corpuscular** (kor-**pus**-kew-ler) *adjective*

**corral** (kŏ-**rahl**) (*Amer.*) *noun* an enclosure for horses, cattle, etc. ● *verb* (**corralled**, **corralling**) put into a corral.

**correct** *adjective* **1** true, accurate. **2** proper, in accordance with an approved way of behaving or working. ● *verb* **1** make correct, set right. **2** mark the errors in. **3** point out faults in (a person); punish (a person or a fault). □ **correctly** *adverb*, **correctness** *noun*, **corrector** *noun*

**correction** *noun* **1** correcting; being corrected. **2** an alteration made to something that was incorrect.

**correctitude** *noun* being correct; consciously correct behaviour.

**corrective** *adjective* correcting what is bad or harmful. ● *noun* something that corrects.

**Correggio** (ko-**rej**-i-oh), Antonio Allegri (*c.*1489–1534), Italian painter.

**correlate** (**ko**-rĕl-ayt) *verb* (usually foll. by *with*) **1** compare or connect systematically. **2** have a systematic connection. ● *noun* each of two related or complementary things. □ **correlation** *noun*, **correlative** (kŏ-**rel**-ătiv) *adjective*

**correspond** *verb* **1** (usually foll. by *with*, *to*) be in harmony or agreement; *this corresponds with what I've heard*. **2** (usually foll. by *to*) be similar or equivalent; *an assembly that corresponds to our parliament*. **3** write letters to each other.

**correspondence** *noun* **1** corresponding; harmony. **2** communicating by writing letters; the letters themselves. □ **correspondence course** instruction by means of materials sent by post.

**correspondent** *noun* **1** a person who writes letters. **2** a person employed to contribute news reports to a newspaper or radio station etc.

**corridor** *noun* a long narrow passage, especially one from which doors open into rooms or compartments. □ **corridors of power** institutions and people said to have hidden influence on government.

**corrie** *noun* (*Scottish*) a round hollow on a mountainside.

**corrigendum** (ko-rig-**en**-dŭm) *noun* (*plural* **corrigenda**) an error, especially in a printed book, for which a correction is printed.

**corrigible** (ko-ri-ji-bŭl) *adjective* **1** able to be corrected. **2** docile. □ **corrigibly** *adverb*, **corrigibility** *noun*

**corroborate** (kŏ-**rob**-er-ayt) *verb* get or give supporting evidence. □ **corroboration** *noun*, **corroborative** (kŏ-**rob**-er-ătiv) *adjective*, **corroborator** *noun*, **corroboratory** (kŏ-**rob**-er-ă-ter-i) *adjective*

**corrode** *verb* destroy gradually by chemical action; *rust corrodes metal*.

**corrosion** *noun* **1** corroding or being corroded. **2** a corroded area. □ **corrosive** *adjective*

**corrugated** *adjective* shaped into alternate ridges and grooves; *corrugated iron*. □ **corrugation** *noun*

**corrupt** *adjective* **1** dishonest, accepting bribes. **2** immoral, wicked. **3** (of a text or computer data) made unreliable by errors, alterations, electrical faults, etc. ● *verb* **1** cause to become dishonest or immoral, persuade to accept bribes. **2** spoil, taint. □ **corruption** *noun*, **corruptive** *adjective*, **corruptible** *adjective*, **corruptibility** *noun*

**corsair** (**kor**-sair) *noun* (*old use*) **1** a pirate ship. **2** a pirate.

**corselette** (**kor**-slit) *noun* a combined corset and bra.

**corset** *noun* a close-fitting undergarment worn to shape or support the body. □ **corsetry** *noun*

**Corsica** an island off the west coast of Italy, belonging to France. □ **Corsican** *adjective & noun*

**cortège** (kor-**tay**zh) *noun* a funeral procession.

**Cortés** (**kor**-tez), Hernando (1485–1547), Spanish conqueror of Mexico.

**cortex** *noun* (*plural* **cortices**, *pronounced* **kor**-ti-seez) **1** an outer layer of tissue (e.g. of a kidney or a plant stem); the bark of a tree. **2** the outer grey matter of the brain.

**cortical** *adjective* of the cortex.

**cortisone** (**kor**-tiz-ohn) *noun* a hormone produced by the adrenal glands or made synthetically, used against inflammation and allergy.

**corundum** (kŏ-**run**-dŭm) *noun* extremely hard alumina, used especially as an abrasive.

**corvette** (kor-**vet**) *noun* a small fast gunboat designed for escorting merchant ships.

**cos** (*pronounced* koss) *noun* a lettuce with long crisp leaves. ● *abbreviation* cosine.

**'cos** (*pronounced* koz) *adverb & conjunction* (*informal*) because.

**cosh** *noun* a weighted weapon for hitting people. ● *verb* hit with a cosh.

**co-signatory** *noun* a person or State signing a treaty etc. jointly with others.

**cosine** (**koh**-syn) *noun* (in a right-angled triangle) the ratio of the length of a side adjacent to one of the acute angles to the length of the hypotenuse.

**cosmetic** *noun* a substance for beautifying the body, especially the face. ● *adjective* for beautifying or improving the appearance; *cosmetic surgery*. □ **cosmetically** *adverb*

**cosmic** *adjective* of the universe. □ **cosmic rays** *or* **radiation** high-energy radiation that reaches the earth from outer space.

**cosmogony** (koz-**mog**-ŏni) *noun* the origin of the universe; a theory about this.

**cosmology** (koz-**mol**-ŏji) *noun* the scientific study of the creation and development of the universe. □ **cosmological** *adjective*, **cosmologist** *noun*

**cosmonaut** *noun* a Russian astronaut.

**cosmopolitan** *adjective* **1** of or from many parts of the world, containing people from many countries; *a cosmopolitan city*. **2** free from national prejudices and at home in all parts of the world; *a cosmopolitan outlook*. ● *noun* a cosmopolitan person. □ **cosmopolitanism** *noun*

**cosmos** (**koz**-moss) *noun* the universe.

**Cossack** (**koss**-ak) *noun* a member of a people of south Russia, famous as horsemen.

**cosset** (**koss**-it) *verb* (**cosseted, cosseting**) pamper.

**cost** *noun* **1** an amount given or required as payment. **2** an expenditure of time or labour; a loss suffered in achieving something. **3** (**costs**) the expenses involved in having something settled in a lawcourt. ● *verb* (in sense 3 **costed**), **costing**) **1** be obtainable at a certain price. **2** require a certain effort or loss etc. **3** estimate the cost involved. □ **at all costs** no matter what the risk or loss involved may be. **at cost** at cost price. **cost accountant** one employed to supervise a firm's expenditure. **cost-effective** *adjective* producing useful results in relation to its cost. **cost of living** the general level of prices. **cost price** the price at which a thing is bought by someone who intends to re-sell or process it. **to one's cost** involving bitter experience.

**Costa Brava** (**brah**-vă) a region of NE Spain, along the Mediterranean coast.

**Costa del Sol** a region of southern Spain, on the Mediterranean Sea.

**costal** *adjective* of the ribs.

**co-star** *noun* a stage or cinema star performing with another or others of equal or greater importance. ● *verb* (**co-starred,**

**co-starring**) perform or include as a co-star.

**Costa Rica** (kostă **ree**-kă) a country in Central America. □ **Costa Rican** *adjective & noun*

**costermonger** (**kost**-er-mung-er) *noun* a person who sells fruit etc. from a barrow.

**costing** *noun* estimation of costs.

**costive** *adjective* constipated.

**costly** *adjective* (**costlier, costliest**) costing much, expensive. □ **costliness** *noun*

**costume** *noun* **1** a style of clothes belonging to a particular place, period, or group, or suitable for a particular activity. **2** special garments worn by an actor. □ **costume jewellery** jewellery made of inexpensive materials.

**costumier** (kos-**tew**-mi-er) *noun* a person who makes or deals in costumes.

**cosy** (*Amer.* **cozy**) *adjective* (**cosier, cosiest**) warm and comfortable. ● *noun* a cover for a teapot or boiled egg to keep it hot. □ **cosily** *adverb*, **cosiness** *noun*

**cot**[1] *noun* a child's bed with high sides. □ **cot-death** *noun* (also **SIDS, sudden infant death syndrome**) the sudden, unexplained death of a sleeping baby.

**cot**[2] *noun* **1** a cote. **2** (*poetic*) a cottage.

**cot**[3] *abbreviation* cotangent.

**cotangent** (koh-**tan**-jĕnt) *noun* the ratio of the side adjacent to an acute angle (in a right-angled triangle) to the opposite side.

**cote** *noun* a small shelter built for birds or animals.

**Côte d'Azur** (koht daz-**yoor**) the Mediterranean coastal region of France which includes the Riviera.

**coterie** (**koh**-ter-i) *noun* an exclusive group of people.

**cotoneaster** (kŏ-toh-ni-**ast**-er) *noun* a shrub with red or orange berries.

**Cotswold Hills** (also **Cotswolds**) a range of hills largely in Gloucestershire.

**cottage** *noun* a small simple house, especially in the country. □ **cottage cheese** soft white cheese made from curds without pressing. **cottage industry** one that can be carried on at home. **cottage pie** a dish of minced meat topped with mashed potato.

**cottager** *noun* a person who lives in a cottage.

**cottaging** *noun* (*slang*) going to public toilets for homosexual sex.

**cotter** *noun* **1** a bolt or wedge for securing parts of machinery etc. **2** (in full **cotter pin**) a split pin that can be opened after passing through a hole.

**cotton** *noun* **1** a soft white substance round the seeds of a tropical plant. **2** the plant itself. **3** thread made from this. **4** fabric made from this thread. □ **cotton on (to)**

(*slang*) **1** understand. **2** form a liking for.
**cotton wool** fluffy wadding of a kind originally made from raw cotton.

**cotyledon** (kot-i-**lee**-dŏn) *noun* the first leaf growing from a seed.

**couch**[1] *noun* **1** an upholstered piece of furniture for several people; a sofa. **2** a long padded seat or bed-like structure with a headrest at one end. ●*verb* express in words of a certain kind; *the request was couched in polite terms.* □ **couch potato** (*slang*) a person who likes lazing at home.

**couch**[2] (*pronounced* kooch, kowch) *noun* (in full **couch grass**) a grass with long creeping roots.

**couchette** (koo-**shet**) *noun* a sleeping-berth in a railway compartment that can be converted to form an ordinary compartment with seats; a railway carriage with such berths.

**cougar** (**koog**-er) *noun* (*Amer.*) a puma.

**cough** *verb* **1** send out air or other matter from the lungs with a sudden sharp sound. **2** (*slang*) reveal information. ●*noun* **1** an act or sound of coughing. **2** an illness causing frequent coughing. □ **cough up 1** eject with coughs. **2** (*slang*) give (money or information) with some reluctance.

**could** *auxiliary verb* **1** used as the past tense of CAN[2]. **2** feel inclined to; *I could laugh for joy.* **3** might; *he could have been delayed.*

**couldn't** (*informal*) = could not.

**coulomb** (**koo**-lom) *noun* a unit of electric charge (*abbreviation* c). (¶ Named after C. A. de Coulomb (1736–1806), French engineer.)

**coulter** (**kohl**-ter) *noun* (*Amer.* **colter**) a vertical blade in front of a ploughshare.

**council** *noun* **1** an assembly of people to advise on, discuss, or organize something. **2** an elected body organizing municipal affairs. □ **council estate** an estate of council houses. **council house** *or* **flat** one owned and let by a municipal council. **council tax** a UK local tax based on the value of a property. The *council tax* replaced the *community charge* in 1993. **Council of Europe** an association of European States, independent of the EC, established to safeguard freedom, the rule of law, human rights, and the political and cultural heritage of Europe.

■**Usage** Do not confuse with **counsel**.

**councillor** *noun* a member of a council.

■**Usage** Do not confuse with **counsellor**.

**counsel** *noun* **1** advice, suggestions; *give counsel.* **2** (*plural* **counsel**) a barrister or group of barristers giving advice in a legal case. ●*verb* (**counselled, counselling**; *Amer.* **counseled, counseling**) **1** advise, recommend. **2** give professional guidance

to (a person in need of psychological help). □ **counsel of despair** advice to be taken when all else fails. **counsel of perfection** advice that is ideal in theory but impossible to follow in practice. **keep one's own counsel** keep one's views or plans secret. **take counsel with** consult.

■**Usage** Do not confuse with **council**.

**counsellor** *noun* (*Amer.* **counselor**) an adviser.

■**Usage** Do not confuse with **councillor**.

**count**[1] *verb* **1** find the total of. **2** say the numbers in order. **3** include or be included in a reckoning; *six of us, counting the dog.* **4** be important; be worth reckoning; *fine words count for nothing.* **5** regard or consider; *I should count it an honour.* ●*noun* **1** counting; a calculation. **2** a number reached by counting, a total. **3** any of the points being considered; each of the charges against an accused person; *he was found guilty on all counts.* □ **count in** include in a reckoning. **count on** rely on; expect confidently. **count noun** *Grammar* a countable noun; *see* COUNTABLE (sense 2). **count one's chickens before they are hatched** assume that something will be successful before this is certain. **count out 1** count one by one from a stock. **2** exclude from a reckoning. **3** (of a referee) count up to ten seconds over (a boxer or wrestler who has been knocked or fallen to the floor). **4** procure an adjournment of (the House of Commons) for lack of a quorum. **count up** find the sum of, add up. **keep** *or* **lose count** know or not know how many there have been. **out for the count 1** defeated. **2** unconscious; asleep.

**count**[2] *noun* a foreign nobleman corresponding to an earl.

**countable** *adjective* **1** able to be counted. **2** *Grammar* (of a noun) that can form a plural or be used with the indefinite article.

**countdown** *noun* counting numerals backwards to zero, as in the procedure for launching a spacecraft etc.

**countenance** *noun* **1** the expression of the face. **2** an appearance of approval; *lending countenance to their plan.* ●*verb* give approval to.

**counter** *noun* **1** a flat-topped fitment over which goods are sold or business is transacted. **2** a small disc used in table-games. **3** a token representing a coin. **4** an apparatus for counting things. ●*adverb* in the opposite direction. ●*adjective* opposed. ●*verb* **1** oppose, contradict. **2** hinder or defeat by an opposing action. □ **under the counter** transacted in an underhand way, especially illegally.

**counter-** *combining form* denoting **1** opposition; rivalry; *a counter-threat.* **2** opposite direction; *counter-clockwise.* **3** correspondence; similarity; *counterpart; countersign.*

**counteract** *verb* reduce or prevent the effects of. □ **counteraction** *noun*, **counteractive** *adjective*

**counter-attack** *noun* an attack directed against an enemy who has already attacked or invaded. ●*verb* make a counter-attack (on).

**counterbalance** *noun* a weight or influence that balances another. ●*verb* act as a counterbalance to.

**counter-claim** *noun* a claim made in opposition to another claim.

**counter-clockwise** *adjective & adverb* anticlockwise.

**counter-espionage** (es-pi-ŏn-ah*zh*) *noun* action taken to uncover and counteract enemy espionage.

**counterfeit** (**kownt**-er-fit) *adjective* fake. ●*noun* a fake. ●*verb* fake.

**counterfoil** *noun* a detachable section of a cheque or receipt etc. kept by the sender as a record.

**counter-intelligence** *noun* = COUNTER-ESPIONAGE.

**countermand** *verb* cancel (a command or order). ●*noun* a command or order cancelling a previous one.

**countermeasure** *noun* action taken to counteract a threat or danger etc.

**countermove** *noun* a move or action taken in opposition to another.

**counter-offensive** *noun* a large-scale counter-attack.

**counterpane** *noun* a bedspread.

**counterpart** *noun* **1** a person or thing corresponding to another in position or use. **2** a duplicate.

**counterpoint** *noun* **1** a melody added as an accompaniment to another. **2** a method of combining melodies according to fixed rules. ●*verb* set in contrast.

**counterpoise** *noun* a counterbalance. ●*verb* counterbalance.

**counter-productive** *adjective* having the opposite of the desired effect.

**Counter-Reformation** *noun* the reformation in the Church of Rome following on the Protestant Reformation (mid-16th to mid-17th century).

**counter-revolution** *noun* a revolution opposing a former one or reversing its results.

**countersign** *noun* a password; a mark of identification. ●*verb* add another signature to (a document) to give it authority.

**countersink** *verb* (**countersunk**, **countersinking**) enlarge the top of (a hole) so that the head of a screw or bolt will lie level with or below the surface; sink (a screw etc.) in such a hole.

**counter-tenor** *noun* a male singing-voice higher than tenor but with its quality; a singer with this.

**countervail** *verb* **1** counterbalance. **2** oppose.

**counterweight** *noun* a counterbalancing weight or influence. ●*verb* **1** counterbalance. **2** fit with a counterweight.

**countess** *noun* **1** the wife or widow of a count or earl. **2** a woman holding the rank of count or earl.

**countless** *adjective* too many to be counted.

**countrified** *adjective* (also **countryfied**) having the characteristics of the country or country life.

**country** *noun* **1** a nation or State; the land it occupies. **2** land consisting of fields and woods with few houses or other buildings. **3** an area of land with certain features; *hill country.* **4** country-and-western. □ **across country** across fields; not keeping to main roads or to a direct road. **country-and-western** *noun* rural or cowboy songs sung to a guitar etc., originating in the southern USA. **country club** a sporting social club in a rural area. **country dance** a traditional British dance, often with couples face to face in lines. **go to the country** (*Brit.*) test public opinion by holding a general election.

**countryman** *noun* (*plural* **countrymen**) **1** a man living or liking to live in the country, not in a town. **2** a man of one's own country.

**countryside** *noun* rural areas; the land, trees, etc. in the country.

**countrywoman** *noun* (*plural* **countrywomen**) **1** a woman living or liking to live in the country. **2** a woman of one's own country.

**county** *noun* **1** each of the main areas into which a country is divided for purposes of local government; (*Amer.*) a political and administrative division next below a State. **2** the people of such an area. **3** the families of high social level long established in a county. □ **county court** a local court where civil cases are tried. **county town** a town that is the administrative centre of a county.

**coup** (*pronounced* koo) *noun* (*plural* **coups**, *pronounced* kooz) **1** a successful stroke or action. **2** a *coup d'état.*

**coup de grâce** (koo dě **grahs**) a stroke or blow that puts an end to something. (¶ French.)

**coup d'état** (koo day-**tah**) (*plural* **coups d'état**, *pronounced* same) the sudden overthrowing of a government by force or by illegal means. (¶ French.)

**coupé** (koo-pay) noun (Amer. **coupe**, pronounced koop) a closed two-door car with a sloping back.

**Couperin** (koo-per-an), François (1668–1733), French composer.

**couple** noun 1 two people or things considered together. 2 a man and woman who are engaged or married to each other. 3 partners in a dance. ●verb 1 fasten or link together; join by a coupling. 2 copulate.

**couplet** (kup-lit) noun two successive lines of verse, especially when these rhyme and have the same metre.

**coupling** noun a device for connecting two railway carriages or parts of machinery.

**coupon** noun 1 a voucher, ticket, etc. that entitles the holder to receive something or that can be used as an application form. 2 an entry form for a football pool or similar competition.

**courage** noun the ability to control fear when facing danger or pain; bravery. □ **have the courage of one's convictions** be brave enough to do what one believes to be right.

**courageous** (kŏ-ray-jŭs) adjective having or showing courage. □ **courageously** adverb

**courgette** (koor-zhet) noun a variety of small vegetable marrow.

**courier** (koor-i-er) noun 1 a messenger carrying news or important papers. 2 a person employed to guide and assist a group of tourists.

**Courrèges** (koor-ezh), André (born 1923), French fashion designer.

**course** noun 1 an onward movement in space or time; in the ordinary course of events. 2 the direction taken or intended; the course of the river; the ship was off course. 3 a series of things one can do to achieve something; your best course is to start again. 4 a series of talks, lessons, or treatment etc. 5 a golf course; a stretch of land or water over which a race takes place. 6 a continuous layer of brick or stone in a wall. 7 each of the successive parts of a meal. ●verb 1 hunt (especially hares) with hounds that follow game by sight not by scent. 2 follow a course. 3 move or flow freely; blood coursed through his veins. □ **in course of** in the process of; the bridge is in course of construction. **in the course of** during. **of course** without a doubt, as was to be expected; admittedly.

**courser** noun (poetic) a fast horse.

**court** noun 1 a courtyard. 2 a yard surrounded by houses, opening off a street. 3 an enclosed area for certain games, e.g. squash, tennis. 4 a sovereign's establishment with attendants, councillors, etc. 5 a lawcourt; the judges in this. ●verb 1 try to win the favour or support of. 2 (old use) try

to win the affection of, especially in order to marry. 3 (of animals) try to attract sexually. 4 behave as though trying to provoke something harmful; courting danger. □ **court card** the king, queen, or jack in playing cards. **court martial** (plural **courts martial**) 1 a court for trying offences against military law. 2 trial by such a court. **court-martial** verb (**court-martialled**, **court-martialling**) try by a court martial. **Court of Session** the supreme civil court in Scotland. **court shoe** a woman's low-cut shoe with no straps, fastenings, etc. **hold court** preside over one's admirers. **put out of court** refuse to consider; make it inappropriate to consider.

**courteous** (ker-ti-ŭs) adjective polite. □ **courteously** adverb

**courtesan** (kor-ti-zan) noun (old use) a prostitute with wealthy or upper-class clients.

**courtesy** (kur-ti-si) noun courteous behaviour. □ **by courtesy of** by the permission or favour of. **courtesy light** a light (in a motor vehicle) that is switched on by opening the door.

**courthouse** noun 1 a building in which lawcourts are held. 2 (Amer.) a building containing the administrative offices of a county.

**courtier** (kor-ti-er) noun one of a sovereign's companions at court.

**courtly** (kort-li) adjective dignified and polite. □ **courtliness** noun

**courtship** noun courting, wooing; the period during which this takes place.

**courtyard** noun a space enclosed by walls or buildings.

**couscous** (koos-koos) noun a North African dish of crushed wheat or coarse flour steamed over broth, often with meat or fruit added.

**cousin** noun 1 (also **first cousin**) a child of one's uncle or aunt. 2 a person of a related race or nation.

**Cousteau** (koo-stoh), Jacques-Yves (born 1910), French oceanographer, who filmed his underwater explorations.

**couture** (koo-tewr) noun the design and making of high-class fashionable clothes.

**couturier** (koo-tewr-i-ay) noun a designer of high-class fashionable clothes.

**covalency** noun 1 the linking of atoms by a bond in which pairs of electrons are shared by two atoms in a molecule. 2 the number of pairs of electrons an atom can share with another. □ **covalent** adjective

**cove** noun 1 a small bay or inlet on a coast. 2 a curved moulding at a junction of a ceiling and a wall. 3 (slang) a man. ●verb

**1** provide (a room etc.) with a cove. **2** slope (the sides of a fireplace) inwards.

**coven** (kuv-ĕn) *noun* an assembly, especially of witches.

**covenant** (kuv-ĕn-ănt) *noun* a formal agreement, a contract. ● *verb* undertake by covenant. □ **covenanter** *noun*

**Covent Garden** a district in central London, the site for 300 years (until 1974) of London's chief fruit and vegetable market, and the home since 1946 of London's chief opera and ballet companies.

**Coventry** (kov-ĕn-tri) a city in the West Midlands. □ **send a person to Coventry** refuse to speak to or associate with him or her.

**cover** *verb* **1** place a thing over or in front of; conceal or protect in this way. **2** spread over. **3** lie or extend over, occupy the surface of; *the factory covers a large area.* **4** travel over (a distance); *we covered ten miles a day.* **5** guard; protect by dominating the approach to; have within range of one's gun(s); keep a gun aimed at. **6** protect by providing insurance or a guarantee; *covering you against fire or theft.* **7** be enough money to pay for. **8** include, deal with (a subject). **9** investigate or report for a newspaper etc.; *who is covering the conference?* ● *noun* **1** a thing that covers. **2** the binding of a book etc.; either half of this. **3** a wrapper or envelope. **4** shelter, protection; *there was no cover.* **5** a supporting force etc. protecting another from attack; *fighter cover.* **6** a screen or pretence; *under cover of friendship.* **7** insurance against loss or damage etc. **8** a place laid at table for a meal. □ **cover charge** a service charge per person in a restaurant. **cover for** deputize temporarily for. **cover girl** a female model appearing on a magazine cover. **cover much ground 1** travel far. **2** deal with a variety of topics. **cover note** a temporary certificate of insurance. **cover point** (in cricket) a fieldsman covering point; this position. **cover story** a magazine article advertised on the front cover. **cover up** conceal (a thing or fact). **cover-up** *noun* concealment, especially of facts. **cover version** a recording of a previously recorded song etc. made by a different artist. **take cover** take shelter. **under separate cover** in a separate envelope or package. **covering letter** an explanatory letter sent with a document or goods.

**coverage** *noun* **1** the act or fact of covering. **2** the area or amount covered. **3** the reporting of events in a newspaper or broadcast.

**coverall** *noun* (especially *Amer.*) **1** a thing that covers something entirely. **2** (**coveralls**) a full-length protective garment.

**Coverdale**, Miles (1488–1568), translator of the first complete printed English Bible (1535).

**coverlet** *noun* a bedspread.

**covert** (kuv-ert) *noun* **1** an area of thick undergrowth in which animals hide. **2** a bird's feather covering the base of another. ● *adjective* concealed, done secretly; *covert glances.* □ **covertly** *adverb*

**covet** (kuv-it) *verb* (**coveted**, **coveting**) desire eagerly, especially something belonging to another person.

**covetous** (kuv-it-ŭs) *adjective* coveting. □ **covetously** *adverb*, **covetousness** *noun*

**covey** (kuv-i) *noun* (*plural* **coveys**) **1** a brood or small flock of partridges. **2** a small group of people.

**cow** *noun* **1** the fully-grown female of cattle or of certain other large animals (e.g. elephant, whale, seal). **2** (*slang, offensive*) a woman one dislikes. **3** (*Austral. slang*) something bad or difficult; *it's a fair cow.* ● *verb* subdue by frightening with threats or force. □ **cow-lick** *noun* a lock of hair that stands out over the forehead. **cow-parsley** *noun* a hedgerow plant with flat umbrella-shaped flower heads. **cow-pat** *noun* a flat round piece of cow-dung.

**Coward**, Sir Noël Pierce (1899–1973), English playwright, actor, and composer.

**coward** *noun* **1** a person who lacks courage. **2** one who attacks only those who cannot retaliate.

**cowardice** *noun* cowardly feelings or actions.

**cowardly** *adjective* of or like a coward. □ **cowardliness** *noun*

**cowbell** *noun* a bell hung round a cow's neck to make a sound by which the cow can be located.

**cowboy** *noun* **1** a man who herds and tends cattle, especially in the western USA. **2** (*informal*) a person who uses reckless or unscrupulous methods in business etc.

**cowcatcher** *noun* (*Amer.*) a fender fitted on the front of a locomotive to push aside cattle or other obstacles on the line.

**cower** *verb* crouch or shrink back in fear.

**Cowes** a town in the Isle of Wight, famous internationally as a yachting centre.

**cowgirl** *noun* a female who herds and tends cattle.

**cowherd** *noun* a person who looks after cows at pasture.

**cowhide** *noun* **1** a cow's hide. **2** leather or a whip made from this.

**cowl** *noun* **1** a monk's hood or hooded robe. **2** a hood-shaped covering, e.g. on a chimney.

**cowling** *noun* a removable metal cover over an engine.

**Cowper** (**koo**-per), William (1731–1800), English poet.

**cowrie** noun a mollusc found in tropical seas, with a glossy often brightly-coloured shell.

**cowslip** noun a wild plant with clusters of small yellow flowers.

**cox** noun a coxswain. ●verb act as cox of a racing-boat.

**coxcomb** noun a conceited young man; a show-off.

**coxswain** (**kok**-sŭn) noun **1** a person who steers a rowing-boat. **2** a sailor in charge of a ship's boat. **3** a senior petty officer on certain naval vessels.

**coy** noun pretending to be shy or embarrassed, bashful. □ **coyly** adverb, **coyness** noun

**coyote** (koi-**oh**-ti) noun a North American wolf-like wild dog.

**coypu** (**koi**-poo) noun a beaver-like water animal, originally from South America.

**cozen** (**kuz**-ĕn) verb (literary) cheat; act deceitfully. □ **cozenage** noun

**cozy** Amer. spelling of COSY.

**cps** abbreviation **1** Computing characters per second. **2** Science cycles per second.

**CPU** abbreviation Computing central processing unit.

**Cr** symbol chromium.

**crab** noun **1** a ten-footed shellfish with the first pair of legs as pincers. **2** its flesh as food. **3** (**the Crab**) a sign of the zodiac, Cancer. ●verb (**crabbed, crabbing**) (informal) find fault with, grumble. □ **catch a crab** get an oar jammed or miss the water by a faulty stroke in rowing. **crab-apple** noun a small sour apple.

**crabbed** (**krab**-id) adjective **1** bad-tempered. **2** (of writing) difficult to read or decipher.

**crabby** adjective bad-tempered. □ **crabbily** adverb, **crabbiness** noun

**crabwise** adjective & adverb sideways or backwards.

**crack** noun **1** a sudden sharp explosive noise. **2** a sharp blow. **3** (informal) a wisecrack, a joke. **4** a chink. **5** a line of division where something is broken but has not come completely apart. **6** a very strong form of cocaine used as a stimulant. ●adjective (informal) first-rate. ●verb **1** make or cause to make a sudden sharp explosive sound; hit sharply; cracked his head against the wall. **2** tell (a joke). **3** break with a sharp sound. **4** break into (a safe etc.). **5** find the solution to (a code or problem). **6** break without coming completely apart. **7** (of a voice) become suddenly harsh, especially with emotion. **8** collapse under strain, cease to resist. **9** break down (heavy oils) in order to produce lighter ones. □ **crackbrained** adjective (informal) crazy. **crack**

**down on** (informal) take severe measures against. **crack-down** noun (informal) severe measures, especially against law-breakers. **crack of dawn** daybreak. **crack up** (informal) **1** praise highly. **2** have a physical or mental breakdown. **get cracking** (informal) get busy on work that is waiting to be done. **have a crack at** (informal) attempt.

**cracked** adjective (slang) crazy.

**cracker** noun **1** a firework that explodes with a sharp crack. **2** a small paper tube that explodes harmlessly when the ends are pulled, releasing a hat, joke, etc. **3** a thin dry biscuit. ●adjective (**crackers**) (slang) crazy.

**cracking** adjective (slang) very good.

**crackle** verb make or cause to make a series of slight cracking sounds. ●noun these sounds.

**crackling** noun crisp skin on roast pork.

**crackpot** adjective (informal) crazy, unpractical. ●noun a person with crazy or unpractical ideas.

**cradle** noun **1** a small bed for a baby, usually on rockers. **2** a place where something originates; the cradle of civilization. **3** a supporting framework or structure. ●verb place in a cradle; hold or support as if in a cradle. □ **cradle-snatcher** noun (slang) a person with a much younger lover or husband.

**craft** noun **1** an occupation in which skill is needed. **2** such a skill. **3** cunning, deceit. **4** (plural **craft**) a boat or raft; an aircraft or spacecraft.

**craftsman** noun (plural **craftsmen**) a person who is skilled in a craft. □ **craftsmanship** noun

**crafty** adjective (**craftier, craftiest**) cunning, using underhand methods; ingenious. □ **craftily** adverb, **craftiness** noun

**crag** noun a steep or rugged rock.

**craggy** adjective (of facial features or landscape) rugged; rough-textured. □ **cragginess** noun

**cram** verb (**crammed, cramming**) **1** force into too small a space so that the container is overfull. **2** overfill in this way. **3** study intensively for an examination.

**cramp** noun **1** sudden painful involuntary tightening of a muscle. **2** a metal bar with bent ends for holding masonry etc. together. ●verb **1** affect with cramp. **2** keep within too narrow limits. **3** fasten with a cramp. □ **cramp a person's style** prevent him or her from acting freely or naturally.

**cramped** adjective **1** without room to move. **2** (of a space) too narrow. **3** (of writing) small and with letters close together.

**crampon** (kram-pŏn) *noun* (*Amer.* **crampoon**) an iron plate with spikes, worn on boots for walking or climbing on ice.

**cranberry** *noun* the small acid red berry of a shrub, used for making jelly and sauce.

**crane** *noun* 1 an apparatus for moving heavy objects, usually by suspending them from a jib by ropes or chains. 2 a large wading bird with long legs, neck, and bill. ●*verb* stretch (one's neck) to see something. □ **crane-fly** *noun* (also **daddy-long-legs**) a flying insect with very long legs.

**cranesbill** *noun* a wild geranium.

**cranium** (kray-ni-ŭm) *noun* (*plural* **craniums** or **crania**) the bones enclosing the brain; the skull. □ **cranial** *adjective*

**crank** *noun* 1 an L-shaped part for converting to-and-fro motion into circular motion. 2 a person with very strange ideas. ●*verb* cause to move by means of a crank.

**crankshaft** *noun* a shaft driven by a crank.

**cranky** *adjective* 1 eccentric; strange. 2 working badly; shaky. 3 (*especially Amer.*) grumpy, irritable. □ **crankiness** *noun*

**Cranmer**, Thomas (1489–1556), Anglican cleric and martyr, chief compiler of the Book of Common Prayer, burnt as a heretic in the reign of Mary Tudor.

**cranny** *noun* a crevice. □ **crannied** *adjective*

**crap** (*vulgar*) *noun* 1 faeces. 2 nonsense, rubbish. ●*verb* (**crapped, crapping**) defecate. □ **crappy** *adjective*

**crape** *noun* black crêpe formerly used for mourning.

**craps** *noun* (*Amer.*) a gambling game played with a pair of dice.

**crapulent** (krap-yoo-lĕnt) *adjective* drunken; caused by drunkenness. □ **crapulence** *noun*, **crapulous** *adjective*

**crash** *noun* 1 a sudden violent noise like that of something breaking by impact. 2 a violent collision or fall. 3 a sudden drop or failure; a financial collapse. ●*verb* 1 make a crash; move or go with a crash. 2 cause (a vehicle or aircraft) to have a collision; be involved in a crash. 3 (*informal*) enter without permission, gatecrash. 4 drop or fail suddenly; collapse financially. 5 (*slang*) (often foll. by *out*) sleep, especially on a floor etc. ●*adjective* involving intense effort to achieve something rapidly; *a crash programme*. □ **crash barrier** a protective fence erected where there is danger of vehicles leaving a road. **crash-dive** (*noun*) a sudden dive by an aircraft or submarine; (*verb*) dive in this way. **crash-helmet** *noun* a padded helmet worn especially by motorcyclists to protect the head in case of a crash. **crash-land** *verb* land (an aircraft) in an emergency, especially with damage to it; be landed in this way.

**crashing** *adjective* (*informal*) overwhelming; *a crashing bore*.

**crass** *adjective* 1 gross; *crass stupidity*. 2 very stupid. □ **crassly** *adverb*, **crassness** *noun*

**crate** *noun* 1 a packing-case made of wooden slats. 2 (*slang*) an old aircraft or car. 3 a divided container for bottles.

**crater** *noun* a bowl-shaped cavity or hollow.

**cravat** (kră-vat) *noun* a man's scarf worn inside an open-necked shirt.

**crave** *verb* 1 long for, have a strong desire. 2 (*old use*) ask earnestly for; *crave mercy*.

**craven** *adjective* cowardly. ●*noun* a cowardly person.

**craving** *noun* a strong desire, a longing.

**craw** *noun* the crop of a bird or insect. □ **stick in one's craw** be unacceptable.

**crawfish** *noun* (*plural* **crawfish**) a large spiny lobster that lives in the sea.

**Crawford**, Joan (original name: Lucille le Sueur) (1908–77), American film actress.

**crawl** *verb* 1 move as snakes or ants do, with the body close to the ground. 2 move on hands and knees. 3 move slowly or with difficulty. 4 (*informal*) seek favour by behaving in a servile way; *he crawls to the boss*. 5 be covered with crawling things; *it was crawling with ants*. ●*noun* 1 a crawling movement. 2 a very slow pace; *at a crawl*. 3 a swimming stroke with an overarm movement of each arm alternately. □ **crawler** *noun*

**crayfish** *noun* (*plural* **crayfish**) a freshwater shellfish like a very small lobster.

**crayon** *noun* a stick of coloured wax etc. for drawing. ●*verb* draw or colour with crayons.

**craze** *noun* 1 a great but short-lived enthusiasm for something. 2 the object of this.

**crazed** *adjective* driven insane; *crazed with grief*.

**crazy** *adjective* (**crazier, craziest**) 1 insane. 2 foolish, not sensible; *this crazy plan*. □ **crazy paving** paving made up of oddly-shaped pieces fitted together. □ **crazily** *adverb*, **craziness** *noun*

**creak** *noun* a harsh squeak like that of an unoiled hinge. ●*verb* make such a sound.

**cream** *noun* 1 the fatty part of milk. 2 its colour, yellowish white. 3 a food containing or like cream. 4 a soft cream-like substance, especially as a cosmetic. 5 the best part of something; *the cream of society*. ●*adjective* cream-coloured. ●*verb* 1 remove the cream from. 2 make creamy; beat (ingredients) to a creamy consistency. 3 apply a cream to. 4 form cream, froth, or scum. □ **cream cheese** soft rich cheese made from curds of cream and unskimmed milk. **cream cracker** a light unsweetened biscuit. **cream off** remove (the best or a required part). **cream of tartar** a compound of potassium used in medicine and in baking powder. **cream soda** a fizzy vanilla-flavoured drink. **cream tea** afternoon tea with scones, jam, and cream.

**creamery** noun **1** a factory producing butter and cheese. **2** a dairy.

**creamy** adjective (**creamier, creamiest**) **1** rich in cream. **2** like cream. □ **creaminess** noun

**crease** noun **1** a line caused by crushing, folding, or pressing. **2** a line marking the limit of the bowler's and batsman's positions in cricket. ●verb **1** make a crease or creases in. **2** develop creases. **3** (slang) (often foll. by up) make (a person) laugh uncontrollably.

**create** verb **1** bring into existence; originate. **2** give rise to; produce by what one does; create a good impression. **3** give a new rank or position to; he was created Duke of Edinburgh. **4** (slang) make a fuss, grumble.

**creation** noun **1** creating or being created. **2** (**the Creation**) God's creating of the universe. **3** (**Creation**) the universe; all things. **4** a product of the imagination, art, fashion, etc.; something created.

**creative** adjective **1** having the power or ability to create things. **2** showing imagination and originality; creative work. □ **creative accounting** modification of accounts so as to create a favourable (perhaps misleading) impression. □ **creatively** adverb

**creator** noun **1** one who creates something. **2** (**the Creator**) God.

**creature** noun **1** a living being, especially an animal. **2** a person; a poor creature. □ **creature comforts** things that make one's life comfortable. **creature of habit** a person who does things from force of habit.

**crèche** (pronounced kresh) noun a day nursery.

**credence** (kree-děns) noun belief.

**credentials** (kri-**den**-shǎlz) plural noun **1** letters or papers showing that a person is who or what he or she claims to be. **2** evidence of achievements or trustworthiness.

**credibility** noun the quality of being credible. □ **credibility gap** people's disinclination to trust official statements or the person(s) making these.

**credible** adjective that can be believed; convincing. □ **credibly** adverb

**credit** noun **1** honour or acknowledgement given for some achievement or good quality. **2** a source of honour; a credit to the firm. **3** credibility, confidence in a person or his or her actions etc. **4** a system of doing business by trusting that a person will pay at a later date for goods or services supplied; buy on credit. **5** the power to buy

in this way. **6** the amount of money in a person's bank account or entered in an account-book as paid to the holder. **7** an educational course counting towards a degree or other qualification. **8** (**credits**) a list of acknowledgements shown at the end of a film or television programme. ●verb (**credited, crediting**) **1** believe. **2** attribute; scholars credit Strauss with this waltz. **3** enter as credit in an account-book. □ **credit card** a card authorizing a person to buy on credit. **credit note** a document crediting a sum of money to a customer e.g. for goods returned. **credit rating** an estimate of a person's suitability for credit or a loan.

**creditable** adjective deserving praise. □ **creditably** adverb

**creditor** noun a person to whom money is owed.

**creditworthy** adjective considered suitable to receive credit or a loan.

**credo** (kree-doh) noun (plural **credos**) a creed.

**credulous** (kred-yoo-lŭs) adjective too ready to believe things. □ **credulously** adverb, **credulity** (krid-**yoo**-liti) noun

**creed** noun **1** a formal summary of Christian beliefs. **2** a set of beliefs or principles.

**creek** noun **1** a narrow inlet of water, especially on the coast. **2** (Amer., Austral., & NZ) a small stream, a tributary to a river. □ **up the creek** (slang) **1** in difficulties. **2** crazy.

**creel** noun a fisherman's wicker basket for carrying fish.

**creep** verb (**crept, creeping**) **1** move with the body close to the ground. **2** move timidly, slowly, or stealthily; come on gradually. **3** (of plants) grow along the ground. **4** feel as if covered with crawling things; it will make your flesh creep. ●noun **1** creeping. **2** (slang) a person one dislikes; one who seeks favour by behaving in a servile way. **3** a gradual change in the shape of metal under stress. **4** (**the creeps**) (informal) a nervous feeling produced by fear or dislike.

**creeper** noun **1** a person or thing that creeps. **2** a creeping or climbing plant.

**creepy** adjective (**creepier, creepiest**) making one's flesh creep; feeling this sensation. □ **creepy-crawly** noun (informal) a crawling insect. □ **creepily** adverb, **creepiness** noun

**cremate** verb burn (a corpse) to ashes. □ **cremation** noun

**crematorium** (krem-ǎ-**tor**-iǔm) noun (plural **crematoria** or **crematoriums**) a place where corpses are cremated.

**crème** (pronounced krem) noun **1** a food containing or like cream. **2** used in the names of various liqueurs. □ *crème brûlée* (**broo**-lay) baked cream or custard pudding coated with caramel. *crème caramel* custard coated with caramel. *crème de la crème* the very best; the best part. *crème de menthe* (*pronounced* mahnt or mahnth) peppermint liqueur.

**crenellated** (kren-ĕl-ay-tid) *adjective* (*Amer.* **crenelated**) (of a tower etc.) having battlements. □ **crenellation** (kren-ĕl-ay-shŏn) *noun*

**Creole** (**kree**-ohl) *noun* **1** a descendant of European settlers in the West Indies or Central or South America; a white descendant of French settlers in the southern USA. **2** a person of mixed European and Black descent. **3** a language formed from a European language and another (especially African) language. ●*adjective* **1** of Creole or Creoles. **2** (**creole**) of local origin or descent.

**creosote** (**kree**-ŏ-soht) *noun* **1** a thick brown oily liquid obtained from coal tar, used as a preservative for wood. **2** a colourless liquid obtained from wood tar, used as an antiseptic. ●*verb* treat with creosote.

**crêpe** (*pronounced* krayp) *noun* **1** fabric with a wrinkled surface. **2** rubber with a wrinkled texture, used for shoe-soles. **3** (also *pronounced* krep) a thin pancake with a sweet or savoury filling. □ **crêpe de Chine** (*pronounced* sheen) fine silk crêpe. **crêpe paper** thin crinkled paper. **crêpe Suzette** a small sweet pancake flamed in alcohol.

**crept** *see* CREEP.

**crepuscular** (kri-**pus**-kew-ler) *adjective* of twilight; appearing or active at dusk or dawn.

**Cres.** *abbreviation* Crescent.

**crescendo** (kri-**shen**-doh) *adjective & adverb* gradually becoming louder. ●*noun* (*plural* **crescendos**) a gradual increase in loudness.

**crescent** *noun* **1** the waxing moon, seen as a narrow curved shape tapering to a point at each end. **2** something shaped like this. **3** a curved street.

**cress** *noun* a plant with small leaves used in salads.

**Cressida** (in medieval legends of the Trojan War) a woman of Troy, who was unfaithful to her lover Troilus.

**crest** *noun* **1** a tuft or fleshy outgrowth on a bird's or animal's head. **2** a plume on a helmet. **3** the top of a slope or hill; the white top of a large wave. **4** a design above the shield on a coat of arms, or used separately on a seal or notepaper etc.

**crested** *adjective* having or bearing a crest.

**crestfallen** *adjective* downcast, disappointed at failure.

**cretaceous** (kri-**tay**-shŭs) *adjective* **1** of or like chalk. **2** (**Cretaceous**) of the geological period in the Mesozoic era when chalk was deposited. ●*noun* (**Cretaceous**) this period.

**Crete** a Greek island in the eastern Mediterranean. □ **Cretan** *adjective & noun*

**cretin** (**kret**-in) *noun* **1** a person who is deformed and mentally undeveloped through lack of thyroid hormone. **2** (*informal*) a very stupid person. □ **cretinism** *noun*, **cretinous** *adjective*

**cretonne** (kret-**on**) *noun* heavy cotton cloth with a printed pattern, used in furnishings.

**crevasse** (kri-**vass**) *noun* a deep open crack, especially in the ice of a glacier.

**crevice** (**krev**-iss) *noun* a narrow opening or crack, especially in a rock or wall.

**crew**[1] *see* CROW[2].

**crew**[2] *noun* **1** the people working a ship or aircraft. **2** all these except the officers. **3** a group of people working together; *the camera crew.* **4** a gang. ●*verb* **1** act as crew (for). **2** supply a crew for. □ **crew cut** a closely cropped style of haircut. **crew neck** a closely fitting round neckline of a knitted garment.

**crewel** (**kroo**-ĕl) *noun* fine worsted yarn used for tapestry and embroidery.

**crib** *noun* **1** a wooden framework from which animals can pull out fodder. **2** a baby's cot. **3** a model of the manger scene at Bethlehem. **4** the cards given by other players to the dealer at cribbage. **5** (*informal*) cribbage. **6** something copied from another person's work. **7** a literal translation (for use by students) for something written in a foreign language. ●*verb* (**cribbed**, **cribbing**) **1** copy unfairly or without acknowledgement; pilfer. **2** confine in a small space.

**cribbage** *noun* a card game in which the dealer scores also from cards in the crib (*see* CRIB sense 4).

**Crick**, Francis Henry Compton (born 1916), British biophysicist, who together with J. D. Watson proposed a structure for the DNA molecule.

**crick** *noun* a painful stiffness in the neck or back. ●*verb* cause a crick in.

**cricket**[1] *noun* an outdoor summer game played with a ball, bats, and wickets, between two sides of 11 players. □ **not cricket** (*informal*) not fair play. □ **cricketer** *noun*

**cricket**[2] *noun* a brown grasshopper-like insect that makes a shrill chirping sound.

*cri de cœur* (kree dĕ ker) (*plural* **cris de cœur** *pronounced* same) a passionate appeal, complaint, or protest. (¶ French, = cry from the heart.)

**crier** noun (also **cryer**) one who cries, especially an official making public announcements in lawcourts or (**town crier**) in the streets.

**crikey** interjection (slang) an exclamation of astonishment.

**crime** noun 1 a serious offence, one for which there is punishment by law. 2 such offences, serious law-breaking; the detection of crime. 3 (informal) a shame, a senseless act; it would be a crime to miss such a chance.

**Crimea** (kry-mee-ă) a peninsula in southern Ukraine. □ **Crimean** adjective

**Crimean War** a war fought mainly in the Crimea in 1853–6, between Russia and an alliance of Great Britain, France, Sardinia, and Turkey.

**criminal** noun a person who is guilty of crime. ● adjective 1 of or involving crime; a criminal offence. 2 concerned with crime and its punishment; criminal law.

**criminology** noun the scientific study of crime. □ **criminologist** noun

**crimp** verb press into small folds or ridges.

**crimson** adjective & noun deep red.

**cringe** verb 1 shrink back in fear, cower. 2 behave in a servile fawning way.

**crinkle** verb make or become wrinkled. ● noun a wrinkle, a crease. □ **crinkle-cut** adjective with wavy edges. □ **crinkly** adjective

**crinoline** (krin-ŏ-lin) noun a light framework formerly worn to make a long skirt stand out; a skirt shaped by this.

**cripple** noun a person who is permanently lame. ● verb 1 make a cripple of. 2 disable; weaken or damage seriously; the business was crippled by lack of money.

**crisis** noun (plural **crises**, pronounced kry-seez) 1 a decisive time. 2 a time of acute difficulty or danger.

**crisp** adjective 1 brittle, breaking with a snap; crisp pastry. 2 slightly stiff; a crisp £5 note. 3 cold and bracing; a crisp winter morning. 4 brisk and decisive; a crisp manner. ● noun a thin fried slice of potato (usually sold in packets). ● verb make or become crisp. □ **burnt to a crisp** burnt until it is crisp, badly burnt. □ **crisply** adverb, **crispness** noun

**crispbread** noun a thin crisp biscuit of crushed rye etc.

**crispy** adjective (**crispier**, **crispiest**) crisp.

**criss-cross** noun a pattern of crossing lines. ● adjective with crossing lines. ● verb mark or form or move in this pattern.

**criterion** (kry-teer-iŏn) noun (plural **criteria**) a standard of judgement.

---

■**Usage** Note that criteria is a plural; it is incorrect to speak of a criteria or this criteria, or of criterias.

---

**critic** noun 1 a person who finds fault with something. 2 a person who forms and expresses judgements about books, art, musical works, etc.

**critical** adjective 1 looking for faults. 2 expressing criticism; critical remarks. 3 of or at a crisis; at an important point when there will be a decisive change; risky; dangerous; the patient's condition is critical. 4 (of a nuclear reactor) having reached the stage of maintaining a self-sustaining chain reaction. □ **critical path** a sequence of stages determining the minimum time needed for an operation. □ **critically** adverb

**criticism** noun 1 finding fault; a remark pointing out a fault. 2 the work of a critic; judgements about books, art, music, etc.

**criticize** verb (also **criticise**) 1 find fault (with). 2 examine critically; express judgements about.

**critique** (kri-teek) noun a critical essay or review.

**croak** noun a deep hoarse cry or sound, like that of a frog. ● verb 1 utter or speak with a croak. 2 (slang) die; kill.

**Croat** (kroh-at) noun 1 a native or inhabitant of Croatia. 2 the language of the Croats.

**Croatia** (kroh-ay-shă) a republic in SE Europe, formerly part of Yugoslavia. □ **Croatian** adjective & noun

**crochet** (kroh-shay) noun a kind of needlework in which thread is looped into a lacy pattern of connected stitches by means of a hooked needle. ● verb (**crocheted**, **crocheting**) do this needlework; make (an article) by this.

**crock** noun 1 an earthenware pot or jar. 2 a broken piece of this. 3 (informal) an old, worn-out person or vehicle.

**crockery** noun household china.

**Crockett**, Davy (David) (1786–1836), American politician and soldier, killed at the battle of Alamo fighting against the Mexicans.

**Crockford** short for Crockford's Clerical Directory, a reference book listing Anglican clergy.

**crocodile** noun 1 a large tropical reptile with a thick skin, long tail, and huge jaws. 2 its skin, used to make bags, shoes, etc. 3 a long line of schoolchildren walking in pairs. □ **crocodile tears** insincere sorrow (¶ so called from the belief that the crocodile wept while devouring its victim or to allure it.)

**crocus** noun (plural **crocuses**) a small plant growing from a corm, with yellow, purple, or white flowers.

**croft** noun (especially in Scotland) a small enclosed field; a small rented farm. ●verb farm a croft.

**crofter** noun the tenant of a croft.

**Crohn's disease** a chronic inflammatory disease of the digestive tract.

**croissant** (**krwass**-ahn) noun a rich crescent-shaped bread roll.

**cromlech** (**krom**-lek) noun **1** = DOLMEN. **2** a circle of upright prehistoric stones.

**Cromwell**[1], Oliver (1599–1658), English general and statesman, Puritan leader during the English Civil War, who became Lord Protector of the Commonwealth after the execution of Charles I.

**Cromwell**[2], Thomas (c.1485–1540), chief minister to Henry VIII.

**crone** noun a withered old woman.

**Cronin** (**kroh**-nin), A(rchibald) J(oseph) (1896–1981), Scottish novelist.

**crony** noun a close friend or companion.

**crook** noun **1** a hooked stick or staff, used by a shepherd or bishop. **2** something bent or curved; _carried it in the crook of her arm._ **3** (_informal_) a dishonest person; a criminal. ●adjective (_Austral. & NZ_) unsatisfactory, unpleasant; ailing, injured. ●verb bend into the shape of a crook.

**crooked** adjective **1** not straight or level; having curves, bends, or twists. **2** dishonest, not straightforward. □ **crookedly** adverb, **crookedness** noun

**Crookes**, Sir William (1832–1919), English scientist, who invented a lens that protects the eyes from ultraviolet radiation.

**croon** verb sing softly and gently. ●noun singing of this kind. □ **crooner** noun

**crop** noun **1** a batch of plants grown for their produce. **2** the harvest from this. **3** a group or quantity appearing or produced at one time; _this year's crop of students._ **4** the bag-like part of a bird's throat where food is broken up for digestion before passing into the stomach. **5** the handle of a whip; a whip with a loop instead of a lash. **6** a very short haircut. ●verb (**cropped**, **cropping**) **1** cut or bite off; _sheep crop the grass closely._ **2** cut (hair) very short. **3** (of land) bear a crop. □ **crop circle** an inexplicable circular pattern of flattened crops in a field. **crop up** occur unexpectedly or by chance.

**cropper** noun a plant producing a crop of a specified quality. □ **come a cropper** (_slang_) fall heavily; fail badly.

**croquet** (**kroh**-kay) noun a game played on a lawn with wooden balls that are driven through hoops with mallets.

**croquette** (krŏ-**ket**) noun a fried ball or roll of potato, meat, or fish.

**crore** noun (in India) ten million, 100 lakhs.

**Crosby**, Bing (original name; Harry Lillis) (1904–77), American singer and film actor.

**crosier** (**kroh**-zi-er) noun (also **crozier**) a hooked staff carried by a bishop as a symbol of office.

**cross** noun **1** a mark made by drawing one line across another, (×) or (+). **2** an upright post with another piece of wood across it, used in ancient times for crucifixion; (**the Cross**) that on which Christ died. **3** a model of this as a Christian emblem. **4** an annoying thing one has to bear. **5** a cross-shaped emblem or medal; _the Victoria Cross._ **6** an animal or plant produced by cross-breeding. **7** a mixture of two different things. ●verb **1** go or extend across. **2** place crosswise. **3** draw a line across; _cross the t's._ **4** mark (a cheque) with two parallel lines so that it must be paid into a bank or building-society account. **5** make the sign of the Cross on or over; _cross oneself._ **6** oppose the wishes or plans of. **7** cross-breed (animals); cross-fertilize (plants). ●adjective **1** passing from side to side. **2** annoyed, showing bad temper. **3** contrary, opposed; reciprocal. □ **at cross purposes** misunderstanding or conflicting with each other. **cross off** cross out. **cross one's mind** come briefly into one's mind. **cross out** draw a line through (an item on a list) to show that it is no longer valid. **cross swords** (**with**) argue or disagree (with). **keep one's fingers crossed** hope that nothing unfortunate will happen, crooking one finger over another to bring good luck. **crossed line** a faulty telephone link in which another person's conversation can be heard. **on the cross** crosswise, on the bias. □ **crossly** adverb, **crossness** noun

**crossbar** noun a horizontal bar, e.g. over a pair of goalposts or on a bicycle.

**cross-bench** noun a bench in Parliament for members not belonging to the government or main opposition.

**crossbill** noun a bird with a bill whose jaws cross when closed.

**crossbow** noun a powerful bow with mechanism for drawing and releasing the string.

**cross-breed** verb (**cross-bred**, **cross-breeding**) produce by mating an animal with one of a different kind. ●noun an animal produced in this way.

**cross-check** verb check by a different method. ●noun a check of this kind.

**cross-country** adjective & adverb across fields, not keeping to main roads or to a direct road.

**cross-dressing** *noun* the practice of dressing in the clothes of the opposite sex.

**crosse** *noun* a lacrosse stick.

**cross-examine** *verb* cross-question, especially in a lawcourt. □ **cross-examination** *noun*

**cross-eyed** *adjective* having one or both eyes turned towards the nose.

**cross-fertilize** *verb* (also **cross-fertilise**) fertilize (an animal or plant) from one of a different kind. □ **cross-fertilization** *noun*

**crossfire** *noun* the firing of guns from two or more points so that the lines of fire cross.

**cross-grained** *adjective* 1 (of wood) with the grain in crossing directions. 2 bad-tempered.

**cross-hatch** *verb* shade with crossing parallel lines.

**crossing** *noun* 1 a journey across water; *we had a smooth crossing.* 2 a place where things cross. 3 a place at which one may cross; a place for pedestrians to cross a road.

**cross-legged** *adjective & adverb* (sitting) with legs folded one across the other.

**crosspatch** *noun* (*informal*) a bad-tempered person.

**crosspiece** *noun* a transverse beam, bar, section, etc.

**cross-ply** *adjective* (of tyres) having fabric layers with cords lying crosswise (compare *radial-ply*).

**cross-question** *verb* question closely in order to test answers given to previous questions.

**cross-refer** *verb* (**cross-referred**, **cross-referring**) refer from one part of a book, document, etc. to another.

**cross-reference** *noun* a note directing people to another part of a book, index, etc. for further information.

**crossroads** *noun* a place where two or more roads intersect.

**cross-section** *noun* 1 a diagram showing the internal structure of something as though it has been cut through. 2 a representative sample.

**cross stitch** a stitch formed by two crossing stitches.

**crosstalk** *noun* 1 conversation heard on a crossed telephone line. 2 dialogue, especially between two comedians in an entertainment.

**crossways** *adverb* = CROSSWISE.

**crosswind** *noun* a wind blowing across the direction of travel.

**crosswise** *adjective & adverb* 1 in the form of a cross; intersecting. 2 diagonal or diagonally.

**crossword** *noun* a puzzle in which intersecting words, indicated by clues, have to be inserted into blank squares in a grid.

**crotch** *noun* 1 a place where things fork. 2 the part of the body or of a garment where the legs fork.

**crotchet** (**kroch**-it) *noun* a note in music, equal to half a minim.

**crotchety** *adjective* peevish, irritable.

**crouch** *verb* lower the body with the limbs bent and close to it; be in this position.

**croup** (*pronounced* kroop) *noun* 1 a children's disease in which inflammation of the windpipe causes a hard cough and difficulty in breathing. 2 the rump, especially of a horse.

**croupier** (**kroop**-i-er) *noun* a person who rakes in the money at a gambling-table and pays out winnings.

**croûton** (**kroo**-ton) *noun* a small piece of fried or toasted bread served with soup etc.

**crow**[1] *noun* a large black bird of a family that includes the jackdaw, raven, and rook. □ **as the crow flies** in a straight line. **crow's-feet** *plural noun* wrinkles in the skin at the side of the eyes. **crow's-nest** *noun* a protected lookout platform high on the mast of a ship.

**crow**[2] *verb* (**crowed** *or* **crew**, **crowing**) 1 (of a cock) make a loud shrill cry. 2 (of a baby) make sounds of pleasure. 3 express gleeful triumph. ●*noun* a crowing cry or sound.

**crowbar** *noun* a bar of iron with a flattened or beak-like end, used as a lever.

**crowd** *noun* a large number of people in one place. ●*verb* 1 come together in a crowd. 2 fill or occupy fully; cram with people or things. 3 inconvenience by crowding or coming aggressively close. □ **crowd out** keep out by crowding. □ **crowded** *adjective*

**crown** *noun* 1 an ornamental headdress worn by a king or queen. 2 (**the Crown**) the sovereign; his or her authority. 3 a wreath worn on the head, especially as a symbol of victory. 4 a crown-shaped object or ornament. 5 the top part of something (e.g. of the head or a hat); the highest part of something arched. 6 the part of a tooth visible above the gum; an artificial replacement for this. 7 a former British coin worth 5 shillings. ●*verb* 1 place a crown on as a symbol of royal power or victory. 2 form, cover, or ornament the top part of. 3 make a successful conclusion to; *our efforts were crowned with success.* 4 put an artificial top on (a tooth). 5 (*slang*) hit on the head. □ **Crown Colony** a colony subject to direct control by the British government. **Crown Court** a court where criminal cases are tried in England and Wales. **Crown Derby** china made at Derby and often marked with a crown. **crown jewels** the sovereign's crown, sceptre, orb, etc. used at coronations. **Crown prince**

the male heir to a throne. **Crown princess 1** the wife of a Crown prince. **2** the female heir to a throne.

**crozier** alternative spelling of CROSIER.

**CRT** *abbreviation* cathode-ray tube.

**cru** (*pronounced* kroo) *noun* **1** a French vine-yard or wine region. **2** a grade of wine.

**cruces** *see* CRUX.

**crucial** (**kroo**-shăl) *adjective* **1** decisive, critical. **2** (*informal*) very important. **3** (*slang*) excellent. □ **crucially** *adverb*

**crucible** (**kroo**-si-bŭl) *noun* a pot in which metals are melted.

**cruciferous** (kroo-**sif**-er-ŭs) *adjective* of the family of plants bearing flowers with four equal petals arranged crosswise.

**crucifix** *noun* a model of the Cross or of Christ on the Cross.

**crucifixion** *noun* crucifying, being crucified; (**the Crucifixion**) that of Christ.

**cruciform** (**kroo**-si-form) *adjective* cross-shaped.

**crucify** *verb* (**crucified**, **crucifying**) **1** put to death by nailing or binding to a cross. **2** persecute, torment. **3** (*slang*) defeat thoroughly; humiliate.

**crud** *noun* (*slang*) a deposit of dirt, grease, etc. □ **cruddy** *adjective*

**crude** *adjective* **1** in a natural state, not refined; *crude oil*. **2** not well finished or worked out, rough; *a crude attempt*. **3** without good manners, vulgar. ●*noun* crude oil. □ **crudely** *adverb*, **crudity** *noun*

**crudités** (**kroo**-di-tay) *plural noun* a starter of mixed raw vegetables cut into small pieces, often with a sauce to dip them in.

**cruel** *adjective* (**crueller**, **cruellest**) **1** feeling pleasure in another's suffering. **2** causing pain or suffering; *this cruel war*. □ **cruelly** *adverb*, **cruelty** *noun*

**cruet** *noun* **1** a set of small salt, pepper, etc. containers for use at the table. **2** such a container.

**Crufts** an annual dog-show held in London, first organized in 1886 by Charles Cruft, British dog-breeder.

**cruise** *verb* **1** sail about for pleasure or on patrol. **2** (of a vehicle or aircraft) travel at a moderate speed that is economical of fuel. **3** drive at moderate speed, or at random when looking for passengers etc. ●*noun* a cruising voyage. □ **cruise missile** a missile that is able to fly at low altitude and guide itself by reference to the features of the region traversed.

**cruiser** *noun* **1** a fast warship. **2** = CABIN CRUISER.

**cruiserweight** = LIGHT HEAVYWEIGHT.

**crumb** *noun* **1** a small fragment, especially of bread or other food. **2** the soft inner part of bread. ●*verb* **1** cover with breadcrumbs. **2** crumble (bread).

**crumble** *verb* break or fall into small fragments. ●*noun* fruit cooked with a crumbly topping; *apple crumble*.

**crumbly** *adjective* easily crumbled.

**crumbs** *interjection* an exclamation of dismay or surprise.

**crumby** *adjective* **1** like or covered in crumbs. **2** = CRUMMY.

**crumhorn** alternative spelling of KRUMM-HORN.

**crummy** *adjective* (**crummier**, **crummiest**) (also **crumby**) (*slang*) **1** dirty, squalid. **2** inferior, worthless. □ **crumminess** *noun*

**crumpet** *noun* **1** a soft cake of yeast mixture, eaten toasted and buttered. **2** (*slang*) sexually attractive women.

**crumple** *verb* **1** crush or become crushed into creases. **2** collapse loosely.

**crunch** *verb* **1** crush noisily with the teeth. **2** walk or move with a sound of crushing; make such a sound. ●*noun* **1** crunching; a crunching sound. **2** (*informal*) a decisive event, a showdown. □ **crunchy** *adjective*

**crupper** *noun* a strap for holding a harness back, passing under a horse's tail.

**crusade** (kroo-**sayd**) *noun* **1** any of the military expeditions made by Europeans in the Middle Ages to recover the Holy Land from the Muslims. **2** a vigorous campaign for a cause. ●*verb* take part in a crusade. □ **crusader** *noun*

**cruse** *noun* (*old use*) an earthenware pot or jar.

**crush** *verb* **1** press so as to break, injure, or wrinkle; squeeze tightly. **2** pound into small fragments. **3** become crushed. **4** defeat or subdue completely. ●*noun* **1** a crowd of people pressed together. **2** a drink made from crushed fruit. **3** (*slang*) an infatuation. □ **crush barrier** a temporary barrier for restraining a crowd. □ **crushable** *adjective*

**crust** *noun* **1** the hard outer layer of something, especially bread. **2** the rocky outer portion of the earth. **3** a deposit, especially from wine on a bottle.

**crustacean** (krus-**tay**-shăn) *noun* an animal that has a hard shell (e.g. crab, lobster, shrimp).

**crusty** *adjective* (**crustier**, **crustiest**) **1** having a crisp crust. **2** having a harsh manner. ●*noun* (*slang*) a homeless or vagrant young person, generally of untidy appearance and living by begging. □ **crustily** *adverb*, **crustiness** *noun*

**crutch** *noun* **1** a support for a lame person, usually fitting under the armpit. **2** the crotch of the body or of a garment.

**crux** *noun* (*plural* **cruxes** or **cruces**, *pronounced* **kroo**-seez) the vital part of a problem; a decisive point.

**cruzado** *noun* (*plural* **cruzados**) the chief monetary unit of Brazil.

**cry** *noun* **1** a loud wordless sound expressing pain, grief, joy, etc. **2** a shout. **3** the call of a bird or animal. **4** an appeal, a demand. **5** a battle-cry. **6** a spell of weeping; *have a good cry.* ●*verb* (**cried, crying**) **1** shed tears. **2** call out loudly in words. **3** appeal, demand. **4** (of an animal) utter its cry. □ **crybaby** *noun* a person who weeps easily without good cause. **a crying shame** a terrible injustice; one demanding attention. **cry off** withdraw from a promise or arrangement. **cry out for** need as an obvious requirement or solution.

**cryer** *noun* alternative spelling of CRIER.

**cryogenics** (kry-ŏ-jen-iks) *noun* the scientific study of very low temperatures and their effects. □ **cryogenic** *adjective*

**crypt** (*pronounced* kript) *noun* a room below the floor of a church; a vault used as a burial place.

**cryptic** (**krip**-tik) *adjective* concealing its meaning in a puzzling way. □ **cryptically** *adverb*

**cryptogam** (**krip**-tŏ-gam) *noun* a flowerless plant such as a fern, moss, or fungus. □ **cryptogamous** (krip-tog-ă-mŭs) *adjective*

**cryptogram** (**krip**-tŏ-gram) *noun* something written in code or cipher.

**cryptography** (krip-tog-ră-fi) *noun* the art of writing in codes or ciphers or of deciphering these. □ **cryptographer** *noun*, **cryptographic** *adjective*

**crystal** *noun* **1** a clear transparent colourless mineral. **2** very clear glass of high quality. **3** each of the pieces into which certain substances solidify; *crystals of ice.* ●*adjective* made of crystal; like or clear as crystal. □ **crystal ball** a globe of glass used in crystal-gazing. **crystal-gazing** *noun* looking into a crystal ball in an attempt to see future events pictured there.

**crystalline** (**krist**-ă-lyn) *adjective* **1** like or containing crystals. **2** transparent, very clear.

**crystallize** *verb* (also **crystallise**) **1** form crystals. **2** (of ideas or plans) become clear and definite in form. □ **crystallized fruit** fruit preserved in and coated with sugar. □ **crystallization** *noun*

**crystallography** *noun* the science of crystal formation and structure. □ **crystallographer** *noun*

**crystalloid** *noun* a substance that in solution is able to pass through a semi-permeable membrane.

**Crystal Palace** a large building of iron and glass, designed by (Sir) Joseph Paxton for the Great Exhibition in London (1851), burnt down in 1936.

**Cs** *symbol* caesium.

**c/s** *abbreviation* cycles per second.

**CSE** *abbreviation* (*Brit.*) Certificate of Secondary Education; an examination replaced in 1988 by GCSE.

**CS gas** *noun* tear-gas used to control riots etc.

**CT** *abbreviation* Connecticut.

**CTC** *abbreviation* (*Brit.*) City Technology College.

**Cu** *symbol* copper.

**cu.** *abbreviation* cubic.

**cub** *noun* **1** the young of certain animals, e.g. fox, bear, lion. **2** (**Cub**) (in full **Cub Scout**) a member of the junior branch of the Scout Association. **3** (*informal*) a young newspaper reporter. ●*verb* (**cubbed, cubbing**) give birth to (cubs).

**Cuba** an island in the West Indies. □ **Cuban** *adjective & noun*

**cubby-hole** *noun* a small room or compartment.

**cube** *noun* **1** a solid body with six equal square faces. **2** a block shaped like this. **3** the product of a number multiplied by itself twice; *the cube of 3 is 27* $(3 \times 3 \times 3 = 27)$. ●*verb* **1** cut (food) into small cubes. **2** find the cube of (a number). □ **cube root** a number which produces a given number when cubed; *the cube root of 27 is 3.*

**cubic** *adjective* of three dimensions. □ **cubic metre** etc., the volume of a cube with sides one metre etc. long.

**cubical** *adjective* cube-shaped.

**cubicle** *noun* a small division of a large room; an enclosed space screened for privacy.

**cubism** *noun* a style in art in which objects are represented as geometrical shapes. □ **cubist** *noun & adjective*

**cubit** (**kew**-bit) *noun* an ancient measure of length, approximately equal to the length of the arm from elbow to fingertips.

**cuboid** (**kew**-boid) *adjective* cube-shaped, like a cube. ●*noun* a solid body with six rectangular sides.

**cuckold** (**kuk**-ŏld) *noun* a man whose wife has committed adultery during their marriage. ●*verb* make a cuckold of (a married man).

**cuckoo** *noun* **1** a bird with a call sounding similar to its name, which lays its eggs in the nests of other birds. **2** a related bird with or without this habit. □ **cuckoo clock** a clock that strikes the hours with a sound like a cuckoo's call. **cuckoo-pint** *noun* wild arum. **cuckoo-spit** *noun* a froth exuded by the larvae of certain insects on leaves, stems, etc.

**cucumber** *noun* **1** a long green-skinned fleshy fruit eaten as salad or pickled. **2** the plant producing this.

**cud** *noun* the food that cattle etc. bring back from the stomach into the mouth and chew again.

**cuddle** *verb* hold closely and lovingly in one's arms. ●*noun* an affectionate hug.

**cuddlesome**, **cuddly** *adjective* pleasant to cuddle.

**cudgel** (**kuj**-ĕl) *noun* a short thick stick used as a weapon. ●*verb* (**cudgelled**, **cudgelling**; *Amer.* **cudgeled**, **cudgeling**) beat with a cudgel.

**cue¹** *noun* something said or done which serves as a signal for something else to be done, e.g. for an actor to speak in a play. ●*verb* (**cued**, **cueing**) give a cue to. □ **on cue** at the correct moment.

**cue²** *noun* a long rod for striking the ball in billiards and similar games. □ **cue-ball** *noun* the ball to be struck with a cue.

**cuff¹** *noun* **1** the end part of a sleeve. **2** (*Amer.*) a trouser turn-up. **3** (**cuffs**) (*informal*) handcuffs. □ **cuff-link** *noun* each of a pair of fasteners for shirt-cuffs, used instead of buttons. **off the cuff** (*informal*) without rehearsal or preparation.

**cuff²** *verb* strike with the open hand. ●*noun* a cuffing blow.

**Cufic** alternative spelling of Kufic.

**cuirass** (kwi-**ras**) *noun* a piece of armour consisting of a breastplate and a similar plate protecting the back.

**cuisine** (kwi-**zeen**) *noun* a style of cooking.

**Culbertson**, Ely (1891–1955), American authority on contract bridge.

**cul-de-sac** (**kul**-dĕ-sak) *noun* (*plural* **culs-de-sac** pronounced same, or **cul-de-sacs**) a street with an opening at one end only.

**culinary** (**kul**-in-er-i) *adjective* of a kitchen or cooking; used in cooking; *culinary herbs*.

**cull** *verb* **1** pick (flowers). **2** select. **3** pick out and kill (surplus animals) from a herd or flock. ●*noun* culling; things culled.

**Culloden** (kŭ-**lod**-ĕn) a moor in NE Scotland, site of a Jacobite defeat in 1746.

**culminate** *verb* reach its highest point or degree; *the argument culminated in a fight.* □ **culmination** *noun*

**culottes** (kew-**lots**) *plural noun* women's trousers or shorts styled to look like a skirt.

**culpable** (**kul**-pă-bŭl) *adjective* deserving blame. □ **culpably** *adverb*, **culpability** *noun*

**culprit** *noun* a person who has done something wrong.

**cult** *noun* **1** a system of religious worship. **2** devotion to or admiration of a person or thing. **3** (often used as *adjective*) fashionable; *a cult film.*

**cultivar** *noun* a variety of plant produced by cultivation.

**cultivate** *verb* **1** prepare and use (land) for crops. **2** produce (crops) by tending them. **3** spend time and care in developing and encouraging (a friendship, person, etc.). □ **cultivation** *noun*

**cultivator** *noun* **1** a device for breaking up ground for cultivation. **2** a person who cultivates.

**cultural** *adjective* of culture. □ **Cultural Revolution** a political upheaval in China (1966–8) in support of the theories of Mao Tse-tung. □ **culturally** *adverb*

**culture** *noun* **1** the appreciation and understanding of literature, arts, music, etc. **2** the customs and civilization of a particular people or group; *West Indian culture.* **3** improvement by care and training. **4** the cultivating of plants, the rearing of bees, silkworms, etc. **5** a quantity of bacteria grown for study. ●*verb* grow (bacteria) for study. □ **culture shock** confusion and discomfort felt by a person subjected to an unfamiliar way of life.

**cultured** *adjective* educated to appreciate literature, arts, music, etc. □ **cultured pearls** pearls formed by an oyster when a foreign body is inserted artificially into its shell.

**culvert** (**kul**-vert) *noun* a drain that crosses under a road or railway etc.

**cum** *preposition* with; combined with; also used as; *a bedroom-cum-study.*

**Cumberland**, William Augustus, Duke of (1721–65), third son of George III, known as 'the Butcher' for the severity of his suppression of the Jacobites after his victory at Culloden.

**cumbersome** (**kum**-ber-sŏm) *adjective* (also **cumbrous**) clumsy to carry, wear, or manage.

**Cumbria** a county of NW England.

**cumin** (**kum**-in) *noun* (also **cummin**) a plant with fragrant seeds that are used for flavouring.

**cummerbund** *noun* a sash worn round the waist.

**Cummings**, E(dward) E(stlin) (1894–1962), American poet, noted for his experimental style and typography.

**cumquat** alternative spelling of Kumquat.

**cumulative** (**kew**-mew-lă-tiv) *adjective* increasing in amount by one addition after another. □ **cumulatively** *adverb*

**cumulus** *noun* (*plural* **cumuli**) a form of cloud consisting of rounded masses heaped on a horizontal base.

**Cunard** (kew-**nard**), Sir Samuel (1787–1865), British-Canadian ship-owner.

**cuneiform** (**kew**-ni-form) *adjective* of or written in the wedge-shaped strokes used in the inscriptions of ancient Assyria, Persia, etc. ●*noun* cuneiform writing.

**cunnilingus** *noun* oral stimulation of the female genitals.

**cunning** *adjective* **1** skilled at deceiving people, crafty. **2** ingenious; *a cunning device*. **3** (*Amer.*) attractive, quaint. ● *noun* craftiness. □ **cunningly** *adverb*

**cunt** *noun* (*vulgar*) **1** the female genitals, the vagina. **2** (*scornful*) an unpleasant person.

**cup** *noun* **1** a small open container for drinking from. **2** its contents; the amount it contains (used as a measure in cookery). **3** something shaped like a cup. **4** an ornamental goblet-shaped vessel awarded as a prize. **5** flavoured wine or cider etc.; *claret cup*. ● *verb* (**cupped, cupping**) **1** form into a cup-like shape; *cupped his hands*. **2** hold as if in a cup; *with her chin cupped in her hands*. □ **Cup Final** (especially in football) the final match in a competition. **not my cup of tea** (*informal*) not what I like; not what interests me. **cup-tie** *noun* a match in a competition for a cup.

**cupboard** *noun* a recess or piece of furniture with a door, in which things may be stored. □ **cupboard love** a display of false affection put on in the hope of obtaining a reward.

**cupful** *noun* (*plural* **cupfuls**) **1** an amount held by a cup; especially in America, a standard half-pint or 8 ounce measure. **2** a full cup.

**Cupid** the Roman god of love. ● *noun* a picture or statue of a beautiful boy with wings and a bow and arrows. □ **play Cupid** indulge in matchmaking.

**cupidity** (kew-**pid**-iti) *noun* greed for gain.

**cupola** (**kew**-pŏ-lă) *noun* **1** a small dome on a roof. **2** a revolving dome protecting mounted guns.

**cuppa** *noun* (*informal*) a cup of tea.

**cupreous** (**kew**-pri-ŭs) *adjective* of or like copper.

**cupric** (**kew**-prik) *adjective* of copper.

**cupro-nickel** *noun* an alloy of copper and nickel.

**cur** *noun* **1** a bad-tempered or worthless dog. **2** a contemptible person.

**curable** *adjective* able to be cured.

**curaçao** (**kewr**-ă-soh) *noun* an orange-flavoured liqueur.

**curacy** *noun* the position of a curate.

**curare** (kewr-**ar**-i) *noun* a bitter substance obtained from certain South American plants, used by American Indians to poison arrows.

**curate** *noun* a member of the clergy who assists a parish priest. □ **curate's egg** something that is good in parts.

**curative** (**kewr**-ă-tiv) *adjective* helping to cure illness.

**curator** (kewr-**ay**-ter) *noun* a person in charge of a museum or other collection. □ **curatorship** *noun*

**curb** *noun* **1** something that restrains; *put a curb on spending*. **2** a chain or strap passing under a horse's lower jaw, used to restrain it. ● *verb* restrain.

**curd** *noun* **1** (often **curds**) the thick soft substance formed when milk turns sour. **2** the edible head of a cauliflower. □ **curd cheese** soft smooth cheese made from skimmed milk curds.

**curdle** *verb* form or cause to form curds. □ **make one's blood curdle** fill one with horror.

**cure** *verb* **1** restore to health. **2** rid (of a disease or troublesome condition). **3** preserve (meat, fruit, tobacco, or skins) by salting, drying, etc. **4** vulcanize (rubber). ● *noun* **1** curing, being cured. **2** a substance or treatment that cures a disease; a remedy.

**curettage** (kewr-et-ij) *noun* scraping surgically to remove tissue or growths.

**curette** (kewr-et) *noun* a surgeon's small scraping-instrument. ● *verb* scrape with this.

**curfew** *noun* **1** a signal or time after which people must remain indoors until the next day. **2** (*hist.*) a signal at a fixed time for all fires to be extinguished.

**Curia** *noun* (also **curia**) the papal court, the government department of the Vatican.

**Curie**, Marie (1867–1934) and Pierre (1859–1906), French pioneers of the study of radioactivity.

**curie** *noun* **1** a unit of radioactivity (symbol Ci). **2** a quantity of radioactive substance having this. (¶ Named after Pierre Curie.)

**curio** *noun* (*plural* **curios**) an object that is interesting because it is rare or unusual.

**curiosity** *noun* **1** a desire to find out and know things. **2** something that is of interest because it is rare or unusual.

**curious** *adjective* **1** eager to learn or know something. **2** strange, unusual. □ **curiously** *adverb*

**curium** *noun* an artificially made radioactive metallic element (symbol Cm).

**curl** *verb* **1** bend, coil into a spiral. **2** move in a spiral form; *smoke curled upwards*. ● *noun* **1** something curved inwards or coiled. **2** a coiled lock of hair. **3** a curling movement. □ **curl up 1** lie or sit with the knees drawn up comfortably. **2** writhe with horror or embarrassment.

**curler** *noun* a pin or roller for curling hair.

**curlew** (**kerl**-yoo) *noun* a wading bird with a long slender curved bill.

**curlicue** (**kerl**-i-kew) *noun* a curly ornamental line.

**curling** *noun* a game played with large flat round stones which are sent along ice towards a mark.

**curly** *adjective* (**curlier, curliest**) curling, full of curls. □ **curliness** *noun*

**curmudgeon** (ker-**muj**-ŏn) *noun* a bad-tempered person. □ **curmudgeonly** *adjective*

**currant** *noun* **1** the dried fruit of a small seedless grape. **2** a small round red, white, or black berry; the shrub that produces it.

**currency** *noun* **1** money in actual use in a country. **2** the state of being in common use or generally accepted; *the rumour gained currency*.

**current** *adjective* **1** belonging to the present time, happening now; *current events*. **2** in general use; *words that are no longer current*. ● *noun* **1** water or air etc. moving in a certain direction; a running stream. **2** the flow of electricity through something or along a wire or cable. **3** a general tendency or course; *current of opinion*. □ **current account** a bank account offering instant access to one's money and the use of a cheque book.

**currently** *adverb* at the present time.

**curriculum** (kŭ-**rik**-yoo-lŭm) *noun* (*plural* **curricula**) subjects included in a course of study. □ **curriculum vitae** (*pronounced* **vee**-ty), a brief account of one's education and previous career. (¶ Latin, = course of life.)

**curry**[1] *noun* a dish of vegetables, meat, etc. cooked with spices. ● *verb* (**curried, currying**) flavour with curry. □ **curry powder** a mixture of spices used for making curry.

**curry**[2] *verb* (**curried, currying**) **1** groom (a horse) with a curry-comb. **2** treat (tanned leather) to improve its properties. □ **curry-comb** *noun* a pad with rubber or plastic projections. **curry favour** win favour by flattery.

**curse** *noun* **1** a call for evil to come upon a person or thing. **2** the evil produced by this. **3** a violent exclamation of anger. **4** something that causes evil or harm. ● *verb* **1** utter a curse against. **2** exclaim violently in anger. □ **the curse** (*informal*) menstruation. **be cursed with** be afflicted or burdened with.

**cursed** (**ker**-sid) *adjective* damnable.

**cursive** *adjective* (of writing) done with joined letters. ● *noun* cursive writing.

**cursor** *noun* **1** an indicator on a VDU screen showing a specific position, usually the point at which the next keystroke will be entered. **2** the transparent slide, bearing the reference line, on a slide-rule.

**cursory** (**ker**-ser-i) *adjective* hasty and not thorough; *a cursory inspection*. □ **cursorily** *adverb*

**curt** *adjective* noticeably or rudely brief. □ **curtly** *adverb*, **curtness** *noun*

**curtail** *verb* cut short, reduce. □ **curtailment** *noun*

**curtain** *noun* **1** a piece of cloth or other material hung up as a screen, especially at a window or between the stage and auditorium of a theatre. **2** the fall of a stage-curtain at the end of an act or scene. **3** a curtain-call. **4** (**curtains**) (*slang*) the end. ● *verb* provide or shut off with a curtain or curtains. □ **curtain-call** *noun* applause calling for an actor etc. to take a bow after the curtain has been lowered. **curtain-raiser** *noun* a short piece before the main performance; a preliminary event.

**Curtiss**, Glen Hammond (1878–1930), pioneer American pilot and designer of aircraft and engines.

**curtsy** *noun* (also **curtsey**) a movement of respect made by women and girls, bending the knees and lowering the body with one foot forward. ● *verb* (**curtsied, curtsying**) make a curtsy.

**curvaceous** (ker-**vay**-shŭs) *adjective* (*informal*) (of a woman) having a shapely figure.

**curvature** (ker-**vă**-cher) *noun* curving; a curved form; *the curvature of the earth*.

**curve** *noun* **1** a line of which no part is straight. **2** a smooth continuous surface of which no part is flat. **3** a curved form *or* thing. ● *verb* bend or shape so as to form a curve. □ **curvy** *adjective*

**curvet** (ker-**vet**) *noun* a horse's short frisky leap. ● *verb* (**curvetted, curvetting** *or* **curveted, curveting**) make a curvet.

**curvilinear** *adjective* contained by or consisting of curved lines.

**Cushing** (**kuush**-ing), Harvey Williams (1869–1939), American surgeon, the first to describe a hormonal disorder named after him.

**cushion** *noun* **1** a bag filled with soft material, used to make a seat more comfortable. **2** a soft pad or other means of support or of protection against jarring or shock. **3** the padded border round a billiard table, from which the balls rebound. **4** the body of air supporting a hovercraft etc. ● *verb* **1** provide or protect with a cushion or cushions. **2** lessen the impact of (a blow, shock, or something harmful).

**Cushitic** *noun* a group of East African languages spoken mainly in Ethiopia and Somalia. ● *adjective* of these languages.

**cushy** *adjective* (**cushier, cushiest**) (*informal*) pleasant and easy; *a cushy job*.

**cusp** *noun* a pointed end where two curves meet, e.g. the horn of a crescent moon.

**cuss** (*informal*) *verb* curse. ● *noun* **1** a curse. **2** a difficult person; *an awkward cuss*.

**cussed** (**kus**-id) *adjective* (*informal*) awkward and stubborn. □ **cussedness** *noun*

**custard** *noun* **1** a dish or sauce made with beaten eggs and milk. **2** a sweet sauce made with milk and flavoured cornflour.

**Custer**, George Armstrong (1839–76), American cavalry general in the American Civil War.

**custodian** (kus-**toh**-diăn) *noun* a guardian or keeper, especially of a public building.

**custody** *noun* **1** the right or duty of taking care of something; guardianship. **2** imprisonment. □ **take into custody** arrest. □ **custodial** *adjective*

**custom** *noun* **1** a usual way of behaving or of doing something. **2** the regular support given to a business by customers. **3** = CUSTOMS. □ **custom-built** *adjective* made according to a customer's order. **custom car** one built or modified to the owner's design.

**customary** *adjective* in accordance with custom, usual. □ **customarily** *adverb*

**customer** *noun* **1** a person who buys goods or services from a shop or business. **2** a person one has to deal with.

**customize** *verb* (also **customise**) make or modify to personal requirements.

**customs** *noun* (treated as *plural* or *singular*) **1** duty charged on goods imported from other countries. **2** the government department dealing with these. **3** the area at a port or airport where officials examine goods and baggage. □ **customs union** a group of countries that have arranged to charge the same amount of duty on imported goods.

**cut** *verb* (**cut, cutting**) **1** divide, wound, or detach with an edged instrument. **2** shape, make, or shorten in this way. **3** be able to be cut. **4** have (a tooth) appear through the gum. **5** cross, intersect; go (through or across), especially as a shorter way. **6** reduce by removing part; *cut taxes; two scenes were cut by the censor*. **7** go directly to another shot in a film. **8** switch off (electric power, an engine, etc.). **9** lift and turn up part of a pack of cards, e.g. in deciding who is to deal. **10** hit a ball with a chopping movement in cricket etc. **11** (especially *Amer.*) stay away deliberately from; *cut the lecture*. **12** ignore (a person) deliberately. **13** (*Amer.*) dilute (spirits for drinking). ● *noun* **1** the act of cutting; a division or wound made by this. **2** a stroke with a sword, whip, or cane. **3** a stroke made by cutting a ball in cricket etc. **4** a piece of meat cut from the carcass of an animal. **5** the way a thing is cut; the style in which clothes are made by cutting. **6** a cutting remark. **7** a reduction; a temporary stoppage. **8** the cutting out of part of a play or film etc. **9** (*slang*) a share of profits. □ **a cut above** noticeably superior to. **cut and dried** planned or prepared in advance. **cut and run** (*slang*) run away. **cut back** reduce; prune. **cut-back** *noun* a reduction. **cut both ways** have two appropriate and opposite ways of being applied. **cut a corner** pass round it as closely as possible. **cut corners** fail to do something properly, especially to save time. **cut a dash** make a

brilliant show in appearance and behaviour. **cut glass** glass with patterns cut in it. **cut in 1** interrupt. **2** return too soon to one's own side of the road, obstructing the path of an overtaken vehicle. **cut it out!** (*slang*) stop doing that. **cut no ice** (*slang*) have no influence or effect. **cut off 1** prevent from continuing. **2** keep from union or contact. **3** leave (a person) a very small amount in a will instead of a large inheritance. **cut one's losses** abandon an unprofitable scheme before one loses too much. **cut out 1** shape by cutting. **2** outdo (a rival). **3** cease or cause to cease functioning; *the engine cut out*. **cut-out** *noun* **1** a shape cut out of paper etc. **2** a device that disconnects an appliance automatically. **cut out for** having the qualities and abilities needed for. **cut-price** *adjective* (also **cut-rate**) for sale at a reduced price. **cut up 1** cut into pieces. **2** cut in on (a vehicle) in driving. **3** (usually as **be cut up**) be greatly distressed. **cut up rough** (*informal*) show anger or resentment.

**cutaneous** (kew-**tay**-niŭs) *adjective* of the skin.

**cutaway** *adjective* (of a diagram, model, etc.) with parts of the outside missing to reveal the interior.

**cute** *adjective* (*informal*) **1** (especially *Amer.*) attractive, quaint. **2** ingenious, clever. □ **cutely** *adverb*, **cuteness** *noun*

**cuticle** (**kew**-ti-kŭl) *noun* hardened skin at the base of a fingernail or toenail.

**cutis** (**kew**-tiss) *noun* the true skin beneath the epidermis.

**cutlass** *noun* a short sword with a slightly curved blade.

**cutler** *noun* a maker or seller of cutlery.

**cutlery** *noun* knives, forks, and spoons used in eating and serving food.

**cutlet** *noun* **1** a neck-chop of mutton or lamb. **2** a piece of veal etc. for frying. **3** minced meat or nuts and breadcrumbs etc. cooked in the shape of a cutlet.

**cutter** *noun* **1** a person or tool that cuts; a tailor who takes measurements and cuts cloth. **2** a small fast sailing-ship. **3** a small boat carried by a large ship.

**cutthroat** *noun* a person who cuts throats, a murderer. ● *adjective* **1** intense and merciless; *cutthroat competition*. **2** (of card games) three-handed. **3** (of a razor) having a long blade set in a handle.

**cutting** *see* CUT. ● *adjective* (of words) hurtful; *cutting remarks*. ● *noun* **1** a piece cut from something; a section cut from a newspaper etc. and kept for reference. **2** an excavation through high ground for a road or railway. **3** a piece cut from a plant for replanting to form a new plant.

**cuttlefish** *noun* (*plural* **cuttlefish** *or* **cuttlefishes**) a mollusc similar to a squid which squirts out a black liquid when attacked.

**Cutty Sark** a British clipper, launched in 1869, preserved as a museum ship at Greenwich, London. (¶ Named from the witch in Robert Burns's poem *Tam O'Shanter*, who wore only a 'cutty sark' (= short shift).)

**cutwater** *noun* **1** the forward edge of a ship's prow. **2** a wedge-shaped projection from a pier or bridge.

**cuvée** (**kyoo**-vay) *noun* a blend or batch of wine.

**Cuvier** (**koo**-vi-ay), Georges, Baron (1769–1832), French naturalist who founded the science of palaeontology.

**Cuzco** (**kus**-koh) a city in the Andes in southern Peru, capital of the Inca empire until the Spanish conquest (1533).

**c.v.** *abbreviation* (also **CV**) curriculum vitae.

**cwm** (*pronounced* koom) *noun* (in Wales) = COOMB; a valley.

**cwt** *abbreviation* hundredweight.

**cyan** (**sy**-ăn) *adjective & noun* (in photography) greenish-blue.

**cyanic** (**sy**-**an**-ik) *adjective* of or containing cyanogen. □ **cyanic acid** an unstable colourless strong-smelling acid gas.

**cyanide** (**sy**-ă-nyd) *noun* a very poisonous chemical substance used in the extraction of gold and silver.

**cyanogen** (**sy**-**an**-ŏ-jĕn) *noun* an inflammable poisonous gas.

**cyanosis** (**sy**-ă-**noh**-sis) *noun* a condition in which the skin appears blue, caused by lack of oxygen in the blood.

**cybernetics** (**sy**-ber-**net**-iks) *noun* the science of communication and control in animals (e.g. by the nervous system) and in machines (e.g. computers). □ **cybernetic** *adjective*

**Cyclades** (**sik**-lă-deez) *plural noun* a group of islands in the Aegean Sea.

**cyclamen** (**sik**-lă-mĕn) *noun* a plant with pink, red, or white flowers with petals that turn back.

**cycle** *noun* **1** a series of events or operations that are regularly repeated in the same order; *the cycle of the seasons.* **2** the time needed for one such series. **3** one complete occurrence of a continually recurring process such as electrical oscillation or alternation of electric current. **4** a complete set or series, e.g. of songs or poems. **5** a bicycle or motorcycle. ● *verb* **1** ride a bicycle or tricycle. **2** move in cycles. □ **cycle-track**, **cycle-way** *noun* a path or road for bicycles.

**cyclic** (**sy**-klik) *adjective* (also **cyclical**) **1** recurring in cycles or series. **2** forming a cycle. □ **cyclically** *adverb*

**cyclist** *noun* a person who rides a bicycle.

**cyclone** (**sy**-klohn) *noun* **1** a system of winds rotating round a calm central area. **2** a violent destructive form of this. □ **cyclonic** (sy-**klon**-ik) *adjective*

**cyclopedia** (sy-klŏ-**pee**-diă) *noun* (also **cyclopaedia**) an encyclopaedia.

**Cyclops** (**sy**-klops) (*plural* **Cyclops** *or* **Cyclopes**) (*Gk. myth.*) a member of a race of one-eyed giants.

**cyclotron** (**sy**-klŏ-tron) *noun* an apparatus for accelerating charged particles by making them move spirally in a magnetic field.

**cygnet** (**sig**-nit) *noun* a young swan.

**cylinder** *noun* **1** a solid or hollow object with straight sides and circular ends. **2** a machine-part shaped like this; the chamber in which a piston moves in an engine. □ **cylindrical** *adjective*

**cymbal** *noun* a percussion instrument consisting of a brass plate struck with another or with a stick. □ **cymbalist** *noun*

**cyme** (*pronounced* sym) *noun* a flower cluster with one flower on the end of each stem. □ **cymose** *adjective*

**Cymric** (**kim**-rik) *adjective* Welsh.

**cynic** (**sin**-ik) *noun* **1** a person who believes people's motives are bad or selfish and shows this by sneering at them. **2** (**Cynic**) a member of a sect of ancient Greek philosophers who despised ease and wealth. □ **cynical** *adjective*, **cynically** *adverb*

**cynicism** (**sin**-i-sizm) *noun* the attitude of a cynic.

**cynosure** (**sy**-nŏz-yoor) *noun* a centre of attraction or admiration.

**cypher** alternative spelling of CIPHER.

**cypress** *noun* a coniferous evergreen tree with dark feathery leaves.

**Cypriot** (**sip**-ri-ŏt) (also **Cypriote**) (**sip**-ri-oht) *noun* a native or national of Cyprus. ● *adjective* of Cyprus.

**Cyprus** an island in the East Mediterranean.

**Cyrano de Bergerac** (si-**rah**-noh de **bair**-zhĕ-rak), Savinien (1619–55), French soldier, libertine, and writer, famous for his grotesque appearance and long nose.

**Cyrillic** (si-**ril**-ik) *adjective* of the alphabet used by Slavonic peoples of the Eastern Church, named after St Cyril (9th c.), Greek missionary, who is said to have introduced it; now used chiefly for Russian and Bulgarian. ● *noun* this alphabet.

**Cyrus** king of Persia 559–529 BC, who conquered Asia Minor and a large part of the Middle East.

**cyst** (*pronounced* sist) *noun* an abnormal sac formed in or on the body, containing fluid or semi-solid matter.

**cystic** (sis-tik) *adjective* **1** of the bladder. **2** like a cyst. □ **cystic fibrosis** a hereditary disease, usually causing breathing disorders.

**cystitis** (sis-ty-tiss) *noun* inflammation of the bladder.

**cytology** (sy-tol-ŏji) *noun* the scientific study of biological cells. □ **cytological** *adjective*

**cytoplasm** (sy-tŏ-plazm) *noun* the content of a biological cell other than the nucleus. □ **cytoplasmic** *adjective*

**czar** alternative spelling of TSAR.

**Czech** (*pronounced* chek) *noun* **1** a native or the language of the Czech Republic. **2** (formerly) a citizen of Czechoslovakia. □ **Czech Republic** the western of the two republics into which the former Czechoslovakia is divided.

**Czechoslovakia** a former country in central Europe which divided into the independent Czech and Slovak Republics in 1993. □ **Czechoslovak** (chek-ŏ-**sloh**-vak) *or* **Czechoslovakian** *adjective & noun*

# Dd

**D** *noun* (*plural* **Ds** *or* **D's**) **1** *Music* the second note of the scale of C major. **2** (as a Roman numeral) 500. **3** the fourth highest class or category (of academic marks etc.); the fourth example, item in a list, etc. ● *symbol* deuterium.

**d.** *abbreviation* (until 1971) penny, pence (¶ short for the Latin *denarius*.)

**'d** (*informal*) had; would; *I'd; she'd*.

**dab** *noun* **1** a light or feeble blow, a tap. **2** quick gentle pressure on a surface with something soft; *a dab with a sponge*. **3** a small amount of a soft substance applied to a surface. **4** a kind of flatfish. ● *verb* (**dabbed, dabbing**) **1** strike lightly or feebly. **2** press quickly and lightly. □ **dab hand** (*informal*) an expert; *she's a dab hand at fixing computers*.

**dabble** *verb* **1** wet by splashing or by putting in and out of water. **2** move the feet, hands, etc. lightly in water. □ **dabble in** study or work at casually, not seriously. □ **dabbler** *noun*

**dabchick** *noun* a small water-bird of the grebe family.

**da capo** (da **cap**-oh) *adverb Music* repeat from the beginning.

**dace** (*pronounced* dayss) *noun* (*plural* **dace**) a small freshwater fish related to the carp.

**dacha** *noun* a Russian country cottage.

**dachshund** (**daks**-huund) *noun* a small dog with a long body and very short legs.

**dactyl** (**dak**-til) *noun* a metrical foot with one long or stressed syllable followed by two short or unstressed syllables. □ **dactylic** (dak-**til**-ik) *adjective*

**dad** *noun* (*informal*) father.

**Dada** (**dah**-dah) *noun* an international movement in art and literature about 1915–20, mocking conventions. □ **Dadaism** *noun*, **Dadaist** *noun & adjective*

**daddy** *noun* (*informal*) father.

**daddy-long-legs** *noun* a crane-fly.

**dado** (**day**-doh) *noun* (*plural* **dados**) **1** the lower part of the wall of a room or corridor when it is coloured or faced differently from the upper part. **2** the plinth of a column. **3** the cube of a pedestal.

**Dadra and Nagar Haveli** (**dah**-dră, **nah**ger hă-**vay**-li) a Union Territory in western India.

**daffodil** *noun* a yellow flower with a trumpet-shaped central part, growing from a bulb.

**daft** *adjective* (*informal*) silly, foolish, crazy.

**da Gama** *see* GAMA.

**dagger** *noun* a short pointed two-edged weapon used for stabbing. □ **at daggers drawn** hostile and on the point of quarrelling. **look daggers** stare angrily.

**dago** (**day**-goh) *noun* (*plural* **dagos**) (*offensive slang*) a foreigner, especially one from southern Europe.

**daguerreotype** (dă-**ge**-rŏ-typ) *noun* an early kind of photograph taken on a silver-coated copper plate, giving an image of white on silver. (¶ Named after its French inventor, Louis Daguerre (died 1851).)

**Dahl**, Roald (1916–90), writer noted especially for his children's stories, born in Wales of Norwegian parents.

**dahlia** (**day**-liă) *noun* a garden plant with large brightly-coloured flowers and tuberous roots.

**Dáil** (*pronounced* doil) *noun* (in full **Dáil Éireann**, *pronounced* **air**-ăn) the lower house of parliament in the Republic of Ireland.

**daily** *adjective* happening or appearing on every day (or every weekday). ● *adverb* **1** once a day. **2** progressively. ● *noun* **1** a daily newspaper. **2** (*informal*) a charwoman. □ **daily bread** one's livelihood.

**Daimler** (**dym**-ler), Gottlieb (1834–90), German engineer, original designer of the car (*pronounced* **daym**-ler) named after him.

**dainty** *adjective* (**daintier, daintiest**) **1** small and pretty, delicate. **2** fastidious, especially about food. **3** (**dainties**) choice foods, delicacies. □ **daintily** *adverb*, **daintiness** *noun*

**daiquiri** (da-ki-ri) *noun* (*plural* **daiquiris**) a cocktail of rum, lime juice, etc.

**dairy** *noun* **1** a room or building where milk and milk products are processed. **2** a shop where these are sold. ● *adjective* of milk or milk products; *dairy cream; a dairy farm*.

**dais** (**day**-iss) *noun* a low platform, especially at one end of a hall.

**daisy** *noun* a flower with many petal-like rays surrounding a centre. □ **daisy wheel** a spoked disc with characters arranged round the circumference, used in electric typewriters, printers, etc. **pushing up the daisies** (*slang*) dead and buried.

**Dakar** (**dak**-ar) the capital of Senegal.

**Dakota** *see* NORTH DAKOTA, SOUTH DAKOTA.

**dal** alternative spelling of DHAL.

**Dalai Lama** (dal-**I** lah-mă) the chief lama of Tibet.

**dale** noun a valley, especially in northern England.

**Dali** (dah-li), Salvador (1904–89), Spanish painter, whose pictures are claimed to be paranoiac in content and deriving from the subconscious.

**dally** verb (**dallied, dallying**) **1** idle, dawdle. **2** amuse oneself; flirt. □ **dalliance** noun

**Dalmatian** (dal-may-shăn) adjective of Dalmatia, a coastal region of southern Croatia. ●noun a large white dog with dark spots.

**dal segno** (dal sayn-yoh) Music repeat from the point marked by a sign.

**Dalton** (dawl-tŏn), John (1766–1844), English chemist, founder of modern atomic theory. He also described colour-blindness, from which he suffered, which became known as 'Daltonism'.

**dam**[1] noun a barrier built across a river etc. to hold back water and control its flow or form a reservoir. ●verb (**dammed, damming**) **1** hold back with a dam. **2** obstruct (a flow).

**dam**[2] noun the mother of a four-footed animal.

**damage** noun **1** harm or injury. **2** (slang) the cost or charge; what's the damage? **3** (**damages**) money claimed or paid as compensation for an injury. ●verb cause damage to.

**damascene** (dam-ă-seen) verb decorate (metal) with inlaid or wavy patterns.

**Damascus** the capital of Syria.

**damask** (dam-ăsk) noun silk or linen material woven with a pattern that is visible on either side. ●adjective **1** made of damask. **2** coloured like a damask rose, velvety pink. □ **damask rose** an old sweet-scented variety of rose.

**dame** noun **1** (**Dame**) the title of a woman who has been awarded an order of knighthood (corresponding to the title of Sir for a knight). **2** (old use or Amer. slang) a woman. **3** a comic female character in pantomime, usually played by a man.

**damn** verb **1** condemn to eternal punishment in hell. **2** condemn as a failure. **3** swear at, curse. ●interjection an exclamation of anger or annoyance. ●noun 'damn' said as a curse. ●adjective & adverb damned. □ **damn with faint praise** praise feebly and so imply disapproval. **not give a damn** (informal) not care at all. **I'll be damned** (informal) I am astonished. **I'm damned if I know** (informal) I certainly do not know.

**damnable** adjective hateful, annoying. □ **damnably** adverb

**damnation** noun being damned or condemned to hell. ●interjection an exclamation of anger or annoyance.

**damned** adjective (informal) damnable. ●adverb damnably, extremely; it's damned hot. □ **do one's damnedest** do one's very best.

**Damocles** (dam-ŏ-kleez) □ **sword of Damocles** imminent danger. (¶ From the story of Damocles, a Greek of the 4th century BC, above whose head a sword was once hung by a hair while he ate.)

**damp** noun **1** slight moisture, especially when unwelcome. **2** foul or explosive gas in a mine. ●adjective slightly or moderately wet. ●verb **1** make damp. **2** make sad or dull; discourage; damped their enthusiasm. **3** reduce the vibration of (a string in music). □ **damp course** (also **damp-proof course**) a layer of damp-proof material built into a wall near the ground to prevent damp from rising. **damp down** heap ashes on (a fire) to make it burn more slowly. **damp squib** an unsuccessful attempt to impress etc. □ **damply** adverb, **dampness** noun

**dampen** verb damp.

**damper** noun **1** a movable metal plate that regulates the flow of air into the fire in a stove or furnace. **2** an influence that discourages enthusiasm; cast a damper over the proceedings. **3** a small pad that presses against a piano string to stop it vibrating.

**damsel** (dam-zĕl) noun (old use) a young woman.

**damselfly** noun an insect like a dragonfly but with wings that fold while it rests.

**damson** noun **1** a small dark purple plum. **2** dark purple.

**dan** noun **1** a grade of proficiency in judo. **2** one who reaches this.

**dance** verb **1** move with rhythmical steps or movements, usually to music; perform in this way. **2** move in a quick or lively way; bob up and down. ●noun **1** a piece of dancing. **2** a piece of music for dancing to. **3** a social gathering for the purpose of dancing. □ **dance attendance on** follow about and help dutifully. □ **dancer** noun

**d. and c.** abbreviation dilatation (of the cervix) and curettage (of the womb); a minor operation to remove matter from the womb.

**dandelion** noun a wild plant with bright yellow flowers.

**dander** noun (informal) fighting spirit. □ **get one's dander up** become angry.

**dandified** adjective like a dandy.

**dandle** verb dance (a child) in one's arms or on one's knee.

**dandruff** noun flakes of dead skin on the scalp and amongst the hair.

**dandy** noun a man who pays excessive attention to the smartness of his appearance and clothes. ●adjective (informal) very good; splendid.

**dandy-brush** *noun* a stiff brush for cleaning horses.

**Dane** *noun* **1** a native of Denmark. **2** a Scandinavian invader of England in the 9th–11th centuries.

**Danegeld** *noun* a land-tax levied in Anglo-Saxon England, originally to bribe the invading Danes to go away.

**Danelaw** *noun* the north-eastern part of England that was held by the Danes from the late 9th century and administered according to their laws until after the Norman Conquest.

**danger** *noun* **1** liability or exposure to harm or death. **2** a thing that causes this. □ **danger money** payment above basic wages for people doing dangerous work.

**dangerous** *adjective* involving or causing danger. □ **dangerously** *adverb*

**dangle** *verb* **1** hang loosely. **2** hold or carry (a thing) so that it swings loosely. **3** hold out (hopes) to a person temptingly.

**Daniel** **1** a Hebrew prophet, said to have been saved by God when he was thrown into the lions' den. **2** the book of the Old Testament named after him.

**Danish** *adjective* of Denmark or its people or language. ●*noun* the language of Denmark. □ **Danish blue** soft white cheese with veins of blue mould. **Danish pastry** a yeast cake topped with icing, nuts, etc.

**dank** *adjective* unpleasantly damp and cold.

**d'Annunzio** (dah-**nuun**-tsi-oh), Gabriele (1863–1938), Italian poet, novelist, and playwright, a fervent patriot.

**Dante** (**dan**-ti) (full name: Dante Alighieri) (1265–1321), Italian poet and philosopher.

**Danube** a river in central and south-east Europe, that rises in the Black Forest and flows into the Black Sea.

**daphne** (**daf**-ni) *noun* a flowering shrub.

**dapper** *adjective* neat and smart in dress and appearance; *a dapper little man*.

**dapple** *verb* mark with spots or patches of shade or a different colour. □ **dapple-grey** *adjective* grey with darker markings.

**Darby and Joan** a devoted old married couple. □ **Darby and Joan Club** a social club for elderly people.

**Dardanelles** (dar-dă-**nelz**) a narrow strait between Europe and Asiatic Turkey, in ancient times called the Hellespont.

**dare** *verb* **1** have the courage or impudence to do something. **2** take the risk of, face as a danger. **3** challenge (a person) to do something risky. ●*noun* a challenge to do something risky. □ **I dare say** I am prepared to believe; it is very likely.

**daredevil** *noun* a recklessly daring person.

**Dar es Salaam** the former capital and chief port of Tanzania.

**daring** *noun* boldness. ●*adjective* **1** bold, taking risks boldly. **2** boldly dramatic or unconventional. □ **daringly** *adverb*

**dariole** (da-ri-ohl) *noun* a dish cooked in a small mould.

**Darius** (dă-**ry**-ŭs) king of Persia 521–486 BC.

**Darjeeling** *noun* a type of tea grown in Darjeeling, a town and district of West Bengal.

**dark** *adjective* **1** with little or no light. **2** (of colour) of a deep shade. **3** (of people) having a brown or black skin; having dark hair. **4** gloomy, cheerless, dismal; *the long dark years of the war*. **5** secret; *keep it dark*. **6** mysterious; remote and unexplored; *in darkest Africa*. ●*noun* **1** absence of light. **2** a time of darkness, night or nightfall; *out after dark*. **3** a dark colour. □ **Dark Ages** the early part of the Middle Ages in Europe (about 500–1100), when learning and culture were in decline. **Dark Continent** Africa, at the time when the continent was relatively unexplored. **dark horse** a successful competitor of whose abilities little was known before the contest. **in the dark** having no information about something. □ **darkly** *adverb*, **darkness** *noun*

**darken** *verb* make or become dark or darker. □ **never darken a person's door** stay away from him or her because one is unwelcome.

**darkroom** *noun* a room where light is excluded so that photographs can be processed.

**darling** *noun* a dearly loved or lovable person or thing; a favourite. ●*adjective* dearly loved; (*informal*) charming.

**Darling River** a river of SE Australia that joins the Murray River.

**darn¹** *verb* mend by weaving yarn across a hole. ●*noun* a place mended by darning.

**darn²** *interjection & adjective* = DAMN, DAMNED.

**darned** *adjective* = DAMNED.

**darnel** *noun* a grass that grows as a weed among corn.

**dart** *noun* **1** a small pointed missile. **2** a small metal-tipped object used in the game of darts. **3** (**darts**) an indoor game in which darts are thrown at a target. **4** a darting movement. **5** a tapering stitched tuck in a garment. ●*verb* **1** move suddenly and rapidly. **2** send out rapidly; *darted an angry look at him*.

**dartboard** *noun* a circular board used as a target in the game of darts.

**Dartmoor** **1** a moorland district of Devon. **2** a prison near Princetown in this district, originally built to hold French prisoners from the Napoleonic Wars.

**Darwin¹** the capital of the Northern Territory, Australia.

**Darwin²**, Charles Robert (1809–82), English naturalist who put forward the theory of evolution by natural selection. □ **Darwinian** *adjective & noun*, **Darwinism** *noun*, **Darwinist** *noun*

**dash** *verb* **1** run rapidly, rush. **2** strike or fling forcefully, especially so as to shatter. **3** destroy; ruin; *our hopes were dashed.* ●*interjection* (*informal*) damn. ●*noun* **1** a short rapid run; a rush. **2** a small amount of liquid or flavouring added. **3** a dashboard. **4** lively spirit or appearance. **5** a punctuation mark (—) used to show a break in sense. **6** the longer of the two signals used in the Morse code. □ **dash off** write or draw hurriedly.

**dashboard** *noun* a panel below the windscreen of a motor vehicle, carrying various instruments and controls.

**dashing** *adjective* spirited, showy.

**dastardly** *adjective* contemptible and cowardly.

**DAT** *abbreviation* digital audio tape.

**data** (day-tă) *plural noun* facts or information to be used as a basis for discussing or deciding something, or prepared for being processed by a computer etc. □ **data bank** a store or source of computerized data. **data capture** the entering of data into a computer. **data processing** the performance of operations on data, especially using a computer, to obtain information, solutions to problems, etc.

∎**Usage** This word is now often used with a singular verb (like 'information'), especially in the context of computers, e.g. *the data is entered here*, but it is by origin a Latin plural (the singular is *datum*) and in other contexts should be used (like 'facts') with a plural verb, *these data are from official sources*.

**database** *noun* an organized store of computerized data.

**datable** *adjective* able to be dated.

**date¹** *noun* **1** the day on which something happened or was written or is to happen etc.; a statement of this in terms of day, month, and year (or any of these). **2** the period to which something belongs; *objects of prehistoric date.* **3** (*informal*) an appointment to meet socially. **4** (*informal*) a person of the opposite sex with whom one has a social engagement. ●*verb* **1** mark with a date. **2** assign a date to. **3** originate from a particular date; *the custom dates from Victorian times.* **4** show signs of becoming out of date; *some fashions date quickly.* **5** (*informal*) make a social engagement (with). □ **date-stamp** *noun* **1** an adjustable rubber stamp for marking the date of receipt etc. on a document. **2** its mark. ●*verb* mark with a date-stamp. **out of date** *see* OUT. **to date**

until now; *here are our sales figures to date.* **up to date** *see* UP.

**date²** *noun* a small brown sweet edible fruit. □ **date-palm** *noun* a palm tree of North Africa and SW Asia bearing this fruit.

**dateless** *adjective* **1** having no date. **2** not becoming out of date.

**dateline** *noun* **1** a line from north to south roughly along the meridian 180° from Greenwich, east and west of which the date differs (east being one day earlier). **2** a line at the head of a newspaper report etc, showing the date and place of writing.

**dative** *noun* the grammatical case of a word expressing the indirect object or a recipient, e.g. *me* in 'give me the book'.

**datum** (day-tŭm) *noun* (*plural* **data**; see the entry for DATA) an item of information; a unit of data.

**daub** *verb* cover or smear roughly with a soft substance; paint clumsily. ●*noun* **1** a clumsily-painted picture. **2** a covering or smear of something soft.

**daughter** *noun* **1** a female child in relation to her parents. **2** a female descendant; *daughters of Eve.* □ **daughter-in-law** *noun* (*plural* **daughters-in-law**) a son's wife.

**daunt** *verb* make afraid or discouraged. □ **daunting** *adjective*

**dauntless** *adjective* brave, not to be daunted.

**dauphin** (daw-fin) *noun* the title of the eldest son of the king of France in the days when France was ruled by a king.

**Davenport** *noun* **1** a small writing desk with a sloping top. **2** (*Amer.*) a large sofa.

**David¹** king of the Hebrews after Saul.

**David²**, Elizabeth (1913–92), English writer on cookery.

**David³** (dah-veed), Jacques-Louis (1748–1825), French neoclassical painter.

**David⁴**, St (6th century), the patron saint of Wales. Feast day, 1 March.

**Davies**, Peter Maxwell (born 1934), English composer.

**Davis¹**, Bette (Ruth Elizabeth) (1908–89), American film actress.

**Davis²**, Miles Dewey (1926–91), American jazz trumpeter and composer.

**Davis³**, Steve (born 1957), English World Championship snooker player.

**Davis Cup** an annual award for a men's international lawn tennis team competition, donated by a leading American player, Dwight F. Davis, in 1900.

**davit** (dav-it) *noun* a small crane on board ship.

**Davy**, Sir Humphry (1778–1829), English chemist. □ **Davy lamp** an early type of safety lamp for miners, invented by Davy in 1816.

**Davy Jones** (*slang*) the evil spirit of the sea. □ **Davy Jones's locker** the bottom of the sea as the graveyard of those who are drowned or buried at sea.

**dawdle** *verb* walk slowly and idly; take one's time. □ **dawdler** *noun*

**dawn** *noun* **1** the first light of day. **2** the beginning; *the dawn of civilization.* ●*verb* **1** begin to grow light. **2** (often foll. by *on*) begin to appear or become evident (to). □ **dawn chorus** early-morning bird-song.

**Day**, Doris (original name: Doris Kappelhoff) (born 1924), American film actress and singer.

**day** *noun* **1** the time during which the sun is above the horizon. **2** the time for one rotation of the earth; a period of 24 hours. **3** the hours given to work; *an eight-hour day.* **4** a specified or appointed day; *Coronation day.* **5** a period or era; *in Queen Victoria's day; in my young days.* **6** a period of success; *colonialism has had its day.* **7** victory in a contest; *win the day.* □ **day-boy**, **day-girl** *noun* a pupil attending a boarding-school but living at home. **day by day** each day; progressively. **day centre** a place where social and other facilities are provided for elderly or handicapped people during the day. **day in**, **day out** every day, unceasingly. **day nursery** a place where young children are looked after while their parents are at work. **day release** a system of allowing employees to have days off work for education. **day return** a ticket sold at a reduced rate for a journey both ways in one day. **day room** a communal room e.g. in a hospital for relaxation during the day. **day school** a school for pupils living at home. **day-to-day** *adjective* routine; ordinary.

**daybreak** *noun* the first light of day, dawn.

**daydream** *noun* idle and pleasant thoughts. ●*verb* have day-dreams.

**Day-Lewis**, Cecil (1904–72), British poet and critic, born in Ireland, Poet Laureate 1968–72.

**daylight** *noun* **1** the light of day. **2** dawn. **3** understanding or knowledge that has dawned. **4** (**daylights**) (*slang*) life, consciousness; *beat the daylights out of him.* □ **daylight robbery** unashamed swindling. **daylight saving** longer summer evening daylight achieved by putting clocks forward.

**daytime** *noun* the time of daylight.

**daze** *verb* make (a person) feel stunned or bewildered. ●*noun* a dazed state.

**dazzle** *verb* **1** make (a person) unable to see clearly because of too much bright light. **2** amaze and impress or confuse (a person) by a splendid display. ●*noun* bright confusing light. □ **dazzling** *adjective*, **dazzlingly** *adverb*

**dB** *abbreviation* decibel(s).

**DBS** *abbreviation* direct-broadcasting satellite; direct broadcasting by satellite.

**DC** *abbreviation* **1** (also **dc**) direct current. **2** District of Columbia. **3** *Music* da capo.

**DD** *abbreviation* Doctor of Divinity.

**D-Day** *noun* **1** the day (6 June 1944) on which British, American, and Canadian forces invaded northern France in the Second World War. **2** the date on which an important operation is planned to begin.

**DDT** *noun* a white chlorinated hydrocarbon used as an insecticide.

**DE** *abbreviation* Delaware.

**deacon** *noun* **1** a member of the clergy ranking below a priest in Episcopal churches. **2** a layman attending to church business in Nonconformist churches.

**deaconess** *noun* a woman with duties similar to those of a deacon.

**deactivate** *verb* make inactive or less reactive.

**dead** *adjective* **1** no longer alive. **2** numb, without feeling. **3** no longer used; *a dead language.* **4** lifeless and without lustre, resonance, or warmth. **5** no longer active or functioning; *the microphone went dead.* **6** dull; without interest, movement, or activity. **7** (of a ball in games) out of play. **8** complete, abrupt, exact; *dead silence; a dead stop; dead centre.* ●*adverb* completely, exactly; *dead drunk; dead level.* ●*noun* an inactive or silent time; *the dead of night.* □ **dead beat** (*informal*) tired out. **deadbeat** *noun* (*informal*) a down-and-out. **dead duck** (*slang*) something useless or unsuccessful. **dead end** the closed end of a road or passage; a blind alley. **dead-end job** a job with no prospects of advancement. **dead heat** the result of a race in which two or more competitors finish exactly even. **dead letter** a rule or law that is no longer observed. **dead loss** (*informal*) a useless person or thing. **dead man's handle** *or* **pedal** a controlling device (on a train etc.) that disconnects the driving power if it is released. **dead march** a funeral march. **dead-nettle** *noun* a plant with nettle-like leaves that does not sting. **dead reckoning** calculating a ship's position by log and compass etc. when observations are impossible. **dead set** a determined attack. **dead weight** a heavy inert weight. **dead wood** a useless person or persons.

**deaden** *verb* deprive of or lose vitality, loudness, feeling, etc.

**dead-head** *verb* remove dead flower heads from (rose bushes etc.). ●*noun* **1** a non-paying passenger or spectator. **2** a useless person.

**deadline** *noun* a time-limit. (¶ Originally this meant the line round a military prison beyond which a prisoner was liable to be shot.)

**deadlock** *noun* a complete standstill or lack of progress. ●*verb* reach a deadlock; cause to do this.

**deadly** *adjective* (**deadlier, deadliest**) **1** causing or capable of causing fatal injury, death, or serious damage. **2** death-like; *a deadly silence*. **3** (*informal*) very dreary. ●*adverb* **1** as if dead; *deadly pale*. **2** extremely; *deadly serious*. □ **deadly nightshade** a plant with poisonous black berries. **the seven deadly sins** those that result in damnation for a person's soul (traditionally pride, covetousness, lust, envy, gluttony, anger, sloth). □ **deadliness** *noun*

**deadpan** *adjective & adverb* (*informal*) with an expressionless face.

**Dead Sea** an inland salt lake in the Jordan valley on the Israel-Jordan border. □ **Dead Sea scrolls** a collection of Hebrew and Aramaic manuscripts discovered (chiefly in fragments) in caves near the Dead Sea.

**deaf** *adjective* **1** wholly or partly without the sense of hearing; unable to hear. **2** refusing to listen; *deaf to all advice*; *turned a deaf ear to our requests*. □ **deaf aid** a hearing-aid. **deaf mute** a person who is both deaf and dumb. □ **deafness** *noun*

**deafen** *verb* make deaf or unable to hear by a very loud noise.

**deal**[1] *verb* (**dealt, dealing**) **1** distribute among several people; hand out (cards) to players in a card game. **2** give, inflict; *dealt him a severe blow*. **3** do business; trade; *they deal in fancy goods*. ●*noun* **1** dealing; a player's turn to deal; a round of play after dealing. **2** a business transaction. **3** treatment; *didn't get a fair deal*. **4** (*informal*) a large amount. □ **a good deal, a great deal** a large amount. **deal with 1** do business with. **2** take action about or be what is needed by (a problem etc.); discuss (a subject) in a book or speech etc.

**deal**[2] *noun* **1** sawn fir or pine timber. **2** a deal board of standard size.

**dealer** *noun* **1** a person who deals. **2** one who deals at cards. **3** a trader; one who deals in second-hand goods. **4** a jobber on the Stock Exchange.

■**Usage** In sense 4, in Britain from October 1986 the term has been merged with *broker*.

**dealings** *plural noun* a person's transactions with another.

**dealt** *see* DEAL.

**Dean**, Christopher Colin (born 1958), English skater and championship ice-dancer in partnership with Jayne Torvill.

**dean**[1] *noun* **1** a member of the clergy who is head of a cathedral chapter. **2** (usually **rural dean**) a member of the clergy with authority over a group of parishes. **3** an official in certain universities, responsible for the organization of studies or for discipline.

**dean**[2] alternative spelling of DENE.

**deanery** *noun* **1** the position of dean. **2** a dean's official residence. **3** a rural dean's area of office.

**dear** *adjective* **1** much loved, cherished. **2** esteemed; as a polite expression beginning a letter; *Dear Sir*. **3** costing more than it is worth, not cheap. ●*noun* a dear person. ●*adverb* dearly, at a high price. ●*interjection* an exclamation of surprise or distress. □ **dearly** *adverb*, **dearness** *noun*

**dearth** (*pronounced* derth) *noun* a scarcity.

**death** *noun* **1** the process of dying, the end of life; final cessation of vital functions. **2** the state of being dead. **3** a cause of death; *drink was the death of him*. **4** the ending or destruction of something; *the death of our hopes*. □ **at death's door** close to death. **death blow 1** a blow etc. causing death. **2** an event or action that destroys something. **death certificate** an official statement of the date, place, and cause of a person's death. **death duty** tax levied on property after the owner's death (replaced in 1975 by *capital transfer tax* and in 1986 by *inheritance tax*). **death penalty** punishment for a crime by being put to death. **death rate** the number of deaths in one year for every 1000 persons. **death row** a prison area housing prisoners sentenced to death. **death's head** a picture of a skull as a symbol of death. **death trap** a dangerous place, vehicle, etc. **death warrant 1** an order for the execution of a condemned person. **2** something that causes the end of an established practice etc. **death-watch beetle** a beetle whose larva bores holes in old wood and makes a ticking sound formerly supposed to be a sign of an imminent death. **death wish** a desire (usually unconscious) for the death of oneself or another person. **put to death** kill, execute. **to death** extremely, to the utmost limit; *bored to death*.

**deathbed** *noun* the bed on which a person dies.

**deathly** *adjective & adverb* like death; *a deathly hush*; *deathly pale*.

**deb** *abbreviation* (*informal*) a debutante.

**debacle** (day-**bahk**l) *noun* (also **débâcle**) a sudden disastrous collapse, defeat, or failure.

**debag** *verb* (**debagged, debagging**) (*slang*) remove the trousers of (a person) as a joke.

**debar** *verb* (**debarred, debarring**) exclude, prohibit. □ **debarment** *noun*

**debark** *verb* disembark. □ **debarkation** *noun*

**debase** *verb* lower in quality or value; reduce the value of (coins) by using an alloy or inferior metal. ☐ **debasement** *noun*

**debatable** *adjective* questionable, open to dispute.

**debate** *noun* a formal discussion. ●*verb* **1** hold a debate about. **2** discuss, consider.

**debauch** (di-bawch) *verb* make dissolute, lead into debauchery.

**debauchery** (di-bawch-er-i) *noun* over-indulgence in harmful or immoral pleasures.

**debenture** (di-ben-cher) *noun* a certificate or bond acknowledging a debt on which fixed interest is being paid.

**debilitate** *verb* cause debility in.

**debility** *noun* feebleness, weakness.

**debit** *noun* **1** an entry in an account-book of a sum owed by the holder. **2** the sum itself; the total of such sums. ●*verb* (**debited, debiting**) enter as a debit in an account.

**debonair** (deb-ŏn-**air**) *adjective* having a carefree self-confident manner.

**Debrett** (di-bret) (in full **Debrett's Peerage of England, Scotland and Ireland**) a book listing members of the peerage.

**debrief** *verb* (*informal*) question (a person) in order to obtain information about a mission just completed.

**debris** (deb-ree) *noun* scattered broken pieces.

**de Broglie** (dĕ brohl-yee), Louis (1892–1987), French physicist, noted for his work in wave mechanics.

**debt** *noun* something owed by one person to another. ☐ **in debt** owing something.

**debtor** *noun* a person who owes money to another.

**debug** *verb* (**debugged, debugging**) (*informal*) **1** remove concealed listening devices from (a room etc.). **2** remove defects from (a computer program). **3** = DELOUSE.

**debunk** *verb* (*informal*) show up (a claim or theory, or a good reputation) as exaggerated or false.

**Debussy** (dĕ-bew-si), Achille-Claude (1862–1918), French composer.

**debut** (day-bew) *noun* (also **début**) a first public appearance.

**debutante** (deb-yoo-tahnt) *noun* (also **débutante**) a young woman making her first appearance in society.

**Dec.** *abbreviation* December.

**deca-** *combining form* ten.

**decade** (dek-ayd *or* dĕ-kayd) *noun* a period of ten years.

**decadent** (dek-ă-dĕnt) *adjective* **1** becoming less worthy; deteriorating in standard. **2** self-indulgent; immoral. ☐ **decadence** *noun*

**decaffeinated** (di-kaf-in-ayt-id) *adjective* with the caffeine removed or reduced.

**decagon** *noun* a geometric figure with ten sides. ☐ **decagonal** (di-kag-ŏn-ăl) *adjective*

**decahedron** (deka-hee-drŏn) *noun* a solid geometric figure with ten faces. ☐ **decahedral** *adjective*

**decalitre** *noun* (*Amer.* **decaliter**) a unit of 10 litres.

**Decalogue** (dek-ă-log) *noun* the Ten Commandments.

**decametre** (dek-ă-mee-ter) *noun* (*Amer.* **decameter**) a unit of length equal to 10 metres.

**decamp** *verb* **1** break up camp; leave camp. **2** go away suddenly or secretly.

**decanal** (di-kay-năl) *adjective* **1** of a dean. **2** of the south side of the choir in a church (where the dean sits).

**decant** (di-kant) *verb* **1** pour (liquid) gently from one container into another without disturbing the sediment. **2** (*informal*) transfer from one place to another.

**decanter** (di-kant-er) *noun* a stoppered glass bottle into which wine etc. may be decanted.

**decapitate** (di-kap-it-ayt) *verb* behead. ☐ **decapitation** *noun*

**decapod** (dek-ă-pod) *noun* a crustacean with ten feet, e.g. a crab.

**decarbonize** *verb* (also **decarbonise**) remove the carbon deposit from (an engine etc.). ☐ **decarbonization** *noun*

**decathlete** *noun* a competitor in a decathlon.

**decathlon** (dik-ath-lŏn) *noun* an athletic contest in which each competitor takes part in the ten events it includes.

**decay** *verb* **1** become rotten; cause to rot. **2** lose quality or strength. **3** (of a substance) undergo change by radioactivity. ●*noun* **1** decaying, rot. **2** decline in health or quality. **3** radioactive change.

**Deccan** (dek-ăn) a triangular plateau in southern India.

**decease** (di-seess) *noun* (*formal*) death.

**deceased** *adjective* dead. ●*noun* (**the deceased**) the person(s) who died recently.

**deceit** *noun* deceiving; a deception.

**deceitful** *adjective* deceiving people. ☐ **deceitfully** *adverb*, **deceitfulness** *noun*

**deceive** *verb* **1** cause (a person) to believe something that is not true. **2** be sexually unfaithful to. ☐ **deceive oneself** persist in a mistaken belief. ☐ **deceiver** *noun*

**decelerate** (dee-sel-er-ayt) *verb* cause to slow down; decrease one's speed. ☐ **deceleration** *noun*

**December** the twelfth month of the year.

**decency** noun **1** being decent. **2** (**decencies**) the requirements of respectable behaviour in society.

**decennial** (di-sen-iăl) adjective **1** lasting for ten years. **2** happening every tenth year.

**decent** adjective **1** conforming to the accepted standards of what is proper; not immodest or obscene. **2** respectable; ordinary decent people. **3** (informal) quite good; earns a decent salary. **4** (informal) kind, generous, obliging. □ **decently** adverb

**decentralize** verb (also **decentralise**) divide and distribute (powers etc.) from a central authority to places or branches away from the centre. □ **decentralization** noun

**deception** noun **1** deceiving; being deceived. **2** something that deceives people.

**deceptive** adjective deceiving; easily mistaken for something else. □ **deceptively** adverb

**decibel** (dess-i-bel) noun a unit for measuring the relative loudness of sound or power levels of electrical signals.

**decide** verb **1** think about and make a choice or judgement; come to a decision. **2** settle by giving victory to one side; this goal decided the match. **3** cause to reach a decision; that decided me.

**decided** adjective **1** having clear opinions; determined. **2** clear, definite; a decided difference. □ **decidedly** adverb

**decider** noun a game or race to decide which of the competitors who finished equal in a previous contest should be the final winner.

**deciduous** (di-sid-yoo-ŭs) adjective **1** (of a tree) shedding its leaves annually. **2** falling off or shed after a time; a deer has deciduous antlers.

**decigram** noun (also **decigramme**) one-tenth of a gram.

**decilitre** noun (Amer. **deciliter**) one-tenth of a litre.

**decimal** (dess-im-ăl) adjective reckoned in tens or tenths. ●noun a decimal fraction. □ **decimal currency** currency in which each unit is ten or one hundred times the value of the one next below it. **decimal fraction** a fraction whose denominator is a power of 10, expressed in figures after a dot (the **decimal point**), e.g. $0.5 = 5/10$, $0.52 = 52/100$. **decimal system** a system of weights and measures with each unit ten times that immediately below it. **go decimal** adopt a decimal currency or system.

**decimalize** verb (also **decimalise**) **1** express as a decimal. **2** convert to a decimal system. □ **decimalization** noun

**decimate** (dess-im-ayt) verb **1** destroy one-tenth of. **2** destroy a large proportion of.

□ **decimation** noun (¶ From the practice of putting to death one in every ten of a body of soldiers guilty of mutiny or other crime—a practice in the ancient Roman army, sometimes followed in later times.)

---

■**Usage** The looser and more general use in terms of 'a large proportion' is now widespread, but strictly speaking is incorrect.

---

**decimetre** noun (Amer. **decimeter**) one-tenth of a metre.

**decipher** (di-sy-fer) verb make out the meaning of (a coded message, bad handwriting, or something difficult to interpret). □ **decipherable** adjective

**decision** noun **1** deciding, making a reasoned judgement about something. **2** the judgement itself. **3** the ability to form clear opinions and act on them.

**decisive** (di-sy-siv) adjective **1** settling something conclusively; a decisive battle. **2** showing decision and firmness. □ **decisively** adverb, **decisiveness** noun

**deck** noun **1** any of the horizontal floors in a ship. **2** a similar floor or platform, especially one of two or more; the top deck of a bus. **3** a piece of equipment for playing discs or tapes as part of a sound system. **4** (especially Amer.) a pack of cards. ●verb decorate; dress up; decked with flags; decked out in her finest clothes.

**deckchair** noun a portable folding chair of canvas on a wood or metal frame.

**deckhand** noun a cleaner on a ship's deck.

**deckle edge** a ragged edge like that on hand-made paper. □ **deckle-edged** adjective

**declaim** (di-klaym) verb speak or say impressively or dramatically. □ **declamation** (deklă-may-shŏn) noun, **declamatory** adjective

**declaration** noun **1** declaring. **2** a formal or emphatic statement.

**declare** verb **1** make known; announce openly, formally, or explicitly. **2** state firmly; he declares that he is innocent. **3** inform customs officials that one has (goods) on which duty may be payable. **4** choose to close one's side's innings at cricket before ten wickets have fallen. **5** name the trump suit in a card game. □ **declarative** adjective, **declaratory** adjective

**declassify** verb declare (information, documents, etc.) to be no longer secret. □ **declassification** noun

**declension** noun **1** variation of the form of a noun etc. to give its grammatical case; the class by which a noun etc. is declined. **2** decrease, deterioration.

**declination** (dek-lin-ay-shŏn) noun **1** a downward turn or bend. **2** the angle between the true north and the magnetic north. **3** the angle between the direction of a star etc. and the celestial equator.

**decline** *verb* **1** refuse; *decline the invitation*. **2** slope downwards. **3** decrease, lose strength or vigour; *one's declining years*. **4** give the forms of (a noun or adjective) corresponding to the grammatical cases. ● *noun* a gradual decrease or loss of strength. □ **in decline** decreasing.

**declivity** (di-**kliv**-iti) *noun* a downward slope.

**declutch** *verb* disengage the clutch of a motor vehicle.

**decoction** *noun* boiling down to extract an essence; the extract itself.

**decode** *verb* put (a coded message) into plain language; translate (coded characters in a computer).

**decoder** *noun* **1** a person or machine that decodes messages etc. **2** a device for analysing stereophonic signals and passing them to separate amplifier-channels.

**decoke** *verb* (*informal*) decarbonize.

*décolletage* (day-**kol**-tah*zh*) *noun* a low neckline. (¶ French.)

*décolleté* (day-**kol**-tay) *adjective* having a low neckline. (¶ French.)

**decompose** *verb* **1** decay; cause to decay. **2** separate (a substance) into its elements. □ **decomposition** *noun*

**decompress** *verb* subject to decompression.

**decompression** *noun* **1** release from compression. **2** the gradual and safe reduction of air pressure on a person who has been in compressed air. □ **decompression chamber** an enclosed space where this can be done. **decompression sickness** a painful condition caused by the sudden lowering of air pressure and the formation of bubbles in the blood.

**decongestant** (dee-kŏn-**jest**-ănt) *noun* a medicinal substance that relieves congestion.

**decontaminate** *verb* rid of radioactive or other contamination. □ **decontamination** *noun*

**decor** (**day**-kor) *noun* (also **décor**) the style of furnishings and decoration used in a room etc.

**decorate** *verb* **1** make (a thing) look attractive or festive by adding objects or details. **2** put fresh paint or paper on the walls etc. of (a room). **3** confer a medal or other award upon.

**decoration** *noun* **1** decorating. **2** something that decorates. **3** a medal etc. awarded and worn as an honour. **4** (**decorations**) flags and other decorative objects put up on festive occasions.

**decorative** (**dek**-er-ătiv) *adjective* ornamental, pleasing to look at. □ **decoratively** *adverb*

**decorator** *noun* a person who decorates, especially one whose job is to paint and paper houses.

**decorous** (**dek**-er-ŭs) *adjective* polite and well-behaved; decent. □ **decorously** *adverb*

**decorum** (di-**kor**-ŭm) *noun* correctness and dignity of behaviour or procedure etc.

**decoy** *noun* (*pronounced* **dee**-koi) something used to lure an animal or person into a trap. ● *verb* (*pronounced* di-**koi**) lure by means of a decoy.

**decrease** *verb* make or become shorter, smaller, or fewer. ● *noun* **1** decreasing. **2** the amount by which something decreases. □ **decreasingly** *adverb*

**decree** *noun* **1** an order given by a government or other authority and having the force of a law. **2** a judgement or decision of certain lawcourts. ● *verb* (**decreed, decreeing**) order by decree. □ **decree absolute** a final order for completion of a divorce. **decree nisi** (*pronounced* **ny**-sy), a provisional order for divorce, made absolute unless good cause to the contrary is shown within a fixed period.

**decrepit** (di-**krep**-it) *adjective* made weak by old age or hard use; dilapidated. □ **decrepitude** *noun*

**decrescendo** = DIMINUENDO.

**decretal** (di-**kree**-tăl) *noun* a papal decree.

**decriminalize** *verb* (also **decriminalise**) pass a law causing (an action, etc.) to cease to be treated as a crime. □ **decriminalization** *noun*

**decry** (di-**kry**) *verb* (**decried, decrying**) disparage.

**dedicate** *verb* **1** devote to a sacred person or use; *they dedicated the church to St Peter*. **2** devote (one's time and energy) to a special purpose. **3** (of an author etc.) address (a book or piece of music etc.) to a person as a compliment, putting his or her name at the beginning. □ **dedication** *noun*, **dedicator** *noun*

**dedicated** *adjective* **1** devoted to a vocation, cause, etc.; *a dedicated scientist*. **2** having single-minded loyalty.

**dedicatory** (**ded**-i-kayt-er-i) *adjective* making a dedication; *a dedicatory inscription*.

**deduce** (di-**dewss**) *verb* arrive at (knowledge or a conclusion) by reasoning from observed facts. □ **deducible** *adjective*

**deduct** *verb* take away (an amount or quantity); subtract.

**deductible** *adjective* able to be deducted, especially from tax or taxable income.

**deduction** *noun* **1** deducting; something that is deducted. **2** deducing; a conclusion reached by reasoning. **3** logical reasoning that something must be true because it is a particular case of a general law that is known to be true.

**deductive** *adjective* based on reasoning.

**deed** *noun* **1** something done, an act. **2** a legal agreement, especially one giving ownership or rights, bearing the giver's signature and seal. □ **deed-box** *noun* a strong-box for holding deeds and other documents. **deed of covenant** an undertaking to make an annual subscription for a period of years to a society etc. which is allowed to reclaim, in addition, the tax paid on this amount by the contributor. **deed poll** a deed made by one party only, making a formal declaration, especially to change a name.

**deem** *verb* (*formal*) believe, consider, or judge.

**deemster** *noun* either of the two judges in the Isle of Man.

**deep** *adjective* **1** going or situated far down or back or in; *a deep cut; deep cupboards; a deep sigh*. **2** (in cricket) distant from the batsman. **3** intense, extreme. **4** low-pitched and resonant, not shrill; *a deep voice*. **5** fully absorbed or overwhelmed; *deep in thought*. **6** heartfelt; *deep sympathy*. **7** difficult to understand, obscure; *that's too deep for me*. ●*adverb* deeply far down or in. ●*noun* **1** a deep place or state. **2** (**the deep**) (*poetic*) the sea. □ **deep-freeze** (*noun*) a freezer; (*verb*) freeze or store in a deep-freeze. **deep-fry** *verb* fry (food) in fat that covers it. **deep-rooted**, **deep-seated** *adjective* (of opinions, beliefs, etc.) firmly established; not superficial; *a deep-seated distrust*. **Deep South** the States in the south-eastern USA. **go off the deep end** (*informal*) become very angry or emotional. **in deep water** in trouble or difficulty. □ **deeply** *adverb*, **deepness** *noun*

**deepen** *verb* make or become deep or deeper.

**deer** *noun* (*plural* **deer**) a grazing animal, the male of which usually has antlers.

**deerstalker** *noun* a soft cloth peaked cap with ear-flaps.

**de-escalate** *verb* (of a dispute, crisis, etc.) make or become less intense or dangerous. □ **de-escalation** *noun*

**def** *adjective* (*slang*) excellent.

**deface** *verb* spoil or damage the surface of. □ **defacement** *noun*

**de facto** (day **fak**-toh) existing in fact (whether by right or not). (¶ Latin.)

**defalcate** (dee-fal-kayt) *verb* (*formal*) misappropriate funds. □ **defalcator** *noun*

**defalcation** (dee-fal-**kay**-shŏn) *noun* (*formal*) misappropriation of funds; a breach of trust concerning money.

**defamatory** (di-**fam**-ă-ter-i) *adjective* defaming.

**defame** (di-**faym**) *verb* attack the good reputation of, speak ill of. □ **defamation** (def-ă-**may**-shŏn) *noun*

**default** *verb* fail to fulfil one's obligations. ●*noun* **1** failure to fulfil an obligation or to appear. **2** a preselected choice or action taken by a computer program when no alternative is specified. □ **by default** because there is no alternative or opposition. **in default of** because of the absence of. □ **defaulter** *noun*

**defeat** *verb* **1** win a victory over. **2** cause to fail, frustrate; *this defeats our hopes for reform*. **3** baffle; *the problem defeats me*. ●*noun* **1** defeating others. **2** being defeated; a lost battle or contest.

**defeatist** *noun* a person who expects to be defeated or accepts defeat too easily. □ **defeatism** *noun*

**defecate** (dee-fik-ayt) *verb* discharge waste matter from the bowels. □ **defecation** *noun*

**defect** *noun* (*pronounced* **dee**-fekt) a deficiency; an imperfection. ●*verb* (*pronounced* di-**fekt**) desert one's country; abandon one's allegiance to a cause. □ **defection** *noun*, **defector** *noun*

**defective** *adjective* having defects; imperfect; incomplete. □ **defectively** *adverb*, **defectiveness** *noun*

**defence** *noun* (*Amer.* **defense**) **1** defending from or resistance against attack. **2** something that defends or protects against attack. **3** a justification put forward in response to an accusation. **4** the defendant's case in a lawsuit; the lawyer(s) representing an accused person. **5** the players in a defending position in a game. □ **defenceless** *adjective*

**defend** *verb* **1** protect by warding off an attack. **2** try to preserve; *the champion is defending his title*. **3** uphold by argument, put forward a justification of. **4** represent the defendant in a lawsuit.

**defendant** *noun* a person accused or sued in a lawsuit (opposed to the *plaintiff*).

**defender** *noun* a person who defends something. □ **Defender of the Faith** a title (translation of Latin *Fidei defensor*) conferred by the Pope on Henry VIII in 1521 and borne by all subsequent sovereigns.

**defense** Amer. spelling of DEFENCE.

**defensible** *adjective* able to be defended. □ **defensibly** *adverb*, **defensibility** *noun*

**defensive** *adjective* used or done for defence, protective. □ **on the defensive** in an attitude of defence; ready to defend oneself against criticism. □ **defensively** *adverb*, **defensiveness** *noun*

**defer**[1] *verb* (**deferred**, **deferring**) put off to a later time, postpone. □ **deferred shares** shares on which dividends are paid only after they have been paid on all other shares. □ **deferment** noun, **deferral** noun

**defer**[2] verb (**deferred**, **deferring**) (foll. by to) give way to a person's wishes or authority; yield.

**deference** (def-er-ĕns) noun polite respect; compliance with another person's wishes. □ **in deference to** out of respect for.

**deferential** (def-er-**en**-shăl) adjective showing deference. □ **deferentially** adverb

**defiance** noun defying, open disobedience, bold resistance.

**defiant** adjective showing defiance. □ **defiantly** adverb

**deficiency** (di-**fish**-ĕn-si) noun **1** being deficient. **2** a lack or shortage; a thing lacking, the amount by which something falls short of what is required. □ **deficiency disease** a disease caused by lack of vitamins or other essential elements in food.

**deficient** (di-**fish**-ĕnt) adjective **1** not having enough; deficient in vitamins. **2** insufficient or not present at all.

**deficit** (**def**-i-sit) noun **1** the amount by which a total falls short of what is required. **2** the excess of expenditure over income, or of liabilities over assets.

**defile**[1] (di-**fyl**) verb make dirty, pollute. □ **defilement** noun

**defile**[2] (di-**fyl**) noun a narrow gorge or pass. ● verb march in file.

**define** verb **1** give the exact meaning of (a word etc.). **2** state or explain the scope of; customers' rights are defined by the law. **3** outline clearly, mark out the boundary of. □ **definable** adjective

**definite** adjective **1** having exact limits. **2** clear and unmistakable, not vague; I want a definite answer. **3** certain, settled; is it definite that we are to move? ● **definite article** Grammar the word 'the'. □ **definitely** adverb

■**Usage** See the note under **definitive**.

**definition** noun **1** a statement of the exact meaning of a word or phrase, or of the nature of a thing. **2** making or being distinct; clearness of outline.

**definitive** (di-**fin**-itiv) adjective finally fixing or settling something; conclusive.

■**Usage** This word is sometimes confused with **definite**. A definite offer is one that is clearly stated. A definitive offer is one that must be accepted or refused without trying to alter its terms. A definitive edition is one with authoritative status.

**deflate** verb **1** let out air or gas from (an inflated tyre etc.). **2** cause (a person) to lose confidence or self-esteem. **3** counteract inflation in (a country's economy), e.g. by reducing the amount of money in circulation. **4** become deflated. □ **deflation** noun, **deflationary** adjective

**deflect** verb turn or cause to turn aside. □ **deflection** (also **deflexion**) noun, **deflector** noun

**deflower** verb (literary) **1** deprive (a woman) of virginity. **2** spoil the perfection of, ravage.

**Defoe** (di-**foh**), Daniel (1660–1731), English novelist, author of Robinson Crusoe.

**defoliant** (dee-**foh**-li-ănt) noun a chemical substance that destroys foliage.

**defoliate** (dee-**foh**-li-ayt) verb strip of leaves; destroy the foliage of by chemical means. □ **defoliation** noun

**deforest** verb clear of trees. □ **deforestation** noun

**deform** verb spoil the form or appearance of; put out of shape. □ **deformation** (dee-for-**may**-shŏn) noun

**deformed** adjective badly or abnormally shaped.

**deformity** noun **1** being deformed. **2** a deformed part of the body.

**defraud** verb deprive by fraud.

**defray** verb provide money to pay (costs or expenses). □ **defrayal** noun

**defrock** verb dismiss (a priest) from office.

**defrost** verb **1** remove frost or ice from. **2** unfreeze; defrost the chicken; let the chicken defrost.

**deft** adjective skilful; handling things neatly. □ **deftly** adverb, **deftness** noun

**defunct** (di-**funkt**) adjective **1** dead. **2** no longer existing, used, or functioning.

**defuse** verb **1** remove the fuse of; make (an explosive) unable to explode. **2** reduce the dangerous tension in (a situation).

**defy** verb (**defied**, **defying**) **1** refuse to obey. **2** challenge (a person) to try and do something that one believes he or she cannot or will not do; I defy you to prove this. **3** offer difficulties that cannot be overcome by; the door defied all attempts to open it.

**Degas** (dĕ-**gah**), Edgar (1834–1917), French impressionist painter.

**de Gaulle** see GAULLE.

**degenerate** verb (pronounced di-**jen**-er-ayt) become worse or lower in standard; lose good qualities. ● adjective (pronounced di-**jen**-er-ăt) having degenerated. ● noun (pronounced di-**jen**-er-ăt) a degenerate person or animal. □ **degeneration** noun, **degeneracy** noun

**degradable** adjective able to be broken down by chemical or biological processes.

**degrade** verb **1** reduce to a lower rank or status. **2** bring disgrace or contempt on. **3** reduce to a lower organic type or a simpler structure. **4** decompose. □ **degradation** (deg-ră-**day**-shŏn) noun

**degrading** *adjective* shaming, humiliating.

**degree** *noun* **1** a step or stage in an ascending or descending series. **2** a stage in intensity or amount; *a high degree of skill*. **3** an academic rank awarded to a person who has successfully completed a course of study or as an honour. **4** a unit of measurement for angles or arcs, indicated by the symbol °, e.g. 45°. **5** a unit of measurement in a scale e.g. of temperatures. □ **by degrees** step by step, gradually.

**dehisce** (di-**hiss**) *verb* (especially of seed-vessels) gape, burst open. □ **dehiscence** *noun*, **dehiscent** *adjective*

**dehumanize** *verb* (also **dehumanise**) take away human qualities from; make impersonal or machine-like. □ **dehumanization** *noun*

**dehydrate** *verb* **1** remove the moisture content from. **2** lose moisture. □ **dehydration** *noun*

**de-ice** *verb* remove or prevent the formation of ice on (a windscreen or other surface). □ **de-icer** *noun*

**deify** (**dee**-i-fy or **day**-i-fy) *verb* (**deified**, **deifying**) make a god of; treat as a god. □ **deification** *noun*

**deign** (*pronounced* dayn) *verb* condescend; be kind or gracious enough to do something; *she did not deign to reply*.

**deism** (**dee**-izm or **day**-izm) *noun* belief in the existence of a god (creator of the world) without accepting revelation (*see* THEISM). □ **deist** *noun*, **deistic** *adjective*

**deity** (**dee**-iti or **day**-iti) *noun* **1** a god or goddess; *Roman deities*. **2** divinity. **3** (**the Deity**) God.

**déjà vu** (day-*zh*a) a feeling of having experienced the present situation before. (¶ French, = already seen.)

**dejected** *adjective* in low spirits; depressed. □ **dejectedly** *adverb*, **dejection** *noun*

**de jure** (dee **joor**-i) rightful, by right. (¶ Latin.)

**dekko** *noun* (*slang*) a look.

**de Klerk**, F(rederik) W(illem) (born 1936), South African statesman, President 1989–94, and a Vice-President from 1994.

**Del.** *abbreviation* Delaware.

**Delacroix** (del-ă-krwah), Ferdinand-Victor-Eugène (1798–1863), French Romantic painter.

**de la Mare**, Walter (1873–1956), English poet and novelist, who wrote for both adults and children.

**Delaware** a State on the east coast of the USA.

**delay** *verb* **1** make or be late; hinder. **2** put off until later, postpone. **3** wait, linger. ● *noun* **1** delaying, being delayed. **2** the amount of time for which something is delayed; *a two-hour delay*. □ **delayed-action** *adjective* operating after an interval of time.

**delectable** *adjective* delightful, enjoyable. □ **delectably** *adverb*

**delectation** (dee-lek-**tay**-shŏn) *noun* enjoyment, delight; *for your delectation*.

**delegate** *noun* (*pronounced* **del**-i-găt) a person who represents others and acts according to their instructions. ● *verb* (*pronounced* **del**-i-gayt) **1** entrust (a task, power, or responsibility) to an agent. **2** appoint or send as a representative.

**delegation** (del-i-**gay**-shŏn) *noun* **1** delegating. **2** a body of delegates.

**delete** (di-**leet**) *verb* cross out (something written or printed). □ **deletion** *noun*

**deleterious** (del-i-**teer**-iŭs) *adjective* harmful to the body or mind.

**delft** *noun* (also **delftware**) glazed earthenware, usually decorated in blue, made at Delft in Holland.

**Delhi** (**del**-i) **1** a Union Territory of India. **2** (in full **New Delhi**) the capital of India.

**deli** *noun* (*plural* **delis**) (*informal*) a delicatessen.

**deliberate** *adjective* (*pronounced* di-**lib**-er-ăt) **1** done or said on purpose, intentional; *a deliberate insult*. **2** slow and careful, unhurried; *entered with deliberate steps*. ● *verb* (*pronounced* di-**lib**-er-ayt) think over or discuss carefully before reaching a decision. □ **deliberately** *adverb*

**deliberation** *noun* **1** careful consideration or discussion. **2** careful slowness.

**deliberative** (di-**lib**-er-ătiv) *adjective* for the purpose of deliberating or discussing things; *a deliberative assembly*.

**Delibes** (dĕ-**leeb**), (Clément Philibert) Léo (1836–91), French composer.

**delicacy** *noun* **1** delicateness. **2** avoidance of what is immodest or offensive or hurtful to others. **3** a special food.

**delicate** *adjective* **1** fine in texture; soft; slender. **2** of fine quality or workmanship. **3** (of colour or flavour) pleasant and not strong or intense. **4** easily injured; liable to illness; (of plants) unable to withstand cold. **5** requiring careful handling; *a delicate operation*; *the situation is delicate*. **6** skilful and sensitive; *has a delicate touch*. **7** taking great care to avoid what is immodest, offensive, or hurtful to others. □ **delicately** *adverb*, **delicateness** *noun*

**delicatessen** (del-i-kă-**tess**-ĕn) *noun* a shop selling high quality speciality grocery goods, cheeses, cooked meats, etc.

**delicious** *adjective* delightful, especially to the senses of taste or smell. □ **deliciously** *adverb*

**delight** *verb* **1** please greatly. **2** (foll. by *in*) take great pleasure in; *she delights in giving* *surprises.* ●*noun* **1** great pleasure. **2** something that causes this.

**delightful** *adjective* giving delight. □ **delightfully** *adverb*

**Delilah** (di-**ly**-lă) *noun* a seductive and treacherous woman. (¶ Named after a woman in the Bible, who betrayed Samson to the Philistines.)

**delimit** (dee-**lim**-it) *verb* fix the limits or boundaries of. □ **delimitation** *noun*

**delineate** (di-**lin**-i-ayt) *verb* show by drawing or by describing. □ **delineation** *noun*

**delinquent** (di-**link**-wěnt) *adjective* committing an offence; failing to perform a duty. ●*noun* a delinquent person, especially a young offender against the law. □ **delinquency** *noun*

**deliquesce** (del-i-**kwess**) *verb* **1** become liquid, melt. **2** dissolve in moisture absorbed from the air. □ **deliquescence** *noun*, **deliquescent** *adjective*

**delirious** (di-**li**-ri-ŭs) *adjective* **1** affected with delirium, raving. **2** wildly excited. □ **deliriously** *adverb*

**delirium** (di-**li**-ri-ŭm) *noun* **1** a disordered state of mind, especially during feverish illness. **2** wild excitement or emotion. □ **delirium tremens** (**tree**-menz), a form of delirium with tremors and terrifying delusions, caused by heavy drinking.

**Delius** (**dee**-li-ŭs), Frederick (1862–1934), English composer.

**deliver** *verb* **1** take (letters, goods, etc.) to the addressee or purchaser. **2** hand over; present. **3** utter (a speech). **4** aim or launch (a blow, an attack); bowl (a ball) in cricket etc. **5** rescue, save, or set free. **6** assist at the birth of or in giving birth. **7** give birth to. □ **deliverer** *noun*

**deliverance** *noun* rescue, setting free; being rescued.

**delivery** *noun* **1** delivering; being delivered. **2** a periodical distribution of letters or goods etc. **3** the manner of delivering a speech. **4** the manner of bowling a ball in cricket etc.

**dell** *noun* a small wooded hollow or valley.

**Delors**, Jacques (born 1925), French politician, President of the European Commission from 1985.

**delouse** *verb* remove lice from (a person or animal).

**Delphi** (**del**-fi) an ancient Greek city on the southern slopes of Mount Parnassus, site of the most famous oracle of Apollo.

**Delphic** *adjective* (also **Delphian**) of or like the ancient Greek oracle at Parnassus, which often gave obscure and enigmatic prophecies.

**delphinium** *noun* a garden plant with tall spikes of flowers, usually blue.

**delta** *noun* **1** the fourth letter of the Greek alphabet (Δ, δ). **2** a triangular patch of land accumulated at the mouth of a river between two or more of its branches; *the Nile Delta.* □ **delta wing** a triangular swept-back wing of an aircraft.

**delude** (di-**lood**) *verb* deceive.

**deluge** (**del**-yooj) *noun* **1** a great flood; a heavy fall of rain. **2** (**the Deluge**) the flood in Noah's time. **3** anything coming in a heavy rush; *a deluge of questions.* ●*verb* flood, come down on like a deluge.

**delusion** *noun* **1** a false belief or opinion. **2** a hallucination. □ **delusory** *adjective*

**delusive** *adjective* deceptive, raising vain hopes.

**de luxe** of very high quality, luxurious.

**delve** *verb* **1** (*old use*) dig. **2** search deeply for information.

**demagnetize** *verb* (also **demagnetise**) remove the magnetization of. □ **demagnetization** *noun*

**demagogue** (**dem**-ă-gog) *noun* (*Amer.* **demagog**) a leader or agitator who wins support by appealing to people's feelings and prejudices rather than by reasoning. □ **demagogic** *adjective*, **demagogy** *noun*

**demand** *noun* **1** a request made imperiously or as if one had a right. **2** a desire for goods or services by people who wish to buy or use these; *an increased demand for new houses.* **3** an urgent claim; *there are many demands on my time.* ●*verb* **1** make a demand for. **2** need; *the work demands great skill.* □ **in demand** sought after. **on demand** as soon as the demand is made; *payable on demand.*

**demanding** *adjective* **1** making many demands. **2** requiring a great deal of skill or effort; *a demanding job.*

**demarcation** (dee-mar-**kay**-shŏn) *noun* marking of the boundary or limits of something. □ **demarcation dispute** a dispute between trade unions about work they consider to belong to different trades.

**dematerialize** *verb* (also **dematerialise**) vanish; make or become non-material.

**demean** *verb* lower the dignity of; *I wouldn't demean myself to ask for it.*

**demeanour** *noun* (*Amer.* **demeanor**) the way a person behaves.

**demented** *adjective* driven mad, crazy. □ **dementedly** *adverb*

**dementia** (di-**men**-shă) *noun* severe or persistent mental disorder. □ **dementia praecox** (**pree**-koks) (*formal*) schizophrenia.

**demerara** (dem-er-**air**-ă) *noun* brown raw cane sugar.

**demerit** *noun* a fault, a defect.

**demesne** (di-**meen**) *noun* **1** a domain. **2** a landed estate.

**Demeter** (di-mee-ter) (*Gk. myth.*) the corn-goddess, mother of Persephone.

**demi-** *combining form* half; partly.

**demigod** *noun* **1** a partly divine being. **2** a person regarded as godlike.

**demijohn** *noun* a large bottle, often in a wicker case.

**demilitarize** *verb* (also **demilitarise**) remove military installations or forces from (an area). □ **demilitarization** *noun*

**De Mille** (dĕ mil), Cecil B(lount) (1881–1959), American film producer-director.

*demi-monde* (dem-i-mond) *noun* **1** women of doubtful repute in society. **2** a group behaving with doubtful legality or respectability. (¶ French, = half-world.)

**demise** (di-myz) *noun* (*formal*) **1** death. **2** termination; failure.

**demisemiquaver** *noun* a note in music, equal to half a semiquaver.

**demist** *verb* clear mist from (a windscreen etc.). □ **demister** *noun*

**demo** *noun* (*plural* **demos**) (*informal*) a demonstration.

**demob** *verb* (**demobbed, demobbing**) (*informal*) demobilize.

**demobilize** *verb* (also **demobilise**) release from military service. □ **demobilization** *noun*

**democracy** *noun* **1** government by the whole people of a country, especially through representatives whom they elect. **2** a country governed in this way. **3** a form of society etc. characterized by social equality and tolerance.

**democrat** *noun* **1** a person who favours democracy. **2** (**Democrat**) a member or supporter of a political party with 'Democrat' or 'Democratic' in its title.

**democratic** *adjective* **1** of, like, or supporting democracy. **2** in accordance with the principle of equal rights for all; *a democratic decision.* □ **Democratic Party** the more liberal of the two main political parties in the USA. □ **democratically** *adverb*

**democratize** (di-mok-ră-tyz) *verb* (also **democratise**) make democratic. □ **democratization** *noun*

**demodulation** *noun* the process of extracting a modulating radio signal from a modulated wave etc.

**demography** (di-mog-răfi) *noun* the study of statistics of births, deaths, diseases, etc., as illustrating the conditions of life in communities. □ **demographic** *adjective*, **demographically** *adverb*

**demolish** *verb* **1** pull or knock down (a building). **2** destroy (a person's argument or theory etc.); put an end to (an institution). **3** (*informal*) eat up. □ **demolition** (dem-ŏ-lish-ŏn) *noun*

**demon** *noun* **1** a devil or evil spirit. **2** a cruel person. **3** (usually used as *adjective*) very skilful or forceful; *a demon bowler.* □ **demonic** (di-mon-ik) *adjective*

**demonetize** (dee-mun-i-tyz) *verb* (also **demonetise**) withdraw (a coin etc.) from use as money. □ **demonetization** *noun*

**demoniac** (di-moh-ni-ak) *adjective* (also **demoniacal**, *pronounced* dee-mŏn-I-ăkăl) **1** of or like a demon. **2** possessed by an evil spirit. **3** fiercely energetic, frenzied. □ **demoniacally** *adverb*

**demonolatry** (dee-mŏ-nol-ă-tri) *noun* worship of demons.

**demonology** *noun* the study of beliefs about demons.

**demonstrable** (dem-ŏn-stră-bŭl) *adjective* able to be shown or proved. □ **demonstrably** *adverb*

**demonstrate** *verb* **1** show evidence of, prove. **2** describe and explain by showing (a machine) in practical use, doing an experiment, etc. **3** take part in a public demonstration. □ **demonstrator** *noun*

**demonstration** *noun* **1** demonstrating. **2** a show of feeling. **3** an organized gathering or procession to express the opinion of a group publicly. **4** a display of military force.

**demonstrative** (di-mon-stră-tiv) *adjective* **1** showing or proving. **2** expressing one's feelings openly. **3** *Grammar* (of an adjective or pronoun) indicating the person or thing referred to (e.g. *this, those*). □ **demonstratively** *adverb*, **demonstrativeness** *noun*

**demoralize** *verb* (also **demoralise**) weaken the morale of, dishearten. □ **demoralization** *noun*

**Demosthenes** (di-moss-thĕ-neez) (384–322 BC), Athenian orator.

**demote** (dee-moht) *verb* reduce to a lower rank or category. □ **demotion** *noun*

**demotic** (di-mot-ik) *adjective* (of language or writing) of the popular form. ●*noun* **1** a cursive script of ancient Egypt. **2** the popular form of modern Greek.

**Dempsey**, 'Jack' (William Harrison) (1895–1983), American boxer, world heavyweight champion 1919–26.

**demur** (di-mer) *verb* (**demurred, demurring**) (often foll. by *to, at*) raise objections; *they demurred at working on Sundays.* ●*noun* an objection raised; *they went without demur.*

**demure** (di-mewr) *adjective* quiet and serious or pretending to be so. □ **demurely** *adverb*, **demureness** *noun*

**demurrer** (di-mu-rer) *noun* a legal objection to the relevance of an opponent's point.

**demystify** *verb* remove the mystery from; make simple.

**den** noun **1** a wild animal's lair. **2** a place where people gather for some illegal activity; *an opium den; a den of vice.* **3** a small private room where a person goes to work or relax.

**denarius** (di-**nair**-iŭs) noun (*plural* **denarii**) an ancient Roman silver coin.

**denary** (**dee**-ner-i) adjective of ten; decimal.

**denationalize** verb (also **denationalise**) transfer (an industry) from national to private ownership. □ **denationalization** noun

**denature** verb **1** change the natural qualities of. **2** make (alcohol) unfit for drinking.

**Dench**, Dame Judi Olivia (born 1934), British actress and director.

**dendrochronology** noun a method of dating timber by study of its annual growth-rings.

**dendrology** noun the study of trees.

**dene** (*pronounced* deen) noun (also **dean**) a narrow wooded valley.

**dengue** (**deng**-i) noun an infectious tropical fever causing acute pain in the joints.

**Deng Xiaoping** (deng show-**ping**) (born 1904), Chinese Communist leader, who remained influential following his official retirement in 1987.

**deniable** adjective able to be denied.

**denial** noun **1** denying. **2** a statement that a thing is not true. **3** refusal of a request or wish.

**denier** (**den**-yer) noun a unit of weight by which the fineness of silk, rayon, or nylon yarn is measured.

**denigrate** (**den**-i-grayt) verb blacken the reputation of; sneer at. □ **denigration** noun

**denim** noun **1** a strong twilled cotton fabric used for making clothes. **2** (**denims**) trousers made of denim.

**De Niro**, Robert (born 1943), American film actor.

**Denis**, St (*c.*250), the patron saint of France. Feast day, 9 October.

**denizen** (**den**-i-zěn) noun **1** an inhabitant or occupant. **2** a foreigner having certain rights in an adopted country. **3** a naturalized foreign word, animal, or plant.

**Denmark** a country in northern Europe.

**denominate** verb give a name to; call or describe as.

**denomination** noun **1** a name or title. **2** a distinctively named Church or religious sect; *Baptists and other Protestant denominations.* **3** a unit of measurement or money; *coins of small denomination.*

**denominational** adjective of a particular religious denomination.

**denominator** noun the number written below the line in a fraction, e.g. 4 in ¾, showing how many parts the whole is divided into.

**denote** (di-**noht**) verb be the sign, symbol, or name of, indicate; *in road signs,* P *denotes a parking place.* □ **denotation** (dee-noh-tay-shŏn) noun

**denouement** (day-**noo**-mahn) noun (also **dénouement**) the clearing up, at the end of a play or story, of the complications of the plot.

**denounce** verb **1** speak publicly against. **2** give information against; *denounced him as a spy.* **3** announce that one is ending (a treaty or agreement).

**dense** adjective **1** thick, not easy to see through; *dense fog.* **2** massed closely together; *dense crowds.* **3** stupid. □ **densely** adverb, **denseness** noun

**density** noun **1** a dense or concentrated condition; *the density of the fog.* **2** stupidity. **3** *Physics* the relation of mass to volume.

**dent** noun a depression left by a blow or by pressure. ● verb **1** make a dent in. **2** become dented.

**dental** adjective **1** of or for the teeth. **2** of dentistry; *a dental practice.* □ **dental floss** strong thread used for cleaning between the teeth. **dental surgeon** a dentist.

**dentate** adjective (in botany and zoology) having teeth or toothlike notches.

**dentifrice** (**dent**-i-friss) noun toothpaste or tooth powder.

**dentine** (**den**-teen) noun (*Amer.* **dentin**, *pronounced* **den**-tin) the hard dense tissue forming the main part of teeth.

**dentist** noun a person who is qualified to treat the teeth, fit artificial ones, etc.

**dentistry** noun the work or profession of a dentist.

**dentition** noun **1** the type and arrangement of teeth in a species etc. of animals. **2** teething.

**denture** noun a set of artificial teeth.

**denude** verb **1** make naked or bare, strip the cover from; *the trees were denuded of their leaves.* **2** take all of something away from (a person); *creditors denuded him of every penny.* □ **denudation** (dee-new-**day**-shŏn) noun

**denunciation** (di-nun-si-**ay**-shŏn) noun denouncing.

**deny** verb (**denied, denying**) **1** say that (a thing) is not true or does not exist. **2** disown, refuse to acknowledge; *Peter denied Christ.* **3** refuse to give what is asked for or needed, prevent from having; *no one can deny you your rights.* □ **deny oneself** restrict one's food, drink, or pleasure.

**deodar** (**dee**-ŏ-dar) noun the Himalayan cedar, with slightly drooping branches and barrel-shaped cones.

**deodorant** (dee-**oh**-der-ănt) noun a substance that removes or conceals unwanted smells. ● adjective deodorizing.

**deodorize** *verb* (also **deodorise**) destroy the odour of. □ **deodorization** *noun*

**deoxyribonucleic acid** (dee-oksī-ry-boh-new-**klay**-ik) *see* DNA.

**depart** *verb* **1** go away, leave. **2** (of trains or buses) start, begin a journey. **3** cease following a particular course; *departing from our normal procedure.*

**departed** *adjective* **1** bygone; *departed glories.* **2** (**the departed**) the dead.

**department** *noun* **1** any of the units, each with a specialized function, into which a business, shop, or organization is divided. **2** an administrative district in France etc. **3** an area of activity. □ **department store** a large shop with many departments dealing in different goods.

**departmental** (dee-part-**men**-tăl) *adjective* of a department. □ **departmentally** *adverb*

**departure** *noun* **1** departing, going away. **2** setting out on a new course of action or thought.

**depend** *verb* (often foll. by *on* or *upon*) **1** be controlled or determined by; *whether we can picnic depends on the weather.* **2** be unable to do without; *she depends on my help.* **3** trust confidently, feel certain about; *you can depend on John to be there when he's needed.*

**dependable** *adjective* able to be relied on. □ **dependably** *adverb*, **dependability** *noun*

**dependant** *noun* (*Amer.* **dependent**) one who depends on another for financial support; *he has four dependants.*

**dependence** *noun* depending, being dependent.

**dependency** *noun* a country that is controlled by another.

**dependent** *adjective* **1** (usually foll. by *on*, *upon*) depending, conditional; *promotion is dependent on ability.* **2** (usually foll. by *on*, *upon*) needing the help of; unable to do without; *he is dependent on drugs.* **3** maintained at another's cost; controlled by another, not independent; *our dependent territories.* **4** (of a clause, phrase, or word) in a subordinate relation to a sentence or word. ● *noun* Amer. spelling of DEPENDANT.

**depict** *verb* **1** show in the form of a picture. **2** describe in words. □ **depiction** *noun*

**depilate** (**dep**-il-ayt) *verb* remove hair from. □ **depilation** *noun*

**depilatory** (di-**pil**-ă-ter-i) *noun* a substance that removes hair. ● *adjective* removing hair.

**deplete** (di-**pleet**) *verb* use up large quantities of; reduce in number or quantity. □ **depletion** *noun*

**deplorable** *adjective* **1** regrettable. **2** exceedingly bad, shocking. □ **deplorably** *adverb*

**deplore** *verb* **1** regret deeply. **2** find deplorable; *we deplore their incompetence.*

**deploy** *verb* spread out; bring or come into action systematically; *deploying troops*; *deploying resources in the most effective way.* □ **deployment** *noun*

**deponent** (di-**poh**-něnt) *noun* a person making a deposition under oath.

**depopulate** *verb* reduce the population of. □ **depopulation** *noun*

**deport** *verb* remove (an unwanted person) from a country. □ **deport oneself** behave in a specified manner. □ **deportation** *noun*

**deportee** *noun* a deported person.

**deportment** *noun* behaviour; a person's way of holding himself or herself in standing and walking.

**depose** *verb* **1** remove from power; *the king was deposed.* **2** testify or bear witness, especially on oath in court.

**deposit** *noun* **1** a thing deposited for safe keeping. **2** a sum of money paid into an account. **3** a sum paid as a guarantee or a first instalment. **4** a layer of matter deposited or accumulated naturally; *new deposits of copper were found.* ● *verb* (**deposited**, **depositing**) **1** lay or put down; *she deposited the books on the desk.* **2** store or entrust for safe keeping; pay (money) into an account. **3** pay as a guarantee or first instalment. **4** leave as a layer or covering of matter; *floods deposited mud on the land.* □ **deposit account** a bank account paying interest but not offering a cheque book, overdraft facilities, etc. **on deposit** in an account; as a deposit of money.

**depositary** *noun* a person to whom a thing is entrusted.

**deposition** *noun* **1** deposing or being deposed from power. **2** a statement made on oath. **3** depositing. **4** the taking down of Christ from the Cross.

**depositor** *noun* a person who deposits money or property.

**depository** *noun* **1** a storehouse. **2** = DEPOSITARY.

**depot** (**dep**-oh) *noun* **1** a storehouse, especially for military supplies. **2** the headquarters of a regiment. **3** a place where goods are deposited or from which goods, vehicles, etc. are dispatched. **4** a bus station; (*Amer.*) a railway station.

**deprave** (di-**prayv**) *verb* make morally bad, corrupt. □ **depravation** (dep-ră-**vay**-shŏn) *noun*

**depraved** *adjective* immoral, wicked; *a depraved character.*

**depravity** (di-**prav**-iti) *noun* moral corruption, wickedness.

**deprecate** (**dep**-ri-kayt) *verb* **1** feel and express disapproval of. **2** try to turn aside (praise or blame etc.) politely. □ **depreca-**

**tion** *noun*, **deprecatory** (dep-ri-kay-ter-i) *adjective*

■**Usage** Do not confuse with **depreciate**.

**depreciate** (di-pree-shi-ayt) *verb* **1** make or become lower in value. **2** belittle, disparage. □ **depreciatory** *adjective*

■**Usage** Do not confuse with **deprecate**.

**depreciation** *noun* **1** a decline in value, especially that due to wear and tear. **2** the allowance made for this.

**depredation** (dep-ri-**day**-shŏn) *noun* plundering; damage.

**depress** *verb* **1** make sad, lower the spirits of. **2** reduce the activity of (trade, businesses, etc.). **3** press down; lower; *depress the lever*.

**depressant** *noun* a substance that reduces the activity of the nervous system, a sedative.

**depression** *noun* **1** a state of excessive sadness or hopelessness, often with physical symptoms. **2** a long period of inactivity in business and trade, with widespread unemployment. **3** (**the Depression**) the severe worldwide economic depression of 1929–34. **4** a lowering of atmospheric pressure; an area of low pressure which may bring rain. **5** a sunken place or hollow on a surface. **6** pressing down.

**depressive** *adjective* **1** depressing. **2** involving mental depression. ●*noun* a person suffering from mental depression.

**deprival** (di-**pry**-văl) *noun* depriving; being deprived.

**deprivation** (dep-ri-vay-shŏn) *noun* **1** deprival. **2** a keenly felt loss.

**deprive** *verb* **1** take a thing away from; prevent from using or enjoying something; *the prisoner had been deprived of food*. **2** (as **deprived** *adjective*) lacking what is needed; underprivileged; *a deprived child*; *deprived areas*.

**Dept.** *abbreviation* Department.

**depth** *noun* **1** being deep. **2** the distance from the top down, or from the surface inwards, or from front to back. **3** deep learning, thought, or feeling. **4** intensity of colour or darkness. **5** lowness of pitch in a voice or sound. **6** the deepest or most central part; *living in the depths of the country*. □ **depth charge** a bomb that will explode under water. **in depth** with thorough and intensive investigations; *studied it in depth*. **in-depth** *adjective* thorough and intensive. **out of one's depth** **1** in water that is too deep to stand in. **2** attempting something that is beyond one's ability.

**deputation** *noun* a body of people appointed to go on a mission on behalf of others.

**depute** (di-pewt) *verb* **1** delegate (a task) to a person. **2** appoint (a person) to act as one's representative.

**deputize** *verb* (also **deputise**) act as deputy.

**deputy** *noun* **1** a person appointed to act as substitute for another. **2** a member of a parliament in certain countries; *the Chamber of Deputies*.

**derail** *verb* (**derailed**, **derailing**) cause (a train) to leave the rails. □ **derailment** *noun*

**derange** *verb* **1** throw into confusion, disrupt. **2** make insane. □ **derangement** *noun*

**Derby** (**dar**-bi) *noun* **1** an annual flat horse race for three-year-olds, run on Epsom Downs. **2** a similar race elsewhere. **3** an important sporting contest. **4** (**derby**) (*Amer.*) (*pronounced* **der**-bi) a bowler hat.

**Derbyshire** a north midland county of England (*abbreviation* Derbys.).

**deregulate** *verb* free from regulations or controls. □ **deregulation** *noun*

**derelict** *adjective* deserted and left to fall into ruin. ●*noun* **1** an abandoned property, especially a ship. **2** a vagrant; a tramp.

**dereliction** (derri-**lik**-shŏn) *noun* **1** neglect of duty. **2** abandoning; being abandoned.

**derestrict** *verb* remove restrictions from. □ **derestricted road** one where a speed limit has been removed or has not been imposed. □ **derestriction** *noun*

**deride** (di-**ryd**) *verb* laugh at scornfully, treat with scorn.

**de rigueur** (dĕ rig-**er**) required by custom or etiquette; *evening dress is de rigueur*. (¶ French, = of strictness.)

**derision** (di-**rizh**-ŏn) *noun* scorn, ridicule.

**derisive** (di-**ry**-siv) *adjective* scornful, showing derision; *derisive cheers*. □ **derisively** *adverb*

**derisory** (di-**ry**-ser-i) *adjective* **1** showing derision. **2** deserving derision; too insignificant for serious consideration; *a derisory offer*.

**derivation** (derri-**vay**-shŏn) *noun* **1** deriving. **2** origin.

**derivative** (di-**riv**-ătiv) *adjective* derived from a source. ●*noun* **1** a thing that is derived from another. **2** (in mathematics) a quantity measuring the rate of change of another.

**derive** *verb* (usually foll. by *from*) **1** get or trace from a source; *she derived great pleasure from music*. **2** arise from, originate in; *happiness derives from many things*. **3** show or state the origin of (a word, phrase, etc.).

**dermatitis** (der-mă-**ty**-tiss) *noun* inflammation of the skin.

**dermatology** (der-ma-**tol**-ŏji) *noun* the study of the skin and its diseases. □ **dermatologist** *noun*

**dermis** *noun* the layer of skin below the epidermis.

**derogate** (derrŏ-gayt) *verb* detract (from a merit or right etc.). □ **derogation** *noun*

**derogatory** (di-**rog**-ă-ter-i) *adjective* critical, scornful, insulting.

**derrick** *noun* **1** a crane with an arm pivoted to the base of a central post or to a floor. **2** a framework over an oil well or bore-hole, holding the drilling machinery.

**derring-do** *noun* (*literary*) heroic courage or action.

**derris** *noun* **1** a tropical climbing plant. **2** an insecticide made from its powdered root.

**derv** *noun* fuel oil for diesel engines. (¶ From the initials of *d*iesel-*e*ngined *r*oad *v*ehicle.)

**dervish** *noun* a member of a Muslim religious order, vowed to poverty.

**DES** *abbreviation* (*Brit.*) Department of Education and Science.

**desalinate** *verb* remove the salt from (sea water etc.). □ **desalination** *noun*

**descale** *verb* remove scale from (a kettle or boiler etc.).

**descant** *noun* a harmonizing higher-pitched melody sung or played in accompaniment to the main melody.

**Descartes** (day-**kart**), René (1596–1650), French philosopher, mathematician, and scientist.

**descend** *verb* **1** come or go down. **2** slope downwards. **3** (usually foll. by *on*) make a sudden attack or visit; *the whole family descended on us for Easter.* **4** sink or stoop to unworthy behaviour; *they would never descend to cheating.* **5** be passed down by inheritance; *the title descended to his son.* □ **be descended from** come by descent from (a specified person, family, or people).

**descendant** *noun* a person who is descended from another.

**descendent** *adjective* descending.

**descent** *noun* **1** descending. **2** a way by which one may descend. **3** a downward slope. **4** a sudden attack or invasion; *the Danes made descents upon the English coast.* **5** ancestry, family origin; *they are of French descent.*

**describe** *verb* **1** set forth in words; say what something is like. **2** mark out or draw the outline of; move in a certain pattern; *described a complete circle.*

**description** *noun* **1** describing. **2** an account or picture in words. **3** a kind or class of thing; *there's no food of any description.*

**descriptive** *adjective* giving a description.

**descry** (di-**skry**) *verb* catch sight of, discern.

**desecrate** (**dess**-i-krayt) *verb* treat (a sacred thing) with irreverence or disrespect. □ **desecration** *noun*, **desecrator** *noun*

**desegregate** *verb* end segregation of (people, classes, races, etc.). □ **desegregation** *noun*

**deselect** *verb* reject (a sitting MP) as one's constituency candidate for a forthcoming election. □ **deselection** *noun*

**desensitize** *verb* (also **desensitise**) reduce or destroy the sensitivity of.

**desert**[1] (**dez**-ert) *noun* a dry barren often sand-covered area of land. ● *adjective* barren and uncultivated; uninhabited. □ **desert boots** suede ankle-high boots. **desert island** an uninhabited island (usually tropical).

**desert**[2] (di-**zert**) *verb* **1** abandon; leave without intending to return; forsake. **2** leave service in the armed forces without permission. □ **deserter** *noun*, **desertion** *noun*

**desertification** *noun* making or becoming a desert.

**deserts** (di-**zerts**) *plural noun* what one deserves.

**deserve** *verb* be worthy of or entitled to (a thing) because of actions or qualities.

**deservedly** (di-**zerv**-idli) *adverb* according to what is deserved, justly.

**deserving** *adjective* worthy, worth rewarding or supporting; *a deserving charity*; *those who are deserving of our sympathy.*

**déshabillé** (day-za-**bee**-ay) *noun* (also **déshabille** (*pronounced* day-za-**beel**), **dishabille** (*pronounced* disĕ-**beel**)) the state of being only partly dressed. (¶ French.)

**desiccate** *verb* (**dess**-i-kayt) dry out the moisture from; dry (solid food) in order to preserve it; *desiccated coconut.* □ **desiccation** *noun*

**desideratum** (di-sid-er-**ah**-tŭm) *noun* (*plural* **desiderata**) something that is lacking but needed or desired.

**design** *noun* **1** a drawing that shows how something is to be made. **2** the art of making such drawings; *she studied design.* **3** the general form or arrangement of something; *the design of the building is good.* **4** a combination of lines or shapes to form a decoration. **5** a mental plan, a purpose. ● *verb* **1** prepare a drawing or design for (a thing). **2** plan, intend for a specific purpose; *the book is designed for students.* □ **have designs on** plan to get possession of.

**designate** *verb* (*pronounced* **dez**-ig-nayt) **1** mark or point out clearly, specify; *the river was designated as the western boundary.* **2** describe as; give a name or title to. **3** appoint to a position; *designated Smith as his successor.* ● *adjective* (*pronounced* **dez**-ig-năt) appointed but not yet installed in office; *the bishop designate.*

**designation** (dez-ig-**nay**-shŏn) *noun* **1** designating. **2** a name or title.

**designedly** (di-**zyn**-id-li) *adverb* intentionally.

**designer** *noun* **1** a person who designs things. **2** (used as *adjective*) designed by a famous, fashionable designer; *designer T-shirts.* □ **designer drug** a drug that has the narcotic effects of an illegal drug, but is sufficiently different to be outside legal control.

**designing** *adjective* crafty, scheming.

**desirable** *adjective* **1** arousing desire; attractive; *a desirable riverside house.* **2** advisable, worth doing; *it is desirable that you should be present.* □ **desirably** *adverb*, **desirability** *noun*

**desire** *noun* **1** a feeling that one would get pleasure or satisfaction by obtaining or possessing something. **2** an expressed wish, a request; *at the desire of Her Majesty.* **3** an object of desire; *all your heart's desires.* **4** sexual urge. ●*verb* **1** have a desire for. **2** ask for. □ **leave much to be desired** be very imperfect.

**desirous** *adjective* having a desire, desiring.

**desist** (di-**zist**) *verb* (often foll. by *from*) cease (from an action etc.).

**desk** *noun* **1** a piece of furniture with a flat top and often drawers, used when reading or writing etc. **2** a counter behind which a cashier or receptionist etc. sits; *ask at the information desk.* **3** the section of a newspaper office dealing with specified topics. **4** a unit of two orchestral players sharing a stand.

**desktop** *noun* **1** the working surface of a desk. **2** (often used as *adjective*) (especially of a computer) small enough for use on a desk. □ **desktop publishing** designing and printing documents, booklets, etc. with a desktop computer and a high-quality printer.

**desolate** (**dess**-ŏ-lăt) *adjective* **1** solitary, lonely. **2** deserted, uninhabited, barren, dismal; *a desolate landscape.* **3** forlorn and unhappy.

**desolated** (**dess**-ŏ-lay-tid) *adjective* feeling lonely and wretched.

**desolation** *noun* **1** a desolate or barren condition. **2** loneliness. **3** grief, wretchedness.

**despair** *noun* **1** complete loss or lack of hope. **2** a thing that causes this. ●*verb* lose all hope.

**despatch** alternative spelling of DISPATCH.

**desperado** (dess-per-**ah**-doh) *noun* (*plural* **desperadoes**; *Amer.* **desperados**) a reckless criminal.

**desperate** *adjective* **1** leaving little or no hope, extremely serious; *the situation is desperate.* **2** made reckless by despair or urgency; *a desperate criminal; they are desperate for food.* **3** done or used in a nearly

hopeless situation; *a desperate remedy.* □ **desperately** *adverb*

**desperation** *noun* **1** hopelessness. **2** being desperate; recklessness caused by despair.

**despicable** (**dess**-pik-ăbŭl *or* di-**spik**-ăbŭl) *adjective* deserving to be despised, contemptible. □ **despicably** *adverb*

**despise** *verb* regard as inferior or worthless, feel disrespect for.

**despite** *preposition* in spite of.

**despoil** *verb* (*literary*) plunder, rob. □ **despoliation** *noun*

**despondent** *adjective* in low spirits, dejected. □ **despondently** *adverb*, **despondency** *noun*

**despot** (**dess**-pot) *noun* a tyrant, a ruler who has unrestricted power.

**despotic** (dis-**pot**-ik) *adjective* having unrestricted power. □ **despotically** *adverb*

**despotism** (**dess**-pŏt-izm) *noun* **1** tyranny, government by a despot. **2** a country ruled by a despot.

**des res** (dez **rez**) (*slang*) a desirable residence.

**dessert** (di-**zert**) *noun* the sweet or fruit course of a meal.

**dessertspoon** *noun* a medium-sized spoon used in eating puddings etc. □ **dessertspoonful** *noun* (*plural* **dessertspoonfuls**).

**destabilize** *verb* (also **destabilise**) **1** make unstable. **2** overthrow or weaken (a government).

**destination** *noun* the place to which a person or thing is going.

**destine** *verb* settle or determine the future of, set apart for a purpose; *he was destined to become President.*

**destiny** *noun* **1** fate considered as a power. **2** that which happens to a person or thing, thought of as determined in advance by fate.

**destitute** *adjective* **1** penniless, without the necessaries of life. **2** lacking in something; *a landscape destitute of trees.*

**destitution** *noun* being destitute; extreme poverty.

**destroy** *verb* **1** pull or break down; reduce to a useless form; spoil completely. **2** kill (a sick or unwanted animal) deliberately; *the dog had to be destroyed.* **3** put out of existence; *it destroyed our chances.*

**destroyer** *noun* **1** a person or thing that destroys. **2** a fast warship designed to protect other ships.

**destruct** *verb* destroy (one's own vehicle, equipment, etc.) or be destroyed deliberately, especially for safety.

**destructible** *adjective* able to be destroyed.

**destruction** *noun* **1** destroying, being destroyed. **2** a cause of destruction or ruin; *gambling was his destruction.*

**destructive** *adjective* **1** destroying; causing destruction. **2** (of criticism etc.) disproving or discrediting something without offering amendments or alternatives.

**desuetude** (dis-yoo-i-tewd) *noun* (*formal*) a state of disuse; *the custom fell into desuetude.*

**desultory** (dez-ŭl-ter-i) *adjective* going constantly from one subject to another, not systematic. □ **desultorily** *adverb*

**detach** *verb* release or remove from something else or from a group. □ **detachable** *adjective*

**detached** *adjective* **1** (of a house) not joined to another. **2** (of the mind or opinions) free from bias or emotion.

**detachment** *noun* **1** detaching; being detached. **2** freedom from bias or emotion; aloofness, lack of concern. **3** a group of people or ships etc. detached from a larger group for a special duty.

**detail** *noun* **1** an individual item; a small or subordinate particular. **2** a number of such particulars; *the description is full of detail.* **3** the minor decoration in a building or picture etc.; *look at the detail in the carvings.* **4** a small military detachment assigned to special duty. ●*verb* **1** give particulars of, describe fully. **2** assign to special duty. □ **go into details** explain things in detail. **in detail** describing the individual parts or events etc. fully.

**detailed** *adjective* giving or showing many details.

**detain** *verb* **1** keep in confinement or under restraint. **2** keep waiting; cause delay to; keep from proceeding.

**detainee** (di-tayn-ee) *noun* a person who is detained by the authorities.

**detect** *verb* **1** discover the existence or presence of. **2** find (a person) doing something bad or secret. □ **detectable** *adjective*

**detection** *noun* **1** detecting, being detected. **2** the work of a detective.

**detective** *noun* a person, especially a police officer, whose job is to investigate crimes.

**detector** *noun* a device for detecting the presence of something; *a smoke detector.*

**détente** (day-tahnt) *noun* the easing of strained relations between countries.

**detention** *noun* **1** detaining; being detained. **2** being kept in custody. **3** being kept in school after hours as a punishment. □ **detention centre** an institution where young offenders are kept in detention for a short time.

**deter** *verb* (**deterred, deterring**) discourage or prevent from doing something through fear of the consequences. □ **determent** *noun*

**detergent** *noun* a cleansing substance, especially a synthetic substance other than soap. ●*adjective* having a cleansing effect.

**deteriorate** *verb* become worse. □ **deterioration** *noun*

**determinable** *adjective* able to be settled or calculated; *its age is not determinable.*

**determinant** *adjective* determining, decisive. ●*noun* **1** a decisive factor. **2** *Maths* the quantity obtained by adding the products of the elements of a square matrix according to a certain rule.

**determinate** (di-ter-min-ăt) *adjective* limited, of fixed and definite scope or nature.

**determination** *noun* **1** firmness of purpose. **2** the process of deciding or calculating.

**determine** *verb* **1** find out or calculate precisely; *we must determine the height of the mountain.* **2** settle, decide; *determine what is to be done.* **3** be the decisive factor or influence on; *income determines one's standard of living.* **4** decide firmly; *he determined to become a doctor.* □ **be determined** be firmly resolved.

**determined** *adjective* showing determination; firm and resolute. □ **determinedly** *adverb*

**determinism** *noun* the theory that human action is not free but is determined by external forces acting on the will. □ **determinist** *noun*, **deterministic** *adjective*

**deterrent** (di-te-rĕnt) *adjective* deterring. ●*noun* a thing that deters; a weapon that deters countries from attacking the one who has it. □ **deterrence** *noun*

**detest** *verb* dislike intensely, hate. □ **detestation** *noun*

**detestable** *adjective* intensely disliked, hateful.

**dethrone** *verb* remove from a throne; depose. □ **dethronement** *noun*

**detonate** (det-ŏn-ayt) *verb* explode or cause to explode. □ **detonation** *noun*

**detonator** *noun* a device for detonating an explosive.

**detour** (dee-toor) *noun* a deviation from one's direct or intended course.

**detoxify** *verb* remove poison or harmful substances from. □ **detoxification** *noun*

**detract** *verb* (foll. by *from*) take away a part or amount from, lessen (a quantity, value, etc.); *it will not detract from our pleasure.* □ **detraction** *noun*

**detractor** *noun* a person who criticizes something; *the plan has its detractors.*

**detriment** (det-ri-mĕnt) *noun* **1** harm, damage; *worked long hours to the detriment of his health.* **2** something causing this.

**detrimental** (det-ri-men-tăl) *adjective* causing harm; *smoking is detrimental to health.* □ **detrimentally** *adverb*

**detritus** (di-try-tŭs) *noun* debris; loose matter (e.g. gravel) produced by erosion.

**de trop** (dĕ **troh**) not wanted; in the way. (¶ French, = excessive.)

**deuce**[1] *noun* **1** (in tennis) the score of 40 all. **2** the two on dice.

**deuce**[2] *noun* (*informal*, in exclamations of surprise or annoyance) the Devil; *where the deuce is it?*

**deus ex machina** (**day**-ŭs eks **mak**-in-ă) an unexpected power or event that saves a seemingly impossible situation. (¶ Latin, = god from the machinery, with reference to the machinery by which, in ancient Greek theatre, gods were shown in the air.)

**deuterium** (dew-**teer**-iŭm) *noun* a heavy form of hydrogen (symbol D or $^2$H), used as a moderator in nuclear reactors and a fuel in thermonuclear bombs.

**Deuteronomy** (dew-ter-**on**-ŏmi), the fifth book of the Old Testament.

**Deutschmark** (**doich**-mark) *noun* (also **Deutsche Mark**) the unit of money in Germany.

**de Valera** (dĕ vă-**lair**-ă), Eamon (1882–1975), Irish statesman, a leader of the Easter 1916 uprising against the British, who formed the Fianna Fáil party and served several times as President and as Prime Minister of his country.

**devalue** *verb* reduce the value of (currency) in relation to other currencies or to gold. □ **devaluation** *noun*

**Devanagari** (day-vă-**nah**-ger-i) *noun* the alphabet in which Sanskrit, Hindi, and several North Indian languages are usually written.

**devastate** *verb* **1** lay waste; cause great destruction to. **2** overwhelm with shock or grief. □ **devastation** *noun*

**devastating** *adjective* **1** causing destruction. **2** overwhelming; *a devastating handicap*.

**develop** *verb* (**developed**, **developing**) **1** make or become larger, fuller, or more mature or organized. **2** bring or come gradually into existence; *a storm developed*. **3** begin to exhibit or suffer from, acquire gradually; *develop measles*; *develop bad habits*. **4** convert (land) to a new purpose so as to use its resources; use (an area) for the building of houses, shops, factories, etc. **5** treat (a photographic film or plate etc.) so as to make the picture visible. □ **developing country** a poor or primitive country that is developing better economic and social conditions.

**developer** *noun* **1** one who develops. **2** a person or firm that develops land. **3** a substance used for developing photographic film etc.

**development** *noun* **1** developing; being developed. **2** something that has developed or been developed; *the latest developments in foreign affairs*. □ **development area** an area where new industries are encouraged by government to counteract unemployment. □ **developmental** *adjective*

**Devi** (**day**-vi) the supreme Hindu goddess, often identified with Parvati.

**deviant** (**dee**-vi-ănt) *adjective* deviating from what is accepted as normal or usual. ●*noun* a person who deviates from accepted standards in beliefs or behaviour.

**deviate** (**dee**-vi-ayt) *verb* turn aside or diverge from a course of action, a rule, truth, etc. □ **deviation** *noun*, **deviator** *noun*

**device** *noun* **1** a thing that is made or used for a particular purpose; *a device for opening tins*. **2** a plan or scheme for achieving something. **3** a design used as a decoration or emblem. □ **left to one's own devices** left to do as one wishes without interference or help.

**devil** *noun* **1** (**the Devil**) (in Jewish and Christian teaching) the supreme spirit of evil and enemy of God. **2** an evil spirit. **3** a wicked or annoying person. **4** a mischievously clever person. **5** (*informal*) something difficult or hard to manage. **6** (*informal*) a person; *poor devil*; *lucky devil*. **7** (*informal*) used in exclamations of surprise or annoyance; *where the devil is it?* **8** a person who devils for an author etc.; a junior legal counsel. ●*verb* (**devilled**, **devilling**; *Amer.* **deviled**, **deviling**) **1** cook (food) with hot seasoning; *devilled kidneys*. **2** do research or other work for an author or barrister. □ **devil-may-care** *adjective* cheerful and reckless. **devil's advocate** one who tests a theory by putting forward possible objections to it. **like the devil** with great energy, intensely. **play the devil with** cause severe damage to. **the devil to pay** trouble to be expected.

**devilish** *adjective* **1** of or like a devil. **2** mischievous. ●*adverb* (*informal*) very.

**devilment** *noun* mischief.

**devilry** *noun* **1** wickedness. **2** devilment.

**Devil's Island** an island off the coast of French Guiana, formerly used as a leper colony, then (1895–1938) as a French penal colony.

**devious** (**dee**-vi-ŭs) *adjective* **1** winding, roundabout. **2** not straightforward, underhand. □ **deviously** *adverb*, **deviousness** *noun*

**devise** (di-**vyz**) *verb* **1** think out, plan, invent. **2** *Law* leave (real estate) by will.

**devoid** (di-**void**) *adjective* (foll. by *of*) lacking or free from something; *devoid of merit*.

**devolution** (dee-vŏ-**loo**-shŏn) *noun* **1** the delegation or transference of work or power from a central administration to a local or regional one. **2** the handing down of property etc. to an heir. □ **devolutionist** *adjective & noun*

**devolve** *verb* pass or be passed on to a deputy or successor; *this work will devolve on the new manager.*

**Devon, Devonshire** a county of SW England.

■ **Usage** *Devon* is the official name.

**Devonian** (di-**voh**-ni-ăn) *Geol. adjective* of the fourth period of the Palaeozoic era. ● *noun* this period.

**devote** *verb* give or use for a particular activity or purpose; *devoted himself to sport.*

**devoted** *adjective* showing devotion, very loyal or loving. □ **devotedly** *adverb*

**devotee** (dev-ŏ-**tee**) *noun* a person who is devoted to something, an enthusiast; *devotees of sport.*

**devotion** *noun* **1** great love or loyalty; enthusiastic zeal. **2** religious worship. **3** (**devotions**) prayers.

**devotional** *adjective* used in religious worship.

**devour** *verb* **1** eat hungrily or greedily. **2** destroy completely, consume; *fire devoured the forest.* **3** take in greedily with the eyes or ears; *they devoured the story.* **4** absorb the attention of; *she was devoured by curiosity.*

**devout** *adjective* **1** earnestly religious. **2** earnest, sincere; *a devout supporter.* □ **devoutly** *adverb*, **devoutness** *noun*

**dew** *noun* **1** small drops of moisture that condense on cool surfaces during the night from water vapour in the air. **2** moisture in small drops on a surface.

**dewberry** *noun* a bluish fruit resembling a blackberry.

**dewclaw** *noun* a small claw on the inner side of a dog's leg, not reaching the ground in walking.

**dewdrop** *noun* a drop of dew.

**Dewey system** a decimal system for classifying books in libraries. (¶ Named after Melville Dewey (1851–1931), the American librarian who devised it.)

**dewlap** *noun* a fold of loose skin that hangs from the throat of cattle and other animals.

**dewy** *adjective* wet with dew. □ **dewy-eyed** *adjective* innocently trusting or sentimental.

**dexter** *adjective* (in heraldry) of or on the right-hand side (the observer's left) of a shield etc.

**dexterity** (deks-**te**-riti) *noun* skill in handling things.

**dexterous** (deks-trŭs) *adjective* (also **dextrous**) showing dexterity. □ **dexterously** *adverb*

**dextrin** *noun* a sticky substance used as a thickening agent, adhesive, etc.

**dextrose** *noun* a form of glucose.

**DFC** *abbreviation* Distinguished Flying Cross.

**DFM** *abbreviation* Distinguished Flying Medal.

**Dhaka** (**dak**-ă) the capital of Bangladesh.

**dhal** (*pronounced* dahl) *noun* (also **dal**) **1** a small pea-like pulse, used in Indian cooking. **2** a dish made with this.

**dharma** (**dar**-mă) *noun* **1** the Hindu moral law; correct behaviour. **2** the Buddhist truth.

**dhoti** (**doh**-ti) *noun* (*plural* **dhotis**) a loincloth worn by male Hindus.

**di-** *combining form* two; double.

**diabetes** (dy-ă-**bee**-teez) *noun* a disease in which sugar and starch are not properly absorbed by the body.

**diabetic** (dy-ă-**bet**-ik) *adjective* of diabetes. ● *noun* a person suffering from diabetes.

**diabolical** (dy-ă-**bol**-ikăl) *adjective* (also **diabolic**) **1** like a devil, very cruel or wicked. **2** fiendishly clever, cunning, or annoying. □ **diabolically** *adverb*

**diabolism** (dy-**ab**-ŏl-izm) *noun* **1** worship of the Devil. **2** sorcery.

**diachronic** (dy-ă-**kron**-ik) *adjective* of or studying the historical development of a subject.

**diaconal** (dy-**ak**-ŏn-ăl) *adjective* of a deacon.

**diaconate** (dy-**ak**-ŏn-ăt) *noun* **1** the office of a deacon. **2** the body of deacons.

**diacritic** (dy-ă-**kri**-tik) *noun* a sign (e.g. an accent or cedilla) indicating different sounds or values of a letter.

**diacritical** *adjective* distinguishing, distinctive. □ **diacritical mark** *or* **sign** = DIA-CRITIC.

**diadem** (**dy**-a-dem) *noun* a crown or headband worn as a sign of sovereignty.

**diaeresis** (dy-**eer**-i-sis) *noun* (*plural* **diaereses**) (*Amer.* **dieresis**) a mark placed over a vowel to show that it is sounded separately, as in *naïve.*

**Diaghilev** (di-**ag**-i-lef), Serge Pavlovich (1872–1929), Russian ballet impresario, who introduced Russian ballet to western Europe.

**diagnose** (dy-ăg-nohz) *verb* make a diagnosis of; *the doctor diagnosed measles.*

**diagnosis** (dy-ăg-**noh**-sis) *noun* (*plural* **diagnoses**) a statement of the nature of a disease or other condition made after observing its signs and symptoms.

**diagnostic** (dy-ăg-**noss**-tik) *adjective* of or used in diagnosis; *diagnostic procedures.* □ **diagnostically** *adverb*

**diagonal** (dy-**ag**-ŏn-ăl) *adjective* slanting, crossing from corner to corner. ● *noun* a straight line joining two opposite corners. □ **diagonally** *adverb*

**diagram** *noun* an outline drawing or plan that shows the parts of something or how it works.

**diagrammatic** (dy-ă-gră-**mat**-ik) *adjective* in the form of a diagram. □ **diagrammatically** *adverb*

**dial** *noun* **1** the face of a clock or watch. **2** a marked scale indicating measurements, selections, etc. by means of a pointer. **3** a selection disc, control knob, etc. on a piece of equipment. **4** a movable numbered disc on a telephone used for selecting the correct number. ●*verb* (**dialled, dialling**; *Amer.* **dialed, dialing**) **1** select or regulate by means of a dial. **2** make a telephone connection by using a dial or numbered buttons. □ **dialling tone** a sound heard on a telephone indicating that a caller may dial.

**dialect** (**dy-ă-lekt**) *noun* the words and pronunciation that are used in a particular area and differ from what is regarded as standard language. □ **dialectal** *adjective*

**dialectic** (dy-ă-**lek**-tik) *noun* investigation of truths in philosophy etc. by systematic reasoning.

**dialectical** (dy-ă-**lek**-tik-ăl) *adjective* of dialectic. □ **dialectical materialism** the theory, put forward by Marx and Engels, that political and social conditions result from a conflict of social forces (the 'class struggle') produced by economic factors. □ **dialectically** *adverb*

**dialogue** (**dy**-ă-log) *noun* (*Amer.* **dialog**) **1** a conversation or discussion. **2** the words spoken by characters in a play or story.

**dialysis** (dy-**al**-i-sis) *noun* purification of the blood by causing it to flow through a suitable membrane.

**diamanté** (dee-ă-**mahn**-tay) *adjective* decorated with fragments of crystal or other sparkling substance. (¶ French.)

**diameter** (dy-**am**-it-er) *noun* **1** a straight line passing from side to side through the centre of a circle or sphere. **2** the length of this.

**diametrical** (dy-ă-**met**-rik-ăl) *adjective* (also **diametric**) **1** of or along a diameter. **2** (of opposites) complete; absolutely opposed. □ **diametrically** *adverb*

**diamond** *noun* **1** a very hard brilliant precious stone of pure crystallized carbon. **2** a figure with four equal sides and with angles that are not right angles. **3** something shaped like this. **4** a playing card of the suit (**diamonds**) marked with red figures of this shape. ●*adjective* made of or set with diamonds. □ **diamond wedding** the 60th (or 75th) anniversary of a wedding.

**Diana**[1] (*Rom. myth.*) an early Italian goddess identified with Artemis.

**Diana**[2], Princess (originally Lady Diana Frances Spencer), Princess of Wales (born 1961).

**dianthus** *noun* a flowering plant of a kind that includes the carnation.

**diapason** (dy-ă-**pay**-zŏn) *noun* **1** the entire range of a musical instrument or a voice.

**2** a fixed standard of musical pitch. **3** either of the two main organ stops extending through the whole range.

**diaper** (**dy**-ă-per) *noun* (*Amer.*) a baby's nappy.

**diaphanous** (dy-**af**-ăn-ŭs) *adjective* (of fabric) light, delicate, and almost transparent.

**diaphragm** (**dy**-ă-fram) *noun* **1** the midriff, the internal muscular partition that separates the chest from the abdomen and is used in breathing. **2** a vibrating disc in a microphone or telephone receiver etc. **3** a device for varying the aperture of a camera lens. **4** a thin contraceptive cap fitting over the neck of the womb.

**diapositive** *noun* a positive photographic slide or transparency.

**diarist** (**dy**-er-ist) *noun* one who keeps a diary.

**diarrhoea** (dy-ă-**ree**-ă) *noun* (especially *Amer.* **diarrhea**) a condition in which bowel movements are excessively frequent and fluid.

**diary** *noun* **1** a daily record of events or thoughts. **2** a book for this or for noting engagements.

**Diaspora** (dy-**ass**-per-ă) *noun* **1** the Dispersion of the Jews after their exile in 538 BC. **2** the Jews dispersed in this.

**diastase** (**dy**-ă-stayz) *noun* the enzyme (important in digestion) that converts starch into sugar.

**diastole** (dy-**ass**-tŏli) *noun* the rhythmical dilatation of the chambers of the heart, alternating with systole to form the pulse. □ **diastolic** (dy-ă-**stol**-ik) *adjective*

**diatom** (**dy**-ă-tŏm) *noun* a microscopic alga found as plankton and forming fossil deposits.

**diatomic** (dy-ă-**tom**-ik) *adjective* consisting of two atoms.

**diatonic** (dy-ă-**tonn**-ik) *adjective* (in music) using the notes of the major or minor scale only, not of the chromatic scale.

**diatribe** (**dy**-ă-tryb) *noun* a violent attack in words, abusive criticism.

**dibble** *noun* (also **dibber**) a hand tool used to make holes in the ground for seeds or young plants. ●*verb* plant with a dibble.

**dice** *noun* **1** (properly the plural of DIE[2], but often used as a singular, *plural* **dice**) a small cube marked on each side with a number of spots (usually 1–6), used in games of chance. **2** a game played with these. ●*verb* **1** take great risks; *dicing with death*. **2** cut into small cubes; *diced carrots*.

**dicey** *adjective* (**dicier, diciest**) (*slang*) risky, unreliable.

**dichotomy** (dy-**kot**-ŏmi) *noun* division into two parts or kinds.

**dichromatic** (dy-krŏ-**mat**-ik) *adjective* **1** two-coloured. **2** having vision that is sensitive to only two of the three primary colours.

**dick** noun **1** (*informal*) (in certain set phrases) person; *clever dick*. **2** (*vulgar slang*) the penis. **3** (*slang*) a detective.

**Dickens**, Charles Huffham (1812–70), English novelist.

**dickens** noun (*informal*) (in exclamations of surprise or annoyance) deuce, the Devil; *where the dickens is it?*

**Dickensian** (dik-en-siăn) *adjective* of Charles Dickens, his works, or the conditions portrayed in them, especially poverty and social injustice.

**dicky** noun (*informal*) a false shirt-front. ● *adjective* (*slang*) unsound, likely to collapse or fail; *a dicky heart*. □ **dicky bow** a bow-tie.

**dicotyledon** (dy-kot-i-lee-dŏn) noun a flowering plant that has two cotyledons. □ **dicotyledonous** *adjective*

**dicta** *see* DICTUM.

**Dictaphone** noun (*trade mark*) a machine that records and plays back dictation.

**dictate** *verb* **1** say or read aloud (words) to be written down by a person or recorded by a machine. **2** state or order with the force of authority; *dictate terms to a defeated enemy*. **3** give orders officiously; *I will not be dictated to*. ● *plural noun* (**dictates**) authoritative commands; *the dictates of conscience*. □ **dictation** noun

**dictator** noun **1** a ruler who has unrestricted authority, especially one who has taken control by force. **2** a person with supreme authority in any sphere. **3** a domineering person. □ **dictatorship** noun

**dictatorial** (dik-tă-tor-iăl) *adjective* **1** of or like a dictator. **2** domineering. □ **dictatorially** *adverb*

**diction** (dik-shŏn) noun a person's manner of uttering or pronouncing words.

**dictionary** noun a book that lists and explains the words of a language or a particular subject, or that gives their equivalents in another language, usually in alphabetical order.

**dictum** noun (*plural* **dicta** *or* **dictums**) **1** a formal expression of opinion. **2** a saying.

**did** *see* DO.

**didactic** (dy-dak-tik) *adjective* **1** giving instruction. **2** having the manner of one who is lecturing pupils. □ **didactically** *adverb*, **didacticism** noun

**diddle** *verb* (*slang*) cheat, swindle.

**Diderot** (dee-der-oh), Denis (1713–84), French philosopher.

**didgeridoo** noun a long tubular Australian Aboriginal musical instrument.

**didn't** (*informal*) = did not.

**Dido** (dy-doh) (*Rom. legend*) queen of Carthage, who fell in love with the shipwrecked Aeneas and killed herself when he deserted her.

**die**[1] *verb* (**died**, **dying**) **1** cease to be alive; have one's vital functions cease finally. **2** cease to exist. **3** cease to function; stop; *the engine sputtered and died*. **4** (of a fire or flame) go out. **5** become exhausted; *we were dying with laughter*. **6** (*informal*) feel an intense longing; *we are dying to go*; *dying for a drink*. □ **die away** become fainter or weaker and then cease; *the noise died away*. **die back** (of plants) decay from the tip towards the root. **die down** become less loud or less violent; *the excitement died down*. **die off** die one by one. **die out** pass out of existence; *the custom has died out*; *the family has died out*. **never say die** keep up courage, do not give in.

**die**[2] noun **1** a dice (*see* DICE). **2** an engraved device that stamps a design on coins or medals etc.; a device that stamps or cuts or moulds material into a particular shape. □ **as straight as a die 1** quite straight. **2** very honest. **die-cast** *adjective* made by casting metal in a mould. **die-casting** noun this process. **the die is cast** a step has been taken and its consequences must follow.

**diehard** noun a person who obstinately refuses to abandon old theories or policies, one who resists change.

**dielectric** *adjective* that does not conduct electricity. ● noun a dielectric substance usable for insulating things.

**dieresis** Amer. spelling of DIAERESIS.

**diesel** (dee-zĕl) noun **1** a diesel engine; a vehicle driven by this. (¶ Named after the German engineer Rudolf Diesel, died 1913.) **2** fuel for a diesel engine. □ **diesel-electric** *adjective* driven by electric current from a generator driven by a diesel engine.

**diesel engine** an oil-burning engine in which ignition is produced by the heat of highly compressed air.

**diet**[1] noun **1** the foods usually eaten by a person, animal, or community. **2** a selection of food to which a person is restricted. ● *verb* (**dieted**, **dieting**) **1** restrict oneself to a special diet, especially in order to control one's weight. **2** restrict (a person) to a special diet. □ **dieter** noun

**diet**[2] noun a congress; a parliamentary assembly in certain countries, e.g. Japan.

**dietary** (dy-it-er-i) *adjective* of or involving diet; *special dietary requirements*.

**dietetic** (dy-i-tet-ik) *adjective* of diet and nutrition. ● *plural noun* (**dietetics**) the study of diet and nutrition.

**dietitian** (dy-i-tish-ăn) noun an expert in dietetics.

**Dietrich** (dee-trik), Marlene (original name: Maria Magdalene von Losch)

(1901–90), German-born American film actress.

**differ** verb **1** be unlike, be distinguishable from something else. **2** disagree in opinion.

**difference** noun **1** the state of being different or unlike. **2** the point in which things differ; the amount or degree of unlikeness. **3** the quantity by which amounts differ; the remainder left after subtraction; *the difference between 8 and 5 is 3*. **4** a disagreement in opinion, a quarrel. □ **make all the difference** have a significant effect.

**different** adjective **1** unlike, of other nature or form or quality; *different from others*.

---

■**Usage** *Different from* is the preferred phrase; *different to* is acceptable when it feels natural in a particular context, e.g. when *similar to* occurs near by; *different than* is common in American use.

---

**2** separate, distinct; *several different people*. **3** unusual. □ **differently** adverb

**differential** (dif-er-**en**-shăl) adjective **1** of, showing, or depending on a difference. **2** (in mathematics) relating to infinitesimal differences. ●noun **1** an agreed difference in wages between industries or between different classes of workers in the same industry. **2** a differential gear. □ **differential calculus** a method of calculating rates of change, maximum or minimum values, etc. **differential gear** an arrangement of gears that allows a motor vehicle's driven wheels to revolve at different speeds in rounding corners.

**differentiate** (dif-er-**en**-shi-ayt) verb **1** be a difference between, make different; *the features that differentiate one breed from another*. **2** recognize as different, distinguish; discriminate; *the pension scheme does not differentiate between male and female employees*. **3** develop differences, become different. **4** (in mathematics) calculate the derivative of. □ **differentiation** noun

**difficult** adjective **1** needing much effort or skill, not easy. **2** troublesome, perplexing; *these are difficult times*. **3** not easy to please or satisfy; *a difficult employer*.

**difficulty** noun **1** being difficult. **2** a difficult problem or thing. **3** a difficult state of affairs, trouble; *in financial difficulties*.

**diffident** (**dif**-i-děnt) adjective lacking self-confidence, hesitating to put oneself or one's ideas forward. □ **diffidently** adverb, **diffidence** noun

**diffract** verb **1** break up (a beam of light) into a series of dark and light bands or the coloured bands of the spectrum. **2** break up (a beam of radiation or particles) into a series of high and low intensities. □ **diffraction** noun, **diffractive** adjective

**diffuse** adjective (*pronounced* di-**fewss**) **1** spread out, diffused, not concentrated; *diffuse light*. **2** wordy, not concise; *a diffuse style*. ●verb (*pronounced* dif-**fewz**) **1** spread (light, heat, knowledge, etc.) widely or thinly throughout something. **2** mix (liquids or gases) slowly, become intermingled. □ **diffused lighting** lighting that is spread or filtered so that there is no glare. □ **diffusely** adverb, **diffusible** adjective, **diffusive** adjective

**diffusion** noun **1** diffusing or being diffused. **2** *Physics* the natural random movement and mingling of atoms and particles through a substance.

**dig** verb (**dug**, **digging**) **1** break up and move (ground) with a tool, claws, etc.; make (a way or a hole) by doing this. **2** remove by digging; *dig potatoes*. **3** excavate archaeologically. **4** (often foll. by *up* or *out*) seek or discover by investigation; *dug up some useful information*. **5** thrust, plunge; prod; *dig a knife into it*; *dug him in the ribs*. **6** (*slang*) appreciate, enjoy, understand. ●noun **1** a piece of digging. **2** an archaeological excavation. **3** a thrust, a poke; *a dig in the ribs*. **4** a cutting remark; *that was a dig at me*. **5** (**digs**) (*informal*) lodgings. □ **dig in** (*informal*) begin eating or working energetically. **dig one's heels in** become obstinate, refuse to give way.

**digest** verb (*pronounced* dy-**jest**) **1** dissolve (food) in the stomach etc. so that it can be absorbed by the body. **2** think over, absorb into the mind; *digesting the information*. **3** summarize methodically. ●noun (*pronounced* **dy**-jest) **1** a methodical summary. **2** a periodical publication giving excerpts and summaries of news, writings, etc.

**digestible** adjective able to be digested. □ **digestibility** noun

**digestion** noun **1** the process of digesting. **2** the power of digesting food; *has a good digestion*.

**digestive** adjective **1** of or aiding digestion. **2** having the function of digesting food; *the digestive system*. ●noun **1** (in full **digestive biscuit**) a wholemeal biscuit. **2** a drink or substance that aids digestion.

**digger** noun **1** one who digs. **2** a mechanical excavator. **3** (*informal*) an Australian or New Zealander.

**digit** (**dij**-it) noun **1** any numeral from 0 to 9. **2** a finger or toe.

**digital** (**dij**-it-ăl) adjective **1** of digits. **2** (of a clock, watch, etc.) showing the time by displaying a row of figures. **3** (of a computer) operating on data represented as a series of digits. **4** (of a recording) converting sound into electrical pulses (representing binary digits). □ **digital au-**

**dio tape** magnetic tape used for digital recording. **digital signal compression** a method of reformulating the information contained in a digital signal so that it can be transmitted more quickly. □ **digitally** adverb

**digitalis** (dij-i-tay-lis) noun a drug prepared from dried foxglove leaves, used as a heart stimulant.

**digitize** verb (also **digitise**) convert data into digital form, especially for a computer. □ **digitization** noun

**dignified** adjective having or showing dignity.

**dignify** verb (**dignified**, **dignifying**) 1 give dignity to. 2 make (a thing) sound more important than it is; they dignified the school with the name of 'college'.

**dignitary** (dig-ni-ter-i) noun a person holding a high rank or position.

**dignity** noun 1 a calm and serious manner or style. 2 worthiness; the dignity of labour. 3 a high rank or position. □ **beneath one's dignity** not worthy enough for one to do. **stand on one's dignity** insist on being treated respectfully.

**digraph** (dy-grahf) noun two letters representing one sound (as ph in phone, ea in bean).

**digress** (dy-gress) verb depart from the main subject temporarily in speaking or writing. □ **digression** noun

**dike** alternative spelling of DYKE.

**diktat** noun a firm statement or decree.

**dilapidated** adjective falling to pieces, in a state of disrepair.

**dilapidation** noun a state of disrepair; bringing or being brought into this state.

**dilatation** (dy-lă-tay-shŏn) noun 1 dilation. 2 widening of the neck of the womb, e.g. for surgical curettage.

**dilate** (dy-layt) verb 1 make or become wider or larger. 2 speak or write at length; dilating upon this subject. □ **dilation** noun

**dilatory** (dil-ă-ter-i) adjective 1 slow in doing something. 2 designed to cause delay. □ **dilatorily** adverb, **dilatoriness** noun

**dildo** (dil-doh) noun (plural **dildos**) an artificial erect penis used for sexual stimulation.

**dilemma** (dil-em-ă) noun 1 a perplexing situation, in which a choice has to be made between alternatives that are equally undesirable. 2 a problem or difficult choice; what to do with one's spare time is a modern dilemma.

■**Usage** Many people regard the use in sense 2 as unacceptable.

**dilettante** (dili-tan-ti) noun (plural **dilettantes** or **dilettanti**) a person who dabbles in a subject for enjoyment and without serious study. □ **dilettantism** noun

**diligent** (dil-i-jĕnt) adjective 1 hard-working, putting care and effort into what one does. 2 done with care and effort; a diligent search. □ **diligently** adverb, **diligence** noun

**dill** noun a herb with feathery leaves and spicy seeds used for flavouring.

**dilly-dally** verb (informal) 1 dawdle. 2 waste time by not making up one's mind.

**dilute** (dy-lewt) verb 1 thin down, make (a liquid) less concentrated by adding water or other liquid. 2 weaken or reduce the forcefulness of. ●adjective diluted; a dilute acid. □ **dilution** noun

**diluvial** (dy-loo-vi-ăl) adjective of a flood, especially the Flood in Genesis.

**dim** adjective (**dimmer**, **dimmest**) 1 faintly lit, luminous but not bright. 2 indistinct, not clearly seen, heard, or remembered. 3 not seeing clearly; eyes dim with tears. 4 (informal) stupid. ●verb (**dimmed**, **dimming**) make or become dim. □ **take a dim view of** (informal) disapprove of. □ **dimly** adverb, **dimness** noun

**dime** noun a ten-cent coin of the USA.

**dimension** (dy-men-shŏn) noun 1 a measurable extent such as length, breadth, thickness, area, or volume. 2 size. 3 extent, scope; aspect; gave the problem a new dimension. □ **dimensional** adjective

**diminish** verb make or become smaller or less.

**diminuendo** (dim-in-yoo-en-doh) adjective & adverb (in music) gradually becoming quieter. ●noun (plural **diminuendos**) a gradual decrease in loudness.

**diminution** (dim-in-yoo-shŏn) noun 1 diminishing; being diminished. 2 a decrease.

**diminutive** (dim-in-yoo-tiv) adjective remarkably small. ●noun a word for a small specimen of something (e.g. booklet, duckling), or an affectionate form of a name etc. (e.g. Johnnie).

**dimity** noun a cotton fabric woven with checks or stripes of heavier thread.

**dimmer** noun a device for varying the brightness of electric lights.

**dimple** noun a small hollow or dent, especially a natural one on the skin of the cheek or chin. ●verb 1 produce dimples in. 2 show dimples.

**dimwit** noun (informal) a stupid person. □ **dim-witted** adjective

**DIN** noun any of a series of German technical standards for electrical connections, film speeds, and paper sizes.

**din** noun a loud, resonant, and annoying noise. ●verb (**dinned**, **dinning**) 1 make a din. 2 force (information) into a person by continually repeating it; din it into him.

**dinar** (dee-nar) noun a unit of currency in the former Yugoslavia and in various countries of the Middle East and North Africa.

**dine** *verb* **1** eat dinner. **2** entertain to dinner; *we were wined and dined.* □ **dining car** a railway carriage in which meals are served. **dining room** a room in which meals are eaten.

**diner** *noun* **1** a person who dines. **2** a dining car on a train. **3** a small dining room.

**dinette** (dy-**net**) *noun* a small room or part of a room used for meals.

**ding** *verb* make a ringing sound. ● *noun* a ringing sound.

**dingbat** *noun* (*Amer. & Austral. slang*) a stupid or eccentric person.

**ding-dong** *noun* the sound of a clapper bell or alternate strokes of two bells. ● *adjective & adverb* with vigorous and alternating action; *a ding-dong argument.*

**dinghy** (**ding**-i) *noun* (*plural* **dinghies**) **1** a small open boat driven by oars or sails. **2** a small inflatable rubber boat.

**dingle** *noun* a deep wooded valley or hollow.

**dingo** *noun* (*plural* **dingoes**) a wild Australian dog.

**dingy** (**din**-ji) *adjective* (**dingier, dingiest**) dirty-looking, not fresh or cheerful. □ **dingily** *adverb*, **dinginess** *noun*

**dinkum** *adjective* (*Austral. & NZ informal*) true, real. □ **dinkum oil** the truth.

**dinky** *adjective* (*informal*) attractively small and neat.

**dinner** *noun* **1** the chief meal of the day, either at midday or in the evening. **2** a formal evening meal. □ **dinner jacket** a man's short (usually black) jacket for evening wear. **dinner lady** (*Brit.*) a woman who supervises school dinners. **dinner service** a set of matching crockery for dinner.

**dinosaur** (**dy**-nŏ-sor) *noun* an extinct reptile of the Mesozoic era, often of enormous size.

**dint** *noun* a dent. ● *verb* mark with dints. □ **by dint of** by means of.

**diocese** (**dy**-ŏ-sis) *noun* a district under the pastoral care of a bishop. □ **diocesan** (dy-**oss**-i-săn) *adjective*

**Diocletian** (dy-ŏ-**klee**-shăn) (died 316), Roman emperor 284–305, noted for his persecution of the Christians.

**diode** (**dy**-ohd) *noun* **1** a simple thermionic valve with only two electrodes. **2** a rectifier made of semiconducting materials and having two terminals.

**Diogenes** (dy-**oj**-in-eez) (4th c. BC), Cynic philosopher, noted for his ostentatious disregard of conventions.

**Dionysian** (dy-ŏ-**niz**-iăn) *adjective* wildly sensual; unrestrained.

**Dionysus** (dy-ŏ-**ny**-sŭs) (*Gk. myth.*) the god of wine and fertility, also known as Bacchus.

**dioptre** (dy-**op**-ter) *noun* (*Amer.* **diopter**) a unit of refractive power of a lens.

**Dior** (**dee**-or), Christian (1905–57), French fashion designer.

**diorama** (dy-ŏ-**rah**-mă) *noun* **1** a small model of a scene etc. with three-dimensional figures, viewed through a window. **2** any small-scale model (e.g. of a building project); a miniature film-set. **3** a scenic painting in which changing lighting simulates sunrise etc.

**dioxide** (dy-**ok**-syd) *noun* an oxide with two atoms of oxygen to one of a metal or other element.

**dip** *verb* (**dipped, dipping**) **1** put or lower into liquid. **2** go under water and emerge quickly. **3** go down; *the sun dipped below the horizon.* **4** put a hand or ladle etc. into something in order to take something out. **5** lower; *dip the flag; dip headlights.* **6** slope or extend downwards; *the path dips down to the river.* **7** (foll. by *into*) read short passages here and there in a book; *I've dipped into 'War and Peace'.* **8** (foll. by *into*) use part of (one's savings, resources, etc.). **9** wash (sheep) in disinfectant. ● *noun* **1** dipping; being dipped. **2** a quick plunge; (*informal*) a short bathe. **3** a downward slope. **4** a liquid into which something is dipped; *sheep-dip.* **5** a creamy mixture in which food is dipped. □ **dip switch** a switch for dipping a vehicle's headlights.

**Dip. Ed.** *abbreviation* Diploma in Education.

**diphtheria** (dif-**theer**-iă or dip-**theer**-iă) *noun* an acute infectious disease causing severe inflammation of a mucous membrane, especially in the throat.

**diphthong** (**dif**-thong) *noun* a compound vowel sound produced by combining two simple ones, e.g. *oi* in *point, ou* in *loud.*

**diplodocus** (di-**plod**-ŏ-kŭs) *noun* a giant plant-eating dinosaur.

**diploma** *noun* a certificate awarded by a college etc. to a person who has successfully completed a course of study.

**diplomacy** (dip-**loh**-mă-si) *noun* **1** the handling of international relations; skill in this. **2** tact.

**diplomat** (**dip**-lŏ-mat) *noun* **1** a member of the diplomatic service. **2** a tactful person.

**diplomatic** (diplŏ-**mat**-ik) *adjective* **1** of or engaged in diplomacy. **2** tactful; *a diplomatic reply.* □ **diplomatic bag** a container for sending official documents to and from an embassy, usually exempt from customs inspection. **diplomatic immunity** the exemption of diplomatic staff abroad from arrest, taxation, etc. **diplomatic service**

officials who represent their country abroad. □ **diplomatically** adverb

**diplomatist** (di-**ploh**-mă-tist) noun a diplomat.

**dipole** noun **1** two equal and oppositely charged or magnetized poles separated by a distance. **2** a molecule in which a concentration of positive charges is separated from a concentration of negative charges. **3** an aerial consisting of a horizontal rod with a connecting wire at its core.

**dipper** noun **1** a diving bird, especially the water ouzel. **2** a ladle.

**dipsomania** (dip-sŏ-**may**-niă) noun an uncontrollable craving for alcohol. □ **dipsomaniac** noun

**dipstick** noun a rod for measuring the depth of oil in a vehicle's engine.

**dipterous** (**dip**-ter-ŭs) adjective **1** (of insects) having two wings. **2** (of seeds) having two wing-like parts.

**diptych** (**dip**-tik) noun a painting, especially an altarpiece, on two surfaces that fold like a book.

**Dirac** (di-**rak**), Paul Adrian Maurice (1902–84), English physicist.

**dire** adjective **1** dreadful, terrible; in dire peril. **2** ominous, predicting trouble; dire warnings. **3** extreme and urgent; in dire need.

**direct** adjective **1** going in a straight line; not curved or roundabout; the direct route. **2** with nothing or no one in between; in an unbroken line; in direct contact. **3** straightforward, frank, going straight to the point; a direct way of speaking. **4** exact, complete; the direct opposite. ● adverb by a direct route; travelled to Rome direct. ● verb **1** tell or show how to do something or get somewhere; can you direct me to the station? **2** address (a letter or parcel etc.). **3** cause to have a specified direction or target. **4** control, manage; there was no one to direct the workmen. **5** command, order; directed his men to advance. **6** supervise the acting, filming, etc. of (a film, play, etc.). □ **direct access** the direct and immediate retrieval of data from any part of a computer file. **direct current** electric current flowing in one direction only. **direct debit** a system of regularly debiting a person's bank account at the request of the creditor. **direct object** Grammar the primary object of the action of a transitive verb; the person or thing that is directly affected. **direct speech** words actually spoken, not as they are reported. **direct tax** tax paid directly to the government (e.g. on income) as opposed to tax on goods and services. □ **directness** noun

**direction** noun **1** directing, aiming, guiding, managing. **2** the line along which something moves or faces; in the direction of London. **3** (**directions**) instructions. □ **sense of direction** the ability to get one's bearings without guidance.

**directional** adjective **1** of or indicating direction. **2** operating or sending radio signals in one direction only.

**directive** noun a general instruction issued by authority.

**directly** adverb **1** in a direct line, in a direct manner. **2** without delay. **3** very soon. ● conjunction (informal) as soon as; I went directly I knew.

**director** noun **1** a person who supervises or manages things, especially a member of the board managing a business company on behalf of shareholders. **2** a person who directs a film or play. □ **director-general** noun the chief executive of a large organization. □ **directorial** adjective, **directorship** noun

**directorate** noun **1** the position of director. **2** a board of directors.

**directory** noun a book containing a list of telephone subscribers, inhabitants of a district, members of a profession, business firms, etc. □ **directory enquiries** a telephone service providing a subscriber's number on request.

**dirge** (pronounced derj) noun a slow mournful song; a lament for the dead.

**dirham** (**deer**-am) noun the main unit of money in Morocco and the United Arab Emirates.

**dirigible** (**di**-rij-ibŭl) adjective capable of being guided. ● noun a dirigible balloon or airship.

**dirk** noun a short dagger.

**dirndl** (**dern**-d'l) noun a full skirt gathered into a tight waistband.

**dirt** noun **1** unclean matter that soils something. **2** earth, soil. **3** anything worthless or not deserving respect. **4** foul words or talk, scandal. **5** excrement. □ **dirt cheap** (informal) very cheap. **dirt track** a racing track made of earth or rolled cinders etc.

**dirty** adjective (**dirtier, dirtiest**) **1** soiled, unclean; (of a job etc.) causing the doer to become dirty. **2** not having clean habits. **3** dishonourable, mean, unfair; a dirty trick; a dirty fighter. **4** (of weather) rough and stormy. **5** lewd, obscene; dirty jokes. ● verb (**dirtied, dirtying**) make or become dirty. □ **dirty look** a disapproving look. **dirty weekend** (informal) a weekend spent with a lover. **dirty word 1** an obscene word. **2** a word denoting something that is regarded as discreditable; charity became a dirty word. **dirty work** dishonourable dealings. **do the dirty on** play a mean trick on. □ **dirtily** adverb, **dirtiness** noun

**disability** noun something that disables or disqualifies a person, a physical incapacity caused by injury or disease etc.

**disable** verb deprive of some ability, make unfit or useless. □ **disablement** noun

**disabled** adjective having a physical disability.

**disabuse** (dis-ă-bewz) verb (usually foll. by of) disillusion, free from a false idea; he was soon disabused of this notion.

**disadvantage** noun **1** an unfavourable condition or circumstance; at a disadvantage. **2** damage to one's interest or reputation; to our disadvantage. ●verb put at a disadvantage.

**disadvantaged** adjective suffering from unfavourable conditions of life.

**disadvantageous** (dis-ad-văn-tay-jŭs) adjective causing disadvantage.

**disaffected** adjective discontented, having lost one's feelings of loyalty. □ **disaffection** noun

**disagree** verb (**disagreed**, **disagreeing**) **1** have a different opinion. **2** be unlike, fail to correspond. **3** quarrel. □ **disagree with 1** differ in opinion from. **2** (of food or climate) have bad effects on.

**disagreeable** adjective **1** unpleasant. **2** bad-tempered. □ **disagreeably** adverb

**disagreement** noun **1** disagreeing. **2** a quarrel; a dispute.

**disallow** verb refuse to allow or accept as valid; the judge disallowed the claim.

**disappear** verb cease to be visible, pass from sight or from existence. □ **disappearance** noun

**disappoint** verb fail to do or be equal to what was hoped, desired, or expected. □ **disappointed** adjective, **disappointing** adjective

**disappointment** noun **1** a person or thing that disappoints. **2** being disappointed.

**disapprobation** (dis-ap-rŏ-bay-shŏn) noun (formal) disapproval.

**disapprove** verb have or express an unfavourable opinion. □ **disapproval** noun

**disarm** verb **1** deprive of weapons or of the means of defence. **2** disband or reduce armed forces. **3** defuse (a bomb). **4** make less angry, hostile, etc.; charm, win over.

**disarmament** noun reduction of a country's armed forces or weapons of war.

**disarrange** verb put into disorder, disorganize. □ **disarrangement** noun

**disarray** noun disorder. ●verb disarrange.

**disassociate** = DISSOCIATE.

**disaster** noun **1** a sudden great misfortune. **2** a complete failure; the performance was a disaster. □ **disaster area** an area in which a major disaster (e.g. an earthquake) has recently occurred. □ **disastrous** (diz-ah-strŭs) adjective, **disastrously** adverb

**disavow** verb disclaim. □ **disavowal** noun

**disband** verb break up, separate; disbanded the choir; the troops disbanded. □ **disbandment** noun

**disbar** verb (**disbarred**, **disbarring**) deprive (a barrister) of the right to practise law. □ **disbarment** noun

**disbelieve** verb refuse or be unable to believe. □ **disbelief** noun

**disburse** verb pay out (money). □ **disbursal** noun, **disbursement** noun

**disc** noun (also especially Amer. **disk**) **1** a thin circular plate of any material. **2** something shaped or looking like this; the sun's disc. **3** a layer of cartilage between vertebrae. **4** a gramophone record. **5** (in full **optical disc**) a disc for data recorded and read by laser. **6** a compact disc. **7** Computing = DISK. □ **disc brake** one in which a flat plate presses against a plate at the centre of a wheel. **disc jockey** a person who plays and introduces pop records on radio, at a disco, etc.

**discard** (dis-**kard**) verb throw away, put aside as useless or unwanted.

**discern** (di-**sern**) verb perceive clearly with the mind or senses. □ **discernible** adjective, **discernment** noun

**discerning** (di-**sern**-ing) adjective perceptive, showing good judgement.

**discharge** verb (pronounced dis-**charj**) **1** give or send out; the pipes discharge their contents into the river; the river discharges into the sea. **2** give out an electric charge; cause to do this. **3** fire (a missile or gun). **4** dismiss from employment; a discharged servant. **5** allow to leave; the patient was discharged from hospital. **6** pay (a debt); perform or fulfil (a duty or contract). ●noun (pronounced dis-**charj**) **1** discharging; being discharged. **2** something that is discharged; the discharge from the wound. **3** the release of an electric charge, especially with a spark. **4** a written certificate of release or dismissal.

**disciple** (di-sy-pŭl) noun **1** any of the original followers of Christ. **2** a person who follows the teachings of a leader.

**disciplinarian** (dis-i-plin-**air**-iăn) noun one who enforces or believes in strict discipline.

**disciplinary** (dis-i-plin-er-i) adjective of or for discipline.

**discipline** (dis-i-plin) noun **1** training that produces obedience, self-control, or a particular skill. **2** controlled behaviour produced by such training. **3** punishment given to correct a person or enforce obedience. **4** a branch of instruction or learning. ●verb **1** train to be obedient and orderly. **2** punish.

**disclaim** verb disown; deny; they disclaim responsibility for the accident.

**disclaimer** noun a statement disclaiming something.

**disclose** verb expose to view, reveal, make known. □ **disclosure** noun

**disco** noun (plural **discos**) (informal) a discothèque.

**discolour** verb (Amer. **discolor**) **1** spoil the colour of, stain. **2** become changed in colour or stained. □ **discoloration** noun

**discomfit** (dis-**kum**-fit) verb (**discomfited**, **discomfiting**) disconcert; frustrate. □ **discomfiture** (dis-**kum**-fi-cher) noun

**discomfort** noun **1** being uncomfortable in body or mind. **2** something that causes this.

**discompose** verb disturb the composure of, agitate. □ **discomposure** noun

**disconcert** (dis-kŏn-**sert**) verb upset the composure of; fluster.

**disconnect** verb break the connection of, put out of action by disconnecting certain parts. □ **disconnection** noun

**disconnected** adjective lacking orderly connection between its parts; a disconnected speech.

**disconsolate** (dis-kon-sŏ-lăt) adjective unhappy at the loss of something, disappointed. □ **disconsolately** adverb

**discontent** noun dissatisfaction, lack of contentment. □ **discontented** adjective, **discontentment** noun

**discontinue** verb put an end to, come to an end. □ **discontinuance** noun

**discontinuous** adjective not continuous. □ **discontinuity** (dis-kon-tin-**yoo**-iti) noun

**discord** (**dis**-kord) noun **1** disagreement, quarrelling. **2** a combination of musical notes producing a harsh or unpleasant sound. □ **discordance** noun, **discordant** (dis-**kor**-dănt) adjective, **discordantly** adverb

**discothèque** (**dis**-kŏ-tek) noun **1** a club or party etc. where amplified recorded music is played for dancing. **2** the equipment used for this.

**discount** noun (pronounced **dis**-kownt) an amount of money taken off the full price or total. ● verb (pronounced dis-**kownt**) **1** disregard partly or wholly; we cannot discount this possibility. **2** deduct an amount from (a price, goods, etc.). □ **at a discount 1** below the nominal or usual price. **2** not valued as it used to be; is honesty at a discount nowadays?

**discountenance** verb **1** fluster, confuse, worry. **2** refuse to approve.

**discourage** verb **1** dishearten. **2** dissuade. **3** deter. □ **discouragement** noun

**discourse** noun (pronounced **dis**-korss) **1** a speech or lecture. **2** a written treatise on a subject. ● verb (pronounced dis-**korss**) utter or write a discourse.

**discourteous** (dis-**ker**-ti-ŭs) adjective lacking courtesy. □ **discourteously** adverb, **discourtesy** noun

**discover** verb **1** obtain sight or knowledge of, especially by searching or other effort. **2** be the first to do this; Herschel discovered a new planet. □ **discoverer** noun

**discovery** noun **1** discovering; being discovered. **2** something that is discovered.

**discredit** verb (**discredited**, **discrediting**) **1** damage the good reputation of. **2** refuse to believe. **3** cause to be disbelieved. ● noun **1** damage to reputation. **2** something that causes this. **3** doubt, lack of credibility.

**discreditable** adjective bringing discredit, shameful. □ **discreditably** adverb

**discreet** adjective **1** showing caution and good judgement in what one does; not giving away secrets. **2** not showy or obtrusive. □ **discreetly** adverb

∎**Usage** Do not confuse with **discrete**.

**discrepancy** (dis-**krep**-ănsi) noun difference, inconsistency, failure to tally; there were several discrepancies between the two accounts. □ **discrepant** adjective

**discrete** (dis-**kreet**) adjective discontinuous, individually distinct. □ **discretely** adverb

∎**Usage** Do not confuse with **discreet**.

**discretion** (dis-**kresh**-ŏn) noun **1** being discreet in one's speech, keeping secrets. **2** good judgement; he acted with discretion. **3** freedom or authority to act according to one's judgement; the treasurer has full discretion. □ **at a person's discretion** in accordance with his or her decision. **years** or **age of discretion** the age at which a person is considered capable of managing his or her own affairs.

**discretionary** (dis-**kresh**-ŏn-er-i) adjective done or used at a person's discretion; discretionary powers.

**discriminate** verb **1** (often foll. by between) make or see a distinction. **2** (usually foll. by against or in favour of) treat unfairly, especially on the basis of race, gender, etc.; employers who discriminate against women. □ **discriminatory** adjective

**discriminating** adjective showing good judgement or taste.

**discrimination** noun **1** unfair treatment based on racial, sexual, etc. prejudice. **2** good taste or judgement.

**discursive** adjective rambling from one subject to another.

**discus** noun a heavy thick-centred disc, thrown in athletic contests.

**discuss** verb examine by means of argument; talk or write about. □ **discussion** noun

**disdain** noun scorn, contempt. ● verb **1** regard with disdain, treat as unworthy of notice.

**2** refrain out of disdain; *she disdained to reply.* □ **disdainful** *adjective*, **disdainfully** *adverb*

**disease** *noun* an unhealthy condition caused by infection or diet or by faulty functioning of a bodily process.

**diseased** *adjective* affected with disease.

**disembark** *verb* put or go ashore. □ **disembarkation** *noun*

**disembodied** *adjective* (of the soul or spirit) freed from the body. □ **disembodiment** *noun*

**disembowel** *verb* (**disembowelled**, **disembowelling**; *Amer.* **disemboweled**, **disemboweling**) take out the bowels or entrails of.

**disenchant** *verb* free from enchantment, disillusion; *they are disenchanted with the government.* □ **disenchantment** *noun*

**disenfranchise** *verb* (also **disfranchise**) deprive (a person) of the right to vote, the right to be represented, or other rights of a citizen. □ **disenfranchisement** *noun*

**disengage** *verb* free from engagement; detach. □ **disengagement** *noun*

**disengaged** *adjective* not engaged in attending to another person or to business; free.

**disentangle** *verb* free from tangles or confusion, extricate. □ **disentanglement** *noun*

**disestablish** *verb* end the established state of; deprive (the Church) of its official connection with the State. □ **disestablishment** *noun*

**disfavour** (*Amer.* **disfavor**) *noun* dislike, disapproval. ●*verb* regard or treat with disfavour.

**disfigure** *verb* spoil the appearance of. □ **disfigurement** *noun*

**disfranchise** = DISENFRANCHISE.

**disgorge** *verb* **1** throw out from the throat; *the whale swallowed Jonah and then disgorged him.* **2** pour forth; *the river disgorges itself into the sea.* **3** (*informal*) hand over; *made him disgorge the stolen property.*

**disgrace** *noun* **1** loss of favour or respect. **2** something that causes this. ●*verb* bring disgrace upon, humiliate.

**disgraceful** *adjective* causing disgrace. □ **disgracefully** *adverb*

**disgruntled** *adjective* discontented, resentful. □ **disgruntlement** *noun*

**disguise** *verb* **1** conceal the identity of. **2** conceal; *there's no disguising the fact.* ●*noun* **1** something worn or used for disguising. **2** disguising; a disguised condition.

**disgust** *noun* a strong feeling of dislike; finding a thing very unpleasant or against one's principles. ●*verb* cause disgust in.

**disgusted** *adjective* feeling disgust.

**disgusting** *adjective* revolting, repugnant; terrible, awful. □ **disgustingly** *adverb*

**dish** *noun* **1** a shallow flat-bottomed container for holding or serving food; (**dishes**) crockery and utensils in general. **2** the amount a dish contains. **3** the food itself; a particular kind of food. **4** a shallow concave object. **5** = SATELLITE DISH. **6** (*slang*) an attractive person. ●*verb* **1** make dishshaped. **2** (*informal*) ruin, spoil; *it has dished our chances.* □ **dish out** (*informal*) distribute. **dish up 1** serve (food). **2** (*slang*) serve up as facts etc.; *they dished up the usual excuses.*

**dishabille** = **déshabillé**.

**disharmony** *noun* lack of harmony. □ **disharmonious** *adjective*

**dishcloth** *noun* a cloth for washing dishes.

**dishearten** *verb* cause to lose hope or confidence. □ **disheartened** *adjective*, **disheartening** *adjective*

**dishevelled** (dish-ev-ĕld) *adjective* (*Amer.* **disheveled**) ruffled and untidy. □ **dishevelment** *noun*

**dishonest** *adjective* not honest. □ **dishonestly** *adverb*, **dishonesty** *noun*

**dishonour** (*Amer.* **dishonor**) *noun* **1** loss of honour or respect, disgrace. **2** something that causes this. ●*verb* **1** bring dishonour on, disgrace. **2** refuse to accept or pay (a cheque etc.).

**dishonourable** *adjective* (*Amer.* **dishonorable**) not honourable, shameful. □ **dishonourably** *adverb*

**dishwasher** *noun* a machine for washing dishes etc.

**dishy** *adjective* (**dishier**, **dishiest**) (*informal*) attractive; good-looking.

**disillusion** *verb* set free from pleasant but mistaken beliefs. ●*noun* the state of being disillusioned. □ **disillusionment** *noun*

**disincentive** *noun* something that discourages an action or effort.

**disincline** *verb* make (a person) feel reluctant or unwilling to do something. □ **disinclination** *noun*

**disinfect** *verb* clean (something) with disinfectant. □ **disinfection** *noun*

**disinfectant** *noun* a substance that destroys germs etc.

**disinformation** *noun* deliberately false information.

**disingenuous** (dis-in-jen-yoo-ŭs) *adjective* insincere, not frank. □ **disingenuously** *adverb*

**disinherit** *verb* deprive (a person) of an inheritance. □ **disinheritance** *noun*

**disintegrate** *verb* break or cause to break into small parts or pieces. □ **disintegration** *noun*

**disinter** (dis-in-ter) *verb* (**disinterred**, **disinterring**) dig up (something buried).

**disinterest** noun **1** impartiality. **2** lack of interest.

■**Usage** See the note on **disinterested**; a similar objection applies here.

**disinterested** adjective **1** impartial, unbiased, not influenced by self-interest. **2** uninterested, uncaring.

■**Usage** The use in sense 2 is widely regarded as unacceptable because it obscures a useful distinction between *disinterested* and *uninterested*.

□ **disinterestedly** adverb

**disinvest** verb reduce or dispose of one's investment in a company etc. □ **disinvestment** noun

**disjointed** adjective (of talk) disconnected.

**disjunction** noun disjoining, separation.

**disjunctive** adjective **1** involving separation. **2** (of a conjunction) expressing an alternative, e.g. *or* in *is it wet or dry?*

**disk** noun **1** (in full **magnetic disk**) a flat circular device coated with magnetic material on which computer data can be stored. **2** alternative spelling (especially *Amer.*) of DISC. □ **disk drive** *Computing* a mechanism for spinning a disk and reading data from or writing data to it.

**diskette** noun *Computing* a floppy disk.

**dislike** noun **1** a feeling of not liking some person or thing. **2** the object of this. ●verb feel dislike for.

**dislocate** verb **1** put (a thing) out of place in relation to connecting parts; displace (a bone) from its proper position in a joint. **2** put out of order, disrupt; *fog dislocated traffic.* □ **dislocation** noun

**dislodge** verb move or force from an established position. □ **dislodgement** noun

**disloyal** adjective not loyal. □ **disloyally** adverb, **disloyalty** noun

**dismal** adjective **1** causing or showing gloom; dreary. **2** (*informal*) feeble; *a dismal attempt at humour.* □ **dismally** adverb

**dismantle** verb **1** take to pieces; pull down. **2** deprive of defences or equipment.

**dismay** noun a feeling of surprise and discouragement. ●verb fill with dismay.

**dismember** verb **1** remove the limbs of. **2** divide into parts; partition (a country etc.). □ **dismemberment** noun

**dismiss** verb **1** send away from one's presence or employment. **2** put out of one's thoughts; mention or discuss only briefly. **3** reject without further hearing; *the case was dismissed for lack of evidence.* **4** put (a batsman or side) out in cricket; *dismissed him for 6 runs.* □ **dismissal** noun

**dismissive** adjective dismissing rudely or casually; disdainful. □ **dismissively** adverb, **dismissiveness** noun

**dismount** verb **1** get off or down from something on which one is riding. **2** cause to fall off, unseat. **3** remove (a gun etc.) from its mounting.

**Disney**, Walt (Walter Elias) (1901–66), American animator and film producer, famous for the creation of cartoon characters such as Mickey Mouse and Donald Duck and pioneer of feature-length cartoon films. □ **Disneyland, Disney World** amusement parks incorporating the elements of the Disney fantasy.

**disobedient** adjective not obedient. □ **disobediently** adverb, **disobedience** noun

**disobey** verb (**disobeyed, disobeying**) disregard orders, fail to obey.

**disoblige** verb refuse to help or cooperate with (a person).

**disorder** noun **1** lack of order, untidiness. **2** a disturbance of public order, a riot. **3** disturbance of the normal working of body or mind; *a nervous disorder.* ●verb throw into disorder, upset. □ **disorderly** adjective

**disorganize** verb (also **disorganise**) throw into confusion, upset the orderly system or arrangement of. □ **disorganization** noun

**disorganized** adjective (also **disorganised**) lacking organization or an orderly system.

**disorient** = DISORIENTATE.

**disorientate** (dis-or-i-ĕn-tayt) verb (also **disorient**) confuse and make (a person) lose his or her bearings. □ **disorientation** noun

**disown** verb refuse to acknowledge as one's own, reject all connection with.

**disparage** (dis-pa-rij) verb speak of in a slighting way, belittle. □ **disparagingly** adverb, **disparagement** noun

**disparate** (dis-per-ăt) adjective different in kind.

**disparity** (dis-pa-riti) noun inequality, difference.

**dispassionate** adjective free from emotion, calm, impartial. □ **dispassionately** adverb

**dispatch** (also **despatch**) verb **1** send off to a destination or for a purpose. **2** kill. **3** complete or dispose of quickly. ●noun **1** dispatching; being dispatched. **2** promptness, speed; *he acted with dispatch.* **3** an official message or report sent with speed. **4** a news report sent to a newspaper or news agency etc. □ **dispatch box** a container for carrying official documents. **dispatch rider** a messenger who travels by motor cycle.

**dispel** verb (**dispelled, dispelling**) drive away, scatter; *wind dispelled the fog; how can we dispel their fears?*

**dispensable** adjective not essential.

**dispensary** noun a place where medicines are dispensed; *the hospital dispensary.*

**dispensation** *noun* **1** dispensing, distributing. **2** ordering or management, especially of the world by Providence. **3** exemption from a penalty, rule, or duty.

**dispense** *verb* **1** distribute, deal out; *dispense justice*. **2** prepare and give out (medicines etc.) according to prescriptions. □ **dispense with** do without; make unnecessary. **dispensing chemist** one who is qualified to dispense medicines.

**dispenser** *noun* **1** a person who dispenses medicines. **2** a device that deals out a quantity of something; *a soap dispenser*.

**disperse** *verb* scatter, go, drive, or send in different directions. □ **dispersal** *noun*

**dispersion** *noun* **1** dispersing; being dispersed. **2** (**the Dispersion**) = DIASPORA.

**dispirited** *adjective* depressed, disheartened.

**displace** *verb* **1** shift from its place. **2** take the place of, oust. □ **displaced person** a refugee in war or from persecution.

**displacement** *noun* **1** displacing or being displaced. **2** the amount of fluid displaced by an object placed in it.

**display** *verb* **1** show, arrange (a thing) so that it can be seen. **2** (of birds and animals) make a display (see sense 3 below). ●*noun* **1** displaying; being displayed. **2** something displayed conspicuously. **3** a special pattern of behaviour used by birds and animals as a means of visual communication.

**displease** *verb* offend, arouse the disapproval or anger of.

**displeasure** *noun* a displeased feeling, dissatisfaction.

**disport** *verb* (*formal*) (usually **disport oneself**) play; amuse oneself; *disporting themselves on the beach*.

**disposable** *adjective* **1** able to be disposed of. **2** at one's disposal. **3** designed to be thrown away after being used once. □ **disposable income** income remaining after tax and other fixed payments.

**disposal** *noun* disposing of something. □ **at one's disposal** available for one's use.

**dispose** *verb* **1** place suitably or in order; *disposed the troops in two lines*. **2** determine the course of events; *man proposes, God disposes*. **3** make willing or ready to do something, incline; *their friendliness disposed us to accept the invitation; we felt disposed to accept*. □ **be well disposed towards** be friendly towards, favour. **dispose of** get rid of; deal with.

**disposition** *noun* **1** setting in order, arrangement; *the disposition of troops*. **2** a person's natural qualities of mind and character; *he has a cheerful disposition*. **3** a natural tendency or inclination.

**dispossess** *verb* deprive (a person) of the possession of something. □ **dispossession** *noun*

**disproof** *noun* disproving; a refutation.

**disproportion** *noun* lack of proper proportion; being out of proportion.

**disproportionate** *adjective* out of proportion, relatively too large or too small. □ **disproportionately** *adverb*

**disprove** *verb* show to be false or wrong.

**disputable** (dis-**pewt**-ăbŭl) *adjective* able to be disputed, questionable. □ **disputably** *adverb*

**disputant** (dis-**pew**-tănt) *noun* a person engaged in a dispute.

**disputation** *noun* argument, debate.

**disputatious** *adjective* argumentative.

**dispute** (dis-**pewt**) *verb* **1** argue, debate. **2** quarrel. **3** question the truth or validity of; *dispute a claim; the disputed territory*. ●*noun* **1** an argument or debate. **2** a quarrel. □ **in dispute 1** being argued about. **2** involved in a dispute.

**disqualify** *verb* (**disqualified**, **disqualifying**) **1** debar from a competition because of an infringement of the rules. **2** make unsuitable or ineligible; *weak eyesight disqualifies him for military service*. □ **disqualification** *noun*

**disquiet** *noun* uneasiness, anxiety. ●*verb* make uneasy or anxious.

**disquietude** *noun* disquiet.

**disquisition** (dis-kwi-**zish**-ŏn) *noun* a long elaborate spoken or written account of something.

**Disraeli** (diz-**ray**-li), Benjamin, 1st Earl of Beaconsfield (1804–81), British statesman and novelist, Prime Minister 1868 and 1874–80.

**disregard** *verb* pay no attention to, treat as of no importance. ●*noun* lack of attention; treating something as of no importance; *complete disregard for his own safety*.

**disrepair** *noun* a bad condition caused by lack of repairs; *in a state of disrepair*.

**disreputable** (dis-**rep**-yoo-tăbŭl) *adjective* having a bad reputation, not respectable. □ **disreputably** *adverb*

**disrepute** (dis-ri-**pewt**) *noun* lack of good reputation, discredit; *fell into disrepute*.

**disrespect** *noun* lack of respect, rudeness. □ **disrespectful** *adjective*, **disrespectfully** *adverb*

**disrobe** *verb* take off official or ceremonial robes; undress.

**disrupt** *verb* cause to break up, throw into disorder, interrupt the flow or continuity of; *party quarrels disrupted the coalition; floods disrupted traffic*. □ **disruption** *noun*

**disruptive** *adjective* causing disruption.

**dissatisfaction** *noun* lack of satisfaction.

**dissatisfied** *adjective* not satisfied, feeling dissatisfaction.

**dissect** (dis-**sekt**) *verb* **1** cut apart, especially in order to examine internal structure. **2** examine (a theory etc.) critically and in detail. □ **dissection** *noun*, **dissector** *noun*

**dissemble** *verb* conceal (one's feelings); be insincere.

**disseminate** (dis-**sem**-in-ayt) *verb* spread (ideas etc.) widely. □ **dissemination** *noun*

**dissension** *noun* disagreement that gives rise to strife.

**dissent** *verb* have or express a different opinion. ●*noun* a difference in opinion.

**dissenter** *noun* **1** a person who dissents. **2** (**Dissenter**) a Protestant dissenting from the Church of England.

**dissentient** (dis-**sen**-shĕnt) *adjective* dissenting from the majority. ●*noun* one who dissents.

**dissertation** *noun* **1** a lengthy essay or a thesis, especially as part of a course of study. **2** a speech.

**disservice** *noun* a harmful action.

**dissident** (dis-i-dĕnt) *adjective* disagreeing. ●*noun* one who disagrees; one who opposes the authorities. □ **dissidence** *noun*

**dissimilar** *adjective* unlike. □ **dissimilarity** *noun*

**dissimulate** *verb* dissemble. □ **dissimulation** *noun*

**dissipate** (dis-i-payt) *verb* **1** dispel, disperse. **2** squander or fritter away.

**dissipated** *adjective* indulging one's vices, living a dissolute life.

**dissipation** *noun* **1** dissipating; being dissipated. **2** dissipated living.

**dissociate** (dis-**soh**-shi-ayt) *verb* **1** separate in one's thoughts; *it is difficult to dissociate the man from his work.* **2** become disconnected. □ **dissociate oneself from** declare that one has no connection with (a person, organization, activity, etc.). □ **dissociation** *noun,* **dissociative** *adjective*

**dissoluble** *adjective* able to be disintegrated, loosened, or disconnected.

**dissolute** (dis-ŏ-loot) *adjective* lacking moral restraint or self-discipline.

**dissolution** *noun* **1** the dissolving of an assembly or partnership. **2** death; destruction. **3** the ending of the existence of monasteries in the reign of Henry VIII.

**dissolve** *verb* **1** make or become liquid; disperse or cause to be dispersed in a liquid. **2** cause to disappear; disappear gradually. **3** dismiss or disperse (an assembly, e.g. parliament); annul or put an end to (a partnership, e.g. a marriage). **4** give way to emotion; *she dissolved into tears.*

**dissonant** (dis-ŏn-ănt) *adjective* harsh-toned; unharmonious. □ **dissonance** *noun*

**dissuade** *verb* discourage or persuade against a course of action; *dissuaded him from going.* □ **dissuasion** *noun*

**dissuasive** *adjective* dissuading.

**distaff** (dis-tahf) *noun* a cleft stick holding wool etc. for spinning. □ **the distaff side** the mother's side of a family.

**distance** *noun* **1** the length of space between one point and another. **2** a distant part; *in the distance.* **3** being distant, remoteness. ●*verb* outdistance in a race. □ **at a distance** far off, not very near. **keep one's distance 1** remain at a safe distance. **2** behave aloofly, be unfriendly.

**distant** *adjective* **1** at a specified or considerable distance away; *three miles distant.* **2** remote, much apart in space, time, or relationship etc.; *the distant past; a distant cousin.* **3** not friendly, aloof. □ **distantly** *adverb*

**distaste** *noun* dislike.

**distasteful** *adjective* unpleasant, arousing distaste. □ **distastefully** *adverb*

**distemper** *noun* **1** a disease of dogs and certain other animals, with coughing and weakness. **2** a paint made from powdered colouring matter mixed with glue or size. ●*verb* paint with this.

**distend** *verb* swell or become swollen by pressure from within. □ **distension** *noun*

**distil** *verb* (*Amer.* **distill**) (**distilled**, **distilling**) **1** treat by distillation; make, produce, or purify in this way. **2** undergo distillation.

**distillate** *noun* a substance produced by distillation.

**distillation** *noun* **1** the process of turning a substance to vapour by heat, then cooling the vapour so that it condenses and collecting the resulting liquid, in order to purify it, separate its constituents, or extract an essence. **2** something distilled.

**distiller** *noun* a person who distils; one who makes alcoholic liquor by distillation.

**distillery** *noun* a place where alcoholic liquor is distilled.

**distinct** *adjective* **1** able to be perceived clearly by the senses or the mind, definite and unmistakable; *a distinct improvement.* **2** different in kind, separate; *his hobbies are quite distinct from his work.* □ **distinctly** *adverb,* **distinctness** *noun*

**distinction** *noun* **1** seeing or making a difference between things. **2** a difference seen or made. **3** a thing that differentiates one thing from another. **4** a mark of honour. **5** excellence; *a person of distinction.*

**distinctive** *adjective* characteristic, serving to distinguish a thing by making it different from others.

■**Usage** Do not confuse with **distinct**. A *distinct* sign is one that can be seen clearly; a *distinctive* sign is one not commonly found elsewhere.

**distingué** (dis-**tang**-gay) *adjective* distinguished or dignified in appearance, manner, etc. (¶ French.)

**distinguish** *verb* **1** see or point out a difference between; draw distinctions; *we must distinguish facts from rumours.* **2** make different, be a characteristic mark or property of; *speech distinguishes man from animals.* **3** make out by listening or looking; *unable to distinguish distant objects.* **4** make notable, bring honour to; *he distinguished himself by his bravery.* □ **distinguishable** *adjective*

**distinguished** *adjective* **1** showing excellence. **2** famous for great achievements. **3** having an air of distinction and dignity.

**distort** *verb* **1** pull or twist out of its usual shape. **2** misrepresent, alter (facts). **3** transmit (sound or pictures) inaccurately. □ **distortion** *noun*

**distract** *verb* **1** draw away the attention of. **2** confuse, bewilder. **3** amuse, entertain.

**distracted** *adjective* distraught; confused.

**distraction** *noun* **1** something that distracts the attention and prevents concentration. **2** an amusement or entertainment. **3** mental upset or distress. □ **to distraction** almost to a state of madness.

**distrain** *verb* levy a distraint (upon a person or goods).

**distraint** *noun* seizure of a person's possessions as payment for what he or she owes, or in order to sell them to meet his or her debts.

**distrait** (dis-**tray**) *adjective* (of a woman **distraite**, *pronounced* dis-**trayt**) **1** inattentive. **2** distraught. (¶ French.)

**distraught** (dis-**trawt**) *adjective* greatly upset, nearly crazy with grief or worry.

**distress** *noun* **1** suffering caused by pain, worry, illness, or exhaustion. **2** poverty. **3** *Law* = DISTRAINT. ●*verb* make worried, upset, or unhappy. □ **in distress** suffering or in danger.

**distressed** *adjective* **1** upset, unhappy, worried. **2** impoverished. **3** (of furniture or fabric) made to look old and worn. □ **distressed area** a region of high unemployment and poverty.

**distributary** *noun* a branch of a river or glacier that does not return to it after leaving the main stream (e.g. in a delta).

**distribute** *verb* **1** divide and give a share to each of a number, deal out. **2** spread or scatter; place at different points. □ **distribution** *noun*

**distributive** *adjective* of or concerned with distribution.

**distributor** *noun* **1** one who distributes things; an agent who markets goods. **2** a device for passing current to each of the spark plugs in an engine.

**district** *noun* part of a country, city, or county having a particular feature or regarded as a unit for a special purpose; *the Lake District*; *a postal district.* □ **district attorney** (in the USA) the prosecuting officer of a district. **district nurse** a nurse who makes home visits in an area.

**distrust** *noun* lack of trust, suspicion. ●*verb* feel distrust in. □ **distrustful** *adjective*

**disturb** *verb* **1** break the rest, quiet, or calm of. **2** cause to move from a settled position.

**disturbance** *noun* **1** disturbing; being disturbed. **2** a commotion; an outbreak of social or political disorder.

**disturbed** *adjective* emotionally or mentally unstable or abnormal.

**disunion** *noun* **1** separation, lack of union. **2** discord.

**disunite** *verb* **1** remove unity from. **2** cause to separate. **3** experience separation.

**disunity** *noun* lack of unity.

**disuse** *noun* the state of not being used; *rusty from disuse.* □ **disused** *adjective*

**ditch** *noun* a trench to hold or carry off water or to serve as a boundary. ●*verb* **1** make or repair ditches; *hedging and ditching.* **2** drive (a vehicle) into a ditch. **3** (*informal*) make a forced aircraft landing on the sea. **4** (*slang*) abandon, discard, leave in the lurch.

**dither** *verb* **1** tremble, quiver. **2** hesitate indecisively. ●*noun* a state of dithering; nervous excitement or fear; *all of a dither.*

**ditto** *noun* (used in lists to avoid repeating something) the same again. □ **ditto marks** two small marks (") placed under the item to be repeated.

**ditty** *noun* a short simple song.

**diuretic** (dy-yoor-et-ik) *noun* a substance that causes more urine to be secreted.

**diurnal** (dy-**ern**-ăl) *adjective* **1** of the day, not nocturnal. **2** occupying one day.

**diva** (**dee**-vă) *noun* a great woman opera singer, a prima donna.

**divalent** (dy-**vay**-lĕnt) *adjective Chem.* having a valency of two.

**divan** (div-**an**) *noun* a low couch without a raised back or ends; a bed resembling this.

**dive** *verb* (**dived** or *Amer.* **dove**, *pronounced* dohv) **1** plunge head first into water. **2** (of an aircraft) plunge steeply downwards. **3** (of a submarine or diver) go under water. **4** go down or out of sight suddenly; rush headlong; *dived into a shop.* **5** move (a thing, e.g. one's hand) quickly downwards into something. ●*noun* **1** an act of diving. **2** a sharp downward movement or fall. **3** (*informal*) a disreputable place. □ **dive-bomb** *verb* bomb (a target) from a diving aircraft. **dive-bomber** *noun* an aircraft designed to dive-bomb. **diving bell** an open-bottomed structure supplied with air, in which a diver can be lowered into deep water. **diving board** a board for diving from. **diving suit** a watertight suit, usually with a helmet and air supply, for work under water.

**diver** *noun* **1** one who dives. **2** a person who works underwater in a diving suit. **3** a diving bird.

**diverge** (dy-**verj**) *verb* **1** go in different directions from a common point or from each other; become further apart. **2** go aside from a path; *diverge from the truth.* □ **divergent** *adjective*, **divergence** *noun*

**divers** (**dy**-verz) *adjective* (*old use*) several, various.

**diverse** (dy-**verss**) *adjective* of different kinds.

**diversify** *verb* (**diversified**, **diversifying**) introduce variety into, vary. □ **diversification** *noun*

**diversion** *noun* **1** diverting something from its course. **2** diverting of attention; *create a diversion.* **3** a recreation, an entertainment. **4** an alternative route when a road is temporarily closed to traffic. □ **diversionary** *adjective*

**diversity** (dy-**vers**-iti) *noun* variety.

**divert** *verb* **1** turn (a thing) from its course; *divert the stream*; *divert attention*; *divert traffic.* **2** entertain or amuse with recreations.

**diverticulitis** (dy-ver-tik-yoo-**ly**-tiss) *noun* inflammation of a side-branch (*diverticulum*) of a cavity or passage in the body, especially in the alimentary tract.

**divertimento** *noun* (*plural* **divertimentos** or **divertimenti**) a light entertaining piece of music, often for a chamber orchestra.

**diverting** *adjective* entertaining, amusing.

**divest** (dy-**vest**) *verb* **1** strip of clothes; *divested himself of his robes.* **2** take away, deprive; *divested him of his power.*

**divide** *verb* **1** separate into parts, split or break up; *divide the money between you*; *the river divides into two channels.* **2** separate from something else; *the Pyrenees divide France from Spain.* **3** arrange in separate groups, classify. **4** cause to disagree; *this controversy divided the party.* **5** (in Parliament) part in order to vote; *the House divided.* **6** find how many times one number contains another; *divide 12 by 3.* **7** be able to be divided. ●*noun* a dividing line; a watershed. □ **Great Divide** the main range of the Rocky Mountains which forms the

watershed between eastern and western drainage systems in North America.

**dividend** *noun* **1** a number that is to be divided. **2** a share of profits paid to shareholders or winners in a football pool. **3** a benefit from an action; *his long training paid dividends.*

**divider** *noun* **1** something that divides; a screen or piece of furniture to divide a room into two parts. **2** (**dividers**) measuring-compasses.

**divination** (div-in-ay-shŏn) *noun* divining, foretelling future events or discovering hidden knowledge.

**divine** *adjective* **1** of, from, or like God or a god. **2** (*informal*) excellent, very beautiful; *this divine weather.* ●*noun* a theologian; a member of the clergy. ●*verb* discover or learn about future events by what are alleged to be magical means, or by inspiration or guessing. □ **divining rod** a forked stick or rod used in dowsing. □ **divinely** *adverb*, **diviner** *noun*

**divinity** *noun* **1** being divine. **2** a god. **3** theology.

**divisible** (di-**viz**-ibŭl) *adjective* able to be divided. □ **divisibility** *noun*

**division** *noun* **1** dividing; being divided. **2** (in Parliament) separation of members into two sections for counting votes. **3** a dividing line, a partition. **4** one of the parts into which a thing is divided. **5** a major unit of an organization; *our export division.* □ **division sign** a sign (÷) (as in 12 ÷ 4) indicating that one quantity is to be divided by another. □ **divisional** *adjective*

**divisive** (di-**vy**-siv) *adjective* tending to cause disagreement among members of a group.

**divisor** (di-**vy**-zer) *noun* a number by which another is divided.

**divorce** *noun* **1** the legal termination of a marriage. **2** the separation of things that were together. ●*verb* **1** end a marriage with (one's husband or wife) by divorce. **2** separate, especially in thought or organization.

**divorcee** (div-or-**see**) *noun* a divorced person.

**divot** (**div**-ŏt) *noun* a piece of turf cut out by a golf club in making a stroke.

**divulge** (dy-**vulj**) *verb* reveal (information). □ **divulgence** *noun*

**divvy** *noun* (*informal*) a dividend. ●*verb* (**divvied**, **divvying**) (often foll. by *up*) (*informal*) share out.

**Diwali** (di-**wah**-li) *noun* a Hindu religious festival at which lamps are lit, held in October or November.

**Dixie** *noun* the southern States of the USA.

**dixie** *noun* a large iron cooking pot used by campers etc.

**Dixieland** *noun* **1** Dixie. **2** a kind of jazz with a strong two-beat rhythm.

**DIY** *abbreviation* do-it-yourself.

**dizzy** *adjective* (**dizzier, dizziest**) **1** giddy, feeling confused. **2** causing giddiness; *dizzy heights*. □ **dizzily** *adverb*, **dizziness** *noun*

**DJ** *abbreviation* **1** disc jockey. **2** dinner jacket.

**Djakarta** (also **Jakarta**) the capital of Indonesia.

**djellaba** (jel-ăbă) *noun* (also **jellaba**) a loose hooded cloak as worn by Arab men.

**Djibouti** (ji-boo-ti) **1** a country on the NE coast of Africa. **2** its capital city.

**djinn** = JINNEE.

**D.Litt.** *abbreviation* Doctor of Letters.

**DM** *abbreviation* Deutschmark.

**D.Mus.** *abbreviation* Doctor of Music.

**DNA** *abbreviation* deoxyribonucleic acid, a substance in chromosomes that stores genetic information.

**Dnieper** (dnee-per) a river flowing through Belorussia and Ukraine into the Black Sea.

**D-notice** *noun* an official notice to news editors not to publish items on specified subjects, for reasons of security.

**do** *verb* (**did, done, doing**) **1** perform, carry out, fulfil or complete (a work, duty, etc.). **2** produce, make; *do five copies*; *we do meals*. **3** deal with, set in order, solve; *do a crossword*; *do the flowers*. **4** cover (a distance) in travelling. **5** (*informal*) visit, see the sights of; *we did Rome last year*. **6** (*informal*) undergo; *did time for robbery*. **7** (*informal*) provide food etc. for; *they do you well here*. **8** act or proceed; *do as you like*. **9** fare, get on, achieve something; *they did well out of it*. **10** be suitable or acceptable. **11** be in progress; be happening. **12** (*slang*) rob, swindle; *you were done!* **13** (*slang*) prosecute, convict; *done for shoplifting*. **14** (*slang*) take (drugs). ● *auxiliary verb* **1** used to indicate present or past tense; *what does he think?*, *what did he think?* **2** used for emphasis; *I do like nuts*. **3** used to avoid repetition of a verb just used; *we work as hard as they do*. ● *noun* (*plural* **dos** or **do's**) **1** (*informal*) an entertainment, a party. **2** alternative spelling of DOH. □ **do away with** abolish, get rid of. **do down** (*informal*) get the better of; swindle. **do for** (*informal*) **1** ruin, destroy, kill. **2** do housework for. **do-gooder** *noun* a person who is well-meaning but unrealistic or officious in trying to promote social work or reform. **do in 1** (*slang*) ruin, kill. **2** (*informal*) tire out. **do-it-yourself** *noun* work (on a house etc.) done by an amateur handyman. **dos and don'ts** rules of behaviour. **do up 1** fasten, wrap up. **2** repair or redecorate. **do with** need or want; find useful; *I could do with a rest*. **do without** manage without.

**Dobermann pinscher** a large dog of a German breed with a smooth coat.

**doc** *noun* (*informal*) doctor.

**docile** (doh-syl) *adjective* willing to obey. □ **docilely** *adverb*, **docility** (dŏ-sil-iti) *noun*

**dock¹** *noun* a weed with broad leaves.

**dock²** *verb* **1** cut short (an animal's tail). **2** reduce or take away part of (wages, supplies, etc.).

**dock³** *noun* **1** an artificially enclosed body of water where ships are admitted for loading, unloading, or repair. **2** (**docks**) a dockyard. ● *verb* **1** bring or come into dock. **2** join (two or more spacecraft) together in space; become joined thus.

**dock⁴** *noun* an enclosure in a criminal court for a prisoner on trial.

**docker** *noun* a labourer who loads and unloads ships in a dockyard.

**docket** *noun* a document or label listing goods delivered, the contents of a package, or recording payment of customs dues etc. ● *verb* (**docketed, docketing**) enter on a docket; label with a docket.

**dockland** *noun* the district near a dockyard.

**dockyard** *noun* an area with docks and equipment for building and repairing ships.

**doctor** *noun* **1** a person who is qualified to be a practitioner of medicine, a physician. **2** a person who holds a doctorate; *Doctor of Civil Law*. ● *verb* **1** treat medically. **2** castrate or spay. **3** patch up (machinery etc.). **4** tamper with or falsify; *doctored the evidence*.

**doctoral** *adjective* of or for the degree of doctor.

**doctorate** (dok-ter-ăt) *noun* the highest degree at a university, entitling the holder to the title of 'doctor'.

**doctrinaire** (dok-trin-air) *adjective* applying theories or principles without regard for practical considerations.

**doctrine** (dok-trin) *noun* a principle or set of principles and beliefs held by a religious, political, or other group. □ **doctrinal** (dok-try-năl) *adjective*

**docudrama** *noun* a television drama based on real events.

**document** *noun* a paper giving information or evidence about something. ● *verb* prove by or support with documents; *a heavily documented report*.

**documentary** (dok-yoo-ment-er-i) *adjective* **1** consisting of documents; *documentary evidence*. **2** giving a factual filmed report of a subject or activity. ● *noun* a documentary film.

**documentation** *noun* **1** collection and classification of information. **2** the documents collected in this way. **3** booklets or other material explaining how to use a computer, piece of software, etc.

**dodder** verb tremble or totter because of age or frailty. □ **dodderer** noun, **doddery** adjective

**doddle** noun (slang) an easy task.

**dodecagon** (doh-**dek**-ă-gŏn) noun a geometric figure with twelve sides.

**dodecahedron** (doh-dekă-**hee**-drŏn) noun a solid body with twelve faces.

**Dodecanese** (doh-dekă-**neez**) a group of twelve Greek islands in the south-east Aegean, of which the largest is Rhodes.

**dodge** verb **1** move quickly to one side; change position or direction in order to avoid something. **2** evade by cunning or trickery; dodged military service. ●noun **1** a quick movement to avoid something. **2** (informal) a clever trick. □ **dodger** noun

**dodgem** (doj-ĕm) noun small electrically driven car in an enclosure at a funfair, in which the driver tries to bump other cars.

**Dodgson** see CARROLL.

**dodgy** adjective (**dodgier**, **dodgiest**) (informal) awkward, difficult.

**dodo** (**doh**-doh) noun (plural **dodos**) a large non-flying bird that formerly lived in Mauritius but has been extinct since the 18th century.

**Dodoma** (dŏ-**doh**-mă) the capital of Tanzania.

**DOE** abbreviation (Brit.) Department of the Environment.

**doe** noun (plural **doe** or **does**) the female of the fallow deer, reindeer, hare, or rabbit.

**doer** noun a person who does something; one who takes action rather than just thinking or talking about things.

**doesn't** (informal) = does not.

**doff** verb take off (one's hat).

**dog** noun **1** a four-legged carnivorous animal, commonly kept as a pet or trained for use in hunting etc. **2** the male of this or of the wolf or fox. **3** (informal) a person; lucky dog. **4** a mechanical device for gripping things. **5** (**the dogs**) (informal) greyhound racing. ●verb (**dogged**, **dogging**) follow closely or persistently; dogged his footsteps. □ **dog-collar** noun (informal) a clerical collar. **dog days** the hottest period of the year. **dog-eared** adjective (of a book) having the corners of the pages turned down through use. **dog-eat-dog** noun ruthless competition. **dog-end** noun (slang) a cigarette end. **dog in the manger** a person who stops others using something for which he or she has no use. **dog-leg** noun a sharp bend. **dog-paddle** noun = DOGGY-PADDLE. **dog rose** a wild rose with single flowers. **dog's breakfast**, **dog's dinner** (informal) a mess. **dog's life** a life of misery or harassment. **dog-star** noun the star Sirius. **dog-tired** adjective tired out. **go to the dogs** (slang) become worthless, be ruined.

**dogcart** noun a light horse-drawn two-wheeled vehicle with cross seats back to back.

**doge** (pronounced dohj) noun (hist.) the former ruler of Venice or of Genoa.

**dogfight** noun **1** a rough fight. **2** close combat between fighter aircraft.

**dogfish** noun (plural **dogfish** or **dogfishes**) a small shark.

**dogged** (**dog**-id) adjective determined, not giving up easily. □ **doggedly** adverb

**doggerel** (**dog**-er-ĕl) noun bad verse.

**doggo** adverb □ **lie doggo** (slang) lie motionless or hidden.

**doggy** adjective **1** of dogs. **2** (informal) fond of dogs. ●noun (also **doggie**) (informal) a child's name for a dog. □ **doggy bag** a bag provided at a restaurant so that customers may take home leftovers. **doggy-paddle** noun (also **dog-paddle**) a simple swimming stroke like that of a dog.

**doghouse** noun (Amer. & Austral.) a dog's kennel. □ **in the doghouse** (slang) in disgrace.

**dogma** noun a doctrine or doctrines put forward by some authority, especially the Church or a political party, to be accepted as true without question.

**dogmatic** (dog-**mat**-ik) adjective putting forward opinions in an authoritative, intolerant, or arrogant way. □ **dogmatically** adverb

**dogmatism** (dog-mă-tizm) noun being dogmatic.

**dogmatize** (dog-mă-tyz) verb (also **dogmatise**) make dogmatic statements.

**dogsbody** noun (informal) a person who runs errands and does boring jobs for others.

**dogtrot** noun a gentle easy trot.

**dogwatch** noun either of two short watches on a ship (4–6 or 6–8 p.m.).

**dogwood** noun a shrub with dark red branches, greenish-white flowers, and purple berries.

**doh** noun (also **do**) Music the first note of a major scale in music, or the note C.

**Doha** (doh-hă) the capital of Qatar.

**doily** noun (also **doyley**) a small ornamental paper or lace mat placed under cakes etc. on a dish.

**doings** noun **1** (treated as plural) things done or being done. **2** (treated as singular) (informal) something unspecified; used to mention something when its name is not known.

**Dolby** noun (trade mark) a system used in tape-recording to reduce unwanted sounds at high frequency.

**doldrums** plural noun (usually as **the doldrums**) **1** the ocean regions near the equator where there is little or no wind. **2** a period of inactivity. □ **in the doldrums** in low spirits.

**dole** verb (usually foll. by out) distribute. ●noun (informal) unemployment benefit. □ **on the dole** (informal) receiving unemployment benefit.

**doleful** adjective mournful, sad. □ **dolefully** adverb

**doll** noun **1** a small model of a human figure, especially as a child's toy. **2** a ventriloquist's dummy. **3** (slang) a young woman, especially a pretty one. ●verb (foll. by up) (informal) dress smartly; dolled herself up.

**dollar** noun the unit of money in the USA, Australia, and certain other countries.

**dollop** noun (informal) a shapeless lump of something soft.

**dolly** noun **1** a child's name for a doll. **2** a movable platform for a cine-camera. □ **dolly-bird** noun (informal) an attractive young woman.

**dolman sleeve** a loose sleeve cut in one piece with the body of a garment.

**dolmen** (dol-men) noun a prehistoric tomb with a large flat stone laid on upright ones.

**dolomite** (dol-ŏ-myt) noun a mineral or rock of calcium magnesium carbonate.

**Dolomite Mountains** (also **the Dolomites**) a rocky mountain range in north Italy.

**dolour** (dol-er) noun (Amer. **dolor**) (literary) sorrow, distress. □ **dolorous** adjective

**dolphin** noun a sea mammal like a porpoise but larger and with a beak-like snout.

**dolphinarium** noun a public aquarium for dolphins.

**dolt** (pronounced dohlt) noun a stupid person. □ **doltish** adjective

**Dom** noun **1** a title put before the names of some Roman Catholic dignitaries and of Benedictine and Carthusian monks. **2** a Portuguese title put before a man's Christian name.

**domain** (dŏm-**ayn**) noun **1** a district or area under someone's control; a range of influence. **2** a field of thought or activity; the domain of science.

**dome** noun **1** a rounded roof with a circular base. **2** something shaped like this. ●verb shape into a dome. □ **domed** adjective

**Dome of the Rock** an Islamic shrine in Jerusalem.

**Domesday Book** (**doomz**-day) a record of the ownership of lands in England made in 1086 by order of William the Conqueror.

**domestic** adjective **1** of the home or household or family affairs. **2** of one's own country, not foreign or international; domestic air services. **3** (of animals) kept by humans, not wild. ●noun a servant in a household. □ **domestic science** home

economics; the study of household management. □ **domestically** adverb

**domesticated** adjective **1** (of animals) trained to live with and be kept by humans. **2** (of people) enjoying household work and home life.

**domesticity** (dom-es-**tiss**-iti) noun being domestic; domestic or home life.

**domicile** (dom-i-syl) noun a person's place of residence. ●verb (usually as **domiciled** adjective) living (in a place).

**domiciliary** (dom-i-sil-yer-i) adjective **1** of a dwelling-place. **2** visiting a patient etc. at home; domiciliary physiotherapist.

**dominant** adjective dominating. ●noun (in music) the fifth note of the diatonic scale of any key. □ **dominance** noun, **dominantly** adverb

**dominate** verb **1** have a commanding influence over. **2** be the most influential or conspicuous person or thing. **3** (of a high place) tower over; the mountain dominates the whole valley. □ **domination** noun

**domineer** verb behave in a forceful way, making others obey.

**Dominica** (dom-in-**eek**-ă) an island in the West Indies. □ **Dominican** (dom-in-eek-ăn) adjective & noun

**Dominican** (dŏm-**in**-ikăn) noun a member of an order of friars (also called **Black Friars**) founded by a Spanish priest, St Dominic (died 1221), or of a corresponding order of nuns.

**Dominican Republic** (dŏm-**in**-ikăn) a country in the West Indies. □ **Dominican** adjective & noun

**Domingo**, Placido (born 1941), Spanish tenor singer.

**dominion** noun **1** authority to rule; control. **2** territory controlled by a ruler or government; a domain.

**domino** noun (plural **dominoes**) **1** each of the small oblong pieces marked with up to 6 pips on each half, used in the game of **dominoes**. **2** a loose cloak with a mask for the upper part of the face, formerly worn at masquerades. □ **domino effect** an effect compared to a row of dominoes falling, when an event triggers off a cascading series of related events.

**Don**[1] a river of southern Russia, flowing into the Sea of Azov.

**Don**[2] noun a Spanish title put before a man's Christian name.

**don**[1] verb (**donned**, **donning**) put on.

**don**[2] noun a head, fellow, or tutor of a college, especially at Oxford or Cambridge.

**Donald Duck** a cartoon character created by Walt Disney.

**donate** verb give as a donation.

**Donatello** (don-ă-**tel**-oh), Donato di Niccolo (1386–1466), Florentine sculptor.

**donation** noun **1** an act of donating. **2** a gift of money etc. to a fund or institution.

**done** see DO. ● adjective **1** cooked sufficiently. **2** (informal) tired out. **3** (informal) socially acceptable; the done thing; it isn't done. ● interjection (in reply to an offer) I accept. □ **done for** (informal) in serious trouble. **done with** finished with; it's over and done with.

**doner Kebab** (**do**-ner, **doh**-ner) spiced lamb cooked on a spit and served in slices, often with pitta bread.

**Donizetti** (don-its-et-i), Gaetano (1797–1848), Italian opera composer.

**donjon** noun the great tower or keep of a castle.

**Don Juan** (joo-ăn) **1** legendary Spanish nobleman of dissolute life. **2** a seducer of women.

**donkey** noun (plural **donkeys**) an animal of the horse family, with long ears. □ **donkey jacket** a worker's thick weatherproof jacket. **donkey's years** (informal) a very long time. **donkey-work** noun drudgery, the laborious part of a job.

**Donna** noun the title of an Italian, Spanish, or Portuguese lady.

**Donne** (pronounced dun), John (1572–1631), English poet and cleric.

**donnish** adjective like a college don.

**donor** noun **1** one who gives or donates something. **2** one who provides blood for transfusion, semen for insemination, or tissue for transplantation. □ **donor card** an official card authorizing the use of the card carrier's organs for transplants in the event of his or her death.

**Don Quixote** see QUIXOTIC.

**don't** (informal) = do not. ● noun a prohibition; do's and don'ts.

**donut** Amer. spelling of DOUGHNUT.

**doodle** verb scribble aimlessly or absentmindedly. ● noun a drawing or marks made by doodling.

**doom** noun a grim fate; death or ruin. ● verb destine to a grim fate.

**doomsday** noun the day of the Last Judgement, the end of the world.

**door** noun **1** a hinged, sliding, or revolving barrier that closes an entrance or exit. **2** a doorway. **3** a means of obtaining or approaching something; closed the door to any agreement. □ **door-keeper** noun a doorman. **door-to-door** adjective (of selling etc.) done at each house in turn.

**doorbell** noun a bell inside a house, rung from outside by visitors as a signal.

**doorman** (plural **doormen**) noun a person on duty at the entrance to a hotel or large building.

**doormat** noun **1** a mat placed at a door, for wiping dirt from shoes. **2** (informal) a very submissive person.

**doorstep** noun **1** a step or area just outside a door. **2** (slang) a thick slice of bread.

**doorstop** noun a device for keeping a door open or preventing it from striking a wall when it opens.

**doorway** noun an opening filled by a door.

**dope** noun **1** (informal) a medicine or drug; a narcotic; a drug given to an athlete, horse, etc. to affect performance. **2** (slang) information. **3** (slang) a stupid person. **4** a thick liquid used as a lubricant etc. ● verb **1** treat with dope. **2** give a narcotic or stimulant to.

**dopey** adjective (also **dopy**) (informal) **1** half asleep, stupefied by a drug. **2** stupid. □ **dopiness** noun

**doppelgänger** (**dop**-ĕl-geng-er) noun an apparition or double of a living person. (¶ German, = double-goer.)

**Doppler effect** the apparent increase (or decrease) in the frequency of light or other radiation, e.g. the pitch of sound, when the source and the observer are becoming closer (or more distant). (¶ Named after the Austrian physicist C. J. Doppler (died 1853).)

**dorado** (dor-**ah**-doh) noun (plural **dorado** or **dorados**) a sea fish with brilliant blue and silver coloration, which changes colour when out of water.

**Dordogne** (dor-**doin**) an inland department of south-west France.

**Doric** (rhymes with historic) adjective of the oldest and simplest of the five classical orders of architecture.

**dormant** adjective **1** sleeping; lying inactive as if in sleep. **2** (of plants) alive but not actively growing. **3** temporarily inactive; a dormant volcano.

**dormer** noun (in full **dormer window**) an upright window under a gable built out from a sloping roof.

**dormitory** noun **1** a room with a number of beds, especially in a school or institution. **2** (in full **dormitory town**, **village**, etc.) one from which people travel to work elsewhere.

**Dormobile** noun (trade mark) a motor caravan.

**dormouse** noun (plural **dormice**) a mouselike animal that hibernates in winter.

**dorsal** adjective of or on the back of an animal or plant; a dorsal fin.

**Dorset** a county of south-west England.

**dory** noun (also **John Dory**) an edible sea fish.

**DOS** noun Computing one of the operating systems available for manipulating information on a disk. (¶ An abbreviation of *disk operating system*.)

**dosage** *noun* **1** the giving of medicine in doses. **2** the size of a dose.

**dose** *noun* **1** an amount of medicine to be taken at one time. **2** an amount of radiation received. **3** (*informal*) an amount of flattery, punishment, etc. **4** (*slang*) a venereal infection. ●*verb* give a dose of medicine to.

**do-se-do** *noun* (also **do-si-do**) a dance figure in which two dancers pass round each other back to back.

**dosh** *noun* (*slang*) money.

**doss** *verb* (*slang*) sleep, especially in a doss-house. □ **doss down** (*slang*) sleep on a makeshift bed. **doss-house** *noun* (*slang*) a cheap lodging-house for vagrants. □ **dosser** *noun*

**dossier** (**dos-i-ay** or **dos-i-er**) *noun* a set of documents containing information about a person or event.

**Dostoevsky** (dost-oi-**ef**-ski), Fedor Mikhailovich (1821–81), Russian novelist.

**DoT** *abbreviation* (*Brit.*) Department of Transport.

**dot** *noun* **1** a small round mark, a point. **2** the shorter of the two signals used in the Morse code. ●*verb* (**dotted, dotting**) **1** mark with a dot or dots, place a dot over a letter. **2** scatter here and there; *dot them about; the sea was dotted with ships.* □ **dot-matrix printer** a printer in which each printed letter or number is made up of dots printed by the tips of small wires selected from a rectangular array. **dotted line** a line of dots showing where a signature etc. is to be entered on a document. **dot the i's and cross the t's** (*informal*) be minutely accurate and explicit about details. **on the dot** exactly on time. **the year dot** (*informal*) a very long time ago.

**dotage** (**doh**-tij) *noun* a state of weakness of mind caused by old age; *in his dotage.*

**dotard** (**doh**-terd) *noun* a person who is in his or her dotage.

**dote** *verb* (often foll. by *on*) show great fondness; *he dotes on that cat; a doting husband.*

**doth** (*old use*) does.

**dotterel** *noun* a small migrant plover.

**dottle** *noun* unburnt tobacco left in a pipe.

**dotty** *adjective* (**dottier, dottiest**) (*informal*) crazy, eccentric. □ **dottiness** *noun*

**double** *adjective* **1** consisting of two things or parts that form a pair. **2** twice as much or as many; twice the standard portion. **3** designed for two people or things; *a double bed.* **4** combining two things or qualities; *it has a double meaning.* **5** (of flowers) having more than one circle of petals. ●*adverb* **1** twice the amount or quantity; *it costs double what it cost last year.* **2** in twos; *see* double. ●*noun* **1** a double quantity or thing. **2** a person or thing that looks very like another. **3** a hit between the two outer circles of the board in darts, scoring double. **4** a bet where the winnings and stake from one race are re-staked on another. ●*verb* **1** make or become twice as much or as many. **2** bend or fold in two. **3** (often foll. by *back*) turn sharply back from a course; *the fox doubled back on its tracks.* **4** sail round; *the ship doubled the Cape.* **5** act two parts in the same play. **6** (**doubles**) a game between two pairs of players. □ **at the double** running, hurrying. **double agent** one who spies for two rival countries. **double-barrelled** *adjective* **1** (of a gun) having two barrels. **2** (of a surname) having two parts. **double bass** the largest lowest-pitched instrument of the violin family. **double-breasted** *adjective* (of a coat) having fronts that overlap to fasten across the breast. **double-check** *verb* verify twice or in two ways. **double chin** a chin with a fold of loose flesh below it. **double cream** thick cream with a high fat content. **double-cross** *verb* deceive or cheat a person with whom one pretends to be collaborating. **double-dealing** *noun* deceit, especially in business. **double-decker** *noun* a bus with two decks. **double Dutch** (*informal*) unintelligible talk. **double-edged** *adjective* having advantages and disadvantages. **double entry** a system of bookkeeping in which each transaction is entered as a debit in one account and a credit in another. **double figures** any number from 10 to 99 inclusive. **double glazing** two layers of glass in a window, with an air space between. **double helix** a pair of parallel helices with a common axis, especially in the structure of a DNA molecule. **double-jointed** *adjective* having very flexible joints that allow the fingers, arms, or legs to bend in unusual ways. **double knitting** a grade of knitting wool of medium thickness. **double negative** *Grammar* a negative statement containing two negative elements, considered incorrect in standard English (e.g. *he didn't say nothing*). **double-park** *verb* park a car alongside one already parked at the side of a street. **double pneumonia** pneumonia affecting both lungs. **double-quick** *adjective* & *adverb* very quick, very quickly. **double take** a delayed reaction to a situation etc., coming immediately after one's first reaction. **double-talk** *noun* talk that means something very different from its apparent meaning. **double time** payment of an employee at twice the normal rate. □ **doubly** *adverb*

**double entendre** (doobl ahn-**tahndr**) a phrase with two meanings, one of which is usually indecent. (¶ French.)

**doublet** (**dub**-lit) *noun* **1** a man's close-fitting jacket, with or without sleeves, worn in the 15th–17th centuries. **2** either of a pair of similar things.

**doubloon** (dub-**loon**) *noun* a former Spanish gold coin.

**doubt** *noun* **1** a feeling of uncertainty about something, an undecided state of mind. **2** a feeling of disbelief. **3** an uncertain state of affairs. ●*verb* **1** feel uncertain or undecided about. **2** hesitate to believe. □ **no doubt** certainly. **without doubt** *or* **without a doubt** certainly. □ **doubter** *noun*

**doubtful** *adjective* **1** feeling doubt. **2** causing doubt; unreliable. □ **doubtfully** *adverb*

**doubtless** *adverb* no doubt.

**douche** (*pronounced* doosh) *noun* **1** a jet of liquid applied to a part of the body to cleanse it or for medical purposes. **2** a device for applying this. ●*verb* treat with a douche; use a douche.

**dough** (*rhymes with* go) *noun* **1** a thick mixture of flour etc. and liquid, to be baked as bread, cake, or pastry. **2** (*slang*) money. □ **doughy** *adverb*

**doughnut** *noun* (*Amer.* **donut**) a small sweetened fried cake of dough.

**doughty** (**dow**-ti) *adjective* (*old use* or *humorous*) valiant, stout-hearted.

**dour** (**doo**-er) *adjective* stern, severe, gloomy-looking. □ **dourness** *noun*

**douse** (*rhymes with* mouse) *verb* (also **dowse**) **1** put into water; throw water over. **2** extinguish; *douse the light.*

**dove** *noun* **1** a bird with short legs, a small head, and a thick body, that makes a cooing sound. **2** a person who favours a policy of peace and negotiation rather than violence.

**dovecote** *noun* (also **dovecot**) a shelter for domesticated pigeons.

**dovetail** *noun* a wedge-shaped joint interlocking two pieces of wood. ●*verb* **1** join by such a joint. **2** fit closely together, combine neatly; *my plans dovetailed with hers.*

**dowager** (**dow**-ă-jer) *noun* **1** a woman who holds a title or property from her dead husband; *the dowager duchess.* **2** (*informal*) a dignified elderly woman.

**dowdy** *adjective* (**dowdier, dowdiest**) **1** (of clothes) unattractively dull, not stylish. **2** dressed in dowdy clothes. □ **dowdily** *adverb*, **dowdiness** *noun*

**dowel** (*rhymes with* fowl) *noun* a headless wooden or metal pin for holding two pieces of wood or stone together by fitting into a corresponding hole in each. ●*verb*

(**dowelled, dowelling**; *Amer.* **doweled, doweling**) fasten with a dowel.

**dowelling** *noun* round rods for cutting into dowels.

**dower** *noun* a widow's share of her husband's estate. □ **dower house** a smaller house near a large one, forming part of a widow's dower.

**Dow-Jones index** (also **Dow-Jones average**) a figure indicating the relative price of shares on the New York Stock Exchange. (¶ Named after C. H. Dow (died 1902) and E. D. Jones (died 1920), American economists.)

**Down** a district and former county of Northern Ireland.

**down**[1] *adverb* **1** from an upright position to a horizontal one; *fell down.* **2** to, in, or at a lower place, level, value, or condition; to a smaller size; further south; *they are two goals down; we are £5 down on the transaction; I'm down to my last penny.* **3** so as to be less active; *quieten down.* **4** incapacitated by illness; *is down with flu.* **5** (of a computer) out of action. **6** away from a central place or a university; *he is down from headquarters.* **7** from an earlier to a later time; *down to the present day.* **8** in writing; listed. **9** to the source or the place where something is; *track it down.* **10** as a payment at the time of purchase; *paid £5 down.* ●*preposition* **1** downwards along or through or into, along, from top to bottom of. **2** at a lower part of; *Oxford is further down the river.* ●*adjective* **1** directed downwards; *a down draught.* **2** travelling away from a central place; *a down train.* ●*verb* (*informal*) **1** knock or bring down. **2** swallow. ●*noun* **1** misfortune; *ups and downs.* **2** a throw in wrestling. **3** (*informal*) a dislike, a grudge against someone; *has a down on him.* □ **down and out** completely destitute. **down-and-out** *noun* a destitute person. **down in the mouth** unhappy. **down-market** *adjective & adverb* of or towards the cheaper end of the market. **down on one's luck** suffering misfortune. **down payment** a partial payment made at the time of purchase. **down to** attributable to; the responsibility of. **down-to-earth** *adjective* sensible and practical. **down under** (*informal*) in Australia or other countries of the antipodes. **down with** may (a person or party etc.) be overthrown.

**down**[2] *noun* very fine soft furry feathers or short hairs.

**down**[3] *noun* **1** (also **downland**) an area of open rolling land. **2** (**the downs**) the chalk uplands of south England.

**downbeat** *adjective* **1** dismal, depressing. **2** relaxed, casual. ●*noun Music* an accented beat, usually the first of the bar.

**downcast** *adjective* **1** looking downwards; *downcast eyes*. **2** (of a person) dejected.

**downer** *noun* (*slang*) **1** a depressant or tranquillizing drug. **2** a depressing person or experience; a failure. □ **on a downer** depressed.

**downfall** *noun* a fall from prosperity or power; something that causes this.

**downgrade** *verb* reduce to a lower grade or status.

**downhearted** *adjective* dejected, disappointed. □ **downheartedly** *adverb*, **downheartedness** *noun*

**downhill** *adverb* in a downward direction; further down a slope. ●*adjective* going or sloping downwards. □ **go downhill** (*informal*) deteriorate.

**Downing Street** a street in London containing the official residences of the Prime Minister and other members of the government.

**downpipe** *noun* a pipe for carrying rainwater from a roof to a drain.

**downpour** *noun* a great fall of rain.

**downright** *adjective* **1** frank, straightforward. **2** thorough, complete; *a downright lie*. ●*adverb* thoroughly; *felt downright scared*.

**downside** *noun* a negative or adverse aspect of a situation etc.

**Down's syndrome** an abnormal congenital condition in which a person has a broad flattened skull, slanting eyes, and mental deficiency. (¶ Named after J. L. H. Down, physician (died 1896).)

**downstage** *adjective & adverb* nearer the front of a theatre stage.

**downstairs** *adverb* down the stairs; to or on a lower floor. ●*adjective* situated downstairs.

**downstream** *adjective & adverb* in the direction in which a stream or river flows.

**downtown** (especially *Amer.*) *adjective* of a lower or more central part of a city. ●*adverb* in or into this part. ●*noun* a downtown area.

**downtrodden** *adjective* trampled underfoot; oppressed.

**downturn** *noun* a decline in activity or prosperity.

**downward** *adjective* moving, leading, or pointing towards what is lower, less important, or later. ●*adverb* (also **downwards**) towards what is lower, less important, or later.

**downwind** *adjective & adverb* in the direction towards which the wind is blowing.

**downy** *adjective* (**downier**, **downiest**) like or covered with soft down.

**dowry** (*rhymes with floury*) *noun* property or money brought by a bride to her husband.

**dowse** (*rhymes with cows*) *verb* **1** search for underground water or minerals by using a Y-shaped stick or rod which dips abruptly when it is over the right spot. **2** alternative spelling of DOUSE. □ **dowser** *noun*

**doxology** *noun* a formula of praise to God used in prayer.

**doyen** (**doy-ĕn**) *noun* a man who is the senior member of his staff, profession, etc.

**doyenne** *noun* a woman who is the senior member of her profession, staff, etc.

**Doyle**, Sir Arthur Conan (1859–1930), Scottish-born novelist, creator of the fictional private detective Sherlock Holmes and his friend Dr Watson.

**doyley** alternative spelling of DOILY.

**doze** *verb* sleep lightly. ●*noun* a short light sleep. □ **doze off** fall into a doze.

**dozen** *noun* **1** a set of twelve; *pack them in dozens*. **2** (**dozens**) very many; *dozens of things*. □ **talk nineteen to the dozen** talk incessantly.

■**Usage** Correct use is *ten dozen* (not *ten dozens*).

**dozy** *adjective* **1** drowsy. **2** (*informal*) stupid; lazy.

**D.Phil.** *abbreviation* Doctor of Philosophy.

**DPP** *abbreviation* Director of Public Prosecutions.

**Dr** *abbreviation* Doctor.

**drab** *adjective* **1** dull, uninteresting. **2** of a dull greyish-brown colour. ●*noun* drab colour. □ **drably** *adverb*, **drabness** *noun*

**Drabble**, Margaret (born 1939), English novelist.

**drachm** (*pronounced* dram) *noun* one-eighth of an ounce or of a fluid ounce.

**drachma** (**drak-mă**) *noun* the unit of money in Greece.

**Draconian** (**dră-koh-niăn**) *adjective* very harsh; *Draconian laws*. (¶ Named after *Draco*, who is said to have established severe laws in ancient Athens in the 6th century BC.)

**Dracula, Count** the chief of the vampires in Bram Stoker's novel *Dracula* (1897).

**draft** *noun* **1** a rough preliminary written version; *a draft of a speech*. **2** a written order for the payment of money by a bank; the drawing of money by this. **3** a group detached from a larger group for special duty; the selection of these. **4** (*Amer.*) conscription. **5** Amer. spelling of DRAUGHT. ●*verb* **1** prepare a written draft of. **2** select for a special duty; *he was drafted to the Paris branch*. **3** (*Amer.*) conscript.

**draftsman** *noun* (*plural* **draftsmen**) **1** a person who drafts documents. **2** = DRAUGHTSMAN (sense 1).

**drafty** Amer. spelling of DRAUGHTY.

**drag** *verb* (**dragged, dragging**) **1** pull along with effort or difficulty. **2** trail or allow to trail along the ground; move slowly and with effort. **3** search the bottom of water

with grapnels, nets, etc.; *drag the river.*
**4** continue slowly in a dull manner; *the speeches dragged on.* **5** draw on a cigarette etc. ●*noun* **1** something that is made for pulling along the ground, e.g. a heavy harrow, a drag-net. **2** something that slows progress; something boring. **3** (*slang*) women's clothes worn by men. **4** (*slang*) a draw on a cigarette etc. □ **drag in** introduce (a subject) unnecessarily or in an artificial way. **drag-net** *noun* a net drawn through a river or across ground to trap fish or game. **drag one's feet** *or* **heels** be deliberately slow or reluctant. **drag out** prolong unnecessarily. **drag queen** (*scornful slang*) a male homosexual who dresses in women's clothes. **drag race** a race between cars to see which can accelerate fastest from a standstill. **drag up** (*informal*) revive (a forgotten scandal or unpleasant subject).

**draggle** *verb* make wet or dirty by trailing on the ground.

**dragon** *noun* **1** a mythical monster resembling a reptile, usually with wings and able to breathe out fire. **2** a fierce woman.

**dragonfly** *noun* a large insect with a long body and two pairs of transparent wings.

**dragoon** *noun* **1** a cavalryman. **2** a fierce person. ●*verb* force into doing something.

**drain** *verb* **1** draw off (liquid) by means of channels or pipes etc. **2** flow or trickle away. **3** dry or become dried when liquid flows away. **4** deprive gradually of (strength or resources). **5** drink; empty (a glass etc.) by drinking its contents. ●*noun* **1** a channel or pipe through which liquid or sewage is carried away. **2** something that drains one's strength or resources. □ **down the drain** (*informal*) lost, wasted.

**drainage** *noun* **1** draining. **2** a system of drains. **3** what is drained off.

**draining-board** *noun* a sloping surface beside a sink, on which washed dishes are put to drain.

**drainpipe** *noun* **1** a pipe used in a system of drains. **2** (**drainpipes**) very narrow trousers.

**Drake**, Sir Francis (*c.*1540–96), Elizabethan sailor and explorer, who sailed round the world in his ship the *Golden Hind*, and played an important part in the defeat of the Spanish Armada (1588).

**drake** *noun* a male duck.

**Dralon** *noun* (*trade mark*) a synthetic acrylic fibre; velvety furnishing fabric made from this.

**dram** *noun* **1** a drachm. **2** a small drink of spirits.

**drama** (**drah-**mă) *noun* **1** a play for acting on the stage or for broadcasting. **2** plays as a branch of literature; their composition and performance. **3** a dramatic series of events. **4** dramatic quality; *the drama of the situation.*

**dramatic** *adjective* **1** of drama. **2** exciting; impressive; *a dramatic change.* ●*noun* (**dramatics**) (often treated as *singular*) **1** the performance of plays. **2** exaggerated behaviour. □ **dramatically** *adverb*

**dramatis personae** (dra-mă-tiss per-**soh-**ny) *plural noun* the characters in a play. (¶ Latin.)

**dramatist** *noun* a writer of plays.

**dramatize** *verb* (also **dramatise**) **1** make (a story etc.) into a play. **2** make (a thing) seem dramatic. □ **dramatization** *noun*

**drank** *see* DRINK.

**drape** *verb* **1** cover loosely or decorate with cloth etc. **2** arrange loosely or in graceful folds. ●*noun* **1** the way a fabric hangs in folds. **2** (**drapes**) (*Amer.*) curtains.

**draper** *noun* a retailer of fabrics.

**drapery** *noun* **1** a draper's trade or fabrics. **2** fabric arranged in loose folds.

**drastic** *adjective* having a strong or violent effect. □ **drastically** *adverb*

**drat** *interjection* (*informal*) an expression of annoyance or frustration.

**dratted** *adjective* (*informal*) cursed; damn; *the dratted thing won't work!*

**draught** (*rhymes with* craft) *noun* (*Amer.* **draft**) **1** a current of air in an enclosed place. **2** pulling. **3** the pulling in of a net of fish; the fish caught in this. **4** the depth of water needed to float a ship. **5** the drawing of liquor from a cask etc. **6** one continuous process of swallowing liquid; the amount swallowed. **7** (**draughts**) a game for two players using 24 round pieces, played on a draughtboard. □ **draught beer** beer drawn from a cask, not bottled. **draught horse** a horse used for pulling heavy loads.

**draughtboard** *noun* a chequered games board of 64 squares.

**draughtsman** (*rhymes with* craftsman) *noun* (*plural* **draughtsmen**) **1** one who makes drawings, plans, or sketches. **2** a piece used in the game of draughts. □ **draughtsmanship** *noun*

**draughty** (*rhymes with* crafty) *adjective* (**draughtier, draughtiest**) (*Amer.* **drafty**) letting in sharp currents of air. □ **draughtiness** *noun*

**Dravidian** (dră-**vid-**iăn) *noun* **1** a member of a dark-skinned people of southern India and Sri Lanka. **2** the group of languages spoken by them (including Tamil, Telugu, and Kanarese). ●*adjective* of the Dravidians or their languages.

**draw** *verb* (**drew, drawn, drawing**) **1** pull; *draw a bow; draw the curtains.* **2** attract; *draw attention.* **3** take in; *draw breath.* **4** take out; *drew the cork; draw water; draw*

£10 *from the account.* **5** draw lots; select (a raffle ticket). **6** get information from; *tried to draw him about his plans.* **7** finish a contest with neither side winning. **8** require (a certain depth of water) in which to float; *the ship draws 10 feet.* **9** produce a picture or diagram by making marks on a surface. **10** formulate; *draw a conclusion.* **11** write out (a cheque etc.) for encashment. **12** search (a covert) for game. **13** make one's way; *draw near; the train drew in.* **14** (of tea) infuse. ●noun **1** the act of drawing. **2** a person or thing that draws custom, an attraction. **3** the drawing of lots. **4** a drawn game. □ **draw a blank** get no response or result. **draw in** (of the time of daylight) become shorter. **draw in one's horns** become less aggressive or less ambitious. **draw out 1** prolong (a discussion etc.); encourage (a person) to talk. **2** (of the time of daylight) become longer. **draw the line at** refuse to do or tolerate. **draw up 1** come to a halt. **2** compose (a contract etc.). **3** make (oneself) stiffly erect. **quick on the draw** quick to react.

**drawback** *noun* a disadvantage.

**drawbridge** *noun* a bridge over a moat, hinged at one end so that it can be drawn up.

**drawer** *noun* **1** a person who draws something; one who writes out a cheque. **2** a boxlike compartment without a lid, that can be slid horizontally in and out of a piece of furniture. **3** (**drawers**) (*old use*) knickers; underpants.

**drawing** *noun* a picture etc. drawn but not coloured. □ **drawing-board** *noun* a flat board on which paper is stretched while a drawing is made. **go back to the drawing-board** begin planning afresh. **drawing-pin** *noun* (*Brit.*) a flat-headed pin for fastening paper etc. to a surface. **drawing-room** *noun* a sitting-room in a private house.

**drawl** *verb* speak lazily or with drawn-out vowel sounds. ●noun a drawling manner of speaking.

**drawn** *see* DRAW. ●*adjective* (of a person's features) looking strained from tiredness or worry.

**drawstring** *noun* a cord threaded through a waistband, bag opening, etc. and pulled to tighten it.

**dray** *noun* a strong low flat cart for heavy loads.

**dread** *noun* great fear. ●*verb* fear greatly. ●*adjective* (*old use*) dreaded, dreadful.

**dreadful** *adjective* **1** causing dread. **2** (*informal*) troublesome, very bad; *dreadful weather.* □ **dreadfully** *adverb*

**dreadlocks** *plural noun* a Rastafarian hairstyle with hair hanging in tight braids.

**dream** *noun* **1** a series of pictures or events in a sleeping person's mind. **2** the state of mind of one dreaming or daydreaming; *he goes round in a dream.* **3** an ambition, an ideal. **4** a beautiful person or thing. ●*verb* (**dreamt** (*pronounced* dremt) *or* **dreamed**, **dreaming**) **1** have a dream or dreams while sleeping. **2** have an ambition; *dream of being champion.* **3** think of as a possibility; *never dreamt it would happen.* □ **dream up** imagine, invent. **like a dream** (*informal*) easily, effortlessly. □ **dreamer** *noun*

**dreamboat** *noun* (*informal*) a very attractive person.

**dreamy** *adjective* **1** daydreaming. **2** (*informal*) wonderful. □ **dreamily** *adverb*, **dreaminess** *noun*

**dreary** *adjective* (**drearier**, **dreariest**) dull, boring; (of places etc.) gloomy. □ **drearily** *adverb*, **dreariness** *noun*

**dredge** *noun* an apparatus for scooping things from the bottom of a river or the sea. ●*verb* **1** bring up or clean out (mud etc.) with a dredge. **2** (often foll. by *up*) bring up (something forgotten); *dredging up old memories.* **3** sprinkle with flour, sugar, etc.

**dredger** *noun* **1** a boat with a dredge; the dredge itself. **2** a container with a perforated lid for sprinkling flour, sugar, etc.

**dregs** *plural noun* **1** bits of worthless matter that sink to the bottom of a liquid. **2** the worst and most useless part; *the dregs of society.*

**Dreiser** (**dry-ser**), Theodore Herman Albert (1871–1945), American novelist.

**drench** *verb* make wet through.

**Dresden china** fine china made at Meissen, near Dresden in Germany.

**dress** *noun* **1** clothing, especially the visible part of it. **2** a woman's or girl's garment with a bodice and skirt. ●*verb* **1** put clothes upon; put on one's clothes; provide clothes for. **2** put on evening dress; *they dress for dinner.* **3** decorate; *dress a shop window.* **4** put a dressing on (a wound etc.). **5** groom and arrange (hair). **6** finish or treat the surface of; *to dress leather.* **7** prepare (poultry, crab, etc.) for cooking or eating; coat (salad) with dressing. **8** arrange (soldiers) into a straight line. □ **dress circle** the first gallery in theatres, where evening dress was formerly required. **dress coat** a man's swallow-tailed evening coat. **dress rehearsal** a rehearsal in full costume. **dress shirt** a shirt suitable for wearing with evening dress. **dress up 1** put on special clothes. **2** make (a thing) look more interesting.

**dressage** (**dress**-ah*z*h) *noun* the management of a horse to show its obedience and deportment.

**dresser** *noun* **1** one who dresses a person or thing. **2** a sideboard with shelves above for dishes etc.

**dressing** *noun* **1** a sauce or stuffing for food. **2** manure etc. spread over land. **3** a bandage, ointment, etc. for a wound. **4** a substance used to stiffen fabrics during manufacture. □ **dressing down** a scolding. **dressing gown** a loose gown worn when one is not fully dressed. **dressing room** a room for dressing or changing one's clothes. **dressing table** a piece of bedroom furniture with a mirror and drawers.

**dressmaker** *noun* a person who makes women's clothes. □ **dressmaking** *noun*

**dressy** *adjective* (**dressier**, **dressiest**) **1** wearing stylish clothes. **2** (of clothes) elegant, elaborate.

**drew** *see* DRAW.

**drey** (*pronounced* dray) *noun* (*plural* **dreys**) a squirrel's nest.

**Dreyfus**, Alfred (1859–1935), French Jewish army officer, falsely accused of spying for Germany (1894), whose trial, imprisonment, and eventual rehabilitation (1906) polarized anti-militarist and anti-Semitic trends in France.

**dribble** *verb* **1** allow saliva to flow from the mouth. **2** flow or allow to flow in drops. **3** move the ball forward in football or hockey with slight touches of the feet or stick. ●*noun* **1** an act of dribbling. **2** a dribbling flow.

**driblet** *noun* a small amount.

**dribs and drabs** (*informal*) small amounts.

**dried** *see* DRY. ●*adjective* (of foods) preserved by drying; *dried apricots*.

**drier** *noun* (also **dryer**) a device for drying hair, laundry, etc. ●*adjective see* DRY.

**drift** *verb* **1** be carried by or as if by a current of water or air. **2** move casually or aimlessly. **3** be piled into drifts by wind; *the snow had drifted*. **4** cause to drift. ●*noun* **1** a drifting movement. **2** a mass of snow or sand piled up by wind. **3** deviation from a set course. **4** the general tendency or meaning of a speech etc. **5** (in mining) a horizontal passage following a mineral vein. □ **drift-net** *noun* a large net for sea fishing, allowed to drift with the tide.

**drifter** *noun* **1** a boat used for fishing with a drift-net. **2** an aimless person.

**driftwood** *noun* wood floating on the sea or washed ashore by it.

**drill**[1] *noun* **1** a pointed tool or a machine used for boring holes or sinking wells. **2** training in military exercises. **3** thorough training by practical exercises, usually with much repetition. **4** (*informal*) a routine procedure to be followed; *what's the drill?* ●*verb* **1** use a drill; make (a hole) with a drill. **2** train or be trained by means of drill.

**drill**[2] *noun* **1** a furrow. **2** a machine for making or sowing seed in furrows. **3** a row of seeds sown in this way. ●*verb* plant in drills.

**drill**[3] *noun* strong twilled linen or cotton cloth.

**drill**[4] *noun* a baboon found in West Africa, related to the mandrill.

**drily** *adverb* (also **dryly**) in a dry way.

**drink** *verb* (**drank**, **drunk**, **drinking**) **1** swallow (liquid). **2** (of plants, the soil, etc.) take in or absorb liquid. **3** take alcohol, especially in excess; *drank himself to death*. **4** pledge good wishes to by drinking; *drank his health*. ●*noun* **1** liquid for drinking. **2** alcoholic liquor; excessive use of this. **3** (*slang*) the sea. □ **drink-driver** *noun* a person who drives having drunk more than the legal limit of alcohol. **drink in** watch or listen to with delight or eagerness. □ **drinker** *noun*

**drip** *verb* (**dripped**, **dripping**) fall or let fall in drops. ●*noun* **1** liquid falling in drops; each of these drops. **2** the sound of this. **3** a drip-feed. **4** (*slang*) a weak or dull person.

**drip-dry** *verb* (**drip-dried**, **drip-drying**) dry when hung up wet, without wringing or ironing. ●*adjective* made of fabric that will drip-dry.

**drip-feed** *noun* **1** feeding by liquid a drop at a time, especially intravenously. **2** apparatus for this. ●*verb* feed in this way.

**dripping** *noun* fat melted from roasted meat.

**drive** *verb* (**drove**, **driven**, **driving**) **1** urge or send in some direction, especially in a forceful way. **2** strike and propel (a ball etc.) forcibly. **3** force to penetrate; *drove a stake into the ground*. **4** operate (a vehicle or locomotive) and direct its course; travel or convey in a vehicle; *he drove me to the station*. **5** (of steam or other power) keep (machinery) going. **6** cause, compel; *was driven by hunger to steal*; *drove him mad*. **7** rush, move or be moved rapidly; *driving rain*. ●*noun* **1** a journey in a vehicle. **2** a stroke made by driving in cricket or golf etc. **3** the transmission of power to machinery; *front-wheel drive*; *left-hand drive*. **4** energy, persistence; a psychological urge. **5** an organized effort; *a sales drive*. **6** a social gathering to play card games etc., changing partners and tables. **7** a road, especially a private one serving as an approach to a house etc. □ **drive a hard bargain** conclude one without making concessions. **drive at** intend to convey as a meaning; *what was he driving at?* **drive-in** *adjective* (of a cinema, bank, etc.) able to be used without getting out of one's car. ●*noun* a cinema, bank, etc., of this kind. **driving licence** a licence permitting one to drive a vehicle. **driving wheel** a wheel that communicates motive power in machinery, or to which driving power is applied.

**drivel** *noun* silly talk, nonsense. ●*verb* (**drivelled, drivelling;** *Amer.* **driveled, driveling**) talk or write drivel.

**driven** *see* DRIVE.

**driver** *noun* **1** a person who drives, especially one who drives a motor vehicle. **2** a golf-club for driving from a tee.

**driveway** *noun* = DRIVE (*noun* sense 7).

**drizzle** *noun* very fine rain. ●*verb* rain in very fine drops. □ **drizzly** *adjective*

**droll** (*pronounced* drohl) *adjective* amusing in an odd way. □ **drolly** *adverb*

**drollery** (**drohl-er-i**) *noun* droll humour.

**dromedary** (**drom-ĕd-er-i**) *noun* a one-humped camel bred for riding.

**drone** *noun* **1** a male honey-bee. **2** an idler. **3** a deep humming sound. **4** the bass-pipe of a bagpipe; its continuous note. ●*verb* **1** make a deep humming sound. **2** speak or utter monotonously.

**drool** *verb* **1** water at the mouth, dribble. **2** (often foll. by *over*) show gushing appreciation.

**droop** *verb* bend or hang downwards through tiredness or weakness. ●*noun* a drooping attitude. □ **droopy** *adjective*

**drop** *noun* **1** a small rounded or pear-shaped portion of liquid. **2** something shaped like this, e.g. a sweet or a hanging ornament. **3** a very small quantity. **4** (**drops**) liquid medicine to be measured and given in drops. **5** the act of dropping; a fall; *a drop in prices.* **6** a steep or vertical descent; the distance of this; *a drop of 10 feet from the window.* ●*verb* **1** fall by force of gravity through not being held; allow to fall. **2** sink from exhaustion; *feel ready to drop.* **3** form a steep or vertical descent; *the cliff drops sharply to the sea.* **4** lower, become lower or weaker; *drop the hem; prices dropped.* **5** allow oneself to move to a position further back; *dropped behind the others.* **6** utter or send casually; *drop a hint; drop me a note.* **7** omit, fail to pronounce or insert; *drop one's h's.* **8** set down (a passenger or parcel etc.). **9** give up; reject; cease to associate with; *dropped the habit; has dropped his friends.* **10** (of animals) give birth to (offspring). **11** lose (a game or point). □ **drop by** or **drop in** pay a casual visit. **drop-kick** *noun* a kick made by dropping a football and kicking it as it falls to the ground. **drop off** fall asleep. **drop out** cease to participate. **drop-out** *noun* one who drops out from a course of study or from conventional society. **drop**

**scone** a scone made by dropping a spoonful of batter on a cooking-surface.

**drop-shot** *noun* (in tennis) a shot which drops abruptly just over the net.

**droplet** *noun* a small drop of liquid.

**dropper** *noun* a device for releasing liquid in drops.

**droppings** *plural noun* dung of animals or birds.

**dropsy** *noun* a disease in which watery fluid collects in the body. □ **dropsical** *adjective*

**dross** *noun* **1** scum on molten metal. **2** impurities; rubbish.

**drought** (*rhymes with* out) *noun* continuous dry weather.

**drove** *see* DRIVE. ●*noun* **1** a moving herd, flock, or crowd. **2** (**droves**) very many; a great number; *they came in droves.*

**drover** *noun* a person who herds cattle.

**drown** *verb* **1** kill or be killed by suffocating in water or other liquid. **2** flood, drench. **3** deaden (grief etc.) with drink; *drown one's sorrows.* **4** overpower (a sound) with greater loudness.

**drowse** (*rhymes with* cows) *verb* be half asleep.

**drowsy** *adjective* (**drowsier, drowsiest**) sleepy, half asleep. □ **drowsily** *adverb*, **drowsiness** *noun*

**drub** *verb* (**drubbed, drubbing**) **1** thrash. **2** defeat thoroughly.

**drubbing** *noun* a beating; a severe defeat.

**drudge** *noun* a person who does dull, laborious, or menial work. ●*verb* do such work. □ **drudgery** *noun*

**drug** *noun* **1** a substance used in medicine. **2** a substance that acts on the nervous system, e.g. a narcotic or stimulant, especially one causing addiction. ●*verb* (**drugged, drugging**) **1** add a drug to (food or drink). **2** give drugs to, stupefy. □ **drug on the market** something that is plentiful but not in demand.

**drugget** (**drug-it**) *noun* coarse woven fabric used for floor coverings.

**druggist** *noun* a pharmaceutical chemist.

**drugstore** *noun* (*Amer.*) a chemist's shop also selling light refreshments and many kinds of goods.

**Druid** (**droo-id**) *noun* **1** a priest of an ancient Celtic religion. **2** a member of a modern Druidic order, especially the Gorsedd. □ **Druidism** *noun*, **Druidic** *adjective*, **Druidical** *adjective*

**drum** *noun* **1** a percussion instrument consisting of a skin stretched tightly across a round frame. **2** the sound of this being struck; a similar sound. **3** a cylindrical structure or object or container. **4** the eardrum. ●*verb* (**drummed, drumming**) **1** play a drum or drums. **2** make a drumming sound; tap or thump continuously or rhythmically. **3** drive (facts etc.) into a person's mind by constant repetition. □ **drum brake** one in which curved pads on a vehicle press against the inner cylindrical part of a wheel. **drum kit** a set of drums. **drum machine** an electronic device that simulates the sound of drums. **drum major** the leader of a marching band. **drum majorette** a female baton-twirling member of a parading group. **drum out** dismiss in disgrace. **drum up** obtain through vigorous effort; *drum up support*.

**drumhead** *noun* the part of a drum that is struck.

**drummer** *noun* a person who plays drums.

**drumstick** *noun* **1** a stick for beating a drum. **2** the lower part of a cooked fowl's leg.

**drunk** *see* DRINK. ● *adjective* **1** excited or stupefied with alcoholic drink. **2** (often foll. by *with*) overcome with joy, power, etc.; *drunk with success*. ● *noun* a drunken person.

■**Usage** See the note under DRUNKEN.

**drunkard** *noun* a person who is often drunk.

**drunken** *adjective* **1** intoxicated; frequently in this condition. **2** happening during or because of drunkenness; *a drunken brawl*. □ **drunkenly** *adverb*, **drunkenness** *noun*

■**Usage** This word is used before a noun (e.g. *a drunken man*), whereas *drunk* is usually used after a verb (e.g. *he is drunk*).

**drupe** (*pronounced* droop) *noun* a fruit with juicy flesh round a stone with a kernel, e.g. a peach.

**Druse** *noun* a member of a political and religious sect of Muslim origin, concentrated in Lebanon, with smaller groups in Syria and Israel, considered heretics by the general Muslim community.

**dry** *adjective* (**drier, driest**) **1** without water or moisture. **2** (of cows) not producing milk. **3** eaten without butter etc.; *dry bread*. **4** thirsty. **5** (of wine) not sweet. **6** uninteresting; *a dry book*. **7** expressed with pretended seriousness; *dry humour*. **8** not allowing the sale of alcohol. ● *verb* (**dried, drying**) **1** make or become dry. **2** preserve (food) by removing its moisture. □ **dry battery** (also **dry cell**) an electric battery or cell in which the electrolyte is absorbed in a solid. **dry-clean** *verb* clean (clothes etc.) by a solvent which evaporates very quickly, not by water. **dry dock** a dock which can be emptied of water, used for repairing ships. **dry-fly** *adjective* (of fishing) using an artificial fly that floats. **dry ice** solid carbon dioxide used as a refrigerant. **dry measure** a measure for dry goods (e.g. corn). **dry rot** decay of wood that is not well ventilated; the fungi that cause

this. **dry run** (*informal*) a dummy run; a rehearsal. **dry up 1** dry washed dishes. **2** (*informal*) cease talking; (of an actor) forget one's lines. **3** become unproductive. □ **dryness** *noun*

**dryad** *noun* a wood nymph.

**Dryden**, John (1631–1700), English poet, critic, and playwright.

**dryer** alternative spelling of DRIER.

**dryly** alternative spelling of DRILY.

**drystone** *adjective* (of a stone wall) built without mortar.

**DSC** *abbreviation* Distinguished Service Cross.

**D.Sc.** *abbreviation* Doctor of Science.

**DSM** *abbreviation* Distinguished Service Medal.

**DSO** *abbreviation* Distinguished Service Order.

**DSS** *abbreviation* (*Brit.*) Department of Social Security (formerly DHSS).

**DT** *abbreviation* (also **DT's**) delirium tremens.

**DTI** *abbreviation* Department of Trade and Industry.

**DTP** *abbreviation* desktop publishing.

**dual** *adjective* composed of two parts, double. □ **dual carriageway** a road with a dividing strip between traffic flowing in opposite directions. **dual control** two linked sets of controls, enabling either of two persons to operate a car or aircraft. □ **duality** (dew-al-iti) *noun*

**dub**[1] *verb* (**dubbed, dubbing**) **1** make (a man) a knight by touching him on the shoulder with a sword. **2** give a nickname to. **3** smear (leather) with grease.

**dub**[2] *verb* (**dubbed, dubbing**) **1** replace the soundtrack of (a film), especially in a different language. **2** add (sound effects or music) to a film or broadcast. **3** copy (a recording).

**Dubai** (dew-by) an emirate belonging to the federation of United Arab Emirates.

**dubbin** *noun* (also **dubbing**) thick grease for softening and waterproofing leather.

**Dubček** (duub-chek), Alexander (born 1921), Czech Communist statesman, whose liberalizing reforms led to the Russian occupation of Czechoslovakia (1968) and his removal from office. He returned to public life in 1989.

**dubiety** (dew-by-iti) *noun* (*literary*) doubt.

**dubious** (dew-bi-ŭs) *adjective* doubtful. □ **dubiously** *adverb*, **dubiousness** *noun*

**Dublin** the capital of the Republic of Ireland.

**ducal** *adjective* of or like a duke.

**ducat** (duk-ăt) *noun* a gold coin formerly current in most European countries.

**Duchamp** (doo-shahn), Marcel (1887–1968), French painter and sculptor, a leader of the Dada movement in the USA.

**duchess** noun **1** a duke's wife or widow. **2** a woman whose rank is equal to that of a duke.

**duchy** noun the territory of a duke or duchess; the royal dukedom of Cornwall or Lancaster.

**duck** noun **1** a swimming bird of various kinds. **2** the female of this. **3** its flesh as food. **4** (informal) dear. **5** a batsman's score of 0. **6** a ducking movement. ●verb **1** dip the head briefly under water; push (a person) under water. **2** bob down, especially to avoid being seen or hit. **3** dodge, avoid (a task etc.). □ **ducks and drakes** a game of making a flat stone skim the surface of water.

**duckbill** noun (also **duck-billed platypus**) = PLATYPUS.

**duckboards** plural noun a path of wooden slats over muddy ground, a trench, etc.

**duckling** noun a young duck.

**duckweed** noun a plant that grows on the surface of ponds etc.

**ducky** noun (informal) dear.

**duct** noun **1** a tube or channel for conveying liquid, gas, cable, etc. **2** a tube in the body through which fluid passes; tear ducts. ●verb convey through a duct.

**ductile** adjective **1** (of metal) able to be drawn out into fine strands. **2** easily moulded. □ **ductility** noun

**ductless** adjective without a duct. □ **ductless glands** glands that pour their secretions directly into the blood, not through a duct.

**dud** (slang) noun **1** something that is useless or counterfeit or that fails to work. **2** (**duds**) clothes. ●adjective useless, defective.

**dude** (pronounced dood) noun (Amer.) **1** a dandy. **2** a city-dweller staying on a ranch. **3** a fellow.

**dudgeon** (duj-ŏn) noun resentment, indignation. □ **in high dudgeon** very angry.

**due** adjective **1** owed as a debt or obligation. **2** payable immediately; it has become due. **3** that ought to be given to a person; rightful, adequate; with due respect. **4** scheduled to do something or to arrive; he is due to speak tonight; the train is due at 7.30. ●adverb exactly; sailed due east. ●noun **1** a person's right; what is owed to a person. **2** (**dues**) a fee; what one owes; pay one's dues. □ **in due course** in the proper order; at the appropriate time. **due to** caused by.

■**Usage** The phrase due to is often used to mean because of, e.g. play was stopped due to rain. Some people regard this usage as unacceptable and maintain that due to should be used only after a noun (often

with a linking verb), e.g. the stoppage was due to rain.

**duel** noun **1** a fight with weapons between two people. **2** a contest between two people or sides. ●verb (**duelled, duelling**; Amer. **dueled, dueling**) fight a duel. □ **duellist** noun

**duet** noun a musical composition for two performers.

**duff** noun a boiled pudding. ●adjective (slang) worthless, useless; counterfeit. □ **duff up** (slang) beat (a person) up.

**duffer** noun (informal) an inefficient or stupid person.

**duffle** noun (also **duffel**) heavy woollen cloth. □ **duffle bag** a cylindrical canvas bag closed by a drawstring. **duffle-coat** noun a hooded overcoat made of duffle, fastened with toggles.

**Dufy** (doo-fi), Raoul (1877–1953), French painter and textile designer.

**dug**[1] see DIG.

**dug**[2] noun an udder, a teat.

**dugong** (dew-gong) noun (plural **dugong** or **dugongs**) an Asian sea mammal.

**dugout** noun **1** an underground shelter. **2** a canoe made by hollowing a tree trunk.

**duke** noun **1** a nobleman of the highest hereditary rank. **2** the male ruler of a duchy or of certain small countries.

**dukedom** noun the position or lands of a duke.

**dulcet** (dul-sit) adjective sweet-sounding.

**dulcimer** (dul-sim-er) noun a musical instrument with strings struck by two handheld hammers.

**dull** adjective **1** not bright or clear. **2** slow in understanding, stupid. **3** not sharp; (of sound) not resonant. **4** not interesting or exciting, boring. ●verb make or become dull. □ **dully** adverb, **dullness** noun

**dullard** noun a mentally dull person.

**duly** (dew-li) adverb in a correct or suitable way.

**Dumas** (dew-mah), Alexandre (1802–70), French novelist and dramatist, famous especially for his historical novels, which include The Three Musketeers and The Count of Monte Cristo. His son Alexandre (1824–95) won fame with his novel La Dame aux camélias.

**Du Maurier** (dew mo-ri-ay), Dame Daphne (1907–89), English novelist, author of Rebecca.

**dumb** adjective **1** unable to speak. **2** temporarily silent. **3** (informal) stupid. **4** giving no sound. □ **dumb-bell** noun a short bar with a weight at each end, lifted to exercise the muscles. **dumb show** gestures without words. **dumb waiter** a stand with shelves for holding food ready to be served; a lift for conveying food etc. □ **dumbly** adverb, **dumbness** noun

**dumbfound** verb astonish, strike dumb with surprise.

**dumbstruck** adjective speechless with surprise.

**dumdum** noun (in full **dumdum bullet**) a soft-nosed bullet that expands on impact.

**Dumfries and Galloway** (dum-**freess**, gal-ŏ-way) a local government region of SW Scotland.

**dummy** noun **1** a sham article. **2** a model of the human figure, used to display clothes. **3** a rubber teat for a baby to suck. **4** a stupid person. **5** a person taking no real part, a figurehead. **6** (in card games) a player whose cards are placed upwards on the table and played by a partner. ● adjective sham. □ **dummy run** a trial run, a practice.

**dump** verb **1** deposit as rubbish. **2** put down carelessly. **3** get rid of (something unwanted). **4** market goods abroad at a lower price than is charged in the home market. ● noun **1** a rubbish-heap; a place where rubbish may be deposited. **2** a temporary store; *ammunition dump*. **3** (*informal*) a dull or unattractive place. □ **down in the dumps** (*informal*) miserable, gloomy. **dump truck** a small truck that tilts its load to unload it.

**dumpling** noun **1** a ball of dough cooked in stew etc. or baked with fruit inside it. **2** a small fat person.

**dumpy** adjective short and fat. □ **dumpiness** noun

**dun**[1] adjective & noun greyish-brown.

**dun**[2] verb (**dunned**, **dunning**) ask persistently for payment of a debt.

**Dunbar**, William (*c.*1456–*c.*1513), Scottish poet and priest in the time of James IV.

**Duncan**, Isadora (1878–1927), American dancer and teacher, who developed a form of barefoot dancing thought to be akin to that of classical Greece.

**dunce** noun a person who is slow at learning.

**dunderhead** noun a stupid person.

**dune** (*pronounced* dewn) noun a mound or ridge of sand formed by the wind.

**dung** noun animal excrement. □ **dung-beetle** noun a beetle whose larvae develop in dung.

**dungarees** (dung-er-**eez**) plural noun overalls or trousers of coarse cotton cloth.

**dungeon** (**dun**-jŏn) noun a strong underground cell for prisoners.

**dunghill** noun a heap of dung.

**dunk** verb dip (a biscuit etc.) into liquid.

**Dunkirk** (French **Dunquerque**) a seaport in northern France from which British troops were evacuated in 1940.

**dunlin** noun the red-backed sandpiper.

**Dunlop**, John Boyd (1840–1921), Scottish veterinary surgeon, the first person to devise a successful pneumatic tyre (1888).

**Dunne**, John William (1875–1949), English philosopher, who developed a theory that all time exists simultaneously.

**dunnock** noun the hedge sparrow.

**Dunstan**, St (*c.*909–88), Benedictine abbot of Glastonbury and Archbishop of Canterbury. Feast day, 19 May.

**duo** (**dew**-oh) noun (*plural* **duos**) **1** a pair of performers. **2** a duet.

**duodecimal** (dew-ŏ-**dess**-imăl) adjective based on 12; reckoning by twelves.

**duodenum** (dew-ŏ-**deen**-ŭm) noun the first part of the small intestine, immediately below the stomach. □ **duodenal** adjective

**duologue** (**dew**-ŏ-log) noun a dialogue between two people.

**dupe** noun a person who is deceived or tricked. ● verb deceive, trick.

**duple** (**dew**-pŭl) adjective of or having two parts. □ **duple time** (in music) rhythm with two beats to the bar.

**duplex** (**dew**-pleks) adjective **1** having two parts. **2** *Computing* (of a circuit) allowing simultaneous two-way transmission of signals. ● noun (especially *Amer.*) **1** a flat on two floors. **2** a house divided for two families; a semi-detached house.

**duplicate** noun (*pronounced* **dew**-plik-ăt) **1** one of two or more things that are exactly alike. **2** an exact copy. ● adjective (*pronounced* **dew**-plik-ăt) exactly like another thing; being a duplicate. ● verb (*pronounced* **dew**-plik-ayt) **1** make or be an exact copy of. **2** repeat or do twice. □ **in duplicate** as two identical copies. □ **duplication** noun

**duplicator** noun a machine for copying documents.

**duplicity** (dew-**pliss**-iti) noun doubledealing, deceitfulness.

**du Pré** (doo **pray**), Jacqueline (1945–87), English cellist.

**Dur.** abbreviation Durham (county).

**durable** adjective likely to last, not wearing out or decaying quickly. ● plural noun (**durables**) durable goods. □ **durably** adverb, **durability** noun

**dura mater** (joorǎ **may**-ter) the tough outermost membrane covering the brain and the spinal cord.

**duration** noun the time during which a thing continues.

**duress** (dewr-**ess**) noun the use of force or threats to procure something.

**Dürer** (**dewr**-er), Albrecht (1471–1528), German painter and engraver.

**Durex** noun (*trade mark*) a condom.

**Durga** a fierce Hindu goddess (often identified with Kali), wife of Siva.

**Durham** a town and county of NE England.

**during** *preposition* throughout or at a point in the continuance of.

**Durkheim** (derk-hym), Émile (1858–1917), French philosopher, a founder of modern sociology.

**Durrell**, Gerald Malcolm (born 1925), English writer and naturalist; his brother Lawrence George (1912–90), English novelist.

**dusk** *noun* the darker stage of twilight.

**dusky** *adjective* (**duskier**, **duskiest**) **1** shadowy, dim. **2** dark-coloured. □ **duskiness** *noun*

**dust** *noun* fine particles of earth or other matter. ●*verb* **1** sprinkle with dust or powder. **2** clear (furniture etc.) of dust by wiping. □ **dust bowl** an arid or unproductive dry region. **dust cover 1** = DUST-SHEET. **2** = DUST-JACKET. **dust-jacket** *noun* a paper cover on a book. **dust-sheet** *noun* a sheet put over furniture to protect it from dust. **dust-up** *noun* (*informal*) a noisy argument; a fight.

**dustbin** *noun* a bin for household rubbish.

**dustcart** *noun* a vehicle collecting household rubbish.

**duster** *noun* a cloth for dusting furniture etc.

**dustman** *noun* (*plural* **dustmen**) a person employed to collect household refuse.

**dustpan** *noun* a pan into which dust is brushed from a floor.

**dusty** *adjective* (**dustier**, **dustiest**) **1** full of dust; covered with dust. **2** (of a colour) greyish; *dusty pink*. □ **dusty answer** a sharp rejection of a request. □ **dustiness** *noun*

**Dutch** *adjective* of the Netherlands or its people or language. ●*noun* **1** the Dutch language. **2** (**the Dutch**) Dutch people. □ **Dutch auction** one in which the price asked is gradually reduced until a buyer is found. **Dutch barn** one consisting of a roof supported on poles. **Dutch cap** a flexible dome-shaped contraceptive device inserted to fit over a woman's cervix. **Dutch courage** that obtained by drinking alcohol. **Dutch elm disease** a disease of elm trees, caused by a fungus. **Dutch oven** a covered dish for cooking meat etc. slowly. **Dutch treat** an outing where people pay for themselves. **Dutch uncle** a kind but firm adviser. **go Dutch** share expenses on an outing. □ **Dutchman** *noun*, **Dutchwoman** *noun*

**dutch** *noun* (*slang*) a wife.

**duteous** (dew-ti-ŭs) *adjective* (*literary*) dutiful.

**dutiable** (dew-ti-ăbŭl) *adjective* on which customs or other duties must be paid.

**dutiful** *adjective* doing one's duty, showing due obedience. □ **dutifully** *adverb*

**duty** *noun* **1** a moral or legal obligation. **2** a task that must be done, action required from a particular person. **3** a tax charged on certain goods or on imports. □ **do duty for** serve as (something else). **in duty bound, duty-bound** *adjective* obliged by duty. **duty-free** *adjective* (of goods) on which duty is not charged. **duty-free shop** a shop on a ferry, at an airport, etc. selling duty-free goods. **on** (*or* **off**) **duty** actually engaged (or not engaged) in one's regular work.

**duvet** (doo-vay) *noun* a thick soft quilt used instead of bedclothes.

**DVLC** *abbreviation* Driver Vehicle Licensing Centre.

**Dvořák** (dvor-zhak), Antonin (1841–1904), Czech composer.

**dwarf** *noun* (*plural* **dwarfs** *or* **dwarves**) **1** a person, animal, or plant much below the usual size. **2** (in fairy tales) a small being with magic powers. ●*adjective* of a kind that is very small in size. ●*verb* **1** stunt. **2** make seem small by contrast or distance.

■**Usage** In sense 1, with regard to people, *person of restricted growth* is now often preferred.

**dweeb** *noun* (*Amer. slang*) a studious or tedious person.

**dwell** *verb* (**dwelt**, **dwelling**) live as an inhabitant. □ **dwell on** think, speak, or write lengthily about; *dwell on a subject*. □ **dweller** *noun*

**dwelling** *noun* (*formal*) a house etc. to live in.

**dwindle** *verb* become gradually less or smaller.

**Dy** *symbol* dysprosium.

**dybbuk** (dib-ŭk) *noun* (in Jewish folklore) the malevolent spirit of a dead person that enters and controls the body of a living person until exorcized.

**dye** *verb* (**dyed**, **dyeing**) **1** colour, especially by dipping in a liquid. **2** absorb dye; *this fabric dyes well*. ●*noun* **1** a substance used for dyeing. **2** a colour given by dyeing. □ **dyed-in-the-wool** *adjective* unchangeable, confirmed in one's beliefs; *a dyed-in-the-wool socialist*. □ **dyer** *noun*

**Dyfed** (duv-id) a county of Wales.

**dying** *see* DIE¹.

**dyke** *noun* (also **dike**) **1** an embankment built to prevent flooding. **2** a ditch. **3** a low wall of turf or stone. **4** (*slang*) a lesbian.

**Dylan** (dil-ĕn), Bob (original name; Robert Allen Zimmerman) (born 1941), American rock singer and songwriter.

**dynamic** *adjective* **1** (of force) producing motion (as opposed to *static*). **2** (of a person) energetic, having force of character. ●*noun* (**dynamics**) **1** (usually treated as *singular*) a branch of physics that deals with matter in motion. **2** *Music* (treated as *plural*) varying degrees of loudness. □ **dynamically** *adverb*

**dynamism** (**dy**-nă-mizm) *noun* energizing or dynamic action or power.

**dynamite** *noun* **1** a powerful explosive made of nitroglycerine. **2** something likely to cause violent or dangerous reactions; *the frontier question is dynamite.* **3** a person or thing with great vitality or effectiveness. ● *verb* fit with a charge of dynamite, blow up with dynamite.

**dynamo** *noun* (*plural* **dynamos**) **1** a generator producing electric current. **2** (*informal*) an energetic dynamic person.

**dynamometer** (dy-nă-**mom**-it-er) *noun* an instrument measuring energy expended.

**dynast** (**din**-ăst) *noun* **1** a ruler. **2** a member of a dynasty.

**dynasty** (**din**-ă-sti) *noun* a line of hereditary rulers. □ **dynastic** *adjective*

**dyne** *noun* *Physics* the force required to give a mass of one gram an acceleration of one centimetre per second per second.

**dysentery** (**dis**-ĕn-tri) *noun* a disease with inflammation of the intestines, causing severe diarrhoea.

**dysfunction** (dis-**funk**-shŏn) *noun* failure to function normally.

**dyslexia** (dis-**leks**-iă) *noun* abnormal difficulty in reading and spelling. □ **dyslexic** *adjective & noun*

**dysmenorrhoea** (dis-menŏ-**ree**-ă) *noun* (*Amer.* **dysmenorrhea**) painful or difficult menstruation.

**dyspepsia** (dis-**pep**-siă) *noun* indigestion. □ **dyspeptic** *adjective & noun*

**dysphasia** (dis-**fay**-ziă) *noun* difficulty in coordinating speech as a result of brain damage.

**dysprosium** (dis-**proh**-ziŭm) *noun* a chemical element (symbol Dy), a soft metal used in certain magnetic alloys.

**dystrophy** (**dis**-trŏ-fi) *noun* defective nutrition. See also *muscular dystrophy*.

**Dzongkha** (**zonk**-ă) *noun* a Tibetan dialect that is the official language of Bhutan.

# Ee

**E** *noun* (*plural* **Es** *or* **E's**) *Music* the third note of the scale of C major. ● *abbreviation* (also **E.**) **1** East; Eastern. **2** *see* E-NUMBER.

**e** *symbol* conforming with EC standards for the indicated weights or volume of certain pre-packaged products.

**each** *adjective* every one of two or more people or things; *each child.* ● *pronoun* each person or thing; *each of them*; *give them two each.* □ **each other** one another. **each way** (of a bet) backing a horse etc. to win and to be placed.

**eager** *adjective* full of strong desire, enthusiastic. □ **eager beaver** (*informal*) a very diligent or keen person. □ **eagerly** *adverb*, **eagerness** *noun*

**eagle** *noun* **1** a large bird of prey. **2** a score of two strokes under par or bogey for a hole at golf. □ **eagle eye** very sharp eyesight; keen watchfulness.

**eaglet** *noun* a young eagle.

**ear**¹ *noun* **1** the organ of hearing in humans and certain animals; the external part of this. **2** the ability to distinguish sounds accurately or with great sensitivity; *she has an ear for music.* **3** an ear-shaped thing. □ **be all ears** listen attentively. **ear-piercing** *adjective* loud and shrill. **ear-splitting** *adjective* piercingly loud. **have one's ear to the ground** be alert to rumours or trends of opinion. **up to one's ears** (*informal*) deeply involved or occupied in something.

**ear**² *noun* the seed-bearing part of corn.

**earache** *noun* pain in the eardrum.

**eardrum** *noun* a membrane inside the middle ear that vibrates when sound waves strike it.

**earful** *noun* (*informal*) **1** a large amount of talk. **2** a strong reprimand.

**earl** *noun* a British nobleman ranking between marquis and viscount. □ **Earl Grey** scented tea flavoured with bergamot. **Earl Marshal** the president of the College of Heralds, with ceremonial duties.

**earldom** *noun* the position or lands of an earl.

**early** *adjective & adverb* (**earlier, earliest**) **1** before the usual or expected time. **2** not far on in a period of time or development or a series; *his early years.* □ **early bird** a person who gets up early or arrives early. **early on** at an early stage. □ **earliness** *noun*

**earmark** *noun* a distinguishing mark. ● *verb* **1** put a distinguishing mark on. **2** set aside for a particular purpose.

**earn** *verb* (**earned, earning**) **1** get or deserve as a reward for one's work or merit. **2** (of money lent or invested) gain as interest. □ **earned income** income derived from paid employment. □ **earner** *noun*

**earnest** *adjective* showing serious feeling or intentions. □ **in earnest** seriously, not jokingly; with determination, intensively. □ **earnestly** *adverb*, **earnestness** *noun*

**earnings** *plural noun* money earned.

**earphone** *noun* (usually as **earphones**) a device applied to the ear to receive radio or telephone communications.

**earplug** *noun* a piece of wax or other material placed in the ear to keep out noise or water.

**earring** *noun* a piece of jewellery worn on the ear.

**earshot** *noun* range of hearing; *within earshot.*

**earth** *noun* **1** (also **Earth**) the planet on which we live; the world in which we live. **2** its surface, dry land, the ground. **3** soil. **4** the hole of a fox or badger. **5** an oxide with little taste or smell. **6** connection to the ground as completion of an electrical circuit. ● *verb* **1** cover (roots of plants) with heaped-up earth. **2** connect (an electrical circuit) to earth. □ **cost the earth** cost a huge amount of money. **earth mother** a sensual and maternal woman. **earth science** a science such as geology or geography concerned with the structure and age of the earth. **earth-shattering** *adjective* (*informal*) shocking; having a devastating effect. **go to earth** go into hiding. **on earth** (used for emphasis in questions) ever; *what on earth is that?* **run to earth** find after a long search.

**earthbound** *adjective* **1** attached to or on the earth. **2** moving towards the earth.

**earthen** *adjective* **1** made of earth. **2** made of baked clay.

**earthenware** *noun* pottery made of coarse baked clay.

**earthling** *noun* an inhabitant of the earth, especially in science fiction.

**earthly** *adjective* of this earth; of human life on it. □ **no earthly use** (*informal*) no use at all. **not an earthly** (*slang*) no chance at all. □ **earthliness** *noun*

**earthquake** *noun* a violent natural movement of a part of the earth's crust.

**earthwork** *noun* an artificial bank of earth.

**earthworm** *noun* a common worm that lives in the soil.

**earthy** *adjective* **1** like earth or soil. **2** gross, coarse; *earthy humour*. □ **earthiness** *noun*

**earwig** *noun* a small insect with pincers at the end of its body.

**ease** *noun* **1** freedom from pain, trouble, or anxiety. **2** relief from pain. **3** absence of painful effort; *did it with ease*. ● *verb* **1** relieve from pain or anxiety. **2** make less tight, forceful, or burdensome. **3** move gently or gradually; *ease it in*. **4** slacken, reduce in severity or pressure etc.; *it will ease off*. □ **at ease 1** free from anxiety, in comfort. **2** (of a soldier) standing with feet apart rather than to attention. **at one's ease** relaxed, not feeling awkward or embarrassed.

**easel** *noun* a wooden frame to support a painting or a blackboard etc.

**easement** *noun* a legal right of way or similar right over another person's ground or property.

**easily** *adverb* **1** in an easy way, with ease. **2** by far; *easily the best*.

**east** *noun* **1** the point on the horizon where the sun rises; the direction in which this point lies. **2** the eastern part of something. **3** (**the East**) the part of the world lying east of Europe. ● *adjective* **1** towards or in the east. **2** (of a wind) blowing from the east. ● *adverb* towards or in the east. □ **East End** the eastern part of London. **East Side** the eastern part of Manhattan.

**East Anglia** an area of eastern England comprising the counties of Norfolk and Suffolk.

**eastbound** *adjective* travelling or leading eastwards.

**East China Sea** see CHINA SEA.

**Easter** *noun* the Christian festival (celebrated on a Sunday in March or April) commemorating Christ's resurrection; the period about this time. □ **Easter egg** a chocolate artificial egg given as a gift at Easter.

**Easter Island** an island in the SE Pacific west of Chile.

**easterly** *adjective* **1** in or towards the east. **2** (of a wind) blowing from the east. ● *noun* an easterly wind.

**eastern** *adjective* of or in the east. □ **Eastern Church** the Orthodox Church.

**easterner** *noun* a native or inhabitant of the east.

**easternmost** *adjective* furthest east.

**East India Company** a company, formed in 1600 to trade in the East Indies, which administered British India until the Indian Mutiny (1857).

**East Indies** the many islands off the SE coast of Asia, now often called the Malay Archipelago.

**East Sussex** a county of SE England.

**eastward** *adjective & adverb* (also **eastwards**) towards the east.

**Eastwood**, Clint (born 1930), American film actor and director.

**easy** *adjective* (**easier, easiest**) **1** not difficult, done or obtained without great effort. **2** free from pain, trouble, or anxiety; *with an easy mind; in easy circumstances*. ● *adverb* in an easy way, with ease. □ **easy chair** a large comfortable chair. **easy on the eye** (*informal*) pleasant to look at. **Easy Street** (*informal*) a state of affluence. **go easy with** *or* **on** be sparing or cautious with. **I'm easy** (*informal*) I do not mind. □ **easiness** *noun*

**easygoing** *adjective* placid and tolerant, not strict.

**eat** *verb* (**ate, eaten, eating**) **1** take food into the mouth and swallow it; chew and swallow. **2** have a meal; *when do we eat?* **3** destroy gradually, consume; *acids eat into metals*. ● *plural noun* (**eats**) (*informal*) food. □ **eating apple** an apple suitable for eating raw. **eat one's heart out** suffer greatly with vexation or longing. **eat one's words** be obliged to withdraw what one has said. **eat out** eat at a restaurant.

**eatable** *adjective* fit to be eaten (because of its condition). ● *plural noun* (**eatables**) food.

**eater** *noun* **1** one who eats. **2** an eating apple.

**eau-de-Cologne** (oh-dĕ-kŏ-**lohn**) *noun* a delicate perfume originally made at Cologne.

**eau-de-vie** (oh-dĕ-**vee**) *noun* spirits, especially brandy.

**eaves** *plural noun* the overhanging edge of a roof.

**eavesdrop** *verb* (**eavesdropped, eavesdropping**) listen secretly to a private conversation. □ **eavesdropper** *noun*

**ebb** *noun* **1** the outward movement of the tide, away from the land. **2** a condition of lowness or decline. ● *verb* **1** (of tides) flow away from the land. **2** become lower, weaken; *his strength ebbed*.

**ebonite** *noun* vulcanite.

**ebony** *noun* the hard black wood of a tropical tree. ● *adjective* black as ebony.

**ebullient** (i-**bul**-iĕnt) *adjective* exuberant, bubbling over with high spirits. □ **ebullience** *noun*, **ebulliency** *noun*, **ebulliently** *adverb*

**EC** *abbreviation* **1** European Community. **2** European Commission.

**eccentric** *adjective* **1** unconventional in appearance or behaviour. **2** (of circles) not concentric; (of orbits) not circular; (of a pivot) not placed centrally. ● *noun* **1** an eccentric person. **2** a disc fixed off centre on a revolving shaft, for changing rotary motion to to-and-fro motion. □ **eccentrically** adverb, **eccentricity** noun

**Eccles cake** (ek-ŭlz) a round cake of pastry filled with currants. (¶ Named after a town in NW England.)

**Ecclesiastes** (i-kleez-i-**ast**-eez) a book of the Old Testament traditionally ascribed to Solomon.

**ecclesiastic** (i-kleez-i-**ast**-ik) noun a member of the clergy.

**ecclesiastical** (i-kleez-i-**ast**-ikăl) adjective of the Church or the clergy.

**Ecclesiasticus** (i-kleez-i-**ast**-ikŭs) a book of the Apocrypha containing moral and practical maxims.

**ECG** abbreviation electrocardiogram.

**echelon** (**esh**-ĕ-lon) noun **1** a wedge-shaped formation of troops, aircraft, etc. **2** a level of rank or authority; *the upper echelons of the Civil Service.*

**echidna** (i-**kid**-nă) noun (also **spiny anteater**) an Australian egg-laying animal resembling a hedgehog.

**echinoderm** (i-**ky**-nŏ-derm) noun an animal of the group that includes starfish and sea urchins.

**echo** noun (plural **echoes**) **1** repetition of sound by the reflection of sound waves; a secondary sound produced in this way. **2** a reflected radio or radar beam. **3** a close imitation or imitator. ●verb (**echoed**, **echoing**) **1** repeat (sound) by echo, resound. **2** repeat or imitate. □ **echo-sounder** noun a sounding apparatus for finding the depth of the sea beneath a ship by measuring the time taken for an echo to be received.

**echoic** (ek-**oh**-ik) adjective (of a word) imitating the sound it represents.

**echolocation** noun location of objects by means of reflected sound.

**éclair** (i-**klair**) noun a finger-shaped cake of choux pastry with cream filling.

**eclampsia** (i-**klamp**-siă) noun a kind of epileptic convulsion affecting women in pregnancy or childbirth.

**éclat** (ay-**klah**) noun **1** brilliant effect. **2** social distinction, conspicuous success; *with great éclat.* (¶ French.)

**eclectic** (i-**klek**-tik) adjective choosing or accepting ideas, beliefs, etc. from various sources. □ **eclectically** adverb, **eclecticism** noun

**eclipse** noun **1** the blocking of light from one heavenly body by another. **2** a loss of brilliance, power, or reputation. ●verb **1** cause an eclipse of. **2** outshine, throw into obscurity.

**ecliptic** (i-**klip**-tik) noun the sun's apparent path among stars during the year.

**eclogue** (**ek**-log) noun a short usually pastoral poem.

**eco-** combining form relating to ecology and environmental issues.

**ecology** (ee-**kol**-ŏji) noun **1** the scientific study of living things in relation to each other and to their environment. **2** this relationship. □ **ecological** (ee-kŏ-**loj**-ikăl) adjective, **ecologically** adverb, **ecologist** noun

**economic** (ee-kŏ-**nom**-ik) adjective **1** of economics; *the government's economic policies.* **2** sufficient to give a good return for the money or effort laid out; *an economic rent.* ●noun (**economics**) **1** (treated as singular) the science concerned with the production and consumption or use of goods and services. **2** (treated as plural) the financial aspects of something; *the economics of farming.*

**economical** (ee-kŏ-**nom**-ikăl) adjective thrifty, avoiding waste. □ **economically** adverb

**economist** (i-**kon**-ŏmist) noun an expert in economics.

**economize** verb (also **economise**) be economical, use or spend less than before; *economize on fuel.*

**economy** noun **1** being economical; *practise economy.* **2** an instance of this, a saving; *make economies.* **3** a community's system of wealth creation; *a capitalist economy.* **4** (**the economy**) the state of a country's prosperity; *this could have a disastrous effect on the economy.* □ **economy class** the cheapest class of air travel.

**ecosystem** noun a biological community of interacting organisms and their environment.

**ecru** (**ay**-kroo) noun light fawn colour.

**ecstasy** noun **1** a feeling of intense delight. **2** (*slang*) a drug used as a stimulant and hallucinogen. □ **ecstatic** adjective, **ecstatically** adverb

**ECT** abbreviation electroconvulsive therapy.

**ectopic** (ek-**top**-ik) adjective in an abnormal place. □ **ectopic pregnancy** an unsuccessful pregnancy in which the fertilized egg develops outside the womb.

**ectoplasm** (**ek**-tŏ-plazm) noun **1** the outer portion of the matter of an animal or vegetable cell. **2** a substance supposed to be exuded from a spiritualist medium during a trance.

**ecu** (**ay**-kew) noun (also **Ecu**) European currency unit, a unit of currency based on the value of several currencies of the EC.

**Ecuador** (**ek**-wă-dor) a country in South America, on the Pacific coast. □ **Ecuadorean** adjective & noun

**ecumenical** (ee-kew-**men**-ikăl) adjective **1** of the whole Christian Church, not only of separate sects. **2** seeking worldwide Christian unity; *the ecumenical movement.*

**eczema** (ek-zim-ă) *noun* a skin disease causing scaly itching patches.

**Edam** (ee-dam) *noun* a round Dutch cheese, usually with a red rind.

**Edda** (ed-ă) a body of ancient Icelandic literature compiled in the 13th century, chief source of our knowledge of Scandinavian mythology.

**Eddington**, Sir Arthur Stanley (1882–1944), English astronomer, founder of the modern science of astrophysics.

**eddy** *noun* a swirling patch of water, air, fog, etc. ● *verb* (**eddied, eddying**) swirl in eddies.

**edelweiss** (ay-děl-vys) *noun* an alpine plant with woolly white bracts round the flowers.

**edema** Amer. spelling of OEDEMA.

**Eden**[1] (also **the Garden of Eden**) **1** In the biblical account of the creation, the place where Adam and Eve lived. **2** a place or state of great happiness and innocence.

**Eden**[2], (Robert) Anthony, 1st Earl of Avon (1897–1977), British statesman, Prime Minister 1955–7.

**edge** *noun* **1** the sharpened side of a blade. **2** its sharpness; *the knife has lost its edge.* **3** the line where two surfaces meet at an angle. **4** a rim, the narrow surface of a thin or flat object; *the pages have gilt edges.* **5** the outer limit or boundary of an area. ● *verb* **1** supply with a border; form the border of. **2** move gradually; *edging towards the door.* □ **be on edge** be tense and irritable. **have the edge on** (*informal*) have an advantage over. **set a person's teeth on edge** upset his or her nerves by causing an unpleasant sensation. **take the edge off** dull or soften (a feeling); *a couple of drinks should take the edge off the pain.*

**edgeways** *adverb* with the edge forwards or outwards. □ **get a word in edgeways** contribute to a conversation during a pause by the dominant speaker.

**edging** *noun* something placed round an edge to define or strengthen or decorate it.

**edgy** *adjective* with nerves on edge, irritable. □ **edginess** *noun*

**edible** *adjective* fit to be eaten. □ **edibility** *noun*

**edict** (ee-dikt) *noun* an order proclaimed by an authority.

**edifice** (ed-i-fis) *noun* a large or imposing building.

**edify** (ed-i-fy) *verb* (**edified, edifying**) be an uplifting moral or intellectual influence on; *an edifying discussion.* □ **edification** *noun*

**Edinburgh** the capital of Scotland.

**Edison**, Thomas Alva (1847–1931), American inventor, among whose most important inventions were the carbon microphone for telephones, the phonograph (precursor of the gramophone), and the carbon filament lamp.

**edit** *verb* (**edited, editing**) **1** act as editor of (a newspaper etc.). **2** prepare (written material) for publication. **3** reword in order to correct or to change the emphasis. **4** prepare (data) for processing by computer. **5** alter or add to (a text entered in a word processor). **6** prepare (a film or recording) by selecting individual sections and arranging them in sequence.

**edition** *noun* **1** the form in which something is published; *a pocket edition.* **2** the copies of a book or newspaper printed from one set of type. **3** the total number of a product (e.g. a commemorative medal) issued at one time; *a limited edition.*

**editor** *noun* **1** a person who is responsible for the content and writing of a newspaper etc. or a section of this; *our financial editor.* **2** one who edits written material for publication. **3** one who edits cinema film or recording tape. □ **editorship** *noun*

**editorial** *adjective* of an editor; *editorial work.* ● *noun* a newspaper article giving the editor's comments on current affairs. □ **editorially** *adverb*

**EDP** *abbreviation* electronic data processing.

**educable** *adjective* able to be educated.

**educate** *verb* train the mind and abilities of, provide education for. □ **educator** *noun*

**education** *noun* systematic training and instruction designed to impart knowledge and develop skill. □ **educational** *adjective*, **educationally** *adjective*

**educationist** *noun* (also **educationalist**) an expert in educational methods.

**educative** (ed-yoo-kă-tiv) *adjective* informative or instructive.

**Edward**[1] the name of six kings of England since the Conquest and two of the United Kingdom, who reigned as Edward I 1272–1307, II 1307–27, III 1327–77, IV 1461–83, V 1483, VI 1547–53, VII 1901–10, VIII 1936.

**Edward**[2], Prince (other names: Antony Richard Louis) (born 1964), youngest son of Queen Elizabeth II and Prince Philip.

**Edwardian** (ed-wor-diăn) *adjective* of the time of King Edward VII's reign (1901–10). ● *noun* a person living at this time.

**Edward the Confessor** (*c.*1003–66), king of England 1042–66.

**EEC** *abbreviation* European Economic Community.

■**Usage** The group of member countries is now normally referred to as the EC or European Community.

**EEG** *abbreviation* electroencephalogram.

**eel** *noun* a snake-like fish.

**eerie** *adjective* (**eerier**, **eeriest**) causing a feeling of mystery and fear. □ **eerily** *adverb*, **eeriness** *noun*

**eff** *verb* (*vulgar*) fuck; *eff off.* □ **eff and blind** swear emphatically and frequently. □ **effing** *adjective*

**efface** *verb* rub out, obliterate. □ **effacement** *noun*

**effect** *noun* **1** a change produced by an action or cause, a result. **2** an impression produced on a spectator or hearer etc.; *special lighting gave the effect of moonlight.* **3** a state of being operative; *the law came into effect last week.* **4** a physical phenomenon; *Doppler effect*; *greenhouse effect.* **5** (**effects**) property; *personal effects.* **6** (**effects**) sounds and lighting etc. provided to accompany a broadcast or film. ●*verb* bring about, accomplish; *effect one's purpose*; *effect a cure.*

■**Usage** See the note under **affect**.

□ **for effect** in order to impress people; *he only does it for effect.* **in effect** in fact, really; *it is, in effect, a refusal.* **take effect** produce its effect(s); become operative. **to that effect** with that implication; *words to that effect.* **with effect from** coming into operation at (a stated time).

**effective** *adjective* **1** producing an effect, powerful in its effect. **2** making a striking impression. **3** actual, existing; *the effective membership is higher than one would expect.* **4** operative; *the law is effective from 1 April.* □ **effectively** *adverb*, **effectiveness** *noun*

**effectual** *adjective* answering its purpose, sufficient to produce an effect. □ **effectually** *adverb*

**effeminate** (i-**fem**-in-ăt) *adjective* (of a man) unmanly, having qualities associated with women. □ **effeminately** *adverb*, **effeminacy** *noun*

**effervesce** (ef-er-**vess**) *verb* **1** give off small bubbles of gas. **2** (of a person) be lively or energetic. □ **effervescent** *adjective*, **effervescence** *noun*

**effete** (ef-**eet**) *adjective* feeble; having lost its vitality. □ **effeteness** *noun*

**efficacious** (ef-i-**kay**-shŭs) *adjective* producing the desired result. □ **efficacy** (**ef**-ik-ăsi) *noun*

**efficient** (i-**fish**-ĕnt) *adjective* acting effectively, producing results with little waste of effort. □ **efficiently** *adverb*, **efficiency** *noun*

**effigy** (**ef**-iji) *noun* a sculpture or model of a person.

**effloresce** (ef-lor-**ess**) *verb* **1** burst into flower. **2** turn to fine powder when exposed to air; (of salts) come to the surface and crystallize. **3** (of a surface) become covered with such salt particles. □ **efflorescence** *noun*, **efflorescent** *adjective*

**effluence** *noun* **1** a flowing out of light or electricity etc. **2** that which flows out.

**effluent** (**ef**-loo-ĕnt) *adjective* flowing out. ●*noun* something that flows out, especially sewage.

**effluvium** (e-**floo**-viŭm) *noun* (*plural* **effluvia**) an unpleasant or harmful outflow of a substance.

**effort** *noun* **1** the use of physical or mental energy to achieve something. **2** the energy exerted; *it was quite an effort to give up smoking.* **3** something produced by this; *this painting is a good effort.*

**effortless** *adjective* done without effort. □ **effortlessly** *adverb*, **effortlessness** *noun*

**effrontery** (i-**frunt**-er-i) *noun* shameless insolence.

**effulgent** (i-**ful**-jĕnt) *adjective* (*literary*) radiant, bright. □ **effulgence** *noun*

**effuse** (i-**fewz**) *verb* pour forth; flow out.

**effusion** (i-**few**-zhŏn) *noun* **1** a pouring forth. **2** an unrestrained outpouring of thought or feeling.

**effusive** (i-**few**-siv) *adjective* expressing emotions in an unrestrained way. □ **effusively** *adverb*, **effusiveness** *noun*

**EFL** *abbreviation* English as a Foreign Language.

**EFTA** *abbreviation* European Free Trade Association.

**e.g.** *abbreviation* = for example. (¶ From the Latin *exempli gratia.*)

**egalitarian** (i-gal-it-**air**-iăn) *adjective* holding the principle of equal rights for all persons. ●*noun* one who holds this principle. □ **egalitarianism** *noun*

**egg** *noun* **1** a reproductive cell produced by the female of birds, fish, reptiles, etc. **2** the hard-shelled egg of a domestic hen, used as food. □ **bad egg** (*informal*) a worthless or dishonest person. **egg-flip** *noun* (also **eggnog**) a drink made from rum or brandy with beaten egg, milk, sugar, and spices. **egg on** encourage to do something daring or foolish. **good egg** (*informal*) a decent person. **have egg on one's face** (*informal*) be made to look foolish. □ **eggy** *adjective*

**eggcup** *noun* a cup for holding a boiled egg.

**egghead** *noun* (*informal*) an intellectual person.

**eggplant** *noun* **1** a plant with deep purple fruit used as a vegetable. **2** its fruit, aubergine.

**eggshell** *noun* the shell of an egg. ●*adjective* **1** (of china) very fragile. **2** (of paint) with a slightly glossy finish.

**eglantine** (**eg**-lăn-tyn) *noun* sweet-brier.

**ego** (**ee**-goh) *noun* (*plural* **egos**) **1** the self. **2** self-esteem, conceit. □ **ego-trip** *noun* (*informal*) an activity devoted to boosting one's self-esteem or indulging one's feelings.

**egocentric** (eg-oh-**sen**-trik) *adjective* self-centred. □ **egocentricity** *noun*

**egoism** (eg-oh-izm) *noun* self-centredness, self-interests. □ **egoist** *noun*, **egoistic** *adjective*, **egoistically** *adverb*

**egotism** (eg-oh-tizm) *noun* the practice of talking too much about oneself; conceit. □ **egotist** *noun*, **egotistic** *adjective*, **egotistical** *adjective*, **egotistically** *adverb*

**egregious** (i-**gree**-jŭs) *adjective* outstandingly bad.

**egress** (ee-gress) *noun* an exit.

**egret** (ee-grit) *noun* a kind of heron with long white feathers.

**Egypt** a country in NE Africa. □ **Egyptian** *adjective & noun*

**Egyptology** *noun* the study of Egyptian antiquities. □ **Egyptologist** *noun*

**eh** (*pronounced* ay) *interjection* (*informal*) an exclamation of enquiry or surprise.

**Ehrlich** (**er**-lik), Paul (1854–1915), German scientist, a founder of immunology and pioneer of chemotherapy.

**eider** (**I**-der) *noun* a large northern duck.

**eiderdown** *noun* a quilt stuffed with soft material.

**Eiffel Tower** (**I**-fĕl) a wrought-iron structure 300m tall that is a landmark in Paris, designed and built by the French engineer A. G. Eiffel for the exhibition of 1889.

**eight** *adjective & noun* **1** one more than seven (8, VIII). **2** an eight-oared rowing-boat or its crew. □ **have had one over the eight** (*informal*) be slightly drunk.

**eighteen** *adjective & noun* **1** one more than seventeen (18, XVIII). **2** (**18**) (of films) suitable only for people of 18 years of age and older. □ **eighteenth** *adjective & noun*

**eightfold** *adjective & adverb* **1** eight times as much or as many. **2** consisting of eight parts.

**eighth** *adjective & noun* **1** next after seventh. **2** one of eight equal parts of a thing. □ **eighthly** *adverb*

**eightsome** *noun* (in full **eightsome reel**) a lively Scottish reel for eight dancers.

**eighty** *adjective & noun* **1** eight times ten (80, LXXX). **2** (**eighties**) the numbers or years or degrees of temperature from 80 to 89. □ **eightieth** *adjective & noun*

**Einstein** (**I**n-styn), Albert (1879–1955), German-born theoretical physicist, founder of the theory of relativity.

**einsteinium** (I'n-**sty**-niŭm) *noun* an artificially made radioactive metallic element (symbol Es).

**Eire** (**air**-ĕ) a former name of the Republic of Ireland, still often used to distinguish the country from Northern Ireland.

**Eisenhower** (**I**-zĕn-how-er), Dwight David (1890–1969), American general and statesman, President of the USA 1953–61.

**Eisenstein** (**I**-zĕn-styn), Sergei Mikhailovich (1898–1948), Russian film director.

**eisteddfod** (I-**sted**-fod) *noun* an annual Welsh festival of music, poetry, and dance.

**either** (**I**-ther *or* **ee**-ther) *adjective & pronoun* **1** one or the other of two; *either of you can go.* **2** each of two; *there are fields on either side of the river.* ● *adverb & conjunction* **1** as one alternative; *he is either mad or drunk.* **2** likewise, any more than the other; *the new lid doesn't fit, either.*

**ejaculate** (i-**jak**-yoo-layt) *verb* **1** say suddenly and briefly. **2** eject fluid (especially semen) during orgasm. □ **ejaculation** *noun*, **ejaculatory** *adjective*

**eject** *verb* **1** thrust or send out forcefully; *the gun ejects the spent cartridges.* **2** expel, compel to leave. **3** exit from an aircraft using an ejector seat. □ **ejection** *noun*

**ejector** *noun* a device for ejecting. □ **ejector seat** a seat that can eject the occupant out of an aircraft in an emergency to descend by parachute.

**eke** (*pronounced* eek) *verb* (foll. by *out*) **1** supplement; *eke out the meat with lots of vegetables.* **2** make (a living) laboriously; *eke out a living.*

**elaborate** *adjective* (*pronounced* i-**lab**-er-ăt) with many parts or details, complicated; *an elaborate pattern.* ● *verb* (*pronounced* i-**lab**-er-ayt) work out or describe in detail. □ **elaborately** *adverb*, **elaborateness** *noun*, **elaboration** *noun*

**El Alamein** (al-ă-**mayn**) the site of the British victory of the North African campaign of 1940–3, 90 km (60 miles) west of Alexandria.

**élan** (ay-**lahn**) *noun* vivacity. (¶ French.)

**eland** (ee-lănd) *noun* (*plural* **eland** *or* **elands**) a large African antelope with spirally twisted horns.

**elapse** *verb* (of time) pass by.

**elastic** *adjective* **1** going back to its original length or shape after being stretched or squeezed. **2** adaptable, not rigid; *the rules are somewhat elastic.* ● *noun* cord or material made elastic by interweaving strands of rubber etc. □ **elastic band** a rubber band. □ **elastically** *adverb*, **elasticity** (el-ass-**tiss**-iti) *noun*

**elasticated** *adjective* made elastic by being interwoven with elastic thread.

**elastomer** (i-**last**-ŏ-mer) *noun* a natural or synthetic rubber or rubber-like plastic.

**elate** *verb* make intensely delighted or proud. □ **elated** *adjective*, **elation** *noun*

**Elba** a small island off the west coast of Italy, famous as the place of Napoleon's first exile 1814–15.

**elbow** *noun* **1** the joint between the forearm and upper arm; its outer part. **2** a sharp bend in a pipe etc. ●*verb* thrust with one's elbow. □ **elbow-grease** *noun* vigorous polishing; hard work. **elbow-room** *noun* enough room to work or move.

**elder**[1] *adjective* older; *elder sister*. ●*noun* **1** an older person; *respect your elders*. **2** an official in certain Churches. □ **elder statesman** an influential and experienced older person, especially a politician.

**elder**[2] *noun* a tree or shrub with white flowers and dark berries.

**elderberry** *noun* the berry of the elder tree.

**elderly** *adjective* rather old; past middle age.

**eldest** *adjective* oldest, first-born; *eldest son*.

**eldorado** (el-dor-**ah**-doh) *noun* (*plural* **eldorados**) a place of great wealth, abundance, or opportunity. (¶ From the name of a fictitious country or city rich in gold, once believed to exist on the River Amazon.)

**elect** *verb* **1** choose by voting; *elect a treasurer*. **2** choose as a course, decide; *he elected to become a lawyer*. ●*adjective* chosen. □ **president elect** a president who has been elected but is not yet in office.

**election** *noun* **1** choosing or being chosen by voting. **2** the process of electing representatives, especially Members of Parliament.

**electioneer** *verb* take part in an election campaign. □ **electioneering** *noun*

**elective** *adjective* **1** having the power to elect; *an elective assembly*. **2** chosen or filled by election; *an elective office*.

**elector** *noun* one who has the right to vote in an election.

**electoral** *adjective* of electors.

**electorate** *noun* the whole body of electors.

**electric** *adjective* **1** of or producing electricity. **2** worked by electricity. **3** causing sudden excitement; *the news had an electric effect*. ●*plural noun* (**electrics**) electrical fittings. □ **electric chair** a chair in which criminals are executed by electrocution. **electric eel** an eel-like fish able to give an electric shock. **electric eye** a photoelectric cell. **electric field** a region of electrical influence. **electric guitar** a solid-bodied guitar that is amplified electrically rather than acoustically. **electric shock** the painful effect of a sudden discharge of electricity through the body. **electric storm** a violent disturbance of the electrical condition of the atmosphere.

**electrical** *adjective* of or concerned with electricity; *electrical engineering*. □ **electrically** *adverb*

**electrician** (i-lek-**trish**-ăn) *noun* a person whose job is installing and maintaining electricity supplies and electrical equipment.

**electricity** *noun* **1** a form of energy produced by the flow of electrons in matter and causing it to accumulate a charge. **2** a supply of electric current for lighting, heating, etc.

**electrify** *verb* (**electrified**, **electrifying**) **1** charge with electricity. **2** convert (a place) to the use of electric power. **3** startle or excite. □ **electrification** *noun*

**electrocardiogram** *noun* the pattern traced by an electrocardiograph.

**electrocardiograph** *noun* an instrument for detecting and recording the electric currents generated by heartbeats.

**electroconvulsive therapy** treatment of mental illness by means of electric shocks that produce convulsions.

**electrocute** *verb* kill by electricity. □ **electrocution** *noun*

**electrode** (i-**lek**-trohd) *noun* **1** a solid conductor through which electricity enters or leaves a vacuum tube etc. **2** a small electrical conductor attached to a person's skin enabling pulse rate, heartbeat, etc. to be monitored on a machine.

**electrodynamics** *noun* the study of the interactions between electrical and mechanical forces.

**electroencephalogram** *noun* the pattern traced by an electroencephalograph.

**electroencephalograph** *noun* an instrument for detecting and recording the electric currents generated by activity of the brain.

**electrolyse** (i-**lek**-trŏ-lyz) *verb* (*Amer.* **electrolyze**) subject to or treat by electrolysis.

**electrolysis** (i-lek-**trol**-ĭ-sis) *noun* **1** chemical decomposition by electric current. **2** the breaking up of tumours, hair-roots, etc. by electric current. □ **electrolytic** (i-lek-trŏ-**lit**-ik) *adjective*

**electrolyte** (i-**lek**-trŏ-lyt) *noun* a solution that conducts electric current, especially in an electric cell or battery.

**electromagnet** *noun* a magnet consisting of a metal core magnetized by a coil, carrying electric current, wound round it.

**electromagnetic** *adjective* having both electrical and magnetic properties. □ **electromagnetically** *adverb*

**electromagnetism** *noun* **1** magnetic forces produced by electricity. **2** the study of these.

**electromotive** *adjective* producing electric current. □ **electromotive force** a force set up in an electric circuit by a difference in potential.

**electron** (i-**lek**-tron) *noun* a negatively charged particle that occurs in all atoms and is the primary carrier of electricity. □ **electron microscope** a high-powered microscope that uses a beam of electrons instead of light.

**electronic** (i-lek-**tron**-ik) *adjective* **1** produced or worked by a flow of electrons. **2** of or concerned with electronics; *electronic engineering.* ●*noun* (**electronics**) **1** (treated as *singular*) the development and application of electronic devices, e.g. in transistors, computers, etc. **2** (treated as *plural*) electronic circuits. □ **electronic mail** messages transmitted within and between networks of computer users and displayed on-screen. **electronic publishing** publication of books in machine-readable form rather than on paper. □ **electronically** *adverb*

**electronvolt** *noun* a unit of energy, the amount of energy gained by an electron when accelerated through a potential difference of one volt.

**electroplate** *verb* coat with a thin layer of silver etc. by electrolysis. ●*noun* objects plated in this way.

**electro-shock** *adjective* (of medical treatment) by means of electric shocks; *electro-shock therapy.*

**electrostatics** *noun* the study of static electricity.

**electrotechnology** *noun* the science of the application of electricity in technology.

**electrotherapy** *noun* the treatment of diseases by the use of electricity.

**elegant** *adjective* tasteful, refined, and dignified in appearance or style. □ **elegantly** *adverb*, **elegance** *noun*

**elegiac** (el-i-**jy**-ăk) *adjective* used for elegies; mournful. □ **elegiacally** *adverb*

**elegy** (**el**-i-ji) *noun* a sorrowful or serious poem.

**element** *noun* **1** any of the parts that make up a whole. **2** any of the 100 or so substances that cannot be chemically separated into simpler substances. **3** any of the four basic substances (earth, water, air, and fire) in ancient and medieval philosophy. **4** the natural environment or habitat for a particular creature; *air is the element of the birds.* **5** a trace; *there's an element of truth in the story.* **6** the wire that gives out heat in an electric heater, cooker, etc. **7** (**the elements**) atmospheric forces, e.g. wind, rain; *exposed to the elements.* **8** (**elements**) the basic or elementary principles of a subject. **9** (**elements**) the bread and wine used in the Eucharist. □ **in one's element** absorbed in doing what one enjoys most.

**elemental** *adjective* **1** of or like the elements or the forces of nature; powerful. **2** basic, essential.

**elementary** *adjective* dealing with the simplest facts of a subject. □ **elementary particle** any of the subatomic particles that are not known to be composed of simpler particles.

**elephant** *noun* the largest living land animal, with grey skin, a trunk, and ivory tusks.

**elephantiasis** (eli-făn-**ty**-ă-sis) *noun* a tropical disease in which parts of the body, especially the limbs, become grossly enlarged.

**elephantine** (el-i-**fan**-tyn) *adjective* **1** of or like elephants. **2** very large or clumsy.

**elevate** *verb* **1** raise to a higher place or position, lift up. **2** raise to a higher moral or intellectual level.

**elevation** *noun* **1** elevating; being elevated. **2** the altitude of a place. **3** a piece of rising ground, a hill. **4** the angle that the direction of something (e.g. a gun) makes with the horizontal. **5** a drawing or diagram showing a structure or object as viewed from the side (compare PLAN).

**elevator** *noun* **1** something that hoists or raises things. **2** the movable part of a tailplane, used for changing an aircraft's altitude. **3** (*Amer.*) a lift.

**eleven** *adjective & noun* **1** one more than ten (11, XI). **2** a team of eleven players at cricket, football, etc. □ **eleven-plus** *noun* (*Brit.*) an examination formerly taken at the age of 11 to determine the type of secondary school a child would attend.

**elevenses** *plural noun* light refreshments at about 11 a.m.

**eleventh** *adjective & noun* **1** next after tenth. **2** one of eleven equal parts of a thing. □ **the eleventh hour** the latest possible moment.

**elf** *noun* (*plural* **elves**) an imaginary small being with magic powers. □ **elfish** *adjective*

**elfin** *adjective* elf-like; small and delicate.

**Elgar**, Sir Edward William (1857–1934), English composer.

**El Greco** (grek-oh) (1541–1614), (= 'the Greek') Spanish painter of Greek origin (original name: Domenikos Theotokopoulos), noted for his use of elongated human forms and bright discordant colour.

**elicit** (i-**lis**-it) *verb* draw out (information, a response, etc.).

**eligible** (**el**-i-ji-bŭl) *adjective* **1** qualified to be chosen for a position or allowed a privilege etc.; *he is eligible for a pension.* **2** regarded as suitable or desirable, especially for marriage. □ **eligibility** *noun*

**Elijah** (i-**ly**-jă) a Hebrew prophet of the 9th century BC.

**eliminate** (i-lim-in-ayt) *verb* **1** get rid of; remove; *eliminate errors*; *he must be eliminated.* **2** exclude from a further stage of a competition etc. through defeat; *was eliminated in the fourth round.* □ **elimination** *noun*, **eliminator** *noun*

**Eliot¹**, George (pseudonym of Mary Ann Evans) (1819–80), English novelist.

**Eliot²**, T(homas) S(tearns) (1888–1965), Anglo-American poet, critic, and dramatist.

**Elisha** (i-ly-shă) a Hebrew prophet, disciple and successor of Elijah.

**elision** (i-lizh-ŏn) *noun* omission of part of a word in pronouncing it (e.g. *I'm* = I am).

**élite** (ay-leet) *noun* **1** a group of people regarded as superior in some way and therefore favoured. **2** a size of letters in typewriting (12 per inch).

**élitist** (ay-leet-ist) *noun* one who advocates selecting and treating certain people as an élite. ● *adjective* advocating the selection and treatment of certain people as an élite. □ **élitism** *noun*

**elixir** (i-liks-eer) *noun* **1** a fragrant liquid used as a medicine. **2** a remedy believed to cure all ills.

**Elizabeth I** (1533–1603), queen of England and Ireland 1558–1603.

**Elizabeth II** (born 1926), queen of the United Kingdom from 1952.

**Elizabeth, the Queen Mother** (original name: Lady Elizabeth Bowes-Lyon) (born 1900), wife of George VI, mother of Elizabeth II.

**Elizabethan** *adjective* of the time of Queen Elizabeth I's reign (1558–1603). ● *noun* a person living at this time.

**elk** *noun* a large deer of northern Europe and Asia.

**ell** *noun* (*old use*) a measure of length, = 45 inches.

**Ellington**, 'Duke' (Edward Kennedy) (1899–1974), American composer, pianist, and jazz band-leader.

**ellipse** (i-lips) *noun* a regular oval that can be divided into four identical quarters.

**ellipsis** (i-lip-sis) *noun* (*plural* **ellipses**, *pronounced* i-lip-seez) the omission of words needed to complete a meaning or a grammatical construction.

**elliptical** (i-lip-ti-kăl) *adjective* **1** of or shaped like an ellipse. **2** containing an ellipsis, having omissions. □ **elliptically** *adverb*

**elm** *noun* **1** a deciduous tree with rough serrated leaves. **2** its wood.

**elocution** (el-ŏ-kew-shŏn) *noun* a person's style of speaking; the art of speaking expressively. □ **elocutionary** *adjective*, **elocutionist** *noun*

**elongate** (ee-long-ayt) *verb* lengthen, prolong. □ **elongation** *noun*

**elope** (i-lohp) *verb* run away secretly with a lover, especially in order to get married. □ **elopement** *noun*

**eloquence** (el-ŏ-kwĕns) *noun* fluent and effective use of language.

**eloquent** (el-ŏ-kwĕnt) *adjective* **1** using language fluently and effectively. **2** expressive. □ **eloquently** *adverb*

**El Salvador** (el sal-vă-dor) a country in Central America, on the Pacific coast.

**else** *adverb* **1** besides, other; *someone else.* **2** otherwise, if not; *run or else you'll be late.*

**elsewhere** *adverb* somewhere else.

**elucidate** (i-loo-sid-ayt) *verb* throw light on (a problem); make clear. □ **elucidation** *noun*, **elucidatory** *adjective*

**elude** (i-lood) *verb* **1** escape skilfully from, avoid; *eluded his pursuers.* **2** baffle (a person or memory etc.); *the answer eludes me.* □ **elusion** *noun*

**elusive** (i-loo-siv) *adjective* **1** difficult to find or catch. **2** difficult to remember. □ **elusiveness** *noun*

**elver** *noun* a young eel.

**elves** *see* ELF.

**Elysium** (i-liz-iŭm) **1** (*Gk. myth.*) the place where certain favoured heroes, exempted from death, were taken by the gods. **2** a place of ideal happiness. □ **Elysian** *adjective*

**em** *noun* (in printing) a unit of measurement equal to the width of an M.

**'em** *pronoun* (*informal*) = THEM.

**emaciated** (i-may-si-ayt-id) *adjective* very thin from illness or starvation. □ **emaciation** *noun*

**email** *noun* (also **e-mail**) = ELECTRONIC MAIL.

**emanate** (em-ăn-ayt) *verb* **1** issue or originate from a source; *pleasant smells emanated from the kitchen.* **2** cause to do this. □ **emanation** *noun*

**emancipate** (i-man-sip-ayt) *verb* liberate, set free from slavery or some form of restraint. □ **emancipation** *noun*, **emancipator** *noun*, **emancipatory** *adjective*

**emasculate** (i-mas-kew-layt) *verb* **1** castrate. **2** deprive of force; *an emasculated law.* □ **emasculation** *noun*

**embalm** (im-bahm) *verb* preserve (a corpse) from decay. □ **embalmment** *noun*

**embankment** *noun* a long mound of earth or a stone structure to keep a river from spreading or to carry a road or railway.

**embargo** (im-bar-goh) *noun* (*plural* **embargoes**) **1** an order forbidding ships to enter or leave a country's ports. **2** an official suspension of commerce or other activity.

**embark** *verb* **1** put or go on board a ship or aircraft at the start of a journey. **2** (usually foll. by *on*) begin an undertaking; *they*

*embarked on a programme of expansion.*
□ **embarkation** *noun*

**embarrass** *verb* make (a person) feel awkward or ashamed. □ **embarrassment** *noun*

**embassy** *noun* **1** an ambassador and his or her staff. **2** the official headquarters of an ambassador. **3** a deputation sent to a foreign government.

**embattled** *adjective* **1** prepared for battle; *embattled troops*. **2** fortified against attack. **3** under pressure or in trying circumstances.

**embed** *verb* (also **imbed**) (**embedded**, **embedding**) fix firmly in a surrounding mass.

**embellish** (im-**bel**-ish) *verb* **1** ornament. **2** improve (a story etc.) by adding details that are entertaining but invented. □ **embellishment** *noun*

**embers** *plural noun* small pieces of live coal or wood in a dying fire.

**embezzle** *verb* take fraudulently for one's own use (money or property placed in one's care). □ **embezzlement** *noun*, **embezzler** *noun*

**embitter** *verb* arouse bitter feelings in. □ **embitterment** *noun*

**emblazon** (im-**blay**-zŏn) *verb* ornament with heraldic or other devices.

**emblem** *noun* a symbol, a device that represents something.

**emblematic** (em-blim-**at**-ik) *adjective* serving as an emblem, symbolic.

**embody** *verb* (**embodied**, **embodying**) **1** express (principles or ideas) in a visible form; *the house embodied her idea of a home*. **2** incorporate, include; *parts of the old treaty are embodied in the new one*. □ **embodiment** *noun*

**embolden** *verb* make bold, encourage.

**embolism** (em-**bŏl**-izm) *noun* obstruction of an artery or vein by a clot of blood, air bubble, etc.

**embolus** (em-**bŏl**-ŭs) *noun* (*plural* **emboli**) a thing causing an embolism.

**emboss** *verb* decorate with a raised design. □ **embossment** *noun*

**embrace** *verb* **1** hold closely and affectionately in one's arms; (of two people) do this to each other. **2** accept eagerly; *embraced the opportunity*. **3** adopt (a religion etc.). **4** include. ●*noun* the act of embracing, a hug.

**embrasure** (im-**bray**-zher) *noun* **1** an opening in a wall for a door or window, with splayed sides. **2** a similar opening for a gun, widening towards the outside.

**embrocation** *noun* liquid for rubbing on the body to relieve aches or bruises.

**embroider** *verb* **1** ornament with needlework. **2** embellish (a story).

**embroidery** *noun* **1** embroidering. **2** embroidered material.

**embroil** *verb* involve in an argument or quarrel etc. □ **embroilment** *noun*

**embryo** (em-bri-oh) *noun* (*plural* **embryos**) **1** an animal in the early stage of its development, before birth or emergence from an egg (used of a child in the first eight weeks of its development in the womb). **2** a rudimentary plant contained in a seed. **3** something in its very early stages. □ **in embryo** existing but undeveloped.

**embryology** (em-bri-**ol**-ŏji) *noun* the study of embryos.

**embryonic** (em-bri-**on**-ik) *adjective* existing in embryo.

**emend** (i-**mend**) *verb* alter (something written) in order to remove errors. □ **emendation** (ee-men-**day**-shŏn) *noun*

---

■ **Usage** See note at **amend**.

---

**emerald** *noun* **1** a bright green precious stone. **2** its colour. □ **the Emerald Isle** (*poetic*) Ireland.

**emerge** (i-**merj**) *verb* **1** come up or out into view. **2** (of facts or ideas) be revealed by investigation, become obvious. □ **emergence** *noun*, **emergent** *adjective*

**emergency** *noun* **1** a serious happening or situation needing prompt action. **2** a condition needing immediate treatment; a patient with this.

**emeritus** (i-**merri**-tŭs) *adjective* retired and retaining a title as an honour; *emeritus professor*.

**Emerson**, Ralph Waldo (1803–82), American philosopher and poet, who evolved the concept of transcendentalism.

**emery** (em-er-i) *noun* coarse abrasive used for polishing metal or wood etc. □ **emery-board** *noun* a small stiff strip of wood or cardboard coated with emery, used for filing the nails.

**emetic** (i-**met**-ik) *noun* medicine used to cause vomiting.

**EMF** *abbreviation* electromotive force.

**emigrant** *noun* a person who emigrates.

**emigrate** *verb* leave one country and go to settle in another. □ **emigration** *noun*

**émigré** (em-i-gray) *noun* an emigrant, especially a political exile.

**eminence** (em-in-ĕns) *noun* **1** the state of being famous or distinguished; *a surgeon of great eminence*. **2** a piece of rising ground. **3** a cardinal's title; *His Eminence*.

**éminence grise** (ay-mi-nawnss greez) (*plural* **éminences grises**, *pronounced* same) a person who exercises power or influence without holding office. (¶ French.)

**eminent** (em-in-ĕnt) *adjective* **1** famous, distinguished. **2** conspicuous, outstanding;

*a man of eminent goodness.* □ **eminently** *adverb*

**emir** (em-**eer**) *noun* (also **amir**) the title of various Muslim rulers.

**emirate** (em-er-ăt) *noun* the territory of an emir.

**emissary** (em-**iss**-er-i) *noun* a person sent on a diplomatic mission.

**emit** (i-**mit**) *verb* (**emitted**, **emitting**) **1** send out (light, heat, fumes, lava, etc.). **2** utter; *she emitted a shriek.* □ **emission** *noun*, **emissive** *adjective*, **emitter** *noun*

**Emmental** (em-ĕn-tahl) *noun* (also **Emmenthal**) a hard Swiss cheese with holes in it.

**Emmy** *noun* a statuette awarded to a television programme or performer by the American Academy of Television Arts and Sciences at their annual award ceremony.

**emollient** (i-**mol**-iĕnt) *adjective* softening or soothing the skin. ●*noun* an emollient substance.

**emolument** (i-**mol**-yoo-mĕnt) *noun* a fee received, a salary.

**emote** (i-**moht**) *verb* act with a show of emotion.

**emotion** *noun* a strong instinctive feeling, e.g. love or fear.

**emotional** *adjective* **1** of emotions. **2** showing emotion excessively. □ **emotionally** *adverb*, **emotionalism** *noun*

**emotive** (i-**moh**-tiv) *adjective* rousing emotion.

**empanel** (im-**pan**-ĕl) *verb* (also **impanel**) (**empanelled**, **empanelling**; *Amer.* **empaneled**, **empaneling**) list or select for service on a jury.

**empathize** (em-pă-thyz) *verb* (also **empathise**) feel empathy.

**empathy** (em-păthi) *noun* the ability to identify oneself mentally with a person or thing and so understand his or her feelings or its meaning. □ **empathetic** *adjective*, **empathic** (em-pa-thik) *adjective*,

**emperor** *noun* the male ruler of an empire. □ **emperor penguin** a penguin of the largest known species.

**emphasis** (em-fă-sis) *noun* (*plural* **emphases**, *pronounced* em-fă-seez) **1** special importance given to something; prominence; *the emphasis is on quality.* **2** vigour of expression, feeling, or action; *nodded his head with emphasis.* **3** the extra force used in speaking a particular syllable or word, or on a sound in music.

**emphasize** (em-fă-syz) *verb* (also **emphasise**) lay emphasis on.

**emphatic** (im-**fat**-ik) *adjective* using or showing emphasis, expressing oneself with emphasis. □ **emphatically** *adverb*

**emphysema** (em-fi-see-mă) *noun* a condition in which the air sacs in the lungs become enlarged, causing breathlessness.

**empire** *noun* **1** a group of countries ruled by a single supreme authority. **2** supreme power. **3** a large commercial organization controlled by one person or group. □ **empire-building** *noun* the process of deliberately acquiring extra territory or authority etc.

**Empire State Building** a skyscraper in New York city, for many years the tallest building in the world, named after the Empire State (= New York).

**empirical** (im-**pi**-ri-kăl) *adjective* (also **empiric**) (of knowledge) based on observation or experiment, not on theory. □ **empirically** *adverb*

**empiricism** (im-**pi**-ri-sizm) *noun* **1** the use of empirical methods. **2** the theory that regards sensory experience as the only source of knowledge. □ **empiricist** *noun*

**emplacement** *noun* a place or platform for a gun or battery of guns.

**employ** *verb* **1** give work to, use the services of. **2** make use of; *how do you employ your spare time?* □ **in the employ of** employed by.

**employable** *adjective* able to be employed or worth employing.

**employee** (im-**ploi**-ee) *noun* a person who works for another in return for wages.

**employer** *noun* a person or firm that employs people.

**employment** *noun* **1** employing. **2** the state of being employed. **3** work done as an occupation or to earn a livelihood.

**emporium** (em-**por**-iŭm) *noun* (*plural* **emporia** or **emporiums**) **1** a centre of commerce. **2** a large shop.

**empower** *verb* give power or authority to; *police are empowered to arrest people.*

**empress** *noun* **1** the female ruler of an empire. **2** the wife or widow of an emperor.

**empty** *adjective* **1** containing nothing; *empty boxes; empty trucks.* **2** without occupants; *an empty chair; empty streets.* **3** ineffective or insincere; *empty threats; empty promises.* **4** without purpose or value; *an empty existence.* **5** lacking good sense or intelligence; *an empty head.* **6** (*informal*) hungry; *feel rather empty.* ●*verb* (**emptied**, **emptying**) **1** make or become empty. **2** transfer (the contents of one thing) into another; discharge itself or its contents. ●*plural noun* (**empties**) emptied boxes, bottles, etc. □ **empty-handed** *adjective* bringing or taking away nothing. **empty-headed** *adjective* lacking good sense or intelligence. □ **emptily** *adverb*, **emptiness** *noun*

**EMS** *abbreviation* European Monetary System, a system aimed at coordinating the exchange rates of currencies in the EC.

**EMU** *abbreviation* economic and monetary union; European Monetary Union, an EC programme aimed at economic unity and the introduction of a common European currency.

**emu** (ee-mew) *noun* a large Australian flightless bird rather like an ostrich.

**emulate** (em-yoo-layt) *verb* try to do as well as or better than; imitate. □ **emulation** *noun*, **emulative** *adjective*, **emulator** *noun*

**emulous** (em-yoo-lŭs) *adjective* **1** imitating in an eager or jealous way. **2** motivated by rivalry.

**emulsify** (i-mul-si-fy) *verb* (**emulsified**, **emulsifying**) convert or be converted into an emulsion.

**emulsion** (i-mul-shŏn) *noun* **1** a creamy liquid in which particles of oil or fat are evenly distributed. **2** a medicine or paint in this form. **3** the light-sensitive coating on photographic film.

**enable** *verb* **1** give the means or authority to do something. **2** make possible.

**enact** *verb* **1** decree, make into a law. **2** perform, act (a play etc.). □ **enactive** *adjective*

**enactment** *noun* a law enacted.

**enamel** *noun* **1** a glass-like substance used for coating metal or pottery. **2** paint that dries hard and glossy. **3** the hard outer covering of teeth. **4** a painting done in enamel. ● *verb* (**enamelled**, **enamelling**; *Amer.* **enameled**, **enameling**) coat or decorate with enamel.

**enamoured** (i-nam-erd) *adjective* (*Amer.* **enamored**) (usually foll. by *of*) feeling great fondness or love; *he was very enamoured of the sound of his own voice.*

**en bloc** (ahn **blok**) in a block, all at the same time. (¶ French.)

**encamp** *verb* settle in a camp.

**encampment** *noun* a camp.

**encapsulate** *verb* **1** enclose in or as if in a capsule. **2** summarize. **3** isolate. □ **encapsulation** *noun*

**encase** *verb* enclose in a case. □ **encasement** *noun*

**encephalitis** (en-sef-ă-ly-tis) *noun* inflammation of the brain.

**encephalogram** (en-sef-ăl-ŏ-gram) *noun* an electroencephalogram.

**encephalograph** (en-sef-ăl-ŏ-grahf) *noun* an electroencephalograph.

**enchant** *verb* **1** put under a magic spell. **2** fill with intense delight. □ **enchantment** *noun*, **enchanter** *noun*

**enchantress** *noun* a woman who enchants.

**enchilada** (en-chi-lah-dă) *noun* a tortilla with chilli sauce and usually containing a filling, especially meat.

**encircle** *verb* surround. □ **encirclement** *noun*

**enclave** (en-klayv) *noun* a small territory belonging to one State but lying wholly within the boundaries of another.

**enclose** *verb* **1** put a wall or fence etc. round; shut in on all sides. **2** shut up in a receptacle; put into an envelope along with a letter or into a parcel along with the contents.

**enclosed** *adjective* (of a religious community) living in isolation from the outside world.

**enclosure** *noun* **1** enclosing. **2** an enclosed area. **3** something enclosed with a letter etc.

**encode** *verb* put into code; put (data) into a coded form for processing by computer. □ **encoder** *noun*

**encomium** (en-koh-miŭm) *noun* (*plural* **encomiums**) high praise given in a speech or writing.

**encompass** *verb* **1** surround, encircle. **2** contain.

**encore** (ong-kor) *interjection* a call for repetition of a performance or for a further item. ● *noun* **1** this call. **2** the item performed in response to it. ● *verb* call for such a repetition of (an item); call back (a performer) for this.

**encounter** *verb* **1** meet, especially by chance or unexpectedly. **2** find oneself faced with; *encounter difficulties.* **3** meet in battle. ● *noun* **1** a sudden or unexpected meeting. **2** a battle.

**encourage** *verb* **1** give hope or confidence to. **2** urge; *encouraged him to try.* **3** stimulate, help to develop; *competitiveness will help to encourage exports.* □ **encouragement** *noun*

**encroach** *verb* **1** intrude on someone's territory, rights, or time. **2** advance beyond the original or proper limits; *the sea encroached gradually upon the land.* □ **encroachment** *noun*

**encrust** *verb* **1** cover with a crust of hard material. **2** ornament with a layer of jewels etc. □ **encrustation** *noun*

**encumber** *verb* be a burden to, hamper.

**encumbrance** *noun* a burden or hindrance.

**encyclical** (en-sik-lik-ăl) *adjective* for wide circulation. ● *noun* a letter written by the pope for wide circulation.

**encyclopedia** *noun* (also **encyclopaedia**) a book or set of books giving information on all branches of knowledge or of one subject, usually arranged alphabetically.

**encyclopedic** *adjective* (also **encyclopaedic**) giving or possessing information about many subjects or branches of one subject.

**end** *noun* **1** the extreme limit of something. **2** the part or surface forming an extremity; *a plank split at one end.* **3** (**the end**) (*informal*) the limit of what one can endure. **4** either half of a sports pitch or court, defended or occupied by one side or player. **5** the finish or conclusion of something, the latter or final part. **6** destruction, downfall, death. **7** a purpose or aim; *to gain his own ends.* ● *verb* **1** bring to an end, put an end to. **2** come to an end. □ **end it all** (*informal*) commit suicide. **end on** with the end facing one or adjoining the end of the next object. **end product** *noun* the final product of a manufacturing process. **end up** reach a specified place or state eventually; *ended up at Dave's house; he ended up a millionaire.* **keep one's end up** do one's part in spite of difficulties. **make ends meet** keep one's expenditure within one's income. **no end** (*informal*) to a great extent. **no end of** (*informal*) much or many of. **put an end to** abolish, stop, or destroy.

**endanger** *verb* cause danger to.

**endear** *verb* cause to be loved; *endeared herself to us all.*

**endearing** *adjective* inspiring affection.

**endearment** *noun* **1** a word or words expressing love. **2** liking, affection.

**endeavour** (in-**dev**-er) (*Amer.* **endeavor**) *verb* attempt, try. ● *noun* an attempt.

**endemic** (en-**dem**-ik) *adjective* commonly found in a particular country, district, or group of people; *the disease is endemic in Africa.* □ **endemically** *adverb*

**ending** *noun* the final part.

**endive** (en-dyv) *noun* **1** a curly-leaved plant used as salad. **2** (*Amer.*) chicory.

**endless** *adjective* without end, never stopping; *endless patience.*

**endmost** *adjective* nearest the end.

**endocrine** (end-o-kryn) *adjective* (of a gland) secreting straight into the blood, not through a duct.

**endogenous** (en-**doj**-in-ŭs) *adjective* originating from within.

**endorse** *verb* **1** sign or add a comment on (a document); sign the back of (a cheque) in order to obtain the money indicated. **2** make an official entry on (a driving licence) about a motoring offence by the holder. **3** confirm (a statement); declare one's approval of. □ **endorsement** *noun*

**endoscope** (end-ŏ-skohp) *noun* an instrument for viewing the internal parts of the body.

**endow** *verb* **1** provide with a permanent income; *endow a school.* **2** provide with a power, ability, or quality; *was endowed with great talents.*

**endowment** *noun* **1** endowing. **2** an endowed income. **3** a natural ability. ● *adjective* denoting forms of life insurance with payment of a fixed sum on a specified date, or on the death of the insured person if earlier. □ **endowment mortgage** a mortgage linked to endowment insurance.

**endpaper** *noun* a strong leaf of paper fixed across the beginning or end of a book and the inside of the cover.

**endue** *verb* (*formal*) provide with a talent or quality etc.; *endue us with gentleness.*

**endurable** *adjective* able to be endured.

**endurance** *noun* ability to withstand pain or hardship or prolonged use or strain.

**endure** *verb* **1** experience (pain or hardship), bear patiently. **2** tolerate. **3** remain in existence, last.

**endways** *adverb* (also **endwise**) **1** with its end foremost. **2** end to end.

**enema** (en-im-ă) *noun* **1** the insertion of liquid into the rectum through the anus by means of a syringe, especially to flush out its contents. **2** this liquid or syringe.

**enemy** *noun* **1** a person who is actively hostile towards another. **2** a member of a hostile army or nation etc. **3** (**the enemy**) an opposing military force, ship, aircraft, etc. or a group or organization considered to be hostile. **4** an opponent of something; *enemy of progress.* ● *adjective* of or belonging to the enemy.

**energetic** *adjective* full of energy, done with energy. □ **energetically** *adverb*

**energize** (en-er-jyz) *verb* (also **energise**) **1** give energy to. **2** cause electricity to flow to.

**energy** *noun* **1** the capacity for vigorous activity. **2** the ability of matter or radiation to do work because of its motion, its mass, or its electric charge. **3** fuel and other resources used for the operation of machinery etc.; *the country's energy requirements.*

**enervate** (en-er-vayt) *verb* cause to lose vitality; *an enervating climate.* □ **enervation** *noun*

**enfant terrible** (ahn-fahn te-**reebl**) (*plural* **enfants terribles**, *pronounced* same) a person whose behaviour is embarrassing, indiscreet, or irresponsible. (¶ French, = terrible child.)

**enfeeble** *verb* make feeble. □ **enfeeblement** *noun*

**enfilade** (en-fil-**ayd**) *noun* gunfire directed along a line from end to end. ● *verb* rake with gunfire.

**enfold** *verb* **1** wrap up. **2** clasp.

**enforce** *verb* compel obedience to; impose by force or compulsion; *the law was firmly enforced.* □ **enforcement** *noun*

**enforceable** *adjective* able to be enforced.

**enfranchise** verb 1 give (a person) the right to vote in elections. 2 give municipal rights to (a town). □ **enfranchisement** noun

**Eng.** abbreviation 1 English. 2 England.

**engage** verb 1 take into one's employment; *engage a typist.* 2 arrange beforehand to occupy (a seat etc.). 3 promise, pledge. 4 occupy the attention of; *engaged her in conversation.* 5 occupy oneself; *he engages in politics.* 6 begin a battle against; *engaged the enemy troops.* 7 interlock (parts of a gear) so that it transmits power; become interlocked in this way.

**engaged** adjective 1 having promised to marry; *an engaged couple.* 2 occupied or reserved by a person, occupied with business etc.; *I'm afraid the manager is engaged.* 3 (of a telephone line) already in use.

**engagement** noun 1 engaging something; being engaged. 2 an appointment made with another person. 3 a promise to marry a specified person. 4 a battle.

**engaging** adjective attractive, charming.

**Engels** (eng-ĕlz), Friedrich (1820–95), German socialist, founder with Karl Marx of modern Communism.

**engender** (in-jen-der) verb give rise to.

**engine** noun 1 a mechanical device consisting of several parts working together, especially as a source of power. 2 the engine of a railway train. 3 a fire-engine. 4 (*old use*) a machine of war. 5 (*old use*) an instrument or means.

**engineer** noun 1 a person who is skilled in a branch of engineering. 2 one who is in charge of machines and engines, e.g. on a ship. 3 one who plans or organizes something. ●verb 1 construct or control as an engineer. 2 (*informal*) contrive or bring about; *he engineered a meeting between them.*

**engineering** noun the application of scientific knowledge to the design, building, and use of machines (**mechanical engineering**), roads and bridges (**civil engineering**), or electrical equipment (**electrical engineering**).

**England** the country forming the southern part of Great Britain.

**English** adjective of England or its people or language. ●noun 1 the English language, used in Britain and most Commonwealth countries and the USA. 2 (**the English**) English people. □ **Englishman** noun (plural **Englishmen**), **Englishwoman** noun (plural **Englishwomen**).

**English Channel** the sea channel separating southern England from northern France.

**engorged** adjective 1 crammed full. 2 congested with blood.

**engraft** verb 1 insert (a shoot) as a graft. 2 implant. 3 incorporate.

**engrave** verb 1 cut or carve (a design) into a hard surface; ornament with a design in this way. 2 fix deeply in the mind or memory. □ **engraver** noun

**engraving** noun a print made from an engraved plate.

**engross** (in-grohs) verb 1 occupy fully by absorbing the attention. 2 express in legal form. □ **engrossment** noun

**engulf** verb 1 surround or cause to disappear by flowing round or over, swamp. 2 overwhelm.

**enhance** verb increase the attractiveness or other qualities of; improve. □ **enhancement** noun

**enigma** (in-ig-mă) noun something mysterious or puzzling.

**enigmatic** (en-ig-mat-ik) adjective mysterious or puzzling. □ **enigmatically** adverb

**enjoin** verb 1 order, command. 2 prohibit (from doing something) by an official injunction.

**enjoy** verb 1 get pleasure from. 2 have as an advantage or benefit; *to enjoy good health.* □ **enjoy oneself** experience pleasure from what one is doing. □ **enjoyment** noun

**enjoyable** adjective giving enjoyment, pleasant. □ **enjoyably** adverb

**enkephalin** (en-kef-ălin) noun either of two morphine-like substances found in the brain and thought to be concerned with the control of pain.

**enkindle** verb cause to flare up, arouse.

**enlarge** verb 1 make or become larger. 2 reproduce (a photograph) on a larger scale. 3 say more about something; *enlarge upon this matter.*

**enlargement** noun 1 enlarging; being enlarged. 2 something enlarged; a photograph printed larger than its negative.

**enlarger** noun an apparatus for making photographic enlargements.

**enlighten** verb give knowledge to, inform. □ **enlightenment** noun

**enlightened** adjective freed from ignorance or prejudice, progressive; *in these enlightened days.*

**enlist** verb 1 take into or join the armed forces; *enlist as a soldier.* 2 secure as a means of help or support; *enlisted their sympathy.* □ **enlistment** noun

**enliven** verb make more lively. □ **enlivenment** noun

**en masse** (ahn mass) all together. (¶ French.)

**enmesh** verb entangle as if in a net.

**enmity** noun hostility between opposing people, groups, nations, etc.

**ennoble** verb 1 make (a person) a noble. 2 make (a person or thing) noble or more dignified. □ **ennoblement** noun

**ennui** (on-wee *or* on-**wee**) *noun* boredom. (¶ French.)

**enormity** (in-**orm**-iti) *noun* **1** great wickedness; *the enormity of this crime.* **2** a serious crime or error. **3** enormous size, magnitude; *the enormity of their task.*

■**Usage** Many people regard the use in sense 3 as unacceptable.

**enormous** *adjective* very large, huge. □ **enormously** *adverb*

**enough** *adjective, noun & adverb* as much or as many as necessary.

**en passant** (ahn **pas**-ahn) in passing; by the way. (¶ French.)

**enquire** *verb* ask. □ **enquiry** *noun*

■**Usage** Although these words are often used in exactly the same way as *inquire* and *inquiry*, there is a tendency to use *enquire* as a formal word for 'ask' and *inquire* to refer to an investigation, especially an official one.

**enrage** *verb* make furious.

**enrapture** *verb* fill with intense delight.

**enrich** *verb* **1** make richer. **2** improve the quality of by adding things; *this food is enriched with vitamins.* □ **enrichment** *noun*

**enrobe** *verb* put a robe on.

**enrol** *verb* (*Amer.* **enroll**) (**enrolled, enrolling**) **1** become a member of a society, institution, etc. **2** admit as a member. □ **enrolment** *noun*

**en route** (ahn **root**) on the way; *met him en route from Rome to London.* (¶ French.)

**ensconce** (in-**skons**) *verb* establish or settle comfortably.

**ensemble** (ahn-**sahmbl**) *noun* **1** a thing viewed as a whole. **2** a group of musicians who perform together; a passage of music for such a group. **3** a set of clothes worn together.

**enshrine** *verb* **1** enclose in a shrine. **2** serve as a shrine for. **3** preserve and cherish, as at a shrine; *the memory of Elvis, enshrined at Graceland.*

**enshroud** *verb* (*literary*) cover or hide.

**ensign** (**en**-syn) *noun* **1** a military or naval flag; a special form of the national flag flown by ships. **2** a standard-bearer. **3** (*old use*) the lowest commissioned infantry officer. **4** (*Amer.*) the lowest commissioned officer in the navy.

**ensilage** (**en**-sil-ij) *noun* silage.

**enslave** *verb* make a slave of. □ **enslavement** *noun*

**ensnare** *verb* catch as if in a snare.

**ensue** (ins-**yoo**) *verb* happen afterwards or as a result; *a quarrel ensued.*

**en suite** (ahn **sweet**) *adverb* forming a single unit; *bedroom with bathroom en suite.* ●*adjective* **1** forming a single unit; *an en suite bath-*

room. **2** with a bathroom attached; *an en suite bedroom.* (¶ French.)

**ensure** *verb* make safe or certain, secure; *good food will ensure good health.*

**ENT** *abbreviation* ear, nose, and throat.

**entablature** (in-**tab**-lǎ-cher) *noun Archit.* the section including the architrave, frieze, and cornice of a building or structure, above the supporting columns.

**entail** (in-**tayl**) *verb* **1** make necessary, involve; *these plans entail great expense.* **2** *Law* leave (land) to a line of heirs so that none of them can give it away or sell it. ●*noun* the entailing of landed property; the property itself.

**entangle** *verb* **1** tangle. **2** entwine in something that it is difficult to escape from. **3** involve in something complicated. □ **entanglement** *noun*

**entente** (ahn-**tahnt**) *noun* (also **entente cordiale**, *pronounced* cord-**yahl**) a friendly understanding between countries.

**enter** *verb* **1** go or come in or into. **2** come on stage. **3** penetrate; *the bullet entered his lung.* **4** become a member of; *he entered the Navy.* **5** put (a name, details, etc.) on a list or in a book. **6** register as a competitor. **7** record formally, present for consideration; *entered a plea of not guilty; entered a protest.* □ **enter into 1** take part in (a conversation, an agreement, etc.). **2** form part of (calculations, plans, etc.). **enter on 1** begin (a process, stage of work, etc.). **2** take possession of (an inheritance, an appointment, etc.). **enter up** record (names or details) in a book.

**enteric** (en-**te**-rik) *adjective* of the intestines.

**enteritis** (en-ter-**I**-tiss) *noun* inflammation of the intestines.

**enterprise** *noun* **1** an undertaking, especially a bold or difficult one. **2** initiative. **3** business activity; *private enterprise.*

**enterprising** *adjective* full of initiative.

**entertain** *verb* **1** amuse, occupy agreeably. **2** receive (a person) with hospitality; *they entertained me to lunch.* **3** have in the mind; *entertain doubts.* **4** consider favourably; *refused to entertain the idea.*

**entertainer** *noun* one who performs in entertainments, especially as an occupation.

**entertainment** *noun* **1** entertaining; being entertained. **2** amusement. **3** something performed before an audience to amuse or interest them.

**enthral** (in-**thrawl**) *verb* (*Amer.* **enthrall**) (**enthralled, enthralling**) captivate, please greatly.

**enthrone** *verb* place on a throne, especially ceremonially. □ **enthronement** *noun*

**enthuse** (in-**thewz**) *verb* **1** show enthusiasm. **2** fill with enthusiasm.

**enthusiasm** *noun* **1** a feeling of eager liking for or interest in something. **2** the object of this; *one of my enthusiasms.*

**enthusiast** *noun* one who is full of enthusiasm for something; *a sports enthusiast.*

**enthusiastic** *adjective* full of enthusiasm. □ **enthusiastically** *adverb*

**entice** *verb* attract or persuade by offering something pleasant. □ **enticement** *noun*

**entire** *adjective* whole, complete. □ **entirely** *adverb*

**entirety** (in-tyr-ĕti) *noun* completeness, the total. □ **in its entirety** in its complete form.

**entitle** *verb* **1** give a title to (a book etc.). **2** give a right; *the ticket entitles you to a seat.* □ **entitlement** *noun*

**entity** (en-titi) *noun* something that exists as a separate thing.

**entomb** (in-toom) *verb* place in a tomb, bury. □ **entombment** *noun*

**entomology** (en-tŏ-mol-ŏji) *noun* the study of insects. □ **entomological** (en-tŏm-ŏ-loj-ikăl) *adjective*, **entomologist** *noun*

**entourage** (on-toor-ahzh) *noun* the people accompanying an important person.

**entr'acte** (on-trakt) *noun* **1** an interval between the acts of a play. **2** a dance or music etc. performed then.

**entrails** (en-traylz) *plural noun* the intestines.

**entrance**[1] (en-trăns) *noun* **1** entering. **2** a door or passage by which one enters. **3** the right of admission; the fee charged for this.

**entrance**[2] (in-trahns) *verb* fill with intense delight. □ **entrancement** *noun*

**entrant** *noun* one who enters, especially as a competitor.

**entrap** *verb* (**entrapped**, **entrapping**) **1** catch as if in a trap. **2** trick, beguile. □ **entrapment** *noun*

**entreat** *verb* request earnestly or emotionally. □ **entreaty** *noun*

**entrecôte** (on-trĕ-koht) *noun* boned steak cut off the sirloin.

**entrée** (on-tray) *noun* **1** the right or privilege of admission. **2** a dish served between the fish and meat courses of a meal. **3** (*Amer.*) the main course of a meal.

**entrench** (in-trench) *verb* **1** establish firmly in a well-defended position. **2** surround with a trench for defence.

**entrenched** *adjective* (of attitudes, ideas, etc.) firmly established and not easily modified.

**entrenchment** *noun* **1** entrenching; being entrenched. **2** a trench made for defence.

**entrepôt** (on-trĕ-poh) *noun* a warehouse for temporary storage of goods in transit.

**entrepreneur** (on-trĕ-prĕn-er) *noun* **1** a person who organizes and manages a commercial undertaking, especially one involving commercial risk. **2** a contractor acting as intermediary. □ **entrepreneurial** *adjective*

**entropy** (en-trŏp-i) *noun* *Physics* a measure of disorder indicating the amount of energy that, rather than being concentrated, has become more evenly distributed and so cannot be used to do work (within a particular system, or in the universe as a whole).

**entrust** *verb* give as a responsibility, place (a person or thing) in a person's care.

**entry** *noun* **1** entering. **2** a place of entrance. **3** an alley between buildings. **4** an item entered in a list, diary, etc. **5** a person or thing entered in a race or competition. **6** the number of entrants in a competition.

**entryism** *noun* infiltration into a political organization to change or subvert its policies or objectives. □ **entryist** *noun*

**Entryphone** *noun* (*trade mark*) a telephone at the entrance to a building, for visitors to use in order to identify themselves before they are allowed to enter.

**entwine** *verb* twine round, interweave.

**E-number** *noun* E plus a number, the EC designation for permitted food additives.

**enumerate** (i-new-mer-ayt) *verb* count, mention (items) one by one. □ **enumeration** *noun*

**enumerator** (i-new-mer-ayter) *noun* a person employed in census-taking.

**enunciate** (i-nun-si-ayt) *verb* **1** pronounce (words). **2** state clearly. □ **enunciation** *noun*

**enuresis** (en-yoor-ee-sis) *noun* involuntary passing of urine.

**envelop** (in-vel-ŏp) *verb* (**enveloped**, **enveloping**) wrap up, cover on all sides; *the hill was enveloped in mist.* □ **envelopment** *noun*

**envelope** (en-vĕ-lohp) *noun* **1** a wrapper or covering, especially a folded paper container for a letter. **2** the gas container of a balloon or airship.

**enviable** (en-vi-ăbŭl) *adjective* desirable enough to arouse envy. □ **enviably** *adverb*

**envious** *adjective* full of envy. □ **enviously** *adverb*

**environment** *noun* **1** physical surroundings and conditions, especially those affecting people's lives; *an urban environment.* **2** (**the environment**) the external conditions affecting the growth, development, and well-being of plants, animals, and humans; *a threat to the environment.* □ **environmental** (in-vyr-ŏn-men-tăl) *adjective*

**environmentalist** *noun* a person who seeks to protect or improve the environment.

**environs** (in-vyr-ŏnz) *plural noun* the surrounding districts, especially round a town.

**envisage** (in-**viz**-ăj) *verb* **1** visualize, imagine. **2** foresee; *changes are envisaged.*

**envoy** (**en**-voi) *noun* **1** a messenger or representative. **2** (in full **envoy extraordinary**) a diplomatic minister ranking below an ambassador.

**envy** *noun* **1** a feeling of discontent aroused by someone else's possession of things one would like to have oneself. **2** the object of this; *his car is the envy of the neighbourhood.* ●*verb* (**envied**, **envying**) feel envy of (a person, their circumstances); *I envy you your good luck.*

**enzyme** (**en**-zym) *noun* **1** a protein formed in living cells and assisting chemical processes (e.g. in digestion). **2** a similar substance produced synthetically for use in chemical processes, household detergents, etc.

**EOC** *abbreviation* Equal Opportunities Commission.

**Eocene** (ee-oh-seen) *adjective* of the second epoch of the Tertiary period of geological time, about 55 million years ago. ●*noun* this epoch.

**eon** alternative spelling of AEON.

**EP** *abbreviation* extended-play (record).

**epaulette** (ep-ă-let) *noun* an ornamental shoulder-piece on a jacket, shirt, etc., especially on a uniform.

**épée** (**ay**-pay) *noun* a sharp-pointed sword used (with the end blunted) in fencing.

**epergne** (i-**pern**) *noun* an ornament for a dinner table, with small bowls or vases on branched supports.

**ephedrine** (**ef**-i-drin) *noun* an alkaloid drug used to relieve asthma, hay fever, etc.

**ephemera** (if-**em**-er-ă) *plural noun* things of only short-lived usefulness.

**ephemeral** (if-**em**-er-ăl) *adjective* lasting only a very short time.

**Ephesians** (i-**fee**-*zh*ĕnz) □ **Epistle to the Ephesians** a book of the New Testament, an epistle to the Church at Ephesus on the coast of Asia Minor.

**epic** *noun* **1** a long poem or other literary work telling of great events or heroic deeds. **2** a book or film resembling this. **3** a subject fit to be told in an epic. ●*adjective* of or like an epic, on a grand scale.

**epicene** (**ep**-i-seen) *adjective* **1** of or for both sexes. **2** having the characteristics of both sexes or of neither sex.

**epicentre** *noun* (*Amer.* **epicenter**) the point at which an earthquake reaches the earth's surface.

**epicure** (**ep**-i-kewr) *noun* a person with refined tastes, especially in food and drink. □ **epicurism** *noun*

**Epicurean** (ep-i-kewr-ee-ăn) *adjective* **1** of the Greek philosopher Epicurus (*c.*300 BC), who sought freedom from anxiety and disturbance. **2** (**epicurean**) devoted to sensuous pleasure and luxury. ●*noun* **1** a follower or student of Epicurus. **2** (**epicurean**) an epicurean person.

**epidemic** *noun* an outbreak of a disease etc. spreading rapidly through a community.

**epidemiology** (epi-deem-i-ol-ŏji) *noun* the branch of medicine concerned with the control of epidemics.

**epidermis** (epi-**der**-mis) *noun* the outer layer of the skin. □ **epidermal** *adjective*

**epidiascope** (epi-**dy**-ă-skohp) *noun* a projector giving images of both opaque and transparent objects.

**epidural** (epi-**dewr**-ăl) *adjective* (of an anaesthetic) injected round the nerves of the spinal cord and having the effect of anaesthetizing the lower part of the body. ●*noun* an epidural injection, used especially in childbirth.

**epiglottis** (epi-**glot**-iss) *noun* the cartilage at the root of the tongue, that descends to cover the windpipe in swallowing.

**epigram** *noun* a short witty saying. □ **epigrammatic** *adjective*

**epigraph** *noun* an inscription.

**epilepsy** *noun* a disorder of the nervous system causing convulsions, sometimes with loss of consciousness.

**epileptic** *noun* a person with epilepsy. ●*adjective* of epilepsy.

**epilogue** (**ep**-i-log) *noun* a short concluding section in a literary work.

**Epiphany** (i-**pif**-ăni) *noun* the Christian festival commemorating the showing of Christ to the Magi, celebrated on 6 January.

**episcopacy** (ip-**iss**-kŏ-pă-si) *noun* **1** government by bishops. **2** (**the episcopacy**) bishops.

**episcopal** (ip-**iss**-kŏ-păl) *adjective* of a bishop or bishops; governed by bishops.

**Episcopal Church** the Anglican Church in Scotland and the U.S.

**episcopalian** (i-piss-kŏ-**pay**-li-ăn) *noun* **1** a member of an episcopal church. **2** (**Episcopalian**) a member of the Episcopal Church. ●*adjective* **1** of an episcopal church. **2** (**Episcopalian**) of the Episcopal Church.

**episcopate** (ip-**iss**-kŏ-păt) *noun* **1** the office of bishop. **2** (**the episcopate**) bishops.

**episiotomy** (epi-si-ot-ŏmi) *noun* a cut made at the opening of the vagina during childbirth, to aid delivery of the baby.

**episode** *noun* **1** an incident or event forming one part of a sequence. **2** an incident in a story; one part of a serial.

**episodic** (epi-**sod**-ik) *adjective* **1** occurring irregularly. **2** consisting of episodes. □ **episodically** *adverb*

**epistle** (i-**piss**-ŭl) *noun* **1** (*humorous*) a letter. **2** (**Epistle**) any of the books in the New Testament written as Letters by the Apostles.

**epistolary** (ip-**iss**-tŏl-ări) *adjective* of letters; in the form of a letter.

**epitaph** (**ep**-i-tahf) *noun* words inscribed on a tomb or describing a dead person.

**epithelium** (ep-ith-**ee**-liŭm) *noun* (*plural* **epithelia** or **epitheliums**) the tissue forming the outer layer of the body or of an open cavity. □ **epithelial** *adjective*

**epithet** (**ep**-i-thet) *noun* a descriptive word or phrase added to a name, e.g. 'the Great' in *Alfred the Great*.

**epitome** (ip-**it**-ŏmi) *noun* **1** a person or thing embodying perfectly a stated quality or idea; *she is the epitome of common sense*. **2** a thing that shows well on a small scale the qualities of something much larger; *a car that was the very epitome of Las Vegas*.

**epitomize** (ip-**it**-ŏ-myz) *verb* (also **epitomise**) be an epitome of.

**EPNS** *abbreviation* electroplated nickel silver.

**epoch** (**ee**-pok) *noun* **1** a particular period of history. **2** a division of a geological period. □ **epoch-making** *adjective* very important or remarkable.

**eponym** (**ep**-ŏ-nim) *noun* **1** a word, place-name, etc. derived from a person's name. **2** a person's name that is used in this way. □ **eponymous** (i-**pon**-i-mŭs) *adjective*

**Epsom salts** magnesium sulphate, used as a purgative.

**Epstein** (**ep**-styn), Sir Jacob (1880–1959), American-born British sculptor, noted for his statues of the famous.

**equable** (**ek**-wă-bŭl) *adjective* **1** moderate or unvarying; *an equable climate*. **2** (of a person) not easily disturbed or angered. □ **equably** *adverb*

**equal** *adjective* **1** the same in size, amount, value, etc. **2** evenly balanced; *an equal contest*. **3** having the same rights or status. ●*noun* a person or thing that is equal to another. ●*verb* (**equalled, equalling**; *Amer.* **equaled, equaling**) **1** be equal to. **2** produce or achieve something to match; *no one has equalled this score*. □ **be equal to** have enough strength, courage, or ability etc. for. **equal opportunity** (often as **equal opportunities**) the opportunity or right to be offered employment, pay, and living standards without discrimination on grounds of gender, race, age, disability, etc. □ **equally** *adverb*

**equality** *noun* being equal.

**equalize** *verb* (also **equalise**) **1** make or become equal. **2** (in games) equal an opponent's score. □ **equalization** *noun*

**equalizer** *noun* (also **equaliser**) an equalizing goal etc.

**equanimity** (ek-wă-**nim**-iti) *noun* calmness of mind or temper.

**equate** (i-**kwayt**) *verb* consider to be equal or equivalent. □ **equatable** *adjective*

**equation** (i-**kway**-zhŏn) *noun* **1** a mathematical statement that two expressions (connected by the sign =) are equal. **2** a formula indicating a chemical reaction by the use of symbols. **3** making equal.

**equator** (i-**kway**-ter) *noun* an imaginary line round the earth at an equal distance from the North and South Poles.

**equatorial** (ek-wă-**tor**-iăl) *adjective* of or near the equator.

**Equatorial Guinea** a country on the west coast of Africa.

**equerry** (**ek**-wer-i) *noun* an officer attending the British royal family.

**equestrian** (i-**kwest**-riăn) *adjective* of or relating to horses and horse-riding.

**equiangular** *adjective* having equal angles.

**equidistant** (ee-kwi-**dis**-tănt) *adjective* at an equal distance.

**equilateral** (ee-kwi-**lat**-er-ăl) *adjective* having all sides equal.

**equilibrium** (ee-kwi-**lib**-riŭm) *noun* (*plural* **equilibria** or **equilibriums**) **1** a state of physical balance. **2** a state of mental or emotional stability.

**equine** (**ek**-wyn) *adjective* of or like a horse.

**equinoctial** (ek-wi-**nok**-shăl) *adjective* occurring at an equinox. ●*noun* (in full **equinoctial line**) = CELESTIAL EQUATOR.

**equinox** (**ek**-win-oks) *noun* each time of year when day and night are of equal length (about 22 September and 20 March).

**equip** *verb* (**equipped, equipping**) supply with what is needed.

**equipage** (**ek**-wi-pij) *noun* **1** (*old use*) requisites, an outfit. **2** a carriage and horses with attendants.

**equipment** *noun* **1** the outfit, tools, and other things needed for a particular job or expedition etc. **2** equipping.

**equipoise** (**ek**-wi-poiz) *noun* **1** equilibrium. **2** a counterbalance.

**equitable** (**ek**-wit-ăbŭl) *adjective* **1** fair and just. **2** *Law* valid in equity as distinct from law. □ **equitably** *adverb*

**equitation** *noun* horse-riding.

**equity** (**ek**-wi-ti) *noun* **1** fairness, impartiality. **2** (**Equity**) the actors' trade union. **3** (**equities**) stocks and shares not bearing fixed interest.

**equivalent** *adjective* equal in value, importance, meaning, etc. ●*noun* an equivalent thing, amount, or word. □ **equivalence** *noun*

**equivocal** (i-**kwiv**-ŏkăl) *adjective* **1** able to be interpreted in two ways, ambiguous. **2** questionable, suspicious; *an equivocal character*. □ **equivocally** *adverb*

**equivocate** (i-**kwiv**-ŏkayt) *verb* use ambiguous words in order to conceal the truth; avoid committing oneself. □ **equivocation** *noun*

**ER** *abbreviation* Elizabetha Regina. (¶ Latin, = Queen Elizabeth.)

**Er** *symbol* erbium.

**er** *interjection* an expression of hesitation.

**era** (**eer**-ă) *noun* **1** a distinct period of history; *the pre-Roman era.* **2** a division of geological time; *the mesozoic era.*

**eradicable** *adjective* able to be eradicated.

**eradicate** (i-**rad**-ik-ayt) *verb* get rid of, remove all traces of. □ **eradication** *noun,* **eradicator** *noun*

**erase** (i-**rayz**) *verb* **1** rub or scrape out (marks, writing, etc.). **2** wipe out a recorded signal from (magnetic tape or disk). **3** remove all traces of.

**eraser** *noun* a thing that erases, especially a piece of rubber for rubbing out marks or writing.

**Erasmus** (i-**raz**-mŭs), Desiderius (*c.*1469–1536), Dutch Christian humanist and writer.

**erasure** (i-**ray**-*zh*er) *noun* **1** erasing. **2** a word etc. that has been erased.

**erbium** (**er**-bi-ŭm) *noun* a soft metallic element (symbol Er).

**ere** (*pronounced* air) *preposition & conjunction* (*old use*) before.

**erect** *adjective* **1** standing on end, upright, vertical. **2** (of the penis, nipples, or clitoris) enlarged and rigid from sexual excitement. ●*verb* set up, build. □ **erectly** *adverb,* **erector** *noun*

**erectile** (i-**rek**-tyl) *adjective* (of parts of the body) able to become enlarged and rigid from sexual excitement.

**erection** *noun* **1** erecting; being erected. **2** something erected, such as a building. **3** swelling and hardening (especially of the penis) in sexual excitement.

**erg** *noun* a unit of work or energy.

**ergo** *adverb* therefore. (¶ Latin.)

**ergonomics** (ergŏ-**nom**-iks) *noun* study of work and its environment and conditions in order to achieve maximum efficiency. □ **ergonomic** *adjective,* **ergonomically** *adverb*

**ergot** (**er**-got) *noun* a fungus affecting rye and other cereals.

**Erie** (**eer**-i), **Lake** one of the five Great Lakes of North America.

**Erin** (**e**-rin) an ancient or poetic name for Ireland.

**Eritrea** (e-ri-**tray**-ă) a province of Ethiopia, on the Red Sea.

**ERM** *abbreviation* Exchange Rate Mechanism, a system for controlling exchange rates within the EMS.

**ermine** *noun* **1** an animal of the weasel family, with brown fur that turns white in winter. **2** this white fur.

**Ernie** *noun* (in Britain) a device for drawing the prize-winning numbers of Premium Bonds. (¶ Named from the initial letters of *e*lectronic *r*andom *n*umber *i*ndicator *e*quipment.)

**Ernst**, Max (1891–1976), German-born artist, one of the major figures of the surrealist movement.

**erode** (i-**rohd**) *verb* wear away gradually, especially by rubbing or corroding. □ **erosion** (i-roh-*zh*ŏn) *noun,* **erosive** *adjective*

**erogenous** (i-**roj**-in-ŭs) *adjective* (of a part of the body) particularly sensitive to sexual stimulation.

**Eros** (**eer**-oss) **1** (*Gk. myth.*) the god of love, Cupid. **2** the winged figure of an archer over the fountain in Piccadilly Circus, London (1899).

**erotic** (i-**rot**-ik) *adjective* of sexual love; arousing sexual desire. □ **erotically** *adverb*

**erotica** (i-**rot**-ik-ă) *plural noun* erotic literature or art.

**eroticism** (i-**rot**-i-sizm) *noun* erotic nature or character.

**err** (*pronounced* er) *verb* (**erred, erring**) **1** make a mistake, be incorrect. **2** sin.

**errand** *noun* **1** a short journey on which a person goes or is sent to carry a message or deliver goods etc. **2** the purpose of a journey. □ **errand of mercy** a journey to bring help or relieve distress etc.

**errant** (**e**-rănt) *adjective* **1** erring, misbehaving. **2** (*literary*) travelling in search of adventure; *a knight errant.*

**erratic** (i-**rat**-ik) *adjective* irregular or uneven in movement, quality, habit, etc. □ **erratically** *adverb*

**erratum** (e-**rah**-tŭm) *noun* (*plural* **errata**) an error in printing or writing.

**erroneous** (i-**roh**-niŭs) *adjective* mistaken, incorrect. □ **erroneously** *adverb*

**error** *noun* **1** a mistake. **2** the condition of being wrong in opinion or conduct. **3** the amount of inaccuracy in a calculation or a measuring-device; *an error of 2 per cent.*

**ersatz** (**air**-zats) *adjective* made in imitation. ●*noun* an ersatz thing or substance. (¶ German.)

**Erse** *noun & adjective* Gaelic.

**erstwhile** *adjective* former.

**eructation** (ee-ruk-**tay**-shŏn) *noun* (*formal*) belching.

**erudite** (**e**-rew-dyt) *adjective* having or showing great learning. □ **erudition** (e-rew-**dish**-ŏn) *noun*

**erupt** *verb* **1** break out suddenly and violently. **2** (of a volcano) shoot forth lava etc.; (of a geyser) spurt water or steam.

**3** (of a rash or blemish) appear on the skin. □ **eruption** noun, **eruptive** adjective

**erysipelas** (e-ri-**sip**-ilăs) noun a disease causing fever and inflammation of the skin.

**erythrocyte** (i-**rith**-rŏ-syt) noun a red blood cell.

**Es** symbol einsteinium.

**escalate** (**esk**-ă-layt) verb increase or cause to increase in intensity or extent. □ **escalation** noun

**escalator** noun a moving staircase consisting of a circulating belt forming steps.

**escalope** (**esk**-ă-lop) noun a thin slice of boneless meat, especially veal.

**escapade** (esk-ă-**payd**) noun a piece of reckless or mischievous conduct.

**escape** verb **1** get oneself free from confinement or control. **2** (of liquid or gas etc.) get out of a container, leak. **3** succeed in avoiding (capture, punishment, etc.). **4** be forgotten or unnoticed by; *his name escapes me.* **5** (of words, a sigh, etc.) be uttered unintentionally. ●noun **1** the act of escaping, the fact of having escaped. **2** a means of escaping. **3** a leakage of liquid or gas. **4** a temporary distraction or relief from reality or worry. □ **escape clause** a clause releasing a person from a contract under certain conditions. **escape velocity** the minimum velocity needed to escape from the gravitational field of a planet or other body.

**escapee** (ess-kay-**pee**) noun a person who has escaped.

**escapement** noun a mechanism regulating the movement of a watch or clock.

**escapist** noun one who likes to escape from the realities of life by absorbing the mind in entertainment or fantasy. □ **escapism** noun

**escapology** (esk-ă-**pol**-ŏji) noun the methods and technique of escaping from captivity or confinement, especially as entertainment. □ **escapologist** noun

**escarpment** noun a steep slope at the edge of a plateau.

**eschatology** (ess-kă-**tol**-ŏji) noun theology concerning death and final destiny. □ **eschatological** adjective

**eschew** (iss-**choo**) verb (formal) avoid or abstain from (certain kinds of action or food etc.). □ **eschewal** noun

**Escoffier** (es-**kof**-i-ay), Georges-Auguste (1846-1935), French chef of international repute.

**escort** noun (pronounced ess-**kort**) **1** one or more persons or ships etc. accompanying a person or thing to give protection or as an honour. **2** a person accompanying a member of the opposite sex socially. ●verb (pronounced i-**skort**) act as an escort to.

**escritoire** (ess-krit-**wahr**) noun a writing-desk with drawers.

**escudo** (ess-**kew**-doh) noun (plural **escudos**) the chief unit of money in Portugal.

**escutcheon** (i-**skuch**-ŏn) noun a shield or emblem bearing a coat of arms.

**Eskimo** noun (plural **Eskimos** or **Eskimo**) **1** a member of a people living near the Arctic coast of America and eastern Siberia. **2** their language.

■**Usage** The name *Inuit* is now considered preferable.

**ESN** abbreviation educationally subnormal.

**esophagus** Amer. spelling of OESOPHAGUS.

**esoteric** (ess-oh-te-**rik**) adjective intelligible only to people with special knowledge. □ **esoterically** adverb

**ESP** abbreviation extrasensory perception.

**espadrille** (ess-pă-**dril**) noun a canvas shoe with a sole of plaited fibre.

**espalier** (iss-**pal**-i-er) noun **1** a trellis or framework on which fruit trees or ornamental shrubs are trained. **2** a tree etc. trained on this.

**esparto** (iss-**par**-toh) noun (plural **espartos**) (in full **esparto grass**) a coarse grass of Spain and North Africa, used in paper-making.

**especial** adjective **1** special, outstanding; *of especial interest.* **2** belonging chiefly to one person or thing; *for your especial benefit.*

**especially** adverb chiefly, more than in other cases.

**Esperanto** (ess-per-**an**-toh) noun an artificial language designed for international use.

**espionage** (ess-pi-ŏn-ah*zh*) noun spying or using spies to obtain secret information.

**esplanade** (ess-plăn-**ayd**) noun a long open level area for walking, especially beside the sea.

**espouse** (i-**spowz**) verb **1** adopt or support (a cause). **2** marry. □ **espousal** noun

**espresso** noun (also **expresso**) (plural **espressos**) **1** strong coffee made by forcing steam through ground coffee. **2** a machine for making this.

**esprit** (ess-**pree**) noun liveliness, wit. □ **esprit de corps** (dĕ **kor**) loyalty and devotion uniting the members of a group. (¶ French.)

**espy** verb (**espied**, **espying**) catch sight of.

**Esq.** abbreviation Esquire; a courtesy title (in formal use) placed after a man's surname where no title is used before his name.

**essay** noun (pronounced ess-**ay**) **1** a short piece of writing on a given subject. **2** (formal) an attempt. ●verb (pronounced e-**say**) (formal) attempt.

**essayist** noun a writer of essays.

**essence** noun **1** all that makes a thing what it is, its nature. **2** an indispensable quality or element. **3** a concentrated extract of something, often obtained by distillation. **4** a liquid perfume.

**essential** *adjective* **1** indispensable. **2** of or constituting a thing's essence; *its essential qualities*. ●*plural noun* (**essentials**) indispensable elements or things. □ **essential oil** a volatile oil that is extracted from a plant, with its characteristic smell. □ **essentially** *adverb*

**Essex** a county of eastern England.

**establish** *verb* **1** set up (a business or government etc.) on a permanent basis. **2** settle (a person or oneself) in a place or position. **3** cause people to accept (a custom or belief etc.). **4** show to be true, prove; *established his innocence*.

**established** *adjective* (of a Church or religion) officially recognized as a country's national Church or religion.

**establishment** *noun* **1** establishing; being established. **2** an organized body of people maintained for a purpose, a household or staff of servants etc. **3** a business firm or public institution, its members or employees or premises. **4** a Church system established by law. □ **the Establishment** people in positions of power and authority, exercising influence and generally resisting changes.

**estate** *noun* **1** landed property. **2** a residential or industrial district planned as a unit. **3** all that a person owns, especially at his or her death. **4** (*old use*) condition; *the holy estate of matrimony*. □ **estate agent** one whose business is the selling or letting of buildings and land. **estate car** a car with a door at the back and the passenger area extended to provide luggage space. **estate duty** (*hist.*) death duty.

**esteem** *verb* **1** think highly of. **2** (*formal*) consider or regard; *I should esteem it an honour*. ●*noun* favourable opinion, respect.

**ester** (ess-ter) *noun* a chemical compound formed when an acid and an alcohol interact in a certain way.

**Esther** (ess-ter) **1** a beautiful Jewish woman who became the wife of the King of Persia (5th century BC). **2** the book of the Old Testament giving an account of this.

**esthete** Amer. spelling of AESTHETE.

**esthetic** Amer. spelling of AESTHETIC.

**estimable** (ess-tim-ăbŭl) *adjective* worthy of esteem.

**estimate** *noun* (*pronounced* ess-tim-ăt) **1** a judgement of a thing's approximate value or amount etc. **2** a contractor's statement of the approximate charge for work to be undertaken. **3** a judgement of character or qualities. ●*verb* (*pronounced* ess-tim-ayt) form an estimate of. □ **estimator** *noun*

**estimation** *noun* **1** estimating. **2** judgement of a person's or thing's worth.

**Estonia** (ess-toh-niă) a country in eastern Europe on the Gulf of Finland, formerly a republic of the USSR.

**Estonian** *adjective* of Estonia or its people or language. ●*noun* **1** a person from Estonia. **2** the language of Estonia.

**estrange** *verb* cause (people formerly friendly or loving) to become unfriendly or indifferent. □ **estrangement** *noun*

**estrogen** Amer. spelling of OESTROGEN.

**estuary** (ess-tew-er-i) *noun* the tidal mouth of a large river.

**ET** *abbreviation* extraterrestrial.

**ETA** *abbreviation* **1** estimated time of arrival. **2** (*pronounced* et-ă) a Basque separatist movement.

**et al.** *abbreviation* = and others. (¶ Latin *et alii*.)

**etc.** *abbreviation* et cetera, and other similar things, and the rest. ●*plural noun* (**etceteras**) the usual extras. (¶ Latin, = and the rest.)

**etch** *verb* **1** make (a pattern or picture) by engraving a metal plate with acid, especially so that copies can be printed from this. **2** impress deeply; *the scene is etched on my mind*. □ **etcher** *noun*

**etching** *noun* a print made from an etched plate.

**eternal** *adjective* **1** existing always without beginning or end. **2** unchanging, not affected by time. **3** (*informal*) ceaseless, too frequent; *these eternal arguments*. □ **the Eternal City** Rome. **eternal triangle** a complex emotional or sexual relationship involving two men and a woman or two women and a man. □ **eternally** *adverb*

**eternity** *noun* **1** infinite (especially future) time. **2** the endless period of life after death. **3** (*informal*) a very long time. □ **eternity ring** a finger ring with gems set all round it.

**ethane** *noun* a gaseous hydrocarbon of the alkane series, occurring in natural gas.

**ethanoic acid** (eth-ă-**noh**-ik) acetic acid.

**ethanol** (eth-ă-nol) *noun* alcohol.

**Ethelred** (eth-ĕl-red) 'the Unready' (c.969–1016), king of England 978–1016.

**ether** (ee-ther) *noun* **1** the clear sky, the upper regions beyond the clouds. **2** a substance formerly thought to fill all space and act as a medium for transmission of radio waves etc. **3** a colourless volatile liquid used as an anaesthetic and as a solvent.

**ethereal** (i-theer-iăl) *adjective* **1** light and delicate, especially in appearance. **2** of heaven, heavenly. □ **ethereally** *adverb*

**ethic** (eth-ik) *adjective* of or involving morals. ●*noun* a moral principle or set of principles.

**ethical** (eth-ikăl) *adjective* **1** of ethics. **2** morally correct, honourable. **3** (of medicines) not advertised to the general public and usually available only on a doctor's prescription. □ **ethically** adverb

**ethics** noun **1** (treated as singular) moral philosophy. **2** (treated as plural) moral principles; medical ethics.

**Ethiopia** a country of NE Africa. □ **Ethiopian** adjective & noun

**Ethiopic** (ee-thi-op-ik) noun the liturgical language of the Coptic Church of Ethiopia.

**ethnic** adjective **1** of a racial group; relating to race or culture. **2** (of music, clothes, etc.) in the style of exotic, non-European cultures. □ **ethnic cleansing** the practice of mass expulsion or killing of people from opposing ethnic or religious groups within a certain area. **ethnic minority** a group differentiated from the main population by racial origin or cultural background. □ **ethnically** adverb

**ethnologist** noun an expert in ethnology.

**ethnology** (eth-nol-ŏji) noun the study of human races and their characteristics. □ **ethnological** (eth-nŏ-loj-ikăl) adjective

**ethos** (ee-thoss) noun the characteristic spirit and beliefs of a community etc.

**ethyl** (eth-il) noun a radical present in alcohol and ether. □ **ethyl alcohol** alcohol.

**ethylene** (eth-i-leen) noun a hydrocarbon of the alkene series, occurring in natural gas and used in the manufacture of polythene.

**etiolate** (ee-tiŏ-layt) verb make (a plant) pale through lack of light. □ **etiolation** noun

**etiology** Amer. spelling of AETIOLOGY.

**etiquette** (et-i-ket) noun the rules of correct behaviour in society or among the members of a profession.

**Etna** a volcano in Sicily.

**Eton** a British public school near Windsor, Berks. □ **Etonian** adjective & noun

**Etruscan** (i-trus-kăn) noun **1** a native of ancient Etruria (modern Tuscany). **2** the language of the Etruscans.

**étude** (ay-tewd) noun a short musical composition.

**etymology** (et-im-ol-ŏji) noun **1** an account of the origin and development of a word. **2** the study of words and their origins. □ **etymological** (et-im-ŏ-loj-ikăl) adjective, **etymologically** adverb, **etymologist** noun

**Eu** symbol europium.

**eucalypt** (yoo-kă-lipt) noun a eucalyptus.

**eucalyptus** (yoo-kă-lip-tŭs) noun (plural **eucalyptuses** or **eucalypti**) (also **eucalypt**) **1** an Australasian evergreen tree. **2** a strong-smelling oil obtained from its leaves.

**Eucharist** (yoo-kă-rist) noun **1** the Christian sacrament in which bread and wine are consecrated and consumed. **2** the consecrated elements, especially the bread. □ **Eucharistic** adjective

**Euclid** (yoo-klid) (c. 300 BC), Greek mathematician, whose Elements was the standard work on geometry until recent times. □ **Euclidean** (yoo-klid-iăn) adjective

**eugenics** (yoo-jen-iks) noun (treated as singular or plural) the science of developing a human or animal population using controlled breeding. □ **eugenic** adjective, **eugenically** adverb

**eulogize** (yoo-lŏ-jyz) verb (also **eulogise**) write or utter a eulogy of. □ **eulogistic** adjective

**eulogy** (yoo-lŏ-ji) noun a speech or piece of writing in praise of a person or thing.

**eunuch** (yoo-nŭk) noun a castrated man.

**euphemism** (yoo-fim-izm) noun a mild or roundabout expression substituted for one considered improper or too direct; 'pass away' is a euphemism for 'die'. □ **euphemistic** (yoo-fim-ist-ik) adjective, **euphemistically** adverb

**euphonium** (yoo-foh-niŭm) noun a large brass wind instrument of the tuba family.

**euphony** (yoo-fŏni) noun pleasantness of sounds, especially in words. □ **euphonious** (yoo-foh-niŭs) adjective

**euphoria** (yoo-for-iă) noun an intense feeling of well-being and excitement. □ **euphoric** (yoo-fo-rik) adjective

**Euphrates** (yoo-fray-teez) a river of SW Asia, flowing from Turkey through Syria and Iraq to join the Tigris, forming the Shatt al-Arab which flows into the Persian Gulf.

**Eurasian** (yoor-ay-zhăn) adjective **1** of Europe and Asia. **2** of mixed European and Asian parentage. ● noun a Eurasian person.

**Euratom** (yoor-at-ŏm) noun the European Atomic Energy Community.

**eureka** (yoor-eek-ă) interjection I have found it; an exclamation of triumph at a discovery. (¶ Said to have been uttered by the Greek mathematician Archimedes (3rd century BC) on realizing that the volume of an object can be calculated by the amount of water it displaces.)

**eurhythmics** (yoo-rith-miks) noun (treated as singular or plural) (Amer. **eurythmics**) harmony of bodily movement, developed with music and dance into a system of education.

**Euripides** (yoor-ip-i-deez) (5th century BC), Greek dramatist.

**Euro-** combining form Europe; European.

**Eurodollar** noun a dollar held in a bank outside the USA.

**Europa** (yoor-oh-pă) (Gk. myth.) a woman who was wooed by Zeus in the form of a bull and carried off by him to Crete.

**Europe** a continent extending from Asia to the Atlantic Ocean. □ **European** adjective & noun

**European Commission** a group appointed by the member states of the European Community to initiate Community action and safeguard individual national interests.

**European Community** an association of certain European countries committed to economic and political integration (an organization broadened from the earlier European Economic Community).

**europium** (yoor-**oh**-piŭm) *noun* a soft metallic element (symbol Eu).

**Eurydice** (yoor-**id**-i-si) (*Gk. myth.*) wife of Orpheus.

**eurythmics** Amer. spelling of EURHYTH-MICS.

**Eustachian tube** (yoo-**stay**-shăn) the narrow passage from the pharynx to the cavity of the middle ear.

**euthanasia** (yoo-thă-**nay**-ziă) *noun* the bringing about of a gentle death for a person suffering from a painful incurable disease.

**eV** *abbreviation* electronvolt.

**evacuate** *verb* 1 send (people) away from a place considered dangerous; remove the occupants of (a place). 2 empty (a vessel) of air etc. 3 empty (the bowels etc.). □ **evacuation** *noun*

**evacuee** *noun* an evacuated person.

**evade** (i-**vayd**) *verb* avoid by cleverness or trickery; *evade the police*; *evade arrest*.

**evaluate** *verb* find out or state the value of, assess. □ **evaluation** *noun*

**evanesce** (e-văn-**ess**) *verb* (*literary*) fade from sight, disappear. □ **evanescent** *adjective*, **evanescence** *noun*

**evangelical** (ee-van-**jel**-ikăl) *adjective* 1 according to the teaching of the gospel or the Christian religion. 2 (in the Church of England) of a group believing that salvation is achieved by faith in the Atonement through Christ. ●*noun* a member of this group. □ **evangelicalism** *noun*, **evangelically** *adverb*

**evangelism** (i-**van**-jĕl-izm) *noun* preaching or spreading of the gospel.

**evangelist** (i-**van**-jĕl-ist) *noun* 1 any of the authors of the four Gospels (Matthew, Mark, Luke, John). 2 a person who preaches the gospel. □ **evangelistic** *adjective*

**evangelize** *verb* (also **evangelise**) preach or spread the gospel to, win over to Christianity. □ **evangelization** *noun*

**Evans**, Dame Edith Mary Booth (1888–1976), English actress.

**evaporate** *verb* 1 turn or be turned into vapour. 2 lose or cause to lose moisture in this way. 3 cease to exist; *their enthusiasm evaporated*. □ **evaporated milk** unsweetened milk thickened by partial evaporation and tinned. □ **evaporation** *noun*

**evasion** (i-**vay**-zhŏn) *noun* 1 evading; *tax evasion*. 2 an evasive answer or excuse.

**evasive** (i-**vay**-siv) *adjective* evading, not frank or straightforward. □ **evasively** *adverb*, **evasiveness** *noun*

**Eve** (in Biblical tradition) the first woman.

**eve** *noun* 1 the evening or day before a festival; *Christmas Eve*. 2 the time just before an event; *on the eve of an election*. 3 (*old use*) evening.

**even¹** *adjective* 1 level, free from irregularities, smooth. 2 uniform in quality. 3 (of temper) calm, not easily upset. 4 equally balanced or matched. 5 equal in number or amount. 6 (of a number) exactly divisible by two. 7 (of money or time or quantity) exact, not involving fractions; *an even dozen*. ●*adverb* 1 (used to emphasize a comparison) to a greater degree; *ran even faster*. 2 (used to introduce a particularly extreme case or example); *does he even suspect the danger?*; *even a child could understand that*. ●*verb* (often foll. by *out* or *up*) make or become even. ●*plural noun* (**evens**) = EVEN MONEY. □ **be** *or* **get even with** have one's revenge on. **even-handed** *adjective* impartial. **even money** betting odds offering the chance to win the amount one has staked. **even now** now as well as before; at this very moment. **even so** although that is the case. □ **evenly** *adverb*, **evenness** *noun*

**even²** *noun* (*poetic*) evening.

**evening** *noun* the end part of the day between late afternoon and bedtime. □ **evening dress** clothing usually worn for formal occasions in the evening; a woman's long formal dress. **evening primrose** a plant with pale yellow flowers that open in the evening. **evening star** a planet (especially Venus) when conspicuous in the west after sunset.

**evensong** *noun* the service of evening prayer in the Church of England.

**event** *noun* 1 something that happens, especially something important. 2 the fact of a thing happening. 3 an item in a sports programme. □ **at all events**, **in any event** in any case. **in the event** as things turned out. **in the event of** if (a specified thing) happens; *in the event of a gas leak*.

**eventful** *adjective* full of incidents.

**eventide** *noun* (*old use*) evening.

**eventing** *noun* participation in horse-riding competitions, especially dressage and showjumping.

**eventual** *adjective* coming at last, ultimate; *his eventual success*. □ **eventually** *adverb*

**eventuality** (i-ven-tew-**al**-iti) *noun* a possible event; *prepared for every eventuality*.

**eventuate** *verb* result, be the outcome.

**ever** adverb **1** at all times, always; *ever hopeful*. **2** at any time; *the best thing I ever did*. **3** (used for emphasis) in any way, at all; *why ever didn't you say so?* □ **did you ever?** (*informal*) an exclamation of surprise. **ever so** (*informal*) very; very much; *it's ever so easy*; *thanks ever so*.

**Everest, Mount** the world's highest mountain (8,848m.), in the Himalayas on the border of Nepal and Tibet.

**evergreen** adjective (of a tree or shrub) having green leaves throughout the year. ● noun an evergreen tree or shrub.

**everlasting** adjective **1** lasting for ever. **2** lasting a very long time. **3** lasting too long, repeated too often; *his everlasting complaints*. **4** (of flowers) keeping shape and colour when dried. □ **everlastingly** adverb

**evermore** adverb for ever, always.

**Evert**, Chris (Christine Marie) (born 1954), American tennis player.

**every** adjective **1** each single one without exception; *enjoyed every minute*. **2** each in a series; *came every fourth day*. **3** all possible; *she shall be given every care*. □ **every bit as** (*informal*) (in comparisons) quite as. **every one** each one. **every other day** *or* **week** etc. on alternate days or weeks etc. **every so often** occasionally.

**everybody** pronoun every person.

**everyday** adjective **1** worn or used on ordinary days. **2** usual, commonplace.

**Everyman** noun the ordinary or typical person.

**everyone** pronoun everybody.

■**Usage** Do not confuse with *every one* = each one (*see* EVERY).

**everything** pronoun **1** all things. **2** the most important thing; *speed is everything*.

**everywhere** adverb in every place.

**evict** (i-**vikt**) verb expel (a tenant) by legal process. □ **eviction** noun

**evidence** noun **1** anything that establishes a fact or gives reason for believing something. **2** statements made or objects produced in a lawcourt as proof or to support a case. ● verb indicate, be evidence of. □ **be in evidence** be conspicuous.

**evident** adjective plain or obvious. □ **evidently** adverb

**evidential** (ev-i-**den**-shăl) adjective of, based on, or providing evidence.

**evil** adjective **1** morally bad, wicked. **2** harmful, intending to do harm. **3** very unpleasant or troublesome; *an evil temper*. ● noun an evil thing, sin, harm. □ **the evil eye** a gaze or stare superstitiously believed to cause harm. □ **evilly** adverb

**evildoer** noun one who does evil things. □ **evildoing** noun

**evince** (i-**vins**) verb indicate or display (a quality, feeling, etc.).

**eviscerate** (i-**vis**-er-ayt) verb disembowel. □ **evisceration** noun

**evocative** (i-**vok**-ătiv) adjective tending to evoke (especially feelings or memories).

**evoke** (i-**vohk**) verb call up or inspire (memories, feelings, a response, etc.). □ **evocation** (ev-ŏ-**kay**-shŏn) noun

**evolution** (ee-vŏ-**loo**-shŏn) noun **1** the process by which something develops gradually into a different form. **2** the origination of plant and animal species by development from earlier forms, rather than by special creation. □ **evolutionary** adverb

**evolutionist** noun a person who regards evolution as explaining the origin of plant and animal species.

**evolve** (i-**volv**) verb **1** develop or work out gradually; *evolve a plan*. **2** develop or modify by evolution. **3** give off (heat, gas, etc.).

**ewe** noun a female sheep.

**ewer** (**yoo**-er) noun a wide-mouthed waterjug.

**ex** preposition **1** (of goods) as sold from (a ship, factory, etc.); *ex-works*. **2** without, excluding. ● noun (*informal*) a former husband, wife, or partner. □ **ex dividend** (of stocks or shares) not including a dividend that is about to be paid.

**ex-** combining form former; *ex-convict*; *ex-president*.

**exacerbate** (eks-**ass**-er-bayt) verb **1** make (pain, disease, etc.) worse. **2** irritate (a person). □ **exacerbation** noun

**exact** adjective **1** correct in every detail, free from error. **2** giving all details; *gave me exact instructions*. **3** capable of being precise; *the exact sciences*. ● verb insist on and obtain; *exacted payment*. □ **exactness** noun

**exacting** adjective making great demands or requiring great effort; *an exacting task*.

**exaction** noun **1** the exacting of money etc. **2** the thing exacted. **3** an illegal or outrageous demand, extortion.

**exactitude** noun exactness.

**exactly** adverb **1** in an exact manner. **2** (said in agreement) quite so, as you say.

**exaggerate** verb **1** make (a thing) seem greater or more extreme than it really is. **2** (usually as **exaggerated** adjective) beyond what is normal or appropriate; *exaggerated politeness*. □ **exaggeration** noun

**exalt** (ig-**zawlt**) verb **1** raise (a person) in rank, power, or dignity. **2** praise highly.

**exaltation** noun **1** exalting; being exalted. **2** elation, spiritual delight.

**exam** noun (*informal*) an examination.

**examination** noun **1** examining; being examined or looked at. **2** the testing of knowledge or ability by oral or written questions or by exercises. **3** a formal questioning of a witness or an accused person in a lawcourt.

**examine** verb **1** look at closely; inspect, investigate. **2** test formally (a person's knowledge or ability). **3** question formally in order to get information. □ **examiner** noun

**examinee** noun a person being tested in an examination.

**example** noun **1** a fact that illustrates a general rule; a thing that shows the quality or characteristics of others in the same group or of the same kind. **2** something (especially conduct) that is worthy of imitation; *his courage is an example to us all.* □ **for example** by way of illustrating a general rule. **make an example of** punish as a warning to others. **set an example** behave in a way that is worthy of imitation.

**exasperate** verb annoy greatly. □ **exasperation** noun

**Excalibur** (in legend) the name of King Arthur's magic sword.

**ex cathedra** (eks kăth-ee-dră) given by the pope as an infallible judgement; with full authority. (¶ Latin, = from the chair.)

**excavate** verb **1** make (a hole or channel) by digging; dig out (soil). **2** reveal or extract by digging. □ **excavation** noun, **excavator** noun

**exceed** verb **1** be greater or more numerous than. **2** go beyond the limit of, do more than is warranted by; *exceeded his authority.*

**exceedingly** adverb very, extremely.

**excel** verb (**excelled, excelling**) **1** be better than. **2** be very good at something. □ **excel oneself** do better than one has ever done before.

**excellence** noun very great merit or quality.

**Excellency** noun (usually preceded by *Your*, *His*, or *Her*) the title of high officials such as ambassadors and governors.

**excellent** adjective extremely good. □ **excellently** adverb

**except** preposition not including; *they all left except me.* ●verb exclude from a statement or calculation etc.

**excepting** preposition except.

**exception** noun **1** excepting; being excepted. **2** a thing that does not follow the general rule. □ **take exception to** object to. **with the exception of** except.

**exceptionable** adjective open to objection.

**exceptional** adjective **1** forming an exception, very unusual. **2** outstandingly good. □ **exceptionally** adverb

**excerpt** noun (*pronounced* ek-serpt) an extract from a book, film, piece of music, etc. ●verb (*pronounced* ek-**serpt**) select excerpts from. □ **excerption** noun

**excess** noun **1** the exceeding of due limits. **2** the amount by which one number or

quantity etc. exceeds another. **3** an agreed amount subtracted by an insurer from the total payment to be made to an insured person who makes a claim. **4** (**excesses**) immoderation in eating or drinking. **5** (**excesses**) outrageous behaviour. □ **excess baggage** (also **excess luggage**) the amount that is over the weight for free carriage on a plane etc. **in excess of** more than.

**excessive** adjective greater than what is normal or necessary, too much. □ **excessively** adverb

**exchange** verb **1** give or receive (one thing) in place of another. **2** give to and receive from another person; *they exchanged greetings.* ●noun **1** exchanging (goods, prisoners, words, blows, etc.). **2** the exchanging of money for its equivalent in another currency; the relation in value between the money of two or more countries. **3** a place where merchants or brokers etc. assemble to do business; *stock exchange.* **4** the central telephone office of a district. □ **in exchange** as a thing exchanged for something else. **exchange rate** the value of one currency in terms of another. □ **exchangeable** adjective

**exchequer** noun **1** a royal or national treasury. **2** a person's supply of money. □ **Chancellor of the Exchequer** see CHANCELLOR.

**excise** noun (*pronounced* **ek**-syz) duty or tax levied on certain goods and licences etc. ●verb (*pronounced* ik-**syz**) remove by cutting out or away; *excise tissue from the body; excise a passage from a book.* □ **excision** (ik-si-zhŏn) noun

**excitable** adjective (of a person) easily excited. □ **excitability** noun

**excite** verb **1** rouse the feelings of; cause (a person) to feel strongly; make eager. **2** cause (a feeling or reaction); *it excited curiosity.* **3** produce activity in (a nerve or organ of the body etc.).

**excited** adjective feeling or showing excitement. □ **excitedly** adverb

**excitement** noun **1** a state of great emotion, especially that caused by something pleasant. **2** something causing this.

**exciting** adjective causing great interest or eagerness. □ **excitingly** adverb

**exclaim** verb cry out or utter suddenly from pain, pleasure, surprise, etc.

**exclamation** noun **1** exclaiming. **2** a word or words exclaimed. □ **exclamation mark** the punctuation mark (!) placed after an exclamation.

**exclamatory** (iks-**klam**-ă-ter-i) adjective of, containing, or serving as an exclamation.

**exclude** verb **1** keep out (a person or thing) from a place, group, or privilege etc.

**2** omit, ignore as irrelevant; *do not exclude this possibility.* **3** make impossible, prevent. □ **exclusion** *noun*

**exclusive** *adjective* **1** not admitting something else; excluding other things. **2** (of groups or societies) admitting only certain carefully selected people to membership. **3** (of shops or their goods) high-class, catering only for the wealthy, expensive. **4** (of an article in a newspaper or goods in a shop) not published or obtainable elsewhere. **5** done or held etc. so as to exclude everything else, not shared; *we have the exclusive rights.* **6** (foll. by *of*) not including; *20 men exclusive of our own.* ●*noun* an article or story released by only one newspaper, TV channel, etc. □ **exclusively** *adverb*, **exclusiveness** *noun*, **exclusivity** *noun*

**excommunicate** *verb* officially exclude (a person) from participation in a Church, especially in its sacraments. □ **excommunication** *noun*

**excoriate** (eks-**kor**-i-ayt) *verb* **1** remove skin from (a person etc.), e.g. by grazing; strip off (skin). **2** criticize severely. □ **excoriation** *noun*

**excrement** (eks-kri-měnt) *noun* faeces. □ **excremental** *adjective*

**excrescence** (iks-**kress**-ěns) *noun* **1** an abnormal outgrowth on the body or a plant. **2** an ugly or disfiguring addition, e.g. to a building. □ **excrescent** *adjective*

**excreta** (iks-**kree**-tǎ) *plural noun* faeces and urine.

**excrete** (iks-**kreet**) *verb* (of an animal or plant) expel (waste matter). □ **excretion** *noun*, **excretory** *adjective*

**excruciating** (iks-**kroo**-shi-ayting) *adjective* **1** intensely painful. **2** (*informal*) extremely bad.

**exculpate** (eks-kŭl-payt) *verb* free (a person) from blame, clear of a charge of wrongdoing. □ **exculpation** *noun*

**excursion** *noun* a short journey to a place and back; a pleasure-trip, an outing.

**excusable** *adjective* able to be excused. □ **excusably** *adverb*

**excuse** *verb* (*pronounced* iks-**kewz**) **1** forgive or overlook (an offence or the person committing it). **2** (of a thing or circumstance) justify a fault or error; *nothing can excuse such rudeness.* **3** release from an obligation or duty; grant exemption to. ●*noun* (*pronounced* iks-**kewss**) a reason put forward to justify a fault or error. □ **be excused** be allowed to leave. **excuse me** a polite apology for interrupting or disagreeing etc. **excuse oneself** ask permission to leave; apologize for leaving.

**ex-directory** *adjective* (of a telephone number or subscriber) not listed in a telephone directory, at the subscriber's request.

**execrable** (eks-i-krǎ-bǔl) *adjective* abominable. □ **execrably** *adverb*

**execrate** (eks-i-krayt) *verb* detest greatly, utter curses upon. □ **execration** *noun*

**execute** *verb* **1** carry out (an order); put (a plan etc.) into effect. **2** perform (an action or manoeuvre). **3** produce (a work of art). **4** make legally valid e.g. by signing; *execute a will.* **5** inflict capital punishment on.

**execution** *noun* **1** the carrying out or performance of something. **2** skill in playing music. **3** executing a condemned person.

**executioner** *noun* an official who executes a condemned person.

**executive** (ig-**zek**-yoo-tiv) *noun* **1** a person or group that has administrative or managerial powers in a business or commercial organization. **2** the branch of a government or other organization concerned with putting laws, agreements, etc. into effect. ●*adjective* having the powers to execute plans or to put laws or agreements etc. into effect.

**executor** (ig-**zek**-yoo-ter) *noun* a person appointed by a testator to carry out the terms of his or her will.

**exemplar** (ig-**zem**-pler) *noun* **1** a model, a type. **2** an instance.

**exemplary** (ig-**zem**-pler-i) *adjective* **1** outstandingly good; *exemplary conduct.* **2** serving as a warning to others; *exemplary punishment.* **3** illustrative.

**exemplify** (ig-**zem**-pli-fy) *verb* (**exemplified**, **exemplifying**) serve as an example of. □ **exemplification** *noun*

**exempt** *adjective* (often foll. by *from*) free from an obligation or payment etc. that is required of others. ●*verb* make exempt. □ **exemption** *noun*

**exercise** *noun* **1** the using or application of mental powers or of one's rights. **2** activity requiring physical exertion, done for the sake of health. **3** an activity or task designed for bodily or mental training. **4** (often as **exercises**) a military training manoeuvre. ●*verb* **1** use or employ (mental powers, rights, etc.). **2** take or cause to take exercise; train by means of exercises. **3** perplex, worry.

**exert** *verb* bring (a quality or influence etc.) into use; *exert all one's strength.* □ **exert oneself** make an effort.

**exertion** *noun* **1** exerting; being exerted. **2** a great effort.

**exeunt** (eks-i-ŭnt) *verb* (as a stage direction) they leave the stage. (¶ Latin, = they go out.)

**ex gratia** (eks **gray**-shǎ) done or given as a favour; not from legal or other obligation; *an ex gratia payment.* (¶ Latin, = from favour.)

**exhale** *verb* breathe out. □ **exhalation** *noun*

**exhaust** verb **1** use up completely. **2** empty, draw out the contents of; *exhaust a well.* **3** tire out; *exhaust oneself.* **4** find out or say all there is to say about (a subject); *exhaust the possibilities.* ● noun **1** waste gases or steam expelled from an engine etc. **2** the system through which they are sent out. □ **exhaustible** adjective

**exhaustion** (ig-zaws-chŏn) noun **1** exhausting something; being exhausted. **2** total loss of strength.

**exhaustive** adjective thorough, trying all possibilities; *we made an exhaustive search.* □ **exhaustively** adverb

**exhibit** (ig-zib-it) verb display, present for the public to see. ● noun a thing or collection of things exhibited. □ **exhibitor** noun

**exhibition** noun **1** exhibiting, being exhibited. **2** a display or show; *an exhibition of temper.* **3** a public display of works of art or industrial products etc. or of a skilled performance. **4** a scholarship. □ **make an exhibition of oneself** behave so that one appears ridiculous.

**exhibitioner** noun a student who has been awarded an exhibition.

**exhibitionism** noun **1** a tendency towards attention-seeking behaviour. **2** (*Psychol.*) a compulsion to display one's genitals in public. □ **exhibitionist** noun

**exhilarate** (ig-zil-er-ayt) verb make very happy or lively. □ **exhilaration** noun

**exhort** (ig-zort) verb urge or advise earnestly. □ **exhortation** (eg-zor-tay-shŏn) noun, **exhortative** adjective, **exhortatory** adjective

**exhume** (eks-hewm) verb dig up (especially a dead body). □ **exhumation** noun

**exigency** (eks-i-jěn-si) noun **1** an urgent need; *the exigencies of the situation.* **2** an emergency; *in this exigency.*

**exigent** (eks-i-jěnt) adjective **1** urgent. **2** exacting, requiring much.

**exiguous** (eg-zig-yoo-ŭs) adjective very small, scanty. □ **exiguity** noun

**exile** noun **1** being sent away from one's country as a punishment. **2** long absence from one's country or home. **3** an exiled person. ● verb send (a person) into exile.

**exist** verb **1** have a place as part of what is real; *do fairies exist?* **2** occur or be found. **3** continue living; *we cannot exist without food.*

**existence** noun **1** the state of existing, occurrence, presence. **2** continuance in life or being; *the struggle for existence.* **3** all that exists.

**existent** adjective existing, actual, current.

**existential** (eg-zis-ten-shăl) adjective **1** of existence. **2** of human experience as viewed by existentialism. □ **existentially** adverb

**existentialism** (eg-zis-ten-shăl-izm) noun a philosophical theory emphasizing that people are responsible for their own actions and free to choose their development and destiny. □ **existentialist** noun & adjective

**exit** noun **1** the act of going away or out, departure from a place or position. **2** a passage or door to go out by. **3** an actor's or performer's departure from the stage. ● verb (**exited, exiting**) make one's exit, leave.

**exocrine** (eks-ŏ-kryn) adjective (of a gland) secreting through a duct.

**exodus** noun **1** a mass departure of people. **2** (**Exodus**) the second book of the Old Testament, telling of the exodus of the Jews from Egypt.

**ex officio** (eks ŏ-fish-i-oh) because of one's official position; *the director is a member of this committee ex officio; an ex-officio member.* (¶ Latin.)

**exonerate** (ig-zon-er-ayt) verb free from blame, declare (a person) to be blameless. □ **exoneration** noun

**exorbitant** (ig-zorb-i-tănt) adjective (of a price or demand) much too great.

**exorcize** (eks-or-syz) verb (also **exorcise**) **1** drive out (an evil spirit) by prayer. **2** free (a person or place) of evil spirits. □ **exorcism** noun, **exorcist** noun

**exoskeleton** noun an external bony or leathery covering on an animal, e.g. the shell of a lobster.

**exotic** (ig-zot-ik) adjective **1** (of plants, words, or fashions) introduced from abroad, not native. **2** striking and attractive through being colourful or unusual. □ **exotically** adverb

**exotica** plural noun strange or rare objects, especially as a collection.

**expand** verb **1** make or become larger, increase in bulk or importance. **2** unfold or spread out. **3** give a fuller account of, write out in full (what is condensed or abbreviated). **4** become genial, throw off one's reserve. □ **expandable** adjective

**expanse** noun a wide area or extent of open land or space.

**expansible** adjective able to be expanded.

**expansion** noun **1** expanding, increase, extension. **2** enlargement or development of a business.

**expansionism** noun the practice of expanding (especially a State's) territory or area of influence. □ **expansionist** noun & adjective

**expansive** adjective **1** able or tending to expand. **2** (of a person or manner) genial, communicating thoughts and feelings readily. □ **expansively** adverb, **expansiveness** noun

**expat** noun (*informal*) an expatriate.

**expatiate** (iks-**pay**-shi-ayt) *verb* speak or write about (a subject) at length. □ **expatiation** *noun*, **expatiatory** *adjective*

**expatriate** *verb* (*pronounced* eks-**pat**-ri-ayt) banish; withdraw (oneself) from one's native country and live abroad. ●*adjective* (*pronounced* eks-**pat**-ri-ăt) expatriated, living abroad. ●*noun* (*pronounced* eks-**pat**-ri-ăt) an expatriate person. □ **expatriation** *noun*

**expect** *verb* **1** regard as likely. **2** regard as appropriate or due to one; *he expects obedience.* **3** think, suppose. □ **be expecting** (*informal*) be pregnant.

**expectancy** *noun* **1** a state of expectation. **2** a prospect; *a life expectancy of 70 years.* **3** (foll. by *of*) an expected chance.

**expectant** *adjective* **1** filled with expectation. **2** pregnant. □ **expectantly** *adverb*

**expectation** *noun* **1** expecting, looking forward with hope or pleasure. **2** a thing that is expected to happen. **3** the probability that a thing will happen.

**expectorant** *noun* a medicine that causes a person to expectorate. ●*adjective* causing expectoration.

**expectorate** *verb* cough and spit out phlegm from the throat or lungs; spit. □ **expectoration** *noun*

**expedient** (iks-**pee**-diĕnt) *adjective* **1** suitable for a particular purpose. **2** advantageous rather than right or just. ●*noun* a means of achieving something. □ **expediently** *adverb*, **expedience** *noun*, **expediency** *noun*

**expedite** (**eks**-pi-dyt) *verb* help or hurry the progress of (business etc.), perform (business) quickly.

**expedition** *noun* **1** a journey or voyage for a particular purpose. **2** the people or ships etc. making this. **3** promptness, speed; *solved it with expedition.*

**expeditionary** *adjective* of or used in an expedition; *an expeditionary force.*

**expeditious** (eks-pi-**dish**-ŭs) *adjective* acting or done speedily or efficiently. □ **expeditiously** *adverb*

**expel** *verb* (**expelled**, **expelling**) **1** force or drive out. **2** compel (a person) to leave a school or country etc.

**expend** *verb* spend (money, time, etc.), use up.

**expendable** *adjective* **1** able to be expended. **2** not worth preserving, suitable for sacrificing in order to gain an objective.

**expenditure** *noun* **1** spending of money etc. **2** the amount expended.

**expense** *noun* **1** the cost or price of an activity. **2** a cause of spending money; *the car was a great expense.* **3** (**expenses**) the amount spent in doing a job etc. **4** (**expenses**) the amount paid to reimburse what has been spent; *£40 per day in*

*expenses.* □ **at the expense of** so as to cause loss, damage, or discredit to; *succeeded but at the expense of his health; had a good laugh at my expense.* **expense account** a record of an employee's expenses to be paid by his or her employer.

**expensive** *adjective* costing or charging a great deal. □ **expensively** *adverb*, **expensiveness** *noun*

**experience** *noun* **1** actual observation of facts or events; activity or practice in doing something. **2** skill or knowledge gained in this way. **3** an event or activity that gives one experience. ●*verb* **1** observe or share in (an event etc.) personally. **2** be affected by (a feeling).

**experienced** *adjective* having knowledge or skill gained from much experience.

**experiential** (eks-peer-i-**en**-shăl) *adjective* involving or based on experience.

**experiment** *noun* a test or trial carried out to see how something works, to find out what happens, or to demonstrate a known fact. ●*verb* conduct an experiment. □ **experimentation** *noun*

**experimental** *adjective* **1** of, used in, or based on experiments. **2** still being tested. □ **experimentally** *adverb*, **experimentalism** *noun*

**expert** *noun* a person with great knowledge or skill in a particular thing. ●*adjective* having great knowledge or skill. □ **expertly** *adverb*

**expertise** (eks-per-**teez**) *noun* expert knowledge, skill, or judgement.

**expiable** (**eks**-pi-ăbŭl) *adjective* able to be expiated.

**expiate** (**eks**-pi-ayt) *verb* make amends for (wrongdoing). □ **expiation** *noun*

**expire** *verb* **1** breathe out (air). **2** breathe one's last, die. **3** come to the end of its period of validity; *this licence has expired.* □ **expiration** (eks-per-**ay**-shŏn) *noun*

**expiry** *noun* the end of a period of validity, e.g. of a licence or contract.

**explain** *verb* **1** make plain or clear, show the meaning of. **2** account for; *that explains his absence.* □ **explain away** minimize the significance of by offering reasons or excuses. **explain oneself 1** make one's meaning clear. **2** give an account of one's motives or conduct.

**explanation** *noun* **1** explaining. **2** a statement or fact that explains something.

**explanatory** (iks-**plan**-ă-ter-i) *adjective* serving or intended to explain something.

**expletive** (iks-**plee**-tiv) *noun* a swear-word or exclamation.

**explicable** (**eks**-plik-ăbŭl) *adjective* able to be explained.

**explicate** (eks-plik-ayt) *verb* bring out the implicit meaning of (an idea or statement) more fully or clearly. □ **explication** *noun*

**explicit** (iks-**pliss**-it) *adjective* **1** stated or shown directly rather than being implied. **2** detailed and definite. □ **explicitly** *adverb*, **explicitness** *noun*

**explode** *verb* **1** expand or burst violently and with a loud noise; cause to do this. **2** (of feelings) burst out; (of a person) show sudden violent emotion; *exploded with laughter*. **3** (of a population, supply of goods, etc.) increase suddenly or rapidly. **4** destroy (a theory) by showing it to be false. □ **exploded diagram** one showing the parts of a structure in their relative positions but slightly separated from each other.

**exploit** *noun* (*pronounced* **eks**-ploit) a bold or notable deed. ● *verb* (*pronounced* iks-**ploit**) **1** work or develop (mines and other natural resources). **2** take full advantage of, use (employees etc.) for one's own advantage and their disadvantage. □ **exploitation** *noun*

**exploratory** (iks-**plo**-ră-ter-i) *adjective* for the purpose of exploring.

**explore** *verb* **1** travel into or through (a country etc.) in order to learn about it. **2** examine by touch. **3** examine or investigate (a problem, possibilities, etc.). □ **exploration** *noun*, **explorer** *noun*

**explosion** *noun* **1** exploding; being exploded; a loud noise caused by this. **2** a sudden outburst of anger, laughter, etc. **3** a sudden great increase; *the population explosion*.

**explosive** *adjective* **1** able to explode, tending to explode. **2** likely to cause violent and dangerous reactions, dangerously tense; *an explosive situation*. ● *noun* an explosive substance. □ **explosively** *adverb*

**Expo** *noun* (also **expo**) (*plural* **Expos**) a large international exhibition.

**exponent** (iks-**poh**-něnt) *noun* **1** a person who sets out the facts or interprets something. **2** one who favours a particular theory or policy. **3** *Maths* a raised figure or other symbol beside a number etc. indicating how many times the number is to be multiplied by itself.

**exponential** *adjective* **1** of or indicated by a mathematical exponent. **2** (of an increase) more and more rapid.

**export** *verb* (*pronounced* iks-**port** *or* eks-port) send (goods etc.) to another country for sale. ● *noun* (*pronounced* **eks**-port) **1** exporting. **2** a thing exported. □ **exporter** *noun*, **exportation** *noun*, **exportable** *adjective*

**expose** *verb* **1** leave (a person or thing) uncovered or unprotected, especially from the weather. **2** (often foll. by *to*) subject to a risk etc. **3** allow light to reach (photographic film or plate). **4** make visible, reveal. **5** make known or reveal (a crime, impostor, etc.); reveal the wrongdoings of (a person). □ **expose oneself** expose one's body indecently.

**exposé** (eks-**poh**-zay) *noun* **1** an orderly statement of facts. **2** revelation of a discreditable thing.

**exposed** *adjective* **1** (of a place) not sheltered. **2** vulnerable to danger or criticism.

**exposition** *noun* **1** expounding; an explanatory account of a plan or theory etc. **2** a large public exhibition. **3** (in music) the part of a movement in which themes are presented.

**expostulate** (iks-**poss**-tew-layt) *verb* make a protest, reason or argue with a person. □ **expostulation** *noun*, **expostulatory** *adjective*

**exposure** *noun* **1** exposing or being exposed. **2** a physical condition resulting from being exposed to the elements; *died of exposure*. **3** the exposing of photographic film or plate to the light; the length of time for which this is done. **4** a section of film exposed as a unit. **5** publicity. □ **exposure meter** a device measuring light and indicating the length of time needed for a photographic exposure.

**expound** *verb* set forth or explain in detail.

**express** *adjective* **1** definitely stated, not merely implied. **2** going or sent quickly; designed for high speed; (of a train etc.) travelling rapidly to its destination with few or no intermediate stops. **3** (of a letter or parcel) delivered quickly by a special messenger or service. ● *adverb* at high speed, by express service. ● *noun* an express train. ● *verb* **1** make known (feelings or qualities). **2** put (a thought etc.) into words. **3** represent by means of symbols, e.g. in mathematics. **4** press or squeeze out. **5** send by express service. □ **express oneself** communicate one's thoughts or feelings. □ **expressible** *adjective*

**expression** *noun* **1** expressing, being expressed. **2** a word or phrase. **3** a look that expresses one's feelings. **4** speaking or playing music in a way that shows feeling for the meaning. **5** a collection of mathematical symbols expressing a quantity.

**expressionism** *noun* a style of painting, drama, or music seeking to express the artist's or writer's emotional experience rather than to represent the physical world realistically. □ **expressionist** *noun & adjective*

**expressionless** *adjective* without positive expression, not revealing one's thoughts or feelings; *an expressionless face*.

**expressive** *adjective* **1** serving to express; *a tone expressive of contempt*. **2** full of expression; *an expressive voice*. □ **expressively** *adverb*, **expressiveness** *noun*

**expressly** *adverb* **1** explicitly. **2** for a particular purpose.

**expresso** = ESPRESSO.

**expressway** *noun* an urban motorway.

**expropriate** (eks-**proh**-pri-ayt) *verb* **1** take away (property) from its owner. **2** dispossess (a person). □ **expropriation** *noun*

**expulsion** *noun* expelling; being expelled. □ **expulsive** *adjective*

**expunge** (iks-**punj**) *verb* wipe or rub out, delete.

**expurgate** (**eks**-per-gayt) *verb* remove objectionable matter from (a book etc.); remove (such matter). □ **expurgation** *noun*, **expurgator** *noun*

**exquisite** (eks-**kwiz**-it) *adjective* **1** having special beauty. **2** having excellent discrimination; *exquisite taste in dress*. **3** acute, keenly felt; *exquisite pain*. □ **exquisitely** *adverb*

**ex-serviceman** *noun* (*plural* **ex-servicemen**) a man formerly a member of the armed services.

**ex-servicewoman** *noun* (*plural* **ex-servicewomen**) a woman formerly a member of the armed forces.

**extant** (eks-**tant**) *adjective* still existing.

**extemporaneous** (eks-tem-per-ay-niŭs) *adjective* spoken or done without preparation. □ **extemporaneously** *adverb*

**extemporary** (eks-**tem**-per-er-i) *adjective* extemporaneous.

**extempore** (eks-**tem**-per-i) *adverb* & *adjective* (spoken or done) without preparation, impromptu.

**extemporize** (eks-**tem**-peryz) *verb* (also **extemporise**) speak or produce extempore. □ **extemporization** *noun*

**extend** *verb* **1** make longer in space or time. **2** stretch out (a hand, foot, etc.). **3** reach, be continuous over an area or from one point to another; *our land extends to the river*. **4** enlarge, increase the scope of. **5** offer or grant; *extend a welcome*. **6** (of a task) stretch the ability of (a person) fully. □ **extended family** a family including all relatives living near. **extended-play** *adjective* (of a gramophone record) playing for longer than most singles. □ **extendible** *adjective*, **extensible** *adjective*

**extension** *noun* **1** extending; being extended. **2** extent, range. **3** an addition or section extended from the main part of a building etc. **4** an additional period. **5** a subsidiary telephone on the same line as the main one; its number. **6** extramural instruction by a university or college; *extension lectures*.

**extensive** *adjective* **1** large in area; *extensive gardens*. **2** wide-ranging, large in scope; *extensive knowledge*. □ **extensively** *adverb*, **extensiveness** *noun*

**extent** *noun* **1** the space over which a thing extends. **2** the range or scope of something; *the full extent of his power*. **3** a large area; *an extent of marsh*.

**extenuate** (iks-**ten**-yoo-ayt) *verb* make (a person's guilt or offence) seem less serious by providing an explanation or excuse; *there were extenuating circumstances*. □ **extenuation** *noun*

**exterior** *adjective* on or coming from the outside. ●*noun* an external surface, part, or appearance.

**exterminate** *verb* destroy utterly (especially a living thing). □ **extermination** *noun*, **exterminator** *noun*

**external** *adjective* **1** of or on the outside or visible part of something. **2** of or on the outside of the body; *for external use only*. **3** coming or obtained from an independent source; *external influences*. **4** belonging to the world outside a person or people, not in the mind. ●*plural noun* (**externals**) outward appearances; external circumstances. □ **externally** *adverb*

**externalize** *verb* (also **externalise**) give or attribute external existence to. □ **externalization** *noun*

**extinct** *adjective* **1** having died out; *extinct animals*. **2** (of a volcano) no longer active. **3** no longer burning.

**extinction** *noun* **1** extinguishing, being extinguished. **2** making or becoming extinct.

**extinguish** *verb* **1** put out (a light, fire, or flame). **2** end the existence of (hope, passion, etc.).

**extinguisher** *noun* = FIRE EXTINGUISHER.

**extirpate** (**eks**-ter-payt) *verb* root out and destroy completely. □ **extirpation** *noun*

**extol** (iks-**tohl**) *verb* (**extolled, extolling**) praise enthusiastically.

**extort** *verb* obtain (especially money) by force, threats, or intimidation. □ **extortion** *noun*, **extortioner** *noun*

**extortionate** (iks-**tor**-shŏn-ăt) *adjective* excessively high in price, (of demands) excessive. □ **extortionately** *adverb*

**extra** *adjective* additional, more than is usual or expected. ●*adverb* **1** more than usually; *extra strong*. **2** in addition; *postage extra*. ●*noun* **1** an extra thing, something additional. **2** a thing for which an additional charge is made. **3** a run in cricket scored otherwise than from a hit by the bat. **4** a special issue of a newspaper etc. **5** a person engaged temporarily for a minor part or to form one of a crowd in a cinema film.

**extra-** *combining form* outside or beyond (a boundary); not coming within the scope of.

**extract** *verb* (*pronounced* iks-**trakt**) **1** take out by force or effort (something firmly fixed). **2** obtain (money, information, etc.) from someone unwilling to give it. **3** obtain (juice) by suction or pressure; obtain (a substance) as an extract. **4** obtain (information from a book etc.); take or copy passages from (a book). **5** derive (pleasure etc.). ●*noun* (*pronounced* eks-trakt) **1** a substance separated from another by dissolving it or by other treatment. **2** a concentrated substance prepared from another. **3** a passage from a book, play, film, or piece of music.

**extraction** *noun* **1** extracting. **2** descent, lineage; *he is of Indian extraction.* **3** a removal of a tooth.

**extractive** *adjective* of or involving extraction; extracting minerals from the ground.

**extractor** *noun* **1** a person or machine that extracts. **2** (usually used as *adjective*) (of a device) extracting stale or polluted air; *extractor fan.*

**extracurricular** (eks-tră-kŭ-**rik**-yoo-lăr) *adjective* not part of the normal curriculum.

**extraditable** (eks-tră-**dy**-tăbŭl) *adjective* liable to extradition; (of a crime) warranting extradition.

**extradite** (eks-tră-dyt) *verb* **1** hand over (a person accused or convicted of a crime) to the country where the crime was committed. **2** obtain (such a person) for trial or punishment. □ **extradition** (eks-tră-**dish**-ŏn) *noun*

**extramarital** (eks-tră-**ma**-ri-t'l) *adjective* (especially of sexual relationships) occurring outside marriage.

**extramural** (eks-tră-**mewr**-ăl) *adjective* (of university teaching or studies) for students who are non-resident or who are not members of the university.

**extraneous** (iks-**tray**-niŭs) *adjective* **1** of external origin. **2** not belonging to the matter or subject in hand. □ **extraneously** *adverb*

**extraordinary** *adjective* **1** very unusual or remarkable. **2** beyond what is usual or ordinary; *an extraordinary general meeting.* □ **extraordinarily** *adverb*

**extrapolate** (iks-**trap**-ŏ-layt) *verb* make an estimate of (something unknown and outside the range of one's data) on the basis of available data. □ **extrapolation** *noun*

**extrasensory** *adjective* achieved by some means other than the known senses. □ **extrasensory perception** the supposed faculties of telepathy, clairvoyance, etc.

**extraterrestrial** *adjective* **1** of or from outside the earth or its atmosphere. **2** of or from outer space. ●*noun* a being from outer space.

**extravagant** *adjective* **1** spending much more than is necessary. **2** (of prices) excessively high. **3** (of ideas, praise, behaviour, etc.) going beyond what is reasonable, not properly controlled. □ **extravagantly** *adverb*, **extravagance** *noun*

**extravaganza** (iks-trav-ă-**gan**-ză) *noun* **1** a lavish spectacular film or theatrical production. **2** a fanciful composition in music.

**extreme** *adjective* **1** very great or intense; *extreme cold.* **2** at the end(s), furthest, outermost; *the extreme edge.* **3** going to great lengths in actions or views, not moderate. ●*noun* **1** either end of anything. **2** an extreme degree, act, or condition. □ **extreme unction** the last rites in the Roman Catholic and Orthodox Churches. **go to extremes** take an extreme course of action. **in the extreme** to an extreme degree. □ **extremely** *adverb*

**extremist** *noun* a person who holds extreme views, especially in politics. □ **extremism** *noun*

**extremity** (iks-**trem**-iti) *noun* **1** an extreme point, the end of something. **2** an extreme degree of feeling, need, danger, etc. **3** (**extremities**) the hands and feet.

**extricate** (eks-trik-ayt) *verb* disentangle or release from an entanglement or difficulty etc. □ **extrication** *noun*, **extricable** *adjective*

**extrovert** (eks-trŏ-vert) *noun* **1** a person more interested in the people and things around him or her than in his or her own thoughts and feelings. **2** a lively sociable person. ●*adjective* (also **extroverted**) having these characteristics. □ **extroversion** *noun*

**extrude** *verb* **1** thrust or squeeze out. **2** shape (metal or plastic etc.) by forcing through a die. □ **extrusion** *noun*

**exuberant** (ig-zew-ber-ănt) *adjective* **1** full of high spirits, very lively. **2** growing profusely; *plants with exuberant foliage.* □ **exuberantly** *adverb*, **exuberance** *noun*

**exude** (ig-zewd) *verb* **1** ooze out (a liquid) or emit (a smell). **2** show (pleasure, confidence, etc.) freely. □ **exudation** (eks-yoo-**day**-shŏn) *noun*

**exult** (ig-zult) *verb* rejoice greatly. □ **exultation** *noun*

**exultant** *adjective* exulting.

**eye** *noun* **1** the organ of sight in humans and animals. **2** the iris; *blue eyes.* **3** the region round the eye; *gave him a black eye.* **4** (also as **eyes**) the power of seeing, observation; *sharp eyes; a good eye.* **5** a thing like an eye; a spot on a peacock's tail; a leaf bud on a potato. **6** the calm region at the centre of a storm or hurricane. **7** the hole in a needle, through which thread is passed. ●*verb* (**eyed**, **eyeing** or **eying**) look at, watch. □ **all eyes** watching intently. **an eye for an eye** retaliation in the same form as the injury done. **cast** or **run an eye over** examine quickly. **eye up** look at (a person) with interest, especially sexual interest. **have an eye for** be capable of recognizing or appreciating. **have eyes for** be interested in. **in the eyes of** in the opinion or judgement of. **keep an eye on** watch carefully; take care of. **keep one's eyes open** or **skinned** or **peeled** watch carefully, be observant. **make eyes at** gaze at flirtatiously. **see eye to eye** be in full agreement with a person. **up to one's eyes** deeply involved or occupied in something. **with an eye to** with the aim or intention of. **with one's eyes open** with full awareness. **with one's eyes shut** with great ease.

**eyeball** noun the ball of the eye, within the lids. ● verb (Amer. slang) stare at. □ **eyeball to eyeball** (informal) confronting a person closely.

**eyebath** noun a small cup shaped to fit round the eye, used for applying liquid to the eyeball.

**eyebrow** noun the line of hair growing on the ridge above the eye-socket. □ **raise one's eyebrows** show surprise or disapproval.

**eye-catching** adjective (informal) striking.

**eyeful** noun (plural **eyefuls**) **1** something thrown or blown into one's eye; got an eyeful of sand. **2** (informal) a thorough look; having an eyeful. **3** (informal) a remarkable or attractive sight.

**eyeglass** noun a lens to aid defective sight.

**eyehole** noun **1** the socket containing the eye. **2** a hole to look through.

**eyelash** noun one of the fringe of hairs on the edge of each eyelid.

**eyelet** noun **1** a small hole through which a rope or cord is passed. **2** a metal ring strengthening this.

**eyelid** noun either of the two folds of skin that can be moved together to cover the eyeball.

**eyeliner** noun a cosmetic applied as a line round the eye.

**eye-opener** noun (informal) a fact or circumstance that brings enlightenment or great surprise.

**eyepiece** noun the lens or lenses to which the eye is applied at the end of a telescope or other optical instrument.

**eye-shade** noun a device to protect eyes from strong light.

**eye-shadow** noun a cosmetic applied to the eyelids and skin round the eyes.

**eyesight** noun **1** the ability to see. **2** range of vision; within eyesight.

**eyesore** noun a thing that is ugly to look at.

**eye-tooth** noun (plural **eye-teeth**) a canine tooth in the upper jaw, under the eye.

**eyewash** noun **1** a lotion for the eyes. **2** (slang) nonsense; insincere talk.

**eyewitness** noun a person who saw an event and can describe it.

**eyrie** (ee-ri) noun **1** the high nest of an eagle or other bird of prey. **2** a house etc. perched high up.

**Ezekiel** (i-zee-ki-ĕl) **1** a Hebrew prophet of the 6th century BC who prophesied the destruction of Jerusalem and the Jewish nation. **2** the book of the Old Testament containing his prophecies.

**Ezra 1** a Jewish priest and scribe of the 5th or 4th century BC. **2** the book of the Old Testament dealing with the return of the Jews from Babylon.

# Ff

**F** *noun* (*plural* **Fs** *or* **F's**) *Music* the fourth note of the scale of C major. ● *abbreviation* Fahrenheit. ● *symbol* flourine.

**f** *abbreviation* (also **f.**) **1** female; feminine. **2** *Music* forte.

**FA** *abbreviation* Football Association.

**fa** alternative spelling of FAH.

**fab** *adjective* (*informal*) fabulous, marvellous.

**Fabergé** (**fah**-bair-*zh*ay), Peter Carl (1846–1920), Russian jeweller, famed for his small intricate ornaments.

**Fabian** (**fay**-bi-ăn) *noun* a member of the Fabian Society, an English socialist society founded in 1884, seeking social change through gradual reform. (¶ Named after the Roman general Fabius (*c*.200 BC) whose strategy of caution and delay was successful against the Carthaginian invaders.)

**fable** *noun* **1** a short (usually supernatural) story not based on fact, often with animals as characters and conveying a moral. **2** these stories or legends collectively. **3** untrue statements; *sort out fact from fable.*

**fabled** *adjective* told of in fables, legendary.

**fabric** *noun* **1** cloth; woven or knitted or felted material. **2** a plastic resembling this. **3** the frame or structure of something; the walls, floors, and roof of a building.

**fabricate** *verb* **1** construct, manufacture. **2** invent (a story); forge (a document). □ **fabrication** *noun*, **fabricator** *noun*

**fabulous** *adjective* **1** told of in fables; legendary. **2** incredibly great; *fabulous wealth*. **3** (*informal*) wonderful, marvellous. □ **fabulously** *adverb*

**façade** (fă-**sahd**) *noun* **1** the face or front of a building. **2** an outward appearance, especially a deceptive one.

**face** *noun* **1** the front part of the head from forehead to chin. **2** the expression shown by its features; *a cheerful face*; *make a face*. **3** the outward show or aspect of something. **4** the front, façade, or right side of something; the dial of a clock; the distinctive side of a playing card. **5** a coalface. **6** the striking-surface of a bat etc.; the working-surface of a tool. ● *verb* **1** have or turn the face towards (a certain direction). **2** be opposite to. **3** meet confidently or defiantly; accept and be prepared to deal with (unpleasant facts or problems). **4** meet (an opponent) in a contest. **5** present itself to; *the problem that faces us*. **6** cover (a surface) with a layer of different material; put a facing on (a garment etc.).

□ **face-lift** *noun* **1** cosmetic surgery to remove wrinkles. **2** an alteration etc. that improves the appearance, e.g. of a building. **face-pack** *noun* a skin preparation for the face. **face the music** face unpleasant consequences bravely. **face to face** (often foll. by *with*) facing; confronting a person or danger etc. **face up to** accept (a difficulty etc.) bravely. **face value 1** the value printed or stamped on money. **2** the superficial appearance or outward impression of a thing. **have the face** be shameless enough. **in the face of** despite. **lose face** be humiliated. **on the face of it** judging by appearances. **put a brave face on it** accept difficulty cheerfully. **save face** avoid humiliation. **to a person's face** openly in his or her presence.

**faceless** *adjective* **1** without identity or character. **2** deliberately not identifiable.

**facer** *noun* (*informal*) a sudden great difficulty.

**facet** (**fas**-it) *noun* **1** each of the many sides of a cut stone or jewel. **2** each aspect of a situation or problem.

**facetious** (fă-**see**-shŭs) *adjective* intended or intending to be amusing, especially inappropriately. □ **facetiously** *adverb*, **facetiousness** *noun*

**facia** alternative spelling of FASCIA.

**facial** (**fay**-shăl) *adjective* of or for the face. ● *noun* a beauty treatment for the face. □ **facially** *adverb*

**facile** (**fa**-syl) *adjective* **1** easily achieved but of little value; *a facile solution*. **2** glib, fluent.

**facilitate** (fă-**sil**-i-tayt) *verb* make easier. □ **facilitation** *noun*

**facility** (fă-**sil**-iti) *noun* **1** the quality of being easy; absence of difficulty. **2** ease in doing something, aptitude; *facility of expression*. **3** (often as **facilities**) an opportunity, the equipment, or the resources for doing something; *sports facilities*.

**facing** *noun* **1** an outer layer covering a surface. **2** a layer of material covering part of a garment etc. for contrast or strengthening.

**facsimile** (fak-**sim**-ili) *noun* an exact copy of a document, book, painting, etc.

**fact** *noun* **1** something known to have happened, to be true, or to exist. **2** a thing asserted to be true as a basis for reasoning; *his facts are disputed*. □ **fact of life** something that must be accepted. **facts and figures** precise details. **facts of life** information about sexual functions and practices. **in fact 1** in reality. **2** (in summarizing) in short.

**faction** (fak-shŏn) *noun* **1** a small united group within a larger one, especially in politics. **2** dissent within a group. □ **factional** *adjective,* **factionally** *adverb*

**factious** (fak-shŏs) *adjective* characterized by or inclined to faction.

**factitious** (fak-**tish**-ŭs) *adjective* made for a special purpose, contrived. □ **factitiously** *adverb*

**factor** *noun* **1** a circumstance or influence that contributes towards a result; *safety factor.* **2** any of the numbers or mathematical expressions by which a larger number etc. can be divided exactly; *2, 3, 4, and 6 are factors of 12.* **3** (in Scotland) a land-agent, a steward.

**factorize** *verb* (also **factorise**) convert into factors. □ **factorization** *noun*

**factory** *noun* a building or buildings in which goods are manufactured. □ **factory farm** one organized on industrial lines.

**factotum** (fak-**toh**-tŭm) *noun* an employee who does all kinds of work.

**factual** *adjective* based on or concerning facts. □ **factually** *adverb*

**faculty** (fak-**ŭl**-ti) *noun* **1** a power of the body or mind; *the faculty of sight.* **2** a particular aptitude or ability; *a faculty for learning languages.* **3** a department teaching a particular subject or group of related subjects in a university or college; *the law faculty.* **4** authorization given by Church authorities.

**fad** *noun* **1** a particular like or dislike, a craze. **2** a peculiar notion. □ **faddish** *adjective*

**faddy** *adjective* having petty likes and dislikes, e.g. about food. □ **faddiness** *noun*

**fade** *verb* **1** lose or cause to lose colour, freshness, or vigour. **2** (often foll. by *away*) disappear gradually, become indistinct. **3** cause (the sound or picture in broadcasting or cinema) to decrease or increase gradually. ● *noun* an act or sound of fading.

**faeces** (fee-seez) *plural noun* (*Amer.* **feces**) waste matter discharged from the bowels. □ **faecal** (fee-kăl) *adjective*

**Faeroe Islands** (fair-oh) (also **Faeroes**) a group of islands in the North Atlantic between Iceland and Shetland, belonging to Denmark but partly autonomous. □ **Faeroese** *adjective & noun*

**faff** *verb* (*informal*) (often foll. by *about* or *around*) fuss, dither.

**fag** *verb* (**fagged, fagging**) **1** (of work) make tired. **2** (at public schools) run errands for a senior pupil. ● *noun* **1** (*informal*) tiring work, drudgery; *what a fag!* **2** exhaustion; *brain-fag.* **3** (at public schools) a junior pupil who has to fag for a senior. **4** (*slang*) a cigarette. **5** (*Amer. offensive slang*) a male homosexual. □ **fag-end** *noun* (*slang*) a

cigarette-end. **fagged** *or* **fagged out** tired out.

**faggot** *noun* (*Amer.* **fagot**) **1** a bundle of sticks or twigs bound together. **2** a ball of chopped seasoned liver, served baked. **3** (*slang*) an unpleasant woman. **4** (*Amer. offensive slang*) a male homosexual.

**fah** *noun* (also **fa**) *Music* the fourth note of a major scale.

**Fahrenheit** (fa-rěn-hyt) *adjective* of a temperature scale with the freezing point of water at 32° and the boiling point at 212°. (¶ Named after the German physicist G. Fahrenheit (died 1736).)

**faience** (fy-ahns) *noun* pottery decorated with an opaque glaze.

**fail** *verb* **1** be unsuccessful in what is attempted. **2** be or become insufficient; (of crops) produce a very poor harvest. **3** become weak or ineffective, cease functioning; *the engine failed.* **4** neglect, forget, or be unable to do something; *he failed to appear.* **5** disappoint the hopes of. **6** become bankrupt. **7** judge (a candidate) not to have passed an examination. ● *noun* failure in an examination. □ **fail-safe** *adjective* (of equipment) reverting to a danger-free condition in the event of a breakdown or other failure. **without fail** for certain, whatever happens.

**failed** *adjective* unsuccessful; *a failed author.*

**failing** *noun* a weakness or fault. ● *preposition* if (a thing) does not happen; if (a person) is not available.

**failure** *noun* **1** failing, non-performance of something, lack of success. **2** breakdown of a mechanism; the ceasing of a part of the body etc. to function; *heart failure.* **3** bankruptcy, collapse. **4** an unsuccessful person, thing, or attempt.

**fain** *adjective & adverb* (*old use*) willing or willingly under the circumstances.

**faint** *adjective* **1** not clearly perceived by the senses, indistinct; not intense in colour, sound, or smell. **2** weak, vague; *a faint hope.* **3** timid, feeble. **4** about to lose consciousness. ● *verb* lose consciousness temporarily through failure in the supply of blood to the brain. ● *noun* an act or state of fainting. □ **faint-hearted** *adjective* timid. □ **faintly** *adverb,* **faintness** *noun*

**fair** *noun* **1** a periodical gathering for the sale of goods, often with entertainments. **2** an exhibition of commercial or industrial goods. **3** a funfair. ● *adjective* **1** (of the hair or skin) light in colour; (of a person) having fair hair. **2** (*old use*) beautiful. **3** (of weather) fine, (of winds) favourable. **4** just, unbiased, in accordance with the rules. **5** of moderate quality or amount. ● *adverb* in a fair manner. □ **fair and square** straightforwardly; exactly. **a fair crack of**

**the whip** (*informal*) a fair chance to share in something. **fair enough** (*informal*) that is reasonable or satisfactory. **fair game** a legitimate target or object. **fair play** reasonable treatment or behaviour. **fairweather friend** an unreliable friend or ally. **the fair sex** women. □ **fairness** *noun*

**fairground** *noun* an outdoor space where a fair is held.

**fairing** *noun* a structure added to the exterior of a ship or aircraft etc. to streamline it.

**Fair Isle** one of the Shetland Islands, noted for its knitting designs in coloured wools.

**fairly** *adverb* **1** in a fair manner. **2** moderately; *fairly difficult*. **3** actually; *fairly jumped for joy*. □ **fairly and squarely** = FAIR AND SQUARE.

**fairway** *noun* **1** a navigable channel. **2** part of a golf course between tee and green, kept free of rough grass.

**fairy** *noun* **1** a small imaginary being supposed to have magical powers. **2** (*offensive slang*) a male homosexual. □ **fairy cake** a small iced sponge cake. **fairy godmother** a benefactress who provides a sudden unexpected gift. **fairy lights** small decorative coloured lights. **fairy ring** a ring of darker grass caused by fungi. **fairy story** *or* **tale 1** a tale about fairies or magic. **2** an incredible story; a falsehood.

**fairyland** *noun* **1** the world of fairies. **2** a very beautiful place.

*fait accompli* (fayt ah-**kom**-pli) a thing that is already done and not reversible. (¶ French.)

**faith** *noun* **1** reliance or trust. **2** belief in a religious doctrine. **3** a system of religious belief; *the Christian faith*. **4** a promise; loyalty, sincerity. **5** (used as *adjective*) concerned with curing by faith and prayer rather than medical treatment; *faith healing*. □ **in bad faith** with intent to deceive. **in good faith** with honest intention.

**faithful** *adjective* **1** loyal, trustworthy, conscientious. **2** true to the facts, accurate. **3** (**the faithful**) true believers (especially Muslims); loyal supporters. □ **faithfully** *adverb*, **faithfulness** *noun*

**faithless** *adjective* **1** lacking religious faith. **2** false to promises, disloyal.

**fake** *noun* a person or thing that is not genuine. ● *adjective* faked, not genuine. ● *verb* **1** make (a thing) that looks genuine, in order to deceive people. **2** pretend; *he faked illness*. □ **faker** *noun*

**fakir** (fay-keer) *noun* a Muslim or Hindu religious beggar regarded as a holy man.

**Falangist** (fă-**lan**-jist) *noun* a member of a Spanish Fascist and right-wing political party, officially abolished in 1977.

**Falasha** (fă-lah-shă) *noun* (*plural* **Falasha**) a member of a group in Ethiopia holding the Jewish faith, who (after much persecution) were airlifted to Israel in 1984–5.

**falcon** (fawl-kŏn) *noun* a small long-winged hawk.

**falconry** *noun* the breeding and training of hawks.

**Faldo**, Nick (Nicholas Alexander) (born 1957), British golfer.

**Falkland Islands** (fawlk-lănd *or* folk-) (also **Falklands**) a group of islands in the South Atlantic, a British dependency but claimed by Argentina.

**fall** *verb* (**fell**, **fallen**, **falling**) **1** come or go down freely, e.g. by force of weight, loss of balance, or becoming detached. **2** come as if by falling; *silence fell*. **3** lose one's position or office; *fell from power*. **4** hang down. **5** decrease in amount, number, or intensity; *prices fell*; *her spirits fell*; *the barometer is falling*. **6** slope downwards. **7** (of the face) show dismay. **8** cease to stand; *six wickets fell*. **9** die in battle. **10** (of a fortress or city) be captured. **11** take a specified direction or place; *his glance fell on me*. **12** come by chance or be assigned as what one must have or do; *the honour falls to you*. **13** happen to come; *fell into bad company*. **14** pass into a specified state, become; *fall in love*; *fell asleep*; *she fell pregnant*. **15** occur, have as a date; *Easter fell early*. ● *noun* **1** the act of falling. **2** giving way to temptation. **3** the amount by which something falls. **4** (*Amer.*) autumn. **5** a wrestling-bout; a throw that causes the opponent to remain on the ground for a specified time. **6** (**falls**) a waterfall. □ **fall back on** retreat to; turn to for help when something else has failed. **fall down on** fail in. **fall flat** fail to produce a result. **fall for 1** fall in love with. **2** be taken in by (a deception). **fall foul of** come into conflict with. **fall guy** (*slang*) an easy victim; a scapegoat. **fall in 1** take one's place in military formation. **2** (of a building) collapse inwards. **falling star** a meteor. **fall in with 1** meet by chance. **2** agree to. **fall off** decrease in size, number, or quality. **fall on one's feet** get out of a difficulty successfully. **fall out 1** quarrel. **2** happen. **3** leave one's place in a military formation. **fall over oneself** (*informal*) **1** be very awkward. **2** be very hasty or eager. **fall short** be insufficient or inadequate. **fall short of** fail to obtain or reach. **fall through** (of a plan) fail, come to nothing. **fall to** begin working, fighting, or eating. **the Fall (of man)** Adam's sin and its results.

**Falla**, Manuel de (1876–1946), Spanish composer and pianist.

**fallacious** (fă-lay-shŭs) *adjective* containing a fallacy. □ **fallaciously** *adverb*, **fallaciousness** *noun*

**fallacy** (fal-ăsi) *noun* **1** a false or mistaken belief. **2** faulty reasoning.

**fallible** (fal-ibŭl) *adjective* liable to make mistakes. □ **fallibly** *adverb*, **fallibility** (fal-i-bil-iti) *noun*

**fallout** *noun* radioactive debris from a nuclear explosion.

**Fallopian tubes** (fă-loh-piăn) the two tubes in female mammals carrying ova from the ovaries to the womb.

**fallow** (fal-oh) *adjective* (of land) ploughed but left unplanted in order to restore its fertility. □ **fallow deer** a small deer, white-spotted in summer.

**false** *adjective* **1** wrong, incorrect. **2** deceitful, lying, unfaithful. **3** not genuine, illusory; sham, artificial; *false teeth*; *false economy*. **4** improperly so called; *the false acacia*. □ **false alarm** an alarm raised needlessly. **false pretences** acts intended to deceive. □ **falsely** *adverb*, **falseness** *noun*

**falsehood** *noun* **1** an untrue statement, a lie. **2** telling lies.

**falsetto** (fol-set-oh) *noun* (*plural* **falsettos**) a high-pitched voice above one's natural range, especially when used by male singers. ● *adverb* in a falsetto voice.

**falsies** *plural noun* (*informal*) pads worn to make the breasts seem larger.

**falsify** *verb* (**falsified**, **falsifying**) **1** alter (a document) fraudulently. **2** misrepresent (facts). □ **falsification** *noun*

**falsity** *noun* **1** falseness. **2** a falsehood, an error.

**falter** *verb* **1** go or function unsteadily. **2** become weaker, begin to give way; *his courage faltered*. **3** speak or utter hesitatingly, stammer.

**fame** *noun* **1** the condition of being known to many people. **2** reputation.

**famed** *adjective* famous.

**familial** (fă-mil-iăl) *adjective* of a family or its members.

**familiar** *adjective* **1** well known, often seen or experienced; *a familiar sight*. **2** (foll. by *with*) knowing well, well acquainted with; *am familiar with all the problems*. **3** lacking formality, friendly and informal; *addressed him in familiar terms*. **4** too informal, assuming a greater degree of informality or friendship than is proper. ● *noun* (in full **familiar spirit**) a demon serving a witch etc. □ **familiarly** *adverb*, **familiarity** *noun*

**familiarize** *verb* (also **familiarise**) make well acquainted (with a person or thing). □ **familiarization** *noun*

**family** *noun* **1** parents and their children. **2** a person's children; *they have a large family*. **3** a set of relatives. **4** all the descendants of a common ancestor; their line of descent. **5** a group of things that are alike in some way. **6** a group of related plants or animals; *lions belong to the cat family*. □ **family man** a man who has a wife and children, especially one fond of family life. **family planning** birth control. **family tree** a diagram showing how people in a family are related. **in the family way** (*informal*) pregnant.

**famine** *noun* extreme scarcity (especially of food) in a region.

**famished**, **famishing** *adjective* (*informal*) extremely hungry.

**famous** *adjective* **1** known to very many people. **2** (*informal*) excellent. □ **famously** *adverb*

**fan**[1] *noun* **1** a device waved in the hand or operated mechanically to create a current of air. **2** anything spread out like a semicircular fan. ● *verb* (**fanned**, **fanning**) **1** drive a current of air upon, with, or as if with a fan. **2** stimulate (flames etc.) in this way. **3** (usually foll. by *out*) spread from a central point; *troops fanned out*. □ **fan belt** a belt driving the fan that cools the radiator of a motor vehicle.

**fan**[2] *noun* an enthusiastic admirer or supporter. (¶ Originally short for *fanatic*.) □ **fan club** an organized group of a person's admirers. **fan mail** letters from fans to the person they admire.

**fanatic** (fă-nat-ik) *noun* a person filled with excessive enthusiasm for something. □ **fanatical** *adjective*, **fanatically** *adverb*

**fanaticism** (fă-nat-i-sizm) *noun* excessive enthusiasm.

**fancier** *noun* a person with special knowledge of and love for something, a connoisseur; *a dog fancier*.

**fanciful** *adjective* **1** (of people) using the imagination freely, imagining things. **2** imaginary. **3** designed in a quaint or imaginative style. □ **fancifully** *adverb*

**fancy** *noun* **1** the power of imagining things, especially of an unreal or fantastic sort. **2** something imagined, an unfounded idea or belief. **3** an unreasoning desire for something. **4** a liking. ● *adjective* **1** ornamental, not plain, elaborate. **2** based on imagination, not fact. ● *verb* (**fancied**, **fancying**) **1** imagine. **2** be inclined to believe or suppose. **3** (*informal*) take a fancy to, like, desire; find (a person) sexually attractive. □ **fancy dress** a costume worn for a party etc. where the guests dress to represent characters of history or fiction etc. **fancy-free** *adjective* not in love. **fancy man** (*slang*) **1** a woman's lover. **2** a pimp. **fancy oneself** (*informal*) be rather conceited, admire oneself. **fancy prices** excessively high prices. **fancy woman** (*slang*) a man's mistress. **take a person's fancy** attract or please him or her.

**fandango** *noun* (*plural* **fandangoes** *or* **fandangos**) a lively Spanish dance for two people.

**fanfare** *noun* a short showy or ceremonious sounding of trumpets.

**fang** *noun* **1** a long sharp tooth, especially of dogs and wolves. **2** a snake's tooth with which it injects venom. **3** the root of a tooth; either of its prongs.

**fanlight** *noun* a small, originally semicircular window above a door or another window.

**fanny** *noun* **1** (*Amer. slang*) the buttocks. **2** (*vulgar*) the female genitals.

**fantail** *noun* a pigeon with a semi-circular tail.

**fantasia** (fan-**tay**-ziă) *noun* an imaginative musical or other composition.

**fantasize** (fan-tă-syz) *verb* (also **fantasise**) imagine in fantasy; day-dream.

**fantastic** *adjective* (also **fantastical**) **1** absurdly fanciful. **2** designed in a very imaginative style. **3** (*informal*) remarkable, excellent. □ **fantastically** *adverb*

**fantasy** *noun* **1** imagination, especially when producing very fanciful ideas. **2** a wild or fantastic product of the imagination, a daydream. **3** a fanciful design; a fantasia.

**fanzine** (fan-zeen) *noun* a magazine for fans, especially of science fiction.

**FAO** *abbreviation* Food and Agriculture Organization (of the United Nations).

**far** *adverb* (**farther** *or* **further**, **farthest** *or* **furthest**; *see also* the note at **farther**) at, to, or by a great distance. ●*adjective* distant, remote. □ **a far cry from** greatly different from. **as far as 1** right up to. **2** to the extent that. **by far** by a great amount. **far and away** by far. **far and wide** over a large area. **far-away** *adjective* **1** remote. **2** (of a look) dreamy. **3** (of the voice) sounding as if from a distance. **Far East** China, Japan, and other countries of East Asia. **far-fetched** *adjective* (of an explanation etc.) unconvincing, incredible. **far-flung** *adjective* **1** widely scattered. **2** remote. **far from** very different from; almost the opposite of. **far gone** (*informal*) very ill or drunk. **far-off** *adjective* remote. **far-out** *adjective* **1** distant. **2** (*slang*) unconventional, avant-garde. **3** (*slang*) excellent. **far-reaching** *adjective* having a wide range, influence, or effect. **far-seeing** *adjective* showing great foresight. **far-sighted** *adjective* **1** having foresight. **2** (especially *Amer.*) long-sighted. **go far 1** achieve much. **2** contribute greatly. **go too far** overstep reasonable limits. **in so far as** *see* IN. **so**

**far 1** to this point. **2** until now. **so far so good** satisfactory up to now.

**farad** (fa-răd) *noun* a unit of electric capacitance. (¶ Named after **Faraday**.)

**Faraday**, Michael (1791–1867), English physicist and chemist, discoverer of electromagnetic induction (the condition under which a permanent magnet can generate electricity), the key to the development of the electric dynamo and motor.

**farce** *noun* **1** a light comedy. **2** this kind of drama. **3** absurd and useless proceedings; a pretence. □ **farcical** (**far**-sik-ăl) *adjective*, **farcically** *adverb*

**fare** *noun* **1** the price charged for a passenger to travel. **2** a passenger who pays a fare, especially for a hired vehicle. **3** food provided. ●*verb* progress, get on; *how did they fare?* □ **fare-stage** *noun* a stopping-place marking one of the sections of a bus route that are regarded as units in calculating fares.

**farewell** *interjection* goodbye. ●*noun* leave-taking.

**farina** (fă-**ry**-nă) *noun* flour or meal of corn, nuts, or starchy roots.

**farinaceous** (fa-rin-**ay**-shŭs) *adjective* of or like farina, starchy.

**farm** *noun* **1** an area of land and its buildings used under one management for raising crops or livestock. **2** a farmhouse. **3** a stretch of water used for raising fish etc. ●*verb* **1** grow crops or raise livestock. **2** use (land) for this purpose. **3** breed (fish etc.) commercially. **4** take the proceeds of (a tax) in return for a fixed sum. □ **farm-hand** *noun* a worker on a farm. **farm out** send out or delegate (work) to be done by others.

**farmer** *noun* a person who owns or manages a farm.

**farmhouse** *noun* the farmer's house on a farm.

**farmstead** (**farm**-sted) *noun* a farm and its buildings.

**farmyard** *noun* the enclosed area round farm buildings.

**Farquhar** (**far**-ker), George (1678–1707), Irish writer of comedies.

**farrago** (fă-**rah**-goh) *noun* (*plural* **farragos** *or* *Amer.* **farragoes**) a hotchpotch.

**farrier** (**fa**-ri-er) *noun* a smith who shoes horses.

**farrow** (**fa**-roh) *verb* (of a sow) give birth to young pigs. ●*noun* **1** farrowing. **2** a litter of young pigs.

**Farsi** *noun* the Persian language.

**fart** (*vulgar*) *verb* send out wind through the anus. ●*noun* an emission of wind in this way.

**farther** *adverb & adjective* at or to a greater distance, more remote. □ **farthest** *adverb & adjective*

> ■ **Usage** *Further* and *furthest* are used more commonly than these words except where the sense of physical distance is involved.

**farthing** *noun* a former British coin worth one-quarter of an old penny.

**farthingale** *noun* a hooped petticoat formerly worn under a skirt to make it stand out.

**fasces** (fa-seez) *plural noun* (in ancient Rome) a bundle of rods with a projecting axe-blade, as a symbol of a magistrate's power.

**fascia** (fay-shă) *noun* (also **facia**) **1** the instrument panel of a vehicle or other machine. **2** a strip with a name etc. over a shop-front. **3** a long flat vertical surface of wood or stone, e.g. under eaves or a cornice.

**fascicle** (fas-ikŭl) *noun* each section of a book that is published in instalments.

**fascinate** *verb* **1** attract and hold the interest of; charm greatly. **2** deprive (a victim) of the power of escape by a fixed look, as a snake does. □ **fascination** *noun*, **fascinator** *noun*

**fascinating** *adjective* having great attraction or charm.

**Fascism** (fash-izm) *noun* (also **fascism**) a system of extreme right-wing dictatorial government. □ **Fascist** *noun*, **Fascistic** *adjective*

**fashion** *noun* **1** a manner or way of doing something; *continue working in this fashion.* **2** the popular style of dress, customs, etc. at a given time. ● *verb* make into a particular form or shape. □ **after** *or* **in a fashion** to some extent but not very satisfactorily. **in fashion** fashionable. **out of fashion** no longer fashionable.

**fashionable** *adjective* **1** in or adopting a style that is currently popular. **2** frequented or used by stylish people; *a fashionable hotel.* □ **fashionably** *adverb*

**fast¹** *adjective* **1** moving or done quickly. **2** producing or allowing quick movement; *a fast road.* **3** (of a clock etc.) showing a time ahead of the correct one. **4** (of a person) spending too much time and energy on pleasure, immoral. **5** (of photographic film) very sensitive to light; (of a lens) having a large aperture, allowing a short exposure to be used. **6** firmly fixed or attached. **7** (of colours or dyes) unlikely to fade or run. ● *adverb* **1** quickly. **2** firmly, tightly, securely; *stuck fast; fast asleep.* □ **fast breeder reactor** one using fast neutrons to produce the same fissile material it uses. **fast food** quickly-prepared food, especially that served or cooked in a restaurant. **fast-forward** *adjective* producing accelerated onward motion of a tape etc., especially in order to reach a particular place in a recording. **fast neutron** one with high kinetic energy. **pull a fast one** (*informal*) try to deceive or gain an unfair advantage.

**fast²** *verb* go without food or without certain kinds of food, especially as a religious duty. ● *noun* **1** fasting. **2** a day or season appointed for this.

**fastback** *noun* a car with a long sloping back; the back itself.

**fasten** *verb* **1** fix firmly, tie or join together. **2** fix (one's glance or attention) intently. **3** become fastened; *the door fastens with a latch.* □ **fasten off** tie or secure the end of a thread etc. **fasten on 1** lay hold of. **2** single out for attack. **3** seize as a pretext.

**fastener** *noun* (also **fastening**) a device for fastening something.

**fastidious** (fas-tid-iŭs) *adjective* **1** selecting carefully, choosing only what is good. **2** easily disgusted. □ **fastidiously** *adverb*, **fastidiousness** *noun*

**fastness** *noun* **1** the state of being fast or secure; *colour fastness.* **2** a stronghold, a fortress.

**fat** *noun* **1** a natural oily substance, insoluble in water, found in animal bodies and certain seeds. **2** this substance prepared for use in cooking. ● *adjective* (**fatter, fattest**) **1** containing much fat, covered with fat. **2** excessively plump. **3** (of an animal) made plump for slaughter. **4** thick; *a fat book.* **5** fertile; *fat lands.* **6** richly rewarded; *a nice fat job.* □ **fat cat** (*Amer. slang*) a wealthy person. **a fat lot** *or* **chance** (*informal*) none, no chance at all. **the fat is in the fire** trouble is imminent. **live off the fat of the land** have the best of everything. □ **fatness** *noun*

**fatal** *adjective* **1** causing or ending in death. **2** causing disaster; *a fatal mistake.* **3** fateful; *the fatal day.* □ **fatally** *adverb*

**fatalist** *noun* a person who accepts and submits to what happens, regarding it as inevitable. □ **fatalism** *noun*, **fatalistic** *adjective*

**fatality** (fă-tal-iti) *noun* **1** death caused by accident or in war etc. **2** a person killed in this way. **3** a fatal influence; a liability to disaster.

**fate** *noun* **1** a power thought to control all events and impossible to resist. **2** a person's destiny. **3** (**the Fates**) (*Gk. myth.*) the three goddesses who presided over people's lives and deaths.

**fated** *adjective* destined by fate, doomed.

**fateful** *adjective* bringing or producing great and usually unpleasant events. □ **fatefully** *adverb*

**fat-head** noun (informal) a stupid person. □ **fat-headed** adjective

**father** noun 1 a male parent. 2 a male ancestor; land of our fathers. 3 the founder or originator of something. 4 (**the Father**) God, the first person of the Trinity. 5 the title of certain priests, especially those belonging to religious orders. ● verb 1 beget, be the father of. 2 found or originate (an idea or plan etc.). □ **Father Christmas** an old man dressed in a red robe, symbolic of Christmas festivities and identified with Santa Claus. **father-figure** noun an older man who is respected and trusted like a father. **father-in-law** noun (plural **fathers-in-law**) the father of one's wife or husband. **Father's Day** a day (usually the third Sunday in June) on which special tribute is paid to fathers. □ **fatherly** adjective, **fatherhood** noun, **fatherless** adjective

**fatherland** noun one's native country.

**fathom** noun a measure of 6 feet, used in stating the depth of water. ● verb 1 measure the depth of. 2 get to the bottom of, understand.

**fathomless** adjective too deep to fathom.

**fatigue** noun 1 tiredness resulting from hard work or exercise. 2 weakness in metals etc. caused by repeated stress. 3 any of the non-military duties of soldiers, e.g. cooking, cleaning. 4 (**fatigues**) clothing worn for these duties. ● verb cause fatigue to.

**fatso** noun (plural **fatsoes**) (informal) a fat person.

**fatstock** noun livestock fattened for slaughter as food.

**fatted** adjective (of animals) fattened as food. □ **kill the fatted calf** celebrate, especially at someone's return.

**fatten** verb make or become fat.

**fattish** adjective rather fat.

**fatty** adjective like fat, containing fat. ● noun (informal) a fat person.

**fatuous** (fat-yoo-ŭs) adjective foolish, silly. □ **fatuously** adverb, **fatuousness** noun, **fatuity** (fă-tew-iti) noun

**fatwa** noun a legal decision or ruling by an Islamic religious leader.

**faucet** (faw-sit) noun 1 a tap for a barrel. 2 (Amer.) any kind of tap.

**Faulkner** (fawk-ner), William (1897–1962), American novelist and writer of short stories.

**fault** noun 1 a defect or imperfection. 2 an offence, something wrongly done. 3 the responsibility for something wrong. 4 a break in the continuity of layers of rock, caused by movement of the earth's crust. 5 an incorrect serve in tennis etc. ● verb 1 find fault with, criticize. 2 Geol. break the continuity of (strata). □ **at fault** responsible for a mistake or shortcoming. **find fault with** criticize, complain about. **to a fault** excessively; generous to a fault. □ **faultless** adjective, **faultlessly** adverb

**faulty** adjective (**faultier**, **faultiest**) having a fault or faults, imperfect. □ **faultily** adverb, **faultiness** noun

**faun** (pronounced fawn) noun (Rom. myth.) any of a class of gods of the woods and fields, with a goat's horns, legs, and tail. (¶ From the name of the Latin god Faunus, identified with the Greek Pan.)

**fauna** noun (plural **faunae** or **faunas**) the animals of an area or period of time.

**Fauré** (faw-ray), Gabriel (1845–1924), French composer, noted for his songs and Requiem Mass.

**Faust** (pronounced fowst) a wandering astronomer and magician who lived in Germany c.1488–1541, and was reputed to have sold his soul to the Devil. He was the hero of dramas by Marlowe and Goethe and of an opera by Gounod.

**faux pas** (foh pah) (plural **faux pas**, pronounced foh **pahz**) an embarrassing blunder. (¶ French, = false step.)

**favour** noun (Amer. **favor**) 1 liking, goodwill, approval. 2 an act of kindness. 3 support or preference given to one person or group at the expense of another. 4 an ornament or badge etc. worn to show that one supports a certain political or other party. ● verb 1 regard or treat with favour. 2 be in favour of. 3 (foll. by with) oblige; favour us with a song. 4 (of events or circumstances) make possible or easy, be advantageous to. 5 resemble (one parent etc.); the boy favours his father. □ **in** or **out of favour** approved or disapproved of. **in favour of** 1 in support of. 2 to the advantage of.

**favourable** adjective (Amer. **favorable**) 1 giving or showing approval. 2 pleasing, satisfactory; made a favourable impression. 3 helpful, advantageous; favourable winds. □ **favourably** adverb

**favourite** adjective (Amer. **favorite**) liked or preferred above others. ● noun 1 a favoured person or thing. 2 a competitor generally expected to win.

**favouritism** noun (Amer. **favoritism**) unfair favouring of one person or group at the expense of another.

**Fawkes**, Guy (1570–1606), a conspirator in the Gunpowder Plot of 1605 (see BONFIRE NIGHT).

**fawn** noun 1 a fallow deer in its first year. 2 light yellowish brown. ● adjective fawn-coloured. ● verb 1 (of a dog etc.) show extreme affection. 2 try to win favour by obsequious behaviour.

**fax** noun 1 transmission of exact copies of documents electronically. 2 a copy produced by this. 3 (also **fax machine**) a machine for sending and receiving faxes. ●*verb* transmit (a document) by this process.

**fay** *noun* (*poetic*) a fairy.

**faze** *verb* fluster; daunt.

**FBI** *abbreviation* Federal Bureau of Investigation.

**FC** *abbreviation* Football Club.

**FCO** *abbreviation* Foreign and Commonwealth Office.

**Fe** *symbol* iron.

**fealty** (feel-ti) *noun* loyalty, allegiance (originally the duty of a feudal tenant or vassal to his lord).

**fear** *noun* **1** an unpleasant emotion caused by the nearness of danger or expectation of pain etc. **2** reverence or awe. **3** a danger, a likelihood. ●*verb* **1** feel fear of, be afraid. **2** show reverence towards (God). **3** have an uneasy feeling; be politely regretful; *I fear there's none left.* □ **for fear of** because of the risk of. **no fear** (*informal*) certainly not!

**fearful** *adjective* **1** causing horror. **2** feeling fear. **3** (*informal*) very great, extremely bad. □ **fearfully** *adverb*

**fearless** *adjective* feeling no fear. □ **fearlessly** *adverb*, **fearlessness** *noun*

**fearsome** *adjective* frightening or alarming in appearance, very great; *a fearsome task.*

**feasible** (fee-zi-bŭl) *adjective* **1** able to be done, possible. **2** likely, plausible; *a feasible explanation.* □ **feasibly** *adverb*, **feasibility** (fee-zi-bil-iti) *noun*

**feast** *noun* **1** a large elaborate meal. **2** a religious festival. ●*verb* **1** eat heartily. **2** give a feast to. □ **feast one's eyes on** look with pleasure at.

**feat** *noun* a remarkable action or achievement.

**feather** *noun* **1** any of the structures that grow from a bird's skin and cover its body, consisting of a central shaft with a fringe of fine strands on each side. **2** plumage. **3** game birds. ●*verb* **1** cover or fit with feathers. **2** turn (an oar) so that the blade passes through the air edgeways. **3** make (propeller blades) rotate in such a way as to lessen the resistance of the air or water. □ **a feather in one's cap** an achievement one can be proud of. **feather bed** a mattress stuffed with feathers. **feather-bed** *verb* (**feather-bedded, feather-bedding**) make things financially easy for, pamper. **feather-brained** *adjective* empty-headed, silly. **feather one's nest** enrich oneself when an opportunity occurs. **in fine** or **high feather** in good spirits. □ **feathery** *adjective*

**feathering** *noun* **1** plumage. **2** the feathers of an arrow. **3** a feather-like structure or marking.

**featherweight** *noun* **1** a weight in certain sports between bantamweight and lightweight, in amateur boxing 54–7 kg. **2** a very lightweight thing or person. **3** (usually used as *adjective*) of little or no influence.

**feature** *noun* **1** any of the parts of the face (e.g. mouth, nose, eyes) which together make up its appearance. **2** a distinctive or noticeable quality of a thing. **3** a prominent article in a newspaper etc. **4** (in full **feature film**) the main film in a cinema programme. **5** a broadcast based on one specific theme. ●*verb* **1** give special prominence to. **2** be a feature. □ **featureless** *adjective*

**Feb.** *abbreviation* February.

**febrile** (fee-bryl) *adjective* of or involving fever, feverish.

**February** the second month of the year.

**feces** Amer. spelling of FAECES.

**feckless** *adjective* feeble and incompetent; irresponsible. □ **fecklessly** *adverb*, **fecklessness** *noun*

**fecund** (fek-ŭnd) *adjective* **1** producing many offspring. **2** producing many ideas etc. □ **fecundity** (fi-kund-iti) *noun*

**fecundate** (fek-ŭn-dayt) *verb* make fecund, fertilize. □ **fecundation** *noun*

**fed** *see* FEED. □ **fed up** (*informal*) bored or discontented.

**federal** *adjective* **1** of a system of government in which several States unite under a central authority but remain independent in internal affairs. **2** belonging to this group as a whole (not to its separate parts); *federal laws.* **3** of an association of units that are largely independent. □ **Federal Bureau of Investigation** a section of the Department of Justice in the USA, responsible for investigating violations of federal law and safeguarding national security. **Federal Reserve System** the central banking system of the USA. □ **federally** *adverb*

**federalism** *noun* **1** being federal. **2** favouring a federal system. □ **federalist** *noun*

**federalize** *verb* (also **federalise**) make federal, organize in a federal system. □ **federalization** *noun*

**federate** *verb* (*pronounced* fe-dĕ-rayt) organize or be organized on a federal basis. ●*adjective* (*pronounced* fe-dĕ-răt) federally organized.

**federation** *noun* **1** federating. **2** a federated society or group of States.

**federative** *adjective* federated, federal.

**fee** *noun* **1** a sum payable to an official or a professional person for advice or services. **2** a sum payable for membership of a society, entrance for an examination, etc. **3** (**fees**) charges for instruction at a school or university.

**feeble** *adjective* weak, without strength, force, or effectiveness. □ **feeble-minded** *adjective* mentally deficient. □ **feebly** *adverb*, **feebleness** *noun*

**feed** *verb* (**fed, feeding**) **1** give food to; put food into the mouth of. **2** give as food to animals; *feed oats to horses*. **3** (often foll. by *on*) (of animals) take food; *feed on nuts and seeds*. **4** serve as food for, nourish. **5** supply, pass a supply of material to. **6** send passes to (a player) in football etc. ●*noun* **1** an amount of food (chiefly for animals or babies). **2** a pipe or channel etc. by which material is carried to a machine; the material itself.

**feedback** *noun* **1** *Electronics* return of part of the output of a system to its source, especially so as to modify the output. **2** the return of information about a product etc.; response.

**feeder** *noun* **1** (of plants and animals) one that takes in food in a certain way; *a dainty feeder*. **2** a baby's feeding-bottle or bib. **3** a hopper or feeding apparatus in a machine. **4** a branch railway line, airline, canal, etc., linking outlying areas with a central line or service.

**feel** *verb* (**felt, feeling**) **1** explore or perceive by touch. **2** be conscious of, be aware of being; *feel a pain*; *feel happy*. **3** be affected by; *feels the cold badly*. **4** give a certain sensation or impression; *the water feels warm*. **5** have a vague conviction or impression of something. **6** have as an opinion, consider; *we felt it was necessary to do this*. **7** (foll. by *for*) sympathize with. ●*noun* **1** the sense of touch. **2** the act of feeling. **3** the sensation produced by something touched; *silk has a soft feel*. □ **feel free** (*informal*) an expression of permission. **feel like** (*informal*) be in the mood for. **feel one's way** proceed cautiously. **get the feel of** become accustomed to using.

**feeler** *noun* **1** a long slender part or organ in certain animals, used for testing things by touch. **2** a cautious proposal or suggestion put forward to test people's reactions. □ **feeler gauge** a gauge with blades that can be inserted to measure gaps.

**feeling** *noun* **1** the power and capacity to feel; *lost all feeling in his legs*. **2** mental or physical awareness, emotion. **3** an idea or belief not wholly based on reason; *had a feeling of safety*. **4** sensitivity, sympathy; *showed no feeling for the sufferings of others*. **5** opinion, attitude; *the feeling of the meeting was against it*. **6** (**feelings**) the emotional side of a person's nature (contrasted with the intellect); *hurt my feelings*; *had strong feelings about it*.

**feet** *see* FOOT.

**feign** (*pronounced* fayn) *verb* pretend.

**feint** (*pronounced* faynt) *noun* a slight attack or movement made to divert attention from the main attack coming elsewhere. ●*verb* make a feint. ●*adjective* (of ruled lines) faint.

**feisty** (fy-sti) *adjective* (*Amer. slang*) aggressive, excitable.

**feldspar** *noun* (also **felspar**) any of a group of usually white or red rock-forming minerals that are aluminium silicates combined with various other metallic ions.

**felicitate** (fi-liss-i-tayt) *verb* congratulate. □ **felicitation** *noun*

**felicitous** (fi-liss-i-tŭs) *adjective* (of words or remarks) well chosen, apt. □ **felicitously** *adverb*

**felicity** *noun* **1** being happy, great happiness. **2** a pleasing manner or style; *expressed himself with great felicity*.

**feline** (fee-lyn) *adjective* of cats, catlike. ●*noun* an animal of the cat family. □ **felinity** (fi-lin-iti) *noun*

**fell**[1] *noun* a stretch of moorland or hilly land in north England. ●*verb* **1** strike down by a blow. **2** cut (a tree) down. **3** stitch down (the edge of a seam) so that it lies flat. ●*adjective* (*poetical*) ruthless, cruel, destructive. □ **at one fell swoop** in a single deadly action.

**fell**[2] *see* FALL.

**fellatio** (fi-lay-shi-oh) *noun* sexual stimulation of the penis by the partner's mouth.

**felloe** *noun* (also **felly**) the outer circle (or a section of it) of a wheel.

**fellow** *noun* **1** one who is associated with another, a comrade. **2** a thing of the same class or kind, the other of a pair. **3** a member of a learned society. **4** a member of the governing body of certain colleges. **5** (*informal*) a man or boy. □ **fellow-feeling** *noun* sympathy. **fellow-traveller** *noun* a sympathizer with the Communist Party.

**fellowship** *noun* **1** friendly association with others, companionship. **2** a number of people associated together, a society; membership of this. **3** the position of a college fellow.

**felly** = FELLOE.

**felon** (fel-ŏn) *noun* a person who has committed a felony.

**felony** (fel-ŏni) *noun* serious, usually violent, crime. □ **felonious** (fi-loh-niŭs) *adjective*

**felspar** = FELDSPAR.

**felt**[1] *noun* a kind of cloth made by matting and pressing fibres. ●*verb* **1** make or become matted together like felt. **2** cover with felt. □ **felt-tipped** (*or* **felt-tip**) **pen** one with a writing-point made of fibre.

**felt**[2] *see* FEEL.

**felucca** (fi-luk-ă) *noun* a small Mediterranean ship with lateen sails and/or oars.

**female** *adjective* **1** of the sex that can bear offspring or produce eggs. **2** (of plants) fruit-bearing, having a pistil and no stamens. **3** of a woman or women. **4** (of parts of machinery etc.) made hollow to receive a corresponding inserted (male) part. ●*noun* a female person, animal, or plant.

**feminine** *adjective* **1** of, like, or suitable for women; having the qualities or appearance considered characteristic of a woman. **2** having the grammatical form suitable for the names of females or for words corresponding to these; *'lioness' is the feminine noun corresponding to 'lion'*. ●*noun* a feminine word or gender. □ **femininity** *noun*

**feminist** *noun* a supporter of women's claims to be given rights equal to those of men. □ **feminism** *noun*

**femme fatale** (fam fa-tahl) (*plural* **femmes fatales**, *pronounced* same) a dangerously seductive woman. (¶ French.)

**femur** (fee-mer) *noun* (*plural* **femurs** *or* **femora**; *pronounced* fem-ŏ-rǎ) the thigh-bone. □ **femoral** *adjective*

**fen** *noun* **1** a low-lying marshy or flooded tract of land. **2** (**the Fens**) those in Cambridgeshire and nearby regions.

**fence** *noun* **1** a barrier, railing, or other upright structure put round a field or garden to mark a boundary or keep animals from straying. **2** a raised structure for a horse to jump. **3** (*slang*) a person who knowingly buys and resells stolen goods. ●*verb* **1** surround with a fence. **2** (*slang*) act as a fence for (stolen goods). **3** engage in fencing. □ **sit on the fence** *see* SIT. □ **fencer** *noun*

**fencing** *noun* **1** fences; a length of fence. **2** the sport of fighting with foils or other kinds of sword.

**fend** *verb* □ **fend for** provide a livelihood for; look after. **fend off** ward off.

**fender** *noun* **1** a low frame bordering a fireplace to keep in falling coals etc. **2** (*Amer.*) the bumper or mudguard of a motor vehicle. **3** a pad or a bundle of rope hung over a vessel's side to prevent damage when it is alongside a wharf or another vessel.

**fennel** *noun* a fragrant aniseed-flavoured herb; its bulbous stem, used as a vegetable.

**fenugreek** (fen-yoo-greek) *noun* a plant with white flowers and fragrant seeds used for flavouring.

**feoff** (*pronounced* fef) *noun* = FIEF.

**feral** (fe-rǎl *or* feer-ǎl) *adjective* **1** (of plants and animals) wild. **2** brutal.

**Ferdinand** (1452–1516), king of Spain, who by succeeding to the thrones of Aragon and Castile effectively united Spain as one country.

**ferial** (feer-iǎl) *adjective* (of a day) not a festival or a fast.

**Fermanagh** (fer-man-ǎ) a district and former county of Northern Ireland.

**Fermat** (fair-mah), Pierre de (1601–65), French lawyer and counsellor, famous as a mathematician.

**ferment** *verb* (*pronounced* fer-ment) **1** undergo fermentation; cause fermentation in. **2** seethe with excitement or agitation. ●*noun* (*pronounced* fer-ment) **1** fermentation. **2** something that causes this. **3** excitement or agitation.

**fermentation** *noun* a chemical change caused by the action of an organic substance such as yeast, involving effervescence and the production of heat, e.g. when sugar is converted into alcohol. □ **fermentative** (fer-ment-ǎ-tiv) *adjective*

**Fermi** (fer-mi), Enrico (1901–54), Italian-born American atomic physicist, a key figure in the development of the atomic bomb and nuclear energy.

**fermium** *noun* an artificially made radioactive metallic element (symbol Fm).

**fern** *noun* a flowerless plant with feathery green leaves. □ **ferny** *adjective*

**ferocious** *adjective* fierce, savage. □ **ferociously** *adverb*, **ferocity** (fi-ross-iti) *noun*

**Ferranti** (fer-ran-ti), Sebastian Ziani de (1864–1930), English electrical engineer, a pioneer of electricity generation and distribution in Britain.

**ferrel** = FERRULE.

**ferret** *noun* a small animal of the weasel family kept for driving rabbits from burrows, killing rats, etc. ●*verb* (**ferreted, ferreting**) search, rummage. □ **ferret out** discover by searching or rummaging.

**ferreting** *noun* hunting with ferrets.

**ferric** *adjective* of or containing iron.

**Ferrier**, Kathleen (1912–53), English contralto singer.

**Ferris wheel** a giant revolving vertical wheel with passenger cars on its rim, used for rides at funfairs etc. (¶ Named after its American inventor G. W. G. Ferris (died 1896).)

**ferroconcrete** *noun* reinforced concrete.

**ferrous** (fe-rǔs) *adjective* containing iron; *ferrous metals*.

**ferrule** (fe-rool) *noun* (also **ferrel**) a metal ring or cap strengthening the end of a stick or tube.

**ferry** *verb* (**ferried, ferrying**) **1** convey (people or things) in a boat etc. across a stretch of water. **2** transport from one place to another, especially as a regular service. ●*noun* **1** a boat etc. used for ferrying. **2** the place where it operates. **3** the service it provides. □ **ferryman** *noun*

**fertile** *adjective* **1** (of soil) rich in the materials needed to support vegetation. **2** (of plants) able to produce fruit; (of animals) able or likely to conceive young. **3** (of seeds or eggs) capable of developing into a new plant or animal, fertilized. **4** (of the mind) able to produce ideas, inventive. **5** (of nuclear material) able to become fissile by the capture of neutrons. □ **fertility** *noun*

**fertilize** *verb* (also **fertilise**) **1** make (soil etc.) fertile or productive. **2** introduce pollen or sperm into (a plant, egg, or female animal) so that it develops seed or young. □ **fertilization** *noun*

**fertilizer** *noun* (also **fertiliser**) material (natural or artificial) added to soil to make it more fertile.

**fervent** (fer-věnt) *adjective* showing warmth of feeling; intense. □ **fervently** *adverb*, **fervency** *noun*

**fervid** *adjective* fervent. □ **fervidly** *adverb*

**fervour** *noun* (*Amer.* **fervor**) warmth and intensity of feeling, zeal.

**fescue** (fess-kew) *noun* a grass used as pasture and fodder.

**festal** *adjective* of a festival.

**fester** *verb* **1** make or become septic and filled with pus. **2** cause continuing resentment. **3** rot, stagnate.

**festival** *noun* **1** a day or time of religious or other celebration. **2** a series of performances of music, drama, etc., given periodically; *the Edinburgh Festival*.

**festive** *adjective* of or suitable for a festival.

**festivity** *noun* a festive occasion or celebration.

**festoon** *noun* a chain of flowers, ribbons, etc., hung in a curve or loop as a decoration. ●*verb* decorate with hanging ornaments.

**feta** (fe-tă) *noun* a soft white salty cheese made especially in Greece.

**fetch** *verb* **1** go for and bring back; *fetch a doctor*. **2** cause to come out; *fetched a sigh*; *fetch tears to the eyes*. **3** (of goods) sell for (a price); *your books won't fetch much*. **4** (*informal*) give (a blow) to; *fetched him a slap*. ●*noun* a dodge, a trick. □ **fetch up** (*informal*) **1** arrive or end up at a place or in a certain position. **2** vomit.

**fetching** *adjective* attractive. □ **fetchingly** *adverb*

**fête** (*pronounced* fayt) *noun* **1** a festival. **2** an outdoor entertainment or sale, usually to raise funds for a cause or charity. ●*verb* (**fêted**, **fêting**) honour or entertain (a person) lavishly.

**fetid** (fet-id *or* fee-tid) *adjective* (also **foetid**) stinking.

**fetish** (fet-ish) *noun* **1** an object worshipped by primitive peoples. **2** an abnormal object

of sexual desire. **3** anything to which abnormally excessive attention is given. □ **fetishism** *noun*, **fetishist** *noun*

**fetlock** *noun* the part of a horse's leg above and behind the hoof.

**fetter** *noun* a chain or shackle for a prisoner's ankles. ●*verb* **1** put into fetters. **2** impede or restrict.

**fettle** *noun* condition, trim; *in fine fettle*.

**fetus** *Amer.* spelling of FOETUS.

**feu** (*pronounced* few) *noun* (*Scottish*) **1** a perpetual lease at a fixed rent. **2** land held in this way.

**feud** (*pronounced* fewd) *noun* lasting hostility between people or groups. ●*verb* carry on a feud.

**feudal** (few-dăl) *adjective* of or according to the **feudal system**, a method of holding land (during the Middle Ages in Europe) by giving one's services to the owner. □ **feudalism** *noun*, **feudalistic** *adjective*

**fever** *noun* **1** an abnormally high body temperature. **2** a disease characterized by this; *typhoid fever*. **3** a state of nervous excitement or agitation. □ **fever pitch** a high level of excitement.

**fevered** *adjective* affected with fever; excited.

**feverfew** *noun* a low-growing aromatic plant with white, daisy-like flowers.

**feverish** *adjective* **1** having a fever; caused or accompanied by a fever. **2** restless with excitement or agitation. □ **feverishly** *adverb*, **feverishness** *noun*

**few** *adjective & noun* not many.

■**Usage** See the note under **less**.

□ **a few** some but not many. **a good few** (*informal*) a fairly large number. **few and far between** scarce.

**fey** (*pronounced* fay) *adjective* **1** clairvoyant. **2** having a strange other-worldly charm; whimsical. **3** (*Scottish*) doomed.

**fez** *noun* (*plural* **fezzes**) a high flat-topped red cap with a tassel, worn by men in certain Muslim countries.

**ff** *abbreviation Music* fortissimo.

**ff.** *abbreviation* the following pages etc.

**fiancé, fiancée** (fee-ahn-say) *noun* a man (*fiancé*) or woman (*fiancée*) to whom one is engaged to be married.

**Fianna Fáil** (fee-ănă foil) an Irish political party formed by de Valera in 1926. (¶ Irish, interpreted by its founders to mean 'soldiers of destiny'.)

**fiasco** (fi-ass-koh) *noun* (*plural* **fiascos**) a ludicrous or humiliating failure.

**fiat** (fy-at) *noun* an order or decree. (¶ Latin, = let it be done.)

**fib** *noun* an unimportant lie. ●*verb* (**fibbed**, **fibbing**) tell a fib. □ **fibber** *noun*

**fiber** *Amer.* spelling of FIBRE.

**Fibonacci** (fib-ŏn-**ah**-chi), Leonardo (*c*.1200), Italian mathematician, after whom is named the series of numbers (1, 1, 2, 3, 5, 8, 13, etc.) in which each number after the first two is the sum of the two preceding numbers.

**fibre** *noun* (*Amer.* **fiber**) **1** one of the thin strands of which animal and vegetable tissue or textile substance is made; a threadlike piece of glass. **2** a substance consisting of fibres; fibrous food material in plants, roughage. **3** strength of character; *moral fibre*. □ **fibre optics** the use of thin flexible fibres of glass or other transparent solids to transmit light-signals.

**fibreboard** *noun* (*Amer.* **fiberboard**) board made of compressed fibres.

**fibreglass** *noun* (*Amer.* **fiberglass**) **1** textile fabric made from woven glass fibres. **2** plastic containing glass fibres.

**fibril** (**fy**-bril) *noun* a small fibre.

**fibroid** (**fy**-broid) *adjective* consisting of fibrous tissue. ●*noun* a benign fibroid tumour in the womb.

**fibrosis** (fy-**broh**-sis) *noun* development of excessive fibrous tissue.

**fibrositis** (fy-brŏ-**sy**-tiss) *noun* rheumatic pain in any tissue other than bones and joints.

**fibrous** (**fy**-brŭs) *adjective* like fibres; made of fibres.

**fibula** (**fib**-yoo-lă) *noun* (*plural* **fibulae** or **fibulas**) the bone on the outer side of the lower part of the leg.

**fiche** (*pronounced* feesh) *noun* (*plural* **fiche** or **fiches**) a microfiche.

**fickle** *adjective* often changing, not constant or loyal. □ **fickleness** *noun*

**fiction** *noun* **1** a product of the imagination. **2** an invented story. **3** a class of literature consisting of books containing such stories. □ **fictional** *adjective*, **fictionally** *adverb*

**fictionalize** *verb* (or **fictionalise**) make into a fictional narrative. □ **fictionalization** *noun*

**fictitious** (fik-**tish**-ŭs) *adjective* imagined, not real, not genuine; *gave a fictitious account of his movements*. □ **fictitiously** *adverb*

**fiddle** *noun* **1** (*informal*) a violin. **2** (*informal*) a piece of cheating, a swindle. ●*verb* **1** (*informal*) play the fiddle. **2** (often foll. by *with*) fidget with something, handle a thing aimlessly. **3** (*informal*) cheat or swindle; falsify (accounts etc.); get by cheating. □ **(as) fit as a fiddle** in very good health. **play second fiddle** take a subordinate role. □ **fiddler** *noun*

**fiddle-faddle** *noun* trivial matters.

**fiddlesticks** *interjection* nonsense.

**fiddling** *adjective* petty, trivial.

**fiddly** *adjective* (*informal*) small and awkward to use or do.

**fidelity** (fid-**el**-iti) *noun* **1** faithfulness, loyalty. **2** accuracy, truthfulness. **3** the quality or precision of the reproduction of sound.

**fidget** *verb* (**fidgeted, fidgeting**) **1** make small restless movements. **2** be uneasy, make (a person) uneasy, worry. ●*noun* **1** a person who fidgets. **2** (**fidgets**) fidgeting movements. □ **fidgety** *adjective*

**fiduciary** (fi-**dew**-sher-i) *adjective* of, held, or given in trust. ●*noun* a trustee.

**fie** *interjection* (*old use*) for shame!

**fief** (*pronounced* feef) *noun* **1** land held under a feudal system or in absolute ownership. **2** one's sphere of operation or control.

**field** *noun* **1** a piece of open ground, especially one used for pasture or cultivation. **2** an area rich in some natural product; a coalfield, gasfield, or oilfield. **3** a battlefield. **4** a sports ground; the playing area marked out on this. **5** the space within which an electric, magnetic, or gravitational influence can be felt; the force of that influence. **6** the area that can be seen or observed; *one's field of vision*. **7** the range of a subject or activity or interest; *an expert in the field of music*. **8** (in computers) one section of a record, representing a unit of information. **9** the scene or area of fieldwork; *field archaeology*. **10** all the competitors in an outdoor contest or sport; all except the one(s) specified; the fielding side in cricket. ●*verb* **1** act as a fielder in cricket etc. **2** stop and return (the ball) in cricket etc. **3** select (a player or team) to play in a game. **4** deal successfully with (a series of questions). □ **field-day** *noun* **1** a day of much activity, especially of brilliant and exciting events. **2** a military exercise or review. **field events** athletic sports other than races, e.g. jumping, weight-putting, etc. **field-glasses** *plural noun* binoculars for outdoor use. **field marshal** an army officer of the highest rank. **field mouse** the type of mouse found in open country. **field sports** outdoor sports such as hunting, shooting, and fishing. **play the field** (*informal*) date many partners.

**fielder** *noun* a fieldsman.

**fieldfare** *noun* a kind of thrush that spends the winter (but not summer) in Britain.

**Fielding**, Henry (1707–54), English novelist.

**Fields**[1], Dame Gracie (original name: Grace Stansfield) (1898–1979), English singer and entertainer.

**Fields**[2], W. C. (original name: William Claude Dukenfield) (1880–1946), American film comedian.

**fieldsman** *noun* (*plural* **fieldsmen**) a member of the side not batting in cricket etc.

**fieldwork** *noun* practical work done outside libraries and laboratories, e.g. by surveyors, scientists, and social workers who visit people in their homes. □ **fieldworker** noun

**fiend** (*pronounced* feend) noun **1** an evil spirit. **2** a very wicked or cruel person, one who causes mischief or annoyance. **3** (*informal*) a devotee or addict; *a fresh-air fiend.* □ **fiendish** adjective, **fiendishly** adverb

**fierce** adjective **1** violent in temper, manner, or action; not gentle. **2** eager, intense; *fierce loyalty.* **3** unpleasantly strong or extreme; *fierce heat.* □ **fiercely** adverb, **fierceness** noun

**fiery** adjective **1** consisting of fire, flaming. **2** looking like fire, bright red. **3** intensely hot, producing a burning sensation. **4** intense, passionate; *a fiery speech.* **5** easily roused to anger. □ **fierily** adverb, **fieriness** noun

**fiesta** (fee-est-ă) noun **1** a religious festival in Spanish-speaking countries. **2** a holiday or festivity.

**FIFA** abbreviation International Football Federation. (¶ French, = *Fédération Internationale de Football Association.*)

**Fife** a local government region of east central Scotland.

**fife** noun a small shrill flute used with a drum in military music.

**fifteen** adjective & noun **1** one more than fourteen (15, XV). **2** a Rugby Union football team of fifteen players. **3** (**15**) (of films) for people of 15 and over. □ **fifteenth** adjective & noun

**fifth** adjective & noun **1** next after fourth. **2** one of five equal parts of a thing. □ **fifth column** an organized body working for the enemy within a country at war. (¶ General Mola, leading four columns of troops towards Madrid in the Spanish Civil War, declared that he had a fifth column inside the city.) **fifth columnist** a member of such a group. □ **fifthly** adverb

**fifty** adjective & noun **1** five times ten (50, L). **2** (**fifties**) the numbers or years or degrees of temperature from 50 to 59. □ **fifty-fifty** adjective & adverb (*informal*) shared or sharing equally between two; with equal chances. □ **fiftieth** adjective & noun

**fig** noun **1** a broad-leaved tree bearing a soft sweet fruit. **2** this fruit. **3** dress, equipment; *in full fig.* **4** condition. □ **fig leaf** a representation of a leaf of a fig tree used in art to cover the genitals of nude figures.

**fig.** abbreviation figure.

**fight** verb (**fought**, **fighting**) **1** struggle against (a person or country) in physical combat or in war. **2** carry on (a battle). **3** struggle or contend in any way; strive to obtain or accomplish something. **4** strive to overcome or destroy; *they fought the fire.* **5** make one's way by fighting or effort. ●noun **1** fighting, a battle. **2** a struggle,

contest, or conflict of any kind. **3** a boxing match. □ **fight back 1** show resistance. **2** suppress (feelings etc.). **fighting chance** a chance of succeeding by great effort. **fighting fit** very fit. **fight it out** settle something by fighting or arguing. **fight off** drive away by fighting. **fight shy of** avoid (a task etc.).

**fighter** noun **1** a person who fights. **2** a fast military aircraft designed for attacking other aircraft.

**figment** noun a thing that only exists in the imagination.

**figurative** (fig-yoor-ătiv) adjective using or containing a figure of speech, metaphorical, not literal. □ **figuratively** adverb

**figure** noun **1** the written symbol of a number. **2** a diagram. **3** a decorative pattern; a pattern traced in dancing or skating. **4** a representation of a person or animal in drawing, sculpture, etc. **5** a person as seen or studied; *saw a figure leaning against the door; the most terrible figure in our history.* **6** external form or shape, bodily shape; *has a good figure.* **7** a geometrical shape enclosed by lines or surfaces. **8** (**figures**) arithmetic; *no good at figures.* ●verb **1** represent in a diagram or picture. **2** picture mentally, imagine. **3** form part of a plan etc.; appear or be mentioned; *he figures in all books on the subject.* **4** (*Amer.*) understand; consider. **5** (*Amer. informal*) be likely or understandable. □ **figure of fun** a person who looks ridiculous. **figure of speech** a word or phrase used for vivid or dramatic effect and not literally. **figure on** (*Amer.*) count on, expect. **figure out 1** work out by arithmetic. **2** (*Amer.*) interpret, understand.

**figured** adjective ornamented, decorated; *figured silk.*

**figurehead** noun **1** a carved image at the prow of a ship. **2** a person at the head of an organization etc. but without real power.

**figurine** (fig-yoor-een) noun a statuette.

**Fiji** (fee-jee) a country consisting of a group of islands in the South Pacific. □ **Fijian** (fee-jee-ăn) adjective & noun

**filament** noun **1** a threadlike strand. **2** a fine wire in an electric lamp, giving off light when heated by the current.

**filbert** noun the nut of a cultivated hazel.

**filch** verb pilfer, steal (something of small value).

**file**[1] noun a steel tool with a roughened surface for shaping or smoothing things. ●verb shape or smooth with a file.

**file**[2] noun **1** a holder, cover, or box for keeping papers arranged for reference purposes. **2** its contents. **3** a collection of related data stored under one reference in a computer. **4** a line of people or things

one behind the other; *in single file.* ●*verb*
**1** place in a file. **2** place on record; *file an application.* **3** (of a reporter) send in (a story etc.). **4** march in file; *they filed out.*

**filial** (**fil-iăl**) *adjective* of or due from a son or daughter; *filial duty.*

**filibuster** *noun* **1** a person who obstructs the passage of a bill by making long speeches. **2** this action. ●*verb* obstruct things in this way.

**filigree** (**fil-i-gree**) *noun* ornamental lace-like work in gold or other metal wire. □ **filigreed** *adjective*

**filing cabinet** a metal or wooden container with drawers for filing documents.

**filings** *plural noun* particles rubbed off by a file.

**Filipino** (**fili-pee-noh**) *noun* (*plural* **Filipinos**) a native of the Philippine Islands.

**fill** *verb* **1** make or become full; occupy the whole of. **2** block up (a hole or cavity). **3** spread over or through; *smoke began to fill the room.* **4** hold (a position); appoint a person to (a vacant post). **5** occupy (vacant time). ●*noun* **1** enough to fill something. **2** enough to satisfy a person's appetite or desire; *eat your fill.* □ **fill in 1** complete by writing or drawing inside an outline; complete (an unfinished document etc.). **2** (*informal*) inform (a person) more fully. **3** (often foll. by *for*) act as a substitute. **fill out** enlarge; become enlarged or plumper. **fill the bill** be suitable for what is required. **fill up 1** fill completely. **2** fill in (a document). **3** fill the petrol tank of a car.

**filler** *noun* an object or material used to fill a cavity or to increase the bulk of something.

**fillet** *noun* **1** a piece of boneless meat from near the loins or ribs; a thick boneless piece of fish. **2** a strip of ribbon etc. worn round the head. **3** (in architecture) a narrow flat band between mouldings. ●*verb* (**filleted, filleting**) remove the bones from (fish etc.).

**filling** *noun* **1** material used to fill a tooth-cavity; the process of inserting this. **2** material put into a container, between layers of bread to form a sandwich, etc. □ **filling-station** *noun* a place where petrol is supplied to motorists from pumps.

**fillip** *noun* **1** a quick smart blow or stroke given with a finger. **2** a stimulus or incentive (to trade etc.). ●*verb* (**filliped, filliping**) propel with a fillip.

**filly** *noun* a young female horse.

**film** *noun* **1** a thin coating or covering layer. **2** a rolled strip or sheet coated with light-sensitive material used for taking photographs or making a motion picture; a single roll of this. **3** a motion picture. **4** (**films**) the cinema industry. **5** a fine haze or blur. ●*verb* **1** cover or become

covered with a thin coating or covering layer. **2** make a film of (a story etc.). □ **film star** a star actor or actress in films. **film-strip** *noun* a series of transparencies for projection.

**filmy** *adjective* (**filmier, filmiest**) thin and almost transparent. □ **filminess** *noun*

**Filofax** *noun* (*trade mark*) a portable loose-leaf filing system for personal or office use.

**filter** *noun* **1** a device or substance for holding back the impurities in a liquid or gas passed through it. **2** a screen for preventing light of certain wavelengths from passing through. **3** a device for suppressing electrical or sound waves of frequencies other than the ones required. **4** an arrangement for the filtering of traffic. ●*verb* **1** pass or cause to pass through a filter; remove (impurities) in this way. **2** make a way in or out gradually; *news filtered out*; *people filtered into the hall.* **3** allow (traffic) or be allowed to pass in a certain direction while other traffic is held up. □ **filter-paper** *noun* porous paper for filtering. **filter tip** a cigarette with a filter at the mouth end to remove some impurities.

**filth** *noun* **1** disgusting dirt. **2** obscenity.

**filthy** *adjective* (**filthier, filthiest**) **1** disgustingly dirty. **2** obscene. □ **filthily** *adverb*, **filthiness** *noun*

**filtrate** *noun* filtered liquid. ●*verb* filter. □ **filtration** *noun*

**fin** *noun* **1** a thin flat projection from the body of a fish etc., used by the animal for propelling and steering itself in the water. **2** an underwater swimmer's rubber flipper. **3** a small projection shaped like a fish's fin, e.g. to improve the stability of an aircraft or rocket.

**finagle** (**fin-ay-gŭl**) *verb* (*informal*) behave or obtain dishonestly.

**final** *adjective* **1** at the end, coming last. **2** putting an end to doubt or argument. ●*noun* **1** the last of a series of contests in sports or a competition. **2** the edition of a newspaper published latest in the day. **3** (**finals**) the last set of examinations in a series. □ **finally** *adverb*

**finale** (**fin-ah-li**) *noun* the final section of a musical composition or a drama.

**finalist** *noun* one who competes in the final.

**finality** (**fy-nal-iti**) *noun* the quality of being final.

**finalize** *verb* (also **finalise**) **1** bring to an end. **2** put into its final form. □ **finalization** *noun*

**finance** (**fy-nanss**) *noun* **1** the management of money. **2** money as support for an undertaking. **3** (**finances**) the money resources of a country, company, or person. ●*verb* provide the money for. □ **finance company** or **house** a company concerned mainly with lending money for hire-purchase transactions.

**financial** (fy-**nan**-shăl) *adjective* of finance. □ **financially** *adverb*

**financier** (fy-**nan**-si-er) *noun* a person engaged in financing business etc. on a large scale.

**finch** *noun* any of a number of related birds most of which have short stubby bills, e.g. a chaffinch or greenfinch.

**find** *verb* (**found, finding**) **1** discover by search or effort or by chance. **2** become aware of, discover (a fact). **3** arrive at naturally; *water finds its own level*. **4** succeed in obtaining; *can't find time to do it*. **5** supply, provide; *who will find the money for the expedition?* **6** (of a jury etc.) decide and declare; *found him innocent; found for the plaintiff*. ●*noun* a discovery; a thing found. □ **find favour** be acceptable. **find one's feet 1** become able to stand or walk. **2** become able to act independently. **find oneself** discover one's natural powers or one's vocation. **find out 1** get information about. **2** detect (a person) who has done wrong. **3** discover (a deception or fraud).

**finder** *noun* **1** one who finds something. **2** the viewfinder of a camera. **3** a small telescope attached to a larger one to locate an object for observation.

**findings** *plural noun* the conclusions reached by means of an inquiry.

**fine**¹ *noun* a sum of money fixed as a penalty for an offence. ●*verb* punish by a fine.

**fine**² *adjective* **1** of high quality. **2** excellent, of great merit. **3** (of weather) bright and clear, free from rain and fog etc. **4** of slender thread or thickness; small-sized; consisting of small particles. **5** requiring very skilful workmanship. **6** difficult to perceive; *making fine distinctions*. **7** complimentary, especially in an insincere way; *said fine things about them*. **8** in good health, comfortable; *I'm fine, thank you*. ●*adverb* **1** finely. **2** (*informal*) very well, *that will suit me fine*. ●*verb* make or become finer, thinner, or less coarse. □ **fine arts** those appealing to the sense of beauty, especially painting, sculpture, and architecture. **fine-drawn** *adjective* **1** subtle. **2** extremely thin. **fine-tooth comb** a comb with narrow close-set teeth. **go over with a fine-tooth comb** examine closely and thoroughly. **not to put too fine a point on it** to express it bluntly. □ **finely** *adverb*, **fineness** *noun*

**finery** *noun* fine clothes or decorations.

**fines herbes** (feenz **airb**) mixed herbs used in cooking. (¶ French.)

**finesse** (fin-**ess**) *noun* **1** delicate manipulation. **2** tact and cleverness in dealing with a situation. **3** (in card games) an attempt to win a trick by playing a card that is not the highest held. ●*verb* **1** achieve by finesse. **2** (in card games) make a finesse (with).

**fine-tune** *verb* make delicate adjustments to (a mechanism, plan, etc.) in order to improve it.

**finger** *noun* **1** any of the five parts extending from each hand; any of these other than the thumb. **2** the part of a glove that fits over a finger. **3** a finger-like object. **4** (*informal*) the breadth of a finger (about ¾ inch) as a measure of alcohol in a glass. ●*verb* touch or feel with the fingers. □ **finger-board** *noun* part of the neck of a stringed instrument on which the strings are pressed by the fingers. **finger-bowl** *noun* a small bowl for rinsing one's fingers at the table. **finger-plate** *noun* a plate fastened on a door to prevent finger-marks. **finger-stall** *noun* a sheath to cover an injured finger. **get** (*or* **pull**) **one's finger out** (*informal*) start to act. **put one's finger on** identify exactly.

**fingering** *noun* **1** a method of using the fingers in playing a musical instrument or in typing. **2** indication of this in a musical score, usually by numbers.

**fingernail** *noun* the nail on a finger.

**fingerprint** *noun* an impression of the ridges of the skin on the pad of a finger, especially as a means of identification.

**fingertip** *noun* the tip of a finger. □ **have at one's fingertips** be thoroughly familiar with (facts etc.).

**finial** *noun* an ornamental top to a gable, canopy, etc.

**finical** *adjective* finicky.

**finicking** *adjective & noun* being finicky.

**finicky** *adjective* **1** excessively detailed, fiddly. **2** over-particular, fastidious.

**finis** (**fin**-iss) *noun* the end, especially of a book.

**finish** *verb* **1** bring or come to an end, complete. **2** reach the end of a task or race etc. **3** consume or get through all of; *finish the pie*. **4** put the final touches to; complete the manufacture of (woodwork, cloth, etc.) by surface treatment. ●*noun* **1** the last stage of something. **2** the point at which a race etc. ends. **3** the state of being finished or perfect. **4** the method, texture, or material used for finishing woodwork etc. □ **finishing-school** *noun* a private school preparing girls for fashionable society. **finish off 1** end. **2** (*informal*) kill. **finish with** complete one's use of; end one's association with.

**finite** (**fy**-nyt) *adjective* **1** limited, not infinite. **2** *Grammar* (of a part of a verb) having a specific number and person.

**Finland** a country of NE Europe.

**Finn** *noun* a native of Finland.

**Finnish** *adjective* of the Finns or their language. ● *noun* the language of the Finns.

**fino** (fee-noh) *noun* a light-coloured dry sherry. (¶ Spanish, = fine.)

**fiord** (fi-ord) *noun* (also **fjord**) a long narrow inlet of the sea between high cliffs as in Norway.

**fipple** *noun* the plug at the mouth-end of a wind instrument. □ **fipple flute** a flute played by blowing the end, e.g. a recorder.

**fir** *noun* **1** an evergreen cone-bearing tree with needle-like leaves on its shoots. **2** its wood.

**fire** *noun* **1** combustion producing light and heat. **2** destructive burning; *insured against fire.* **3** burning fuel in a grate or furnace etc.; an electric or gas fire. **4** angry or excited feeling, enthusiasm. **5** the firing of guns; *hold your fire.* ● *verb* **1** send a bullet or shell from a gun etc.; send out (a missile); detonate. **2** deliver or utter in rapid succession. **3** dismiss (an employee) from a job. **4** set fire to. **5** catch fire; (of an internal-combustion engine) undergo ignition. **6** supply (a furnace etc.) with fuel. **7** bake (pottery or bricks); cure (tea or tobacco) by artificial heat. **8** excite, stimulate; *fired them with enthusiasm.* **9** cause to glow, redden. □ **fire-alarm** *noun* a bell or other device giving warning of fire. **fire away** (*informal*) begin, go ahead. **fire-ball** *noun* **1** a large meteor. **2** a ball of flame or lightning. **3** an energetic person. **fire-bomb** *noun* an incendiary bomb. **fire-break** *noun* an obstacle to the spread of fire in a forest etc. **fire-brick** *noun* a fireproof brick used in grates. **fire brigade** an organized body of people trained and employed to extinguish fires. **fire door** a fire-resistant door preventing the spread of fire. **fire-drill** *noun* rehearsal of the procedure to be used in case of fire. **fire-eater** *noun* **1** a conjuror who appears to eat fire. **2** a person who is fond of fighting or quarrelling. **fire-engine** *noun* a vehicle fitted with equipment used for fighting large fires. **fire-escape** *noun* a staircase or apparatus for escape from a building etc. in case of fire. **fire extinguisher** an apparatus for spraying foam etc. to put out a fire. **fire-irons** *plural noun* a poker, tongs, and shovel for tending a domestic fire. **fire-lighter** *noun* a piece of inflammable material to help start a fire in a grate. **fire-power** *noun* the destructive capacity of guns etc. **fire-raising** *noun* arson. **fire station** the headquarters of a fire brigade. **fire-trap** *noun* a building without sufficient exits in case of fire. **on fire** **1** burning. **2** excited. **set the world on fire** do something remarkable or sensational. **under fire** **1** being fired on. **2** being rigorously criticized or questioned.

**firearm** *noun* a gun, especially a rifle or pistol.

**firebrand** *noun* a person who stirs up trouble.

**firecracker** *noun* (*Amer.*) an explosive firework.

**firedamp** *noun* the miners' name for methane, which is explosive when mixed in certain proportions with air.

**firedog** *noun* an iron support (usually one of a pair) for holding logs in a fireplace.

**firefighter** *noun* = FIREMAN (sense 1).

**firefly** *noun* a beetle that gives off a phosphorescent light.

**fireman** *noun* (*plural* **firemen**) **1** a member of a fire brigade. **2** one whose job is to tend a furnace etc.

**fireplace** *noun* **1** an open recess for a domestic fire, at the base of a chimney. **2** the surrounding structure.

**fireproof** *adjective* able to resist fire or great heat; *fireproof dishes.*

**fireside** *noun* the part of a room near a fireplace; this as the centre of one's home.

**firewood** *noun* wood for use as fuel.

**firework** *noun* **1** a device containing chemicals that burn or explode with spectacular effect, used at celebrations. **2** (**fireworks**) an outburst of anger.

**firing line** **1** the front line of a battle, from which troops fire at the enemy. **2** the forefront of an activity.

**firing-squad** *noun* a group ordered to fire a salute during a military funeral, or to shoot a condemned person.

**firm** *noun* a partnership for carrying on a business; a commercial establishment. ● *adjective* **1** not yielding when pressed, hard, solid. **2** steady, not shaking. **3** securely fixed. **4** established, not easily changed or influenced; *a firm belief; a firm offer.* ● *adverb* firmly; *stand firm.* ● *verb* make or become firm or compact; fix firmly.

**firmament** *noun* (*poetic*) the sky with its clouds and stars.

**first** *adjective* coming before all others in time, order, or importance. ● *noun* **1** something that is first; the first day of a month; the first occurrence or achievement of something. **2** first-class honours in a university degree. **3** first gear. ● *adverb* **1** before all others. **2** before another event or time; *finish this work first.* **3** for the first time; *when did you first see him?* **4** in preference; *will see him damned first.* **5** first class; *I usually travel first.* □ **at first** at the beginning. **at first hand** directly from the original source. **first aid** treatment given to an injured person before a doctor comes. **first-born** *adjective & noun* eldest, the eldest child. **first class** **1** a set of persons or things grouped together as better than others. **2** the best accommodation in a train, aircraft, etc. **3** a category of mail that is to be delivered quickly. **4** (used as *adverb*) in or by first-class accommodation etc. **first-class** *adjective* **1** of the best quality; very good. **2** of or using first-class accommodation etc. **first cousin** *see* COUSIN. **first-day cover** an envelope with stamps postmarked on the first day of issue. **first-degree burn** a non-serious surface burn. **first-footing** *noun* (*Scottish*) the custom of being the first to cross the threshold in the New Year. **first-fruits** *plural noun* **1** the first of a season's agricultural products. **2** the first results of work etc. **first-generation** *see* GENERATION. **First Lady** the wife of the President of the USA. **first mate** the second in command on a merchant ship. **first name** a personal or Christian name. **first night** the first public performance of a play etc. **first offender** a criminal with no previous convictions. **first officer** = FIRST MATE. **first person** *see* PERSON. **first-rate** *adjective* of the best class, excellent. ● *adverb* (*informal*) very well. **first thing** (*informal*) before anything else.

**firsthand** *adjective & adverb* directly from the original source.

**firstly** *adverb* first, as a first consideration.

**firth** *noun* (also **frith**) an estuary or a narrow inlet of the sea.

**fiscal** *adjective* of public revenue. ● *noun* a legal official in some countries.

**Fischer** (**fish**-er), Bobby (Robert James) (born 1943), American chess-player, world champion 1972–5.

**fish**[1] *noun* (*plural* **fish** or **fishes**) **1** a cold-blooded animal living wholly in water. **2** its flesh as food. **3** (*informal*) a person; *an odd fish*. **4** (**the Fish** or **Fishes**) a sign of the zodiac, Pisces. ● *verb* **1** try to catch fish. **2** search for something under water or by reaching into something; (*informal*) bring out or up in this way; *fished out his keys*. **3** (usually foll. by *for*) try to obtain by hinting or indirect questioning; *fishing for information*. □ **fish cake** a small cake of shredded fish and mashed potato. **fish-eye lens** a very wide-angled lens producing a distorting effect. **fish finger** a small oblong piece of fish in batter or breadcrumbs. **fish-hook** *noun* a barbed hook for catching fish. **fish-meal** *noun* ground dried fish used as a fertilizer. **fish out of water** a person out of his or her element. **fish-slice** *noun* a flat slotted cooking utensil. **have other fish to fry** have more important business to attend to.

**fish**[2] *noun* a piece of wood or iron etc. to strength a mast or beam. □ **fish-plate** *noun* a flat plate of iron etc. connecting the rails of a railway.

**fisherman** *noun* (*plural* **fishermen**) a person who catches fish for a living or as a sport.

**fishery** *noun* **1** a place where fishing is carried on. **2** the business of fishing.

**fishing** *noun* trying to catch fish. □ **fishing line** a thread with a baited hook for catching fish. **fishing-rod** *noun* a long rod to which a line is attached, used for fishing.

**fishmonger** *noun* a shopkeeper who sells fish.

**fishnet** *adjective* (of fabric) made in a kind of open mesh.

**fishy** *adjective* (**fishier**, **fishiest**) **1** like fish, smelling or tasting of fish. **2** (*informal*) causing disbelief or suspicion; *a fishy story*. □ **fishily** *adverb*, **fishiness** *noun*

**fissile** (**fi**-syl) *adjective* **1** tending to split. **2** capable of undergoing nuclear fission.

**fission** *noun* **1** splitting of the nucleus of certain atoms, with release of energy. **2** splitting or division of biological cells as a method of reproduction.

**fissionable** *adjective* capable of undergoing nuclear fission.

**fissure** (**fish**-er) *noun* a cleft made by splitting or separation of parts.

**fist** *noun* the hand when tightly closed, with the fingers bent into the palm.

**fisticuffs** *plural noun* fighting with the fists.

**fistula** (**fiss**-tew-lă) *noun* (*plural* **fistulas** or **fistulae**) **1** a long pipe-like ulcer. **2** an abnormal or surgically made passage in the body. **3** a natural pipe or spout in whales, insects, etc. □ **fistular** *adjective*

**fit**[1] *noun* **1** a brief spell of an illness or its symptoms; *a fit of coughing*. **2** a sudden violent seizure of epilepsy, apoplexy, etc., with convulsions or loss of consciousness. **3** an attack of strong feeling; *a fit of rage*. **4** a short period of a certain feeling or activity, an impulse; *a fit of energy*. □ **have a fit** (*informal*) be outraged. **in fits and starts** in short bursts of activity, not steadily or regularly.

**fit**[2] *adjective* (**fitter**, **fittest**) **1** suitable or well adapted for something, good enough. **2** right and proper, fitting. **3** feeling in a suitable condition to do something; *worked till they were fit to drop*. **4** in good athletic condition or health. ● *verb* (**fitted**, **fitting**) **1** be the right shape and size for something. **2** put clothing on (a person) and adjust it to the right shape and size. **3** put into place; *fit a lock on the door*. **4** (usually foll. by *for*) make or be suitable or competent; *his training fitted him for the position*. ● *noun* the way a thing fits; *the coat is a good fit*. □ **fit in 1** make room or time etc. for. **2** be or cause to be harmonious or in a suitable relationship. **fit out** *or* **up** supply or equip. **fitted carpet** one cut to fit the floor exactly. **see** *or* **think fit** decide or choose to do something. □ **fitly** *adverb*, **fitness** *noun*

**fitful** *adjective* occurring in short periods, not regularly or steadily. □ **fitfully** *adverb*

**fitment** *noun* a piece of fixed furniture.

**fitter** *noun* **1** a person who supervises the fitting of clothes etc. **2** a mechanic who fits together and adjusts machinery.

**fitting** *adjective* proper, suitable. ● *noun* **1** the process of having a garment etc. fitted. **2** (**fittings**) the fixtures and fitments of a building.

**Fitzgerald¹**, Ella (born 1918), American jazz singer.

**Fitzgerald²**, (Francis) Scott (Key) (1896–1940), American novelist.

**five** *adjective & noun* one more than four (5, V). □ **five o'clock shadow** beard-growth visible towards the end of the day. **five-star** *adjective* of the highest class.

**fivefold** *adjective & adverb* **1** five times as much or as many. **2** consisting of five parts.

**fiver** *noun* (*informal*) £5, a five-pound note.

**fives** *noun* a game in which a ball is struck with gloved hands or a bat against the walls of a court.

**fix** *verb* **1** fasten firmly. **2** implant (facts or ideas) firmly in the mind or memory. **3** direct (the eyes or attention) steadily. **4** establish, specify; *fixed a time for the meeting*; *how are you fixed for cash?* **5** treat (a photographic image or a colour etc.) with a substance that prevents it from fading or changing colour. **6** repair. **7** (*informal*) deal with, get even with. **8** (*informal*) use bribery or deception or improper influence on, arrange (the result of a race etc.) fraudulently. **9** (*slang*) inject a narcotic. ● *noun* **1** (*informal*) an awkward situation; *be in a fix*. **2** the finding of the position of a ship or aircraft etc. by taking bearings; the position found. **3** (*slang*) an addict's dose of a narcotic drug. □ **fixed star** an ordinary star, one that (unlike the sun and planets) is so far from its earth that it seems to have no motion of its own. **fix on** choose, decide on. **fix up 1** arrange; organize. **2** provide for; *fixed him up for the night*.

**fixated** *adjective* having a fixation.

**fixation** *noun* **1** fixing, being fixed. **2** an abnormal emotional attachment to a person or thing. **3** concentration on one idea, an obsession.

**fixative** *adjective* tending to fix or secure. ● *noun* **1** a substance for keeping things in position. **2** a substance for fixing colours etc., or for preventing perfumes from evaporating too quickly.

**fixedly** (**fiks**-id-li) *adverb* in a fixed way; intently.

**fixer** *noun* **1** a person or thing that fixes something. **2** a substance for fixing photographic images.

**fixings** *plural noun* (*Amer.*) **1** apparatus, equipment. **2** the trimmings of a dress or dish.

**fixity** *noun* a fixed state, stability, permanence.

**fixture** *noun* **1** a thing that is fixed in position. **2** a person or thing that is firmly established and unlikely to leave. **3** a date appointed for a match or race etc.; the match or race itself.

**fizz** *verb* make a hissing or spluttering sound as when gas escapes in bubbles from a liquid. ● *noun* **1** this sound. **2** a fizzy drink; *gin fizz*. □ **fizzy** *adjective*, **fizziness** *noun*

**fizzle** *verb* make a feeble fizzing sound. □ **fizzle out** end feebly or unsuccessfully.

**fjord** alternative spelling of FIORD.

**FL, Fla.** *abbreviation* Florida.

**fl.** *abbreviation* **1** floruit. **2** fluid.

**flab** *noun* (*informal*) fat; flabbiness.

**flabbergast** *verb* (*informal*) astonish, astound.

**flabby** *adjective* (**flabbier, flabbiest**) fat and limp, not firm. □ **flabbily** *adverb*, **flabbiness** *noun*

**flaccid** (**flak**-sid) *adjective* hanging loose or wrinkled, not firm. □ **flaccidly** *adverb*, **flaccidity** *noun*

**flag¹** *noun* **1** a piece of cloth attached by one edge to a staff or rope and used as a country's emblem or as a signal. **2** an oblong device used as a signal that a taxi is for hire. **3** a small device of paper etc. resembling a flag. **4** a plant with blade-like leaves, especially an iris. **5** a flagstone. ● *verb* (**flagged, flagging**) **1** mark out with flags. **2** signal with or as if with a flag. **3** hang down limply, droop. **4** lose vigour, become weak; *interest flagged*. **5** pave with flagstones. □ **flag-day** *noun* a day on which money is raised for a cause by the sale of small flags or badges to passers-by. **flag down** signal to stop. **flag of convenience** a foreign flag of the nationality under which a ship is registered to evade taxation or certain regulations. **flag-pole** *noun* a flagstaff.

**flagellate** (**flaj**-ěl-ayt) *verb* whip. □ **flagellation** *noun*

**flageolet** (flaj-ŏ-**let**) *noun* a small pipe like a recorder.

**flagon** *noun* **1** a large rounded bottle in which wine or cider etc. is sold, usually holding twice as much as an ordinary bottle. **2** a vessel with a handle, lip, and lid for serving wine.

**flagrant** (**flay**-gránt) *adjective* (of an offence or an offender) very bad and obvious. □ **flagrantly** *adverb*, **flagrancy** *noun*

**flagship** *noun* **1** a ship that carries an admiral. **2** the principal vessel of a shipping-line. **3** a firm's best or most important product.

**flagstaff** *noun* a pole on which a flag is hoisted.

**flagstone** *noun* a flat slab of rock used for paving.

**flail** *noun* an old-fashioned tool for threshing grain, consisting of a strong stick hinged on a long handle. ●*verb* **1** beat with or as if with a flail. **2** wave or swing about wildly.

**flair** *noun* a natural ability to do something well or to select what is good or useful etc.

**flak** *noun* **1** shells fired by anti-aircraft guns. **2** adverse criticism; abuse. □ **flak jacket** a heavy protective jacket reinforced with metal.

**flake** *noun* **1** a small light piece of snow. **2** a small thin leaf-like piece of something. **3** dogfish or other shark sold as food. ●*verb* **1** come off in flakes. **2** separate into flakes. □ **flake out** (*informal*) faint or fall asleep from exhaustion. □ **flaky** *adjective*

**flambé** (**flahm**-bay) *adjective* (of food) covered with alcohol and served alight. (¶ French, = singed.)

**flamboyant** *adjective* **1** coloured or decorated in a very showy way. **2** (of people) having a very showy appearance or manner. □ **flamboyantly** *adverb*, **flamboyance** *noun*

**flame** *noun* **1** a bright tongue-shaped portion of ignited gases burning visibly. **2** bright red. **3** passion, especially of love. ●*verb* **1** burn with flames, send out flames. **2** become bright or glowing; *his face flamed with anger.* □ **flame-thrower** *noun* a weapon throwing a jet of flame. **old flame** (*informal*) a former boyfriend or girlfriend.

**flamenco** (flă-**menk**-oh) *noun* (*plural* **flamencos**) a Spanish gypsy style of song or dance.

**flaming** *adjective* **1** very hot or bright. **2** (*informal*) damned; *that flaming cat.*

**flamingo** (flă-**ming**-oh) *noun* (*plural* **flamingoes**) a long-legged wading bird with a long neck and pinkish feathers.

**flammable** *adjective* able to be set on fire. □ **flammability** *noun*

▪**Usage** See the note under **inflammable**.

**flan** *noun* an open pastry or sponge case filled with fruit or a savoury filling.

**Flanders** an area in the south-west of the Low Countries, now divided between Belgium, France, and Holland, the scene of much fighting in the First World War. □ **Flanders poppy 1** a red poppy used as an emblem of Allied forces who died in the First World War. **2** an artificial red poppy for wearing on Remembrance Sunday, sold in aid of needy ex-service people.

**flange** (*pronounced* flanj) *noun* a projecting rim or edge.

**flank** *noun* **1** the fleshy part of the side of the body between the last rib and the hip. **2** the side of a building or mountain. **3** the right or left side of a body of troops etc. ●*verb* place or be situated at the side of.

**flannel** *noun* **1** a kind of loosely woven woollen fabric. **2** a cloth used for washing the face etc. **3** (*slang*) nonsense, flattery, bragging. **4** (**flannels**) trousers made of flannel or similar fabric. ●*verb* (**flannelled, flannelling**; *Amer.* **flanneled, flanneling**) **1** wash with a flannel. **2** (*slang*) flatter.

**flannelette** *noun* cotton fabric made to look and feel like flannel.

**flap** *verb* (**flapped, flapping**) **1** sway or be swayed up and down or from side to side, wave about. **2** give a light blow with something flat; *flapped at a fly.* **3** (*informal*) be agitated or in a panic. ●*noun* **1** the action or sound of flapping. **2** a light blow with something flat. **3** a broad piece hinged or attached at one side; a hinged or sliding section on an aircraft wing etc. used to control lift. **4** (*informal*) a state of agitation or fuss; *he is in a flap.* □ **with ears flapping** (*informal*) listening eagerly.

**flapjack** *noun* **1** (especially *Amer.*) a pancake. **2** a sweet oatcake.

**flapper** *noun* **1** a person apt to panic. **2** a frivolous young woman in the 1920s.

**flare** *verb* **1** blaze with a sudden irregular flame. **2** burst into sudden activity or anger; *tempers flared.* **3** widen gradually outwards. ●*noun* **1** a sudden outburst of flame. **2** a device producing a flaring light as a signal or for illumination. **3** a flared shape, a gradual widening. **4** (**flares**) wide-bottomed trousers. □ **flare up 1** burst into flame. **2** become suddenly angry. **flare-up** *noun* a sudden outburst.

**flash** *verb* **1** give out a brief or intermittent bright light. **2** come suddenly into view or into the mind; *the idea flashed upon me.* **3** move rapidly; *the train flashed past.* **4** (of water) rush along, rise and flow. **5** cause to shine briefly. **6** signal with a light or lights. **7** send (news etc.) by radio or telegraph. **8** (*slang*) expose the genitals briefly in an indecent way. ●*noun* **1** a sudden burst of flame or light. **2** a sudden showing of wit or feeling. **3** a very brief time; *in a flash.* **4** a rush of water. **5** a brief news item sent out by radio etc. **6** a device producing a brief bright light in photography. **7** a coloured patch of cloth as an emblem on a military uniform etc. ●*adjective* (*informal*) flashy. □ **flash bulb** a bulb giving a bright light for flashlight photography. **flash-flood** *noun* a sudden destructive flood. **flash in the pan** something that makes a promising start and then fails. (¶ Originally an explosion of gunpowder in the 'pan' of an old gun without actually firing the charge.)

**flashback** noun the changing of the scene in a story or film to a scene at an earlier time.

**flasher** noun **1** an automatic device for flashing a light intermittently. **2** (*slang*) a man who indecently exposes himself.

**flashing** noun a strip of metal to prevent water entering at a joint in roofing etc.

**flashlight** noun **1** an intensely bright flash of light used for photography. **2** *Amer.* an electric torch.

**flashpoint** noun **1** the temperature at which vapour from oil etc. will ignite. **2** the point at which anger is ready to break out.

**flashy** adjective showy, gaudy. □ **flashily** adverb, **flashiness** noun

**flask** noun **1** a narrow-necked bottle. **2** a vacuum flask.

**flat** adjective (**flatter**, **flattest**) **1** horizontal, level. **2** spread out; lying at full length. **3** smooth and even; with a broad level surface and little depth; *a flat cap*. **4** (of a tyre) deflated because of a puncture etc. **5** absolute, unqualified; *a flat refusal*. **6** dull, monotonous. **7** (of drink) having lost its effervescence. **8** (of a battery etc.) unable to generate any more electric current. **9** (in music) below the correct pitch; (as *D flat* etc.) a semitone lower than the note or key stated. ● adverb **1** in a flat manner. **2** (*informal*) completely; *I am flat broke*. **3** (*informal*) exactly; *in ten seconds flat*. **4** below the correct pitch in music; *he was singing flat*. ● noun **1** a flat thing or part, level ground. **2** a set of rooms on one floor, used as a residence. **3** (**the flat**) the season of flat races for horses. **4** (in music) a note that is a semitone lower than the corresponding one of natural pitch; the sign (♭) indicating this. □ **fall flat** fail to win applause or appreciation. **flat feet** feet with less than the normal arch beneath. **flat-footed** adjective **1** having flat feet. **2** (*informal*) resolute. **3** unprepared. **flat-iron** noun (*hist.*) a heavy iron heated by external means. **flat out 1** at top speed. **2** using all one's strength or resources. **flat race** a horse race over level ground, without jumps. **flat rate** a rate that is the same in all cases, not proportional. **that's flat** (*informal*) that is definite. □ **flatly** adverb, **flatness** noun

**flatfish** noun a fish with a flattened, thin body, e.g. sole or plaice.

**flatlet** noun a small flat (sense 2).

**flatmate** noun a person sharing a flat.

**flatten** verb make or become flat.

**flatter** verb **1** compliment (a person) excessively or insincerely, especially in order to win favour. **2** gratify by honouring; *we were flattered to receive an invitation.*

**3** represent (a person or thing) favourably in a portrait etc. so that good looks are exaggerated. □ **flatter oneself** please or delude oneself with a belief. □ **flatterer** noun

**flattery** noun **1** flattering. **2** excessive or insincere compliments.

**flattish** adjective rather flat.

**flatulent** (flat-yoo-lĕnt) adjective **1** causing or suffering from the formation of gas in the digestive tract. **2** (of speech etc.) pretentious. □ **flatulence** noun

**flatworm** noun a worm with a flattened body.

**Flaubert** (floh-bair), Gustave (1821–80), French novelist, author of *Madame Bovary*.

**flaunt** verb **1** display proudly or ostentatiously. **2** wave proudly.

■ **Usage** This word is sometimes used incorrectly in place of **flout**.

**flautist** (flaw-tist) noun a flute-player.

**flavour** noun **1** a distinctive taste. **2** a special quality or characteristic; *the story has a romantic flavour*. ● verb give flavour to, season.

**flavouring** noun a substance used to give flavour to food.

**flaw** noun **1** an imperfection. **2** a squall of wind. ● verb spoil, damage.

**flawless** adjective without a flaw; perfect. □ **flawlessly** adverb

**flax** noun **1** a blue-flowered plant cultivated for the textile fibre obtained from its stem and for its seeds (linseed). **2** its fibre.

**flaxen** adjective **1** made of flax. **2** pale yellow in colour like dressed flax; *flaxen hair*.

**flay** verb **1** strip off the skin or hide of. **2** criticize severely.

**flea** noun a small wingless jumping insect that feeds on human and animal blood. □ **a flea in one's ear** (*informal*) a stinging rebuke. **flea-bite** noun **1** the bite of a flea. **2** a trivial inconvenience or expense. **flea market** a street market selling second-hand goods. **flea-pit** noun a dingy dirty cinema or theatre.

**fleck** noun **1** a very small patch of colour. **2** a small particle, a speck. ● verb mark with specks.

**fled** see FLEE.

**fledged** adjective (of young birds) with fully grown wing-feathers, able to fly. □ **fully-fledged** mature, trained and experienced; *a fully-fledged engineer*.

**fledgling** noun (also **fledgeling**) **1** a young bird that is just fledged. **2** an inexperienced person.

**flee** verb (**fled**, **fleeing**) **1** run or hurry away. **2** run away from; *fled the country*. **3** pass away swiftly, vanish; *all hope had fled*.

**fleece** noun 1 the woolly hair of a sheep or similar animal. 2 a soft fabric used for linings etc. ●verb 1 defraud, rob by trickery. 2 remove the fleece from (a sheep). □ **fleecy** adjective

**fleet** noun 1 the naval force of a country; a number of warships under one commander. 2 a number of ships or aircraft or buses etc. moving or working under one command or ownership. ●adjective (literary) moving swiftly, nimble.

**fleeting** adjective passing quickly, brief; a fleeting glimpse. □ **fleetingly** adverb

**Fleet Street** London newspapers, the English national papers (most of which have or have had headquarters in Fleet Street, London).

**Fleming**[1] noun a native of Flanders or of Flemish-speaking Belgium.

**Fleming**[2], Sir Alexander (1881–1955), Scottish doctor and scientist, who in 1928 discovered the effect of penicillin on bacteria.

**Fleming**[3], Ian (Lancaster) (1908–64), English thriller-writer, creator of the fictional secret agent James Bond.

**Flemish** adjective of Flanders or its people or language. ●noun the Flemish language, one of the two official languages of Belgium.

**flesh** noun 1 the soft substance of an animal body, consisting of muscle and fat. 2 this tissue as food; meat. 3 the body as opposed to mind or soul. 4 the pulpy part of fruits and vegetables. □ **flesh and blood** human nature, people with their emotions and weaknesses. **flesh-coloured** adjective yellowish-pink. **flesh out** make or become substantial. **flesh-wound** noun a wound that does not reach a bone or vital organ. **in the flesh** in person. **one's own flesh and blood** relatives, descendants.

**fleshly** adjective 1 bodily; sensual. 2 worldly rather than spiritual.

**fleshy** adjective 1 of or like flesh. 2 having much flesh, plump; (of plants or fruits etc.) pulpy. □ **fleshiness** noun

**fleur-de-lis** (fler-dĕ-lee) noun (also **fleur-de-lys**) (plural **fleurs-de-lis**, pronounced same) a design of a lily with three petals used in heraldry.

**flew** see FLY[2].

**flews** plural noun the hanging lips of a bloodhound or other dog.

**flex** verb bend (a joint or limb); move (a muscle) so that it bends a joint. ●noun flexible insulated wire used for carrying electric current to a lamp or other appliance.

**flexible** adjective 1 able to bend easily without breaking. 2 adaptable, able to be changed to suit circumstances. □ **flexibly** adverb, **flexibility** noun

**flexion** noun bending, a bent state, especially of a joint or limb.

**flexitime** noun a system of flexible working hours.

**flibbertigibbet** noun a gossiping or frivolous person.

**flick** noun 1 a quick light blow or stroke, e.g. with a whip. 2 (informal) a cinema film. 3 (**the flicks**) (informal) the cinema. ●verb 1 strike or remove with a quick light blow. 2 make a flicking movement. □ **flick-knife** noun a weapon with a blade that springs out when a button is pressed. **flick through** turn over (pages etc.) quickly.

**flicker** verb 1 burn or shine unsteadily. 2 (of hope etc.) occur briefly. 3 quiver, move quickly to and fro. ●noun a flickering movement or light; a brief occurrence of hope etc.

**flier** alternative spelling of FLYER.

**flight** noun 1 the process of flying; the movement or path of a thing through the air. 2 a journey made by air, transport in an aircraft making a particular journey; there are three flights a day to Rome. 3 a flock of birds or insects. 4 a number of aircraft regarded as a unit; an aircraft of the Queen's flight. 5 a series of stairs in a straight line or between two landings; a series of hurdles etc. in a race. 6 swift passage (of time). 7 a mental soaring; a flight of the imagination. 8 the feathers etc. on a dart or arrow. 9 fleeing, running or going away. ●verb 1 shoot (a bird etc.) while it is flying. 2 give (a ball etc.) a certain path through the air. □ **flight-deck** noun the cockpit of a large aircraft. **flight lieutenant** an RAF officer next below squadron leader. **flight path** the planned course of an aircraft. **flight recorder** an electronic device in an aircraft, recording technical details about its flight. **flight sergeant** an RAF rank next above sergeant. **put to flight** cause to flee. **take flight** or **take to flight** flee.

**flightless** adjective (of birds, e.g. penguins) unable to fly.

**flighty** adjective (**flightier, flightiest**) (usually of a woman) irresponsible, frivolous. □ **flightiness** noun

**flimsy** adjective (**flimsier, flimsiest**) 1 light and thin; of loose structure; fragile. 2 unconvincing; a flimsy excuse. □ **flimsily** adverb, **flimsiness** noun

**flinch** verb 1 draw back in fear, wince. 2 shrink from one's duty etc.

**fling** verb (**flung, flinging**) 1 throw violently, angrily, or hurriedly. 2 put or send suddenly or forcefully; flung him into prison. 3 rush, go angrily or violently; she flung out of the room. ●noun 1 the act or movement of flinging. 2 a vigorous Scottish dance; the

*Highland fling.* **3** a spell of indulgence in pleasure; *have a fling.*

**flint** *noun* **1** a very hard kind of stone that can produce sparks when struck against steel. **2** a piece of this. **3** a piece of hard alloy used to produce a spark. □ **flinty** *adjective*

**flintlock** *noun* an old type of gun fired by a spark from a flint.

**flip** *verb* (**flipped, flipping**) **1** flick. **2** toss (a thing) with a sharp movement so that it turns over in the air. **3** (*slang*) show great anger. ● *noun* **1** the action of flipping something. **2** (*informal*) a short flight in an aircraft. **3** a quick tour. ● *adjective* (*informal*) glib, flippant. □ **flip one's lid** (*slang*) show great anger; go mad. **flip side** the reverse side of a gramophone record. **flip through** = FLICK THROUGH.

**flippant** *adjective* not showing proper seriousness; disrespectful. □ **flippantly** *adverb*, **flippancy** *noun*

**flipper** *noun* **1** a limb of certain sea animals (e.g. seals, turtles, penguins), used in swimming. **2** one of a pair of large flat rubber attachments worn on the feet for underwater swimming.

**flipping** *adjective* (*slang*) damned.

**flirt** *verb* **1** (often foll. by *with*) behave in a frivolously amorous manner. **2** (usually foll. by *with*) toy, trifle; *flirted with the idea*; *flirting with death.* ● *noun* a person who flirts. □ **flirtation** *noun*

**flirtatious** *adjective* flirting, fond of flirting. □ **flirtatiously** *adverb*, **flirtatiousness** *noun*

**flit** *verb* (**flitted, flitting**) **1** fly or move lightly and quickly. **2** disappear in a stealthy way. ● *noun* a stealthy move of this kind.

**flitch** *noun* a side of bacon.

**flitter** *verb* flit about.

**float** *verb* **1** rest or drift on the surface of a liquid without sinking; be held up freely in air or gas. **2** cause to do this. **3** move lightly or casually. **4** have or allow (currency) have a variable rate of exchange. **5** launch (a business company or a scheme), especially by getting financial support from the sale of shares. ● *noun* **1** a thing designed to float on liquid; a cork or quill used on a fishing line to show when the bait has been taken; any of the corks supporting the edge of a fishing net. **2** a floating device to control the flow of water, petrol, etc. **3** a structure to enable an aircraft to float on water. **4** a low-bodied cart; a milk-float; a platform on wheels carrying a display in a procession. **5** a sum of money made available for minor expenditures or for giving change. □ **floating kidney** an abnormally movable kidney. **floating rib** a lower rib not joined to the breastbone. **floating voter** a voter not permanently supporting any political party.

**floatation** alternative spelling of FLOTATION.

**floaty** *adjective* (of fabric) light and airy.

**flocculent** *adjective* like tufts of wool; in or showing tufts. □ **flocculence** *noun*

**flock** *noun* **1** a number of sheep, goats, or birds kept together or feeding or travelling together. **2** a large number of people together. **3** a number of people in someone's charge; a Christian congregation. **4** a tuft of wool or cotton etc. **5** wool or cotton waste used for stuffing mattresses etc.; powdered wool or cloth. ● *verb* gather or go in a flock.

**floe** *noun* a sheet of floating ice.

**flog** *verb* (**flogged, flogging**) **1** beat severely with a rod or whip. **2** (*slang*) sell. □ **flog a dead horse** waste one's efforts. **flog to death** (*informal*) talk about or promote at tedious length. □ **flogging** *noun*

**flood** *noun* **1** the coming of a great quantity of water over a place that is usually dry; the water itself. **2** (**the Flood**) that of the time of Noah, described in Genesis. **3** a great outpouring or outburst; *a flood of abuse.* **4** the inflow of the tide. ● *verb* **1** cover or fill with a flood, overflow. **2** (of a river etc.) become flooded. **3** come in great quantities; *letters flooded in.* **4** have a haemorrhage of the womb.

**floodgate** *noun* **1** a gate that can be opened or closed to control the flow of water, especially the lower gate of a lock. **2** (usually as **floodgates**) a last restraint holding back tears, rain, anger, etc.

**floodlight** *noun* a lamp used for producing a broad bright beam of light to light up a stage or building etc. ● *verb* (**floodlit, floodlighting**) illuminate with this.

**floor** *noun* **1** the lower surface of a room, the part on which one stands. **2** the bottom of the sea or of a cave etc. **3** (in legislative assemblies) the part of the assembly hall where members sit. **4** a minimum level for wages or prices. **5** a storey of a building. ● *verb* **1** put a floor into (a building). **2** knock down (a person) in a fight. **3** (*informal*) baffle, overwhelm (a person) with a problem or argument. □ **floor manager** the stage manager of a television production. **floor show** an entertainment in a nightclub. **take the floor 1** begin to dance. **2** speak in a debate.

**floorboard** *noun* one of the wooden boards forming the floor of a room.

**flooring** *noun* boards etc. used as a floor.

**floozie** *noun* (also **floozy**) (*informal*) a woman, especially a disreputable one.

**flop** *verb* (**flopped, flopping**) **1** hang or sway heavily and loosely. **2** fall or move or sit down clumsily. **3** (*slang*) be a failure. ● *noun*

**1** a flopping movement or sound. **2** (*slang*) a failure. ●*adverb* with a flop.

**floppy** *adjective* (**floppier, floppiest**) hanging heavily and loosely, not firm or rigid. ●*noun* (in full **floppy disk**) *Computing* a flexible magnetic disk for the storage of data. □ **floppiness** *noun*

**flora** *noun* the plants of an area or period of time.

**floral** *adjective* decorated with or depicting flowers.

**Florence** a city of north Italy.

**Florentine** (**flo-rĕn-tyn**) *adjective* of Florence. ●*noun* a native of Florence.

**floret** *noun* a small flower.

**floribunda** (**flor-i-bun-dă**) *noun* a rose or other plant bearing dense clusters of flowers.

**florid** *adjective* **1** elaborate and ornate. **2** (of the complexion) ruddy.

**Florida** a State forming a peninsula of the south-eastern USA.

**florin** *noun* **1** a Dutch guilder. **2** a former British coin worth two shillings.

**florist** *noun* a person whose business is the selling or growing of flowers.

**floruit** (**flo-roo-it**) *noun & verb* (the period at which a person) was alive and working. (¶ Latin.)

**floss** *noun* **1** a mass of silky fibres. **2** silk thread with little or no twist, used in embroidery. **3** = DENTAL FLOSS. □ **flossy** *adjective*

**flotation** *noun* (also **floatation**) the launching or financing of a commercial venture.

**flotilla** (**flŏ-til-ă**) *noun* **1** a small fleet. **2** a fleet of boats or small ships.

**flotsam** *noun* wreckage found floating. □ **flotsam and jetsam 1** odds and ends. **2** vagrants, tramps, etc.

**flounce** *verb* go in an impatient annoyed manner; *flounced out of the room*. ●*noun* **1** a flouncing movement. **2** a deep frill of material sewn by its upper edge to a skirt etc.

**flounced** *adjective* trimmed with a flounce.

**flounder** *noun* a small edible flatfish. ●*verb* **1** move clumsily and with difficulty as in mud. **2** make mistakes or become confused when trying to do something.

**flour** *noun* fine meal or powder made from ground wheat or other grain. ●*verb* cover or sprinkle with flour. □ **floury** *adjective*

**flourish** *verb* **1** thrive in growth or development. **2** prosper, be successful. **3** (of famous people) be alive and working at a certain time; *Beethoven flourished in the early 19th century*. **4** wave (a thing) dramatically. ●*noun* **1** a dramatic sweeping gesture. **2** a flowing ornamental curve in writing etc. **3** a fanfare.

**flout** *verb* disobey openly and scornfully.

■**Usage** See the note under **flaunt**.

**flow** *verb* **1** glide along as a stream, move freely like a liquid or gas; circulate. **2** proceed steadily and continuously; *keep the traffic flowing*. **3** (of talk or literary style) proceed smoothly and evenly. **4** hang loosely; (of a line or curve) be smoothly continuous. **5** gush forth; (of the tide) come in, rise. **6** come (from a source), be the result. ●*noun* **1** a flowing movement or mass. **2** the amount that flows. **3** an outpouring, a copious supply. **4** the inward movement of the tide towards the land; *ebb and flow*. □ **flow chart** (*or* **diagram** *or* **sheet**) a diagram showing the movement of things through a series of processes, e.g. in manufacturing.

**flower** *noun* **1** the part of a plant from which seed or fruit develops. **2** a blossom and its stem for use as a decoration etc., usually in groups. **3** a plant that is cultivated or noted for its fine flowers. **4** the best part of something. ●*verb* (of a plant) produce flowers. □ **in flower** with the flowers out. □ **flowered** *adjective*

**flowerpot** *noun* a pot in which a plant may be grown.

**flowery** *adjective* **1** (of language) full of ornamental phrases. **2** full of flowers.

**flown** *see* FLY².

**flu** *noun* (*informal*) influenza.

**fluctuate** *verb* (of levels, prices, etc.) vary irregularly, rise and fall. □ **fluctuation** *noun*

**flue** *noun* **1** a smoke-duct in a chimney. **2** a channel for conveying heat.

**fluent** (**floo-ĕnt**) *adjective* **1** (of a person) able to speak smoothly and readily. **2** (of speech) coming smoothly and readily. □ **fluently** *adverb*, **fluency** *noun*

**fluff** *noun* **1** a light soft downy substance. **2** (*informal*) a bungled attempt; a mistake in speaking. ●*verb* **1** shake into a soft mass. **2** (*informal*) bungle.

**fluffy** *adjective* (**fluffier, fluffiest**) having or covered with a soft mass of fur or fibres. □ **fluffiness** *noun*

**fluid** *noun* a substance that is able to flow freely as liquids and gases do. ●*adjective* **1** able to flow freely, not solid or rigid. **2** (of a situation) not stable. □ **fluid ounce** one-twentieth of a pint; (*Amer.*) one-sixteenth of an American pint. □ **fluidity** (**floo-id-iti**) *noun*

**fluke** *noun* **1** an accidental stroke of good luck. **2** the broad triangular flat end of each arm of an anchor. **3** the barbed head of a harpoon etc. **4** one of the lobes of a whale's tail. **5** a flatfish, especially the flounder. **6** a flatworm found as a parasite in sheep's liver.

**flummery** *noun* **1** a sweet pudding made with milk. **2** nonsense, empty talk.

**flummox** *verb* (*informal*) baffle.

**flung** *see* FLING.

**flunk** *verb* (*Amer. informal*) fail, especially in an examination.

**flunkey** *noun* (also **flunky**) (*plural* **flunkeys** or **flunkies**) (*informal*, usually *scornful*) a liveried servant.

**fluoresce** (floo-er-**ess**) *verb* become fluorescent.

**fluorescent** (floo-er-**ess**-ĕnt) *adjective* (of substances) taking in radiations and sending them out in the form of light; (of lamps) containing such a substance; (of a screen) coated with this. □ **fluorescence** *noun*

**fluoridate** (floo-er-i-dayt) *verb* add traces of fluoride to drinking-water to prevent tooth decay. □ **fluoridation** *noun*

**fluoride** *noun* a compound of fluorine and one other element.

**fluorine** (floo-er-een) *noun* a chemical element (symbol F), a pale yellow corrosive gas.

**flurry** *noun* **1** a short sudden rush of wind, rain, or snow. **2** a commotion. **3** a state of nervous agitation. ● *verb* (**flurried, flurrying**) fluster, agitate.

**flush** *verb* **1** become red in the face because of a rush of blood to the skin. **2** cause (the face) to redden in this way. **3** fill with pride; *flushed with success*. **4** cleanse (a drain or lavatory etc.) with a flow of water; dispose of in this way. **5** (of water) rush out in a flood. **6** cause (a bird) to fly up and away; drive out. ● *noun* **1** flushing of the face, a blush. **2** excitement caused by emotion; *the first flush of victory*. **3** a rush of water. **4** fresh growth of vegetation. **5** (in poker) a hand of cards all of one suit. ● *adjective* **1** level, in the same plane, without projections; *doors that are flush with the walls*. **2** (*informal*) well supplied with money. □ **royal flush** (in poker) a straight flush headed by an ace. **straight flush** (in poker) a flush that is a straight sequence.

**fluster** *verb* make nervous and confused. ● *noun* a flustered state.

**flute** *noun* **1** a wind instrument consisting of a long pipe held sideways with holes stopped by fingers or keys and a mouthhole at the side. **2** an ornamental groove. ● *verb* **1** speak or utter in high flute-like tones. **2** make ornamental grooves in.

**fluting** *noun* ornamental grooves.

**flutter** *verb* **1** move the wings hurriedly in flying or trying to fly. **2** wave or flap quickly and irregularly; (of the heart) beat feebly and irregularly. ● *noun* **1** a fluttering movement or beat. **2** a state of nervous excitement. **3** a stir, a sensation. **4** (*in-*

*formal*) a slight gamble; *have a flutter*. **5** rapid variation in the pitch or loudness of reproduced sound.

**fluvial** (floo-vi-ăl) *adjective* of or found in rivers.

**flux** *noun* **1** a continuous succession of changes; *in a state of flux*. **2** flowing, flowing out. **3** discharge.

**fly¹** *noun* **1** a two-winged insect. **2** a disease in plants and animals caused by one of various flies. **3** a natural or artificial fly used as bait in fishing. ● *adjective* (*slang*) astute, knowing. □ **fly-blown** *adjective* (of meat etc.) tainted by flies' eggs. **fly-fishing** *noun* fishing with flies as bait. **fly in the ointment** one small thing that spoils enjoyment. **fly on the wall** an unnoticed observer. **fly-paper** *noun* sticky paper for trapping or poisoning flies. **like flies** in large numbers; *dying like flies*. **there are no flies on him** (*slang*) he is very astute.

**fly²** *verb* (**flew, flown, flying**) **1** move through the air by means of wings as a bird does. **2** travel through the air or through space. **3** travel in an aircraft. **4** direct or control the flight of (an aircraft etc.); transport in an aircraft. **5** raise (a flag) so that it waves; (of a flag) wave in the air. **6** make (a kite) rise and stay aloft. **7** go or move quickly, rush along; (of time) pass quickly. **8** be scattered violently; *sparks flew in all directions*. **9** become angry etc. quickly; *flew into a rage*. **10** flee from; *must fly the country*. ● *noun* **1** flying. **2** (often as **flies**) a trouser-fastening. **3** a flap at the entrance of a tent. **4** a speed-regulating device in clockwork or machinery. □ **fly a kite** (*informal*) do something to test public opinion. **fly at** attack violently, either physically or with words. **fly-away** *adjective* (of hair) fine and difficult to control. **fly-by-night** *noun* an unreliable person. **fly-half** *noun* a stand-off half in Rugby football. **fly high** behave very ambitiously. **fly in the face of** disregard or disobey openly. **fly off the handle** (*informal*) lose one's temper. **fly-past** *noun* a ceremonial flight of aircraft. **fly-post** *verb* display (posters etc.) in unauthorized places.

**flycatcher** *noun* a type of bird that catches insects in the air.

**flyer** *noun* (also **flier**) **1** a bird etc. that flies. **2** an animal or vehicle that moves very fast. **3** an aviator. **4** a high-flyer.

**flying** *adjective* able to fly. □ **flying buttress** a buttress that springs from a separate structure, usually forming an arch with the wall it supports. **flying colours** great credit gained in a test etc. **flying doctor** a doctor who visits patients (e.g. in the Australian outback) by air. **flying fish** a tropical fish with wing-like fins, able to rise into the air. **flying fox** a fruit-eating bat. **flying**

**officer** an RAF rank next below flight lieutenant. **flying picket** a picket organized for moving from place to place. **flying saucer** an unidentified saucer-shaped object reported as seen in the sky and imagined to come from outer space. **flying squad** a detachment of police etc. organized for rapid movement. **flying start** a vigorous start giving one an initial advantage. **flying visit** a brief or hasty visit.

**flyleaf** *noun* a blank leaf at the beginning or end of a book.

**Flynn**, Errol (1909–59), American film actor, noted for his swashbuckling roles.

**flyover** *noun* a bridge that carries one road or railway over another.

**flysheet** *noun* **1** a cover over a tent for extra protection. **2** a circular with two or four pages.

**flyweight** *noun* a boxing-weight (48–51 kg) below bantamweight.

**flywheel** *noun* a heavy wheel revolving on a shaft to regulate machinery.

**FM** *abbreviation* frequency modulation.

**Fm** *symbol* fermium.

**f-number** *noun* a ratio used in photography to calculate the amount of light passing through the lens.

**foal** *noun* the young of a horse or of a related animal. ● *verb* give birth to a foal. □ **in foal** (of a mare) pregnant.

**foam** *noun* **1** a collection of small bubbles formed in or on a liquid. **2** the froth of saliva or perspiration. **3** rubber or plastic in a light spongy form. ● *verb* form or send out foam. □ **foamy** *adjective*

**fob** *noun* **1** an ornament worn hanging from a watch-chain etc. **2** a tab on a key-ring. □ **fob off** (**fobbed, fobbing**) **1** palm (a thing) off. **2** deceive (a person) into accepting something inferior.

**focal** *adjective* of or at a focus. □ **focal distance** *or* **length** the distance between the centre of a mirror or lens and its focus. **focal point 1** = FOCUS (*noun* sense 1). **2** the centre of interest or activity.

**fo'c's'le** alternative spelling of FORECASTLE.

**focus** (foh-kŭs) *noun* (*plural* **focuses** *or* **foci**, *pronounced* foh-sy) **1** the point at which rays meet or from which they appear to proceed. **2** the point or distance at which an object is most clearly seen by the eye or through a lens; *bring into focus*. **3** an adjustment on a lens to produce a clear image at varying distances. **4** a centre of activity or interest. ● *verb* (**focused, focusing** *or* **focussed, focussing**) **1** adjust the focus of (a lens or the eye). **2** bring into focus. **3** concentrate or be concentrated or directed (on a centre etc.).

**fodder** *noun* dried food, hay, etc. for horses and farm animals.

**foe** *noun* an enemy.

**foetid** alternative spelling of FETID.

**foetus** (fee-tŭs) *noun* (*Amer.* **fetus**) (*plural* **foetuses**) a developed embryo in the womb or egg; a human embryo more than 8 weeks after conception. □ **foetal** *adjective*

**fog** *noun* **1** thick mist that is difficult to see through. **2** cloudiness on a photographic negative etc., obscuring the image. ● *verb* (**fogged, fogging**) **1** cover or become covered with fog or condensed vapour. **2** cause cloudiness on (a negative etc.). **3** bewilder or confuse. □ **fog-lamp** *noun* a lamp for use on a vehicle in fog.

**fogey** alternative spelling of FOGY.

**foggy** *adjective* (**foggier, foggiest**) **1** full of fog. **2** made opaque by condensed vapour etc.; clouded. **3** obscure, vague; *only a foggy idea*. □ **not the foggiest** (*informal*) no idea at all. □ **fogginess** *noun*

**foghorn** *noun* a sounding instrument for warning ships in fog.

**fogy** *noun* (also **fogey**) (*plural* **fogies**) a person with old-fashioned ideas.

**foible** (foi-bŭl) *noun* a harmless peculiarity or minor weakness in a person's character.

**foil** *noun* **1** metal hammered or rolled into a thin sheet; *tin foil*. **2** a person or thing that contrasts strongly with another and therefore makes the other's qualities more obvious. **3** a long thin sword with a button on the point, used in fencing. ● *verb* thwart, frustrate.

**foist** *verb* cause a person to accept (something inferior or unwelcome or undeserved); *the job was foisted on us*.

**Fokine** (foh-keen), Michel (Mikhail Mikhailovich) (1880–1942), Russian dancer and choreographer.

**Fokker**, Anthony Herman Gerard (1890–1939), Dutch pioneer aircraft designer.

**fold** *verb* **1** bend or turn (a flexible thing) so that one part lies on another; close or flatten by pressing parts together. **2** become folded; be able to be folded. **3** clasp (the arms etc.) about; hold close to one's chest. **4** envelop. **5** blend (an ingredient) in cooking by turning it over carefully with a spoon. **6** collapse, cease to function; *the business had folded*. ● *noun* **1** a folded part. **2** a line made by folding. **3** a hollow among hills. **4** an enclosure for sheep. **5** an established body of believers or members of a Church. □ **fold one's arms** place them together or entwined across one's chest. **fold one's hands** clasp them together.

**-fold** *combining form* forming *adjectives & adverbs* from numbers: **1** in an amount multiplied by; *repaid tenfold*. **2** with so many parts; *threefold blessing*.

**folder** *noun* **1** a folding cover for loose papers. **2** a folded leaflet.

**foliaceous** (foh-li-**ay**-shŭs) *adjective* of or like leaves.

**foliage** (**foh**-li-ij) *noun* the leaves of a tree or plant.

**foliar** (**foh**-li-ar) *adjective* of leaves.

**foliate** *adjective* (*pronounced* **foh**-li-ăt) leaflike, having leaves. ●*verb* (*pronounced* **foh**-li-ayt) split or beat into thin layers. □ **foliation** *noun*

**folic acid** (**foh**-lik) a vitamin of the B-group, deficiency of which causes anaemia.

**folio** (**foh**-li-oh) *noun* (*plural* **folios**) **1** a large sheet of paper folded once, making two leaves of a book. **2** a book made of such sheets, the largest-sized volume. **3** the page-number of a printed book.

**folk** *noun* (*plural* **folk** *or* **folks**) **1** (**folk** *as plural*) people in general. **2** the people of a certain group or nation etc.; *country folk*. **3** (**folks**) one's relatives. **4** folk-music. □ **folk-dance**, **folk-music** a dance, music, of popular origin or in the traditional style of a country.

**folklore** *noun* the traditional beliefs and tales of a community. □ **folklorist** *noun*

**folksy** *adjective* **1** of or like folk art or culture. **2** friendly, unpretentious.

**folkweave** *noun* loosely woven fabric used chiefly for furnishings.

**follicle** (**fol**-i-kŭl) *noun* a very small sac or cavity in the body, especially one containing a hair-root. □ **follicular** (fol-**ik**-yoo-ler) *adjective*

**follow** *verb* **1** go or come after. **2** go along (a path or road etc.). **3** provide with a sequel or successor. **4** take as a guide or leader or example; conform to; *follow the fashion*. **5** grasp the meaning of, understand. **6** take an interest in the progress of (events, a team, etc.). **7** happen as a result, result from. **8** be necessarily true in consequence of something else. □ **follow on** (of a side in cricket) have to bat again immediately after the first innings. **follow-on** *noun* an example of this. **follow one's nose** be guided by instinct. **follow out** carry out (instructions etc.). **follow suit 1** play a card of the suit led. **2** follow a person's example. **follow through** continue to a conclusion. **follow up 1** add a further action etc. to a previous one. **2** perform further work or investigation upon. **follow-up** *noun* subsequent or continued action.

**follower** *noun* **1** one who follows. **2** a person who believes in or supports a religion, teacher, or cause.

**following** *noun* a body of believers or supporters. ●*adjective* now to be mentioned; *answer the following questions*. ●*preposition* as a sequel to, after; *following the fall of sterling, prices rose sharply*.

**folly** *noun* **1** foolishness; a foolish act. **2** an ornamental building serving no practical purpose.

**foment** (fŏ-**ment**) *verb* arouse or stimulate (trouble, discontent, etc.).

**fomentation** (foh-men-**tay**-shŏn) *noun* **1** fomenting. **2** hot lotion applied to part of the body to relieve pain or inflammation.

**fond** *adjective* **1** affectionate, loving, doting. **2** (of hopes) cherished but unlikely to be fulfilled; naïve. □ **fond of** having a liking for; much inclined to. □ **fondly** *adverb*, **fondness** *noun*

**Fonda**, Henry (1905–82) and daughter Jane (born 1937), American film actors.

**fondant** *noun* a soft sweet made of flavoured sugar.

**fondle** *verb* touch or stroke lovingly.

**fondue** (**fon**-dew) *noun* a dish of melted cheese.

**font** *noun* a basin or vessel in a church, to hold water for baptism.

**fontanelle** (fon-tăn-**el**) *noun* (*Amer.* **fontanel**) a space under the skin on the top of an infant's head where the bones of the skull have not yet grown together.

**Fonteyn** (fon-**tayn**), Dame Margot (original name: Margaret Hookham) (1919–91), British ballerina.

**food** *noun* **1** any substance that can be taken into an animal or plant to maintain its life and growth. **2** a solid substance of this kind; *food and drink*. □ **food-chain** *noun* a series of organisms each dependent on the next for food. **food for thought** something that needs thinking about. **food poisoning** illness caused by bacteria or toxins in food. **food processor** an electric machine with blades for mixing and chopping food.

**foodie** *noun* (*informal*) a gourmet; one who is specially interested in food.

**foodstuff** *noun* a substance used as food.

**fool** *noun* **1** a person who acts unwisely; one who lacks good sense or judgement. **2** a jester or clown in a household during the Middle Ages. **3** a creamy pudding of fruit purée mixed with cream or custard. ●*verb* **1** behave in a joking or teasing way. **2** play about idly. **3** trick or deceive (a person). □ **fool's paradise** happiness that is based on an illusion. **make a fool of** make (a person) look foolish; trick or deceive.

**foolery** *noun* foolish behaviour.

**foolhardy** *adjective* bold but rash, delighting in taking unnecessary risks. □ **foolhardiness** *noun*

**foolish** *adjective* **1** lacking good sense or judgement. **2** (of actions) unwise. **3** ridiculous; *felt foolish*. □ **foolishly** *adverb*, **foolishness** *noun*

**foolproof** *adjective* **1** (of rules or instructions) plain and simple and unable to be misinterpreted. **2** (of machinery) very simple to operate.

**foolscap** *noun* a large size of paper. (¶ So called from the use of a *fool's cap* (a jester's cap with bells) as a watermark.)

**foot** *noun* (*plural* **feet**) **1** the end part of the leg below the ankle. **2** a similar part in animals, used in moving or to attach itself to things. **3** the lower end of a table or bed etc., the end opposite the head. **4** the part of a stocking covering the foot. **5** a person's step or tread or pace of movement; *fleet of foot*. **6** a lower usually projecting part of something (e.g. of a table-leg); the part of a sewing machine that is lowered on to the material to hold it steady. **7** the lowest part of something that has height or length; the bottom of a hill, ladder, page, list, etc. **8** a measure of length, = 12 inches (30.48 cm); *a ten-foot pole; it is ten feet long*. **9** a unit of rhythm in a line of poetry, usually containing a stressed syllable, e.g. each of the four divisions in *Jack/and Jill/went up/the hill*. ● *verb* go on foot; walk; *shall have to foot it*. □ **feet of clay** a great weakness in a person or thing that is honoured. **foot-and-mouth disease** a contagious disease of cattle etc. **foot-fault** *noun* Tennis putting the foot illegally over the baseline while serving. **foot the bill** pay the bill. **have both feet on the ground** be practical. **have one foot in the grave** be nearing death or very old. **my foot!** an exclamation of scornful contradiction. **on foot** walking. **put one's foot down** (*informal*) **1** insist. **2** accelerate a vehicle. **put one's foot in it** (*informal*) make a tactless blunder. **under foot** on the ground. **under one's feet** in the way.

**footage** *noun* a length measured in feet, especially of cinema or television film.

**football** *noun* **1** a large inflated leather or plastic ball. **2** a game played with this on a field, between two teams of players. □ **football pools** a form of gambling on the results of football matches. □ **footballer** *noun*

**footbrake** *noun* a brake operated by the foot in a motor vehicle.

**footbridge** *noun* a bridge for pedestrians.

**footfall** *noun* the sound of a footstep.

**foothill** *noun* one of the low hills near the bottom of a mountain or range.

**foothold** *noun* **1** a place wide enough for a foot to be placed on when climbing etc. **2** a secure position gained in a business etc.

**footing** *noun* **1** a placing of the feet, a foothold; *lost his footing*. **2** status; conditions; *they were on a friendly footing; put the army on a war footing*. **3** (**footings**) the foundations of a wall.

**footlights** *plural noun* a row of lights along the front of a stage floor.

**footling** (foo-tling) *adjective* (*informal*) trivial, petty.

**footloose** *adjective* independent, without responsibilities.

**footman** *noun* (*plural* **footmen**) a manservant (usually in livery) who admits visitors, waits at table, etc.

**footmark** *noun* a footprint.

**footnote** *noun* a note printed at the bottom of a page.

**footpath** *noun* a path for pedestrians, a pavement.

**footplate** *noun* a platform for the driver etc. operating a locomotive.

**footprint** *noun* an impression left by a foot or shoe.

**footsie** *noun* (*informal*) flirtatious touching of another's feet with one's own.

**footsore** *adjective* having feet that are sore from walking.

**footstep** *noun* a step taken in walking; the sound of this. □ **follow in someone's footsteps** do as an earlier person did.

**footstool** *noun* a stool for resting the feet on when sitting.

**footwear** *noun* shoes, socks, stockings, etc.

**footwork** *noun* the manner of moving the feet in dancing, boxing, football, etc.

**fop** *noun* a dandy. □ **foppery** *noun*, **foppish** *adjective*

**for** *preposition* **1** in place of. **2** as the price or penalty of; *was fined for speeding*. **3** in support or favour of. **4** with a view to, in order to obtain; *went for a walk; looking for a job*. **5** with regard to, in respect of; *ready for dinner*. **6** in the direction of; *set out for home*. **7** intended to be received by or belong to; *bought shoes for the children*. **8** so as to happen at; *an appointment for two o'clock*. **9** on account of; *famous for its cider*. **10** to the extent or duration of; *walked for two miles; it will last for years*. ● *conjunction* because; *they hesitated, for they were afraid*. □ **be for it** (*informal*) be about to meet with punishment or trouble. **for ever** for all time; continually, repeatedly.

**forage** (*rhymes with* porridge) *noun* **1** food for horses and cattle. **2** foraging. ● *verb* go searching, rummage. □ **forager** *noun*

**foray** (fo-ray) *noun* a sudden attack or raid. ● *verb* make a foray.

**forbade** *see* FORBID.

**forbear** *verb* (*old use*) (**forbore**, **forborne**, **forbearing**) refrain; *could not forbear criticizing; forbore to mention it*.

**forbearance** *noun* patience, tolerance.

**forbearing** *adjective* patient or tolerant.

**forbid** *verb* (**forbade** (*pronounced* for-**bad**), **forbidden**, **forbidding**) **1** order (a person) not to do something or not to enter; *forbid him to go*; *forbid him the court*. **2** refuse to allow; *forbid the marriage*; *he is forbidden wine*.

**forbidding** *adjective* uninviting, stern.

**forbore, forborne** *see* FORBEAR.

**force** *noun* **1** strength, power, intense effort. **2** (in scientific use) a measurable influence tending to cause movement of a body; its intensity. **3** a body of troops or police. **4** a body of people organized or available for a purpose; *a labour force*. **5** compulsion. **6** effectiveness, legal validity; *the new rules come into force next week*. ●*verb* **1** use force in order to get or do something, compel, oblige. **2** exert force on, break open by force; *forced the lock*. **3** strain to the utmost, overstrain. **4** impose, inflict. **5** cause or produce by effort; *forced a smile*. **6** cause (plants etc.) to reach maturity earlier than is normal. □ **force a person's hand** compel him or her to take action. **forced landing** an emergency landing of an aircraft. **force the issue** make an immediate decision necessary. **force the pace** adopt a high speed in a race etc. and so tire out others who are taking part. **in force 1** valid, current. **2** in great strength or numbers.

**force-feed** *verb* (**force-fed, force-feeding**) feed (a prisoner etc.) against his or her will.

**forceful** *adjective* powerful and vigorous, effective. □ **forcefully** *adverb*, **forcefulness** *noun*

**force majeure** (mah-*zh*er) **1** irresistible compulsion or coercion. **2** an unforeseeable course of events that excuses a person from the fulfilment of a contract. (¶ French, = superior strength.)

**forcemeat** *noun* finely chopped meat seasoned and used as stuffing.

**forceps** (for-seps) *noun* (*plural* **forceps**) surgical pincers or tongs used for gripping things.

**forcible** *adjective* done by force, forceful. □ **forcibly** *adverb*

**Ford**[1], Gerald Rudolph (born 1913), 38th President of the USA 1974–7.

**Ford**[2], Henry (1863–1947), American pioneer of mass production for motor vehicles.

**ford** *noun* a shallow place where a river may be crossed by wading or riding or driving through. ●*verb* cross in this way. □ **fordable** *adjective*

**fore** *adjective* situated in front. ●*adverb* in, at, or towards the front. ●*noun* the fore part. ●*interjection* a cry to warn a person who may be hit by a golf ball that is about to be played. □ **fore-and-aft** *adjective* (of sails) set lengthwise on a ship or boat (as opposed to *square-rigged*). **to the fore** in front; conspicuous.

**forearm** *noun* (*pronounced* **for**-arm) the arm from elbow to wrist or fingertips. ●*verb* (*pronounced* for-**arm**) arm or prepare in advance against possible danger etc.

**forebears** *plural noun* ancestors.

**forebode** *verb* be an advance sign or token of (trouble).

**foreboding** *noun* a feeling that trouble is coming.

**forecast** *verb* (**forecast, forecasting**) tell in advance (what is likely to happen). ●*noun* a statement that forecasts something.

**forecastle** (**fohk**-sŭl) *noun* (also **fo'c's'le**) the forward part of certain ships, where formerly the crew had their accommodation.

**foreclose** *verb* **1** (of a firm etc. that has lent money on mortgage) take possession of property when the loan is not duly repaid; *the Bank decided to foreclose the mortgage*. **2** bar from a privilege. □ **foreclosure** *noun*

**forecourt** *noun* **1** an enclosed space in front of a building; an outer court. **2** the outer part of a filling station where petrol is sold.

**forefathers** *plural noun* ancestors.

**forefinger** *noun* the finger next to the thumb.

**forefoot** *noun* (*plural* **forefeet**) an animal's front foot.

**forefront** *noun* the very front.

**forego** alternative spelling of FORGO.

**foregoing** *adjective* preceding, previously mentioned.

**foregone conclusion** a result that can be foreseen easily and with certainty.

**foreground** *noun* **1** the part of a scene or picture that is nearest to an observer. **2** the most conspicuous position.

**forehand** *adjective* **1** (of a stroke in tennis etc.) played with the palm of the hand turned forwards. **2** on the side on which this is made. ●*noun* a forehand stroke. □ **forehanded** *adjective*

**forehead** (fo-rid *or* **for**-hed) *noun* the part of the face above the eyebrows.

**foreign** *adjective* **1** of, in, or from another country; not of one's own country. **2** dealing with or involving other countries; *foreign affairs*. **3** not belonging naturally; *jealousy is foreign to her nature*. **4** coming from outside; *a foreign body in the eye*. □ **Foreign and Commonwealth Office** the UK government department dealing with foreign affairs. **Foreign Legion** *see* LEGION. **Foreign Secretary** the head of the Foreign and Commonwealth Office.

**foreigner** *noun* a person who was born in or comes from another country.

**foreknowledge** *noun* knowledge of something before it occurs.

**foreland** *noun* a cape or promontory.

**foreleg** *noun* an animal's front leg.

**forelock** *noun* a lock of hair just above the forehead.

**foreman** *noun* (*plural* **foremen**) **1** a worker who supervises other workers. **2** the member of a jury who acts as president and spokesman.

**foremast** *noun* the mast nearest to the bow in a sailing-ship.

**foremost** *adjective* **1** most advanced in position or rank. **2** most important. ●*adverb* in the foremost position etc.

**forename** *noun* a person's first name, a Christian name.

**forenoon** *noun* (*literary*) the morning.

**forensic** (fer-**en**-sik) *adjective* **1** of or used in lawcourts. **2** of or involving **forensic medicine**, the medical knowledge needed in legal matters or police investigations (e.g. in a poisoning case). □ **forensically** *adverb*

**foreordain** *verb* destine beforehand; *it was foreordained by God.*

**forepaw** *noun* an animal's front paw.

**foreplay** *noun* sexual stimulation before intercourse.

**forerunner** *noun* a person or thing that comes in advance of another; a predecessor.

**foresail** *noun* the principal sail on a foremast.

**foresee** *verb* (**foresaw, foreseen, foreseeing**) be aware of or realize beforehand. □ **foreseeable** *adjective*

**foreshadow** *verb* be a sign of (something that is to come).

**foreshore** *noun* the shore between high-water mark and low-water mark.

**foreshorten** *verb* represent (an object, when drawing it) with shortening of certain lines to give an effect of distance.

**foresight** *noun* **1** the ability to foresee and prepare for future needs. **2** the front sight of a gun.

**foreskin** *noun* the loose skin covering the end of the penis.

**forest** *noun* trees and undergrowth covering a large area.

**forestall** *verb* prevent or foil (a person or his or her plans) by taking action first.

**forestay** *noun* a stay from the head of the mast or foremast to a ship's deck.

**forested** *adjective* covered in forest.

**Forester,** C(ecil) S(cott) (pseudonym of Cecil Troughton Smith) (1899–1966), English novelist.

**forester** *noun* an officer in charge of a forest or of growing timber.

**forestry** *noun* the science or practice of planting and caring for forests.

**foretaste** *noun* an experience of something in advance of what is to come.

**foretell** *verb* (**foretold, foretelling**) forecast, prophesy.

**forethought** *noun* careful thought and planning for the future.

**forever** *adverb* continually; without end.

**forewarn** *verb* warn beforehand.

**forewoman** *noun* (*plural* **forewomen**) **1** a woman who supervises other workers. **2** a woman acting as president and spokeswoman of a jury.

**foreword** *noun* introductory remarks at the beginning of a book, usually written by someone other than the author.

**forfeit** (**for**-fit) *noun* something that has to be paid or given up as a penalty. ●*adjective* paid or given up in this way. ●*verb* pay or give up as a forfeit. □ **forfeiture** (**for**-fi-cher) *noun*

**forgather** *verb* assemble.

**forgave** *see* FORGIVE.

**forge** *noun* **1** a workshop with a fire and an anvil where metals are heated and shaped, especially one used by a smith for shoeing horses and working iron. **2** a furnace or hearth for melting or refining metal; the workshop containing it. ●*verb* **1** shape by heating in fire and hammering. **2** make an imitation or copy of (a thing) in order to pass it off fraudulently as real. **3** make one's way forward gradually or steadily; *forged ahead.* ● **forger** *noun*

**forgery** *noun* **1** forging, imitating fraudulently. **2** a fraudulent copy.

**forget** *verb* (**forgot, forgotten, forgetting**) **1** lose remembrance of (a thing or duty etc.). **2** put out of one's mind, stop thinking about; *decided to forget our quarrels.* □ **forget oneself** behave without suitable dignity.

**forgetful** *adjective* tending to forget things. □ **forgetfully** *adverb*, **forgetfulness** *noun*

**forget-me-not** *noun* a plant with small blue flowers.

**forgive** *verb* (**forgave, forgiven, forgiving**) cease to feel angry or bitter towards (a person) or about (an offence); pardon. □ **forgiveness** *noun*

**forgiving** *adjective* willing to forgive.

**forgo** *verb* (also **forego**) (**forwent, forgone, forgoing**) give up; go without.

**forgot, forgotten** *see* FORGET.

**fork** *noun* **1** a pronged instrument used in eating or cooking. **2** a pronged agricultural implement used for digging or lifting things. **3** a thing shaped like this. **4** a place where something separates into two or more parts; either of these parts. ●*verb* **1** lift or dig with a fork. **2** (of an object or road etc.) form a fork by separating into two branches. **3** follow one of these branches; *fork left.* □ **fork out** (*slang*) hand over; pay out money reluctantly.

**fork-lift truck** a truck with a fork-like mechanical device for lifting and moving heavy objects.

**forlorn** *adjective* left alone and unhappy. □ **forlorn hope** the only faint hope left. □ **forlornly** *adverb*

**form** *noun* **1** the shape of something; its outward or visible appearance. **2** its structure, arrangement, or style. **3** a person or animal as it can be seen or touched. **4** the way in which a thing exists; *ice is a form of water.* **5** a class in a school. **6** a fixed or usual method of doing something, a formality; a set order of words in a ritual etc. **7** a document with blank spaces that are to be filled in with information. **8** (of a horse or athlete) condition of health and training; *is in good form.* **9** details of previous performances; *study form before betting.* **10** a bench. **11** a hare's lair. ● *verb* **1** shape, mould; produce, construct. **2** bring into existence, constitute; *form a committee.* **3** be the material of. **4** come into existence; take shape, become solid; *icicles formed.* **5** develop in the mind; *formed a plan.* **6** arrange in a certain formation.

**formal** *adjective* **1** conforming to accepted rules or customs; showing or requiring formality; *a formal greeting* or *party.* **2** outward; *only a formal resemblance.* **3** regular or geometrical in design; *formal gardens.* □ **formally** *adverb*

**formaldehyde** (for-mal-di-hyd) *noun* a colourless gas used in solution as a preservative and disinfectant.

**formalin** *noun* a solution of formaldehyde in water.

**formalism** *noun* strict or excessive adherence to the outward form (as opposed to the content) of something. □ **formalist** *noun*

**formality** (for-mal-iti) *noun* **1** strict observance of rules and conventions. **2** a formal act, something required by law or custom; *legal formalities; it's just a formality.*

**formalize** *verb* (also **formalise**) make formal or official. □ **formalization** *noun*

**format** (for-mat) *noun* **1** the shape and size of a book etc. **2** a style of arrangement or procedure. **3** an arrangement of data etc. for processing or storage by computer. ● *verb* (**formatted, formatting**) arrange in a format, especially for a computer.

**formation** *noun* **1** forming; being formed. **2** a thing formed. **3** a particular arrangement or order.

**formative** (form-ătiv) *adjective* forming something; *a child's formative years.*

**former** *adjective* **1** of an earlier period; *in former times.* **2** mentioned before another. □ **the former** the first of two.

**formerly** *adverb* in former times.

**Formica** (for-my-kă) *noun* (*trade mark*) a hard heat-resistant plastic used on surfaces.

**formic acid** a colourless acid contained in fluid emitted by ants.

**formidable** (for-mid-ăbŭl, for-**mid**-ăbŭl) *adjective* **1** inspiring fear or awe. **2** difficult to do or overcome; *a formidable task.* □ **formidably** *adverb*

∎**Usage** The second pronunciation given is considered incorrect by some people.

**formless** *adjective* without distinct or regular form.

**formula** *noun* (*plural* **formulas** or *in scientific usage* **formulae,** *pronounced* for-mew-lee) **1** a set of chemical symbols showing the constituents of a substance. **2** a mathematical rule or statement expressed in algebraic symbols. **3** a fixed series of words, especially one used on social or ceremonial occasions. **4** a form or set of words that embody an agreement or enable it to be made. **5** a list of ingredients. **6** the classification of a racing car, especially by its engine capacity. **7** an infant's food made according to a prescribed recipe. □ **formulaic** (for-mew-lay-ik) *adjective*

**formulary** (for-mew-ler-i) *noun* a collection of formulas or set forms.

**formulate** *verb* express in a formula; express clearly and exactly. □ **formulation** *noun*

**fornicate** (for-ni-kayt) *verb* (*old use*) (of people not married to each other) have sexual intercourse. □ **fornication** *noun*, **fornicator** *noun*

**forsake** *verb* (**forsook, forsaken, forsaking**) **1** give up, renounce; *forsaking their former way of life.* **2** withdraw one's help, friendship, or companionship from; *he forsook his wife and children.*

**forsooth** (for-sooth) *adverb* (*old use*, now usually said in irony) indeed, no doubt.

**Forster,** E(dward) M(organ) (1879–1970), English novelist.

**forswear** *verb* (**forswore, forsworn, forswearing**) give up, renounce.

**Forsyth,** Frederick (born 1938), English author of political thrillers.

**forsythia** (for-syth-iă) *noun* a shrub with yellow flowers, blooming in spring.

**fort** *noun* a fortified building or position.

**forte** (for-tay) *noun* a person's strong point. ● *adverb* (in music) loudly.

**forth** *adverb* **1** out. **2** onwards, forwards; *from this day forth.* □ **and so forth** and so on. **back and forth** to and fro.

**forthcoming** *adjective* **1** about to come or appear; *forthcoming events.* **2** made available

when needed; *money was not forthcoming.*
**3** (*informal*) willing to give information, responsive; *the girl was not very forthcoming.*

**forthright** *adjective* frank, outspoken.

**forthwith** *adverb* immediately.

**fortieth** *see* FORTY.

**fortification** *noun* **1** fortifying. **2** a wall or building constructed to defend a place.

**fortify** *verb* (**fortified**, **fortifying**) **1** strengthen (a place) against attack, especially by constructing fortifications. **2** strengthen (a person) mentally or morally; increase the vigour of. **3** increase the food value of (bread etc.) by adding vitamins; strengthen (wine) with alcohol.

**fortissimo** *adverb* (in music) very loudly.

**fortitude** *noun* courage in bearing pain or trouble.

**Fort Knox** an American military reservation in Kentucky, famous as the site of the US Depository which holds the bulk of the nation's gold bullion in its vaults.

**fortnight** *noun* a period of two weeks.

**fortnightly** *adverb & adjective* happening or appearing once a fortnight.

**Fortran** *noun* a high-level computer language used especially in scientific work. (¶ From the first letters of *For*mula *Tran*slation.)

**fortress** *noun* a fortified building or town.

**fortuitous** (for-tew-it-ŭs) *adjective* happening by chance. □ **fortuitously** *adverb*, **fortuitousness** *noun*, **fortuity** *noun*

**fortunate** *adjective* having, bringing, or brought by good fortune. □ **fortunately** *adverb*

**fortune** *noun* **1** the events that chance brings to a person or undertaking. **2** chance as a power in the affairs of mankind. **3** a person's destiny. **4** prosperity, success; *seek one's fortune.* **5** a great amount of wealth; *left him a fortune.* □ **fortune-teller** *noun* a person who claims to foretell future events in people's lives. **tell fortunes** be a fortune-teller.

**forty** *adjective & noun* **1** four times ten (40, XL). **2** (**forties**) the numbers, years, or degrees of temperature from 40 to 49. □ **forty winks** a nap. □ **fortieth** *adjective & noun*

**forum** *noun* **1** the public square or market-place in an ancient Roman city. **2** a place or meeting where a public discussion is held.

**forward** *adjective* **1** continuing in one's line of motion; directed or moving towards the front; situated in the front. **2** of or relating to the future; *forward buying.* **3** having made more than the normal progress. **4** too bold in one's manner, presumptuous. ●*noun* an attacking player near the front in football or hockey (= striker); this position. ●*adverb* forwards, in advance, ahead; to-

wards the future. ●*verb* **1** send on (a letter etc.) to a new address. **2** send or dispatch (goods) to a customer. **3** help to advance (a person's interests). □ **forwardness** *noun*

**forwards** *adverb* **1** towards the front, onward so as to make progress. **2** with the front foremost.

**forwent** *see* FORGO.

**fosse** *noun* a long ditch or trench, especially in fortification.

**fossil** *noun* **1** the remains or impression of a prehistoric animal or plant once buried in earth and now hardened in rock. **2** (*informal*) a person who is out of date and unable to accept new ideas. □ **fossil fuel** natural fuel extracted from the ground, e.g. coal.

**fossilize** *verb* (also **fossilise**) turn or be turned into a fossil. □ **fossilization** *noun*

**foster** *verb* **1** promote the growth or development of. **2** take care of and bring up (a child that is not one's own). □ **foster-brother**, **foster-child**, etc. *noun* a child fostered in this way. **foster home** a family home in which a foster-child is brought up. **foster-mother**, **-parent**, etc. *noun* a person who fosters a child.

**Foucault** (foo-koh), Jean Bernard Léon (1819–68), French physicist, inventor of the gyroscope.

**fought** *see* FIGHT.

**foul** *adjective* **1** causing disgust, having an offensive smell or taste. **2** morally offensive, evil. **3** (of language) disgusting, obscene. **4** (of weather) rough, stormy. **5** clogged, choked; overgrown with barnacles etc. **6** in collision; entangled. **7** unfair, against the rules of a game; *a foul stroke.* ●*noun* a foul stroke or blow etc., breaking the rules of a game. ●*verb* **1** make or become foul. **2** entangle or collide with, obstruct. **3** commit a foul against (a player) in a game. □ **foul-mouthed** *adjective* using foul language. **foul play 1** a foul in sport. **2** a violent crime, especially murder. **foul up 1** become or cause to become entangled or blocked. **2** spoil, bungle. □ **foully** *adverb*

**found¹** *verb* **1** establish, originate; provide money for starting (an institution etc.). **2** base or construct; *a novel that is founded on fact.* **3** melt and mould (metal); fuse (materials for glass). **4** make (an object) in this way. □ **founder** *noun*

**found²** *see* FIND.

**foundation** *noun* **1** the founding of an institution etc. **2** the institution itself; a fund of money established for a charitable purpose. **3** the solid ground or base from which a building is built up; (also **foundations**) the lowest part of a building, usually below ground level. **4** a cosmetic applied to the skin as the first layer of make-up. **5** the underlying principle or idea etc. on which something is based. **6** the material or part on which others are overlaid. **7** a foundation garment. □ **foundation garment** a woman's supporting undergarment, e.g. a corset. **foundation-stone** noun a stone laid ceremonially to celebrate the founding of a building.

**founder¹** verb **1** stumble or fall. **2** (of a ship) fill with water and sink. **3** fail completely; *the plan foundered.*

**founder²** noun a person who has founded an institution, etc.

**foundling** noun a deserted child of unknown parents.

**foundry** noun a factory or workshop where metal or glass is founded.

**fount** noun **1** a set of printing-type of one style and size. **2** a source. **3** (*poetic*) a spring; a fountain.

**fountain** noun **1** a spring of water, especially a jet of water made to spout artificially as an ornament. **2** a structure providing a supply of drinking-water in a public place. **3** the source; *the fountain of wisdom.* □ **fountain-head** noun the source. **fountain pen** a pen that can be filled with a supply of ink.

**four** adjective & noun **1** one more than three (4, IV). **2** a four-oared boat or its crew. □ **four figures** a figure with four digits, e.g. 1000. **four-letter word** a short word referring to sexual or excretory functions and regarded as obscene. **four-poster** noun a bed with four posts to support a canopy. **foursquare** (adjective) solidly based, steady; (adverb) squarely. **four-stroke** adjective (of an engine) having a cycle of four strokes of the piston with the cylinder firing once. **fourwheel** adjective applied to all four wheels of a vehicle; *four-wheel drive.*

**fourfold** adjective & adverb **1** four times as much or as many. **2** consisting of four parts.

**foursome** noun **1** a company of four people. **2** a golf match between two pairs, with partners playing the same ball. ● adjective for four people; *a foursome reel.*

**fourteen** adjective & noun one more than thirteen (14, XIV). □ **fourteenth** adjective & noun

**fourth** adjective next after third. ● noun **1** something that is fourth. **2** one of four equal parts of a thing. □ **fourthly** adverb

**fowl** noun (plural **fowls** or **fowl**) **1** a kind of bird often kept to supply eggs and flesh for food. **2** the flesh of birds as food.

**Fowles** (*pronounced* fowlz), John Robert (born 1926), English novelist.

**fowling** noun catching, shooting, or snaring wildfowl. □ **fowler** noun

**Fox**, George (1624–91), founder of the Society of Friends.

**fox** noun **1** a wild animal of the dog family with a pointed snout, reddish fur, and a bushy tail. **2** its fur. **3** a crafty person. ● verb deceive or puzzle by acting craftily.

**foxed** adjective (of things) discoloured by brown spots caused by damp.

**foxglove** noun a tall plant with purple or white flowers like glove-fingers.

**foxhound** noun a hound bred and trained to hunt foxes.

**fox-terrier** noun a short-haired terrier.

**foxtrot** noun a ballroom dance with slow and quick steps. ● verb (**foxtrotted, foxtrotting**) dance a foxtrot.

**foxy** adjective (**foxier, foxiest**) **1** reddishbrown. **2** crafty. **3** looking like a fox. □ **foxily** adverb, **foxiness** noun

**foyer** (foi-ay) noun the entrance hall of a theatre or cinema or of a hotel.

**Fr** symbol francium.

**Fr.** abbreviation **1** Father. **2** French.

**fracas** (frak-ah) noun (plural **fracas**, *pronounced* frak-ahz) a noisy quarrel or disturbance.

**fraction** noun **1** a number that is not a whole number, e.g. ⅓, 0.5. **2** a very small part, piece, or amount.

**fractional** adjective **1** of a fraction. **2** very small; *a fractional difference.* □ **fractional distillation** separation of a mixture into its constituent parts by making use of their different physical properties. □ **fractionally** adverb

**fractious** (frak-shŭs) adjective irritable, peevish. □ **fractiously** adverb, **fractiousness** noun

**fracture** noun breakage, especially of a bone. ● verb cause a fracture in; suffer a fracture.

**fragile** adjective **1** easily damaged or broken. **2** of delicate constitution, not strong. □ **fragilely** adverb, **fragility** (frǎ-jil-iti) noun

**fragment** noun (*pronounced* frag-měnt) **1** a piece broken off something. **2** an isolated part; *a fragment of the conversation.* ● verb (*pronounced* frag-**ment**) break or be broken into fragments. □ **fragmentation** noun

**fragmentary** (frag-měnt-er-i) adjective consisting of fragments.

**fragrance** noun **1** sweetness of smell. **2** something fragrant; perfume.

**fragrant** adjective having a pleasant smell. □ **fragrantly** adverb

**frail** adjective not strong, physically weak.

**frailty** noun **1** being frail, weakness. **2** moral weakness, liability to yield to temptation.

**frame** noun **1** a rigid structure forming a support for other parts e.g. of a building, vehicle, or piece of furniture. **2** an open case or a border in which a picture, door, pane of glass, etc. may be set. **3** the human or an animal body with reference to its size; *a small frame*. **4** a single exposure on a strip of cinema film. **5** a boxlike structure used for protecting plants from the cold. **6** a triangular structure for setting up balls in snooker etc.; a round of play using this. ●*verb* **1** put or form a frame round. **2** construct. **3** compose, express in words; *frame a treaty*. **4** (*informal*) arrange false evidence against. □ **frame of mind** a temporary state of mind. **frame of reference** a set of principles or standards by which ideas and behaviour etc. are evaluated. **frame-up** *noun* (*informal*) the arrangement of false evidence against an innocent person.

**framework** *noun* **1** the supporting frame of a building or other construction. **2** the structural basis of an organization, the structure of a plan etc.

**franc** *noun* the unit of money in France, Belgium, Switzerland, and certain other countries.

**France** a country in western Europe.

**franchise** (fran-chyz) *noun* **1** the right to vote at public elections. **2** authorization to sell a company's goods or services in a particular area. ●*verb* grant a franchise to.

**Francis**, St, of Assisi (1181/2–1226), Italian friar, founder of the Franciscan order, noted for his simple faith and love of nature.

**Franciscan** (fran-sis-kăn) *noun* a member of an order of friars (also called *Grey Friars*) founded by St Francis of Assisi, or of a corresponding order of nuns.

**francium** (fran-si-ŭm) *noun* a radioactive metallic element (symbol Fr).

**Franck**, César (1822–90), Belgian composer.

**Franco**, Francisco (1892–1975), Spanish dictator 1939–75.

**Franco-** *combining form* French; *a Franco-German treaty*.

**Frank**[1] *noun* a member of a Germanic people that conquered Gaul in the 6th century. □ **Frankish** *adjective*

**Frank**[2], Anne (1929–45), German-Jewish girl, whose diary records the experiences of her family living for two years in hiding from the Nazis in Amsterdam.

**frank** *adjective* showing one's thoughts and feelings openly. ●*verb* mark (a letter) to record the payment of postage. ●*noun* a franking signature or mark. □ **frankly** *adverb*, **frankness** *noun*

**Frankenstein** (frank-in-styn) *noun* (in full **Frankenstein's monster**) a thing that becomes terrifying to its creator. (¶ The name of a person in Mary Shelley's novel *Frankenstein* (1818), who constructed a human monster and endowed it with life.

It became filled with hatred for its creator and eventually killed him.)

**frankfurter** *noun* a smoked sausage (¶ originally made at Frankfurt in Germany).

**frankincense** *noun* a sweet-smelling gum resin burnt as incense.

**Franklin**, Benjamin (1706–90), American statesman, inventor, and scientist, one of the signatories to the peace between the USA and Great Britain after the War of American Independence.

**frantic** *adjective* wildly excited or agitated by anxiety etc.; frenzied. □ **frantically** *adverb*

**fraternal** (fră-ter-năl) *adjective* of a brother or brothers. □ **fraternal twins** twins developed from separate ova and not necessarily similar. □ **fraternally** *adverb*

**fraternity** (fră-tern-iti) *noun* **1** being fraternal, brotherly feeling. **2** a religious brotherhood. **3** a group or company of people with common interests.

**fraternize** (frat-er-nyz) *verb* (also **fraternise**) (often foll. by *with*) associate with others in a friendly way. □ **fraternization** *noun*

**fratricide** (frat-ri-syd) *noun* **1** the act of killing one's own brother or sister. **2** a person who is guilty of this. □ **fratricidal** *adjective*

**Frau** (*rhymes with* brow) *noun* (*plural* **Frauen**) (the title of) a German married woman; Mrs.

**fraud** *noun* **1** criminal deception; a dishonest trick. **2** a person or thing that is not what it seems or pretends to be; an impostor.

**fraudulent** (fraw-dew-lĕnt) *adjective* acting with fraud; obtained by fraud. □ **fraudulently** *adverb*, **fraudulence** *noun*

**fraught** (*pronounced* frawt) *adjective* **1** (foll. by *with*) filled, involving; *fraught with danger*. **2** anxious; distressing.

**Fräulein** (froi-lyn) *noun* (the title of) a German unmarried woman; Miss.

**Fraunhofer** (frown-hoh-fer), Joseph von (1787–1826), German pioneer in spectroscopy.

**fray** *noun* a fight, a conflict; *ready for the fray*. ●*verb* (**frayed**, **fraying**) **1** make worn so that there are loose threads, especially at the edge. **2** strain or upset (nerves or temper). **3** become frayed.

**Frazer**, Sir James George (1854–1941), Scottish anthropologist.

**frazzle** *noun* (*informal*) a completely exhausted state; *worn to a frazzle*. □ **frazzled** *adjective*

**freak** *noun* **1** a person or thing that is abnormal in form. **2** (usually used as *adjective*) very unusual or irregular; *a freak storm*. **3** a person who dresses absurdly. **4** one who freaks out; a drug addict. **5** a person who is obsessed with something specified; *a health* *freak*. □ **freak out 1** have hallucinations from narcotic drugs; have a strong emotional experience. **2** adopt an unconventional lifestyle. □ **freakish** *adjective*, **freaky** *adjective*

**freckle** *noun* a light brown spot on the skin. ● *verb* become or cause to become spotted with freckles.

**Frederick**[1] the name of three Holy Roman Emperors, including Frederick I 'Barbarossa' (= 'Redbeard', emperor 1152–90).

**Frederick**[2] the name of three kings of Prussia, including Frederick II 'the Great' (reigned 1740–86).

**free** *adjective* (**freer, freest**) **1** (of a person) not a slave, not in the power of another or others; having social and political liberty. **2** (of a country or its citizens or institutions) not controlled by a foreign or despotic government; having representative government; having private rights which are respected. **3** not fixed or held down, able to move without hindrance. **4** unrestricted, not controlled by rules. **5** (foll. by *from* or *of*) without, not subject to or affected by *from* or blame; *the harbour is free of ice*. **6** without payment, costing nothing. **7** (of place or time) not occupied, not being used; (of a person) without engagements or things to do. **8** coming, given, or giving readily; *he is very free with his advice*. ● *verb* (**freed, freeing**) **1** make free, liberate. **2** (foll. by *from* or *of*) relieve, rid or ease; *freed him from suspicion*. **3** clear, disengage or disentangle. □ **for free** provided without payment. **free and easy** informal. **Free Church** a nonconformist Church. **free enterprise** freedom of private business to operate without government control. **free fall** the unrestricted fall of a body towards earth under the force of gravity. **free fight** a general fight in which anyone present can join. **free-for-all** *noun* **1** a free fight. **2** a discussion in which anyone present may join. **free hand** the right of taking what action one chooses. **free house** a public house not controlled by a brewery and therefore able to stock any brand of beer etc. **free kick** a kick allowed to be taken in football as a minor penalty. **free port** one open to all traders alike, or free from duty on goods in transit. **free-range** *adjective* (of hens) allowed to range freely in search of food, not kept in a battery; (of eggs) from such hens. **free speech** the right to express opinions freely. **free-standing** *adjective* not supported by another structure. **free vote** a parliamentary vote in which members are not subject to party discipline. **free will** the power of choosing one's own course of action. □ **freely** *adverb*

**freebie** *noun* (*informal*) something that is provided free.

**freedom** *noun* **1** the condition of being free; independence. **2** frankness, outspokenness. **3** exemption from a defect or duty etc. **4** (foll. by *of*) unrestricted use; *has the freedom of the library*. □ **freedom fighter** one who takes part in violent resistance to an established political regime.

**freefone** *noun* (also **Freefone, freephone**) a system whereby certain telephone calls can be made free of charge.

**freehand** *adjective* (of a drawing) done without ruler or compasses etc.

**freehold** *noun* the holding of land or property in absolute ownership. □ **freeholder** *noun*

**freelance** *noun* (also **freelancer**) a self-employed person who works for several businesses on particular assignments. ● *verb* work as a freelance.

**freeloader** (*slang*) a sponger.

**freeman** *noun* (*plural* **freemen**) **1** a free person, one who is not a slave or serf. **2** a holder of the freedom of a city.

**Freemason** *noun* a member of an international fraternity for mutual help and fellowship, with elaborate secret rituals. □ **Freemasonry** *noun*

**freephone** alternative spelling of FREEFONE.

**freepost** *noun* a system of business post where postage is paid by the addressee.

**freesia** *noun* a fragrant flowering plant growing from a bulb.

**freestyle** *noun* **1** a swimming race in which any stroke may be used. **2** wrestling allowing almost any hold.

**Freetown** the capital of Sierra Leone.

**freeway** *noun* (*Amer.*) a motorway on which there are no tolls.

**freeze** *verb* (**froze, frozen, freezing**) **1** be so cold that water turns to ice; *it was freezing last night*. **2** change or be changed from a liquid to a solid by extreme cold; become full of ice or covered in ice. **3** become very cold, or rigid from cold or fear etc.; chill by cold or fear etc. **4** preserve (food) by refrigeration to below freezing point. **5** make (credits or assets) unable to be realized. **6** hold (prices, wages, etc.) at a fixed level. ● *noun* **1** a period of freezing weather. **2** the freezing of prices, wages, etc. **3** (in full **freeze-frame**) a still film-shot. □ **freeze-dry** *verb* freeze and dry by evaporation of ice in a vacuum. **freeze up** obstruct by the formation of ice. **freeze-up** *noun* a period or condition of extreme cold. **freezing point** the temperature at which a liquid, especially water, freezes.

**freezer** *noun* a refrigerated container for preserving and storing perishable goods by keeping them at a very low temperature.

**freewheel** verb **1** ride a bicycle without pedalling. **2** act without constraint.

**Frege** (fray-gĕ), Gottlob (1848–1925), German philosopher and mathematician, the founder of modern logic.

**freight** (pronounced frayt) noun **1** the transport of goods in containers or by water or air (in the USA also by land). **2** the goods transported, cargo. **3** the charge for this. ● verb load (a ship) with cargo; send or carry as cargo.

**freighter** (frayt-er) noun a ship or aircraft carrying mainly freight.

**French** adjective of France or its people or language. ● noun **1** the French language. **2** (informal) bad language; excuse my French. **3** (the French) (as plural) French people. □ **French bean** a kidney bean or haricot bean, used as a vegetable both as unripe pods and as ripe seeds. **French bread** white bread in a long crisp loaf. **French Canadian** a native of the French-speaking area of Canada. **french chalk** finely powdered talc used as a lubricant etc. **French dressing** salad dressing of seasoned oil and vinegar. **French fries** potato chips. **French horn** a coiled brass wind instrument with a wide bell. **French kiss** one with the mouth open and using the tongue. **French leave** absence without permission. **French letter** (informal) a condom. **french-polish** verb polish (wood) with shellac polish. **French window** one of a pair of long windows used as doors. □ **Frenchman** noun (plural **Frenchmen**), **Frenchwoman** noun (plural **Frenchwomen**)

**French Guiana** an overseas department of France in the north of South America.

**frenetic** (frĕ-net-ik) adjective **1** frantic, frenzied. **2** fanatic. □ **frenetically** adverb

**frenzied** adjective in a state of frenzy, wildly excited or agitated. □ **frenziedly** adverb

**frenzy** noun violent excitement or agitation.

**frequency** noun **1** the state of being frequent, frequent occurrence. **2** the rate of the occurrence or repetition of something. **3** the number of cycles per second of a carrier wave; a band or group of similar frequencies. □ **frequency modulation** Electronics a modulation in which the frequency of the carrier wave is varied; used especially in broadcasting.

**frequent** verb (pronounced fri-**kwent**) go frequently to, be often in (a place). ● adjective (pronounced **free**-kwĕnt) happening or appearing often. □ **frequently** adverb

**frequentative** (fri-kwent-ă-tiv) adjective Grammar (of a verb) expressing frequent repetition or intensity of an action. ● noun a frequentative verb.

**fresco** (fress-koh) noun (plural **frescos**) a picture painted on a wall or ceiling before the plaster is dry.

**fresh** adjective **1** newly made, produced, or gathered; not stale. **2** newly arrived. **3** new or different, not previously known or used. **4** (of food) not preserved by salting, pickling, tinning, or freezing etc. **5** not salty, not bitter. **6** (of air or weather) cool, refreshing; (of wind) moderately strong. **7** bright and pure in colour, not dull or faded. **8** not weary; feeling vigorous. **9** (informal) presumptuous, forward. □ **freshly** adverb, **freshness** noun

**freshen** verb make or become fresh.

**fresher** noun (informal) a first-year student at a university or (in the USA) high school.

**freshet** noun **1** a stream of fresh water flowing into the sea. **2** a flood of a river.

**freshman** noun (plural **freshmen**) = FRESHER.

**freshwater** adjective of fresh water, not of the sea; freshwater fish.

**Fresnel** (frĕ-nel), Augustin Jean (1788–1827), French physicist and civil engineer, inventor of a large lens for lighthouses and searchlights.

**fret¹** verb (**fretted, fretting**) **1** make or become unhappy, worry, vex. **2** wear away by gnawing or rubbing. ● noun a state of unhappiness or worry.

**fret²** noun **1** a bar or ridge on the fingerboard of a guitar, banjo, etc., as a guide for the fingers to press the strings at the correct place. **2** an ornamental pattern of straight lines joined usually at right angles. ● verb (**fretted, fretting**) ornament with this or with carved or embossed work. □ **fretted** adjective

**fretful** adjective anxious or distressed. □ **fretfully** adverb, **fretfulness** noun

**fretsaw** noun a narrow saw fixed in a frame, used for cutting thin wood in patterns.

**fretwork** noun carved work in decorative patterns, especially in wood cut with a fretsaw.

**Freud** (pronounced froid), Sigmund (1856–1939), Austrian psychiatrist, the founder of psychoanalysis.

**Freudian** (froi-di-ăn) adjective of Sigmund Freud or his theories. □ **Freudian slip** an absent-minded remark that seems to reveal subconscious feelings.

**Fri.** abbreviation Friday.

**friable** (fry-ă-bŭl) adjective easily crumbled. □ **friability** noun

**friar** noun a member of certain Roman Catholic male religious orders (especially the Franciscans, Augustinians, Dominicans, and Carmelites), working among people in the outside world and not as enclosed orders. □ **friar's balsam** an oil used as an inhalant.

**friary** noun a monastery of friars.

**fricassee** (frik-ă-say) noun a dish of pieces of meat served in a thick sauce.

**fricative** noun Phonetics a consonant sounded by the friction of breath in a narrow opening, e.g. f, th.

**friction** noun 1 the rubbing of one thing against another. 2 the resistance of one surface to another that moves over it. 3 conflict between people with different ideas or personalities. □ **frictional** adjective

**Friday** the day of the week following Thursday. □ **girl** or **man Friday** an assistant doing general duties in an office etc. (¶ Named after Man Friday in Defoe's Robinson Crusoe.)

**fridge** noun (informal) a refrigerator. □ **fridge-freezer** noun an upright unit comprising a refrigerator and a freezer.

**fried** see FRY.

**Friedman**, Milton (born 1912), American economist, exponent of monetarism.

**friend** noun 1 a person with whom one is on terms of mutual affection independently of sexual or family love. 2 a helpful thing or quality; darkness was our friend. 3 a helper, sympathizer, or patron; Friends of the cathedral. 4 (**Friend**) a member of the Society of Friends, a Quaker. □ **friendship** noun, **friendless** adjective

**friendly** adjective (**friendlier, friendliest**) 1 like a friend, kindly. 2 (of things) favourable, helpful. ●noun a friendly match. □ **friendly fire** gunfire from one's own side in a conflict. **friendly match** a match played for enjoyment rather than competition. **Friendly Society** a society for the mutual benefit of its members e.g. during illness or old age. □ **friendliness** noun

**Friendly Islands** Tonga.

**frier** alternative spelling of FRYER.

**Friesian** (free-zhăn) noun an animal of a breed of large black-and-white dairy cattle originally from Friesland, a province of the Netherlands.

**frieze** noun a band of sculpture or decoration round the top of a wall or building.

**frigate** (frig-ăt) noun a small fast naval escort vessel or a small destroyer.

**Frigga** (Scand. myth.) wife of Odin and goddess of married love and the hearth.

**frigging** adjective (vulgar) damned.

**fright** noun 1 sudden great fear. 2 a grotesque or ridiculous-looking person or thing.

**frighten** verb 1 cause fright to. 2 feel fright; he doesn't frighten easily. 3 drive or compel by fright; frightened them into concealing it. □ **frightened of** afraid of.

**frightful** adjective 1 causing horror. 2 ugly. 3 (informal) very great, extremely bad; a

frightful expense; frightful weather. □ **frightfully** adverb

**frigid** (frij-id) adjective 1 intensely cold. 2 very cold and formal in manner. 3 (of a woman) unresponsive sexually. □ **frigidly** adverb, **frigidity** (fri-jid-iti) noun

**frill** noun 1 a gathered or pleated strip of trimming attached at one edge. 2 (often as **frills**) an unnecessary extra; simple accommodation with no frills. □ **frilled** adjective, **frilly** adjective

**fringe** noun 1 an ornamental edging of hanging threads or cords etc. 2 something resembling this. 3 front hair cut short to hang over the forehead. 4 the edge of an area or group. ●verb 1 decorate with a fringe. 2 form a fringe to. □ **fringe benefits** benefits that are provided for an employee in addition to wages or salary.

**Frink**, Dame Elisabeth (1930–93), English sculptor.

**frippery** noun showy unnecessary finery or ornaments.

**Frisbee** noun (trade mark) a plastic disc for skimming through the air as an outdoor game.

**Frisian** (friz-iăn) adjective of Friesland, a province of the Netherlands, or its people or language. ●noun 1 a native of Friesland. 2 the Germanic language spoken there.

**frisk** verb 1 leap or skip playfully. 2 (informal) pass one's hands over (a person) in order to search for concealed weapons etc.

**frisky** adjective (**friskier, friskiest**) lively, playful. □ **friskily** adverb, **friskiness** noun

**frisson** (free-son) noun an emotional thrill. (¶ French, = shiver.)

**frith** = FIRTH.

**fritillary** (fri-til-er-i) noun 1 a plant with speckled bell-shaped flowers. 2 a kind of spotted butterfly.

**fritter** noun a small flat fried cake of batter containing sliced fruit or meat etc. ●verb (usually foll. by away) waste little by little, especially on trivial things; fritter away one's money.

**frivolous** adjective lacking a serious purpose, pleasure-loving. □ **frivolously** adverb, **frivolity** noun

**frizz** verb curl into a wiry mass. ●noun a frizzed condition; frizzed hair. □ **frizzy** adjective, **frizziness** noun

**frizzle** verb 1 burn or cook with a sizzling noise. 2 burn or shrivel by burning. 3 frizz. ●noun frizzed hair. □ **frizzly** adjective

**fro** adverb □ **to and fro** see TO.

**Frobisher** (froh-bish-er), Sir Martin (c.1535–94), English sailor and explorer, who made expeditions to Canada and the West Indies.

**frock** noun 1 a woman's or girl's dress. 2 a smock.

**Froebel** (**frer-bĕl**), Friedrich Wilhelm (1782–1852), German educationist, founder of the kindergarten system.

**frog** noun **1** a small cold-blooded jumping animal living both in water and on land. **2** a horny substance in the sole of a horse's foot. **3** a fastener consisting of a button and an ornamentally looped cord. **4** (**Frog**) (slang, offensive) a Frenchman. □ **have a frog in one's throat** (informal) be unable to speak except hoarsely.

**frogman** noun (plural **frogmen**) a swimmer equipped with a rubber suit, flippers, and an oxygen supply for swimming and working under water.

**frogmarch** verb hustle (a person) forward forcibly with his or her arms held fast; carry (a person) face downwards by means of four people each holding a limb. ●noun this process.

**frolic** verb (**frolicked, frolicking**) play about in a lively cheerful way. ●noun lively cheerful playing or entertainment.

**from** preposition expressing separation or origin: **1** indicating the place, time, or limit that is the starting-point; travelled from London; from ten o'clock. **2** indicating source or origin; took water from the well. **3** indicating separation, prevention, escape, etc.; was released from prison; cannot refrain from laughing. **4** indicating difference or discrimination; can't tell red from green. **5** indicating cause, agent, or means; died from starvation. **6** indicating material used in a process; wine is made from grapes. □ **from time to time** at intervals, occasionally.

**fromage frais** (fro-mah*zh* fray) smooth low-fat soft cheese.

**frond** noun a leaflike part of a fern or other flowerless plant or of a palm tree.

**front** noun **1** the foremost or most important side or surface. **2** the part normally nearer or towards the spectator or line of motion; the front of a bus. **3** the area where fighting is taking place in a war; the foremost line of an army etc. **4** an outward appearance or show; something serving as a cover for secret activities. **5** the forward edge of an advancing mass of cold or warm air. **6** the promenade of a seaside resort. **7** the part of a garment covering the front of the body. **8** the part of a theatre where the audience sits, in front of the stage. **9** (in names) an organized political group; the Patriotic Front. ●adjective of the front; situated in front. ●verb **1** face, have the front towards; a hotel fronting the sea. **2** (slang) serve as a front or cover for secret activities. □ **frontbencher** noun an MP entitled to sit on the front benches in Parliament, which are reserved for government ministers and members of the Shadow Cabinet (compare BACKBENCHER). **front runner** the contest-

ant who seems most likely to succeed. **in front** at the front of something. **in front of 1** ahead of. **2** in the presence of.

**frontage** noun **1** the front of a building. **2** the land bordering its front.

**frontal** adjective **1** of or on the front. **2** of the forehead.

**frontier** noun **1** the land-border of a country. **2** the limit of attainment or knowledge in a subject.

**frontispiece** (**frunt-iss-peess**) noun an illustration placed opposite the title-page of a book.

**Frost**, Robert Lee (1874–1963), American poet.

**frost** noun **1** a weather condition with temperature below the freezing point of water. **2** a white powder-like coating of frozen vapour produced by this. **3** a chilling influence; great coolness of manner, unfriendliness. ●verb **1** injure (a plant etc.) with frost. **2** cover with frost or frosting. **3** make (glass) opaque by roughening the surface.

**frostbite** noun injury to tissue of the body from freezing. □ **frostbitten** adjective

**frosting** noun sugar icing.

**frosty** adjective (**frostier, frostiest**) **1** cold with frost. **2** covered by frost. **3** unfriendly in manner. □ **frostily** adverb, **frostiness** noun

**froth** noun **1** foam. **2** idle talk or ideas. ●verb cause froth in, foam. □ **frothy** adjective

**frown** verb wrinkle one's brow in thought or disapproval. ●noun a frowning movement or look. □ **frown at** or **on** disapprove of.

**frowsty** adjective fusty, stuffy.

**frowzy** adjective (also **frowsy**) **1** fusty. **2** slatternly, dingy.

**frozen** see FREEZE.

**FRS** abbreviation Fellow of the Royal Society.

**fructose** noun a simple sugar found in honey and fruits.

**frugal** (**froo-găl**) adjective **1** careful and economical. **2** scanty, costing little; a frugal meal. □ **frugally** adverb, **frugality** (froo-gal-iti) noun

**fruit** noun **1** the seed-containing part of a plant. **2** this used as food. **3** any plant product used as food; the fruits of the earth. **4** the product or rewarding outcome of labour. **5** currants etc. used in food. ●verb **1** (of a plant) produce fruit. **2** cause (a plant) to produce fruit. □ **fruit machine** a coin-operated gambling machine, often using symbols representing fruit. **fruit salad** various fruits cut up and mixed.

**fruiterer** noun a shopkeeper who deals in fruit.

**fruitful** adjective **1** producing much fruit. **2** producing good results. □ **fruitfully** adverb

**fruition** (froo-**ish**-ŏn) *noun* the fulfilment of hopes; results attained by work.

**fruitless** *adjective* producing little or no result. □ **fruitlessly** *adverb*

**fruity** *adjective* (**fruitier, fruitiest**) **1** like fruit in smell or taste. **2** of full rich quality; *a fruity voice*. **3** (*informal*) full of rough humour or scandal; *fruity stories*.

**frump** *noun* a dowdily-dressed unattractive woman. □ **frumpish** *adjective*, **frumpy** *adjective*

**frustrate** *verb* prevent (a person) from achieving a purpose; make (efforts) useless. □ **frustrated** *adjective* discontented because of being unable to achieve something; unfulfilled. □ **frustration** *noun*

**frustum** *noun* (*plural* **frusta** or **frustums**) the lower part of a cone or pyramid whose top is cut off parallel to the base.

**Fry**[1], Christopher Harris (born 1907), English author of poetic dramas.

**Fry**[2], Elizabeth (1780–1845), English Quaker prison reformer.

**fry** *verb* (**fried, frying**) cook or be cooked in boiling fat. ● *noun* **1** various internal parts of animals usually fried; *lamb's fry*. **2** (as *plural*) young or newly hatched fishes. □ **frying-pan** *noun* a shallow pan used in frying. **out of the frying-pan into the fire** from a bad situation to a worse one. **small fry** people of little importance; children.

**Frye**, (Herman) Northrop (1912–91), Canadian writer and critic.

**fryer** *noun* (also **frier**) **1** a person who fries things. **2** a vessel for frying fish etc.

**ft** *abbreviation* foot or feet (as a measure).

**FT-SE** *abbreviation* Financial Times-Stock Exchange 100 share index, based on the share values of Britain's 100 largest public companies.

**Fuchs** (*pronounced* fuuks), Sir Vivian Ernest (born 1908), English Antarctic explorer and geologist.

**fuchsia** (**few**-shă) *noun* an ornamental shrub with red, purple, or white drooping flowers.

**fuck** (*vulgar*) *verb* **1** have sexual intercourse with. **2** (expressing annoyance) damn, curse. ● *noun* **1** sexual intercourse. **2** a damn; *doesn't care a fuck*. □ **fuck off** go away.

**fucking** *adjective & adverb* (*vulgar*) damned.

**fuddle** *verb* stupefy, especially with alcoholic drink.

**fuddy-duddy** (*informal*) *adjective* old-fashioned; quaintly fussy. ● *noun* a person of this kind.

**fudge** *noun* a soft sweet made of milk, sugar, and butter. ● *verb* put together in a makeshift or dishonest way; fake.

**fuehrer** alternative spelling of FÜHRER.

**fuel** *noun* **1** material for burning or lighting as a source of warmth, light, or energy, or used as a source of nuclear energy. **2** something that increases anger or other strong feelings. ● *verb* (**fuelled, fuelling**; *Amer.* **fueled, fueling**) supply with fuel.

**fug** *noun* (*informal*) fustiness of air in a room. □ **fuggy** *adjective*

**fugitive** (**few**-ji-tiv) *noun* a person fleeing or escaping from something. ● *adjective* **1** fleeing, escaping. **2** transient.

**fugue** (*pronounced* fewg) *noun* a musical composition in which one or more themes are introduced and then repeated in a complex pattern. □ **fugal** *adjective*

**führer** (**few**-rer) *noun* (also **fuehrer**) a tyrannical leader. (¶ German, = leader: the title taken by Hitler.)

**Fujairah** an emirate belonging to the federation of United Arab Emirates.

**Fujiyama** (foo-ji-**yah**-mă) the highest mountain in Japan, a cone-shaped dormant or extinct volcano.

**fulcrum** (**ful**-krŭm) *noun* (*plural* **fulcra** or **fulcrums**) the point on which a lever turns.

**fulfil** *verb* (*Amer.* **fulfill**) (**fulfilled, fulfilling**) **1** accomplish, carry out (a task). **2** do what is required by (a treaty etc.); satisfy the requirements of. **3** make (a prophecy) come true. □ **fulfil oneself** or **be fulfilled** (of persons) develop and use one's abilities etc. fully. □ **fulfilment** *noun*

**full** *adjective* **1** holding or having as much as the limits will allow. **2** (often foll. by *of*) having much or many, crowded; *full of vitality*. **3** (foll. by *of*) completely occupied with, engrossed in; *full of himself*; *full of the news*. **4** fed to satisfaction; *ate till he was full*. **5** copious; *give full details*. **6** complete, reaching the usual or specified extent or limit; *in full bloom*; *waited a full hour*. **7** plump, rounded; *a full figure*. **8** (of clothes) fitting loosely, made with much material hanging in folds. **9** (of tone) deep and mellow. ● *adverb* **1** completely. **2** exactly; *hit him full on the nose*. ● *verb* clean and thicken freshly-woven cloth. □ **full back** one of the defensive players near the goal in football, hockey, etc. **full-blooded** *adjective* vigorous, hearty; sensual. **full-blown** *adjective* fully developed. **full board** provision of bed and all meals at a hotel etc. **full-bodied** *adjective* rich in quality, tone, or flavour. **full-frontal** *adjective* (of a nude figure) fully exposed at the front. **full house 1** maximum attendance at a theatre. **2** (in poker) a hand with three of a kind and a pair. **full moon** the moon with its whole disc illuminated; the time when this occurs. **full-scale** *adjective* of the actual size, not reduced. **full speed ahead!** an order to move or work with maximum speed. **full stop 1** the punctuation mark (.) used at the end of a sentence or abbreviation. **2** a complete cessation. **full time 1** the whole of a working day or week. **2** the end of a football match etc. **full-time** adjective for or during the whole of the working day or week. **full-timer** noun a person employed to work a full working week. **in full 1** with nothing omitted. **2** for the whole amount; *paid in full*. **to the full** thoroughly, completely.

**fuller** noun a person who fulls cloth. □ **fuller's earth** a type of clay used for this process.

**fully** adverb **1** completely, entirely. **2** no less than. □ **fully-fashioned** shaped to fit the body closely.

**fullness** noun being full. □ **in the fullness of time** at the proper or destined time.

**fulmar** noun an Arctic sea bird related to the petrel.

**fulminant** (ful-min-ănt) adjective **1** fulminating. **2** (of a disease) developing suddenly.

**fulminate** (ful-min-ayt) verb protest loudly and bitterly. □ **fulmination** noun

**fulsome** (fuul-sŏm) adjective praising something excessively and sickeningly.

■**Usage** It is regarded as unacceptable to use this word in current English to mean 'full' or 'plentiful'.

**Fulton**, Robert (1765–1815), American pioneer of the steamship.

**fumble** verb **1** touch or handle awkwardly. **2** grope about.

**fume** noun (usually as **fumes**) strong-smelling smoke, gas, or vapour. ●verb **1** treat with chemical fumes, especially to darken wood; *fumed oak*. **2** emit fumes. **3** seethe with anger.

**fumigate** (few-mig-ayt) verb disinfect by means of fumes. □ **fumigation** noun, **fumigator** noun

**fun** noun **1** light-hearted amusement. **2** a source of this. □ **for** or **in fun** as a source of amusement, not seriously. **fun run** an organized non-competitive long-distance run, often for charity. **make fun of, poke fun at** ridicule, tease.

**function** noun **1** the special activity or purpose of a person or thing. **2** an important social or official gathering. **3** any of the basic operations of a computer etc. **4** *Maths* a quantity whose value depends on the varying values of others. ●verb **1** perform a function. **2** work properly.

**functional** adjective **1** of a function or functions. **2** designed to perform a particular function without being decorative or luxurious; practical. □ **functionally** adverb

**functionalism** noun belief in or stress on the practical application of a thing, especially in architecture and furniture design. □ **functionalist** noun & adjective

**functionary** noun an official.

**fund** noun **1** a stock of money, especially that available for a particular purpose. **2** an available stock or supply; *a fund of jokes*. ●verb provide with money. □ **in funds** (*informal*) having money to spend.

**fundamental** adverb **1** of the basis or foundation of a subject etc., serving as a starting-point. **2** very important, essential. ●plural noun (**fundamentals**) fundamental facts or principles. □ **fundamentally** adverb

**fundamentalism** noun strict maintenance of traditional orthodox religious beliefs; belief that the Bible contains accurate historical records and should be accepted strictly and literally as the basis of Protestant Christianity. □ **fundamentalist** noun & adjective

**fundholder** noun a GP or medical practice which controls its own budget. □ **fundholding** noun

**funeral** noun **1** the ceremony of burying or cremating the dead. **2** a procession to this. **3** (*slang*) a person's unpleasant responsibility or concern; *that's your funeral*. □ **funeral director** an undertaker.

**funerary** (few-ner-er-i) adjective of or used for burial or a funeral.

**funereal** (few-neer-iăl) adjective suitable for a funeral; dismal, dark. □ **funereally** adverb

**funfair** noun a fair with amusements and sideshows.

**fungal** adjective of a fungus.

**fungicide** (fun-ji-syd) noun a fungus-destroying substance. □ **fungicidal** adjective

**fungoid** (fung-oid) adjective like a fungus. ●noun a fungoid plant.

**fungous** (fung-ŭs) adjective like a fungus.

**fungus** noun (plural **fungi**, *pronounced* **fung-I**) plant without leaves, flowers, or green colouring matter, growing on other plants or on decaying matter and including mushrooms, toadstools, and moulds.

**funicular** (few-nik-yoo-ler) noun a cable railway with ascending and descending cars counterbalancing each other.

**funk** noun (*slang*) **1** fear. **2** a coward. **3** funky music. ●verb (*slang*) show fear; fear and shirk.

**funky** adjective (*slang*) (of jazz etc.) earthy, soulful, emotional, with a heavy rhythm.

**funnel** noun **1** a tube or pipe, wide at the top and narrow at the bottom, for pouring liquids or powders into small openings. **2** a metal chimney on a steam engine or steamship. ●verb (**funnelled, funnelling**; *Amer.* **funneled, funneling**) move through a funnel or a narrowing space.

**funny** *adjective* (**funnier, funniest**) **1** causing amusement. **2** puzzling, hard to account for. **3** (*informal*) slightly unwell or insane. □ **funny bone** part of the elbow over which a very sensitive nerve passes. **funny business** trickery. □ **funnily** *adverb*

**fur** *noun* **1** the short fine soft hair covering the bodies of certain animals. **2** animal skin with the fur on it, especially when used for making or trimming clothes. **3** fabric imitating this. **4** a coat or other garment of real or imitation fur. **5** a coating formed on a sick or unhealthy person's tongue. **6** the coating formed by hard water on the inside of a kettle or pipes. ● *verb* (**furred, furring**) cover or become covered with fur.

**furbelows** *plural noun* showy trimmings; *frills and furbelows.*

**furbish** *verb* polish, clean or renovate.

**furcate** (**fer**-kayt) *adjective* forked, branched. ● *verb* fork, divide. □ **furcation** *noun*

**furious** *adjective* **1** full of anger. **2** violent, intense; *a furious pace.* □ **furiously** *adverb*

**furl** *verb* (**furled, furling**) roll up and fasten (a sail, flag, or umbrella).

**furlong** *noun* one-eighth of a mile, 220 yards.

**furlough** (**fer**-loh) *noun* leave of absence, especially military. ● *verb* (*Amer.*) **1** grant furlough to. **2** spend furlough.

**furnace** *noun* **1** an enclosed structure for intense heating by fire, especially of metals or water. **2** a very hot place.

**furnish** *verb* **1** equip (a room or house etc.) with furniture. **2** provide or supply.

**furnishings** *plural noun* furniture and fitments, curtains, etc. in a room or house.

**furniture** *noun* **1** the movable articles (such as tables, chairs, beds) needed in a room or house etc. **2** a ship's equipment. **3** accessories, e.g. the handles and lock on a door.

**furore** (fewr-or-i) *noun* (*Amer.* **furor**) an uproar of enthusiastic admiration or fury.

**furrier** (**fu**-ri-er) *noun* a person who deals in furs or fur clothes.

**furrow** *noun* **1** a long cut in the ground made by a plough or other implement. **2** a groove resembling this; a deep wrinkle in the skin. ● *verb* make furrows in.

**furry** *adjective* (**furrier, furriest**) **1** like fur. **2** covered with fur.

**further** *adverb & adjective* **1** more distant in space or time. **2** to a greater extent, more, additional; *shall enquire further, made further enquiries.*

■**Usage** See the note under **farther**.

● *verb* help the progress of; *further someone's interests.* □ **further education** education for people above school age.

**furtherance** *noun* the furthering of someone's interests etc.

**furthermore** *adverb* in addition, moreover.

**furthermost** *adjective* most distant.

**furthest** *adjective* most distant. ● *adverb* to or at the greatest distance.

■**Usage** See the note under **farther**.

**furtive** *adjective* sly, stealthy. □ **furtively** *adverb*, **furtiveness** *noun*

**fury** *noun* **1** wild anger, rage. **2** violence of weather etc.; *the storm's fury.* **3** a violently angry person, especially a woman. **4** (**Furies**) (*Gk. myth.*) snake-haired goddesses sent from the underworld to punish crime. □ **like fury** (*informal*) intensely, powerfully.

**furze** *noun* gorse.

**fuse**[1] *noun* (in an electric circuit) a short piece of wire designed to melt and break the circuit if the current exceeds a safe level. ● *verb* **1** blend or amalgamate (metals, living bones, institutions, etc.) into a whole. **2** fit (a circuit or appliance) with a fuse. **3** cease or cause to cease functioning through the melting of a fuse. □ **fuse-box** *noun* a box containing the fuses of an electrical system.

**fuse**[2] *noun* (also **fuze**) a length of easily burnt material for igniting a bomb or an explosive charge. ● *verb* fit a fuse to.

**fuselage** (**few**-zěl-ah*zh*) *noun* the body of an aeroplane.

**fusible** *adjective* able to be fused. □ **fusibility** *noun*

**fusil** (**few**-zil) *noun* (*hist.*) a light musket.

**fusiliers** (few-zi-**leerz**) *plural noun* any of several infantry regiments formerly armed with fusils.

**fusillade** (few-zi-**layd**) *noun* **1** a continuous firing of guns. **2** a great outburst of questions, criticism, etc.

**fusion** (**few**-*zh*ŏn) *noun* **1** fusing, the blending or uniting of different things into a whole. **2** the union of atomic nuclei to form a heavier nucleus, usually with release of energy.

**fuss** *noun* **1** unnecessary excitement or activity. **2** a display of worry about something unimportant. **3** a vigorous protest or dispute. ● *verb* make a fuss; bother (a person) with unimportant matters or by fussing. □ **make a fuss of** *or* **over** treat with a great display of attention or affection.

**fusspot** *noun* (*informal*) a person who fusses habitually.

**fussy** *adjective* (**fussier, fussiest**) **1** often fussing. **2** fastidious. **3** full of unnecessary detail or decoration. □ **fussily** *adverb*, **fussiness** *noun*

**fustian** *noun* **1** a thick twilled cotton (usually dark) cloth. **2** pompous language.

**fusty** *adjective* (**fustier, fustiest**) **1** musty, stuffy. **2** old-fashioned in ideas etc. □ **fustiness** *noun*

**futile** (few-tyl) *adjective* producing no result, useless. □ **futility** (few-**til**-iti) *noun*

**futon** (foo-tonn) *noun* a Japanese quilted mattress used as a bed; this with a wooden frame, convertible into a couch.

**future** *adjective* belonging or referring to the time coming after the present; *Grammar* (of a tense) describing an event yet to happen. ●*noun* future time, events, or condition. □ **future perfect** *Grammar* a tense giving the sense 'will have done'. **in future** from this time onwards.

**futurism** *noun* an artistic movement launched in Italy in 1909 that departed from traditional forms so as to express movement, growth, and celebration of new technology. □ **futurist** *noun*

**futuristic** (few-tewr-**ist**-ik) *adjective* **1** looking suitable for the future, not traditional. **2** of futurism.

**futurity** (few-**tewr**-iti) *noun* (*literary*) future time.

**futurology** *noun* the forecasting of the future especially from present trends in society.

**fuze** alternative spelling of FUSE².

**fuzz** *noun* **1** fluff, something fluffy or frizzy. **2** (*slang*) the police.

**fuzzy** *adjective* (**fuzzier**, **fuzziest**) **1** like fuzz; covered with fuzz. **2** frizzy. **3** blurred, indistinct. □ **fuzzily** *adverb*, **fuzziness** *noun*

# Gg

**G** noun (plural **Gs** or **G's**) *Music* the fifth note of the scale of C major.

**g** abbreviation (also **g**) **1** gram(s). **2** gravity; the acceleration due to this.

**GA, Ga.** abbreviation Georgia (USA).

**Ga** symbol gallium.

**gab** noun (*informal*) chatter. □ **have the gift of the gab** be good at talking.

**gabardine** (gab-er-deen) noun (also **gaberdine**) **1** a strong fabric woven in a twill pattern. **2** a coat made of this.

**gabble** verb talk quickly and indistinctly. ●noun gabbled talk. □ **gabbler** noun

**gaberdine** alternative spelling of GABARDINE.

**Gable**, (William) Clark (1901–60), American film actor.

**gable** noun the triangular upper part of an outside wall at the end of a ridged roof. □ **gabled** adjective

**Gabon** (gă-**bon**) a country on the west coast of Africa. □ **Gabonese** (gab-ŏn-**eez**) adjective & noun (plural **Gabonese**).

**Gaborone** (kab-oo-**roh**-ni) the capital of Botswana.

**gad** verb (**gadded**, **gadding**) (usu. foll. by *about*) go about aimlessly or in search of pleasure.

**gadabout** noun a person who gads about.

**Gadaffi** (gă-**dah**-fi), Muammar al- (born 1942), head of the State of Libya since 1970.

**gadfly** noun a fly that bites horses and cattle.

**gadget** noun a small mechanical device or tool. □ **gadgetry** noun

**gadolinium** (gad-ŏ-**lin**-iŭm) noun a metallic element (symbol Gd) resembling steel in appearance.

**Gael** (*pronounced* gayl) noun a Scottish or Irish Celt.

**Gaelic** (gay-lik) noun **1** (also *pronounced* gal-ik) the Celtic language of the Scots. **2** the Irish language. ●adjective of or in Gaelic.

**gaff** noun a stick with an iron hook for landing large fish caught with rod and line. ●verb seize with a gaff; *gaffing a salmon*. □ **blow the gaff** (*slang*) reveal a plot or secret.

**gaffe** noun a blunder.

**gaffer** noun (*informal*) **1** an elderly man. **2** (*informal*) a boss or foreman. **3** the chief electrician in a film or television production unit.

**gag** noun **1** something put into a person's mouth or tied across it to prevent speaking

or crying out. **2** anything that prevents freedom of speech or of writing. **3** a joke or funny story, especially as part of a comedian's act. ●verb (**gagged, gagging**) **1** put a gag into or over the mouth of. **2** prevent from having freedom of speech or of writing; *we cannot gag the press*. **3** retch or choke.

**gaga** (**gah**-gah) adjective (*slang*) **1** senile. **2** crazy.

**Gagarin** (gă-**gar**-in), Yuri Alekseevich (1934–68), Russian cosmonaut, who in 1961 made the first manned space flight.

**gage**[1] noun a pledge, a thing given as security.

**gage**[2] Amer. spelling of GAUGE.

**gaggle** noun **1** a flock of geese. **2** (*informal*) a disorderly group.

**gaiety** noun (*Amer.* **gayety**) **1** cheerfulness, a happy and lighthearted manner. **2** merrymaking.

**gaily** adverb **1** in a cheerful light-hearted manner. **2** in bright colours.

**gain** verb **1** obtain, especially something desirable. **2** make a profit. **3** acquire gradually, get more of; *gained strength after illness*. **4** (of a clock etc.) become ahead of the correct time. **5** (often foll. by *on*) get nearer in racing or pursuit; *our horse was gaining on the favourite*. **6** reach (a desired place); *gained the shore*. ●noun **1** an increase in wealth or possessions. **2** an improvement, an increase in amount or power. □ **gain ground 1** advance. **2** (foll. by *on*) catch up with (a person). **gain time** improve one's chances by arranging or accepting a delay. □ **gainer** noun

**gainful** adjective profitable. □ **gainfully** adverb

**gainsay** verb (**gainsaid, gainsaying**) (*formal*) deny or contradict; *there is no gainsaying it*.

**Gainsborough** (gaynz-bŏrŏ), Thomas (1727–88), English painter of portraits and landscapes.

**gait** noun a manner of walking or running.

**gaiter** noun a covering of cloth or leather for the lower leg.

**gal** noun (*informal*) a girl.

**gala** (**gah**-lă) noun **1** a festive occasion. **2** a sports gathering; *a swimming gala*.

**galactic** (gă-**lak**-tik) adjective of a galaxy or galaxies.

**Galahad** (in legends of King Arthur) a knight of immaculate purity, destined to retrieve the Holy Grail.

**galantine** (gal-ăn-teen) *noun* white meat or fish boned and spiced and cooked in the form of a roll, served cold.

**Galapagos Islands** (gă-lap-ă-gŏs) a group of islands in the Pacific on the Equator, west of Ecuador (to which they belong).

**Galatians** (gă-lay-shănz) □ **Epistle to the Galatians** a book of the New Testament.

**galaxy** (gal-ăk-si) *noun* **1** any of the large independent systems of stars existing in space. **2** a brilliant company of beautiful or famous people. **3** (**the Galaxy**) the galaxy containing the Earth. **4** (**the Galaxy**) the Milky Way.

**Galbraith,** J(ohn) K(enneth) (born 1908), Canadian-born American economist.

**gale** *noun* **1** a very strong wind; *gale-force winds*. **2** a noisy outburst; *gales of laughter*.

**Galen** (gay-lin) (129–99), ancient Greek physician.

**Galilean** *adjective* of Galileo.

**Galilee** the northern part of ancient Palestine west of the Jordan, now in Israel. □ **Sea of Galilee** (also called **Lake Tiberias**) an inland lake in northern Israel.

**Galileo Galilei** (gal-i-lay-oh gal-i-lay-ee) (1564–1642), Italian astronomer and physicist, one of the founders of modern science.

**gall**¹ (*pronounced* gawl) *noun* **1** bile. **2** bitterness of feeling. **3** (*slang*) impudence. □ **gall bladder** an organ attached to the liver, storing and releasing bile.

**gall**² (*pronounced* gawl) *noun* **1** a sore spot, especially on the skin of an animal. **2** an abnormal growth produced by an insect, fungus, etc. on a plant, especially on an oak tree. ● *verb* **1** rub and make sore. **2** vex or humiliate.

**gallant** (gal-ănt) *adjective* **1** brave, chivalrous. **2** fine, stately; *our gallant ship.* □ **gallantly** *adverb*, **gallantry** *noun*

**galleon** (gal-i-ŏn) *noun* a large Spanish sailing-ship used in the 15th–17th centuries.

**galleria** (gal-ĕ-ree-ă) *noun* a collection of small shops under one roof.

**gallery** *noun* **1** a room or building for showing works of art. **2** a balcony, especially in a church or hall; *minstrels' gallery*. **3** the highest balcony in a theatre. **4** a raised covered platform or passage along the wall of a building. **5** a long room or passage, especially one used for a special purpose; *a shooting gallery*. **6** the spectators at a golf match. **7** an underground passage in a mine. □ **play to the gallery** try to win favour by appealing to the taste of the general public.

**galley** *noun* (*plural* **galleys**) **1** a long low medieval ship, usually rowed by slaves or criminals. **2** an ancient Greek or Roman warship propelled by oars. **3** the kitchen in a ship or aircraft. **4** an oblong tray for holding type for printing. □ **galley proof** a printed proof made from type set in a galley.

**Gallic** (gal-ik) *adjective* **1** of ancient Gaul. **2** of France, typically French; *Gallic wit*.

**Gallicism** (gal-i-sizm) *noun* a French idiom.

**gallinaceous** (gal-in-ay-shŭs) *adjective* of the group of birds that includes domestic poultry and pheasants.

**galling** (gawl-ing) *adjective* vexing, humiliating.

**Gallipoli** (gă-lip-ŏli) a peninsula on the European side of the Dardanelles, the scene of heavy fighting in 1915–16 during the First World War.

**gallium** *noun* a soft bluish-white metallic element (symbol Ga).

**gallivant** *verb* (*informal*) gad about.

**gallon** *noun* a measure for liquids, = 8 pints (4.546 litres, or 3.785 litres in the USA).

**gallop** *noun* **1** a horse's fastest pace, with all four feet off the ground simultaneously in each stride. **2** a ride at this pace. ● *verb* (**galloped, galloping**) **1** go at a gallop, cause a horse to do this. **2** progress very fast; *galloping inflation*.

**Galloway** (gal-ŏ-way) *see* DUMFRIES AND GALLOWAY.

**gallows** *noun* **1** a framework with a suspended noose for the hanging of criminals. **2** (**the gallows**) execution by hanging.

**gallstone** *noun* a small hard mass that sometimes forms in the gall bladder.

**Gallup poll** an opinion poll, used especially to forecast how people will vote in an election. (¶ Named after G. H. Gallup (1901–84), American statistician who devised it.)

**galore** *adverb* in plenty; *whisky galore*.

**galosh** *noun* (also **golosh**) an overshoe, usually made of rubber.

**Galsworthy** (gawlz-wer-thi), John (1867–1933), English novelist and dramatist.

**galumph** (gă-lumf) *verb* (*informal*) move noisily or clumsily.

**Galvani** (gal-vah-ni), Luigi (1737–98), Italian anatomist, pioneer of research into the electrical properties of living things. (¶ The words *galvanic*, *galvanize*, and *galvanometer* embody his name.)

**galvanic** (gal-van-ik) *adjective* producing an electric current by chemical action; *a galvanic cell*. □ **galvanically** *adverb*

**galvanize** *verb* (also **galvanise**) **1** stimulate into sudden activity. **2** coat (iron) with zinc in order to protect it from rust; *galvanized iron*. □ **galvanization** *noun*

**galvanometer** (gal-vă-**nom**-it-er) *noun* an instrument for measuring small electric currents.

**Gama** (gah-mă), Vasco da (*c.*1469–1524), Portuguese explorer, the first European to sail round the Cape of Good Hope.

**Gambia** (also **the Gambia**) a country in West Africa. □ **Gambian** *adjective & noun*

**gambit** *noun* **1** an opening sequence of moves in chess in which a player deliberately sacrifices a pawn or piece in order to gain an advantage. **2** an action or statement intended to secure some advantage.

**gamble** *verb* **1** play games of chance for money. **2** stake or risk money etc. in the hope of great gain. **3** (foll. by *on*) stake one's hopes; *gambled on its being a fine day.* ●*noun* **1** a spell of gambling. **2** a risky attempt or undertaking. □ **gambler** *noun*

**gamboge** (gam-**bohj**) *noun* a gum resin used as a yellow pigment and as a purgative.

**gambol** *verb* (**gambolled**, **gambolling**; *Amer.* **gamboled**, **gamboling**) jump or skip about in play. ●*noun* a gambolling movement.

**game¹** *noun* **1** a form of play or sport, especially one with rules. **2** a single section forming a scoring unit in some games (e.g. in tennis or bridge). **3** a scheme or plan, a trick; *so that's his little game!* **4** a type of activity or business; *she has been in the antiques game a long time.* **5** (**games**) a series of athletics or sports contests; *the Olympic Games.* **6** wild animals or birds hunted for sport or food. **7** their flesh as food; *game pie.* ●*verb* gamble for money stakes. ●*adjective* **1** brave. **2** having spirit or energy; *are you game for a lark?* □ **game laws** laws regulating the killing and preservation of game. **game point** the stage in a game when one side will win if it gains the next point. **give the game away** reveal a secret or scheme. **on the game** (*slang*) involved in prostitution or thieving. **the game is up** the secret or deception is revealed. □ **gamely** *adverb*

**game²** *adjective* lame; *a game leg.*

**gamekeeper** *noun* a person employed to protect and breed game.

**gamelan** (gam-ĕl-an) *noun* **1** the standard instrumental group of Indonesia, consisting of sets of tuned gongs and other percussion instruments as well as string and woodwind instruments. **2** a type of xylophone used in this group.

**gamesmanship** *noun* the art of winning contests by upsetting the confidence of one's opponent.

**gamester** *noun* a gambler.

**gamete** (gam-eet) *noun* a sexual cell capable of fusing with another in reproduction. □ **gametic** (gă-met-ik) *adjective*

**gamin** (gam-an) *noun* **1** a street urchin. **2** an impudent child.

**gamine** (gam-een) *noun* **1** a female gamin. **2** a girl with mischievous charm.

**gamma** *noun* **1** the third letter of the Greek alphabet (Γ, γ). **2** a third-class mark in an examination. □ **gamma radiation** *or* **rays** X-rays of very short wavelength emitted by radioactive substances.

**gammon** *noun* **1** the bottom piece of a flitch of bacon, including a hind leg. **2** cured or smoked ham.

**gammy** *adjective* (*slang*) = GAME².

**gamut** (gam-ŭt) *noun* the whole series, range, or scope of anything; *the whole gamut of emotion.*

**gamy** (gay-mi) *adjective* tasting or smelling like game does when it is high.

**Ganapati** (găn-ă-pă-ti) = GANESHA.

**gander** *noun* a male goose.

**Gandhi¹** (gahn-di), Indira (1917–84), Indian stateswoman, Prime Minister 1966–77 and 1980–4; and son Rajiv (1944–91), Indian statesman, Prime Minister 1984–9.

**Gandhi²** (gahn-di), Mahatma (Mohandas Karamchand) (1869–1948), Indian statesman, who became the leader and symbol of the nationalist movement in opposition to British rule.

**Ganesha** (gă-nay-shă) (also **Ganapati**) an elephant-headed Hindu god, worshipped as the remover of obstacles and as patron of learning.

**gang** *noun* **1** a band of people going about or working together, especially for some criminal purpose. **2** a group of friends who go about together. **3** a group of workers; *a road gang.* **gang rape** the rape of one person by several men in succession. **gang up** (*informal*) combine in a group (against a person); *they ganged up on him.*

**Ganges** (gan-jeez) a river in the north of India, held sacred by Hindus, flowing from the Himalayas through Bangladesh to the Bay of Bengal.

**gangling** *adjective* tall, thin, and awkward-looking.

**ganglion** *noun* (*plural* **ganglia** *or* **ganglions**) **1** a group of nerve cells from which nerve fibres radiate. **2** a cyst on a tendon sheath. □ **ganglionic** (gang-li-on-ik) *adjective*

**gangplank** *noun* a movable plank used as a bridge for walking onto or off a boat.

**gangrene** *noun* death and decay of body tissue, usually caused by blockage of the blood supply. □ **gangrenous** (gang-rin-ŭs) *adjective*

**gangster** *noun* a member of a gang of violent criminals.

**gangue** (*pronounced* gang) *noun* valueless earth or other material in which ore is found.

**gangway** *noun* **1** a passage, especially between rows of seats. **2** a movable bridge from a ship to the land; the opening in a ship's side into which this fits. ● *interjection* make way!

**ganja** *noun* marijuana.

**gannet** (gan-it) *noun* **1** a large diving sea bird. **2** *slang* a greedy person.

**gantry** *noun* a light bridge-like overhead framework for supporting a travelling crane, railway signals over several tracks, etc.

**Ganymede** (gan-i-meed) **1** (*Gk. myth.*) a Trojan youth who was so beautiful that he was carried off to be Zeus' cup-bearer. **2** the largest satellite of the planet Jupiter.

**gaol** alternative spelling of JAIL.

**gaolbird** alternative spelling of JAILBIRD.

**gaolbreak** alternative spelling of JAILBREAK.

**gaoler** alternative spelling of JAILER.

**gap** *noun* **1** a break or opening in something continuous such as a hedge or fence, or between hills. **2** an unfilled space or interval; *a gap between programmes*. **3** something lacking; *a gap in one's education*. **4** a wide difference in ideas. □ **gappy** *adjective*

**gape** *verb* **1** open the mouth wide. **2** stare in surprise or wonder. **3** open or be open wide; *a gaping chasm*. ● *noun* an open-mouthed stare.

**garage** (ga-rah*zh* or ga-rij) *noun* **1** a building in which to keep a motor vehicle or vehicles. **2** a commercial establishment where motor vehicles are repaired and serviced. **3** a roadside establishment selling petrol and oil etc. ● *verb* put or keep in a garage. □ **garage sale** a sale of household goods, often held in the garage of a private house.

**garb** *noun* clothing, especially of a distinctive kind; *a man in clerical garb*. ● *verb* clothe.

**garbage** *noun* rubbish or refuse.

**garble** *verb* give a confused account of something, so that a message or story is distorted or misunderstood.

**Garbo**, Greta (original name: Greta Gustafsson) (1905–90), Swedish film actress.

**García Lorca** *see* LORCA.

**Garda** *noun* (*plural* **Gardai**) the police force of the Republic of Ireland.

**garden** *noun* **1** a piece of cultivated ground, especially attached to a house. **2** (**gardens**) ornamental public grounds. ● *verb* tend a garden. □ **garden centre** a place where plants and gardening tools are sold. **garden city** a town laid out with many open spaces and planted with numerous trees. **garden party** a party held on a lawn or in a garden or park. **lead up the garden path** (*informal*) entice, mislead deliberately.

**gardener** *noun* a person who tends a garden, either as a job or as a hobby.

**gardenia** (gar-deen-iă) *noun* a tree or shrub with large fragrant white or yellow flowers.

**gargantuan** (gar-gan-tew-ăn) *adjective* gigantic.

**gargle** *verb* wash or rinse the inside of the throat with liquid held there by air breathed out from the lungs. ● *noun* a liquid used for this.

**gargoyle** *noun* a grotesque carved face or figure, especially as a gutter-spout carrying water clear of a wall.

**Garibaldi** (ga-ri-bawl-di), Giuseppe (1807–82), Italian patriot and military leader, who played a vital part in the unification of Italy.

**garibaldi** (ga-ri-bawl-di) *noun* a biscuit containing a layer of currants.

**garish** (gair-ish) *adjective* excessively bright, gaudy, over-decorated. □ **garishly** *adverb*

**Garland**, Judy (original name: Frances Gumm) (1922–69), American film actress and singer.

**garland** *noun* a wreath of flowers etc. worn or hung as a decoration. ● *verb* adorn with a garland or garlands.

**garlic** *noun* **1** an onion-like plant. **2** its bulbous root that has a strong taste and smell, used for flavouring. □ **garlicky** *adjective*

**garment** *noun* an article of clothing.

**garner** *verb* store up, collect. ● *noun* (*literary*) a storehouse.

**garnet** *noun* a semiprecious stone of deep transparent red.

**garnish** *verb* decorate (especially food for the table). ● *noun* something used for garnishing.

**garotte** alternative spelling of GARROTTE.

**garret** *noun* an attic.

**Garrick** (ga-rik), David (1717–79), English actor, who became manager of Drury Lane theatre.

**garrison** *noun* **1** troops stationed in a town or fort to defend it; *a garrison town*. **2** the building or fort they occupy. ● *verb* **1** place a garrison in. **2** occupy and defend; *troops garrisoned the town*.

**garrotte** (gă-rot) (also **garotte**; *Amer.* **garrote**) *verb* execute or kill by strangulation, especially with a wire around the neck. ● *noun* a device used for this.

**garrulous** (ga-roo-lŭs) *adjective* talkative. □ **garrulously** *adverb*, **garrulousness** *noun*, **garrulity** (gă-roo-liti) *noun*

**garter** noun **1** a band especially of elastic worn round the leg to keep a stocking up. **2** (**the Garter**) the highest order in English knighthood. □ **garter stitch** rows of plain stitch in knitting.

**gas** noun (plural **gases**) **1** an airlike substance with particles that can move freely, i.e. not a liquid or solid. **2** any of the gases or mixtures of gases used for lighting, heating, or cooking; gas cooker; gas fire. **3** poisonous gas used to disable an enemy in war. **4** nitrous oxide or other gas used as an anaesthetic. **5** (slang) idle talk. **6** (Amer. informal) petrol. ●verb (**gassed, gassing**) **1** expose to gas, poison or overcome by gas. **2** (informal) talk idly for a long time. □ **gas chamber** a room that can be filled with poisonous gas to kill animals or prisoners. **gas-fired** adjective heated by burning gas. **gas mask** a device worn over the face to protect the wearer against poisonous gas. **gas permeable** adjective (especially of contact lenses) capable of penetration by gases. **gas ring** a hollow perforated ring through which gas flows for cooking on.

**gasbag** noun (informal) a person who talks too much.

**gaseous** (gas-ius) adjective of or like a gas.

**gash** noun a long deep slash, cut, or wound. ●verb make a gash in.

**gasholder** noun a gasometer.

**gasify** verb (**gasified, gasifying**) change into gas. □ **gasification** noun

**Gaskell**, Mrs Elizabeth Cleghorn (1810–65), English novelist.

**gasket** noun a flat sheet or ring of rubber or other soft material used for sealing a joint between metal surfaces to prevent gas, steam, or liquid from entering or escaping.

**gaslight** noun light given by a jet of burning gas.

**gasoline** noun (also **gasolene**) (Amer.) petrol.

**gasometer** (gas-om-it-er) noun a large tank in which gas is stored and from which it is distributed through pipes.

**gasp** verb **1** struggle for breath with the mouth open. **2** draw in the breath sharply in astonishment etc. **3** speak in a breathless way. ●noun a breath drawn in sharply.

**gassy** adjective **1** of or like a gas. **2** (informal) using too many words.

**gasteropod** alternative spelling of GASTROPOD.

**gastric** adjective of the stomach. □ **gastric flu** sickness and diarrhoea of unknown cause. **gastric juice** digestive fluid secreted by the stomach.

**gastritis** (gas-try-tiss) noun inflammation of the stomach.

**gastroenteritis** (gas-troh-en-ter-I-tiss) noun inflammation of the stomach and intestines.

**gastronomy** (gas-**tron**-ŏmi) noun the science or art of good eating and drinking. □ **gastronomic** (gas-trŏ-**nom**-ik) adjective

**gastropod** (gas-trŏ-pod) noun (also **gasteropod**) a mollusc (such as a snail or limpet) that moves by means of a muscular organ on its ventral surface.

**gastroscope** (gas-trŏ-skohp) noun an instrument that can be passed down the throat for looking inside the stomach.

**gasworks** noun a place where gas for lighting and heating is manufactured.

**gate** noun **1** a movable barrier, usually on hinges, serving as a door in a wall or fence, or regulating the passage of water etc. **2** a means of entrance or exit. **3** a numbered place of access to aircraft at an airport. **4** an arrangement of slots controlling the movement of a gear lever in a motor vehicle. **5** an electrical device that controls the passage of electrical signals; (in computers) a circuit with one output that is activated only by a combination of input signals. **6** the number of spectators entering by payment to see a football match etc.; the amount of money taken. ●verb confine to college or school as a punishment.

**-gate** combining form describing scandals comparable in some way to the Watergate scandal of 1972; Irangate; Dianagate.

**gateau** (gat-oh) noun (plural **gateaus** or **gateaux**, pronounced gat-ohz) a large rich cream cake.

**gatecrash** verb go to a private party etc. without being invited. □ **gatecrasher** noun

**gatehouse** noun a house built at the side of or over a large gate.

**gatekeeper** noun a person on duty at a gate.

**gateleg** noun (in full **gateleg table**) a table with folding flaps supported by legs swung open like a gate. □ **gatelegged** adjective

**gateway** noun **1** an opening or structure framing a gate. **2** any means of access; the gateway to success.

**gather** verb **1** bring or come together. **2** collect, especially as harvest; pick. **3** increase gradually; gather speed. **4** understand or conclude; I gather your proposal was accepted. **5** draw (parts) together; his brow was gathered in thought. **6** pull fabric into gathers; a gathered skirt. **7** (of a sore) swell up and form pus. ●noun a fold or pleat.

**gathering** noun **1** an assembly of people. **2** an inflamed swelling with pus in it.

**GATT** abbreviation General Agreement on Tariffs and Trade; a treaty to which more than 100 countries are parties, to promote trade and economic development.

**gauche** (*pronounced* **goh**sh) *adjective* **1** socially awkward. **2** tactless.

**gaucherie** (**goh**-sher-i) *noun* gauche manners; a gauche action.

**gaucho** (**gow**-choh) *noun* (*plural* **gauchos**) a cowboy from the South American pampas.

**gaudy** *adjective* (**gaudier**, **gaudiest**) showy or bright in a tasteless way. □ **gaudily** *adverb*, **gaudiness** *noun*

**gauge** (*pronounced* gayj) *noun* (*Amer.* **gage**) **1** a standard measure of contents, fineness of textiles, thickness of sheet metal, or diameter of bullets. **2** the distance between pairs of rails or between opposite wheels. **3** an instrument used for measuring, marked with regular divisions or units of measurement. **4** capacity, extent. **5** a means of estimating something. ●*verb* **1** measure exactly. **2** estimate, form a judgement of.

**Gauguin** (**goh**-gan), Paul (1848-1903), French painter.

**Gaul** an ancient region of Europe corresponding roughly to modern France and Belgium. ●*noun* a native or inhabitant of Gaul.

**Gaulle** (*pronounced* gohl), Charles Joseph de (1890-1970), French general and statesman, President of the French Republic 1959-69.

**gaunt** *adjective* **1** lean and haggard. **2** grim or desolate-looking. □ **gauntness** *noun*

**gauntlet** *noun* **1** a glove with a wide cuff covering the wrist. **2** a glove with metal plates worn by soldiers in the Middle Ages. □ **run the gauntlet** be exposed to continuous severe criticism or risk. (¶ The phrase is derived from a former military and naval punishment in which the victim was made to pass between two rows of men who struck him as he passed.) **throw down** (*or* **take up**) **the gauntlet** issue (or accept) a challenge.

**gauss** (*rhymes with* house) *noun* (*plural* **gauss**) a unit of magnetic flux density. (¶ Named after K. F. Gauss (1777-1855), German mathematician, astronomer, and physicist.)

**Gautama** (**gow**-tă-mă) the family name of the Buddha.

**gauze** *noun* **1** thin transparent woven material of silk or cotton etc. **2** fine wire mesh. □ **gauzy** *adjective*

**Gavaskar** (gă-vas-kar), Sunil Manohar (born 1949), Indian cricketer.

**gave** *see* GIVE.

**gavel** (gav-ĕl) *noun* a hammer used by an auctioneer, chairman, or judge to call for attention or order.

**gavotte** (gă-vot) *noun* an old French dance.

**gawk** *verb* (*informal*) gawp. ●*noun* an awkward or bashful person.

**gawky** *adjective* awkward and ungainly. □ **gawkiness** *noun*

**gawp** *verb* (*informal*) stare stupidly.

**Gay**, John (1685-1732), English poet and dramatist, best known for *The Beggar's Opera*.

**gay** *adjective* **1** light-hearted and cheerful. **2** brightly coloured. **3** careless, thoughtless; *gay abandon*. **4** homosexual. ●*noun* a homosexual (especially male). □ **gayness** *noun*

**gayety** Amer. spelling of GAIETY.

**Gay-Lussac** (gay-**loo**-sak), Joseph Louis (1778-1850), French chemist and physicist, famous for his work on gases.

**Gaza Strip** (gah-ză) a strip of coastal territory on the SE Mediterranean, including the town of Gaza.

**gaze** *verb* look long and steadily. ●*noun* a long steady look.

**gazebo** (gă-zee-boh) *noun* (*plural* **gazebos**) a structure, such as a raised turret or summer-house, with a wide view.

**gazelle** *noun* a small graceful Asian or African antelope.

**gazette** *noun* the title of certain newspapers, or of official journals that contain public notices and lists of government appointments.

**gazetteer** (gaz-it-**eer**) *noun* an index of geographical names and statistics.

**gazpacho** (gahs-pa-choh) *noun* Spanish cold vegetable soup.

**gazump** *verb* (*informal*) raise the price of a property after accepting an offer from (a buyer).

**gazunder** *verb* (*informal*) lower an offer made to (a seller) for a property just before the exchange of contracts.

**GB** *abbreviation* Great Britain.

**GBH** *abbreviation* (*Brit.*) grievous bodily harm.

**GC** *abbreviation* (*Brit.*) George Cross.

**GCE** *abbreviation* (*Brit.*) General Certificate of Education.

**GCHQ** *abbreviation* (*Brit.*) Government Communications Headquarters.

**GCSE** *abbreviation* (*Brit.*) General Certificate of Secondary Education.

**Gd** *symbol* gadolinium.

**GDP** *abbreviation* gross domestic product.

**GDR** *abbreviation* (*hist.*) German Democratic Republic.

**Ge** *symbol* germanium.

**gear** *noun* **1** (often as **gears**) a set of toothed wheels working together in a machine to transmit rotary motion, especially those connecting the engine of a motor vehicle to the road wheels. **2** a particular setting of these; *first gear*. **3** apparatus or equipment; *aircraft landing gear*. **4** (*informal*) clothes. ●*verb* **1** provide with or connect by gears. **2** (foll. by *to*) adjust or adapt; *a factory* *geared to the export trade.* **3** (foll. by *up*) get ready; *the resort is gearing up for the tourist season.* □ **gear lever** (*Amer.* **gear shift**) a lever used to engage or change a gear. **in gear** with gear mechanism engaged. **out of gear** with it disengaged.

**gearbox** *noun* a case enclosing a gear mechanism.

**gearing** *noun* a set or arrangement of gears.

**gecko** (gek-oh) *noun* (*plural* **geckos**) a lizard of warm climates, able to climb walls by the adhesive pads on its toes.

**gee** *interjection* (also **gee whiz**) (*Amer. informal*) a mild exclamation of surprise or admiration.

**geese** *see* GOOSE.

**gee-up** *interjection* a command to a horse to move on or go faster.

**geezer** *noun* (*slang*) a person, an old man.

**Geiger counter** (gy-ger) a device for detecting and measuring radioactivity. (¶ Named after H. J. W. Geiger (1882–1945), German nuclear physicist, who developed the first device of this kind.)

**geisha** (gay-shă) *noun* a Japanese hostess trained to entertain men by dancing and singing.

**gel** (*pronounced* jel) *noun* a jelly-like substance. ●*verb* (**gelled, gelling**) set as a gel.

**gelatin** *noun* (also **gelatine**) a clear tasteless substance made by boiling the bones, skins, and connective tissue of animals, used in foods, medicine, and photographic film.

**gelatinize** (jil-at-i-nyz) *verb* (also **gelatinise**) make or become gelatinous. □ **gelatinization** *noun*

**gelatinous** (jil-at-in-ŭs) *adjective* of or like gelatine, jelly-like.

**geld** *verb* castrate (an animal).

**gelding** *noun* a gelded animal, especially a horse.

**gelignite** (jel-ig-nyt) *noun* an explosive containing nitroglycerine.

**gem** *noun* **1** (also **gemstone**) a precious stone, especially when cut and polished. **2** something valued because of its excellence or beauty; *the gem of the collection.*

**geminate** (jem-in-ayt) *verb* **1** double, repeat. **2** arrange in pairs. □ **gemination** *noun*

**Gemini** (jem-in-I) the third sign of the zodiac, the Twins. □ **Geminian** *adjective & noun*

**Gen.** *abbreviation* General.

**gen** (*pronounced* jen) *noun* (*slang*) information. ●*verb* □ **gen up** (**genned, genning**) (*slang*) gain information; give information to.

**gendarme** (*zh*on-darm) *noun* a French police officer.

**gender** *noun* **1** the class in which a noun is placed in grammatical grouping in certain languages, in particular masculine, feminine, or neuter. **2** a person's sex.

**gene** (*pronounced* jeen) *noun* each of the factors controlling heredity, carried by a chromosome. □ **gene therapy** the introduction of normal genes into cells in place of defective or missing ones in order to correct genetic disorders.

**genealogy** (jeen-i-al-ŏji) *noun* **1** an account of descent from an ancestor given by listing the intermediate persons; pedigree. **2** the science or study of family pedigrees. □ **genealogical** (jeeni-ă-loj-ikăl) *adjective*, **genealogist** *noun*

**genera** *see* GENUS.

**general** *adjective* **1** of or affecting all or nearly all; not partial, local, or particular. **2** involving various kinds, not specialized; *a general education.* **3** involving only main features, not detailed or specific; *spoke only in general terms.* **4** chief, head; *the general secretary.* ●*noun* **1** an army officer ranking below a Field Marshal. **2** a lieutenant general or major-general. **3** the chief of the Jesuits or other religious order. □ **general anaesthetic** one affecting the whole body, usually with loss of consciousness. **General Certificate of Education** an examination set especially for secondary school pupils at advanced level (and formerly, ordinary level) in England, Wales, and Northern Ireland. **General Certificate of Secondary Education** an examination replacing and combining the GCE ordinary level and CSE examinations. **general election** an election for representatives in Parliament from the whole country. **general knowledge** knowledge of a wide variety of subjects. **general meeting** one open to all members. **general practitioner** a community doctor who treats cases of all kinds. **general staff** officers assisting a military commander at headquarters. **general strike** a simultaneous strike by workers in all or most trades. **in general** as a general rule, usually; for the most part.

**generalissimo** *noun* (*plural* **generalissimos**) a commander of combined military, naval, and air forces, or of several armies.

**generality** (jen-er-al-iti) *noun* **1** being general. **2** a general statement lacking precise details.

**generalize** *verb* (also **generalise**) **1** draw a general conclusion from particular instances. **2** speak in general terms, use generalities. **3** bring into general use. □ **generalization** *noun*

**generally** *adverb* **1** usually, as a general rule. **2** widely, for the most part; *the plan was generally welcomed.* **3** in a general sense, without regard to details; *speaking generally.*

**generate** verb bring into existence, produce.

**generation** noun **1** generating; being generated. **2** a single stage in descent or pedigree, for example, children, parents, or grandparents. **3** all people born about the same time and therefore of the same age. **4** the average period (regarded as about 30 years) in which children grow up and take the former place of their parents. **5** (of machinery etc.) a set of models at one stage of development; *a new generation of computers*. □ **first-generation, second-generation**, etc. adjective being of the first, second, etc. generation within a family to exhibit a particular characteristic or to adopt a new nationality, allegiance, etc.; *first-generation Americans*. **generation gap** lack of understanding between people of different generations.

**generator** noun **1** an apparatus for producing gases, steam, etc. **2** a machine for converting mechanical energy into electricity.

**generic** (jin-e-rik) adjective of a whole genus or group. □ **generically** adverb

**generous** adjective **1** giving or ready to give freely, free from meanness or prejudice. **2** given freely, plentiful; *a generous gift*; *a generous portion*. □ **generously** adverb, **generosity** noun

**genesis** (jen-i-sis) noun **1** a beginning or origin. **2** (**Genesis**) the first book of the Old Testament, telling of the creation of the world.

**genetic** (ji-net-ik) adjective **1** of genes. **2** of genetics. **3** (**genetics**) the scientific study of heredity. □ **genetic code** the system of storage of genetic information in chromosomes. **genetic engineering** deliberate modification of hereditary features by treatment to transfer certain genes. **genetic fingerprinting** (or **profiling**) an analysis of body tissue or fluid to discover its cell-structure, used for identifying criminals or for proving a family relationship. □ **genetically** adverb

**geneticist** (ji-net-i-sist) noun an expert in genetics.

**Geneva** (ji-nee-vă) a city in SW Switzerland, on the Lake of Geneva. □ **Geneva Conventions** a series of international agreements made at Geneva between 1846 and 1949 governing the status and treatment of hospitals, ambulances, wounded persons, etc. during times of war.

**Genghis Khan** (geng-is kahn) (1162–1227), founder of the Mongol empire, which by the time of his death stretched from the Pacific to the Black Sea.

**genial** (jee-niăl) adjective **1** kindly, pleasant, and cheerful. **2** mild, pleasantly warm; *a genial climate*. □ **genially** adverb, **geniality** (jee-ni-al-iti) noun

**genie** (jee-ni) noun (in Arabian tales) a spirit or goblin with strange powers.

**genital** (jen-i-t'l) adjective of animal reproduction or reproductive organs. ● plural noun (**genitals**) (also **genitalia**, pronounced gen-i-tay-liă) noun the external sex organs of people and animals.

**genitive** (jen-i-tiv) noun the grammatical case showing source or possession in certain languages, corresponding to the use of *of* or *from* in English.

**genius** noun (plural **geniuses**) **1** exceptionally great mental ability; any great natural ability. **2** a person possessing this. **3** a guardian spirit; *one's evil genius*.

**Genoa** (jen-oh-ă) a city and seaport of NW Italy. □ **Genoese** (jen-oh-eez) adjective & noun

**genocide** (jen-ŏ-syd) noun deliberate extermination of a race of people. □ **genocidal** adjective

**genre** (pronounced zhahnr) noun **1** a particular kind or style of art or literature. **2** painting of scenes from ordinary life.

**gent** noun (informal) **1** a man, a gentleman. **2** (**the Gents**) a men's public lavatory.

**genteel** (jen-teel) adjective affectedly polite and refined. □ **genteelly** adverb

**gentian** (jen-shăn) noun a mountain plant usually with blue bell-like flowers. □ **gentian violet** a dye used as an antiseptic.

**Gentile** (jen-tyl) noun a person who is not Jewish. ● adjective of Gentiles.

**gentility** (jen-til-iti) noun good manners and elegance.

**gentle** adjective **1** mild, moderate, not rough or severe; *a gentle breeze*. **2** (old use) of good family; *of gentle birth*. □ **gently** adverb, **gentleness** noun

**gentlefolk** plural noun people of good family.

**gentleman** noun (plural **gentlemen**) **1** a man of honourable and kindly behaviour. **2** a man of good social position. **3** (in polite use) a man. □ **gentleman's agreement** one that is regarded as binding in honour but not enforceable at law. □ **gentlemanly** adjective

**gentlewoman** noun (plural **gentlewomen**) (old use) a lady.

**gentrify** verb (**gentrified, gentrifying**) renovate or convert (housing in a working-class area) so that it conforms to middle-class taste. □ **gentrification** noun

**gentry** plural noun **1** people next below the nobility in position and birth. **2** (scornful) people; *these gentry*.

**genuflect** (jen-yoo-flekt) verb bend the knee and lower the body, especially in worship. □ **genuflection** noun (also **genuflexion**)

**genuine** *adjective* really what it is said to be; *genuine pearls; with genuine pleasure.* □ **genuinely** *adverb,* **genuineness** *noun*

**genus** (**jee**-nŭs) *noun* (*plural* **genera,** *pronounced* **jen**-er-ă) **1** a group of animals or plants with common characteristics, usually containing several species. **2** (*informal*) a kind or sort. **3** (in logic) a class of things including subordinate kinds or species.

**geocentric** (jee-oh-**sen**-trik) *adjective* **1** considered as viewed from the earth's centre. **2** having the earth as its centre. □ **geocentrically** *adverb*

**geode** (**jee**-ohd) *noun* **1** a small cavity lined with crystals. **2** a rock containing this.

**geodesic** *adjective* (jee-oh-**dee**-zik) (also **geodetic,** *pronounced* jee-oh-**det**-ik) of geodesy. □ **geodesic dome** a dome built of short struts holding flat or triangular polygonal pieces, fitted together to form a rough hemisphere. **geodesic line** the shortest possible line between two points on a curved surface.

**geodesy** (jee-**od**-i-si) *noun* the scientific study of the earth's shape and size.

**geographical** *adjective* (also **geographic**) of geography. □ **geographical mile** a distance of one minute of longitude or latitude of the equator (about 1.85 km). □ **geographically** *adverb*

**geography** *noun* **1** the scientific study of the earth's surface and its physical features, climate, products, and population. **2** the physical features and arrangement of a place. □ **geographer** *noun*

**geologist** *noun* an expert in geology.

**geology** (jee-**ol**-ŏji) *noun* **1** the scientific study of the earth's crust, strata, origins of its rocks, etc. **2** the geological features of an area. □ **geological** *adjective,* **geologically** *adverb*

**geometric** *adjective* (also **geometrical**) **1** of geometry. **2** (of a design etc.) having regular lines and shapes. □ **geometric progression** a progression with a constant ratio between successive quantities (as 1, 3, 9, 27). □ **geometrically** *adverb*

**geometry** (jee-**om**-itri) *noun* the branch of mathematics dealing with the properties and relations of lines, angles, surfaces, and solids.

**Geordie** (**jor**-di) *noun* **1** a person from Tyneside. **2** the dialect of Tyneside.

**George**[1] the name of six kings of Great Britain and Ireland, who reigned as George I 1714–27, II 1727–60, III 1760–1820, IV 1820–30, V 1910–36, and VI 1936–52. □ **George Cross** a decoration for bravery (chiefly in civilian life) instituted by George VI in 1940.

**George**[2], St (possibly martyred in Palestine some time before the end of the 3rd century), the patron saint of England.

**Georgetown** the capital of Guyana.

**georgette** (jor-**jet**) *noun* a thin dress-material similar to crêpe.

**Georgia 1** a State of the south-eastern USA. **2** a republic between the Black Sea and the Caspian Sea.

**Georgian** (**jor**-jăn) *adjective* **1** of the time of Kings George I–IV or of George V and VI. **2** of Georgia. ●*noun* **1** a native or the language of Georgia in eastern Europe. **2** a native of Georgia in the USA.

**geothermal** (jee-oh-**ther**-măl) *adjective* of or using the heat produced in the earth's interior.

**geranium** *noun* **1** (in general use) a cultivated garden plant with showy red, pink, or white flowers, properly known as PELARGONIUM. **2** a small bushy plant with pink, purple, or blue flowers.

**gerbil** (**jer**-bil) *noun* (also **jerbil**) a mouse-like desert rodent with long hind legs.

**geriatric** *adjective* (je-ri-**at**-rik) **1** of old people. **2** (*informal*) old, outdated. ●*noun* **1** an old person. **2** (**geriatrics**) the branch of medicine dealing with the diseases and care of old people.

**geriatrician** (je-ri-ă-**trish**-ăn) *noun* a specialist in geriatrics.

**germ** *noun* **1** a micro-organism, especially one causing disease. **2** a portion of a living organism capable of becoming a new organism, the embryo of a seed; *wheat germ.* **3** a beginning or basis from which something may develop; *the germ of an idea.* □ **germ warfare** the use of germs to spread disease in war.

**German** *adjective* of Germany or its people or language. ●*noun* **1** a native of Germany. **2** the language of Germany. □ **German measles** a contagious disease like mild measles; rubella. **German shepherd dog** an Alsatian.

**german** *adjective* □ **brother, sister german** one having the same parents, not a half-brother etc. **cousin german** a first cousin.

**germander** *noun* a plant of the mint family.

**germane** (jer-**mayn**) *adjective* relevant.

**Germanic** (jer-**man**-ik) *adjective* **1** having German characteristics. **2** of the Scandinavians, Anglo-Saxons, or Germans. ●*noun* the branch of Indo-European languages which includes English, German, Dutch, and the Scandinavian languages.

**germanium** (jer-**may**-nium) *noun* a brittle greyish-white semi-metallic element (symbol Ge).

**Germany** a country in Europe. The Federal Republic of Germany (= West Germany) and the German Democratic Republic (= East Germany) united in October 1990.

**germicide** (jerm-i-syd) *noun* a substance that kills germs or micro-organisms. □ **germicidal** *adjective*

**germinal** *adjective* **1** of germs. **2** in the earliest stage of development. **3** productive of new ideas.

**germinate** *verb* **1** begin to develop and grow, put forth shoots. **2** cause to do this. □ **germination** *noun*

**gerontology** (je-ron-tol-ŏji) *noun* the study of the process of ageing and of old people's special problems.

**gerrymander** (je-ri-**man**-der) *verb* arrange the boundaries of constituencies so as to give unfair advantages to one party or class in an election. (¶ Named after Governor Gerry of Massachusetts, who rearranged boundaries for this purpose in 1812.)

**Gershwin**, George (1898–1937), American composer and pianist, of Russian-Jewish family (Gershovitz).

**gerund** (je-rŭnd) *noun* a verbal noun, in English ending in *-ing*, as in *I'll do the cooking.*

**gesso** (jes-oh) *noun* gypsum as used in painting or sculpture.

**Gestapo** (ges-**tah**-poh) *noun* the German secret police of the Nazi regime.

**gestation** (jes-**tay**-shŏn) *noun* **1** the process or period of carrying or being carried in the womb. **2** development of a plan etc.

**gesticulate** (jes-**tik**-yoo-layt) *verb* make expressive movements of the hands and arms. □ **gesticulation** *noun*

**gesture** (jes-cher) *noun* **1** an expressive movement of any part of the body. **2** something done to convey one's intentions or attitude; *a gesture of friendship.* ● *verb* make a gesture.

**get** *verb* (**got, getting**) **1** come into possession of, obtain or receive. **2** fetch; *get your coat.* **3** suffer (a punishment etc.); *she got ten years in prison.* **4** contract (an illness). **5** go to reach or catch (a bus, train, etc.). **6** catch, punish or have revenge on; *I'll get him for that.* **7** hit; *the bullet got him in the leg.* **8** (*informal*) understand; *I don't get your meaning.* **9** prepare (a meal). **10** bring or come into a certain condition; *get your hair cut; got wet.* **11** move in a particular direction, succeed in coming or going or bringing; *get off the grass; we got from here to London in an hour.* **12** succeed in bringing or persuading; *got a message to her; got her to agree.* **13** (*informal*) annoy; *what really gets me.* **14** begin; *get going.* □ **get about** or **around** travel extensively; go from place to place. **get across** communicate, convey (an idea, etc.). **get along** get on. **get at 1** reach. **2** (*informal*) mean, imply; *what are*

*you getting at?* **3** (*slang*) criticize; *he keeps getting at the trade unions.* **get away** escape; leave. **get away with** escape blame or punishment for. **get by** (*informal*) pass, be accepted; manage to survive. **get down 1** swallow (a thing). **2** record in writing. **3** (*informal*) cause depression in (a person). **get down to** begin working on. **get in** arrive; obtain a place in a college, job, etc. **get off 1** begin a journey. **2** escape with little or no punishment; obtain an acquittal for; *a clever lawyer got him off.* **get off with** (*informal*) form a romantic or sexual relationship with (a person), especially quickly. **get on 1** manage; make progress. **2** be on friendly or harmonious terms. **3** advance in age; *he is getting on in years.* **get one's own back** (*informal*) have one's revenge. **get out of** avoid or get round. **get-out** *noun* a means of evading something. **get over** overcome (a difficulty); recover from (an illness or shock etc.). **get round 1** influence in one's favour, coax. **2** evade (a law or rule) without actually breaking it. **get round to** find time to deal with. **get through 1** finish or use up. **2** pass an examination. **3** make contact by telephone. **get through to** make (a person) understand. **get to** (*informal*) affect (a person) emotionally; *the baby's crying was really getting to him.* **get-together** *noun* (*informal*) a social gathering. **get up** stand after sitting or kneeling etc., get out of bed or from one's chair. **get-up** *noun* (*informal*) an outfit or costume. **get up to** become involved in (mischief etc.).

**get-at-able** *adjective* (*informal*) able to be reached.

**getaway** *noun* an escape, especially after committing a crime.

**Getty**, Jean Paul (1892–1976), American industrialist who made his immense fortune in the oil industry and was also a noted art collector.

**Gettysburg** (get-iz-berg) a small town in Pennsylvania, scene of a decisive battle of the American Civil War.

**get-up-and-go** *noun* (*informal*) energy, enthusiasm.

**geyser** *noun* (gee-zer) **1** a natural spring sending up a column of hot water or steam at intervals. **2** a kind of water-heater.

**Ghana** (gah-nă) a country in West Africa. □ **Ghanaian** (gah-**nay**-ăn) *adjective & noun*

**ghastly** *adjective* **1** causing horror or fear; *a ghastly accident.* **2** (*informal*) very unpleasant, very bad; *a ghastly mistake.* **3** pale and ill-looking. □ **ghastliness** *noun*

**ghat** (*pronounced* gaht) *noun* (in India) **1** a flight of steps down to a river, a landing-place. **2** a mountain pass. □ **Eastern**

**Ghats, Western Ghats** mountains along the east and west coasts of south India.

**ghee** (*pronounced* g'ee) *noun* Indian clarified butter.

**gherkin** (**ger**-kin) *noun* a small pickled cucumber.

**ghetto** (**get**-oh) *noun* (*plural* **ghettos**) **1** part of a city occupied by a minority group. **2** (*hist.*) a Jewish quarter in a city. **3** a segregated group or area. □ **ghetto-blaster** *noun* a large portable stereo radio etc., especially for playing loud pop music.

**ghillie** alternative spelling of GILLIE.

**ghost** *noun* **1** a dead person's spirit or apparition. **2** something very slight; *he hasn't the ghost of a chance*. **3** a duplicated image in a defective telescope or television picture. ● *verb* write as a ghost-writer. □ **ghost town** a town abandoned by all or most of its former inhabitants. **ghost-writer** *noun* a person who writes a book, article, or speech for another to pass off as his or her own. **give up the ghost** die. □ **ghostly** *adjective*, **ghostliness** *noun*

**ghoul** (*pronounced* gool) *noun* **1** a person who enjoys gruesome things. **2** an evil spirit or phantom. **3** (in Muslim folklore) a spirit that robs graves and devours the corpses in them. □ **ghoulish** *adjective*, **ghoulishly** *adverb*

**GHQ** *abbreviation* General Headquarters.

**GI** *noun* a soldier in the US Army. (¶ Short for *government* (or *general*) *issue*.)

**giant** *noun* **1** (in fairy tales) a man of very great height and size. **2** a person, animal, or plant that is much larger than the usual size. **3** a person of outstanding ability or influence. **4** (**Giants**) (*Gk. myth.*) a race of monstrous appearance and great strength who tried unsuccessfully to overthrow the Olympian gods. ● *adjective* gigantic; of a very large kind.

**giantess** *noun* a female giant.

**gibber** (**jib**-er) *verb* make unintelligible or meaningless sounds, especially when shocked or terrified.

**gibberish** (**jib**-er-ish) *noun* unintelligible talk or sounds, nonsense.

**gibbet** (**jib**-it) *noun* **1** a gallows. **2** an upright post with an arm from which executed criminals were formerly hung.

**Gibbon**, Edward (1737–94), English historian, author of *The History of the Decline and Fall of the Roman Empire*.

**gibbon** *noun* a long-armed ape of SE Asia.

**gibbous** (**gib**-ŭs) *adjective* **1** convex, protuberant, humped. **2** (of a moon or planet) having more than half (but less than the whole) of its disc illuminated.

**gibe** (*pronounced* jyb) (also **jibe**) *verb* jeer. ● *noun* a jeering remark.

**giblets** (**jib**-lits) *plural noun* the edible parts of the inside of a bird, taken out before it is cooked.

**Gibraltar** a fortified town and rocky headland at the southern tip of Spain on the Strait of Gibraltar that forms the outlet of the Mediterranean Sea to the Atlantic, a British naval and airbase. □ **Gibraltarian** (jib-rawl-**tair**-iăn) *adjective* & *noun*

**giddy** *adjective* (**giddier, giddiest**) **1** having the feeling that everything is spinning round. **2** causing this feeling; *giddy heights*. **3** frivolous, flighty. □ **giddily** *adverb*, **giddiness** *noun*

**Gide** (*pronounced* zheed), André (1869–1951), French novelist and critic.

**Gielgud** (**geel**-guud), Sir (Arthur) John (born 1904), English actor.

**gift** *noun* **1** a thing given or received without payment. **2** a natural ability; *has a gift for languages*. **3** (*informal*) an easy task. ● *verb* give as a gift. □ **gift token** *or* **voucher** a voucher (given as a gift) for money to buy something. **look a gift-horse in the mouth** accept something ungratefully, examining it for faults.

**gifted** *adjective* having great natural ability.

**gift-wrap** *verb* (**gift-wrapped, gift-wrapping**) wrap attractively as a gift.

**gig** (g- *as in* get) *noun* **1** a light two-wheeled horse-drawn carriage. **2** a light ship's boat for rowing or sailing. **3** a rowing-boat chiefly used for racing. **4** an engagement to play music etc., especially for a single performance.

**giga-** *combining form* one thousand million (10⁹).

**gigantic** *adjective* very large. □ **gigantically** *adverb*

**giggle** *verb* laugh in a silly or nervous way. ● *noun* **1** this kind of laugh. **2** (*informal*) something amusing, a joke; *did it for a giggle*.

**gigolo** (**jig**-ŏ-loh) *noun* (*plural* **gigolos**) a man who is paid by an older woman to be her escort or lover.

**Gilbert**, Sir William Schwenck (1836–1911), English comic dramatist and writer of humorous verse, who collaborated with the composer Sir Arthur Sullivan, writing the libretti for 14 comic operas.

**gild¹** *verb* cover with a thin layer of gold or gold paint. □ **gild the lily** spoil something already beautiful by trying to improve it.

**gild²** alternative spelling of GUILD.

**gill** (*pronounced* jil) *noun* one quarter of a pint.

**Gillespie** (gil-**esp**-i), Dizzy (John Birks) (1917–93), American jazz trumpet-player.

**gillie** (gil-i) *noun* (also **ghillie**) (*Scottish*) a man or boy attending someone shooting or fishing.

**gills** (g- *as in* get) *plural noun* **1** the organ with which a fish breathes in water. **2** the vertical plates on the underside of a mushroom cap. **3** the flesh below a person's jaws and ears. □ **green about the gills** looking sickly.

**gillyflower** *noun* a clove-scented flower, e.g. the wallflower or clove-scented pink.

**gilt** *adjective* gilded, gold-coloured. ●*noun* **1** a substance used for gilding. **2** (**gilts**) gilt-edged securities. **3** a young sow. □ **gilt-edged** *adjective* (of investments) considered to be very safe.

**gimbals** (jim-bălz) *plural noun* a contrivance of rings and pivots for keeping instruments horizontal in a moving ship etc.

**gimcrack** (jim-krak) *adjective* showy, worthless, and flimsy; *gimcrack ornaments.*

**gimlet** (gim-lit) *noun* a small tool with a screw-like tip for boring holes.

**gimmick** (gim-ik) *noun* a trick or device, used especially for attracting notice or publicity. □ **gimmickry** *noun*, **gimmicky** *adjective*

**gin**[1] (*pronounced* jin) *noun* **1** a trap or snare for catching animals. **2** a machine for separating raw cotton from its seeds. **3** a kind of crane and windlass. ●*verb* (**ginned, ginning**) **1** treat (cotton) in a gin. **2** snare.

**gin**[2] (*pronounced* jin) *noun* a colourless alcoholic spirit flavoured with juniper berries. □ **gin rummy** a form of rummy for two players.

**ginger** *noun* **1** the hot-tasting root of a tropical plant. **2** liveliness. **3** light reddish yellow. ●*verb* (foll. by *up*) make more lively; *ginger things up.* ●*adjective* ginger-coloured. □ **ginger ale**, **ginger beer** ginger-flavoured fizzy drinks. **ginger group** a group within a larger group, urging a more active or livelier policy. **ginger-nut** *noun* a ginger-flavoured biscuit. □ **gingery** *adjective*

**gingerbread** *noun* ginger-flavoured treacle cake.

**gingerly** *adverb* cautiously. ●*adjective* cautious.

**gingham** (ging-ăm) *noun* a cotton fabric often with a striped or checked pattern.

**gingivitis** (jin-ji-vy-tiss) *noun* inflammation of the gums.

**ginkgo** (gink-oh) *noun* (*plural* **ginkgos** or **ginkgoes**) a tree with fan-shaped leaves and yellow flowers, originally from China and Japan.

**ginormous** *adjective* (*informal*) enormous.

**Ginsberg** (ginz-berg), Allen (born 1926), American poet.

**ginseng** (jin-seng) *noun* the root of a plant found in eastern Asia and North America, used in medicine.

**Giotto** (jot-oh) di Bondone (*c*.1267–1337), Florentine painter.

**gippy tummy** (jip-i) (*informal*) diarrhoea affecting visitors to hot countries. (¶ Humorous alteration of *Egyptian.*)

**Gipsy** *noun* alternative spelling of GYPSY.

**giraffe** *noun* a long-necked African animal.

**gird** *verb* encircle or attach with a belt or band; *he girded on his sword.* □ **gird** (or **gird up**) **one's loins** prepare for action.

**girder** *noun* a metal beam supporting part of a building or a bridge.

**girdle**[1] *noun* **1** a belt or cord worn round the waist. **2** an elastic corset. **3** a connected ring of bones in the body; *the pelvic girdle.* ●*verb* surround.

**girdle**[2] (in Scotland and N. England) = GRIDDLE.

**girl** *noun* **1** a female child, a daughter. **2** (*informal*) a young woman. **3** (*informal*) a girlfriend. □ **girl Friday** *see* FRIDAY. □ **girlhood** *noun*

**girlfriend** *noun* a female friend, especially a man's usual companion or lover.

**girlie** *noun* (*informal*) a girl. □ **girlie magazine** a magazine containing erotic pictures of young women.

**girlish** *adjective* like a girl. □ **girlishly** *adverb*, **girlishness** *noun*

**giro** (jy-roh) *noun* (*plural* **giros**) **1** a system, used in banking or operated by the Post Office, by which one customer can make a payment to another by transferring credit from his or her own account to the other person's, instead of paying directly. **2** a cheque or payment by giro.

**girt** *adjective* (*poetic*) girded.

**girth** *noun* **1** the distance round a thing. **2** a band passing under a horse's belly, holding the saddle in place.

**Giscard d'Estaing**, Valéry (born 1926), French statesman, President 1974–81.

**gismo** *noun* (also **gizmo**) (*plural* **gismos**) (*slang*) a gadget.

**gist** (*pronounced* jist) *noun* the essential points or general sense of anything.

**git** *noun* (*slang*) a silly or contemptible person.

**gîte** (*pronounced* zheet) *noun* (in France) a furnished holiday home in a country district.

**give** *verb* (**gave, given, giving**) **1** cause another person to receive or have, hand over, supply. **2** deliver (a message). **3** (*informal*) tell what one knows. **4** utter; *gave a laugh.* **5** pledge; *give one's word.* **6** make over in exchange or payment. **7** make or perform (an action or effort), affect another person or thing with this; *gave him a scolding*; *gave the door a kick*; *I was given to understand.* **8** provide (a meal or party) as host. **9** perform or present (a play etc.) in public.

**10** yield as a product or result. **11** be the source of. **12** permit a view of or access to; *the window gives on to the street.* **13** declare (judgement) authoritatively; *the umpire gave the batsman out.* **14** be flexible, yield when pressed or pulled; *woollen fabric gives.* **15** (*informal*) be happening; *what gives?* ●*noun* springiness, elasticity. □ **give and take 1** an exchange of talk and ideas. **2** willingness on both sides to make concessions. **give away 1** give as a present. **2** hand over (the bride) to the groom at a wedding. **3** reveal (a secret etc.) unintentionally. **give-away** *noun* (*informal*) **1** a thing given without charge. **2** something that reveals a secret. **give in 1** hand in (a document etc.). **2** acknowledge that one is defeated. **give off** produce and emit; *petrol gives off fumes.* **give or take** (*informal*) add or subtract (an amount) in estimating. **give out 1** distribute; announce; emit; *chimney was giving out smoke.* **2** become exhausted or used up. **give over 1** devote; *afternoons are given over to sport.* **2** (*informal*) cease doing something. **give up 1** cease (doing something). **2** part with; surrender. **3** abandon hope. **4** declare a person to be incurable or a problem to be too difficult for oneself to solve. **give up the ghost** (*informal*) die; (of machinery) break down. **give way 1** yield, allow other traffic to go first. **2** collapse. □ **giver** *noun*

**given** *see* GIVE. ●*adjective* **1** specified or stated; assumed or granted; *all the people in a given area; given the circumstances.* **2** (foll. by *to*) having a certain tendency; *he is given to swearing.* □ **given name** a Christian name, a first name (given in addition to a family name).

**Giza** (g'ee-ză), **El** a city south-west of Cairo in northern Egypt, site of three great pyramids and of the Sphinx.

**gizmo** alternative spelling of GISMO.

**gizzard** *noun* a bird's second stomach, in which food is ground.

**glacé** (gla-say) *adjective* iced with sugar, preserved in sugar; *glacé fruits.* □ **glacé icing** icing made from icing sugar and water.

**glacial** (glay-shăl) *adjective* **1** icy. **2** of or from glaciers or other ice; *glacial deposits.* □ **glacial period** the period when a large part of the earth's surface was covered by ice. □ **glacially** *adverb*

**glaciated** (glas-i-ayt-id) *adjective* covered with glaciers; affected by their action. □ **glaciation** *noun*

**glacier** (glas-i-er) *noun* a river of ice moving very slowly, formed by an accumulation of snow.

**glad** *adjective* (**gladder**, **gladdest**) **1** pleased, expressing joy. **2** giving joy; *the glad news.*

□ **be glad of** be grateful for. **glad eye** (*slang*) an inviting or seductive look. **glad rags** (*informal*) dressy clothes. □ **gladly** *adverb*, **gladness** *noun*

**gladden** *verb* make glad.

**glade** *noun* an open space in a forest.

**gladiator** (glad-i-ay-ter) *noun* a trained fighter in ancient Roman shows. □ **gladiatorial** (gladi-ă-**tor**-iăl) *adjective*

**gladiolus** *noun* (*plural* **gladioli**), (*pronounced* glad-i-**oh**-ly) a garden plant with spikes of brightly coloured flowers.

**Gladstone**, William Ewart (1809–98), British statesman, Prime Minister 1868–74, 1880–5, 1886, and 1892–4. □ **Gladstone bag** a small case hinged so that it opens into two compartments.

**glair** *noun* white of egg; a thick substance made of or resembling this.

**Glam.** *abbreviation* Glamorgan.

**glam** *adjective* (*informal*) glamorous. □ **glam rock** a kind of rock music highly dependent on showy theatrical effects.

**Glamorgan** a former county of Wales, now divided into *Mid*, *South*, and *West Glamorgan.*

**glamorize** *verb* (also **glamorise**) make glamorous or attractive.

**glamour** *noun* (*Amer.* **glamor**) **1** alluring beauty. **2** attractive and exciting qualities that arouse envy. □ **glamorous** *adjective*, **glamorously** *adverb*

**glance** *verb* **1** look briefly. **2** strike at an angle and glide off an object; *a glancing blow; the ball glanced off his bat.* ●*noun* **1** a brief look. **2** a stroke in cricket with the bat's face turned slantwise to the ball.

**gland** *noun* an organ that separates from the blood substances that are to be used by the body or expelled from it.

**glanders** *noun* a contagious disease of horses and related animals.

**glandular** (glan-dew-ler) *adjective* of or like a gland. □ **glandular fever** a feverish illness in which the lymph glands are swollen.

**glare** *verb* **1** shine with an unpleasant dazzling light. **2** stare angrily or fiercely. ●*noun* **1** a strong unpleasant light. **2** oppressive attention; *the glare of publicity.* **3** an angry or fierce stare.

**glaring** *adjective* **1** bright and dazzling. **2** very obvious; *a glaring error.* □ **glaringly** *adverb*

**glasnost** (glaz-nost) *noun* (in the former USSR) a policy of more openness in the reporting of news etc. (¶ Russian, = openness.)

**Glass**, Philip (born 1937), American composer.

**glass** *noun* **1** a hard brittle substance (as used in windows), usually transparent. **2** an object made of this, e.g. a mirror. **3** a glass container for drinking from. **4** a barometer. **5** (**glasses**) spectacles; binoculars. ●*verb* fit or enclose with glass. □ **glass-blowing** *noun* shaping semi-molten glass by blowing air into it through a tube. **glass ceiling** an invisible barrier which prevents progress upwards (especially of women in a career). **glass fibre** fabric woven from glass filaments; plastic reinforced with glass filaments. **glass-paper** *noun* paper coated with glass particles, used for smoothing things. **under glass** (of plants) in a greenhouse, cold-frame, etc.

**glasshouse** *noun* **1** a greenhouse. **2** (*slang*) a military prison.

**glassy** *adjective* **1** like glass in appearance. **2** with a dull expressionless stare; *glassy-eyed*. □ **glassily** *adverb*, **glassiness** *noun*

**Glaswegian** (glaz-**wee**-jăn) *adjective* of Glasgow, a city in western Scotland. ●*noun* a native or inhabitant of Glasgow.

**glaucoma** (glaw-**koh**-mă) *noun* a condition caused by increased pressure of the fluid within the eyeball, causing weakening or loss of sight.

**glaze** *verb* **1** fit or cover with glass. **2** coat with a glossy surface. **3** become glassy. ●*noun* a shiny surface or coating especially on pottery.

**glazier** (**glay**-zi-er) *noun* a person whose trade is to fit glass in windows etc.

**gleam** *noun* **1** a beam or ray of soft light, especially one that comes and goes. **2** a brief show of some quality; *a gleam of hope*. ●*verb* send out gleams.

**glean** *verb* **1** pick up (grain left by harvesters). **2** gather (information) in small amounts. □ **gleaner** *noun*

**gleanings** *plural noun* things gleaned, especially facts.

**glebe** (*pronounced* gleeb) *noun* a portion of land going with a clergyman's benefice and providing revenue.

**glee** *noun* **1** lively or triumphant joy. **2** a part-song, especially for male voices. □ **glee club** a type of choral society.

**gleeful** *adjective* full of glee. □ **gleefully** *adverb*

**glen** *noun* a narrow valley.

**Glendower** (glen-**dow**-er), Owen (*c.*1355– *c.*1417), Welsh chieftain, whose leadership made him a legendary symbol of Welsh nationalism.

**glengarry** (glen-ga-ri) *noun* a Scottish cap with a crease down the centre and usually ribbons hanging from the back.

**glib** *adjective* ready with words but insincere or superficial; *a glib tongue*; *a glib excuse*. □ **glibly** *adverb*, **glibness** *noun*

**glide** *verb* **1** move along smoothly. **2** fly in a glider or in an aeroplane without engine power. ●*noun* a gliding movement.

**glider** *noun* an aircraft without an engine.

**glimmer** *noun* a faint gleam. ●*verb* gleam faintly.

**glimpse** *noun* a brief view. ●*verb* catch a glimpse of.

**glint** *noun* a very brief flash of light. ●*verb* send out a glint.

**glissade** (glis-**ayd**) *verb* **1** glide or slide skilfully down a steep slope, especially in mountaineering. **2** make a gliding step in ballet. ●*noun* a glissading movement or step.

**glisten** *verb* shine like something wet or polished.

**glitch** *noun* (*informal*) a malfunction, a hitch.

**glitter** *verb* sparkle. ●*noun* a sparkle.

**glitterati** (gli-tĕ-**rah**-ti) *plural noun* (*slang*) rich and famous people.

**glitz** *noun* (*slang*) showy glamour. □ **glitzy** *adjective*

**gloaming** *noun* (*Scottish* or *poetic*) the evening twilight.

**gloat** *verb* be full of greedy or malicious delight.

**global** *adjective* **1** of the whole world, worldwide. **2** relating to the whole of a set of data; total. □ **global warming** the increase in the temperature of the earth's atmosphere caused by the greenhouse effect. □ **globally** *adverb*

**globe** *noun* **1** an object shaped like a ball, especially one with a map of the earth on it. **2** the world; *travelled all over the globe*. **3** a hollow round glass object. □ **globe artichoke** the edible flower of an artichoke. **globe-trotting** *noun & adjective* travelling all over the world as a tourist. **globe-trotter** *noun* a person who travels widely.

**Globe Theatre** a theatre in London, erected in 1599, in which Shakespeare had a share and where he acted.

**globular** (**glob**-yoo-ler) *adjective* shaped like a globe.

**globule** (**glob**-yool) *noun* a small rounded drop.

**globulin** (**glob**-yoo-lin) *noun* a kind of protein found in animal and plant tissue.

**glockenspiel** (**glok**-ĕn-speel) *noun* a musical instrument consisting of bells or metal bars struck by hammers.

**gloom** *noun* **1** semi-darkness. **2** a feeling of sadness and depression.

**gloomy** *adjective* (**gloomier**, **gloomiest**) **1** almost dark, unlighted. **2** depressed, sullen. **3** dismal, depressing. □ **gloomily** *adverb*, **gloominess** *noun*

**Gloriana** the nickname of Elizabeth I of England.

**glorify** *verb* (**glorified**, **glorifying**) **1** praise highly. **2** worship. **3** make something seem more splendid than it is; *their patio is only a glorified backyard*. □ **glorification** *noun*

**glorious** adjective **1** possessing or bringing glory. **2** splendid, great; a glorious view; a glorious muddle. □ **gloriously** adverb

**glory** noun **1** fame and honour won by great deeds. **2** adoration and praise. **3** beauty, magnificence; the glory of a sunset. **4** a thing deserving praise and honour. ●verb (**gloried, glorying**) (foll. by in) rejoice or pride oneself; glorying in their success. □ **gloryhole** noun (slang) an untidy room or cupboard etc.

**Glos.** abbreviation Gloucestershire.

**gloss** noun **1** the shine on a smooth surface. **2** an explanatory comment. ●verb **1** make glossy. **2** provide an explanatory comment in (a text). □ **gloss over** cover up (a mistake or fault). **gloss paint** a paint with a glossy finish.

**glossary** (glos-er-i) noun a list of technical or special words with their definitions.

**glossy** adjective (**glossier, glossiest**) shiny. □ **glossy magazine** one printed on glossy paper, with many illustrations. □ **glossily** adverb, **glossiness** noun

**glottal** adjective of the glottis. □ **glottal stop** a sound in speech made by suddenly opening or shutting the glottis.

**glottis** noun the opening of the upper end of the windpipe between the vocal cords.

**Gloucester** (glos-ter) noun (usually **double Gloucester**) a kind of cheese originally made in Gloucestershire.

**Gloucestershire** a county of SW England.

**glove** noun a covering for the hand, usually with separate divisions for each finger and the thumb. □ **fit like a glove** fit exactly. **glove compartment** a recess for small articles in the dashboard of a car. **glove puppet** one fitting over the hand so that the fingers can move it.

**gloved** adjective wearing a glove or gloves.

**glover** noun a glove-maker.

**glow** verb **1** send out light and heat without flame. **2** have a warm or flushed look, colour, or feeling. **3** (as **glowing** adjective) very enthusiastic or favourable; a glowing account. ●noun a glowing state, look, or feeling. □ **glow-worm** noun a kind of beetle whose female can give out a greenish light at its tail.

**glower** (rhymes with flower) verb scowl, stare angrily.

**gloxinia** (glok-sin-iă) noun a tropical plant with large bell-shaped flowers.

**Gluck** (pronounced gluuk), Christoph Willibald von (1714–87), German composer of operas.

**glucose** (gloo-kohz) noun a form of sugar found in fruit juice.

**glue** noun a sticky substance used for joining things. ●verb (**glued, gluing**) **1** fasten with glue. **2** attach or hold closely; his ear was glued to the keyhole. □ **glue ear** a blocking of the Eustachian tube, especially in children. **glue-sniffing** noun inhaling the fumes of plastic glue for their narcotic effects. **glue-sniffer** noun a person who sniffs glue. □ **gluey** adjective

**glum** adjective (**glummer, glummest**) sad and gloomy. □ **glumly** adverb, **glumness** noun

**glut** verb (**glutted, glutting**) **1** supply with much more than is needed; glut the market. **2** satisfy fully with food; glut oneself; glut one's appetite. ●noun an excessive supply; a glut of apples.

**glutamate** (gloo-tă-mayt) noun a substance used to bring out the flavour in food.

**gluten** (gloo-těn) noun a sticky protein substance present in cereal grains, which remains when starch is washed out of flour.

**glutinous** (gloo-tin-ŭs) adjective glue-like, sticky.

**glutton** noun **1** a person who eats far too much. **2** a person with a great desire or capacity for something; a glutton for punishment. **3** an animal of the weasel family. □ **gluttonous** adjective, **gluttony** noun

**glycerine** (glis-er-een or glis-er-in) noun (Amer. **glycerin**) a thick sweet colourless liquid used in ointments, medicines, and explosives.

**glycerol** = GLYCERINE.

**Glyndebourne** (glynd-born) an estate in Sussex, England, where an annual festival of opera is held.

**gm** abbreviation gram(s).

**G-man** noun (plural **G-men**) (Amer. slang) an agent of the Federal Bureau of Investigation.

**GMT** abbreviation Greenwich Mean Time.

**GMWU** abbreviation General and Municipal Workers' Union.

**gnarled** (pronounced narld) adjective (of a tree or hands) covered with knobbly lumps; twisted and misshapen.

**gnash** verb **1** grind (one's teeth). **2** (of teeth) strike together.

**gnat** noun a small biting fly.

**gnaw** verb (**gnawed, gnawed** or **gnawn, gnawing**) **1** bite persistently at something hard. **2** (as **gnawing** adjective) hurting continuously; a gnawing pain.

**gneiss** (pronounced nyss) noun a kind of coarse-grained rock.

**gnome** noun **1** a kind of dwarf in fairy tales, living underground. **2** a model of such a dwarf as a garden ornament. **3** (informal) a person with secret influence, especially in finance.

**gnomic** (noh-mik) adjective consisting of or using aphorisms or maxims.

**gnomon** (noh-mon) noun the rod of a sundial, showing the time by its shadow.

**gnostic** (nos-tik) *adjective* **1** of knowledge. **2** having special mystical knowledge. ●*noun* (**Gnostic**) an early Christian heretic claiming mystical knowledge. □ **Gnosticism** *noun*

**GNP** *abbreviation* gross national product.

**gnu** (*pronounced* noo) *noun* an ox-like antelope.

**go**[1] *verb* (**goes, went, gone, going**) **1** begin to move; be moving; pass from one point to another; make a trip for a specific purpose; *we must go at one o'clock; go shopping.* **2** extend or lead from one place to another; *the road goes to York.* **3** be in a specified state; *they went hungry.* **4** be functioning; *that clock doesn't go.* **5** make a movement or sound, often of a specified kind; *the gun went bang; the whistle has gone.* **6** (of time) pass; (of a distance) be traversed or accomplished; *ten miles to go.* **7** be allowable or acceptable; *anything goes; what she says, goes; that goes without saying.* **8** belong in some place or position; *plates go on the shelf.* **9** (of a story or tune etc.) have a certain wording or content; *I forget how the chorus goes.* **10** pass into a certain condition; *the fruit went bad.* **11** make progress, fare; *all went well.* **12** be sold; *it's going cheap.* **13** (of money or supplies) be spent or used up. **14** be given up, dismissed, abolished, or lost; *some luxuries must go; my sight is going.* **15** fail, give way; die; *the fuse has gone.* **16** carry an action to a certain point; *that's going too far; I'll go to £50 for it.* **17** be able to be put; *your clothes won't go into that suitcase; 3 into 12 goes 4.* **18** be given or allotted; *his estate went to his nephew.* **19** contribute, serve; *it all goes to prove what I said.* ●*noun* (*plural* **goes**) **1** energy; *full of go.* **2** a turn or try; *(informal)* a success; *make a go of it.* **4** vigorous activity; *it's all go.* ●*adjective* (*informal*) functioning properly; *all systems are go.* □ **go about 1** be socially active. **2** set to work at. **go ahead** proceed immediately. **go-ahead** (*noun*) a signal to proceed immediately; (*adjective*) energetic, willing to try new methods. **go a long way** go far; last long or buy much; have a great effect towards achieving something. **go along with** agree with. **go back on one's word** fail to keep a promise. **go-between** *noun* one who acts as a messenger or negotiator. **go down 1** (of a ship) sink, (of the sun) appear to descend towards the horizon, set. **2** be written down. **3** be swallowed. **4** be received or accepted; *the suggestion went down very well.* **5** (*slang*) go to prison. **go down with** become ill with (a disease). **go far** achieve much; contribute greatly towards something. **go for 1** like, prefer, choose. **2** (*slang*) attack. **go-getter** *noun* (*informal*) one who is successful through being ag-

gressive or energetic. **go-go** *adjective* (*informal*) (of dancers, music, etc.) in a modern style; lively, erotic, and rhythmic. **go in for** compete in; engage in (an activity). **go into 1** become a member or occupant or patient in (an institution). **2** investigate (a problem). **go it alone** take action by oneself without assistance. **go off 1** explode. **2** lose quality, become stale. **3** fall asleep. **4** proceed; *the party went off well.* **5** dislike what one liked formerly; *I've gone off tea lately.* **go on 1** continue. **2** talk lengthily. **go on at** (*informal*) nag. **go out 1** leave (a house, room, etc.). **2** be broadcast; *the programme goes out live.* **3** be extinguished. **4** cease to be fashionable. **5** (*Amer. informal*) lose consciousness. **go out with** have (a person) as a regular (usually sexual) partner. **go round** be enough for everyone. **go slow** work at a deliberately slow pace as a form of industrial protest. **go-slow** *noun* a deliberately slow pace of this kind. **go through with** complete; not leave unfinished. **go up 1** rise in price. **2** explode or burn rapidly. **go with** match, harmonize with. **go without** put up with the lack of something. **on the go** in constant motion, active. **to go** (*Amer.*) (of foods) to be taken away for consumption; *two ham sandwiches to go.*

**go**[2] *noun* a Japanese board game.

**Goa** (goh-ă) a state on the west coast of India. □ **Goan** *adjective & noun*, **Goanese** *adjective & noun*

**goad** *noun* **1** a pointed stick for prodding cattle to move onwards. **2** something stimulating a person to activity. ●*verb* act as a stimulus to; *goaded her into answering back.*

**goal** *noun* **1** a structure or area into which players try to send a ball in certain games. **2** a point scored in this way. **3** an objective. □ **goal line** the end line of a football or hockey pitch.

**goalie** *noun* (*informal*) a goalkeeper.

**goalkeeper** *noun* a player whose task is to keep the ball out of the goal.

**goalpost** *noun* either of the pair of upright posts of a goal.

**goat** *noun* **1** a small horned animal kept for its milk. **2** (**the Goat**) a sign of the zodiac, Capricorn. □ **get someone's goat** (*slang*) annoy him or her.

**goatee** (goh-tee) *noun* a short pointed beard.

**goatherd** *noun* a person who looks after a herd of goats.

**gob** (*slang*) *noun* **1** a clot of a slimy substance. **2** the mouth. ●*verb* (**gobbed, gobbing**) spit. □ **gob-stopper** *noun* a large sweet for sucking.

**gobbet** *noun* **1** a lump or piece. **2** an extract from a text.

**Gobbi**, Tito (1915–84), Italian operatic baritone.

**gobble** *verb* **1** eat quickly and greedily. **2** (of a turkeycock) to make a throaty sound.

**gobbledegook** *noun* (also **gobbledygook**) (*slang*) pompous or unintelligible language used by officials.

**Gobi Desert** (goh-bi) a barren plateau of southern Mongolia and northern China.

**goblet** *noun* a drinking-glass with a stem and a foot.

**goblin** *noun* a mischievous ugly dwarflike creature in fairy tales etc.

**gobsmacked** *adjective* (*slang*) astonished.

**goby** (goh-bi) *noun* a small fish with the ventral fins joined to form a disc or sucker.

**go-cart** alternative spelling of GO-KART.

**god** *noun* **1** a superhuman being regarded and worshipped as having power over nature and human affairs; *Mars was the Roman god of war.* **2** (**God**) the creator and ruler of the universe in Christian, Jewish, and Muslim teaching. **3** an image of a god, an idol. **4** a person or thing that is greatly admired or adored; *money is his god.* **5** (**the gods**) the gallery of a theatre. □ **God-fearing** *adjective* sincerely religious. **God forbid** I wish that this may not happen. **God-forsaken** *adjective* wretched, dismal. **God knows 1** this is something we cannot hope to know. **2** I call God to witness. **God Save the King** *or* **Queen** the British national anthem. **God willing** if circumstances allow it. **good God!**, **my God!** exclamations of surprise or pain.

**Godard**, Jean-Luc (born 1930), French film director.

**godchild** *noun* (*plural* **godchildren**) a child in relation to its godparent(s).

**god-daughter** *noun* a female godchild.

**goddess** *noun* a female god.

**godetia** (gŏ-dee-shă) *noun* an annual garden plant with brightly coloured flowers.

**godfather** *noun* **1** a male godparent. **2** the mastermind behind an illegal organization.

**godhead** *noun* **1** divine nature. **2** (**the Godhead**) God.

**Godiva** (gŏ-dy-vă) the wife of an 11th-century earl of Mercia, who (according to a later legend) rode naked through Coventry as a condition of her husband's remitting some unpopular taxes.

**godless** *adjective* **1** not having belief in God. **2** wicked. □ **godlessly** *adverb*, **godlessness** *noun*

**godlike** *adjective* like God or a god.

**godly** *adjective* (**godlier**, **godliest**) sincerely religious. □ **godliness** *noun*

**godmother** *noun* a female godparent.

**godparent** *noun* a person who undertakes, when a child is baptized, to see that it is brought up as a Christian.

**godsend** *noun* a piece of unexpected good fortune.

**godson** *noun* a male godchild.

**Godspeed** *noun* an expression of good wishes to a person starting a journey.

**Godunov** (god-ŭ-nof), Boris (1550–1605), tsar of Russia 1598–1605.

**Godwin-Austen, Mount** *see* K2.

**Goebbels**, (Paul) Joseph (1897–1945), German Nazi leader and politician, who became Hitler's propaganda minister in 1933.

**goer** *noun* **1** a person or thing that goes; *car is a nice goer*; *churchgoers*. **2** (*informal*) a lively or persevering person.

**Goering**, Hermann Wilhelm (1893–1946), German Nazi leader, who became the commander of the German air force in 1934 and founded the Gestapo.

**Goethe** (ger-tĕ), Johann Wolfgang von (1749–1832), German writer, scholar, and statesman.

**goggle** *verb* stare with wide-open eyes. □ **goggle-box** *noun* (*slang*) a television set. **goggle-eyed** *adjective* with wide-open eyes.

**goggles** *plural noun* spectacles for protecting the eyes from wind, dust, water, etc.

**go-go** *see* GO[1].

**Gogh** (*pronounced* gof) *see* VAN GOGH.

**Gogol** (goh-gol), Nikolai Vasilievich (1809–52), Russian writer.

**going** *see* GO[1]. ● *noun* **1** moving away, departing; *comings and goings*. **2** the state of the ground for walking or riding on; *rough going.* **3** rate of progress; *it was good going to get there by lunchtime.* ● *adjective* **1** moving away, departing. **2** existing, available; *there is cold beef going.* **3** current; *the going rate.* **4** active and prosperous; *a going concern.* □ **be going to** be about to, be likely to. **going-over** *noun* **1** (*informal*) an inspection or overhaul. **2** (*slang*) a thrashing. **goings-on** *plural noun* surprising or mysterious behaviour or events. **while the going is good** while conditions are favourable.

**goitre** (goi-ter) *noun* (*Amer.* **goiter**) an enlarged thyroid gland, often showing as a swelling in the neck.

**go-kart** *noun* (also **go-cart**) a miniature racing car with a skeleton body.

**gold** *noun* **1** a chemical element (symbol Au), a yellow metal of very high value. **2** coins or other articles made of gold. **3** its colour. **4** a gold medal (awarded as first prize). **5** something very good or precious. ● *adjective* made of gold; coloured like gold. □ **gold card** a preferential charge card giving privileges not available to holders of the standard card. **gold-digger** *noun* (*informal*) a woman who uses her attractions to obtain money from men. **gold-dust** *noun* gold found naturally in fine particles. **gold-mine** *noun* **1** a place where gold is mined. **2** a source of great wealth; *the shop was a little gold-mine.* **gold-plated** *adjective* coated with gold. **gold reserve** gold held by a central bank to guarantee the value of a country's currency. **gold-rush** *noun* a rush to a region where gold has been found. **gold standard** a system by which the value of money is based on that of gold.

**Gold Coast** (*hist.*) the name given by European traders to a coastal area of West Africa (now Ghana) that was an important source of gold.

**goldcrest** *noun* a very small bird with a golden crest.

**golden** *adjective* **1** made of gold. **2** coloured like gold. **3** precious, excellent; *a golden opportunity.* □ **golden age** a time of great prosperity. **golden boy** or **girl** a popular or successful person. **Golden Fleece** (*Gk. legend*) the fleece of a winged golden ram, sought by Jason and the Argonauts. **golden handshake** (*informal*) money given by a firm to an employee as compensation for being dismissed or forced to retire. **golden jubilee** a 50th anniversary, e.g. of a sovereign's accession. **golden mean** neither too much nor too little. **golden retriever** a retriever dog with a thick golden coat. **golden rod** a plant with spikes of yellow flowers, blooming in late summer. **golden rule** a basic principle of action. **golden share** the controlling interest in a company, especially as retained by the government after an industry is privatized. **golden syrup** a kind of pale treacle. **golden wedding** the 50th anniversary of a wedding.

**Golden Gate** a channel of water in California between San Francisco Bay and the Pacific, spanned by a suspension bridge.

**Golden Horn** the harbour at Istanbul.

**goldfinch** *noun* a songbird with a band of yellow across each wing.

**goldfish** *noun* (*plural* **goldfish** or **goldfishes**) a small reddish Chinese carp kept in a bowl or pond.

**Golding**, Sir William Gerald (1911–93), English novelist.

**Goldsmith**, Oliver (*c.*1730–74), Anglo-Irish novelist, poet, essayist, and dramatist.

**goldsmith** *noun* a person whose trade is making articles in gold.

**Goldwyn**, Samuel (original name; Schmuel Gelbfisz) (1882–1974), American film producer.

**golf** *noun* a game in which a small hard ball is struck with clubs towards and into a series of holes. ● *verb* play golf. □ **golf club 1** a club used in golf. **2** an association for playing golf; its premises. **golf course, golf links** an area of land on which golf is played. □ **golfer** *noun*

**Golgotha** (gol-gŏth-ă) the Aramaic name of Calvary.

**Goliath** (gŏ-ly-ăth) (in the Old Testament) a Philistine giant, traditionally slain by David with a stone from a sling.

**golliwog** *noun* a black-faced soft doll with fuzzy hair.

**golly** (*informal*) *interjection* an exclamation of surprise. ● *noun* a golliwog.

**golosh** alternative spelling of GALOSH.

**gonad** (goh-nad) *noun* an animal organ (such as a testis or ovary) producing gametes.

**gondola** (gon-dŏl-ă) *noun* **1** a boat with high pointed ends, used on the canals in Venice. **2** a basket-like structure suspended beneath a balloon or airship, or attached to a ski-lift, for carrying passengers etc.

**gondolier** (gond-ŏ-leer) *noun* a person who propels a gondola by means of a pole.

**gone** *see* GO¹. ● *adjective* **1** departed; past; *it's gone six o'clock.* **2** dead. **3** (*informal*) pregnant for a specified time; *she is six months gone.* □ **gone on** (*slang*) infatuated with.

**goner** *noun* (*slang*) a person or thing that is dead, ruined, or doomed.

**gong** *noun* **1** a round metal plate that resounds when struck. **2** (*slang*) a medal.

**gonorrhoea** (gon-ŏ-ree-ă) *noun* a venereal disease causing a thick discharge from the sexual organs.

**goo** *noun* (*informal*) **1** sticky wet material. **2** sickly sentiment.

**good** *adjective* (**better, best**) **1** having the right or desirable properties, satisfactory. **2** right, proper, expedient. **3** morally correct, virtuous, kindly. **4** (of a child) well-behaved. **5** gratifying, enjoyable, beneficial; *have a good time; good morning.* **6** efficient, suitable, competent; *a good driver, good at chess.* **7** thorough, considerable; *a good beating.* **8** not less than, full; *walked a good ten miles.* **9** used in exclamations; *good God!* ● *adverb* (*Amer. informal*) well; *doing pretty good.* ● *noun* **1** that which is morally right. **2** profit, benefit; *it will do him good.* **3** (**the good**) virtuous people. (*See also* GOODS.) □ **as good as** practically, almost; *the war was as good as over.* **for good (and all)** permanently, finally. **good for** beneficial to; able to pay or undertake; *he is good for £100; they are good for a 10-mile walk.* **good-for-nothing** (*adjective*) worthless; (*noun*) a worthless person. **good for you!** well done. **Good Friday** the Friday before Easter, commemorating the Crucifixion. **good-looking** *adjective* having a pleasing appearance. **good-tempered** *adjective* not easily annoyed. **good will** an intention that good shall result. **in good faith** with honest or sincere intentions. **in good time 1** with no risk of being late. **2** (also **all in good time**) in due course but without haste.

**goodbye** *interjection & noun* farewell, an expression used when parting or at the end of a telephone call.

**goodly** *adjective* **1** good-looking. **2** of imposing size etc. □ **goodliness** *noun*

**Goodman**, Benny (Benjamin David) (1909–86), American jazz clarinettist.

**goodness** *noun* **1** the quality of being good; kindness. **2** the good part of something; *the goodness is in the gravy*. **3** used instead of 'God' in exclamations; *goodness knows; for goodness' sake; thank goodness*.

**goods** *plural noun* **1** movable property. **2** articles of trade; *leather goods*. **3** things to be carried by road and rail; *goods train*. **4** (**the goods**) (*informal*) the genuine article, the real thing. □ **deliver the goods** (*informal*) produce what one has promised. **have the goods on** (*slang*) have evidence of (a person's) guilt.

**goodwill** *noun* **1** a friendly feeling. **2** the established custom or popularity of a business, considered as an asset.

**goody** *noun* (also **goodie**) (*informal*) **1** something good or attractive, especially to eat. **2** a person of good character; *the goodies and the baddies*. ● *interjection* (*children's use*) an exclamation of delight.

**goody-goody** (*informal*) *adjective* smugly virtuous. ● *noun* a goody-goody person.

**gooey** *adjective* (*slang*) **1** wet and sticky. **2** sickly and sentimental.

**goof** (*slang*) *noun* **1** a stupid person. **2** a mistake. ● *verb* bungle; blunder.

**goofy** *adjective* (*slang*) **1** stupid. **2** having protruding or crooked front teeth.

**googly** *noun* a ball bowled in cricket so that it bounces in an unexpected direction.

**goon** *noun* (*slang*) **1** a stupid person. **2** (especially *Amer.*) a hired ruffian.

**goose** *noun* (*plural* **geese**) **1** a large waterbird with webbed feet and a broad bill. **2** its flesh as food. **3** a female goose (compare GANDER). **4** (*informal*) a stupid person. □ **goose-flesh** *or* **goose-pimples** *noun* (*Amer.* **goose-bumps**) rough bristling skin caused by cold or fear. **goose-step** *noun* a way of marching without bending the knees.

**gooseberry** *noun* **1** a thorny shrub. **2** its edible berry. □ **play gooseberry** (*informal*) be an unwanted third person accompanying a couple.

**gopher** (**goh**-fer) *noun* an American burrowing rodent, ground squirrel, or burrowing tortoise.

**Gorbachev** (gor-bă-chof), Mikhail Sergeevich (born 1931), Soviet statesman, general secretary of the Communist Party of the USSR 1985–1991, President 1988–1991.

**Gordian** *adjective* □ **cut the Gordian knot** to solve a problem forcefully or by some unexpected means. (¶ An intricate knot was tied by Gordius, king of ancient Phrygia; it was eventually cut, rather than untied, by Alexander the Great.)

**Gordon**, Charles George (1833–85), British general and colonial administrator.

**gore** *noun* **1** thickened blood from a cut or wound. **2** a triangular or tapering section of a skirt, sail, or umbrella. ● *verb* pierce with a horn or tusk.

**gorge** *noun* a narrow steep-sided valley. ● *verb* **1** eat greedily. **2** fill full, choke up. □ **make a person's gorge rise** sicken or disgust him or her.

**gorgeous** *adjective* **1** richly coloured, magnificent. **2** (*informal*) very pleasant, beautiful. □ **gorgeously** *adverb*

**gorgon** *noun* **1** (*Gk. myth.*) any of three snake-haired sisters whose looks turned to stone anyone who saw them. **2** a terrifying woman.

**Gorgonzola** (gor-gŏn-**zoh**-lă) *noun* a rich strong blue-veined cheese, originally from Gorgonzola in north Italy.

**gorilla** *noun* a large powerful African ape.

**Gorky**, Maxim (pseudonym of Alexei Maximovich Peshkov) (1868–1936), Russian novelist, playwright, and revolutionary.

**gormless** *adjective* (*informal*) stupid.

**gorse** *noun* a wild evergreen shrub with yellow flowers and sharp thorns. □ **gorsy** *adjective*

**Gorsedd** (gor-se*th*) *noun* a meeting of Welsh bards and Druids, especially before an eisteddfod. (¶ Welsh, = throne.)

**gory** *adjective* **1** covered with blood. **2** involving bloodshed; *a gory battle*. □ **gorily** *adverb*, **goriness** *noun*

**gosh** *interjection* an exclamation of surprise.

**goshawk** (**goss**-hawk) *noun* a large hawk with short wings.

**gosling** (**goz**-ling) *noun* a young goose.

**gospel** *noun* **1** the teachings of Christ recorded in the first four books of the New Testament. **2** (**Gospel**) any of these books. **3** (also **gospel truth**) a thing one may safely believe; *you can take it as gospel*. **4** (in full **gospel music**) Black American religious singing.

**gossamer** *noun* **1** a fine filmy piece of cobweb made by small spiders. **2** any flimsy delicate material. ● *adjective* light and flimsy as gossamer.

**gossip** *noun* **1** casual talk, especially about other people's affairs. **2** a person who is fond of gossiping. ● *verb* engage in or spread gossip. □ **gossip column** a section of a newspaper containing titbits of information about people or social incidents. □ **gossipy** *adjective*

**got** *see* GET. □ **have got** possess; *she has got a car.* **have got to** must.

**Goth** *noun* a member of a Germanic tribe which invaded the Roman Empire from the east in the 3rd–5th centuries.

**goth** *noun* **1** a style of rock music with an intense or droning sound and mystical lyrics. **2** a performer or follower of this music, often favouring black clothing and a white-painted face with black make-up.

**Gothic** (**goth**-ik) *adjective* **1** of the Goths. **2** of the style of architecture common in western Europe in the 12th–16th centuries, with pointed arches and rich stone carving. ● *noun* this style. □ **Gothic novel** a kind of novel with sensational or horrifying events, popular in the 18th–19th centuries.

**gotten** (*Amer.*) = GOT.

■ **Usage** Not now used in British English, except in *ill-gotten*.

**Götterdämmerung** (ger-ter-**dem**-er-uung) *noun* the twilight of the gods (*see* TWILIGHT); the complete downfall of a regime etc. (¶ German.)

**gouache** (goo-**ahsh**) *noun* painting with opaque pigments ground in water and thickened with gum and honey.

**Gouda** (gow-dă) *noun* a flat round Dutch cheese.

**gouge** (*pronounced* gowj) *noun* a chisel with a concave blade, used for cutting grooves. ● *verb* **1** cut out with a gouge. **2** scoop or force out.

**goujons** (goo-*zh*awn) *plural noun* narrow deep-fried strips of fish or meat.

**goulash** (goo-lash) *noun* a stew of meat and vegetables, seasoned with paprika.

**Gounod** (goo-noh), Charles François (1818–93), French composer.

**gourd** (*pronounced* goord) *noun* **1** the hard-skinned fleshy fruit of a climbing plant. **2** a bowl or container made from the dried hollowed-out rind of this fruit.

**gourmand** (goor-mănd) *noun* a lover of food; a glutton.

■ **Usage** This word is often applied to a person contemptuously, whereas *gourmet* is not.

**gourmandise** (goor-mahn-deez) *noun* love of food, gluttony.

**gourmet** (goor-may) *noun* a connoisseur of good food and drink.

■ **Usage** See the note under **gourmand**.

**gout** *noun* a disease causing inflammation of the joints, especially the toes. □ **gouty** *adjective*

**govern** *verb* **1** rule with authority; conduct the affairs of a country or an organization. **2** keep under control; *to govern one's temper.* **3** influence or direct; *be governed by the experts' advice.*

**governance** *noun* governing, control.

**governess** *noun* a woman employed to teach children in a private household.

**government** *noun* **1** governing, the system or method of governing. **2** the group or organization governing a country. **3** (usually **Government**) a particular ministry in office. **4** the State as an agent; *a government grant.* □ **governmental** *adjective*

**governor** *noun* **1** a person who governs a province or colony. **2** the head of each State in the USA. **3** the head or a member of the governing body of an institution; *the governor of the prison.* **4** (*slang*) one's employer. **5** (*slang*) one's father. **6** (*slang*) a form of address to a man regarded as being of superior status. **7** a mechanism that automatically controls speed or the intake of gas or water etc. in a machine. □ **Governor-General** *noun* the representative of the Crown in a Commonwealth country that recognizes the Queen as head of the State. □ **governorship** *noun*

**gown** *noun* **1** a loose flowing garment, especially a woman's long dress. **2** a loose outer garment that is the official robe of members of a university, judges, etc. **3** a surgeon's overall.

**gowned** *adjective* wearing a gown.

**goy** *noun* (*plural* **goyim** *or* **goys**) a Jewish name for a person who is not a Jew.

**Goya** (in full Francisco José de Goya y Lucientes) (1746–1828), Spanish painter and etcher.

**GP** *abbreviation* general practitioner.

**GPO** *abbreviation* General Post Office.

**grab** *verb* (**grabbed**, **grabbing**) **1** grasp suddenly. **2** take something greedily. **3** operate harshly or jerkily; *the brakes are grabbing.* **4** (*slang*) make an impression on; *how does that music grab you?* ● *noun* **1** a sudden clutch or an attempt to seize. **2** a mechanical device for gripping or lifting things. □ **up for grabs** (*slang*) available for anyone to take.

**Grace**, Dr W(illiam) G(ilbert) (1848–1915), English cricketer.

**grace** *noun* **1** the quality of being attractive, especially in movement, manner, or design. **2** elegance of manner, politeness; *he had the grace to apologize.* **3** favour, goodwill. **4** a delay granted as a favour; *give him a week's grace.* **5** (in Christianity) the unmerited favour of God. **6** a short prayer of thanks before or after a meal. ●*verb* confer honour or dignity on, be an ornament to. □ **grace and favour house** a house occupied by permission of the British sovereign. **grace note** a music note that is added as an embellishment. **His Grace, Your Grace**, etc. the title used in speaking of or to a duke, duchess, or archbishop. **with a good grace** as if willingly.

**graceful** *adjective* having or showing grace. □ **gracefully** *adverb*, **gracefulness** *noun*

**graceless** *adjective* **1** inelegant. **2** ungracious.

**Graces** *plural noun* (*Gk. myth.*) three beautiful goddesses, givers of beauty, charm, and skill.

**gracious** *adjective* **1** kind and pleasant in manner to inferiors. **2** showing divine grace, merciful. **3** showing qualities associated with good taste and breeding; *gracious living*. ●*interjection* an exclamation of surprise; *good gracious!* □ **graciously** *adverb*, **graciousness** *noun*

**gradate** (grā-dayt) *verb* **1** pass or cause to pass by gradations into the next colour or stage etc. **2** arrange in gradations.

**gradation** (grā-day-shŏn) *noun* **1** a series following successive stages in rank, merit, intensity, etc. **2** arrangement in this way. **3** a process of gradual change; a stage in such a process; *the gradations of colour between blue and green*. □ **gradational** *adjective*

**grade** *noun* **1** a step, stage, or degree in some rank, quality, or value; *Grade A eggs*. **2** a class of people or things of the same rank or quality etc. **3** a mark indicating the quality of a student's work. **4** gradient, slope. **5** (*Amer.*) a class in school. ●*verb* **1** arrange in grades. **2** give a grade to a student. **3** adjust the gradient of (a road). **4** pass gradually into a grade or between grades. □ **grade school** (*Amer.*) an elementary school. **make the grade** reach the desired standard.

**gradient** (gray-di-ĕnt) *noun* **1** the amount of slope in a road, railway, or line or curve on a graph; *the road has a gradient of 1 in 10*. **2** a sloping road or railway.

**gradual** *adjective* taking place by degrees, not sudden or steep. □ **gradually** *adverb*

**graduate** *noun* (*pronounced* **grad**-yoo-ăt) a person who holds a university degree. ●*verb* (*pronounced* **grad**-yoo-ayt) **1** take a university degree. **2** divide into graded sections. **3** mark into regular divisions or units of measurement. □ **graduation** *noun*

**Graeco-Roman** (greek-oh-**roh**-măn) *adjective* of the ancient Greeks and Romans.

**Graf**, Steffi (Stephanie) (born 1969), German tennis player.

**graffiti** (grǎ-**fee**-tee) *plural noun* (*singular* **graffito**) words or a drawing roughly scratched, scribbled, or sprayed on a wall.

▪**Usage** *Graffiti* is often used as a singular form although this is considered incorrect by some people.

**graft** *noun* **1** a shoot from one tree fixed into a cut in another to form a new growth. **2** a piece of living tissue transplanted surgically to replace diseased or damaged tissue. **3** (*slang*) hard work. **4** advantage in business or politics obtained by bribery, unfair influence, or other shady means. ●*verb* **1** put a graft in or on. **2** join (a thing) inseparably to another. **3** (*slang*) work hard.

**Graham**, Billy (William Franklin) (born 1918), American evangelistic preacher.

**Grahame**, Kenneth (1859–1932), Scottish author of books for children, including *The Wind in the Willows*.

**Grail** *noun* (in full **Holy Grail**) the cup or platter used (according to legend) by Christ at the Last Supper and in which Joseph of Arimathea received drops of Christ's blood at the Crucifixion, sought in prolonged quests by knights in medieval legends.

**grain** *noun* **1** a small hard seed of a food plant such as wheat or rice. **2** such plants themselves. **3** a small hard particle; *a grain of sand*. **4** a unit of weight, about 65 milligrams. **5** the smallest possible amount; *he hasn't a grain of sense*. **6** the texture produced by the particles in flesh, stone, etc. or in photographic prints. **7** the pattern of lines made by fibres in wood or by layers in rock or coal etc.; the direction of threads in woven fabric. □ **against the grain** contrary to one's natural inclinations. □ **grainy** *adjective*

**gram** *noun* (also **gramme**) a unit of mass in the metric system, one-thousandth of a kilogram.

**graminaceous** (gram-in-**ay**-shŭs) *adjective* of or like grass.

**graminivorous** (gram-in-**iv**-er-ŭs) *adjective* feeding on grass.

**grammar** *noun* **1** the study of words and of the rules for their formation and their relationships to each other in sentences. **2** the rules themselves. **3** a book about these. **4** speech or writing judged as good or bad according to these rules; *his grammar is appalling*. □ **grammar school** (mainly *hist.*) a selective secondary school with a mainly academic curriculum.

**grammatical** *adjective* in accordance with the rules of grammar. □ **grammatically** *adverb*

**gramme** alternative spelling of GRAM.

**gramophone** *noun* a record player, especially the kind that is not operated electrically.

**Grampian** a local government region of Scotland.

**grampus** *noun* (*plural* **grampuses**) a large dolphin-like sea animal with a blunt snout.

**gran** *noun* (*informal*) grandmother.

**granadilla** (gran-ă-**dil**-ă) *noun* passion-fruit.

**granary** *noun* a storehouse for grain.

**grand** *adjective* **1** splendid, magnificent. **2** (**Grand**) of the highest rank; *the Grand Duke Alexis*. **3** dignified, imposing; *she puts on a grand manner*. **4** (*informal*) very enjoyable or satisfactory; *we had a grand time*. **5** including everything, final; *the grand total*. ●*noun* **1** a grand piano. **2** (*slang*) a thousand pounds or dollars; *five grand*. □ **grand opera** opera in which everything is sung and there are no spoken parts. **grand piano** a large full-toned piano with horizontal strings. **grand slam** *see* SLAM. □ **grandly** *adverb*, **grandness** *noun*

**Grand Canyon** a deep gorge through which the Colorado River runs in Arizona.

**grandad** *noun* (*informal*) **1** grandfather. **2** an elderly man.

**grandchild** *noun* (*plural* **grandchildren**) the child of a person's son or daughter.

**granddaughter** *noun* the daughter of a person's son or daughter.

**grandee** (gran-**dee**) *noun* **1** a Spanish or Portuguese noble. **2** a person of high rank.

**grandeur** (**grand**-yer) *noun* splendour, magnificence, grandness.

**grandfather** *noun* the father of a person's father or mother. □ **grandfather clock** a clock in a tall wooden case, worked by weights.

**grandiloquent** (gran-**dil**-ŏ-kwĕnt) *adjective* using pompous, flowery language. □ **grandiloquently** *adverb*, **grandiloquence** *noun*

**grandiose** (gran-di-ohss) *adjective* **1** imposing, planned on a large scale. **2** trying to be grand, pompous. □ **grandiosity** (grandi-**oss**-iti) *noun*

**grandma** *noun* (*informal*) grandmother.

**grand mal** (grahn mal) epilepsy with loss of consciousness. (¶ French, = great sickness.)

**grandmother** *noun* the mother of a person's father or mother.

**Grand National** a steeplechase with 30 jumps run annually at Aintree, Liverpool.

**grandpa** *noun* (*informal*) grandfather.

**grandparent** *noun* a grandfather or grandmother.

**Grand Prix** (grahn pree) any of various important motor or motor-cycle racing events. (¶ French, = great or chief prize.)

**grandsire** *noun* (*old use*) grandfather.

**grandson** *noun* the son of a person's son or daughter.

**grandstand** *noun* the principal roofed building with rows of seats for spectators at a racetrack or sports ground.

**grange** *noun* a country house with farm buildings that belong to it.

**graniferous** (grăn-**if**-er-ŭs) *adjective* producing grain or grainlike seed.

**granite** *noun* a hard grey stone for building.

**granivorous** (grăn-**iv**-er-ŭs) *adjective* feeding on grains.

**granny** *noun* (*informal*) grandmother. □ **granny flat** a flat in someone's house where an elderly relative can live independently but close to the family. **granny knot** a reef-knot with the strings crossed the wrong way and therefore likely to slip.

**grant** *verb* **1** give or allow as a privilege; *grant a request*. **2** give formally, transfer legally. **3** admit or agree that something is true; *I grant that your offer is generous*. ●*noun* something granted, especially a sum of money. □ **take for granted** assume that (a thing) is true or sure to happen; be so used to having (a thing) that one no longer appreciates it.

**Grant**, Cary (original name: Alexander Archibald Leach) (1904–86), American film actor, born in England.

**Granth** = ADI GRANTH.

**grantor** *noun* a person by whom something is legally transferred.

**granular** (**gran**-yoo-ler) *adjective* like grains or granules. □ **granularity** *noun*

**granulate** (**gran**-yoo-layt) *verb* **1** form into grains or granules; *granulated sugar*. **2** make rough and grainy on the surface. □ **granulation** *noun*

**granule** (**gran**-yool) *noun* a small grain.

**grape** *noun* a green or purple berry growing in clusters on vines, used for making wine. □ **grape hyacinth** a small hyacinth-like plant with clusters of rounded usually blue flowers.

**grapefruit** *noun* (*plural* **grapefruit**) a large round yellow citrus fruit with an acid juicy pulp.

**grapevine** *noun* **1** a vine on which grapes grow. **2** a way by which news is passed on unofficially; *heard it on the grapevine*.

**graph** *noun* a diagram consisting of a line or lines showing the relationship between corresponding values of two quantities. ●*verb* draw a graph of. □ **graph paper** paper ruled into small squares, used for plotting graphs.

**graphic** (**graf**-ik) *adjective* **1** of drawing, painting, lettering, or engraving; *the graphic arts*; *a graphic artist*. **2** giving a vivid description; *a graphic account of the fight*.

●*noun* (**graphics**) **1** (as *singular*) the use of diagrams in calculation or in design. **2** (as *plural*) lettering and drawings; *the graphics are by John James.* □ **graphic equalizer** a device for varying the quality of an audio signal by controlling the strength of individual radio frequency bands.

**graphical** (graf-ikǎl) *adjective* **1** using diagrams or graphs. **2** = GRAPHIC (sense 1). □ **graphically** *adverb*

**graphite** *noun* a soft black form of carbon used in lubrication, as a moderator in nuclear reactors, and in lead pencils.

**graphology** (grǎ-**fol**-ŏji) *noun* the study of handwriting, especially as a guide to the writer's character. □ **graphological** *adjective*, **graphologist** *noun*

**grapnel** *noun* **1** a hooked grappling instrument used in dragging the bed of a lake or river. **2** a small anchor with three or more flukes.

**grapple** *verb* **1** seize or hold firmly. **2** (often foll. by *with*) struggle at close quarters. **3** (foll. by *with*) try to manage or deal with; *grapple with a problem.* □ **grappling-iron** *noun* a grapnel.

**grasp** *verb* **1** seize and hold firmly, especially with one's hands or arms. **2** understand; *he couldn't grasp what we meant.* ●*noun* **1** a firm hold or grip; *within her grasp.* **2** a mental hold, understanding; *a thorough grasp of the subject.* □ **grasp at** snatch at. **grasp the nettle** tackle a difficulty boldly.

**grasping** *adjective* greedy for money or possessions.

**Grass**, Günter Wilhelm (born 1927), German novelist.

**grass** *noun* **1** any of a group of common wild low-growing plants with green blades and stalks that are eaten by animals. **2** a plant of the family which includes cereal plants, reeds, and bamboos. **3** ground covered with grass, lawn, or pasture. **4** (*slang*) marijuana. **5** (*slang*) a person who grasses, an act of betraying. ●*verb* **1** cover with grass. **2** (*slang*) betray a conspiracy, turn informer. □ **grass roots 1** the fundamental level or source. **2** ordinary people, the rank and file of a political party or other group. **grass snake** a small harmless European snake. **grass widow** (*or* **widower**) a wife or husband whose spouse is absent for some time. **let the grass grow under one's feet** waste time; miss an opportunity.

**grasshopper** *noun* a jumping insect that makes a shrill chirping noise.

**grassland** *noun* a wide area covered in grass and with few trees.

**grassy** *adjective* like grass; covered with grass.

**grate** *noun* **1** a metal framework that keeps fuel in a fireplace. **2** a fireplace or furnace.

●*verb* **1** shred into small pieces by rubbing against a jagged surface. **2** make a harsh noise by rubbing, sound harshly; *a grating laugh.* **3** have an unpleasant irritating effect.

**grateful** *adjective* feeling or showing that one values a kindness or benefit received. □ **gratefully** *adverb*

**grater** *noun* a device with a jagged surface for grating food.

**gratify** *verb* (**gratified, gratifying**) give pleasure to, satisfy (wishes etc.). □ **gratification** *noun*

**grating** *noun* a screen of spaced metal or wooden bars placed across an opening.

**gratis** (**grah**-tiss) *adverb* & *adjective* free of charge; *you can have the leaflet gratis.*

**gratitude** *noun* being grateful.

**gratuitous** (grǎ-**tew**-it-ŭs) *adjective* **1** given or done without payment. **2** given or done without good reason; *a gratuitous insult.* □ **gratuitously** *adverb*

**gratuity** (grǎ-**tew**-iti) *noun* money given in recognition of services rendered, a tip.

**grave** *noun* **1** a hole dug in the ground to bury a corpse; a mound or memorial stone placed over this. **2** (**the grave**) death, being dead. ●*adjective* **1** serious, causing great anxiety; *grave news.* **2** solemn, not smiling. □ **grave accent** (*pronounced* grahv), a mark (`) over a vowel, as over *a* in *à la carte.* □ **gravely** *adverb*

**gravel** *noun* **1** coarse sand with small stones, as used for roads and paths. **2** *Med.* hard crystals forming in the urinary tract. ●*verb* (**gravelled, gravelling**; *Amer.* **graveled, graveling**) cover with gravel.

**gravelly** *adverb* **1** like gravel. **2** rough-sounding; *a gravelly voice.*

**graven** *adjective* **1** carved; *a graven image.* **2** firmly fixed; *graven on my memory.*

**Graves**[1] (*pronounced* grahv) *noun* a light usually white French wine.

**Graves**[2], Robert Ranke (1895–1985), English poet, writer, and critic.

**gravestone** *noun* a stone monument over a grave.

**graveyard** *noun* a burial ground.

**gravid** (**grav**-id) *adjective Med.* pregnant.

**gravitate** *verb* move or be attracted towards.

**gravitation** *noun* **1** gravitating. **2** the force of gravity. □ **gravitational** *adjective*

**gravity** *noun* **1** the force that attracts bodies towards the centre of the earth; the intensity of this. **2** seriousness; *the gravity of the situation.* **3** solemnity. □ **centre of gravity** *see* CENTRE.

**gravy** *noun* **1** juice that comes out of meat while it is cooking. **2** sauce made from this. **3** (*slang*) money or profit easily or unexpectedly acquired. □ **gravy train** (*slang*) a source of easy money.

**Gray**, Thomas (1716–71), English poet.

**gray** Amer. spelling of GREY.

**grayling** *noun* a silver-grey freshwater fish.

**graze**[1] *verb* **1** eat growing grass; *cattle grazing in the fields.* **2** put (animals) into a field to eat the grass.

**graze**[2] *verb* **1** touch or scrape lightly in passing. **2** scrape the skin from. ●*noun* a raw place where the skin has been scraped.

**grazier** (gray-zi-er) *noun* **1** a person who feeds cattle for market. **2** (*Austral.*) a sheep-farmer.

**grazing** *noun* grassland suitable for animals to feed on.

**grease** *noun* **1** oily or fatty matter, especially as a lubricant. **2** the melted fat of an animal. ●*verb* put grease on or in. □ **grease the palm of** (*slang*) bribe.

**greasepaint** *noun* make-up used by actors and other performers.

**greaseproof** *adjective* impervious to grease.

**greaser** *noun* (*slang*) a member of a gang of youths with long hair and motor cycles.

**greasy** *adjective* (**greasier**, **greasiest**) **1** covered with or containing much grease. **2** slippery. **3** oily in manner; unctuous. □ **greasily** *adverb*, **greasiness** *noun*

**great** *adjective* **1** much above average in size, amount, or intensity. **2** larger than others of similar kind; *the great auk.* **3** of remarkable ability or character, important; *one of the great painters; Peter the Great.* **4** elaborate, intense; *told in great detail.* **5** doing something frequently or intensively or very well; *a great reader.* **6** (*informal*) very enjoyable or satisfactory; *we had a great time.* **7** of a family relationship that is one generation removed in ancestry or descent; *great-aunt; great-niece; great-great-grandfather.* □ **great circle** a circle on the surface of a sphere whose plane passes through the sphere's centre. **Great Dane** a very large powerful smooth-haired breed of dog. **Great Seal** the official seal affixed to important State papers in Britain. **Great Trek** the northward migration in 1835–7 of large numbers of Boers to the areas where they eventually founded the Transvaal Republic and the Orange Free State. **Great War** the First World War. □ **greatness** *noun*

**Great Australian Bight** a wide bay on the south coast of Australia.

**Great Barrier Reef** the largest coral reef in the world, roughly parallel to the NE coast of Australia.

**Great Britain** England, Wales, and Scotland considered as a unit.

**greatcoat** *noun* a heavy overcoat.

**Great Dividing Range** the crest of the eastern highlands of Australia, roughly parallel to the coast for most of its north–south length.

**Greater London** an administrative area comprising London and the surrounding regions.

**Greater Manchester** a metropolitan county of NW England.

**Great Lakes** five large interconnected lakes (Superior, Michigan, Huron, Erie, Ontario) in North America.

**greatly** *adverb* by a considerable amount.

**Great Plains** a vast area of plains in Canada and the USA between the Rocky Mountains and the Mississippi River.

**Great Rift Valley** the extensive rift valley system running from the Jordan valley in Syria, along the Red Sea into Ethiopia, and southwards to Mozambique.

**Great Salt Lake** a heavily saline lake in northern Utah.

**Great Wall of China** a long defensive wall in northern China.

**greave** *noun* a piece of armour worn on the leg to protect the shin.

**grebe** (*pronounced* greeb) *noun* a diving bird.

**Grecian** (gree-shăn) *adjective* Greek. □ **Grecian nose** a straight nose that continues the line of the forehead without a dip.

**Greece** a country in SE Europe.

**greed** *noun* an excessive desire for food or wealth.

**greedy** *adjective* (**greedier**, **greediest**) **1** showing greed. **2** very eager or keen for something. □ **greedily** *adverb*, **greediness** *noun*

**Greek** *adjective* of Greece or its people or language. ●*noun* **1** a member of the people living in ancient or modern Greece. **2** their language. □ **Greek cross** a cross with four equal arms. **it's Greek to me** (*informal*) I cannot understand its meaning.

**green** *adjective* **1** of the colour between blue and yellow, the colour of growing grass. **2** covered with grass or with growing leaves. **3** unripe, not seasoned. **4** not smoked or cured; *green bacon.* **5** immature, inexperienced, easily deceived. **6** pale and sickly-looking. **7** concerned with protection of the environment; (of a product) not harmful to the environment. ●*noun* **1** green colour. **2** a green substance or material; green clothes. **3** a green light. **4** a piece of grassy public land; *the village green.* **5** a grassy area; *a putting-green.* **6** (**Greens**) the Green Party (see below). **7** (**greens**) green vegetables. □ **green belt** an area of open land round a town, where the amount of building is restricted. **green card 1** an international insurance document for motorists. **2** a permit for a foreigner to work in the USA. **green fingers** skill in making plants grow. **green light 1** a signal to proceed on a road. **2** (*informal*) permission to go ahead with a project. **Green Paper** a government report of proposals which are being considered but are not yet accepted. **Green Party** a political party of environmentalists and ecologists. **green pound** the agreed value of the £ according to which payments to agricultural producers are reckoned in the EC. **green revolution** greatly increased crop production in developing countries. **green-room** *noun* a room in a theatre, for the use of actors when they are not on the stage. **green salad** salad consisting of leafy vegetables. **green tea** tea made from leaves that are steam-dried, not fermented (compare BLACK TEA). □ **greenish** *adjective*, **greenly** *adverb*, **greenness** *noun*

**Greene**, (Henry) Graham (1904–91), English novelist.

**greenery** *noun* green foliage or growing plants.

**greenfinch** *noun* a finch with green and yellow feathers.

**greenfly** *noun* (*plural* **greenfly**) a small green insect that sucks juices from plants.

**greengage** *noun* a round plum with a greenish skin.

**greengrocer** *noun* a shopkeeper selling vegetables and fruit. □ **greengrocery** *noun*

**greenhorn** *noun* an inexperienced person.

**greenhouse** *noun* a building with glass sides and roof, for growing plants. □ **greenhouse effect** the trapping of the sun's warmth in the lower atmosphere of the earth, caused by an increase in carbon dioxide, methane, etc. **greenhouse gas** any of the gases, especially carbon dioxide and methane, that contribute to the greenhouse effect.

**Greenland** an island lying north-east of North America and mostly within the Arctic Circle, a part of Denmark but with internal autonomy. □ **Greenlander** *noun*

**Greenpeace** an international organization concerned with the general conservation and safety of the environment.

**greenstick fracture** a kind of fracture, usually in children, in which the bone is partly broken and partly only bent.

**greensward** *noun* (*poetic*) an expanse of grassy turf.

**Greenwich** (gren-ich) a suburb of London, the former site of the Royal Observatory. □ **Greenwich Mean Time** time on the line of longitude which passes through Greenwich, used as a basis for calculating time throughout the world.

**Greer**, Germaine (born 1939), Australian feminist writer.

**greet**[1] *verb* **1** address (a person) on meeting or arrival. **2** receive with a certain reaction;

*the news was greeted with dismay.* **3** present itself to one's sight or hearing; *the sight that greeted our eyes.*

**greet**[2] *verb* (*Scottish*) weep.

**greeting** *noun* **1** words or gestures used to greet a person. **2** (often in *plural*) an expression of goodwill; *birthday greetings.* □ **greetings card** a decorative card sent to convey greetings.

**gregarious** (gri-gair-iŭs) *adjective* **1** living in flocks or communities. **2** fond of company. □ **gregariously** *adverb*, **gregariousness** *noun*

**Gregorian calendar** (gri-gor-iăn) the calendar introduced by Pope Gregory XIII in 1582, replacing the Julian calendar and still in general use.

**Gregorian chant** plainsong church music, named after Pope Gregory I.

**Gregory**, St, 'the Great' (*c.*540–604), pope from 590, who sent St Augustine as head of a mission to convert England to the Christian faith, and is credited with the invention of plainsong.

**gremlin** *noun* (*slang*) a mischievous sprite said to cause mishaps to machinery.

**Grenada** (gren-ay-dă) an island country in the West Indies. □ **Grenadian** *adjective & noun*

**grenade** *noun* a small bomb thrown by hand or fired from a rifle.

**Grenadier Guards** (gren-ă-deer) the first regiment of the royal household infantry.

**Grenadine Islands** (gren-ă-deen) (also **Grenadines**) a chain of small islands in the West Indies, divided between St Vincent and Grenada.

**Gretna Green** a village just north of the Scottish/English border near Carlisle, formerly a popular place for runaway couples from England to be married according to Scots law.

**grew** *see* GROW.

**Grey**[1], Sir George (1812–98), British statesman and colonial administrator, Prime Minister of New Zealand 1877–9.

**Grey**[2], Lady Jane (1537–54), queen of England for nine days, after Edward VI had been persuaded to name her as his successor.

**grey** (*Amer.* **gray**) *adjective* **1** of the colour between black and white, coloured like ashes or lead. **2** having hair which is turning white with age. **3** dull in character, boring. ●*noun* **1** grey colour. **2** a grey substance or material; *grey clothes.* **3** a grey horse. ●*verb* make or become grey. □ **grey area** a situation or topic not clearly defined. **Grey Friars** Franciscan friars, so called from their grey cloaks. **grey matter 1** the material of the brain and spinal cord. **2** (*informal*) intelligence. □ **greyish** *adjective*, **greyness** *noun*

**greyhound** *noun* a slender smooth-haired dog noted for its swiftness, used in racing.

**greylag** *noun* (in full **greylag goose**) a grey wild European goose.

**grid** *noun* **1** a grating. **2** a network of squares on maps, numbered for reference. **3** any network of lines; an arrangement of electric-powered cables or gas-supply lines for distributing current or supplies over a large area. **4** a pattern of lines marking the starting-places on a motor-racing track. **5** a perforated electrode controlling the flow of electrons in a valve.

**gridded** *adjective* marked with a grid.

**griddle** *noun* a circular iron plate placed over a source of heat for baking etc.

**gridiron** (**grid**-I-ern) *noun* **1** a framework of metal bars for grilling food on. **2** a field on which American football is played, with parallel lines marking the area of play.

**gridlock** *noun* an urban traffic jam caused by continuous intersecting lines of traffic. □ **gridlocked** *adjective*

**grief** *noun* **1** deep sorrow. **2** something causing this. □ **come to grief** meet with disaster.

**Grieg** (*pronounced* greeg), Edvard (1843–1907), Norwegian composer.

**grievance** *noun* a real or imagined cause of complaint.

**grieve** *verb* **1** cause grief to. **2** feel grief.

**grievous** (**gree**-vŭs) *adjective* **1** causing grief. **2** serious. □ **grievous bodily harm** *Law* serious injury afflicted intentionally. □ **grievously** *adverb*

**griffin** *noun* (also **gryphon**) a mythical creature with an eagle's head and wings on a lion's body.

**griffon** *noun* **1** one of a breed of terrier-like dogs with coarse hair. **2** a large vulture. **3** = GRIFFIN.

**grill** *noun* **1** a device on a cooker for radiating heat downwards. **2** meat, fish, or vegetables cooked under this or on a gridiron. **3** a gridiron for cooking on. **4** (in full **grill room**) a restaurant specializing in grilled food. ●*verb* **1** cook under a grill or on a gridiron. **2** be exposed to great heat. **3** question closely and severely.

**grille** *noun* (also **grill**) **1** a grating, especially in a door or window. **2** a metal grid protecting the radiator of a vehicle.

**grilse** *noun* (*plural* **grilse** *or* **grilses**) a young salmon returning from the sea to fresh water to spawn for the first time.

**grim** *adjective* (**grimmer**, **grimmest**) **1** stern or severe in appearance. **2** severe, unrelenting, merciless; *held on like grim death.* **3** without cheerfulness, unattractive; *a grim prospect.* □ **grimly** *adverb*, **grimness** *noun*

**grimace** (**grim**-ăs *or* grim-**ayss**) *noun* a contortion of the face expressing pain or disgust, or intended to cause amusement. ●*verb* make a grimace.

**Grimaldi** (grim-**al**-di), Joseph (1779–1837), English actor, creator of the English clown.

**grime** *noun* dirt or soot ingrained in a surface or in the skin. ●*verb* blacken with grime. □ **grimy** *adjective*, **griminess** *noun*

**Grimm**, Jacob Ludwig Carl (1785–1863) and brother Wilhelm Carl (1786–1859), German linguistics scholars who inaugurated a dictionary of German on historical principles and are remembered also for the anthology of fairy tales which they compiled.

**grin** *verb* (**grinned**, **grinning**) **1** smile broadly, showing the teeth. **2** express by a grin; *he grinned his approval.* ●*noun* a broad smile. □ **grin and bear it** endure something without complaining.

**grind** *verb* (**ground**, **grinding**) **1** crush or be crushed into grains or powder. **2** produce in this way. **3** oppress or crush by cruelty. **4** sharpen or smooth by friction. **5** rub harshly together; *grind one's teeth.* **6** work something by turning a handle. **7** (often foll. by *away*) study hard; *grinding away at his algebra.* ●*noun* **1** the act of grinding. **2** the size of ground particles; *a coarse grind.* **3** (*informal*) hard monotonous work. □ **grind out** produce with effort. **grind to a halt** stop laboriously.

**grinder** *noun* **1** a person or thing that grinds. **2** a molar tooth.

**grindstone** *noun* a thick revolving disc used for sharpening or grinding things. □ **keep one's nose to the grindstone** work hard without rest.

**grip** *verb* (**gripped**, **gripping**) **1** take a firm hold of. **2** hold a person's attention; *a gripping story.* ●*noun* **1** a firm grasp or hold. **2** the power of gripping; a way of grasping or holding. **3** understanding, mental hold or control; *has a good grip of her subject.* **4** the part of a tool or machine etc. that grips things. **5** the part (of a weapon or device) designed to be held. **6** a hairgrip. **7** a travelling bag. □ **come** (*or* **get**) **to grips with** begin to cope with, deal with (a problem) firmly.

**gripe** *verb* **1** (*informal*) grumble. **2** affect with gastric pain. ●*noun* (*informal*) a grumble. □ **Gripe Water** (*trade mark*) a medicine to relieve colic in babies.

**grisly** *adjective* causing fear, horror, or disgust; *all the grisly details.* □ **grisliness** *noun*

**grist** *noun* grain to be ground or already ground. □ **grist to one's mill** a source of profit or advantage.

**gristle** *noun* tough flexible tissue of animal bodies, especially in meat. □ **gristly** *adjective*

**grit** *noun* **1** particles of stone or sand. **2** courage and endurance. ●*verb* (**gritted**,

**gritting**) **1** clench; *grit one's teeth.* **2** spread grit on. **3** make a grating sound. □ **gritty** *adjective*, **grittiness** *noun*

**grits** *plural noun* **1** coarsely ground grain, especially oatmeal. **2** oats that have been husked but not ground.

**grizzle** *verb* (*informal*) whimper or whine, complain. □ **grizzly** *adjective*

**grizzled** *adjective* grey-haired or partly so.

**grizzly** *adjective* **1** grey, grey-haired. **2** in a whining or complaining mood. ●*noun* (in full **grizzly bear**) a large variety of brown bear of North America.

**groan** *verb* **1** make a long deep sound expressing pain, grief, or disapproval. **2** make a creaking noise resembling this. ●*noun* the sound made in groaning.

**groats** *plural noun* crushed grain, especially oats.

**grocer** *noun* a shopkeeper who sells foods and household stores.

**grocery** *noun* **1** a grocer's shop or goods. **2** (**groceries**) goods sold by a grocer.

**grog** *noun* **1** a drink of spirits mixed with water. **2** (*Austral.*) any alcoholic drink.

**groggy** *adjective* weak and unsteady. □ **groggily** *adverb*, **grogginess** *noun*

**groin**[1] *noun* **1** the part of the body where each thigh joins the trunk. **2** *Archit.* the curved edge where two vaults meet in a roof; an arch supporting a vault.

**groin**[2] Amer. spelling of GROYNE.

**groined** *adjective* built with groins.

**grommet** *noun* (also **grummet**) **1** a metal, plastic, or rubber eyelet placed in a hole to protect or insulate a rope or cable passed through it. **2** a tube passed through the eardrum in surgery to drain and ventilate the middle ear.

**Gromyko** (grŏ-**mee**-koh), Andrei Andreievich (1909–89), Soviet statesman, Foreign Minister 1957–85, President of the USSR 1985–8.

**groom** *noun* **1** a person employed to look after horses. **2** the title of certain officers of the royal household, chiefly in the Lord Chamberlain's department. **3** a bridegroom. ●*verb* **1** clean and brush (an animal). **2** make neat and trim. **3** prepare (a person) for a career or position.

**groove** *noun* **1** a long narrow channel in the surface of hard material. **2** a spiral cut on a gramophone record for the needle or stylus. **3** a way of living that has become a habit, a rut. ●*verb* make a groove or grooves in.

**groovy** *adjective* (*slang*) excellent.

**grope** *verb* **1** feel about as one does in the dark; (foll. by *for*) seek by feeling. **2** search mentally with some uncertainty; *groping for an answer.*

**Gropius** (groh-pi-ŭs), Walter (1883–1969), German-born American architect, director of the Bauhaus 1919–28.

**grosgrain** (**groh**-grayn) *noun* corded fabric of silky thread, used for ribbons etc.

**gross** (*pronounced* grohss) *adjective* **1** thick, large-bodied. **2** not refined, vulgar; *gross manners.* **3** glaringly obvious, outrageous; *gross negligence.* **4** total, whole, without deductions; *gross income.* ●*noun* (*plural* **gross**) twelve dozen (144) items. ●*verb* produce or earn as total profit. □ **gross domestic product** the total value of goods produced and services provided in a country in one year. **gross national product** the gross domestic product plus the total of net income from abroad.

**grotesque** (groh-**tesk**) *adjective* very odd or unnatural, fantastically ugly or absurd. ●*noun* **1** a comically distorted figure. **2** a design using fantastic human, animal, and plant forms. □ **grotesquely** *adverb*, **grotesqueness** *noun*

**Grotius** (**groh**-ti-ŭs), Hugo (1583–1645), Dutch jurist, author of a legal treatise that established the basis of modern international law.

**grotto** (**grot**-oh) *noun* (*plural* **grottoes** or **grottos**) a picturesque cave.

**grotty** *adjective* (*slang*) unpleasant, dirty, or useless.

**grouch** (*informal*) *verb* grumble. ●*noun* **1** a grumble. **2** a grumbler. □ **grouchy** *adjective*

**ground**[1] *noun* **1** the solid surface of the earth, especially contrasted with the air surrounding it. **2** an area, position, or distance on the earth's surface; *gain ground.* **3** a foundation or reason for a theory or action; *there are no grounds for suspicion.* **4** soil, earth; *marshy ground.* **5** an area used for a particular purpose; *a football ground.* **6** the underlying part; a surface worked upon in embroidery or painting. **7** (**grounds**) an area of enclosed land belonging to a large house or an institution. **8** (**grounds**) solid particles that sink to the bottom of a liquid; *coffee grounds.* ●*verb* **1** run aground. **2** prevent (an aircraft) from flying; *all aircraft were grounded because of the fog.* **3** teach thoroughly, give good basic training to. **4** base; *it is grounded on fact.* □ **break new ground** achieve something new. **down to the ground** completely; *the job suits me down to the ground.* **get off the ground 1** rise in the air. **2** make a successful start. **ground bass** *Music* a short bass line constantly repeated. **ground floor** the floor at ground level in a building. **ground frost** frost on the surface of the ground or in the top layer of soil. **ground-plan** *noun* **1** a plan of a building at ground level. **2** an outline or general design of a scheme. **ground-rent**

*noun* the rent paid for land that is leased for building. **ground squirrel** a burrowing rodent related to the squirrel. **ground swell** heavy slow-moving waves caused by a distant or recent storm.

**ground²** *see* GRIND. □ **ground glass** glass made non-transparent by grinding.

**grounding** *noun* thorough teaching, basic training; *a good grounding in arithmetic*.

**groundless** *adjective* without basis, without good reason; *your fears are groundless*. □ **groundlessly** *adverb*

**groundnut** *noun* a peanut.

**groundsel** *noun* a weed with small yellow flowers.

**groundsheet** *noun* a waterproof sheet for spreading on the ground.

**groundsman** *noun* (*plural* **groundsmen**) a man employed to look after a sports ground.

**groundwork** *noun* preliminary or basic work.

**group** *noun* **1** a number of people or things gathered, placed, or classed together, or working together for some purpose. **2** a number of commercial companies under one owner. **3** a pop group. ●*verb* **1** form or gather into a group or groups. **2** place in a group; organize into groups. □ **group captain** an officer in the RAF. **group therapy** therapy in which patients with a similar condition are brought together to assist one another psychologically.

**groupie** *noun* (*slang*) an ardent follower of touring pop groups.

**grouse¹** *noun* (*plural* **grouse**) **1** a game bird with feathered feet. **2** its flesh as food.

**grouse²** (*informal*) *verb* grumble. ●*noun* a grumble. □ **grouser** *noun*

**grout** *noun* thin fluid mortar used to fill narrow cavities such as joints between stones or wall-tiles. ●*verb* fill with grout.

**grove** *noun* a group of trees, a small wood.

**grovel** *verb* (**grovelled**, **grovelling**; *Amer.* **groveled**, **groveling**) **1** humble oneself; behave obsequiously. **2** lie or crawl with the face downwards in a show of humility or fear.

**grow** *verb* (**grew**, **grown**, **growing**) **1** increase in size or quantity; become greater. **2** develop; *the seeds are growing*. **3** be capable of developing as a plant, flourish; *rice grows in warm climates*. **4** become gradually; *she grew rich*. **5** cause or allow to grow, produce by cultivation; *grow a beard*; *grow roses*. □ **growing pains 1** neuralgic pain in children's legs, usually caused by tiredness. **2** problems arising because a project or development is in its early stages. **grow on** (of an idea etc.) become more acceptable to. **grow out of 1** (of a growing child) become too large to wear (certain clothes).

**2** become too mature for; *grew out of childish habits*. **3** have as a source, arise or develop from. **grow up** develop, become adult or mature.

**grower** *noun* **1** a person who grows plants, fruit, or vegetables commercially. **2** a plant that grows in a certain way; *a rapid grower*.

**growl** *verb* **1** make a low threatening sound. **2** speak or say in a growling manner, grumble. ●*noun* **1** a growling sound. **2** a grumble.

**grown** *see* GROW. ●*adjective* **1** fully developed, adult; *a grown man*. **2** (foll. by *over*) covered with a growth; *a wall grown over with ivy*. □ **grown-up** (*adjective*) adult; (*noun*) an adult person.

**growth** *noun* **1** the process of growing, development. **2** cultivation of produce. **3** something that grows or has grown; *a thick growth of weeds*. **4** an abnormal formation of tissue in the body, a tumour. □ **growth industry** one developing rapidly.

**groyne** *noun* (*Amer.* **groin**) a structure of wood, stone, or concrete projecting towards the sea, preventing sand and pebbles from being washed away by the current.

**grub** *noun* **1** the thick-bodied worm-like larva of certain insects. **2** (*slang*) food. ●*verb* (**grubbed**, **grubbing**) **1** dig the surface of the soil. **2** search laboriously, rummage. **3** (foll. by *up*) clear away (roots) by digging; dig up by the roots.

**grubby** *adjective* (**grubbier**, **grubbiest**) dirty, unwashed. □ **grubbily** *adverb*, **grubbiness** *noun*

**grudge** *verb* resent having to give or allow something; *I don't grudge him his success*. ●*noun* a feeling of resentment or ill will. □ **grudging** *adjective*, **grudgingly** *adverb*

**gruel** (groo-ĕl) *noun* a thin porridge made by boiling oatmeal in milk or water.

**gruelling** (groo-ĕl-ing) *adjective* (*Amer.* **grueling**) very tiring, exhausting.

**gruesome** (groo-sŏm) *adjective* horrifying, disgusting, revolting; *the gruesome details of the murder*.

**gruff** *adjective* **1** (of the voice) low and harsh, hoarse. **2** having a gruff voice. **3** surly in manner. □ **gruffly** *adverb*, **gruffness** *noun*

**grumble** *verb* **1** complain in a bad-tempered way. **2** rumble; *thunder was grumbling in the distance*. ●*noun* **1** a complaint, especially a bad-tempered one. **2** a rumble. □ **grumbling appendix** (*informal*) one that causes pain from time to time without developing into appendicitis. □ **grumbler** *noun*

**grummet** = GROMMET.

**grumpy** *adjective* bad-tempered and gloomy. □ **grumpily** *adverb*, **grumpiness** *noun*

**grunge** *noun* (*slang*) a raucous style of rock music; a ragged style of clothing associated with this music.

**grunt** *verb* **1** make the gruff snorting sound characteristic of a pig. **2** speak or utter with such a sound; *he grunted a reply*. **3** grumble. ● *noun* a grunting sound.

**Gruyère** (groo-yair) *noun* a firm pale cheese with holes.

**gryphon** = GRIFFIN.

**G7** *abbreviation* the 'Group of Seven' principal industrial nations, consisting of the USA, Japan, Germany, France, the UK, Italy, and Canada.

**G-string** *noun* **1** a string on a musical instrument, tuned to the note G. **2** a narrow strip of cloth covering the genitals, attached to a string round the waist.

**G-suit** *noun* a close-fitting inflatable suit worn by pilots and astronauts flying at high speed to prevent blood from draining away from the head and causing blackouts (G = gravity).

**GT** *abbreviation* gran turismo; a high-performance saloon car. (¶ Italian, = grand touring.)

**guano** (gwah-noh) *noun* **1** excrement of sea birds, used as manure. **2** an artificial manure, especially made from fish.

**guarantee** *noun* **1** a formal promise to do what has been agreed, or that a thing is of specified quality and durability, with penalties for failure. **2** = GUARANTY. **3** = GUARANTOR. ● *verb* (**guaranteed, guaranteeing**) **1** give or be a guarantee for. **2** promise, state with certainty.

**guarantor** *noun* a person who gives a guarantee.

**guaranty** *noun* **1** a formal promise given by one person to another that he or she will be responsible for something that is to be done or a debt that is to be paid by a third person. **2** something offered or accepted as security.

**guard** *verb* **1** watch over and protect, keep safe. **2** watch over and supervise or prevent from escaping. **3** keep in check, restrain; *guard your tongue*. **4** take precautions; *guard against errors*. ● *noun* **1** a state of watchfulness or alertness for possible danger. **2** a defensive attitude in boxing, fencing, cricket, etc. **3** a protector, a sentry. **4** a railway official in charge of a train. **5** a body of soldiers or others guarding a place or a person, serving as escort, or forming a separate part of an army. **6** a protecting part or device. **7** (**the Guards**) the royal household troops. □ **off (one's) guard** unprepared against attack or surprise. **on (one's) guard** alert for possible danger etc. **stand guard** act as a protector or sentry, keep watch.

**guarded** *adjective* cautious, discreet; *a guarded statement*.

**guardhouse** *noun* a building accommodating a military guard or securing prisoners.

**guardian** *noun* **1** one who guards or protects. **2** a person who undertakes legal responsibility for someone who is not able to manage his or her own affairs, such as an orphaned child. □ **guardian angel** an angel thought of as watching over a person or place. □ **guardianship** *noun*

**guardsman** *noun* (*plural* **guardsmen**) **1** a soldier acting as guard. **2** a member of the Guards.

**Guatemala** (gwati-**mah**-lă) **1** a country in the north of Central America. **2** its capital city. □ **Guatemalan** *adjective & noun*

**guava** (gwah-vă) *noun* the edible orange-coloured fruit of a tropical American tree.

**gubernatorial** (gew-ber-na-**tor**-iăl) *adjective* (especially *Amer.*) of a governor.

**gudgeon[1]** (guj-ŏn) *noun* a small freshwater fish used as bait.

**gudgeon[2]** (guj-ŏn) *noun* **1** a kind of pivot. **2** a socket for a rudder. **3** the tubular part of a hinge. **4** a pin holding two blocks of stone etc. together.

**guelder rose** (geld-er) a shrub with bunches of round white flowers.

**Guernsey** (gern-zi) **1** the second largest of the Channel Islands. **2** an animal of a breed of dairy cattle originally from the island of Guernsey. **3** (**guernsey**) a thick knitted woollen sweater.

**guerrilla** (gĕ-**ril**-ă) *noun* (also **guerilla**) a person who takes part in fighting or harassment by small groups acting independently.

**guess** *verb* **1** form an opinion, make a statement, or give an answer without calculating or measuring and without definite knowledge. **2** think likely. **3** (*Amer.*) suppose; *I guess we ought to be going.* ● *noun* an opinion formed by guessing. □ **keep a person guessing** (*informal*) keep him or her uncertain of one's feelings or future actions etc. □ **guesser** *noun*

**guesstimate** alternative spelling of GUESTIMATE.

**guesswork** *noun* the process of guessing; an example of this.

**guest** *noun* **1** a person staying at another's house or visiting by invitation or being entertained to a meal. **2** a person lodging at a hotel. **3** a visiting performer taking part in an entertainment; *a guest artist.* □ **guest house** a private house offering paid accommodation.

**guestimate** (gess-tim-ăt) *noun* (also **guesstimate**) (*informal*) an estimate based on guesswork and reasoning.

**Guevara** (gĕv-ar-ă), Ernesto (known as 'Che Guevara') (1928–67), Argentinian revolutionary, guerrilla leader, and a principal supporter of Castro.

**guff** *noun* (*slang*) empty talk, nonsense.

**guffaw** *noun* a coarse noisy laugh. ● *verb* give a guffaw.

**guidance** *noun* **1** guiding, being guided. **2** advising or advice on problems.

**guide** *noun* **1** a person who shows others the way. **2** one employed to point out interesting sights on a journey or visit. **3** an adviser; a person or thing that directs or influences one's behaviour. **4** a book of information about a place or a subject; *A Guide to Italy.* **5** a thing that marks a position, guides the eye, or steers moving parts. **6** (**Guide**) a member of a girls' organization corresponding to the Scout Association. ● *verb* act as guide to. □ **guided missile** a missile that is under remote control or directed by equipment within itself. **guide-dog** *noun* a dog trained to guide a blind person.

**guidebook** *noun* a book of information about a place, for travellers or visitors.

**guideline** *noun* a statement of principle giving general guidance.

**Guider** *noun* an adult leader of Guides.

**guild** *noun* (also **gild**) **1** a society of people with similar interests and aims. **2** any of the associations of craftsmen or merchants in the Middle Ages.

**guilder** (**gild**-er) *noun* a unit of money in the Netherlands, a florin.

**guildhall** *noun* **1** a hall built or used as a meeting-place by a guild or corporation. **2** a town hall. **3** (**Guildhall**) the hall of the Corporation of the City of London, used for official banquets and receptions.

**guile** (*rhymes with* mile) *noun* treacherous cunning, craftiness. □ **guileful** *adjective*, **guileless** *adjective*

**guillemot** (**gil**-i-mot) *noun* a fast-flying sea bird nesting on cliffs etc.

**guillotine** (**gil**-ŏ-teen) *noun* **1** a machine with a heavy blade sliding down in grooves, used for beheading people. **2** a machine with a long blade for cutting paper or metal. **3** a method of preventing delay in the discussion of a bill in Parliament by fixing times at which various parts of it must be voted on. ● *verb* use a guillotine on.

**guilt** *noun* **1** the fact of having committed some offence. **2** a feeling that one is to blame for something.

**guiltless** *adjective* innocent.

**guilty** *adjective* (**guiltier**, **guiltiest**) **1** having done wrong. **2** feeling or showing guilt. □ **guiltily** *adverb*, **guiltiness** *noun*

**Guinea** a country on the west coast of Africa. □ **Gulf of Guinea** a large inlet of the Atlantic Ocean south-east of Guinea.

**guinea** *noun* a former British gold coin worth 21 shillings (£1.05).

**Guinea-Bissau** (**bis**-ow) a country on the west coast of Africa between Guinea and Senegal.

**guinea-fowl** *noun* a domestic fowl of the pheasant family, with grey feathers spotted with white.

**guinea pig 1** a short-eared animal like a large rat, kept as a pet or for biological experiments. **2** a person or thing used as a subject for experiment.

**Guinevere** (**gwin**-i-veer) (in legends of King Arthur) the wife of King Arthur and mistress of Lancelot.

**Guinness**, Sir Alec (born 1914), English actor.

**guipure** (g'ee-pyoor) *noun* a heavy lace of linen pieces joined by embroidery.

**guise** (*pronounced as* guys) *noun* an outward manner or appearance put on in order to conceal the truth, a pretence; *they exploited him under the guise of friendship.*

**guitar** (gi-**tar**) *noun* a stringed musical instrument, played by plucking with the fingers or a plectrum. □ **electric guitar** one with a built-in microphone. □ **guitarist** *noun*

**Gujarat** (goo-jer-**aht**) a State in western India.

**Gujarati** (goo-jer-**ah**-ti) *noun* **1** a native of Gujarat. **2** a language descended from Sanskrit and spoken mainly in Gujarat.

**Gulag** *noun* the system of detention camps which operated in the former Soviet Union 1930–55.

**Gulbenkian** (guul-**benk**-iăn), Calouste Sarkis (1869–1955), British oil magnate and philanthropist, born in Turkey of Armenian family, who endowed an international foundation for the advancement of social and cultural projects.

**gulch** *noun* (*Amer.*) a ravine, especially one containing a torrent.

**gulf** *noun* **1** an area of sea (larger than a bay) that is partly surrounded by land. **2** (**the Gulf**) the Persian Gulf. **3** a deep hollow. **4** a wide difference in opinions or outlook.

**Gulf Stream** a warm ocean current flowing from the Gulf of Mexico towards Newfoundland and across to Europe.

**Gulf War 1** the war between Iraq and Iran, in the general area of the Persian Gulf, 1980–8. **2** the war of Jan.–Feb. 1991, between Iraq and an international coalition of forces based in Saudia Arabia, after Iraq's invasion of Kuwait in Aug. 1990.

**gull** *noun* a large sea bird with long wings.

**gullet** *noun* the passage by which food goes from the mouth to the stomach, the throat.

**gullible** (**gul**-i-bŭl) *adjective* easily deceived. □ **gullibility** (gul-i-**bil**-iti) *noun*

**gully** noun **1** a narrow channel cut by water or made for carrying rainwater away from a building. **2** (in cricket) a fieldsman between point and slips.

**gulp** verb **1** swallow (food or drink) hastily or greedily. **2** (foll. by *back*, *down*) suppress; *he gulped back his rage.* **3** make a gulping movement, choke or gasp; *gulping for breath.* ●noun **1** the act of gulping. **2** a large mouthful of liquid.

**gum**[1] noun the firm flesh in which the teeth are rooted.

**gum**[2] noun **1** a sticky substance exuded by some trees and shrubs, used for sticking things together. **2** chewing gum. **3** a gumdrop. **4** a gum-tree. ●verb (**gummed**, **gumming**) smear or cover with gum; stick together with gum. □ **gum arabic** gum exuded by some kinds of acacia. **gum-tree** noun a tree that exudes gum, a eucalyptus. **gum up** (*informal*) cause confusion or delay in, spoil. **gum up the works** interfere with the smooth running of something. **up a gum-tree** (*slang*) in great difficulties.

**gumboil** noun a small abscess on the gum.

**gumboot** noun a rubber boot, a wellington.

**gumdrop** noun a hard transparent sweet made of gelatin or gum arabic.

**gummy** adjective **1** sticky with gum. **2** showing the gums, toothless.

**gumption** (**gump-**shŏn) noun (*informal*) **1** common sense. **2** initiative.

**gun** noun **1** a firearm that sends shells or bullets from a metal tube. **2** a starting pistol. **3** a device that forces out a substance through a tube; *a grease-gun.* **4** a person using a sporting gun as a member of a shooting-party. **5** (*Amer.*) a gunman; *a professional gun.* ●verb (**gunned**, **gunning**) **1** (foll. by *down*) shoot with a gun; *gunned him down.* **2** (foll. by *for*) search for determinedly in order to attack or rebuke (a person); *she was really gunning for him after his gambling spree.* □ **go great guns** (*informal*) proceed vigorously or intensively. **gun cotton** an explosive made of acid-soaked cotton. **gun dog** a dog trained to retrieve game shot in a hunt. **gun metal** adjective & noun dull bluish-grey, like the colour of metal formerly used for guns.

**gunboat** noun a small armed vessel with heavy guns. □ **gunboat diplomacy** diplomacy backed by the threat of force.

**gunfire** noun the firing of guns.

**gunge** noun (*informal*) a sticky or messy mass of a substance. □ **gungy** adjective

**gung-ho** adjective arrogantly eager; over-zealous.

**gunman** noun (*plural* **gunmen**) a man armed with a gun.

**gunnel** alternative spelling of GUNWALE.

**gunner** noun **1** a soldier in an artillery unit, the official term for a private. **2** a warrant officer in the navy, in charge of a battery of guns. **3** a member of an aircraft crew who operates a gun; *rear gunner.*

**gunnery** noun the construction and operating of large guns.

**gunny** noun **1** a coarse material used for making sacks. **2** a sack made from this.

**gunpoint** noun □ **at gunpoint** under threat of being shot by a gun held ready.

**gunpowder** noun an explosive of saltpetre, sulphur, and charcoal. □ **Gunpowder Plot** an unsuccessful plot to blow up James I and Parliament (5 November 1605).

**gunrunner** noun a person engaged in smuggling guns and ammunition into a country. □ **gunrunning** noun

**gunshot** noun **1** a shot fired from a gun. **2** the range of a gun; *within gunshot.*

**gunslinger** noun (especially *Amer. slang*) a gunman.

**gunsmith** noun a maker and repairer of small firearms.

**gunwale** (gun-ăl) noun (also **gunnel**) the upper edge of a ship's or boat's side.

**guppy** noun a small freshwater West Indian fish, often kept in aquariums.

**Gupta** (guup-tă) a Hindu dynasty established in Bihar in 320 and ruling most of northern India until near the end of the 5th century. □ **Guptan** adjective

**gurdwara** (gerd-wah-ră) noun a Sikh temple.

**gurgle** noun a low bubbling sound. ●verb make this sound.

**Gurkha** (ger-kă) noun **1** a member of a Hindu people in Nepal. **2** a Nepalese soldier serving in the British army.

**gurnard** noun a sea fish with a large head.

**guru** (goor-oo) noun (*plural* **gurus**) **1** a Hindu spiritual teacher or head of a religious sect. **2** an influential or revered teacher.

**gush** verb **1** flow or pour out suddenly or in great quantities. **2** talk with extravagant enthusiasm or emotion, especially in an affected manner. ●noun **1** a sudden or great outflow. **2** an outpouring of feeling, effusiveness.

**gusher** noun **1** an effusive person. **2** an oil well from which oil flows strongly without needing to be pumped.

**gusset** noun a piece of cloth inserted in a garment to strengthen or enlarge it.

**gust** noun **1** a sudden rush of wind. **2** a burst of rain, smoke, emotion, etc. ●verb blow in gusts. □ **gusty** adjective, **gustily** adverb

**Gustavus Adolphus** (guus-**tah**-vŭs ă-**dol**-fŭs) (1594–1632), king of Sweden 1611–32, known as the 'Lion of the North'.

**gusto** *noun* zest, great enjoyment in doing something.

**gut** *noun* **1** the lower part of the alimentary canal, the intestine. **2** (*slang*) the stomach, the belly. **3** a thread made from the intestines of animals, used surgically and for violin and racket strings. **4** (**guts**) the internal organs of the abdomen. **5** (**guts**) the contents or essence of something. **6** (**guts**) (*informal*) courage and determination. ●*adjective* **1** fundamental, basic; *a gut issue*. **2** instinctive; *a gut reaction*. ●*verb* (**gutted, gutting**) **1** remove the guts from (a fish). **2** remove or destroy the internal fittings or parts of (a building); *the factory was gutted by fire*. □ **gut-rot** (*informal*) a stomach upset.

**Gutenberg** (**goo-těn**-berg), Johann (*c.*1400–68), German printer, inventor of movable type.

**gutless** *adjective* (*informal*) lacking courage and determination.

**gutsy** *adjective* (*informal*) **1** greedy. **2** courageous.

**gutta-percha** *noun* a tough rubber-like substance made from the juice of various Malayan trees.

**gutted** *adjective* (*informal*) utterly exhausted; overcome by emotion.

**gutter** *noun* **1** a shallow trough under the eaves of a building, or a channel at the side of a street, for carrying off rainwater. **2** (**the gutter**) a poor or degraded background or environment. ●*verb* (of a candle) burn unsteadily so that melted wax flows freely down the sides. □ **gutter press** newspapers seeking sensationalism, e.g. concerning people's private lives.

**guttering** *noun* gutters; a length of gutter.

**guttersnipe** *noun* a dirty badly-dressed child who plays in slum streets.

**guttural** (**gut**-er-ăl) *adjective* **1** throaty, harsh-sounding; *a guttural voice*. **2** *Phonetics* pronounced in the back of the throat. □ **gutturally** *adverb*

**guv** *noun* (*slang*) governor.

**guy¹** *noun* a rope or chain used to keep something steady or secured. ●*verb* secure with a guy or guys.

**guy²** *noun* **1** (*informal*) a man; a fellow. **2** a figure in the form of a man dressed in old clothes, representing Guy Fawkes and burnt on 5 November in memory of the Gunpowder Plot. ●*verb* ridicule, especially by comic imitation.

**Guyana** (gy-**an**-ă) a country on the NE coast of South America. □ **Guyanese** (gy-ăn-**eez**) *adjective & noun* (*plural* **Guyanese**).

**guzzle** *verb* eat or drink greedily. □ **guzzler** *noun*

**Gwent** a county of SE Wales.

**Gwynedd** (**gwin**-*eth*) a county of NW Wales.

**Gwynn**, Nell (1650–87), an actress who became one of Charles II's many mistresses.

**gybe** (*pronounced* j-) *verb* (*Amer.* **jibe**) **1** (of a sail or boom) swing across. **2** make (a sail) do this. **3** change course; change the course of (a ship) so that this happens.

**gym** (*pronounced* jim) *noun* (*informal*) **1** a gymnasium. **2** gymnastics.

**gymkhana** (jim-**kah**-nă) *noun* a horse-riding competition.

**gymnasium** *noun* (*plural* **gymnasiums** or **gymnasia**) a room or building equipped for gymnastics.

**gymnast** (**jim**-nast) *noun* an expert performer of gymnastics.

**gymnastic** *adjective* of gymnastics. □ **gymnastically** *adverb*

**gymnastics** *plural noun* (also treated as *singular*) exercises performed to develop the muscles or demonstrate agility. □ **mental gymnastics** mental agility, elaborate reasoning.

**gymnosperm** (**jim**-noh-sperm) *noun* a member of the group of plants (mainly trees) that have seeds not enclosed in an ovary.

**gymslip** *noun* a sleeveless tunic worn (especially formerly) as a part of girls' school uniform.

**gynaecology** (gy-ni-**kol**-ŏji) *noun* (*Amer.* **gynecology**) the science of the female reproductive system and functions and diseases specific to women. □ **gynaecological** *adjective*, **gynaecologist** *noun*

**gyp** (*pronounced* jip) *noun* □ **give a person gyp** (*informal*) cause pain to him or her.

**gypsum** (**jip**-sŭm) *noun* a chalk-like mineral from which plaster of Paris is made.

**Gypsy** *noun* (also **Gipsy**) a member of a travelling people with dark skin and hair.

**gyrate** (jy-**rayt**) *verb* move round in circles or spirals, revolve. □ **gyration** (jy-**ray**-shŏn) *noun*

**gyratory** (jy-ră-ter-i) *adjective* gyrating, following a circular or spiral path.

**gyrfalcon** (jer-**fawl**-kŏn) *noun* a large falcon of northern countries.

**gyro** (jy-roh) *noun* (*plural* **gyros**) (*informal*) a gyroscope.

**gyrocompass** (jy-rŏ-kum-păs) *noun* a navigation compass using a gyroscope and so independent of the earth's rotation.

**gyroscope** (jy-rŏ-skohp) *noun* a device consisting of a heavy wheel which, when spinning fast, keeps the direction of its axis unchanged, used in navigation instruments in ships and in spacecraft etc.

**H** *abbreviation* (of a pencil lead) hard. ●*symbol* hydrogen.

**h.** *abbreviation* (also **h**) **1** height. **2** hour.

**Ha** *symbol* hahnium.

**ha** *interjection* (also **hah**) an exclamation of triumph, derision, or surprise. ●*abbreviation* hectare(s).

**Habakkuk** (**hab**-ă-kŭk *or* hă-**bak**-ŭk) **1** a Hebrew minor prophet probably of the 7th century BC. **2** the book of the Old Testament bearing his name.

**habeas corpus** (**hay**-bi-ăs **kor**-pŭs) an order requiring a person to be brought before a judge or into court, especially in order to investigate the right of the authorities to keep him or her imprisoned. (¶ Latin, = you must have the body.)

**haberdasher** *noun* a shopkeeper dealing in accessories for dress and in sewing-goods. □ **haberdashery** *noun*

**habiliments** (hă-**bil**-i-měnts) *plural noun* (*old use*) clothing, garments.

**habit** *noun* **1** a settled way of behaving. **2** something done frequently and almost without thinking. **3** something that is hard to give up. **4** the long dress worn by a monk or nun. □ **habit-forming** *adjective* causing addiction.

**habitable** *adjective* suitable for living in.

**habitat** (**hab**-i-tat) *noun* the natural environment of an animal or plant.

**habitation** *noun* **1** a place to live in. **2** inhabiting, being inhabited.

**habitual** *adjective* **1** done constantly, like or resulting from a habit. **2** regular, usual, *in his habitual place*. **3** doing something as a habit; *a habitual smoker*. □ **habitually** *adverb*

**habituate** *verb* accustom. □ **habituation** *noun*

**habitué** (hă-**bit**-yoo-ay) *noun* one who visits a place frequently or lives there. (¶ French.)

**háček** a mark (ˇ) placed over a letter to modify its sound in some languages.

**hachures** (ha-**shoor**) *plural noun* parallel lines used on maps to indicate the degree of slope in hills.

**hacienda** (ha-si-**en**-dă) *noun* (in Spanish-speaking countries) a large estate with a dwelling-house.

**hack**¹ *verb* **1** cut or chop roughly. **2** deal a rough blow or kick; *hacked at his shins*. **3** (*informal*) gain unauthorized access to (computer files).

**hack**² *noun* **1** a horse for ordinary riding; one that may be hired. **2** a person paid to do hard and uninteresting work, especially as a writer. ●*verb* ride on horseback at an ordinary pace, especially along roads.

**hacker** *noun* **1** a person or thing that hacks or cuts roughly. **2** (*informal*) a computer enthusiast, especially one who gains unauthorized access to a computer network.

**hacking** *adjective* (of a cough) short, dry, and frequent.

**hackles** *plural noun* **1** hairs on the back of an animal's neck which rise when it is angry or alarmed. **2** the long feathers on the neck of a domestic cock and other birds. □ **make one's hackles rise** cause one to be angry or indignant.

**hackney** a horse for ordinary riding. □ **hackney carriage** a taxi.

**hackneyed** (**hak**-nid) *adjective* (of a saying) having lost its original impact through long overuse.

**hacksaw** *noun* a saw for cutting metal, with a short blade in a frame.

**had** *see* HAVE.

**haddock** *noun* (*plural* **haddock**) a North Atlantic sea fish like cod but smaller, used for food.

**Hades** (**hay**-deez) *noun* (*Gk. myth.*) the underworld, the place where the spirits of the dead go.

**Hadith** (**had**-ith) *noun* a collection of sayings of the Prophet Muhammad and of traditions about him, now forming a supplement to the Koran.

**hadj** alternative spelling of HAJJ.

**hadji** alternative spelling of HAJJI.

**hadn't** (*informal*) = had not.

**Hadrian** (**hay**-dri-ăn) Roman emperor 117–38. □ **Hadrian's Wall** a Roman defensive wall across northern England.

**haemal** (**hee**-măl) *adjective* (*Amer.* **hemal**) of the blood.

**haematic** (hee-**mat**-ik) *adjective* (*Amer.* **hematic**) of or containing blood.

**haematite** (**hee**-mă-tyt) *noun* (*Amer.* **hematite**) ferric oxide as ore.

**haematology** (hee-mă-**tol**-ŏji) *noun* (*Amer.* **hematology**) the study of blood and its diseases. □ **haematologist** *noun*

**haemoglobin** (heem-ŏ-**gloh**-bin) *noun* (*Amer.* **hemoglobin**) the red oxygen-carrying substance in the blood.

**haemophilia** (heem-ŏ-**fil**-iă) *noun* (*Amer.* **hemophilia**) a tendency (usually inherited) to bleed severely from even slight injury, through failure of the blood to clot quickly.

**haemophiliac** (heem-ŏ-**fil**-iak) *noun* (*Amer.* **hemophiliac**) a person suffering from haemophilia.

**haemorrhage** (**hem**-er-ij) *noun* (*Amer.* **hemorrhage**) bleeding, especially when this is heavy. ●*verb* bleed heavily.

**haemorrhoids** (**hem**-er-oidz) *plural noun* (*Amer.* **hemorrhoids**) swollen veins in the wall of the anus; piles.

**hafnium** (**haf**-ni-ŭm) *noun* a metallic element (symbol Hf), used in control rods of nuclear reactors.

**haft** *noun* the handle of a knife, dagger, or cutting tool.

**hag** *noun* **1** an ugly old woman. **2** a witch.

**Haggai** (**hag**-i-I) **1** a Hebrew minor prophet of the 6th century BC. **2** a book of the Old Testament containing his prophecies.

**Haggard**, Sir Henry Rider (1856–1925), English novelist, famous for his adventure stories which include *King Solomon's Mines*.

**haggard** *adjective* looking exhausted and distraught.

**haggis** *noun* a Scottish dish made from offal boiled in a sheep's stomach with suet, oatmeal, etc.

**haggle** *verb* argue about price or terms when settling a bargain.

**hagiography** (hag-i-og-ră-fi) *noun* writing about saints' lives. □ **hagiographer** *noun*

**hagiology** *noun* literature about the lives and legends of saints.

**hagridden** *adjective* afflicted by nightmares or fear.

**Hague** (*pronounced* hayg), **The** the seat of government of the Netherlands.

**hah** alternative spelling of HA.

**ha ha** *interjection* representing an outburst of laughter.

**ha-ha** *noun* a ditch with a wall in it, forming a boundary or fence without interrupting the view.

**Hahn**, Otto (1879–1968), German chemist, one of the discoverers of nuclear fission.

**hahnium** (**hah**-ni-ŭm) *noun* an artificially produced radioactive element (symbol Ha).

**Haig**, Douglas, 1st Earl (1861–1928), commander of the British armies in France 1915–18 during the First World War.

**haiku** (**hy**-koo) *noun* a Japanese three-line poem of 17 syllables.

**hail¹** *verb* **1** greet, call to (a person or ship) in order to attract his or her attention. **2** signal to and summon (a taxi, etc.). **3** originate, have come; *where does he hail from?* ●*interjection* (*old use*) an exclamation of greeting. □ **hail-fellow-well-met** *adjective* over-friendly towards strangers. **Hail Mary**

a prayer to the Virgin Mary beginning with these words.

**hail²** *noun* **1** pellets of frozen rain falling in a shower. **2** something coming in great numbers; *a hail of blows*. ●*verb* **1** send down hail; *it is hailing*. **2** come or send down like hail.

**Haile Selassie** (**hy**-li sĕ-**las**-i) (1892–1975), emperor of Ethiopia 1930–74, exiled during the Italian occupation 1936–41.

**hailstone** *noun* a pellet of hail.

**hailstorm** *noun* a storm of hail.

**hair** *noun* **1** each of the fine threadlike strands that grow from the skin of people and animals or on certain plants. **2** a mass of these, especially on the human head. □ **get in a person's hair** (*informal*) encumber or annoy him or her. **hair-drier** *noun* (also **hair-dryer**) a device for drying wet hair with warm air. **hair of the dog** a further alcoholic drink taken to cure a hangover. **hair-raising** *adjective* terrifying. **hair's breadth** a tiny amount. **hair-slide** *noun* a clip for keeping the hair in place. **hair-splitting** *noun* splitting hairs (*see below*). **hair-trigger** *noun* a trigger that causes a gun to fire at the very slightest pressure. **let one's hair down** (*informal*) enjoy oneself without restraint. **not turn a hair** remain unmoved or unaffected. **split hairs** make distinctions of meaning that are too small to be of any real importance.

**hairbrush** *noun* a brush for tidying the hair.

**haircloth** *noun* stiff cloth woven from hair.

**haircut** *noun* **1** shortening the hair by cutting it. **2** the style in which it is cut.

**hairdo** *noun* (*plural* **hairdos**) a hair-style; the process of styling hair.

**hairdresser** *noun* a person who cuts and styles hair. □ **hairdressing** *noun*

**hairgrip** *noun* a flat hairpin with the ends close together.

**hairless** *adjective* without hair, bald.

**hairline** *noun* **1** the edge of a person's hair around the face. **2** a very narrow line, especially a crack.

**hairpin** *noun* a U-shaped pin for keeping the hair in place. □ **hairpin bend** a sharp U-shaped bend in a road.

**hairspring** *noun* a fine spring regulating the balance wheel in a watch.

**hairstyle** *noun* a style in which hair is arranged.

**hairy** *adjective* (**hairier, hairiest**) **1** having much hair. **2** (*slang*) hair-raising; difficult. □ **hairiness** *noun*

**Haiti** (**hay**-ti) a country in the West Indies. □ **Haitian** (hay-shăn) *adjective & noun*

**hajj** *noun* (also **hadj**) an Islamic pilgrimage to Mecca.

**hajji** (haj-i) (also **hadji**) a Muslim who has made the pilgrimage to Mecca.

**haka** (hah-kă) *noun* (*New Zealand*) a Maori war dance with chanting; an imitation of this by a sports team before a match.

**hake** *noun* (*plural* **hake**) a fish of the cod family, used as food.

**halal** (hah-lahl) *noun* (also **hallal**) meat from an animal killed according to Muslim law.

**halberd** *noun* an ancient weapon that is a combined spear and battleaxe.

**halcyon** (hal-si-ŏn) *adjective* (of a period) happy and peaceful; *halcyon days*. (¶ Named after a bird formerly believed to have the power of calming wind and waves while it nested on the sea.)

**hale** *adjective* strong and healthy; *hale and hearty*.

**half** *noun* (*plural* **halves**) **1** each of two equal or corresponding parts into which a thing is divided. **2** a half-price ticket for a child on a bus or train. **3** (*informal*) a half-back. **4** (*informal*) a half-pint. **5** *Sport* either of two equal periods of play. ● *adjective* amounting to a half; *half the men*. ● *adverb* **1** to the extent of a half, partly; *half-cooked*; *I'm half inclined to agree*. **2** (in reckoning time) by the amount of half (an hour); *half past two*. **3** (*informal*) half past; *half seven*. □ **at half cock** when only half-ready. **by half** excessively; *too clever by half*. **by halves** lacking thoroughness; *they never do things by halves*. **go halves** share a thing equally. **half and half** half one thing and half another. **half-back** *noun Sport* a player between the forwards and the full backs. **half-baked** *adjective* (*informal*) not competently planned; foolish. **half board** provision of bed, breakfast, and one main meal. **half-breed** *noun* = HALF-CASTE. **half-brother** *noun* a brother with whom one has only one parent in common. **half-caste** *noun* (*offensive*) a person of mixed race. **half-crown** *noun*, **half a crown** a former British coin worth 2s 6d. (12½p). **half-cut** (*slang*) fairly drunk. **half-dozen** *noun*, **half a dozen** six. **half-hearted** *adjective* lacking in enthusiasm. **half hitch** a knot for tying a rope round a post etc., formed by passing the short end round the main length of rope and then through the loop. **half-hour** *noun*, **half an hour 1** thirty minutes. **2** a point of time 30 minutes after any hour o'clock. **half-life** *noun* the time it takes the radioactivity of a substance to fall to half its original value. **half-light** *noun* a dim imperfect light. **half-mast** *noun* a position of a flag halfway down a mast, as a mark of respect for a dead person. **half measures** a policy lacking thoroughness. **half-moon** *noun* the moon when half its surface is illuminated. **half nelson** a hold in wrestling, with an arm under the arm and behind the back of the opponent. **half-sister** *noun* a sister with whom one has only one parent in common. **half-term** *noun* a short holiday halfway through a school term. **half-timbered** *adjective* (of a building) having a timber frame with the spaces filled in by brick or plaster. **half-time** *noun* the interval between the two halves of a game. **half-truth** *noun* a statement conveying only part of the truth. **half-volley** *noun* (in ball games) a return of the ball as soon as it has reached the ground. **not half 1** not nearly; *not half enough*. **2** (*slang*) extremely, violently; *he didn't half swear*.

**halfpenny** (hayp-ni) *noun* (*plural* **halfpennies** for separate coins, **halfpence** for a sum of money) a former British coin worth half a penny.

**halftone** *noun* a black-and-white illustration in which light and dark shades are reproduced by means of small and large dots.

**halfway** *adverb* **1** at a point between and equally distant from two others; *halfway there*. **2** to some extent, more or less; *halfway acceptable*. ● *adjective* situated halfway. □ **halfway house** a compromise.

**halfwit** *noun* a foolish or stupid person. □ **halfwitted** *adjective*

**halibut** *noun* (*plural* **halibut**) a large flatfish used for food.

**halitosis** (hal-i-toh-sis) *noun* breath that smells unpleasant.

**hall** *noun* **1** a large room or a building for meetings, meals, concerts, etc. **2** a large country house, especially one with a landed estate. **3** a space or passage into which the front entrance of a house etc. opens. □ **hall of residence** a building for university students to live in.

**hallal** alternative spelling of HALAL.

**hallelujah** = ALLELUIA.

**Halley** (hal-i), Edmond (1656–1742), English astronomer. □ **Halley's comet** a bright comet that orbits the sun in about 76 years, whose reappearance in 1758 was predicted by Halley.

**halliard** alternative spelling of HALYARD.

**hallmark** *noun* **1** a mark indicating the standard of gold, silver, and platinum. **2** a distinguishing characteristic; *the bombing bears the hallmark of recent guerrilla attacks*.

**hallmarked** *adjective* marked with a hallmark.

**hallo** alternative spelling of HELLO.

**halloo** *interjection & noun* a cry to urge on hounds or attract a person's attention.

**hallow** *verb* **1** make holy. **2** honour as holy.

**Hallowe'en** *noun* 31 October, the eve of All Saints' Day.

**hallucinate** (ha-loo-sin-ayt) *verb* experience hallucinations. □ **hallucinant** *adjective & noun*

**hallucination** (hă-loo-sin-**ay**-shŏn) *noun* the illusion of seeing or hearing something when no such thing is present. □ **hallucinatory** (hă-**loo**-sin-ă-ter-i) *adjective*

**hallucinogen** (hă-**loo**-sin-ŏ-jen) *noun* a drug causing hallucinations. □ **hallucinogenic** (hă-loo-sin-ŏ-**jen**-ik) *adjective*

**hallway** *noun* an entrance area or corridor.

**halm** alternative spelling of HAULM.

**halo** *noun* (*plural* **haloes**) **1** a disc or ring of light shown round the head of a sacred figure in paintings etc. **2** glory associated with an idealized person etc. **3** a disc of diffused light round a luminous body such as the sun or moon. □ **haloed** *adjective*

**halogen** (**hal**-ŏ-jĕn) *noun* any of the five chemically related elements fluorine, chlorine, bromine, iodine, and astatine, which form salts when combined with a metal.

**halon** (**hay**-lon) *noun* any of various gaseous compounds of carbon, bromine, and other halogens, used to extinguish fires.

**Hals**, Frans (1581/5–1666), Dutch painter, who specialized in portraits.

**halt** *noun* **1** a temporary stop, an interruption of progress; *work came to a halt.* **2** a minor stopping-place on a railway line. ● *verb* come or bring to a halt.

**halter** *noun* **1** a length of rope or a leather strap for leading or tying up a horse. **2** (also **halter-neck**) a strap passing round the back of the neck holding a dress or top up and leaving the back and shoulders bare. ● *verb* put a halter on (a horse).

**halting** *adjective* hesitant; *a halting explanation.* □ **haltingly** *adverb*

**halve** *verb* **1** divide or share equally between two. **2** reduce by half. **3** *Golf* use the same number of strokes as an opponent in (a hole or match).

**halves** *see* HALF.

**halyard** (**hal**-yerd) *noun* (also **halliard**) a rope or tackle for raising or lowering a sail, yard, or flag.

**ham** *noun* **1** the upper part of a pig's leg, dried and salted or smoked for food. **2** the back of the thigh and buttock. **3** (*informal*) a poor actor or performer. **4** (*informal*) the operator of an amateur radio station; *a radio ham.* ● *verb* (**hammed**, **hamming**) (*informal*) overact, exaggerate one's actions deliberately; *hamming it up.* □ **ham-fisted, ham-handed** *adjective* (*informal*) clumsy.

**hamburger** *noun* a flat round cake of minced beef served fried, often eaten in a bread roll.

**Hamite** (**ha**-myt) *noun* a member of a group of North African peoples including the an-

cient Egyptians and the Berbers. □ **Hamitic** (ha-**mit**-ik) *adjective*

**hamlet** *noun* a small village, usually without a church.

**hammer** *noun* **1** a tool with a heavy metal head used for breaking things, driving nails in, etc. **2** something shaped or used like this, e.g. an auctioneer's mallet, part of the firing device in a gun, a lever striking the string in a piano. **3** a metal ball attached to a wire for throwing as an athletic contest. ● *verb* **1** hit or beat with a hammer, strike loudly. **2** impress (an idea etc.) strongly upon a person; *hammer an idea into her.* **3** (*informal*) defeat utterly. □ **come under the hammer** be sold by auction. **hammer and sickle** the symbols of manual worker and peasant used as the emblem of the former USSR and international communism. **hammer and tongs** with great energy and noise. **hammer out** devise (a plan) with great effort. **hammer-toe** *noun* a toe that is permanently bent downwards.

**hammerlock** *noun* a hold in which a wrestler's arm is bent behind the back.

**hammock** *noun* a hanging bed of canvas or rope network.

**hamper** *noun* a large basket, usually with a hinged lid and containing food. ● *verb* prevent the free movement or activity of, hinder.

**Hampshire** a county of southern England.

**Hampton Court** a palace in Richmond, London, built by Cardinal Wolsey and presented by him to Henry VIII.

**hamster** *noun* a small mouselike rodent with cheek-pouches for storing food.

**hamstring** *noun* **1** any of the five tendons at the back of the human knee. **2** the great tendon at the back of an animal's hock. ● *verb* (**hamstrung, hamstringing**) **1** cripple by cutting the hamstring(s). **2** cripple the activity or efficiency of.

**hand** *noun* **1** the end part of the arm below the wrist. **2** part of an animal's foreleg. **3** possession, control, care; *the child is in good hands.* **4** influence, activity; *many people had a hand in it.* **5** active help; *give him a hand.* **6** a pledge of marriage; *asked for her hand.* **7** a manual worker in a factory or farm etc.; a member of a ship's crew. **8** skill or style of workmanship, a person with reference to skill; *has a light hand with pastry; an old hand at this.* **9** style of handwriting. **10** a pointer on a clock etc. **11** side or direction; each of two contrasted sides in an argument etc.; *on the left hand side; on the other hand.* **12** a unit of 4 inches used in measuring a horse's height. **13** the cards dealt to a player in a card game. **14** (*informal*) applause; *got a big hand.* **15** done, operated, or carried etc. by hand; *hand-knitted*; *hand luggage*. ●*verb* give or pass with one's hand(s) or otherwise. □ **at hand 1** close by. **2** about to happen. **by hand** by a person (not a machine); delivered by a messenger, not through the post. **from hand to mouth** satisfying only one's immediate needs. **hand in glove with** working in close association with. **hand in hand 1** holding each other's hand. **2** closely associated, linked together. **hand it to** (*informal*) award praise to, admire. **hand-me-down** *noun* an article of clothing etc. passed on from another person. **hand over** put (a person or thing) into the custody or control of another person, present. **hand over fist** (*informal*) with rapid progress; *making money hand over fist*. **hand-picked** *adjective* carefully chosen. **hands down** (of a victory won) easily, completely. **hands off!** do not touch or interfere. **hands-off** *adjective* not requiring the manual use of controls. **hands-on** *adjective* (of experience etc.) practical, working or operating a thing (especially a keyboard) directly. **hands up!** an order to raise one's hand (e.g. in agreement) or both hands in surrender. **hand-to-hand** *adjective* (of fighting) at close quarters. **in hand 1** in one's possession. **2** in control. **3** (of business) being dealt with. **on hand** available. **on one's hands** resting on one as a responsibility. **out of hand 1** out of control. **2** without delay or preparation; *rejected it out of hand*. **show one's hand** reveal one's plans. **to hand** within reach; available. **turn one's hand to** undertake (a new activity).

**handbag** *noun* a small bag for holding a purse and personal articles.

**handball** *noun* **1** a game with a ball thrown by hand among players or against a wall. **2** *Football* intentional touching of the ball, constituting a foul.

**handbell** *noun* a small bell rung by hand.

**handbill** *noun* a printed notice circulated by hand.

**handbook** *noun* a small book giving useful facts.

**handbrake** *noun* a brake operated by hand.

**h. & c.** *abbreviation* hot and cold water.

**handcraft** *verb* make by handicraft.

**handcuff** *noun* each of a pair of linked metal rings for securing a prisoner's wrists. ●*verb* put handcuffs on (a prisoner).

**Handel**, George Frederick (1685–1759), German-born composer who settled in England.

**handful** *noun* (*plural* **handfuls**) **1** a quantity that fills the hand. **2** a small number of people or things. **3** (*informal*) a person who is difficult to control; a troublesome task.

**handicap** *noun* **1** a physical or mental disability. **2** a disadvantage imposed on a superior competitor in order to equalize chances; a race or contest in which this is imposed. **3** the number of strokes by which a golfer normally exceeds par for the course. **4** anything that lessens one's chance of success or makes progress difficult. ●*verb* (**handicapped**, **handicapping**) impose or be a handicap on.

**handicapped** *adjective* suffering from a physical or mental disability.

**handicraft** *noun* work that needs both skill with the hands and artistic design, e.g. woodwork, needlework, pottery.

**handiwork** *noun* something done or made by the hands, or by a named person.

**handkerchief** *noun* (*plural* **handkerchiefs** or **handkerchieves**) a small square of cloth for wiping the nose etc.

**handle** *noun* **1** the part of a thing by which it is to be held, carried, or controlled. **2** a fact that may be taken advantage of; *gave a handle to his critics*. **3** (*informal*) a personal title or name. ●*verb* **1** touch, feel, or move with the hands. **2** be able to be operated; *the car handles well*. **3** manage, deal with; *knows how to handle people*. **4** deal in (goods). **5** discuss or write about (a subject). □ **fly off the handle** *see* FLY².

**handlebar** *noun* the steering-bar of a bicycle etc. □ **handlebar moustache** a thick moustache with curved ends.

**handler** *noun* **1** a person who handles or deals in something. **2** a person who trains and looks after an animal (especially a police dog).

**handmade** *adjective* made by hand.

**handmaid** *noun* (also **handmaiden**) (*old use*) a female servant.

**handout** *noun* **1** something distributed free of charge. **2** notes given out in a class etc. **3** a statement issued to the press etc.

**handrail** *noun* a narrow rail for people to hold as a support.

**handset** *noun* a telephone mouthpiece and earpiece as one unit.

**handshake** *noun* grasping and shaking a person's hand with one's own as a greeting.

**handsome** *adjective* **1** good-looking. **2** generous; *a handsome present*. **3** (of a price or fortune etc.) very large. □ **handsomely** *adverb*

**handspring** *noun* a gymnastic feat consisting of a handstand, somersaulting, and landing in a standing position.

**handstand** *noun* balancing on one's hands with the feet in the air.

**handwriting** *noun* **1** writing done by hand with a pen or pencil. **2** a person's style of this.

**handwritten** *adjective* written by hand.

**handy** *adjective* (**handier, handiest**) **1** convenient to handle or use. **2** conveniently placed for being reached or used. **3** clever with one's hands. □ **handily** *adverb*, **handiness** *noun*

**handyman** *noun* (*plural* **handymen**) a person who is clever at doing household repairs etc. or who is employed to do odd jobs.

**hang** *verb* (**hung** (in senses 5 and 6 **hanged**), **hanging**) **1** support or be supported from above so that the lower end is free. **2** cause (a door or gate) to rest on hinges so that it swings freely to and fro; be placed in this way. **3** stick (wallpaper) to a wall. **4** decorate with drapery or hanging ornaments. **5** kill by suspending from a rope that tightens round the neck; be executed in this way. **6** (*informal*) damn; *I'm hanged if I know.* **7** droop, lean over; *people hung over the gate.* **8** be present, especially oppressively or threateningly; *smoke hung over the area; the threat is hanging over him.* ●*noun* the way something hangs or falls. ●**get the hang of** (*informal*) get the knack of. **hang about** or **around** loiter, linger. **hang back** show reluctance to take action or to advance. **hang fire** (of a gun) be slow in going off; (of events) be slow in developing. **hang on 1** hold tightly; depend on; *much hangs on this decision.* **2** attend closely to; *they hung on his words.* **3** remain in office, to stick to one's duty etc. **4** (*slang*) wait for a short time; *hang on a minute.* **hang out** (*slang*) frequent a place. **hang-out** *noun* (*slang*) a place in which a person is usually found. **hang together** (of people) help or support one another; (of statements) fit well together, be consistent. **hang up** end a telephone conversation by replacing the receiver. **hang-up** *noun* (*slang*) an emotional problem or inhibition.

**hangar** *noun* a building for housing aircraft.

**hangdog** *adjective* shamefaced.

**hanger** *noun* **1** a person who hangs things. **2** a loop or hook by which something is hung. **3** (in full **coat-hanger**) a shaped piece of wood etc. for hanging a garment on. □ **hanger-on** *noun* (*plural* **hangers-on**) an unwanted follower or dependant.

**hang-glider** *noun* the frame used in hanggliding.

**hang-gliding** *noun* the sport of being suspended in an airborne frame controlled by one's own movements.

**hanging** *noun* **1** execution by suspending a person by the neck. **2** a drapery hung on a wall.

**hangman** *noun* a man whose job is to hang persons condemned to death.

**hangnail** *noun* a piece of torn skin at the base of a fingernail.

**hangover** *noun* **1** a severe headache or other unpleasant after-effects from drinking too much alcohol. **2** something left from an earlier time.

**Hang Seng index** an index based on the average price of selected securities on the Hong Kong stock exchange.

**hank** *noun* a coil or length of wool or thread etc.

**hanker** *verb* (usually foll. by *for* or *after*) crave, feel a longing.

**hanky** *noun* (also **hankie**) (*informal*) a handkerchief.

**hanky-panky** *noun* (*slang*) **1** trickery, dishonest dealing. **2** naughtiness, especially sexual.

**Hannibal** (**han**-i-băl) (247–183/2 BC), Carthaginian general who led an army over the Alps into Italy and inflicted a number of defeats on the Romans.

**Hanoi** the capital of Vietnam.

**Hanover 1** a city in the north of Germany. **2** a former German State, whose ruler succeeded to the British throne in 1714 as George I. **3** the name of the British royal house from 1714 to the death of Queen Victoria in 1901. □ **Hanoverian** (han-ŏ-**veer**-iăn) *adjective*

**Hansard** *noun* the official report of proceedings of the Houses of Parliament. (¶ Named after the English printer whose firm originally compiled it.)

**Hanseatic League** (han-si-at-ik) a medieval association of north German cities, formed in 1241 as a commercial alliance, that developed into an independent political power.

**Hansen's disease** leprosy. (¶ Named after the Norwegian physician G. H. A. Hansen (died 1912), who discovered the leprosy bacillus.)

**hansom** *noun* (in full **hansom cab**) (*old use*) a two-wheeled horse-drawn cab.

**Hants** *abbreviation* Hampshire.

■**Usage** No full stop is used after 'Hants' because it is not a shortening of the modern spelling.

**Hanukka** (**hah**-nŭk-ă) *noun* an eight-day Jewish festival of lights, beginning in December, commemorating the rededication of the Temple at Jerusalem in 165 BC after its desecration by the Syrian king.

**hanuman** (hăn-oo-**mahn**) *noun* **1** an Indian monkey venerated by Hindus. **2** (**Hanuman**) (in Hinduism) a semi-divine monkey-like creature to whom extraordinary powers are attributed.

**haphazard** (hap-**haz**-erd) *adjective* done or chosen at random, without planning. □ **haphazardly** *adverb*

**hapless** *adjective* unlucky.

**happen** *verb* **1** occur (by chance or otherwise). **2** have the (good or bad) fortune to do something; *we happened to see him.* **3** be the fate or experience of; *what happened to you?* **4** (foll. by *on*) find by chance.

**happening** *noun* **1** an event. **2** an improvised or spontaneous performance.

**happy** *adjective* (**happier**, **happiest**) **1** feeling or showing pleasure or contentment. **2** fortunate. **3** (of words or behaviour) very suitable, pleasing. □ **happy-go-lucky** *adjective* cheerfully casual. **happy hour** a time in the day when drinks are served at reduced prices. **happy medium** something that achieves satisfactory avoidance of extremes; a compromise. □ **happily** *adverb*, **happiness** *noun*

**Hapsburg** the name of a German family to which belonged rulers of various countries of Europe from medieval times onwards.

**hara-kiri** (ha-ră-**ki**-ri) *noun* suicide involving disembowelment, formerly practised by Japanese samurai when in disgrace or under sentence of death.

**harangue** (hă-**rang**) *noun* a lengthy earnest speech. ● *verb* make a harangue to; lecture.

**Harare** (hă-**rah**-ri) the capital of Zimbabwe.

**harass** (**ha**-răs or hă-**ras**) *verb* **1** trouble and annoy continually. **2** make repeated attacks on (an enemy). □ **harassed** *adjective*, **harassment** (**ha**-răs-měnt) *noun*

---

■**Usage** The second pronunciation given, with the stress on the second syllable, is common, but is considered incorrect by some people.

---

**harbinger** (**har**-bin-jer) *noun* a person or thing whose presence announces the approach of another.

**harbour** (*Amer.* **harbor**) *noun* a place of shelter for ships. ● *verb* **1** give shelter to, conceal (a criminal etc.). **2** keep in one's mind; *harbour a grudge.*

**hard** *adjective* **1** firm, not yielding to pressure; not easily cut. **2** difficult to do or understand or answer. **3** causing unhappiness, difficult to bear. **4** severe, harsh, unsympathetic. **5** energetic; *a hard worker.* **6** (of currency) not likely to drop suddenly in value. **7** (of drinks) strongly alcoholic. **8** (of drugs) strong and likely to cause addiction. **9** (of water) containing mineral salts that prevent soap from lathering freely and cause a hard coating to form inside kettles, water-tanks, etc. **10** (of colours or sounds) harsh to the eye or ear. **11** (of consonants) sounding sharp not soft; *the letter 'g' is hard in 'gun' and soft in 'gin'.* **12** (in politics) extreme; most radical; *hard right.* ● *adverb* **1** with great effort, intensively; *worked hard; it's raining hard.* **2** with difficulty; *hard-earned money.* **3** so as

to be hard; *hard-baked.* □ **hard and fast rules** rules that cannot be altered to fit special cases. **hard bargaining** bargaining making few concessions. **hard-boiled** *adjective* **1** (of eggs) boiled until white and yolk have become solid. **2** (of people) callous. **hard by** close by. **hard cash** coins and banknotes, not a cheque or a promise to pay later. **hard copy** material printed, especially by a computer, on paper. **hard core 1** the stubborn unyielding nucleus of a group. **2** rubble or other heavy material as a road-foundation. **hard-core** *adjective* (of pornography) explicit, obscene. **hard disk** (in computers) a rigid disk, installed permanently, capable of holding more data than a floppy disk. **hard-headed** *adjective* practical, not sentimental. **hard-hearted** *adjective* unsympathetic. **hard labour** heavy manual work as a punishment, especially in a prison. **hard line** unyielding adherence to a firm policy. **hard luck** worse luck than is deserved. **hard of hearing** slightly deaf. **hard-on** *noun* (*slang*) an erection of the penis. **hard pad** a form of distemper causing abnormal thickening of the foot pads in dogs etc. **hard palate** the bony front part of the palate. **hard-pressed** *adjective* **1** in difficulty; burdened. **2** closely pursued. **hard sell** aggressive salesmanship. **hard shoulder** a hard surface beside a motorway for stopping on in an emergency. **hard up** (*informal*) short of money. **hard-wearing** *adjective* able to stand much wear. □ **hardness** *noun*

**hardback** *adjective* bound in stiff covers. ● *noun* a book bound in this way.

**hardbitten** *adjective* tough and realistic.

**hardboard** *noun* stiff board made of compressed wood pulp.

**harden** *verb* **1** make or become hard or hardy. **2** make or become unyielding; *attitudes have hardened in the dispute.* **3** (of prices etc.) cease to fall or fluctuate. □ **hardening of the arteries** = ARTERIOSCLEROSIS.

**Hardie**, James Keir (1856–1915), Scottish labour leader and politician, first chairman of the Labour Party.

**hardihood** *noun* boldness, daring.

**hardly** *adverb* **1** only with difficulty; *can hardly see.* **2** scarcely; *hardly recognized me.* **3** surely not; *can hardly have realized.*

**hardship** *noun* **1** severe discomfort or lack of the necessities of life. **2** a circumstance causing this.

**hardware** *noun* **1** tools and household implements etc. sold by a shop. **2** weapons, machinery. **3** the mechanical and electronic parts of a computer.

**hardwood** *noun* the hard heavy wood obtained from deciduous trees, e.g. oak and teak.

**Hardy**[1], Oliver, *see* LAUREL AND HARDY.

**Hardy**[2], Thomas (1840–1928), English novelist and poet, whose most popular novels are set in 'Wessex' (his native Dorset).

**hardy** *adjective* (**hardier, hardiest**) **1** capable of enduring cold or difficult conditions. **2** (of plants) able to grow in the open air all the year round. □ **hardiness** *noun*

**hare** *noun* a field animal like a rabbit but larger. ● *verb* run rapidly. □ **hare-brained** *adjective* wild and foolish, rash.

**harebell** *noun* a wild plant with blue bell-shaped flowers on a slender stalk.

**Hare Krishna** (**hah**-ri **krish**-nă) the title of a love-chant or mantra based on the name of the Hindu god Vishnu, used as an incantation by members of a religious sect founded in the USA in 1966.

**harelip** *noun* (often *offensive*) a deformed lip (usually the upper lip) with a vertical slit in it.

**harem** (**har**-eem) *noun* **1** the women of a Muslim household, living in a separate part of the house. **2** their quarters.

**haricot** (**ha**-rik-oh) *noun* (in full **haricot bean**) the edible white dried seed of a kind of bean.

**hark** *verb* (*old use*) listen. □ **hark back** return to an earlier subject.

**harlequin** *noun* (**Harlequin**) a mute pantomime character, usually masked and dressed in a diamond-patterned costume. ● *adjective* in varied colours.

**harlequinade** (har-li-kwin-**ayd**) *noun* **1** a play in which Harlequin plays the leading role. **2** a piece of buffoonery.

**Harley Street** a London street associated with eminent medical specialists.

**harlot** *noun* (*old use*) a prostitute. □ **harlotry** *noun*

**harm** *noun* damage, injury. ● *verb* cause harm to.

**harmattan** (har-**ma**-tăn) *noun* a dry dusty wind that blows on the coast of West Africa from December to February.

**harmful** *adjective* causing harm. □ **harmfully** *adverb*

**harmless** *adjective* **1** unlikely to cause harm. **2** inoffensive. □ **harmlessly** *adverb*, **harmlessness** *noun*

**harmonic** *adjective* **1** of harmony in music. **2** harmonious. ● *noun* a tone produced by vibration of a string etc. in any of certain fractions (half, third, quarter, fifth, etc.) of its length.

**harmonica** *noun* a small rectangular musical instrument played by blowing and sucking air through it.

**harmonious** *adjective* **1** forming a pleasing or consistent whole. **2** free from disagreement or ill feeling. **3** sweet-sounding, tuneful. □ **harmoniously** *adverb*

**harmonium** *noun* a musical instrument with a keyboard, in which notes are produced by air pumped through reeds.

**harmonize** *verb* (also **harmonise**) **1** make or be harmonious. **2** produce an agreeable artistic effect. **3** add notes to (a melody) to form chords. □ **harmonization** *noun*

**harmony** *noun* **1** the state of being harmonious. **2** the combination of musical notes to produce chords. **3** a sweet or melodious sound.

**harness** *noun* **1** the straps and fittings by which a horse is controlled and fastened to the cart etc. that it pulls. **2** fastenings resembling this for attaching a thing to a person's body. ● *verb* **1** put harness on (a horse); attach by a harness. **2** control and use (a river or other natural force), especially to produce power. □ **in harness** in the routine of daily work.

**Harold** the name of two kings of England: Harold I (reigned 1035–40), Harold II (reigned 1066).

**harp** *noun* a large upright musical instrument consisting of strings stretched on a roughly triangular frame, played by plucking with the fingers. □ **harp on** talk repeatedly and tiresomely (about a subject). □ **harpist** *noun*

**harpoon** *noun* a spear-like missile with a rope attached, for catching whales etc. ● *verb* spear with a harpoon.

**harpsichord** (**harp**-si-kord) *noun* a keyboard instrument with horizontal strings plucked mechanically. □ **harpsichordist** *noun*

**harpy** *noun* a grasping unscrupulous person. (¶ Named after the Harpies, creatures in Greek mythology with a woman's head and body and a bird's wings and claws.)

**harridan** (**ha**-rid-ăn) *noun* a bad-tempered old woman.

**harrier** *noun* **1** a hound used for hunting hares. **2** a kind of falcon. **3** a group of cross-country runners.

**harrow** *noun* a heavy frame with metal spikes or discs for breaking up clods of soil. ● *verb* **1** draw a harrow over (land). **2** distress greatly.

**harry** *verb* (**harried, harrying**) harass.

**harsh** *adjective* **1** rough and disagreeable, especially to the senses; *a harsh texture*; *a harsh voice*. **2** severe, cruel; *harsh treatment*. □ **harshly** *adverb*, **harshness** *noun*

**hart** *noun* (*plural* **hart** *or* **harts**) an adult male deer.

**hartebeest** (**hart**-i-beest) *noun* a large African antelope with curving horns.

**Hartnell**, Sir Norman (1901–79), English fashion designer.

**harum-scarum** (*informal*) *adjective* wild and reckless. ● *noun* a wild and reckless person.

**Harvard** the oldest American university, founded in 1636 at Cambridge, Massachusetts.

**harvest** *verb* **1** the gathering of a crop or crops; the season when this is done. **2** the season's yield of any natural product. **3** the product of any action. ● *verb* gather a crop, reap. □ **harvest festival** a Christian festival of thanksgiving for the harvest. **harvest moon** the full moon nearest to the autumnal equinox (22 or 23 September). **harvest mouse** a very small mouse that nests in the stalks of standing corn.

**harvester** *noun* **1** a reaper. **2** a reaping-machine.

**Harvey**, William (1578–1657), English physician who discovered that blood circulates in the veins and is not (as contemporary theory held) absorbed as food.

**Haryana** (hurri-ah-nă) a State of northern India.

**has** *see* HAVE. □ **has-been** *noun* (*plural* **has-beens**) (*informal*) a person or thing that is no longer as famous or successful as formerly.

**hash** *noun* **1** a dish of cooked or preserved meat cut into small pieces and recooked. **2** a jumble, a mixture. **3** recycled material. **4** (*informal*) hashish. □ **make a hash of** (*informal*) make a mess of, bungle. **settle a person's hash** (*informal*) deal with and subdue him or her.

**hashish** *noun* the resinous product of the top leaves and tender parts of hemp, smoked or chewed as a narcotic.

**Hasid** (**has**-id) *noun* (*plural* **Hasidim**) a member of an orthodox Jewish sect which originated as a mystical Jewish movement in 18th century Poland. □ **Hasidic** *adjective*, **Hasidism** *noun*

**haslet** (**haz**-lit) *noun* a meat loaf made from pig's offal, eaten cold.

**hasn't** (*informal*) = has not.

**hasp** *noun* a hinged metal strip with a slit in it that fits over a U-shaped staple through which a pin or padlock is then passed.

**hassle** (*informal*) *noun* a quarrel or struggle. ● *verb* **1** quarrel. **2** annoy; harass.

**hassock** *noun* a thick firm cushion for kneeling on in church.

**hast** (*old use*) the present tense of HAVE, used with *thou*.

**haste** *noun* urgency of movement or action, hurry. □ **in haste** quickly, hurriedly. **make haste** hurry.

**hasten** *verb* **1** hurry. **2** cause (a thing) to be done earlier or to happen earlier.

**Hastings** a town on the coast of East Sussex, scene of William the Conqueror's victory over the Anglo-Saxon king Harold II in 1066.

**hasty** *adjective* (**hastier, hastiest**) **1** hurried, acting quickly. **2** done too quickly. □ **hastily** *adverb*, **hastiness** *noun*

**hat** *noun* **1** a covering for the head, worn out of doors. **2** this thought of as symbolizing a person's official position; *wearing her managerial hat*. □ **hat trick** the taking of 3 wickets in cricket by 3 successive balls from the same bowler; the scoring of 3 goals or winning of 3 victories by one person. **keep it under one's hat** keep it secret. **pass the hat round** collect contributions of money. **take one's hat off to** (*informal*) admire, congratulate.

**hatband** *noun* a band of ribbon etc. round a hat just above the brim.

**hatch**[1] *noun* **1** an opening in a wall between two rooms. **2** an opening or door in an aircraft etc. **3** a hatchway; a movable cover for this.

**hatch**[2] *verb* **1** (of a young bird or fish etc.) emerge from an egg; (of an egg) produce a young animal. **2** cause (eggs) to produce young by incubating them. **3** devise (a plot). ● *noun* hatching; a brood hatched.

**hatch**[3] *verb* mark with close parallel lines. □ **hatching** *noun*

**hatchback** *noun* a car with a sloping back hinged at the top to form a door.

**hatchery** *noun* a place for hatching eggs, especially of fish; *a trout hatchery*.

**hatchet** *noun* a light short-handled axe. □ **hatchet man** (*informal*) a person employed to attack, dismiss, or otherwise harm others.

**hatchway** *noun* an opening in a ship's deck for cargo.

**hate** *noun* **1** hatred. **2** (*informal*) a hated person or thing. ● *verb* **1** feel hatred towards. **2** dislike greatly. **3** (*informal*) be reluctant; *I hate to interrupt you, but it's time to go*.

**hateful** *adjective* arousing hatred.

**hath** (*old use*) has.

**hatred** *noun* extreme dislike or enmity.

**hatter** *noun* a person whose trade is making or selling hats.

**haughty** (**haw**-ti) *adjective* (**haughtier, haughtiest**) proud of oneself and looking down on other people. □ **haughtily** *adverb*, **haughtiness** *noun*

**haul** *verb* **1** pull or drag forcibly. **2** transport by a truck etc. **3** turn a ship's course. ● *noun* **1** hauling. **2** the amount gained as a result of effort, booty; *made a good haul*. **3** a distance to be travelled; *it's only a short haul from here*.

**haulage** *noun* transport of goods; the charge for this.

**haulier** (**hawl**-i-er) *noun* a person or firm whose trade is transporting goods by road.

**haulm** (*pronounced* hawm) *noun* (also **halm**) **1** a stalk or stem. **2** the stems of plants such as potatoes, beans, and peas.

**haunch** *noun* **1** the fleshy part of the buttock and thigh. **2** the leg and loin of deer etc. as food.

**haunt** *verb* **1** (of ghosts) be frequently in (a place) with manifestations of their presence and influence. **2** be persistently in (a place). **3** linger in the mind of; *the memory haunts me.* ● *noun* a place often visited by the person(s) named; *the inn is a favourite haunt of fishermen.*

**haunted** *adjective* frequented by a ghost or ghosts.

**haunting** *adjective* (of a memory, melody, etc.) lingering in the mind; evocative.

**Hausa** (**how**-să) *noun* (*plural* **Hausa** or **Hausas**) **1** a member of a people of the Sudan and northern Nigeria. **2** their language, which is widely used in West Africa.

**haute couture** (oht koo-**tewr**) high-class fashion; products of the leading fashion houses. (¶ French.)

**haute cuisine** (oht kwee-**zeen**) high-class cookery. (¶ French.)

**hauteur** (oh-**ter**) *noun* haughtiness.

**Havana** (hă-**van**-ă) the capital of Cuba.

**have** *verb* (**has, had, having**) **1** be in possession of (a thing or quality); possess in a certain relationship; *he has many enemies.* **2** contain; *the house has six rooms.* **3** experience, undergo; *had a shock.* **4** give birth to. **5** put into a certain condition; *you had me worried.* **6** defeat; have at a disadvantage; *you have me there.* **7** (*slang*) cheat or deceive; *we've been had.* **8** have sexual intercourse with. **9** engage in, carry on; *had a talk with him.* **10** eat; *had breakfast.* **11** allow, tolerate; *won't have him bullied.* **12** show (a quality); *have mercy on us.* **13** receive, accept; *we had news of her; will you have a cigarette?* **14** cause a thing to be done; *have one's hair cut; have three copies made.* ● *auxiliary verb*, used to form past tenses of verbs; *he has gone; we had expected it.* □ **had better** would find it wiser to. **have had it** (*informal*) **1** have missed one's chance. **2** be near death, no longer usable, etc. **have it 1** have a sudden inspiration about a problem etc.; *I have it!.* **2** win a decision in a vote; *the ayes have it.* **have it away** (*or* **off**) (*slang*) have sexual intercourse. **have it coming** (*informal*) deserve one's punishment or bad luck. **have it in for** (*informal*) show ill will towards (a person). **have it out** (**with a person**) settle a problem by frank discussion. **have on** (*informal*) hoax. **haves and have-nots** people with and without wealth or privilege. **have**

**to** be obliged to, must. **have up** bring (a person) before a court of justice or an interviewer.

**Havel** (**hah**-vel), Václav (born 1936), Czech writer and President of the former Czechoslovakia 1989–92.

**haven** *noun* a refuge.

**haven't** (*informal*) = have not.

**haver** (**hay**-ver) *verb* **1** hesitate. **2** (*Scottish & N. England*) talk foolishly.

**haversack** *noun* a strong bag carried on the back or over the shoulder.

**havoc** (**hav**-ŏk) *noun* widespread destruction, great disorder. □ **play havoc with** create havoc in.

**haw**[1] *noun* a hawthorn berry; *hips and haws.*

**haw**[2] *verb see* HUM.

**Hawaii** (hă-**wy**-i) a State of the USA consisting of a group of islands in the Pacific. □ **Hawaiian** (hă-**wy**-ăn) *adjective & noun*

**hawfinch** *noun* a large finch with a powerful beak.

**hawk**[1] *noun* **1** a bird of prey with rounded wings shorter than a falcon's. **2** a person who favours an aggressive policy. □ **hawk-eyed** *adjective* keen-sighted.

**hawk**[2] *verb* **1** clear the throat of phlegm noisily. **2** carry (goods) about for sale.

**hawker** *noun* a person who hawks goods for a living.

**Hawking**, Stephen William (born 1942), English theoretical physicist.

**Hawksmoor**, Nicholas (1661–1736), English architect, whose works include six London churches.

**hawser** (**haw**-zer) *noun* a heavy rope or cable for mooring or towing a ship.

**hawthorn** *noun* a thorny tree or shrub with small red berries.

**Hawthorne**, Nathaniel (1804–64), American novelist.

**hay** *noun* grass mown and dried for fodder. □ **hay fever** an allergy with asthmatic symptoms caused by pollen or dust. **make hay while the sun shines** seize opportunities for profit.

**Haydn** (**hy**-děn), Franz Joseph (1732–1809), Austrian-born composer.

**haymaking** *noun* mowing grass and spreading it to dry. □ **haymaker** *noun*

**hayrick** *noun* a haystack.

**haystack** *noun* a regularly shaped pile of hay firmly packed for storing, with a pointed or ridged top.

**haywire** *adjective* (*informal*) badly disorganized, out of control.

**hazard** (**haz**-erd) *noun* **1** risk, danger; a source of this. **2** an obstacle (e.g. a pond or bunker) on a golf course. ● *verb* risk, venture; *hazard a guess.*

**hazardous** *adjective* risky.

**haze** *noun* **1** thin mist. **2** mental confusion or obscurity.

**hazel** *noun* **1** a bush with small edible nuts. **2** greenish-brown.

**hazelnut** *noun* the nut of the hazel.

**Hazlitt**, William (1778–1830), British essayist and critic.

**hazy** *adjective* (**hazier**, **haziest**) **1** misty. **2** vague, indistinct. **3** feeling confused or uncertain. □ **hazily** *adverb*, **haziness** *noun*

**HB** *abbreviation* (of a pencil lead) hard black.

**H-bomb** *noun* a hydrogen bomb.

**HCF** *abbreviation* highest common factor.

**HDTV** *abbreviation* high-definition television.

**HE** *abbreviation* **1** His or Her Excellency. **2** His Eminence. **3** high explosive.

**He** *symbol* helium.

**he** *pronoun* **1** the male person or animal mentioned. **2** a person (male or female); *he who hesitates is lost.* ● *noun* male; *a he-goat.* □ **he-man** *noun* a masterful or muscular man.

**head** *noun* **1** the part of the human body containing the eyes, nose, mouth, and brain; the corresponding part of an animal's body. **2** this as a measure of length; *the horse won by a head.* **3** the intellect, the imagination, the mind; *use your head.* **4** a mental ability or faculty; *has a good head for figures; no head for heights.* **5** the side of a coin on which the ruler's head appears; (**heads**) this side turned upwards after being tossed. **6** (*informal*) a headache. **7** a person, an individual person or animal; *it costs £1 per head.* **8** (*plural* **head**) a number of animals; *20 head of cattle.* **9** a thing like a head in form or position, e.g. the rounded end of a pin, the cutting or striking part of a tool etc., a rounded mass of leaves or petals etc. at the top of a stem, the flat surface of a drum or cask. **10** foam on top of beer etc. **11** the top of something long (e.g. a stair or mast) or of a list. **12** the top part of a boil where it tends to break. **13** the upper end or part of a table (where the host sits) or of a lake (where a river enters) or of a bed etc. (where a person's head rests). **14** a confined body of steam for exerting pressure in an engine. **15** the leading part in a procession or army. **16** (in place-names) a promontory; *Beachy Head.* **17** the chief person of a group or organization etc.; a headmaster or headmistress. **18** the part of a tape recorder that touches the moving tape and converts signals. ● *verb* **1** be at the head or top of. **2** strike (a ball) with one's head in football. **3** move in a certain direction; *we headed south*; *heading for disaster.* **4** (often foll. by *off*) force to turn back or aside by getting in front of; *head him off.* □ **come to a head** (of matters) reach a crisis. **give a**

person his or her head let him or her act freely. **go to a person's head 1** (of alcohol) make him or her dizzy or slightly drunk. **2** (of success) make him or her conceited. **head-on** *adjective & adverb* with the head pointed directly towards something; colliding head to head. **head over heels 1** turning one's body upside down in a circular movement. **2** very much; *he is head over heels in love.* **head start** an early advantage. **heads will roll** some people will be punished or dismissed. **head teacher** the principal teacher in a school, responsible for organizing it. **head wind** a wind blowing from directly in front. **keep one's head** remain calm in a crisis. **lose one's head** act foolishly. **make head or tail of** be able to understand. **off** (*or* **out of**) **one's head** crazy. **over one's head 1** beyond one's understanding. **2** without one's rightful knowledge or involvement, especially of action taken by a subordinate consulting one's own superior. **put heads together** pool ideas. **turn a person's head** make him or her vain.

**headache** *noun* **1** a continuous pain in the head. **2** (*informal*) a worrying problem.

**headbanger** *noun* (*slang*) **1** a person who shakes his or her head violently to loud rock music. **2** a crazy or eccentric person.

**headboard** *noun* an upright panel along the head of a bed.

**head-butt** *noun* a thrust with the head into the chin or body of another person. ● *verb* attack with a head-butt.

**headcount** *noun* **1** a counting of individual people. **2** the total number of a group, especially of employees.

**headdress** *noun* an ornamental covering for the head.

**header** *noun* **1** heading of the ball in football. **2** a dive or plunge with head first. **3** a brick laid at right angles to the face of a wall.

**headgear** *noun* a hat or headdress.

**head-hunt** *verb* **1** cut off and preserve the heads of enemies as trophies. **2** seek to recruit experienced staff, especially as senior managers. □ **head-hunter** *noun*, **head-hunting** *noun*

**heading** *noun* **1** a word or words put at the top of a section of printed or written matters as a title etc. **2** a horizontal passage in a mine.

**headlamp** *noun* = HEADLIGHT.

**headland** *noun* a promontory.

**headlight** *noun* a powerful light mounted on the front of a vehicle.

**headline** *noun* **1** a heading in a newspaper, especially the largest one at the top of the front page. **2** (**headlines**) a brief broadcast summary of news.

**headlong** adverb & adjective **1** falling or plunging with the head first. **2** in a hasty and rash way.

**headmaster** noun a male head teacher.

**headmistress** noun a female head teacher.

**headphones** plural noun a set of earphones fitting over the head, for listening to audio equipment etc.

**headquarters** noun (as singular or plural) the place from which an organization is controlled.

**headroom** noun clearance above the head of a person or the top of a vehicle etc.

**headship** noun the position of chief or leader, especially as a head teacher.

**headshrinker** noun (slang) a psychiatrist.

**headstall** noun the part of a bridle or halter fitting round a horse's head.

**headstone** noun a stone set up at the head of a grave.

**headstrong** noun self-willed and obstinate.

**headwaters** plural noun the streams forming the sources of a river.

**headway** noun **1** progress. **2** headroom.

**headword** noun a word forming a heading especially to an entry in a dictionary.

**heady** adjective (**headier, headiest**) **1** (of drinks) likely to intoxicate people. **2** (of success etc.) exciting. **3** rash, impulsive. □ **headily** adverb, **headiness** noun

**heal** verb **1** (of sore or wounded parts) form healthy flesh again. **2** cause to do this. **3** cure; healing the sick. **4** put right (differences etc.). □ **healer** noun

**health** noun **1** the state of being well and free from illness; was restored to health. **2** the condition of the body; ill health. □ **health centre** the headquarters of a group of local medical services. **health farm** an establishment where improved health is sought by dieting etc. **health food** food thought to have health-giving qualities; natural unprocessed foods. **health service** a public service providing medical care. **health visitor** a trained person visiting babies or sick or elderly people at their homes.

**healthful** adjective producing good health, beneficial.

**healthy** adjective (**healthier, healthiest**) **1** having, showing, or producing good health. **2** beneficial. **3** (of things) functioning well. **4** substantial; a healthy amount. □ **healthily** adverb, **healthiness** noun

**Heaney** (hee-ni), Seamus Justin (born 1939), Irish poet.

**heap** noun **1** a number of things lying on one another; a mass of material so shaped. **2** (**heaps**) (informal) a great amount; plenty; there's heaps of time. **3** (slang) a dilapidated vehicle. ●verb **1** pile or become piled in a heap. **2** load with large quantities, give large quantities of; heaped the plate with food; they heaped insults on him.

**hear** verb (**heard, hearing**) **1** perceive (sounds) with the ear. **2** listen or pay attention to. **3** listen to and try (a case) in a lawcourt. **4** receive information or a message or letter etc. □ **have heard of** have knowledge or information about; we have never heard of this firm. **hear a person out** listen to the whole of what he or she wishes to say. **hear! hear!** I agree. **not hear of** refuse to allow; won't hear of my paying for it. □ **hearer** noun

**hearing** noun **1** the ability to hear. **2** the range within which sounds may be heard; within hearing. **3** an opportunity of being heard; trial of a case in a lawcourt (especially before a judge without a jury); got a fair hearing. □ **hearing-aid** noun a small sound-amplifier worn by a partially deaf person to improve the hearing.

**hearken** (har-kĕn) verb (old use) listen.

**hearsay** noun rumour or gossip.

**hearse** (pronounced herss) noun a vehicle for carrying the coffin at a funeral.

**heart** noun **1** the hollow muscular organ that keeps blood circulating in the body by contracting rhythmically. **2** the part of the body where this is, the breast. **3** the centre of a person's emotions or affections or inmost thoughts; knew it in her heart. **4** the ability to feel emotion; a tender heart. **5** courage; take heart. **6** enthusiasm; his heart isn't in it. **7** a mood or feeling; a change of heart. **8** the innermost part of a thing; the close compact head of a cabbage etc.; the heart of the matter. **9** a symmetrical figure conventionally representing a heart. **10** a red figure shaped like this on playing cards; a playing card of the suit (**hearts**) marked with these. □ **after one's own heart** exactly to one's liking. **at heart 1** in one's inmost feelings. **2** basically. **break a person's heart** overwhelm him or her with sorrow. **by heart** memorized thoroughly. **have one's heart in one's mouth** feel very alarmed or frightened. **have the heart to** be hard-hearted enough to (do something). **heart attack** or **heart failure** sudden failure of the heart to function normally. **heart-rending** adjective very distressing. **heart-searching** noun examination by oneself of one's feelings and motives. **heart-to-heart** adjective frank and personal; a heart-to-heart talk. **heart-warming** adjective emotionally uplifting. **set one's heart on** desire eagerly. **take to heart** be deeply troubled by. **to one's heart's content** as much as one wishes. **with all one's heart** sincerely, with the greatest goodwill.

**heartache** noun mental pain, deep sorrow.

**heartbeat** noun the pulsation of the heart.

**heartbreak** noun overwhelming unhappiness. □ **heartbreaking** adjective, **heartbroken** adjective

**heartburn** noun a burning sensation in the lower part of the chest from indigestion.

**hearten** verb make (a person) feel encouraged.

**heartfelt** adjective felt deeply or earnestly.

**hearth** (pronounced harth) noun 1 the floor of a fireplace. 2 the home.

**heartily** adverb 1 in a hearty way. 2 very; heartily sick of it.

**heartland** noun the central or most important part of an area etc.

**heartless** adjective not feeling pity or sympathy. □ **heartlessly** adverb, **heartlessness** noun

**heartstrings** plural noun one's deepest feelings of love or pity.

**heartthrob** noun (informal) a person for whom one has romantic feelings.

**heartwood** noun the dense inner part of a tree trunk, yielding the hardest timber.

**hearty** adjective (**heartier, heartiest**) 1 showing warmth of feeling, enthusiastic. 2 vigorous, strong; hale and hearty. 3 (of meals or appetites) large. □ **heartiness** noun

**heat** noun 1 a form of energy produced by the movement of molecules. 2 the sensation produced by this, hotness. 3 hot weather. 4 an intense feeling (especially of anger), tension. 5 the most intense part or period of activity; the heat of battle. 6 a preliminary race etc. whose winners take part in further contests or the final. ●verb make or become hot or warm. □ **on heat** (of mammals, especially females) sexually receptive; ready to mate.

**heated** adjective (of a person or discussion) angry. □ **heatedly** adverb

**heater** noun a stove or other heating device.

**heath** noun 1 an area of flat uncultivated land with low shrubs. 2 a small shrubby plant of the heather kind.

**Heath**, Sir Edward Richard George (born 1916), British Conservative statesman, Prime Minister 1970–4.

**heathen** (hee-thĕn) noun 1 a person who is not a believer in any of the world's chief religions, especially one who is neither Christian, Jew, nor Muslim. 2 a person regarded as lacking culture or moral principles. ●adjective of heathens.

**heather** noun an evergreen plant or shrub with small purple, pinkish, or white bell-shaped flowers, growing on uplands.

**Heath Robinson** (of equipment) absurdly elaborate and impracticable. (¶ Named after the English cartoonist W. Heath Robinson (died 1944), who drew machines of this kind.)

**heatstroke** noun a feverish condition caused by excessive exposure to heat.

**heatwave** noun a period of very hot weather.

**heave** verb (**heaved** (in sense 6 **hove**), **heaving**) 1 lift or haul (something heavy) with great effort. 2 utter with effort; heaved a sigh. 3 (informal) throw; heave a brick at him. 4 rise and fall regularly like waves at sea. 5 pant; retch. 6 (in nautical use) come; hove in sight. ●noun the act of heaving. □ **heave to** bring (a ship) or come to a standstill without anchoring or mooring.

**heaven** noun 1 the place regarded in some religions as the abode of God and the angels, and of the blessed after death. 2 (**Heaven**) God, Providence. 3 a place or state of supreme bliss. 4 (**the heavens**) the sky as seen from the earth, in which the sun, moon, and stars appear. ●interjection (**heavens**) an exclamation of surprise. □ **heaven-sent** adjective providential, fortunate.

**heavenly** adjective 1 of heaven, divine. 2 of the heavens or sky. 3 (informal) very pleasing. □ **heavenly bodies** the sun and stars etc.

**heavy** adjective (**heavier, heaviest**) 1 having great weight, difficult to lift, carry, or move. 2 of more than average amount or force; heavy artillery; heavy rain. 3 (of work) needing much physical effort. 4 severe, intense; a heavy sleeper. 5 dense; a heavy mist. 6 (of ground) clinging, difficult to travel over. 7 (of food) stodgy and difficult to digest. 8 clumsy or ungraceful in appearance, effect, or movement. 9 dull and tedious; serious in tone. 10 oppressive; heavy demands. ●noun 1 (informal) a large violent person; a hired thug. 2 a villainous role or actor. 3 (**heavies**) (informal) serious newspapers. □ **heavy-duty** adjective intended to withstand hard use. **heavy going** progress made only with difficulty. **heavy-handed** adjective 1 clumsy. 2 overbearing, oppressive. **heavy hydrogen** = DEUTERIUM. **heavy industry** industry producing metal, machines, etc. **heavy metal** a type of loud rock music with a heavy beat. **heavy water** deuterium oxide, a substance with the same chemical properties as water but greater density. **make heavy weather of** find (a thing) more difficult than it really is. □ **heavily** adverb, **heaviness** noun

**heavyweight** noun 1 a person of more than average weight. 2 a weight in certain sports, in amateur boxing over 81 kg. 3 (informal) a person of great influence.

**hebdomadal** (heb-**dom**-ă-dăl) adjective (formal) weekly.

**Hebe** (hee-bee) (Gk. myth.) the gods' cupbearer, daughter of Zeus and Hera.

**hebe** (**hee**-bee) *noun* a small shrub with blue, violet, or white flowers in spikes.

**Hebraic** (hee-**bray**-ik) *adjective* of Hebrew or the Hebrews.

**Hebraist** (**hee**-bray-ist) *noun* an expert in Hebrew.

**Hebrew** *noun* **1** a member of a Semitic people in ancient Palestine; an Israelite. **2** their language; a modern form of this used in Israel. ● *adjective* **1** of the Hebrews or the Jews. **2** of or in Hebrew.

**Hebrides** (**heb**-ri-deez) two groups of islands off the north-west coast of Scotland. □ **Hebridean** (heb-ri-**dee**-ăn) *adjective & noun*

**Hecate** (**hek**-ă-ti) (*Gk. myth.*) a goddess associated with uncanny things, the ghost-world, and witchcraft.

**heck** *interjection* (*informal*) a mild exclamation of surprise or dismay.

**heckle** *verb* interrupt and harass (a public speaker) with aggressive questions and abuse. □ **heckler** *noun*

**hectare** (**hek**-tair) *noun* a unit of area, 10,000 sq. metres (2.471 acres).

**hectic** *adjective* involving feverish activity; *a hectic day*. □ **hectically** *adverb*

**hectogram** *noun* one hundred grams.

**Hector** (*Gk. legend*) a Trojan prince, killed by Achilles at the siege of Troy.

**hector** *verb* intimidate by bullying.

**Hecuba** (**hek**-yoo-bă) (*Gk. legend*) wife of Priam, king of Troy.

**he'd** (*informal*) **1** he had. **2** he would.

**hedge** *noun* **1** a fence of closely planted bushes or shrubs. **2** a means of protecting oneself against possible loss; *bought diamonds as a hedge against inflation*. ● *verb* **1** surround or bound with a hedge. **2** make or trim hedges; *hedging and ditching*. **3** reduce the possible loss on (a bet etc.) by another speculation. **4** avoid giving a direct answer or commitment. □ **hedge-hop** *verb* fly at a very low altitude. **hedge sparrow** a common British bird resembling a small thrush. □ **hedger** *noun*

**hedgehog** *noun* a small insect-eating animal with a piglike snout and a back covered in stiff spines, able to roll itself up into a ball when attacked.

**hedgerow** *noun* a row of bushes etc. forming a hedge.

**hedonist** (**hee**-dŏn-ist) *noun* one who believes that pleasure is the chief good in life. □ **hedonism** *noun*, **hedonistic** *adjective*

**heebie-jeebies** *plural noun* (preceded by *the*) (*slang*) nervous anxiety.

**heed** *verb* pay attention to. ● *noun* careful attention; *take heed*. □ **heedful** *adjective*, **heedless** *adjective*, **heedlessly** *adverb*

**hee-haw** *noun* a donkey's bray. ● *verb* bray like a donkey.

**heel**[1] *noun* **1** the rounded back part of the human foot. **2** the part of a sock etc. covering this. **3** a built-up part of a boot or shoe that supports a person's heel. **4** something like a heel in shape or position; *the heel of the hand*. **5** (*informal*) a scoundrel. ● *verb* **1** repair the heels of (shoes etc.). **2** (foll. by *out*) (in Rugby football) pass the ball with the heel. □ **at** *or* **to heel** (of a dog) close behind; under control. **at** *or* **on the heels of** following closely after. **down at heel** (of a person) shabby. **take to one's heels** run away. **well-heeled** *adjective* rich.

**heel**[2] *verb* tilt (a ship) or become tilted to one side; *heeled over*. ● *noun* the act or amount of this.

**heelball** *noun* **1** a mixture of hard wax and lampblack used by shoemakers for polishing. **2** a similar mixture used in brass-rubbing.

**hefty** *adjective* (**heftier, heftiest**) large and heavy; powerful. □ **heftily** *adverb*, **heftiness** *noun*

**Hegel** (**hay**-gĕl), Georg Wilhelm Friedrich (1770–1831), German idealist philosopher. □ **Hegelian** (hi-**gay**-liăn) *adjective*

**hegemony** (hig-**em**-ŏn-i) *noun* leadership, especially by one country.

**Hegira** (**hej**-i-ră) *noun* (also **Hejira**) the flight of Muhammad from Mecca (AD 622), from which the Muslim era is reckoned.

**Heidegger** (**hy**-de-ger), Martin (1889–1976), German philosopher.

**heifer** (**hef**-er) *noun* a young cow, especially one that has not had more than one calf.

**height** *noun* **1** measurement from base to top or head to foot. **2** the distance (of an object or position) above ground level or sea level. **3** a high place or area; *afraid of heights*. **4** the highest degree of something; *the height of fashion*. **5** the most intense part or period; *the height of the tourist season*.

**heighten** *verb* make or become higher or more intense.

**Heine** (**hy**-nĕ), Heinrich (1797–1856), German poet.

**heinous** (**hay**-nŭs) *adjective* very wicked.

**heir** (*pronounced* air) *noun* a person who inherits property or rank etc. from its former owner. □ **heir apparent** the legal heir whose claim cannot be set aside by the birth of another heir. **heir presumptive** one whose claim may be set aside in this way.

**heiress** (**air**-ess) *noun* a female heir.

**heirloom** (**air**-loom) *noun* a possession that has been handed down in a family for several generations.

**heist** (*rhymes with* sliced) *noun* (*Amer. slang*) a robbery.

**Hejira** alternative spelling of HEGIRA.

**held** see HOLD¹.

**Helen** (*Gk. legend*) wife of Menelaus king of Sparta, whose abduction by Paris led to the Trojan War.

**helical** (**hel**-i-kăl) *adjective* like a helix.

**helicopter** (**hel**-i-kop-ter) *noun* a wingless aircraft obtaining lift and propulsion from horizontal revolving overhead blades.

**heliocentric** (hee-li-ŏ-**sen**-trik) *adjective* **1** considered as viewed from the sun's centre. **2** regarding the sun as the centre.

**heliograph** (**hee**-li-ŏ-graf) *noun* **1** a signalling device reflecting the sun's rays in flashes. **2** a message sent by this.

**heliotrope** (**hee**-li-ŏ-trohp) *noun* a plant with small sweet-smelling purple flowers.

**heliport** (**hel**i-port) *noun* a place where helicopters take off and land.

**helium** (**hee**-li-ŭm) *noun* a chemical element (symbol He), a light colourless gas that does not burn, used in airships and as a coolant.

**helix** (**hee**-liks) *noun* (*plural* **helices**, *pronounced* **hee**-li-seez) a spiral, especially a three-dimensional one, either like a corkscrew or flat like a watch spring.

**hell** *noun* **1** a place regarded in some religions as the abode of the dead, or of devils and condemned sinners. **2** a place or state of supreme misery, something extremely unpleasant. **3** (*informal*) used to express anger or intensify a meaning or indicate something extreme; *what the hell does he want?*; *ran like hell*. ●*interjection* an exclamation of anger or surprise. □ **a** (*or* **one**) **hell of a** (*informal*) an outstanding example of; *a hell of a mess*; *one hell of a party*. **come hell or high water** no matter what the obstacles. **for the hell of it** just for fun. **hell-bent** *adjective* recklessly determined. **hell-fire** *noun* the fire(s) of hell. **hell for leather** at full speed. **Hell's Angel** a member of a gang of motor cycle enthusiasts notorious for disorderly or violent behaviour.

**he'll** (*informal*) = he will.

**Hellas** (**hel**-as) the ancient and modern Greek name for Greece.

**hellebore** (**hel**-i-bor) *noun* a poisonous plant with white, purple, or greenish flowers; the Christmas rose.

**Hellene** (**hel**-een) *noun* a Greek. □ **Hellenic** (hě-**len**-ik) *adjective*

**Hellenistic** *adjective* of the Greek language and culture of the 4th–1st centuries BC.

**Heller**, Joseph (born 1923), American novelist, whose most famous novel was *Catch-22* (see entry).

**Hellespont** (**hel**-iss-pont) the ancient name for the Dardanelles.

**hellish** *adjective* (*informal*) very unpleasant.

**hello** *interjection & noun* (also **hallo, hullo**) (*plural* **hellos**) an expression used in greeting or to call attention or express surprise.

**helm** *noun* the tiller or wheel by which a ship's rudder is controlled. □ **at the helm** at the head of an organization etc., in control.

**helmet** *noun* a protective head-covering worn by a policeman, motor cyclist, etc.

**helmsman** *noun* (*plural* **helmsmen**) a person who steers a ship.

**helot** (**hel**-ŏt) *noun* a serf in ancient Sparta.

**help** *verb* **1** make it easier for (a person) to do something or for (a thing) to happen. **2** do something for the benefit of (someone in need). **3** prevent, refrain from, remedy; *it can't be helped*; *I couldn't help myself*. ●*noun* **1** the action of helping or being helped. **2** a person or thing that helps. **3** a person employed to help with housework. □ **help oneself to 1** serve oneself with (food) at a meal. **2** take without seeking assistance or permission. **help out** give help (especially in a crisis). □ **helper** *noun*

**helpful** *adjective* giving help, useful. □ **helpfully** *adverb*, **helpfulness** *noun*

**helping** *noun* a portion of food given to one person at a meal.

**helpless** *adjective* **1** unable to manage without help, dependent on others. **2** incapable of action, indicating this; *helpless with laughter*; *gave him a helpless glance*. □ **helplessly** *adverb*, **helplessness** *noun*

**helpline** *noun* a telephone service providing help with problems.

**helpmate** *noun* a helper, a companion or partner who helps.

**Helsinki** (**hel**-sink-i) the capital of Finland.

**helter-skelter** *adverb* in disorderly haste. ●*noun* a tower-shaped structure at a fairground with a spiral track outside it down which people slide on a mat.

**Helvetian** (hel-**vee**-shăn) *adjective* Swiss. ●*noun* a Swiss person.

**hem¹** *noun* the border of cloth where the edge is turned under and sewn or fixed down. ●*verb* (**hemmed, hemming**) turn and sew a hem on. □ **hem in** surround and restrict the movement of; *enemy forces hemmed them in*.

**hem²** *interjection* = AHEM.

**hemal** etc. Amer. spelling of HAEMAL etc.

**hemi-** *combining form* half.

**Hemingway**, Ernest Miller (1899–1961), American novelist and writer of short stories, whose works include *A Farewell to Arms*, *For Whom the Bell Tolls*, and *The Old Man and the Sea*.

**hemiplegia** *noun* paralysis of one side of the body.

**hemipterous** (hem-**ip**-ter-ŭs) *adjective* of those insects (such as aphids, bugs, and cicadas) with piercing or sucking mouthparts.

**hemisphere** noun **1** half a sphere. **2** either of the halves into which the earth is divided either by the equator (the *northern* and *southern hemisphere*) or by a line passing through the poles (the *eastern* and *western hemisphere*).

**hemispherical** (hem-iss-**fe**-ri-kăl) adjective shaped like a hemisphere.

**hemline** noun the lower edge of a skirt or dress.

**hemlock** noun a poisonous plant with small white flowers.

**hemp** noun **1** a plant from which coarse fibres are obtained for the manufacture of rope and cloth. **2** a narcotic drug made from this plant. □ **hempen** adjective

**hemstitch** noun a decorative stitch used for hems.

**hen** noun a female bird, especially of a domestic fowl. □ **hen-party** noun (*informal*) a party of women only.

**henbane** noun a poisonous plant with an unpleasant smell.

**hence** adverb **1** from this time; *five years hence*. **2** for this reason. **3** (*old use*) from here.

**henceforth** adverb (also **henceforward**) from this time on, in future.

**henchman** noun (*plural* **henchmen**) a faithful supporter.

**Hendrix**, Jimi (original name: James Marshall) (1942–70), Black American rock guitarist and singer.

**henge** noun a prehistoric monument of wood or stone such as the circle of stones at Stonehenge.

**henna** noun a reddish-brown dye used especially on the hair, obtained from a tropical shrub. □ **hennaed** (**hen**-ăd) adjective

**henpecked** adjective (of a husband) nagged by a domineering wife.

**Henry**[1] the name of eight kings of England, who reigned as Henry I 1100–35, II 1154–89, III 1216–72, IV 1399–1413, V 1413–22, VI 1422–61, 1470–1, VII 1485–1509, and VIII 1509–47.

**Henry**[2] Prince (other names: Charles Albert David) (born 1984), second son of the Prince and Princess of Wales.

**henry** noun (*plural* **henries**) a unit of electric inductance. (¶ Named after the American physicist J. Henry (died 1878).)

**hep** = HIP[4].

**hepatic** (hip-**at**-ik) adjective of the liver.

**hepatitis** (hep-ă-**ty**-tiss) noun inflammation of the liver.

**Hepburn**, Katharine (born 1909), American stage and film actress.

**Hephaestus** (hi-**fy**-stŭs) (*Gk. myth.*) the god of fire, called Vulcan by the Romans.

**Hepplewhite** noun a light and graceful style of furniture named after George Hepplewhite, an 18th-century cabinet-maker.

**hepta-** *combining form* seven.

**heptagon** (**hep**-tă-gŏn) noun a geometric figure with seven sides. □ **heptagonal** (hep-**tag**-ŏn-ăl) adjective

**heptathlon** noun an athletic contest in which each competitor takes part in the seven events it includes.

**Hepworth**, Dame (Jocelyn) Barbara (1903–75), English sculptor.

**her** pronoun **1** the objective case of SHE; *we saw her*. **2** (*informal*) = SHE; *it's her all right*. ● adjective of or belonging to her.

**Hera** (**heer**-ă) (*Gk. myth*) a goddess, sister and wife of Zeus and queen of the Olympian gods, identified by the Romans with Juno.

**Heracles** (**herr**ă-kleez) the Greek form of the name Hercules.

**herald** noun **1** an official in former times who made announcements and carried messages from a ruler. **2** a person or thing indicating the approach of something; *heralds of spring*. **3** an official who records people's pedigrees and grants coats of arms. ● verb proclaim the approach of.

**heraldic** (hi-**ral**-dik) adjective of heralds or heraldry.

**heraldry** noun the study of coats of arms and the right to bear them.

**herb** noun **1** a soft-stemmed plant that dies down to the ground after flowering. **2** a plant with leaves or seeds etc. that are used as food or in medicine or for flavouring. □ **herby** adjective

**herbaceous** (her-**bay**-shŭs) adjective of or like herbs. □ **herbaceous border** a garden border containing perennial flowering plants.

**herbage** noun grass and other field plants.

**herbal** adjective of herbs used in medicine or for flavouring. ● noun a book with descriptions of these.

**herbalist** noun a dealer in medicinal herbs.

**herbarium** (her-**bair**-iŭm) noun (*plural* **herbaria**) **1** a systematic collection of dried plants. **2** a book, case, or room for these.

**herbicide** noun a substance that is poisonous to plants, used to destroy unwanted vegetation.

**herbivore** (**her**-biv-or) noun a herbivorous animal.

**herbivorous** (her-**biv**-er-ŭs) adjective feeding on plants.

**herculean** (her-kew-**lee**-ăn) adjective having or needing great strength or effort; *a herculean task*.

**Hercules** (**her**-kew-leez) (*Gk. myth.*) a hero, noted for his great strength and courage, who performed twelve immense tasks ('labours') imposed upon him.

**herd** noun **1** a number of cattle or other animals feeding or staying together. **2** a mob. ●verb **1** gather, stay, or drive as a group. **2** tend (a herd of animals). □ **herd instinct** the instinct to think and behave like the majority of people.

**herdsman** noun (plural **herdsmen**) a person who tends a herd of animals.

**here** adverb **1** in, at, or to this place. **2** at this point in a process or a series of events. ●interjection an exclamation calling attention to something or making a protest, or used as a reply (= I am here) in answer to a roll-call. □ **here and there** in or to various places. **here goes** I am about to begin. **here's to** I drink to the health of. **neither here nor there** of no importance.

**hereabouts** adverb (also **hereabout**) somewhere near here.

**hereafter** adverb in future, from now on. ●noun (**the hereafter**) the future; life after death.

**hereby** adverb by this means, as a result of this.

**hereditable** (hi-**red**-it-ăbŭl) adjective able to be inherited.

**hereditary** (hi-**red**-it-er-i) adjective **1** inherited, able to be passed or received from one generation to another; hereditary characteristics. **2** holding a position by inheritance; hereditary ruler.

**heredity** (hi-**red**-iti) noun inheritance of physical or mental characteristics from parents or ancestors.

**Hereford** noun an animal of a breed of red and white beef cattle.

**Hereford and Worcester** a west midland county of England.

**herein** adverb (formal) in this place, document, etc.

**hereinafter** adverb (formal) from this point on; in a later part of this document etc.

**hereof** adverb (formal) of this.

**heresy** (**herri**-si) noun **1** an opinion that is contrary to the accepted beliefs of a religion, especially of the Roman Catholic Church. **2** opinion contrary to what is normally accepted.

**heretic** (**herri**-tik) noun a person believing in or practising heresy. □ **heretical** (hi-**ret**-ikăl) adjective

**hereto** adverb (formal) to this.

**heretofore** adverb (formal) formerly.

**hereupon** adverb after or in consequence of this.

**herewith** adverb with this; enclosed herewith.

**heritable** adjective able to be inherited or to inherit.

**heritage** noun **1** that which has been or may be inherited. **2** inherited circumstances or

benefits. **3** a nation's historic buildings, monuments, etc.

**hermaphrodite** (her-**maf**-rŏ-dyt) noun an animal or plant that has both male and female sexual organs in one individual. □ **hermaphroditic** (her-maf-rŏ-**dit**-ik) adjective

**Hermes** (**her**-meez) (Gk. myth.) the messenger of the gods, identified by the Romans with Mercury.

**hermetic** adjective with an airtight closure; hermetic seal. □ **hermetically** adverb

**hermit** noun a person (especially an early Christian) who has withdrawn from human society and lives in solitude. □ **hermit-crab** noun a crab that lives in a cast-off shell to protect its soft hinder parts.

**Hermitage, the** an art museum in St Petersburg.

**hermitage** noun a hermit's dwelling.

**hernia** noun a protrusion of a part or organ of the body through a wall of the cavity (especially the abdomen) that normally contains it; a rupture.

**hero** noun (plural **heroes**) **1** a person admired for nobility, courage, outstanding achievements, etc. **2** the chief male character in a story, play, or poem. □ **hero-worship** noun excessive devotion to an admired person.

**Herod** the name of four rulers in ancient Palestine, including Herod the Great, in whose reign Christ was born.

**Herodotus** (hi-**rod**-ŏ-tŭs) (5th century BC), Greek historian, who wrote an account of the wars between the Greeks and Persians in the early 5th century BC.

**heroic** adjective having the characteristics of a hero, very brave. ●plural noun (**heroics**) overdramatic talk or behaviour. □ **heroically** adverb

**heroin** noun a highly addictive analgesic drug prepared from morphine.

**heroine** noun a female hero.

**heroism** noun heroic conduct or qualities.

**heron** noun a long-legged long-necked wading bird.

**herpes** (**her**-peez) noun a virus disease causing blisters on the skin. □ **herpes simplex** a form of this. **herpes zoster** shingles.

**herpetology** (her-pi-**tol**-ŏji) noun the study of reptiles. □ **herpetologist** noun

**Herr** (pronounced hair) noun (plural **Herren**) the title of a German man; Mr.

**herring** noun (plural **herring** or **herrings**) a North Atlantic fish used for food. □ **herring-bone** noun a zigzag pattern or arrangement.

**hers** possessive pronoun the one or ones of or belonging to her; it is hers; hers are best. □ **of hers** belonging to her.

**Herschel** (**her**-shěl), Sir William (1738–1822), German-born astronomer, who settled in England and became court astronomer to George III.

**herself** *pronoun* **1** the emphatic and reflexive form of *she* and *her*; *she herself went*; *she hurt herself.* **2** in her normal state; *not herself today.* □ **by herself** see ONESELF.

**Hertfordshire** (**har**-ferd-sher) a county of England, bordering on north London.

**Herts** *abbreviation* Hertfordshire.

**Hertz** (*pronounced* herts), Heinrich Rudolf (1857–94), German physicist, a pioneer of radio communication.

**hertz** *noun* (*plural* **hertz**) a unit of frequency of electromagnetic waves, = one cycle per second. (¶ Named after H. R. Hertz (see entry).)

**Herzl** (**hert**-sĕl), Theodor (1860–1904), Austrian Jewish writer, born in Hungary, who built up the Zionist movement.

**he's** (*informal*) **1** he is. **2** he has.

**Hesiod** (**hee**-si-ŏd) (*c.*700 BC) one of the oldest known Greek poets.

**hesitant** *adjective* hesitating. □ **hesitantly** *adverb*, **hesitancy** *noun*

**hesitate** *verb* **1** show or feel indecision or uncertainty, pause in doubt. **2** be reluctant, scruple; *wouldn't hesitate to break the rules if it suited him.* □ **hesitation** *noun*

**hessian** *noun* strong coarse cloth made of hemp or jute; sackcloth.

**heterodox** (**het**-er-ŏ-doks) *adjective* not orthodox. □ **heterodoxy** *noun*

**heterodyne** (**het**-er-ŏ-dyn) *adjective* of or involved in the production of a lower radio frequency from a combination of two high frequencies.

**heterogeneous** (het-er-ŏ-**jee**-niŭs) *adjective* made up of people or things that are unlike each other. □ **heterogeneity** (het-er-ŏ-jin-ee-iti) *noun*

**heteromorphic** (het-er-ŏ-**mor**-fik) *adjective* (also **heteromorphous**) *Biology* of dissimilar forms. □ **heteromorphism** *noun*

**heterosexual** *adjective* feeling or involving sexual attraction to people of the opposite sex. ●*noun* a heterosexual person. □ **heterosexuality** *noun*

**het up** *adjective* (*informal*) excited, overwrought.

**heuristic** (hewr-**iss**-tik) *adjective* **1** serving or helping to find out or discover something. **2** proceeding by trial and error.

**hew** *verb* (**hewed**, **hewn** or **hewed**, **hewing**) **1** chop or cut with an axe or sword etc. **2** cut into shape.

**hex** *noun* a magic spell, a curse. ●*verb* **1** bewitch. **2** practise witchcraft.

**hexa-** *combining form* six.

**hexadecimal** (heks-ă-**des**-i-măl) *adjective* *Computing* of a number system that has 16 (the figures 0 to 9 and the letters A to F) rather than 10 as a base.

**hexagon** (**heks**-ă-gŏn) *noun* a geometric figure with six sides. □ **hexagonal** (heks-**ag**-ŏn-ăl) *adjective*

**hexagram** *noun* a six-pointed star formed by two intersecting equilateral triangles.

**hexameter** (heks-**am**-it-er) *noun* a line of verse with six metrical feet.

**hey** *interjection* an exclamation calling attention or expressing surprise or enquiry.

**heyday** *noun* the time of greatest success or prosperity; *it was in its heyday.*

**Hezbollah** (hez-bŏ-**lah**) *noun* (also **Hizbollah**) an extreme Shiite Muslim group, active especially in Lebanon. (¶ From Arabic, = party of God.)

**HF** *abbreviation* high frequency.

**Hf** *symbol* hafnium.

**Hg** *symbol* mercury.

**hg** *abbreviation* hectogram(s).

**HGV** *abbreviation* heavy goods vehicle.

**HH** *abbreviation* (of a pencil lead) double-hard.

**HI** *abbreviation* Hawaii.

**hi** *interjection* an exclamation calling attention or expressing greeting.

**hiatus** (hy-**ay**-tŭs) *noun* (*plural* **hiatuses**) a break or gap in a sequence or series.

**hibernate** (**hy**-ber-nayt) *verb* (of certain animals) spend the winter in a state like deep sleep. □ **hibernation** *noun*

**Hibernian** (hy-**ber**-niăn) *adjective* (*poetic*) of Ireland. ●*noun* an Irish person.

**hibiscus** (hib-**isk**-ŭs) *noun* (*plural* **hibiscuses**) a cultivated shrub with large brightly coloured flowers.

**hiccup** (also **hiccough**) *noun* **1** a sudden spasm of the diaphragm causing a characteristic sound 'hic'. **2** (**hiccups**) an attack of hiccuping. **3** a brief hitch. ●*verb* (**hiccuped**, **hiccuping**) make a hiccup.

**hick** *noun* (*Amer. informal*) a country bumpkin, a provincial.

**hickory** *noun* **1** a North American tree related to the walnut. **2** its hard wood.

**hid** see HIDE[2].

**hide**[1] *noun* an animal's skin, especially when tanned or dressed.

**hide**[2] *verb* (**hid**, **hidden**, **hiding**) **1** put or keep out of sight, prevent from being seen. **2** keep secret. **3** conceal oneself. ●*noun* a place of concealment used when observing wildlife. □ **hidden agenda** a secret motivation behind a policy, statement, etc.; an ulterior motive. **hide-and-seek** *noun* a children's game in which some players conceal themselves and others try to find them. **hide-out** *noun* (*informal*) a hiding-place.

**hidebound** *adjective* narrow-minded, refusing to abandon old customs and prejudices.

**hideous** *adjective* very ugly; revolting. □ **hideously** *adverb*

**hiding**[1] *noun* (*informal*) a thrashing. □ **on a hiding to nothing** (*slang*) bound to lose or fail.

**hiding**[2] *noun* the state of being or remaining hidden; *went into hiding.* □ **hiding place** a place where a person or thing is or could be hidden.

**hie** *verb* (also **hie oneself**) (*old use*) go quickly.

**hierarchy** (**hyr**-ark-i) *noun* a system with grades of status or authority ranking one above another in a series. □ **hierarchical** (hyr-**ark**-ikăl) *adjective*

**hieratic** (hy-er-at-ik) *adjective* of priests. ●*noun* a form of hieroglyphs used in ancient Egypt, originally for religious texts.

**hieroglyph** (**hyr**-ŏ-glif) *noun* **1** one of the pictures or symbols used in ancient Egypt and elsewhere to represent sounds, words, or ideas. **2** a written symbol with a secret or cryptic meaning.

**hieroglyphic** (hyr-ŏ-**glif**-ik) *adjective* of or written in hieroglyphs. ●*plural noun* (**hieroglyphics**) hieroglyphs.

**hi-fi** (*informal*) *adjective* high-fidelity. ●*noun* a set of hi-fi equipment.

**higgledy-piggledy** *adjective & adverb* mixed up, in disorder.

**high** *adjective* **1** extending far upwards, extending above the normal or average level. **2** situated far above the ground or above sea level. **3** measuring a specified distance from base to top; *one inch high*; *waist-high*. **4** ranking above others in importance or quality; *High Admiral*. **5** extreme, intense, greater than what is normal or average; *high temperatures*; *high prices*; *formed a high opinion of her.* **6** (of a time or period) fully reached, at its peak; *high noon*; *it's high time we left*; *High Renaissance*. **7** noble, virtuous; *high ideals*. **8** (of a sound or voice) of high frequency; shrill. **9** (of meat) beginning to go bad; (of game) hung until slightly decomposed and ready to cook. **10** (*slang*) intoxicated; under the influence of drugs. ●*noun* **1** a high level or figure; *exports reached a new high*. **2** an area of high barometric pressure. **3** a state of great excitement or happiness; *I'm on a high.* ●*adverb* **1** in, at, or to a high level or position. **2** in or to a high degree. **3** at a high price. **4** (of a sound) at or to a high pitch. □ **high altar** the chief altar of a church. **high and dry** aground; stranded, isolated. **high and low** everywhere; *searched high and low*. **high and mighty** arrogant. **high chair** an infant's chair with long legs and a tray for meals. **High Church** that section of the Church of England that gives an important place to ritual and to the authority of bishops and priests. **high-class** *adjective* of high quality or social class. **high colour** a flushed complexion. **High Commission** an embassy from one Commonwealth country to another. **High Commissioner** the head of this. **High Court** (also in England **High Court of Justice**) the supreme court for civil cases. **high explosive** explosive with a violently shattering effect. **high fidelity** reproduction of sound with little or no distortion. **high-flown** *adjective* (of language etc.) extravagant, pretentious. **high-flyer** *noun* (also **high-flier**) **1** an ambitious person. **2** a person or thing with capacity for great achievements. **high frequency** (in radio) 3 to 30 megahertz. **high-handed** *adjective* disregarding others' feelings. **high hat** a pair of cymbals supported on a stand. **high jump 1** an athletic competition of jumping over a high horizontal bar. **2** (*informal*) drastic punishment; *you're for the high jump*. **high-level** *adjective* **1** (of negotiations) conducted by people of high rank. **2** (of a computer language) not machine-dependent and usually close to natural language. **high-minded** *adjective* having high moral principles. **high-pitched** *adjective* (of a voice or sound) high. **high-powered** *adjective* **1** using great power or energy. **2** important or influential. **high pressure 1** a high degree of activity or exertion. **2** an atmospheric condition with the pressure above average. **high priest** a chief priest. **high-rise** *adjective* (of a building) with many storeys. **high road** a main road. **high school** a secondary school. **high sea** or **seas** the open seas not under any country's jurisdiction. **high season** the busiest period at a resort etc. **high-speed** *adjective* operating at great speed. **high-spirited** *adjective* lively, cheerful. **high spot** an important place or feature. **high street** the principal shopping street of a town. **high table** a table at a public dinner or in a college etc. for the most important guests or members. **high tea** an evening meal with tea and cooked food. **high-tech** *adjective* using or involving advanced technological development, especially in electronics. **high tide** the tide at its highest level. **high treason** treason against one's country or ruler. **high voltage** electrical potential large enough to injure or damage. **high water** high tide. **high water mark** the level reached at high water. **high wire** a high tightrope.

**highball** *noun* (*Amer.*) a drink with spirits and soda etc. served with ice in a tall glass.

**highbrow** *adjective* intellectual, cultured. ●*noun* a highbrow person.

**higher** *adjective & adverb* more high. ●*adverb* in or to a higher position etc. □ **higher**

**animals** or **plants** those which are highly developed and of complex structure.

**higher education** education above the level given in schools, e.g. at university.

**highfalutin** *adjective* (also **highfaluting**) pompous, pretentious.

**Highland** a local government region of northern Scotland.

**highland** *adjective* **1** of or in upland or mountainous country. **2** (**Highland**) of the Scottish Highlands. ●*plural noun* **1** (**highlands**) mountainous country. **2** (**Highlands**) the mountainous area of northern Scotland. □ **Highland cattle** shaggy-haired cattle with long curved horns. **Highland fling** a lively Scottish dance.

**highlander** *noun* **1** a native or inhabitant of highlands. **2** (**Highlander**) a native of the Scottish Highlands.

**highlight** *noun* **1** a light or bright area in a painting etc. **2** the brightest or most outstanding feature of something; *the highlight of the tour*. **3** (usually as **highlights**) a light streak in the hair produced by bleaching. ●*verb* **1** draw special attention to. **2** mark with a bright colour.

**highlighter** *noun* a marker pen for emphasizing a printed word etc. by overlaying it with colour.

**highly** *adverb* **1** in a high degree, extremely; *highly amusing*; *highly commended*. **2** very favourably; *thinks highly of her*. □ **highly-strung** *adjective* (of a person) easily upset.

**Highness** *noun* the title used in speaking of or to a prince or princess; *Her Highness*; *Your Royal Highness*.

**highway** *noun* **1** a public road. **2** a main route. **3** a direct course of action; *on the highway to success*. □ **Highway Code** a set of rules issued officially for the guidance of road-users.

**highwayman** *noun* (*plural* **highwaymen**) a man (usually on horseback) who robbed passing travellers in former times.

**hijack** *verb* seize control of (a vehicle) in order to steal its goods, take its passengers hostage, or force it to a new destination. ●*noun* a hijacking. □ **hijacker** *noun*

**hike** *noun* **1** a long walk, especially a cross-country walk taken for pleasure. **2** (*informal*) an increase; *a price hike*. ●*verb* **1** go for a hike. **2** walk laboriously. **3** (*informal*) raise; increase. □ **hiker** *noun*

**hilarious** *adjective* **1** noisily merry. **2** extremely funny. □ **hilariously** *adverb*, **hilarity** (hi-**la**-riti) *noun*

**Hilary**, St (*c*.315–*c*.367), bishop of Poitiers. Feast day, 13 or 14 January.

**hill** *noun* **1** a natural elevation of the earth's surface not as high as a mountain. **2** a slope in a road etc. **3** a heap or mound.

□ **over the hill** (*informal*) past the prime of life.

**Hillary**, Sir Edmund (born 1919), New Zealand mountaineer, who (with Tenzing Norgay) was the first to reach the summit of Mount Everest (1953).

**hill-billy** *noun* **1** folk-music like that of the southern USA. **2** (*Amer. informal*) a person from a remote mountain area in a southern State.

**hillock** *noun* a small hill, a mound.

**hillside** *noun* the sloping side of a hill.

**hilly** *adjective* full of hills. □ **hilliness** *noun*

**hilt** *noun* the handle of a sword or dagger etc. □ **to the hilt** completely; *his guilt was proved up to the hilt*.

**him** *pronoun* **1** the objective case of HE; *we saw him*. **2** (*informal*) = HE; *it's him all right*.

**Himachal Pradesh** (him-**ah**-chăl prǎ-desh) a State in northern India.

**Himalayas** (him-ă-**lay**-ăz) *plural noun* a system of high mountains in Nepal and adjacent countries. □ **Himalayan** *adjective*

**himself** *pronoun* **1** the emphatic and reflexive form of *he* and *him*; *he told me himself*; *he cut himself*. **2** in his normal state; *he is not himself today*. □ **by himself** *see* ONESELF.

**hind** *noun* a female deer. ●*adjective* situated at the back; *hind legs*.

**Hindemith** (**hin**-dĕ-mit), Paul (1895–1963), German composer, living in the USA from the 1930s.

**hinder**[1] (**hin**-der) *verb* keep (a person or thing) back by delaying progress.

**hinder**[2] (**hynd**-er) *adjective* hind; *the hinder part*.

**Hindi** (**hin**-di) *noun* **1** one of the official languages of India, a literary form of Hindustani. **2** a group of spoken languages of northern India.

**hindmost** *adjective* furthest behind.

**hindquarters** *plural noun* the hind legs and parts adjoining these of a four-legged animal.

**hindrance** *noun* **1** something that hinders. **2** hindering, being hindered; *went forward without hindrance*.

**hindsight** *noun* wisdom about an event after it has occurred.

**Hindu** *noun* a person whose religion is Hinduism. ●*adjective* of the Hindus.

**Hinduism** (**hin**-doo-izm) *noun* a religion and philosophy of India, with a caste system and belief in reincarnation.

**Hindu Kush** (*pronounced* kuush) a range of high mountains in northern Pakistan and Afghanistan which forms a westward continuation of the Himalayas.

**Hindustani** (hin-dŭ-**stah**-ni) *noun* the language of much of northern India and (as colloquial Urdu) Pakistan.

**hinge** noun **1** a joint on which a lid, door, etc. turns or swings. **2** a principle on which all depends. ●verb **1** attach or be attached by a hinge or hinges. **2** (foll. by *on*) depend; *everything hinges on this meeting.*

**hinny** noun the offspring of a female donkey and a male horse.

**hint** noun **1** a slight indication, a suggestion made indirectly. **2** a small piece of practical information; *household hints.* ●verb make a hint. □ **hint at** refer indirectly to.

**hinterland** noun **1** a district lying behind a coast etc. **2** an area served by a port or other centre. **3** a remote or fringe area.

**hip**[1] noun the projection formed by the pelvis and upper part of the thigh-bone on each side of the body. □ **hip-bath** noun a small portable bath in which a person can sit immersed to the hips. **hip-bone** noun the bone forming the hip. **hip-flask** noun a small flask for spirits etc.

**hip**[2] noun the fruit (red when ripe) of the wild rose.

**hip**[3] interjection used in cheering; *hip, hip, hooray.*

**hip**[4] adjective (also **hep**) (*slang*) trendy, stylish. □ **hip hop** a youth culture combining rap music, graffiti art, and break-dancing.

**hippie** noun (also **hippy**) (*informal*) (especially in the 1960s) a person rejecting conventional ideas and clothes, typically with long hair, beads, etc., and using hallucinogenic drugs.

**hippo** noun (*plural* **hippos**) (*informal*) a hippopotamus.

**Hippocratic** (hip-ŏ-**krat**-ik) adjective of Hippocrates, a Greek physician of the 5th century BC. □ **Hippocratic oath** an oath (formerly taken by those beginning medical practice) to observe the code of professional behaviour.

**hippodrome** noun **1** (in names) a music-hall or dancehall. **2** (in classical antiquity) a course for chariot races etc.

**hippopotamus** noun (*plural* **hippopotamuses** or **hippopotami**) a large African river animal with tusks, short legs, and thick dark skin.

**hippy** alternative spelling of HIPPIE.

**hipsters** plural noun trousers hanging from the hips rather than from the waist.

**hire** verb **1** purchase the temporary use of (a thing); *hired a van.* **2** (especially *Amer.*) employ (a person). ●noun hiring; payment for this. □ **for hire** available to be hired. **hire out** grant the temporary use of (a thing) for payment. **hire purchase** a system of purchase by payment in instalments. □ **hirer** noun

**hireable** adjective able to be hired.

**hireling** noun (*scornful*) a person who works (only) for money.

**Hirohito** (heer-ŏ-**hee**-toh) (1901–1989), emperor of Japan 1926–89.

**Hiroshima** (hi-**rosh**-im-ă) a Japanese city, target of the first atomic bomb (6 August 1945).

**hirsute** (**herss**-yoot) adjective hairy, shaggy.

**his** adjective & possessive pronoun **1** of or belonging to him; the thing(s) belonging to him. **2** used in men's titles; *His Majesty.*

**Hispanic** (hiss-**pan**-ik) adjective of Spain and other Spanish-speaking countries. ●noun a Hispanic person.

**Hispaniola** (hiss-pan-i-**oh**-lă) an island in the West Indies, divided into the States of Haiti and the Dominican Republic.

**hiss** noun a sound like that of *s.* ●verb **1** make this sound. **2** express disapproval in this way.

**histamine** (**hist**-ă-meen) noun a chemical compound present in body tissues, associated with some allergic reactions.

**histogram** (**hist**-ŏ-gram) noun a diagram used in statistics, showing the value of a number of variables by means of columns.

**histology** (hist-**ol**-ŏji) noun the study of organic tissues. □ **histological** adjective

**historian** noun an expert in history; a writer of history.

**historic** adjective famous or important in history.

**historical** adjective **1** belonging to or dealing with history or past events (as opposed to legend or prehistory); *historical novels.* **2** concerned with history; *a historical society.* □ **historically** adverb

**historicism** (hiss-**torri**-sizm) noun **1** the belief that historical events occur in accordance with certain laws of development. **2** a tendency to stress the importance of historical development and the influence of the past.

**historicity** (hiss-ter-**iss**-iti) noun the historical genuineness of an alleged event etc.

**historiography** (hiss-torri-og-**ră**fi) noun the writing of history; the study of this. □ **historiographer** noun

**history** noun **1** a continuous methodical record of important or public events. **2** the study of past events, especially of human affairs. **3** past events; those connected with a person or thing. **4** an interesting or eventful past; *the house has a history.* □ **make history** do something memorable.

**histrionic** (histri-**on**-ik) adjective dramatic or theatrical in manner. ●plural noun (**histrionics**) insincere and dramatic behaviour intended to impress people.

**hit** verb (**hit, hitting**) **1** strike with a blow or missile; aim a blow etc.; come against (a thing) with force. **2** propel (a ball etc.) with a bat or club; score runs or points in this way. **3** have an effect on (a person); cause to suffer. **4** get at, come to (a thing aimed at), find or reach (what is sought); *can't hit the high notes.* ●*noun* **1** a blow, a stroke. **2** a shot etc. that hits its target. **3** a success. □ **hit-and-run** *adjective* causing harm or damage and making off immediately. **hit back** retaliate. **hit it off** get on well (with a person). **hit list** (*slang*) **1** a list of people to be killed or eliminated. **2** a list of things against which action is planned. **hit man** (*slang*) a hired assassin. **hit on** discover suddenly or by chance. **hit-or-miss** *adjective* erratic; random. **hit the bottle** (*slang*) drink alcohol heavily. **hit the nail on the head** guess right, express the truth exactly. **hit the road** (*slang*) depart.

**hitch** *verb* **1** fasten or be fastened with a loop or hook etc. **2** move (a thing) with a slight jerk. **3** = HITCHHIKE. ●*noun* **1** a noose or knot of various kinds. **2** a temporary stoppage, a snag. **3** a slight jerk. □ **get hitched** (*informal*) get married.

**Hitchcock**, Sir Alfred Joseph (1899–1980), British film director, specializing in suspense thrillers.

**hitchhike** *verb* travel by seeking free rides in passing vehicles. □ **hitchhiker** *noun*

**hi-tech** = HIGH-TECH.

**hither** *adverb* (*formal*) to or towards this place. □ **hither and thither** to and fro.

**hitherto** *adverb* until this time.

**Hitler**, Adolf (1889–1945), Austrian-born German dictator, leader of the National Socialist (Nazi) party, whose expansionist foreign policy led to the Second World War.

**Hittite** *noun* **1** a member of a powerful people in Asia Minor and Syria *c.*1900–700 BC. **2** their language.

**HIV** *abbreviation* human immunodeficiency virus, the virus which causes Aids.

**hive** *noun* **1** a box or other container for bees to live in. **2** the bees living in this. **3** (**hives**) a skin eruption, especially nettlerash. ●*verb* gather or live in a hive. □ **hive off** separate from a larger group.

**Hizbollah** alternative spelling of HEZBOLLAH.

**HM** *abbreviation* Her (or His) Majesty('s).

**HMG** *abbreviation* Her (or His) Majesty's Government.

**HMI** *abbreviation* Her (or His) Majesty's Inspector (of Schools).

**HMS** *abbreviation* Her (or His) Majesty's Ship.

**HMSO** *abbreviation* Her (or His) Majesty's Stationery Office.

**HNC** *abbreviation* (*Brit.*) Higher National Certificate.

**HND** *abbreviation* (*Brit.*) Higher National Diploma.

**Ho** *symbol* holmium.

**ho** *interjection* an exclamation of triumph or scorn, or calling attention.

**hoard** *noun* a carefully saved and guarded store of money, food, or treasured objects. ●*verb* save and store away. □ **hoarder** *noun*

**hoarding** *noun* a fence of light boarding, often used for displaying advertisements.

**hoar-frost** *noun* a white frost.

**hoarse** *adjective* **1** (of the voice) sounding rough, as if from a dry throat. **2** (of a person) having a hoarse voice. □ **hoarsely** *adverb*, **hoarseness** *noun*

**hoary** *adjective* (**hoarier, hoariest**) **1** white or grey; *hoary hair.* **2** with hoary hair, aged. **3** (of a joke etc.) old.

**hoax** *verb* deceive jokingly. ●*noun* a joking deception. □ **hoaxer** *noun*

**hob** *noun* **1** a flat heating surface on a cooker. **2** a flat metal shelf at the side of a fireplace, where a pan etc. can be heated.

**Hobart** the capital of Tasmania.

**hobble** *verb* **1** walk lamely. **2** fasten the legs of (a horse etc.) so as to limit movement and prevent it from straying. ●*noun* **1** a hobbling walk. **2** a rope etc. for hobbling a horse.

**hobby** *noun* an activity pursued for pleasure in one's spare time.

**hobby-horse** *noun* **1** a stick with a horse's head, used as a toy. **2** a topic that a person is especially fond of discussing.

**hobgoblin** *noun* a mischievous imp.

**hobnail** *noun* a heavy-headed nail for boot-soles.

**hobnob** *verb* (**hobnobbed, hobnobbing**) spend time together, socialize; *hobnobbing with the rich and famous.*

**Hobson's choice** a situation in which there is no alternative to the thing offered. (¶ Thomas Hobson (17th century) hired out horses and made people take the one nearest the stable door.)

**Ho Chi Minh** (original name: Nguyen That Thanh) (1890–1969), Vietnamese Communist statesman, who led his country in its struggle for independence.

**Ho Chi Minh City** a city (formerly called Saigon) in southern Vietnam.

**hock**[1] *noun* the middle joint of an animal's hind leg.

**hock**[2] *noun* a German white wine from the Rhineland.

**hock**[3] *verb* (especially *Amer. informal*) pawn. □ **in hock 1** in pawn. **2** in prison. **3** in debt.

**hockey** *noun* **1** a game played on a field between two teams of players with curved sticks and a small hard ball. **2** = ICE HOCKEY.

**Hockney**, David (born 1937), English painter and draughtsman.

**hocus-pocus** *noun* trickery.

**hod** *noun* **1** a trough on a pole used by bricklayers for carrying mortar or bricks. **2** a cylindrical container for shovelling and holding coal.

**hodgepodge** = HOTCHPOTCH.

**Hodgkin's disease** a malignant disease of the lymphatic tissues, usually characterized by enlargement of the lymph nodes. (¶ Named after T. Hodgkin (died 1866), English physician.)

**hoe** *noun* a tool with a blade on a long handle, used for loosening soil or scraping up weeds. ●*verb* (**hoed, hoeing**) dig or scrape with a hoe.

**Hoffman**, Dustin Lee (born 1937), American stage and film actor.

**hog** *noun* **1** a castrated male pig reared for meat. **2** (*informal*) a greedy person. ●*verb* (**hogged, hogging**) (*informal*) take more than one's fair share of; hoard selfishly. □ **go the whole hog** (*informal*) do something thoroughly. □ **hoggish** *adjective*

**Hogarth** (**hoh**-garth), William (1697–1764), English painter and engraver.

**hogmanay** (hog-mǎ-nay) *noun* (*Scottish*) New Year's Eve.

**hogshead** *noun* **1** a large cask. **2** a liquid or dry measure (about 50 gallons).

**hogwash** *noun* (*informal*) nonsense, rubbish.

**ho-ho** *interjection* **1** representing a deep laugh. **2** expressing surprise.

**hoick** *verb* (*informal*) lift or bring out, especially with a jerk.

*hoi polloi* (hoi pǒ-**loi**) the common people, the masses. (¶ Greek, = the many.)

**hoist** *verb* raise or haul up, lift with ropes and pulleys etc. ●*noun* **1** an apparatus for hoisting things. **2** a pull or haul up; *give it a hoist*. □ **hoist with one's own petard** caught by one's own trick etc.

**hoity-toity** *adjective* haughty.

**hokum** (**hoh**-kǔm) *noun* (especially *Amer. slang*) **1** sentimental, sensational, or unreal material in a play, film, etc. **2** nonsense.

**Holbein** (**hol**-byn), Hans (1497/8–1543), German painter, who worked at the court of Henry VIII in London and is noted for his portraits.

**hold**[1] *verb* (**held, holding**) **1** take and keep in one's arms, hand(s), etc. **2** keep in a particular position or condition; grasp or keep so as to control; detain in custody. **3** be able to contain; *this jug holds two pints*. **4** have in one's possession or as something one has gained; *he holds the record for the high jump*. **5** support, bear the weight of. **6** remain unbroken under strain; *the rope failed to hold*. **7** continue, remain valid; *will the fine weather hold?*; *the law still holds*. **8** keep possession of (a place or position etc.) against attack. **9** keep (a person's at-

tention) by being interesting. **10** have the position of, occupy (a job etc.); *held the directorship*. **11** cause to take place, conduct; *hold a meeting*. **12** restrain, cause to cease action or movement etc. **13** believe, consider; assert. **14** (in telephoning) hold the line (see below and *on hold*). ●*noun* **1** the act or manner of holding something. **2** an opportunity or means of holding. **3** (foll. by *on, over*) a means of exerting influence on a person. □ **get hold of 1** acquire. **2** make contact with (a person). **hold back 1** prevent (a person) from doing something. **2** hesitate; refrain. **hold down** be competent enough to keep (one's job). **hold forth** speak lengthily. **hold good** remain valid. **hold it!** cease action etc. **hold off** wait, not begin; *the rain held off*. **hold on 1** keep one's grasp of something. **2** refrain from ringing off (on the telephone). **3** (*informal*) wait! **hold one's ground** *or* **hold one's own** stand firm, refuse to yield. **hold one's peace** (*or* **tongue**) keep silent. **hold out 1** offer (an inducement or hope). **2** last; *if supplies hold out*. **hold out for** refuse to accept anything other than. **hold out on** (*informal*) conceal something from; refuse the requests etc. of. **hold over** postpone. **hold the fort** act as a temporary substitute; cope in an emergency. **hold the line** refrain from ringing off (on the telephone). **hold up 1** hinder. **2** stop by the use of threats or force for the purpose of robbery. **hold-up** *noun* **1** a stoppage or delay. **2** robbery by armed robbers. **hold water** (of reasoning) be sound. **hold with** (*slang*) approve of; *we don't hold with bribery*. **no holds barred** all methods are permitted. **on hold 1** postponed; awaiting action. **2** (of a telephone connection) held open automatically until the person called is free to deal with the call. **take hold** grasp; become established. □ **holder** *noun*

**hold**[2] *noun* a cavity in the lower part of a ship or aircraft, where cargo is stored.

**holdall** *noun* a large soft travelling bag.

**holding** *noun* something held or owned; land held by an owner or tenant. □ **holding company** one formed to hold the shares of other companies which it then controls.

**hole** *noun* **1** an empty place in a solid body or mass; a sunken place on a surface. **2** an animal's burrow. **3** a small, dark, or wretched place. **4** (*informal*) an awkward situation. **5** a hollow or cavity into which a ball etc. must be sent in various games. **6** a section of a golf course between tee and hole; a point scored by a player who reaches the hole with the fewest strokes. **7** an opening through something. ●*verb* make a hole or holes in; *the ship was holed*. □ **hole-and-corner** *adjective* underhand.

**hole in the heart** (*informal*) a congenital defect in the heart membrane. **hole-in-the-wall** noun **1** a small dingy establishment. **2** (*informal*) a cash dispensing machine in the wall of a bank etc. **hole out** get the ball into the hole in golf. **hole up** (*Amer. informal*) hide oneself. **make a hole in** (*informal*) use a large amount of (one's supply).

**holey** *adjective* full of holes.

**Holi** (**hoh**-li) *noun* a Hindu spring festival celebrated in February or March.

**Holiday**, Billie (original name: Eleanora Fagan) (1915–59), American jazz singer.

**holiday** *noun* **1** (also **holidays**) an extended period of recreation, especially spent away from home or travelling; a break from work. **2** a day of festivity or recreation, when no work is done. ● *verb* (**holidayed**, **holidaying**) spend a holiday. □ **holidaymaker** *noun* a person who is on holiday.

**holiness** *noun* being holy or sacred. □ **His Holiness** the title of the pope.

**holism** (**hoh**-lizm) *noun* (also **wholism**) **1** the theory that certain wholes are greater than the sum of their parts. **2** *Med.* treating of the whole person rather than the symptoms of a disease. □ **holistic** (hŏ-**lis**-tik) *adjective*

**Holland** the Netherlands.

**hollandaise sauce** (hol-ăn-**dayz**) a creamy sauce containing butter, egg yolks, and vinegar.

**holler** (*informal*) *verb* shout. ● *noun* a shout.

**hollow** *adjective* **1** having a hole inside, not solid. **2** sunken; *hollow cheeks*. **3** (of sound) echoing, as if from something hollow. **4** empty, worthless; *a hollow triumph*. **5** insincere; *a hollow laugh*. ● *noun* a hollow or sunken place, a hole, a valley. ● *adverb* completely; *beat them hollow*. ● *verb* (often foll. by *out*) make or become hollow. □ **hollowly** *adverb*, **hollowness** *noun*

**holly** *noun* an evergreen shrub with prickly leaves and red berries.

**hollyhock** *noun* a plant with large showy flowers on a tall stem.

**Hollywood** a district of Los Angeles, centre of the American film-making industry.

**holm** (*pronounced* as home) *noun* (in full **holm-oak**) an evergreen oak with holly-like leaves.

**Holmes**, Sherlock, a fictional private detective, the central figure in a number of stories by Conan Doyle.

**holmium** (**hohl**-mi-ŭm) *noun* a silvery soft metallic element (symbol Ho).

**holocaust** (**hol**-ŏ-kawst) *noun* **1** large-scale destruction, especially by fire. **2** (**the Holocaust**) the mass murder of Jews by Nazis in 1939–45.

**Holocene** (**hol**-ŏ-seen) *adjective Geol.* of the second of the two epochs of the Quaternary period, lasting from about 10,000 years ago to the present day. ● *noun* this epoch.

**hologram** (**hol**-ŏ-gram) *noun* an image produced (without using lenses) on photographic film in such a way that under suitable illumination a three-dimensional representation of an object is seen. □ **holographic** *adjective*, **holography** *noun*

**holograph** (**hol**-ŏ-grahf) *noun* a document that is handwritten by its author.

**hols** *plural noun* (*informal*) holidays.

**Holst** (*pronounced* hohlst), Gustav (1874–1934), English composer, best known for his orchestral suite *The Planets*.

**holster** (**hohl**-ster) *noun* a leather case for a pistol or revolver, worn fixed to a belt.

**holy** *adjective* (**holier**, **holiest**) **1** morally and spiritually excellent or perfect, and to be revered. **2** consecrated, sacred; *holy water*. **3** devoted to God; *a holy man*. □ **holier-than-thou** *adjective* self-righteous. **Holy Communion** *see* COMMUNION. **Holy Ghost** = HOLY SPIRIT. **Holy Grail** *see* GRAIL. **holy of holies 1** a place or thing regarded as most sacred. **2** the sacred inner chamber of the Jewish temple. **holy orders** the status of a bishop, priest, or deacon. **Holy Shroud** a relic venerated as the winding-sheet in which Christ's body was wrapped for burial, preserved at Turin in Italy since 1578. **Holy Spirit** the Third Person of the Trinity, God acting spiritually. **Holy Week** the week before Easter Sunday. **Holy Writ** the Bible.

**Holy Island** *see* LINDISFARNE.

**Holy Land** the part of Palestine west of the Jordan, revered by Christians.

**Holy Roman Empire** the empire set up in western Europe following the coronation of Charlemagne (800) and ruled by Frankish or German rulers bearing the title of Emperor until abolished by Napoleon in 1806.

**Holy See** the papacy or papal court; those people associated with the pope in the government of the Roman Catholic Church at its headquarters in Rome.

**homage** *noun* **1** things said as a mark of respect; *paid homage to his achievements*. **2** a formal expression of loyalty to a ruler.

**Homburg** *noun* a man's felt hat with a narrow curled brim and a lengthwise dent in the crown.

**home** *noun* **1** the place where one lives, especially with one's family. **2** one's native land; the district where one was born or where one has lived for a long time or to which one feels attached. **3** a dwelling-house. **4** an institution where those needing care may live; *an old people's home*. **5** the natural environment of an animal or plant. **6** the place to be reached by a runner in a race or in certain games. **7** *Sport* a home match or win. ●*adjective* **1** of or connected with one's own home or country; done or produced there; *home industries; home produce.* **2** played on one's own ground; *a home match.* ●*adverb* **1** to or at one's home; *go home.* **2** to the point aimed at; right in; *the thrust went home; drive a nail home.* ●*verb* **1** (of a trained pigeon) fly home. **2** (often foll. by *in on*) be guided to a target; make for a particular destination. □ **at home 1** in one's own home or country. **2** at ease; comfortable or familiar. **3** available to visitors. **bring home to** cause to realize fully. **home and dry** having achieved one's aim. **home-bird** *noun* a person who enjoys home life and staying at home. **homecoming** *noun* arrival at home. **Home Counties** the counties nearest to London. **home economics** the study of household management, e.g. cookery and needlework. **home farm** a farm worked by the owner of an estate on which there are other farms. **home from home** a place (other than home) where one feels comfortable and at home. **home-grown** *adjective* grown at home. **Home Guard** (*hist.*) a British part-time volunteer army organized for defence in 1940. **home help** a person who helps with housework etc., especially in a service organized by local authorities. **home-made** *adjective* made at home. **home movie** a film made at home or of one's own activities. **Home Office** the British government department dealing with law and order and immigration in England and Wales. **home rule** government of a country by its own citizens. **home run** a hit in baseball that allows the batter to make a complete circuit of the bases. **Home Secretary** the government minister in charge of the Home Office. **home straight** or **stretch** the stretch of a racecourse between the last turn and the finishing line. **home truth** an unpleasant truth that a person is made to realize about himself or herself.

**homeland** *noun* **1** one's native land. **2** (formerly) any of the partially self-governing areas in South Africa reserved under the apartheid system for Black South Africans (the official name for a Bantustan).

**homeless** *adjective* lacking a home. □ **homelessness** *noun*

**homely** *adjective* **1** simple and informal, not pretentious. **2** (*Amer.*) (of a person's appearance) plain, not beautiful. **3** comfortable, cosy. □ **homeliness** *noun*

**homeopathy** Amer. spelling of HOMOEOPATHY.

**Homer** (?*c.*700 BC) Greek epic poet, traditionally the author of the *Iliad* and the *Odyssey.*

**Homeric** (hoh-**merrik**) *adjective* of the writings or heroes of Homer.

**homesick** *adjective* feeling depressed through longing for one's home when one is away from it. □ **homesickness** *noun*

**homespun** *adjective* **1** made of yarn spun at home. **2** plain, simple. ●*noun* homespun fabric.

**homestead** (**hohm**-sted) *noun* a farmhouse or similar building with the land and buildings round it.

**homeward** *adjective* going towards home. ●*adverb* (also **homewards**) towards home.

**homework** *noun* **1** work that a pupil is required to do away from school. **2** preparatory work to be done before a discussion etc. takes place.

**homey** *adjective* (also **homy**) like home, homely.

**homicide** (**hom**-i-syd) *noun* **1** the killing of one person by another. **2** a person who kills another. □ **homicidal** *adjective*

**homily** *noun* a sermon, a moralizing lecture. □ **homiletic** (hom-i-**let**-ik) *adjective*

**homing** *adjective* **1** (of a pigeon) trained to fly home. **2** (of a device) for guiding to a target etc.

**hominid** (**hom**-in-id) *noun* a member of the zoological family that includes humans and their extinct ancestors. ●*adjective* of this family.

**hominoid** (**hom**-in-oid) *noun* an animal resembling a human. ●*adjective* like a human.

**homo** (**hoh**-moh) *noun* (*plural* **homos**) (*informal, offensive*) a homosexual.

**homoeopathy** (hohm-i-**op**-ă-thi) *noun* (*Amer.* **homeopathy**) treatment of disease with very small doses of drugs etc. that in a healthy person would produce symptoms like those of the disease itself. □ **homoeopath** (**hohm**-i-ŏ-path) *noun,* **homeopathic** *adjective,* **homoeopathist** *noun*

**homogeneous** (hom-ŏ-**jee**-niŭs) *adjective* of the same kind as the others; formed of parts that are all of the same kind. □ **homogeneity** (hom-ŏ-jin-ee-iti) *noun*

**homogenize** (hŏ-**moj**-i-nyz) *verb* (also **homogenise**) treat (milk) so that the particles of fat are broken down and the cream does not separate. □ **homogenization** *noun*

**homograph** (**homo**-ŏ-grahf) *noun* a word that is spelt like another but has a different meaning or origin, e.g. *bat* (a flying animal) and *bat* (for striking a ball).

**homologous** (hŏm-**ol**-ŏ-gŭs) *adjective* **1** having the same relation or relative position, corresponding. **2** *Biology* (of organs etc.) similar in position or structure but not in function.

**homology** (hŏm-**ol**-ŏji) *noun* a homologous state or relation.

**homonym** (hom-ŏ-nim) *noun* a word of the same spelling or sound as another but with a different meaning, e.g. *grate* (= fire-place), *grate* (= to rub), *great* (= large).

**homophobia** (hom-ŏ-**fohb**-i-ă) *noun* hatred or fear of homosexuals. □ **homophobe** *noun*, **homophobic** *adjective*

**homophone** (hom-ŏ-fohn) *noun* a word with the same sound as another, e.g. *son*, *sun*.

**Homo sapiens** (hoh-moh **sap**-i-enz) modern humans regarded as a species. (¶ Latin, = wise man.)

**homosexual** (hoh-mŏ-**seks**-yoo-ăl) *adjective* feeling sexually attracted only to people of the same sex as oneself. ●*noun* a homo-sexual person. □ **homosexuality** *noun*

**homy** alternative spelling of HOMEY.

**Hon.** *abbreviation* **1** Honorary. **2** Honourable.

**Honduras** (hon-**dewr**-ăs) a country in Central America. □ **Honduran** *adjective* & *noun*

**hone** (*rhymes with* stone) *noun* a fine-grained stone used for sharpening razors and tools. ●*verb* **1** sharpen on this. **2** polish or refine (reasoning etc.).

**Honecker** (hon-ĕk-er), Erich (born 1912), East German head of State 1976–89.

**honest** *adjective* **1** fair and just; not cheating or stealing. **2** free of deceit and lies; sincere. **3** (of gain etc.) got by fair means; *earn an honest living.* □ **honest-to-goodness** *adjective* (*informal*) genuine, straightforward.

**honestly** *adverb* **1** in an honest way. **2** really; *that's all I know, honestly.*

**honesty** *noun* **1** being honest. **2** a plant with seeds that form in round translucent pods.

**honey** *noun* (*plural* **honeys**) **1** a sweet sticky yellowish substance made by bees from nectar. **2** its colour. **3** sweetness, pleasantness; a sweet thing. **4** (especially *Amer.*) darling. □ **honey-bee** *noun* the common bee that lives in a hive.

**honeycomb** *noun* **1** a bees' wax structure of six-sided cells for holding their honey and eggs. **2** a pattern or arrangement of six-sided sections. ●*verb* **1** fill with holes or tunnels; *the rock was honeycombed with passages.* **2** mark or sew in a honeycomb pattern.

**honeydew** *noun* **1** a sweet sticky substance found on leaves and stems, secreted by aphids. **2** a variety of melon with pale skin and sweet green flesh.

**honeyed** *adjective* flattering, pleasant; *honeyed words.*

**honeymoon** *noun* **1** a holiday spent together by a newly-married couple. **2** an initial period of enthusiasm or goodwill. ●*verb* spend a honeymoon. □ **honeymooner** *noun*

**honeysuckle** *noun* a climbing shrub with fragrant yellow and pink flowers.

**Hong Kong** a British dependency on the SE coast of China, over which China will resume sovereignty in 1997.

**Honiara** (hoh-ni-**ar**-ă) the capital of the Solomon Islands.

**honk** *noun* a loud harsh sound; the cry of the wild goose; the sound made by an old-style motor horn. ●*verb* make a honk, sound (a horn).

**honky-tonk** *noun* **1** ragtime piano music. **2** a cheap or disreputable nightclub.

**Honolulu** the capital of Hawaii.

**honor** Amer. spelling of HONOUR.

**honorable** Amer. spelling of HONOURABLE.

**honorarium** (on-er-**air**-iŭm) *noun* (*plural* **honorariums** *or* **honoraria**) a voluntary payment made for services where no fee is legally required.

**honorary** (**on**-er-ă-ri) *adjective* **1** given as an honour; *an honorary degree.* **2** (of an office or its holder) unpaid; *the honorary treasurer.*

**honorific** (on-er-**if**-ik) *adjective* conferring honour; implying respect.

**honour** *noun* (*Amer.* **honor**) **1** great respect, high public regard. **2** a mark of this; a privilege given or received; *had the honour of being invited.* **3** a source of this; a person or thing that brings honour; *an honour to her profession.* **4** good personal character; a reputation for honesty and loyalty etc. **5** a title of respect given to certain judges or people of importance; *your Honour.* **6** the right of driving off first in golf, held by the player who won the previous hole. **7** (in certain card games) any of the four or five cards of the highest value. **8** (**honours**) a specialized degree course or special distinction in an examination. ●*verb* **1** respect highly. **2** confer honour on. **3** acknowledge and pay (a cheque etc. when it is due). **4** observe the terms of (an agreement). □ **do the honours** perform the usual civilities to guests or visitors etc. **honours degree** a university degree requiring a higher level of attainment than a pass degree. **honours list** a list of people awarded honours by the sovereign. **in honour bound** *or* **on one's honour** under a moral obligation to do something.

**honourable** *adjective* (*Amer.* **honorable**) **1** deserving honour. **2** possessing or showing honour. ●*adjective* (**Honourable**) the courtesy title of certain high officials and judges, also of the children of viscounts and barons, the younger sons of earls, and used during debates by MPs to one another. □ **honourably** adverb

**hooch** noun (Amer. informal) alcohol, especially illicitly distilled whisky.

**hood** noun **1** a covering for the head and neck, especially as part of a garment. **2** a separate hoodlike garment. **3** something resembling a hood in shape or use, e.g. a folding roof over a car, a canopy over a machine etc. **4** (Amer.) the bonnet of a car. **5** (Amer. slang) a gangster or gunman.

**hooded** adjective **1** having a hood. **2** (of animals) having a hoodlike part.

**hoodlum** noun **1** a hooligan, a young thug. **2** a gangster.

**hoodoo** noun (Amer.) **1** a thing or person thought to cause bad luck. **2** = VOODOO.

**hoodwink** verb deceive.

**hooey** noun (slang) nonsense.

**hoof** noun (plural **hoofs** or **hooves**) the horny part of the foot of a horse and other animals. □ **hoof it** (slang) go on foot.

**hoo-ha** noun (slang) a commotion.

**hook** noun **1** a bent or curved piece of metal etc. for catching hold or for hanging things on. **2** something shaped like this, e.g. a projecting point of land; the Hook of Holland. **3** a curved cutting tool; reaping hook. **4** (in cricket or golf) a hooked stroke. **5** (in boxing) a short swinging blow with the elbow bent. ●verb **1** grasp or catch with a hook; fasten with a hook or hooks. **2** (slang) obtain; steal. **3** propel (a ball) in a curving path. **4** (in Rugby) pass (the ball) backward with the foot. □ **by hook or by crook** by some means no matter what happens. **hook and eye** a small metal hook and loop for fastening a garment. **hook, line, and sinker** entirely. **hook-up** noun (informal) interconnection of broadcasting equipment. **off the hook** **1** (informal) freed from a difficulty. **2** (of a telephone receiver) not on its rest.

**hookah** (**huuk**-ă) noun an oriental tobacco pipe with a long tube passing through a glass container of water that cools the smoke as it is drawn through.

**Hooke,** Robert (1635–1703), English scientist and inventor.

**hooked** adjective **1** hook-shaped; a hooked nose. **2** (often foll. by on) (slang) addicted or captivated.

**hooker** noun **1** Rugby a player in the front row of the scrum, who tries to get the ball by hooking it. **2** (slang) a prostitute.

**hookey** noun □ **play hookey** (Amer. slang) play truant.

**hookworm** noun a worm with hook like mouth parts, which can infest the intestines of humans and animals.

**hooligan** noun a young ruffian. □ **hooliganism** noun

**hoop** noun **1** a band of metal or wood etc. forming part of a framework. **2** this used as a child's toy for bowling along the ground, or for circus performers to jump through. **3** a small iron arch used in croquet. ●verb bind or encircle with hoops. □ **be put** (or **go**) **through the hoops** undergo a test or ordeal.

**hoop-la** noun a game in which rings are thrown to encircle a prize.

**hoopoe** (**hoo**-poo) noun a bird with a fan-like crest and striped wings and tail.

**hooray** = HURRAH. □ **Hooray Henry** (Brit. slang) a loud upper-class young man.

**hoot** noun **1** the cry of an owl. **2** the sound made by a vehicle's horn or a steam whistle. **3** a cry expressing scorn or disapproval. **4** (informal) laughter; a cause of this. ●verb **1** make a hoot or hoots. **2** receive or drive away with scornful hoots. **3** sound (a horn). □ **not care** or **give a hoot** or **two hoots** (slang) not care at all.

**hooter** noun **1** a thing that hoots, e.g. a car horn. **2** (slang) a nose.

**Hoover**[1] noun (trade mark) a vacuum cleaner. ●verb (**hoover**) clean (a carpet etc.) with a vacuum cleaner.

**Hoover**[2], Herbert Clark (1874–1964), 31st President of the USA 1929–33.

**Hoover**[3] J(ohn) Edgar (1895–1972), American lawyer and FBI director.

**hooves** see HOOF.

**hop**[1] verb (**hopped, hopping**) **1** (of an animal) spring from all feet at once. **2** (of a person) jump on one foot. **3** cross by hopping. **4** move or go quickly. ●noun **1** a hopping movement. **2** an informal dance. **3** a short journey, especially a flight. □ **hop in** or **out** (informal) get into or out of a car. **hopping mad** (informal) very angry. **hop it** (slang) go away. **on the hop** (informal) unprepared; we were caught on the hop.

**hop**[2] noun **1** a climbing plant cultivated for its cones which are used for giving a bitter flavour to beer. **2** (**hops**) the ripe cones of this plant.

**Hope,** Bob (original name: Leslie Townes) (born 1903), American film actor and comedian.

**hope** noun **1** a feeling of expectation and desire combined; a desire for certain events to happen. **2** a person, thing, or circumstance that gives cause for this. **3** what is hoped for. ●verb feel hope, expect and desire, feel fairly confident. □ **hoping against hope** hoping for something that is barely possible.

**hopeful** adjective **1** feeling hope. **2** causing hope, seeming likely to be favourable or successful. ●noun a person who hopes or seems likely to succeed; young hopefuls.

**hopefully** adverb **1** in a hopeful way. **2** it is to be hoped; *hopefully, we shall be there by one o'clock*.

▪**Usage** Many people regard the use in sense 2 as unacceptable.

**hopeless** adjective **1** feeling no hope. **2** admitting no hope; *a hopeless case*. **3** inadequate, incompetent; *is hopeless at tennis*. □ **hopelessly** adverb, **hopelessness** noun

**Hopkins**, Gerard Manley (1844–89), English poet.

**hopper** noun **1** a hopping insect. **2** a V-shaped container with an opening at the base through which its contents can be discharged into a machine etc.

**hopscotch** noun a children's game of hopping and jumping over marked squares to retrieve a stone tossed into these.

**Horace** (Quintus Horatius Flaccus) (65–8 BC), Roman poet, whose works include lyric verse and satires.

**horde** noun a large group or crowd.

**horehound** noun a herb with woolly leaves and white flowers, producing a bitter juice used against coughs.

**horizon** noun **1** the line at which earth and sky appear to meet. **2** the limit of a person's experience, knowledge, or interests. □ **on the horizon** (of an event) about to happen, just becoming apparent.

**horizontal** adjective parallel to the horizon; at right angles to the vertical. □ **horizontally** adverb

**hormone** (**hor**-mohn) noun a regulatory substance produced within the body of an animal or plant (or made synthetically) and carried by the blood or sap to stimulate cells or tissues into action. □ **hormone replacement therapy** treatment to relieve menopausal symptoms by boosting a woman's oestrogen levels. □ **hormonal** (hor-**moh**-năl) adjective

**Hormuz** (hor-**muuz**), **Strait of** a strait separating Iran from the Arabian peninsula, through which sea traffic from the oil-rich States of the Persian Gulf must pass.

**horn** noun **1** a hard pointed outgrowth on the heads of certain animals. **2** the hard smooth substance of which this consists. **3** a projection resembling a horn. **4** any of various wind instruments (originally made of horn, now usually of brass) with a trumpet-shaped end; the French horn (*see* FRENCH). **5** a device for sounding a warning signal. **6** (**the Horn**) Cape Horn. □ **Horn of Africa** (also called the Somali Peninsula) the peninsula of NE Africa comprising Somalia and parts of Ethiopia, separating the Gulf of Aden from the main part of the Indian Ocean. **horn of plenty** a cornucopia. **horn-rimmed** adjective (of

spectacles) with frames made of a material like horn or tortoiseshell. □ **horned** adjective

**hornbeam** noun a tree with hard tough wood, often used in hedges.

**hornbill** noun a tropical bird with a hornlike projection on its beak.

**hornblende** noun a black, green, or dark brown mineral.

**hornet** noun a large kind of wasp inflicting a serious sting. □ **stir up a hornets' nest** cause an outbreak of angry feeling.

**hornpipe** noun a lively dance usually for one person, traditionally associated with sailors.

**horny** adjective (**hornier**, **horniest**) **1** of or like horn. **2** hardened and calloused; *horny hands*. **3** (*slang*) sexually excited.

**horology** (hŏ-**rol**-ŏji) noun the art of measuring time or of making clocks and watches. □ **horological** adjective

**horoscope** noun a forecast of a person's future, based on an astrologer's diagram showing the relative positions of the planets and stars at a particular time.

**horrendous** adjective horrifying. □ **horrendously** adverb

**horrible** adjective **1** causing horror. **2** (*informal*) unpleasant. □ **horribly** adverb

**horrid** adjective horrible. □ **horridly** adverb

**horrific** adjective horrifying. □ **horrifically** adverb

**horrify** verb (**horrified**, **horrifying**) arouse horror in, shock. □ **horrifying** adjective

**horror** noun **1** a feeling of loathing and fear. **2** intense dislike or dismay. **3** a person or thing causing horror. **4** (**the horrors**) a fit of horror or depression. □ **horror film** one full of violence presented sensationally for entertainment.

**hors d'oeuvre** (or-**dervr**) noun food served as an appetizer at the start of a meal. (¶ French.)

**horse** noun **1** a four-legged animal with a flowing mane and tail, used for riding on or to carry or pull loads. **2** an adult male horse. **3** cavalry. **4** a frame on which something is supported, a clothes-horse. **5** a vaulting-block. □ **horse around** (*informal*) fool about. **horse brass** a brass ornament originally for a horse's harness. **horse-drawn** adjective (of a vehicle) pulled by a horse. **Horse Guards** (*Brit.*) a cavalry brigade of the household troops. **horse-laugh** noun a loud coarse laugh. **horse race** a race between horses with riders. **horse racing** the sport of conducting horse races. **horse sense** (*informal*) plain common sense. **straight from the horse's mouth** (of information) from a first-hand source.

**horseback** noun □ **on horseback** mounted on a horse.

**horsebox** *noun* a closed vehicle for transporting a horse.

**horse chestnut 1** a large tree with conical clusters of white, pink, or red flowers. **2** its dark brown fruit.

**horseflesh** *noun* **1** the flesh of horses, as food. **2** horses; *a good judge of horseflesh*.

**horsefly** *noun* a large biting fly, especially troublesome to horses.

**horsehair** *noun* hair from a horse's mane or tail, used for padding furniture etc.

**horseman** *noun* (*plural* **horsemen**) a rider on horseback, especially a skilled one. □ **horsemanship** *noun*

**horseplay** *noun* boisterous play.

**horsepower** *noun* (*plural* **horsepower**) a unit for measuring the power of an engine (550 foot-pounds per second, about 750 watts).

**horseradish** *noun* a plant with a strong-tasting root used to make a sauce.

**horseshoe** *noun* **1** a U-shaped strip of metal nailed to a horse's hoof. **2** anything shaped like this.

**horsewhip** *noun* a whip for horses. ●*verb* (**horsewhipped**, **horsewhipping**) beat with a horsewhip.

**horsewoman** *noun* (*plural* **horsewomen**) a woman rider on horseback, especially a skilled one.

**horsy** *adjective* **1** of or like a horse. **2** interested in horses.

**hortative** (**hor-tă-tiv**) *adjective* = HORTATORY.

**hortatory** (**hor-tă-teri**) *adjective* exhorting, encouraging.

**horticulture** *noun* the art of garden cultivation. □ **horticultural** *adjective*, **horticulturist** *noun*

**hosanna** *interjection & noun* a cry of adoration.

**hose** *noun* **1** (also **hose-pipe**) a flexible tube for conveying water etc. **2** stockings and socks. **3** (*old use*) breeches; *doublet and hose*. ●*verb* (often foll. by *down*) water or spray with a hose; *hose the car down*.

**Hosea** (**hoh-zee-ă**) **1** a Hebrew minor prophet of the 8th century BC. **2** a book of the Old Testament containing his prophecies.

**hosier** *noun* a dealer in hosiery.

**hosiery** *noun* stockings and socks.

**hospice** (**hos-pis**) *noun* **1** a home for destitute or sick people, especially the terminally ill. **2** a lodging-house for travellers, especially one kept by a religious order.

**hospitable** (**hos-pit-ăbŭl**) *adjective* giving hospitality, welcoming. □ **hospitably** *adverb*

**hospital** *noun* **1** an institution providing medical and surgical treatment for people who are ill or injured. **2** (*old use*) a hospice.

**hospitality** *noun* friendly and generous reception and entertainment of guests.

**hospitalize** (**hos-pit-ă-lyz**) *verb* (also **hospitalise**) send or admit (a patient) to a hospital. □ **hospitalization** *noun*

**host**[1] *noun* a large number of people or things.

**host**[2] *noun* **1** a person who receives and entertains another as a guest. **2** a compère. **3** an organism on which another organism lives as a parasite. ●*verb* act as host to (a person) or at (an event).

**host**[3] *noun* (often **the Host**) the bread consecrated in the Eucharist.

**hostage** *noun* a person held as security that the holder's demands will be satisfied.

**hostel** *noun* a lodging-house for young travellers, students, or other special groups.

**hostelling** *noun* (*Amer.* **hosteling**) the practice of staying in youth hostels. □ **hosteller** *noun*

**hostelry** *noun* (*old use*) an inn.

**hostess** *noun* **1** a woman who receives and entertains a person as her guest. **2** a woman employed to welcome and entertain people at a nightclub etc.

**hostile** *adjective* **1** of an enemy; *hostile aircraft*. **2** unfriendly, opposed; *a hostile glance; they are hostile towards reform.* □ **hostilely** *adverb*

**hostility** *noun* **1** being hostile, enmity. **2** (**hostilities**) acts of warfare.

**hot** *adjective* (**hotter, hottest**) **1** having great heat or high temperature; giving off heat; feeling heat. **2** producing a burning sensation to the taste. **3** angry; excited, excitable; *a hot temper*. **4** (often foll. by *on*) eager, keen; *in hot pursuit; he's hot on punctuality.* **5** (of the scent in hunting) fresh and strong; (of news) fresh. **6** (*informal*) (of a player) very skilful. **7** (*informal*) (foll. by *on*) knowledgeable about. **8** (of jazz etc.) strongly rhythmical and emotional. **9** (*slang*) radioactive. **10** (*slang*) (of goods etc.) recently stolen, difficult to dispose of because identifiable. □ **have the hots for** (*slang*) be sexually attracted to. **hot air** (*slang*) empty or boastful talk. **hot-blooded** *adjective* excitable; passionate. **hot cross bun** a bun marked with a cross, traditionally eaten hot on Good Friday. **hot dog** a hot sausage sandwiched in a roll of bread. **hot gospeller** (*informal*) an eager and enthusiastic preacher of the gospel. **hot potato** (*informal*) a situation etc. likely to cause trouble to the person handling it. **hot rod** a motor vehicle modified to have extra power and speed. **hot seat** (*slang*) **1** the position of someone who has difficult responsibilities. **2** the electric chair. **hot stuff** (*informal*) **1** a person or thing of high spirit or skill or passions. **2** a sexually attractive person. **3** an erotic book, film, etc. **hot-tempered** *adjective* easily becoming angry. **hot under the collar** angry, resentful, or embarrassed. **hot up** (**hotted, hotting**) (*informal*) **1** make or become hot. **2** make or become more active, exciting, or dangerous. **hot-water bottle** a rubber container filled with hot water for warmth in bed. **in hot water** (*informal*) in trouble or disgrace. **make it** (*or* **things**) **hot for a person** make it uncomfortable for him or her by persecution. **sell like hot cakes** sell very readily. □ **hotly** adverb, **hotness** noun

**hotbed** noun **1** a bed of earth heated by fermenting manure. **2** a place favourable to the growth of vice, intrigue, etc.

**hotchpotch** noun (also **hodgepodge**) a jumble.

**hotel** noun a building where meals and rooms are provided for payment.

**hotelier** (hoh-**tel**-i-er) noun a hotel-keeper.

**hotfoot** adverb in eager haste.

**hothead** noun an impetuous person. □ **hotheaded** adjective

**hothouse** noun a heated building made of glass, for growing plants in a warm temperature.

**hotline** noun a direct exclusive telephone line, especially for emergencies.

**hotplate** noun a heated surface for cooking food or keeping it hot.

**hotpot** noun a stew containing meat with potatoes and other vegetables.

**Hottentot** noun **1** a member of a people of SW Africa. **2** their language.

**hotting** noun (*informal*) stunt-driving, especially in stolen cars in urban areas.

**Houdini** (hoo-**dee**-ni), Harry (original name: Eric Weiss) (1874–1926), American escapologist.

**houmous** alternative spelling of HUMMUS.

**hound** noun a dog used in hunting. ● verb harass or pursue.

**hour** noun **1** a twenty-fourth part of a day and night, 60 minutes. **2** a time of day, a point of time; *always comes at the same hour.* **3** a short period of time; *the time for action; the hour has come.* **4** (in the RC Church) prayers to be said at one of the seven times of day appointed for prayer; *a book of hours.* **5** a period for a specified activity; *the lunch hour.* **6** an hour's travelling time; *we are an hour from London.* **7** (**hours**, preceded by numerals in the form 18.00, 20.30, etc.) this number of hours and minutes past midnight on the 24-hour clock; *assemble at 20.00 hours.* **8** (**hours**) a fixed period for daily work; *office hours are 9 to 5; after hours.* □ **on the hour** when the clock indicates a whole number of hours after midnight; *buses leave on the hour.*

**hourglass** noun a wasp-waisted glass container holding a quantity of fine sand that takes one hour to trickle from the upper to the lower section.

**houri** (**hoor**-i) noun a young and beautiful woman of the Muslim Paradise.

**hourly** adjective **1** done or occurring once an hour; *an hourly bus service.* **2** continual, frequent; *lives in hourly dread of discovery.* **3** per hour; *hourly wage.* ● adverb every hour.

**house** noun (*pronounced* howss) **1** a building made for people to live in, a home. **2** the people living in this, a household. **3** a building used for a particular purpose; *the opera house.* **4** a boarding-school residence; the pupils in this; each of the divisions of a day-school for sports competitions etc. **5** a building used by an assembly, the assembly itself; *the Houses of Parliament.* **6** (**the House**) the House of Commons or House of Lords. **7** a business firm; *a banking house.* **8** the audience of a theatre or cinema; *a full house.* **9** a family or dynasty; *the House of Windsor.* **10** each of the twelve parts into which the heavens are divided in astrology. ● verb (*pronounced* howz) **1** provide accommodation for. **2** store (goods etc.). **3** encase (a part or fixture). □ **house arrest** detention in one's own house, not in prison. **house lights** lights in a theatre auditorium. **house-martin** noun a black and white bird that builds a mud nest on house walls. **house music** a style of pop music, typically using drum machines and synthesized bass lines with sparse repetitive vocals and a fast beat. **house of cards** an insecure scheme. **House of Commons** the assembly of elected representatives in the British Parliament. **House of Keys** (in the Isle of Man) the assembly of elected members of the Tynwald. **House of Lords** the assembly of members of the nobility and bishops in the British Parliament. **House of Representatives** see REPRESENTATIVE. **house party** a number of guests staying at a house. **house plant** a plant for growing indoors. **house-proud** adjective giving attention to the care and appearance of the home. **house-to-house** adjective calling at each house in turn. **house-trained** adjective **1** (of animals) trained to be clean in the house. **2** (*informal*) well-mannered. **house-warming** noun a party to celebrate a move to a new home. **like a house on fire** vigorously; excellently. **on the house** (of drinks) free. **put** (*or* **set**) **one's house in order** make the necessary reforms.

**houseboat** noun a boat fitted up for living in.

**housebound** adjective confined to one's house through illness etc.

**housebreaking** noun the act of breaking into a building to commit a crime. □ **housebreaker** noun

**housecoat** noun a woman's informal coat or gown for wear in the house.

**housefly** noun a common fly often found in houses.

**household** noun 1 all the occupants of a house living as a family. 2 a house and its affairs. □ **household troops** (*Brit.*) the troops nominally employed to guard the sovereign. **household word** (*or* **name**) a familiar saying or name.

**householder** noun a person owning or renting a house.

**housekeeper** noun a person, especially a woman, employed to look after a household.

**housekeeping** noun 1 management of household affairs. 2 money to be used for this. 3 operations of maintenance, record-keeping, etc., in an organization.

**housemaid** noun a female servant in a house, especially one who cleans rooms. □ **housemaid's knee** inflammation of the kneecap, often caused by excessive kneeling.

**houseman** noun (plural **housemen**) a resident junior doctor at a hospital.

**housemaster** noun a male teacher in charge of a house at a boarding-school.

**housemistress** noun a female teacher in charge of a house at a boarding-school.

**houseroom** noun space or accommodation in one's house. □ **not give houseroom to** not have under any circumstances.

**housewife** noun (plural **housewives**) a woman managing a household. □ **housewifely** adverb

**housework** noun the cleaning and cooking etc. done in housekeeping.

**housing** noun 1 accommodation. 2 a rigid casing enclosing machinery. 3 a shallow trench or groove cut in a piece of wood to receive an insertion. □ **housing estate** a number of houses in an area planned as a unit.

**Housman**, Alfred Edward (1859–1936), English poet and classical scholar.

**Houston** (**hew**-stŏn) an inland port of Texas, an important centre for space research and manned space-flight.

**hove** see HEAVE.

**hovel** (**hov**-ĕl) noun a miserable dwelling.

**hover** verb 1 (of a bird etc.) remain in one place in the air. 2 wait about, linger, wait close at hand.

**hovercraft** noun a vehicle that travels over land or water supported on an air cushion provided by a downward blast from its engines.

**hoverport** noun a port used by hovercraft.

**how** adverb 1 by what means, in what way. 2 to what extent or amount etc. 3 in what condition; *how are you?* ●conjunction (*in-formal*) that; *he told us how he'd been in India*. □ **and how!** (*slang*) very much so. **how about** what is your feeling about (this thing)?; would you like (this)? **how come** (*informal*) why, how did it happen? **how do you do?** a formal greeting. **how many** what total. **how much** what amount, what price. **how's that** 1 what is your opinion or explanation? 2 *Cricket* (also **howzat**) (an appeal to the umpire) is the batsman out?

**Howard**, Catherine (died 1542), the fifth wife of Henry VIII.

**howdah** (**how**-dă) noun a seat, usually with a canopy, for riding on an elephant or camel.

**however** adverb 1 in whatever way, to whatever extent; *he'll not succeed, however hard he tries.* 2 all the same, nevertheless; *later, however, she decided to go.*

**howitzer** noun a short gun firing shells, with a steep angle of fire.

**howl** noun 1 the long loud wailing cry of a dog etc. 2 a loud cry of amusement, pain, or scorn. 3 a similar noise made by a strong wind or in an electrical amplifier. ●verb 1 make a howl. 2 weep loudly. 3 utter with a howl. □ **howl down** prevent (a speaker) from being heard by shouting disapprovingly.

**howler** noun (*informal*) a glaring mistake.

**hoy** interjection an exclamation used to call attention.

**hoyden** noun a girl who behaves boisterously.

**h.p.** abbreviation (also **hp**) 1 hire purchase. 2 horsepower.

**HQ** abbreviation headquarters.

**hr.** abbreviation hour.

**HRH** abbreviation His or Her Royal Highness.

**HRT** abbreviation hormone replacement therapy.

**HT** abbreviation high tension.

**hub** noun 1 the central part of a wheel, from which spokes radiate. 2 a central point of activity; *the hub of the universe.* □ **hub-cap** noun a round metal cover over the hub of a car wheel.

**Hubble**, Edwin Powell (1889–1953), American astronomer, whose researches established that the universe is continually expanding so that the galaxies are carried further apart.

**hubble-bubble** noun 1 a simple hookah. 2 a bubbling sound. 3 confused talk.

**hubbub** noun a loud confused noise of voices.

**hubby** noun (*informal*) a husband.

**hubris** (**hew**-bris) noun arrogant pride or presumption. □ **hubristic** adjective

**huckleberry** noun a low shrub of North America with blue or black fruit.

**huckster** noun an aggressive salesman; a hawker.

**huddle** verb **1** heap or crowd together into a small space. **2** (often foll. by up) curl one's body closely, nestle. ●noun a confused mass. □ **go into a huddle** hold a close or secret conference.

**Hudson**, Henry (died 1611), English explorer, discoverer of the North American bay, river, and strait which bear his name.

**Hudson Bay** an inland sea of NE Canada, linked to the North Atlantic by Hudson Strait.

**hue** noun a colour, a tint. □ **hue and cry** a general outcry of alarm, demand, or protest.

**huff** noun a fit of annoyance. ●verb **1** blow. **2** (especially as **huff and puff**) bluster self-importantly but ineffectually. **3** (in draughts) remove (an opponent's piece) as a forfeit. □ **in a huff** annoyed and offended.

**huffy** adjective (also **huffish**) **1** apt to take offence. **2** offended. □ **huffily** adverb

**hug** verb (**hugged**, **hugging**) **1** squeeze tightly in one's arms. **2** keep close to; the ship hugged the shore. ●noun a strong clasp with the arms.

**huge** adjective extremely large, enormous. □ **hugely** adverb

**hugger-mugger** adjective & adverb **1** in secret. **2** in disorder. ●noun **1** confusion. **2** secrecy.

**Hughes**[1], Howard Robard (1905–76), American industrialist, aviator, and film producer who lived in seclusion for the last 25 years of his life.

**Hughes**[2], Ted (Edward James) (born 1930), English poet, Poet Laureate from 1984.

**Hugo**, Victor-Marie (1802–85), French poet, novelist, and dramatist, whose novels include Notre Dame de Paris and Les Misérables.

**Huguenot** (hew-gĕ-noh) noun a member of the Calvinist French Protestants c.1560 who were involved in almost continuous civil war with the Catholic majority.

**huh** interjection an expression of disgust or surprise.

**hula** noun a Polynesian dance performed by women.

**hulk** noun **1** the body of an old ship. **2** a large clumsy-looking person or thing.

**hulking** adjective (informal) bulky, clumsy.

**hull** noun **1** the framework of a ship or airship. **2** the cluster of leaves on a strawberry. **3** the pod of peas and beans. ●verb remove the hulls of (strawberries etc.).

**hullabaloo** noun an uproar.

**hullo** alternative spelling of HELLO.

**hum** verb (**hummed**, **humming**) **1** make a low steady continuous sound like that of a bee. **2** utter a slight sound in hesitating. **3** sing with closed lips. **4** (informal) be in a state of activity; things started humming; make things hum. **5** (slang) give off a bad smell. ●interjection an exclamation of hesitation. ●noun **1** a humming sound. **2** an exclamation of hesitation. **3** (slang) a bad smell. □ **hum and haw** (or **ha**) hesitate.

**human** adjective **1** of or consisting of human beings; the human race. **2** having the qualities that distinguish mankind, not divine, animal, or mechanical. **3** of or characteristic of humans, especially as being weak, fallible, etc.; he's only human. **4** kind, sympathetic, etc.; very human. ●noun a human being. □ **human being** a man, woman, or child. **human interest** something that appeals to personal emotions (in a newspaper story etc.). **human rights** those held to be claimable by any living person. **human shield** a person (or people) placed in a line of fire in order to discourage attack.

**humane** (hew-mayn) adjective **1** kind-hearted, compassionate, merciful. **2** inflicting the minimum of pain. **3** (of learning etc.) tending to civilize. □ **humanely** adverb

**humanism** (hew-măn-izm) noun a non-religious philosophy based on liberal human values. □ **humanist** noun, **humanistic** adjective

**humanitarian** (hew-man-i-tair-iăn) adjective concerned with human welfare and the reduction of suffering. ●noun a humanitarian person. □ **humanitarianism** noun

**humanity** noun **1** the human race, people; crimes against humanity. **2** being human, human nature. **3** being humane, kindheartedness. **4** (**humanities**) subjects concerned with human culture, e.g. language, literature, and history, as opposed to the sciences.

**humanize** verb (also **humanise**) make human or humane. □ **humanization** noun

**humankind** noun human beings collectively.

**humanly** adverb **1** in a human way. **2** by human means, with human limitations; as accurate as is humanly possible.

**humanoid** adjective having a human form or human characteristics. ●noun a humanoid thing.

**Humberside** a county of NE England.

**humble** adjective **1** having or showing a modest estimate of one's own importance, not proud. **2** of low social or political rank. **3** (of a thing) not large or showy or elaborate; a humble cottage. ●verb make humble, lower the rank or self-importance of. □ **eat humble pie** make a humble apology; accept humiliation. (¶ From umble pie, that made with 'umbles', the edible offal of deer.) □ **humbly** adverb, **humbleness** noun

**humbug** noun **1** deceptive or false talk or behaviour. **2** an impostor, a hypocrite. **3** a hard, boiled, striped sweet, usually flavoured with peppermint.

**humdinger** noun (slang) a remarkable person or thing.

**humdrum** adjective dull, commonplace, monotonous.

**Hume**, David (1711–76), Scottish philosopher and historian.

**humerus** (**hew**-mer-ŭs) noun (plural **humeri**, pronounced **hew**-mer-I) the bone in the upper arm, from shoulder to elbow. □ **humeral** adjective

**humid** (**hew**-mid) adjective (of the air or climate) damp.

**humidifier** (hew-**mid**-i-fy-er) noun a device for keeping the air moist in a room or enclosed space.

**humidify** (hew-**mid**-i-fy) verb (**humidified**, **humidifying**) make humid.

**humidity** (hew-**mid**-iti) noun dampness of the air.

**humiliate** verb cause (a person) to feel disgraced. □ **humiliation** noun

**humility** noun a humble condition or attitude of mind.

**hummingbird** noun a small tropical bird that vibrates its wings rapidly, producing a humming sound.

**hummock** noun a hump in the ground.

**hummus** (**huu**-mŭs) noun (also **houmous**) a dip or appetizer made from ground chick peas and sesame oil flavoured with lemon and garlic.

**humor** Amer. spelling of HUMOUR.

**humoresque** (hew-mer-**esk**) noun a light and lively musical composition.

**humorist** noun a writer or speaker noted for his or her humour.

**humorous** adjective full of humour. □ **humorously** adverb

**humour** noun (Amer. **humor**) **1** the quality of being amusing. **2** (in full **sense of humour**) the ability to perceive and enjoy amusement. **3** a state of mind; in a good humour. **4** (in full **cardinal humour**) (old use) each of the four bodily fluids (blood, phlegm, choler, and melancholy) formerly believed to determine a person's physical and mental qualities. ● verb keep (a person) contented by giving way to his or her wishes. □ **aqueous humour** the clear fluid between the lens of the eye and the cornea. **vitreous humour** the transparent jelly-like tissue filling the eyeball.

**hump** noun **1** a rounded projecting part. **2** a deformity on a person's back, where there is abnormal curvature of the spine. **3** (**the hump**) (slang) a fit of depression or annoyance; gave me the hump. ● verb **1** form into a hump. **2** hoist or carry (one's pack etc.).

**humpback** noun **1** a hunchback. **2** a whale with a hump on its back. □ **humpback bridge** a small steeply-arched bridge. □ **humpbacked** adjective

**humph** interjection & noun a sound expressing doubt or dissatisfaction.

**humus** (**hew**-mŭs) noun a rich dark organic material, formed by the decay of dead leaves and plants etc. and essential to the fertility of soil.

**Hun** noun **1** (offensive) a German. **2** a member of an Asiatic people who ravaged Europe in the 4th–5th centuries.

**hunch** verb bend into a hump. ● noun **1** a hump. **2** a feeling based on intuition.

**hunchback** noun **1** a person with a hump on his or her back. **2** this hump.

**hundred** adjective & noun (plural **hundreds** or **hundred**) ten times ten (100, C); a few hundred. □ **hundred per cent** entirely, completely. **hundreds and thousands** tiny coloured sugar strands used for decorating cakes etc. **Hundred Years War** an intermittent conflict between France and England between the 1340s and 1450s, a series of attempts by English kings to dominate France. □ **hundredth** adjective & noun

**hundredfold** adjective & adverb one hundred times as much or as many.

**hundredweight** noun (plural **hundredweight** or **hundredweights**) **1** a measure of weight, 112 lb (50.802 kg), or in America 100 lb (45.359 kg). **2** a metric unit of weight equal to 50 kg.

**hung** see HANG. □ **hung-over** adjective (informal) having a hangover. **hung parliament** one that cannot reach decisions because there is no clear majority in voting.

**Hungarian** (hung-**air**-iăn) adjective of Hungary or its people or language. ● noun **1** a person from Hungary. **2** the language of Hungary.

**Hungary** a country of central Europe.

**hunger** noun **1** need for food, the uncomfortable sensation felt when one has not eaten for some time. **2** a strong desire for something. ● verb feel hunger. □ **hunger strike** refusal of food as a form of protest.

**hungry** adjective (**hungrier**, **hungriest**) feeling hunger. □ **hungrily** adverb

**hunk** noun **1** a large roughly cut piece. **2** (informal) a sexually attractive man. □ **hunky** adjective

**hunkers** plural noun the haunches.

**hunky-dory** adjective (informal) excellent.

**Hunt**, William Holman (1827–1910), English painter, a co-founder of the Pre-Raphaelite Brotherhood in 1848.

**hunt** *verb* **1** pursue (wild animals) for food or sport. **2** make a search (for); *hunted for it everywhere; hunt it out.* **3** search (a district) for game. **4** use (a horse or hounds) in hunting. **5** (of an engine) run too fast and too slow alternately. ●*noun* **1** hunting. **2** an association of people hunting with a pack of hounds; the district where they hunt. □ **hunt down** pursue and capture.

**hunted** *adjective* (of a look etc.) terrified as if being hunted.

**hunter** *noun* **1** one who hunts. **2** a horse used for hunting. **3** a watch with a hinged metal cover over the dial. □ **hunter's moon** the first full moon after the harvest moon.

**huntsman** *noun* (*plural* **huntsmen**) **1** a man who hunts. **2** a man in charge of a pack of hounds.

**hurdle** *noun* **1** one of a series of light upright frames to be jumped over by athletes in a race. **2** a portable rectangular frame with bars, used for a temporary fence. **3** an obstacle or difficulty. **4** (**hurdles**) a hurdle race.

**hurdler** *noun* a person who runs in hurdle races.

**hurdy-gurdy** *noun* **1** a musical instrument with a droning sound, played by turning a handle. **2** (*informal*) a barrel organ.

**hurl** *verb* **1** throw violently. **2** utter vehemently; *hurl insults.*

**hurley** *noun* (also **hurling**) an Irish form of hockey played with broad sticks.

**hurly-burly** *noun* a rough bustle of activity.

**Huron** (hewr-ŏn), **Lake** one of the five Great Lakes of North America.

**hurrah** *interjection & noun* (also **hooray**, **hurray**) an exclamation of joy or approval.

**hurricane** (hurri-kǎn) *noun* **1** a storm with a violent wind, especially a West Indian cyclone. **2** a wind of 75 m.p.h. or more. □ **hurricane lamp** a paraffin lamp with the flame protected from violent wind.

**hurried** *adjective* done with great haste. □ **hurriedly** *adverb*

**hurry** *noun* great haste; the need for this. ●*verb* (**hurried**, **hurrying**) **1** move or do something with eager haste or too quickly. **2** cause to move etc. in this way. □ **hurry up** (*or* **along**) (*informal*) make haste. **in a hurry 1** hurrying. **2** easily or willingly; *you won't beat that in a hurry; shan't ask again in a hurry.* □ **hurriedly** *adverb*

**hurt** *verb* (**hurt**, **hurting**) **1** cause pain, damage, or injury to. **2** cause mental pain to, distress. **3** suffer pain; *my leg hurts.* ●*noun* **1** injury. **2** harm, wrong.

**hurtful** *adjective* causing hurt, especially mental. □ **hurtfully** *adverb*

**hurtle** *verb* move rapidly or noisily.

**husband** *noun* a married man in relation to his wife. ●*verb* use economically, try to save; *husband one's resources.*

**husbandry** *noun* **1** farming. **2** management of resources.

**hush** *verb* **1** make or become silent or quiet. **2** (foll. by *up*) prevent (a thing) from becoming generally known. ●*interjection* a call for silence. ●*noun* silence. □ **hush-hush** *adjective* (*informal*) kept very secret. **hush money** money paid to prevent something from being revealed.

**husk** *noun* the dry outer covering of certain seeds and fruits. ●*verb* remove the husk(s) from.

**husky¹** *adjective* (**huskier**, **huskiest**) **1** (of a person or voice) dry in the throat, hoarse. **2** big and strong, burly. □ **huskily** *adverb*, **huskiness** *noun*

**husky²** *noun* a dog of a powerful breed used in the Arctic for pulling sledges.

**hussar** (hŭ-zar) *noun* a member of a light cavalry regiment.

**Hussein**, Saddam (in full Saddam bin Hussein at-Takriti) (born 1937), Iraqi leader, President from 1979.

**hussy** *noun* (*scornful*) an impudent or promiscuous girl or woman.

**hustings** *noun* parliamentary election proceedings. (¶ Originally a temporary platform from which candidates for parliament could address the electors.)

**hustle** *verb* **1** jostle, push roughly. **2** hurry. **3** make (a person) act quickly and without time to consider things; *hustled him into a decision.* ●*noun* hustling; bustle. □ **hustler** *noun*

**hut** *noun* a small roughly-made house or shelter.

**hutch** *noun* a box or cage for rabbits or other small animals.

**Huxley¹**, Aldous Leonard (1894–1963), English novelist and essayist (brother of Julian Huxley), whose works include *Brave New World.*

**Huxley²**, Sir Julian (1887–1975), English biologist, grandson of T. H. Huxley and first director-general of UNESCO (1946–8).

**Huxley³**, Thomas Henry (1825–95), English biologist, a firm supporter of Darwin.

**Huygens** (hy-gĕnz), Christiaan (1629–95), Dutch physicist, mathematician, and astronomer, best known for his pendulum-regulated clock invented in 1656.

**hyacinth** *noun* **1** a plant with fragrant bell-shaped flowers, growing from a bulb. **2** purplish blue.

**hyaena** alternative spelling of HYENA.

**hybrid** *noun* **1** an animal or plant that is the offspring of two different species or varieties. **2** something made by combining two different elements. ●*adjective* produced in this way, cross-bred. □ **hybridism** *noun*

**hybridize** *verb* (also **hybridise**) **1** subject (a species etc.) to cross-breeding. **2** produce hybrids. **3** (of animals or plants) interbreed. □ **hybridization** *noun*

**Hyde**, Edward, *see* JEKYLL.

**hydra** *noun* **1** a freshwater polyp with a tubular body and tentacles round the mouth. **2** a thing that is hard to get rid of. (¶ Named after the Hydra in Greek mythology, a water-snake with many heads that grew again if cut off.)

**hydrangea** (hy-**drayn**-jă) *noun* a shrub with white, pink, or blue flowers growing in clusters.

**hydrant** *noun* a pipe from a water-main (especially in a street) with a nozzle to which a hose can be attached for firefighting etc.

**hydrate** *noun* (*pronounced* **hy**-drayt) a chemical compound of water with another compound or element. ●*verb* (*pronounced* hy-**drayt**) combine chemically with water; cause to absorb water. □ **hydration** *noun*

**hydraulic** (hy-**draw**-lik) *adjective* **1** of water conveyed through pipes or channels. **2** operated by the movement of water or other fluid; *a hydraulic lift*. **3** concerned with the use of water etc. in this way; *hydraulic engineer*. **4** hardening under water; *hydraulic cement*. **5** (**hydraulics**) the science of the conveyance of liquids through pipes etc., especially as motive power. □ **hydraulically** *adverb*

**hydride** *noun* a compound of hydrogen with an element.

**hydro** *noun* (*plural* **hydros**) (*informal*) **1** a hotel etc. providing hydrotherapy. **2** a hydroelectric power plant.

**hydrocarbon** *noun* any of a class of compounds of hydrogen and carbon which are found in petrol, coal, and natural gas.

**hydrocephalus** (hy-drŏ-**sef**-ă-lŭs) *noun* a condition (especially of children) in which fluid accumulates on the brain. □ **hydrocephalic** *adjective*

**hydrochloric acid** (hy-drŏ-**klor**-ik) a colourless corrosive acid, a solution of hydrogen chloride gas in water.

**hydrodynamics** *noun* the science of forces exerted by a moving liquid, especially water. □ **hydrodynamic** *adjective*

**hydroelectric** *adjective* using water-power to produce electricity. □ **hydroelectricity** *noun*

**hydrofoil** *noun* a boat equipped with a structure designed to raise the hull out of the water when the boat is in motion, enabling it to travel fast and economically.

**hydrogen** *noun* a chemical element (symbol H), a colourless odourless tasteless gas, the lightest substance known, combining with oxygen to form water. □ **hydrogen bomb** an immensely powerful bomb releasing energy by fusion of hydrogen nuclei. **hydrogen peroxide** a viscous unstable liquid with strong oxidizing properties, used as a bleach. **hydrogen sulphide** a poisonous unpleasant-smelling gas formed by rotting animal matter.

**hydrogenate** (hy-**droj**-in-ayt) *verb* charge with or cause to combine with hydrogen. □ **hydrogenation** *noun*

**hydrogenous** (hy-**droj**-in-ŭs) *adjective* of or containing hydrogen.

**hydrography** (hy-**drog**-răfi) *noun* the scientific study of seas, lakes, rivers, etc. □ **hydrographer** *noun*, **hydrographic** *adjective*

**hydrology** (hy-**drol**-ŏji) *noun* the study of the properties of water, especially of its movement in relation to the land. □ **hydrological** *adjective*, **hydrologist** *noun*

**hydrolyse** (hy-drŏ-lyz) *verb* (*Amer.* **hydrolyze**) decompose by hydrolysis.

**hydrolysis** (hy-**drol**-i-sis) *noun* a chemical reaction of a substance with water, usually resulting in decomposition.

**hydrometer** (hy-**drom**-it-er) *noun* an instrument that measures the density of liquids.

**hydropathy** (hy-**drop**-ă-thi) *noun* the use of water (internally and externally) in the treatment of disease and abnormal physical conditions. □ **hydropathic** (hy-drŏ-**path**-ik) *adjective*

**hydrophilic** (hy-drŏ-**fil**-ik) *adjective* having a tendency to combine with water; able to be wetted by water.

**hydrophobia** (hy-drŏ-**foh**-biă) *noun* **1** abnormal fear of water, especially as a symptom of rabies in humans. **2** rabies. □ **hydrophobic** *adjective*

**hydroplane** *noun* **1** a light fast motor boat designed to skim over the surface of water. **2** a finlike attachment enabling a submarine to rise and descend.

**hydroponics** (hy-drŏ-**pon**-iks) *noun* the art of growing plants without soil in sand, gravel, or liquid to which nutrients have been added.

**hydrosphere** *noun* the waters of the earth's surface.

**hydrostatic** *adjective* of the pressure and other characteristics of water or other liquid at rest. ●*noun* (**hydrostatics**) the study of these characteristics.

**hydrotherapy** *noun* the use of water externally in the treatment of disease and abnormal physical conditions.

**hydrous** (**hy**-drŭs) *adjective* (of substances) containing water.

**hydroxide** *noun* a compound containing oxygen and hydrogen either as a hydroxide ion or a hydroxyl group.

**hydroxyl** (hy-**droks**-il) *noun* a univalent group containing hydrogen and oxygen.

**hyena** *noun* (also **hyaena**) a flesh-eating animal like a dog or wolf, with a howl that sounds like wild laughter.

**hygiene** (**hy**-jeen) *noun* the practice or conditions of cleanliness which help to maintain health and prevent disease. □ **hygienic** *adjective*, **hygienically** *adverb*

**hygienist** (**hy**-jeen-ist) *noun* an expert in hygiene.

**hygrometer** (hy-**grom**-it-er) *noun* an instrument that measures humidity.

**hygroscope** (**hy**-grŏ-skohp) *noun* an instrument indicating but not measuring the humidity of the air.

**hygroscopic** (hy-grŏ-**skop**-ik) *adjective* **1** of the hygroscope. **2** (of a substance) having a tendency to absorb moisture from the air.

**hymen** *noun* a membrane partly closing the external opening of the vagina, usually broken at the first occurrence of sexual intercourse.

**hymenopterous** (hy-měn-**op**-ter-ŭs) *adjective* of the kind of insects that includes ants, bees, and wasps, having four transparent wings.

**hymn** *noun* a Christian song of praise.

**hymnal** *noun* a book of hymns.

**hyoscine** (**hy**-ŏ-seen) *noun* a poisonous substance from which a sedative is made, found in plants of the nightshade family.

**hype** (*slang*) *noun* extravagant or intensive promotion of a product etc. ● *verb* publicize or promote with hype.

**hyped up** (*slang*) nervously excited or stimulated.

**hyper** *adjective* (*slang*) hyperactive, highly-strung.

**hyper-** *combining form* above, over; excessively.

**hyperactive** *adjective* (of a person) abnormally and excessively active. □ **hyperactivity** *noun*

**hyperbola** (hy-**per**-bŏlă) *noun* (*plural* **hyperbolas** or **hyperbolae**) the curve produced when a cone is cut by a plane that makes a larger angle with the base than the side of the cone does. □ **hyperbolic** (hy-per-**bol**-ik) *adjective*

**hyperbole** (hy-**per**-bŏli) *noun* an exaggerated statement that is not meant to be taken literally, e.g. *a stack of work a mile high*. □ **hyperbolical** (hy-per-**bol**-ikăl) *adjective*

**hypercritical** *adjective* excessively critical. □ **hypercritically** *adverb*

**hyperglycaemia** (hy-per-gly-see-mi-ă) *noun* (*Amer.* **hyperglycemia**) excess glucose in the bloodstream.

**hypermarket** *noun* a very large supermarket.

**hypermedia** *noun* the provision of several media (e.g. audio, video, and graphics) on one computer system.

**hypersensitive** *adjective* excessively sensitive. □ **hypersensitivity** *noun*

**hypersonic** *adjective* **1** of speeds more than five times that of sound. **2** of sound frequencies above 1,000 megahertz.

**hypertension** *noun* **1** abnormally high blood pressure. **2** great emotional tension.

**hypertext** *noun* the provision of several texts on one computer system.

**hyperventilation** *noun* abnormally rapid breathing. □ **hyperventilate** *verb*

**hyphen** *noun* a sign (-) used to join two words together (e.g. *half-size*) or to divide a word into parts.

**hyphenate** *verb* separate (words) with a hyphen. □ **hyphenation** *noun*

**hypnosis** (hip-**noh**-sis) *noun* a sleep-like state produced in a person who is then very susceptible to suggestion and acts only if told to do so.

**hypnotic** (hip-**not**-ik) *adjective* **1** of or producing hypnosis or a similar condition. **2** (of a drug) producing sleep. ● *noun* a hypnotic drug. □ **hypnotically** *adverb*

**hypnotism** (**hip**-nŏ-tizm) *noun* the production of hypnosis. □ **hypnotist** (**hip**-nŏ-tist) *noun*

**hypnotize** (**hip**-nŏ-tyz) *verb* (also **hypnotise**) **1** produce hypnosis in (a person). **2** fascinate, dominate the mind or will of.

**hypo-** *combining form* under; below normal.

**hypocaust** (**hy**-pŏ-kawst) *noun* a system of under-floor heating by hot air, used in ancient Roman houses.

**hypochondria** (hy-pŏ-**kon**-driă) *noun* abnormal and ill-founded anxiety about one's health.

**hypochondriac** *noun* one who suffers from hypochondria.

**hypocrisy** (hip-**ok**-risi) *noun* falsely pretending to be virtuous, insincerity.

**hypocrite** (**hip**-ŏ-krit) *noun* a person who is given to hypocrisy. □ **hypocritical** (hip-ŏ-**krit**-ikăl) *adjective*, **hypocritically** *adverb*

**hypodermic** *adjective* injected beneath the skin; used for such injections. ● *noun* (in full **hypodermic syringe**) a syringe fitted with a hollow needle through which a liquid can be injected beneath the skin. □ **hypodermically** *adverb*

**hypotension** *noun* abnormally low blood pressure.

**hypotenuse** (hy-**pot**-i-newz) *noun* the side opposite the right angle in a right-angled triangle.

**hypothalamus** *noun* (*plural* **hypothalami**) the part of the brain controlling body temperature, thirst, hunger, etc.

**hypothermia** *noun* the condition of having an abnormally low body temperature.

**hypothesis** (hy-**poth**-i-sis) *noun* (*plural* **hypotheses**, *pronounced* -seez) a supposition or guess put forward to account for certain facts and used as a basis for further investigation by which it may be proved or disproved.

**hypothesize** (hy-**poth**-i-syz) *verb* (also **hypothesise**) form or assume a hypothesis.

**hypothetical** (hy-pŏ-**thet**-ikăl) *adjective* **1** of or based on a hypothesis. **2** supposed but not necessarily true. □ **hypothetically** *adverb*

**hyssop** (**hiss**-ŏp) *noun* **1** a small fragrant bushy herb formerly used in medicine. **2** a plant used for sprinkling in ancient Jewish rites.

**hysterectomy** (hiss-ter-**ek**-tŏmi) *noun* surgical removal of the womb.

**hysteria** (hiss-**teer**-iă) *noun* **1** wild uncontrollable emotion or excitement. **2** a functional disturbance of the nervous system marked by emotional outbursts.

**hysteric** (hiss-**te**-rik) *noun* **1** a hysterical person. **2** (**hysterics**) a hysterical outburst; (*informal*) uncontrollable laughter.

**hysterical** (hiss-**te**-ri-kăl) *adjective* **1** caused by hysteria; suffering from this. **2** (of laughter) uncontrollable. **3** (*informal*) extremely funny. □ **hysterically** *adverb*

**Hz** *abbreviation* hertz.

# Ii

**I** *pronoun* the person who is speaking or writing and referring to himself or herself. ●*noun* (as a Roman numeral) 1. ●*symbol* iodine. ●*abbreviation* (also **I.**) island(s); isle(s).

**IA, Ia** *abbreviation* Iowa.

**iambic** (I-am-bik) *adjective* of or using iambuses. ●*plural noun* (**iambics**) lines of verse in iambic metre.

**iambus** (I-am-bŭs) *noun* (*plural* **iambuses** or **iambi**) a metrical foot with one short or unstressed syllable followed by one long or stressed syllable.

**IBA** *abbreviation* Independent Broadcasting Authority.

**Iberia** (I-beer-iă) the ancient name for the peninsula in SW Europe comprising Spain and Portugal. □ **Iberian** *adjective & noun*

**ibex** (I-beks) *noun* (*plural* **ibexes**) a mountain goat with long curving horns.

**ibid.** *abbreviation* ibidem; in the same book or passage etc. (¶ Latin.)

**ibis** (I-bis) *noun* (*plural* **ibises**) a wading bird with a long curved bill and long legs.

**Ibiza** (i-bee-thă) **1** the westernmost of the Balearic Islands. **2** its capital.

**Ibo** (ee-boh) *noun* (also **Igbo**) (*plural* **Ibo** or **Ibos**) **1** a member of a Black people of SE Nigeria. **2** their language.

**Ibsen** (ib-sĕn), Henrik (1828–1906), Norwegian dramatist.

**ICBM** *abbreviation* intercontinental ballistic missile.

**ice** *noun* **1** frozen water, a brittle transparent solid. **2** a portion of ice cream or water-ice. ●*verb* **1** (foll. by *over* or *up*) become covered with ice; *the pond iced over*. **2** cover or mix with ice; make very cold; *iced beer*. **3** decorate with icing. □ **Ice Age** a period when much of the northern hemisphere was covered with glaciers. **ice blue** *adjective & noun* very pale blue. **ice-cold** *adjective* as cold as ice. **ice cream** a sweet creamy frozen food. **ice field** a large expanse of floating ice. **ice hockey** a form of hockey played on ice. **ice lolly** (also **iced lolly**) a water-ice on a small stick. **ice-pack** *noun* **1** = PACK ICE. **2** ice applied to the body for medical purposes. **ice-plant** *noun* a plant with leaves that glisten as if with ice. **ice-skate** (*noun*) a boot with a blade underneath, for skating on ice; (*verb*) skate on ice.

**iceberg** *noun* a huge mass of ice floating in the sea with the greater part under water. □ **iceberg lettuce** a crisp round type of lettuce. **the tip of the iceberg** a small evident part of something much larger or more complex.

**icebox** *noun* **1** a compartment in a refrigerator for making or storing ice. **2** (*Amer.*) a refrigerator.

**ice-breaker** *noun* a ship designed to break through ice.

**icecap** *noun* the permanent covering of ice in polar regions.

**Iceland** an island country in the North Atlantic. □ **Icelander** *noun*

**Icelandic** *adjective* of Iceland or its people or language. ●*noun* the language of Iceland.

**ichthyology** (ik-thi-ol-ŏji) *noun* the study of fishes. □ **ichthyological** *adjective*, **ichthyologist** *noun*

**ichthyosaurus** (ik-thi-ŏ-sor-ŭs) *noun* (also **ichthyosaur**) (*plural* **ichthyosauruses**) an extinct sea reptile with a long head, four flippers, and a large tail.

**ICI** *abbreviation* Imperial Chemical Industries.

**icicle** *noun* a pointed piece of ice hanging down, formed when dripping water freezes.

**icing** *noun* a coating of sugar etc. on cakes or biscuits. □ **icing on the cake** an attractive addition or bonus. **icing sugar** powdered sugar used for making icing.

**icon** (I-kon) *noun* (also **ikon**) **1** an image or statue. **2** (in the Orthodox Church) a painting or mosaic of a holy figure. **3** *Computing* a symbol on a screen of a program, option, or window for selection.

**iconoclast** (I-kon-ŏ-klast) *noun* **1** a person who attacks cherished beliefs. **2** a destroyer of religious images. □ **iconoclasm** *noun*, **iconoclastic** *adjective*

**iconography** (I-kŏn-og-ră-fi) *noun* **1** the illustration of a subject by drawings. **2** the study of portraits, especially those of one person.

**icosahedron** (I-koss-ă-hee-drŏn) *noun* a solid figure with twenty faces.

**icy** *adjective* (**icier, iciest**) **1** very cold; *icy winds*. **2** covered with ice; *icy roads*. **3** very cold and unfriendly in manner; *an icy voice*. □ **icily** *adverb*, **iciness** *noun*

**ID** *abbreviation* **1** identification, identity. **2** Idaho.

**I'd** (*informal*) **1** I had. **2** I should; I would.

**id** *noun* a person's inherited psychological impulses considered as part of the unconscious. (¶ Latin, = that.)

**Idaho** (I-dă-hoh) a State of the northwestern USA.

**idea** *noun* **1** a plan etc. formed in the mind by thinking. **2** a mental impression; *give* *him an idea of what is needed.* **3** an opinion; *tries to force his ideas on us.* **4** a vague belief or fancy, a feeling that something is likely; *I have an idea that we shall be late.* □ **have no idea** (*informal*) **1** not know. **2** be utterly incompetent.

**ideal** *adjective* **1** satisfying one's idea of what is perfect; *ideal weather for sailing.* **2** existing only in an idea, visionary. ●*noun* a person, thing, or idea that is regarded as perfect or as a standard for attainment or imitation. □ **ideally** *adverb*

**idealist** (I-dee-ăl-ist) *noun* a person who has high ideals and tries in an unrealistic way to achieve these. □ **idealism** *noun*, **idealistic** *adjective*

**idealize** *verb* (also **idealise**) regard or represent as perfect. □ **idealization** *noun*

**idée fixe** (ee-day **feeks**) (*plural* **idées fixes**, *pronounced* same) an idea that is dominant or keeps recurring. (¶ French, = fixed idea.)

**identical** *adjective* **1** the same; *this is the identical place we stayed in last year.* **2** similar in every detail, exactly alike; *no two people have identical fingerprints.* □ **identical twins** twins developed from a single fertilized ovum and therefore of the same sex and very similar in appearance. □ **identically** *adverb*

**identify** *verb* (**identified**, **identifying**) **1** establish the identity of, recognize as being a specified person or thing. **2** consider to be identical, equate; *one cannot identify riches and happiness.* **3** (foll. by *with*) associate very closely in feeling or interest; *he has identified himself with the progress of the firm.* **4** (foll. by *with*) regard oneself as sharing the characteristics or fortunes of another person; *people like to identify with the characters in a film.* □ **identification** *noun*, **identifiable** *adjective*

**Identikit** *noun* (*trade mark*) a set of pictures of features that can be put together to form a likeness (especially of a person who is sought by the police) constructed from descriptions.

**identity** *noun* **1** the state of being identical. **2** the condition of being a specified person or thing; *established his identity.* **3** individuality, personality.

**ideogram** (**id**-i-ŏ-gram) *noun* a symbol indicating the idea (not the sounds forming the name) of a thing, e.g. numerals, Chinese characters, and symbols used in road signs.

**ideograph** (**id**-i-ŏ-grahf) *noun* an ideogram. □ **ideographic** *adjective*, **ideography** *noun*

**ideologue** (I-di-ŏ-log) *noun* a person who supports an ideology.

**ideology** (I-dee-**ol**-ŏji) *noun* the ideas that form the basis of an economic or political

theory etc.; *in Marxist ideology.* □ **ideological** *adjective*, **ideologist** *noun*

**ides** (*rhymes with* tides) *plural noun* the 15th day of March, May, July, and October, the 13th of other months, in the ancient Roman calendar.

**idiocy** *noun* **1** the state of being an idiot. **2** stupid behaviour; a stupid action.

**idiom** (**id**-i-ŏm) *noun* **1** a phrase that must be taken as a whole, usually having a meaning that is not clear from the meanings of the individual words, e.g. *foot the bill* and *a change of heart.* **2** the language used by a people or group; *in the scientific idiom.* **3** a characteristic style of expression in art or music etc.

**idiomatic** (idi-ŏ-**mat**-ik) *adjective* **1** relating to or conforming to idiom. **2** characteristic of a particular language. □ **idiomatically** *adverb*

**idiosyncrasy** (idi-ŏ-**sink**-răsi) *noun* a person's attitude or behaviour that is unlike that of others; an eccentricity. □ **idiosyncratic** (idi-ŏ-sin-**krat**-ik) *adjective*

**idiot** *noun* **1** a mentally deficient person incapable of rational conduct. **2** a stupid person. □ **idiotic** *adjective*, **idiotically** *adverb*

**idle** *adjective* **1** doing no work, not employed; not active or in use. **2** (of time) not spent in doing something. **3** avoiding work, lazy; *an idle fellow.* **4** worthless, having no special purpose; *idle gossip*; *idle curiosity.* ●*verb* **1** pass (time) without working, be idle. **2** (of an engine) run slowly in a neutral gear. □ **idly** *adverb*, **idleness** *noun*, **idler** *noun*

**idol** *noun* **1** an image of a god, used as an object of worship. **2** a person or thing that is the object of intense admiration or devotion.

**idolater** (I-**dol**-ă-ter) *noun* a person who worships an idol or idols. □ **idolatry** *noun*, **idolatrous** *adjective*

**idolize** *verb* (also **idolise**) feel excessive admiration or devotion to (a person or thing). □ **idolization** *noun*

**idyll** (**id**-il) *noun* **1** a short description (usually in verse) of a peaceful or romantic scene or incident, especially in country life. **2** a scene or incident of this kind.

**idyllic** (id-**il**-ik) *adjective* like an idyll, peaceful and happy. □ **idyllically** *adverb*

**i.e.** *abbreviation* = that is. (¶ From the Latin *id est.*)

**if** *conjunction* **1** on condition that; *he'll do it only if you pay him.* **2** in the event that; *if you are tired we will rest.* **3** supposing or granting that; *even if she said it she didn't mean it.* **4** even though; *I'll finish it, if it takes me all day.* **5** whether; *see if you can turn the handle.* **6** in exclamations of wish or surprise; *well, if it isn't Simon!* ●*noun* a condition or supposition; *too many ifs about it.* □ **if only** expressing regret; I wish that.

**Igbo** alternative spelling of IBO.

**igloo** *noun* a dome-shaped Eskimo house built of blocks of hard snow.

**Ignatius Loyola** (ig-nay-shŭs **loy**-ŏlă), St (1491/5–1556), Spanish theologian, founder of the Jesuits and their first superior general.

**igneous** (**ig**-ni-ŭs) *adjective* **1** of fire; fiery. **2** (of rocks) formed when molten matter has solidified; volcanic.

**ignite** (ig-**nyt**) *verb* **1** set fire to. **2** catch fire.

**ignition** (ig-**nish**-ŏn) *noun* **1** igniting; being ignited. **2** the mechanism providing the spark that ignites the fuel in an internal-combustion engine.

**ignoble** *adjective* not noble in character, aims, or purpose. □ **ignobly** *adverb*

**ignominious** (ignŏ-**min**-iŭs) *adjective* bringing contempt or disgrace, humiliating. □ **ignominiously** *adverb*

**ignominy** (**ig**-nŏm-ini) *noun* disgrace, humiliation.

**ignoramus** (ig-ner-**ay**-mŭs) *noun* (*plural* **ignoramuses**) an ignorant person.

**ignorant** *adjective* **1** lacking knowledge. **2** behaving rudely through lack of knowledge of good manners. □ **ignorantly** *adverb*, **ignorance** *noun*

**ignore** *verb* take no notice of, disregard deliberately.

**iguana** (ig-**wah**-nă) *noun* a large tree-climbing lizard of the West Indies and tropical America.

**iguanodon** (ig-**wah**-nŏ-dŏn) *noun* a large dinosaur that fed on plants.

**ikebana** (i-ki-**bah**-nă) *noun* the art of Japanese flower arrangement.

**ikon** alternative spelling of ICON.

**IL** *abbreviation* Illinois.

**ileum** (**il**-iŭm) *noun* (*plural* **ilea**) the lowest part of the small intestine.

**ilex** (**I**-leks) *noun* **1** holly. **2** holm-oak.

**Iliad** (**il**-i-ăd) a Greek epic poem, traditionally ascribed to Homer, telling of the climax of the war at Troy (Ilium) between Greeks and Trojans.

**ilk** *noun* a sort, a type. □ **of that ilk 1** (*Scottish*) of the ancestral estate with the same name as a family. **2** of that kind.

**I'll** (*informal*) = I shall, I will.

**ill** *adjective* **1** physically or mentally unwell. **2** (of health) unsound, not good. **3** harmful; *no ill effects.* **4** not favourable; *ill luck.* **5** hostile, unkind; *no ill feelings.* ● *adverb* **1** badly, wrongly. **2** unfavourably. **3** imperfectly, scarcely; *ill provided for; can ill afford to do this.* ● *noun* evil, harm, injury. □ **ill-advised** *adjective* unwise. **ill at ease** uncomfortable, embarrassed. **ill-bred** *adjective* having bad manners. **ill-fated** *adjective*

unlucky. **ill-favoured** *adjective* unattractive. **ill-gotten** *adjective* gained by evil or unlawful means. **ill-mannered** *adjective* having bad manners. **ill-natured** *adjective* unkind. **ill-timed** *adjective* done or occurring at an unfortunate time. **ill-treat, ill-use** *verb* treat badly or cruelly. **ill will** hostility, unkind feeling.

**Ill.** *abbreviation* Illinois.

**illegal** *adjective* against the law. □ **illegally** *adverb*, **illegality** (ili-**gal**-iti) *noun*

**illegible** (i-**lej**-ibŭl) *adjective* not legible. □ **illegibly** *adverb*, **illegibility** *noun*

**illegitimate** (ili-**jit**-im-ăt) *adjective* **1** born of parents not married to each other. **2** contrary to law or to rules. **3** (of a conclusion in an argument etc.) not logical, wrongly inferred. □ **illegitimately** *adverb*, **illegitimacy** *noun*

**illiberal** (i-**lib**-er-ăl) *adjective* **1** intolerant, narrow-minded. **2** without liberal culture; vulgar. **3** stingy. □ **illiberally** *adverb*, **illiberality** *noun*

**illicit** (i-**lis**-it) *adjective* unlawful, not allowed. □ **illicitly** *adverb*

**Illinois** (il-in-**oi**) a State of the Middle West of the USA.

**illiterate** (i-**lit**-er-ăt) *adjective* unable to read and write; showing lack of education. ● *noun* an illiterate person. □ **illiterately** *adverb*, **illiteracy** *noun*

**illness** *noun* **1** the state of being ill in body or mind. **2** a particular form of ill health.

**illogical** *adjective* not logical, contrary to logic. □ **illogically** *adverb*, **illogicality** (i-loj-i-**kal**-iti) *noun*

**illuminate** *verb* **1** light up, make bright. **2** throw light on (a subject), make understandable. **3** decorate (a street or building etc.) with lights. **4** decorate (a manuscript) with coloured designs. □ **illumination** *noun*, **illuminative** *adjective*

**illumine** *verb* (*literary*) **1** light up. **2** enlighten spiritually.

**illusion** (i-loo-**zh**ŏn) *noun* **1** something that a person wrongly supposes to exist. **2** a false belief about the nature of something.

**illusionist** *noun* a person who produces illusions, a conjuror.

**illusive** (i-loo-siv) *adjective* illusory.

**illusory** (i-loo-ser-i) *adjective* based on illusion, not real.

**illustrate** *verb* **1** supply (a book or newspaper etc.) with drawings or pictures. **2** make clear or explain by examples or pictures. **3** serve as an example of. □ **illustrator** *noun*

**illustration** *noun* **1** illustrating. **2** a drawing or picture in a book etc. **3** an example used to explain something.

**illustrative** (il-ŭs-tră-tiv) *adjective* serving as an illustration or example. □ **illustratively** *adverb*

**illustrious** (i-lus-triŭs) *adjective* famous and distinguished. □ **illustriousness** *noun*

**Illyria** (i-**li**-riă) an ancient region along the east coast of the Adriatic Sea.

**Ilyushin** (il-**yoo**-shin), Sergei Vladimirovich (1894–1977), Russian aeronautical engineer and designer of aircraft.

**I'm** (*informal*) = I am.

**image** *noun* **1** a representation of the outward form of a person or thing, e.g. a statue (especially as an object of worship). **2** the optical appearance of something, produced in a mirror or through a lens etc. **3** a mental picture. **4** the general impression of a person, firm, etc. as perceived by the public; a reputation. □ **be the image of** look exactly like.

**imagery** *noun* **1** the use of metaphorical language to produce pictures in the minds of readers or hearers. **2** images; statuary, carving.

**imaginary** *adjective* existing only in the imagination, not real.

**imagination** *noun* imagining, the ability to imagine creatively or to use this ability in a practical way.

**imaginative** *adjective* having or showing imagination. □ **imaginatively** *adverb*

**imagine** *verb* **1** form a mental image of, picture in one's mind. **2** think or believe; suppose; *don't imagine you'll get away with it.* **3** guess; *can't imagine where it has gone.* □ **imaginable** *adjective*

**imago** (i-**may**-goh) *noun* (*plural* **imagos** or **imagines**, *pronounced* i-**ma**-jin-eez) the fully developed stage of an insect's life, e.g. a butterfly.

**imam** (im-**ahm**) *noun* **1** the leader of prayers in a mosque. **2** the title of various Muslim religious leaders.

**imbalance** *noun* lack of balance, disproportion.

**imbecile** (**im**-bi-seel) *noun* **1** a mentally deficient person; an adult whose intelligence is equal to that of an average five-year-old child. **2** a stupid person. ● *adjective* idiotic. □ **imbecility** (imbi-**sil**-iti) *noun*

**imbed** alternative spelling of EMBED.

**imbibe** (im-**byb**) *verb* **1** drink. **2** absorb (ideas etc.) into the mind. **3** inhale (air).

**imbroglio** (im-**brohl**-yoh) *noun* (*plural* **imbroglios**) **1** a confused situation, usually involving a disagreement. **2** a confused heap.

**imbue** (im-**bew**) *verb* **1** fill (a person) with certain feelings, qualities, or opinions. **2** saturate or dye (with a colour etc.).

**IMF** *abbreviation* International Monetary Fund.

**imitable** *adjective* able to be imitated.

**imitate** *verb* **1** copy the behaviour of, take as an example that should be followed. **2** mimic playfully or for entertainment.

**3** make a copy of; be like (something else). □ **imitator** *noun*

**imitation** *noun* **1** imitating. **2** something produced by this, a copy. **3** (usually used as *adjective*) fake, counterfeit; *imitation leather.* **4** the act of mimicking a person or thing for entertainment; *he does imitations.*

**imitative** (**im**-it-ătiv) *adjective* imitating.

**immaculate** *adjective* **1** spotlessly clean. **2** free from moral blemish. **3** free from fault, right in every detail. □ **Immaculate Conception** the Roman Catholic doctrine that the Virgin Mary, from the moment of her conception by her mother, was and remained free from original sin. □ **immaculately** *adverb*

**immanent** (**im**-ă-nĕnt) *adjective* **1** (of qualities) inherent. **2** (of God) permanently pervading the universe. □ **immanence** *noun*

■**Usage** Do not confuse with **imminent**.

**Immanuel** (i-**man**-yoo-ĕl) the name given to Christ as the deliverer of Judah prophesied by the prophet Isaiah.

**immaterial** *adjective* **1** having no physical substance; *as immaterial as a ghost.* **2** of no importance or relevance; *it is now immaterial whether he goes or stays.* □ **immateriality** *noun*

**immature** *adjective* not mature; undeveloped. □ **immaturity** *noun*

**immeasurable** *adjective* not measurable; immense. □ **immeasurably** *adverb*

**immediate** *adjective* **1** occurring or done at once, without delay. **2** nearest, next; direct; *the immediate neighbourhood; my immediate family.* **3** most pressing or urgent; *our immediate concern.* □ **immediacy** *noun*

**immediately** *adverb* **1** without delay. **2** without an intermediary. ● *conjunction* as soon as.

**immemorial** *adjective* existing from before what can be remembered or found recorded; *from time immemorial.*

**immense** *adjective* exceedingly great. □ **immensely** *adverb*, **immensity** *noun*

**immerse** *verb* (often foll. by *in*) **1** put completely into water or other liquid. **2** absorb or involve deeply in thought or business etc. **3** embed.

**immersion** *noun* **1** immersing; being immersed. **2** baptism by putting the whole body into water. □ **immersion heater** an electric heating-element designed to be placed in the liquid that is to be heated, especially as a fixture in a hot-water tank.

**immigrant** *adjective* **1** immigrating. **2** of immigrants. ● *noun* a person who immigrates.

**immigrate** *verb* come into a foreign country as a permanent resident. □ **immigration** *noun*

**imminent** *adjective* (of events) about to occur, likely to occur at any moment. □ **imminence** *noun*

■**Usage** Do not confuse with **immanent**.

**immiscible** (i-mis-ibŭl) *adjective* (often foll. by *with*) not able to be mixed with another substance.

**immobile** *adjective* **1** immovable. **2** not moving. □ **immobility** *noun*

**immobilize** *verb* (also **immobilise**) make or keep immobile. □ **immobilization** *noun*

**immoderate** *adjective* excessive, lacking moderation. □ **immoderately** *adverb*

**immodest** *adjective* **1** lacking in modesty, indecent. **2** conceited. □ **immodestly** *adverb*, **immodesty** *noun*

**immolate** (im-ŏ-layt) *verb* sacrifice. □ **immolation** *noun*

**immoral** *adjective* not conforming to the accepted rules of morality, morally wrong (especially in sexual matters). □ **immorally** *adverb*, **immorality** (im-er-al-iti) *noun*

**immortal** *adjective* **1** living for ever, not mortal. **2** famous for all time. ●*noun* an immortal being or person. □ **immortality** *noun*

**immortalize** *verb* (also **immortalise**) make immortal.

**immovable** *adjective* (also **immoveable**) **1** unable to be moved. **2** unyielding, not changing in one's purpose; not moved emotionally. **3** (of property) consisting of land, houses, etc. □ **immovably** *adverb*, **immovability** *noun*

**immune** *adjective* having immunity; protected, exempt; *immune from infection.*

**immunity** *noun* **1** the ability of an animal or plant to resist infection. **2** special exemption from a tax, duty, or penalty.

**immunize** *verb* (also **immunise**) make immune, especially against infection by inoculation. □ **immunization** *noun*

**immunodeficiency** *noun* reduction in the body's normal immune defences.

**immunology** (im-yoo-**nol**-ŏji) *noun* the scientific study of resistance to infection. □ **immunological** *adjective*, **immunologist** *noun*

**immure** (im-**yoor**) *verb* imprison, shut in.

**immutable** (i-**mewt**-ăbŭl) *adjective* unchangeable. □ **immutably** *adverb*, **immutability** *noun*

**imp** *noun* **1** a small devil. **2** a mischievous child.

**impact** *noun* (*pronounced* **im**-pakt) **1** a collision. **2** the force exerted when one body collides with another. **3** the force exerted by the influence of new ideas. ●*verb* (*pronounced* im-**pakt**) pack, drive, or wedge firmly into something or together. □ **impaction** *noun*

**impacted** *adjective* (of a tooth) wedged between another tooth and the jaw.

**impair** *verb* damage, cause weakening of; *impair one's health.* □ **impairment** *noun*

**impala** (im-**pah**-lă) *noun* (*plural* **impala** or **impalas**) a small African antelope.

**impale** *verb* fix or pierce through with a sharp-pointed object. □ **impalement** *noun*

**impalpable** (im-**palp**-ăbŭl) *adjective* **1** unable to be felt by touch. **2** not easily grasped by the mind. **3** (of a powder) so fine that grains cannot be felt. □ **impalpably** *adverb*, **impalpability** *noun*

**impanel** alternative spelling of EMPANEL.

**impart** *verb* **1** give. **2** reveal or make (information etc.) known.

**impartial** (im-**par**-shăl) *adjective* not favouring one more than another. □ **impartially** *adverb*, **impartiality** (im-par-shi-al-iti) *noun*

**impassable** *adjective* (of roads or barriers) impossible to travel on or over. □ **impassably** *adverb*, **impassability** *noun*

**impasse** (**am**-pahss) *noun* a deadlock.

**impassible** *adjective* incapable of feeling, emotion, or injury; impassive. □ **impassibly** *adverb*, **impassibility** *noun*

**impassioned** (im-**pash**-ŏnd) *adjective* full of deep feeling; *an impassioned appeal.*

**impassive** *adjective* not feeling or showing emotion. □ **impassively** *adverb*, **impassiveness** *noun*, **impassivity** *noun*

**impasto** *noun* a technique in art of laying on paint thickly.

**impatient** *adjective* **1** unable to wait patiently; restlessly eager. **2** showing lack of patience, irritated; *got an impatient reply.* **3** (foll. by *of*) intolerant; *impatient of delay.* □ **impatiently** *adverb*, **impatience** *noun*

**impeach** *verb* **1** accuse of treason or other serious crime against the State, and bring for trial. **2** (*Amer.*) charge (a public official) with misconduct. **3** call in question, disparage. □ **impeachment** *noun*

**impeccable** *adjective* faultless. □ **impeccably** *adverb*, **impeccability** *noun*

**impecunious** (impi-**kew**-niŭs) *adjective* having little or no money. □ **impecuniosity** *noun*

**impedance** (im-**pee**-dăns) *noun* the total resistance of an electric circuit to the flow of alternating current.

■**Usage** Do not confuse with **impediment**.

**impede** *verb* hinder.

**impediment** *noun* **1** a hindrance, an obstruction. **2** a defect in speech, e.g. a lisp or stammer.

■**Usage** Do not confuse with **impedance**.

**impedimenta** (im-ped-i-ment-ă) *plural noun* encumbrances; baggage.

**impel** *verb* (**impelled, impelling**) **1** urge or drive to do something; *curiosity impelled her to investigate.* **2** send or drive forward, propel.

**impending** *adjective* (of an event or danger) imminent, about to happen.

**impenetrable** *adjective* **1** unable to be penetrated. **2** incomprehensible. **3** inaccessible to ideas etc. □ **impenetrably** *adverb*, **impenetrability** *noun*

**impenitent** *adjective* not sorry, not repentant. □ **impenitence** *noun*

**imperative** (im-pe-ră-tiv) *adjective* **1** expressing a command. **2** essential, obligatory; *further economies are imperative.* ● *noun* **1** a command. **2** *Grammar* a form of a verb used in making commands (e.g. *come* in *come here!*). **3** something essential or obligatory; *survival is the first imperative.*

**imperceptible** *adjective* not perceptible; very slight or gradual and therefore difficult to see. □ **imperceptibly** *adverb*, **imperceptibility** *noun*

**imperfect** *adjective* **1** not perfect; incomplete. **2** *Grammar* of the tense of a verb used to denote action going on but not completed, especially in the past, e.g. *she was singing.* ● *noun Grammar* the imperfect tense.

**imperfection** *noun* **1** being imperfect. **2** a mark or fault.

**imperial** *adjective* **1** of an empire or an emperor or empress. **2** majestic. **3** (of weights and measures) used by statute in the UK, formerly for all goods and still for certain goods; *an imperial gallon.* □ **imperially** *adverb*

**imperialism** *noun* **1** belief in the desirability of acquiring colonies and dependencies. **2** imperial rule or authority. □ **imperialist** *noun*, **imperialistic** *adjective*

**imperil** *verb* (**imperilled, imperilling**; *Amer.* **imperiled, imperiling**) endanger.

**imperious** (im-peer-iŭs) *adjective* commanding, bossy. □ **imperiously** *adverb*, **imperiousness** *noun*

**impermanent** *adjective* not permanent. □ **impermanence** *noun*, **impermanency** *noun*

**impermeable** (im-per-mi-ăbŭl) *adjective* not able to be penetrated, especially by liquid. □ **impermeability** *noun*

**impersonal** *adjective* **1** not influenced by personal feeling, showing no emotion. **2** not referring to any particular person. **3** having no existence as a person; *nature's impersonal forces.* **4** *Grammar* (of verbs) used with 'it' to make general statements such as 'it is raining'. □ **impersonally** *adverb*, **impersonality** *noun*

**impersonate** *verb* **1** play the part of. **2** pretend to be (another person) for entertainment or in fraud. □ **impersonation** *noun*, **impersonator** *noun*

**impertinent** *adjective* insolent, not showing proper respect. □ **impertinently** *adverb*, **impertinence** *noun*

**imperturbable** (im-per-terb-ăbŭl) *adjective* not excitable, calm. □ **imperturbably** *adverb*, **imperturbability** *noun*

**impervious** (im-per-viŭs) *adjective* (usually foll. by *to*) **1** not able to be penetrated; *impervious to water.* **2** not influenced, not responsive; *impervious to argument.*

**impetigo** (imp-i-ty-goh) *noun* a contagious skin disease causing spots that form yellowish crusts.

**impetuous** (im-pet-yoo-ŭs) *adjective* **1** moving quickly or violently; *an impetuous dash.* **2** acting or done on impulse. □ **impetuously** *adverb*, **impetuosity** *noun*

**impetus** (im-pit-ŭs) *noun* (*plural* **impetuses**) **1** the force or energy with which a body moves. **2** a driving force; *the treaty gave an impetus to trade.*

**impiety** (im-py-iti) *noun* lack of reverence.

**impinge** *verb* (usually foll. by *on* or *upon*) **1** make an impact. **2** encroach.

**impious** (imp-iŭs) *adjective* not reverent; wicked. □ **impiously** *adverb*

**impish** *adjective* of or like an imp; mischievous. □ **impishly** *adverb*, **impishness** *noun*

**implacable** (im-plak-ăbŭl) *adjective* not able to be placated, relentless. □ **implacably** *adverb*, **implacability** *adverb*

**implant** *verb* (*pronounced* im-plahnt) **1** plant, insert. **2** insert or fix (ideas etc.) in the mind. **3** insert (tissue or other substance) in a living thing. ● *noun* (*pronounced* im-plahnt) a thing implanted, implanted tissue etc. □ **implantation** *noun*

**implausible** *adjective* not plausible. □ **implausibly** *adverb*, **implausibility** *noun*

**implement** *noun* (*pronounced* im-pli-měnt) a tool or instrument for working with. ● *verb* (*pronounced* im-pli-ment) put into effect; *we implemented the scheme.* □ **implementation** *noun*

**implicate** *verb* **1** involve or show (a person) to be involved in a crime etc. **2** lead to as a consequence or inference; imply.

**implication** *noun* **1** implicating; being implicated. **2** implying; being implied. **3** something that is implied.

**implicit** (im-pliss-it) *adjective* **1** implied though not made explicit. **2** absolute, unquestioning; *expect implicit obedience.* □ **implicitly** *adverb*

**implode** *verb* burst or cause to burst inwards. □ **implosion** *noun*

**implore** *verb* request earnestly, entreat. □ **imploringly** *adverb*

**imply** verb (**implied, implying**) **1** suggest without stating directly, hint. **2** mean. **3** involve the truth or existence of; *the beauty of the carving implies that they had skilled craftsmen.*

**impolite** adjective ill-mannered, rude. □ **impolitely** adverb

**impolitic** (im-**pol**-i-tik) adjective unwise, inexpedient.

**imponderable** (im-**pon**-der-ăbŭl) adjective **1** not able to be estimated. **2** weightless, very light. ●noun (usually as **imponderables**) something difficult or impossible to assess.

**import** verb (pronounced im-**port**) **1** bring in from abroad or from an outside source. **2** imply, indicate. ●noun (pronounced **im**-port) **1** the importing of goods etc., something imported. **2** meaning. **3** importance. □ **importation** noun, **importer** noun

**important** adjective **1** having or able to have a great effect. **2** (of a person) having great authority or influence. **3** pompous; *he has an important manner.* □ **importantly** adverb, **importance** noun

**importunate** (im-**por**-tew-năt) adjective making persistent or pressing requests. □ **importunity** noun

**importune** (im-per-**tewn**) verb **1** make insistent requests to. **2** solicit as a prostitute.

**impose** verb **1** (often foll. by *on*) put (a tax or obligation etc.); *imposed heavy duties on tobacco.* **2** (often foll. by *on*) inflict; *imposed a great strain on our resources.* **3** force to be accepted; *imposed his ideas on the group.* **4** (foll. by *on*) take unfair advantage of; *we don't want to impose on your hospitality.* **5** lay (pages of type) in proper order.

**imposing** adjective impressive.

**imposition** noun **1** the act of imposing something. **2** something imposed, e.g. a tax or duty. **3** a burden imposed unfairly.

**impossible** adjective **1** not possible, unable to be done or to exist. **2** (*informal*) outrageous, unendurable; *an impossible person.* □ **impossibly** adverb, **impossibility** noun

**impost** (**im**-pohst) noun **1** a tax or duty levied. **2** the upper course of a pillar, carrying an arch.

**impostor** noun a person who fraudulently pretends to be someone else.

**imposture** noun a fraudulent deception.

**impotent** (**im**-pŏ-těnt) adjective **1** powerless, unable to take action. **2** (of a man) unable to perform sexual intercourse. □ **impotence** noun

**impound** verb **1** take (another person's property) into legal custody, confiscate. **2** shut up (cattle etc.) in a pound.

**impoverish** verb **1** cause to become poor. **2** exhaust the natural strength or fertility of; *impoverished soil.* □ **impoverishment** noun

**impracticable** adjective incapable of being put into practice. □ **impracticably** adverb, **impracticability** noun

**impractical** adjective not practical, unwise. □ **impracticality** noun

**imprecation** (impri-**kay**-shŏn) noun a spoken curse.

**imprecise** adjective not precise. □ **imprecisely** adverb, **imprecision** noun

**impregnable** (im-**preg**-năbŭl) adjective safe against attack; *an impregnable fortress.* □ **impregnably** adverb, **impregnability** noun

**impregnate** (**im**-preg-nayt) verb **1** introduce sperm or pollen into and fertilize (a female animal or plant); make pregnant. **2** penetrate all parts of (a substance), fill or saturate; *the water was impregnated with salts.* □ **impregnation** noun

**impresario** (impri-**sar**-i-oh) noun (plural **impresarios**) an organizer of public entertainment; the manager of a theatre or music company.

**impress** verb (pronounced im-**press**) **1** make (a person) form a strong (usually favourable) opinion of something. **2** (often foll. by *on*) fix firmly in the mind; *impressed on them the need for haste.* **3** press a mark into, stamp with a mark. ●noun (pronounced **im**-press) an impressed mark.

**impression** noun **1** an effect produced on the mind. **2** an uncertain idea, belief, or memory. **3** an imitation of a person or sound, done for entertainment. **4** the impressing of a mark; an impressed mark. **5** a reprint of a book etc. made with few or no alterations to its contents. □ **be under the impression** think (that something is a fact).

**impressionable** adjective easily influenced. □ **impressionably** adverb, **impressionability** noun

**impressionism** noun **1** a style of painting in the late 19th century giving the general impression of a subject, especially by using the effects of light, without elaborate detail. **2** a similar style in music or literature. □ **impressionist** noun, **impressionistic** adjective

**impressive** adjective making a strong impression; arousing admiration and approval. □ **impressively** adverb

**imprimatur** (im-prim-**ah**-ter) noun authoritative permission or approval, especially from the RC Church, for a book etc. to be printed.

**imprint** noun (pronounced **im**-print) **1** a mark made by pressing or stamping a surface; *the imprint of a foot.* **2** a publisher's name etc. printed in a book. ●verb (pronounced im-

**print) 1** impress or stamp a mark etc. on. **2** establish firmly in the mind.

**imprison** verb **1** put into prison. **2** keep in confinement. □ **imprisonment** noun

**improbable** adjective not likely to be true or to happen. □ **improbably** adverb, **improbability** noun

**improbity** (im-**proh**-biti) noun dishonesty, wickedness.

**impromptu** (im-**promp**-tew) adverb & adjective without preparation or rehearsal. ●noun **1** a short instrumental composition, often improvisatory in style. **2** an impromptu performance or speech.

**improper** adjective **1** wrong, incorrect; made improper use of the blade. **2** not conforming to the rules of social or lawful conduct. **3** indecent. □ **improper fraction** one with the numerator greater than the denominator, e.g. ⅗. □ **improperly** adverb

**impropriety** (im-prŏ-**pry**-iti) noun being improper; an improper act or remark.

**improve** verb **1** make or become better. **2** make good or better use of; improved the occasion. □ **improve on** produce something better than. □ **improvable** adjective

**improvement** noun **1** improving, being improved. **2** an addition or alteration that improves something or adds to its value.

**improvident** (im-**prov**-idĕnt) adjective not providing for future needs; wasteful. □ **improvidently** adverb, **improvidence** noun

**improvise** (im-prŏ-vyz) verb **1** compose (a thing) impromptu. **2** provide or construct using whatever materials are at hand; improvised a bed from cushions and rugs. □ **improvisation** noun, **improviser** noun, **improvisatory** adjective

**imprudent** (im-**proo**-dĕnt) adjective unwise, rash. □ **imprudently** adverb, **imprudence** noun

**impudent** adjective impertinent, cheeky. □ **impudently** adverb, **impudence** noun

**impugn** (im-**pewn**) verb express doubts about the truth or honesty of; try to discredit; we do not impugn their motives. □ **impugnment** noun

**impulse** noun **1** a push or thrust; impetus. **2** a stimulating force in a nerve, causing a muscle to react. **3** a sudden inclination to act, without thought for the consequences; did it on impulse. □ **impulse buying** buying of goods on impulse and not because of previous planning.

**impulsion** noun **1** impelling, a push; impetus. **2** a mental impulse.

**impulsive** adjective **1** (of a person) habitually acting on impulse. **2** (of an action) done on impulse. □ **impulsively** adverb, **impulsiveness** noun

**impunity** (im-**pewn**-iti) noun freedom from punishment or injury.

**impure** adjective **1** adulterated, not pure. **2** dirty. **3** unchaste; obscene.

**impurity** noun **1** being impure. **2** an impure substance or element.

**impute** (im-**pewt**) verb attribute or ascribe (a fault etc.). □ **imputation** (im-pew-**tay**-shŏn) noun

**IN** abbreviation Indiana.

**In** symbol indium.

**in** preposition expressing position or state. **1** of inclusion within the limits of space, time, circumstance, or surroundings. **2** of quantity or proportion; they are packed in tens. **3** of form or arrangement; hanging in folds. **4** of activity, occupation, or membership; he is in the army. **5** wearing as dress or colour etc.; in gumboots. **6** of method or means of expression; spoke in French. **7** with the instrument or means of; written in ink. **8** of identity; found a friend in Mary. **9** under the influence of; spoke in anger. **10** with respect to; lacking in courage. **11** as the content of; there's not much in it. **12** after the time of; back in ten minutes. **13** into. ●adverb **1** expressing position bounded by certain limits, or motion to a point enclosed by these; come in. **2** at home; will you be in? **3** on or towards the inside; with the fur side in. **4** in fashion, season, or office; elected; in effective or favourable action; my luck was in; the tide was in. **5** (in cricket and baseball) batting; which side is in? **6** having arrived or been gathered or received; the train is in; harvest is in. ●adjective **1** internal; living etc. inside. **2** fashionable; it's the in thing to do. □ **be in for** be about to experience; she is in for a surprise. **be in on** (informal) be aware of or sharing in (a secret or activity). **in all** in total number. **ins and outs** the details of an activity or procedure. **in so far as** to the extent that; he carried out orders only in so far as he did not openly disobey them. **in with** on good terms with.

**in.** abbreviation inch(es).

**inability** noun being unable.

**in absentia** (ab-sent-iă) in his, her, or their absence. (¶ Latin.)

**inaccessible** adjective not accessible; unapproachable. □ **inaccessibly** adverb, **inaccessibility** noun

**inaccurate** adjective not accurate. □ **inaccurately** adverb, **inaccuracy** noun

**inaction** noun lack of action, doing nothing.

**inactive** adjective not active, showing no activity. □ **inactively** adverb, **inactivity** noun

**inadequate** adjective **1** not adequate, insufficient. **2** not sufficiently able or competent; felt inadequate. □ **inadequately** adverb, **inadequacy** noun

**inadmissible** adjective not allowable. □ **inadmissibly** adverb, **inadmissibility** noun

**inadvertent** (in-ăd-ver-těnt) *adjective* unintentional. □ **inadvertently** *adverb*, **inadvertence** *noun*

**inadvisable** *adjective* not advisable. □ **inadvisability** *noun*

**inalienable** (in-ay-li-ĕn-ăbŭl) *adjective* not able to be given away or taken away; *an inalienable right*.

**inamorata** *noun* (*literary*) a female lover.

**inamorato** (in-am-er-**ah**-toh) *noun* (*plural* **inamoratos**) (*literary*) a male lover.

**inane** *adjective* silly, lacking sense. □ **inanely** *adverb*, **inanity** (in-**an**-iti) *noun*

**inanimate** (in-**an**-im-ăt) *adjective* **1** (of rocks and other objects) lifeless; (of plants) lacking animal life. **2** showing no sign of life.

**inapplicable** (in-ap-lik-ăbŭl) *adjective* not applicable.

**inapposite** (in-ap-ŏ-sit) *adjective* not apposite, unsuitable. □ **inappositely** *adverb*

**inappropriate** (in-ă-**proh**-pri-ăt) *adjective* unsuitable. □ **inappropriately** *adverb*, **inappropriateness** *noun*

**inarticulate** (in-ar-**tik**-yoo-lăt) *adjective* **1** not expressed in words; *an inarticulate cry*. **2** unable to speak distinctly; *was inarticulate with rage*. **3** unable to express one's ideas clearly. □ **inarticulately** *adverb*

**inasmuch as 1** since, because. **2** in so far as.

**inattention** *noun* lack of attention, neglect.

**inattentive** *adjective* not attentive, not paying attention. □ **inattentively** *adverb*, **inattentiveness** *noun*

**inaudible** (in-aw-dibŭl) *adjective* not audible, unable to be heard. □ **inaudibly** *adverb*

**inaugural** (in-**awg**-yoor-ăl) *adjective* of or for an inauguration; *the inaugural ceremony*.

**inaugurate** (in-**awg**-yoor-ayt) *verb* **1** admit (a person) to office with a ceremony. **2** enter ceremonially upon (an undertaking); open (a building or exhibition etc.) formally. **3** be the beginning of, introduce. □ **inauguration** *noun*, **inaugurator** *noun*

**inauspicious** (in-aw-**spish**-ŭs) *adjective* not auspicious. □ **inauspiciously** *adverb*, **inauspiciousness** *noun*

**inboard** *adjective & adverb* within the sides of or towards the centre of a ship, aircraft, or vehicle.

**inborn** *adjective* existing in a person or animal from birth; natural; *an inborn ability*.

**inbred** *adjective* **1** produced by inbreeding. **2** inborn.

**inbreeding** *noun* breeding from closely related individuals.

**inbuilt** *adjective* built-in.

**Inc.** *abbreviation* (*Amer.*) Incorporated.

**Inca** *noun* a member of an American Indian people in Peru before the Spanish conquest.

**incalculable** *adjective* unable to be calculated. □ **incalculably** *adverb*, **incalculability** *noun*

**incandesce** (in-kan-**dess**) *verb* glow with heat; cause to do this.

**incandescent** (in-kan-**dess**-ĕnt) *adjective* glowing with heat, shining. □ **incandescent lamp** a lamp in which a white-hot filament gives off light. □ **incandescence** *noun*

**incantation** (in-kan-**tay**-shŏn) *noun* words or sounds to be uttered as a magic spell.

**incapable** *adjective* **1** not capable. **2** helpless, powerless. □ **incapably** *adverb*, **incapability** *noun*

**incapacitate** (in-kă-**pas**-i-tayt) *verb* **1** disable. **2** make ineligible.

**incapacity** *noun* inability, lack of sufficient strength or power.

**incarcerate** (in-**kar**-ser-ayt) *verb* imprison. □ **incarceration** *noun*

**incarnate** *adjective* (*pronounced* in-**kar**-năt) embodied in flesh, especially in human form; *a devil incarnate*. ●*verb* (*pronounced* in-**kar**-nayt) **1** embody in flesh. **2** put (an idea etc.) into concrete form. **3** be a living embodiment of (a quality etc.).

**incarnation** (in-kar-**nay**-shŏn) *noun* **1** embodiment, especially in human form. **2** (**the Incarnation**) the embodiment of God in human form as Christ.

**incautious** (in-**kaw**-shŭs) *adjective* not cautious, rash. □ **incautiously** *adverb*, **incautiousness** *noun*

**incendiary** (in-**sen**-di-er-i) *adjective* **1** (of a bomb etc.) designed to cause a fire; containing chemicals that ignite. **2** of arson; guilty of arson. **3** tending to stir up strife, inflammatory. ●*noun* **1** an incendiary bomb. **2** an arsonist.

**incense**[1] (**in**-sens) *noun* **1** a substance that produces a sweet smell when burning. **2** its smoke, used especially in religious ceremonies.

**incense**[2] (in-**sens**) *verb* make angry.

**incentive** (in-**sen**-tiv) *noun* something that rouses or encourages a person to some action or effort. ●*adjective* acting as an incentive, inciting.

**inception** (in-**sep**-shŏn) *noun* the beginning of the existence of something.

**inceptive** (in-**sep**-tiv) *adjective* beginning, initial.

**incessant** (in-**sess**-ănt) *adjective* unceasing, continually repeated. □ **incessantly** *adverb*

**incest** (**in**-sest) *noun* sexual intercourse between people regarded as too closely related to marry each other.

**incestuous** (in-**sess**-tew-ŭs) *adjective* **1** involving incest. **2** guilty of incest.

**inch** *noun* **1** a measure of length, one twelfth of a foot (= 2.54 cm). **2** an amount of rainfall that would cover a surface to a depth of 1 inch. **3** a very small amount; *would not yield an inch.* ●*verb* move slowly and gradually; *they inched forward.* □ **every inch** entirely; *looked every inch a soldier.* **within an inch of** almost to the point of.

**inchoate** (in-koh-ăt) *adjective* **1** just begun. **2** not yet fully developed. □ **inchoation** *noun*

**incidence** (in-si-dĕns) *noun* **1** the rate at which something occurs or affects people or things; *studied the incidence of the disease.* **2** the falling of something (e.g. a ray of light) on a surface.

**incident** *noun* **1** an event, especially a minor one. **2** a piece of hostile activity; *frontier incidents.* **3** a public disturbance or accident; *the protest march took place without incident.* **4** an event that attracts general attention. ●*adjective* **1** (often foll. by *to*) liable to happen; accompanying something; *the risks incident to a pilot's career.* **2** (of rays of light etc.) falling on a surface.

**incidental** *adjective* **1** occurring as a minor accompaniment; *incidental expenses.* **2** liable to occur in consequence of or in connection with something; *the incidental hazards of exploration.* **3** casual, occurring by chance. □ **incidental music** music played as a background to the action of a film or play.

**incidentally** *adverb* **1** in an incidental way. **2** as an unconnected comment; by the way.

**incinerate** (in-sin-er-ayt) *verb* burn to ashes. □ **incineration** *noun*

**incinerator** (in-sin-er-ayt-er) *noun* a furnace or enclosed device for burning rubbish.

**incipient** (in-sip-iĕnt) *adjective* in its early stages, beginning; *incipient decay.*

**incise** (in-syz) *verb* **1** make a cut in (a surface). **2** engrave by cutting.

**incision** (in-si-zhŏn) *noun* **1** incising. **2** a cut, especially one made surgically into the body.

**incisive** (in-sy-siv) *adjective* clear and decisive; *made incisive comments.* □ **incisively** *adverb*, **incisiveness** *noun*

**incisor** (in-sy-zer) *noun* a sharp-edged cutting tooth at the front of the mouth.

**incite** (in-syt) *verb* urge on to action, stir up. □ **incitement** *noun*

**incivility** *noun* **1** lack of civility. **2** an impolite act or remark.

**inclement** (in-klem-ĕnt) *adjective* (of weather) cold, wet, or stormy. □ **inclemency** *noun*

**inclination** *noun* **1** a slope or slant; a leaning or bending movement. **2** a tendency. **3** a liking or preference.

**incline** *verb* (*pronounced* in-klyn) **1** lean, slope. **2** bend (the head or body) forward. **3** have or cause a certain tendency,

influence; *his manner inclines me to believe him.* ●*noun* (*pronounced* in-klyn) a slope. □ **be inclined** have a certain tendency or willingness; *the door is inclined to bang; I'm inclined to agree.*

**include** *verb* **1** have or regard or treat as part of a whole. **2** put into a certain category or list etc. □ **inclusion** *noun*

**inclusive** *adjective* **1** including the limits mentioned and the part between; *pages 7 to 26 inclusive.* **2** (often foll. by *of*) including. □ **inclusively** *adverb*

**incognito** (in-kog-nee-toh) *adjective & adverb* with one's identity kept secret; *she was travelling incognito.* ●*noun* (*plural* **incognitos**) the identity assumed by one who is incognito.

**incognizant** (in-kog-ni-zănt) *adjective* unaware. □ **incognizance** *noun*

**incoherent** (in-koh-heer-ĕnt) *adjective* rambling in speech or in reasoning. □ **incoherently** *adverb*, **incoherence** *noun*

**incombustible** *adjective* not able to be burnt.

**income** *noun* money received during a certain period (especially a year) as wages or salary, interest on investments, etc. □ **income tax** tax that must be paid on annual income.

**incoming** *adjective* **1** coming in; *the incoming tide.* **2** succeeding another person; *the incoming president.*

**incommensurable** *adjective* not commensurable. □ **incommensurability** *noun*

**incommensurate** *adjective* **1** not commensurate; disproportionate, inadequate. **2** incommensurable.

**incommode** (in-kŏ-mohd) *verb* inconvenience, disturb.

**incommodious** (in-kŏ-moh-diŭs) *adjective* (*formal*) too small for comfort; inconvenient.

**incommunicable** *adjective* unable to be communicated.

**incommunicado** (in-kŏ-mew-ni-kah-doh) *adjective* not allowed to communicate with others; *the prisoner was held incommunicado.*

**incomparable** (in-komp-er-ăbŭl) *adjective* without an equal, beyond comparison. □ **incomparably** *adverb*, **incomparability** *noun*

**incompatible** (in-kŏm-pat-ibŭl) *adjective* not compatible; conflicting or inconsistent; *the two statements are incompatible.* □ **incompatibly** *adverb*, **incompatibility** *noun*

**incompetent** (in-kom-pi-tĕnt) *adjective* not competent, lacking the necessary skill. ●*noun* an incompetent person. □ **incompetently** *adverb*, **incompetence** *noun*

**incomplete** *adjective* not complete. □ **incompletely** *adverb*, **incompleteness** *noun*

**incomprehensible** (in-kom-pri-**hen**-sibŭl) *adjective* not able to be understood. □ **incomprehensibly** *adverb*

**incomprehension** (in-kom-pri-**hen**-shŏn) *noun* failure to understand.

**inconceivable** *adjective* 1 unable to be imagined. 2 (*informal*) impossible to believe, most unlikely. □ **inconceivably** *adverb*

**inconclusive** *adjective* (of evidence or an argument etc.) not fully convincing, not decisive. □ **inconclusively** *adverb*

**incongruous** (in-**kong**-roo-ŭs) *adjective* unsuitable; out of place. □ **incongruously** *adverb*, **incongruity** (in-kong-**roo**-iti) *noun*

**inconsequent** (in-**kon**-si-kwěnt) *adjective* not following logically; irrelevant. □ **inconsequently** *adverb*, **inconsequence** *noun*

**inconsequential** (in-kon-si-**kwen**-shǎl) *adjective* 1 not following logically; irrelevant. 2 unimportant. □ **inconsequentially** *adverb*

**inconsiderable** *adjective* not worth considering, of small size, amount, or value. □ **inconsiderably** *adverb*

**inconsiderate** *adjective* not considerate towards other people; thoughtless. □ **inconsiderately** *adverb*, **inconsiderateness** *noun*

**inconsistent** *adjective* not consistent. □ **inconsistently** *adverb*, **inconsistency** *noun*

**inconsolable** (in-kŏn-**soh**-lă-bŭl) *adjective* not able to be consoled. □ **inconsolably** *adverb*

**inconspicuous** *adjective* not conspicuous, not easily noticed. □ **inconspicuously** *adverb*, **inconspicuousness** *noun*

**inconstant** *adjective* 1 fickle, changeable. 2 variable, not fixed. □ **inconstancy** *noun*

**incontestable** (in-kŏn-**test**-ăbŭl) *adjective* indisputable. □ **incontestably** *adverb*

**incontinent** *adjective* 1 unable to control the bladder or bowels. 2 lacking self-restraint in sexual desire. □ **incontinence** *noun*

**incontrovertible** (in-kon-trŏ-**vert**-ibŭl) *adjective* indisputable, undeniable. □ **incontrovertibly** *adverb*

**inconvenience** *noun* 1 being inconvenient. 2 a circumstance that is inconvenient. ● *verb* cause inconvenience or slight difficulty to.

**inconvenient** *adjective* not convenient, not suiting one's needs or requirements; slightly troublesome. □ **inconveniently** *adverb*

**incorporate** *verb* (*pronounced* in-**kor**-per-ayt) 1 include as a part; *your suggestions will be incorporated in the plan*. 2 form into a legal corporation. ● *adjective* (*pronounced* in-

kor-per-ăt) incorporated. □ **incorporation** *noun*

**incorrect** *adjective* 1 wrong; not true. 2 improper, unsuitable. □ **incorrectly** *adverb*, **incorrectness** *noun*

**incorrigible** (in-ko-ri-jibŭl) *adjective* (of a person or habit) not able to be reformed or improved; *an incorrigible liar.* □ **incorrigibly** *adverb*, **incorrigibility** *noun*

**incorruptible** (in-kŏ-**rupt**-ibŭl) *adjective* 1 not able to be corrupted morally, e.g. by bribes. 2 not liable to decay. □ **incorruptibility** *noun*

**increase** *verb* (*pronounced* in-**kreess**) make or become greater in size, amount, or intensity. ● *noun* (*pronounced* **in**-kreess) 1 the process of increasing. 2 the amount by which something increases. □ **on the increase** increasing.

**increasingly** *adverb* more and more.

**incredible** *adjective* 1 unbelievable. 2 (*informal*) hard to believe, very surprising. □ **incredibly** *adverb*

**incredulous** (in-**kred**-yoo-lŭs) *adjective* unbelieving, showing disbelief. □ **incredulously** *adverb*, **incredulity** (in-kri-**dew**-liti) *noun*

**increment** (**in**-kri-měnt) *noun* an increase, an added amount; *a salary with annual increments of £400.* □ **incremental** (in-kri-**men**-tăl) *adjective*

**incriminate** *verb* 1 indicate as involved in wrongdoing; *his statement incriminated the guard.* 2 charge with a crime. □ **incrimination** *noun*, **incriminatory** *adjective*

**incrustation** *noun* 1 encrusting, being encrusted. 2 a crust or deposit formed on a surface.

**incubate** *verb* 1 hatch (eggs) by warmth of a bird's body as it sits on them or by artificial heat. 2 cause (bacteria) to develop in suitable conditions. 3 develop slowly.

**incubation** *noun* incubating. □ **incubation period** the time it takes for symptoms of a disease to become apparent in an infected person.

**incubator** *noun* 1 an apparatus for hatching eggs or developing bacteria by artificial warmth. 2 an apparatus in which babies born prematurely can be kept in a constant controlled heat and supplied with oxygen etc.

**incubus** (**ink**-yoo-bŭs) *noun* (*plural* **incubuses** *or* **incubi**) 1 a burdensome person or thing. 2 an evil spirit visiting a sleeping person.

**inculcate** (**in**-kul-kayt) *verb* implant (ideas or habits) by persistent urging; *desiring to inculcate obedience in the young.* □ **inculcation** *noun*

**incumbency** (in-**kum**-běn-si) *noun* the position of an incumbent.

**incumbent** (in-**kum**-bĕnt) *adjective* (often foll. by *on*) forming an obligation or duty; *it is incumbent on you to warn people of the danger*. ●*noun* the holder of an office or post, especially a church benefice; a rector or vicar.

**incur** *verb* (**incurred, incurring**) bring (something unpleasant) on oneself; *incurred great expense*.

**incurable** *adjective* unable to be cured. ●*noun* a person with an incurable disease. □ **incurably** *adverb*, **incurability** *noun*

**incurious** *adjective* feeling or showing no curiosity. □ **incuriously** *adverb*

**incursion** *noun* a raid or brief invasion. □ **incursive** *adjective*

**Ind.** *abbreviation* Indiana.

**indebted** *adjective* owing money or gratitude. □ **indebtedness** *noun*

**indecent** *adjective* **1** offending against recognized standards of decency. **2** unseemly; *with indecent haste*. □ **indecent assault** sexual assault not involving rape. **indecent exposure** exposing one's genitals in public. □ **indecently** *adverb*, **indecency** *noun*

**indecipherable** *adjective* unable to be deciphered.

**indecision** *noun* inability to make up one's mind; hesitation.

**indecisive** *adjective* not decisive. □ **indecisively** *adverb*, **indecisiveness** *noun*

**indecorous** (in-**dek**-er-ŭs) *adjective* improper; not in good taste. □ **indecorously** *adverb*

**indeed** *adverb* **1** truly, really; *it was indeed remarkable*. **2** used to intensify a meaning; *very nice indeed*. **3** admittedly; *it is, indeed, his first attempt*. **4** used to express surprise or contempt; *does she indeed!*

**indefatigable** (indi-**fat**-ig-ăbŭl) *adjective* untiring, unflagging. □ **indefatigably** *adverb*

**indefeasible** (in-di-**fee**-zibŭl) *adjective* (*literary*) (of a right or possession) unable to be annulled or forfeited. □ **indefeasibly** *adverb*

**indefensible** *adjective* unable to be defended or justified. □ **indefensibly** *adverb*, **indefensibility** *noun*

**indefinable** (indi-**fy**-năbŭl) *adjective* unable to be defined or described clearly. □ **indefinably** *adverb*

**indefinite** *adjective* not clearly defined, stated, or decided; vague. □ **indefinite article** *Grammar* the word 'a' or 'an'.

**indefinitely** *adverb* **1** in an indefinite way. **2** for an unlimited period.

**indelible** *adjective* **1** (of a mark, stain, or feeling) unable to be removed or washed away. **2** (of ink etc.) making an indelible mark. □ **indelibly** *adverb*

**indelicate** *adjective* **1** slightly indecent; coarse, unrefined. **2** tactless. □ **indelicately** *adverb*, **indelicacy** *noun*

**indemnify** (in-**dem**-ni-fy) *verb* (**indemnified, indemnifying**) **1** protect or insure (a person) against penalties incurred by his or her actions etc. **2** compensate (a person) for injury suffered. □ **indemnification** *noun*

**indemnity** *noun* **1** protection or insurance against penalties incurred by one's actions. **2** compensation for damage done.

**indent** *verb* (*pronounced* in-**dent**) **1** make recesses or tooth-like notches in; *an indented coastline*. **2** start (a line of print or writing) further from the margin than the others; *indent the first line of each paragraph*. **3** place an indent for goods or stores. ●*noun* (*pronounced* **in**-dent) **1** an official order for goods or stores. **2** an indentation. **3** an indenture. □ **indentation** *noun*

**indenture** (in-**den**-cher) *noun* **1** a written contract or agreement. **2** (**indentures**) an agreement binding an apprentice to work for someone. ●*verb* bind by indentures.

**independence** *noun* being independent. □ **Independence Day** 4 July, celebrated in the USA as the anniversary of the date in 1776 when the American colonies formally declared themselves free and independent of Britain. **2** a similar festival celebrating national independence elsewhere.

**independent** *adjective* **1** (often foll. by *of*) not dependent on or controlled by another person or thing; *he is now independent of his parents*. **2** (of broadcasting) not financed by licence fees. **3** not depending on something else for its validity or operation; *independent proof*. **4** self-governing. **5** having or providing a sufficient income to make it unnecessary for the possessor to earn a living; *he has independent means*. **6** not influenced by others in one's ideas or conduct. **7** unwilling to be under an obligation to others. ●*noun* a politician who is not committed to any political party. □ **independent school** one that is not controlled by a local authority and does not receive a government grant. □ **independently** *adverb*

**in-depth** *adjective* thorough, very detailed; *an in-depth survey*.

**indescribable** *adjective* unable to be described, too great or bad etc. to be described. □ **indescribably** *adverb*

**indestructible** *adjective* unable to be destroyed. □ **indestructibly** *adverb*, **indestructibility** *noun*

**indeterminable** *adjective* impossible to discover or decide. □ **indeterminably** *adverb*

**indeterminate** *adjective* not fixed in extent or character etc.; vague, left doubtful.

□ **indeterminately** *adverb*, **indeterminacy** *noun*

**index** *noun* (*plural* **indexes** or (in sense 2, and always in sense 3) **indices**, *pronounced* in-di-seez) **1** a list of names, titles, subjects, etc., especially an alphabetical list indicating where in a book etc. each can be found. **2** a figure indicating the relative level of prices or wages compared with that at a previous date. **3** *Maths* the exponent of a number. ● *verb* **1** make an index to (a book or collection of books etc.). **2** enter in an index. **3** make (wages, pensions, etc.) index-linked. □ **index finger** the forefinger. **index-linked** *adjective* (of wages, pensions, etc.) increased according to increases in the cost-of-living index. □ **indexer** *noun*

**indexation** *noun* the practice of making wages, pensions, etc. index-linked.

**India 1** a large peninsula of Asia south of the Himalayas, forming a subcontinent. **2** a country consisting of the greater part of this. □ **India paper** thin tough opaque paper used for printing.

**Indian** *adjective* of India or Indians. ● *noun* **1** a native of India. **2** (in full **American Indian**) any of the original inhabitants of the continent of America (other than Eskimos) or their descendants. □ **Indian clubs** a pair of heavy bottle-shaped clubs for swinging to exercise the arms. **Indian corn** maize. **Indian file** single file. **Indian ink** ink made with a black pigment (made originally in China and Japan). **Indian summer 1** a period of dry sunny weather in late autumn. **2** a period of tranquil enjoyment late in life.

**Indiana** (indi-**an**-ă) a State in the Middle West of the USA.

**Indian Ocean** the ocean to the south of India, extending from the east coast of Africa to the East Indies and Australia.

**indiarubber** *noun* (*old use*) a rubber for rubbing out pencil or ink marks.

**Indic** *adjective* of the branch of Indo-European languages consisting of Sanskrit and the modern Indian languages which are its descendants. ● *noun* this group of languages.

**indicate** *verb* **1** point out, make known. **2** be a sign of, show the presence of. **3** show the need of, require. **4** state briefly. □ **indication** *noun*

**indicative** (in-**dik**-ătiv) *adjective* **1** (foll. by *of*) giving an indication; *the style is indicative of the author's origin.* **2** *Grammar* (of a form of a verb) used in making a statement, not in a command or wish etc., e.g. *he said* or *he is coming.* ● *noun* this form of a verb.

**indicator** *noun* **1** a thing that indicates or points to something. **2** a meter or other device giving information about the functioning of a machine etc. **3** a board giving information about something that is constantly changing, e.g. the arrival or departure of trains or aircraft. **4** a flashing light on a vehicle showing the direction in which it is to turn.

**indices** *see* INDEX.

**indict** (in-**dyt**) *verb* make an indictment against (a person).

**indictable** (in-**dyt**-ăbŭl) *adjective* (of an action) making the doer liable to be charged with a crime; (of a person) liable to this.

**indictment** (in-**dyt**-měnt) *noun* **1** a written statement of charges against an accused person. **2** an accusation, especially of serious wrongdoing.

**indie** *noun* (*informal*) an independent record company.

**Indies, the** (*old use*) India and adjacent regions. □ **East Indies, West Indies** see separate entries.

**indifferent** *adjective* **1** feeling or showing no interest or sympathy; unconcerned. **2** neither good nor bad. **3** not of good quality or ability; *he is an indifferent footballer.* □ **indifferently** *adverb*, **indifference** *noun*

**indigenous** (in-**dij**-in-ŭs) *adjective* (of plants, animals, or inhabitants) native.

**indigent** (in-dij-ěnt) *adjective* needy, poverty-stricken. □ **indigence** *noun*

**indigestible** (indi-**jest**-ibŭl) *adjective* difficult or impossible to digest. □ **indigestibility** *noun*

**indigestion** (indi-**jes**-chŏn) *noun* pain caused by difficulty in digesting food.

**indignant** *adjective* feeling or showing indignation. □ **indignantly** *adverb*

**indignation** *noun* anger aroused by something thought to be unjust or wrong.

**indignity** *noun* **1** the quality of being humiliating. **2** treatment that makes a person feel undignified or humiliated.

**indigo** *noun* a deep blue dye or colour.

**indirect** *adjective* not direct. □ **indirect object** *Grammar* a person or thing indirectly affected by the action of a verb, e.g. *him* in *give him the book.* **indirect speech** = REPORTED SPEECH. **indirect taxes** those paid in the form of increased prices for goods and services, not on income or capital. □ **indirectly** *adverb*

**indiscernible** (indi-**sern**-ibŭl) *adjective* not discernible.

**indiscipline** *noun* lack of discipline.

**indiscreet** *adjective* **1** not discreet, revealing secrets. **2** not cautious, unwise. □ **indiscreetly** *adverb*

**indiscretion** (in-dis-**kresh**-ŏn) *noun* **1** lack of discretion. **2** an indiscreet action or statement.

**indiscriminate** *adjective* showing no discrimination; doing or giving things without making a careful choice. □ **indiscriminately** *adverb*, **indiscrimination** *noun*

**indispensable** *adjective* not able to be dispensed with; essential. □ **indispensably** *adverb*, **indispensability** *noun*

**indisposed** *adjective* **1** slightly ill. **2** unwilling; *they seem indisposed to help us.* □ **indisposition** *noun*

**indisputable** (in-dis-**pewt**-ăbŭl) *adjective* not able to be disputed; undeniable. □ **indisputably** *adverb*, **indisputability** *noun*

**indissoluble** (indi-**sol**-yoo-bŭl) *adjective* firm and lasting; not able to be dissolved or destroyed; *indissoluble bonds of friendship.* □ **indissolubly** *adverb*

**indistinct** *adjective* not distinct; unclear, obscure. □ **indistinctly** *adverb*, **indistinctness** *noun*

**indistinguishable** *adjective* not distinguishable. □ **indistinguishably** *adverb*

**indite** (in-**dyt**) *verb* (*old use*) put into words, compose and write (a letter etc.).

**indium** (**in**-di-ŭm) *noun* a soft silvery metallic element (symbol In), used in alloys and semiconductor devices.

**individual** *adjective* **1** single, separate; *each individual strand.* **2** of or for one person; *baked in individual portions.* **3** characteristic of one particular person or thing; *has a very individual style.* ● *noun* **1** one person, plant, or animal considered separately. **2** (*informal*) a person; *a most unpleasant individual.* □ **individually** *adverb*, **individuality** (indi-vid-yoo-**al**-iti) *noun*

**individualist** *noun* a person who is very independent in thought or action. □ **individualism** *noun*, **individualistic** *adjective*

**indivisible** (indi-**viz**-ibŭl) *adjective* not divisible. □ **indivisibly** *adverb*, **indivisibility** *noun*

**Indo-** *combining form* Indian (and).

**Indo-China 1** the peninsula of SE Asia between India and China, containing Myanmar (Burma), Thailand, Malaya, Laos, Cambodia, and Vietnam. **2** a former French dependency, the region that now consists of Laos, Cambodia, and Vietnam. □ **Indo-Chinese** *adjective & noun*

**indoctrinate** (in-**dok**-trin-ayt) *verb* teach (a person) to accept a particular belief uncritically. □ **indoctrination** *noun*

**Indo-European** *adjective* of the family of languages spoken over most of Europe and Asia as far as north India. ● *noun* this family of languages.

**indolent** (**in**-dŏl-ĕnt) *adjective* lazy. □ **indolently** *adverb*, **indolence** *noun*

**indomitable** (in-**dom**-it-ăbŭl) *adjective* having an unyielding spirit, stubbornly per-

sistent when faced with difficulty or opposition. □ **indomitably** *adverb*

**Indonesia** (indŏ-**nee**-*zh*ă) a country consisting of a large group of islands in SE Asia. □ **Indonesian** *adjective & noun*

**indoor** *adjective* situated, used, or done inside a building; *indoor games; an indoor aerial.*

**indoors** *adverb* inside a building.

**indrawn** *adjective* (of breath etc.) drawn in.

**indubitable** (in-**dew**-bit-ăbŭl) *adjective* that cannot reasonably be doubted. □ **indubitably** *adverb*

**induce** (in-**dewss**) *verb* **1** persuade. **2** produce or cause. **3** bring on (labour in childbirth) by artificial means. □ **inducible** *adjective*

**inducement** *noun* **1** inducing; being induced. **2** an attraction or incentive.

**induct** *verb* install (a clergyman) ceremonially into a benefice.

**inductance** *noun* the property of producing an electric current by induction.

**induction** *noun* **1** inducting. **2** inducing. **3** logical reasoning that a general law exists because particular cases that seem to be examples of it exist. **4** production of an electric or magnetic state in an object by bringing an electrified or magnetic object close to but not touching it. **5** the drawing of a fuel mixture into the cylinders of an internal-combustion engine. **6** production of an electric current in a circuit by varying the magnetic field. **7** formal introduction to a new job or position.

**inductive** *adjective* **1** of or using induction; *inductive reasoning.* **2** of electric or magnetic induction.

**inductor** *noun* a component in an electric circuit having inductance.

**indulge** *verb* **1** allow (a person) to have what he or she wishes. **2** gratify (a wish). **3** (*informal*) take alcoholic drink. □ **indulge in** allow oneself the pleasure of; *he indulges in a cigar after lunch.*

**indulgence** *noun* **1** indulging. **2** being indulgent. **3** something allowed as a pleasure or privilege. **4** (in the RC Church) remission of the punishment still due for sins even after absolution has been given.

**indulgent** *adjective* indulging a person's wishes too freely; kind and lenient. □ **indulgently** *adverb*

**industrial** *adjective* **1** of or engaged in industries; *industrial workers.* **2** for use in industries. **3** having many highly developed industries; *an industrial country.* □ **industrial action** a strike or other disruptive activity by workers as a protest. **industrial estate** an area of land developed for industrial and business enterprises. **industrial relations** relations between management and workers. **Industrial Revolution** the rapid development of British industry by use of machines in the early 19th century. □ **industrially** *adverb*

**industrialism** *noun* a system in which manufacturing industries are predominant.

**industrialist** *noun* a person who owns or manages an industrial business.

**industrialized** *adjective* (also **industrialised**) (of a country or area) made industrial. □ **industrialization** *noun*

**industrious** *adjective* hard-working. □ **industriously** *adverb*, **industriousness** *noun*

**industry** *noun* **1** the manufacture or production of goods. **2** a particular branch of this; any business activity; *the tourist industry.* **3** the quality of being industrious; diligence.

**inebriate** (in-ee-bri-ăt) *adjective* drunken. ● *noun* a drunken person; a drunkard.

**inebriated** (in-ee-bri-ayt-id) *adjective* drunken. □ **inebriation** *noun*

**inedible** *adjective* not edible, not suitable for eating.

**ineducable** (in-ed-yoo-kăbŭl) *adjective* incapable of being educated, especially through mental inadequacy.

**ineffable** (in-ef-ăbŭl) *adjective* too great to be described; unutterable; *ineffable joy.* □ **ineffably** *adverb*

**ineffective** *adjective* **1** not effective. **2** (of a person) inefficient. □ **ineffectively** *adverb*

**ineffectual** *adjective* having no effect. □ **ineffectually** *adverb*

**inefficient** *adjective* not efficient; wasteful. □ **inefficiently** *adverb*, **inefficiency** *noun*

**inelegant** *adjective* not elegant; unrefined. □ **inelegantly** *adverb*, **inelegance** *noun*

**ineligible** *adjective* not eligible or qualified. □ **ineligibility** *noun*

**ineluctable** (in-i-luk-tăbŭl) *adjective* inescapable, unavoidable.

**inept** *adjective* **1** unsuitable, absurd. **2** unskilful. □ **ineptly** *adverb*, **ineptitude** *noun*

**inequable** (in-ek-wă-bŭl) *adjective* **1** unfair. **2** not uniform.

**inequality** *noun* **1** lack of equality in size, standard, etc. **2** unevenness.

**inequitable** (in-ek-wit-ăbŭl) *adjective* unfair, unjust. □ **inequitably** *adverb*

**inequity** (in-ek-witi) *noun* unfairness.

**ineradicable** (in-i-rad-ik-ăbŭl) *adjective* unable to be removed or rooted out. □ **ineradicably** *adverb*

**inert** *adjective* **1** (of matter) without power to move or act. **2** without active chemical or other properties, incapable of reacting; *an inert gas.* **3** not moving; slow to move or take action. □ **inertly** *adverb*, **inertness** *noun*

**inertia** (in-er-shă) *noun* **1** inertness, slowness to take action. **2** *Physics* the property of matter by which it remains in its existing state of rest or motion unless acted upon by an external force. □ **inertia reel** a reel round which one end of a safety-belt is wound so that the belt will tighten automatically over the wearer if it is pulled suddenly. **inertia selling** the sending of goods to a person who has not ordered them, in the hope that he or she will not take action to refuse them and must later make payment. □ **inertial** *adjective*

**inescapable** *adjective* unavoidable. □ **inescapably** *adverb*

**inessential** *adjective* not essential. ● *noun* an inessential thing.

**inestimable** (in-est-im-ăbŭl) *adjective* too great, precious, etc. to be estimated. □ **inestimably** *adverb*

**inevitable** (in-ev-it-ăbŭl) *adjective* **1** not able to be prevented, sure to happen or appear. **2** (*informal*) tiresomely familiar; *the tourist with his inevitable camera.* ● *noun* (**the inevitable**) something that is unavoidable. □ **inevitably** *adverb*, **inevitability** *noun*

**inexact** *adjective* not exact. □ **inexactly** *adverb*, **inexactitude** *noun*

**inexcusable** *adjective* unable to be excused or justified. □ **inexcusably** *adverb*

**inexhaustible** *adjective* not able to be totally used up; available in unlimited quantity.

**inexorable** (in-eks-er-ăbŭl) *adjective* relentless; unable to be persuaded by request or entreaty. □ **inexorably** *adverb*

**inexpedient** *adjective* not expedient.

**inexpensive** *adjective* not expensive, offering good value for the price.

**inexperience** *noun* lack of experience. □ **inexperienced** *adjective*

**inexpert** *adjective* not expert, unskilful. □ **inexpertly** *adverb*

**inexpiable** (in-eks-pi-ăbŭl) *adjective* unable to be expiated or appeased.

**inexplicable** (in-iks-**plik**-ăbŭl) *adjective* unable to be explained or accounted for. □ **inexplicably** *adverb*

**inexpressible** *adjective* unable to be expressed in words.

*in* **extremis** (in eks-**tree**-meess) **1** at the point of death. **2** in very great difficulties. (¶ Latin.)

**inextricable** (in-eks-**trik**-ăbŭl) *adjective* **1** inescapable. **2** unable to be disentangled or sorted out. □ **inextricably** *adverb*

**infallible** (in-fal-ibŭl) *adjective* **1** incapable of making a mistake or being wrong. **2** never failing; *an infallible remedy.* **3** (of the Pope) incapable of doctrinal error. □ **infallibly** *adverb*, **infallibility** (in-fali-**bil**-iti) *noun*

**infamous** (in-fă-mŭs) *adjective* having or deserving a very bad reputation; notorious. □ **infamy** (in-fă-mi) *noun*

**infancy** *noun* **1** early childhood, babyhood. **2** an early stage of development.

**infant** *noun* **1** a child during the earliest period of its life. **2** a schoolchild under seven. **3** (also **minor**) *Law* a person under 18.

**infanta** (in-**fant**-ă) *noun* (*hist.*) a daughter of the Spanish or Portuguese king.

**infanticide** (in-**fant**-i-syd) *noun* **1** the act of killing an infant soon after its birth. **2** a person who is guilty of this.

**infantile** (in-**făn**-tyl) *adjective* **1** of infants or infancy. **2** childish. □ **infantile paralysis** polio.

**infantry** *noun* troops who fight on foot.

**infantryman** *noun* (*plural* **infantrymen**) a member of an infantry regiment.

**infatuated** *adjective* temporarily filled with an intense unreasoning love for a person or thing. □ **infatuation** *noun*

**infect** *verb* **1** affect or contaminate with a germ, virus, or disease. **2** inspire with one's feeling, especially bad feeling.

**infection** *noun* **1** infecting, being infected. **2** the spreading of disease, especially by air or water etc. **3** a disease that is spread in this way; a diseased condition.

**infectious** *adjective* **1** (of a disease) able to spread by air or water etc. **2** infecting with disease. **3** quickly spreading to others; *his fear was infectious.*

**infelicity** (in-fi-**lis**-iti) *noun* **1** an inapt remark or expression. **2** unhappiness; misfortune. □ **infelicitous** *adjective*

**infer** *verb* (**inferred, inferring**) **1** reach (an opinion) from facts or reasoning; deduce. **2** imply. □ **inferable** *adjective*

∎**Usage** The use in sense 2 is often considered incorrect and conceals a useful distinction between *infer* and *imply*.

**inference** (in-fer-ĕns) *noun* **1** inferring. **2** a thing inferred. □ **inferential** (in-fer-**en**-shăl) *adjective*

**inferior** *adjective* low or lower in rank, importance, quality, or ability. ●*noun* a person who is inferior to another, especially in rank.

**inferiority** *noun* being inferior. □ **inferiority complex** a feeling of general inferiority, sometimes with aggressive behaviour in compensation.

**infernal** *adjective* **1** of hell; *the infernal regions.* **2** (*informal*) detestable, tiresome; *an infernal nuisance.* □ **infernally** *adverb*

**inferno** (in-**fer**-noh) *noun* (*plural* **infernos**) **1** a raging fire. **2** somewhere intensely hot. **3** a place resembling hell.

**infertile** *adjective* **1** not fertile. **2** unable to have offspring. □ **infertility** *noun*

**infest** *verb* (of pests or vermin etc.) be numerous and troublesome in (a place); overrun. □ **infestation** *noun*

**infidel** (in-fid-ĕl) *noun* a person who does not believe in a religion. ●*adjective* **1** of infidels. **2** unbelieving.

**infidelity** *noun* unfaithfulness, especially adultery.

**infield** *noun* (in cricket) the part of the ground near the wicket.

**infighting** *noun* **1** conflict within an organization. **2** boxing with an opponent nearer than arm's length.

**infilling** *noun* **1** placing of buildings to occupy gaps between earlier ones. **2** material used to fill a gap.

**infiltrate** (in-fil-trayt) *verb* **1** enter gradually and without being noticed, e.g. as settlers or spies. **2** cause to do this. **3** pass (fluid) by filtration. □ **infiltration** *noun*, **infiltrator** *noun*

**infinite** (in-fin-it) *adjective* **1** having no limit, endless. **2** very great or many. □ **infinitely** *adverb*

**infinitesimal** (in-fini-**tess**-imăl) *adjective* extremely small. □ **infinitesimally** *adverb*

**infinitive** (in-**fin**-itiv) *noun* a form of a verb that does not indicate a particular tense or number or person, in English used with or without *to*, e.g. *go* in *let him go* or *allow him to go.*

**infinitude** *noun* (*literary*) being infinite; infinity.

**infinity** (in-**fin**-iti) *noun* **1** an infinite number, extent, or time. **2** being infinite; boundlessness.

**infirm** *adjective* physically weak, especially from old age.

**infirmary** *noun* **1** a hospital. **2** a room or rooms for sick people in a school etc.

**infirmity** *noun* **1** being infirm. **2** a particular physical weakness.

**infix** *verb* fasten or fix in.

***in flagrante delicto*** (in flă-**gran**-ti di-**lik**-toh) in the very act of committing an offence. (¶ Latin, = in blazing crime.)

**inflame** *verb* **1** provoke to strong feeling or emotion; arouse anger in. **2** cause inflammation in. **3** aggravate, intensify. **4** catch or set on fire.

**inflammable** *adjective* able to be set on fire or excited.

∎**Usage** This word means the same as *flammable.* Its opposite is *non-inflammable.*

**inflammation** *noun* **1** redness, heat, and pain produced in the body, especially as a reaction to injury or infection. **2** inflaming.

**inflammatory** (in-**flam**-ă-ter-i) *adjective* **1** likely to arouse strong feeling or anger; *inflammatory speeches.* **2** causing or involving inflammation.

**inflatable** (in-**flayt**-ăbul) *adjective* able to be inflated. ●*noun* an inflatable plastic or rubber object.

**inflate** *verb* **1** fill or become filled with air or gas and swell up. **2** exaggerate the importance of; puff up (with pride etc.). **3** increase (a price etc.) artificially. **4** resort to inflation (of currency).

**inflation** *noun* **1** inflating; being inflated. **2** a general increase of prices and fall in the purchasing value of money. □ **inflationary** *adjective*

**inflect** *verb* **1** change the pitch of (the voice) in speaking. **2** change the ending or form of (a word) to show its grammatical relation or number etc., e.g. *sing* to *sang* or *sung; child* to *children*. □ **inflection** *or* **inflexion** *noun*

**inflective** *adjective* of or involving grammatical inflexion.

**inflexible** *adjective* **1** not flexible, unable to be bent. **2** not able to be altered; *an inflexible rule*. **3** refusing to alter one's demands etc., unyielding. □ **inflexibly** *adverb*, **inflexibility** *noun*

**inflict** *verb* **1** deal out (a blow or wound). **2** (usually foll. by *on*) impose (something unpleasant); *shall not inflict myself on you any longer*. □ **infliction** *noun*, **inflictor** *noun*

**inflorescence** (in-flor-ess-ěns) *noun* **1** flowering. **2** the flowers of a plant; their arrangement on a stem etc.

**inflow** *noun* an inward flow; the amount that flows in; *a large inflow of cash*.

**influence** *noun* **1** the power to produce an effect; *the influence of the moon on the tides*. **2** the ability to affect someone's character or beliefs or actions. **3** a person or thing with this ability. ●*verb* exert influence on. □ **under the influence** (*informal*) drunk.

**influential** (in-floo-en-shǎl) *adjective* having great influence. □ **influentially** *adverb*

**influenza** *noun* a virus disease causing fever, muscular pain, and catarrh.

**influx** *noun* an inflow, especially of people or things into a place.

**info** *noun* (*informal*) information.

**inform** *verb* **1** give information to. **2** (usually foll. by *against* or *on*) give incriminating information about a person to the authorities.

**informal** *adjective* not formal; without formality or ceremony. □ **informally** *adverb*, **informality** (in-for-mal-iti) *noun*

▪**Usage** In this dictionary, words marked *informal* are used in everyday speech but should not be used when speaking or writing formally.

**informant** *noun* a person who gives information.

**information** *noun* **1** facts told or discovered. **2** facts fed into a computer etc.; data. □ **information science** *or* **technology** the study or use of processes (especially

computers, microelectronics, and telecommunications) for storing, retrieving, and sending information (e.g. words, numbers, pictures).

**informative** *adjective* giving information; instructive.

**informed** *adjective* having good or sufficient knowledge of something; *informed opinion*.

**informer** *noun* a person who informs against someone.

*infra* *adverb* below or further on in a book etc. (¶ Latin, = below.)

**infraction** (in-frak-shŏn) *noun* infringement.

**infra dig** (*informal*) beneath one's dignity. (¶ From the Latin *infra dignitatem*.)

**infrared** *adjective* of or using rays with a wavelength slightly longer than the red end of the visible spectrum.

**infrastructure** *noun* **1** the basic structural foundations of a society or enterprise. **2** the facilities (such as roads, sewers, etc.) regarded as a country's economic foundation.

**infrequent** *adjective* not frequent. □ **infrequently** *adverb*, **infrequency** *noun*

**infringe** *verb* **1** break or act against (a rule or agreement etc.); violate. **2** (foll. by *on* or *upon*) encroach; *do not infringe on his privacy*. □ **infringement** *noun*

**infuriate** *verb* enrage. □ **infuriating** *adjective*, **infuriatingly** *adverb*

**infuse** *verb* **1** imbue, instil; *infused them with courage; infused life into them*. **2** steep (tea or herbs etc.) in a liquid in order to make flavour or soluble constituents pass into the liquid; (of tea etc.) undergo this process.

**infusible** *adjective* not able to be melted. □ **infusibility** *noun*

**infusion** *noun* **1** infusing, being infused. **2** a liquid made by infusing. **3** something added or introduced into a stock; *an infusion of new blood to improve the breed*.

**ingenious** *adjective* **1** clever at inventing new things or methods. **2** cleverly contrived; *an ingenious machine*. □ **ingeniously** *adverb*, **ingenuity** (in-jin-yoo-iti) *noun*

*ingénue* (an-zhe-new) *noun* an unsophisticated or innocent young woman, especially as a role in a play. (¶ French.)

**ingenuous** (in-jen-yoo-ŭs) *adjective* **1** unsophisticated, innocent; *an ingenuous manner*. **2** frank. □ **ingenuously** *adverb*

▪**Usage** Do not confuse with **ingenious**.

**ingest** (in-jest) *verb* take in as food. □ **ingestion** *noun*

**inglenook** *noun* a nook forming a place for sitting beside a deeply recessed fireplace.

**inglorious** *adjective* **1** ignominious. **2** not famous; obscure.

**ingoing** *adjective* going in.

**ingot** (ing-ŏt) *noun* a brick-shaped lump of cast metal, especially gold.

**ingrained** *adjective* **1** (of habits, feelings, or tendencies) firmly fixed. **2** (of dirt) marking a surface deeply.

**ingratiate** (in-gray-shi-ayt) *verb* (**ingratiate oneself**) (usually foll. by *with*) bring oneself into a person's favour, especially in order to gain an advantage. □ **ingratiating** *adjective*, **ingratiatingly** *adverb*

**ingratitude** *noun* lack of due gratitude.

**ingredient** *noun* any of the parts or elements in a mixture.

**ingress** *noun* **1** going in. **2** the right to go in.

**ingrowing** *adjective* growing abnormally into the flesh; *an ingrowing toenail*. □ **ingrown** *adjective*

**inhabit** *verb* live in (a place) as one's home; occupy. □ **inhabitable** *adjective*

**inhabitant** *noun* one who inhabits a place.

**inhalant** (in-hay-lănt) *noun* a medicinal substance to be inhaled.

**inhale** *verb* breathe in, draw into the lungs by breathing. □ **inhalation** (in-hă-lay-shŏn) *noun*

**inhaler** *noun* a device that sends out a medicinal vapour to be inhaled, especially to relieve asthma.

**inharmonious** *adjective* not harmonious; discordant.

**inhere** (in-heer) *verb* be inherent.

**inherent** (in-heer-ĕnt) *adjective* existing in something as a natural or permanent characteristic or quality. □ **inherently** *adverb*, **inherence** *noun*

**inherit** *verb* **1** receive (property or a title etc.) by legal right of succession or by a will when its previous owner or holder has died. **2** receive from a predecessor; *this government inherited many problems from the last one*. **3** receive (a characteristic) from one's parents or ancestors. □ **inheritable** *adjective*, **inheritor** *noun*

**inheritance** *noun* **1** inheriting. **2** a thing that is inherited. □ **inheritance tax** a tax on property acquired by gift or inheritance (introduced in 1986 to replace *capital transfer tax*).

**inhibit** *verb* **1** restrain, prevent; *this substance inhibits the growth of moss*. **2** hinder the impulses of (a person); cause inhibitions in.

**inhibition** (in-hib-ish-ŏn) *noun* **1** inhibiting; being inhibited. **2** *Psychol.* repression of or resistance to an instinct, impulse, or feeling.

**inhospitable** (in-hoss-pit-ăbŭl) *adjective* **1** not hospitable. **2** (of a place or climate) giving no shelter or no favourable conditions.

**in-house** *adverb & adjective* within an institution or company.

**inhuman** *adjective* brutal; lacking normal human qualities of kindness, pity, etc. □ **inhumanity** (in-hew-man-iti) *noun*

**inhumane** (in-hew-mayn) *noun* = INHUMAN.

**inimical** (in-im-ikăl) *adjective* **1** hostile. **2** harmful. □ **inimically** *adverb*

**inimitable** (in-im-it-ăbŭl) *adjective* impossible to imitate. □ **inimitably** *adverb*

**iniquitous** (in-ik-wit-ŭs) *adjective* very unjust.

**iniquity** (in-ik-witi) *noun* **1** great injustice. **2** wickedness.

**initial** *adjective* of or at the beginning; *the initial stages of the work*. ● *noun* the first letter of a word, especially of a person's name. ● *verb* (**initialled, initialling**; *Amer.* **initialed, initialing**) sign or mark with initials. □ **initially** *adverb*

**initiate** *verb* (*pronounced* in-ish-i-ayt) **1** cause to begin, start (a scheme) working; *he initiated certain reforms*. **2** admit (a person) into membership of a society etc., often with special ceremonies. **3** give (a person) basic instruction or information about something. ● *noun* (*pronounced* in-ish-i-ăt) an initiated person. □ **initiation** *noun*, **initiator** *noun*, **initiatory** *adjective*

**initiative** (in-ish-ă-tiv) *noun* **1** the first step in a process. **2** the power or right to begin something. **3** the ability to initiate things; enterprise; *he lacks initiative*. □ **have the initiative** be in a position to control the course of events, e.g. in a war. **on one's own initiative** without being prompted by others.

**inject** *verb* **1** force or drive (a liquid etc.) into something, especially by means of a syringe; administer medicine etc. to (a person) in this way. **2** (foll. by *into*) introduce (a new element or quality); *inject some new ideas into the committee*. □ **injector** *noun*

**injection** *noun* injecting; an instance of this. □ **fuel injection** the spraying of liquid fuel into the cylinders of an internal-combustion engine.

**injudicious** (in-joo-dish-ŭs) *adjective* showing lack of good judgement, unwise. □ **injudiciously** *adverb*

**injunction** *noun* an order or command, especially an order from a lawcourt restraining a person or group from some act.

**injure** *verb* **1** hurt. **2** do wrong to.

**injurious** (in-joor-iŭs) *adjective* **1** hurtful. **2** insulting.

**injury** *noun* **1** damage, harm. **2** a particular form of this; *a leg injury*. **3** a wrong or unjust act.

**injustice** *noun* **1** lack of justice. **2** an unjust action or treatment. □ **do a person an**

**injustice** make an unfair judgement about him or her.

**ink** *noun* **1** a coloured liquid or paste used in writing, printing, etc. **2** a black liquid squirted by a cuttlefish or octopus for concealment. ●*verb* mark or cover with ink. □ **ink-well** *noun* a small pot for holding ink, fitted into a hole in a desk.

**Inkatha** (in-**kah**-tă) a Zulu political organization in South Africa.

**inkling** *noun* a hint, a slight knowledge or suspicion.

**inkstand** *noun* a stand for one or more bottles of ink.

**inky** *adjective* **1** covered or stained with ink. **2** black like ink; *inky darkness*. □ **inkiness** *noun*

**INLA** *abbreviation* Irish National Liberation Army, an organization seeking to achieve union between Northern Ireland and the Irish Republic.

**inlaid** *see* INLAY.

**inland** *adjective & adverb* in or towards the interior of a country. □ **Inland Revenue** (*Brit.*) the government department responsible for assessing and collecting taxes and inland duties.

**in-laws** *plural noun* (*informal*) a person's relatives by marriage.

**inlay** *verb* (*pronounced* in-lay) (**inlaid, inlaying**) set (pieces of wood or metal etc.) into a surface so that they lie flush with it and form a design. ●*noun* (*pronounced* **in**-lay) **1** inlaid material. **2** a design formed by this. **3** a dental filling shaped to fit a tooth-cavity.

**inlet** *noun* **1** a strip of water extending into the land from a sea or lake, or between islands. **2** a way in, e.g. for water into a tank; *the inlet pipe*.

*in loco parentis* (in **loh**-koh pă-**ren**-tis) acting in place of a parent. (¶ Latin.)

**inmate** *noun* one of a number of inhabitants of a hospital, prison, or other institution.

**in memoriam** (mi-**mor**-i-am) in memory of (a dead person). (¶ Latin.)

**inmost** *adjective* furthest inward.

**inn** *noun* **1** a small hotel, especially in the country. **2** a public house. □ **Inn of Court** any of the four law societies in London with the exclusive right of admitting people to practise as barristers in England.

**innards** *plural noun* (*informal*) the stomach and bowels; entrails.

**innate** (in-**ayt**) *adjective* inborn. □ **innately** *adverb*

**inner** *adjective* **1** nearer to the centre or inside, interior, internal. **2** (of thoughts etc.) deeper. ●*noun* (in archery) the division of a target next to the bull's-eye; a shot that strikes this. □ **inner city** the central area of a city, often with overcrowding and pov-

erty. **inner tube** a separate inflatable tube inside a pneumatic tyre.

**innermost** *adjective* furthest inward.

**innings** *noun* (*plural* **innings**) **1** a batsman's or side's turn at batting in cricket. **2** a period of power or of opportunity to show one's ability.

**innkeeper** *noun* a person who keeps an inn.

**innocent** *adjective* **1** not guilty of a particular crime etc. **2** free of all evil or wrongdoing; *as innocent as a new-born babe*. **3** harmless, not intended to be harmful; *innocent amusements*; *an innocent remark*. **4** foolishly trustful. ●*noun* a person (especially a child) who is free of all evil or who is foolishly trustful. □ **innocently** *adverb*, **innocence** *noun*

**innocuous** (in-**ok**-yoo-ŭs) *adjective* harmless. □ **innocuously** *adverb*

**innovate** *verb* introduce a new process or way of doing things. □ **innovation** *noun*, **innovator** *noun*, **innovatory** *adjective*

**innuendo** (in-yoo-**en**-doh) *noun* (*plural* **innuendoes** or **innuendos**) an unpleasant insinuation.

**Innuit** alternative spelling of INUIT.

**innumerable** *adjective* too many to be counted. □ **innumerably** *adverb*

**innumerate** *adjective* having no knowledge of basic mathematics. □ **innumeracy** *noun*

**inoculate** *verb* treat (a person or animal) with vaccine or serum as a protection against a disease. □ **inoculation** *noun*

**inoffensive** *adjective* not offensive, harmless.

**inoperable** (in-**op**-er-ăbŭl) *adjective* unable to be cured by surgical operation.

**inoperative** *adjective* not functioning.

**inopportune** (in-op-er-**tewn**) *adjective* coming or happening at an unsuitable time. □ **inopportunely** *adverb*

**inordinate** (in-**or**-din-ăt) *adjective* excessive. □ **inordinately** *adverb*

**inorganic** (in-or-**gan**-ik) *adjective* **1** of mineral origin, not organic. **2** without organized physical structure. □ **inorganic chemistry** a branch of chemistry dealing with inorganic compounds.

**in-patient** *noun* a patient who remains resident in a hospital while undergoing treatment.

**input** *noun* **1** what is put in. **2** the place where energy or information etc. enters a system. **3** the data, programs, etc. supplied to a computer. ●*verb* (**input** or **inputted, inputting**) put in; supply (data, programs, etc.) to a computer.

**inquest** *noun* **1** a judicial investigation to establish facts, especially about a death which may not be the result of natural causes. **2** (*informal*) a detailed discussion of something that is over, e.g. a game.

**inquietude** (in-**kwy**-i-tewd) *noun* uneasiness of mind.

**inquire** *verb* make an inquiry, seek information. □ **inquirer** *noun*

■**Usage** See the note under **enquire**.

**inquiry** *noun* an investigation, especially an official one.

**inquisition** (inkwi-**zish**-ŏn) *noun* **1** a detailed questioning or investigation. **2** (**the Inquisition**) (*hist.*) a tribunal of the Roman Catholic Church in the Middle Ages, especially the very severe one in Spain, to discover and punish heretics. □ **inquisitional** *adjective*

**inquisitive** *adjective* **1** eagerly seeking knowledge. **2** prying. □ **inquisitively** *adverb*

**inquisitor** (in-**kwiz**-it-er) *noun* **1** a person who questions another searchingly. **2** (*hist.*) an officer of the Inquisition.

**inquisitorial** (in-kwiz-i-**tor**-iǎl) *adjective* of or like an inquisitor, prying. □ **inquisitorially** *adverb*

**inroad** *noun* a sudden attack made into a country. □ **make inroads on** *or* **into** use up large quantities of (resources etc.).

**inrush** *noun* a rush in, a violent influx.

**insalubrious** (in-sǎ-**loo**-briŭs) *adjective* (of a place or climate) unhealthy.

**insane** *adjective* **1** not sane, mad. **2** extremely foolish. □ **insanely** *adverb*, **insanity** *noun*

**insanitary** *adjective* unclean and likely to be harmful to health.

**insatiable** (in-**say**-shǎ-bŭl) *adjective* unable to be satisfied; *an insatiable appetite.* □ **insatiably** *adverb*, **insatiability** *noun*

**inscribe** *verb* **1** write or cut (words etc.) on (a surface); *inscribed their names on the stone*; *inscribed it with their names.* **2** draw (one geometrical figure) within another so that certain points of their boundaries coincide. **3** enter (a name) on a list or in a book.

**inscription** *noun* **1** words inscribed on a monument, coin, etc. **2** inscribing.

**inscrutable** (in-**skroot**-ǎbŭl) *adjective* impossible to understand or interpret; mysterious. □ **inscrutably** *adverb*, **inscrutability** *noun*

**insect** *noun* a small animal with six legs, no backbone, and a body divided into three parts (head, thorax, abdomen).

**insecticide** *noun* a substance for killing insects.

**insectivore** (in-**sek**-ti-vor) *noun* an animal or plant that feeds on insects. □ **insectivorous** (in-sek-**tiv**-er-ŭs) *adjective*

**insecure** *adjective* not secure or safe. □ **insecurely** *adverb*, **insecurity** *noun*

**inseminate** (in-**sem**-in-ayt) *verb* insert semen into. □ **insemination** *noun*

**insensate** (in-**sen**-sayt) *adjective* **1** without sensibility, unfeeling. **2** stupid. **3** without physical sensation.

**insensible** *adjective* **1** unconscious. **2** without feeling, unaware; *seemed insensible of his danger.* **3** callous. **4** (of changes) imperceptible. □ **insensibly** *adverb*, **insensibility** *noun*

**insensitive** *adjective* not sensitive; unfeeling. □ **insensitively** *adverb*, **insensitivity** *noun*

**inseparable** *adjective* **1** unable to be separated. **2** liking to be constantly together; *inseparable companions.* □ **inseparably** *adverb*, **inseparability** *noun*

**insert** *verb* (*pronounced* in-**sert**) put (a thing) in or between or among other things. ●*noun* (*pronounced* **in**-sert) a thing inserted. □ **insertion** *noun*

**in-service** *adjective* (of training) for people actively working in the profession or activity concerned.

**inset** *verb* (*pronounced* in-**set**) (**inset** *or* **insetted, insetting**) set or place in; decorate with an inset; *the crown was inset with jewels.* ●*noun* (*pronounced* **in**-set) something set into a larger thing, e.g. a small map within the border of a larger one.

**inshore** *adverb & adjective* at sea but near to the shore.

**inside** *noun* **1** the inner side, surface, or part. **2** (usually as **insides**) (*informal*) the organs in the abdomen; the stomach and bowels. ●*adjective* on or coming from the inside. ●*adverb* **1** on, in, or to the inside. **2** (*slang*) in prison. ●*preposition* on the inner side of, within; *inside an hour.* □ **inside information** information that is not available to outsiders. **inside job** (*informal*) a crime committed by someone living or working on the premises where it occurred. **inside left** *or* **right** (in football etc.) a player on the forward line near to the centre on the left or right side. **inside out 1** with the inner surface turned to face the outside. **2** thoroughly; *know a subject inside out.*

**insider** *noun* an accepted member of a certain group or profession etc. □ **insider dealing** the illegal practice of trading on the stock exchange to one's own advantage through having access to confidential information.

**insidious** (in-**sid**-iŭs) *adjective* spreading, developing, or acting inconspicuously but with harmful effect. □ **insidiously** *adverb*, **insidiousness** *noun*

**insight** *noun* **1** the ability to perceive and understand the true nature of something. **2** knowledge obtained by this.

**insignia** (in-**sig**-niǎ) *noun* (treated as *singular* or *plural*) a badge or emblem.

**insignificant** *adjective* having little or no importance, value, or influence.

□ **insignificantly** adverb, **insignificance** noun

**insincere** adjective not sincere; hypocritical. □ **insincerely** adverb, **insincerity** noun

**insinuate** (in-**sin**-yoo-ayt) verb **1** hint artfully or unpleasantly. **2** introduce gradually or craftily; *insinuate oneself into a person's good graces.* □ **insinuation** noun

**insipid** (in-**sip**-id) adjective **1** lacking in flavour. **2** lacking in interest or liveliness. □ **insipidity** (in-si-**pid**-iti) noun

**insist** verb declare or demand emphatically; *insist on your being there.*

**insistent** adjective **1** insisting, declaring or demanding something emphatically. **2** forcing itself on one's attention; *the insistent throb of the engines.* □ **insistently** adverb, **insistence** noun

**in situ** (**sit**-yoo) in its original place. (¶ Latin.)

**insobriety** (in-sŏ-**bry**-iti) noun lack of sobriety, drunkenness.

**insofar as** = in so far as (*see* IN).

**insole** noun **1** the inner sole of a boot or shoe. **2** a loose piece of material laid in the bottom of a shoe for warmth or comfort.

**insolent** adjective behaving insultingly; arrogant, contemptuous. □ **insolently** adverb, **insolence** noun

**insoluble** adjective **1** unable to be dissolved. **2** unable to be solved; *an insoluble problem.* □ **insolubly** adverb, **insolubility** noun

**insolvent** adjective unable to pay one's debts; bankrupt. □ **insolvency** noun

**insomnia** noun habitual inability to sleep.

**insomniac** noun a person who suffers from insomnia.

**insomuch** adverb **1** (foll. by *that*) to such an extent. **2** (foll. by *as*) inasmuch as.

**insouciant** (in-**soo**-si-ănt) adjective carefree, unconcerned. □ **insouciance** noun

**inspect** verb **1** look at closely, especially looking for flaws. **2** examine officially; visit in order to make sure that rules and standards are being observed. □ **inspection** noun

**inspector** noun **1** a person whose job is to inspect things or supervise services etc. **2** a police officer above sergeant and below superintendent. □ **inspector of taxes** an official assessing the amount of income tax to be paid. □ **inspectorate** noun

**inspiration** noun **1** inspiring. **2** an inspiring influence. **3** a sudden brilliant idea.

**inspire** verb **1** stimulate (a person) to creative or other activity or to express certain ideas. **2** fill or arouse with (a certain feeling or reaction); *he inspires confidence in us; inspired me with determination.*

**inspiriting** adjective encouraging.

**inst.** abbreviation instant, = of the current month; *on the 6th inst.*

**instability** noun lack of stability.

**install** verb (also **instal**) **1** place (a person) in office, especially with ceremonies. **2** set (apparatus) in position and ready for use. **3** settle in a place; *he was comfortably installed in an armchair.* □ **installation** (in-stă-**lay**-shŏn) noun

**instalment** noun (*Amer.* **installment**) **1** any of a number of payments made to clear a debt over a period of time. **2** any of several parts, especially of a broadcast or published story.

**instance** noun a case or example of something. ●verb mention as an instance. □ **for instance** as an example. **in the first instance** firstly.

**instant** adjective **1** occurring immediately; *there was instant relief.* **2** (of food) designed to be prepared quickly and easily. **3** (in commerce) of the current month; *the 6th instant.* ●noun **1** an exact moment; *come here this instant!* **2** a very short space of time, a moment; *not an instant too soon.*

**instantaneous** (in-stăn-**tay**-niŭs) adjective occurring or done instantly; *death was instantaneous.* □ **instantaneously** adverb

**instantly** adverb immediately.

**instead** adverb as an alternative or substitute. □ **instead of** in place of.

**instep** noun **1** the upper surface of the foot between toes and ankle. **2** the part of a shoe etc. over or under this.

**instigate** verb urge or incite; bring about by persuasion; *instigated them to strike; instigated an inquiry.* □ **instigation** noun, **instigator** noun

**instil** verb (*Amer.* **instill**) (**instilled, instilling**) introduce (ideas etc.) into a person's mind gradually. □ **instillation** noun, **instilment** noun

**instinct** noun **1** an inborn impulse or tendency to perform certain acts or behave in certain ways. **2** a natural ability; *has an instinct for finding a good place.* **3** intuition. □ **instinctive** adjective, **instinctively** adverb

**instinctual** adjective instinctive. □ **instinctually** adverb

**institute** noun **1** a society or organization for promotion of a scientific, educational, or social etc. activity. **2** the building used by this. ●verb **1** establish, found. **2** cause (an inquiry or a custom) to be started. **3** appoint to a benefice or other office.

**institution** noun **1** instituting; being instituted. **2** an institute, especially for a charitable or social activity. **3** an established law, custom, or practice. **4** (*informal*) a person who has become a familiar figure in some activity.

**institutional** adjective **1** of or like an institution. **2** typical of institutions; *institutional food.* □ **institutionally** adverb

**institutionalize** *verb* (also **institutionalise**) **1** make (a thing) institutional. **2** place or keep (a person) in an institution that will provide the care needed. □ **institutionalization** *noun*

**institutionalized** *adjective* so used to living in an institution that one cannot live independently.

**instruct** *verb* **1** give (a person) instruction in a subject or skill. **2** inform; *we are instructed by our agents that you owe us £50.* **3** give instructions to. **4** authorize (a solicitor or counsel) to act on one's behalf. □ **instructor** *noun*

**instruction** *noun* **1** teaching; education. **2** (often as **instructions**) a direction; an order. **3** an expression in a computer program defining and effecting an operation. □ **instructional** *adjective*

**instructive** *adjective* giving or containing instruction; enlightening. □ **instructively** *adverb*

**instrument** *noun* **1** a tool or implement, especially for delicate or scientific work. **2** a measuring-device giving information about the operation of an engine etc. or used in navigation. **3** (in full **musical instrument**) a device designed for producing musical sounds. **4** a person or thing used or controlled to perform an action; *was made the instrument of another's crime.* **5** a formal or legal document; *signed the instrument of abdication.*

**instrumental** *adjective* **1** serving as an instrument or means of doing something; *was instrumental in finding her a job.* **2** performed on musical instruments; *instrumental music.* **3** of or done with an instrument; *instrumental error.*

**instrumentalist** *noun* a person who plays a musical instrument.

**instrumentation** *noun* **1** the arrangement or composition of music for instruments. **2** the provision or use of mechanical or scientific instruments.

**insubordinate** *adjective* disobedient, rebellious. □ **insubordination** *noun*

**insubstantial** *adjective* **1** not existing in reality, imaginary. **2** not made of a strong or solid substance; flimsy; *insubstantial evidence.*

**insufferable** *adjective* **1** unbearable. **2** unbearably conceited or arrogant. □ **insufferably** *adverb*

**insufficient** *adjective* not sufficient; inadequate. □ **insufficiently** *adverb*, **insufficiency** *noun*

**insular** (ins-yoo-ler) *adjective* **1** of or on an island. **2** narrow-minded; *insular prejudices.* □ **insularity** (ins-yoo-**la**-riti) *noun*

**insulate** (ins-yoo-layt) *verb* **1** cover or protect (a thing) with a substance or device

that prevents the passage of electricity or sound or the loss of heat; *insulating tape.* **2** isolate (a person or place) from influences. □ **insulation** *noun*, **insulator** *noun*

**insulin** (ins-yoo-lin) *noun* a hormone produced in the pancreas, controlling the absorption of sugar by the body.

**insult** *verb* (*pronounced* in-**sult**) speak or act in a way that hurts the feelings or pride of (a person). ●*noun* (*pronounced* **in**-sult) an insulting remark or action. □ **insulting** *adjective*, **insultingly** *adverb*

**insuperable** (in-**soop**-er-ăbŭl) *adjective* unable to be overcome; *an insuperable difficulty.* □ **insuperably** *adverb*, **insuperability** *noun*

**insupportable** *adjective* unbearable.

**insurance** *noun* **1** a contract undertaking to provide compensation for loss, damage, or injury etc., in return for a payment made in advance once or regularly. **2** the business of providing such contracts. **3** the amount payable to the company etc. providing the contract; a premium. **4** the amount payable by the company etc. in compensation. **5** anything done as a safeguard against loss or failure etc.

∎**Usage** See the note under **assurance**.

**insure** *verb* **1** protect by a contract of insurance. **2** (*Amer.*) ensure. □ **insurer** *noun*, **insurable** *adjective*

**insurgent** (in-**ser**-jĕnt) *adjective* rebellious, rising in revolt. ●*noun* a rebel. □ **insurgence** *noun*

**insurmountable** (in-ser-**mownt**-ăbŭl) *adjective* unable to be surmounted, insuperable.

**insurrection** (in-ser-**ek**-shŏn) *noun* rising against established authority, rebellion. □ **insurrectionist** *noun*

**intact** *adjective* undamaged; complete.

**intaglio** (in-**tal**-yoh) *noun* (*plural* **intaglios**) **1** a carving in which the design is sunk below the surface. **2** a gem carved in this way.

**intake** *noun* **1** the process of taking something in. **2** the place where liquid or air etc. is channelled into something. **3** the number of people or things accepted or received; *a school's annual intake of pupils.*

**intangible** (in-**tan**-jibŭl) *adjective* **1** unable to be touched. **2** unable to be grasped mentally. □ **intangibly** *adverb*

**integer** (**in**-ti-jer) *noun* a whole number, not a fraction.

**integral** (**in**-ti-grăl) *adjective* **1** (of a part) constituent, necessary to the completeness of a whole; *Cornwall is an integral part of England.* **2** complete, forming a whole; *an integral design.* **3** of or denoted by an integer. ●*noun Maths* a quantity of which a given function is the derivative. □ **integrally** *adverb*

**integrate** (**in**-ti-grayt) *verb* **1** combine or form (a part or parts) into a whole. **2** bring or come into equal membership of a community. **3** desegregate, especially racially (e.g. a school). **4** *Maths* calculate the integral of. □ **integrated circuit** a small chip of material replacing a conventional electronic circuit of many components. □ **integration** *noun*

**integrity** (in-**teg**-riti) *noun* **1** honesty, incorruptibility. **2** wholeness, soundness.

**integument** (in-**teg**-yoo-měnt) *noun* skin or other natural outer covering.

**intellect** (**in**-ti-lekt) *noun* **1** the mind's power of reasoning and acquiring knowledge. **2** a clever or knowledgeable person.

**intellectual** (inti-**lek**-tew-ăl) *adjective* **1** of the intellect. **2** needing use of the intellect; *an intellectual occupation*. **3** having a well-developed intellect and a taste for advanced knowledge. ●*noun* an intellectual person. □ **intellectually** *adverb*, **intellectuality** *noun*

**intelligence** *noun* **1** mental ability; the power of learning and understanding. **2** information, especially that of military value. **3** the people engaged in collecting this. □ **intelligence quotient** (also **IQ**) a number that shows how a person's intelligence compares with the average.

**intelligent** *adjective* **1** having great mental ability. **2** (of a device in a computer system) containing in itself a capacity to process information. □ **intelligently** *adverb*

**intelligentsia** (in-tel-i-**jent**-siă) *noun* intellectual people regarded as a class.

**intelligible** (in-**tel**-i-jibŭl) *adjective* able to be understood. □ **intelligibly** *adverb*, **intelligibility** *noun*

**intemperate** *adjective* **1** drinking alcohol excessively. **2** immoderate. □ **intemperance** *noun*

**intend** *verb* **1** have in mind as what one wishes to do or achieve. **2** plan that (a thing) shall be used or interpreted in a particular way; *we intended this room for you*; *the remark was intended as an insult*.

**intended** *adjective* done on purpose. ●*noun* (*informal*) one's fiancé or fiancée.

**intense** *adjective* **1** strong in quality or degree; *intense heat*. **2** (of a person) emotional. □ **intensely** *adverb*, **intenseness** *noun*

**intensifier** *noun Grammar* a word used to give force or emphasis, e.g. *really* in *I'm really hot*.

**intensify** *verb* (**intensified**, **intensifying**) make or become more intense. □ **intensification** *noun*

**intensity** *noun* **1** intenseness. **2** the amount of some quality such as force or brightness.

**intensive** *adjective* **1** employing much effort; concentrated. **2** serving to increase production; *intensive farming*. **3** *Grammar* (of a word) used to give force or emphasis, e.g. *really* in *I'm really hot*. □ **intensive care** medical treatment with constant supervision of a seriously ill patient. □ **intensively** *adverb*, **intensiveness** *noun*

**intent** *noun* intention; *with intent to kill*. ●*adjective* **1** (foll. by *on* or *upon*) intending, having one's mind fixed on some purpose; *intent on killing*. **2** with one's attention concentrated; *an intent gaze*. □ **to all intents and purposes** practically, virtually. □ **intently** *adverb*, **intentness** *noun*

**intention** *noun* what one intends to do or achieve; one's purpose.

**intentional** *adjective* done on purpose; not accidental. □ **intentionally** *adverb*

**inter** (in-**ter**) *verb* (**interred**, **interring**) bury (a dead body) in the earth or in a tomb.

**inter-** *combining form* between, among.

**interact** *verb* have an effect upon each other. □ **interaction** *noun*

**interactive** *adjective* **1** interacting. **2** (in computers) allowing information to be transferred immediately both to and from a computer system and its user.

*inter alia* (**ay**-liă) among other things. (¶ Latin.)

**interbreed** *verb* (**interbred**, **interbreeding**) breed with each other; cross-breed.

**intercede** (inter-**seed**) *verb* intervene on behalf of another person or as a peacemaker.

**intercept** (inter-**sept**) *verb* stop or catch (a person or thing) on the way from one place to another. □ **interception** *noun*, **interceptor** *noun*

**intercession** (inter-**sesh**-ŏn) *noun* interceding. □ **intercessor** *noun*

**interchange** *verb* (*pronounced* inter-**chaynj**) **1** put (each of two things) into the other's place. **2** make an exchange of, give and receive (one thing for another). **3** alternate. ●*noun* (*pronounced* **in**-ter-chaynj) **1** interchanging. **2** alternation. **3** a road junction designed so that streams of traffic do not intersect on the same level. □ **interchangeable** *adjective*, **interchangeability** *noun*

**inter-city** *adjective* existing or travelling between cities.

**intercom** (**in**-ter-kom) *noun* a system of communication by radio or telephone.

**interconnect** *verb* connect with each other. □ **interconnection** *noun*

**intercontinental** *adjective* connecting or travelling between continents.

**intercourse** *noun* **1** dealings or communication between people or countries. **2** sexual intercourse (*see* SEXUAL), copulation.

**interdenominational** *adjective* of or involving more than one religious denomination.

**interdepartmental** *adjective* of or involving more than one department.

**interdependent** *adjective* dependent on each other. □ **interdependence** *noun*

**interdict** *verb* (*pronounced* inter-**dikt**) prohibit or forbid authoritatively. ●*noun* (*pronounced* **in**-ter-dikt) **1** an authoritative prohibition. **2** (in the RC Church) a sentence excluding a person or place from certain ecclesiastical functions and privileges. □ **interdiction** *noun*

**interdisciplinary** *adjective* of or involving different branches of learning.

**interest** *noun* **1** curiosity or concern about something. **2** the quality of arousing such a feeling; *the subject has no interest for me.* **3** a subject or hobby in which one is concerned; *music is one of his interests.* **4** advantage, benefit; *she looks after her own interests.* **5** a legal right to a share in something; a financial stake in a business etc. **6** money paid for the use of money lent. ●*verb* **1** arouse the interest of. **2** cause to take an interest in; *interested herself in welfare work.*

**interested** *adjective* **1** feeling or showing interest or curiosity. **2** having a private interest in something; *interested parties.*

**interesting** *adjective* arousing interest. □ **interestingly** *adverb*

**interface** *noun* **1** a surface forming a boundary between two regions. **2** a place or piece of equipment where interaction occurs between two processes etc. **3** *Computing* a program or apparatus for connecting two pieces of equipment so that they can be operated jointly or for enabling a user to access a program. ●*verb* connect by means of an interface.

**interfacing** *noun* stiffish material between two layers of fabric in collars etc.

**interfere** *verb* **1** (usually foll. by *with*) meddle; obstruct a process etc. **2** intervene, especially without invitation. **3** (foll. by *with*) molest sexually. **4** *Physics* cause interference.

**interference** *noun* **1** interfering. **2** the fading of received radio signals because of atmospherics or unwanted signals. **3** *Physics* the meeting of wave motions to form a wave in which the displacement is reinforced or cancelled.

**interferon** (inter-**feer**-on) *noun* a protein substance that prevents the development of a virus in living cells.

**interfuse** *verb* **1** intersperse. **2** blend or fuse together. □ **interfusion** *noun*

**intergalactic** *adjective* between galaxies.

**interim** (**in**-ter-im) *noun* an intervening period of time; *in the interim.* ●*adjective* temporary, provisional; *an interim report.*

**interior** *adjective* **1** nearer to the centre, inner. **2** internal; domestic. ●*noun* **1** an interior part or region; the central or inland part of a country. **2** the inside of a building or room. □ **interior decoration** *or* **design** decoration or design of the interior of a building.

**interject** *verb* put in (a remark) when someone is speaking.

**interjection** *noun* **1** interjecting. **2** an interjected remark. **3** an exclamation such as *oh!* or *good heavens!*

**interlace** *verb* weave or lace together.

**interlard** *verb* insert contrasting remarks throughout (a speech etc.); *interlarded his speech with quotations.*

**interleave** *verb* insert leaves (usually blank) between the pages of (a book).

**interline** *verb* put an extra layer of material between the fabric of (a garment) and its lining. □ **interlining** *noun*

**interlink** *verb* connect together.

**interlock** *verb* fit into each other, especially so that parts engage. ●*noun* **1** machine-knitted fabric with fine stitches. **2** a mechanism for preventing a set of operations from being performed in the wrong sequence.

**interlocutor** (inter-**lok**-yoo-ter) *noun* a person who takes part in a conversation.

**interloper** *noun* **1** an intruder. **2** one who interferes in the affairs of others.

**interlude** *noun* **1** an interval between parts of a play etc. **2** something (such as a piece of music) performed during this. **3** an intervening time or event etc. of a different kind from the main one.

**intermarry** *verb* (**intermarried, intermarrying**) **1** (of races, families, etc.) become connected by marriage. **2** marry within one's own family. □ **intermarriage** *noun*

**intermediary** (inter-**meed**-i-er-i) *noun* a mediator, a go-between. ●*adjective* **1** acting as an intermediary. **2** intermediate.

**intermediate** *adjective* coming between two things in time, place, or order. ●*noun* an intermediate thing.

**interment** (in-ter-**ment**) *noun* burial.

▪**Usage** Do not confuse with **internment**.

**intermezzo** (inter-**mets**-oh) *noun* (*plural* **intermezzi** *or* **intermezzos**) a short musical composition to be played between acts of a play etc. or between sections of a larger work, or independently.

**interminable** (in-ter-min-ăbŭl) *adjective* endless; long and boring. □ **interminably** *adverb*

**intermingle** *verb* mix together.

**intermission** *noun* an interval; a pause in work or action.

**intermittent** *adjective* occurring at intervals, not continuous; *intermittent rain*. □ **intermittently** *adverb*

**intern** *verb* (*pronounced* in-**tern**) compel (an enemy alien or prisoner of war etc.) to live in a special area or camp. ●*noun* (*pronounced* **in**-tern) (also **interne**) (especially *Amer.*) a resident junior doctor at a hospital.

**internal** *adjective* **1** of or in the inside of a thing. **2** of or in the interior of the body; *internal organs*. **3** of the domestic affairs of a country. **4** used or applying within an organization. **5** of the mind or soul. □ **internal-combustion engine** an engine that produces power by the explosion of gases or vapour with air in a cylinder. **internal evidence** evidence contained in the thing being discussed. **internal market** an economic market operating within a group or organization, especially within the European Community and the National Health Service. □ **internally** *adverb*

**internalize** *verb* (also **internalise**) learn, absorb into the mind as a fact, attitude, etc. □ **internalization** *noun*

**international** *adjective* of or existing or agreed between two or more countries. ●*noun* **1** a sports contest between players representing different countries. **2** any of these players. **3** (**International**) any of several international socialist organizations, of which the first was formed by Karl Marx in London in 1864. □ **International Court of Justice** a judicial court of the United Nations which meets at The Hague. **International Monetary Fund** an international organization, with headquarters in Washington, DC, for promoting international trade and monetary cooperation and the stabilization of exchange rates. **International Phonetic Alphabet** a set of phonetic symbols for international use. **International System (of Units)** *see* SI. □ **internationally** *adverb*

**internationalism** *noun* **1** being international. **2** support and cooperation between nations.

**internationalize** *verb* (also **internationalise**) make international.

**interne** alternative spelling of INTERN *noun*.

**internecine** (inter-**nee**-syn) *adjective* destructive to each of the parties involved; *internecine war*.

**internee** (in-ter-**nee**) *noun* a person who is interned.

**internment** *noun* interning; being interned.

━**Usage** Do not confuse with **interment**.

**interpenetrate** *verb* **1** penetrate each other. **2** pervade. □ **interpenetration** *noun*

**interpersonal** *adjective* between persons; social.

**interplanetary** *adjective* between planets.

**interplay** *noun* interaction; reciprocal action.

**Interpol** International Criminal Police Commission, an organization that coordinates investigations made by the police forces of member countries into crimes with an international basis.

**interpolate** (in-ter-pŏl-ayt) *verb* **1** interject. **2** insert (new material) into a book etc. **3** estimate (values) between known ones in the same range. □ **interpolation** *noun*, **interpolator** *noun*

**interpose** *verb* **1** insert between; interject. **2** intervene. □ **interposition** *noun*

**interpret** *verb* **1** explain the meaning of. **2** understand in a specified way. **3** act as interpreter. □ **interpretation** *noun*

**interpretative** (in-ter-prit-ătiv) *adjective* interpreting.

**interpreter** *noun* a person whose job is to translate a speech etc. into another language orally.

**interpretive** *adjective* interpretative.

**interracial** *adjective* between or affecting different races.

**interregnum** (inter-reg-nŭm) *noun* **1** a period between the rule of two successive rulers. **2** an interval, a pause.

**interrelated** *adjective* related to each other. □ **interrelation** *noun*

**interrogate** (in-te-rŏ-gayt) *verb* question closely or formally. □ **interrogation** *noun*, **interrogator** *noun*

**interrogative** (inter-**rog**-ătiv) *adjective* questioning; having the form of a question; *an interrogative tone*. ●*noun* an interrogative word.

**interrogatory** (inter-**rog**-ă-ter-i) *adjective* questioning. ●*noun* a formal set of questions.

**interrupt** *verb* **1** break the continuity of. **2** break the flow of a speech etc. by inserting a remark. **3** obstruct (a view etc.). □ **interruption** *noun*

**interrupter** *noun* (also **interruptor**) **1** a person or thing that interrupts. **2** a device for opening and closing an electric circuit.

**intersect** *verb* **1** divide (a thing) by passing or lying across it. **2** (of lines or roads etc.) cross each other.

**intersection** *noun* **1** intersecting. **2** a place where lines or roads etc. intersect.

**intersperse** *verb* insert contrasting material here and there in (a thing); scatter.

**interstate** *adjective* existing or carried on between States, especially of the USA.

**interstellar** *adjective* between stars.

**interstice** (in-**ter**-stiss) *noun* a small intervening space; a crevice.

**intertwine** *verb* twine together, entwine.

**interval** *noun* **1** a time between two events or parts of an action. **2** a pause between two parts of a performance. **3** a space between two objects or points. **4** the difference in musical pitch between two notes. □ **at intervals** with some time or distance between; now and then.

**intervene** (inter-**veen**) *verb* **1** occur in the time between events; *in the intervening years*. **2** cause hindrance by occurring; *we should have finished harvesting but a storm intervened*. **3** enter a discussion or dispute etc. in order to change its course or resolve it.

**intervention** (inter-**ven**-shŏn) *noun* intervening, especially by a State in another's affairs.

**interventionist** *noun* a person who favours intervention.

**interview** *noun* a formal meeting or conversation with a person, held in order to assess his or her merits as a candidate etc. or to obtain comments and information. ● *verb* hold an interview with. □ **interviewer** *noun*

**interviewee** *noun* a person who is interviewed.

**interwar** *adjective* in the period between two wars.

**interweave** *verb* (**interwove**, **interwoven**, **interweaving**) **1** weave together. **2** blend intimately.

**intestate** (in-**test**-ăt) *adjective* not having made a valid will before death; *he died intestate*. □ **intestacy** (in-**test**-ăsi) *noun*

**intestine** (in-**test**-in) *noun* the long tubular section of the alimentary canal, extending from the outlet of the stomach to the anus. □ **large intestine** the broader and shorter part of this, including the colon and rectum. **small intestine** the narrower and longer part. □ **intestinal** *adjective*

**intifada** (in-ti-**fah**-dă) *noun* an uprising by Arabs.

**intimate**[1] (**in**-tim-ăt) *adjective* **1** having a close acquaintance or friendship with a person. **2** having a sexual relationship with a person, especially outside marriage. **3** private and personal. **4** (of knowledge) detailed and obtained by much study or experience. ● *noun* an intimate friend. □ **intimately** *adverb*, **intimacy** *noun*

**intimate**[2] (**in**-tim-ayt) *verb* make known, especially by hinting. □ **intimation** *noun*

**intimidate** (in-**tim**-i-dayt) *verb* subdue or influence by frightening with threats or force. □ **intimidation** *noun*

**into** *preposition* **1** to the inside of, to a point within; *went into the house; fell into the river; far into the night*. **2** to a particular state, condition, or occupation; *got into trouble; grew into an adult; went into banking*. **3** (*informal*) actively interested and participating in; *he is into rock music*. **4** *Maths* indicating division; *4 into 20 is 5*.

**intolerable** *adjective* unbearable. □ **intolerably** *adverb*

**intolerant** *adjective* not tolerant, especially of ideas or beliefs etc. that differ from one's own; *intolerant of opposition*. □ **intolerantly** *adverb*, **intolerance** *noun*

**intonation** (in-tŏn-**ay**-shŏn) *noun* **1** intoning. **2** the tone or pitch of the voice in speaking. **3** a slight accent; *a Welsh intonation*.

**intone** *verb* recite in a chanting voice, especially on one note.

*in toto* completely. (¶ Latin.)

**intoxicant** *adjective* causing intoxication. ● *noun* an intoxicating substance.

**intoxicated** *adjective* **1** (of a person) drunk. **2** made greatly excited or reckless; *intoxicated by success*. □ **intoxication** *noun*

**intra-** *combining form* within.

**intractable** (in-**trakt**-ăbŭl) *adjective* unmanageable, hard to deal with or control; *an intractable difficulty; intractable children*. □ **intractability** *noun*

**intramural** (intră-**mewr**-ăl) *adjective* **1** situated or done within the walls of an institution etc. **2** forming part of ordinary university work.

**intransigent** (in-**trans**-i-jĕnt) *adjective* unwilling to compromise, stubborn. □ **intransigence** *noun*

**intransitive** (in-**trans**-itiv) *adjective* (of a verb) used without being followed by a direct object, e.g. *hear* in *we can hear* (but not in *we can hear you*). □ **intransitively** *adverb*

**intrauterine** *adjective* within the uterus.

**intravenous** (intră-**vee**-nŭs) *adjective* within or into a vein. □ **intravenously** *adverb*

**in-tray** *noun* a tray to hold incoming documents awaiting attention.

**intrepid** (in-**trep**-id) *adjective* fearless, brave. □ **intrepidly** *adverb*, **intrepidity** (in-trip-**id**-iti) *noun*

**intricate** *adjective* very complicated. □ **intricately** *adverb*, **intricacy** (**in**-trik-ăsi) *noun*

**intrigue** *verb* (*pronounced* in-**treeg**) **1** plot with someone in an underhand way; use secret influence. **2** rouse the interest or curiosity of; *the subject intrigues me*. ● *noun* (*pronounced* **in**-treeg) **1** underhand plotting; an underhand plot. **2** (*old use*) a secret love affair. □ **intriguing** *adjective*, **intriguingly** *adverb*

**intrinsic** (in-**trin**-sik) *adjective* belonging to the basic nature of a person or thing. □ **intrinsically** *adverb*

**introduce** *verb* **1** make (a person) known by name to others. **2** announce (a speaker or broadcast programme etc.) to an audience. **3** bring (a bill) before Parliament. **4** cause (a person) to become acquainted with a subject. **5** bring (a custom or idea etc.) into use or into a system. **6** bring or put in; *introduce the needle into a vein.*

**introduction** *noun* **1** introducing; being introduced. **2** the formal presentation of one person to another. **3** an introductory or explanatory section at the beginning of a book, speech, etc. **4** an introductory treatise.

**introductory** *adjective* introducing a person or subject; preliminary.

**introit** (**in**-troit) *noun* a psalm or antiphon sung or said while the priest approaches the altar for the Eucharist.

**introspection** *noun* examination of one's own thoughts and feelings. □ **introspective** *adjective*

**introvert** (in-trŏ-vert) *noun* **1** a person concerned more with his or her own thoughts and feelings than with the people and things round him or her. **2** a shy person. ● *adjective* (also **introverted**) having these characteristics. □ **introversion** *noun*

**intrude** *verb* come or join in without being invited or wanted.

**intruder** *noun* **1** a person who intrudes. **2** a burglar.

**intrusion** *noun* **1** intruding. **2** influx of molten rock between existing strata. □ **intrusive** *adjective*

**intuition** (in-tew-**ish**-ŏn) *noun* the power of knowing or understanding something immediately without reasoning or being taught. □ **intuitional** *adjective*

**intuitive** (in-tew-itiv) *adjective* of, possessing, or based on intuition. □ **intuitively** *adverb*

**Inuit** (**in**-yoo-it) *noun* (also **Innuit**) (*plural* **Inuit** *or* **Inuits**) a North American Eskimo.

**inundate** (**in**-ŭn-dayt) *verb* **1** flood, cover with water. **2** overwhelm. □ **inundation** *noun*

**inure** (in-**yoor**) *verb* **1** accustom, especially to something unpleasant. **2** (in law) take effect. □ **inurement** *noun*

**invade** *verb* **1** enter (territory) with armed forces in order to attack or occupy it. **2** crowd into; *tourists invaded the city.* **3** penetrate harmfully; *the disease had invaded all parts of the body.* □ **invader** *noun*

**invalid**[1] (**in**-vă-lid) *noun* a person who is weakened by illness or injury. ● *verb* **1** remove from active service because of ill health or injury; *he was invalided out of the army.* **2** disable by illness.

**invalid**[2] (in-**val**-id) *adjective* not valid.

**invalidate** (in-**val**-i-dayt) *verb* make (a claim, argument, law, etc.) ineffective or not valid. □ **invalidation** *noun*

**invalidity** (in-vă-**lid**-iti) *noun* **1** lack of validity. **2** being an invalid.

**invaluable** *adjective* having a value that is too great to be measured; priceless. □ **invaluably** *adverb*

**invariable** (in-**vair**-i-ăbŭl) *adjective* not variable; always the same. □ **invariably** *adverb*

**invasion** *noun* invading, being invaded.

**invasive** (in-**vay**-siv) *adjective* invading; tending to spread; *an invasive plant.*

**invective** (in-**vek**-tiv) *noun* a violent attack in words; abusive language.

**inveigh** (in-**vay**) *verb* (foll. by *against*) attack violently or bitterly in words.

**inveigle** (in-**vay**-gŭl) *verb* entice. □ **inveiglement** *noun*

**invent** *verb* **1** create by thought; make or design (something original). **2** construct (a false or fictional story); *invented an excuse.* □ **inventor** *noun*

**invention** *noun* **1** inventing; being invented. **2** something invented. **3** a false story. **4** inventiveness.

**inventive** *adjective* able to invent things; imaginative. □ **inventiveness** *noun*

**inventory** (**in**-věn-ter-i) *noun* a detailed list of goods or furniture etc. ● *verb* (**inventoried, inventorying**) make an inventory of; enter in an inventory.

**inverse** *adjective* reversed in position, order, or relation. ● *noun* **1** an inverse state. **2** a thing that is the exact opposite of another. □ **in inverse proportion** with one quantity increasing in proportion as the other decreases. □ **inversely** *adverb*

**inversion** *noun* **1** inverting; being inverted. **2** something that is inverted.

**invert** *verb* turn (a thing) upside down; reverse the position, order, or relationship of. □ **inverted commas** quotation marks ('' or "").

**invertebrate** (in-**vert**-ibrăt) *adjective* not having a backbone. ● *noun* an invertebrate animal.

**invest** *verb* **1** use (money) to buy stocks, shares, or property in order to earn interest or bring profit for the buyer. **2** (often foll. by *in*) spend money, time, or effort on something that will be useful; *invest in a freezer.* **3** confer a rank, office, or power upon (a person). **4** endow with a quality. □ **investor** *noun*

**investigate** *verb* **1** make a careful study of (a thing) in order to discover the facts about it. **2** make a search or systematic inquiry. □ **investigation** *noun*, **investig-**

**ator** *noun,* **investigative** (in-vest-i-găt-iv) *adjective,* **investigatory** *adjective*

**investiture** (in-vest-i-cher) *noun* the process of investing a person with honours or rank.

**investment** *noun* **1** investing. **2** a sum of money invested. **3** something in which money, time, or effort is invested. □ **investment trust** a trust that buys and sells shares in selected companies to make a profit for its members.

**inveterate** (in-vet-er-ăt) *adjective* **1** habitual; *an inveterate smoker.* **2** firmly established; *inveterate prejudices.* □ **inveteracy** *noun*

**invidious** (in-vid-iŭs) *adjective* likely to cause resentment or anger.

**invigilate** (in-vij-i-layt) *verb* supervise people taking an examination. □ **invigilation** *noun,* **invigilator** *noun*

**invigorate** (in-vig-er-ayt) *verb* give vigour or strength to. □ **invigorating** *adjective*

**invincible** (in-vin-si-bŭl) *adjective* unconquerable. □ **invincibly** *adverb,* **invincibility** *noun*

**inviolable** (in-vy-ŏl-ăbŭl) *adjective* not to be violated or dishonoured. □ **inviolably** *adverb,* **inviolability** *noun*

**inviolate** (in-vy-ŏ-lăt) *adjective* not violated; safe. □ **inviolacy** *noun*

**invisible** *adjective* not visible, unable to be seen. □ **invisible exports** *or* **imports** payment for services (such as insurance or shipping) made to or by another country. □ **invisibly** *adverb,* **invisibility** *noun*

**invite** *verb* (*pronounced* in-vyt) **1** ask (a person) in a friendly way to come to one's house or to a gathering etc. **2** ask (a person) formally to do something. **3** ask for (comments, suggestions, etc.). **4** act so as to be likely to cause (a thing) unintentionally; *you are inviting disaster.* **5** attract, tempt. ●*noun* (*pronounced* in-vyt) (*informal*) an invitation. □ **invitation** *noun*

**inviting** *adjective* attracting one to do something, pleasant and tempting. □ **invitingly** *adverb*

**in vitro** (vee-troh) (of biological processes) taking place in a test-tube or other laboratory environment; *in vitro fertilization.* (¶ Latin, = in glass.)

**invocation** (invŏ-kay-shŏn) *noun* invoking; calling upon God in prayer. □ **invocatory** *adjective*

**invoice** *noun* a list of goods sent or services performed, with prices and charges. ●*verb* **1** make an invoice of (goods). **2** send an invoice to (a person).

**invoke** (in-vohk) *verb* **1** call upon (a deity) in prayer. **2** call for the help or protection of; *invoked the law.* **3** summon up (a spirit) with words. **4** ask earnestly for (vengeance etc.).

**involuntary** *adjective* done without intention or without conscious effort of the will; *an involuntary twitch.* □ **involuntarily** *adverb*

**involute** (in-vŏ-loot) *adjective* **1** complex, intricate. **2** curled spirally.

**involve** *verb* **1** contain within itself, make necessary as a condition or result; *the plan involves much expense.* **2** cause to share in an experience or effect; include or affect in its operation; *the safety of the nation is involved.* **3** bring into difficulties; *it will involve us in much expense.* **4** show (a person) to be concerned in a crime etc. □ **involvement** *noun*

**involved** *adjective* **1** complicated. **2** concerned in something.

**invulnerable** (in-vul-ner-ăbŭl) *adjective* unable to be wounded or damaged. □ **invulnerability** *noun*

**inward** *adjective* **1** situated on the inside. **2** going towards the inside. **3** in the mind or spirit; *inward happiness.* ●*adverb* (also **inwards**) **1** towards the inside. **2** in the mind or spirit.

**inwardly** *adverb* **1** on the inside. **2** in the mind or spirit.

**inwrought** (in-rawt) *adjective* **1** (of fabric etc.) with a pattern worked into it. **2** (of a pattern) worked into something.

**iodine** (I-ŏ-deen) *noun* a bluish-black chemical element (symbol I), found in sea water and seaweed and used in solution as an antiseptic.

**iodize** (I-ŏ-dyz) *verb* (also **iodise**) treat or impregnate with iodine.

**IOM** *abbreviation* Isle of Man.

**ion** (I-ŏn) *noun* an electrically charged atom or group of atoms that has lost or gained one or more electrons.

**Iona** (I-oh-nă) an island in the Inner Hebrides, site of a monastery founded *c.*563 by St Columba.

**Ionesco** (yon-esk-oh), Eugène (1912–94), Romanian-born French dramatist.

**Ionia** (I-oh-niă) the ancient Greek name for the central part of the west coast of Asia Minor. □ **Ionian** *adjective & noun*

**Ionic** (I-on-ik) *adjective* of the **Ionic order**, one of the five classical orders of architecture, characterized by columns with a scroll-like ornamentation at the top.

**ionic** (I-on-ik) *adjective* of or using ions.

**ionize** (I-ŏ-nyz) *verb* (also **ionise**) convert or be converted into ions. □ **ionization** *noun,* **ionizer** *noun*

**ionosphere** (I-on-ŏ-sfeer) *noun* an ionized region of the upper atmosphere, able to reflect radio waves for transmission to another part of the earth. □ **ionospheric** *adjective*

**iota** (I-oh-tă) *noun* **1** the ninth letter of the Greek alphabet (I, ι). **2** the smallest possible amount; a jot; *it doesn't make an iota of difference.*

**IOU** *noun* a signed paper acknowledging that one owes a sum of money to the holder (= *I owe you*).

**IOW** *abbreviation* Isle of Wight.

**Iowa** (I-ŏ-wă) a State in the Middle West of the USA.

**IPA** *abbreviation* International Phonetic Alphabet.

**ipecacuanha** (ipi-kak-yoo-**an**-ă) *noun* the dried root of a South American plant, used as an emetic or purgative.

**ipso facto** (ip-soh **fak**-toh) by that very fact. (¶ Latin.)

**IQ** *abbreviation* intelligence quotient.

**Ir** *symbol* iridium.

**IRA** *abbreviation* Irish Republican Army, an organization seeking to achieve by force a united Ireland independent of Britain.

**Iran** (i-**rahn**) a country in SW Asia, formerly called Persia. □ **Iranian** (i-ray-niăn) *adjective & noun*

**Irangate** a US political scandal of 1987 involving the sale of arms to Iran (and subsequent release of American hostages) and use of the proceeds to supply arms to the anti-Communist Contras in Nicaragua.

**Iraq** (i-**rahk**) a country lying between Iran and Saudi Arabia. □ **Iraqi** (i-**rah**-ki) *adjective & noun* (*plural* **Iraqis**).

**irascible** (i-**ras**-ibŭl) *adjective* irritable, hot-tempered. □ **irascibly** *adverb*, **irascibility** *noun*

**irate** (I-**rayt**) *adjective* angry, enraged. □ **irately** *adverb*

**ire** *noun* (*literary*) anger.

**Ireland** an island west of Great Britain, divided into Northern Ireland (which forms part of the UK) and the Republic of Ireland.

**iridaceous** (i-ri-**day**-shŭs) *adjective* of the iris family.

**iridescent** (i-ri-**dess**-ĕnt) *adjective* **1** showing rainbow-like colours. **2** showing a change of colour when its position is altered. □ **iridescence** *noun*

**iridium** (i-**rid**-iŭm) *noun* a hard white metallic element (symbol Ir).

**Iris** (*Gk. myth.*) the goddess of the rainbow.

**iris** *noun* **1** the circular coloured membrane in the eye, with a circular opening (the pupil) in the centre. **2** a plant with sword-shaped leaves and showy flowers.

**Irish** *adjective* of Ireland or its people or language. ●*noun* **1** the Celtic language of Ireland. **2** (**the Irish**) Irish people. □ **Irish coffee** coffee with cream and Irish whiskey. **Irish stew** a stew of mutton, potatoes, and onions. □ **Irishman** *noun* (*plural* **Irishmen**), **Irishwoman** *noun* (*plural* **Irishwomen**).

**Irish Sea** the sea separating Ireland from England and Wales.

**irk** *verb* annoy, be tiresome to.

**irksome** *adjective* tiresome.

**iron** *noun* **1** a metallic element (symbol Fe), a very common hard grey metal capable of being magnetized. **2** a tool made of this; *branding-iron.* **3** a golf club with an iron or steel head. **4** an implement with a flat base that is heated for smoothing clothes etc. **5** a metal splint or support worn on the leg. **6** (**irons**) fetters. **7** great strength; *a will of iron.* ●*adjective* **1** made of iron. **2** strong or unyielding; *an iron constitution; an iron will.* ●*verb* smooth (clothes etc.) with an iron. □ **Iron Age** the prehistoric period when weapons and tools were made of iron. **Iron Cross** a German military decoration. **Iron Curtain** (*hist.*) a former barrier of secrecy and restriction preventing the free passage of people and information between the USSR (and countries under its influence) and the Western world. **iron lung** a rigid case fitting over a patient's body, used for administering artificial respiration for a prolonged period by means of mechanical pumps. **iron out** deal with and remove (difficulties etc.). **iron rations** a small emergency supply of food. **many irons in the fire** many undertakings or opportunities.

**ironclad** *adjective* covered or protected with iron. ●*noun* (*old use*) a ship cased with plates of iron.

**ironic** (I-**ron**-ik) *adjective* (also **ironical**) using or expressing irony. □ **ironically** *adverb*

**ironing-board** *noun* a narrow flat stand on which clothes etc. are ironed.

**ironmaster** *noun* a manufacturer of iron.

**ironmonger** (I-ern-mung-er) *noun* a person who sells tools and household implements etc. □ **ironmongery** *noun*

**ironstone** *noun* **1** rock containing iron ore. **2** a kind of hard white pottery.

**ironware** *noun* things made of iron.

**ironwork** *noun* articles made of iron, such as gratings or railings.

**ironworks** *noun* a place where iron is smelted or iron goods are made.

**irony** (I-rŏn-i) *noun* **1** the expression of one's meaning by using words of the opposite meaning in order to make one's remarks forceful; sarcasm. **2** the quality of an occurrence being so unexpected or ill-timed that it appears to be deliberately perverse.

**irradiate** (i-**ray**-di-ayt) *verb* **1** shine on. **2** subject to radiation. **3** throw light on (a subject). □ **irradiation** *noun*

**irrational** (i-**rash**-ŏn-ăl) *adjective* **1** not rational, not guided by reasoning, illogical; *irrational fears* or *behaviour.* **2** not capable of reasoning. □ **irrationally** adverb, **irrationality** noun

**irreconcilable** adjective unable to be reconciled; opposed or incompatible. □ **irreconcilably** adverb, **irreconcilability** noun

**irrecoverable** adjective unable to be recovered or remedied. □ **irrecoverably** adverb

**irredeemable** adjective **1** unable to be redeemed. **2** hopeless. □ **irredeemably** adverb

**irreducible** (i-ri-dew-sibŭl) adjective unable to be reduced or simplified; *an irreducible minimum.*

**irrefutable** (i-ref-yoo-tăbŭl) adjective unable to be refuted. □ **irrefutably** adverb

**irregular** adjective **1** not regular; uneven; varying. **2** contrary to rules or to established custom. **3** (of troops) not belonging to the regular armed forces. **4** (of a word) not inflected according to the usual rules. □ **irregularly** adverb, **irregularity** noun

**irrelevant** (i-rel-i-vănt) adjective not relevant. □ **irrelevance** noun, **irrelevancy** noun

**irreligious** (i-ri-lij-ŭs) adjective not religious; irreverent.

**irremediable** (i-ri-meed-i-ăbŭl) adjective not able to be remedied. □ **irremediably** adverb

**irremovable** (i-ri-moo-văbŭl) adjective unable to be removed. □ **irremovably** adverb

**irreparable** (i-rep-er-ăbŭl) adjective unable to be repaired or made good; *irreparable damage.* □ **irreparably** adverb

**irreplaceable** adjective unable to be replaced.

**irrepressible** (i-ri-press-ibŭl) adjective unable to be repressed or restrained. □ **irrepressibly** adverb

**irreproachable** adjective blameless, faultless. □ **irreproachably** adverb

**irresistible** adjective too strong, convincing, or delightful to be resisted. □ **irresistibly** adverb

**irresolute** (i-rez-ŏ-loot) adjective showing uncertainty; hesitating. □ **irresolutely** adverb, **irresoluteness** noun, **irresolution** noun

**irrespective** adjective (foll. by *of*) not taking into account; *prizes are awarded to winners irrespective of nationality.*

**irresponsible** adjective not showing a proper sense of responsibility. □ **irresponsibly** adverb, **irresponsibility** noun

**irretrievable** adjective unable to be retrieved or restored. □ **irretrievably** adverb

**irreverent** adjective not reverent, not respectful. □ **irreverently** adverb, **irreverence** noun

**irreversible** adjective not reversible, unable to be altered or revoked. □ **irreversibly** adverb

**irrevocable** (i-rev-ŏk-ăbŭl) adjective unable to be revoked; final and unalterable. □ **irrevocably** adverb

**irrigate** verb **1** supply (land or crops) with water by means of streams, channels, etc. **2** wash (a wound) with a constant flow of liquid. □ **irrigation** noun, **irrigator** noun

**irritable** adjective **1** easily annoyed, bad-tempered. **2** (of an organ etc.) sensitive. □ **irritable bowel syndrome** recurrent abdominal pain and constipation or diarrhoea, often associated with stress. □ **irritably** adverb, **irritability** noun

**irritant** adjective causing irritation. ●noun something that causes irritation.

**irritate** verb **1** annoy, rouse impatience or slight anger in (a person). **2** cause itching or other discomfort in (a part of the body). **3** *Biology* stimulate (an organ) to action. □ **irritation** noun

**irrupt** verb enter forcibly or violently. □ **irruption** noun

**is** see BE.

**Isaiah** (I-zy-ă) **1** a Hebrew major prophet of the 8th century BC. **2** a book of the Old Testament that bears his name.

**ISBN** abbreviation international standard book number.

**Isherwood**, Christopher William Bradshaw (1904–86), English novelist.

**isinglass** (I-zing-glahs) noun **1** a kind of gelatin obtained from fish. **2** mica.

**Islam** (iz-lahm) noun **1** the Muslim religion, based on the teaching of Muhammad. **2** the Muslim world. □ **Islamic** (iz-lam-ik) adjective

**Islamabad** (iz-lahm-ă-bad) the capital of Pakistan.

**island** (I-lănd) noun **1** a piece of land surrounded by water. **2** something detached or isolated. □ **traffic island** a paved or raised area in the middle of a road, for pedestrians to use in crossing.

**islander** (I-lăn-der) noun an inhabitant of an island.

**isle** (rhymes with mile) noun (poetic and in place-names) an island.

**Isle of Man** an island in the Irish Sea, a British Crown possession with home rule.

**Isle of Wight** an island off the south coast of England, a county of England.

**islet** (I-lit) noun a small island. □ **islets of Langerhans** groups of pancreatic cells secreting insulin.

**ism** noun (informal, usually scornful) a doctrine or practice, especially one with a name ending in -ism.

**Ismaili** (iz-my-li) noun a member of any of various Shiite Muslim sects, of which the best known is that headed by the Aga Khan.

**isn't** (informal) = is not.

**isobar** (**I**-sŏ-bar) *noun* a line on a map connecting places that have the same atmospheric pressure. □ **isobaric** *adjective*

**isochronous** (I-**sok**-rŏn-ŭs) *adjective* **1** occupying an equal time. **2** occurring at the same time.

**isolate** *verb* **1** place apart or alone. **2** separate (an infectious person) from others. **3** separate (a substance) from a mixture. □ **isolation** *noun*

**isolationism** *noun* the policy of holding aloof from other countries or groups. □ **isolationist** *noun*

**isomer** (**I**-sŏm-er) *noun* one of two or more substances whose molecules have the same atoms in different arrangements. □ **isomeric** (I-sŏ-**merrik**) *adjective*, **isomerism** (I-**som**-er-izm) *noun*

**isometric** (I-sŏ-**met**-rik) *adjective* **1** (of muscle action) developing tension while the muscle is prevented from contracting. **2** (of a drawing or projection) drawing a three-dimensional object, without perspective, so that equal lengths along the three axes are drawn equal. **3** of equal measure.

**isomorph** (**I**-sŏ-morf) *noun* a substance having the same form or composition as another. □ **isomorphic** *adjective*, **isomorphism** *noun*

**isosceles** (I-**sos**-i-leez) *adjective* (of a triangle) having two sides of equal length.

**isotherm** (**I**-sŏ-therm) *noun* a line on a map connecting places that have the same temperature. □ **isothermal** *adjective*

**isotope** (**I**-sŏ-tohp) *noun* one of two or more forms of a chemical element with different atomic weight and different nuclear properties but the same chemical properties. □ **isotopic** (I-sŏ-**top**-ik) *adjective*

**isotropic** (I-sŏ-**trop**-ik) *adjective* having the same physical properties in all directions. □ **isotropy** (I-**so**-trŏ-pi) *noun*

**Israel**[1] the Hebrew nation or people (also called **children of Israel**) traditionally descended from Jacob. □ **Israelite** *adjective & noun*

**Israel**[2] a country in SW Asia, at the eastern end of the Mediterranean Sea. □ **Israeli** (iz-**ray**-li) *adjective & noun* (*plural* **Israelis**)

**Issigonis** (iss-i-**goh**-nis), Alec Arnold Constantine (1906–88), British car designer, of Greek parentage, whose most famous designs were the Morris Minor and the Mini.

**issue** *noun* **1** an outgoing or outflow. **2** the giving out of things for use or for sale. **3** one set of publications in a regular series; *the May issue*. **4** a result, an outcome. **5** the point in question; an important topic for discussion; *what are the real issues?* **6** offspring; *died without male issue*. ● *verb*

**1** come or flow out. **2** supply or distribute for use; *campers were issued with blankets*. **3** put out for sale; publish. **4** send out; *issue orders*. **5** result, originate. □ **at issue** being discussed or disputed. **join** *or* **take issue** argue or disagree.

**Istanbul** a port and the former capital of Turkey.

**isthmus** (iss-mŭs) *noun* (*plural* **isthmuses**) a narrow strip of land connecting two masses of land.

**it** *pronoun* **1** the thing or animal mentioned or being discussed. **2** the person in question; *who is it?*; *it's me*. **3** used as the subject of a verb making a general statement about the weather (e.g. *it is raining*) or about circumstances etc. (e.g. *it is 6 miles to Oxford*), or as an indefinite object (*run for it!*). **4** used as the subject or object of a verb, with reference to a following clause or phrase, e.g. *it is seldom that he fails*; *I take it that you agree*. **5** exactly what is needed. **6** (in children's games) the player who has to catch others. **7** (*informal*) sexual intercourse. **8** (*informal*) sex appeal.

■**Usage** See the note under **its**.

**Italian** *adjective* of Italy or its people or language. ● *noun* **1** a native of Italy. **2** the Italian language.

**Italianate** (i-**tal**-yăn-ayt) *adjective* Italian in style or appearance.

**italic** (i-**tal**-ik) *adjective* **1** (of printed letters) sloping *like this*. **2** (of handwriting) compact and pointed like an early form of Italian handwriting. **3** (**Italic**) of ancient Italy. ● *plural noun* (**italics**) sloping printed letters *like these*.

**italicize** (i-**tal**-i-syz) *verb* (also **italicise**) put into italics.

**Italy** a country in southern Europe.

**itch** *noun* **1** an irritation or tickling feeling in the skin. **2** a restless desire or longing. ● *verb* **1** have or feel a tickling sensation in the skin, causing a desire to scratch the affected part. **2** feel a restless desire or longing.

**itchy** *adjective* having or causing an itch. □ **have itchy feet** (*informal*) be restless; have a desire to travel. □ **itchiness** *noun*

**it'd** (*informal*) **1** it had. **2** it would.

**item** *noun* **1** a single thing in a list or number of things. **2** a single piece of news.

**itemize** *verb* (also **itemise**) list, state item by item. □ **itemization** *noun*

**iterate** (**it**-er-ayt) *verb* repeat, state repeatedly. □ **iteration** *noun*, **iterative** *adjective*

**Ithaca** (**ith**-ă-kă) an island off the western coast of Greece, legendary home of Odysseus.

**itinerant** (i-**tin**-er-ănt) *adjective* travelling from place to place; *an itinerant preacher.* • *noun* an itinerant person.

**itinerary** (I-**tin**-er-er-i) *noun* **1** a route, a list of places to be visited on a journey. **2** a record of travel. **3** a guidebook.

**it'll** (*informal*) = it will.

**its** *possessive pronoun* of or belonging to it.

■**Usage** Do not confuse with *it's*, which has a different meaning (see the next entry). The word *its* is the possessive form of *it*, and (like *hers, ours, theirs, yours*) has no apostrophe; correct usage is *the dog wagged its tail* (not *it's*), *the dog is hers* (not *her's*), *these are ours* (not *our's*).

**it's 1** it is; *it's very hot.* **2** it has; *it's broken all records.*

■**Usage** Do not confuse with **its**.

**itself** *pronoun* the emphatic and reflexive form of *it; the meal itself was good; the money doubled itself.* □ **in itself** viewed in its essential qualities; *not in itself a bad thing.*

**ITV** *abbreviation* Independent Television.

**IUD** *abbreviation* intrauterine device; a coil placed inside the womb as a contraceptive.

**Ivan** (**I**-văn) the name of several rulers of Russia, including Ivan III 'the Great' (reigned 1462–1505) and Ivan IV 'the Terrible' (reigned 1533–84).

**I've** (*informal*) = I have.

**Ives** (*rhymes with* hives), Charles Edward (1874–1954), American composer.

**IVF** *abbreviation in vitro* fertilization.

**ivory** *noun* **1** the hard creamy-white substance forming the tusks of elephants etc. **2** a creamy-white colour. • *adjective* creamy-white. □ **ivory tower** a place or situation where people live secluded from the harsh realities of everyday life.

**Ivory Coast** (official name **Côte d'Ivoire**) a country in West Africa.

**ivy** *noun* a climbing evergreen shrub with shiny five-pointed leaves.

**Ivy League** a group of eight long-established universities of the eastern USA (including Harvard, Yale, Princeton, and Columbia) of high academic prestige.

**ixia** (**iks**-iă) *noun* a plant of the iris family.

# Jj

**J** *abbreviation* joule(s).

**jab** *verb* (**jabbed**, **jabbing**) poke roughly, thrust. ●*noun* **1** a rough blow or thrust, especially with something pointed. **2** (*informal*) a hypodermic injection.

**jabber** *verb* **1** speak or say rapidly and unintelligibly. **2** chatter continuously. ●*noun* jabbering talk or sound.

**jabot** (*zh*ab-oh) *noun* an ornamental frill down the front of a shirt, blouse, or dress.

**jacaranda** (jak-ă-ran-dă) *noun* a tropical American tree with hard scented wood and blue flowers.

**jacinth** (jas-inth) *noun* a reddish-orange gem, a variety of zircon.

**jack** *noun* **1** a portable device for raising heavy weights off the ground, especially one for raising the axle of a motor vehicle so that a wheel may be changed. **2** a ship's flag (smaller than an ensign) flown at the bow of a ship to show its nationality. **3** a playing card with a picture of a soldier, page, etc., ranking below a queen in card games. **4** a small white ball aimed at in the game of bowls. **5** a device using a single-pronged plug to connect an electrical circuit. ●*verb* (usually foll. by *up*) **1** raise with a jack. **2** (*informal*) raise (prices etc.). □ **every man Jack** every individual person. **Jack Frost** frost personified. **jack in** (*slang*) abandon (an attempt etc.). **jack-in-the-box** *noun* a toy figure that springs out of a box when the lid is lifted. **jack of all trades** one who can do many different kinds of work. **Jack Russell** a short-legged breed of terrier. **Jack tar** a sailor.

**jackal** (jak-awl) *noun* a wild flesh-eating animal of Africa and Asia, related to the dog, scavenging in packs for food.

**jackanapes** *noun* (*old use*) a rascal.

**jackass** *noun* **1** a male donkey. **2** a stupid or foolish person.

**jackboot** *noun* **1** a military boot reaching above the knee. **2** military oppression, bullying behaviour.

**jackdaw** *noun* a grey-headed bird of the crow family.

**jacket** *noun* **1** a short coat, usually reaching to the hips. **2** an outer covering round a boiler etc. to lessen loss of heat. **3** = DUST-JACKET. **4** the skin of a potato. □ **jacket potato** a potato baked in its skin.

**jackknife** *noun* **1** a large clasp-knife. **2** a dive in which the body is first bent double and then straightened. ●*verb* (of an articulated vehicle) fold against itself in an accident.

**jackpot** *noun* a large prize, especially the accumulated stakes in various games, increasing in value until won. □ **hit the jackpot** (*informal*) have sudden great success or good fortune.

**jackrabbit** *noun* (*Amer.*) a large prairie hare.

**Jackson¹**, Andrew (1767–1845), 7th President of the USA 1829–37, known as 'Old Hickory'.

**Jackson²**, Michael (born 1958), American singer and songwriter.

**Jack the Ripper** a notorious Victorian murderer, never identified, who carried out a series of grisly murders of women in the East End of London in 1888–9.

**Jacob** a Hebrew patriarch also called Israel (*see* ISRAEL¹).

**Jacobean** (jak-ŏ-bee-ăn) *adjective* **1** of the reign of James I of England (1603–25). **2** (of furniture) heavy and dark in style.

**Jacobite** (jak-ŏ-byt) *noun* a supporter of James II of England after his abdication (1688), or of the exiled Stuarts.

**Jacquard** (jak-ard) *noun* a fabric woven with an intricate figured pattern.

**Jacuzzi** (ja-koo-zi) *noun* (*trade mark*) a large bath with underwater jets of water which massage the body.

**jade¹** *noun* **1** a hard green, blue, or white stone from which ornaments are carved. **2** its green colour.

**jade²** *noun* **1** a poor worn-out horse. **2** a disreputable or bad-tempered woman.

**jaded** *adjective* tired and bored; lacking zest.

**Jaffa** *noun* a large oval thick-skinned variety of orange, originally grown near the port of Jaffa in Israel.

**jag** *noun* (*slang*) **1** a drinking bout. **2** a period of indulgence in a particular activity, emotion, etc.

**jagged** (jag-id) *adjective* having an uneven edge or outline with sharp projections.

**jaguar** *noun* a large flesh-eating animal of the cat family, found in tropical America.

**jail** (*pronounced* jayl) *noun* (also **gaol**) **1** a public prison. **2** confinement in this; *sentenced to three years' jail.* ●*verb* put into jail.

**jailbird** *noun* (also **gaolbird**) a person who is or has been in prison; a habitual criminal.

**jailbreak** *noun* (also **gaolbreak**) an escape from jail.

**jailer** *noun* (also **gaoler**) a person in charge of a jail or its prisoners.

**Jain** (*rhymes with* mine) *noun* a member of an Indian religion with doctrines like those of

Buddhism. ● *adjective* of this religion. □ **Jainism** *noun*, **Jainist** *noun & adjective*

**Jakarta** alternative spelling of DJAKARTA.

**jalap** *noun* a purgative drug obtained from the tubers of a Mexican plant.

**jalapeno** (hal-ă-**peen**-oh) *noun* (*plural* **jalapenos**) a very hot green chilli pepper, used in Mexican cooking.

**jalopy** (jă-**lop**-i) *noun* a battered old car.

**jalousie** (*zh*al-oo-zi) *noun* a slatted blind or shutter that lets in air and light but not rain etc.

**jam¹** *verb* (**jammed**, **jamming**) **1** squeeze or wedge into a space; become wedged. **2** make (part of a machine) immovable so that the machine will not work; become unworkable in this way. **3** crowd or block (a passage, road, etc.) with people or things. **4** (usually foll. by *on*) thrust or apply forcibly; *jammed the brakes on*. **5** cause interference to (a radio transmission), making it unintelligible. **6** (*informal*) (in jazz and popular music) improvise with other musicians. ● *noun* **1** a squeeze, crush, or stoppage caused by jamming. **2** a crowded mass making movement difficult; *traffic jams*. **3** (*informal*) a difficult situation; *I'm in a jam*. □ **jam-packed** *adjective* (*informal*) packed full and tightly. **jam session** (*informal*) improvised playing by a group of jazz musicians.

**jam²** *noun* **1** a sweet substance made by boiling fruit with sugar to a thick consistency. **2** (*informal*) something easy or pleasant; *money for jam*. □ **jam tomorrow** a pleasant thing continually promised but never produced.

**Jamaica** an island in the Caribbean Sea. □ **Jamaican** *adjective & noun*

**jamb** (*pronounced* jam) *noun* the vertical side post of a doorway or window frame.

**jamboree** (jam-ber-**ee**) *noun* **1** a celebration. **2** a large rally of Scouts.

**James¹** the name of two kings of England and Scotland, James I (James VI of Scotland), king of Scotland 1567–1625 and England 1603–25, James II (James VII of Scotland), reigned 1685–8.

**James²**, Henry (1843–1916), American novelist and critic.

**James³**, St **1** 'the Great', an Apostle, martyred in AD 44; feast day, 25 July. **2** 'the Less', an Apostle; feast day, 1 May. **3** a person described as 'the Lord's brother', put to death in AD 62, to whom is ascribed the **Epistle of St James**, a book of the New Testament. □ **Court of St James's** the official title of the British sovereign's court. **St James's Palace** a Tudor palace in London, the chief royal residence from 1697 to 1837.

**Jammu and Kashmir** (jum-oo, kash-meer) a State in NW India.

**jammy** *adjective* **1** smeared with jam. **2** (*informal*) lucky.

**Jan.** *abbreviation* January.

**Janáček** (yan-ă-chek), Leoš (1854–1928), Czech composer and conductor.

**jangle** *noun* a harsh metallic sound. ● *verb* **1** make or cause to make this sound. **2** cause irritation to (nerves etc.) by discord.

**janitor** (jan-it-er) *noun* the caretaker of a building.

**January** the first month of the year.

**Janus** (jay-nŭs) (*Rom. myth.*) a god who was the guardian of doorways, gates, and beginnings, usually shown with two faces that look in opposite directions. January is named after him.

**Jap** *noun & adjective* (*informal*, often *offensive*) = JAPANESE.

**Japan** a country in eastern Asia. □ **Japanese** *adjective & noun* (*plural* **Japanese**).

**japan** *noun* a hard usually black varnish, originally from Japan. ● *verb* (**japanned**, **japanning**) coat with japan.

**jape** *noun* a practical joke. ● *verb* play a joke.

**japonica** (jă-**pon**-ikă) *noun* an ornamental variety of quince, with red or pink flowers.

**jar¹** *noun* **1** a cylindrical container made of glass or earthenware. **2** (*informal*) a glass of beer.

**jar²** *verb* (**jarred**, **jarring**) **1** (often foll. by *on*) make a sound that has a discordant or painful effect. **2** (often foll. by *with*) (of an action etc.) be out of harmony, have a harsh or disagreeable effect. **3** (often foll. by *against* or *on*) cause an unpleasant jolt or a sudden shock. ● *noun* a jarring movement or effect.

**jardinière** (*zh*ar-din-**yair**) *noun* **1** a large ornamental pot for holding indoor plants. **2** a dish of mixed vegetables.

**jargon** *noun* **1** words or expressions developed for use within a particular group, hard for outsiders to understand; *scientists' jargon*. **2** ugly or pretentious language.

**jasmine** *noun* a shrub with yellow or white flowers.

**Jason** (*Gk. legend*) the leader of the Argonauts in quest of the Golden Fleece.

**jasper** *noun* an opaque variety of quartz, usually red, yellow, or brown.

**Jat** (*pronounced* jaht) *noun* a member of an Indian people widely distributed in NW India.

**Jataka** (jah-tă-kă) *noun* any of the various stories of the Buddha found in Buddhist literature.

**jaundice** (**jawn**-dis) *noun* a condition in which the skin becomes abnormally yellow as a result of excessive bile in the blood-stream.

**jaundiced** adjective **1** discoloured by jaundice. **2** filled with resentment or jealousy.

**jaunt** noun a short trip, especially one taken for pleasure. □ **jaunting car** noun a light two-wheeled horse-drawn vehicle formerly common in Ireland.

**jaunty** adjective (**jauntier, jauntiest**) **1** cheerful and self-confident in manner. **2** (of clothes) stylish and cheerful. □ **jauntily** adverb, **jauntiness** noun

**Java** (jah-vă) an island of Indonesia. □ **Javanese** adjective & noun (plural **Javanese**).

**javelin** (jav-ĕ-lin) noun a light spear thrown in sport or, formerly, as a weapon.

**jaw** noun **1** either of the two bones that form the framework of the mouth and in which the teeth are set. **2** the lower of these; the part of the face covering it. **3** (**jaws**) the narrow mouth of a valley, channel, etc. **4** (**jaws**) the gripping parts of a tool etc. **5** (**jaws**) a grip; in the jaws of death. **6** (informal) tedious talk; hold your jaw. ● verb (slang) talk long and boringly; gossip. □ **jaw-breaker** noun a word that is very long or difficult to pronounce.

**jawbone** noun the lower jaw in most mammals.

**jay** noun a noisy European bird of the crow family with pinkish-brown plumage, a black tail, and a small blue barred patch on each wing.

**jaywalk** verb walk carelessly in a road, without regard for traffic or signals. □ **jaywalker** noun

**jazz** noun **1** a type of music with strong rhythm and syncopation, often improvised. **2** (slang) a matter, especially something regarded as pretentious or as nonsense; talked of the honour of the firm and all that jazz. ● verb play or dance to jazz. □ **jazz up** brighten, enliven.

**jazzy** adjective **1** of or like jazz. **2** flashy, showy; a jazzy sports car.

**JCB** noun (trade mark) a mechanical excavator with a shovel at the front and a digging arm at the rear. (¶ Named after the makers, J. C. Bamford.)

**jealous** (jel-ŭs) adjective **1** feeling or showing resentment towards a person whom one thinks of as a rival (especially in love) or as having advantages. **2** possessive and taking watchful care; is very jealous of his own rights. □ **jealously** adverb, **jealousy** noun

**Jeans**, Sir James Hopwood (1877–1946), English physicist, mathematician, and writer on astronomy, the first to propose (1928) that matter is continuously created throughout the universe.

**jeans** plural noun casual trousers, especially made of denim.

**Jeep** noun (trade mark) a small sturdy motor vehicle, especially in military use, with four-wheel drive.

**jeer** verb laugh or shout at rudely and scornfully. ● noun a jeering remark or shout.

**Jefferson**, Thomas (1743–1826), 3rd President of the USA 1801–9, who drafted the Declaration of Independence (1775–6).

**jehad** alternative spelling of JIHAD.

**Jehovah** (ji-hoh-vă) the name of God in the Old Testament (compare YAHWEH).

**Jehovah's Witness** a member of a Christian sect of American origin, denying many traditional Christian doctrines and refusing the claims of the State when these conflict with their own principles.

**jejune** (ji-joon) adjective **1** scanty, poor; (of land) barren. **2** unsatisfying to the mind.

**Jekyll and Hyde** a person in whom two personalities (one good, one evil) alternate. (¶ Named after the hero of a story (by R. L. Stevenson) who could transform himself from the respectable Dr Jekyll into the evil Mr Hyde by means of a potion which he drank.)

**jell** verb (informal) **1** set as jelly. **2** take definite form; our ideas began to jell.

**jellaba** alternative spelling of DJELLABA.

**jellied** adjective set in jelly; jellied eels.

**jelly** noun **1** a soft solid food made of liquid set with gelatin, especially one prepared in a mould as a sweet dish. **2** a kind of jam made of strained fruit juice and sugar. **3** a substance of similar consistency; petroleum jelly. **4** (slang) gelignite. □ **jelly baby** a jelly-like sweet made in the shape of a baby.

**jellyfish** noun (plural **jellyfish** or **jellyfishes**) a sea animal with a jelly-like body and stinging tentacles.

**jemmy** noun a short crowbar used by burglars to force doors, windows, and drawers.

**Jenner**, Edward (1749–1823), English physician, the pioneer of vaccination.

**jenny** noun a female donkey.

**jeopardize** (jep-er-dyz) verb (also **jeopardise**) endanger.

**jeopardy** (jep-er-di) noun danger.

**jerbil** alternative spelling of GERBIL.

**jerboa** (jer-boh-ă) noun a small desert rodent with long hind legs used for leaping.

**jeremiad** (je-ri-my-ad) noun a long mournful lament about one's troubles. (¶ Named after Jeremiah.)

**Jeremiah** (je-ri-my-ă) **1** a Hebrew major prophet (c.650–c.585 BC). **2** the book of the Old Testament containing his account of the troubles of the Jews at that time. ●*noun* a pessimistic person.

**Jerez** (**he**-reth) a town in Andalusia, Spain, centre of the sherry-making industry.

**Jericho** an ancient city north of the Dead Sea, on the West Bank.

**jerk** *noun* **1** a sudden sharp movement; an abrupt pull, push, or throw. **2** (*slang*) a stupid or insignificant person. ●*verb* **1** pull, throw, or stop with a jerk; move with a jerk or in short uneven movements. **2** cure (beef etc.) by cutting it into long slices and drying it in the sun.

**jerkin** *noun* a sleeveless jacket.

**jerky** *adjective* making abrupt starts and stops, not moving or acting smoothly. ●*noun* (*Amer.*) sun-dried strips of beef. □ **jerkily** *adverb*, **jerkiness** *noun*

**jeroboam** (je-rŏ-**boh**-ăm) *noun* a wine bottle of 4–12 times the ordinary size. (¶ Named after a king of Israel (10th century BC) whose name means 'mighty man of valour'.)

**Jerome**[1] (jĕ-**rohm**), Jerome K(lapka) (1859–1927), English novelist and playwright, author of the humorous novel *Three Men in a Boat*.

**Jerome**[2] (jĕ-**rohm**), St (*c.*342–420), scholar and monk, who translated the Bible from the original Hebrew and Greek into the language (Latin) of the people of his own time.

**Jerry** *noun* (*slang*) **1** a German. **2** Germans collectively.

**jerry** *noun* (*slang*) a chamber pot.

**jerry-built** *adjective* built badly and with poor materials. □ **jerry-builder** *noun*, **jerry-building** *noun*

**jerrycan** *noun* a kind of can for petrol or water.

**Jersey** the largest of the Channel Islands. ●*noun* an animal of a breed of light brown dairy cattle, originally from Jersey.

**jersey** *noun* **1** plain machine-knitted fabric used for making clothes. **2** (*plural* **jerseys**) a close-fitting woollen pullover with sleeves.

**Jerusalem** the holy city of the Jews, sacred also to Christians and Muslims, the capital of Israel. □ **Jerusalem artichoke** a kind of sunflower with edible underground tubers; this tuber as a vegetable.

**jess** *noun* a short strap put round the leg of a hawk used in falconry.

**jest** *noun* a joke. ●*verb* make jokes. □ **in jest** in fun, not seriously.

**jester** *noun* a professional clown employed at a royal court in the Middle Ages.

**Jesu** (*old use*) Jesus.

**Jesuit** (**jez**-yoo-it) *noun* a member of the Society of Jesus, a Roman Catholic religious order.

**Jesuitical** (jez-yoo-**it**-ikăl) *adjective* **1** of or like Jesuits. **2** (*scornful*) using clever but false reasoning (such as the Jesuits were accused of by their enemies).

**Jesus** (also **Jesus Christ**) the central figure of the Christian religion believed by Christians to be the Son of God, a Jew living in Palestine at the beginning of the 1st century AD. ●*interjection* (*slang*) an exclamation of surprise, dismay, etc.

**jet**[1] *noun* a hard black mineral that can be polished, used as a gem. □ **jet black** *adjective & noun* deep glossy black.

**jet**[2] *noun* **1** a stream of water, gas, flame, etc., shot out from a small opening. **2** a spout or opening from which this comes, e.g. a burner on a gas cooker. **3** a jet engine or jet plane. ●*verb* (**jetted**, **jetting**) **1** spurt in jets. **2** (*informal*) travel or convey by jet-propelled aircraft. □ **jet engine** an engine using jet propulsion to give forward thrust. **jet lag** delayed physical effects of tiredness etc. felt after a long flight by aircraft across time zones. **jet-propelled** *adjective* propelled by jet engines. **jet propulsion** propulsion by engines that give forward thrust by sending out a high-speed jet of gases at the back. **jet set** wealthy people who travel widely, especially for pleasure. **jet stream 1** a jet from a jet engine. **2** a strong wind blowing in a narrow range of altitudes in the upper atmosphere.

**jetsam** *noun* goods thrown overboard from a ship in distress to lighten it, especially those that are washed ashore.

**jettison** *verb* **1** throw (goods) overboard or (goods or fuel) from an aircraft, especially to lighten a ship or aircraft in distress. **2** discard (what is unwanted).

**jetty** *noun* **1** a breakwater built to protect a harbour, coast, etc. **2** a landing-pier.

**Jew** *noun* a person of Hebrew descent, or one whose religion is Judaism. □ **jew's harp** a musical instrument held in the teeth while a projecting metal strip is twanged with a finger.

**jewel** *noun* **1** a precious stone. **2** an ornament for wearing, containing one or more precious stones. **3** a person or thing that is highly valued.

**jewelled** *adjective* (*Amer.* **jeweled**) ornamented or set with jewels.

**jeweller** *noun* (*Amer.* **jeweler**) a person who makes or deals in jewels or jewellery.

**jewellery** (**joo**-ĕl-ri) *noun* (also **jewelry**) jewels or similar ornaments to be worn.

**Jewess** *noun* (often *offensive*) a female Jew.

**Jewish** *adjective* of Jews or Judaism.

**Jewry** *noun* Jews collectively.

**Jezebel** (**jez**-ĕ-bĕl) *noun* a shameless or immoral woman. (¶ From Jezebel in the

Old Testament, wife of Ahab, king of Israel.)

**jib¹** *noun* **1** a triangular sail stretching forward from the mast. **2** the projecting arm of a crane.

**jib²** *verb* (**jibbed, jibbing**) **1** (especially of a horse) stop and refuse to go on. **2** (foll. by *at*) show unwillingness and dislike for (a course of action).

**jibe 1** alternative spelling of GIBE. **2** Amer. spelling of GYBE.

**jiff** *noun* (also **jiffy**) (*informal*) a moment; *in a jiffy*.

**Jiffy bag** (*trade mark*) a padded envelope.

**jig** *noun* **1** a lively jumping dance; the music for this. **2** a device that holds a piece of work and guides the tools working on it. ● *verb* (**jigged, jigging**) **1** dance a jig. **2** move up and down rapidly and jerkily. **3** work on or equip with a jig or jigs.

**jigger** *noun* **1** a measure of spirits etc.; a glass holding this amount. **2** (*informal*) a cue-rest used in billiards.

**jiggered** *adjective* □ **I'll be jiggered** (*informal*) an exclamation of astonishment.

**jiggery-pokery** *noun* (*informal*) trickery, underhand dealing.

**jiggle** *verb* rock or jerk lightly.

**jigsaw** *noun* **1** a mechanical fretsaw with a fine blade. **2** (in full **jigsaw puzzle**) a picture pasted on board and cut with a jigsaw into irregular pieces which are then shuffled and reassembled as a pastime.

**jihad** (ji-**had**) *noun* (also **jehad**) (in Islam) a holy war.

**jilt** *verb* abruptly reject or abandon (especially a lover).

**Jim Crow** (*Amer.*) **1** the policy of segregating Blacks. **2** (*offensive*) a Black person.

**jim-jams** *plural noun* **1** (*slang*) = DELIRIUM TREMENS. **2** (*informal*) nervousness; depression.

**Jimmu** (**jim**-oo) the legendary first emperor of Japan (660 BC).

**jingle** *verb* make or cause to make a metallic ringing or clinking sound. ● *noun* **1** a jingling sound. **2** a verse or words with simple catchy rhymes or repetitive sounds.

**jingo** *noun* (*plural* **jingoes**) a supporter of war; an overenthusiastic patriot. □ **by jingo!** (*old use*) an exclamation of surprise.

**jingoism** (**jing**-oh-izm) *noun* aggressive patriotism. □ **jingoist** *noun*, **jingoistic** *adjective*

**jink** *verb* dodge by turning suddenly and sharply. ● *noun* an act of jinking. □ **high jinks** noisy merrymaking, boisterous fun.

**Jinnah** (**jin**-ă), Muhammad Ali (1876–1948), founder and first Governor-General of Pakistan.

**jinnee** *noun* (also **jinn, djinn**) (*plural* **jinn** or **djinn**) (*Islamic myth.*) any of the supernatural beings able to appear in human and animal form and to help or hinder human beings.

**jinx** (*informal*) *noun* a person or thing that is thought to bring bad luck. ● *verb* (usually used as **jinxed** *adjective*) subjected to bad luck.

**jitter** (*informal*) *verb* feel nervous, behave nervously. ● *plural noun* (**the jitters**) nervousness. □ **jittery** *adjective*, **jitteriness** *noun*

**jitterbug** *noun* **1** a nervous person. **2** a fast dance popular in the early 1940s. ● *verb* (**jitterbugged, jitterbugging**) dance the jitterbug.

**jiu-jitsu** alternative spelling of JU-JITSU.

**jive** *noun* fast lively jazz music; dancing to this. ● *verb* dance to such music. □ **jiver** *noun*

**Jnr.** *abbreviation* Junior.

**Joachim** (joh-ă-kim), St, the husband of St Anne and father of the Virgin Mary.

**Joan of Arc**, St (1412–31), French national heroine, who led French forces against the English in the Hundred Years War, and relieved Orleans. After being captured she was tried and burnt at the stake as a heretic. Feast day, 30 May.

**Job** (*pronounced* johb) **1** a prosperous Hebrew leader who, despite enduring many undeserved misfortunes, ultimately remained convinced of the goodness of God. **2** a book of the Old Testament giving an account of this. □ **Job's comforter** a person who aggravates the distress of the person he or she is supposed to be comforting, like those who counselled Job.

**job** *noun* **1** a piece of work to be done. **2** a paid position of employment; *got a job at the factory*. **3** something one has to do, a responsibility; *it's your job to lock the gates*. **4** something completed, a product of work; *a neat little job*. **5** (*slang*) a crime, especially a robbery. **6** (*informal*) a difficult task; *you'll have a job to move it*. **7** a state of affairs; *gave it up as a bad job*. ● *verb* (**jobbed, jobbing**) **1** do jobs, do piece-work. **2** buy or sell (stock or goods) as a middleman. □ **job lot** a collection of miscellaneous articles bought together. **jobs for the boys** (*informal*) the assurance of gain or profitable positions for one's friends. **job-sharing** *noun* sharing of a full-time job by two or more people. **just the job** (*informal*) exactly what is wanted. **make a good job of** do thoroughly or successfully. **on the job** at work.

**jobber** *noun* **1** a principal or wholesaler dealing on the Stock Exchange (¶ up to October 1986 permitted to deal only with brokers, not directly with the public; from that date the name has ceased to be in official use). **2** one who jobs.

**jobbery** *noun* corrupt dealing.

**jobbing** *adjective* doing single specific pieces of work for payment; *a jobbing gardener.*

**jobcentre** *noun* (*Brit.*) a government office in a town centre where information about jobs available is displayed.

**jobless** *adjective* unemployed, out of work.

**Jock** (*slang*) a nickname for a Scotsman.

**jockey** *noun* (*plural* **jockeys**) a person who rides horses in horse races, especially a professional rider. ●*verb* (**jockeyed**, **jockeying**) manoeuvre in order to gain an advantage; *jockeying for position*; *jockeyed him into doing it.*

**Jockey Club** a club whose stewards are the central authority for the administration and control of horse racing in England.

**jockstrap** *noun* a support or protective covering for the male genitals, worn especially for sport.

**jocose** (jŏk-**ohss**) *adjective* joking, playful. □ **jocosely** *adverb*, **jocosity** *noun*

**jocular** (**jok**-yoo-ler) *adjective* joking, avoiding seriousness. □ **jocularly** *adverb*, **jocularity** (jok-yoo-**la**-riti) *noun*

**jocund** (**jok**-ŭnd) *adjective* (*literary*) merry, cheerful. □ **jocundity** (jŏ-**kund**-iti) *noun*

**jodhpurs** (**jod**-perz) *plural noun* long breeches for riding, fitting closely below the knee and loosely above it.

**Jodrell Bank** (**jod**-rĕl) the site in Cheshire of an astronomical observatory which has a radio telescope with a giant reflector.

**Joe Bloggs** a hypothetical average person.

**Joel** (*pronounced* **joh**-ĕl) **1** a Hebrew minor prophet. **2** a book of the Old Testament containing his prophecies.

**joey** *noun* (*Austral.*) **1** a young kangaroo. **2** a young animal.

**jog** *verb* (**jogged**, **jogging**) **1** give a slight knock or push to; shake with a push or jerk. **2** rouse or stimulate; *jogged his memory.* **3** (of a horse) trot. **4** run at a leisurely pace with short strides, as a form of exercise. ●*noun* **1** a slight shake or push, a nudge. **2** a slow run or trot; a spell of jogging. □ **jog on** *or* **along** proceed slowly or laboriously. □ **jogger** *noun*

**joggle** *verb* shake slightly; move by slight jerks. ●*noun* a joggling movement, a slight shake.

**jogtrot** *noun* a slow regular trot.

**Johannesburg** a city of Transvaal, the centre of the South African gold-mining industry.

**John**[1] king of England 1199–1216.

**John**[2], St **1** an Apostle, credited with the authorship of the fourth Gospel, the Apocalypse, and three epistles of the New Testament. Feast days, 27 December and 6 May. **2** the fourth Gospel. **3** any of the three epistles attributed to St John.

**john** *noun* (*Amer. slang*) a lavatory.

**John Bull** a typical Englishman; England.

**John Dory** = DORY.

**johnny** *noun* **1** (*slang*) a condom. **2** (*informal*) a fellow. □ **johnny-come-lately** *noun* a recently arrived person, an upstart.

**John o' Groats** a place near the extreme NE point of the Scottish mainland.

**John Paul II** (Karol Józef Wojtyła) (born 1920), Polish-born cleric, pope from 1978.

**Johnson**[1], Amy (1903–41), English aviator, who established several records with her solo flights to Australia (1930), Tokyo (1932), and the Cape of Good Hope (1936).

**Johnson**[2], Samuel (1709–84), English poet, critic, and lexicographer, whose celebrated *Dictionary* was published in 1755.

**John the Baptist**, St, a preacher who was the cousin of Jesus Christ, whom he baptized, and was beheaded by Herod Antipas. Feast days, 24 June and 29 August.

**joie de vivre** (zh**wah dĕ veevr**) a feeling of great enjoyment of life. (¶ French, = joy of living.)

**join** *verb* **1** put together; fasten, unite, or connect. **2** come together, become united with; *the Moselle joins the Rhine at Koblenz.* **3** take part with others in doing something; *joined in the chorus.* **4** come into the company of; *join us for lunch.* **5** become a member of; *joined the Navy.* **6** take or resume one's place in; *joined his ship.* ●*noun* a point, line, or surface where things join. □ **join battle** begin fighting. **join forces** combine efforts. **join hands 1** clasp each other's hands. **2** combine in an action etc. **join in** take part in (an activity). **join up 1** enlist in the armed forces. **2** connect, unite.

**joiner** *noun* a person who makes furniture, house fittings, and other finished woodwork.

**joinery** *noun* the work of a joiner.

**joint** *adjective* **1** shared, held, or done by two or more people together; *a joint account.* **2** sharing in an activity etc.; *joint authors.* ●*noun* **1** a place or device at which two parts of a structure are joined. **2** a structure in an animal body by which bones are fitted together. **3** any of the parts into which a butcher divides a carcass as meat. **4** (*slang*) a place where people meet for gambling or drinking etc. **5** (*slang*) a marijuana cigarette. ●*verb* **1** connect by a joint or joints. **2** divide (meat) into joints. □ **joint-stock company** a business company with capital contributed and held jointly by a number of people. **out of joint 1** (of a bone) dislocated. **2** in disorder.

**jointly** *adverb* so as to be shared or done by two or more people together.

**jointure** *noun* an estate settled on a wife by her husband for use after his death.

**joist** *noun* any of the parallel beams, extending from wall to wall, on which floorboards or ceiling laths are fixed.

**jojoba** (hoh-**hoh**-bă) *noun* a plant with seeds yielding an oily extract used in cosmetics etc.

**joke** *noun* **1** something said or done to cause laughter. **2** a ridiculous person, thing, or circumstance. ●*verb* make jokes. □ **it's no joke** it is a serious matter. □ **jokingly** *adverb*

**joker** *noun* **1** a person who jokes. **2** (*slang*) a fellow. **3** an extra playing card used in certain games as the highest trump.

**joky** *adjective* (also **jokey**) joking, not serious.

**Joliot-Curie** (zhol-yoh-**kewr**-i), Jean-Frédéric (1900–58), French nuclear physicist, who with his wife Irène (1897–1956), daughter of Marie Curie, discovered artificial radioactivity.

**jollify** *verb* (**jollified**, **jollifying**) be or cause to be jolly. □ **jollification** *noun*

**jollity** *noun* being jolly, merriment, merrymaking.

**jolly** *adverb* (**jollier**, **jolliest**) **1** cheerful, merry. **2** festive, jovial. **3** very pleasant, delightful. ●*adverb* (*informal*) very; *jolly good*. □ **jolly along** (**jollied**, **jollying**) (*informal*) keep (a person) in a good humour, especially in order to win cooperation. **jolly boat** a clinker-built ship's boat smaller than a cutter. **Jolly Roger** a black flag, usually with a white skull and crossbones, traditionally associated with pirates.

**Jolson** (**johl**-sŏn), Al (original name: Asa Yoelson) (1886–1950), Russian-born American singer and film actor.

**jolt** *verb* **1** shake or dislodge with a jerk. **2** move along jerkily, as on a rough road. **3** give a mental shock to. ●*noun* **1** a jolting movement or effect. **2** a surprise or shock.

**Jonah** (**joh**-nă) **1** a Hebrew minor prophet. **2** a book of the Old Testament telling of his attempted escape from God's call, in which he was thrown overboard, swallowed by a great fish, and vomited out on to dry land. ●*noun* a person who is believed to bring bad luck.

**Jones**, Inigo (1573–1652), English architect and stage designer, who introduced the Palladian style into England.

**jonquil** (**jon**-kwil) *noun* a narcissus with fragrant yellow or white flowers.

**Jonson**, Ben(jamin) (1572/3–1637), English playwright and poet, whose comedies include *Volpone* and *The Alchemist*.

**Jordan** **1** a river rising in Syria and Lebanon and flowing south through the Sea of Galilee to the Dead Sea. **2** (in full

**Hashemite Kingdom of Jordan**) a country in the Middle East, bordering on the east of Israel. □ **Jordanian** (jor-**day**-niăn) *adjective & noun*

**Joseph**, St, a carpenter of Nazareth, husband of the Virgin Mary to whom he was betrothed at the time of the Annunciation.

**Josephine** (1763–1814), empress of France (as wife of Napoleon) from 1804 until their divorce in 1809.

**josh** (*Amer. slang*) *verb* hoax, tease in a good-natured way. ●*noun* good-natured teasing.

**Joshua** **1** the Israelite leader who succeeded Moses and led his people into the Promised Land. **2** the sixth book of the Old Testament, telling of the conquest of Canaan by the Israelites.

**joss** *noun* a Chinese idol. □ **joss-stick** *noun* a thin stick that burns to give off a smell of incense.

**jostle** *verb* **1** push roughly, especially when in a crowd. **2** (foll. by *with*) struggle roughly. ●*noun* the act of jostling.

**jot** *noun* a very small amount; *not one jot*. ●*verb* (**jotted**, **jotting**) write briefly or hastily; *jot it down*.

**jotter** *noun* a small pad or notebook.

**jottings** *plural noun* jotted notes.

**joule** (*pronounced* jool) *noun* a unit of work or energy (*symbol* J). (¶ Named after the English physicist J. P. Joule (1818–89).)

**journal** (**jer**-năl) *noun* **1** a daily record of news, events, or business transactions. **2** a newspaper or periodical.

**journalese** (jer-năl-eez) *noun* a style of language used in inferior newspaper writing, full of hackneyed or artificially elaborate phrases.

**journalist** (**jer**-năl-ist) *noun* a person employed in writing for a newspaper or magazine. □ **journalism** *noun*, **journalistic** *adjective*

**journey** *noun* (*plural* **journeys**) **1** an act of going from one place to another, especially at a long distance. **2** the distance travelled or the time required for this; *a day's or 4 days' journey*. ●*verb* (**journeyed**, **journeying**) make a journey.

**journeyman** *noun* (*plural* **journeymen**) **1** a qualified mechanic or artisan who works for another. **2** a reliable but not outstanding worker.

**joust** (*pronounced* jowst) *verb* (*hist.*) fight on horseback with lances.

**Jove** Jupiter, the king of the gods in Roman mythology. □ **by Jove!** (*old use*) an exclamation of surprise.

**jovial** (**joh**-viăl) *adjective* full of cheerful good humour. □ **jovially** *adverb*, **joviality** (joh-vi-al-iti) *noun*

**jowl** (*rhymes with* howl) *noun* **1** the jaw or jawbone. **2** the cheek. **3** an animal's dewlap; similar loose skin on a person's throat.

**joy** *noun* **1** pleasure, extreme gladness. **2** a thing that causes this. □ **no joy** (*informal*) no satisfaction or success. □ **joyful** *adjective*, **joyfully** *adverb*, **joyfulness** *noun*, **joyless** *adjective*

**Joyce**, James Augustine Aloysius (1882–1941), Irish novelist, whose most important novels, *Ulysses* and *Finnegans Wake*, revolutionized the form and structure of the modern novel. □ **Joycean** *adjective*

**joyous** *adjective* joyful. □ **joyously** *adverb*

**joyride** *noun* a ride taken for pleasure in a stolen car. □ **joyrider** *noun*, **joyriding** *noun*

**joystick** *noun* **1** the control lever of an aircraft. **2** a device for moving a cursor on a VDU screen.

**JP** *abbreviation* Justice of the Peace.

**Jr.** *abbreviation* Junior.

**jubilant** *adjective* showing joy, rejoicing.

**jubilation** *noun* rejoicing.

**jubilee** *noun* **1** a special anniversary, especially the 25th (*silver*), 50th (*golden*), or 60th (*diamond jubilee*). **2** a time of rejoicing.

**Judaea** (joo-dee-ă) (*hist.*) the name for the southern district of ancient Palestine, west of the Jordan. □ **Judaean** *adjective*

**Judaic** (joo-day-ik) *adjective* of or characteristic of the Jews or Judaism.

**Judaism** (joo-day-izm) *noun* the religion of the Jewish people, with belief in one God and based on the teachings of Moses and the Talmud.

**Judas** *noun* a betrayer or traitor. (¶ Named after Judas Iscariot who betrayed Christ.)

**judder** *verb* shake noisily or violently. ● *noun* a juddering movement or effect.

**Jude**, St, an Apostle (martyred in Persia with St Simon) to whom the last epistle in the New Testament is ascribed. Feast day (with St Simon), 28 October.

**judge** *noun* **1** a public officer appointed to hear and try legal cases. **2** a person appointed to decide who has won a contest. **3** a person who is able to give an authoritative opinion on the merits of something. **4** (in ancient Israel) any of the leaders with temporary authority in the period between Joshua and the kings. ● *verb* **1** try (a case) in a lawcourt. **2** act as judge of (a contest). **3** form and give an opinion about. **4** estimate; *judged the distance accurately.*

**judgement** *noun* (also **judgment**) **1** judging, being judged. **2** the decision of a judge etc. in a lawcourt; *the judgement was in his favour.* **3** ability to judge wisely, good sense; *he lacks judgement.* **4** misfortune considered or jokingly said to be a punishment sent by God; *it's a judgement on you!* **5** an opinion; *in the judgement of most people.* □ **against one's better judgement** contrary to what one really thinks to be advisable. **Judgement Day** *or* **Day of Judgement** the day of the **Last Judgement**, when God will judge all mankind.

**judgemental** (juj-men-t'l) *adjective* **1** involving judgement. **2** condemning, critical.

**Judges** the seventh book of the Old Testament.

**judgment** alternative spelling of JUDGEMENT.

**judicature** (joo-dik-ă-choor) *noun* **1** the administration of justice. **2** a judge's position. **3** a body of judges.

**judicial** (joo-dish-ăl) *adjective* **1** of lawcourts or the administration of justice. **2** of a judge or judgement. **3** able to judge things wisely; *a judicial mind.* □ **judicially** *adverb*

**judiciary** (joo-dish-er-i) *noun* the whole body of judges in a country.

**judicious** (joo-dish-ŭs) *adjective* judging wisely, showing good sense. □ **judiciously** *adverb*

**judo** *noun* a Japanese sport of unarmed combat, developed from ju-jitsu.

**Judy** *see* PUNCH.

**jug** *noun* **1** a vessel for holding and pouring liquids, with a handle and a shaped lip. **2** (*slang*) prison. ● *verb* (**jugged**, **jugging**) cook (hare) by stewing it (formerly in a jug or jar). □ **jugful** *noun* (*plural* **jugfuls**).

**juggernaut** *noun* **1** a very large heavy lorry. **2** an overwhelming force or object.

**juggle** *verb* **1** toss and catch a number of objects skilfully, keeping one or more in the air at one time. **2** deal with (several activities) at once. **3** rearrange (facts or figures) in order to achieve something or to deceive people. □ **juggler** *noun*

**jugular** (jug-yoo-ler) *adjective* of the neck or throat. ● *noun* (in full **jugular vein**) a large vein in the neck carrying blood from the head.

**juice** *noun* **1** the liquid content of fruits, vegetables, or meat. **2** liquid secreted by an organ of the body; *digestive juices.* **3** (*slang*) electricity. **4** (*slang*) petrol.

**juicy** *adjective* (**juicier**, **juiciest**) **1** full of juice. **2** (*informal*) interesting, especially because of its scandalous nature; *juicy stories.* □ **juicily** *adverb*, **juiciness** *noun*

**ju-jitsu** (joo-jit-soo) *noun* (also **jiu-jitsu**, **ju-jutsu**) a Japanese method of unarmed self-defence using throws, punches, etc.

**ju-ju** (joo-joo) *noun* **1** an object venerated in parts of West Africa as a charm or fetish. **2** the magic attributed to this.

**jujube** *noun* a jelly-like sweet.

**ju-jutsu** alternative spelling of JU-JITSU.

**jukebox** *noun* a machine that automatically plays a selected musical recording when a coin is inserted.

**Jul.** *abbreviation* July.

**julep** (joo-lep) *noun* **1** a medicated drink. **2** (*Amer.*) a drink of iced and flavoured spirits and water; *mint julep.*

**Julian calendar** the calendar introduced by Julius Caesar, replaced by the Gregorian calendar.

**julienne** (joo-li-en) *noun* vegetables or other food cut into thin strips. ●*adjective* cut into thin strips.

**Julius Caesar**, Gaius (100–44 BC), Roman general and statesman, who completed the conquest of Gaul and established himself in supreme authority in Rome. July, the month in which he was born, is named after him.

**July** the seventh month of the year.

**jumble** *verb* mix in a confused way. ●*noun* **1** articles jumbled together, a muddle. **2** articles for a jumble sale. ▢ **jumble sale** a sale of miscellaneous second-hand goods to raise money, especially for a charity.

**jumbo** *noun* (*plural* **jumbos**) **1** something very large of its kind. **2** (in full **jumbo jet**) a very large jet aircraft able to carry several hundred passengers (usually specifically a Boeing 747).

**jump** *verb* **1** move up off the ground etc. by bending and then extending the legs or (of fish) by a movement of the tail. **2** move suddenly with a jump or bound; get quickly into a car etc. **3** pass over by jumping; use (a horse) for jumping. **4** pass over (a thing) to a point beyond; skip (part of a book etc.) in reading or studying. **5** give a sudden movement from shock or excitement. **6** rise suddenly in amount or in price or value. **7** leave (rails or a track) accidentally. **8** pounce on, attack suddenly. **9** pass (a red traffic light etc.). ●*noun* **1** a jumping movement. **2** a sudden movement caused by shock etc. **3** a sudden rise in amount or price or value. **4** a sudden change to a different condition or set of circumstances; a gap in a series etc. **5** an obstacle to be jumped over. ▢ **jump at** accept eagerly. **jump bail** fail to come for trial when summoned after being released on bail. **jump down a person's throat** reprimand or contradict him or her severely. **jumped-up** *adjective* having risen suddenly from a low position or status and appearing arrogant. **jump-jet** *noun* a jet aircraft that can take off directly upwards. **jump-lead** *noun* a cable for conveying current from one battery through another. **jump-off** *noun* a deciding round between competitors with equal scores in show-jumping. **jump ship** (of a seaman) desert one's ship. **jump-start** *verb* start (a vehicle) by pushing it or with jump-leads. **jump suit** a one-piece garment for the whole body. **jump the gun** start or act prematurely. **jump the queue** obtain something without waiting for one's proper turn. **jump to conclusions** reach them too hastily. **jump to it** (*informal*) make an energetic start. **one jump ahead** one stage ahead of one's rival.

**jumper¹** *noun* **1** a person or animal that jumps. **2** a short wire used to make or break an electrical circuit.

**jumper²** *noun* **1** a knitted pullover. **2** a loose outer jacket worn by sailors. **3** (*Amer.*) a pinafore dress.

**jumpy** *adjective* **1** nervous. **2** making sudden movements.

**Jun.** *abbreviation* **1** June. **2** Junior.

**junction** *noun* **1** a place where things join. **2** a place where roads or railways lines etc. meet and unite. ▢ **junction box** a box containing a junction of electric cables etc.

**juncture** (junk-cher) *noun* **1** a point of time; a critical convergence of events. **2** joining; a joining-point.

**June** the sixth month of the year.

**Jung** (*pronounced* yuung), Carl Gustav (1875–1961), Swiss psychologist, who originated the concepts of two types of personality (introvert and extrovert) and of the existence of a 'collective unconscious' derived from ancestral experiences. ▢ **Jungian** *adjective & noun*

**Jungfrau** (yuung-frow) a mountain in the Swiss Alps.

**jungle** *noun* **1** land overgrown with tangled vegetation, especially in the tropics. **2** a wild tangled mass. **3** a scene of bewildering complexity or confusion, or of ruthless struggle; *the concrete jungle.* ▢ **jungly** *adjective*

**junior** *adjective* **1** younger in age. **2** added to a son's name to distinguish him from his father when the names are the same; *Tom Brown junior.* **3** lower in rank or authority. **4** for younger children; *junior school.* ●*noun* **1** a person younger than oneself; *he is two years my junior.* **2** a person employed to work in a junior capacity; *the office junior.* **3** a member of a junior school.

**juniper** (joo-nip-er) *noun* an evergreen shrub with prickly leaves and dark purplish berries.

**junk¹** *noun* **1** discarded material, rubbish. **2** (*informal*) anything regarded as useless or of little value. **3** (*slang*) a narcotic drug, especially heroin. ●*verb* discard as junk. ▢ **junk bond** (*Amer.*) a bond bearing high interest but considered to be a very risky investment. **junk food** food that is not nutritious. **junk mail** unrequested advertising matter sent by post. **junk shop** a shop selling miscellaneous cheap second-hand goods.

**junk²** *noun* a flat-bottomed ship with sails, used in the China seas.

**junket** *noun* **1** a sweet custard-like food made of milk curdled with rennet and flavoured. **2** a feast, merrymaking. **3** a pleasure outing. **4** an official's tour at public expense. ● *verb* (**junketed, junketing**) **1** feast, make merry. **2** hold a picnic or outing.

**junkie** *noun* (*slang*) a drug addict.

**Juno** (jew-noh) (*Rom. myth.*) a great goddess of the Roman State, identified with Hera.

**Junoesque** (jew-noh-esk) *adjective* resembling the goddess Juno in stately beauty.

**junta** *noun* a group of people who combine to rule a country, especially having seized power after a revolution.

**Jupiter** (jew-pit-er) **1** (*Rom. myth.*) the chief of the gods, identified with Zeus. **2** the largest planet of the solar system.

**jural** (joor-ăl) *adjective* **1** of the law. **2** of (moral) rights and obligations.

**Jurassic** (joor-ass-ik) *adjective Geol.* of the second period of the Mesozoic era. ● *noun* this period.

**juridical** (joor-id-ikăl) *adjective* of the law or judicial proceedings.

**jurisdiction** (joor-iss-**dik**-shŏn) *noun* **1** the administration of justice. **2** official power exercised within a particular sphere of activity. **3** the extent or territory over which legal or other power extends.

**jurisprudence** (joor-iss-**proo**-děns) *noun* the science or philosophy of law. □ **jurisprudential** *adjective* (joor-iss-proo-**den**-shăl)

**jurist** (joor-ist) *noun* a person who is skilled in the law. □ **juristic** *adjective*

**juror** (joor-er) *noun* **1** a member of a jury. **2** a person taking an oath.

**jury** *noun* **1** a body of people sworn to give a verdict on a case presented to them in a court of law. **2** a body of people appointed to judge a competition. □ **jury-box** *noun* an enclosure for the jury in a lawcourt.

**jury-rigged** *adjective* (of a ship) having temporary makeshift rigging.

**Jussieu** (*zhoo*-si-er), Antoine Laurent de (1748–1836), French botanist, who developed the system on which modern plant classification is based.

**just** *adjective* **1** giving proper consideration to the claims of everyone concerned. **2** deserved, right in amount etc.; *a just reward.* **3** well grounded in fact. ● *adverb* **1** exactly; *just at that spot.* **2** barely, no

more than, by only a short distance; *I just managed it*; *just below the knee*. **3** at this moment or only a little time ago; *he has just gone*. **4** (*informal*) simply, merely; *we are just good friends*. **5** quite; *not just yet*. **6** (*slang*) really, positively; *it's just splendid*. □ **just about** (*informal*) almost exactly or completely. **just now 1** at this moment. **2** a little time ago. **just so 1** exactly arranged; *she likes everything just so*. **2** it is exactly as you say. □ **justly** *adverb*, **justness** *noun*

**justice** *noun* **1** just treatment, fairness. **2** legal proceedings; *a court of justice*. **3** a judge or magistrate; the title of a judge; *Mr Justice Humphreys*. □ **do justice to 1** show (a thing) to advantage. **2** show appreciation of. **Justice of the Peace** a non-professional magistrate.

**justiciary** (jus-**tish**-er-i) *noun* one who administers justice.

**justifiable** *adjective* able to be justified. □ **justifiably** *adverb*

**justify** *verb* (**justified, justifying**) **1** show (a person, statement, or act etc.) to be right or just or reasonable. **2** be a good or sufficient reason for; *increased production justifies an increase in wages*. **3** adjust (a line of type in printing) so that it fills a space neatly. □ **justification** *noun*, **justificatory** *adjective*

**Justinian** (jus-**tin**-iăn) (483–565), Roman emperor from 527, noted for his codification of the law and the construction of many buildings (including Santa Sophia) throughout the empire.

**jut** *verb* (**jutted, jutting**) (often foll. by *out*) protrude, project.

**Jute** *noun* a member of a Low German tribe that invaded southern England in the 5th century and settled in Kent.

**jute** *noun* fibre from the bark of certain tropical plants, used for making sacks etc.

**Jutland** a peninsula that forms the mainland part of Denmark.

**Juvenal** (joo-věn-ăl) (*c.*60–*c.*130), Roman satirist, who attacked the vice and folly of Roman society.

**juvenile** (joo-vě-nyl) *adjective* **1** youthful, childish. **2** for young people. ● *noun* **1** a young person. **2** an actor playing the parts of young people. □ **juvenile delinquent** a young offender against the law, below the age when he or she may be held legally responsible for his or her actions. **juvenile delinquency** offences of this kind.

**juxtapose** (juks-tă-**pohz**) *verb* put (things) side by side. □ **juxtaposition** *noun*

# Kk

**K** *abbreviation* **1** kelvin(s). **2** King, King's. **3** one thousand; *32 K.* **4** the unit of core-memory size in computers, = 1,024 (often taken as 1,000) words, bits, or bytes. ● *symbol* potassium.

**Kaaba** (**kah**-ă-bă) *noun* a shrine at Mecca containing a sacred black stone.

**kabuki** (kă-**boo**-ki) *noun* a form of classical Japanese theatre.

**Kabul** (**kah**-buul) the capital of Afghanistan.

**Kaddish** (**kad**-ish) *noun* **1** a Jewish mourner's prayer. **2** a doxology recited in the synagogue service.

**Kaffir** *noun* **1** (*hist.*) a member or language of a Bantu people of South Africa. **2** (*South African, offensive*) a Black African.

**Kafka**, Franz (1883–1924), German-speaking Jewish novelist born in Prague, whose works often portray an enigmatic reality where the individual is seen as lonely, perplexed, and threatened. □ **Kafkaesque** *adjective*

**kaftan** alternative spelling of CAFTAN.

**kaiser** (**ky**-zer) *noun* (*hist.*) an emperor, especially of Germany, Austria, or the Holy Roman Empire.

**Kalahari Desert** (kal-ă-**hah**-ri) a high barren plateau in southern Africa, mainly in Botswana.

**kalashnikov** (kă-**lash**-ni-kof) *noun* a Russian-made rifle or sub-machine-gun.

**kale** *noun* a kind of cabbage with curly leaves that do not form a compact head.

**kaleidoscope** (kă-**ly**-dŏ-skohp) *noun* a toy consisting of a tube containing small brightly coloured fragments of glass etc. and mirrors which reflect these to form changing patterns. □ **kaleidoscopic** (kă-ly-dŏ-**skop**-ik) *adjective*

**kalends** alternative spelling of CALENDS.

**kaleyard** *noun* (*Scottish*) a kitchen garden.

**Kali** (**kah**-li) (in Hinduism) the most terrifying goddess, wife of Siva, often identified with Durga and usually portrayed as black, naked, old, and hideous, with a protruding bloodstained tongue.

**Kama** (**kah**-mă) (in Hinduism) the god of sexual love, usually portrayed as a beautiful youth with a bow of sugar cane, a bowstring of bees, and arrows of flowers.

**Kama Sutra** (kah-mă **soo**-tră) an ancient Sanskrit treatise on the art of love and sexual technique.

**kamikaze** (kam-i-**kah**-zi) *noun* (in the Second World War) **1** a Japanese aircraft laden with explosives and suicidally crashed on a target by its pilot. **2** the pilot of this. ● *adjective* reckless, especially suicidal.

**Kampala** (kam-**pah**-lă) the capital of Uganda.

**Kampuchea** (kam-puu-**chee**-ă) the former name for Cambodia. □ **Kampuchean** *adjective & noun*

**Kan.** *abbreviation* Kansas.

**Kanarese** (kan-ă-**reez**) *adjective* of Kanara, a district in SW India, or its people or language. ● *noun* **1** (*plural* **Kanarese**) a native of Kanara. **2** the language spoken there (now generally and officially called *Kannada*).

**Kanchenjunga** (kan-chen-**juung**-ă) the third-highest peak in the world, situated east of Mount Everest in the Himalayas.

**Kandinsky**, Wassily (1866–1944), Russian painter and theorist, usually considered the originator of abstract painting.

**kangaroo** *noun* an Australian animal with strong hind legs used for jumping, the female having a pouch on the front of the body in which young are carried. □ **kangaroo court** a court formed illegally by a group of people (e.g. prisoners or strikers) to settle disputes among themselves.

**Kannada** (**kan**-ă-dă) *noun* the Kanarese language.

**Kans.** *abbreviation* Kansas.

**Kansas** a State in the Middle West of the USA.

**Kant** (*pronounced* kahnt), Immanuel (1724–1804), German philosopher, who sought to establish the limitations of human knowledge of the external world, and held that there was an absolute moral law which can never be modified.

**kaolin** (**kay**-ŏ-lin) *noun* a fine white clay used in making porcelain and in medicine.

**kapok** (**kay**-pok) *noun* a substance resembling cotton wool, used for padding.

**kaput** (kă-**puut**) *adjective* (*slang*) ruined, broken; out of order.

**Karachi** (kă-**rah**-chi) a seaport and former capital of Pakistan.

**Karakoram** (ka-ră-**kor**-ăm) a great chain of mountains north of the west end of the Himalayas.

**karakul** (**ka**-ră-kuul) *noun* **1** an Asian sheep whose lambs have a dark curled fleece. **2** a fur made from or resembling this.

**Karaoke** (ka-ri-**oh**-ki) *noun* a form of entertainment in pubs, clubs, etc., in which customers sing along to a backing track.

**karate** (kă-**rah**-ti) *noun* a Japanese system of unarmed combat in which the hands and feet are used as weapons.

**karma** *noun* (in Buddhism and Hinduism) the sum of a person's actions in a previous existence, thought to decide his or her fate in future existences.

**Karnataka** (kă-**nah**-tă-kă) a State in southern India, formerly called Mysore.

**karoo** (kă-**roo**) *noun* (also **karroo**) a high plateau in southern Africa, waterless in the dry season.

**Karpov**, Anatoli (born 1951), Russian chess-player, world champion 1975–85.

**karst** *noun* a limestone region with underground streams and many cavities.

**kasbah** (**kaz**-bah) *noun* (also **casbah**) the citadel of an Arab city in North Africa, or the old crowded part near this.

**Kashmir** a former State on the northern border of India, since 1947 disputed between India and Pakistan.

**Kasparov**, Gary (original name: Gary Weinstein) (born 1963), Russian chess-player, world champion from 1985.

**Kathmandu** (kat-man-**doo**) the capital of Nepal.

**katydid** (**kay**-ti-did) *noun* a large green grasshopper of the USA.

**Kaunda** (kah-**uun**-dă), Kenneth David (born 1924), Zambian statesman, first President of his country after it became an independent republic (1964).

**kauri** (**kowr**-i) *noun* a coniferous tree of New Zealand, yielding a resin.

**kayak** (**ky**-ak) *noun* **1** an Eskimo canoe with a sealskin covering. **2** a small covered canoe resembling this.

**Kazakhstan** (kaz-ahk-**stahn**) an independent republic in central Asia (formerly part of the USSR), lying east of the Caspian Sea.

**KBE** *abbreviation* Knight Commander of the Order of the British Empire.

**KC** *abbreviation* King's Counsel.

**KCB** *abbreviation* Knight Commander of the Order of the Bath.

**kc/s** *abbreviation* kilocycles per second.

**kea** (**kay**-ă) *noun* a green New Zealand parrot with brownish-green and red plumage.

**Keating**, Paul John, Australian statesman, Prime Minister from 1991.

**Keaton**, Buster (Joseph Francis) (1895–1966), American comic silent-film actor and director.

**Keats**, John (1795–1821), English poet, a principal figure of the Romantic movement.

**kebab** (ki-**bab**) *noun* small pieces of meat, vegetables, etc. cooked on a skewer.

**kedge** *verb* move (a boat) or be moved by means of a hawser attached to a small anchor. ●*noun* this anchor.

**kedgeree** (kej-e-**ree**) *noun* a cooked dish of rice, fish, and hard-boiled eggs.

**keel** *noun* the timber or steel structure along the base of a ship, on which the ship's framework is built up. ●*verb* **1** (often foll. by *over*) become tilted; overturn, collapse. **2** turn keel upwards. □ **on an even keel** steady, balanced.

**keelhaul** *verb* **1** haul (a person) under the keel of a ship as a punishment. **2** rebuke severely.

**Keeling Islands** = COCOS ISLANDS.

**keelson** *noun* (also **kelson**) the line of timber fixing a ship's floor-timbers to the keel.

**keen**[1] *adjective* **1** sharp, having a sharp edge or point. **2** (of sound or light) acute, penetrating. **3** piercingly cold; *keen wind*. **4** (of prices) low because of competition. **5** intense; *keen interest*. **6** showing or feeling intense interest or desire; *a keen swimmer; is keen to go*. **7** perceiving things very distinctly; *keen sight*. □ **keen on** (*informal*) much attracted to. □ **keenly** *adverb*, **keenness** *noun*

**keen**[2] *noun* an Irish funeral song accompanied by wailing. ●*verb* wail mournfully.

**keep** *verb* (**kept, keeping**) **1** remain or cause to remain in a specified state, position, or condition. **2** prevent or hold back from doing something, detain; *what kept you?* **3** put aside for a future time. **4** respect, honour, abide by; *keep the law; keep a promise*. **5** celebrate (a feast or ceremony). **6** guard or protect (a person or place), keep safe. **7** continue to have, have and not give away; *keep the change*. **8** provide with the necessities of life; maintain (a person) as one's lover etc.; *a kept woman*. **9** own and look after (animals) for one's use or enjoyment; *keep hens*. **10** manage; *keep a shop*. **11** have (a commodity) regularly in stock or for sale. **12** make entries in (a diary or accounts etc.). **13** continue doing something, do frequently or repeatedly; *the strap keeps breaking*. **14** continue in a specified direction; *keep straight on*. **15** (of food) remain in good condition. **16** be able to be put aside for later; *the news will keep*. ●*noun* **1** provision of the necessities of life, the food required for this; *he earns his keep*. **2** the central tower or other strongly fortified structure in a castle. □ **for keeps** (*informal*) permanently. **how are you keeping?** how are you? **keep a secret** not tell it to others. **keep at** persist or cause to persist with. **keep back 1** remain or keep at a distance. **2** conceal, withhold; *kept back £50*. **keep down 1** keep low in amount or number; *it keeps the weeds down*. **2** eat and not vomit (food). **keep fit**

to be and remain healthy. **keep-fit** noun regular physical exercises. **keep house** look after a house or a household. **keep in with** remain on good terms with. **keep on** 1 continue doing something. 2 continue to employ. 3 nag; *she keeps on at me.* **keep the peace** obey the laws and refrain from causing trouble. **keep to oneself** 1 keep (a thing) secret. 2 avoid meeting people; *keeps himself to himself.* **keep up** 1 progress at the same pace as others. 2 continue to observe, carry on; *keep up old customs.* 3 continue; *our troops kept up the attack all day.* 4 maintain in proper condition; *the cost of keeping up a large house.* **keep up with the Joneses** strive to remain in terms of obvious social equality with one's neighbours.

**keeper** noun 1 a person who looks after or is in charge of animals, people, or a thing. 2 the custodian of a museum, forest, etc. 3 a wicket-keeper.

**keeping** noun 1 custody, charge; *in safe keeping.* 2 harmony, conformity; *a style that is in keeping with his dignity.*

**keepsake** noun a thing that is kept in memory of the giver.

**keg** noun a small barrel. □ **keg beer** beer kept in a metal keg under pressure.

**Keller**, Helen Adams (1880–1968), American author who, although she became blind and deaf before she was two years old, graduated in 1904 and became a prominent social reformer.

**kelp** noun a large brown seaweed suitable for manure.

**kelpie** noun 1 (*Scottish*) a malevolent water-spirit usually in the form of a horse. 2 an Australian sheepdog of Scottish origin.

**kelson** = KEELSON.

**Kelt** alternative spelling of CELT.

**kelt** noun a salmon or sea trout after spawning.

**kelter** = KILTER.

**Kelvin**, William Thomson, 1st Baron (1824–1907), British physicist, noted for his work in thermodynamics, introduction of an absolute temperature scale, and involvement in laying the first transatlantic telephone cable.

**kelvin** noun a degree (equivalent to the Celsius degree) of the **Kelvin scale** of temperature (with zero at absolute zero, −273.15°C). (¶ Named after Lord Kelvin.)

**ken** noun the range of sight or knowledge; *beyond my ken.* ●*verb* (*Scottish* & *N. England*) know.

**kendo** noun the Japanese art of fencing with two-handed bamboo swords.

**Kennedy**, John Fitzgerald (1917–63), 35th President of the USA 1961–3, assassinated at Dallas, Texas.

**kennel** noun 1 a shelter for a dog. 2 (**kennels**) a breeding or boarding place for dogs. ●*verb* (**kennelled**, **kennelling**; *Amer.* **kenneled**, **kenneling**) put into a kennel.

**Kent** a county of SE England. □ **Kentish** adjective

**Kentucky** a State of the central southeastern USA. □ **Kentucky Derby** an annual horse race for three-year-olds at Louisville, Kentucky.

**Kenya** (ken-yǎ) a country in East Africa. □ **Kenyan** adjective & noun

**Kenyatta** (ken-yat-ǎ), Jomo (*c.*1894–1978), Kenyan statesman, first President of his country 1964–78.

**kepi** (kay-pi) noun a French military cap with a horizontal peak.

**kept** *see* KEEP.

**Kerala** (ke-rǎ-lǎ) a State in SW India. □ **Keralite** adjective & noun

**keratin** (ke-rǎ-tin) noun a strong protein substance forming the basis of horns, claws, nails, feathers, hair, etc.

**kerb** noun a stone edging to a pavement or raised path. □ **kerb-crawling** noun (*informal*) driving slowly in order to engage a prostitute.

**kerbstone** noun a stone forming part of a kerb.

**kerchief** noun 1 a headscarf or neckerchief. 2 (*poetic*) a handkerchief.

**kerfuffle** noun (*informal*) fuss, commotion.

**kermes** (ker-miz) noun 1 the female of an insect (formerly taken to be a berry) that feeds on a kind of evergreen oak. 2 a red dye made from the dried bodies of such insects.

**Kern**, Jerome (1885–1945), American composer of popular melodies and songs, including 'Ol' Man River'.

**kernel** noun 1 the softer (usually edible) part inside the shell of a nut or fruit stone. 2 the part of a grain or seed within the husk. 3 the central or important part of a subject, plan, problem, etc.

**kerosene** (ke-rǒ-seen) noun (also **kerosine**) (especially *Amer.*) a fuel oil distilled from petroleum etc.; paraffin oil.

**kestrel** noun a kind of small falcon.

**ketch** noun a small sailing-boat with two masts.

**ketchup** noun (*Amer.* **catsup**) a thick sauce made from tomatoes and vinegar etc., used as a seasoning.

**ketone** (kee-tohn) noun any of a class of organic compounds including acetone.

**kettle** noun a container with a spout and handle, for boiling water in. □ **a fine** (*or* **pretty**) **kettle of fish** an awkward state of affairs.

**kettledrum** noun a large bowl-shaped drum.

**Kew Gardens** the Royal Botanic Gardens at Kew near Richmond upon Thames, London.

**key**¹ *noun* **1** a small piece of metal shaped so that it will move the bolt of a lock and so lock or unlock something. **2** a similar instrument for grasping and turning something, e.g. for winding a clock or tightening a spring. **3** something that provides access or control or insight; *the key to success*. **4** a set of answers to problems; a word or set of symbols for interpreting a map, code, etc., or for extracting items of data from a computer. **5** a system of related notes in music, based on a particular note; *the key of C major*. **6** the general tone or degree of intensity of something; *low-key discussions*. **7** roughness of surface helping plaster or paint to adhere to it. **8** a piece of wood or metal inserted between others to hold them secure. **9** each of a set of levers to be pressed by the fingers in playing a musical instrument or operating a typewriter etc. **10** a device for making or breaking an electric circuit, e.g. in telegraphy or to operate the ignition in a motor vehicle. **11** the winged fruit of certain trees, e.g. sycamore. ● *adjective* essential; *a key element in the plan*. ● *verb* (**keyed**, **keying**) **1** fasten with a pin, bolt, etc. **2** (often foll. by *in*) enter (data) by means of a computer keyboard. **3** roughen (a surface) so that plaster or paint will adhere well. **4** (foll. by *to*) link closely with something else; *the factory is keyed to the export trade*. □ **keyed up** stimulated, nervously tense. **key grip** a person in charge of moving equipment to the correct positions in a film or television studio. **key money** payment demanded from an incoming tenant, nominally for the provision of the key to the premises. **key signature** *Music* any of several combinations of sharps or flats indicating the key of a composition.

**key**² *noun* a reef, a low island.

**keyboard** *noun* **1** the set of keys on a piano, typewriter, etc. **2** an electronic musical instrument with keys arranged as on a piano. ● *verb* enter (data) by means of a computer keyboard. □ **keyboarder** *noun*

**keyhole** *noun* the hole by which a key is put into a lock. □ **keyhole surgery** surgery carried out through a very small incision.

**Keynes** (*pronounced* kaynz), John Maynard, 1st Baron (1883–1946), English economist, advocate of the planned economy with positive intervention by the State. □ **Keynesian** *adjective*

**keynote** *noun* **1** the note on which a key in music is based. **2** the prevailing tone or idea of a speech etc.

**keypad** *noun* a small keyboard of numbered buttons on a telephone, remote control device, etc.

**keyring** *noun* a ring on which keys are threaded.

**keystone** *noun* **1** the central wedge-shaped stone at the summit of an arch, locking the others in position. **2** the central principle of a system, policy, etc.

**keystroke** *noun* a single depression of a key on a keyboard, especially as a measure of work.

**keyword** *noun* **1** the key to a cipher etc. **2** a significant word, especially when used in indexing.

**KG** *abbreviation* Knight of the Order of the Garter.

**kg** *abbreviation* kilogram(s).

**KGB** *abbreviation* the secret police of the former USSR.

**khaki** (**kah**-ki) *adjective & noun* dull brownish-yellow, the colour used for some military uniforms.

**khan** (*pronounced* kahn) *noun* the title of rulers and officials in Central Asia.

**Khartoum** (kar-**toom**) the capital of Sudan.

**Khmer** (*pronounced* kmair) *noun* **1** a native or inhabitant of the ancient kingdom of Khmer in SE Asia or of the Khmer Republic (the official name in 1970–5 of what is now Cambodia). **2** their language, the official language of Cambodia. □ **Khmer Rouge** (*pronounced* roozh) the Communist guerrilla organization in the wars there in the 1960s and 1970s, holding power 1975–9.

**Khomeini** (hom-**ay**-ni), Ruhollah (1900–89), known as Ayatollah Khomeini, Iranian Shiite Muslim leader who in 1979 established a fundamentalist Islamic regime after the overthrow of the Shah.

**Khrushchev** (kroos-**chof**), Nikita Sergeevich (1894–1971), Russian statesman, Premier of the USSR 1958–64.

**Khufu** (**koo**-foo) (also known as **Cheops**) (*c*.2551–2528 BC), a pharaoh in ancient Egypt, who commissioned the building of the great pyramid at Giza.

**Khyber Pass** (**ky**-ber) the major mountain pass on the border between northern Pakistan and Afghanistan.

**kHz** *abbreviation* kilohertz.

**kibbutz** (kib-**uuts**) *noun* (*plural* **kibbutzim**, *pronounced* kib-uuts-**eem**) a communal (especially farming) settlement in Israel.

**kibbutznik** *noun* a member of a kibbutz.

**kibosh** (**ky**-bosh) *noun* □ **put the kibosh on** (*slang*) put an end to.

**kick** *verb* **1** strike, thrust, or propel with the foot. **2** move the legs about vigorously. **3** *Football* score by kicking the ball into goal. **4** (of a gun) recoil when fired. **5** (*in-*

*formal*) object. **6** (*informal*) give up (a habit). ●*noun* **1** an act of kicking; a blow from being kicked. **2** (*informal*) a thrill, a pleasurable effect. **3** (*informal*) an interest or activity; *the health food kick*. **4** the recoil of a gun when it is fired. **5** (*informal*) a sharp stimulant effect, especially of alcohol. □ **alive and kicking** (*informal*) fully active. **kick about** *or* **around** (*informal*) **1** treat roughly or inconsiderately. **2** discuss unsystematically. **3** go idly from place to place. **4** be unused or unwanted. **kick off 1** start a football game by kicking the ball. **2** (*informal*) begin proceedings. **kick-off** *noun* kicking off in football. **kick one's heels** be kept waiting. **kick out** (*informal*) drive out forcibly; dismiss. **kick the bucket** (*slang*) die. **kick up** (*informal*) create (a fuss or noise). **kick upstairs** promote (a person) to a higher position in order to get rid of him or her.

**kickback** *noun* **1** a recoil. **2** (*informal*) payment for help in making a profit etc.

**kickstand** *noun* a rod for supporting a bicycle or motor cycle when stationary.

**kick-start** *verb* **1** start (the engine of a motor cycle etc.) by pushing down a lever with one's foot. **2** start or restart (a process etc.) by providing some initial impetus. ●*noun* (also **kick-starter**) a device for starting an engine in this way.

**kid** *noun* **1** a young goat. **2** leather made from its skin. **3** (*informal*) a child. ●*verb* (**kidded**, **kidding**) deceive (especially for fun), tease. □ **handle with kid gloves** treat tactfully. **no kidding** (*informal*) that is the truth.

**kiddie** *noun* (*informal*) a child.

**kidnap** *verb* (**kidnapped**, **kidnapping**; *Amer.* **kidnaped**, **kidnaping**) carry off (a person) by force or fraud in order to obtain a ransom. □ **kidnapper** *noun*

**kidney** *noun* (*plural* **kidneys**) **1** either of a pair of glandular organs that remove waste products from the blood and secrete urine. **2** an animal's kidney as food. □ **kidney bean** a red-skinned dried bean. **kidney machine** an apparatus able to take over the functions of a damaged kidney.

**Kierkegaard** (**keer**-kĕ-gard), Soren (1813–55), Danish philosopher and theologian.

**Kiev** (**kee**-ef) the capital of Ukraine.

**Kigali** (ki-**gah**-li) the capital of Rwanda.

**Kilimanjaro** (kili-măn-**jar**-oh) an extinct volcano in Tanzania, with twin peaks, the higher of which is the highest mountain in Africa.

**kill** *verb* **1** cause the death of (a person or animal); destroy the vitality of (a plant etc.). **2** put an end to (a feeling etc.). **3** make (a colour, noise, etc.) ineffective. **4** spend (time) while waiting for some-

thing; *an hour to kill*. **5** (*informal*) cause severe pain to; *my feet are killing me*. **6** (*informal*) overwhelm with amusement etc. **7** switch off (a light, engine, etc.). **8** *Computing* (*informal*) delete. ●*noun* **1** the act of killing. **2** the animal(s) killed by a hunter. □ **dressed to kill** dressed showily or alluringly. **in at the kill** present at the time of victory. **kill off** get rid of by killing. **kill oneself** (*informal*) overexert oneself. **kill two birds with one stone** achieve two purposes with one action. **kill with kindness** harm with excessive kindness. **make a killing** have a great financial success.

**killer** *noun* **1** a person, animal, or thing that kills. **2** (*informal*) an impressive, formidable, or excellent thing; a hilarious joke. □ **killer instinct 1** an inborn tendency to kill. **2** a ruthless streak. **killer whale** a black and white whale with a prominent dorsal fin.

**killing** *adjective* (*informal*) **1** very amusing. **2** exhausting. ●*noun* an act of causing death. □ **make a killing** (*informal*) have a great financial success.

**killjoy** *noun* a person who spoils or questions the enjoyment of others.

**kiln** *noun* an oven for hardening or drying things such as pottery, bricks, or hops, or for burning lime.

**kilo** (**kee**-loh) *noun* (*plural* **kilos**) a kilogram.

**kilo-** (kil-ŏ) *combining form* one thousand.

**kilobyte** *noun Computing* 1,024 bytes as a measure of memory size etc.

**kilocalorie** *noun* the amount of heat needed to raise the temperature of 1kg of water by 1°C.

**kilocycle** *noun* (*hist.*) a kilohertz.

**kilogram** *noun* the basic unit of mass in the International System of Units (approx. 2.205 lb).

**kilohertz** *noun* a unit of frequency of electromagnetic waves, = 1,000 cycles per second.

**kilojoule** *noun* 1,000 joules, especially as a measure of the energy value of foods.

**kilolitre** *noun* (*Amer.* **kiloliter**) 1,000 litres (220 imperial gallons).

**kilometre** (**kil**-ŏ-meet-er *or* kil-**om**-it-er) *noun* (*Amer.* **kilometer**) a distance of 1,000 metres (approx. 0.62 miles). □ **kilometric** *adjective*

**kiloton** (**kil**-ŏ-tun) *noun* (also **kilotonne**) a unit of explosive force equal to 1,000 tons of TNT.

**kilovolt** *noun* 1,000 volts.

**kilowatt** *noun* 1,000 watts. □ **kilowatt-hour** *noun* an amount of energy equal to a power consumption of 1,000 watts for one hour.

**kilt** *noun* a knee-length pleated skirt of tartan wool, worn as part of a Highland man's dress or by women and children. ●*verb*

**1** tuck up (skirts) round the body. **2** arrange in vertical pleats.

**kilted** *adjective* wearing a kilt.

**kilter** *noun* (also **kelter**) good working order; *out of kilter.*

**kimono** (kim-oh-noh) *noun* (*plural* **kimonos**) **1** a long loose Japanese robe with wide sleeves, worn with a sash. **2** a dressing gown resembling this.

**kin** *noun* a person's relatives.

**kind** *noun* a class of similar things or animals, a type. ●*adjective* friendly, generous, or considerate. □ **kind-hearted** *adjective* of a kind nature, sympathetic. **a kind of** something that belongs (approximately) to the class named. **in kind 1** in the same form; *repaid his insolence in kind.* **2** (of payment) in goods or labour, not money. **kind of** (*informal*) slightly; *I felt kind of sorry for him.* **of a kind** similar. □ **kindness** *noun*

**kindergarten** *noun* a school for very young children.

**kindle** *verb* **1** set on fire; cause (a fire) to begin burning. **2** arouse or stimulate; *kindled our hopes.* **3** become kindled.

**kindling** *noun* small pieces of wood for lighting fires.

**kindly** *adjective* (**kindlier, kindliest**) kind in character, manner, or appearance. ●*adverb* **1** in a kind way. **2** please; *kindly shut the door.* □ **not take kindly to** be displeased by. □ **kindliness** *noun*

**kindred** (kin-drid) *noun* **1** a person's relatives. **2** blood relationship. **3** resemblance in character. ●*adjective* **1** related. **2** of a similar kind; *chemistry and kindred subjects.* □ **kindred spirit** a person whose tastes are similar to one's own.

**kine** *plural noun* (*old use*) cows, cattle.

**kinematic** (kin-i-mat-ik) *adjective* of motion considered abstractly without reference to force or mass. ●*noun* (**kinematics**) the science of pure motion.

**kinetic** (kin-et-ik) *adjective* of or produced by movement; characterized by movement. ●*noun* (**kinetics**) **1** the science of the relations between the motions of objects and the forces acting upon them. **2** the study of the mechanisms and rates of chemical reactions or other processes. □ **kinetic art** art that depends for its effect on the movement of some of its parts. **kinetic energy** energy of motion.

**King**[1], Billie Jean (born 1943), American tennis-player.

**King**[2], Martin Luther (1929–68), Black Baptist minister and American civil rights leader.

**king** *noun* **1** a man who is the supreme ruler of an independent country by right of succession to the throne. **2** a person or thing regarded as supreme in some way.

**3** a large species of animal; *king penguin.* **4** the piece in chess that has to be protected from checkmate. **5** a piece in draughts that has been crowned on reaching the opponent's end of the board. **6** a playing card bearing a picture of a king and ranking next above queen. **7** (**Kings**) either of two books of the Old Testament recording Jewish history of the 10th–6th centuries BC. □ **King Charles spaniel** a small black and tan spaniel. **King of Arms** the title of the chief heralds at the College of Arms and in Scotland. **king of beasts** the lion. **king of birds** the eagle. **king-size** *or* **king-sized** *adjective* extra large. □ **kingly** *adjective*, **kingship** *noun*

**kingcup** *noun* the marsh marigold.

**kingdom** *noun* **1** a country ruled by a king or queen. **2** the spiritual reign of God; *thy Kingdom come.* **3** a division of the natural world; *the animal kingdom.* **4** a specified mental or emotional province; *kingdom of the heart.* □ **kingdom come** (*informal*) the next world, the afterlife.

**kingfisher** *noun* a small bird with bright bluish plumage, which dives to catch fish.

**kingpin** *noun* **1** a vertical bolt used as a pivot. **2** an indispensable person or thing.

**Kingsley**, Charles (1819–75), English novelist, whose works include the historical novel *Westward Ho!* and the children's book *The Water-Babies.*

**Kingston** the capital of Jamaica.

**kink** *noun* **1** a short twist in a wire, rope, hair etc. **2** a mental or moral peculiarity. ●*verb* form or cause to form kinks.

**kinky** *adjective* (**kinkier, kinkiest**) **1** full of kinks. **2** (*informal*) bizarre, eccentric, especially in sexual behaviour.

**kinsfolk** *plural noun* a person's relatives. □ **kinsman** *noun* (*plural* **kinsmen**), **kinswoman** *noun* (*plural* **kinswomen**)

**Kinshasa** (kin-shah-să) the capital of Zaïre.

**kinship** *noun* **1** blood relationship. **2** likeness; sympathy.

**kiosk** (kee-osk) *noun* **1** a small light open structure where newspapers, refreshments, tickets, etc. are sold. **2** a public telephone booth.

**kip** *noun* (*slang*) **1** a sleep, a nap. **2** a bed or cheap lodgings. ●*verb* (**kipped, kipping**) sleep.

**Kipling**, Rudyard (1865–1936), English writer and poet, the first English writer to be awarded the Nobel Prize for literature (1907).

**kipper** *noun* a fish, especially a herring, cured by splitting, cleaning, and drying it in the open air or in smoke. ●*verb* cure (a fish) in this way.

**Kirchhoff** (**keerk**-hof), Gustav Robert (1824–87), German physicist, who (with Bunsen) developed a technique of spectrum analysis.

**Kirghizia** (ker-geez-iă) an independent republic (formerly part of the USSR) in Asia, on the Chinese frontier.

**Kiribati** (ki-ri-bas) a group of islands in the Pacific north-east of Australia. ● *adjective* of Kiribati or its inhabitants.

**kirk** *noun* (*Scottish*) a church.

**kirsch** (*pronounced* keersh) *noun* a colourless brandy made from the juice of cherries.

**Kirundi** (ki-**ruun**-di) *noun* a Bantu language, the official language of Burundi.

**kismet** (**kiz**-met) *noun* destiny, fate.

**kiss** *noun* 1 a touch or caress given with the lips. 2 a light touch. ● *verb* 1 touch with the lips in affection or as a greeting or in reverence. 2 greet each other in this way. 3 touch gently. □ **kiss and tell** recount one's sexual exploits. **kiss-curl** *noun* a small curl of hair on the forehead, cheek, or nape. **kiss of death** an apparently friendly act causing ruin. **kiss of life** mouth-to-mouth resuscitation.

**kisser** *noun* (*slang*) the mouth or face.

**kissogram** *noun* (also **Kissagram** (*trade mark*)) a novelty telegram or greetings message delivered with a kiss.

**Kiswahili** (kis-wah-**hee**-li) *noun* the Swahili language.

**kit** *noun* 1 specialized clothing or uniform; *football kit*. 2 the equipment needed for a particular activity or situation; *a first-aid kit*. 3 a set of parts sold together to be assembled; *in kit form*. ● *verb* (**kitted**, **kitting**) (often foll. by *out* or *up*) equip with kit.

**kitbag** *noun* a large usually cylindrical bag for holding a soldier's or traveller's kit.

**kitchen** *noun* a room in which meals are prepared. □ **kitchen garden** a garden for growing one's own fruit and vegetables.

**Kitchener**, Horatio Herbert, 1st Earl (1850–1916), British soldier and statesman, who organized the large volunteer army at the outbreak of the First World War.

**kitchenette** *noun* a small room or alcove used as a kitchen.

**kite** *noun* 1 a large bird of prey of the hawk family. 2 a toy consisting of a light framework to be flown in a strong wind on the end of a long string.

**Kitemark** *noun* an official kite-shaped mark affixed to goods approved by the British Standards Institution.

**kith** *noun* □ **kith and kin** kinsfolk; friends and relations.

**kitsch** (*pronounced* kich) *noun* pretentiousness and lack of good taste in art; art of this type.

**kitten** *noun* the young of a cat, ferret, etc. □ **have kittens** (*slang*) be very agitated or nervous.

**kittenish** *adjective* playful, lively, or flirtatious.

**kittiwake** *noun* a kind of small seagull.

**kitty** *noun* 1 the pool of stakes to be played for in some card games. 2 a fund of money for communal use.

**kiwi** (**kee**-wee) *noun* 1 a New Zealand bird that does not fly, with a long bill and no tail. 2 (**Kiwi**) (*informal*) a New Zealander. □ **kiwi fruit** the fruit of a kind of vine, with thin hairy skin and green flesh.

**kJ** *abbreviation* kilojoule(s).

**kl** *abbreviation* kilolitre(s).

**Klaxon** *noun* (*trade mark*) a powerful electric horn.

**Klee** (*pronounced* klay), Paul (1879–1940), Swiss modernist painter.

**Kleenex** *noun* (*trade mark*) a disposable paper handkerchief.

**Klemperer**, Otto (1885–1973), German-born conductor.

**kleptomania** (kleptŏ-**may**-niă) *noun* an uncontrollable tendency to steal things, with no desire to use or profit by them. □ **kleptomaniac** *noun*

**Klondike** a river and district in Yukon, Canada, where gold was discovered in 1896.

**km** *abbreviation* kilometre(s).

**knack** *noun* 1 the ability to do something skilfully. 2 a habit; *it has a knack of going wrong*.

**knacker** *noun* a person who buys and slaughters useless horses, selling the meat and hides.

**knackered** *adjective* (*slang*) exhausted, worn out.

**knapsack** *noun* a hiker's or soldier's usually canvas bag worn strapped on the back.

**knapweed** *noun* a common weed like a thistle but without prickles.

**knave** *noun* 1 (*old use*) a rogue. 2 the jack in playing cards. □ **knavish** *adjective*, **knavery** *noun*

**knead** *verb* 1 work (moist flour or clay) into dough by pressing and stretching it with the hands. 2 make (bread etc.) in this way. 3 massage with kneading movements.

**knee** *noun* 1 the joint between the thigh and the lower part of the human leg; the corresponding joint in animals. 2 the part of a garment covering this. 3 the upper surface of the thigh of a sitting person; *sit on my knee*. ● *verb* touch or strike with the knee. □ **bring a person to his** *or* **her knees** reduce him or her to submission or a state of weakness. **knee-breeches** *plural noun* breeches reaching to or just below the knee. **knee-deep** *adjective* **1** of or in sufficient depth to cover a person up to the knees. **2** deeply involved; *knee-deep in work*. **knee-jerk** *noun* an involuntary jerk of the leg when a tendon below the knee is struck. **knee-jerk reaction** one that is automatic, predictable, or stereotyped. **knee-length** *adjective* reaching to the knees. **knees-up** *noun* (*informal*) a lively party.

**kneecap** *noun* **1** the small bone covering the front of the knee-joint. **2** a protective covering for the knee. ● *verb* (**kneecapped, kneecapping**) (*slang*) shoot (a person) in the knee or leg as a punishment.

**kneel** *verb* (**knelt** or (especially *Amer.*) **kneeled, kneeling**) fall or rest on the knees or a knee.

**kneeler** *noun* a cushion for kneeling on.

**knell** *noun* **1** the sound of a bell tolled solemnly after a death or at a funeral. **2** an announcement, event, etc., regarded as an ill omen. ● *verb* **1** ring a knell. **2** announce by a knell.

**knelt** *see* KNEEL.

**Knesset** (**knes**-it) *noun* the parliament of the State of Israel.

**knew** *see* KNOW.

**knickerbockers** *plural noun* loose-fitting breeches gathered in at the knee or calf.

**knickers** *plural noun* a woman's or girl's undergarment covering the lower part of the body and having separate legs or leg-holes (= *Amer.* panties).

**knick-knack** *noun* (also **nick-nack**) a small ornamental article.

**knife** *noun* (*plural* **knives**) **1** a cutting instrument or weapon consisting of a sharp blade with a handle. **2** the cutting-blade of a machine. ● *verb* cut or stab with a knife. □ **at knife-point** threatened with a knife or ultimatum etc. **knife-pleats** *plural noun* narrow flat pleats. **on a knife-edge** in a situation involving extreme tension or anxiety about the outcome.

**knight** *noun* **1** a man awarded a non-hereditary title (*Sir*) by a sovereign. **2** (*hist.*) a man raised to an honourable military rank by a sovereign. **3** a chess piece, usually shaped like a horse's head. **4** a man devoted to a cause, woman, etc. ● *verb* confer a knighthood on. □ **knight errant** a medieval knight or chivalrous man in search of adventures. **Knights Hospitallers** a military religious order founded in the 11th century. **Knights Templars** a military order founded in 1118 to protect pilgrims from bandits in the Holy Land. □ **knighthood** *noun*, **knightly** *adjective* (*poetic*)

**knit** *verb* (**knitted** or **knit, knitting**) **1** make (a garment or fabric etc.) from yarn formed into interlocking loops either by long hand-held needles or on a machine. **2** form (yarn) into fabric etc. in this way. **3** make a plain (not purl) stitch in knitting. **4** unite or grow together; *the broken bones had knit well*. □ **knit one's brow** frown. □ **knitter** *noun*

**knitting** *noun* work in the process of being knitted. □ **knitting-needle** *noun* each of the long needles used for knitting by hand.

**knitwear** *noun* knitted garments.

**knives** *see* KNIFE.

**knob** *noun* **1** a rounded projecting part, especially one forming the handle of a door or drawer or for turning to adjust a dial-setting etc. **2** a small lump of butter etc. □ **with knobs on** (*slang*) that and more. □ **knobby** *adjective*

**knobbly** *adjective* hard and lumpy.

**knock** *verb* **1** strike with an audible sharp blow. **2** make a noise by striking something, e.g. at a door to gain admittance. **3** (of an engine) make a thumping or rattling noise while running, pink. **4** drive by striking; *knock a nail in*. **5** (*slang*) criticize; *stop knocking Britain*. **6** (*slang, offensive*) have sexual intercourse with (a woman). ● *noun* **1** an act or sound of knocking. **2** a sharp blow. **3** (in an engine) knocking, pinking. □ **knock about** (*informal*) **1** treat roughly. **2** wander casually; be present, especially by chance. **knock back** (*slang*) swallow (a drink). **knock down 1** dispose of (an article) at auction. **2** lower the price of (an article). **knock-down** *adjective* **1** overwhelming. **2** (of prices) very low. **3** (of furniture) easy to dismantle and re-assemble. **knocking-shop** *noun* (*slang*) a brothel. **knock knees** an abnormal inward curving of the legs at the knees. **knock off** (*informal*) **1** cease work. **2** complete (work) quickly. **3** deduct (an amount) from a price. **4** (*slang*) steal. **knock-on effect** an alteration that causes similar alterations elsewhere. **knock on the head** (*informal*) put an end to (a scheme etc.). **knock out 1** make unconscious by hitting on the head. **2** defeat (a boxer) by knocking him down for a count of 10. **3** defeat in a knockout competition; exhaust or disable. **4** (*informal*) astonish. **knock spots off** (*informal*) be easily superior to. **knock up 1** rouse by knocking at the door. **2** make or arrange hastily. **3** (*slang*) make pregnant. **4** practise tennis etc. before formal play begins. **knock-up** *noun* a practice or casual game at tennis etc.

**knockabout** *adjective* **1** rough, boisterous. **2** (of clothes) hard-wearing.

**knocker** *noun* **1** a hinged metal instrument on a door for knocking with. **2** (**knockers**) (*vulgar slang*) women's breasts.

**knockout** *adjective* **1** that knocks a boxer etc. out; *a knockout blow*. **2** (of a competition) in which the loser of each successive round is eliminated. ● *noun* **1** a blow that knocks a boxer out. **2** a knockout competition. **3** (*informal*) an outstanding or irresistible person or thing.

**knoll** (*pronounced* nohl) *noun* a hillock, a mound.

**Knossos** (knos-ŏs) the principal city of Crete in Minoan times, containing the remains of the Palace of Minos.

**knot** *noun* **1** an intertwining of one or more pieces of thread or rope etc. to fasten them together; knotted ribbon etc. as an ornament. **2** a tangle. **3** a hard mass in something, especially on a tree trunk where a branch joins it. **4** a round cross-grained spot in timber where a branch joined. **5** a cluster of people or things. **6** a unit of speed used by ships at sea and by aircraft, = one nautical mile per hour. **7** the central point in a problem etc. ● *verb* (**knotted**, **knotting**) **1** tie or fasten with a knot. **2** entangle. □ **at a rate of knots** (*informal*) very rapidly. **knot-hole** *noun* a hole in timber where a knot has fallen out. **tie in knots** (*informal*) baffle or confuse.

**knotgrass** *noun* a common weed with creeping stems and small pale pink flowers.

**knotty** *adjective* (**knottier, knottiest**) **1** full of knots. **2** puzzling, full of problems or difficulties.

**know** *verb* (**knew, known, knowing**) **1** have in one's mind or memory as a result of experience, learning, or information. **2** feel certain; *I know I left it here!* **3** recognize (a person); have had social contact with; be familiar with (a place). **4** recognize with certainty; *knows a bargain when she sees one.* **5** understand and be able to use (a subject, language, or skill). **6** experience; be subject to; *her joy knew no bounds.* □ **in the know** (*informal*) having inside information. **know-all** *noun* (*informal*) a person who behaves as if he or she knows everything. **know-how** *noun* practical knowledge or skill. **know one's own mind** know firmly what one wants or intends. **know what's what** have knowledge of the world, life, etc. **you never know** it is always possible. □ **knowable** *adjective*

**knowing** *adjective* showing knowledge or awareness; showing that one has inside information. □ **knowingly** *adverb*

**knowledge** *noun* **1** knowing. **2** all that a person knows. **3** all that is known, an organized body of information. □ **to my knowledge** as far as I know.

**knowledgeable** *adjective* (also **knowledgable**) well-informed.

**known** *see* KNOW.

**Knox** (*pronounced* noks), John (*c.*1505–72), Scottish Protestant reformer.

**knuckle** *noun* **1** a finger-joint. **2** the knee-joint of an animal, or the part joining the leg to the foot, especially as a joint of meat. ● *verb* strike, press, or rub with the knuckles. □ **knuckle down** begin to work earnestly. **knuckle under** yield, submit.

**knuckleduster** *noun* a metal device worn over the knuckles to protect them and increase the injury done by a blow.

**knurl** (*pronounced* nerl) *noun* a small projecting ridge or knob.

**KO** *abbreviation* knockout. □ **KO'd** knocked out.

**koala** (koh-ah-lă) *noun* (in full **koala bear**) an Australian tree-climbing animal (a marsupial) with thick grey fur and large ears.

**Koch** (*pronounced* kok), Robert (1843–1910), German bacteriologist, who identified the organisms causing anthrax, tuberculosis, and cholera.

**Kodály** (koh-dy), Zoltán (1882–1967), Hungarian composer.

**Koestler** (kerst-ler), Arthur (1905–83), Hungarian-born essayist and novelist, whose best-known novel *Darkness at Noon* exposed the Stalinist purges of the 1930s.

**Koh-i-noor** (koh-i-noor) an Indian diamond, famous for its size, now one of the British Crown jewels.

**Kohl**, Helmut (born 1930), German statesman, Chancellor of the Federal Republic of Germany from 1982, and of the united Germany from 1990.

**kohl** *noun* a black powder used as eye make-up, especially in Eastern countries.

**kohlrabi** (kohl-rah-bi) *noun* (*plural* **kohlrabies**) a cabbage with an edible turnip-shaped stem.

**kola** alternative spelling of COLA.

**kolkhoz** (kul-horz) *noun* a collective farm in the former USSR.

**koodoo** alternative spelling of KUDU.

**kook** *noun* (*Amer. slang*) a crazy or eccentric person. □ **kooky** *adjective*

**kookaburra** *noun* a large kingfisher of Australia with a strange laughing cry.

**kopeck, kopek** alternative spelling of CO-PECK.

**koppie** *noun* (also **kopje**) (in South Africa) a small hill.

**Koran** (kor-ahn) *noun* the sacred book of Islam containing the revelations of Muhammad, written in Arabic.

**Korda**, Sir Alexander (original name; Sándor Kellner) (1893–1956), Hungarian-born film producer and director, noted for his extravagant films.

**Korea** (kŏ-ree-ă) a country in Asia, divided between the Republic of Korea (= South Korea) and the Democratic People's Republic of Korea (= North Korea).

**Korean** adjective of Korea or its people or language. ●noun **1** a person from North or South Korea. **2** the language of Korea.

**kosher** (koh-sher) adjective **1** (of food etc.) conforming to the requirements of Jewish dietary laws. **2** (informal) genuine, correct, legitimate. ●noun kosher food.

**kowhai** (koh-I) noun a New Zealand tree or shrub with golden flowers.

**kowtow** verb behave with exaggerated respect towards a person. (¶ The kowtow was a former Chinese custom of touching the ground with one's forehead as a sign of worship or submission.)

**k.p.h.** abbreviation kilometres per hour.

**Kr** symbol krypton.

**kraal** (pronounced krahl) noun (in South Africa) **1** a village of huts enclosed by a fence. **2** an enclosure for cattle or sheep.

**Kraut** (rhymes with trout) noun (slang, offensive) a German.

**kremlin** noun **1** a citadel within a Russian town. **2** (**the Kremlin**) that of Moscow; the Russian government.

**krill** noun the mass of tiny planktonic crustaceans that forms the principal food of certain whales.

**Krishna** (in Hinduism) one of the most popular gods, the eighth and most important avatar of Vishnu.

**krona** (kroh-nă) noun the unit of money in Sweden (plural **kronor**) and Iceland (plural **kronur**).

**krone** (kroh-nĕ) noun (plural **kroner**) the unit of money in Denmark and Norway.

**Kruger** (kroo-ger), Stephanus Johannes Paulus (1825–1904), South African soldier and statesman, President of the Transvaal 1883–99.

**krugerrand** (kroog-er-ahnt) noun a South African gold coin bearing a portrait of President Kruger.

**krummhorn** noun (also **crumhorn**) a medieval wind instrument with a double reed.

**krypton** (krip-ton) noun a chemical element (symbol Kr), a colourless odourless gas used in various types of lamps and bulbs.

**KS** abbreviation Kansas.

**Kshatriya** (kshah-tri-ă) noun a member of the second of the four great Hindu classes, the warrior or baronial caste.

**Kt.** abbreviation Knight.

**kt.** abbreviation knot.

**K2** the second-highest peak in the world, in the western Himalayas.

**Ku** symbol Kurchatovium.

**Kuala Lumpur** (kwah-lă luum-poor) the capital of Malaysia.

**Kublai Khan** (koo-bly kahn) (1216–94), Mongol emperor of China from 1259, grandson of Genghis Khan.

**kudos** (kew-doss) noun (informal) honour and glory.

**kudu** (koo-doo) noun (also **koodoo**) a large African antelope with white stripes and spiral horns.

**Kufic** (kew-fik) noun (also **Cufic**) an early form of the Arabic alphabet, found especially in inscriptions.

**Ku Klux Klan** an American secret society of racist Whites using terrorism against Blacks, originally formed in the southern States after the Civil War.

**kukri** (kuuk-ri) noun a heavy curved knife broadening towards the point, used by Gurkhas.

**kulak** (koo-lak) noun (hist.) (in the former USSR) a peasant proprietor working for his or her own profit.

**kümmel** (kuu-mĕl) noun a sweet liqueur flavoured with caraway and cumin seeds.

**kumquat** (kum-kwot) noun (also **cumquat**) a plum-sized orange-like fruit used in preserves.

**kung fu** (kung foo) a Chinese form of unarmed combat, similar to karate.

**Kuomintang** (kwoh-min-tang) noun a nationalist party founded in China in 1912, eventually defeated by the Communist Party in 1949 and subsequently forming the central administration of Taiwan.

**kurchatovium** (ker-chă-toh-viŭm) noun the Russian name for the element also called rutherfordium (symbol Ku).

**Kurd** noun a member of a pastoral people of Kurdistan.

**Kurdish** adjective of the Kurds or their language. ●noun the language of the Kurds.

**Kurdistan** a mountainous region inhabited by the Kurds, covering parts of Turkey, Iraq, Iran, Syria, and the former USSR.

**Kurosawa** (koor-ă-sah-wă), Akira (born 1910), Japanese film director.

**Kuwait** (koo-wayt) **1** a country bordering on the Persian Gulf. **2** its capital city. □ **Kuwaiti** adjective & noun

**kV** abbreviation kilovolt(s).

**kwashiorkor** (kwash-i-or-kor) noun a form of malnutrition caused by lack of protein in the diet, especially in young children in the tropics.

**kW** abbreviation kilowatt(s).

**kWh** abbreviation kilowatt-hour(s).

**KWIC** abbreviation key word in context.

**KY, Ky.** abbreviation Kentucky.

**kyle** noun a narrow channel between an island and the mainland (or another island) in Scotland.

**Kyoto** (kee-oh-toh) a city of Japan, the imperial capital 794–1868.

# LI

**L** *abbreviation* learner driver. ● *noun* (as a Roman numeral) 50.

**l** *abbreviation* (also **l.**) litre(s).

**LA** *abbreviation* **1** Los Angeles. **2** Louisiana.

**La** *symbol* lanthanum.

**La.** *abbreviation* Louisiana.

**la** alternative spelling of LAH.

**lab** *noun* (*informal*) a laboratory.

**label** *noun* **1** a slip of paper or other material fixed on or beside an object and showing its nature, owner, name, destination, or other information about it. **2** a descriptive word or phrase classifying people etc. ● *verb* (**labelled**, **labelling**; *Amer.* **labeled**, **labeling**) **1** attach a label to. **2** describe or classify; *he was labelled as a troublemaker.*

**labia** (**lay**-bi-ă) *plural noun* the lips of the female genitals.

**labial** (**lay**-bi-ăl) *adjective* of the lips. ● *noun* a speech sound involving closure of the lips (e.g. *p*, *m*).

**labor** etc. *Amer.* spelling of LABOUR etc.

**laboratory** (lă-**bo**-ră-ter-i) *noun* a room or building equipped for scientific experiments or research etc.

**laborious** *adjective* **1** needing much effort or perseverance. **2** showing signs of great effort, not spontaneous, forced. □ **laboriously** *adverb*

**labour** *noun* (*Amer.* **labor**) **1** physical or mental work, exertion. **2** a task. **3** the pains or contractions of the womb at childbirth. **4** workers, working people distinguished from management or considered as a political force. **5** (**Labour**) the Labour Party. ● *verb* **1** exert oneself, work hard. **2** have to make a great effort, operate or progress only with difficulty; *the engine was labouring.* **3** treat at great length or in excessive detail; *I will not labour the point.* □ **labour camp** a penal settlement with forced labour by prisoners. **Labour Day 1** a day celebrated in honour of workers, often 1 May. **2** (in the USA) a public holiday on the first Monday in September. **Labour Exchange** (*informal*) an employment exchange. **labour force** the body of workers employed, especially in a particular place or area. **labour-intensive** *adjective* **1** (of an industry) needing to employ many people. **2** (of a job or type of manual work) time-consuming. **labour of love** a demanding task done for satisfaction rather than payment. **Labour Party** a political party committed to democratic socialism.

**labour-saving** *adjective* designed to reduce the amount of work or effort needed.

**laboured** *adjective* (*Amer.* **labored**) showing signs of great effort, not spontaneous.

**labourer** *noun* (*Amer.* **laborer**) a person employed to do unskilled manual work or to assist a skilled worker; *a bricklayer's labourer.*

**Labrador** (**lab**-ră-dor) a region of NE Canada. ● *noun* a retriever dog of a breed with a smooth black or golden coat.

**laburnum** *noun* an ornamental tree with hanging clusters of yellow flowers.

**labyrinth** (**lab**-er-inth) *noun* **1** a complicated network of paths through which it is difficult to find one's way. **2** the complex cavity of the inner ear. □ **labyrinthine** (lab-ĕr-**in**-thyn) *adjective*

**lac** *noun* a resinous substance secreted by an insect of SE Asia as a protective covering and used to make shellac.

**lace** *noun* **1** fabric or trimming made in an ornamental openwork design. **2** a cord or narrow leather strip threaded through holes or hooks for pulling opposite edges together and securing them. ● *verb* **1** fasten with a lace or laces. **2** pass (a cord) through; intertwine. **3** add spirits to (a drink or food). □ **lace-up** (*noun*) a shoe fastened with a lace; (*adjective*) (of a shoe etc.) fastened by a lace or laces.

**lacerate** (**las**-er-ayt) *verb* **1** injure (flesh) by tearing. **2** wound (feelings). □ **laceration** *noun*

**lachrymal** (**lak**-rim-ăl) *adjective* (also **lacrimal**) of tears, secreting tears; *lachrymal ducts.*

**lachrymose** (**lak**-rim-ohs) *adjective* (*formal*) tearful.

**lack** *noun* the state or fact of not having something. ● *verb* be without or not have (a thing) when it is needed. □ **be lacking 1** be undesirably absent; *money was lacking.* **2** be deficient; *he is lacking in courage.* **lack for nothing** have plenty of everything.

**lackadaisical** (lak-ă-**day**-zikăl) *adjective* lacking vigour or determination, unenthusiastic. □ **lackadaisically** *adverb*

**lackey** *noun* (*plural* **lackeys**) **1** a footman, a servant. **2** a person's servile follower.

**lacklustre** *adjective* (*Amer.* **lackluster**) lacking in force or vitality; dull; *a lacklustre performance.*

**laconic** (lă-**kon**-ik) *adjective* using few words, terse. □ **laconically** *adverb*

**lacquer** (lak-er) *noun* a hard glossy varnish. ●*verb* coat with lacquer.

**lacrimal** alternative spelling of LACHRYMAL.

**lacrosse** (lă-**kross**) *noun* a game resembling hockey but with players using a netted crook (a crosse) to catch, carry, or throw the ball.

**lactate** *verb* (*pronounced* lak-**tayt**) secrete milk. ●*noun* (*pronounced* **lak**-tayt) a salt or ester of lactic acid.

**lactation** (lak-**tay**-shŏn) *noun* the secreting of milk in breasts or udder; the period during which this occurs.

**lacteal** *adjective* of milk. ●*plural noun* (**lacteals**) vessels in the intestine which absorb fats.

**lactic** *adjective* of milk. □ **lactic acid** the acid found in sour milk and produced in the muscles during strenuous exercise.

**lactose** *noun* a sugar present in milk.

**lacuna** (lă-**kew**-nă) *noun* (*plural* **lacunas** or **lacunae**, *pronounced* lă-**kew**-nee) a gap, a section missing from a book or argument etc.

**lacy** *adjective* like lace.

**lad** *noun* **1** a boy or youth. **2** (*informal*) a man.

**ladder** *noun* **1** a set of horizontal bars fixed between two uprights, used for climbing up or down. **2** a vertical strip of unravelled stitching in a stocking etc. **3** a means or series of stages by which a person may advance in his or her career etc.; *the political ladder*. ●*verb* cause a ladder in (a stocking etc.); develop a ladder. □ **ladder-back** *noun* a chair with the back made of horizontal bars between uprights.

**lade** *verb* (**laded**, **laden**, **lading**) load (a ship); (of a ship) take on cargo.

**laden** *adjective* loaded with a cargo or burden.

**la-di-da** *adjective* (*informal*) having an affected manner or pronunciation.

**lading** (**lay**-ding) *noun* cargo.

**ladle** *noun* a deep long-handled spoon used for serving liquids. ●*verb* (often foll. by *out*) transfer with a ladle.

**Ladoga** (**lah**-dŏ-gă) the largest European lake, in north-west Russia near the Finnish border.

**lady** *noun* **1** a woman considered to be of good social position or to have refined manners. **2** (often used as *adjective*) a woman; *a lady doctor*. **3** (*old use*) a wife or girl friend. **4** (**Lady**) a title used by peeresses, female relatives of peers, wives and widows of knights, etc. **5** a woman with authority over a household etc.; *the lady of the house*. □ **the Ladies** (or **Ladies'**) a women's public lavatory. **ladies' man** (or **lady's man**) a man who is fond of female society. **Lady chapel** a chapel within a large church, dedicated to the Virgin Mary. **Lady Day** the Feast of the Annunciation, 25 March.

**lady-in-waiting** *noun* a lady attending a queen or princess. **lady-killer** *noun* a man who seeks to attract women. **lady's slipper** a flower of the orchid family, with a bloom shaped like a slipper or pouch. **Our Lady** the Virgin Mary.

**ladybird** *noun* a small flying beetle, usually red with black spots (= *Amer.* LADYBUG).

**ladylike** *adjective* polite and suitable for a lady; *ladylike manners*.

**ladyship** *noun* a title used in speaking to or about a woman of the rank of Lady; *your ladyship*.

**La Fontaine** (lah fon-**tayn**), Jean de (1621–95), French poet, author of *Fables*.

**lag**[1] *verb* (**lagged**, **lagging**) go too slow, fail to keep up with others. ●*noun* lagging; a delay.

**lag**[2] *verb* (**lagged**, **lagging**) encase (pipes or a boiler etc.) in a layer of insulating material to prevent loss of heat.

**lag**[3] *noun* (*slang*) a convict; *old lags*.

**lager** (**lah**-ger) *noun* a light beer. □ **lager lout** (*informal*) a drunken rowdy youth.

**laggard** *noun* a person who lags behind.

**lagging** *noun* material used to lag pipes etc.

**lagoon** *noun* a salt-water lake separated from the sea by a sandbank or coral reef etc.

**Lagos** (**lay**-goss) the chief port and former capital of Nigeria.

**lah** *noun* (also **la**) *Music* the sixth note of a major scale.

**laid** *see* LAY[3]. □ **laid-back** *adjective* (*slang*) easygoing, relaxed. **laid paper** paper with the surface marked in fine ribs.

**lain** *see* LIE[2].

**lair** *noun* **1** a sheltered place where a wild animal regularly sleeps or rests. **2** a person's hiding-place.

**laird** *noun* (*Scottish*) a landowner.

**laissez-faire** (less-ay-**fair**) *noun* (also **laisser-faire**) the policy of non-interference, especially in politics or economics. (¶ French, = let act.)

**laity** (**lay**-iti) *noun* lay people as distinct from the clergy.

**lake**[1] *noun* a large body of water entirely surrounded by land. □ **the Lake District** (also **the Lakes**) a region of lakes and mountains in Cumbria, NW England.

**lake**[2] *noun* a kind of pigment, especially a reddish pigment originally made from lac.

**lakh** (*pronounced* lak) *noun* (in India) a hundred thousand; *a lakh of rupees*.

**Lakshadweep** (lak-shad-**weep**) a group of islands in the Indian Ocean off the Malabar coast, constituting a Union Territory of India.

**Lakshmi** (**luk**-shmi) (in Hinduism) the goddess of prosperity, consort of Vishnu.

**Lallan** adjective (*Scottish*) of the Lowlands of Scotland. ●*noun* (also **Lallans**) Lowland Scots dialect.

**lam** verb (**lammed, lamming**) (*slang*) hit hard, thrash.

**lama** (**lah**-mă) noun a priest or monk of the form of Buddhism found in Tibet and Mongolia.

**Lamarck** (la-**mark**), Jean Baptiste de (1744–1829), French botanist and zoologist who (among others) anticipated Darwin's theory of organic evolution.

**lamasery** (**lah**-mă-ser-i) noun a monastery of lamas.

**lamb** noun **1** a young sheep. **2** its flesh as food. **3** a gentle or endearing person. ●*verb* give birth to a lamb. □ **Lamb of God** Christ (compared to the lamb sacrificed by Jews at the Passover).

**lambada** (lam-**bah**-dă) noun a fast erotic Brazilian dance in which couples dance with their stomachs touching each other.

**lambaste** (lam-**bayst**) (also **lambast**) verb (*informal*) beat or reprimand severely.

**lambent** adjective **1** (of a flame or light) playing about a surface. **2** (of the eyes, wit, etc.) gently brilliant. □ **lambency** noun

**Lambeth Palace** a palace in the London borough of Lambeth, residence of the archbishop of Canterbury.

**lambswool** noun soft fine wool from a young sheep.

**lame** adjective **1** unable to walk normally because of an injury or defect, especially in a foot or leg. **2** (of an excuse or argument) weak, unconvincing. ●*verb* make lame. □ **lame duck** a person or firm etc. that is in difficulties and unable to manage without help. □ **lamely** adverb, **lameness** noun

**lamé** (**lah**-may) noun a fabric in which gold or silver thread is interwoven.

**lament** noun **1** a passionate expression of grief. **2** a song or poem expressing grief. ●*verb* feel or express grief or regret.

**lamentable** (lam-ĕn-tă-bŭl) adjective regrettable, deplorable. □ **lamentably** adverb

**lamentation** (lam-en-**tay**-shŏn) noun **1** lamenting. **2** a lament, an expression of grief. **3** (**Lamentations**) a book of the Old Testament telling of the desolation after the destruction of the Temple in 586 BC.

**lamented** adjective (especially of a dead person) mourned for.

**lamina** (**lam**-in-ă) noun (*plural* **laminae**) a thin plate, scale, or layer. □ **laminar** adjective

**laminate** verb (*pronounced* **lam**-in-ayt) **1** flatten or split (a material) into thin sheets or layers. **2** form (a sheet of material) by pressing together several layers. **3** overlay (a surface or material) with a thin sheet or layer of another material. ●*noun* (*pronounced* **lam**-in-ăt) a material formed from several layers pressed together. □ **lamination** noun

**laminated** adjective made of layers joined one upon the other; *laminated plastic*.

**Lammas** noun the first day of August, formerly observed as a harvest festival.

**lamp** noun **1** a device for giving light, either by the use of electricity or gas or by burning oil or spirit. **2** a glass container enclosing a filament that is made to glow by electricity. **3** an electrical device producing radiation; *an infrared lamp*.

**lampblack** noun a pigment made from soot.

**lampoon** (lam-**poon**) noun a piece of writing that attacks a person by ridiculing him or her. ●*verb* ridicule in a lampoon.

**lamppost** noun a tall post supporting a street lamp.

**lamprey** noun (*plural* **lampreys**) a small eel-like water animal with a round mouth used as a sucker for attaching itself to things.

**lampshade** noun a shade placed over a lamp to soften or screen its light.

**Lancashire** a county of NW England.

**Lancaster 1** a city in Lancashire. **2** the name of the English royal house that ruled England from 1399 (Henry IV) until the death of Henry VI (1471).

**Lancastrian** adjective **1** of Lancashire or Lancaster. **2** of the Lancaster family or of the Red Rose party supporting it in the Wars of the Roses. ●*noun* a Lancastrian person.

**lance** noun a long spear used especially by horsemen. ●*verb* **1** pierce with a lance. **2** prick or cut open with a surgical lancet. □ **lance-corporal** noun an NCO ranking below a corporal.

**Lancelot** (**lahn**-sĕ-lot) (in legends of King Arthur) the most famous of Arthur's knights, lover of Queen Guinevere.

**lancer** noun (*hist.*) a soldier of a certain cavalry regiment formerly armed with lances.

**lancet** noun a pointed two-edged knife used by surgeons. □ **lancet arch or window** a tall narrow pointed arch or window.

**Lancs.** abbreviation Lancashire.

**land** noun **1** the solid part of the earth's surface, the part not covered by water. **2** the ground or soil as used for farming. **3** an expanse of country; *forest land*. **4** a country, State, or nation. **5** property consisting of land. ●*verb* **1** arrive or put on land from a ship. **2** bring (an aircraft or its passengers etc.) down to the ground or other surface; come down in this way. **3** alight after a jump or fall. **4** bring (a fish) to land; win (a prize) or obtain (an appointment etc.); *landed an excellent job*. **5** (often foll. by *up*) arrive or cause to arrive at a certain place, stage, or position; *landed up in gaol*; *landed us all in a mess*. **6** strike with a blow; *landed* *him one in the eye.* **7** present with a problem etc.; *landed us with the job of sorting it out.* □ **landmass** a large continuous area of land. **land-mine** *noun* an explosive mine laid in or on the ground.

**landau** (**lan**-daw) *noun* a four-wheeled horse-drawn carriage with a divided top.

**landed** *adjective* **1** owning land; *landed gentry.* **2** consisting of land; *landed estates.*

**landfall** *noun* approach to land after a journey by sea or air.

**landfill** *noun* **1** waste material etc. used for land reclamation or buried in large pits. **2** this process of waste disposal. □ **landfill site** a place where rubbish is disposed of by burying it in the ground.

**landing** *noun* **1** the process of coming or bringing something to land. **2** a place where people and goods may be landed from a boat etc. **3** a level area at the top of a flight of stairs or between flights. □ **landing-craft** *noun* a vehicle designed for putting ashore troops and equipment. **landing-gear** *noun* the undercarriage of an aircraft. **landing-stage** *noun* a platform on which people and goods are landed from a boat.

**landlady** *noun* **1** a woman who lets rooms etc. to tenants. **2** a woman who keeps an inn or boarding house.

**landlocked** *adjective* almost or entirely surrounded by land.

**landlord** *noun* **1** a person who lets land or a house or room etc. to a tenant. **2** one who keeps an inn or boarding house.

**landlubber** *noun* a person who is unfamiliar with the sea or sailing.

**landmark** *noun* **1** a conspicuous and easily recognized feature of a landscape. **2** an event that marks a stage or change in the history of something.

**landowner** *noun* a person who owns a large area of land. □ **landowning** *adjective & noun*

**landscape** *noun* **1** the scenery of a land area. **2** a picture of this. ●*verb* lay out (an area) attractively, with natural features. □ **landscape gardening** the laying out of grounds to resemble natural scenery.

**Landseer**, Sir Edwin (1802–73), English painter and sculptor, known for his animal subjects, whose works include the bronze lions in Trafalgar Square, London.

**Land's End** a rocky promontory in Cornwall forming the SW promontory of England.

**landslide** *noun* **1** a landslip. **2** an overwhelming majority of votes for one side in an election.

**landslip** *noun* the sliding down of a mass of land from a slope or mountain.

**Landsteiner** (**land**-sty-ner), Karl (1868–1943), Austrian physician, who devised the classification of the main blood groups.

**landward** *adjective & adverb* towards the land. □ **landwards** *adverb*

**lane** *noun* **1** a narrow road. **2** a strip of road for a single line of traffic. **3** a strip of track or water for a runner, rower, or swimmer in a race. **4** a route prescribed for or regularly followed by ships or aircraft; *shipping lanes.* **5** a passage made or left between rows of people.

**language** *noun* **1** words and their use. **2** a system of words used in one or more countries or regions. **3** a system of signs or symbols used for conveying information. **4** a system of words, phrases, and symbols by means of which a computer can be programmed. **5** a particular style of wording. **6** the vocabulary of a particular group of people; *medical language.* □ **language laboratory** a room equipped with tape recorders etc. for learning a foreign language.

**languid** (**lang**-wid) *adjective* lacking vigour or vitality. □ **languidly** *adverb*

**languish** (**lang**-wish) *verb* **1** lose or lack vitality. **2** live under miserable conditions, be neglected. **3** pine.

**languor** (**lang**-er) *noun* **1** tiredness, listlessness, lack of vitality. **2** a languishing expression. **3** oppressive stillness of the air. □ **languorous** *adjective*

**lank** *adjective* **1** tall and lean. **2** (of hair or grass) long and limp.

**lanky** *adjective* (**lankier, lankiest**) ungracefully lean and long or tall. □ **lankiness** *noun*

**lanolin** (**lan**-ŏ-lin) *noun* fat extracted from sheep's wool and used as a basis for ointments.

**lantern** *noun* **1** a transparent case for holding a light and shielding it against wind etc. outdoors. **2** the light-chamber of a lighthouse. **3** a projection with windows on each side, on top of a dome or room. □ **lantern-jawed** *adjective* having long thin jaws so that the face has a hollow look.

**lanthanide** (**lan**-thă-nyd) *noun* any of a series of chemically related elements from lanthanum to lutetium (atomic numbers 57–71).

**lanthanum** (**lan**-thă-nŭm) *noun* a silvery-white metallic element (symbol La).

**lanyard** *noun* **1** a short rope or line used on a ship to fasten something or secure it. **2** a cord worn round the neck or on the shoulder, to which a knife or whistle etc. may be attached.

**Laodicean** (lay-oh-di-**see**-ăn) *adjective* half-hearted, especially in religion or politics.

**Laos** (*rhymes with* mouse) a small landlocked country in SE Asia. □ **Laotian** (lah-**oh**-shăn) *adjective & noun*

**Lao-tzu** (lah-oh-**tsoo**) **1** the legendary founder of Taoism and traditional author of its most sacred scripture. **2** this scripture.

**lap¹** noun **1** the flat area formed by the upper part of the thighs of a seated person. **2** the part of a dress etc. covering this. □ **in a person's lap** as his or her responsibility. **in the lap of the gods** beyond human control. **in the lap of luxury** in great luxury. **lap-dog** noun a small pet dog.

**lap²** noun **1** an overlapping part; the amount of overlap. **2** a single circuit e.g. of a racecourse. **3** one section of a journey; *the last lap*. ●verb (**lapped, lapping**) **1** fold or wrap round. **2** overlap. **3** be one or more laps ahead of (another competitor) in a race. □ **lap of honour** a ceremonial circuit of a racetrack etc. by the winner.

**lap³** verb (**lapped, lapping**) **1** take up (liquid) by movements of the tongue, as a cat does. **2** flow with ripples making a gentle splashing sound; *waves lapped the shore*. □ **lap up 1** drink (liquid) greedily. **2** consume (gossip, praise, etc.) eagerly.

**laparoscope** (lap-er-ŏ-skohp) noun a fibre optic instrument inserted through the abdomen to view the internal organs. □ **laparoscopy** (lap-er-os-kŏ-pi) noun

**laparotomy** (lap-er-ot-ŏmi) noun surgical cutting through the abdominal wall for access to the internal organs.

**La Paz** the capital of Bolivia.

**lapel** (lă-**pel**) noun a flap at the edge of each front of a coat etc., folded back to lie against its outer surface. □ **lapelled** adjective

**lapidary** (lap-id-er-i) adjective of stones, engraved on stone. ●noun a cutter, polisher, or engraver of gems.

**lapis lazuli** (lap-iss laz-yoo-li) a bright blue semi-precious stone.

**Lapland** a region at the north of Scandinavia. □ **Laplander** noun

**Lapp** noun **1** a Laplander. **2** the language of Lapland. □ **Lappish** adjective

**lappet** noun a flap or fold of a garment etc. or of flesh.

**lapse** noun **1** a slight error, especially one caused by forgetfulness, weakness, or inattention. **2** backsliding, a decline into an inferior state. **3** the passage of a period of time; *after a lapse of six months*. **4** the termination of a privilege or legal right through disuse. ●verb **1** fail to maintain one's position or standard. **2** (of rights and privileges) be lost or no longer valid because not used, claimed, or renewed.

**laptop** noun (often used as *adjective*) (of a microcomputer) portable and suitable for use while travelling.

**lapwing** noun a peewit.

**larboard** noun (*old use*) = PORT³.

**larceny** (lar-sĕn-i) noun theft of personal goods. □ **larcenous** adjective

**larch** noun a tall cone-bearing deciduous tree of the pine family.

**lard** noun a white greasy substance prepared from pig fat and used in cooking. ●verb **1** place strips of fat or bacon in or on (meat) before cooking, in order to prevent it from becoming dry while roasting. **2** garnish (talk or writing) with strange terms.

**larder** noun a room or cupboard for storing food.

**lardy** adjective like lard. □ **lardy-cake** noun cake made with lard and containing currants.

**large** adjective **1** of considerable size or extent. **2** of the larger kind; *the large intestine*. **3** acting on a large scale; *large farmers*. ●adverb in a large way, on a large scale; *loom large*. □ **at large 1** free to roam about, not in confinement. **2** in a general way, at random. **3** as a whole, in general; *is popular with the country at large*. **large as life** in person, especially when prominent. **larger than life** seeming extreme or exaggerated. **large-scale** adjective **1** drawn to a large scale so that many details can be shown; *a large-scale map*. **2** extensive, involving large quantities etc.; *large-scale operations*. □ **largeness** noun, **largish** adjective

**largely** adverb to a great extent; *his success was largely due to luck*.

**largesse** (lar-**jess**) noun money or gifts generously given.

**largish** adjective fairly large.

**largo** adjective & adverb Music in a slow tempo and dignified style. ●noun (plural **largos**) a largo passage or movement.

**lariat** (la-ri-ăt) noun **1** a lasso. **2** a rope used to tether a horse etc.

**lark¹** noun **1** any of several small sandy-brown songbirds, especially the skylark. □ **rise with the lark** get up early.

**lark²** (*informal*) noun **1** a playful adventurous action. **2** an amusing incident. ●verb play light-heartedly; *larking about*.

**Larkin**, Philip Arthur (1922–85), English poet and novelist.

**larkspur** noun a plant with spur-shaped blue or pink flowers.

**Larousse** (lah-**rooss**), Pierre (1817–75), French lexicographer and encyclopedia compiler.

**larva** noun (plural **larvae**, *pronounced* **lar**-vee) an insect in the first stage of its life after coming out of the egg. □ **larval** adjective

**laryngeal** (lă-**rin**-ji-ăl) adjective of the larynx.

**laryngitis** (la-rin-jy-tiss) noun inflammation of the larynx.

**larynx** (**la**-rinks) noun the part of the throat containing the vocal cords.

**lasagne** (lă-**san**-yă) *noun* **1** pasta formed into sheets. **2** a dish of this pasta layered with minced meat and cheese sauce.

**Lascar** (**lask**-er) *noun* a seaman from the countries south-east of India.

**lascivious** (lă-**siv**-i-ŭs) *adjective* lustful. □ **lasciviously** *adverb*, **lasciviousness** *noun*

**laser** (**lay**-zer) *noun* a device that generates an intense and highly concentrated beam of light or other electromagnetic radiation. □ **laser printer** a computer printer that uses a laser beam to print quietly and accurately.

**lash** *verb* **1** move in a whip-like movement; *lashed its tail*. **2** strike with a whip; beat or strike violently; *rain lashed against the windows*. **3** attack violently in words. **4** fasten or secure with cord etc.; *lashed them together*. ●*noun* **1** a stroke with a whip etc. **2** the flexible part of a whip. **3** an eyelash. □ **lash out 1** attack with blows or words. **2** spend lavishly.

**lashings** *plural noun* (*informal*) a lot; *lashings of cream*.

**lass** *noun* (*Scottish & N. England*, or *poetic*) a girl, a young woman.

**Lassa fever** a serious disease of tropical Africa, caused by a virus. (¶ Named after Lassa in Nigeria.)

**lassitude** *noun* tiredness, listlessness.

**lasso** (la-**soo**) *noun* (*plural* **lassos** or **lassoes**) a rope with a running noose, used for catching cattle. ●*verb* (**lassoed**, **lassoing**) catch with a lasso.

**last¹** *adjective & adverb* **1** after all others in position or time, coming at the end. **2** latest, most recent, most recently; *last night*. **3** remaining as the only one(s) left; *our last hope*. **4** least likely or suitable; *she is the last person I'd have chosen*. ●*noun* **1** a person or thing that is last. **2** the last performance of certain actions; *breathe one's last*. **3** the last mention or sight of something; *shall never hear the last of it*. □ **at last** *or* **at long last** in the end, after much delay. **last-ditch** *adjective* (of an attempt etc.) final, desperate. **the Last Judgement** *see* JUDGEMENT. **last-minute** *adjective* at the latest possible time. **last post** a military bugle call sounded at sunset and at military funerals. **last rites** a religious ritual for a person who is about to die. **last straw** a slight addition to one's difficulties that makes them unbearable. **Last Supper** the meal eaten by Christ and his disciples on the eve of the Crucifixion. **last trump** a trumpet-call to wake the dead on Judgement Day. **last word 1** the final statement in a dispute. **2** a definitive statement. **3** the latest fashion.

**last²** *verb* **1** continue for a period of time, endure; *the rain lasted all day*. **2** be

sufficient for one's needs; *enough food to last us for three days*. □ **last out** be strong enough or sufficient to last.

**last³** *noun* a block of wood or metal shaped like a foot, used in making and repairing shoes.

**lasting** *adjective* able to last for a long time.

**lastly** *adverb* in the last place, finally.

**Las Vegas** a city in Nevada, famous for its casinos and nightclubs.

**lat.** *abbreviation* latitude.

**latch** *noun* **1** a small bar fastening a door or gate, lifted from its catch by a lever. **2** a spring-lock that catches when a door is closed. ●*verb* fasten or be fastened with a latch. □ **latch on to** (*informal*) **1** cling to. **2** take in as an idea. **on the latch** fastened by a latch but not locked.

**latchkey** *noun* the key of an outer door. □ **latchkey child** a child who is alone at home after school until a parent returns from work.

**late** *adjective & adverb* **1** after the proper or usual time. **2** flowering or ripening late in the season. **3** far on in the day or night or a period of time or a series etc.; *in the late 1920s*. **4** of recent date or time; *the latest news*. **5** no longer alive; no longer holding a certain position; *the late president*. □ **late in the day** at a late stage in the proceedings. **of late** lately. □ **lateness** *noun*

**latecomer** *noun* a person who arrives late.

**lateen** (lă-**teen**) *adjective* (of a sail) triangular and hung on a long spar at an angle of 45° to the mast.

**lately** *adverb* in recent times, not long ago.

**latent** (**lay**-tĕnt) *adjective* existing but not active, developed, or visible. □ **latent heat** *Physics* heat required to turn a solid into a liquid or vapour, or a liquid into a vapour, without change of temperature. □ **latency** *noun*

**lateral** (**lat**-er-ăl) *adjective* of, at, or towards the side(s). □ **lateral thinking** a method of solving problems without using conventional logic. □ **laterally** *adverb*

**latex** (**lay**-teks) *noun* **1** a milky fluid exuded from the cut surfaces of certain plants, e.g. the rubber plant. **2** a synthetic product resembling this, used in paints and adhesives.

**lath** *noun* a narrow thin strip of wood, used in trellises or as a support for plaster etc.

**lathe** (*pronounced* layth) *noun* a machine for holding and turning pieces of wood or metal etc. against a tool that shapes them.

**lather** (**lah**-ther) *noun* **1** a froth produced by soap or detergent mixed with water. **2** frothy sweat. **3** a state of agitation. ●*verb* **1** cover with lather. **2** form a lather. **3** thrash.

**Latin** *noun* the language of the ancient Romans. ● *adjective* **1** of or in Latin. **2** of the countries or peoples (e.g. France, Spain, Portugal, Italy) using languages developed from Latin. **3** of the Roman Catholic Church. □ **Latin America** the parts of Central and South America where Spanish or Portuguese is the main language. **Latin American** (*adjective*) of these parts; (*noun*) a native of these parts.

**latish** *adjective & adverb* rather late.

**latitude** *noun* **1** the distance of a place from the equator, measured in degrees. **2** (usually as **latitudes**) a region or climate. **3** freedom from restrictions on actions or opinions.

**latitudinarian** (lat-i-tew-din-**air**-iăn) *adjective* allowing great freedom of belief or opinion, especially in religion. ● *noun* a person of this kind.

**latrine** (lă-**treen**) *noun* a communal lavatory in a camp or barracks etc.

**latter** *adjective* **1** the second of two (people, things etc.) mentioned. **2** nearer to the end; *the latter half of the twentieth century.* □ **latter-day** *adjective* modern, recent. **Latter-day Saints** the Mormons' name for themselves.

▪**Usage** When referring to the last of three or more, *the last*, not *the latter*, should be used.

**latterly** *adverb* of late, nowadays.

**lattice** (**lat**-iss) *noun* **1** a framework of crossed laths or bars with spaces between, used as a screen or fence etc. **2** a structure resembling this. □ **lattice window** one made with a lattice or with small panes set in strips of lead.

**Latvia** a country in eastern Europe on the shore of the Baltic Sea, formerly a republic of the USSR.

**Latvian** *adjective* of Latvia or its people or language. ● *noun* **1** a person from Latvia. **2** the language of Latvia.

**laud** *verb* (*formal*) praise. ● *noun* **1** praise; a hymn of praise. **2** (**lauds**) the first service of the day in the Roman Catholic Church.

**laudable** (law-dă-bŭl) *adjective* praiseworthy, commendable. □ **laudably** *adverb*

**laudanum** (**lawd**-nŭm) *noun* a solution containing opium, prepared for use as a sedative.

**laudatory** (law-dă-ter-i) *adjective* expressing praise.

▪**Usage** Do not confuse with **laudable**.

**laugh** *verb* **1** make the sounds and movements that express lively amusement or amused scorn. **2** express (a feeling) by laughing. **3** (foll. by *at*) ridicule, make fun of. ● *noun* **1** an act, sound, or manner of laughing. **2** (*informal*) an amusing incident.

□ **be laughing** (*informal*) be in a fortunate or successful position. **laughing-gas** *noun* nitrous oxide used as an anaesthetic, which can cause involuntary laughter when inhaled. **laughing jackass** the kookaburra. **laughing stock** a person or thing that is ridiculed. **laugh off** get rid of (embarrassment) by joking. **laugh on the other side of one's face** change from amusement to dismay. **laugh out of court** deprive (a thing) of serious consideration by ridicule. **laugh up one's sleeve** laugh secretly. **no laughing matter** not a fit subject for laughter.

**laughable** *adjective* so ridiculous as to be amusing.

**laughter** *noun* the act, sound, or manner of laughing.

**Laughton** (**law**-tŏn), Charles (1899–1962), English-born stage and film actor.

**launch** *verb* **1** send on its course by hurling or thrusting; *launch a rocket.* **2** set (a vessel) afloat. **3** put into action; *launch an attack.* **4** publicly introduce (a new product etc.) or begin (a new enterprise). **5** enter boldly or freely into a course of action. ● *noun* **1** the process of launching a ship or spacecraft. **2** a large motor boat. **3** a warship's largest boat. **4** the occasion of launching a new product, business, etc. □ **launching pad** *or* **launch pad** a concrete platform from which spacecraft are launched. **launch out** spend money freely; start on an ambitious enterprise.

**launder** *verb* **1** wash and iron (clothes etc.). **2** transfer (funds etc.) to conceal their origin.

**launderette** (lawn-der-et) *noun* (also **laundrette**) an establishment with coin-operated washing machines and driers for public use.

**laundress** *noun* a woman whose job is to launder clothes.

**laundry** *noun* **1** a place where clothes etc. are laundered; a business establishment that launders things for customers. **2** clothes etc. for washing, especially those sent to or from a laundry.

**laureate** (**lo**-rri-ăt) *adjective* (*poetic*) wreathed with laurel as an honour. ● *noun* a Poet Laureate. □ **Poet Laureate** the poet officially appointed to write poems for State occasions. □ **laureateship** *noun*

**laurel** (*rhymes with* quarrel) *noun* **1** an evergreen shrub with smooth glossy leaves. **2** (also **laurels**) a wreath of laurel leaves as an emblem of victory or poetic merit. □ **look to one's laurels** beware of losing one's position of superiority. **rest on one's laurels** be satisfied with what one has done and not seek further success. (¶ From the ancient use of a branch or wreath of laurel as a token of victory.)

**Laurel and Hardy** a team of film comedians, English-born Stan Laurel (1890-1965) and American Oliver Hardy (1892-1957).

**lav** noun (informal) a lavatory.

**lava** (lah-vă) noun flowing molten rock discharged from a volcano; the solid substance formed when this cools.

**lavatorial** adjective (especially of humour) relating to or preoccupied with excretion.

**lavatory** noun **1** a large receptacle for the disposal of urine and faeces, usually by means of running water. **2** a room, building, or compartment equipped with this.

**lave** (pronounced layv) verb (literary) wash; flow against.

**lavender** noun **1** a shrub with fragrant purple flowers that are dried and used to scent linen etc. **2** light purple. □ **lavender-water** noun a light perfume made from lavender.

**laver** (lay-ver) noun edible seaweed.

**lavish** (lav-ish) adjective **1** giving or producing something in large quantities. **2** plentiful; a lavish display. ● verb bestow lavishly. □ **lavishly** adverb, **lavishness** noun

**Lavoisier** (lah-vwah-zi-ay), Antoine Laurent (1743-94), French scientist, regarded as the father of modern chemistry.

**law** noun **1** a rule established among a community by authority or custom. **2** a body of such rules. **3** their controlling influence, their operation as providing a remedy against wrongs; law and order. **4** the subject or study of such rules. **5** (the law) (informal) the police. **6** something that must be obeyed; his word was law. **7** a general statement about consistently-occurring natural events; the laws of nature; the law of gravity. □ **go to law** use a lawcourt to resolve a particular issue or dispute. **law-abiding** adjective obeying the law. **Law Lord** a member of the House of Lords qualified to perform its legal work. **a law unto oneself** or **itself** a person or thing that does not behave in the accepted fashion. **take the law into one's own hands** right a wrong oneself without legal sanction.

**lawbreaker** noun a person who breaks the law.

**lawcourt** noun a room or building in which legal cases are heard and judged.

**lawful** adjective permitted or recognized by law; lawful business; his lawful wife. □ **lawfully** adverb

**lawless** adjective **1** (of a country) where laws do not exist or are not applied. **2** disregarding the law, uncontrolled; law-

less hooligans. □ **lawlessly** adverb, **lawlessness** noun

**lawmaker** noun one who makes laws, a legislator.

**lawn** noun **1** an area of closely-cut grass in a garden or park. **2** fine woven cotton or synthetic material. □ **lawn tennis** tennis played with a soft ball on outdoor grass or a hard court.

**lawnmower** noun a machine for cutting lawns.

**Lawrence¹**, D(avid) H(erbert) (1885-1930), English novelist, poet, critic, and painter.

**Lawrence²**, T(homas) E(dward) (1888-1935), English soldier and writer, known as 'Lawrence of Arabia', who helped to organize and lead the Arab revolt against the Turks during the First World War.

**lawrencium** (lă-ren-siŭm) noun a radioactive metallic element (symbol Lw).

**lawsuit** noun the process of bringing a dispute or claim before a court of law for settlement.

**lawyer** noun a person who is trained and qualified in legal matters.

**lax** adjective slack, not strict or severe; discipline was lax. □ **laxly** adverb, **laxity** noun

**laxative** (laks-ă-tiv) noun a medicine that stimulates the bowels to empty. ● adjective having this effect.

**lay¹** noun (old use) a poem meant to be sung, a ballad.

**lay²** adjective **1** not ordained into the clergy. **2** not professionally qualified, especially in law or medicine; lay opinion. □ **lay reader** a lay person licensed to conduct certain religious services.

**lay³** verb (**laid**, **laying**) **1** place on a surface, especially horizontally or in a particular place. **2** put down into the required place; lay a carpet. **3** make by putting down; lay foundations. **4** (of a hen bird) produce (an egg). **5** cause to subside or lie flat. **6** (usually foll. by on) attribute or place; laid the blame on me. **7** prepare (a plan or trap). **8** prepare (a table) for a meal. **9** arrange the materials for (a fire). **10** put down as a bet; stake. **11** (foll. by with) coat or scatter over (a surface). **12** (vulgar slang) have sexual relations with (a person). ● noun **1** the way in which something lies. **2** (vulgar slang) sexual intercourse; a partner in this. □ **lay bare** expose, reveal. **lay claim to** claim as one's right. **lay down 1** put on a flat surface. **2** give up (office). **3** establish as a rule or instruction. **4** store (wine) in a cellar for future use. **5** sacrifice (one's life). **lay down the law** talk authoritatively or as if sure of being right. **lay in** provide oneself with a stock of. **lay into** (informal) thrash; reprimand harshly. **lay it on the line** (*informal*) offer without reserve; speak frankly. **lay it on thick** *or* **with a trowel** (*informal*) exaggerate greatly; flatter a person excessively. **lay low 1** overthrow; humble. **2** incapacitate by illness. **lay off 1** discharge (workers) temporarily owing to shortage of work. **2** (*informal*) cease, especially from causing trouble or annoyance. **lay-off** *noun* a temporary discharge. **lay on 1** provide. **2** inflict blows forcefully. **lay open** expose to criticism. **lay out 1** arrange according to a plan. **2** prepare (a body) for burial. **3** spend (money) for a purpose. **4** knock unconscious. **lay to rest** bury. **lay up 1** store or save. **2** cause to be confined to bed or unfit for work. **lay waste** destroy or ruin (a place or area).

■**Usage** Do not confuse *lay* (= put down; past tense is *laid*) with *lie* (= recline; past tense is *lay*). Correct uses are as follows: *go and lie down; she went and lay down; please lay it on the floor; they laid it on the floor.* Incorrect use is *go and lay down.*

**lay⁴** *see* LIE².

**layabout** *noun* a habitually idle person.

**lay-by** *noun* (*plural* **lay-bys**) an area along the side of a main road where vehicles may stop.

**layer** *noun* **1** a thickness of material (often one of several) covering a surface. **2** a person etc. that lays something. **3** a hen that lays eggs. **4** a shoot of a plant fastened down for propagation by layering. ●*verb* **1** arrange in layers. **2** cut (hair) in layers. **3** propagate (a plant) by fastening down a shoot to take root while still attached to the parent plant.

**layette** *noun* the clothes and bedding etc. prepared for a newborn baby.

**lay figure** a jointed wooden figure of the human body, used by artists for arranging drapery on etc. (¶ From an old Dutch word *led* = joint.)

**layman** *noun* (*plural* **laymen**) a lay person (*see* LAY²).

**layout** *noun* the way in which a thing or place is arranged or set out.

**laze** *verb* **1** spend time idly. **2** (foll. by *away*) pass (time) idly. ●*noun* an act or period of lazing.

**lazy** *adjective* (**lazier, laziest**) **1** unwilling to work; doing little work. **2** showing or characterized by lack of energy; *a lazy yawn.* □ **lazily** *adverb*, **laziness** *noun*

**lazybones** *noun* (*plural* **lazybones**) (*informal*) a lazy person.

**lb** *abbreviation* = pound(s) weight. (¶ From the Latin *libra*.)

**l.b.w.** *abbreviation* leg before wicket.

**LCD** *abbreviation* **1** liquid crystal display. **2** lowest common denominator.

**LCM** *abbreviation* lowest common multiple.

**LEA** *abbreviation* Local Education Authority.

**lea** *noun* (*poetic*) a piece of meadow, pasture, or arable land.

**leach** *verb* make (liquid) percolate through soil or ore etc.; remove (soluble matter) in this way.

**lead¹** (*pronounced* leed) *verb* (**led, leading**) **1** cause to go with oneself; guide, especially by going in front. **2** influence the actions or opinions of; *what led you to believe this?* **3** be a route or means of access; *the door leads into a passage.* **4** have as its result; *this led to confusion.* **5** live or pass (one's life); *he was leading a double life.* **6** be in first place or position in, be ahead; *they lead the world in electronics.* **7** be the leader or head of, control. **8** (foll. by *with* or *on*) (of a newspaper or news programme) have as its main story or feature; *led with the unemployment figures.* **9** (in card games) play as one's first card; be the first player. ●*noun* **1** guidance given by going in front, an example. **2** a clue; *it gave us a lead.* **3** a leading place, leadership; *take the lead.* **4** the amount by which one competitor is in front; *a lead of 5 points.* **5** an electrical cable or wire carrying current to an appliance. **6** a strap or cord etc. for leading and restraining a dog or other animal. **7** the act or right of playing one's card first in a card game; the card played. **8** the chief part in a play or other performance, one who takes this part; *play the lead; the lead singer.* □ **lead by the nose** control the actions of (a person) completely. **lead-in** *noun* an introduction or opening. **lead on** entice. **lead up the garden path** mislead. **lead up to 1** serve as an introduction to or preparation for. **2** direct the conversation towards.

**lead²** (*pronounced* led) *noun* **1** a chemical element (symbol Pb), a heavy soft greyish metal. **2** a thin stick of graphite in a pencil. **3** a lump of lead used in taking soundings in water. **4** (**leads**) strips of lead used to cover a roof. **5** (**leads**) a piece of lead-covered roof. **6** (**leads**) a framework of lead strips holding pieces of glass in a window. □ **lead pencil** a pencil of graphite in wood. **lead-poisoning** *noun* poisoning by absorption of lead into the body.

**leaded** (led-id) *adjective* **1** covered or framed with lead. **2** (especially of petrol) containing lead.

**leaden** (led'n) *adjective* **1** made of lead. **2** heavy, slow as if weighted with lead. **3** lead-coloured, dark grey; *leaden skies.*

**leader** *noun* **1** a person or thing that leads. **2** one who has the principal part in something; the head of a group etc.; (in an orchestra) the principal first-violin player. **3** one whose example is followed; *a leader of fashion*. **4** a leading article in a newspaper. **5** a shoot of a plant growing from the stem or main branch. □ **Leader of the House** a member of the government in the House of Commons or House of Lords who arranges and announces the business of the House.

**leadership** *noun* **1** being a leader. **2** ability to be a leader. **3** the leaders of a group.

**leading¹** (leed-ing) *see* LEAD¹. □ **leading aircraftman** one ranking above aircraftman in the RAF. **leading article** a long article in a newspaper, giving editorial opinions. **leading lady** *or* **man** one taking the chief part in a play etc. **leading light** a prominent member of a group. **leading question** a question that prompts a person to give the desired answer (not the same as a *searching question*).

**leading²** (led-ing) *noun* a covering or framework of lead (metal).

**leaf** *noun* (*plural* **leaves**) **1** a flat organ (usually green) growing from the stem or branch of a plant or directly from the root. **2** the state of having leaves out; *the trees are in leaf*. **3** a single thickness of the paper forming the pages of a book. **4** a very thin sheet of metal; *gold leaf*. **5** a hinged flap of a table; an extra section inserted to extend a table. ●*verb* put forth leaves. □ **leaf-mould** *noun* soil or compost consisting chiefly of decayed leaves. **leaf through** turn over the leaves of a book. **take a leaf out of someone's book** follow his or her example. □ **leafage** *noun*, **leafy** *adjective*, **leafless** *adjective*

**leaflet** *noun* **1** a sheet of paper or pamphlet giving information. **2** a young leaf. **3** a division of a compound leaf. ●*verb* (**leafleted, leafleting**) distribute leaflets to.

**league¹** *noun* **1** a group of people or countries who combine formally for a particular purpose. **2** a group of sports clubs which compete against each other for a championship. **3** a class of contestants; *he is out of his league*. ●*verb* form a league. □ **in league with** allied with; conspiring with. **league table** a table of contestants etc. in order of merit.

**league²** *noun* (*old use*) a measure of distance, usually about 3 miles.

**League of Nations** (*hist.*) an association of countries with the aim of achieving international peace, security, and co-operation, established in 1919 and superseded by the United Nations.

**leak** *noun* **1** a hole or crack etc. through which liquid or gas may accidentally pass in or out. **2** the liquid or gas passing

through this. **3** such an escape of liquid or gas. **4** a similar escape of an electric charge; the charge itself. **5** a disclosure of secret information. ●*verb* **1** (of liquid or gas etc.) escape through an opening. **2** (of a container) allow such an escape, let out (liquid or gas). **3** disclose; *he leaked the news to a reporter*. □ **leak out** (of a secret) become known despite efforts to keep it secret.

**leakage** *noun* **1** leaking. **2** a thing or amount that has leaked out.

**leaky** *adjective* liable to leak.

**Lean,** Sir David (1908–91), British film director.

**lean¹** *adjective* **1** (of a person or animal) without much flesh. **2** (of meat) containing little or no fat. **3** scanty; *a lean harvest*. ●*noun* the lean part of meat. □ **lean years** years of scarcity. □ **leanness** *noun*

**lean²** *verb* (**leaned** or **leant, leaning**) **1** put or be in a sloping position. **2** rest against or on something for support. **3** rely or depend for help. □ **lean on** (*informal*) seek to influence by intimidation. **lean-to** *noun* a building with its roof resting against the side of a larger building.

**leaning** *noun* a tendency or preference; *she has leanings towards socialism*.

**leap** *verb* (**leaped** or **leapt, leaping**) jump vigorously. ●*noun* a vigorous jump. □ **leap in the dark** an uninformed act of daring. **by leaps and bounds** with very rapid progress. **leap year** a year with an extra day (29 February), occurring every four years.

**leap-frog** *noun* a game in which each player in turn vaults with parted legs over another who is bending down. ●*verb* (**leap-frogged, leap-frogging**) **1** perform this vault. **2** overtake alternately.

**Lear,** Edward (1812–88), English artist and poet, noted for his nonsense verses.

**learn** *verb* (**learned** (*pronounced* lernt *or* lernd) or **learnt, learning**) **1** gain knowledge of or skill in (a subject etc.) by study or experience or by being taught. **2** become aware by information or from observation.

**learned** (lern-id) *adjective* **1** having much knowledge acquired by study; *learned men*. **2** of or for learned people; *a learned society*. □ **learnedly** *adverb*

**learner** *noun* a person who is learning a subject or skill. □ **learner driver** one who is learning to drive a motor vehicle but has not yet passed the driving test.

**learning** *noun* knowledge obtained by study.

**lease** *noun* a contract by which the owner of land or a building etc. allows another person to use it for a specified time, usually in return for payment. ●*verb* **1** grant the use of (a property) by lease. **2** obtain or hold (a property) by lease. □ **a new lease of life** a longer and better prospect of life, or of use after repair.

**leasehold** *noun* the holding of land or a house or flat etc. by means of a lease. □ **leaseholder** *noun*

**leash** *noun* a strap for holding a dog etc.; a lead. ● *verb* hold on a leash. □ **straining at the leash** eager to begin something.

**least** *adjective* **1** smallest in amount or degree. **2** lowest in rank or importance. ● *noun* the least amount or degree. ● *adverb* in the least degree. □ **at least 1** not less than what is stated. **2** anyway. **in the least** at all, in the smallest degree. **to say the least** putting the case moderately.

**leather** *noun* **1** material made from animal skins by tanning or a similar process. **2** the leather part(s) of something. **3** a piece of leather for polishing with. **4** (often as **leathers**) leather clothing, especially for motor cyclists. ● *verb* **1** wipe or polish with a leather. **2** cover with leather. **3** thrash. □ **leather-jacket** *noun* a crane-fly grub with a tough skin.

**leatherback** *noun* a large marine turtle with a leathery shell.

**leatherette** (le*th*-er-et) *noun* imitation leather.

**leathery** *adjective* as tough as leather.

**leave**[1] *verb* (**left**, **leaving**) **1** go away from; go away finally or permanently. **2** cease to belong to (a group) or live at (a place); cease working for an employer. **3** cause or allow to remain; *left the door open*; *left my gloves in the bus*. **4** give as a legacy. **5** have remaining after one's death; *he leaves a wife and two children*. **6** allow to stay or proceed without interference; *left him to get on with it*; *leave the dog alone*. **7** refrain from consuming or dealing with; *left all the fat*; *let's leave the washing-up*. **8** entrust or commit to another person; *leave it to me*. **9** deposit for collection, repair, or transmission; *leave a message*. **10** abandon, desert; *was left to clear up the mess*. □ **leave off** cease; cease to wear. **leave out** omit, not include.

**leave**[2] *noun* **1** permission. **2** official permission to be absent from duty; the period for which this lasts. □ **leave-taking** *noun* taking one's leave, departure. **on leave** absent with official permission. **take leave of one's senses** go mad. **take one's leave** say farewell and go away.

**leaven** (lev-ĕn) *noun* **1** a substance (e.g. yeast) that produces fermentation in dough. **2** a quality or influence that lightens or enlivens something. ● *verb* **1** add leaven to. **2** modify by an addition; enliven.

**leavings** *plural noun* what is left.

**Lebanon** (leb-ă-nŏn) a country at the eastern end of the Mediterranean Sea.

□ **Lebanese** *adjective* & *noun* (*plural* **Lebanese**).

**Lebrun** (lĕ-**brern**), Charles (1619–90), French painter, designer, and decorator, responsible for much of the decoration at Versailles.

**Le Carré** (lĕ ka-ray), John (pseudonym of David John Moore Cornwell) (born 1931), English novelist, noted for his thrillers and spy novels.

**lech** *verb* (*informal*) (often foll. by *after*) lust.

**lecher** *noun* a lecherous person.

**lecherous** *adjective* of or characterized by lechery.

**lechery** *noun* unrestrained sexual desire.

**lecithin** (less-i-thin) *noun* a compound found in plant and animal tissue and used as an emulsifier and stabilizer in food products.

**Le Corbusier** (lĕ kor-bew-zi-ay) (real name; Charles Édouard Jeanneret) (1887–1965), French modernist architect.

**lectern** *noun* a stand with a sloping top to hold a Bible in a church or a lecturer's notes etc.

**lecture** *noun* **1** a speech giving information about a subject to an audience or class. **2** a long serious speech, especially one giving reproof or warning. ● *verb* **1** give a lecture or series of lectures. **2** talk to (a person) seriously or reprovingly. □ **lecturer** *noun*

**LED** *abbreviation* light-emitting diode.

**led** *see* LEAD[1].

**Leda** (lee-dă) (*Gk. myth.*) queen of Sparta, loved by Zeus who visited her in the form of a swan.

**lederhosen** (lay-dĕr-hoh-zĕn) *plural noun* leather shorts traditionally worn by men in Bavaria. (¶ German.)

**ledge** *noun* a narrow horizontal projection, a narrow shelf.

**ledger** *noun* a tall narrow book used as an account book or to record transactions.

**Lee**, Robert E(dward) (1807–70), American Confederate general in the American Civil War.

**lee** *noun* shelter, the sheltered side or part of something; *under the lee of the hedge*.

**leech** *noun* **1** a small blood-sucking worm usually living in water. **2** a person who drains the resources of another.

**leek** *noun* a plant related to the onion but with broader leaves and a cylindrical white bulb.

**leer** *verb* look slyly, maliciously, or lustfully. ● *noun* a leering look.

**leery** *adjective* (*slang*) wary, suspicious.

**lees** *plural noun* sediment that settles at the bottom of wine etc.

**leeward** (lee-werd; *in nautical use* loo-erd) *adjective* situated on the side turned away from the wind. ●*noun* the leeward side or region.

**Leeward Islands** (lee-werd) a group of islands in the West Indies, of which the largest are Guadeloupe, Antigua, St Kitts, and Montserrat.

**leeway** *noun* **1** a ship's sideways drift from its course. **2** a degree of freedom of action; *these instructions give us plenty of leeway.*

**left**[1] *see* LEAVE[1]. □ **left luggage** luggage deposited temporarily at a railway station etc.

**left**[2] *adjective & adverb* on or towards the left-hand side. ●*noun* **1** the left-hand side or region. **2** the left hand; a blow with this. **3** (in marching) the left foot. **4** (often **Left**) the left wing of a political party or other group. □ **have two left feet** be extremely clumsy. **left hand** the hand that in most people is less used, on the west side of the body when facing north. **left-hand** *adjective* of or towards this side of a person or the corresponding side of a thing. **left-handed** *adjective* **1** naturally using the left hand for writing etc. **2** (of a blow or tool) made with or operated by the left hand. **3** (of a screw) to be tightened by turning towards the left. **4** (of a compliment) ambiguous in meaning, backhanded. **left-hander** *noun* a left-handed person or blow. **left wing 1** those who support a more extreme form of socialism than others. **2** the left side of a football etc. team on the field.

**leftist** *noun* a supporter of socialism; one who belongs to the left of a socialist group. ●*adjective* of the left wing in politics etc. □ **leftism** *noun*

**leftover** *plural noun* (**leftovers**) food left at the end of a meal. ●*adjective* left at the end of a meal; *leftover food.*

**leftward** *adverb & adjective* towards or facing the left. □ **leftwards** *adverb*

**lefty** *noun* (*informal*) **1** a left-handed person. **2** a left-winger.

**leg** *noun* **1** each of the limbs on which a human or animal stands or walks. **2** the leg of a bird or animal as food. **3** the part of a garment covering a leg. **4** a projecting support beneath a chair, table, etc. **5** a section of a journey. **6** a stage of a competition. **7** (in cricket) the half of the field, when divided lengthways, in which the batsman's feet are placed. □ **give a leg up** help to mount a horse etc., or to get over an obstacle or difficulty. **leg before wicket** (of a batsman in cricket) out because of illegally obstructing the ball. **leg it** (*informal*) **1** walk or run rapidly. **2** go on foot. **leg-pull** *noun* (*informal*) a hoax. **leg-room** *noun* space for the legs of a seated person. **leg warmer** each of a pair of usually knitted garments resembling footless

stockings. **not have a leg to stand on** be unable to explain or justify one's position. **on one's last legs** near death or the end of being useful.

**legacy** (leg-ăsi) *noun* **1** money or an article left to someone in a will. **2** something received from a predecessor or because of earlier events etc.; *a legacy of distrust.*

**legal** *adjective* **1** of or based on law. **2** in accordance with the law; authorized or required by law. □ **legal aid** payment from public funds towards the cost of legal advice or proceedings. **legal tender** officially recognized currency that cannot be refused in payment of a debt. □ **legally** *adverb*, **legality** (lig-al-iti) *noun*

**legalese** *noun* (*informal*) the technical style of language used in legal documents.

**legalistic** *adjective* adhering too closely to laws or rules. □ **legalism** *noun*

**legalize** *verb* (also **legalise**) make legal. □ **legalization** *noun*

**legate** (leg-ăt) *noun* an envoy, especially one representing the Pope.

**legatee** (leg-ă-tee) *noun* a person who receives a legacy.

**legation** (lig-ay-shŏn) *noun* **1** a diplomatic minister and staff. **2** his or her official residence.

**legato** (lig-ah-toh) *adverb* (in music) in a smooth even manner.

**legend** (lej-ĕnd) *noun* **1** a traditional story or myth. **2** a famous or remarkable person or event; *became a rock legend.* **3** an inscription on a coin or medal. **4** an explanation on a map etc. of the symbols used.

**legendary** (lej-ĕn-der-i) *adjective* **1** of or based on legends; described in a legend. **2** famous, often talked about.

**legerdemain** (lej-er-dĕ-mayn) *noun* sleight of hand, conjuring tricks.

**leger line** (lej-er) a short line added in a musical score for notes above or below the range of the stave.

**leggings** *plural noun* **1** close-fitting knitted trousers worn by women and children. **2** protective outer coverings for each leg from knee to ankle.

**leggy** *adjective* **1** having noticeably long legs. **2** (of a plant) long-stemmed and weak.

**leghorn** *noun* **1** fine plaited straw. **2** a hat of this. **3** (**Leghorn**) one of a small hardy breed of domestic fowl.

**legible** (lej-i-bŭl) *adjective* (of print or handwriting) clear enough to read, readable. □ **legibly** *adverb*, **legibility** *noun*

**legion** (lee-jŏn) *noun* **1** a division of the ancient Roman army. ●*adjective* great in number; *such stories are legion.* □ **American Legion** an American association of ex-service men and women. **Foreign Legion** a body of foreign volunteers in the French army. **Legion of Honour** a French order of distinction. **Royal British Legion** a British organization of ex-service men and women.

**legionary** (lee-jŏn-er-i) *adjective* of legions or a legion. ● *noun* a member of a legion.

**legionnaire** (lee-jŏn-**air**) *noun* a member of the Foreign Legion or of the American or Royal British Legion. □ **legionnaires' disease** a form of bacterial pneumonia first identified in an outbreak at a meeting of the American Legion in 1976.

**legislate** (lej-iss-layt) *verb* make laws.

**legislation** (lej-iss-**lay**-shŏn) *noun* **1** legislating. **2** the laws themselves.

**legislative** (lej-iss-lă-tiv) *adjective* making laws; *a legislative assembly*.

**legislator** (lej-iss-layt-er) *noun* a member of a legislative assembly.

**legislature** (lej-iss-lă-cher) *noun* a country's legislative assembly.

**legit** (li-**jit**) *adjective* (*informal*) legitimate.

**legitimate** (li-**jit**-i-măt) *adjective* **1** in accordance with the law or rules. **2** logical, justifiable; *a legitimate reason for absence.* **3** (of a child) born of parents who are married to each other. □ **legitimately** *adverb*, **legitimacy** *noun*

**legitimatize** (li-**jit**-im-ă-tyz) *verb* (also **legitimatise**) legitimize.

**legitimize** (li-**jit**-i-myz) *verb* (also **legitimise**) make legitimate.

**legless** *adjective* **1** without legs. **2** (*slang*) extremely drunk.

**Lego** *noun* (*trade mark*) a toy consisting of interlocking studded plastic bricks.

**legume** (leg-yoom) *noun* **1** a leguminous plant. **2** a fruit or pod of this, especially when edible.

**leguminous** (lig-yoo-min-ŭs) *adjective* of the family of plants that bear their seeds in pods, e.g. peas and beans.

**lei** (*pronounced* lay) *noun* (in Polynesian countries) a garland of flowers worn round the neck.

**Leibniz** (**lyb**-nits), Gottfried Wilhelm (1646–1716), German philosopher and mathematician.

**Leicestershire** a midland county of England.

**Leics.** *abbreviation* Leicestershire.

**Leipzig** (**lyp**-zig) a city in Germany, a centre of the publishing and music trade.

**leisure** (le*zh*-er) *noun* free time. □ **at leisure** not occupied; in an unhurried way. **at one's leisure** when one has time. **leisure centre** a public building containing sports and recreational facilities.

**leisured** *adjective* having plenty of leisure.

**leisurely** (le*zh*-er-li) *adjective & adverb* unhurried, relaxed. □ **leisureliness** *noun*

**leisurewear** *noun* casual clothing, especially sportswear.

**leitmotif** (lyt-moh-teef) *noun* (also **leitmotiv**) a theme associated with a particular person or idea etc. throughout a musical, literary, or cinematic work.

**lemming** *noun* a small rodent of Arctic regions, one species of which migrates in large numbers and is said to rush into the sea and drown.

**lemon** *noun* **1** a yellow oval citrus fruit with acidic juice. **2** the tree that bears it. **3** its pale yellow colour. **4** (*slang*) a person or thing regarded as a failure. □ **lemon cheese** *or* **curd** a thick creamy-textured jam made with lemons. **lemon sole** a kind of plaice. □ **lemony** *adjective*

**lemonade** *noun* a lemon-flavoured soft drink.

**lemur** (lee-mer) *noun* a monkey-like animal of Madagascar.

**lend** *verb* (**lent, lending**) **1** give or allow the use of (a thing) temporarily on the understanding that it or its equivalent will be returned. **2** provide (money) temporarily in return for payment of interest. **3** contribute as a temporary help or effect etc.; *lend dignity to the occasion.* □ **lend a hand** help. **lend an ear** listen. **lend itself to** be suitable for. □ **lender** *noun*

**Lendl**, Ivan (born 1960), American tennis-player, born in Czechoslovakia.

**length** *noun* **1** measurement or extent from end to end. **2** the amount of time occupied by something; *the length of our holiday.* **3** the distance a thing extends, used as a unit of measurement; the length of a horse or boat etc. as a measure of the lead in a race. **4** the degree of thoroughness in an action; *went to great lengths.* **5** a piece of cloth or other material from a larger piece; *a length of wire.* □ **at length 1** after a long time. **2** taking a long time. **3** in detail.

**lengthen** *verb* make or become longer.

**lengthways** *adverb & adjective* (also **lengthwise**) in the direction of the length of something.

**lengthy** *adjective* (**lengthier, lengthiest**) very long; long and boring. □ **lengthily** *adverb*, **lengthiness** *noun*

**lenient** (lee-ni-ĕnt) *adjective* merciful, not severe (especially in awarding punishment); mild. □ **leniently** *adverb*, **lenience** *noun*

**Lenin** (original name: Vladimir Ilyich Ulyanov) (1870–1924), Russian revolutionary statesman, Premier and virtual dictator of the Communist State which he established after the fall of the Tsar.

**Leningrad** a city of the former USSR on the Gulf of Finland, the Russian capital under the name St. Petersburg until 1918, recently renamed St. Petersburg.

**Lennon**, John (1940–80), English singer, guitarist, and songwriter, a member of the Beatles.

**Le Nôtre** (lĕ **nohtr**), André (1613–1700), French landscape gardener, whose greatest achievement was the gardens at Versailles.

**lens** noun (plural **lenses**) **1** a piece of glass or glass-like substance with one or both sides curved, for use in optical instruments. **2** a combination of lenses used in photography etc. **3** the transparent part of the eye, behind the iris.

**Lent** noun the period from Ash Wednesday to Easter Eve, of which the 40 weekdays are observed as a time of fasting and penitence. □ **Lenten** adjective

**lent** see LEND.

**lentil** noun **1** a kind of bean plant. **2** its edible seed; lentil soup.

**lento** adjective & adverb (in music) slow or slowly.

**Leo** (lee-oh) noun the fifth sign of the zodiac, the Lion.

**Leonardo da Vinci** (li-ŏ-**nar**-doh dah **vin**-chi) (1452–1519), Italian painter and designer, whose most famous paintings include the Last Supper fresco and the Mona Lisa.

**leonine** (lee-ŏ-nyn) adjective of or like a lion.

**leopard** (lep-erd) noun a large African and South Asian flesh-eating animal of the cat family (also called a panther), having a yellowish coat with dark spots or a black coat.

**leopardess** noun a female leopard.

**leotard** (lee-ŏ-tard) noun a close-fitting one-piece garment worn by dancers, gymnasts, etc.

**leper** noun **1** a person with leprosy. **2** a person who is shunned; an outcast; social leper.

**lepidopterous** (lep-i-**dop**-ter-ŭs) adjective of the group of insects that includes moths and butterflies. □ **lepidopterist** noun

**leprechaun** (lep-rĕ-kawn) noun (in Irish folklore) an elf resembling a little old man.

**leprosy** noun an infectious disease affecting skin and nerves, causing disfigurement and deformities. □ **leprous** adjective

**lesbian** noun a homosexual woman. ●adjective of lesbians; of homosexuality in women. □ **lesbianism** noun

**Lesbos** (lez-boss) the largest of the Greek islands, off the western coast of Turkey.

**lese-majesty** (pronounced leez) noun **1** an insult to a sovereign or ruler; treason. **2** (humorous) presumptuous behaviour.

**lesion** (lee-zhŏn) noun a physical change in the tissue or an organ of the body, caused by injury or disease.

**Lesotho** (lĕ-**soo**-too) a country surrounded by the Republic of South Africa.

**less** adjective **1** not so much, a smaller quantity; eat less meat. **2** smaller in amount or degree etc.; of less importance. ●adverb to a smaller extent. ●noun a smaller amount or quantity etc.; will not take less. ●preposition minus, deducting; a year less three days; was paid £100, less tax.

■**Usage** The word less is used of things that are measured by amount (e.g. in eat less butter; use less fuel). Its use of things measured by number is often regarded as incorrect (e.g. in we need less workers; correct usage is fewer workers).

**lessee** (less-ee) noun a person who holds a property by lease.

**lessen** verb make or become less.

**lesser** adjective not so great as the other; the lesser evil.

**Lessing**, Doris May (born 1919), English novelist and short-story writer.

**lesson** noun **1** a thing to be learnt by a pupil. **2** an amount of teaching given at one time; give lessons in French. **3** an example or experience by which one can learn; let this be a lesson to you! **4** a passage from the Bible read aloud during a church service.

**lessor** (less-or) noun a person who lets a property on lease.

**lest** conjunction **1** in order not to, to avoid the risk that; lest we forget. **2** that; were afraid lest we should be late.

**let¹** noun **1** stoppage; without let or hindrance. **2** (in tennis etc.) an obstruction of a ball or player, requiring the ball to be served again.

**let²** verb (**let**, **letting**) **1** allow to, not prevent or forbid; let me see it. **2** cause to; let us know what happens. **3** allow or cause to pass in, out, up, etc.; let the dog in; let the rope down. **4** allow the use of (rooms or land) for payment; house to let. **5** used as an auxiliary verb in requests or commands (let's try; let us pray), assumptions (let x equal 7), and challenges (let him do his worst). ●noun the letting of property etc.; a long let. □ **let alone 1** leave; refrain from interfering with or doing. **2** never mind; we can't afford one, let alone three; I'm too tired to walk, let alone run. **let be** leave; refrain from interfering with or doing. **let down 1** let out air from (a balloon or tyre etc.). **2** fail to support or satisfy, disappoint. **3** lengthen (a garment) by adjusting the hem. **let-down** noun a disappointment. **let fly** release or emit violently; let fly a punch; let fly a stream of abuse. **let go 1** set at liberty; loose one's hold of. **2** cease discussion of, ignore. **let oneself go 1** behave freely or spontaneously. **2** neglect one's usual standards of appearance, hygiene, etc. **let in for** involve in (loss or difficulty). **let loose** release. **let off 1** fire (a gun); cause (a bomb) to explode; ignite (a firework). **2** excuse from doing (duties etc.); give little or no punishment to. **let off steam** release one's pent-up energy or feelings. **let on** (*informal*) reveal a secret. **let one's hair down** abandon conventional restraint in one's behaviour. **let out 1** release from restraint or obligation. **2** make (a garment) looser by adjusting the seams. **3** let (rooms etc.) to tenants. **let-out** *noun* a way of escaping an obligation. **let slip 1** reveal (a secret) accidentally. **2** miss (an opportunity). **let up** (*informal*) become less intense; relax one's efforts. **let-up** *noun* a reduction in intensity; relaxation of effort.

**lethal** (lee-thăl) *adjective* causing or able to cause death. □ **lethally** *adverb*

**lethargy** (leth-er-ji) *noun* extreme lack of energy or vitality. □ **lethargic** (lith-ar-jik) *adjective*, **lethargically** *adverb*

**let's** (*informal*) = let us.

**letter** *noun* **1** a symbol representing a sound used in speech. **2** a written or printed message, usually sent by post. ●*verb* inscribe letters on; draw or inscribe letters. □ **letter bomb** a terrorist explosive device in the form of a postal packet. **letter box 1** a slit in a door, with a movable flap, through which letters are delivered. **2** a postbox. **letter of credit** a letter from a bank authorizing the bearer to draw money from another bank. **letter of the law** the law's exact requirements (as opposed to its spirit or true purpose). **man** (*or* **woman**) **of letters** a scholar or author. **to the letter** paying strict attention to every detail.

**lettered** *adjective* well-read, well-educated.

**letterhead** *noun* a printed heading on stationery; stationery with this.

**letterpress** *noun* **1** the printed words in an illustrated book. **2** printing from raised type.

**lettuce** *noun* a plant with broad crisp leaves used in salads.

**leucocyte** (lew-kŏ-syt) *noun* a white blood cell.

**leukaemia** (lew-kee-miă) *noun* (*Amer.* **leukemia**) a disease in which the white blood cells multiply uncontrollably.

**Levant** (li-vant) *noun* the countries and islands in the eastern part of the Mediterranean Sea. □ **Levantine** (lev-ăn-tyn) *adjective & noun*

**levee** (lev-i) *noun* (*Amer.*) an embankment put up to prevent a river flooding, or one built up by the river itself.

**level** *noun* **1** a horizontal line or plane joining points of equal height. **2** a measured height or value etc., position on a scale; *the level of alcohol in the blood*. **3** relative position in rank or class or authority; *decisions at Cabinet level*. **4** a flat surface, layer, or area. **5** an instrument for testing a horizontal line. ●*adjective* **1** horizontal. **2** (of ground)

flat, without hills or hollows. **3** on a level with; at the same height, rank, or position on a scale. **4** steady, uniform, (of a voice) not changing in tone. ●*verb* (**levelled**, **levelling**; *Amer.* **leveled**, **leveling**) **1** (also foll. by *out*) make or become level, even, or uniform. **2** flatten (an area or its buildings) by demolition; raze. **3** aim (a gun or missile). **4** direct (an accusation or criticism) at a person. □ **do one's level best** (*informal*) make all possible efforts. **level crossing** a place where a road and a railway (or two railways) cross each other. **level-headed** *adjective* mentally well-balanced, sensible. **level pegging** equal scores or achievements. **on the level** (*informal*) with no dishonesty or deception.

**leveller** *noun* (*Amer.* **leveler**) **1** something that removes social distinctions; *unemployment is a great leveller*. **2** a person or thing that levels.

**lever** (lee-ver) *noun* **1** a bar or other device pivoted on a fulcrum or fixed point in order to lift something or force something open. **2** a projecting handle used to operate machinery etc. ●*verb* use a lever; lift or move by means of this.

**leverage** *noun* **1** the action or power of a lever. **2** power, influence.

**leveret** (lev-er-it) *noun* a young hare.

**leviathan** (li-vy-ăth-ăn) *noun* something of enormous size and power. (¶ Named after a sea monster in the Bible.)

**Levis** (lee-vyz) *plural noun* (*trade mark*) denim jeans.

**levitate** *verb* rise or cause to rise and float in the air in defiance of gravity. □ **levitation** *noun*

**Leviticus** (li-vit-i-kŭs) the third book of the Old Testament, containing details of laws and ritual.

**levity** (lev-iti) *noun* a humorous attitude, especially towards matters that should be treated with respect.

**levy** *verb* (**levied**, **levying**) **1** impose or collect (a payment etc.) by authority or by force. **2** enrol (troops etc.). **3** wage (war). ●*noun* **1** levying. **2** the payment etc. levied. **3** (**levies**) troops enrolled.

**lewd** *adjective* **1** indecent, treating sexual matters in a vulgar way. **2** lascivious. □ **lewdly** *adverb*, **lewdness** *noun*

**Lewis**[1], Carl (Frederick Carleton) (born 1961), American track and field athlete.

**Lewis**[2], C(live) S(taples) (1898–1963), English literary scholar, whose writings include Christian and moral themes and science fiction.

**Lewis**[3], (Harry) Sinclair (1885–1951), American novelist, the first American writer to win a Nobel Prize for literature.

**lexical** *adjective* **1** of the words of a language. **2** of a lexicon or dictionary.

**lexicography** (leksi-**kog**-răfi) *noun* the process of compiling dictionaries. □ **lexicographer** *noun*, **lexicographical** *adjective*

**lexicology** (leksi-**kol**-ŏji) *noun* the study of words and their form, history, and meaning. □ **lexicologist** *noun*

**lexicon** *noun* **1** a dictionary, especially of certain ancient languages such as Greek and Hebrew. **2** the vocabulary of a person, language, branch of knowledge, etc.

**lexis** *noun* words, vocabulary; a total stock of words.

**ley** (*pronounced* lay) *noun* (*plural* **leys**) land that is temporarily sown with grass.

**Leyden jar** (**ly**-děn) a kind of electrical condenser with a glass jar as a dielectric between sheets of tin foil, invented in 1745 at Leyden (now Leiden) in Holland.

**LF** *abbreviation* low frequency.

**l.h.** *abbreviation* left hand.

**Lhasa** (lah-să) the capital of Tibet.

**Li** *symbol* lithium.

**liability** *noun* **1** being liable. **2** a handicap, a disadvantage. **3** (**liabilities**) debts, obligations.

**liable** (**ly**-ăbŭl) *adjective* **1** held responsible by law; legally obliged to pay a tax or penalty. **2** able or likely (to do or suffer something); *the cliff is liable to crumble*; *she is liable to colds.*

**liaise** (lee-ayz) *verb* (often foll. by *with*) act as a link or go-between.

**liaison** (lee-ay-zŏn) *noun* **1** communication and cooperation between units of an organization. **2** an illicit sexual relationship.

**liana** (lee-**ar**-nă) *noun* a thick vine found in tropical forests.

**liar** *noun* a person who tells lies.

**lib** *noun* (*informal*) (in names of political movements) liberation; *Women's Lib.*

**Lib.** *abbreviation* Liberal.

**libation** *noun* (*literary*) **1** a drink poured out in offering to a god. **2** the pouring out of this.

**libel** (**ly**-běl) *noun* **1** a published false statement that damages a person's reputation. **2** the act of publishing it; *was charged with libel.* **3** a statement or anything that brings discredit on a person or thing, *the programme is a libel on him.* ● *verb* (**libelled**, **libelling**; *Amer.* **libeled**, **libeling**) utter or publish a libel against. □ **libellous** *adjective*

**liberal** *adjective* **1** giving generously. **2** ample, given in large amounts. **3** not strict or literal; *a liberal interpretation of the rules.* **4** (of education) broadening the mind in a general way rather than training it in technical subjects. **5** tolerant, openminded, especially in religion and politics. **6** (**Liberal**) of the Liberal Party. ● *noun* **1** a person who

is tolerant or open-minded, especially in religion and politics. **2** (**Liberal**) a member of the Liberal Party. □ **Liberal Democrat** (*Brit.*) a member of a party formed from the Liberal Party and members of the Social Democratic Party, formerly known as the Social and Liberal Democrats. **Liberal Party 1** a political party advocating liberal policies. **2** a British political party, formerly the Whig Party, advocating a mild form of socialism. It is now part of the Liberal Democrat party. **Liberal** *noun* a member of the **Liberal Party**, a political party more socialist than the Conservative Party but less so than the Labour Party. **Liberal Democrat** a member of a UK political party formerly called the Social and Liberal Democrats. □ **liberalism** *noun.*

**liberalize** *verb* (also **liberalise**) make less strict. □ **liberalization** *noun*

**liberate** *verb* set free, especially from oppressive authority. □ **liberation** *noun*, **liberator** *noun*

**Liberia** (ly-**beer**-iă) a country on the coast of West Africa. □ **Liberian** *adjective* & *noun*

**libertarian** (lib-er-**tair**-iăn) *noun* a person who favours absolute liberty of thought and action. □ **libertarianism** *noun*

**libertine** (**lib**-er-teen) *noun* a person who lives an irresponsible and immoral life.

**liberty** *noun* **1** freedom from captivity, slavery, imprisonment, or oppression. **2** the right or power to do as one chooses. **3** a right or privilege granted by authority. **4** the setting aside of convention, improper familiarity. □ **at liberty 1** (of a person) not imprisoned, free. **2** allowed; *you are at liberty to leave.* **Statue of Liberty** the statue at the entrance to New York harbour. **take liberties** behave too familiarly towards a person.

**libidinous** (li-**bid**-in-ŭs) *adjective* lustful.

**libido** (lib-**ee**-doh) *noun* (*plural* **libidos**) emotional energies and urges, especially those associated with sexual desire. □ **libidinal** *adjective*

**Libra** (**lib**-ră) *noun* the seventh sign of the zodiac, the Scales. □ **Libran** *adjective* & *noun*

**librarian** *noun* a person in charge of or assisting in a library. □ **librarianship** *noun*

**library** (**ly**-bră-ri) *noun* **1** a collection of books for reading or borrowing. **2** a room or building where these are kept. **3** a similar collection of records, films, computer programs, etc. **4** a series of books issued in similar bindings as a set.

**libretto** (lib-**ret**-oh) *noun* (*plural* **librettos** or **libretti**) the words of an opera or other long musical work. □ **librettist** *noun*

**Libreville** (**leeb**-rě-vil) the capital of Gabon.

**Libya** a country in North Africa, bordering on the Mediterranean Sea. □ **Libyan** *adjective & noun*

**lice** *see* LOUSE.

**licence** *noun* (*Amer.* **license**) **1** an official permit to own or do something or to carry on a trade. **2** permission. **3** disregard of rules or customs etc.; lack of due restraint in behaviour. **4** a writer's or artist's exaggeration, or disregard of rules etc., for the sake of effect; *poetic licence*.

**license** *verb* **1** grant a licence to or for, authorize; *licensed to sell tobacco*. **2** *Amer.* spelling of LICENCE.

**licensee** *noun* a person who holds a licence, especially to sell alcoholic drinks.

**licentiate** (ly-sen-shi-ăt) *noun* one who holds a certificate showing that he or she is competent to practise a certain profession; *Licentiate in Dental Surgery*.

**licentious** (ly-sen-shŭs) *adjective* disregarding the rules of conduct, especially in sexual matters. □ **licentiousness** *noun*

**lichee** alternative spelling of LYCHEE.

**lichen** (ly-kĕn *or* lich-ĕn) *noun* a small slow-growing plant found on rocks, tree trunks, etc., usually green, grey, or yellow in colour. □ **lichenous** *adjective*

**lich-gate** *noun* (also **lych-gate**) a roofed gateway to a churchyard.

**licit** (lis-it) *adjective* (*formal*) allowed, not forbidden. □ **licitly** *adverb*

**lick** *verb* **1** pass the tongue over; take up or make clean by doing this. **2** (of waves or flames) move like a tongue, touch lightly. **3** (*informal*) defeat. ● *noun* **1** an act of licking with the tongue. **2** a blow with a stick etc. **3** a slight application (of paint etc.). **4** (*informal*) a fast pace; *we were going at quite a lick*. □ **lick a person's boots** be servile towards him or her. **lick into shape** make presentable or efficient. **lick one's lips** look forward eagerly. **lick one's wounds** remain in hiding, recovering after a defeat.

**licking** *noun* (*informal*) **1** a defeat. **2** a thrashing.

**licorice** alternative spelling of LIQUORICE.

**lid** *noun* **1** a hinged or removable cover for a box or pot etc. **2** an eyelid. □ **put the lid on** (*informal*) **1** form a climax to. **2** put a stop to. □ **lidded** *adjective*

**lido** (lee-doh) *noun* (*plural* **lidos**) a public open-air swimming pool or pleasure beach.

**lie¹** *noun* **1** a statement that the speaker knows to be untrue; *tell a lie*. **2** a thing that deceives. ● *verb* (**lied, lying**) **1** tell a lie or lies. **2** be deceptive. □ **give the lie to** show that (something) is untrue. **lie-detector** *noun* an instrument that can supposedly show whether a person is lying by testing for physical changes caused by tension.

**lie²** *verb* (**lay, lain, lying**) **1** be in or adopt a horizontal position on a surface; be at rest on something. **2** (of a thing) rest flat on a surface. **3** exist, be kept, or remain in a specified state; *machinery lay idle*. **4** be situated; *the island lies near the coast*. **5** exist or be found; *the remedy lies in education*. **6** (in law) be admissible or able to be upheld; *the appeal will not lie*. ● *noun* the way or position in which something lies. □ **how the land lies** what the situation is. **it lies with you** it is your business or right. **lie down** have a brief rest in or on a bed etc. **lie-down** *noun* such a rest. **lie in** (*informal*) stay in bed late in the morning. **lie-in** *noun* such a stay. **lie in state** be displayed in a public place of honour before burial or cremation. **lie low** conceal oneself or one's intentions. **take lying down** accept (an insult etc.) without protest.

■**Usage** See the note on LAY³.

**Liebfraumilch** (leeb-frow-milk) *noun* a light white wine from the Rhine region of Germany.

**Liechtenstein** (lik-tĕn-styn) a small country between Austria and Switzerland. □ **Liechtensteiner** *noun*

**lied** (*pronounced* leed) *noun* (*plural* **lieder**) a German song, especially of the Romantic period and usually for solo voice and piano.

**lief** (*pronounced* leef) *adverb* (*old use*) gladly, willingly; *I would as lief stay as go*.

**liege** (*pronounced* leej) *noun* (*hist.*) (also **liege lord**) one's feudal superior; one's king.

**lien** (*pronounced* leen) *noun* *Law* the right to hold another person's property until a debt on it (e.g. for repair) is paid.

**lieu** (*pronounced* lew) *noun* □ **in lieu** instead, in place; *accepted a cheque in lieu of cash*.

**lieutenant** (lef-ten-ănt) *noun* **1** an army officer next below a captain. **2** a navy officer next below a lieutenant commander. **3** an officer ranking just below one specified; *lieutenant colonel*; *lieutenant commander*. **4** a deputy, a chief assistant. □ **lieutenancy** *noun*

**life** *noun* (*plural* **lives**) **1** the capacity for activity, growth, and change in animals and plants that ends at death. **2** living things; *plant life*; *is there life on Mars?* **3** a living form or mode; *portrait is drawn from life*. **4** liveliness, interest; *full of life*. **5** the period for which a person or organism is, has been, or will be alive; *all my life*. **6** this state of existence; *lost their lives*. **7** (*informal*) a life sentence. **8** a person's or people's activities, fortunes, or manner of existence; *in private life*; *village life*. **9** the activities and pleasures of the world; *we do see life!* **10** a biography. **11** a period during which something exists or continues to function;

*the battery has a life of two years.* □ **for life** for the rest of one's life. **for one's life** *or* **for dear life** as if or in order to escape death. **life assurance** = LIFE INSURANCE. **life cycle** the series of changes that characterize the life of an organism or thing. **Life Guards** (*Brit.*) a regiment of the royal household cavalry. **life insurance** insurance for a sum of money to be paid after a set period or on the death of the insured person if earlier. **life-jacket** *noun* a jacket of buoyant or inflatable material to keep a person afloat in water. **life peer** a peer whose title lapses on death and cannot be inherited. **life-preserver** *noun* **1** a short stick with a weighted end, used for self-defence. **2** a lifebelt or life-jacket. **life sciences** biology and related subjects. **life-size, life-sized** *adjective* of the same size as the person or thing represented. **life-support** *adjective* (of equipment) providing and maintaining suitable conditions for life in unnatural circumstances, e.g. severe illness, space travel, etc. **matter of life and death** an event or decision etc. of vital importance. **not on your life** (*informal*) most certainly not.

**lifebelt** *noun* a belt of buoyant or inflatable material to keep a person afloat in water.

**lifeblood** *noun* **1** blood, as necessary for staying alive. **2** a vital factor or influence.

**lifeboat** *noun* **1** a small boat carried on a ship for use if the ship has to be abandoned at sea. **2** a boat specially constructed for going to the help of people in danger at sea along a coast.

**lifebuoy** *noun* a buoyant device to keep a person afloat.

**lifeguard** *noun* an expert swimmer employed to prevent or rescue bathers from drowning.

**lifeless** *adjective* **1** without life, dead or never having had life. **2** unconscious. **3** lacking vitality. □ **lifelessly** *adverb*, **lifelessness** *noun*

**lifelike** *adjective* exactly like a real person or thing.

**lifeline** *noun* **1** a rope etc. used in rescuing people, e.g. one attached to a lifebelt. **2** a diver's signalling-line. **3** a sole means of communication or transport.

**lifelong** *adjective* continued all one's life.

**lifer** *noun* (*slang*) a person sentenced to life imprisonment.

**lifestyle** *noun* the way of life of a particular person or group.

**lifetime** *noun* the duration of a person's life or of a thing's existence.

**lift** *verb* **1** raise to a higher level or position. **2** take up from the ground or from its resting-place. **3** dig up (e.g. potatoes etc. at harvest, or plants for storing). **4** (*informal*) steal; copy from another source. **5** (of fog etc.) disperse. **6** remove or abolish (restrictions). ●*noun* **1** lifting; being lifted. **2** a ride as a passenger without payment. **3** an apparatus for transporting people or goods from one floor of a building to another. **4** a ski-lift or chair-lift. **5** the upward pressure that air exerts on an aircraft in flight. **6** a feeling of elation; *the praise gave me a lift.* □ **lift-off** *noun* the vertical take-off of a rocket or spacecraft.

**ligament** *noun* a piece of the tough flexible tissue that holds bones together or keeps organs in place in the body.

**ligature** (lig-ă-cher) *noun* **1** a thing used in tying, especially in surgical operations. **2** a tie in music. **3** joined printed letters such as œ. ●*verb* tie with a ligature.

**light**[1] *noun* **1** the energy that stimulates the sense of sight and makes things visible. **2** the presence, amount, or effect of this. **3** a source of light, especially an electric lamp; *leave the light on.* **4** (often as **lights**) a traffic light. **5** a flame or spark; something used to produce this. **6** the bright parts of a picture etc. **7** mental or spiritual insight. **8** the way something or someone is regarded; *sees the matter in a different light.* **9** a window or opening to admit light. ●*adjective* **1** full of light, not in darkness. **2** pale; *light blue.* ●*verb* (**lit**, *or* **lighted, lighting**) **1** set burning; begin to burn. **2** cause to give out light. **3** provide with light; guide with a light. **4** brighten. □ **bring** *or* **come to light** reveal or be revealed, make or become known. **in the light of** taking into account. **light bulb** a glass bulb containing a gas and a metal filament, providing light when an electric current is passed through it. **light meter** an exposure meter. **light pen** a pen-shaped device for drawing on or highlighting parts of a computer screen. **light up 1** put lights on at dusk. **2** make or become bright with light or colour. **3** (of a person's face or eyes) suddenly become animated, shine. **4** begin to smoke a cigarette or pipe. **light year** the distance light travels in one year (about 6 million million miles).

**light**[2] *adjective* **1** having little weight, not heavy; easy to lift, carry, or move. **2** of less than average weight, amount, or force; *light rain.* **3** (of work) needing little physical effort. **4** carrying or suitable for carrying small loads; *light aircraft.* **5** (of sleep or a sleeper) easily disturbed. **6** (of food) easy to digest. **7** moving easily and quickly. **8** cheerful, free from worry; *with a light heart.* **9** not profound or serious, intended as entertainment; *light music.* ●*adverb* lightly, with little load; *we travel light.* ●*verb* (**lit** *or* **lighted, lighting**) (foll. by *on* or *upon*) find accidentally; *we lit on this book.*

□ **light-fingered** adjective apt to steal. **light flyweight** an amateur boxing weight up to 48 kg. **light-footed** adjective nimble. **light-headed** adjective feeling slightly faint, dizzy; delirious. **light-hearted** adjective **1** cheerful, without cares. **2** too casual, not treating a thing seriously. **light heavyweight** a weight in certain sports between middleweight and heavyweight, in amateur boxing 75–81 kg. **light industry** industry producing small or light articles. **light middleweight** an amateur boxing weight of 67–71 kg. **make light of** treat as unimportant. **light welterweight** an amateur boxing weight of 60–63.5 kg. □ **lightish** adjective, **lightly** adverb, **lightness** noun

**lighten**[1] verb **1** shed light on. **2** make or become brighter. **3** produce lightning.

**lighten**[2] verb **1** make or become lighter in weight. **2** relieve or be relieved of care or worry. **3** reduce (a penalty).

**lighter**[1] noun a device for lighting cigarettes etc.

**lighter**[2] noun a flat-bottomed boat used in a harbour for loading and unloading ships and transporting goods.

**lighthouse** noun a tower or other structure containing a beacon light to warn or guide ships.

**lighting** noun equipment for providing light to a room or building or street etc.; the light itself. □ **lighting-up time** the time after which vehicles must have their lights on.

**lightning** noun a flash of bright light produced by natural electricity, between clouds or a cloud and the ground. ● adverb very quick; *with lightning speed.* □ **lightning-conductor** noun (also **lightning-rod**) a metal rod or wire fixed to an exposed part of a building etc., to divert lightning into the earth.

**lights** plural noun the lungs of sheep, pigs, etc., used as food for animals.

**lightship** noun a moored or anchored ship with a beacon light, serving the same purpose as a lighthouse.

**lightweight** noun **1** a person of less than average weight. **2** a boxing weight (57–60 kg) between welterweight and featherweight. **3** a person of little influence. ● adjective not having great weight or influence.

**ligneous** (**lig**-ni-ŭs) adjective **1** like wood. **2** (of plants) woody.

**lignite** (**lig**-nyt) noun a brown coal of woody texture.

**lignum vitae** (**lig**-nŭm vy-tee) a kind of tree with hard wood.

**Liguria** (lig-yoor-iă) a region of NW Italy. □ **Ligurian Sea** the part of the Mediterranean Sea between Corsica and NW Italy.

**like**[1] adjective **1** having some or all the qualities or appearance etc. of, similar. **2** characteristic of; *it was just like him to do that.* **3** in a suitable state or the right mood for something; *it looks like rain; we felt like a walk.* **4** such as, for example; *in subjects like music.* ● preposition in the manner of, to the same degree as; *he swims like a fish.* ● conjunction **1** in the same manner as, to the same degree as; *do it like I do.* **2** as if; *she doesn't act like she belongs here.* ● adverb (informal) likely; *as like as not they'll refuse.* ● noun one that is like another, a similar thing; *shall not see his like again.* □ **and the like** and similar things. **like-minded** adjective having similar tastes or opinions. **the likes of** (informal) people like; *we don't want the likes of you here.*

**like**[2] verb **1** find pleasant or satisfactory. **2** wish for; *should like to think it over.* ● plural noun (**likes**) the things one likes or prefers.

**likeable** adjective (also **likable**) pleasant, easy for a person to like.

**likelihood** noun being likely, probability.

**likely** adjective (**likelier**, **likeliest**) **1** such as may reasonably be expected to occur or be true etc.; *he is likely to be late; rain is likely.* **2** seeming to be suitable; *the likeliest place.* **3** showing promise of being successful; *a likely lad.* ● adverb probably. □ **not likely!** (informal) certainly not. □ **likeliness** noun

**liken** verb point out the resemblance of (one thing to another); *he likened the heart to a pump.*

**likeness** noun **1** being like, a resemblance. **2** a copy, portrait, or picture.

**likewise** adverb **1** moreover, also. **2** similarly; *do likewise.*

**liking** noun **1** what one likes, one's taste; *is it to your liking?* **2** (foll. by *for*) a fondness, a taste; *a liking for it.*

**lilac** noun **1** a shrub with fragrant purplish or white flowers. **2** pale purple. ● adjective lilac-coloured.

**liliaceous** (lil-i-ay-shŭs) adjective lily-like; of the lily family.

**Lillee**, Dennis Keith (born 1949), Australian fast bowler.

**lilliputian** (lili-pew-shăn) adjective very small. ● noun a very small person or thing. (¶ Named after the inhabitants of Lilliput, a country in Swift's *Gulliver's Travels*, who were only six inches tall.)

**Lilo** noun (plural **Lilos**) (trade mark) a type of inflatable plastic mattress.

**Lilongwe** (li-**long**-way) the capital of Malawi.

**lilt** noun a light pleasant rhythm; a song or tune having this.

**lilting** adjective having a light pleasant rhythm.

**lily** noun 1 a plant growing from a bulb, with large white or reddish flowers. 2 a plant of this family. □ **lily-livered** adjective cowardly. **lily of the valley** a spring flower with small fragrant white bell-shaped flowers. **lily white** adjective as white as a lily.

**Lima** (lee-mǎ) the capital of Peru.

**limb** noun 1 an arm, leg, or wing. 2 a main branch of a tree. 3 an arm of a cross. □ **out on a limb** isolated, stranded.

**limber¹** adjective flexible, agile. ●verb make limber. □ **limber up** exercise in preparation for athletic activity.

**limber²** noun the detachable front part of a gun carriage. ●verb attach a limber to.

**limbo¹** noun (plural **limbos**) (in medieval Christian theology) the supposed abode of those unbaptized souls not admitted to heaven but not condemned to punishment. 2 an intermediate state or condition (e.g. awaiting a decision), a condition of being neglected or forgotten.

**limbo²** noun (plural **limbos**) a West Indian dance in which the dancer bends backwards to pass under a horizontal bar which is progressively lowered.

**lime¹** noun a white substance (calcium oxide) used in making cement and as a fertilizer. ●verb treat with lime.

**lime²** noun 1 a round green fruit like a lemon but smaller and more acid. 2 (also **lime-green**) its colour.

**lime³** noun (in full **lime tree**) a tree with smooth heart-shaped leaves and fragrant yellow flowers, a linden.

**limelight** noun (**the limelight**) intense publicity. (¶ Named after the brilliant light, obtained by heating lime, formerly used to illuminate the stages of theatres.)

**limerick** noun a type of humorous five-line poem. (¶ Named after *Limerick*, a town in Ireland.)

**limestone** noun a kind of rock (mainly calcium carbonate) from which lime is obtained by heating.

**Limey** noun (plural **Limeys**) (*Amer. slang*) a British person (originally a sailor) or ship. (¶ Named after *lime juice*, which was formerly issued to British sailors as a drink to prevent scurvy.)

**limit** noun 1 the point, line, or level beyond which something does not continue. 2 the greatest amount allowed; *the speed limit*. ●verb 1 set or act as a limit to. 2 (foll. by *to*) restrict to a specified amount; *I'm limited to two drinks*. □ **be the limit** (*informal*) be intolerable.

**limitation** noun 1 limiting; being limited. 2 a limit (of ability etc.); *knows his limitations*.

**limited** adjective 1 confined within limits. 2 few, scanty. 3 (after the name of a company) limited company. □ **limited edition**

a production of a limited number of copies.

**limited company** (also **limited liability company**) a company whose members are liable for its debts only to a specified extent.

**limo** noun (plural **limos**) (*informal*) a limousine.

**limousine** (lim-ŏ-zeen) noun a large luxurious car.

**limp** verb walk or proceed lamely. ●noun a limping walk. ●adjective 1 not stiff or firm. 2 lacking strength or energy, wilting. □ **limply** adverb, **limpness** noun

**limpet** noun a small shellfish that sticks tightly to rocks.

**limpid** adjective (of liquids etc.) clear, transparent. □ **limpidity** noun

**Limpopo** (lim-poh-poh) a river of SE Africa forming the northern boundary of South Africa with Botswana and Zimbabwe, and flowing into the Indian Ocean in Mozambique.

**linage** (ly-nij) noun 1 the number of lines in printed or written matter. 2 payment by the line.

**linchpin** noun 1 a pin passed through the end of an axle to keep the wheel in position. 2 a person or thing that is vital to an organization or plan etc.

**Lincoln**, Abraham (1809–65), 16th President of the USA 1860–5, noted for his policy of emancipation of slaves.

**Lincolnshire** an eastern county of England.

**Lincs.** abbreviation Lincolnshire.

**linctus** noun a soothing syrupy cough mixture.

**Lindbergh** (lind-berg), Charles Augustus (1902–74), American aviator who made the first solo transatlantic flight (20/21 May 1927).

**linden** noun a lime tree.

**Lindisfarne** (lin-dis-farn) a small island (also called Holy Island) off the coast of Northumberland, from the 7th century a missionary centre of the Celtic Church.

**line¹** noun 1 a long continuous mark on a surface. 2 a wrinkle, crease, etc. 3 a continuous extent of length without breadth. 4 a contour or outline; a thing's shape. 5 a limit or boundary; *finishing line*. 6 a row of people or things. 7 a row of words on a page. 8 (**lines**) the words of an actor's part. 9 a short letter or note; *drop me a line*. 10 a length of cord, rope, etc., especially for a specified use; *fishing line*. 11 telephone wire or electrical cable; connection by this; *a bad line*. 12 a single track of a railway, a branch of a system, or the name of the system itself; *a local line*; *Central Line*. 13 a transport service along a particular route; the name of the company providing this. 14 a series, especially successive generations e.g. of a family. 15 an approach or course of action; *along these lines*; *don't take that line with me!* **16** a type of activity or business; *what line are you in?* **17** a type of goods; *a new line of sportswear.* **18** a connected series of military encampments; *enemy lines.* ●*verb* **1** mark with lines. **2** arrange in a line; *line them up.* □ **come** *or* **bring into line** conform or cause to conform. **get a line on** (*informal*) discover information about. **in line** so as to form a straight line. **in line for** likely to get (e.g. promotion). **in line with** in accordance with. **line-drawing** *noun* a drawing in which an image is created using lines. **line of fire** the path of gunfire, a missile, etc. **line-out** *noun* (in Rugby) parallel lines of opposing forwards formed when the ball is thrown in. **line printer** a machine that prints output from a computer a line at a time. **line-up** *noun* a line of people formed for inspection etc. **on the line 1** at risk. **2** speaking on the telephone. **out of line 1** not in line. **2** beyond the accepted bounds of one's position or power.

**line²** *verb* **1** cover the inside surface of (a thing) with a layer of different material. **2** be the lining of. □ **line one's pockets** *or* **purse** make money, especially by underhand or dishonest methods.

**lineage** (**lin**-i-ij) *noun* ancestry, the line of descendants of an ancestor.

**lineal** (**lin**-i-ăl) *adjective* of or in a line, especially as a descendant. □ **lineally** *adverb*

**lineaments** (**lin**-iă-měnts) *plural noun* the features of a face.

**linear** (**lin**-i-er) *adjective* **1** of a line; of length. **2** arranged in a line. □ **linearity** *noun*

**lineation** (lin-i-**ay**-shŏn) *noun* **1** an arrangement of lines. **2** marking with these.

**linen** *noun* **1** cloth made of flax. **2** shirts, sheets, tablecloths, etc. which were formerly made of this.

**liner** *noun* **1** a large passenger or cargo ship travelling on a regular route. **2** a freight train travelling regularly. **3** a removable lining; *nappy-liners.*

**linesman** *noun* (*plural* **linesmen**) an official assisting the referee in certain games, especially in deciding whether or where a ball crosses a line.

**ling** *noun* **1** a kind of heather. **2** a long slender sea fish of northern Europe, used (usually salted) as food.

**linga** *noun* (also **lingam**) a phallus as the symbol of the Hindu god Siva.

**linger** *verb* **1** stay a long time, especially as if reluctant to leave. **2** dawdle. **3** remain alive although continually growing weaker.

**lingerie** (**lan**-*zh*er-ee) *noun* women's underwear and nightclothes.

**lingo** *noun* (*plural* **lingos** *or* **lingoes**) (*informal*) **1** a foreign language. **2** jargon.

**lingua franca** (ling-wă **frank**-ă) a common language used by people whose native languages are different.

**lingual** (**ling**-wăl) *adjective* **1** of or formed by the tongue. **2** of speech or languages. □ **lingually** *adverb*

**linguist** (**ling**-wist) *noun* a person who is skilled in languages or linguistics.

**linguistic** (ling-**wist**-ik) *adjective* of language or linguistics. ●*noun* (**linguistics**) the study of languages and their structure. □ **linguistically** *adverb*

**liniment** *noun* an embrocation, especially one made with oil.

**lining** *noun* a layer of material which lines a surface etc.

**link** *noun* **1** one ring or loop of a chain. **2** a connecting part. **3** a person who is a connection between others. **4** a cuff-link. ●*verb* join; make or be a connection between. □ **link up** (usually foll. by *with*) connect or combine. **link-up** *noun* an act or result of linking up.

**linkage** *noun* linking; a link or system of links.

**linkman** *noun* (*plural* **linkmen**) a person providing continuity in a broadcast programme or between programmes.

**links** *noun* (treated as *singular* or *plural*) a golf course.

**Linnaeus** (lin-ee-ŭs), Carolus (Carl Linné) (1707–78), Swedish naturalist, who established the system of classifying plants by giving each one a Latin name in two parts (the *genus* or group-name, and *species* identifying the individual plant).

**linnet** (**lin**-it) *noun* a brown-grey kind of finch.

**lino** (**ly**-noh) *noun* linoleum.

**linocut** *noun* a design cut in relief on a layer of thick linoleum; a print made from this.

**linoleum** (lin-**oh**-liŭm) *noun* a kind of floor covering made by pressing a thick coating of powdered cork and linseed oil etc. on to a canvas backing.

**Linotype** *noun* (*trade mark*) a machine that produces a line of type as a single strip of metal.

**linseed** *noun* the seed of flax. □ **linseed oil** oil extracted from linseed and used in paint and varnish.

**linsey-woolsey** *noun* a fabric of coarse wool woven on a cotton warp.

**lint** *noun* **1** a soft absorbent material for dressing wounds, consisting of linen or cotton with a raised nap on one side. **2** fluff.

**lintel** *noun* a horizontal piece of timber or stone etc. over a door or other opening.

**lion** *noun* **1** a large powerful flesh-eating animal of the cat family; a male lion. **2** (**the Lion**) a sign of the zodiac, Leo. **3** a brave or celebrated person. **4** (**the Lions**) the British Rugby Union team. □ **lion-hearted** *adjective* very brave. **the lion's share** the largest or best part of something. (¶ In the fable the lion demanded most (or, in one version, all) of the prey in return for his help in the kill.)

**lioness** *noun* a female lion.

**lionize** *verb* (also **lionise**) treat (a person) as a celebrity.

**lip** *noun* **1** either of the fleshy edges of the mouth-opening. **2** (*slang*) impudent talk. **3** the edge of a cup or other hollow container or of an opening. **4** a projecting part of such an edge shaped for pouring. □ **lip-read** *verb* understand (speech) from watching the movements of a speaker's lips. **lip-service** *noun* insincere expression of support or approval. □ **lipped** *adjective*

**Lipari Islands** (**lip**-er-i) a group of volcanic islands (the ancient Aeolian Islands) off the north of Sicily.

**lipid** *noun* any of a group of fat-like compounds including fatty acids, oils, waxes, and steroids.

**liposuction** *noun* a technique in cosmetic surgery for removing excess fat from under the skin by suction.

**Lippizaner** (lip-i-tsah-ner) *noun* a horse of a white breed used especially in dressage.

**lipsalve** *noun* ointment for sore lips.

**lipstick** *noun* a stick of cosmetic for colouring the lips.

**liquefy** *verb* (**liquefied, liquefying**) make or become liquid. □ **liquefaction** *noun*

**liqueur** (lik-yoor) *noun* a strong sweet alcoholic spirit with fragrant flavouring.

**liquid** *noun* a substance like water or oil that flows freely but is not a gas. ● *adjective* **1** in the form of a liquid. **2** having the clearness of water. **3** (of sounds) flowing clearly and pleasantly; *the blackbird's liquid notes*. **4** (of assets) easily converted into cash. □ **liquid crystal** a thick liquid with some of the molecular properties of a crystal. **liquid crystal display** a visual display in electronic devices, consisting of a matrix of liquid crystals whose reflective properties change as an electric signal is applied.

**liquidate** *verb* **1** pay or settle (a debt). **2** close down (a business) and divide its assets between its creditors. **3** get rid of, especially by killing. □ **liquidator** *noun*

**liquidation** *noun* liquidating, especially of a firm. □ **go into liquidation** (of a business) be closed down and have its assets divided, especially in bankruptcy.

**liquidity** (li-kwid-iti) *noun* **1** the state of being liquid. **2** the availability of liquid assets.

**liquidize** *verb* (also **liquidise**) cause to become liquid; crush into a liquid pulp.

**liquidizer** *noun* (also **liquidiser**) a machine for liquidizing fruit and vegetables.

**liquor** (lik-er) *noun* **1** alcoholic drink. **2** juice produced in cooking, liquid in which food has been boiled.

**liquorice** (lik-er-iss) *noun* (also **licorice**) **1** a black substance used in medicine and as a sweet. **2** the plant from whose root it is obtained.

**lira** (leer-ă) *noun* (*plural* **lire**) the unit of money in Italy and Turkey.

**Lisbon** the capital of Portugal.

**lisle** (*rhymes with* mile) *noun* a fine smooth cotton thread used especially for stockings.

**lisp** *noun* a speech defect in which s is pronounced like th (as in *thin*) and z like *th* (as in *they*). ● *verb* speak or utter with a lisp.

**lissom** (liss-ŏm) *adjective* lithe, agile.

**list**[1] *noun* a series of names, items, figures, etc. written or printed. ● *verb* make a list of; enter (a name etc.) in a list. □ **enter the lists** make or accept a challenge, especially in a controversy. **listed building** a building of architectural or historical importance officially protected from demolition or alteration. **list price** the published or advertised price of goods.

**list**[2] *verb* (of a ship) lean over to one side. ● *noun* a listing position, a tilt.

**listen** *verb* **1** concentrate in order to hear something or someone. **2** pay attention. **3** (foll. by *to*) respond to a person, request, advice, etc. □ **listen in 1** overhear a conversation, especially by telephone. **2** listen to a radio broadcast.

**listener** *noun* **1** a person who listens. **2** a person listening to a radio broadcast.

**Lister**, Joseph, 1st Baron (1827–1912), English surgeon, inventor of antiseptic techniques in surgery.

**listeria** *noun* any of several bacteria infecting humans and animals eating contaminated food.

**listeriosis** *noun* food poisoning caused by listeria.

**listing** *noun* a list or catalogue; an item on a list.

**listless** *adjective* without energy or vitality, showing no enthusiasm. □ **listlessly** *adverb*, **listlessness** *noun*

**Liszt** (*pronounced* list), Franz (Ferenc) (1811–86), Hungarian composer and noted pianist.

**lit** *see* LIGHT[1], LIGHT[2].

**Li (Tai) Po** (lee ty poh) (701–62), a major Chinese poet, whose favourite themes include wine, friendship, and the beauties of nature.

**litany** *noun* **1** a form of prayer consisting of a series of supplications to God, recited by a priest and with set responses by the congregation. **2** (**the Litany**) that in the Book of Common Prayer. **3** a long monotonous recital; *a litany of complaints.*

**litchi** alternative spelling of LYCHEE.

**liter** Amer. spelling of LITRE.

**literacy** (lit-er-ăsi) *noun* the ability to read and write.

**literal** *adjective* **1** taking words in their most basic sense without allowing for figurative or metaphorical use of language. **2** corresponding exactly to a given form of words; *literal translation.* **3** unimaginative, matter-of-fact.   □   **literally** *adverb*, **literalness** *noun*

**literary** (lit-er-er-i) *adjective* of or concerned with literature.

**literate** (lit-er-ăt) *adjective* able to read and write. ● *noun* a literate person.

**literati** (lit-er-**ah**-ti) *plural noun* learned people.

**literature** *noun* **1** written works, especially those novels, poems, plays, etc. valued for their artistic worth. **2** the writings of a country or a period, or on a particular subject. **3** (*informal*) printed pamphlets or leaflets etc.; *some literature about coach tours.*

**lithe** (*rhymes with* scythe) *adjective* flexible, supple.

**lithium** (lith-i-ŭm) *noun* a soft silver-white metallic element (symbol Li), the lightest known metal.

**litho** (lyth-oh) *noun* (*informal*) the lithographic process.

**lithograph** *noun* a picture etc. printed by lithography.

**lithography** (lith-og-răfi) *noun* a process of printing using a smooth surface treated so that ink will adhere only to the design to be printed and not to the rest of the surface.   □ **lithographic** *adjective*

**Lithuania** a country in eastern Europe between Latvia and Poland, formerly a republic of the USSR.

**Lithuanian** *adjective* of Lithuania or its people or language. ● *noun* **1** a person from Lithuania. **2** the language of Lithuania.

**litigant** (lit-i-gănt) *noun* a person who is involved in a lawsuit, one who goes to law.

**litigation** (lit-i-gay-shŏn) *noun* a lawsuit; the process of going to law.

**litigious** (lit-ij-ŭs) *adjective* **1** of lawsuits. **2** giving matter for a lawsuit. **3** fond of going to law.

**litmus** *noun* a blue colouring matter that is turned red by acids and can be restored to blue by alkalis.   □ **litmus paper** paper stained with this, used to test whether a solution is acid or alkaline. **litmus test** (*informal*) the real or ultimate test.

**litotes** (ly-toh-teez) *noun* an ironic understatement, e.g. *I shan't be sorry* = I shall be glad.

**litre** (lee-ter) *noun* (*Amer.* **liter**) a metric unit of capacity equal to 1,000 cubic centimetres or 1 cubic decimetre (1.76 pints).

**litter** *noun* **1** odds and ends of rubbish left lying about. **2** the young animals brought forth at a birth. **3** a means of transport consisting of a couch in a frame carried on the shoulders of bearers. **4** granulated material for use by pets, especially cats, as an indoor toilet. **5** straw put down as bedding for animals. ● *verb* **1** make untidy by scattering odds and ends; scatter as litter. **2** give birth to (a litter of young). **3** provide (a horse etc.) with litter as bedding; spread straw etc. on (a floor).

**litterbug** *noun* (also **litter-lout**) (*informal*) a person who drops litter, especially in a public place.

**little** *adjective* **1** small in size, amount, duration, etc. **2** (**a little**) a small amount of; *add a little salt.* **3** trivial; *argues about every little thing.* **4** only a small amount; *had little sleep.* **5** operating or existing only on a small scale; *little shopkeepers.* **6** smaller than others of its kind; *the little hand of the clock.* **7** young, younger; *a little boy; my little sister.* ● *noun* **1** only a small amount; *got little in return.* **2** (**a little**) a definite though small amount, distance, or period of time. ● *adverb* **1** only to a small extent; *a little known fact; little more than a rumour.* **2** (**a little**) rather; *I'm a little deaf.* **3** hardly; *little did they know.*   □ **little by little** gradually. **little end** the smaller end of a connecting rod, attached to a piston. **the little people** the fairies.

**littoral** *adjective* of or on the shore. ● *noun* a region lying along the shore.

■**Usage** Do not confuse with **literal**.

**liturgy** (lit-er-ji) *noun* **1** a fixed form of public worship used in churches. **2** (**the Liturgy**) the Book of Common Prayer.   □ **liturgical** (lit-**er**-ji-kăl) *adjective*, **liturgically** *adverb*

**live¹** (*rhymes with* hive) *adjective* **1** alive. **2** (of a broadcast) heard or seen while taking place rather than being recorded and edited. **3** (of a recording) made in front of an audience rather than in a studio. **4** of current interest or importance; *a live issue.* **5** (of a match, ammunition, etc.) unused. **6** (of a wire etc.) charged with or carrying electricity. **7** glowing or burning; *live coals.* ● *adverb* in the form of a live broadcast; *the show went out live.*   □ **live wire** a highly energetic person.

**live²** (*rhymes with* give) *verb* **1** have life, be or remain alive. **2** have one's home; *she lives up the road.* **3** feed, subsist; *living on fruit.* **4** depend on for survival; *lives on a pension; lives by his wits.* **5** spend or pass; *live a full* *life*. **6** express in one's life; *lives his faith*. **7** lead one's life in a specified way; *live quietly*. **8** enjoy life to the full; *you haven't lived*. □ **lived-in** *adjective* **1** inhabited, (of a room) used frequently. **2** (of a person's face) worn by weather, worry, etc. **live down** live in such a way that (a past guilt or scandal etc.) becomes forgotten. **live in** *or* **out** (of an employee) live on or off the premises. **live-in** *adjective* sharing one's home; *live-in nanny*. **live it up** live extravagantly. **live together 1** live in the same house etc. **2** coexist peacefully. **3** (of a couple) share a home as if married. **live up to** fulfil; *did not live up to his principles*. **live with 1** live together with. **2** tolerate; *you will have to learn to live with it*.

**liveable** (liv-ăbŭl) *adjective* (also **livable**) **1** (*informal*) (also **liveable-in**) (of a house etc.) fit to live in. **2** (of one's life) worth living. **3** (also **liveable-with**) (of a person, idea, etc.) easy to live with.

**livelihood** (lyv-li-huud) *noun* a means of living; a way in which a person earns a living.

**livelong** (liv-long) *adjective* for its entire length. □ **the livelong day** all day.

**lively** *adverb* (**livelier**, **liveliest**) full of life or energy, vigorous and cheerful, full of action. □ **look lively** move more quickly or energetically. □ **liveliness** *noun*

**liven** *verb* (often foll. by *up*) make or become lively; *liven it up*; *things livened up*.

**liver**[1] *noun* **1** a large organ in the abdomen, secreting bile. **2** the liver of certain animals, used as food.

**liver**[2] *noun* a person who lives in a specified way; *a clean liver*.

**liveried** *adjective* wearing a livery.

**liverish** *adjective* **1** suffering from a disorder of the liver. **2** irritable, glum.

**Liverpudlian** *adjective* of Liverpool, a city in NW England. ●*noun* a native or inhabitant of Liverpool.

**liverwort** (liv-er-wert) *noun* a small mosslike or leafless plant, some varieties of which are liver-shaped.

**livery** *noun* **1** a distinctive uniform worn by servants or by members of the London trade guilds. **2** the distinctive colour scheme in which a company's vehicles are painted. □ **livery stables** stables where horses are kept in return for a fee, or where they may be hired.

**lives** *see* LIFE.

**livestock** *noun* animals kept for use or profit, e.g. cattle or sheep on a farm.

**livid** *adjective* **1** of the colour of lead, bluish-grey. **2** (*informal*) furiously angry.

**living** *adjective* **1** contemporary, now alive. **2** (of a likeness) exact, true to life. ●*noun* **1** being alive. **2** a livelihood. **3** a position

held by a member of the clergy and providing him or her with an income. □ **living-room** *noun* a room for general use during the day. **living wage** a wage on which it is possible to live. **living will** a written statement of a person's desire not to be kept alive by artificial means in the event of terminal illness or accident. **within living memory** within the memory of people who are still alive.

**Livingstone**, David (1813–73), Scottish missionary and explorer of Africa.

**Livy** (Titus Livius) (59 BC–AD 17), Roman historian, who wrote a history of Rome from its foundation to his own time.

**lizard** *noun* a reptile with a rough or scaly hide, four legs, and a long tail.

**llama** (lah-mă) *noun* a South American animal related to the camel, kept as a beast of burden and for its soft woolly hair.

**LLB** *abbreviation* Bachelor of Laws.

**Lloyd George**, David, 1st Earl (1863–1945), British Liberal statesman, Prime Minister 1916–22, whose social reforms included the introduction of old-age pensions and national insurance.

**Lloyd's** a corporation of underwriters in London. □ **Lloyd's Register** an annual classified list of ships.

**Lloyd Webber**, Sir Andrew (born 1948), English composer, whose works include the musical plays *Evita*, *Cats*, and *The Phantom of the Opera*.

**lo** *interjection* (*old use*) look. □ **lo and behold** (*humorous*) an expression used to introduce something unexpected or surprising.

**loach** *noun* (*plural* **loach** *or* **loaches**) a small edible freshwater fish.

**load** *noun* **1** something carried. **2** the amount carried; *a lorry-load of bricks*. **3** a commitment or responsibility. **4** (often as **loads**) a lot; *loads of money*; *what a load of rubbish!* **5** the amount of power carried by an electric circuit or supplied by a generating station. ●*verb* **1** put a load in or on; fill with goods; take a load. **2** (often foll. by *with*) burden, load heavily. **3** put ammunition into (a firearm). **4** insert (a cassette, film, computer program, etc.) into a device; fill (a tape recorder, camera, computer, etc.). **5** tamper with (dice, a roulette wheel, etc.) by weighting; give bias to. **6** add an extra charge to (an insurance premium) because of poor risk. □ **get a load of** (*slang*) take notice of. **load line** a Plimsoll line.

**loaded** *adjective* **1** (*slang*) very rich. **2** (*slang*) under the influence of drink or drugs. **3** (of dice, a roulette wheel, etc.) weighted, given bias. **4** (of a question or statement) having some hidden implication.

**loader** *noun* **1** a person who loads things; an attendant loading a sportsman's guns. **2** a device for loading something. **3** a gun, machine, lorry, etc. loaded in a certain way; *breech-loader; front-loader*.

**loadstone** *noun* alternative spelling of LODESTONE.

**loaf** *noun* (*plural* **loaves**) **1** a mass of bread shaped in one piece. **2** minced or chopped meat moulded into an oblong shape. **3** (*slang*) the head; *use your loaf!* ● *verb* spend time idly, hang about. □ **loafer** *noun*

**loam** *noun* rich soil containing clay, sand, and decayed vegetable matter. □ **loamy** *adjective*

**loan** *noun* **1** something lent, especially a sum of money. **2** lending, being lent; *books on loan.* ● *verb* lend. □ **loan shark** (*informal*) a person who lends money at extremely high rates of interest.

**loath** (*rhymes with* both) *adjective* (also **loth**) reluctant; *was loath to depart.*

**loathe** (*rhymes with* clothe) *verb* feel great hatred and disgust for.

**loathing** *noun* hatred, disgust.

**loathsome** *adjective* arousing loathing, repulsive.

**loaves** *see* LOAF.

**lob** *verb* (**lobbed, lobbing**) send or strike (a ball) slowly or in a high arc in cricket or tennis etc. ● *noun* a lobbed ball in tennis etc.; a slow underarm delivery in cricket.

**lobar** (**loh**-ber) *adjective* of a lobe, especially of the lung; *lobar pneumonia.*

**lobate** (**loh**-bayt) *adjective* having a lobe or lobes.

**lobby** *noun* **1** a porch or entrance hall; an ante-room. **2** (in the House of Commons) a large hall open to the public and used for interviews with MPs etc. **3** (also **division lobby**) either of two corridors to which MPs retire when a vote is taken in the House. **4** a body of people lobbying an MP etc. or seeking to influence legislation; *the anti-abortion lobby.* ● *verb* (**lobbied, lobbying**) mount a campaign to influence (an MP or other person).

**lobe** *noun* **1** a rounded flattish part or projection (especially of an organ of the body). **2** the lower soft part of the ear. □ **lobed** *adjective*

**lobelia** (lŏ-**bee**-liă) *noun* a garden plant with blue, red, white, or purple flowers.

**lobotomy** (lŏ-**bot**-ŏmi) *noun* an incision into the frontal lobe of the brain, formerly used in some cases of mental disorder.

**lobster** *noun* **1** a large shellfish with eight legs and two long claws. **2** its flesh as food. □ **lobster pot** a basket for trapping lobsters.

**lobworm** *noun* a large earthworm used as fishing-bait.

**local** *adjective* **1** belonging to a particular place or neighbourhood; *local history; the local paper.* **2** affecting a particular place, not general; *local disturbances.* ● *noun* **1** an inhabitant of a particular district. **2** (*informal*) the public house of a neighbourhood. □ **local anaesthetic** one affecting a specific area of the body and not causing unconsciousness. **local authority** the body of people given responsibility for administration in local government. **local call** a telephone call to a nearby place. **local colour** details characteristic of the scene in which a novel etc. is set, added to make it seem more real. **local government** the system of administration of a district or county etc. by the elected representatives of people who live there.

**locale** (loh-**kahl**) *noun* the scene of an event or occurrence.

**locality** (loh-**kal**-iti) *noun* a thing's position, the site or neighbourhood of something.

**localize** *verb* (also **localise**) make local not general, confine within a particular area; *a localized infection.*

**locate** *verb* **1** discover the place where (a thing) is; *locate the electrical fault.* **2** assign to or establish in a particular location; *the town hall is located in the city centre.*

**location** *noun* **1** the place where something is situated. **2** finding a thing's location; being found. **3** a natural (rather than studio-based) setting for a film or broadcast; *filmed entirely on location.*

**loch** (*pronounced* lok) *noun* (*Scottish*) a lake or narrow inlet of the sea.

**loci** *see* LOCUS.

**lock¹** *noun* **1** a mechanism for fastening shut a door or lid etc., with a bolt that cannot be opened without a key or similar device. **2** a section of a canal or river enclosed by sluice-gates, for raising or lowering boats by changing the water level. **3** the turning of a vehicle's front wheels; the maximum extent of this. **4** the interlocking or jamming of parts. **5** a wrestling hold that prevents an opponent's limb from moving. **6** (in full **lock forward**) a player in the second row of a Rugby scrum. **7** a mechanism for exploding the charge in a gun. ● *verb* **1** fasten or be able to be fastened with a lock. **2** (often foll. by *up* or *away*) secure in a place fastened by a lock; store away securely or inaccessibly; *his capital is locked up in land.* **3** bring or come into a rigidly fixed position, jam. **4** (foll. by *in*) hold fast (in a struggle, embrace, etc.). □ **lock-keeper** *noun* a person in charge of a lock on a canal or river. **lock on to** (of a missile or guidance system) automatically find and track (a target). **lock out** shut out by locking a door. **lock, stock, and barrel** completely, including everything. **lock-up** (*adjective*) able to be locked up; (*noun*) **1** premises that can be locked up. **2** a room or building where prisoners can be detained temporarily.

**lock²** noun **1** a portion of hair that hangs together. **2** (**locks**) the hair of the head.

**Locke**, John (1632–1704), English philosopher, a founder of empiricism and political liberalism.

**locker** noun a small cupboard or compartment where things can be stowed safely, especially for an individual's use in a public place.

**locket** noun a small ornamental case holding a portrait or lock of hair etc., worn on a chain round the neck.

**lockjaw** noun a form of tetanus in which the jaws become rigidly closed.

**lockout** noun an employer's exclusion of employees from the workplace until a dispute is ended.

**locksmith** noun a maker and mender of locks.

**loco** noun (plural **locos**) (informal) a locomotive. ● adjective (Amer. slang) crazy.

**locomotion** noun moving, the ability to move from place to place.

**locomotive** noun an engine for drawing a train along rails. ● adjective of locomotion; locomotive power.

**locum** (loh-kŭm) noun a deputy acting for a doctor or clergyman in his or her absence.

**locus** (loh-kŭs) noun (plural **loci**, pronounced loh-sy) **1** the exact place of something. **2** Maths the line or curve etc. formed by all points satisfying certain conditions or by movement of a point or line etc.

**locust** (loh-kŭst) noun an African or Asian grasshopper that migrates in swarms and eats all vegetation.

**locution** (lŏ-kew-shŏn) noun **1** a word, phrase, or idiom. **2** a style of speech.

**lode** noun a vein of metal ore.

**lodestar** noun a star used as a guide in navigation, especially the pole star.

**lodestone** noun (also **loadstone**) **1** a magnetic oxide of iron. **2** a piece of this used as a magnet. **3** a thing that attracts.

**lodge** noun **1** a small house at the gates of a park or in the grounds of a large house. **2** a country house for use in certain seasons; a hunting lodge. **3** a porter's room in the chief entrance to a block of flats or to a college or factory etc. **4** the members or meeting-place of a branch of a society such as the Freemasons. **5** a beaver's or otter's lair. ● verb **1** provide with temporary accommodation. **2** live as a lodger. **3** deposit; be or become embedded; the bullet lodged in his brain. **4** present formally for attention; lodged a complaint.

**lodger** noun a person paying for accommodation in another's house.

**lodging** noun **1** temporary accommodation; a lodging for the night. **2** (**lodgings**) a room or rooms (not in a hotel) rented for lodging in.

**loess** (loh-iss) noun a layer of fine-grained fertile soil found especially in the basins of large rivers.

**loft** noun **1** a space under the roof of a house. **2** a space under the roof of a stable or barn, used for storing hay etc. **3** a gallery or upper level in a church or hall; the organ-loft. **4** a backward slope in the face of a golf club. **5** a lofted stroke. ● verb send (a ball) in a high arc.

**lofty** adjective (**loftier**, **loftiest**) **1** (of things) very tall, towering. **2** (of thoughts or aims etc.) noble. **3** haughty; a lofty manner. □ **loftily** adverb, **loftiness** noun

**log¹** noun **1** a length of tree trunk that has fallen or been cut down; a short piece of this cut for firewood. **2** (hist.) a floating device for gauging a ship's speed. **3** a detailed record of a ship's voyage or an aircraft's flight; any similar record. **4** = LOGBOOK. ● verb (**logged**, **logging**) **1** enter (facts) in a logbook. **2** achieve (a certain distance, number of hours worked, etc.) as recorded in a logbook; the pilot had logged 200 hours. □ **log-jam** noun a deadlock. **log on** or **off** (also **log in** or **out**) open or close one's online access to a computer system.

**log²** noun a logarithm; log tables.

**logan** (loh-gǎn) noun (in full **logan-stone**) a heavy stone poised so that it rocks at a touch.

**loganberry** noun a large dark red cultivated fruit resembling a blackberry.

**logarithm** (log-er-ith'm) noun one of a series of numbers set out in tables which make it possible to work out arithmetic problems by adding and subtracting numbers instead of multiplying and dividing. □ **logarithmic** adjective

**logbook** noun **1** a book containing a detailed record or log. **2** a vehicle registration document.

**logger** noun (Amer.) a lumberjack.

**loggerheads** plural noun □ **at loggerheads** disagreeing or quarrelling.

**loggia** (loj-ă) noun an open-sided gallery or arcade.

**logging** noun the work of cutting down forest trees for timber.

**logic** (loj-ik) noun **1** the science of reasoning. **2** a particular system or method of reasoning. **3** a chain of reasoning regarded as good or bad. **4** the ability to reason correctly. **5** the principles used in designing a computer or any of its units; the circuit(s) involved in this.

**logical** (loj-ikăl) adjective **1** of or according to logic, correctly reasoned. **2** (of an action etc.) in accordance with what seems reasonable or natural. **3** capable of reasoning correctly. □ **logically** adverb, **logicality** (loj-i-**kal**-iti) noun

**logician** (lŏj-**ish**-ăn) noun a person who is skilled in logic.

**logistics** (lŏj-**ist**-iks) plural noun the organization of a large complex operation, such as a military campaign. □ **logistic** adjective, **logistical** adjective, **logistically** adverb

**logo** (**loh**-goh) noun (plural **logos**) a printed symbol used by an organization as its emblem. (¶ Abbreviation of logotype.)

**loin** noun **1** (**loins**) the side and back of the body between the ribs and the hip-bone. **2** a joint of meat that includes the vertebrae of this part.

**loincloth** noun a piece of cloth worn round the body at the hips, especially as the only garment.

**Loire** (pronounced lwahr) the longest river of France, flowing into the Atlantic Ocean at St Nazaire.

**loiter** verb linger or stand about idly; proceed slowly with frequent stops. □ **loiter with intent** linger in a place in order to commit a crime. □ **loiterer** noun

**loll** verb **1** stand, sit, or lean back in a lazy or relaxed manner. **2** hang loosely; a dog with its tongue lolling out.

**lollipop** noun a large round usually flat boiled sweet on a small stick. □ **lollipop man** or **lady** (informal) a warden using a circular sign on a pole to stop traffic for schoolchildren to cross the road.

**lollop** verb (**lolloped, lolloping**) (informal) flop about, move in clumsy bounds.

**lolly** noun (informal) **1** a lollipop. **2** = ICE LOLLY. **3** (slang) money.

**Lombardy** a region of central northern Italy, mainly between the Alps and the River Po.

**Lomé** (loh-**may**) the capital of Togo.

**London**[1] the capital of England and of the United Kingdom. □ **London pride** a kind of saxifrage with pink flowers.

**London**[2], Jack (John Griffith) (1876–1916), American novelist, author of The Call of the Wild.

**Londonderry** a district and former county of Northern Ireland.

**Londoner** noun a native or inhabitant of London.

**lone** adjective **1** solitary, without companions; a lone horseman. **2** single; a lone parent. □ **play a lone hand** take action without the support of others. **lone wolf** a person who prefers to do this or to be alone.

**lonely** adjective (**lonelier, loneliest**) **1** solitary, without companions. **2** sad because one lacks friends or companions. **3** (of places) far from inhabited places, remote,

not often frequented; a lonely road. □ **lonely hearts** people seeking friendship or marriage through a newspaper column, club, etc. □ **loneliness** noun

**loner** noun one who prefers not to associate with others.

**lonesome** adjective lonely; causing loneliness.

**long**[1] adjective **1** having great length in space or duration in time. **2** having a certain length or duration; two metres long; two hours long. **3** seeming to be longer than it really is; ten long years. **4** lasting, going far into the past or future; a long friendship. **5** (foll. by on) (informal) having plenty of (a quality); long on talk, short on ideas. **6** of elongated shape. **7** (of vowel sounds) having a pronunciation longer than that of a corresponding 'short' vowel (the a in cane is long, in can it is short). **8** (of odds) reflecting a low level of probability. ● adverb **1** for a long time, by a long time; long before. **2** throughout a specified time; all day long. ● noun a long period of time; it won't take long. □ **as** or **so long as** provided that, on condition that. **in the long run** in the end, over a long period. **the long and the short of it 1** all that need be said. **2** the eventual outcome. **long-distance** adjective travelling or operating between distant places. **long division** the process of dividing one number by another with all calculations written down. **long face** a dismal expression. **long haul 1** transport of goods or passengers over a long distance. **2** a prolonged effort or task. **long in the tooth** (informal) old. **long johns** (informal) underpants with long legs. **long jump** an athletic competition of jumping as far as possible along the ground in one leap. **long-life** adjective remaining usable for a long time. **long-lived** adjective having a long life; lasting for a long time. **long-playing** adjective (of a record) playing at 33 rpm, 12 inches in diameter, and lasting about 10 to 25 minutes per side. **long-range** adjective **1** having a long range. **2** relating to a period far into the future; long-range weather forecast. **long shot** a wild guess or venture. **long-sighted** adjective **1** able to see clearly only what is at a distance. **2** far-sighted. **long-standing** adjective having existed for a long time; a long-standing grievance. **long-suffering** adjective bearing provocation patiently. **long-term** adjective of or for a long period. **long wave** a radio wave of frequency less than 300 kHz. **long-winded** adjective talking or writing at tedious length. □ **longish** adjective

**long**[2] verb (often foll. by for) feel a longing.

**longboat** noun the largest boat carried by a sailing ship.

**longbow** noun a large bow drawn by hand and shooting a long feathered arrow.

**longeron** (lon-jer-ŏn) *noun* a lengthwise structural part of an aircraft's fuselage.

**longevity** (lon-jev-iti) *noun* long life.

**Longfellow**, Henry Wadsworth (1807–82), American poet, author of *The Song of Hiawatha*.

**longhand** *noun* ordinary writing, contrasted with shorthand, typing, or printing.

**longing** *noun* an intense persistent wish.

**Long Island** an island of New York State.

**longitude** (lonj-i-tewd) *noun* the distance east or west (measured in degrees) from the meridian of Greenwich.

**longitudinal** (lonji-**tew**-din-ăl) *adjective* **1** of longitude. **2** of or in length, measured lengthwise. □ **longitudinally** *adverb*

**longshore** *adjective* found on the shore; employed along the shore, especially near a port.

**longshoreman** *noun* (*plural* **longshoremen**) (*Amer.*) a docker.

**longways, longwise** *adverb* lengthways.

**loo** *noun* (*informal*) a lavatory.

**loofah** (loo-fă) *noun* the dried pod of a kind of gourd, used as a rough sponge.

**look** *verb* **1** use one's sight, turn one's eyes in a particular direction; *look at that!* **2** turn one's eyes on, examine; *looked me up and down*; *looked him in the eye.* **3** search; *I'll look in the morning*; *looking for some new shoes.* **4** direct one's attention to examine or investigate; *look at the facts*; *when one looks deeper.* **5** have a specified appearance; *you look nice*; *things are looking hopeful.* **6** face (a particular direction); *the room looked across the lake.* **7** indicate (a specified emotion) in one's face and bearing; *he looks miserable.* ●*noun* **1** the act of looking, a gaze or glance. **2** an inspection or search; *have a look at the television.* **3** (**looks**) the appearance of one's face, especially when attractive; *good looks*; *losing his looks.* **4** appearance; *the house had a run-down look.* **5** a style, a fashion; *this summer's look*; *the ethnic look.* □ **look after** take care of; attend to. **look-alike** *noun* a person or thing closely resembling another. **look down on** *or* **look down one's nose at** regard with contempt. **look forward to** be waiting eagerly (or sometimes with anxiety etc.) for an expected thing or event. **look here!** an exclamation of protest. **look in** make a short visit. **look-in** *noun* a chance of participation or success. **look into** investigate. **look on** be a spectator. **look out 1** be vigilant. **2** select or find; *I'll look out some books for you.* **look sharp** make haste. **look to 1** consider, be concerned about; *look to the future.* **2** rely on; *we're looking to you for support.* **3** intend; *I'm looking to have it ready for tomorrow.* **look up 1** search for information about; *look up words in a dic-*

*tionary.* **2** improve in prospects; *things are looking up.* **3** go to visit; *look us up.* **look up to** admire and respect as superior.

**looker** *noun* a person of specified appearance; *a good-looker.* □ **looker-on** *noun* (*plural* **lookers-on**) a spectator.

**looking-glass** *noun* a mirror.

**lookout** *noun* **1** looking out, a watch. **2** one who keeps watch. **3** a place from which observation is kept. **4** a prospect of luck; *it's a poor lookout for us.* **5** a person's own concern; *that's his lookout.*

**loom** *noun* an apparatus for weaving cloth. ●*verb* **1** come into view dimly but appear close and threatening. **2** (of a future event) seem ominously close.

**loon** *noun* **1** a diving bird with a loud wild cry. **2** (*slang*) a crazy person.

**loony** (*slang*) *noun* a lunatic. ●*adjective* crazy. □ **loony-bin** *noun* (*slang*) a mental home or hospital.

**loop** *noun* **1** the shape produced by a curve that crosses itself. **2** anything shaped roughly like this. **3** an attachment or fastener shaped like this. **4** a complete circuit for electrical current. **5** a set of computer operations repeated until some specified condition is satisfied. **6** an endless strip of tape or film allowing continuous repetition. **7** a contraceptive coil. **8** a strip of fabric etc. attached to a garment or object so that it can be hung on a peg. ●*verb* **1** form into a loop or loops. **2** fasten or join with a loop or loops. **3** enclose in a loop. **4** (also **loop the loop**) (of an aircraft) fly in a vertical loop.

**loophole** *noun* **1** a way of evading a rule or contract etc., especially through an omission or inexact wording in its provisions. **2** a narrow vertical slit in the wall of a fort etc.

**loose** *adjective* **1** detached or detachable from its place, not rigidly fixed; *a loose handle.* **2** freed from bonds or restraint; (of an animal) not tethered or shut in. **3** not fastened, packed, or contained in something; *loose papers.* **4** not organized strictly; *a loose confederation.* **5** slack, relaxed, not tense or tight; *loose skin*; *loose bowels.* **6** not compact or dense; *a loose weave.* **7** inexact, vague; *a loose translation.* **8** morally lax; *loose living.* ●*adverb* loosely; *loose-fitting.* ●*verb* **1** release. **2** untie or loosen. **3** fire (a missile). □ **at a loose end** unoccupied. **loose box** a stall in which a horse can move about. **loose-leaf** *adjective* (of a notebook etc.) with each leaf separate and removable. **on the loose 1** escaped from captivity. **2** enjoying oneself without restraint. □ **loosely** *adverb*, **looseness** *noun*

**loosen** *verb* make or become loose or looser. □ **loosen a person's tongue** make him or her talk freely. **loosen up 1** relax. **2** limber up.

**loot** noun **1** goods taken from an enemy or by theft. **2** (informal) money. ●verb **1** plunder; take as loot. **2** steal (goods) or rob (premises) left unprotected, especially after rioting. □ **looter** noun

**lop** verb (**lopped, lopping**) cut away branches or twigs; cut off.

**lope** verb run with a long bounding stride. ●noun a long bounding stride.

**lop-eared** adjective having drooping ears.

**lopsided** adjective with one side lower, smaller, or heavier than the other.

**loquacious** (lŏ-**kway**-shŭs) adjective talkative. □ **loquacity** (lŏ-**kwass**-iti) noun

**Lorca,** Federico García (1898–1936), Spanish poet and playwright.

**lord** noun **1** a master or ruler. **2** a male peer of the realm (entitled to sit in the House of Lords) or a man with the title of Lord. **3** (**Lord**) the title used before the surname of certain male members of nobility, e.g. a marquis, viscount, earl, or baron. **4** (**Lord**) God or Christ. **5** (**the Lords**) the House of Lords. ●interjection (**Lord**) an expression of surprise, dismay, etc. □ **Lord Chamberlain** (in the UK) the official in charge of the Royal Household. **Lord Chancellor** the cabinet minister who is head of the judiciary and speaker of the House of Lords. **Lord Chief Justice** the judge who is president of the Queen's Bench Division of the judiciary and second in rank to the Lord Chancellor. **lord it over** domineer. **Lord Lieutenant** (in the UK) the chief crown representative and head of the magistrates in each county. **Lord Mayor** the title of the mayor in a number of large cities including London. **lord of the manor** (in the Middle Ages) the master from whom men held land and to whom they owed service. **Lord Privy Seal** (in the UK) a senior cabinet minister without official duties. **the Lord's Prayer** the prayer taught by Christ to his disciples, beginning 'Our Father'. **Lords spiritual** the bishops in the House of Lords. **Lord's Supper** the Eucharist. **Lords temporal** the members of the House of Lords who are not bishops.

**lordly** adjective (**lordlier, lordliest**) **1** haughty, imperious. **2** suitable for a lord; a lordly mansion.

**Lord's Cricket Ground** a cricket ground in London, home of the MCC.

**Lordship** noun a title used in speaking to or about a man of the rank of Lord; your Lordship; His Lordship.

**lore** noun a body of traditions and knowledge on a particular subject or possessed by a particular group; herbal lore; gypsy lore.

**Lorelei** (**lor**-ĕ-ly) a rock or cliff on the Rhine with an unusual echo, in German legend the home of a siren of the same name whose song lured boatmen to destruction.

**lorgnette** (lorn-**yet**) noun a pair of spectacles or opera-glasses on a long handle.

**Lorraine** (lŏ-**rayn**) a region and former province of eastern France.

**lorry** noun a large strong motor vehicle for transporting goods etc.

**Los Angeles** (loss **an**-ji-leez) a city on the coast of California, the second largest in the USA.

**lose** verb (**lost, losing**) **1** be deprived of or cease to have, especially through negligence. **2** be deprived of (a person) by death. **3** become unable to find, follow, or understand; lose one's way. **4** cease to have, control, or maintain; lost my balance; lost his temper; we're losing height. **5** be defeated in a contest, lawsuit, etc. **6** succeed in getting rid of; lose weight; lost our pursuers. **7** forfeit; lost his deposit. **8** waste time or effort; lost half an hour in the traffic. **9** suffer loss, be worse off; we lost on the deal. **10** cause (a person) the loss of; delay lost them the contract. **11** (of a clock) become slow; it loses two minutes a day. □ **lose oneself in** become engrossed in. **lose out** (informal) be unsuccessful; not get a full chance or advantage. **losing battle** one in which defeat seems certain.

**loss** noun **1** losing; being lost. **2** a person or thing lost. **3** money lost in a business transaction; the excess of outlay over returns. **4** a disadvantage or suffering caused by losing something; a great loss to me. □ **be at a loss** be puzzled, be unable to know what to do or say. **loss-leader** noun a popular article sold at a loss to attract customers who will then buy other articles.

**lost** see LOSE. ●adjective **1** strayed or separated from its owner; a lost dog. **2** (usually foll. by in) engrossed; lost in thought. □ **be lost on** be unnoticed or unappreciated by; subtlety is lost on him. **be lost without** be extremely dependent on; I'm lost without my diary. **get lost!** (slang) go away! **lost cause 1** a hopeless effort or undertaking. **2** a person one can no longer help or influence.

**lot** noun **1** (**a lot** or **lots**) a large number or amount; a lot of people; lots of gravy. **2** (**a lot** or **lots**) much; laughs a lot; lots to do. **3** (**the lot**) everything; I'll take the lot. **4** a group of people or things; a rowdy lot; that lot's going in the bin. **5** one of a set of things used in making a chance selection; this method of selection; was chosen by lot. **6** a share or responsibility resulting from this.

**7** a person's destiny or fortune. **8** (*Amer.*) a plot of land, or one used for a specified purpose; *parking lot.* **9** an article or group of articles for sale, especially at an auction. □ **a lot** *or* **a whole lot** (*informal*) very much; *a whole lot better.* **bad lot** a person of bad character. **draw** *or* **cast lots** use lots to make a chance selection. **throw in one's lot with** decide to join and share the fortunes of.

**loth** alternative spelling of LOATH.

**Lothario** (lŏ-**thar**-i-oh) *noun* (*plural* **Lotharios**) a libertine. (¶ Named after a character in Rowe's play *The Fair Penitent* (1703).)

**Lothian** (**loh**-*th*i-ăn) a local government region of SE central Scotland.

**lotion** *noun* a medicinal or cosmetic liquid applied to the skin.

**lottery** *noun* **1** a system of raising money by selling numbered tickets and giving prizes to the holders of numbers drawn at random. **2** something where the outcome is governed by luck.

**lotto** *noun* a game resembling bingo but with numbers drawn instead of called.

**lotus** (**loh**-tŭs) *noun* (*plural* **lotuses**) **1** a kind of tropical water lily. **2** a mythical fruit inducing a state of lazy and luxurious dreaminess. □ **lotus-eater** *noun* a person living a life of lazy enjoyment. **lotus position** a cross-legged position adopted in yoga and for meditating.

**loud** *adjective* **1** noisy, having a high volume. **2** (of colours etc.) unpleasantly bright, gaudy. ●*adverb* loudly. □ **loud hailer** a portable electronic device for amplifying one's voice. **out loud** aloud. □ **loudly** *adverb*, **loudness** *noun*

**loudspeaker** *noun* an apparatus that converts electrical impulses into sound.

**lough** (*pronounced* lok) *noun* (*Irish*) a lake or an arm of the sea.

**Louis¹** (**loo**-ee) the name of 18 kings of France, including Louis XIV (reigned 1643–1715), known as the Sun King, whose reign represented the high point of French power in Europe.

**Louis²** (**loo**-ee), Joe (original name: Joseph Louis Barrow) (1914–81), American boxer, known as the 'Brown Bomber', heavyweight champion of the world 1937–49.

**Louisiana** (loo-eez-i-**an**-ă) a State of the south-western USA.

**lounge** *verb* loll, sit or stand about idly. ●*noun* **1** a seated area at an airport etc. **2** a public room (in a hotel) for sitting in. **3** a sitting-room in a house. **4** (also **lounge bar**) a more comfortable seated area in a public house. □ **lounge suit** a man's ordinary suit for day wear.

**lour** (*rhymes with* sour) *verb* (also **lower**) **1** frown or scowl. **2** (of clouds or the sky etc.) look dark and threatening.

**Lourdes** (*pronounced* loord) a town in SW France where in 1858 a peasant girl, Bernadette Soubirous, claimed to have had visions of the Virgin Mary. It is now a major centre of pilgrimage.

**louse** *noun* **1** (*plural* **lice**) a small insect that lives as a parasite on animals or plants. **2** (*plural* **louses**) (*slang*) a contemptible person. □ **louse up** (*slang*) make a mess of.

**lousy** *adjective* (**lousier**, **lousiest**) **1** infested with lice. **2** (*slang*) very bad or ill. **3** (*slang*) well provided, swarming; *he's lousy with money; lousy with tourists.*

**lout** *noun* a noisy badly-behaved youth. □ **loutish** *adjective*

**Louvre** (*pronounced* loovr) the national museum and art gallery of France, in Paris.

**louvre** (**loo**-ver) *noun* one of a set of overlapping slats arranged to admit air but exclude light or rain.

**louvred** (**loo**-verd) *adjective* fitted with louvres.

**lovable** *adjective* easy to love.

**lovage** (**luv**-ij) *noun* a herb with leaves that are used for flavouring.

**lovat** *noun* a muted green colour found especially in tweed and woollen clothing. ●*adjective* of this colour.

**love** *noun* **1** an intense feeling of deep affection or fondness. **2** a great liking; *his love of music.* **3** sexual passion or excitement. **4** sexual relations. **5** a person one loves; *my love; come on, love.* **6** (*informal*) a person one is fond of; *he's a love.* **7** (*informal*) a form of address; *morning, love.* **8** affectionate greetings; *give him my love.* **9** (in certain games) nil, no score; *love thirty.* ●*verb* **1** feel a deep affection or fondness for. **2** have a great liking for; *I love Chinese food.* **3** enjoy greatly, find pleasure or satisfaction in, especially as a habit; *children love dressing up; he loves to find fault.* □ **fall in love** (often foll. by *with*) **1** suddenly and intensely begin to love (a person). **2** begin to live or greatly enjoy (a thing, place etc.). **love affair 1** a romantic or sexual relationship, especially outside marriage. **2** a feeling of growing fondness and pleasure; *my love affair with Greece.* **love bite** a bruise made by a partner's biting during lovemaking. **love-child** *noun* a child of unmarried parents. **love handles** (*slang*) excess fat at the waist. **love-nest** *noun* a secluded, intimate place used by (especially illicit) lovers. **make love 1** (often foll. by *to* or *with*) have sexual intercourse (with). **2** (often foll. by *to*) (*old use*) pay amorous attention (to), court. **not for**

**love or money** (*informal*) not in any circumstances.

**lovebird** *noun* **1** a small African parrot. **2** (**lovebirds**) (*informal*) an affectionate couple.

**loveless** *adjective* without love; *a loveless marriage.*

**Lovell** (**luv-ĕl**), Sir (Alfred Charles) Bernard (born 1913), English physicist and astronomer, a pioneer of radio astronomy, founder and director of Jodrell Bank observatory.

**lovelorn** *adjective* pining with love; forsaken by one's lover.

**lovely** *adjective* (**lovelier, loveliest**) **1** beautiful, attractive. **2** (*informal*) delightful; *having a lovely time.* ● *noun* (*informal*) a pretty woman. □ **loveliness** *noun*

**lover** *noun* **1** someone who is in love with another person. **2** a person with whom another is having sexual relations. **3** (**lovers**) a couple in love or having sexual relations. **4** one who likes or enjoys something; *lover of music; music-lovers.*

**lovesick** *adjective* languishing because of love.

**lovey-dovey** *adjective* (*informal*) fondly affectionate, sentimental.

**loving** *adjective* feeling or showing love. □ **loving cup** a large two-handled drinking cup. □ **lovingly** *adverb*

**low¹** *adjective* **1** not high or tall; *a low wall.* **2** not elevated in position; close to the ground or to sea-level; *low hills; low altitude.* **3** below others in importance; *a low priority; lowest of the low.* **4** less than normal; *low prices.* **5** greatly reduced in amount or quantity; *low on fuel.* **6** below the normal level or position; *low neckline.* **7** sad, depressed; *feeling low.* **8** not loud or high-pitched; *a low voice.* **9** unfavourable; *a low opinion.* **10** mean, common; *low cunning.* ● *noun* **1** a low level or figure; *share prices reached a new low.* **2** an area of low barometric pressure. ● *adverb* **1** in or at or to a low level or position. **2** in or to a low degree. **3** in a low tone, (of sound) at a low pitch. □ **Low Church** the section of the Church of England that attaches little importance to ritual and the authority of the clergy. **low-class** *adjective* of low quality or social class. **Low Countries** the Netherlands, Belgium, and Luxembourg. **low-down** (*adjective*) dishonourable; (*noun*) (*slang*) the true facts, inside information. **low frequency** (in radio) 30 to 300 kilohertz. **low-key** *adjective* restrained, not intense or emotional. **low-level** *adjective* **1** (of a computer language) close in form to machine code. **2** close to the ground or to sea level; *low-level airstrike.* **low-pitched** *adjective* (of a voice or sound) low. **low pro-**

**file** avoidance of attention or publicity. **low-rise** *adjective* (of a building) having few storeys. **low season** the period when a resort etc. has relatively few visitors. **Low Sunday** the Sunday after Easter. **low-tech** *adjective* of or using technology based on the effective use of cheap, simple components and local resources. **low tide** the tide at its lowest level; the time when this occurs. **low water** low tide.

**low²** *noun* the deep sound made by cattle, a moo. ● *verb* make this sound.

**lowbrow** *adjective* not intellectual or cultured. ● *noun* a lowbrow person.

**lower¹** *adjective* **1** less high in place or position. **2** situated below another part; *lower lip.* **3** situated on less high land or to the south; *Lower Egypt.* **4** (of an animal or plant) not highly developed, primitive. ● *adverb* in or to a lower position etc. ● *verb* **1** let or haul down. **2** make or become lower. □ **lower case** (of letters) not capitals. **Lower Chamber** *or* **House** the House of Commons (as opposed to the House of Lords).

**lower²** alternative spelling of LOUR.

**lowest** *adjective* least high in position or status. □ **lowest common denominator** **1** *Maths* the lowest common multiple of the denominators of several fractions. **2** the least attractive or positive features of a group or community. **lowest common multiple** *Maths* the lowest amount that is a multiple of two or more given numbers.

**lowland** *noun* low-lying land. ● *adjective* of or in lowland.

**lowlander** *noun* a native or inhabitant of lowlands.

**lowly** *adjective* (**lowlier, lowliest**) of humble rank or condition. □ **lowliness** *noun*

**Lowry** (*rhymes with floury*), L(awrence) S(tephen) (1887–1976), English artist, famous for his industrial landscapes populated by small matchstick figures.

**loyal** *adjective* true or faithful in one's commitment to one's friends, beliefs, etc. □ **loyally** *adverb*, **loyalty** *noun*

**loyalist** *noun* **1** a person who is loyal, especially to the established government during a revolt. **2** (**Loyalist**) a supporter of the union between Great Britain and Northern Ireland. □ **loyalism** *noun*

**lozenge** *noun* **1** a four-sided diamond-shaped figure. **2** a small tablet or sweet to ‧ be dissolved in the mouth.

**LP** *abbreviation* a long-playing record.

**L-plate** *noun* a sign bearing the letter 'L', fixed to a vehicle that is being driven by a learner.

**Lr** *symbol* lawrencium.

**LSD** *noun* a powerful hallucinogenic drug (= lysergic acid diethylamide).

**LSE** *abbreviation* London School of Economics.

**Lt.** *abbreviation* **1** Lieutenant. **2** light.

**Ltd.** *abbreviation* (*Brit.*) Limited (= 'limited liability company', now used only by private companies; public companies use PLC).

**Lu** *symbol* lutetium.

**Luanda** (loo-**an**-dǎ) the capital of Angola.

**lubber** *noun* a clumsy fellow, a lout.
□ **lubberly** *adjective*

**lubricant** (**loo**-brik-ǎnt) *noun* a lubricating substance.

**lubricate** (**loo**-brik-ayt) *verb* oil or grease (machinery etc.) so that it moves easily.
□ **lubrication** *noun*, **lubricator** *noun*

**lubricious** *adjective* **1** slippery, evasive. **2** lewd. □ **lubricity** *noun*

**lucerne** (loo-**sern**) *noun* alfalfa, a clover-like plant used for fodder.

**lucid** (**loo**-sid) *adjective* **1** clearly expressed, easy to understand. **2** sane. □ **lucidly** *adverb*, **lucidity** (loo-**sid**-iti) *noun*

**Lucifer** (**loo**-si-fer) Satan, the Devil.

**luck** *noun* **1** chance thought of as the bringer of good or bad fortune. **2** the events etc. (favourable or unfavourable) that it brings. **3** good fortune; *it will bring you luck.* □ **no such luck** (*informal*) unfortunately not.

**luckless** *adjective* unlucky.

**Lucknow** the capital of Uttar Pradesh in India.

**lucky** *adjective* (**luckier**, **luckiest**) having or bringing or resulting from good luck.
□ **lucky dip** a tub containing articles of various values, which people may choose at random. □ **luckily** *adverb*

**lucrative** (**loo**-krǎ-tiv) *adjective* profitable, producing much money. □ **lucrativeness** *noun*

**lucre** (**loo**-ker) *noun* (*scornful*) money; money-making as a motive for action.
□ **filthy lucre** (*humorous*) money.

**Luddite** (**lud**-dyt) *noun* **1** (*hist.*) a member of the bands of English workers (1811–16) who destroyed newly introduced machinery which they thought would cause unemployment. **2** a person who opposes the introduction of new technology or working methods. (¶ Probably named after Ned *Lud*, an insane person who destroyed some machinery in about 1779.)
□ **Luddism** *noun*, **Ludditism** *noun*

**ludicrous** (**loo**-dik-rǔs) *adjective* absurd, ridiculous, laughable. □ **ludicrously** *adverb*

**ludo** *noun* a simple board game played with dice and counters.

**luff** *verb* steer (a ship) nearer the wind.

**Luftwaffe** (**luuft**-va-fě) the German air force before and during the Second World War.

**lug** *verb* (**lugged**, **lugging**) **1** drag or carry with great effort. **2** pull hard. ●*noun* **1** a hard or rough pull. **2** a projection on an object by which it may be carried or fixed in place etc.

**luge** (*pronounced* loozh) *noun* a light single or double toboggan, ridden sitting upright.

**luggage** *noun* suitcases and bags etc. containing a traveller's belongings.

**lugger** *noun* a small ship with four-cornered sails.

**lughole** *noun* (*slang*) the ear.

**lugubrious** (lǔ-**goo**-briǔs) *adjective* dismal, mournful. □ **lugubriously** *adverb*

**lugworm** *noun* a large marine worm used as bait.

**Luke, St 1** an evangelist, traditionally the author of the third Gospel and the Acts of the Apostles. Feast day, 18 October. **2** the third Gospel.

**lukewarm** *adjective* **1** only slightly warm. **2** not enthusiastic; *got a lukewarm reception.*

**lull** *verb* **1** soothe or send to sleep. **2** calm (a person) or allay (suspicion etc.), especially by deception. **3** (of a storm or noise) lessen, become quiet. ●*noun* a temporary period of quiet or inactivity.

**lullaby** *noun* a soothing song sung to send a child to sleep.

**lumbago** (lum-**bay**-goh) *noun* rheumatic pain in the muscles of the lower back.

**lumbar** *adjective* of or in the lower back.
□ **lumbar puncture** the extraction of spinal fluid from the lower back for diagnosis, using a hollow needle.

**lumber** *noun* **1** disused or inconvenient articles of furniture etc. **2** partly prepared timber. ●*verb* **1** (usually foll. by *with*) leave (a person etc.) with something unwanted or unpleasant. **2** fill up (space) inconveniently. **3** move in a heavy clumsy way.

**lumberjack** *noun* a person whose trade is the cutting, conveying, or preparing of lumber (= timber).

**Lumière** (loom-**yair**), Auguste (1862–1954) and Louis (1864–1948), French inventors and pioneers of cinema.

**luminary** (**loo**-min-er-i) *noun* **1** a natural light-giving body, especially the sun or moon. **2** an eminent or influential person.

**luminescent** (loo-min-**ess**-ěnt) *adjective* emitting light without being hot. □ **luminescence** *noun*

**luminous** (**loo**-min-ǔs) *adjective* emitting light, glowing in the dark. □ **luminosity** (loo-min-**oss**-iti) *noun*

**lump** *noun* **1** a hard or compact mass, usually one without a regular shape. **2** a protuberance or swelling. **3** a heavy, dull, or clumsy person. **4** (**the lump**) the body of casual workers in the building trade. ●*verb* put or consider together, treat as alike; *lump them together*. □ **lump in the throat** a feeling of pressure there caused by emotion. **lump it** (*informal*) put up with something one dislikes. **lump sugar** sugar in small lumps or cubes. **lump sum** a single payment covering a number of items, or paid all at once rather than by instalments.

**lumpectomy** *noun* surgical removal of a lump of tissue from the breast.

**lumpish** *adjective* heavy and clumsy or stupid.

**lumpy** *adjective* (**lumpier, lumpiest**) full of lumps; covered in lumps. □ **lumpily** *adverb*, **lumpiness** *noun*

**lunacy** *noun* 1 insanity. 2 great folly.

**lunar** *adjective* of the moon. □ **lunar month** 1 the interval between new moons (about 29½ days). 2 four weeks.

**lunate** (**loo**-nayt) *adjective* crescent-shaped.

**lunatic** *noun* 1 an insane person. 2 one who is extremely foolish or reckless. ● *adjective* insane; extremely foolish or reckless. □ **lunatic asylum** (*old use*) a mental home or mental hospital. **lunatic fringe** a few eccentric or fanatical members of a political or other group.

**lunation** (loo-**nay**-shŏn) *noun* the interval between new moons, about 29½ days.

**lunch** *noun* a meal taken in the middle of the day. ● *verb* 1 eat lunch. 2 entertain to lunch. □ **out to lunch** (*informal*) lacking or seeming to lack one's mental faculties.

**luncheon** *noun* (*formal*) lunch. □ **luncheon meat** a block of ground cooked meat, especially pork, mixed with cereal. **luncheon voucher** a voucher given to an employee, exchangeable for food at many restaurants and shops.

**lung** *noun* either of the two organs used for breathing by humans and most other vertebrates.

**lunge** *noun* 1 a sudden forward movement of the body towards something; a thrust. 2 a long rope on which a horse is held by its trainer while it is made to canter in a circle. ● *verb* (**lunged, lunging**) 1 (often foll. by *at* or *out*) make a lunge. 2 exercise (a horse) on a lunge.

**lungfish** *noun* a freshwater fish that has both gills and lungs.

**lupin** *noun* a garden plant with tall tapering spikes of flowers, bearing seeds in pods.

**lupine** (**loo**-pyn) *adjective* of or like wolves.

**lupus** (**loo**-pŭs) *noun* a skin disease producing ulcers, especially tuberculosis of the skin.

**lurch** *noun* an unsteady swaying movement to one side. ● *verb* make such a movement, stagger. □ **leave in the lurch** abandon (a person etc.) in an awkward situation.

**lurcher** *noun* a dog of a breed that is a cross between a sheepdog or retriever and a greyhound.

**lure** (*rhymes with* pure) *noun* 1 something that attracts or entices. 2 its power of attracting. 3 a bait or decoy for wild animals, a device used to attract and recall a trained hawk. ● *verb* entice, attract by the promise of pleasure or gain.

**Lurex** *noun* (*trade mark*) 1 a type of yarn containing glittering metallic threads. 2 fabric made from this.

**lurid** (**lewr**-id) *adjective* 1 in glaring colours or combinations of colour. 2 sensationally and shockingly vivid; *the lurid details*. □ **luridly** *adverb*, **luridness** *noun*

**lurk** *verb* 1 hide or wait stealthily; prowl. 2 lie hidden, waiting or as if waiting to attack. 3 be latent or lingering; *a lurking sympathy for the rebels*.

**Lusaka** (loo-**sah**-kă) the capital of Zambia.

**luscious** (**lush**-ŭs) *adjective* 1 richly sweet in taste or smell. 2 voluptuously attractive; *a luscious blonde*. □ **lusciously** *adverb*, **lusciousness** *noun*

**lush**[1] *adjective* 1 (of grass etc.) growing thickly and strongly. 2 luxurious; *lush furnishings*. □ **lushly** *adverb*, **lushness** *noun*

**lush**[2] *noun* (*slang*) a drunkard.

**lust** *noun* 1 intense sexual desire. 2 any intense desire for something; *lust for power*. ● *verb* (usually foll. by *after* or *for*) feel lust. □ **lustful** *adjective*, **lustfully** *adverb*

**lustre** (**lus**-ter) *noun* (*Amer.* **luster**) 1 the soft brightness of a smooth or shining surface. 2 glory, distinction; *add lustre to the assembly*. 3 a metallic glaze on pottery and porcelain. □ **lustrous** (**lus**-trŭs) *adjective*

**lusty** *adjective* (**lustier, lustiest**) strong and vigorous, full of vitality. □ **lustily** *adverb*, **lustiness** *noun*

**lute** (*pronounced* loot) *noun* a guitar-like instrument with a pear-shaped body, popular in the 14th–17th centuries.

**lutetium** (loo-**tee**-shŭm) *noun* a metallic element, (symbol Lu).

**Luther** (**loo**-ther), Martin (1483–1546), German theologian, founder of the Protestant Reformation in Germany. □ **Lutheran** *adjective & noun*, **Lutheranism** *noun*

**Lutine Bell** (**loo**-teen) the bell of HMS *Lutine*, which sank in 1799, taken from its wreck and kept at Lloyd's, London, where it is rung when an important announcement is about to be made.

**Lutyens** (**lut**-yĕnz), Sir Edwin Landseer (1869–1944), English architect, whose designs include country houses and the Indian capital, New Delhi.

**lux** *noun* a unit of illumination.

**Luxembourg 1** a country lying between France and Germany. **2** its capital city. □ **Luxembourger** noun

**Luxor** a city of Egypt, site of the southern complex of monuments of ancient Thebes.

**luxuriant** adjective growing profusely. □ **luxuriance** noun

■**Usage** Do not confuse with **luxurious**.

**luxuriate** verb feel great enjoyment, enjoy as luxury; *luxuriating in the warm sun.*

**luxurious** adjective supplied with luxuries, very comfortable. □ **luxuriously** adverb, **luxuriousness** noun

■**Usage** Do not confuse with **luxuriant**.

**luxury** noun **1** surroundings and food, dress, etc. that are choice and costly. **2** luxuriousness; self-indulgence. **3** something costly that is enjoyable but not essential.

**LV** abbreviation luncheon voucher.

**Lw** symbol lawrencium.

**lx** abbreviation lux.

**lych-gate** alternative spelling of LICH-GATE.

**lychee** (ly-chi) noun (also **lichee, litchi**) **1** a sweet white fleshy fruit with a brown spiny skin. **2** the tree from which this is obtained, originally Chinese.

**Lycra** noun (*trade mark*) an elastic fabric used especially for close-fitting clothing.

**lye** noun **1** water made alkaline with wood ashes. **2** any alkaline solution for washing things.

**lying** see LIE[1], LIE[2].

**lymph** (*pronounced* limf) noun **1** a colourless fluid containing white blood cells. **2** this fluid used as a vaccine. □ **lymph gland** (or **node**) any of the small glands in the **lymphatic system** (network of vessels carrying lymph) that protect against infection. □ **lymphatic** adjective

**lymphoma** (lim-**foh**-mă) noun (*plural* **lymphomas** or **lymphomata**) a tumour of the lymph glands.

**lynch** (*pronounced* linch) verb (of a mob) kill (a suspected wrongdoer) without a legal trial. □ **lynching** noun

**lynx** (*pronounced* links) noun (*plural* **lynx** or **lynxes**) a wild cat with spotted fur, tufted ears, and a short tail.

**lynx-eyed** adverb keen-sighted.

**lyre** noun an ancient musical instrument with strings fixed in a U-shaped frame. □ **lyrebird** noun an Australian bird, the male of which can spread its tail in the shape of a lyre.

**lyric** (li-rik) adjective of poetry that expresses the poet's thoughts and feelings. ●noun **1** a lyric poem. **2** (**lyrics**) the words of a song.

**lyrical** (li-ri-kăl) adjective **1** lyric; using language suitable for lyric poetry. **2** song-like. **3** (*informal*) expressing oneself enthusiastically. □ **lyrically** adverb

**lyricist** (li-ri-sist) noun a writer of lyrics.

# Mm

**M** *abbreviation* (also **M.**) **1** mega-. **2** motorway (in numbered references, e.g. M1, M25). **3** Master. **4** Monsieur. ● *noun* (as a Roman numeral) 1,000.

**m** *abbreviation* (also **m.**) **1** metre(s). **2** mile(s). **3** million(s). **4** male. **5** married.

**MA** *abbreviation* **1** Master of Arts. **2** Massachusetts.

**ma** *noun* (*informal*) mother.

**ma'am** (*pronounced* mam *or* mahm) *noun* madam (used chiefly in addressing the Queen or a royal lady).

**Maastricht** (**mahs**-trikt) a city of the southern Netherlands. ● *noun* (in full **Maastricht agreement** *or* **treaty**) an agreement promoting increased links and cooperation between members of the European Community.

**mac** *noun* (also **mack**) (*informal*) a mackintosh.

**macabre** (mă-**kahbr**) *adjective* gruesome, suggesting death.

**macadam** (mă-**kad**-ăm) *noun* layers of broken stone used in road-making, each layer being rolled hard before the next is put down.

**macadamize** (mă-**kad**-ă-myz) *verb* (also **macadamise**) surface with macadam.

**macaque** (mă-**kahk**) *noun* a monkey of India and SE Asia, with prominent cheek-pouches.

**macaroni** *noun* short thick tubes of pasta.

**macaroon** *noun* a small sweet biscuit made with ground almonds or coconut.

**MacArthur**, Douglas (1880–1964), American general, who commanded US (later Allied) forces in the SW Pacific during the Second World War.

**Macaulay**, Thomas Babington, 1st Baron (1800–59), English historian, essayist, and philanthropist.

**macaw** (mă-**kaw**) *noun* a brightly coloured American parrot with a long tail.

**Macbeth** (*c.*1005–57), King of Scotland 1040–57, the subject of one of Shakespeare's plays.

**Maccabees** (**mak**-ă-beez) **1** a family of Jewish patriots who led opposition to Syrian oppression from 168 BC. **2** four books of Jewish history, of which the first two are included in the Apocrypha. □ **Maccabean** *adjective*

**McCarthyism** *noun* the policy of hunting out suspected Communists and removing them, especially from public office, prevalent in the USA in the decade following the Second World War. (¶ Named after the American senator J. R. McCarthy (died 1957).)

**McCartney**, (James) Paul (born 1942), English guitarist, singer, and songwriter, a member of the Beatles.

**McCoy** (mă-**koi**) *noun* □ **the real McCoy** (*informal*) the real thing, the genuine article.

**MacDonald**, Ramsay (James Ramsay) (1866–1937), British statesman, who led the Labour governments of 1924 and 1929–31, and the coalition government of 1931–5.

**mace¹** *noun* a ceremonial staff, especially that symbolizing the Speaker's authority in the House of Commons.

**mace²** *noun* a spice made from the dried outer covering of nutmeg.

**macédoine** (**mas**-id-wahn) *noun* a mixture of chopped fruits or vegetables, often served set in jelly.

**Macedon** (**mas**-i-dŏn) ancient Macedonia.

**Macedonia** (mas-i-**doh**-niă) **1** an ancient country at the NE end of the Greek peninsula. **2** a republic of former Yugoslavia. □ **Macedonian** *adjective & noun*

**McEnroe**, John Patrick (born 1959), American tennis-player.

**macerate** (**mas**-er-ayt) *verb* make or become soft by steeping in a liquid. □ **maceration** *noun*

**Mach** (*pronounced* mahk) *noun* (in full **Mach number**) the ratio of the speed of a body to the speed of sound in the same medium; a body travelling at *mach one* is travelling at the speed of sound, *mach two* is twice this. (¶ Named after the Austrian physicist Ernst Mach (1838–1916).)

**machete** (mă-**she**-ti) *noun* a broad heavy knife used in Central America and the West Indies as a tool and weapon.

**machiavellian** (maki-ă-**vel**-iăn) *adjective* elaborately cunning or deceitful. □ **machiavellianism** *noun* (¶ Named after Niccolo dei Machiavelli (1469–1527), an Italian statesman who advised the use of any means, however unscrupulous, that would strengthen the State.)

**machicolation** (mă-chik-ŏ-**lay**-shŏn) *noun* an opening between the supports of a projecting parapet through which missiles could be hurled down on attackers.

**machinate** (**mak**-in-ayt) *verb* scheme cleverly. □ **machination** *noun*

**machine** *noun* **1** an apparatus for applying mechanical power, having several interrelated parts. **2** something operated by such apparatus, e.g. a bicycle or aircraft. **3** a complex controlling system of an organization; *the publicity machine.* ●*verb* make, produce, or work on (a thing) with a machine; stitch with a sewing-machine. □ **machine code, machine language** a computer language to which a particular computer can respond directly without further translation. **machine-gun** (*noun*) an automatic gun giving rapid continuous fire; (*verb*) shoot at with a machine-gun. **machine-readable** *adjective* in a form that a computer can respond to. **machine tool** a power-driven machine such as a lathe or a grinding machine used in engineering to shape metals, plastics, etc. **machine translation** automatic translation by computer from one language into another.

**machinery** *noun* **1** machines. **2** a mechanism. **3** an organized system for doing something.

**machinist** *noun* a person who makes or works machinery; one who operates machine tools.

**machismo** (mă-**kiz**-moh *or* mă-**chiz**-moh) *noun* virility or manly courage; a show of this.

**macho** (**mach**-oh) *adjective* aggressively masculine.

**macintosh** alternative spelling of MACKINTOSH.

**mack** alternative spelling of MAC.

**Mackenzie**, Sir (Edward Montague) Compton (1883–1972), English writer.

**Mackenzie River** the longest river of Canada, flowing NW to a section of the Arctic Ocean. (¶ Named after the Scottish explorer of Canada, Sir Alexander Mackenzie (1764–1820).)

**mackerel** *noun* (*plural* **mackerel** *or* **mackerels**) an edible seafish. □ **mackerel sky** rows of small white fleecy clouds.

**McKinley** (mă-**kin**-li), **Mount** the highest peak in North America, in Alaska.

**mackintosh** *noun* (also **macintosh**) **1** a raincoat. **2** waterproof material of rubber and cloth.

**Maclean**[1] (mă-**klayn**), Alistair (1924–87), British writer of thrillers.

**Maclean**[2] Donald Duart (1913–83), British Foreign Office official and Soviet spy.

**McLuhan** (mă-**kloo**-ăn), (Herbert) Marshall (1911–80), Canadian writer, noted for his studies of mass communications.

**Macmillan**, (Maurice) Harold, 1st Earl of Stockton (1894–1986), British Conservative statesman, Prime Minister 1957–63.

**MacNeice**, (Frederick) Louis (1907–63), British poet and playwright.

**McQueen**, Steve (Terence Steven) (1930–80), American film actor.

**macramé** (mă-**krah**-mi) *noun* **1** the art of knotting cord to make decorative articles. **2** items made in this way.

**macro-** *combining form* **1** large, large scale. **2** long.

**macrobiotic** (mak-roh-by-**ot**-ik) *adjective* of or following a dietary system comprising wholefoods grown in close harmony with the patterns of nature.

**macrocosm** (**mak**-roh-kozm) *noun* **1** the universe. **2** any great whole.

**macroeconomics** *noun* the study of the economy as a whole. □ **macroeconomic** *adjective*

**macromolecule** *noun* a molecule containing a very large number of atoms.

**macron** (**mak**-ron) *noun* a mark placed over a long or stressed vowel (for example, ō).

**macroscopic** (makroh-**skop**-ik) *adjective* **1** visible to the naked eye. **2** regarded in terms of large units. □ **macroscopically** *adverb*

**macula** *noun* (*plural* **maculae**) a dark spot on the skin. □ **maculation** *noun*

**mad** *adjective* (**madder, maddest**) **1** having a disordered mind, not sane. **2** extremely foolish; *a mad scheme.* **3** wildly enthusiastic; *is mad about sport.* **4** (*informal*) very annoyed. **5** frenzied; *a mad scramble.* **6** wildly light-hearted. □ **like mad** (*informal*) with great haste, energy, or enthusiasm. **mad cow disease** (*informal*) = BSE. □ **madly** *adverb*, **madness** *noun*

**Madagascar** an island off the SE coast of Africa.

**madam** *noun* **1** a word used in speaking politely to a woman, or prefixed to the name of her office in formal address; *Madam Chairman.* **2** a conceited or presumptuous young woman. **3** (*informal*) a woman in charge of a brothel.

**Madame** (mă-**dahm**) *noun* (*plural* **Mesdames**, *pronounced* may-**dahm**) the title of a French-speaking woman, = Mrs *or* madam.

**madcap** *adjective* wildly impulsive. ●*noun* a wildly impulsive person.

**madden** *verb* make mad or angry; irritate.

**madder** *noun* **1** a plant with yellowish flowers. **2** a red dye obtained from its root or made synthetically.

**made** *see* MAKE. □ **made to measure** tailor-made; made for a particular person. **made-up** *adjective* **1** wearing make-up. **2** invented, not true. **3** already prepared, ready-made; *made-up salad dressing.* **4** (of a road) surfaced, not rough and stony.

**Madeira** the largest of a group of islands (**the Madeiras**) in the Atlantic Ocean off NW Africa which are in Portuguese possession but partly autonomous. ●noun a fortified white wine produced in Madeira. □ **Madeira cake** a rich plain sponge cake.

**madeleine** (mad-ĕ-layn) noun a small fancy sponge cake.

**Mademoiselle** (mad-mwă-**zel**) noun (plural **Mesdemoiselles**, pronounced mayd-mwă-zel) the title of a French-speaking girl or unmarried woman, = Miss or madam.

**madhouse** noun (informal) **1** (old use) a mental home or mental hospital. **2** a scene of confused uproar.

**Madhya Pradesh** (mahd-yă pră-**desh**) a State in central India.

**madman** noun (plural **madmen**) a man who is mad.

**Madonna** (Madonna Louise Veronica Ciccone) (born 1958), American singer and film actress.

**madonna** noun **1** (**the Madonna**) the Virgin Mary. **2** a picture or statue of her. □ **madonna lily** a tall lily with white flowers.

**Madras** (mă-**dras** or mă-**drahs**) a seaport on the east coast of India, capital of Tamil Nadu.

**Madrid** the capital of Spain.

**madrigal** (**mad**-ri-găl) noun a part-song for voices, usually without instrumental accompaniment.

**madwoman** noun (plural **madwomen**) a woman who is mad.

**maelstrom** (**mayl**-strŏm) noun **1** a great whirlpool. **2** a confused state.

**maestro** (**my**-stroh) noun (plural **maestri** or **maestros**) **1** a great musical composer, teacher, or conductor. **2** a master of any art.

**Mae West** (slang) an inflatable life-jacket. (¶ Named after an American film actress (1892–1980) noted for her large bust.)

**Mafia** (**ma**-fiă) noun **1** (**the Mafia**) an organized group of criminals originating in Sicily, aiming to influence business and politics in Italy and the USA. **2** (**mafia**) a network of people regarded as exerting hidden influence.

**Mafioso** (mah-fi-**oh**-soh) noun (plural **Mafiosi**) a member of the Mafia.

**mag** noun (informal) a magazine.

**magazine** noun **1** a paper-covered illustrated periodical publication containing articles or stories etc. by a number of writers. **2** a store for arms, ammunition, or explosives. **3** a chamber for holding cartridges to be fed into the breech of a gun. **4** a similar device in a camera or slide projector.

**Magellan** (mă-**gel**-ăn), Ferdinand (c. 1480–1521), Portuguese explorer, who reached South America and rounded the continent through the strait which now bears his name.

**magenta** (mă-**jen**-tă) noun & adjective bright purplish red.

**maggot** noun a larva, especially of the housefly or bluebottle. □ **maggoty** adjective

**Magi** (**may**-jy) plural noun **1** see MAGUS. **2** (in Christian belief) the 'wise men' from the East who brought offerings to the infant Christ at Bethlehem.

**magic** noun **1** the supposed art of controlling events or effects etc. by supernatural power. **2** superstitious practices based on belief in this. **3** a mysterious and enchanting quality; the magic of a spring day. ●adjective of magic; used in producing magic; magic words. ●verb (**magicked**, **magicking**) **1** change or create as if by magic. **2** (foll. by away) cause to disappear as if by magic. □ **magic carpet** a mythical carpet able to transport a person on it to any place. **magic eye** noun a photoelectric device that is able to detect movement, used to operate burglar alarms, automatic doors, etc. **magic lantern** a simple form of projector using slides. □ **magical** adjective, **magically** adverb

**magician** (mă-**jish**-ăn) noun **1** a person who is skilled in magic. **2** a conjuror.

**magisterial** (ma-jis-**teer**-iăl) adjective **1** of a magistrate. **2** having or showing authority, imperious. □ **magisterially** adverb

**magistracy** (**maj**-i-stră-si) noun **1** the office of magistrate. **2** magistrates collectively.

**magistrate** noun an official with authority to administer the law, hear and judge minor cases, and hold preliminary hearings. □ **magistrates' court** a court where such cases and hearings are held.

**magma** noun a fluid or semi-fluid material under the earth's crust, from which igneous rock is formed by cooling.

**Magna Carta** (**kar**-tă) (also **Magna Charta**) the charter establishing people's rights concerning personal and political liberty, obtained by the English from King John in 1215.

**magnanimous** (mag-**nan**-imŭs) adjective noble and generous in one's conduct, not petty. □ **magnanimously** adverb, **magnanimity** (mag-nă-**nim**-iti) noun

**magnate** (**mag**-nayt) noun a wealthy and influential person, especially in business.

**magnesia** (mag-**nee**-zhă) noun a white powder that is a compound of magnesium, used as an antacid and mild laxative.

**magnesium** (mag-**nee**-ziŭm) noun a chemical element (symbol Mg), a silvery-white metal that burns with an intensely bright flame.

**magnet** noun **1** a piece of iron or steel etc. that can attract iron and that points north and south when suspended. **2** a person or thing that exerts a powerful attraction.

**magnetic** *adjective* **1** having the properties of a magnet. **2** produced or acting by magnetism. **3** having the power to attract people; *a magnetic personality*. □ **magnetic disk** a computer disk. **magnetic field** the area of force around a magnet. **magnetic mine** an underwater mine detonated by the approach of a mass of metal, e.g. a ship. **magnetic needle** a piece of magnetized steel that points north and south, used as an indicator on the dial of a compass. **magnetic north** the direction indicated by a compass needle, at a slight angle to that of true north. **magnetic pole** either of the two points, in the region of the geographical North and South Poles, indicated by the needle of a magnetic compass. **magnetic storm** disturbance of the earth's magnetic field by charged particles from the sun etc. **magnetic tape** a strip of plastic coated with magnetic particles for recording sound or other signals. □ **magnetically** *adverb*

**magnetism** *noun* **1** the properties and effects of magnetic substances. **2** the scientific study of these. **3** great charm and attraction; *personal magnetism*.

**magnetite** *noun* magnetic iron oxide, a valuable source of iron ore.

**magnetize** *verb* (also **magnetise**) **1** give magnetic properties to. **2** attract as a magnet does. **3** exert attraction on (a person or people). □ **magnetization** *noun*

**magneto** (mag-**nee**-toh) *noun* (*plural* **magnetos**) a small electric generator using permanent magnets, especially one used to produce electricity for the spark in the ignition system of an engine.

**Magnificat** *noun* a canticle beginning 'My soul doth magnify the Lord', the words of the Virgin Mary at the Annunciation.

**magnification** *noun* **1** magnifying. **2** the amount by which a lens etc. magnifies things.

**magnificent** *adjective* **1** splendid in appearance etc. **2** excellent in quality. □ **magnificently** *adverb*, **magnificence** *noun*

**magnify** *verb* (**magnified**, **magnifying**) **1** make (an object) appear larger than it really is, as a lens or microscope does. **2** exaggerate. **3** (*old use*) praise; *My soul doth magnify the Lord*. □ **magnifying glass** a lens (often mounted in a frame) that magnifies things. □ **magnifier** *noun*

**magnitude** *noun* **1** largeness, size. **2** importance. **3** the degree of brightness of a star. □ **of the first magnitude** very important.

**magnolia** (mag-**noh**-liă) *noun* a tree cultivated for its large wax-like usually white or pale pink flowers.

**magnox** *noun* a magnesium-based alloy used to enclose uranium fuel elements in some nuclear reactors.

**magnum** *noun* a wine bottle twice the normal size.

**magnum opus** a great work of art, literature, etc.; an artist's greatest work. (¶ Latin.)

**magpie** *noun* **1** a noisy bird with black and white plumage. **2** a chatterer. **3** a person who collects objects at random.

**Magritte** (mah-**greet**), René François Ghislain (1898–1967), Belgian painter, prominent in the Surrealist movement.

**magus** (**may**-gŭs) *noun* (*plural* **magi**, *pronounced* may-jy) **1** a priest of ancient Persia. **2** a sorcerer. **3** *see* MAGI.

**Magyar** (**mag**-yar) *noun* **1** a member of a people originally from western Siberia, now predominant in Hungary. **2** their language, Hungarian. ● *adjective* of the Magyars.

**Mahabharata** (mah-hă-**bah**-rătă) one of the two great Sanskrit epics of the Hindus (the other is the Ramayana), dating in its present form from *c.*AD 400.

**maharaja** (mah-hă-**rah**-jă) *noun* (also **maharajah**) the former title of certain Indian princes.

**maharanee** (mah-hă-**rah**-nee) *noun* (also **maharani**) (*hist.*) a maharaja's wife or widow.

**Maharashtra** (mah-hă-**rash**-tră) a State in western India bordering on the Arabian Sea. □ **Maharashtrian** *adjective & noun*

**maharishi** (mah-hă-**rish**-i) *noun* a Hindu man of great wisdom.

**mahatma** (mă-**hat**-mă) *noun* (in India etc.) a title of respect for a person regarded with reverence.

**Mahdi** (**mah**-di) *noun* **1** the title of a spiritual and temporal leader expected by Muslims. **2** a claimant of this title, especially a former leader of insurrection in the Sudan. □ **Mahdist** *noun*

**mah-jong** *noun* (also **mah-jongg**) a Chinese game for four people, played with pieces called tiles.

**Mahler** (**mah**-ler), Gustav (1860–1911), Austrian composer and conductor, Director of the Viennese Opera 1897–1907.

**mahlstick** = MAULSTICK.

**mahogany** (mă-**hog**-ăni) *noun* **1** a very hard reddish-brown wood much used for furniture. **2** the tropical tree that produces this. **3** its colour.

**mahonia** *noun* an evergreen shrub with yellow flowers.

**mahout** (mă-**howt**) *noun* (in India etc.) an elephant-driver.

**maid** *noun* **1** (*old use*) a maiden, a girl. **2** a woman servant doing indoor work. □ **maid of honour 1** an unmarried lady attending a queen or princess. **2** (*Amer.*) a principal bridesmaid.

**maiden** *noun* (*old use*) a girl or young unmarried woman; a virgin. ●*adjective* **1** unmarried; *maiden aunt.* **2** (of a horse) not yet having won a prize. **3** first; *a maiden speech; maiden voyage.* □ **maiden name** a woman's surname before she marries. **maiden over** an over in cricket in which no runs are scored. □ **maidenly** *adjective*, **maidenhood** *noun*

**maidenhair** *noun* a fern with fine hairlike stalks and delicate foliage.

**maidenhead** *noun* **1** virginity. **2** the hymen.

**maidservant** *noun* a female servant.

**mail**[1] *noun* **1** post; letters, parcels, etc.; the postal service. **2** messages distributed by a computer system. ●*verb* send by post or electronic mail. □ **mailing list** a list of people to whom advertising matter etc. is to be posted. **mail order** an order for goods to be sent by post. **mail-order firm** a firm doing business mainly by this system.

**mail**[2] *noun* body-armour made of metal rings or chains.

**mailbag** *noun* a large bag for carrying mail.

**mailbox** *noun* (*Amer.*) a letter box.

**Mailer**, Norman (born 1923), American novelist and essayist.

**mailshot** *noun* advertising literature sent to potential customers.

**maim** *verb* wound or injure so that some part of the body is useless.

**main** *adjective* principal, most important; greatest in size or extent. ●*noun* **1** the main pipe, channel, or cable in a public system for conveying water, gas, or (usually **mains**) electricity. **2** (*literary*) the high seas. □ **main clause** *Grammar* a clause that can be a complete sentence in its own right. **in the main** for the most part, on the whole.

**Maine** a State of the north-eastern USA.

**mainframe** *noun* **1** the central processing unit of a large computer. **2** a large computer as distinct from a microcomputer etc.

**mainland** *noun* a country or continent without its adjacent islands.

**mainline** *verb* (*slang*) take or inject drugs intravenously. □ **mainliner** *noun*

**mainly** *adverb* for the most part, chiefly.

**mainmast** *noun* the principal mast of a sailing ship.

**mainsail** *noun* (in a square-rigged ship) the lowest sail on the mainmast; (in a fore-and-aft rigged ship) a sail set on the after part of the mainmast.

**mainspring** *noun* **1** the principal spring of a watch or clock etc. **2** the chief force motivating the actions of a person or group.

**mainstay** *noun* **1** the strong cable that secures a mainmast. **2** the chief support.

**mainstream** *noun* the dominant trend of opinion or style etc.

**maintain** *verb* **1** cause to continue, keep in existence. **2** keep in repair; *the house is well maintained.* **3** support, provide for, bear the expenses of; *maintaining his son at college.* **4** assert as true. □ **maintained school** (*Brit.*) a school supported from public funds; a state school.

**maintenance** *noun* **1** maintaining; being maintained. **2** keeping equipment etc. in repair. **3** provision of the means to support life. **4** financial provision for a spouse after separation or divorce.

**maintop** *noun* a platform above the head of the lower mainmast.

**maiolica** (mă-yo-likă) *noun* (also **majolica**) white pottery decorated with metallic colours.

**maisonette** (may-zŏn-et) *noun* **1** a small house. **2** part of a house (usually not all on one floor) let or used separately as a self-contained dwelling.

**maître d'hôtel** (met-rĕ doh-**tel**) **1** the manager of a hotel. **2** the head waiter.

**maize** *noun* **1** a tall cereal plant bearing grain on large cobs. **2** its grain.

**Maj.** *abbreviation* Major.

**majestic** *adjective* stately and dignified, imposing. □ **majestically** *adverb*

**majesty** *noun* **1** impressive stateliness. **2** sovereign power. **3** the title used in speaking of or to a sovereign or a sovereign's wife or widow; *His* or *Her* or *Your Majesty.*

**majolica** alternative spelling of MAIOLICA.

**Major**, John Roy (born 1943), British Conservative politician, Prime Minister from 1990.

**major** *adjective* **1** greater, very important. **2** (of a surgical operation) serious or life-threatening. **3** (in music) of or based on a scale which has a semitone next above the third and seventh notes and a whole tone elsewhere. ●*noun* **1** an army officer below lieutenant colonel and above captain. **2** an officer in charge of a section of a band; *drum major.* ●*verb* (*Amer.*) specialize (in a certain subject) at college or university. □ **major-general** *noun* an army officer next below lieutenant general.

**Majorca** (mă-**yor**-kă) the largest of the Balearic Islands.

**major-domo** (may-jer-**doh**-moh) *noun* (*plural* **major-domos**) the head steward of a great household.

**majorette** *noun* = DRUM MAJORETTE.

**majority** *noun* **1** the greatest part of a group or class. **2** the number by which votes for one party etc. exceed those for the next or for all combined. **3** (in law) full age; *attained his majority*. □ **majority rule** the principle that the largest group, race, etc. should have the most power. **majority verdict** a verdict supported by more than half of a jury but not unanimous.

**make** *verb* (**made, making**) **1** construct, create, or prepare from parts or from other substances. **2** draw up as a legal document or contract; *make a will*. **3** establish (laws, rules, or distinctions). **4** arrange ready for use; *make the beds*. **5** cause to exist, produce; *make difficulties*. **6** result in, amount to; *two and two make four*. **7** cause to be or become; *it made me happy*. **8** frame in the mind; *made a decision*. **9** succeed in arriving at or achieving a position; *we made London by midnight*. **10** (*slang*) catch (a train etc.). **11** form, serve for; *this makes pleasant reading*. **12** gain or acquire; *make a profit*; *make friends*. **13** consider to be; *what do you make the time?* **14** cause or compel; *make him repeat it*. **15** perform (an action etc.); *make an attempt*. **16** ensure the success of; *wine can make the meal*; *this made my day*. **17** (foll. by *to* + infinitive) act as if intending to do something; *he made to go*. ● *noun* **1** making; the way a thing is made. **2** the origin of manufacture; *British make*; *our own make of shoes*. □ **be made for** be ideally suited to. **be the making of** be the main factor in the success of. **have it made** (*informal*) be sure of success. **have the makings of** have the essential qualities for becoming; *he had the makings of a good manager*. **make believe** pretend. **make-believe** (*adjective*) pretended; (*noun*) pretence. **make conversation** converse only as a social duty. **make do** manage with something that is not really satisfactory. **make for 1** proceed towards, try to reach. **2** tend to bring about; *it makes for domestic harmony*. **make good 1** become successful or prosperous. **2** pay compensation; repair (damage). **3** achieve (a purpose); *he made good his escape*. **make it** achieve what one wanted, be successful. **make it up** become reconciled after a quarrel. **make it up to** compensate. **make love** *see* LOVE. **make much** *or* **little of** treat as important or unimportant. **make off** go away hastily. **make off with** carry away, steal. **make out 1** write out (a list etc.). **2** manage to see or read; *made out a shadowy figure*. **3** understand the nature of; *I can't make him out*. **4** assert, claim, or pretend to be; *made him out to be a fool*. **5** (*informal*) fare; *how did you make out?* **make over 1** transfer the ownership of. **2** convert for a new purpose. **make up 1** form or constitute; put together, prepare (medicine etc.). **2** invent (a story etc.). **3** compensate (for a loss or mistake).

**4** complete (an amount) by supplying what is lacking. **5** apply cosmetics to. **make up one's mind** decide. **make-up** *noun* **1** cosmetics applied to the skin, especially of the face. **2** the way something is made up, its composition or constituent parts; a person's character and temperament. **make up to** curry favour with. **on the make** (*slang*) intent on gain.

**maker** *noun* one who makes something. □ **our Maker** God.

**makeshift** *noun* a temporary or improvised substitute. ● *adjective* serving as this.

**makeweight** *noun* **1** a small quantity added to make up the full weight. **2** anything added to make up for a deficiency.

**mal-** *combining form* **1** bad, badly; *malpractice*, *maltreat*. **2** faulty; *malfunction*.

**Malabar** (**mal-ă-bar**) a coastal district of SW India.

**Malabo** (**mă-lah-boh**) the capital of Equatorial Guinea.

**malacca** (**mă-lak-ă**) *noun* a brown cane made from the stem of a palm tree.

**Malachi** (**mal-a-ky**) the last book of the Old Testament in the English version.

**malachite** (**mal-ă-kyt**) *noun* a green mineral that can be polished.

**maladjusted** *adjective* (of a person) not well adjusted to his or her own circumstances. □ **maladjustment** *noun*

**maladminister** *verb* manage (business or public affairs) badly or improperly. □ **maladministration** *noun*

**maladroit** (**mal-ă-droit**) *adjective* clumsy, bungling. □ **maladroitly** *adverb*, **maladroitness** *noun*

**malady** (**mal-ă-di**) *noun* an illness, a disease.

**Malagasy** (**mală-gas-i**) *adjective* of Madagascar. ● *noun* **1** a native or inhabitant of Madagascar. **2** the official language of Madagascar (related to Malay).

**malaise** (**mal-ayz**) *noun* a feeling of illness or mental uneasiness.

**malapropism** (**mal-ă-prop-izm**) *noun* a comical confusion of words, e.g. *what are you incinerating?* (for *insinuating*). (¶ Named after Mrs Malaprop in Sheridan's play *The Rivals*, who made mistakes of this kind.)

**malaria** (**mă-lair-iă**) *noun* a disease causing fever which recurs at intervals, transmitted by mosquitoes. □ **malarial** *adjective*

**malarkey** (**mă-lar-ki**) *noun* (*slang*) humbug, nonsense.

**Malawi** (**mă-lah-wi**) a country in south central Africa. □ **Malawian** *adjective & noun*

**Malay** (**mă-lay**) *adjective* of a people living in Malaysia and Indonesia. ● *noun* **1** a member of this people. **2** their language.

**Malaya** a group of States forming part of Malaysia. □ **Malayan** *adjective & noun*

**Malayalam** (mal-ay-**ah**-lăm) *noun* the Dravidian language of the Malabar district of southern India.

**Malay Archipelago** a large group of islands, including Sumatra, Java, Borneo, the Philippines, and New Guinea, lying SE of Asia and north of Australia.

**Malaysia** (mă-**lay**-zhă) a country in SE Asia. □ **Malaysian** *adjective & noun*

**Malcolm X** (original name: Malcolm Little) (1925–65), American Black civil rights leader, assassinated by rivals.

**malcontent** (mal-kŏn-tent) *noun* a person who is discontented and inclined to rebel.

**Maldive Islands** (mawl-dyv) (also **the Maldives**) a group of islands south-west of India. □ **Maldivian** (mawl-**div**-iăn) *adjective & noun*

**Male** (mah-lay) the capital of the Maldive Islands.

**male** *adjective* **1** of the sex that can beget offspring by fertilizing egg cells produced by the female. **2** (of plants) having flowers that contain pollen-bearing organs and not seeds. **3** of a man or men; *male voice choir*. **4** (of parts of machinery etc.) designed to enter or fill a corresponding hollow (female) part. ●*noun* a male person, animal, or plant. □ **male chauvinist** a man who believes that men are superior to women. **male menopause** (*informal*) a crisis of potency, confidence, etc. supposed to afflict some middle-aged men.

**malediction** (mali-**dik**-shŏn) *noun* a curse.

**maledictory** (mal-i-**dik**-ter-i) *adjective* expressing a curse.

**malefactor** (**mal**-i-fak-ter) *noun* a criminal, a wrongdoer. □ **malefaction** (mal-i-**fak**-shŏn) *noun*

**malevolent** (mă-**lev**-ŏ-lĕnt) *adjective* wishing harm to others. □ **malevolently** *adverb*, **malevolence** *noun*

**malfeasance** (mal-**fee**-zĕns) *noun* (*formal*) improper or unprofessional behaviour.

**malformation** *noun* faulty formation. □ **malformed** *adjective*

**malfunction** *noun* faulty functioning. ●*verb* function faultily.

**Mali** (**mah**-li) an inland country in West Africa. □ **Malian** *adjective & noun*

**malice** *noun* a desire to harm others or to tease. □ **malice aforethought** *Law* the intention to commit a crime.

**malicious** (mă-**lish**-ŭs) *adjective* feeling, showing, or caused by malice. □ **maliciously** *adverb*

**malign** (mă-**lyn**) *adjective* **1** harmful; *a malign influence*. **2** showing malice. ●*verb* say unpleasant and untrue things about; *maligning an innocent person*. □ **malignity** (mă-**lig**-niti) *noun*

**malignant** (mă-**lig**-nănt) *adjective* **1** (of a tumour) growing uncontrollably. **2** feeling or showing great ill will. □ **malignantly** *adverb*, **malignancy** *noun*

**malinger** (mă-**ling**-er) *verb* pretend to be ill in order to avoid work. □ **malingerer** *noun*

**mall** (*pronounced* mal *or* mawl) *noun* **1** a sheltered walk or promenade. **2** (*Amer.*) a shopping precinct.

**mallard** (**mal**-ard) *noun* (*plural* **mallard**) a wild duck, the male of which has a glossy green head.

**malleable** (**mal**-i-ăbŭl) *adjective* **1** able to be hammered or pressed into shape. **2** easy to influence, adaptable. □ **malleably** *adverb*, **malleability** *noun*

**mallee** (**mal**-i) *noun* (*Austral.*) any of the kinds of eucalyptus tree that flourish in dry areas; scrub formed by these.

**mallet** *noun* **1** a hammer, usually of wood. **2** a similarly shaped instrument with a long handle, for striking the ball in croquet or polo.

**mallow** *noun* a tall plant with hairy stems and leaves, bearing purple, pink, or white flowers.

**malmsey** (**mahm**-zi) *noun* a strong sweet wine.

**malnutrition** *noun* weakness resulting from insufficient nutrition.

**malodorous** (mal-**oh**-der-ŭs) *adjective* stinking.

**Malory** (**mal**-er-i), Sir Thomas (died 1471), English writer, whose major work is a translation of legends of King Arthur.

**malpractice** *noun* **1** wrongdoing. **2** improper or negligent professional behaviour, especially by a doctor.

**malt** *noun* **1** grain (usually barley) that has been allowed to sprout and then dried, used for brewing, distilling, or vinegar-making. **2** (*informal*) malt whisky, malt liquor. ●*verb* make or be made into malt. □ **malted milk** a drink made from dried milk and malt. **malt whisky** whisky made entirely from malted barley. □ **malty** *adjective*

**Malta** an island in the Mediterranean Sea.

**Maltese** *noun* **1** (*plural* **Maltese**) a person from Malta. **2** the language of Malta. ●*adjective* of Malta or its people or language. □ **Maltese cross** a cross with four equal arms broadening outwards, often indented at the ends.

**Malthusian** *adjective* of the doctrine that the population should be restricted to prevent it increasing beyond its ability to feed itself. □ **Malthusianism** *noun* (¶ Named after Thomas Malthus (1766–1834), English clergyman who propounded the theory.)

**maltose** *noun* sugar made from starch by enzymes in malt, saliva, etc.

**maltreat** *verb* ill-treat. □ **maltreatment** *noun*

**Malvern Hills** (**mawl**-věn) (also **Malverns**) a range of hills to the SW of Worcester.

**Malvinas** (mal-**vee**-năs) the name by which the Falkland Islands are known in Argentina.

**mama** (mǎ-**mah**) *noun* (also **mamma**) (*old use*) mother.

**mamba** *noun* a poisonous black or green South African tree-snake.

**Mameluke** (**mam**-i-look) *noun* a member of a military group ruling in Egypt 1254–1811.

**Mamet**, David (born 1947), American playwright and screenplay writer.

**mamma** alternative spelling of MAMA.

**mammal** *noun* a member of the class of animals that suckle their young. □ **mammalian** (mǎ-**may**-liǎn) *adjective*

**mammary** (**mam**-er-i) *adjective* of the breasts. □ **mammary gland** a milk-secreting gland.

**mammography** *noun* an X-ray technique for screening the breasts for tumours etc.

**Mammon** *noun* wealth personified, regarded as an evil influence.

**mammoth** *noun* a large extinct type of elephant with a hairy coat and curved tusks. ● *adjective* huge.

**Man** *see* ISLE OF MAN.

**man** *noun* (*plural* **men**) **1** a human being. **2** mankind. **3** an adult male person. **4** an individual male person considered as an expert or one's assistant or opponent etc.; *if you want a good teacher, he's your man.* **5** a person of unspecified sex, an individual person; *every man for himself.* **6** a manly person; *is he man enough to do it?* **7** a male servant, employee, or workman. **8** an ordinary soldier etc., not an officer. **9** each of the set of small objects moved on a board in playing board games such as chess and draughts. ● *verb* (**manned, manning**) supply with people for service or to operate something; *man the pumps.* □ **be one's own man** be independent. **man about town** a man who spends much of his time in sophisticated social amusements. **man Friday** *see* FRIDAY. **man-hour** *noun* the amount of work that one person can do in an hour, considered as a unit. **man-made** *adjective* made by humans not by nature, synthetic. **man of the house** the male head of a household. **man-of-war** *noun* (*plural* **men-of-war**) a warship. **man to man** with frankness. **to a man** all without exception.

**Man.** *abbreviation* Manitoba.

**manacle** (**man**-ǎ-kǔl) *noun* each of a pair of fetters for the hands. ● *verb* fetter with manacles.

**manage** *verb* **1** have under effective control. **2** be the manager of (a business etc.). **3** operate (a tool or machinery) effectively. **4** succeed in doing or producing something (often with inadequate means); be able to cope; *managed without help.* **5** contrive to persuade (a person) to do what one wants, e.g. by use of tact or flattery. □ **manageable** *adjective*

**management** *noun* **1** managing; being managed. **2** the process of managing a business; people engaged in this.

**manager** *noun* **1** a person who is in charge of the affairs of a business etc. **2** one who deals with the business affairs of a sports team or entertainer etc. **3** one who manages affairs in a certain way; *she is a good manager.* □ **managing director** one having executive control or authority. □ **managerial** (manǎ-**jeer**-iǎl) *adjective*

**manageress** *noun* a woman manager, especially of a shop or hotel.

**Managua** (mǎ-**nag**-wǎ) the capital of Nicaragua.

**Manama** (man-**ah**-mǎ) the capital of Bahrain.

**mañana** (man-**yah**-nǎ) *adverb* tomorrow; (indicating procrastination) at some time in the future. (¶ Spanish.)

**manatee** (man-ǎ-**tee**) *noun* a large tropical aquatic mammal that feeds on plants.

**Manchu** (man-**choo**) *noun* **1** a member of a Tartar people who conquered China and founded the last imperial dynasty (1644–1912). **2** their language, now spoken in part of NE China.

**Manchuria** (man-**choor**-iǎ) a region forming the NE portion of China.

**Mancunian** (man-**kew**-niǎn) *adjective* of Manchester, a city in NW England. ● *noun* a native or inhabitant of Manchester.

**mandala** (**man**-dǎ-lǎ) *noun* a circular religious symbol representing the universe.

**mandarin** (**man**-der-in) *noun* **1** a high-ranking influential official. **2** a small flattened orange grown in China and North Africa. **3** (**Mandarin**) the language formerly used by officials and educated people in China; any of the varieties of this spoken as a common language in China, especially the northern variety (the official language of China). □ **mandarin collar** a high upright collar not quite meeting in front.

**mandate** *noun* authority given to someone to perform a certain task. ● *verb* **1** give authority to (a delegate). **2** commit (a territory) to a mandatary.

**mandatory** (**man**-dǎ-ter-i) *adjective* obligatory, compulsory. □ **mandatorily** *adverb*

**Mandela** (man-**del**-ǎ), Nelson Rolihlahla (born 1918), South African statesman,

President from 1994; leader of the African National Congress.

**mandible** (**man**-dib-ŭl) *noun* **1** a jaw, especially the lower one. **2** either of the parts of a bird's beak. **3** the corresponding part in insects etc.

**mandolin** (**man**-dŏl-in) *noun* a musical instrument rather like a small lute, played with a plectrum.

**mandrake** *noun* a poisonous plant with white or purple flowers and large yellow fruit.

**mandrel** *noun* **1** (in a lathe) the shaft to which work is fixed while being turned etc. **2** a cylindrical rod round which metal or other material is forged or shaped.

**mandrill** *noun* a large baboon of West Africa.

**mane** *noun* **1** the long hair on a horse's or lion's neck. **2** (*informal*) a person's long hair.

**manège** (man-ay*zh*) *noun* (also **manege**) **1** a riding-school. **2** horsemanship. **3** the movements of a trained horse.

**Manet** (ma-**nay**), Édouard (1832–83), French painter.

**maneuver** Amer. spelling of MANOEUVRE.

**manful** *adjective* brave, resolute. □ **manfully** *adverb*

**manganese** (**mang**-ă-neez) *noun* a chemical element (symbol Mn), a hard brittle grey metal; its black oxide.

**mange** (*pronounced* maynj) *noun* a skin disease affecting hairy animals, caused by a parasite.

**mangel-wurzel** *noun* (also **mangold**) a large beet used as cattle food.

**manger** *noun* a long open trough or box in a stable etc. for horses or cattle to eat from.

**mange-tout** (mahn*zh*-**too**) *noun* a variety of pea, the whole pods of which are eaten. (¶ French, = eat all.)

**mangle** *noun* a wringer. ●*verb* **1** press (clothes etc.) in a mangle. **2** damage by cutting or crushing roughly, mutilate.

**mango** *noun* (*plural* **mangoes** or **mangos**) **1** a tropical fruit with yellowish flesh. **2** the tree that bears it.

**mangold** (**mang**-ŏld) *noun* a mangel-wurzel.

**mangrove** *noun* a tropical tree or shrub growing in shore-mud and swamps, with many tangled roots above ground.

**mangy** (**mayn**-ji) *adjective* (**mangier, mangiest**) **1** having mange. **2** squalid; shabby.

**manhandle** *verb* **1** move (a thing) by human effort alone. **2** treat roughly.

**Manhattan** an island at the mouth of the Hudson River, now a borough of the city of New York, with financial, commercial, and cultural establishments.

**Manhattan Project** the code name for an American project set up in 1942 to develop an atomic bomb.

**manhole** *noun* a covered opening through which a person can enter a sewer, pipe, or boiler etc. to inspect or repair it.

**manhood** *noun* **1** the state of being a man. **2** manly qualities, courage. **3** the men of a country.

**manhunt** *noun* an organized search for a criminal.

**mania** (**may**-niă) *noun* **1** violent madness. **2** extreme enthusiasm for something; *a mania for sport*.

**maniac** (**may**-ni-ak) *noun* **1** a person behaving wildly; an idiot. **2** a person affected with mania.

**maniacal** (mă-**ny**-ă-kăl) *adjective* of or like a mania or a maniac. □ **maniacally** *adverb*

**manic** (**man**-ik) *adjective* of or affected with mania. □ **manic-depressive** (*adjective*) of a mental disorder with alternating bouts of excitement and depression; (*noun*) a person suffering from this disorder. □ **maniacally** *adverb*

**manicure** *noun* cosmetic care of the hands and fingernails. ●*verb* apply such treatment to. □ **manicurist** *noun*

**manifest** *adjective* clear and unmistakable. ●*verb* show (a thing) clearly, give signs of; *the crowd manifested its approval by cheering.* ●*noun* a list of cargo or passengers carried by a ship or aircraft etc. □ **manifestly** *adverb*, **manifestation** *noun*

**manifesto** *noun* (*plural* **manifestos**) a public declaration of policy, especially by a political party.

**manifold** *adjective* of many kinds, varied. ●*noun* a pipe or chamber (in a mechanism) with several openings that connect with other parts.

**manikin** *noun* a little man, a dwarf.

**Manila** (mă-**nil**-ă) the capital of the Philippines.

**manila** (mă-**nil**-ă) *noun* brown paper used for wrapping and for envelopes.

**manioc** (**man**-i-ok) *noun* cassava.

**manipulable** *adjective* able to be manipulated.

**manipulate** *verb* **1** handle, manage, or use (a thing) skilfully. **2** arrange or influence cleverly or craftily; alter or adjust (figures, data, etc.) to suit one's purposes. **3** move about (part of a patient's body) to reduce stiffness, pain, etc. □ **manipulation** *noun*, **manipulator** *noun*

**Manipur** (man-i-**poor**) a State of NE India. □ **Manipuri** *adjective & noun*

**Manitoba** (man-i-**toh**-bă) a province of central Canada.

**mankind** *noun* human beings in general, the human race.

**manky** *adjective* (*informal*) **1** bad, of poor quality. **2** dirty.

**manly** *adjective* **1** having qualities associated with a man (e.g. strength and courage). **2** suitable for a man. □ **manliness** *noun*

**Mann**, Thomas (1875–1955), German novelist and essayist.

**manna** *noun* **1** (in the Bible) a substance miraculously supplied as food to the Israelites in the wilderness after the exodus from Egypt. **2** something unexpected and delightful.

**manned** *see* MAN. ● *adjective* (of a spacecraft etc.) containing a human crew; *manned flights.*

**mannequin** (**man**-i-kin) *noun* **1** a woman who models clothes. **2** a window dummy.

**manner** *noun* **1** the way a thing is done or happens. **2** a person's bearing or way of behaving towards others. **3** kind, sort; *all manner of things.* **4** (**manners**) social behaviour; polite social behaviour; *has no manners.* □ **in a manner of speaking** so to speak (used to qualify or weaken what one says).

**mannered** *adjective* **1** having manners of a certain kind; *well-mannered.* **2** full of mannerisms; *a mannered style.*

**mannerism** *noun* a distinctive personal habit or way of doing something; excessive use of these in art etc.

**mannerly** *adjective* polite.

**mannish** *adjective* **1** having masculine characteristics. **2** suitable for a man.

**manoeuvre** (mă-**noo**-ver) (*Amer.* **maneuver**) *noun* **1** a planned and controlled movement of a vehicle or a body of troops etc. **2** a skilful or crafty proceeding, a trick; *the manoeuvres of politicians to achieve their purposes.* **3** (**manoeuvres**) large-scale exercises of troops or ships; *on manoeuvres.* ● *verb* **1** move a thing's position or course etc. carefully; *manoeuvred the car into the garage.* **2** perform manoeuvres. **3** guide skilfully or craftily; *manoeuvred the conversation towards money.* □ **manoeuvrable** *adjective*, **manoeuvrability** *noun*

**manometer** (mă-**nom**-it-er) *noun* a pressure gauge for gases and liquids.

**manor** *noun* **1** a large country house (also **manor house**) or the landed estate belonging to it. **2** (*slang*) an area under the administration of a unit of police. □ **manorial** (man-**or**-iăl) *adjective*

**manpower** *noun* **1** power supplied by human physical effort. **2** the number of people working on a particular task or available for work or service.

**manqué** (**mahn**-kay) *adjective* that might have been but is not what is specified; *a publisher is an author manqué.* (¶ French, = missed.)

**mansard** (**man**-sard) *noun* a roof that has a steep lower part and a less steep upper part on all four sides of a building.

**manse** *noun* a church minister's house, especially in Scotland.

**Mansell**, Nigel Ernest James (born 1953), English championship racing driver.

**manservant** *noun* (*plural* **menservants**) a male servant.

**Mansfield**, Katherine (original name: Kathleen Mansfield Beauchamp) (1888–1923), New Zealand writer of short stories.

**mansion** (**man**-shŏn) *noun* **1** a large stately house. **2** (**Mansions**) a name given to a block of flats; *Victoria Mansions.* □ **the Mansion House** the official residence of the Lord Mayor of London.

**manslaughter** *noun* the act of killing a person unlawfully but not intentionally, or by negligence.

**Mantegna** (man-**ten**-yă), Andrea (1431–1506), Italian painter and engraver.

**mantel** *noun* a mantelpiece.

**mantelpiece** *noun* **1** a structure of wood, marble, etc. above and around a fireplace. **2** (also **mantelshelf**) a shelf above a fireplace.

**mantilla** (man-**til**-ă) *noun* a lace veil worn by Spanish women over the hair and shoulders.

**mantis** *noun* (*plural* **mantis** *or* **mantises**) (in full **praying mantis**) an insect resembling a grasshopper, which holds its forelegs like hands folded in prayer.

**mantissa** *noun* the part of a logarithm after the decimal point.

**mantle** *noun* **1** a loose sleeveless cloak. **2** something likened to this, a covering; *a mantle of secrecy.* **3** a fragile gauzy cover fixed round the flame of a gas lamp, producing a strong light when heated. ● *verb* envelop or cover as if with a mantle.

**mantra** *noun* **1** a special word or phrase repeated as an aid to concentration in Hindu or Buddhist meditation, yoga, etc. **2** a Vedic hymn.

**mantrap** *noun* a trap for catching trespassers, poachers, etc.

**Manu** (mă-**noo**) (*Hindu myth.*) the first man, survivor of the great flood, and father of the human race.

**manual** *adjective* **1** of the hands. **2** done or operated by the hand(s), not automatic; *manual labour; manual gear-change.* ● *noun* **1** a handbook. **2** an organ keyboard that is played with the hands, not with the feet. □ **manually** *adverb*

**manufacture** *verb* **1** make or produce (goods) on a large scale by machinery. **2** invent; *manufactured an excuse.* ● *noun* the process of manufacturing. □ **manufacturer** *noun*

**manure** *noun* any substance (e.g. dung or compost) used as a fertilizer. ●*verb* apply manure to.

**manuscript** (man-yoo-skript) *noun* **1** something written by hand, not typed or printed. **2** an author's work as written or typed, not a printed book.

**Manx** *adjective* of the Isle of Man. ●*noun* **1** the Celtic language of the Manx people. **2** (**the Manx**) Manx people. □ **Manx cat** a tailless variety of domestic cat. □ **Manxman** *noun* (*plural* **Manxmen**), **Manxwoman** *noun* (*plural* **Manxwomen**).

**many** *adjective* (**more, most**) great in number, numerous. ●*noun* many people or things.

**Maoism** (mow-izm); (*rhymes with* cow) *noun* the doctrines of Mao Zedong. □ **Maoist** *noun & adjective*

**Maori** (mow-ri; *first part rhymes with* cow) *noun* **1** (*plural* **Maoris**) a member of the aboriginal people of New Zealand. **2** their language.

**Mao Zedong** (mow (*rhymes with* cow) dzee-**duung**) (also **Mao Tse-tung,** *pronounced* mow tsee-**tuung**) (1893–1976), Chinese Communist statesman, founder of the People's Republic of China (1949) and its President until 1959.

**map** *noun* **1** a representation of the earth's surface or a part of it, or of the sky showing the positions of the stars etc. **2** a diagram of a route etc. ●*verb* (**mapped, mapping**) **1** make a map of. **2** *Maths* associate each element of (a set) with one element of (another set). □ **map out** plan in detail. **put a thing on the map** (*informal*) make it become famous or important.

**maple** *noun* a tree with broad leaves, grown for ornament or for its wood or sugar. □ **maple leaf** a leaf of this, especially as the emblem of Canada. **maple sugar, maple syrup** that made by evaporating the sap of some kinds of maple.

**Maputo** (mă-**poo**-toh) the capital of Mozambique.

**maquette** (mă-**ket**) *noun* a preliminary sketch or model.

**Maquis** (ma-**kee**) *noun* (*plural* **Maquis**) **1** the French resistance movement during the German occupation (1940–45). **2** a member of this.

**mar** *verb* (**marred, marring**) damage, spoil.

**Mar.** *abbreviation* March.

**marabou** (ma-ră-boo) *noun* **1** a large African stork. **2** its down used as a trimming.

**maracas** (mă-**rak**-ăz) *plural noun* a pair of club-like gourds containing beans, beads, etc., held in the hands and shaken as a musical instrument.

**Maradona,** Diego Armando (born 1960), Argentine footballer.

**maraschino** (ma-ră-**skee**-noh) *noun* a strong sweet liqueur made from small black Dalmatian cherries. □ **maraschino cherry** a cherry preserved in this.

**marathon** *noun* **1** a long-distance running race, usually of 26 miles 385 yards (42.195 km). (¶ Named after Marathon in Greece, where an invading Persian army was defeated in 490 BC; a man who fought at the battle ran to Athens, announced the victory, and died.) **2** any very long race or other test of endurance.

**marauding** (mă-**raw**-ding) *adjective* going about in search of plunder or prey. □ **marauder** *noun*

**marble** *noun* **1** crystalline limestone that can be polished, used in sculpture and building. **2** a piece of sculpture in marble. **3** a small ball made of glass or clay etc. used in children's games. ●*adjective* like marble, hard and smooth and white or mottled. □ **lose one's marbles** (*slang*) lose one's mental faculties, go mad.

**marbled** *adjective* having a veined or mottled appearance; (of meat) with alternating layers of lean and fat. □ **marbling** *noun*

**marcasite** (**mark**-ă-syt) *noun* crystallized iron pyrites; a piece of this used in jewellery.

**March** the third month of the year. □ **March hare** a hare in the breeding season when it leaps about and behaves wildly.

**march** *verb* **1** walk in a military manner with regular paces; walk in an organized column. **2** walk purposefully; *marched up to the manager.* **3** cause to march or walk; *he was marched off.* **4** progress steadily; *time marches on.* ●*noun* **1** marching; the distance covered by marching troops etc.; a protest or demonstration. **2** progress; *the march of events.* **3** a piece of music suitable for marching to. □ **get one's marching orders** be told to go; be dismissed. **march past** a ceremonial march past a saluting-point. **on the march** marching, advancing. □ **marcher** *noun*

**marches** *plural noun* border regions.

**marchioness** (mar-shŏn-ess) *noun* **1** the wife or widow of a marquess. **2** a woman holding the rank of marquess in her own right.

**Marconi** (mar-**koh**-ni), Guglielmo (1874–1937), Italian electrical engineer, a pioneer of radio communication.

**Marco Polo** (*c.*1254–*c.*1324), Venetian traveller, famous for his account of his travels in China and central Asia.

**Mardi Gras** (mar-dee-**grah**) Shrove Tuesday in some Catholic countries; celebrations held on this day.

**mare**[1] *noun* the female of a horse or related animal. □ **mare's nest** a discovery that is thought to be interesting but turns out to be false or worthless.

**mare**[2] (**mah**-ray) *noun* (*plural* **maria**, *pronounced* **mah**-riă, *or* **mares**) a large dark flat area on the moon, once thought to be a sea; a similar area on Mars.

**Margaret**, Princess (Margaret Rose) (born 1930), sister of Queen Elizabeth II.

**margarine** (mar-jer-**een**) *noun* a substance used like butter, made from animal or vegetable fats.

**marge** *noun* (*informal*) margarine.

**margin** *noun* **1** an edge or border. **2** a blank space round printed or written matter on a page. **3** an amount over and above the essential minimum; *was defeated by a narrow margin*; *margin of safety*. **4** (in commerce) the difference between cost price and selling price; *profit margins*.

**marginal** *adjective* **1** written in a margin; *marginal notes*. **2** of or at an edge. **3** very slight in amount; *its usefulness is marginal*. **4** (of a parliamentary seat) where an MP has only a small majority and may easily be defeated at the next election. □ **marginal cost** the cost added by making one extra item, copy, etc. □ **marginally** *adverb*

**marginalia** (mar-jin-**ay**-liă) *plural noun* notes written in a margin.

**marginalize** *verb* (*also* **marginalise**) make or treat (a person, issue, etc.) as insignificant.

**marguerite** (marg-er-**eet**) *noun* a large daisy-like flower with a yellow centre and white petals.

**maria** *see* MARE[2].

**Mariana Islands** (ma-ri-**ah**-nă) (*also* **Marianas**) a group of islands in the NW Pacific, administered by the USA.

**Marie Antoinette** (**mah**-ri ahn-twah-**net**) (1755–93), queen of France (as the wife of Louis XVI), executed during the French Revolution.

**marigold** *noun* a garden plant with golden or bright yellow flowers.

**marijuana** (ma-ri-**wah**-nă) *noun* (*also* **marihuana**) the dried leaves, stems, and flowering tops of the hemp plant, used to make a hallucinogenic drug, especially in the form of cigarettes.

**marimba** (mă-**rim**-bă) *noun* **1** a xylophone of Africa and Central America. **2** a modern orchestral instrument evolved from this.

**marina** (mă-**ree**-nă) *noun* a harbour for yachts and pleasure boats.

**marinade** (ma-rin-**ayd**) *noun* a seasoned flavoured liquid in which meat, fish, etc. is soaked before being cooked. ●*verb* soak in a marinade.

**marinate** *verb* = MARINADE.

**marine** (mă-**reen**) *adjective* **1** of or living in the sea; *marine animals*. **2** of shipping, nautical; *marine insurance*. **3** for use at sea. ●*noun* **1** a country's shipping; *the mercantile marine*. **2** a member of a body of troops trained to serve on land or sea.

**Mariner** (**ma**-rin-er) a series of US planetary probes (1962–77), of which 11 and 12 were renamed Voyager 1 and 2.

**mariner** (**ma**-rin-er) *noun* a sailor, a seaman.

**marionette** (ma-ri-ŏn-**et**) *noun* a puppet worked by strings.

**marital** (**ma**-rit'l) *adjective* of marriage, of or between husband and wife. □ **maritally** *adverb*

**maritime** (**ma**-ri-tym) *adjective* **1** living, situated, or found near the sea. **2** of seafaring or shipping; *maritime law*.

**Maritime Provinces** (*also* **Maritimes**) the Canadian Provinces of New Brunswick, Nova Scotia, Prince Edward Island, and sometimes Newfoundland, with coastlines on the Gulf of St Lawrence or the Atlantic.

**marjoram** (**mar**-jer-ăm) *noun* a herb with fragrant leaves, used in cooking.

**Mark**, St **1** an evangelist, traditional author of the second Gospel. Feast day, 25 April. **2** the second Gospel.

**mark**[1] *noun* **1** a line or area that differs in appearance from the rest of a surface, especially one that spoils it. **2** a distinguishing feature or characteristic. **3** something that indicates the presence of a quality or feeling; *as a mark of respect*. **4** a symbol placed on a thing to indicate its origin, ownership, or quality. **5** a written or printed symbol; *punctuation marks*. **6** a lasting impression; *poverty had left its mark*. **7** a unit awarded for the merit or quality of a piece of work or a performance; *got high marks*. **8** a target, a standard to be aimed at; *not up to the mark*. **9** (*usually* **Mark**) (foll. by a number) a particular design or model of a car, aircraft, etc.; *an old Mark 2 Cortina*. **10** a line or object serving to indicate position. ●*verb* **1** make a mark on. **2** distinguish with a mark, characterize. **3** assign marks of merit to. **4** notice, watch carefully; *mark my words!* **5** keep close to (an opposing player) in football etc. so as to prevent him or her receiving the ball. □ **make one's mark** make a significant achievement, become famous. **mark down 1** notice and remember the place etc. of. **2** reduce the price of. **mark off** separate by a boundary. **mark out** mark the boundaries of; destine, single out; *marked her out for promotion*. **mark time 1** move the feet rhythmically as if in marching but without advancing. **2** occupy time in routine work without making progress. **mark up** increase the price of. **mark-up** *noun* the amount a seller adds to the cost price of an article to determine selling price. **off the mark 1** off the point, irrelevant. **2** having made a start.

**mark²** *noun* = DEUTSCHMARK.

**Mark Antony** *see* ANTONY².

**marked** *adjective* clearly noticeable; *a marked improvement*. □ **a marked man** one who is singled out, e.g. as an object of vengeance. □ **markedly** (mark-id-li) *adverb*

**marker** *noun* **1** a person or tool that marks; one who records the score in games etc. **2** a broad felt-tipped pen. **3** something that serves to mark a position.

**market** *noun* **1** a gathering for the sale of goods or livestock. **2** a space or building used for this. **3** the conditions or opportunity for buying or selling; *found a ready market*. **4** a place where goods may be sold; a particular class of buyers; *foreign markets*; *the teenage market*. **5** the stock market. ● *verb* offer for sale; promote the sale of (products) by advertising etc. □ **be in the market for** wish to buy or obtain. **market forces** the influences of business, supply and demand, etc. on prices, wages, jobs, etc. without interference or control from government. **market garden** a small farm where vegetables are grown for market. **market-place** *noun* **1** an open space where a market is held in a town. **2** the commercial world. **market price** the current price; the going rate. **market research** study of consumers' needs and preferences. **market town** one where a market is held regularly. **market value** the amount for which something can be sold, its current value. **on the market** offered for sale. □ **marketer** *noun*, **marketing** *noun*

**marketable** *adjective* able or fit to be sold. □ **marketability** *noun*

**marketeer** *noun* **1** a supporter of the EC and full British membership of it. **2** a marketer.

**marking** *noun* **1** a mark or marks. **2** the colouring of an animal's skin, feathers, or fur.

**Markova** (mar-**koh**-vă), Dame Alicia (original name: Lilian Alicia Marks) (born 1910), English ballerina.

**Marks**, Simon, 1st Baron (1888–1964), English retailer and business innovator, son of Michael Marks, a Polish refugee, whose stall in Leeds market was the nucleus of the company created in 1926 as Marks & Spencer.

**marksman** *noun* (*plural* **marksmen**) a person who is a skilled shot. □ **marksmanship** *noun*

**marl** *noun* a soil consisting of clay and lime, a valuable fertilizer. □ **marly** *adjective*

**Marlborough** (**mawl**-bŏ-rŏ), John Churchill, 1st Duke of (1650–1722), English soldier, noted for his series of victories over the French.

**Marley**, Bob (Robert Nesta) (1945–81), Jamaican reggae musician and songwriter.

**marlin** *noun* (*plural* **marlin** *or* **marlins**) (*Amer.*) a long-nosed sea fish.

**marlinspike** *noun* a pointed metal tool used to separate strands of rope or wire.

**Marlowe** (**mar**-loh), Christopher (1564–93), English dramatist and poet.

**marmalade** *noun* a jam made from citrus fruit, especially oranges.

**Marmara** (**mar**-mă-ră), **Sea of** a small inland sea in Turkey connected by the Bosporus to the Black Sea and by the Dardanelles to the Aegean.

**marmoreal** (mar-**mor**-iăl) *adjective* of or like marble.

**marmoset** (**mar**-mŏ-zet) *noun* a small bushy-tailed monkey of tropical America.

**marmot** (**mar**-mŏt) *noun* a small burrowing animal of the squirrel family.

**marocain** (ma-rŏ-**kayn**) *noun* a ribbed crêpe dress-fabric.

**Maronite** (**ma**-rŏ-nyt) *noun* a member of a Christian sect of Syrian origin, living chiefly in Lebanon.

**maroon¹** *noun* a brownish-red colour. ● *adjective* brownish-red.

**maroon²** *verb* abandon or isolate (a person), e.g. on an island or in a deserted place.

**marque** (*pronounced* mark) *noun* a make of motor car, as opposed to a specific model.

**marquee** (mar-**kee**) *noun* a large tent used for a party or an exhibition etc.

**Marquesas Islands** (mar-**kay**-săs) a group of islands in the Pacific, in French possession.

**marquess** (**mar**-kwis) *noun* a British nobleman ranking between a duke and an earl.

**marquetry** (**mar**-kit-ri) *noun* inlaid work in wood or ivory etc.

**Márquez**, Gabriel García (born 1928), Colombian novelist.

**marquis** (**mar**-kwis) *noun* a foreign nobleman ranking between a duke and a count.

**marquise** (mar-**keez**) *noun* (in foreign nobility) a marchioness.

**marram** (**ma**-răm) *noun* a shore grass that binds sand.

**marriage** *noun* **1** the legal union of a man and woman. **2** the act or ceremony of being married. **3** joining; union; combination. □ **marriage bureau** an agency that arranges meetings between people of opposite sexes who wish to marry. **marriage certificate** a certificate confirming that two people are legally married. **marriage guidance** advice given by authorized counsellors about marital problems. **marriage licence** a licence giving people permission to get married. **marriage lines** plural noun = MARRIAGE CERTIFICATE.

**marriageable** adjective old enough or fit for marriage. □ **marriageability** noun

**marron glacé** (ma-ron **gla**-say) (plural **marrons glacés**, pronounced same) a chestnut preserved in sugar as a sweet.

**marrow** noun **1** the soft fatty substance in the cavities of bones. **2** the large fruit of a plant of the gourd family, used as a vegetable.

**marrowbone** noun a bone containing edible marrow.

**marrowfat** noun a kind of large pea.

**marry** verb (**married, marrying**) **1** unite or give or take in marriage. **2** take a husband or wife in marriage; she never married. **3** unite, put (things) together as a pair.

**Mars 1** (Rom. myth.) the god of war, identified with Ares. **2** one of the planets, with a characteristic red colour.

**Marsala** (mar-**sah**-lă) noun a dark sweet fortified wine of a kind originally made in Sicily.

**Marseillaise** (mar-say-**yayz**) noun the national anthem of France.

**Marseilles** (mar-**say**) a French seaport on the Mediterranean coast.

**marsh** noun low-lying watery ground. □ **marsh gas** methane. **marsh marigold** a golden-flowered plant that grows in moist meadows. □ **marshy** adjective

**marshal** noun **1** an officer of high or the highest rank; Air Marshal; Field Marshal. **2** an official with responsibility for arranging certain public events or ceremonies. **3** an official accompanying a judge on circuit, with secretarial duties. **4** an official at a race. ● verb (**marshalled, marshalling**; Amer. **marshaled, marshaling**) **1** arrange in proper order. **2** cause to assemble. **3** usher; marshalled him into the governor's office. □ **Marshal of the Royal Air Force** the highest rank in the RAF. **marshalling yard** a railway yard in which goods trains etc. are assembled for dispatch.

**Marshall Aid** financial assistance given to certain Western European countries after the Second World War. (¶ Named after G. C. Marshall (1880-1959), the US Secretary of State who initiated this plan in 1947.)

**Marshall Islands** a group of islands in the NW Pacific, administered by the USA under the trusteeship of the UN.

**marshland** noun marshy land.

**marshmallow** noun a soft sweet made from sugar, egg-white, and gelatin.

**marsupial** (mar-**soo**-piăl) noun an animal such as the kangaroo, the female of which has a pouch in which its young are carried until they are fully developed.

**mart** noun a market.

**Martello** noun (also **Martello tower**) any of the small circular forts erected along the coasts of Britain during the Napoleonic Wars to repel the expected French landings.

**marten** noun a weasel-like animal with thick soft fur.

**Martial** (**mar**-shăl) (Marcus Valerius Martialis) (c. AD 40–c.104), Roman writer of epigrams.

**martial** (**mar**-shăl) adjective of war, warlike; martial music. □ **martial arts** fighting sports such as judo and karate. **martial law** military rule imposed on a country, suspending ordinary law.

**Martian** (**mar**-shăn) adjective of the planet Mars. ● noun (in science fiction etc.) an inhabitant of Mars.

**Martin**, St (died 397), a patron saint of France. Feast day, 11 November.

**martin** noun a bird of the swallow family.

**martinet** (mar-tin-**et**) noun a person who demands strict obedience.

**martingale** noun a strap or set of straps fastened from the reins to the girth on a horse to prevent it from rearing etc.

**Martini** (mar-**tee**-ni) noun **1** (trade mark) vermouth. **2** a cocktail of gin and vermouth.

**Martinique** (mar-tin-**eek**) a French West Indian island.

**Martinmas** noun St Martin's day, 11 November.

**martyr** noun **1** a person who undergoes death or great suffering in support of a belief, cause, or principle. **2** a person who makes a show of suffering to get sympathy. **3** (foll. by to) a constant sufferer from (an ailment); is a martyr to rheumatism. ● verb put to death or torment as a martyr. □ **martyrdom** noun

**marvel** noun a wonderful thing. ● verb (**marvelled, marvelling**; Amer. **marveled, marveling**) be filled with wonder.

**Marvell**, Andrew (1621-78), English poet and satirist.

**marvellous** adjective (Amer. **marvelous**) astonishing, excellent. □ **marvellously** adverb

**Marx**, Karl Heinrich (1818-83), German political philosopher and economist, founder of modern Communism.

**Marx Brothers** an American family of film comedians, consisting of Chico (Leonard) (1891-1961), and his brothers Harpo (Adolph, later Arthur) (1893-1964), Groucho (Julius Henry) (1895-1977), and Zeppo (Herbert) (1900-79).

**Marxism** noun the political and economic theory of Karl Marx, on which Communism is based. □ **Marxist** adjective & noun

**Mary**[1] (in the Bible) **1** the Blessed Virgin Mary, mother of Jesus Christ. **2** Mary Magdalene (= of Magdala in Galilee), a follower of Christ. Feast day, 22 July.

**Mary**[2] the name of two queens of England, Mary I (reigned 1553–8), Mary II (reigned, with William III, 1689–94).

*Mary Celeste* (si-**lest**) an American brig that set sail from New York for Genoa and was found abandoned in the North Atlantic in December 1872.

**Maryland** a State on the Atlantic coast of the USA.

**Mary, Queen of Scots** (1542–87), queen of Scotland 1542–67, beheaded after the discovery of a Catholic plot against Elizabeth I of England.

*Mary Rose* a heavily armed ship built for Henry VIII, sunk in July 1545. The hull was raised in 1982.

**marzipan** (**mar**-zi-pan) noun a paste of ground almonds and sugar, made into small cakes or sweets or used to coat large cakes.

**Masada** (mă-**sah**-dă) a fortress on a steep hill west of the Dead Sea, famous as the Jewish stronghold during the revolt against Roman rule, where in AD 73 the defenders committed mass suicide rather than surrender.

**Masai** (**mah**-sy or mă-**sy**) noun (plural **Masai** or **Masais**) **1** a member of a pastoral people of Kenya and Tanzania. **2** their language.

**Masaryk** (**ma**-să-rik), Tomáš Garrigue (1850–1937), Czechoslovakian statesman, a co-founder of the former Czechoslovakia and its first President.

**mascara** noun a cosmetic for darkening the eyelashes.

**mascot** noun **1** a person or thing believed to bring good luck to its owner. **2** a figurine mounted on the bonnet of a car etc.

**masculine** adjective **1** of, like, or suitable for men; having the qualities or appearance considered characteristic of a man. **2** having the grammatical form of the male gender; *'hero' is a masculine noun, 'heroine' is the corresponding feminine noun.* ●noun a masculine word or gender. □ **masculinity** noun

**Masefield**, John Edward (1878–1967), English poet, Poet Laureate from 1930.

**maser** (**may**-zer) noun a device for amplifying microwaves.

**Maseru** (ma-ser-**oo**) the capital of Lesotho.

**mash** noun **1** grain or bran etc. cooked in water to form a soft mixture, used as animal food. **2** (*informal*) mashed potatoes. **3** a mixture of malt and hot water used in

brewing. ●verb beat or crush into a soft mixture.

**mask** noun **1** a covering worn over the face (or part of it) as a disguise or for protection. **2** a carved or moulded replica of a face. **3** a respirator worn over the face to filter air for breathing or to supply gas for inhaling. **4** the face or head of a fox. **5** a screen used in photography to exclude part of the image. ●verb **1** cover with a mask. **2** disguise, screen, or conceal. □ **masking tape** adhesive tape used when painting to protect areas where paint is not wanted.

**masochist** (**mas**-ŏ-kist) noun **1** a person who derives sexual excitement and satisfaction from his or her own pain or humiliation. **2** one who enjoys what seems to be painful or tiresome. □ **masochism** noun, **masochistic** adjective

**Mason** noun a Freemason. □ **Masonic** (mă-**sonn**-ik) adjective

**mason** noun a person who builds or works with stone.

**Mason-Dixon line** the boundary line between Pennsylvania and Maryland, laid out in 1763–7 by the English surveyors Charles Mason and Jeremiah Dixon, popularly regarded as the border between North and South in the USA.

**Masonry** noun Freemasonry.

**masonry** noun stonework.

**masque** (*pronounced* mahsk) noun a musical drama with mime, especially in the 16th and 17th centuries.

**masquerade** (mas-ker-**ayd**) noun a false show or pretence. ●verb pretend to be what one is not; *masqueraded as a policeman.*

**mass**[1] noun **1** a coherent unit of matter with no specific shape. **2** a large quantity or heap, an unbroken extent; *the garden was a mass of flowers.* **3** (in technical usage) the quantity of matter a body contains (called *weight* in non-technical usage). **4** (**the mass**) the majority. **5** (**the masses**) the common people. ●verb gather or assemble into a mass. □ **mass media** = *the media*; see MEDIA (sense 2). **mass meeting** one attended by a large number of people. **mass noun** Grammar a noun that is not normally countable and not used with the indefinite article, e.g. bread. **mass number** the total number of protons and neutrons in a nucleus. **mass-produce** verb manufacture in large numbers of identical articles by standardized processes. **mass production** manufacturing in this way.

**mass**[2] noun (especially in the RC Church) **1** a celebration of the Eucharist. **2** the form of service used in this; a musical setting for the words of it.

**Mass.** abbreviation Massachusetts.

**Massachusetts** a State of the north-eastern USA.

**massacre** *noun* slaughter of a large number of people or animals. ●*verb* slaughter in large numbers.

**massage** (mas-ah*zh*) *noun* rubbing and kneading the body to lessen pain or stiffness. ●*verb* **1** treat in this way. **2** adjust (figures, statistics, etc.) to give an acceptable result.

**masseur** (ma-ser) *noun* a man who practises massage professionally.

**masseuse** (ma-serz) *noun* a woman who practices massage professionally.

**massif** (ma-seef) *noun* mountain heights forming a compact group.

**massive** *adjective* **1** large and heavy or solid. **2** unusually large. **3** considerable, great; *a massive improvement*. □ **massively** *adverb*, **massiveness** *noun*

**mast**¹ *noun* **1** a long upright pole that supports a ship's sails. **2** a tall pole from which a flag is flown. **3** a tall steel structure for the aerials of a radio or television transmitter. □ **before the mast** serving as an ordinary seaman (quartered in the forecastle). □ **masted** *adjective*

**mast**² *noun* the fruit of beech, oak, chestnut, and other forest trees, used as food for pigs.

**mastectomy** (mas-tek-tŏmi) *noun* surgical removal of a breast.

**master** *noun* **1** a person who has control or ownership of people or things. **2** the captain of a merchant ship. **3** an employer; *masters and men*. **4** a male teacher, a schoolmaster. **5** (**Master**) the holder of a university degree as *Master of Arts* etc. **6** a respected teacher. **7** a person with very great skill, a great artist. **8** a chess player of proved ability at international level. **9** a document, film, disk, etc. from which a series of copies is made. **10** (**Master**) a title prefixed to the name of a boy who is not old enough to be called *Mr*. ●*verb* **1** overcome, bring under control. **2** acquire knowledge or skill in. □ **master-class** *noun* a class given by a famous musician, artist, etc. **master-key** *noun* a key that opens a number of locks, each also opened by a separate key. **Master of Arts, Master of Science** a university degree, usually above a first degree, but below a Ph.D. **Master of Ceremonies** a person in charge of a social or other occasion, who introduces the events or performers. **Master of the Rolls** (*Brit.*) the judge who presides over the Court of Appeal. (**United States**) **Masters Tournament** a golf contest for players of the highest standard, held annually at Augusta, Georgia, USA. **master-stroke** *noun* an outstandingly skilful act of

policy etc. **master-switch** *noun* a switch controlling the supply of electricity etc. to an entire system.

**masterful** *adjective* **1** domineering. **2** (of a person) very skilful. □ **masterfully** *adverb*

**masterly** *adjective* (of an achievement or ability) worthy of a master, very skilful.

**mastermind** *noun* **1** a person with outstanding mental ability. **2** the person directing an enterprise. ●*verb* plan and direct; *masterminded the whole scheme*.

**masterpiece** *noun* **1** an outstanding piece of workmanship. **2** a person's best piece of work.

**mastery** *noun* **1** complete control, supremacy. **2** thorough knowledge or skill; *his mastery of Arabic*.

**masthead** *noun* **1** the highest part of a ship's mast. **2** the title details of a newspaper at the head of its front or editorial page.

**mastic** *noun* **1** a gum or resin exuded from certain trees. **2** a type of cement.

**masticate** *verb* chew (food). □ **mastication** *noun*, **masticatory** *adjective*

**mastiff** *noun* a large strong dog with drooping ears.

**mastitis** (mas-ty-tis) *noun* inflammation of the breast or udder.

**mastodon** (mast-ŏ-don) *noun* a large extinct animal resembling the elephant.

**mastoid** *adjective* shaped like a breast. ●*noun* **1** = MASTOID PROCESS. **2** (usually as **mastoids**) inflammation of the mastoid process. □ **mastoid process** a cone-shaped bump on the temporal bone behind the ear.

**masturbate** *verb* excite oneself (or another person) sexually by stimulating the genitals with the hand. □ **masturbation** *noun*

**mat**¹ *noun* **1** a piece of material used as a floor covering, a doormat. **2** a small pad or piece of material placed under an ornament or vase etc. or under a hot dish, to protect the surface on which it stands. **3** a thick pad for landing on in gymnastics etc. ●*verb* (**matted, matting**) make or become entangled to form a thick mass; *matted hair*. □ **on the mat** (*slang*) being reprimanded.

**mat**² alternative spelling of MATT.

**Matabele** (mat-ă-bee-li) *noun* (*plural* **Matabele**) a member of a Bantu-speaking people of Zimbabwe.

**matador** (mat-ă-dor) *noun* a performer whose task is to fight and kill the bull in a bull-fight.

**Mata Hari** (mah-tă hah-ri) (real name: Margaretha Geertruida Zelle) (1876–1917), Dutch dancer, courtesan, and secret agent, who worked for both the French and the German intelligence services before being executed by the French as a spy.

**match¹** *noun* a short piece of wood or pasteboard with a tip that bursts into flame when rubbed on a rough surface.

**match²** *noun* **1** a contest in a game or sport. **2** a person or animal with abilities equalling those of one met in contest; *meet one's match*; *you are no match for him*. **3** a person or thing exactly like or corresponding to another. **4** a marriage. **5** a person considered as a partner for marriage, especially with regard to rank or fortune. ● *verb* **1** (foll. by *against* or *with*) place in competition; *the teams were matched against each other*. **2** equal in ability or skill etc. **3** be alike or correspond in colour, quality, quantity, etc. **4** find something similar to; *I want to match this wool*. **5** put or bring together as corresponding; *matching unemployed workers with vacant posts*. □ **match play** *Golf* scoring by counting the holes won by each side (as opposed to the number of strokes taken). **match point** the stage in a match when one side will win if it gains the next point; this point.

**matchboard** *noun* board with a tongue cut along one edge and a groove along another, so as to fit with similar boards.

**matchbox** *noun* a box for holding matches.

**matchless** *adjective* unequalled.

**matchmaker** *noun* a person who is fond of scheming to bring about marriages. □ **matchmaking** *adjective & noun*

**matchstick** *noun* the stem of a match.

**matchwood** *noun* **1** wood that splinters easily. **2** wood reduced to splinters.

**mate¹** *noun* **1** a companion, a fellow worker (also used informally as a form of address to an equal). **2** each of a mated pair of birds or animals. **3** (*informal*) a partner in marriage. **4** a fellow member or sharer; *team-mate*; *room-mate*. **5** an officer on a merchant ship ranking next below the master. **6** a worker's assistant; *plumber's mate*. ● *verb* **1** put or come together as a pair or as corresponding. **2** put (two birds or animals) together so that they can breed; come together in order to breed.

**mate²** *noun* a situation in chess in which the capture of a king cannot be prevented. ● *verb* put into this situation.

**mater** (**may**-ter) *noun* (*slang* or *old use*) mother. (¶ Latin.)

**material** *noun* **1** the substance or things from which something is or can be made or with which something is done; *writing materials*; *select those regarded as officer material*. **2** cloth, fabric. **3** facts, information, or events etc. to be used in composing something; *gathering material for a book on poverty*. ● *adjective* **1** of matter; consisting of matter; of the physical (as opposed to spiritual) world; *material things*; *had no thought of material gain*. **2** of bodily comfort; *our material well-being*. **3** important, significant, relevant; *is this material to the issue?*

**materialism** *noun* **1** excessive concern with material possessions rather than spiritual or intellectual values. **2** belief that only the material world exists. □ **materialist** *noun*, **materialistic** *adjective*

**materialize** *verb* (also **materialise**) **1** appear or become visible; arrive; *the boy failed to materialize*. **2** become a fact, happen; *if the threatened strike materializes*. □ **materialization** *noun*

**materially** *adverb* substantially, considerably.

**matériel** (*pronounced as* material) *noun* means, especially materials and equipment in warfare.

**maternal** (mă-**ter**-năl) *adjective* **1** of a mother, of motherhood. **2** motherly. **3** related through one's mother; *maternal uncle*. □ **maternally** *adverb*

**maternity** (mă-**ter**-niti) *noun* **1** motherhood. **2** of or suitable or caring for women in pregnancy or childbirth; *maternity dress*; *maternity ward*.

**matey** (also **maty**) *adjective* (**matier**, **matiest**) sociable, friendly. ● *noun* (*informal*) (as a form of address) mate. □ **mateyness** *noun* (also **matiness**), **matily** *adverb*

**math** *noun* (*Amer. informal*) mathematics.

**mathematician** *noun* a person who is skilled in mathematics.

**mathematics** *noun* **1** (usually treated as *singular*) the science of number, quantity, and space. **2** (treated as *plural*) the use of mathematics in calculation; *his mathematics are weak*. □ **mathematical** *adjective*, **mathematically** *adverb*

**maths** *noun* (*informal*) mathematics.

**matinée** (**mat**-in-ay) *noun* (*Amer.* **matinee**) an afternoon performance at a theatre or cinema. □ **matinée coat** *or* **jacket** a baby's short coat.

**matins** *noun* (also **mattins**) (treated as *singular* or *plural*) morning prayer, especially in the Church of England.

**Matisse** (ma-**teess**), Henri Émile Benoît (1869–1954), French painter and sculptor.

**matriarch** (**may**-tri-ark) *noun* a woman who is head of a family or tribe. □ **matriarchal** (may-tri-**ark**-ăl) *adjective*

**matriarchy** (**may**-tri-ark-i) *noun* **1** a social organization in which the mother is head of the family and descent is through the female line. **2** a society in which women have most of the authority.

**matrices** *see* MATRIX.

**matricide** (may-tri-syd) *noun* **1** the act of killing one's mother. **2** a person who is guilty of this. □ **matricidal** *adjective*

**matriculate** (mă-**trik**-yoo-layt) *verb* enrol at a college or university. □ **matriculation** *noun*

**matrilineal** (mat-ri-**lin**-iăl) *adjective* of or based on kinship with the mother or the female line of ancestors.

**matrimony** (**mat**-ri-mŏni) *noun* marriage. □ **matrimonial** (mat-ri-**moh**-niăl) *adjective*, **matrimonially** *adverb*

**matrix** (**may**-triks) *noun* (*plural* **matrices**, *pronounced* **may**-tri-seez, *or* **matrixes**) **1** a mould in which something is cast or shaped. **2** a place in which a thing is developed. **3** an array of mathematical quantities etc. in rows and columns. **4** (in computers) an interconnected array of circuit elements that resembles a lattice or grid.

**matron** *noun* **1** a married woman, especially one who is staid and middle-aged or elderly. **2** a woman managing the domestic affairs of a school etc. **3** a former term for the senior nursing officer in a hospital or other institution. □ **matron of honour** a married woman as the chief attendant of the bride at a wedding.

**matronly** *adjective* like or suitable for a staid married woman.

**matt** *adjective* (also **mat**) (of a colour or surface) having a dull finish, not shiny.

**matter** *noun* **1** that which occupies space in the visible world, as opposed to spirit, mind, or qualities etc. **2** a particular substance or material; *colouring matter*. **3** a discharge from the body; pus. **4** material for thought or expression; the content of a book or speech as distinct from its form; *subject matter*. **5** things of a specified kind; *reading matter*. **6** a situation or business being considered; *it's a serious matter*; *a matter for complaint*. **7** a quantity; *for a matter of 40 years*. ●*verb* be of importance; *it doesn't matter*. □ **the matter** the thing that is amiss, the trouble or difficulty; *what's the matter?* **for that matter** as far as that is concerned. **a matter of course** an event etc. that follows naturally or is to be expected. **a matter of fact** something that is a fact not an opinion etc. **matter-of-fact** *adjective* strictly factual and not imaginative or emotional; down-to-earth. **no matter** it is of no importance.

**Matterhorn** a spectacular Alpine peak on the Swiss-Italian border.

**Matthew**, St **1** an Apostle, to whom the first Gospel is ascribed. Feast day, 21 September. **2** the first Gospel.

**Matthews**, Sir Stanley (born 1915), English footballer.

**matting** *noun* mats; material for making these.

**mattins** alternative spelling of MATINS.

**mattock** *noun* an agricultural tool with the blade set at right angles to the handle, used for loosening soil and digging out roots.

**mattress** *noun* a fabric case filled with soft, firm, or springy material, used on or as a bed.

**maturate** (**mat**-yoor-ayt) *verb* come or bring to maturation, mature.

**maturation** (mat-yoor-**ay**-shŏn) *noun* the process of maturing, ripening.

**mature** *adjective* **1** having reached full growth or development. **2** having or showing fully developed mental powers, capable of reasoning and acting sensibly. **3** (of wine) having reached a good stage of development. **4** (of a bill of exchange, life assurance policy, etc.) due for payment. ●*verb* make or become mature. □ **mature student** an older student, one who has had a break of several years between school and higher education. □ **maturely** *adverb*, **maturity** *noun*

**matutinal** (mă-**tew**-tin-ăl) *adjective* (*formal*) of or occurring in the morning.

**maty** alternative spelling of MATEY.

**matzo** *noun* (*plural* **matzos**) a wafer of unleavened bread, traditionally eaten at Passover.

**maudlin** *adjective* sentimental in a silly or tearful way, especially from drunkenness.

**Maugham** (*pronounced* mawm), (William) Somerset (1874–1965), English novelist, dramatist, and writer of short stories.

**maul** *verb* treat roughly, injure by rough handling or clawing. ●*noun* **1** (in Rugby) a loose scrum. **2** a heavy hammer.

**maulstick** *noun* (also **mahlstick**) a stick used to support the hand in painting.

**maunder** *verb* talk in a rambling way.

**Maundy** *noun* **1** the distribution of Maundy money. **2** (in the RC Church) the ceremony of washing people's feet on Maundy Thursday. □ **Maundy money** specially minted silver coins distributed by the sovereign to the poor on **Maundy Thursday**, the Thursday before Easter, celebrated in commemoration of the Last Supper.

**Maupassant** (**moh**-pass-ahn), Guy de (1850–93), French short-story writer and novelist.

**Mauritania** (mo-ri-**tay**-niă) a country in north-west Africa. □ **Mauritanian** *adjective & noun*

**Mauritius** (mă-**rish**-ŭs) an island in the Indian Ocean. □ **Mauritian** *adjective & noun*

**mausoleum** (maw-sŏ-**lee**-ŭm) *noun* a magnificent tomb. (¶ Named after that erected at Halicarnassus in Asia Minor for King Mausolus in the 4th century BC.)

**mauve** (*pronounced* mohv) *adjective & noun* pale purple.

**maverick** (**mav**-er-ik) *noun* **1** an unconventional or independent-minded person. **2** (*Amer.*) an unbranded calf or other young animal.

**maw** *noun* the jaws, mouth, or stomach of a voracious animal.

**mawkish** *adjective* sentimental in a sickly way. □ **mawkishly** *adverb*, **mawkishness** *noun*

**max.** *abbreviation* maximum.

**maxi** *noun* (*informal*) a full-length skirt, coat, etc.

**maxi-** *combining form* very large or long.

**maxilla** *noun* (*plural* **maxillae**) **1** a jaw, especially the upper one. **2** a corresponding part in insects etc. □ **maxillary** *adjective*

**maxim** *noun* a general truth or rule of conduct, e.g. 'waste not, want not'.

**maxima** *see* MAXIMUM.

**maximal** *adjective* greatest possible. □ **maximally** *adverb*

**maximize** *verb* (also **maximise**) increase to a maximum. □ **maximization** *noun*

**maximum** *noun* (*plural* **maxima**) the greatest or greatest possible number, amount, or intensity etc. ● *adjective* greatest, greatest possible.

**Maxwell**[1], James Clerk (1831–79), Scottish physicist, noted especially for his work on electromagnetism.

**Maxwell**[2], Robert (Ian Robert) (original name: Jan Ludvik Hoch), (1923–1991), British publisher, newspaper proprietor, and entrepreneur, born in Czechoslovakia, whose death revealed massive debts and financial disorder among his business interests.

**May** the fifth month of the year. □ **May Day** 1 May, kept as a festival with dancing or as an international holiday in honour of workers. **May queen** a girl chosen to preside over festivities on May Day.

**may**[1] *auxiliary verb* (*see also* MIGHT[2]) expressing possibility (*it may be true*), permission (*you may go*), wish (*long may she reign*), or uncertainty (*whoever it may be*).

**may**[2] *noun* hawthorn blossom.

**Maya** (**mah**-yă) *noun* **1** (*plural* **Maya** or **Mayas**) a member of an American Indian people living in Mexico until the 15th century. **2** their language. □ **Mayan** *adjective & noun*

**maya** (**mah**-yă) *noun* **1** (in Hinduism) illusion, magic. **2** (in Hindu and Buddhist philosophy) the power by which the universe becomes manifest; the material world, regarded as illusory.

**maybe** *adverb* perhaps, possibly.

**mayday** *noun* an international radio signal of distress. (¶ Representing the pronunciation of French *m'aider* = help me.)

**Mayflower** the ship in which, in 1620, the Pilgrim Fathers sailed from Plymouth to establish the first colony in New England on the coast of North America.

**mayflower** *noun* any of various flowers that bloom in May.

**mayfly** *noun* an insect with two or three long hairlike tails, living briefly in spring.

**mayhem** *noun* violent or damaging action.

**mayn't** (*informal*) = may not.

**mayonnaise** (may-ŏn-**ayz**) *noun* **1** a creamy sauce made with egg yolks, oil, and vinegar. **2** a dish with a dressing of this; *egg mayonnaise*.

**mayor** *noun* the head of the municipal corporation of a city or borough, or of a district council with borough status. □ **mayoral** (**mair**-ăl) *adjective*

**mayoralty** (**mair**-ăl-ti) *noun* the office of mayor; its duration.

**mayoress** *noun* **1** a mayor's wife, or other lady performing her ceremonial duties. **2** a woman mayor.

**maypole** *noun* a tall pole for dancing round on May Day, with ribbons attached to its top.

**Mazdaism** (**maz**-dă-izm) *noun* Zoroastrianism, worship of Ahura Mazda.

**maze** *noun* **1** a complicated network of paths, a labyrinth. **2** a network of paths and hedges designed as a puzzle in which to try and find one's way. **3** a state of bewilderment.

**mazurka** (mă-**zerk**-ă) *noun* a lively Polish dance in triple time; music for this.

**MB** *abbreviation* **1** Bachelor of Medicine. **2** *Computing* (often **Mb**) megabyte.

**Mbabane** (mbah-**bah**-ni) the capital of Swaziland.

**MBE** *abbreviation* Member of the Order of the British Empire.

**MBO** *abbreviation* management buyout.

**MC** *abbreviation* **1** Master of Ceremonies. **2** Military Cross. **3** Member of Congress.

**MCC** *abbreviation* Marylebone Cricket Club, until 1969 the governing body that made the rules of cricket.

**MD** *abbreviation* **1** (also **Md.**) Maryland. **2** Doctor of Medicine. **3** Managing Director.

**Md** *symbol* mendelevium.

**ME** *abbreviation* **1** myalgic encephalomyelitis, a condition with prolonged flu-like symptoms, great fatigue, and depression. **2** (also **Me.**) Maine.

**me**[1] *pronoun* **1** the objective case of I. **2** (*informal*) = I; *it's me*.

**me**[2] *noun* (also **mi**) *Music* the third note of a major scale.

**mea culpa** (may-ă **kuul**-pă) an acknowledgement of error, guilt, etc. (¶ Latin, = by my fault.)

**mead** *noun* an alcoholic drink of fermented honey and water.

**meadow** *noun* a field of grass.

**meadowsweet** *noun* a meadow plant with fragrant creamy-white flowers.

**meagre** (**meeg**-er) *adjective* (*Amer.* **meager**) scanty in amount.

**meal**¹ *noun* **1** an occasion when food is eaten. **2** the food itself. □ **make a meal of** make (a task) seem unnecessarily laborious. **meals on wheels** a service that delivers hot meals by car to elderly or disabled people. **meal-ticket** *noun* (*informal*) a person or thing that is a source of maintenance or income.

**meal**² *noun* coarsely-ground grain or pulse.

**mealie** *noun* (in South Africa) maize.

**mealy** *adjective* **1** like or containing meal, dry and powdery. **2** (of a complexion) pale. □ **mealy-mouthed** *adjective* trying excessively to avoid offending people.

**mean**¹ *verb* (**meant, meaning**) **1** have as one's purpose or intention. **2** design or destine for a purpose; *it was meant for you; are we meant to go this way?* **3** intend to convey (a sense) or to indicate or refer to (a thing). **4** (of words) have as an equivalent in the same or another language; *'maybe' means 'perhaps'.* **5** entail, involve; *it means catching the early train.* **6** be likely or certain to result in; *this means war.* **7** be of a specified importance; *the honour means a lot to me.* □ **mean business** (*informal*) be ready to take action, not merely talk. **mean it** not be joking or exaggerating. **mean well** have good intentions.

**mean**² *adjective* **1** poor in quality or appearance; low in rank. **2** unkind, spiteful; *a mean trick.* **3** not generous, miserly. **4** (*Amer.*) vicious. **5** (*informal*) skilful, formidable. □ **no mean** a very good; considerable; *she's no mean runner; requiring no mean effort.* □ **meanly** *adverb,* **meanness** *noun*

**mean**³ *adjective* (of a point or quantity) equally far from two extremes, average. ● *noun* a middle point, condition, or course etc.

**meander** (mee-an-der) *verb* **1** (of a stream) follow a winding course, flowing slowly and gently. **2** wander in a leisurely way. ● *noun* a winding course.

**meanie** *noun* (also **meany**) (*informal*) a miserly or unkind person.

**meaning** *noun* what is meant; significance. ● *adjective* full of meaning, expressive; *gave him a meaning look.*

**meaningful** *adjective* full of meaning, significant. □ **meaningfully** *adverb*

**meaningless** *adjective* with no meaning. □ **meaninglessly** *adverb*

**means** *plural noun* **1** (often treated as *singular*) that by which a result is brought about; *transported their goods by means of lorries.* **2** resources; money or other wealth considered as a means of supporting oneself; *has private means.* □ **by all means** certainly. **by no means** definitely not; not at all; *it is by no means certain.* **means test** an official inquiry to establish a person's neediness before financial help is given from public funds.

**meant** *see* MEAN¹.

**meantime** *noun* the intervening period; *in the meantime.* ● *adverb* meanwhile.

**meanwhile** *adverb* **1** in the intervening period of time. **2** at the same time, while something else takes place.

**meany** alternative spelling of MEANIE.

**measles** *noun* an infectious disease producing small red spots on the whole body.

**measly** *adjective* **1** affected with measles. **2** (*slang*) meagre.

**measure** *noun* **1** the size or quantity of something, found by measuring. **2** extent, amount; *he is in some measure responsible; had a measure of success.* **3** a unit, standard, or system used in measuring; *the metre is a measure of length.* **4** a device used in measuring, e.g. a container or a marked rod. **5** the rhythm or metre of poetry; the time of a piece of music; a bar of music. **6** suitable action taken for a particular purpose; a law or proposed law; *measures to stop tax evasion.* **7** a layer of rock or mineral. ● *verb* **1** find the size, quantity, or extent of something by comparing it with a fixed unit or with an object of known size. **2** be of a certain size; *it measures two metres by four.* **3** mark or deal out a measured quantity; *measured out their rations.* **4** estimate (a quality etc.) by comparing it with some standard. □ **beyond measure** very much, very great; *kindness beyond measure.* **for good measure** in addition to what was needed; as a finishing touch. **made to measure** made in accordance with measurements taken. **measure up to** reach the standard required by. □ **measurable** *adjective*

**measured** *adjective* **1** rhythmical, regular in movement; *measured tread.* **2** carefully considered; *in measured language.*

**measureless** *adjective* not measurable, infinite.

**measurement** *noun* **1** measuring. **2** size etc. found by measuring and expressed in units.

**meat** *noun* **1** animal flesh as food (usually excluding fish and poultry). **2** informative matter; the chief part; *the meat of the report.* □ **meatless** *adjective*

**meatball** *noun* a small ball of minced meat.

**meaty** *adjective* (**meatier, meatiest**) **1** like meat. **2** full of meat, fleshy. **3** full of informative matter; *a meaty book.*

**Mecca 1** a city in Saudi Arabia, the birthplace of Muhammad and chief place of Muslim pilgrimage. **2** any place that people with particular interests are eager to visit.

**mechanic** *noun* a skilled worker who uses or repairs machines or tools.

**mechanical** *adjective* **1** of machines or mechanism. **2** worked or produced by machinery. **3** (of a person or action) like a machine, as if acting or done without conscious thought. **4** (of work) needing little or no thought. **5** of or belonging to the science of mechanics. □ **mechanical engineer** a person qualified in the design and construction of machines. □ **mechanically** *adverb*

**mechanics** *noun* **1** the scientific study of motion and force. **2** the science of machinery. **3** (treated as *plural*) the processes by which something is done or functions.

**mechanism** *noun* **1** the way a machine works. **2** the structure of parts of a machine. **3** the process by which something is done; *the mechanism of government.*

**mechanize** (**mek-ă-nyz**) *verb* (also **mechanise**) **1** equip with machines, use machines in or for. **2** give a mechanical character to. □ **mechanization** *noun*

**Med** *noun* (*informal*) the Mediterranean Sea.

**medal** *noun* a small flat metal disc bearing a design and commemorating an event or given as an award.

**medallion** (**mid-al-yŏn**) *noun* **1** a large medal. **2** a large circular ornamental design, e.g. on a carpet.

**medallist** *noun* (*Amer.* **medalist**) one who wins a medal as a prize; *gold medallist.*

**Medawar** (**med-ă-wer**), Sir Peter Brian (1915–87), English immunologist, noted for his studies of the transplantation of living tissue.

**meddle** *verb* **1** interfere in people's affairs. **2** tinker. □ **meddler** *noun*

**meddlesome** *adjective* often meddling.

**Mede** *noun* an inhabitant of ancient Persia (Media).

**media** (**meed-iă**) *plural noun* **1** *see* MEDIUM. **2** (**the media**) newspapers and broadcasting, by which information is conveyed to the general public.

---

■**Usage** This word is commonly used with a singular verb (e.g. *the media is biased*), but this is not generally accepted as it is the plural of *medium* and should therefore have a plural verb.

---

**mediaeval** alternative spelling of MEDIEVAL.

**medial** (**mee-di-ăl**) *adjective* situated in the middle, intermediate between two extremes. □ **medially** *adverb*

**median** (**mee-di-ăn**) *adjective* situated in or passing through the middle. ●*noun* **1** a median point or line etc. **2** a medial number or point in a series.

**mediate** (**mee-di-ayt**) *verb* **1** act as negotiator or peacemaker between the opposing sides in a dispute. **2** bring about (a settlement) in this way. □ **mediation** *noun*, **mediator** *noun*

**medic** *noun* (*informal*) a doctor or medical student.

**Medicaid** *noun* (in the USA) a Federal system of health insurance for people who require financial help.

**medical** *adjective* of or involving the science of medicine; of this as distinct from surgery. ●*noun* (*informal*) a medical examination. □ **medical certificate** a certificate giving the results of a medical examination, stating whether a person is fit for work etc. **medical examination** examination by a doctor to determine a person's state of health. **medical officer** a person in charge of the health services of a local authority etc. □ **medically** *adverb*

**medicament** (**mid-ik-ă-měnt**) *noun* any medicine or ointment etc.

**Medicare** *noun* (in the USA) a Federal programme of health insurance for the elderly.

**medicate** *verb* treat or impregnate with a medicinal substance; *medicated gauze.*

**medication** *noun* **1** medicine, drugs, etc. **2** treatment using drugs.

**Medici** (**med-i-chi**) the name of an Italian family prominent especially in Florence and Tuscany in the 15th–17th centuries.

**medicinal** (**mid-iss-in-ăl**) *adjective* of medicine; having healing properties. □ **medicinally** *adverb*

**medicine** (**med-sĭn**) *noun* **1** the scientific study of the prevention and cure of diseases and disorders of the body. **2** this as distinct from surgery. **3** a substance used to treat a disease etc., especially one taken by mouth. □ **medicine man** a witch-doctor. **take one's medicine** submit to something unpleasant.

**medico** *noun* (*plural* **medicos**) (*informal*) a doctor or medical student.

**medieval** (**med-i-ee-văl**) *adjective* (also **mediaeval**) **1** of the Middle Ages. **2** (*informal*) old-fashioned.

**Medina** (**med-een-ă**) a city in Saudi Arabia, the second holiest city of Islam (after Mecca), which contains Muhammad's tomb.

**mediocre** (**meed-i-oh-ker**) *adjective* **1** of medium quality, neither good nor bad.

**2** second-rate. □ **mediocrity** (meed-i-ok-riti) noun

**meditate** verb **1** think deeply and quietly. **2** plan in one's mind. □ **meditation** noun

**meditative** (med-it-ătiv) adjective meditating; accompanied by meditation. □ **meditatively** adverb

**Mediterranean** adjective of or characteristic of the Mediterranean Sea or the regions bordering on it. ●noun (in full **Mediterranean Sea**) a sea lying between Europe and North Africa.

**medium** noun (plural **media** or **mediums**) **1** a middle quality or degree of intensiveness etc. **2** a substance or surroundings in which something exists, moves, or is transmitted; air is the medium through which sound travels. **3** an environment. **4** a liquid (e.g. oil or water) in which pigments are mixed for use in painting. **5** an agency or means by which something is done; the use of television as a medium for advertising. **6** the material or form used by an artist or composer; sculpture is his medium. **7** (plural **mediums**) a person who claims to be able to communicate with the spirits of the dead. ●adjective intermediate between two extremes or amounts, average, moderate. □ **medium wave** a radio wave having a wavelength between 300 kHz and 3 MHz.

■**Usage** See the entry for **media**.

**medlar** noun **1** a fruit like a small brown apple that is not edible until it begins to decay. **2** the tree that bears it.

**medley** noun (plural **medleys**) **1** an assortment of things. **2** a collection of tunes or songs played or performed as one piece.

**medulla** (mi-dul-ă) noun **1** the marrow within a bone; the substance of the spinal cord. **2** the hindmost section of the brain. **3** the central part of certain organs, e.g. that of the kidney. **4** the soft internal tissue of plants. □ **medullary** adjective

**Medusa** (mi-dew-să) (Gk. myth.) one of the Gorgons, slain by Perseus who cut off her head.

**medusa** (mi-dew-să) noun (plural **medusae** or **medusas**) a jellyfish.

**meek** adjective quiet and obedient, making no protest. □ **meekly** adverb, **meekness** noun

**meerkat** noun a South African mongoose.

**meerschaum** (meer-shăm) noun a tobacco pipe with a bowl made from a white clay-like substance.

**meet**[1] verb (**met, meeting**) **1** come face to face with, come together (e.g. socially or for discussion). **2** come into contact, touch. **3** go to a place to be present at the arrival of; I will meet your train. **4** make the acquaintance of, be introduced. **5** come together as opponents in a contest or battle. **6** find oneself faced (with a thing); experience or receive; met with difficulties; met his death. **7** deal with (a problem); satisfy (a demand etc.); pay (the cost or what is owing). ●noun a meeting of people and hounds for a hunt, or of athletes etc. for a competition. □ **meet the case** be adequate or satisfactory. **meet the eye** or **ear** be visible or audible.

**meet**[2] adjective (old use) suitable, proper.

**meeting** noun **1** coming together. **2** an assembly of people for discussion etc. or (of Quakers) for worship. **3** a race meeting.

**mega** (meg-ă) (slang) adjective **1** excellent. **2** enormous. ●adverb extremely.

**mega-** combining form **1** large. **2** one million; megavolts, megawatts. **3** (informal) extremely; very big; mega-stupid.

**megabuck** noun (Amer. slang) a million dollars.

**megabyte** noun Computing a measure of how much data a disk or memory can hold, = 1,048,576 (i.e. $2^{20}$) bytes.

**megacycle** noun **1** one million cycles as a unit of wave frequency. **2** (informal) megahertz.

**megadeath** noun the death of one million people.

**megahertz** noun a unit of frequency of electromagnetic waves, = one million cycles per second.

**megalith** (meg-ă-lith) noun a huge stone used in the building of prehistoric monuments. □ **megalithic** (megă-lith-ik) adjective

**megalomania** (meg-ăl-ŏ-may-niă) noun **1** a form of madness in which a person has exaggerated ideas of his or her own importance etc. **2** an obsessive desire to do things on a grand scale. □ **megalomaniac** noun & adjective

**megalosaurus** noun (plural **megalosauruses**) a large flesh-eating dinosaur with stout hind legs and small front limbs.

**megaphone** noun a funnel-shaped device used for amplifying a speaker's voice.

**megastar** noun (informal) a very famous entertainer.

**megaton** (meg-ă-tun) noun a unit of explosive power equal to that of one million tons of TNT.

**megavolt** noun a unit of electromotive force equal to one million volts.

**megawatt** noun a unit of electrical power equal to one million watts.

**Meghalaya** (meg-ă-lay-ă) a State of NE India.

**megohm** noun a unit of electrical resistance equal to one million ohms.

**meiosis** (my-oh-sis) noun **1** the process of division of the nuclei of cells in which gametes are formed each containing half the normal number of chromosomes. **2** litotes.

**Meir** (may-eer), Golda (original name: Goldie Mabovich) (1898–1978), Israeli stateswoman, Prime Minister 1969–74.

**Meissen** (my-sĕn) a German town near Dresden, famous for its china (often called *Dresden china*).

**Meistersinger** (my-ster-sing-er) *noun* a member of one of the guilds of German lyric poets and musicians that flourished in the 14th–17th centuries.

**Mekong** (mee-kong) the major river of SE Asia, flowing from Tibet along the Burma–Laos and Thailand–Laos borders and across Cambodia and Vietnam to the South China Sea.

**melamine** (mel-ă-meen) *noun* a resilient kind of plastic.

**melancholia** (mel-ăn-koh-liă) *noun* mental depression.

**melancholy** (mel-ăn-kŏli) *noun* **1** mental depression; thoughtful sadness. **2** an atmosphere of gloom. ●*adjective* sad, gloomy, depressing. □ **melancholic** (mel-ăn-kol-ik) *adjective*

**Melanesia** (mel-ă-nee-shă) a group of islands in the SW Pacific containing the Bismarck Archipelago, the Solomon Islands, Santa Cruz, Vanuatu, New Caledonia, Fiji, and the intervening islands. □ **Melanesian** *adjective & noun*

**mélange** (may-lahn*zh*) *noun* a mixture.

**melanin** (mel-ăn-in) *noun* a dark pigment found in skin and hair.

**melanoma** (mel-ă-noh-mă) *noun* a malignant skin tumour.

**Melba**, Dame Nellie (real name: Helen Porter Mitchell) (1859–1931), Australian soprano singer.

**Melba toast** thin crisp toast.

**Melbourne** the capital of Victoria and second-largest city in Australia.

**meld** *verb* merge, blend.

**mêlée** (mel-ay) *noun* (*Amer.* **melee**) **1** a confused fight. **2** a muddle.

**mellifluous** (mel-if-loo-ŭs) *adjective* sweet-sounding. □ **mellifluously** *adverb*, **mellifluousness** *noun*

**mellow** *adjective* **1** sweet and rich in flavour. **2** (of sound or colour) soft and rich, free from harshness or sharp contrast. **3** made kindly and sympathetic by age or experience. **4** genial, jovial (e.g. through the effects of alcohol). **5** (of wines) well-matured, smooth. ●*verb* make or become mellow. □ **mellowly** *adverb*, **mellowness** *noun*

**melodeon** (mi-loh-di-ŏn) *noun* (also **melodion**) **1** a kind of harmonium. **2** a small accordion in which the notes are produced by pressing buttons.

**melodic** (mil-od-ik) *adjective* of melody. □ **melodically** *adverb*

**melodious** (mil-oh-diŭs) *adjective* full of melody. □ **melodiously** *adverb*

**melodrama** (mel-ŏ-drah-mă) *noun* **1** a play full of suspense in a sensational and emotional style. **2** plays of this kind. **3** a situation in real life resembling this. □ **melodramatic** (mel-ŏ-dră-mat-ik) *adjective*, **melodramatically** *adverb*

**melody** *noun* **1** sweet music, tunefulness. **2** a song or tune; *old Irish melodies*. **3** the main part in a piece of harmonized music.

**melon** *noun* the large sweet fruit of various gourds.

**melt** *verb* **1** make into or become liquid by heat. **2** (of food) be softened or dissolved easily; *it melts in the mouth*. **3** make or become gentler through pity or love. **4** dwindle or fade away; pass slowly into something else; *one shade of colour melted into another*. **5** (often foll. by *away*) (of a person) depart unobtrusively. □ **melt down** melt completely; melt (metal articles) in order to use the metal as raw material. **melting point** the temperature at which a solid melts. **melting pot** a place or situation where things are being mixed or reconstructed; *putting ideas into the melting pot*. **melt water** water from melting snow and ice.

**meltdown** *noun* **1** the melting of (and consequent damage to) a structure, e.g. the overheated core of a nuclear reactor. **2** a disastrous event, especially a rapid fall in share prices.

**melton** *noun* heavy woollen cloth with close-cut nap, used for overcoats.

**Melville**, Herman (1819–91), American novelist and poet, author of *Moby Dick*.

**member** *noun* **1** a person or thing that belongs to a particular group of society. **2** (**Member**) (in full **Member of Parliament** or (in the USA) **of Congress**) a person formally elected to take part in the proceedings of a parliament (in the UK the House of Commons, in the USA Congress). **3** a part of a complex structure. **4** a part of the body.

**membership** *noun* **1** being a member. **2** the total number of members.

**membrane** (mem-brayn) *noun* thin flexible skin-like tissue, especially that covering or lining organs or other structures in animals and plants. □ **membranous** (mem-brăn-ŭs) *adjective*

**memento** (mim-ent-oh) *noun* (*plural* **mementoes** *or* **mementos**) a souvenir.

**memento mori** *noun* a warning or reminder of death (e.g. a skull). (¶ Latin, = remember you must die.)

**memo** (mem-oh) *noun* (*plural* **memos**) (*informal*) a memorandum.

**memoir** (mem-wahr) *noun* **1** (**memoirs**) a written account of events that one has lived through or of the life or character of a person whom one knew; *write one's memoirs*. **2** an essay on a learned subject.

**memorabilia** *plural noun* souvenirs and collectors' items relating to a particular period, event, famous person, etc.; *a sale of Beatles memorabilia*.

**memorable** (mem-er-ăbŭl) *adjective* worth remembering; easy to remember. □ **memorably** *adverb*, **memorability** *noun*

**memorandum** (mem-er-an-dŭm) *noun* (*plural* **memorandums** or **memoranda**) **1** a note or record of events written as a reminder, for future use. **2** an informal written communication from one person to another in an office or organization.

**memorial** *noun* an object, institution, or custom established in memory of an event or person. ● *adjective* serving as a memorial.

**memorize** *verb* (also **memorise**) learn (a thing) so as to know it from memory.

**memory** *noun* **1** the ability to keep things in one's mind or to recall them at will. **2** remembering; a thing remembered; *memories of childhood*. **3** the length of time over which people's memory extends; *within living memory*. **4** the storage capacity of a computer. □ **from memory** remembered without the aid of notes etc. **in memory of** in honour of (a person or thing that is remembered with respect).

**memsahib** (mem-sahb) *noun* (*hist.*) an Indian name for a European married woman in India.

**men** *see* MAN.

**menace** *noun* **1** something that seems likely to bring harm or danger; a threatening quality. **2** an annoying or troublesome person or thing. ● *verb* threaten with harm or danger. □ **menacingly** *adverb*

**ménage** (may-nahzh) *noun* a household.

**ménage à trois** (*pronounced* ah trwah) (*plural* **ménages à trois**) a household consisting of husband, wife, and the lover of one of these. (¶ French, = household of three.)

**menagerie** (min-aj-er-i) *noun* a collection of wild animals in captivity, for exhibition.

**Menai Strait** (men-I) the channel separating Anglesey from the mainland of NW Wales.

**mend** *verb* **1** make whole (something that is damaged), repair. **2** make or become better; *mend one's manners*. ● *noun* a repaired place. □ **on the mend** improving in health or condition.

**mendacious** (men-day-shŭs) *adjective* untruthful, telling lies. □ **mendaciously** *adverb*, **mendacity** (men-dass-iti) *noun*

**Mendel** (men-dĕl), Gregor Johan (1822–84), Moravian monk, founder of the science of genetics. □ **Mendelian** (men-dee-li-ăn) *adjective*

**Mendeleev** (men-del-ay-ef), Dmitri Ivanovich (1834–1907), Russian chemist, who developed the periodic table of elements.

**mendelevium** (men-dĕ-lee-viŭm) *noun* an artificially produced radioactive metallic element (symbol Md).

**Mendelssohn** (men-dĕl-sŏn), (Jakob Ludwig) Felix (1809–47), German composer.

**mender** *noun* one who mends things.

**mendicant** (men-dik-ănt) *adjective* begging; depending on alms for a living. ● *noun* a beggar; a mendicant friar.

**menfolk** *plural noun* men in general; the men of one's family.

**menhir** (men-heer) *noun* a tall upright stone set up in prehistoric times.

**menial** (meen-iăl) *adjective* lowly, degrading; *menial tasks*. ● *noun* a domestic servant; a person who does humble tasks. □ **menially** *adverb*

**meninges** (min-in-jeez) *plural noun* the three membranes that enclose the brain and spinal cord.

**meningitis** (men-in-jy-tiss) *noun* inflammation of the meninges.

**meniscus** (min-isk-ŭs) *noun* (*plural* **menisci**, *pronounced* min-iss-I) **1** the curved upper surface of liquid in a tube, caused by surface tension. **2** a lens that is convex on one side and concave on the other.

**menopause** (men-ŏ-pawz) *noun* the time of life during which a woman finally ceases to menstruate (usually between 45 and 55). □ **menopausal** *adjective*

**menorah** (mĕn-or-ă) *noun* a seven-branched Jewish candelabrum.

**Mensa** an organization admitting as members people who pass an intelligence test showing that they have a high IQ.

**menses** (men-seez) *plural noun* the blood etc. discharged in menstruation.

**menstrual** (men-stroo-ăl) *adjective* of or in menstruation. □ **menstrual cycle** the process of ovulation and menstruation.

**menstruate** (men-stroo-ayt) *verb* experience the discharge of blood from the womb that normally occurs in women between puberty and middle age at approximately monthly intervals. □ **menstruation** *noun*

**mensuration** (men-sewr-ay-shŏn) *noun* **1** measuring. **2** the mathematical rules for finding lengths, areas, and volumes.

**menswear** *noun* (in shops) clothes for men.

**mental** *adjective* **1** of the mind; existing in or performed by the mind; *mental arithmetic.* **2** (*informal*) suffering from a disorder of the mind, mad. □ **mental age** the level of a person's mental development expressed as the age at which this level is reached by an average person. **mental deficiency** lack of normal intelligence through imperfect mental development. **mental home** *or* **hospital** an establishment for the care of patients suffering from mental illness. □ **mentally** *adverb*

**mentality** (men-**tal**-iti) *noun* a person's mental ability or characteristic attitude of mind.

**menthol** *noun* a solid white substance obtained from peppermint oil or made synthetically, used as a flavouring and to relieve pain.

**mentholated** *adjective* treated with or containing menthol.

**mention** *verb* **1** speak or write about briefly; refer to by name. **2** (usually as **mention in dispatches**) award a minor military honour to (a person) in war. ●*noun* mentioning, being mentioned; a reference. □ **don't mention it** a polite reply to thanks or to an apology. **not to mention** and as another important thing; let alone.

**mentor** (**men**-tor) *noun* a trusted adviser.

**menu** (**men**-yoo) *noun* **1** a list of dishes to be served or available in a restaurant etc. **2** a list of options, displayed on a screen, from which users select what they require a computer to do.

**Menuhin** (**men**-yoo-in), Yehudi, Baron (born 1916), American-born violinist, living in Britain.

**Menzies** (**men**-ziz), Sir Robert Gordon (1894–1978), Australian statesman and its longest-serving Prime Minister (1939–41, 1949–66).

**meow** (also **miaow**) = mew (*see* MEW[1]).

**MEP** *abbreviation* Member of the European Parliament.

**Mephistopheles** (mef-iss-**tof**-il-eez) (in the legend of Faust) the demon to whom Faust sold his soul.

**mercantile** (**mer**-kǎn-tyl) *adjective* trading; of trade or merchants. □ **mercantile marine** the merchant navy.

**Mercator projection** (mer-**kay**-ter) (also **Mercator's projection**) a map of the world projected so that lines of latitude and longitude are straight lines with lines of latitude the same length as the equator. (¶ Named after its inventor Mercator (1512–94), Flemish geographer.)

**mercenary** (**mer**-sin-er-i) *adjective* **1** working merely for money or other reward; grasping. **2** (of professional soldiers) hired to serve a foreign country. ●*noun* a

professional soldier serving a foreign country. □ **mercenarily** *adverb*, **mercenariness** *noun*

**mercerized** *adjective* (also **mercerised**) (of cotton fabric or thread) treated with a substance that gives greater strength and a slight gloss.

**merchandise** *noun* goods or commodities bought and kept for sale. ●*verb* **1** buy and sell; trade. **2** promote sales of (goods etc.).

**merchant** *noun* **1** a wholesale trader. **2** (*Amer. & Scottish*) a retail trader. **3** (*slang*, usually *scornful*) a person who is fond of a certain activity; *speed merchants.* □ **merchant bank** a bank dealing in commercial loans and the financing of businesses. **merchant navy** shipping employed in commerce. **merchant ship** a ship carrying merchandise.

**merchantable** *adjective* saleable, marketable.

**merchantman** *noun* (*plural* **merchantmen**) a merchant ship.

**merciful** *adjective* **1** showing mercy. **2** giving relief from pain or suffering; *a merciful death.*

**mercifully** *adverb* **1** in a merciful way. **2** fortunately, thank goodness.

**merciless** *adjective* showing no mercy. □ **mercilessly** *adverb*

**mercurial** (mer-**kewr**-iǎl) *adjective* **1** of or caused by mercury; *mercurial eczema.* **2** having a lively temperament. **3** liable to sudden changes of mood.

**Mercury 1** (*Rom. myth.*) the messenger of the gods, identified with Hermes. **2** the innermost planet of the solar system.

**mercury** *noun* a chemical element (symbol Hg), a heavy silvery normally liquid metal, used in thermometers and barometers etc. □ **mercuric** (mer-**kewr**-ik) *adjective*, **mercurous** *adjective*

**mercy** *noun* **1** refraining from inflicting punishment or pain on an offender or enemy etc. who is in one's power. **2** a disposition to behave in this way; *a tyrant without mercy.* **3** a merciful act; a thing to be thankful for; *it's a mercy no one was killed.* ●*interjection* an exclamation of surprise or fear; *mercy on us!* □ **at the mercy of** wholly in the power of; liable to danger or harm from. **mercy killing** euthanasia.

**mere**[1] *adjective* nothing more or better than what is specified; *she is a mere child*; *mere words.* □ **merely** *adverb*

**mere**[2] *noun* (*poetic*) a lake.

**Meredith**, George (1828–1909), English novelist and poet.

**merest** *adjective* very small or insignificant; *the merest trace of colour.*

**meretricious** (merri-**trish**-ŭs) *adjective* showily attractive but cheap or insincere.

**merganser** (mer-**gan**-ser) *noun* (*plural* **merganser** *or* **mergansers**) a diving duck that feeds on fish.

**merge** *verb* **1** unite or combine into a whole; *the two companies merged.* **2** pass slowly into something else, blend or become blended.

**merger** *noun* the combining of two commercial companies etc. into one.

**meridian** (mer-**rid**-iăn) *noun* any of the great semicircles on the globe, passing through a given place and the North and South Poles; *the meridian of Greenwich is shown on maps as 0° longitude.*

**meridional** (mer-**id**-i-ŏn-ăl) *adjective* **1** of the south (especially of Europe) or its inhabitants. **2** of a meridian.

**meringue** (mer-**rang**) *noun* **1** a mixture of sugar and beaten egg white, baked crisp. **2** a small cake of this.

**merino** (mer-**ree**-noh) *noun* (*plural* **merinos**) **1** (in full **merino sheep**) a breed of sheep with long fine wool. **2** fine soft woollen yarn or fabric.

**merit** *noun* **1** the quality of deserving to be praised, excellence. **2** a feature or quality that deserves praise; *judge it on its merits.* ● *verb* (**merited**, **meriting**) deserve.

**meritocracy** (merri-**tok**-răsi) *noun* **1** government or control by people of high ability, selected by some form of competition. **2** these people.

**meritorious** (merri-**tor**-iŭs) *adjective* having merit, deserving praise.

**Merlin** (in legends of King Arthur) a magician who aided King Arthur.

**merlin** *noun* a small falcon.

**mermaid** *noun* an imaginary sea creature, a woman with a fish's tail in place of legs.

**merry** *adjective* (**merrier**, **merriest**) **1** cheerful and lively, joyous. **2** (*informal*) slightly drunk. □ **make merry** be festive.

**merry-go-round** *noun* **1** a fairground ride with revolving model horses, cars, etc.; a roundabout in a playground. **2** a cycle of bustling activity. □ **merrily** *adverb*, **merriment** *noun*

**merrymaking** *noun* lively festivities, fun.

**Mersey** a river of England, flowing into the Irish Sea.

**Merseyside** a metropolitan county of NW England.

**mesa** (**may**-să) *noun* (*Amer.*) a high table-land with steep sides.

**mésalliance** (may-**zal**-i-ahns) *noun* a marriage with a person of lower social position. (¶ French.)

**mescal** (**mes**-kal) *noun* the peyote cactus. □ **mescal buttons** its disc-shaped dried tops used as an intoxicant or drug.

**mescaline** (**mesk**-ă-leen) *noun* (also **mescalin**) a drug that produces hallucinations, made from mescal buttons.

**Mesdames** *see* MADAME.

**Mesdemoiselles** *see* MADEMOISELLE.

**mesembryanthemum** (miz-em-bri-**anth**-imŭm) *noun* a low-growing plant with bright daisy-like flowers opening in sunlight.

**mesh** *noun* **1** one of the spaces between threads in a net, sieve, etc. **2** network fabric. ● *verb* (of a toothed wheel etc.) engage with another or others.

**mesmerism** *noun* hypnosis. □ **mesmeric** (mez-**merrik**) *adjective*

**mesmerize** *verb* (also **mesmerise**) hypnotize; dominate the attention or will of.

**mesolithic** (me-zoh-**lith**-ik) *adjective* of the geological period between palaeolithic and neolithic. ● *noun* this period.

**meson** (**mee**-zon) *noun* an unstable elementary particle intermediate in mass between a proton and an electron.

**Mesopotamia** (mess-ŏ-pŏ-**tay**-miă) a region of SW Asia between the rivers Tigris and Euphrates, now within Iraq.

**mesosphere** (**mess**-ŏ-sfeer) *noun* the region of the earth's atmosphere from the top of the stratosphere to an altitude of about 80 km.

**Mesozoic** (mess-ŏ-**zoh**-ik) *adjective* of the geological era between the Palaeozoic and Cainozoic, lasting from about 248 to 65 million years ago and marked by the development of dinosaurs. ● *noun* this era.

**mess** *noun* **1** a dirty or untidy condition; an untidy collection of things; something spilt. **2** a difficult or confused situation, trouble. **3** any disagreeable substance or concoction; a domestic animal's excreta. **4** (*informal*) a person who looks untidy, dirty, or slovenly. **5** (in the armed forces) a group who take meals together; the place where such meals are eaten. ● *verb* **1** (often foll. by *up*) make untidy or dirty. **2** (often foll. by *up*) muddle or bungle (business etc.); *messed it up.* **3** (*Amer.*) (foll. by *with*) meddle or tinker; *don't mess with the transistor.* **4** take one's meals with a military or other group; *they mess together.* □ **mess about** *or* **around 1** potter; fiddle. **2** (*informal*) make things awkward for (a person) by being indecisive, inconsistent, etc. **mess kit** a soldier's cooking and eating utensils.

**message** *noun* **1** a spoken or written communication. **2** the inspired moral or social teaching of a prophet or writer etc.; *a film with a message.* **3** (**messages**) (*Scottish & N. England*) shopping. □ **get the message** (*informal*) understand what is meant or implied.

**Messeigneurs** *see* MONSEIGNEUR.

**messenger** *noun* the bearer of a message.

**Messiaen** (**mess**-yan), Olivier (1908–92), French composer and teacher.

**Messiah** (mi-sy-ă) *noun* **1** the expected deliverer and ruler of the Jewish people, whose coming was prophesied in the Old Testament. **2** Christ, regarded by Christians as this.

**Messianic** (mess-i-**an**-ik) *adjective* of the Messiah.

**Messieurs** *see* MONSIEUR.

**Messina** (mess-**een**-ă), **Strait of** the strait which separates Sicily from Italy.

**Messrs** (**mess**-erz) *abbreviation* plural of Mr.

**messy** *adjective* (**messier, messiest**) **1** untidy or dirty, slovenly. **2** causing a mess; *a messy job*. **3** complicated and difficult to deal with. □ **messily** *adverb*, **messiness** *noun*

**met**[1] *see* MEET[1].

**met**[2] *adjective* (*informal*) **1** meteorological. **2** metropolitan. ●*noun* (**the Met**) (*informal*) the Meteorological Office; the Metropolitan Opera House (New York); the Metropolitan Police.

**metabolism** (mi-**tab**-ŏl-izm) *noun* the process by which food is built up into living material or used to supply energy in a living organism. □ **metabolic** (met-ă-**bol**-ik) *adjective*

**metabolize** (mi-**tab**-ŏ-lyz) *verb* (also **metabolise**) process (food) in metabolism.

**metacarpus** (met-ă-**kar**-pŭs) *noun* (*plural* **metacarpi**) the part of the hand between the wrist and the fingers; the set of bones in this. □ **metacarpal** *adjective*

**metal** *noun* any of a class of mineral substances such as gold, silver, copper, iron, uranium, etc.. or an alloy of any of these. ●*adjective* made of metal. ●*verb* (**metalled, metalling;** *Amer.* **metaled, metaling**) **1** cover or fit with metal. **2** make or mend (a road) with road-metal. □ **metal detector** an electronic device for locating buried metal items.

**metalanguage** *noun* a form of language used to discuss or describe a language.

**metallic** (mi-**tal**-ik) *adjective* **1** of or like metal. **2** (of sound) like metals struck together, sharp and ringing. □ **metallically** *adverb*

**metalliferous** (met-ăl-**if**-er-ŭs) *adjective* (of rocks etc.) containing metal.

**metallize** *verb* (also **metallise;** *Amer.* **metalize**) **1** make metallic. **2** coat with a thin layer of metal. □ **metallization** *noun*

**metallography** (met-ăl-**og**-răfi) *noun* the scientific study of the internal structure of metals.

**metalloid** *noun* an element that is midway between a metal and a non-metal, e.g. boron, silicon, and germanium.

**metallurgy** (mi-**tal**-er-ji) *noun* **1** the scientific study of the properties of metals

and alloys. **2** the art of working metals or of extracting them from their ores. □ **metallurgical** (met-ăl-**er**-jikăl) *adjective*, **metallurgist** *noun*

**metalwork** *noun* **1** the art of working in metal. **2** metal objects. □ **metalworker** *noun*

**metamorphic** (met-ă-**mor**-fik) *adjective* **1** (of rock) having had its structure or other properties changed by natural agencies (such as heat and pressure), as in the transformation of limestone into marble. **2** of metamorphosis. □ **metamorphism** *noun*

**metamorphose** (met-ă-**mor**-fohs) *verb* change in form or character.

**metamorphosis** (met-ă-**mor**-fŏ-sis) *noun* (*plural* **metamorphoses**) a change of form or character.

**metaphor** (**met**-ă-fer) *noun* the application of a word or phrase to something that it does not apply to literally, in order to indicate a comparison with the literal usage, e.g. the *evening* of one's life, *food* for thought, *cut off one's nose to spite one's face.*

**metaphorical** (met-ă-**fo**-rikăl) *adjective* in a metaphor, not literal. □ **metaphorically** *adverb*

**metaphysics** (met-ă-**fiz**-iks) *noun* **1** a branch of philosophy that deals with the nature of existence and of truth and knowledge. **2** (popularly) abstract or subtle thought; mere theory. □ **metaphysical** *adjective*

**metastasis** (mi-**tas**-tă-sis) *noun* (*plural* **metastases**) the transfer of disease from one part of the body to another.

**metatarsus** (met-ă-**tar**-sŭs) *noun* (*plural* **metatarsi**) the part of the foot between the ankle and the toes; the set of bones in this. □ **metatarsal** *adjective*

**mete** (*pronounced* meet) □ **mete out** give as what is due; *mete out punishment to wrongdoers.*

**meteor** (**meet**-i-er) *noun* a bright moving body seen in the sky, formed by a small mass of matter from outer space that becomes luminous from compression of air as it enters the earth's atmosphere.

**meteoric** (meet-i-o-rik) *adjective* **1** of meteors. **2** like a meteor in brilliance or sudden appearance; *a meteoric career.*

**meteorite** (**meet**-i-er-ryt) *noun* a fallen meteor, a fragment of rock or metal reaching the earth's surface from outer space.

**meteoroid** (**meet**-i-er-oid) *noun* a body moving through space, of the same nature as those which become visible as meteors when they enter the earth's atmosphere.

**meteorological** (meet-i-er-ŏ-**loj**-ikăl) *adjective* of meteorology. □ **Meteorological**

**Office** a government department providing information and forecasts about the weather.

**meteorology** (meet-i-er-**ol**-ŏji) *noun* the scientific study of atmospheric conditions, especially in order to forecast weather. □ **meteorologist** *noun*

**meter**[1] *noun* a device designed to measure and indicate the quantity of a substance supplied, or the distance travelled and fare payable, or the time that has elapsed, etc. ●*verb* (**metered, metering**) measure by meter.

**meter**[2] Amer. spelling of METRE.

**methadone** *noun* a narcotic pain-killing drug, used as a substitute for morphine or heroin.

**methanal** = FORMALDEHYDE.

**methane** (mee-thayn) *noun* a colourless inflammable gas that occurs in coal mines and marshy areas.

**methanol** *noun* a colourless inflammable liquid hydrocarbon, used as a solvent.

**methinks** *verb* (*old use*) I think.

**method** *noun* **1** a procedure or way of doing something. **2** orderliness; *he's a man of method.* **3** a technique of acting based on the actor's complete emotional identification with the character.

**methodical** (mi-**thod**-ikăl) *adjective* orderly, systematic. □ **methodically** *adverb*

**Methodist** *noun* a member of a Protestant religious denomination originating in the 18th century and based on the teachings of John and Charles Wesley and their followers. □ **Methodism** *noun*

**methodology** (meth-ŏ-**dol**-ŏji) *noun* **1** the science of method and procedure. **2** the methods used in a particular activity. □ **methodological** *adjective*, **methodologically** *adverb*

**methought** *verb* (*old use*) I thought.

**meths** *noun* (*informal*) methylated spirit.

**Methuselah** (mi-**thew**-zĕ-lă) a Hebrew patriarch, grandfather of Noah, said to have lived for 969 years.

**methyl** (**meth**-il) *noun* a chemical unit present in methane and in many organic compounds. □ **methyl alcohol** = METHANOL.

**methylated spirit(s)** alcohol (treated to make it unfit for drinking) used as a solvent and a fuel.

**meticulous** (mi-**tik**-yoo-lŭs) *adjective* giving or showing great attention to detail, very careful and exact. □ **meticulously** *adverb*, **meticulousness** *noun*

**métier** (**may**-ti-ay) *noun* one's trade, profession, or field of activity; what one does best. (¶ French.)

**metonymy** (mi-**ton**-imi) *noun* substitution of the word for an attribute for that of the thing meant, e.g. *allegiance to the crown* instead of *to the king.*

**metre** *noun* (*Amer.* **meter**) **1** a unit of length in the metric system (about 39.4 inches). **2** rhythm in poetry; a particular form of this. **3** the basic rhythm of a piece of music.

**metric** *adjective* **1** of or using the metric system. **2** of poetic metre. □ **metric system** a decimal system of weights and measures, using the metre, litre, and gram as units. **metric ton** (also **metric tonne**) a tonne (1,000 kilograms).

**metrical** *adjective* **1** of or composed in rhythmic metre, not prose; *metrical psalms.* **2** of or involving measurement; *metrical geometry.* □ **metrically** *adverb*

**metricate** *verb* change or adapt to the metric system of measurement. □ **metrication** *noun*

**metro** *noun* (*plural* **metros**) (*informal*) an underground railway, especially in Paris.

**metronome** (**met**-rŏ-nohm) *noun* a device that sounds a click repeatedly at a selected interval, used to indicate tempo for a person practising music.

**metropolis** (mi-**trop**-ŏlis) *noun* the chief city of a country or region.

**metropolitan** (metrŏ-**pol**-ităn) *adjective* of a metropolis. □ **metropolitan county** any of the six English counties formed in 1974, treated as a unit for some purposes and divided into districts for others. **metropolitan magistrate** a paid professional magistrate in London. **Metropolitan Police** the police force of London.

**Metropolitan Museum of Art** an important museum of art and archaeology, in New York.

**mettle** *noun* courage or strength of character. □ **on one's mettle** determined to show one's courage or ability.

**mettlesome** *adjective* spirited, courageous.

**Meuse** (*pronounced* merz) a river of NE France, Belgium, and the Netherlands, flowing into the North Sea.

**MeV** *abbreviation* mega-electronvolt(s).

**mew**[1] *noun* the characteristic cry of a cat. ●*verb* make this sound.

**mew**[2] *noun* a gull.

**mewl** *verb* **1** whimper. **2** mew like a cat.

**mews** *noun* (usually treated as *singular*) a group of what were formerly stables in a small square, now converted into houses.

**Mexico** a country in Central America. □ **Mexican wave** a wave-like movement produced when successive sections of a seated crowd of spectators stand, raise their arms, and sit down again. (¶ First observed at World Cup football matches in Mexico City in 1986.) **Mexico City** the capital of Mexico. □ **Mexican** *adjective & noun*

**mezzanine** (mets-ă-neen) *noun* an extra storey between ground floor and first floor, often in the form of a wide balcony.

**mezzo** (met-soh) *adverb* (in music) half; moderately; *mezzo forte*. ●*noun* (in full **mezzo-soprano**) a voice between soprano and contralto; a singer with this voice.

**mezzotint** (met-soh-tint) *noun* **1** a method of engraving in which the plate is roughened to give areas of shadow and smoothed to give areas of light. **2** a print produced by this.

**mf** *abbreviation* (in music) mezzo forte.

**Mg** *symbol* magnesium.

**mg** *abbreviation* milligram(s).

**MHz** *abbreviation* megahertz.

**MI** *abbreviation* Michigan.

**mi** alternative spelling of ME².

**mi.** *abbreviation* (*Amer.*) mile(s).

**miaow** (also **meow**) = mew (*see* MEW¹).

**miasma** (mi-az-mă) *noun* (*plural* **miasmata** or **miasmas**) (*old use*) unpleasant or unwholesome air.

**mica** (my-kă) *noun* a mineral substance used as an electrical insulator.

**Micah** (my-kă) **1** a Hebrew minor prophet. **2** a book of the Old Testament bearing his name.

**Micawber** (mi-kaw-ber) *noun* a person who is perpetually hoping that something good will turn up while making no effort. (¶ Name of a character in Dickens's novel David Copperfield.)

**mice** *see* MOUSE.

**Mich.** *abbreviation* Michigan.

**Michael**, St, one of the archangels. Feast day, 29 September (Michaelmas Day).

**Michaelmas** (mik-ĕl-măs) *noun* a Christian festival in honour of St Michael (29 September). □ **Michaelmas daisy** a perennial aster flowering in autumn, with blue, dark red, pink, or white blooms.

**Michelangelo** (my-kĕl-an-jel-oh) (Michelangelo Buonarroti) (1475–1564), Italian sculptor, painter, architect, and poet, whose most famous works include the decoration of the ceiling of the Sistine chapel.

**Michelin** (mee-shĕ-len), André (1853–1931), French tyre manufacturer, a pioneer of the pneumatic tyre.

**Michigan** (mish-i-găn) a State of the northwestern USA. □ **Lake Michigan** one of the five Great Lakes of North America.

**mickey** *noun* (also **micky**) □ **take the mickey (out of)** (*slang*) tease or ridicule.

**Mickey Finn** (*slang*) a drink containing extra alcohol or a drug of which the drinker is not aware.

**Mickey Mouse** a cartoon character created by Walt Disney.

**mickle** (*Scottish*) *adjective* (also **muckle**) much, great. ●*noun* a large amount.

**micro** *noun* (*plural* **micros**) (*informal*) a microcomputer; a microprocessor.

**micro-** *combining form* **1** very small. **2** one-millionth of a unit; *microgram*.

**microbe** *noun* a micro-organism, especially one that causes disease or fermentation. □ **microbial** *adjective*, **microbic** *adjective*

**microbiology** *noun* the study of micro-organisms. □ **microbiologist** *noun*

**microchip** *noun* a very small piece of silicon or similar material made so as to work like a complex wired electric circuit.

**microcircuit** *noun* an integrated circuit or other small electrical circuit.

**microclimate** *noun* the climatic conditions of a very small area, e.g. of part of a garden.

**microcomputer** *noun* a small computer with a microprocessor as the central processor.

**microcosm** (my-krŏ-kozm) *noun* a world in miniature; something regarded as resembling something else on a very small scale. □ **microcosmic** *adjective*

**microdot** *noun* a photograph of a document etc. reduced to the size of a dot.

**micro-electronics** *noun* the design, manufacture, and use of microcircuits. □ **micro-electronic** *adjective*

**microfiche** (my-kroh-feesh) *noun* (*plural* **microfiche** or **microfiches**) a sheet of microfilm in a form suitable for filing like an index card.

**microfilm** *noun* a length of film on which written or printed material is photographed in greatly reduced size. ●*verb* photograph on this.

**microlight** *noun* a motorized hang-glider.

**micromesh** *noun* fine-meshed material, especially nylon.

**micrometer** (my-krom-it-er) *noun* an instrument for measuring small lengths or angles.

**micron** (my-kron) *noun* one-millionth of a metre.

**Micronesia** (my-krŏ-nee-ziă) part of the western Pacific Ocean including the Mariana, Caroline, and Marshall Islands and Kiribati.

**micro-organism** *noun* an organism that cannot be seen by the naked eye, e.g. bacteria, viruses, and protozoa.

**microphone** *noun* an instrument for picking up sound waves for recording, amplifying, or broadcasting.

**microprocessor** *noun* an integrated circuit containing all the functions of a computer's central processing unit.

**microscope** *noun* an instrument with lenses that magnify objects or details too small to be seen by the naked eye.

**microscopic** *adjective* **1** of the microscope. **2** too small to be visible without the aid of a microscope. **3** extremely small. □ **microscopically** *adverb*

**microscopy** (my-**kros**-kŏ-pi) *noun* use of microscopes.

**microsecond** *noun* one-millionth of a second.

**microsurgery** *noun* surgery using a microscope to see the tissue and instruments involved.

**microwave** *noun* **1** an electromagnetic wave of length between about 30 cm and 1 mm. **2** (in full **microwave oven**) an oven using such waves to heat food very quickly. ● *verb* cook (food) in a microwave oven.

**micturition** (mik-tewr-**ish**-ŏn) *noun* urination.

**mid** *adjective* in the middle of, middle; *in mid-air*; *to mid-August*. □ **mid-life** *noun* middle age. **mid-life crisis** a crisis of self-confidence in early middle age. **mid-off**, **mid-on** *noun* a fielder in cricket near the bowler on the off (or on) side; this position.

**Midas** (my-dăs) □ **the Midas touch** the ability to make money in all one's activities. (¶ Named after a legendary king in Asia Minor, whose touch turned all things to gold.)

**midday** *noun* the middle of the day, noon.

**midden** *noun* **1** a heap of dung. **2** a rubbish heap.

**middle** *adjective* **1** at an equal distance from extremes or outer limits. **2** occurring halfway between beginning and end. **3** intermediate in rank or quality; moderate in size etc.; *a man of middle height*. ● *noun* **1** a middle point, position, time, area, or quality etc. **2** the waist. □ **in the middle of nowhere** (*informal*) in a very remote place. **middle age** the period between youth and old age, about 45 to 60. **middle-aged** *adjective* of middle age. **Middle Ages** about AD 1000–1453 or (in a wider sense) 5th c.–1453. **Middle America 1** Mexico and Central America. **2** the middle class in the USA, especially as a conservative political force. **middle C** the note C that occurs near the middle of the piano keyboard. **middle class** the class of society between the upper and working classes, including business and professional people. **middle-class** *adjective* of or relating to the middle class. **middle distance 1** (of a landscape) the part between the foreground and the background. **2** (in athletics) a race distance of especially 400 or 800 metres. **middle ear** the cavity behind the eardrum. **Middle East** the area covered by countries from Egypt to Iran inclusive. **Middle English** the English language as it was from around 1150 to 1500. **middle-of-the-road** *adjective* favouring a moderate policy, avoiding extremes. **middle school** a school for children aged about 9–13 years. **middle-sized** *adjective* of medium size.

**middlebrow** (*informal*) *adjective* having or appealing to only moderately intellectual tastes. ● *noun* a middlebrow person.

**middleman** *noun* (*plural* **middlemen**) **1** any of the traders handling a commodity between producer and consumer. **2** an intermediary.

**Middlesex** a former county of England.

**middleweight** *noun* a boxing weight between light heavyweight and welterweight, in amateur boxing 71–75kg.

**middling** *adjective* moderately good. ● *adverb* moderately well.

**Middx.** *abbreviation* Middlesex.

**midfield** *noun* the part of a football pitch away from the goals.

**midge** *noun* a small biting gnatlike insect.

**midget** *noun* an extremely small person or thing. ● *adjective* extremely small.

**Mid Glamorgan** a county of South Wales.

**MIDI** *noun* (also **midi**) an interface allowing electronic musical instruments, synthesizers, and computers to be connected and used together. (¶ Abbreviation of *m*usical *i*nstrument *d*igital *i*nterface.)

**midi system** a compact hi-fi system made up of stacking components.

**midland** *adjective* of the Midlands or the middle part of a country. ● *noun* (**the Midlands**) the inland counties of central England.

**midnight** *noun* twelve o'clock at night; the time near this. □ **midnight sun** the sun visible at midnight in polar regions during the summer.

**Midrash** *noun* (*plural* **Midrashim**) an ancient Jewish commentary on part of the Hebrew scriptures.

**midriff** *noun* the front part of the body just above the waist.

**midshipman** *noun* (*plural* **midshipmen**) a naval rank between cadet and sub-lieutenant.

**midst** *noun* the middle.

**midsummer** *noun* the middle of the summer, about 21 June. □ **Midsummer('s) Day** 24 June.

**midway** *adverb* halfway between places.

**Midwest** *noun* the region of the USA near the northern Mississippi.

**midwicket** *noun* a position in cricket on the leg side opposite the middle of the pitch.

**midwife** *noun* (*plural* **midwives**) a person trained to assist women in childbirth. □ **midwifery** (mid-**wif**-ĕri) *noun*

**midwinter** *noun* the middle of the winter, about 22 December.

**mien** (*pronounced* meen) *noun* a person's manner or bearing.

**Mies van der Rohe** (meez, **roh**), Ludwig (1886–1969), German-born architect and designer of furniture.

**miffed** *adjective* (*informal*) offended, put out.

**M.I.5.** the UK military intelligence service covering internal security and counter-intelligence on British territory.

■**Usage** This term is not in official use.

**might**[1] *noun* great strength or power; *with all one's might.* □ **with might and main** with all one's power.

**might**[2] *auxiliary verb* used as the past tense of MAY[1], especially expressing **1** possibility; *it might be true.* **2** permission; *we told him that he might go.* **3** a request; *you might call at the baker's.* **4** a complaint; *you might have offered.* □ **might-have-been** *noun* **1** an event that might have happened but did not. **2** a person who failed to achieve what was expected.

**mightn't** (*informal*) = might not.

**mighty** *adjective* (**mightier, mightiest**) **1** having or showing great strength or power. **2** very great in size. ● *adverb* (*informal*) very; *mighty fine.* □ **mightily** *adverb*, **mightiness** *noun*

**mignonette** (min-yŏn-**et**) *noun* an annual plant with fragrant greyish-green flowers.

**migraine** (**mee**-grayn or **my**-grayn) *noun* a severe form of headache that tends to re-cur.

**migrant** (**my**-grănt) *adjective* migrating. ● *noun* a migrant person or animal.

**migrate** (**my**-grayt) *verb* **1** leave one place and settle in another. **2** (of animals) go periodically from one place to another, living in each place for part of a year. □ **migration** *noun*

**migratory** (**my**-gră-ter-i) *adjective* of or involving migration; migrating.

**mihrab** (**mee**-rahb) *noun* a niche or slab in a mosque, used to show the direction of Mecca.

**mikado** (mi-**kah**-doh) *noun* (*plural* **mikados**) an emperor of Japan.

**mike** *noun* (*informal*) a microphone.

**mil** *noun* one-thousandth of an inch.

**milady** *noun* (especially as a form of address) an English noblewoman.

**milage** alternative spelling of MILEAGE.

**milch** *adjective* giving milk. □ **milch cow 1** a cow kept for its milk rather than for beef. **2** a person or organization from whom money is easily obtained.

**mild** *adjective* **1** moderate in intensity, character, or effect; not severe or harsh or drastic. **2** (of a person) gentle in manner. **3** not strongly flavoured. □ **mild steel** steel that is strong and tough and not readily tempered. □ **mildly** *adverb*, **mildness** *noun*

**mildew** *noun* a minute fungus that forms a white coating on things exposed to damp. □ **mildewy** *adjective*

**mildewed** *adjective* coated with mildew.

**mile** *noun* **1** a measure of length, 1760 yards (about 1.609 kilometres). See also *nautical mile.* **2** (usually as **miles**) (*informal*) a great distance or amount; *miles too big.* **3** a race extending over a mile.

**mileage** *noun* (also **milage**) **1** distance measured in miles. **2** the number of miles a vehicle travels on one gallon of fuel. **3** travelling expenses at a fixed rate per mile. **4** (*informal*) benefit; *he gets a lot of mileage out of his family name.*

**milepost** *noun* a post marking the point one mile from the finish of a race.

**miler** *noun* an athlete or horse specializing in races that are one mile in length.

**milestone** *noun* **1** a stone set up beside a road to show the distance in miles to a given point. **2** a significant event or stage in life or history.

**milfoil** *noun* yarrow.

**milieu** (**meel**-yer) *noun* (*plural* **milieux**, *pronounced same, or* **milieus**) environment, surroundings.

**militant** *adjective* prepared to take aggressive action in support of a cause. ● *noun* a militant person. □ **militancy** *noun*

**Militant Tendency** a movement of people dedicated to upholding Trotskyist principles within the Labour Party, from which they were later excluded.

**militarism** (**mil**-it-er-izm) *noun* aggressive military policy; strong military spirit. □ **militarist** *noun*, **militaristic** *adjective*

**militarize** *verb* (also **militarise**) **1** make military or warlike. **2** equip with military resources. **3** imbue with militarism. □ **militarization** *noun*

**military** *adjective* of soldiers or the army or all armed forces; *military service.* ● *noun* (**the military**) (treated as *singular* or *plural*) the army. □ **military police** an army corps responsible for police and disciplinary duties.

**militate** (**mil**-i-tayt) *verb* (usually foll. by *against*) serve as a strong influence; *several factors militated against the success of our plan.*

■**Usage** Do not confuse with *mitigate.*

**militia** (mil-**ish**-ă) *noun* a military force, especially one consisting of civilians trained as soldiers and available to supplement the regular army in an emergency. □ **militia-man** noun

**milk** noun **1** a white fluid secreted by female mammals as food for their young. **2** the milk of cows, goats, or sheep, used as food. **3** a milklike liquid, e.g. that in a coconut. ●verb **1** draw milk from (a cow, goat etc.). **2** extract juice from (a tree etc.). **3** exploit or get money undeservedly from; *milking the Welfare State*. □ **milk chocolate** chocolate made with milk. **milk float** a light vehicle used in delivering milk. **Milk of Magnesia** (*trade mark*) a mixture of magnesium hydroxide and water, taken as an antacid or laxative. **milk-powder** noun dehydrated milk. **milk pudding** rice, semolina, etc. baked slowly with milk and sugar. **milk round 1** a route on which milk is delivered regularly to houses. **2** a regular trip with calls to several places, especially annual recruitment visits by major industries to colleges and universities. **milk run** a routine expedition. **milk shake** a drink made of milk and flavouring mixed until frothy. **milk tooth** any of the first (temporary) teeth in young mammals.

**milker** noun **1** a person who milks an animal. **2** an animal that gives milk.

**milkmaid** noun a woman who milks cows.

**milkman** noun (plural **milkmen**) a person who delivers milk to customers' houses.

**milksop** noun a weak or timid boy or man.

**milky** adjective (**milkier, milkiest**) **1** of or like milk. **2** made with milk; containing a lot of milk. **3** (of a gem or liquid) cloudy, not clear. □ **Milky Way** the broad faintly luminous band of stars, the Galaxy. □ **milkiness** noun

**Mill**, John Stuart (1806–73), English philosopher and economist.

**mill** noun **1** machinery for grinding corn; a building fitted with this. **2** any machine for grinding or crushing a solid substance into powder or pulp; *coffee-mill*. **3** a machine or a building fitted with machinery for processing material of certain kinds; *cotton-mill*; *paper-mill*; *saw-mill*. ●verb **1** grind or crush in a mill. **2** produce in a mill. **3** produce regular markings on the edge of (a coin); *silver coins with a milled edge*. **4** cut or shape (metal) with a rotating tool. **5** (often foll. by *about* or *around*) (of people or animals) move about in a confused mass. □ **go** or **put through the mill** undergo or subject to training, experience, or suffering. **mill-race** noun a current of water that works a water-wheel. **mill-wheel** noun the wheel that drives a water-mill.

**Millais** (**mil**-ay), Sir John Everett (1829–96), English painter, one of the founders of the Pre-Raphaelite Brotherhood.

*millefeuille* noun layers of puff pastry, jam, and cream.

**millennium** (mil-en-iŭm) noun (plural **millenniums** or **millennia**) **1** a period of 1,000 years. **2** the thousand-year reign of Christ on earth prophesied in the Bible. **3** a period of great happiness and prosperity for everyone. □ **millennial** adjective

**millepede** alternative spelling of MILLIPEDE.

**Miller**[1], Arthur (born 1915), American playwright, whose works include *Death of a Salesman* and *The Crucible*.

**Miller**[2], Glenn (Alton Glenn) (1904–44), American trombonist, arranger, and bandleader.

**miller** noun a person who owns or runs a corn-grinding mill.

**Millet**, (mee-lay) Jean François (1814–75), French painter.

**millet** noun **1** a cereal plant producing a large crop of small seeds. **2** its seeds, used as food.

**milli-** combining form **1** thousand. **2** one-thousandth.

**milliard** noun one thousand million.

■**Usage** *milliard* is now largely superseded by *billion*.

**millibar** noun one-thousandth of a bar as a unit of pressure in meteorology.

**milligram** noun (also **milligramme**) one-thousandth of a gram.

**millilitre** noun (*Amer.* **milliliter**) one-thousandth of a litre.

**millimetre** noun (*Amer.* **millimeter**) one-thousandth of a metre (0.04 inch).

**milliner** noun a person who makes or sells women's hats.

**millinery** noun **1** a milliner's work. **2** women's hats sold in a shop.

**million** adjective & noun **1** one thousand thousand (1,000,000); *a few million*. **2** a million pounds or dollars. **3** (**millions**) (*informal*) an enormous number. □ **millionth** adjective & noun

**millionaire** noun a person who has over a million pounds, dollars, etc.

**millipede** noun (also **millepede**) a small crawling creature like a centipede but with two pairs of legs on each segment of its body.

**millisecond** noun one-thousandth of a second.

**millpond** noun water retained in a dam by a mill to operate a water-wheel. □ **like a millpond** (of water) very calm and flat.

**Mills**, Sir John (born 1908), English actor.

**millstone** noun **1** each of a pair of circular stones between which corn is ground. **2** a great burden that impedes progress; *a millstone round one's neck*.

**millwright** *noun* a person who designs or erects mills.

**Milne**, A(lan) A(lexander) (1882–1956), British writer, author of the *Winnie the Pooh* children's books.

**milometer** (my-**lom**-it-er) *noun* an instrument for measuring the number of miles travelled by a vehicle.

**Milos** (my-loss *or* mee-loss) a Greek island in the Cyclades.

**milt** *noun* the roe of a male fish, fish-sperm discharged into the water over the eggs laid by the female.

**Milton**, John (1608–74), English poet, author of the epics *Paradise Lost* and *Paradise Regained*.

**mimbar** *noun* a pulpit in a mosque.

**mime** *noun* acting with gestures and without words; a performance using this. ● *verb* act with mime.

**mimeograph** (**mim**-i-ŏ-grahf) *noun* an apparatus for making copies from stencils. ● *verb* reproduce by means of this.

**mimetic** (mim-**et**-ik) *adjective* of or using imitation or mimicry.

**mimic** *verb* (**mimicked, mimicking**) **1** copy the appearance or ways of (a person etc.) playfully or for entertainment. **2** pretend to be; (of things) resemble closely. ● *noun* a person who is clever at mimicking others. □ **mimicry** *noun*

**mimosa** (mim-**oh**-ză) *noun* any of several usually tropical trees or shrubs, especially with clusters of small ball-shaped fragrant flowers.

**Min.** *abbreviation* **1** Minister. **2** Ministry.

**min.** *abbreviation* **1** minute(s). **2** minimum.

**mina** alternative spelling of MYNA.

**minaret** (min-er-**et**) *noun* a tall slender tower on or beside a mosque, with a balcony from which a muezzin calls Muslims to prayer.

**minatory** (**min**-ă-ter-i) *adjective* threatening.

**mince** *verb* **1** cut into small pieces in a machine with revolving blades. **2** walk or speak in an affected way, trying to appear refined. ● *noun* minced meat. □ **mince pie** a pie containing mincemeat. **not to mince matters** *or* **one's words** speak bluntly. □ **mincer** *noun*

**mincemeat** *noun* a mixture of currants, raisins, sugar, spices, etc., used in pies. □ **make mincemeat of** defeat utterly; destroy utterly in argument.

**mind** *noun* **1** the ability to be aware of things and to think and reason, originating in the brain. **2** concentration, attention; *keep your mind on the job*. **3** remembrance; *keep it in mind*. **4** opinion; *change one's mind*; *to my mind he's a genius*. **5** a way of thinking and feeling; *state of mind*. **6** sanity, normal mental faculties; *in one's right mind*; *out of one's mind*. ● *verb* **1** take care of, attend to; *minding the baby*. **2** feel annoyance or discomfort at, object to; *she doesn't mind the cold*. **3** bear in mind; give heed to or concern oneself about; *never mind the expense*. **4** remember and take care; *mind you lock the door*. **5** be careful about; *mind the step*. □ **have a good** (*or* **half a**) **mind to** feel tempted or inclined to. **have a mind of one's own** be capable of forming opinions independently of others. **in two minds** undecided. **mind-bending** *adjective* strongly influencing the mind. **mind-blowing** *adjective* (*slang*) **1** mind-boggling, overwhelming. **2** (of drugs) causing hallucinations. **mind-boggling** *adjective* unbelievable, amazing. **mind one's P's and Q's** be careful in one's speech or behaviour. **mind-reader** *noun* a thought-reader. **mind's eye** the faculty of imagination. **on one's mind** constantly in one's thoughts, causing worry. **to my mind** in my opinion.

**minded** *adjective* **1** having a mind of a certain kind; *independent-minded*. **2** having certain interests; *politically minded*. **3** inclined or disposed to do something; *he could do it if he were so minded*.

**minder** *noun* one whose job is to attend to or take care of a person or thing.

**mindful** *adjective* taking thought or care of something; *mindful of his public image*. □ **mindfully** *adverb*

**mindless** *adjective* without a mind, without intelligence. □ **mindlessly** *adverb*, **mindlessness** *noun*

**mine**¹ *adjective & possessive pronoun* of or belonging to me; the thing(s) belonging to me.

**mine**² *noun* **1** an excavation in the earth for extracting metal or coal etc. **2** an abundant source of something; *a mine of information*. **3** a receptacle filled with explosive, placed in the ground or in water ready to explode when something strikes it or passes near it. ● *verb* **1** dig for minerals; extract (metal or coal etc.) in this way. **2** lay explosive mines in (an area). □ **mine-detector** *noun* an instrument for detecting the presence of explosive mines.

**minefield** *noun* **1** an area where explosive mines have been laid. **2** (*informal*) a subject or situation full of difficulties and dangers.

**minelayer** *noun* a ship or aircraft for laying explosive mines.

**miner** *noun* a person who works in a mine.

**mineral** *noun* **1** an inorganic substance that occurs naturally in the earth. **2** an ore or other substance obtained by mining. **3** a non-alcoholic usually fizzy drink. ● *adjective* of or containing minerals. □ **mineral water** water that is found naturally, containing dissolved mineral salts or gases.

**mineralogy** (min-er-al-ŏji) *noun* the scientific study of minerals. □ **mineralogical** *adjective*, **mineralogist** *noun*

**Minerva** (*Rom. myth.*) the goddess of handicrafts, identified with Athene.

**minestrone** (mini-**stroh**-ni) *noun* soup containing vegetables and pasta.

**minesweeper** *noun* a ship for clearing away explosive mines laid in the sea.

**mineworker** *noun* a miner.

**Ming** *noun* porcelain belonging to the time of the Ming dynasty in China (1368–1644).

**mingle** *verb* **1** mix, blend. **2** go about among people; mix socially; *mingled with the crowd*.

**mingy** *adjective* (*informal*) mean, stingy.

**mini** *noun* **1** (*informal*) a miniskirt. **2** (**Mini**) (*trade mark*) a make of small car.

**mini-** *combining form* miniature, small.

**miniature** (**min**-i-cher) *adjective* very small; made or represented on a small scale. ●*noun* **1** a very small and detailed portrait. **2** a small-scale copy or model of something. □ **in miniature** on a very small scale.

**miniaturist** *noun* a person who paints miniatures.

**miniaturize** *verb* (also **miniaturise**) make miniature, produce in a very small version. □ **miniaturization** *noun*

**minibus** *noun* a small bus for about twelve people.

**minicab** *noun* a car like a taxi that can be booked but does not ply for hire.

**minicomputer** *noun* a computer of medium power, bigger than a microcomputer but not as big as a mainframe.

**minim** *noun* **1** a note in music, lasting half as long as a semibreve. **2** one-sixtieth of a fluid drachm, about one drop.

**minima** *see* MINIMUM.

**minimal** *adjective* very small, the least possible. □ **minimally** *adverb*

**minimalism** *noun* the use of simple, basic forms in design, art, etc.; including only the minimum. □ **minimalist** *adjective & noun*

**minimize** *verb* (also **minimise**) **1** reduce to a minimum. **2** estimate at the smallest possible amount; represent at less than the true value or importance.

**minimum** *noun* (*plural* **minima**) the lowest or the lowest possible number, amount, intensity, etc.

**mining** *noun* **1** the process of extracting minerals etc. from the earth. **2** the process of laying explosive mines.

**minion** (**min**-yŏn) *noun* (*scornful*) a subordinate assistant.

**minipill** *noun* a contraceptive pill containing progestogen only (not oestrogen).

**miniskirt** *noun* a very short skirt.

**minister** *noun* **1** a person at the head of a government department or a main branch of this. **2** a diplomatic representative usu-ally ranking below ambassador. **3** a member of the clergy, especially in Presbyterian and Nonconformist Churches. ●*verb* attend to people's needs; *nurses ministered to the wounded*. □ **Minister of State** a government minister, especially holding a rank below Head of Department. **Minister of the Crown** a member of the Cabinet. **Minister without Portfolio** a government minister not in charge of a specific department of State. □ **ministerial** (min-iss-**teer**-iăl) *adjective*

**ministration** *noun* **1** (usually as **ministrations**) help or service. **2** ministering; supplying of help, justice, etc.

**ministry** *noun* **1** a government department headed by a minister; *Ministry of Defence*. **2** a period of government under one premier; his or her body of ministers. **3** the profession or functions of a member of the clergy or a religious leader.

**mink** *noun* **1** a small stoatlike animal of the weasel family. **2** its fur. **3** a coat made of this.

**Minn.** *abbreviation* Minnesota.

**Minnesota** (mini-**soh**-tă) a State of the north central USA.

**minnow** (**min**-oh) *noun* a small freshwater fish of the carp family.

**Minoan** (min-**oh**-ăn) *adjective* of the Bronze Age civilization of Crete (about 3000–1000 BC). ●*noun* a person of this civilization. (¶ Named after *Minos*, a legendary king of Crete.)

**minor** *adjective* **1** lesser, less important; *minor roads*; *a minor operation*. **2** (in music) of or based on a scale which has a semitone next above the second note. ●*noun* a person under full legal age. □ **minor planet** an asteroid.

**Minorca** the second largest of the Balearic Islands.

**Minorite** (my-ner-ryt) *noun* a Franciscan friar.

**minority** *noun* **1** the smallest part of a group or class. **2** a small group differing from others. **3** (in law) the state of being under full age; *during his minority*.

**Minotaur** (my-nŏ-tor) (*Gk. myth.*) a creature, half man and half bull, kept in the labyrinth in Crete and eventually slain by Theseus.

**minster** *noun* a name given to certain large or important churches; *York Minster*.

**minstrel** *noun* a travelling singer and musician in the Middle Ages.

**mint¹** *noun* **1** a place authorized to make a country's coins. **2** a vast amount; *left him a mint of money*. ●*verb* **1** make (coins) by stamping metal. **2** invent or coin (a word etc.). □ **in mint condition** fresh and unsoiled as if newly from the mint.

**mint²** noun **1** a plant with fragrant leaves that are used for flavouring sauces and drinks etc. **2** peppermint; a sweet flavoured with this. □ **minty** adjective

**minuet** (min-yoo-**et**) noun a slow stately dance in triple time; music suitable for this.

**minus** (**my**-nŭs) preposition **1** reduced by the subtraction of; *seven minus three equals four* ($7-3 = 4$). **2** (*informal*) without, deprived of; *returned minus his shoes.* ●*adjective* less than zero (= negative), less than the amount or number indicated; *a minus quantity*; *temperatures of minus ten degrees*; *alpha minus.* ●*noun* **1** = MINUS SIGN. **2** a disadvantage. □ **minus sign** a symbol ($-$), indicating subtraction or a negative value.

**minuscule** (**min**-ŭs-kewl) adjective extremely small.

**minute¹** (**min**-it) noun **1** one-sixtieth of an hour. **2** a very short time, a moment. **3** an exact point of time. **4** one-sixtieth of a degree used in measuring angles. **5** a memorandum. **6** (**minutes**) an official record of the proceedings of an assembly or committee etc. made during a meeting. ●*verb* make a note of; record in the minutes of an assembly's proceedings. □ **minute steak** a thin slice of steak that can be cooked quickly.

**minute²** (my-**newt**) adjective **1** extremely small. **2** very detailed and precise; *a minute examination.* □ **minutely** adverb

**minutiae** (min-**yoo**-shi-ee) plural noun very small details.

**minx** noun a cheeky or mischievous girl.

**Miocene** (**my**-ŏ-seen) Geol. adjective of the fourth epoch of the Tertiary period. ●*noun* this epoch.

**miracle** noun **1** a remarkable and welcome event that seems impossible to explain by the laws of nature and is therefore attributed to a supernatural agency. **2** a remarkable example or specimen; *it's a miracle of ingenuity.* □ **miracle play** a medieval play on biblical themes.

**miraculous** adjective of or like a miracle, wonderful. □ **miraculously** adverb

**mirage** (mi-**rah**zh) noun an optical illusion caused by atmospheric conditions, especially making sheets of water seem to appear in a desert or on a hot road.

**MIRAS** (**my**-răs) abbreviation (*Brit.*) mortgage interest relief at source.

**mire** noun **1** swampy ground, bog. **2** mud or sticky dirt. ●*verb* **1** plunge in mire. **2** involve in difficulties. **3** spatter with mire, soil.

**Miró** (mi-**roh**), Joan (1893–1983), Spanish surrealist painter.

**mirror** noun a piece of glass backed with amalgam so that reflections can be seen in it. ●*verb* reflect in or as if in a mirror. □ **mirror image** a reflection or copy in which the right and left sides of the original are reversed.

**mirth** noun merriment, laughter. □ **mirthful** adjective, **mirthless** adjective

**mis-** combining form badly, wrongly.

**misadventure** noun **1** a piece of bad luck. **2** Law an accident without crime or negligence; *death by misadventure.*

**misalliance** noun an unsuitable alliance; marriage with a person of lower social status.

**misanthrope** (**mis**-ăn-throhp) noun (also **misanthropist** (mis-**an**-thrŏp-ist) a person who hates mankind or avoids people in general. □ **misanthropic** adjective, **misanthropically** adverb, **misanthropy** noun

**misapply** verb (**misapplied, misapplying**) apply wrongly. □ **misapplication** noun

**misapprehend** (mis-apri-**hend**) verb misunderstand. □ **misapprehension** noun

**misappropriate** (mis-ă-**proh**-pri-ayt) verb take dishonestly, especially for one's own use. □ **misappropriation** noun

**misbegotten** adjective **1** contemptible, disreputable. **2** illegitimate, bastard.

**misbehave** verb behave badly. □ **misbehaviour** noun

**misc.** abbreviation miscellaneous.

**miscalculate** verb calculate incorrectly. □ **miscalculation** noun

**miscarriage** (mis-**ka**-rij) noun **1** abortion occurring without being induced. **2** a mistake or failure to achieve the correct result; *a miscarriage of justice.*

**miscarry** verb (**miscarried, miscarrying**) **1** (of a pregnant woman) have a miscarriage. **2** (of a scheme etc.) go wrong, fail.

**miscast** verb (**miscast, miscasting**) cast (an actor) in an unsuitable role.

**miscegenation** (mis-i-jin-ay-shŏn) noun interbreeding of races, especially of Whites with non-Whites.

**miscellaneous** (mis-ĕl-ay-niŭs) adjective **1** of various kinds; *miscellaneous items.* **2** of mixed composition or character; *a miscellaneous collection.*

**miscellany** (mi-**sel**-ăni) noun a collection of various items; a mixture.

**mischance** noun misfortune.

**mischief** noun **1** conduct (especially of children) that is annoying or does slight damage but is not malicious. **2** a tendency to tease or cause annoyance playfully; *full of mischief.* **3** harm or damage; *did a lot of mischief.* □ **make mischief** cause discord or ill feeling.

**mischievous** (mis-chiv-ŭs) *adjective* (of a person) full of mischief; (of an action) brought about by mischief. □ **mischievously** *adverb*

**miscible** (mis-ibŭl) *adjective* able to be mixed. □ **miscibility** *noun*

**misconceive** (mis-kŏn-**seev**) *verb* misunderstand, interpret incorrectly.

**misconception** (mis-kŏn-**sep**-shŏn) *noun* a wrong interpretation.

**misconduct** (mis-**kon**-dukt) *noun* bad, improper, or unprofessional behaviour.

**misconstrue** (mis-kŏn-**stroo**) *verb* misinterpret. □ **misconstruction** *noun*

**miscopy** *verb* (**miscopied, miscopying**) copy incorrectly.

**miscount** *verb* count incorrectly. ●*noun* an incorrect count.

**miscreant** (mis-kri-ănt) *noun* a wrongdoer, a villain.

**misdeal** *verb* (**misdealt, misdealing**) make a mistake in dealing playing cards. ●*noun* an incorrect dealing.

**misdeed** *noun* a wrong or improper act, a crime.

**misdemeanour** (mis-dim-een-er) *noun* (*Amer.* **misdemeanor**) a misdeed, wrongdoing.

**misdirect** *verb* direct incorrectly. □ **misdirection** *noun*

*mise en scène* (meez ahn sayn) **1** the scenery and properties for a play. **2** the surroundings of an event. (¶ French.)

**miser** *noun* a person who hoards money and spends as little as possible. □ **miserly** *adjective,* **miserliness** *noun*

**miserable** *adjective* **1** full of misery, feeling very unhappy or uncomfortable. **2** surly and discontented, disagreeable. **3** unpleasant; *miserable weather.* **4** wretchedly poor in quality or surroundings etc.; *a miserable attempt; miserable slums.* □ **miserably** *adverb*

**misericord** (miz-e-ri-kord) *noun* a small projection on the under side of a hinged seat in the choir stalls of a church, giving support (when the seat is turned up) to a person standing.

**misery** *noun* **1** a feeling of great unhappiness or discomfort. **2** something causing this. **3** (*informal*) a discontented or disagreeable person.

**misfire** *verb* **1** (of a gun) fail to go off correctly. **2** (of an engine etc.) fail to start, fail to function correctly. **3** fail to have the intended effect; *the joke misfired.* ●*noun* a failure of this kind.

**misfit** *noun* **1** a garment etc. that does not fit. **2** a person who is not well suited to his or her environment.

**misfortune** *noun* bad luck; an unfortunate event.

**misgive** *verb* (**misgave, misgiven, misgiving**) fill with misgivings; *his heart misgave him.*

**misgiving** *noun* (often as **misgivings**) a feeling of doubt or slight fear or mistrust.

**misgovern** *verb* govern badly.

**misguided** *adjective* mistaken in one's opinions or actions; ill-judged. □ **misguidedly** *adverb*

**mishandle** *verb* deal with (a thing) badly or inefficiently.

**mishap** (mis-hap) *noun* an unlucky accident.

**mishear** *verb* (**misheard, mishearing**) hear incorrectly.

**mishit** *verb* (**mishit, mishitting**) hit (a ball) faultily or badly. ●*noun* a faulty or bad hit.

**mishmash** *noun* a confused mixture.

**Mishnah** *noun* the collection of decisions on Jewish legal and ritual observance that form the main text of the Talmud.

**misinform** *verb* give wrong information to.

**misinterpret** *verb* interpret incorrectly. □ **misinterpretation** *noun*

**M.I.6** the UK military intelligence operating mainly overseas.

▪**Usage** This term is not in official use.

**misjudge** *verb* form a wrong opinion of; estimate incorrectly. □ **misjudgement** *noun*

**miskey** *verb* key (data) wrongly.

**mislay** *verb* (**mislaid, mislaying**) lose temporarily.

**mislead** *verb* (**misled, misleading**) lead astray; cause (a person) to gain a wrong impression of something. □ **misleading** *adjective*

**mismanage** *verb* manage (affairs) badly or wrongly. □ **mismanagement** *noun*

**mismatch** *verb* match unsuitably or incorrectly. ●*noun* a bad match.

**misnomer** (mis-**noh**-mer) *noun* a name or description that is wrongly applied to something.

**misogynist** (mis-**oj**-in-ist) *noun* a person who hates women. □ **misogynistic** *adjective,* **misogyny** *noun*

**misplace** *verb* **1** put (a thing) in the wrong place; lose temporarily. **2** place (one's confidence etc.) unwisely. **3** use (words or action) in an unsuitable situation; *misplaced humour.* □ **misplacement** *noun*

**misprint** *noun* an error in printing. ●*verb* print wrongly.

**misprision** (mis-**prizh**-ŏn) *noun* *Law* **1** a wrong act or an omission. **2** (in full **misprision of a felony** *or* **of treason**) deliberate concealment of one's knowledge of a crime, treason, etc.

**mispronounce** *verb* pronounce incorrectly. □ **mispronunciation** *noun*

**misquote** *verb* quote incorrectly. □ **misquotation** *noun*

**misread** verb (**misread** (pronounced mis-red), **misreading**) read or interpret incorrectly.

**misrepresent** verb represent in a false or misleading way. □ **misrepresentation** noun

**misrule** noun bad government. ● verb govern badly.

**miss**[1] verb 1 fail to hit, reach, or catch (an object). 2 fail to see, hear, or understand etc.; we missed the signpost; I missed that remark. 3 fail to catch (a train etc.) or keep (an appointment) or meet (a person); fail to seize (an opportunity). 4 omit, lack. 5 notice the absence or loss of. 6 feel regret at the absence or loss of; old Smith won't be missed. 7 avoid; go this way and you'll miss the traffic. 8 (of an engine etc.) misfire. ● noun failure to hit or attain what is aimed at. □ **give a thing a miss** avoid it, leave it alone. **miss out** omit. **miss out on** fail to get benefit or enjoyment from. **miss the boat** (informal) lose an opportunity.

**miss**[2] noun 1 a girl or unmarried woman. 2 (**Miss**) a title used of or to a girl or unmarried woman.

**Miss.** abbreviation Mississippi.

**missal** noun a book containing the prayers used in the Mass in the Roman Catholic Church.

**missel thrush** alternative spelling of MISTLE THRUSH.

**misshapen** adjective badly shaped, distorted.

**missile** noun an object or weapon suitable for throwing or firing at a target; a weapon directed by remote control or automatically.

**missing** adjective 1 lost, not in its place; two pages are missing. 2 not present; he's always missing when there's work to be done. 3 absent from home and with one's whereabouts unknown; she's listed as a missing person. 4 (of a soldier etc.) neither present after a battle nor known to have been killed. □ **missing link** 1 a thing lacking to complete a series. 2 a type of animal supposed to have existed between the anthropoid apes and the development of man.

**mission** noun 1 a body of envoys sent to a foreign country or to an international organization. 2 an establishment of missionaries. 3 an organization for spreading the Christian faith, a series of religious services etc. for this purpose. 4 the work or premises of a religious or other mission. 5 a person's vocation; her mission in life.

**missionary** noun a person who is sent to spread the Christian faith amongst a community. □ **missionary position** (informal) a position for sexual intercourse with the woman lying on her back and the man lying facing her on top.

**missis** noun (also **missus**) (informal) 1 wife; how's the missis? 2 a form of address to a woman, used without her name.

**Mississippi** 1 the greatest river of North America, flowing south from Minnesota to the Gulf of Mexico. 2 a State of the southeastern USA.

**missive** noun a written message, a letter.

**Missouri** 1 one of the main tributaries of the Mississippi. 2 a State of the central USA.

**misspell** verb (**misspelt** or **misspelled**, **misspelling**) spell incorrectly.

**misspend** verb (**misspent**, **misspending**) spend badly or unwisely.

**misstate** verb state wrongly. □ **misstatement** noun

**mist** noun 1 water vapour near the ground in drops smaller than raindrops, clouding the atmosphere less thickly than fog does. 2 condensed vapour clouding a window etc. 3 something resembling mist in its form or effect. ● verb (usually foll. by up or over) cover or become covered with mist; the windscreen misted up.

**mistake** noun an incorrect idea or opinion; something done incorrectly. ● verb (**mistook**, **mistaken**, **mistaking**) 1 misunderstand the meaning or intention of. 2 choose or identify wrongly; mistake one's vocation; she is often mistaken for her sister.

**mistaken** adjective 1 wrong in one's opinion; you are mistaken. 2 applied unwisely; mistaken kindness. □ **mistakenly** adverb

**mister** noun (informal) a form of address to a man, used without his name.

**mistime** verb say or do (a thing) at the wrong time.

**mistle thrush** (also **missel thrush**) a large thrush with a spotted breast, feeding on mistletoe berries.

**mistletoe** noun a plant with white berries that grows as a parasite on trees.

**mistook** see MISTAKE.

**mistral** (mis-trǎl) noun a cold north or north-west wind in southern France.

**mistreat** verb treat badly. □ **mistreatment** noun

**mistress** noun 1 a woman who is in a position of authority or control. 2 the female head of a household. 3 the female owner of a dog or other animal. 4 a female teacher. 5 a man's female lover with whom he has a continuing illicit sexual relationship.

**mistrial** noun a trial invalidated by an error in procedure etc.

**mistrust** verb feel no trust in. ● noun lack of trust. □ **mistrustful** adjective, **mistrustfully** adverb

**misty** adjective (**mistier**, **mistiest**) 1 full of mist. 2 indistinct in form or idea etc. □ **mistily** adverb, **mistiness** noun

**misunderstand** verb (**misunderstood**, **misunderstanding**) form an incorrect interpretation or opinion of.

**misunderstanding** noun **1** failure to understand. **2** a slight disagreement or quarrel.

**misuse** verb (pronounced mis-**yooz**) **1** use wrongly or incorrectly. **2** treat badly. ●noun (pronounced mis-**yooss**) (also **misusage**) wrong or incorrect use.

**MIT** abbreviation Massachusetts Institute of Technology.

**Mitchell**, Margaret (1900–49), American novelist, author of Gone with the Wind.

**mite** noun **1** a very small spider-like animal found in food; cheese-mites. **2** a very small contribution; offered a mite of comfort. **3** a very small creature; a small child.

**miter** Amer. spelling of MITRE.

**Mithras** (mith-ras) (Persian myth.) the god of light, also worshipped in the ancient Roman world. □ **Mithraic** adjective, **Mithraism** noun

**mitigate** (mit-i-gayt) verb make less intense or serious. □ **mitigating circumstances** facts that partially excuse wrongdoing. □ **mitigation** noun

▪Usage Do not confuse with militate.

**mitosis** noun a type of cell division that results in two nuclei each having the same number and kind of chromosomes as the parent nucleus.

**mitre** (my-ter) noun (Amer. **miter**) **1** the tall headdress worn by bishops and abbots. **2** a joint or join of two pieces of wood or cloth etc. with their ends evenly tapered so that together they form a right angle. ●verb (**mitred, mitring**) **1** join in this way; mitred corners. **2** bestow a mitre on.

**mitt** noun a mitten.

**mitten** noun a glove that has no partition between the fingers.

**Mitterrand**, (mee-ter-rahn) François Maurice Marie (born 1916), French socialist statesman, President from 1981.

**Mitty**, Walter, the hero of a story (by James Thurber) who indulged in extravagant daydreams of his own triumphs.

**mix** verb **1** put different things together so that the substances etc. are no longer distinct. **2** be capable of being blended; oil will not mix with water. **3** combine, be able to be combined; mix business with pleasure; drinking and driving don't mix. **4** (of a person) be sociable or harmonious. **5** combine (two or more sound signals) into one. ●noun **1** a mixture. **2** a mixture prepared commercially from suitable ingredients for making something; cake mix; concrete mix. □ **be mixed up in** (or **with**) be involved in. **mix up 1** mix thoroughly. **2** confuse.

**mix-up** noun a misunderstanding; confusion.

**mixed** adjective **1** composed of various qualities or elements. **2** containing people from various races or social classes. **3** for people of both sexes; a mixed school. □ **mixed bag** an assortment of different things or people. **mixed blessing** a thing that has advantages and also disadvantages. **mixed doubles** a doubles game in tennis with a man and woman as partners on each side. **mixed economy** an economic system combining private and state enterprise. **mixed farming** with both crops and livestock. **mixed feelings** a mixture of pleasure and dismay at the same event. **mixed grill** a dish of various grilled meats and vegetables. **mixed marriage** a marriage between people of different race or religion. **mixed metaphor** a combination of metaphors that do not work together; e.g. this tower of strength will forge ahead. **mixed-up** adjective (informal) mentally or emotionally confused; not well-adjusted socially.

**mixer** noun **1** a device that mixes or blends things; food mixers. **2** a person who gets on in a certain way with others; a good mixer. **3** a drink to be mixed with another (stronger) drink. □ **mixer tap** a tap through which both hot and cold water can be drawn together.

**mixture** noun **1** mixing; being mixed. **2** something made by mixing, a combination of things, ingredients, or qualities etc.

**mizen** noun (also **mizzen**) a mizen-sail. □ **mizen-mast** noun the mast that is next aft of the mainmast. **mizen-sail** noun the lowest sail, set lengthways, on a mizen-mast.

**Mizoram** (mi-zor-ăm) a State of NE India.

**ml** abbreviation millilitre(s).

**M.Litt.** abbreviation Master of Letters.

**Mlle** abbreviation (plural **Mlles**) Mademoiselle.

**MM** abbreviation **1** Messieurs. **2** Military Medal.

**mm** abbreviation millimetre(s).

**Mme** abbreviation (plural **Mmes**) Madame.

**MN** abbreviation Minnesota.

**Mn** symbol manganese.

**mnemonic** (nim-on-ik) adjective aiding the memory. ●noun a verse or other aid to help one remember facts. □ **mnemonically** adverb

**MO** abbreviation **1** Medical Officer. **2** Missouri. **3** money order.

**Mo** symbol molybdenum.

**Mo.** abbreviation Missouri.

**mo** noun (plural **mos**) (informal) a moment; half a mo.

**moa** noun an extinct flightless New Zealand bird resembling the ostrich.

**moan** noun **1** a low mournful sound, usually indicating pain or suffering. **2** a grumble. ●verb **1** utter a moan; say with a moan. **2** (of wind etc.) make a sound like a moan. **3** grumble.

**moat** noun a deep wide ditch surrounding a castle, house, etc., usually filled with water.

**mob** noun **1** a large disorderly crowd of people. **2** the common people, the rabble. **3** (slang) a gang. ●verb (**mobbed, mobbing**) crowd round in great numbers either to attack or to admire. □ **mob-cap** noun a large round cap worn indoors by women in the 18th and early 19th centuries. **mob rule** rule imposed and enforced by the mob.

**mobile** (**moh-**byl) adjective **1** movable, not fixed; able to move or be moved easily and quickly. **2** (of the features of the face) readily changing expression. **3** (of a person) able to change social status. ●noun a decorative structure that may be hung so that its parts move freely. □ **mobile home** a large caravan permanently parked and used as a residence. □ **mobility** (moh-**bil**-iti) noun

**mobilize** (**moh**-bi-lyz) verb (also **mobilise**) **1** assemble (troops) for service; prepare for war or other emergency. **2** assemble for a particular purpose; they mobilized support from all parties. □ **mobilization** noun

**mobster** noun (slang) a gangster.

**moccasin** (**mok**-ă-sin) noun a soft leather shoe, stitched round the vamp.

**mocha** (**moh**-kă) noun a kind of coffee; flavouring made with this.

**mock** verb **1** make fun of by imitating, mimic. **2** scoff or jeer; defy contemptuously. ●adjective sham, imitation; a mock battle. □ **mock orange** a shrub with strongly scented white flowers. **mock turtle soup** soup made from calf's head or other meat, to resemble turtle soup. **mock-up** noun a model of something, to be used for testing or study. □ **mockingly** adverb

**mockers** □ **put the mockers on** (slang) **1** bring bad luck to. **2** put a stop to.

**mockery** noun **1** ridicule, contempt. **2** a ridiculous or unsatisfactory imitation, a travesty. **3** a ridiculously futile action etc.

**mockingbird** noun a bird that mimics the notes of other birds.

**MOD** abbreviation Ministry of Defence.

**mod** (informal) noun **1** a modification. **2** a young person (especially in the 1960s) of a group known for its smart modern dress. ●adjective modern. □ **mod cons** (informal) modern conveniences.

**modal** adjective **1** of mode or form, not substance. **2** Grammar of the mood of a verb; (of an auxiliary verb, e.g. would) used to express the mood of another verb. **3** denoting a style of music using a particular mode. □ **modality** (moh-**dal**-iti) noun

**mode** noun **1** the way in which a thing is done. **2** the current fashion. **3** (in music) each of a number of traditional scale systems.

**model** noun **1** a three-dimensional reproduction of something, usually on a smaller scale. **2** a design or style of structure, e.g. of a car; this year's model. **3** a garment by a well-known designer; a copy of this. **4** a person or thing regarded as excellent of its kind and worthy of imitation. **5** a person employed to pose for an artist. **6** a person employed to display clothes by wearing them. ●adjective excellent of its kind, exemplary. ●verb (**modelled, modelling**; Amer. **modeled, modeling**) **1** make a model of (a thing) in clay or wax etc.; shape (clay etc.) into a model. **2** design or plan (a thing) in accordance with a model; the new method is modelled on the old one. **3** work as an artist's model or as a fashion model; display (clothes) in this way.

**modem** (**moh**-děm) noun a device linking a computer system and a telephone line so that data can be transmitted at high speeds.

**moderate** adjective (pronounced **mod**-er-ăt) **1** medium in amount, intensity, or quality etc. **2** keeping or kept within reasonable limits, not extreme or excessive. **3** not holding extremist views. ●noun (pronounced **mod**-er-ăt) a person with moderate views in politics etc. ●verb (pronounced **mod**-er-ayt) make or become moderate or less intense etc. □ **moderately** adverb, **moderateness** noun

**moderation** noun moderating; moderateness. □ **in moderation** in moderate amounts.

**moderato** adjective & adverb Music at a moderate speed.

**moderator** noun **1** an arbitrator, a mediator. **2** a Presbyterian minister presiding over a church court or assembly. **3** a substance used in nuclear reactors to slow down neutrons.

**modern** adjective **1** of the present or recent times; modern history. **2** in current fashion, not antiquated. **3** (of artistic or literary forms) new and experimental, not following traditional styles. ●noun a person of modern times or with modern tastes or style. □ **modern dance** an expressive style of dancing distinct from classical ballet. **modern English** the English language from about 1500. □ **modernity** (mŏ-**dern**-iti) noun

**modernism** noun modern ideas or methods, especially in art. □ **modernist** noun & adjective

**modernize** verb (also **modernise**) make modern, adapt to modern ideas or tastes etc. □ **modernization** noun

**modest** adjective **1** not vain, not boasting about one's merits or achievements. **2** rather shy, not putting oneself forward. **3** moderate in size or amount etc.; not showy or splendid in appearance. □ **modestly** adverb, **modesty** noun

**modicum** (**mod**-i-kŭm) noun a small amount.

**modification** noun **1** modifying or being modified. **2** a change made.

**modificatory** adjective modifying.

**modify** verb (**modified**, **modifying**) **1** make less severe or harsh or violent. **2** make partial changes in; some clauses in the agreement have been modified. **3** (in grammar) qualify by describing; adjectives modify nouns. □ **modifier** noun

**Modigliani** (mod-eel-**yah**-ni), Amedeo (1884–1920), Italian painter and sculptor.

**modish** (**moh**-dish) adjective fashionable. □ **modishly** adverb, **modishness** noun

**modiste** (mod-**eest**) noun a milliner, a dressmaker.

**modular** adjective consisting of independent units.

**modulate** verb **1** adjust or regulate; moderate. **2** vary the tone or pitch of (one's voice). **3** pass from one key to another in music. **4** alter the amplitude, frequency, or phase of (a carrier wave) so as to convey a particular signal. □ **modulation** noun

**module** (**mod**-yool) noun **1** a unit or standard used in measuring. **2** a standardized part or an independent unit in furniture, buildings, or a spacecraft etc.

**modulus** (**mod**-yoo-lŭs) noun (plural **moduli**) a constant factor or ratio.

**modus operandi** (moh-dŭs op-er-**an**-di) (plural **modi operandi**) a method of working. (¶ Latin.)

**modus vivendi** (moh-dŭs viv-**en**-di) (plural **modi vivendi**) an arrangement that enables parties who are in dispute to carry on instead of having their activities paralysed until the dispute has been settled. (¶ Latin, = way of living.)

**mog** noun (also **moggie**) (slang) a cat.

**Mogadishu** (mog-ă-**dish**-oo) the capital of Somalia.

**Mogul** (**moh**-gŭl) noun **1** a member of a Mongolian dynasty in India in the 16th–19th centuries. **2** (**mogul**) (informal) an important or influential person. ● adjective of the Moguls.

**mohair** noun **1** the fine silky hair of the angora goat, or a mixture of it with wool or cotton. **2** yarn or fabric made from this.

**Mohammed** alternative spelling of MU-HAMMAD.

**Mohammedan** alternative spelling of MUHAMMADAN.

**Mohican** (moh-**hee**-kăn) noun a member of a warlike tribe of North American Indians, formerly living in western Connecticut and Massachusetts. ● adjective (**mohican**) (of a hairstyle) in which the sides of the head are shaved and the remaining strip of hair is worn stiffly erect and often brightly coloured.

**Mohs** (pronounced mohz), Friedrich (1773–1839), German mineralogist who devised a scale classifying minerals according to their hardness.

**moiety** (**moy**-ăti) noun (formal) **1** half. **2** each of two parts of something.

**moire** (pronounced mwahr) noun (in full **moire antique**) a fabric that looks like watered silk.

**moiré** (**mwah**-ray) adjective **1** (of silk) watered. **2** (of metal) having a clouded appearance.

**moist** adjective slightly wet, damp.

**moisten** (**moi**-sĕn) verb make or become moist.

**moisture** noun water or other liquid diffused through a substance or present in the air as vapour or condensed on a surface.

**moisturize** verb (also **moisturise**) make (the skin) less dry by use of certain cosmetics. □ **moisturizer** noun

**moksa** noun (in Hinduism) liberation from the chain of births impelled by the law of karma; the bliss attained by this.

**molar** (**moh**-ler) noun any of the teeth at the back of the jaw that have broad tops and are used for grinding food in chewing. ● adjective of these teeth.

**molasses** (mŏ-**las**-iz) noun **1** uncrystallized syrup drained from raw sugar. **2** (Amer.) treacle.

**mold** etc. Amer. spelling of MOULD etc.

**Moldavia** (mol-**day**-viă) **1** a country of Eastern Europe bordering on Romania and Ukraine. **2** a former principality on the Danube. □ **Moldavian** adjective & noun

**mole** noun **1** a small permanent dark spot on the human skin. **2** a small burrowing animal with dark velvety fur and very small eyes. **3** a person working within an organization who secretly passes confidential information to another organization or country. **4** a structure built out into the sea as a breakwater or causeway. **5** Chem. a unit of amount of a substance equal to the quantity containing as many elementary units as there are atoms in 0.012 kg of carbon-12.

**molecular** (mŏ-**lek**-yoo-ler) adjective of, relating to, or consisting of molecules. □ **molecular weight** = RELATIVE MOLECULAR MASS.

**molecule** (mol-i-kewl) *noun* **1** the smallest unit (usually consisting of a group of atoms) into which a substance can be divided while still retaining the substance's chemical qualities. **2** a small particle.

**molehill** *noun* a small mound of earth thrown up by a burrowing mole. □ **make a mountain out of a molehill** behave as if a small difficulty were a very great one.

**molest** (mŏ-lest) *verb* **1** annoy or pester (a person). **2** attack or interfere with (a person), especially sexually. □ **molestation** *noun*, **molester** *noun*

**Molière** (mol-i-air) (real name: Jean-Baptiste Poquelin) (1622–73), French comic dramatist.

**moll** *noun* (*informal*) **1** a prostitute. **2** a gangster's female companion.

**mollify** *verb* (**mollified, mollifying**) soothe the anger of. □ **mollification** *noun*

**mollusc** (mol-ŭsk) *noun* (*Amer.* **mollusk**) any of a group of animals which have soft bodies and hard shells (e.g. snails, oysters, mussels) or no shell (e.g. slugs, octopuses).

**mollycoddle** *verb* coddle excessively, pamper. ●*noun* a mollycoddled person.

**Molotov cocktail** an improvised incendiary bomb, usually a bottle filled with inflammable liquid. (¶ Named after the Russian statesman V. M. Molotov (1890–1986).)

**molt** Amer. spelling of MOULT.

**molten** (mohl-tĕn) *adjective* melted, made liquid by very great heat.

**molto** *adverb* Music very.

**Molucca Islands** (mŏ-luk-ă) (also **Moluccas**) a group of islands in Indonesia. □ **Moluccan** *adjective & noun*

**molybdenum** (mŏ-lib-din-ŭm) *noun* a metallic element (symbol Mo), used as a strengthening agent in steels and other alloys.

**mom** *noun* (*Amer. informal*) mother.

**moment** *noun* **1** a very brief portion of time. **2** an exact point of time; *at that very moment.* **3** importance; *these are matters of great moment.* □ **at the moment** now. **for the moment** for now, temporarily. **in a moment** instantly; very soon. **the man** (*or* **woman**) **of the moment** the one who is important or the centre of attention now. **moment of truth** a time of test or crisis. (¶ from a Spanish phrase referring to the final sword-thrust in a bullfight.)

**momentary** (moh-měn-ter-i) *adjective* lasting only a moment. □ **momentarily** *adverb*

**momentous** (mŏ-ment-ŭs) *adjective* of great importance. □ **momentously** *adverb*, **momentousness** *noun*

**momentum** (mŏ-ment-ŭm) *noun* (*plural* **momenta**) impetus gained by movement; *the sledge gathered momentum as it ran downhill.*

**Mon.** *abbreviation* Monday.

**Monaco** (mon-ă-koh) **1** a country on the French Riviera. **2** its capital city. □ **Monacan** (mon-ă-kăn) *adjective & noun*

**monad** *noun* **1** the number one; a unit. **2** *Philosophy* the ultimate unit of being (e.g. a soul, an atom, a person, God). □ **monadic** *adjective*

**Mona Lisa** (moh-nă lee-ză) a painting (now in the Louvre) by Leonardo da Vinci of a woman with an enigmatic smile.

**monarch** (mon-erk) *noun* **1** a ruler with the title of king, queen, emperor, or empress. **2** a large orange and black butterfly. □ **monarchic** (mŏn-ark-ik), **monarchical** *adjectives*

**monarchist** (mon-er-kist) *noun* a person who favours government by a monarch or who supports a monarch against opponents of this system. □ **monarchism** *noun*

**monarchy** (mon-er-ki) *noun* **1** a form of government in which a monarch is the supreme ruler. **2** a country with this form of government. □ **monarchial** *adjective*

**monastery** (mon-ă-ster-i) *noun* a building in which monks live as a community.

**monastic** (mŏn-ast-ik) *adjective* of monks or monasteries. □ **monastically** *adverb*

**monasticism** (mŏn-ast-i-sizm) *noun* the way of life practised by monks.

**Monday** the day of the week following Sunday.

**Mondrian** (mon-dri-ahn), Piet (Pieter Cornelis Mondriaan) (1872–1944), Dutch painter, who used a geometrical style of abstract painting.

**Monégasque** (mon-i-gask) *adjective & noun* = MONACAN (*see* MONACO).

**Monet** (mon-ay), Claude Oscar (1840–1926), French painter, one of the founders of Impressionism.

**monetarism** (mun-it-er-izm) *noun* control of the supply of money as the chief method of stabilizing the economy. □ **monetarist** *noun & adjective*

**monetary** (mun-it-er-i) *adjective* **1** of a country's currency; *our monetary system.* **2** of or involving money; *its monetary value.* □ **monetarily** *adverb*

**money** *noun* **1** coins and banknotes. **2** (**moneys** *or* **monies**) sums of money. **3** wealth; *there's money in it.* □ **get one's money's worth** get good value for one's money. **in the money** (*informal*) winning money prizes; having plenty of money. **money-back** *adjective* (of a guarantee) promising to return a customer's money if he or she is not satisfied. **money for jam** *or* **for old rope** (*slang*) profit for little or no trouble. **money-grubber** *noun* one who is greedily intent on making money. **money market** trade in short term stocks, loans, etc. **money order** a printed order for the payment of a specified sum of money, issued by a bank or Post Office. **money-spinner** noun something that brings in a profit.

**moneybags** noun (treated as *singular*) (*informal*) a rich person.

**moneyed** (**mun**-id) adjective wealthy.

**moneylender** noun a person who lends money in return for payment of interest.

**moneymaker** noun **1** a person who earns a lot of money. **2** an idea, thing, etc. that produces a lot of money. ☐ **moneymaking** adjective & noun

**-monger** combining form **1** a dealer or trader; *fishmonger; ironmonger.* **2** (usually *scornful*) a person who promotes, encourages, or spreads something; *warmonger; scaremonger.*

**Mongol** (**mong**-ŏl) adjective Mongolian. ● noun a Mongolian person.

**mongol** (**mong**-ŏl) noun (often *offensive*) a person suffering from Down's syndrome.

**Mongolia** (mong-**oh**-liă) a country north of China, formerly extending to eastern Europe. ☐ **Mongolian** adjective & noun

**mongolism** (**mong**-ŏl-izm) noun Down's syndrome.

---

■**Usage** The term *Down's syndrome* is now preferred.

---

**Mongoloid** (**mong**-ŏ-loid) adjective resembling the Mongols in racial characteristics, having yellowish skin, a broad flat face, and straight black hair. ● noun a Mongoloid person.

**mongoose** (**mon**-gooss) noun (plural **mongooses**) a stoat-like tropical animal that can attack and kill venomous snakes.

**mongrel** (**mung**-rĕl) noun **1** a dog of no definable type or breed. **2** an animal of mixed breed. ● adjective of mixed origin or character.

**monism** (**mon**-iz'm) noun *Philosophy* the doctrine that only one ultimate principle or element exists, e.g. mind or matter. ☐ **monist** noun & adjective

**monitor** noun **1** a device used for observing or testing the operation of something. **2** a television screen used to check or select transmissions. **3** a visual display unit, a computer screen. **4** a person who listens to and reports on foreign broadcasts etc. **5** a pupil who is given special duties in a school. ● verb keep watch over; record or test or control the working of.

**monitory** adjective (*literary*) giving a warning.

**monk** noun a member of a community of men living apart from the world under the rules of a religious order.

**monkey** noun (plural **monkeys**) **1** an animal of a group closely related to man, especially one of the small long-tailed species. **2** a mischievous person. ● verb (**monkeyed**, **monkeying**) **1** (often foll. by *about* or *around*) fool around. **2** (often foll. by *with*) tamper; play mischievous tricks. ☐ **monkey business** (*informal*) mischief; underhand dealings. **monkey-nut** noun a peanut. **monkey-puzzle** noun an evergreen tree with needle-like leaves and intertwining branches. **monkey tricks** (*informal*) mischief. **monkey wrench** a wrench with an adjustable jaw.

**monkfish** noun a large edible sea fish.

**monkshood** noun a poisonous plant with blue hood-shaped flowers.

**mono** adjective monophonic. ● noun (plural **monos**) monophonic sound or recording.

**mono-** combining form one, alone, single.

**monochromatic** (mon-ŏ-krŏ-**mat**-ik) adjective **1** (of light or other radiation) containing only one colour or wavelength. **2** (of a picture) monochrome.

**monochrome** (**mon**-ŏ-krohm) adjective done in only one colour or in black and white.

**monocle** (**mon**-ŏ-kŭl) noun an eyeglass for one eye only. ☐ **monocled** adjective

**monocotyledon** (monŏ-kot-i-**lee**-dŏn) noun a flowering plant that has a single cotyledon. ☐ **monocotyledonous** adjective

**monocular** (mŏn-**ok**-yoo-ler) adjective with one eye; using or intended for use with one eye.

**monogamy** (mŏn-**og**-ămi) noun the system of being married to only one person at a time. ☐ **monogamous** adjective

**monogram** (**mon**-ŏ-gram) noun two or more letters (especially a person's initials) combined in one design. ☐ **monogrammed** adjective

**monograph** (**mon**-ŏ-grahf) noun a scholarly treatise on a single subject.

**monolingual** adjective speaking or using one language.

**monolith** (**mon**-ŏ-lith) noun a large single upright block of stone.

**monolithic** (monŏ-**lith**-ik) adjective **1** consisting of one or more monoliths. **2** like a monolith in being single and massive; *a monolithic organization.*

**monologue** (**mon**-ŏ-log) noun a long speech by one performer or by one person in a group.

**monomania** (monŏ-**may**-niă) noun an obsession with one idea or interest. ☐ **monomaniac** noun & adjective

**monophonic** (mon-ŏ-**fon**-ik) adjective (of sound reproduction) using only one transmission channel.

**monoplane** noun an aeroplane with only one set of wings.

**monopolist** (mŏn-op-ŏlist) *noun* one who has or advocates a monopoly. □ **monopolistic** *adjective*

**monopolize** *verb* (also **monopolise**) take exclusive control or use of; *monopolize the conversation.* □ **monopolization** *noun*

**monopoly** (mŏn-op-ŏli) *noun* **1** exclusive possession of the sale of some commodity or service. **2** sole possession or control of anything. **3** (**Monopoly**) (*trade mark*) a board game in which squares represent properties which players 'buy' with imitation money.

**monorail** *noun* a railway in which the track consists of a single rail.

**monosodium glutamate** a substance added to foods to enhance their flavour.

**monosyllable** (mon-ŏ-sil-ăbŭl) *noun* a word of one syllable. □ **monosyllabic** (monŏ-sil-ab-ik) *adjective*

**monotheism** (mon-ŏth-ee-izm) *noun* the doctrine that there is only one God. □ **monotheist** *noun*, **monotheistic** *adjective*

**monotone** (mon-ŏ-tohn) *noun* a level unchanging sound or tone of voice.

**monotonous** (mŏn-ot-ŏn-ŭs) *adjective* lacking in variety or variation; tiring or boring because of this. □ **monotonously** *adverb*

**monotony** (mŏn-ot-ŏn-i) *noun* a monotonous condition.

**monovalent** (mon-ŏ-vay-lĕnt) *adjective* univalent.

**monoxide** (mŏn-ok-syd) *noun* an oxide with one atom of oxygen.

**Monroe¹** (mŏn-roh), James (1758–1831), 5th President of the USA, who formulated the **Monroe Doctrine** which opposed interference of European countries in the affairs of the Americas.

**Monroe²** (mŏn-roh), Marilyn (original name: Norma Jean Mortenson, later Baker) (1926–62), American film actress, promoted as a sex symbol.

**Monrovia** (mŏn-roh-viă) the capital of Liberia.

**Monseigneur** (mon-sen-yer) *noun* (*plural* **Messeigneurs**, *pronounced* me-sen-yer) the title of an eminent Frenchman.

**Monsieur** (mŏs-yer) *noun* (*plural* **Messieurs**, *pronounced* mes-yer) the title of a Frenchman, = Mr *or* sir.

**Monsignor** (mon-seen-yor) *noun* (*plural* **Monsignori**) the title of certain Roman Catholic priests and officials.

**monsoon** *noun* **1** a seasonal wind blowing in South Asia. **2** the rainy season accompanying the south-west monsoon.

**mons pubis** the rounded mass of flesh lying over the joint of a man's pubic bones.

**monster** *noun* **1** a large ugly or frightening creature. **2** an animal or plant that is very

abnormal in form. **3** anything of huge size. **4** an extremely cruel or wicked person. ● *adjective* huge.

**monstrance** (mon-străns) *noun* (in the RC Church) a framed open or transparent holder in which the consecrated bread of the Eucharist is exposed for veneration.

**monstrosity** (mon-stros-iti) *noun* a monstrous thing.

**monstrous** (mon-strŭs) *adjective* **1** like a monster, huge. **2** outrageous, very wrong or absurd. □ **monstrously** *adverb*

**mons veneris** the rounded mass of flesh on a woman's abdomen just above the vulva.

**Mont.** *abbreviation* Montana.

**montage** (mon-tah*zh*) *noun* **1** the process of making a composite picture or piece of music etc. by putting together pieces from other pictures, designs, or compositions. **2** a picture etc. produced in this way. **3** the combination of short disconnected shots in cinematography to compress background information or provide atmosphere etc.

**Montaigne** (mon-tayn), Michel Eyquem de (1533–92), French writer, regarded as the inventor of the modern 'essay'.

**Montana** (mon-tan-ă) a State of the north-western USA.

**Mont Blanc** (mawn blahn) a peak in the Alps on the French–Italian border, the highest mountain in Europe.

**Monte Carlo** one of the three communes of Monaco, famous as a gambling resort and as the terminus of a car rally.

**Montenegro** (monti-nee-groh) a republic of the former Yugoslavia.

**Montessori** (monti-sor-i), Maria (1870–1952), Italian educationist, who devised a system of guided play.

**Monteverdi** (monti-vair-di), Claudio (1567–1643), Italian Renaissance composer of sacred and secular music.

**Montevideo** (monti-vi-day-oh) the capital of Uruguay.

**Montezuma** (monti-zoom-ă) (1466–1520), the last ruler of the Aztec empire in Mexico.

**Montfort**, Simon de (1208–65), Earl of Leicester, leader of the baronial opposition to Henry III.

**Montgolfier** (mon-golf-i-ay), Joseph (1740–1810) and his brother Jacques Étienne (1745–99), French inventors of the first practical hot-air balloons.

**Montgomery**, Bernard Law, Viscount (1887–1976), British soldier, noted for his successes in North Africa in the Second World War.

**month** *noun* **1** (in full **calendar month**) any of the twelve portions into which a year is divided; the period between the same dates in successive months. **2** a period of 28 days. □ **month of Sundays** (*informal*) a very long time.

**monthly** *adjective* happening, published, payable, etc. once a month. ●*adverb* once a month. ●*noun* a monthly magazine etc.

**Montmartre** (mawn-**mahtr**) a district in Paris frequented by artists in the 19th century.

**Montreal** (mon-tri-**awl**) the largest city in Canada, a port on the St Lawrence.

**Montrose**, James Graham, Marquess of (1612–50), Scottish general, who supported Charles I in the English Civil War.

**Montserrat** (mont-sĕ-**rat**) one of the Leeward Islands in the West Indies, a British dependency.

**monument** *noun* **1** anything (especially a structure) designed or serving to celebrate a person, event, etc. **2** a structure that is preserved because of its historical importance. □ **the Monument** a Doric column in the City of London, commemorating the Great Fire of 1666.

**monumental** *adjective* **1** of or serving as a monument; *monumental brasses in the church*. **2** (of a literary work) massive and of permanent importance. **3** extremely great; *a monumental blunder*. □ **monumental mason** a maker of tombstones etc.

**moo** *noun* the low deep sound made by a cow. ●*verb* make this sound.

**mooch** *verb* (*slang*) **1** walk slowly and aimlessly. **2** (especially *Amer.*) cadge; steal.

**mood** *noun* **1** a temporary state of mind or spirits. **2** the feeling or tone conveyed by a literary or artistic work; *the visual mood of a film*. **3** a fit of bad temper or depression; *he's in one of his moods*. **4** a grammatical form of a verb that shows whether it is a statement (e.g. *he stopped*) or a command (e.g. *stop!*) etc. □ **in the mood** in a willing state of mind.

**moody** *adjective* (**moodier, moodiest**) gloomy, sullen; liable to be like this. □ **moodily** *adverb*, **moodiness** *noun*

**mooli** *noun* a large white radish with a mild flavour.

**moon** *noun* **1** the natural satellite of the earth, made visible by light that it reflects from the sun. **2** this when it is visible; *there's no moon tonight*. **3** a natural satellite of any planet. **4** something desirable but unlikely to be attained; *cry for the moon*; *promised us the moon*. ●*verb* move, look, or pass time dreamily or listlessly. □ **moon boot** a warm thickly-padded boot. **moonface** *noun* a round face. **over the moon** (*informal*) ecstatic, greatly excited or pleased. □ **moonless** *adjective*

**moonbeam** *noun* a ray of moonlight.

**Moonie** *noun* (*informal, scornful*) a member of the Unification Church.

**moonlight** *noun* light from the moon. ●*verb* (*informal*) have two paid jobs, one during the day and the other in the evening. □ **moonlight flit** a hurried departure by night, especially to avoid paying a debt. □ **moonlighter** *noun*

**moonlit** *adjective* lit by the moon.

**moonscape** *noun* the surface of the moon; a landscape resembling this.

**moonshine** *noun* **1** foolish ideas. **2** (*slang*) illicitly distilled or smuggled alcoholic liquor.

**moonshot** *noun* the launch of a spacecraft to the moon.

**moonstone** *noun* a semi-precious stone, a form of feldspar with a pearly appearance.

**moonstruck** *adjective* crazy.

**moony** *adjective* listless, dreamy.

**Moor** *noun* a member of a Muslim people of NW Africa. □ **Moorish** *adjective*

**moor**[1] *noun* **1** a stretch of open uncultivated land with low shrubs (e.g. heather). **2** this used for preserving game for shooting; *a grouse moor*.

**moor**[2] *verb* secure (a boat or other floating thing) to a fixed object.

**Moore**, Henry (1898–1986), English sculptor and draughtsman.

**moorhen** *noun* a small waterbird.

**moorings** *plural noun* **1** cables etc. by which something is moored. **2** a place where a boat is moored.

**moorland** *noun* an area of moor.

**moose** *noun* (*plural* **moose**) a large animal of North America closely related to or the same as the European elk.

**moot** *adjective* debatable, undecided; *that's a moot point*. ●*verb* raise (a question) for discussion. ●*noun* (*old use*) an assembly.

**mop** *noun* **1** a bundle of yarn or soft material fastened at the end of a stick, used for cleaning floors. **2** a small device of similar shape for various purposes; *dish-mop*. **3** a thick mass of hair. ●*verb* (**mopped, mopping**) clean or wipe with a mop etc.; wipe away. □ **mop up 1** wipe up with a mop etc. **2** finish off a task; clear (an area) of the remnants of enemy troops etc. after a victory.

**mope** *verb* **1** be in low spirits and listless. **2** wander about listlessly.

**moped** (**moh**-ped) *noun* a low-powered motor cycle.

**moppet** *noun* (*informal*) (as a term of endearment) a baby or young child.

**moquette** (mŏ-**ket**) *noun* a material with raised loops or cut pile used for carpets and upholstery.

**moraine** (mŏ-**rayn**) *noun* a mass of debris carried down and deposited by a glacier.

**moral** adjective **1** of or concerned with the goodness and badness of human character or with the principles of what is right and wrong in conduct; moral philosophy. **2** virtuous. **3** capable of understanding and living by the rules of morality. **4** based on people's sense of what is right or just, not on legal rights and obligations; we had a moral obligation to help. **5** psychological, mental, not physical or concrete; moral courage; moral support. ●noun **1** a moral lesson or principle. **2** (**morals**) a person's moral habits, especially in sexual conduct. □ **moral philosophy** the branch of philosophy concerned with ethics. **moral victory** a triumph, although nothing concrete is obtained by it. □ **morally** adverb

**morale** (mŏ-**rahl**) noun the state of a person's or group's spirits and confidence.

**moralist** noun a person who expresses or teaches moral principles. □ **moralistic** adjective

**morality** (mŏ-**ral**-iti) noun **1** moral principles or rules. **2** a particular system of morals; commercial morality. **3** being moral, conforming to moral principles; goodness or rightness. □ **morality play** a drama popular in the 16th century illustrating a moral lesson with characters that represent virtues and vices.

**moralize** verb (also **moralise**) talk or write about the principles of right and wrong and conduct etc.

**morass** (mo-**rass**) noun **1** a marsh, a bog. **2** an entanglement, something that confuses or impedes people.

**moratorium** (mo-ră-**tor**-iŭm) noun (plural **moratoriums** or **moratoria**) **1** legal authorization to debtors to postpone payment. **2** a temporary ban or suspension on some activity; asked for a moratorium on strikes.

**Moravia** (mŏ-**ray**-viă) a region of the Czech Republic, bordering on Slovakia. □ **Moravian Church** a Protestant sect with the Bible as the only source of faith. □ **Moravian** adjective & noun

**morbid** adjective **1** (of the mind or ideas) unwholesome, preoccupied with gloomy or unpleasant things. **2** caused by or indicating disease, unhealthy; a morbid growth. □ **morbidly** adverb, **morbidity** (mor-**bid**-iti) noun

**mordant** (mor-**dănt**) adjective **1** characterized by a biting sarcasm; mordant wit. **2** corrosive. **3** fixing colouring matter. ●noun a mordant acid or substance.

**More**, Sir Thomas (1478–1535), English statesman and Roman Catholic saint, Lord Chancellor of England 1529–32. Feast day, 22 June.

**more** adjective greater in quantity or intensity etc. ●noun a greater quantity or number. ●adverb **1** in a greater degree. **2** again; once more. □ **more or less** in a greater or less degree; approximately.

**moreish** adjective (also **morish**) (informal) (of food) so tasty that it causes a desire for more.

**morel** (mŏ-**rel**) noun an edible mushroom with a dark conical cap pitted with irregular holes.

**morello** (mŏ-**rel**-oh) noun (plural **morellos**) a bitter dark cherry.

**moreover** adverb besides, in addition to what has already been said.

**mores** (**mor**-ayz) plural noun customs or conventions of a community.

**morganatic** (mor-găn-**at**-ik) adjective (of a marriage) between a man of high rank and a woman of low rank who retains her former status, their children having no claim to the father's possessions or title.

**morgue** (pronounced morg) noun a mortuary.

**moribund** (mo-ri-bund) adjective in a dying state.

**morish** alternative spelling of MOREISH.

**Morland**, George (1763–1804), English painter, especially of rural scenes.

**Mormon** (mor-mŏn) noun a member of a religious organization (the Church of Jesus Christ of Latter-Day Saints) founded in the USA in 1830. □ **Mormonism** noun

**morn** noun (poetic) morning.

**mornay** noun a cheese-flavoured white sauce.

**morning** noun **1** the early part of the day, ending at noon or at the midday meal. **2** sunrise, dawn; when morning broke. **3** (used as adjective) taken or occurring in the morning; morning coffee. □ **morning after** (informal) a hangover. **morning dress** formal dress for a man consisting of a tailcoat, striped trousers, and top hat. **morning glory** a climbing plant with trumpet-shaped flowers that often close after one morning. **morning sickness** sickness felt in the morning during the early months of pregnancy. **morning star** a bright star or planet (especially Venus) seen in the east before sunrise.

**Morocco** a country in North Africa. □ **Moroccan** adjective & noun

**morocco** noun a fine flexible leather made (originally in Morocco) from goatskins.

**moron** (mor-on) noun **1** (informal) a very stupid person. **2** an adult with intelligence equal to that of an average child of 8–12 years. □ **moronic** (mŏ-**ron**-ik) adjective

**Moroni** (mŏ-**roh**-ni) the capital of Comoros.

**morose** (mŏ-**rohss**) adjective sullen, gloomy, and unsociable. □ **morosely** adverb, **moroseness** noun

**morpheme** *noun* *Linguistics* a meaningful unit of language that cannot be further divided (e.g. *in*, *come*, *-ing* are morphemes forming *incoming*).

**Morpheus** (**mor**-fi-ŭs) (*Rom. myth.*) the god of dreams.

**morphia** (**mor**-fiă) *noun* morphine.

**morphine** (**mor**-feen) *noun* a drug made from opium, used for relieving pain.

**morphology** (mor-**fol**-ŏji) *noun* the study of the forms of things. □ **morphological** *adjective*

**Morris**[1], William (1834–96), English writer, artist, and designer.

**Morris**[2], William Richard, *see* NUFFIELD.

**morris dance** a traditional English folk-dance, of various forms, usually performed by people in costume, often with ribbons and bells.

**morrow** *noun* (*poetic*) the following day.

**Morse** *noun* (in full **Morse code**) a code in which letters of the alphabet are represented by combinations of short and long sounds or flashes of light (dots and dashes). (¶ Devised by S. F. B. Morse (1791–1872), American pioneer of the use of the electric telegraph.)

**morsel** *noun* a small quantity; a small amount or piece of food.

**mortal** *adjective* **1** subject to death. **2** causing death, fatal; *a mortal wound*. **3** deadly, lasting until death; *mortal enemies*; *in mortal combat*. **4** intense; *in mortal fear*. **5** (*informal*) without exception; *sold every mortal thing*. ●*noun* a person who is subject to death, a human being. □ **mortal sin** (in RC teaching) sin that causes death of the soul or that is fatal to salvation. □ **mortally** *adjective*

**mortality** (mor-**tal**-iti) *noun* **1** being mortal, subject to death. **2** loss of life on a large scale. **3** a number of deaths in a given period. □ **mortality rate** the death rate.

**mortar** *noun* **1** a mixture of lime or cement with sand and water, for joining bricks or stones. **2** a bowl-shaped container in which substances are pounded with a pestle. **3** a short cannon for firing shells at a high angle. ●*verb* **1** plaster or join (bricks etc.) with mortar. **2** attack with mortars.

**mortarboard** *noun* **1** an academic cap with a stiff flat square top. **2** a flat board for holding mortar.

**mortgage** (**mor**-gij) *verb* give someone a claim on (property) as security for payment of a debt or loan. ●*noun* **1** mortgaging. **2** an agreement giving a claim of this kind. **3** the amount of money borrowed or lent against the security of a property in this way. □ **mortgage rate** the rate of interest charged on a mortgage. □ **mortgageable** *adjective*

**mortgagee** (mor-gij-**ee**) *noun* a person or firm (e.g. a building society) to whom property is mortgaged.

**mortgager** *noun* (also **mortgagor**, *pronounced* mor-gij-**or**) one who mortgages his or her property.

**mortice** alternative spelling of MORTISE.

**mortician** (mor-**tish**-ăn) *noun* (*Amer.*) an undertaker.

**mortify** *verb* (**mortified**, **mortifying**) **1** humiliate greatly. **2** subdue by discipline or self-denial. **3** (of flesh) become gangrenous. □ **mortification** *noun*

**mortise** (**mor**-tiss) *noun* (also **mortice**) a hole in one part of a wooden structure into which the end of another part is inserted so that the two are held together. ●*verb* cut a mortise in; join with a mortise. □ **mortise lock** a lock that is set into (not on) the framework of a door.

**Morton**, 'Jelly Roll' (Ferdinand Joseph) (1885–1941), American jazz pianist, composer, and band-leader.

**mortuary** (**mor**-tew-er-i) *noun* a place where dead bodies may be kept temporarily.

**Mosaic** (mŏ-**zay**-ik) *adjective* of Moses or his teaching; *Mosaic Law*.

**mosaic** (mŏ-**zay**-ik) *noun* a pattern or picture made by placing together small pieces of glass or stone etc. of different colours.

**Moscow** the capital of Russia.

**moselle** (moh-**zel**) *noun* a dry white wine from the Moselle valley in Germany.

**Moses**[1] Hebrew patriarch who led the Jews from bondage in Egypt towards the Promised Land, and gave them the Ten Commandments.

**Moses**[2], Anna Mary Robertson ('Grandma') (1860–1961), American painter, who began painting at the age of 75.

**mosey** *verb* (often foll. by *along*) (*slang*) go in a slow, leisurely way.

**Moslem** = MUSLIM.

**Mosley** (**mohz**-li), Sir Oswald Ernald (1896–1980), English Fascist leader.

**mosque** (*pronounced* mosk) *noun* a Muslim place of worship.

**mosquito** (mos-**kee**-toh) *noun* (*plural* **mosquitoes**) a kind of gnat, the female of which bites and sucks blood.

**Moss**, Stirling (born 1929), English motor-racing driver.

**moss** *noun* a small flowerless plant that forms a dense growth on moist surfaces or in bogs. □ **moss-rose** a cultivated variety of rose with a moss-like growth on the stem and calyx. **moss stitch** a pattern formed of alternating plain and purl stitches in knitting.

**Mossad** (moh-**sad**) the Israeli secret service. (¶ Hebrew, = agency.)

**mossy** *adjective* (**mossier, mossiest**) like moss; covered in moss.

**most** *adjective* greatest in quantity or intensity etc. ●*noun* the greatest quantity or number. ●*adverb* **1** in the greatest degree. **2** very; *a most amusing book.* □ **at most** *or* **at the most** not more than. **for the most part** in most cases; in most of its extent. **make the most of** use to the best advantage. **Most Reverend** the title of an archbishop.

**mostly** *adverb* for the most part.

**MOT** *abbreviation* **1** (*formerly*) Ministry of Transport. **2** (in full **MOT test**) a compulsory annual test of motor vehicles of more than a specified age.

**mote** *noun* a particle of dust.

**motel** (moh-**tel**) *noun* a roadside hotel for motorists.

**motet** (moh-**tet**) *noun* a short religious choral work.

**moth** *noun* **1** an insect resembling a butterfly but usually flying at night. **2** a small similar insect that lays its eggs in cloth or fur fabrics on which its larvae feed. □ **motheaten** *adjective* **1** damaged by moth-larvae. **2** antiquated, decrepit.

**mothball** *noun* a small ball of naphthalene etc. placed in stored clothes to keep away moths. □ **in mothballs** stored out of use for a considerable time.

**mother** *noun* **1** a female parent. **2** a quality or condition that gives rise to another; *necessity is the mother of invention.* **3** (in full **Mother Superior**) the head of a female religious community. ●*verb* look after in a motherly way. □ **Mother Carey's chicken** = STORM PETREL. **mother country** a country in relation to its colonies. **Mother Goose rhyme** (*Amer.*) a nursery rhyme. **Mothering Sunday** = MOTHER'S DAY. **mother-in-law** *noun* (*plural* **mothers-in-law**) the mother of one's wife or husband. **mother-of-pearl** *noun* a pearly substance lining the shells of oysters and mussels etc. **Mother's Day** a day in honour of mothers, (in Britain) the fourth Sunday in Lent, (in the USA) the second Sunday in May. **mother tongue** one's native language. □ **motherhood** *noun*

**motherboard** *noun* a printed circuit board containing the principal components of a microcomputer or other electronic device, to which other boards may be connected.

**motherland** *noun* one's native country.

**motherless** *adjective* without a living mother.

**motherly** *adjective* like a mother, showing a mother's kindliness and tenderness. □ **motherliness** *noun*

**mothproof** *adjective* (of clothes) treated so as to repel moths. ●*verb* treat (clothes) in this way.

**motif** (moh-**teef**) *noun* **1** a recurring design, feature, or theme in a literary, artistic, or musical work. **2** an ornament sewn on a dress etc.

**motion** *noun* **1** moving, change of position. **2** manner of movement. **3** change of posture; a particular movement, a gesture. **4** a formal proposal that is to be discussed and voted on at a meeting. **5** emptying of the bowels; faeces. ●*verb* make a gesture directing (a person) to do something; *motioned him to sit beside her.* □ **go through the motions** do something in a perfunctory or insincere manner. **in motion** moving, not at rest. **motion picture** (especially *Amer.*) a cinema film.

**motionless** *adjective* not moving.

**motivated** *adjective* having a definite and positive desire to do things.

**motivate** *verb* **1** give a motive or incentive to, be the motive of; *she was motivated by kindness.* **2** stimulate the interest of, inspire. □ **motivation** *noun*

**motive** *noun* that which induces a person to act in a certain way. ●*adjective* producing movement or action; *motive power.*

**mot juste** (moh *zh*oost) (*plural* **mots justes**, *pronounced* same) the most appropriate word or phrase. (¶ French.)

**motley** *adjective* **1** multicoloured. **2** made up of various sorts; *a motley collection.* ●*noun* (*old use*) a jester's particoloured costume.

**moto-cross** *noun* a motor cycle race over rough ground.

**motor** *noun* **1** a machine that supplies motive power for a vehicle or boat etc. or for another device with moving parts; an internal-combustion engine. **2** a motor car. ●*adjective* **1** giving or producing motion. **2** driven by a motor; *motor boat; motor mower.* **3** of or for motor vehicles; *the motor show.* **4** relating to muscular movement or the nerves activating it. ●*verb* go or convey in a motor car. □ **motor bike** (*informal*) a motor cycle. **motor car** a short-bodied motor vehicle for a driver and passengers. **motor cycle** a two-wheeled motor-driven road vehicle that cannot be driven by pedals. **motor cyclist** *noun* one who rides a motor cycle. **motor vehicle** a vehicle with a motor engine, for use on ordinary roads.

**motorcade** *noun* a procession or parade of motor vehicles.

**motorist** *noun* the driver of a car.

**motorize** *verb* (also **motorise**) **1** equip with a motor or motors. **2** equip (troops) with motor vehicles.

**motorman** *noun* the driver of a tram, underground train, etc.

**motorway** *noun* a road specially constructed and controlled for fast motor traffic.

**Motown** noun popular music with elements of rhythm and blues, associated with Detroit, USA.

**motte** noun a mound forming the site of an ancient castle or camp etc.

**mottled** adjective marked or patterned with irregular patches of colour.

**motto** noun (plural **mottoes**) **1** a short sentence or phrase adopted as a rule of conduct or as expressing the aims and ideals of a family, country, institution, etc. (often accompanying a coat of arms). **2** a sentence inscribed on an object. **3** a maxim, verse, or riddle inside a paper cracker.

**mould** (Amer. **mold**) noun **1** a hollow container into which a soft or liquid substance is poured to set or cool into a desired shape. **2** a pudding etc. made in a mould. **3** a fine furry growth of very small fungi, forming on things that lie in moist warm air. **4** soft fine loose earth that is rich in organic matter; leaf-mould. ● verb **1** cause to have a certain shape; produce by shaping. **2** guide or control the development of; mould his character.

**moulder** verb (Amer. **molder**) decay into dust, rot away.

**moulding** noun (Amer. **molding**) a moulded object, especially an ornamental strip of plaster or wood etc. decorating or outlining something.

**mouldy** adjective (Amer. **moldy**) (**mouldier, mouldiest**) **1** covered with mould. **2** stale, smelling of mould. **3** (slang) dull, worthless. □ **mouldiness** noun

**moult** (pronounced mohlt) (Amer. **molt**) verb (of a bird, animal, or insect) shed feathers, hair, or skin etc. before a new growth. ● noun the process of moulting.

**mound** noun a mass of piled-up earth or stones; a small hill.

**mount** verb **1** ascend, go upwards; rise to a higher level. **2** get or put on to a horse etc. for riding. **3** increase in amount or intensity; the death toll mounted. **4** put into place on a support; fix in position for use or display or study. **5** take action to effect (something); mount an offensive. **6** place on guard; mount sentries round the palace. ● noun **1** a horse for riding. **2** (also **mounting**) something on which a thing is mounted for support or display etc. **3** (old use, except before a name) a mountain or hill; Mount Everest.

**mountain** noun **1** a mass of land that rises to a great height, especially of over 1000 ft. **2** a large heap or pile; a huge quantity. **3** a large surplus stock; the butter mountain. □ **mountain ash** the rowan tree. **mountain bike** a sturdy bike with thick tyres and many gears for riding over rough ground. **mountain lion** a puma. **mountain**

**sickness** sickness caused by thin air at great heights.

**mountaineer** noun a person who is skilled in mountain climbing. □ **mountaineering** noun

**mountainous** adjective **1** full of mountains; mountainous country. **2** huge.

**Mountbatten**, Louis, 1st Earl (1900–79), British sailor, soldier, and statesman, supreme Allied commander in SE Asia 1943–5, last Viceroy and then Governor-General of India 1947–8.

**mountebank** (mownt-i-bank) noun a swindler or charlatan.

**mounted** adjective serving on horseback; mounted police.

**Mountie** noun (informal) a member of the Royal Canadian Mounted Police.

**mounting** noun = MOUNT (sense 2).

**mourn** verb feel or express sorrow for a person who has died or regret for a thing that is lost or past. □ **mourner** noun

**mournful** adjective sorrowful, showing grief. □ **mournfully** adverb, **mournfulness** noun

**mourning** noun black or dark clothes worn as a conventional sign of bereavement.

**mouse** noun (plural **mice**) **1** a small rodent with a long thin tail. **2** a shy or timid person. **3** (plural **mouses**) a small hand-held device for controlling a cursor on a VDU screen.

**mouser** noun a cat as a hunter of mice.

**mousetrap** noun **1** a trap for catching mice. **2** (informal) cheese of poor quality.

**moussaka** (moo-sah-kă) noun (also **mousaka**) a Greek dish of layers of minced meat, aubergine, etc., usually topped with cheese sauce.

**mousse** (pronounced mooss) noun **1** a dessert of cream or a similar substance flavoured with fruit or chocolate. **2** meat or fish purée mixed with cream etc. and shaped in a mould. **3** a frothy creamy substance, e.g. one used for styling hair.

**moustache** (mŭs-tahsh) noun (Amer. **mustache**) hair left to grow on a man's upper lip.

**mousy** adjective **1** quiet and shy or timid. **2** nondescript light brown.

**mouth** noun (pronounced mowth) **1** the opening through which food is taken into an animal's body. **2** (slang) talkativeness; impudence. **3** the opening of a bag, cave, cannon, trumpet, etc. **4** the place where a river enters the sea. ● verb (pronounced mowth) **1** form (words) with the lips without speaking them aloud. **2** declaim words pompously or with exaggerated distinctness. □ **mouth-organ** noun = HARMONICA. **mouth-watering** adjective (of food) looking or smelling delicious, appetizing. **put words into a person's mouth** represent him or her as having said this. **take words out of a person's mouth** say what he or she was about to say.

**mouthful** noun **1** an amount that fills the mouth. **2** a small quantity of food etc. **3** a lengthy word or phrase; one that is difficult to say.

**mouthpiece** noun **1** the part of a musical instrument or telephone that is placed between or near the lips. **2** a person who speaks on behalf of another or others.

**mouthwash** noun a liquid for cleansing the mouth.

**movable** adjective (also **moveable**) **1** able to be moved. **2** variable in date from year to year; a movable feast.

**move** verb **1** change or cause to change in position, place, or posture. **2** be or cause to be in motion. **3** change one's place of residence. **4** cause (bowels) to empty. **5** make progress; the work moves slowly. **6** make a move in a board game. **7** provoke a reaction or emotion in; I felt very moved. **8** prompt or incline, motivate; what moved them to invite us? **9** put forward formally for discussion and decision at a meeting. **10** initiate some action; unless the employers move quickly, there will be a strike. **11** live or be active in a particular group; she moves in the best circles. ● noun **1** the act or process of moving. **2** the moving of a piece in a board game; a player's turn to do this. **3** a calculated action done to achieve some purpose. □ **get a move on** (informal) hurry. **move in** take up residence in a new home. **move over** or **up** alter position in order to make room for another. **on the move** moving from one place to another; progressing. □ **mover** noun

**moveable** alternative spelling of MOVABLE.

**movement** noun **1** moving; being moved. **2** action, activity; watch every movement. **3** the moving parts in a mechanism, especially of a clock or watch. **4** a series of combined actions by a group to achieve some purpose; the group itself; the Women's Lib movement. **5** a trend; the movement towards more casual styles in fashion. **6** market activity in some commodity; the movement in stocks and shares. **7** one of the principal divisions in a long musical work.

**movie** noun (especially Amer., informal) a cinema film.

**moving** adjective affecting the emotions; a moving story. □ **moving staircase** an escalator.

**mow** verb (**mowed**, **mown**, **mowing**) cut (grass or grain etc.). □ **mow down** kill or destroy at random or in great numbers.

**mower** noun a person or machine that mows.

**Mozambique** (moh-zam-**beek**) a country in East Africa. □ **Mozambican** noun

**Mozart** (**moh**-tsart), Wolfgang Amadeus (1756–91), Austrian composer.

**mozzarella** (mot-să-**rel**-ă) noun soft Italian curd cheese, used especially in cooking.

**MP** abbreviation Member of Parliament.

■**Usage** Note the placing or absence of an apostrophe in MPs (= Members of Parliament), an MP's salary, MPs' salaries.

**mp** abbreviation (in music) mezzo piano.

**m.p.g.** abbreviation miles per gallon.

**m.p.h.** abbreviation miles per hour.

**M.Phil.** abbreviation Master of Philosophy.

**Mr** noun (plural **Messrs**) the title prefixed to a man's name or to the name of his office; Mr Byrne; Mr Speaker.

**Mrs** noun (plural **Mrs**) the title prefixed to a married woman's name.

**MS** abbreviation **1** (plural **MSS**) manuscript. **2** Mississippi. **3** multiple sclerosis.

**Ms** (pronounced miz or mŭz) noun the title of a married or unmarried woman.

**M.Sc.** abbreviation Master of Science.

**MS-DOS** abbreviation (trade mark) Microsoft disk operating system.

**MT** abbreviation Montana.

**Mt.** abbreviation Mount.

**mu** (pronounced myoo) noun **1** the twelfth letter of the Greek alphabet (M, μ). **2** a symbol (μ) = MICRO- (sense 2).

**much** adjective existing in great quantity. ● noun a great quantity. ● adverb **1** in a great degree; much to my surprise. **2** approximately; much the same. □ **I thought as much** I thought so. **much as** even though, however much; I can't go, much as I should like to. **much of a muchness** very alike, very nearly the same.

**mucilage** (mew-sil-ij) noun **1** a sticky substance secreted by certain plants. **2** an adhesive gum.

**muck** noun **1** farmyard manure. **2** (informal) dirt, filth. **3** (informal) untidy things, a mess. ● verb (often foll. by up) make dirty, mess. □ **make a muck of** (slang) bungle. **muck about** or **around** (slang) mess about. **muck in** (slang) share tasks or expenses equally. **muck out** remove manure from; mucking out the stables. **muck up** (slang) spoil.

**muckle** = MICKLE.

**muckraking** noun searching out and revealing scandal. □ **muckraker** noun

**mucky** adjective (**muckier**, **muckiest**) covered with muck, dirty.

**mucous** (mew-kŭs) adjective of or like mucus; covered with mucus. □ **mucous membrane** the moist skin lining the nose, mouth, throat, etc.

**mucus** (*mew-kŭs*) *noun* the moist slimy substance produced by a mucous membrane.

**mud** *noun* wet soft earth. □ **one's name is mud** (*informal*) one is in disgrace. **mud-flat** *noun* a stretch of muddy land left uncovered at low tide. **mud pack** a cosmetic paste applied thickly to the skin and removed after a short period of time. **mud-slinging** *noun* (*slang*) speaking evil of someone, trying to damage someone's reputation.

**muddle** *verb* **1** bring into a state of confusion and disorder. **2** confuse (a person) mentally. **3** confuse or mistake (one thing for another). ●*noun* a muddled condition, disorder. □ **muddle-headed** *adjective* liable to muddle things, mentally confused. **muddle on** *or* **along** work in a haphazard way. **muddle through** succeed in the end in spite of inefficiency.

**muddy** *adjective* (**muddier**, **muddiest**) **1** like mud; full of mud. **2** (of colour, liquid, or sound) not clear or pure. **3** (of thoughts) vague, confused. ●*verb* (**muddied**, **muddying**) make muddy. □ **muddiness** *noun*

**mudflap** *noun* a flap behind the wheel of a vehicle, to prevent splashes.

**mudguard** *noun* a curved cover above the wheel of a cycle etc. to protect the rider from the mud it throws up.

**muesli** (**mooz-li**) *noun* a breakfast food of mixed crushed cereals, dried fruit, nuts, etc., eaten with milk.

**muezzin** (*moo-ez-in*) *noun* a man who proclaims the hours of prayer for Muslims, usually from a minaret.

**muff** *noun* a covering of furry material for keeping the hands or ears warm. ●*verb* (*informal*) bungle or blunder.

**muffin** *noun* **1** a light flat round spongy cake, eaten toasted and buttered. **2** (*Amer.*) a cup-shaped cake made from dough or batter.

**muffle** *verb* **1** wrap or cover for warmth or protection. **2** wrap up or pad in order to deaden its sound. **3** deaden, make less loud or less distinct.

**muffler** *noun* **1** a scarf worn round the neck for warmth. **2** something used to muffle sound. **3** (*Amer.*) the silencer on a vehicle.

**mufti** *noun* plain clothes worn by a person who also wears uniform; *in mufti*.

**mug** *noun* **1** a large drinking-vessel (usually with a handle) for use without a saucer. **2** its contents. **3** (*slang*) the face or mouth. **4** (*slang*) a person who is easily deceived. ●*verb* (**mugged**, **mugging**) attack and rob (a person), especially in a public place. □ **a mug's game** (*informal*) an activity that is unlikely to bring profit or reward. **mug shot** (*slang*) a photograph of a face, especially for police records. **mug up** (*slang*)

learn (a subject) by studying hard. □ **mugger** *noun*

**Mugabe** (*muu-gah-bi*), Robert Gabriel (born 1924), African statesman, first prime minister (1980) of an independent Zimbabwe, President from 1987.

**muggins** *noun* (*informal*) (often used to refer to oneself) a gullible person; *so muggins had to pay as usual*.

**muggy** *adjective* (**muggier**, **muggiest**) oppressively damp and warm; *a muggy day*; *muggy weather*. □ **mugginess** *noun*

**Muhammad** (*mŭ-ham-id*) (also **Mohammed**) (*c.*570–632), the founder of the Islamic faith and community.

**Muhammadan** *noun & adjective* (also **Mohammedan**) = Muslim.

▪**Usage** This term is not used by Muslims, and is often regarded as offensive.

**mujahidin** (*muu-jah-hi-deen*) *plural noun* (also **mujahedin**, **mujahedeen**) guerrilla fighters in Islamic countries, especially Muslim fundamentalists. (¶ Arabic, = one who fights a war.)

**mulatto** (*mew-lat-oh*) *noun* (*plural* **mulattos** *or* **mulattoes**) a person who has one White and one Black parent.

**mulberry** *noun* **1** a purple or white fruit rather like a blackberry. **2** the tree that bears it. **3** dull purplish red.

**mulch** *noun* a mixture of wet straw, leaves, etc., spread on the ground to protect plants or retain moisture. ●*verb* cover with a mulch.

**mule** *noun* **1** an animal that is the offspring of a horse and a donkey, known for its stubbornness. **2** (in full **spinning mule**) a type of spinning machine. **3** a backless slipper.

**muleteer** (*mew-li-teer*) *noun* a mule driver.

**mulish** (*mewl-ish*) *adjective* stubborn. □ **mulishly** *adverb*, **mulishness** *noun*

**mull¹** *verb* heat (wine or beer) with sugar and spices, as a drink. □ **mull over** think over, ponder.

**mull²** *noun* (*Scottish*) a promontory; *Mull of Kintyre*.

**mullah** (*mul-ă*) *noun* a Muslim who is learned in Islamic theology and sacred law.

**mullet** (*mul-it*) *noun* (*plural* **mullet**) an edible sea fish; *red mullet*; *grey mullet*.

**mulligatawny** (*mul-ig-ă-taw-ni*) *noun* a highly seasoned soup flavoured like curry, originally from India.

**mullion** (*mul-iŏn*) *noun* an upright bar between the panes of a window.

**multi-** *combining form* many. □ **multi-access** *adjective* (of a computer) able to serve several terminals at the same time.

**multicoloured** *adjective* (*Amer.* **multicolored**) with many colours.

**multicultural** *adjective* of or involving several cultural groups.

**multifarious** (multi-**fair**-iŭs) *adjective* very varied, of many kinds; *his multifarious duties.* □ **multifariously** *adverb*

**multiform** *adjective* having many forms; of many kinds.

**multilateral** (multi-**lat**-er-ăl) *adjective* (of an agreement etc.) involving three or more parties. □ **multilaterally** *adverb*, **multilateralism** *noun*

**multimedia** the combined use of text, sound, video, and animation on a compact disc.

**multimillionaire** *noun* a person who has several million pounds or dollars etc.

**multinational** *adjective* (of a business company) operating in several countries. ●*noun* a multinational company.

**multiple** *adjective* having several or many parts, elements, or components. ●*noun* a quantity that contains another (a *factor*) a number of times without remainder; *30 is a multiple of 10.* □ **multiple-choice** *adjective* (of an exam question) providing several possible answers from which the correct one must be chosen. **multiple sclerosis** a chronic progressive disease of the nervous system in which patches of tissue in the brain or spinal cord become damaged and harden, causing paralysis, speech difficulties, etc.

**multiplex** *adjective* **1** having many parts or forms; consisting of many elements. **2** (of a cinema) large with many screens showing different films.

**multiplicand** *noun* a quantity to be multiplied by another (compare MULTIPLIER).

**multiplication** *noun* multiplying, being multiplied. □ **multiplication sign** a sign (×) (as in 2 × 3) indicating that one quantity is to be multiplied by another. **multiplication tables** a series of lists showing the results when a number is multiplied by each number (especially 1 to 12) in turn.

**multiplicity** (multi-**plis**-iti) *noun* a great variety.

**multiplier** *noun* the number by which a quantity is multiplied (compare MULTIPLICAND).

**multiply** *verb* (**multiplied**, **multiplying**) **1** (in mathematics) take a specified quantity a specified number of times and find the quantity produced; *multiply 6 by 4 and get 24.* **2** make or become many; increase in number by breeding.

**multiracial** (multi-**ray**-shăl) *adjective* composed of people of many races; *a multiracial society.*

**multi-storey** *adjective* having several storeys; *a multi-storey car park.*

**multitasking** *noun* (in computers) performance of a number of different tasks simultaneously.

**multitude** *noun* a great number of things or people.

**multitudinous** (multi-**tewd**-in-ŭs) *adjective* very numerous.

**multi-user** *adjective* (of a computer system) able to be used by several people at the same time.

**mum** *noun* (*informal*) mother. ●*adjective* (*informal*) silent; *keep mum.* □ **mum's the word** say nothing about this.

**mumble** *verb* speak or utter indistinctly. ●*noun* indistinct speech. □ **mumbler** *noun*

**mumbo-jumbo** *noun* **1** meaningless ritual. **2** words or actions that are deliberately obscure in order to mystify or confuse people.

**mummer** *noun* a disguised actor in a traditional play or mime.

**mummery** *noun* a ceremonial procedure regarded as ridiculous.

**mummify** *verb* (**mummified**, **mummifying**) preserve (a corpse) by embalming it as in ancient Egypt. □ **mummification** *noun*

**mummy¹** *noun* (*informal*) mother.

**mummy²** *noun* **1** the body of a person or animal embalmed for burial so as to preserve it, especially in ancient Egypt. **2** a dried-up body preserved from decay by an accident of nature.

**mumps** *noun* a virus disease that causes painful swellings in the neck.

**Munch** (*pronounced* munk), Edvard (1863–1944), Norwegian expressionist painter and engraver.

**munch** *verb* chew steadily and vigorously.

**mundane** (mun-**dayn**) *adjective* **1** dull, routine. **2** worldly, not spiritual. □ **mundanely** *adverb*, **mundanity** *noun*

**mung** *noun* (in full **mung bean**) a plant producing small pea-like beans that can be cooked or sprouted to produce bean sprouts.

**Munich** (**mew**-nik) a city in the south of Germany, capital of Bavaria. □ **Munich Pact** an agreement between Britain, France, Germany, and Italy, signed at Munich in 1938, ceding part of Czechoslovakia to Germany. It is remembered as an act of appeasement.

**municipal** (mew-**nis**-i-păl) *adjective* of a town or city or its self-government. □ **municipally** *adverb*

**municipality** (mew-nis-i-**pal**-iti) *noun* a self-governing town or district.

**munificent** (mew-**nif**-i-sĕnt) *adjective* splendidly generous. □ **munificently** *adverb*, **munificence** *noun*

**muniments** (mew-ni-měnts) *plural noun* title deeds and similar records kept as evidence of rights or privileges.

**munitions** (mew-**nish**-ŏnz) *plural noun* military weapons, ammunition, equipment, etc.

**muntjac** (**munt**-jak) *noun* (also **muntjak**) a small deer, the male of which has small tusks and antlers.

**muon** (**mew**-on) *noun* an unstable elementary particle like an electron, but with a much greater mass.

**mural** (**mewr**-ăl) *adjective* of or on a wall. ● *noun* a wall-painting, a fresco.

**murder** *noun* 1 the intentional and unlawful killing of one person by another. 2 (*informal*) something very difficult or unpleasant. ● *verb* 1 kill (a person) unlawfully and intentionally. 2 (*informal*) ruin by bad performance or pronunciation etc. □ **murderer** *noun*, **murderess** *noun*

**murderous** *adjective* 1 involving murder; capable of or intent on murder. 2 very angry, suggesting murder; *a murderous look*.

**Murdoch**[1] (**mer**-dok), Dame Iris Jean (born 1919), British novelist.

**Murdoch**[2], Rupert (Keith Rupert) (born 1931), Australian-born entrepreneur whose business interests include newspapers, film and television companies, and publishing.

**Murillo** (mewr-**il**-oh), Bartolomé Esteban (1618–82), Spanish painter.

**murk** *noun* darkness, poor visibility.

**murky** *adjective* (**murkier, murkiest**) 1 dark, gloomy. 2 (of liquid) muddy, full of sediment. 3 secretly scandalous; *his murky past*. □ **murkily** *adverb*, **murkiness** *noun*

**murmur** *noun* 1 a low continuous sound. 2 a low abnormal sound made by the heart. 3 softly spoken words. 4 a subdued expression of feeling; *murmurs of discontent*. ● *verb* make a murmur; speak or utter in a low voice.

**Murphy's law** a humorous expression of the apparent perverseness of things (roughly, 'anything that can go wrong will go wrong').

**murrain** (**mu**-rin) *noun* an infectious disease of cattle.

**Murray**[1] the principal river of Australia, flowing from New South Wales westward to the Southern Ocean.

**Murray**[2], Sir James Augustus Henry (1837–1915), Scottish-born lexicographer, chief editor of the *Oxford English Dictionary*.

**Mus.B.** *abbreviation* (also **Mus.Bac.**) Bachelor of Music.

**Muscadet** (mus-kă-day) *noun* a dry white wine from the Loire region of France; the variety of grape used for this.

**muscadine** (musk-ă-deen) *noun* a musk-flavoured grape.

**Muscat** (musk-at) the capital of Oman.

**muscat** (**musk**-ăt) *noun* 1 a muscadine. 2 wine made from muscadines.

**muscatel** (musk-ă-**tel**) *noun* 1 a muscadine. 2 a wine or a raisin made from this.

**muscle** *noun* 1 a band or bundle of fibrous tissue able to contract and relax and so produce movement in an animal body. 2 a part of the body made chiefly of such tissue. 3 muscular power. 4 strength; *trade unions with plenty of muscle*. □ **muscle-bound** *adjective* with muscles stiff from excessive exercise. **muscle in** (*slang*) force one's way. **muscle-man** *noun* a man with highly developed muscles.

**Muscovite** (musk-ŏ-vyt) *adjective* of Moscow. ● *noun* a native or inhabitant of Moscow.

**Muscovy duck** a crested duck with red markings on its head.

**muscular** *adjective* 1 of or affecting the muscles. 2 having well-developed muscles. □ **muscular dystrophy** a hereditary condition causing progressive wasting of the muscles. □ **muscularity** (mus-kew-**la**-riti) *noun*

**musculature** *noun* the system of muscles of a body or organ.

**Mus.D.** *abbreviation* (also **Mus. Doc.**) Doctor of Music.

**Muse** *noun* (*Gk. & Rom. myth.*) each of the nine sister goddesses presiding over branches of learning and the arts.

**muse** *verb* ponder; say meditatively.

**museum** *noun* a building in which objects of historical or scientific interest are stored and exhibited. □ **museum piece** 1 a fine specimen suitable for a museum. 2 (*scornful*) an antiquated person or thing.

**Musgrave**, Thea (born 1928), Scottish composer and conductor.

**mush** *noun* 1 soft pulp. 2 feeble sentimentality. 3 (*Amer.*) maize porridge.

**mushroom** *noun* 1 an edible fungus with a stem and domed cap. 2 pale creamy brown. ● *verb* 1 spring up rapidly in large numbers. 2 rise and spread in the shape of a mushroom. □ **mushroom cloud** a mushroom-shaped cloud from a nuclear explosion.

**mushy** *adjective* (**mushier, mushiest**) 1 as or like mush. 2 feebly sentimental. □ **mushiness** *noun*

**music** *noun* 1 the art of arranging the sounds of voices or instruments in a pleasing sequence. 2 the sounds produced; a written or printed score for this. 3 any pleasant series of sounds, e.g. birdsong. □ **music centre** a radio, record player, and tape recorder in one piece of equipment.

**music-hall** noun a style of variety entertainment, popular during the late 19th century, including singing, comic turns, dance acts, etc.; a theatre where this took place.

**musical** adjective **1** of music; *musical instruments*. **2** fond of, sensitive to, or skilled in music. **3** accompanied by music; set to music. ●noun a musical film or play. □ **musical box** a box with a mechanical device that produces music by means of a toothed cylinder which strikes a comb-like metal plate. **musical chairs** a game in which players walk round chairs (one fewer than the number of players) till the music stops, when the one who finds no chair is eliminated and a chair is removed before the next round. □ **musically** adverb, **musicality** noun

**musician** noun a person who plays or composes music; one whose profession is music. □ **musicianship** noun

**musicology** noun the study of the history and forms of music. □ **musicologist** noun

**musk** noun **1** a substance secreted by the male musk deer or certain other animals, or produced artificially, used as the basis of perfumes. **2** a plant with a musky smell. □ **musk deer** a small hornless deer of Central Asia. **musk ox** a shaggy North American ox with curved horns. **musk-rose** noun a rambling rose that has a musky fragrance.

**musket** noun a long-barrelled gun formerly used by infantry.

**musketeer** noun a soldier armed with a musket.

**muskrat** noun a large rat-like water animal of North America, valued for its fur.

**musky** adjective smelling like musk. □ **muskiness** noun

**Muslim** (also **Moslem**) noun one who believes in the Islamic faith. ●adjective of Muslims or their faith.

**muslin** noun thin cotton cloth.

**musquash** (mus-**kwosh**) noun **1** the muskrat. **2** its fur.

**muss** verb □ **muss up** (*Amer. informal*) make untidy.

**mussel** noun a bivalve mollusc, the marine variety of which is edible.

**Mussolini** (mus-ŏ-**leen**-i), Benito (1883–1945), Italian Fascist dictator, who took his country into the Second World War on Germany's side.

**Mussorgsky** (mŭ-**sorg**-ski), Modest (1839–81), Russian composer.

**must**[1] auxiliary verb used to express necessity or obligation (*you must go*), certainty (*night must fall*), or insistence (*I must repeat, all precautions were taken*). ●noun (*informal*) a thing that should not be overlooked or missed; *the exhibition is a must*.

**must**[2] noun grape juice undergoing fermentation; new wine.

**mustache** Amer. spelling of MOUSTACHE.

**mustang** (mus-tang) noun a small wild horse of Mexico and California.

**mustard** noun **1** a plant with yellow flowers and with black or white sharp-tasting seeds in long pods. **2** these seeds ground and made into paste as a condiment. **3** a brownish-yellow colour. □ **mustard gas** a poison gas that burns the skin, used in chemical weapons.

**muster** verb **1** assemble; gather together. **2** summon; *muster one's strength*. ●noun an assembly or gathering of people or things. □ **pass muster** be accepted as adequate.

**mustn't** (*informal*) = must not.

**musty** adjective (**mustier, mustiest**) **1** smelling or tasting mouldy or stale. **2** antiquated. □ **mustily** adverb, **mustiness** noun

**mutable** (mew-tă-bŭl) adjective liable to change, fickle. □ **mutability** noun

**mutagen** (mew-tă-jĕn) noun something causing genetic mutation, e.g. radiation. □ **mutagenic** adjective

**mutant** (mew-tănt) noun a living thing that differs basically from its parents as a result of genetic change. ●adjective differing in this way.

**mutate** (mew-**tayt**) verb undergo or cause to undergo mutation.

**mutation** noun **1** a change or alteration in form. **2** a genetic change which, when transmitted to offspring, gives rise to heritable variations. **3** a mutant.

**mutatis mutandis** (moo-tah-teess moo-tan-deess) when the necessary alteration of details has been made (in comparing things). (¶ Latin.)

**mute** adjective **1** silent, refraining from speaking. **2** not having the power of speech, dumb. **3** not expressed in words; *in mute adoration*. **4** (of a letter) not pronounced; *the e in 'house' is mute*. **5** (of colour) subdued. ●noun **1** a dumb person. **2** a device fitted to a musical instrument to deaden its sound. ●verb **1** deaden or muffle the sound of. **2** make less intense. □ **mute button** a device on a telephone to prevent the person at the other end from hearing what is said temporarily; a device to turn off the sound of a TV, video, etc. **mute swan** the common white swan. □ **mutely** adverb, **muteness** noun

**mutilate** verb **1** injure or disfigure by cutting off a part. **2** cut out or damage part of (a book etc.). □ **mutilation** noun, **mutilator** noun

**mutineer** (mew-tin-**eer**) *noun* one who mutinies.

**mutinous** (mew-tin-ŭs) *adjective* rebellious, ready to mutiny. □ **mutinously** *adverb*

**mutiny** (mew-tin-i) *noun* open rebellion against authority, especially by members of the armed forces against their officers. ● *verb* (**mutinied, mutinying**) engage in mutiny.

**mutt** *noun* (*slang*) **1** a stupid person. **2** (*scornful*) a dog.

**mutter** *verb* **1** speak or utter in a low unclear tone. **2** utter subdued grumbles. ● *noun* muttering; muttered words.

**mutton** *noun* the flesh of sheep as food. □ **mutton dressed as lamb** (*informal*) an older woman dressed in too youthful a style. **mutton-head** *noun* (*informal*) a stupid person.

**mutual** (mew-tew-ăl) *adjective* **1** (of a feeling or action) felt or done by each towards or to the other; *mutual affection; mutual aid.* **2** having the same specified relationship to each other; *mutual enemies.* **3** (*informal*) common to two or more people; *our mutual friend.* □ **mutually** *adverb*

▪**Usage** Some people object to the use in sense 3, although it is often found; the alternative word 'common' could be taken to mean 'ill-bred'.

**Muzak** (mew-zak) *noun* (*trade mark*) piped music in public places; recorded light music as a background.

**muzzle** *noun* **1** the projecting nose and jaws of certain animals (e.g. dogs). **2** the open end of a firearm. **3** a strap or wire etc. put over an animal's head to prevent it from biting or feeding. ● *verb* **1** put a muzzle on (an animal). **2** silence, prevent (a person or newspaper etc.) from expressing opinions freely.

**muzzy** *adjective* **1** dazed, feeling stupefied. **2** blurred, hazy. □ **muzzily** *adverb*, **muzziness** *noun*

**MW** *abbreviation* **1** megawatt(s). **2** medium wave.

**my** *adjective* **1** of or belonging to me. **2** used in forms of address (*my lord, my dear*), or exclamations of surprise etc. (*my God!*).

**myalgia** (my-al-jiă) *noun* pain in the muscles. □ **myalgic** *adjective*

**Myanmar** (mee-an-**mar**) the official name (since 1989) of Burma.

**mycelium** *noun* (*plural* **mycelia**) the vegetative part of a fungus consisting of fine threadlike parts.

**Mycenaean** (my-sin-ee-ăn) *adjective* of a Bronze Age civilization of Greece (*c.* 1500–1100 BC), remains of which were found at Mycenae in the Peloponnese and elsewhere. ● *noun* a member of this civilization.

**mycology** (my-kol-ŏji) *noun* the study of fungi. □ **mycologist** *noun*

**myelin** *noun* a white substance which forms a protective sheath around certain nerve-fibres.

**myeloma** *noun* (*plural* **myelomas** *or* **myelomata**) a tumour of the bone marrow.

**myna** (my-nă) *noun* (also **mynah, mina**) a talking bird of the starling family.

**myopia** (my-oh-piă) *noun* short-sightedness.

**myopic** (my-op-ik) *adjective* short-sighted. □ **myopically** *noun*

**myriad** (mi-ri-ăd) (*literary*) *noun* (often as **myriads**) a vast number. ● *adjective* innumerable.

**myriapod** (mi-ri-ă-pod) *noun* a small crawling creature with many legs, such as a centipede or millipede.

**myrmidon** (mer-mid-ŏn) *noun* a henchman.

**myrrh** (*rhymes with* fur) *noun* a gum resin used in perfumes, medicine, and incense.

**myrtle** (mer-t'l) *noun* an evergreen shrub with dark leaves and scented white flowers.

**myself** *pronoun* **1** the emphatic and reflexive form of *I* and *me*; *I went myself; I cut myself.* **2** in my normal state; *not myself today.* □ **by myself** *see* ONESELF.

**mysterious** *adjective* full of mystery, puzzling or obscure. □ **mysteriously** *adverb*

**mystery** *noun* **1** a matter that remains unexplained or secret. **2** the quality of being unexplained or obscure; *its origins are wrapped in mystery.* **3** the practice of making a secret of things. **4** a religious truth that is beyond human powers to understand. **5** a story or play that deals with a puzzling crime. □ **mystery play** a medieval religious drama; a miracle play. **mystery tour** a pleasure trip to an unspecified destination.

**mystic** (mis-tik) *adjective* **1** of hidden or symbolic meaning, especially in religion; *mystic ceremonies.* **2** inspiring a sense of mystery and awe. ● *noun* a person who seeks to obtain union with God by spiritual contemplation and self-surrender.

**mystical** (mis-tik-ăl) *adjective* **1** of mystics or mysticism. **2** having spiritual meaning, value, or symbolism. □ **mystically** *adverb*

**mysticism** (mis-ti-sizm) *noun* **1** mystical quality. **2** being a mystic.

**mystify** *verb* (**mystified, mystifying**) **1** bewilder, cause (a person) to feel puzzled. **2** wrap in mystery. □ **mystification** *noun*

**mystique** (mis-teek) *noun* an aura of mystery or mystical power.

**myth** (*pronounced* mith) *noun* **1** a traditional story containing ideas or beliefs about ancient times or natural events. **2** such stories collectively; *in myth and legend.* **3** an imaginary person or thing. **4** an idea that forms part of the beliefs of a group but is not founded on fact.

**mythical** (**mith**-i-kăl) *adjective* **1** of myths, existing in myths. **2** imaginary, fancied. □ **mythically** *adverb*

**mythology** (mith-**ol**-ŏji) *noun* **1** a body of myths; *Greek mythology*. **2** study of myths. □ **mythological** *adjective*, **mythologist** *noun*

**myxomatosis** (miksŏ-mă-**toh**-sis) *noun* an infectious and usually fatal virus disease of rabbits.

# Nn

**N** *symbol* nitrogen. ●*abbreviation* (also **N.**) **1** North; Northern. **2** New. **3** newton(s). **4** *Chess* knight. **5** nuclear.

**n** *noun* an indefinite number. ●*abbreviation* (also **n.**) **1** name. **2** neuter. □ **to the nth degree** to the utmost.

**Na** *symbol* sodium.

**NAAFI** (**naf**-i) *abbreviation* (also **Naafi**) **1** Navy, Army, and Air Force Institutes. **2** a canteen for servicemen, organized by the NAAFI.

**naan** = NAN².

**nab** *verb* (**nabbed**, **nabbing**) (*slang*) **1** catch (a wrongdoer) in the act, arrest. **2** seize, grab.

**nabob** (**nay**-bob) *noun* (*old use*) **1** a Muslim official under the Mogul empire. **2** a wealthy person.

**Nabokov** (nă-**boh**-kof *or* **nab**-ŏ-kof), Vladimir Vladimirovich (1899–1977), Russian-born novelist and poet, author of *Lolita*.

**nacho** *noun* (*plural* **nachos**) a tortilla chip, usually topped with melted cheese and spices.

**nacre** (**nay**-ker) *noun* mother-of-pearl obtained from shellfish. □ **nacreous** (**nay**-kri-ŭs) *adjective*

**nadir** (**nay**-deer) *noun* **1** the point of the celestial sphere directly under the observer (opposite to the zenith). **2** the lowest point; the time of deepest depression.

**naevus** (**nee**-vŭs) *noun* (*Amer.* **nevus**) (*plural* **naevi**, *pronounced* **nee**-vy) **1** a birthmark consisting of a red patch on the skin. **2** = MOLE (sense 1).

**naff** *adjective* (*slang*) **1** unfashionable. **2** rubbishy. ●*verb* □ **naff off** (*slang*) go away.

**nag¹** *verb* (**nagged**, **nagging**) **1** make scolding remarks to, find fault continually. **2** (of pain or worry) be felt persistently.

**nag²** *noun* (*informal*) a horse.

**Nagaland** (**nah**-gă-land) a State in NE India.

**Nagar Haveli** *see* DADRA.

**Nagasaki** (nag-ă-**sah**-ki) Japanese city, target of the second atomic bomb attack (9 August 1945); *see* HIROSHIMA.

**Nahum** (**nay**-hŭm) **1** a Hebrew minor prophet. **2** a book of the Old Testament containing his prophecies.

**naiad** (**ny**-ad) *noun* a water nymph.

**nail** *noun* **1** the layer of horny substance over the outer tip of a finger or toe. **2** a claw or talon. **3** a small metal spike driven in with a hammer to hold things together or as a peg or protection or ornament. ●*verb* **1** fasten with a nail or nails. **2** catch or arrest; *nailed the intruder*. □ **nail down 1** bind (a person) to a promise etc. **2** define precisely. **3** fasten (a thing) with nails. **nail-file** *noun* a roughened metal or emery strip for shaping and trimming the nails. **nail polish** (*or* **varnish**) varnish, usually coloured, applied to the nails. **on the nail** (especially of payment) without delay.

**Nairobi** (ny-**roh**-bi) the capital of Kenya.

**naïve** (nah-**eev**) *adjective* (also **naive**) showing a lack of experience or of informed judgement. □ **naïvely** *adverb*, **naïvety** *or* **naïveté** (nah-**eev**-tay) *noun*

**naked** *adjective* **1** without clothes on, nude. **2** without the usual coverings, ornamentation, or protection; *a naked sword*. **3** undisguised; *the naked truth*. □ **naked eye** the eye unassisted by a telescope or microscope etc. □ **nakedly** *adverb*, **nakedness** *noun*

**namby-pamby** *adjective* lacking positive character, feeble, sentimental. ●*noun* a person of this kind.

**name** *noun* **1** a word or words by which a person, animal, place, or thing is known or indicated. **2** a reputation; *it has got a bad name*; *made a name for himself*. **3** a famous person; *the film has some big names in it.* ●*verb* **1** give a name to. **2** state the name(s) of. **3** nominate or appoint to an office etc. **4** mention or specify. □ **have to one's name** possess. **in the name of 1** invoking or calling to witness; *in the name of God, what are you doing?* **2** by authority of; *open in the name of the law!* **3** under the designation or pretence of; *did it all in the name of friendship.* **name-day** *noun* the feast day of a saint after whom a person is named. **name-dropping** *noun* mention of famous people's names in order to impress others by implying that one is familiar with such people. **the name of the game** (*informal*) the purpose or essence of an activity. **name-plate** *noun* a plate with a name inscribed on it, identifying the occupant etc. □ **nameable** *adjective*

**nameless** *adjective* **1** having no name or no known name. **2** not mentioned by name, anonymous; *others who shall be nameless.* **3** too bad to be named; *nameless horrors.*

**namely** *adverb* that is to say, specifically.

**namesake** *noun* a person or thing with the same name as another.

**Namibia** (nă-**mib**-iă) a country in SW Africa. □ **Namibian** *adjective & noun*

**nan**[1] *noun* (also **nana, nanna**) (*informal*) grandmother.

**nan**[2] (*pronounced* nahn) *noun* (also **naan**) a type of flat leavened Indian bread.

**nancy** *noun* (in full **nancy boy**) (*offensive slang*) an effeminate man, especially a homosexual.

**Nandi** (in Hinduism) the bull of Siva, which is his vehicle and symbolizes fertility.

**Nanjing** (also **Nanking**) a city of eastern China on the Yangtze River.

**nankeen** (nan-keen) *noun* a kind of cotton cloth, originally made in Nanjing in China from naturally yellow cotton.

**nanna** = NAN[1].

**nanny** *noun* **1** a child's nurse. **2** (*informal*) grandmother. **3** (in full **nanny-goat**) a female goat.

**Nansen**, Fridtjof (1861–1930), Norwegian polar explorer and statesman.

**nap**[1] *noun* a short sleep or doze, especially during the day. ● *verb* (**napped, napping**) have a nap. □ **catch a person napping** catch a person off his or her guard. □ **napper** *noun*

**nap**[2] *noun* short raised fibres on the surface of cloth or leather.

**nap**[3] *noun* **1** a card game in which players have five cards and declare how many tricks they expect to take. **2** a call of five in this game. **3** a racing tip claimed to be almost a certainty. ● *verb* (**napped, napping**) name as a choice for this kind of bet.

**napalm** (nay-pahm) *noun* a jelly-like petrol substance used in incendiary bombs.

**nape** *noun* the back of the neck.

**naphtha** (naf-thă) *noun* an inflammable oil obtained from coal or petroleum.

**naphthalene** (naf-thă-leen) *noun* a strong-smelling white substance obtained from coal tar, used in dyes and as a moth-repellent.

**Napier** (nay-pi-er), John (1550–1617), Scottish inventor of logarithms.

**napkin** *noun* **1** a square piece of cloth or paper used at meals to protect one's clothes or for wiping one's lips or fingers. **2** a baby's nappy.

**Naples** a city and port on the west coast of Italy, south of Rome.

**Napoleon** the name of three rulers of France, including Napoleon I, emperor 1804–15. □ **Napoleonic** *adjective*

**nappy** *noun* a piece of towelling or other absorbent material wrapped around a baby's bottom to absorb or retain urine and faeces.

**narcissism** (nar-sis-izm) *noun* abnormal self-love or self-admiration. □ **narcissistic** (nar-sis-**ist**-ik) *adjective*

**narcissus** (nar-sis-ŭs) *noun* (*plural* **narcissi**) any of a group of flowers including jonquils and daffodils.

**narcosis** (nar-koh-sis) *noun* a state of sleep or drowsiness, esp. one produced by drugs.

**narcotic** (nar-kot-ik) *adjective* causing sleep or drowsiness. ● *noun* a narcotic drug.

**nark** (*slang*) *noun* a police informer or decoy. ● *verb* annoy.

**narrate** (nă-rayt) *verb* tell (a story); give an account of; utter or write a narrative. □ **narration** *noun*, **narrator** *noun*

**narrative** (na-ră-tiv) *noun* a spoken or written account of something. ● *adjective* in the form of narrative.

**narrow** *adjective* **1** of small width in proportion to length. **2** having or allowing little space; *within narrow bounds*. **3** with little scope or variety, small; *a narrow circle of friends*. **4** with little margin; *a narrow escape; a narrow majority*. **5** narrow-minded. ● *verb* make or become narrower. □ **narrow boat** a long narrow boat used on canals. **narrow-minded** *adjective* rigid in one's views and sympathies, not tolerant. □ **narrowly** *adverb*, **narrowness** *noun*

**narwhal** (nar-wăl) *noun* an Arctic animal related to the whale, the male of which has a long tusk with a spiral groove.

**NASA** (nas-ă) *abbreviation* (also **Nasa**) National Aeronautics and Space Administration, a body responsible for organizing US research in extraterrestrial space.

**nasal** (nay-zăl) *adjective* **1** of the nose. **2** (of a voice or speech) sounding as if the breath came out through the nose. □ **nasally** *adverb*

**nasalize** *verb* (also **nasalise**) speak nasally; give a nasal sound to. □ **nasalization** *noun*

**nascent** (nas-ĕnt *or* nay-sĕnt) *adjective* beginning to develop. □ **nascency** *noun*

**Nash**, John (1752–1835), English architect, who designed Regent Street and other parts of London.

**Nassau** (nass-aw) the capital of the Bahamas.

**Nasser**, Gamal Abdel (1918–70), Egyptian statesman, who became president of the new Republic of Egypt (1956) after leading a military coup to depose King Farouk.

**nasturtium** (nă-ster-shŭm) *noun* a trailing plant with bright orange, yellow, or red flowers and round flat edible leaves.

**nasty** *adjective* (**nastier, nastiest**) **1** unpleasant. **2** unkind, spiteful. **3** difficult to deal with; *a nasty problem*. ● *noun* (*informal*) a horror film, especially one on video depicting cruelty and killing. □ **nasty piece of work** (*informal*) an unpleasant person. □ **nastily** *adverb*, **nastiness** *noun*

**Natal** (nă-tal) (also **KwaZulu Natal**) the eastern coastal province of South Africa.

**natal** (nay-t'l) *adjective* of or from one's birth.

**nation** *noun* a large community of people of mainly common descent, language, history, etc., usually inhabiting a particular territory and under one government.

**national** *adjective* of a nation, common to or characteristic of a whole nation. ●*noun* **1** a citizen or subject of a particular country. **2** a fellow-countryman. □ **national anthem** a song of loyalty or patriotism adopted by a country. **national curriculum** a common programme of study for pupils in State schools in England and Wales, with tests at specific ages. **national debt** the total amount owed by the government of a country to those who have lent money to it. **National Front** a political group in Britain holding extreme nationalistic views and opposing immigration. **National Gallery** a gallery in Trafalgar Square, London, holding one of the nation's chief collections of pictures. **national grid** a network of high-voltage electric power lines between major power stations; a metric system of geographical coordinates used in maps of the British Isles. **National Guard** (in the USA) a reserve force available for federal use. **National Health Service** the public service in Britain that provides medical care. **National Insurance** a system of compulsory contributions from employed persons and employers to provide State assistance to people who are ill, unemployed, retired, etc. **national park** an area of natural beauty protected by the State for the use and enjoyment of the public. **national service** a period of compulsory service in a country's armed forces. **National Trust** a trust for the preservation of places of historic interest or natural beauty in England, Wales, and Northern Ireland. □ **nationally** *adverb*

**nationalism** *noun* **1** patriotic feeling or principles or efforts. **2** a movement favouring independence for a country that is controlled by or forms part of another. □ **nationalist** *noun*, **nationalistic** *adjective*

**nationality** *noun* **1** the condition of belonging to a particular nation. **2** an ethnic group forming a part of one or more political nations.

**nationalize** *verb* (also **nationalise**) convert (industries etc.) from private to government ownership. □ **nationalization** *noun*

**nationwide** *adjective* extending over the whole of a nation.

**native** *adjective* **1** belonging to a person or thing by nature, inborn, natural. **2** (of a person) belonging to a particular place by birth; (of a thing) belonging to a person because of his or her place of birth; *one's*

*native land.* **3** (usually foll. by *of*) grown, produced, or originating in a specified place. **4** of the natives of a place. ●*noun* **1** a person who was born in a specified place; *a native of Canada.* **2** a local inhabitant of a place. **3** (often *offensive*) a member of a non-White native people, as regarded by colonial settlers. **4** an animal or plant grown or originating in a specified place.

**nativity** *noun* **1** (especially as **the Nativity**) Christ's birth; the festival celebrating this. **2** birth.

**NATO** (nay-toh) *abbreviation* (also **Nato**) North Atlantic Treaty Organization, an association of European and North American States formed in 1949 for the purposes of collective security.

**natter** (*informal*) *verb* chat. ●*noun* a chat.

**natterjack** *noun* a kind of small toad with a yellow stripe down its back, that runs instead of hopping.

**natty** *adjective* (**nattier, nattiest**) (*informal*) neat and trim, smart. □ **nattily** *adverb*

**natural** *adjective* **1** of, existing in, or produced by nature; *natural landscape.* **2** in accordance with the course of nature, normal; *a natural death.* **3** (of a person) having certain inborn qualities or abilities; *a natural leader.* **4** not looking artificial; not affected in manner etc. **5** not surprising, to be expected. **6** *Music* (of a note) neither sharp nor flat; *B natural.* **7** (of a child) illegitimate. ●*noun* **1** a person or thing that seems to be naturally suited for something. **2** *Music* a natural note; the sign for this (♮). □ **natural childbirth** a system of childbirth in which the mother has been taught to relax and so needs little or no anaesthetic. **natural gas** gas found in the earth's crust, not manufactured. **natural history** the study of animal and vegetable life. **natural number** a whole number greater than 0. **natural resources** materials or conditions occurring in nature which may be exploited economically. **natural science** any of the sciences which study the natural or physical world. **natural selection** survival of the organisms that are best adapted to their environment while the less well adapted ones die out. □ **naturally** *adverb*, **naturalness** *noun*

**naturalism** *noun* realism in art and literature; drawing or representing things as they are in nature. □ **naturalistic** *adjective*

**naturalist** *noun* **1** an expert in natural history. **2** a supporter of naturalism.

**naturalize** *verb* (also **naturalise**) **1** admit (a person of foreign birth) to full citizenship of a country. **2** adopt (a foreign word or custom) into the language or customs of a country. **3** introduce and acclimatize (an animal or plant) into a country where it is not native. **4** cause to appear natural, especially (of a plant) as if growing wild; *daffodil bulbs suitable for naturalizing.* □ **naturalization** *noun*

**nature** *noun* **1** (often **Nature**) the world with all its features and living things; the physical power that produces these. **2** a kind, sort, or class; *things of this nature; the request was in the nature of a command.* **3** the complex of qualities and characteristics innate in a person or animal. **4** a thing's essential qualities, its characteristics. □ **back to nature** returning to what are regarded as the natural conditions of living before the spread of civilization. **by nature** innately. **call of nature** (*informal*) a need to urinate or defecate. **nature reserve** an area of land managed so as to preserve its flora, fauna, physical features, etc. **nature study** (in schools) the practical study of plant and animal life. **nature trail** a path through woods or countryside where interesting natural objects can be seen.

**naturist** *noun* a nudist. □ **naturism** *noun*

**naught** *noun* (*old use*) nothing, = NOUGHT.

**naughty** *adjective* (**naughtier, naughtiest**) **1** behaving badly, disobedient. **2** improper; shocking or amusing people by mild indecency. □ **naughtily** *adverb*, **naughtiness** *noun*

**Nauru** (now-**roo**) an island country in the SW Pacific. □ **Nauruan** *adjective & noun*

**nausea** (**naw**-ziǎ) *noun* **1** a feeling of sickness. **2** disgust.

**nauseate** (**naw**-zi-ayt) *verb* affect with nausea.

**nauseous** (**naw**-zi-ǔs) *adjective* **1** causing or feeling nausea. **2** disgusting.

**nautical** *adjective* of sailors or seamanship. □ **nautical mile** a unit of 1,852 metres (approx. 2,025 yards).

**nautilus** (**naw**-til-ǔs) *noun* (*plural* **nautiluses** or **nautili**) a mollusc with a spiral shell divided into compartments.

**naval** *adjective* of a navy, of ships.

**Navarre** (nǎ-**var**) a former kingdom in the Pyrenees area.

**nave** *noun* **1** the body of a church apart from the chancel, aisles, and transepts. **2** the hub of a wheel.

**navel** (**nay**-věl) *noun* **1** the small hollow in the centre of the abdomen where the umbilical cord was attached. **2** the central point of something. □ **navel orange** a large orange with a navel-like formation at the top.

**navigable** (**nav**-ig-ǎbǔl) *adjective* **1** (of rivers or seas) suitable for ships to sail in. **2** (of a ship etc.) able to be steered and sailed. □ **navigability** *noun*

**navigate** *verb* **1** sail in or through (a sea or river etc.). **2** direct the course of (a ship,

aircraft, or other vehicle), using maps and instruments. □ **navigation** *noun*, **navigator** *noun*

**Navratilova** (navrǎ-til-**oh**-vǎ), Martina (born 1956), American tennis-player, born in Czechoslovakia.

**navvy** *noun* a labourer employed in making roads, railways, canals, etc. where digging is necessary.

**navy** *noun* **1** (often as **the Navy**) a country's warships. **2** the officers and men of these. **3** (in full **navy blue**) very dark blue like that used in naval uniform.

**nawab** (nǎ-**wahb**) *noun* **1** the title of a distinguished Muslim in Pakistan. **2** (*old use*) the title of a governor or nobleman in India.

**nay** *adverb* **1** (*old use*) no. **2** or rather; and even; and more than that; *large, nay, huge.*

**Nazareth** a town of Galilee in Israel, where Christ spent his youth.

**Nazi** (**nah**-tsi) *noun* (*plural* **Nazis**) a member of the National Socialist party in Germany, brought to power by Hitler. ●*adjective* of the Nazis. □ **Nazism** *noun*

**NB** *abbreviation* **1** Nebraska. **2** New Brunswick. **3** note well. (¶ from the Latin *nota bene*.)

**Nb** *symbol* niobium.

**NC** *abbreviation* North Carolina.

**NCO** *abbreviation* non-commissioned officer.

**Nd** *symbol* neodymium.

**ND** *abbreviation* (also **N. Dak.**) North Dakota.

**N'Djamena** (njǎ-**may**-nǎ) the capital of Chad.

**NE** *abbreviation* **1** north-east. **2** north-eastern.

**Ne** *symbol* neon.

**Neanderthal man** (ni-**an**-der-tahl) an extinct type of human being living in the Old Stone Age in Europe, with a retreating forehead and prominent brow ridges.

**neap** *noun* (in full **neap tide**) the tide when there is the least rise and fall of water, halfway between spring tides.

**Neapolitan** (nee-ǎ-**pol**-itǎn) *adjective* of Naples. ●*noun* a native or inhabitant of Naples. □ **Neapolitan ice cream** ice cream made in layers of different colours.

**near** *adverb* **1** at, to, or within a short distance or interval. **2** nearly; *as near as I can guess.* ●*preposition* near to. ●*adjective* **1** with only a short distance or interval between; *in the near future.* **2** closely related, intimate. **3** (of a part of a vehicle, horse, or road) on the left side; *near hind leg.* **4** with little margin; *a near escape.* **5** (*informal*) stingy. ●*verb* draw near. □ **Near East** the Middle East. **near miss 1** a bomb etc. falling close to the target. **2** a narrowly avoided collision. **3** something that missed its objective only narrowly. **near-sighted** *adjective* short-sighted. **near thing** something achieved or missed by only a narrow margin; a narrow escape. □ **nearness** noun

**nearby** adjective near in position; *a nearby house.* ● adverb not far away; close.

**nearly** adverb almost. □ **not nearly** nothing like, far from; *not nearly enough.*

**nearside** noun the side of a vehicle that is normally nearest the kerb, in Britain the left side (compare OFFSIDE).

**neat** adjective **1** simple and clean and orderly in appearance. **2** done or doing things in a precise and skilful way. **3** undiluted; *neat whisky.* □ **neatly** adverb, **neatness** noun

**neaten** verb make or become neat.

**Neb.** abbreviation (also **Nebr.**) Nebraska.

**Nebraska** (nib-**ras**-kǎ) a State of the central USA.

**Nebuchadnezzar** (neb-yoo-kǎd-**nez**-er) king of Babylon 605–562 BC, who captured and destroyed Jerusalem in 586 BC.

**nebula** (**neb**-yoo-lǎ) noun (plural **nebulae**, pronounced **neb**-yoo-lee) a bright or dark patch in the sky caused by a distant galaxy or a cloud of dust or gas. □ **nebular** adjective

**nebulous** (**neb**-yoo-lǔs) adjective indistinct, having no definite form; *nebulous ideas.*

**necessarily** adverb as a necessary result, inevitably.

**necessary** adjective **1** essential in order to achieve something. **2** unavoidable, happening or existing by necessity; *the necessary consequence.* ● noun **1** (**the necessary**) (slang) money or action needed for a purpose. **2** (**necessaries**) things without which life cannot be maintained or is exceedingly harsh.

**necessitate** (ni-**sess**-i-tayt) verb make necessary, involve as a condition or result.

**necessitous** (ni-**sess**-i-tǔs) adjective needy.

**necessity** (ni-**sess**-iti) noun **1** the state or fact of being necessary; *the necessity of adequate food.* **2** a necessary thing. **3** the compelling power of circumstances. **4** a state of need or great poverty or hardship.

**neck** noun **1** the narrow part of the body connecting the head to the shoulders. **2** the part of a garment round this. **3** the length of a horse's head and neck as a measure of its lead in a race. **4** the flesh of an animal's neck as food. **5** the narrow part of anything (especially of a bottle or cavity); a narrow connecting part or channel. **6** (informal) impudence. ● verb (slang) (of couples) kiss and caress each other lovingly. □ **get it in the neck** (informal) suffer a reprimand or a severe blow. **neck and neck** running level in a race. **neck of the woods** (informal) a specific area. **risk** or **save one's neck** risk or save one's own life. **up to one's neck** (**in**) (informal) very deeply involved (in).

**neckband** noun a strip of material round the neck of a garment.

**neckerchief** noun a square of cloth worn round the neck.

**necklace** noun an ornament of precious stones, metal, beads, etc. worn round the neck.

**neckline** noun the outline formed by the edge of a garment at or below the neck.

**necktie** noun (especially *Amer.*) = TIE (noun sense 2).

**necromancy** (**nek**-rǒ-man-si) noun **1** the art of predicting events by allegedly communicating with the dead. **2** witchcraft. □ **necromancer** noun

**necrophilia** noun a morbid and especially erotic attraction to corpses.

**necropolis** (nek-**rop**-ǒ-lis) noun a cemetery, especially an ancient one.

**necrosis** (nek-**roh**-sis) noun the death of a piece of bone or tissue. □ **necrotic** (nek-**rot**-ik) adjective

**nectar** noun **1** a sweet fluid produced by plants and collected by bees for making honey. **2** (*Gk. myth.*) the drink of the gods. **3** any delicious drink.

**nectarine** (**nek**-ter-in) noun a kind of peach that has a thin skin with no down.

**nectary** (**nek**-ter-i) noun the nectar-secreting part of a plant or flower.

**neddy** noun (informal) a donkey.

**née** (pronounced nay) adjective born (used in giving a married woman's maiden name); *Mrs Jane Smith, née Jones.*

**need** noun **1** circumstances in which a thing or course of action is required; *there is no need to worry.* **2** a situation of great difficulty or misfortune; *a friend in need.* **3** lack of necessaries, poverty. **4** a requirement, a thing necessary for life; *my needs are few.* ● verb **1** be in need of, require. **2** be under a necessity or obligation; *need you ask?* □ **if need be** if necessary. **must needs** or **needs must** (old use) of necessity; *must needs do it.*

**needful** adjective necessary. □ **needfully** adverb

**needle** noun **1** a small thin piece of polished steel with a point at one end and a hole for thread at the other, used in sewing. **2** a long thin piece of smooth metal or plastic etc. with one or both ends pointed, used in knitting by hand. **3** the pointer of a compass or dial. **4** the sharp hollow end of a hypodermic syringe. **5** a stylus on a record player. **6** an obelisk; *Cleopatra's Needle.* **7** a pointed rock or peak. **8** one of the long thin leaves of pine trees. **9** (**the needle**) (slang) a fit of bad temper or nervousness. ● verb (informal) annoy or provoke. **needlepoint** noun a kind of fine embroidery on canvas.

**needlecord** noun very fine corduroy fabric.

**needless** adjective not needed, unnecessary. □ **needlessly** adverb

**needlewoman** *noun* **1** a seamstress. **2** a woman with a specified skill in needlework; *a good needlewoman.*

**needlework** *noun* sewing or embroidery.

**needn't** (*informal*) = need not.

**needy** *adjective* (**needier, neediest**) lacking the necessaries of life, extremely poor. □ **neediness** *noun*

**ne'er** *adverb* (*poetic*) never. □ **ne'er-do-well** *noun* a good-for-nothing person.

**nefarious** (ni-**fair**-iŭs) *adjective* wicked. □ **nefariously** *adverb*

**negate** (ni-**gayt**) *verb* nullify, disprove. □ **negation** *noun*

**negative** *adjective* **1** expressing or implying denial, refusal, or prohibition; *a negative answer.* **2** (of a person or attitude) not positive, lacking positive qualities or characteristics. **3** marked by the absence of qualities; *a negative reaction.* **4** (of a quantity) less than zero, minus. **5** of, containing, or producing the kind of electric charge carried by electrons. ●*noun* **1** a negative statement, reply, or word. **2** a negative quality or quantity. **3** *Photography* a developed film or plate containing an image with black and white reversed, or with colours replaced by complementary ones, from which a positive picture may be obtained. ●*verb* **1** veto. **2** disprove. **3** contradict (a statement). **4** neutralize (an effect). □ **negative equity** a discrepancy arising when the value of an asset (especially a property on which a mortgage is secured) falls below that of the debt outstanding on it. **negative pole** the south-seeking pole of a magnet. **negative sign** the sign (−). □ **negatively** *adverb*

**Negev** (**neg**-ev) a triangular semi-desert region of southern Israel.

**neglect** *verb* **1** pay no attention or not enough attention to. **2** fail to take proper care of. **3** omit to do something, e.g. through carelessness or forgetfulness. ●*noun* neglecting; being neglected. □ **neglectful** *adjective*

**negligée** (neg-li-*zh*ay) *noun* (also **negligee, négligé**) a woman's light flimsy ornamental dressing gown.

**negligence** (**neg**-li-jĕns) *noun* lack of proper care or attention, carelessness. □ **negligent** *adjective*, **negligently** *adverb*

**negligible** (**neg**-lij-ibŭl) *adjective* very small in amount etc. and not worth taking into account. □ **negligibly** *adverb*

**negotiable** (nig-**oh**-shă-bŭl) *adjective* **1** able to be modified after discussion; *the salary is negotiable.* **2** able to be negotiated.

**negotiate** (nig-**oh**-shi-ayt) *verb* **1** try to reach an agreement or arrangement by discussion; arrange in this way; *negotiated a treaty.* **2** get over or through (an obstacle or difficulty) successfully. **3** get or give money in exchange for (a cheque or bonds etc.). □ **negotiation** *noun*, **negotiator** *noun*

**Negress** *noun* a female Negro.

■**Usage** Often considered offensive; the term *Black* is usually preferred.

**Negritude** (**neg**-ri-tyood) *noun* **1** the state of being Black. **2** affirmation of Black Culture.

**Negro** *noun* (*plural* **Negroes**) a member of a black-skinned race that originated in Africa.

■**Usage** Often considered offensive; the term *Black* is usually preferred.

**Negroid** *adjective* having the physical characteristics that are typical of Black people. ●*noun* a Black person.

**Nehemiah** (nee-i-**my**-ă) **1** a Jewish leader of the 5th century BC. **2** a book of the Old Testament telling of his reforms.

**Nehru** (**nair**-oo), Pandit Jawaharlal (1889–1964), Indian statesman, first prime minister of an independent India 1947–64.

**neigh** (*pronounced* nay) *noun* the long high-pitched cry of a horse. ●*verb* make this cry.

**neighbour** *noun* (*Amer.* **neighbor**) **1** a person who lives near or next to another. **2** a fellow human being. **3** a person or thing situated near or next to another; *Britain's nearest neighbour is France.* ●*verb* adjoin, border.

**neighbourhood** *noun* (*Amer.* **neighborhood**) **1** a district. **2** the people living in it. □ **in the neighbourhood of** somewhere near, approximately; *in the neighbourhood of £500.* **neighbourhood watch** organized local vigilance by householders in order to discourage crime in their neighbourhood.

**neighbouring** *adjective* (*Amer.* **neighboring**) living or situated near by.

**neighbourly** *adjective* (*Amer.* **neighborly**) like a good neighbour, kind and friendly. □ **neighbourliness** *noun*

**neither** (**ny**-*th*er *or* **nee**-*th*er) *adjective & pronoun* not either; *neither of them likes it.* ●*adverb & conjunction* **1** not either; *she neither knew nor cared.* **2** also not; *you don't know and neither do I.* □ **be neither here nor there** be of no importance or relevance.

**Nelson**, Horatio, Viscount Nelson, Duke of Brontë (1758–1805), British admiral, whose victories at sea made him a national hero, killed at Trafalgar where he defeated the combined fleets of France and Spain.

**nelson** *noun* a kind of hold in wrestling in which the arm is passed under the opponent's arm from behind and the hand applied to the neck.

**nematode** (**nem**-ă-tohd) *noun* a worm with a slender unsegmented cylindrical shape.

**nem. con.** *abbreviation* unanimously. (¶ From the Latin *nemine contradicente* = with nobody disagreeing.)

**nemesis** (**nem**-i-sis) *noun* the infliction of deserved and unavoidable punishment. (¶ Named after Nemesis, goddess of retribution in Greek mythology.)

**neo-** *combining form* new, recent, a new form of.

**neoclassical** *adjective* of or in a style of art, literature, or music that is based on or influenced by classical style. □ **neoclassicism** *noun*

**neodymium** (nee-ŏ-**dim**-iŭm) *noun* a metallic element (symbol Nd), used in certain alloys.

**neo-impressionist** *noun* any of a group of painters whose style was similar to that of the impressionists but with greater detail. □ **neo-impressionism** *noun*

**neolithic** (nee-ŏ-**lith**-ik) *adjective* of the later part of the Stone Age.

**neologism** (ni-**ol**-ŏ-jizm) *noun* a newly coined word.

**neon** (**nee**-on) *noun* a chemical element (symbol Ne), a kind of gas used in illuminated signs because it glows orange-red when electricity is passed through it.

**neonatal** *adjective* of or for the newly born.

**neophyte** (**nee**-ŏ-fyt) *noun* **1** a new convert. **2** a novice of a religious order. **3** a beginner.

**Neoplatonism** (nee-oh-**play**-tŏn-izm) *noun* a philosophy dating from the 3rd century, in which Platonic ideas are combined with oriental mysticism. □ **Neoplatonist** *noun*

**Nepal** (nĕ-**pawl**) a country north-east of India. □ **Nepalese** (nep-ă-**leez**) *adjective & noun* (*plural* **Nepalese**).

**Nepali** (nĕ-**pawl**-i) *noun* the language of Nepal.

**nephew** (**nef**-yoo) *noun* one's brother's or sister's son.

**nephritic** *adjective* **1** of or in the kidneys. **2** of nephritis.

**nephritis** (ni-**fry**-tiss) *noun* inflammation of the kidneys.

***ne plus ultra*** (*pronounced* nay) the furthest point attainable, the highest form of something. (¶ Latin, = not beyond this point.)

**nepotism** (**nep**-ŏ-tizm) *noun* favouritism shown to relatives in appointing them to jobs.

**Neptune** **1** (*Rom. myth.*) the god of water, identified with the sea-god Poseidon. **2** the third-largest of the planets.

**neptunium** (nep-**tewn**-iŭm) *noun* a radioactive metallic element (symbol Np).

**nerd** *noun* (also **nurd**) (*slang*) a foolish, feeble, or uninteresting person.

**Nero** (15–68), Roman emperor 54–68.

**nerve** *noun* **1** any of the fibres or bundles of fibres carrying impulses of sensation or of movement between the brain or spinal cord and all parts of the body. **2** courage, coolness in danger; *lose one's nerve*. **3** (*informal*) impudent boldness; *had the nerve to ask for more*. **4** (**nerves**) nervousness; a condition in which a person suffers from mental stress and easily becomes anxious or upset. ●*verb* give strength, vigour, or courage to; *nerve oneself*. □ **get on a person's nerves** be irritating to him or her. **nerve-centre** *noun* a centre of control from which instructions are sent out. **nerve gas** a poison gas that affects the nervous system. **nerve-racking** *adjective* inflicting great mental strain.

**nerveless** *adjective* incapable of effort or movement; *the knife fell from his nerveless fingers*.

**nervous** *adjective* **1** of the nerves or nervous system; *a nervous disorder*. **2** excitable, easily agitated; timid. **3** uneasy; *a nervous laugh*. □ **nervous breakdown** a period of loss of mental and emotional stability. **nervous system** the system of nerves throughout the body. □ **nervously** *adverb*, **nervousness** *noun*

**nervy** *adjective* (**nervier**, **nerviest**) nervous, easily agitated, uneasy. □ **nerviness** *noun*

**nescient** (**nes**-i-ĕnt) *adjective literary* (foll. by *of*) not having knowledge (of a specified thing). □ **nescience** *noun*

**nest** *noun* **1** a structure or place in which a bird lays its eggs and shelters its young. **2** a place where certain creatures (e.g. mice, wasps) live, or produce and keep their young. **3** a snug place. **4** a secluded shelter or retreat. **5** a set of similar articles designed to fit inside each other in a series; *a nest of tables*. ●*verb* **1** make or have a nest. **2** (of objects) fit together or inside one another. **3** *Computing* make (a set of procedures, commands, etc.) operate within each other in a program. □ **nest egg** a sum of money saved for future use.

**nestle** *verb* **1** curl up or press oneself comfortably into a soft place. **2** press oneself against another in affection. **3** lie half-hidden or sheltered.

**nestling** *noun* a bird too young to leave the nest.

**net**[1] *noun* **1** open-work material of thread, cord, wire, etc. woven or joined at intervals. **2** a piece of this used for a particular purpose, e.g. covering or protecting something, catching fish, dividing a tennis court, or surrounding a goal. ●*verb* (**netted**, **netting**) **1** cover, catch, or confine with or as if with a net. **2** hit (a ball) into the net, especially of a goal.

**net²** *adjective* (also **nett**) **1** remaining when nothing more is to be taken away. **2** (of an effect etc.) positive, excluding unimportant effects or those that cancel each other out; *the net result.* ●*verb* (**netted, netting**) obtain or yield as net profit. □ **net profit** profit after tax etc. has been deducted. **net weight** weight of contents only, excluding wrapping.

**netball** *noun* a team game in which a ball has to be thrown so that it falls into a net hanging from a ring on a high post.

**nether** (**ne***th*-er) *adjective* (*old use*) lower. □ **nether regions** (*or* **world**) hell; the underworld.

**Netherlands, the** a country (often called Holland) in Europe. □ **Netherlander** *noun*

**nett** alternative spelling of NET².

**netting** *noun* fabric of netted thread, cord, wire, etc.

**nettle** *noun* a common wild plant with hairs on its leaves that sting and redden the skin when they are touched. ●*verb* irritate, provoke. □ **nettle-rash** *noun* an eruption on the skin with red patches like those made by nettle stings.

**network** *noun* **1** an arrangement or pattern with intersecting lines; *a network of railways.* **2** a chain of people; connected professionally or socially; *a spy network.* **3** a group of broadcasting stations connected for the simultaneous broadcast of a programme. **4** a chain of interconnected computers. **5** a system of connected electrical conductors. ●*verb* broadcast on a network.

**networking** *noun* the exploitation of social contacts as a business strategy.

**neural** (**newr**-ăl) *adjective* of nerves.

**neuralgia** (**newr-al**-jă) *noun* sharp intermittent pain along the course of a nerve, especially in the head or face. □ **neuralgic** *adjective*

**neuritis** (**newr-I**-tiss) *noun* inflammation of a nerve or nerves.

**neurology** (**newr-ol**-ŏji) *noun* the scientific study of nerve systems and their diseases. □ **neurological** *adjective*, **neurologist** *noun*

**neuron** (**newr**-on) *noun* (also **neurone**, *pronounced* **newr**-ohn) a nerve cell.

**neurosis** (**newr-oh**-sis) *noun* (*plural* **neuroses**) a mental disorder producing depression or abnormal behaviour.

**neurosurgery** *noun* surgery performed on the nervous system. □ **neurosurgeon** *noun*, **neurosurgical** *adjective*

**neurotic** (**newr-ot**-ik) *adjective* **1** of or caused by a neurosis. **2** (*informal*) (of a person) subject to abnormal anxieties or obsessive behaviour. ●*noun* a neurotic person. □ **neurotically** *adverb*

**neuter** (**new**-ter) *adjective* **1** (of a noun) neither masculine nor feminine. **2** (of plants) without male or female parts. **3** (of insects) sexually undeveloped, sterile. ●*noun* **1** a neuter word. **2** a neuter plant or insect. **3** a non-fertile or castrated animal. ●*verb* castrate.

**neutral** *adjective* **1** not supporting or assisting either side in a dispute or conflict. **2** belonging to a country or person etc. that is neutral; *neutral ships.* **3** having no positive or distinctive characteristics; not definitely one thing or the other. **4** (of colours) not strong or positive; grey or beige. **5** (of a gear) in which the engine is disconnected from the moving parts. **6** *Chem.* neither acid nor alkaline. **7** *Electricity* neither positive nor negative. ●*noun* **1** a neutral person or country; one who is a subject of a neutral country. **2** grey or beige colour. **3** neutral gear. □ **neutrally** *adverb*, **neutrality** (new-**tral**-iti) *noun*

**neutralize** *verb* (also **neutralise**) **1** make neutral. **2** make ineffective by means of an opposite force or effect. **3** exempt or exclude (a place) from hostilities. □ **neutralization** *noun*

**neutrino** (new-**tree**-noh) *noun* (*plural* **neutrinos**) an elementary particle with zero electric charge and probably zero mass.

**neutron** (**new**-tron) *noun* an elementary particle of about the same mass as a proton but with no electric charge, present in the nuclei of all atoms except those of ordinary hydrogen. □ **neutron bomb** a nuclear bomb that kills people by intense radiation but does little damage to buildings etc.

**Nev.** *abbreviation* Nevada.

**Nevada** (ně-**vah**-dă) a State of the western USA.

**never** *adverb* **1** at no time, on no occasion. **2** not at all; *never fear.* **3** (*informal*) surely not; *you never left the key in the lock!* **4** not; *never a care in the world.* ●*interjection* (*informal*) surely not. □ **never mind** do not be troubled; you may ignore; *never mind the expense.* **the never-never** *noun* (*informal*) hire purchase or credit. **well I never!** an exclamation of surprise.

**nevermore** *adverb* at no future time.

**nevertheless** *adverb & conjunction* in spite of this.

**nevus** Amer. spelling of NAEVUS.

**new** *adjective* **1** not existing before; recently made, invented, discovered, or experienced. **2** unfamiliar, unaccustomed; *it was new to me; I am new to the job.* **3** recently changed or renewed, different; *the new manager.* ●*adverb* newly, recently, just; *new-laid.* □ **New Age** a set of beliefs designed to replace traditional Western culture, with alternative approaches to religion, medicine, the environment, etc. **New Age traveller** (*Brit.*) a person who holds New Age beliefs and has adopted a travelling way of life. **new blood** a new member or members admitted to a society, company, etc. **new broom** see BROOM. **New Commonwealth** see COMMONWEALTH. **New Deal** the economic measures introduced by Franklin D. Roosevelt as President of the USA in 1933 to counteract the effects of the depression which had gravely affected the American economy. **new look** a fresh and up-to-date appearance. **new mathematics** (*or* **maths**) a system of elementary maths teaching with an emphasis on investigation and set theory. **new moon** the moon when it is seen in the evening as a crescent; (on calendars) the precise moment when the moon is in conjunction with the sun and is not visible. **new potatoes** the earliest potatoes of a new crop. **New Style** dating reckoned by the Gregorian calendar. **New Testament** see TESTAMENT. **new town** a town established as a completely new settlement, with government sponsorship. **New World** the Americas. **new year** the first few days of January. **New Year's Day** 1 January. **New Year's Eve** 31 December. □ **newish** *adjective*, **newness** *noun*

**newborn** *adjective* recently born.

**New Brunswick** a province of SE Canada.

**New Caledonia** an island in the SW Pacific, in French possession.

**newcomer** *noun* a person who has recently arrived or started an activity.

**newel** (**new-ĕl**) *noun* **1** (also **newel post**) a post that supports the handrail of a stair at the top or bottom of a staircase. **2** the centre pillar of a winding stair.

**New England** part of the USA comprising the States of Maine, New Hampshire, Vermont, Massachusetts, Rhode Island, and Connecticut.

**newfangled** *adjective* (*scornful*) objectionably new in method or style.

**Newfoundland** (**new-fŭnd-lănd**) a large island at the mouth of the St Lawrence, united with Labrador as a province of Canada. ● *noun* a dog of a large breed with a thick dark coat. □ **Newfoundlander** *noun*

**New Hampshire** a State of the north-eastern USA.

**New Jersey** a State of the USA, bordering on the Atlantic.

**newly** *adverb* recently, freshly. □ **newly-wed** *noun* a recently-married person.

**Newman**, Paul (born 1925), American film actor and director.

**New Mexico** a State of the south-western USA.

**news** *noun* **1** information about recent events. **2** a broadcast report of this. **3** newsworthy information; *when a man bites a dog, that's news.* □ **news-stand** *noun* a stall where newspapers are sold.

**newsagent** *noun* a shopkeeper who sells newspapers.

**newscast** *noun* a broadcast news report. □ **newscaster** *noun*

**newsflash** *noun* a single item of important news, broadcast urgently and often interrupting other programmes.

**newsletter** *noun* an informal printed report giving information that is of interest to members of a club etc.

**New South Wales** a State in SE Australia.

**newspaper** *noun* **1** a printed publication, usually issued daily or weekly, containing news reports, advertisements, articles on various subjects, etc. **2** the sheets of paper forming this; *wrapped in newspaper.*

**Newspeak** *noun* ambiguous euphemistic language used especially in political propaganda. (¶ The name of an artificial official language in George Orwell's *Nineteen Eighty-Four.*)

**newsprint** *noun* the type of paper on which a newspaper is printed.

**newsreel** *noun* (*hist.*) a cinema film showing current items of news.

**newsvendor** *noun* a newspaper-seller.

**newsworthy** *adjective* important or interesting enough to be mentioned as news.

**newsy** *adjective* (*informal*) full of news.

**newt** *noun* a small lizard-like creature that can live in water or on land.

**Newton**, Sir Isaac (1642–1727), English mathematician and physicist, the greatest single influence on theoretical physics until Einstein.

**newton** *noun* a unit of force. (¶ Named after Sir Isaac Newton.)

**Newtonian** (**new-toh-niăn**) *adjective* of the theories etc. devised by Sir Isaac Newton.

**New York 1** the most populous city of the USA, at the mouth of the Hudson River. **2** a State of the USA, bordering on the Atlantic. □ **New Yorker** *noun*

**New Zealand** a country in the South Pacific east of Australia, consisting of two major islands and several smaller ones. □ **New Zealander** *noun*

**next** *adjective* **1** lying, living, or being nearest to something. **2** coming nearest in order, time, or sequence; soonest come to. ● *adverb* in the next place or degree; on the next occasion. ● *noun* the next person or thing. □ **next-best** *adjective* the next in order of preference. **next door** in the next house or room. **next-door** *adjective* living or situated next door; *my next-door neighbour.* **next of kin** one's closest relative. **next to** almost;

*next to nothing left.* **the next world** life after death.

**nexus** *noun* (*plural* **nexus**) a connected group or series.

**Nfld.** *abbreviation* (also **NF**) Newfoundland.

**NH** *abbreviation* New Hampshire.

**NHS** *abbreviation* National Health Service.

**NI** *abbreviation* **1** Northern Ireland. **2** National Insurance.

**Ni** *symbol* nickel.

**niacin** = NICOTINIC ACID.

**Niagara** a river forming the US-Canada border between Lakes Erie and Ontario, famous for its spectacular waterfalls.

**Niamey** (n'yah-may) the capital of Niger.

**nib** *noun* **1** the point of a pen. **2** (**nibs**) crushed coffee or cocoa beans.

**nibble** *verb* **1** take small quick or gentle bites. **2** eat in small amounts; *no nibbling between meals.* **3** show interest in (an offer etc.) but without being definite. ●*noun* **1** a small quick bite. **2** a very small amount of food. □ **nibbler** *noun*

**Nibelungenlied** (nee-bĕ-luung-ĕn-leed) a 13th-century Germanic poem telling of the life and death of Siegfried, a prince of the Netherlands.

**nibs** *noun* □ **his nibs** (*slang*) a humorous title used in referring to an important or self-important person.

**nicad** (ny-kad) *adjective* nickel and cadmium. ●*noun* a nickel and cadmium battery.

**NICAM** (ny-kam) *noun* (also **Nicam**) (*trade mark*) a digital system used in television to produce high quality stereo sound.

**Nicaragua** (nik-er-ag-yoo-ă) a country in Central America. □ **Nicaraguan** *adjective & noun*

**nice** *adjective* **1** pleasant, satisfactory. **2** (of a person) kind, good-natured. **3** (*ironically*) difficult, bad; *this is a nice mess.* **4** fine or subtle; *nice distinctions.* **5** fastidious. □ **nicely** *adverb,* **niceness** *noun*

**Nicene Creed** (ny-seen) a formal statement of Christian belief based on that adopted at the Council of Nicaea (325).

**nicety** (ny-sit-i) *noun* **1** a subtle distinction or detail. **2** precision. □ **to a nicety** exactly.

**niche** (*pronounced* neesh) *noun* **1** a shallow recess, especially in a wall. **2** a position in life or employment to which the holder is well suited; *has found his niche.*

**Nicholas**[1] the name of two emperors of Russia, of whom Nicholas II was forced to abdicate after the Russian Revolution (1917) and was murdered along with his family by the Bolsheviks a year later.

**Nicholas**[2], St (4th century), bishop of Myra in Lycia, patron saint of children, sailors, and Russia. Feast day, 6 December.

**Nichrome** *noun* (*trade mark*) a group of nickel-chromium alloys used for making wire in heating elements etc.

**nick** *noun* **1** a small cut or notch. **2** (*slang*) a police station or a prison. ●*verb* **1** make a nick in. **2** (*slang*) steal. **3** (*slang*) catch or arrest (a criminal). □ **in good nick** (*slang*) in good condition. **in the nick of time** only just in time.

**nickel** *noun* **1** a chemical element (symbol Ni), a hard silvery-white metal used in alloys. **2** (*Amer.*) a 5-cent coin. □ **nickel silver** an alloy of nickel, zinc, and copper.

**nickelodeon** (nik-el-oh-diăn) *noun* (*Amer. informal*) a jukebox.

**nicker** *noun* (*plural* **nicker**) (*slang*) £1.

**Nicklaus** (nik-lowss), Jack William (born 1940), American golfer.

**nick-nack** alternative spelling of KNICK-KNACK.

**nickname** *noun* a name given humorously to a person instead of or as well as his or her real name. ●*verb* give a nickname to.

**Nicobar Islands** *see* ANDAMAN.

**Nicosia** (nik-ŏ-see-ă) the capital of Cyprus.

**nicotine** (nik-ŏ-teen) *noun* a poisonous substance found in tobacco. □ **nicotinic acid** a vitamin of the B group obtained from nicotine.

**nictitate** *verb* blink. □ **nictitating membrane** a transparent third eyelid in amphibians, birds, and some other animals. □ **nictitation** *noun*

**niece** *noun* one's brother's or sister's daughter.

**Nietzsche** (nee-chĕ), Friedrich Wilhelm (1844–1900), German philosopher of Polish descent, who divided mankind into a small dominant 'master-class' and a large dominated 'herd'.

**niff** (*slang*) *noun* a smell. ●*verb* smell, stink. □ **niffy** *adjective*

**nifty** *adjective* (*informal*) **1** smart, stylish. **2** excellent, clever.

**Niger 1** (*pronounced* ny-jer) a river of West Africa, flowing into the Gulf of Guinea. **2** (*pronounced* nee-zhair) a landlocked country of West Africa.

**Nigeria** a country in West Africa. □ **Nigerian** *adjective & noun*

**niggard** *noun* a stingy person. □ **niggardly** (nig-erd-li) *adjective,* **niggardliness** *noun*

**nigger** *noun* (*offensive*) a Black or dark-skinned person.

**niggle** *verb* **1** fuss over details, find fault in a petty way. **2** nag. □ **niggling** *adjective*

**nigh** (*rhymes with* by) *adverb & preposition* (*old use & dialect*) near.

**night** *noun* **1** the dark hours between sunset and sunrise. **2** nightfall. **3** darkness of night. **4** a specified or appointed night; an evening on which a performance or other

activity occurs; *the first night of the play*.
□ **night-life** *noun* entertainment available in towns at night. **night-light** *noun* a faint light kept burning in a bedroom at night. **night-long** *adjective & adverb* throughout the night. **night safe** a safe with access from the outer wall of a bank so that money etc. can be deposited when the bank is closed. **night school** classes provided in the evening for people who are at work during the day. **night-time** *noun* night, the time of darkness. **night-watchman** *noun* **1** a person employed to keep watch at night in a building that is closed. **2** *Cricket* an inferior batsman sent in when a wicket falls near the close of a day's play.

**nightcap** *noun* **1** (*hist.*) a soft cap for wearing in bed. **2** an alcoholic or hot drink taken at bedtime.

**nightclub** *noun* a club that is open at night, providing food, drink, and entertainment.

**nightdress** *noun* a woman's or child's loose garment for wearing in bed.

**nightfall** *noun* the coming of darkness at the end of the day.

**nightgown** *noun* a nightdress or nightshirt.

**nightie** *noun* (*informal*) a nightdress.

**Nightingale**, Florence (1820–1910), British nurse and medical reformer who became famous during the Crimean War, where she became known as the 'Lady of the Lamp'.

**nightingale** *noun* a small reddish-brown thrush, the male of which sings melodiously, especially at night.

**nightjar** *noun* a night-flying bird with a harsh cry.

**nightly** *adjective* **1** happening, done, or existing etc. in the night. **2** happening every night. ● *adverb* every night.

**nightmare** *noun* **1** a bad dream. **2** (*informal*) a terrifying or very unpleasant experience. □ **nightmarish** *adjective*

**nightshade** *noun* any of several wild plants with poisonous berries.

**nightshirt** *noun* a long shirt for wearing in bed.

**nightspot** *noun* a nightclub.

**nihilism** (**ny**-il-izm) *noun* **1** rejection of all religious and moral principles. **2** the theory that nothing has real existence. □ **nihilist** *noun*, **nihilistic** *adjective*

**Nijinsky** (ni-*zh*in-ski), Vaslav Fomich (1890–1950), Russian dancer and choreographer.

**Nikkei index** an index of shares traded on the Tokyo Stock Exchange.

**nil** *noun* nothing.

**Nile** a river flowing from east central Africa through Egypt to the Mediterranean Sea.

**nimble** *adjective* **1** able to move quickly, agile. **2** (of the mind or wits) able to think quickly. □ **nimbly** *adverb*, **nimbleness** *noun*

**nimbus** *noun* (*plural* **nimbi** or **nimbuses**) **1** a halo. **2** a rain-cloud.

**Nimby** *adjective* objecting to the siting of unpleasant developments in one's own locality. ● *noun* a person who objects in this way. (¶ From the initials of *not in my back yard*.)

**nincompoop** *noun* a foolish person.

**nine** *adjective & noun* one more than eight (9, IX). □ **dressed up to the nines** dressed very elaborately. **nine days' wonder** something that attracts much attention at first but is soon forgotten.

**ninepins** *noun* the game of skittles played with nine objects to be knocked down by rolling a ball.

**nineteen** *adjective & noun* one more than eighteen (19, XIX). □ **talk nineteen to the dozen** talk continually. □ **nineteenth** *adjective & noun*

**ninety** *adjective & noun* **1** nine times ten (90, XC). **2** (**nineties**) the numbers, years, or degrees of temperature from 90 to 99. □ **ninetieth** *adjective & noun*

**Nineveh** (**nin**-i-vĕ) the capital of Assyria from *c.*700 BC to 612 BC.

**ninny** *noun* a foolish person.

**ninth** *adjective & noun* **1** next after eighth. **2** one of nine equal parts of a thing. □ **ninthly** *adverb*

**niobium** (ny-**oh**-biŭm) *noun* a metallic element (symbol Nb) used in alloys.

**nip**[1] *verb* (**nipped**, **nipping**) **1** pinch or squeeze sharply; bite quickly with the front teeth. **2** (often foll. by *off*) break off by doing this; *nip off the side-shoots*. **3** pain or harm with biting cold; *a nipping wind*. **4** (*informal*) go quickly; *nip out to the shop*. ● *noun* **1** a sharp pinch, squeeze, or bite. **2** biting coldness; *a nip in the air*. □ **nip in the bud** destroy at an early stage of development.

**nip**[2] *noun* a small drink of spirits.

**nipper** *noun* **1** (*informal*) a young child. **2** the claw of a lobster or similar animal. **3** (**nippers**) pincers or forceps for gripping or cutting things.

**nipple** *noun* **1** a small projection in the centre of a male or female mammal's breasts, containing (in females) the outlets of the milk-secreting organs. **2** the teat of a feeding-bottle. **3** a nipple-like projection.

**Nipponese** (nip-ŏn-**eez**) *adjective & noun* (*plural* **Nipponese**) Japanese.

**nippy** *adjective* (*informal*) **1** nimble, quick. **2** bitingly cold. □ **nippiness** *noun*

**nirvana** (neer-**vah**-nă) *noun* (in Buddhist and Hindu teaching) the state of perfect bliss attained when the soul is freed from all suffering and absorbed into the supreme spirit.

**nisi** *see* DECREE NISI.

**Nissen hut** a tunnel-shaped hut of corrugated iron with a cement floor.

**nit** *noun* **1** the egg of a louse or other parasite; the insect laying this. **2** (*slang*) a stupid person. □ **nit-picking** *noun* fault-finding in a petty way.

**nitrate** *noun* (*pronounced* **ny**-trayt) **1** a salt or ester of nitric acid. **2** potassium or sodium nitrate used as a fertilizer. ●*verb* (*pronounced* ny-**trayt**) treat, combine, or impregnate with nitric acid. □ **nitration** *noun*

**nitre** (**ny**-ter) *noun* (*Amer.* **niter**) saltpetre.

**nitric** (**ny**-trik) *adjective* of or containing nitrogen. □ **nitric acid** a colourless caustic highly corrosive acid.

**nitride** *noun* a binary compound of nitrogen.

**nitrify** *verb* **1** impregnate with nitrogen. **2** convert into nitrites or nitrates. □ **nitrification** *noun*

**nitrite** *noun* any salt or ester of nitrous acid.

**nitrobenzene** (ny-trŏ-**ben**-zeen) *noun* a poisonous yellow oil used as a solvent and in making certain dyes.

**nitrogen** (**ny**-trŏ-jĕn) *noun* a chemical element (symbol N), a colourless odourless gas forming about four-fifths of the atmosphere. □ **nitrogenous** (ny-**troj**-in-ŭs) *adjective*

**nitroglycerine** (ny-troh-**gliss**-er-in) *noun* (*Amer.* **nitroglycerin**) a powerful explosive made by adding glycerine to a mixture of nitric and sulphuric acids.

**nitrous** (**ny**-trŭs) *adjective* of or containing nitrogen. □ **nitrous oxide** a colourless gas used as an anaesthetic, laughing-gas.

**nitty-gritty** *noun* (*slang*) the basic facts or realities of a matter.

**nitwit** *noun* (*informal*) a stupid person.

**Nixon**, Richard Milhous (1913–94), 37th President of the USA 1969–1974.

**NJ** *abbreviation* New Jersey.

**Nkruma** (n-**kroo**-mă), Kwame (1909–72), African statesman, the first leader of Ghana after it gained independence (1957–66).

**NM** *abbreviation* (also **N. Mex.**) New Mexico.

**No¹** *symbol* nobelium.

**No²** alternative spelling of NOH.

**No.** *abbreviation* (also **no.**) number.

**no** *adjective* **1** not any. **2** not a, quite other than; *she is no fool.* ●*adverb* **1** used as a denial or refusal of something. **2** not at all; *no better than before.* ●*noun* (*plural* **noes**) a negative reply or vote; a person voting against something. □ **no-ball** *noun* Cricket an unlawfully delivered ball. **no-claim** (*or* **no-claims**) **bonus** a reduction of an insurance premium after an agreed period without a claim. **no go** the task is impossible, the situation is hopeless. **no-go area** an area to which entry is forbidden to certain people or groups. **no man's land** an area not firmly assigned to any one owner; a space between the fronts of two opposing armies in war. **no one** no person, nobody. **no way** (*informal*) that is impossible.

**Noah** a Hebrew patriarch, said to have made the ark which saved his family and specimens of every animal from the flood sent by God to destroy the world.

**nob** (*slang*) *noun* **1** the head. **2** a person of high rank.

**nobble** *verb* (*slang*) **1** tamper with (a racehorse) to prevent its winning. **2** try to influence (especially a judge) by underhand means. **3** steal. **4** seize, catch.

**nobelium** (noh-bee-liŭm) *noun* a radioactive metallic element (symbol No).

**Nobel prize** (noh-**bel**) any of six international prizes awarded annually for outstanding achievements in physics, chemistry, physiology or medicine, literature, economics, and the promotion of peace, from the bequest of Alfred Nobel (1833–96), the Swedish inventor of dynamite.

**nobility** (noh-**bil**-iti) *noun* **1** nobleness of mind, character, or rank. **2** (**the nobility**) people of aristocratic birth or rank, titled people.

**noble** *adjective* **1** belonging to the aristocracy by birth or rank. **2** possessing excellent qualities, especially character; free from pettiness or meanness. **3** imposing in appearance; *a noble edifice.* ●*noun* a nobleman or noblewoman. □ **noble gas** any of a group of gaseous elements that almost never combine with other elements. □ **nobleness** *noun*, **nobly** *adverb*

**nobleman** *noun* (*plural* **noblemen**) a male member of the nobility.

**noblesse oblige** (noh-bless ŏ-blee*zh*) noble people must behave nobly, privilege entails responsibility. (¶ French.)

**noblewoman** *noun* (*plural* **noblewomen**) a female member of the nobility.

**nobody** *pronoun* no person. ●*noun* a person of no importance or authority. □ **like nobody's business** (*informal*) very much, intensively.

**nock** *noun* a notch on a bow or arrow for the bowstring.

**nocturnal** (nok-**ter**-năl) *adjective* **1** of or in the night. **2** active in the night; *nocturnal animals.* □ **nocturnally** *adverb*

**nocturne** (**nok**-tern) *noun* a short romantic piece of music.

**nod** *verb* (**nodded**, **nodding**) **1** move the head down and up again quickly as a sign of agreement or casual greeting; indicate

(agreement etc.) in this way. **2** let the head
fall forward in drowsiness; be drowsy. **3** (of
plumes, flowers, etc.) bend downwards
and sway. **4** make a mistake due to a
momentary lack of alertness. ●*noun* a nodding movement in agreement or greeting.
□ **a nodding acquaintance** a slight acquaintance with a person or subject. **land
of Nod** sleep. **nod off** fall asleep.

**noddle** *noun* (*informal*) the head.

**noddy** *noun* **1** a simpleton. **2** a tropical
seabird resembling the tern.

**node** (*rhymes with* load) *noun* **1** a knob-like
swelling. **2** the point on the stem of a plant
where a leaf or bud grows out. **3** either of
two points at which a planet's orbit
intersects the plane of the ecliptic or the
celestial equator. **4** the point of minimum
disturbance in a standing wave system. **5** a
point at which a curve intersects itself. **6** a
component in a computer network.

**nodule** (**nod**-yool) *noun* a small rounded
lump, a small node. □ **nodular** *adjective*

**Noel** (noh-**el**) *noun* (in carols) Christmas.

**noggin** *noun* **1** a small mug. **2** a small
measure of alcohol, usually ¼ pint.
**3** (*slang*) the head.

**nogging** *noun* brickwork in a wooden frame.

**Noh** (*pronounced* noh) *noun* (also **No**) a form
of traditional Japanese drama.

**noise** *noun* a sound, especially one that is
loud, harsh, or confused or undesired.
●*verb* make public; *noised it abroad.*
□ **noiseless** *adjective*, **noiselessly** *adverb*

**noisome** (**noi**-sŏm) *adjective* (*literary*)
**1** harmful. **2** evil-smelling; objectionable.

**noisy** *adjective* (**noisier, noisiest**) making
much noise. □ **noisily** *adverb*, **noisiness**
*noun*

**nomad** (**noh**-mad) *noun* **1** a member of a
tribe that roams from place to place
seeking pasture for its animals. **2** a wanderer. □ **nomadism** *noun*, **nomadic** (nŏ-
**mad**-ik) *adjective*

**nom de plume** (nom dĕ **ploom**) (*plural*
**noms de plume**, *pronounced* same) a
writer's pseudonym. (¶ French, = pen-
name.)

**nomenclature** (nŏ-**men**-klă-cher) *noun* a
system of names, e.g. those used in a particular science.

**nominal** (**nomin**-ăl) *adjective* **1** in name only;
*nominal ruler of that country.* **2** (of an
amount or sum of money) very small but
charged or paid as a token that payment is
required; *a nominal fee.* □ **nominal value**
the face value of a coin etc. □ **nominally**
*adverb*

**nominalism** *noun* the doctrine that
universals or general ideas are merely
names. □ **nominalist** *noun*, **nominalistic**
*adjective*

**nominate** (**nom**-in-ayt) *verb* **1** name as
candidate for or future holder of an office.
**2** appoint as a place or date for a meeting
etc. □ **nomination** *noun*, **nominator** *noun*

**nominative** (**nom**-in-ă-tiv) *noun* *Grammar*
the form of a noun used when it is the
subject of a verb.

**nominee** (nom-in-**ee**) *noun* a person who is
nominated by another.

**non-** *combining form* not.

**nonagenarian** (noh-nă-jin-**air**-iăn) *noun* a
person who is in his or her nineties.

**nonagon** *noun* a plane figure with nine sides
and angles.

**non-aligned** (non-ă-**lynd**) *adjective* not in alliance with another (especially major)
power. □ **non-alignment** *noun*

**nonce** *noun* □ **for the nonce** for the time
being. **nonce-word** *noun* a word coined for
one occasion only.

**nonchalant** (**non**-shă-lănt) *adjective* not
feeling or showing anxiety or excitement,
calm and casual. □ **nonchalantly** *adverb*,
**nonchalance** *noun*

**non-combatant** (non-**com**-bă-tănt) *noun*
**1** a member of an army etc. whose duties
do not involve fighting, e.g. a doctor or
chaplain. **2** a civilian during a war.

**non-commissioned** *adjective* not holding a
commission; *non-commissioned officers.*

**noncommittal** (non-kŏ-**mi**-t'l) *adjective* not
committing oneself, not showing what one
thinks or which side one supports.

**non compos mentis** not in one's right
mind. (¶ Latin, = not in control of one's
mind.)

**non-conductor** *noun* a substance that does
not conduct heat or electricity.

**nonconformist** *noun* **1** a person who does
not conform to established principles.
**2** (**Nonconformist**) a member of certain
Protestant sects that do not conform to the
teaching or practices of the Church of
England or other established Churches.
□ **nonconformity** *noun*

**non-contributory** *adjective* not involving
payment of contributions; *a non-
contributory pension scheme.*

**non-cooperation** *noun* failure or refusal to
cooperate, especially as a protest.

**nondescript** (**non**-dis-kript) *adjective* lacking
in distinctive characteristics and therefore
not easy to classify. ●*noun* a nondescript
person or thing.

**none** *pronoun* **1** not any. **2** no person(s), no
one; *none can tell.* ●*adverb* by no amount,
not at all; *is none the worse for it.* □ **none
other** no other person. **none the less** *see*
NONETHELESS. **none too** not very, not at
all; *he's none too pleased.*

▪**Usage** In sense 1, *none* may be followed
by either a singular or a plural verb. The

singular construction is preferred (*none of the candidates has failed*), but the plural is very common (*none of them are required*).

**nonentity** (non-**en**-titi) *noun* a person or thing of no importance.

**nonetheless** *adverb* (also **none the less**) nevertheless.

**non-event** *noun* an event that was expected or intended to be important but proves to be disappointing.

**non-existent** *adjective* not existing.

**non-ferrous** *adjective* (of a metal) not iron or steel.

**non-fiction** *noun* literature other than fiction.

**non-flammable** *adjective* unable to be set on fire.

■**Usage** See the note under **inflammable**.

**non-intervention** *noun* the policy of not interfering in other people's disputes.

**nonpareil** (non-pě-**rayl** or non-per-el) *adjective* unrivalled. ●*noun* an unrivalled person or thing.

**non-party** *adjective* not belonging to or supported by a political party.

**nonplus** (non-**plus**) *verb* (**nonplussed**, **nonplussing**) perplex completely.

**non-proliferation** *noun* limitation of the increase in number especially of nuclear weapons.

**non-resident** *adjective* **1** not living on the premises; *a non-resident caretaker*. **2** (of a job) not requiring the holder to live in. ●*noun* a person not staying at a hotel etc.; *open to non-residents*.

**nonsense** *noun* **1** words put together in a way that does not make sense. **2** absurd or foolish talk, ideas, or behaviour. □ **nonsensical** (non-**sens**-ikǎl) *adjective*, **nonsensically** *adverb*

**non sequitur** (non **sek**-wit-er) a conclusion that does not logically follow from the evidence given. (¶ Latin, = it does not follow.)

**non-smoker** *noun* **1** a person who does not smoke. **2** a train compartment where smoking is forbidden. □ **non-smoking** *adjective*

**non-starter** *noun* **1** a horse which is entered for a race but does not run in it. **2** (*informal*) a person or scheme that is unlikely to succeed and not worth considering.

**non-stick** *adjective* coated with a substance that does not allow things to stick to it.

**non-stop** *adjective* **1** (of a train etc.) not stopping at intermediate places. **2** not ceasing; *non-stop chatter*. ●*adverb* without stopping or pausing.

**non-U** (non-**yoo**) *adjective* (*informal*) not characteristic of upper-class speech or behaviour.

**non-union** *adjective* not belonging to a trade union.

**non-voter** *noun* a person who does not vote or is not entitled to vote.

**non-voting** *adjective* (of shares) not entitling the holder to a vote.

**non-White** *adjective* not White. ●*noun* a non-White person.

**noodle** *noun* **1** (**noodles**) pasta in narrow strips. **2** a foolish person. **3** (*slang*) the head.

**nook** *noun* a secluded place or corner, a recess.

**nooky** *noun* (also **nookie**) (*slang*) sexual intercourse.

**noon** *noun* twelve o'clock in the day, midday.

**noonday** *noun* midday.

**noose** *noun* a loop of rope etc. with a knot that tightens when pulled.

**nor** *conjunction* and not.

**Nordic** *adjective* **1** of or relating to a physical type of northern Germanic people who are often tall and fair with a long head. **2** of Scandinavia, Finland, or Iceland. **3** (of skiing) involving cross-country work and jumping. ●*noun* a Nordic person.

**Norfolk** (**nor**-fŏk) a county of eastern England. □ **Norfolk jacket** a man's loose belted jacket with box pleats.

**norm** *noun* **1** a standard, pattern, or type considered to be representative of a group. **2** a standard amount of work etc. to be done or produced. **3** customary behaviour.

**normal** *adjective* **1** conforming to what is standard or usual. **2** free from mental or emotional disorders. **3** (of a line) at right angles, perpendicular. ●*noun* **1** the normal value or standard etc. **2** a line at right angles. □ **normal distribution** a function that represents the distribution of many random variables as a symmetrical bell-shaped graph. □ **normalcy** *noun* (especially *Amer.*), **normally** *adverb*, **normality** *noun*

**normalize** *verb* (also **normalise**) make or become normal. □ **normalization** *noun*

**Norman**[1] *adjective* of the Normans or the style of architecture found in Britain under the Normans. ●*noun* a native or inhabitant of Normandy in northern France, especially one of those who conquered England in 1066. □ **Norman Conquest** *see* CONQUEST. **Norman French** French as spoken by the Normans or (after 1066) in English lawcourts.

**Norman**[2], Jessye (born 1945), American operatic soprano.

**Normandy** **1** a region of NW France bordering on the English Channel. **2** the name of the royal house including William I and II, Henry I, and Stephen, which ruled England 1066–1154.

**normative** (norm-ă-tiv) *adjective* of or establishing a norm.

**Norn** *noun* (*Scand. myth.*) any of the virgin goddesses of fate or destiny.

**Norse** *adjective* of ancient Norway or Scandinavia. ●*noun* **1** the Norwegian language. **2** the Scandinavian group of languages.

**Norseman** *noun* (*plural* **Norsemen**) a Viking.

**north** *noun* **1** the point or direction to the left of a person facing east. **2** the northern part of something. ●*adjective* **1** towards or in the north. **2** (of a wind) blowing from the north. ●*adverb* towards or in the north. □ **north country** northern England. **North Pole** the northernmost point of the earth. **north pole** (of a magnet) the pole that is attracted to the north. **North Star** the pole star.

**North America** the northern half of the American land mass (*see* AMERICA).

**Northamptonshire** an east midland county of England.

**Northants** *abbreviation* Northamptonshire.

**northbound** *adjective* travelling or leading northwards.

**North Carolina** (ka-rŏ-ly-nă) a State of the USA on the Atlantic coast.

**North Dakota** (dă-koh-tă) a State of the north central USA.

**north-east** *noun* the point or direction midway between north and east. ●*adjective* of, towards, or coming from the north-east. ●*adverb* towards, in, or near the north-east. □ **north-easterly** *adjective & noun*, **north-eastern** *adjective*

**northeaster** *noun* a north-east wind.

**northerly** *adjective* **1** in or towards the north. **2** (of a wind) blowing from the north. ●*noun* a northerly wind.

**northern** *adjective* of or in the north. □ **Northern hemisphere** the half of the earth north of the equator. **northern lights** the aurora borealis.

**northerner** *noun* a native or inhabitant of the north.

**Northern Ireland** a unit of the UK comprising the six north-eastern districts (and former counties) of Ireland.

**northernmost** *adjective* furthest north.

**Northern Territory** a territory in central north Australia.

**North Sea** that part of the Atlantic Ocean between the mainland of Europe and the east coast of Britain.

**Northumb.** *abbreviation* Northumberland.

**Northumberland** a county of England.

**Northumbrian** *adjective* **1** of ancient Northumbria (= England north of the Humber). **2** of modern Northumberland.

**northward** *adjective & adverb* (also **northwards**) towards the north.

**north-west** *noun* the point or direction midway between north and west. ●*adjective* of, towards, or coming from the north-west. ●*adverb* towards, in, or near the north-west. □ **north-westerly** *adjective & adverb*, **north-western** *adjective*

**northwester** *noun* a north-west wind.

**Northwest Territories** part of Canada lying north of the 60th parallel.

**North Yorkshire** a county of NE England.

**Norway** a country in northern Europe.

**Norwegian** *adjective* of Norway or its people or language. ●*noun* **1** a native or inhabitant of Norway. **2** the language of Norway.

**Nos.** *abbreviation* (also **nos.**) numbers.

**nose** *noun* **1** the organ at the front of the head in man and animals, containing the nostrils and used for breathing and smelling. **2** a sense of smell. **3** the ability to detect things of a particular kind; *has a nose for scandal.* **4** the odour or perfume of wine etc. **5** the front end or projecting front part of something, e.g. of a car or aircraft. ●*verb* **1** detect or search by using one's sense of smell. **2** smell at; rub with the nose; push the nose against or into. **3** push one's way cautiously ahead; *the car nosed past the obstruction.* □ **by a nose** by a very narrow margin. **get up a person's nose** (*slang*) annoy him or her. **keep one's nose clean** (*slang*) stay out of trouble. **pay through the nose** pay an unfairly high price. **put a person's nose out of joint** (*informal*) make him or her envious because of another's success or promotion etc. **rub a person's nose in it** (*informal*) remind him or her humiliatingly of an error. **turn up one's nose at** (*informal*) reject or ignore contemptuously. **under a person's nose** where he or she can or should see it clearly. **with one's nose in the air** haughtily.

**nosebag** *noun* a bag containing fodder, for hanging on a horse's head.

**nosebleed** *noun* bleeding from the nose.

**nosedive** *noun* **1** a steep downward plunge by an aircraft. **2** any sudden drop or plunge. ●*verb* make a nosedive.

**nosegay** *noun* a small bunch of flowers.

**nosh** (*slang*) *noun* food. ●*verb* eat. □ **nosh-up** *noun* (*slang*) a large meal.

**nostalgia** (noss-tal-jă) *noun* sentimental memory of or longing for things of the past. □ **nostalgic** (noss-tal-jik) *adjective*, **nostalgically** *adverb*

**Nostradamus** (nostră-dah-mŭs), Michel de Notredame (1503–66), Provençal astrologer whose extensive prophecies were widely believed in the mid-16th century at the French court.

**nostril** *noun* either of the two openings in the nose through which air is admitted.

**nostrum** (noss-trŭm) *noun* **1** a quack remedy. **2** a pet scheme, especially for political or social reform.

**nosy** *adjective* (**nosier**, **nosiest**) (*informal*) inquisitive. □ **Nosy Parker** an inquisitive person, a busybody. □ **nosily** *adverb*, **nosiness** *noun*

**not** *adverb* expressing a negative, denial, or refusal. □ **not at all** a polite reply to thanks.

**notable** *adjective* worthy of notice, remarkable, eminent. ● *noun* an eminent person. □ **notability** *noun*, **notably** *adverb*

**notary** (noh-ter-i) *noun* (in full **notary public**, *plural* **notaries public**) a solicitor or other public official who is legally authorized to witness the signing of documents and to perform other formal transactions. □ **notarial** *adjective*

**notation** *noun* a system of signs or symbols representing numbers, quantities, musical notes, etc.

**notch** *noun* **1** a V-shaped cut or indentation. **2** each of the levels in a graded system; *everyone moved up a notch.* ● *verb* **1** make a notch or notches in. **2** (usually foll. by *up*) score; *notched up another win.*

**note** *noun* **1** a brief record of something, written down to aid the memory. **2** a short or informal letter; a memorandum; a formal diplomatic communication. **3** a short comment on or explanation of a word or passage in a book etc. **4** a written or printed promise to pay money; a banknote; *£5 notes.* **5** a tone of definite pitch made by a voice, instrument, engine, etc. **6** a written sign representing the pitch and duration of a musical sound. **7** any of the keys on a piano etc. **8** a significant sound or indication of feelings etc.; *a note of optimism.* **9** eminence, distinction; *a family of note.* **10** notice, attention; *take note of what he says.* ● *verb* **1** notice, pay attention to. **2** (often foll. by *down*) write down, record. □ **strike the right note** speak or act in the appropriate manner.

**notebook** *noun* a small book with blank pages for making notes.

**notecase** *noun* a wallet for holding banknotes.

**noted** *adjective* famous, well-known.

**notelet** *noun* a piece of small folded ornamental notepaper, for informal letters.

**notepaper** *noun* paper for writing letters on.

**noteworthy** *adjective* worthy of notice, remarkable.

**nothing** *noun* **1** no thing, not anything. **2** no amount, nought. **3** non-existence; what does not exist. **4** a person or thing of no importance. ● *adverb* not at all, in no way; *it's nothing like as good.* □ **be** (or **have**) **nothing to do with 1** have no connection

with. **2** not be involved or associated with. **for nothing 1** without payment, free. **2** without a reward or result. **nothing doing** (*informal*) a statement of refusal or failure.

**nothingness** *noun* **1** non-existence; *faded into nothingness.* **2** worthlessness, triviality.

**notice** *noun* **1** news or information of what has happened or is about to happen. **2** a formal announcement that one is to end an agreement or leave a job at a specified time; *gave her a month's notice.* **3** written or printed information; instructions displayed publicly. **4** attention, observation; *it escaped my notice.* **5** an account or review in a newspaper. ● *verb* **1** perceive, become aware of; take notice of. **2** remark upon, speak of. □ **at short notice** with little warning. **notice-board** *noun* a board on which notices may be displayed. **take notice** show signs of interest; pay attention.

**noticeable** *adjective* easily seen or noticed. □ **noticeably** *adverb*

**notifiable** *adjective* (of a disease etc.) that must be reported to the public health authorities.

**notify** *verb* (**notified**, **notifying**) **1** inform. **2** report, make (a thing) known. □ **notification** *noun*

**notion** *noun* **1** an idea or opinion, especially one that is vague or probably incorrect. **2** an understanding or intention; *has no notion of discipline.*

**notional** (**noh**-shŏn-ăl) *adjective* hypothetical; assumed to be correct or valid for a particular purpose; *an estimate based on notional figures.* □ **notionally** *adverb*

**notorious** (noh-**tor**-iŭs) *adjective* well-known, especially in an unfavourable way. □ **notoriously** *adverb*, **notoriety** (noh-ter-**I**-iti) *noun*

**Notre-Dame** (not-rĕ-**dahm**) the cathedral church of Paris, dedicated to the Virgin Mary.

**Nottinghamshire** a midland county of England.

**Notts.** *abbreviation* Nottinghamshire.

**notwithstanding** *preposition* in spite of. ● *adverb* nevertheless.

**Nouakchott** (nwak-shot) the capital of Mauritania.

**nougat** (noo-gah) *noun* a chewy sweet made of nuts, sugar or honey, and egg white.

**nought** (*pronounced* nawt) *noun* **1** the figure 0. **2** (*poetic* or *old use*) nothing. □ **noughts and crosses** a pencil-and-paper game in which players seek to complete a row of three noughts or three crosses.

**noun** *noun* a word or phrase used as the name of a person, place, or thing. □ **common nouns** words such as *man*, *dog*, *table*, and *sport*, which are used of whole classes of people or things. **proper nouns** words such as *John*, *Smith*, and *London* which name a particular person or thing.

**nourish** (**nu**-rish) *verb* **1** keep (a person, animal, or plant) alive and well by means of food. **2** foster or cherish (a feeling etc.). □ **nourishment** *noun*

**nous** (*rhymes with* house) *noun* (*informal*) common sense.

**nouveau riche** (noo-voh **reesh**) (*plural* **nouveaux riches**, *pronounced* same) a person who has acquired wealth only recently, especially one who makes a display of it. (¶ French, = new rich.)

**nouvelle cuisine** (noo-vel kwi-**zeen**) a style of cooking that avoids traditional rich sauces and emphasizes fresh ingredients and attractive presentation. (¶ French, = new cookery.)

**Nov.** *abbreviation* November.

**nova** (**noh**-vă) *noun* (*plural* **novae** or **novas**) a star that suddenly becomes much brighter for a short time.

**Nova Scotia** (noh-vă **skoh**-shă) a province of Canada. □ **Nova Scotian** *adjective & noun*

**novel** *noun* a book-length fictional story. ● *adjective* of a new kind; *a novel experience*.

**novelette** *noun* a short novel.

**novelist** *noun* a writer of novels.

**novella** (nŏ-**vel**-ă) *noun* a short novel or narrative story.

**Novello** (nŏ-**vel**-oh), Ivor (original name; David Ivor Davies) (1893–1951), Welsh-born composer, actor, and playwright, noted for his romantic musicals and popular songs.

**novelty** *noun* **1** the quality of being novel. **2** a novel thing or occurrence. **3** a small toy or trinket.

**November** the eleventh month of the year.

**novena** (nŏ-**vee**-nă) *noun* (in the RC Church) a devotion consisting of special prayers or services on nine successive days.

**novice** (**nov**-iss) *noun* **1** a beginner. **2** one who has been accepted into a religious order but has not yet taken the final vows.

**noviciate** (nŏ-**vish**-i-ăt) *noun* **1** the period of being a novice in a religious order. **2** the novices' quarters in a monastery or convent.

**now** *adverb* **1** at the time when or of which one is writing or speaking. **2** by this time. **3** immediately; *must go now*. **4** (with no reference to time, giving various tones to a sentence) surely, *I wonder, I am telling you, etc.; now why didn't I think of that?* ● *conjunction* as a consequence of the fact, simultaneously with it; *now that you have come, we'll start*; *I do remember, now you mention it*. ● *noun* the present time; *they ought to be here by now*. □ **for now** until a

later time; *goodbye for now*. **now and again** *or* **now and then** occasionally.

**nowadays** *adverb* at the present time (contrasted with years ago).

**nowhere** *adverb* not anywhere. ● *pronoun* no place. □ **come from nowhere** be suddenly present. **get nowhere** make no progress. **nowhere near** not nearly.

**nowise** *adverb* in no way, not at all.

**nowt** *noun* (*informal* or *dialect*) nothing.

**noxious** (**nok**-shŭs) *adjective* unpleasant and harmful.

**nozzle** *noun* the vent or spout of a hose etc. through which a stream of liquid or air is directed.

**Np** *symbol* neptunium.

**nr.** *abbreviation* near.

**NS** *abbreviation* **1** Nova Scotia. **2** New Style.

**NSPCC** *abbreviation* National Society for the Prevention of Cruelty to Children.

**NSW** *abbreviation* New South Wales.

**NT** *abbreviation* **1** New Testament. **2** Northern Territory (of Australia). **3** National Trust.

**nth** *see* N.

**nuance** (**new**-ahns) *noun* a subtle difference in meaning, a shade of meaning.

**nub** *noun* **1** (also **nubble**) a small knob or lump. **2** the central point or core of a matter or problem. □ **nubbly** *adjective*

**Nubia** (**new**-biă) a region of southern Egypt and northern Sudan. □ **Nubian** *adjective & noun*

**nubile** (**new**-byl) *adjective* (of a young woman) marriageable or sexually attractive. □ **nubility** (new-**bil**-iti) *noun*

**nuclear** *adjective* **1** of a nucleus. **2** of or using nuclear energy; *nuclear weapons*. □ **nuclear bomb** a bomb using the release of energy by nuclear fission or fusion or both. **nuclear energy** energy that is released or absorbed during reactions taking place in the nuclei of atoms. **nuclear family** a father, mother, and their child or children. **nuclear fission** the splitting of a heavy nucleus spontaneously or on impact with another particle, with the release of energy. **nuclear fusion** the union of atomic nuclei to form a heavier nucleus with the release of energy. **nuclear physics** the branch of physics dealing with atomic nuclei and their reactions. **nuclear power 1** power generated by a nuclear reactor. **2** a country that has nuclear weapons. **nuclear reactor** *see* REACTOR.

**nucleate** (**new**-kli-ayt) *verb* form or form into a nucleus. ● *adjective* having a nucleus.

**nucleic acid** (new-**klee**-ik) a complex organic molecule of either of the two types (DNA and RNA) present in all living cells.

**nucleon** *noun* a proton or neutron.

**nucleonics** (new-kli-**on**-iks) *noun* the branch of science and engineering that deals with the practical uses of nuclear energy. □ **nucleonic** adjective

**nucleus** (**new**-kli-ŭs) noun (plural **nuclei**, pronounced **new**-kli-I) **1** the central part or thing round which others are collected. **2** something established that will receive additions; *this collection of books will form the nucleus of a new library.* **3** the central positively charged portion of an atom. **4** the central part of a seed or of a plant or animal cell.

**nude** adjective not clothed, naked. ● noun a nude human figure in a painting etc. □ **in the nude** not clothed, naked. □ **nudity** noun

**nudge** verb **1** poke (a person) gently with the elbow to attract attention quietly. **2** push slightly or gradually. ● noun this movement.

**nudist** (**newd**-ist) noun a person who is in favour of or enjoys going unclothed. □ **nudism** noun

**Nuer** (**noo**-er) noun **1** (plural **Nuer**) a member of an African people living in SE Sudan. **2** their language.

**Nuffield**, William Richard Morris, 1st Viscount (1877–1963), British motor manufacturer and philanthropist.

**nugatory** (**new**-gă-ter-i) adjective **1** futile, trivial. **2** inoperative, not valid.

**nugget** (**nug**-it) noun **1** a lump of gold or platinum as found in the earth. **2** something small and valuable; *nuggets of information.*

**nuisance** noun a source of annoyance, an annoying person or thing.

**nuke** (slang) noun a nuclear weapon. ● verb attack with nuclear weapons.

**Nuku'alofa** (noo-koo-ă-**loh**-fă) the capital of Tonga.

**null** adjective **1** (especially as **null and void**) having no legal force; *declared the agreement null and void.* **2** non-existent; amounting to nothing. **3** without character or expression. □ **nullity** noun

**nullify** verb (**nullified**, **nullifying**) **1** make (a thing) null. **2** cancel or neutralize the effect of. □ **nullification** noun

**numb** adjective deprived of the power to feel or move; *numb with cold.* ● verb make numb. □ **numbly** adverb, **numbness** noun

**number** noun **1** a symbol or word indicating how many, a numeral. **2** a numeral identifying a person or thing (e.g. a telephone or a house in a street) by its position in a series. **3** a single issue of a magazine. **4** a song or piece of music, especially as an item in a theatrical performance. **5** (informal) an object (such as a garment or car) considered as an item. **6** a group of people; *among our number.* **7** a total of people or things. **8** (**numbers**) very many. **9** the category 'singular' or 'plural' in grammar.

**10** (**Numbers**) the fourth book of the Old Testament, telling of the wanderings of the Israelites in the desert. ● verb **1** count, find out how many. **2** amount to. **3** assign a number to (each in a series); distinguish in this way. **4** include or regard as; *I number him among my friends.* □ **a number of** several. **one's days are numbered** one does not have long to live or to remain in one's position. **have a person's number** (informal) understand his or her real character or motives. **number crunching** (informal) the process of making complicated calculations. **number one** (informal) oneself; *always takes care of number one.* **number plate** a plate on a motor vehicle, bearing its registration number. **Number Ten** 10 Downing Street, the official London home of the British Prime Minister.

**numberless** adjective innumerable.

**numerable** adjective able to be counted.

**numeral** (**new**-mer-ăl) noun a symbol that represents a certain number, a figure.

**numerate** (**new**-mer-ăt) adjective having a good basic knowledge and understanding of mathematics. □ **numeracy** noun

**numeration** (new-mer-**ay**-shŏn) noun **1** numbering. **2** calculation.

**numerator** (**new**-mer-ayter) noun the number written above the line in a vulgar fraction, showing how many of the parts indicated by the denominator are to be taken (e.g. 2 in ⅔).

**numerical** (new-**merri**-kăl) adjective of a number or series of numbers; *placed in numerical order.* □ **numerically** adverb

**numerology** (new-mer-**ol**-ŏji) noun the study of the occult significance of numbers.

**numerous** (**new**-mer-ŭs) adjective **1** many. **2** consisting of many items.

**numinous** (**new**-min-ŭs) adjective **1** indicating the presence of a divinity. **2** spiritual; awe-inspiring.

**numismatics** (new-miz-**mat**-iks) noun the study of coins and similar objects (e.g. medals). □ **numismatic** adjective, **numismatist** (new-**miz**-mă-tist) noun

**numskull** noun a stupid person.

**nun** noun a member of a community of women living apart from the world under the rules of a religious order.

**nuncio** (**nun**-si-oh) noun (plural **nuncios**) a diplomatic representative of the pope.

**nunnery** noun a convent for nuns.

**nuptial** (**nup**-shăl) adjective of marriage; of a wedding ceremony. ● plural noun (**nuptials**) a wedding.

**nurd** alternative spelling of NERD.

**Nureyev** (**newr**-i-ef), Rudolf (1939–93), Russian ballet dancer, who defected to the West in 1961.

**nurse** *noun* **1** a person trained to care for sick, injured, or infirm people. **2** a person employed to take charge of young children. ●*verb* **1** work as a nurse; look after in this way. **2** feed or be fed at the breast. **3** hold carefully. **4** give special care or attention to. **5** harbour or foster (a grievance etc.). □ **nursing home** a privately run hospital or home for invalids or old people.

**nurseling** alternative spelling of NURSLING.

**nursemaid** *noun* a young woman employed to take charge of young children.

**nursery** *noun* **1** a room set apart for young children. **2** = DAY NURSERY. **3** a place where young plants are reared for sale. □ **nursery rhyme** a simple traditional song or rhyme for children. **nursery school** a school for children below normal school age (usually between three and five). **nursery slopes** gentle slopes suitable for beginners at a ski resort. **nursery stakes** a race for two-year-old horses.

**nurseryman** *noun* (*plural* **nurserymen**) one who owns or works in a plant nursery.

**nursling** *noun* (also **nurseling**) a baby or young animal that is being suckled.

**nurture** (ner-cher) *verb* **1** nourish and rear. **2** bring up. ●*noun* nurturing; nourishment.

**nut** *noun* **1** a fruit consisting of a hard shell round an edible kernel. **2** this kernel. **3** (*slang*) the head. **4** (*slang*) a crazy or eccentric person. **5** a small piece of metal with a threaded hole through it for screwing on the end of a bolt to secure it. **6** a small lump of a solid substance, e.g. coal or butter. **7** (**nuts**) (*vulgar slang*) the testicles. □ **do one's nut** (*slang*) be extremely angry. **nuts and bolts** (*informal*) the practical details.

**nut case** (*slang*) a crazy person.

**nutcracker** *noun* (usually as **nutcrackers**) a device for cracking nuts.

**nuthatch** *noun* a small climbing bird that feeds on nuts and insects.

**nutmeg** *noun* the hard fragrant seed of a tropical tree, ground or grated as spice.

**nutria** (new-tri-ă) *noun* the skin or fur of a coypu.

**nutrient** (new-tri-ĕnt) *noun* a substance that provides nourishment. ●*adjective* nourishing.

**nutriment** (new-trim-ĕnt) *noun* nourishing food.

**nutrition** (new-trish-ŏn) *noun* nourishment. □ **nutritional** *adjective*, **nutritionally** *adverb*

**nutritious** (new-trish-ŭs) *adjective* nourishing, efficient as food. □ **nutritiousness** *noun*

**nutritive** (new-tri-tiv) *adjective* nourishing, nutritious.

**nuts** *adjective* (*slang*) crazy. □ **be nuts about** or **on** (*slang*) be very fond of or enthusiastic about.

**nutshell** *noun* the hard outer shell of a nut. □ **in a nutshell** expressed in the briefest possible way.

**nutter** *noun* (*slang*) a crazy person.

**nutty** *adjective* **1** full of nuts. **2** tasting like nuts. **3** (*slang*) crazy. □ **nuttiness** *noun*

**nuzzle** *verb* press or rub gently with the nose.

**NV** *abbreviation* Nevada.

**NW** *abbreviation* **1** north-west. **2** north-western.

**NWT** *abbreviation* Northwest Territories.

**NY** *abbreviation* New York.

**Nyerere** (n'ye-**rair**-i), Julius Kambarage (born 1922), African statesman, first premier and then President of Tanganyika following its independence in 1961, President of Tanzania 1964–85.

**nylon** *noun* **1** a synthetic fibre of great lightness and strength. **2** fabric made from this. **3** (**nylons**) stockings made of nylon.

**nymph** (*pronounced* nimf) *noun* **1** (in mythology) a semi-divine maiden associated with nature and living in the sea or woods etc. **2** (*poetic*) a beautiful young woman. **3** a young insect that resembles its parents in form.

**nympho** (**nim**-foh) *noun* (*plural* **nymphos**) (*informal*) a nymphomaniac.

**nymphomania** (nim-fŏ-**may**-niă) *noun* excessive and uncontrollable sexual desire in women. □ **nymphomaniac** *noun & adjective*

**nystagmus** (nis-**tag**-mŭs) *noun* abnormal continual rapid involuntary movement of the eyeballs.

**NZ** *abbreviation* New Zealand.

# Oo

**O** *interjection* = OH. ● *symbol* oxygen. ● *noun* (**0**) nought, zero. ● *abbreviation* (also **O.**) Old.

**o'** *preposition* of; *six o'clock*; *will-o'-the wisp*.

**oaf** *noun* (*plural* **oafs**) a clumsy or stupid person. □ **oafish** *adjective*

**oak** *noun* **1** a deciduous forest tree with irregularly-shaped leaves, bearing acorns. **2** its wood. **3** (**the Oaks**) an annual race held three days after the Derby at Epsom in Surrey for three-year-old fillies. □ **oak-apple** *noun* (also **oak-gall**) a growth formed on oak trees by the larvae of certain wasps. □ **oaken** *adjective*

**oakum** *noun* loose fibre obtained by picking old rope to pieces.

**OAP** *abbreviation* old-age pensioner.

**oar** *noun* **1** a pole with a flat blade at one end, used to row or steer a boat. **2** a rower. □ **put one's oar in** interfere.

**oarsman** *noun* (*plural* **oarsmen**) a male rower.

**oarsmanship** *noun* skill in rowing.

**oarswoman** *noun* (*plural* **oarswomen**) a female rower.

**oasis** (oh-ay-sis) *noun* (*plural* **oases**, *pronounced* oh-ay-seez) **1** a fertile spot in a desert, where water is found. **2** an area or period of tranquillity.

**oast** *noun* a kiln for drying hops. □ **oast house** a building containing this.

**oatcake** *noun* a thin biscuit made of oatmeal.

**oath** *noun* **1** a solemn undertaking or declaration, naming God or a revered object as witness. **2** a use of the name of God etc. as a swear word; a curse. □ **on** *or* **under oath** having made a solemn oath.

**oatmeal** *noun* **1** meal prepared from oats, used to make porridge etc. **2** a greyish-fawn colour flecked with brown.

**oats** *plural noun* **1** a hardy cereal plant grown in cool climates for food. **2** its grain. **3** (*slang*) sexual gratification; *get one's oats*. □ **sow one's wild oats** lead a life of excess or promiscuity while young.

**OAU** *abbreviation* Organization of African Unity.

**ob.** *abbreviation* (before the date of a person's death) he or she died. (¶ Latin *obiit*.)

**Obadiah** (oh-bă-dy-ă) **1** a Hebrew minor prophet. **2** the shortest book of the Old Testament, bearing his name.

**obbligato** (obli-gah-toh) *noun* (*plural* **obbligatos**) an important accompanying part in a musical composition.

**obdurate** (ob-dewr-ăt) *adjective* stubborn and unyielding. □ **obduracy** *noun*

**OBE** *abbreviation* Order of the British Empire.

**obedient** *adjective* doing what one is told to do, willing to obey. □ **obediently** *adverb*, **obedience** *noun*

**obeisance** (ŏ-bay-săns) *noun* **1** a deep bow or curtsy. **2** homage, deference. □ **obeisant** *adjective*

**obelisk** (ob-ĕl-isk) *noun* **1** a tall pillar, usually with four sides and a tapering top, set up as a monument or landmark. **2** = OBELUS.

**obelus** (ob-il-ŭs) *noun* (*plural* **obeli**, *pronounced* ob-i-ly) a dagger-shaped reference mark (†).

**obese** (oh-beess) *adjective* very fat. □ **obesity** *noun*

**obey** *verb* (**obeyed, obeying**) do what is commanded by (a person, law, instinct, etc.); be obedient.

**obfuscate** (ob-fŭs-kayt) *verb* **1** make (a subject) obscure. **2** bewilder. □ **obfuscation** *noun*

**obituary** (ŏ-bit-yoo-eri) *noun* a notice of a person's death, especially in a newspaper, often with a short account of his or her life and achievements.

**object** *noun* (*pronounced* ob-jikt) **1** something solid that can be seen or touched. **2** a person or thing to which some action or feeling is directed; *an object of pity*. **3** a purpose, an intention; *the object of our mission*. **4** (in grammar) a noun or its equivalent acted upon by a transitive verb or by a preposition (e.g. 'him' is the object in *the dog bit him* and *against him*). ● *verb* (*pronounced* ŏb-**jekt**) say that one is not in favour of something, protest. □ **no object** not acting as a restriction or limitation; *expense is no object*. **object-lesson** *noun* a striking practical illustration of some principle. □ **objector** *noun*

**objectify** *verb* **1** make objective. **2** embody.

**objection** *noun* **1** a feeling of disapproval or opposition; a statement of this. **2** a reason for objecting; a drawback in a plan etc.

**objectionable** *adjective* **1** unpleasant, offensive. **2** open to objection. □ **objectionably** *adverb*

**objective** (ŏb-jek-tiv) *adjective* **1** having real existence outside the mind, not subjective. **2** not influenced by personal feelings or opinions; *an objective account of the problem.* **3** (in grammar) (of a case or word) expressed as the object of a verb or preposition; see OBJECT (sense 4). ● *noun* something one is trying to achieve, reach, or capture. □ **objectively** *adverb*, **objectivity** *noun*

**objet d'art** (ob-*zh*ay **dar**) (*plural* **objets d'art**, *pronounced* same) a small decorative object. (¶ French, = object of art.)

**oblate** (**ob**-layt) *adjective* (of a spheroid) flattened at the poles.

**oblation** (ŏb-**lay**-shŏn) *noun* an offering to a divine being.

**obligate** (**ob**-li-gayt) *verb* oblige (a person) legally or morally to do a specified thing.

**obligation** *noun* **1** being obliged to do something. **2** what one must do in order to comply with an agreement or law etc., one's duty. □ **under an obligation** indebted to another person for some service or benefit.

**obligatory** (ŏ-**blig**-ă-ter-i) *adjective* required by law, rule, or custom; compulsory not optional.

**oblige** *verb* **1** compel by law, agreement, custom, or necessity. **2** help or gratify by performing a small service; *oblige me with a loan.* □ **be obliged to a person** be indebted to him or her for some service. **much obliged** thank you.

**obliging** *adjective* courteous and helpful. □ **obligingly** *adverb*

**oblique** (ŏ-**bleek**) *adjective* **1** slanting. **2** expressed indirectly, not going straight to the point; *an oblique reply.* □ **oblique angle** an acute or obtuse angle. □ **obliquely** *adverb*, **obliqueness** *noun*

**obliterate** (ŏ-**blit**-er-ayt) *verb* blot out, destroy leaving no trace. □ **obliteration** *noun*

**oblivion** (ŏ-**bliv**-iŏn) *noun* **1** the state of being forgotten. **2** the state of being oblivious.

**oblivious** (ŏ-**bliv**-iŭs) *adjective* unaware or unconscious of something; *oblivious of her surroundings.*

**oblong** *noun* a rectangular shape with one pair of sides longer than the other. ● *adjective* having this shape.

**obloquy** (**ob**-lŏ-kwi) *noun* **1** abuse intended to damage a person's reputation. **2** shame, etc. caused by this abuse.

**obnoxious** (ŏb-**nok**-shŭs) *adjective* offensive, objectionable. □ **obnoxiously** *adverb*

**oboe** (**oh**-boh) *noun* a woodwind instrument of treble pitch. □ **oboist** *noun*

**obscene** (ŏb-**seen**) *adjective* **1** offensive or indecent, especially sexually; *an obscene film.* **2** offensive or repugnant, especially morally; *an obscene amount of money.* □ **obscenely** *adverb*

**obscenity** (ŏb-**sen**-iti) *noun* **1** being obscene. **2** an obscene action or word etc.

**obscurantism** (ob-skewr-**ant**-izm) *noun* opposition to knowledge and enlightenment. □ **obscurantist** *noun & adjective*

**obscure** *adjective* **1** dark, indistinct. **2** remote from people's observation. **3** not famous; *an obscure poet.* **4** not easily understood, not clearly expressed. ● *verb* make obscure, conceal from view. □ **obscurely** *adverb*, **obscurity** *noun*, **obscuration** *noun*

**obsequies** (**ob**-si-kwiz) *plural noun* funeral rites.

**obsequious** (ŏb-**see**-kwi-ŭs) *adjective* servile, sickeningly respectful. □ **obsequiously** *adverb*, **obsequiousness** *noun*

**observable** *adjective* able to be observed.

**observance** *noun* **1** the keeping of a law, rule, or custom etc. **2** the keeping or celebrating of a religious festival or of a holiday.

**observant** *adjective* quick at noticing things. □ **observantly** *adverb*

**observation** *noun* **1** observing; being observed. **2** a comment or remark. □ **observational** *adjective*

**observatory** (ŏb-**zerv**-ă-ter-i) *noun* a building designed and equipped for scientific observation of the stars or weather.

**observe** *verb* **1** see and notice; watch carefully. **2** follow or keep (rules etc.). **3** keep or celebrate; *not all countries observe New Year's Day.* **4** remark.

**observer** *noun* **1** a person who observes. **2** an interested spectator. **3** a person attending an event in order to note what happens rather than to participate.

**obsess** (ŏb-**sess**) *verb* occupy the thoughts of (a person) continually.

**obsession** (ŏb-**sesh**-ŏn) *noun* **1** obsessing; being obsessed. **2** a persistent idea that dominates a person's thoughts. □ **obsessional** *adjective*

**obsessive** *adjective* of, causing, or showing obsession. □ **obsessively** *adverb*, **obsessiveness** *noun*

**obsidian** *noun* a dark glassy rock formed from lava.

**obsolescent** (obsŏ-**less**-ĕnt) *adjective* becoming obsolete, going out of use or out of fashion. □ **obsolescence** *noun*

**obsolete** (**ob**-sŏ-leet) *adjective* no longer used, out of date.

**obstacle** *noun* a thing that obstructs progress.

**obstetrician** (ob-stit-**rish**-ăn) *noun* a specialist in obstetrics.

**obstetrics** (ŏb-**stet**-riks) *noun* the branch of medicine and surgery that deals with childbirth. □ **obstetric** *adjective*

**obstinate** *adjective* **1** keeping firmly or stubbornly to an opinion or course of action against advice. **2** not easily removed or treated; *an obstinate cold.* □ **obstinately** *adverb*, **obstinacy** *noun*

**obstreperous** (ŏb-**strep**-er-ŭs) *adjective* noisy, unruly. □ **obstreperously** *adverb*

**obstruct** *verb* **1** block; make movement along or through (a place) difficult or impossible; *obstructing the road.* **2** prevent or hinder the movement or progress of; *obstructing the police.*

**obstruction** *noun* **1** obstructing; being obstructed. **2** a thing that obstructs. **3** (in sport) the act of unlawfully obstructing another player.

**obstructionist** *noun* a person who seeks to obstruct proceedings, legislation, etc.

**obstructive** *adjective* causing or intended to cause obstruction.

**obtain** *verb* **1** get, come into possession of (a thing) by effort or as a gift. **2** be established or in use as a rule or custom; *this custom still obtains in some districts.* □ **obtainable** *adjective*

**obtrude** (ŏb-**trood**) *verb* **1** force (oneself or one's ideas) on others. **2** be or become obtrusive. □ **obtrusion** *noun*

**obtrusive** (ŏb-**troo**-siv) *adjective* obtruding oneself; unpleasantly noticeable. □ **obtrusively** *adverb*

**obtuse** (ŏb-**tewss**) *adjective* **1** of blunt shape, not sharp or pointed. **2** stupid, slow at understanding. □ **obtuse angle** an angle of more than 90° but less than 180°. □ **obtusely** *adverb*, **obtuseness** *noun*

**obverse** (**ob**-verss) *noun* **1** the side of a coin or medal etc. that bears the head or the principal design. **2** the counterpart or opposite of something. **3** the front or top side of a thing.

**obviate** (**ob**-vi-ayt) *verb* get round or do away with (an inconvenience or need).

**obvious** *adjective* easy to see, recognize, or understand. □ **obviously** *adverb*, **obviousness** *noun*

**ocarina** (o-kă-**ree**-nă) *noun* a small egg-shaped musical wind instrument with a mouthpiece and holes for the fingers.

**occasion** *noun* **1** the time at which a particular event takes place. **2** a special event; *this is quite an occasion.* **3** a suitable time for doing something, an opportunity. **4** a need, reason, or cause; *had no occasion to be alarmed.* ● *verb* cause. □ **on occasion** when the need arises, occasionally.

**occasional** *adjective* **1** happening from time to time but not regular or frequent; *occasional showers.* **2** used or meant for a special event; *occasional verses.* □ **occasional table** a small table for use as required. □ **occasionally** *adverb*

**Occident** (**oks**-i-děnt) *noun* (**the Occident**) the West as opposed to the Orient.

**occidental** (oksi-**den**-t'l) *adjective* western. ● *noun* (**Occidental**) a native of the West.

**occiput** (**ok**-si-put) *noun* the back of the head. □ **occipital** (ok-**sip**-i-t'l) *adjective*

**occlude** *verb* **1** stop up, obstruct. **2** *Chem.* absorb and retain (gases). □ **occluded front** a front formed when a cold front overtakes a warm front, driving warm air upwards and producing a long period of steady rain. □ **occlusion** *noun*

**occult** (o-**kult** or **o**-kult) *adjective* **1** involving the supernatural; mystical; *occult powers.* **2** secret, esoteric. ● *noun* (**the occult**) the knowledge and study of supernatural phenomena.

**occupant** *noun* a person occupying a place, dwelling, or position. □ **occupancy** *noun*

**occupation** *noun* **1** occupying; being occupied. **2** taking or holding possession by force, especially of a defeated country or district. **3** an activity that keeps a person busy; one's employment.

**occupational** *adjective* of or caused by one's occupation; *an occupational hazard.* □ **occupational therapy** activity designed to assist recovery from illness or injury.

**occupier** *noun* a person living in a house as its owner or tenant.

**occupy** *verb* (**occupied, occupying**) **1** dwell in, inhabit. **2** take military possession of (a country or strategic position etc.). **3** place oneself in (a building etc.) forcibly or without authority as a protest. **4** take up or fill (space or a position). **5** hold as one's official position; *he occupies the post of manager.* **6** keep (a person or his or her time) busy.

**occur** *verb* (**occurred, occurring**) **1** come into being as an event or process. **2** be found to exist in some place or conditions; *these plants occur in marshy areas.* □ **occur to** come into the mind of.

**occurrence** (ŏ-**ku**-rĕns) *noun* **1** occurring. **2** an incident or event.

**ocean** *noun* **1** the seas surrounding the continents of the earth, especially one of the very large named areas of this, *the Atlantic, Pacific, Indian, Arctic, and Antarctic Oceans.* **2** an immense expanse or amount. □ **ocean-going** *adjective* (of ships) made for crossing the sea, not for coastal or river journeys.

**Oceania** (oh-shi-**ah**-niă) the islands of the Pacific Ocean and adjacent seas. □ **Oceanian** *adjective & noun*

**oceanic** (oh-shi-**an**-ik) *adjective* of the ocean.

**oceanography** (oh-shăn-og-**răfi**) *noun* the scientific study of the ocean. □ **oceanographer** *noun*

**ocelot** (**oh**-sil-ot) *noun* a leopard-like cat of Central and South America.

**oche** (ok-i) *noun* the line from which the player throws in the game of darts.

**ochre** (oh-ker) *noun* (*Amer.* **ocher**) **1** a yellow, red, or brownish mineral consisting of clay and iron oxide, used as a pigment. **2** pale brownish-yellow. □ **ochreous** *adjective*, **ochrous** *adjective*

**o'clock** *adverb* of the clock (used in specifying the hour); *six o'clock.*

**OCR** *abbreviation* optical character recognition (or reader).

**Oct.** *abbreviation* October.

**octagon** (ok-tă-gŏn) *noun* a geometric figure with eight sides. □ **octagonal** (ok-**tag**-ŏn-ăl) *adjective*

**octahedron** (oktă-**hee**-drŏn) *noun* a solid geometric shape with eight faces.

**octane** (ok-tayn) *noun* a hydrocarbon compound occurring in petrol. □ **high-octane** *adjective* (of fuel) having a high octane number and therefore good antiknock properties. **octane number** *or* **rating** a measure of the antiknock properties of a petrol.

**octave** (ok-tiv) *noun* **1** a series of eight consecutive notes on a scale, between and including the upper and lower note. **2** the interval between the upper and lower note. **3** each of these two notes. **4** these two notes played together. **5** a verse of eight lines.

**octavo** (ok-**tay**-voh) *noun* (*plural* **octavos**) **1** the size of a book or page given by folding a sheet of standard size three times to form eight leaves. **2** a book or page of this size.

**octet** (ok-tet) *noun* a group of eight instruments or voices; a musical composition for these.

**octo-** *combining form* eight.

**October** the tenth month of the year.

**octogenarian** (ok-toh-jin-**air**-iăn) *noun* a person who is in his or her eighties.

**octopus** *noun* (*plural* **octopuses**) a sea animal with a soft body and eight long tentacles.

**ocular** (ok-yoo-ler) *adjective* of, for, or by the eyes; visual.

**oculist** (ok-yoo-list) *noun* a specialist in the treatment of diseases and defects of the eyes.

**OD** (*slang*) *noun* a drug overdose. ● *verb* (**OD'd**, **OD'ing**) take a drug overdose.

**odalisque** (oh-dăl-isk) *noun* (*old use*) a female slave in a harem.

**odd** *adjective* **1** unusual, strange, eccentric; *a very odd idea.* **2** casual, occasional; *odd jobs; at odd moments.* **3** unexpected, unconnected; *picks up odd bargains.* **4** (of a number) not even, not divisible by two. **5** remaining from a pair or set; *an odd glove.* **6** (following a number) somewhat more than; *forty-odd people.* □ **odd man** *or*

**one out** a person or thing differing in some way from others of a group. □ **oddly** *adverb*, **oddness** *noun*

**oddball** *noun* (*informal*) an eccentric person.

**oddity** *noun* **1** strangeness. **2** an unusual person, thing, or event.

**oddment** *noun* something left over, an isolated article.

**odds** *plural noun* **1** the probability that a certain thing will happen; this expressed as a ratio; *the odds are 5 to 1 against throwing a six.* **2** the ratio between amounts staked by parties to a bet; *gave odds of 3 to 1.* □ **at odds with** in disagreement or conflict with. **make** *or* **be no odds** make no difference. **odds and ends** oddments. **odds-on** *adjective* with success more likely than failure; with betting odds in favour of its success; *the odds-on favourite.* **over the odds** above the normal price etc.

**ode** *noun* a poem expressing noble feelings, often addressed to a person or celebrating an event.

**Odessa** (oh-**dess**-ă) a Ukrainian city and seaport on the NW coast of the Black Sea.

**Odin** (oh-din) (*Scand. myth.*) the supreme god and creator.

**odious** (oh-di-ŭs) *adjective* hateful, detestable. □ **odiously** *adverb*, **odiousness** *noun*

**odium** (oh-di-ŭm) *noun* widespread hatred or disgust felt towards a person or actions.

**odometer** (od-**om**-it-er) *noun* (*Amer.*) = MILOMETER.

**odoriferous** (oh-der-**if**-er-ŭs) *adjective* bearing a fragrant odour.

**odour** (oh-der) *noun* (*Amer.* **odor**) a smell. □ **in good** (*or* **bad**) **odour** in good (or bad) repute or favour. □ **odorous** *adjective*, **odourless** *adjective*

**Odysseus** (ŏ-**dis**-iŭs) (*Gk. legend*) king of Ithaca (called Ulysses by the Romans) whose ten-year journey home after the Trojan Wars is the subject of the Odyssey.

**odyssey** (od-iss-i) *noun* (*plural* **odysseys**) **1** a long adventurous journey. **2** (**the Odyssey**) a Greek epic poem telling of the wanderings of Odysseus.

**OECD** *abbreviation* Organization for Economic Cooperation and Development.

**oedema** (i-dee-mă) *noun* (*Amer.* **edema**) excess of fluid in the tissues, causing swelling.

**Oedipus complex** (ee-dip-ŭs) sexual feeling towards one's parents, involving attraction to the parent of the opposite sex (especially the mother) and jealousy of the other parent. □ **Oedipal** *adjective* (¶ Named after Oedipus in Greek legend, who, unaware of his own identity, unknowingly killed his father and married his mother.)

**o'er** *preposition & adverb* (*poetic*) over.

**oesophagus** (ee-sof-ă-gŭs) noun (Amer. **esophagus**) (plural **oesophagi** or **oesophaguses**) the canal from the mouth to the stomach; the gullet.

**oestrogen** (ees-trŏ-jĕn) noun (Amer. **estrogen**) a sex hormone responsible for developing and maintaining female bodily characteristics.

**of** preposition used to indicate relationships. **1** originating from or caused by; the works of Shakespeare; died of starvation. **2** containing or made from; built of bricks. **3** belonging to or connected with; the car of the future; items of clothing; chief of police. **4** identified or specified as; the city of Glasgow; a pint of milk; a giant of a man. **5** removed or separated from; north of the border; got rid of them; robbed her of £100. **6** referring to; beware of the dog; accused of murder; short of money. **7** specifying an object; a love of music; in search of happiness. **8** dividing, classifying, or including; part of the story; this sort of thing. **9** representing a quality or condition; a woman of good taste; a boy of seven; on the point of leaving. **10** (Amer.) before a specified hour; a quarter of three. □ **of itself** by itself or in itself.

**off** adverb **1** away, at or to a distance; rode off; 3 years off. **2** out of position, not touching or attached, separate; take the lid off. **3** disconnected, not functioning, no longer obtainable, cancelled; turn the gas off; the wedding is off; take the day off. **4** to the end, completely, so as to be clear; finish off; sell them off. **5** situated as regards money or supplies; well off. **6** (in a theatre) behind or at the side(s) of the stage; noises off. **7** (of food) beginning to decay. ●preposition **1** from, away from, not on; fell off a ladder. **2** not attracted to or involved with for the time being; off his food; off duty. **3** leading from, not far from; in a street off the Strand. **4** deducted from; £5 off the price. **5** at sea a short distance from; sank off Cape Horn. ●adjective **1** (of a part of a vehicle, horse, or road) on the right-hand side; the off front wheel. **2** of the side of a cricket field to the right-hand side of the wicket-keeper, opposite the leg side. ●noun **1** the off side in cricket. **2** the start of a race etc.; ready for the off. □ **off and on** now and then. **off chance** a slight possibility. **off colour** **1** unwell. **2** (Amer.) indelicate or indecent. **off-day** noun a day when a person is not at his or her best. **off-key** adjective out of tune. **off-licence** noun **1** a shop selling alcoholic drinks. **2** the licence to do this. **off-peak** adjective in or used outside times when demand is greatest; off-peak electricity. **off-putting** adjective repellent, disconcerting. **off-roading** noun driving on dirt tracks and other unmetalled surfaces as a sport or leisure activity. **off-season** noun the time

when business etc. is slack. **off-stage** adjective & adverb not on the stage; not visible to the audience. **off white** white with a grey or yellowish tinge.

■**Usage** Avoid the use of off of for the preposition off (e.g. picked it up off of the floor).

**offal** noun **1** the less valuable edible parts of an animal, especially the entrails and internal organs. **2** rubbish, scraps.

**offbeat** adjective unusual, unconventional. ●noun Music an unaccented beat in a bar.

**offcut** noun a remnant of timber etc.

**Offenbach** (off-ĕn-bahk), Jacques (original name: Jacques Eberst) (1819–80), German-born French composer, noted especially for his opera Orpheus in the Underworld.

**offence** noun (Amer. **offense**) **1** breaking of the law, an illegal act. **2** a feeling of annoyance or resentment; take offence.

**offend** verb **1** cause offence or displeasure to. **2** do wrong; offend against the law. □ **offender** noun

**offensive** adjective **1** causing offence, insulting; offensive remarks. **2** disgusting, repulsive; an offensive smell. **3** used in attacking, aggressive; offensive weapons. ●noun an aggressive action or campaign; go on the offensive. □ **offensively** adverb, **offensiveness** noun

**offer** verb (**offered, offering**) **1** present (a thing) so that it may be accepted, rejected, or considered. **2** state what one is willing to do, pay, or give. **3** show for sale. **4** provide, give opportunity; the job offers prospects of promotion. **5** show an intention; the dog didn't offer to bark. ●noun **1** an expression of willingness to give, do, or pay something. **2** an amount offered; offers above £500. □ **on offer** for sale at a certain price or at a reduced price.

**offering** noun a gift or contribution etc. that is offered.

**offertory** noun **1** the act of offering bread and wine for consecration at the Eucharist. **2** money collected in a religious service.

**offhand** adjective (of behaviour etc.) casual or curt. ●adverb without previous thought or preparation; I couldn't say offhand. □ **offhanded** adjective, **offhandedly** adverb, **offhandedness** noun

**office** noun **1** a room or building used as a place of business, especially for clerical and administrative work. **2** the staff working there. **3** a particular room or area of a business; ticket office; our London office. **4** (**Office**) the premises, staff, or authority of certain government departments; the Foreign Office. **5** a position of authority or trust, the holding of an official position; hold office. **6** an authorized form of Chris-

tian worship; *the Office for the Dead.*
**7** (usually as **offices**) a piece of kindness
or a service; *through the good offices of his
friends.* □ **office block** a large building
designed to contain business offices. **office
hours** the hours or times during which a
business is open.

**officer** *noun* **1** a person holding a position of
authority or trust, an official; *customs
officers.* **2** a person who holds authority in
any of the armed services (especially with a
commission), in the emergency services, in
the Merchant Navy, or on a passenger
ship. **3** a policeman or policewoman.

**official** *adjective* **1** of an office or position of
authority; *in his official capacity.* **2** suitable
for or characteristic of officials and bureaucracy; *official red tape.* **3** properly
authorized; *the news is official.* ● *noun* a person holding office. □ **official secrets**
protected information involving national
security. □ **officially** *adverb*

**officialdom** *noun* officials collectively.

**officialese** *noun* (*scornful*) the formal long-
winded language used in official
documents.

**officiate** (ŏ-**fish**-i-ayt) *verb* act in an official
capacity, be in charge.

**officious** (ŏ-**fish**-ŭs) *adjective* asserting one's
authority, bossy. □ **officiously** *adverb*

**offing** *noun* □ **in the offing** not far away in
distance or future time.

**offline** *adjective & adverb* (of a computer terminal or process) not online; not directly
controlled by or connected to a central
processor.

**offload** *verb* get rid of (something unwelcome or unpleasant) by passing responsibility to someone else.

**offprint** *noun* a printed copy of an article etc.
originally forming part of a larger publication.

**offset** *verb* (**offset**, **offsetting**) counterbalance or compensate for. ● *noun* **1** an
offshoot. **2** a method of printing in which
the ink is transferred to a rubber surface
and from this to paper; *offset lithography.*

**offshoot** *noun* **1** a side-shoot. **2** a subsidiary
product, organization, etc.

**offshore** *adjective & adverb* **1** at sea some distance from the shore. **2** (of wind) blowing
from the land towards the sea.

**offside** *adjective & adverb* (of a player in football
etc.) in a position where he or she may not
legally play the ball. ● *noun* the side of a
vehicle that is normally furthest from the
kerb, in Britain the right side (compare
NEARSIDE).

**offspring** *noun* (*plural* **offspring**) **1** the child
or children of a person. **2** the young of an
animal. **3** a result or outcome.

**oft** *adverb* (*old use*) often.

**often** *adverb* **1** frequently, many times, at
short intervals. **2** in many instances.

**ogee** (**oh**-jee) *noun* **1** the line of a double
continuous curve, as in S. **2** a moulding
with such a section.

**ogive** (**oh**-jyv) *noun* **1** a diagonal groin or rib
of a vault. **2** a pointed arch.

**ogle** (**oh**-gŭl) *verb* look flirtatiously or lustfully (at). ● *noun* such a look.

**ogre** *noun* **1** a cruel or man-eating giant in
fairy tales and legends. **2** a terrifying person.

**ogress** *noun* a female ogre.

**OH** *abbreviation* Ohio.

**oh** *interjection* **1** an exclamation of surprise,
pain, entreaty, etc.

**Ohio** (oh-**hy**-oh) a State of the north-eastern
USA.

**ohm** (*rhymes with* Rome) *noun* a unit of electrical resistance. (¶ Named after the German physicist G. S. Ohm (1789–1854).)

**OHMS** *abbreviation* On Her (or His) Majesty's
Service.

**oho** *interjection* an exclamation of surprise or
delight.

**OHP** *abbreviation* overhead projector.

**oi** *interjection* an exclamation to attract
someone's attention, express alarm, etc.

**oil** *noun* **1** a thick slippery liquid that will not
dissolve in water and is often inflammable.
**2** petroleum; a form of this used as fuel;
*oil-heater.* **3** (also **oils**) oil paint. **4** an oil
painting. **5** (**oils**) oilskins. ● *verb* apply oil
to, lubricate or treat with oil. □ **oil-fired**
*adjective* using oil as fuel. **oil paint** paint
made by mixing powdered pigment in oil.
**oil painting 1** the practice or technique of
using oil-paint. **2** a picture painted using
oil paints. **oil rig** a structure equipped for
drilling oil wells and extracting oil. **oil
slick** a patch of oil, especially on the sea.
**oil-tanker** *noun* a ship for transporting fuel
oil in bulk. **oil the wheels** make things go
smoothly by tactful behaviour or flattery
etc. **oil well** a well yielding mineral oil.

**oilcake** *noun* cattle food made from linseed
or similar seeds after the oil has been
pressed out.

**oilcan** *noun* a can with a long nozzle through
which oil flows, used for oiling machinery.

**oilcloth** *noun* strong fabric treated with oil to
make it waterproof.

**oiled** *adjective* (*slang*) drunk.

**oilfield** *noun* an area where oil is found in the
ground or beneath the sea.

**oilskin** *noun* **1** cloth waterproofed by treatment with oil. **2** (**oilskins**) waterproof
clothing made of this.

**oily** *adjective* (**oilier**, **oiliest**) **1** of or like oil;
covered in oil; containing much oil.
**2** unpleasantly smooth in manner; trying to
win favour by flattery. □ **oiliness** *noun*

**ointment** *noun* a smooth greasy paste rubbed on the skin as a medicine or cosmetic.

**Oireachtas** (eer-ăk-thăs) *noun* the legislature of the Republic of Ireland, consisting of the President, Dáil, and Seanad. (¶ Irish, = assembly.)

**OK¹** (also **okay**) (*informal*) *adjective* all right, satisfactory. ●*adverb* well, satisfactorily. ●*noun* (*plural* **OKs**) approval, agreement to a plan etc. ●*verb* (**OK'd**, **OK'ing**) give one's approval or agreement to.

**OK²** *abbreviation* Oklahoma.

**okapi** (ŏ-kah-pi) *noun* (*plural* **okapis**) an animal of Central Africa, like a giraffe but with a shorter neck and a striped body.

**okay** alternative spelling of OK.

**O'Keeffe**, Georgia (1887–1986), American artist.

**Okla.** *abbreviation* Oklahoma.

**Oklahoma** a State of the south central USA.

**okra** (oh-kră) *noun* a tropical plant with seed pods that are used as a vegetable.

**old** *adjective* **1** having lived or existed for a long time. **2** made long ago; used, established, or known for a long time. **3** shabby from age or wear. **4** of a specified age; *ten years old*; *a ten-year-old*. **5** belonging to the past; not recent or modern; *in the old days*. **6** former, original; *in its old place*. **7** skilled through long experience; *an old campaigner*. **8** (*informal*) used for emphasis in friendly or casual mention; *good old Winnie*. □ **the old** people. **of old** of, in, or from former times; *we know him of old*. **old age** the period of a person's life from about 65 or 70 onwards. **old-age pension** a State pension paid to people above retirement age. **old-age pensioner** a person receiving this. **Old Bailey** the Central Criminal Court in London. **Old Bill** (*slang*) the police. **old boy 1** a former member of a school. **2** (*informal*) an elderly man. **3** a man or male animal regarded affectionately. **old boy network** discrimination in employment, especially favouring fellow ex-pupils of public schools. **old country** a native country. **Old English** = ANGLO-SAXON (sense 2). **old-fashioned** *adjective* **1** in a fashion that is no longer in style. **2** having the ways or tastes of former times. **old girl 1** a former member of a school. **2** (*informal*) an elderly woman. **3** a woman or female animal regarded affectionately. **Old Glory** (*Amer.*) the US national flag. **old gold** dull gold colour. **old guard** the original or most conservative members of a group. **old hand** an experienced or well-practised person. **old hat** (*informal*) tediously familiar or outdated. **old maid** an elderly spinster. **old-maidish** *adjective* fussy and prim. **old man** (*informal*) one's employer, manager, husband, or father. **old man's beard** a kind of clematis with masses of grey fluffy hairs round the seeds. **old master 1** a great painter of former times (especially the 13th–17th centuries in Europe). **2** a painting by such a painter. **Old Nick** the Devil. **old school** traditional attitudes or those people having them. **old school tie** excessive loyalty to traditional values and to those having them, especially amongst ex-pupils of public schools. **Old Testament** *see* TESTAMENT. **old-time** *adjective* belonging to former times. **old-timer** *noun* a person with long experience or standing. **old wives' tale** an old and superstitious or foolish belief. **old woman 1** (*informal*) one's wife or mother. **2** a fussy or timid man. **Old World** Europe, Asia, and Africa, as distinct from the Americas. □ **oldish** *adjective*, **oldness** *noun*

**olden** *adjective* (*old use*) old; of old.

**oldie** *noun* (*informal*) an old person or thing.

**Olduvai Gorge** (ol-duuv-I) a gorge in northern Tanzania, famous for its fossils of the Pleistocene period, including those of early humans.

**oleaginous** (oh-li-aj-in-ŭs) *adjective* **1** like oil; producing oil. **2** oily in texture or in manner.

**oleander** (oh-li-an-der) *noun* a poisonous evergreen shrub of Mediterranean regions, with red, white, or pink flowers.

**O level** = ORDINARY LEVEL.

**olfactory** (ol-fak-ter-i) *adjective* concerned with smelling; *olfactory organs*.

**oligarch** (ol-i-gark) *noun* a member of an oligarchy.

**oligarchy** (ol-i-gar-ki) *noun* **1** a form of government in which power is in the hands of a few people. **2** these people. **3** a country governed in this way. □ **oligarchic** *adjective*, **oligarchical** *adjective*

**Oligocene** (ol-ig-ŏ-seen) *adjective* of the third geological epoch of the Tertiary period. ●*noun* this period.

**olive** *noun* **1** a small oval fruit with a hard stone and bitter pulp from which an oil (*olive oil*) is obtained. **2** the evergreen tree that bears it. **3** = OLIVE GREEN. ●*adjective* **1** = OLIVE GREEN. **2** (of the complexion) yellowish-brown. □ **olive branch** something done or offered to show one's desire to make peace. **olive green** dull yellowish green.

**Olivier** (ŏ-liv-i-ay), Laurence Kerr, Baron (1907–89), English stage and film actor and director.

**olivine** (ol-i-veen) *noun* a mineral that is usually olive green in colour.

**Olympiad** (ŏ-**limp**-i-ad) *noun* **1** a period of four years between Olympic Games, used by the ancient Greeks in dating events. **2** a staging of the modern Olympic Games. **3** a regular international contest in chess etc.

**Olympian** (ŏ-**limp**-i-ăn) *adjective* **1** of Olympus; celestial. **2** (of manners etc.) majestic and imposing. **3** Olympic. •*noun* **1** any of the Greek gods dwelling on Olympus. **2** a person of superhuman attainments or great calm.

**Olympic** (ŏ-**limp**-ik) *adjective* of the Olympic Games. •*plural noun* (**the Olympics**) the Olympic Games. □ **Olympic Games** an ancient Greek sporting and cultural festival held at Olympia every four years and revived since 1896 as a four-yearly international athletic and sports meeting.

**Olympus** (ŏ-**limp**-ŭs) a mountain in NE Greece, the home of the gods in Greek mythology.

**OM** *abbreviation* Order of Merit.

**om** (in Buddhism and Hinduism etc.) a mystic syllable considered the most sacred mantra.

**Oman** (ŏ-**mahn**) a country in Arabia. □ **Omani** (ŏ-**mah**-ni) *adjective & noun* (*plural* **Omanis**).

**Omar Khayyám** (oh-mar ky-**ahm**) (died 1123), Persian poet, mathematician, and astronomer.

**ombudsman** (om-buudz-măn) *noun* (*plural* **ombudsmen**) an official appointed to investigate complaints by individuals against public authorities.

**omega** (oh-mig-ă) *noun* **1** the last letter of the Greek alphabet (Ω, ω). **2** the last of a series; the final development.

**omelette** (**om**-lit) *noun* a dish made of beaten eggs fried and often served with a filling.

**omen** (oh-men) *noun* an event regarded as a prophetic sign of good or evil.

**ominous** (**om**-in-ŭs) *adjective* **1** looking or seeming as if trouble is at hand; *an ominous silence*. **2** giving or being an omen, predictive. □ **ominously** *adverb*

**omission** *noun* **1** omitting; being omitted. **2** something that has been omitted or not done.

**omit** *verb* (**omitted, omitting**) **1** leave out, not insert or include. **2** leave undone, neglect or fail to do.

**omnibus** *noun* **1** (*formal*) a bus. **2** a volume containing a number of books or stories previously published separately. •*adjective* comprising several items; *omnibus edition*.

**omnipotent** (ŏm-**nip**-ŏ-tĕnt) *adjective* having unlimited or very great power. □ **omnipotence** *noun*

**omnipresent** *adjective* present everywhere. □ **omnipresence** *noun*

**omniscient** (om-**niss**-i-ĕnt) *adjective* knowing everything, having very extensive knowledge. □ **omniscience** *noun*

**omnivorous** (om-**niv**-er-ŭs) *adjective* **1** feeding on both plants and animal flesh. **2** reading, observing, etc. everything indiscriminately.

**on** *preposition* **1** supported by, attached to, covering, or around; *sat on a chair; a fly on the wall; rings on her fingers*. **2** about one's person; *have you got a pen on you?* **3** at or during a specified time or event; *on 11 March; on my birthday*. **4** immediately after or before; *I was met on my arrival*. **5** as a result of; *on further investigation*. **6** in a specified group or location; *on the committee; on the Continent*. **7** living or operating by means of; *living on a grant; lives on chips; runs on gas*. **8** close to or alongside; *a house on the sea; lives on the main road*. **9** against; *marched on Rome; pulled a gun on me*. **10** with a specified basis or reason; *on good authority; arrested on suspicion of murder*. **11** concerning or about; *a book on computers*. **12** involved in a specified process; *on holiday; on strike*. **13** using (a drug); *on antibiotics; on heroin*. **14** played or broadcast by means of; *a tune on the piano; a programme on television*. **15** so as to affect (a person, group, etc.); *walked out on her; burst in on them*. **16** paid for by; *this round is on me*. **17** added to; *5p on a pint of beer*. •*adverb* **1** (so as to be) covering or in contact; *put your coat on*. **2** in the appropriate direction; towards something; *looked on from the balcony; come on in*. **3** forward; *head on; side on*. **4** further forward or advanced; *time is getting on; later on*. **5** continuing in an activity; *the band played on; keeps on complaining*. **6** operating or active; *leave the light on; the search is on*. **7** due to take place as planned; *is the party still on?* **8** (of a person making an offer or challenge) accepted; *you're on!* **9** (of an idea or suggestion) unacceptable or impracticable; *it's just not on*. **10** being broadcast or performed; *a good film on tonight*. **11** (of an actor) on stage; (of an employee) on duty. •*adjective* of the part of a cricket field to the striker's side and in front of the wicket. •*noun Cricket* the on side. □ **be on at** (*informal*) nag. **be on to** realize the significance of (a thing) or the intentions of (a person). **on and off** from time to time, not continually. **on and on** continuing, continually. **on to** to a position on (*see* ONTO).

**onager** (**on**-ăg-er) *noun* a wild ass.

**onanism** *noun* (*literary*) masturbation.

**Onassis** (ŏ-**nas**-iss), Aristotle Socrates (1906–75), Greek shipping magnate and international businessman.

**ONC** *abbreviation* (*Brit.*) Ordinary National Certificate.

**once** *adverb* **1** on one occasion only; *only read it once.* **2** at some time in the past; *I once had a car.* **3** ever or at all; *once a thief, always a thief.* **4** multiplied by one. ● *conjunction* as soon as; *once he had gone she cheered up.* ● *noun* one time or occasion; *just this once.* □ **all at once 1** suddenly. **2** all together. **at once 1** immediately. **2** simultaneously. **for once** on one particular occasion, even if at no other time. **once and for all** finally, especially after hesitation. **once** (*or* **every once**) **in a while** from time to time. **once or twice** a few times. **once-over** *noun* (*informal*) a quick inspection. **once upon a time** at some unspecified time in the past.

**oncogene** (on-kŏ-jeen) *noun* a gene which can transform a cell into a cancer cell.

**oncology** (onk-ol-ŏji) *noun* the scientific study of tumours.

**oncoming** *adjective* approaching.

**OND** *abbreviation* (*Brit.*) Ordinary National Diploma.

**one** *adjective* **1** single in number. **2** a particular person or thing of the kind described; *that's a nice one.* **3** particular but undefined; *one thing led to another; one day.* **4** only; *the one thing I can't stand.* **5** forming a unity. **6** identical, the same; *of one mind.* ● *noun* **1** the smallest whole number. **2** a single thing or person; *the red shirt and the green one.* **3** (*informal*) a joke or story; *the one about the piano player's monkey.* ● *pronoun* **1** a person; *loved ones.* **2** any person; the speaker or writer as representing people in general; *one doesn't want to seem mean.* □ **at one** in agreement. **one and all** everyone. **one another** each other. **one-armed bandit** a fruit machine worked by a long handle at the side. **one by one** singly; one at a time. **one-horse** *adjective* (*informal*) small or insignificant; *a one-horse town.* **one-liner** *noun* a joke or witty remark consisting of a single short sentence. **one-man** *adjective* involving or operated by one person. **one-night stand 1** a single performance in a place by actors, musicians, etc. **2** a sexual encounter lasting only one night. **one-off** (*adjective*) made or done as the only one, not reproduced or repeated; (*noun*) a one-off event, object, achievement, etc. **one or two** a few. **one-sided** *adjective* **1** unfair; favouring only one side. **2** uneven; having all the advantage on one side. **one-up** *adjective* having a particular advantage. **one-upmanship** *noun* the practice or skill of maintaining a psychological advantage over others. **one-way** *adjective* allowing movement or travel in one direction only; *one-way street; one-way ticket.*

**O'Neill**, Eugene Gladstone (1888–1953), American playwright.

**oneness** *noun* **1** singleness. **2** uniqueness. **3** agreement. **4** sameness.

**onerous** (oh-ner-ŭs) *adjective* burdensome.

**oneself** *pronoun* the emphatic and reflexive form of one; *do it oneself; ask oneself.* □ **be oneself** act in one's normal manner. **by oneself** alone; unaided.

**ongoing** *adjective* continuing to exist or progress.

**onion** *noun* a vegetable with an edible rounded bulb that has a strong smell and strong flavour. □ **know one's onions** (*slang*) know one's subject or one's job thoroughly. □ **oniony** *adjective*

**online** *adjective* & *adverb* *Computing* directly controlled by or connected to a central processor allowing information to be sent, received, or processed immediately.

**onlooker** *noun* a spectator. □ **onlooking** *adjective*

**only** *adjective* **1** existing alone, with no others of its or their kind; *the only coat I've got; an only child.* **2** the best, with no others worth considering; *it's the only place to eat.* ● *adverb* **1** solely, merely, with nothing or no one else; *I'm only looking; it's only me.* **2** no longer ago than; *saw him only yesterday.* **3** not until; *arrives only on Monday.* **4** with no better result than; *hurried home only to find her gone.* ● *conjunction* but, except that; *I would go, only I'm too tired.* □ **only too** extremely; *we'll be only too pleased.*

**o.n.o.** *abbreviation* or near offer.

**onomatopoeia** (on-ŏ-mat-ŏ-pee-ă) *noun* the formation of words that imitate or suggest the sounds that they stand for, e.g. *cuckoo, plop, sizzle.* □ **onomatopoeic** *adjective*

**onrush** *noun* an onward rush.

**onscreen** *adjective* & *adverb* **1** appearing on a cinema, television, or computer screen. **2** within the range of a film camera; being filmed.

**onset** *noun* **1** a beginning; *the onset of winter.* **2** an attack or assault.

**onshore** *adjective* **1** (of wind) blowing from the sea towards the land. **2** on land.

**onside** *adjective* & *adverb* not offside.

**onslaught** (on-slawt) *noun* a fierce attack.

**Ont.** *abbreviation* Ontario.

**Ontario** (on-tair-i-oh) a province of SE Canada. □ **Lake Ontario** one of the Great Lakes between Canada and the USA.

**onto** *preposition* to a position on.

■**Usage** Many people prefer not to use *onto*, and write *on to* in all cases. Note that *onto* cannot be used where *on* is an adverb, e.g. *we walked on to the river* (= continued walking until we reached it).

**ontology** (on-**tol**-ŏji) *noun* a branch of philosophy dealing with the nature of being. □ **ontological** *adjective*

**onus** (oh-nŭs) *noun* (*plural* **onuses**) the duty or responsibility of doing something.

**onward** *adjective & adverb* (also **onwards**) with an advancing motion; further on.

**onyx** (on-iks) *noun* a stone like marble with different colours in layers.

**oodles** *noun* (*informal*) a great quantity.

**ooh** *interjection* an exclamation of surprise, pleasure, or pain.

**oolite** (oh-ŏ-lyt) *noun* a granular form of limestone. □ **oolitic** *adjective*

**oompah** *noun* (*informal*) a rhythmical sound of deep brass instruments.

**oomph** *noun* (*informal*) energy or enthusiasm.

**oops** *interjection* an exclamation on falling or making an obvious mistake etc.

**ooze** *verb* **1** (of liquid) trickle or flow out slowly. **2** (of a substance or wound etc.) exude a liquid; allow to trickle out slowly. **3** show (a feeling) freely; *ooze confidence.* ● *noun* wet mud.

**op** *noun* (*informal*) an operation.

**op.** *abbreviation* opus.

**opacity** (ŏ-**pas**-iti) *noun* being opaque.

**opal** *noun* a semiprecious stone usually of a milky or bluish colour with iridescent reflections.

**opalescent** (oh-pă-**less**-ĕnt) *adjective* iridescent like an opal. □ **opalescence** *noun*

**opaque** (ŏ-**payk**) *adjective* **1** not transparent, not allowing light to pass through. **2** (of a statement etc.) not clear.

**op art** art in a style using geometric patterns and optical effects to give an illusion of movement. (¶ The word *op* is short for *optical*.)

**op. cit.** *abbreviation* in the work already quoted.

**OPEC** (oh-pek) *abbreviation* Organization of Petroleum Exporting Countries.

**open** *adjective* **1** not closed or blocked up; not sealed or locked. **2** not enclosed or confined; *the open road.* **3** uncovered or unprotected; *open drain*; *open goal.* **4** undisguised, public; *open hostility.* **5** spread out, unfolded. **6** with wide spaces between solid parts; *open texture.* **7** honest, direct, open-minded. **8** admitting visitors or customers, ready for business. **9** not restricted to particular categories of people, or to members; *open scholarship*; *open meeting.* **10** (foll. by *to*) available; *three options are open to us*; *I'm open to offers.* **11** vulnerable; *open to abuse.* **12** (of a return ticket) not restricted in the date of travel. ● *noun* an open championship or competition. ● *verb* **1** make or become open or more open. **2** (of a door, room etc.) give access as specified; *opened on to a patio.* **3** begin or

establish, make a start; *open a business*; to *open fire.* **4** ceremonially declare (a building etc.) to be open to the public. □ **the open** open space; open country; open air. **in the open air** not inside a house or building. **open-air** *adjective* taking place in the open air. **open-and-shut** *adjective* perfectly straightforward. **open day** a day when the public may visit a place that is not normally open to them. **open-door** *adjective* open, accessible to all; *open-door management.* **open-ended** *adjective* with no fixed limit; *an open-ended discussion.* **open-handed** *adjective* generous. **open-heart surgery** surgery with the heart exposed and with blood circulating temporarily through a bypass. **open house** hospitality to all comers. **open letter** a letter of comment or protest addressed to a person by name but printed in a newspaper. **open mind** a mind that is unprejudiced or undecided. **open-minded** *adjective* accessible to new ideas, unprejudiced. **open-mouthed** *adjective* having an expression of surprise or shock. **open-plan** *adjective* (of a house, office, etc.) having large undivided rooms. **open prison** a prison with few physical restraints on the prisoners. **open question** a matter on which no final verdict has yet been made or on which none is possible. **open sandwich** a sandwich without a top slice of bread. **open secret** one known to so many people that it is no longer a secret. **Open University** (*Brit.*) a university teaching mainly by broadcasts and correspondence, open to all, including those without academic qualifications. **open up 1** unlock. **2** make accessible. **3** speak freely. **4** accelerate. **5** begin shooting. **open verdict** a verdict that does not specify whether a crime is involved in the case of a person's death. **with open arms** with an enthusiastic welcome. □ **openness** *noun*

**opencast** *adjective* (of a mine or mining) with layers of earth removed from the surface and worked from above, not from shafts.

**opener** *noun* **1** a person or thing that opens something. **2** a device for opening tins or bottles.

**opening** *noun* **1** a space or gap; a place where something opens. **2** the beginning of something. **3** an opportunity.

**openly** *adverb* without concealment, publicly, frankly.

**openwork** *noun* a pattern with spaces between threads or strips of metal etc.

**opera** *noun* **1** a play in which the words are sung to a musical accompaniment. **2** dramatic works of this kind. **3** an opera house. ● *plural noun see* OPUS. □ **opera-glasses** *plural noun* small binoculars for use at the opera or theatre. **opera house** a theatre for operas.

**operable** *adjective* **1** able to be operated. **2** able to be treated by a surgical operation.

**operate** *verb* **1** be in action; produce an effect; *the new tax operates to our advantage.* **2** control the functioning of; *he operates the lift.* **3** perform a surgical operation. **4** conduct a military or similar operation. □ **operating system** the basic software that enables a computer program to be run. **operating theatre** a room for surgical operations.

**operatic** *adjective* of or like opera.

**operation** *noun* **1** operating; being operated. **2** the way a thing works. **3** a piece of work, something to be done. **4** strategic military activities in war or during manoeuvres. **5** an act of surgery performed on a patient.

**operational** *adjective* **1** of, engaged in, or used in operations. **2** able to function; *is the system operational yet?* □ **operational research** the analysis of problems encountered in business and industry.

**operative** *adjective* **1** having an effect, working or functioning. **2** of surgical operations. ●*noun* a worker, especially in a factory.

**operator** *noun* **1** a person who operates a machine; one who engages in business or runs a business etc. **2** one who makes connections of lines at a telephone exchange. **3** (*informal*) a person acting in a specified way; *a smooth operator.* **4** a symbol or function denoting an operation in maths, computing, etc.

**operculum** (ŏ-**per**-kyoo-lŭm) *noun* (*plural* **opercula**) a flap covering the gills of a fish; any other flap-like cover on a plant or animal.

**operetta** *noun* a short or light opera.

**ophthalmia** (off-**thal**-miă) *noun* inflammation of the eye, conjunctivitis.

**ophthalmic** (off-**thal**-mik) *adjective* of or for the eyes. □ **ophthalmic optician** an optician qualified to prescribe as well as dispense spectacles, etc.

**ophthalmology** (off-thal-**mol**-ŏji) *noun* the study of the eye and its diseases. □ **ophthalmologist** *noun*

**ophthalmoscope** (off-**thal**-mŏ-skohp) *noun* an instrument for examining the retina and other parts of the eye.

**opiate** (**oh**-piăt) *noun* **1** a sedative drug containing opium. **2** a thing that soothes the feelings or dulls activity.

**opine** (oh-**pyn**) *verb* (*literary*) express or hold as one's opinion.

**opinion** *noun* **1** an unproven belief or judgement; a view held as probable. **2** what one thinks on a particular point; *your opinion on capital punishment.* **3** a judgement or

observation given by an expert. **4** an estimation; *have a low opinion of him.* □ **opinion poll** an assessment of public opinion made by questioning a representative sample of people.

**opinionated** *adjective* having strong opinions and holding them obstinately.

**opium** *noun* an addictive drug made from the juice of certain poppies and used in medicine as a sedative and pain-killer.

**opossum** (ŏ-**poss**-ŭm) *noun* a small furry American or Australian marsupial that lives in trees.

**opp.** *abbreviation* opposite.

**Oppenheimer** (**op**-ĕn-hy-mer), Julius Robert (1904–67), American theoretical physicist who led the team which designed and built the first atomic bomb during the Second World War.

**opponent** *noun* a person or group opposing another.

**opportune** (op-er-**tewn**) *adjective* **1** (of time) suitable or favourable for a purpose. **2** (of an action or event) well-timed. □ **opportunely** *adverb*

**opportunist** (op-er-**tewn**-ist) *noun* one who grasps opportunities, often in an unprincipled way. □ **opportunism** *noun*

**opportunity** *noun* a time or set of circumstances that are suitable for a particular purpose.

**opposable** *adjective* **1** (of the thumb in primates) facing and able to touch the fingers of the same hand and so grip objects. **2** able to be opposed.

**oppose** *verb* **1** show resistance to, argue or fight against. **2** place opposite; place or be in opposition to. **3** represent (things) as contrasting. □ **as opposed to** in contrast with.

**opposite** *adjective* **1** having a position on the other or further side, facing. **2** of a contrary kind, as different as possible from; *opposite opinion; opposite directions.* ●*noun* an opposite thing or person. ●*adverb & preposition* in an opposite place, position, or direction to (a person or thing). □ **opposite number** a person holding a similar position to oneself in another group or organization.

**opposition** *noun* **1** resistance, being hostile or in conflict or disagreement. **2** the people who oppose a proposal etc.; one's competitors or rivals. **3** placing or being placed opposite; contrast. **4** (**the Opposition**) the chief parliamentary party opposed to the one that is in office.

**oppress** *verb* **1** govern harshly, treat with continual cruelty or injustice. **2** weigh down with cares or unhappiness. □ **oppression** *noun*, **oppressor** *noun*

**oppressive** *adjective* **1** oppressing. **2** difficult to endure. **3** (of weather) sultry and tiring.

□ **oppressively** *adverb*, **oppressiveness** *noun*

**opprobrious** (ŏ-**proh**-briŭs) *adjective* (of language) showing scorn or reproach, abusive.

**opprobrium** (ŏ-**proh**-briŭm) *noun* great disgrace brought by shameful conduct.

**oppugn** (ŏ-**pewn**) *verb* dispute the truth or validity of.

**opt** *verb* (often foll. by *for*) make a choice. □ **opt out** choose not to participate.

**optic** *adjective* of the eye or the sense of sight. ●*noun* (**optics**) the scientific study of light and vision.

**optical** *adjective* 1 of the sense of sight. 2 aiding sight. 3 relating to optics. □ **optical character reader** a computer device enabling written and printed material to be scanned optically and then stored. **optical character recognition** a process by which written and printed material is scanned electronically and letters and numbers are recognized by a computer. **optical fibre** thin glass fibre used in fibre optics to transmit signals. **optical illusion** 1 an image which deceives the eye. 2 the mental misinterpretation that this causes. □ **optically** *adverb*

**optician** (op-**tish**-ăn) *noun* a maker or seller of spectacles and other optical equipment.

**optimal** *adjective* best or most favourable.

**optimism** *noun* a tendency to take a hopeful view of things, or to expect that results will be good. □ **optimist** *noun*

**optimistic** *adjective* showing optimism, hopeful. □ **optimistically** *noun*

**optimize** *verb* (also **optimise**) make the best or most effective use of. □ **optimization** *noun*

**optimum** *adjective* best, most favourable. ●*noun* (*plural* **optima**) the best or most favourable conditions or amount etc.

**option** *noun* 1 freedom to choose; *had no option but to go.* 2 a thing that is or may be chosen; *none of the options is satisfactory.* 3 the right to buy or sell something at a certain price within a limited time. □ **keep** (*or* **leave**) **one's options open** avoid committing oneself so that one still has a choice.

**optional** *adjective* not compulsory. □ **optionally** *adverb*

**optometrist** (op-**tom**-ĕ-trist) *noun* an ophthalmic optician. □ **optometry** *noun*

**opulent** (op-yoo-lĕnt) *adjective* 1 wealthy, rich. 2 abundant, luxuriant. □ **opulently** *adverb*, **opulence** *noun*

**opus** (oh-pŭs) *noun* (*plural* **opera**, *pronounced* **op**-er-ă) a musical composition numbered as one of a composer's works (usually in order of publication); *Beethoven opus 15.*

**OR** *abbreviation* Oregon.

**or** *conjunction* 1 as an alternative; *are you coming or not?* 2 also known as; *hydrophobia or rabies.* □ **or else** 1 otherwise; *run or else you'll be late.* 2 (*informal*) expressing a warning or threat; *do what you're told or else.*

**oracle** *noun* 1 one of the places where the ancient Greeks consulted their gods for advice or prophecy. 2 the reply given. 3 a person or thing regarded as a source of wisdom or knowledge. 4 (**Oracle**) (*trade mark*) a teletext service provided by the IBA. □ **oracular** (or-**ak**-yoo-ler) *adjective*

**oral** (or-ăl) *adjective* 1 spoken not written; *oral evidence.* 2 of the mouth; done or taken by mouth; *oral contraceptives; oral sex.* ●*noun* (*informal*) a spoken (not written) examination. □ **orally** *adverb*

**Orange** 1 the name of the Dutch royal house ruling since 1815. 2 of the Orangemen. □ **William of Orange** William III.

**orange** *noun* 1 a round juicy citrus fruit with reddish-yellow peel. 2 reddish yellow. ●*adjective* orange-coloured.

**orangeade** *noun* an orange-flavoured soft drink, usually fizzy.

**Orange Free State** an inland province of the Republic of South Africa.

**Orangeman** *noun* (*plural* **Orangemen**) a member of a political society formed in 1895 to support Protestantism in Ireland. (¶ Named after William of Orange (William III).)

**Orange River** the longest river in South Africa, flowing westward across almost the whole continent into the Atlantic.

**orangery** *noun* a building or hothouse for orange trees.

**orang-utan** (or-ang-oo-**tan**) *noun* (also **orang-outang**) a large long-armed ape of Borneo and Sumatra.

**oration** (ŏ-**ray**-shŏn) *noun* a long speech, especially of a ceremonial kind.

**orator** (o-ră-ter) *noun* a person who makes public speeches; one who is good at public speaking.

**oratorio** (o-ră-**tor**-i-oh) *noun* (*plural* **oratorios**) a musical composition for solo voices, chorus, and orchestra, usually with a biblical theme.

**oratory** (o-ră-ter-i) *noun* 1 the art or skill of public speaking. 2 a small chapel or place for private worship. □ **oratorical** *adjective*

**orb** *noun* 1 a sphere or globe. 2 an ornamental globe surmounted by a cross, forming part of the royal regalia. 3 (*poetic*) the eye.

**orbicular** (or-**bik**-yoo-ler) *adjective* (*formal*) spherical, circular.

**orbit** *noun* 1 the curved path of a planet, satellite, or spacecraft etc. round another body. 2 a sphere of influence. ●*verb* move in an orbit; travel in an orbit round (a body). □ **orbiter** noun

**orbital** (or-bit'l) adjective **1** (of a road) passing round the outside of a city. **2** of an orbit; orbital velocity. □ **orbitally** adverb

**Orcadian** (or-kay-diǎn) adjective of Orkney. ● noun a native or inhabitant of Orkney.

**orchard** noun a piece of land planted with fruit trees.

**orchestra** noun **1** a large body of people playing various musical instruments, including stringed and wind instruments. **2** (in full **orchestra pit**) the part of a theatre where these sit, in front of the stalls and lower than the stage. □ **orchestral** (or-kess-trǎl) adjective

**orchestrate** (or-kis-trayt) verb **1** compose or arrange (music) for performance by an orchestra. **2** coordinate (things) deliberately; an orchestrated series of protests. □ **orchestration** noun

**orchid** (or-kid) noun a plant with showy often irregularly-shaped flowers.

**ordain** verb **1** appoint ceremonially to perform spiritual functions in the Christian Church. **2** (of God or fate) order, decree; providence ordained that they should meet. **3** appoint or decree authoritatively.

**ordeal** (or-deel) noun a difficult experience that tests a person's character or power of endurance.

**order** noun **1** the way in which things are placed in relation to one another; tidiness. **2** a proper or customary sequence. **3** a condition in which every part or unit is in its right place or in a normal or efficient state; in good working order; out of order. **4** the condition brought about by good and firm government and obedience to the laws; law and order. **5** a system of rules or procedure. **6** a command, an instruction given with authority. **7** a request to supply goods; the goods themselves. **8** a written direction (especially to a bank or post office) to pay money, or giving authority to do something; a postal order; an estate agent's order to view property. **9** a rank or class in society; the lower orders. **10** a kind, sort, or quality; showed courage of the highest order. **11** a monastic organization or institution; the Franciscan Order. **12** a company of people distinguished by a particular honour; the insignia worn by its members; the Order of the Garter. **13** a style of ancient Greek or Roman architecture distinguished by the type of column used. **14** a scientifically classified group of plants or animals. ● verb **1** put in order, arrange methodically. **2** issue a command to, command that (something shall be done). **3** give an order for (goods etc.); direct a waiter to serve (certain food). □ **in order**

to or that with the intention that, with the purpose of. of (or in) the order of approximately. on order (of goods) ordered but not yet received. to order according to the buyer's instructions. order about keep on giving commands to. **order-paper** noun a written or printed programme of the day's business, especially in Parliament.

**orderly** adjective **1** well arranged, in good order, tidy. **2** methodical; an orderly mind. **3** obedient, well-behaved; an orderly crowd. ● noun **1** a soldier who carries orders or does errands for a senior officer. **2** a male attendant in a hospital. □ **orderly officer** the officer on duty on a particular day. **orderly room** a room where business is conducted in a military barracks. □ **orderliness** noun

**ordinal** noun (in full **ordinal number**) a number defining a thing's position in a series (e.g. first, fifth, twentieth).

**ordinance** noun **1** a rule made by authority, a decree. **2** a religious rite.

**ordinand** (or-din-and) noun a candidate for ordination.

**ordinary** adjective usual, customary, not exceptional. □ **in the ordinary way** if the circumstances were not exceptional. **ordinary level** (also **O level**) (hist., Brit.) the lowest level of the GCE examination. **ordinary seaman** a seaman of the lowest rank. **out of the ordinary** unusual. □ **ordinarily** adverb

**ordinate** (or-din-ǎt) noun (in mathematics) a coordinate measured usually vertically.

**ordination** noun ordaining or being ordained as a member of the clergy.

**ordnance** noun military supplies and materials; the government service dealing with these. □ **Ordnance Survey** an official surveying organization preparing accurate and detailed maps of the British Isles.

**Ordovician** (ordǒ-vish-iǎn) Geol. adjective of the second period of the Palaeozoic era. ● noun this period.

**ordure** (or-dewr) noun (literary) dung.

**ore** noun solid rock or mineral, found in the earth's crust, from which metal or other useful or valuable substances can be extracted; iron ore.

**Oreg.** abbreviation Oregon.

**oregano** (o-ri-gah-noh) noun dried wild marjoram used as a seasoning.

**Oregon** (o-ri-gǒn) a State of the USA on the Pacific coast.

**organ** noun **1** a musical instrument consisting of pipes that sound notes when air is forced through them, operated by keyboards and pedals. **2** a distinct part of an animal or plant body, adapted for a particular function; digestive organs. **3** a medium of communication (e.g. a newspaper) giving the views of a particular group. □ **organ-grinder** *noun* a person who plays a barrel organ. **organ-loft** *noun* a gallery for an organ.

**organdie** (or-gan-di) *noun* a kind of fine translucent usually stiffened cotton fabric.

**organic** (or-gan-ik) *adjective* **1** of or affecting an organ or organs of the body; *organic diseases*. **2** of or formed from living things; *organic matter*. **3** (of food etc.) produced without the use of artificial fertilizers or pesticides. **4** organized or arranged as a system of related parts; *the business forms an organic whole*. □ **organic chemistry** chemistry of carbon compounds, present in all living matter.

**organism** *noun* a living being, an individual animal or plant.

**organist** *noun* one who plays the organ.

**organization** *noun* (also **organisation**) **1** organizing; being organized. **2** an organized body of people; an organized system. □ **organizational** *adjective*

**organize** *verb* (also **organise**) **1** arrange in an orderly or systematic way. **2** make arrangements for; *organize a picnic*. **3** form (people) into an association for a common purpose. **4** make organic, make into living tissue. □ **organizer** *noun*

**organza** (or-gan-ză) *noun* thin stiff transparent dress fabric of silk or synthetic fibre.

**orgasm** (or-gazm) *noun* the climax of sexual excitement. □ **orgasmic** (or-gaz-mik) *adjective*

**orgy** *noun* **1** a wild party, especially one involving excessive drinking and indiscriminate sexual activity. **2** excessive indulgence in an activity; *an orgy of destruction*. □ **orgiastic** *adjective*

**oriel window** (or-i-ĕl) a projecting window in an upper storey.

**orient** (or-i-ĕnt) *noun* (**the Orient**) the East, countries east of the Mediterranean, especially East Asia. ● *verb* **1** place or determine the position of (a thing) with regard to the points of the compass. **2** face or direct (towards a certain direction). □ **Orient Express** the name of a train which ran (1883–1961) between Paris and Istanbul and other Balkan cities, via Vienna, and of its successors. **orient oneself** get one's bearings; become accustomed to a new situation.

**oriental** (or-i-en-t'l) (often **Oriental**) *adjective* *ive* of the Orient, of the eastern or Asian world or its civilization. ● *noun* a native of the Orient.

**orientate** (or-i-ĕn-tayt) *verb* orient.

**orientation** (or-i-ĕn-tay-shŏn) *noun* **1** orienting; being oriented. **2** position relative to surroundings. **3** an introduction to

a subject or situation; a briefing or short course.

**orienteering** (or-i-ĕn-teer-ing) *noun* the sport of finding one's way on foot across rough country by map and compass.

**orifice** (o-ri-fiss) *noun* an opening, especially the mouth of a cavity.

**origami** (o-ri-gah-mi) *noun* the Japanese art of folding paper into decorative shapes.

**origan** (o-ri-găn) *noun* (also **origanum**) = OREGANO.

**origin** *noun* **1** the point, source, or cause from which a thing begins its existence. **2** (often as **origins**) a person's ancestry or parentage; *a man of humble origins*.

**original** *adjective* **1** existing from the beginning, earliest. **2** inventive, creative; new in character or design; *an original idea*. **3** not a copy or a translation; by the artist rather than being a reproduction; *the original Greek text*; *an original Rembrandt*. ● *noun* the first form of something, the thing from which another is copied. □ **original sin** the condition of innate wickedness thought to be common to all humanity because of Adam's sin. □ **originally** *adverb*, **originality** *noun*

**originate** *verb* **1** give origin to, cause to begin. **2** have origin, begin; *from what country did the custom originate?* □ **origination** *noun*, **originator** *noun*

**Orinoco** (o-ri-noh-koh) a river in the north of South America, flowing through Venezuela to the Atlantic Ocean.

**oriole** (or-i-ohl) *noun* (in full **golden oriole**) a bird of which the male has black and yellow plumage.

**Orion** (ŏ-ry-ŏn) **1** (*Gk. legend*) a giant and hunter, said to have been turned into a constellation on his death. **2** a constellation containing many bright stars including **Orion's belt**, three stars in a short line.

**Orissa** (o-ris-ă) a State in eastern India.

**Orkney** an island area of Scotland consisting of the **Orkney Islands** (or **Orkneys**), situated off the NE tip of the Scottish mainland.

**Orleans** (or-lee-ănz) a French city on the River Loire, scene of Joan of Arc's first victory over the English in the Hundred Years War.

**ormolu** (or-mŏ-loo) *noun* **1** gilded bronze or a gold-coloured alloy of copper, used in decorating furniture. **2** articles made of or decorated with this.

**ornament** *noun* **1** a decorative object or detail. **2** decoration, adornment; *rich in ornament*. **3** a person or thing that adds distinction. ● *verb* decorate, be an ornament to. □ **ornamentation** *noun*, **ornamental** *adjective*

**ornate** (or-**nayt**) *adjective* elaborately ornamented.

**ornithology** (orni-**thol**-ŏji) *noun* the scientific study of birds. □ **ornithologist** *noun*, **ornithological** *adjective*

**orotund** (o-rŏ-tund) *adjective* (of speech) dignified and imposing, pompous.

**orphan** *noun* a child whose parents are dead. ●*verb* make (a child) an orphan.

**orphanage** *noun* an institution where orphans are housed and cared for.

**orrery** (o-rer-i) *noun* a clockwork model of the solar system.

**orris** (o-riss) *noun* a kind of iris that has a fragrant root which is dried for use in perfumery and medicine.

**orthodontics** (orthŏ-**don**-tiks) *noun* correction of irregularities in the teeth and jaws. □ **orthodontist** *noun*, **orthodontic** *adjective*

**orthodox** *adjective* 1 of or holding conventional or widely accepted beliefs, especially in religion or morals. 2 (also **Orthodox**) (of Judaism) strictly traditional. □ **Orthodox Church** the Eastern or Greek Church (recognizing the Patriarch of Constantinople as its head), and the national Churches of Russia, Romania, etc., in communion with it. □ **orthodoxy** *noun*

**orthography** (or-**thog**-ră-fi) *noun* spelling, especially with reference to its correctness. □ **orthographic** *adjective*, **orthographical** *adjective*

**orthopaedics** (orthŏ-**pee**-diks) *noun* (*Amer.* **orthopedics**) the branch of surgery dealing with the correction of deformities in bones or muscles. □ **orthopaedic** *adjective*, **orthopaedist** *noun*

**ortolan** (or-tŏ-lăn) *noun* a European bunting with a pink bill and pink legs, eaten as a delicacy.

**Orton**, Joe (John Kingsley) (1933–67), English playwright, author of bizarre black comedies.

**Orwell**, George (real name: Eric Arthur Blair) (1903–50), English novelist and essayist, whose novels include *Animal Farm* and *Nineteen Eighty-Four*.

**oryx** (o-riks) *noun* a large African antelope with straight horns.

**OS** *abbreviation* 1 old style. 2 ordinary seaman. 3 Ordnance Survey. 4 outsize.

**Os** *symbol* osmium.

**Osborne**, John James (born 1929), English playwright, author of *Look Back in Anger*.

**Oscar** *noun* any of the statuettes awarded by the Academy of Motion Picture Arts and Sciences for excellence in the acting or directing of films.

**oscillate** (oss-i-layt) *verb* 1 move to and fro like a pendulum. 2 vary between extremes of opinion or condition etc. 3 (of an electric current) undergo high-frequency alternations. □ **oscillation** *noun*, **oscillator** *noun*

**oscilloscope** (ŏ-**sil**-ŏ-skohp) *noun* a device for showing oscillations as a display on the screen of a cathode-ray tube.

**osier** (oh-zi-er) *noun* 1 a kind of willow with flexible twigs used in basketwork. 2 a twig from this.

**Oslo** (oz-loh) the capital of Norway.

**osmium** (oz-mi-ŭm) *noun* a hard metallic element (symbol Os) used chiefly in alloys with platinum etc.

**osmosis** (oz-**moh**-sis) *noun* the passage of fluid through a porous partition into a more concentrated solution. □ **osmotic** (oz-**mot**-ik) *adjective*

**osprey** (oss-pri) *noun* (*plural* **ospreys**) a large bird preying on fish in inland waters.

**osseous** (oss-i-ŭs) *adjective* 1 of bone. 2 having bones, bony.

**ossify** *verb* (**ossified**, **ossifying**) 1 change into bone; make or become hard like bone. 2 make or become rigid and unprogressive; *their ideas had ossified.* □ **ossification** *noun*

**ostensible** (oss-**ten**-sibŭl) *adjective* pretended, put forward as a reason etc. to conceal the real one; *their ostensible motive was humanitarian.* □ **ostensibly** *adverb*

**ostensive** (oss-**ten**-siv) *adjective* showing something directly.

**ostentation** *noun* a pretentious display of wealth etc. intended to impress people. □ **ostentatious** (oss-ten-**tay**-shŭs) *adjective*, **ostentatiously** *adverb*

**osteoarthritis** *noun* a form of arthritis in which the joints degenerate.

**osteopathy** (oss-ti-**op**-ăthi) *noun* the treatment of disease or illness by manipulation of the bones and muscles. □ **osteopath** *noun*, **osteopathic** *adjective*

**osteoporosis** (oss-ti-oh-pŏ-**roh**-sis) *noun* a painful condition in which the bones become brittle, often caused by hormonal changes or calcium deficiency.

**ostler** (oss-ler) *noun* a person in charge of stabling horses at an inn.

**Ostmark** *noun* the unit of money in the former East Germany.

**ostracize** (oss-tră-syz) *verb* refuse to associate with, exclude from a group or from society. □ **ostracism** *noun*

**ostrich** *noun* 1 a swift-running flightless African bird, said to bury its head in the sand when pursued, in the belief that it then cannot be seen. 2 a person who refuses to face an awkward truth.

**OT** *abbreviation* Old Testament.

**other** *adjective* 1 alternative, additional, being the remaining one or set of two or more; *has no other income*; *try the other shoe*; *my other friends.* 2 further, additional; *some other examples.* 3 not the same. ●*noun & pro-*

*noun* the other person or thing; *where are the others?* ● *adverb* otherwise. □ **other than 1** apart from; except; *has no friends other than me.* **2** different from; *wouldn't want her to be other than she is.* **the other day** etc., a few days etc. ago. **other-worldly** *adjective* **1** of another world. **2** dreamy, remote, impractical.

**otherwise** *adverb* **1** in a different way; *could not have done otherwise.* **2** in other respects; *is otherwise correct.* **3** if circumstances were different; or else; *write it down, otherwise you'll forget.* **4** as an alternative; *otherwise known as Jacko.* ● *adjective* in a different state, not as supposed; *the truth is quite otherwise.*

**otiose** (oh-ti-ohss) *adjective* serving no practical purpose.

**OTT** *abbreviation* (*informal*) over-the-top.

**Ottawa** the capital of Canada.

**otter** *noun* a fish-eating water animal with webbed feet, a flat tail, and thick brown fur.

**Otto**, Nikolaus August (1832–91), German engineer. □ **Otto cycle** the four-stroke cycle on which most internal-combustion engines work.

**Ottoman** *adjective* of the Turkish dynasty founded by Osman or Othman (1259–1326), his branch of the Turks, or the empire ruled by his descendants (late 13th–early 20th century). ● *noun* **1** a Turk of the Ottoman period. **2** (**ottoman**) a long cushioned seat without back or arms, sometimes a storage box with a padded top.

**OU** *abbreviation* **1** Open University. **2** Oxford University.

**Ouagadougou** (wah-gă-**doo**-goo) the capital of Burkina.

**oubliette** (oo-bli-et) *noun* a secret dungeon with a trapdoor entrance.

**ouch** *interjection* an exclamation of sudden pain.

**ought** *auxiliary verb* expressing duty, rightness, advisability, or strong probability.

**oughtn't** (*informal*) = ought not.

**Ouija** (we-jă) *noun* (*trade mark*) (in full **Ouija board**) a board marked with the alphabet and other signs, used with a movable pointer to indicate messages in seances.

**ounce** *noun* **1** a unit of weight equal to one-sixteenth of a pound (about 28 grams). **2** a very small amount; *hasn't an ounce of common sense.*

**our** *adjective* of or belonging to us. □ **Our Father** the Lord's Prayer. **Our Lady** (used by Catholics) the Virgin Mary. **Our Lord** (used by Catholics) Christ.

**ours** *possessive pronoun* belonging to us; the thing(s) belonging to us.

**ourselves** *pronoun* **1** the emphatic and reflexive form of *we* and *us*; *we did it ourselves; hurt ourselves.* **2** in our normal state; *not ourselves today.* □ **by ourselves** see ONESELF.

**oust** (*pronounced* ow- *as in* cow) *verb* drive out, eject from office or a position or employment etc.

**out** *adverb* **1** away from or not in a place; *keep out; the tide is out.* **2** dispersed; *share it out; spread out.* **3** indicating a need for alertness; *look out.* **4** not in one's home, place of work, etc. **5** to or at an end; completely; *write it out; die out; tired out.* **6** (of a fire etc.) no longer burning. **7** in error; *3% out.* **8** (*informal*) unconscious, asleep. **9** (of a jury) deciding on a verdict. **10** (of workers) on strike. **11** (of a secret) revealed. **12** (of a flower) open. **13** (of a book, record, etc.) just published or on sale. **14** (of a star) visible after dark. **15** no longer in fashion. **16** (in a game or sport) dismissed, at the end of one's turn. **17** not worth considering; *that idea is definitely out.* **18** (of a stain etc.) removed; *it won't wash out.* ● *preposition* (*informal*) out of; *looked out the window.* ● *noun* a means of escape. ● *verb* **1** come or go out; *the truth will out.* **2** (*informal*) publicly expose a person's homosexuality. □ **out for** intent on obtaining. **out to** acting with the intention of; *out to cause trouble.* **out-and-out** *adjective* thorough, complete; *an out-and-out bigot.* **out of 1** from within or among. **2** beyond the range of. **3** so as to be without a supply of. **out of date** no longer fashionable, current, or valid; *this passport is out of date.* **out of doors** in the open air. **out of it 1** excluded, left out. **2** (*informal*) dazed, intoxicated, or unconscious. **out of the way 1** no longer an obstacle. **2** remote. **3** unusual. **out of this world** incredibly good, indescribable. **out of work** having no work, unable to find paid employment. **out with it** say what you are thinking.

**out-** *combining form* **1** out of, away from, outward; *outcast.* **2** external, separate; *outhouse.* **3** more than, so as to exceed; *outbid, outgrow, out-talk.*

**outback** *noun* remote inland areas of Australia.

**outbalance** *verb* outweigh.

**outbid** *verb* (**outbid, outbidding**) bid higher than (another person).

**outboard** *adjective & adverb* on or towards the outside of a ship, aircraft, or vehicle. □ **outboard motor** a portable motor attached to the rear of a boat.

**outbreak** *noun* a sudden breaking out of anger, war, disease, etc.

**outbuilding** *noun* an outhouse.

**outburst** *noun* a bursting out, especially of strong or violent emotion.

**outcast** *noun* a person who has been driven out of a group or rejected by society. ● *adjective* rejected; homeless.

**outclass** *verb* surpass greatly.

**outcome** *noun* the result or effect of an event etc.

**outcrop** *noun* **1** part of an underlying layer of rock that projects on the surface of the ground. **2** a breaking out.

**outcry** *noun* a strong public protest.

**outdated** *adjective* out of date.

**outdistance** *verb* get far ahead of (a person) in a race etc.

**outdo** *verb* (**outdid, outdone, outdoing**) do better than (another person etc.); surpass.

**outdoor** *adjective* **1** of or for use in the open air. **2** enjoying open-air activities; *she's not an outdoor type.*

**outdoors** *adverb* in or to the open air. ● *noun* the open air.

**outer** *adjective* further from the centre or from the inside; exterior, external. ● *noun* the division of a target furthest from the bull's-eye; a shot that strikes this. □ **outer space** the universe beyond the earth's atmosphere.

**outermost** *adjective* furthest outward, most remote.

**outface** *verb* disconcert (a person) by one's confident manner or by staring.

**outfall** *noun* an outlet where water falls or flows out.

**outfield** *noun* the outer part of a cricket or baseball field.

**outfit** *noun* **1** a set of equipment. **2** a set of clothes to be worn together. **3** (*informal*) an organization, a group of people regarded as a unit.

**outfitter** *noun* a supplier of men's clothing.

**outflank** *verb* **1** get round the flank of (an enemy). **2** outmanoeuvre, outwit.

**outflow** *noun* an outward flow; the amount that flows out.

**outfox** *verb* outwit.

**outgoing** *adjective* **1** sociable, friendly. **2** retiring from office; *the outgoing president.* **3** going out. ● *plural noun* (**outgoings**) expenditure.

**outgrow** *verb* (**outgrew, outgrown, outgrowing**) **1** grow too big for (clothes etc.). **2** grow out of (childish behaviour etc.). **3** grow faster than.

**outgrowth** *noun* **1** something that grows out of another thing. **2** a natural development, an effect.

**outhouse** *noun* a building (e.g. a shed or barn) belonging to but separate from a house.

**outing** *noun* a pleasure trip, an excursion.

**outlandish** *adjective* looking or sounding strange or foreign. □ **outlandishly** *adverb*, **outlandishness** *noun*

**outlast** *verb* last longer than.

**outlaw** *noun* **1** a fugitive from the law. **2** (*hist.*) a person formally deprived of the protection of the law. ● *verb* **1** make illegal. **2** declare (a person) an outlaw.

**outlay** *noun* what is spent on something.

**outlet** *noun* **1** a way out for water or steam etc. **2** a means or occasion for giving vent to one's feelings or energies. **3** a market for goods.

**outline** *noun* **1** a line or lines showing the shape or boundary of something. **2** a statement or summary of the chief facts about something. ● *verb* draw or describe in outline; mark the outline of. □ **in outline** giving only an outline.

**outlive** *verb* live longer than.

**outlook** *noun* **1** a view on which one looks out; *a pleasant outlook over the lake.* **2** a person's mental attitude or way of looking at something. **3** future prospects.

**outlying** *adjective* situated far from a centre, remote.

**outmanoeuvre** *verb* (*Amer.* **outmaneuver**) outdo in manoeuvring.

**outmatch** *verb* be more than a match for.

**outmoded** (owt-**moh**-did) *adjective* no longer fashionable or acceptable.

**outnumber** *verb* exceed in number.

**outpace** *verb* go faster than.

**outpatient** *noun* a person who visits a hospital for treatment but does not remain resident there.

**outpost** *noun* **1** a detachment of troops stationed at a distance from the main army. **2** any distant branch or settlement.

**outpouring** *noun* an intense expressing of one's emotions.

**output** *noun* **1** the amount produced (by a machine, worker etc.). **2** the electrical power etc. delivered by a machine or apparatus. **3** the printout or results from a computer. ● *verb* (**output** *or* **outputted, outputting**) (of a computer) supply (results).

**outrage** *noun* **1** an act that shocks public opinion. **2** great anger. **3** violation of rights; *safe from outrage.* ● *verb* commit an outrage against; shock and anger greatly.

**outrageous** *adjective* greatly exceeding what is moderate or reasonable, shocking. □ **outrageously** *adverb*

**outrank** *verb* be of higher rank than.

**outré** (oo-tray) *adjective* eccentric; unseemly. (¶ French.)

**outrider** *noun* a mounted guard or motor cyclist riding ahead of or beside a carriage or procession.

**outrigger** *noun* **1** a spar or framework projecting from the side of a ship or canoe to give stability. **2** a boat fitted with this.

**outright** *adverb* **1** completely, entirely, not gradually; *bought the house outright.* **2** openly, frankly; *told him outright.* ● *adjective* thorough, complete; *an outright fraud.*

**outrun** *verb* (**outran, outrun, outrunning**) **1** run faster or further than. **2** go beyond (a specified point or limit).

**outsell** *verb* (**outsold, outselling**) sell or be sold in greater quantities than.

**outset** *noun* □ **at** (*or* **from**) **the outset** from the beginning.

**outshine** *verb* (**outshone, outshining**) surpass in splendour or excellence.

**outside** *noun* the outer side, surface, or part. ● *adjective* **1** of or coming from the outside. **2** (of a player in football etc.) positioned nearest to the edge of the field; *outside left.* **3** greatest possible; *the outside price.* ● *adverb* on or at or to the outside. ● *preposition* on the outer side of; at or to the outside of; other than; *has no interests outside his work.* □ **at the outside** (of amounts) at most. **outside broadcast** one that is not made from a studio. **outside chance** a remote possibility.

**outsider** *noun* **1** a non-member of a certain group or profession. **2** a competitor thought to have little chance.

**outsize** *adjective* much larger than average.

**outskirts** *plural noun* the outer districts or outlying parts, especially of a town.

**outsmart** *verb* (*informal*) outwit.

**outspan** *verb* (**outspanned, outspanning**) (in South Africa) unyoke, unharness. ● *noun* an area on a farm for travellers and their animals to rest.

**outspoken** *adjective* speaking or spoken without reserve, very frank. □ **outspokenly** *adverb*, **outspokeness** *noun*

**outspread** *adjective* spread out.

**outstanding** *adjective* **1** conspicuous. **2** exceptionally good. **3** not yet paid or settled; *some of his debts are still outstanding.* □ **outstandingly** *adverb*

**outstay** *verb* stay longer than; *outstayed his welcome.*

**outstretched** *adjective* stretched out.

**outstrip** *verb* (**outstripped, outstripping**) **1** outrun. **2** surpass.

**out-tray** *noun* a tray to hold documents that have been dealt with.

**outvote** *verb* defeat by a majority of votes.

**outward** *adjective* **1** situated on the outside. **2** going towards the outside. **3** in one's expression or actions etc. as distinct from in one's mind or spirit. ● *adverb* (also **outwards**) towards the outside. □ **outward bound** travelling away from home.

**outwardly** *adverb* on the outside.

**outweigh** *verb* be greater in weight, importance, or significance than.

**outwit** *verb* (**outwitted, outwitting**) get the better of (a person) by one's cleverness or craftiness.

**outwork** *noun* **1** an advanced or detached part of a fortification. **2** work done for an employer off the premises.

**outworn** *adjective* worn out, damaged by wear.

**ouzel** (oo-zĕl) *noun* **1** (in full **ring ouzel**) a small bird of the thrush family. **2** (in full **water ouzel**) a kind of diving bird.

**ouzo** (oo-zoh) *noun* a Greek drink of aniseed-flavoured spirits.

**ova** *see* OVUM.

**oval** *noun* a rounded symmetrical shape longer than it is broad. ● *adjective* having this shape.

**ovary** (oh-ver-i) *noun* **1** either of the two organs in which egg cells are produced in female animals. **2** part of the pistil in a plant, from which fruit is formed. □ **ovarian** (ŏ-vair-iăn) *adjective*

**ovate** (oh-vayt) *adjective* egg-shaped, oval.

**ovation** (ŏ-vay-shŏn) *noun* enthusiastic applause.

**oven** *noun* an enclosed chamber in which things are cooked or heated.

**ovenware** *noun* dishes for cooking food in the oven.

**over** *adverb* **1** with movement outwards and downwards from the brink or from an upright position; *knocked me over.* **2** with movement from one side to the other or so that a different side is showing; *turn it over.* **3** across a street or other space or distance; *she is over here from America.* **4** passing above or across something; *climb over; fly over.* **5** so as to cover or touch a whole surface; *the lake froze over, paint it over.* **6** changing or transferring from one hand, side, etc. to another; *went over to the enemy; hand it over.* **7** (in radio conversation) it is your turn to speak. **8** besides, in addition or excess. **9** with repetition; *ten times over.* **10** thoroughly, with detailed consideration; *think it over.* **11** at an end; *the battle is over.* ● *noun* a series of 6 balls bowled in cricket. ● *preposition* **1** in or to a position higher than. **2** out and downwards from; *fell over the cliff.* **3** so as to cover; *hat over his eyes.* **4** above and across, so as to clear. **5** throughout the length or extent of, during; *over the years; stayed over the weekend.* **6** so as to visit or examine all parts; *saw over the house; went over the plan again.* **7** transmitted by; *heard it over the radio.* **8** while engaged with; *we can talk over dinner.* **9** concerning; *quarrelling over money.* **10** more than; *it's over a mile away.* **11** in superiority or preference to; *their victory* *over United.* **12** recovered from; *I'm over it now.* □ **over and above** besides. **over and over** repeatedly. **over-the-top** adjective (*informal*) excessive. **over to you** it is your turn to act.

**over-** combining form **1** above; *overlay.* **2** too much, excessively; *over-anxious.*

**overact** verb act one's part in an exaggerated manner.

**overall** noun **1** a garment worn to protect other clothing, which it covers. **2** (**overalls**) a one-piece garment covering body and legs, worn as protective clothing. ● adjective **1** including everything, total. **2** taking all aspects into account. ● adverb in all parts, taken as a whole.

**overarm** adjective & adverb with the hand raised above the shoulder.

**overawe** verb overcome with awe.

**overbalance** verb lose balance and fall.

**overbear** verb (**overbore, overborne, overbearing**) **1** bear down by weight or force. **2** repress by power or authority.

**overbearing** adjective domineering.

**overblown** adjective **1** pretentious or inflated. **2** (of a flower etc.) past its prime.

**overboard** adverb from a ship into the water. □ **go overboard** (*informal*) **1** be very enthusiastic. **2** behave immoderately. **throw overboard** abandon, discard.

**overbook** verb book too many passengers or visitors for (an aircraft flight, hotel, etc.).

**overburden** verb burden excessively.

**overcast** adjective (of the sky) covered with cloud. ● verb (**overcast, overcasting**) stitch over (an edge) to prevent it from fraying.

**overcharge** verb **1** charge too high a price. **2** fill too full.

**overcoat** noun a warm outdoor coat.

**overcome** verb (**overcame, overcome, overcoming**) **1** win a victory over, succeed in subduing. **2** be victorious. **3** make helpless or weak; *overcome by gas fumes; overcome by grief.* **4** find a way of dealing with (a problem etc.).

**overcompensate** verb **1** (usually foll. by *for*) compensate excessively for. **2** try excessively hard to make amends.

**overcrowd** verb crowd too many people into (a place or vehicle etc.). □ **overcrowding** noun

**overdo** verb (**overdid, overdone, overdoing**) **1** do (a thing) excessively. **2** cook (food) too long. □ **overdo it** or **things** work too hard; exaggerate.

**overdose** noun too large a dose of a drug etc. ● verb take an overdose.

**overdraft** noun **1** overdrawing of a bank account. **2** the amount by which an account is overdrawn.

**overdraw** verb (**overdrew, overdrawn, overdrawing**) **1** draw more from (a bank account) than the amount credited. **2** (as **overdrawn** adjective) having drawn more money than is in one's account.

**overdress** verb dress too formally.

**overdrive** noun **1** a mechanism providing an extra gear above the normal top gear in a vehicle. **2** a state of great activity.

**overdue** adjective not paid or arrived etc. by the due or expected time.

**overeat** verb (**overate, overeaten, overeating**) eat too much.

**overestimate** verb form too high an estimate of. □ **overestimation** noun

**overexpose** verb **1** expose to the public for too long. **2** expose (film) for too long. □ **overexposure** noun

**overfeed** verb (**overfed, overfeeding**) feed too much.

**overfill** verb fill too full or to overflowing.

**overfish** verb catch so many fish from (a certain area) that next season's supply is reduced.

**overflow** verb (*pronounced* oh-ver-**floh**) **1** flow over (the edge, limits, or banks etc.). **2** (of a crowd) spread beyond the limits of (a room etc.). ● noun (*pronounced* **oh**-ver-floh) **1** what overflows. **2** an outlet for excess liquid.

**overfly** verb (**overflew, overflown, overflying**) fly over or beyond (a place or territory).

**overfond** adjective having too great a fondness; *an overfond parent.*

**overfull** adjective overfilled, too full.

**overgrown** adjective **1** having grown too large. **2** covered with weeds etc. □ **overgrowth** noun

**overhang** verb (**overhung, overhanging**) jut out over. ● noun an overhanging part.

**overhaul** verb **1** examine and make any necessary repairs or changes. **2** overtake. ● noun an examination and repair etc.

**overhead** adverb & adjective above the level of one's head, in the sky. ● plural noun (**overheads**) the expenses involved in running a business. □ **overhead projector** a projector on which a large transparency is laid flat over a light source, and an enlarged image produced using a reflector and lens combined.

**overhear** verb (**overheard, overhearing**) hear accidentally or without the speaker's knowledge or intention.

**overheat** verb **1** make or become too hot or too intensive. **2** (as **overheated** adjective) excessively excited; *an overheated discussion.*

**overjoyed** adjective filled with very great joy.

**overkill** noun **1** a surplus of capacity for destruction above what is needed to defeat or destroy an enemy. **2** excess.

**overland** *adverb & adjective* by land, not by sea.

**overlap** *verb* (**overlapped, overlapping**) **1** extend beyond the edge of (a thing) and partly cover it. **2** coincide partially; *our holidays overlap.* ●*noun* overlapping; an overlapping part or amount.

**overlay** (*pronounced* oh-ver-**lay**) *verb* (**overlaid, overlaying**) **1** cover with a surface layer. **2** lay on top of. ●*noun* (*pronounced* **oh**-ver-lay) a thing laid over another; a coverlet.

**overleaf** *adverb* on the other side of a leaf of a book etc.

**overlie** *verb* (**overlay, overlain, overlying**) lie on top of; smother by doing this.

**overload** *verb* (*pronounced* oh-ver-**lohd**) put too great a load on or into. ●*noun* (*pronounced* **oh**-ver-lohd) a load that is too great.

**overlook** *verb* **1** have a view of or over (a place) from above. **2** oversee. **3** fail to observe or consider. **4** take no notice of, allow (an offence) to go unpunished.

**overlord** *noun* a supreme lord.

**overly** *adverb* excessively; too.

**overman** *verb* (**overmanned, overmanning**) provide with too many people as workers or crew etc.

**over-much** *adverb* too much.

**overnight** *adverb* **1** for a night; *stayed overnight.* **2** during the night. **3** instantly; *won't happen overnight.* ●*adjective* **1** done or used overnight; *overnight bag.* **2** instant; *an overnight success.*

**overpass** *noun* a road that crosses another by means of a bridge.

**overpay** *verb* (**overpaid, overpaying**) pay too highly. □ **overpayment** *noun*

**overplay** *verb* give too much importance to. □ **overplay one's hand** take unjustified risks by overestimating one's strength.

**overpopulated** *adjective* having too large a population. □ **overpopulation** *noun*

**overpower** *verb* overcome by greater strength or numbers.

**overpowering** *adjective* (of heat or feelings) extremely intense.

**overprint** *verb* (*pronounced* oh-ver-**print**) **1** print (a photograph) darker than was intended. **2** print further matter on (an already printed surface, e.g. a postage stamp); print (further matter) thus. ●*noun* (*pronounced* **oh**-ver-print) material that is overprinted.

**overqualified** *adjective* too highly qualified for a particular job or type of work.

**overrate** *verb* **1** have too high an opinion of. **2** assess the rates of (a place) too highly.

**overrated** *adjective* not as good as it is generally believed to be.

**overreach** *verb* outwit. □ **overreach oneself** fail through being too ambitious.

**overreact** *verb* respond more strongly than is justified. □ **overreaction** *noun*

**override** *verb* (**overrode, overridden, overriding**) **1** set aside (an order) by having, or behaving as if one had, superior authority. **2** prevail over; *considerations of safety override all others.* **3** intervene and cancel the operation of (an automatic mechanism).

**overrider** *noun* a vertical attachment on the bumper of a car to prevent another bumper from becoming locked behind it.

**overripe** *adjective* too ripe.

**overrule** *verb* **1** set aside (a decision etc.) by using one's authority. **2** reject a proposal of (a person) in this way.

**overrun** *verb* (**overran, overrun, overrunning**) **1** spread over and occupy or injure; *the place is overrun with mice.* **2** exceed (a limit or time allowed); *the broadcast overran its allotted time.*

**overseas** *adverb & adjective* across or beyond the sea, abroad.

**oversee** *verb* (**oversaw, overseen, overseeing**) officially supervise; superintend. □ **overseer** *noun*

**oversew** *verb* (**oversewed, oversewn, oversewing**) sew together (two edges) so that each stitch lies over the edges.

**oversexed** *adjective* having unusually great sexual desires.

**overshadow** *verb* **1** cast a shadow over. **2** make (a person or thing) seem unimportant in comparison.

**overshoe** *noun* a shoe worn over an ordinary one as a protection against wet etc.

**overshoot** *verb* (**overshot, overshooting**) pass beyond (a target or limit); *the plane overshot the runway.*

**oversight** *noun* **1** supervision. **2** an unintentional omission or mistake.

**oversimplify** *verb* (**oversimplified, oversimplifying**) misrepresent (a problem etc.) by stating it in terms that are too simple. □ **oversimplification** *noun*

**oversize** *adjective* (also **oversized**) of more than the usual size.

**oversleep** *verb* (**overslept, oversleeping**) sleep longer than one intended.

**overspend** *verb* (**overspent, overspending**) spend too much or more than one can afford.

**overspill** *noun* **1** what spills over or overflows. **2** the surplus population of a town etc., who seek accommodation in other districts.

**overstate** *verb* state too strongly; exaggerate. □ **overstatement** *noun*

**overstay** *verb* stay longer than; *overstay one's welcome.*

**oversteer** verb (of a car etc.) have a tendency to turn more sharply than was intended. ●noun this tendency.

**overstep** verb (**overstepped, overstepping**) go beyond (a limit).

**overstretch** verb **1** stretch too much or too far. **2** make excessive demands on (a person, resources, etc.).

**overstrung** adjective **1** (of a piano) with strings in sets crossing each other obliquely. **2** (of a person, nerves, etc.) too highly strung; tense.

**oversubscribed** adjective with applications for (an issue of shares etc.) in excess of the number offered.

**overt** (oh-**vert**) adjective done or shown openly; overt hostility. □ **overtly** adverb

**overtake** verb (**overtook, overtaken, overtaking**) **1** catch up with and pass (a person or vehicle). **2** (of misfortune etc.) come suddenly upon.

**overtax** verb **1** levy excessive taxes on. **2** put too heavy a burden or strain on.

**overthrow** verb (pronounced oh-ver-**throh**) (**overthrew, overthrown, overthrowing**) cause the downfall of; overthrew the government. ●noun (pronounced **oh**-ver-throh) **1** downfall, defeat. **2** a fielder's throwing of a ball beyond an intended point.

**overtime** adverb in addition to regular working hours. ●noun **1** time worked in this way. **2** payment for this.

**overtone** noun **1** an additional quality or implication; overtones of malice in his comments. **2** (in music) any of the tones above the lowest in a harmonic series.

**overtook** see OVERTAKE.

**overture** noun **1** an orchestral composition forming a prelude to an opera or ballet etc. **2** a composition resembling this. **3** (**overtures**) a friendly approach showing willingness to begin negotiations; a formal proposal or offer.

**overturn** verb **1** turn over; cause to turn over. **2** reverse or overthrow.

**overuse** verb (pronounced oh-ver-**yooz**) use excessively. ●noun (pronounced oh-ver-**yoos**) excessive use.

**overweening** adjective arrogant, presumptuous.

**overweight** adjective weighing more than is normal, required, or permissible.

**overwhelm** verb **1** make helpless with emotion. **2** overcome completely, especially by force of numbers. **3** bury or drown beneath a huge mass.

**overwhelming** adjective **1** too great to resist; an overwhelming desire to laugh. **2** by a great number; an overwhelming majority.

**overwind** verb (**overwound, overwinding**) wind (a watch etc.) beyond the proper stopping point.

**overwork** verb **1** work or cause to work so hard that one becomes exhausted. **2** make excessive use of; an overworked phrase. ●noun excessive work causing exhaustion.

**overwrought** (oh-ver-**rawt**) adjective in a state of nervous agitation.

**Ovid** (**ov**-id) (Publius Ovidus Naso) (43 BC–c. AD 17), Roman poet in the age of Augustus.

**oviduct** (**oh**-vi-dukt) noun a canal through which ova pass from the ovary.

**oviform** adjective egg-shaped.

**ovine** (**oh**-vyn) adjective of or like sheep.

**oviparous** (oh-**vip**-er-ŭs) adjective producing young from eggs that are expelled from the body and then hatched (compare VIVIPAROUS).

**ovoid** (**oh**-void) adjective egg-shaped.

**ovulate** (**ov**-yoo-layt) verb produce or discharge an ovum or ova from an ovary. □ **ovulation** noun

**ovule** (**oh**-vewl) noun a small part in a plant's ovary that develops into a seed when fertilized.

**ovum** (**oh**-vŭm) noun (plural **ova**) a female egg-cell capable of developing into a new individual when fertilized.

**ow** interjection an exclamation of sudden pain.

**owe** verb **1** be under an obligation to pay or repay (money etc.), be in debt. **2** have a duty to render; owe allegiance to the Queen. **3** (usually foll. by to) have (a thing) as a result of the work or action of another person or cause; we owe this discovery to Newton; he owes his success to luck.

**Owen**, Wilfrid (1893–1918), English poet of the First World War.

**Owens**, Jesse (James Cleveland) (1913–80), Black American athlete of track and field events, famed for his spectacular performance at the 1936 Olympic Games in Berlin.

**owing** adjective owed and not yet paid. □ **owing to** caused by; because of.

**owl** noun a bird of prey with a large head, large eyes, and a hooked beak, usually flying at night. □ **owlish** adjective

**owlet** noun a small or young owl.

**own** adjective belonging to oneself or itself. ●verb **1** have as one's property, possess. **2** acknowledge that one is the author, possessor, father, etc. of. **3** (old use) confess; she owns to having said it. □ **come into one's own** receive one's due; achieve recognition. **get one's own back** have one's revenge. **hold one's own** succeed in holding one's position; not lose strength. **of one's own** belonging to oneself exclusively. **on one's own** alone; independently. **own brand** a class of goods marked with the trade mark of the retailer instead of that of the manufacturer. **own**

**goal 1** a goal scored accidentally by a member of a team against his or her own side. **2** an act that unintentionally damages one's own interests. **own up** confess, admit that one is guilty.

**owner** *noun* one who owns something. □ **owner-occupier** *noun* a person who owns the house that he or she lives in. □ **ownership** *noun*

**ox** *noun* (*plural* **oxen**) **1** an animal of the kind kept as domestic cattle or related to these. **2** a fully grown bullock, used as a draught animal or as food.

**oxalic acid** a poisonous acid found in sorrel and rhubarb leaves.

**Oxbridge** *noun* the universities of Oxford and Cambridge regarded together.

**ox-eye daisy** a daisy with a large yellow centre from which white petals radiate.

**Oxfam** *abbreviation* Oxford Committee for Famine Relief.

**Oxford** a midland city on the River Thames, seat of a major English university. □ **Oxford blue** dark blue.

**Oxfordshire** a south midland county of England.

**oxhide** *noun* **1** the hide of an ox. **2** leather made from this.

**oxidant** *noun* an oxidizing agent.

**oxidation** *noun* the process of combining or causing to combine with oxygen.

**oxide** *noun* a compound of oxygen and one other element.

**oxidize** *verb* (also **oxidise**) **1** combine or cause to combine with oxygen. **2** coat with an oxide. **3** make or become rusty. □ **oxidation** *noun*

**Oxon.** *abbreviation* **1** Oxfordshire. **2** of Oxford University.

**Oxonian** (oks-**oh**-niăn) *adjective* of Oxford University. ●*noun* **1** a member of Oxford University. **2** a native or inhabitant of Oxford.

**oxtail** *noun* the tail of an ox, used to make soup or stew.

**oxyacetylene** (oksi-ă-set-i-leen) *adjective* using a mixture of oxygen and acetylene, especially in the cutting and welding of metals.

**oxygen** *noun* a chemical element (symbol O), a colourless odourless tasteless gas essential to plant and animal life, existing in air and combining with hydrogen to form water. □ **oxygen tent** a tentlike cover over a patient's bed supplying air rich in oxygen.

**oxygenate** *verb* supply, treat, or mix with oxygen. □ **oxygenation** *noun*

**oxymoron** (oksi-**mor**-ŏn) *noun* putting together words which seem to contradict one another, e.g. *bitter-sweet*.

**oxytocin** (oksi-**toh**-sin) *noun* a hormone controlling contractions of the womb, used in synthetic form to induce labour in childbirth.

**oyez** (oh-**yess**) *interjection* (also **oyes**) a cry uttered (usually three times) by a public crier or court officer to call for attention.

**oyster** *noun* a kind of shellfish used as food, some types of which produce pearls inside their shells. □ **oyster-catcher** *noun* a wading seabird with black and white plumage and a long beak. **oyster white** greyish white. **the world is your oyster** you have every opportunity for satisfaction or success.

**oz.** *abbreviation* ounce(s).

**ozone** (oh-zohn) *noun* **1** a form of oxygen with a sharp smell, formed by an electrical discharge in the atmosphere. **2** (*humorous*) invigorating air at the seaside. □ **ozone-friendly** *adjective* not containing chemicals destructive to the ozone layer. **ozone hole** an area of the ozone layer in which depletion has occurred through atmospheric pollution. **ozone layer** a layer of ozone in the earth's upper atmosphere that absorbs most of the sun's ultraviolet radiation.

# Pp

**P** *abbreviation* **1** (on road signs) parking. **2** (in chess) pawn. ●*symbol* phosphorus.

**p** *abbreviation* **1** penny or pence (in decimal coinage). **2** *Music* piano (softly).

**p.** *abbreviation* page.

**PA** *abbreviation* **1** Pennsylvania. **2** personal assistant. **3** public address system.

**Pa** *symbol* protactinium.

**Pa.** *abbreviation* Pennsylvania.

**pa** *noun* (*informal*) father.

**p.a.** *abbreviation* per annum, yearly.

**pace¹** *noun* **1** a single step made in walking or running. **2** the distance passed in this. **3** a style of walking or running. **4** speed in walking or running. **5** the rate of progress in some activity. ●*verb* **1** walk with a slow or regular pace. **2** walk to and fro across (a room etc.). **3** (foll. by *out*) measure by pacing. **4** set the pace for (a runner etc.). □ **keep pace** (**with**) advance at an equal rate (to). **put a person through his** *or* **her paces** test his or her ability. **set the pace** set the speed, especially by leading.

**pace²** (pay-si *or* pah-chay) *preposition* although (a named person) may not agree; with due respect to. (¶ Latin.)

**pacemaker** *noun* **1** a runner who sets the pace in a race. **2** an electrical device placed on the heart to stimulate contractions.

**pachyderm** (pak-i-derm) *noun* a thick-skinned mammal, especially an elephant or rhinoceros.

**Pacific** *noun* (in full **Pacific Ocean**) the world's largest ocean, separating North and South America from Asia and Australia. ●*adjective* **1** of the Pacific Ocean. **2** (**pacific**) peaceful; making or loving peace.

**pacifier** *noun* **1** a person or thing that pacifies. **2** (*Amer.*) a baby's dummy.

**pacifist** (pas-i-fist) *noun* a person who totally opposes war, believing that disputes should be settled by peaceful means. □ **pacifism** *noun*

**pacify** (pas-i-fy) *verb* (**pacified, pacifying**) **1** calm and quieten. **2** establish peace in. □ **pacification** *noun*, **pacificatory** *adjective*

**pack¹** *noun* **1** a collection of things wrapped or tied together for carrying. **2** a set of things packed for selling. **3** a rucksack. **4** a complete set of playing cards (usually 52). **5** a group of hounds or wolves etc. **6** a gang of people; an organized group of Cub Scouts or Brownies; a Rugby football team's forwards. **7** a large amount or collection; *a pack of lies*. **8** a face-pack. ●*verb*

**1** put (things) into a container for transport or storing or for marketing; fill with things in this way. **2** be able to be packed; *this dress packs easily.* **3** cram, press, or crowd together into; fill (a space) in this way; *the hall was packed out.* **4** cover or protect (a thing) with something pressed tightly on, in, or round it. □ **pack a punch** (*slang*) be capable of delivering a powerful blow. **pack ice** crowded pieces of floating ice in the sea. **pack in** (*slang*) stop doing (something). **pack off** send (a person) away. **pack up 1** put one's things together in readiness for departing or stopping work. **2** (*informal*) (of machinery etc.) break down. **send packing** dismiss abruptly. □ **packer** *noun*

**pack²** *verb* select (a jury or committee) fraudulently so that their decisions will be in one's favour.

**package** *noun* **1** a parcel; a box in which things are packed. **2** (in full **package deal**) a set of items or proposals considered as a whole. **3** *Computing* a piece of software designed for a wide range of users. ●*verb* put together in a package. □ **package holiday** *or* **tour** one offering travel, hotels, etc. at an inclusive price.

**packaging** *noun* wrapping or containers for goods.

**packet** *noun* **1** a small package. **2** (*informal*) a considerable sum of money. **3** a mail-boat. □ **catch a packet** (*slang*) be severely injured or reprimanded.

**packhorse** *noun* a horse for carrying loads.

**packing** *noun* material used as padding to pack fragile articles.

**pact** *noun* an agreement, a treaty.

**pad¹** *noun* **1** a thick piece of soft material used to protect, add bulk, absorb fluid, etc. **2** a set of sheets of blank paper fastened together at one edge. **3** the fleshy underpart of an animal's foot or at the end of a finger. **4** a flat surface for helicopter take-off or rocket launching. **5** (*slang*) a person's home; a flat or bedsitter. ●*verb* (**padded, padding**) **1** provide with a pad or padding; stuff. **2** lengthen (a piece of writing or speech) by adding unnecessary material. □ **padded cell** a room with padded walls in a mental hospital.

**pad²** *verb* (**padded, padding**) walk with soft steady steps.

**padding** *noun* soft material used to pad things.

**paddle¹** *noun* **1** a short oar with a broad blade, used without a rowlock. **2** an instrument shaped like this. **3** one of the boards on a paddle-wheel. ●*verb* **1** propel by using a paddle or paddles. **2** row gently. □ **paddle-boat** *or* **paddle-steamer** *noun* a boat propelled by a paddle-wheel. **paddle-wheel** *noun* a wheel, with boards round its rim, attached to the side of a boat as a means of propulsion.

**paddle²** *verb* **1** walk with bare feet in shallow water. **2** dabble (the feet or hands) in shallow water. ●*noun* a spell of paddling.

**paddock** *noun* **1** a small field where horses are kept. **2** an enclosure at a racecourse for horses or racing-cars.

**paddy¹** *noun* (*informal*) a rage, a temper.

**paddy²** *noun* **1** (in full **paddy field**) a field where rice is grown. **2** rice that is still growing or in the husk.

**padlock** *noun* a detachable lock with a U-shaped bar that fastens through the loop of a staple or ring. ●*verb* fasten with a padlock.

**padre** (pah-dray) *noun* (*informal*) a chaplain in the armed forces.

**paean** (pee-ăn) *noun* (*Amer.* **pean**) a song of praise or triumph.

**paederast** alternative spelling of PEDERAST.

**paediatrician** (peed-i-ă-**trish**-ăn) *noun* (*Amer.* **pediatrician**) a specialist in paediatrics.

**paediatrics** (peed-i-**at**-triks) *noun* (*Amer.* **pediatrics**) the branch of medicine dealing with children and their diseases. □ **paediatric** *adjective*

**paedophilia** (peed-ŏ-**fil**-iă) *noun* (*Amer.* **pedophilia**) sexual attraction felt by an adult towards a child.

**paella** (pah-**el**-ă) *noun* a Spanish dish of rice, chicken, seafood, etc. cooked in a large shallow pan.

**paeony** alternative spelling of PEONY.

**pagan** (**pay**-găn) *adjective* **1** heathen. **2** holding the belief that deity exists in natural forces; nature-worshipping, especially in contrast to believing in Christianity, Judaism, etc. ●*noun* a pagan person. □ **paganism** *noun*

**Paganini** (pag-ă-**nee**-ni), Niccolò (1782–1840), Italian violinist and composer.

**Page**, Sir Frederick Handley (1885–1962), English aircraft designer and manufacturer.

**page¹** *noun* **1** a leaf in a book, newspaper, etc. **2** one side of this.

**page²** *noun* **1** a liveried boy or man employed to go on errands, act as door attendant, etc. **2** a boy attendant of a person of rank or a bride. ●*verb* summon (a person) by making an announcement or using a pager. □ **page-boy** *noun* **1** a page. **2** a woman's hairstyle with the hair rolled under at the ends.

**pageant** (**paj**-ĕnt) *noun* an elaborate procession, play, or tableau, especially on a historical theme. □ **pageantry** *noun*

**pager** *noun* a radio device with a bleeper, used to contact the wearer.

**paginate** *verb* number the pages of (a book etc.). □ **pagination** *noun*

**pagoda** (pă-**goh**-dă) *noun* a Hindu or Buddhist temple, especially a pyramid-shaped tower with many tiers.

**pah** *interjection* an exclamation of disgust or contempt.

**paid** *see* PAY. ●*adjective* receiving money in exchange for goods or services; *a paid assistant; paid holidays.* □ **paid-up** *adjective* having paid one's subscription; recognized as a full member of a particular group. **put paid to** (*informal*) destroy the hopes, chances, or activities of.

**pail** *noun* a bucket.

**pain** *noun* **1** an unpleasant feeling caused by injury or disease of the body. **2** mental suffering. **3** (**pains**) careful effort, trouble taken; *take pains with the work.* ●*verb* cause pain to. □ **a pain in the neck** (*informal*) an annoying or tiresome person or thing. **on** (*or* **under**) **pain of death** with the threat of this punishment.

**pained** *adjective* distressed and annoyed; *a pained look.*

**painful** *adjective* **1** causing pain. **2** (of a part of the body) suffering pain. **3** causing trouble or difficulty; laborious. □ **painfully** *adverb*

**painkiller** *noun* a drug for lessening pain.

**painless** *adjective* not causing pain. □ **painlessly** *adverb*

**painstaking** *adjective* careful, thorough.

**paint** *noun* colouring matter for applying in liquid form to a surface. ●*verb* **1** cover or decorate with paint. **2** make a picture or portray using paint(s). **3** describe vividly; *he's not so black as he is painted.* □ **painted lady** an orange-red spotted butterfly. **paint the town red** (*informal*) go out and enjoy oneself flamboyantly.

**paintbrush** *noun* a brush for applying paint.

**painter** *noun* **1** a person who paints; an artist or decorator. **2** a rope attached to the bow of a boat for tying it up.

**painting** *noun* a painted picture.

**paintwork** *noun* a painted surface.

**pair** *noun* **1** a set of two things or people, a couple. **2** something consisting of two joined corresponding parts; *a pair of scissors.* **3** the other member of a pair; *can't find a pair to this sock.* **4** either or both of two MPs of opposite parties who agree not to vote on certain occasions. ●*verb* **1** (often foll. by *off*) arrange or be arranged in couples. **2** (of animals) mate. **3** partner (a person) with a member of the opposite sex.

**Paisley** *adjective* having a pattern of curved feather-shaped figures with much detail.

**pajamas** Amer. spelling of PYJAMAS.

**Paki** (**pak**-i) *noun* (*slang, offensive*) a Pakistani.

**Pakistan** (pah-kis-**tahn**) a country in southern Asia. □ **Pakistani** *adjective & noun* (*plural* **Pakistanis**).

**pal** *noun* (*informal*) a friend. □ **pal up** (**palled, palling**) become friends.

**palace** *noun* **1** the official residence of a sovereign, archbishop, or bishop. **2** a splendid building.

**Palaeocene** (**pal**-i-ŏ-seen) *adjective* (*Amer.* **Paleocene**) *Geol.* of the first epoch of the Tertiary period. ● *noun* this epoch.

**palaeography** (pal-i-**og**-răfi) *noun* (*Amer.* **paleography**) the study of ancient writing and documents. □ **palaeographer** *noun*, **palaeographic** *adjective*

**palaeolithic** (pal-i-ŏ-**lith**-ik) *adjective* (*Amer.* **paleolithic**) of the early part of the Stone Age. ● *noun* this period.

**palaeontology** (pal-i-on-**tol**-ŏji) *noun* (*Amer.* **paleontology**) the study of life in the geological past. □ **palaeontologist** *noun*

**Palaeozoic** (pal-i-ŏ-**zoh**-ik) *adjective* (*Amer.* **Paleozoic**) of the geological era between the Precambrian and Mesozoic, marked by the appearance of plants and animals. ● *noun* this era.

**palais** (**pal**-ay) *noun* a public dance hall.

**palanquin** (pal-ăn-**keen**) *noun* (*also* **palankeen**) a covered litter for one passenger, used in India and the East.

**palatable** (**pal**-ă-tă-bŭl) *adjective* **1** pleasant to the taste. **2** (of an idea) acceptable.

**palate** (**pal**-ăt) *noun* **1** the roof of the mouth. **2** the sense of taste.

**palatial** (pă-**lay**-shăl) *adjective* like a palace; spacious and splendid. □ **palatially** *adverb*

**palaver** (pă-**lah**-ver) *noun* (*informal*) tedious fuss and bother.

**pale**[1] *adjective* **1** (of a person's face) having little colour, lighter than normal. **2** (of colour or light) faint, not bright or vivid. ● *verb* turn pale. □ **palely** *adverb*, **paleness** *noun*

**pale**[2] *noun* **1** a stake forming part of a fence. **2** a boundary. □ **beyond the pale** outside the bounds of acceptable behaviour.

**Paleocene** Amer. spelling of PALAEOCENE.

**paleography** Amer. spelling of PALAEOGRAPHY.

**paleolithic** Amer. spelling of PALAEOLITHIC.

**paleontology** Amer. spelling of PALAEONTOLOGY.

**Paleozoic** Amer. spelling of PALAEOZOIC.

**Palestine** the former name of a country at the eastern end of the Mediterranean Sea, now divided between Israel and Jordan.

□ **Palestine Liberation Organization** *see* PLO. □ **Palestinian** *adjective & noun*

**Palestrina** (pal-es-**tree**-nă), Giovanni Pierluigi da (1525/6–1594), Italian composer, known for his sacred music.

**palette** (**pal**-it) *noun* a thin board on which an artist mixes colours when painting. □ **palette-knife** *noun* **1** an artist's knife for mixing or spreading paint. **2** a kitchen knife with a flexible blade for spreading or smoothing soft substances.

**Pali** (**pah**-li) *noun* a language closely related to Sanskrit in which many sacred Buddhist texts are written.

**palimony** *noun* (*Amer. informal*) an allowance paid by one partner of a separated unmarried couple to the other. *See* ALIMONY.

**palimpsest** (**pal**-imp-sest) *noun* **1** writing-material on which the original writing has been removed to make room for other writing. **2** a monumental brass turned and re-engraved on the reverse side.

**palindrome** (**pal**-in-drohm) *noun* a word or phrase that reads the same backwards as forwards, e.g. *rotator, nurses run.*

**paling** *noun* **1** fencing made of wooden posts or railings. **2** one of its uprights.

**palisade** (pal-i-**sayd**) *noun* a fence of pointed stakes.

**pall** (*pronounced* pawl) *noun* **1** a cloth spread over a coffin. **2** something forming a dark heavy covering; *a pall of smoke.* ● *verb* become uninteresting or boring.

**Palladio** (pă-**lah**-di-oh), Andrea (1508–80), Italian architect, whose designs show classical influence. □ **Palladian** (pă-**lay**-diăn) *adjective*

**palladium** (pă-**lay**-diŭm) *noun* a rare white metallic element (symbol Pd), used as a catalyst and in jewellery.

**pallbearer** *noun* a person helping to carry the coffin or walking beside it at a funeral.

**pallet**[1] *noun* **1** a mattress stuffed with straw. **2** a hard narrow bed; a makeshift bed. **3** a portable platform for carrying or storing goods.

**palliasse** (**pal**-i-ass) *noun* a straw mattress.

**palliate** (**pal**-i-ayt) *verb* **1** make less intense or severe. **2** excuse (an offence etc.).

**palliative** (**pal**-i-ătiv) *adjective* reducing the bad effects of something. ● *noun* something that does this.

**pallid** (**pal**-id) *adjective* pale, especially from illness.

**pallor** (**pal**-er) *noun* paleness.

**pally** *adjective* (*informal*) friendly.

**palm** *noun* **1** the inner surface of the hand between the wrist and the fingers; this part of a glove. **2** a palm tree. ● *verb* conceal in one's hand. □ **palm off 1** get (a thing) accepted fraudulently; *palmed it off on them.* **2** cause (a person) to accept unwillingly or unknowingly; *palmed him off with my old car*. **Palm Sunday** the Sunday before Easter, commemorating Christ's entry into Jerusalem. **palm tree** a tree growing in warm climates, with no branches and a mass of pointed or fan-shaped leaves at the top.

**palmate** (pal-mayt) *adjective* shaped like a hand with the fingers spread out.

**Palmerston** (pahm-er-stŏn), Henry John Temple, 3rd Viscount (1784–1865), British Prime Minister 1855–8, 1859–65.

**palmetto** (pal-met-oh) *noun* (*plural* **palmettos**) a small palm tree with fan-shaped leaves.

**palmistry** (pahm-ist-ri) *noun* telling a person's future or character by examining the lines in the palm of his or her hand. □ **palmist** *noun*

**palmy** (pahm-i) *adjective* (**palmier**, **palmiest**) **1** full of palms. **2** flourishing; *in their former palmy days*.

**palomino** (pal-ŏ-meen-oh) *noun* (*plural* **palominos**) a golden or cream-coloured horse with a light-coloured mane and tail.

**palpable** (pal-pă-bŭl) *adjective* **1** able to be touched or felt. **2** easily perceived, obvious. □ **palpably** *adverb*

**palpate** (pal-payt) *verb* examine by feeling with the hands, especially as part of a medical examination. □ **palpation** *noun*

**palpitate** (pal-pit-ayt) *verb* **1** pulsate, throb rapidly. **2** (of a person) quiver with fear or excitement.

**palpitation** *noun* **1** throbbing, quivering. **2** (often as **palpitations**) increased heartbeat due to agitation or disease.

**palsied** (pawl-zid) *adjective* affected with palsy.

**palsy** (pawl-zi) *noun* paralysis, especially with involuntary tremors.

**paltry** (pol-tri) *adjective* (**paltrier**, **paltriest**) worthless, trivial, contemptible.

**pampas** (pam-păs) *noun* (treated as *singular* or *plural*) vast grassy plains in South America. □ **pampas-grass** *noun* tall ornamental grass with feathery plumes.

**pamper** *verb* treat very indulgently.

**pamphlet** (pamf-lit) *noun* a leaflet or booklet containing information.

**Pan** (*Gk. myth.*) the god of flocks and herds.

**pan¹** *noun* **1** a metal or earthenware vessel with a handle, used for cooking. **2** any similar shallow container, e.g. the bowl of a pair of scales. **3** a lavatory bowl. ●*verb* (**panned**, **panning**) **1** wash (gravel) in a pan in search of gold. **2** (*informal*) criticize severely. □ **pan out** (of circumstances or events) work out well or in a specified way.

**pan²** *verb* (**panned**, **panning**) **1** swing (a camera) horizontally to give a panoramic effect or follow a moving object. **2** (of a camera) swing in this way.

**pan-** *combining form* all-, of the whole of a continent, racial group etc.; *pan-African*; *pan-American*.

**panacea** (pan-ă-see-ă) *noun* a remedy for all kinds of diseases or troubles.

**panache** (păn-ash) *noun* a confident stylish manner.

**Panama** (pan-ă-mah) a country in Central America. □ **Panamanian** (pană-may-niăn) *adjective & noun*

**panama** (pan-ă-mah) *noun* a straw hat with a brim and indented crown.

**Panama Canal** a canal across the isthmus of Panama, connecting the Atlantic and Pacific Oceans.

**Panama City** the capital of Panama.

**panatella** (pan-ă-tel-ă) *noun* a thin cigar.

**pancake** *noun* **1** a thin round cake of batter fried on both sides, sometimes rolled up with filling. **2** make-up in the form of a flat cake. □ **Pancake Day** Shrove Tuesday, on which pancakes are traditionally eaten. **pancake landing** an emergency landing in which an aircraft lands horizontally with the undercarriage still retracted.

**panchromatic** (pan-krŏ-mat-ik) *adjective* sensitive to all colours of the visible spectrum; *panchromatic film*.

**pancreas** (pank-ri-ăs) *noun* a gland near the stomach discharging a digestive secretion into the duodenum and insulin into the blood. □ **pancreatic** (pank-ri-at-ik) *adjective*

**panda** *noun* **1** (also **giant panda**) a large rare bearlike black and white animal living in the mountains of south-west China. **2** (also **red panda**) a reddish-brown racoon-like animal of India. □ **panda car** a police patrol car.

**pandemic** (pan-dem-ik) *adjective* (of a disease) occurring over a whole country or the whole world; widespread.

**pandemonium** (pandi-moh-niŭm) *noun* uproar; confusion and chaos.

**pander** *verb* (foll. by *to*) gratify (weakness or a person's wishes); *pandering to the public interest in scandal*. ●*noun* a pimp.

**pandit** = PUNDIT (sense 2).

**Pandora** (*Gk. myth.*) the first woman, who opened a store-jar which let loose all kinds of misfortunes. □ **Pandora's box** something that once begun will generate many unmanageable problems.

**p. & p.** *abbreviation* postage and packing.

**pane** *noun* a single sheet of glass in a window or door.

**panegyric** (pan-i-ji-rik) *noun* a speech or piece of writing praising a person or thing.

**panel** *noun* **1** a strip of board or other material forming a separate section of a wall, door, or cabinet; a section of the metal bodywork of a vehicle; a distinct section of a surface. **2** a strip of material set lengthwise in a garment. **3** a group of people assembled to discuss or decide something. **4** a list of jurors; a jury. ●*verb* (**panelled, panelling;** *Amer.* **paneled, paneling**) cover or decorate with panels. ☐ **panel game** a broadcast quiz or game in which a panel of people take part.

**panelling** *noun* (*Amer.* **paneling**) **1** a series of panels in a wall. **2** wood used for making panels.

**panellist** *noun* (*Amer.* **panelist**) a member of a panel.

**pang** *noun* a sudden sharp feeling of pain or painful emotion; *pangs of jealousy.*

**pangolin** (**pang-ŏ-lin**) *noun* a scaly anteater.

**panic** *noun* sudden uncontrollable terror, infectious fear. ●*verb* (**panicked, panicking**) affect or be affected with panic. ☐ **panic stations** (*informal*) a state of emergency. **panic-stricken, panic-struck** *adjective* affected with panic. ☐ **panicky** *adjective*

**panicle** *noun* a loose branching cluster of flowers, as in oats.

**panjandrum** *noun* **1** a mock title of an important person. **2** a pompous official.

**Pankhurst**, Mrs Emmeline (1858–1928), British suffragette leader.

**pannier** *noun* a large basket, bag, or box, especially one of a pair carried on either side of a pack animal, bicycle, or motor cycle.

**panoply** (**pan-ŏ-pli**) *noun* a splendid array.

**panorama** *noun* **1** a view of a wide area; a picture or photograph of this. **2** a view of a constantly changing scene or series of events. ☐ **panoramic** (**pan-er-am-ik**) *adjective*

**pan-pipes** *plural noun* a musical instrument made of a series of pipes of graduated lengths fixed together. (¶ Named after the Greek god Pan.)

**pansy** *noun* **1** a garden plant of the violet family, with large richly-coloured petals. **2** (*informal, offensive*) an effeminate or homosexual man.

**pant** *verb* **1** breathe with short quick breaths. **2** utter breathlessly. **3** (usually foll. by *for*) be extremely eager. ●*noun* a panting breath.

**pantaloons** *plural noun* baggy trousers gathered at the ankles.

**pantechnicon** (**pan-tek-nik-ŏn**) *noun* a large lorry used for transporting furniture etc.

**pantheism** (**pan-thi-izm**) *noun* **1** the belief that God is in everything. **2** worship that accepts all gods. ☐ **pantheist** *noun*, **pantheistic** *adjective*

**pantheon** (**pan-thi-ŏn**) *noun* **1** a temple dedicated to all the gods. **2** the gods of a people collectively.

**panther** *noun* **1** a leopard, especially a black one. **2** (*Amer.*) a puma.

**panties** *plural noun* (*informal*) underpants for women or children.

**pantihose** *noun* (*Amer.* **panty hose**) (usually treated as *plural*) women's tights.

**pantile** (**pan-tyl**) *noun* a curved roof-tile.

**panto** *noun* (*plural* **pantos**) (*informal*) a pantomime (sense 1).

**pantograph** *noun* **1** an instrument with jointed rods for copying drawings on a different scale. **2** a jointed framework conveying a current to an electric vehicle from overhead wires.

**pantomime** *noun* **1** a Christmas theatre show based on a fairy tale. **2** expressive movements of the face and body used to convey a story or meaning. **3** (*informal*) a ridiculous situation.

**pantry** *noun* **1** a room in which crockery, cutlery, table linen, etc. are kept. **2** a larder.

**pants** *plural noun* **1** underpants or knickers. **2** (*Amer.*) trousers. ☐ **caught with one's pants down** caught in an embarrassing situation.

**pap** *noun* **1** soft or semi-liquid food for infants or invalids. **2** light or trivial reading matter. **3** (*old use* or *dialect*) a nipple.

**papa** *noun* (*old use*) father.

**papacy** (**pay-pă-si**) *noun* the position or authority of the pope; the system of Church government by popes.

**papal** (**pay-păl**) *adjective* of the pope or the papacy.

**paparazzo** (**pap-a-ra-tsoh**) *noun* (*plural* **paparazzi**) a freelance photographer who pursues celebrities to photograph them.

**papaw** (**pă-paw**) = PAWPAW.

**papaya** = PAWPAW.

**paper** *noun* **1** a substance manufactured in thin sheets from wood fibre etc., used for writing or printing on or for wrapping things. **2** a newspaper. **3** wallpaper. **4** a set of examination questions; *the biology paper.* **5** (**papers**) official documents, identification, etc.; *a ship's papers.* **6** an essay or dissertation. ●*adjective* **1** made of paper. **2** only theoretical; not actual; *paper profits.* ●*verb* **1** cover (walls etc.) with wallpaper. **2** (foll. by *over*) try to hide (faults etc.). ☐ **on paper** in writing; in theory, when judged from written or printed evidence; *the scheme looks good on paper.* **paper-boy, paper-girl** *noun* one who delivers newspapers. **paper-clip** *noun* a piece of bent wire for holding sheets of paper together. **paper-knife** *noun* a blunt knife for slitting open envelopes. **paper**

**money** banknotes as distinct from coins.
**paper tiger** a person or thing that seems threatening but can do no harm.

**paperback** *noun* a book bound in a flexible paper binding, not in a stiff cover.

**paperweight** *noun* a small heavy object placed on top of loose papers to keep them in place.

**paperwork** *noun* routine clerical or administrative work.

**papery** *adjective* like paper in texture; thin and flimsy.

**papier mâché** (pap-yay ma-shay) *noun* paper pulp used for making boxes and ornaments. (¶ French, = chewed paper.)

**papilla** *noun* (*plural* **papillae**) a small protuberance at the base of a hair, feather, or tooth. □ **papillary** *adjective*

**papist** (pay-pist) *noun* (often *scornful*) a Roman Catholic.

**papoose** (pă-pooss) *noun* a North American Indian baby.

**paprika** (pap-rik-ă) *noun* mild red pepper.

**Pap test** a cervical smear test.

**Papua New Guinea** (pap-oo-ă) a country consisting of a group of islands between Asia and Australia.

**papyrus** (pă-py-rŭs) *noun* (*plural* **papyri**) **1** a reed-like water plant with thick fibrous stems. **2** a type of paper made from this plant by the ancient Egyptians. **3** a manuscript written on this.

**par** *noun* **1** an average or normal amount, degree, condition, etc.; *feeling below par.* **2** (in golf) the number of strokes that a first-class player should normally require for a hole or course. **3** the face value of stocks and shares. **4** (in full **par of exchange**) the recognized value of one country's currency in terms of another's. □ **on a par with** on an equal footing with; similar to. **par for the course** (*informal*) what is normal or expected.

**para** *noun* (*informal*) **1** a paratrooper. **2** a paragraph.

**parable** *noun* a story told to illustrate a moral lesson.

**parabola** (pă-rab-ŏ-lă) *noun* a curve like the path of an object that is thrown into the air and falls back to earth; an open plane curve formed by the intersection of a cone with a plane parallel to its side. □ **parabolic** (pa-ra-bol-ik) *adjective*

**paracetamol** (pa-ră-see-tă-mol) *noun* drug used to relieve pain and reduce fever.

**parachute** *noun* a rectangular or umbrella-shaped device that allows a person to jump from an aircraft and descend safely; a similar device used as a brake; *parachute troops.* ●*verb* descend or drop (supplies) by parachute. □ **parachutist** *noun*

**parade** *noun* **1** a public procession or display. **2** a ceremonial assembly of troops for inspection, roll-call, etc. **3** a boastful display; *makes a parade of his virtues.* **4** a public square, promenade, or row of shops. ●*verb* **1** march ceremonially; walk in procession through (streets etc.). **2** (of troops) assemble for parade. **3** display boastfully. □ **on parade** taking part in a parade.

**paradigm** (pa-ră-dym) *noun* an example, pattern, or model that serves as an explanation.

**paradise** *noun* **1** heaven. **2** the garden of Eden. **3** a place or state of complete happiness.

**paradox** (pa-ră-doks) *noun* **1** a statement which seems contradictory or absurd, but which expresses a truth. **2** a person or thing having contradictory qualities. □ **paradoxical** (pa-ră-doks-ikăl) *adjective*, **paradoxically** *adverb*

**paraffin** *noun* an oil obtained from petroleum or shale, used as a fuel. □ **liquid paraffin** a tasteless form of this used as a mild laxative. **paraffin wax** paraffin in solid form.

**paragon** (pa-ră-gŏn) *noun* a model of excellence; an apparently perfect person or thing.

**paragraph** *noun* one or more sentences forming a distinct section of a piece of writing and beginning on a new (often indented) line. ●*verb* arrange in paragraphs.

**Paraguay** (pa-ră-gwy) an inland country in South America. □ **Paraguayan** (pa-ră-gwy-ăn) *adjective & noun*

**parakeet** (pa-ră-keet) *noun* a small parrot, usually with a long tail.

**parallax** (pa-ră-laks) *noun* an apparent difference in the position or direction of an object when it is viewed from different points. □ **parallactic** (pa-ră-lak-tik) *adjective*

**parallel** *adjective* **1** (of lines or planes) continually at the same distance from each other or from another line or plane; *parallel lines; the road runs parallel to the railway.* **2** (of circumstances) similar; having features that correspond. **3** (of processes) occurring or performed simultaneously. ●*noun* **1** a person or situation that is comparable or similar to another. **2** a comparison; *drew a parallel between the two situations.* **3** (in full **parallel of latitude**) an imaginary line on the earth's surface, or a corresponding line on a map, parallel to the equator. ●*verb* (**paralleled**, **paralleling**) **1** be parallel to. **2** mention something parallel or corresponding; compare. □ **in parallel** (of electronic circuits) arranged so as to join at common points at each end. □ **parallelism** *noun*

**parallelepiped** (pa-ră-lel-i-**py**-ped) *noun* a solid body of which each face is a parallelogram.

**parallelogram** (pa-ră-**lel**-ŏ-gram) *noun* a plane four-sided figure with its opposite sides parallel to each other.

**Paralympics** *plural noun* an international athletic competition modelled on the Olympic Games, for paraplegics and other disabled athletes.

**paralyse** *verb* (*Amer.* **paralyze**) **1** affect with paralysis; make unable to move or act normally. **2** bring to a standstill.

**paralysis** *noun* **1** inability to move normally, especially when caused by disease or injury to nerves. **2** powerlessness; inability to function normally.

**paralytic** (pa-ră-**lit**-ik) *adjective* **1** affected with paralysis. **2** (*slang*) very drunk.

**Paramaribo** (pa-ră-**ma**-ri-boh) the capital of Suriname.

**paramedic** *noun* a paramedical worker, especially a member of an ambulance crew with advanced medical training.

**paramedical** *adjective* supplementing and supporting medical work.

**parameter** (pă-**ram**-it-er) *noun* **1** *Maths* a quantity that is constant in the case considered but varies in different cases. **2** a variable quantity or quality that restricts or gives a particular form to the thing it characterizes. **3** a specification that is used in a computer program or routine and that can be given a different value whenever this is repeated. **4** a limit or boundary, especially of a subject of discussion.

**paramilitary** *adjective* organized like a military force but not part of the official armed services. ●*noun* a member of a paramilitary organization.

**paramount** *adjective* chief in importance; supreme.

**paramour** (pa-ră-moor) *noun* a married person's secret or illicit lover.

**paranoia** (pa-ră-**noi**-ă) *noun* **1** *Psychol.* a mental disorder in which a person has delusions, e.g. of grandeur or persecution. **2** an abnormal tendency to suspect and mistrust others.

**paranoiac** = PARANOID.

**paranoid** (pa-ră-noid) *adjective* of, like, or suffering from paranoia. ●*noun* a person suffering from paranoia.

**paranormal** *adjective* (of occurrences or powers) operating according to laws and influences that cannot be explained scientifically; supernatural.

**parapet** (pa-ră-pit) *noun* a low protective wall along the edge of a balcony, roof, or bridge.

**paraphernalia** (pa-ră-fer-**nay**-liă) *noun* (treated as *plural* or *singular*) miscellaneous articles or pieces of equipment.

**paraphrase** (**pa**-ră-frayz) *verb* express the meaning of (a passage) in other words. ●*noun* rewording in this way; a reworded passage.

**paraplegia** (pa-ră-**plee**-jiă) *noun* paralysis of the legs and part or all of the trunk.

**paraplegic** (pa-ră-**plee**-jik) *adjective* of or suffering from paraplegia. ●*noun* a person suffering from paraplegia.

**parapsychology** (pa-ră-sy-**kol**-ŏji) *noun* the study of mental phenomena that seem to be beyond normal mental abilities (e.g. clairvoyance and telepathy).

**paraquat** (**pa**-ră-kwot) *noun* a highly poisonous weedkiller.

**parasailing** *noun* a sport in which participants wearing open parachutes are towed behind a motor boat.

**parascending** *noun* a sport in which the participant is attached to a parachute and towed through the air behind a motor boat or vehicle.

**parasite** *noun* **1** an animal or plant that lives on or in another and feeds on it. **2** a person who lives off another and gives nothing in return. □ **parasitic** (pa-ră-**sit**-ik) *adjective*

**parasol** *noun* a light umbrella giving shade from the sun.

**paratrooper** *noun* a member of the paratroops.

**paratroops** *plural noun* parachute troops.

**paratyphoid** (pa-ră-**ty**-foid) *noun* a fever resembling typhoid but milder.

**parboil** *verb* boil (food) until it is partly cooked.

**parcel** *noun* **1** something wrapped up in a package for posting or carrying. **2** a quantity of something considered as a distinct unit; a piece of land. ●*verb* (**parcelled**, **parcelling**; *Amer.* **parceled**, **parceling**) **1** (foll. by *up*) wrap up as a parcel. **2** (foll. by *out*) divide into portions; *parcelled it out.*

**parch** *verb* make hot and dry or thirsty.

**parchment** *noun* **1** a heavy paper-like material made from animal skins. **2** a manuscript written on this. **3** high-grade paper resembling parchment.

**pardon** *noun* **1** forgiveness for an offence, discourtesy, or error; *I beg your pardon.* **2** cancellation of the punishment incurred through a crime or conviction; *a free pardon.* ●*verb* (**pardoned**, **pardoning**) forgive; overlook (a slight discourtesy, error, etc.) kindly. □ **pardonable** *adjective*

**pare** (*pronounced* pair) *verb* **1** trim by cutting away the edges. **2** (often foll. by *down* or *away*) reduce little by little; *pared down their expenses.*

**parent** *noun* **1** a person who has a child; a father or mother. **2** an animal or plant from which others are derived. **3** the source or origin of something. ●*verb* be a parent (of). □ **parent company** a company of which others are subsidiaries. □ **parenthood** *noun*

**parentage** (**pair**-ĕn-tij) *noun* ancestry, lineage; descent from parents.

**parental** (pă-**ren**-t'l) *adjective* of parents; *parental guidance*.

**parenthesis** (pă-**ren**-thi-sis) *noun* (*plural* **parentheses**) **1** an additional word, phrase, or sentence inserted into a sentence or paragraph and marked off by brackets, dashes, or commas. **2** either of a pair of round brackets (like these) used for this. □ **in parenthesis** between brackets as a parenthesis; as an aside or digression in a speech.

**parenthetic** (pa-rĕn-**thet**-ik) *adjective* **1** of or as a parenthesis. **2** inserted as an aside or digression. □ **parenthetical** *adjective*, **parenthetically** *adverb*

**parenting** *noun* bringing up children.

**par excellence** (par **eks**-el-ahns) being a supreme example of its kind; *a restaurant par excellence*. (¶ French.)

**parfait** (**par**-fay) *noun* **1** a rich iced pudding made of eggs and cream or ice cream. **2** layers of ice cream, fruit, meringue, etc., served in a tall glass.

**pariah** (pă-**ry**-ă) *noun* a social outcast.

**parietal** (pă-**ry**-ĕt'l) *noun* either of the **parietal bones**, those forming part of the sides and top of the skull.

**parings** (**pair**-ingz) *plural noun* strips that have been cut off.

**Paris**[1] the capital of France. □ **Parisian** (pă-**riz**-iăn) *adjective & noun*

**Paris**[2] (*Gk. legend*) a Trojan prince, whose abduction of Helen (the wife of the king of Sparta) provoked the Trojan War.

**parish** *noun* **1** an area within a diocese, having its own church and minister. **2** a distinct area within a county, constituted for purposes of local government. **3** the people of a parish. □ **parish clerk** an official performing various duties in connection with a parish church. **parish council** an administrative body in a civil parish. **parish register** a record of the christenings, marriages, and burials in a parish church.

**parishioner** (pă-**rish**-ŏn-er) *noun* an inhabitant of a parish.

**parity** (**pa**-riti) *noun* **1** equality; equal status or pay. **2** equivalence of one currency with another; being valued at par.

**park** *noun* **1** a public garden or recreation ground in a town. **2** an enclosed area of grassland attached to a large country house. **3** a large protected area where wild animals are kept in captivity; *a wildlife park*. **4** a parking area for vehicles; *a lorry park*. **5** an area of land planned for industry or business; *a science park*. **6** (*Amer.*) a sports ground. ●*verb* **1** position and leave (a vehicle) temporarily. **2** (*informal*) deposit temporarily; *just park it on the table*. □ **parking lot** (*Amer.*) a car park. **parking-meter** *noun* a coin-operated meter allocating a length of time for which a vehicle may be parked beside it. **parking ticket** a notice of a fine for parking illegally.

**parka** *noun* **1** a long canvas jacket with fur round the hood. **2** a hooded skin jacket worn by Eskimos.

**Parker**, Charlie (Christopher) (1920–55), American jazz saxophonist.

**parkin** *noun* ginger cake made with oatmeal and treacle.

**Parkinson's disease** a disease of the nervous system causing trembling and weakness of the muscles. (¶ Named after the English surgeon J. Parkinson, who described it in 1817.)

**Parkinson's law** the humorous notion that work expands to fill the time available for its completion. (¶ Formulated by C. Northcote Parkinson (born 1909), English writer.)

**parkland** *noun* open grassland with groups of trees.

**parky** *adjective* (*informal*) (of weather) chilly.

**parlance** (**par**-lăns) *noun* the vocabulary or expressions of a particular subject or group.

**parley** *noun* (*plural* **parleys**) a discussion to settle a dispute. ●*verb* (**parleyed, parleying**) hold a parley.

**parliament** (**par**-lă-mĕnt) *noun* **1** an assembly that makes the laws of a country. **2** (**Parliament**) (in the UK) the House of Commons and the House of Lords.

**parliamentarian** (parlă-men-**tair**-iăn) *noun* a person skilled at debating in parliament.

**parliamentary** (parlă-**ment**-eri) *adjective* **1** of parliament; enacted by parliament. **2** (of language, behaviour) polite; acceptable according to the rules of a parliament. □ **Parliamentary Commissioner for Administration** (in the UK) the official name of the ombudsman. **parliamentary private secretary** a member of parliament who assists a government minister.

**parlour** *noun* (*Amer.* **parlor**) **1** (*old use*) a sitting-room in a private house. **2** a shop providing specific items; *beauty parlour*; *ice cream parlour*.

**parlourmaid** *noun* a maid who waits on a household at meals.

**parlous** (**par**-lŭs) *adjective* (*formal*) (of a state of affairs) difficult or dangerous.

**Parmesan** (par-mi-**zan**) *noun* a hard dry cheese made originally at Parma in Italy, usually grated.

**Parnassus** a mountain of central Greece, in antiquity sacred to the Muses. □ **Parnassian** *adjective*

**Parnell** (par-**nel**), Charles Stewart (1846–91), Irish Nationalist leader.

**parochial** (pă-**roh**-kiăl) *adjective* **1** of a church parish. **2** showing interest only in local affairs; limited, narrow. □ **parochially** *adverb*, **parochialism** *noun*

**parody** (**pa**-rŏ-di) *noun* **1** a comic imitation of a well-known person, literary work, style of writing, etc. **2** a feeble imitation, a travesty. ● *verb* (**parodied, parodying**) write a parody of; mimic humorously. □ **parodist** *noun*

**parole** (pă-**rohl**) *noun* **1** temporary or permanent release of a prisoner before his or her sentence has expired, on the promise of good behaviour. **2** such a promise. ● *verb* release (a prisoner) on parole.

**parotid** (pă-**rot**-id) *adjective* situated near the ear. ● *noun* (in full **parotid gland**) the salivary gland in front of the ear.

**paroxysm** (**pa**-rŏk-sizm) *noun* a spasm; a sudden attack or outburst of pain, rage, laughter, etc. □ **paroxysmal** (pa-rok-**siz**-m'l) *adjective*

**parquet** (par-**kay**) *noun* flooring of wooden blocks arranged in a pattern.

**Parr**, Catherine (1512–48), sixth wife of Henry VIII, who married him in 1543 and survived him.

**parr** *noun* a young salmon.

**parricide** (**pa**-ri-syd) *noun* **1** the act of killing one's own parent or other near relative. **2** a person who is guilty of this.

**parrot** *noun* **1** a tropical bird with a hooked bill and often brightly coloured plumage. **2** a person who mechanically repeats another's words. ● *verb* (**parroted, parroting**) repeat mechanically.

**parry** *verb* (**parried, parrying**) **1** ward off (a blow) using a weapon, one's arm, etc. to block the thrust. **2** deal skilfully with (an awkward question).

**parse** (*pronounced* parz) *verb* identify the grammatical form and function of (the words in a sentence).

**parsec** (**par**-sek) *noun* a unit of distance used in astronomy; about 3.25 light years.

**Parsee** (par-**see**) *noun* a follower of Zoroastrianism.

**parsimonious** (par-si-**moh**-niŭs) *adjective* stingy; too careful with money. □ **parsimoniously** *adverb*, **parsimony** (**par**-sim-ŏni) *noun*

**parsley** *noun* a herb with crinkly leaves used for flavouring and garnishing food.

**parsnip** *noun* a plant with a large yellowish tapering root used as a vegetable.

**parson** *noun* a rector or vicar. □ **parson's nose** the rump of a cooked fowl.

**parsonage** *noun* a rectory or vicarage.

**part** *noun* **1** some but not all of something. **2** a section or portion; *a story broadcast in three parts; this part of the country; parts of the body.* **3** a component of a machine or structure. **4** each of several equal portions of a whole; *three parts sugar to two parts butter.* **5** one's share or duty; *I've done my part; I want no part in it.* **6** an integral element; *feel part of the family.* **7** the role of a character in a play. **8** the tune or line of music assigned to a particular voice or instrument. ● *verb* **1** separate or divide. **2** leave one another's company. □ **for my part** as far as I am concerned. **in good part** without taking offence. **in part** partly. **part and parcel of** an essential part of. **part-exchange** *noun* a transaction in which goods are given as part of the payment. **part of speech** one of the grammatical classes into which words are divided (in English noun, adjective, pronoun, verb, etc.). **part-song** *noun* a song with three or more voice-parts. **part-time** *adjective & adverb* for only part of the working week. **part-timer** *noun* one employed in part-time work. **part with** give up, hand over.

**partake** *verb* (**partook, partaken, partaking**) **1** (foll. by *of* or *in*) participate; take a share or part. **2** (foll. by *of*) eat or drink (something).

**parterre** (par-**tair**) *noun* **1** a level space in a formal garden, occupied by flower beds. **2** the pit of a theatre.

**parthenogenesis** (par-thin-ŏ-**jen**-i-sis) *noun* reproduction without fertilization, especially in invertebrates and lower plants.

**Parthenon** (par-thin-ŏn) the temple of Athene Parthenos built on the Acropolis at Athens in 447–432 BC.

**Parthian** (par-thi-ăn) *adjective* of the ancient kingdom of Parthia, SE of the Caspian Sea, or its people. ● *noun* a native of Parthia. □ **Parthian shot** a sharp remark made by a person as he or she departs. (¶ The horsemen of Parthia were renowned for firing arrows at the enemy while retreating.)

**partial** (par-shăl) *adjective* **1** in part but not complete or total; *a partial eclipse.* **2** biased, unfair. □ **be partial to** have a strong liking for. □ **partially** *adverb*

**partiality** (par-shi-**al**-iti) *noun* **1** bias, favouritism. **2** a strong liking.

**participant** (par-**tiss**-i-pănt) *noun* one who participates.

**participate** (par-**tiss**-i-payt) *verb* take part or share in something. □ **participation** *noun*, **participator** *noun*

**participle** (par-**tiss**-ipŭl) *noun* a word formed from a verb (e.g. *going, gone; burning, burnt*) and used in compound verb-forms (*she is going* or *has gone*) or as an adjective (*a going concern*). □ **past participle**, e.g. *burnt, frightened, wasted*. **present participle**, e.g. *burning, frightening, wasting*. □ **participial** (par-ti-**sip**-iăl) *adjective*

**particle** *noun* **1** a very small portion of matter. **2** the smallest possible amount; *he hasn't a particle of sense*. **3** a minor part of speech or a common prefix or suffix, e.g. *non-, un-, -ness*.

**particoloured** *adjective* (*Amer.* **particolored**) of more than one colour; variegated; multicoloured.

**particular** *adjective* **1** relating to one person or thing as distinct from others, individual; *this particular case*. **2** special, exceptional; *took particular trouble*. **3** insisting on high standards; fussy; *is very particular about what he eats*. ● *noun* a detail; a piece of information; *gave particulars of the stolen property*. □ **in particular 1** particularly, especially; *we liked this one in particular*. **2** specifically; *did nothing in particular*. □ **particularity** (per-tik-yoo-la-riti) *noun*

**particularize** *verb* (also **particularise**) specify, name specially or one by one. □ **particularization** *noun*

**particularly** *adverb* **1** especially, very. **2** specifically; *particularly asked for vegetarian food*.

**parting** *noun* **1** leave-taking. **2** a line where hair is combed away in different directions. □ **parting shot** = PARTHIAN SHOT.

**partisan** (parti-**zan**) *noun* (also **partizan**) **1** a strong and often uncritical supporter of a person, cause, etc. **2** a guerrilla. □ **partisanship** *noun*

**partition** (par-**tish**-ŏn) *noun* **1** division into parts. **2** a structure that divides a room or space; a thin wall. ● *verb* **1** divide into parts; share out in this way. **2** divide (a room) with a partition.

**partitive** *adjective Grammar* (of a word or form) denoting part of a group or quantity. ● *noun* a partitive word or form, e.g. *some, any*.

**partly** *adverb* to some extent but not completely or wholly.

**partner** *noun* **1** one who shares with another or others in some activity, especially in a business where he or she shares risks and profits. **2** either of two people dancing together or playing on the same side in a game. **3** a husband or wife; either member of an unmarried couple. ● *verb* be the partner of. □ **partnership** *noun*

**partook** *see* PARTAKE.

**partridge** *noun* a game bird with brown feathers and a plump body.

**parturition** (par-tewr-**ish**-ŏn) *noun* (*formal*) giving birth to young, childbirth.

**party** *noun* **1** a social gathering, usually of invited guests. **2** a number of people travelling or working together as a unit; *a search party*. **3** a political group organized on a national basis to put forward its policies and candidates for office. **4** the person(s) forming one side in an agreement or dispute. **5** a person who participates in, knows of, or supports an action or plan etc.; *refused to be a party to the conspiracy*. **6** (*humorous*) a person. □ **party line 1** a shared telephone line. **2** the set policy of a political party. **party wall** a dividing wall that is common to two rooms or buildings.

**Parvati** (par-vă-ti) (in Hinduism) a benevolent goddess, wife of Siva.

**parvenu** (par-věn-yoo) *noun* an upstart.

**parvenue** *noun* a female upstart.

**Pascal**[1] (pas-**kahl**) *noun* a computer language. (¶ Named after Blaise Pascal.)

**Pascal**[2] (pas-**kahl**), Blaise (1623–62), French mathematician, physicist, and religious philosopher.

**pascal** (pas-kăl) *noun* a unit of pressure. (¶ Named after Blaise Pascal.)

**paschal** (pas-kăl) *adjective* **1** of the Jewish Passover. **2** of Easter.

**pas de deux** (pah dě **der**) a dance for two. (¶ French, = step for two.)

**pasha** *noun* a former Turkish title (placed after a name) for an official of high rank.

**Pashto** (pu'sh-toh) *noun* (also **Pushto**) the Iranian language of the Pathans.

**paso doble** (pass-oh **doh**-blay) a Latin-American ballroom dance. (¶ Spanish, = double step.)

**pasque-flower** *noun* a perennial plant with feathery leaves and purple bell-shaped flowers.

**pass** *verb* (**passed, passing**) **1** go, proceed, or move onward or past something. **2** cause to move across, over, or past. **3** be transferred from one person to another; *his title passed to his eldest son*. **4** hand or transfer; (in football etc.) send the ball to another player. **5** discharge from the body as or with excreta. **6** change from one state into another. **7** come to an end. **8** happen, be done or said; *we heard what passed between them*. **9** occupy (time). **10** circulate, be accepted or currently known in a certain way. **11** be tolerated or allowed. **12** examine and declare satisfactory; approve (a law etc.), especially by vote. **13** achieve the required standard in performing (a test). **14** go beyond. **15** utter; pronounce as a decision; *passed some remarks*; *pass judgement*. **16** (in cards) refuse one's turn (e.g. in bidding). ●*noun* **1** passing, especially of an examination or at cards; a university degree without honours. **2** a movement made with the hand(s) or something held. **3** a permit to go into or out of a place or to be absent from one's quarters. **4** transference of the ball to another player in football etc. **5** a critical state of affairs; *things have come to a pretty pass*. **6** a narrow road or path over a mountain range. □ **make a pass at** (*informal*) make sexual advances to. **pass away, pass on** die. **pass off 1** disappear gradually. **2** (of an event) take place and be completed; *the meeting passed off smoothly*. **3** (foll. by *as*) offer or dispose of (a thing) under false pretences; *passed it off as his own*. **4** evade or dismiss (an awkward remark etc.) lightly. **pass out 1** complete one's military training. **2** (*informal*) faint. **pass over** disregard; ignore the claims of (a person) to promotion etc. **pass the buck** *see* BUCK. **pass up** (*informal*) refuse to accept (an opportunity etc.). **pass water** urinate.

**passable** *adjective* **1** able to be passed. **2** fairly good but not outstanding. □ **passably** *adverb*

**passage** *noun* **1** the process of passing. **2** the right to pass through. **3** a journey by sea or air. **4** a way through, a passageway. **5** a tube-like structure through which air or secretions pass in the body. **6** a particular section of a literary or musical work.

**passageway** *noun* a narrow path, alley, or corridor.

**passbook** *noun* a book recording deposits and withdrawals from a bank or building society account.

**passé** (**pas**-ay) *adjective* old-fashioned; past its prime. (¶ French.)

**passenger** *noun* **1** a person (other than the driver, pilot, or crew) travelling in a vehicle, ship, or aircraft. **2** a member of a team who does no work.

**passer-by** *noun* (*plural* **passers-by**) a person who happens to be going past.

**passerine** (**pas**-er-ryn) *adjective* of perching birds, whose feet are adapted for gripping. ●*noun* a bird of this kind.

**passim** (**pas**-im) *adverb* throughout or at many points in a book, article, etc. (¶ Latin, = everywhere.)

**passing** *adjective* not lasting long; casual; *a passing interest*. ●*noun* the end of something; a death.

**passion** *noun* **1** strong emotion, especially anger or love. **2** great enthusiasm for something; the object of this; *chess is his passion*. **3** (**Passion**) the sufferings of Christ on the Cross. □ **passion-flower** *noun*

a climbing plant with flowers thought to resemble the crown of thorns and symbolize the Passion of Christ. **passion-fruit** *noun* the edible fruit of some kinds of passion-flower. **Passion Sunday** the fifth Sunday in Lent.

**passionate** *adjective* **1** full of passion, showing or moved by strong emotion. **2** (of emotion) intense. □ **passionately** *adverb*

**passive** *adjective* **1** acted upon and not active. **2** not resisting, submissive. **3** lacking initiative or forceful qualities. **4** (of substances) inert, not active. ●*noun* the form of a verb used when the subject of the sentence receives the action, e.g. *was seen* in *he was seen there*. □ **passive resistance** non-violent resistance by refusal to cooperate. **passive smoking** breathing in smoke from other people's cigarettes etc., considered as a health risk. □ **passively** *adverb*, **passiveness** *noun*, **passivity** (pa-**siv**-iti) *noun*

**passkey** *noun* **1** a key to a door or gate. **2** a master-key.

**Passover** *noun* a Jewish festival commemorating the liberation of the Jews from slavery in Egypt.

**passport** *noun* **1** an official document identifying the holder as a citizen of a particular country and entitling him or her to travel abroad under its protection. **2** (foll. by *to*) a thing that enables one to obtain something; *such ability is a passport to success*.

**password** *noun* a secret prearranged word or phrase used as a code to gain admission, as proof of identity, etc.

**past** *adjective* **1** belonging or referring to the time before the present; (of time) gone by. **2** *Grammar* (of a tense or form) expressing a past action or state. ●*noun* **1** time that is gone by; past events. **2** a person's past life, especially if discreditable; *a man with a past*. **3** *Grammar* the past tense. ●*preposition* **1** beyond in time or place; *hurried past me*. **2** beyond the limits, power, range, or stage of; *past belief*; *she's past caring what happens*. ●*adverb* beyond in time or place; up to and further; *drove past*. □ **past it** (*slang*) too old or decrepit. **past master** an expert. **would not put it past someone** (*informal*) regard him or her as capable of doing it.

**pasta** (**pas**-tă) *noun* dried flour paste used in various shapes in cooking (e.g. macaroni, spaghetti).

**paste** *noun* **1** a moist fairly stiff mixture, especially of a powder and a liquid. **2** an adhesive. **3** an easily spread preparation of ground meat or fish etc.; *anchovy paste*. **4** a hard glasslike substance used in making imitation gems. ●*verb* **1** fasten or coat with paste. **2** (*slang*) beat or thrash.

**pasteboard** noun thin board made of layers of paper or wood-fibres pasted together.

**pastel** (pas-t'l) noun 1 a chalk-like crayon. 2 a drawing made with this. 3 a light delicate shade of colour.

**pastern** (pas-tern) noun the part of a horse's foot between fetlock and hoof.

**Pasternak** (pas-ter-nak), Boris Leonidovich (1890–1960), Russian poet and novelist, author of *Doctor Zhivago*.

**Pasteur** (pas-ter), Louis (1822–95), French chemist and bacteriologist, whose work led to the process now known as pasteurization.

**pasteurize** (pahs-chĕryz) verb (also **pasteurise**) sterilize (milk etc.) partially by heating and then chilling it. □ **pasteurization** noun (¶ Named after Louis Pasteur.)

**pastiche** (pas-teesh) noun 1 a musical or other composition made up of selections from various sources. 2 a work composed in the style of a well-known author, composer, etc.

**pastille** (pas-til) noun a small flavoured sweet for sucking; a lozenge.

**pastime** noun something done to pass time pleasantly; a recreation, a hobby.

**pastor** (pah-ster) noun a member of the clergy in charge of a church or congregation.

**pastoral** (pah-ster-ăl) adjective 1 of shepherds or country life; *a pastoral scene.* 2 of a pastor; concerned with spiritual guidance.

**pastoralist** (pah-ster-ăl-ist) noun (*Austral.*) a sheep-farmer or cattle-farmer.

**pastrami** (pas-trah-mi) noun seasoned smoked beef.

**pastry** noun 1 dough made of flour, fat, and water, used for making pies etc. 2 a cake etc. made of sweetened or filled pastry.

**pasturage** (pahs-cher-ij) noun 1 pastureland. 2 the right to graze animals on this.

**pasture** noun 1 land covered with grass suitable for grazing cattle. 2 grass on such land. ● verb put (animals) to graze in a pasture.

**pasty¹** (pas-ti) noun an individual portion of pastry wrapped around a filling of meat and vegetables.

**pasty²** (pay-sti) adjective 1 of or like paste. 2 unhealthily pale; *pasty-faced.* □ **pastiness** noun

**Pat.** abbreviation Patent.

**pat** verb (**patted, patting**) 1 tap gently with the open hand or with something flat. 2 flatten or shape by doing this. ● noun 1 a patting movement. 2 the sound of this. 3 a small mass of butter or other soft substance. ● adverb & adjective known and ready for any occasion; *had his answer pat.* □ **a pat on the back** praise, congratulations.

**Patagonia** the southernmost region of South America, chiefly a dry barren plateau in southern Argentina and Chile. □ **Patagonian** adjective & noun

**patch** noun 1 a piece of material or metal etc. put over a hole to mend it. 2 a piece of plaster or a pad placed over a wound etc. to protect it. 3 an area on a surface, differing in colour or texture from the rest. 4 a piece of ground; an area assigned to a specific policeman etc. 5 a small area of anything; *patches of fog.* 6 a short period; *went through a bad patch last summer.* ● verb 1 put a patch or patches on. 2 serve as a patch for. 3 piece (things) together. □ **not a patch on** (*informal*) not nearly as good as. **patch up 1** repair with patches. 2 settle (a quarrel etc.).

**patchouli** (pa-choo-li) noun a fragrant plant grown in the Far East.

**patchwork** noun 1 needlework in which assorted small pieces of cloth are joined, often in a pattern. 2 anything made of assorted pieces.

**patchy** adjective (**patchier, patchiest**) 1 having patches, existing in patches; *patchy fog.* 2 uneven in quality. □ **patchily** adverb

**pate** (*pronounced* payt) noun (*humorous or old use*) the head.

**pâté** (pa-tay) noun paste of meat etc. □ **pâté de foie gras** (dĕ fwah **grah**) fatted goose liver pâté.

**patella** (pă-tel-ă) noun (*plural* **patellae**) the kneecap.

**paten** (pat-ĕn) noun a metal plate on which bread is placed at the Eucharist.

**patent** noun (*pronounced* **pay**-tĕnt or **pat**-ĕnt) 1 an official document conferring a right or title, especially the sole right to make, use, or sell an invention. 2 an invention or process protected in this way. ● adjective (*pronounced* **pay**-tĕnt) 1 obvious, plain, unconcealed; *her patent dislike of him.* 2 protected by patent. ● verb (*pronounced* **pay**-tĕnt *or* **pat**-ĕnt) obtain a patent for (an invention). □ **patent leather** leather with a glossy varnished surface. **patent medicine** a medicine made under a patent and available without a prescription. **Patent Office** the government office that issues patents.

**patentee** (pay-tĕn-**tee** *or* pat-ĕn-**tee**) noun one who holds a patent.

**patently** adverb clearly, obviously; *he was patently jealous.*

**pater** (pay-ter) noun (*humorous or old use*) father. (¶ Latin.)

**paternal** (pă-ter-năl) adjective 1 of a father; of fatherhood. 2 fatherly. 3 related through one's father; *paternal grandmother*. □ **paternally** *adverb*

**paternalism** (pă-ter-năl-izm) *noun* the policy of governing in a paternal way, providing for people's needs but giving them no responsibility. □ **paternalistic** *adjective*

**paternity** (pă-tern-iti) *noun* **1** fatherhood, being a father. **2** descent from a father. □ **paternity test** a test to determine from blood samples whether a man may be the father of a particular child.

**paternoster** (pat-er-**nost**-er) *noun* the Lord's Prayer, especially in Latin.

**path** *noun* **1** a way by which people pass on foot, a track. **2** a line along which a person or thing moves. **3** a course of action.

**Pathan** (pă-tahn) *noun* a member of a people living in parts of Afghanistan and Pakistan.

**pathetic** (pă-thet-ik) *adjective* **1** arousing pity or sadness. **2** miserably inadequate. □ **pathetically** *adverb*

**pathfinder** *noun* an explorer.

**pathogen** *noun* something causing disease. □ **pathogenic** *adjective*

**pathological** (pa-thŏ-**loj**-ikăl) *adjective* **1** of pathology. **2** of or caused by a physical or mental disorder; *a pathological liar*. □ **pathologically** *adverb*

**pathology** (pă-**thol**-ŏji) *noun* **1** the study of diseases of the body. **2** abnormal changes in body tissue, caused by disease. □ **pathologist** *noun*

**pathos** (**pay**-thoss) *noun* a quality that arouses pity or sadness.

**pathway** *noun* a footway or track.

**patience** *noun* **1** calm endurance of hardship, inconvenience, delay, etc. **2** perseverance. **3** a card game for one player.

**patient** *adjective* having or showing patience. ●*noun* a person receiving treatment (or registered to receive treatment) by a doctor, dentist, etc. □ **patiently** *adverb*

**patina** (pat-in-ă) *noun* **1** a green incrustation on the surface of old bronze. **2** a gloss on the surface of woodwork, produced by age.

**patio** (**pat**-i-oh) *noun* (*plural* **patios**) **1** a paved area beside a house. **2** an inner courtyard in a Spanish or Spanish-American house.

**patisserie** (pă-**teess**-er-i) *noun* **1** fancy pastries. **2** a shop selling these.

**Patna** the capital of Bihar. □ **Patna rice** rice with long firm grains.

**patois** (**pat**-wah) *noun* (*plural* **patois**, *pronounced* **pat**-wahz) a dialect.

**Paton**, Alan Stewart (1903–88), South African writer and Liberal politician; author of *Cry the Beloved Country*.

**patrial** (**pay**-tri-ăl) (*hist., Brit.*) *adjective* having the right to live in the UK. ●*noun* a person with this status.

**patriarch** (**pay**-tri-ark) *noun* **1** the male head of a family or tribe. **2** (**the Patriarchs**) men named in the Bible as the ancestors of mankind or of the tribes of Israel. **3** a bishop of high rank in certain Churches. **4** a venerable old man. □ **patriarchal** (pay-tri-**ar**-kăl) *adjective*

**patriarchy** *noun* a male-dominated social system with descent through the male line.

**patrician** (pă-**trish**-ăn) *noun* a member of the aristocracy, especially in ancient Rome. ●*adjective* aristocratic.

**patricide** (pat-ri-syd) *noun* **1** the crime of killing one's own father. **2** a person who is guilty of this. □ **patricidal** *adjective*

**Patrick**, St (5th century), an apostle; the patron saint of Ireland. Feast day, 17 March.

**patrimony** (pat-rim-ŏni) *noun* **1** property inherited from one's father or ancestors; a heritage. **2** a church's endowed income or property.

**patriot** (**pay**-tri-ŏt *or* pat-ri-ŏt) *noun* a patriotic person.

**patriotic** (pat-ri-ot-ik) *adjective* loyally supporting one's country. □ **patriotically** *adverb*, **patriotism** (**pat**-riŏ-tizm) *noun*

**patrol** *verb* (**patrolled**, **patrolling**) walk or travel around (an area or building) to see that all is secure and orderly. ●*noun* **1** patrolling; *on patrol*. **2** the person(s), ship(s), or aircraft whose job is to patrol an area. **3** a unit of usually six members of a Scout troop or Guide company. □ **patrol car** a police car used for patrolling streets.

**patrolman** *noun* (*plural* **patrolmen**) (*Amer.*) a policeman of the lowest rank.

**patron** (**pay**-trŏn) *noun* **1** a person who gives encouragement or financial support to an activity or cause. **2** a regular customer of a shop, restaurant, etc. □ **patron saint** a saint regarded as giving special protection to a person, place, or activity.

**patronage** (pat-rŏn-ij) *noun* **1** support given by a patron. **2** the right of appointing a person to a benefice or other position. **3** patronizing behaviour.

**patronize** (**pat**-rŏ-nyz) *verb* (also **patronise**) **1** act as a patron towards, support or encourage. **2** be a regular customer at (a shop etc.). **3** treat in a condescending way.

**patronizing** *adjective* (also **patronising**) condescending. □ **patronizingly** *adverb*

**patronymic** (pat-rŏ-**nim**-ik) *noun* a person's name taken from the name of the father or a male ancestor.

**patter**[1] *verb* **1** make a series of light quick taps. **2** run with short quick steps. ●*noun* a series of light quick tapping sounds.

**patter²** *noun* rapid and often glib or deceptive speech, e.g. that used by a conjuror or salesman. ● *verb* talk or repeat glibly.

**pattern** *noun* **1** an arrangement of lines, shapes, or colours; a decorative design. **2** a model, design, or instructions for making something. **3** a sample of cloth or other material. **4** an excellent example, a model. **5** the regular form or order in which a series of actions or qualities occur; *behaviour patterns*. ● *verb* **1** model according to a pattern. **2** decorate with a pattern.

**patty** *noun* a small pie or pasty.

**paucity** (paw-siti) *noun* smallness of supply or quantity.

**Paul**, St (original name; Saul) (1st century AD), the first great Christian missionary, whose journeys are described in the Acts of the Apostles. Feast day, 29 June.

**Pauli** (**paw**-li), Wolfgang (1900–58), Austrian physicist, noted for his work on atomic and subatomic particles.

**Pauling**, Linus Carl (born 1901), American chemist noted for his work on molecular structure and for his opposition to nuclear weapons.

**paunch** *noun* a large stomach or belly. □ **paunchy** *adjective*

**pauper** *noun* a very poor person.

**pause** *noun* **1** a temporary stop or silence. **2** *Music* a mark (⌒) over a note or rest that is to be lengthened. ● *verb* make a pause. □ **give pause to** cause (a person) to hesitate.

**pavane** (pă-**van**) *noun* (also **pavan**) a stately dance; the music for this.

**Pavarotti**, Luciano (born 1935), Italian operatic tenor.

**pave** *verb* cover (a road or path etc.) with a hard surface. □ **pave the way** prepare the way (for changes etc.). **paving-stone** *noun* a slab of stone for paving.

**pavement** *noun* **1** (*Brit.*) a path for pedestrians at the side of a road. **2** (*Amer.*) the hard surface of a roadway, on which vehicles are driven.

**pavilion** *noun* **1** a structure used as a shelter, e.g. in a park. **2** an ornamental building used for dances and concerts etc. **3** a building on a sports ground for use by players and spectators.

**Pavlov** (**pav**-lof), Ivan Petrovich (1849–1936), Russian physiologist, noted for his study of conditioned reflexes in dogs.

**Pavlova** (pav-**loh**-vă), Anna (1881–1931), Russian ballerina.

**pavlova** (pav-**loh**-vă) *noun* a meringue cake with cream and fruit. (¶ Named after Anna Pavlova.)

**paw** *noun* **1** the foot of an animal that has claws. **2** (*informal*) a person's hand. ● *verb*

**1** strike with a paw. **2** scrape (the ground) with a hoof. **3** (*informal*) touch awkwardly or rudely with the hands.

**pawl** *noun* a lever with a catch that engages with the notches of a ratchet.

**pawn¹** *noun* **1** a chess piece of the smallest size and value. **2** a person whose actions are controlled by others.

**pawn²** *verb* deposit (a thing) with a pawnbroker as security for money borrowed. ● *noun* something deposited as a pledge. □ **in pawn** deposited as a pawn.

**pawnbroker** *noun* a person licensed to lend money on the security of personal property deposited. □ **pawnbroking** *noun*

**pawnshop** *noun* a pawnbroker's place of business.

**pawpaw** *noun* (also **papaw**, **papaya**) a fruit like a long melon with orange flesh.

**pax** *noun* a kiss of peace. ● *interjection* a call for a truce, especially in children's games.

**pay** *verb* (**paid**, **paying**) **1** give (money) in return for goods or services. **2** give what is owed as wages, a debt, ransom, etc.; undergo (a penalty). **3** bear the cost of something. **4** be profitable or worthwhile; *it would pay you to get a computer.* **5** bestow, render, or express; *pay attention; paid them a visit; paid them a compliment.* ● *noun* **1** payment. **2** wages. □ **in the pay of** employed by. **pay-as-you-earn** *noun* a method of collecting income tax by deducting it at source from wages, interest, etc. **pay-claim** *noun* a demand for an increase of wages. **pay for** suffer or be punished because of (a mistake etc.). **pay its way** make enough profit to cover expenses. **pay off 1** pay in full and be free from (a debt) or discharge (an employee). **2** (*informal*) yield good results; *the risk paid off.* **pay-off** *noun* (*slang*) **1** payment. **2** reward or retribution. **3** a climax, especially of a joke or story. **pay one's way** not get into debt. **pay out 1** punish or be revenged on (a person). **2** let out (a rope) by slackening it. **pay up** pay in full; pay what is demanded. □ **payer** *noun*

**payable** *adjective* which must or may be paid.

**PAYE** *abbreviation* pay-as-you-earn.

**payee** (pay-**ee**) *noun* a person to whom money is paid or is to be paid.

**payload** *noun* **1** the part of an aircraft's load from which revenue is derived (e.g. passengers or cargo). **2** the total weight of bombs carried by an aircraft or rocket.

**paymaster** *noun* an official who pays troops, workers, etc. □ **Paymaster General** a Treasury Minister responsible for payments.

**payment** *noun* **1** paying. **2** money paid. **3** reward, compensation.

**payola** (pay-oh-lă) *noun* a bribe offered to one who promotes a commercial product by dishonestly making use of his or her position or influence.

**payroll** *noun* a list of a firm's employees receiving regular pay.

**Pb** *symbol* lead.

**PC** *abbreviation* **1** police constable. **2** Privy Counsellor. **3** personal computer.

**p.c.** *abbreviation* **1** per cent. **2** postcard.

**PCB** *abbreviation* **1** polychlorinated biphenyl; a toxic compound formed as a waste product of industrial processes. **2** *Computing* printed circuit board.

**Pd** *symbol* palladium.

**pd.** *abbreviation* paid.

**p.d.q.** *abbreviation* (*slang*) pretty damn quick.

**PE** *abbreviation* physical education.

**pea** *noun* a climbing plant bearing seeds in pods; its seed used as a vegetable. □ **pea green** bright green. **pea-souper** *noun* (*informal*) a thick yellowish fog.

**peace** *noun* **1** a state of freedom from war; ending of war. **2** a state of harmony between people; freedom from civil disorder; *a breach of the peace*. **3** quiet, calm. □ **peace dividend** public money which becomes available when defence spending is reduced. **peace-offering** *noun* something offered to show that one is willing to make peace.

**peaceable** *adjective* **1** not quarrelsome, desiring to be at peace with others. **2** peaceful, without strife; *a peaceable settlement*. □ **peaceably** *adverb*

**peaceful** *adjective* **1** characterized by peace. **2** belonging to a state of peace not of war; *peaceful uses of atomic energy*. □ **peacefully** *adverb*, **peacefulness** *noun*

**peacemaker** *noun* a person who brings about peace.

**peach** *noun* **1** a round juicy fruit with downy yellowish-pink skin and a rough stone. **2** the tree that bears this. **3** (*informal*) a person or thing that is greatly admired. **4** yellowish-pink colour. ●*adjective* yellowish-pink. □ **peach Melba** ice cream and peaches with raspberry syrup. □ **peachy** *adjective*

**Peacock**, Thomas Love (1785–1866), English novelist and poet.

**peacock** *noun* a large male bird with greenish-blue plumage and long tail-feathers that can be spread upright like a fan.

**peahen** *noun* the female of a peacock.

**peak** *noun* **1** a pointed top, especially of a mountain. **2** the mountain itself. **3** a projecting part of the edge of a cap. **4** the point of highest value, achievement, intensity, etc.; *at the peak of his career; peak hours*. ●*verb* reach its peak in value or in-tensity etc. □ **Peak District** an area in Derbyshire where there are many peaks.

**peak-load** *noun* the maximum of electric power demand.

**peaked** *adjective* having a peak; pointed.

**peaky** *adjective* having a pale sickly appearance.

**peal** *noun* **1** the loud ringing of bells. **2** a set of bells with different notes. **3** a loud burst of thunder or laughter. ●*verb* sound or cause to sound in a peal.

**pean** Amer. spelling of PAEAN.

**peanut** *noun* **1** a plant bearing pods that ripen underground, containing edible seeds. **2** this seed. **3** (**peanuts**) (*informal*) a trivial or contemptibly small amount, especially of money. □ **peanut butter** a paste of ground roasted peanuts.

**pear** *noun* **1** a rounded fleshy fruit that tapers towards the stalk. **2** the tree that bears this.

**pearl** *noun* **1** a round lustrous white solid formed inside the shells of certain oysters, valued as a gem. **2** something resembling this. **3** something valued because of its excellence or beauty. ●*adjective* (of an electric light bulb) made of opaque glass. □ **cast pearls before swine** offer a good thing to someone who is incapable of appreciating it. **pearl barley** barley grains ground small.

**pearled** *adjective* formed into or covered with pearl-like drops.

**Pearl Harbor** a harbour on the island of Oahu, Hawaii, site of an American naval base attacked by the Japanese on 7 December 1941, an event which brought America into the Second World War.

**pearling** *noun* fishing or diving for pearls.

**pearly** *adjective* **1** like pearls. **2** with pearls. □ **Pearly Gates** (*informal*) the gates of heaven. **pearly king and queen** a London costermonger and his wife wearing clothes covered with pearl buttons.

**peasant** (pez-ănt) *noun* **1** (in some countries) a farm labourer or small farmer. **2** (*informal*) a lout, an ill-mannered person.

**peasantry** *noun* peasants.

**pease-pudding** *noun* boiled split peas (traditionally served with boiled ham).

**peat** *noun* vegetable matter decomposed by the action of water in bogs etc. and partly carbonized, used in horticulture or cut in pieces as fuel. □ **peaty** *adjective*

**pebble** *noun* a small stone worn smooth by the action of water. □ **pebble-dash** *noun* mortar with pebbles in it, used as a coating for an outside wall. □ **pebbly** *adjective*

**pecan** (pee-kăn *or* pi-kan) *noun* the smooth pinkish-brown nut of a kind of hickory.

**peccadillo** (pek-ă-dil-oh) *noun* (*plural* **peccadilloes** *or* **peccadillos**) a trivial offence.

**peccary** (pek-er-i) *noun* a wild pig of tropical America.

**peck**[1] *verb* **1** strike or nip or pick up with the beak. **2** kiss lightly and hastily. ● *noun* **1** a stroke or nip made with the beak. **2** a light hasty kiss. □ **pecking order** a system of rank or status in which people dominate those below themselves and are dominated by those above (as observed among domestic fowls).

**peck**[2] *noun* a measure of capacity for dry goods, = 2 gallons or 8 quarts.

**pecker** *noun* (*Amer. vulgar*) the penis. □ **keep your pecker up** (*informal*) stay cheerful.

**peckish** *adjective* (*informal*) hungry.

**pectin** *noun* a gelatinous substance found in ripe fruits etc., causing jams to set.

**pectoral** (pek-ter-ăl) *adjective* **1** of, in, or on the chest or breast; *pectoral muscles*. **2** worn on the breast; *a pectoral cross*.

**peculate** (pek-yoo-layt) *verb* embezzle (money). □ **peculation** *noun*, **peculator** *noun*

**peculiar** *adjective* **1** strange, eccentric. **2** belonging exclusively to a particular person, place, or thing; *customs peculiar to the 18th century*. **3** particular, special; *a point of peculiar interest*.

**peculiarity** *noun* **1** being peculiar. **2** a characteristic. **3** something unusual, an eccentricity.

**peculiarly** *adverb* **1** in a peculiar way. **2** especially; *peculiarly annoying*.

**pecuniary** (pi-kew-ni-er-i) *adjective* of or in money; *pecuniary aid*.

**pedagogue** (ped-ă-gog) *noun* (*scornful or old use*) a teacher.

**pedal** *noun* a lever operated by the foot. ● *verb* (**pedalled, pedalling**; *Amer.* **pedaled, pedaling**) **1** work the pedal(s) of. **2** move or operate by means of pedals; ride a bicycle.

**pedalo** (ped-ă-loh) *noun* (*plural* **pedalos**) a small pleasure-boat operated by pedals.

**pedant** (ped-ănt) *noun* (*scornful*) a person who insists unimaginatively on strict observance of formal rules and details. □ **pedantry** (ped-ăn-tri) *noun*, **pedantic** (pid-an-tik) *adjective*, **pedantically** *adverb*

**peddle** *verb* **1** sell (goods) as a pedlar. **2** advocate or promote (ideas etc.). **3** sell (drugs) illegally.

**peddler** *noun* **1** a person who sells drugs illegally. **2** Amer. spelling of PEDLAR.

**pederast** (peed-er-ast) *noun* (also **paederast**) a man who has anal intercourse with a boy. □ **pederasty** *noun*

**pedestal** *noun* a base supporting a column, statue, etc. □ **pedestal table** one with a single central support. **put a person on a pedestal** admire or respect him or her greatly.

**pedestrian** *noun* a person who is walking, especially in a street. ● *adjective* **1** of walking; of or for pedestrians. **2** unimaginative, dull. □ **pedestrian crossing** a street crossing where pedestrians have priority over traffic.

**pedestrianize** *verb* (also **pedestrianise**) convert (a street or area) for the use of pedestrians only.

**pediatrician, pediatrics** Amer. spelling of PAEDIATRICIAN, PAEDIATRICS.

**pedicure** (ped-i-kewr) *noun* care or treatment of the feet and toenails.

**pedigree** *noun* a line of ancestors, especially a distinguished one. ● *adjective* (of animals) having a recorded line of descent that shows pure breeding; *pedigree dogs*.

**pediment** (ped-i-měnt) *noun* a triangular part crowning the front of a building.

**pedlar** *noun* (*Amer.* **peddler**) a person who goes from house to house selling small articles.

**pedometer** (pid-om-it-er) *noun* a device that calculates the distance a person walks by counting the number of steps taken.

**pedophilia** Amer. spelling of PAEDOPHILIA.

**peduncle** (pi-dunk-ěl) *noun* the stalk of a flower, fruit, or cluster. □ **peduncular** *adjective*

**pee** (*informal*) *verb* (**pees, peed**) urinate. ● *noun* **1** urination. **2** urine.

**peek** *verb* peep or glance. ● *noun* a peep or glance.

**Peel**, Sir Robert (1788–1850), British statesman, who established the Metropolitan Police.

**peel** *noun* the skin of certain fruits and vegetables. ● *verb* **1** remove the peel of. **2** strip away, pull off (a skin or covering). **3** come off in strips or layers; lose skin or bark etc. in this way. □ **peel off** veer away from a formation. □ **peeler** *noun*

**peelings** *plural noun* strips of skin peeled from potatoes etc.

**peen** *noun* the wedge-shaped or curved end of a hammer-head, opposite the striking face.

**peep**[1] *verb* **1** look through a narrow opening; look quickly or surreptitiously. **2** come briefly or partially into view, show slightly. ● *noun* a brief or surreptitious look. □ **peephole** *noun* a small hole to peep through. **peeping Tom** a man who furtively watches someone undressing or engaging in sexual activities. (¶ Named after the Coventry tailor in the story of Lady Godiva.) **peepshow** *noun* a box with a small eyepiece, inside which a series of pictures can be seen.

**peep**[2] *noun* a high chirping sound like that made by young birds. ● *verb* make this sound.

**peer**[1] *verb* look searchingly or with difficulty.

**peer**[2] *noun* **1** a member of the peerage in Britain, a duke, marquis, earl, viscount, or baron. **2** one who is the equal of another in rank, quality, ability, etc. □ **peer group** a group of people who are associated and of equal status; a group of children of similar age and ability. **peer of the realm** a peer entitled to sit in the House of Lords.

**peerage** *noun* **1** peers, the nobility. **2** the rank of peer or peeress.

**peeress** *noun* a female peer; a peer's wife.

**peerless** *adjective* without equal; superb.

**peeve** (*informal*) *verb* annoy. ●*noun* a cause of annoyance; a feeling of irritation. □ **peeved** *adjective*

**peevish** *adjective* irritable. □ **peevishly** *adverb*

**peewit** *noun* (also **pewit**) a plover named from its cry; a lapwing.

**peg** *noun* **1** a wooden or metal pin or bolt for fixing, hanging, or marking things. **2** a clothes-peg. **3** a wooden screw for tightening or loosening the strings of a violin etc. **4** a drink or measure of spirits. ●*verb* (**pegged**, **pegging**) **1** fix or mark by means of a peg or pegs. **2** keep (wages or prices) at a fixed amount. □ **off the peg** (of clothes) ready-made. **peg away** (often foll. by *at*) work diligently, be persistent in doing something. **peg-leg** *noun* (*informal*) an artificial leg; a person with this. **peg out** (*slang*) **1** die. **2** mark the boundaries of. **take a person down a peg** reduce his or her pride.

**Pegasus** (peg-ă-sŭs) **1** (*Gk. myth.*) an immortal winged horse. **2** a northern constellation.

**pegboard** *noun* a board with small holes for pegs, used for games and displays.

**pejorative** (pij-o-ră-tiv) *adjective* expressing disapproval; disparaging, derogatory. □ **pejoratively** *adverb*

**peke** *noun* (*informal*) a Pekingese dog.

**Peking** (pee-king) (official form **Beijing**) the capital of China.

**Pekingese** *noun* (*plural* **Pekingese**) a dog with short legs, flat face, and long silky hair.

**pelargonium** (pel-er-goh-niŭm) *noun* a plant with showy flowers and fragrant leaves (often called *geranium*).

**Pelé** (pel-ay) (original name; Edson Arantes do Nascimento) (born 1940), Brazilian footballer.

**pelf** *noun* (*humorous or scornful*) money, wealth.

**pelican** *noun* a large water-bird with a pouch in its long bill for storing fish. □ **pelican crossing** a pedestrian crossing with traffic lights operated by pedestrians.

**pelisse** (pel-eess) *noun* (*hist.*) **1** a woman's long cloak-like garment with armholes or sleeves. **2** a fur-lined cloak as part of a hussar's uniform.

**pellagra** (pil-ag-ră) *noun* a deficiency disease causing cracking of the skin, often ending in insanity.

**pellet** *noun* **1** a small rounded closely-packed mass of a soft substance. **2** a piece of small shot. **3** a pill.

**pell-mell** *adverb* & *adjective* in a hurried disorderly manner; headlong.

**pellucid** (pil-oo-sid) *adjective* very clear.

**pelmet** (pel-mit) *noun* a valance or ornamental strip above a window to conceal a curtain rail.

**Peloponnese** (pel-ŏ-pŏn-eess) the mountainous southern peninsula of Greece, connected to the mainland by the isthmus of Corinth. □ **Peloponnesian** (pel-ŏ-pŏn-ee-shăn) *adjective*

**pelt**[1] *noun* an animal skin, especially with the fur or hair still on it. ●*verb* **1** throw missiles at. **2** (of rain etc.) come down fast. **3** run fast. □ **at full pelt** as fast as possible.

**pelvis** *noun* the basin-shaped framework of bones at the lower end of the body. □ **pelvic** *adjective*

**pen**[1] *noun* a small fenced enclosure, especially for cattle, sheep, poultry, etc. ●*verb* (**penned**, **penning**) shut in or as if in a pen.

**pen**[2] *noun* a device with a metal point for writing with ink. ●*verb* (**penned**, **penning**) write (a letter etc.). □ **pen-name** *noun* an author's pseudonym. □ **pen-pushing** *noun* (*informal*) clerical work.

**pen**[3] *noun* **1** a female swan. **2** (*Amer. informal*) a penitentiary.

**penal** (pee-năl) *adjective* of or involving punishment, especially according to law.

**penalize** *verb* (also **penalise**) **1** inflict a penalty on. **2** place at a serious disadvantage. □ **penalization** *noun*

**penalty** *noun* **1** a punishment for breaking a law, rule, or contract. **2** a disadvantage or hardship brought on by some action or quality; *the penalties of fame*. **3** a disadvantage to which a sports player or team must submit for breaking a rule. □ **penalty area** an area in front of the goal on a football field in which a foul by the defenders involves the award of a penalty kick. **penalty box** a place for penalized players and some officials in ice hockey. **penalty kick** a free kick at goal awarded as a penalty in football.

**penance** (pen-ăns) *noun* **1** an act performed as an expression of penitence. **2** (in the RC and Orthodox Church) a sacrament including confession, absolution, and an act of penitence. □ **do penance** perform a penance.

**Penang** (pin-ang) a State of Malaysia.

**pence** see PENNY.

**penchant** (pahn-shahn) *noun* a liking or inclination; *he has a penchant for Indian music.* (¶ French.)

**pencil** *noun* **1** an instrument for drawing or writing, usually a thin stick of graphite enclosed in a cylinder of wood. **2** something used or shaped like this. ● *verb* (**pencilled, pencilling**; *Amer.* **penciled, penciling**) write or draw or mark with a pencil. □ **pencil in** enter (a suggested date, estimate, etc.) provisionally.

**pendant** *noun* a hanging ornament, especially one attached to a necklace.

**pendent** *adjective* hanging. □ **pendency** *noun*

**pending** *adjective* **1** waiting to be decided or settled. **2** about to come into existence; *patent pending.* ● *preposition* **1** during; *pending these negotiations.* **2** until; *pending his return.*

**pendulous** (pen-dew-lŭs) *adjective* hanging downwards; hanging so as to swing freely.

**pendulum** (pen-dew-lŭm) *noun* a weight hung so that it can swing freely, especially a rod with a weighted end that regulates the movement of a clock.

**Penelope** (pi-**nel**-ŏ-pi) (*Gk. legend*) the wife of Odysseus, who remained faithful to him during his long years of absence.

**penetrable** (pen-i-tră-bŭl) *adjective* able to be penetrated. □ **penetrability** *noun*

**penetrate** *verb* **1** make a way into or through, pierce. **2** enter and permeate. **3** see into or through; *our eyes could not penetrate the darkness.* **4** discover or understand; *penetrated their secrets.* **5** be absorbed by the mind; *my hint didn't penetrate.* □ **penetration** *noun*

**penetrating** *adjective* **1** having or showing great insight. **2** (of a voice or sound) loud and carrying; piercing.

**penetrative** (pen-i-tră-tiv) *adjective* able to penetrate; penetrating.

**penfriend** *noun* a friend with whom a person corresponds without meeting.

**penguin** *noun* a seabird of the Antarctic regions, with wings developed into scaly flippers used for swimming.

**penicillin** (pen-i-**sil**-in) *noun* an antibiotic of the kind obtained from mould fungi.

**peninsula** (pěn-**ins**-yoo-lă) *noun* a piece of land that is almost surrounded by water or projecting far into the sea. □ **peninsular** *adjective*

**penis** (**pee**-nis) *noun* the organ by which a male animal copulates and (in mammals) urinates.

**penitent** *adjective* feeling regret that one has done wrong. ● *noun* a penitent person. □ **penitently** *adverb*, **penitence** *noun*

**penitential** (pen-i-**ten**-shăl) *adjective* of penitence or penance.

**penitentiary** (pen-i-**ten**-sher-i) *noun* (*Amer.*) a federal or State prison. ● *adjective* **1** of penance. **2** of reformatory treatment.

**penknife** *noun* (*plural* **penknives**) a small folding knife.

**Penn.** *abbreviation* Pennsylvania.

**pennant** (**pen**-ănt) *noun* a long tapering flag, especially one flown on a ship.

**penniless** *adjective* having no money; destitute.

**Pennines** *plural noun* (also **Pennine Chain**) a range of hills in England running northwards from Derbyshire to the Scottish border.

**pennon** *noun* **1** a long narrow triangular or swallow-tailed flag. **2** a long pointed streamer on a ship.

**Pennsylvania** a State of the north-eastern USA. □ **Pennsylvanian** *adjective & noun*

**penny** *noun* (*plural* **pennies** *for separate coins*, **pence** *for a sum of money*) **1** a British bronze coin worth ¹⁄₁₀₀ of £1; a former coin worth ¹⁄₁₂ of a shilling. **2** (*Amer.*) a cent. **3** a very small sum of money; *it won't cost you a penny.* □ **in for a penny, in for a pound** if one is going to be involved, one might as well be totally involved. **penny black** the first adhesive postage stamp (1840), printed in black. **the penny drops** (*informal*) one understands at last. **penny-farthing** *noun* an old type of bicycle with a very large front wheel and a small rear one. **penny-pinching** (*adjective*) mean, miserly; (*noun*) meanness. **penny whistle** a musical instrument, a tin pipe with six holes. **a pretty penny** a large sum of money.

**pennyroyal** *noun* a creeping mint, used in medicine.

**pennywort** (**pen**-i-wert) *noun* a wild plant with rounded leaves.

**pennyworth** *noun* the amount a penny will buy.

**penology** (pee-**nol**-ŏji) *noun* the scientific study of crime, its punishment, and prison management. □ **penological** *adjective*

**pension¹** (**pen**-shŏn) *noun* a periodic payment made by the State to people who are above a certain age or widowed, or to certain disabled people, or by an employer to a retired employee. ● *verb* pay a pension to. □ **pension off** dismiss or allow to retire with a pension.

**pension²** (**pahn**-si-awn) a boarding house in Europe, especially France. (¶ French.)

**pensionable** *adjective* **1** entitled to receive a pension. **2** (of a job) entitling a person to receive a pension.

**pensioner** *noun* a person who receives a retirement or other pension.

**pensive** *adjective* deep in thought. □ **pensively** *adverb*, **pensiveness** *noun*

**pent** *adjective* (often foll. by *in* or *up*) shut in a confined space; shut in; *pent-up anger*.

**penta-** *combining form* five.

**pentagon** (pen-tă-gŏn) *noun* **1** a geometric figure with five sides. **2** (**the Pentagon**) a five-sided building near Washington, headquarters of the USA Department of Defense.

**pentagonal** (pen-**tag**-ŏn-ăl) *adjective* five-sided.

**pentagram** (**pen**-tă-gram) *noun* a five-pointed star.

**pentameter** (pen-**tam**-it-er) *noun* a line of verse with five metrical feet.

**Pentateuch** (**pen**-tă-tewk) *noun* the first five books of the Old Testament.

**pentathlon** (pen-**tath**-lŏn) *noun* an athletic contest in which each competitor takes part in the five events it includes.

**Pentecost** (**pen**-ti-kost) *noun* **1** the Jewish harvest festival, fifty days after the second day of the Passover. **2** Whit Sunday.

**Pentecostal Church** (pen-ti-kos-t'l) any of the Churches of a 20th-century religious movement emphasizing the gifts of the Holy Spirit as at Pentecost.

**penthouse** *noun* **1** a sloping roof (especially for a shelter or shed) attached to the wall of a main building. **2** a flat (especially a luxurious one) on the roof or top floor of a tall building.

**penultimate** (pĕn-**ul**-tim-ăt) *adjective* last but one.

**penumbra** (pin-**um**-bră) *noun* (*plural* **penumbras** *or* **penumbrae**) a partly shaded region around the shadow of an opaque body, especially that around the shadow of the earth or room in an eclipse. □ **penumbral** *adjective*

**penurious** (pin-**yoor**-iŭs) *adjective* **1** poverty-stricken. **2** stingy, mean.

**penury** (**pen**-yoor-i) *noun* extreme poverty.

**peony** (**pee**-ŏni) *noun* (also **paeony**) a garden plant with large round red, pink, or white flowers.

**people** *plural noun* **1** human beings in general. **2** the persons belonging to a place or forming a group or social class; the subjects or citizens of a State. **3** ordinary persons, those who are not nobles or not in high office etc. **4** a person's parents or other relatives. **5** (treated as *singular*) the persons composing a community, tribe, race, or nation; *the English-speaking peoples*; *a warlike people*. ●*verb* fill (a place) with people, populate.

**PEP** *abbreviation* personal equity plan.

**pep** *noun* (*informal*) vigour, energy, spirit. □ **pep pill** a pill containing a stimulant drug. **pep talk** a talk urging the hearer(s) to great effort or courage. **pep up**

(**pepped**, **pepping**) (*informal*) fill with vigour, enliven.

**peplum** *noun* a short flounce from the waist of a garment.

**pepper** *noun* **1** a hot-tasting powder made from the dried berries of certain plants, used to season food. **2** a capsicum grown as a vegetable. ●*verb* **1** sprinkle with pepper. **2** pelt with small missiles. **3** sprinkle here and there; *a speech peppered with jokes*. □ **pepper-and-salt** *adjective* woven with light and dark threads producing a speckled effect. **pepper-mill** *noun* a mill for grinding peppercorns by hand. **pepper pot** a small container with a perforated lid for sprinkling pepper.

**peppercorn** *noun* the dried berry from which pepper is made. □ **peppercorn rent** a very low rent, virtually nothing.

**peppermint** *noun* **1** a mint grown for its strong fragrant oil, used in medicine, sweets, etc. **2** a sweet flavoured with this.

**pepperoni** *noun* beef and pork sausage seasoned with pepper.

**peppery** *adjective* **1** like pepper, containing much pepper. **2** hot-tempered.

**pepsin** *noun* an enzyme contained in gastric juice, helping to digest food.

**peptic** *adjective* of digestion. □ **peptic ulcer** an ulcer in the stomach or duodenum.

**peptide** *noun* a compound consisting of a chain of amino acids, chemically linked.

**Pepys** (*pronounced* peeps), Samuel (1633–1703), English diarist, whose writings are an important document of contemporary life.

**per** *preposition* **1** for each; *£2 per gallon*. **2** (in full **as per**) in accordance with; *as per instructions*; *as per usual*. **3** by means of; *per post*. □ **per annum** for each year. **per capita** for each person. **per cent** in or for every hundred; *three per cent* (3%).

**peradventure** *adverb* (*old use*) perhaps.

**perambulate** (per-**am**-bew-layt) *verb* **1** walk through, over, or round (an area), travel through and inspect. **2** walk about. □ **perambulation** *noun*

**perambulator** *noun* (*old use*) a pram.

**percale** *noun* closely woven cotton fabric.

**perceive** *verb* become aware of, see or notice.

**percent** Amer. spelling of PER CENT.

**percentage** (per-**sen**-tij) *noun* **1** the rate or proportion per hundred. **2** a proportion or part.

**percentile** *noun* each of 99 points at which a range of data is divided to make 100 groups of equal size.

**perceptible** *adjective* able to be perceived. □ **perceptibly** *adverb*, **perceptibility** *noun*

**perception** *noun* perceiving; ability to perceive.

**perceptive** *adjective* having or showing insight and sensitive understanding. □ **perceptively** *adverb*, **perceptiveness** *noun*

**perceptual** *adjective* of or involving perception.

**perch¹** *noun* **1** a bird's resting place, e.g. a branch or rod. **2** a high place or narrow ledge used as a resting place, viewing point, etc. **3** a former measure of length equal to 5½ yards. ●*verb* rest or place on or as if on a perch.

**perch²** *noun* (*plural* **perch** or **perches**) an edible freshwater fish with spiny fins.

**perchance** *adverb* (*poetic or old use*) perhaps.

**percipient** (per-**sip**-i-ĕnt) *adjective* perceiving; perceptive. □ **percipience** *noun*

**percolate** (per-kŏl-ayt) *verb* **1** filter or cause to filter, especially through small holes. **2** prepare (coffee) in a percolator. **3** (of ideas etc.) spread gradually. □ **percolation** *noun*

**percolator** *noun* a coffee-making pot, in which boiling water circulates repeatedly up a central tube and downwards through ground coffee held in a perforated drum.

**percussion** (per-**kush**-ŏn) *noun* **1** the striking of one object against another. **2** percussion instruments in an orchestra. □ **percussion cap** a small metal or paper device containing explosive powder that explodes when it is struck, used as a detonator or in a toy pistol. **percussion instrument** a musical instrument (e.g. drum, cymbals) played by striking. □ **percussionist** *noun*, **percussive** *adjective*

**perdition** (per-**dish**-ŏn) *noun* eternal damnation.

**peregrination** (pe-ri-grin-ay-shŏn) *noun* (*old use*) travelling; a journey.

**peregrine** (pe-ri-grin) *noun* (in full **peregrine falcon**) a falcon that can be trained to hunt and catch small animals and birds.

**peremptory** (per-**emp**-ter-i) *adjective* imperious; insisting on obedience. □ **peremptorily** *adverb*, **peremptoriness** *noun*

**perennial** (per-**en**-yăl) *adjective* **1** lasting a long time or for ever; constantly recurring; *a perennial problem*. **2** (of a plant) living for several years; producing new growth each year which dies back in winter. ●*noun* a perennial plant. □ **perennially** *adverb*

**perestroika** (pe-res-**troi**-kă) *noun* (in the former USSR) restructuring of the Russian economic and political system under Gorbachev. (¶ Russian.)

**perfect** *adjective* (*pronounced* **per**-fikt) **1** complete, having all its essential qualities. **2** faultless, excellent. **3** exact, precise; *a perfect circle*. **4** entire, total; *a perfect stranger*. **5** *Grammar* of a tense of a verb used to denote an action or event that is completed, e.g. *he has gone*. ●*verb* (*pronounced* per-**fekt**) make perfect. □ **perfect pitch** the ability to recognize or sing any given note.

**perfection** *noun* **1** making or being perfect. **2** a person or thing considered perfect.

**perfectionist** *noun* a person who is satisfied with nothing less than what he or she thinks is perfect. □ **perfectionism** *noun*

**perfectly** *adverb* **1** in a perfect way. **2** completely, quite; *perfectly satisfied*.

**perfidious** (per-**fid**-iŭs) *adjective* treacherous, disloyal. □ **perfidiously** *adverb*, **perfidy** (**per**-fid-i) *noun*

**perforate** *verb* **1** make a hole or holes through, especially a row of tiny holes so that part(s) can be torn off easily. **2** penetrate. □ **perforation** *noun*

**perforce** *adverb* (*old use*) by force of circumstances, necessarily.

**perform** *verb* **1** carry into effect, accomplish, do; go through (a particular proceeding). **2** function; *the car performed well when tested*. **3** act in a play etc.; play an instrument, sing, do tricks, etc. before an audience. □ **performer** *noun*

**performance** *noun* **1** the act, process, or manner of performing. **2** the performing of a play or other entertainment. **3** (*informal*) a fuss; a scene; a difficult or complicated task.

**perfume** *noun* **1** a sweet smell. **2** a fragrant liquid for giving a pleasant smell, especially to the body. ●*verb* give a sweet smell to; apply perfume to.

**perfumery** (per-**fewm**-er-i) *noun* perfumes; the preparation of these.

**perfunctory** (per-**funk**-ter-i) *adjective* done as a duty or routine but without much care or interest. □ **perfunctorily** *adverb*, **perfunctoriness** *noun*

**pergola** (per-**gŏl**ă) *noun* an arbour or covered walk formed of climbing plants trained over trellis-work.

**perhaps** *adverb* it may be; possibly.

**pericardium** *noun* (*plural* **pericardia**) the membranous sac enclosing the heart.

**pericarp** (pe-ri-karp) *noun* a seed-vessel such as a pea pod.

**Pericles** (pe-ri-kleez) (*c*.495–429 BC), Athenian statesman and general.

**perigee** (pe-ri-jee) *noun* the point in the orbit of the moon or any planet when it is nearest to earth.

**perihelion** (pe-ri-**hee**-li-ŏn) *noun* (*plural* **perihelia**) the point in a planet's or comet's orbit when it is closest to the sun.

**peril** *noun* serious danger.

**perilous** *adjective* full of risk, dangerous. □ **perilously** *adverb*

**perimeter** (per-**im**-it-er) *noun* **1** the outer edge or boundary of a closed geometric figure or of an area. **2** the length of this.

**perinatal** *adjective* relating to the time immediately before and after birth.

**perineum** (pe-ri-nee-ŭm) *noun* the region of the body between the anus and the scrotum or vulva. □ **perineal** *adjective*

**period** *noun* **1** a length or portion of time. **2** a time with particular characteristics; *the colonial period.* **3** the time allocated for a lesson in school. **4** an occurrence of menstruation. **5** a complete sentence. **6** a full stop in punctuation. ● *adjective* (of furniture, dress, or architecture) belonging to a past age.

**periodic** *adjective* occurring or appearing at intervals. □ **periodic table** a table of the elements in order of their atomic numbers, in which chemically related elements tend to appear in the same column or row.

**periodical** *adjective* periodic. ● *noun* a magazine etc. published at regular intervals. □ **periodically** *adverb*

**periodicity** (peer-i-ŏ-**diss**-iti) *noun* being periodic, the tendency to recur at intervals.

**periodontics** *noun* the branch of dentistry concerned with the gums and structures surrounding the teeth. □ **periodontal** *adjective*

**peripatetic** (pe-ri-pă-**tet**-ik) *adjective* **1** going from place to place. **2** (of a teacher) working in more than one school or college etc. ● *noun* a peripatetic person.

**peripheral** (per-**if**-er-ăl) *adjective* **1** of or on the periphery. **2** of minor but not central importance to something. ● *noun* any input, output, or storage device that can be controlled by the central processing unit of a computer (e.g. a magnetic tape, floppy disk, line printer).

**periphery** (per-**if**-er-i) *noun* **1** the boundary of a surface or area; the region immediately inside or beyond this. **2** the fringes of a subject.

**periphrasis** (per-**if**-ră-sis) *noun* (*plural* **periphrases**) a roundabout phrase or way of speaking; a circumlocution.

**periscope** *noun* an apparatus with a tube and mirror(s) by which a person can see things that are otherwise out of sight, e.g. in a submarine or a trench. □ **periscopic** *adjective*

**perish** *verb* **1** suffer destruction; become extinct; die a violent or untimely death. **2** rot, lose or cause (rubber or other fabric) to lose its normal qualities.

**perishable** *adjective* liable to decay or go bad in a short time. ● *plural noun* (**perishables**) perishable foods.

**perisher** *noun* (*slang*) an annoying person.

**perishing** *adjective* (*slang*) **1** damned. **2** very cold.

**peritoneum** (pe-ri-tŏn-**ee**-ŭm) *noun* (*plural* **peritoneums** or **peritonea**) the membrane lining the abdomen. □ **peritoneal** *adjective*

**peritonitis** (pe-ri-tŏn-**I**-tiss) *noun* inflammation of the peritoneum.

**periwig** *noun* (*old use*) a wig.

**periwinkle** *noun* **1** an evergreen trailing plant with blue or white flowers. **2** a winkle.

**perjure** (per-jer) *verb* □ **perjure oneself** give false evidence while on oath. □ **perjurer** *noun*

**perjured** *adjective* **1** involving perjury; *perjured evidence.* **2** guilty of perjury.

**perjury** (per-jer-i) *noun* the deliberate giving of false evidence while on oath.

**perk** *noun* (*informal*) a perquisite. □ **perk up** **1** regain or cause to regain courage, confidence, or vitality. **2** smarten up. **3** raise (the head etc.) briskly or jauntily.

**perky** *adjective* (**perkier, perkiest**) lively and cheerful. □ **perkily** *adverb*, **perkiness** *noun*

**perm¹** *noun* a permanent wave. ● *verb* give a perm to.

**perm²** *noun* (in football pools) a permutation. ● *verb* make a perm of.

**permafrost** *noun* the permanently frozen subsoil in polar regions.

**permanent** *adjective* lasting or meant to last indefinitely. □ **permanent wave** a long-lasting artificial wave in the hair. □ **permanently** *adverb*, **permanence** *noun*, **permanency** *noun*

**permanganate** (per-**mang**-ăn-ayt) *noun* a salt of an acid containing manganese.

**permeable** (per-mi-ăbŭl) *adjective* able to be permeated by fluids etc. □ **permeability** *noun*

**permeate** (per-mi-ayt) *verb* pass, flow, or spread into every part of. □ **permeation** *noun*

**Permian** (per-mi-ăn) *adjective* Geol. of the final period of the Palaeozoic era. ● *noun* this period.

**permissible** *adjective* such as may be permitted; allowable. □ **permissibly** *adverb*, **permissibility** *noun*

**permission** *noun* consent or authorization to do something.

**permissive** *adjective* **1** giving permission. **2** tolerant, allowing much freedom in social conduct and sexual matters. □ **permissiveness** *noun*

**permit** *verb* (*pronounced* per-**mit**) (**permitted, permitting**) **1** give permission or consent to; authorize. **2** give opportunity, make possible; *weather permitting.* ● *noun* (*pronounced* **per**-mit) a written order giving permission, especially for entry.

**permutation** (per-mew-**tay**-shŏn) *noun*
**1** variation of the order of a set of things.
**2** any one of these arrangements. **3** a selection of specified items from a larger
group, to be arranged in a number of
combinations (e.g. in a football pool).

**pernicious** (per-**nish**-ŭs) *adjective* very
harmful or destructive. □ **pernicious anaemia** defective formation of red blood
cells through lack of vitamin B.

**pernickety** *adjective* (*informal*) fastidious,
scrupulous; too fussy.

**Perón** (pair-**on**), Juan Domingo
(1895–1974), Argentinian soldier and
statesman, President 1946–55 and 1973–4;
and his second wife Eva ('Evita')
(1919–52), actress and a popular figure
with powerful political influence.

**peroration** (pe-rer-**ay**-shŏn) *noun* **1** the
rhetorical ending of a speech. **2** a lengthy
speech.

**peroxide** *noun* a compound containing the
maximum proportion of oxygen, especially
hydrogen peroxide which is used as an antiseptic or to bleach hair. ●*verb* bleach (the
hair) with hydrogen peroxide.

**perpendicular** *adjective* **1** at a right angle
(90°) to another line or surface. **2** upright,
at right angles to the horizontal. **3** (of a
cliff etc.) having a vertical face. **4** (**Perpendicular**) of the style of English Gothic
architecture in the 14th–15th centuries,
with vertical tracery in large windows.
●*noun* a perpendicular line or direction.
□ **perpendicularly** *adverb*, **perpendicular-
ity** *noun*

**perpetrate** (per-**pit**-rayt) *verb* commit (a
crime or error); be guilty of (a blunder
etc.). □ **perpetration** *noun*, **perpetrator**
*noun*

**perpetual** *adjective* **1** lasting for a long time,
not ceasing. **2** (*informal*) frequent, often
repeated; *this perpetual quarrelling.* □ **perpetual motion** motion of a hypothetical
machine which would continue for ever
unless subject to an external force. □ **perpetually** *adverb*

**perpetuate** *verb* preserve from being forgotten or from going out of use; *his invention will perpetuate his memory.* □ **perpetu-
ation** *noun*

**perpetuity** (per-pi-**tew**-iti) *noun* the state or
quality of being perpetual. □ **in perpetuity**
for ever.

**perplex** *verb* **1** bewilder, puzzle. **2** make
more complicated.

**perplexedly** (per-**pleks**-idli) *adverb* in a
perplexed way.

**perplexity** *noun* bewilderment.

**per pro.** *see* P.P.

**perquisite** (per-**kwiz**-it) *noun* a profit, allowance, or privilege given in addition to
wages or salary.

**Perrault** (pe-**roh**), Charles (1628–1703),
French author, noted for his fairy tales
which include 'The Sleeping Beauty',
'Little Red Riding Hood', and 'Cinderella'.

**Perry**, Frederick John (born 1909), English
championship lawn tennis and table tennis
player.

**perry** *noun* an alcoholic drink made from the
fermented juice of pears.

**per se** by or in itself; intrinsically. (¶ Latin.)

**persecute** *verb* **1** subject to constant hostility or cruel treatment, especially because of
religious or political beliefs. **2** harass.
□ **persecution** *noun*, **persecutor** *noun*

**Persephone** (per-**sef**-ŏni) (*Gk. myth.*) the
daughter of the corn-goddess Demeter,
carried off by Pluto and made queen of the
Underworld, but allowed to return to earth
for part of each year.

**Perseus** (per-siŭs) (*Gk. myth.*) the son of
Zeus and Danae, who cut off the head of
Medusa and rescued Andromeda.

**persevere** *verb* continue steadfastly, especially in something that is difficult or tedious. □ **perseverance** *noun*

**Persia** the ancient and now the alternative
name of Iran.

**Persian** *adjective* of Persia or its people or
language. ●*noun* **1** a native or inhabitant of
Persia. **2** the language of Persia (preferred
terms are *Iranian* and *Farsi*). **3** (in full
**Persian cat**) a cat of a breed that has long
silky fur. □ **Persian lamb** the silky tightly
curled fur of lambs of a kind of Asian
sheep.

**Persian Gulf** an arm of the Arabian Sea,
between the Arabian peninsula and mainland Asia.

**persiflage** (per-si-flah*zh*) *noun* banter.

**persimmon** (per-**sim**-ŏn) *noun* **1** the edible
sweet tomato-like fruit of an American or
East Asian tree. **2** this tree.

**persist** *verb* **1** (often foll. by *in*) continue
firmly or obstinately. **2** continue to exist;
*the custom persists in some areas.* □ **persistent** *adjective*, **persistently** *adverb*, **persistence** *noun*

**person** *noun* **1** an individual human being.
**2** the living body of a human being; *offences
against the person.* **3** (in Christianity) God
as the Father (*First Person*), the Son (*Second Person*), or the Holy Spirit (*Third Person*). **4** *Grammar* any of the three classes of
personal pronouns and verb-forms, referring to the person speaking (*first person*, =
I, me, we, us), or spoken to (*second person*,
= thou, thee, you), or spoken of (*third person*, = he, him, she, her, it, they, them).
□ **in person** physically present.

**persona** (per-soh-nă) *noun* (*plural* **personae**) the personality that a person presents to other people.

**personable** (per-sŏn-ăbŭl) *adjective* attractive in appearance and personality.

**personage** (per-sŏn-ij) *noun* a person, especially one of importance or distinction.

***persona grata*** (per-soh-nă grah-tă) (*plural* **personae gratae**) a person who is acceptable, especially a diplomat acceptable to a foreign government. □ ***persona non grata*** one who is not acceptable. (¶ Latin.)

**personal** *adjective* 1 one's own; *will give it my personal attention.* 2 designed for use by one person only; *a personal stereo.* 3 of one's private life; *a personal matter.* 4 making critical remarks about a person's appearance or private affairs; *don't let us become personal.* 5 done or made etc. in person; *several personal appearances.* 6 of the body and clothing; *personal hygiene.* 7 existing as a person; *a personal God.* □ **personal assistant** a confidential assistant helping an official or manager etc. **personal column** a column of private messages or advertisements in a newspaper. **personal computer** a computer designed for use by a single individual (*abbreviation* **PC**). **personal equity plan** a scheme for tax-free personal investments through financial institutions (*abbreviation* **PEP**). **personal identification number** *see* PIN. **personal organizer** a means of keeping track of personal affairs, especially a loose-leaf notebook divided into sections. **personal pronoun** *see* PRONOUN.

**personality** *noun* 1 a person's own distinctive character. 2 a person with distinctive qualities, especially pleasing ones. 3 a celebrity. 4 (**personalities**) personal remarks of a critical or hostile kind.

**personalize** *verb* (also **personalise**) 1 make personal, especially by marking as one's own property. 2 personify.

**personally** *adverb* 1 in person, not through an agent; *showed us round personally.* 2 as a person, in a personal capacity; *we don't know him personally.* 3 in a personal manner; *don't take it personally.* 4 as regards oneself; *personally, I like it.*

**personate** *verb* impersonate. □ **personation** *noun*

**personify** (per-sonn-i-fy) *verb* (**personified, personifying**) 1 represent (an idea) in human form or (a thing) as having human characteristics; *Justice is personified as a blindfolded woman holding a pair of scales.* 2 embody in one's life or behaviour; *he was meanness personified.* □ **personification** *noun*

**personnel** (per-sŏn-el) *noun* 1 the body of people employed in any work, staff. 2 the department (in a business firm etc.) dealing with employees and their problems and welfare.

**perspective** *noun* 1 the art of drawing solid objects on a flat surface so as to give the impression of depth, solidity, etc. 2 the apparent relationship between visible objects as to position, distance, etc. 3 a view of a visible scene or of facts and events. 4 a mental picture of the relative importance of things. □ **in perspective** 1 drawn according to the rules of perspective. 2 with its relative importance understood.

**Perspex** *noun* (*trade mark*) a tough transparent plastic material.

**perspicacious** (per-spi-kay-shŭs) *adjective* showing great insight. □ **perspicaciously** *adverb*, **perspicacity** (per-spi-kas-iti) *noun*

**perspicuous** (per-spik-yoo-ŭs) *adjective* expressed or expressing things clearly. □ **perspicuity** (per-spi-kew-iti) *noun*

**perspiration** *noun* 1 sweat. 2 sweating.

**perspire** *verb* sweat.

**persuade** *verb* cause (a person) to believe or do something by reasoning; convince or induce. □ **persuadable** *adjective*, **persuasible** *adjective*

**persuasion** *noun* 1 persuading, being persuaded. 2 persuasiveness. 3 belief, especially religious belief; *people of the same persuasion.*

**persuasive** *adjective* able or trying to persuade people. □ **persuasively** *adverb*, **persuasiveness** *noun*

**pert** *adjective* 1 cheeky, saucy. 2 lively, jaunty. □ **pertly** *adverb*, **pertness** *noun*

**pertain** (per-tayn) *verb* (usually foll. by *to*) 1 be relevant; *evidence pertaining to the case.* 2 belong as part; *the mansion and lands pertaining to it.*

**Perth** the capital of the State of Western Australia.

**pertinacious** (per-tin-ay-shŭs) *adjective* holding firmly to an opinion or course of action, persistent and determined. □ **pertinaciously** *adverb*, **pertinacity** (per-tin-ass-iti) *noun*

**pertinent** *adjective* pertaining, relevant. □ **pertinently** *adverb*, **pertinence** *noun*, **pertinency** *noun*

**perturb** *verb* 1 disturb greatly, make anxious or uneasy. 2 throw into confusion. □ **perturbation** *noun*

**Peru** a country in South America on the Pacific coast. □ **Peruvian** (per-oo-viăn) *adjective & noun*

**peruke** (per-ook) *noun* (*old use*) a wig.

**peruse** (per-ooz) *verb* 1 read or study carefully. 2 browse, read casually. □ **perusal** (per-oo-zăl) *noun*

**pervade** *verb* spread or be present throughout, permeate; *a pervading atmosphere of optimism.* □ **pervasion** *noun*

**pervasive** (per-**vay**-siv) *adjective* pervading; able to pervade. □ **pervasiveness** *noun*

**perverse** (per-**verss**) *adjective* **1** obstinately doing something different from what is reasonable or required; intractable. **2** indicating or characterized by a tendency of this kind; *a perverse satisfaction.* □ **perversely** *adverb*, **perverseness** *noun*, **perversity** *noun*

**perversion** *noun* **1** perverting; being perverted. **2** a perverted form of something. **3** preference for a form of sexual activity that is considered abnormal or unacceptable.

**pervert** *verb* (*pronounced* per-**vert**) **1** turn (a thing) from its proper course or use; *pervert the course of justice.* **2** lead astray from right behaviour or beliefs, corrupt. ● *noun* (*pronounced* **per**-vert) a perverted person; one showing perversion of sexual instincts.

**pervious** (**per**-vi-ŭs) *adjective* **1** permeable, allowing something to pass through. **2** accessible, receptive; *pervious to new ideas.*

**peseta** (pĕ-**say**-tă) *noun* the unit of money in Spain.

**pesky** *adjective* (especially *Amer. informal*) annoying.

**peso** (**pay**-soh) *noun* (*plural* **pesos**) the unit of money in several Latin-American countries, and the Philippines.

**pessary** (**pess**-er-i) *noun* **1** a device placed in the vagina to prevent displacement of the womb or as a contraceptive. **2** a vaginal suppository.

**pessimism** *noun* a tendency to take a gloomy view of things or to expect the worst. □ **pessimist** *noun*

**pessimistic** *adjective* showing pessimism. □ **pessimistically** *adverb*

**pest** *noun* **1** a troublesome or annoying person or thing. **2** an insect or animal that is destructive to plants, stored food, etc.

**pester** *verb* make persistent requests; annoy with frequent requests or questions.

**pesticide** *noun* a substance for destroying harmful insects.

**pestilence** *noun* (*old use*) a deadly epidemic disease.

**pestilent** *adjective* **1** deadly. **2** harmful or morally destructive. **3** annoying, troublesome. □ **pestilential** (pest-i-**len**-shăl) *adjective*

**pestle** *noun* a club-shaped instrument for pounding substances in a mortar.

**pet**[1] *noun* **1** a tame animal kept for companionship or amusement. **2** a darling or favourite. ● *adjective* **1** kept or treated as a pet; *pet lamb.* **2** favourite. ● *verb* (**petted**, **petting**) **1** treat with affection. **2** fondle

erotically. □ **pet hate** something one particularly dislikes. **pet name** a name (other than the real name) used affectionately.

**pet**[2] *noun* a fit of ill temper.

**petal** *noun* any of the coloured outer parts of a flower head.

**petard** (pit-**ard**) *noun* (*old use*) a small bombshell. □ **hoist with one's own petard** injured by one's own schemes against others.

**Peter**, St (died *c.* AD 67), an Apostle to whom two of the epistles in the New Testament are ascribed. Feast day, 29 June.

**Peter I** 'the Great' (1672–1725), emperor of Russia 1682–1725.

**peter** *verb* □ **peter out** diminish gradually and cease to exist.

**Peter Pan 1** the hero of J. M. Barrie's play of the same name (1904), a boy who never grew up. **2** a youthful or immature person.

**petersham** *noun* strong corded ribbon used to strengthen waistbands etc.

**Peterson**, Oscar Emmanuel (born 1925), Canadian jazz pianist and singer.

**pethidine** (**peth**-i-deen) *noun* a soluble synthetic drug used for relieving pain.

**petiole** (**pet**-i-ohl) *noun* a slender stalk joining a leaf to a stem.

**petit** (pĕ-**tee**) *adjective* □ **petit bourgeois** (*pronounced* **boor**-*zh*wah) a member of the lower middle classes. **petit four** (*pronounced* foor) (*plural* **petits fours**, *pronounced* same) very small fancy cakes. **petit mal** a mild form of epilepsy without loss of consciousness. **petit point** (*pronounced* pwan) embroidery on canvas using small stitches. (¶ French, = small.)

**petite** (pĕ-**teet**) *adjective* (of a woman) of small dainty build.

**petition** *noun* **1** an earnest request. **2** a formal document appealing to an authority for a right or benefit etc., especially one signed by a large number of people. **3** a formal application made to a court of law for a writ, order, etc. ● *verb* make or address a petition to. ● **petitioner** *noun*

**Petra** an ancient city in southern Jordan.

**Petrarch** (**pet**-rark), Francesco Petrarca (1304–74), Italian lyric poet and scholar.

**petrel** *noun* a seabird that flies far from land.

**Petri dish** a shallow covered dish used in laboratories for growing bacteria.

**petrify** *verb* (**petrified**, **petrifying**) **1** change or cause to change into a stony mass. **2** paralyse or stun with astonishment, fear, etc. □ **petrification** *noun*, **petrifaction** *noun*

**petrochemical** *noun* a chemical substance obtained from petroleum or natural gas.

**petrodollar** *noun* a dollar earned by a country that exports petroleum.

**petrol** noun an inflammable liquid made from petroleum, used as fuel in internal-combustion engines. □ **petrol pump** a machine for transferring petrol from a storage tank into the tank of a motor vehicle.

**petroleum** (pi-**troh**-liŭm) noun a mineral oil found underground, refined for use as fuel (e.g. petrol, paraffin) or for use in dry-cleaning etc. □ **petroleum jelly** a greasy translucent substance obtained from petroleum, used as a lubricant.

**petticoat** noun a woman's or girl's dress-length undergarment hanging from the shoulders or waist.

**pettifogging** adjective trivial, paying too much attention to unimportant details.

**pettish** adjective peevish, irritably impatient. □ **pettishness** noun

**petty** adjective (**pettier**, **pettiest**) **1** unimportant, trivial; petty details. **2** minor, on a small scale. **3** small-minded; petty spite. □ **petty cash** a small amount of money kept by an office etc. for small payments. **petty officer** an NCO in the navy. □ **pettily** adverb, **pettiness** noun

**petulant** (**pet**-yoo-lănt) adjective peevish. □ **petulantly** adverb, **petulance** noun

**petunia** noun a garden plant with large funnel-shaped flowers.

**pew** noun **1** a long bench-like seat with a back and sides, usually in a church. **2** (informal) a seat; take a pew.

**pewit** alternative spelling of PEEWIT.

**pewter** noun **1** a grey alloy of tin with lead or other metal, used for making mugs and dishes etc. **2** articles made of this.

**peyote** (pay-**oh**-ti) noun **1** a Mexican cactus. **2** a hallucinogenic drug made from this.

**pfennig** noun a German coin worth ¹/₁₀₀ of a mark.

**PG** abbreviation parental guidance; a film classification indicating that parents should decide whether the film is suitable for their children.

**pH** (pee-**aych**) noun a measure of the acidity or alkalinity of a solution.

▪**Usage** An alkaline solution or soil has a pH of greater than 7, while an acid solution has a pH of less than 7.

**phaeton** (**fay**-tŏn) noun an old type of open horse-drawn carriage with four wheels.

**phagocyte** (**fag**-ŏ-syt) noun a leucocyte or other cell that can absorb foreign matter (e.g. bacteria) in the body.

**phalanger** (fă-**lan**-jer) noun a tree-dwelling marsupial of Australia, with webbed hind feet.

**phalanx** noun (plural **phalanxes** or **phalanges**) **1** a number of people forming a compact mass or banded together for a common purpose. **2** an ancient Greek line of battle with infantry in close ranks.

**phallic** (**fal**-ik) adjective of or resembling a phallus.

**phallus** (**fal**-ŭs) noun (plural **phalluses** or **phalli**) a penis, especially when erect.

**phantasm** (**fan**-tazm) noun a phantom, an illusion. □ **phantasmal** adjective

**phantasmagoria** (fan-taz-mă-**gor**-iă) noun a shifting scene of real or imagined figures. □ **phantasmagoric** adjective

**phantom** noun **1** a ghost, an apparition. **2** something without reality, as seen in a dream or vision.

**Pharaoh** (**fair**-oh) noun the title of a king of ancient Egypt.

**Pharisee** noun **1** a member of an ancient Jewish sect represented in the New Testament as making a show of sanctity and piety. **2** a hypocritical self-righteous person. □ **pharisaical** (fa-ri-**say**-ikăl) adjective

**pharmaceutical** (farm-ă-**sewt**-ikăl) adjective of or engaged in pharmacy, of medicinal drugs; a pharmaceutical chemist.

**pharmaceutics** (farm-ă-**sew**-tiks) noun = PHARMACY (sense 1).

**pharmacist** (**farm**-ă-sist) noun a person who is skilled in pharmacy; a pharmaceutical chemist.

**pharmacology** (farm-ă-**kol**-ŏji) noun the study of medicinal drugs and their effects on the body. □ **pharmacological** adjective, **pharmacologist** noun

**pharmacopoeia** (farm-ă-kŏ-**pee**-ă) noun **1** a book containing a list of medicinal drugs with directions for their use. **2** a stock of medicinal drugs.

**pharmacy** (**farm**-ăsi) noun **1** the preparation and dispensing of medicinal drugs. **2** a shop where these are sold; a dispensary.

**Pharos** (**fair**-oss) a large lighthouse, one of the Seven Wonders of the World, erected c.280 BC on the island of Pharos off the coast of Egypt and destroyed in 1375.

**pharyngitis** (fa-rin-**jy**-tiss) noun inflammation of the pharynx.

**pharynx** (**fa**-rinks) noun the cavity at the back of the nose and throat. □ **pharyngeal** (fa-rin-**jee**-ăl) adjective

**phase** noun **1** a stage in a process of change or development. **2** any of the forms in which the moon or a planet appears as part or all of its disc is seen illuminated (new moon, first quarter, full moon, last quarter). **3** Physics a stage in a recurring sequence, especially the wave form of alternating electric currents or light. ●verb carry out (a programme etc.) in stages. □ **phase in** or **out** bring gradually into or out of use.

**Ph.D.** *abbreviation* Doctor of Philosophy; a higher degree awarded for a piece of original research usually taking three or more years to complete.

**pheasant** (**fez**-ănt) *noun* **1** a long-tailed game bird with bright feathers in the male. **2** its flesh as food.

**phenobarbitone** (feen-ŏ-**bar**-bit-ohn) *noun* a medicinal drug used to treat insomnia and epilepsy.

**phenol** (**fee**-nol) *noun* a hydroxyl derivative of benzene, used as an antiseptic and disinfectant.

**phenomenal** *adjective* extraordinary, remarkable. □ **phenomenally** *adverb*

**phenomenon** (fin-om-inŏn) *noun* (*plural* **phenomena**) **1** a fact, occurrence, or change perceived by any of the senses or by the mind; *snow is a common phenomenon in winter.* **2** a remarkable person or thing, a wonder.

---

■**Usage** Note that *phenomena* is a plural but is often used mistakenly for the singular. This should be avoided.

---

**pheromone** (ferrŏ-mohn) *noun* a substance, secreted by an animal, that is detected by others of the same species and produces a response in them.

**phew** *interjection* an exclamation of relief, surprise, discomfort, etc.

**phial** (**fy**-ăl) *noun* a small glass bottle, especially for perfume or liquid medicine.

**Phi Beta Kappa** (fy bee-tă **kap**-ă) the oldest American college fraternity, an honorary society to which distinguished scholars may be elected. (¶ Named from the initials of its Greek motto, = 'philosophy the guide to life'.)

**Philadelphia** the chief city of Pennsylvania.

**philadelphus** *noun* a large shrub with fragrant white flowers.

**philander** (fil-**and**-er) *verb* (of a man) flirt. □ **philanderer** *noun*

**philanthropic** (fil-ăn-**throp**-ik) *adjective* **1** benevolent. **2** concerned with human welfare and the reduction of suffering. □ **philanthropically** *adverb*

**philanthropist** (fil-**an**-thrŏp-ist) *noun* a philanthropic person.

**philanthropy** (fil-**an**-thrŏp-i) *noun* love of mankind, benevolence; philanthropic acts and principles.

**philately** (fil-**at**-ĕl-i) *noun* stamp-collecting. □ **philatelist** *noun*

**Philemon** (fi-lee-mŏn) □ **Epistle to Philemon** a book of the New Testament, an epistle of St Paul to a wealthy Christian of Phrygia in Asia Minor.

**philharmonic** (fil-ar-**mon**-ik) *adjective* (in names of symphony orchestras and music societies) devoted to music.

**Philip¹**, Prince, Duke of Edinburgh (born 1921), husband of Queen Elizabeth II.

**Philip²**, St **1** an Apostle, commemorated with St James the Less on 1 May. **2** 'the Evangelist', one of seven deacons appointed by the early Church at Jerusalem.

**Philippians** (fil-**ip**-i-ănz) □ **Epistle to the Philippians** a book of the New Testament, an epistle of St Paul to the Church at Philippi in Macedonia.

**Philippine** (**fil**-i-peen) *adjective* of the Philippines, Filipino. ●*plural noun* (**Philippines**) the Philippine Islands, a group of islands in the western Pacific.

**philistine** (**fil**-i-styn) *noun* **1** (**Philistine**) a member of a people in ancient ·Palestine who were enemies of the Israelites. **2** an uncultured person, one whose interests are material and commonplace. ●*adjective* having or showing uncultured tastes.

**philology** (fil-**ol**-ŏji) *noun* the study of languages and their development. □ **philological** *adjective*, **philologist** *noun*

**philosopher** *noun* **1** an expert in philosophy. **2** one who expounds a particular philosophical system. **3** one who speaks or behaves philosophically.

**philosophical** *adjective* **1** of philosophy. **2** calmly reasonable, bearing unavoidable misfortune unemotionally. □ **philosophically** *adverb*

**philosophize** *verb* (also **philosophise**) reason like a philosopher; moralize.

**philosophy** *noun* **1** the search, by logical reasoning, for understanding of the basic truths and principles of the universe, life, and morals, and of human perception and understanding of these. **2** a system of ideas concerning this or a particular subject; a system of principles for the conduct of life. **3** calm endurance of misfortune.

**philtre** (**fil**-ter) *noun* (*Amer.* **philter**) a magic potion; a love potion.

**phlebitis** (fli-by-tiss) *noun* inflammation of the walls of a vein.

**phlegm** (*pronounced* flem) *noun* **1** thick mucus in the throat and bronchial passages, ejected by coughing. **2** (*old use*) one of the four bodily humours.

**phlegmatic** (fleg-**mat**-ik) *adjective* **1** not easily excited or agitated. **2** sluggish, apathetic. □ **phlegmatically** *adverb*

**phloem** (**floh**-em) *noun* tissue conducting sap in plants.

**phlox** (*pronounced* floks) *noun* (*plural* **phlox** or **phloxes**) a plant with reddish, purple, or white flowers, either tall-growing with clusters of flowers or a low-growing rockery plant.

**Phnom Penh** (nom **pen**) the capital of Cambodia.

**phobia** (foh-biă) *noun* a lasting abnormal fear or great dislike of something.

**Phoenician** (fin-ish-ăn) *noun* a member of an ancient Semitic people of the eastern Mediterranean.    ●*adjective* of the Phoenicians.

**phoenix** (fee-niks) *noun* a mythical bird of the Arabian desert, said to live for hundreds of years and then burn itself on a funeral pile, rising from its ashes to live for another cycle.

**phone** *noun* (*informal*) a telephone. ●*verb* (*informal*) telephone. □ **on the phone** using the telephone; having an instrument connected to a telephone system. **over the phone** by use of the telephone. **phone-in** *noun* a broadcast programme in which listeners telephone the studio and participate.

**phonecard** *noun* a card containing prepaid units for use in a card phone.

**phoneme** (foh-neem) *noun* a unit of significant sound in a language (e.g. the sound of *c* in *cat*, which differs from the *b* in *bat* and distinguishes the two words). □ **phonemic** (foh-neem-ik) *adjective*

**phonetic** (fŏ-net-ik) *adjective* **1** representing each speech sound by a particular symbol which is always used for that sound; *the phonetic alphabet.* **2** (of spelling) corresponding to pronunciation. **3** of phonetics. ●*noun* (**phonetics**) (usu. treated as *singular*) speech sounds; the study of these. □ **phonetically** *adverb*

**phonetician** (foh-ni-tish-ăn) *noun* an expert in phonetics.

**phoney** *adjective* (also **phony**) (**phonier**, **phoniest**) (*slang*) sham, not genuine; insincere. ●*noun* (*slang*) a phoney person or thing.

**phonograph** (fohn-ŏ-grahf) *noun* (*Amer.*) a record player.

**phonology** (fŏ-nol-oji) *noun* the study of the sounds in a language. □ **phonological** *adjective*

**phony** alternative spelling of PHONEY.

**phosphate** (foss-fayt) *noun* a salt or ester of phosphoric acid; an artificial fertilizer composed of or containing this.

**phosphor** (foss-fer) *noun* a synthetic fluorescent or phosphorescent substance.

**phosphoresce** (foss-fer-ess) *verb* be phosphorescent.

**phosphorescent** (foss-fer-ess-ĕnt) *adjective* luminous, glowing with a faint light without burning or perceptible heat. □ **phosphorescence** *noun*

**phosphoric** (foss-fo-rik) *adjective* of or containing phosphorus.

**phosphorus** (foss-fer-ŭs) *noun* a chemical element (symbol P) existing in several forms; a yellowish wax-like form of it that appears luminous in the dark. □ **phosphorous** *adjective*

**photo** *noun* (*plural* **photos**) (*informal*) a photograph. □ **photo-call** *noun* = PHOTO OPPORTUNITY. **photo finish** a very close finish of a race, photographed to decide the winner. **photo opportunity** an organized opportunity for the press etc. to photograph a celebrity.

**photochemistry** *noun* the study of the chemical effects of light.

**photocopier** *noun* a machine for photocopying documents etc.

**photocopy** *noun* a copy (of a document etc.) made by photographing the original. ●*verb* (**photocopied**, **photocopying**) make a photocopy of.

**photoelectric** *adjective* of or using the electrical effects of light. □ **photoelectric cell** an electronic device which emits an electric current when light falls on it, used e.g. to measure light for photography or to cause a door to open when someone approaches it. □ **photoelectricity** *noun*

**photofit** *noun* a likeness of a person (especially one who is sought by the police) that is put together by assembling photographs of separate features.

**photogenic** (foh-tŏ-jen-ik) *adjective* **1** looking attractive in photographs. **2** *Biology* producing or emitting light.

**photograph** *noun* a picture formed by the chemical action of light or other radiation on a sensitive surface. ●*verb* **1** take a photograph of. **2** come out in a certain way when photographed; *it photographs badly.*

**photographer** *noun* a person who takes photographs.

**photographic** *adjective* **1** of or used in or produced by photography. **2** (of the memory) recalling accurately what was seen. □ **photographically** *adverb*

**photography** *noun* the taking and processing of photographs.

**photogravure** (foh-toh-gră-vewr) *noun* a picture produced from a photographic negative transferred to a metal plate and etched in.

**photojournalism** *noun* the relating of news by photographs, especially in magazines.

**photolithography** (foh-toh-lith-og-răfi) *noun* lithography with plates made photographically.

**photometer** (foh-tom-it-er) *noun* an instrument for measuring light. □ **photometric** *adjective*, **photometry** *noun*

**photon** (foh-tonn) *noun* an indivisible unit of electromagnetic radiation.

**photosensitive** *adjective* reacting to light.

**Photostat** *noun* (*trade mark*) **1** a photocopier. **2** a photocopy. ●*verb* (**photostat**) (**photostatted, photostatting**) make a photostat of.

**photosynthesis** (foh-toh-**sin**-thi-sis) *noun* the process by which green plants use sunlight to convert carbon dioxide (taken from the air) and water into complex substances. □ **photosynthesize** *verb*, **photosynthetic** *adjective*

**phototropic** (foh-tŏ-**trop**-ik) *adjective* (of the movement or growth of a plant) responding to the direction from which light falls on it. □ **phototropism** *noun*

**phrase** *noun* **1** a group of words forming a unit, especially as an idiom or a clever way of saying something. **2** a group of words (usually without a finite verb) forming a unit within a sentence or clause, e.g. *in the garden.* **3** the way something is worded; *we didn't like his choice of phrase.* **4** *Music* a short distinct passage forming a unit in a melody. ●*verb* **1** express in words. **2** divide (music) into phrases. □ **phrase book** a book listing common phrases and their equivalents in a foreign language. □ **phrasal** *adjective*

**phraseology** (fray-zi-**ol**-ŏji) *noun* wording, the way something is worded.

**phrenetic** alternative spelling of FRENETIC.

**phrenology** (frin-**ol**-ŏji) *noun* study of the external shape of a person's skull as a supposed indication of character and abilities. □ **phrenological** *adjective*

**phut** *noun* a sound like air escaping in a short burst. □ **go phut** (*informal*) come to nothing, break down.

**phylactery** (fi-**lak**-ter-i) *noun* a small leather box containing Hebrew texts, worn by Jews at weekday morning prayer.

**phylum** (**fy**-lŭm) *noun* (*plural* **phyla**) any of the larger groups into which plants and animals are divided, containing species with the same general form.

**physic** (**fiz**-ik) *noun* (*old use*) medicine.

**physical** *adjective* **1** of the body; *physical fitness; a physical examination.* **2** of matter or the laws of nature (as opposed to moral, spiritual, or imaginary things); *the physical world.* **3** of physics. ●*noun* (*informal*) a physical examination. □ **physical chemistry** a branch of chemistry in which physics is used to study substances and their reactions. **physical geography** a branch of geography dealing with the natural features of the earth's surface (e.g. mountains, lakes, rivers). **physical science** science concerned with inanimate natural objects. □ **physically** *adverb*

**physician** (fiz-**ish**-ăn) *noun* a doctor, especially one who practises medicine (as distinct from surgery) or is a specialist in this (as distinct from a general practitioner).

**physicist** (**fiz**-i-sist) *noun* an expert in physics.

**physics** (**fiz**-iks) *noun* **1** the scientific study of the properties and interactions of matter and energy. **2** these properties etc.

**physiognomy** (fiz-i-**on**-ŏmi) *noun* the features of a person's face.

**physiology** (fiz-i-**ol**-ŏji) *noun* **1** the study of the bodily functions of living organisms and their parts. **2** these functions. □ **physiological** (fizi-ŏ-**loj**-ikăl) *adjective*, **physiologist** *noun*

**physiotherapy** (fiz-i-oh-the-**ră**-pi) *noun* treatment of a disease, injury, deformity, or weakness by massaging, exercises, heat, etc. □ **physiotherapist** *noun*

**physique** (fiz-**eek**) *noun* a person's physical build and muscular development.

**pi** (*rhymes with* my) *noun* a letter of the Greek alphabet (Π, π) used as a symbol for the ratio of the circumference of a circle to its diameter (approximately 3.14159).

**Piaf** (p'yahf), Edith (original name: Edith Giovanna Gassion) (1915–63), French singer and songwriter.

**Piaget** (**pi**-ă-zhay), Jean (1897–1980), Swiss psychologist, noted for his work on the mental development of children.

**pia mater** (py-ă **may**-ter) a delicate membrane surrounding the brain and spinal cord.

**pianissimo** *adverb* (in music) very softly.

**pianist** *noun* a person who plays the piano.

**piano**[1] (pee-**an**-oh) *noun* (*plural* **pianos**) a musical instrument in which metal strings are struck by hammers operated by pressing the keys of a keyboard. □ **piano-accordion** *noun* an accordion in which the melody is played on a small piano-like keyboard.

**piano**[2] (pee-**ah**-noh) *adverb* (in music) softly.

**pianoforte** (pi-ah-noh-**for**-ti) *noun* (*formal* or *old use*) a piano.

**Pianola** (pee-ă-**noh**-lă) *noun* (*trade mark*) an automatic piano operated by a perforated paper roll.

**piastre** (pee-**ast**-er) *noun* a small coin of various Middle Eastern countries.

**piazza** (pee-**ats**-ă) *noun* a public square in a town. (¶ Italian.)

**pibroch** (**pee**-brok) *noun* a series of variations on a theme, for bagpipes.

**pica** (**py**-kă) *noun* **1** a size of letters in typewriting (10 per inch). **2** a unit of length for measuring printing-type, about one-sixth of an inch.

**picador** (**pik**-ă-dor) *noun* a mounted man with a lance in bullfighting.

**Picardy** a former province of northern France, the scene of heavy fighting in the First World War.

**picaresque** (pik-er-**esk**) *adjective* (of a style of fiction) dealing with the adventures of rogues.

■**Usage** *Picaresque* is sometimes used to mean 'transitory' or 'roaming', but this is considered incorrect in standard English.

**Picasso**, Pablo (1881–1973), Spanish painter, living in France, highly inventive and a founder of cubism.

**picayune** (pik-ă-**yoon**) *noun* (*Amer.*) **1** a small coin. **2** an insignificant person or thing. ●*adjective* (*Amer. informal*) petty, contemptible.

**piccalilli** *noun* pickle of chopped vegetables, mustard, and hot spices.

**piccaninny** *noun* (*Amer.* **pickaninny**) (often *offensive*) **1** a Black child. **2** an Australian Aboriginal child.

**piccolo** *noun* (*plural* **piccolos**) a small flute sounding an octave higher than the ordinary one.

**pick**[1] *verb* **1** use a pointed instrument, the fingers, beak, etc. to make a hole in or remove bits from (a thing). **2** detach (a flower or fruit) from the plant bearing it. **3** select carefully; choose; *pick a winner*. ●*noun* **1** picking. **2** selection; *have first pick*. **3** (usually foll. by *of*) the best part; *the pick of the bunch*. **pick a lock** use a piece of wire or a tool to open it without a key. **pick and choose** select with excessive care. **pick a person's brains** extract ideas or information from him or her. **pick a person's pocket** steal its contents while he or she is wearing the garment. **pick a quarrel** provoke a quarrel deliberately. **pick at** eat (one's food) in small bits without interest. **pick holes in** find fault with (an idea, suggestion etc.). **pick-me-up** *noun* a tonic to restore health or relieve depression. **pick off 1** pluck off. **2** select and shoot or destroy one by one as opportunity arises. **pick on** single out, especially as a target for nagging or harassment. **pick out 1** take from among a number of things. **2** recognize; distinguish from surrounding objects or areas. **3** play (a tune) by searching for the right notes. **pick over** select the best of. **pick up 1** lift or take up. **2** call for and take with one, take aboard (passengers or freight etc.). **3** (of police etc.) catch, find and take into custody. **4** get or acquire by chance or casually. **5** meet casually and become acquainted with. **6** succeed in seeing or hearing by means of apparatus. **7** recover health, show an improvement. **pick-up** *noun* **1** picking up. **2** an acquaintance met informally. **3** a small open motor truck. **4** the part carrying the stylus in a record player. **pick up speed** accelerate. **pick up the bill** be the

one who pays it. □ **pickable** *adjective*, **picker** *noun*

**pick**[2] *noun* **1** a pickaxe. **2** a plectrum.

**pickaback** *adverb* = PIGGYBACK.

**pickaninny** Amer. spelling of PICCANINNY.

**pickaxe** *noun* a tool consisting of a curved iron bar with sharpened ends mounted at right angles to its handle, used for breaking hard ground, stones, etc.

**picket** *noun* **1** one or more persons stationed by strikers outside their place of work to dissuade others from entering. **2** an outpost of troops; a party of sentries. **3** a pointed stake set into the ground, e.g. as part of a fence. ●*verb* (**picketed**, **picketing**) **1** station or act as a picket during a strike. **2** post as a military picket. **3** secure or enclose with a stake or stakes. □ **picket line** a line of workers on strike at their workplace, which others are asked not to go past.

**pickings** *plural noun* **1** scraps of good food etc. remaining. **2** odd gains or perquisites; profits from pilfering.

**pickle** *noun* **1** food (especially a vegetable) preserved in vinegar or brine. **2** vinegar or brine used for this. **3** (*informal*) a plight; a mess. ●*verb* preserve in pickle.

**pickled** *adjective* (*slang*) drunk.

**pickpocket** *noun* a thief who picks people's pockets.

**picnic** *noun* **1** an informal meal taken in the open air for pleasure; an excursion for this. **2** (*informal*) something very agreeable or easily done. ●*verb* (**picnicked**, **picnicking**) take part in a picnic. □ **picnicker** *noun*

**pico-** *combining form* denoting a factor of $10^{-12}$; *picometre*.

**Pict** *noun* a member of an ancient people of northern Britain. □ **Pictish** *adjective*

**pictograph** *noun* (also **pictogram**) **1** a pictorial symbol used as a form of writing. **2** a chart using pictures to represent statistical information. □ **pictographic** *adjective*

**pictorial** *adjective* **1** of or expressed in a picture or pictures. **2** illustrated by pictures. ●*noun* a newspaper or magazine in which pictures are the main feature. □ **pictorially** *adverb*

**picture** *noun* **1** a representation of a person or people or object(s) etc. made by painting, drawing, or photography. **2** a portrait. **3** something that looks beautiful; *the garden is a picture*. **4** a scene, the total impression produced on one's sight or mind. **5** a perfect example; *she is a picture of health*. **6** (**the pictures**) cinema; a cinema film. **7** the image on a television screen. ●*verb* **1** represent in a picture. **2** describe vividly. **3** form a mental picture of; *picture yourself on a deserted beach*. □ **in the picture** (*informal*) fully informed. **picture window** a large window of one pane of glass, usually facing an attractive view.

**picturesque** (pik-cher-**esk**) *adjective* **1** forming a striking and pleasant scene; *picturesque villages*. **2** (of words or a description) very expressive, vivid.

**piddle** *verb* (*informal*) urinate.

**piddling** *adjective* (*informal*) trivial, unimportant.

**pidgin** (**pij**-in) *noun* a simplified form of English or another language, containing elements of the local language(s) and used for communication between people speaking different languages. □ **pidgin English** a pidgin in which the chief language is English.

**pie** *noun* a baked dish of meat, fruit, etc. enclosed in or covered with pastry or other crust. □ **pie chart** a diagram representing quantities as sectors of a circle. **pie in the sky** a prospect (considered unrealistic) of future happiness.

**piebald** *adjective* (of a horse etc.) with irregular patches of white and black or other dark colour. ●*noun* a piebald animal.

**piece** *noun* **1** one of the distinct portions of which a thing is composed or into which it is divided or broken. **2** one of a set of things; *a three-piece suite*. **3** something regarded as a unit; *a fine piece of work*. **4** a musical, literary, or artistic composition. **5** a coin; *a ten-cent piece*. **6** one of the set of objects used to make moves in board games; a chessman other than a pawn. ●*verb* (usually foll. by *together*) make by joining or adding pieces together. □ **go to pieces** lose one's strength or ability; collapse emotionally. **in one piece** not broken. **of a piece** of the same kind, consistent. **a piece of cake** (*informal*) something very easy. **a piece of one's mind** a reproach or scolding. **piece-work** *noun* work paid according to the quantity done, not by the time spent on it. **say one's piece** make a prepared statement; give one's opinion.

**pièce de résistance** (pee-ess dĕ ray-zee-stahns) (*plural* **pièces de résistance**, *pronounced* same) **1** the principal dish at a meal. **2** the most important or remarkable item. (¶ French.)

**piecemeal** *adjective & adverb* done piece by piece; gradually; unsystematically.

**pied** (*rhymes with* tide) *adjective* particoloured, piebald; *a pied wagtail*. □ **Pied Piper** (in German legend) a piper who rid the town of Hamelin of its rats by luring them away with his music and, when refused the promised fee, lured away all the children.

***pied-à-terre*** (pee-ayd-ah-**tair**) *noun* (*plural **pieds-à-terre***, *pronounced* same) a small flat or house kept for occasional use. (¶ French, = foot to earth.)

**Piedmont** (**peed**-mont) a district of NW Italy.

**pie-eyed** *adjective* (*slang*) drunk.

**pier** (*pronounced* peer) *noun* **1** a structure built out into the sea to serve as a breakwater, landing-stage, or promenade. **2** each of the pillars supporting an arch or bridge. **3** solid masonry between windows etc.

**pierce** *verb* **1** go into or through like a sharp-pointed instrument; make a hole in (a thing) in this way. **2** force one's way into or through.

**piercing** *adjective* **1** (of cold or wind etc.) penetrating sharply. **2** (of a voice or sound) shrilly audible.

**Pierrot** (**peer**-oh) a male character from French pantomime with a whitened face and loose white clown's costume.

**pietism** (**py**-e-tizm) *noun* pious sentiment.

**piety** (**py**-iti) *noun* piousness.

**piffle** (*informal*) *noun* nonsense, worthless talk. ●*verb* talk nonsense.

**piffling** *adjective* (*informal*) trivial, worthless.

**pig** *noun* **1** a domestic or wild animal with short legs, cloven hooves, and a broad blunt snout. **2** (*informal*) a greedy, dirty, or unpleasant person; a difficult or unpleasant thing. **3** (*slang, scornful*) a policeman. **4** an oblong mass of metal from a smelting-furnace; pig-iron. □ **buy a pig in a poke** buy a thing without seeing it or knowing whether it will be satisfactory. **pig-iron** *noun* crude iron from a smelting-furnace. **pig it** (**pigged, pigging**) (*informal*) live in dirty conditions or in a disorderly way. **pig oneself, pig out** (*informal*) eat greedily, overeat.

**pigeon** *noun* **1** a bird of the dove family. **2** (*informal*) a person's business or responsibility; *that's your pigeon* (¶ from a Chinese pronunciation of the word *business*). □ **pigeon-toed** *adjective* having the toes turned inwards.

**pigeon-hole** *noun* one of a set of small compartments in a desk or on a wall, used for holding papers, letters, etc. ●*verb* **1** put away for future consideration or indefinitely. **2** classify mentally as belonging to a particular group or kind.

**piggery** *noun* **1** a pig-breeding establishment. **2** a pigsty.

**piggish** *adjective* like a pig; dirty or greedy.

**Piggott**, Lester Keith (born 1935), English flat-racing jockey.

**piggy** *adjective* like a pig or those of a pig; *piggy eyes*. □ **piggy bank** a money-box made in the shape of a hollow pig.

**piggyback** (also **pickaback**) *noun* a ride on a person's shoulders and back. ●*adverb* carried in this way.

**pigheaded** *adjective* stubborn, obstinate.

**piglet** *noun* a young pig.

**pigment** *noun* colouring matter. ●*verb* colour (skin or other tissue) with natural pigment. □ **pigmentation** *noun*

**pigmy** alternative spelling of PYGMY.

**pigskin** *noun* leather made from the skin of a pig.

**pigsty** *noun* **1** a partly-covered pen for pigs. **2** a very dirty or untidy place.

**pigtail** *noun* long hair worn hanging in a plait at the back of the head.

**pike** *noun* **1** (*hist.*) a long wooden shaft with a pointed metal head. **2** (*plural* **pike**) a large voracious freshwater fish with a long narrow snout.

**piked** *adjective* (of a position in acrobatics etc.) with the legs straight and forming an angle with the body at the hips; *piked somersault.*

**pikestaff** *noun* the wooden shaft of a pike. □ **plain as a pikestaff** quite plain or obvious.

**pilaff, pilaf** = PILAU.

**pilaster** (pil-**ast**-er) *noun* a rectangular column, especially an ornamental one that projects from a wall into which it is set.

**Pilate**, Pontius (1st century AD), the Roman governor of Judaea who presided at the trial of Jesus Christ.

**pilau** (pi-**low**) *noun* (also **pilaff, pilaf**) a Middle Eastern or Indian dish of rice boiled with meat, vegetables, spices, etc.

**pilchard** *noun* a small sea fish related to the herring.

**pile**¹ *noun* a heavy beam of metal, concrete, or timber driven vertically into the ground as a foundation or support for a building or bridge. □ **pile-driver** *noun* a machine for driving piles into the ground.

**pile**² *noun* **1** a number of things lying one upon another. **2** a funeral pyre. **3** (*informal*) a large quantity; *a pile of work.* **4** (*informal*) a large quantity of money; *made a pile.* **5** a large imposing building. **6** *Physics* a nuclear reactor. ●*verb* **1** heap, stack, or load. **2** crowd; *they all piled into one car.* □ **pile it on** (*informal*) exaggerate. **pile up 1** accumulate. **2** cause (a vehicle) to crash. **pile-up** *noun* a collision of several motor vehicles.

**pile**³ *noun* the projecting surface on velvet, carpets, etc.

**piles** *plural noun* haemorrhoids.

**pilfer** *verb* steal small items or in small quantities.

**pilgrim** *noun* a person who travels to a sacred place as an act of religious devotion. □ **Pilgrim Fathers** the English Puritans who founded the colony of Plymouth, Massachusetts, in 1620.

**pilgrimage** *noun* a pilgrim's journey; a journey made to a place as a mark of respect (e.g. to a person's birthplace).

**Pilipino** (pili-**peen**-oh) *noun* the national language of the Philippines, based on Tagalog.

**pill** *noun* **1** a small solid medicinal substance for swallowing whole. **2** (**the pill**) (*informal*) a contraceptive pill. **3** an unpleasant or painful necessity; *a bitter pill.*

**pillage** *verb* plunder. ●*noun* plunder. □ **pillager** *noun*

**pillar** *noun* **1** a vertical structure used as a support or ornament. **2** something resembling this in shape; *a pillar of rock.* **3** a person regarded as one of the chief supporters of something; *a pillar of the community.* □ **from pillar to post** from one place or situation to another. **pillar-box** *noun* a postbox.

**pillbox** *noun* **1** a small round box for holding pills. **2** a hat shaped like this. **3** a small concrete shelter for a gun emplacement.

**pillion** *noun* a saddle for a passenger behind the driver of a motor cycle. □ **ride pillion** ride on this as a passenger.

**pillory** *noun* a wooden framework with holes for the head and hands, into which offenders were formerly locked for exposure to public ridicule. ●*verb* (**pilloried, pillorying**) **1** hold up to public ridicule or scorn. **2** put into the pillory as a punishment.

**pillow** *noun* a cushion used (especially in bed) for supporting the head. ●*verb* rest or prop up on or as if on a pillow.

**pillowcase** *noun* (also **pillowslip**) a washable cloth cover for a pillow.

**pilot** *noun* **1** a person who operates the controls of an aircraft. **2** a person qualified to take charge of ships entering or leaving a harbour or travelling through certain waters. **3** a guide. ●*verb* (**piloted, piloting**) **1** act as pilot of. **2** conduct as a test or pilot project. ●*adjective* experimental, testing (on a small scale) how a scheme etc. will work; *a pilot project.* □ **pilot-light** *noun* **1** a small jet of gas kept alight to light a larger burner when this is turned on. **2** an electric indicator light. **pilot officer** an officer of the lowest commissioned rank in the RAF.

**pimento** (pim-**ent**-oh) *noun* (*plural* **pimentos**) **1** allspice; the West Indian tree yielding this. **2** = PIMIENTO.

**pi meson** = PION.

**pimiento** *noun* (*plural* **pimientos**) a sweet pepper.

**pimp** *noun* a man who solicits clients for a prostitute or brothel. ●*verb* be a pimp.

**pimpernel** (**pimp**-er-nel) *noun* a wild plant with small scarlet, blue, or white flowers that close in cloudy or wet weather.

**pimple** *noun* a small hard inflamed spot on the skin.

**pimply** *adjective* covered with pimples, especially on the face.

**PIN** *abbreviation* personal identification number; a number allocated by a bank etc. to a customer, e.g. for use with a card for obtaining cash from a machine.

**pin** *noun* **1** a short thin stiff piece of metal with a sharp point and a round head, used for fastening fabrics or papers together or (with an ornamental head) as a decoration. **2** a peg of wood or metal used for various purposes. **3** a stick with a flag on it, placed in a hole on a golf course to mark its position. **4** a drawing-pin, hairpin, ninepin, or safety pin. **5** (**pins**) (*informal*) legs; *quick on his pins*. ● *verb* (**pinned, pinning**) **1** fasten with a pin or pins. **2** transfix with a weapon or arrow etc. and hold fast; restrict and make unable to move; *he was pinned under the wreckage*. **3** (foll. by *on*) put (blame, responsibility, hopes, etc.) on (a person); *pinned the blame on her.* □ **pin down 1** establish clearly. **2** make (a person) agree to keep to a promise or arrangement, or declare his or her intentions definitely. **pin-money** *noun* a very small sum of money. **pins and needles** a tingling sensation. **pin-table** *noun* a board on which pinball is played. **pin-tuck** *noun* a very narrow ornamental tuck. **pin-up** *noun* (*informal*) a picture of an attractive or famous person, for pinning on a wall; the subject of this.

**pina colada** (pee-nǎ kǒ-**lah**-dǎ) a cocktail made from pineapple juice, rum, and coconut.

**pinafore** *noun* **1** an apron. **2** (in full **pinafore dress**) a dress without collar or sleeves, worn over a blouse or jumper.

**pinball** *noun* a game in which balls are shot across a sloping board to strike pins or targets.

**pince-nez** (panss-nay) *noun* (*plural* **pince-nez**) a pair of glasses with a spring that clips on the nose and no side-pieces. (¶ French, = pinch-nose.)

**pincers** *plural noun* **1** a tool for gripping and pulling things, consisting of a pair of pivoted jaws with handles that are pressed together to close them. **2** the front claw-like parts of lobsters etc. □ **pincer movement** an attack in which forces converge from each side on an enemy position.

**pinch** *verb* **1** squeeze tightly or painfully between two surfaces, especially between finger and thumb. **2** (usually as **pinched** *adjective*) having a drawn appearance from feeling unpleasantly cold or hungry. **3** stint, be niggardly; *pinching and scrimping*. **4** (*slang*) steal. **5** (*slang*) arrest.

● *noun* **1** pinching, squeezing. **2** stress or pressure of circumstances; *began to feel the pinch*. **3** as much as can be held between the tips of the thumb and forefinger. □ **at a pinch** in time of difficulty or necessity.

**pinchbeck** *noun* an alloy of copper and zinc used as imitation gold in cheap jewellery. ● *adjective* sham.

**pincushion** *noun* a small pad into which pins are stuck to keep them ready for use.

**Pindar** (518–438 BC), Greek lyric poet.

**pine¹** *noun* **1** an evergreen tree with needle-shaped leaves growing in clusters. **2** its wood. □ **pine cone** the fruit of the pine. **pine marten** a dark brown weasel-like mammal with a white throat and stomach. **pine nut** the edible seed of various pine trees.

**pine²** *verb* **1** waste away through grief or yearning. **2** feel an intense longing.

**pineapple** *noun* **1** a large juicy tropical fruit with yellow flesh and a tough prickly segmented skin. **2** the plant that bears it.

**ping** *noun* a short sharp ringing sound. ● *verb* make or cause to make this sound.

**ping-pong** *noun* (*informal*) table tennis.

**pinion¹** (**pin**-yǒn) *noun* a bird's wing, especially the outer segment. ● *verb* **1** clip the wings of (a bird) to prevent it from flying. **2** restrain (a person) by holding or binding his or her arms or legs.

**pinion²** (**pin**-yǒn) *noun* a small cog-wheel that engages with a larger one or with a rack.

**pink¹** *noun* **1** a pale red colour. **2** a garden plant with fragrant white or pink flowers. **3** the best or most perfect condition; *the pink of perfection*. ● *adjective* **1** of pale red colour. **2** (*informal*) mildly left-wing. □ **in the pink** (*informal*) in very good health. □ **pinkish** *adjective*, **pinkness** *noun*

**pink²** *verb* **1** pierce slightly. **2** cut a zigzag edge on. □ **pinking shears** dressmaker's scissors with serrated blades for cutting a zigzag edge.

**pink³** *verb* (of an engine) make slight high-pitched explosive sounds caused by faulty combustion.

**pinkie** *noun* (especially *Amer.* & *Scottish*) the little finger.

**pinnace** (**pin**-iss) *noun* a ship's small boat.

**pinnacle** *noun* **1** a pointed ornament on a roof. **2** a peak. **3** the highest point; *the pinnacle of his fame*.

**pinnate** *adjective* (of a compound leaf) having leaflets on either side of the leaf-stalk.

**pinny** *noun* (*informal*) an apron or pinafore.

**Pinochet** (**pin**-ǒ-shay), Augusto (born 1915), Chilean general and statesman, President of Chile 1974–90 after his overthrow of Allende (1973).

**pinpoint** noun **1** the point of a pin. **2** something very small or sharp. ● adjective precise, accurate; *with pinpoint accuracy.* ● verb locate or identify precisely.

**pinprick** noun a small annoyance.

**pinstripe** noun a very narrow stripe on cloth; a suit made from cloth of this kind. □ **pinstriped** adjective

**pint** noun **1** a measure for liquids, ⅛ of a gallon (in Britain 568 ml, in the USA 473 ml). **2** this quantity of liquid, especially milk or beer. □ **pint-sized** adjective (*informal*) very small.

**pinta** noun (*informal*) a pint of milk.

**pintail** noun a duck or grouse with a pointed tail.

**Pinter** (**pin**-ter), Harold (born 1930), English playwright.

**pintle** (**pin**-t'l) noun a pin or bolt, especially one on which another part turns.

**Pinyin** noun a system of romanized spelling used for the Chinese language.

**pion** noun (also **pi meson**) a sub-atomic particle with a mass many times greater than that of an electron.

**pioneer** (py-ŏn-**eer**) noun a person who is one of the first to enter or settle in a new region or to investigate a new subject or method. ● verb be a pioneer; take part in (a course of action etc.) that leads the way for others to follow.

**pious** adjective **1** devout in religion. **2** too virtuous, sanctimonious. □ **piously** adverb, **piousness** noun

**pip** noun **1** one of the small seeds of an apple, pear, orange, etc. **2** a spot on a domino, dice, or playing card. **3** a star (indicating rank) on the shoulder of an army officer's uniform. **4** a short high-pitched sound, usually one produced mechanically; *the six pips of the time-signal.* **5** a disease of poultry and other birds. **6** (**the pip**) (*slang*) a feeling of disgust, depression, or bad temper; *he gives me the pip.* ● verb (**pipped**, **pipping**) (*informal*) **1** hit with a shot. **2** defeat. □ **pip at the post** defeat at the last moment.

**pipe** noun **1** a tube through which something can flow. **2** a wind instrument consisting of a single tube. **3** each of the tubes by which sound is produced in an organ. **4** (**the pipes**) bagpipes. **5** a boatswain's whistle; its sounding. **6** a narrow tube with a bowl at one end in which tobacco burns for smoking. ● verb **1** convey (water etc.) through pipes. **2** transmit (music or a broadcast programme etc.) by wire or cable. **3** play (music) on a pipe. **4** lead, bring, or summon by sounding a pipe. **5** utter in a shrill voice. **6** decorate (a dress etc.) with piping. **7** force (icing, cream, etc.) through an aperture to make orna-

mental shapes. □ **pipe down** (*informal*) become less noisy or less insistent. **pipe-cleaner** noun a length of flexible tufted wire for cleaning a tobacco pipe. **pipe up** begin to play, sing, or speak.

**pipeclay** noun a fine white clay for tobacco pipes or for whitening leather.

**pipedream** noun an impractical hope or scheme.

**pipeline** noun **1** a pipe for conveying oil etc. over a distance. **2** a channel of supply or information. □ **in the pipeline** on the way; in the process of being prepared.

**piper** noun a person who plays a pipe or bagpipes.

**pipette** (pip-**et**) noun a slender tube, usually filled by suction, used in a laboratory for transferring or measuring small quantities of liquids.

**piping** noun **1** pipes; a length of pipe. **2** a pipelike fold (often enclosing a cord) decorating edges or seams of clothing or upholstery. **3** a decorative line of icing etc. piped on food. □ **piping hot** (of water or food) very hot.

**pipistrelle** (pip-iss-**trel**) noun a small bat.

**pipit** noun a small bird resembling a lark.

**pippin** noun a variety of apple.

**pipsqueak** noun (*slang*) a small, unimportant, or contemptible person.

**piquant** (**pee**-kănt) adjective **1** pleasantly sharp in taste or smell. **2** pleasantly stimulating or exciting to the mind. □ **piquancy** noun

**pique** (*pronounced* peek) verb (**piqued**, **piquing**) **1** hurt the pride or self-respect of. **2** stimulate; *their curiosity was piqued.* ● noun a feeling of hurt pride.

**piqué** (**pee**-kay) noun a firm fabric especially of cotton, with a lengthwise corded effect.

**piquet** (pi-**ket**) noun a card game for two players with a pack of 32 cards.

**piracy** (**pyr**-ăsi) noun **1** robbery of ships at sea. **2** hijacking. **3** infringement of copyright; use of material without authorization.

**Pirandello** (peer-ăn-**del**-oh), Luigi (1867–1936), Italian dramatist and novelist.

**piranha** (pi-**rahn**-ă) noun a fierce tropical South American freshwater fish, with sharp teeth.

**pirate** noun **1** a person on a ship who unlawfully attacks and robs another ship at sea. **2** a ship used by pirates. **3** (often used as adjective) infringing another's copyright or business rights, or broadcasting without authorization; *a pirate radio station.* ● verb reproduce (a book, video, or computer software) or trade (goods) without due authorization. □ **piratical** adjective

**pirouette** (pi-roo-et) *noun* a dancer's spinning movement while balanced on tiptoe. ●*verb* perform a pirouette.

**Pisa** (pee-ză) a city in northern Italy, noted for its 'Leaning Tower', the campanile of its cathedral (12th century).

**piscatorial** (pisk-ă-**tor**-iăl) *adjective* of fishing or fishermen.

**Pisces** (py-seez) *noun* the twelfth sign of the zodiac, the Fishes. □ **Piscean** *adjective & noun*

**piscina** (pi-**seen**-ă) *noun* (*plural* **piscinae** *or* **piscinas**) **1** a stone basin near the altar in a church, used for rinsing the chalice etc. **2** a fish-pond.

**piss** (*vulgar*) *verb* urinate. ●*noun* **1** urination. **2** urine. □ **piss artist 1** a drunkard. **2** a person who fools about. **piss about** mess about, fool around. **piss off 1** go away. **2** annoy, depress. **take the piss** mock, make fun of.

**pissed** *adjective* (*vulgar*) drunk.

**pistachio** (pis-**tash**-i-oh) *noun* (*plural* **pistachios**) a nut with an edible green kernel.

**piste** (*pronounced* peest) *noun* a ski run of compacted snow.

**pistil** *noun* the seed-producing part of a flower, comprising ovary, style, and stigma. □ **pistillate** *adjective*

**pistol** *noun* a small handgun.

**piston** *noun* **1** a sliding disc or cylinder fitting closely inside a tube in which it moves up and down as part of an engine or pump. **2** the sliding valve in a trumpet or other brass wind instrument.

**pit** *noun* **1** a hole in the ground, especially one from which material is dug out; *chalk-pit*. **2** a coalmine. **3** a depression in the skin or in any surface. **4** seats on the ground floor of a theatre behind the stalls. **5** a sunken area in a workshop floor, giving access to the underside of motor vehicles. **6** an area at the side of a racetrack where cars are serviced and refuelled during a race. ●*verb* (**pitted, pitting**) **1** make pits or depressions in, become marked with hollows; *pitted with craters*. **2** (usually foll. by *against*) set (one's wits, strength, etc.) in competition. **3** (usually as **pitted** *adjective*) remove stones from (olives, cherries, etc.). □ **the pits** (*slang*) the worst or most despicable person, place, or thing. **pit bull terrier** a small stocky American dog noted for ferocity. **pit-head** *noun* the top of a mine shaft; the area surrounding this. **pit of the stomach** the depression between the ribs below the breastbone.

**pita** alternative spelling of PITTA.

**pit-a-pat** *noun* (also **pitter-patter**) a quick tapping sound. ●*adverb* with this sound.

**Pitcairn Islands** a British dependency comprising a group of islands in the South Pacific, north-east of New Zealand.

**pitch¹** *noun* a dark resinous tarry substance that sets hard, used for caulking seams of ships etc. ●*verb* coat with pitch. □ **pitch-black, pitch-dark** *adjective* completely black, with no light at all. **pitch pine** a pine tree that yields much resin.

**pitch²** *verb* **1** throw or fling. **2** erect and fix (a tent or camp). **3** set at a particular degree, slope, or level; *pitched their hopes high*. **4** fall heavily. **5** (in cricket) cause the ball to strike the ground near the wicket in bowling; (of a bowled ball) strike the ground. **6** (in baseball) throw (the ball) to the batter. **7** (of a ship or vehicle) plunge forward and backward alternately. ●*noun* **1** the act or process of pitching. **2** the steepness of a slope. **3** the intensity of a quality etc. **4** the degree of highness or lowness of a musical note or a voice. **5** a place at which a street performer or trader etc. is stationed. **6** a playing field for football, hockey, etc.; the area between and near the wickets in cricket. **7** a salesman's persuasive talk. □ **pitched battle** a battle fought by troops in prepared positions, not a skirmish. **pitched roof** a sloping roof. **pitch in** (*informal*) begin to work vigorously. **pitch into** (*informal*) attack or reprimand vigorously.

**pitchblende** *noun* a mineral ore (uranium oxide) that yields radium.

**pitcher** *noun* **1** the baseball player who delivers the ball to the batter. **2** a large jug. □ **pitcher-plant** *noun* a plant with pitcher-shaped leaves holding a secretion in which insects become trapped.

**pitchfork** *noun* a long-handled fork with two prongs, used for pitching hay. ●*verb* **1** lift or move (a thing) with a pitchfork. **2** thrust (a person) forcibly into a position or office.

**piteous** *adjective* deserving or arousing pity. □ **piteously** *adverb*

**pitfall** *noun* an unsuspected danger or difficulty.

**pith** *noun* **1** the spongy tissue in the stems of certain plants or lining the rind of oranges etc. **2** the essential part; *the pith of the argument*.

**pithy** *adjective* (**pithier, pithiest**) **1** like pith; containing much pith. **2** brief and full of meaning; *pithy comments*.

**pitiable** *adjective* deserving or arousing pity or contempt. □ **pitiably** *adverb*

**pitiful** *adjective* pitiable. □ **pitifully** *adverb*

**pitiless** *adjective* showing no pity. □ **pitilessly** *adverb*

**piton** (pee-tonn) *noun* a peg with a hole through which a rope can be passed, driven into rock as a support in rock-climbing.

**Pitt¹**, William, 'the Elder', Earl of Chatham (1708–78), British statesman.

**Pitt²**, William, 'the Younger' (1759–1806), British statesman, Prime Minister 1783–1801 and 1804–6, the youngest ever to hold this office.

**pitta** noun (also **pita**) a flat bread with a hollow inside, originally from Greece and the Middle East.

**pittance** noun a very small allowance or wage.

**pitter-patter** = PIT-A-PAT.

**pituitary** (pit-yoo-it-eri) noun (also **pituitary gland**) a small ductless gland at the base of the brain, with important influence on growth and bodily functions.

**pity** noun **1** a feeling of sorrow for another person's suffering. **2** a cause for regret; *what a pity.* ● verb (**pitied, pitying**) feel pity for. □ **take pity on** feel concern for and help (a person who is in difficulty).

**pivot** noun **1** a central point or shaft etc. on which something turns or swings. **2** a pivoting movement. ● verb (**pivoted, pivoting**) turn or place to turn on a pivot.

**pivotal** adjective **1** of a pivot. **2** vitally important.

**pixel** noun any of the minute illuminated areas which make up an image displayed on a screen.

**pixie** noun (also **pixy**) a small supernatural being in fairy tales.

**Pizarro** (pi-zar-oh), Francisco (c.1478–1541), Spanish conqueror of the Inca empire in Peru.

**pizza** (peets-ă) noun an Italian dish of a layer of dough baked with a savoury topping.

**pizzazz** (pi-zaz) noun (informal) **1** zest, liveliness. **2** showiness.

**pizzeria** noun a pizza restaurant.

**pizzicato** (pits-i-kah-toh) adverb plucking the string of a musical instrument (instead of using the bow).

**pl.** abbreviation **1** plural. **2** (usually **Pl.**) place. **3** plate.

**placable** (plak-ă-bŭl) adjective able to be placated, forgiving. □ **placability** noun

**placard** noun a poster or other notice for displaying. ● verb post up placards on (a wall etc.).

**placate** (plă-kayt) verb pacify, conciliate. □ **placatory** adjective

**place** noun **1** a particular part of space or of an area. **2** a particular town, district, building, etc.; *one of the places we visited.* **3** (in names) a short street; a square or the buildings round it; a country mansion. **4** the part one has reached in a book etc.; *lose one's place.* **5** a proper position for a thing; a position in a series; one's rank or position in a community; a duty appropriate to this. **6** a position of employment. **7** a space or seat or accommodation for a person; *keep me a place on the train.* **8** one's home or dwelling. **9** (in racing) a position among placed competitors, especially second or third. **10** the position of a figure after a decimal point etc.; *correct to 3 decimal places.* ● verb **1** put into a particular place, rank, position, or order; find a place for. **2** locate, identify in relation to circumstances etc.; *I know his face but can't place him.* **3** put or give; *placed an order with the firm.* □ **be placed** (in a race) be among the first three. **go places** (informal) become successful. **in place** in the right position; suitable. **in place of** instead of. **out of place** in the wrong position or environment; unsuitable. **place-kick** noun a kick in football with the ball placed on the ground. **place-setting** noun a set of dishes or cutlery for one person at table.

**placebo** (plă-see-boh) noun (plural **placebos**) a harmless substance given as if it were medicine, to humour a patient or as a dummy pill etc. in a controlled experiment.

**placement** noun placing; a position.

**placenta** (plă-sent-ă) noun an organ that develops in the womb during pregnancy and supplies the developing foetus with nourishment. □ **placental** adjective

**placid** adjective calm and peaceful, not easily made anxious or upset. □ **placidly** adverb, **placidity** (plă-sid-iti) noun

**placket** an opening or slit in a garment for fastenings or access to a pocket.

**plagiarize** (play-ji-ă-ryz) verb (also **plagiarise**) take and use (another person's ideas, writings, or inventions) as one's own. □ **plagiarism** noun, **plagiarist** noun

**plague** (pronounced playg) noun **1** a deadly contagious disease. **2** an infestation of a pest; *a plague of caterpillars.* **3** (informal) a nuisance. ● verb (**plagued, plaguing**) annoy, pester.

**plaice** noun (plural **plaice**) a kind of flatfish used as food.

**plaid** (pronounced plad) noun tartan cloth; a long piece of this worn over the shoulder as part of Highland dress.

**Plaid Cymru** (plyd kum-ri) the Welsh nationalist party. (¶ Welsh, = party of Wales.)

**plain** adjective **1** unmistakable, easy to see or hear or understand. **2** not elaborate or intricate, not luxurious, without flavouring etc.; *plain cooking; plain water.* **3** straightforward, candid; *some plain speaking.* **4** ordinary; homely in manner, without affectation. **5** lacking beauty. ● adverb plainly, simply; *it's plain stupid.* ● noun **1** a large area of level country. **2** the basic stitch in knitting, made by pushing the point of the working needle away from the knitter. □ **plain chocolate** dark chocolate without added milk. **plain clothes** civilian clothes as distinct from uniform or official dress. **plain flour** flour that does not contain a raising agent. **plain sailing** a course of action that is free from difficulties. **plain-spoken** adjective frank. □ **plainly** adverb, **plainness** noun

**plainsong** noun (also **plainchant**) medieval church music for voices singing in unison, without regular rhythm.

**plaint** noun 1 Law a charge, an accusation. 2 (old use) a complaint or lamentation.

**plaintiff** noun the party that brings an action in a court of law (opposed to the defendant).

**plaintive** adjective sounding sad. □ **plaintively** adverb

**plait** (pronounced plat) verb weave or twist (three or more strands) into one rope-like length. ● noun something plaited.

**plan** noun 1 a drawing showing the relative position and size of parts of a building etc. 2 a map of a town or district. 3 a drawing or diagram showing a structure or object as viewed from above (compare ELEVATION). 4 a method or course of action thought out in advance; it all went according to plan. ● verb (**planned, planning**) 1 make a plan or design of. 2 arrange a method etc. for, make plans. □ **plan on** (informal) have as (part of) one's plan, intend. □ **planner** noun

**planchette** (plahn-**shet**) noun a small board on castors with a vertical pencil said to trace messages on paper at spiritualist seances.

**Planck**, Max Karl Ernst Ludwig (1858–1947), German theoretical physicist, the originator of the quantum theory.

**plane¹** noun a tall spreading tree with broad leaves.

**plane²** noun 1 a flat or level surface. 2 an imaginary surface of this kind. 3 a level of thought, existence, or development; on the same plane as a savage. 4 an aeroplane. ● adjective lying in a plane, level; a plane figure; a plane surface.

**plane³** noun 1 a tool with a blade projecting from the base, used for smoothing the surface of wood by paring shavings from it. 2 a similar tool for smoothing metal. ● verb smooth or pare with a plane.

**planet** noun a celestial body orbiting round a star. □ **planetary** adjective

**planetarium** (plan-i-**tair**-iŭm) noun (plural **planetariums** or **planetaria**) a room with a domed ceiling on which lights are projected to show the appearance of the stars and planets.

**plangent** (plan-jĕnt) adjective (literary) (of sounds) 1 resonant, reverberating. 2 loud and mournful.

**plank** noun 1 a long flat piece of timber. 2 one of the policies in a political programme. ● verb lay with planks. □ **walk the plank** (hist.) be forced by pirates to walk to one's death off a plank over the side of a ship.

**planking** noun a structure or floor of planks.

**plankton** noun the forms of organic life (chiefly microscopic) that float in the sea or fresh water.

**planning** noun making plans, especially with reference to the controlled design of buildings and development of land. □ **planning permission** formal approval for the construction or alteration of a building or structure, granted by a local authority.

**plant** noun 1 a living organism that makes its own food from inorganic substances and has neither the power of movement nor special organs of sensation and digestion. 2 a small plant (distinguished from a tree or shrub). 3 a factory or its machinery and equipment. 4 (informal) something deliberately placed so as to incriminate a person. ● verb 1 put (plants or seeds) into ground or soil for growing. 2 set or place firmly in position; planted his foot on the ladder. 3 station (a person) as a spy. 4 conceal (stolen or incriminating articles) in a place where they will be discovered and mislead the discoverer. □ **plant out** transfer (a plant) from a pot or frame to open ground.

**Plantagenet** (plan-**taj**-in-it) noun any of the kings of England from Henry II to Richard III (1154–1485).

**plantain** (plan-tin) noun 1 a common wild plant with broad leaves spread close to the ground, bearing seeds used as food for birds. 2 a tropical tree and fruit resembling the banana.

**plantation** noun 1 a number of cultivated plants or trees; the area of land on which they grow. 2 an estate on which cotton, tobacco, tea, etc. is cultivated.

**planter** noun 1 a person who owns or manages a plantation. 2 a container for house plants.

**plaque** (pronounced plak) noun 1 a flat plate fixed on a wall as an ornament or memorial. 2 a substance that forms on teeth, encouraging the growth of harmful bacteria.

**plasma** (plaz-mă) noun 1 the colourless fluid part of blood, in which the corpuscles are suspended. 2 a kind of gas containing positively and negatively charged particles in approximately equal numbers.

**plaster** noun 1 a soft mixture of lime, sand, and water, etc. applied to walls and ceilings to dry as a smooth hard surface. 2 a plaster of Paris; a cast made of this fitted round a broken limb etc. 3 sticking-plaster; a piece of this. ● verb 1 cover (a wall etc.) with plaster or a similar substance. **2** coat or daub; cover thickly. **3** make smooth with a fixative etc.; *his hair was plastered down.* □ **plaster cast 1** a cast of a statue etc. made in plaster. **2** plaster moulded round a broken limb etc. to keep it rigid. **plaster of Paris** white paste made from gypsum, used for making moulds or casts. □ **plasterer** *noun*

**plasterboard** *noun* board with a core of plaster, used for making partitions etc.

**plastered** *adjective* (*slang*) drunk.

**plastic** (plass-tik) *noun* **1** a synthetic resinous substance that can be given any permanent shape, e.g. by moulding it under pressure while heated. **2** = PLASTIC MONEY. ●*adjective* **1** made of plastic; *plastic bag.* **2** able to be shaped or moulded; *clay is a plastic substance.* **3** giving form to clay or wax etc. □ **plastic arts** arts involving modelling, e.g. sculpture or ceramics. **plastic bullet** a solid plastic cylinder fired as a riot-control device rather than to kill. **plastic explosive** a soft putty-like explosive. **plastic money** (*informal*) credit cards as opposed to cash or cheques. **plastic surgeon** a specialist in **plastic surgery**, the repairing or replacing of damaged or unsightly skin, muscle, etc. □ **plasticity** (plas-tiss-iti) *noun*

**Plasticine** *noun* (*trade mark*) a plastic substance used for modelling things.

**plasticize** (plast-i-syz) *verb* (also **plasticise**) make or become plastic. □ **plasticizer** *noun*

**Plate**, River, an estuary on the eastern side of South America between Uruguay and Argentina.

**plate** *noun* **1** an almost flat usually circular utensil from which food is eaten or served; its contents. **2** a similar shallow vessel for the collection of money in church. **3** dishes and other domestic utensils made of gold, silver, or other metal. **4** plated metal; objects made of this. **5** a silver or gold cup as a prize for a horse race etc.; the race itself. **6** a flat thin sheet of metal, glass, or other rigid material. **7** this coated with material sensitive to light or other radiation, for use in photography etc. **8** a flat piece of metal on which something is engraved or bearing a name, registration number, etc. **9** an illustration on special paper in a book. **10** a thin flat structure or formation in a plant or animal body. **11** a piece of plastic material moulded to the shape of the gums or roof of the mouth for holding artificial teeth; (*informal*) a denture. **12** each of several rigid layers of rock thought to form the earth's crust. ●*verb* **1** cover with plates of metal. **2** coat (metal) with a thin layer of silver, gold, or tin. □ **on a plate** (*informal*) available without the re-

cipient having to make an effort. **on one's plate** (*informal*) for one to deal with. **plate glass** thick glass of fine quality for shop windows etc. □ **plateful** *noun*

**plateau** (plat-oh) *noun* (*plural* **plateaux** or **plateaus**) **1** an area of fairly level high ground. **2** a state in which there is little variation following an increase; *the firm's export trade reached a plateau.*

**platelayer** *noun* a person employed to fix and repair railway rails.

**platelet** *noun* a small colourless disc found in the blood and involved in clotting.

**platen** (plat-ĕn) *noun* **1** a plate in a printing press which presses the paper against the type. **2** the roller of a typewriter, against which the paper is held.

**platform** *noun* **1** a level surface raised above the surrounding ground or floor, especially one from which a speaker addresses an audience. **2** a raised area along the side of the line at a railway station, where passengers get on and off trains. **3** a floor area at the entrance to a bus or tram. **4** the declared policy or programme of a political party.

**Plath**, Sylvia (1932–63), American poet and novelist, married in 1956 to the English poet Ted Hughes.

**platinum** *noun* a chemical element (symbol Pt), a silver-white metal that does not tarnish. □ **platinum blonde** a woman with silvery-blonde hair.

**platitude** (plat-i-tewd) *noun* a commonplace remark, especially one uttered solemnly as if it were new. □ **platitudinous** (plat-i-tewd-in-ŭs) *adjective*

**Plato** (play-toh) (429–347 BC), Greek philosopher, a disciple of Socrates.

**Platonic** (plă-tonn-ik) *adjective* **1** of Plato or his doctrines. **2** (**platonic**) (of love or friendship) not sexual.

**Platonism** (play-tŏn-izm) *noun* the doctrines of Plato or his followers.

**platoon** *noun* a subdivision of a military company.

**platter** *noun* a large flat dish or plate.

**platypus** (plat-i-pŭs) *noun* (*plural* **platypuses**) an Australian animal with a ducklike bill and a flat tail, that lays eggs but suckles its young.

**plaudit** (plaw-dit) *noun* (usually as **plaudits**) a round of applause; an emphatic expression of approval.

**plausible** (plaw-zib-ŭl) *adjective* **1** (of a statement) reasonable or probable but not proved. **2** (of a person) persuasive but deceptive. □ **plausibly** *adverb*, **plausibility** *noun*

**play** *verb* **1** occupy oneself in a game or other recreational activity. **2** take part in (a game); compete against (a player or team);

occupy (a specified position) in a game; assign (a player) to a particular position. **3** move (a piece), put (a card) on the table, or strike (a ball etc.) in a game. **4** act in a drama etc.; act the part of; *play the politician.* **5** perform (a part in a process). **6** perform on (a musical instrument); perform (a piece of music). **7** cause (a tape, CD, etc.) to produce sound. **8** move lightly or irregularly; emit light, water, etc.; *fountains gently playing.* **9** allow (a hooked fish) to exhaust itself by pulling against the line. ●*noun* **1** playing. **2** activity, operation; *other influences came into play.* **3** a literary work written for performance on the stage, television, or radio. **4** free movement; *bolts should have half an inch of play.* □ **in** or **out of play** (of a ball) being used, or temporarily out of use, in a game. **play about** or **around** behave irresponsibly. **play-acting** *noun* playing a part in a play; pretending. **play along** pretend to cooperate. **play at** perform in a trivial or half-hearted way. **play back** play (what has recently been recorded) on a tape recorder etc. **playback** *noun* playing back sound; a device for doing this. **play ball** (*informal*) cooperate. **play by ear 1** perform (music) without having seen a written score. **2** (also **play it by ear**) proceed step by step, going by one's instinct or by results. **play down** minimize the importance of. **played out** exhausted. **play fast and loose** act unreliably; ignore one's obligations. **play for time** seek to gain time by delaying. **play into someone's hands** do something that unwittingly gives him or her an advantage. **play off 1** play an extra match to decide a drawn position. **2** oppose (one person against another) in order to serve one's own interests. **play-off** *noun* a match played to decide a draw or tie. **play on** affect and make use of (a person's sympathy etc.). **play on words** a pun. **play one's cards right** or **well** make good use of one's opportunities. **play-pen** *noun* a portable enclosure for a young child to play in. **play safe** avoid taking risks. **play the game** keep the rules; behave honourably. **play the market** speculate in stocks etc. **play up 1** be mischievous and unruly, annoy by doing this. **2** cause trouble, go wrong; *my leg's playing up.* **play up to** try to win the favour of (a person) by flattery etc. **play with fire** take foolish risks.

**playbill** *noun* a poster advertising a play.

**playboy** *noun* a pleasure-loving usually rich man.

**player** *noun* **1** a person who takes part in a game. **2** a performer on a musical instrument. **3** an actor. **4** a record player.

**playful** *adjective* **1** full of fun. **2** in a mood for play, not serious. □ **playfully** *adverb,* **playfulness** *noun*

**playground** *noun* a piece of ground for children to play on.

**playgroup** *noun* a group of young children who play together regularly under supervision.

**playing card** each of a pack or set of 52 oblong cards used to play a variety of games, marked on one side to show one of 13 ranks in one of 4 suits.

**playing field** a field used for outdoor games.

**playmate** *noun* a child's companion in play.

**plaything** *noun* **1** a toy. **2** a person treated as a thing to play with.

**playtime** *noun* time assigned for children to play.

**playwright** *noun* a person who writes plays, a dramatist.

**plaza** (plah-ză) *noun* a public square, especially in a Spanish town.

**PLC** *abbreviation* (*Brit.*) (also **plc**) Public Limited Company.

**plea** *noun* **1** a formal statement (especially of 'guilty' or 'not guilty') made by or on behalf of a person charged in a lawcourt. **2** an appeal or entreaty; *a plea for mercy.* **3** an excuse; *on the plea of ill health.*

**plead** *verb* (**pleaded** (*Scottish* & *Amer.* **pled**), **pleading**) **1** put forward as a plea in a lawcourt. **2** address a lawcourt as an advocate; put forward (a case) in court. **3** make an appeal or entreaty. **4** put forward as an excuse; *pleaded a previous engagement.* □ **plead with** entreat.

**pleasant** *adjective* **1** pleasing, giving pleasure to the mind or feelings or senses. **2** having an agreeable manner. □ **pleasantly** *adverb,* **pleasantness** *noun*

**pleasantry** *noun* being humorous; a humorous remark.

**please** *verb* **1** give pleasure to, make (a person etc.) feel satisfied or glad. **2** think fit; have the desire; *take what you please.* ●*adverb* a polite phrase of request. □ **if you please** (*formal*) please; an ironical phrase, pointing out unreasonableness; *and so, if you please, we're to get nothing!* **please oneself** do as one chooses.

**pleased** *adjective* feeling or showing pleasure or satisfaction.

**pleasurable** *adjective* causing pleasure. □ **pleasurably** *adverb*

**pleasure** *noun* **1** a feeling of satisfaction or joy, enjoyment. **2** a source of pleasure; *it's a pleasure to talk to him.* **3** choice, desire; *at your pleasure.* ●*adjective* done or used for pleasure; *a pleasure trip.* □ **with pleasure** willingly, gladly.

**pleat** *noun* a flat fold made by doubling cloth on itself. ●*verb* make a pleat or pleats in.

**pleb** *noun* (*informal*, often *scornful*) a coarse uncultured person.

**plebeian** (pli-**bee**-ăn) *adjective* **1** of the lower social classes. **2** uncultured, vulgar; *plebeian tastes*. ●*noun* **1** a member of the lower classes, especially in ancient Rome. **2** a coarse uncultured person.

**plebiscite** (**pleb**-i-sit) *noun* a referendum, a vote by all the people of a country on an important public matter.

**plectrum** (*plural* **plectrums** *or* **plectra**) a small piece of plastic etc. for plucking the strings of a musical instrument.

**pled** *see* PLEAD.

**pledge** *noun* **1** a thing deposited as security for payment of a debt or fulfilment of a contract etc., and liable to be forfeited in case of failure. **2** a token of something; *as a pledge of his devotion*. **3** a toast drunk to someone's health. **4** a solemn promise; *under pledge of secrecy*. ●*verb* **1** deposit (an article) as a pledge. **2** promise solemnly. **3** drink to the health of.

**Pleiades** (**ply**-ă-deez) *plural noun* the 'Seven Sisters', a group of seven stars in the constellation Taurus.

**Pleistocene** (**play**-stŏ-seen) *adjective Geol.* of the first of the two epochs forming the Quaternary period. ●*noun* this epoch.

**plenary** (**pleen**-er-i) *adjective* attended by all members; *a plenary session of the assembly*.

**plenipotentiary** (plen-i-pŏ-**ten**-sher-i) *noun* an envoy with full powers to take action on behalf of the government he or she represents. ●*adjective* having these powers.

**plenitude** (**plen**-i-tewd) *noun* (*literary*) **1** fullness, completeness. **2** abundance.

**plenteous** (**plen**-ti-ŭs) *adjective* (*literary*) plentiful.

**plentiful** *adjective* in large quantities or numbers, abundant. □ **plentifully** *adverb*

**plenty** *noun* quite enough, as much as one could need or desire. ●*adverb* (*informal*) quite, fully; *it's plenty big enough*.

**pleonasm** (**plee**-ŏn-azm) *noun* an expression in which a word is redundant, as in 'a sure certainty'. □ **pleonastic** *adjective*

**plethora** (**pleth**-er-ă) *noun* an overabundance; a glut.

**pleura** (**ploor**-ă) *noun* (*plural* **pleurae**) the membrane surrounding the lungs.

**pleurisy** (**ploor**-i-si) *noun* inflammation of the pleura, causing painful breathing. □ **pleuritic** *adjective*

**plexus** *noun* (*plural* **plexus** *or* **plexuses**) a network of nerves or vessels.

**pliable** *adjective* **1** bending easily, flexible. **2** easily influenced. □ **pliability** *noun*

**pliant** (**ply**-ănt) *adjective* pliable. □ **pliancy** *noun*

**pliers** *plural noun* pincers having jaws with flat surfaces that can be brought together for gripping small objects, bending wire, etc.

**plight** *noun* a serious and difficult situation. ●*verb* (*old use*) pledge. □ **plight one's troth** (*old use*) promise to marry.

**plimsoll** *noun* a rubber-soled canvas sports shoe.

**Plimsoll line** *or* **mark** a mark on a ship's side showing how far it may legally go down in the water when loaded. (¶ Named after the English politician Samuel Plimsoll, whose agitation in the 1870s put an end to the practice of sending to sea overloaded and heavily insured old ships.)

**plinth** *noun* a block or slab forming the base of a column or a support for a vase.

**Pliny**[1] 'the Elder' (Gaius Plinius Secundus) (23/4–79), Roman statesman, author of the encyclopedic *Natural History*.

**Pliny**[2] 'the Younger' (Gaius Plinius Caecilius Secundus) (*c*.61–*c*.112), nephew of Pliny the Elder, Roman statesman, writer, and provincial governor.

**Pliocene** (**ply**-ŏ-seen) *adjective Geol.* of the final epoch of the Tertiary period. ●*noun* this epoch.

**PLO** *abbreviation* Palestine Liberation Organization, a political and military organization campaigning for the rights of Palestinian Arabs in the Middle East.

**plod** *verb* (**plodded**, **plodding**) **1** walk doggedly or laboriously, trudge. **2** work at a slow but steady rate. ●*noun* plodding. □ **plodder** *noun*

**plonk** *verb* place or drop down heavily. ●*noun* (*informal*) cheap or inferior wine.

**plop** *noun* a sound like that of something dropping into water without a splash.

**plot** *noun* **1** a small measured piece of land; *building-plots*. **2** the story in a play, novel, or film. **3** a conspiracy, a secret plan; *Gunpowder Plot*. ●*verb* (**plotted**, **plotting**) **1** make a plan or map of. **2** mark on a chart or diagram. **3** plan secretly, contrive a secret plan. □ **plotter** *noun*

**Plotinus** (plŏ-**ty**-nŭs) (*c*.205–70), Greek philosopher, the founder of Neoplatonism.

**plough** (*rhymes with* cow) (*Amer.* **plow**) *noun* **1** an implement for cutting furrows and turning the soil. **2** an implement resembling a plough; *snow-plough*. **3** (**the Plough**) a constellation also called the Great Bear. ●*verb* **1** turn (earth) or cut (a furrow) with a plough. **2** progress laboriously; *ploughed through the snow*; *ploughing through a book*. **3** advance violently; *the lorry ploughed into the barrier*. □ **plough back** **1** turn (growing grass etc.) into the soil to enrich it. **2** reinvest (profits) in the business that produced them.

**ploughman** *noun* (*plural* **ploughmen**) a person who guides a plough. □ **ploughman's lunch** a meal of bread and cheese with pickle and salad.

**ploughshare** *noun* the cutting blade of a plough.

**plover** (pluv-er) *noun* a wading bird.

**plow** *Amer.* spelling of PLOUGH.

**ploy** *noun* a cunning manoeuvre to gain an advantage.

**PLR** *abbreviation* Public Lending Right.

**pluck** *verb* **1** pick (a flower or fruit); pull out (a hair or feather etc.). **2** strip (a bird) of its feathers. **3** pull at or twitch. **4** sound (the string of a musical instrument) by pulling and then releasing it with the finger(s) or a plectrum. ●*noun* **1** plucking, a pull. **2** courage, spirit. **3** an animal's heart, liver, and lungs as food. □ **pluck up courage** summon up one's courage.

**plucky** *adjective* (**pluckier**, **pluckiest**) showing pluck, brave. □ **pluckily** *adverb*

**plug** *noun* **1** something fitting into and stopping or filling a hole or cavity. **2** a device with metal pins that fit into a socket to make an electrical connection. **3** (*informal*) a spark plug. **4** (*informal*) a piece of free publicity for an idea, product, etc. **5** a cake of tobacco; a piece of this cut off for chewing. ●*verb* (**plugged**, **plugging**) **1** put a plug into, stop with a plug. **2** (*slang*) shoot or hit (a person etc.). **3** (*informal*) advertise (a song, product, policy, etc.) by constant commendation. □ **plug away** (**at**) work steadily (at). **plug in** connect electrically by inserting a plug into a socket. **plug-in** *adjective* able to be connected in this way.

**plum** *noun* **1** a fleshy fruit with sweet pulp and a flattish pointed stone. **2** the tree that bears it. **3** (*old use*) a dried grape or raisin used in cooking. **4** reddish-purple colour. **5** (usually used as *adjective*) very good; highly desirable; *a plum job*. □ **plum pudding** a rich suet pudding with raisins, currants, and spices.

**plumage** (ploo-mij) *noun* a bird's feathers.

**plumb** (*pronounced* plum) *noun* a piece of lead tied to the end of a cord, used for finding the depth of water or testing whether a wall etc. is vertical. ●*adverb* **1** exactly; *plumb in the middle*. **2** (*Amer. informal*) completely; *plumb crazy*. ●*verb* **1** provide with a plumbing system; fit (a thing) as part of this. **2** work as a plumber. **3** measure or test with a plumb line. **4** reach; experience (an intense feeling); *plumb the depths of misery*. **5** get to the bottom of (a matter). □ **plumb line** a cord with a plumb attached.

**plumber** (plum-er) *noun* a person whose job is to fit and repair plumbing.

**plumbing** (plum-ing) *noun* **1** a system of water-pipes, cisterns, and drainage pipes in a building. **2** the work of a plumber. **3** (*informal*) lavatory installations.

**plume** (*pronounced* ploom) *noun* **1** a feather, especially a large ornamental one. **2** an ornament of feathers or similar material. **3** something resembling this; *a plume of smoke*. ●*verb* (of a bird) preen (itself or its feathers). □ **plume oneself** pride oneself, especially on something trivial.

**plumed** *adjective* ornamented with plumes.

**plummet** *noun* **1** a plumb or plumb line. **2** a weight attached to a fishing line to keep a float upright. ●*verb* (**plummeted**, **plummeting**) fall or plunge steeply.

**plummy** *adjective* **1** full of or like plums. **2** (of the voice) sounding affectedly full and rich in tone.

**plump**[1] *adjective* having a full rounded shape. ●*verb* (often foll. by *up* or *out*) make or become plump. □ **plumpness** *noun*

**plump**[2] *verb* drop or plunge abruptly; *plumped down*. ●*adverb* with a sudden or heavy fall. □ **plump for** choose, decide on.

**plunder** *verb* rob (a place or person) forcibly or systematically, steal or embezzle. ●*noun* **1** the taking of goods or money in this way. **2** the goods etc. acquired. □ **plunderer** *noun*

**plunge** *verb* **1** thrust or go forcefully into something. **2** descend suddenly. **3** jump or dive into water. **4** change the circumstances of (a person) suddenly; embark impetuously on a new course; *plunged the world into war*. **5** (of a horse) start forward violently; (of a ship) thrust its bows down into the water; pitch. **6** gamble heavily; run deeply into debt. ●*noun* a plunging movement; a dive. □ **take the plunge** take a bold decisive step.

**plunger** *noun* **1** the part of a mechanism that works with a plunging or thrusting movement. **2** a rubber cup on a handle for removing blockages by alternate thrusting and suction.

**pluperfect** (ploo-per-fikt) *adjective Grammar* of the tense of a verb used to denote an action completed before some past point of time, e.g. *we had arrived*.

**plural** (ploor-ăl) *noun* the form of a noun or verb used with reference to more than one person or thing; *the plural of 'child' is 'children'*. ●*adjective* **1** of this form. **2** of more than one. □ **plurality** *noun*

**pluralism** *noun* **1** a form of society with many minority groups and cultures. **2** the holding of more than one office at a time. □ **pluralist** *noun*, **pluralistic** *adjective*

**pluralize** *verb* (also **pluralise**) make or become plural.

**plus** *preposition* **1** with the addition of; *two plus four equals 6* (2 + 4 = 6). **2** (of temperature) above zero; *plus 2°.* **3** (*informal*) with, having gained, possessing; *arrived plus dog.* ● *adjective* **1** (after a number) at least; more than the amount indicated; *we're expecting thirty plus.* **2** (after a grade etc.) slightly better than; *beta plus.* **3** above zero, positive. ● *noun* **1** = PLUS SIGN. **2** an advantage. ● *conjunction* also, furthermore; *they arrived late, plus they wanted a meal.* □ **plus-fours** *plural noun* knickerbockers worn especially by golfers. (¶ So named because the length is increased by 4 inches to produce the overhang.) **plus sign** the symbol (+), indicating addition or a positive value.

▪ **Usage** The use of *plus* as a conjunction is considered incorrect by some people.

**plush** *noun* a kind of cloth with long soft nap, used in furnishings. ● *adjective* **1** made of plush. **2** plushy.

**plushy** *adjective* (*informal*) luxurious. □ **plushiness** *noun*

**Plutarch** (**ploo**-tark) (Lucius Mestrius Plutarchus) (*c.*46–*c.*120), Greek Platonist philosopher and biographer.

**Pluto** (**ploo**-toh) **1** (*Gk. myth.*) a title of Hades, lord of the Underworld. **2** the ninth planet of the solar system.

**plutocracy** (ploo-**tok**-răsi) *noun* **1** government by the wealthy. **2** a wealthy élite.

**plutocrat** (**ploo**-tŏ-krat) *noun* a person who is powerful because of his or her wealth. □ **plutocratic** *adjective*

**plutonic** *adjective Geol.* formed as igneous rock by solidification below the earth's surface.

**plutonium** (ploo-**toh**-niŭm) *noun* a chemical element (symbol Pu), a radioactive substance used in nuclear weapons and reactors.

**pluvial** (**ploo**-vi-ăl) *adjective* of or caused by rain, rainy.

**ply**[1] *noun* **1** a thickness or layer of wood or cloth etc. **2** a strand in yarn; *3-ply wool.* **3** plywood.

**ply**[2] *verb* (**plied, plying**) **1** use or wield (a tool or weapon). **2** work steadily at; *ply one's trade.* **3** keep offering or supplying; *plied her with questions.* **4** go to and fro regularly; *the boat plies between the two harbours.* **5** (of a taxi driver, boatman, etc.) look for custom; *ply for hire.*

**Plymouth Brethren** (**plim**-ŭth) a Calvinistic religious body formed about 1830 at Plymouth in Devon.

**Plymouth Rock** (**plim**-ŭth) a granite boulder at Plymouth, Mass., on which the Pilgrim Fathers are supposed to have stepped from the *Mayflower.*

**plywood** *noun* strong thin board made by gluing layers with the grain crosswise.

**PM** *abbreviation* **1** Prime Minister. **2** postmortem.

**Pm** *symbol* promethium.

**p.m.** *abbreviation* after noon. (¶ From the Latin *post meridiem.*)

**PMS** *abbreviation* premenstrual syndrome.

**PMT** *abbreviation* premenstrual tension.

**pneumatic** (new-**mat**-ik) *adjective* filled with or operated by compressed air; *pneumatic drills.* □ **pneumatically** *adverb*

**pneumonia** (new-**moh**-niă) *noun* inflammation of one or both lungs.

**PO** *abbreviation* **1** postal order. **2** Post Office. **3** Petty Officer. **4** Pilot Officer.

**Po**[1] the longest river of Italy, flowing from the Alps to the Adriatic Sea.

**Po**[2] *symbol* polonium.

**po** *noun* (*plural* **pos**) (*informal*) a chamber pot.

**poach**[1] *verb* **1** cook (an egg removed from its shell) in boiling water. **2** cook (fish, fruit, etc.) by simmering it in a small amount of liquid.

**poach**[2] *verb* **1** take (game or fish) illegally from private land or water. **2** trespass or encroach on something that belongs to another person; take (another's ideas, staff, etc.). □ **poacher** *noun*

**pock** *noun* (also **pock-mark**) **1** one of the spots that erupt on the skin in smallpox. **2** a scar left by this. □ **pock-marked** *adjective* marked by scars or pits.

**pocket** *noun* **1** a small baglike part sewn into a garment for holding money or small articles. **2** one's financial resources; what one can afford; *beyond my pocket.* **3** a pouchlike compartment in a suitcase, on a car door, etc. **4** any of the pouches at the edges of a billiard or snooker table, into which balls are driven. **5** an isolated group or area; *small pockets of resistance.* ● *adjective* of a size or shape suitable for carrying in a pocket; *pocket calculators.* ● *verb* **1** put into one's pocket. **2** take for oneself (especially dishonestly). **3** (in billiards and snooker) drive (a ball) into a pocket. **4** suppress or hide (one's feelings); *pocketing his pride.* □ **in a person's pocket** intimate with him or her; completely under his or her control. **in pocket** having gained in a transaction. **out of pocket** having lost in a transaction. **pocket knife** a penknife. **pocket money** money for small expenses; money allowed regularly to children.

**pocketbook** *noun* **1** a notebook. **2** a small folding case for money or papers carried in a pocket.

**pocketful** *noun* (*plural* **pocketfuls**) the amount that a pocket will hold.

**poco** *adverb Music* a little; rather. (¶ Italian.)

**pod** *noun* **1** a long seed-vessel like that of a pea or bean. ● *verb* (**podded, podding**) **1** bear or form pods. **2** remove (peas etc.) from their pods.

**podgy** adjective (**podgier**, **podgiest**) short and fat; chubby.

**podium** (**poh-di-ŭm**) noun (plural **podiums** or **podia**) a pedestal or platform.

**Poe**, Edgar Allan (1809–49), American short-story writer, poet, and critic, famous for his macabre tales.

**poem** noun a literary composition in verse, especially one expressing deep feeling in an imaginative way.

**poesy** (**poh-si**) noun (old use) poetry.

**poet** noun a writer of poems. □ **Poet Laureate** see LAUREATE.

**poetaster** (**poh-i-tas-ter**) noun a trivial or inferior poet.

**poetess** noun (sometimes scornful) a female poet.

**poetic** adjective of or like poetry; of poets. □ **poetic justice** suitable and well-deserved punishment or reward.

**poetical** adjective poetic, written in verse; poetical works. □ **poetically** adverb

**poetry** noun **1** poems; a poet's art or work. **2** a quality that pleases the mind as poetry does; the poetry of motion.

**po-faced** adjective solemn-faced; not showing amusement.

**pogo stick** a stiltlike toy with a spring, used for jumping about on.

**pogrom** (**pog-rŏm**) noun an organized massacre.

**poignant** (**poin-yănt**) adjective arousing sympathy; deeply moving to the feelings; keenly felt; poignant grief. □ **poignantly** adverb, **poignancy** noun

**poinsettia** (**poin-set-iă**) noun a plant with large usually scarlet petal-like bracts.

**point** noun **1** the tapered or sharp end of something, the tip. **2** a projection, a promontory of land. **3** (in geometry) that which has position but not magnitude, e.g. the intersection of two lines. **4** a dot used as a punctuation mark; a decimal point. **5** a particular place, position, stage, or moment. **6** each of the directions marked on a compass. **7** a unit of measurement, value, or scoring. **8** a detail; an item being discussed; we differ on several points. **9** a distinctive feature; it has its good points. **10** the essential thing; the main issue; the important feature of a story or remark; come to the point. **11** effectiveness, purpose, value; there's no point in wasting time. **12** a fielder in cricket near the batsman on the off side; this position. **13** an electrical socket; power points. **14** (**points**) electrical contacts in the distributor of a vehicle. **15** (**points**) the tapering movable rails by which a train is directed from one line to another. ●verb **1** (usually foll. by to or at)

direct or aim (a finger, weapon, etc.); pointed a gun at her. **2** (foll. by at or towards) be directed or aimed to. **3** (foll. by to) direct attention to; indicate; be evidence of; it all points to a conspiracy. **4** fill in the joints of (brickwork etc.) with mortar. □ **a case in point** one that is relevant to what has just been said. **make a point of** take care to do; regard as important; call attention to. **on the point of** on the verge of (an action). **point-duty** noun traffic control by a police officer at a road junction. **point of no return** the point after which one cannot withdraw from an action. **point of order** a query in a debate as to whether correct procedure is being followed. **point of view** a way of looking at an issue. **point out** indicate; draw attention to. **point-to-point** noun a steeplechase for hunting horses. **point up** emphasize. **to the point** relevant; relevantly.

**point-blank** adjective **1** (of a shot) aimed or fired at very close range. **2** (of a remark) direct, straightforward; a point-blank refusal. ●adverb directly; bluntly; refused point-blank.

**pointed** adjective **1** tapering or sharpened to a point. **2** (of a remark or manner) direct; cutting. □ **pointedly** adverb

**pointer** noun **1** a thing that points or is used to point to something; an indicator on a dial or scale. **2** (informal) a hint or indication. **3** a dog of a breed that on scenting game stands rigidly looking towards it.

**pointing** noun **1** the cement filling the joints of brickwork. **2** the facing produced by this.

**pointless** adjective having no purpose, point, or meaning. □ **pointlessly** adverb

**poise** verb **1** balance or be balanced. **2** hold suspended or supported. ●noun **1** balance, the way something is poised. **2** a dignified and self-assured manner.

**poised** adjective **1** (of a person) having poise; dignified and self-assured. **2** ready for action; poised to strike.

**poison** noun **1** a substance that can cause death or injury when absorbed by a living thing. **2** a harmful influence. ●verb **1** give poison to; kill with poison. **2** put poison on or in. **3** corrupt or pervert; spoil; poisoned their minds. □ **poison ivy** a North American climbing plant which causes an itching rash when touched. **poison-pen letter** a malicious or libellous anonymous letter. □ **poisoner** noun

**poisonous** adjective **1** containing or having the effect of poison. **2** likely to corrupt people; a poisonous influence.

**poke** verb **1** push, prod, or lever with the end of a finger, stick, etc. **2** (usually foll. by out or up) thrust or be thrust forward; protrude. **3** produce by poking; *poked a hole in it.* **4** (often foll. by *about* or *around*) search; pry; *poking about in the attic.* ● *noun* a poking movement, a thrust or nudge. □ **poke fun at** ridicule. **poke one's nose into** pry or intrude into.

**poker** *noun* **1** a metal rod for poking a fire. **2** a card game in which players bet on whose hand of cards has the highest value. □ **poker-face** *noun* an expression that does not reveal thoughts or feelings.

**poky** *adjective* (**pokier**, **pokiest**) small and cramped; *poky little rooms.* □ **pokiness** *noun*

**Poland** a country in eastern Europe.

**polar** *adjective* **1** of or near the North Pole or South Pole. **2** of one of the poles of a magnet. **3** directly opposite in character or tendency. □ **polar bear** a white bear living in the Arctic regions. **polar circle** each of the circles parallel to the equator at 23° 27′ from either pole; the Arctic or Antarctic circle.

**Polaris** *noun* **1** the North Star or pole star. **2** an intermediate-range nuclear missile, fired from a submarine.

**polarity** (poh-**la**-riti) *noun* **1** the possessing of negative and positive poles. **2** the electrical condition of a body (positive or negative). **3** the state of having two opposite opinions, tendencies, etc.

**polarize** *verb* (also **polarise**) **1** confine similar vibrations of (light waves etc.) to a single direction or plane. **2** give polarity to. **3** set or become set at opposite extremes of opinion; *public opinion had polarized.* □ **polarization** *noun*

**Polaroid** *noun* (*trade mark*) **1** a material that polarizes the light passing through it, used in sunglasses to protect the eyes from glare. **2** a camera that prints a photograph as soon as it has been taken.

**polder** (**pohl**-der) *noun* a piece of low-lying land reclaimed from the sea or a river, especially in the Netherlands.

**Pole** *noun* a Polish person.

**pole**[1] *noun* **1** a long slender rounded piece of wood or metal, especially one used as a support. **2** a measure of land, 5½ yds. or 30¼ sq. yds. ● *verb* push along using a pole. □ **pole-jump**, **pole-vault** (*noun*) a vault over a high crossbar with the help of a pole held in the hands; (*verb*) perform this vault. **pole position** = POLL POSITION. **up the pole** (*slang*) **1** in difficulty. **2** crazy.

**pole**[2] *noun* **1** (in full **north pole**, **south pole**) either extremity of the earth's or other body's axis; either of two points in the sky about which the stars appear to rotate. **2** each of the two points of a magnet which attract or repel magnetic bodies. **3** the positive or negative terminal of an electric cell or battery. **4** each of two opposed principles. □ **be poles apart** differ greatly. **pole star 1** a star in the Little Bear, near the North Pole in the sky. **2** a thing serving as a guide.

■**Usage** The spelling is *North Pole* and *South Pole* when used as geographical designations.

**poleaxe** *noun* (*Amer.* **poleax**) **1** a battleaxe with a long handle. **2** a butcher's implement for slaughtering cattle. ● *verb* strike down with or as if with a poleaxe.

**polecat** *noun* **1** a small dark brown animal of the weasel family. **2** (*Amer.*) a skunk.

**polemic** (pŏl-**em**-ik) *noun* a verbal attack on a belief or opinion. ● *adjective* (also **polemical**) **1** controversial. **2** argumentative. □ **polemically** *adverb*

**polenta** *noun* porridge made from maize meal.

**police** *noun* **1** a civil force responsible for the keeping of public order; its members. **2** a force responsible for enforcing the regulations of an organization etc.; *military police; railway police.* ● *verb* keep order by means of police; provide with police. □ **police officer** a policeman or policewoman. **police State** a country (usually a totalitarian State) controlled by political police. **police station** the office of a local police force.

**policeman** *noun* (*plural* **policemen**) a male member of a police force.

**policewoman** *noun* (*plural* **policewomen**) a female member of a police force.

**policy**[1] *noun* **1** the plan of action adopted by a person or organization. **2** wisdom, prudence.

■**Usage** Do not confuse with *polity.*

**policy**[2] *noun* a contract of insurance; the document containing this.

**policyholder** *noun* a person or body holding an insurance policy.

**polio** (**poh**-li-oh) *noun* poliomyelitis.

**poliomyelitis** (poh-li-oh-my-il-**I**-tiss) *noun* an infectious disease caused by a virus, producing temporary or permanent paralysis.

**Polish** *adjective* of Poland or its people or language. ● *noun* the language of Poland.

**polish** *verb* **1** make or become smooth and glossy by rubbing. **2** improve by correcting or putting finishing touches. ● *noun* **1** a substance used for polishing. **2** smoothness and glossiness. **3** elegance and refinement. □ **polish off** finish off.

**polished** *adjective* elegant, refined, perfected; *polished manners; a polished performance.*

**Politburo** (pol-it-**bewr**-oh) *noun* the principal policy-making committee of a Communist Party, especially in the former USSR.

**polite** *adjective* **1** having good manners, socially correct. **2** refined; *polite society*. □ **politely** *adverb*, **politeness** *noun*

**politic** (**pol-i-tik**) *adjective* showing good judgement, prudent. ●*verb* (**politicked**, **politicking**) engage in politics. □ **the body politic** the State or similar organized system.

**political** *adjective* **1** of or engaged in politics. **2** of the way a country is governed; *its political system*. □ **political asylum** refuge in foreign territory for people fleeing from political persecution. **political correctness** avoidance of expressions or actions that may be considered discriminatory or pejorative to any minority. **political prisoner** a person imprisoned for a political offence. □ **politically** *adverb*

**politician** *noun* an MP or other political representative.

**politicize** *verb* (also **politicise**) **1** engage in or talk politics. **2** give a political character to. □ **politicization** *noun*

**politics** *noun* (treated as *singular* or *plural*) **1** the science and art of governing a country. **2** political affairs or life. **3** manoeuvring for power etc. within a group; *office politics*. **4** (usually treated as *plural*) political principles or affairs or tactics.

**polity** (**pol-iti**) *noun* **1** the form or process of civil government. **2** an organized society, a State.

▪**Usage** Do not confuse with *policy*.

**polka** *noun* a lively dance for couples, of Bohemian origin. □ **polka dots** round dots evenly spaced to form a pattern on fabric.

**poll** (*rhymes with* hole) *noun* **1** voting at an election; the counting of votes; the number of votes recorded; *a heavy poll*. **2** the place where voting is held. **3** (in full (**public**) **opinion poll**) an estimate of public opinion made by questioning a representative sample of people. **4** (*old use*) the head. ●*verb* **1** vote at an election. **2** (of a candidate) receive as votes. **3** cut off the horns of (cattle) or the top of (a tree). □ **polling booth**, **polling station** *noun* a place where votes are recorded. **poll position** (originally *pole position* next to the inside boundary fence) the most favourable position on the starting-grid in a motor race. **poll tax** a tax on each (or on each adult) person; (*informal*) (in Britain) the community charge (replaced by the *council tax* in 1993).

**pollack** (**pol-ăk**) *noun* (also **pollock**) a sea fish related to the cod, used as food.

**pollard** (**pol-erd**) *noun* **1** a tree that is polled so as to produce a close head of young branches. **2** an animal that has cast or lost its horns; an ox or sheep or goat of a hornless breed. ●*verb* make (a tree) into a pollard; *pollarded willows*.

**pollen** *noun* a fine powdery substance produced by the anthers of flowers, containing the fertilizing element. □ **pollen count** an index of the amount of pollen in the air, published as a warning to those who are allergic to it.

**pollinate** *verb* shed pollen on; fertilize with pollen. □ **pollination** *noun*

**Pollock**, Jackson (1912–56), American abstract expressionist painter.

**pollock** alternative spelling of POLLACK.

**pollster** *noun* a person conducting a public opinion poll.

**pollutant** *noun* a substance causing pollution.

**pollute** *verb* **1** make dirty or impure, especially by adding harmful or offensive substances. **2** corrupt; *polluting the mind*. □ **polluter** *noun*, **pollution** *noun*

**Pollux 1** (*Gk. myth.*) the immortal twin brother of Castor (who was mortal), sons of Zeus and Leda. **2** a bright star in the constellation Gemini.

**polo** *noun* a game like hockey, played by teams on horseback with long-handled mallets. □ **polo-neck** a high turned-over collar on a jumper.

**polonaise** (pol-ŏ-**nayz**) *noun* a stately dance of Polish origin; music for this or in this style.

**polonium** (pŏ-**loh**-niŭm) *noun* a radioactive metallic element (symbol Po).

**Pol Pot** (born 1925), Cambodian Communist leader, Prime Minister 1976–9, leader of the Khmer Rouge guerilla forces.

**poltergeist** (**pol**-ter-gyst) *noun* a ghost or spirit that throws things about noisily.

**poltroon** (pol-**troon**) *noun* (*old use*) a coward.

**poly** (**pol**-i) *noun* (*plural* **polys**) (*informal*) a polytechnic.

**poly-** *combining form* **1** many (as in *polyhedron*). **2** (in names of plastics) polymerized.

**polyandry** (**pol**-i-an-dri) *noun* the system of having more than one husband at a time. □ **polyandrous** *adjective*

**polyanthus** *noun* (*plural* **polyanthuses**) a flowering plant cultivated from hybridized primulas.

**polychromatic** (poli-krŏ-**mat**-ik) *adjective* **1** many-coloured. **2** (of radiation) consisting of more than one wavelength.

**polychrome** (**pol**-i-krohm) *adjective* painted, printed, or decorated in many colours.

**polyester** *noun* a polymerized substance, especially as a synthetic resin or fibre.

**polyethylene** = POLYTHENE.

**polygamy** (pŏ-**lig**-ămi) *noun* the system of having more than one wife at a time. □ **polygamous** *adjective*, **polygamist** *noun*

**polyglot** (**pol**-i-glot) *adjective* knowing, using, or written in several languages. ●*noun* a person who knows several languages.

**polygon** (**pol**-i-gŏn) *noun* a geometric figure with many (usually five or more) sides. □ **polygonal** (pŏ-**lig**-ŏn-ăl) *adjective*

**polygraph** (**pol**-i-grahf) *noun* a machine for reading the pulse-rate and other variable physical features, used as a lie-detector.

**polyhedron** (poli-**hee**-drŏn) *noun* (*plural* **polyhedra**) a solid figure with many (usually seven or more) faces. □ **polyhedral** *adjective*

**polymath** (**pol**-i-math) *noun* a person with knowledge of many subjects.

**polymer** (**pol**-im-er) *noun* a compound of one or more large molecules formed from repeated units of smaller molecules.

**polymerize** (**pol**-im-er-ryz) *verb* (also **polymerise**) combine or become combined into a polymer. □ **polymerization** *noun*

**polymorphous** *adjective* (also **polymorphic**) passing through various forms in successive stages of development.

**Polynesia** (poli-**nee**-zhă) the islands of the central and western Pacific Ocean, including New Zealand, Hawaii, and Samoa. □ **Polynesian** *adjective & noun*

**polynomial** (poli-**noh**-miăl) *adjective* (of an algebraic expression) consisting of three or more terms. ●*noun* a polynomial expression.

**polyp** (**pol**-ip) *noun* **1** a simple organism with a tube-shaped body, e.g. one of the organisms of which coral is composed. **2** a small growth on a mucous membrane, e.g. in the nose.

**polyphony** (pŏ-**lif**-ŏni) *noun* contrapuntal music. □ **polyphonic** (poli-**fon**-ik) *adjective*

**polypropylene** *noun* (also **polypropene**) any polymer of propylene, including thermoplastic materials used for films, fibres, or moulding materials.

**polystyrene** (poli-**styr**-een) *noun* a plastic, a polymer of styrene, used for packaging and insulating.

**polysyllabic** (poli-sil-**ab**-ik) *adjective* having many syllables; *polysyllabic words*.

**polytechnic** (poli-**tek**-nik) *noun* a college offering courses in many subjects up to degree level.

**polytheism** (**pol**-ith-ee-ism) *noun* belief in or worship of more than one god. □ **polytheist** *noun*, **polytheistic** *adjective*

**polythene** *noun* a tough light plastic.

**polyunsaturated** *adjective* (of a fat or oil) having a chemical structure capable of further reaction and (unlike animal and dairy fats) not thought to contribute to the formation of cholesterol in the blood.

**polyurethane** (poli-**yoor**-i-thayn) *noun* a synthetic resin or plastic.

**polyvinyl** (poli-**vy**-nil) *adjective* made from polymerized vinyl. □ **polyvinyl chloride** a plastic used for insulation and as fabric (*abbreviation* **PVC**).

**pom** *noun* (*Austral.* & *NZ slang*) a pommy.

**pomace** *noun* crushed apples in cider-making.

**pomade** *noun* scented ointment for the hair and head.

**pomander** (pŏm-**an**-der) *noun* a ball of sweet-smelling substances or a round container for this.

**pomegranate** (**pom**-i-gran-it) *noun* **1** a tropical fruit with tough rind, reddish pulp, and many seeds. **2** the tree that produces it.

**pomelo** (**pum**-i-loh) *noun* (*plural* **pomelos**) a shaddock or grapefruit.

**pommel** (**pum**-ĕl) *noun* **1** a knob on the handle of a sword. **2** an upward projection at the front of a saddle. ●*verb* (**pommelled**, **pommelling**; *Amer.* **pommeled**, **pommeling**) pummel.

**pommy** *noun* (also **pommie**) (*Austral.* & *NZ slang*) a British person, especially a recent immigrant.

**pomp** *noun* stately and splendid display.

**Pompeii** (pom-**pay**-i) an ancient town south-east of Naples, buried in volcanic ash from the eruption of Vesuvius in AD 69.

**Pompey** (Gnaeus Pompeius) (106–48 BC), Roman general and politician, an opponent of Julius Caesar.

**pom-pom** *noun* an automatic quick-firing gun.

**pompon** *noun* (also **pompom**) **1** a decorative tuft or ball. **2** a form of flower with small tightly-clustered petals.

**pompous** *adjective* full of ostentatious dignity and self-importance. □ **pompously** *adverb*, **pomposity** (pom-**poss**-iti) *noun*

**ponce** *noun* **1** a man who lives off a prostitute's earnings. **2** (*offensive*) a homosexual or effeminate man. ●*verb* act as a ponce. □ **ponce about** walk or move in an effeminate or ineffectual way.

**poncho** *noun* (*plural* **ponchos**) a blanket-like piece of cloth with a slit in the centre for the head, worn as a cloak.

**pond** *noun* a small area of still water.

**ponder** *verb* **1** be deep in thought. **2** think something over thoroughly.

**ponderable** *adjective* having an appreciable weight or significance.

**ponderous** *adjective* **1** heavy, unwieldy. **2** laborious in style. □ **ponderously** *adverb*

**Pondicherry** a Union Territory in SE India.

**pondweed** *noun* a plant that grows in still water.

**pong** (*slang*) *noun* a stink. ●*verb* stink.

**poniard** (**pon**-yerd) *noun* (*old use*) a dagger.

**pontiff** noun the Pope.

**pontifical** (pon-**tif**-ikăl) adjective 1 pompously dogmatic. 2 papal. □ **pontifically** adverb

**pontificate** verb (pronounced pon-**tif**-i-kayt) talk pompously and at length. ●noun (pronounced pon-**tif**-i-kăt) the office of bishop or pope. □ **pontificator** noun

**pontoon** noun 1 a flat-bottomed boat. 2 each of a number of floats used to support a temporary bridge. 3 a card game in which players try to acquire cards with face value totalling 21.

**pony** noun a small horse. □ **pony-tail** noun hair drawn back and tied at the back of the head so that it hangs down. **pony-trekking** noun travelling across country on ponies for pleasure.

**poodle** noun a dog with a curly coat often clipped in a pattern.

**poof** noun (also **poofter**) (slang, offensive) an effeminate or homosexual man.

**pooh** interjection an exclamation of impatience, contempt, or disgust at a bad smell. □ **pooh-pooh** verb dismiss (a suggestion) scornfully; ridicule.

**pool¹** noun 1 a small area of still water. 2 a shallow patch of liquid; a puddle. 3 a swimming pool. 4 a deep place in a river.

**pool²** noun 1 a common fund, e.g. that containing the total stakes in a gambling venture. 2 a common supply of vehicles, commodities, or services for sharing between a number of people. 3 a game resembling snooker. ●verb put into a common fund or supply, for sharing. □ **the pools** football pools.

**poop** noun 1 the stern of a ship. 2 a raised deck at the stern.

**poor** adjective 1 having little money or means. 2 deficient in something; poor in minerals. 3 scanty, inadequate, less good than is expected; a poor crop; he is a poor driver. 4 deserving pity or sympathy, unfortunate; poor fellow! □ **poor law** noun (hist., Brit.) a law providing public support for the poor. **poor man's** an inferior or cheaper substitute for (something). □ **poorness** noun

**poorhouse** = WORKHOUSE.

**poorly** adverb in a poor way, badly. ●adjective unwell; feeling poorly.

**pop¹** noun 1 a small sharp explosive sound. 2 a fizzy drink. ●verb (**popped**, **popping**) 1 make or cause to make a pop. 2 put, come, or go quickly or suddenly; pop it in the oven; popped out for coffee. 3 (informal) swallow or inject as a drug. 4 (slang) pawn. □ **pop-eyed** adjective with bulging eyes. **pop off** (informal) die. **pop the question** (informal) propose marriage. **pop-up** adjective operating so that something comes upwards automatically.

**pop²** noun (especially Amer. informal) father.

**pop³** adjective in a popular modern style. ●noun pop music. □ **pop art** art that uses themes drawn from popular culture. **pop music** modern popular music (e.g. rock music) appealing particularly to younger people.

**popadam** alternative spelling of POPPADAM.

**popcorn** noun maize heated so that it bursts to form fluffy balls.

**Pope**, Alexander (1688–1744), English poet, whose works include The Rape of the Lock.

**pope** noun (also **Pope**) the bishop of Rome, head of the Roman Catholic Church.

**popery** noun (scornful) the papal system, the Roman Catholic religion.

**popgun** noun a child's toy gun that shoots a pellet or cork with a popping sound.

**popinjay** noun a fop; a conceited person.

**popish** adjective (scornful) of Roman Catholicism or the papal system.

**poplar** noun a tall slender tree, often with leaves that quiver easily.

**poplin** noun a plain woven fabric usually of cotton.

**poppadam** (pop-ă-dăm) noun (also **popadam**, **poppadom**) a thin crisp fried bread, eaten especially with Indian food.

**popper** noun (informal) a press-stud.

**poppet** noun (informal) (especially as a term of endearment) a small or dainty person.

**popping-crease** noun a line marking the limit of the batsman's position in cricket.

**poppy** noun a plant with large especially scarlet flowers on tall stems. □ **Poppy Day** Remembrance Sunday, on which artificial poppies are worn.

**poppycock** noun (slang) nonsense.

**populace** (pop-yoo-lăs) noun the general public.

**popular** adjective 1 liked or enjoyed by many people. 2 of or for the general public. 3 (of a belief etc.) held by many people; popular superstitions. □ **popular front** a political party representing left-wing groups. □ **popularly** adverb, **popularity** noun

**popularize** verb (also **popularise**) 1 make generally liked. 2 present (a subject) so that it can be understood by ordinary people. □ **popularization** noun

**populate** verb supply with inhabitants; form the population of.

**population** noun the inhabitants of a place; the total number of these.

**populist** noun a person who claims to support the interests of ordinary people.

**populous** adjective thickly populated.

**porcelain** (por-sĕl-in) noun 1 a hard fine translucent ceramic. 2 objects made of this.

**porch** noun a covered entrance to a building.

**porcine** (por-syn) *adjective* of or like a pig.

**porcupine** *noun* a rodent with a body and tail covered in protective spines.

**pore** *noun* one of the tiny openings on an animal's skin or on a leaf, through which moisture may pass (e.g. as sweat). □ **pore over** study (a thing) with close attention.

**pork** *noun* unsalted pig-flesh as food. □ **pork pie** a raised pie of minced pork etc., eaten cold. **pork pie hat** a hat with a flat crown and a brim turned up all round.

**porker** *noun* a pig raised for food.

**porky** *adjective* **1** (*informal*) fat. **2** of or like pork.

**porn** *noun* (also **porno**) (*informal*) pornography.

**pornography** *noun* writings, pictures, or films intended to stimulate erotic feelings by portrayal of sexual activity. □ **pornographic** *adjective*

**porous** (por-ŭs) *adjective* **1** containing pores. **2** letting through fluid or air. □ **porosity** (por-oss-iti) *noun*

**porphyry** (por-fi-ri) *noun* a rock containing crystals of minerals. □ **porphyritic** *adjective*

**porpoise** (por-pŭs) *noun* a sea mammal resembling a dolphin, with a blunt rounded snout.

**porridge** *noun* **1** a food made by boiling oatmeal or other cereal to a thick paste in water or milk. **2** (*slang*) imprisonment.

**porringer** *noun* a small bowl, often with a handle, for soup, porridge, etc.

**Porsche** (*pronounced* porsh), Ferdinand (1875–1952), Austrian designer of cars, including the original German Volkswagen.

**port¹** *noun* **1** a harbour. **2** a town with a harbour, especially one where goods are imported or exported.

**port²** *noun* **1** an opening in a ship's side for entrance, loading, etc. **2** a porthole. **3** a place where signals enter or leave a data-transmission system or device.

**port³** *noun* the left-hand side (when facing forward) of a ship or aircraft. ● *verb* turn this way; *port your helm.*

**port⁴** *noun* a sweet, usually dark red fortified wine.

**portable** *adjective* able to be carried; *portable typewriters.* ● *noun* a portable kind of typewriter, television set, etc. □ **portability** *noun*

**portage** *noun* the carrying of goods overland between two navigable waters.

**Portakabin** *noun* (*trade mark*) a small portable building designed for quick assembly.

**portal** *noun* an imposing doorway or gateway.

**Port-au-Prince** (port-oh-**prins**) the capital of Haiti.

**portcullis** *noun* a strong heavy vertical grating that can be lowered to block the gateway to a fortress.

**portend** (por-tend) *verb* foreshadow; be an omen of.

**portent** (por-tent) *noun* an omen, a significant sign of something to come.

**portentous** (por-tent-ŭs) *adjective* ominous, being a sign of some extraordinary (usually terrible) event.

**Porter**, Cole (1891–1964), American composer and songwriter.

**porter** *noun* **1** a gatekeeper or doorman of a large building. **2** a person employed to carry luggage or other goods. **3** a type of dark beer.

**porterage** *noun* the services of a porter; the charge for this.

**porterhouse steak** a choice cut of beefsteak.

**portfolio** *noun* (*plural* **portfolios**) **1** a case for holding loose sheets of paper or drawings. **2** a set of investments held by one investor. **3** the position of a minister of State. □ **Minister without portfolio** a Cabinet Minister who is not in charge of any department of State.

**porthole** *noun* a window-like structure in the side of a ship or aircraft.

**portico** (port-i-koh) *noun* (*plural* **porticoes** or **porticos**) a structure consisting of a roof supported on columns, usually forming a porch to a building.

**portion** *noun* **1** a part or share of something. **2** the amount of food allotted to one person. **3** one's destiny or lot. ● *verb* divide up and distribute in portions; *portion it out.*

**Portland cement** cement made from chalk and clay.

**portly** *adjective* (**portlier**, **portliest**) stout and dignified. □ **portliness** *noun*

**portmanteau** (port-man-toh) *noun* (*plural* **portmanteaux** or **portmanteaus**) a trunk for clothes that opens into two equal parts. □ **portmanteau word** a word combining the sounds and meanings of two others, e.g. *motel*, *Oxbridge.*

**Port of Spain** the capital of Trinidad and Tobago.

**Porto Novo** (noh-voh) the capital of Benin.

**portrait** *noun* **1** a picture of a person or animal. **2** a description in words. □ **portraitist** *noun*

**portraiture** *noun* **1** making portraits. **2** a portrait.

**portray** (por-tray) *verb* **1** make a picture of. **2** describe in words or represent in a play etc.; *she is portrayed as a pathetic character.* □ **portrayal** *noun*

**Port Said** (*rhymes with* hide) a seaport of Egypt, at the north end of the Suez Canal.

**Portsmouth** a city and naval port in Hampshire.

**Portugal** a country in SW Europe.

**Portuguese** *adjective* of Portugal or its people or language. ●*noun* **1** (*plural* **Portuguese**) a native of Portugal. **2** the language of Portugal. □ **Portuguese man-of-war** a jellyfish with tentacles that have a poisonous sting.

**pose** *verb* **1** take up a position for a portrait or photograph etc. **2** take a particular attitude for effect. **3** (foll. by *as*) pretend to be; *posed as an expert.* **4** put forward; present; *pose a question.* ●*noun* **1** an attitude in which a person is posed. **2** an affectation, a pretence.

**Poseidon** (pŏ-sy-dŏn) (*Gk. myth.*) the god of earthquakes and the sea.

**poser** *noun* a puzzling question or problem.

**poseur** (poh-**zer**) *noun* a person who behaves affectedly.

**posh** *adjective* (*informal*) **1** very smart, luxurious. **2** upper-class.

**posit** (**poz**-it) *verb* assume as a fact, postulate.

**position** *noun* **1** the place occupied by a person or thing. **2** the proper place for something; *in* or *out of position.* **3** an advantageous location; *manoeuvring for position.* **4** the way in which a thing or its parts are placed or arranged. **5** a situation in relation to others; *this puts me in a difficult position.* **6** a point of view; *what is their position on tax reform?* **7** rank or status; high social standing; *people of position.* **8** paid employment, a job. ●*verb* place in a certain position.

**positive** *adjective* **1** explicit; definite, with no doubt; *we have positive proof.* **2** holding an opinion confidently. **3** (*informal*) clear, out-and-out; *it's a positive miracle.* **4** constructive and helpful; *some positive suggestions.* **5** indicating the presence of qualities or features tested for; *the result of the test was positive.* **6** (of a number) greater than zero. **7** containing or producing the kind of electrical charge produced by rubbing glass with silk; lacking electrons. **8** (of a photograph) having the lights and shades or colours as in the actual scene photographed, not as in a negative. **9** *Grammar* (of an adjective or adverb) in the primary form (e.g. *big*) as distinct from the comparative (*bigger*) or superlative (*biggest*). ●*noun* a positive quality, quantity, photograph, etc. □ **positive discrimination** the policy of deliberately favouring members of an underprivileged group. **positive pole** the north-seeking pole of a magnet. **positive sign** the sign (+). **positive vetting** an intensive inquiry into the background and character of a candidate for a senior post. □ **positively** *adverb*, **positiveness** *noun*

**positivism** *noun* a philosophical system recognizing only facts and observable phenomena. □ **positivist** *noun & adjective*

**positron** (**poz**-i-tron) *noun Physics* an elementary particle with the mass of an electron and a charge the same as an electron's but positive.

**posse** (**poss**-i) *noun* a group of law-enforcers; a strong force or company.

**possess** *verb* **1** have or own. **2** occupy or dominate the mind of; *be possessed by a devil.* □ **be possessed of** own, have. □ **possessor** *noun*

**possession** *noun* **1** possessing; being possessed. **2** a thing possessed. □ **take possession of** become the owner of; take.

**possessive** *adjective* **1** wanting to retain what one possesses; reluctant to share. **2** of or indicating possession; *the possessive form of a word*, e.g. *John's, the baker's.* ●*noun* (in full **possessive case**) a grammatical case of nouns and pronouns expressing possession. □ **possessive pronoun** *see* PRONOUN. □ **possessively** *adverb*, **possessiveness** *noun*

**possibility** *noun* **1** the fact or condition of being possible. **2** something that may exist or happen; *thunder is a possibility today.* **3** a capability of being used or of producing good results; *the plan has distinct possibilities.*

**possible** *adjective* capable of existing, happening, or of being done or used. ●*noun* a candidate who may be successful.

**possibly** *adverb* **1** in accordance with possibility; *can't possibly do it.* **2** perhaps.

**possum** *noun* **1** (*informal*) an opossum. **2** (*Austral. & NZ*) a phalanger resembling an American opossum. □ **play possum** pretend to be unconscious or unaware of something (¶ from the possum's habit of feigning death when in danger).

**post**[1] *noun* **1** a piece of timber or metal set upright and used as a support or marker. **2** the starting post or winning post in a race. ●*verb* **1** put up (a notice). **2** announce by means of a notice; *the ship was posted as missing.*

**post**[2] *noun* **1** the place where a soldier is on duty; *the sentries are at their posts.* **2** a place occupied by soldiers, especially a frontier fort. **3** = TRADING POST. **4** a position of paid employment; *got a post with a textile firm.* ●*verb* **1** place or station; *we posted sentries.* **2** appoint to a post or command.

**post**[3] *noun* (= *Amer.* MAIL) **1** the official conveyance of letters and parcels; *sent by post.* **2** the letters etc. conveyed; a single collection or delivery of these. **3** the place where letters etc. are collected. ●*verb* **1** put (a letter etc.) in the post. **2** enter in an official ledger. □ **keep a person posted** keep him or her informed. **post-free** *adject-*

*ive & adverb* carried by post without charge. **Post Office** the organization responsible for postal services. **post office** a building where postal business is carried on. **post office box** a numbered place in a post office where letters are kept until called for. **post-** *combining form* after.

**postage** *noun* the charge for sending something by post. □ **postage stamp** a small adhesive stamp for sticking on things to be posted, showing the amount paid.

**postal** *adjective* **1** of the post. **2** by post; *a postal vote.* □ **postal code** = POSTCODE. **postal order** a money order issued by the Post Office.

**postbox** *noun* a public box where letters are posted.

**postcard** *noun* a card for sending by post without an envelope.

**postcode** *noun* a group of letters and figures included in a postal address to assist sorting.

**postdate** *verb* **1** put a date on (a document or cheque) that is later than the actual one. **2** occur later than.

**poster** *noun* a large sheet of paper announcing or advertising something, for display in a public place.

**poste restante** (pohst ress-**tahnt**) a department in a post office where letters are kept until called for. (¶ French, = letters remaining.)

**posterior** *adjective* situated behind or at the back. ●*noun* the buttocks.

**posterity** (poss-**te**-riti) *noun* **1** future generations. **2** a person's descendants.

**postern** (**poss**-tern) *noun* a back or side entrance.

**postgraduate** *adjective* (of studies) carried on after taking a first degree. ●*noun* a student engaged on such studies.

**post-haste** *adverb* with great speed or haste.

**posthumous** (**poss**-tew-mŭs) *adjective* **1** happening or awarded after a person's death. **2** published after the author's death; *a posthumous novel.* **3** (of a child) born after its father's death. □ **posthumously** *adverb*

**postilion** (poss-**til**-yŏn) *noun* (also **postillion**) a rider on a near-side horse drawing a coach when there is no coach-driver.

**post-impressionism** *noun* a movement in French painting in the late 19th century seeking to express the individual artist's conception of the objects represented. □ **post-impressionist** *noun & adjective*

**postman** *noun* (*plural* **postmen**) (= Amer. MAILMAN) a person employed to deliver and collect letters and parcels.

**postmark** *noun* an official mark on mail giving the place and date of posting. ●*verb* mark with a postmark.

**postmaster** *noun* a male official in charge of a post office.

**postmistress** *noun* a female official in charge of a post office.

**post-mortem** *adverb & adjective* after death, ●*noun* **1** an examination made after death to determine its cause. **2** (*informal*) a detailed discussion of something that is over.

**postnatal** *adjective* existing or occurring after birth or childbirth.

**postpone** *verb* rearrange (an event) so that it takes place at a later time; *postpone the meeting.* □ **postponement** *noun*

**postprandial** *adjective* (*formal* or *humorous*) taking place after lunch or after dinner.

**postscript** *noun* a note added at the end of something, especially in a letter, after the signature and introduced by 'PS'.

**post-traumatic stress disorder** (*or* **syndrome**) a group of characteristic symptoms that develop following exposure to a stressful situation.

**postulant** (**poss**-tew-lănt) *noun* a candidate for admission to a religious order.

**postulate** *verb* (*pronounced* **poss**-tew-layt) **1** assume (a thing) to be true, especially as a basis for reasoning. **2** claim. ●*noun* (*pronounced* **poss**-tew-lăt) something postulated. □ **postulation** *noun*

**posture** (**poss**-cher) *noun* the way a person stands, sits, or walks. ●*verb* assume a posture, especially for effect. □ **postural** *adjective*, **posturer** *noun*

**postwar** *adjective* existing or occurring after a war.

**posy** *noun* a small bunch of flowers.

**pot¹** *noun* **1** a rounded vessel for holding liquids or solids, or for cooking in; a teapot, flowerpot, etc. **2** the contents of a pot. **3** (*slang*) a silver cup as a trophy. **4** (*informal*) a large amount; *pots of money.* **5** (*slang*) a pot-belly. **6** the total amount bet in a game. ●*verb* (**potted, potting**) **1** plant in a pot. **2** pocket (a ball) in billiards etc. **3** abridge; *a potted edition.* **4** shoot; kill with a potshot. □ **go to pot** (*informal*) deteriorate, become ruined. **pot-belly** *noun* a protuberant belly. **pot-boiler** *noun* a piece of art, writing, etc. done merely to make money. **pot-bound** *adjective* (of a plant) with roots filling a flower-pot tightly and lacking room to spread. **pot-herb** *noun* a herb used in cooking. **pot luck** whatever is available; *take pot luck with us.* **pot plant** a plant grown in a flowerpot; a house plant. **pot-roast** *noun* a piece of meat cooked slowly in a covered dish. **pot-shot** *noun* a shot aimed casually.

**pot²** *noun* (*slang*) marijuana.

**potable** (**poh**-tă-bŭl) *adjective* drinkable.

**potage** (po-**tah***zh*) *noun* thick soup. (¶ French.)

**potash** *noun* any of various salts of potassium, especially potassium carbonate.

**potassium** (pŏ-tas-iŭm) *noun* a soft silvery-white metallic element (symbol K).

**potation** (pŏ-tay-shŏn) *noun* drinking; a drink.

**potato** *noun* (*plural* **potatoes**) **1** a plant with starchy edible tubers. **2** one of these tubers used as a vegetable.

**poteen** (poch-een) *noun* (in Ireland) whisky from an illicit still.

**Potemkin** (pŏ-tem-kin), Grigori Alexandrovich (1739–91), Russian soldier and statesman; favourite of Catherine the Great.

**potent** (poh-tĕnt) *adjective* **1** powerful, strong; *potent drugs*; *a potent argument*. **2** (of a male) capable of having sexual intercourse. □ **potency** *noun*

**potentate** (poh-tĕn-tayt) *noun* a monarch or ruler.

**potential** (pŏ-ten-shăl) *adjective* capable of coming into being or of being developed or used; *a potential source of energy*. ●*noun* **1** an ability or capacity for development or use. **2** *Physics* the quantity determining the energy of mass in a gravitational field or of charge in an electric field. □ **potential difference** the difference of electric potential between two points, measured in volts. □ **potentially** *adverb*, **potentiality** *noun*

**pother** *noun* (*literary*) a commotion.

**pothole** *noun* **1** a deep cylindrical hole formed in rock (e.g. in limestone) by the action of water; an underground cave. **2** a hole in the surface of a road. □ **potholer** *noun*, **potholing** *noun*

**potion** (poh-shŏn) *noun* a liquid medicine, poison, or drug.

**pot-pourri** (poh-poor-ee) *noun* **1** a scented mixture of dried petals and spices. **2** a literary or musical medley.

**potsherd** (pot-sherd) *noun* a broken piece of earthenware, especially in archaeology.

**pottage** *noun* (*old use*) a soup; a stew.

**potted** *see* POT[1]. ●*adjective* (of food) preserved in a sealed pot.

**Potter**, (Helen) Beatrix (1866–1943), English writer of children's books, which she illustrated herself.

**potter**[1] *noun* a person who makes ceramic pots, vases, etc. □ **potter's wheel** a horizontal revolving disc to carry clay for shaping.

**potter**[2] *verb* (*Amer.* **putter**) **1** (often foll. by *about* or *around*) work on trivial tasks in a leisurely way. **2** go slowly, dawdle.

**pottery** *noun* **1** vessels and other objects made of fired clay. **2** a potter's work or workshop. □ **the Potteries** a district in north Staffordshire famous for its pottery industry.

**potting shed** a shed where plants are potted and tools are stored.

**potty** *adjective* (**pottier**, **pottiest**) (*slang*) crazy. ●*noun* (*informal*) a chamber-pot for a child.

**pouch** *noun* a small bag or pocket; a similar structure in various animals.

**pouffe** (*pronounced* poof) *noun* a large firm cushion used as a seat or footstool.

**Poulenc** (poo-lahnk), Francis (1899–1963), French composer.

**poult** (*pronounced* pohlt) *noun* a young domestic fowl, turkey, or game bird.

**poulterer** *noun* a dealer in poultry and game.

**poultice** (pohl-tiss) *noun* a soft heated mass applied to an inflamed area of skin.

**poultry** (pohl-tri) *noun* domestic fowls (ducks, geese, turkeys, etc.), especially as a source of food.

**pounce** *verb* **1** spring or swoop down on and grasp; attack suddenly. **2** seize eagerly on a mistake, remark, etc. ●*noun* a pouncing movement.

**Pound**, Ezra Weston Loomis (1885–1972), American poet and critic.

**pound**[1] *noun* **1** a measure of weight, 16 oz avoirdupois (0.4536 kg) or 12 oz troy (0.3732 kg). **2** the unit of money of Britain and certain other countries. □ **pound coin** (also **pound note**) a coin or note worth £1.

**pound**[2] *noun* a place where stray animals, or motor vehicles left in unauthorized places, are taken and kept until claimed.

**pound**[3] *verb* **1** crush or beat with repeated blows. **2** make one's way heavily; *pounding along*. **3** (of the heart) beat quickly and heavily.

**poundage** *noun* **1** a charge or allowance for each £. **2** payment per pound weight.

**pour** *verb* **1** flow or cause to flow in a stream or shower. **2** pour tea etc. into cups. **3** rain heavily. **4** come or go in large numbers; *refugees poured out of the country*; *letters poured in*. **5** (foll. by *out*) say or write rapidly; *he poured out his story*. □ **pour cold water on** *see* COLD.

**pout** *verb* push out one's lips; (of lips) be pushed out, especially as a sign of annoyance or sulking. ●*noun* a pouting expression.

**pouter** *noun* a kind of pigeon that can inflate its crop greatly.

**poverty** *noun* **1** being poor; great lack of money or resources. **2** scarcity, lack. **3** inferiority, poorness. □ **poverty line** the minimum income needed for the necessities of life. **poverty-stricken** *adjective* extremely poor. **poverty trap** a situation in which it is a disadvantage to work because the wage is less than the State benefits lost by taking the job.

**POW** *abbreviation* prisoner of war.

**powder** *noun* **1** a mass of fine dry particles. **2** a medicine or cosmetic in this form. **3** gunpowder. ●*verb* apply powder to. □ **powder blue** pale blue. **powder-puff** *noun* a soft pad for applying powder to the skin. **powder-room** *noun* a ladies' toilet.

**powdered** *adjective* made into powder.

**powdery** *adjective* like powder.

**Powell** (poh-ĕl), Anthony Dymoke (born 1905), English novelist and satirist.

**power** *noun* **1** the ability to do something. **2** vigour, energy, strength. **3** a property, quality, or function; *great heating power*. **4** control, influence; *the party in power*. **5** what one has authority to do; *their powers are defined by law*. **6** an influential person, country, or organization. **7** (*informal*) a large amount; *did me a power of good*. **8** (in mathematics) the product of a number multiplied by itself a given number of times; *2 to the power of 3 = 8*. **9** mechanical or electrical energy as opposed to manual labour; *power tools*. **10** the electricity supply; *a power failure*. **11** the magnifying capacity of a lens. ●*verb* **1** equip with mechanical or electrical power. **2** (*informal*) travel with great speed or strength. □ **power of attorney** authority to act for another person in legal and financial matters. **power point** a socket on a wall where electrical appliances can be connected to the mains. **power station** a building where electrical power is generated. **the powers that be** people in authority.

**powerful** *adjective* having great power, strength, or influence. □ **powerfully** *adjective*

**powerhouse** *noun* **1** a power station. **2** a person or thing of great energy.

**powerless** *adjective* without power to take action; wholly unable.

**powwow** *noun* a meeting for discussion.

**Powys** (poh-iss *or* pow-iss) an inland county of Wales.

**pox** *noun* **1** a virus disease leaving pockmarks. **2** (*informal*) syphilis.

**pp** *abbreviation Music* pianissimo.

**pp.** *abbreviation* pages.

**p.p.** *abbreviation* (also **pp**) by proxy, through an agent (Latin *per procurationem*); used in signatures.

∎**Usage** The correct sequence is A p.p. B, where B is signing on behalf of A.

**PPS** *abbreviation* **1** Parliamentary Private Secretary. **2** post-postscript, = an additional postscript.

**PR** *abbreviation* **1** public relations. **2** proportional representation.

**Pr** *symbol* praseodymium.

**pr.** *abbreviation* pair.

**practicable** *adjective* able to be done. □ **practicability** *noun*

**practical** *adjective* **1** involving activity as distinct from study or theory; *has had practical experience*. **2** suitable for use; *an ingenious but not very practical invention*. **3** (of people) clever at doing and making things; *a practical handyman*. **4** virtual; *he has practical control of the firm*. ●*noun* a practical examination; practical study. □ **practical joke** a humorous trick played on a person. □ **practicality** (prakti-**kal**-iti) *noun*

**practically** *adverb* **1** in a practical way. **2** virtually, almost.

**practice** *noun* **1** action as opposed to theory; *it works well in practice*. **2** a habitual action, custom; *it is our practice to supply good material*. **3** repeated exercise to improve one's skill. **4** the professional work, business, or place of business of a doctor, lawyer, etc. □ **out of practice** no longer possessing a former skill.

**practise** *verb* (*Amer.* **practice**) **1** do something repeatedly to improve one's skill. **2** do something actively; *a practising Catholic*; *practise what you preach*.

**practised** *adjective* (*Amer.* **practiced**) experienced, expert.

**practitioner** (prak-**tish**-ŏn-er) *noun* a professional or practical worker, especially in medicine.

**Prado** (**prah**-doh) the Spanish national art gallery, in Madrid.

**praesidium** alternative spelling of PRESIDIUM.

**pragmatic** (prag-**mat**-ik) *adjective* treating things from a practical point of view; *a pragmatic approach to the problem*. □ **pragmatically** *adverb*

**pragmatism** (**prag**-mă-tizm) *noun* **1** treating things in a pragmatic way. **2** philosophy that evaluates assertions solely by their practical consequences. □ **pragmatist** *noun*

**Prague** (*pronounced* prahg) the capital of the Czech Republic (formerly of Czechoslovakia).

**prairie** *noun* a large treeless tract of grassland. □ **prairie dog** a North American rodent that makes a barking sound. **prairie oyster** a raw egg seasoned and swallowed whole. **prairie wolf** a wolflike animal of the North American prairies and deserts; a coyote.

**praise** *verb* **1** express approval or admiration of. **2** honour (God) in words. ●*noun* praising, approval.

**praiseworthy** *adjective* deserving praise.

**praline** (**prah**-leen) *noun* a sweet made by browning nuts in boiling sugar.

**pram** *noun* a four-wheeled conveyance for a baby, pushed by a person walking.

**prance** *verb* **1** (of horses) raise the forelegs and spring from the hind legs. **2** walk or behave in an elated or arrogant manner.

**prang** (*slang*) *verb* crash an aircraft or vehicle. ● *noun* a crash; damage by impact.

**prank** *noun* a practical joke, a piece of mischief.

**prankster** *noun* a person who plays pranks.

**praseodymium** (pray-si-ŏ-**dim**-iŭm) *noun* a metallic element (symbol Pr).

**prat** *noun* (*slang*) **1** a fool. **2** the buttocks.

**prate** *verb* chatter, talk too much; talk foolishly.

**prattle** *verb* chatter in a childish way. ● *noun* childish chatter.

**prawn** *noun* an edible shellfish like a large shrimp.

**pray** *verb* **1** say prayers. **2** entreat. **3** (*old use*) please; *pray be seated.*

**prayer** *noun* **1** a solemn request or thanksgiving to God or to an object of worship. **2** a set form of words used in this; *the Lord's Prayer.* **3** a religious service; *morning prayer.* **4** the act of praying. **5** entreaty to a person. □ **prayer-mat** *noun* a small carpet on which Muslims kneel to pray. **prayer wheel** a revolving cylindrical box containing prayers, used especially by Tibetan Buddhists. **praying mantis** *see* MANTIS.

**pre-** *combining form* before, beforehand.

**preach** *verb* **1** deliver (a sermon or religious address). **2** advocate or encourage (a practice, quality, etc.); *they preached economy.* **3** give moral advice in an obtrusive way. □ **preacher** *noun*

**preamble** (pree-**am**-bŭl) *noun* an introductory or preliminary statement.

**preamplifier** *noun* an electronic device that amplifies a weak signal and transmits it to the main amplifier.

**prearrange** *verb* arrange beforehand. □ **prearrangement** *noun*

**prebend** (**preb**-ĕnd) *noun* **1** an allowance paid to a canon or member of chapter. **2** the land or tithe from which this is paid.

**prebendary** (**preb**-ĕn-der-i) *noun* **1** a clergyman receiving a prebend from a cathedral revenue. **2** an honorary canon (not receiving a prebend).

**Precambrian** (pree-**kam**-briăn) *adjective* of the earliest geological era, preceding the Cambrian period and Palaeozoic era. ● *noun* this era.

**precarious** (pri-**kair**-iŭs) *adjective* unsafe, not secure. □ **precariously** *adverb*

**precast** *adjective* (of concrete) cast in its final shape before use.

**precaution** *noun* something done in advance to avoid a risk; *take precautions.* □ **precautionary** *adjective*

**precede** (pri-**seed**) *verb* come, go, or place before in time or order.

**precedence** (**press**-i-dĕnss) *noun* priority in time or order. □ **take precedence** have priority.

**precedent** (**press**-i-dĕnt) *noun* a previous case that is taken as an example to be followed.

**precentor** (pri-**sent**-er) *noun* a person who leads the singing or (in a synagogue) the prayers of a congregation.

**precept** (**pree**-sept) *noun* a command; a rule of conduct.

**preceptor** (pri-**sept**-er) *noun* a teacher, an instructor. □ **preceptorial** (pree-sep-**tor**-iăl) *adjective*

**precession** (pri-**sesh**-ŏn) *noun* the slow movement of the axis of a spinning body round another axis. □ **precession of the equinoxes** the apparent slow backward movement of the equinoctial points along the ecliptic; the resulting earlier occurrences of the equinoxes in each successive year.

**pre-Christian** *adjective* before Christianity.

**precinct** (**pree**-sinkt) *noun* **1** an enclosed area, e.g. around a cathedral or college. **2** an area where traffic is prohibited in a town; *a pedestrian precinct.* **3** (*Amer.*) an administrative subdivision of a county, city, or ward. **4** (**precincts**) the area surrounding a place.

**preciosity** (presh-i-**oss**-iti) *noun* affected refinement, especially in choice of words.

**precious** *adjective* **1** of great value or worth. **2** affectedly refined. **3** (*informal*, used ironically) considerable; *did him a precious lot of good.* **4** expressing irritation or scorn; *him and his precious car!* ● *adverb* (*informal*) very; *there's precious little money left.* □ **precious metals** gold, silver, and platinum. **precious stone** a valuable mineral used in jewellery, e.g. a diamond or ruby. □ **preciously** *adverb*, **preciousness** *noun*

**precipice** (**press**-i-piss) *noun* a very steep or vertical cliff or rock-face.

**precipitate** *verb* (*pronounced* pri-**sip**-i-tayt) **1** cause to happen suddenly or prematurely; *this action precipitated a crisis.* **2** send rapidly into a certain state or condition; *precipitated the country into war.* **3** throw down headlong. **4** cause (a substance) to be deposited in solid form from a solution. **5** condense (vapour) into drops which fall as rain, dew, etc. ● *noun* (*pronounced* pri-**sip**-i-tăt) a substance precipitated from a solution; moisture condensed from vapour (e.g. rain, dew). ● *adjective* (*pronounced* pri-**sip**-i-tăt) headlong, hasty; rash; *a precipitate departure.* □ **precipitately** adverb

**precipitation** noun **1** rain or snow; the amount of this. **2** precipitating or being precipitated.

**precipitous** (pri-sip-itŭs) adjective **1** like a precipice, steep. **2** hasty, precipitate.

**précis** (**pray**-see) noun (plural **précis**, pronounced **pray**-seez) a summary. ● verb (**précised, précising**) make a précis of.

**precise** adjective **1** exact; correctly and clearly stated. **2** taking care to be exact; *she is very precise.*

**precisely** adverb **1** in a precise manner, exactly. **2** (as a reply) I agree entirely.

**precision** (pri-si*zh*-ŏn) noun **1** great accuracy. **2** (used as adjective) adapted for precision; *precision tools.*

**preclude** (pri-**klood**) verb exclude the possibility of; prevent.

**precocious** (pri-**koh**-shŭs) adjective **1** (of a child) having developed certain abilities earlier than is usual. **2** (of abilities or knowledge) showing such development. □ **precociously** adverb, **precocity** (pri-**koss**-iti) noun

**precognition** (pree-kog-**nish**-ŏn) noun (supposed) foreknowledge, especially of a supernatural kind.

**preconceived** adjective (of an idea or opinion) formed before full knowledge or evidence is available.

**preconception** noun a preconceived idea.

**precondition** noun a condition that must be fulfilled before something else can happen.

**precursor** (pri-**ker**-ser) noun **1** a person or thing that precedes another, a forerunner. **2** a thing that precedes a later and more developed form; *rocket bombs were the precursors of space probes.*

**predate** verb exist or occur at an earlier time than.

**predator** (**pred**-ă-ter) noun a predatory animal.

**predatory** (**pred**-ă-ter-i) adjective **1** (of animals) preying upon others. **2** plundering or exploiting others.

**predecease** (pree-di-**seess**) verb die earlier than (another person).

**predecessor** (**pree**-di-sess-er) noun **1** the former holder of a position. **2** an ancestor. **3** a thing to which another has succeeded; *it will share the fate of its predecessor.*

**predestination** noun the doctrine that God has determined in advance all that happens.

**predestine** verb destine beforehand, appoint as if by fate.

**predetermine** verb determine in advance, predestine. □ **predetermination** noun

**predicament** (pri-**dik**-ă-měnt) noun a difficult or unpleasant situation.

**predicate** noun (pronounced **pred**-i-kăt) *Grammar* the part of a sentence that says something about the subject, e.g. 'is short' in *life is short.* ● verb (pronounced **pred**-i-kayt) assert that (a thing) belongs as a quality or property; *we cannot predicate honesty of his motives.*

**predicative** (pri-**dik**-ătiv) adjective *Grammar* forming part or the whole of the predicate, e.g. 'old' in *the dog is old.*

**predict** verb forecast, prophesy. □ **prediction** noun, **predictor** noun

**predictable** adjective able to be predicted; expected. □ **predictably** adverb, **predictability** noun

**predilection** (pree-di-**lek**-shŏn) noun a special liking, a preference.

**predispose** verb **1** influence in advance; *circumstances predispose us to be lenient.* **2** make susceptible or liable, e.g. to a disease.

**predisposition** noun a state of mind or body that makes a person liable to act or behave in a certain way, or to be subject to certain diseases; *a predisposition to bronchitis.*

**predominant** adjective predominating. □ **predominantly** adverb, **predominance** noun

**predominate** verb **1** be greater than others in number or intensity etc., be the main element. **2** (foll. by *over*) have or exert control.

**pre-eminent** adjective excelling others, outstanding. □ **pre-eminently** adverb, **pre-eminence** noun

**pre-empt** verb obtain (a thing) before anyone else can do so; forestall.

■**Usage** *Pre-empt* is sometimes used to mean *prevent*, but this is considered incorrect by many people.

**pre-emption** noun purchase of property etc. by one person before the opportunity is offered to others.

**pre-emptive** adjective **1** pre-empting. **2** (of military action) intended to disable an enemy and prevent an attack.

**preen** verb (of a bird) smooth (its feathers) with its beak. □ **preen oneself 1** groom oneself. **2** congratulate oneself.

**prefab** noun (informal) a prefabricated building.

**prefabricate** verb manufacture (a building) in sections that are ready for assembly on a site. □ **prefabrication** noun

**preface** (**pref**-ăs) noun an introductory statement at the beginning of a book or speech. ● verb **1** provide or introduce with a preface. **2** lead up to (an event); *the music that prefaced the ceremony.*

**prefatory** (**pref**-ă-ter-i) adjective serving as a preface; preliminary; *prefatory remarks.*

**prefect** *noun* **1** a senior pupil in a school, authorized to maintain discipline. **2** the chief administrative official of a district in France, Japan, and other countries.

**prefecture** (**pree**-fek-cher) *noun* the office or district of authority of a prefect.

**prefer** *verb* (**preferred**, **preferring**) **1** choose as more desirable; like better. **2** put forward (an accusation etc.) for consideration by an authority; *they preferred charges of forgery against him.* **3** promote (a person).

**preferable** (**pref**-er-ăbŭl) *adjective* more desirable. □ **preferably** *adverb*

**preference** (**pref**-er-ĕns) *noun* **1** preferring; being preferred. **2** a thing preferred. **3** a prior right to something. **4** the favouring of one person or country etc. rather than another. □ **preference shares** *or* **stock** that on which dividend is paid before profits are distributed to holders of ordinary shares.

**preferential** (pref-er-en-shăl) *adjective* giving or receiving preference; *preferential treatment.* □ **preferentially** *adverb*

**preferment** *noun* (*formal*) promotion.

**prefigure** *verb* represent or imagine beforehand.

**prefix** *noun* (*plural* **prefixes**) **1** a word or syllable (e.g. *co-*, *ex-*, *non-*, *out-*, *pre-*) placed in front of a word to change its meaning. **2** a title (e.g. *Mr*) before a name. ●*verb* **1** put as a prefix. **2** add as an introduction.

**pregnant** *adjective* **1** having a child or young developing in the womb. **2** full of meaning, significant; *a pregnant pause.* □ **pregnancy** *noun*

**prehensile** (pri-**hen**-syl) *adjective* (of an animal's foot, tail, etc.) able to grasp things.

**prehistoric** *adjective* **1** of the ancient period before written records of events were made. **2** (*informal*) completely out of date. □ **prehistorically** *adverb*

◾**Usage** The prehistoric era is divided into a Stone Age, Bronze Age, and Iron Age.

**prehistory** *noun* prehistoric events or times.

**prejudge** *verb* form a judgement before full information is available.

**prejudice** *noun* **1** an unreasoning opinion or like or dislike of something; *racial prejudice.* **2** harm to someone's rights. ●*verb* **1** cause (a person) to have a prejudice. **2** cause harm to; *it may prejudice our rights.* □ **without prejudice** *Law* without detriment (to an existing right or claim). □ **prejudiced** *adjective*

**prejudicial** (prej-oo-**dish**-ăl) *adjective* harmful to someone's rights or claims.

**prelacy** (**prel**-ă-si) *noun* **1** church government by prelates. **2** prelates collectively; the rank of prelate.

**prelate** (**prel**-ăt) *noun* a high ranking member of the clergy, e.g. a bishop.

**prelim** *noun* (*informal*) **1** a preliminary examination. **2** (**prelims**) the pages preceding the main text of a book.

**preliminary** *adjective* coming before a main action or event and preparing for it; *some preliminary negotiations.* ●*noun* a preliminary action, event, or examination.

**prelude** (**prel**-yood) *noun* **1** an action or event that precedes another and leads up to it. **2** an introductory section of a poem or piece of music.

**premarital** (pree-**ma**-rit'l) *adjective* of the time before marriage; *premarital sex.*

**premature** (**prem**-ă-tewr) *adjective* **1** happening before the proper time; too early. **2** (of a baby) born three or more weeks before the expected time. □ **prematurely** *adverb*

**premed** *noun* (*informal*) premedication.

**premedication** *noun* medication in preparation for a surgical operation.

**premeditated** (pree-**med**-i-tayt-id) *adjective* planned beforehand; *a premeditated crime.* □ **premeditation** *noun*

**premenstrual** (pree-**men**-stroo-ăl) *adjective* of the time immediately before each menstruation; *premenstrual tension.*

**premier** (**prem**-i-er) *adjective* first in importance, order, or time. ●*noun* a prime minister or other head of government. □ **premiership** *noun*

**première** (**prem**-yair) *noun* the first public performance of a play or film. ●*verb* give a première of.

**premise** = PREMISS.

**premises** (**prem**-i-siz) *plural noun* a house or other building with its grounds and outbuildings etc.; *not allowed on the premises.*

**premiss** (**prem**-iss) *noun* a statement on which reasoning is based.

**premium** (**pree**-mi-ŭm) *noun* **1** an amount or instalment to be paid for an insurance policy. **2** an additional sum of money. □ **at a premium 1** above the nominal or usual price; highly valued or esteemed. **2** scarce and in demand. **Premium Bond** a government security that pays no interest but offers a regular chance of a cash prize. **put a premium on** attach especial value to.

**premolar** (pree-**moh**-ler) *noun* a tooth between the canines and the molars.

**premonition** (pree-mŏn-**ish**-ŏn) *noun* a feeling that something (bad) is going to happen. □ **premonitory** (pri-**mon**-it-er-i) *adjective*

**preoccupation** *noun* **1** the state of being preoccupied. **2** a thing that fills one's thoughts.

**preoccupied** *adjective* deep in thought; inattentive because of this.

**preordain** *verb* ordain beforehand.

**prep** *noun* **1** school work that a child is required to do outside lessons, homework. **2** a school period during which this is done. □ **prep school** a preparatory school.

**prepack** *verb* (also **pre-package**) pack (goods) ready for sale before distributing them.

**preparation** *noun* **1** preparing; being prepared. **2** a thing done to make ready for something. **3** (*formal*) prep. **4** a substance or mixture prepared for use, e.g. as medicine.

**preparatory** (pri-**pa**-ră-ter-i) *adjective* preparing for something; *preparatory training.* ●*adverb* in a preparatory way. □ **preparatory school** a private primary school or (in America) secondary school.

**prepare** *verb* make or get ready. □ **be prepared to** be ready and willing to (do something).

**preparedness** (pri-**pair**-id-ness) *noun* readiness.

**prepay** *verb* (**prepaid, prepaying**) pay (a charge) beforehand; pay the postage of (a letter etc.) beforehand. □ **prepayment** *noun*

**preponderant** (pri-**pond**-er-ănt) *adjective* greater in number, importance, or power; predominant. □ **preponderantly** *adverb*, **preponderance** *noun*

**preponderate** (pri-**pond**-er-ayt) *verb* (often foll. by *over*) be greater than others in number or intensity etc.

**preposition** *noun Grammar* a word used with a noun or pronoun to show place, position, time, or means, e.g. *at* home, *in* the hall, *on* Sunday, *by* train. □ **prepositional** *adjective*

**prepossessing** *adjective* attractive; making a good impression.

**preposterous** (pri-**poss**-ter-ŭs) *adjective* utterly absurd, outrageous. □ **preposterously** *adverb*

**prepuce** (**pree**-pewss) *noun* **1** the foreskin. **2** a similar fold of skin at the tip of the clitoris.

**Pre-Raphaelite** (pree-**raf**-ĕ-lyt) *noun* a member of a group of 19th-century artists who produced work in the style of Italian artists of before the time of Raphael. ●*adjective* **1** of the Pre-Raphaelites. **2** (**pre-Raphaelite**) (especially of a woman) like a type painted by the Pre-Raphaelites (with long curly auburn hair).

**prerequisite** (pree-**rek**-wiz-it) *adjective* required as a condition or in preparation for something else. ●*noun* a prerequisite thing.

**prerogative** (pri-**rog**-ătiv) *noun* a right or privilege.

**Pres.** *abbreviation* President.

**presage** *noun* (*pronounced* **pres**-ij) **1** an omen. **2** a presentiment. ●*verb* (*pronounced* pri-**sayj**) **1** foreshadow, be an advance sign of. **2** predict.

**presbyter** (**prez**-bit-er) *noun* **1** (in the Episcopal Church) a minister of the second order, a priest. **2** (in the Presbyterian Church) an elder.

**Presbyterian** (prezbi-**teer**-iăn) *adjective* (of a church) governed by **elders** who are all of equal rank, especially the national Church of Scotland. ●*noun* a member of the Presbyterian Church. □ **Presbyterianism** *noun*

**presbytery** (**prez**-bit-er-i) *noun* **1** a body of presbyters. **2** the eastern part of a chancel. **3** the house of a Roman Catholic priest.

**preschool** *adjective* of the time before a child is old enough to go to school.

**prescient** (**pres**-i-ĕnt) *adjective* having foreknowledge or foresight. □ **prescience** *noun*

**prescribe** *verb* **1** advise the use of (a medicine etc.). **2** lay down as a course or rule to be followed.

---

■**Usage** Do not confuse with *proscribe.*

---

**prescript** (**pree**-skript) *noun* a law or command.

**prescription** *noun* **1** a doctor's written instruction for the supply of a medicine; the medicine itself. **2** prescribing.

**prescriptive** *adjective* **1** laying down rules. **2** prescribed by custom.

**presence** *noun* **1** being present in a place; *your presence is required.* **2** a person's bearing, impressiveness of bearing; *has a fine presence.* **3** a person or thing that is or seems to be present in a place; *felt a presence in the room.* □ **presence of mind** ability to act quickly and sensibly in an emergency.

**present**[1] (**prez**-ĕnt) *adjective* **1** being in the place in question; *no one else was present.* **2** being dealt with or discussed; *in the present case.* **3** existing or occurring now; *the present Duke.* ●*noun* present time, the time now passing. □ **at present** now. **for the present** for now, temporarily. **present-day** *adjective* of present times, modern.

**present**[2] (**prez**-ĕnt) *noun* a gift.

**present**[3] (pri-**zent**) *verb* **1** give as a gift or award. **2** introduce (a person) to another or others. **3** bring (a play, new product, etc.) to the public. **4** (of a compère, broadcaster, etc.) introduce (a show). **5** show, reveal; *presented a brave front to the world.* **6** send (a cheque) to the bank or (a bill) to a customer for payment. □ **present arms** hold a rifle etc. vertically in front of the body as a salute. **present oneself**

appear or attend, e.g. for an examination. □ **presenter** noun

**presentable** adjective fit to be presented to someone; neat and tidy.

**presentation** noun **1** presenting; being presented. **2** something that is presented. **3** the way in which something is presented.

**presentiment** (pri-**zent**-i-měnt) noun a feeling of something that is about to happen, a foreboding.

**presently** adverb **1** soon, after a short time. **2** (especially Amer. & Scottish) now.

**preservation** noun preserving; being preserved.

**preservative** adjective preserving things. ●noun a substance that preserves perishable foods, wood, etc.

**preserve** verb **1** keep safe; keep in an unchanged condition. **2** keep from decay; treat (food) so that it can be kept for future use. **3** keep (game, or a river etc.) undisturbed, for private use. ●noun **1** (also **preserves**) preserved fruit; jam. **2** an area where game or fish are preserved. **3** activities or interests regarded as belonging to a particular person. □ **preserver** noun

**pre-set** verb (**pre-set, pre-setting**) set beforehand.

**preshrunk** adjective (of fabric) subjected to a shrinking process before being used or sold.

**preside** verb be president or chairman; be in authority or control.

**president** noun **1** the head of a club, society, or council. **2** the head of a republic. □ **presidency** noun, **presidential** (prez-i-den-shăl) adjective

**presidium** (pri-**sid**-iŭm) noun (also **praesidium**) the standing committee in a Communist organization.

**Presley** (**prez**-li), Elvis (Aaron) (1935–77), American rock and roll singer.

**press¹** verb **1** apply weight or force steadily to (a thing). **2** squeeze juice from. **3** make by pressing. **4** flatten or smooth; iron (clothes etc.). **5** exert pressure on (an enemy etc.); urge, entreat, or demand; press for a 35-hour week. **6** offer insistently; they pressed sweets upon us. **7** insist upon; don't press that point. **8** throng closely. ●noun **1** pressing; give it a press. **2** a throng of people. **3** hurry, pressure of affairs; the press of modern life. **4** an instrument or machinery for compressing, flattening, or shaping something. **5** a printing press; a printing or publishing firm. **6** newspapers and periodicals, the people involved in writing or producing these; a press photographer. **7** a large cupboard with shelves for linen or books. □ **be pressed for** have barely enough of; we are pressed for time. **press conference** an interview given to journalists by a person who wishes to publicize something. **press-stud** noun a small fastener for clothes etc., with two parts that are pressed together. **press-up** noun an exercise in which a person lies face downwards and presses down on the hands to lift the shoulders and trunk.

**press²** verb (old use) force to serve in the army or navy. □ **press-gang** (noun) a group who coerce people into doing something; (verb) force into doing something. **press into service** bring into use as a makeshift.

**pressie** noun (also **prezzie**) (informal) a present.

**pressing** adjective **1** urgent; a pressing need. **2** urging something strongly; a pressing invitation. ●noun a thing made by pressing; a record, CD, or series of these made at one time.

**pressure** noun **1** the exertion of continuous force upon something. **2** the force exerted; that of the atmosphere; pressure is high in eastern areas. **3** a compelling or oppressive influence; is under pressure to resign; the pressures of business life. ●verb pressurize (a person etc.). □ **pressure-cooker** noun a pan designed for cooking things quickly under high pressure. **pressure group** an organized group seeking to influence policy by concerted action and intensive propaganda.

**pressurize** verb (also **pressurise**) **1** try to compel (a person) into some action. **2** keep (a closed compartment, e.g. an aircraft cabin) at a constant atmospheric pressure. □ **pressurized water reactor** a nuclear reactor in which the coolant is water at high pressure. □ **pressurization** noun

**Prestel** noun (trade mark) (in the UK) a computerized information system that can be viewed on a television or computer screen via the telephone network.

**prestidigitator** (presti-**dij**-i-tayt-er) noun (formal) a conjuror. □ **prestidigitation** noun

**prestige** (press-**tee**zh) noun respect or good reputation gained from success, power, etc.

**prestigious** (press-**tij**-ŭs) adjective having or bringing prestige.

**presto** adverb (especially in music) very quickly. □ **hey presto!** a conjuror's words used at a moment of sudden change.

**prestressed** adjective (of concrete) strengthened by stretched wires within it.

**presumably** adverb as may reasonably be presumed; I presume.

**presume** verb **1** take for granted; suppose to be true. **2** take the liberty of doing something, venture; may we presume to advise you?. **3** (foll. by on) make unscrupulous use of, take unwarranted liberties because of; they are presuming on her good nature.

**presumption** *noun* **1** supposing a thing to be true; something presumed. **2** presumptuous behaviour.

**presumptive** *adjective* giving grounds for presumption. □ **heir presumptive** *see* HEIR.

**presumptuous** (pri-**zump**-tew-ŭs) *adjective* behaving with impudent boldness; acting without authority. □ **presumptuously** *adverb*, **presumptuousness** *noun*

**presuppose** *verb* **1** take for granted. **2** require as a prior condition; *effects presuppose causes*. □ **presupposition** *noun*

**pre-tax** *adjective* before tax has been deducted; *pre-tax profits*.

**pretence** *noun* (*Amer.* **pretense**) **1** pretending, make-believe. **2** a claim, e.g. to merit or knowledge. **3** pretentiousness.

**pretend** *verb* **1** create a false appearance or impression, either playfully or deceitfully. **2** (foll. by *to*) lay claim to; *he pretended to the title*.

**pretender** *noun* **1** a person who pretends. **2** a person who claims a throne, title, etc.

**pretense** Amer. spelling of PRETENCE.

**pretension** *noun* **1** the assertion of a claim to something. **2** pretentiousness.

**pretentious** (pri-**ten**-shŭs) *adjective* too showy; pompous. □ **pretentiously** *adverb*, **pretentiousness** *noun*

**preterite** (*Amer.* **preterit**) *adjective Grammar* expressing a past action or state. ●*noun* a preterite tense or form.

**preterm** *adjective & adverb* born or occurring prematurely.

**preternatural** (pree-ter-**nach**-er-ăl) *adjective* extraordinary, unusual; supernatural.

**pretext** (**pree**-tekst) *noun* a reason put forward to conceal one's true reason.

**Pretoria** (pri-**tor**-iă) the capital of Transvaal and administrative capital of South Africa.

**prettify** *verb* (**prettified**, **prettifying**) make (a thing) look superficially attractive.

**pretty** *adjective* (**prettier**, **prettiest**) **1** attractive in a delicate way. **2** considerable; *cost me a pretty penny*. ●*adverb* fairly, moderately; *pretty good*. □ **pretty much** *or* **nearly** *or* **well** almost. **pretty-pretty** *adjective* too pretty or dainty. □ **prettily** *adverb*, **prettiness** *noun*

**pretzel** (**pret**-zĕl) *noun* a crisp knot-shaped biscuit flavoured with salt.

**prevail** *verb* **1** be victorious, gain the mastery. **2** be more usual or frequent than others; occur generally; *the prevailing wind*. **3** (foll. by *on* or *upon*) persuade.

**prevalent** (**prev**-ă-lĕnt) *adjective* occurring generally; widespread. □ **prevalently** *adverb*, **prevalence** *noun*

**prevaricate** (pri-**va**-ri-kayt) *verb* speak evasively or misleadingly. □ **prevarication** *noun*, **prevaricator** *noun*

■**Usage** *Prevaricate* is often confused with *procrastinate* which means 'to defer or put off action'.

**prevent** *verb* (often foll. by *from*) **1** stop from happening; make impossible. **2** keep (a person) from doing something. □ **prevention** *noun*, **preventable** *adjective*

■**Usage** the use of *prevent* without 'from' as in *prevented me going* is informal.

**preventive** (also **preventative**) *adjective* preventing something. ●*noun* a thing that prevents something. □ **preventive medicine** the branch of medicine concerned with the prevention of disease.

**preview** *noun* an advance showing of a film, play, etc. before it is shown to the general public.

**Previn**, André George (original name: Andreas Ludwig Priwin) (born 1929), German-born American pianist, conductor, and composer.

**previous** *adjective* **1** coming before in time or order. **2** (*informal*) done or acting prematurely; hasty; *you have been a little too previous*. □ **previously** *adverb*

**pre-war** *adjective* existing or occurring before a war, especially before that of 1914–18 or 1939–45.

**prey** (*pronounced* pray) *noun* **1** an animal that is hunted by another for food. **2** a person or thing that falls victim to an enemy, fear, disease etc. ●*verb* (**preyed**, **preying**) (foll. by *on* or *upon*) **1** seek or take as prey. **2** have a harmful influence on; *the problem preyed on his mind*. □ **bird** *or* **beast of prey** one that kills and eats other birds or animals.

**prezzie** alternative spelling of PRESSIE.

**Priam** (**pry**-am) (*Gk. legend*) the king of Troy at the time of the Trojan War.

**price** *noun* **1** the amount of money for which a thing is bought or sold. **2** the odds in betting. **3** what must be given or done in order to achieve something; *peace at any price*. ●*verb* fix or estimate the price of. □ **a price on someone's head** a reward offered for his or her capture or killing. **at a price** at a high cost. **price oneself out of the market** charge such a high price for one's goods or services that no one will buy them. **price tag 1** a label on an item showing its price. **2** the cost of an undertaking.

**priceless** *adjective* **1** invaluable. **2** (*informal*) very amusing or absurd.

**pricey** *adjective* (**pricier**, **priciest**) (*informal*) expensive.

**prick** *verb* **1** pierce slightly, make a tiny hole in. **2** worry; make one feel guilty; *my conscience is pricking me.* **3** feel a pricking sensation. ●*noun* **1** pricking; a mark or puncture made by this. **2** (*vulgar*) the penis. **3** (*scornful*) a stupid man. □ **prick out** plant out (seedlings) in small holes pricked in soil. **prick up one's ears** (of a dog) raise the ears erect when alert; (of a person) become suddenly attentive. □ **pricker** *noun*

**prickle** *noun* **1** a small thorn. **2** one of the hard pointed spines on a hedgehog etc. **3** a pricking sensation. ●*verb* feel or cause a sensation of pricking.

**prickly** *adjective* (**pricklier, prickliest**) **1** having prickles. **2** (of a person) irritable, touchy. □ **prickly pear** a cactus with pear-shaped edible fruit. □ **prickliness** *noun*

**pride** *noun* **1** pleasure or satisfaction at one's actions, qualities, possessions, etc. **2** a person or thing that is a source of pride. **3** a proper sense of what is fitting for one's position or character; self-respect. **4** an unduly high opinion of one's own worth. **5** a group (of lions). □ **pride oneself on** be proud of. **pride of place** the most prominent position.

**prie-dieu** (pree-di-**er**) *noun* (*plural* **prie-dieux,** *pronounced* same) a desk at which one kneels to pray.

**priest** *noun* **1** a member of the clergy; (in the Anglican Church) one ranking above deacon and below bishop. **2** a person appointed to perform religious rites in a non-Christian religion. □ **priesthood** *noun*

**priestess** *noun* a female priest of a non-Christian religion.

**Priestley[1]**, J(ohn) B(oynton) (1894–1984), English novelist, playwright, and broadcaster.

**Priestley[2]**, Joseph (1733–1804), English chemist, noted for his work on gases and for the discovery of oxygen.

**priestly** *adjective* of, like, or suitable for a priest.

**prig** *noun* a self-righteous person. □ **priggish** *adjective,* **priggishness** *noun*

**prim** *adjective* (**primmer, primmest**) stiffly formal and precise; disliking what is rough or improper. □ **primly** *adverb,* **primness** *noun*

**prima ballerina** (pree-mǎ) the chief female dancer in a ballet.

**primacy** (pry-mǎ-si) *noun* **1** pre-eminence. **2** the office of a primate of the Church.

**prima donna** *noun* (*plural* **prima donnas**) **1** the chief female singer in an opera. **2** a temperamental and self-important person.

**prima facie** (pry-mǎ **fay**-shee) at first sight, based on a first impression; *made out a prima facie case against him.* (¶ Latin.)

**primal** (pry-mǎl) *adjective* **1** primitive, primeval. **2** chief, fundamental.

**primary** *adjective* **1** earliest in time or order; first in a series; *the primary meaning of a word.* **2** most important; chief. ●*noun* (in full **primary election**) (in the USA) a preliminary election to elect party conference delegates or select candidates for a presidential election. □ **primary colours** those colours from which all others can be made by mixing, (of paint) red, yellow, and blue, (of light) red, green, and blue. **primary education** *or* **school** for children below the age of 11. **primary feather** a large flight feather of a bird's wing. □ **primarily** (pry-mer-ili) *adverb*

**primate** (pry-mayt) *noun* **1** an archbishop. **2** a member of the highly developed order of animals that includes man, apes, and monkeys. □ **Primate of England** the Archbishop of York. **Primate of All England** the Archbishop of Canterbury.

**prime[1]** *adjective* **1** chief, most important; *the prime cause.* **2** first-rate, excellent; *prime beef.* **3** basic, fundamental. ●*noun* the state of greatest perfection, the best part; *in the prime of life.* □ **prime minister** the head of a parliamentary government. **prime number** a number (e.g. 2, 3, 5, 7, 11) that can be divided exactly only by itself and 1. **prime time** the time at which a TV or radio audience is at its largest.

**prime[2]** *verb* **1** prepare (a thing or person) for use or action; *prime a pump.* **2** prepare (a surface) for painting by coating it with a substance that prevents the first coat of paint from being absorbed. **3** equip (a person) with information.

**primer** (pry-mer) *noun* **1** a substance used to prime a surface for painting. **2** an elementary textbook.

**primeval** (pry-**mee**-vǎl) *adjective* of the earliest times of the world; ancient. □ **primevally** *adverb*

**primitive** *adjective* **1** of or at an early stage of civilization; *primitive tribes.* **2** simple or crude, using unsophisticated techniques; *primitive tools.* □ **primitively** *adjective*

**primogeniture** (pry-mŏ-**jen**-i-cher) *noun* **1** the fact of being a first-born child. **2** the system by which the eldest child (especially the eldest son) inherits all his parents' property.

**primordial** (pry-**mor**-di-ǎl) *adjective* existing at or from the beginning, primeval.

**primp** *verb* make (the hair etc.) tidy; smarten.

**primrose** *noun* **1** a plant bearing pale yellow flowers in spring. **2** pale yellow. □ **primrose path** a life of ease and pleasure.

**primula** *noun* a perennial plant of the family which includes the primrose and polyanthus.

**Primus** (pry-mŭs) *noun* (*trade mark*) a portable cooking stove burning vaporized oil.

**prince** *noun* **1** a male member of a royal family; (in Britain) a son or grandson of the sovereign. **2** a ruler, especially of a small State; *Prince Rainier of Monaco*. **3** a nobleman of various countries. □ **Prince Consort** a title conferred on the husband (who is himself a prince) of a reigning queen. **Prince Charming** a fairy-tale prince and hero. **Prince of Wales** a title usually conferred on the heir apparent to the British throne; *see* CHARLES[4]. **Prince Regent** a prince who acts as regent.

**Prince Edward Island** a province of Canada, an island in the Gulf of St Lawrence.

**princeling** *noun* a young or petty prince.

**princely** *adjective* **1** of or worthy of a prince; (of a State) ruled by a prince. **2** splendid, generous.

**princess** *noun* **1** the wife of a prince. **2** a female member of a royal family; (in Britain) a daughter or granddaughter of the sovereign. □ **Princess Royal** a title conferred on the eldest daughter of the British sovereign; *see* ANNE[2].

**principal** *adjective* first in rank or importance, chief. ●*noun* **1** the person with highest authority in an organization; the head of certain schools or colleges. **2** a person who takes a leading part in an activity, play, etc. **3** a person for whom another acts as agent; *I must consult my principal.* **4** a capital sum as distinguished from the interest or income on it. □ **principal boy** the leading male part in a pantomime, traditionally played by a woman.

■**Usage** Do not confuse with *principle*.

**principality** (prin-si-**pal**-iti) *noun* a country ruled by a prince. □ **the Principality** Wales.

**principally** *adverb* for the most part; chiefly.

**principle** *noun* **1** a basic truth or a general rule used as a basis of reasoning or a guide to behaviour. **2** a personal code of right conduct; *a man of principle*; *has no principles*. **3** a general or scientific law shown in the way something works. □ **in principle** in theory; as regards the main elements but not necessarily the details. **on principle** because of the principles of conduct one accepts; *we refused on principle*.

■**Usage** Do not confuse with *principal*.

**print** *verb* **1** press (a mark or design etc.) on a surface. **2** produce (a book, newspaper, etc.) by applying inked type to paper.

**3** express or publish in print. **4** write (letters) without joining them up. **5** produce a positive picture from (a photographic negative or transparency) by transmission of light. **6** (often foll. by *out*) produce a printed copy of (a document stored on computer). ●*noun* **1** a mark or indentation left where something has pressed on a surface. **2** printed lettering or writing; words in printed form. **3** a printed picture or design. **4** printed cotton fabric. □ **in print 1** in printed form. **2** available from a publisher. **out of print** no longer available from the publisher. **printed circuit** an electric circuit with thin strips of conducting material on a flat insulating sheet. **printing press** a machine for printing.

**printer** *noun* **1** a person whose job or business is the printing of books, newspapers, etc. **2** a machine that prints, especially one linked to a computer.

**printout** *noun* material produced in printed form from a computer or teleprinter.

**prior**[1] *adjective* earlier, coming before another or others in time, order, or importance. ●*adverb* **prior to** before; *prior to that date*.

**prior**[2] *noun* **1** the superior of a religious house or order. **2** (in an abbey) the deputy of an abbot.

**prioress** *noun* a female prior.

**prioritize** *verb* (also **prioritise**) give priority to. □ **prioritization** *noun*

**priority** *noun* **1** being earlier or more important; precedence in rank etc., the right to be first. **2** something that is (or that a person considers to be) more important than other things; *he has got his priorities wrong*.

**priory** *noun* a monastery governed by a prior; a nunnery governed by a prioress.

**prise** *verb* (also **prize**) force out or open by leverage.

**prism** *noun* **1** a solid geometric shape with ends that are similar, equal, and parallel. **2** a transparent body of this form, usually triangular and made of glass, that breaks up light into the colours of the rainbow.

**prismatic** (priz-**mat**-ik) *adjective* **1** of or like a prism. **2** (of colours) formed or distributed as if by a prism, rainbow-like.

**prison** *noun* **1** a building used to confine people who are convicted or awaiting trial. **2** imprisonment as a punishment.

**prisoner** *noun* **1** a person kept in prison. **2** a person who is in custody and on trial for a criminal offence; *prisoner at the bar*. **3** a captive. □ **prisoner of war** an enemy captured in a war.

**prissy** *adjective* prim, prudish. □ **prissily** *adverb*, **prissiness** *noun*

**pristine** (pris-teen) *adjective* **1** in its original condition; unspoilt. **2** fresh and clean as if new; *a pristine layer of snow.*

■**Usage** Some people consider the use in sense 2 incorrect.

**privacy** (priv-ăsi) *noun* being private, seclusion.

**private** *adjective* **1** of or belonging to a particular person; personal; *private property.* **2** not holding public office; *speaking as a private citizen.* **3** not to be made known publicly, confidential. **4** (of a place) secluded. **5** of or belonging to a profession conducted outside the state system; not run by government; *private medicine; private patient.* ●*noun* a soldier of the lowest rank. □ **in private** in the presence only of the person(s) directly concerned, not in public. **private company** a company with restricted membership and no public share issue. **private detective** one who undertakes investigations for a fee. **private enterprise** management of business by private companies (contrasted with State control). **private eye** (*informal*) a private detective. **private hotel** a hotel that is not obliged to accept all comers. **private means** an income from investments etc., not as an earned salary. **private member** an' MP not holding a government appointment. **private parts** the genitals. **private school** a school supported wholly by pupils' fees or endowments. **private sector** the part of a country's economy that is not owned by the State. **private soldier** an ordinary soldier, other than officers. □ **privately** *adverb*

**privateer** (pry-vă-teer) *noun* **1** an armed vessel owned and commanded by private persons commissioned by a government to act against a hostile nation. **2** its commander.

**privation** (pry-vay-shŏn) *noun* loss or lack of the necessities of life.

**privatize** (pry-vă-tyz) *verb* (also **privatise**) transfer (a business) from State to private ownership. □ **privatization** *noun*

**privet** (priv-it) *noun* a bushy evergreen shrub with small leaves, used for hedges.

**privilege** *noun* a special right or advantage granted to one person or group. ●*verb* grant a privilege to, give priority to.

**privileged** *adjective* having a privilege or privileges.

**privy** *adjective* (*old use*) hidden, secret. ●*noun* (*old use & Amer.*) a lavatory. □ **be privy to** share in the secret of (a person's plans etc.). **Privy Council** a body of people advising the sovereign on matters of State. **Privy Councillor** (or **Counsellor**) (in Britain) a member of the Privy Council. **privy purse** an allowance from public revenue for the sovereign's private expenses. **privy seal** a State seal formerly affixed to documents of minor importance.

**prize¹** *noun* **1** something that can be won in a competition; an award given as a symbol of victory or superiority. **2** something striven for or worth striving for. **3** a ship or property captured at sea during a war. ●*adjective* winning or likely to win a prize; excellent of its kind; *a prize bull.* ●*verb* value highly.

**prize²** *verb* alternative spelling of PRISE.

**prizefight** *noun* a boxing match fought for a prize of money. □ **prizefighter** *noun*

**pro¹** *noun* (*plural* **pros**) (*informal*) a professional.

**pro²** *adjective & preposition* (of an argument or reason) for, in favour (of). ●*noun* (*plural* **pros**) a reason for or in favour. □ **pros and cons** reasons for and against something.

**proactive** *adjective* (of a person, policy, etc.) taking the initiative.

**probability** *noun* **1** being probable. **2** something that is probable. **3** a ratio expressing the chances that a certain event will occur. □ **in all probability** most probably.

**probable** *adjective* likely to happen or be true. ●*noun* a candidate likely to be successful. □ **probably** *adverb*

**probate** (proh-bayt) *noun* **1** the official process of proving that a will is valid. **2** a copy of a will with a certificate that it is valid, handed to executors.

**probation** *noun* **1** the testing of a person's behaviour or abilities, especially those of a new employee. **2** the supervision of an offender by an official (**probation officer**) as an alternative to imprisonment. □ **on probation** undergoing probation. □ **probationary** *adjective*

**probationer** *noun* a person who is undergoing a probationary period of testing.

**probative** (proh-bă-tiv) *adjective* (*formal*) providing proof.

**probe** *noun* **1** a device for exploring an otherwise inaccessible place or object; a blunt-ended surgical instrument for exploring a wound. **2** (in full **space probe**) an unmanned exploratory spacecraft transmitting information about its environment. **3** a penetrating investigation. ●*verb* **1** explore with a probe. **2** make a penetrating investigation of.

**probity** (proh-biti) *noun* honesty, integrity.

**problem** *noun* **1** a difficult situation that needs to be resolved. **2** something that is hard to understand or accomplish.

**problematic** *adjective* (also **problematical**) difficult to deal with or understand. □ **problematically** *adverb*

**proboscis** (prŏ-boss-iss) *noun* (*plural* **prosbosces**) **1** a long flexible snout, e.g. an elephant's trunk. **2** an elongated mouthpart in certain insects, used for sucking things.

**procedure** *noun* a series of actions done or appointed to be done in order to accomplish something. □ **procedural** *adjective*

**proceed** (prŏ-**seed**) *verb* **1** go forward or onward, make one's way. **2** continue, carry on an activity; *please proceed with your work.* **3** (foll. by *against*) start a lawsuit. **4** come forth, originate; *the evils that proceed from war.*

**proceedings** *plural noun* **1** a lawsuit; *start proceedings for divorce.* **2** what takes place at a formal meeting. **3** a published report of discussions; *Proceedings of the Royal Society.*

**proceeds** (**proh**-seedz) *plural noun* the amount of money produced by a sale or performance.

**process**[1] (**proh**-sess) *noun* **1** a series of actions or operations used in making or achieving something. **2** a series of changes, a natural function; *the digestive process.* **3** a course of events or time; *the process of growing old.* **4** a lawsuit; a summons or writ. **5** a natural projection on the body or a plant. ●*verb* **1** put through a manufacturing or other process. **2** perform operations on (data).

**process**[2] (prŏ-**sess**) *verb* go in procession.

**procession** *noun* a number of people, vehicles, etc. going along in an orderly line. □ **processional** *adjective*

**processor** *noun* a machine that processes things; *a food processor.*

**proclaim** *verb* **1** announce officially, declare publicly. **2** make known unmistakably as being; *his accent proclaimed him a Scot.* □ **proclamation** *noun*

**proclivity** (prŏ-**kliv**-iti) *noun* a tendency.

**procrastinate** (prŏ-**kras**-tin-ayt) *verb* postpone action. □ **procrastination** *noun*, **procrastinator** *noun*

■**Usage** *Procrastinate* is often confused with *prevaricate* which means 'to be evasive, quibble'.

**procreate** (**proh**-kri-ayt) *verb* produce (offspring) by the natural process of reproduction. □ **procreation** *noun*, **procreative** *adjective*

**Procrustean** (proh-**krust**-iăn) *adjective* seeking to enforce conformity by ruthless or violent methods. (¶ Named after Procrustes, a robber in Greek legend, who fitted victims to his bed by stretching them or lopping bits off.)

**proctor** *noun* either of two disciplinary officials at certain universities. □ **Queen's** or **King's Proctor** an official with the right to intervene in certain legal cases (e.g.

probate and divorce) where suppression of facts is alleged. □ **proctorial** *adjective*

**procurator** (**prok**-yoor-ayt-er) *noun* an agent or proxy. □ **procurator fiscal** (in Scotland) the public prosecutor and coroner of a district.

**procure** *verb* **1** obtain by care or effort; acquire. **2** obtain (women) for prostitution. □ **procurement** *noun*

**procurer** *noun* one who procures something; a pimp.

**procuress** (prŏ-**kewr**-ess) *noun* a female pimp.

**prod** *verb* (**prodded, prodding**) **1** poke. **2** urge or stimulate into action. ●*noun* **1** a poke. **2** a stimulus to action.

**prodigal** *adjective* **1** recklessly wasteful or extravagant. **2** lavish. ●*noun* **1** a recklessly extravagant person. **2** (in full **prodigal son**) a wanderer who has returned home. □ **prodigality** (prod-i-**gal**-iti) *noun*

**prodigious** (prŏ-**dij**-us) *adjective* **1** marvellous, amazing; *a prodigious achievement.* **2** enormous; *spent a prodigious amount.* □ **prodigiously** *adverb*

**prodigy** (**prod**-iji) *noun* **1** a person with exceptional qualities or abilities; a child with abilities very much beyond his or her age. **2** a marvellous thing, a wonderful example of something.

**produce** *verb* (*pronounced* prŏ-**dewss**) **1** bring forward for inspection, consideration, or use; *will produce evidence.* **2** bring (a play or performance etc.) before the public. **3** bring into existence; cause (a reaction or sensation etc.); bear or yield (offspring or products). **4** manufacture. **5** (in geometry) extend (a line). ●*noun* (*pronounced* **prod**-yewss) **1** an amount or thing produced. **2** agricultural and natural products; *dairy produce.*

**producer** *noun* **1** a person producing articles, agricultural products, etc. (contrasted with a *consumer*). **2** one who directs the acting of a play. **3** one who is responsible for control of expenditure, schedule, and quality in the production of a film or a broadcast programme.

**product** *noun* **1** something produced, especially by a natural process or by agriculture or manufacture. **2** *Maths* the result obtained by multiplying two quantities together.

**production** *noun* **1** producing; being produced. **2** a thing produced, especially a play or film. **3** the amount produced. □ **production line** a sequence of machines and workers through which things pass during manufacture.

**productive** *adjective* able to produce things, especially in large quantities.

□ **productively** *adverb*, **productiveness** *noun*

**productivity** *noun* productiveness; efficiency in industrial production.

**profane** (prŏ-**fayn**) *adjective* **1** not concerned with religion; not sacred. **2** irreverent, blasphemous. ●*verb* treat (a thing) with irreverence or lack of due respect. □ **profanely** *adverb*, **profanity** (prŏ-**fan**-iti) *noun*

**profess** *verb* **1** state that one has (a quality or feeling etc.); pretend; *she professed ignorance of this law*. **2** affirm one's faith in (a religion).

**professed** *adjective* **1** avowed, openly acknowledged by oneself; *a professed Christian*. **2** falsely claiming to be something; *a professed friend*. □ **professedly** (prŏ-**fess**-idli) *adverb*

**profession** *noun* **1** an occupation, especially one that involves knowledge and training in a branch of advanced learning; *the dental profession*. **2** the people engaged in an occupation of this kind. **3** a declaration or avowal; *made professions of loyalty*.

**professional** *adjective* **1** of or belonging to a profession or its members. **2** having or showing the skill of a professional. **3** doing a certain kind of work to make a living. ●*noun* **1** a person working or performing for payment. **2** someone highly skilled. □ **professional foul** a deliberate foul committed to halt the game when a member of the opposing team seems certain to score. □ **professionally** *adverb*

**professionalism** *noun* the qualities or skills of a profession or professionals.

**professor** *noun* **1** a university teacher of the highest rank. **2** (in the USA) a university lecturer. □ **professorship** *noun*, **professorial** (prof-i-**sor**-iăl) *adjective*

**proffer** (**prof**-er) *verb* offer.

**proficient** (prŏ-**fish**-ĕnt) *adjective* doing something correctly and competently; skilled. □ **proficiently** *adverb*, **proficiency** *noun*

**profile** (**proh**-fyl) *noun* **1** a side view, especially of the human face; a drawing or other representation of this. **2** a short account of a person's character or career. ●*verb* represent in profile; give a profile of. □ **keep a low profile** avoid being noticed; avoid attention.

**profit** *noun* **1** an advantage or benefit obtained from doing something. **2** money gained in a business transaction, the excess of returns over outlay. ●*verb* (**profited**, **profiting**) **1** bring advantage to. **2** obtain an advantage or benefit. □ **profit and loss account** an account showing net profit or loss at any time. **profit margin** profit after the deduction of costs. **profit-sharing** *noun*

allowing a company's employees to share directly in its profits.

**profitable** *adjective* bringing profit or benefits. □ **profitably** *adverb*, **profitability** *noun*

**profiteer** *noun* a person who makes excessive profits, especially by taking advantage of times of difficulty or scarcity. ●*verb* make excessive profits.

**profiterole** (prŏ-**fit**-er-ohl) *noun* a small hollow cake of choux pastry, usually filled with cream and covered with chocolate.

**profligate** (**prof**-lig-ăt) *adjective* **1** recklessly wasteful or extravagant. **2** of low morality. ●*noun* a profligate person. □ **profligacy** *noun*

**pro forma** **1** as a matter of form. **2** a standard form or other document. (¶ Latin.)

**profound** *adjective* **1** deep, intense; *takes a profound interest in it*. **2** having or showing great knowledge of or insight into a subject. **3** requiring much study or thought. □ **profoundly** *adverb*, **profundity** *noun*

**profuse** (prŏ-**fewss**) *adjective* **1** lavish, extravagant; *profuse gratitude*. **2** plentiful; *a profuse variety*. □ **profusely** *adverb*, **profuseness** *noun*

**profusion** (prŏ-**few**-zhŏn) *noun* abundance, a plentiful supply; *a profusion of roses*.

**progenitor** (prŏ-**jen**-it-er) *noun* an ancestor.

**progeny** (**proj**-ini) *noun* **1** offspring, descendants. **2** an outcome.

**progesterone** (prŏ-**jest**-er-ohn) *noun* a hormone that prevents ovulation and prepares the uterus for pregnancy.

**progestogen** *noun* any of a group of hormones (including progesterone) that maintain pregnancy.

**prognosis** (prog-**noh**-sis) *noun* (*plural* **prognoses**) a forecast or advance indication, especially of the course of a disease.

**prognostic** (prog-**nost**-ik) *noun* **1** a prediction. **2** an advance indication. ●*adjective* making or giving this.

**prognosticate** (prog-**nost**-i-kayt) *verb* **1** predict. **2** be an advance indication of. □ **prognostication** *noun*, **prognosticator** *noun*

**program** *noun* **1** Amer. spelling of PROGRAMME. **2** a series of coded instructions for a computer. ●*verb* (**programmed**, **programming**; *Amer.* **programed**, **programing**) instruct (a computer) by means of a program. □ **programmer** *noun*, **programmable** *adjective*

**programmatic** *adjective* of or involving a programme.

**programme** *noun* (*Amer.* **program**) **1** a plan of action or events. **2** a descriptive notice or list of a series of planned events (e.g. of a concert or a course of study). **3** a radio or television broadcast.

**progress** noun (pronounced **proh**-gress) **1** forward or onward movement. **2** an advance or development; an improvement. ●verb (pronounced prŏ-**gress**) **1** move forward or onward. **2** advance, develop, or improve. □ **in progress** taking place, in the course of occurring. □ **progression** noun

**progressive** adjective **1** making continuous forward movement. **2** proceeding steadily or in regular degrees; a progressive improvement. **3** (of a card game, dance, etc.) with a periodic change of partners. **4** (of a disease) gradually increasing in its effect. **5** advancing in social conditions or efficiency; a progressive company. **6** favouring rapid progress or reform; a progressive policy. ●noun (also **Progressive**) one who favours a progressive political policy. □ **progressively** adverb, **progressiveness** noun

**prohibit** verb (**prohibited**, **prohibiting**) forbid or prevent. □ **prohibitor** noun

**prohibition** noun **1** forbidding or being forbidden. **2** (usually **Prohibition**) a ban on the manufacture and sale of alcohol, especially in the USA 1920-33.

**prohibitive** adjective preventing or intended to prevent the use, abuse, or purchase of something; prohibitive taxes. □ **prohibitively** adverb

**project** verb (pronounced prŏ-**jekt**) **1** extend outward from a surface; a projecting balcony. **2** cast or throw outward. **3** cause (a picture or shadow) to fall on a surface. **4** imagine (a thing or oneself) in another situation or having another person's feelings. **5** plan (a scheme or course of action). **6** represent (a solid thing) on a plane surface, as maps of the earth are made. ●noun (pronounced **proj**-ekt) **1** a plan or scheme. **2** a detailed study, piece of research, etc. by a student.

**projectile** (prŏ-**jek**-tyl) noun a missile (e.g. a bullet, arrow, or rocket) that can be projected forcefully.

**projection** noun **1** projecting; being projected. **2** something that projects from a surface. **3** a thing that is projected. **4** a representation of the surface of the earth on a plane surface. **5** an estimate of future situations or trends based on a study of present ones.

**projectionist** noun a person who operates a projector.

**projector** noun an apparatus for projecting photographs or film on to a screen.

**Prokofiev** (prŏ-**kof**-i-ef), Sergei Sergeevich (1891-1953), Russian composer.

**prolactin** noun a hormone that stimulates milk production after childbirth.

**prolapse** (**proh**-laps) verb (of an organ of the body) slip forward or down out of its place. ●noun (also **prolapsus**) the prolapsing of an organ of the body.

**prole** noun (informal) a member of the proletariat.

**proletarian** (proh-li-**tair**-iăn) adjective of the proletariat. ●noun a member of the proletariat.

**proletariat** (proh-li-**tair**-iăt) noun the working class (contrasted with the bourgeoisie).

**pro-life** adjective in favour of preserving life, especially in opposition to abortion.

**proliferate** (prŏ-**lif**-er-ayt) verb produce new growth or offspring rapidly, multiply. □ **proliferation** noun

**prolific** (prŏ-**lif**-ik) adjective producing a great amount; a prolific writer. □ **prolifically** adverb

**prolix** (**proh**-liks) adjective lengthy, tediously wordy. □ **prolixity** (prŏ-**liks**-iti) noun

**prologue** (**proh**-log) noun **1** an introduction to a poem or play. **2** an act or event serving as an introduction.

**prolong** (prŏ-**long**) verb lengthen (a thing) in extent or duration. □ **prolongation** (proh-long-ay-shŏn) noun

**prolonged** adjective continuing for a long time; tedious.

**prom** noun (informal) **1** a promenade along a sea front. **2** a promenade concert.

**promenade** (prom-ĕn-**ahd**) noun **1** a leisurely walk in a public place. **2** a paved public walk (especially along a sea front), an esplanade. ●verb go or take for a promenade. □ **promenade concert** one at which part of the audience is not seated and can move about. **promenade deck** an upper deck on a ship, where passengers may promenade.

**Prometheus** (prŏ-**mee**-thiŭs) (Gk. myth.) a Titan, who stole fire from the gods and was punished by being chained to a rock where an eagle fed on his liver.

**promethium** (prŏ-**mee**-thiŭm) noun a radioactive metallic element (symbol Pm).

**prominent** adjective **1** jutting out, projecting. **2** conspicuous. **3** important, well-known; prominent citizens. □ **prominently** adverb, **prominence** noun

**promiscuous** (prŏ-**miss**-kew-ŭs) adjective **1** having sexual relations with many people. **2** indiscriminate. □ **promiscuously** adverb, **promiscuity** (prom-iss-**kew**-iti) noun

**promise** noun **1** a declaration that one will give or do a certain thing. **2** a sign of future success or good results; his work shows promise. ●verb **1** make a promise. **2** make (a thing) seem likely; it promises to be a good investment. □ **Promised Land** Canaan, the land promised by God to Abraham and his descendants; any place of expected happiness.

**promising** *adjective* likely to turn out well. □ **promisingly** *adverb*

**promissory** (prom-iss-er-i) *adjective* conveying a promise. □ **promissory note** a signed promise to pay a sum of money.

**promo** (proh-moh) *noun* (*plural* **promos**) (*informal*) a film or other thing used to promote a product, advertise a programme, etc.

**promontory** (prom-ŏn-ter-i) *noun* high land jutting out into the sea; a headland.

**promote** *verb* 1 raise (a person) to a higher rank or office. 2 encourage the progress of; *promote friendship between nations.* 3 publicize (a product) in order to sell it. □ **promoter** *noun*

**promotion** *noun* 1 promoting; being promoted. 2 an advertising campaign; a special offer. □ **promotional** *adjective*

**prompt** *adjective* 1 made, done, or doing something without delay. 2 punctual. ● *adverb* punctually. ● *verb* 1 stimulate (a person) to action. 2 cause (a feeling, thought, or action). 3 assist by supplying forgotten words to (an actor or speaker). ● *noun* 1 an act of prompting; something said to prompt an actor or speaker. 2 a sign on a computer screen showing that the system is ready for input. □ **promptly** *adverb*, **promptness** *noun*

**prompter** *noun* a person (out of sight of the audience) who prompts actors on the stage.

**promulgate** (prom-ul-gayt) *verb* make widely known; promote. □ **promulgation** *noun*, **promulgator** *noun*

**prone** *adjective* 1 lying face downwards. 2 likely to do or suffer something; *prone to feelings of jealousy; strike-prone industries.* □ **proneness** *noun*

**prong** *noun* each of the projecting pointed parts of a fork.

**pronoun** (proh-nown) *noun* a word used as a substitute for a noun; *demonstrative pronouns,* this, that, these, those; *interrogative pronouns,* who? what? which? etc.; *personal pronouns,* I, me, we, us, thou, thee, you, ye, he, him, she, her, it, they, them; *possessive pronouns,* my, your, etc.; *reflexive pronouns,* myself, oneself, etc.; *relative pronouns,* who, what, which, that.

**pronounce** *verb* 1 utter (a speech sound) correctly or in a certain way; *can't pronounce the letter r.* 2 declare formally; *I now pronounce you man and wife; the wine was pronounced excellent.*

**pronounced** *adjective* definite, noticeable; *he walks with a pronounced limp.*

**pronouncement** *noun* a declaration.

**pronto** *adverb* (*slang*) immediately, quickly.

**pronunciation** *noun* 1 the way a word is pronounced. 2 the way a person pronounces words.

**proof** *noun* 1 a fact or thing that shows or helps to show that something is true or exists. 2 a demonstration of the truth of something; *in proof of my statement.* 3 a standard of strength for distilled alcohol; *80% proof.* 4 a trial impression of printed matter, produced so that corrections can be made. ● *adjective* able to resist or withstand penetration or damage; *bullet-proof; proof against the severest weather.* ● *verb* 1 make a proof of (printed matter etc.). 2 make (a fabric) proof against water or bullets.

**proofreader** *noun* a person employed to read and correct proofs. □ **proofreading** *noun*

**prop**[1] *noun* 1 a rigid support. 2 a person or thing providing support or help. ● *verb* (**propped, propping**) support with or as if with a prop; *prop it up.*

**prop**[2] *noun* (*informal*) a stage property.

**prop**[3] *noun* (*informal*) an aircraft propeller.

**propaganda** *noun* publicity intended to spread ideas or information that will influence public opinion. □ **propagandist** *noun & adjective*

**propagate** *verb* 1 breed or reproduce (a plant) from parent stock; *propagating plants from cuttings.* 2 spread (news or ideas). 3 transmit; *the vibrations are propagated through the rock.* □ **propagation** *noun*, **propagator** *noun*

**propane** (proh-payn) *noun* a hydrocarbon found in petroleum and used as a fuel.

**propel** *verb* (**propelled, propelling**) drive or push forward; urge on. □ **propelling pencil** one with a lead that can be moved forwards by turning the outer case. □ **propellant** *noun & adjective*

**propeller** *noun* a revolving device with blades for propelling a ship or aircraft.

**propensity** (prŏ-pen-siti) *noun* a tendency or inclination; *a propensity to laziness.*

**proper** *adjective* 1 suitable, appropriate; correct, according to rules; *the proper way to hold the bat.* 2 strictly so called; *we drove from the suburbs to the city proper.* 3 (*informal*) thorough, complete; *a proper mess.* □ **proper fraction** one that is less than unity, with the numerator less than the denominator, e.g. ¾. **proper name** or **noun** the name of an individual person or thing, e.g. *Jane, London.* □ **properly** *adverb*

**property** *noun* 1 a thing or things owned. 2 real estate, someone's land; *their property borders on ours.* 3 a movable object (other than furniture or scenery) used on stage. 4 a quality or characteristic; *it has the property of dissolving grease.*

**prophecy** (prof-i-si) *noun* **1** the power of prophesying; *the gift of prophecy.* **2** a statement that tells what will happen.

**prophesy** (prof-i-sy) *verb* (**prophesied, prophesying**) declare beforehand (what will happen) as if by divine inspiration.

**prophet** *noun* **1** a person who foretells the future. **2** a religious teacher inspired by God. □ **the Prophet** Muhammad.

**prophetess** *noun* a female prophet.

**prophetic** *adjective* **1** prophesying the future. **2** of a prophet or prophets. □ **prophetically** *adverb*

**prophylactic** (proh-fil-**ak**-tik) *adjective* tending to prevent a disease or misfortune. ●*noun* **1** a preventive medicine or action. **2** (especially *Amer.*) a condom.

**prophylaxis** (proh-fil-**aks**-iss) *noun* preventive treatment against a disease.

**propinquity** (prŏ-**pink**-witi) *noun* nearness; similarity.

**propitiate** (prŏ-**pish**-i-ayt) *verb* win the favour or forgiveness of; placate. □ **propitiation** *noun*, **propitiator** *noun*, **propitiatory** (prŏ-**pish**-ă-ter-i) *adjective*

**propitious** (prŏ-**pish**-ŭs) *adjective* favourable, giving a good omen or a suitable opportunity. □ **propitiously** *adverb*

**proponent** (prŏ-**poh**-nĕnt) *noun* a person who puts forward a theory or proposal.

**proportion** *noun* **1** a fraction or share of a whole. **2** a ratio; *the proportion of skilled workers to unskilled.* **3** the correct relation in size, amount, or degree between one thing and another or between parts of a thing. **4** (**proportions**) size, dimensions; *a ship of majestic proportions.* ●*verb* give correct proportions to; make (one thing) proportionate to another.

**proportional** *adjective* in correct proportion, corresponding in size or amount or degree. □ **proportional representation** an electoral system in which each party has a number of seats in proportion to the number of votes for its candidates. □ **proportionally** *adverb*

**proportionate** *adjective* in proportion, corresponding; *the cost is proportionate to the quality.* □ **proportionately** *adverb*

**proposal** *noun* **1** the proposing of something. **2** the thing proposed. **3** an offer of marriage.

**propose** *verb* **1** put forward for consideration. **2** have and declare as one's intention; *we propose to wait.* **3** nominate as a candidate. **4** make a proposal of marriage. □ **propose a toast** ask people formally to drink a toast. □ **proposer** *noun*

**proposition** *noun* **1** a statement, an assertion. **2** a proposal; a scheme proposed. **3** (*informal*) an undertaking; something to be dealt with; *not an attractive proposition.*

●*verb* (*informal*) put a proposal to (a person); suggest sexual intercourse to.

**propound** *verb* put forward for consideration.

**proprietary** (prŏ-**pry**-et-er-i) *adjective* **1** manufactured and sold by one particular firm, usually under a patent; *proprietary medicines.* **2** of an owner or ownership.

**proprietor** (prŏ-**pry**-ĕt-er) *noun* the owner of a business.

**proprietorial** (prŏ-pry-ĕ-**tor**-iăl) *adjective* of or indicating ownership.

**proprietress** *noun* a female proprietor.

**propriety** (prŏ-**pry**-ĕti) *noun* **1** being proper or suitable. **2** correctness of behaviour or morals.

**propulsion** *noun* the process of propelling or being propelled.

**propylene** *noun* a gaseous hydrocarbon used in the manufacture of chemicals.

**pro rata** (proh **rah**-tă) *adjective* proportional; *if costs increase, there will be a pro rata increase in prices.* ●*adverb* proportionally; *prices will increase pro rata.* (¶ Latin = according to the rate.)

**prorogue** (prŏ-**rohg**) *verb* (**prorogued, proroguing**) **1** discontinue the meetings of (a parliament etc.) without dissolving it. **2** (of a parliament etc.) have its meetings discontinued in this way. □ **prorogation** (proh-rŏ-**gay**-shŏn) *noun*

**prosaic** (prŏ-**zay**-ik) *adjective* **1** lacking poetic beauty. **2** unimaginative, plain, and ordinary. □ **prosaically** *adverb*

**proscenium** (prŏ-**seen**-iŭm) *noun* (*plural* **prosceniums** *or* **proscenia**) the part of a theatre stage in front of the curtain, with its enclosing arch.

**proscribe** *verb* **1** forbid by law. **2** reject or denounce as dangerous etc. □ **proscription** *noun*, **proscriptive** *adjective*

■**Usage** Do not confuse with *prescribe.*

**prose** *noun* **1** written or spoken language not in verse form. **2** a passage of prose for translation into another language. **3** dull or tedious talk.

**prosecute** *verb* **1** take legal proceedings against (a person) for a crime. **2** carry on or conduct; *prosecuting their trade.* □ **prosecutor** *noun*

**prosecution** *noun* **1** prosecuting; being prosecuted. **2** the party prosecuting another for a crime.

**proselyte** (**pross**-i-lyt) *noun* a convert to a religion or opinion, especially to the Jewish faith.

**proselytism** (**pross**-il-it-izm) *noun* **1** being a proselyte. **2** proselytizing.

**proselytize** (**pross**-il-i-tyz) *verb* (also **proselytise**) try to convert people to one's beliefs or opinions.

**Proserpine** (prŏ-**ser**-pini) (*Roman myth.*) the Roman name for Persephone.

**prosody** (**pross**-o-di) *noun* the study of verse-forms and poetic metres. □ **prosodic** *adjective*, **prosodist** *noun*

**prospect** *noun* (*pronounced* pross-pekt) **1** an extensive view of a landscape etc.; a mental view of matters. **2** something one is expecting; *I don't relish the prospect of telling him.* **3** (usually as **prospects**) a chance of success or advancement; *a job with prospects.* **4** a possible customer or client; a person likely to be successful. ● *verb* (*pronounced* prŏ-**spekt**) explore in search of something; *prospecting for gold.* □ **prospector** *noun*

**prospective** (prŏ-**spek**-tiv) *adjective* expected to be or to occur; future, possible; *prospective customers.*

**prospectus** (prŏ-**spek**-tŭs) *noun* (*plural* **prospectuses**) a printed document describing and advertising the chief features of a school or business.

**prosper** *verb* be successful, thrive.

**prosperous** *adjective* financially successful. □ **prosperously** *adverb*, **prosperity** *noun*

**Prost**, Alain (born 1955), French championship racing driver.

**prostate** (**pross**-tayt) *noun* (in full **prostate gland**) a gland round the neck of the bladder in males. □ **prostatic** (prŏ-**stat**-ik) *adjective*

**prosthesis** (pros-thĕ-sis) *noun* (*plural* **prostheses**) an artificial limb or similar appliance. □ **prosthetic** *adjective*

**prostitute** *noun* a woman who engages in sexual intercourse for payment; (usually **male prostitute**) a man who engages in homosexual acts for payment. ● *verb* **1** make a prostitute of; *prostitute oneself.* **2** put to an unworthy use; *prostituting their artistic abilities.* □ **prostitution** *noun*

**prostrate** *adjective* (*pronounced* **pross**-trayt) **1** face downwards. **2** lying horizontally. **3** overcome, exhausted; *prostrate with grief.* ● *verb* (*pronounced* pross-**trayt**) cause to be prostrate; *prostrate oneself.* □ **prostration** *noun*

**prosy** (**proh**-zi) *adjective* prosaic, dull. □ **prosily** *adverb*, **prosiness** *noun*

**protactinium** (proh-tak-**tin**-iŭm) *noun* a radioactive metallic element (symbol Pa).

**protagonist** (proh-**tag**-ŏn-ist) *noun* **1** the chief person in a drama. **2** one of the chief contenders in a contest. **3** an advocate or champion of a cause etc.

---

∎**Usage** The use in sense 3 is considered incorrect by some people.

---

**protea** (**proh**-ti-ă) *noun* a South African shrub with many species, having spectacular flower-heads.

**protean** (proh-**tee**-ăn) *adjective* variable, versatile; taking many forms. (¶ Named after *Proteus*, a Greek sea-god who took various shapes.)

**protect** *verb* keep from harm or injury.

**protection** *noun* **1** protecting or being protected. **2** = PROTECTIONISM. **3** (*informal*) protection from violence etc. obtained by payment to gangsters or terrorists. □ **protection money** money paid for protection from violence.

**protectionism** *noun* the policy of protecting home industries from foreign competition, e.g. by controlling imports. □ **protectionist** *noun* & *adjective*

**protective** *adjective* protecting, giving protection. □ **protectively** *adverb*

**protector** *noun* **1** a person or thing that protects something. **2** (*hist.*) a person who ruled during the minority or absence of the sovereign.

**protectorate** *noun* **1** a country that is under the official protection and partial control of a stronger one. **2** (*hist.*) the office or period of rule of a protector.

**protégé** (**prot**-ezh-ay) *noun* a person who is helped and protected by another.

**protégée** *noun* a female protégé.

**protein** (**proh**-teen) *noun* an organic compound containing nitrogen, occurring in plant and animal tissue and forming an essential part of the food of animals.

**pro tem** (*informal*) for the time being, temporarily. (¶ From the Latin *pro tempore.*)

**Proterozoic** *adjective* *Geol.* of the later part of the Precambrian era.

**protest** *noun* (*pronounced* **proh**-test) a statement or action showing one's disapproval. ● *verb* (*pronounced* prŏ-**test**) **1** express one's disapproval; *protesting against the cuts.* **2** declare firmly or solemnly; *protesting their innocence.* **3** (especially *Amer.*) object to (a decision etc.). □ **under protest** unwillingly. □ **protester** *noun*

**Protestant** (**prot**-i-stănt) *noun* a member of any of the Christian bodies that separated from the Church of Rome after the Reformation. ● *adjective* of the Protestants. □ **Protestantism** *noun*

**protestation** (prot-i-**stay**-shŏn) *noun* a firm declaration; *protestations of loyalty.*

**protium** *noun* the most common isotope of hydrogen.

**protocol** (**proh**-tŏ-kol) *noun* **1** etiquette with regard to people's rank or status. **2** the first or original draft of an agreement (especially between States) in preparation for a treaty.

**proton** (**proh**-ton) *noun* an elementary particle with a positive electric charge equal to that of an electron.

**protoplasm** (**proh**-tŏ-plazm) *noun* the living part of a cell, consisting of a nucleus enclosed in cytoplasm. □ **protoplasmic** adjective

**prototype** (proh-tŏ-typ) noun a first or original example of something from which others are developed; a trial model (e.g. of an aircraft).

**protozoan** (proh-tŏ-**zoh**-ăn) noun (also **protozoon**) (plural **protozoa** or **protozoans**) a minute usually microscopic animal, such as the amoeba.

**protract** (prŏ-**trakt**) verb prolong in duration; protracted talks. □ **protraction** noun

**protractor** noun an instrument for measuring angles, usually a semicircle marked off in degrees.

**protrude** verb project from a surface; stick out. □ **protrusion** noun, **protrusive** adjective

**protuberance** noun a protuberant part.

**protuberant** (prŏ-**tew**-ber-ănt) adjective bulging outwards from a surface.

**proud** adjective **1** feeling or showing justifiable pride. **2** marked by such feeling; a proud day for us. **3** full of self-respect and independence; too proud to ask for help. **4** having an unduly high opinion of one's own qualities or merits. **5** slightly projecting. ● adverb (informal) proudly; they did us proud. □ **proudly** adverb

**Proust** (pronounced proost), Marcel (1871–1922), French novelist, essayist, and critic.

**prove** verb (**proved** or **proven**, **proving**) **1** give or be proof of. **2** establish the validity of (a will). **3** be found to be; it proved to be a good thing. **4** (of dough) rise because of the action of yeast, before being baked. □ **prove oneself** show that one has the required character or abilities. □ **provable** adjective

**proven** (**proo**-vĕn) adjective proved; a person of proven ability. □ **not proven** (in Scottish law) the evidence is insufficient to establish either guilt or innocence.

**provenance** (**prov**-in-ăns) noun origin or a place of origin.

**Provence** (prov-**ahns**) a district of SE France containing Marseilles and the French Riviera. □ **Provençal** (prov-ahn-**sahl**) adjective & noun

**provender** (**prov**-in-der) noun **1** fodder. **2** (humorous) food.

**proverb** noun **1** a short well-known saying stating a general truth, e.g. many hands make light work. **2** (**Proverbs**) a book of the Old Testament, ascribed to Solomon.

**proverbial** (prŏ-**verb**-iăl) adjective **1** of or like a proverb; mentioned in a proverb. **2** well-known, notorious; his meanness is proverbial. □ **proverbially** adverb

**provide** verb **1** give or supply; they will provide office space; provided me with an opportunity. **2** (foll. by for) take care of (a person) by supplying money, food, etc.; has to provide for his family. **3** make suitable preparation for something; try to provide against emergencies. □ **provider** noun

**provided** conjunction on the condition; we will come provided that our expenses are paid.

**providence** noun **1** being provident. **2** God's or nature's care and protection. **3** (**Providence**) God.

**provident** adjective showing wise forethought for future needs or events; thrifty. □ **Provident Society** a Friendly Society.

**providential** (prov-i-**den**-shăl) adjective fortunate, lucky; by divine intervention. □ **providentially** adverb

**providing** conjunction = PROVIDED.

**province** noun **1** one of the principal administrative divisions in certain countries. **2** a district under the charge of an archbishop. **3** a range of learning, knowledge, responsibility, or concern; estimates of expenditure are the treasurer's province. □ **the Province** (in recent use) Northern Ireland. **the provinces** the areas of a country outside its capital city, often regarded as uncultured.

**provincial** (prŏ-**vin**-shăl) adjective **1** of a province or provinces; provincial government. **2** having only limited interests and narrow-minded views; provincial attitudes. ● noun a native or inhabitant of a province or of the provinces. □ **provincialism** noun

**provision** noun **1** providing; preparation of resources etc. for future need; made provision for their old age. **2** (**provisions**) food and drink. **3** a statement or clause in a treaty or contract stipulating something; under the provisions of his will. ● verb supply with provisions of food etc.

**provisional** adjective arranged or agreed upon temporarily but possibly to be altered later. ● noun (**Provisional**) a member of the Provisional unofficial wing of the IRA. □ **provisionally** adverb

**proviso** (prŏ-**vy**-zoh) noun (plural **provisos**) something insisted upon as a condition of an agreement.

**provisory** (prŏ-**vy**-zeri) adjective **1** conditional. **2** making provision for something.

**Provo** (**proh**-voh) (plural **Provos**) (informal) a member of the Provisionals.

**provocation** noun **1** provoking; being provoked. **2** a cause of annoyance.

**provocative** (prŏ-**vok**-ătiv) adjective **1** arousing or likely to arouse anger, interest, or sexual desire. **2** deliberately annoying. □ **provocatively** adverb

**provoke** verb **1** make angry. **2** rouse or incite (a person) to action. **3** produce as a reaction or effect; the joke provoked laughter. □ **provoking** adjective

**provost** (**prov**-ŏst) *noun* **1** the head of certain colleges. **2** the head of the chapter in certain cathedrals.

**prow** (*rhymes with* cow) *noun* the projecting front part of a ship or boat.

**prowess** (-ow- *as in* cow) *noun* great ability or daring.

**prowl** *verb* **1** go about stealthily in search of prey or plunder. **2** pace or wander restlessly. ●*noun* prowling; *on the prowl*. □ **prowler** *noun*

**prox.** *abbreviation* proximo.

**proximate** (**proks**-im-ăt) *adjective* **1** nearest, next before or after. **2** approximate.

**proximity** (proks-**im**-iti) *noun* **1** nearness in space or time. **2** neighbourhood; *in the proximity of the station*.

**proximo** *adjective* (in commerce) of the next month; *the 3rd proximo*. (¶ Latin, = in the next.)

**proxy** *noun* a person authorized to represent or act for another; the use of such a person; *voted by proxy*.

**prude** (*pronounced* prood) *noun* a person of extreme or exaggerated propriety; one who is easily shocked by sexual matters. □ **prudery** *noun*

**prudent** *adjective* wise and cautious. □ **prudently** *adverb*, **prudence** *noun*

**prudential** (proo-**den**-shǎl) *adjective* showing or involving prudence. □ **prudentially** *adverb*

**prudish** (**proo**-dish) *adjective* like a prude, showing prudery. □ **prudishness** *noun*

**prune**[1] *noun* a dried plum.

**prune**[2] *verb* **1** trim and shape by cutting away branches or shoots. **2** shorten or reduce and improve (a speech, book, etc.) by removing unnecessary parts.

**prurient** (**proor**-i-ěnt) *adjective* having or exciting sexual or lustful thoughts. □ **prurience** *noun*

**Prussian** *adjective* of Prussia, a former country of north Europe. ●*noun* a native of Prussia. □ **Prussian blue** a deep blue.

**prussic acid** a highly poisonous acid, hydrocyanic acid.

**pry** *verb* (**pried**, **prying**) inquire or investigate or peer impertinently (and often furtively).

**PS** *abbreviation* postscript.

**psalm** (*pronounced* sahm) *noun* a sacred song, especially one of those in the Book of Psalms in the Old Testament.

**psalmist** (**sahm**-ist) *noun* a writer of psalms.

**psalter** (**sol**-ter) *noun* a copy of the Book of Psalms.

**psaltery** *noun* an early instrument like a dulcimer but played by plucking the strings.

**PSBR** *abbreviation* public sector borrowing requirement; the amount of money that has to be borrowed by the government to make up the difference between its receipts from taxation etc. and its expenditure.

**psephology** (sef-**ol**-ŏji) *noun* the study of trends in elections and voting. □ **psephologist** *noun*

**pseudo** (s'**yoo**-doh) *adjective* false, insincere.

**pseudo-** (s'yoo-doh) *combining form* false.

**pseudonym** (s'**yoo**-dŏn-im) *noun* a fictitious name used by an author.

**psi** *abbreviation* pounds per square inch.

**psittacosis** *noun* an infectious viral disease, especially of parrots, also affecting humans.

**psoriasis** (sŏr-**I**-ă-sis) *noun* a skin disease causing red scaly patches.

**psst** *interjection* (also **pst**) a whispered exclamation to attract someone's attention.

**PSV** *abbreviation* public service vehicle.

**psych** (*pronounced* syk) *verb* (*informal*) **1** work out the intentions of (a person) or the solution of (a problem). **2** intimidate (a person) by making him or her feel uneasy. □ **psych up** make (oneself or another person) ready emotionally.

**psyche** (**sy**-ki) *noun* the human soul, spirit, or mind.

**psychedelic** (sy-ki-**del**-ik) *adjective* **1** (of a drug) producing hallucinations. **2** vivid, colourful, and bold; involving abstract patterns.

**psychiatry** (sy-**ky**-ă-tri) *noun* the study and treatment of mental disease. □ **psychiatric** (sy-ki-**at**-rik) *adjective*, **psychiatrist** *noun*

**psychic** (**sy**-kik) *adjective* **1** of the soul or mind. **2** having or involving extrasensory perception or occult powers. □ **psychically** *adverb*

**psychical** (**sy**-kik-ǎl) *adjective* psychic; *psychical research*. □ **psychically** *adverb*

**psycho** (**sy**-koh) (*informal*) *noun* (*plural* **psychos**) a psychopath. ●*adjective* psychopathic.

**psychoanalyse** *verb* treat (a person) by psychoanalysis.

**psychoanalysis** *noun* a method of examining or treating mental conditions that involves bringing to light certain things in a person's unconscious mind that may be influencing behaviour and mental state. □ **psychoanalytic** *adjective*, **psychoanalytical** *adjective*

**psychoanalyst** *noun* a specialist in psychoanalysis.

**psychological** *adjective* **1** of or affecting the mind and its workings. **2** of psychology. □ **psychological moment** the best time for achieving a particular effect or purpose. **psychological warfare** actions or propaganda designed to weaken an enemy's morale. □ **psychologically** *adverb*

**psychology** *noun* **1** the study of the mind (as deduced from behaviour) and how it works. **2** mental characteristics. □ **psychologist** noun

**psychopath** (sy-kŏ-path) noun a person suffering from a severe mental disorder, especially with aggressive antisocial behaviour. □ **psychopathic** (sy-kŏ-pa-thik) adjective

**psychopathology** (sy-koh-pă-**thol**-ŏji) noun the scientific study of mental disorders.

**psychosis** (sy-**koh**-sis) noun (plural **psychoses**) a severe mental disorder affecting the whole personality.

**psychosomatic** (sy-kŏ-sŏ-**mat**-ik) adjective **1** of or involving both the mind and the body. **2** (of an illness) caused or aggravated by mental stress. □ **psychosomatically** adverb

**psychotherapy** (sy-kŏ-th'e-răpi) noun treatment of mental disorders by the use of psychological methods. □ **psychotherapeutic** adjective, **psychotherapist** noun

**psychotic** (sy-**kot**-ik) adjective of or suffering from a psychosis. ●noun a person suffering from a psychosis.

**PT** abbreviation physical training.

**Pt** symbol platinum.

**pt** abbreviation **1** pint. **2** part. **3** point.

**PTA** abbreviation parent-teacher association.

**ptarmigan** (**tar**-mig-ăn) noun a bird of the grouse family with plumage that turns white in winter.

**Pte.** abbreviation Private (soldier).

**pterodactyl** (te-rŏ-**dak**-til) noun a large extinct reptile with wings.

**PTO** abbreviation please turn over.

**Ptolemaic** (tol-ĕ-**may**-ik) adjective of Ptolemy or his theories (see PTOLEMY²).

**Ptolemy¹** (**tol**-ĕ-mi) **1** the friend and general of Alexander the Great, who declared himself king of Egypt in 304 BC. **2** the name of all the Macedonian kings of Egypt in the dynasty that he founded.

**Ptolemy²** (**tol**-ĕ-mi) (2nd century), Greek astronomer and geographer, who conceived a theory that the earth was the stationary centre of the universe.

**ptomaine** (**toh**-mayn) noun any of various substances (some of which are poisonous) that occur in rotting animal and vegetable matter.

**Pu** symbol plutonium.

**pub** noun (informal) a public house. □ **pubcrawl** noun a drinking tour of several pubs.

**puberty** (**pew**-ber-ti) noun the stage at which a person's reproductive organs mature and he or she becomes capable of producing offspring. □ **pubertal** adjective

**pubes** see PUBIS. ●noun **1** (pronounced pyoo-beez, plural **pubes**) the lower part of the abdomen at the front of the pelvis. **2** (pronounced pewbs) (informal) pubic hair.

**pubescence** noun **1** the beginning of puberty. **2** a soft down on plants, insects, etc. □ **pubescent** adjective

**pubic** (**pew**-bik) adjective of the pubes or pubis; pubic hair.

**pubis** noun (plural **pubes**) either of the pair of bones forming the sides of the pelvis.

**public** adjective of, for, or known to people in general, not private. ●noun members of the community in general or a particular section of this; the British public. □ **in public** openly, not in private. **public address system** a system of loudspeakers to make something audible over a wide area. **public company** a company that sells shares on the open market. **public convenience** a public toilet. **public enemy** a notorious wanted criminal. **public health** protection of the public from disease, by means of hygienic living conditions and environment. **public house** a building (not a hotel) licensed to sell alcohol to the general public for consumption on the premises. **public lending right** the right of authors to payment when their books are lent by public libraries. **public ownership** State ownership and control (of an industry, service, etc.). **public prosecutor** a law officer conducting prosecutions on behalf of the State or in the public interest. **public relations** the promotion of a favourable public image, especially by a company, political party, etc. **public school** (Brit.) a secondary school (usually a boarding-school) for fee-paying pupils; (in Scotland, USA, etc.) a school managed by public authorities. **public sector** the part of a country's economy that is owned and controlled by the State. **public servant** a State official, e.g. an employee of the civil service or local government. **public spirit** readiness to do things for the benefit of people in general. **public-spirited** adjective showing public spirit.

**publican** noun the keeper of a public house.

**publication** noun **1** publishing; being published. **2** something published, e.g. a book or newspaper.

**publicist** (**pub**-li-sist) noun **1** an expert in publicity. **2** a journalist.

**publicity** noun **1** public attention directed upon a person or thing. **2** the process of drawing public attention to a person or thing; the material used for this.

**publicize** verb (also **publicise**) bring to the attention of the public; advertise.

**publicly** adverb in public, openly.

**publish** verb **1** prepare and issue copies of (a book etc.) to the public. **2** make generally known. **3** announce formally; *publish the banns of marriage*.

**publisher** *noun* a person or firm that publishes books, newspapers, etc.

**Puccini** (puu-**chee**-ni), Giacomo (1858–1924), Italian operatic composer.

**puce** (*pronounced* pewss) *adjective & noun* brownish-purple.

**puck**¹ *noun* a mischievous or evil sprite. □ **puckish** *adjective*

**puck**² *noun* a hard rubber disc used in ice hockey.

**pucker** *verb* gather into wrinkles. ●*noun* a wrinkle or bulge made in this way.

**pud** *noun* (*informal*) pudding.

**pudding** *noun* **1** a sweet cooked dish, especially a cake-like mixture made with flour, suet, etc. **2** a savoury dish containing flour, suet, etc.; *steak and kidney pudding*. **3** the sweet course of a meal. **4** a kind of sausage; *black pudding*. **5** (*informal*) a fat, stupid, or lazy person.

**puddle** *noun* **1** a small pool of rainwater or other liquid on a surface. **2** wet clay and sand used as a watertight covering for embankments etc. ●*verb* **1** stir (molten iron) to expel carbon and produce wrought iron. **2** work (clay and sand) into a wet mixture.

**pudenda** (pew-**den**-dă) *plural noun* the genitals, especially of a woman. □ **pudendal** *adjective*

**pudgy** *adjective* (**pudgier**, **pudgiest**) podgy, plump.

**pueblo** (**pweb**-loh) *noun* (*plural* **pueblos**) a communal village dwelling built by American Indians in Mexico and the south-west USA.

**puerile** (**pew**-er-ryl) *adjective* childish, immature; *asking puerile questions*. □ **puerility** (pew-er-**il**-iti) *noun*

**puerperal** (pew-**er**-per-ăl) *adjective* of or caused by childbirth; *puerperal fever*.

**Puerto Rico** (pwer-toh **ree**-koh) an island in the West Indies. □ **Puerto Rican** *adjective & noun*

**puff** *noun* **1** a short light breath or wind; smoke or vapour sent out by this. **2** a powder-puff. **3** a cake of puff pastry or choux pastry filled with cream etc.; *cream puffs*. **4** an over-enthusiastic review or advertisement. ●*verb* **1** send out a puff or puffs; blow (smoke etc.) in puffs; smoke (a pipe etc.) in puffs. **2** breathe hard, pant. **3** make or become inflated, swell. **4** advertise with extravagant praise. □ **puff-adder** *noun* a large poisonous African viper that inflates the upper part of its body when excited. **puff pastry** light flaky pastry. **puff sleeve** *or* **puffed sleeve** a sleeve that is very full at the shoulder.

**puffball** *noun* a fungus with a ball-shaped spore-case that bursts open when ripe.

**puffin** *noun* a black and white seabird with a brightly coloured bill.

**puffy** *adjective* (**puffier**, **puffiest**) puffed out, swollen. □ **puffiness** *noun*

**pug** *noun* a dog of a dwarf breed with a broad flat nose and wrinkled face. □ **pug-nosed** *adjective* having a short flattish nose.

**pugilist** (**pew**-jil-ist) *noun* a professional boxer. □ **pugilism** *noun*, **pugilistic** *adjective*

**pugnacious** (pug-**nay**-shŭs) *adjective* eager to fight; aggressive. □ **pugnaciously** *adverb*, **pugnacity** (pug-**nas**-iti) *noun*

**puissance** (**pwee**-săns) *noun* (in show-jumping) a test of a horse's ability to jump high obstacles.

**puke** *verb* (*slang*) vomit.

**pukka** (**puk**-ă) *adjective* (*informal*) real, genuine.

**pulchritude** (**pul**-kri-tewd) *noun* (*literary*) beauty. □ **pulchritudinous** *adjective*

**Pulitzer** (**puul**-it-ser), Joseph (1847–1911), American newspaper owner and editor. □ **Pulitzer Prize** any of a group of money prizes established under his will and offered annually to Americans for work in music, journalism, American history, and literature.

**pull** *verb* **1** exert force upon (a thing) so as to move it towards oneself or towards the source of the force. **2** remove by pulling; *pull the cork*. **3** propel (a boat) by pulling on its oars. **4** (in cricket) strike the ball to the leg side; (in golf) hit the ball widely to the left. **5** exert a pulling or driving force; *the engine is pulling well*. **6** attract; *attractions that pull the crowds*. **7** damage (a muscle) by straining or twisting it awkwardly. **8** draw (beer, liquor) from a barrel. ●*noun* **1** the act of pulling; the force exerted by this. **2** a means of exerting influence. **3** a deep draught of a drink; a draw at a pipe etc. **4** a prolonged effort in walking etc.; *the long pull up the hill*. □ **pull a fast one** (*slang*) trick or deceive someone. **pull a person's leg** tease him or her. **pull back** retreat or withdraw; cause to do this. **pull down** demolish. **pull in 1** (of a train) enter and stop at a station. **2** (of a vehicle) move into a slower lane; move to the side of the road and stop. **3** (*informal*) take into custody. **4** obtain as wages or profit. **pull off** succeed in achieving. **pull oneself together** regain one's self-control. **pull one's punches** avoid using one's full force. **pull one's weight** do one's fair share. **pull out 1** withdraw or cause to withdraw. **2** (of a train) move out of a station. **3** (of a vehicle) move away from the side of a road, or from behind another vehicle to overtake it. **pull-out** *noun* a middle section of a magazine etc., detachable by pulling. **pull over** (of a vehicle) pull in. **pull rank** make unfair use of one's senior rank in demanding obedience or a privilege. **pull round** recover or cause to recover from illness. **pull strings** use one's influence, often secretly. **pull the other one** (*informal*) used to express disbelief. **pull through** come or bring successfully through an illness or difficulty. **pull together** cooperate. **pull up 1** stop or cause (a person, vehicle, etc.) to stop. **2** reprimand.

**pullet** *noun* a young domestic hen less than one year old.

**pulley** *noun* (*plural* **pulleys**) a wheel over which a rope or belt passes, used in lifting things or to drive a circular belt.

**Pullman** *noun* a luxurious railway carriage or motor coach.

**pullover** *noun* a knitted garment (with no fastenings) for the upper part of the body, put on over the head.

**pulmonary** (pul-mŏn-er-i) *adjective* of or affecting the lungs.

**pulp** *noun* **1** the soft moist part of fruit. **2** the soft tissue inside a tooth. **3** any soft moist mass of material, especially of wood-fibre, rags, etc. as used for making paper. ●*verb* reduce to pulp; become pulpy. □ **pulp magazines**, **pulp fiction** cheap popular magazines or books (originally printed on rough paper). □ **pulpy** *adjective*

**pulpit** *noun* a raised enclosed platform in a church, used by a preacher.

**pulsar** *noun* a source (in space) of radio signals that pulsate in a rapid regular rhythm.

**pulsate** (pul-sayt) *verb* expand and contract rhythmically; vibrate; quiver. □ **pulsation** *noun*, **pulsator** *noun*

**pulse**[1] *noun* **1** the rhythmical throbbing of the arteries as blood is propelled along them; this as felt in the wrists, temples, etc. **2** any steady throb. **3** a single beat or throb. ●*verb* pulsate.

**pulse**[2] *noun* the edible seed of peas, beans, lentils, etc.

**pulverize** *verb* (also **pulverise**) **1** crush or crumble into powder. **2** defeat thoroughly. □ **pulverization** *noun*

**puma** (pew-mă) *noun* a large greyish brown American animal of the cat family.

**pumice** (pum-iss) *noun* (in full **pumice-stone**) a light porous kind of lava used for removing hard skin or as powder for polishing.

**pummel** *verb* (**pummelled**, **pummelling**; *Amer.* **pummeled**, **pummeling**) strike repeatedly, especially with the fists.

**pump**[1] *noun* a machine or device for forcing liquid, air, or gas into or out of something. ●*verb* **1** raise, move, or inflate by means of a pump. **2** use a pump. **3** empty by using a pump; *pump the ship dry*. **4** move vigorously up and down. **5** pour or cause to pour forth as if by pumping. **6** question (a person) persistently to obtain information.

**pump**[2] *noun* **1** a plimsoll. **2** a light dancing shoe. **3** (*Amer.*) a court shoe.

**pumpernickel** *noun* German wholemeal rye bread.

**pumpkin** *noun* a large round orange-coloured fruit used as a vegetable.

**pun** *noun* a humorous use of a word to suggest another that sounds the same, e.g. 'the sole has no feet and therefore no sole, poor soul'. ●*verb* (**punned**, **punning**) make a pun or puns.

**Punch** a character in the puppet show **Punch and Judy**, a bullying puppet with a humped back and hooked nose. □ **as pleased as Punch** extremely pleased.

**punch**[1] *verb* **1** strike with the fist. **2** (*Amer.*) herd; *cattle-punching*. ●*noun* **1** a blow with the fist. **2** (*slang*) vigour, effective force; *a speech with plenty of punch in it*. □ **punch-drunk** *adjective* stupefied from or as if from being punched. **punch-up** *noun* (*informal*) a fight with fists, a brawl.

**punch**[2] *noun* a device for making holes in metal or leather, or for stamping a design on material. ●*verb* perforate with a punch; make (a hole etc.) with a punch.

**punch**[3] *noun* a drink made of wine or spirits mixed with fruit juices etc.

**punchline** *noun* words that give the point of a joke or story.

**punchy** *adjective* having vigour, forceful.

**punctilio** (punk-til-i-oh) *noun* (*plural* **punctilios**) **1** a delicate point of ceremony or honour. **2** the etiquette of such points. **3** petty formality.

**punctilious** (punk-til-iŭs) *adjective* very careful to carry out duties correctly; conscientious. □ **punctiliously** *adverb*, **punctiliousness** *noun*

**punctual** *adjective* arriving or doing things at the appointed time, neither early nor late. □ **punctually** *adverb*, **punctuality** *noun*

**punctuate** *verb* **1** insert punctuation marks in. **2** interrupt at intervals; *his speech was punctuated with cheers.*

**punctuation** *noun* punctuating; the marks used for this. □ **punctuation mark** any of the marks (e.g. full stop, comma, question mark) used in written or printed material.

**puncture** *noun* a small hole made by something sharp, especially one made accidentally in a tyre. ●*verb* **1** make a puncture in; suffer a puncture. **2** reduce the pride or confidence of; *punctured his conceit.*

**pundit** *noun* **1** an expert. **2** (also **pandit**) a learned Hindu.

**pungent** (**pun**-jĕnt) *adjective* **1** having a strong sharp taste or smell. **2** (of remarks) penetrating, biting. **3** mentally stimulating. □ **pungently** *adverb*, **pungency** *noun*

**Punic Wars** three wars between Rome and Carthage in the 3rd and 2nd centuries BC, ending in the defeat of Carthaginian power and the destruction of the city of Carthage.

**punish** *verb* **1** cause (an offender) to suffer for his or her offence. **2** inflict a punishment for; *vandalism should be severely punished.* **3** treat roughly, test severely; *the race was run at a punishing pace.*

**punishable** *adjective* liable to be punished, especially by law; *punishable offences.*

**punishment** *noun* **1** punishing; being punished. **2** a penalty for an offence. **3** (*informal*) severe treatment.

**punitive** (**pew**-nit-iv) *adjective* inflicting or intended to inflict punishment.

**Punjab** (**pun**-jahb) a State of NW India. □ **Punjabi** *adjective & noun*

**punk** *noun* **1** (in full **punk rock**) an anti-establishment and deliberately outrageous style of rock music, popular in the late 1970s. **2** (in full **punk rocker**) a follower of this. **3** (especially *Amer.*) a hooligan, a lout.

**punnet** (**pun**-it) *noun* a small container for fruit etc.

**punster** *noun* a person who makes puns.

**punt**[1] *noun* a flat-bottomed boat propelled by pushing a pole on the river-bottom. ●*verb* **1** propel (a punt) with a pole in this way. **2** carry or travel in a punt.

**punt**[2] *verb* kick (a ball, especially in Rugby) after it has dropped from the hands and before it touches the ground. ●*noun* a kick of this kind.

**punt**[3] *verb* **1** lay a stake against the bank in certain card games. **2** (*informal*) bet on a horse etc.; speculate in shares.

**punter** *noun* **1** a person who punts. **2** (*informal*) the victim of a swindler or confidence trickster. **3** (*informal*) a customer or client; a member of the public.

**puny** (**pew**-ni) *adjective* (**punier, puniest**) undersized; feeble.

**pup** *noun* **1** a young dog. **2** a young wolf, rat, or seal. ●*verb* (**pupped, pupping**) give birth to pups.

**pupa** (**pew**-pă) *noun* (plural **pupae**, *pronounced* **pew**-pee) a chrysalis. □ **pupal** *adjective*

**pupate** (pew-**payt**) *verb* become a pupa. □ **pupation** *noun*

**pupil** *noun* **1** a person taught by another. **2** an opening in the centre of the iris of the eye, through which light passes to the retina.

**puppet** *noun* **1** a kind of doll that can be made to move by various means as an entertainment. **2** a person who is entirely controlled by another.

**puppeteer** *noun* a person who works puppets.

**puppetry** *noun* manipulation of puppets.

**puppy** *noun* a young dog. □ **puppy-fat** *noun* temporary fatness of a child or adolescent. **puppy love** romantic adolescent love.

**purblind** (per-blynd) *adjective* **1** partially blind, dim-sighted. **2** stupid, dim-witted.

**Purcell** (per-sĕl), Henry (1659–95), English composer.

**purchase** *verb* buy. ●*noun* **1** buying. **2** something bought. **3** a firm hold to pull or raise something or prevent it from slipping; leverage. **4** an annual rent or return from land. □ **purchaser** *noun*

**purdah** (per-dă) *noun* the system in Muslim or Hindu communities of keeping women from the sight of men or strangers.

**pure** *adjective* **1** not mixed with any other substance; free from impurities. **2** mere, nothing but; *pure nonsense.* **3** free from evil or sin. **4** chaste. **5** dealing with theory only, not with practical applications; *pure mathematics.* □ **pureness** *noun*

**purée** (**pewr**-ay) *noun* pulped fruit, vegetables, etc. ●*verb* make into purée.

**purely** *adverb* **1** in a pure way. **2** entirely; only; *came purely out of interest.*

**purgative** (per-gă-tiv) *adjective* **1** purifying. **2** strongly laxative. ●*noun* a purgative thing; a strong laxative.

**purgatory** (per-gă-ter-i) *noun* **1** (in RC and Orthodox belief) a place or condition in which souls undergo purification by temporary punishment. **2** a place or condition of suffering. □ **purgatorial** (per-gă-**tor**-iăl) *adjective*

**purge** (*pronounced* perj) *verb* **1** empty the bowels of (a person) by means of a purgative. **2** rid (an organization) of undesirable members. **3** atone for (an offence, especially contempt of court). ●*noun* **1** purging. **2** a purgative.

**purify** *verb* (**purified, purifying**) make pure, cleanse from impurities. □ **purifier** *noun*, **purification** *noun*, **purificatory** *adjective*

**purist** (**pewr**-ist) *noun* a stickler for correctness, especially in language. □ **purism** *noun*

**puritan** *noun* **1** (**Puritan**) a member of the party of English Protestants in the 16th and 17th centuries who wanted simpler forms of church ceremony and strict standards of behaviour. **2** a strict person who regards many forms of pleasure as sinful. ●*adjective* **1** (**Puritan**) of the Puritans. **2** characteristic of a puritan.

**puritanical** (pewr-i-tan-ikăl) *adjective* strictly religious or moral in behaviour. □ **puritanically** *adverb*

**purity** *noun* pureness.

**purl¹** *noun* a knitting stitch formed by inserting the needle with its point towards the knitter. ● *verb* make this stitch.

**purl²** *verb* (of a brook) flow with a swirling motion and babbling sound.

**purler** *noun* (*informal*) a headlong fall.

**purlieu** (**perl**-yoo) *noun* **1** one's bounds, limits, or usual haunts. **2** (*old use*) a tract on the border of a forest. **3** (**purlieus**) outskirts, an outlying region.

**purlin** *noun* a horizontal beam along a roof.

**purloin** (per-**loin**) *verb* (*formal* or *humorous*) steal.

**purple** *noun* a colour obtained by mixing red and blue. ● *adjective* of this colour. ● *verb* become purple. □ **born into the purple** born into an aristocratic or influential family. **purple emperor** a large butterfly with purple wings. **purple passage** (*or* **patch**) a very ornate passage in a literary work. □ **purplish** *adjective*

**purport** *noun* (*pronounced* **per**-port) the meaning or intention of something said or written. ● *verb* (*pronounced* per-**port**) pretend, be intended to seem; *the letter purports to come from you.* □ **purportedly** *adverb*

**purpose** *noun* **1** an intended result; *this will serve our purpose.* **2** intention to act, determination. ● *verb* intend. □ **on purpose** by intention, not by chance. **purpose-built** *adjective* built for a particular purpose. **to no purpose** with no result.

**purposeful** *adjective* having or showing a particular purpose; with determination. □ **purposefully** *adverb*, **purposefulness** *noun*

**purposeless** *adjective* without a purpose.

**purposely** *adverb* on purpose.

**purposive** (**per**-pŏ-siv) *adjective* having or done with a purpose; purposeful.

**purr** *verb* **1** (of a cat) make a low vibrant sound expressing contentment. **2** (of machinery etc.) make a similar sound. ● *noun* a purring sound.

**purse** *noun* **1** a small pouch for carrying money. **2** (*Amer.*) a handbag. **3** money, funds; a sum of money as a prize. ● *verb* pucker; *pursing her lips.* □ **hold the purse-strings** have control of expenditure.

**purser** *noun* a ship's officer in charge of accounts, especially on a passenger ship.

**pursuance** *noun* performance or carrying out of something; *in pursuance of my duties.*

**pursuant** *adverb* (foll. by *to*) in accordance with.

**pursue** *verb* (**pursued, pursuing**) **1** follow or chase. **2** afflict continually; *was pursued by misfortunes.* **3** continue, proceed along;

*we pursued our course.* **4** engage in; *pursuing her hobby.* □ **pursuer** *noun*

**pursuit** *noun* **1** pursuing; *in pursuit of the fox.* **2** an activity or occupation.

**purvey** (per-**vay**) *verb* (**purveyed, purveying**) supply (food) as a trader. □ **purveyor** *noun*

**purview** (**per**-vew) *noun* **1** the scope or range of a document, scheme, occupation, etc. **2** the range of physical or mental vision.

**pus** *noun* thick yellowish matter produced from an infected wound.

**push** *verb* **1** exert force upon (a thing) so as to move it away from oneself or from the source of the force. **2** thrust or cause to thrust outwards. **3** extend by effort; *the frontier was pushed further north.* **4** move forward or make (one's way) by pushing. **5** make a vigorous effort in order to succeed or to surpass others. **6** press (a person) to do something; *don't push him for payment.* **7** urge the use or adoption of (goods or ideas etc.), e.g. by advertisement. **8** (*informal*) sell (illegal drugs). ● *noun* **1** the act of pushing; the force exerted by this. **2** a vigorous effort; a military attack made in order to advance. **3** enterprise, self-assertion, determination to get on. □ **pusher** *noun* □ **at a push** (*informal*) just about; if a big effort were made. **be pushed for** (*informal*) have barely enough of; *I'm pushed for time.* **give** *or* **get the push** (*slang*) dismiss or be dismissed (from one's job etc.). **push around** treat contemptuously and unfairly; bully. **push-bike** *noun* a bicycle worked by pedalling. **push-button** *adjective* operated by pressing a button. **push off** (*slang*) go away. **push one's luck** (*informal*) take undue risks. **push-start** (*verb*) start (a motor vehicle) by pushing it along to turn the engine; (*noun*) a start made in this way. **push the boat out** (*informal*) celebrate. **push through** get (a proposal) accepted quickly. **push-up** *noun* a press-up.

**pushchair** *noun* a folding chair on wheels, for pushing a young child along in.

**pusher** *noun* a person who sells illegal drugs.

**pushing** *adjective* (of a person) **1** pushy. **2** (*informal*) having nearly reached (a specified age); *pushing forty.*

**Pushkin**, Alexander Sergeevich (1799–1837), Russian poet.

**pushover** *noun* (*informal*) **1** something that is easily done. **2** a person who is easily convinced.

**Pushtu** (**pu**'sh-too) *noun* = PASHTO.

**pushy** *adjective* too assertive and determined; not patient or considerate.

**pusillanimous** (pew-si-**lan**-imŭs) *adjective* timid, cowardly.

**puss** *noun* (*informal*) a cat.

**pussy** *noun* **1** (also **pussy-cat**) (*informal*) a cat. **2** (*vulgar*) the vulva. □ **pussy willow** a willow with furry catkins.

**pussyfoot** *verb* (*informal*) **1** move stealthily. **2** act too cautiously; avoid committing oneself.

**pustule** (pus-tewl) *noun* a pimple or blister containing pus. □ **pustular** *adjective*

**put** *verb* (**put, putting**) **1** move (a thing) to a specified place; cause to occupy a certain place or position; send. **2** cause to be in a certain state or relationship; *put the machine out of action*; *put her at her ease*. **3** subject; *put it to the test*. **4** estimate; *I put the cost at £400*. **5** express or state; *put it tactfully*. **6** impose as a tax etc. **7** place as an investment or bet; *put his money into land*. **8** lay (blame) on. **9** (of ships) proceed; *put to sea*. ●*noun* a throw of the shot. □ **put about 1** spread (information, a rumour, etc.). **2** *Nautical* turn round; put (a ship) on the opposite tack. **put across** communicate (an idea etc.). **put away** (*informal*) **1** put into prison or a mental home. **2** consume as food or drink. **put back 1** return to its former place. **2** change to a later time. **put by** save for future use. **put down 1** suppress by force or authority. **2** snub. **3** have (an animal) destroyed. **4** enter (a person's name) on a list. **5** reckon or consider; *put him down as a fool*. **6** attribute; *put it down to nervousness*. **put-down** *noun* a snub. **put forward 1** suggest, propose. **2** change to an earlier time. **put in 1** make (an appearance). **2** enter (a claim). **3** spend (time) working. **put in for** apply for. **put it on** (*informal*) pretend an emotion. **put off 1** postpone; postpone an engagement with (a person). **2** make excuses and try to avoid. **3** dissuade, repel; *the smell puts me off*. **put on 1** stage (a play etc.). **2** increase; *putting on weight*. **3** cause to operate; *put the radio on*. **put out 1** disconcert, annoy, or inconvenience (a person). **2** extinguish (a light or fire). **3** dislocate (a joint). **put over** = PUT ACROSS. **put the shot** hurl it as an athletic exercise. **put through 1** complete (a business transaction) successfully. **2** connect by telephone. **3** cause to undergo; *put it through severe tests*. **put up 1** construct or build. **2** raise the price of. **3** provide or contribute; *the firm will put up the money*. **4** offer for sale. **5** display (a notice). **6** present as an idea or proposal. **7** give or receive accommodation. **8** attempt or offer; *they put up no resistance*. **put-up** *adjective* concocted fraudulently; *a put-up job*. **put up to** encourage (a person) to do something wrong; *who put him up to it?* **put up with** endure, tolerate.

**putative** (pew-tă-tiv) *adjective* reputed, supposed; *his putative father*.

**putrefy** (pew-tri-fy) *verb* (**putrefied, putrefying**) rot, decay or cause to decay. □ **putrefaction** (pew-tri-**fak**-shŏn) *noun*

**putrescent** (pew-**tress**-ĕnt) *adjective* decaying, rotting. □ **putrescence** *noun*

**putrid** (pew-trid) *adjective* **1** decomposed, rotting. **2** foul-smelling. **3** (*slang*) very distasteful or unpleasant. □ **putridity** *noun*

**putt** (*rhymes with* cut) *verb* strike (a golf ball) lightly to make it roll along the ground. ●*noun* a stroke of this kind. □ **putting green** (in golf) a smooth area of grass round a hole.

**puttee** *noun* (*hist.*) a strip of cloth wound round the leg from ankle to knee for support or protection.

**putter**[1] *noun* a golf club used in putting.

**putter**[2] *verb* (*Amer.*) = POTTER[2].

**putty** *noun* a soft paste that sets hard, used for fixing glass in window frames, filling holes, etc.

**puzzle** *noun* **1** a question that is difficult to answer; a problem. **2** a problem or toy designed to test one's knowledge, ingenuity, or patience. ●*verb* confuse (a person); cause doubt and uncertainty to. □ **puzzle over** be uncertain and think hard about. **puzzle out** solve or understand by patient thought or ingenuity. □ **puzzlement** *noun*

**puzzler** *noun* a puzzling problem.

**PVC** *abbreviation* polyvinyl chloride.

**PW** *abbreviation* policewoman.

**PWR** *abbreviation* pressurized-water reactor.

**pyaemia** (py-eem-iă) *noun* (*Amer.* **pyemia**) blood-poisoning with formation of abscesses in the internal organs of the body.

**pye-dog** *noun* a stray mongrel in Eastern countries.

**Pygmalion** (pig-may-li-ŏn) (*Gk. legend*) a king of Cyprus who made an ivory statue of a beautiful woman and loved it so deeply that at his request Aphrodite gave it life.

**pygmy** (pig-mi) *noun* (also **pigmy**) **1** a person or thing of unusually small size. **2** a member of a dwarf Black people of equatorial Africa. ●*adjective* very small.

**pyjamas** *plural noun* (*Amer.* **pajamas**) a loose-fitting jacket and trousers for sleeping in.

**pylon** *noun* a tall metal structure for carrying overhead electricity cables.

**Pyongyang** the capital of North Korea.

**pyorrhoea** (py-ŏ-ree-ă) *noun* (*Amer.* **pyorrhea**) a disease of the tooth-sockets causing discharge of pus and loosening of the teeth.

**pyracantha** (py-ră-**kan**-thă) *noun* an evergreen thorny shrub with scarlet or orange berries.

**pyramid** *noun* a structure with a flat (usually square) base and sloping sides that meet at the top, especially one built by the ancient Egyptians as a tomb or by the Aztecs and Mayas as a platform for a temple. □ **pyramid selling** a method of selling goods whereby distributors pay a premium for the right to sell a company's goods and then sell part of that right to a number of others. □ **pyramidal** (pi-**ram**-id'l) *adjective*

**pyre** (*rhymes with fire*) *noun* a pile of wood etc. for burning a corpse at a funeral.

**Pyrenees** *plural noun* a range of mountains between France and Spain. □ **Pyrenean** (pi-ri-**nee**-ăn) *adjective*

**pyrethrum** (py-**ree**-thrŭm) *noun* **1** a chrysanthemum with finely divided leaves. **2** an insecticide made from its dried flowers.

**pyretic** (py-**ret**-ik) *adjective* of or producing fever.

**Pyrex** *noun* (*trade mark*) a hard heat-resistant glass.

**pyrexia** (py-**reks**-iă) *noun Med.* fever.

**pyrites** (py-**ry**-teez) *noun* a mineral that is a sulphide of iron (*iron pyrites*) or copper and iron (*copper pyrites*).

**pyromania** (pyr-ŏ-**may**-niă) an uncontrollable impulse to set things on fire. □ **pyromaniac** *noun & adjective*

**pyrotechnic** (py-rŏ-**tek**-nik) *adjective* of or like fireworks. ● *plural noun* (**pyrotechnics**) **1** the art of making fireworks. **2** a firework display. **3** any loud or brilliant display.

**Pyrrhic victory** (**pi**-rik) a victory gained at too great a cost, like that of Pyrrhus (king of Epirus) over the Romans in 279 BC.

**Pythagoras** (py-**thag**-er-ăs) (late 6th century BC), Greek philosopher and mathematician. □ **Pythagoras' theorem** the mathematical theorem that the square on the hypotenuse of a right-angled triangle is equal to the sum of the squares on the other two sides. □ **Pythagorean** *adjective & noun*

**Pythia** (**pith**-iă) the priestess of Apollo at Delphi in ancient Greece, who delivered the oracles.

**python** (**py**-thŏn) *noun* a large tropical snake that squeezes its prey so as to suffocate it.

**pyx** (*pronounced* piks) *noun* a vessel in which bread consecrated for Holy Communion is kept.

**Q** *abbreviation* (also **Q.**) **1** Queen. **2** question.

**Qatar** (**kat**-ar) a country on the west coast of the Persian Gulf. □ **Qatari** *adjective & noun* (*plural* **Qataris**).

**QC** *abbreviation* Queen's Counsel.

**QED** *abbreviation* quod erat demonstrandum. (¶ Latin, = which was the thing that had to be proved.)

**Qld.** *abbreviation* Queensland.

**QM** *abbreviation* quartermaster.

**qr.** *abbreviation* quarter(s).

**qt** *abbreviation* quart(s).

**q.t.** *noun* □ **on the q.t.** (*informal*) on the quiet, secretly.

**qua** (*pronounced* kwah *or* kway) *conjunction* in the capacity or character of; *put his duty qua citizen above other loyalties.* (¶ Latin.)

**quack**[1] *noun* the harsh cry of a duck. ● *verb* utter this sound.

**quack**[2] *noun* **1** a person who falsely claims to have medical skill or to have remedies which will cure disease etc. **2** (*informal*) a doctor.

**quad** (*pronounced* kwod) *noun* (*informal*) **1** a quadrangle. **2** a quadruplet. **3** quadraphonics. ● *adjective* quadraphonic.

**Quadragesima** (kwod-ră-**jess**-imă) *noun* the first Sunday in Lent.

**quadrangle** (**kwod**-rang-ŭl) *noun* a four-sided court bordered by large buildings. □ **quadrangular** *adjective*

**quadrant** (**kwod**-rănt) *noun* **1** a quarter of a circle or of its circumference. **2** an instrument with an arc of 90° marked off in degrees, for measuring angles.

**quadraphonic** (kwod-ră-**fon**-ik) *adjective* (also **quadrophonic**) (of sound reproduction) using four transmission channels. ● *plural noun* (**quadraphonics**) quadraphonic transmission. □ **quadraphonically** *adverb*

**quadrate** *noun* a rectangular object. ● *verb* make square.

**quadratic** (kwod-**rat**-ik) *noun* (also **quadratic equation**) an equation involving the square (and no higher power) of one or more of the unknown quantities or variables.

**quadrennial** (kwod-**ren**-iăl) *adjective* **1** lasting for four years. **2** happening every fourth year.

**quadri-** *combining form* four.

**quadrilateral** (kwod-ri-**lat**-er-ăl) *noun* a geometric figure with four sides. ● *adjective* having four sides.

**quadrille** (kwod-**ril**) *noun* a square dance for four couples; the music for this.

**quadriplegia** (kwod-ri-**plee**-jiă) *noun* paralysis of both arms and both legs. □ **quadriplegic** *adjective & noun*

**quadruped** (**kwod**-ruu-ped) *noun* a four-footed animal.

**quadruple** *adjective* **1** consisting of four parts; involving four people or groups; *a quadruple alliance.* **2** four times as much as; *we shall need quadruple that number of lights.* ● *verb* multiply or become multiplied by four; *costs had quadrupled.*

**quadruplet** (**kwod**-ruu-plit) *noun* each of four children born at one birth.

**quadruplicate** *adjective* (*pronounced* kwod-**roo**-plik-ăt) fourfold; of which four copies are made. ● *verb* (*pronounced* kwod-**roo**-plik-ayt) multiply by four.

**quaff** (*pronounced* kwof) *verb* drink (a thing) in long draughts.

**quagmire** (**kwag**-myr) *noun* **1** a bog or marsh. **2** a complex or dangerous situation.

**Quai d'Orsay** (kay dor-**say**) a riverside street on the left bank of the Seine in Paris, containing the headquarters of the French ministry for foreign affairs.

**quail** *noun* (*plural* **quail** *or* **quails**) a small game bird related to the partridge. ● *verb* flinch, show fear.

**quaint** *adjective* attractive through being unusual or old-fashioned. □ **quaintly** *adverb*, **quaintness** *noun*

**quake** *verb* shake or tremble from unsteadiness; shake with fear. ● *noun* **1** a quaking movement. **2** (*informal*) an earthquake.

**Quaker** *noun* a member of the Society of Friends (*see* SOCIETY). □ **Quakerism** *noun*

**qualification** *noun* **1** qualifying; being qualified. **2** a thing that qualifies a person to do something. **3** something that restricts a meaning; *this statement needs certain qualifications.*

**qualificatory** *adjective* of, giving, or involving qualifications.

**qualify** *verb* (**qualified**, **qualifying**) **1** make or become competent, eligible, or legally entitled to do something. **2** make (a statement etc.) less general or extreme; limit its meaning; *'in all cases' needs to be qualified as 'in all known cases'; we gave it only qualified approval.* **3** describe, attribute some quality to; *adjectives qualify nouns.* □ **qualifier** *noun*

**qualitative** (**kwol**-i-tă-tiv) *adjective* of or concerned with quality rather than quantity.

**quality** *noun* **1** a degree or level of excellence; *goods of high quality*. **2** general excellence. **3** a characteristic, something that is special in a person or thing; *she has the quality of inspiring confidence*. □ **quality control** maintenance of standards in products or services by testing samples.

**qualm** (*pronounced* kwahm) *noun* **1** a misgiving; a pang of conscience. **2** a sudden feeling of sickness or faintness.

**quandary** (**kwon**-der-i) *noun* a state of perplexity; a difficult situation.

**quango** *noun* (*plural* **quangos**) an administrative body with financial support from and senior appointments made by the government but not controlled by it. (¶ From the initials of *quasi-autonomous non-governmental organization*.)

**Quant** (*pronounced* kwont), Mary (born 1934), English fashion designer, whose most famous innovation was the miniskirt (1965).

**quanta** *see* QUANTUM.

**quantify** (**kwon**-ti-fy) *verb* (**quantified**, **quantifying**) express as a quantity. □ **quantification** *noun*, **quantifiable** *adjective*

**quantitative** (**kwon**-ti-tă-tiv) *adjective* of or concerned with quantity; *quantitative analysis*.

**· quantity** *noun* **1** an amount or number of things; a specified or considerable amount or number. **2** ability to be measured through having size, weight, amount, or number. **3** a thing that has this ability; a figure or symbol representing it. □ **quantity surveyor** a person who measures and prices building work.

**quantum** (**kwon**-tŭm) *noun* (*plural* **quanta**) **1** *Physics* a minimum amount of a physical quantity (such as energy) which can exist in a given situation. **2** the amount required, desired, or allowed. □ **quantum leap** (*or* **jump**) a sudden great advance. **quantum mechanics** (also **quantum theory**) a theory of physics based on the assumption that energy exists in indivisible units.

**quarantine** (**kwo**-răn-teen) *noun* **1** isolation imposed on people or animals who may have been exposed to an infectious or contagious disease. **2** the period of this isolation. ● *verb* put into quarantine.

**quark** *noun* **1** *Physics* any of a group of hypothetical components of elementary particles. **2** a low-fat curd cheese.

**quarrel** *noun* **1** a violent disagreement; breaking of friendly relations. **2** a cause for complaint against a person; *we have no quarrel with him*. ● *verb* (**quarrelled**, **quarrelling**; *Amer.* **quarreled**, **quarreling**) **1** engage in a quarrel. **2** disagree or complain; *we are not quarrelling with this decision*.

**quarrelsome** *adjective* liable to quarrel with people.

**quarry** *noun* **1** an intended prey or victim being hunted. **2** something that is sought or pursued. **3** an open excavation from which stone or slate etc. is obtained. ● *verb* (**quarried**, **quarrying**) **1** obtain (stone etc.) from a quarry. **2** search laboriously in order to extract information. □ **quarry tile** an unglazed floor-tile.

**quart** *noun* a measure of capacity for liquids, 2 pints or a quarter of a gallon (0.946 litre).

**quarter** *noun* **1** each of the four equal parts into which a thing is divided. **2** a quarter of a US or Canadian dollar, 25 cents. **3** a grain measure of 8 bushels; one-quarter of a hundredweight. **4** a fourth part of a year. **5** a fourth part of a lunar month. **6** a point of time 15 minutes before or after every hour. **7** a direction or point of the compass; a district; a division of a town. **8** a person or group regarded as a possible source of help or information; *got no sympathy from that quarter*. **9** mercy towards an enemy or opponent; *gave no quarter*. **10** (**quarters**) lodgings, accommodation. ● *verb* **1** divide into quarters. **2** put (soldiers etc.) into lodgings. **3** (of a dog etc.) search (ground) in every direction. **4** (in heraldry) place (a symbol) in one of the divisions of a shield or coat of arms. □ **quarter day** each of the four days regarded as beginning the quarters of a year for financial purposes or tenancies etc. **quarter-final** *noun* a match or round preceding a semifinal. **quarterlight** *noun* a small triangular pivoted window in a car. **quarter sessions** (formerly) a court of limited criminal and civil jurisdiction, usually held quarterly.

**quarterback** *noun* a player in American football who directs attacking play.

**quarterdeck** *noun* the part of the upper deck of a ship nearest the stern, usually reserved for the ship's officers.

**quarterly** *adjective & adverb* produced or occurring once in every quarter of a year. ● *noun* a quarterly periodical.

**quartermaster** *noun* **1** (in the army) a regimental officer in charge of stores and assigning quarters etc. **2** a naval petty officer in charge of steering and signals.

**quarterstaff** *noun* a stout pole 6–8 ft. long formerly used as a weapon.

**quartet** *noun* **1** a group of four instruments or voices; a musical composition for these. **2** a set of four.

**quarto** *noun* (*plural* **quartos**) the size of a book or sheet of paper given by folding a sheet of standard size twice to form four leaves.

**quartz** (*pronounced* kwortz) *noun* a hard mineral occurring in various forms. □ **quartz clock** *or* **watch** one operated by electric vibrations of a quartz crystal.

**quasar** (**kway**-zar) *noun* a starlike object that is the source of intense electromagnetic radiation.

**quash** *verb* **1** annul; reject (by legal authority) as not valid; *quashed the conviction.* **2** suppress or crush (a rebellion etc.).

**quasi-** (**kwayz**-I) *combining form* seeming to be something but not really so; *a quasi-scientific explanation.*

**Quasimodo** (kway-si-**moh**-doh) the deformed bell-ringer of Notre Dame in Victor Hugo's novel *Notre Dame de Paris* (1831).

**quassia** (**kwosh**-ă) *noun* a South American tree with bitter bark, wood, and root, used to make a medicinal tonic and insecticide.

**quaternary** (kwă-**tern**-eri) *adjective* **1** having four parts. **2** (**Quaternary**) *Geol.* of the second period of the Cainozoic era. ● *noun* (**Quaternary**) this period.

**quatrain** (**kwot**-rayn) *noun* a stanza or poem of four lines.

**quatrefoil** (**kat**-rĕ-foil) *noun* **1** a leaf or flower with four lobes. **2** (in architecture) an ornament resembling this.

**quattrocento** (kwah-troh-**chen**-toh) *noun* Italian art of the 15th century.

**quaver** *verb* **1** tremble, vibrate. **2** speak in a trembling voice. ● *noun* **1** a quavering sound. **2** a note in music, lasting half as long as a crotchet.

**quay** (*pronounced* kee) *noun* a man-made landing-place alongside which ships can be tied up for loading and unloading.

**quayside** *noun* land forming or beside a quay.

**queasy** *adjective* (**queasier**, **queasiest**) **1** feeling slightly sick. **2** having a digestion that is easily upset. **3** uneasy, squeamish. □ **queasiness** *noun*

**Quebec** a province of eastern Canada.

**Quechua** (**kech**-wă) *noun* **1** (*plural* **Quechua**) a member of an Indian people of Peru and adjacent regions. **2** their language.

**queen** *noun* **1** (as a title, usually **Queen**) a woman who is the supreme ruler of an independent country by right of succession to the throne. **2** a king's wife. **3** a woman, place, or thing regarded as supreme; *Venice, the queen of the Adriatic.* **4** a playing card bearing a picture of a queen. **5** (*slang, offensive*) a male homosexual. **6** a piece in chess. **7** a fertile female of a bee or ant etc. ● *verb* convert (a pawn in chess) to a queen when it reaches the opponent's end of the board. □ **Queen-Anne** *adjective* in the style of furniture and architecture popular in the early 18th century, characterized by careful proportions, lack of ornament, and the curved cabriole leg. **queen mother** a dowager queen who is the mother of a reigning king or queen. **Queen's Counsel** (*Brit.*) counsel to the Crown, taking precedence over other barristers. **Queen's Guide** *or* **Scout** one who has reached the highest standard of proficiency. **queen-size** *adjective* extra large, but smaller than king-size.

**queenly** *adjective* like a queen in appearance or manner. □ **queenliness** *noun*

**Queensberry Rules** the standard rules of boxing.

**Queensland** a State comprising the NE part of Australia.

**queer** *adjective* **1** strange, odd, eccentric. **2** causing one to feel suspicious; of questionable character. **3** slightly ill or faint; *felt queer.* **4** (*slang, offensive*) homosexual. ● *noun* (*slang, offensive*) a homosexual. ● *verb* spoil. □ **in Queer Street** (*slang*) in difficulties, in debt or trouble. **queer a person's pitch** (*informal*) spoil his or her chances. □ **queerly** *adverb*, **queerness** *noun*

**quell** *verb* suppress, reduce to submission; *quelled the rebellion.*

**quench** *verb* **1** extinguish (a fire or flame). **2** satisfy (one's thirst) by drinking. **3** cool (a heated thing) by water.

**quern** *noun* a hand-mill for grinding corn.

**querulous** (**kwe**-rew-lŭs) *adjective* complaining peevishly. □ **querulously** *adverb*

**query** *noun* **1** a question. **2** a question mark. ● *verb* (**queried**, **querying**) ask a question or express doubt about.

**quest** *noun* a search; the thing being sought.

**question** *noun* **1** a sentence requesting information or an answer. **2** something being discussed or for discussion; a problem requiring solution. **3** the raising of doubt; *whether we shall win is open to question.* ● *verb* **1** ask questions of (a person). **2** express doubt about. □ **in question** being referred to or discussed; being disputed; *his honesty is not in question.* **no question of** no possibility of. **out of the question** completely impracticable. **question mark** a punctuation mark (?) placed after a question. **question-master** *noun* the person who puts the questions to people in a quiz game. **question time** a period in Parliament when MPs may question ministers. □ **questioner** *noun*, **questioning** *adjective* & *noun*

**questionable** *adjective* open to doubt or suspicion. □ **questionably** *adverb*

**questionnaire** (kwes-chŏn-**air**) *noun* a list of questions seeking information about people's opinions or customs etc.

**queue** *noun* a line or series of people awaiting their turn for something. ●*verb* (**queued, queuing** or **queueing**) wait in a queue; *queuing up.*

**quibble** *noun* a petty objection. ●*verb* make petty objections. □ **quibbler** *noun*

**quiche** (*pronounced* keesh) *noun* an open tart, usually with a savoury egg filling.

**quick** *adjective* **1** taking only a short time. **2** able to notice, learn, or think quickly. **3** (of temper) easily roused. **4** (*old use*) alive; *the quick and the dead.* ●*noun* the sensitive flesh below the nails. ●*adverb* quickly; *quick-drying.* □ **be cut to the quick** have one's feelings deeply hurt. **quick-fire** *adjective* rapid, in quick succession. **quick-freeze** *verb* freeze (food) rapidly. **quick-tempered** *adjective* easily angered. **quick-witted** *adjective* quick at understanding a situation or making jokes. □ **quickly** *adverb*

**quicken** *verb* **1** make or become quicker. **2** stimulate, make or become livelier; *our interest quickened.* **3** reach a stage in pregnancy when the foetus makes movements that can be felt by the mother.

**quickie** *noun* (*informal*) something done or made quickly or hastily.

**quicklime** *noun* = LIME[1].

**quicksand** *noun* an area of loose wet deep sand into which heavy objects will sink.

**quickset** *adjective* (of a hedge) formed of plants (especially hawthorn) grown as hedging.

**quicksilver** *noun* mercury.

**quickstep** *noun* a ballroom dance with quick steps; music for this.

**quid** *noun* **1** (*plural* **quid**) (*slang*) £1. **2** a lump of tobacco for chewing. □ **quids in** (*slang*) in a position of profit.

**quiddity** *noun* **1** the essence of a thing. **2** a quibble.

**quid pro quo** (*plural* **quid pro quos**) a thing given or done in return for something else. (¶ Latin, = something for something.)

**quiescent** (kwi-**ess**-ĕnt) *adjective* inactive, quiet. □ **quiescence** *noun*

**quiet** *adjective* **1** with little or no sound, not loud or noisy. **2** with little or no movement. **3** free from disturbance or vigorous activity, peaceful. **4** silent; *be quiet!* **5** unobtrusive, done in a restrained manner; *had a quiet laugh about it.* **6** (of colours or dress etc.) subdued, not showy. ●*noun* quietness. ●*verb* make or become quiet, calm. □ **on the quiet** unobtrusively; secretly. □ **quietly** *adverb,* **quietness** *noun*

**quieten** *verb* make or become quiet.

**quietism** (**kwy**-ĕ-tizm) *noun* a passive contemplative attitude to life, as a form of religious mysticism. □ **quietist** *noun & adjective*

**quietude** (**kwy**-i-tewd) *noun* quietness.

**quietus** (kwy-ee-tūs) *noun* release from life; final riddance, death.

**quiff** *noun* an upright tuft of hair brushed upward above the forehead.

**quill** *noun* **1** one of the large feathers on a bird's wing or tail. **2** (in full **quill pen**) an old type of pen made from this. **3** each of a porcupine's spines. **4** the hollow stem of a feather.

**quilt** *noun* a padded bed-cover. ●*verb* line with padding and fix with patterns of stitching.

**quin** *noun* a quintuplet.

**quince** *noun* **1** a hard yellowish pear-shaped fruit used for making jam. **2** the shrub bearing it.

**quincentenary** (kwin-sen-**teen**-er-i) *noun* a 500th anniversary.

**quincunx** *noun* five objects in the shape of a square or rectangle with one in each corner and one in the middle.

**quinine** (kwin-**een**) *noun* a bitter-tasting drug obtained from cinchona bark, used to treat malaria and in tonics.

**Quinquagesima** (kwinkwă-**jess**-imă) *noun* the Sunday before Lent (50 days before Easter).

**quinquennial** (kwin-**kwen**-iăl) *adjective* **1** lasting for five years. **2** happening every fifth year. □ **quinquennially** *adverb*

**quinquereme** *noun* an ancient Roman galley with five rows of oarsmen on each side.

**quinsy** (**kwin**-zi) *noun* a severe inflammation of the throat, often with an abscess on one of the tonsils.

**quintessence** (kwin-**tess**-ĕns) *noun* **1** an essence of a substance. **2** the essence or essential part of a theory, speech, condition, etc. **3** a perfect example of a quality. □ **quintessential** (kwin-ti-**sen**-shăl) *adjective,* **quintessentially** *adverb*

**quintet** *noun* **1** a group of five instruments or voices; a musical composition for these. **2** a set of five.

**quintuple** (**kwin**-tew-pŭl) *adjective* **1** consisting of five parts; involving five people. **2** five times as much. ●*verb* multiply by five.

**quintuplet** (**kwin**-tew-plit) *noun* each of five children born at one birth.

**quip** *noun* a witty or sarcastic remark. ●*verb* (**quipped, quipping**) utter as a quip.

**quire** *noun* a set of 25 (formerly 24) sheets of paper.

**quirk** *noun* **1** a peculiarity of a person's behaviour. **2** a trick of fate. □ **quirky** *adjective*

**quisling** (**kwiz**-ling) *noun* a traitor, especially one who collaborates with an enemy occupying his or her country. (¶ Named after V. Quisling, a pro-Nazi Norwegian leader in the Second World War.)

**quit** *verb* (**quitted** or **quit, quitting**) **1** go away from, leave; *gave him notice to quit.* **2** give up or abandon (a task etc.). **3** (especially *Amer.*) cease; *quit grumbling.* ●*adjective* (foll. by *of*) rid; *glad to be quit of the trouble.*

**quitch** *noun* (in full **quitch-grass**) couch grass.

**quite** *adverb* **1** completely, entirely; *quite finished.* **2** to some extent, somewhat; *quite a long time.* **3** really, actually; *it's quite a change.* **4** (as an answer) I agree; *quite so.* □ **quite a few** a considerable number. **quite something** a remarkable thing or person.

**Quito** (**kee**-toh) the capital of Ecuador.

**quits** *adjective* even with; on even terms as a result of retaliation or repayment. □ **call it quits** acknowledge that things are now even; agree to cease quarrelling.

**quitter** *noun* (*informal*) a person who gives up too easily.

**quiver**[1] *noun* a case for holding arrows.

**quiver**[2] *verb* shake or vibrate with a slight rapid motion. ●*noun* a quivering movement or sound.

**quixotic** (kwik-**sot**-ik) *adjective* chivalrous and unselfish to an extravagant or impractical extent. □ **quixotically** *adverb* (¶ Named after Don Quixote, hero of a Spanish story by Cervantes.)

**quiz** *noun* (*plural* **quizzes**) **1** a series of questions testing people's knowledge, as a form of entertainment. **2** an interrogation or examination. ●*verb* (**quizzed, quizzing**) examine by questioning.

**quizzical** (**kwiz**-ikăl) *adjective* **1** done in a questioning way. **2** gently amused. □ **quizzically** *adverb*

**quod** *noun* (*slang*) prison; *in quod.*

**quoin** (*pronounced* koin) *noun* **1** an external angle of a building. **2** a cornerstone.

**quoit** (*pronounced* koit) *noun* a ring of metal, rubber, or rope thrown to encircle a peg in the game of **quoits**.

**quondam** *adjective* that once was; former; *his quondam friend.*

**quorate** (**kwor**-ayt) *adjective* having or constituting a quorum.

**quorum** (**kwor**-ŭm) *noun* the minimum number of people that must be present at a meeting before its proceedings are valid.

**quota** *noun* **1** a fixed share that must be done, contributed, or received. **2** the maximum number or amount of people or things that may be admitted e.g. to a country or institution or allowed as exports.

**quotable** *adjective* worth quoting.

**quotation** *noun* **1** quoting; being quoted. **2** a passage quoted. **3** an amount stated as the current price of stocks or commodities. **4** a contractor's statement of the sum for which he or she is willing to do a job. □ **quotation marks** punctuation marks (either single ' ' or double " ") enclosing words quoted or put round a slang or similar word.

**quote** *verb* **1** repeat or write out words from a book or speech; *quote from the Bible; quoting Shakespeare.* **2** mention in support of a statement; *can you quote a recent example?* **3** state the price of (goods or services); give a quotation or estimate. **4** (in dictation etc.) begin the quotation, open the inverted commas (compare UNQUOTE).

**quoth** (*rhymes with* both) *verb* (*old use*) (only used with *I, he,* or *she*) said.

**quotidian** (kwŏ-**tid**-iăn) *adjective* **1** daily; (of a fever) recurring every day. **2** everyday, commonplace.

**quotient** (**kwoh**-shĕnt) *noun* the result obtained when one amount is divided by another (e.g. 3 in '12 ÷ 4 = 3').

**q.v.** *abbreviation* which see (used as an indication that the reader should look at the reference given). (¶ From the Latin *quod vide.*)

**qwerty** *adjective* denoting the standard layout of English-language keyboards, with these letters as the first keys on the top row of letters.

# Rr

**R** *abbreviation* (also **R.**) **1** Regina; *Elizabeth R.* **2** Rex; *George R.* **3** (in names) river. **4** (also ®) registered as a trade mark. **5** *Chess* rook.

**r.** *abbreviation* **1** right. **2** radius.

**RA** *abbreviation* **1** Royal Academician. **2** Royal Academy. **3** Royal Artillery.

**Ra** (*pronounced* rah) (*Egyptian myth.*) the sun-god.

**Ra** *symbol* radium.

**Rabat** the capital of Morocco.

**rabbet** *noun* a step-shaped channel cut along the edge of a piece of wood etc. to receive another piece or the glass of a window etc. ●*verb* (**rabbeted, rabbeting**) **1** join or fix with a rabbet. **2** cut a rabbet in.

**rabbi** (**rab-I**) *noun* (*plural* **rabbis**) **1** the religious leader of a Jewish congregation. **2** a Jewish scholar or teacher, especially of the law.

**rabbinical** (**ră-bin-**ikăl) *adjective* of rabbis or Jewish doctrines or law.

**rabbit** *noun* **1** a burrowing animal with long ears and a short fluffy tail. **2** (*informal*) a person who is a poor performer at a game, especially tennis. ●*verb* (**rabbited, rabbiting**) **1** hunt rabbits. **2** (often foll. by *on*) talk lengthily or in a rambling way. □ **rabbit punch** a short chop with the edge of the hand on the back of a person's neck. **Welsh rabbit** *see* WELSH.

**rabble** *noun* **1** a disorderly crowd; a mob. **2** (**the rabble**) the common people, the lowest social classes.

**Rabelais** (**rab-**ĕ-lay), François (*c.* 1494– 1553), French writer.

**rabid** (**rab-**id) *adjective* **1** furious; fanatical; *rabid hate; a rabid Socialist.* **2** affected with rabies. □ **rabidly** *adverb*, **rabidity** (ră-**bid-**iti) *noun*

**rabies** (**ray-**beez) *noun* a contagious fatal virus disease affecting dogs and similar animals, transmitted to humans by the bite of an infected animal.

**Rabin** (ra-**been**), Yitzhak (born 1922), Israeli statesman, Prime Minister from 1992.

**RAC** *abbreviation* Royal Automobile Club.

**raccoon** alternative spelling of RACOON.

**race¹** *noun* **1** a contest of speed in reaching a certain point or in doing or achieving something. **2** (**the races**) a series of races for horses or dogs at fixed times on a regular course. **3** a strong fast current of water. **4** a channel of a stream etc. ●*verb* **1** compete in a race; have a race with. **2** move or cause to move or operate at full speed. □ **race meeting** a horse-racing fixture. □ **racer** *noun*

**race²** *noun* **1** any of the great divisions of humankind with certain inherited physical characteristics in common; a number of people related by common descent. **2** a genus, species, breed, or variety of animals or plants. □ **the human race** human beings collectively. **race relations** relations between members of different races in the same country.

**racecourse** *noun* a ground where horse races are run.

**racehorse** *noun* a horse bred or kept for racing.

**raceme** (ră-**seem**) *noun* flowers evenly spaced along a central stem, with the ones at the base opening first (as in lupins, laburnum, etc.).

**racetrack** *noun* **1** = RACECOURSE. **2** a motor-racing circuit.

**Rachmaninov** (rak-**man-**in-off), Sergei Vasilyevich (1873–1943), Russian composer, noted especially for his piano music.

**racial** (**ray-**shăl) *adjective* of or based on race. □ **racially** *adverb*

**racialism** (**ray-**shăl-izm) *noun* = RACISM. □ **racialist** *noun & adjective*

**Racine** (ra-**seen**), Jean (1639–99), French dramatist.

**racism** (**ray-**sizm) *noun* **1** belief in the superiority of a particular race; prejudice based on this. **2** antagonism towards people of other races. □ **racist** *noun & adjective*

**rack** *noun* **1** a framework with bars or pegs for holding things or for hanging things on. **2** a bar or rail with teeth or cogs into which those of a wheel or gear etc. fit. **3** an instrument of torture on which people were tied and stretched. ●*verb* **1** inflict great torment on; *was racked with pain.* **2** draw off (wine or beer) from the lees. □ **go to rack and ruin** be destroyed; disintegrate; break down. **rack one's brains** think hard about a problem. **rack-railway** *noun* a railway having a cogged rail with which a cogged wheel on the train engages. **rack-rent** *noun* an excessively high rent.

**racket¹** *noun* (also **racquet**) **1** a stringed bat used in tennis and similar games. **2** (**rackets**) a ball game for two or four people played with rackets in a four-walled court.

**racket²** *noun* **1** a din, a noisy fuss. **2** a business or other activity in which dishonest methods are used. **3** (*slang*) a line of business; a dodge. ●*verb* move about noisily; engage in wild social activities; *racketing about.*

**racketeer** *noun* a person who runs a dishonest business. □ **racketeering** *noun*

**raconteur** (rak-on-**ter**) *noun* a person who is good at telling entertaining stories.

**racoon** *noun* (also **raccoon**) (*plural* **racoon** or **racoons**) a North American animal with a bushy tail, sharp snout, and greyish-brown fur.

**racquet** alternative spelling of RACKET[1].

**racy** *adjective* (**racier**, **raciest**) spirited and vigorous in style; *a racy description of his adventures.* □ **racily** *adverb*, **raciness** *noun*

**rad** *noun* a unit of absorbed dose of ionizing radiation.

**RADA** *abbreviation* Royal Academy of Dramatic Art.

**radar** *noun* **1** a system for detecting the presence, position, or movement of objects by sending out short radio waves which they reflect. **2** apparatus used for this. □ **radar trap** a device using radar to detect vehicles travelling faster than the speed limit.

**raddle** *noun* red ochre. ●*verb* colour with raddle or too much rouge.

**raddled** *adjective* worn out.

**radial** (**ray**-di-ăl) *adjective* of rays or radii; having spokes or lines etc. that radiate from a central point. ●*noun* a radial-ply tyre. □ **radial-ply** *adjective* (of a tyre) having fabric layers with cords lying radial to the hub of the wheel (compare CROSS-PLY). □ **radially** *adverb*

**radian** (**ray**-di-ăn) *noun* an SI unit of plane angle; the angle at the centre of a circle formed by the radii of an arc equal in length to the radius.

**radiant** *adjective* **1** giving out rays of light. **2** looking very bright and happy. **3** transmitting heat by radiation; (of heat) transmitted in this way. □ **radiantly** *adverb*, **radiance** *noun*

**radiate** *verb* **1** spread outwards (especially in lines or rays) from a central point. **2** send out (light or heat etc.) in rays; be sent out as radiation. **3** give out a feeling of; *she radiated confidence.*

**radiation** *noun* **1** radiating; being radiated. **2** the sending out of the rays and atomic particles characteristic of radioactive substances; these rays and particles. □ **radiation sickness** sickness caused by exposure to radiation.

**radiator** *noun* **1** a device for heating a room, consisting of a metal case through which steam or hot water circulates, or one heated electrically. **2** an engine-cooling apparatus in a motor vehicle or aircraft.

**radical** *adjective* **1** going to the root or foundation of something, fundamental. **2** drastic, thorough; *radical changes.* **3** desiring radical reforms; holding extremist views. ●*noun* **1** a person desiring radical reforms or holding extremist views. **2** a group of atoms forming part of a compound and remaining unaltered during the compound's ordinary chemical changes. **3** the root of a word. **4** a mathematical quantity forming or expressed as the root of another. □ **radically** *adverb*, **radicalism** *noun*

**radicchio** (ră-**dee**-kioh) *noun* (*plural* **radicchios**) a variety of chicory with reddish-purple leaves.

**radicle** *noun* an embryo root (e.g. of a pea or bean).

**radii** *see* RADIUS.

**radio** *noun* (*plural* **radios**) **1** the process of sending and receiving messages etc. by invisible electromagnetic radiation. **2** an apparatus for sending or receiving messages etc. in this way; a transmitter or receiver. **3** sound broadcasting; a sound-broadcasting station; *Radio Oxford.* ●*adjective* **1** of or using radio. **2** of or involving stars etc. from which radio waves are received or reflected; *radio astronomy.* ●*verb* (**radioed**, **radioing**) send, signal, or communicate with by radio. □ **radio-controlled** *adjective* controlled from a distance by radio signals. **radio frequency** the frequency band of telecommunication, ranging from $10^4$ to $10^{11}$ or $10^{12}$ Hz. **radiotelephone** *noun* a telephone operating by radio signals rather than electronic signals sent along cables. **radio telescope** an instrument used to detect radio emissions from the sky, whether from natural celestial objects or from artificial satellites.

**radioactive** *adjective* of or showing radioactivity.

**radioactivity** *noun* the property of having atoms that break up spontaneously and send out radiation capable of penetrating opaque bodies and producing electrical and chemical effects.

**radiocarbon** *noun* a radioactive form of carbon that is present in organic materials and is used in carbon dating (*see* CARBON).

**radiogram** *noun* an old-fashioned piece of furniture incorporating a radio and a record player.

**radiograph** *noun* **1** an instrument recording the intensity of radiation. **2** an X-ray picture.

**radiography** (ray-di-**og**-răfi) *noun* the production of X-ray photographs. □ **radiographer** *noun*

**radioisotope** *noun* a radioactive isotope that decays spontaneously.

# radiology | raillery

**radiology** (ray-di-**ol**-ŏji) *noun* the scientific study of X-rays and similar radiation. □ **radiologist** *noun*

**radiophonic** *adjective* relating to electronically produced sound, music, etc.

**radioscopy** *noun* examination by X-rays of opaque objects.

**radiotherapy** *noun* treatment of disease etc. by X-rays or similar forms of radiation.

**radish** *noun* **1** a plant with a crisp root that is eaten raw. **2** its root.

**radium** *noun* a radioactive metallic element (symbol Ra), obtained from pitchblende.

**radius** *noun* (*plural* **radii**, *pronounced* **ray**-di-I, *or* **radiuses**) **1** a straight line extending from the centre of a circle or sphere to its circumference. **2** the length of this line; the distance from a centre; *within a radius of 20 miles*. **3** the thicker of the two long bones in the forearm; the corresponding bone in animals.

**radix** (**ray**-diks) *noun* (*plural* **radices**) a number or symbol used as the basis of a numeration scale (e.g. ten in the decimal system).

**radon** (**ray**-don) *noun* a chemical element, a radioactive gas (symbol Rn).

**RAF** *abbreviation* Royal Air Force.

**raffia** *noun* soft fibre from the leaves of a palm tree, used for tying plants, making mats, etc.

**raffish** *adjective* vulgarly flashy, disreputable, or rakish. □ **raffishness** *noun*

**raffle** *noun* a lottery with an object as the prize, especially as a method of raising money for a charity. ● *verb* offer (a thing) as the prize in a raffle.

**Raffles**, Sir Thomas Stamford Bingley (1781–1826), English colonial administrator, founder of Singapore.

**Rafsanjani**, Ali Akbar Hashemi (born 1934), Iranian cleric and statesman, President from 1989.

**raft** *noun* **1** a flat floating structure used especially as a substitute for a boat. **2** a large collection; *a raft of unions*.

**rafter** *noun* one of the sloping beams forming the framework of a roof.

**rag**[1] *noun* **1** a torn or worn piece of fabric. **2** (**rags**) old torn clothes. **3** rags used as material for stuffing things, making paper etc. **4** (*informal, scornful*) a newspaper. □ **rag-and-bone man** an itinerant dealer in old clothes and discarded articles. **rag-bag** *noun* **1** a bag for scraps of fabric etc. **2** a miscellaneous collection. **rag trade** (*informal*) the clothing business.

**rag**[2] *verb* (**ragged**, **ragging**) tease, play practical jokes on (a person). ● *noun* **1** a practical joke, a piece of fun. **2** a programme of stunts, parades, and entertainment organized by students to collect money for charity.

**rag**[3] *noun* a piece of ragtime music.

**raga** (**rah**-gă) *noun* (in Indian music) **1** notes used as a basis for improvisation. **2** a piece of music using a particular raga.

**ragamuffin** *noun* **1** a child in ragged dirty clothes. **2** = RAGGA.

**rage** *noun* violent anger; a fit of this. ● *verb* **1** show violent anger. **2** (of a storm or battle etc.) be violent; continue furiously. □ **all the rage** very popular or fashionable.

**ragga** *noun* (also **ragamuffin**) a style of pop music derived from reggae but with faster more electronic elements; a follower of this style.

**ragged** (**rag**-id) *adjective* **1** torn, frayed. **2** wearing torn clothes. **3** jagged. **4** faulty, lacking finish, smoothness, or uniformity; *a ragged performance*. □ **ragged robin** a crimson-flowered campion with ragged petals. □ **raggedly** *adverb*, **raggedness** *noun*

**raglan** *noun* a sleeve that continues to the neck and is joined to the body of the garment by sloping seams.

**ragout** (ra-**goo**) *noun* a stew of meat and vegetables.

**ragtag and bobtail** riff-raff, common people.

**ragtime** *noun* a form of jazz music with much syncopation.

**ragwort** *noun* a wild plant with yellow flowers and ragged leaves.

**raid** *noun* **1** a sudden military attack and withdrawal. **2** an attack made in order to steal. **3** a surprise visit by police etc. to arrest suspected people or seize illicit goods. ● *verb* make a raid on (a place etc.). □ **raider** *noun*

**rail**[1] *noun* **1** a horizontal or sloping bar forming part of a fence or barrier or for hanging things on. **2** one of the metal lines on which trains or trams run. **3** railways as a means of transport; *send it by rail*. **4** a horizontal piece in the frame of a panelled door etc. ● *verb* fit or enclose with a rail; *rail it off*. □ **go off the rails** (*informal*) become disorganized, out of control or crazy.

**rail**[2] *noun* a small wading bird.

**rail**[3] *verb* (often foll. by *at* or *against*) complain or protest strongly; *railing at him*.

**railcar** *noun* a self-propelled railway coach.

**railcard** *noun* (*Brit.*) a pass entitling the holder to reduced rail fares.

**railhead** *noun* **1** the furthest point yet reached by a railway under construction. **2** the point on a railway at which goods are transferred to and from road transport.

**railing** *noun* a fence of rails supported on upright metal bars.

**raillery** *noun* good-humoured joking or teasing.

**railman** noun (plural **railmen**) a railwayman.

**railroad** noun (Amer.) a railway. ●verb rush or force into hasty action; railroaded him into accepting.

**railway** noun **1** a set of rails on which trains run. **2** a system of transport using these; the organization required for its working.

**railwayman** noun (plural **railwaymen**) a railway employee.

**raiment** noun (old use) clothing.

**rain** noun **1** condensed moisture of the atmosphere falling in drops. **2** a fall of this. **3** (**the rains**) the rainy season in tropical countries. **4** a shower of things. ●verb send down rain; fall as or like rain. □ **be rained off** (Amer. **rained out**) (of an event) be prevented by rain from taking place. **rain check** (especially Amer.) a ticket for an outdoor event allowing a refund or readmission should the event be interrupted by rain. **take a rain check** (informal) defer one's acceptance of an offer.

**rainbow** noun an arch of colours formed in rain or spray by the sun's rays. □ **rainbow trout** a large trout, originally from North America.

**raincoat** noun a water-resistant coat.

**raindrop** noun a single drop of rain.

**rainfall** noun the total amount of rain falling within a given area in a given time.

**rainforest** noun thick forest in tropical areas where there is heavy rainfall.

**rainwater** noun water collected from fallen rain, not obtained from wells etc.

**rainy** adjective (**rainier**, **rainiest**) in or on which much rain falls. □ **save for a rainy day** save (money etc.) for a time when one may need it.

**raise** verb **1** bring to or towards a higher or upright position. **2** increase the amount or level of; raise prices. **3** cause, rouse, or produce; raise doubts; raise a laugh; raise a loan. **4** breed, rear, or grow; raise sheep; raise a family. **5** put forward; raise objections. ●noun (Amer.) an increase in wages or salary. □ **raise Cain** or **raise the roof** (informal) make an uproar; show great anger. **raise from the dead** restore to life. **raise the alarm** give a warning of imminent danger. **raising agent** a substance (e.g. yeast or baking powder) that makes bread or cake swell and become light in texture.

**raisin** noun a dried grape.

**raison d'être** (ray-zawn **detr**) (plural **raisons d'être**, pronounced same) the reason for or purpose of a thing's existence. (¶ French.)

**raj** (pronounced rahj) noun the period of British rule in India.

**raja** (rah-jä) noun (also **rajah**) (in former times) an Indian king or prince.

**Rajasthan** (rah-jä-stahn) a State in NW India. □ **Rajasthani** adjective & noun

**rake¹** noun **1** a long-handled tool with prongs used for drawing together hay, fallen leaves, etc. or for smoothing loose soil. **2** an implement resembling this, used e.g. by a croupier at a gaming-table. ●verb **1** gather or smooth with a rake. **2** search; have been raking through old records. **3** direct gunfire along (a line) from end to end; direct one's eyes or a camera in this way. □ **rake-off** noun (informal) a commission or share of profits. **rake up** revive the memory of (an unpleasant incident).

**rake²** noun a slope (e.g. of a ship's mast or funnel, or of a driver's seat). ●verb set at a sloping angle.

**rake³** noun (old use) a man of fashion who lives an irresponsible and immoral life.

**rakish** adjective dashing, jaunty, and perhaps immoral. □ **rakishly** adverb, **rakishness** noun

**Raleigh** (rah-li or raw-li), Sir Walter (c.1552–1618), Elizabethan explorer, who organized several voyages to North America.

**rallentando** adverb & adjective Music with a gradual decrease in speed.

**rally¹** verb (**rallied**, **rallying**) **1** bring or come together for a united effort. **2** rouse or revive; recover one's strength after illness. **3** (of share prices etc.) increase after falling. ●noun **1** an act of rallying; a recovery of energy or spirits. **2** (in tennis etc.) a lengthy series of strokes before a point is scored. **3** a mass meeting of people with a common interest. **4** a driving competition for cars or motor cycles over public roads.

**rally²** verb (**rallied**, **rallying**) tease, ridicule in a good-humoured way.

**RAM** abbreviation **1** Computing random-access memory; a temporary working memory that can be read from and written to. All data in RAM is lost when the computer is turned off. **2** Royal Academy of Music.

**ram** noun **1** an uncastrated male sheep. **2** (**the Ram**) a sign of the zodiac, Aries. **3** a battering-ram. **4** a striking or plunging device in various machines. ●verb (**rammed**, **ramming**) **1** force or drive into place by pressure. **2** crash against. □ **ram-raider** noun a criminal who carries out ram-raiding. **ram-raiding** noun robbery by ramming the front of a shop using a large vehicle, looting the shop, and escaping in the vehicle.

**Ramadan** (ram-ä-dan) noun the ninth month of the Muslim year, when Muslims fast between sunrise and sunset.

**Raman** (rah-män), Sir Chandrasekhara Venkata (1888–1970), Indian physicist.

**Ramayana** (rah-**my**-ănă) *noun* a Sanskrit epic poem composed *c.*300 BC.

**Rambert** (**rahm**-bair), Dame Marie (1888–1982), British dancer, teacher, and ballet director, born in Poland.

**ramble** *verb* **1** walk for pleasure. **2** talk or write disconnectedly; wander from the subject. ●*noun* a walk taken for pleasure.

**rambler** *noun* **1** a person who rambles; one who goes for a ramble. **2** a climbing rose.

**rambling** *adjective* **1** wandering. **2** speaking, spoken, or written disconnectedly, wandering from one subject to another. **3** (of a plant) straggling, climbing. **4** (of a house, street, village, etc.) extending in various directions irregularly.

**Rambo** the violent hero of David Morrell's novel *First Blood* (popularized in films).

**Rameau**, Jean-Philippe (1683–1764), French composer.

**ramekin** (**ram**-i-kin) *noun* a small mould for baking and serving an individual portion of food.

**Rameses** (**ram**-seez) the name of 11 Egyptian pharaohs, of whom the most famous are **Rameses II** 'the Great' (1290–1224 BC) and **Rameses III** (1194–1163 BC).

**ramification** *noun* (usually as **ramifications**) **1** an arrangement of branching parts; a part of a complex structure. **2** a consequence; an indirect result.

**ramify** *verb* (**ramified**, **ramifying**) form or cause to form into branching parts.

**ramp** *noun* **1** a slope joining two levels. **2** a movable set of stairs put beside an aircraft. **3** a ridge across a road.

**rampage** *verb* (*pronounced* ram-**payj**) rush about wildly or destructively. ●*noun* (*pronounced* **ram**-payj) violent behaviour. □ **on the rampage** rampaging.

**rampant** *adjective* **1** unrestrained, flourishing excessively; *disease was rampant in the poorer districts.* **2** (in heraldry) (of an animal) standing on one hind leg with the opposite foreleg raised; *a lion rampant.* □ **rampancy** *noun*

**rampart** *noun* a broad bank of earth built as a fortification, usually topped with a parapet.

**ramrod** *noun* an iron rod formerly used for ramming a charge into muzzle-loading guns. □ **like a ramrod** stiff and straight.

**Ramsay** (**ram**-zi), Sir William (1852–1916), Scottish chemist, noted for his work on gases.

**ramshackle** *adjective* tumbledown, rickety.

**ran** *see* RUN.

**ranch** *noun* **1** a cattle-breeding establishment, especially in North America. **2** a farm where certain other animals are bred; *a mink ranch.* ●*verb* farm on a ranch. □ **rancher** *noun*

**rancid** (**ran**-sid) *adjective* smelling or tasting unpleasant like stale fat. □ **rancidity** (ran-**sid**-iti) *noun*

**rancour** (**rank**-er) *noun* (*Amer.* **rancor**) bitter feeling or ill will. □ **rancorous** *adjective*

**rand** *noun* the unit of money in South Africa.

**R & B** *abbreviation* rhythm and blues.

**R & D** *abbreviation* research and development.

**random** *adjective* done, made, or taken etc. at random; *a random choice.* □ **at random** without a particular aim, purpose, or principle. **random-access** *Computing* (of a memory or file) having all parts directly accessible, so that it need not be read sequentially; *see also* RAM. □ **randomly** *adverb*

**randy** *adjective* (**randier**, **randiest**) lustful, sexually aroused. □ **randiness** *noun*

**ranee** (**rah**-nee) *noun* (also **rani**) a raja's wife or widow.

**rang** *see* RING².

**range** *noun* **1** a line or tier or series of things; *a range of mountains.* **2** an extent, the limits between which something operates or varies. **3** the distance over which one can see or hear, or to which a sound, signal, or missile can travel; the distance that a ship or aircraft etc. can travel without refuelling. **4** the distance to a thing being aimed at or looked at; *at close range.* **5** a large open stretch of grazing or hunting ground. **6** a place with targets for shooting-practice. **7** a fireplace with ovens etc. for cooking in. ●*verb* **1** arrange in a row or ranks or in a specified way. **2** extend, reach. **3** vary between limits. **4** wander or go about a place.

**rangefinder** *noun* a device for calculating the distance of an object to be shot at or photographed.

**ranger** *noun* **1** a keeper of a royal or national park or forest. **2** a member of a body of mounted troops policing a thinly populated area. **3** (**Ranger**) a senior Guide.

**Rangoon** (rang-**oon**) (from 1989 officially called **Yangon**) the capital of Burma.

**rangy** (**rayn**-ji) *adjective* tall and thin.

**rani** alternative spelling of RANEE.

**Rank**, Joseph Arthur, 1st Baron (1888–1972), English industrialist and film executive, founder of the Rank Organization.

**rank¹** *noun* **1** a line of people or things. **2** a place where taxis stand to await hire. **3** a place in a scale of quality or value etc.; a position or grade; *ministers of Cabinet rank.* **4** high social position; *people of rank.* **5** (the **ranks**) ordinary soldiers, not officers. ●*verb* **1** arrange in a rank. **2** assign a rank to. **3** have a certain rank or place; *he ranks among the great statesmen.* □ **close ranks** maintain solidarity. **the rank and file** the ordinary undistinguished people of an organization.

**rank²** *adjective* **1** growing too thickly and coarsely. **2** (of land) full of weeds. **3** foul-smelling. **4** unmistakably bad; out-and-out; *rank injustice*.

**rankle** *verb* cause lasting and bitter annoyance or resentment.

**ransack** *verb* **1** search thoroughly or roughly. **2** rob or pillage (a place).

**ransom** *noun* the release of a captive in return for payment demanded by the captors; the payment itself. ● *verb* **1** obtain the release of (a captive) in return for payment. **2** hold (a captive) to ransom. □ **hold to ransom** hold (a captive) and demand ransom for his or her release; demand concessions from (a person etc.) by threatening some damaging action.

**rant** *verb* make a speech loudly and violently and theatrically.

**rap** *noun* **1** a quick sharp blow or knock. **2** (*slang*) blame, punishment. **3** (*slang*) a chat. **4** a rhyming monologue recited rhythmically to rock music. ● *verb* (**rapped, rapping**) **1** strike quickly and sharply. **2** reprimand. **3** (*slang*) chat. **4** perform a rap. □ **not care** *or* **give a rap** not care at all. **take the rap** (*slang*) suffer the consequences.

**rapacious** (ră-**pay**-shŭs) *adjective* greedy and grasping; plundering and robbing others. □ **rapaciously** *adverb*, **rapacity** (ră-**pas**-iti) *noun*

**rape¹** *noun* the crime of forcing a person (especially a woman) to have sexual intercourse against his or her will. ● *verb* commit rape on (a person).

**rape²** *noun* a plant grown as food for sheep and for its seed from which oil is obtained.

**Raphael** (**raf**-ay-ĕl) Raffaello Sanzio (1483–1520), Italian Renaissance painter and architect.

**rapid** *adjective* **1** quick, swift. **2** (of a slope) descending steeply. **3** (**rapids**) a swift current in a river, caused by a steep downward slope in the river bed. □ **rapid eye movement** jerky eye movements during dreaming. □ **rapidly** *adverb*, **rapidity** (ră-**pid**-iti) *noun*

**rapier** (**rayp**-i-er) *noun* a thin light double-edged sword.

**rapine** (**ra**-pyn) *noun* plundering.

**rapist** (**ray**-pist) *noun* a person who commits rape.

**rapport** (rap-**or**) *noun* a harmonious and understanding relationship between people.

**rapprochement** (ra-**prosh**-mahn) *noun* a resumption of friendly relations, especially between countries. (¶ French.)

**rapscallion** *noun* a rascal.

**rapt** *adjective* very intent and absorbed, enraptured. □ **raptly** *adverb*

**raptorial** (rap-**tor**-iăl) *adjective* predatory.

**rapture** *noun* intense delight. □ **in raptures** feeling or expressing rapture. □ **rapturous** *adjective*, **rapturously** *adverb*

**rare¹** *adjective* **1** seldom found; very uncommon. **2** (*informal*) exceptionally good; *had a rare time*. **3** of low density; thin; *the rare atmosphere in the Himalayas*. □ **rare earth** a lanthanide element, any of a group of metallic elements with similar chemical properties. □ **rarely** *adverb*, **rareness** *noun*

**rare²** *adjective* (of meat) cooked very lightly so that the inside is still red.

**rarebit** *noun* = WELSH RAREBIT.

**rarefied** (**rair**-i-fyd) *adjective* **1** (of air etc.) less dense than is normal; thin, like that on high mountains. **2** (of an idea etc.) very subtle.

**raring** (**rair**-ing) *adjective* (*informal*) enthusiastic; *raring to go*.

**rarity** (**rair**-iti) *noun* **1** rareness. **2** something uncommon; a thing valued because it is rare.

**Ras al Khaimah** (ras al ky-**mă**) an emirate belonging to the federation of United Arab Emirates.

**rascal** *noun* **1** a dishonest person. **2** a mischievous person. □ **rascally** *adjective*

**rase** alternative spelling of RAZE.

**rash** *noun* an eruption of spots or patches on the skin. ● *adjective* acting or done without due consideration of the possible consequences or risks. □ **rashly** *adverb*, **rashness** *noun*

**rasher** *noun* a slice of bacon or ham.

**rasp** *noun* **1** a coarse file with raised sharp points on its surface. **2** a rough grating sound. ● *verb* **1** scrape with a rasp. **2** make a rough grating sound; *a rasping voice*; *he rasped out orders*.

**raspberry** *noun* **1** an edible sweet red conical berry. **2** the bush that bears it. **3** (*slang*) a vulgar sound or expression of disapproval or rejection.

**Rasputin** (ras-**pew**-tin), Grigori Efimovich (1871–1916), Russian religious fanatic, who exerted great influence over the Tsar and his family during the First World War.

**Rastafarian** (ras-tă-**fair**-iăn) *noun* (also **Rasta**) a member of a Jamaican sect regarding the late Emperor Haile Selassie of Ethiopia as God and their true homeland as Africa. ● *adjective* of Rastafarians.

**rat** *noun* **1** a rodent resembling a mouse but larger. **2** an unpleasant or treacherous person. ● *verb* (**ratted, ratting**) withdraw treacherously from an undertaking; break a promise; *he ratted on us*. □ **rat race** a fiercely competitive struggle to maintain one's position in work or life.

**ratable** alternative spelling of RATEABLE.

**rat-a-tat** = RAT-TAT.

**ratatouille** (rah-tah-**too**-i) *noun* a Provençal dish of stewed vegetables (chiefly aubergines, tomatoes, onions, and peppers). (¶ French.)

**ratbag** *noun* (*slang*) an obnoxious person.

**ratchet** (**rach**-it) *noun* **1** a series of notches on a bar or wheel in which a catch engages to prevent backward movement. **2** the bar or wheel bearing these.

**rate** *noun* **1** a standard of reckoning, obtained by expressing the quantity or amount of one thing with respect to another; *walked at a rate of four miles per hour*. **2** a measure of value or charge or cost; *postal rates*. **3** speed; *drove at a great rate*. **4** (**rates**) (*Brit.*) a tax levied by local authorities on businesses (and formerly on private individuals) according to the value of buildings and land; *see also* COUNCIL TAX. ●*verb* **1** estimate the worth or value of. **2** assign a value to. **3** consider, regard as; *we rate him among our benefactors*. **4** rank or be regarded in a certain way; *he rates as a benefactor*. **5** (*informal*) consider to be successful, of high quality etc. **6** (*Amer.*) deserve; *that joke didn't rate a laugh*. **7** levy rates on (property); value (property) for the purpose of assessing rates. **8** scold angrily. □ **at any rate** in any possible case, no matter what happens; at least. **at this** *or* **that rate** if this is true or a typical specimen. **rate-capped** *adjective* (*Brit.*) subjected to **rate-capping**, the imposition by central government of an upper limit on rates that may be levied by local authorities.

**rateable** *adjective* (also **ratable**) liable to rates (*see* RATE *noun* sense 4). □ **rateable value** the value at which a business etc. is assessed for rates.

**ratepayer** *noun* a person liable to pay rates.

**rather** *adverb* **1** slightly; more so than not; *rather dark*. **2** more precisely; as a better alternative; as opposed to; *he is lazy rather than incompetent*. **3** more willingly; by preference; *would rather not go*. **4** (*informal*) emphatically yes; *do you like it? Rather!* □ **had rather** would rather.

**ratify** *verb* (**ratified, ratifying**) confirm or accept (an agreement, treaty, etc.), especially by signing it. □ **ratification** *noun*

**rating** *noun* **1** the classification assigned to a person or thing in respect of quality, popularity, etc. **2** the amount payable as a local rate. **3** a non-commissioned sailor. **4** an angry reprimand.

**ratio** (**ray**-shi-oh) *noun* (*plural* **ratios**) the relationship between two amounts reckoned as the number of times one contains the other.

**ratiocinate** (rat-i-**oss**-in-ayt) *verb* (*literary*) reason, especially in a formal way. □ **ratiocination** *noun*

**ration** *noun* a fixed quantity (especially of food) allowed to one person. ●*verb* limit (food etc.) to a fixed ration; allow (a person) only a certain amount.

**rational** *adjective* **1** able to reason. **2** sane. **3** based on reasoning, using reason or logic and rejecting explanations that involve the supernatural etc. □ **rationally** *adverb*, **rationality** (rash-ŏn-**al**-iti) *noun*

**rationale** (rash-ŏn-**ahl**) *noun* the logical basis of something; the fundamental reason for it.

**rationalism** *noun* using rational explanations as the basis of belief and knowledge. □ **rationalist** *noun & adjective*, **rationalistic** *adjective*

**rationalize** *verb* (also **rationalise**) **1** make logical and consistent; *tried to rationalize English spelling*. **2** put forward a rational explanation of; *tried to rationalize their fears*. **3** make (a process or an industry) more efficient by reorganizing so as to eliminate waste of labour, time, or materials. □ **rationalization** *noun*

**ratline** (**rat**-lin) *noun* (also **ratlin**) any of the small lines fastened across a ship's shrouds like rungs of a ladder.

**ratsbane** *noun* anything poisonous to rats, especially a plant.

**rattan** (rat-**an**) *noun* **1** a climbing palm with long thin jointed pliable stems, used for furniture-making. **2** a piece of this stem used as a walking stick etc.

**rat-tat** *noun* (also **rat-a-tat**) a rapping sound, especially of a knocker.

**ratter** *noun* a dog as a hunter of rats.

**Rattigan**, Sir Terence Mervyn (1911–77), English playwright.

**ratting** *noun* hunting rats.

**rattle** *verb* **1** make or cause to make a rapid series of short sharp hard sounds especially by shaking. **2** move or travel with a rattling noise. **3** (usually foll. by *off*) utter rapidly; *rattled off the oath*. **4** (usually foll. by *on*) chatter idly. **5** (*informal*) alarm, agitate, or fluster. ●*noun* **1** a rattling sound. **2** a device or toy for making a rattling sound.

**rattlesnake** *noun* a poisonous American snake with a rattling structure in its tail.

**rattletrap** *noun* a rickety old vehicle.

**rattling** *adjective* **1** that rattles. **2** vigorous, brisk; *a rattling pace*. ●*adverb* (*informal*) very; *a rattling good story*.

**ratty** *adjective* (**rattier, rattiest**) (*informal*) angry, irritable.

**raucous** (**raw**-kŭs) *adjective* loud and harsh-sounding. □ **raucously** *adverb*, **raucousness** *noun*

**raunchy** *adjective* (**raunchier, raunchiest**) (*informal*) coarse, earthy, sexually boisterous. □ **raunchily** *adverb*, **raunchiness** *noun*

**ravage** *verb* do great damage to; devastate. ●*plural noun* (**ravages**) damage, devastation.

**rave** *verb* **1** talk wildly or furiously; talk nonsensically in delirium. **2** (of the wind or sea) howl, roar. **3** (foll. by about, over) talk with great enthusiasm. ●*noun* **1** (*informal*) a very enthusiastic review of a book or play etc. **2** (*slang*) a craze. **3** an all-night party with loud rock music attended by large numbers of young people. □ **rave-up** *noun* (*slang*) a lively party.

**Ravel** (ră-**vel**), Maurice (1875–1937), French composer.

**ravel** *verb* (**ravelled, ravelling**; *Amer.* **raveled, raveling**) **1** tangle; become tangled. **2** (usually foll. by *out*) disentangle, unravel.

**raven** *noun* a large bird with glossy black feathers and a hoarse cry. ●*adjective* (especially of hair) glossy black.

**ravening** (rav-ĕn-ing) *adjective* hungrily seeking prey.

**ravenous** (rav-ĕn-ŭs) *adjective* very hungry. □ **ravenously** *adverb*

**raver** *noun* **1** (*informal*) an uninhibited pleasure-loving person. **2** a person attending a rave (*noun* sense 3).

**ravine** (ră-**veen**) *noun* a deep narrow gorge or cleft between mountains.

**raving** *noun* (usually as **ravings**) wild or delirious talk. ●*adjective & adverb* as an intensifier; *raving mad; a raving beauty.*

**ravioli** (rav-i-**oh**-li) *noun* small square pasta cases containing meat or other savoury fillings.

**ravish** *verb* **1** rape. **2** fill with delight, enrapture. □ **ravishment** *noun*

**ravishing** *adjective* very beautiful. □ **ravishingly** *adverb*

**raw** *adjective* **1** not cooked. **2** in its natural state, not yet or not fully processed or manufactured; *raw hides.* **3** crude in artistic quality, lacking finish. **4** inexperienced, untrained; *raw recruits.* **5** stripped of skin and with the underlying flesh exposed. **6** (of an edge of cloth) not a selvage and not hemmed. **7** (of weather) damp and chilly. □ **in the raw 1** naked. **2** in a raw state; crude, without a softening or refining influence; *life in the raw.* **touch on the raw** upset (a person) by raising a sensitive issue. **raw-boned** *adjective* gaunt. **raw deal** unfair treatment. **raw material** any material from which something is made. □ **rawness** *noun*

**rawhide** *noun* untanned leather.

**Rawlplug** *noun* (*trade mark*) a thin cylindrical plug for holding a screw or nail in masonry.

**Ray¹**, John (1627–1705), English naturalist, who developed early systematic classifications of plants and animals.

**Ray²**, Satyajit (1921–92), Indian film director.

**ray** *noun* **1** a single line or narrow beam of light or other radiation. **2** a trace of something good; *a ray of hope.* **3** one of a set of radiating lines, parts, or things. **4** any of several large sea fish related to the shark and used as food, especially the skate. **5** (also **re**) (in music) the second note of a major scale.

**rayon** *noun* a synthetic fibre or fabric made from cellulose.

**raze** *verb* (also **rase**) destroy completely, tear down to the ground.

**razor** *noun* an instrument with a sharp blade used for shaving. □ **razor wire** wire set with small sharp pieces of metal, used as fencing.

**razorbill** *noun* a black and white auk with a sharp bill.

**razzle** *noun* □ **on the razzle** (*slang*) out having a good time. **razzle-dazzle** *noun* (*slang*) excitement, bustle; showy advertising.

**razzmatazz** *noun* (*informal*) showy publicity or display.

**Rb** *symbol* rubidium.

**RC** *abbreviation* Roman Catholic.

**Rd.** *abbreviation* Road.

**RDA** *abbreviation* recommended daily allowance (of vitamins, minerals, etc.).

**RE** *abbreviation* **1** Religious Education. **2** Royal Engineers.

**Re** *symbol* rhenium.

**re¹** (*pronounced* ree) *preposition* in the matter of; about, concerning (in business correspondence).

**re²** alternative spelling of RAY (sense 5).

**re-** *combining form* **1** again (as in *redecorate, revisit*). **2** back again, with return to a previous state (as in *re-enter, reopen*).

■**Usage** A hyphen is normally used when the word begins with *e* (*re-enact*), or to distinguish the compound from a more familiar one-word form (*re-cover* = cover again).

**reach** *verb* **1** stretch out or extend. **2** go as far as, arrive at. **3** stretch out one's hand in order to touch or take something; *reached for his gun.* **4** establish communication with; *you can reach me by phone.* **5** achieve; *reached a speed of 100 m.p.h.; reached a conclusion.* **6** sail with the wind blowing at right angles to the ship's course. ●*noun* **1** an act of reaching. **2** the distance over which a person or thing can reach; the extent covered by one's mental abilities. **3** a continuous extent of a river between two bends or of a canal between two locks. □ **reach-me-down** adjective (informal) ready-made or second-made. □ **reachable** adjective

**react** verb respond to a stimulus; cause or undergo a reaction.

**reaction** noun 1 a response to a stimulus or act or situation etc. 2 a chemical change produced by two or more substances acting upon each other. 3 the occurrence of one condition after a period of the opposite, e.g. of depression after excitement. 4 a bad physical response to a drug.

**reactionary** adjective opposed to progress or reform. ●noun a person who favours reactionary policies.

**reactivate** verb restore to a state of activity. □ **reactivation** noun

**reactive** adjective 1 showing reaction. 2 reacting rather than taking the initiative. 3 susceptible to chemical reaction.

**reactor** noun (also **nuclear reactor**) an apparatus for the controlled production of nuclear energy.

**read** (pronounced reed) verb (**read** (pronounced red), **reading**) 1 be able to understand the meaning of (written or printed words or symbols). 2 speak (written words etc.) aloud; read to the children. 3 carry out a course of study; she's reading Philosophy at Oxford; reading for a degree in French. 4 interpret mentally, find implications; don't read too much into it. 5 have a certain wording; the sign reads 'Keep Left'. 6 (of a computer) copy, extract, or transfer (data). 7 (of a measuring instrument) indicate or register; the thermometer reads 20°. ●noun (informal) 1 a session of reading; had a nice quiet read. 2 a thing in regard to its readability; an interesting read. □ **read between the lines** discover a hidden or implicit meaning. **read-only** adjective (of a computer memory) with contents that can be copied, searched, extracted, or transferred but not changed. **read up** study (a subject) by reading. **well read** adjective (of a person) having knowledge of a subject, especially literature, through reading.

**readable** adjective 1 pleasant and interesting to read. 2 legible. □ **readability** noun

**reader** noun 1 a person who reads. 2 (also **Reader**) a university lecturer of the highest grade below professor. 3 a book containing passages for practice in reading.

**readership** noun 1 the readers of a newspaper etc.; the number of these. 2 (also **Readership**) the position of reader at a university.

**readily** adverb 1 without reluctance, willingly. 2 without difficulty.

**readiness** noun being ready.

**reading** noun 1 the act of one who reads. 2 being read; the way something is read; an occasion when something is read. 3 books etc. intended to be read. 4 the amount that is indicated or registered by a measuring instrument.

**readjust** verb 1 adjust (a thing) again. 2 adapt oneself again. □ **readjustment** noun

**ready** adjective (**readier, readiest**) 1 in a fit state for immediate action or use. 2 willing; always ready to help a friend. 3 about or inclined to do something; looked ready to collapse. 4 quick; a ready wit. 5 easily available; found a ready market. ●adverb beforehand; ready cooked. □ **at the ready** ready for action. **ready-made** adjective (of clothes) made in standard shapes and sizes, not to individual customers' orders; (of opinions or excuses etc.) not original. **ready money** actual coins or notes; payment on the spot, not credit. **ready reckoner** a collection of answers to calculations commonly needed in business etc.

**reafforest** verb (also **reforest**) replant (former forest land) with trees. □ **reafforestation** noun

**Reagan** (ray-găn), Ronald Wilson (born 1911), American Republican statesman, 40th President of the USA 1981-9.

**reagent** (ree-ay-jĕnt) noun a substance used to produce a chemical reaction.

**real** adjective 1 existing as a thing or occurring as a fact, not imaginary. 2 genuine, not imitation; real pearls. 3 true, complete; there's no real cure. 4 (of income or value etc.) with regard to its purchasing power. 5 consisting of immovable property such as land or houses; real estate. ●adverb (Scottish & Amer. informal) really, very. □ **real ale** beer brewed in a traditional way. **real estate** (especially Amer.) immovable property such as land and houses. **real tennis** the original form of tennis played on an indoor court. **real-time** adjective (of a computer system) able to respond immediately to input data, as in an air-traffic-control system.

**realign** verb 1 align again. 2 regroup in politics etc. □ **realignment** noun

**realise** alternative spelling of REALIZE.

**realism** noun 1 (in art and literature) representing things as they are in reality. 2 the attitude of a realist.

**realist** noun a person whose ideas and practices are based on facts not on ideals or illusions.

**realistic** adjective 1 true to nature, closely resembling what is imitated or portrayed. 2 facing facts, based on facts not on ideals or illusions. 3 (of wages, or prices) high enough to pay the worker or seller adequately. □ **realistically** *adverb*

**reality** *noun* **1** the quality of being real; resemblance to an original. **2** all that is real, the real world as distinct from imagination or fantasy; *lost his grip on reality.* **3** something that exists or that is real; *the realities of the situation.*

**realize** *verb* (also **realise**) **1** be fully aware of, accept as a fact; *realized his mistake.* **2** convert (a hope or plan) into a fact; *our hopes were realized.* **3** convert (securities or property) into money by selling. **4** obtain or bring in as profit; (of goods) fetch as a price. □ **realization** *noun*

**really** *adverb* **1** in fact. **2** truly; very; *a really nice girl.* **3** an expression of interest, surprise, or mild protest.

**realm** (*pronounced* relm) *noun* **1** a kingdom. **2** a field of activity or interest; *the realms of science.*

**realty** (**ree-ăl**-ti) *noun* (*Amer.*) real estate.

**ream** *noun* **1** a quantity of paper (about 500 sheets) of the same size. **2** (**reams**) a great quantity of writing.

**reap** *verb* **1** cut (grain or a similar crop) as a harvest. **2** receive as the consequence of actions; *reaped great benefit from their training.* □ **reaper** *noun*

**reappear** *verb* appear again. □ **reappearance** *noun*

**reappraisal** (ree-ă-**pray**-zăl) *noun* a new appraisal.

**rear**[1] *noun* the back part of something. ● *adjective* situated at or in the rear. □ **bring up the rear** come last. **Rear Admiral** *see* AD-MIRAL. **rear-view mirror** a mirror placed so that the driver of a vehicle can see traffic behind.

**rear**[2] *verb* **1** bring up (children); breed and look after (animals); cultivate (crops). **2** build or set up (a monument etc.). **3** (of a horse etc.) raise itself on its hind legs. **4** (of a building) extend to a great height.

**rearguard** *noun* a body of troops whose job is to protect the rear of the main force. □ **rearguard action** a defensive stand or struggle, especially when losing.

**rearm** *verb* arm again. □ **rearmament** *noun*

**rearmost** *adjective* furthest back.

**rearrange** *verb* arrange in a different way or order. □ **rearrangement** *noun*

**rearward** *adjective* to the rear. ● *adverb* (also **rearwards**) towards the rear.

**reason** *noun* **1** a motive, cause, or justification. **2** the ability to think, understand, and draw conclusions. **3** sanity; *lost his reason.* **4** good sense or judgement; what is right, practical, or possible; *will do anything within reason.* ● *verb* **1** use one's ability to think and draw conclusions; *reasoning that the burglar was familiar with*

*the house.* **2** try to persuade someone; *reasoned with the rebels.*

━━━━━━━━━━━━━━━━━━━━━━

■**Usage** The phrase *the reason is…* should not be followed by *because* (which means the same thing). Correct usage is *We are unable to come; the reason is that we both have flu* (not 'the reason is because we have flu').

━━━━━━━━━━━━━━━━━━━━━━

**reasonable** *adjective* **1** ready to use or listen to reason; sensible; *a reasonable person.* **2** in accordance with reason, not absurd, logical. **3** moderate, not expensive or extortionate; *reasonable prices.* □ **reasonably** *adverb*, **reasonableness** *noun*

**reassemble** *verb* assemble again.

**reassure** (ree-ă-**shoor**) *verb* restore confidence to; remove the fears or doubts of. □ **reassurance** *noun*, **reassuring** *adjective*

**Réaumur scale** (ray-oh-**mewr**) a scale of temperature (now obsolete) with 80 divisions between 0° (the melting point of ice) and 80° (the boiling point of water). (¶ Named after the French scientist R. A. F. de Réaumur (1683–1757).)

**rebate**[1] (**ree**-bayt) *noun* a reduction in the amount to be paid, a partial refund.

**rebate**[2] = RABBET.

**rebel** *verb* (*pronounced* ri-**bel**) (**rebelled**, **rebelling**; *Amer.* **rebeled**, **rebeling**) **1** refuse to continue allegiance to an established government; take up arms against it. **2** resist authority or control; refuse to obey. ● *noun* (*pronounced* **reb**-ĕl) a person who rebels.

**rebellion** *noun* open resistance to authority, especially organized armed resistance to an established government.

**rebellious** *adjective* rebelling, insubordinate. □ **rebelliously** *adverb*, **rebelliousness** *noun*

**rebirth** *noun* a return to life or activity, a revival.

**reboot** *verb* start up (a computer) again; switch it off and on again.

**rebound** *verb* (*pronounced* ri-**bownd**) **1** spring back after an impact. **2** have an adverse effect upon the originator. ● *noun* (*pronounced* **ree**-bownd) an act or instance of rebounding. □ **on the rebound 1** (of a hit or catch) made to a ball that is rebounding. **2** while still recovering from an emotional shock, especially rejection by a lover.

**rebuff** *noun* an unkind or contemptuous refusal, a snub. ● *verb* give a rebuff to.

**rebuild** *verb* (**rebuilt**, **rebuilding**) build again after destruction or demolition.

**rebuke** *verb* reprove sharply or severely. ● *noun* a sharp or severe reproof.

**rebus** (ree-bŭs) *noun* (*plural* **rebuses**) a representation of a name or word by means of pictures suggesting its syllables.

**rebut** (ri-**but**) *verb* (**rebutted, rebutting**) refute or disprove (evidence or an accusation). □ **rebuttal** *noun*

**recalcitrant** (ri-**kal**-si-trănt) *adjective* disobedient; resisting authority or discipline. □ **recalcitrance** *noun*

**recall** *verb* **1** summon (a person) to return from a place. **2** bring back into the mind, remember or cause to remember. ●*noun* recalling, being recalled.

**recant** (ri-**kant**) *verb* formally withdraw one's former statement or belief, rejecting it as wrong or heretical. □ **recantation** *noun*

**recap** (ree-kap) (*informal*) *verb* (**recapped, recapping**) recapitulate. ●*noun* a recapitulation.

**recapitulate** (ree-kă-**pit**-yoo-layt) *verb* state again the main points of what has been said. □ **recapitulation** *noun*

**recapture** *verb* **1** capture (a person or thing that has escaped or been lost to an enemy). **2** succeed in experiencing (a former state or emotion) again. ●*noun* recapturing.

**recast** *verb* (**recast, recasting**) cast again, put into a different form; *recast the question in different words.*

**recce** (**rek**-i) (*informal*) *noun* a reconnaissance. ●*verb* reconnoitre.

**recede** *verb* **1** go or shrink back from a certain point; seem to go away from the observer; *the floods receded; the shore receded as we sailed away.* **2** slope backwards.

**receipt** (ri-**seet**) *noun* **1** receiving; being received; *on receipt of your letter.* **2** a written acknowledgement that something has been received or that money has been paid. **3** (*old use*) a recipe. ●*verb* mark (a bill) as having been paid.

**receive** *verb* **1** acquire, accept, or take in (something offered, sent, or given). **2** experience; be treated with; *it received close attention.* **3** take the force, weight, or impact of. **4** serve as a receptacle for. **5** allow to enter as a member or guest. **6** greet on arrival. □ **be on the receiving end** be the one who has to submit to something unpleasant. **received pronunciation** the form of English spoken by educated people in southern England, regarded as the standard.

**receiver** *noun* **1** a person or thing that receives something. **2** one who accepts stolen goods while knowing them to be stolen. **3** (in full **official receiver**) an official who administers property under a receiving-order. **4** a radio or television apparatus that receives broadcast signals and converts them into sound or a picture.

**5** the part of a telephone that is held to the ear.

**receivership** *noun* the office of official receiver; the state of being dealt with by a receiver; *in receivership.*

**receiving** *noun* the crime of accepting stolen goods while knowing them to be stolen. □ **receiving-order** *noun* a lawcourt's order to an official (the receiver) to take charge of the property of a bankrupt or insane person or property that is the subject of litigation.

**recent** *adjective* not long past, happening or begun in a time shortly before the present. □ **recently** *adverb*

**receptacle** *noun* something for holding or containing what is put into it.

**reception** *noun* **1** receiving; being received. **2** the way something is received; *the speech got a cool reception.* **3** an assembly held to receive guests; *wedding reception.* **4** a place where hotel guests or a firm's clients are received on arrival. **5** the receiving of broadcast signals, the efficiency of this; *reception was poor.* □ **reception room** a room where visitors are received; (in estate agents' use) a living-room as distinct from a bedroom or kitchen etc.

**receptionist** *noun* a person employed to receive and direct callers or clients.

**receptive** *adjective* able or quick or willing to receive knowledge, ideas, or suggestions etc. □ **receptiveness** *noun*, **receptivity** *noun*

**receptor** *noun* an organ of the body that is able to respond to a stimulus (such as light or pressure) and transmit a signal through a sensory nerve.

**recess** (ri-**sess** or **ree**-sess) *noun* **1** a part or space set back from the line of a wall etc.; a small hollow place inside something. **2** temporary cessation from business, a time of this; *while parliament is in recess.* ●*verb* make a recess in or of (a wall etc.); set back.

**recession** *noun* **1** receding from a point or level. **2** a temporary decline in economic activity or prosperity.

**recessional** *noun* a hymn sung while clergy and choir withdraw after a church service.

**recessive** *adjective* **1** tending to recede. **2** (of inherited characteristics) remaining latent when a dominant characteristic is present.

**recharge** *verb* charge (a battery or gun etc.) again. □ **recharge one's batteries** (*informal*) have a period of rest and recovery. □ **rechargeable** *adjective*

**recherché** (rĕ-**shair**-shay) *adjective* **1** devised or selected with care. **2** rare or exotic. **3** far-fetched. (¶ French.)

**rechristen** *verb* christen again; give a new name to.

**recidivist** (ri-sid-i-vist) *noun* a person who constantly commits crimes and seems unable to be cured; a persistent offender. □ **recidivism** *noun*

**recipe** *noun* **1** directions for preparing a dish in cookery. **2** a way of achieving something; *a recipe for success.*

**recipient** (ri-sip-iĕnt) *noun* a person who receives something.

**reciprocal** (ri-sip-rŏ-kăl) *adjective* **1** given or received in return; *reciprocal help.* **2** given or felt by each towards the other, mutual; *reciprocal affection.* **3** corresponding but the other way round; *I thought he was a waiter, while he made the reciprocal mistake and thought that I was.* ●*noun* a mathematical expression related to another in the way that ⅔ is related to ³/₂. □ **reciprocally** *adverb*

**reciprocate** (ri-sip-rŏ-kayt) *verb* **1** give and receive; make a return for something done, given, or felt. **2** (of a machine part) move backward and forward alternately. □ **reciprocation** *noun*

**reciprocity** (ress-i-pross-iti) *noun* a reciprocal condition or action; the giving of privileges in return for similar privileges.

**recital** *noun* **1** reciting. **2** a long account of a series of events. **3** a musical entertainment given by one performer or group.

**recitation** *noun* **1** reciting. **2** a thing recited.

**recitative** (ress-i-tă-teev) *noun* a narrative or conversational part of an opera or oratorio, sung in a rhythm imitating that of ordinary speech.

**recite** *verb* **1** repeat (a passage) aloud from memory, especially before an audience. **2** state (facts) in order.

**reckless** *adjective* wildly impulsive, rash. □ **recklessly** *adverb*, **recklessness** *noun*

**reckon** *verb* **1** count up. **2** include in a total or as a member of a particular class. **3** have as one's opinion, feel confident; *I reckon we'll win.* **4** (foll. by *on*) rely or base one's plans on; *we reckoned on your support.* □ **day of reckoning** the time when one must atone for one's actions or be punished. **reckon with** take into account.

**reclaim** *verb* **1** take action so as to recover possession of. **2** make (flooded or waste land) usable, e.g. by draining or irrigating it. □ **reclamation** (rek-lă-may-shŏn) *noun*

**recline** *verb* have or put one's body in a horizontal or leaning position.

**recluse** (ri-klooss) *noun* a person who lives alone and avoids mixing with people.

**recognition** *noun* recognizing; being recognized; *a presentation in recognition of his services.*

**recognizance** (ri-kog-ni-zăns) *noun* a pledge made to a lawcourt or magistrate that a person will observe some condition (e.g. keep the peace) or appear when summoned; a sum of money pledged as surety for this.

**recognize** *verb* (also **recognise**) **1** know again, identify from one's previous knowledge or experience. **2** realize or admit the nature of; *recognized the hopelessness of the situation.* **3** acknowledge or accept formally as genuine or valid; *France has recognized the island's new government.* **4** show appreciation of (ability or service etc.) by giving an honour or reward. **5** (of a chairman in a formal debate) allow (a particular person) the right to speak next. □ **recognizable** *adjective*, **recognizably** *adverb*

**recoil** *verb* **1** move or spring back suddenly, rebound. **2** draw oneself back in fear or disgust. **3** have an adverse effect on the originator. ●*noun* the act or sensation of recoiling.

**recollect** *verb* remember. □ **recollection** *noun*

**recommence** (ree-kŏ-menss) *verb* begin again. □ **recommencement** *noun*

**recommend** *verb* **1** advise (a course of action or a treatment etc.). **2** praise as worthy of employment, favour, or trial etc. **3** (of qualities or conduct) make acceptable or desirable; *this plan has much to recommend it.* □ **recommendation** *noun*

**recompense** (rek-ŏm-penss) *verb* repay or reward, compensate. ●*noun* payment or reward etc. in return for something.

**reconcile** (rek-ŏn-syl) *verb* **1** restore friendship between (people) after an estrangement or quarrel. **2** induce (a person or oneself) to accept an unwelcome fact or situation; *this reconciled him to living far from home.* **3** bring (facts or statements etc.) into harmony or compatibility when they appear to conflict. □ **reconciliation** *noun*, **reconcilable** *adjective*

**recondite** (rek-ŏn-dyt) *adjective* (of a subject) obscure; (of an author) writing about an obscure subject.

**recondition** *verb* overhaul, replace any worn parts, and make any necessary repairs to.

**reconnaissance** (ri-kon-i-săns) *noun* an exploration or examination of an area to obtain information about it (especially for military purposes).

**reconnoitre** (rek-ŏn-oi-ter) *verb* (*Amer.* **reconnoiter**) make a reconnaissance of (an area); make a preliminary survey.

**reconsider** *verb* consider again, especially with the possibility of changing one's former decision. □ **reconsideration** *noun*

**reconstitute** *verb* **1** reconstruct; reorganize. **2** add water to (dried food) to restore it to its previous condition. □ **reconstitution** *noun*

**reconstruct** *verb* **1** construct or build again. **2** create or enact (past events) again, e.g. in investigating the circumstances of a crime. □ **reconstruction** *noun*

**record** *noun* (*pronounced* **rek**-ord) **1** information preserved in a permanent form, especially in writing. **2** a document etc. bearing this. **3** a disc bearing recorded sound. **4** facts known about a person's past; *has a good record of service.* **5** (in full **police record**) a list of a person's previous criminal convictions. **6** the best performance or most remarkable event etc. of its kind that is known; *hold the record.* ● *adjective* (*pronounced* **rek**-ord) best, highest, or most extreme hitherto recorded; *a record crop.* ● *verb* (*pronounced* ri-**kord**) **1** set down in writing or other permanent form. **2** preserve (sound or visual scenes, especially television pictures) on disc or tape etc. for later reproduction. **3** (of a measuring-instrument) register. □ **for the record** so that facts may be recorded. **off the record** stated unofficially or not for publication. **on record** preserved in written records. **record-breaking** *adjective* surpassing all previous records. **recorded delivery** a postal delivery in which a receipt is obtained from the recipient as proof of delivery. **record player** an apparatus for reproducing sound from discs on which it is recorded.

**recorder** *noun* **1** a person or thing that records something. **2** (also **Recorder**) a barrister or solicitor of at least ten years standing, serving as a part-time judge. **3** a wooden or plastic wind instrument with holes covered by the fingers, held downwards from the mouth as it is played.

**recording** *noun* **1** a process by which audio or video signals are recorded for later reproduction. **2** the disc or tape etc. produced. **3** the recorded material.

**recordist** *noun* a person who makes recordings.

**recount** (ri-**kownt**) *verb* narrate; tell in detail; *recounted his adventures.*

**re-count** *verb* (*pronounced* ree-**kownt**) count again. ● *noun* (*pronounced* **ree**-kownt) a second counting, especially of election votes to check the totals.

**recoup** (ri-**koop**) *verb* **1** recover what one has lost or its equivalent; *recoup one's losses.* **2** reimburse or compensate; *recoup him for his losses.* □ **recoupment** *noun*

**recourse** (ri-**korss**) *noun* a source of help. □ **have recourse to** turn to (a person or thing) for help.

**recover** *verb* **1** regain possession, use, or control of. **2** obtain as compensation; *sought to recover damages from the company.* **3** return to a normal condition after illness or unconsciousness. □ **recover oneself** regain consciousness or calmness, or one's balance. □ **recoverable** *adjective*, **recovery** *noun*

**re-create** *verb* create again, reproduce.

**recreation** (rek-ri-**ay**-shŏn) *noun* the process or means of entertaining oneself or relaxing. □ **recreation ground** a public playground or sports field. □ **recreational** *adjective*

**recriminate** *verb* make recriminations.

**recrimination** *noun* an angry retort or accusation made in retaliation.

**recriminatory** *adjective* making recriminations.

**recrudesce** (ree-kroo-**dess**) *verb* (*formal*) (of a disease or sore or discontent) break out again. □ **recrudescent** *adjective*, **recrudescence** *noun*

**recruit** *noun* **1** a person who has just joined the armed forces and is not yet trained. **2** a new member of a group. ● *verb* **1** form (an army or other group) by enlisting recruits. **2** enlist (a person) as a recruit. **3** refresh; *recruit one's strength.* □ **recruitment** *noun*

**rectal** *adjective* of the rectum.

**rectangle** *noun* a four-sided geometric figure with four right angles, especially one with adjacent sides unequal in length.

**rectangular** *adjective* shaped like a rectangle.

**rectifier** *noun* a device that converts alternating current to direct current.

**rectify** *verb* (**rectified, rectifying**) **1** put right, correct; *rectify the error.* **2** purify or refine, especially by distillation. **3** convert (alternating current) to direct current. □ **rectifiable** *adjective*, **rectification** *noun*

**rectilinear** (rek-ti-**lin**-i-er) *adjective* **1** bounded by straight lines; *a rectilinear figure.* **2** in or forming a straight line.

**rectitude** *noun* moral goodness; correctness of behaviour or procedure.

**recto** *noun* (*plural* **rectos**) **1** the right-hand page of an open book. **2** the front of a leaf of a manuscript etc. (compare VERSO).

**rector** *noun* **1** a member of the clergy in charge of a parish (in the Church of England; one formerly entitled to receive all the tithes of the parish). **2** the head of certain universities, colleges, schools, and religious institutions. **3** the students' elected representative on the governing body of a Scottish university. □ **rectorship** *noun*

**rectory** *noun* the house of a rector.

**rectum** *noun* the last section of the large intestine, between colon and anus.

**recumbent** *adjective* lying down, reclining.

**recuperate** (ri-**koo**-per-ayt) *verb* **1** recover, regain (one's health or strength) after illness or exhaustion. **2** recover (losses). □ **recuperation** *noun*, **recuperative** *adjective*

**recur** verb (**recurred, recurring**) happen again, keep occurring. □ **recurring decimal** a decimal fraction in which the same figures are repeated indefinitely, e.g. 3.999... or 4.014014...

**recurrent** (ri-ku-rĕnt) adjective recurring; a recurrent problem. □ **recurrence** noun

**recusant** (**rek**-yoo-zănt) noun a person who refuses to submit to authority or to comply with a regulation. □ **recusancy** noun

**recycle** verb convert (waste material) into a form in which it can be reused. □ **recyclable** adjective

**red** adjective (**redder, reddest**) **1** of the colour of blood. **2** (of the face) flushed with anger or shame; (of the eyes) bloodshot or reddened with weeping. **3** (of the hair) reddish-brown, ginger. **4** (informal) Communist; favouring Communism. ● noun **1** red colour. **2** a red substance or material; red clothes. **3** (informal) a Communist. □ **in the red** having a debit balance, in debt. **red admiral** a butterfly with red, black, and white markings. **Red Army** the army of China and other Communist countries. (¶ Originally the Russian Bolshevik army.) **Red Army Faction** a left-wing urban guerrilla group in former West Germany, active from 1968. It was originally led by Andreas Baader (1943–77) and Ulrike Meinhof (1934–76), after whom it was sometimes called the Baader-Meinhof Group. **red-blooded** adjective full of vigour. **red card** such a card shown by a football referee to a player who is being sent off the field. **red carpet** privileged treatment given to an important visitor. **red cell** (also **red corpuscle**) an erythrocyte, a blood cell which contains haemoglobin and carries oxygen and carbon dioxide to and from the tissues. **Red Crescent** the equivalent of the Red Cross in Muslim countries. **Red Cross** an international organization for the treatment of the sick and wounded in war and for helping those affected by large-scale natural disasters. **red ensign** the flag of the merchant navy; a red flag with a Union Jack in the corner. **red flag 1** a flag used as a warning of danger. **2** the symbol of a left-wing revolutionary group. **Red Guard** any of various radical groups and their members, especially (i) an organized detachment of workers during the Russian Bolshevik revolution of 1917, (ii) a youth movement during the Cultural Revolution in China, 1966–76. **red-handed** adjective in the act of crime; caught red-handed. **red herring** a misleading clue; something that draws attention away from the matter under consideration. **red-hot** adjective **1** so hot that it glows red. **2** (of news) fresh, completely new. **red-hot poker** a garden plant with spikes of red or yellow flowers. **Red Indian** (old use, offensive) a native American, North American Indian. **red lead** red oxide of lead, used as a pigment. **red-letter day** a day that is memorable because of a success, happy event, etc. **red light** a signal to stop on a road or railway; a danger-signal. **red-light district** a district containing many brothels. **red pepper 1** the ripe red fruit of the capsicum plant. **2** cayenne pepper. **red rose** the emblem of Lancashire or the Lancastrians. **red shift** displacement of the spectrum to longer wavelengths in the light coming from receding galaxies. **red squirrel** a native British squirrel with reddish brown fur. **red tape** excessive formalities in official transactions. □ **reddish** adjective, **redness** noun

**redbreast** noun a robin.

**redbrick** adjective of English universities founded in the 19th century or later, as distinct from Oxford and Cambridge.

**redcap** noun a member of the military police.

**redcurrant** noun a small round edible berry; the bush bearing it.

**redden** verb make or become red.

**Redding**, Otis (1941–67), American soul singer and songwriter.

**redecorate** verb decorate freshly. □ **redecoration** noun

**redeem** verb **1** buy back, recover (a thing) by payment or by doing something. **2** clear (a debt etc.) by paying it off; redeem the mortgage. **3** convert (tokens etc.) into goods or cash. **4** obtain the freedom of (a person) by payment. **5** save from damnation or from the consequences of sin. **6** make up for faults or deficiencies; it has one redeeming feature. □ **redeem oneself** make up for one's former fault. □ **redeemable** adjective

**redeemer** noun **1** one who redeems something. **2** (**the Redeemer**) Christ.

**redemption** noun redeeming; being redeemed.

**redeploy** verb send (troops or workers etc.) to a new place or task. □ **redeployment** noun

**redevelop** verb (**redeveloped, redeveloping**) replan or rebuild (an urban area). □ **redevelopment** noun

**Redford**, Robert (Charles Robert) (born 1937), American film actor.

**Redgrave**, Sir Michael Scudamore (1908–85), English actor; daughter Vanessa (born 1937), English actress.

**redhead** noun a person with reddish hair.

**rediffusion** noun relaying of broadcast programmes from a central receiver.

**redirect** verb direct or send to another place. □ **redirection** noun

**redistribute** *verb* distribute again or differently. □ **redistribution** *noun*

**redneck** *noun* (*Amer.*, often *scornful*) a right-wing working-class White person in the southern USA.

**redo** (ree-**doo**) *verb* (**redid**, **redone**, **redoing**) **1** do again. **2** redecorate.

**redolent** (**red**-ŏ-lĕnt) *adjective* **1** smelling strongly; *redolent of onions.* **2** (foll. by *of*) suggestive of, full of memories of; *a town redolent of age and romance.* □ **redolence** *noun*

**redouble** *verb* **1** double again. **2** make or become more intense; *redoubled their efforts.*

**redoubt** (ri-**dowt**) *noun* a temporary or outer fortification with no defences flanking it.

**redoubtable** *adjective* formidable, especially as an opponent.

**redound** *verb* come back as an advantage or disadvantage; accrue; *this will redound to our credit.*

**redpoll** *noun* a bird with a red forehead, similar to a linnet.

**redress** (ri-**dress**) *verb* set right, rectify; *redress the balance.* ●*noun* reparation, amends for a wrong done; *has no chance of redress for this damage.*

**Red Sea** a long narrow landlocked sea between North Africa and the Arabian Peninsula.

**redshank** *noun* a large sandpiper with bright red legs.

**redskin** *noun* (*old use, offensive*) a native American, American Indian.

**redstart** *noun* a songbird with a red tail.

**reduce** *verb* **1** make or become less. **2** make lower in rank or status. **3** slim. **4** subdue; bring by force or necessity into a specified state or condition; *was reduced to despair*; *reduced to begging.* **5** convert into a simpler or more general form; *reduce the fraction to its lowest terms*; *the problem may be reduced to two main elements.* **6** restore (a fractured or dislocated bone) to its proper position. **7** *Chem.* combine or cause to combine with hydrogen; undergo or cause to undergo addition of electrons; convert (oxide) into metal. **8** (in cookery) boil off excess liquid from (a sauce) to thicken it. □ **reduced circumstances** poverty after a period of prosperity. □ **reducible** *adjective*

**reductio ad absurdum** proof that a premiss is false by showing that its logical consequence is absurd. (¶ Latin).

**reduction** *noun* **1** reducing; being reduced. **2** the amount by which something is reduced, especially in price.

**reductive** *adjective* causing reduction.

**redundant** *adjective* **1** superfluous. **2** (of workers) no longer needed and therefore unemployed. **3** (of apparatus etc.) being a duplicate in case of failure of the corresponding part or unit. □ **redundancy** *noun*

**reduplicate** *verb* double (a letter or syllable), e.g. *bye-bye, goody-goody, super-duper.* □ **reduplication** *noun*

**redwing** *noun* a thrush with red flanks and underwings.

**redwood** *noun* **1** a very tall evergreen coniferous tree of California. **2** its reddish wood.

**re-echo** *verb* (**re-echoed, re-echoing**) echo; echo repeatedly, resound.

**reed** *noun* **1** a water or marsh plant with tall straight hollow stems. **2** its stem. **3** a vibrating part (often a strip of cane) that produces the sound in certain wind instruments.

**re-educate** *verb* educate again, especially to change a person's views.

**reedy** *adjective* (**reedier, reediest**) **1** full of reeds. **2** like a reed in slenderness or (of grass) thickness. **3** (of the voice) having the thin high tone of a reed instrument. □ **reediness** *noun*

**reef** *noun* **1** a ridge of rock, shingle, or sand that reaches to or close to the surface of water. **2** each of several strips at the top or bottom of a sail that can be drawn in to reduce the area of sail exposed to the wind. ●*verb* shorten (a sail) by drawing in a reef or reefs. □ **reef-knot** *noun* a symmetrical double knot that is very secure.

**reefer** *noun* **1** a thick double-breasted jacket. **2** (*slang*) a marijuana cigarette.

**reek** *noun* a foul or stale smell. ●*verb* smell strongly or unpleasantly.

**reel** *noun* **1** a cylinder or similar device on which something is wound; the amount held by a reel. **2** a lively folk-dance, especially of Scottish or Irish origin. ●*verb* **1** wind on or off a reel. **2** pull (a thing) in using a reel. **3** stagger; have a violent swinging or spinning motion. □ **reel off** recite (a list, story, etc.) rapidly.

**re-elect** *verb* elect again. □ **re-election** *noun*

**re-enter** *verb* enter again.

**re-entry** *noun* the act of entering again, especially of a spacecraft returning into the earth's atmosphere.

**reeve** *noun* **1** (*old use*) the chief magistrate of a town or district. **2** a female ruff (*see* RUFF[1] *sense* 3). ●*verb* (**rove** *or* **reeved, reeving**) (in nautical use) **1** thread (a rope or rod etc.) through a ring or other opening. **2** fasten (a rope or block etc.) in this way.

**re-examine** *verb* examine again. □ **re-examination** *noun*

**ref** *noun* **1** (*informal*) a referee in sports. **2** (in commerce) reference, reference number.

**reface** *verb* put a new facing on (a building).

**refectory** (ri-**fek**-teri) *noun* the dining-room of a monastery, college, etc. □ **refectory table** a long narrow table.

**refer** *verb* (**referred**, **referring**) (usually foll. by *to*) **1** make an allusion, direct people's attention by words; *I wasn't referring to you*. **2** send on or direct (a person) to some authority, specialist, or source of information. **3** turn to (a thing) for information; *we referred to the list of rules*. **4** (of a statement etc.) be relevant; relate; *these figures refer to last year*. **5** return (a document) to its sender. □ **referred pain** one felt in a part of the body other than its true source. □ **referable** *adjective*

**referee** *noun* **1** an umpire, especially in football and boxing. **2** a person to whom disputes are referred for decision, an arbitrator. **3** a person willing to testify to the character or ability of someone applying for a job. ●*verb* (**refereed**, **refereeing**) act as referee in (a football match etc.).

**reference** *noun* **1** the act of referring. **2** something that can be referred to as an authority or standard. **3** a statement referring to or mentioning something; *made no reference to recent events*. **4** a direction to a book or page or file etc. where information can be found; the book or passage etc. cited in this way. **5** a testimonial. **6** a person willing to testify to someone's character, ability, or financial circumstances. □ **in** or **with reference to** in connection with, about. **reference book** a book providing information for reference but not designed to be read straight through. **reference library** one containing books that can be consulted but not taken away.

**referendum** *noun* (*plural* **referendums** or **referenda**) the referring of a question to the people of a country etc. for direct decision by a general vote; a vote taken in this way.

**referral** (ri-**fer**-ăl) *noun* referring; being referred.

**refill** *verb* (*pronounced* ree-**fil**) fill again. ●*noun* (*pronounced* **ree**-fil) **1** a second or later filling. **2** the material used for this; a thing that replaces something used up. □ **refillable** *adjective*

**refine** *verb* **1** remove impurities or defects from. **2** make elegant or cultured.

**refinement** *noun* **1** refining; being refined. **2** elegance of behaviour or manners etc. **3** an added improvement or development; *the oven has automatic cleaning and other refinements*. **4** a piece of subtle reasoning, a fine distinction.

**refiner** *noun* one whose business is to refine crude oil, metal, sugar, etc.

**refinery** *noun* a factory where crude substances are refined.

**refit** *verb* (*pronounced* ree-**fit**) (**refitted**, **refitting**) renew or repair the fittings of. ●*noun* (*pronounced* **ree**-fit) refitting.

**reflate** *verb* cause reflation of (a financial system).

**reflation** *noun* the process of restoring a financial system to its previous condition when deflation has been carried out too fast or too far. □ **reflationary** *adjective*

**reflect** *verb* **1** throw back (light, heat, or sound). **2** be thrown back in this way. **3** (of a mirror etc.) show an image of. **4** correspond to (a thing) because of its influence; *improved methods of agriculture were soon reflected in larger crops*. **5** bring (credit or discredit). **6** (usually foll. by *on*, *upon*) bring discredit on; *this failure reflects upon the whole industry*. **7** think deeply, consider; remind oneself of past events.

**reflection** *noun* (also **reflexion**) **1** reflecting; being reflected. **2** reflected light or heat etc.; a reflected image. **3** discredit; a thing that brings this. **4** deep thought; an idea or statement produced by this.

**reflective** *adjective* **1** reflecting. **2** thoughtful; *in a reflective mood*. □ **reflectively** *adverb*

**reflector** *noun* **1** a thing that reflects light or heat or images. **2** a red fitment on the back of a vehicle that reflects the lights of vehicles behind it.

**reflex** (**ree**-fleks) *noun* **1** a reflex action. **2** a reflected light or image. □ **reflex action** an involuntary or automatic movement in response to a stimulus. **reflex angle** an angle of more than 180°. **reflex camera** one in which the image given by the lens is reflected by an angled mirror to the viewfinder.

**reflexion** alternative spelling of REFLECTION.

**reflexive** *adjective* (of a word or form) referring back to the subject of the verb, in which the action of the verb is performed on its subject, e.g. *he washed himself*. ●*noun* a reflexive word or form. □ **reflexive pronoun** any of the pronouns *myself*, *himself*, *itself*, *themselves*, etc.

**reflexology** *noun* the practice of massaging points on the feet to relieve tension and treat illness. □ **reflexologist** *noun*

**refloat** *verb* set (a stranded ship) afloat again.

**reforest** = REAFFOREST.

**reform** *verb* make or become better by removal or abandonment of imperfections or faults. ●*noun* **1** reforming; being reformed. **2** a change to improve something. □ **Reformed Church** a Protestant Church, especially the Calvinist Church. □ **reformer** *noun*

**re-form** *verb* form again.

**reformation** (ref-er-**may**-shŏn) *noun*
**1** reforming; being reformed; a great change for the better in public affairs. **2** (**the Reformation**) the 16th-century movement for reform of certain doctrines and practices of the Church of Rome, resulting in the establishment of Reformed or Protestant Churches.

**reformative** *adjective* producing or intended to produce reform.

**reformatory** (ri-**form**-ă-ter-i) *adjective* reformative. ● *noun* (*Amer.* or *hist.*) an institution where young offenders are sent to be reformed.

**refract** (ri-**frakt**) *verb* bend (a ray of light) at the point where it enters water or glass etc. obliquely. □ **refraction** *noun*, **refractive** *adjective*

**refractor** *noun* **1** a refracting medium or lens. **2** a telescope using a lens to produce an image.

**refractory** *adjective* **1** resisting control or discipline, stubborn; *a refractory child*. **2** (of a disease etc.) not yielding to treatment. **3** (of a substance) resistant to heat; hard to fuse or work.

**refrain** **1** the lines of a song that are repeated at the end of each verse. **2** the main part of a song, after the verse. ● *verb* (foll. by *from*) keep oneself from doing something; *please refrain from talking*.

**refrangible** (ri-**franj**-ibŭl) *adjective* able to be refracted.

**refresh** *verb* **1** restore the strength and vigour of (a person etc.) by food, drink, or rest. **2** stimulate (the memory) by reminding.

**refresher** *noun* **1** an extra fee paid to counsel while a case is proceeding in a lawcourt. **2** a drink. □ **refresher course** a course of instruction enabling a qualified person to keep abreast of recent developments in the subject.

**refreshing** *adjective* **1** restoring strength and vigour. **2** welcome and interesting because of its novelty.

**refreshment** *noun* **1** refreshing; being refreshed. **2** something that refreshes, especially food and drink.

**refrigerant** *noun* a substance used for cooling things in refrigeration. ● *adjective* refrigerating.

**refrigerate** *verb* make extremely cold, especially in order to preserve and store food. □ **refrigeration** *noun*

**refrigerator** *noun* a cabinet or room in which food is stored at a very low temperature.

**refuel** *verb* (**refuelled, refuelling**; *Amer.* **refueled, refueling**) replenish the fuel supply of (a ship or aircraft).

**refuge** *noun* shelter from pursuit, danger, or trouble; a place giving this.

**refugee** *noun* a person who has left home and seeks refuge elsewhere e.g. from war, persecution, or some natural disaster.

**refulgent** (ri-**ful**-jĕnt) *adjective* (*literary*) shining; gloriously bright. □ **refulgence** *noun*

**refund** *verb* (*pronounced* ri-**fund**) pay back (money received, or expenses that a person has incurred). ● *noun* (*pronounced* **ree**-fund) money refunded, repayment.

**refurbish** *verb* make clean or bright again; restore and redecorate. □ **refurbishment** *noun*

**refusal** *noun* refusing; being refused. □ **first refusal** the right to accept or refuse something before the choice is offered to others.

**refuse¹** (ri-**fewz**) *verb* **1** indicate that one is unwilling to accept, give, or do something; *I refused to go; she refused my request; the car refused to start*. **2** (of a horse) be unwilling to jump (a fence).

**refuse²** (**ref**-yooss) *noun* what is rejected as worthless, waste material.

**refusenik** *noun* (*old use*) a Soviet Jew who had been refused permission to emigrate to Israel.

**refutable** (ri-**fewt**-ăbŭl) *adjective* able to be refuted.

**refute** *verb* **1** prove that (a statement or opinion or person) is wrong. **2** deny; contradict. □ **refutation** (ref-yoo-**tay**-shŏn) *noun*

■**Usage** The use of *refute* in sense 2 is generally considered incorrect.

**regain** *verb* **1** obtain possession, use, or control of (a thing) again after losing it. **2** reach again; *regained the shore*.

**regal** (**ree**-găl) *adjective* like or fit for a monarch. □ **regally** *adverb*, **regality** (ri-**gal**-iti) *noun*

**regale** (ri-**gayl**) *verb* feed or entertain well; *regaled them with stories of the campaign*.

**regalia** (ri-**gay**-li-ă) *plural noun* **1** the emblems of royalty used at coronations; *the regalia include crown, sceptre, and orb*. **2** the emblems or costumes of an order (e.g. the Order of the Garter) or of a certain rank or office; *the mayoral regalia*.

**regard** *verb* **1** look steadily at. **2** consider to be; *we regard the matter as serious*. **3** concern or have a connection with; *he is innocent as regards the first charge*. ● *noun* **1** a steady gaze. **2** heed, consideration; *acted without regard to the safety of others*. **3** respect; *we have a great regard for him as our chairman*. **4** (**regards**) kindly greetings conveyed in a message; *give him my regards*. □ **in** (or **with**) **regard to** regarding, in respect of.

**regardful** *adjective* mindful.

**regarding** *preposition* concerning, with reference to; *laws regarding picketing*.

**regardless** *adjective & adverb* paying no attention to something; *regardless of expense*.

**regatta** *noun* a number of boat or yacht races organized as a sporting event.

**regency** *noun* 1 being a regent; a regent's period of office. 2 a group of people acting as regent. 3 (**the Regency**) the period 1811–20 in England, when George, Prince of Wales, acted as regent.

**regenerate** *verb* (*pronounced* ri-jen-er-ayt) 1 give new life or vigour to. 2 reform spiritually or morally. ● *adjective* (*pronounced* ri-jen-er-ăt) spiritually born again, reformed. □ **regeneration** *noun*, **regenerative** *adjective*

**regent** *noun* a person appointed to rule a country while the monarch is too young or unable to rule, or is absent. ● *adjective* acting as regent; *Prince Regent*.

**reggae** (**reg**-ay) *noun* a West Indian style of music with a strongly accented subsidiary beat.

**regicide** (**rej**-i-syd) *noun* 1 the killing of a king. 2 a person guilty of or involved in this.

**regime** (ray-*zh*eem) *noun* 1 a method or system of government. 2 a particular government. 3 a regimen.

**regimen** (**rej**-i-měn) *noun* a prescribed course of exercise, way of life, and especially diet.

**regiment** *noun* 1 a permanent unit of an army, usually divided into companies, troops, or battalions. 2 an operational unit of artillery, tanks, armoured cars, etc. 3 a large array or number of things. ● *verb* organize (people, work, data, etc.) rigidly into groups or into a pattern. □ **regimentation** *noun*

**regimental** *adjective* of an army regiment. ● *plural noun* (**regimentals**) the uniform of an army regiment.

***Regina*** (ri-**jy**-nă) *noun* 1 (after the name) a reigning queen; *Elizabeth Regina*. 2 *Law* (in titles of lawsuits) the Crown; *Regina v. Jones*. (¶ Latin, = queen.)

**region** *noun* 1 a continuous part of a surface or space or body, with more or less definite boundaries or with certain characteristics. 2 an administrative division of a country. □ **in the region of** approximately. □ **regional** *adjective*, **regionally** *adverb*

**register** *noun* 1 an official list of names, items, etc. 2 the book or other document(s) in which this is kept. 3 a mechanical device for indicating or recording speed, force, numbers, etc. automatically. 4 an adjustable plate for widening or narrowing an opening, e.g. for regulating the draught in a fire-grate.

5 exact correspondence of position; *out of register*. 6 the range of a human voice or of a musical instrument. 7 a particular style of language (e.g. informal, literary) used in appropriate circumstances. ● *verb* 1 enter or cause to be entered in a register. 2 set down formally in writing; present for consideration. 3 notice and remember. 4 (of an instrument) indicate or record something automatically. 5 make an impression on a person's mind; *his name did not register with me*. 6 express (an emotion) on one's face or by gesture. □ **registered nurse** (*Brit.*) a nurse with a state certificate of competence. **registered post** a postal service with special precautions for safety and compensation in case of loss. **register office** a place where civil marriages are performed and where records of births, marriages, and deaths are made.

■ **Usage** *Register office* is the official term, although *registry office* is often used instead.

**registrar** (rej-i-**strar**) *noun* 1 an official with responsibility for keeping written records or registers. 2 a chief administrator in a university or college. 3 a doctor undergoing hospital training to be a specialist.

**registration** *noun* registering; being registered. □ **registration document** an official document recording the details of a particular vehicle and its owners. **registration number** (*or* **mark**) a combination of letters and figures identifying a motor vehicle.

**registry** *noun* 1 registration. 2 a place where written records or registers are kept. □ **registry office** a register office.

**Regius professor** (ree-ji-ŭs) (*Brit.*) a professor holding a chair that was founded by a sovereign or that is filled by Crown appointment.

**regress** *verb* (*pronounced* ri-gress) go back to an earlier or more primitive form or state. ● *noun* (*pronounced* ree-gress) regressing. □ **regression** *noun*, **regressive** *adjective*

**regret** *noun* a feeling of sorrow for the loss of a person or thing, or of disappointment or repentance. ● *verb* (**regretted, regretting**) feel regret about.

**regretful** *adjective* feeling regret. □ **regretfully** *adverb*

**regrettable** *adjective* to be regretted; *a regrettable incident*. □ **regrettably** *adverb*

**regroup** *verb* form into new groups.

**regular** *adjective* 1 acting, recurring, or done in a uniform manner, or constantly at a fixed time or interval; *his pulse is regular*. 2 conforming to a principle or to a standard of procedure. 3 even, symmetrical; *a regular pentagon*. 4 usual, normal, habitual;

*has no regular occupation.* **5** belonging to the permanent armed forces of a country; *regular soldiers; the regular navy.* **6** (of a verb or noun etc.) having inflexions that are of a normal type. **7** (*informal*) complete, out-and-out; *it's a regular mess.* **8** (*informal*) not constipated. ●*noun* **1** a member of the permanent armed forces of a country. **2** (*informal*) a regular customer or client etc. □ **regularly** *adverb,* **regularity** *noun*

**regularize** *verb* (also **regularise**) **1** make regular. **2** make lawful or correct; *the company wishes to regularize the situation.* □ **regularization** *noun*

**regulate** *verb* **1** control or direct by means of rules and restrictions. **2** adjust or control (a thing) so that it works correctly or according to one's requirements. □ **regulator** *noun*

**regulation** *noun* **1** regulating; being regulated. **2** a rule or restriction.

**regulo** *noun* (usually foll. by a number) a point on a scale indicating the temperature of a gas oven; *cook at regulo 4 for 45 minutes.*

**regurgitate** (ri-**gerj**-it-ayt) *verb* **1** bring (swallowed food) up again to the mouth. **2** cast or pour out again. □ **regurgitation** *noun*

**rehabilitate** *verb* **1** restore (a person) to a normal life by training, after a period of illness or imprisonment. **2** reinstate. **3** restore (a building etc.) to a good condition or for a new purpose. □ **rehabilitation** *noun*

**rehash** *verb* (*pronounced* ree-**hash**) put (old material) into a new form with no great change or improvement. ●*noun* (*pronounced* ree-hash) **1** rehashing. **2** something made of rehashed material; *the programme was a rehash of old newsreels.*

**rehearsal** *noun* **1** rehearsing. **2** a practice or trial performance.

**rehearse** *verb* **1** practise before performing in public. **2** train (a person) by doing this. **3** say over, give an account of; *rehearsing his grievances.*

**rehoboam** (ree-hŏ-**boh**-ăm) *noun* a large wine bottle, twice the size of a jeroboam. (¶ Named after Rehoboam, son of Solomon.)

**rehouse** (ree-**howz**) *verb* provide with accommodation elsewhere.

**Reich** (*rhymes with* like) *noun* the former German State. □ **Third Reich** Germany under the Nazi regime (1933–45).

**reign** (*pronounced* rayn) *noun* **1** a sovereign's rule; the period of this. **2** the controlling or dominating effect of a person or thing; *a reign of terror.* ●*verb* **1** rule as king or queen. **2** be supreme, dominate; prevail; *silence reigned.* **3** (as **reigning** *adjective*) (of a champion) currently holding the title.

**reimburse** *verb* repay, refund. □ **reimbursement** *noun*

**Reims** (*pronounced* reemz) (also **Rheims**) an ancient cathedral city of northern France.

**rein** *noun* (also **reins**) **1** a long narrow strap fastened to the bit of a bridle and used to control a horse. **2** a similar device to restrain a toddler. ●*verb* (often foll. by *in*) check or control with reins. □ **give free rein to** allow freedom to; *give one's imagination free rein.* **keep a tight rein on** allow little freedom to.

**reincarnate** *verb* (*pronounced* ree-in-**kar**-nayt) bring back (a soul after death) into another body. ●*adjective* (*pronounced* ree-in-**kar**-năt) reincarnated. □ **reincarnation** *noun*

**reindeer** *noun* (*plural* **reindeer** *or* **reindeers**) a deer with large antlers, living in Arctic regions.

**reinforce** *verb* strengthen or support by additional persons or material or an added quantity. □ **reinforced concrete** concrete with metal bars or wire embedded in it to increase its strength.

**reinforcement** *noun* **1** reinforcing; being reinforced. **2** a thing that reinforces. **3** (**reinforcements**) additional personnel, ships, etc. sent to reinforce armed forces.

**reinstate** *verb* restore to a previous position. □ **reinstatement** *noun*

**reinsure** *verb* insure again (especially of an insurer transferring risk to another insurer). □ **reinsurance** *noun*

**reissue** *verb* issue (a thing) again. ●*noun* something reissued, e.g. a new issue of a book.

**reiterate** (ree-**it**-er-ayt) *verb* say or do again or repeatedly. □ **reiteration** *noun*

**Reith** (*pronounced* reeth), John Charles Walsham, 1st Baron (1889–1971), first General Manager and later first Director-General of the BBC.

**reject** *verb* (*pronounced* ri-**jekt**) **1** refuse to accept; put aside or send back as not to be chosen, used, or done etc. **2** react against; *the body may reject the transplanted tissue.* **3** fail to give due affection to; *the child was rejected by both his parents.* ●*noun* (*pronounced* **ree**-jekt) a person or thing that is rejected, especially as being below standard. □ **rejection** *noun*

**rejig** *verb* (**rejigged, rejigging**) **1** re-equip (a factory etc.) for a new type of work. **2** (*informal*) rearrange.

**rejoice** *verb* feel or show great joy.

**rejoin**[1] (ree-**join**) *verb* join again.

**rejoin**[2] (ri-**join**) *verb* say in answer; retort.

**rejoinder** *noun* something said in answer or retort.

**rejuvenate** (ri-joo-věn-ayt) *verb* restore youthful appearance or vigour to. □ **rejuvenation** *noun*

**relapse** *verb* fall back into a previous condition, or into a worse state after improvement. ●*noun* relapsing, especially after partial recovery from illness.

**relate** *verb* **1** narrate; tell in detail. **2** (often foll. by *to*) connect (two things) in thought or meaning. **3** (foll. by *to*) have reference to; be concerned with. **4** (foll. by *to*) establish a sympathetic or successful relationship with (a person or thing); *learning to relate to children*.

**related** *adjective* having a common descent or origin.

**relation** *noun* **1** the way in which one thing is related to another; a similarity, correspondence, or contrast between people, things, or events. **2** being related. **3** a person who is a relative. **4** narrating, being narrated. **5** (**relations**) dealings with others; *the country's foreign relations*. **6** (**relations**) sexual intercourse; *had relations with him*.

**relationship** *noun* **1** the state of being related; a connection or association. **2** an emotional (especially sexual) association between two people.

**relative** *adjective* **1** considered in relation or proportion to something else; *the relative merits of the two plans*; *lived in relative comfort*. **2** having a connection with; *facts relative to the matter in hand*. **3** *Grammar* (especially of a pronoun) referring or attached to an earlier noun, clause, or sentence; *'who' in 'the man who came to dinner' is a relative pronoun*. ●*noun* **1** a person who is related to another by parentage, descent, or marriage. **2** *Grammar* a relative pronoun or adverb. □ **relative atomic mass** the ratio of the average mass of one atom of an element to one-twelfth of the mass of an atom of carbon-12. **relative density** the ratio between the mass of a substance and that of the same volume of a substance used as a standard (usually water or air). **relative molecular mass** the ratio of the average mass of one molecule of an element or compound to one-twelfth of the mass of an atom of carbon-12. □ **relatively** *adverb*

**relativity** *noun* **1** relativeness. **2** one of two theories developed by Einstein; (**special theory of relativity**) based on the principle that all motion is relative and that light has a constant speed; (**general theory of relativity**) a theory extending this to gravitation and accelerated motion.

**relax** *verb* **1** become or cause to become less tight or tense. **2** make or become less strict; *relax the rules*. **3** make or become less

anxious or formal; cease work or effort and indulge in recreation. □ **relaxation** *noun*

**relay** *noun* (*pronounced* ree-lay) **1** a fresh set of people or animals taking the place of others who have completed a spell of work; *operating in relays*. **2** a fresh supply of material to be used or worked on. **3** a relay race. **4** a relayed message or transmission. **5** an electronic device that receives and passes on a signal, often strengthening it. ●*verb* (*pronounced* ree-**lay**) (**relayed**, **relaying**) receive and pass on or retransmit (a message, broadcast, etc.). □ **relay race** a race between teams in which each person in turn covers a part of the total distance.

**re-lay** *verb* (**re-laid, re-laying**) lay again.

**release** *verb* **1** set free. **2** remove from a fixed position; allow to fall, fly, etc.; *released an arrow*. **3** issue (a film) for general exhibition; make (information or a recording etc.) available to the public. ●*noun* **1** releasing; being released. **2** a handle or catch that unfastens a device or machine-part. **3** a news item released to the public; *a press release*. **4** a new film, recording, etc. issued for sale or public showing.

**relegate** (rel-i-gayt) *verb* **1** send or consign to a less important place or condition. **2** transfer (a sports team) to a lower division of a league. □ **relegation** *noun*

**relent** *verb* abandon one's harsh intentions and be more lenient.

**relentless** *adjective* **1** not relenting. **2** unceasing in its severity; *the relentless pressure of business life*. □ **relentlessly** *adverb*, **relentlessness** *noun*

**relevant** (rel-i-vănt) *adjective* related to the matter in hand. □ **relevance** *noun*

**reliable** *adjective* **1** able to be relied on. **2** consistently good in quality or performance. □ **reliably** *adverb*, **reliability** *noun*

**reliance** *noun* **1** relying. **2** trust or confidence. □ **reliant** *adjective*

**relic** (rel-ik) *noun* **1** something that survives from an earlier age. **2** a surviving trace of a custom or practice. **3** part of a holy person's body or belongings kept after his or her death as an object of reverence. **4** (**relics**) remnants, residue.

**relict** (rel-ikt) *noun* **1** (*old use*) a person's widow. **2** a geological or other object surviving in a primitive form.

**relief** *noun* **1** ease given by reduction or removal of pain, anxiety, or a burden. **2** something that relaxes tension or breaks up monotony; *a humorous scene serving as comic relief*. **3** assistance given to people in special need; *a relief fund for the earthquake victims*. **4** a person taking over another's turn of duty. **5** a bus etc. supplementing an ordinary service. **6** the raising of the siege

of a besieged town; *the relief of Mafeking.*
**7** a method of carving or moulding in
which the design projects from the surface.
**8** a piece of carving etc. done in this way.
**9** a similar effect achieved by the use of
colour or shading. □ **relief map** a map
showing hills and valleys either by shading
or by their being moulded in relief. **relief
road** a bypass by which traffic can avoid a
congested area.

**relieve** *verb* **1** give relief to; bring or be a relief to. **2** introduce variation into, make less
monotonous. **3** (foll. by *of*) take a thing
from (a person); *the thief had relieved him of
his watch.* **4** raise the siege of (a town).
**5** (foll. by *of*) release (a person) from a
duty or task by taking his or her place or
providing a substitute. □ **relieve oneself**
urinate or defecate.

**relievo** *noun* (*plural* **relievos**) = RELIEF
(senses 7, 8, 9).

**religion** *noun* **1** belief in and worship of a
superhuman controlling power, especially a
God or gods. **2** a particular system of faith
and worship; *the Christian religion.* **3** a controlling influence on a person's life; *football
is his religion.* **4** life under monastic vows.

**religious** *adjective* **1** of religion; *a religious
service.* **2** believing firmly in a religion and
paying great attention to its practices. **3** of
a monastic order. **4** very conscientious;
*with religious attention to detail.* ● *noun* (*plural*
**religious**) a person bound by monastic
vows. □ **religiously** *adverb*

**relinquish** *verb* **1** give up or cease from (a
plan, habit, or belief etc.). **2** surrender
possession of. **3** relax one's hold of; let go;
*relinquished the reins.* □ **relinquishment** *noun*

**reliquary** (**rel**-i-kwer-i) *noun* a receptacle for
a relic or relics of a holy person.

**relish** *noun* **1** great enjoyment of food or
other things. **2** an appetizing flavour or attractive quality. **3** a strong-tasting substance or food eaten with plainer food to
add flavour. ● *verb* enjoy greatly.

**relive** *verb* live (an experience etc.) over
again, especially in the imagination.

**reload** *verb* load again.

**relocate** (ree-lŏ-**kayt**) *verb* move (a person
or thing) to a different place. □ **relocation**
*noun*

**reluctant** *adjective* unwilling, grudging one's
consent. □ **reluctantly** *adverb*, **reluctance**
*noun*

**rely** *verb* (**relied**, **relying**) (foll. by *on*) trust
confidently, depend on for help etc.

**REM** *abbreviation* rapid eye movement;
movement of the eyeballs during sleep, indicating a period of dreaming.

**remain** *verb* **1** be there after other parts have
been removed or used or dealt with. **2** be
in the same place or condition during fur-

ther time, continue to be; *remained in
London; remained faithful.*

**remainder** *noun* **1** the remaining people,
things, or part. **2** the quantity left after
subtraction or division. ● *verb* dispose of
unsold copies of (a book) at a reduced
price.

**remains** *plural noun* **1** what remains after
other parts or things have been removed or
used. **2** ancient buildings or objects that
have survived when others are destroyed;
relics. **3** a dead body; *his mortal remains.*

**remake** *verb* (*pronounced* ree-**mayk**) (**remade**, **remaking**) make again. ● *noun*
(*pronounced* **ree**-mayk) something remade,
especially a new version of an old film.

**remand** *verb* return (a prisoner) to custody
while further evidence is sought. ● *noun*
remanding, being remanded. □ **on remand**
held in custody after being remanded.
**remand centre** a place where accused
people are sent to await trial.

**remark** *noun* a written or spoken comment.
● *verb* **1** make a remark, say. **2** notice.

**remarkable** *adjective* worth noticing, exceptional, unusual. □ **remarkably** *adverb*

**remarry** *verb* (**remarried**, **remarrying**)
marry again. □ **remarriage** *noun*

**Rembrandt** (**rem**-brănt) (Rembrandt
Harmensz van Rijn) (1606–69), Dutch
painter.

**REME** *abbreviation* Royal Electrical and
Mechanical Engineers.

**remediable** (ri-**meed**-i-abŭl) *adjective* able
to be remedied.

**remedial** (ri-**meed**-iăl) *adjective* **1** providing
a remedy for a disease or deficiency; *remedial exercises.* **2** (of teaching) for slow or
disadvantaged pupils. □ **remedially** *adverb*

**remedy** *noun* something that cures or
relieves a disease or that puts a matter
right. ● *verb* (**remedied**, **remedying**) be a
remedy for, put right.

**remember** *verb* **1** keep in one's mind. **2** recall knowledge or experience to one's
mind; be able to do this. **3** think of (a
person), especially in making a gift;
*remembered me in his will.* **4** mention as
sending greetings; *remember me to your
mother.*

**remembrance** *noun* **1** remembering; being
remembered; memory. **2** something that
reminds people, a memento or memorial.
□ **Remembrance Sunday** (also **Remembrance Day**) the Sunday nearest to 11
November, when those killed in the two
World Wars and in later conflicts are
commemorated.

**remind** *verb* cause to remember or think of
something.

**reminder** *noun* a thing that reminds someone; a note written to remind someone.

**reminisce** (rem-in-iss) *verb* think or talk about past events and experiences.

**reminiscence** (rem-in-iss-ĕns) *noun* **1** thinking or talking about past events. **2** an account of what one remembers; *wrote his reminiscences*. **3** a thing that is reminiscent of something else.

**reminiscent** (rem-in-iss-ĕnt) *adjective* **1** inclined to reminisce; *she was in a reminiscent mood*. **2** (foll. by *of*) having characteristics that recall something to one's mind; *his style is reminiscent of Picasso's*. □ **reminiscently** *adverb*

**remiss** (ri-miss) *adjective* negligent; *you have been remiss in your duties*.

**remission** *noun* **1** God's pardon or forgiveness of sins. **2** the remitting of a debt or penalty; the shortening of a convict's prison sentence for good behaviour. **3** reduction of the force or intensity of something; *slight remission of the pain*.

**remit** *verb* (**remitted, remitting**) **1** cancel (a debt); refrain from inflicting (a punishment). **2** make or become less intense; *we must not remit our efforts*. **3** send (money, a document, etc.) to a person or place; *please remit the interest to my home address*. **4** postpone. **5** forgive (sins).

**remittance** *noun* **1** the sending of money to a person. **2** the money sent.

**remittent** *adjective* (of a fever or disease) abating at intervals.

**remix** *verb* (ree-**miks**) mix again. ●*noun* (ree-miks) a remixed recording.

**remnant** *noun* **1** a small remaining quantity or trace of something. **2** a small piece of cloth left when the rest of the roll has been used or sold.

**remodel** *verb* (**remodelled, remodelling**; *Amer.* **remodeled, remodeling**) model again or differently; reconstruct or reorganize.

**remold** Amer. spelling of REMOULD.

**remonstrance** (ri-**mon**-străns) *noun* remonstrating, a protest.

**remonstrate** (rem-ŏn-strayt) *verb* make a protest; *remonstrated with him about his behaviour*.

**remorse** *noun* **1** deep regret for one's wrongdoing. **2** compassion, pity. □ **remorseful** *adjective*, **remorsefully** *adverb*

**remorseless** *adverb* relentless; without compassion. □ **remorselessly** *adverb*

**remortgage** *verb* mortgage again; revise the terms of an existing mortgage on (a property).

**remote** *adjective* **1** far away in place or time; *the remote past*. **2** far from civilization; *a remote village*. **3** not close in relationship or connection; *a remote ancestor; remote causes*. **4** slight; *I haven't the remotest idea*. **5** aloof; not friendly. □ **remote control** control of

apparatus from a distance, usually by means of electricity or radio. □ **remotely** *adverb*, **remoteness** *noun*

**remould** (*Amer.* **remold**) *verb* (*pronounced* ree-**mohld**) mould again; reconstruct the tread of (a tyre). ●*noun* (*pronounced* ree-mohld) a remoulded tyre.

**removable** *adjective* able to be removed.

**removal** *noun* **1** removing; being removed. **2** transfer of furniture etc. to a different house.

**remove** *verb* **1** take off or away from the place occupied. **2** dismiss from office. **3** get rid of; *this removes the last of my doubts*. ●*noun* **1** a form or division in some schools. **2** a stage or degree; a degree of difference; *this is several removes from the truth*. □ **remover** *noun*

**removed** *adjective* distant, remote; *a dialect not far removed from Cockney*. □ **cousin once removed** a cousin's child or parent. **cousin twice removed** a cousin's grandchild or grandparent.

**remunerate** (ri-**mewn**-er-ayt) *verb* pay (a person) for services rendered. □ **remuneration** *noun*, **remunerative** *adjective*

**Remus** (ree-mŭs) (*Rom. legend*) the twin brother of Romulus.

**Renaissance** (rĕ-**nay**-săns) *noun* **1** the revival of art and literature in Europe (influenced by classical forms) in the 14th–16th centuries; the period of this. **2** (**renaissance**) any similar revival. □ **Renaissance man** a person with many talents or interests.

**renal** (ree-năl) *adjective* of the kidneys.

**rename** *verb* give a fresh name to.

**renascent** (ri-nas-ĕnt) *adjective* springing up anew; being reborn. □ **renascence** *noun*

**rend** *verb* (**rent, rending**) (*old use*) tear, wrench.

**Rendell,** Ruth (born 1930), English writer of crime and psychological suspense novels.

**render** *verb* **1** give, especially in return or exchange or as something due; *a reward for services rendered*. **2** present or send in; *account rendered*. **3** cause to become; *rendered him helpless*. **4** give a performance of (a play or character). **5** translate; *rendered into English*. **6** melt down (fat). **7** cover (stone or brick) with a coat of plaster.

**rendezvous** (**ron**-day-voo) *noun* (*plural* **rendezvous,** *pronounced* **ron**-day-vooz) **1** a prearranged meeting. **2** a prearranged or regular meeting-place. ●*verb* (**rendezvoused, rendezvousing**) meet at a rendezvous.

**rendition** (ren-**dish**-ŏn) *noun* **1** a performance of a dramatic role or musical piece etc. **2** a translation.

**renegade** (ren-i-gayd) *noun* someone who deserts from a group, cause, or faith.

**renege** (ri-**neeg** or ri-**nayg**) *verb* **1** (often foll. by *on*) go back on (one's word etc.), fail to keep (a promise etc.). **2** (in card games) revoke.

**renew** *verb* **1** restore to its original state. **2** replace with a fresh supply; *the tyres need renewing*. **3** get or make or give again; *renewed their acquaintance*. **4** arrange for a continuation or continued validity of; *renew one's subscription*. □ **renewable** *adjective*, **renewal** *noun*

**rennet** (ren-it) *noun* a substance made from the stomach membrane of a calf or from certain fungi, used to curdle milk in making cheese or junket.

**Renoir**[1] (rě-**nwahr** or ren-wahr), Jean (1894–1979), French film director.

**Renoir**[2] (rě-**nwahr** or ren-wahr), Pierre Auguste (1841–1919), French impressionist painter.

**renounce** *verb* **1** give up (a claim or right etc.) formally; *renounced his title.* **2** reject; refuse to abide by (an agreement etc.).

**renovate** (ren-ŏ-vayt) *verb* repair; renew. □ **renovation** *noun*, **renovator** *noun*

**renown** (*rhymes with* down) *noun* fame.

**renowned** *adjective* famous, celebrated.

**rent**[1] *see* REND. ● *noun* a tear in a garment etc.

**rent**[2] *noun* payment made periodically for the use of land or accommodation or for equipment such as a telephone. ● *verb* **1** pay rent for temporary use of. **2** allow to be used in return for payment of rent. □ **rent-boy** *noun* (*slang*) a young male prostitute.

**rental** *noun* **1** the amount paid or received as rent. **2** renting.

**rentier** (**rahn**-ti-ay) *noun* a person living on income from property, investments, etc.

**renumber** *verb* change the numbering of.

**renunciation** (ri-nun-si-**ay**-shŏn) *noun* renouncing; giving something up.

**reopen** *verb* open again.

**reorder** *verb* **1** order again; order further supplies of. **2** put into a different sequence.

**reorient** *verb* **1** change or adjust (a person's ideas or outlook). **2** help (a person) find his or her bearings again.

**reorientate** *verb* = REORIENT. □ **reorientation** *noun*

**reorganize** *verb* (*also* **reorganise**) organize in a new way. □ **reorganization** *noun*

**rep** *noun* (*informal*) **1** a business firm's travelling representative. **2** repertory; *a rep theatre.*

**repaint** *verb* paint again or differently. ● *noun* **1** repainting. **2** a repainted thing.

**repair** *verb* **1** restore to good condition after damage or the effects of wear and tear. **2** put right, make amends for. **3** go; *repaired to the coffee room.* ● *noun* **1** the act or process of repairing something. **2** condition as regards being repaired; *keep it in good repair.* □ **repairable** *adjective*, **repairer** *noun*

**reparable** (**rep**-er-ăbŭl) *adjective* (of a loss etc.) able to be made good.

**reparation** (rep-er-ay-shŏn) *noun* **1** making amends. **2** (**reparations**) compensation for war damage, demanded by the victor from a defeated enemy.

**repartee** (rep-ar-tee) *noun* a witty reply; ability to make witty replies.

**repast** (ri-**pahst**) *noun* (*formal*) a meal.

**repatriate** (ree-**pat**-ri-ayt) *verb* return (a person) to his or her own country. □ **repatriation** *noun*

**repay** *verb* (**repaid**, **repaying**) **1** pay back (money). **2** do, make, or give in return; *repaid kindness with kindness.* □ **repayment** *noun*

**repayable** *adjective* able or needing to be repaid.

**repeal** *verb* withdraw (a law) officially. ● *noun* the repealing of a law.

**repeat** *verb* **1** say, do, or occur again. **2** say aloud (something heard or learnt); *repeat the oath after me.* **3** (of food) produce a taste in one's mouth after being eaten due to belching. **4** supply a further consignment of; *we cannot repeat this article.* ● *noun* **1** repeating. **2** something that is repeated; *a repeat order.* □ **repeat oneself** say or do the same thing again.

**repeatable** *adjective* able to be repeated; suitable for being repeated.

**repeatedly** *adverb* again and again.

**repeater** *noun* a device that repeats a signal.

**repel** *verb* (**repelled**, **repelling**) **1** drive away; *repelled the attackers.* **2** refuse to accept; *repelled all offers of help.* **3** be impossible for (a substance) to penetrate; *the surface repels moisture.* **4** push away from itself by an unseen force; *one north magnetic pole repels another.* **5** be repulsive or distasteful to.

**repellent** *adjective* **1** repelling, arousing distaste. **2** not penetrable by a specified substance; *the fabric is water-repellent.* ● *noun* a substance that repels something; *insect repellents.*

**repent** *verb* feel regret about (what one has done or failed to do). □ **repentance** *noun*, **repentant** *adjective*

**repercussion** (ree-per-kush-ŏn) *noun* **1** the recoil of something after impact. **2** an echo. **3** an indirect effect or reaction.

**repertoire** (rep-er-twar) *noun* a stock of songs, plays, acts, etc. that a person or company knows and is prepared to perform.

**repertory** (rep-er-ter-i) *noun* **1** a repertoire. **2** theatrical performances of various plays for short periods (not for long runs as in

London theatres). □ **repertory company** or **theatre** one giving such performances.

**repetition** noun repeating, being repeated; an instance of this.

**repetitious** (rep-i-**tish**-ŭs) adjective repetitive.

**repetitive** (ri-**pet**-it-iv) adjective characterized by repetition. □ **repetitive strain injury** a painful condition affecting the hands or arms, caused by prolonged repetitive movements. □ **repetitively** adverb

**rephrase** verb express using different words.

**repine** (ri-**pyn**) verb fret, be discontented.

**replace** verb **1** put back in place. **2** take the place of. **3** find or provide a substitute for. □ **replaceable** adjective

**replacement** noun **1** replacing or being replaced. **2** a person or thing that replaces another.

**replant** verb plant again or differently.

**replay** verb (pronounced ree-**play**) play (a match or recording etc.) again. ●noun (pronounced **ree**-play) the replaying of a match or recorded incident.

**replenish** verb fill (a thing) again; renew (a supply etc.). □ **replenishment** noun

**replete** (ri-**pleet**) adjective **1** well stocked or supplied. **2** full, gorged. □ **repletion** noun

**replica** (**rep**-lik-ă) noun an exact copy or reproduction of something.

**replicate** (**rep**-lik-ayt) verb make a replica of; reproduce; repeat. □ **replication** noun

**reply** verb (**replied, replying**) answer; say in answer. ●noun **1** replying. **2** what is replied, an answer.

**report** verb **1** give an account of (something seen, done, or studied); tell as news. **2** make a formal accusation about (an offence or offender). **3** present oneself to a person when one arrives or returns. **4** be responsible to a certain person as one's superior or supervisor. ●noun **1** a spoken or written account of something seen, done, or studied. **2** a description for publication or broadcasting. **3** a periodical statement about a pupil's or employee's work and conduct. **4** rumour, a piece of gossip. **5** an explosive sound like that made by a gun. □ **reported speech** a speaker's words as reported by another person (e.g. Tom said, "I will go" becomes in reported speech Tom said that he would go).

**reportage** (rep-or-**tah**zh) noun the reporting of news for the press etc.; a particular style of doing this.

**reportedly** adverb according to reports.

**reporter** noun a person employed to report news etc. for publication or broadcasting.

**repose** noun **1** rest, sleep. **2** a peaceful state or effect, tranquillity. ●verb **1** rest, lie. **2** place (trust etc.).

**reposeful** adjective inducing or showing repose. □ **reposefully** adverb

**repository** noun a place where things are stored.

**repossess** verb regain possession of (goods on which credit payments have not been kept up). □ **repossession** noun

**reprehend** (rep-ri-**hend**) verb rebuke.

**reprehensible** (rep-ri-**hen**-sibŭl) adjective deserving rebuke. □ **reprehensibly** adverb

**represent** (re-pri-**zent**) verb **1** show (a person, thing, or scene) in a picture or play etc. **2** describe or declare to be; representing himself as an expert. **3** state in polite protest or remonstrance; we must represent to them the risks involved. **4** symbolize; in Roman numerals C represents 100. **5** be an example or embodiment of; the election results represent the views of the electorate. **6** act as a deputy, agent, or spokesman for. **7** (pronounced ree-pri-**zent**) present or submit (a cheque) again for payment.

**representation** noun **1** representing or being represented. **2** something that represents another, e.g. a picture or diagram. **3** (**representations**) statements made in the form of an appeal, protest, or allegation.

**representational** adjective (in art) portraying a subject as it appears to the eye.

**representative** adjective **1** typical of a group or class. **2** containing examples of a number of types; a representative selection. **3** consisting of elected representatives; based on representation by these; representative government. ●noun **1** a sample or specimen of something. **2** a person's or firm's agent. **3** a person chosen to represent another or others, or to take part in a legislative assembly on their behalf. □ **House of Representatives** the lower house of Congress in the USA and of other national parliaments.

**repress** verb keep down, suppress; keep (emotions etc.) from finding an outlet. □ **repression** noun

**repressed** adjective suffering from repression of the emotions.

**repressive** adjective serving or intended to repress a person or thing. □ **repressively** adverb

**reprieve** (ri-**preev**) noun **1** postponement or cancellation of a punishment, especially of the death sentence. **2** temporary relief from danger; postponement of trouble. ●verb give a reprieve to.

**reprimand** (**rep**-ri-mahnd) noun a rebuke, especially a formal or official one. ●verb give a reprimand to.

**reprint** verb (pronounced ree-**print**) print again in the same or a new form. ●noun (*pronounced* **ree**-print) the reprinting of a book; a book reprinted.

**reprisal** (ri-**pry**-zǎl) *noun* an act of retaliation.

**reprise** (ri-**preez**) *noun* **1** a repeated passage in music. **2** a repeated song etc. in a musical performance.

**reproach** *verb* express disapproval to (a person) for a fault or offence. ●*noun* **1** reproaching; an instance of this. **2** a thing that brings disgrace or discredit. □ **above** *or* **beyond reproach** deserving no blame; perfect.

**reproachful** *adjective* expressing reproach. □ **reproachfully** *adverb*

**reprobate** (**rep**-rǒ-bayt) *noun* an immoral or unprincipled person.

**reprobation** (rep-rǒ-**bay**-shǒn) *noun* strong condemnation.

**reproduce** *verb* **1** produce a copy of (a picture etc.). **2** cause to be seen or heard again or to occur again. **3** have a specified quality when reproduced; *some colours don't reproduce well.* **4** produce (offspring). □ **reproducible** *adjective*

**reproduction** *noun* **1** reproducing; being reproduced. **2** a copy of a painting etc. □ **reproduction furniture** furniture made in imitation of an earlier style.

**reproductive** *adjective* of or belonging to reproduction; *the reproductive system.*

**reproof** *noun* an expression of condemnation for a fault or offence.

**reprove** *verb* rebuke, reprimand, tell off.

**reptile** *noun* a member of the class of cold-blooded animals with a backbone and relatively short legs or no legs at all, e.g. snakes, lizards, crocodiles, tortoises. □ **reptilian** (rep-**til**-iǎn) *adjective & noun*

**republic** *noun* a country in which the supreme power is held by the people or their elected representatives, or by an elected or nominated president, not by a king or queen.

**republican** *adjective* of, like, or advocating a republic. ●*noun* **1** a person advocating republican government. **2** (**Republican**) a member of the Republican Party, one of the two main political parties in the USA.

**repudiate** (ri-**pew**-di-ayt) *verb* reject or disown utterly, deny; *repudiate the accusation.* □ **repudiation** *noun*, **repudiator** *noun*

**repugnant** (ri-**pug**-nǎnt) *adjective* distasteful, objectionable. □ **repugnance** *noun*

**repulse** *verb* **1** drive back (an attacking force). **2** reject (an offer or help etc.) firmly.

**repulsion** *noun* **1** repelling; being repelled. **2** a feeling of strong distaste, revulsion.

**repulsive** *adjective* **1** arousing disgust. **2** repelling things; *a repulsive force.* □ **repulsively** *adverb*, **repulsiveness** *noun*

**reputable** (**rep**-yoo-tǎbǔl) *adjective* having a good reputation, respected. □ **reputably** *adverb*

**reputation** *noun* **1** what is generally said or believed about a person or thing; *she has a reputation for honesty.* **2** public recognition for one's abilities or achievements; *built up a reputation.*

**repute** (ri-**pewt**) *noun* reputation; *I know him by repute.*

**reputed** (ri-**pewt**-id) *adjective* said or thought to be; *his reputed father.* □ **reputedly** *adverb*

**request** *noun* **1** the act of asking for something; *at my request.* **2** a thing asked for. ●*verb* make a request for. □ **by** *or* **on request** in response to a request. **request stop** a place where a bus etc. stops only on request.

**requiem** (**rek**-wi-em) *noun* a special mass for the repose of the souls of the dead; a musical setting for this.

**require** *verb* **1** need, depend on for success or fulfilment etc.; *cars require regular servicing.* **2** order or oblige; *Civil Servants are required to sign the Official Secrets Act.* **3** wish to have; *will you require tea?*

**requirement** *noun* a thing required; a need.

**requisite** (**rek**-wiz-it) *adjective* required by circumstances, necessary to success. ●*noun* a thing needed for some purpose.

**requisition** *noun* an official order laying claim to the use of property or materials; a formal written demand for something that is needed. ●*verb* demand or order by a requisition.

**requite** (ri-**kwyt**) *verb* **1** make a return for (a service) or to (a person). **2** avenge (a wrong or injury etc.). □ **requital** *noun*

**reredos** (**reer**-doss) *noun* an ornamental screen covering the wall above the back of an altar.

**re-route** (ree-**root**) *verb* (**re-routed, re-routeing**) send or carry by a different route.

**rerun** *verb* (*pronounced* ree-**run**) (**reran, rerunning**) run again. ●*noun* (*pronounced* **ree**-run) **1** an act of rerunning. **2** a repeat of a film etc.

**resale** *noun* sale to another person of something one has bought.

**rescind** (ri-**sind**) *verb* repeal or cancel (a law or rule etc.). □ **rescission** *noun*

**rescript** (**ree**-skript) *noun* **1** a pope's written reply to an appeal for a decision. **2** any papal decision. **3** an official edict or announcement.

**rescue** *verb* save from attack, capture, danger, etc. ●*noun* rescuing, being rescued. □ **rescuer** *noun*

**research** (ri-**serch** *or* **ree**-serch) *noun* careful study and investigation, especially in order to discover new facts or information. ●*verb* do research into; *the subject has been fully researched.* □ **researcher** *noun*

■**Usage** The second pronunciation, with stress on the first syllable, is considered incorrect by some people.

**resell** *verb* (**resold, reselling**) sell (what one has bought) to another person.

**resemble** *verb* be like (another person or thing). □ **resemblance** *noun*

**resent** (ri-zent) *verb* feel displeased and indignant about; feel insulted by (something said or done). □ **resentment** *noun*

**resentful** *adjective* feeling resentment. □ **resentfully** *adverb*

**reservation** *noun* **1** reserving; being reserved. **2** a reserved seat or accommodation etc.; a record of this; *our hotel reservations.* **3** a limitation on one's agreement or acceptance of an idea; *we accept the plan in principle but have certain reservations; without reservation.* **4** (in full **central reservation**) a strip of land between the carriageways of a road. **5** an area of land set apart by a government for some special purpose or for the exclusive use of certain people, e.g. American or Canadian Indians.

**reserve** *verb* **1** put aside or order for a later occasion or for special use. **2** retain; *the company reserves the right to offer a substitute.* **3** postpone; *reserve judgement.* ●*noun* **1** something reserved for future use; an extra amount or stock kept available for use when needed. **2** (also **reserves**) forces outside the regular armed services and liable to be called out in an emergency. **3** an extra player chosen in case a substitute should be needed in a team. **4** an area of land reserved for some special purpose; *a nature reserve.* **5** a limitation on one's agreement or acceptance of an idea etc. **6** a reserve price. **7** a tendency to avoid showing one's feelings; lack of friendliness. □ **in reserve** in a state of being unused but available. **reserve price** the lowest price that will be accepted for something sold at an auction or exhibition.

**reserved** *adjective* (of a person) showing reserve of manner; uncommunicative.

**reservist** *noun* a member of a country's reserve forces.

**reservoir** (rez-er-vwar) *noun* **1** a natural or artificial lake that is a source of water. **2** a container for a supply of fuel or other liquid. **3** a supply or collection of information etc.

**reshuffle** *verb* **1** shuffle (cards) again. **2** change the posts or responsibilities of (a group of people). ●*noun* reshuffling; *a Cabinet reshuffle.*

**reside** *verb* **1** have one's home (in a certain place). **2** be present or vested in a person; *supreme authority resides in the President.*

**residence** *noun* **1** a place where one lives. **2** a house; *desirable residence for sale.* **3** residing; *take up residence.* □ **in residence** living in a specified place for the performance of one's work or duties. □ **residency** *noun*

**resident** *adjective* residing, in residence. ●*noun* **1** a permanent inhabitant of a place, not a visitor. **2** (at a hotel) a person staying overnight.

**residential** (rez-i-**den**-shăl) *adjective* **1** containing or suitable for private houses; *a residential area.* **2** connected with or based on residence; *residential qualifications for voters.*

**residual** (ri-**zid**-yoo-ăl) *adjective* left over as a residue. □ **residually** *adverb*

**residuary** (ri-**zid**-yoo-er-i) *adjective* **1** residual. **2** of the residue of an estate. □ **residuary legatee** the one who inherits the remainder of an estate after specific items have been allotted to others.

**residue** (**rez**-i-dew) *noun* the remainder, what is left over.

**residuum** (ri-**zid**-yoo-ŭm) *noun* (*plural* **residua**) a residue, especially after combustion or evaporation.

**resign** *verb* give up or surrender (one's job, property, claim, etc.). □ **resign oneself to** be ready to accept and endure, accept as inevitable.

**resignation** *noun* **1** resigning. **2** a statement conveying that one wishes to resign. **3** a resigned attitude or expression.

**resigned** *adjective* showing patient acceptance of an unwelcome task or situation. □ **be resigned to** resign oneself to. □ **resignedly** (ri-**zyn**-idli) *adverb*

**resilient** (ri-**zil**-iĕnt) *adjective* **1** springing back to its original form after being bent or stretched; springy. **2** (of a person) readily recovering from shock or depression etc. □ **resiliently** *adverb*, **resilience** *noun*

**resin** (**rez**-in) *noun* **1** a sticky substance that oozes from pine trees and many other plants, used in making varnish etc. **2** a similar substance made synthetically, used in making plastics. □ **resinous** *adjective*

**resist** *verb* **1** oppose; use force to prevent something from happening or being successful. **2** regard (a plan or idea) unfavourably. **3** be undamaged or unaffected by; prevent from penetrating; *pans that resist heat.* **4** refrain from accepting or yielding to; *can't resist chocolates.*

**resistance** *noun* **1** resisting; the power to resist something. **2** an influence that hinders or stops something. **3** the property of not conducting heat or electricity; the measure of this. **4** (also **Resistance**) a secret organization resisting the authorities, especially in an enemy-occupied country. □ **the line of least resistance** the easiest method or course.

**resistant** *adjective* offering resistance, capable of resisting; *heat-resistant plastics*.

**resistivity** (rez-iss-**tiv**-iti) *noun* the power of a specified material to resist the passage of electric current.

**resistor** *noun* a device having resistance to the passage of electric current.

**resit** *verb* (**resat**, **resitting**) sit (an examination) again after a failure.

**resoluble** (ri-zol-yoo-bŭl) *adjective* able to be resolved or analysed.

**resolute** (**rez**-ŏ-loot) *adjective* showing great determination. □ **resolutely** *adverb*, **resoluteness** *noun*

**resolution** *noun* **1** the quality of being resolute, great determination. **2** a mental pledge, something one intends to do; *New Year resolutions*. **3** a formal statement agreed on by a committee or assembly. **4** the solving of a problem. **5** the process of separating something or being separated into constituent parts.

**resolve** *verb* **1** decide firmly. **2** solve or settle (a problem or doubts etc.). **3** separate into constituent parts. ●*noun* **1** something one has decided to do, a resolution; *and she kept her resolve*. **2** great determination.

**resolved** *adjective* (of a person) resolute.

**resonant** (**rez**-ŏn-ănt) *adjective* **1** resounding, echoing. **2** tending to emphasize or prolong sound, especially by vibration. □ **resonance** *noun*

**resonate** (**rez**-ŏn-ayt) *verb* produce or show resonance; resound. □ **resonator** *noun*

**resort** (ri-**zort**) *verb* **1** turn for help; adopt as an expedient; *resorted to violence*. **2** go, especially as a frequent or customary practice; *police watched the bars to which he was known to resort*. ●*noun* **1** an expedient or measure; *resorting to this; compulsion is our only resort; without resort to violence*. **2** a popular holiday place. □ **in the last resort** when everything else has failed.

**resound** (ri-**zownd**) *verb* **1** (of a voice or sound etc.) fill a place with sound; produce echoes. **2** (of a place) be filled with sound; echo.

**resounding** *adjective* (of an event etc.) notable; *a resounding victory*. □ **resoundingly** *adverb*

**resource** *noun* **1** something to which one can turn for help or support or to achieve one's purpose. **2** a means of relaxation or amusement. **3** ingenuity, quick wit. **4** (**resources**) available assets; *we pooled our resources*. **5** (**resources**) a source of

wealth to a country; *natural resources such as minerals*.

**resourceful** *adjective* clever at finding ways of doing things. □ **resourcefully** *adverb*, **resourcefulness** *noun*

**respect** *noun* **1** admiration felt towards a person or thing that has good qualities or achievements; politeness arising from this. **2** attention, consideration; *showing respect for people's feelings*. **3** relation, reference; *this is true with respect to English but not to French*. **4** a particular detail or aspect; *in this one respect*. **5** (**respects**) polite greetings; *pay one's respects*. ●*verb* feel or show respect for. □ **respecter** *noun*

**respectable** *adjective* **1** of good social standing; honest and decent; proper in appearance or behaviour. **2** of a moderately good standard or size etc., not bringing disgrace or embarrassment; *a respectable score*. □ **respectably** *adverb*, **respectability** *noun*

**respectful** *adjective* showing respect. □ **respectfully** *adverb*, **respectfulness** *noun*

**respecting** *preposition* concerning, with respect to.

**respective** *adjective* of or relating to each as an individual; *were given places according to their respective ranks*.

**respectively** *adverb* for each separately in the order mentioned; *she and I gave £10 and £5 respectively*.

**respiration** *noun* **1** breathing. **2** (in living organisms) the absorption of oxygen and release of energy and carbon dioxide.

**respirator** *noun* **1** a device worn over the nose and mouth to filter or purify the air. **2** an apparatus for giving artificial respiration.

**respiratory** (ri-**spir**-ă-ter-i) *adjective* of or involving respiration.

**respire** *verb* breathe; (of plants) perform the process of respiration.

**respite** (**ress**-pyt) *noun* **1** an interval of rest or relief. **2** delay permitted before an obligation must be fulfilled or a penalty suffered.

**resplendent** *adjective* brilliant with colour or decorations. □ **resplendently** *adverb*

**respond** *verb* **1** answer. **2** (foll. by *to*) act or behave in answer to or because of; *the horse responds to the bridle*; *the disease did not respond to treatment*.

**respondent** *noun* the defendant in a lawsuit, especially in a divorce case.

**response** *noun* **1** an answer. **2** any part of the liturgy said or sung in answer to the priest. **3** an act, feeling, or movement produced by a stimulus or by another's action.

**responsibility** *noun* **1** being responsible. **2** something for which one is responsible.

**responsible** *adjective* **1** legally or morally obliged to take care of something or to carry out a duty; liable to be blamed for loss or failure. **2** having to account for one's actions; *you will be responsible to the president himself.* **3** capable of rational conduct; trustworthy; *a responsible person.* **4** involving important duties; *a responsible position.* **5** being the cause of something; *the plague was responsible for many deaths.* □ **responsibly** *adverb*

**responsive** *adjective* responding warmly and favourably to an influence. □ **responsiveness** *noun*

**respray** *verb* spray again. ● *noun* the act or process of respraying.

**rest**[1] *verb* **1** be still; stop moving or working, especially to regain one's vigour. **2** cause or allow to do this; *sit down and rest your feet.* **3** (of a matter under discussion) be left without further investigation. **4** place or be placed for support; *rested the parcel on the table.* **5** (foll. by *on*) rely on, be based on; *the case rests on evidence of identification.* **6** (of a look) alight, be directed; *his gaze rested on his son.* ● *noun* **1** inactivity or sleep as a way of regaining one's vigour; a period of this. **2** a prop or support for an object. **3** an interval of silence between notes in music; a sign indicating this. □ **at rest** not moving; free from trouble or anxiety. **come to rest** stop moving. **rest-cure** *noun* a prolonged period of rest as medical treatment. **be resting** (of an actor) be out of work. **rest room** (*Amer.*) a toilet in a public building.

**rest**[2] *verb* **1** remain in a specified state; *rest assured, it will be a success.* ● *noun* (**the rest**) the remaining part; the others. □ **rest with** be left in the hands or charge of; *it rests with you to suggest terms.*

**restaurant** (**rest**-er-ont) *noun* a place where meals can be bought and eaten.

**restaurateur** (rest-er-ă-**ter**) *noun* a restaurant-keeper.

**rested** *adjective* refreshed by resting.

**restful** *adjective* giving rest or a feeling of rest; quiet and relaxing. □ **restfully** *adverb*, **restfulness** *noun*

**restitution** *noun* **1** restoration of a thing to its proper owner or its original state. **2** reparation for injury or damage.

**restive** *adjective* restless; resisting control. □ **restively** *adverb*, **restiveness** *noun*

**restless** *adjective* **1** unable to rest or to be still. **2** without rest or sleep; *a restless night.* □ **restlessly** *adverb*, **restlessness** *noun*

**restock** *verb* stock again; renew one's stock.

**restoration** *noun* **1** restoring; being restored. **2** a model, drawing, or reconstruction of an extinct animal, ruined building, etc. □ **the Restoration** the re-establishment of

the monarchy in Britain in 1660 when Charles II became king.

**restorative** (ri-**sto**-ră-tiv) *adjective* tending to restore health or strength. ● *noun* a restorative food or medicine or treatment.

**restore** *verb* **1** bring back to its original state, e.g. by repairing or rebuilding. **2** bring back to good health or vigour. **3** put back in its former position, reinstate. □ **restorer** *noun*

**restrain** *verb* hold back from movement or action; keep under control.

**restrained** *adjective* showing restraint.

**restraint** *noun* **1** restraining; being restrained. **2** something that restrains, a limiting influence. **3** avoidance of exaggeration; moderation; reserve.

**restrict** *verb* put a limit on; subject to limitations. □ **restricted area** an area where there is a special speed limit for motor vehicles, lower than that applied elsewhere. □ **restriction** *noun*

**restrictive** *adjective* restricting. □ **restrictive practice** an industrial agreement that limits competition or output.

**restructure** *verb* give a new structure to.

**result** *noun* **1** that which is produced by an activity or operation, an effect. **2** a statement of the score or the name of the winner in a sporting event, competition, etc. **3** an answer or formula obtained by calculation. ● *verb* **1** (often foll. by *from*) occur as a result; *the troubles that resulted from the merger.* **2** (often foll. by *in*) have a specified result; *the match resulted in a draw.*

**resultant** *adjective* occurring as a result; *the resultant profit.*

**resume** *verb* **1** get, take, or occupy again; *resume one's seat.* **2** begin to speak or work or use again. □ **resumption** *noun*

**résumé** (**rez**-yoom-ay) *noun* **1** a summary. **2** *Amer.* = CURRICULUM VITAE.

**resumptive** *adjective* resuming.

**resurgence** (ri-**ser**-jĕns) *noun* a rise or revival after defeat, destruction, or disappearance etc. □ **resurgent** *adjective*

**resurrect** *verb* bring back into use; *resurrect an old custom.*

**resurrection** *noun* **1** rising from the dead. **2** (**the Resurrection**) that of Christ. **3** revival after disuse.

**resuscitate** (ri-**sus**-i-tayt) *verb* **1** bring back from unconsciousness. **2** revive (a custom, institution, etc.). □ **resuscitation** *noun*

**retail** *noun* the selling of goods to the general public. ● *adjective & adverb* in the retail trade. ● *verb* **1** sell or be sold in the retail trade. **2** recount, relate details of. □ **retailer** *noun*

**retain** *verb* **1** keep in one's possession or use. **2** continue to have, not to lose; *the fire had retained its heat.* **3** keep in one's memory; *she retained a clear impression of the building.*

**4** hold in place; *a retaining wall.* **5** book the services of (a barrister).

**retainer** *noun* **1** a fee paid to secure a person's services. **2** a reduced rent paid to retain unoccupied accommodation. **3** (*old use*) an attendant of a person of rank. □ **old retainer** a faithful old servant.

**retake** *verb* (*pronounced* ree-**tayk**) (**retook**, **retaken**, **retaking**) take (an exam, photograph, etc.) again. ●*noun* (*pronounced* **ree**-tayk) **1** an act of filming a scene again. **2** an act of taking an exam etc. again.

**retaliate** (ri-**tal**-i-ayt) *verb* repay an injury, attack, insult, etc. with a similar one. □ **retaliation** *noun*, **retaliatory** (ri-**tal**-yă-ter-i) *adjective*

**retard** (ri-**tard**) *verb* delay, slow the progress of. □ **retardant** *noun*, **retardation** *noun*

**retarded** *adjective* backward in mental or physical development.

**retch** (*rhymes with* fetch) *verb* strain one's throat as if vomiting.

**retell** *verb* (**retold**, **retelling**) tell (a story etc.) again.

**retention** *noun* **1** retaining or being retained. **2** the condition of retaining urine or other body fluid that would normally be expelled.

**retentive** *adjective* able to retain things; *a retentive memory.* □ **retentiveness** *noun*

**rethink** *verb* (**rethought**, **rethinking**) think about again; plan again and differently.

**reticent** (**ret**-i-sĕnt) *adjective* not revealing one's thoughts and feelings readily. □ **reticently** *adverb*, **reticence** *noun*

**reticulated** (ri-**tik**-yoo-layt-id) *adjective* divided into a network or into small squares with intersecting lines. □ **reticulation** *noun*

**reticule** (**ret**-i-kewl) *noun* (*old use*) a woman's small bag of woven or other material.

**retina** (**ret**-in-ă) *noun* (*plural* **retinas** or **retinae**) a layer of membrane at the back of the eyeball, sensitive to light.

**retinue** (**ret**-in-yoo) *noun* a number of attendants accompanying an important person.

**retire** *verb* **1** give up one's regular work because of advancing age; cause (an employee) to do this. **2** withdraw, retreat. **3** go to bed or to one's private room. □ **retirement** *noun*

**retired** *adjective* **1** having retired from work. **2** withdrawn from society or from observation, secluded.

**retiring** *adjective* shy, avoiding company.

**retort**¹ *verb* make a quick or witty or angry reply. ●*noun* retorting; a reply of this kind.

**retort**² *noun* **1** a vessel (usually of glass) with a long downward-bent neck, used in distilling liquids. **2** a receptacle used in making gas or steel.

**retouch** *verb* improve (a picture or photograph) by making minor alterations.

**retrace** *verb* trace back to the source or beginning; *retrace one's steps.* □ **retraceable** *adjective*

**retract** *verb* **1** pull (a thing) back or in; *the snail retracts its horns.* **2** withdraw (a statement or promise). □ **retractable** *adjective*, **retraction** *noun*, **retractor** *noun*

**retractile** (ri-**trak**-tyl) *adjective* (of a part of the body) retractable.

**retrain** *verb* train again or for something different, especially for new work.

**retread** *verb* (*pronounced* ree-**tred**) put a fresh tread on (a tyre) by moulding rubber to a used foundation. ●*noun* (*pronounced* **ree**-tred) a retreaded tyre.

**retreat** *verb* withdraw when faced with defeat, danger, or difficulty; go away to a place of shelter. ●*noun* **1** retreating; the military signal for this. **2** a military bugle call at sunset. **3** withdrawal into privacy or seclusion, especially for prayer and meditation; a place for this.

**retrench** *verb* reduce (one's expenditure or operations). □ **retrenchment** *noun*

**retrial** *noun* the trying of a lawsuit again.

**retribution** (ret-ri-**bew**-shŏn) *noun* a deserved punishment.

**retributive** (ri-**trib**-yoo-tiv) *adjective* happening or inflicted as retribution.

**retrieve** *verb* **1** regain possession of. **2** find again or extract (stored information etc.). **3** (of a dog) find and bring in (killed game). **4** rescue, restore to a flourishing state; *retrieve one's fortunes.* **5** set right (a loss or error or a bad situation). ●*noun* possibility of recovery; *beyond retrieve.* □ **retrievable** *adjective*, **retrieval** *noun*

**retriever** *noun* a dog of a breed traditionally used to retrieve game.

**retro** (*slang*) *adjective* reviving or harking back to the past; *retro fashion.*

**retroactive** *adjective* effective as from a past date. □ **retroactively** *adverb*

**retrograde** *adjective* **1** going backwards; *retrograde motion.* **2** reverting to a less good condition. ●*verb* **1** move backwards, recede. **2** revert, especially to a less good condition.

**retrogress** (ret-rŏ-**gress**) *verb* move backwards; deteriorate. □ **retrogression** *noun*, **retrogressive** *adjective*

**retrorocket** *noun* an auxiliary rocket discharging its exhaust in the opposite direction to the main rockets, used for slowing a spacecraft.

**retrospect** *noun* □ **in retrospect** when one looks back on a past event or situation.

**retrospection** noun looking back, especially on the past.

**retrospective** adjective **1** looking back on the past. **2** applying to the past as well as the future; *the law could not be made retrospective*. ●noun an exhibition, recital, etc. showing an artist's development over his or her lifetime. □ **retrospectively** adjective

**retroussé** (rĕ-troo-say) adjective (of the nose) turned up at the tip. (¶ French, = tucked up.)

**retroverted** (ret-roh-ver-tid) adjective turned backwards. □ **retroversion** noun

**retry** verb (**retried, retrying**) try (a lawsuit or a defendant) again.

**retsina** (ret-seen-ă) noun Greek white wine flavoured with resin.

**return** verb **1** come or go back. **2** bring, give, put, or send back. **3** say in reply. **4** elect as an MP; *she was returned as MP for Finchley*. ●noun **1** coming or going back. **2** bringing, giving, putting, or sending back. **3** the proceeds or profits of a transaction; *brings a good return on one's investment*. **4** a return ticket. **5** a return match or game. **6** a formal report, e.g. of a set of transactions; *income-tax return*. □ **in return** in exchange. **many happy returns (of the day)** a greeting on a person's birthday. **returning officer** the official conducting an election in a constituency and announcing the result. **return match** or **game** a second match or game between the same opponents. **return ticket** a ticket for a journey to a place and back to one's starting point. □ **returnable** adjective

**reunify** verb restore (especially separated territories) to a political unity. □ **reunification** noun

**reunion** noun **1** reuniting; being reunited. **2** a social gathering of people who were formerly associated.

**reunite** verb unite again after separation.

**reusable** adjective able to be reused.

**reuse** verb (*pronounced* ree-yooz) use again. ●noun (*pronounced* ree-yooss) using or being used again.

**Reuters** (roi-terz) an international news agency. (¶ Established by Baron von Reuter (1816–99).)

**rev** noun a revolution of an engine. ●verb (**revved, revving**) **1** (of an engine) revolve. **2** (often foll. by *up*) cause (an engine) to run quickly, especially when starting.

**Rev.** abbreviation Reverend; *the Rev. John Smith*.

**revalue** verb **1** reassess the value of. **2** give a new (higher) value to (a currency). □ **revaluation** noun

**revamp** verb renovate; give a new appearance to.

**Revd** abbreviation Reverend.

**reveal** verb make known; uncover and allow to be seen.

**reveille** (ri-val-i) noun a military waking-signal sounded on a bugle or drums.

**revel** verb (**revelled, revelling**; *Amer.* **reveled, reveling**) **1** (foll. by *in*) take great delight; *some people revel in gossip*. **2** have a good time; be festive. ●plural noun (**revels**) lively festivities or merrymaking. □ **reveller** noun

**revelation** noun **1** revealing, making known something that was secret or hidden. **2** something revealed, especially something surprising. **3** (**Revelation** or (*informal*) **Revelations**) the last book of the New Testament.

**revelry** noun revelling; revels.

**revenge** noun **1** punishment or injury inflicted in return for what one has suffered. **2** a desire to inflict this. **3** the defeat in a return game of an opponent who won the first game. ●verb avenge. □ **be revenged** or **revenge oneself** get satisfaction by inflicting vengeance. □ **revengeful** adjective, **revengefully** adjective

**revenue** (rev-ĕn-yoo) noun a country's annual income from taxes, duties, etc.

**reverberate** (ri-verb-er-ayt) verb echo, resound. □ **reverberant** adjective, **reverberation** noun, **reverberative** adjective

**revere** (ri-veer) verb feel deep respect for religious veneration for.

**reverence** noun **1** a feeling of awe and respect or veneration; *hold in reverence*; *feel reverence for*. **2** (**Reverence**) a title used for certain members of the clergy. ●verb feel or show reverence towards.

**reverend** adjective **1** deserving to be treated with respect. **2** (**the Reverend**) the title of a member of the clergy (**Very Reverend**, of a dean, **Right Reverend**, of a bishop, **Most Reverend**, of an archbishop or Irish Roman Catholic bishop). ●noun (*informal*) a clergyman. □ **Reverend Mother** the Mother Superior of a convent.

**reverent** adjective feeling or showing reverence. □ **reverently** adjective

**reverential** adjective full of respect, awe, and admiration. □ **reverentially** adverb

**reverie** (rev-er-i) noun a daydream; daydreaming.

**revers** (ri-veer) noun (*plural* **revers**, *pronounced* ri-veerz) a turned-back front edge of the neck of a jacket or bodice.

**reversal** noun reversing; being reversed.

**reverse** adjective facing or moving in the opposite direction; opposite in character or order; upside down. ●verb **1** turn the other way round or up, or inside out. **2** convert to the opposite kind or effect; *reversed the tendency*. **3** annul (a decree or decision etc.). **4** move in the opposite direction; travel backwards; make (something) move or work backwards. ●*noun* **1** the reverse side or effect. **2** the opposite of the usual manner; *the name was printed in reverse*. **3** a piece of misfortune; a setback or defeat. **4** reverse gear. □ **reverse gear** a gear used to make a vehicle travel backwards. **reverse the charges** make the recipient (not the caller) pay for a telephone call. **reversing light** a white light at the rear of a vehicle showing that it is in reverse gear.

**reversible** *adjective* able to be reversed; (of a garment) able to be worn with either side turned outwards.

**reversion** *noun* **1** reverting. **2** the legal right to possess something when its present holder relinquishes it; the returning of a right or property in this way. □ **reversionary** *adjective*

■**Usage** Note that *reversion* does not mean *reversal*.

**revert** *verb* **1** return to a former condition, habit or type. **2** return to a subject in talk or thought. **3** (of property etc.) return or pass to another owner by reversion.

**review** *noun* **1** a general survey of past events or of a subject. **2** a re-examination or reconsideration; *the salary scale is under review*. **3** a ceremonial inspection of troops or a fleet etc. **4** a published report assessing the merits of a book, play, etc. ●*verb* **1** survey. **2** re-examine or reconsider. **3** inspect (troops or a fleet etc.) ceremonially. **4** write a review of (a book, play, etc.). □ **reviewer** *noun*

■**Usage** Do not confuse with **revue**.

**revile** *verb* criticize angrily in abusive language.

**revise** *verb* **1** re-examine and alter or correct. **2** go over (work already studied) in preparation for an examination. □ **Revised Standard Version** a revision of the American Standard Version of the Bible published in 1946–57. **Revised Version** the revision published in 1881–95 of the Authorized Version of the Bible.

**revision** *noun* **1** revising; being revised. **2** a revised version or form.

**revisionist** (ri-vizh-ŏn-ist) *noun* a person who insists on modifying theories or practices that are considered authoritative. □ **revisionism** *noun*

**revisit** *verb* pay another visit to.

**revisory** *adjective* revising; of revision.

**revitalize** *verb* (also **revitalise**) give new life and vitality to.

**revival** *noun* **1** reviving; being revived. **2** something brought back into use or fashion. **3** a reawakening of interest in religion; a special effort with meetings etc. to promote this.

**revivalist** *noun* a person who organizes or conducts meetings to promote a religious revival. □ **revivalism** *noun*

**revive** *verb* **1** come or bring back to life, consciousness, or strength. **2** come or bring back into use, activity, or fashion etc.

**revivify** *verb* restore the vigour of; bring back to life. □ **revivification** *noun*

**revocable** (rev-ŏ-kǎ-bŭl) *adjective* able to be revoked.

**revoke** (ri-vohk) *verb* **1** withdraw or cancel (a decree or licence etc.). **2** fail to follow suit in a card game when able to do so. ●*noun* revoking in a card game.

**revolt** *verb* **1** take part in a rebellion. **2** be in a mood of protest or defiance. **3** feel strong disgust. **4** cause a feeling of strong disgust in (a person). ●*noun* **1** an act or state of rebelling or defying authority. **2** a sense of disgust.

**revolting** *adjective* disgusting, horrible. □ **revoltingly** *adverb*

**revolution** *noun* **1** the overthrow of a government or social order, especially by force. **2** any complete change of method, conditions, etc.; *a revolution in the treatment of burns*. **3** revolving, rotation; a single complete orbit or movement of this kind.

**revolutionary** *adjective* **1** of political revolution. **2** involving a great change; *revolutionary new ideas*. ●*noun* a person who begins or supports a political revolution.

**revolutionize** *verb* (also **revolutionise**) alter (a thing) completely; *the discovery will revolutionize our lives*.

**revolve** *verb* **1** turn or cause to turn round, rotate. **2** move in a circular orbit. **3** turn over (a problem etc.) in one's mind. **4** (foll. by *around*) have as its chief concern, be centred upon; *our lives revolve around the baby*. □ **revolving door** a door with several partitions revolving round a central axis.

**revolver** *noun* a pistol with a revolving mechanism that makes it possible to fire it a number of times without reloading.

**revue** *noun* an entertainment consisting of a series of items such as sketches and songs.

■**Usage** Do not confuse with **review**.

**revulsion** *noun* **1** a feeling of strong disgust. **2** a sudden violent change of feeling; *a revulsion of public feeling in favour of the accused woman*.

**reward** *noun* **1** something given or received in return for what is done or for a service or merit. **2** a sum of money offered for the detection of a criminal or return of lost property etc. ●*verb* give a reward to.

**rewarding** *adjective* (of an occupation) well worth doing; satisfying.

**rewind** verb (**rewound, rewinding**) wind (a film or tape etc.) back to the beginning. ● noun rewinding.

**rewire** verb renew the electrical wiring of.

**reword** verb change the wording of.

**rework** verb revise; remake.

**rewrite** verb (**rewrote, rewritten, rewriting**) write (a thing) again in a different form or style.

**Rex** noun a reigning king. (¶ Latin, = king.)

■**Usage** Used in the same ways as REGINA.

**Reykjavik** (**rayk**-yă-vik) the capital of Iceland.

**Reynolds** (**ren**-ŏldz), Sir Joshua (1723–92), English painter, first President of the Royal Academy.

**Rf** symbol rutherfordium.

**RFC** abbreviation Rugby Football Club.

**Rh** abbreviation Rhesus. ● symbol rhodium.

**r.h.** abbreviation right hand.

**rhapsodize** verb (also **rhapsodise**) talk or write about something in an ecstatic way.

**rhapsody** noun **1** an ecstatic written or spoken statement. **2** a romantic musical composition in an irregular form.

**rhea** noun a South American flightless ostrich-like bird.

**Rheims** alternative spelling of REIMS.

**rhenium** (**reen**-iŭm) noun a rare metallic element occurring naturally in molybdenum ores (symbol Re).

**rheostat** (**ree**-ŏ-stat) noun an instrument used to control the current in an electrical circuit by varying the amount of resistance in it.

**rhesus** (**ree**-sŭs) noun (in full **rhesus monkey**) a small monkey common in northern India. □ **rhesus factor** a substance present in the blood of most people and some animals, causing a blood disorder in a newborn baby whose blood is **rhesus-positive** (= containing this substance) while its mother's blood is **rhesus-negative** (= not containing it).

**rhetoric** (**ret**-er-ik) noun **1** the art of using words impressively, especially in public speaking. **2** language used for its impressive sound; affected or exaggerated expressions.

**rhetorical** (rit-o-ri-kăl) adjective expressed in a way that is designed to be impressive. □ **rhetorical question** something phrased as a question only for dramatic effect and not to seek an answer, e.g. who cares? (= nobody cares). □ **rhetorically** adverb

**rheumatic** (roo-**mat**-ik) adjective of or affected with rheumatism. ● noun (**rheumatics**) (informal) rheumatism. □ **rheumatic fever** a serious form of rheumatism with fever, chiefly in children.

□ **rheumaticky** adjective, **rheumatically** adverb

**rheumatism** (**room**-ă-tizm) noun a disease causing pain in the joints, muscles, or fibrous tissue, especially rheumatoid arthritis.

**rheumatoid** (**room**-ă-toid) adjective of rheumatism. □ **rheumatoid arthritis** a disease causing inflammation and stiffening of the joints.

**rheumatology** (roo-mă-**tol**-ŏji) noun the study of rheumatic diseases. □ **rheumatologist** noun

**Rhine** a river of western Europe, flowing from the Alps through Germany and the Netherlands to the North Sea.

**Rhineland** the region of Germany lying west of the Rhine.

**rhinestone** noun an imitation diamond.

**rhino** noun (plural **rhino** or **rhinos**) (informal) a rhinoceros.

**rhinoceros** noun (plural **rhinoceros** or **rhinoceroses**) a large thick-skinned animal of Africa and south Asia, with a horn or two horns on its nose.

**rhizome** (**ry**-zohm) noun a rootlike stem growing along or under the ground and sending out both roots and shoots.

**Rhode Island** a State of the north-eastern USA.

**Rhodes**[1] a Greek island in the Aegean Sea, off the coast of Turkey.

**Rhodes**[2], Cecil John (1853–1902), British statesman in South Africa, who was instrumental in the development of Rhodesia. □ **Rhodes Scholar** the holder of any of a number of **Rhodes Scholarships** tenable at Oxford University by students from certain overseas countries.

**Rhodesia** (roh-**dee**-shă) the former name of Zimbabwe. □ **Rhodesian** adjective & noun

**rhodium** (**roh**-di-ŭm) noun a metallic element (symbol Rh), used in alloys to increase hardness.

**rhododendron** (roh-dŏ-**den**-drŏn) noun an evergreen shrub with large clusters of trumpet-shaped flowers.

**rhomboid** (**rom**-boid) adjective (also **rhomboidal**) like a rhombus. ● noun a quadrilateral of which only the opposite sides and angles are equal.

**rhombus** (**rom**-bŭs) noun a geometric figure shaped like the diamond on playing cards.

**Rhône** a river rising in the Alps and flowing through France to the Mediterranean Sea.

**rhubarb** noun **1** a garden plant with fleshy reddish leaf-stalks that are used like fruit. **2** (slang) nonsense. **3** (informal) indistinct conversation from a crowd.

**rhyme** noun **1** the similarity of sound between words or syllables or the endings of lines of verse (e.g. line/mine/pine, visit/is it).

**2** a poem with rhymes. **3** a word providing a rhyme to another. ●*verb* form a rhyme; have rhymes. □ **rhyming slang** slang in which words are replaced by words that rhyme with them, e.g. *apples and pears* = stairs. **without rhyme or reason** with no sensible or logical reason.

**rhymester** (**rym**-ster) *noun* a writer of rhymes.

**rhythm** (**rith**-ĕm) *noun* **1** the pattern produced by emphasis and length of notes in music or by long and short or stressed syllables in words. **2** a movement with a regular succession of strong and weak elements; *the rhythm of the heart beating.* **3** a constantly recurring sequence of events. □ **rhythm and blues** popular music with a blues theme and a strong rhythm. **rhythm method** contraception by avoiding sexual intercourse near the time of ovulation (which recurs regularly). **rhythm section** piano (or guitar etc.), bass, and drums in a dance or jazz band. □ **rhythmic** *adjective*, **rhythmical** *adjective*, **rhythmically** *adverb*

**RI** *abbreviation* Rhode Island.

**rib** *noun* **1** each of the curved bones round the chest. **2** a cut of meat from this part of an animal. **3** a curved structural part resembling a rib. **4** each of the hinged rods forming the framework of an umbrella. **5** a knitting stitch of alternating plain and purl stitches producing a raised pattern of vertical lines. ●*verb* (**ribbed**, **ribbing**) **1** support (a structure) with ribs. **2** knit in rib. **3** (*informal*) tease.

**ribald** (**rib**-ăld) *adjective* humorous in a vulgar or disrespectful way. □ **ribaldry** *noun*

**riband** (**rib**-ănd) *noun* a ribbon.

**ribbed** *adjective* **1** with raised ridges. **2** knitted in rib.

**ribbon** *noun* **1** a narrow band of ornamental material used for decoration or for tying something. **2** a ribbon of special colour or pattern worn to indicate the award of a medal or order etc. **3** a long narrow strip of material, e.g. an inked strip used in a typewriter. **4** (**ribbons**) ragged strips. □ **ribbon development** the building of houses along a main road, extending outwards from a town or village.

**ribcage** *noun* the framework of ribs round the chest.

**riboflavin** *noun* (also **riboflavine**) a vitamin of the B complex found in liver, milk, and eggs.

**ribonucleic acid** a nucleic acid in living cells, involved in protein synthesis.

**rice** *noun* **1** a grass grown in marshes in hot countries, producing seeds that are used as food. **2** these seeds. □ **rice-paper** *noun* edible paper made from the pith of an oriental tree, used for painting and in cookery.

**rich** *adjective* **1** having much wealth. **2** having a large supply of something; *the country is rich in natural resources.* **3** splendid, made of costly materials, elaborate; *rich furniture.* **4** producing or produced abundantly; *rich soil; a rich harvest.* **5** (of food) containing a large proportion of fat, butter, eggs, etc. **6** (of a mixture in an internal-combustion engine) containing more than the normal proportion of fuel. **7** (of colour, sound, or smell) pleasantly deep or strong. **8** highly amusing or outrageous. □ **richness** *noun*

**Richard**[1] the name of three kings of England, who reigned as Richard I 1189–99, Richard II 1377–99, Richard III 1483–5.

**Richard**[2], Cliff (original name: Harry Rodger Webb) (born 1940), English pop singer.

**Richardson**, Sir Ralph David (1902–83), English stage and screen actor.

**Richelieu** (**reesh**-li-er) Armand Jean du Plessis (1585–1642), French Cardinal and statesman.

**riches** *plural noun* a great quantity of money, property, or valuable possessions.

**richly** *adjective* **1** in a rich way. **2** thoroughly; *the book richly deserves its success.*

**Richter scale** (**rik**-ter) a scale for measuring the strength of earthquakes. (¶ Named after the American seismologist C. F. Richter (1900–85).)

**rick**[1] *noun* a stack of hay etc.

**rick**[2] (also **wrick**) *noun* a slight sprain or strain. ●*verb* sprain or strain slightly.

**rickets** *noun* a children's disease caused by deficiency of vitamin D, resulting in softening and deformity of the bones.

**rickety** *adjective* shaky, insecure. □ **ricketiness** *noun*

**rickrack** alternative spelling of RICRAC.

**rickshaw** *noun* a light two-wheeled hooded vehicle used in countries of the Far East, pulled along by one or more people.

**ricochet** (**rik**-ŏ-shay) *verb* (**ricocheted** (*pronounced* **rik**-ŏ-shayd), **ricocheting** (*pronounced* **rik**-ŏ-shay-ing)) rebound from a surface as a missile does when it strikes with a glancing blow. ●*noun* a rebound of this kind; a hit made by it.

**ricotta** *noun* soft Italian cheese.

**ricrac** *noun* (also **rickrack**) a zigzag braid trimming.

**rid** *verb* (**rid**, **ridding**) free from something unpleasant or unwanted; *rid the house of mice; was glad to be rid of him.* □ **get rid of** cause to go away; (*informal*) succeed in selling.

**riddance** *noun* ridding. □ **good riddance** an expression of relief at getting rid of something.

**ridden** *see* RIDE. ●*adjective* full of or dominated by; *rat-ridden cellars*; *guilt-ridden*.

**riddle**¹ *noun* **1** a question or statement designed to test ingenuity or give amusement in finding its answer or meaning. **2** something puzzling or mysterious.

**riddle**² *noun* a coarse sieve for gravel or cinders etc. ●*verb* **1** pass (gravel etc.) through a riddle; *riddle the ashes*. **2** pierce with many holes; *riddled the car with bullets*. **3** permeate thoroughly; *be riddled with disease*.

**ride** *verb* (**rode**, **ridden**, **riding**) **1** travel in or be carried on a bicycle, vehicle, horse, etc. **2** sit on and manage a horse. **3** be supported on, float or seem to float; *the ship rode at anchor*; *the moon was riding high*. **4** yield to (a blow) so as to reduce its impact. ●*noun* **1** a spell of riding; a journey in a vehicle; *only a short ride into town*. **2** a track for horse-riding, especially through woods. **3** the feel of a ride; *the car gives a smooth ride*. **4** a piece of equipment on which people ride at a funfair. □ **let it ride** take no further action. **ride high** be elated or successful. **ride out the storm** survive a storm or difficulty successfully. **ride up** (of a garment) work upwards when worn. **take for a ride** (*informal*) deceive or swindle.

**rider** *noun* **1** a person who rides a horse or bicycle etc. **2** an additional clause supplementing a statement etc.; an expression of opinion added to a verdict.

**riderless** *adjective* without a rider.

**ridge** *noun* **1** a narrow raised strip; a line where two upward-sloping surfaces meet. **2** an elongated region of high barometric pressure. □ **ridge-pole** *noun* a horizontal pole supporting the top of a tent.

**ridged** *adjective* formed into ridges.

**ridgeway** *noun* a road along the ridge of a hilltop.

**ridicule** *noun* the process of making a person or thing appear ridiculous. ●*verb* subject to ridicule; make fun of.

**ridiculous** *adjective* **1** deserving to be laughed at, especially in a scornful way. **2** not worth serious consideration, preposterous. □ **ridiculously** *adverb*

**Riding** *noun* each of the former divisions of Yorkshire, **East**, **North**, and **West Riding**.

**riding-light** *noun* a light shown by a ship at anchor.

**Riemann** (**ree**-măn), (Georg Friedrich) Bernhard (1826–66), German mathematician, whose geometry is fundamental to the general theory of relativity.

**Riesling** (**rees**-ling) *noun* a medium-dry white wine.

**rife** *adjective* **1** occurring frequently, widespread; *crime was rife in the city*. **2** (foll. by *with*) abounding in, full of; *the country was rife with rumours of war*.

**riff** *noun* a short repeated phrase in jazz etc.

**riffle** *verb* **1** turn (pages) in quick succession, leaf through quickly; *riffled through the book*. **2** shuffle (playing cards) rapidly by flexing and combining two halves of the pack.

**riff-raff** *noun* the rabble; disreputable people.

**rifle** *noun* a gun, usually fired from the shoulder, with a long barrel cut with spiral grooves to make the bullet spin and so travel more accurately. ●*verb* **1** search and rob; *rifled the safe*. **2** cut spiral grooves in (a gun barrel).

**rift** *noun* **1** a cleft in earth or rock. **2** a crack or split; a break in cloud. **3** a disagreement; a breach in friendly relations. □ **rift-valley** *noun* a steep-sided valley formed by subsidence of the earth's crust.

**rig**¹ *verb* (**rigged**, **rigging**) **1** provide with clothes or equipment; *rigged them out*. **2** fit (a ship) with spars, ropes, sails, etc. **3** set up (a structure) quickly or with makeshift materials. ●*noun* **1** the way a ship's masts and sails etc. are arranged. **2** equipment for a special purpose, e.g. for drilling an oil well; *a test rig*; *an oil rig*. **3** (*informal*) an outfit of clothes. □ **rig-out** *noun* (*informal*) an outfit of clothes.

**rig**² *verb* (**rigged**, **rigging**) manage or control fraudulently; *the election was rigged*.

**Riga** (**Ree**-gă) the capital of Latvia.

**rigger** *noun* a worker on an oil rig.

**rigging** *noun* the ropes etc. used to support masts and control the sails on a ship.

**right** *adjective* **1** (of conduct or actions etc.) morally good, in accordance with justice. **2** proper, correct, true; *the right answer*. **3** suitable; preferable; *the right person for the job*. **4** (*informal*) real; complete; *made a right old mess of it*. **5** of the right-hand side. ●*noun* **1** what is just; a fair claim or treatment; something one is entitled to. **2** the right-hand part or region. **3** the right hand; a blow with this. **4** (in marching) the right foot. **5** (often **Right**) the right wing of a political party or other group. ●*verb* **1** restore to a proper or correct or upright position; *managed to right the boat*. **2** set right, make amends or take vengeance for; *the fault will right itself*; *right a wrong*. ●*adverb* **1** on or towards the right-hand side; *turn right*. **2** straight; *go right on*. **3** (*informal*) immediately; *I'll be right back*. **4** all the way, completely; *went right round it*. **5** exactly; *right in the middle*. **6** very, fully; *dined right royally*. **7** rightly; *you did right to come*. **8** all right; that is correct; I agree. □ **by right** *or* **rights** if right were done. **in the right** having justice or truth on one's side. **on the right side of** in the favour of or liked by (a person). **right angle** an angle of 90°. **at right angles** placed at or turning through a right angle. **right-angled** adjective having a right angle. **right away** immediately. **right hand** the hand that in most people is used more than the left, on the east side of the body when facing north. **right-hand** adjective of or towards this side of a person or the corresponding side of a thing. **right-hand man** a person's indispensable or chief assistant. **right-handed** adjective **1** naturally using the right hand for writing etc. **2** (of a blow or tool) made with or operated by the right hand. **3** (of a screw) be tightened by turning towards the right. **right-hander** noun a right-handed person or blow. **Right Honourable** the title of earls, viscounts, barons, Privy Counsellors, and certain other high officials. **right-minded** adjective having proper or honest principles. **right of way** the right to pass over another's land, a path that is subject to such a right; the right to proceed, while another vehicle must wait. **right oh!, right ho!** = RIGHTO. **Right Reverend** see REVEREND. **right wing 1** those who support more conservative or traditional policies than others. **2** the right side of a football etc. team on the field.

**righteous** adjective **1** doing what is morally right; making a show of this. **2** morally justifiable; *full of righteous indignation.* □ **righteously** adverb, **righteousness** noun

**rightful** adjective in accordance with what is just or proper or legal. □ **rightfully** adverb

**rightist** noun a member of the right wing of a political party. ● adjective of the right wing in politics etc. □ **rightism** noun

**rightly** adverb justly, correctly, properly, justifiably.

**rightmost** adjective furthest to the right.

**rightness** noun being just, correct, proper, or justifiable.

**righto** interjection (*informal*) an expression of agreement.

**rightward** adverb & adjective towards or facing the right. □ **rightwards** adverb

**rigid** adjective **1** stiff, not bending or yielding. **2** strict, inflexible; *rigid rules.* □ **rigidly** adverb, **rigidity** (ri-jid-iti) noun

**rigmarole** (rig-mă-rohl) noun **1** a long rambling statement. **2** a complicated formal procedure.

**rigor** Amer. spelling of RIGOUR.

**rigor mortis** stiffening of the body after death. (¶ Latin.)

**rigorous** (rig-er-ŭs) adjective **1** strict, severe; *rigorous discipline.* **2** thorough, detailed; *a rigorous search.* **3** harsh, unpleasant; *a rigorous climate.* □ **rigorously** adverb

**rigour** (rig-er) noun (*Amer.* **rigor**) **1** severity, strictness. **2** harshness of weather or conditions; *the rigours of famine.*

**rile** (*rhymes with* mile) verb (*informal*) annoy, irritate.

**Riley**¹ □ **the life of Riley** (*informal*) a carefree luxurious existence.

**Riley**², Bridget Louise (born 1931), English painter of op art.

**rill** noun a small stream.

**rim** noun **1** the edge or border of something more or less circular. **2** the outer edge of a wheel, on which a tyre is fitted.

**rime** noun frost.

**rimless** adjective (of spectacles) made without frames.

**rimmed** adjective edged, bordered; *red-rimmed eyes.*

**Rimsky-Korsakov**, Nikolai Andreievich (1844–1908), Russian composer.

**rind** (*rhymes with* mind) noun a tough outer layer or skin on fruit, cheese, bacon, etc.

**ring**¹ noun **1** the outline of a circle. **2** something shaped like this, a circular band, especially as worn on the finger. **3** an enclosure for a circus, sports event, cattle-show etc. **4** a combination of people acting together for control of operations or policy. ● verb **1** enclose with a ring, encircle. **2** put a ring on (a bird etc.) to identify it. **3** cut a ring in the bark of (a tree), especially to retard its growth and improve fruit production. □ **the ring** bookmakers. **make** or **run rings round** do things much better than (another person). **ring-binder** noun a loose-leaf binder with ring-shaped clasps. **ring-dove** noun a wood pigeon. **ring-fence** verb protect or guarantee (funds). **ring finger** the third finger, especially of the left hand, on which a wedding ring is worn. **ring-pull** adjective (of a can) having a seal that can be broken by pulling the attached ring. **ring road** a bypass encircling a town.

**ring**² verb (**rang, rung, ringing**) **1** give out a loud clear resonant sound, like that of a bell when struck. **2** cause (a bell) to do this; signal by ringing; *bells rang out the old year.* **3** be filled with sound; *the stadium rang with cheers.* **4** telephone (a person). ● noun **1** the act of ringing a bell. **2** a ringing sound or tone. **3** a tone or feeling of a particular kind; *it has the ring of truth.* **4** (*informal*) a telephone call. □ **ring a bell** (*informal*) arouse a vague memory, sound faintly familiar. **ring off** end a telephone call by replacing the receiver. **ring the changes** vary things. **ring the curtain up** or **down 1** signal that the curtain on a theatre stage should be raised or lowered. **2** mark the beginning or end of an enterprise etc. **ring up 1** telephone (a person). **2** record (an amount) on a cash register.

**ringer** noun a person who rings bells. □ **be a ringer** (or **dead ringer**) **for** look exactly like (a person).

**ringleader** *noun* a person who leads others in wrongdoing or in opposition to authority.

**ringlet** *noun* a long tubular curl.

**ringmaster** *noun* the person in charge of a circus performance.

**ringside** *noun* the area immediately beside a boxing or circus ring etc. □ **ringside seat** a position from which one has a clear view of the scene of action.

**ringworm** *noun* a skin disease producing round scaly patches on the skin, caused by a fungus.

**rink** *noun* **1** a skating-rink. **2** a strip of bowling green. **3** a team in bowls or curling.

**rinse** *verb* **1** wash lightly with water. **2** wash out soap or impurities from. ● *noun* **1** rinsing. **2** a solution washed through hair to tint it.

**Rio de Janeiro** (jĕ-**neer**-oh) the chief port and former capital of Brazil.

**Rio de la Plata** (plah-tă) the River Plate.

**Rio Grande** (*pronounced* grand) a river of North America flowing south-east from Colorado to the Gulf of Mexico, forming the border between the USA and Mexico.

**Rioja** (ree-**oh**-hă) *noun* a wine produced in the region around the River Ebro in northern Spain.

**riot** *noun* **1** a wild disturbance by a crowd of people. **2** a profuse display of something; *a riot of colour*. **3** (*informal*) a very amusing thing or person. ● *verb* take part in a riot or in disorderly revelry. □ **read the Riot Act** caution or reprimand sternly. **run riot 1** throw off all restraint. **2** (of plants) grow or spread rapidly in an uncontrolled way. □ **rioter** *noun*

**riotous** *adjective* **1** disorderly, unruly. **2** boisterous, unrestrained; *riotous laughter*. □ **riotously** *adverb*

**RIP** *abbreviation* rest in peace. (¶ From the Latin, *requiescat* (or *requiescant*) *in pace*.)

**rip**[1] *verb* (**ripped, ripping**) **1** tear apart, remove by pulling roughly. **2** become torn. **3** rush along. ● *noun* ripping; a torn place. □ **let rip** (*informal*) say or do something forcefully and without restraint. **rip-cord** *noun* a cord for pulling to release a parachute from its pack. **rip into** (*informal*) criticize or scold severely. **rip off** (*slang*) defraud; steal. **rip-off** *noun* (*slang*) something fraudulent; a swindle. **rip-roaring** *adjective* wildly noisy and exciting. □ **ripper** *noun*

**rip**[2] *noun* **1** a dissolute person. **2** a worthless horse.

**riparian** (ry-**pair**-iăn) *adjective* of or on a riverbank.

**ripe** *adjective* **1** (of fruit or grain etc.) matured and ready to be gathered, used, eaten or drunk. **2** (of a person's age) advanced; *lived to a ripe old age*. **3** ready; prepared or able to undergo something; *the time is ripe for revolution; the land is ripe for development*. □ **ripely** *adverb*, **ripeness** *noun*

**ripen** *verb* make or become ripe.

**riposte** (ri-**posst**) *noun* **1** a quick retort. **2** a quick return thrust in fencing. ● *verb* deliver a riposte.

**ripple** *noun* **1** a small wave or series of waves. **2** something resembling this in appearance or movement. **3** a gentle sound that rises and falls; *a ripple of laughter*. ● *verb* form or cause ripples.

**ripsaw** *noun* a coarse saw for sawing wood along the grain.

**Rip van Winkle** a character in a story (by Washington Irving) who slept for 20 years and awoke to find the world completely changed.

**rise** *verb* (**rose, risen, rising**) **1** come or go upwards; grow or extend upwards. **2** get up from lying, sitting, or kneeling; get out of bed. **3** (of a meeting, Parliament, etc.) come to the end of a session; adjourn. **4** become upright or erect. **5** come to life again after death; *Christ is risen*. **6** rebel; *rise in revolt*. **7** (of the wind) begin to blow more strongly. **8** (of the sun etc.) become visible above the horizon. **9** increase in amount, number, or intensity; *prices are rising; her spirits rose*. **10** achieve a higher position or status; *rose to the rank of colonel*. **11** (of bread or cake etc.) swell by the action of yeast or other raising agent. **12** have its origin, begin or begin to flow; *the Thames rises in the Cotswolds*. ● *noun* **1** rising, an upward movement. **2** an upward slope; a small hill. **3** an increase in amount, number, or intensity; an increase in wages. **4** an upward movement in rank or status. □ **get** *or* **take a rise out of** (*informal*) draw (a person) into a display of annoyance or into making a retort. **give rise to** cause. **rise to the occasion** *or* **challenge** prove oneself able to deal with an unexpected situation. **rising damp** moisture absorbed upwards from the ground into a wall. **rising five** etc. (of a child) nearing the age of five. **rising generation** young people, those who are growing up.

**riser** *noun* **1** a person or thing that rises; *an early riser*. **2** a vertical piece between treads of a staircase.

**risible** *adjective* laughable; ludicrous.

**rising** *noun* a revolt.

**risk** *noun* **1** the possibility of meeting danger or suffering harm or loss; exposure to this. **2** a person or thing insured or similarly representing a source of risk; *not a good risk*. ● *verb* expose to the chance of injury or loss; accept the risk of.

**risky** *adjective* (**riskier, riskiest**) full of risk. □ **riskily** *adverb*, **riskiness** *noun*

**Risorgimento** (ri-sorj-i-**ment**-oh) *noun* a movement in the 19th century to unite Italy.

**risotto** (ri-**zot**-oh) *noun* (*plural* **risottos**) an Italian dish of rice cooked in stock with chopped meat or cheese and vegetables.

**risqué** (**risk**-ay) *adjective* (of a story) slightly indecent. (¶ French.)

**rissole** *noun* a mixture of minced meat, vegetables, etc. formed into a round shape, coated in breadcrumbs and fried.

**rit.** *abbreviation* (in music) ritardando.

**ritardando** = RALLENTANDO.

**rite** *noun* a religious or other solemn ritual. □ **rites of passage** ritual events marking stages in life e.g. marriage.

**ritual** *noun* **1** the series of actions used in a religious or other ceremony. **2** a procedure regularly followed. ● *adjective* of or done as a ritual. □ **ritually** *adverb*, **ritualistic** *adjective*

**ritzy** *adjective* (**ritzier**, **ritziest**) (*informal*) high-class, luxurious, ostentatiously smart. (¶ From *Ritz*, the name of luxurious hotels, named after C. Ritz (died 1918), Swiss hotel-owner.)

**rival** *noun* **1** a person or thing competing with another. **2** a person or thing that can equal another in quality. ● *adjective* being a rival or rivals. ● *verb* (**rivalled**, **rivalling**; *Amer.* **rivaled**, **rivaling**) be comparable to, seem or be as good as. □ **rivalry** *noun*

**riven** (**riv**-ĕn) *adjective* split; torn violently.

**river** *noun* **1** a large natural stream of water flowing in a channel. **2** a great flow; *rivers of blood*.

**riverside** *noun* the land along a river-bank.

**rivet** (**riv**-it) *noun* a nail or bolt for holding two pieces of metal together, its headless end being beaten or pressed down to form a head when it is in place. ● *verb* (**riveted**, **riveting**) **1** fasten with a rivet. **2** flatten (the end of a bolt) when it is in place. **3** fix, make immovable; *she stood riveted to the spot*. **4** (especially as **riveting** *adjective*) fascinating; holding one's attention. □ **riveter** *noun*

**Riviera** (rivi-**air**-ă), **the** the region along the Mediterranean coast, of SE France, Monaco, and NW Italy. ● *noun* (**riviera**) a region thought to resemble this.

**rivulet** (**riv**-yoo-lit) *noun* a small stream.

**Riyadh** (ree-**ad**) the capital of Saudi Arabia.

**RM** *abbreviation* Royal Marines.

**RN** *abbreviation* Royal Navy.

**Rn** *symbol* radon.

**RNA** *abbreviation* ribonucleic acid.

**RNLI** *abbreviation* Royal National Lifeboat Institution.

**roach** *noun* (*plural* **roach** or **roaches**) a small freshwater fish related to the carp.

**road** *noun* **1** a way with a prepared surface by which people, animals, or vehicles may pass between places. **2** a way of reaching or achieving something; *the road to success*. **3** (**roads**) (also **roadstead**) a piece of water near a shore in which ships can ride at anchor. □ **on the road** travelling. **road fund licence** a disc displayed on a vehicle certifying payment of road tax. **road-hog** *noun* (*informal*) a reckless or inconsiderate driver. **road-holding** *noun* the stability of a moving vehicle; its ability to travel round bends at speed. **road-metal** *noun* broken stone for the foundation of a road or railway. **road sense** ability to behave safely on roads. **road tax** a regular tax payable on road vehicles. **road test** a test of a vehicle by using it on a road. **road-test** *verb* test in this way.

**roadblock** *noun* a barrier set up to stop traffic.

**roadhouse** *noun* an inn or restaurant on a major road.

**roadie** *noun* (*informal*) a person who helps a touring band with their equipment.

**roadshow** *noun* a touring radio show, political campaign, etc.

**roadside** *noun* the border of a road.

**roadstead** (**rohd**-sted) *noun* = roads (*see* ROAD sense 3).

**roadster** *noun* an open car without rear seats.

**roadway** *noun* a road; the part of this intended for vehicles.

**roadworks** *plural noun* the construction or repair of roads.

**roadworthy** *adjective* (of a vehicle) fit to be used on a road. □ **roadworthiness** *noun*

**roam** *verb* wander. ● *noun* a wander.

**roan** *adjective* (of an animal) having a coat thickly sprinkled with white or grey hairs. ● *noun* a roan horse or other animal.

**roar** *noun* **1** a long deep loud sound, like that made by a lion. **2** loud laughter. ● *verb* **1** give a roar. **2** express in this way; *the crowd roared its approval*. **3** be full of din. **4** drive a vehicle at high speed. □ **roaring drunk** *adjective* very drunk and noisy. **roaring forties** stormy ocean tracts between latitudes 40° and 50° S. **roaring success** a great success. **roaring trade** very brisk trade. □ **roarer** *noun*

**roast** *verb* **1** cook (meat etc.) in an oven or by exposure to heat. **2** expose to great heat. ● *adjective* roasted; *roast beef*. ● *noun* roast meat; a joint of meat for roasting.

**roaster** *noun* **1** a fowl etc. suitable for roasting. **2** an apparatus that will roast meat etc.

**roasting** *adjective* very hot. ● *noun* severe criticism.

**rob** *verb* (**robbed**, **robbing**) **1** steal from; commit robbery. **2** deprive of what is due or normal; *robbing us of our sleep.* □ **robber** *noun,* **robbery** *noun*

**robe** *noun* **1** a long loose garment, especially a ceremonial one. **2** (especially *Amer.*) a dressing gown. ● *verb* dress in a robe.

**Robert** the name of three kings of Scotland, including Robert I 'the Bruce' (reigned 1306–29).

**Robeson** (**rohb**-sŏn), Paul Le Roy (1898–1976), American Black actor and bass singer.

**Robespierre** (**rohbs**-pi-air), Maximilien de (1758–94), French revolutionary leader.

**robin** *noun* **1** (also **robin redbreast**) a small brown red-breasted European bird. **2** (*Amer.*) a red-breasted thrush.

**Robin Hood** a semi-legendary English medieval outlaw, said to have robbed the rich and helped the poor.

**robot** (**roh**-bot) *noun* **1** a machine programmed to move automatically and perform certain tasks. **2** a person who seems to act like a machine. **3** (in South Africa) traffic lights.

**robotic** (rŏ-**bot**-ik) *adjective* of or using robots. ● *noun* (**robotics**) the study and development of robots; the use of robots in industry.

**Rob Roy** (Robert MacGregor) (1671–1734), Scottish Highland bandit.

**robust** (rŏ-**bust**) *adjective* strong, vigorous. □ **robustly** *adverb,* **robustness** *noun*

**roc** *noun* a gigantic bird of Eastern legend.

**rock**[1] *noun* **1** the hard part of the earth's crust, underlying the soil. **2** a mass of this; a large stone or boulder. **3** a hard sweet made in cylindrical sticks. □ **the Rock** Gibraltar. **on the rocks** (*informal*) **1** short of money. **2** (of a marriage, business, etc.) in difficulties, about to collapse. **3** (of a drink) served neat with ice-cubes. **rock-bottom** *adjective* (of prices etc.) very low. **rock-cake** *noun* a small fruit cake with a rugged surface. **rock crystal** transparent colourless quartz. **rock-garden** *noun* a mound or bank containing large stones and planted with rock plants. **rock plant** a plant suitable for growing on or among rocks. **rock salmon** dogfish or catfish sold as food.

**rock**[2] *verb* **1** move or be moved gently to and fro; sway or shake. **2** disturb greatly by shock; *the scandal rocked the country.* ● *noun* **1** a rocking movement. **2** modern music with a heavy beat popular with young people, performed by bands or solo singers. □ **rock and roll** (also **rock 'n' roll**) a style of popular dance-music originating in the 1950s with a strong beat and elements of blues. **rock the boat** (*informal*) do something that upsets plans or progress.

**Rockefeller** (rok-ĕ-fel-er), John Davison (1839–1937), American industrialist and philanthropist.

**rocker** *noun* **1** a thing that rocks something or is rocked. **2** each of the curved bars on which a rocking-chair etc. is mounted. **3** a rocking-chair. **4** a switch that pivots between the 'on' and 'off' positions.

**rockery** *noun* a rock-garden.

**rocket** *noun* **1** a firework or signalling device that rises into the air when ignited and then explodes. **2** a structure that flies by expelling gases that are the products of combustion, used to propel a warhead or spacecraft; a missile, spacecraft, etc. propelled by this. **3** (*slang*) a reprimand. ● *verb* (**rocketed, rocketing**) move rapidly upwards or away.

**rocketry** *noun* the science or practice of using rockets for propelling missiles or spacecraft.

**rocking-chair** *noun* a chair mounted on rockers or with springs so that it can be rocked by the sitter.

**rocking-horse** *noun* a toy horse mounted on rockers or springs.

**rocky** *adjective* (**rockier, rockiest**) **1** of or like rock. **2** full of rocks. **3** unsteady. □ **rockily** *adverb,* **rockiness** *noun*

**Rocky Mountains** (also **Rockies**) the great mountain system running north-south in western North America.

**rococo** (rŏ-**koh**-koh) *noun* an ornate style of decoration common in Europe in the 18th century. ● *adjective* of or in this style.

**rod** *noun* **1** a slender straight round stick or metal bar. **2** a cane or birch used for flogging people. **3** a fishing-rod. **4** a former measure of length equal to 5½ yards.

**rode** *see* RIDE.

**rodent** *noun* an animal (e.g. rat, mouse, squirrel) with strong front teeth used for gnawing.

**rodeo** (**roh**-di-oh *or* roh-**day**-oh) *noun* (*plural* **rodeos**) **1** a round-up of cattle on a ranch, for branding etc. **2** an exhibition of cowboys' skill in handling animals.

**Rodin** (**roh**-dan), Auguste (1840–1917), French sculptor.

**rodomontade** (rod-ŏ-mon-**tayd**) *noun* boastful talk or behaviour.

**roe**[1] *noun* **1** (also **hard roe**) a mass of eggs in a female fish's ovary. **2** (also **soft roe**) a male fish's milt.

**roe**[2] *noun* (*plural* **roe** *or* **roes**) (also **roe-deer**) a kind of small deer.

**roebuck** *noun* a male roe-deer.

**roentgen** (**runt**-yĕn) *noun* (also **röntgen**) a unit of ionizing radiation. (¶ Named after RÖNTGEN.)

**rogations** *plural noun* a special litany for use on **Rogation Days**, the three days before Ascension Day.

**roger** *interjection* (in signalling) your message has been received and understood.

**rogue** *noun* **1** a dishonest or unprincipled person. **2** a mischievous person. **3** a wild animal driven away from the herd or living apart from it; *a rogue elephant*. **4** an inferior or defective specimen. □ **rogues' gallery** a collection of photographs of criminals. □ **roguery** *noun*

**roguish** *adjective* mischievous, affectedly playful. □ **roguishly** *adverb*, **roguishness** *noun*

**roister** *verb* make merry noisily. □ **roisterer** *noun*

**role** *noun* **1** an actor's part. **2** a person's or thing's function. □ **role model** a person regarded by others as an ideal to be copied. **role-playing** *noun* (also **role-play**) acting as an aid in teaching, psychotherapy, etc.

**roll** *verb* **1** move or cause to move along in contact with a surface, either on wheels or by turning over and over. **2** turn on an axis or over and over; revolve. **3** form into a cylindrical or spherical shape. **4** flatten by means of a roller; *roll out the pastry*. **5** rock from side to side, e.g. in walking. **6** move or pass steadily; *the years rolled on*. **7** undulate; *rolling hills*. **8** make a long continuous vibrating sound; *the thunder rolled*. **9** start functioning or moving; *the cameras rolled*. ● *noun* **1** a cylinder formed by turning flexible material over and over upon itself without creasing it. **2** something having this shape, an undulation; *rolls of fat*. **3** a small individual portion of bread baked in a rounded shape. **4** an official list or register. **5** a rolling movement. **6** a long steady vibrating sound. □ **be rolling in** (*informal*) have a large supply of. **Master of the Rolls** one of the judges in the Court of Appeal, in charge of the Public Record Office. **roll-call** *noun* the calling of a list of names, to check that all are present. **rolled gold** a thin coating of gold applied to another metal. **roll in** arrive in great numbers. **rolled oats** husked and crushed oats. **rolling-mill** *noun* a machine or factory for rolling metal into various shapes. **rolling-pin** *noun* a cylinder used to flatten pastry or dough. **rolling-stock** *noun* railway engines, carriages, and wagons. **rolling stone** a person who does not settle in one place. **roll-neck** *adjective* (of a sweater) having a high turned-over neck. **roll of honour** a list of people whose achievements are honoured. **roll-on** *adjective* (of deodorant etc.) applied by means of a ball that rotates in the neck of a container. **roll-on, roll-off** (of a ferry) that vehicles can be driven on to and off. **roll-top desk**

a desk with a flexible cover that slides in curved grooves. **roll up 1** (*informal*) arrive in a vehicle; arrive casually. **2** wind or make into a roll. **roll-up** *noun* (also **roll-your-own**) a hand-rolled cigarette. **strike off the rolls** debar (especially a solicitor) from practising his or her profession.

**roller** *noun* **1** a cylinder used for flattening or spreading things, or on which something is wound. **2** a long swelling wave. □ **roller coaster** a switchback at a fair. **roller skate** a boot or frame for the foot with small wheels attached for gliding on a hard surface. **roller towel** a towel with its ends joined so that it is continuous, hung over a roller.

**rollicking** *adjective* full of boisterous high spirits.

**Rolling Stones** a British rock group formed in 1962, with Mick Jagger as the lead vocalist.

**rollmop** *noun* a rolled uncooked pickled herring fillet.

**Rolls**[1], Charles Stewart (1877–1910), English motoring and aviation pioneer, founder (with Royce) of Rolls-Royce Ltd.

**Rolls**[2] *noun* a Rolls-Royce car.

**roly-poly** *noun* a pudding consisting of suet pastry spread with jam, rolled up, and boiled. ● *adjective* plump, podgy.

**ROM** *abbreviation Computing* read-only memory (*see* READ).

**Roman** *adjective* **1** of ancient or modern Rome. **2** of the ancient Roman republic or empire. **3** of the Christian Church of Rome, Roman Catholic. ● *noun* **1** a member of the ancient Roman republic or empire. **2** a native or inhabitant of Rome. **3** a Roman Catholic. **4** (**Romans**) (in full the **Epistle to the Romans**) an epistle of St Paul to the Church at Rome. **5** (**roman**) plain upright type (not italic), like that used for the definitions in this dictionary. □ **Roman candle** a tubular firework that sends out coloured sparks. **Roman Catholic** of the Church that acknowledges the Pope as its head; a member of this Church. **Roman Catholicism** the faith of the Roman Catholic Church. **Roman Empire** a powerful empire established by Augustus in 27 BC, eventually extending into western and southern Europe, northern Africa, and south-west Asia. It was divided by Theodosius in AD 395. **Roman nose** a nose with a high bridge. **Roman numerals** letters representing numbers (I = 1, V = 5, X = 10, L = 50, C = 100, D = 500, M = 1,000).

**romance** (roh-**manss**) *noun* **1** an imaginative story; literature of this kind; *medieval romances*. **2** a romantic situation, event, or atmosphere. **3** a love story; a love affair resembling this. **4** a picturesque exaggeration or falsehood. ●*verb* exaggerate or distort the truth in an imaginative way. □ **Romance languages** the group of European languages descended from Latin (French, Italian, Spanish, etc.).

**Romanesque** (roh-măn-**esk**) *noun* a style of art and architecture in Europe in about 900–1200, with massive vaulting and round arches. ●*adjective* of this style.

**Romania** (also **Rumania**) a country in eastern Europe.

**Romanian** (also **Rumanian**) *noun* **1** a person from Romania. **2** the language of Romania. ●*adjective* of Romania or its people or language.

**Romanov** (roh-mă-nof) the name of a dynasty that ruled in Russia from 1613 to 1917.

**romantic** *adjective* **1** appealing to the emotions by its imaginative, heroic, or picturesque quality. **2** involving a love affair. **3** enjoying romantic situations. **4** (also **Romantic**) (of music or literature) richly imaginative, not conforming to classical conventions. ●*noun* a person who enjoys romantic situations etc. □ **romantically** *adverb*

**romanticism** *noun* (also **Romanticism**) the romantic style in art, music, etc. □ **romanticist** *noun*

**romanticize** *verb* (also **romanticise**) make romantic; indulge in romantic thoughts.

**Romany** (**rom**-ă-ni) *noun* **1** a gypsy. **2** the language of gypsies. ●*adjective* of Romanies or their language.

**Rome 1** the capital of Italy. **2** the ancient Roman republic or empire. **3** Roman Catholicism.

**Romeo** *noun* (*plural* **Romeos**) a romantic male lover. (¶ Named after the hero of Shakespeare's romantic tragedy *Romeo and Juliet*.)

**Rommel**, Erwin (1891–1944), German general, commander of the Afrika Korps in the Second World War.

**romp** *verb* **1** play about in a lively way, as children do. **2** (*informal*) get along easily; *romped home*. ●*noun* a spell of romping.

**rompers** *plural noun* (also **romper suit**) a child's one-piece garment covering the legs and trunk.

**Romulus** (*Rom. legend*) the founder of Rome, twin brother of Remus.

**rondeau** (**ron**-doh) *noun* (*plural* **rondeaux**, *pronounced* same or **ron**-dohz) a short poem with only two rhymes throughout and the opening words used twice as a refrain.

**rondel** *noun* a rondeau.

**rondo** *noun* (*plural* **rondos**) a piece of music with a theme that recurs several times.

**Röntgen** (**runt**-yĕn), Wilhelm Conrad von (1845–1923), German physicist, the discoverer of X-rays.

**röntgen** alternative spelling of ROENTGEN.

**rood** *noun* **1** a crucifix, especially one raised on the middle of the rood-screen. **2** a quarter of an acre. □ **Holy Rood** (*old use*) the Cross of Christ. **rood-screen** *noun* a carved wooden or stone screen separating the nave from the chancel in a church.

**roof** *noun* **1** a structure covering the top of a building. **2** the top of a car or tent etc. ●*verb* cover with a roof; be the roof of. □ **hit** or **go through the roof** (*informal*) become very angry. **roof-garden** *noun* a garden on the flat roof of a building. **roof of the mouth** the upper part of the mouth cavity, the palate. **roof-rack** *noun* a framework to carry luggage on the roof of a car.

**roofing** *noun* material used for a roof.

**rook** *noun* **1** a black crow that nests in colonies. **2** a chess piece with a top shaped like battlements. ●*verb* swindle, charge (a person) an extortionate price.

**rookery** *noun* **1** a colony of rooks; a place where these nest. **2** a colony or breeding place of penguins or seals.

**rookie** *noun* (*slang*) a new recruit.

**room** *noun* **1** space that is or could be occupied by something. **2** a part of a building enclosed by walls or partitions; the people present in this. **3** opportunity or scope or ability to allow something; *there is room for improvement*. □ **room-mate** *noun* a person sharing a room with another. **room service** provision of food etc. to a hotel guest in his or her room.

**roomy** *adjective* (**roomier**, **roomiest**) having plenty of room, spacious. □ **roominess** *noun*

**Roosevelt¹** (roh-zĕ-velt), Franklin D(elano) (1882–1945), 32nd President of the USA 1932–1945, whose 'New Deal' lifted America out of the 1930s depression.

**Roosevelt²** (roh-zĕ-velt), Theodore (1858–1919), 26th President of the USA 1901–8.

**roost** *noun* a place where birds perch or where they settle for sleep. ●*verb* (of birds) perch; settle for sleep. □ **come home to roost** (of an action) react unfavourably on the doer.

**rooster** *noun* a male domestic cock.

**root¹** *noun* **1** the part of a plant that supports it in the earth and absorbs water and nourishment from the soil. **2** (**roots**) a person's emotional attachment to a place in which the person or his or her family has lived for a long time. **3** a small plant with root attached, for transplanting. **4** an edible root, a plant with this (e.g. carrot, turnip); *root crops*. **5** the part of a bodily organ or structure that is embedded in tissue; *the root of a tooth*. **6** a source or basis; *the root of all evil*; *get to the root of the matter*. **7** a number in relation to a given number which it produces when multiplied by itself once (= *square root*) or a specified number of times; *2 is the cube root of 8* (2 × 2 × 2 = 8). ●*verb* **1** take root; cause to do this. **2** cause to stand fixed and unmoving; *was rooted to the spot by fear*. **3** establish deeply and firmly; *the feeling is deeply rooted*. □ **root out** or **up** find and get rid of. **take root 1** send down roots. **2** (of an idea etc.) become established.

**root²** *verb* **1** (of an animal) turn up ground with its snout or beak in search of food. **2** rummage; find or extract by doing this; *root out some facts and figures*. □ **root for** (*slang*) support actively by applause etc.; *rooting for their team*.

**rootless** *adjective* **1** having no root or roots. **2** (of a person) having no roots in a community.

**rootstock** *noun* **1** a rhizome. **2** a plant into which a graft is inserted.

**rope** *noun* **1** strong thick cord; a length of this. **2** a quantity of similar things strung together; *a rope of pearls*. ●*verb* **1** fasten, secure, or catch with rope. **2** fence off with rope. □ **rope in** persuade to take part in an activity. **rope-ladder** *noun* a ladder made of two ropes connected by cross-pieces. **the ropes** the procedure for doing something; *know the ropes*.

**ropy** *adjective* (also **ropey**) (**ropier, ropiest**) (*informal*) poor in quality. □ **ropiness** *noun*

**Roquefort** (**rok**-for) *noun* (*trade mark*) a soft blue cheese made from ewes' milk.

**ro-ro** *adjective* (of a ferry) roll-on roll-off.

**rorqual** (**ror**-kwăl) *noun* a whale with a dorsal fin.

**Rorschach test** (**raw**-shahk) a personality test based on a person's interpretation of a standard set of ink-blots.

**rosaceous** (roh-**zay**-shŭs) *adjective* of the large family of plants including the rose.

**rosary** *noun* **1** a set series of prayers used in the Roman Catholic Church. **2** a string of beads for keeping count of these prayers as they are recited.

**rose¹** *noun* **1** a bush or shrub bearing ornamental usually fragrant flowers. **2** its flower. **3** deep pink colour. **4** the perforated sprinkling-nozzle of a watering-can. ●*adjective* deep pink. □ **rose-hip** *noun* the fruit of a rose. **roses in one's cheeks** a healthy rosy complexion. **see through rose-coloured spectacles** have an unrealistically cheerful view of things. **rose-water** *noun* a fragrant liquid perfumed with roses. **rose window** a circular patterned

window in a church. **Wars of the Roses** *see* WAR.

**rose²** *see* RISE.

**rosé** (**roh**-zay) *noun* a light pink wine. (¶ French, = pink.)

**roseate** (**roh**-zi-ăt) *adjective* deep pink, rosy.

**Roseau** (roh-**zoh**) the capital of Dominica.

**rosebud** *noun* the bud of a rose.

**rosemary** (**rohz**-mer-i) *noun* an evergreen shrub with fragrant leaves used for flavouring food.

**Rosetta stone** a basalt stone found in Egypt in 1799, dating from *c.*200 BC, with parallel inscriptions in hieroglyphs, demotic Egyptian, and Greek, providing the key to the decipherment of ancient Egyptian texts.

**rosette** *noun* **1** a rose-shaped badge or ornament made of ribbon etc. **2** a rose-shaped carving.

**rosewood** *noun* any of several fragrant close-grained woods used for making furniture.

**Rosh Hashana** the Jewish New Year.

**rosin** (**roz**-in) *noun* a kind of resin.

**RoSPA** *abbreviation* (*Brit.*) Royal Society for the Prevention of Accidents.

**Ross**, Sir James Clark (1800–62), English polar explorer, after whom the Ross Sea, Ross Barrier, and Ross Island in the Antarctic are named.

**Rossetti** (rŏ-**zet**-i), Christina Georgina (1830–94), English poet, sister of Dante Gabriel (1828–82), English poet and painter, a founder of the Pre-Raphaelite Brotherhood.

**Rossini** (rŏ-**seen**-i), Gioacchino Antonio (1792–1868), Italian composer of operas.

**roster** (**ros**-ter) *noun* a list showing people's turns of duty etc. ●*verb* place on a roster.

**Rostropovich**, Mstislav Leopoldovich (born 1927), Russian-born cellist, conductor, and composer.

**rostrum** (**ros**-trŭm) *noun* (*plural* **rostra** or **rostrums**) a platform for public speaking or for an orchestral conductor.

**rosy** *adjective* (**rosier, rosiest**) **1** rose-coloured, deep pink. **2** promising, hopeful; *a rosy future*. □ **rosily** *adverb*, **rosiness** *noun*

**rot** *verb* (**rotted, rotting**) **1** (of animal or vegetable matter) lose its original form by chemical action caused by bacteria or fungi etc.; decay. **2** perish or become weak through lack of use or activity. ●*noun* **1** rotting; rottenness. **2** (*slang*) nonsense. **3** a series of failures; *the rot set in*.

**rota** (**roh**-tă) *noun* a list of duties to be done or people to do them in rotation.

**Rotarian** (roh-**tair**-iăn) *noun* a member of a Rotary Club.

**rotary** *adjective* rotating; acting by rotating; *a rotary drill*. □ **Rotary Club** a local branch of an international association (**Rotary In-**

ternational) formed by businessmen for the purpose of rendering service to the community.

**rotate** *verb* **1** turn round an axis or central point; revolve. **2** arrange or deal with in a recurrent series. **3** take turns; be used in turn; *the crews rotate every three weeks*. □ **rotation** *noun*, **rotator** *noun*

**rotatory** (roh-tă-ter-i) *adjective* rotating.

**Rotavator** *noun* (also **Rotovator**) (*trade mark*) a machine with rotating blades for breaking up and turning over rough uncultivated ground.

**rote** *noun* □ **by rote** by memory without thought of the meaning.

**Roth** (*rhymes with* both), Philip (born 1933), American Jewish novelist.

**Rothschild** the name of a family of European Jewish bankers, who first established a banking-house in Frankfurt at the end of the 18th century.

**rotisserie** (rŏ-**tiss**-er-i) *noun* a revolving spit for roasting meat.

**rotor** *noun* **1** a rotating part of a machine. **2** a horizontally-rotating vane of a helicopter.

**Rotovator** alternative spelling of ROTA-VATOR.

**rotten** *adjective* **1** rotting; rotted; breaking easily or falling to pieces from age or use. **2** morally corrupt. **3** (*informal*) contemptible, worthless. **4** (*informal*) unpleasant; *rotten weather*. □ **rottenly** *adverb*, **rottenness** *noun*

**rotter** *noun* (*slang*) a contemptible person.

**Rotterdam** a city and the principal port of the Netherlands.

**Rottweiler** (**rot**-vy-ler) *noun* a dog of a tall black-and-tan breed, used as a guard dog.

**rotund** (roh-**tund**) *adjective* rounded, plump. □ **rotundity** *noun*

**rotunda** (rŏ-**tun**-dă) *noun* a circular domed building or hall.

**rouble** (**roo**-bŭl) *noun* (also **ruble**) the unit of money in Russia.

**roué** (**roo**-ay) *noun* a dissolute elderly man.

**rouge** (*pronounced* roozh) *noun* a reddish cosmetic for colouring the cheeks. ● *verb* colour with rouge.

**rough** *adjective* **1** having an uneven or irregular surface, coarse in texture, not level or smooth. **2** not gentle or restrained or careful; violent; *rough weather*. **3** lacking finish or delicacy; not perfected or detailed. ● *adverb* roughly; in rough conditions. ● *noun* **1** something rough; rough ground. **2** hardship; *take the rough with the smooth*. **3** an unfinished state. A rough drawing or design etc. **5** a ruffian or hooligan. ● *verb* **1** make rough. **2** shape or plan or sketch roughly; *roughed out a scheme*. □ **rough-and-ready** *adjective* not refined; rough or crude but effective. **rough-and-tumble**

*noun* a disorderly fight or struggle. **rough diamond 1** a diamond not yet cut. **2** a person of good nature but lacking polished manners. **rough house** (*slang*) a disturbance with violent behaviour or fighting. **rough it** do without ordinary comforts. **rough justice** treatment that is only approximately fair or not fair at all. **rough up** (*slang*) attack violently. □ **roughly** *adverb*, **roughness** *noun*

**roughage** *noun* indigestible material in plants used as food (e.g. bran, green vegetables, and certain fruits), that stimulates the action of the intestines.

**roughcast** *noun* plaster of lime and gravel, used for covering the outsides of buildings. ● *verb* (**roughcast**, **roughcasting**) coat with this.

**roughen** *verb* make or become rough.

**roughneck** *noun* (*informal*) **1** a worker in an oil-drilling crew. **2** a rough or rowdy person.

**roughshod** *adjective* (of a horse) having shoes with the nail-heads left projecting to prevent slipping. □ **ride roughshod over** treat inconsiderately or arrogantly.

**roulette** (roo-**let**) *noun* a gambling game in which a small ball falls at random into one of the compartments on a revolving disc.

**round** *adjective* **1** having a curved shape or outline; shaped like a circle, sphere, or cylinder. **2** full, complete; *a round dozen*. ● *noun* **1** a round object. **2** a circular or recurring course or series; *the daily round*. **3** a route on which things are to be inspected or delivered. **4** a musical composition for two or more voices in which each sings the same melody but starts at a different time. **5** a single shot or volley of shots from one or more firearms; ammunition for this. **6** one stage in a competition or struggle; one section of a boxing match; one circuit of a golf course playing all the holes once. **7** a drink for each person in a group. **8** a slice of bread; a sandwich made of two slices. ● *preposition* **1** so as to circle or enclose. **2** at points on or near the circumference of; *sat round the table*. **3** having as its axis or central point; *the earth moves round the sun*. **4** visiting in a series or all over, to all points of interest in; *went round the cafés; were shown round the museum*. **5** on or to the further side of; *the shop round the corner*. ● *adverb* **1** in a circle or curve; by a circuitous route. **2** so as to face in a different direction. **3** round a place or group; in every direction. **4** to a person's house etc.; *I'll be round in an hour*. ● *verb* **1** make or become round. **2** make into a round figure or number; *round it up to 100*. **3** travel round; *the car rounded the corner*. □ **in the round** (of sculpture) with all sides shown, not attached to a background; (of a

theatre) with seats on all sides of the stage.
**round about 1** near by. **2** approximately.
**round and round** turning or going round
several times. **round brackets** brackets of
the form ( ). **round figure** *or* **number** one
without odd units. **round game** a game for
any number of players, with no teams or
partners. **round off** bring (a thing) into a
complete state; finish off. **round on** make
an attack or retort in retaliation, especially
unexpectedly. **round robin 1** a statement
signed by a number of people (often with
signatures in a circle to conceal who signed
first). **2** a tournament in which each competitor plays every other. **Round Table
1** that at which King Arthur and his
knights sat so that none might have precedence. **2** an international charitable association. **round the clock** continuously
throughout day and night. **round trip** a
trip to one or more places and back again.
**round up** gather (animals, people, or
things) into one place. **round-up** *noun* **1** a
systematic rounding up. **2** a summary (of
news etc.). □ **roundish** *adjective*, **roundness**
*noun*

**roundabout** *noun* **1** a merry-go-round at a
funfair. **2** a road junction with a circular
structure round which traffic has to pass in
the same direction. ●*adjective* indirect, not
using the shortest or most direct route or
phrasing etc.; *heard the news in a roundabout
way.*

**roundel** *noun* **1** a circular identifying mark
on an aircraft etc. **2** a small disc, e.g. a
medallion.

**rounder** *noun* the unit of scoring in rounders.

**rounders** *noun* a team game played with bat
and ball, in which players have to run
round a circuit.

**Roundhead** *noun* (*hist.*) a supporter of the
Parliament party in the English Civil War.
(¶ so called because they wore their hair
cut short at a time when long hair was in
fashion for men.)

**roundly** *adverb* **1** thoroughly, severely; *was
roundly scolded.* **2** in a rounded shape.

**roundsman** *noun* (*plural* **roundsmen**) a
tradesman's employee delivering goods.

**roundworm** *noun* a worm with a rounded
body.

**rouse** *verb* **1** cause (a person) to wake; wake
up. **2** cause to become active or excited.

**rousing** *adjective* vigorous, stirring.

**Rousseau¹** (**roo**-soh), Henri Julien (called
'douanier Rousseau' (customs-officer
Rousseau)) (1844–1910), French painter
noted for his bold naïve style.

**Rousseau²** (**roo**-soh), Jean-Jacques
(1712–78), Swiss-born French philosopher.

**Rousseau³** (**roo**-soh), Théodore
(1812–67), French landscape painter.

**roustabout** *noun* a labourer on an oil rig.

**rout¹** *noun* utter defeat; a disorderly retreat of
defeated troops. ●*verb* defeat completely;
put to flight.

**rout²** *verb* **1** fetch or force out; *routed him out
of bed.* **2** rummage.

**route** (*pronounced* root) *noun* the course or
way taken to get to a place. ●*verb* (**routed,
routeing**) send by a certain route. □ **route
march** a training-march for troops.

**routine** (roo-**teen**) *noun* **1** a standard course
of procedure; a series of acts performed
regularly in the same way. **2** a set sequence
of movements in a dance or other performance. **3** a sequence of instructions to a
computer. ●*adjective* in accordance with
routine. □ **routinely** *adverb*

**roux** (*pronounced* roo) *noun* a mixture of
heated fat and flour used as a basis for a
sauce.

**rove¹** *verb* roam. □ **roving commission** authority to travel as may be necessary in
connection with one's inquiries or other
work. **roving eye** a tendency to flirt or to
be unfaithful. □ **rover** *noun*

**rove²** *see* REEVE.

**row¹** (*rhymes with* go) *noun* **1** a number of
people or things in a line. **2** a line of seats
across a theatre etc.

**row²** (*rhymes with* go) *verb* **1** propel (a boat)
using oars. **2** carry in a boat that one rows.
●*noun* a spell of rowing; an excursion in a
rowing-boat. □ **row-boat** *noun* (*Amer.*) a
rowing-boat. **rowing-boat** *noun* a boat for
rowing.

**row³** (*rhymes with* cow) (*informal*) *noun* **1** a
loud noise. **2** a quarrel, a heated argument.
**3** a severe reprimand. ●*verb* quarrel or argue heatedly.

**rowan** (**roh**-ăn) *noun* a tree that bears
hanging clusters of scarlet berries; the
mountain ash.

**rowdy** (*rhymes with* cloudy) *adjective* (**row-
dier, rowdiest**) noisy and disorderly.
●*noun* a rowdy person. □ **rowdily** *adverb*,
**rowdiness** *noun*, **rowdyism** *noun*

**rowel** (*rhymes with* towel) *noun* a spiked revolving disc at the end of a spur.

**rowlock** (**rol**-ŏk) *noun* a device on the side
of a boat for holding an oar in place.

**royal** *adjective* **1** of, suitable for, or worthy of
a king or queen. **2** belonging to the family
of a king or queen; in the service or under
the patronage of royalty. **3** splendid, first-
rate; of exceptional size etc. ●*noun* (*informal*) a member of a royal family. □ **royal
blue** deep vivid blue. **Royal Commission**
(*Brit.*) a body of people appointed by the
Crown to investigate and report on something. **royal flush** *see* FLUSH. **royal icing**

hard icing for cakes, made with icing sugar and egg white. **royal jelly** a substance secreted by worker bees and fed to future queen bees; believed by some people to be beneficial to health. **royal warrant** (*Brit.*) a warrant authorizing a tradesperson to supply goods to a member of the royal family. **royal 'we'** the use of 'we' instead of 'I' by a single person. □ **royally** *adverb*

**Royal Academy of Arts** an institution established in 1768 to foster the arts of painting, sculpture, and architecture in Britain.

**Royal Air Force** the British air force.

**Royal British Legion** a national association of ex-members of the British armed forces, founded in 1921.

**Royal Canadian Mounted Police** the Canadian police force.

**Royal Institution** a society founded in London in 1799 for the dissemination of scientific knowledge.

**royalist** *noun* **1** a person who favours monarchy. **2** (**Royalist**) a supporter of the monarchy in the English Civil War.

**Royal Marines** a British armed force for service on land and at sea.

**Royal Mint** the establishment for the manufacture of British coins.

**Royal Navy** the British navy.

**Royal Society** the oldest and most prestigious scientific society in Britain, founded in 1662.

**royalty** *noun* **1** being royal. **2** a royal person; royal people; *in the presence of royalty*. **3** payment to an author etc. for each copy of the book sold or for each public performance of his or her work; payment to a patentee for the use of the patent. **4** payment by a mining or oil company to the owner of the land used.

**Royce**, Sir Frederick Henry (1863–1933), English engine designer, co-founder (with C. S. Rolls) of Rolls-Royce Ltd (1906).

**RP** *abbreviation* received pronunciation.

**RPI** *abbreviation* retail price index; a list published monthly showing the variations in price of basic retail goods.

**rpm.** *abbreviation* revolutions per minute.

**RSA** *abbreviation* **1** Royal Society of Arts. **2** Royal Scottish Academy. **3** Republic of South Africa.

**RSC** *abbreviation* Royal Shakespeare Company.

**RSI** *abbreviation* repetitive strain injury.

**RSJ** *abbreviation* rolled steel joist; a load-bearing beam in a building.

**RSM** *abbreviation* Regimental Sergeant-Major.

**RSPB** *abbreviation* Royal Society for the Protection of Birds.

**RSPCA** *abbreviation* Royal Society for the Prevention of Cruelty to Animals.

**RSVP** *abbreviation* (in an invitation) please reply. (¶ From the French, *répondez s'il vous plaît*.)

**rt.** *abbreviation* right.

**Rt. Hon.** *abbreviation* Right Honourable.

**Rt. Rev., Rt. Revd** *abbreviation* Right Reverend.

**RU** *abbreviation* Rugby Union.

**Ru** *symbol* ruthenium.

**rub** *verb* (**rubbed, rubbing**) **1** press something against (a surface) and slide it to and fro; apply in this way. **2** polish or clean by rubbing; make or become dry, smooth, or sore etc. in this way. ●*noun* **1** the act or process of rubbing. **2** a difficulty or impediment; *there's the rub*. □ **rub along** (*informal*) manage to get on without undue difficulty. **rub down** dry, smooth, or reduce the level of (a thing) by rubbing. **rub it in** (or **rub a person's nose in it**) emphasize or remind a person constantly of an unpleasant fact. **rub off** (usually foll. by *on*) be removed or transferred by or as if by rubbing. **rub out** remove (marks etc.) by using a rubber. **rub shoulders with** associate with (certain people). **rub up 1** polish. **2** brush up (a subject etc.). **rub up the wrong way** irritate or annoy (a person).

**rubato** *noun* (*plural* **rubatos** *or* **rubati**) (in music) a temporary disregarding of strict tempo.

**rubber¹** *noun* **1** a tough elastic substance made from the latex of certain plants or synthetically. **2** a piece of this or other substance for rubbing out pencil or ink marks. **3** (*informal*) a condom. □ **rubber band** a loop of thin rubber for holding papers etc. together. **rubber plant** a tropical plant with large leathery leaves, often grown as a house-plant. **rubber stamp 1** a device for imprinting a mark on to a surface. **2** a person who mechanically gives approval to the actions of another person or group. **rubber-stamp** *verb* approve automatically without due consideration.

**rubber²** *noun* a match of three successive games at bridge or whist etc.

**rubberize** *verb* (also **rubberise**) treat or coat with rubber.

**rubberneck** (*informal*) *noun* a gaping sightseer; an inquisitive person. ●*verb* behave as a rubberneck.

**rubbery** *adjective* like rubber.

**rubbing** *noun* a reproduction made of a memorial brass or other relief design by placing paper over it and rubbing with pigment.

**rubbish** *noun* **1** waste or worthless material. **2** nonsense. ●*verb* criticize severely, disparage. □ **rubbishy** *adjective*

**rubble** *noun* waste or rough fragments of stone or brick etc.

**rubella** *noun* German measles.

**Rubens** (**roo**-binz), Sir Peter Paul (1577–1640), Flemish painter.

**Rubicon** (**roo**-bi-kŏn) □ **cross the Rubicon** take a decisive step that commits one to an enterprise. (¶ The river Rubicon, in NE Italy, was the ancient boundary between Gaul and Italy; by crossing it into Italy Julius Caesar committed himself to war against the Senate and Pompey.)

**rubicund** (**roo**-bik-ŭnd) *adjective* (of the complexion) red, ruddy.

**rubidium** (roo-**bid**-iŭm) *noun* a soft silvery metallic element (symbol Rb).

**Rubik's cube** a cube-shaped puzzle formed of coloured sections which are rotated until each face is a single colour.

**Rubinstein** (**roo**-bin-styn), Artur (1886–1982), Polish-born American pianist.

**ruble** alternative spelling of ROUBLE.

**rubric** (**roo**-brik) *noun* words put as a heading, explanation, or direction as to how something must be done.

**ruby** *noun* **1** a red precious stone. **2** deep red colour. ● *adjective* deep red. □ **ruby wedding** the 40th anniversary of a wedding.

**RUC** *abbreviation* Royal Ulster Constabulary.

**ruche** (*pronounced* roosh) *noun* a gathered trimming. ● *verb* gather (fabric) ornamentally.

**ruck** *verb* crease, wrinkle. ● *noun* **1** a crease or wrinkle. **2** an undistinguished crowd of people or things. **3** (in Rugby football) a loose scrum with the ball on the ground.

**rucksack** *noun* a bag worn slung by straps from both shoulders and resting on the back, used especially by walkers and climbers.

**ruckus** *noun* (especially *Amer. informal*) a row, a commotion.

**ructions** *plural noun* (*informal*) protests and noisy argument.

**rudder** *noun* a vertical piece of metal or wood hinged to the stern of a boat or rear of an aeroplane and used for steering.

**ruddy** *adjective* (**ruddier**, **ruddiest**) **1** reddish; (of a person's face) having a fresh healthy reddish colour. **2** (*slang*) bloody, damned, wretched. □ **ruddily** *adverb*, **ruddiness** *noun*

**rude** *adjective* **1** impolite, showing no respect or consideration. **2** primitive, roughly made; *rude stone implements.* **3** vigorous, hearty; *rude health.* **4** violent, startling; *a rude awakening.* □ **rudely** *adverb*, **rudeness** *noun*

**rudiment** (**roo**-dim-ĕnt) *noun* **1** a part or organ that is incompletely developed. **2** (**rudiments**) basic or elementary principles; *learning the rudiments of chem-*

*istry.* □ **rudimentary** (roodi-**ment**-er-i) *adjective*

**rue** *noun* an evergreen shrub with bitter leaves formerly used in medicine. ● *verb* (**rued**, **ruing**) repent or regret; *he'll live to rue the day.*

**rueful** *adjective* showing good-humoured regret. □ **ruefully** *adverb*, **ruefulness** *noun*

**ruff**[1] *noun* **1** a deep starched pleated frill worn around the neck in the 16th century. **2** a projecting or coloured ring of feathers or fur round the neck of a bird or animal. **3** a wading bird of the sandpiper family.

**ruff**[2] *verb* trump in a card game. ● *noun* trumping.

**ruffian** *noun* a violent lawless person.

**ruffle** *verb* **1** disturb the smoothness or evenness of. **2** upset the calmness or even temper of (a person). **3** become ruffled. ● *noun* a gathered ornamental frill.

**rufous** (**roo**-fŭs) *adjective* (especially of animals) reddish-brown.

**rug** *noun* **1** a thick floor-mat. **2** a thick warm blanket or coverlet. □ **pull the rug from under** remove the support of (a theory etc.); weaken.

**Rugby** *noun* (in full **Rugby football**) a kind of football played with an oval ball which may be kicked or carried. □ **Rugby League** a partly professional form of the game with teams of 13. **Rugby Union** an amateur form with teams of 15. (¶ Named after Rugby School in Warwickshire, where it was first played.)

**rugged** *adjective* **1** having an uneven surface or an irregular outline, craggy. **2** rough but kindly and honest; *a rugged individualist.* □ **ruggedly** *adverb*, **ruggedness** *noun*

**rugger** *noun* (*informal*) Rugby football.

**ruin** *noun* **1** severe damage or destruction. **2** complete loss of one's fortune, resources, or prospects. **3** the remains of something decayed or destroyed; *the house was a ruin; the ruins of Pompeii.* **4** a cause of ruin. ● *verb* damage (a thing) so severely that it is useless; bring into a ruined condition. □ **ruination** *noun*

**ruinous** *adjective* **1** bringing or likely to bring ruin. **2** in ruins, ruined; *the house is in a ruinous condition.* □ **ruinously** *adverb*

**Ruisdael** (**rois**-dahl), Jacob Isaacksz van (1628/9–82), Dutch landscape painter.

**rule** *noun* **1** a statement of what can, must, or should be done. **2** the general custom or normal state of things; *seaside holidays became the rule.* **3** exercise of authority, control, governing; *countries that were under French rule.* **4** a straight often jointed measuring device used by carpenters etc. ● *verb* **1** have authoritative control over people or a country; govern. **2** keep (a person or feeling etc.) under control, dominate. **3** give a decision as judge or other authority; *the chairman ruled that the question was out of order.* **4** draw (a line) using a ruler or other straight edge; mark parallel lines on (paper etc.). □ **as a rule** usually. **rule of thumb** a rough practical method. **rule out** exclude as irrelevant or ineligible. **rule the roost** be in control.

**ruler** *noun* **1** a person who rules by authority. **2** a straight strip of wood, plastic, etc. used for measuring or drawing straight lines.

**ruling** *noun* an authoritative decision.

**rum** *noun* alcoholic spirit distilled from sugar cane or molasses. ● *adjective* (*informal*) strange, odd. □ **rum baba** a sponge cake soaked in rum syrup.

**Rumania, Rumanian** alternative spelling of ROMANIA, ROMANIAN.

**rumba** *noun* a ballroom dance of Cuban origin; music for this.

**rumble** *verb* **1** make a deep heavy continuous sound, like thunder. **2** utter in a deep voice. **3** (*slang*) detect the true character of; see through (a deception). ● *noun* a rumbling sound.

**rumbustious** *adjective* (*informal*) boisterous, uproarious.

**ruminant** (**roo-min-ănt**) *noun* an animal that chews the cud. ● *adjective* **1** ruminating. **2** meditative.

**ruminate** (**roo-min-ayt**) *verb* **1** chew the cud. **2** meditate, ponder. □ **rumination** *noun*

**ruminative** (**roo-min-ătiv**) *adjective* meditative, pondering.

**rummage** *verb* search by turning things over or disarranging them. ● *noun* a search of this kind. □ **rummage sale** (especially *Amer.*) a jumble sale.

**rummy** *noun* a card game in which players try to form sets or sequences of cards.

**rumour** (*Amer.* **rumor**) *noun* information spread by word of mouth but not certainly true. □ **be rumoured** be spread as a rumour.

**rump** *noun* **1** the buttocks; the corresponding part of a bird. **2** a cut of meat from an animal's hindquarters.

**rumple** *verb* make or become crumpled; make (something smooth) untidy.

**rumpus** *noun* (*informal*) an uproar; an angry dispute.

**run** *verb* (**ran, run, running**) **1** move with quick steps, never having both or all feet on the ground at once. **2** go or travel smoothly or swiftly; (of salmon) go up river in large numbers from the sea. **3** compete in a race, contest, or election; *ran for President.* **4** spread rapidly or beyond the intended limit; *the dye has run.* **5** flow or cause to flow, exude liquid; *run some water into it; smoke makes my eyes run.* **6** function,

be in action; *left the engine running.* **7** travel or convey from point to point; *the bus runs every hour; we'll run you home.* **8** extend; *a fence runs round the estate.* **9** be current, operative, or valid; *the lease runs for 20 years.* **10** pass or cause to pass (into a specified condition); *supplies are running low; run a temperature.* **11** cause to run, go, extend, or function. **12** manage, organize; *who runs the country?* **13** own and use (a vehicle etc.). **14** (of a newspaper) print as an item. ● *noun* an act or spell or course of running. **2** a point scored in cricket or baseball. **3** a ladder in a stocking or knitted fabric. **4** a continuous stretch, sequence, or spell. **5** a general demand for goods etc.; *there has been a run on tinned meat.* **6** a large number of salmon going up river from the sea. **7** a general type or class of things. **8** an enclosure where domestic animals can range. **9** a track for some purpose; *a ski run.* **10** (foll. by *of*) permission to make unrestricted use of something; *he has the run of the house.* **11** (**the runs**) (*informal*) diarrhoea. □ **give a person the run-around** (*informal*) deceive or inconvenience him or her. **on the run** fleeing from pursuit. **run across** happen to meet or find. **run after** seek the company or attentions of. **run away** leave quickly or secretly. **run away with 1** elope with (a person). **2** win (a prize etc.) easily. **3** accept (an idea) too hastily. **run down 1** stop because not re- wound. **2** reduce the numbers of. **3** knock down with a moving vehicle or ship. **4** discover after searching. **5** speak of in a slighting way. **run-down** (*adjective*) weak or exhausted; (*noun*) a detailed analysis. **run dry 1** stop flowing; become dry. **2** run out; become used up. **run high** (of feelings) become strong or fierce. **run in** (*informal*) **1** arrest and take into custody. **2** rún (a new engine) carefully into good working order. **run in the family** (of a feature, ability etc.) be common in a family. **run into** collide with; happen to meet. **run off** produce (copies) on a machine. **run-of- the-mill** *adjective* ordinary, not special. **run out 1** (of time or a stock of something) become used up, (of a person) have used up one's stock. **2** put down the wicket of (a running batsman). **run over 1** knock down or crush with a vehicle. **2** study or repeat quickly. **run risks** take risks. **run through** study or repeat quickly. **run to 1** have the money, resources, or ability for. **2** (of a person) have a tendency to; *runs to fat.* **run up 1** raise (a flag) on a mast. **2** allow (a bill) to mount. **3** make quickly by sewing; *run up some curtains.* **run-up** *noun* the period leading to an event.

**runaway** *noun* a person who has run away. ● *adjective* **1** having run away or become out of control. **2** won easily; *a runaway victory*.

**Runcie**, Robert Alexander Kennedy, Baron (born 1921), Archbishop of Canterbury 1980–91.

**rune** (*pronounced* roon) *noun* **1** any of the letters in an alphabet used by early Germanic peoples. **2** a similar mark used as a mystical symbol. □ **runic** *adjective*

**rung**¹ *noun* one of the crosspieces of a ladder etc.

**rung**² *see* RING².

**runner** *noun* **1** a person or animal that runs; one taking part in a race. **2** a messenger. **3** a creeping stem that grows from the main stem and takes root. **4** a groove, rod, or roller for a thing to move on; each of the long strips on which a sledge etc. slides. **5** a long narrow strip of carpet, or of ornamental cloth for a table etc. □ **do a runner** (*slang*) leave hastily; run away. **runner bean** a climbing bean. **runner-up** *noun* (*plural* **runners-up**) a person or team finishing second in a competition.

**running** *see* RUN. ● *adjective* **1** performed while running; *a running jump*. **2** following each other without interval; *for four days running*. **3** continuous; *a running battle*; *running commentary*. □ **in** or **out of the running** with a good chance or with no chance of winning. **make the running** set the pace. **running-board** *noun* a footboard on either side of a vehicle. **running mate** (*Amer.*) **1** a candidate for the secondary position in an election e.g. for vice-president. **2** a horse intended to set the pace for another horse in a race. **running stitch** a line of evenly spaced straight stitches.

**runny** *adjective* **1** semi-liquid. **2** tending to flow or to exude fluid.

**runt** *noun* an undersized person or animal; *the runt of the litter*.

**runway** *noun* a prepared surface on an airfield, on which aircraft take off and land.

**Runyon**, (Alfred) Damon (1884–1946), American journalist and short-story writer.

**rupee** (roo-**pee**) *noun* the unit of money in India, Pakistan, and certain other countries.

**rupture** *noun* **1** breaking; a breach. **2** an abdominal hernia. ● *verb* **1** burst or break (tissue etc.); become burst or broken. **2** affect with a hernia.

**rural** *adjective* of, in, or like the countryside. □ **rural dean** *see* DEAN (sense 2).

**ruse** (*pronounced* rooz) *noun* a deception or trick.

**rush**¹ *noun* a marsh plant with a slender pithy stem used for making mats, chair-seats, baskets, etc.

**rush**² *verb* **1** go, come, or convey with great speed. **2** act hastily; force into hasty action. **3** attack with a sudden assault. ● *noun* **1** rushing; an instance of this. **2** a period of great activity. **3** a sudden great demand for goods etc. **4** (**rushes**) (*informal*) the first prints of a cinema film before it is cut and edited. ● *adjective* done with haste or with minimum delay; *a rush job*. □ **rush hour** the time each day when traffic is busiest.

**Rushdie**, Salman (Ahmed Salman) (born 1947), Indian-born British novelist.

**Rushmore**, **Mount** a mountain in South Dakota with gigantic faces of US Presidents Washington, Lincoln, Jefferson, and Theodore Roosevelt carved into it.

**rusk** *noun* a biscuit, especially one for babies.

**Ruskin**, John (1819–1900), English art and social critic.

**Russell**¹, Bertrand Arthur William (1873–1970), 3rd Earl (though he rejected the title), British philosopher, mathematician, and reformer.

**Russell**², Ken (born 1927), British film and television director.

**russet** *adjective* soft reddish-brown. ● *noun* **1** russet colour. **2** an apple with a rough skin of this colour.

**Russia** a country in northern Asia and eastern Europe.

**Russian** *adjective* of Russia (or more widely the former USSR) or its people or language. ● *noun* **1** a native or inhabitant of Russia or the former USSR. **2** the language of Russia, the official language of the former USSR. □ **Russian roulette** an act of bravado in which a person holds to his or her head a revolver of which one (unknown) chamber contains a bullet, and pulls the trigger. **Russian salad** salad of mixed diced vegetables in mayonnaise.

**Russo-** *combining form* Russian; Russian and; *Russo-Japanese*.

**rust** *noun* **1** a reddish-brown or yellowish-brown coating formed on iron or other metal by the effect of moisture, and gradually corroding it. **2** reddish-brown. **3** a plant disease with rust-coloured spots; the fungus causing this. ● *verb* **1** affect or be affected with rust. **2** lose quality or efficiency by lack of use.

**rustic** *adjective* **1** having the qualities ascribed to country people or peasants, simple and unsophisticated. **2** made of rough timber or untrimmed branches; *a rustic seat*. ● *noun* a country person, a peasant.

**rusticate** *verb* **1** settle in the country and live a rural life. **2** make or become rustic. **3** send down (a student) temporarily from university as punishment. □ **rustication** *noun*

**rustle** *verb* **1** make a sound like that of paper being crumpled; cause to do this. **2** steal (horses or cattle). ●*noun* a rustling sound. □ **rustle up** (*informal*) prepare or produce quickly; *rustle up a meal*. □ **rustler** *noun*

**rustproof** *adjective* not susceptible to corrosion by rust. ●*verb* make rustproof.

**rusty** *adjective* (**rustier, rustiest**) **1** affected with rust. **2** rust-coloured. **3** having lost quality or efficiency by lack of use. □ **rustiness** *noun*

**rut¹** *noun* **1** a deep track made by wheels in soft ground. **2** a dull tedious routine or way of life; *getting into a rut*.

**rut²** *noun* the periodic sexual excitement of a male deer, goat, etc. ●*verb* (**rutted, rutting**) be affected with this.

**Ruth¹** a book of the Old Testament.

**Ruth²**, 'Babe' (George Herman) (1895–1948), American professional baseball player.

**ruthenium** (roo-theen-iŭm) *noun* a metallic element (symbol Ru), used in certain alloys to increase hardness.

**Rutherford**, Sir Ernest, 1st Baron (1871–1937), British physicist, born in New Zealand, widely regarded as the founder of nuclear physics.

**rutherfordium** (ru-ther-ford-iŭm) *noun* the American name for an artificially produced radioactive element (symbol Rf).

**ruthless** *adjective* having no pity or compassion. □ **ruthlessly** *adverb*, **ruthlessness** *noun*

**rutted** *adjective* marked with ruts.

**RV** *abbreviation* Revised Version (of the Bible).

**Rwanda** (roo-an-dǎ) a country in East Africa. □ **Rwandan** *adjective & noun*

**Ryder Cup** a golf tournament played between teams of male professionals, held every second year in September.

**rye** *noun* **1** a cereal used for making flour or as food for cattle. **2** (in full **rye whisky**) a whisky made from rye.

**ryegrass** *noun* forage grass or coarse lawn grass.

# Ss

**S¹** *abbreviation* siemens. ●*symbol* sulphur.

**S²** *abbreviation* (also **S.**) **1** Saint. **2** South, Southern.

**s.** *abbreviation* **1** second(s). **2** (*hist.*) shilling(s) (¶ originally short for the Latin *solidus*).

**-s'** *combining form* denoting the possessive case of plural nouns and sometimes of singular nouns ending in *s*; *the boys' shoes*; *Charles' book*.

**'s** *abbreviation* **1** is; has; *he's coming*; *she's got it*. **2** us; *let's go*.

**-'s** *combining form* denoting the possessive case of singular nouns and of plural nouns not ending in *s*; *Tom's book*; *the book's cover*; *children's shoes*.

**SA** *abbreviation* **1** South Africa. **2** South Australia. **3** Salvation Army.

**Sabah** (sah-bah) a State of Malaysia, comprising North Borneo and some offshore islands.

**sabbath** *noun* a religious day of rest kept by Christians on Sunday and Jews on Saturday.

**sabbatical** (să-bat-ikăl) *adjective* (of leave) granted at intervals to a university teacher for study or travel. ●*noun* a period of sabbatical leave.

**saber** Amer. spelling of SABRE.

**Sabin** (say-bin), Albert Bruce (born 1906), Russian-born American biologist who developed an oral vaccine against poliomyelitis.

**Sabine** (sa-byn) *noun* a member of a people of ancient Italy north-east of Rome.

**sable** *noun* a small weasel-like animal of Arctic and adjacent regions, valued for its dark brown fur. ●*adjective* black; gloomy.

**sabot** (sab-oh) *noun* a shoe hollowed out from one piece of wood, or with a wooden sole.

**sabotage** (sab-ŏ-tahzh) *noun* deliberate damage to machinery, materials, etc. in order to prevent work or plans going ahead. ●*verb* commit sabotage on; destroy or spoil; *sabotaged my plans*.

**saboteur** (sab-ŏ-ter) *noun* a person who commits sabotage.

**sabre** (say-ber) *noun* (*Amer.* **saber**) **1** a cavalry sword with a curved blade. **2** a light fencing-sword with a tapering blade. □ **sabre-rattling** *noun* a display or threat of force.

**sac** *noun* a bag-like part in an animal or plant.

**saccharin** (sak-er-in) *noun* a very sweet substance used as a substitute for sugar.

**saccharine** (sak-er-een) *adjective* intensely and unpleasantly sweet or sentimental.

**sacerdotal** (sak-er-doh-tăl) *adjective* of priests or priestly office.

**sachet** (sash-ay) *noun* **1** a small bag filled with a sweet-smelling substance for laying among clothes etc. **2** a sealed plastic or paper pack containing a single portion of a substance.

**sack¹** *noun* **1** a large bag of strong coarse fabric; this with its contents. **2** (**the sack**) (*informal*) dismissal from one's employment or position; *got the sack*. ●*verb* (*informal*) dismiss from a job. □ **sack-race** *noun* a race in which each competitor stands in a sack and moves by jumping. □ **sackful** *noun* (*plural* **sackfuls**).

**sack²** *verb* plunder (a captured town etc.) in a violent destructive way. ●*noun* the act or process of sacking a place.

**sack³** *noun* (*old use*) a white wine formerly imported from Spain and the Canary Islands.

**sackbut** *noun* an early form of trombone.

**sackcloth** *noun* **1** coarse fabric for making sacks. **2** clothing made from coarse fabric; *sackcloth and ashes*. (¶ From the ancient custom of wearing sackcloth and sprinkling ashes on one's head in penitence or mourning.)

**sacking** *noun* material for making sacks.

**sacral** (say-krăl) *adjective* **1** of the sacrum. **2** of or for sacred rites.

**sacrament** *noun* **1** any of the symbolic Christian religious ceremonies, especially baptism and the Eucharist. **2** the consecrated elements in the Eucharist, especially the bread. □ **sacramental** *adjective*

**sacred** *adjective* **1** associated with or dedicated to God or a god; regarded with reverence because of this. **2** dedicated to some person or purpose; *sacred to the memory of those who fell in battle*. **3** connected with religion, not secular; *sacred music*. **4** sacrosanct. □ **sacred cow** (*informal*) an idea or institution which its supporters will not allow to be criticized. (¶ The phrase refers to Hindu respect for the cow as a sacred animal.)

**sacrifice** *noun* **1** the slaughter of a victim or the presenting of a gift to win the favour of a god. **2** the giving up of a valued thing for the sake of another that is more worthy. **3** the thing offered or given up. ●*verb* **1** offer or give up as a sacrifice. **2** give up (a thing) in order to achieve something else. □ **sacrificial** (sak-ri-fish-ăl) *adjective*

**sacrilege** (sak-ri-lij) *noun* disrespect or damage to something regarded as sacred. □ **sacrilegious** (sak-ri-lij-ŭs) *adjective*

**sacristan** (sak-ri-stăn) *noun* the person in charge of the contents of a church, especially the sacred vessels etc.

**sacristy** (sak-rist-i) *noun* the place in a church where sacred vessels etc. are kept.

**sacrosanct** (sak-roh-sankt) *adjective* sacred or respected and therefore secure from violation or damage.

**sacrum** (say-krŭm) *noun* (*plural* **sacra** or **sacrums**) the triangular bone that forms the back of the pelvis.

**sad** *adjective* (**sadder, saddest**) **1** showing or causing sorrow; unhappy. **2** regrettable. **3** shameful, deplorable. □ **sadly** *adverb*, **sadness** *noun*

**Sadat** (să-dat), (Muhammad) Anwar el (1918–81), Egyptian statesman, President of Egypt 1970–81.

**sadden** *verb* make sad.

**saddle** *noun* **1** a seat for a rider on a horse, bicycle, etc. **2** a saddle-shaped thing, a ridge of high land between two peaks. **3** a joint of meat consisting of the two loins. ●*verb* **1** put a saddle on (an animal). **2** burden (a person) with a task. □ **in the saddle 1** on horseback. **2** in a controlling position. **saddle-bag** *noun* a strong bag fixed behind a saddle or as one of a pair slung over a horse etc.

**saddleback** *noun* **1** a black pig with a white stripe round its body. **2** a hill with a concave upper outline.

**saddler** *noun* one who makes or sells saddles and harnesses.

**saddlery** *noun* a saddler's goods or business.

**Sadducee** (sad-yoo-see) *noun* a member of a Jewish sect at the time of Christ.

**sadhu** (sah-doo) *noun* (in India) a holy man, sage, or ascetic.

**sadism** (say-dizm) *noun* enjoyment of inflicting or watching cruelty; this as a form of sexual perversion. □ **sadist** *noun*, **sadistic** (să-dis-tik) *adjective*, **sadistically** *adverb*

**sadomasochism** *noun* sadism and masochism in one person. □ **sadomasochist** *noun*, **sadomasochistic** *adjective*

**s.a.e.** *abbreviation* stamped addressed envelope.

**safari** (să-far-i) *noun* (*plural* **safaris**) an expedition, especially in Africa, to observe or hunt wild animals; *go on safari*. □ **safari jacket** a belted jacket in linen or similar fabric. **safari park** a park where exotic wild animals are kept in the open for visitors to view from vehicles.

**safe** *adjective* **1** free from risk or danger, not dangerous. **2** providing security or protection. ●*adverb* safely; *play safe*. ●*noun* **1** a strong locked cupboard or cabinet for valuables. **2** a ventilated cabinet for storing food. □ **on the safe side** allowing a margin of security against risks. **safe conduct** the right to pass through a district without risk of arrest or harm (e.g. in time of war); a document guaranteeing this. **safe deposit** a building containing safes and strongrooms for hire. **safe period** (in birth control) the time in a woman's menstrual cycle when sexual intercourse is least likely to result in conception. **safe sex** sexual activity in which people use condoms etc. as a precaution against sexually transmitted diseases, especially Aids. □ **safely** *adverb*, **safeness** *noun*

**safeguard** *noun* a means of protection. ●*verb* protect.

**safety** *noun* being safe, freedom from risk or danger. □ **safety belt** a seat belt; a belt or strap worn to prevent injury. **safety-catch** *noun* a device that prevents a mechanism from being operated accidentally or dangerously; a locking device on a gun-trigger. **safety curtain** a fireproof curtain that can be lowered to cut off a theatre stage from the auditorium. **safety lamp** a miner's lamp with the flame protected so that it will not ignite firedamp. **safety match** a match that will light only on a special surface. **safety net** a net placed to catch an acrobat etc. in case of a fall. **safety pin** a brooch-like pin with a guard covering the point. **safety razor** a razor with a guard to prevent the blade from cutting the skin deeply. **safety-valve** *noun* **1** a valve that opens automatically to relieve excessive pressure in a steam boiler. **2** a means of releasing anger, excitement, etc. harmlessly.

**safflower** *noun* a thistle-like plant yielding a red dye and an oil.

**saffron** *noun* **1** the orange-coloured stigmas of a kind of crocus, used for colouring and flavouring food. **2** the colour of these.

**sag** *verb* (**sagged, sagging**) **1** sink or curve down in the middle under weight or pressure. **2** hang loosely and unevenly, droop. **3** fall in price. ●*noun* sagging.

**saga** (sah-gă) *noun* a long story with many episodes.

**sagacious** (să-gay-shŭs) *adjective* showing insight or wisdom. □ **sagaciously** *adverb*, **sagacity** (să-gas-iti) *noun*

**sage**[1] *noun* a herb with fragrant greyish-green leaves used to flavour food.

**sage**[2] *adjective* profoundly wise; having wisdom gained from experience. ●*noun* a profoundly wise man. □ **sagely** *adverb*

**Sagittarius** (saj-i-**tair**-iŭs) the ninth sign of the zodiac, the Archer. □ **Sagittarian** *adjective & noun*

**sago** *noun* a starchy food in the form of hard white grains, used in puddings, obtained from the pith of a palm tree (the **sago palm**).

**Sahara** a great desert of North Africa extending from the Atlantic to the Red Sea.

**Sahel** (să-**hel**) the belt of dry savannah south of the Sahara in West Africa, comprising parts of Senegal, Mauritania, Mali, Niger, and Chad.

**sahib** (**sah**-ib *or* sahb) *noun* a former title of address to European men in India.

**said** *see* SAY.

**sail** *noun* **1** a piece of fabric spread on rigging to catch the wind and drive a ship or boat along. **2** a journey by ship or boat; *Haifa is three days' sail from Naples.* **3** something resembling a sail in function; *the sails of a windmill.* ● *verb* **1** travel on water by use of sails or engine-power. **2** start on a voyage; *we sail next week.* **3** travel on or over (water) in a ship or boat; *sailed the seas.* **4** control the navigation of (a ship); set (a toy boat) afloat. **5** move swiftly and smoothly; walk in a stately manner. **6** (usually foll. by *through*) progress or succeed easily; *sailed through the exams.* □ **sail into** (*informal*) attack violently. **sailing boat** *or* **ship** a vessel driven by sails.

**sailboard** *noun* a board with a mast and sail, used in windsurfing. □ **sailboarding** *noun*

**sailcloth** *noun* **1** canvas for sails. **2** a strong canvas-like dress material.

**sailor** *noun* **1** a person who works as a member of a ship's crew; a member of a country's navy, especially one below the rank of officer. **2** a traveller considered as liable or not liable to seasickness; *I'm not a good sailor.*

**sailplane** *noun* a glider designed for soaring.

**sainfoin** (**san**-foin) *noun* a fodder plant with pink flowers.

**saint** *noun* **1** a holy person, one declared (in the RC or Orthodox Church) to have won a high place in heaven and to be worthy of veneration. **2** (**Saint** *or* **St**) the title of such a person or of one receiving veneration, or used in the name of a church not called after a saint (e.g. *St Saviour's; St Cross*). **3** a very good, patient, or unselfish person. □ **sainthood** *noun*, **saintlike** *adjective*

**St Bernard** (in full **St Bernard dog**) a very large dog of a breed originally kept in the Alps to rescue travellers.

**St Helena** (hil-**een**-ă) a solitary island in the South Atlantic, famous as the place of Napoleon's exile (1815–21) and death.

**St John Ambulance** an organization providing first aid, nursing, ambulance, and welfare services.

**St John's wort** a yellow-flowered plant.

**St Kitts and Nevis** (**nee**-vis) a State consisting of two adjoining islands in the West Indies.

**St Laurent** (san law-**rahn**), Yves (born 1936), French fashion designer.

**St Lawrence** a river of North America flowing from Lake Ontario to the Atlantic Ocean.

**St Leger** (**lej**-er) an annual horse race for 3-year-old colts and fillies, held in September at Doncaster, S. Yorks.

**St Lucia** (**loo**-shă) an island State of the West Indies.

**saintly** *adjective* (**saintlier, saintliest**) like a saint, very virtuous. □ **saintliness** *noun*

**St Mark's Cathedral** the cathedral church of Venice.

**St Paul's Cathedral** a cathedral on Ludgate Hill, London, built between 1675 and 1711 by Sir Christopher Wren.

**St Peter's Basilica** the Roman Catholic basilica in the Vatican City, Rome.

**St Petersburg** (formerly **Leningrad**) a major city and port in Russia.

**Saint-Saëns** (san-**sahn**), (Charles) Camille (1835–1921), French composer.

**St Swithin's Day** 15 July; according to tradition, if it rains on this day, it will rain for the next 40 days.

**St Vincent** an island State in the West Indies.

**St Vitus's dance** a disease causing the limbs to twitch uncontrollably.

**saithe** (*rhymes with* faith) *noun* a fish related to the cod, with a skin which soils the fingers.

**sake¹** *noun* □ **for the sake of** in order to please or honour (a person) or get or keep (a thing).

**sake²** (**sah**-ki) *noun* a Japanese alcoholic drink made from rice.

**Sakharov** (**sak**-ă-rof), Andrei Dimitrievich (1921–89), Russian nuclear physicist and dissident.

**salaam** (să-**lahm**) *noun* **1** an Oriental salutation meaning 'Peace'. **2** a Muslim greeting consisting of a low bow with the right palm on the forehead. ● *verb* make a salaam to.

**salacious** (să-**lay**-shŭs) *adjective* lewd, erotic. □ **salaciously** *adverb*, **salaciousness** *noun*, **salacity** (să-**lass**-iti) *noun*

**salad** *noun* a cold dish consisting of one or more vegetables (usually raw), often with a dressing. □ **salad days** a period of youth and inexperience. **salad dressing** a mixture of oil and vinegar or lemon juice with flavourings, poured over salads.

**salamander** (sal-ă-mand-er) *noun* **1** a lizard-like animal related to the newt. **2** (in mythology) a lizard-like animal living in fire.

**salami** (să-lah-mi) *noun* a strongly flavoured Italian sausage.

**sal ammoniac** ammonium chloride, a white crystalline salt.

**salaried** *adjective* receiving a salary.

**salary** *noun* a fixed payment made by an employer at regular intervals (usually monthly) to a person doing other than manual or mechanical work.

**sale** *noun* **1** selling; being sold. **2** an instance of this; the amount sold; *made a sale; our sales were enormous.* **3** an event at which goods are sold. **4** disposal of a shop's stock at reduced prices. □ **for** or **on sale** offered for purchase. **sales talk** persuasive talk designed to make people buy goods or accept an idea.

**saleable** *adjective* fit for sale, likely to find a purchaser. □ **saleability** *noun*

**saleroom** *noun* a room where goods are displayed for sale; an auction room.

**Salesian** (să-lee-zhăn) *noun* a member of a Roman Catholic religious order engaged in teaching, named after St Francis de Sales (died 1622), French bishop of Geneva. ●*adjective* of this order.

**salesman** *noun* (*plural* **salesmen**) a man employed to sell goods.

**salesmanship** *noun* skill in selling.

**salesperson** *noun* a salesman or saleswoman.

**saleswoman** *noun* (*plural* **saleswomen**) a woman employed to sell goods.

**salicylic acid** a chemical used as a fungicide and in aspirin and dyes.

**salient** (say-li-ĕnt) *adjective* prominent; most noticeable; *the salient features of the plan.* ●*noun* a projecting part, especially of a battle-line.

**saline** (say-lyn) *adjective* salty, containing salt or salts. □ **salinity** (să-lin-iti) *noun*

**Salinger** (sal-in-jer), J(erome) D(avid) (born 1919), American novelist, author of *The Catcher in the Rye.*

**saliva** (să-ly-vă) *noun* the colourless liquid discharged into the mouth by various glands, assisting in chewing and digestion.

**salivary** (să-ly-ver-i) *adjective* of or producing saliva; *salivary glands.*

**salivate** (sal-i-vayt) *verb* produce saliva. □ **salivation** *noun*

**Salk**, Jonas Edward (born 1914), American microbiologist, who developed the first effective vaccine against poliomyelitis.

**sallow**[1] *adjective* (of a person's skin or complexion) yellowish. □ **sallowness** *noun*

**sallow**[2] *noun* a willow tree, especially of a low-growing or shrubby kind.

**sally** *noun* **1** a sudden rush forward in attack; a sortie. **2** an excursion. **3** a lively or witty remark. ●*verb* (**sallied**, **sallying**) (usually foll. by *out* or *forth*) make a sally (in attack) or an excursion.

**salmon** *noun* **1** (*plural* **salmon** or **salmons**) a large fish with pinkish flesh, valued for food and sport. **2** salmon pink. □ **salmon pink** an orange-pink colour like the flesh of salmon. **salmon trout** a large silver-coloured trout resembling salmon.

**salmonella** *noun* (*plural* **salmonellae**) food poisoning caused by bacteria; the bacterium itself.

**Salome** (să-loh-mi) the daughter of Herod Antipas (son of Herod the Great) and Herodias, who asked for John the Baptist to be beheaded.

**salon** (sal-on) *noun* **1** a room or establishment where a hairdresser, beauty specialist, etc. works. **2** an elegant room used for receiving guests.

**Salonica** (să-lon-ikă) a seaport in NE Greece, the capital of Macedonia.

**saloon** *noun* **1** a public room for a specified purpose; *billiard saloon.* **2** a public room on a ship. **3** (*Amer.*) a place where alcoholic drinks may be bought and drunk. **4** a saloon car. □ **saloon bar** a more comfortable bar in a public house. **saloon car** a car with a closed body and no partition behind the driver.

**salsa** *noun* **1** dance music of Cuban origin with jazz and rock elements. **2** a spicy sauce served with meat or as a dip.

**salsify** (sal-si-fi) *noun* a plant with a long fleshy root cooked as a vegetable.

**SALT** *abbreviation* Strategic Arms Limitations Talks (*or* Treaty), aimed at the reduction of nuclear armaments.

**salt** *noun* **1** sodium chloride obtained from mines or by evaporation of sea water, used to flavour and preserve food. **2** a chemical compound of a metal and an acid. **3** (**salts**) a substance resembling salt in form, especially a laxative. **4** piquancy, wit. ●*adjective* tasting of salt; impregnated with or preserved in salt. ●*verb* **1** season with salt. **2** preserve in salt. **3** put aside for the future; *salt it away.* □ **old salt** an experienced sailor. **salt-cellar** *noun* a dish or perforated pot holding salt for use at meals. **salt-lick** *noun* a place where animals go to lick rock or earth impregnated with salt. **salt of the earth** admirable and honest people. **salt-pan** *noun* a vessel or hollow by the sea where salt is obtained from sea water by evaporation. **salt-water** *adjective* of or living in the sea. **take with a grain** or **pinch of salt** not believe wholly. **worth**

**one's salt** competent; deserving one's position.

**saltire** (sal-tyr) *noun* an X-shaped cross dividing a shield into four compartments.

**saltpetre** (solt-**peet**-er) *noun* (*Amer.* **saltpeter**) a salty white powder (potassium nitrate) used in gunpowder, medicines, and preserving meat.

**salty** *adjective* (**saltier, saltiest**) containing or tasting of salt. □ **saltiness** *noun*

**salubrious** (să-**loo**-bri-ŭs) *adjective* health-giving, healthy. □ **salubrity** *noun*

**saluki** (să-**loo**-ki) *noun* (*plural* **salukis**) a tall slender silky-coated dog.

**salutary** (sal-yoo-ter-i) *adjective* producing a beneficial or wholesome effect.

**salutation** (sal-yoo-**tay**-shŏn) *noun* a word or gesture of greeting; an expression of respect.

**salute** *noun* **1** a formal military movement of the body, or a signal by guns or flags, as a sign of respect. **2** a gesture of respect, greeting, or polite recognition. ● *verb* **1** perform a salute; greet with this. **2** express respect or admiration for.

**Salvador** *see* EL SALVADOR. □ **Salvadorean** (sal-vă-**dor**-iăn) *adjective & noun*

**salvage** *noun* **1** rescue of a wrecked or damaged ship or its cargo; rescue of property from fire or other disaster. **2** the goods or property saved. **3** the saving and use of waste paper, scrap metal, etc. **4** the items saved. ● *verb* save from loss or for use as salvage. □ **salvageable** *adjective*

**salvation** *noun* **1** saving of the soul from sin; the state of being saved. **2** preservation from loss or calamity; a person or thing that preserves from these; *the loan was our salvation*.

**Salvation Army** an international Christian organization founded on military lines to do charitable work and spread Christianity.

**salve**[1] *noun* **1** a soothing ointment. **2** something that soothes conscience or wounded feelings. ● *verb* soothe (conscience etc.).

**salve**[2] *verb* save from a wreck or fire. □ **salvable** *adjective*

**salver** *noun* a tray (usually of metal) on which letters, cards, or refreshments are placed.

**salvia** (sal-viă) *noun* a plant with spikes of red or blue flowers.

**salvo** *noun* (*plural* **salvoes** or **salvos**) **1** the firing of a number of guns simultaneously, especially as a salute. **2** a round of applause.

**sal volatile** (sal vŏ-**lat**-ili) a strong-smelling solution of ammonium carbonate used as a remedy for faintness. (¶ Latin).

**Salyut** (**sal**-yuut) any of a series of manned space stations launched by the former USSR.

**Salzburg** a city in Austria.

**SAM** *abbreviation* surface-to-air missile.

**Samaritan** *noun* **1** (in full **good Samaritan**) someone who readily gives help to a person in distress. (¶ Named after the parable of the Good Samaritan in the Bible.) **2** a member of an organization (**the Samaritans**) offering help and friendship to those in despair.

**samarium** (să-**mair**-iŭm) *noun* a metallic element (symbol Sm).

**samba** *noun* a ballroom dance of Brazilian origin; music for this.

**Sam Browne belt** a belt with a supporting strap that passes over the right shoulder.

**same** *adjective* **1** being of one kind, not changed or changing or different. **2** previously mentioned. **3** (**the same**) the same person or thing; *would do the same again*. **4** (**the same**) in the same manner; *we still feel the same about it*. ● *pronoun & adjective* (*informal*) = the same (senses 3 and 4 above); *same for me, please*. □ **all** (*or* **just**) **the same** nevertheless. **same here** (*informal*) the same applies to me.

**sameness** *noun* being the same; lack of variety.

**samizdat** (**sam**-iz-dat) *noun* secret publication of banned literature. (¶ Russian.)

**Samoa** (să-**moh**-ă) a group of islands in the Pacific Ocean, of which the eastern part is a territory of the USA (*see also* WESTERN SAMOA). □ **Samoan** *adjective & noun*

**Samos** (**say**-moss) a Greek island in the Aegean Sea.

**samosa** (să-**moh**-să) *noun* a fried triangular pastry containing spiced vegetables or meat.

**samovar** (**sam**-ŏ-var) *noun* a metal urn with an interior heating-tube to keep water at boiling point for making tea. (¶ Russian.)

**Samoyed** (**sam**-ŏ-yed) *noun* **1** a member of a people of northern Siberia. **2** (also **samoyed**) a dog of a white Arctic breed.

**sampan** *noun* a small flat-bottomed boat used in China.

**samphire** (**sam**-fyr) *noun* a plant with fragrant fleshy edible leaves, growing on cliffs.

**sample** *noun* a small separated part showing the quality of the whole; a specimen. ● *verb* test by taking a sample or getting an experience of.

**sampler** *noun* **1** a thing that takes samples. **2** a piece of embroidery worked in various stitches to display skill in needlework.

**sampling** *noun* the technique of digitally encoding a piece of sound and reusing it as part of a recording.

**Samson** (probably 11th century BC) an Israelite leader famous for his strength, betrayed by Delilah to the Philistines. ● *noun* a person of great strength.

**Samuel 1** a Hebrew prophet of the 11th century BC. **2** either of two historical books of the Old Testament.

**samurai** (sam-oor-I) *noun* (*plural* **samurai**) **1** a Japanese army officer. **2** a member of the former military caste in Japan.

**Sana'a** (sah-nă) the capital of the Yemen Arab Republic.

**sanatorium** *noun* (*plural* **sanatoriums** or **sanatoria**) **1** an establishment for treating chronic diseases (e.g. tuberculosis) or convalescents. **2** a room for sick people in a school etc.

**sanctify** *verb* (**sanctified, sanctifying**) make holy or sacred. □ **sanctification** *noun*

**sanctimonious** (sank-ti-moh-niŭs) *adjective* too righteous or pious. □ **sanctimoniously** *adverb*, **sanctimoniousness** *noun*, **sanctimony** *noun*

**sanction** *noun* **1** permission or approval. **2** action taken by a country to penalize and coerce a country or organization that has violated a law or code of practice or basic human rights. ● *verb* **1** give sanction or approval to; authorize. **2** attach a penalty or reward to (a law).

**sanctity** *noun* sacredness, holiness.

**sanctuary** *noun* **1** a sacred place. **2** the holiest part of a temple; the part of a chancel containing the altar. **3** an area where birds or wild animals are protected. **4** refuge; a place of refuge; *seek sanctuary*.

**sanctum** *noun* **1** a holy place. **2** a person's private room.

**Sand** (*pronounced* sahn), George (pseudonym of Amandine-Aurore Lucille Dupin, Baronne Dudevant) (1804–76), French novelist, advocate of women's rights.

**sand** *noun* **1** very fine loose fragments resulting from the wearing down of rock, found in deserts, seashores, river beds, etc. **2** an expanse of sand; a sandbank; *Goodwin Sands*. **3** light brown colour like that of sand. ● *verb* **1** smooth or polish with sand or sandpaper. **2** sprinkle or cover with sand. □ **sand-dune** or **sand-hill** *noun* loose sand formed into a mound by wind. **sand-martin** *noun* a swallow-like bird nesting in sandy banks. **sand-shoe** *noun* a light canvas shoe.

**sandal** *noun* a light shoe with straps over the foot.

**sandalled** *adjective* (*Amer.* **sandaled**) wearing sandals.

**sandalwood** *noun* a scented wood from a tropical tree.

**sandbag** *noun* a bag filled with sand, used to protect a wall or building (e.g. in war, or as a defence against rising flood-water). ● *verb* (**sandbagged, sandbagging**) **1** protect with sandbags. **2** hit with a sandbag.

**sandbank** *noun* a deposit of sand under water forming a shallow area.

**sandblast** *verb* clean or treat with a jet of sand driven by compressed air or steam. □ **sandblaster** *noun*

**sandcastle** *noun* a structure of sand made on the seashore.

**sander** *noun* a device for sanding things.

**Sandinista** (san-din-eest-ă) *noun* a member of a revolutionary guerrilla organization in Nicaragua, in power 1979–90. (¶ Named after A. C. Sandino (1893–1934), Nicaraguan nationalist leader.)

**sandman** *noun* an imaginary person causing sleepiness in children.

**sandpaper** *noun* paper with a coating of sand or other abrasive substance, used for smoothing or polishing surfaces. ● *verb* smooth or polish with sandpaper.

**sandpiper** *noun* a wading bird with a long pointed bill, living in open wet sandy places.

**sandpit** *noun* a shallow pit containing sand for children to play in.

**Sandringham House** a holiday house of the British royal family, in Norfolk.

**sandstone** *noun* rock formed of compressed sand.

**sandstorm** *noun* a desert storm of wind with clouds of sand.

**sandwich** *noun* two or more slices of bread with a filling between. ● *verb* insert (a thing) between two others. □ **sandwich-boards** *plural noun* two advertising boards hanging front and back from the shoulders. **sandwich course** a course of training with alternating periods of study and practical work.

**sandy** *adjective* (**sandier, sandiest**) **1** like sand; covered with sand. **2** (of hair) reddish-yellow. □ **sandiness** *noun*

**sane** *adjective* **1** having a sound mind; not mad. **2** showing good judgement; sensible and practical. □ **sanely** *adverb*

**San Francisco** a city and seaport on the coast of California.

**sang** see SING.

**sang-froid** (sahn-frwah) *noun* calmness in danger or difficulty. (¶ French, = cold blood.)

**sangha** (sang-ă) *noun* the Buddhist monastic order, including monks, nuns, and novices.

**sangria** *noun* a Spanish drink of red wine with lemonade, fruit, etc.

**sanguinary** (sang-win-er-i) *adjective* **1** full of bloodshed. **2** bloodthirsty.

**sanguine** (sang-win) *adjective* **1** hopeful, optimistic; *they are not very sanguine about their chances of winning*. **2** (of the complexion) ruddy.

**Sanhedrin** (san-i-drin) *noun* the supreme Jewish council and court of justice at Jerusalem in New Testament times.

**sanitarium** (san-i-**tair**-iŭm) *noun* (*plural* **sanitariums** or **sanitaria**) (*Amer.*) a sanatorium.

**sanitary** (san-it-er-i) *noun* **1** of hygiene; hygienic. **2** of sanitation. □ **sanitary towel** (*Amer.* **sanitary napkin**) an absorbent pad worn during menstruation.

**sanitation** *noun* arrangements to protect public health, especially by drainage and the efficient disposal of sewage.

**sanitize** *verb* (also **sanitise**) **1** make hygienic. **2** (*informal*) censor (information) to make it more acceptable. □ **sanitization** *noun*

**sanity** *noun* the state or condition of being sane.

**San José** (hoh-**zay**) the capital of Costa Rica.

**San Juan** (*pronounced* hwahn) the capital of Puerto Rico.

**sank** *see* SINK.

**San Marino** (mă-**ree**-noh) a small independent republic in NE Italy.

**San Martín** (mar-**teen**), José de (1778–1850), South American soldier and statesman, who liberated Chile and Peru from Spanish rule.

**San Salvador** the capital of El Salvador.

**Sanskrit** *noun* the ancient language of the Hindus in India, one of the oldest known Indo-European languages.

**sans serif** (also **sanserif**) (san-se-rif) a form of typeface without serifs.

**Santa Claus** Father Christmas. (¶ From the Dutch name *Sante Klaas* = St Nicholas.)

**Santiago** (san-ti-**ah**-goh) the capital of Chile.

**Santo Domingo** (dŏ-**ming**-oh) the capital of the Dominican Republic.

**São Paulo** (sah-oo **pow**-loh) the largest city in Brazil.

**São Tomé** (sah-oo tom-**ay**) the capital of **São Tomé and Principe** (*pronounced* **prin**-sipi), a country consisting of two islands off the west coast of Africa.

**sap** *noun* **1** the liquid that circulates in plants, carrying food to all parts. **2** vigour, vitality. **3** (*slang*) a foolish person. **4** a trench or tunnel made to get closer to an enemy. ●*verb* (**sapped**, **sapping**) **1** exhaust (strength) gradually. **2** drain of sap. **3** dig saps.

**sapient** (say-pi-ĕnt) *adjective* (*literary*) wise; pretending to be wise. □ **sapience** *noun*

**sapling** *noun* a young tree.

**sapper** *noun* **1** a soldier (especially a private) of the Royal Engineers. **2** a person who digs saps.

**sapphire** *noun* **1** a transparent blue precious stone. **2** its colour. ●*adjective* bright blue.

**Sappho** (**saf**-oh) (early 7th century BC) Greek lyric poetess from the island of Lesbos.

**sappy** *adjective* **1** full of sap. **2** young and vigorous.

**saprophyte** (sap-rŏ-fyt) *noun* a fungus or similar plant living on dead organic matter. □ **saprophytic** (sap-rŏ-**fit**-ik) *adjective*

**saraband** (sa-ră-band) *noun* a slow Spanish dance; the music for this.

**Saracen** (sa-ră-sĕn) *noun* an Arab or Muslim of the time of the Crusades.

**Sarajevo** (sa-ră-**yay**-voh) a city in former Yugoslavia, capital of Bosnia and Hercegovina.

**Sarawak** (să-**rah**-wak) a State of Malaysia, on the NW coast of Borneo.

**sarcasm** (**sar**-kazm) *noun* ironically scornful language.

**sarcastic** (sar-**kas**-tik) *adjective* using or showing sarcasm. □ **sarcastically** *adverb*

**sarcoma** (sar-**koh**-mă) *noun* (*plural* **sarcomas** or **sarcomata**) a malignant tumour on connective tissue.

**sarcophagus** (sar-**kof**-ă-gŭs) *noun* (*plural* **sarcophagi**) a stone coffin, often decorated with carvings.

**sardine** *noun* a young pilchard or similar small fish, often tinned as food tightly packed in oil.

**Sardinia** a large island in the Mediterranean Sea, west of Italy, an administrative region of Italy. □ **Sardinian** *adjective & noun*

**sardonic** (sar-**don**-ik) *adjective* humorous in a grim or sarcastic way. □ **sardonically** *adverb*

**sardonyx** (**sar**-dŏn-iks) *noun* onyx with alternate layers of white and yellow or orange.

**sargasso** (sar-**gas**-oh) *noun* (*plural* **sargassos** or **sargassoes**) (also **sargassum**, *plural* **sargassa**) a seaweed with berry-like air-vessels, found floating in masses.

**Sargasso Sea** (sar-**gas**-oh) a region of the western Atlantic Ocean, so called from the masses of sargasso found in it.

**sarge** *noun* (*slang*) sergeant.

**Sargent** (**sar**-jĕnt), John Singer (1856–1925), American portrait painter.

**sari** (**sar**-i) *noun* (*plural* **saris**) a length of cloth draped round the body, traditionally worn by women of the Indian subcontinent.

**sarky** *adjective* (*slang*) sarcastic.

**sarnie** *noun* (*informal*) a sandwich.

**sarong** (să-**rong**) *noun* a Malay and Javanese skirt-like garment worn by both sexes, consisting of a strip of cloth tucked round the waist or under the armpits.

**sarsaparilla** (sar-să-pă-**ril**-ă) *noun* a preparation of the dried roots of various plants, especially smilax, used to flavour drinks and medicines; formerly used as a tonic.

**sarsen** (sar-sĕn) *noun* sandstone boulder carried by ice during a glacial period.

**sarsenet** (sar-snit) *noun* a soft silk fabric used mainly for linings.

**sartorial** (sar-tor-iăl) *adjective* of tailoring; of men's clothing; *sartorial elegance*.

**Sartre** (*pronounced* sartr), Jean-Paul (1905–80), French existentialist philosopher, novelist, and dramatist.

**SAS** *abbreviation* Special Air Service, a regiment of the British armed services trained in commando techniques.

**sash**[1] *noun* a long strip of cloth worn round the waist or over one shoulder and across the body.

**sash**[2] *noun* either of the frames holding the glass in a sash-window. □ **sash-cord** *noun* strong cord used for attaching a weight to each end of a sash so that it can be balanced at any height. **sash-window** *noun* a window sliding up and down in grooves.

**sashay** *verb* (especially *Amer. informal*) walk in a showy casual way.

**Sask** *abbreviation* Saskatchewan.

**Saskatchewan** (să-skach-i-wăn) a province of Canada.

**sass** (*Amer. informal*) *noun* impudence, cheek. ● *verb* be cheeky to. □ **sassy** *adjective*

**Sassenach** (sas-ĕn-ak) *noun* (*Scottish & Irish, usually scornful*) an Englishman.

**Sassoon** (să-soon), Siegfried Louvain (1886–1967), English writer and First World War poet.

**Sat.** *abbreviation* Saturday.

**sat** *see* SIT.

**Satan** the Devil.

**satanic** (să-tan-ik) *adjective* of Satan; devilish, hellish. □ **satanically** *adverb*

**Satanism** *noun* worship of Satan, using distorted forms of Christian worship. □ **Satanist** *noun & adjective*

**satchel** *noun* a small shoulder bag for carrying light articles (especially schoolbooks).

**sate** (*pronounced* sayt) *verb* satiate.

**sateen** (să-teen) *noun* a closely-woven cotton fabric resembling satin.

**satellite** *noun* **1** a heavenly body revolving round a planet; an artificial body placed in orbit to revolve similarly. **2** (in full **satellite State**) a country that is subservient to another and follows its lead. ● *adjective* transmitted by satellite; *satellite television*. □ **satellite dish** a dish-shaped aerial for receiving satellite television. **satellite town** a smaller town dependent on a larger one near it.

**Sati** (să-ti) (in Hinduism) the wife of Siva, reborn as Parvati.

**satiable** (say-shă-bul) *adjective* able to be satiated.

**satiate** (say-shi-ayt) *verb* satisfy fully; glut or cloy with an excess of something. □ **satiation** *noun*

**Satie** (sah-ti), Erik (Alfred Leslie) (1866–1925), French composer.

**satiety** (să-ty-ĕti) *noun* (*formal*) the condition or feeling of being satiated.

**satin** *noun* a silky material woven in such a way that it is glossy on one side only. ● *adjective* smooth as satin. □ **satiny** *adjective*

**satinwood** *noun* the smooth hard wood of various tropical trees, used for making furniture.

**satire** *noun* **1** ridicule, irony, or sarcasm in speech or writing. **2** a novel, play, etc. that ridicules people's hypocrisy or foolishness in this way.

**satirical** (să-ti-ri-kăl) *adjective* using satire, criticizing in a humorous or sarcastic way. □ **satirically** *adverb*

**satirist** (sat-i-rist) *noun* a person who writes satires or uses satire.

**satirize** (sat-i-ryz) *verb* (also **satirise**) attack with satire; describe satirically.

**satisfaction** *noun* **1** satisfying; being satisfied. **2** something that satisfies a desire or gratifies a feeling. **3** compensation for injury or loss; *demand satisfaction*.

**satisfactory** *adjective* satisfying expectations or needs; adequate. □ **satisfactorily** *adverb*

**satisfy** *verb* (**satisfied**, **satisfying**) **1** give (a person) what he or she wants or needs; make pleased or contented. **2** put an end to (a demand or craving) by giving what is required; *satisfy one's hunger*. **3** provide with sufficient proof, convince; *the police are satisfied that his death was accidental*.

**satsuma** (sat-soo-mă) *noun* a small variety of orange similar to a mandarin.

**saturate** *verb* **1** make thoroughly wet, soak. **2** cause to absorb or accept as much as possible; *the market for used cars is saturated*. **3** cause (a substance) to combine with or absorb the greatest possible amount of another substance. □ **saturation** *noun*

**saturation point** the stage beyond which no more can be absorbed or accepted.

**Saturday** the day of the week following Friday.

**Saturn 1** (*Rom. myth*) a god of agriculture. **2** a large planet of the solar system, with 'rings' composed of small icy particles.

**saturnalia** (sat-er-nay-liă) *noun* (*plural* **saturnalia** *or* **saturnalias**) **1** wild revelry. **2** (usually **Saturnalia**) an ancient Roman festival of Saturn in December, the predecessor of Christmas.

**saturnine** (sat-er-nyn) *adjective* (of a person or looks) having a gloomy forbidding appearance.

**satyr** (sat-er) *noun* **1** (*Gk. & Rom. myth.*) a woodland god in human form but having a goat's ears, tail, and legs. **2** a grossly lustful man.

**sauce** *noun* **1** a liquid or semi-liquid preparation served with food to add flavour or richness. **2** (*informal*) impudence. □ **sauce-boat** *noun* a shallow jug for serving sauces, gravy, etc.

**saucepan** *noun* a metal cooking pan with a long handle, used over heat.

**saucer** *noun* **1** a small shallow curved dish on which a cup stands. **2** something shaped like this. □ **saucerful** *noun*

**saucy** *adjective* (**saucier, sauciest**) **1** impudent. **2** jaunty. □ **saucily** *adverb*, **sauciness** *noun*

**Saudi** (*rhymes with* dowdy) *noun* (*plural* **Saudis**) a native or inhabitant of Saudi Arabia.

**Saudi Arabia** a country in the Middle East, occupying most of the Arabian peninsula. □ **Saudi Arabian** *adjective & noun*

**sauerkraut** (**sowr**-krowt, *rhymes with* our, out) *noun* a German dish of chopped pickled cabbage.

**Saul** (11th century BC) the first king of Israel.

**sauna** (**saw**-nă) *noun* a period spent in a specially-designed very hot room to clean the body; the room itself. (¶ Finnish.)

**saunter** *verb* walk in a leisurely way. ● *noun* a leisurely walk or walking-pace.

**saurian** (**sor**-iăn) *adjective* of or like a lizard.

**sausage** *noun* minced seasoned meat enclosed in a cylindrical edible skin. □ **sausage meat** meat prepared for this or as a stuffing etc. **sausage roll** sausage meat enclosed in a cylindrical roll of pastry.

**sauté** (**soh**-tay) *adjective* fried quickly in a small amount of fat; *sauté potatoes.* ● *verb* (**sautéd** *or* **sautéed, sautéing**) cook in this way.

**Sauternes** (soh-**tern**) *noun* a sweet white French wine.

**savage** *adjective* **1** in a primitive or uncivilized state; *savage tribes.* **2** wild and fierce; *savage animals.* **3** cruel and hostile; *savage criticism.* **4** (*informal*) very angry. ● *noun* a member of a savage tribe. ● *verb* attack savagely, maul. □ **savagely** *adverb*, **savagery** *noun*

**savannah** (să-**van**-ă) *noun* a grassy plain in hot regions, with few or no trees.

**savant** (**sav**-ănt) *noun* a learned person.

**savarin** (**sav**-er-in) *noun* a sponge-like cake made with yeast, often baked in a ring mould and filled with fruit.

**save** *verb* **1** rescue; keep from danger, harm, or capture. **2** free from the power of sin. **3** avoid wasting; *save fuel.* **4** keep for future use or enjoyment; put aside (money) for future use. **5** make unnecessary; relieve (a person) from (trouble, expense, etc.); *did it to save you a journey.* **6** (in sports) prevent an opponent from scoring. ● *noun* the act of saving in football etc. ● *preposition* except; in *all cases save one.* □ **save-as-you-earn** *noun* a method of saving money by having an amount deducted regularly from one's income. **save one's breath** keep silent because it would be useless to speak. □ **savable** *or* **saveable** *adjective*

**saveloy** (**sav**-ĕl-oi) *noun* a seasoned dried smoked sausage.

**saver** *noun* **1** a person who saves (money). **2** (often as *combining form*) something that saves; *a real time-saver.* **3** a special cheap fare.

**saving** *noun* **1** the act of rescuing or keeping from danger etc. **2** (**savings**) money put aside for future use. ● *adjective* that saves. ● *preposition* except. □ **saving grace** a good quality that redeems a person or thing whose other qualities are not good.

**savings certificate** a document issued by the government in return for a deposit of savings on which it will pay interest.

**saviour** *noun* **1** a person who rescues or delivers people from harm or danger. **2** (**the** *or* **our Saviour**) Christ as the saviour of mankind.

**savoir-faire** (sav-wahr-**fair**) *noun* knowledge of how to behave in any situation that may arise; social tact. (¶ French, = knowing how to do.)

**savory** *noun* a low-growing herb with a spicy smell and flavour.

**savour** *noun* (*Amer.* **savor**) **1** the taste or smell of something. **2** the power to arouse enjoyment; *felt that life had lost its savour.* ● *verb* **1** have a certain taste or smell. **2** taste or smell (a thing) with enjoyment. **3** (foll. by *of*) give a certain impression; *the reply savours of impertinence.*

**savoury** *adjective* (*Amer.* **savory**) **1** having an appetizing taste or smell. **2** having a salt or piquant and not sweet flavour. ● *noun* a savoury dish, especially one served at the end of a meal. □ **savouriness** *noun*

**Savoy** (să-**voi**) a region in SE France bordering on Italy.

**savoy** *noun* a cabbage with wrinkled leaves.

**savvy** (*slang*) *noun* common sense, understanding. ● *verb* understand.

**saw¹** *noun* a tool with a zigzag edge for cutting wood etc. ● *verb* (**sawed, sawn** *or* **sawed, sawing**) **1** cut with a saw. **2** make a to-and-fro movement like that of sawing.

**saw²** *noun* an old saying, a maxim.

**saw³** *see* SEE¹.

**sawdust** *noun* powdery fragments of wood produced when timber is sawn.

**sawfish** *noun* a large sea fish having a bladelike snout with jagged edges.

**sawmill** *noun* a factory with power-operated saws where timber is cut into planks.

**sawn** *see* SAW¹. □ **sawn-off** *adjective* (*Amer.* **sawed-off**) (of a gun) with part of the barrel removed by sawing.

**sawyer** *noun* a person who saws timber.

**sax** *noun* (*informal*) a saxophone.

**saxe** *noun* (in full **saxe blue**) light blue with a greyish tinge.

**Saxe-Coburg-Gotha** (saks-koh-berg-**goh**-thă) the name of the British royal house from the accession of Edward VII (1901), whose father was Prince Albert, until the family name was changed to Windsor in 1917.

**saxifrage** (saks-i-frij) *noun* a rock plant with clusters of small white, yellow, or red flowers.

**Saxon** *noun* **1** a member of a Germanic people who occupied parts of England in the 5th–6th centuries. **2** (usually **Old Saxon**) their language. ●*adjective* of the Saxons or their language.

**Saxony** a former province of east central Germany.

**saxophone** *noun* a brass wind instrument with a reed in the mouthpiece, and with keys operated by the player's fingers.

**saxophonist** (saks-**off**-ŏn-ist) *noun* a person who plays the saxophone.

**say** *verb* (**said, saying**) **1** utter or recite in a speaking voice. **2** state, express in words; have a specified wording; *the notice says 'keep out'.* **3** give as an argument or excuse; *there's much to be said on both sides.* **4** give as one's opinion or decision; *I say we should accept.* **5** suppose as a possibility; take (a specified amount) as being near enough; *let's allow, say, an hour for the meeting.* **6** convey artistically (inner meaning etc.); *what is the poem saying?* ●*noun* the power to decide; *has no say in the matter.* ●*interjection* (*Amer. informal*) = I SAY. □ **go without saying** be too obvious to need mention. **I'll say** (*informal*) yes indeed. **I say** (*Brit.*) an expression of surprise or admiration, or calling attention, or opening a conversation. **say-so** *noun* **1** the power to decide something; a command. **2** a mere assertion without proof.

**SAYE** *abbreviation* save-as-you-earn.

**Sayers**, Dorothy L(eigh) (1893–1957), English writer of detective fiction.

**saying** *noun* a well-known phrase or proverb.

**Sb** *symbol* antimony.

**SC** *abbreviation* South Carolina.

**Sc** *symbol* scandium.

**sc.** *abbreviation* scilicet.

**scab** *noun* **1** a crust forming over a wound or sore as it heals. **2** a skin disease or plant disease that causes scab-like roughness. **3** (*informal, scornful*) a blackleg. ●*verb* (**scabbed, scabbing**) **1** form a scab; heal by doing this. **2** (*informal, scornful*) act as a blackleg. □ **scabby** *adjective*

**scabbard** *noun* the sheath of a sword or dagger.

**scabies** (skay-beez) *noun* a contagious skin disease causing itching.

**scabious** (skay-bi-ŭs) *noun* a herbaceous plant with flowers shaped like a pincushion surrounded by a frill of blue or white petals.

**scabrous** (skayb-rŭs) *adjective* **1** (of the surface of a plant or animal) rough, scaly. **2** indecent, salacious.

**Scafell** (**Pike**) (skaw-**fel**) a mountain in the Lake District; the highest peak in England.

**scaffold** *noun* **1** a wooden platform for the execution of criminals. **2** scaffolding. ●*verb* fit scaffolding to (a building).

**scaffolding** *noun* **1** a temporary structure of poles and planks providing workers with platforms to stand on while building or repairing a house etc. **2** the poles etc. from which this is made.

**scalar** (skay-ler) *adjective* (in mathematics) having magnitude but not direction. ●*noun* a scalar quantity.

**scalawag** = SCALLYWAG.

**scald** *verb* **1** injure with hot liquid or steam. **2** heat (milk) to near boiling point. **3** clean (pans etc.) with boiling water. ●*noun* an injury to the skin by scalding.

**scale¹** *noun* **1** each of the thin overlapping plates of horny membrane or hard substance that protect the skin of many fish and reptiles. **2** something resembling this (e.g. on a plant); a flake of skin. **3** a white deposit formed inside a boiler or kettle etc. in which hard water is regularly used. **4** tartar formed on teeth. ●*verb* **1** remove scales or scale from. **2** come off in scales or flakes.

**scale²** *noun* **1** (**scales**) an instrument for weighing things. **2** (also **scale-pan**) each of the dishes on a simple balance. **3** (**the Scales**) a sign of the zodiac, Libra. □ **tip** *or* **turn the scales** be the decisive factor in a situation. **turn the scales at** weigh; *turned the scales at 12 stone.*

**scale³** *noun* **1** an ordered series of units, degrees, qualities, etc. for measurement or classification. **2** an arrangement of notes in music, ascending or descending by fixed intervals. **3** the ratio of the actual measurements of something to those of a drawing, map, or model of it; a line with marks showing this; *the scale is 1 inch to the* *mile; a scale model.* **4** the relative size or extent of something; *entertainment on a grand scale.* ●*verb* **1** climb; *scaled the cliff.* **2** represent in measurements or extent in proportion to the size of the original. □ **to scale** in exact proportion throughout. **scale up** *or* **down** make larger or smaller in proportion.

**scalene** (skay-leen) *adjective* (especially of a triangle) having unequal sides.

**scallion** *noun* **1** a shallot. **2** a bulbous onion with a long neck, e.g. a spring onion.

**scallop** (skal-ŏp *or* skol-ŏp) *noun* (also **scollop**) **1** a shellfish with two hinged fan-shaped shells. **2** either shell of this, often used for cooking and serving food. **3** each of a series of semicircular curves used as an ornamental edging. ●*verb* (**scalloped**, **scalloping**) **1** cook in a scallop shell. **2** ornament with scallops. □ **scalloping** *noun*

**scallywag** *noun* (also **scalawag**) (*informal*) a rascal.

**scalp** *noun* **1** the skin of the head excluding the face. **2** this with the hair, formerly cut as a trophy from an enemy's head by American Indians. ●*verb* **1** take the scalp of. **2** (*Amer. informal*) resell (shares etc.) at a high or quick profit.

**scalpel** (skal-pĕl) *noun* a surgeon's small sharp knife.

**scaly** *adjective* (**scalier**, **scaliest**) covered in scales or scale (*see* SCALE¹).

**scam** *noun* (*Amer. slang*) **1** a fraudulent trick; a swindle. **2** a rumour; information.

**scamp** *noun* a rascal.

**scamper** *verb* run hastily; run and skip playfully. ●*noun* a scampering run.

**scampi** (skamp-i) (treated as *plural* or *singular*) large prawns.

**scan** *verb* (**scanned**, **scanning**) **1** look at all parts of (a thing) intently. **2** glance at quickly and not thoroughly. **3** sweep a radar or electronic beam over (an area) in search of something. **4** resolve (a picture) into elements of light and shade for television transmission. **5** analyse the rhythm of (a line of verse). **6** (of verse) be correct in rhythm. ●*noun* scanning.

**scandal** *noun* **1** something shameful or disgraceful. **2** gossip about other people's faults and wrongdoing.

**scandalize** *verb* (also **scandalise**) shock by something shameful or disgraceful.

**scandalmonger** *noun* a person who invents or spreads scandal.

**scandalous** *adjective* shameful, disgraceful; containing scandal; *scandalous reports.* □ **scandalously** *adverb*

**Scandinavia** Norway, Sweden, and Denmark (sometimes also Finland, Ice-land, and the Faeroe Islands) considered as a unit. □ **Scandinavian** *adjective* & *noun*

**scandium** *noun* a metallic element (symbol Sc).

**scanner** *noun* **1** a device for scanning or systematically examining all parts of something. **2** (in medicine) a machine using X-ray, ultrasound, etc. to examine internal areas of the body.

**scansion** (skan-shŏn) *noun* the scanning of lines of verse; the way verse scans.

**scant** *adjective* scanty, insufficient; *was treated with scant courtesy.*

**scanty** *adjective* (**scantier**, **scantiest**) **1** of small amount or extent; *scanty vegetation.* **2** barely enough. □ **scantily** *adverb*, **scantiness** *noun*

**scapegoat** *noun* a person who is made to bear blame or punishment that should rightly fall on others. (¶ Named after the goat which, in ancient Jewish religious custom, was allowed to escape into the wilderness after the high priest had symbolically laid the sins of the people upon it.)

**scapula** (skap-yoo-lă) *noun* (*plural* **scapulae**, *pronounced* skap-yoo-lee, *or* **scapulas**) the shoulder blade.

**scapular** (skap-yoo-ler) *adjective* of the scapula. ●*noun* a monk's short cloak.

**scar¹** *noun* **1** a mark left where a wound or sore has healed, or on a plant from which a leaf has fallen. **2** a mark left by damage. **3** a lasting effect produced by grief etc. ●*verb* (**scarred**, **scarring**) mark with a scar; form a scar or scars.

**scar²** *noun* (also **scaur**) a steep craggy part of a mountainside or cliff.

**scarab** (ska-răb) *noun* **1** a kind of beetle. **2** the sacred dung-beetle of ancient Egypt. **3** a carving of a beetle, used in ancient Egypt as a charm.

**scarce** *adjective* not enough to supply a demand or need, rare. □ **make oneself scarce** (*informal*) go away; keep out of the way.

**scarcely** *adverb* **1** only just, almost not; *she is scarcely 17 years old; I scarcely know him.* **2** not, surely not; *you can scarcely expect me to believe that.*

**scarcity** *noun* being scarce; a shortage.

**scare** *verb* frighten or become frightened suddenly. ●*noun* a sudden fright; alarm caused by a rumour; *a bomb scare.*

**scarecrow** *noun* **1** a figure dressed in old clothes, set up to scare birds away from crops. **2** (*informal*) a badly-dressed or grotesque person.

**scaremonger** *noun* a person who spreads alarming rumours. □ **scaremongering** *noun*

**scarf¹** *noun* (*plural* **scarves** *or* **scarfs**) **1** a long strip of material worn for warmth or ornament round the neck. **2** a square of material worn round the neck or over the head.

**scarf²** noun (plural **scarfs**) a joint made by thinning the ends of two pieces of timber etc., so that they overlap without an increase of thickness, and fastening them with bolts etc. ●verb join in this way.

**scarify** (**skair**-i-fy) verb (**scarified, scarifying**) **1** loosen the surface of (soil etc.). **2** make slight cuts in (skin or tissue) surgically. **3** hurt by severe criticism. **4** (informal) scare.

**scarlatina** (skar-lă-**teen**-ă) noun scarlet fever.

**Scarlatti** (skar-**lat**-i), Alessandro (1660–1725) and his son Domenico (1685–1757), Italian composers.

**scarlet** adjective of brilliant red colour. ●noun **1** scarlet colour. **2** a scarlet substance or material; scarlet clothes. □ **scarlet fever** an infectious fever caused by bacteria, producing a scarlet rash. **scarlet pimpernel** a wild plant with small red flowers. **scarlet woman** (old use) a prostitute.

**scarp** noun a steep slope on a hillside.

**scarper** verb (slang) run away.

**scarves** see SCARF¹.

**scary** adjective (**scarier, scariest**) frightening.

**scat¹** interjection (informal) go away quickly.

**scat²** noun wordless jazz singing using the voice as an instrument. ●verb (**scatted, scatting**) sing in this way.

**scathing** (skay-*th*'ing) adjective (of criticism) severe and scornful. □ **scathingly** adverb

**scatology** noun an excessive interest in excrement or obscene things. □ **scatological** adjective

**scatter** verb **1** throw or put here and there, cover in this way. **2** go or send in different directions. ●noun scattering; the extent over which something is scattered.

**scatterbrain** noun a person who is unable to concentrate or do things systematically. □ **scatterbrained** adjective

**scatty** adjective (**scattier, scattiest**) (informal) scatterbrained; crazy. □ **scattily** adverb, **scattiness** noun

**scaur** = SCAR².

**scavenge** verb **1** (of an animal) search for decaying flesh as food. **2** search for usable objects or material among rubbish or discarded things. □ **scavenger** noun

**Sc.D.** abbreviation Doctor of Science.

**SCE** abbreviation Scottish Certificate of Education.

**scenario** (sin-**ar**-i-oh) noun (plural **scenarios**) **1** the outline of a film, play, etc. **2** a possible sequence of events suggested for consideration.

**scene** noun **1** the place of an actual or fictional event; the scene of the crime. **2** a piece of continuous action in a play or film; a subdivision of an act. **3** an incident thought of as resembling this. **4** a dramatic outburst of temper or emotion; a stormy argument; made a scene. **5** stage scenery. **6** a landscape or view as seen by a spectator; the rural scene before us. **7** (informal) an area of action, a way of life; the drug scene; not my scene. □ **behind the scenes** **1** backstage. **2** in secret. **be on the scene** be present.

**scenery** noun **1** the general appearance of a landscape. **2** picturesque features of a landscape. **3** structures used on a theatre stage to represent features in the scene of the action.

**scenic** (**seen**-ik) adjective **1** having fine natural scenery; the scenic road along the coast. **2** of or on a theatre stage. □ **scenically** adverb

**scent** noun **1** the characteristic pleasant smell of something. **2** a sweet-smelling liquid made from essence of flowers or aromatic chemicals; perfume. **3** a perceptible smell left by an animal, by which it can be traced. **4** clues leading to a discovery. ●verb **1** discover by sense of smell; the dog scented a rat. **2** begin to suspect the presence or existence of; she scented trouble. **3** put scent on (a thing); make fragrant. □ **scented** adjective

**scepter** Amer. spelling of SCEPTRE.

**sceptic** (**skep**-tik) noun (Amer. **skeptic**) a sceptical person; one who doubts the truth of religious doctrines. □ **scepticism** (**skep**-ti-sizm) noun

**sceptical** (**skep**-tik-ăl) adjective (Amer. **skeptical**) inclined to disbelieve things; doubting or questioning the truth of claims or statements etc. □ **sceptically** adverb

**sceptre** (**sep**-ter) noun (Amer. **scepter**) a staff carried by a king or queen as a symbol of sovereignty.

**schadenfreude** (**shah**-děn-froi-dě) noun malicious enjoyment of another's misfortunes. (¶ German.)

**schedule** (**shed**-yool) noun a programme or timetable of planned events or of work. ●verb **1** include in a schedule, appoint for a certain time; the train is scheduled to stop at Bletchley. **2** list (a building) for preservation. □ **on schedule** punctual according to the timetable. **scheduled flight** (also **scheduled service**) a regular public flight; not a chartered flight.

**schema** noun (plural **schemata** or **schemas**) a summary, outline, or diagram.

**schematic** (skee-**mat**-ik) adjective in the form of a diagram or chart. □ **schematically** adverb

**schematize** (skee-mă-tyz) *verb* (also **schematise**) put into schematic form; formulate in regular order. □ **schematization** *noun*

**scheme** (*pronounced* skeem) *noun* **1** a plan of work or action. **2** a secret or underhand plan. **3** an orderly planned arrangement; *a colour scheme.* ●*verb* make plans; plan in a secret or underhand way. □ **schemer** *noun*

**scherzo** (skairts-oh) *noun* (*plural* **scherzos**) a lively vigorous musical composition or independent section of a longer work.

**Schiller** (shil-er), Johann Christoph Friedrich von (1759-1805), German dramatist and poet.

**schism** (*pronounced* skizm *or* sizm) *noun* division into opposing groups because of a difference in belief or opinion, especially in a religious body. □ **schismatic** *adjective & noun*

**schist** (*pronounced* shist) *noun* a crystalline rock formed in layers.

**schizo** (skits-oh) *adjective & noun* (*plural* **schizos**) (*informal*) = SCHIZOPHRENIC.

**schizoid** (skits-oid) *adjective* resembling or suffering from schizophrenia. ●*noun* a schizoid person.

**schizophrenia** (skits-ŏ-**freen**-iă) *noun* a mental disorder in which a person becomes unable to act or think in a rational way, often with delusions and withdrawal from social relationships.

**schizophrenic** (skits-ŏ-**fren**-ik) *adjective* of or suffering from schizophrenia. ●*noun* a schizophrenic person.

**Schleswig-Holstein** (shles-vik-**hol**-shtyn) a province of West Germany.

**Schliemann** (shlee-măn), Heinrich (1822-90), German archaeologist, excavator of Troy and Mycenae, the discoverer of the Mycenaean civilization.

**schmaltz** (*pronounced* shmawlts) *noun* (*informal*) sugary sentimentality, especially in music or literature.

**schmuck** *noun* (*slang*, especially *Amer.*) a foolish or contemptible person.

**schnapps** (*pronounced* shnaps) *noun* any of various strong spirits drunk in northern Europe.

**schnitzel** (shnits-ĕl) *noun* a fried veal cutlet.

**Schoenberg** (shern-berg), Arnold (1874-1951), Austrian composer, living in the USA from 1933, who invented serial composition and developed atonality and the twelve-tone technique.

**scholar** *noun* **1** a person with great learning in a particular subject. **2** a person who is skilled in academic work. **3** a person who holds a scholarship. □ **scholarly** *adjective*

**scholarship** *noun* **1** a grant of money towards education, usually gained by means of a competitive examination. **2** great

learning in a particular subject. **3** the methods and achievements characteristic of scholars and academic work.

**scholastic** (skŏl-**ast**-ik) *adjective* of schools or education; academic. □ **scholastically** *adverb*

**scholasticism** *noun* (*hist.*) medieval western church philosophy, based on the works of Aristotle.

**school**[1] *noun* **1** an institution for educating pupils up to 19 years of age; in America including college and university. **2** its buildings; its pupils. **3** the time during which teaching is done there; *school ends at 4.30 p.m.* **4** the department of one branch of study in a university; *the history school.* **5** experience that gives discipline or instruction; *learned his tactics in a hard school.* **6** a group or succession of philosophers, artists, etc. following the same teachings or principles. ●*verb* train or discipline. □ **of the old school** according to old standards.

**school**[2] *noun* a shoal, e.g. of fish or whales.

**schoolboy** *noun* a boy at school.

**schoolchild** *noun* (*plural* **schoolchildren**) a child at school.

**schoolgirl** *noun* a girl at school.

**schooling** *noun* education, training.

**schoolmaster** *noun* a male schoolteacher.

**schoolmistress** *noun* a female schoolteacher.

**schoolteacher** *noun* a teacher in a school.

**schooner** (skoo-ner) *noun* **1** a sailing ship with two or more masts. **2** a measure or glass for sherry. **3** (*Amer. & Austral.*) a tall beer glass.

**Schopenhauer** (shoh-pĕn-howr), Arthur (1788-1860), German philosopher.

**schottische** (shot-**eesh**) *noun* a slow polka; the music for this.

**Schrödinger** (shrer-ding-er), Erwin (1887-1961), Austrian physicist, who developed the theory of wave mechanics.

**Schubert** (shoo-bert), Franz (1797-1828), Austrian composer.

**Schumann** (shoo-măn), Robert Alexander (1810-56), German composer.

**Schweitzer** (shvy-tser), Albert (1875-1965), German theologian, musician, and medical missionary.

**sciatic** (sy-at-ik) *adjective* of the hip or the sciatic nerve. □ **sciatic nerve** the largest nerve in the human body, running from pelvis to thigh.

**sciatica** (sy-at-ik-ă) *noun* neuralgia of the hip and thigh, pain in the sciatic nerve.

**science** *noun* **1** a branch of knowledge requiring systematic study and method, especially one of those dealing with substances, animal and vegetable life, and natural laws. **2** an expert's skilful technique; *with skill and science.* □ **science fiction** stories based on imaginary future scientific discoveries, changes of the environment, or space travel and life on other planets. **science park** an area allocated to science-based industries and scientific research.

**scientific** *adjective* **1** of or used in a science; *scientific apparatus.* **2** of scientists. **3** using careful and systematic study, observations, and tests of conclusions etc. □ **scientifically** *adverb*

**scientist** *noun* an expert in or student of a science.

**Scientology** *noun* a quasi-religious philosophy based on self-improvement and courses of study and training. □ **Scientologist** *noun*

**sci-fi** (sy-fy) *noun* (*informal*) science fiction.

**scilicet** (sy-li-set) *adverb* that is to say (used especially in explaining an ambiguity). (¶ Latin.)

**Scilly Islands** (sil-i) (also **Scillies** *or* **Isles of Scilly**) a group of about 40 small islands off the west coast of Cornwall. □ **Scillonian** (sil-oh-niăn) *adjective & noun*

**scimitar** (sim-it-er) *noun* a short curved oriental sword.

**scintilla** (sin-til-ă) *noun* a trace; *not a scintilla of evidence.*

**scintillate** (sin-til-ayt) *verb* **1** sparkle, give off sparks. **2** be brilliant; *a scintillating discussion.* □ **scintillation** *noun*

**sciolism** (sy-ŏ-lizm) *noun* superficial knowledge; a display of this. □ **sciolist** *noun*, **sciolistic** *adjective*

**scion** (sy-ŏn) *noun* **1** a descendant of a family, especially a noble one. **2** a shoot of a plant cut for grafting or planting.

**Scipio** (**skip**-i-oh) the name of two Roman generals and politicians, of whom the first (236–184/3 BC) successfully concluded the second Punic War, and the second (185/4–129 BC) fought in the third Punic War and destroyed Carthage in 146 BC.

**scirocco** alternative spelling of SIROCCO.

**scissors** *plural noun* a cutting instrument made of two blades with handles for the thumb and fingers.

**sclerosis** (skler-**oh**-sis) *noun* a diseased condition in which soft tissue (e.g. of arteries) hardens; *see also* MULTIPLE SCLEROSIS. □ **sclerotic** (skler-ot-ik) *adjective*

**scoff**[1] *verb* jeer, speak contemptuously. ● *noun* a taunt; mocking words.

**scoff**[2] (*slang*) *verb* eat (food) quickly or greedily. ● *noun* food, a meal.

**scold** *verb* rebuke; tell off harshly. □ **scolding** *noun*

**scollop** alternative spelling of SCALLOP.

**sconce** *noun* an ornamental wall-bracket for holding a candle or electric light.

**scone** (*pronounced* skon *or* skohn) *noun* a small soft cake of flour, fat, and milk, baked quickly and eaten buttered.

**scoop** *noun* **1** a deep shovel-like tool for taking up and moving grain, sugar, etc. **2** a ladle; a device with a small round bowl and a handle used for serving ice cream etc. **3** a scooping movement. **4** a piece of news discovered and published by one newspaper in advance of its rivals. ● *verb* **1** lift or hollow with or as if with a scoop. **2** forestall (a rival newspaper) with a news scoop.

**scoot** *verb* (*informal*) go away hastily.

**scooter** *noun* **1** a child's toy vehicle with a footboard on wheels and a long steering-handle. **2** (in full **motor scooter**) a lightweight motor cycle with a protective shield at the front.

**scope** *noun* **1** the range of something; *the subject is outside the scope of this inquiry.* **2** opportunity, outlet; *a kind of work that gives scope for her abilities.*

**scorbutic** (skor-**bew**-tik) *adjective* of, like, or affected with scurvy.

**scorch** *verb* burn or become burnt on the surface; make or become discoloured in this way. ● *noun* a mark made by scorching.

**scorcher** *noun* (*informal*) a very hot day.

**scorching** *adjective* (*informal*) **1** (of the weather) very hot. **2** (of criticism etc.) harsh, severe.

**score** *noun* **1** the number of points made by each player or side in a game or competition. **2** a record of this, a reckoning. **3** a reason or motive; *rejected on that score.* **4** a set of twenty. **5** (**scores**) a great many; *scores of things.* **6** a line or mark cut into something. **7** a copy of a musical composition showing the notes on sets of staves. **8** the music for a film, musical, etc. **9** a record of money owing. ● *verb* **1** gain (a point or points) in a game etc.; make a score. **2** keep a record of the score. **3** be worth as points in a game; *a goal scores 6 points.* **4** achieve; *scored a great success.* **5** have an advantage; *he scores by knowing the language well.* **6** make a clever retort that puts an opponent at a disadvantage. **7** cut a line or mark(s) into (a thing). **8** write out as a musical score; arrange (a piece of music) for instruments. □ **know the score** (*informal*) be aware of the essential facts. **score off** (*informal*) defeat in argument or repartee. **score out** *or* **through** cancel by drawing a line through (words etc.). □ **scorer** *noun*

**scoria** (skor-iă) *noun* (*plural* **scoriae**) **1** a mass of lava with many holes. **2** slag or dross of metals. □ **scoriaceous** (skor-i-ay-shŭs) *adjective*

**scorn** *noun* strong contempt. ● *verb* **1** feel or show strong contempt for. **2** reject or refuse scornfully; *would scorn to ask for favours*.

**scornful** *adjective* (often foll. by *of*) feeling or showing scorn. □ **scornfully** *adverb*

**Scorpio** *noun* the eighth sign of the zodiac, the Scorpion. □ **Scorpian** *adjective & noun*

**scorpion** *noun* 1 a small animal of the spider group with pincers and a jointed stinging tail. 2 (**the Scorpion**) a sign of the zodiac, Scorpio.

**Scot** *noun* a native of Scotland; a person of Scottish descent.

**Scotch** *adjective* of Scotland or Scottish people or their form of English. ●*noun* 1 the Scottish dialect. 2 Scotch whisky, the kind distilled in Scotland especially from malted barley. □ **Scotch broth** meat soup containing pearl barley and vegetables. **Scotch egg** a hard-boiled egg enclosed in sausage meat. **scotch mist** thick drizzly mist. **Scotch terrier** a small terrier with rough hair and short legs.

■**Usage** Modern Scots prefer to use the words *Scots* and *Scottish*, not *Scotch*, except when the word is applied to whisky and in the compounds listed above.

**scotch** *verb* put an end to; *scotched the rumour*.

**scot-free** *adjective & adverb* unharmed; not punished.

**Scotland** the country forming the northern part of Great Britain.

**Scotland Yard** (in full **New Scotland Yard**) 1 the headquarters of the London Metropolitan Police. 2 its Criminal Investigation Department.

**Scots** *adjective* Scottish. ●*noun* the Scottish dialect. □ **Scotsman** *noun* (*plural* **Scotsmen**), **Scotswoman** *noun* (*plural* **Scotswomen**).

**Scott¹**, Sir George Gilbert (1811–78), English architect, who designed the Albert Memorial.

**Scott²**, Sir Peter Markham (1909–89), English naturalist, conservationist, and bird-painter.

**Scott³**, Robert Falcon (1868–1912), English explorer of the Antarctic, who died on the return journey from the South Pole.

**Scott⁴**, Sir Walter (1771–1832), Scottish novelist and poet.

**Scotticism** (skot-i-sizm) *noun* a Scottish word or phrase.

**Scottie** *noun* (*informal*) a Scotch terrier.

**Scottish** *adjective* of Scotland or its people or their form of the English language. □ **Scottish National Party** a political party seeking autonomous government for Scotland.

**scoundrel** *noun* a dishonest or unprincipled person; a rogue.

**scour** *verb* 1 clean by rubbing with something abrasive. 2 clear out (a channel or pipe etc.) by the force of water flowing through it. 3 travel over (an area) in search of something; search thoroughly. ●*noun* scouring; the action of water on a channel etc. □ **scourer** *noun*

**scourge** (*pronounced* skerj) *noun* 1 a whip for flogging. 2 a person or thing regarded as a cause of suffering. ●*verb* 1 flog with a whip. 2 afflict greatly; punish.

**Scouse** (*rhymes with* house) *noun* (*slang*) 1 (also **scouser**) a native of Liverpool. 2 Liverpool dialect. ●*adjective* (*slang*) of Liverpool.

**scout** *noun* 1 a person sent out to gather information, e.g. about an enemy's movements or strength. 2 a search for information etc. 3 (also **Scout**) a member of the Scout Association, an (originally boys') organization intended to develop character by outdoor activities. ●*verb* act as scout; make a search. □ **scouting** *noun*

**Scouter** *noun* an adult leader in the Scout Association.

**scow** (*rhymes with* now) *noun* (especially *Amer.*) a flat-bottomed boat.

**scowl** *noun* a sullen or angry frown. ●*verb* make a scowl.

**Scrabble** *noun* (*trade mark*) a game played on a board in which words are built up from letters printed on small square counters.

**scrabble** *verb* 1 make a scratching movement or sound with the hands or feet. 2 grope busily or struggle to find or obtain something.

**scrag** *noun* the bony part of an animal's carcass as food; neck of mutton or the less meaty end (**scrag-end**) of this. ●*verb* (**scragged**, **scragging**) (*slang*) 1 seize roughly by the neck; handle roughly. 2 strangle, hang.

**scraggy** *adjective* (**scraggier**, **scraggiest**) lean and bony. □ **scragginess** *noun*

**scram** *verb* (**scrammed**, **scramming**) (*slang*) go away.

**scramble** *verb* 1 clamber, crawl, climb, etc., especially hurriedly and awkwardly. 2 struggle eagerly to do or obtain something. 3 (of aircraft or their crew) take off quickly in an emergency or to attack an invading enemy. 4 mix together indiscriminately. 5 cook (egg) by stirring and heating it in a pan until it thickens. 6 make (a radio broadcast, telephone conversation, etc.) unintelligible except to a person with a special receiver, by altering the frequencies on which it is transmitted. ●*noun* 1 a climb or walk over rough ground. 2 an eager struggle to do or obtain something. 3 a motor-cycle race over rough ground. **4** an emergency take-off by aircraft.

**scrambler** *noun* an electronic device for scrambling telephone conversations.

**scrap**[1] *noun* **1** a small detached piece of something, a fragment; a remnant. **2** rubbish, waste material; discarded metal suitable for being reprocessed. ● *verb* (**scrapped, scrapping**) discard as useless. □ **scrap heap** a heap of waste material. **scrap merchant** a dealer in scrap.

**scrap**[2] (*informal*) *noun* a fight or quarrel. ● *verb* (**scrapped, scrapping**) fight; quarrel.

**scrapbook** *noun* a blank book for sticking cuttings, drawings, etc. in.

**scrape** *verb* **1** make (a thing) clean, smooth, or level by passing the hard edge of something across it. **2** pass (an edge) across in this way. **3** remove by doing this; *scrape mud off shoes.* **4** excavate by scraping; *scrape a hole.* **5** damage by scraping. **6** make the sound of scraping. **7** pass along or through something with difficulty, with or without touching it. **8** obtain or amass with difficulty or by careful saving; *scrape a living.* **9** be very economical. ● *noun* **1** a scraping movement or sound. **2** a scraped mark or injury. **3** (*informal*) an awkward situation resulting from rashness. **4** (*informal*) a fight. □ **scrape the barrel** be reduced to using one's last and inferior resources. **scrape through** get through a testing situation with great difficulty.

**scraper** *noun* a device used for scraping.

**scrapie** *noun* a viral disease of sheep, causing loss of coordination.

**scrapings** *plural noun* fragments produced by scraping.

**scrappy** *adjective* (**scrappier, scrappiest**) made up of scraps or odds and ends or disconnected elements. □ **scrappily** *adverb*, **scrappiness** *noun*

**scrapyard** *noun* a place where metal scrap, old vehicles, etc. are collected for recycling.

**scratch** *verb* **1** make a shallow mark or wound on (a surface) with something sharp. **2** form by scratching. **3** scrape with the fingernails to relieve itching. **4** make a thin scraping sound. **5** obtain with difficulty; *scratch a living.* **6** cancel by drawing a line through; *scratch it out.* **7** withdraw from a race or competition; *was obliged to scratch; scratched his horse.* ● *noun* **1** a mark or wound made by scratching. **2** a spell of scratching. **3** a line from which competitors start in a race when they receive no handicap. ● *adjective* **1** collected from whatever is available; *a scratch team.* **2** with no handicap given; *a scratch race.* □ **from scratch** from the very beginning. **2** with no advantage or preparation. **scratch card** a game card with panels which can be scratched off to reveal answers or details of prizes printed beneath. **scratch my back and I will scratch yours** do me a favour and I will return it. **up to scratch** up to the required standard.

**scratchy** *adjective* (**scratchier, scratchiest**) **1** tending to make scratches or a scratching sound. **2** (of a drawing) looking like a series of scratches. **3** tending to cause itching. □ **scratchily** *adverb*, **scratchiness** *noun*

**scrawl** *noun* bad handwriting; something written in this. ● *verb* write in a scrawl. □ **scrawly** *adjective*

**scrawny** *adjective* (**scrawnier, scrawniest**) scraggy and thin.

**scream** *verb* **1** make a long piercing cry of pain, terror, annoyance, or excitement. **2** utter in a screaming tone. **3** (of the wind or a machine etc.) make a loud piercing sound. **4** be blatantly obvious. ● *noun* **1** a screaming cry or sound. **2** (*informal*) an extremely amusing person or thing.

**screamingly** *adverb* so as to cause screams of laughter; *screamingly funny.*

**scree** *noun* a mass of loose stones on a mountainside.

**screech** *noun* a harsh high-pitched scream or sound. ● *verb* make a screech. □ **screech-owl** *noun* an owl that makes a screeching cry (not a hoot), especially a barn owl.

**screed** *noun* **1** a tiresomely long list, letter, or other document. **2** a strip of plaster, wood, etc. fixed to a wall or floor as a guide to the correct thickness of a coat of plaster or concrete to be laid. **3** a finishing layer of mortar, cement, etc. ● *verb* level by means of a screed; apply (material) as a screed.

**screen** *noun* **1** an upright structure used to conceal, protect, or divide something. **2** anything serving a similar purpose; *under the screen of night.* **3** a windscreen. **4** a blank surface on which pictures, cinema films, or television transmissions etc. are projected. **5** a large sieve or riddle, especially one used for sorting grain or coal etc. into sizes. ● *verb* **1** shelter, conceal, or protect. **2** protect (a person) from discovery or deserved blame by diverting suspicion from him or her. **3** show (images or a cinema film etc.) on a screen. **4** pass (grain or coal etc.) through a screen. **5** examine systematically in order to discover something, e.g. a person's suitability for a post, or the presence or absence of a substance or disease. □ **screen printing** a process like stencilling with ink or dye forced through a prepared sheet of fine fabric. **screen test**

a test of a person's suitability for taking part in a film.

**screenplay** *noun* the script of a film.

**screenwriter** *noun* a person who writes for the cinema.

**screw** *noun* 1 a metal pin with a spiral ridge or thread round its length, used for holding things together by being twisted in under pressure, or secured by a nut. 2 a thing turned like a screw and used for tightening something or exerting pressure. 3 (in full **screw-propeller**) a propeller, especially of a ship or motor boat. 4 the act of screwing. 5 (*slang*) a prison officer. 6 (*vulgar*) sexual intercourse; a partner in this. ●*verb* 1 fasten or tighten with a screw or screws; fasten by twisting like a screw. 2 turn (a screw); twist or become twisted. 3 oppress; extort; *screwed a promise out of her*. 4 (*slang*) extort money from; *how much did they screw you for?* 5 (*vulgar*) have sexual intercourse (with). □ **have a screw loose** (*informal*) be slightly mad. **put the screws on** (*informal*) put pressure on, intimidate. **screw cap**, **screw top** a cap that screws on to the opening of a container. **screw up** 1 contract (one's eyes); twist (one's face) out of the natural expression, e.g. in disgust. 2 summon up (one's courage). 3 (*slang*) bungle, mismanage.

**screwball** *noun* (*Amer. slang*) a crazy person.

**screwdriver** *noun* a tool with a tip that fits into the head of a screw to turn it.

**screwy** *adjective* (**screwier**, **screwiest**) (*slang*) crazy, eccentric; ridiculous, absurd.

**Scriabin** (skri-ah-bin) (also **Skryabin**), Alexander (1872–1915), Russian composer.

**scribble** *verb* 1 write hurriedly or carelessly. 2 make meaningless marks. ●*noun* something scribbled; hurried or careless writing; scribbled meaningless marks.

**scribe** *noun* 1 a person who (before the invention of printing) made copies of writings. 2 (in New Testament times) a professional religious scholar. 3 a pointed instrument for making marks on wood, metal, etc. □ **scribal** *adjective*

**scrim** *noun* a loosely-woven cotton fabric.

**scrimmage** *noun* a confused struggle; a skirmish.

**scrimp** *verb* skimp.

**scrip** *noun* 1 a provisional certificate of money subscribed, entitling the holder to dividends; such certificates collectively. 2 an extra share or shares (in a business company) issued instead of a dividend; *a scrip issue*.

**script** *noun* 1 handwriting. 2 a style of printed or typewritten characters resembling this. 3 the text of a play, film, or broadcast talk. 4 a candidate's written answer-paper in an examination. ●*verb* write a script for (a film etc.).

**scripture** *noun* 1 any sacred writings. 2 (**Scripture** *or* **the Scriptures**) the sacred writings of the Christians (the Old and New Testaments) or the Jews (the Old Testament). □ **scriptural** *adjective*

**scriptwriter** *noun* a person who writes scripts for films, TV, etc. □ **scriptwriting** *noun*

**scrofula** (skrof-yoo-lă) *noun* a disease causing glandular swellings. □ **scrofulous** *adjective*

**scroll** *noun* 1 a roll of paper or parchment. 2 an ornamental design resembling a scroll or in spiral form. ●*verb* (often foll. by *down* or *up*) move gradually upwards or downwards through the text of a computer document, viewing successive sections on the screen.

**Scrooge** *noun* a miser. (¶ Named after a character in Dickens's novel *A Christmas Carol*.)

**scrotum** (skroh-tŭm) *noun* (*plural* **scrota** *or* **scrotums**) the pouch of skin that encloses the testicles in most male mammals, behind the penis. □ **scrotal** *adjective*

**scrounge** *verb* (*informal*) cadge; borrow; get without paying. □ **scrounger** *noun*

**scrub**[1] *noun* vegetation consisting of stunted trees or shrubs; land covered with this.

**scrub**[2] *verb* (**scrubbed**, **scrubbing**) 1 rub hard with something coarse or bristly; clean in this way with a wet brush. 2 (*informal*) cancel, scrap; *we'll have to scrub our plans*. ●*noun* scrubbing, being scrubbed; *give it a scrub*. □ **scrub up** (of a surgeon etc.) clean the hands and arms by scrubbing, before an operation.

**scrubber** *noun* 1 (*slang*) a promiscuous woman. 2 an apparatus for purifying gases.

**scrubby** *adjective* (**scrubbier**, **scrubbiest**) small and mean or shabby.

**scruff** *noun* the back of the neck as used to grasp, lift, or drag a person or animal.

**scruffy** *adjective* (**scruffier**, **scruffiest**) shabby and untidy. □ **scruffily** *adverb*, **scruffiness** *noun*

**scrum** *noun* 1 a scrummage. 2 a milling crowd; a confused struggle. □ **scrum-half** *noun* a half-back who puts the ball into the scrum.

**scrummage** *noun* (in Rugby football) the grouping of the forwards of each side to push against each other and seek possession of the ball thrown on the ground between them.

**scrumping** *noun* (*informal*) stealing apples from trees.

**scrumptious** *adjective* (*informal*) delicious; delightful.

**scrumpy** *noun* (*informal*) rough cider.

**scrunch** *verb* crunch or crumple.

**scruple** *noun* a feeling of doubt or hesitation produced by one's conscience or principles. ●*verb* hesitate because of scruples.

**scrupulous** (skroo-pew-lŭs) *adjective* **1** very conscientious; painstakingly careful and thorough. **2** strictly honest or honourable. □ **scrupulously** *adverb*

**scrutineer** *noun* a person who scrutinizes ballot papers.

**scrutinize** *verb* (also **scrutinise**) look at or examine carefully.

**scrutiny** *noun* a careful look or examination of something.

**scuba** *noun* an aqualung; self-contained underwater breathing apparatus. (¶ Named from the initials of these words.) □ **scuba-diving** *noun* swimming underwater using a scuba.

**scud** *verb* (**scudded, scudding**) move along straight, fast, and smoothly; *clouds were scudding across the sky.* ●*noun* clouds or spray driven by the wind; a short shower of driving rain.

**scuff** *verb* **1** scrape or drag (one's feet) in walking. **2** mark or wear away by doing this. **3** scrape (a thing) with one's foot or feet. ●*noun* a mark made by scuffing.

**scuffle** *noun* a confused struggle or fight at close quarters. ●*verb* take part in a scuffle.

**scull** *noun* **1** each of a pair of small oars used by a single rower. **2** an oar that rests on the stern of a boat, worked with a twisting movement. ●*verb* row with sculls.

**sculler** *noun* **1** one who uses a scull or sculls. **2** a boat for sculling.

**scullery** *noun* a room where dishes etc. are washed up.

**scullion** *noun* (*old use*) a cook's boy assistant; one who washes dishes.

**sculpt** *verb* sculpture.

**sculptor** *noun* a person who makes sculptures.

**sculptress** *noun* a female sculptor.

**sculpture** *noun* **1** the art of carving in wood or stone or producing shapes in cast metal. **2** a work made in this way. ●*verb* represent in sculpture; decorate with sculptures. □ **sculptural** *adjective*

**scum** *noun* **1** impurities that rise to the surface of a liquid; a film of material floating on the surface of water. **2** people regarded as the most worthless part of the population. ●*verb* (**scummed, scumming**) **1** remove the scum from. **2** form a scum. □ **scummy** *adjective*

**scumbag** *noun* (*slang*) a contemptible person.

**scuncheon** *noun* the inside face of a doorjamb or window frame.

**scupper** *noun* an opening in a ship's side to carry off water from the deck. ●*verb* **1** sink (a ship) deliberately. **2** (*informal*) wreck (plans etc.).

**scurf** *noun* **1** flakes of dry skin, especially from the scalp. **2** any dry scaly matter on a surface. □ **scurfy** *adjective*

**scurrilous** (sku-ril-ŭs) *adjective* **1** abusive and insulting. **2** coarsely humorous. □ **scurrilously** *adverb*, **scurrility** (sku-**ril**-iti) *noun*

**scurry** *verb* (**scurried, scurrying**) move hurriedly with quick short steps; hurry. ●*noun* **1** scurrying, a rush. **2** a flurry of rain or snow.

**scurvy** *noun* a disease caused by lack of vitamin C in the diet. ●*adjective* paltry; dishonourable, contemptible.

**scut** *noun* a short tail, especially that of a hare, rabbit, or deer.

**scutter** (*informal*) *verb* scurry. ●*noun* a scurrying movement or sound.

**scuttle**[1] *noun* **1** = COAL-SCUTTLE. **2** the part of a car body between the windscreen and the bonnet. **3** a small opening with a lid, on a ship's deck or side or in a roof or wall. ●*verb* let water into (a ship) to sink it.

**scuttle**[2] *verb* scurry; hurry away. ●*noun* a scuttling run; a hasty departure.

**scuzzy** *adjective* (*slang*) disgusting, abhorrent.

**Scylla** (sil-ă) (*Gk. myth.*) a female sea monster who devoured men from ships when they tried to navigate the narrow channel between her cave and the whirlpool Charybdis.

**scythe** (*pronounced* syth) *noun* an implement with a curved blade and a long handle, used for cutting long grass or grain. ●*verb* cut with a scythe.

**Scythia** (si-*th*iă) the ancient Greek name for a country on the north shore of the Black Sea. □ **Scythian** *adjective & noun*

**SD, S. Dak.** *abbreviation* South Dakota.

**SDI** *abbreviation* Strategic Defence Initiative.

**SDLP** *abbreviation* Social Democratic and Labour Party, a political party in Northern Ireland.

**SDP** *abbreviation* (*hist.*) Social Democratic Party.

**SE** *abbreviation* **1** south-east. **2** south-eastern.

**Se** *symbol* selenium.

**sea** *noun* **1** the expanse of salt water that covers most of the earth's surface. **2** any part of this as opposed to dry land or fresh water; a named section of it partly enclosed by land; *the Mediterranean Sea.* **3** a large inland lake of either salt or fresh water; *the Sea of Galilee.* **4** the waves of the sea; the movement or state of these; *a heavy sea.* **5** a vast expanse of something; *a sea of faces.* □ **at sea 1** in a ship on the sea. **2** perplexed, confused. **sea anchor** a bag dragged in the water to slow the drifting of a vessel. **sea anemone** a tube-shaped sea animal with petal-like tentacles round its mouth. **sea change** a significant or unexpected transformation. **sea dog** an old sailor. **sea fish** a fish living in the sea, not a freshwater fish. **sea front** the part of a town facing the sea. **sea green** *adjective & noun* bluish-green. **sea horse** *noun* a small upright fish with a horse-like head. **sea legs** ability to walk steadily and avoid seasickness at sea. **sea level** the level corresponding to that of the surface of the sea halfway between high and low water. **sea lion** a large eared seal of the Pacific Ocean. **Sea Lord** a naval member of the Admiralty Board. **sea mile** a unit varying between 1,842 metres (2,014 yds) and 1,861 metres (2,035 yds). **sea salt** salt obtained from sea water by evaporation. **Sea Scout** a member of the maritime branch of the Scout Association. **sea urchin** a sea animal with a round spiny shell.

**seaboard** *noun* the coast or its outline.

**seafarer** *noun* **1** a sailor. **2** a traveller by sea.

**seafaring** *adjective & noun* working or travelling on the sea, especially as one's regular occupation.

**seafood** *noun* fish or shellfish from the sea eaten as food.

**seagoing** *adjective* (of ships) fit for crossing the sea.

**seagull** *noun* a gull.

**seakale** *noun* a maritime plant, the young shoots of which are used as a vegetable.

**seal**¹ *noun* an amphibious fish-eating sea mammal with flippers.

**seal**² *noun* **1** a gem or piece of metal etc. with an engraved design that is pressed on wax or other soft material to leave an impression. **2** this impression or a piece of wax bearing it, attached to a document as a guarantee of authenticity, or to an envelope, box, etc. to show that (while the seal is unbroken) the contents have not been tampered with. **3** a mark, event, action, etc. serving to confirm or guarantee something; *gave it their seal of approval.* **4** a small decorative paper sticker resembling a postage stamp. **5** a substance or fitting used to close an opening and prevent air or liquid from passing through it. ●*verb* **1** affix a seal to. **2** stamp or certify as authentic in this way. **3** close securely so as to prevent penetration; coat or surface with a protective substance or sealant; stick down (an envelope etc.). **4** settle or decide; *his fate was sealed.*

**sealant** *noun* a substance used for coating a surface to make it watertight or airtight.

**sealing** *noun* hunting seals.

**sealing wax** a substance that is soft when heated but hardens when cooled, used for sealing letters or for impressing with a raised design.

**sealskin** *noun* the skin or prepared fur of a seal used as a clothing material.

**seam** *noun* **1** the line or groove where two edges of cloth, wood, etc. join. **2** a surface line such as a wrinkle or scar. **3** a layer of coal etc. in the ground. ●*verb* **1** join by means of a seam. **2** mark with a wrinkle or scar etc. □ **seam bowler** a bowler in cricket who makes the ball bounce off its seam.

**seaman** *noun* (*plural* **seamen**) **1** a sailor, especially one below the rank of officer. **2** a person who is skilled in seafaring.

**seamanship** *noun* skill in seafaring.

**seamstress** (**sem**-stris) *noun* (also **sempstress**) a woman who sews, especially for a living.

**seamy** *adjective* (**seamier, seamiest**) showing seams. □ **seamy side** the less presentable or less attractive aspect of life.

**Seanad** (**shan**-ăd) *noun* the upper house of parliament in the Republic of Ireland.

**seance** (**say**-ahns) *noun* a meeting at which a spiritualist attempts to make contact with spirits of the dead.

**seaplane** *noun* an aeroplane designed to alight on and take off from water.

**seaport** *noun* a port on the coast.

**sear** *verb* **1** scorch or burn the surface of. **2** (as **searing** *adjective*) burning; severe and sharp; *a searing pain.*

**search** *verb* **1** look through or go over (a place etc.) in order to find something. **2** examine thoroughly; *search your conscience.* ●*noun* the act or process of searching. □ **search party** a group of people organized to look for a lost person or thing. **search warrant** a warrant allowing officials to enter a building and search it. □ **searcher** *noun*

**searching** *adjective* (of a scrutiny or examination) thorough.

**searchlight** *noun* an outdoor electric lamp with a powerful beam that can be turned in any direction.

**seascape** *noun* a picture or view of the sea.

**seashell** *noun* the shell of a mollusc living in salt water.

**seashore** *noun* the land next to the sea.

**seasick** *adjective* made sick or queasy by the motion of a ship. □ **seasickness** *noun*

**seaside** *noun* the sea-coast, especially as a place for holidays.

**season** *noun* **1** a section of the year with distinct characteristics of temperature and rainfall. **2** the time of year when something is common or plentiful, or when an activity takes place; *the hunting season.* **3** (*informal*) a season ticket. ●*verb* **1** give extra flavour to (food) by adding salt, pepper, spices, etc. **2** bring (wood etc.) into a fit condition for use by drying, treating, or allowing to mature; become seasoned in this way. **3** make (people) competent by training and experience; *seasoned soldiers.* □ **in season 1** (of food) available as a freshly-gathered crop at the normal time of year. **2** (of an animal) on heat. **out of season** (of food) not in season. **season ticket** a ticket that allows a person to travel between certain destinations, or to attend performances etc., for a specified period.

**seasonable** *adjective* **1** suitable for the season; *seasonable weather.* **2** timely, opportune. □ **seasonably** *adverb*

▪**Usage** Do not confuse with **seasonal**.

**seasonal** *adjective* of a season or seasons, varying according to these; *the seasonal migration of geese; fruit-picking is seasonal work.*

▪**Usage** Do not confuse with **seasonable**.

**seasoning** *noun* salt, pepper, herbs, etc. added to food.

**seat** *noun* **1** a thing made or used for sitting on. **2** a place where one sits. **3** the right to sit as a member of a council or committee or parliament etc. **4** the horizontal part of a chair etc. on which a sitter's body rests. **5** the part supporting another part in a machine. **6** the buttocks; the part of a skirt or trousers covering these. **7** the place where something is based or located; *seats of learning, such as Oxford and Cambridge.* **8** a country mansion; *the family seat in Norfolk.* **9** the manner in which a person sits on a horse etc. ●*verb* **1** cause to sit. **2** provide sitting accommodation for; *the hall seats 500.* **3** put (machinery) on its support. □ **seat belt** a strap securing a person to a seat in a vehicle or aircraft, for safety. □ **seated** *adjective*

**seaward** *adverb* (also **seawards**) towards the sea. ●*adjective* going or facing towards the sea.

**seaweed** *noun* a plant that grows in the sea or on rocks in a shore.

**seaworthy** *adjective* (of a ship) in a fit state for a sea voyage. □ **seaworthiness** *noun*

**sebaceous** (si-**bay**-shŭs) *adjective* secreting an oily or greasy substance; *sebaceous glands.*

**sebum** *noun* the oily substance secreted by sebaceous glands.

**Sec.** *abbreviation* (also **sec.**) secretary.

**sec** *noun* (*informal*) moment, second; *wait a sec.* ●*adjective* (of wine) dry. (¶ French.) ●*abbreviation* secant.

**sec.** *abbreviation* second(s).

**secant** (see-**kănt**) *Maths* **1** the ratio of the hypotenuse to the shorter side adjacent to an acute angle (in a right-angled triangle). **2** a line cutting a curve at one or more points.

**secateurs** (sek-ă-**terz** or sek-ă-terz) *plural noun* clippers used with one hand for pruning plants.

**secede** (si-**seed**) *verb* withdraw formally from membership of an organization.

**secession** (si-**sesh**-ŏn) *noun* seceding. □ **secessionist** *noun & adjective*

**seclude** *verb* keep (a person) apart from others.

**secluded** *adjective* (of a place) screened or sheltered from view.

**seclusion** (si-**kloo**-zhŏn) *noun* secluding; being secluded, privacy.

**second¹** (sek-ŏnd) *adjective* **1** next after first. **2** another after the first; *a second chance.* **3** of a secondary kind, subordinate, inferior; *second quality; the second eleven.* ●*noun* **1** something that is second; the second day of a month. **2** second-class honours in a university degree. **3** second gear. **4** an attendant of a person taking part in a duel or boxing match. **5** a sixtieth part of a minute of time or angular measurement. **6** (*informal*) a short time; *wait a second.* **7** (**seconds**) goods rated second-class in quality, having some flaws. **8** (**seconds**) (*informal*) a second helping of food; a second course at a meal. ●*adverb* **1** in second place, rank, or position. **2** second class; *travelling second.* ●*verb* **1** assist. **2** state formally that one supports a motion that has been put forward by another person as a means of bringing it to be voted on. □ **second-best** *adjective* of second or inferior quality or status. **second childhood** childishness caused by mental weakness in old age. **second class** a group of persons or things, or a standard of accommodation etc., less good than first class (but better than third); a category of mail that is to be given lower priority than first-class mail; (used adverbially) in or by second-class accommodation etc.; *we travelled second class.* **second-class** *adjective* of second or inferior quality; of or using less good accommodation etc. than first-class. **second cousin** *see* COUSIN. **second-degree burn** a burn causing blistering but not scars. **second fiddle** a subsidiary or secondary role; *had to play second fiddle to his brother.* **second-guess** *verb* (*informal*) **1** anticipate by guesswork. **2** criticize with hindsight. **at second hand** obtained indirectly, not from the original source. **second-hand** *adjective & adverb* **1** bought after use by a previous owner. **2** dealing in used goods; *a second-hand shop.* **3** at second hand, obtained or experienced in this way. **sec-**

**ond in command** the person next in rank to the commanding or chief officer or official. **second lieutenant** an army officer immediately below lieutenant. **second name** a surname. **second nature** a habit or characteristic that has become automatic; *secrecy is second nature to him.* **second officer** the assistant mate on a merchant ship. **second person** *see* PERSON. **second-rate** *adjective* not of the best quality, mediocre; rated second-class. **second sight** the supposed power to foresee future events. **second thoughts** a change of mind after reconsideration. **second wind** recovery of one's ease of breathing after having become out of breath; renewed energy. □ **seconder** *noun*

**second²** (si-**kond**) *verb* transfer (a person) temporarily to another post or department. □ **secondment** *noun*

**secondary** *adjective* **1** coming after what is primary. **2** of lesser importance or rank etc. than the first. **3** derived from what is primary or original; *secondary sources.* **4** (of education or school) following primary, especially from the age of 11. □ **secondary colours** colours obtained by mixing two primary colours. **secondary picketing** (during an industrial dispute) picketing of firms that are not directly involved in order to increase the effect of a strike etc. □ **secondarily** *adverb*

**secondly** *adverb* second, as a second consideration.

**secrecy** *noun* **1** being kept secret. **2** keeping things secret; *was pledged to secrecy.*

**secret** *adjective* **1** kept or intended to be kept from the knowledge or view of others, to be known only by specified people. **2** working or operating secretly. ● *noun* **1** something kept or intended to be kept secret. **2** a mystery, a thing no one properly understands; *the secrets of nature.* **3** a method for attaining something; *the secret of good health.* □ **in secret** secretly. **secret agent** a spy acting for a country. **secret ballot** one in which individual voters' choices are not made public. **secret police** a police force operating in secret for political purposes. **secret service** a government department responsible for conducting espionage. **secret society** a society whose members are sworn to secrecy about it. □ **secretly** *adverb*

**secretaire** (sek-ri-**tair**) *noun* an escritoire.

**secretarial** (sek-ri-**tair**-iăl) *adjective* of or involving the work of a secretary.

**secretariat** (sek-ri-**tair**-i-at) *noun* an administrative office or department headed by a government Secretary or by a Secretary-General; its premises.

**secretary** (**sek**-rĕ-tri) *noun* **1** a person employed to help deal with correspondence, typing, filing, making appointments, etc. **2** an official in charge of the correspondence and records of an organization. **3** the principal assistant of a government minister or ambassador. □ **secretary bird** a long-legged African bird with a crest likened to quill pens placed behind a writer's ear. **Secretary-General** *noun* the principal administrator of a large organization. **Secretary of State 1** the head of a major government department. **2** (in the USA) the government minister in charge of foreign affairs.

**secrete** (si-**kreet**) *verb* **1** hide or conceal (an object). **2** form and send out (a substance) into the body, either for excretion or for use within the body; *the liver secretes bile.* □ **secretor** *noun*

**secretion** (si-**kree**-shŏn) *noun* **1** secreting; being secreted. **2** a substance secreted by an organ or cell of the body.

**secretive** (**seek**-rit-iv) *adjective* making a secret of things unnecessarily; uncommunicative. □ **secretively** *adverb*, **secretiveness** *noun*

**secretory** (si-**kree**-ter-i) *adjective* of bodily secretion.

**sect** *noun* a group of people with religious or other beliefs that differ from those more generally accepted.

**sectarian** (sek-**tair**-iăn) *adjective* **1** of or belonging to a sect or sects. **2** narrow-mindedly putting the beliefs or interests of one's sect before more general interests. ● *noun* a member of a sect. □ **sectarianism** *noun*

**section** *noun* **1** a distinct part or portion of something. **2** a subdivision. **3** the process of cutting or separating something surgically. **4** a plane surface formed by cutting a solid. ● *verb* **1** divide into sections. **2** commit (a person) to a psychiatric hospital.

**sectional** *adjective* **1** of a section or sections. **2** of one section of a group or community as distinct from others or from the whole. **3** made in sections.

**sector** *noun* **1** any of the parts into which a battle area is divided for the purpose of controlling operations. **2** a similar division of an activity; *the private sector of industry.* **3** a section of a circular area between two lines drawn from its centre to its circumference.

**secular** (**sek**-yoo-ler) *adjective* **1** concerned with worldly affairs rather than spiritual ones; not involving religion; *secular music.* **2** (of clergy) not members of a monastic community. □ **secularity** (sek-yoo-**la**-riti) *noun*

**secure** *adjective* safe (especially against attack); certain not to slip or fail, reliable. ●*verb* **1** make secure. **2** fasten securely. **3** obtain. **4** guarantee by pledging something as security; *the loan is secured on landed property*. □ **securely** *adverb*

**security** *noun* **1** a state or feeling of being secure; something that gives this. **2** the safety of a country or organization against espionage, theft, or other danger. **3** a thing that serves as a guarantee or pledge; *offered the deeds of his house as security for the loan*. **4** a certificate showing ownership of financial stocks, bonds, or shares. □ **Security Council** a permanent body of the UN established to maintain world peace, consisting of five permanent members (China, France, UK, USA, the former USSR) and ten members elected for two-year terms.

**sedan** (si-**dan**) *noun* **1** (*Amer.*) a saloon car. **2** (in full **sedan chair**) an enclosed chair for one person (used in the 17th–18th centuries), mounted on two poles and carried by two bearers.

**sedate** (si-**dayt**) *adjective* calm and dignified, not lively. ●*verb* treat (a person) with sedatives. □ **sedation** *noun*, **sedately** *adverb*, **sedateness** *noun*

**sedative** (**sed**-ă-tiv) *adjective* having a calming or soothing effect. ●*noun* a sedative medicine or influence.

**sedentary** (**sed**-ĕn-ter-i) *adjective* **1** spending much time seated; *sedentary workers*. **2** requiring much sitting; *sedentary work*.

**sedge** *noun* a grass-like plant growing in marshes or near water.

**sediment** *noun* **1** fine particles of solid matter suspended in a liquid or settling to the bottom of it. **2** solid matter (e.g. sand, gravel) that is carried by water or wind and settles on land.

**sedimentary** (sed-i-**ment**-er-i) *adjective* **1** of or like sediment. **2** (of rock) formed from layers of sediment carried by water or wind.

**sedition** (si-**dish**-ŏn) *noun* words or actions that make people rebel against authority. □ **seditious** (si-**dish**-ŭs) *adjective*

**seduce** (si-**dewss**) *verb* **1** persuade (especially into wrongdoing) by offering temptations; *was seduced into betraying his country*. **2** tempt (a person) into sexual intercourse. □ **seducer** *noun*

**seduction** *noun* **1** seducing; being seduced. **2** a tempting and attractive feature; *the seductions of country life*.

**seductive** *adjective* tending to seduce, alluring. □ **seductively** *adjective*, **seductiveness** *noun*

**sedulous** (**sed**-yoo-lŭs) *adjective* diligent and persevering. □ **sedulously** *adverb*, **sedulity** *noun*

**sedum** (**see**-dŭm) *noun* a plant with fleshy leaves, often with pink, white, or yellow flowers.

**see**[1] *verb* (**saw, seen, seeing**) **1** perceive with the eyes; have or use the power of doing this. **2** perceive with the mind, understand; *I can't see why not*. **3** have a certain opinion about; *as I see it*. **4** consider; take time to do this; *must see what can be done; let me see, how can we fix it?* **5** watch; be a spectator of; *went to see a film*. **6** look at for information; *see page 310*. **7** meet; be near and recognize; *saw her in church*. **8** discover; *see who is at the door*. **9** experience, undergo; *saw service during the war*. **10** grant or obtain an interview with, consult; *I must see the doctor about my wrist*. **11** escort, conduct; *see her to the door*. **12** make sure; *see that this letter goes today*. □ **see about** attend to. **see off 1** accompany to the point of departure for a journey and take leave of (a person). **2** chase away (an intruder). **see red** be suddenly angry. **see the back of** be rid of. **see the light** understand after failing to do so; realize one's mistakes. **see things** have hallucinations. **see through 1** understand the true nature of, not be deceived by. **2** finish (a project) completely. **see-through** *adjective* transparent. **see to** attend to.

**see**[2] *noun* the position or district of a bishop or archbishop; *the see of Canterbury*. □ **See of Rome** the papacy.

**seed** *noun* (*plural* **seeds** *or* **seed**) **1** a fertilized ovule of a plant, capable of developing into a plant like its parent. **2** seeds as collected for sowing; *to be kept for seed*. **3** semen; milt. **4** something from which a tendency or feeling etc. can develop; *sowing the seeds of doubt in their minds*. **5** (*informal*) a seeded player. ●*verb* **1** plant seeds in; sprinkle with seeds. **2** place particles in (a cloud) to cause condensation and produce rain. **3** remove seeds from (fruit). **4** name (a strong player) as not to be matched against another named in this way in the early rounds of a knockout tournament, so as to increase the interest of later rounds. □ **go** *or* **run to seed 1** cease flowering as seed develops. **2** deteriorate in appearance or efficiency. **seed-bed** *noun* a bed of fine soil in which seeds are sown. **seed-pearl** *noun* a very small pearl. **seed-potato** *noun* a potato kept for seed. □ **seedless** *adjective*

**seedling** *noun* a very young plant growing from a seed.

**seedy** *adjective* (**seedier, seediest**) **1** full of seeds. **2** looking shabby and disreputable.

**3** (*informal*) feeling slightly ill. □ **seedily** *adverb*, **seediness** *noun*

**seeing** *see* SEE[1]. □ **seeing that** in view of the fact that, because.

**seek** *verb* (**sought**, **seeking**) make a search or inquiry for; try to find, obtain, or do. □ **seek out** seek specially, make a special effort to meet and address (a person).

**seem** *verb* appear to be or to exist or to be true.

**seeming** *adjective* having an appearance of being something but not necessarily being this in fact. □ **seemingly** *adverb*

**seemly** *adjective* proper, suitable, in accordance with accepted standards of good taste. □ **seemliness** *noun*

**seen** *see* SEE[1].

**seep** *verb* ooze slowly out or through.

**seepage** (seep-ij) *noun* seeping; the amount that seeps out.

**seer** *noun* **1** a prophet, a person who sees visions. **2** one who sees.

**seersucker** *noun* fabric woven with a puckered surface.

**see-saw** *noun* **1** a long board balanced on a central support so that when a child sits on each end the two can go up and down alternately. **2** an up-and-down change that is constantly repeated. ●*verb* ride on a see-saw; make this movement.

**seethe** *verb* **1** bubble or surge as in boiling. **2** be very angry or resentful.

**segment** (seg-měnt) *noun* a part cut off or marked off as separable from the other parts of a thing. □ **segmental** (seg-men-tăl) *adjective*

**segmented** (seg-ment-id) *adjective* divided into segments. □ **segmentation** *noun*

**Segovia** (seg-oh-viă), Andrés (1893–1987), Spanish guitarist and composer.

**segregate** (seg-ri-gayt) *verb* **1** put apart from the rest, isolate. **2** separate (people) according to their race. □ **segregation** *noun*, **segregationist** *noun & adjective*

**seigneur** (sayn-yer) *noun* a feudal lord. □ **seigneurial** *adjective*

**Seine** (*pronounced* sayn) a river of northern France, flowing through Paris to the English Channel.

**seine** (*pronounced* sayn) *noun* a large fishing-net that hangs vertically with floats at the top and weights at the bottom, the ends being drawn together to enclose fish as it is hauled ashore.

**seise** *see* SEIZE (sense 5).

**seismic** (sy-zmik) *adjective* **1** of an earthquake or earthquakes. **2** of or using vibrations produced artificially by explosions, e.g. to explore the structure of underground rock formations; *seismic survey*. □ **seismically** *adverb*

**seismogram** (syz-mŏ-gram) *noun* the record given by a seismograph.

**seismograph** (sy-zmŏ-grahf) *noun* an instrument for detecting, recording, and measuring earthquakes.

**seismography** (syz-mog-ră-fi) *noun* the study or recording of seismic effects. □ **seismographer** *noun*, **seismographic** *adjective*

**seismology** (syz-mol-ŏji) *noun* the study of earthquakes. □ **seismological** *adjective*, **seismologist** *noun*

**seize** *verb* **1** take hold of (a thing) forcibly, suddenly, or eagerly. **2** take possession of (a thing) forcibly or by legal right; *seize smuggled goods*. **3** have a sudden overwhelming effect on; *panic seized us*. **4** seize up. **5** (also **seise**) (usually foll. by *of*) *Law* put in possession of. □ **seize on** make use of (an excuse etc.) eagerly. **seize up** (of a moving part or the machine containing it) become stuck or jammed.

**seizure** (see-zher) *noun* **1** seizing; being seized. **2** a sudden attack of epilepsy or apoplexy etc., a stroke.

**seldom** *adverb* rarely, not often.

**select** *verb* pick out as best or most suitable. ●*adjective* **1** chosen for excellence. **2** (of a society) exclusive, admitting only certain people as members. □ **select committee** a small committee appointed to make a special investigation.

**selection** *noun* **1** selecting, being selected. **2** the people or things selected. **3** a collection of things from which a choice can be made; *they stock a large selection of goods*.

**selective** *adjective* **1** choosing; involving choice. **2** chosen or choosing carefully. □ **selectively** *adverb*, **selectivity** *noun*

**selector** *noun* **1** a person who selects; a member of a committee selecting a sports team. **2** a device that selects the appropriate gear or circuit etc. in machinery.

**selenium** (si-leen-iŭm) *noun* a chemical element (symbol Se) that is a semiconductor and has various applications in electronics.

**self** *noun* (*plural* **selves**) **1** a person as an individual. **2** a person's special nature; *she is her old self again*. **3** one's own interests, advantage, or pleasure; *always puts self first*. **4** (*humorous* or in commerce) myself, herself, himself, etc.; *the cheque is payable to self*.

**self-** *combining form* of, to, or done by oneself or itself.

**self-abuse** *noun* (*old use*) masturbation.

**self-addressed** *adjective* (of an envelope for containing a reply) addressed to oneself.

**self-appointed** *adjective* designated or described as such by oneself, not by others.

**self-assembly** *adjective* made by the buyer from a kit.

**self-assertive** *adjective* asserting oneself confidently. □ **self-assertion** *noun*

**self-assured** *adjective* self-confident. □ **self-assurance** *noun*

**self-aware** *adjective* conscious of one's feelings, motives, etc. □ **self-awareness** *noun*

**self-catering** *adjective* catering for oneself (instead of having meals provided in rented accommodation), especially while on holiday.

**self-centred** *adjective* thinking chiefly of oneself or one's own affairs, selfish.

**self-confessed** *adjective* openly admitting oneself to be.

**self-confident** *adjective* having confidence in one's own abilities. □ **self-confidence** *noun*

**self-conscious** *adjective* embarrassed or unnatural in manner from knowing that one is being observed by others. □ **self-consciously** *adverb*, **self-consciousness** *noun*

**self-contained** *adjective* **1** complete in itself; (of accommodation) having all the necessary facilities and not sharing these. **2** (of a person) able to do without the company of others.

**self-control** *noun* ability to control one's behaviour and not act emotionally. □ **self-controlled** *adjective*

**self-defeating** *adjective* (of a course of action etc.) achieving the opposite of what was intended; doomed to failure because of internal inconsistencies.

**self-defence** *noun* (*Amer.* **self-defense**) defence of oneself, or of one's rights or good reputation etc., against attack.

**self-denial** *noun* deliberately going without the things one would like to have.

**self-destruct** *verb* (of a spacecraft, bomb, etc.) destroy itself.

**self-determination** *noun* **1** determination of one's own fate or course of action; free will. **2** a nation's determination of its own form of government or its allegiance.

**self-discipline** *noun* the ability to control one's feelings, apply oneself to a task, etc.

**self-drive** *adjective* (of a hired vehicle) driven by the hirer.

**self-effacing** *adjective* modest, retiring. □ **self-effacement** *noun*

**self-employed** *adjective* working independently and not for an employer. □ **self-employment** *noun*

**self-esteem** *noun* one's good opinion of oneself.

**self-evident** *adjective* obvious; clear without proof or explanation or further evidence.

**self-explanatory** *adjective* so easy to understand that it needs no further explanation.

**self-fulfilling** *adjective* (of a prophecy, forecast, etc.) bound to come true by the very fact of it having been made.

**self-governing** *adjective* (of a country) governing itself. □ **self-government** *noun*

**self-help** *noun* use of one's own powers to achieve things, without dependence on aid from others.

**self-important** *adjective* having a high opinion of one's own importance, pompous. □ **self-importance** *noun*

**self-indulgent** *adjective* greatly indulging one's own desires for comfort and pleasure. □ **self-indulgence** *noun*

**self-interest** *noun* one's own personal advantage.

**selfish** *adjective* acting or done according to one's own interests and needs without regard for others; keeping things for oneself and not sharing. □ **selfishly** *adverb*, **selfishness** *noun*

**selfless** *adjective* unselfish. □ **selflessly** *adverb*, **selflessness** *noun*

**self-made** *adjective* having risen from poverty or obscurity and achieved success by one's own efforts; *a self-made man.*

**self-perpetuating** *adjective* reproducing itself or continuing without help or intervention.

**self-pity** *noun* pity for oneself.

**self-portrait** *noun* a portrait of himself or herself by an artist; an account of himself or herself by a writer.

**self-possessed** *adjective* calm and dignified. □ **self-possession** *noun*

**self-preservation** *noun* protection of oneself from harm or injury; the instinct to ensure one's own survival.

**self-raising** *adjective* (of flour) containing a raising agent and for use without additional baking powder.

**self-regard** *noun* regard for oneself.

**self-reliant** *adjective* independent, relying on one's own abilities and resources. □ **self-reliance** *noun*

**self-respect** *noun* proper regard for oneself and one's own dignity and principles etc. □ **self-respecting** *adjective*

**self-righteous** *adjective* smugly sure of one's own righteousness.

**self-sacrifice** *noun* sacrifice of one's own interests and desires so that others may benefit. □ **self-sacrificing** *adjective*

**selfsame** *adjective* the very same; *died in the selfsame house where he was born.*

**self-satisfied** *adjective* pleased with oneself and one's own achievements, conceited. □ **self-satisfaction** *noun*

**self-sealing** *adjective* **1** (of a tyre) automatically able to seal small punctures. **2** (of an envelope) adhesive without being moistened.

**self-seed** verb (of a plant) propagate itself by seed.

**self-seeking** adjective & noun seeking to promote one's own interests rather than those of others.

**self-service** adjective (of a restaurant, shop, or filling-station) at which customers help themselves and pay a cashier for what they have taken.

**self-starter** noun **1** an electric device for starting an internal-combustion engine. **2** an ambitious person who can act on his or her own initiative.

**self-styled** adjective using a name or description one has adopted without right; *one of these self-styled fast safe drivers.*

**self-sufficient** adjective able to provide what one needs without outside help. □ **self-sufficiency** noun

**self-supporting** adjective able to support oneself or itself without help.

**self-taught** adjective having taught oneself without formal teaching.

**self-willed** adjective obstinately doing what one wishes, stubborn.

**Seljuk** (sel-juuk) noun a member of the Turkish dynasty ruling Asia Minor in the 11th–13th centuries. ●adjective of the Seljuks.

**sell** verb (**sold**, **selling**) **1** transfer the ownership of (goods etc.) in exchange for money. **2** keep a stock of (goods) for sale, be a dealer in. **3** promote sales of; *the author's name alone will sell many copies.* **4** (of goods) find buyers; *the book is selling well.* **5** be on sale at a certain price; *it sells for £1.50.* **6** persuade a person into accepting (a thing); *tried to sell him the idea.* ●noun **1** the manner of selling something. **2** (*informal*) a deception, a disappointment. □ **sell-by date** the date by which something should be sold, after which it may no longer be fresh or safe. **sell down the river** betray; defraud. **sell off** dispose of by selling, especially at a reduced price. **sell out 1** dispose of (all one's stock etc.) by selling. **2** betray. **sell-out** noun **1** the selling of all tickets for a show etc.; a great commercial success. **2** a betrayal. **sell short** underestimate the value or worth of; make (a person or thing) seem insignificant. **sell up** sell one's house or business etc.

**Sellafield** (formerly **Windscale**) a nuclear power plant in south Cumbria.

**seller** noun **1** a person who sells something. **2** a thing that sells well or badly; *those sandals were good sellers.* □ **seller's market** a state of affairs when goods are scarce and prices are high.

**Sellers**, Peter (1925–80), English actor and comedian.

**Sellotape** noun (*trade mark*) an adhesive usually transparent tape. ●verb (**sellotape**) fix or seal with this.

**selvage** noun (also **selvedge**) **1** an edge of cloth so woven that it does not unravel. **2** a tape-like border along the edge of cloth, intended to be removed or hidden.

**selves** *see* SELF.

**semantic** (sim-an-tik) adjective of meaning and connotations in language; of semantics. ●noun (**semantics**) the branch of linguistics concerned with meanings. □ **semantically** adverb

**semaphore** (sem-ă-for) noun **1** a system of signalling by holding the arms in certain positions to indicate letters of the alphabet. **2** a device with mechanically moved arms, used for signalling on railways. ●verb signal by semaphore.

**semblance** (sem-blăns) noun **1** an outward appearance (either real or pretended); a show; *spoke with a semblance of friendship.* **2** a resemblance or likeness to something.

**semen** (see-měn) noun the whitish sperm-bearing fluid produced by male animals.

**semester** (sim-est-er) noun (especially in America) a half-year course or term in a university.

**semi** noun (*plural* **semis**) (*informal*) a semi-detached house.

**semi-** combining form half; partly.

**semibreve** (sem-i-breev) noun the longest note in common use in music, equal to two minims in length.

**semicircle** noun half of a circle; something arranged in this shape. □ **semicircular** adjective

**semicolon** (sem-i-koh-lŏn) noun the punctuation-mark (;) used to separate parts of a sentence where there is a more distinct break than that represented by a comma.

**semiconductor** noun a substance that (in certain conditions) conducts electricity but not as well as most metals do.

**semi-detached** adjective (of a house) being one of a pair of houses that have one wall in common but are detached from other houses.

**semifinal** noun the match or round preceding the final. □ **semifinalist** noun

**seminal** (sem-in-ăl) adjective **1** of seed or semen. **2** giving rise to new developments; *seminal ideas.*

**seminar** (sem-in-ar) noun **1** a small discussion class at a university etc. **2** a short intensive course of study. **3** a small conference of specialists.

**seminary** (sem-in-er-i) noun a training college for priests or rabbis. □ **seminarist** noun

**semiotics** (sem-i-o-tiks) *noun* the branch of linguistics concerned with signs and symbols. □ **semiotic** *adjective*

**semipermeable** *adjective* (of a membrane) allowing small molecules to pass through.

**semiprecious** *adjective* (of a gemstone) less valuable than those called precious.

**semi-professional** *adjective* **1** (of a footballer, musician, etc.) paid for an activity but not relying on it for a living. **2** involving semi-professionals. ●*noun* a semi-professional person.

**semiquaver** *noun* a note in music equal to half a quaver.

**semi-skilled** *adjective* having or requiring some training but less than that needed for skilled work.

**semi-skimmed** *adjective* (of milk) from which some of the cream has been removed.

**Semite** (see-myt) *noun* a member of the group of races that includes the Jews and Arabs and formerly the Phoenicians and Assyrians.

**Semitic** (sim-it-ik) *adjective* of the Semites or their languages.

**semitone** *noun* the smallest interval used in classical European music, half of a tone.

**semitropical** *adjective* subtropical.

**semivowel** *noun* **1** a sound that is intermediate between a vowel and a consonant (e.g. that of *w* or *y*). **2** a letter representing this.

**semolina** *noun* hard round grains left when wheat has been ground and sifted, used to make puddings and pasta.

**sempstress** *noun* = SEAMSTRESS.

**Semtex** *noun* (*trade mark*) a soft plastic explosive.

**SEN** *abbreviation* (*Brit.*) State Enrolled Nurse.

**Sen.** *abbreviation* **1** senior. **2** senator.

**senate** (sen-ăt) *noun* **1** (**Senate**) the upper house of the parliamentary assemblies of the USA, France, and certain other countries. **2** the governing body of certain universities. **3** the governing council in ancient Rome.

**senator** (sen-ă-ter) *noun* a member of a senate. □ **senatorial** (sen-ă-**tor**-iăl) *adjective*

**send** *verb* (**sent, sending**) **1** order, cause, or enable to go to a certain destination; have (a thing) conveyed. **2** send a message or letter; *she sent to say she was coming.* **3** cause to move, go, or become; *sent his temperature up; the sermon sent us to sleep.* □ **send away for** order (goods etc.) by post. **send down** expel from a university. **send for** order (a person or thing) to come or be brought. **send-off** *noun* a demonstration of goodwill etc. at a person's departure. **send up** (*informal*) make fun of (a thing) by imitating it. **send-up** *noun* (*informal*) a humorous im-

itation. **send word** send information. □ **sender** *noun*

**Seneca** (sen-i-kă) (died AD 65), Roman writer and statesman, a Stoic philosopher.

**Senegal** (sen-i-gawl) a country in West Africa. □ **Senegalese** (sen-i-gawl-**eez**) *adjective & noun* (*plural* **Senegalese**).

**senescent** (sin-ess-ĕnt) *adjective* growing old. □ **senescence** *noun*

**seneschal** (sen-i-shăl) *noun* the steward of a medieval great house.

**senile** (see-nyl) *adjective* suffering from bodily or mental weakness because of old age; (of illness etc.) characteristic of elderly people. □ **senile dementia** an illness of older people with loss of memory and control of bodily functions. □ **senility** (sin-il-iti) *noun*

**senior** *adjective* **1** older in age. **2** added to a father's name to distinguish him from a son with the same name; *Tom Brown senior.* **3** higher in rank or authority. **4** for older children, especially over the age of 11; *senior school.* ●*noun* **1** a senior person; a member of a senior school. **2** a person older than oneself; *he is three years my senior.* □ **senior citizen** an elderly person, one who has retired. **senior nursing officer** a person in charge of nurses in a hospital. **senior service** the Royal Navy. □ **seniority** *noun*

**senna** *noun* the dried pods or leaves of a tropical tree, used as a laxative.

**señor** (sen-yor) *noun* (*plural* **señores**) the title used of or to a Spanish-speaking man.

**señora** (sen-yor-ă) *noun* the title used of or to a Spanish-speaking woman, especially one who is married.

**señorita** (sen-yor-eet-ă) *noun* the title used of or to a young (especially unmarried) Spanish-speaking woman.

**sensation** *noun* **1** an awareness or feeling produced by stimulation of a sense organ or of the mind. **2** ability to feel such stimulation; *loss of sensation in the fingers.* **3** a condition of eager interest, excitement, or admiration aroused in a number of people; a person or thing arousing this.

**sensational** *adjective* **1** producing or intended to produce eager interest, excitement, or admiration in many people. **2** (*informal*) wonderful. □ **sensationally** *adverb*, **sensationalize** (also **sensationalise**) *verb*

**sensationalism** *noun* use of subject-matter, words, or style etc. to produce excessive emotional excitement in people. □ **sensationalist** *noun & adjective*

**sense** *noun* **1** any of the special powers by which a living thing becomes aware of things; the faculties of sight, hearing, smell, taste, and touch, by which the external world is perceived. **2** ability to perceive or feel or be conscious of a thing; awareness or recognition of something; *has no sense of shame*. **3** the power of making a good judgement; practical wisdom; *had the sense to get out of the way*. **4** the way in which a word or phrase or passage etc. is to be understood, its meaning. **5** possession of a meaning or of reasonableness. **6** (**senses**) sanity. ●*verb* **1** perceive by one of the senses. **2** become aware of (a thing) by getting a mental impression; *sensed that he was unwelcome*. **3** (of a machine) detect. □ **come to one's senses 1** regain consciousness. **2** become sensible after behaving stupidly. **in a sense** *or* **in one sense** if the statement is understood in a particular way; *what you say is true in a sense*. **make sense** be understandable or practicable. **sense organ** any of the organs (e.g. the eye or ear) by which the body becomes aware of stimuli from the external world.

**senseless** *adjective* **1** not showing good sense, foolish. **2** unconscious. □ **senselessness** *noun*

**sensibility** *noun* the ability to feel things mentally, sensitiveness; delicacy of feeling.

---

■**Usage** This word does not mean 'possession of good sense'.

---

**sensible** *adjective* **1** having or showing good sense. **2** (*old use*) (foll. by *of*) aware; *we are sensible of the honour you have done us*. **3** (of clothing) practical rather than fashionable; *sensible shoes*. □ **sensibly** *adverb*

**sensitive** *adjective* **1** affected by something, responsive to stimuli; *plants are sensitive to light*. **2** receiving impressions quickly and easily; *sensitive fingers*. **3** alert and considerate about other people's feelings. **4** easily hurt or offended. **5** (of an instrument etc.) readily responding to or recording slight changes of condition. **6** (of a subject) requiring tactful treatment. □ **sensitively** *adverb*, **sensitivity** *noun*

**sensitize** *verb* (also **sensitise**) make sensitive or abnormally sensitive. □ **sensitization** *noun*

**sensor** *noun* a device (e.g. a photoelectric cell) that reacts to a certain stimulus.

**sensory** (sen-ser-i) *adjective* of the senses, receiving or transmitting sensations; *sensory nerves*.

**sensual** (sens-yoo-ăl) *adjective* **1** of physical, especially sexual, pleasure. **2** indulging oneself with physical pleasures, showing that one does this; *a sensual face*. □ **sensually** *adverb*, **sensuality** (sens-yoo-al-iti) *noun*

---

■**Usage** See the note under SENSUOUS.

---

**sensuous** (sens-yoo-ŭs) *adjective* affecting or appealing to the senses, especially by beauty or delicacy. □ **sensuously** *adverb*

---

■**Usage** This word does not have the sexual overtones that *sensual* can have.

---

**sent** *see* SEND.

**sentence** *noun* **1** a set of words containing a verb, which is complete in itself and conveys a statement, question, exclamation, or command. **2** the punishment awarded by a lawcourt to a person convicted in a criminal trial; declaration of this. ●*verb* pass sentence on (a person); condemn (to punishment).

**sententious** (sen-ten-shŭs) *adjective* putting on an air of wisdom; dull and moralizing. □ **sententiously** *adverb*, **sententiousness** *noun*

**sentient** (sen-shĕnt) *adjective* capable of perceiving and feeling things; *sentient beings*.

**sentiment** *noun* **1** a mental attitude produced by one's feeling about something; an opinion. **2** emotion as opposed to reason; sentimentality.

**sentimental** *adjective* **1** showing or influenced by romantic or nostalgic feeling. **2** characterized by emotions as opposed to reason. □ **sentimentally** *adverb*, **sentimentality** (senti-men-tal-iti) *noun*

**sentinel** *noun* a sentry.

**sentry** *noun* a soldier posted to keep watch and guard something. □ **sentry-box** *noun* a wooden structure to shelter a standing sentry.

**Seoul** (*pronounced as* sole) the capital of South Korea.

**sepal** (sep-ăl) *noun* one of the leaf-like parts forming the calyx of a flower.

**separable** (sep-er-ăbŭl) *adjective* able to be separated. □ **separably** *adverb*, **separability** *noun*

**separate** *adjective* (*pronounced* sep-er-ăt) forming a unit by itself, not joined or united with others. ●*plural noun* (**separates**) (*pronounced* sep-er-ăts) individual items of outer clothing for wearing together in various combinations. ●*verb* (*pronounced* sep-er-ayt) **1** divide, make separate; keep apart. **2** be between; *the Channel separates England from France*. **3** become separate; go different ways; withdraw oneself from a union; cease to live together as a married couple. □ **separately** *adverb*

**separation** *noun* **1** separating; being separated. **2** (in full **judicial** *or* **legal separation**) a legal arrangement by which a married couple live apart but without ending the marriage.

**separatist** (sep-er-ă-tist) *noun* a person who favours separation from a larger unit, e.g.

so as to achieve political independence. □ **separatism** noun

**separator** noun a machine that separates things (e.g. cream from milk).

**Sephardi** (si-**far**-di) noun (plural **Sephardim**) a Jew of Spanish or Portuguese descent, as distinct from an Ashkenazi. □ **Sephardic** adjective

**sepia** (**seep**-iă) noun **1** brown colouring matter originally made from the black fluid of the cuttlefish, used in inks and paints. **2** rich reddish-brown colour. ● adjective of sepia colour.

**sepoy** (**see**-poi) noun (old use) a native Indian soldier under British or other European discipline.

**sepsis** noun a septic condition.

**Sept.** abbreviation September.

**September** the ninth month of the year.

**septet** noun a group of seven instruments or voices; a musical composition for these.

**septic** adjective infected with harmful microorganisms that cause pus to form. □ **septic tank** a tank into which sewage is conveyed and in which it remains until the activity of bacteria makes it liquid enough to drain away.

**septicaemia** (septi-**seem**-iă) noun (Amer. **septicemia**) blood-poisoning.

**septuagenarian** (sep-tew-ă-jin-**air**-iăn) noun a person in his or her seventies.

**Septuagesima** (sep-tew-ă-**jess**-imă) noun the Sunday before Sexagesima.

**Septuagint** (**sep**-tew-ă-jint) noun the Greek version of the Old Testament.

**septum** noun (plural **septa**) a partition between two cavities, e.g. that in the nose between the nostrils.

**septuple** (**sep**-tew-pŭl) adjective sevenfold. ● noun a sevenfold quantity.

**sepulchral** (sip-**ul**-krăl) adjective **1** of a tomb; sepulchral monument. **2** looking or sounding dismal, funereal; a sepulchral voice.

**sepulchre** (**sep**-ŭl-ker) noun (Amer. **sepulcher**) a tomb.

**sepulture** (**sep**-ŭl-cher) noun burying, placing in a grave.

**sequel** noun **1** what follows or arises out of an earlier event. **2** a novel or film etc. that continues the story of an earlier one.

**sequence** noun **1** the following of one thing after another in an orderly or continuous way. **2** a series without gaps, a set of things that belong next to each other in a particular order. **3** a section dealing with one scene or topic in a film.

**sequencer** noun a programmable electronic device for storing sequences of musical notes and transmitting them to an electronic musical instrument. □ **sequencing** noun

**sequential** (si-**kwen**-shăl) adjective **1** forming a sequence, following in succession. **2** occurring as a result. □ **sequentially** adverb

**sequester** (si-**kwest**-er) verb **1** seclude. **2** confiscate.

**sequestrate** (see-kwis-trayt or si-**kwes**-trayt) verb **1** confiscate. **2** take temporary possession of (a debtor's estate etc.). □ **sequestration** noun, **sequestrator** noun

**sequin** (**see**-kwin) noun a circular spangle ornamenting clothing or other material. □ **sequinned** adjective

**sequoia** (si-**kwoi**-ă) noun a coniferous tree of California, growing to a great height.

**seraglio** (si-**rahl**-yoh) noun (plural **seraglios**) **1** a harem. **2** (hist.) a Turkish palace.

**seraph** noun (plural **seraphim** or **seraphs**) a member of the highest order of angels in ancient Christian belief. □ **seraphic** adjective

**Serb** noun a native or inhabitant of Serbia. ● adjective Serbian.

**Serbia** a republic in SE Europe, formerly part of Yugoslavia.

**Serbian** noun **1** a Serb. **2** the dialect of the Serbs. ● adjective of Serbia or its people or language.

**Serbo-Croat** (ser-boh-**kroh**-at) noun the language of the Serbs and Croats.

**serenade** noun **1** a song or tune performed at night, especially beneath a lover's window. **2** an orchestral suite for a small ensemble. ● verb sing or play a serenade to.

**serendipity** (se-rĕn-**dip**-iti) noun the making of pleasant discoveries by accident; the knack of doing this. □ **serendipitous** adjective

**serene** adjective **1** calm and cheerful. **2** the title used in speaking of or to members of certain European royal families; His or Her or Your Serene Highness. □ **serenely** adverb, **serenity** (ser-**en**-iti) noun

**serf** noun **1** a farm labourer who was forced to work for his landowner in the Middle Ages. **2** an oppressed labourer. □ **serfdom** noun

**serge** noun a strong twilled worsted fabric used for making clothes.

**sergeant** noun **1** a non-commissioned army officer ranking above corporal. **2** a police officer ranking just below inspector. □ **(regimental) sergeant major** a warrant officer assisting the adjutant of a regiment or battalion.

**serial** noun a story presented in a series of instalments. ● adjective of or forming a series. □ **serial composition** serialism. **serial killer** a person who murders continually with no apparent motive. **serial number** a number that identifies one item in a series of things. □ **serially** adverb

**serialism** *noun* a technique of musical composition using the twelve notes of the chromatic scale arranged in a fixed order.

**serialize** *verb* (also **serialise**) produce as a serial. □ **serialization** *noun*

**series** *noun* (*plural* **series**) **1** a number of similar things occurring or arranged in order. **2** a set of stamps or coins etc. issued at one time or in one reign.

**serif** (se-rif) *noun* a slight projection finishing off the stroke of a printed letter (as in T, contrasted with sans serif T).

**serio-comic** *adjective* partly serious and partly comic.

**serious** *adjective* **1** solemn and thoughtful, not smiling. **2** sincere, in earnest; not casual or light-hearted; *made a serious attempt*. **3** important; *this is a serious decision*. **4** causing great concern, not slight; *serious illness*. □ **seriously** *adverb*, **seriousness** *noun*

**serjeant-at-arms** *noun* an official of a parliament, court, or city, with ceremonial duties.

**sermon** *noun* **1** a talk on a religious or moral subject, especially one delivered during a religious service. **2** a long moralizing talk.

**sermonize** *verb* (also **sermonise**) give a long moralizing talk.

**serous** (seer-ŭs) *adjective* of, like, or producing serum.

**serpent** *noun* **1** a snake, especially a large one. **2** a sly or treacherous person.

**serpentine** *adjective* twisting and curving; *a serpentine road*.

**SERPS** *abbreviation* (*Brit.*) state earnings-related pension scheme.

**serrated** (ser-ay-tid) *adjective* having a series of small projections like the teeth of a saw. □ **serration** *noun*

**serried** (*rhymes with* buried) *adjective* (of rows of people or things) arranged in a close series.

**serum** (seer-ŭm) *noun* (*plural* **sera** *or* **serums**) **1** the thin yellowish fluid that remains from blood when the rest has clotted. **2** this taken from an immunized animal and used for inoculations. **3** any watery fluid from animal tissue (e.g. in a blister).

**servant** *noun* **1** a person employed to do domestic work in a household or as a personal attendant. **2** a devoted follower or employee; *a faithful servant of the company*.

**serve** *verb* **1** perform services for (a person or community etc.), work for; *served his country*. **2** be employed or performing a spell of duty; *served in the Navy*. **3** be suitable for, do what is required; *it will serve our purpose; it will serve*. **4** provide a facility for; *the area is served by a number of buses*. **5** spend time in; undergo; *served his apprenticeship; served a prison sentence*. **6** (of a male animal) copulate with. **7** set out (food etc.) for others to consume; attend to (customers in a shop). **8** (of a quantity of food) be enough for; *this recipe serves six people*. **9** set the ball in play at tennis etc. **10** assist the priest officiating in a religious service. **11** deliver (a legal writ etc.) to the person named; *served him with the writ; served the writ on him*. **12** treat in a certain way; *she was most unjustly served*. ● *noun* a service in tennis etc.; a person's turn for this; the ball served. □ **serve a person right** be his or her deserved punishment. □ **server** *noun*

**servery** *noun* a room or counter from which meals are served.

**service** *noun* **1** being a servant, a servant's status; *be in service*. **2** the occupation or process of working for an employer or of assisting others. **3** a department of people employed by the Crown or by a public organization. **4** a system or arrangement that performs work for customers or supplies public needs; *laundry services are available; the bus service*. **5** a branch of the armed forces; *the services*. **6** use, assistance; a helpful or beneficial act; *did me a service; be of service*. **7** a religious ceremony. **8** the serving of a legal writ. **9** the serving of food or goods; provision of help for customers or clients; *quick service*. **10** a service charge. **11** a set of dishes, plates, etc. for serving a meal; *a dinner service*. **12** the act or manner or turn of serving in tennis etc.; the game in which one serves; *lost his service*. **13** maintenance and repair of a car or of machinery or appliances at intervals. **14** the serving of a mare etc. by a male animal. ● *verb* **1** maintain or repair (a piece of machinery etc.). **2** supply with service(s). **3** pay the interest on; *the amount needed to service this loan*. □ **service area** (also **services**) an area beside a motorway where petrol and refreshments etc. are available. **service charge** an additional charge for service in a restaurant etc. **service flat** a flat in which domestic service and sometimes meals are provided. **service industry** an industry providing services (e.g. gas, electricity) not goods. **service road** a road giving access to houses etc. but not intended for through traffic. **service station** a place where petrol etc. is available, beside a road.

**serviceable** *adjective* **1** usable. **2** suitable for ordinary use or wear; hard-wearing. □ **serviceably** *adverb*, **serviceability** *noun*

**serviceman** *noun* (*plural* **servicemen**) **1** a man in the armed services. **2** a man providing service or maintenance.

**servicewoman** *noun* (*plural* **servicewomen**) a woman in the armed services.

**serviette** *noun* a table-napkin.

**servile** (ser-vyl) *adjective* **1** suitable for a servant; menial; *servile tasks*. **2** excessively submissive; lacking independence; *servile flattery*. □ **servility** (ser-**vil**-iti) *noun*

**serving** *noun* a helping.

**servitor** (ser-vit-er) *noun* (*old use*) a servant, an attendant.

**servitude** *noun* the condition of being forced to work for others and having no freedom.

**servo** *noun* (*plural* **servos**) a servo-motor or -mechanism.

**servo-** *combining form* power-assisted.

**sesame** (sess-ă-mi) *noun* **1** a plant of tropical Asia with seeds that are used as food or as a source of oil. **2** its seeds. □ **open sesame** a magic phrase for obtaining access to something that is usually inaccessible. (¶ These words were used, in one of the Arabian Nights stories, to cause a door to open.)

**Sesotho** (ses-oo-too) *noun* a Bantu language; one of the official languages of Lesotho.

**sessile** (ses-syl) *adjective* **1** (of a flower, leaf, eye, etc.) attached directly at the base without a stalk. **2** fixed in one position.

**session** *noun* **1** a meeting or series of meetings. **2** a period spent continuously in an activity. **3** the academic year in certain universities; (*Amer.*) a university term. **4** the governing body of a Presbyterian church. □ **Court of Session** *see* COURT. **in session** assembled for business.

**set** *verb* (**set**, **setting**) **1** put or place; cause to stand in position. **2** put in contact with; *set pen to paper*. **3** fix in position; adjust the hands of (a clock) or the mechanism of (a trap etc.). **4** represent as happening in a certain place, or at a certain time; *the story is set in Egypt in 2000 BC*. **5** provide a tune for; *set it to music*. **6** make or become hard, firm, or established. **7** fix, decide, or appoint; *set a date for the wedding*. **8** arrange (a broken bone) so that it will heal. **9** fix (hair) while it is damp so that it will dry in the desired style. **10** place (a jewel) in a surrounding framework; *the bracelet is set with emeralds*. **11** (of blossom) form into fruit; (of fruit) develop from blossom. **12** establish; *set a new record for the high jump*. **13** offer or assign as something to be done; *set them a task*. **14** put into a specified state; *set them free; set it swinging*. **15** have a certain movement; *the current sets strongly eastwards*. **16** be brought towards or below the horizon by the earth's movement; *the sun sets*. ● *noun* **1** a number of people or things regarded as a group or unit. **2** a group of games forming part of a match in tennis etc. **3** (in mathematics) a collection of things having a common property. **4** a radio or television receiver.

**5** the way something is set or arranged; *the set of his shoulders*. **6** the process or style of setting hair. **7** the scenery in use for a play or film. **8** (also **sett**) a badger's burrow. **9** (also **sett**) a paving-block. **10** a slip or shoot for planting; *onion sets*. □ **be set on** be determined about. **set about** begin (a task); attack with blows or words. **set back 1** halt or slow the progress of. **2** (*slang*) cost; *it set me back £50*. **set-back** *noun* something that sets back progress. **set eyes on** catch sight of. **set forth** set out. **set in** become established; *depression had set in*. **set off 1** begin a journey; start; *set off a chain reaction*. **2** ignite or cause to explode. **3** improve the appearance of (a thing) by providing a contrast. **set out 1** declare or make known; *set out the terms of the agreement*. **2** begin a journey. **3** make a start with the intention of doing something. **set piece** a formal or elaborate arrangement, especially in art or literature. **set sail** hoist sail(s); begin a voyage. **set square** a draughtsman's right-angled triangular plate for drawing lines in a certain relation to each other. **set theory** the study of sets in mathematics, without regard to the nature of their individual constituents. **set to** begin doing something vigorously; begin fighting or arguing. **set-to** *noun* a fight; an argument. **set up 1** place in view. **2** arrange; begin or create (a business etc.); establish in some capacity; begin making (a loud sound). **3** supply; *set yourself up with a computer*. **4** (*informal*) lead on in order to fool, cheat, or incriminate (a person). **set-up** *noun* the structure of an organization.

**sett** alternative spelling of SET (*noun senses* 8 and 9).

**settee** *noun* a long upholstered seat with a back, for two or more people.

**setter** *noun* **1** a person or thing that sets something. **2** a dog of a long-haired breed that is trained to stand rigid when it scents game.

**setting** *noun* **1** the way or place in which something is set. **2** music for the words of a song etc. **3** a set of cutlery or crockery for one person.

**settle¹** *verb* **1** place (a thing) so that it stays in position. **2** establish or become established more or less permanently; make one's home. **3** sink or come to rest; *dust settled on the shelves; let the earth settle after digging*. **4** arrange as desired; deal with; *settled the dispute*. **5** make or become calm or orderly. **6** pay (a debt, bill, claim, etc.). **7** bestow legally; *settled all his property on his wife*. □ **settle down** become settled after wandering, movement, disturbance, etc. **settle up** pay what is owing.

**settle²** *noun* a wooden seat for two or more people, with a high back and arms.

**settlement** *noun* **1** settling; being settled. **2** a business or financial arrangement. **3** an amount or property settled legally on a person. **4** a place occupied by settlers.

**settler** *noun* a person who goes to live permanently in a previously unoccupied land.

**Seurat** (ser-**ah**), Georges (1859–91), French painter, the founder of neo-impressionism.

**seven** *adjective & noun* one more than six (7, VII). □ **seven deadly sins** *see* DEADLY. **seven seas** all the oceans of the world; the Arctic, Antarctic, North and South Atlantic, North and South Pacific, and Indian Oceans. **Seven Sisters** the Pleiades. **Seven Wonders of the World** the seven most spectacular man-made structures of the ancient world, traditionally the pyramids of Egypt, the Hanging Gardens of Babylon, the Mausoleum of Halicarnassus, the temple of Diana at Ephesus, the Colossus of Rhodes, the statue of Zeus at Olympia in Greece, and the Pharos of Alexandria. **Seven Years War** a war (1756–63) which ranged Britain, Prussia, and Hanover against Austria, France, Russia, Saxony, Sweden, and Spain.

**sevenfold** *adjective & adverb* **1** seven times as much or as many. **2** consisting of seven parts.

**seventeen** *adjective & noun* one more than sixteen (17, XVII). □ **seventeenth** *adjective & noun*

**seventh** *adjective & noun* **1** next after sixth. **2** each of seven equal parts of a thing. □ **Seventh-day Adventist** a member of a strict Protestant sect who observe the sabbath on Saturday; they originally expected the second coming of Christ in 1844 and still preach that his return is imminent. **seventh heaven** a state of intense delight. □ **seventhly** *adverb*

**seventy** *adjective & noun* **1** seven times ten (70, LXX). **2** (**seventies**) the numbers, years, or degrees of temperature from 70 to 79. □ **seventieth** *adjective*

**sever** (sev-er) *verb* (**severed, severing**) cut or break off from a whole.

**several** *adjective* **1** a few, more than two but not many. **2** separate, individual; *we all went our several ways*. ●*pronoun* several people or things.

**severally** *adverb* separately.

**severance** (sev-er-ăns) *noun* severing; being severed. □ **severance pay** an amount of money paid to an employee on termination of his or her contract.

**severe** (si-**veer**) *adjective* **1** strict, without sympathy, imposing harsh rules on others. **2** intense, forceful; *severe gales*. **3** making great demands on endurance or energy or ability etc.; *the pace was severe*. **4** plain and without decoration; *a severe style of dress*. □ **severely** *adverb*, **severity** (si-ve-riti) *noun*

**Severn** the longest river of Britain, flowing from eastern Wales to the Bristol Channel.

**Seville orange** (sev-il *or* sĕ-**vil**) a bitter orange used for making marmalade. (¶ Named after Seville in Spain.)

**Sèvres** (*pronounced* sayvr) *noun* fine porcelain made at Sèvres in France.

**sew** *verb* (**sewed, sewn** *or* **sewed, sewing**) fasten, join, make, etc. by passing thread through material, using a needle or a sewing machine.

**sewage** *noun* waste matter from houses, factories, etc. □ **sewage farm, sewage works** a place where sewage is purified.

**sewer** (**soo**-er) *noun* a pipe for carrying away sewage.

**sewerage** *noun* a system of sewers; drainage by this.

**sewing machine** a machine for sewing or stitching things.

**sewn** *see* SEW. □ **have a thing sewn up** (*informal*) have it all arranged.

**sex** *noun* **1** either of the two main groups (male and female) into which living things are placed according to their reproductive functions; the fact of belonging to one of these. **2** sexual feelings or impulses. **3** sexual intercourse; *have sex with someone*. ●*verb* judge the sex of; *to sex chickens*. □ **sex appeal** sexual attractiveness. **sex change** an apparent change of sex by hormone treatment and surgery. **sex life** a person's sexual activities. **sex object** a person regarded only in terms of sexual attractiveness. **sex symbol** a person who is for many people an epitome of sexual attraction.

**sexagenarian** (seks-ă-jin-**air**-iăn) *noun* a person in his or her sixties.

**Sexagesima** (seks-ă-**jes**-imă) *noun* the Sunday before Quinquagesima.

**sexed** *adjective* having specified sexual characteristics or impulses; *highly sexed*.

**sexist** *adjective* **1** discriminating in favour of members of one sex. **2** assuming that a person's abilities and social functions are predetermined by his or her sex. ●*noun* a person who does this. □ **sexism** *noun*

**sexless** *adjective* **1** lacking sex, neuter. **2** not involving sexual feelings.

**sexology** *noun* study of human sexual relationships. □ **sexological** *adjective*, **sexologist** *noun*

**sextant** *noun* an instrument used in navigating and surveying, for finding one's position by measuring the altitude of the sun etc.

**sextet** *noun* a group of six instruments or voices; a musical composition for these.

**sexton** *noun* a person who takes care of a church and churchyard.

**sextuple** (seks-tew-pŭl) *adjective* sixfold. ● *noun* a sixfold quantity.

**sextuplet** (seks-tew-plit) *noun* each of six children born at one birth.

**sexual** *adjective* 1 of sex or the sexes or the relationship or feelings etc. between them. 2 (of reproduction) occurring by fusion of male and female cells. □ **sexual intercourse** copulation (especially of man and woman), insertion of the penis into the vagina. □ **sexually** *adverb*

**sexuality** (seks-yoo-al-iti) *noun* 1 the fact of belonging to one of the sexes. 2 sexual characteristics or impulses.

**sexy** *adjective* (**sexier, sexiest**) sexually attractive or stimulating. □ **sexiness** *noun*

**Seychelles** (say-shelz) a country consisting of a group of islands in the Indian Ocean. □ **Seychellois** (say-shel-wah) *adjective & noun*

**Seymour** (see-mor), Jane (*c*.1509–37), the third wife of Henry VIII, mother of Edward VI.

**SF** *abbreviation* science fiction.

**sf** *abbreviation* sforzando.

**sforzando** *adjective & adverb Music* with sudden emphasis.

**Sgt.** *abbreviation* sergeant.

**sh** *interjection* hush.

**shabby** *adjective* (**shabbier, shabbiest**) 1 worn and threadbare, not kept in good condition; (of a person) poorly dressed. 2 unfair, dishonourable; *a shabby trick*. □ **shabbily** *adverb*, **shabbiness** *noun*

**shack** *noun* a roughly-built hut or shed. □ **shack up with** (*slang*) live with (a person) as a lover.

**shackle** *noun* one of a pair of iron rings joined by a chain, for fastening a prisoner's wrists or ankles. ● *verb* 1 put shackles on. 2 impede or restrict; *shackled by tradition*.

**Shackleton**, Sir Ernest Henry (1874–1922), Irish-born explorer of the Antarctic.

**shad** *noun* (*plural* **shads** or **shad**) a large edible sea fish.

**shade** *noun* 1 comparative darkness or coolness where something blocks rays of light. 2 the darker part of a picture. 3 a colour; a degree or depth of colour; *in shades of blue*. 4 a different variety; *all shades of opinion*. 5 a small amount; *she's a shade better today*. 6 (*literary*) a ghost. 7 a screen used to block light or heat; a cover for a lamp. 8 (**shades**) sunglasses. 9 (**shades**) reminders of some person or

thing; *shades of the 1930s*. ● *verb* 1 block the rays of. 2 give shade to; make dark. 3 pass gradually into another colour or variety; *the blue here shades into green; where socialism shaded into communism*. □ **put in the shade** cause to appear inferior by contrast; outshine.

**shadow** *noun* 1 shade. 2 a patch of this with the shape of the body that is blocking the rays. 3 a person's inseparable attendant or companion. 4 a slight trace; *no shadow of doubt*. 5 gloom; *the news cast a shadow over the proceedings*. 6 something weak or unsubstantial; *worn to a shadow*. 7 (used as *adjective*) denoting members of the opposition party holding posts parallel to those of the government; *the shadow cabinet; the shadow Chancellor*. ● *verb* 1 cast shadow over. 2 follow and watch secretly. □ **shadow-boxing** *noun* boxing against an imaginary opponent as a form of training.

**shadowy** *adjective* 1 like a shadow. 2 full of shadows.

**shady** *adjective* (**shadier, shadiest**) 1 giving shade; situated in the shade. 2 disreputable; not completely honest; *shady dealings*. □ **shadily** *adverb*, **shadiness** *noun*

**shaft** *noun* 1 a spear or arrow; its long slender stem. 2 a remark aimed or striking like an arrow; *shafts of wit*. 3 a ray (of light); a bolt (of lightning). 4 any long narrow straight part of something, e.g. of a supporting column or a golf club. 5 a large axle. 6 each of a pair of long bars between which a horse is harnessed to draw a vehicle. 7 a vertical or sloping passage or opening giving access to a mine or providing an outlet for air, smoke, etc.

**shag** *noun* 1 a rough mass of hair or fibre. 2 a strong coarse tobacco. 3 a cormorant. ● *verb* (*vulgar slang*) 1 have sexual intercourse with. 2 (as **shagged** *adjective*, often foll. by *out*) exhausted, tired out.

**shaggy** *adjective* (**shaggier, shaggiest**) 1 having long rough hair or fibre. 2 rough, thick, and untidy; *shaggy hair*. □ **shaggy-dog story** a lengthy tale with a peculiar twist of humour at the end. □ **shagginess** *noun*

**shagreen** (shag-reen) *noun* 1 untanned leather with a granulated surface. 2 sharkskin used for rasping and polishing things.

**shah** *noun* the former ruler of Iran.

**shake** *verb* (**shook, shaken, shaking**) 1 move quickly and jerkily up and down or to and fro. 2 dislodge by doing this; *shook snow off his hat*. 3 shock or disturb; upset the calmness of. 4 make less firm. 5 (of a voice) tremble or falter. 6 shake hands; *let's shake on it*. ● *noun* 1 shaking; being shaken. 2 a jolt or shock. 3 a milk shake. 4 a moment; *shall be there in two shakes.* □ **no great shakes** (*slang*) not very good. **shake down 1** become adjusted to new conditions. **2** sleep in an improvised bed. **shake hands** clasp right hands in greeting, parting, or agreement. **shake one's head** turn it from side to side in refusal, denial, or disapproval. **shake up 1** mix by shaking. **2** restore to shape by shaking. **3** rouse from sluggishness or a set habit. **shake-up** *noun* an upheaval; a reorganization.

**shaker** *noun* **1** a person or thing that shakes something. **2** a container in which cocktails are mixed by being shaken. **3** (**Shaker**) a member of an American religious sect, believing in the need for celibacy and a very simple life.

**Shakespeare**, William (1564–1616), English playwright and poet, born at Stratford-upon-Avon in Warwickshire. □ **Shakespearian** (also **Shakespearean**) *adjective*

**shako** (**shak**-oh) *noun* (*plural* **shakos**) a cylindrical military hat with a peak and an upright plume.

**shaky** *adjective* (**shakier**, **shakiest**) **1** shaking, unsteady, trembling. **2** unreliable, wavering. □ **shakily** *adverb*, **shakiness** *noun*

**shale** *noun* stone that splits easily into fine pieces. □ **shaly** *adjective*

**shall** *auxiliary verb* (*past* **should**) (*old use* **shalt**, used with *thou*) **1** used with *I* and *we* to express the future tense in statements and questions (but *will* is used with other words); *I shall arrive tomorrow* (but *they will arrive*); *shall I open the window?* **2** used with words other than *I* and *we* in promises or statements of intention or obligation; *you shall have it*; *thou shalt not kill.* **3** sometimes *shall* is used in questions with words other than *I* and *we* because *will* would look like a request, e.g. *shall you take the children?*

**shallot** (shă-**lot**) *noun* an onion-like plant that forms clusters of bulbs as it grows.

**shallow** *adjective* **1** not deep. **2** not thinking or thought out deeply; not capable of deep feelings. ●*noun* a shallow place. ●*verb* make or become shallow. □ **shallowly** *adverb*, **shallowness** *noun*

**shalom** (shă-**lom**) *noun & interjection* a Jewish expression of greeting or leave-taking.

**shalt** *see* SHALL.

**sham** *noun* a pretence; a thing, feeling, or person that is not genuine. ●*adjective* pretended, not genuine. ●*verb* (**shammed**, **shamming**) pretend or pretend to be.

**shaman** (**sham**-ăn) *noun* (in primitive religions) a witch-doctor or priest regarded as having access to the spiritual world. □ **shamanism** *noun*

**shamble** *verb* walk or run in an awkward or lazy way. ●*noun* **1** a shambling movement.

**2** (**shambles**) (treated as *singular*) a mess; a scene of chaos or slaughter.

**shambolic** (sham-**bol**-ik) *adjective* (*informal*) chaotic, very disorganized.

**shame** *noun* **1** a painful mental feeling aroused by a sense of having done something wrong or ridiculous. **2** ability to feel this; *he has no shame.* **3** something regrettable, a pity; *it's a shame you can't come.* ●*verb* bring shame on, make ashamed; compel by arousing feelings of shame; *they were shamed into contributing more.*

**shamefaced** *adjective* looking ashamed.

**shameful** *adjective* causing shame, disgraceful. □ **shamefully** *adverb*

**shameless** *adjective* having or showing no feeling of shame. □ **shamelessly** *adverb*

**Shamir**, Yitzhak (Yitzhak Jazernicki) (born 1915), Israeli statesman, prime minister 1983–4 and 1986–92.

**shammy** *noun* a chamois leather.

**shampoo** *noun* **1** a liquid used to wash hair. **2** a liquid or chemical for cleaning carpets or upholstery, or for washing a car. **3** shampooing; *a shampoo and set.* ●*verb* wash or clean with a shampoo.

**shamrock** *noun* a clover-like plant with three leaves on each stem, the national emblem of Ireland.

**shandy** *noun* a mixed drink of beer and ginger beer or lemonade.

**shanghai** (shang-**hy**) *verb* (**shanghaied**, **shanghaiing**) (*slang*) take (a person) by force or trickery and compel him or her to do something. (¶ Named after Shanghai, a seaport in China.)

**shank** *noun* **1** the leg. **2** the leg from knee to ankle; the corresponding part of an animal's leg (especially as a cut of meat). **3** a long narrow part of something; a shaft. □ **shanks's mare** or **pony** one's own legs as a means of transport.

**Shankar**, Ravi (born 1920), Indian sitar player and composer.

**Shannon** the chief river of Ireland, flowing into the Atlantic Ocean.

**shan't** = shall not.

**shantung** *noun* a soft untreated Chinese silk.

**shanty** *noun* **1** a shack. **2** a sailors' traditional song. □ **shanty town** an area with makeshift housing of rough shacks.

**shape** *noun* **1** an area or form with a definite outline. **2** the form or condition in which something appears; *a monster in human shape.* **3** the proper form or condition of something; *get it into shape.* **4** a pattern or mould. ●*verb* **1** give a certain shape to. **2** develop into a certain shape or condition; *the plans are shaping up well.* **3** adapt or modify (one's plans or ideas etc.). □ **take shape** take on a definite form.

**shapeless** *adjective* **1** having no definite shape. **2** not shapely. □ **shapelessly** *adverb*

**shapely** *adjective* (**shapelier**, **shapeliest**) having a pleasing shape; well proportioned. □ **shapeliness** *noun*

**shard** *noun* a broken piece of pottery or glass.

**share**[1] *noun* **1** a part given to an individual out of a larger amount which is being divided; the part one is entitled to have or do. **2** any of the equal parts forming a business company's capital and entitling the holder to a proportion of the profits. ●*verb* **1** give portions of (a thing) to two or more people; *share it out*. **2** give away part of; *would share his last crust*. **3** have a share of; use, possess, endure, or benefit from (a thing) jointly with others; *share a room; we share the credit*. □ **go shares** share things equally.

**share**[2] *noun* a ploughshare.

**shareholder** *noun* a person who owns a share or shares in a business company.

**shareware** *noun* computer programs available on trial to any user free of charge (but if used regularly a fee should be paid to the author).

**shariah** (sha-**ree**-ă) *noun* the sacred law of Islam, prescribing religious and other duties.

**Sharjah** an emirate, a member state of the United Arab Emirates.

**shark** *noun* **1** a large sea fish with a triangular fin on its back, some kinds of which are dangerous to bathers. **2** a person who ruthlessly extorts money from others, a swindler.

**sharkskin** *noun* **1** the skin of a shark. **2** wool, silk, or rayon fabric with a smooth slightly shiny finish.

**sharp** *adjective* **1** having a fine edge or point that is capable of cutting or piercing. **2** narrowing to a point or edge; *a sharp ridge*. **3** steep, angular, not gradual; *a sharp slope; a sharp turn*. **4** well-defined, distinct; *in sharp focus*. **5** intense, forceful; loud and shrill; (of temper) irritable. **6** (of tastes and smells) producing a smarting sensation. **7** quick to see or hear or notice things; intelligent. **8** unscrupulous. **9** (in music) above the correct pitch; a semitone higher than the specified pitch; *C sharp; F sharp*. ●*adverb* **1** punctually; *at six o'clock sharp*. **2** suddenly; *stopped sharp*. **3** at a sharp angle; *turn sharp right at the junction*. **4** above the correct pitch in music; *was singing sharp*. ●*noun* **1** (in music) a note that is a semitone higher than the corresponding one of natural pitch; a sign (♯) indicating this. **2** (*informal*) a swindler. □ **sharp practice** business dealings that

are dishonest or dubious. □ **sharply** *adverb*, **sharpness** *noun*

**sharpen** *verb* make or become sharp. □ **sharpener** *noun*

**sharper** *noun* a swindler, especially at cards.

**sharpish** *adjective* rather sharp. ●*adverb* (*informal*) quickly, briskly.

**sharpshooter** *noun* a skilled marksman.

**shat** *see* SHIT.

**Shatt al-Arab** a river of SE Iraq, flowing to the Persian Gulf.

**shatter** *verb* **1** break violently into small pieces. **2** destroy utterly; *shattered our hopes*. **3** disturb or upset the calmness of; *we were shattered by the news*.

**shave** *verb* **1** scrape (growing hair) off the skin with a razor. **2** cut thin slices from the surface of (wood etc.). **3** graze gently in passing. **4** reduce or remove; *shave ten per cent off our estimates*. ●*noun* the shaving of hair from the face. □ **close shave** (*informal*) a narrow escape.

**shaven** *adjective* shaved.

**shaver** *noun* **1** a person or thing that shaves. **2** an electric razor. **3** (*informal*) a youngster.

**Shavian** (**shay**-viăn) *adjective* of G. B. Shaw. ●*noun* an admirer of Shaw.

**shavings** *plural noun* thin strips of wood etc. shaved off the surface of a piece.

**Shaw**, George Bernard (1856–1950), Irish playwright and critic.

**shawl** *noun* a large piece of fabric worn round the shoulders or head, or wrapped round a baby.

**she** *pronoun* the female person or animal mentioned; a thing (e.g. a vehicle, ship, or aircraft) personified as female. ●*noun* a female animal; *she-bear*.

**s/he** *pronoun* a written representation of 'he or she', used to indicate either sex.

**sheaf** *noun* (*plural* **sheaves**) **1** a bundle of stalks of corn etc. tied together after reaping. **2** a bundle of arrows, papers, or other things laid lengthwise together.

**shear** *verb* (**sheared**, **shorn** *or* **sheared**, **shearing**) **1** cut or trim with shears, scissors, etc.; remove (a sheep's wool) in this way. **2** strip bare, deprive; *shorn of his glory*. **3** break or distort, or become broken or distorted. ●*noun* **1** (**shears**) a large scissor-shaped instrument for cutting or clipping. **2** a type of fracture or distortion produced by pressure, in which each successive layer (e.g. of a mass of rock) slides over the next. □ **shearer** *noun*

**sheath** *noun* (*plural* **sheaths**, *pronounced* sheeths *or* sheeth*z*) **1** a close-fitting covering; a cover for a blade or tool. **2** a covering for wearing on the penis during sexual intercourse as a contraceptive. **3** a close-fitting dress. □ **sheath knife** a dagger-like knife carried in a sheath.

**sheathe** (*pronounced* sheeth) *verb* **1** put into a sheath. **2** encase in a covering.

**sheave** *verb* make into sheaves.

**sheaves** *see* SHEAF.

**Sheba** (shee-bǎ) the biblical name of Saba, an ancient country in SW Arabia.

**shebeen** (shi-been) *noun* (*Irish*) an unlicensed house selling alcoholic drinks.

**shed¹** *noun* a one-storeyed building for storing things, sheltering livestock, for use as a workshop, etc.

**shed²** *verb* (**shed, shedding**) **1** lose (a thing) by a natural falling off; *trees shed their leaves.* **2** take off; *shed one's clothes.* **3** allow to pour forth; *shed tears.* □ **shed light on** help to explain.

**she'd** (*informal*) **1** she had. **2** she would.

**sheen** *noun* gloss, lustre.

**sheep** *noun* (*plural* **sheep**) a grass-eating animal with a thick fleecy coat, kept for its fleece and meat. □ **like sheep** (of people) easily led or influenced. **separate the sheep from the goats** separate the good from the bad. **sheep-dip** *noun* a liquid for cleansing sheep of vermin by dipping.

**sheepdog** *noun* a dog of a breed often trained to guard and herd sheep, e.g. a border collie.

**sheepfold** *noun* an enclosure for sheep.

**sheepish** *adjective* bashful, embarrassed. □ **sheepishly** *adverb*, **sheepishness** *noun*

**sheepshank** *noun* a knot used to shorten a rope without cutting it.

**sheepskin** *noun* **1** a coat or rug made of sheep's skin with the wool on. **2** leather made from sheep's skin.

**sheer¹** *adjective* **1** pure, absolute; *sheer luck.* **2** (of a rock etc.) having a vertical or almost vertical surface. **3** (of fabric) very thin, transparent. ● *adverb* directly, straight up or down; *the cliff rises sheer from the sea.*

**sheer²** *verb* **1** swerve from a course. **2** (foll. by *off* or *away*) turn away, especially from a person or topic that one dislikes or wishes to avoid.

**sheet¹** *noun* **1** a large rectangular piece of fabric, used as part of bedclothes. **2** a large thin piece of any material (e.g. glass, metal). **3** a piece of paper. **4** a wide expanse of water, snow, flame, etc. ● *verb* **1** provide or cover with sheets. **2** form into sheets. **3** (of rain etc.) fall in sheets. □ **sheet music** music published on loose sheets of paper and not bound into a book.

**sheet²** *noun* a rope or chain attached to the lower corner of a sail, to secure or adjust it. □ **sheet anchor 1** an emergency reserve anchor. **2** a thing on which one depends for security or stability.

**sheeting** *noun* material for making sheets.

**sheikh** (*pronounced* shayk) *noun* **1** the leader of an Arab family, tribe, or village. **2** a Muslim leader. □ **sheikhdom** *noun*

**sheila** *noun* (*Austral. & NZ slang*) a young woman; a girl.

**shekel** (shek-ĕl) *noun* **1** the unit of money in Israel. **2** (**shekels**) (*informal*) money, riches.

**sheldrake** *noun* (*plural* **sheldrake** or **sheldrakes**) a male shelduck.

**shelduck** *noun* (*plural* **shelduck** or **shelducks**) a wild duck with bright plumage, living on coasts.

**shelf** *noun* (*plural* **shelves**) **1** a flat rectangular piece of wood, glass, etc. fastened horizontally for things to be placed on. **2** something resembling this, a ledge or step-like projection. □ **on the shelf** put aside or abandoned as no longer of use; (of an unmarried woman) past the age when she is regarded as likely to be sought in marriage. **shelf-life** *noun* the time for which a stored item remains usable. **shelf-mark** *noun* a number marked on a book to show its place in a library.

**shell** *noun* **1** the hard outer covering of eggs, nut-kernels, and of animals such as snails, crabs, and tortoises. **2** the walls of an unfinished or burnt-out building or ship. **3** any structure that forms a firm framework or covering. **4** a light rowing boat for racing. **5** a metal case filled with explosive, to be fired from a large gun. **6** a group of electrons in an atom, with almost equal energy. ● *verb* **1** remove the shell of; *shell peas.* **2** fire explosive shells at. □ **come out of one's shell** become more sociable and less shy. **shell out** (*informal*) pay out (money). **shell-shock** *noun* nervous breakdown resulting from exposure to battle conditions. **shell suit** a track suit with a soft lining and a nylon outer 'shell'.

**she'll** (*informal*) = she will.

**shellac** (shěl-ak) *noun* thin flakes of a resinous substance used in making varnish. ● *verb* (**shellacked, shellacking**) varnish with shellac.

**Shelley**, Percy Bysshe (1792–1822), English Romantic poet.

**shellfish** *noun* a water animal that has a shell, especially one of edible kinds such as oysters, crabs, and shrimps.

**Shelta** *noun* an ancient secret language used by Irish Gypsies, tinkers, etc.

**shelter** *noun* **1** something that serves as a shield or barrier against attack, danger, heat, wind, etc. **2** a structure built to keep rain etc. off people; *a bus shelter.* **3** refuge; a shielded condition; *seek shelter from the rain.* ● *verb* **1** provide with shelter. **2** protect from blame, trouble, or competition. **3** find or take shelter. □ **sheltered housing** that provided for people who are elderly or handicapped, with special facilities or services.

**shelve** *verb* **1** arrange on a shelf or shelves. **2** fit (a wall or cupboard etc.) with shelves. **3** put aside for later consideration. **4** slope; *the river bottom shelves here.*

**shelves** *see* SHELF.

**shelving** *noun* shelves; material for making these.

**shemozzle** *noun* (*slang*) a rumpus; a brawl.

**shenanigans** (shin-**an**-i-gänz) *plural noun* (*slang*) **1** high-spirited behaviour. **2** trickery.

**shepherd** *noun* a person who looks after sheep. ●*verb* guide or direct (people). □ **shepherd's pie** a pie of minced meat topped with mashed potato.

**shepherdess** *noun* a woman who looks after sheep.

**Sheraton** (sh'e-ră-tŏn) *noun* a late 18th-century style of English furniture, named after its designer Thomas Sheraton (died 1806).

**sherbet** *noun* **1** a cooling Oriental drink of weak sweet fruit juice. **2** a fizzy sweet drink or the powder from which this is made. **3** (*Amer.*) a flavoured water-ice.

**sherd** *noun* = POTSHERD.

**Sheridan**, Richard Brinsley (1751–1816), Anglo-Irish playwright.

**sheriff** *noun* **1** (also **High Sheriff**) the chief executive officer of the Crown in a county, with certain legal and ceremonial duties. **2** (also **sheriff-depute**) the chief judge of a district in Scotland. **3** (*Amer.*) the chief law-enforcing officer of a county.

**Sherman**, William Tecumseh (1820–91), a general commanding union forces in the American Civil War.

**Sherpa** *noun* a member of a Himalayan people living on the borders of Nepal and Tibet.

**Sherrington**, Sir Charles Scott (1857–1952), English physiologist, noted for his researches on the central nervous system.

**sherry** *noun* a fortified wine, originally from southern Spain.

**she's** (*informal*) **1** she is. **2** she has.

**Shetland** *adjective* of Shetland or the Shetland Islands. □ **Shetland Islands** (also **Shetlands**) a group of about 100 Scottish islands north-east of the Orkneys, constituting an islands area (**Shetland**) of Scotland. **Shetland pony** a pony of a very small rough-coated breed.

**Shetlander** *noun* a native or inhabitant of the Shetland Islands.

**shew** (*old use*) = SHOW.

**Shiah** *noun* the Shiites group in Islam.

**shiatsu** (shi-**at**-soo) *noun* Japanese therapy in which pressure is applied with the hands to specific points on the body.

**shibboleth** (**shib**-ŏ-leth) *noun* an old slogan or principle that is still considered essential by some members of a group. (¶ From a story in the Bible, in which 'shibboleth' was a kind of password.)

**shield** *noun* **1** a piece of armour carried on the arm to protect the body. **2** a drawing or model of a triangular shield used for displaying a coat of arms; a trophy in the form of this. **3** an object, structure, or layer of material that protects something. **4** a mass of ancient rock under a land area. ●*verb* protect or screen; protect from discovery.

**shift** *verb* **1** change or move from one position to another. **2** change form or character. **3** transfer (blame or responsibility etc.). **4** (*slang*) move quickly. **5** remove; *can't shift this stain.* ●*noun* **1** a change of place, form, character, etc. **2** a set of workers who start work as another set finishes; the time for which they work; *the night shift.* **3** a piece of evasion. **4** a scheme for achieving something. **5** a straight-cut dress.

**shiftless** *adjective* lazy; lacking resourcefulness. □ **shiftlessness** *noun*

**shifty** *adjective* (**shiftier, shiftiest**) evasive, not straightforward in manner or character; untrustworthy. □ **shiftily** *adverb*, **shiftiness** *noun*

**Shiite** (shee-**I**'t) *noun* a member of the Shiah, one of the two major groups in Islam (the other is Sunni), centred chiefly in Iran.

**shillelagh** (shi-**lay**-li) *noun* an Irish cudgel.

**shilling** *noun* **1** a former British coin, worth one twentieth of a pound. **2** a unit of money in Kenya, Tanzania, and Uganda.

**shilly-shally** *verb* (**shilly-shallied, shilly-shallying**) be unable to make up one's mind.

**shim** *noun* a thin wedge or slip of material used in machinery to make parts fit together. ●*verb* (**shimmed, shimming**) fit or fill up in this way.

**shimmer** *verb* shine with a soft light that appears to quiver. ●*noun* a shimmering effect.

**shin** *noun* **1** the front of the leg below the knee. **2** the lower part of the foreleg in cattle, especially as a cut of beef. ●*verb* (**shinned, shinning**) climb using arms and legs.

**shindig** *noun* (*informal*) **1** a lively noisy party. **2** a shindy.

**shindy** *noun* (*informal*) a din; a brawl.

**shine** *verb* (**shone** (in sense 5 **shined**), **shining**) **1** give out or reflect light, be bright, glow. **2** (of the sun etc.) be visible and not obscured by clouds. **3** excel in some way; *does not shine in maths; a shining example.* **4** direct the light of; *shine the torch on it.* **5** (*informal*) polish. ●*noun* **1** brightness. **2** a high polish. □ **take a shine to** (*informal*) take a liking to.

**shiner** *noun* (*informal*) a black eye.

**shingle** *noun* **1** a rectangular slip of wood used as a roof-tile. **2** (*old use*) shingled hair; shingling the hair. **3** small round pebbles, especially on the seashore. **4** (**shingles**) a painful disease caused by a virus, with a rash often encircling the body. ●*verb* **1** roof with shingles. **2** (*old use*) cut (a woman's hair) in a short tapering style at the back, with all ends exposed.

**Shinto** *noun* (also **Shintoism**) a Japanese religion revering ancestors and nature-spirits.

**shinty** *noun* a game resembling hockey.

**shiny** *adjective* (**shinier, shiniest**) shining, rubbed until glossy. □ **shininess** *noun*

**ship** *noun* a large seagoing vessel. ●*verb* (**shipped, shipping**) **1** put, take, or send on a ship. **2** transport.

**shipboard** *adjective* used or occurring on board a ship.

**shipbuilding** *noun* the business of constructing ships. □ **shipbuilder** *noun*

**shipmate** *noun* a sailor working on the same ship as another.

**shipment** *noun* **1** the putting of goods on a ship. **2** the amount shipped; a consignment.

**shipowner** *noun* a person who owns a ship or holds shares in a shipping company.

**shipper** *noun* a person or firm whose business is transporting goods by ship.

**shipping** *noun* **1** ships. **2** transporting goods by ship.

**shipshape** *adverb & adjective* in good order, tidy.

**shipwreck** *noun* the destruction of a ship by storm or striking a rock etc. □ **shipwrecked** *adjective*

**shipwright** *noun* a shipbuilder.

**shipyard** *noun* a shipbuilding establishment.

**shire** *noun* **1** a county. **2** (*Austral.*) a rural area with its own elected council. □ **the Shires** the band of English counties with names (formerly) ending in *-shire*, extending northwards from Hampshire to Yorkshire; the midland counties of England. **shire-horse** *noun* a heavy powerful breed of horse used for pulling loads.

**shirk** *verb* avoid (a duty or work etc.) selfishly or unfairly. □ **shirker** *noun*

**shirr** *verb* gather (cloth) with parallel elastic threads run through it. □ **shirring** *noun*

**shirt** *noun* a garment of cotton or silk etc. for the upper part of the body. □ **put one's**

**shirt on** (*slang*) bet all one has on (a horse etc.); be sure of.

**shirtsleeve** *noun* the sleeve of a shirt. □ **in one's shirtsleeves** without one's jacket on.

**shirtwaister** *noun* a woman's dress with the bodice shaped like a shirt.

**shirty** *adjective* (**shirtier, shirtiest**) (*slang*) annoyed, angry. □ **shirtily** *adverb*, **shirtiness** *noun*

**shish kebab** (shish ki-**bab**) pieces of meat and vegetable grilled on skewers.

**shit** (*vulgar*) *noun* **1** faeces. **2** a contemptible person or thing. ●*verb* (**shitted** *or* **shat** *or* **shit, shitting**) empty the bowels, defecate. ●*interjection* an exclamation of anger etc.

**Shiva** (shee-vă) = SIVA.

**shiver**[1] *verb* tremble slightly, especially with cold or fear. ●*noun* a shivering movement. □ **shivery** *adjective*

**shiver**[2] *verb* shatter. ●*plural noun* (**shivers**) shattered fragments.

**shoal**[1] *noun* a great number of fish swimming together. ●*verb* form shoals.

**shoal**[2] *noun* **1** a shallow place; an underwater sandbank. **2** (**shoals**) hidden dangers or difficulties. ●*verb* become shallow.

**shock**[1] *noun* **1** the effect of a violent impact or shake. **2** a violent shake of the earth's crust in an earthquake. **3** a sudden violent effect upon a person's mind or emotions (e.g. by news of a disaster). **4** an acute state of weakness caused by physical injury or pain or by mental shock. **5** an electric shock (*see* ELECTRIC). ●*verb* **1** affect with great indignation, horror, or disgust. **2** give an electric shock to. **3** cause an acute state of weakness in (a person or animal). □ **shock absorber** a device for absorbing vibration in a vehicle. **shock tactics** sudden violent action taken to achieve one's purpose. **shock therapy** *or* **treatment** treatment of psychiatric patients by means of an electric shock or a drug causing a similar effect. **shock troops** troops specially trained for violent assaults. **shock wave** a sharp wave of increased atmospheric pressure, caused by an explosion or by a body moving faster than sound.

**shock**[2] *noun* a bushy untidy mass of hair.

**shock**[3] *noun* an arrangement of sheaves of corn standing propped against each other in a field for drying. ●*verb* arrange in shocks.

**shocker** *noun* (*informal*) a shocking person or thing; a very bad specimen.

**shocking** *adjective* **1** causing great shock, indignation, or disgust; scandalous. **2** (*informal*) very bad; *shocking weather.* □ **shocking pink** very bright pink. □ **shockingly** *adverb*

**shod** *see* SHOE. ●*adjective* having shoes of a specified kind; *sensibly shod*.

**shoddy** *adjective* (**shoddier, shoddiest**) of poor quality or workmanship. □ **shoddily** *adverb*, **shoddiness** *noun*

**shoe** *noun* **1** an outer covering for a person's foot, with a fairly stiff sole. **2** a horseshoe. **3** an object like a shoe in appearance or use. **4** the part of a brake that presses against the wheel or its drum in a vehicle. ●*verb* (**shod, shoeing**) fit with a shoe or shoes. □ **be in a person's shoes** be in his or her situation or difficulty. **shoe-tree** *noun* a shaped block for keeping a shoe in shape.

**shoehorn** *noun* a curved implement for easing one's heel into the back of a shoe.

**shoelace** *noun* a cord for fastening shoes.

**shoemaker** *noun* a person whose trade is making or mending boots and shoes.

**shoestring** *noun* a shoelace. □ **on a shoestring** with only a small amount of money.

**shogun** (shoh-gŭn) *noun* (*hist.*) the hereditary commander of the army in feudal Japan.

**shone** *see* SHINE.

**shoo** *interjection* an exclamation used to frighten animals away. ●*verb* (**shooed, shooing**) drive away by this.

**shook** *see* SHAKE.

**shoot** *verb* (**shot, shooting**) **1** fire (a gun, missile, etc.). **2** kill or wound with a missile from a gun etc. **3** hunt with a gun for sport. **4** move or send out swiftly or violently; *the car shot past*. **5** (of a plant) put forth buds or shoots. **6** slide (the bolt of a door) into or out of its fastening. **7** take a shot at goal. **8** photograph or film. ●*interjection* say what you have to say. ●*noun* **1** a young branch or new growth of a plant. **2** an expedition for shooting game; land where this is held. □ **have shot one's bolt** have made one's last possible effort. **shooting star** a small meteor appearing like a star, moving rapidly, and then disappearing. **shooting stick** a walking stick with a small folding seat at the handle end. **shoot one's mouth off** (*slang*) talk too freely. **shoot up 1** rise suddenly; (of a person) grow rapidly. **2** (*slang*) inject oneself with a drug.

**shop** *noun* **1** a place where goods or services are on sale. **2** a workshop. **3** one's own work or profession as a subject of conversation; *she is always talking shop*. ●*verb* (**shopped, shopping**) **1** go to shops to buy things. **2** (*slang*) inform against (a person), especially to the police. □ **all over the shop** (*informal*) in great disorder, scattered everywhere. **shop around** look for the best bargain. **shop-floor** *noun* **1** the production area in a factory. **2** workers as distinct from management. **shop-soiled** *adjective* soiled or faded from being on display in a shop. **shop steward** a trade-union official elected by fellow workers as their representative. □ **shopper** *noun*

**shopaholic** *noun* (*informal*) a compulsive shopper.

**shopkeeper** *noun* a person who owns or manages a shop.

**shoplifter** *noun* a person who steals goods on display in a shop. □ **shoplifting** *noun*

**shopping** *noun* **1** buying goods in shops. **2** the goods bought. □ **shopping centre** an area where shops are concentrated.

**shopwalker** *noun* a supervisor in a large shop.

**shore**[1] *noun* the land along the edge of the sea or a lake.

**shore**[2] *verb* prop or support with a length of timber set at a slant. ●*noun* a support of this kind.

**shoreline** *noun* the line of a shore.

**shorn** *see* SHEAR.

**short** *adjective* **1** measuring little from end to end in space or time. **2** seeming to be shorter than it really is; *for one short hour*. **3** not lasting, not going far into the past or future; *a short memory*. **4** insufficient, having an insufficient supply; *water is short; we are short of water*. **5** (*informal*) having little of a certain quality; *he's short on tact*. **6** concise, brief. **7** curt. **8** (of vowel sounds) relatively brief or light (*see* LONG[1], sense 7). **9** (of an alcoholic drink) small and concentrated, made with spirits. **10** (of temper) easily lost. **11** (of pastry) rich and crumbly. ●*adverb* suddenly, abruptly; *stopped short*. ●*noun* **1** a short drink. **2** a short circuit. ●*verb* short-circuit. □ **for short** as an abbreviation; *Raymond is called Ray for short*. **in short** briefly. **in short supply** scarce. **short-change** *verb* give insufficient change; cheat (a person). **short circuit** a connection (usually a fault) in an electrical circuit in which current flows by a shorter route than the normal one. **short-circuit** *verb* cause a short circuit in; bypass. **short cut** a route or method that is quicker than the usual one. **short for** an abbreviation of; *'Ray' is short for 'Raymond'*. **short-handed** *adjective* having an insufficient number of workers or helpers. **short list** a list of selected candidates from whom the final choice will be made. **short-list** *verb* put on a short list. **short-lived** *adjective* not lasting long. **short odds** nearly even odds in betting. **short of 1** without going so far as; *will do anything for her short of having her to stay*. **2** distant from; having failed to reach; *two miles short of home*. (See also sense 4 of *adjective*.) **short shrift** curt treatment. **short-sighted** adjective **1** able to see clearly only what is close. **2** lacking foresight. **short-staffed** adjective with insufficient staff. **short-tempered** adjective easily becoming angry. **short-term** adjective of or for a short period. **short wave** a radio wave of frequency greater than 3 MHz. □ **shortish** adjective, **shortness** noun

**shortage** noun a lack of something that is needed.

**shortbread** noun a rich sweet biscuit.

**shortcake** noun shortbread.

**shortcoming** noun failure to reach a required standard; a fault.

**shortcrust pastry** crumbly pastry with an even texture.

**shorten** verb make or become shorter.

**shortening** noun fat used to make pastry etc.

**shortfall** noun a deficit.

**shorthand** noun a system of rapid writing using special symbols.

**shorthorn** noun one of a breed of cattle with short horns.

**shortly** adverb **1** in a short time, not long, soon; *coming shortly*; *shortly afterwards*. **2** in a few words. **3** curtly.

**shorts** plural noun **1** trousers that do not reach to the knee. **2** (*Amer.*) underpants.

**shorty** noun (*informal*) a person or garment that is shorter than average.

**Shostakovich** (shost-ă-**koh**-vich), Dmitri (1906–75), Russian composer.

**shot** see SHOOT. ●adjective (of fabric) woven or dyed so that different colours show at different angles. ●noun **1** the firing of a gun etc.; the sound of this. **2** a person with regard to skill in shooting; *he's a good shot*. **3** (*plural* **shot**) a single missile for a cannon or gun, a non-explosive projectile. **4** lead pellets for firing from small guns. **5** a heavy metal ball thrown as a sport. **6** the launching of a rocket or spacecraft. **7** a stroke in tennis, cricket, billiards, etc. **8** an attempt to hit something or reach a target. **9** an attempt to do something; *have a shot at this crossword*. **10** an injection. **11** (*informal*) a measure of spirits. **12** a photograph; the scene photographed; a single continuous photographed scene in a cinema film. □ **like a shot** without hesitation; willingly. **shot in the arm** a stimulus, an encouragement. **shot in the dark** a mere guess. **shot-put** noun an athletic contest in which a shot is thrown.

**shotgun** noun a gun for firing small shot at close range. □ **shotgun wedding** a wedding that has been enforced, especially because the bride is pregnant.

**should** auxiliary verb, used to express **1** duty or obligation; *you should have told me*. **2** an expected future event; *they should be here by ten*. **3** a possible event; *if you should happen*

*to see him*. **4** with *I* and *we* to form a polite statement or a conditional clause; *I should like to come*; *I should say it's about right*.

**shoulder** noun **1** the part of the body at which an arm, foreleg, or wing is attached; the part of the human body between this and the neck. **2** the part of a garment covering a shoulder. **3** a strip of land bordering a road. ●verb **1** push with one's shoulder. **2** put or carry on one's shoulders. **3** take (blame or responsibility) upon oneself. □ **put one's shoulder to the wheel** make an effort. **shoulder arms** hold a rifle with the barrel against one's shoulder. **shoulder bag** a handbag hung on a strap over the shoulder. **shoulder blade** either of the two large flat bones at the top of the back. **shoulder to shoulder** side by side and close together.

**shouldn't** (*informal*) = should not.

**shout** noun **1** a loud cry calling attention or expressing joy, excitement, or disapproval. **2** (*informal*) a person's turn to buy a round of drinks. ●verb utter a shout; utter or call loudly. □ **shout down** silence (a person) by shouting.

**shove** (*pronounced* shuv) noun a rough push. ●verb **1** push roughly. **2** (*informal*) put; *shove it in the drawer*. □ **shove off 1** push a boat so that it moves from the shore. **2** (*informal*) go away.

**shovel** noun **1** a tool for scooping up earth or snow etc., shaped like a spade with the edges turned up. **2** a large mechanically-operated device used for the same purpose. ●verb (**shovelled**, **shovelling**; *Amer.* **shoveled**, **shoveling**) **1** shift or clear with or as if with a shovel. **2** scoop or thrust roughly; *shovelling food into his mouth*. □ **shovelful** noun

**shoveller** noun (also **shoveler**) a duck with a broad shovel-like beak.

**show** verb (**showed**, **shown**, **showing**) **1** allow or cause to be seen; offer for inspection or viewing. **2** demonstrate; point out; prove; cause (a person) to understand; *show us how it works*. **3** conduct; *show them in*. **4** present an image of; *this picture shows the hotel*. **5** treat in a certain way; *showed us much kindness*. **6** be able to be seen; *the lining is showing*. **7** (*informal*) appear, come when expected. ●noun **1** showing; being shown. **2** a display; a public exhibition for competition, entertainment, or advertisement; *a dog show*; *a puppet show*; *the motor show*. **3** (*slang*) any business or undertaking; *he runs the whole show*. **4** an outward appearance, an insincere display; *under a show of friendship*. **5** a discharge of blood from the vagina at the start of childbirth. □ **bad show!** (*informal*) that was badly done or unfortunate. **good show!** (*informal*) well done. **show business** the entertainment or theatrical profession. **show house** or **flat** one prepared as a sample of those available. **show off** display well, proudly, or ostentatiously; try to impress people. **show-off** noun a person who tries to impress others. **show of hands** raising of hands to vote. **show-piece** noun an excellent specimen used for exhibition. **showplace** noun a place that tourists etc. go to see. **show-stopper** noun a spectacular act in a show receiving prolonged applause. **show trial** a judicial trial designed to frighten or impress the public. **show up** **1** make or be clearly visible. **2** expose or humiliate. **3** (informal) appear, come when expected.

**showbiz** noun (informal) = SHOW BUSINESS.

**showcase** noun **1** a glass case for exhibiting items. **2** an event designed to show someone or something to advantage.

**showdown** noun a final test or confrontation.

**shower** noun **1** a brief fall of rain or snow etc., or of bullets, dust, etc. **2** a sudden influx of letters or gifts etc. **3** (also **shower-bath**) a device or cabinet in which water is sprayed so as to wash a person's body; a wash in this. **4** (Amer.) a party for giving presents to a prospective bride or mother. **5** (slang) a contemptible or unpleasant person. ●verb **1** pour down or come in a shower. **2** send or give (many letters or gifts etc.) to. **3** wash oneself in sprayed water.

**showerproof** adjective (of fabric) able to keep out slight rain. ●verb make showerproof.

**showery** adjective (of weather) with many showers.

**showing** noun the evidence or quality that a person shows; on today's showing, he will fail.

**showjumping** noun the sport of riding and jumping horses around a course of fences.

**showman** noun (plural **showmen**) **1** an organizer of circuses or similar entertainments. **2** a person who is good at showmanship.

**showmanship** noun skill in presenting an entertainment or one's abilities to the best advantage.

**shown** see SHOW.

**showroom** noun a room in which goods are displayed for inspection.

**showy** adjective (**showier**, **showiest**) **1** making a good display. **2** brilliant, gaudy. □ **showily** adverb, **showiness** noun

**shrank** see SHRINK.

**shrapnel** noun **1** an artillery shell containing bullets or pieces of metal which it scatters as it explodes. **2** the pieces it scatters.

**shred** noun **1** a small piece torn or cut from something. **2** a small amount; not a shred of evidence. ●verb (**shredded**, **shredding**) tear or cut into shreds. □ **shredder** noun

**shrew** noun **1** a small mouselike animal. **2** a sharp-tempered scolding woman.

**shrewd** adjective having sound judgement and common sense; clever. □ **shrewdly** adverb, **shrewdness** noun

**shriek** noun a shrill cry or scream. ●verb make a shriek; utter with a shriek.

**shrift** noun (old use) confession and absolution. □ **short shrift** see SHORT.

**shrike** noun a bird with a strong hooked beak that impales its prey on thorns.

**shrill** adjective piercing and high-pitched in sound. ●verb sound or utter shrilly. □ **shrilly** adverb, **shrillness** noun

**shrimp** noun **1** a small edible shellfish, pink when boiled. **2** (informal) a very small person.

**shrine** noun an altar, chapel, or other place that is hallowed because of its special associations.

**shrink** verb (**shrank**, **shrunk** or (especially as adjective) **shrunken**, **shrinking**) **1** make or become smaller, especially by the action of moisture, heat, or cold; it shrank in the wash. **2** draw back so as to avoid something; be unwilling to do something (e.g. because of shame or dislike). ●noun (slang, short for head-shrinker) a psychiatrist. □ **shrink fit** an extremely tight fit formed by shrinking one metal part round another. **shrink-wrap** verb wrap (an article) in plastic that shrinks tightly round it.

**shrinkage** noun **1** the process of shrinking; the amount by which something shrinks. **2** (in commerce) loss by theft, wastage, etc.

**shrive** verb (**shrove**, **shriven**) (old use) hear the confession of and give absolution to (a penitent).

**shrivel** verb (**shrivelled**, **shrivelling**; Amer. **shriveled**, **shriveling**) shrink and wrinkle from great heat or cold or lack of moisture.

**Shropshire** a county in central England, bordering on Wales.

**shroud** noun **1** a sheet or garment in which a dead body is wrapped for burial. **2** something that conceals; wrapped in a shroud of secrecy. **3** one of a set of ropes supporting the mast of a ship. ●verb **1** wrap in a shroud; conceal in wrappings. **2** hide; cover; obscure; his past life is shrouded in mystery.

**shrove** see SHRIVE. □ **Shrove Tuesday** the day before Ash Wednesday.

**shrovetide** noun Shrove Tuesday and the two days preceding it when it was formerly customary to be shriven.

**shrub** *noun* a woody plant smaller than a tree, usually with several main stems. □ **shrubby** *adjective*

**shrubbery** *noun* an area planted with shrubs.

**shrug** *verb* (**shrugged, shrugging**) raise (the shoulders) as a gesture of indifference, doubt, or helplessness. ●*noun* this movement. □ **shrug off** dismiss (a thing) as unimportant.

**shrunk** *see* SHRINK.

**shrunken** *adjective* having shrunk.

**shudder** *verb* **1** shiver violently with horror, fear, or cold. **2** make a strong shaking movement. ●*noun* a shuddering movement.

**shuffle** *verb* **1** walk without lifting the feet clear of the ground. **2** rearrange; change the order of (cards, papers, etc.). **3** keep shifting one's position. **4** get rid of (a burden etc.) shiftily; *shuffled off the responsibility on to others*; *shuffled out of it.* ●*noun* **1** a shuffling movement, walk, or dance. **2** shuffling of cards etc. **3** a rearrangement; *the latest Cabinet shuffle.*

**shufti** *noun* (*informal*) a look; a brief inspection.

**shun** *verb* (**shunned, shunning**) avoid, keep away from.

**shunt** *verb* **1** move (a train) on to a sidetrack. **2** divert onto an alternative course. ●*noun* **1** shunting; being shunted. **2** (*slang*) a collision of vehicles, especially one behind another; *a rear-end shunt.* **3** *Electricity* a conductor joining two points of a circuit, through which current may be diverted. **4** (in surgery) an alternative path for the circulation of the blood. □ **shunter** *noun*

**shush** *interjection & verb* (*informal*) hush.

**shut** *verb* (**shut, shutting**) **1** move or be moved into a closed position; seal. **2** (of a shop, office, etc.) close for business. **3** bring or fold the parts of (a thing) together; *shut the book.* **4** keep in or out by shutting a door etc.; *shut out the noise.* **5** trap (a finger or dress etc.) by shutting something on it. □ **be** (*or* **get**) **shut of** (*slang*) be (or get) rid of. **shut down** cease working or business, either for the day or permanently; cause to do this. **shut-down** *noun* this process. **shut-eye** *noun* (*slang*) sleep. **shut off** stop the flow of (water or gas etc.). **shut up 1** shut securely; shut all the doors and windows of (a house). **2** put away in a box etc. **3** (*informal*) stop talking or making a noise; cause to do this, silence. **shut up shop** close a business or shop. **shut your mouth** (*slang*) be silent.

**Shute**, Nevil (Nevil Shute Norway) (1899–1960), English novelist.

**shutter** *noun* **1** a panel or screen that can be closed over a window. **2** a device that opens and closes the aperture of a camera lens to allow light to fall on the film.

**shuttered** *adjective* **1** fitted with shutters. **2** with the shutters closed.

**shuttle** *noun* **1** a holder carrying the weft-thread to and fro across the loom in weaving. **2** a holder carrying the lower thread in a sewing machine. **3** a bus, aircraft, etc. used in a shuttle service. **4** = SPACE SHUTTLE. **5** a shuttlecock. ●*verb* move, travel, or send to and fro. □ **shuttle diplomacy** diplomacy that involves travelling between countries involved in a dispute. **shuttle service** a transport service operating to and fro over a relatively short distance.

**shuttlecock** *noun* a cork with a ring of feathers, or a similar plastic device struck to and fro in badminton.

**shy**[1] *adjective* (**shyer, shyest**) **1** (of a person) timid and lacking self-confidence in the presence of others. **2** (of behaviour) showing shyness; *a shy smile.* **3** (of an animal) timid and avoiding observation. ●*verb* (**shied, shying**) jump or move suddenly in alarm. □ **shyly** *adverb*, **shyness** *noun*

**shy**[2] *verb* (**shied, shying**) fling or throw (a stone etc.). ●*noun* a throw.

**shylock** *noun* a hard-hearted money-lender. (¶ Name of a character in Shakespeare's *Merchant of Venice.*)

**shyster** *noun* (*informal*) a person who acts unscrupulously or unprofessionally.

**SI** *abbreviation* Système International d'Unités; the international system of units of measurement. (¶ French.)

**Si** *symbol* silicon.

**Siamese** *adjective* of Siam (now called Thailand) or its people or language. ●*noun* (*plural* **Siamese**) **1** a native of Siam. **2** the language of Siam. **3** (in full **Siamese cat**) a cat of a breed that has short cream-coloured fur with darker face, ears, tail, and feet. □ **Siamese twins** twins whose bodies are joined in some way at birth.

**Sibelius** (si-bay-liŭs), Jean (1865–1957), Finnish composer.

**Siberia** a region of the former USSR in northern Asia, noted for its harsh winters. □ **Siberian** *adjective*

**sibilant** *adjective* having a hissing sound. ●*noun* one of the speech sounds that sound like hissing, e.g. *s, sh.* □ **sibilance** *noun*

**sibling** *noun* a child in relation to another or others of the same parent; a brother or sister.

**sibyl** (sib-il) *noun* (in ancient times) a woman acting as the reputed mouthpiece of a god, uttering prophecies and oracles.

**sibylline** (sib-i-lyn) *adjective* issuing from a sibyl; oracular, mysteriously prophetic.

**sic** (*pronounced* seek) *adverb* used or spelt in that way. (¶ Latin, = thus.)

■**Usage** This word is placed in brackets after a word that seems odd or is wrongly spelt, to show that one is quoting it exactly as it was given.

**Sicily** a large island in the Mediterranean Sea, off the 'toe' of Italy. □ **Sicilian** *adjective & noun*

**sick** *adjective* **1** physically or mentally unwell. **2** likely to vomit; *feel sick.* **3** distressed; disgusted; *their attitude makes me sick.* **4** bored with something through having already had too much of it; *I'm sick of cricket.* **5** finding amusement in misfortune or in morbid subjects; *sick jokes.* ●*verb* (*informal*) vomit; *sicked it up.* ●*noun* (*informal*) vomit. □ **be sick** vomit. **sick leave** leave of absence because of illness. **sick pay** pay given to an employee who is absent through illness.

**sickbay** *noun* a room, cabin, etc. for people who are ill at school, on board ship, etc.

**sickbed** *noun* the bed of a sick person.

**sicken** *verb* **1** begin to be ill; *be sickening for a disease.* **2** make or become distressed or disgusted.

**sickening** *adjective* annoying; disgusting.

**Sickert**, Walter Richard (1860–1942), English painter.

**sickle** *noun* **1** a tool with a curved blade and a short handle, used for cutting corn etc. **2** something shaped like this, e.g. the crescent moon. □ **sickle-cell** *noun* a sickle-shaped blood cell, especially as found in a type of severe hereditary anaemia.

**sickly** *adjective* (**sicklier, sickliest**) **1** often ill; *a sickly child.* **2** unhealthy-looking. **3** causing ill health; *a sickly climate.* **4** causing sickness or distaste; *a sickly smell; sickly sentimentality.*

**sickness** *noun* **1** illness. **2** a disease. **3** vomiting.

**Siddons**, Sarah (1755–1831), English tragic actress.

**side** *noun* **1** any of the more or less flat inner or outer surfaces of an object, especially as distinct from the top and bottom, front and back, or ends. **2** any of the bounding lines of a plane figure such as a triangle or square. **3** either of the two halves into which an object can be divided by a line down its centre. **4** the part near the edge and away from the centre of something. **5** a slope of a hill or ridge. **6** the region next to a person or thing; *he stood at my side.* **7** one aspect or view of something; *study all sides of the problem.* **8** one of two opposing groups, teams, etc. **9** the line of descent through father or mother; *his mother's side of the family.* ●*adjective* at or on the side; *side door.* ●*verb* take the side of a

person in a dispute; *he sided with his son.* □ **on one side** not in the main or central position; apart from the rest. **on the side** as a sideline; as a surreptitious or illicit activity. **on the…side** rather, somewhat; *prices are on the high side.* **side by side** close together. **side drum** a small double-headed drum. **side effect** a secondary (usually undesirable) effect. **side issue** an issue that is not the main one. **side road** a road leading off a main road; a minor road. **side-saddle** (*noun*) a saddle for a woman rider to sit on with both legs on the same side of the horse, not astride; (*adverb*) sitting in this way. **side street** = SIDE ROAD. **side-whiskers** *plural noun* whiskers on the cheeks.

**sideboard** *noun* **1** a flat-topped piece of dining-room furniture with drawers and cupboards for china etc. **2** (**sideboards**) (*informal*) hair grown by a man down the sides of his face.

**sideburns** *plural noun* sideboards.

**sidecar** *noun* a passenger compartment attached to the side of a motor cycle.

**sidekick** *noun* (*informal*) a close friend or associate; a subordinate member of a pair or group.

**sidelight** *noun* **1** light from one side (not front or back). **2** each of a pair of small lights at the front of a vehicle. **3** a light at either side of a moving ship.

**sideline** *noun* **1** something done in addition to one's main work or activity. **2** (**sidelines**) the lines bounding a football pitch etc. at its sides; the space just outside these; a place for spectators.

**sidelong** *adverb & adjective* to one side, sideways; *a sidelong glance.*

**sidereal** (sy-**deer**-iăl) *adjective* of or measured by the stars.

**sideshow** *noun* **1** a small show or stall forming part of a fair, exhibition, etc. **2** a minor incident or issue.

**sidesman** *noun* (*plural* **sidesmen**) one who assists a churchwarden and acts as an usher at a church service.

**sidestep** *noun* a step to the side. ●*verb* (**sidestepped, sidestepping**) **1** avoid by stepping sideways. **2** evade (a question, responsibility, etc.).

**sideswipe** *noun* **1** a glancing blow on or from the side. **2** incidental criticism.

**sidetrack** *verb* divert from the main course or issue.

**sidewalk** *noun* (*Amer.*) a pavement.

**sideways** *adverb & adjective* **1** to or from one side. **2** with one side facing forward; *sat sideways.*

**siding** *noun* a short track by the side of a railway, used for shunting.

**sidle** (*rhymes with* bridle) *verb* move in a timid, furtive, or cringing manner; edge.

**SIDS** *abbreviation* sudden infant death syndrome; cot-death.

**siege** *noun* the surrounding and blockading of a town or fortified place, to capture it or the people inside. □ **lay siege to** begin besieging.

**Siemens** (see-mĕnz), Ernst Werner von (1816–92), German electrical engineer.

**siemens** (see-mĕnz) *noun* the SI unit of electrical conductance, the reciprocal of the ohm. (¶ Named after E. W. von Siemens.)

**sienna** (si-**en**-ă) *noun* a kind of earth used as colouring matter. □ **burnt sienna** reddish-brown. **raw sienna** yellowish-brown.

**sierra** (si-e-ră) *noun* a long jagged chain of mountains especially in Spain or Spanish America.

**Sierra Leone** (si-e-ră li-**ohn**) a country in West Africa. □ **Sierra Leonean** *adjective & noun*

**siesta** (si-**est**-ă) *noun* an afternoon nap or rest, especially in hot countries.

**sieve** (*pronounced* siv) *noun* a utensil consisting of a frame with mesh, used for straining, sifting, or pulping food or other material. ● *verb* put through a sieve.

**sift** *verb* **1** sieve. **2** sprinkle lightly from a perforated container. **3** examine carefully and select or analyse. **4** (of snow or light) fall as if from a sieve.

**sigh** *noun* a long audible breath expressing sadness, tiredness, relief, etc. ● *verb* **1** give a sigh; express with a sigh. **2** (of wind etc.) make a similar sound.

**sight** *noun* **1** the faculty of seeing; ability to see. **2** seeing, being seen; *lost sight of it*. **3** the range over which a person can see or an object can be seen; *within sight of the castle*. **4** a thing seen or visible or worth seeing, a display; *the tulips are a wonderful sight*. **5** something regarded as unsightly or looking ridiculous; *he looks a sight in those clothes*. **6** (*informal*) a great quantity; *a darned sight better*. **7** a device looked through to help aim or observe with a gun or telescope etc.; aim or observation using this. ● *verb* **1** get a sight of; *we sighted land*. **2** aim or observe by using the sight in a gun, telescope, etc. □ **at** *or* **on sight** as soon as a person or thing has been seen. **play music at sight** play without preliminary practice or study of the score. **in sight** visible; clearly near at hand; *victory was in sight*. **lower one's sights** adopt a less ambitious policy. **sight-read** *verb* play or sing music at sight. **sight-screen** *noun* a large movable white structure placed to help the batsman see the ball in cricket. **sight unseen** without previous inspection.

**sighted** *adjective* having sight, not blind.

**sightless** *adjective* blind.

**sightseeing** *noun* visiting places of interest in a place. □ **sightseer** *noun*

**sign** *noun* **1** something perceived that suggests the existence of a fact or quality or condition; *it shows signs of being a success*. **2** a mark with a special meaning, a symbol. **3** a signboard or other visual object used similarly; a notice. **4** an action or gesture conveying information or a command etc. **5** any of the twelve divisions of the zodiac; a symbol representing one of these. ● *verb* **1** make a sign; *signed to me to come*. **2** write (one's name) on a document etc. to guarantee that it has one's authority or consent; *signed the letter; sign here*. **3** convey by signing a document; *signed away her right to the house*. **4** engage or be engaged as an employee by signing a contract of employment. **5** use sign language. □ **sign language** a series of gestures used by deaf or dumb people for communication. **sign off 1** (in broadcasting) announce the end of one's programme or transmission. **2** withdraw one's claim to unemployment benefit after finding work. **sign on** sign a contract (of employment etc.); register oneself (e.g. as unemployed). **sign up 1** engage (a person). **2** enrol; enlist in the armed forces.

**signal** *noun* **1** a sign, object, or gesture giving information or a command; a message made up of such signs. **2** an act or event that immediately produces a general reaction; *his arrival was the signal for an outburst of cheering*. **3** a sequence of electrical impulses or radio waves transmitted or received. ● *verb* (**signalled**, **signalling**; *Amer.* **signaled**, **signaling**) make a signal or signals; direct, communicate with, or announce in this way. ● *adjective* remarkably good or bad; *a signal success*. □ **signal-box** *noun* a small railway building with signalling apparatus. □ **signaller** *noun*, **signally** *adverb*

**signalize** *verb* (also **signalise**) make noteworthy.

**signalman** *noun* (*plural* **signalmen**) one who is responsible for operating railway signals.

**signatory** (sig-nă-ter-i) *noun* any of the parties signing a treaty or other agreement.

**signature** *noun* **1** a person's name or initials written by himself or herself in signing something. **2** a key signature or time signature in music. **3** a section of a book made from one sheet folded and cut, often marked with a letter or figure as a guide to the binder. □ **signature tune** a tune used to announce a particular programme or performer.

**signboard** *noun* a board bearing the name of a shop or inn etc.

**signet** (sig-nit) *noun* a person's seal used with or instead of a signature. □ **signet ring** a finger-ring with an engraved design, formerly used as a seal.

**significance** *noun* **1** what is meant by something; *what is the significance of this symbol?* **2** being significant, importance; *the event is of no significance.*

**significant** *adjective* **1** having a meaning. **2** full of meaning; *a significant glance.* **3** important, noteworthy; *significant developments.* □ **to three, four,** etc. **significant figures** (of a number) expressed to the specified degree of accuracy, with the final figure rounded up or down, ignoring zeros at the beginning; e.g. 7.63186 to four significant figures is 7.632. □ **significantly** *adverb*

**signification** *noun* meaning.

**signify** *verb* (**signified, signifying**) **1** be a sign or symbol of. **2** have as a meaning. **3** make known; *signified her approval.* **4** be of importance, matter; *it doesn't signify.*

**signor** (seen-yor) *noun* the title used of or to an Italian-speaking man.

**signora** (seen-yor-ă) *noun* the title used of or to an Italian-speaking woman.

**signorina** (seen-yor-een-ă) *noun* the title used of or to an Italian-speaking young woman (especially one who is unmarried).

**signpost** *noun* a post at a road junction etc. showing the names of places along each of the roads. ●*verb* provide with a post or posts of this kind.

**signwriter** *noun* a person who paints signboards etc.

**Sikh** (*pronounced* seek) *noun* a member of an Indian religious sect, combining elements of Hinduism and Islam. □ **Sikhism** *noun*

**Sikkim** (sik-im) a State of India, in the eastern Himalayas. □ **Sikkimese** *adjective & noun*

**Sikorsky** (si-kor-ski), Igor Ivan (1889–1972), Russian-born American aeronautical engineer.

**silage** (sy-lij) *noun* green fodder stored and fermented in a silo.

**silence** *noun* **1** absence of sound. **2** avoidance or absence of speaking or of making a sound. **3** avoidance of mentioning something, refusal to betray a secret. ●*verb* make silent.

**silencer** *noun* a device for reducing the sound made by a gun or a vehicle's exhaust etc.

**silent** *adjective* **1** not speaking, not making or accompanied by a sound. **2** saying little. □ **silent majority** people of moderate opinions who rarely make themselves heard. □ **silently** *adverb*

**Silesia** (sy-lee-ziă) a region of central Europe, now largely in SW Poland. □ **Silesian** *adjective & noun*

**silhouette** (sil-oo-et) *noun* **1** a dark shadow or outline seen against a light background. **2** a profile portrait in solid black. ●*verb* show as a silhouette; *she was silhouetted against the screen.*

**silica** (sil-i-kă) *noun* a compound of silicon occurring as quartz or flint and in sandstone and other rocks. □ **silica gel** hydrated silica in the form of granules, used as a drying agent. □ **siliceous** (sil-ish-ŭs) *adjective*

**silicate** (sil-i-kayt) *noun* any of the insoluble compounds of silica.

**silicon** (sil-i-kŏn) *noun* a chemical element (symbol Si), found widely in the earth's crust in its compound forms. □ **silicon chip** a microchip made of silicon. **Silicon Valley** an area with a high concentration of electronics industries, especially the Santa Clara valley south-east of San Francisco.

**silicone** (sil-i-kohn) *noun* any of the organic compounds of silicon, widely used in paints, varnish, and lubricants.

**silicosis** (sil-i-koh-sis) *noun* an abnormal condition of the lungs caused by inhaling dust that contains silica.

**silk** *noun* **1** the fine strong soft fibre produced by a silkworm in making its cocoon, or by certain other insects or spiders. **2** thread or cloth made from it; fabric resembling this. **3** (**silks**) clothing made from silk. **4** (*informal*) a Queen's Counsel, entitled to wear a silk gown. **5** fine soft strands like threads of silk. □ **Silk Road** a trade route from China through Central Asia to Europe, used in ancient times by traders in silk (now a tourist route by rail). **silk-screen printing** = SCREEN PRINTING. **take silk** become a Queen's Counsel.

**silken** *adjective* made of or like silk.

**silkworm** *noun* a caterpillar which feeds on mulberry leaves and spins its cocoon of silk.

**silky** *adjective* (**silkier, silkiest**) as soft, fine, or smooth as silk. □ **silkily** *adverb*, **silkiness** *noun*

**sill** *noun* a strip of stone, wood, or metal at the base of a window or door.

**sillabub** alternative spelling of SYLLABUB.

**Sillitoe**, Alan (born 1928), British writer.

**silly** *adjective* (**sillier, silliest**) **1** lacking good sense, foolish, unwise. **2** feeble-minded. **3** (of a fieldsman's position in cricket) close to the batsman; *silly mid-on.* ●*noun* (*informal*) a foolish person. □ **silliness** *noun*

**silo** (sy-loh) *noun* (*plural* **silos**) **1** a pit or airtight structure in which green crops are pressed and undergo fermentation for use as fodder. **2** a pit or tower for storing grain, cement, or radioactive waste. **3** an underground place where a missile is kept ready for firing.

**silt** *noun* sediment deposited by water in a channel or harbour etc. ●*verb* (often foll. by *up*) block or become blocked with silt; *the harbour is silted up.*

**Silurian** (sy-**lewr**-iăn) *adjective Geol.* of the third period of the Palaeozoic era. ●*noun* this period.

**silvan** alternative spelling of SYLVAN.

**silver** *noun* **1** a chemical element (symbol Ag), a shiny white precious metal. **2** coins made of this or of an alloy resembling it. **3** silver dishes or ornaments; household cutlery of any metal. **4** a silver medal (awarded as second prize). **5** the colour of silver. ●*adjective* made of silver; coloured like silver. ●*verb* **1** coat or plate with silver. **2** give a silvery appearance to; become silvery; (of hair) turn grey or white. □ **born with a silver spoon in one's mouth** destined to be wealthy. **silver birch** a birch tree with silver-coloured bark. **silver-grey** *adjective & noun* very pale grey. **silver jubilee** the 25th anniversary of a sovereign's accession or other event. **silver lining** a consolation or hopeful prospect in the midst of misfortune. **silver paper** aluminium or tin foil. **silver-plated** *adjective* coated with silver. **silver sand** very fine sand used in gardening. **the silver screen** cinema films; the film industry. **silver wedding** the 25th anniversary of a wedding.

**silverfish** *noun* a small silvery wingless insect.

**silverside** *noun* a joint of beef cut from the haunch, below topside.

**silversmith** *noun* a person whose trade is making articles in silver.

**silverware** *noun* articles made of silver.

**silvery** *adjective* **1** like silver in colour or appearance. **2** having a clear gentle ringing sound.

**silviculture** *noun* (also **sylviculture**) the cultivation of forest trees.

**Simenon** (**seem**-ĕn-awn), Georges (1903–89), Belgian-French novelist, noted for his detective novels featuring Commissaire Maigret.

**simian** (**sim**-iăn) *adjective* monkey-like.

**similar** *adjective* **1** like, alike, resembling something but not the same. **2** of the same kind, nature, or amount. □ **similarly** *adverb*, **similarity** (sim-i-**la**-riti) *noun*

**simile** (**sim**-i-li) *noun* a figure of speech in which one thing is compared to another; e.g. *he's as fit as a fiddle*; *went through it like a hot knife through butter.*

**similitude** (sim-**il**-i-tewd) *noun* similarity.

**simmer** *verb* **1** keep (a pan or its contents) almost at boiling point; be kept like this; boil very gently. **2** be in a state of excitement or anger which is only just kept under control. □ **simmer down** become less excited or agitated.

**simnel cake** a rich cake (especially for Easter), covered with marzipan and decorated.

**Simon**, St (1st century AD), one of the twelve Apostles. Feast day (with St Jude), 28 October.

**simony** (**sy**-mŏn-i) *noun* the buying or selling of ecclesiastical privileges.

**simoom** (sim-**oom**) *noun* a hot dry dust-laden desert wind.

**simper** *verb* smile in an affected way. ●*noun* an affected smile.

**simple** *adjective* **1** understood or done easily; not difficult. **2** of one element or kind, not compound. **3** not elaborate, showy or luxurious; plain. **4** foolish; inexperienced. **5** feeble-minded. **6** of humble rank; *simple ordinary people.* □ **simple fracture** a fracture of a bone without a wound on the skin. **simple interest** interest paid only on the original capital, not on the interest added to it. Compare COMPOUND INTEREST.

**simpleton** *noun* a foolish or easily-deceived person; a halfwit.

**simplicity** *noun* being simple.

**simplify** *verb* (**simplified**, **simplifying**) make simple, make easy to do or understand. □ **simplification** *noun*

**simplistic** *adjective* made to appear too simple; ignoring significant issues.

**simply** *adverb* **1** in a simple manner. **2** absolutely, without doubt. **3** merely.

**Simpson**[1], Sir James Young (1811–71), Scottish surgeon and obstetrician, who discovered the usefulness of chloroform as an anaesthetic.

**Simpson**[2], Wallis (1896–1986), wife of the Duke of Windsor, formerly Edward VIII.

**simulate** *verb* **1** reproduce the conditions of (a situation), e.g. by means of a model, for study, testing, training etc. **2** pretend to have or feel. **3** imitate the form or condition of. □ **simulation** *noun*, **simulator** *noun*

**simulated** *adjective* (of furs, pearls, etc.) manufactured to look like natural products.

**simultaneous** (sim-ŭl-**tayn**-iŭs) *adjective* occurring or operating at the same time. □ **simultaneously** *adverb*, **simultaneity** (simŭl-tăn-**ay**-iti) *noun*

**sin**[1] *noun* **1** the breaking of a religious or moral law; an act which does this. **2** a serious fault or offence. **3** something contrary to common sense; *it's a sin to stay indoors on this fine day.* ●*verb* (**sinned**, **sinning**) commit a sin. □ **live in sin** (*old use*) cohabit without marrying. **sin bin** (*informal*) the penalty box in ice hockey.

**sin**² *abbreviation* sine.

**Sinai** (**sy**-ny *or* sy-ni-I) a peninsula, mostly desert, at the north end of the Red Sea, now part of Egypt.

**Sinatra** (sin-**ah**-trǎ), Frank (Francis Albert) (born 1915), American singer and film actor.

**since** *adverb, preposition, & conjunction* **1** after (a certain event or past time), between then and now. **2** ago, before now; *it happened long since.* **3** for the reason that; because; *since we have no money, we can't buy it.*

**sincere** *adjective* free from pretence or deceit; genuine, honest. □ **sincerely** *adverb*, **sincerity** (sin-**se**-ri-ti) *noun*

**sine** (*rhymes with* mine) *noun* (in a right-angled triangle) the ratio of the length of a side opposite one of the acute angles to the length of the hypotenuse.

**sinecure** (**sy**-ni-kewr) *noun* an official position that gives the holder profit or honour with no work attached.

**sine die** (**sy**-ni **dy**-i) indefinitely, with no appointed date; *the business was adjourned sine die.* (¶ Latin, = without a day.)

**sine qua non** (sin-ay kwah **nohn**) an indispensable condition or qualification. (¶ Latin, = without which not.)

**sinew** (**sin**-yoo) *noun* **1** tough fibrous tissue uniting muscle to bone. **2** a tendon. **3** (**sinews**) muscles; strength. □ **sinewy** *adjective*

**sinful** *adjective* full of sin, wicked. □ **sinfully** *adverb*, **sinfulness** *noun*

**sing** *verb* (**sang**, **sung**, **singing**) **1** make musical sounds with the voice, especially in a set tune. **2** perform (a song). **3** make a humming, buzzing, or whistling sound; *the kettle sings.* **4** (*slang*) turn informer. □ **sing the praises of** praise greatly. **sing out** call out loudly.

**Singapore** an island forming (with others) a country south of the Malay peninsula. □ **Singaporean** *adjective & noun*

**singe** (*pronounced* sinj) *verb* (**singed**, **singeing**) burn slightly; burn the ends or edges of. ●*noun* a slight burn.

**singer** *noun* a person who sings, especially as a professional.

**Singh**, V(ishwanath) P(ratap) (born 1931), Indian Prime Minister from 1990.

**Singhalese** alternative spelling of SINHALESE.

**single** *adjective* **1** one only, not double or multiple. **2** designed for one person or thing; *single beds.* **3** taken separately; *every single thing.* **4** unmarried. **5** (of a ticket) valid for a one-way journey only, not to return. **6** (of a flower) having only one circle of petals. ●*noun* **1** one person or thing, a single one. **2** a room etc. for one person. **3** a single ticket. **4** a pop record with one piece of music on each side. **5** a hit for one run in cricket. **6** (**singles**) a game with one player on each side. ●*verb* (foll. by *out*) choose or distinguish from others; *singled him out.* □ **single-breasted** *adjective* (of a coat) fastening but not overlapping widely across the breast. **single combat** a duel. **single cream** thin cream containing less fat than double cream. **single-decker** *noun* a bus with only one deck. **single figures** any number from 1 to 9 inclusive. **single file** a line of people one behind the other. **single-handed** *adjective* without help from others. **single market** an association of countries trading without restrictions, especially as a basis for the European Community. **single-minded** *adjective* with one's mind set on a single purpose. **single parent** a person bringing up a child or children alone. □ **singly** *adverb*

**singlet** *noun* a sleeveless vest.

**singleton** (**sing**-ěl-tǒn) *noun* something occurring singly, not as one of a group.

**Sing Sing** a New York State prison built in 1825–8, now called the Ossining Correctional Facility.

**singsong** *adjective* with a rise and fall of the voice in speaking. ●*noun* an informal singing of well-known songs by a group of people.

**singular** *noun* the form of a noun or verb used with reference to one person or thing; *the singular is 'man', the plural is 'men'.* ●*adjective* **1** of this form. **2** uncommon; extraordinary; *spoke with singular shrewdness.* □ **singularly** *adverb*, **singularity** (sing-yoo-la-riti) *noun*

**Sinhalese** (sin-hǎ-**leez**) *adjective* (also **Singhalese**) of Sri Lanka or its people or language. ●*noun* (*plural* **Sinhalese**) **1** a Sinhalese person. **2** the Sinhalese language.

**sinister** *adjective* **1** suggestive of evil. **2** involving wickedness, criminal; *sinister motives.*

**sink** *verb* (**sank**, **sunk** or (as *adjective*) **sunken**, **sinking**) **1** fall slowly downwards, come gradually to a lower level or pitch. **2** become wholly or partly submerged in water etc.; (of a ship) go to the bottom of the sea. **3** pass into a less active condition; *she sank into sleep.* **4** lose value or strength etc. gradually. **5** cause or allow to sink. **6** dig (a well) or bore (a shaft). **7** engrave (a die). **8** send (a ball) into a pocket or hole in billiards, golf, etc. **9** invest (money). **10** overlook or forget; *they decided to sink their differences.* ●*noun* **1** a fixed basin with a drainage pipe and water supply, in a kitchen etc. **2** a cesspool. □ **sink in** penetrate; become understood.

**sinking fund** a fund set aside for the purpose of wiping out a country's or business company's debt gradually.

**sinker** noun a weight used to sink a fishing-line or a line used in taking soundings.

**sinner** noun a person who sins.

**Sinn Fein** (shin-**fayn**) a nationalist political party in Ireland, linked to the IRA. (¶ Irish, = we ourselves.)

**Sino-** (sy-noh-) combining form Chinese and; Sino-Japanese; Sino-Tibetan.

**sinuous** (sin-yoo-ŭs) adjective with many curves, undulating. □ **sinuously** adverb, **sinuosity** noun

**sinus** (sy-nŭs) noun (plural **sinuses**) a cavity in bone or tissue, especially that in the skull connecting with the nostrils.

**sinusitis** (sy-nŭs-I-tiss) noun inflammation of a sinus.

**sip** verb (**sipped, sipping**) take a sip; drink in small mouthfuls. ● noun **1** the act of sipping. **2** a small mouthful of liquid.

**siphon** (sy-fŏn) noun **1** a pipe or tube in the form of an upside-down U, used for forcing liquid to flow from one container to another by utilizing atmospheric pressure. **2** a bottle from which aerated water is forced out through a tube by pressure of gas. ● verb (often foll. by off) **1** flow or draw out through a siphon. **2** divert, take, or set aside (funds, resources, etc.).

**sir** noun **1** a polite form of address to a man. **2** (**Sir**) a title prefixed to the name of a knight or baronet; Sir John Moore; Sir J. Moore; Sir John. ● verb address as sir; don't sir me.

**sire** noun **1** (old use) a father or male ancestor. **2** (old use) a title of respect, used to a king. **3** the male parent of an animal. ● verb (of an animal) be the sire of, beget.

**siren** noun **1** a device that makes a loud prolonged sound as a signal. **2** a dangerously fascinating woman. (¶ Named after the Sirens in Greek legend, women who lived on an island and by their singing lured seafarers to destruction on the rocks.)

**sirenian** (sy-**reen**-iǎn) noun a member of a group of large plant-eating animals that live in water, e.g. the dugong and the manatee. ● adjective of this group.

**Sirius** (si-ri-ŭs) the Dog Star, the brightest of the fixed stars, apparently following on the heels of the hunter Orion.

**sirloin** noun the upper (best) part of loin of beef.

**sirocco** (si-**rok**-oh) noun (also **scirocco**) (plural **siroccos**) a hot wind that reaches Italy from Africa.

**sirup** Amer. spelling of SYRUP.

**sis** noun (informal) sister.

**sisal** (sy-sǎl) noun **1** rope-fibre made from the leaves of a tropical plant. **2** the plant itself.

**siskin** noun a greenish songbird related to the goldfinch.

**sissy** noun (also **cissy**) (informal) an effeminate boy; a cowardly person. ● adjective effeminate; cowardly.

**sister** noun **1** a daughter of the same parents as another person. **2** a fellow woman; one who is a fellow member of a group or sect. **3** a nun; (**Sister**) the title of a nun. **4** a female hospital nurse in authority over others. □ **sister-in-law** noun (plural **sisters-in-law**) the sister of one's husband or wife; the wife of one's brother. **sister ship** a ship built in the same design as another. □ **sisterly** adjective

**sisterhood** noun **1** the relationship of sisters. **2** an order of nuns; a society of women doing religious or charitable work.

**Sistine Chapel** (sis-teen) a chapel in the Vatican, built by Sixtus IV (pope 1471–84), containing Michelangelo's painted ceiling and his fresco of the Last Judgement.

**Sisyphean** (sis-i-fee-ǎn) adjective (of toil) endless and fruitless. (¶ From SISYPHUS.)

**Sisyphus** (sis-i-fŭs) (Gk. myth.) a king of Corinth whose punishment in Hades for his misdeeds was to roll a large stone up a hill from which it continually rolled back.

**sit** verb (**sat, sitting**) **1** take or be in a position in which the body rests more or less upright on the buttocks; we were sitting gossiping. **2** cause to sit, place in a sitting position; sat him down. **3** pose for a portrait. **4** (of birds) perch. **5** (of birds) remain on the nest to hatch eggs. **6** be situated, lie. **7** be a candidate for; sit an examination. **8** occupy a seat as a member of a committee etc. **9** (of Parliament or a lawcourt or committee) be in session. **10** (of clothes) fit in a certain way; the coat sits badly on the shoulders. **11** babysit. □ **be sitting pretty** be in an advantageous situation. **sit back** relax one's efforts. **sit down** take a seat after standing. **sit-down** adjective (of a meal) taken seated. **sit-down strike** one in which strikers refuse to leave their place of work. **sit-in** noun occupation of a building etc. as a form of protest. **sit in on** be present as an observer at (a meeting etc.) **sit on** (informal) **1** delay action concerning; the Government has been sitting on the report. **2** (slang) repress or snub; he wants sitting on. **sit on the fence** avoid taking sides in a dispute. **sit out 1** take no part in (a dance etc.). **2** stay till the end of; had to sit the concert out. **sit tight** (informal) remain firmly where one is; take no action and not yield.

**sitar** (sit-ar *or* si-**tar**) *noun* an Indian musical instrument resembling a long-necked lute.

**sitcom** *noun* (*informal*) a situation comedy.

**site** *noun* **1** the ground on which a town or building stood, stands, or is to stand. **2** the place where some activity or event takes place or took place; *camping site*; *the site of the battle.* ●*verb* locate, provide with a site.

**Sitka** *noun* (in full **Sitka spruce**) a fast-growing spruce tree grown for its timber.

**sits vac** *abbreviation* situations vacant.

**sitter** *noun* **1** a person who is seated. **2** one who is sitting for a portrait. **3** a babysitter. **4** (*slang*) an easy catch or shot; something easy to do.

**sitting** *see* SIT. ●*adjective* (of an animal) not running; (of a game bird) not flying; *shot a sitting pheasant.* ●*noun* **1** a continuous period spent on one activity; *finished the book in one sitting.* **2** the time during which an assembly is engaged in business. **3** a session during which a meal is served. □ **sitting duck** *or* **target** a person or thing that is a helpless victim of attack. **sitting room** a room used for sitting in; a lounge. **sitting tenant** one already in occupation of rented accommodation.

**situate** *verb* place or put in a certain position.

**situation** *noun* **1** a place (with its surroundings) that is occupied by something. **2** a set of circumstances. **3** a position of employment. □ **situation comedy** a broadcast comedy in which humour derives from characters' misunderstandings and embarrassments in everyday situations.

**Sitwell**, Dame Edith (Louisa) (1887–1964), English poet and critic.

**Siva** (see-vă *or* shee-vă) (also **Shiva**) (in Hinduism) one of the major gods, usually depicted with a third eye in the middle of his forehead, wearing a crescent moon and a necklace of skulls.

**six** *adjective & noun* one more than five (6, VI). □ **at sixes and sevens** in disorder. **hit** *or* **knock for six** (*informal*) surprise or defeat utterly. **six-shooter** a revolver with six chambers.

**sixer** *noun* the leader of a group of six Brownies or Cub Scouts.

**sixfold** *adjective & adverb* **1** six times as much or as many. **2** consisting of six parts.

**sixpence** *noun* **1** the sum of 6p. **2** (*old use*) the sum of 6d.; a coin worth this.

**sixpenny** *adjective* costing sixpence.

**sixteen** *adjective & noun* one more than fifteen (16, XVI). □ **sixteenth** *adjective & noun*

**sixth** *adjective & noun* **1** next after fifth. **2** one of six equal parts of a thing. □ **sixth form** a form for pupils aged 16–18 in a secondary school. **sixth-form college** a college for pupils between 16 and 18 years of age.

**sixth sense** a supposed extra power of perception other than the five physical ones; intuition. □ **sixthly** *adverb*

**sixty** *adjective & noun* six times ten (60, LX). ●*plural noun* (**sixties**) the numbers, years, or degrees of temperature from 60 to 69. □ **sixtieth** *adjective & noun*

**sizable** alternative spelling of SIZEABLE.

**size¹** *noun* **1** the measurements or extent of something. **2** any of the standard measurements in which things are made and sold. ●*verb* group or sort according to size. □ **size up** estimate the size of; (*informal*) form a judgement of (a person or situation etc.). **the size of it** (*informal*) the way it is, the truth of the matter.

**size²** *noun* a gluey solution used to glaze paper, stiffen textiles, etc. ●*verb* treat with size.

**sizeable** *adjective* (also **sizable**) large or fairly large.

**sizzle** *verb* **1** make a hissing sound like that of frying. **2** (*informal*) be very hot; be angry or resentful.

**SJ** *abbreviation* Society of Jesus.

**ska** *noun* a type of fast pop music, originally from Jamaica.

**skate¹** *noun* (*plural* **skate** *or* **skates**) a large flat sea fish used as food.

**skate²** *noun* **1** an ice-skate. **2** a roller skate. ●*verb* glide over ice or a hard surface wearing skates; perform (a specified figure) in this way. □ **get one's skates on** (*slang*) make haste. **skate over a subject** make only a passing reference to it. □ **skater** *noun*

**skateboard** *noun* a small board with wheels like those of roller skates, for riding on while standing. □ **skateboarding** *noun*, **skateboarder** *noun*

**skating-rink** *noun* a stretch of artificial ice used for skating; a smooth floor used for roller skating.

**skedaddle** *verb* (*slang*) go away quickly.

**skein** (*pronounced* skayn) *noun* **1** a loosely-coiled bundle of yarn or thread. **2** a number of wild geese etc. in flight.

**skeletal** (skel-i-t'l) *adjective* of or like a skeleton.

**skeleton** *noun* **1** the framework of bones supporting an animal body. **2** the shell or other hard structure covering or supporting an invertebrate animal. **3** a very lean person or animal. **4** any supporting structure or framework, e.g. of a building. **5** an outline of a literary work etc. ●*adjective* reduced to a minimum; *a skeleton crew*; *a skeleton staff.* □ **skeleton in the cupboard** a discreditable secret. **skeleton key** a key made so as to fit many locks.

**skeptic, skeptical** Amer. spelling of SCEPTIC, SCEPTICAL.

**skerry** *noun* (*Scottish*) a rocky island; a reef.

**sketch** noun **1** a rough drawing or painting. **2** a brief account of something. **3** a short usually comic play. ●verb make a sketch or sketches; make a sketch of. □ **sketch-book** noun a pad of drawing-paper for sketching on. **sketch-map** noun a roughly-drawn map.

**sketchy** adjective (**sketchier, sketchiest**) rough and not detailed or careful. □ **sketchily** adverb, **sketchiness** noun

**skew** adjective slanting, askew. ●verb make skew, turn or twist round. □ **on the skew** askew.

**skewbald** adjective (of an animal) with irregular patches of white and another colour (strictly, not including black; compare PIEBALD).

**skewer** noun a pin thrust through meat to hold it together while it is cooked. ●verb pierce or hold in place with a skewer or other pointed object.

**ski** (pronounced skee) noun (plural **skis**) one of a pair of long narrow strips of wood etc. fixed under the feet for travelling over snow. ●verb (**ski'd** or **skied, skiing**) travel on skis. □ **ski-jump** noun a steep snow-covered slope levelling off before a sharp drop to allow skiers to leap through the air. **ski-lift** noun a device for carrying skiers up a slope, usually on seats slung from an overhead cable. **ski pants** stretch trousers with straps under the feet. **ski run** a slope suitable for skiing down as a sport. □ **skier** noun

**skid** verb (**skidded, skidding**) (of a vehicle or its wheels) slide on slippery ground. ●noun **1** a skidding movement. **2** a log or plank etc. used to make a track over which heavy objects may be dragged or rolled. **3** a runner on a helicopter, for use when landing. **4** a wedge or a wooden or metal shoe that acts as a braking device on the wheel of a cart. □ **on the skids** (informal) about to be discarded or defeated. **put the skids under** (slang) cause to hurry; hasten the downfall of. **skid-pan** noun a slippery surface used for practice in controlling skidding vehicles. **skid row** (Amer.) a slum area where vagrants live.

**skiff** noun a small light boat for rowing or sculling.

**skilful** adjective (Amer. **skillful**) having or showing great skill. □ **skilfully** adverb

**skill** noun ability to do something well.

**skilled** adjective **1** skilful. **2** (of work) needing great skill; (of a worker) highly trained or experienced in such work.

**skillet** noun **1** a metal cooking pot with a long handle. **2** (Amer.) a frying-pan.

**skillful** Amer. spelling of SKILFUL.

**skim** verb (**skimmed, skimming**) **1** take (floating matter) from the surface of a li-
quid; clear (a liquid) in this way. **2** move or throw lightly and quickly over a surface; glide through air. **3** read quickly, noting only the chief points; skim through a newspaper. □ **skim milk** (also **skimmed milk**) milk from which the cream has been removed.

**skimp** verb supply, use, or do less than is needed.

**skimpy** adjective (**skimpier, skimpiest**) scanty, meagre, insufficient. □ **skimpily** adverb, **skimpiness** noun

**skin** noun **1** the flexible covering of the body. **2** an animal's skin removed from its body, with or without the hair still attached. **3** a vessel for water or wine, made from an animal's whole skin. **4** a person's complexion. **5** an outer layer or covering. **6** the film that forms on the surface of certain liquids. ●verb (**skinned, skinning**) strip or scrape the skin from. □ **by the skin of one's teeth** only just, barely. **get under a person's skin** (informal) interest or annoy him or her greatly. **save one's skin** avoid injury or loss. **skin-deep** adjective superficial. **skin-diver** noun one who engages in **skin-diving**, the sport of swimming deep under water with flippers and breathing apparatus.

**skinflint** noun a miserly person.

**skinful** noun (informal) enough alcohol to make a person very drunk.

**skinhead** noun a youth with close-cropped hair.

**skinny** adjective (**skinnier, skinniest**) (of a person or animal) very thin. □ **skinny-dipping** noun (informal) swimming naked. □ **skinniness** noun

**skint** adjective (slang) having no money left.

**skintight** adjective (of clothing) very close-fitting.

**skip¹** verb (**skipped, skipping**) **1** move along lightly, especially by taking two steps with each foot in turn. **2** jump with a skipping-rope. **3** pass quickly from one subject or point to another. **4** omit in reading or dealing with a thing. **5** (slang) go away hastily or secretly. ●noun a skipping movement.

**skip²** noun **1** a cage or bucket in which people or materials are raised and lowered in mines and quarries. **2** a large metal container for holding and carrying away builders' rubbish etc.

**skipper** noun the captain of a ship, aircraft, or sports team. ●verb captain.

**skipping-rope** noun a length of rope, turned over the head and under the feet as a person jumps.

**skirl** noun the shrill sound characteristic of bagpipes. ●verb make this sound.

**skirmish** *noun* a minor fight or conflict. ● *verb* take part in a skirmish.

**skirt** *noun* **1** a woman's garment hanging from the waist; this part of a garment. **2** the flap of a saddle. **3** the hanging part round the base of a hovercraft. **4** a cut of beef from the lower flank. ● *verb* (often foll. by *around*) **1** go or be situated along the edge of. **2** avoid dealing directly with (an issue etc.). □ **bit of skirt** (*offensive slang*) a woman.

**skirting** *noun* (also **skirting-board**) a narrow board round the wall of a room, close to the floor.

**skit** *noun* a short play or piece of writing that is a humorous imitation of a serious one; a piece of humorous mimicry.

**skittish** *adjective* frisky. □ **skittishly** *adverb*, **skittishness** *noun*

**skittle** *noun* **1** (**skittles**) a game of trying to knock down a group of wooden pins by rolling a ball at them. **2** a pin used in this game.

**skive** *verb* (often foll. by *off*) (*slang*) dodge a duty; play truant. □ **skiver** *noun*

**skivvy** *noun* (*informal*) a lowly female servant. ● *verb* work as a skivvy.

**Skryabin** alternative spelling of SCRIABIN.

**skua** (skew-ä) *noun* a predatory seabird like a large gull.

**skulduggery** *noun* (*informal*) trickery.

**skulk** *verb* loiter or move stealthily; lurk, hide.

**skull** *noun* the bony framework of the head; the part of this protecting the brain. □ **skull and cross-bones** a picture of a skull with two thigh-bones crossed below it as an emblem of death or piracy.

**skullcap** *noun* a small close-fitting cap with no peak, for the crown of the head.

**skunk** *noun* **1** a black bushy-tailed American animal about the size of a cat, able to spray an evil-smelling liquid from glands near its tail. **2** (*informal*) a contemptible person.

**sky** *noun* the region of the clouds or upper air. ● *verb* (**skied, skying**) hit (a ball) to a great height. □ **sky blue** *adjective & noun* bright clear blue. **sky-high** *adjective & adverb* very high. **sky-rocket** (*noun*) a rocket that rises high into the air before exploding; (*verb*) rise sharply.

**skydiving** *noun* the sport of performing acrobatic movements in the sky before opening a parachute. □ **skydiver** *noun*

**Skye** the largest island of the Inner Hebrides in NW Scotland.

**skyjack** *verb* (*slang*) hijack (an aircraft).

**skylark** *noun* a lark that soars while singing. ● *verb* play about light-heartedly.

**skylight** *noun* a window in a roof or ceiling.

**skyline** *noun* the outline of hills, buildings, etc. seen against the sky.

**skyscraper** *noun* a very tall building.

**skyward** *adverb* (also **skywards**) towards the sky. ● *adjective* moving skyward.

**slab** *noun* a flat broad fairly thick piece of something solid.

**slack**[1] *adjective* **1** loose, not tight or tense. **2** slow, sluggish; negligent. **3** (of trade or business) with little happening; not busy. ● *noun* the slack part of a rope etc.; *haul in the slack*. ● *verb* **1** slacken. **2** be idle or lazy about work. □ **slackly** *adverb*, **slackness** *noun*

**slack**[2] *noun* coal-dust or very small pieces of coal.

**slacken** *verb* make or become slack.

**slacker** *noun* a lazy person; a shirker.

**slacks** *plural noun* informal trousers.

**slag** *noun* **1** solid non-metallic waste matter left when metal has been separated from ore by smelting. **2** (*slang*) an immoral woman; a prostitute. □ **slag-heap** *noun* a mound of waste matter from a mine etc.

**slain** *see* SLAY.

**slake** *verb* **1** satisfy or make less strong; *slake one's thirst*. **2** combine (lime) chemically with water.

**slalom** (slah-lŏm) *noun* **1** a ski race down a zigzag course. **2** an obstacle race in canoes.

**slam** *verb* (**slammed, slamming**) **1** shut forcefully with a loud noise. **2** put, knock, or hit forcefully. **3** (*slang*) criticize severely. ● *noun* **1** a slamming noise. **2** the winning of 12 or 13 tricks in the game of bridge. □ **grand slam** the winning of all 13 tricks in the game of bridge; the winning of all of a group of championships in tennis or golf etc.

**slander** *noun* **1** a false statement uttered maliciously that damages a person's reputation. **2** the crime of uttering this. ● *verb* utter a slander about. □ **slanderous** *adjective*, **slanderously** *adverb*

**slang** *noun* words, phrases, or particular meanings of these, that are used very informally, often by a specific class or profession, and are not regarded as standard. ● *verb* use abusive language to. □ **slanging match** a prolonged exchange of insults. □ **slangy** *adjective*

**slant** *verb* **1** slope. **2** present (news etc.) from a particular point of view. ● *noun* **1** a slope. **2** the way something is presented, an attitude or bias.

**slantwise** *adverb* in a slanting position.

**slap** *verb* (**slapped, slapping**) **1** strike with the open hand or with something flat. **2** lay forcefully; *slapped the money on the counter*. **3** place hastily or carelessly; *slapped paint on the walls*. ● *noun* a blow with the open hand or with something flat. ● *adverb* with a slap; directly; *ran slap into him*. □ **slap and tickle** light-hearted sexual play. **slap**

**down** snub or reprimand. **slap-happy** adjective (informal) cheerfully casual or irresponsible. **slap-up** adjective (informal) first-class, lavish; a slap-up meal.

**slapdash** adjective hasty and careless. ●adverb in a slapdash way.

**slapstick** noun boisterous comedy based on actions rather than words.

**slash** verb 1 make a sweeping stroke with a sword, knife, etc.; cut or gash in this way. 2 reduce (prices etc.) drastically. 3 criticize vigorously. ●noun a slashing cut; a wound made by this.

**slat** noun one of the thin narrow strips of wood, metal, or plastic overlapping to form a screen, e.g. in a Venetian blind.

**slate** noun 1 a kind of rock that is easily split into flat smooth plates. 2 a piece of this used as roofing-material or (formerly) for writing on. 3 the bluish-grey colour of slate. 4 a list of nominees for office etc. ●verb 1 cover or roof with slates. 2 (informal) criticize severely, scold. □ **a clean slate** a record of good conduct with nothing discreditable. **on the slate** (informal) recorded as a debt; on credit. □ **slaty** adjective

**slattern** noun a slovenly woman. □ **slatternly** adjective

**slaughter** noun 1 the killing of animals for food. 2 the ruthless killing of a great number of people or animals; a massacre. ●verb 1 kill (animals) for food. 2 kill ruthlessly or in great numbers. 3 (informal) defeat utterly. □ **slaughterer** noun

**slaughterhouse** noun a place where animals are killed for food.

**Slav** noun a member of any of the peoples of East and Central Europe who speak a Slavonic language.

**slave** noun 1 a person who is the property of another and obliged to work for him or her. 2 one who is dominated by another person or by an influence; a slave to duty. 3 a mechanism directly controlled by another mechanism. ●verb work very hard. □ **slave-driver** noun a person who makes others work very hard. **slave labour** forced labour. **slave trade** the procuring, transporting, and selling of slaves, especially (formerly) African Blacks.

**slaver**[1] noun a ship or person engaged in the slave-trade.

**slaver**[2] (slav-er) verb 1 have saliva flowing from the mouth. 2 (foll. by over) drool over. ●noun 1 dribbling saliva. 2 drivel.

**slavery** noun 1 the condition of a slave. 2 the practice of having slaves; to abolish slavery. 3 very hard work, drudgery.

**Slavic** adjective & noun = SLAVONIC.

**slavish** adjective 1 like a slave, excessively submissive. 2 showing no independence or

originality. □ **slavishly** adverb, **slavishness** noun

**Slavonic** (slă-von-ik) adjective of the group of languages including Russian and Polish. ●noun this group of languages.

**slay** verb (**slew**, **slain**, **slaying**) (literary) kill.

**sleazy** adjective (**sleazier**, **sleaziest**) (informal) dirty and slovenly; squalid. □ **sleaziness** noun

**sled** noun (Amer.) a sports sledge.

**sledge** noun a narrow cart with runners, used for travelling on snow. □ **sledging** noun

**sledgehammer** noun a large heavy hammer used with both hands.

**sleek** adjective 1 smooth and glossy; sleek hair. 2 looking well-fed and thriving. ●verb make sleek by smoothing. □ **sleekly** adverb, **sleekness** noun

**sleep** noun 1 the natural recurring condition of rest in animals, with the eyes closed and muscles relaxed. 2 a spell of this; a long sleep. 3 the inert condition of hibernating animals. ●verb (**slept**, **sleeping**) 1 be in a state of sleep. 2 stay somewhere for a night's sleep. 3 provide with sleeping accommodation; the cottage sleeps four. □ **sleep around** (informal) be sexually promiscuous. **sleep in** sleep late. **sleeping bag** a padded bag for sleeping in, especially while camping. **sleeping car** or **sleeping carriage** a railway coach fitted with berths or beds. **sleeping partner** a partner in a business firm who does not take part in its actual work. **sleeping pill** a pill to help a person to sleep. **sleeping policeman** a ramp in the road to make traffic slow down. **sleeping sickness** a tropical disease with symptoms that include extreme sleepiness, spread by the bite of the tsetse fly. **sleep on it** delay deciding about something until the next day. **sleep with** have sexual intercourse with.

**sleeper** noun 1 one who sleeps. 2 each of the beams on which the rails of a railway etc. rest. 3 a sleeping car; a berth in this. 4 a ring worn in a pierced ear to keep the hole from closing.

**sleepless** adjective unable to sleep; without sleep. □ **sleeplessly** adverb, **sleeplessness** noun

**sleepwalk** verb walk about while asleep. □ **sleepwalker** noun

**sleepy** adjective (**sleepier**, **sleepiest**) 1 feeling or showing a desire to sleep. 2 inactive, without stir or bustle; a sleepy little town. □ **sleepily** adverb, **sleepiness** noun

**sleepyhead** noun a sleepy person.

**sleet** noun snow and rain falling at the same time; hail or snow that melts while falling.

● *verb* send down sleet; *it is sleeting.* □ **sleety** *adjective*

**sleeve** *noun* **1** the part of a garment covering the arm. **2** a tube enclosing a rod or another tube. **3** the cover of a gramophone record. □ **up one's sleeve** concealed but available for use; in reserve. □ **sleeved** *adjective*

**sleeveless** *adjective* without sleeves.

**sleigh** (*pronounced* slay) *noun* a sledge, especially a passenger vehicle drawn by horses.

**sleight of hand** (*rhymes with* bite) great skill in using the hands to perform conjuring tricks etc.

**slender** *adjective* **1** slim and graceful. **2** small in amount, scanty; *slender means.*

**slept** *see* SLEEP.

**sleuth** (*pronounced* slooth) *noun* (*informal*) a detective.

**slew**[1] *verb* (also **slue**) turn or swing round.

**slew**[2] *see* SLAY.

**slice** *noun* **1** a piece cut from something. **2** a portion or share. **3** an implement with a thin broad blade for lifting or serving fish etc. **4** a slicing stroke in golf, tennis, etc. ● *verb* **1** cut into slices. **2** cut from a larger piece. **3** cut cleanly or easily. **4** strike (a ball) so that it spins away or travels at an angle. □ **slicer** *noun*

**slick** *adjective* **1** done or doing things smoothly and cleverly but perhaps with some trickery. **2** smooth in manner or speech. **3** smooth and slippery. ● *noun* a slippery place; a thick patch of oil floating on the sea. ● *verb* make sleek or smart.

**slicker** *noun* (*Amer. informal*) a stylish city-dweller with a smooth but deceptive manner.

**slide** *verb* (**slid**, **sliding**) **1** move or cause to move along a smooth surface with the same area in continuous contact with this. **2** move or cause to move quietly or unobtrusively; *slid a coin into his hand.* **3** pass gradually into a condition or habit. ● *noun* **1** the act of sliding. **2** a smooth surface for sliding on. **3** a chute for goods etc. or for children to play on. **4** a sliding part of a machine or instrument. **5** a small glass plate on which things are placed for examination under a microscope. **6** a mounted picture or transparency for showing on a blank surface by means of a projector. **7** a hair-slide. □ **slide-rule** *noun* a ruler with a sliding central strip, marked with logarithmic scales and used for making calculations. **sliding scale** a scale of fees, taxes, wages, etc. that varies in accordance with the variation of some standard.

**slight** *adjective* **1** not much, not great; not thorough. **2** (**the slightest**) any whatever; *if there were the slightest chance.* **3** slender,

not heavily built. ● *verb* treat or speak of (a person etc.) as not worth one's attention; insult by lack of respect or courtesy. ● *noun* an insult given in this way. □ **slightly** *adverb*, **slightness** *noun*

**slim** *adjective* (**slimmer**, **slimmest**) **1** of small girth or thickness, not heavily built. **2** small, insufficient; *only a slim chance of success.* ● *verb* (**slimmed**, **slimming**) **1** make oneself slimmer by dieting, exercise, etc. **2** reduce in numbers or scale; *slim down the workforce.* □ **slimly** *adverb*, **slimness** *noun*, **slimmer** *noun*

**slime** *noun* a slippery thick mud or liquid substance.

**slimline** *adjective* of slender design.

**slimy** *adjective* (**slimier**, **slimiest**) **1** like slime; covered or smeared with slime. **2** disgustingly dishonest, meek, or flattering. □ **slimily** *adverb*, **sliminess** *noun*

**sling**[1] *noun* **1** a belt, strap, etc. looped round an object to support or lift it. **2** a bandage looped round the neck to form a support for an injured arm. **3** a looped strap used to throw a stone or other missile. ● *verb* (**slung**, **slinging**) **1** suspend or lift with a sling. **2** hurl (a stone) with a sling. **3** (*informal*) throw. □ **sling-back** *adjective* (of a shoe) with a strap round the back of the foot. **sling one's hook** (*slang*) run away.

**sling**[2] *noun* a sweetened drink of gin or other spirits and water.

**slink** *verb* (**slunk**, **slinking**) move in a stealthy, guilty, or shamefaced way.

**slinky** *adjective* **1** moving in a slinking way. **2** smooth and sinuous. **3** (of clothes) close-fitting.

**slip**[1] *verb* (**slipped**, **slipping**) **1** slide accidentally; lose one's balance in this way. **2** go, put, or be put with a smooth movement, especially without being observed. **3** detach or release. **4** escape; become detached from; *the ship slipped her moorings*; *it slipped my memory.* ● *noun* **1** the act of slipping. **2** a mistake. **3** a loose covering or garment; a petticoat; a pillow-case. **4** a slipway. **5** a fieldsman in cricket stationed on the off side just behind the wicket; this position; (**the slips**) this part of the field. □ **give a person the slip** escape; avoid him or her skilfully. **let slip 1** release accidentally or deliberately. **2** miss (an opportunity). **3** reveal (news etc.) unintentionally or thoughtlessly. **slip a stitch** (in knitting) transfer it to the other needle without looping the yarn through it. **slip-knot** *noun* a knot that can slide easily or be undone by pulling. **slip of the pen** *or* **tongue** a small mistake in what is written or said. **slip-on** *adjective* (of clothes) easily slipped on, usually without fastenings. **slipped disc** a displaced disc between vertebrae, causing back pain. **slip-road** noun a road for entering or leaving a motorway or other main road. **slip up** (informal) make a mistake. **slip-up** noun (informal) a mistake.

**slip²** noun **1** a small piece of paper. **2** a cutting taken from a plant for grafting or planting. □ **a slip of a girl** a small slim girl.

**slip³** noun a thin liquid containing fine clay and water, used for decorating pottery.

**slipper** noun a light loose comfortable shoe for indoor wear.

**slippery** adjective **1** smooth and difficult to hold; causing slipping by its wetness or smoothness. **2** (of a person) not to be trusted; a slippery customer. □ **slipperiness** noun

**slippy** adjective (informal) slippery. □ **look slippy** (informal) make haste.

**slipshod** adjective careless; badly done or arranged.

**slipstream** noun a current of air driven backward by a vehicle moving forward.

**slipway** noun a sloping structure used as a landing-stage or on which ships are built or repaired.

**slit** noun a narrow straight cut or opening. ●verb (**slit, slitting**) **1** cut a slit in. **2** cut into strips.

**slither** verb (informal) slide unsteadily. □ **slithery** adjective

**sliver** (sliv-er) noun a thin strip cut or split from wood or glass etc.

**Sloane**, Sir Hans (1660–1753), English physician and naturalist, whose collections formed the basis of the Natural History Museum in South Kensington, London.

**Sloane Ranger** (also **Sloane**) a fashionable upper-class conventional young person. (¶ Named after Sloane Square in London and the Lone Ranger, hero of Western stories and films.)

**slob** noun (slang, scornful) a lazy, untidy person.

**slobber** verb **1** slaver or dribble. **2** (foll. by over) behave with repulsively excessive affection. ●noun slaver.

**sloe** (rhymes with go) noun blackthorn; its small bluish-black plum-like fruit. □ **sloe-eyed** adjective with eyes of this colour. **sloe gin** a liqueur of gin in which sloes have been steeped.

**slog** verb (**slogged, slogging**) **1** hit hard. **2** work or walk hard and steadily. ●noun **1** a hard hit. **2** a spell of hard steady work or walking.

**slogan** noun a word or phrase adopted as a motto; a short catchy phrase used in advertising.

**sloop** noun a sailing ship with one mast.

**slop** verb (**slopped, slopping**) **1** spill over or cause to spill; splash liquid on. **2** plod clumsily, especially through mud or puddles etc. ●noun **1** (also **slops**) weak unappetizing drink or liquid food. **2** a quantity of slopped liquid. **3** (**slops**) household liquid refuse; dregs from teacups. □ **slop out** (in prison) remove slops, urine, etc. in buckets from cells which have no sanitation.

**slope** verb lie, turn, or place at an angle from the horizontal or vertical. ●noun **1** a sloping surface or direction; a stretch of rising or falling ground. **2** the amount by which something slopes. □ **slope off** (slang) go away.

**sloppy** adjective (**sloppier, sloppiest**) **1** having a liquid consistency that splashes easily; excessively liquid. **2** careless, untidy. **3** weakly sentimental. □ **sloppily** adverb, **sloppiness** noun

**slosh** verb **1** (slang) hit; sloshed him on the chin. **2** pour (liquid) clumsily. **3** splash; move with a splashing sound. ●noun **1** (slang) a blow. **2** a splashing sound. **3** slush.

**sloshed** adjective (slang) drunk.

**slot** noun **1** a narrow opening through which something is to be put. **2** a groove, channel, or slit into which something fits. **3** a position in a series or scheme; the programme has its regular slot. ●verb (**slotted, slotting**) **1** make a slot or slots in. **2** put into a slot. □ **slot machine** a machine operated by a coin put in a slot.

**sloth** (rhymes with both) noun **1** laziness. **2** a slow-moving animal of tropical America that lives in trees.

**slothful** adjective lazy. □ **slothfully** adverb

**slouch** verb stand, sit, or move in a lazy awkward way, not with an upright posture. ●noun a slouching movement or posture. □ **slouch hat** a hat with a wide flexible brim.

**slough¹** (rhymes with cow) noun a swamp or marshy place. □ **Slough of Despond** a state of hopeless depression.

**slough²** (pronounced sluf) verb shed; a snake sloughs its skin periodically. ●noun a snake's cast skin; dead tissue that drops away.

**Slovak** (sloh-vak) noun a native or the language of the Slovak Republic. ●adjective of the Slovaks or their language. □ **Slovak Republic** the eastern of the two republics into which the former Czechoslovakia is divided.

**sloven** (sluv-ĕn) noun a slovenly person.

**Slovenia** (slŏ-veen-iă) a republic of former Yugoslavia. □ **Slovenian** adjective & noun

**slovenly** (sluv-ĕn-li) adjective careless and untidy; not methodical. □ **slovenliness** noun

**slow** adjective **1** not quick or fast. **2** (of a clock) showing a time earlier than the correct one. **3** (of a person) not able to understand or learn easily. **4** lacking liveliness, sluggish; *business is slow today*. **5** (of photographic film) not very sensitive to light; (of a lens) having only a small aperture, needing a long exposure. **6** tending to cause slowness. ●*adverb* slowly; *go slow*. ●*verb* reduce the speed of, go more slowly; *slow down*. □ **slow motion** (of a film) making movements appear to be performed much more slowly than in real life. **slow-worm** noun a small European lizard with no legs. □ **slowish** adjective, **slowly** adverb, **slowness** noun

**slowcoach** noun a person who is slow in actions or work.

**sludge** noun thick greasy mud; something resembling this.

**slue** alternative spelling of SLEW[1].

**slug[1]** noun **1** a small slimy animal like a snail without a shell. **2** a roundish lump of metal; a bullet of irregular shape; a pellet for firing from an airgun.

**slug[2]** verb (**slugged, slugging**) strike with a hard heavy blow. ●*noun* a blow of this kind.

**sluggard** noun a slow or lazy person.

**sluggish** adjective slow-moving; not alert or lively. □ **sluggishly** adverb, **sluggishness** noun

**sluice** (*pronounced* slooss) noun **1** a sliding gate for controlling the volume or flow of water in a stream etc. **2** the water controlled by this. **3** a channel carrying off water. **4** a place where objects are rinsed. **5** the act of rinsing. ●*verb* **1** let out (water) by means of a sluice. **2** flood, scour, or rinse with a flow of water.

**slum** noun an overcrowded, run-down district with buildings of poor quality. ●*verb* (**slummed, slumming**) visit slums, especially out of curiosity. □ **slum it** (*informal*) put up with uncomfortable conditions for a short period. □ **slummy** adjective

**slumber** (*poetic*) noun sleep. ●*verb* sleep.

**slump** noun a sudden great fall in prices or in the demand for goods etc. ●*verb* **1** undergo a slump. **2** sit or flop down heavily and slackly.

**slung** see SLING[1].

**slunk** see SLINK.

**slur** verb (**slurred, slurring**) **1** write or pronounce indistinctly with each letter or sound running into the next. **2** mark (notes) with a slur in music; perform in the way indicated by this. **3** pass lightly over (a fact etc.). **4** (*Amer.*) speak ill of. ●*noun* **1** a slurred letter or sound. **2** a curved line placed over notes in music to show that they are to be sung to one syllable or played smoothly without a break. **3** discredit; *a slur on his reputation*.

**slurp** (*informal*) verb make a noisy sucking sound in eating or drinking. ●*noun* this sound.

**slurry** (*rhymes with* hurry) noun thin mud; thin liquid cement; liquid manure.

**slush** noun **1** partly melted snow on the ground. **2** silly sentimental talk or writing. □ **slush fund** a fund of money for corrupt purposes such as bribing officials. □ **slushy** adjective

**slut** noun a slovenly or promiscuous woman. □ **sluttish** adjective

**sly** adjective (**slyer, slyest**) **1** done or doing things in an unpleasantly cunning and secret way. **2** mischievous and knowing; *with a sly smile*. □ **on the sly** secretly. □ **slyly** adverb, **slyness** noun

**Sm** symbol samarium.

**smack[1]** noun **1** a slap. **2** a hard hit. **3** a loud kiss. ●*verb* slap, hit hard. ●*adverb* (*informal*) with a smack, directly; *went smack through the window*. □ **smack one's lips** close and then part them noisily in enjoyment.

**smack[2]** noun a slight flavour or trace of something. ●*verb* have a slight flavour or trace of something; *his manner smacks of conceit*.

**smack[3]** noun a boat with a single mast used for coasting or fishing.

**smack[4]** noun (*slang*) a hard drug, especially heroin.

**smacker** noun (*slang*) **1** a loud kiss; a sounding blow. **2** £1; (*Amer.*) a dollar.

**small** adjective **1** not large or big. **2** not great in size, importance, number, etc. **3** of the smaller kind; *the small intestine*. **4** doing things on a small scale; *a small farmer*. **5** petty. ●*noun* **1** the most slender part of something. **2** (**smalls**) small articles of laundry, especially underwear. ●*adverb* in a small size or way; into small pieces; *chop it small*. □ **look** or **feel small** be humiliated. **small beer** something trivial. **small change** coins as opposed to notes. **small fry** unimportant people; children. **small hours** the hours soon after midnight. **small-minded** adjective narrow or selfish in outlook. **small of the back** the part at the back of the waist. **small print** matter printed in small type; limitations (in a contract etc.) stated inconspicuously in this way. **small talk** social conversation on unimportant subjects. **small-time** adjective unimportant, minor; *small-time crooks*. □ **smallness** noun

**smallholder** noun the owner or tenant of a smallholding.

**smallholding** noun an agricultural holding smaller than a farm.

**smallpox** *noun* a contagious disease (now eliminated) caused by a virus, with pustules that often left disfiguring scars.

**smarm** *verb* (*informal*) **1** (often foll. by *down*) smooth flat, plaster down (hair) with grease. **2** flatter obsequiously.

**smarmy** *adjective* (*informal*) trying to win favour by flattery or excessive politeness. □ **smarmily** *adverb*, **smarminess** *noun*

**smart** *adjective* **1** forceful, brisk; *a smart pace*. **2** clever, ingenious. **3** neat and elegant. **4** (of a device) capable of some independent and seemingly intelligent action (e.g. through having a built-in microprocessor); *a smart card*. ●*verb* feel a stinging pain (bodily or mental). ●*noun* a stinging pain. □ **smart alec** (also **smart aleck**) (*informal*) a know-all. **smart money** money invested by people with expert knowledge. □ **smartly** *adverb*, **smartness** *noun*

**smarten** *verb* make or become smarter.

**smash** *verb* **1** break or become broken suddenly and noisily into pieces. **2** strike or move with great force; crash. **3** strike (a ball) forcefully downwards in tennis etc. **4** overthrow or destroy; *police smashed the drug ring*. ●*noun* **1** the act or sound of smashing. **2** a collision. □ **smash-and-grab raid** a robbery done by smashing a shop window and grabbing goods. **smash hit** (*slang*) an extremely successful play, song, etc. **smash-up** *noun* a violent collision.

**smasher** *noun* (*informal*) an excellent person or thing.

**smashing** *adjective* (*informal*) excellent.

**smattering** *noun* a slight superficial knowledge of a language or subject.

**smear** *verb* **1** spread with a greasy, sticky, or dirty substance. **2** try to damage the reputation of. ●*noun* **1** something smeared on a surface; a mark made by this. **2** a specimen of material smeared on a microscope slide for examination. **3** an attempt to damage a reputation; *a smear campaign*. □ **smear test** = CERVICAL SMEAR.

**smeary** *adjective* **1** smeared. **2** tending to smear things.

**smell** *noun* **1** the faculty of perceiving things by the sense organs of the nose. **2** the quality that is perceived in this way. **3** an unpleasant quality of this kind. **4** an act of smelling something. ●*verb* (**smelt**, **smelling**) **1** perceive the smell of; detect or test by one's sense of smell. **2** give off a smell. **3** give off an unpleasant smell. □ **smelling salts** a strong-smelling substance sniffed to relieve faintness.

**smelly** *adjective* (**smellier**, **smelliest**) having a strong or unpleasant smell.

**smelt¹** *see* SMELL.

**smelt²** *verb* heat and melt (ore) so as to obtain the metal it contains; obtain (metal) in this way.

**smelt³** *noun* (*plural* **smelt** or **smelts**) a small silvery fish related to salmon.

**Smetana** (smet-ăn-ă) Bedřich (1824–84), Czech (Bohemian) composer.

**smidgen** *noun* (also **smidgin**) (*informal*) a very small amount.

**smile** *noun* a facial expression indicating pleasure or amusement with the corners of the mouth turned up. ●*verb* **1** give a smile; express by smiling. **2** look bright or favourable; *fortune smiled on us*.

**smirch** *verb* **1** smear or soil. **2** bring discredit upon (a reputation). ●*noun* a smear; discredit.

**smirk** *noun* a self-satisfied smile. ●*verb* give a smirk.

**smite** *verb* (**smote, smitten, smiting**) **1** hit hard. **2** have a sudden effect on; *his conscience smote him*.

**Smith¹**, Adam (1723–90), Scottish philosopher and economist.

**Smith²**, Bessie (1895–1937), American blues singer.

**Smith³**, Ian Douglas (born 1919), Rhodesian statesman, Prime Minister 1964–79, who unilaterally declared independence from Britain in 1965.

**Smith⁴**, John (1938–94), British politician, leader of the Labour Party 1992–4.

**Smith⁵**, Joseph (1805–44), American founder of the Mormon sect.

**Smith⁶**, Dame Maggie (born 1934), British actress.

**Smith⁷**, William (1769–1839), English surveyor, one of the founders of stratigraphical geology.

**smith** *noun* **1** a person who makes things in metal. **2** a blacksmith.

**smithereens** *plural noun* small fragments.

**Smithsonian Institution** the oldest US foundation for scientific research, named after the English chemist and mineralogist James Smithson (1765–1829), with whose bequest it originated.

**smithy** *noun* a blacksmith's workshop.

**smitten** *see* SMITE. □ **smitten with** affected by (a disease, desire, fascination, etc.).

**smock** *noun* **1** a loose shirtlike garment, often decorated with smocking and embroidery. **2** a loose overall. ●*verb* ornament with smocking.

**smocking** *noun* a decoration of close gathers stitched into a honeycomb pattern.

**smog** *noun* fog polluted by smoke.

**smoke** *noun* **1** the visible vapour given off by a burning substance. **2** the act of smoking tobacco; *wanted a smoke*. **3** (*informal*) a cigarette or cigar. **4** (**the Smoke**) (*informal*) London. ●*verb* **1** give out smoke or steam or other visible vapour. **2** (of a fireplace) send smoke into a room instead of up the chimney. **3** darken with smoke; *smoked glass*. **4** preserve by treating with smoke; *smoked salmon*. **5** draw into the mouth the smoke from a cigarette, cigar, or tobacco pipe; do this as a habit. □ **go up in smoke** (*informal*) come to nothing. **smoke bomb** a bomb that gives out dense smoke when it explodes. **smoke out** drive out by means of smoke.

**smokeless** *adjective* **1** free from smoke. **2** producing little or no smoke; *smokeless fuel*. □ **smokeless zone** a district where only smokeless fuel may be used.

**smoker** *noun* **1** a person who smokes tobacco as a habit. **2** a compartment on a train where smoking is permitted.

**smokescreen** *noun* **1** a mass of smoke used to conceal the movement of troops. **2** something intended to conceal or disguise one's activities.

**smokestack** *noun* a tall chimney; the funnel of a locomotive or steamer.

**smoky** *adjective* (**smokier, smokiest**) **1** giving off much smoke. **2** covered or filled with smoke. **3** greyish; *smoky blue*.

**smolder** Amer. spelling of SMOULDER.

**Smollett**, Tobias George (1721–71), Scottish novelist.

**smolt** *noun* a young salmon at the stage when it is covered with silvery scales and migrates to the sea for the first time.

**smooch** (*informal*) *verb* **1** kiss and caress. **2** dance slowly, holding one's partner closely. ● *noun* a spell of smooching.

**smooth** *adjective* **1** having an even surface with no projections, free from roughness. **2** not harsh in sound or taste. **3** moving evenly without jolts or bumping. **4** pleasantly polite but perhaps insincere. ● *adverb* smoothly; *the course of true love never did run smooth*. ● *verb* **1** make or become smooth. **2** remove problems or dangers from; *smooth a person's path*. ● *noun* a smoothing touch or stroke. □ **smooth-tongued** *adjective* pleasantly polite or convincing but insincere. □ **smoothly** *adverb*, **smoothness** *noun*

**smoothie** *noun* (*informal*, often *scornful*) a charming but perhaps insincere person.

**smorgasbord** (smor-găs-bord) *noun* Swedish hors d'oeuvres; a buffet meal with a variety of dishes.

**smote** *see* SMITE.

**smother** *verb* **1** suffocate or stifle; be suffocated. **2** put out (a fire) by covering it. **3** cover thickly. **4** restrain or suppress; *she smothered her anger*.

**smoulder** *verb* (*Amer.* **smolder**) **1** burn slowly with smoke but no flame. **2** burn inwardly with concealed anger or jealousy

etc. **3** (of feelings) exist in a suppressed state.

**smudge** *noun* a dirty or blurred mark. ● *verb* **1** make a smudge on or with. **2** become smudged or blurred. □ **smudgy** *adjective*

**smug** *adjective* (**smugger, smuggest**) self-satisfied. □ **smugly** *adverb*, **smugness** *noun*

**smuggle** *verb* **1** convey secretly. **2** bring (goods) into or out of a country illegally, especially without paying customs duties. □ **smuggler** *noun*

**smut** *noun* **1** a small flake of soot; a small black mark made by this. **2** indecent talk, pictures, or stories. **3** a disease of cereal plants in which parts of the plant turn to black powder. ● *verb* (**smutted, smutting**) mark with smuts.

**smutty** *adjective* (**smuttier, smuttiest**) **1** marked with smuts. **2** (of talk, pictures, or stories) indecent.

**Smuts**, Jan Christiaan (1870–1950), South African soldier, statesman, and philosopher, one of the founders of the Union of South Africa.

**Sn** *symbol* tin.

**snack** *noun* **1** a small, casual, or hurried meal. **2** a small amount of food eaten between meals. □ **snack bar** a place where snacks are sold.

**snaffle** *noun* a horse's bit without a curb. ● *verb* **1** put a snaffle on. **2** (*slang*) take for oneself, steal.

**snafu** (sna-**foo**) (*slang*) *adjective* in total confusion. ● *noun* a state of total confusion. (¶ From the initial letters of 'situation normal: all fouled (or fucked) up'.)

**snag** *noun* **1** a jagged projection. **2** a tear in fabric that has caught on a snag. **3** an unexpected difficulty. ● *verb* (**snagged, snagging**) catch, tear, or be caught on a snag.

**snail** *noun* a soft-bodied animal with a spiral shell. □ **snail's pace** a very slow pace.

**snake** *noun* **1** a reptile with a long narrow body and no legs. **2** (also **snake in the grass**) a treacherous person. ● *verb* move or twist like a snake. □ **snake-charmer** *noun* an entertainer who seems to make snakes move to music. **snakes and ladders** a game with counters moved along a board, with sudden advances up 'ladders' or descents down 'snakes'. □ **snaky** *adjective*

**snap** *verb* (**snapped, snapping**) **1** make or cause to make a sharp cracking sound. **2** break suddenly or with a cracking sound. **3** bite or try to bite with a snatching movement. **4** take or accept eagerly; *snapping up bargains*. **5** speak with sudden irritation. **6** move smartly; *snapped to attention*. **7** take a snapshot of. ● *noun* **1** the act or sound of snapping. **2** a small crisp brittle biscuit; *brandy snaps*. **3** a sudden

brief spell of cold weather. **4** a snapshot.
**5** a card game in which players call 'snap'
when two similar cards are exposed. ●*adverb*
with a snapping sound. ●*adjective* sudden;
done or arranged at short notice; *a snap
election.* □ **snap-fastener** *noun* = PRESS-
STUD. **snap one's fingers at** defy; regard
with contempt. **snap out of it** (*slang*)
make oneself recover quickly from a bad
mood.

**snapdragon** *noun* a garden plant with
flowers that have a mouth-like opening.

**snapper** *noun* **1** a person or thing that snaps.
**2** any of several sea fish used as food.

**snappish** *adjective* bad-tempered and
inclined to snap at people. □ **snappishly**
*adverb*

**snappy** *adjective* (**snappier, snappiest**) (*informal*) **1** brisk, vigorous. **2** neat and elegant. □ **make it snappy** (*informal*) be quick.
□ **snappily** *adverb*

**snapshot** *noun* a photograph taken informally or casually.

**snare** *noun* **1** a trap for catching birds or
animals, usually with a noose. **2** something
liable to entangle a person or expose him
or her to danger or failure. **3** each of the
strings of gut or hide stretched across a
side drum to produce a rattling effect. **4** (in
full **snare drum**) a drum with snares. ●*verb*
trap in a snare.

**snarl**[1] *verb* **1** growl angrily with the teeth
bared. **2** speak in a bad-tempered way.
●*noun* the act or sound of snarling.

**snarl**[2] *verb* tangle; become entangled. ●*noun* a
tangle. □ **snarl up** make or become
jammed or tangled; *traffic was snarled up.*
**snarl-up** *noun* (*informal*) a traffic jam; a
muddle.

**snatch** *verb* **1** seize quickly or eagerly. **2** take
quickly or when a chance occurs; *snatched
a few hours' sleep.* ●*noun* **1** the act of
snatching. **2** a short or brief part; *snatches
of song.*

**snazzy** *adjective* (*slang*) smart, stylish.
□ **snazzily** *adverb*, **snazziness** *noun*

**sneak** *verb* **1** go or convey furtively. **2** (*slang*)
steal furtively. **3** (*school slang*) tell tales.
●*noun* (*school slang*) a tell-tale. ●*adjective* acting or done without warning; *sneak raider.*
□ **sneak-thief** *noun* a burglar who enters by
sneaking or reaching through an open door
or window. □ **sneaky** *adjective*

**sneakers** *plural noun* soft-soled canvas shoes.

**sneaking** *adjective* persistent but not openly
acknowledged; *a sneaking feeling.*

**sneer** *noun* a scornful expression or remark.
●*verb* show contempt by a sneer.

**sneeze** *noun* a sudden audible involuntary
expulsion of air through the nose and
mouth. ●*verb* give a sneeze. □ **not to be**

**sneezed at** (*informal*) not to be despised;
worth having.

**snick** *noun* **1** a small cut or notch. **2** a
batsman's light glancing stroke. ●*verb* **1** cut
a snick in. **2** hit with a light glancing
stroke.

**snicker** *verb* snigger. ●*noun* a snigger.

**snide** *adjective* sneering in a sly way.

**sniff** *verb* **1** draw up air audibly through the
nose. **2** draw in through the nose as one
breathes; try the smell of. ●*noun* the act or
sound of sniffing. □ **sniff at** (*informal*) show
contempt for. **sniffer-dog** *noun* a dog
trained to scent the presence of drugs or
explosives.

**sniffle** *verb* sniff slightly or repeatedly. ●*noun*
the act or sound of sniffling.

**sniffy** *adjective* (*informal*) contemptuous.
□ **sniffily** *adverb*

**snifter** *noun* (*slang*) a small alcoholic drink.

**snigger** *noun* a sly or suppressed giggle. ●*verb*
give a snigger.

**snip** *verb* (**snipped, snipping**) cut with
scissors or shears in small quick strokes.
●*noun* **1** the act or sound of snipping. **2** a
piece snipped off. **3** (*slang*) a bargain; a
certainty; something very easy to do.

**snipe** *noun* (*plural* **snipe** *or* **snipes**) a wading
bird with a long straight bill, frequenting
marshes. ●*verb* **1** fire shots from a hiding-
place. **2** (often foll. by *at*) make sly critical
remarks attacking a person or thing.
□ **sniper** *noun*

**snippet** *noun* **1** a small piece cut off. **2** a
fragment of information or news; a brief
extract.

**snitch** *verb* (*slang*) **1** steal. **2** inform on a
person.

**snivel** *verb* (**snivelled, snivelling**; *Amer.*
**sniveled, sniveling**) cry or complain in a
miserable whining way.

**snob** *noun* a person who has an exaggerated
respect for social position, wealth, etc., and
who despises people whom he or she
considers inferior. □ **snobbery** *noun*

**snobbish** *adjective* of or like a snob.
□ **snobbishly** *adverb*, **snobbishness** *noun*

**snog** (*slang*) *verb* (**snogged, snogging**) kiss
and caress. ●*noun* a kissing session.

**snood** *noun* a loose bag-like ornamental net
in which a woman's hair is held at the
back.

**snook** *noun* (*slang*) a contemptuous gesture
with thumb to nose and fingers spread out.
□ **cock a snook** make this gesture; show
cheeky contempt.

**snooker** *noun* **1** a game played on a billiard
table with 15 red and 6 other coloured
balls. **2** a position in snooker where a direct
shot would lose points. ●*verb* **1** subject to a
snooker. **2** (*slang*) thwart, defeat.

**snoop** (*informal*) *verb* pry inquisitively. ●*noun* the act of snooping. □ **snooper** *noun*

**snooty** *adjective* (**snootier, snootiest**) (*informal*) haughty and snobbish. □ **snootily** *adverb*

**snooze** *noun* a nap. ●*verb* take a snooze.

**snore** *noun* a snorting or grunting sound made during sleep. ●*verb* make such sounds. □ **snorer** *noun*

**snorkel** *noun* **1** a breathing-tube to enable a person to swim under water. **2** a device by which a submerged submarine can take in and expel air.

**snorkelling** *noun* (*Amer.* **snorkeling**) swimming with the aid of a snorkel.

**snort** *noun* **1** a rough sound made by forcing breath suddenly through the nose, usually expressing annoyance or disgust. **2** (*informal*) a small alcoholic drink. ●*verb* **1** utter a snort. **2** (*slang*) inhale (cocaine).

**snot** *noun* (*slang*) mucous discharge from the nose.

**snotty** *adjective* (*slang*) **1** running or covered with nasal mucus. **2** snobbish. **3** mean, nasty.

**snout** *noun* **1** an animal's long projecting nose or nose and jaws. **2** the projecting front part of something.

**Snow**, C(harles) P(ercy), 1st Baron (1905–80), English novelist and scientist.

**snow** *noun* **1** crystals of ice that form from atmospheric vapour and fall to earth in light white flakes. **2** a fall or layer of snow. **3** something resembling snow. **4** (*slang*) cocaine. ●*verb* **1** send down snow; *it is snowing*. **2** scatter or fall like snow. □ **snowed under 1** covered with snow. **2** overwhelmed with a mass of work. **snowed up** snowbound; blocked with snow. **snow goose** a white goose of Arctic areas. **snow-white** *adjective* pure white.

**snowball** *noun* snow pressed into a small compact mass for throwing in play. ●*verb* grow quickly in size or intensity, as a snowball does when rolled in more snow; *opposition to the war snowballed*.

**snowberry** *noun* a shrub with white berries.

**snowbound** *adjective* prevented by snow from leaving or travelling; blocked by snow.

**Snowdon** the highest mountain of Wales, in Gwynedd.

**snowdrift** *noun* a bank of snow heaped up by the wind.

**snowdrop** *noun* a small flower growing from a bulb, with hanging white flowers blooming in early spring.

**snowfall** *noun* a fall of snow; the amount that falls.

**snowflake** *noun* a flake of snow.

**snowline** *noun* the level above which there is permanent snow.

**snowman** *noun* (*plural* **snowmen**) a figure made in snow in the shape of a human.

**snowmobile** (snoh-mŏ-beel) *noun* a motor vehicle designed for travel over snow.

**snowplough** *noun* (*Amer.* **snowplow**) a machine that clears snow by pushing it out of the way.

**snowshoe** *noun* a racket-shaped device attached to each shoe to prevent a person from sinking into deep snow.

**snowstorm** *noun* a storm in which snow falls.

**snowy** *adjective* (**snowier, snowiest**) **1** with snow falling; *snowy weather*. **2** covered with snow. **3** as white as snow.

**SNP** *abbreviation* Scottish National Party.

**Snr.** *abbreviation* Senior.

**snub** *verb* (**snubbed, snubbing**) reject or humiliate (a person) by speaking sharply or behaving coldly. ●*noun* treatment of this kind. □ **snub nose** a short turned-up nose.

**snuff**[1] *noun* powdered tobacco for sniffing into the nostrils.

**snuff**[2] *noun* the charred part of a candle wick. ●*verb* **1** put out (a candle) by covering or pinching the flame. **2** (foll. by *out*) put an end to (hopes etc.). □ **snuff it** (*slang*) die. □ **snuffer** *noun*

**snuffle** *verb* sniff in a noisy way; breathe noisily through a partly blocked nose. ●*noun* a snuffling sound.

**snug** *adjective* (**snugger, snuggest**) **1** cosy. **2** (of a garment) close-fitting. ●*noun* a small room in a pub, with comfortable seating. □ **snugly** *adverb*

**snuggery** *noun* a snug place, a cosy room.

**snuggle** *verb* nestle, cuddle.

**so**[1] *adverb* & *conjunction* **1** to the extent or in the manner or with the result indicated; *it was so dark that we could not see.* **2** very; *we are so pleased.* **3** for that reason; *and so they ran away.* **4** also; *if you go, so shall I.* ●*pronoun* that; the same thing; *do you think so?*; *and so say all of us.* □ **and so on** and others of the same kind. **or so** or about that number or amount; *two hundred or so.* **so-and-so** *noun* (*plural* **so-and-so's**) **1** a person or thing that need not be named. **2** (*informal*) (to avoid using a vulgar word) an unpleasant or objectionable person. **so-called** *adjective* called by that name or description but perhaps not correctly. **so long** (*informal*) goodbye. **so much** nothing but; *melted like so much snow.* **so much for that** no more need be said of it. **so-so** *adjective* & *adverb* (*informal*) only moderately good or well. **so that** in order that; with the result that. **so what?** that fact has no importance.

**so**[2] alternative spelling of SOH.

**soak** *verb* **1** place or lie in a liquid so as to become thoroughly wet. **2** (of liquid) penetrate gradually; (of rain etc.) drench.

**3** absorb; *soak it up with a sponge; soak up knowledge.* **4** (*slang*) extract a lot of money from (a person). ●*noun* **1** the act or process of soaking. **2** (*slang*) a heavy drinker.

**soap** *noun* **1** a substance used for washing and cleaning things, made of fat or oil combined with an alkali. **2** (*informal*) a soap opera. ●*verb* apply soap to. □ **soap flakes** soap prepared in small flakes for washing clothes. **soap opera** a sentimental broadcast serial with a domestic setting. (¶ A type of broadcast originally sponsored by soap manufacturers in the USA.)

**soapbox** *noun* a makeshift stand for a speaker in the street.

**soapstone** *noun* steatite.

**soapsuds** *plural noun* froth of soapy water.

**soapy** *adjective* **1** like soap. **2** covered or impregnated with soap. **3** (*informal*) trying to win favour by flattery or excessive politeness. □ **soapiness** *noun*

**soar** *verb* **1** rise high in flight. **2** rise very high; *prices soared.*

**sob** *noun* an uneven drawing of breath in weeping. ●*verb* (**sobbed, sobbing**) weep or utter with sobs. □ **sob story** (*informal*) a story or explanation meant to arouse sympathy.

**sober** *adjective* **1** not intoxicated. **2** serious and self-controlled; not frivolous. **3** (of colour) not bright or conspicuous. ●*verb* (often foll. by *up*) make or become sober. □ **soberly** *adverb*

**Sobers**, Gary (Sir Garfield St Aubrun) (born 1936), West Indian cricketer.

**sobriety** (sŏ-**bry**-ĕti) *noun* being sober.

**sobriquet** (soh-brik-ay) *noun* (also **soubriquet**) a nickname.

**Soc.** *abbreviation* **1** Socialist. **2** Society.

**soccer** *noun* Association football.

**sociable** (soh-**shă**-bŭl) *adjective* fond of company; characterized by friendly companionship. □ **sociably** *adverb*, **sociability** *noun*

**social** *adjective* **1** living in an organized community, not solitary. **2** of society or its organization; of the relationships of people living in an organized community; *social problems.* **3** of or designed for companionship and sociability; *a social club.* **4** sociable. ●*noun* a social gathering. □ **Social and Liberal Democrats** a UK political party formed by a merger of the Liberal Party and some Social Democrats. **social climber** a person seeking to gain a higher rank in society. **social democracy** a political system favouring a mixed economy and democratic social change. **Social Democratic Party** a UK political party (1981–90) with moderate socialist aims, founded by a group of former Labour MPs. **social science** the study of

human society and social relationships. **social security** State financial assistance for those who are unemployed, ill, disabled, etc. **social services** welfare services provided by the State. **social worker** a person trained to help people with social problems. □ **socially** *adverb*

**socialism** *noun* a political and economic theory advocating that the community as a whole should own and control the means of production, transport, property, etc. □ **socialist** *noun*, **socialistic** *adjective*

**socialite** (soh-shă-lyt) *noun* a person who is prominent in fashionable society.

**socialize** *verb* (also **socialise**) **1** organize in a socialistic manner. **2** behave sociably, take part in social activities. □ **socialization** *noun*

**society** *noun* **1** an organized community; the system of living in this. **2** people of the higher social classes. **3** company, companionship; *always enjoy his society; he is at his best in society.* **4** a group of people organized for some common purpose. □ **Society of Friends** a Christian sect (also called **Quakers**) with no written creed or ordained ministers, who believe in the 'Inner Light' or Christ's direct working in the soul and have a strong commitment to pacifism. **Society of Jesus** Jesuits.

**Society Islands** a group of islands in French Polynesia, including Tahiti, named by Captain Cook in honour of the Royal Society.

**socio-** *combining form* of society or sociology and; *socio-economic; socio-political.*

**sociology** (soh-si-ol-ŏji) *noun* the scientific study of human society or of social problems. □ **sociological** *adjective*, **sociologist** (soh-si-ol-ŏ-jist) *noun*

**sock**[1] *noun* **1** a short stocking not reaching the knee. **2** a loose insole. □ **pull one's socks up** (*informal*) make an effort to do better. **put a sock in it** (*slang*) be quiet.

**sock**[2] (*slang*) *verb* hit forcefully. ●*noun* a forceful blow. □ **sock it to** (*slang*) attack or address (a person) forcefully.

**socket** *noun* **1** a hollow into which something fits. **2** a device into which an electric plug, bulb, etc. is inserted to make a connection.

**Socratic** *adjective* of Socrates or his philosophy. □ **Socratic method** the investigation of truth by discussion or question and answer.

**Socrates** (sok-ră-teez) (469–399 BC), Athenian moral philosopher.

**sod**[1] *noun* turf; a piece of this.

**sod**[2] (*vulgar*) *noun* **1** an unpleasant or awkward person or thing. **2** a person; *lucky sod.* ●*verb* damn. □ **sod off** go away. **Sod's Law** = MURPHY'S LAW.

**soda** *noun* **1** a compound of sodium in common use, especially sodium carbonate (*washing soda*), bicarbonate (*baking soda*), or hydroxide (*caustic soda*). **2** soda water; *whisky and soda*. □ **soda bread** bread made with baking soda (not yeast). **soda fountain** an apparatus containing soda water under pressure, ready to be squirted out. **soda water** water made fizzy by being charged with carbon dioxide under pressure.

**sodden** *adjective* made very wet.

**sodium** (soh-di-ŭm) *noun* a chemical element (symbol Na), a soft silver-white metal. □ **sodium chloride** common salt. **sodium hydroxide** a strongly alkaline compound used in soap; caustic soda. **sodium lamp** a lamp using an electrical discharge in sodium vapour and giving a yellow light, often used in street lighting.

**Sodom** a town of ancient Palestine, said to have been destroyed (along with Gomorrah) by fire from heaven for the wickedness of its inhabitants.

**sodomite** *noun* a person who practises sodomy.

**sodomy** (sod-ŏ-mi) *noun* **1** anal intercourse. **2** = BESTIALITY (sense 2).

**sofa** *noun* a long upholstered seat with a back and arms. □ **sofa bed** a sofa that can be converted into a bed.

**soffit** *noun* the undersurface of an arch or architrave.

**Sofia** (soh-fee-ă) the capital of Bulgaria.

**soft** *adjective* **1** not hard or firm. **2** not rough or stiff. **3** not loud. **4** gentle, soothing. **5** not physically robust, feeble. **6** easily influenced, tender-hearted. **7** (*slang*) easy, comfortable; *a soft job*; *soft living*. **8** (of currency) likely to drop suddenly in value. **9** (of water) free from mineral salts that prevent soap from lathering. **10** (of colour or light) not bright or dazzling; (of an outline) not sharp. **11** (of consonants) not hard (*see* HARD, sense 11). ● *adverb* softly. □ **soft-boiled** *adjective* (of eggs) boiled but without allowing the yolk to set. **soft-core** *adjective* (of pornography) not highly obscene. **soft drink** a non-alcoholic drink. **soft drugs** drugs that are not likely to cause addiction. **soft fruit** small stoneless fruits such as strawberries and currants. **soft furnishings** curtains, cushions, rugs, etc. **soft-hearted** *adjective* compassionate. **soft option** the easier alternative. **soft on 1** lenient towards. **2** romantically attracted to. **soft palate** the rear of the roof of the mouth. **soft-pedal** *verb* (*informal*) refrain from emphasizing; be restrained. **soft sell** restrained sales talk. **soft soap** (*informal*) persuasive talk; flattery. **soft spot** a feeling of affection towards a person or thing. **soft**

**touch** (*informal*) a person who is easy to persuade or from whom it is easy to obtain money. □ **softly** *adverb*, **softness** *noun*

**softball** *noun* a form of baseball using a large soft ball.

**soften** *verb* make or become soft or softer. □ **soften up** make weaker by attacking repeatedly; make less able to resist (salesmanship etc.) by making preliminary approaches. □ **softener** *noun*

**softie** *noun* (also **softy**) (*informal*) a person who is physically weak or not hardy, or who is soft-hearted.

**software** *noun* computer programs (as distinct from *hardware*).

**softwood** *noun* wood from coniferous trees, which is easily sawn.

**softy** alternative spelling of SOFTIE.

**soggy** *adjective* **1** sodden. **2** moist and heavy in texture. □ **soggily** *adverb*, **sogginess** *noun*

**soh** *noun* (also **so**) *Music* the fifth note of a major scale.

**soigné** (swahn-yay) *adjective* (of a woman, **soignée**) well-groomed and sophisticated. (¶ French, = taken care of.)

**soil** *noun* **1** the loose upper layer of earth in which plants grow. **2** ground as territory; *on British soil*. ● *verb* make or become dirty. □ **soil pipe** the pipe that carries waste from a toilet.

**soirée** (swah-ray) *noun* a social gathering in the evening, e.g. for music.

**sojourn** (soj-ern) *noun* a temporary stay. ● *verb* stay at a place temporarily.

**solace** (sol-ăs) *noun* comfort in distress; something that gives this. ● *verb* give solace to.

**solar** (soh-ler) *adjective* **1** of or derived from the sun; *solar energy*. **2** reckoned by the sun; *solar time*. □ **solar battery** *or* **cell** a device converting solar radiation into electricity. **solar heating** heating derived from solar energy. **solar panel** a panel that absorbs the sun's rays to power a heating system etc. **solar plexus** the network of nerves at the pit of the stomach; this area. **solar system** the sun with the heavenly bodies that revolve round it. **solar year** the time taken for the earth to travel once round the sun.

**solarium** (sŏl-**air**-iŭm) *noun* (*plural* **solaria**) a room with sunlamps or enclosed with glass so that people can benefit from exposure to sunlight.

**sold** *see* SELL. □ **sold on** (*informal*) enthusiastic about.

**solder** (sohl-der) *noun* a soft alloy used to cement metal parts together. ● *verb* join with solder. □ **soldering iron** a tool used hot for applying solder.

**soldier** *noun* a member of an army, especially a private or NCO. ● *verb* serve as a soldier. □ **soldier of fortune** a person ready to serve any country or person for money. **soldier on** (*informal*) persevere doggedly.

**soldierly** *adjective* like a soldier.

**soldiery** *noun* soldiers collectively or as a class.

**sole**[1] *noun* **1** the undersurface of a foot. **2** the part of a shoe or stocking that covers this (often excluding the heel). **3** the lower surface of an object. ● *verb* put a sole on (a shoe).

**sole**[2] *noun* (*plural* **sole** *or* **soles**) a flatfish used as food.

**sole**[3] *adjective* **1** one and only; *our sole objection is this.* **2** belonging exclusively to one person or group; *we have the sole right to sell these cars.* □ **solely** *adverb*

**solecism** (sol-i-sizm) *noun* **1** a mistake in the use of language. **2** an offence against good manners or etiquette. □ **solecistic** (sol-i-**sist**-ik) *adjective*

**solemn** *adjective* **1** not smiling or cheerful. **2** dignified and impressive; *a solemn occasion.* **3** formal; accompanied by a religious or other ceremony. □ **solemnly** *adverb*, **solemnity** (sol-**em**-niti) *noun*

**solemnize** (sol-ĕm-nyz) *verb* (also **solemnise**) **1** celebrate (a festival etc.). **2** perform (a marriage ceremony) with formal rites. □ **solemnization** *noun*

**solenoid** (soh-lin-oid) *noun* a coil of wire that becomes magnetic when an electric current is passed through it.

**Solent** (soh-lĕnt) the west part of the channel between the Isle of Wight and the mainland of England.

**sol-fa** (sol-fah) *noun* a system of syllables representing musical notes.

**soli** *see* SOLO.

**solicit** (sŏl-iss-it) *verb* **1** seek to obtain, ask earnestly; *solicit votes.* **2** (of a prostitute) offer sexual services; look for business, especially in a public place. □ **solicitation** *noun*

**solicitor** *noun* a lawyer qualified to advise clients, represent them in court, and instruct barristers. □ **Solicitor-General** *noun* (*plural* **Solicitors-General**) a law officer below the Attorney-General (or in Scotland the Lord Advocate).

**solicitous** (sŏl-iss-it-ŭs) *adjective* anxious and concerned about a person's welfare or comfort. □ **solicitously** *adverb*

**solicitude** (sŏl-iss-i-tewd) *noun* solicitous concern.

**solid** *adjective* **1** keeping its shape, firm; not liquid or gas. **2** not hollow. **3** of the same substance throughout; *solid silver.* **4** continuous, without a break; *for two solid hours.* **5** strongly constructed, not flimsy. **6** having three dimensions; concerned with solids; *solid geometry.* **7** sound and reliable; *there are solid arguments against it.* **8** unanimous; undivided; determined; *the miners are solid on this issue.* ● *noun* **1** a solid substance or body or food. **2** a body or shape with three dimensions. □ **solid state** a state of matter in which the constituent atoms or molecules occupy fixed positions with respect to each other and cannot move freely (other states are the liquid, gas, and plasma states). **solid-state** *adjective* using transistors (which make use of the electronic properties of solids) instead of valves. □ **solidly** *adverb*, **solidity** (sŏl-**id**-iti) *noun*

**Solidarity** an organization which began as an independent trade-union movement in Poland and became involved in government following political reform and elections.

**solidarity** *noun* unity resulting from common interests, feelings, or sympathies.

**solidify** (sŏl-id-i-fy) *verb* (**solidified**, **solidifying**) make or become solid.

**solidus** *noun* (*plural* **solidi**) an oblique stroke (/).

**soliloquize** (sŏl-il-ŏ-kwyz) *verb* (also **soliloquise**) utter a soliloquy.

**soliloquy** (sŏl-il-ŏ-kwi) *noun* a speech in which a person expresses his or her thoughts aloud without addressing anyone.

**solipsism** (sol-ip-sizm) *noun* the theory that the self is all that exists or can be known. □ **solipsist** *noun*

**solitaire** (sol-i-tair) *noun* **1** a diamond or other gem set by itself. **2** a game for one person, in which marbles or pegs are removed from their places on a special board after jumping others over them. **3** (*Amer.*) a card game for one person.

**solitary** *adjective* **1** alone, without companions. **2** single; *a solitary example.* **3** not frequented, lonely; *a solitary valley.* ● *noun* **1** a recluse. **2** (*slang*) solitary confinement. □ **solitary confinement** isolation in a separate prison cell as a punishment. □ **solitarily** *adverb*

**solitude** *noun* being solitary.

**solo** *noun* (*plural* **solos**) **1** (*plural* **solos** *or* **soli**) a musical composition or passage for a single voice or instrument. **2** a pilot's flight in an aircraft without an instructor or companion. **3** solo whist. ● *adjective & adverb* unaccompanied, alone; *for solo flute; flying solo.* □ **solo whist** a card game like whist in which one player may oppose the others.

**soloist** *noun* a person who performs a solo.

**Solomon** king of Israel *c.*970–930 BC, son of David, famous for his wisdom and magnificence. □ **Song of Solomon** (also called the **Song of Songs** or **Canticles**) a book of the Old Testament, an anthology of love poems ascribed to Solomon but dating from a much later period. **Wisdom of Solomon** a book of the Apocrypha containing a meditation on wisdom. **Solomon's seal** a plant with arching stems bearing drooping green and white flowers.

**Solomon Islands** a country consisting of a group of islands in the South Pacific.

**solstice** (sol-stis) *noun* either of the times in the year when the sun is furthest from the equator; the point reached by the sun at these times (**summer solstice** about 21 June; **winter solstice** about 22 December).

**soluble** (sol-yoo-bŭl) *adjective* **1** able to be dissolved in liquid. **2** able to be solved. □ **solubly** *adverb,* **solubility** (sol-yoo-bil-iti) *noun*

**solute** *noun* a dissolved substance.

**solution** *noun* **1** a liquid in which something is dissolved. **2** dissolving or being dissolved into liquid form. **3** the process of solving a problem etc.; the answer found.

**solve** *verb* find the answer to (a problem or puzzle) or the way out of (a difficulty). □ **solvable** *adjective,* **solver** *noun*

**solvent** *adjective* **1** having enough money to pay one's debts. **2** able to dissolve another substance. ●*noun* a liquid used for dissolving something. □ **solvency** *noun*

**Solzhenitsyn** (sol-zhĕn-it-sin), Alexander (born 1918), Russian novelist, imprisoned and later deported to the West (1974) for his criticisms of the former Soviet regime.

**Som.** *abbreviation* Somerset.

**Somalia** (sŏm-ah-liǎ) a country in East Africa. □ **Somali** *adjective & noun* (*plural* **Somalis**).

**somatic** (sŏ-mat-ik) *adjective* of the body, physical as distinct from mental or spiritual. □ **somatically** *adverb*

**sombre** (som-ber) *adjective* (*Amer.* **somber**) dark, gloomy, dismal. □ **sombrely** *adverb*

**sombrero** (som-**brair**-oh) *noun* (*plural* **sombreros**) a felt or straw hat with a very wide brim, worn especially in Latin America.

**some** *adjective & pronoun* **1** an unspecified quantity; *buy some apples.* **2** an amount that is less than the whole; *some of them were late.* **3** an unspecified person or thing; *some fool locked the door; come round some time.* **4** a considerable quantity; *that was some years ago.* **5** approximately; *waited some 20 minutes.* **6** (*informal*) remarkable; *that was some storm!*

**somebody** *noun & pronoun* **1** an unspecified person. **2** a person of importance.

**someday** *adverb* at some time in the future.

**somehow** *adverb* **1** in some unspecified or unexplained manner; *I never liked him,* somehow. **2** by one means or another; *must get it finished somehow.*

**someone** *noun & pronoun* somebody.

**someplace** *adverb* (*Amer.*) somewhere.

**somersault** (**sum**-er-solt) *noun* an acrobatic movement in which a person rolls head over heels on the ground or in the air. ●*verb* turn a somersault.

**Somerset** (**sum**-er-set) a county of SW England.

**something** *noun & pronoun* **1** an unspecified thing. **2** an important or praiseworthy thing. □ **something else** (*informal*) something excellent or remarkable. **something like** approximately; *it cost something like £10.* **something of** to some extent; *something of an expert.*

**sometime** *adjective* former; *her sometime friend.* ●*adverb* formerly.

**sometimes** *adverb* at some times, occasionally.

**somewhat** *adverb* to some extent; *it is somewhat difficult.*

**somewhere** *adverb* at, in, or to an unspecified place or position. □ **get somewhere** (*informal*) achieve some success.

**Somme** a river of NE France, flowing into the English Channel, the scene of a First World War battle (1916) in which thousands of soldiers were killed.

**somnambulist** (som-**nam**-bew-list) *noun* a sleepwalker. □ **somnambulism** *noun,* **somnambulant** *adjective*

**somnolent** (som-nŏl-ĕnt) *adjective* sleepy, drowsy. □ **somnolence** *noun*

**son** *noun* **1** a male child in relation to his parents. **2** a male descendant. **3** a form of address to a boy or young man. □ **son-in-law** *noun* (*plural* **sons-in-law**) a daughter's husband. **son of a bitch** (*vulgar*) an unpleasant person. **son of a gun** (*humorous*) a person.

**sonar** (**soh**-ner) *noun* a device for detecting objects under water by reflection of sound waves.

**sonata** (sŏn-**ah**-tǎ) *noun* a musical composition for one instrument or two, usually with three or four movements.

**sonatina** (sonn-ǎ-**teen**-ǎ) *noun* a simple or short sonata.

**Sondheim**, Stephen Joshua (born 1930), American composer and songwriter, famous for his musicals.

**son et lumière** (sonn ay **loom**-yair) an entertainment given at night, a dramatic account of the history of a building or place, with lighting effects and recorded sound. (¶ French, = sound and light.)

**song** *noun* **1** singing. **2** a musical composition for singing. **3** the cry of some birds. □ **going for a song** being sold very cheaply. **make a song and dance** (*informal*) make a great fuss.

**songbird** *noun* a bird with a musical cry.

**songster** *noun* **1** a singer. **2** a songbird.

**songwriter** *noun* a person who writes songs or the music for them.

**sonic** *adjective* of or involving sound waves. □ **sonic barrier** = SOUND BARRIER. **sonic boom** *or* **bang** a loud noise heard when the shock wave caused by an aircraft travelling at supersonic speed reaches the hearer.

**sonnet** *noun* a poem of 14 lines with lengths and rhymes in accordance with any of several patterns.

**sonny** *noun* (*informal*) a form of address to a boy or young man.

**sonorous** (sonn-er-ŭs) *adjective* resonant, giving a deep powerful sound.

**soon** *adverb* **1** in a short time, not long after the present or a specified time. **2** early, quickly; *spoke too soon*. □ **as soon** as readily, as willingly. **as soon as** at the moment that, as early as; as readily or willingly as. **sooner or later** at some time, eventually.

**soot** *noun* the black powdery substance that rises in the smoke of coal or wood etc. ●*verb* cover with soot.

**sooth** *noun* (*old use*) truth.

**soothe** *verb* calm; ease (pain etc.). □ **soothing** *adjective*

**soothsayer** *noun* a person who foretells the future.

**sooty** *adjective* (**sootier**, **sootiest**) **1** full of soot; covered with soot. **2** like soot, black.

**sop** *noun* **1** a piece of bread dipped in liquid before being eaten or cooked. **2** a concession made to pacify or bribe a troublesome person. ●*verb* (**sopped, sopping**) **1** dip (a thing) in liquid. **2** soak up (liquid) with something absorbent.

**sophism** (sof-izm) *noun* a clever but false or misleading argument.

**sophist** (sof-ist) *noun* a person who uses sophistry. (¶ Named after the Sophists, Greek philosophers of the 5th century BC, who taught rhetoric and skilled reasoning.)

**sophisticated** (sŏf-ist-i-kaytid) *adjective* **1** characteristic of fashionable life and its ways; experienced in this and lacking natural simplicity. **2** complicated, elaborate; *sophisticated electronic devices*. □ **sophistication** *noun*

**sophistry** (sof-ist-ri) *noun* clever and subtle but misleading reasoning.

**Sophocles** (sof-ŏ-kleez) (*c.*496–406 BC), Greek playwright.

**sophomore** (sof-ŏ-mor) *noun* (*Amer.*) a second-year student at a university or high school.

**soporific** (sop-er-**if**-ik) *adjective* tending to cause sleep. ●*noun* a drug that causes sleep. □ **soporifically** *adverb*

**sopping** *adjective* very wet, drenched.

**soppy** *adjective* (**soppier, soppiest**) (*informal*) sentimental in a sickly way. □ **soppily** *adverb*, **soppiness** *noun*

**soprano** (sŏ-**prah**-noh) *noun* (*plural* **sopranos**) **1** the highest female or boy's singing-voice. **2** a singer with such a voice; a part written for it.

**sorbet** (sor-bay) *noun* a flavoured water-ice.

**Sorbonne** (sor-**bon**), **the** a part of the University of Paris containing the faculties of science and literature.

**sorcerer** *noun* a male magician, a wizard.

**sorceress** *noun* a female magician, a witch.

**sorcery** *noun* a sorcerer's art or practices.

**sordid** *adjective* **1** dirty, squalid. **2** (of motives or actions) lacking dignity; not honourable. □ **sordidly** *adverb*, **sordidness** *noun*

**sore** *adjective* **1** causing or suffering pain. **2** causing mental pain or annoyance; *a sore subject*. **3** (*old use*) dire, serious; *in sore need*. **4** distressed, vexed. ●*noun* **1** a sore place, especially where the skin is raw. **2** a source of distress or annoyance. □ **soreness** *noun*

**sorely** *adverb* seriously, very; *I was sorely tempted*.

**sorghum** (sor-gŭm) *noun* a tropical cereal grass.

**sorority** *noun* (*Amer.*) a female students' society in a university or college.

**sorrel** (*rhymes with* coral) *noun* **1** a herb with sharp-tasting leaves used in salads. **2** light reddish-brown; a horse of this colour.

**sorrow** *noun* **1** mental suffering caused by loss or disappointment. **2** something that causes this. ●*verb* feel sorrow; grieve.

**sorrowful** *adjective* feeling or showing sorrow. □ **sorrowfully** *adverb*

**sorry** *adjective* (**sorrier, sorriest**) **1** feeling pity, regret, or sympathy. **2** wretched; *in a sorry plight*. ●*interjection* an expression of apology.

**sort** *noun* **1** a particular kind or variety. **2** (*informal*) a person with regard to character; *she's a good sort*. ●*verb* arrange according to sort, size, destination, etc. □ **of a sort** *or* **of sorts** not fully deserving the name given; *a holiday of sorts*. **out of sorts** slightly unwell; in a bad mood. **sort of** (*informal*) somewhat, rather. **sort out** **1** disentangle; select from others. **2** (*informal*) deal with or punish.

**sortie** (sor-tee) *noun* **1** an attack by troops, especially from a besieged place. **2** a flight of an aircraft on a military operation.

**SOS** *noun* **1** the international code-signal of extreme distress. **2** (*plural* **SOSs**) an urgent appeal for help or response.

**sostenuto** *adverb & adjective Music* in a sustained or prolonged way. (¶ Italian.)

**sot** *noun* a drunkard. □ **sottish** *adjective*

**Sotheby's** (su*th*-i-biz) a firm of fine-art auctioneers in London.

**Sotho** (soo-too) *noun* **1** a member of a Bantu people living chiefly in Botswana, Lesotho, and the Transvaal. **2** their language.

*sotto voce* (sot-oh **voh**-chi) in an undertone. (¶ Italian.)

**sou** (*pronounced* soo) *noun* **1** a former French coin of low value. **2** (*informal*) a very small amount of money.

**soubrette** (soo-**bret**) *noun* a pert maidservant or similar character in comedy.

**soubriquet** (soo-bri-kay) = SOBRIQUET.

**soufflé** (soo-flay) *noun* a light spongy dish made with beaten egg white.

**sough** (*pronounced* suf *or rhyming with* cow) *verb* make a moaning or whispering sound as the wind does in trees. ● *noun* this sound.

**sought** *see* SEEK. □ **sought-after** *adjective* much sought for purchase or use etc.

**souk** (*pronounced* sook) *noun* a market-place in Muslim countries of the Middle East and North Africa.

**soul** *noun* **1** the spiritual or immortal element in a person. **2** a person's mental, moral, or emotional nature; *his whole soul revolted from it*. **3** a personification or pattern; *she is the soul of discretion*. **4** a person; *there's not a soul about*. **5** soul music. □ **soul-destroying** *adjective* deadeningly monotonous or depressing. **soul food** traditional food of American Blacks. **soul mates** people ideally suited to each other. **soul music** Black American music with rhythm and blues, gospel, and rock influences. **soul-searching** *noun* examination of one's conscience.

**soulful** *adjective* **1** having or showing deep feeling. **2** emotional. □ **soulfully** *adverb*

**soulless** *adjective* **1** lacking sensitivity or noble qualities. **2** dull, uninteresting.

**sound¹** *noun* **1** vibrations that travel through the air and are detectable (at certain frequencies) by the ear. **2** the sensation produced by these vibrations; a particular kind of it. **3** the mental impression produced by a statement or description etc.; *we don't like the sound of the new scheme*. ● *verb* **1** produce or cause to produce sound; *sound the trumpet*. **2** utter, pronounce; *the 'h' in 'hour' is not sounded*. **3** give an impression when heard; *it sounds like an owl; the news sounds good*. **4** test by noting the sound produced; *the doctor sounds a patient's lungs with a stethoscope*. □ **sound barrier** the high resistance of air to objects moving at speeds near that of sound. **sound bite** a very short, snappy extract from an interview, speech, etc., used e.g. as part of a news broadcast to convey a forceful message. **sound effects** sounds (other than speech or music) made

artificially for use in a play or film etc. **sound off** (*informal*) express one's opinions loudly and freely. **sound out** question cautiously. **sound system** a hi-fi, PA system, or other equipment for sound reproduction. **sound wave** a wave by which sound is transmitted through the air etc.

**sound²** *adjective* **1** healthy, not diseased or damaged. **2** correct, logical, well-founded; *sound reasoning*. **3** financially secure; *a sound investment*. **4** thorough; *a sound thrashing; sound sleep*. ● *adverb* soundly; *is sound asleep*. □ **soundly** *adverb*, **soundness** *noun*

**sound³** *verb* **1** test or measure the depth or quality of the bottom of (the sea or a river etc.). **2** examine with a probe. ● *noun* a surgeon's probe. □ **sounder** *noun*

**sound⁴** *noun* a strait (of water).

**soundbox** *noun* the hollow body of a stringed instrument.

**sounding** *noun* **1** measurement of the depth of water (*see* SOUND³). **2** (**soundings**) discreet enquiries. □ **sounding-balloon** *noun* a balloon used to obtain information about the upper atmosphere. **sounding-board** *noun* **1** a person or group used to test opinion. **2** a canopy directing sound towards an audience.

**soundproof** *adjective* not able to be penetrated by sound. ● *verb* make soundproof.

**soundtrack** *noun* **1** a strip on cinema film or recording-tape for recording sound. **2** the sound itself.

**soup** *noun* liquid food made by boiling meat, vegetables, etc. □ **in the soup** (*slang*) in difficulties. **soup-kitchen** *noun* a place where soup and other food is supplied free to the needy. **soup-plate** *noun* a large deep plate for soup. **soup up** (*informal*) increase the power of (an engine); enliven.

**soupçon** (soop-son) *noun* a very small quantity; a trace; *add a soupçon of garlic*. (¶ French.)

**sour** *adjective* **1** tasting sharp like vinegar. **2** not fresh, tasting or smelling sharp or unpleasant from fermentation or staleness. **3** (of soil) excessively acid, deficient in lime. **4** bad-tempered, disagreeable; *gave me a sour look*. ● *verb* make or become sour; *was soured by misfortune*. □ **sour cream** cream deliberately fermented by the action of bacteria. **sour grapes** said when a person pretends to despise something he or she cannot have. (¶ From the fable of the fox who wanted some grapes but found that they were out of reach and so pretended that they were sour and undesirable anyway.) □ **sourly** *adverb*, **sourness** *noun*

**source** noun **1** the place from which something comes or is obtained. **2** the starting point of a river.

**sourpuss** noun (informal) a sour-tempered person.

**Sousa** (soo-ză), John Philip (1854–1932), American conductor and composer of over 100 marches, including The Stars and Stripes.

**souse** (rhymes with mouse) verb **1** steep in pickle; soused herrings. **2** plunge or soak in liquid; drench, throw (liquid) over a thing.

**soused** adjective (slang) drunk.

**soutane** (soo-tahn) noun the cassock of a Roman Catholic priest.

**south** noun **1** the point or direction opposite north. **2** the southern part of something. ●adjective **1** towards or in the south. **2** (of a wind) blowing from the south. ●adverb towards or in the south. □ **South Pole** the southernmost point of the earth. **south pole** (of a magnet) the pole that is attracted to the south.

**South Africa** a country occupying the southernmost part of the continent of Africa. □ **South African** adjective & noun

**South America** the southern half of the American land mass (see AMERICA).

**South Australia** a State comprising the central southern part of Australia.

**southbound** adjective travelling or leading southwards.

**South Carolina** (ka-rŏ-ly-nă) a State of the USA on the Atlantic coast.

**South China Sea** see CHINA SEA.

**South Dakota** (dă-koh-tă) a State in the north central USA.

**south-east** noun the point or direction midway between south and east. ●adjective of, towards, or coming from the south-east. ●adverb towards, in, or near the south-east. □ **south-easterly** adjective & noun, **south-eastern** adjective

**southeaster** noun a south-east wind.

**southerly** adjective **1** in or towards the south. **2** (of a wind) blowing from the south. ●noun a southerly wind.

**southern** adjective of or in the south. □ **Southern Cross** a constellation in the southern sky. **Southern hemisphere** the half of the earth south of the equator. **southern lights** the aurora australis.

**southerner** noun a native or inhabitant of the south.

**southernmost** adjective furthest south.

**Southern Ocean** the body of water surrounding the continent of Antarctica.

**Southey** (su**th**-i), Robert (1774–1843), English poet and prose writer.

**South Glamorgan** a county of South Wales.

**southpaw** noun (informal) a left-handed person, especially in sports.

**southward** adjective & adverb (also **southwards**) towards the south.

**south-west** noun the point or direction midway between south and west. ●adjective of, towards, or coming from the south-west. ●adverb towards, in, or near the south-west. □ **south-westerly** adjective & noun, **south-western** adjective

**southwester** noun a south-west wind.

**South Yorkshire** a metropolitan county of northern England.

**souvenir** (soo-věn-**eer**) noun something bought or kept as a reminder of an incident or a place visited.

**sou'wester** noun a waterproof hat with a broad flap at the back.

**sovereign** (sov-rin) noun **1** a king or queen who is the supreme ruler of a country. **2** (hist.) a British gold coin, nominally worth £1. ●adjective **1** supreme; sovereign power. **2** possessing sovereign power, independent; sovereign states. **3** very effective; a sovereign remedy. □ **sovereignty** noun

**soviet** (soh-vi-ět or sov-i-ět) noun **1** a citizen of the former USSR. **2** (**Soviet**) an elected council in the former USSR. ●adjective of the former Soviet Union.

**Soviet Union** (hist.) the Union of Soviet Socialist Republics.

**sow**[1] (rhymes with go) verb (**sowed, sown** or **sowed, sowing**) **1** plant or scatter (seed) for growth; plant seed in (a field etc.). **2** implant or spread (feelings or ideas). □ **sow one's wild oats** (of a young person) behave wildly or promiscuously.

**sow**[2] (rhymes with cow) noun a fully-grown female pig.

**Soweto** (sŏ-wayt-oh) a group of townships near Johannesburg in South Africa.

**soy** noun (in full **soy bean**) the soya bean. □ **soy sauce** a sauce made by fermenting soya beans in brine.

**soya** noun (in full **soya bean**) a bean (originally from SE Asia) from which an edible oil and flour are obtained, often used to replace animal protein.

**Soyinka** (shoi-**ink**-ă), Wole (born 1934), Nigerian playwright and novelist.

**Soyuz** (soi-uuz) any of a series of manned spacecraft launched by the former USSR.

**sozzled** adjective (slang) very drunk.

**spa** (pronounced spah) noun a curative mineral spring; a place with such a spring.

**space** noun **1** the boundless expanse in which all objects exist and move. **2** a portion of this, an area or volume for a particular purpose; the box takes too much space; parking spaces. **3** an interval between points or objects, an empty area; separated by a space of 10 ft; there's a space for your *signature.* **4** the area of paper used in writing or printing something; *would take too much space to explain in detail.* **5** a large area; *the wide open spaces.* **6** outer space (*see* OUTER). **7** an interval of time; *within the space of an hour.* ●*verb* arrange with spaces between; *space them out.* □ **space age** the era of space travel. **space-age** *adjective* very modern. **Space Invaders** (*trade mark*) a computer game in which players have to destroy landing aliens. **space probe** an unmanned rocket with instruments to detect conditions in outer space. **space shuttle** a spacecraft for repeated use e.g. between earth and a space station. **space station** an artificial satellite used as a base for operations in space. **space-time** (**continuum**) fusion of the concepts of space and time, with time as a fourth dimension.

**spacecraft** *noun* (*plural* **spacecraft**) a vehicle for travelling in outer space.

**spaceman** *noun* (*plural* **spacemen**) a person who travels in outer space; an astronaut.

**spaceship** *noun* a spacecraft.

**spacesuit** *noun* a sealed pressurized suit allowing the wearer to leave a spacecraft and move about in outer space.

**spacewoman** *noun* (*plural* **spacewomen**) a female astronaut.

**spacious** (**spay-shŭs**) *adjective* providing much space, roomy. □ **spaciousness** *noun*

**spade** *noun* **1** a tool for digging ground, with a broad metal blade and a wooden handle. **2** a playing card of the suit (**spades**) marked with black figures shaped like an inverted heart with a short stem. **3** (*slang, offensive*) a Black person. □ **call a spade a spade** call a thing by its proper name; speak plainly or bluntly. □ **spadeful** *noun* (*plural* **spadefuls**).

**spadework** *noun* hard work done in preparation for something.

**spaghetti** (**spă-get-i**) *noun* pasta made in solid strands, between macaroni and vermicelli in thickness. □ **spaghetti Bolognese** (**bol-ŏn-ayz**) spaghetti with a meat and tomato sauce. **spaghetti junction** a complex multi-level road junction, especially on a motorway. **spaghetti western** a cowboy film made cheaply in Italy.

**Spain** a country in SW Europe.

**Spam** *noun* (*trade mark*) tinned meat made mainly from ham.

**span¹** *noun* **1** the extent from end to end or across. **2** the distance (reckoned as 9 inches or 23 cm) between the tips of a person's thumb and little finger when these are stretched apart. **3** the distance or part between the uprights supporting an arch or bridge. **4** the distance between the tips of the wings of an aeroplane or the outspread wings of a bird. ●*verb* (**spanned, spanning**) extend across, bridge.

**span²** *see* SPICK AND SPAN.

**spandrel** *noun* the space between the curve of an arch and the surrounding rectangular moulding or framework, or between the curves of adjoining arches and the moulding above.

**spangle** *noun* one of many thin pieces of glittering material ornamenting a dress etc. ●*verb* cover with spangles or sparkling objects.

**Spaniard** *noun* a native of Spain.

**spaniel** *noun* a dog with long drooping ears and a silky coat.

**Spanish** *adjective* of Spain or its people or language. ●*noun* **1** the language of Spain. **2** (**the Spanish**) (as *plural*) Spanish people. □ **Spanish Main** (*hist.*) the north-east coast of South America and adjoining parts of the Caribbean Sea.

**spank** *verb* slap on the buttocks.

**spanking** *adjective* (*informal*) brisk, lively; *a spanking pace.*

**spanner** *noun* a tool for gripping and turning the nut on a bolt etc. □ **throw a spanner in the works** sabotage a scheme.

**spar¹** *noun* **1** a strong pole used for a ship's mast, boom, etc. **2** the main lengthwise beam of an aeroplane wing.

**spar²** *noun* any of several kinds of non-metallic mineral that split easily.

**spar³** *verb* (**sparred, sparring**) **1** box, especially for practice. **2** quarrel or argue. □ **sparring partner 1** a boxer employed to give another boxer practice. **2** a person with whom one enjoys frequent arguments.

**spare** *verb* **1** be merciful towards, refrain from hurting or harming. **2** use with great restraint. **3** part with; afford to give; *we can't spare him until next week*; *can you spare me a moment?* ●*adjective* **1** additional to what is usually needed or used; in reserve for use when needed; *a spare wheel*; *spare time.* **2** thin; lean. **3** small in quantity. ●*noun* a spare part or thing kept in reserve for use when needed. □ **go spare** (*slang*) become very annoyed. **spare-rib** *noun* a cut of pork from the lower ribs. **spare tyre** (*informal*) a roll of fat round the waist. □ **sparely** *adverb*, **spareness** *noun*

**sparing** (**spair-ing**) *adjective* economical, not generous or wasteful. □ **sparingly** *adverb*

**Spark**, Muriel (born 1918), Scottish novelist.

**spark** *noun* **1** a fiery particle thrown off by a burning substance or caused by friction. **2** a flash of light produced by an electrical discharge. **3** a short burst or flash of genius, wit, generosity, energy, etc. **4** a lively young person. ●*verb* give off a spark or sparks. □ **spark plug** *or* **sparking plug**

a device producing an electrical spark to fire the mixture in an internal-combustion engine. **spark off** trigger off.

**sparkle** *verb* **1** shine brightly with tiny flashes of light. **2** show brilliant wit or liveliness. ●*noun* a sparkling light or brightness. □ **sparkling wine** wine that is effervescent.

**sparkler** *noun* a hand-held sparkling firework.

**sparrow** *noun* a small brownish-grey bird.

**sparrowhawk** *noun* a small hawk.

**sparse** *adjective* thinly scattered, not dense. □ **sparsely** *adverb*, **sparsity** *noun*, **sparseness** *noun*

**Sparta** a city in the southern Peloponnese in Greece, whose citizens in ancient times were renowned for hardiness. □ **Spartan** *adjective & noun*

**spartan** *adjective* (of conditions) simple and sometimes harsh, without comfort or luxuries. (¶ *See* SPARTA.)

**spasm** *noun* **1** a strong involuntary contraction of a muscle. **2** a sudden brief spell of activity or emotion.

**spasmodic** (spaz-mod-ik) *adjective* **1** occurring at irregular intervals. **2** of or like a spasm; characterized by spasms. □ **spasmodically** *adverb*

**spastic** *adjective* physically disabled because of a condition (especially cerebral palsy) in which there are faulty links between the brain and the motor nerves, causing jerky or involuntary movements. ●*noun* a person suffering from this condition.

**spat**[1] *see* SPIT[1].

**spat**[2] *noun* **1** a short gaiter covering the instep and ankle, formerly worn by men. **2** (*informal*) a slight quarrel.

**spate** (*pronounced* spayt) *noun* a sudden flood or rush; *a spate of orders*. □ **in spate** (of a river) flowing strongly at an abnormally high level.

**spathe** (*pronounced* spay*th*) *noun* a large petal-like part of a flower, surrounding a central spike.

**spatial** (spay-shăl) *adjective* of or relating to space; existing in space. □ **spatially** *adverb*

**spatter** *verb* scatter or fall in small drops; splash. ●*noun* a splash or splashes; the sound of spattering.

**spatula** (spat-yoo-lă) *noun* **1** a tool with a broad blunt flexible blade for spreading, mixing, etc. **2** a strip of stiff material used by a doctor for pressing down the tongue etc.

**spawn** *noun* **1** the eggs of fish or frogs or shellfish. **2** (*scornful*) offspring. **3** the thread-like matter from which fungi grow; *mushroom spawn*. ●*verb* **1** deposit spawn; produce from spawn. **2** generate, especially in large numbers; *the reports spawned by that committee*.

**spay** *verb* sterilize (a female animal) by removing the ovaries.

**speak** *verb* (**spoke**, **spoken**, **speaking**) **1** utter words in an ordinary voice (not singing); hold a conversation; make a speech; express in words. **2** use or be able to use (a specified language) in speaking; *we speak French.* **3** make a polite or friendly remark; *she always speaks when we meet.* **4** be evidence of something; *it speaks volumes for his patience; the facts speak for themselves.* □ **not** *or* **nothing to speak of** very little, only very slightly. **so to speak** if I may express it this way. **speak one's mind** give one's opinion frankly. **speak out** speak loudly or freely; speak one's mind. **speak up** speak more loudly; speak out.

**-speak** *combining form* jargon; *computerspeak; marketing-speak.*

**speaker** *noun* **1** a person who speaks; one who makes a speech. **2** a loudspeaker. **3** (**the Speaker**) the person presiding over the House of Commons or a similar assembly.

**spear** *noun* **1** a weapon for hurling, with a long shaft and a pointed tip. **2** a pointed stem, e.g. of asparagus. ●*verb* pierce with or as if with a spear.

**spearhead** *noun* the foremost part of an attacking or advancing force. ●*verb* be the spearhead of.

**spearmint** *noun* a common garden mint used in cookery and to flavour chewing gum.

**spec** *noun* (*informal*) a detailed description of a design, materials used, etc.; a specification. □ **on spec** (*slang*) as a speculation, without being certain of achieving what one wants.

**special** *adjective* **1** of a particular kind; for a particular purpose, not general; *a special key; special training.* **2** exceptional in amount, quality, or intensity; *take special care of it.* ●*noun* a special thing; a special train or edition etc.; a special constable. □ **Special Branch** the police department that deals with political security. **special constable** a person trained to assist the police. **special correspondent** a journalist reporting on a specific subject. **special effects** (in TV, film, etc.) illusions created by props, camera-work, etc. **special licence** a licence allowing a marriage to take place at very short notice or at a place other than one duly authorized. **special pleading** (in Law) pleading with particular reference to the circumstances of a case, as opposed to general pleading; (in popular use) persuasive but unfair reasoning. **special school** a school for children with learning difficulties. □ **specially** *adverb*

**specialist** *noun* an expert in a special branch of a subject, especially of medicine.

**speciality** (spesh-i-al-iti) *noun* a special quality, characteristic, or product; an activity in which a person specializes.

**specialize** *verb* (also **specialise**) **1** (often foll. by *in*) study a subject etc. with special intensity; become a specialist. **2** (often foll. by *in*) have a product etc. to which one devotes special attention; *the shop specializes in sports goods.* **3** adapt for a particular purpose; *specialized organs such as the ear.* □ **specialization** *noun*

**specie** (spee-shee) *noun* coin as opposed to paper money.

**species** (spee-shiz) *noun* (*plural* **species**) **1** a group of animals or plants within a genus, differing only in minor details from the others. **2** a kind or sort.

**specific** (spi-sif-ik) *adjective* **1** particular, clearly distinguished from others; *the money was given for a specific purpose.* **2** expressing oneself in exact terms, not vague; *please be specific about your requirements.* ●*noun* a specific aspect or influence; a remedy for a specific disease or condition. □ **specific gravity** = RELATIVE DENSITY. □ **specifically** *adverb*

**specification** *noun* **1** specifying; being specified. **2** the details describing something to be done or made.

**specify** *verb* (**specified, specifying**) mention (details, ingredients, etc.) clearly and definitely; include in a list of specifications.

**specimen** *noun* **1** a part or individual taken as an example of a whole or of a class, especially for experiments. **2** a quantity of a person's urine etc. taken for testing. **3** (*informal*) a person of a special sort.

**specious** (spee-shŭs) *adjective* seeming good or sound at first sight but lacking real merit; *specious reasoning.* □ **speciously** *adverb*

**speck** *noun* a small spot or particle.

**speckle** *noun* a small spot, a speck, especially as a natural marking.

**speckled** *adjective* marked with speckles.

**specs** *plural noun* (*informal*) spectacles.

**spectacle** *noun* **1** a striking or impressive sight; *a magnificent spectacle.* **2** a ridiculous sight; *made a spectacle of himself.* **3** (**spectacles**) a pair of lenses set in a frame, worn in front of the eyes. □ **spectacled** *adjective*

**spectacular** *adjective* striking, impressive, amazing. ●*noun* a spectacular show. □ **spectacularly** *adverb*

**spectator** *noun* a person who watches a show, game, incident, etc. □ **spectator sports** sports that attract many spectators.

**specter** *Amer.* spelling of SPECTRE.

**spectra** *see* SPECTRUM.

**spectral** *adjective* **1** of or like a spectre. **2** of the spectrum. □ **spectrally** *adverb*

**spectre** (spek-ter) *noun* (*Amer.* **specter**) **1** a ghost. **2** a haunting fear of future trouble; *the spectre of defeat.*

**spectrometer** (spek-trom-it-er) *noun* a spectroscope that can be used for measuring spectra.

**spectroscope** (spek-trŏ-skohp) *noun* an instrument for producing and examining spectra. □ **spectroscopic** *adjective*

**spectroscopy** (spek-tros-kŏpi) *noun* the examination and investigation of spectra.

**spectrum** *noun* (*plural* **spectra**) **1** the bands of colour as seen in a rainbow, forming a series according to their wavelengths. **2** a similar series of bands of sound. **3** an entire range of related qualities, ideas, etc.

**specula** *see* SPECULUM.

**speculate** *verb* **1** form opinions without definite knowledge or evidence. **2** buy or sell goods or stocks and shares etc. in the hope of making a profit but with risk of loss. □ **speculation** *noun*, **speculator** *noun*

**speculative** (spek-yoo-lă-tiv) *adjective* **1** of or based on speculation; *speculative reasoning.* **2** involving financial speculation and risk of loss. □ **speculatively** *adverb*

**speculum** (spek-yoo-lŭm) *noun* (*plural* **specula**) **1** a medical instrument for looking inside cavities of the body. **2** a mirror of polished metal in a telescope.

**sped** *see* SPEED.

**speech** *noun* **1** the act, power, or manner of speaking. **2** words spoken; a spoken communication to an audience. □ **speech day** an annual celebration at a school, with speeches, prizes, etc. **speech therapy** treatment to improve speech defects.

**speechifying** *noun* (*informal*) making a long or boring speech.

**speechless** *adjective* silent; unable to speak because of great emotion. □ **speechlessly** *adverb*

**speed** *noun* **1** the rate at which something moves or operates. **2** rapidity of movement. **3** the sensitivity of photographic film to light; the power of a lens to admit light. **4** (*slang*) an amphetamine drug. ●*verb* (**sped** (in senses **3** and **4 speeded**), **speeding**) **1** move or pass quickly. **2** send quickly; *speed you on your way.* **3** travel at an illegal or dangerous speed. **4** (foll. by *up*) move or work at greater speed. □ **speed limit** the maximum permitted speed on a road etc.

**speedboat** *noun* a fast motor boat.

**speedo** *noun* (*plural* **speedos**) (*informal*) a speedometer.

**speedometer** (spee-dom-it-er) *noun* a device in a motor vehicle, showing its speed.

**speedway** noun **1** an arena for motor-cycle racing. **2** (*Amer.*) a road or track reserved for fast traffic.

**speedwell** noun a low-growing wild plant with small blue flowers.

**speedy** adjective (**speedier, speediest**) **1** moving quickly. **2** done without delay. □ **speedily** adverb

**speleology** (spel-i-ol-ŏji) noun the exploration and scientific study of caves. □ **speleological** adjective, **speleologist** noun

**spell**[1] noun **1** words supposed to have magic power; their magical effect. **2** fascination, attraction; *the spell of eastern countries.*

**spell**[2] verb (**spelt** or **spelled, spelling**) **1** put in their correct sequence the letters that form (a word). **2** (of letters) form as a word; *c a t spells 'cat'.* **3** result in; *these changes spell ruin.* □ **spell out 1** spell aloud. **2** state explicitly; explain in detail.

**spell**[3] noun **1** a period of time. **2** a period of a certain type of weather; *a cold spell.* **3** a period of a certain activity. **4** (*Austral.*) a rest period. ● verb relieve (a person) in work etc. by taking one's turn.

**spellbound** adjective with the attention held as if by a spell; entranced.

**spelt**[1] see SPELL[2].

**spelt**[2] noun a kind of wheat.

**Spencer**[1], Herbert (1820–1903), English philosopher, a leading agnostic.

**Spencer**[2], Sir Stanley (1891–1959), English painter.

**spend** verb (**spent, spending**) **1** pay out (money) in buying something. **2** use up; *don't spend too much time on it.* **3** pass; *spent a holiday in Greece.* □ **spend a penny** (*informal*) go to the toilet.

**Spender**, Sir Stephen Harold (born 1909), English poet.

**spendthrift** noun a person who spends money extravagantly and wastefully.

**Spenser**, Edmund (*c.*1552–99), English poet, author of *The Faerie Queene.*

**spent** see SPEND. ● adjective used up, having lost its force or strength.

**sperm** noun **1** (plural **sperms** or **sperm**) a spermatozoon. **2** semen. □ **sperm count** the number of sperm in a measured amount of semen. **sperm whale** a large whale yielding spermaceti.

**spermaceti** noun a white waxy substance from a sperm whale, used in ointments, soap, etc.

**spermatozoon** (sper-mǎ-tŏ-**zoh**-ŏn) noun (plural **spermatozoa**) a male reproductive cell in semen, capable of fertilizing an ovum.

**spermicide** (sperm-i-syd) noun a substance that kills sperm. □ **spermicidal** adjective

**spew** verb (also **spue**) **1** vomit. **2** cast out in a stream.

**sphagnum** (sfag-nŭm) noun (in full **sphagnum moss**) a moss that grows in bogs.

**sphere** (pronounced sfeer) noun **1** a perfectly round solid geometric figure. **2** something shaped like this. **3** a field of action or influence or existence; a person's place in society; *it took him out of his sphere.*

**spherical** (sfe-ri-kǎl) adjective shaped like a sphere. □ **spherically** adverb

**spheroid** (**sfeer**-oid) noun a spherelike but not perfectly spherical solid. □ **spheroidal** adjective

**sphincter** (sfink-ter) noun a ring of muscle surrounding an opening in the body and able to close it by contracting.

**sphinx** noun **1** (**the Sphinx**) (*Gk. myth.*) a winged monster at Thebes that killed all who could not answer a riddle. **2** any of the ancient stone statues in Egypt with a recumbent lion's body and a human or animal's head, especially the one at Giza. **3** a person who does not reveal his or her thoughts and feelings.

**spice** noun **1** a plant substance, especially ground seeds or roots, with a strong taste or smell, used for flavouring food. **2** a thing that adds zest or excitement; *variety is the spice of life.* ● verb flavour with spice.

**Spice Islands** the Moluccas.

**spick and span** neat and clean; new-looking.

**spicy** adjective (**spicier, spiciest**) **1** like spice; flavoured with spice. **2** (of stories) slightly scandalous or improper. □ **spiciness** noun

**spider** noun an animal (not an insect) with a segmented body and eight jointed legs, spinning webs to trap insects. □ **spider monkey** a monkey with long limbs and a prehensile tail. **spider plant** a house plant with long narrow arching striped leaves.

**spidery** adjective having long thin angular lines like a spider's legs.

**spiel** (pronounced shpeel) noun (*slang*) a glib or lengthy speech, usually intended to persuade.

**Spielberg**, Steven (born 1947), American film director.

**spigot** (spig-ŏt) noun a peg or plug used to stop the vent-hole of a cask or to control the flow of a tap.

**spike** noun **1** a sharp projecting point; a pointed piece of metal. **2** an ear of corn. **3** a long cluster of flowers on a central stem. ● verb **1** put spikes on; *spiked running shoes.* **2** pierce or fasten with a spike. **3** (*informal*) add alcohol to (a drink). □ **spike a person's guns** spoil his or her plans. □ **spiky** adjective

**spikenard** (spyk·nard) noun **1** a tall sweet-smelling Indian plant. **2** a fragrant ointment formerly made from this.

**spill**[1] noun a thin strip of wood or of twisted paper used for lighting a fire or pipe.

**spill**[2] verb (**spilt** or **spilled, spilling**) **1** cause or allow (a liquid etc.) to run over the edge of its container. **2** (of liquid etc.) become spilt. **3** (*slang*) make known; *spilt the news.* ● noun **1** spilling; being spilt. **2** a fall. □ **spill blood** kill or wound. **spill over** overflow. **spill the beans** (*slang*) let out information.

**spillage** noun **1** spilling; **2** the amount spilt.

**spillikin** noun **1** a splinter of wood etc. **2** (**spillikins**) a game in which such splinters must be moved one at a time from a heap without disturbing the others.

**spin** verb (**spun, spinning**) **1** turn or cause to turn rapidly on its axis. **2** draw out and twist (raw cotton or wool etc.) into threads. **3** (of a spider or silkworm) make from a fine threadlike material emitted from the body; *spinning its web.* ● noun **1** a spinning movement. **2** a rotating dive of an aircraft. **3** a secondary twisting motion, e.g. of a ball in flight. **4** (*informal*) a short drive in a vehicle. □ **spin a yarn** tell an invented story. **spin bowler** (in cricket) a bowler who gives the ball a spinning movement. **spin doctor** a person employed to promote a favourable impression of political events to the media. **spin-drier** noun (also **spin-dryer**) a machine with a rapidly rotating drum in which moisture is removed from washed articles. **spin-dry** verb dry in a spin-drier. **spin-off** noun a benefit or product produced incidentally from a larger process. **spin out** cause to last a long time.

**spina bifida** (spy·nă bif·id·ă) an abnormal congenital condition in which certain bones of the spine are not properly developed and the spinal cord protrudes.

**spinach** noun a vegetable with dark green leaves.

**spinal** adjective of the spine. □ **spinal column** the spine. **spinal cord** the rope-like mass of nerve fibres enclosed within the spinal column.

**spindle** noun **1** a slender rod on which thread is wound in spinning. **2** a pin or axis that revolves or on which something revolves. **3** a spindle tree. □ **spindle tree** a shrub or small tree with pink or red berries and hard wood formerly used for spindles.

**spindly** adjective long or tall and thin.

**spindrift** noun spray blown along the surface of the sea.

**spine** noun **1** the backbone. **2** any of the sharp needle-like projections on certain plants (e.g. cacti) and animals (e.g. hedgehogs). **3** the part of a book where the pages are hinged. □ **spine-chiller** noun a spine-chilling book, film, etc. **spine-chilling** adjective causing a thrill of terror.

**spineless** adjective **1** having no backbone. **2** lacking determination or strength of character. □ **spinelessness** noun

**spinet** (spin·et) noun a small harpsichord.

**spinnaker** (spin·ă·ker) noun a large triangular extra sail on a racing yacht.

**spinner** noun **1** a person or thing that spins. **2** a spin bowler. **3** (in fishing) revolving bait.

**spinneret** noun **1** a spinning organ in a spider or silkworm. **2** a device for making synthetic fibre.

**spinney** noun (*plural* **spinneys**) a small wood; a thicket.

**spinning** noun the act of spinning yarn. □ **spinning-jenny** noun (*hist.*) a machine for spinning yarn using more than one spindle at a time. **spinning wheel** a household device for spinning fibre into yarn, with a spindle driven by a wheel.

**Spinoza** (spin·oh·ză), Baruch (Benedict) de (1632–77), Dutch philosopher.

**spinster** noun an unmarried woman.

**spiny** adjective full of spines, prickly. □ **spiny anteater** = ECHIDNA.

**spiraea** (spy·ree·ă) noun (*Amer.* **spirea**) a shrub with small white or pink flowers.

**spiracle** (spy·ră·kŭl) noun **1** any of the openings through which an insect breathes. **2** the blowhole of a whale etc.

**spiral** adjective advancing or ascending in a continuous curve that winds round a central point or axis. ● noun **1** a spiral line; a thing of spiral form. **2** a continuous increase or decrease in two or more quantities alternately because of their dependence on each other; *the spiral of rising wages and prices.* ● verb (**spiralled, spiralling;** *Amer.* **spiraled, spiraling**) move in a spiral course. □ **spirally** adverb

**spire** noun a pointed structure in the form of a tall cone or pyramid, especially on a church.

**spirea** Amer. spelling of SPIRAEA.

**spirit** noun **1** a person's mind, feelings, or soul as distinct from the body. **2** a ghost. **3** a person's nature. **4** a person with specified mental or moral qualities; *a few brave spirits went swimming.* **5** the characteristic quality or mood of something; *the spirit of the times.* **6** the real purpose (of a law) as distinct from a strict interpretation of its words. **7** liveliness, readiness to assert oneself; *answered with spirit.* **8** (**spirits**) a person's feeling of cheerfulness or depression. **9** a strong distilled alcoholic drink, e.g. whisky or gin. ● verb carry off swiftly and secretly; *spirited him away.* □ **spirit gum** quick-drying gum for attaching false hair. **spirit-lamp** noun a lamp that burns methylated spirit or a similar fluid. **spirit-level** noun a glass tube nearly filled with liquid and containing an air bubble, used to test whether something is level.

**spirited** adjective 1 full of spirit, lively; ready to assert oneself. 2 having spirits of a specified kind; in a specified mood; *high-spirited*. □ **spiritedly** adverb

**spiritless** adjective lacking vigour or energy.

**spiritual** adjective 1 of the human spirit or soul. 2 of the Church or religion. ●noun (also **Negro spiritual**) a religious folk-song of American Blacks. □ **Lords spiritual** see LORD. □ **spiritually** adverb, **spirituality** noun

**spiritualism** noun the belief that spirits of the dead can communicate with the living; practices based on this. □ **spiritualist** noun, **spiritualistic** adjective

**spirituous** adjective (of alcoholic drink) 1 very alcoholic. 2 distilled and not only fermented.

**spirogyra** (spy-rŏ-jy-rä) noun a freshwater alga with spiral bands of chlorophyll.

**spit¹** verb (**spat** or **spit**, **spitting**) 1 eject from the mouth; eject saliva. 2 (of a cat) make a noise like spitting when angry or hostile; (of a person) show anger; *spitting with fury*. 3 (of a fire etc.) throw out sparks etc. explosively. 4 fall lightly; *it's spitting with rain*. ●noun 1 spittle. 2 the act of spitting. □ **spit and polish** cleaning and polishing of equipment etc., especially by soldiers. **spit it out** (slang) say it quickly. **spitting image** an exact likeness.

**spit²** noun 1 a long thin metal spike thrust through meat to hold it while it is roasted. 2 a long narrow strip of land projecting into the sea. ●verb (**spitted**, **spitting**) pierce with or as if with a spit.

**spite** noun a malicious desire to hurt, annoy, or humiliate another person. ●verb hurt or annoy etc. from spite. □ **in spite of** not being prevented by; *we enjoyed ourselves in spite of the weather*.

**spiteful** adjective full of spite; showing or caused by spite. □ **spitefully** adverb, **spitefulness** noun

**spitfire** noun a fiery-tempered person.

**Spitfire** a type of British fighter aircraft used in World War II.

**Spitsbergen** an archipelago in the Arctic Ocean north of Norway, under Norwegian sovereignty.

**spittle** noun saliva, especially that ejected from the mouth.

**spittoon** noun a vessel for spitting into.

**spiv** noun (slang) a smartly-dressed person who makes money by shady dealings.

**splash** verb 1 cause (liquid) to fly about in drops; wet with such drops. 2 (of liquid) be splashed. 3 move or fall with splashing;

*we splashed through the puddles*. 4 decorate with irregular patches of colour etc. 5 display prominently; *the news was splashed across the Sunday papers*. 6 (often foll. by out) spend (money) freely; be extravagant. ●noun 1 splashing; a sound or mark made by this. 2 a quantity of liquid splashed. 3 (informal) a small quantity of soda water or other liquid in a drink. 4 a patch of colour or light. 5 a striking or ostentatious display or effect.

**splashback** noun a panel behind a sink etc. to protect a wall from splashes.

**splashdown** noun the landing of a spacecraft on the sea.

**splat** (informal) noun a sharp sound of something squashy hitting a hard surface. ●adverb with a splat.

**splatter** verb splash noisily. ●noun a noisy splashing sound.

**splay** verb spread apart; bend outwards; slant (the sides of an opening).

**spleen** noun 1 an organ of the body situated at the left of the stomach and involved in maintaining the proper condition of the blood. 2 bad temper, peevishness.

**splendid** adjective 1 magnificent, displaying splendour. 2 excellent; *a splendid achievement*. □ **splendidly** adverb

**splendiferous** adjective (informal) splendid.

**splendour** noun (Amer. **splendor**) brilliance; magnificent display or appearance, grandeur.

**splenetic** (splin-et-ik) adjective bad-tempered, peevish. □ **splenetically** adverb

**splenic** (spleen-ik or splen-ik) adjective of or in the spleen.

**splice** verb 1 join (two ends of rope) by untwisting and interweaving the strands of each. 2 join (pieces of film or timber etc.) by overlapping the ends. ●noun a join made by splicing. □ **get spliced** (informal) get married. **splice the main brace** (in nautical use) serve a free drink of spirits.

**splint** noun a strip of rigid material bound to an injured part of the body to prevent movement, e.g. while a broken bone heals. ●verb secure with a splint.

**splinter** noun a thin sharp piece of wood or stone etc. broken off from a larger piece. ●verb break or become broken into splinters. □ **splinter group** a small group that has broken away from a larger one, e.g. in a political party. □ **splintery** adjective

**split** verb (**split**, **splitting**) 1 break or become broken into parts, especially lengthwise or along the grain of wood etc. 2 divide into parts; divide and share. 3 come apart, tear; *this coat has split at the seams*. 4 divide or become divided into hostile groups. 5 (usually foll. by on) (informal) betray, inform; *split on his mates*. ●noun

**1** splitting; being split. **2** the place where something has split or torn. **3** a dish of split fruit with cream or ice cream etc.; *banana split*. **4** (**splits**) an acrobatic position in which the legs are stretched in opposite directions and at right angles to the trunk. □ **split infinitive** an infinitive with a word or words placed between *to* and the verb (disliked and avoided by many people), e.g. *to thoroughly understand*. **split-level** *adjective* (of a building) having adjoining rooms at a level midway between successive storeys in other parts; (of a cooker) having the oven placed separately from the burners or hotplates, not below them, so that it can be at a convenient height. **split one's sides** laugh heartily. **split pea** a dried pea split in half. **split personality** schizophrenia. **split pin** a metal pin with split ends that hold it in position when they are splayed. **split second** a very brief moment. **split-second** *adjective* extremely rapid; accurate to a very small fraction of time; *split-second timing*. **split shift** a shift in which there are two or more periods of duty. **split the difference** decide on an amount halfway between two proposed amounts. **split up** split, separate; (of a married couple) cease to live together.

**splitting** *adjective* (of a headache) severe, feeling as if it will split one's head.

**splodge** (*informal*) *noun* a daub, blot, or smear. ●*verb* make a splodge on. □ **splodgy** *adjective*

**splosh** (*informal*) *verb* splash. ●*noun* a splash.

**splotch** *noun & verb* = SPLODGE.

**splurge** *noun* **1** a sudden extravagance; a spending spree. **2** an ostentatious display. ●*verb* make a splurge, spend money freely.

**splutter** *verb* **1** make a rapid series of spitting sounds. **2** speak or utter rapidly or indistinctly (e.g. in rage). ●*noun* a spluttering sound.

**Spock**, Benjamin McLane (born 1903), American paediatrician, whose ideas on child-rearing had worldwide influence.

**Spode** *noun* fine pottery or porcelain named after the English potter Josiah Spode (1754–1827), its original maker.

**spoil** *verb* (**spoilt** *or* **spoiled**, **spoiling**) **1** damage, make useless or unsatisfactory. **2** become unfit for use. **3** harm the character of (a person) by lack of discipline, excessive generosity, or pampering. ●*noun* (usually as **spoils**) **1** plunder; benefits gained by a victor. **2** profitable advantages of an official position. □ **be spoiling for** desire eagerly; *he is spoiling for a fight*.

**spoilage** *noun* **1** paper spoilt in printing. **2** the spoiling of food etc. by decay.

**spoiler** *noun* **1** a device on an aircraft to slow it down by interrupting the airflow. **2** a

similar device on a vehicle to prevent it from being lifted off the road when travelling very fast.

**spoilsport** *noun* a person who spoils others' enjoyment.

**spoke¹** *noun* each of the rods that connect the centre of a wheel to its rim. □ **put a spoke in a person's wheel** thwart his or her intentions.

**spoke²**, **spoken** *see* SPEAK.

**spokeshave** *noun* a tool for planing something curved.

**spokesman** *noun* (*plural* **spokesmen**) a person who speaks on behalf of a group.

**spokesperson** *noun* (*plural* **spokespersons** *or* **spokespeople**) a spokesman or spokeswoman.

**spokeswoman** *noun* (*plural* **spokeswomen**) a woman who speaks on behalf of a group.

**spoliation** (spoh-li-ay-shŏn) *noun* pillaging.

**spondee** *noun* Poetry a metrical foot with two long or stressed syllables.

**sponge** *noun* **1** a sea animal with a porous structure. **2** the skeleton of this, or a substance of similar texture, used for washing, cleaning, or padding. **3** sponge cake. **4** sponging; a wash with a sponge. ●*verb* **1** wipe or wash with a sponge. **2** (often foll. by *on* or *off*) live off the generosity of others, cadge. □ **sponge bag** a waterproof bag for toilet articles. **sponge cake** a cake with a light, open texture. **sponge pudding** a pudding like a sponge cake.

**sponger** *noun* a person who sponges on others.

**spongiform** *adjective* of or like a sponge, especially the sea animal.

**spongy** *adjective* (**spongier**, **spongiest**) like a sponge in texture, soft and springy. □ **sponginess** *noun*

**sponson** *noun* a projection on the side of a ship, tank, or seaplane; an air-filled structure fitted along the gunwale of a canoe to make it more stable and buoyant.

**sponsor** *noun* **1** a person who makes himself or herself responsible for another who is undergoing training etc. **2** a godparent. **3** a person who puts forward a proposal, e.g. for a new law. **4** a person or firm that provides funds for a musical, artistic, or sporting event. **5** a person who subscribes to charity in return for a specified activity by another person. ●*verb* act as sponsor for. □ **sponsorship** *noun*

**spontaneous** (spon-**tay**-niŭs) *adjective* resulting from natural impulse; not caused or suggested from outside; not forced. □ **spontaneous combustion** the bursting into flame of a substance because of heat produced by its own rapid oxidation and not by flame etc. from an external source.

□ **spontaneously** *adverb*, **spontaneity** (spon-tăn-ee-iti) *noun*

**spoof** *noun* (*informal*) a hoax; a humorous imitation.

**spook** (*informal*) *noun* a ghost. ● *verb* frighten, unnerve.

**spooky** *adjective* (*informal*) ghostly, eerie. □ **spookily** *adverb*, **spookiness** *noun*

**spool** *noun* a reel on which something is wound, e.g. yarn or photographic film. ● *verb* wind or become wound on a spool.

**spoon** *noun* **1** a utensil consisting of a rounded bowl and a handle, used for eating, stirring, or measuring things. **2** the amount it contains. ● *verb* **1** take or lift with a spoon. **2** hit (a ball) feebly upwards. **3** (*informal*) kiss and cuddle.

**spoonbill** *noun* a wading bird with a very broad flat tip to its bill.

**spoonerism** *noun* interchange of the initial sounds of two words, usually as a slip of the tongue, e.g. *he's a boiled sprat* (= spoiled brat). (¶ Named after the Rev. W. A. Spooner (1844–1930), said to have made such errors in speaking.)

**spoonfeed** *verb* (**spoonfed**, **spoonfeeding**) **1** feed with liquid food from a spoon. **2** give excessive help to (a person etc.) so that the recipient does not need to make any effort.

**spoonful** *noun* (*plural* **spoonfuls**) as much as a spoon will hold.

**spoor** *noun* the track or scent left by an animal.

**sporadic** (sper-ad-ik) *adjective* occurring here and there, scattered. □ **sporadically** *adverb*

**spore** *noun* one of the tiny reproductive cells of plants such as fungi and ferns.

**sporran** (spo-răn) *noun* a pouch worn in front of the kilt as part of Highland dress.

**sport** *noun* **1** a competitive activity; a game or pastime involving physical exertion; these collectively. **2** (**sports**) athletic activities; a meeting for competition in these; *the school sports.* **3** amusement, fun; *we said it in sport.* **4** (*informal*) a sportsmanlike person. **5** an animal or plant that is strikingly different from its parent(s). ● *verb* **1** play, amuse oneself. **2** wear or display; *he sported a gold tie-pin.* □ **sports car** an open low-built fast car. **sports coat** *or* **jacket** a man's jacket for informal wear (not part of a suit).

**sporting** *adjective* **1** interested in sport, concerned with sport; *a sporting man.* **2** sportsmanlike. □ **a sporting chance** a reasonable chance of success.

**sportive** *adjective* playful. □ **sportively** *adverb*

**sportsman** *noun* (*plural* **sportsmen**) **1** a man who takes part in sports. **2** a fair and generous person.

**sportsmanlike** *adjective* behaving fairly and generously.

**sportswear** *noun* clothes for sports.

**sportswoman** *noun* (*plural* **sportswomen**) a woman who takes part in sports.

**sporty** *adjective* (*informal*) **1** fond of sport. **2** dashing. □ **sportily** *adverb*, **sportiness** *noun*

**spot** *noun* **1** a roundish area different in colour from the rest of a surface; a roundish mark. **2** a pimple. **3** a particular place. **4** (*informal*) a small amount of something; *a spot of leave.* **5** a drop; *a few spots of rain.* **6** a spotlight. ● *verb* (**spotted**, **spotting**) **1** mark with a spot or spots. **2** (*informal*) catch sight of; detect or recognize. □ **in a spot** (*informal*) in difficulties. **on the spot** without delay or change of place; at the scene of action. **put on the spot** put (a person) in a difficult position; compel to take action. **spot check** a check made suddenly on something chosen at random. **spot on** (*informal*) precisely. **spotted dick** suet pudding containing currants. **spot welding** welding of small areas that are in contact. □ **spotter** *noun*

**spotless** *adjective* free from stain or blemish, perfectly clean. □ **spotlessly** *adverb*

**spotlight** *noun* **1** a beam of light directed on a small area; a lamp giving this. **2** full publicity or attention. ● *verb* (**spotlighted**, **spotlighting**) **1** direct a spotlight on. **2** draw attention to, make conspicuous.

**spotty** *adjective* (**spottier**, **spottiest**) marked with spots. □ **spottiness** *noun*

**spouse** *noun* a person's husband or wife.

**spout** *noun* **1** a projecting tube through which liquid is poured or conveyed. **2** a jet of liquid. ● *verb* **1** come or send out forcefully as a jet of liquid. **2** utter or speak lengthily. □ **up the spout** (*slang*) **1** broken or ruined, in a hopeless condition. **2** pregnant.

**sprain** *verb* injure (a joint or its muscles or ligaments) by wrenching it violently. ● *noun* an injury caused in this way.

**sprang** *see* SPRING.

**sprat** *noun* a small herring-like fish.

**sprawl** *verb* **1** sit, lie, or fall with the arms and legs spread out loosely. **2** spread out in an irregular or straggling way. ● *noun* a sprawling attitude, movement, or arrangement.

**spray**¹ *noun* **1** a single shoot or branch with its leaves, twigs, and flowers. **2** a bunch of cut flowers etc. arranged decoratively. **3** an ornament in similar form.

**spray**² *noun* **1** water or other liquid dispersed in very small drops. **2** a liquid preparation for spraying. **3** a device for spraying liquid. ● *verb* **1** send out (liquid) or be sent out in very small drops; wet with liquid in this way. **2** (of an animal) mark its territory with urine. □ **spray-gun** *noun* a device for spraying paint or other liquid. □ **sprayer** *noun*

**spread** *verb* (**spread, spreading**) **1** open out, unroll or unfold. **2** become longer or wider; *the stain began to spread.* **3** cover the surface of, apply as a layer; *spread the bread with jam.* **4** be able to be spread; *it spreads like butter.* **5** make or become more widely distributed, known, felt, or suffered; *spread the news; panic spread.* **6** distribute over a period; *spread the payments over 12 months.* ●*noun* **1** spreading; being spread. **2** the extent, expanse, or breadth of something. **3** expansion. **4** a bedspread. **5** (*informal*) a lavish meal. **6** the range of something. **7** a sweet or savoury paste for spreading on bread. □ **spread eagle** the figure of an eagle with legs and wings extended, as an emblem. **spread-eagle** *verb* **1** spread out (a person's body) in this way. **2** defeat utterly. **spread oneself** talk lengthily; spend or provide things lavishly.

**spreadsheet** *noun* a computer program that manipulates figures in tabulated form; used in financial planning and accounting.

**spree** *noun* (*informal*) a lively extravagant outing; some fun; *a shopping spree.*

**sprig** *noun* **1** a small branch, a shoot. **2** an ornament or decoration in this form.

**sprigged** *adjective* (of fabric) having a pattern of sprigs.

**sprightly** *adjective* (**sprightlier, sprightliest**) lively, full of energy. □ **sprightliness** *noun*

**spring** *verb* (**sprang, sprung, springing**) **1** jump; move rapidly or suddenly in a single movement. **2** grow or issue; arise; *weeds sprang up; their discontent springs from distrust of their leaders.* **3** become warped or split. **4** rouse (game) from an earth or covert. **5** (*slang*) arrange the escape of (a prisoner). **6** cause to operate suddenly; *sprang the trap.* **7** produce or develop suddenly or unexpectedly; *sprang a surprise on us.* ●*noun* **1** the act of springing, a jump. **2** a device (usually of bent or coiled metal) that reverts to its original position after being compressed or stretched. **3** elasticity. **4** a place where water or oil comes up naturally from the ground; the flow of this. **5** the season in which vegetation begins to appear, from March to May in the Northern hemisphere. □ **spring a leak** develop a leak. **spring balance** a device that measures weight by the tension of a spring. **spring chicken 1** a young fowl for eating. **2** a young person. **spring-clean** *verb* clean one's home thoroughly. **spring equinox** (also **vernal equinox**) the equinox occurring about 20 March. **spring greens** a type of cabbage eaten when the leaves are

very young. **spring onion** a young onion eaten raw. **spring roll** a Chinese fried pancake filled with vegetables and sometimes meat. **spring tide** the tide when there is the largest rise and fall of water, occurring shortly after the new and full moon.

**springboard** *noun* a flexible board for giving impetus to a person who jumps on it, used in gymnastics and in diving.

**springbok** *noun* **1** (*plural* **springbok** or **springboks**) a South African gazelle that can spring high into the air. **2** (**Springboks**) a South African national sporting team or touring party.

**springer** *noun* **1** a small spaniel of a breed used to spring game. **2** the part of an arch where the curve begins; the lowest stone of this.

**springtime** *noun* the season of spring.

**springy** *adjective* (**springier, springiest**) able to spring back easily after being squeezed or stretched. □ **springiness** *noun*

**sprinkle** *verb* scatter or fall in small drops or particles; scatter small drops etc. on (a surface). ●*noun* a sprinkling.

**sprinkler** *noun* a device for sprinkling water.

**sprinkling** *noun* **1** something sprinkled. **2** a few here and there.

**sprint** *verb* run at full speed, especially over a short distance. ●*noun* a run of this kind; a similar spell of maximum effort in swimming, cycling, etc. □ **sprinter** *noun*

**sprit** *noun* a small spar reaching diagonally from a mast to the upper outer corner of a sail.

**sprite** *noun* an elf, fairy, or goblin.

**spritsail** (**sprit**-săl) *noun* a sail extended by a sprit.

**spritzer** *noun* a drink of white wine mixed with soda water.

**sprocket** *noun* each of a series of teeth on a wheel, engaging with links on a chain.

**sprout** *verb* **1** begin to grow or appear; put forth shoots. **2** cause to spring up as a growth; *has sprouted horns.* ●*noun* **1** the shoot of a plant. **2** a Brussels sprout (*see* BRUSSELS).

**spruce**¹ *adjective* neat and trim in appearance, smart. ●*verb* smarten; *spruce oneself up.* □ **sprucely** *adverb*, **spruceness** *noun*

**spruce**² *noun* a fir with dense foliage; its wood.

**sprung** *see* SPRING. ●*adjective* fitted with springs; *a sprung mattress.*

**spry** *adjective* (**spryer, spryest**) active, nimble, lively. □ **spryly** *adverb*, **spryness** *noun*

**spud** *noun* **1** a small narrow spade for digging up weeds or cutting their roots. **2** (*informal*) a potato. ●*verb* (**spudded, spudding**) dig with a spud.

**spue** alternative spelling of SPEW.

**spumante** (spoo-**man**-ti) *noun* Italian sparkling white wine.

**spume** *noun* froth, foam. ●*verb* foam.

**spun** *see* SPIN. □ **spun silk** yarn or fabric made from waste silk. **spun sugar** a fluffy mass made from boiled sugar drawn into long threads.

**spunk** *noun* (*informal*) courage. □ **spunky** *adjective*

**spur** *noun* **1** a pricking device with a projecting point or toothed wheel, worn on a horse-rider's heel. **2** a stimulus or incentive. **3** something shaped like a spur; a hard projection on a cock's leg; a slender hollow projection on a flower. **4** a ridge projecting from a mountain. **5** a branch road or railway. ●*verb* (**spurred, spurring**) **1** urge (one's horse) on by pricking it with spurs. **2** urge on, incite, stimulate; *he spurred the men to greater effort.* □ **on the spur of the moment** on an impulse. **win one's spurs** prove one's ability; win distinction.

**spurge** *noun* a plant or bush with a bitter milky juice.

**spurious** (spewr-iŭs) *adjective* not genuine or authentic.

**spurn** *verb* reject scornfully.

**spurt** *verb* **1** gush, send out (a liquid) suddenly. **2** increase one's speed suddenly. ●*noun* **1** a sudden gush. **2** a short burst of activity; a sudden increase in speed.

**sputnik** (spuut-nik) *noun* a Russian artificial satellite orbiting the earth.

**sputter** *verb* splutter; make a series of quick explosive sounds; *sausages sputtered in the pan.* ●*noun* a sputtering sound.

**sputum** (spew-tŭm) *noun* spittle; matter that is spat out.

**spy** *noun* (*plural* **spies**) a person who secretly collects and reports information, especially for a government or organization. ●*verb* (**spied, spying**) **1** see, catch sight of. **2** be a spy, keep watch secretly. **3** pry.

**spyglass** *noun* a small telescope.

**spyhole** *noun* a peep-hole.

**sq.** *abbreviation* square.

**squab** (*pronounced* skwob) *noun* **1** a young pigeon. **2** a stuffed seat or cushion, especially as part (usually the back) of a car seat. **3** a short fat person.

**squabble** *verb* quarrel in a petty or noisy way. ●*noun* a quarrel of this kind.

**squad** *noun* a small group of people working or being trained together. □ **squad car** a police car.

**squaddie** *noun* (also **squaddy**) (*plural* **squaddies**) (*Brit. slang*) an ordinary soldier.

**squadron** *noun* **1** a division of a cavalry unit or armoured formation, consisting of two troops. **2** a detachment of warships. **3** a unit of the RAF (10 to 18 aircraft). □ **squadron leader** a commander of an RAF squadron, next below Wing Commander.

**squalid** *adjective* **1** dirty and unpleasant, especially because of neglect or poverty. **2** morally degrading. □ **squalidly** *adverb*

**squall** *noun* **1** a harsh cry or scream, especially of a baby. **2** a sudden storm of wind, especially with rain, snow, or sleet. ●*verb* utter a squall. □ **squally** *adjective*

**squalor** *noun* a filthy or squalid state.

**squander** *verb* spend wastefully.

**square** *noun* **1** a geometric figure with four equal sides and four right angles. **2** an area or object shaped like this. **3** a four-sided area surrounded by buildings. **4** (in astrology) the aspect of two planets 90° apart, regarded as having an unfavourable influence. **5** an L-shaped or T-shaped instrument for obtaining or testing right angles. **6** the product obtained when a number is multiplied by itself; *9 is the square of 3 (9 = 3 × 3).* **7** (*slang*) a person considered old-fashioned or conventional. ●*adjective* **1** of square shape. **2** right-angled; *the desk has square corners.* **3** of or using units that express the measure of an area (e.g. *one square metre* is an area equal to that of a square with sides one metre long). **4** of comparatively broad sturdy shape; *a man of square frame.* **5** properly arranged; tidy; *get things square.* **6** (also **all square**) equal, with no balance of advantage or debt etc. on either side. **7** straightforward, uncompromising; *a square refusal.* **8** fair, honest; *a square deal.* **9** (*slang*) old-fashioned, conventional. ●*adverb* squarely, directly; *hit him square on the jaw.* ●*verb* **1** make right-angled; *square the corners.* **2** mark with squares; *squared paper.* **3** place evenly or squarely; *he squared his shoulders.* **4** multiply (a number) by itself; *3 squared is 9 (3² = 9), 3 × 3 = 9.* **5** settle or pay; *that squares the account.* **6** (*informal*) secure the cooperation of (a person) by payment or bribery; *try and square the porter.* **7** be or make consistent; *his story doesn't square with yours.* □ **back to square one** back to the starting point with no progress made. **square-bashing** *noun* (*slang*) military drill. **square brackets** brackets of the form [ ]. **square the circle 1** construct a square equal in area to a given circle. **2** do what is impossible. **square dance** a dance in which four couples face inwards from four sides. **square leg** a fielder in cricket on the batsman's leg side and nearly in line with the wicket; this position. **square meal** a large satisfying meal. **square peg in a round hole** a person who is not fitted for his or her job. **square-rigged** *adjective* with the principal sails at right angles to the length of the ship. **square root** a number of which the given number is the square (*see noun sense 6*); *3 is the square root of 9*. **square up to** assume a boxer's fighting attitude; face and tackle (a difficulty) resolutely. □ **squarely** *adverb*, **squareness** *noun*

**squash**[1] *verb* 1 crush; squeeze or become squeezed flat or into pulp. 2 pack tightly; squeeze into a small space. 3 suppress; *squashed the rebellion*. 4 silence with a crushing reply. ●*noun* 1 a crowd of people squashed together. 2 the sound of something being squashed. 3 a crushed mass. 4 a fruit-flavoured soft drink. 5 (in full **squash rackets**) a game played with rackets and a small ball in a closed court. □ **squashy** *adjective*

**squash**[2] *noun* a gourd used as a vegetable; the plant that bears it.

**squat** *verb* (**squatted**, **squatting**) 1 sit on one's heels or crouch with knees drawn up closely. 2 (of an animal) crouch close to the ground. 3 (*informal*) sit. 4 be a squatter; occupy as a squatter. ●*noun* 1 a squatting posture. 2 occupying a place as a squatter; the place itself. ●*adjective* short and thick, dumpy.

**squatter** *noun* 1 one who sits in a squatting posture. 2 a person who settles on unoccupied land in order to acquire a legal right to it. 3 a person who takes temporary possession of unoccupied buildings for living in, without authority. 4 (*Austral.*) a sheep-farmer.

**squaw** *noun* a North American Indian woman or wife.

**squawk** *noun* a loud harsh cry. ●*verb* 1 utter a squawk. 2 (*informal*) complain.

**squeak** *noun* a short high-pitched cry or sound. ●*verb* 1 utter or make a squeak. 2 (*slang*) become an informer. □ **a narrow squeak** (*informal*) a narrow escape. □ **squeaker** *noun*

**squeaky** *adjective* (**squeakier**, **squeakiest**) making a squeaking sound. □ **squeaky clean** (*informal*) 1 completely clean. 2 above criticism; beyond reproach. □ **squeakily** *adverb*, **squeakiness** *noun*

**squeal** *noun* a long shrill cry or sound. ●*verb* 1 make this cry or sound. 2 (*informal*) protest sharply. 3 (*slang*) become an informer.

**squeamish** *adjective* 1 easily sickened, disgusted, or shocked. 2 excessively scrupulous about principles. □ **squeamishly** *adverb*, **squeamishness** *noun*

**squeegee** (skwee-**jee**) *noun* a tool with a rubber blade, used for sweeping or squeezing away water or moisture.

**squeeze** *verb* 1 exert pressure on, especially to extract moisture or juice; extract (moisture etc.) by squeezing. 2 force into or through; *we squeezed six people into the car; she squeezed through the gap*. 3 produce or obtain by pressure or compulsion; *squeeze a promise from them*. 4 extort money etc. from; harass in this way; *heavy taxation is squeezing small firms*. ●*noun* 1 squeezing; being squeezed. 2 an affectionate clasp or hug. 3 a small amount of liquid produced by squeezing; *a squeeze of lemon juice*. 4 a crowd or crush; *we all got in, but it was a tight squeeze*. 5 hardship or difficulty caused by shortage of money or time etc. 6 restrictions on borrowing etc. during a financial crisis. □ **squeeze-box** *noun* (*informal*) an accordion or concertina.

**squeezer** *noun* a device for squeezing juice from fruit.

**squelch** *verb* make a sound like someone treading in thick mud. ●*noun* this sound.

**squib** *noun* a small hissing firework that explodes. □ **damp squib** something intended to impress people but failing to do so.

**squid** *noun* (*plural* **squid** or **squids**) a sea creature related to the cuttle-fish, with ten arms round the mouth.

**squidgy** *adjective* (*informal*) squashy, soggy.

**squiffy** *adjective* (*slang*) slightly drunk.

**squiggle** *noun* a short curly line, especially in handwriting. □ **squiggly** *adverb*

**squill** *noun* a bulbous plant resembling a bluebell.

**squint** *verb* 1 have an eye that is turned abnormally from the line of gaze of the other; be cross-eyed. 2 look at a thing with the eyes turned sideways or half shut, or through a narrow opening. ●*noun* 1 a squinting position of the eyeballs. 2 a stealthy or sideways glance. 3 (*informal*) a look; *have a squint at this*. ●*adjective* (*informal*) askew.

**squire** *noun* 1 a country gentleman, especially the chief landowner in a district. 2 (as an informal form of address) sir.

**squirearchy** *noun* landowners collectively, especially as having political or social influence.

**squirm** *verb* 1 wriggle or writhe. 2 feel embarrassment or uneasiness. ●*noun* a squirming movement.

**squirrel** *noun* 1 a small tree-climbing animal with a bushy tail and red or grey fur. 2 its fur. ●*verb* (**squirrelled**, **squirrelling**; *Amer.* **squirreled**, **squirreling**) (often foll. by *away*) put away in a hoard.

**squirt** *verb* send out (liquid) or be sent out in a jet to wet in this way. ●*noun* 1 a syringe. 2 a jet of liquid. 3 (*informal*) a small or unimportant but self-assertive person.

**squish** *noun* a slight squelching sound. ●*verb* move with a squish. □ **squishy** *adjective*

**Sr** *symbol* strontium.

**Sr.** *abbreviation* **1** senior. **2** señor. **3** signor.

**Sri Lanka** a country consisting of a large island (formerly called Ceylon) south of India. □ **Sri Lankan** *adjective & noun*

**SRN** *abbreviation* State Registered Nurse.

**SS** *abbreviation* **1** saints. **2** steamship. **3** (*hist.*) the Nazi special police force (¶ German *Schutz-Staffel*).

**St** *abbreviation* Saint.

**St.** *abbreviation* Street.

**st.** *abbreviation* stone (in weight).

**stab** *verb* (**stabbed, stabbing**) **1** pierce or wound with a pointed tool or weapon. **2** aim a blow with or as if with a pointed weapon. **3** cause a sensation of being stabbed; *a stabbing pain.* ●*noun* **1** the act of stabbing; a blow, thrust, or wound made by stabbing. **2** a sensation of being stabbed; *she felt a stab of fear.* **3** (*informal*) an attempt; *have a stab at it.* □ **a stab in the back** an act of betrayal.

**stability** (stǎ-**bil**-iti) *noun* being stable.

**stabilize** (stay-bǐ-lyz) *verb* (also **stabilise**) make or become stable. □ **stabilization** *noun*

**stabilizer** *noun* (also **stabiliser**) **1** a device to prevent a ship from rolling or to aid in keeping a child's bicycle upright. **2** an arrangement for stabilizing an amount, effect, etc.

**stable¹** *adjective* firmly fixed or established; not readily changing or fluctuating; not easily destroyed or decomposed. □ **stably** *adverb*

**stable²** *noun* **1** a building in which horses are kept. **2** an establishment for training racehorses; the horses from a particular establishment. **3** racing-cars, products, or people originating from or working for the same establishment. ●*verb* put or keep in a stable.

**stabling** *noun* accommodation for horses.

**staccato** (stǎ-**kah**-toh) *adjective & adverb* (especially in music) in a sharp disconnected manner, not running on smoothly.

**stack** *noun* **1** an orderly pile or heap. **2** a haystack. **3** (*informal*) a large quantity; *have stacks of work to do.* **4** a number of aircraft stacked for landing. **5** a tall factory chimney; a chimney or funnel on a steamer etc. ●*verb* **1** pile in a stack or stacks. **2** arrange (cards) secretly for cheating. **3** manipulate (circumstances etc.) to suit one. **4** instruct (aircraft) to fly round the same point at different altitudes while waiting to land.

**stadium** *noun* (*plural* **stadiums**) a sports ground surrounded by tiers of seats for spectators.

**staff** *noun* **1** a stick or pole used as a weapon, support, symbol of authority, etc. **2** a body of officers assisting a commanding officer and concerned with an army, regiment, or fleet etc. as a whole. **3** the people employed in a particular business or organization. **4** a stave in music. ●*verb* provide with a staff of employees or assistants. □ **staff nurse** a nurse ranking just below a sister. **staff officer** an officer serving on the staff of an army etc. **staff sergeant** a senior sergeant of a non-infantry company.

**Staffordshire** a midland county of England.

**Staffs.** *abbreviation* Staffordshire.

**stag** *noun* a fully-grown male deer. □ **stag beetle** a beetle with branched projecting mouth-parts that resemble a stag's antlers. **stag-party** *noun* a party for men only, held for a man who is about to marry.

**stage** *noun* **1** a platform on which plays etc. are performed before an audience. **2** the profession of actors and actresses. **3** a raised floor or platform, e.g. on scaffolding. **4** a point or period in the course or development of something; *the talks have reached a critical stage.* **5** a section of a space rocket with a separate engine, jettisoned when its fuel is exhausted. ●*verb* **1** present (a play etc.) on the stage. **2** arrange and carry out; *decided to stage a sit-in.* □ **stage fright** nervousness on facing an audience. **stage-manage** *verb* organize things as or like a stage-manager. **stage manager** the person responsible for the scenery and other practical arrangements in the production of a play. **stage-struck** *adjective* having an obsessive desire to become an actor. **stage whisper** a whisper that is meant to be overheard.

**stagecoach** *noun* (*hist.*) a large closed horse-drawn coach running on a regular route by stages.

**stagecraft** *noun* skill in writing or staging plays.

**stagey** alternative spelling of STAGY.

**stagflation** *noun* a state of inflation without a corresponding increase in demand and employment.

**stagger** *verb* **1** move or go unsteadily, as if about to fall. **2** shock deeply; amaze; *we were staggered by the news.* **3** place or organize in a zigzag or alternating arrangement. ●*noun* an unsteady staggering movement.

**staggering** *adjective* bewildering, astonishing; *the total cost is staggering.*

**staghound** *noun* a large dog used in hunting deer.

**staging** *noun* **1** scaffolding; a temporary platform or support. **2** a platform of boards for plants to stand on in a greenhouse.

□ **staging post** a regular stopping place on a long route.

**stagnant** *adjective* **1** (of water) not flowing, still and stale. **2** showing no activity; *business was stagnant*. □ **stagnancy** *noun*

**stagnate** (stag-**nayt**) *verb* **1** be stagnant. **2** (of a person) become dull through inactivity. □ **stagnation** *noun*

**stagy** (stay-ji) *adjective* (also **stagey**) theatrical and exaggerated in style or manner.

**staid** (*pronounced* stayd) *adjective* steady and serious in manner, tastes, etc.; sedate.

**stain** *verb* **1** discolour or become discoloured by a substance. **2** spoil, damage; *it stained his good reputation*. **3** colour with a pigment that penetrates. ●*noun* **1** a mark caused by staining. **2** a blemish; *without a stain on his character*. **3** a liquid used for staining things. □ **stained glass** glass coloured with transparent colouring.

**stainless** *adjective* free from stains or blemishes. □ **stainless steel** steel containing chromium making it resistant to rust and tarnishing.

**stair** *noun* **1** each of a flight of fixed indoor steps. **2** (**stairs**) a set of these. □ **stair-rod** *noun* a rod for securing a stair-carpet in the angle between two stairs.

**staircase** *noun* a flight of stairs (often with banisters) and its supporting structure.

**stairway** *noun* a staircase.

**stairwell** *noun* a shaft or space for a staircase.

**stake** *noun* **1** a stick or post sharpened at one end for driving into the ground. **2** the post to which a person was bound for execution by being burnt alive. **3** money etc. wagered on the result of a race or other event. **4** something invested in an enterprise and giving a share or interest in it. **5** (**stakes**) (in horse races) money offered as a prize; the race itself; *the Queen Anne Stakes*. ●*verb* **1** fasten, support, or mark with stakes. **2** wager or risk (money etc.) on an event. **3** (*Amer. informal*) give financial or other support to. □ **at stake** being risked, depending on the outcome of an event. **stake a claim** claim or obtain a right to something. **stake out** (*informal*) place under surveillance.

**stakeholder** *noun* a third party with whom money etc. wagered is deposited.

**Stakhanovite** (stǎ-**kahn**-ŏ-vyt) *noun* a worker whose output wins special awards. (¶ Originally in the former USSR, named after a Russian coalminer, A. G. Stakhanov, who achieved an immense output in 1935.)

**stalactite** (stal-ǎk-tyt) *noun* a deposit of calcium carbonate hanging like an icicle from the roof of a cave etc.

**stalagmite** (stal-ǎg-myt) *noun* a deposit like a stalactite but standing like a pillar on the floor of a cave etc.

**stale** *adjective* **1** lacking freshness; dry, musty. **2** uninteresting because not new; *stale jokes*. **3** having one's ability to perform spoilt by too much practice. ●*verb* make or become stale. □ **stalely** *adverb*, **staleness** *noun*

**stalemate** *noun* **1** a drawn position in chess, in which a player can make no move without putting the king in check. **2** a deadlock, a drawn contest. ●*verb* bring to a position of stalemate or deadlock.

**Stalin**, Joseph (real name: Dzhugashvili) (1879–1953), Russian dictator.

**stalk**[1] *noun* **1** the main stem of a plant. **2** a stem attaching a leaf, flower, or fruit to another stem. **3** a similar support of a part or organ in animals or of a device.

**stalk**[2] *verb* **1** walk in a stately or imposing manner. **2** track or pursue (game etc.) stealthily. □ **stalking-horse** *noun* a person or thing used to conceal one's real intentions. □ **stalker** *noun*

**stall**[1] *noun* **1** a stable or cowhouse; a compartment for one animal in this. **2** a compartment for one person. **3** a seat with its back and sides more or less enclosed, in a church etc. **4** (**stalls**) the seats in a theatre nearest to the stage. **5** a stand from which things are sold. **6** stalling of an engine or aircraft. ●*verb* **1** (of an engine) stop suddenly because of an overload or insufficient fuel. **2** (of an aircraft) begin to drop because the speed is too low for the plane to respond to its controls. **3** cause (an engine or aircraft) to stall.

**stall**[2] *verb* use delaying tactics in order to gain time; stave off (a person or request) in this way.

**stallion** (stal-yŏn) *noun* an uncastrated male horse, especially one kept for breeding.

**stalwart** (**stawl**-wert) *adjective* **1** sturdy. **2** strong and faithful; *stalwart supporters*. ●*noun* a stalwart person.

**stamen** (stay-měn) *noun* the male fertilizing-organ of flowering plants, bearing pollen.

**stamina** (stam-in-ǎ) *noun* staying power, ability to withstand prolonged physical or mental strain.

**stammer** *verb* speak or utter with involuntary pauses or rapid repetitions of the same syllable. ●*noun* stammering speech; a tendency to stammer. □ **stammerer** *noun*

**stamp** *verb* **1** bring one's foot down heavily on the ground. **2** walk with loud heavy steps. **3** strike or press with a device that leaves a mark or pattern etc.; cut or shape in this way. **4** fix a postage or other stamp to. **5** give a certain character to; *this*

*achievement stamps him as a genius.* ●*noun*
**1** the act or sound of stamping. **2** an instrument for stamping a pattern or mark; the mark itself. **3** a piece of paper for affixing to an envelope or document to indicate that postage or duty has been paid. **4** a distinguishing mark, a clear indication; *the story bears the stamp of truth.* □ **stamping ground** (*informal*) a person's or animal's usual haunt. **stamp on** crush by stamping; quell. **stamp out** extinguish by stamping; suppress (a rebellion etc.) by force.

**stampede** *noun* **1** a sudden rush of a herd of frightened animals. **2** a rush of people under a sudden common impulse. ●*verb* take part or cause to take part in a stampede; cause to act hurriedly.

**stance** *noun* the position in which a person or animal stands; a player's attitude for making a stroke.

**stanch** *verb* (also **staunch**) restrain the flow of (blood etc.) or the flow from (a wound).

**stanchion** (**stan-**shŏn) *noun* an upright bar or post forming a support.

**stand** *verb* (**stood, standing**) **1** have, take, or keep an upright position; *we were standing talking about the weather.* **2** be situated. **3** place; set upright. **4** remain firm or valid or in a specified condition; *the offer still stands; the thermometer stood at 90°.* **5** remain stationary or unused. **6** offer oneself for election; *she stood for Parliament.* **7** undergo; *he stood trial for murder.* **8** steer a specified course in sailing. **9** put up with, endure; *I can't stand that noise.* **10** provide at one's own expense; *stood him a drink.* ●*noun* **1** a stationary condition. **2** a position taken up; *took his stand near the door.* **3** resistance to attack, the period of this; *made a stand.* **4** a halt to give a performance; *the band did a one-night stand.* **5** a rack or pedestal etc. on which something may be placed. **6** a raised structure with seats at a sports ground etc. **7** a table, booth, or other (often temporary) structure where things are exhibited or sold. **8** a standing-place for vehicles; *taxi stand.* **9** (*Amer.*) a witness-box. □ **as it stands** in the present state of affairs; in its present condition, unaltered. **it stands to reason** it is obvious or logical. **stand a chance** have a chance of success. **stand alone** be unequalled. **stand by 1** look on without interfering. **2** support or side with (a person) in a difficulty or dispute. **3** stand ready for action. **4** keep to (a promise or agreement). **stand-by** (*adjective*) ready for use or action as a substitute etc.; (*noun*) a person or thing available as a substitute or in an emergency. **stand down** withdraw (e.g. from a competition). **stand for 1** represent; *'US' stands for 'United States'.* **2** (*informal*) toler-

ate. **stand in** deputize. **stand-in** *noun* a person who takes the place of another; a substitute or deputy. **stand off 1** remain at a distance. **2** lay off (employees) temporarily. **stand-off** *adjective* (of a missile) launched by an aircraft but having a long range and its own guidance system. **stand-off half** a half-back in Rugby football who forms the link between scrum-half and three-quarters. **stand on** insist on formal observance of; *stand on ceremony.* **stand on one's own feet** be independent. **stand out 1** be conspicuous. **2** (foll. by *for*) persist in opposition or in one's demands; *they stood out for a ten per cent rise.* **stand to** stand ready for action. **stand up 1** be valid; *that argument won't stand up.* **2** (*informal*) fail to keep an appointment with. **stand-up** *adjective* (of a collar) not turned down; (of a fight) vigorous, actual; (of a meal) eaten while standing. **stand up for** defend or support (a person or opinion). **stand up to** resist courageously; remain durable in (hard use or wear).

**standard** *noun* **1** a thing, quality, or specification by which something may be tested or measured. **2** the required level of quality; *rejected as being below standard.* **3** the average quality; *the standard of her work is high.* **4** a distinctive flag; *the royal standard.* **5** an upright support. **6** a shrub that has been grafted on a tall upright stem; *standard roses.* ●*adjective* **1** serving as or conforming to a standard; *standard measures of length.* **2** of average or usual quality, not of special design etc.; *the standard model of this car.* **3** of recognized merit or authority; *the standard book on spiders.* **4** (of language) of the type used by educated speakers; regarded as correct. □ **standard assessment task** a national test given to schoolchildren in Britain when they reach a specified age. **standard lamp** a household lamp set on a tall pillar on a base. **standard of living** the level of material comfort enjoyed by a person or group.

**standardize** *verb* (also **standardise**) cause to conform to a standard. □ **standardization** *noun*

**standing** *adjective* **1** upright. **2** (of a jump) performed without a run. **3** permanent, remaining effective or valid; *a standing invitation.* ●*noun* **1** status; *people of high standing.* **2** past duration; *a friendship of long standing.* □ **standing committee** a committee that is permanent for the duration of the appointing body. **standing joke** an object of permanent ridicule. **standing order** an instruction to a bank to make regular payments, or to a retailer for a regular supply of goods. **standing orders** rules governing the procedures of a committee, parliament, etc. **standing ovation** an ovation by people rising from their seats to applaud. **standing room** space for people to stand in.

**standoffish** *adjective* cold, aloof, distant in manner.

**standpipe** *noun* a vertical pipe for fluid to rise in, e.g. to provide a temporary water supply.

**standpoint** *noun* a point of view.

**standstill** *noun* a stoppage, inability to proceed.

**Stanislaus** (stan-iss-lawss), St (1030–79), the patron saint of Poland. Feast day, 7 May.

**Stanislavsky**, Konstantin (1863–1938), Russian director, actor, and teacher of acting.

**stank** *see* STINK.

**Stanley**, Sir Henry Morton (1841–1904), British explorer of central Africa, who led an expedition (1869–71) in search of Livingstone.

**stannary** *noun* a tin-mine.

**stanza** *noun* a verse of poetry.

**staphylococcus** *noun* (*plural* **staphylococci**, *pronounced* staf-il-ŏ-**kok**-I) a microorganism that causes pus to form.

**staple**[1] *noun* **1** a U-shaped piece of metal or wire for holding something in place. **2** a piece of wire driven into papers to fasten them. ●*verb* secure with a staple or staples. □ **stapler** *noun*

**staple**[2] *adjective* principal, standard; *rice is their staple food.* ●*noun* a staple food or product etc.

**star** *noun* **1** a celestial body appearing as a point of light in the night sky. **2** (in astronomy) any large light-emitting gaseous ball, such as the sun. **3** a celestial body regarded as influencing a person's fortunes; *thank your lucky stars.* **4** a figure, object, or ornament with rays or radiating points; an asterisk; a star-shaped mark indicating a category of excellence. **5** a brilliant person; a famous performer. ●*verb* (**starred, starring**) **1** put an asterisk or star symbol beside (a name or item). **2** present or perform as a star actor. □ **Star Chamber 1** an apartment in the royal palace at Westminster where in the 14th–15th centuries the Privy Council tried civil and criminal cases. **2** (*informal*) a committee that arbitrates between the Treasury and the spending departments of the British Government. **star-gazing** *noun* studying the stars as an astronomer or astrologer. **Star of David** the six-pointed star used as a Jewish and Israeli symbol. **Stars and Stripes** the national flag of the USA. **Star-Spangled Banner** the national anthem of the USA. **star-studded** *adjective* featuring many

famous performers. **star turn** the principal item in an entertainment. **Star Wars** (*informal*) the US Strategic Defense Initiative (*see* STRATEGIC).

**starboard** *noun* the right-hand side (when facing forward) of a ship or aircraft. ●*verb* turn this way.

**starch** *noun* **1** a white carbohydrate that is an important element in human food. **2** a preparation for stiffening fabrics. **3** stiffness of manner. ●*verb* stiffen with starch.

**starchy** *adjective* (**starchier, starchiest**) **1** of or like starch. **2** containing much starch. **3** stiff and formal in manner. □ **starchiness** *noun*

**stardom** *noun* being a star actor or performer.

**stardust** *noun* **1** a mass of stars looking like dust. **2** romance; a magical feeling.

**stare** *verb* **1** gaze fixedly with the eyes wide open. **2** (of the eyes) be wide open with fixed gaze. ●*noun* a staring gaze. □ **stare a person in the face** be glaringly obvious or clearly imminent; *ruin stared him in the face.*

**starfish** *noun* a star-shaped sea creature.

**stark** *adjective* **1** desolate; bare; cheerless; *stark prison conditions.* **2** absolute; sharply evident; *in stark contrast.* ●*adverb* completely, wholly; *stark raving mad.* □ **starkly** *adverb*, **starkness** *noun*

**starlight** *noun* light from the stars.

**starling** *noun* a noisy bird with glossy blackish speckled feathers.

**starlit** *adjective* lit by starlight.

**starry** *adjective* (**starrier, starriest**) **1** set with stars. **2** shining like stars. □ **starry-eyed** *adjective* romantically enthusiastic; enthusiastic but impractical.

**START** *abbreviation* Strategic Arms Reduction Treaty (or Talks).

**start** *verb* **1** begin or cause to begin; (of an engine) begin running. **2** begin a journey. **3** make a sudden movement from pain, surprise etc. **4** spring suddenly; *started from his seat.* **5** (of timber) spring from its proper position. **6** rouse (game etc.) from its lair or covert. ●*noun* **1** the beginning of a journey, activity, or race; the place where a race starts. **2** an opportunity for or assistance in starting; an advantage gained or allowed in starting; the amount of this. **3** a sudden movement of surprise or pain etc. □ **starting-block** *noun* a shaped block for a runner's feet at the start of a race. **starting price** the final odds on a horse etc. at the start of a race. **start out** begin, begin a journey; intend when starting; *started out to write a novel.*

**starter** *noun* **1** a person or thing that starts something. **2** a horse or competitor at the start of a race; *list of probable starters.* **3** the first course of a meal. □ **for starters** (*in-*

*formal*) to start with. **under starter's orders** awaiting the signal to start (a race).

**startle** *verb* surprise or alarm.

**starve** *verb* **1** die or suffer acutely from lack of food; cause to do this. **2** suffer or cause to suffer for lack of something; *was starved of affection.* **3** (*informal*) feel very hungry. ▫ **starvation** *noun*

**starveling** (starv-ling) *noun* a starving or ill-fed person or animal.

**stash** (*informal*) *verb* hide away; hoard. ●*noun* a hidden store of things.

**stasis** (stay-sis) *noun* (*plural* **stases**) **1** inactivity, stagnation. **2** stoppage of circulation.

**state** *noun* **1** the quality of a person's or thing's characteristics or circumstances. **2** an excited or agitated condition of mind; *he got into a state.* **3** a grand imposing style; *arrived in state.* **4** (often **State**) an organized community under one government (*the State of Israel*) or forming part of a federal republic (*States of the USA*). **5** civil government; *matters of state.* ●*adjective* **1** of, for, or run by the State. **2** involving ceremony, used or done on ceremonial occasions; *the state apartments.* ●*verb* **1** express in spoken or written words. **2** fix or specify; *must be inspected at stated intervals.* ▫ **lie in state** see LIE². **State Department** the department of foreign affairs in the government of the USA. **state of emergency** a national situation of danger or disaster, with normal procedures suspended. **state of the art** the current stage of development. **state-of-the-art** *adjective* absolutely up-to-date. **the States** the USA.

**stateless** *adjective* (of a person) not a citizen or subject of any country.

**stately** *adjective* (**statelier**, **stateliest**) dignified, imposing, grand. ▫ **stately home** a large historic house, especially one open to the public. ▫ **stateliness** *noun*

**statement** *noun* **1** stating. **2** something stated. **3** a formal account of facts; a written report of a financial account.

**stateroom** *noun* **1** a state apartment. **2** a passenger's private compartment on a ship.

**statesman** *noun* (*plural* **statesmen**) a person who is skilled or prominent in State affairs. ▫ **statesmanlike** *adjective*, **statesmanship** *noun*

**stateswoman** *noun* (*plural* **stateswomen**) a woman who is skilled or prominent in State affairs.

**static** *adjective* **1** (of force) acting by weight without motion (as opposed to *dynamic*). **2** not moving, stationary. **3** not changing. ●*noun* **1** atmospherics. **2** (in full **static electricity**) electricity present in a body and not flowing as current. **3** (**statics**) (usually treated as *singular*) a branch of

physics that deals with bodies at rest or forces in equilibrium.

**station** *noun* **1** a place where a person or thing stands or is stationed. **2** an establishment or building where a public service is based or which is equipped for certain activities; *the fire station; an agricultural research station.* **3** a broadcasting establishment with its own frequency. **4** a stopping place on a railway with buildings. **5** position in life, status; *she had ideas above her station.* **6** (*Austral.*) a large sheep or cattle farm. ●*verb* put at or in a certain place for a purpose; *the regiment was stationed in Germany.* ▫ **Stations of the Cross** a series of locations on the traditional route in Jerusalem from Pilate's house to Calvary, followed by pilgrims; a series of 14 images or pictures representing events in Christ's Passion. **station wagon** (especially *Amer.*) an estate car.

**stationary** *adjective* **1** not moving; not movable. **2** not changing in condition or quantity etc.

**stationer** *noun* one who sells writing materials (paper, pens, ink, etc.).

**stationery** *noun* writing paper, envelopes, and other articles sold by a stationer. ▫ **Stationery Office** the UK government publishing house.

**stationmaster** *noun* an official in charge of a railway station.

**statistic** (stă-**tist**-ik) *noun* **1** an item of information expressed in numbers. **2** (**statistics**) the science of collecting, classifying, and interpreting information based on the numbers of things. ▫ **statistical** *adjective*, **statistically** *adverb*

**statistician** (stat-iss-**tish**-ăn) *noun* an expert in statistics.

**statuary** (stat-yoo-er-i) *noun* statues collectively.

**statue** *noun* a sculptured, cast, or moulded figure of a person or animal.

**statuesque** (stat-yoo-**esk**) *adjective* like a statue in size or dignity or stillness.

**statuette** (stat-yoo-et) *noun* a small statue.

**stature** (stat-yer) *noun* **1** the natural height of the body. **2** greatness gained by ability or achievement.

**status** (stay-tŭs) *noun* (*plural* **statuses**) **1** a person's position or rank in relation to others; a person's or thing's legal position. **2** high rank or prestige. ▫ **status symbol** a possession or activity etc. regarded as evidence of a person's high status.

**status quo** (stay-tŭs **kwoh**) the existing state of affairs; *restore the status quo.* (¶ Latin, = the state in which.)

**statute** (stat-yoot) *noun* **1** a law passed by Parliament or a similar body. **2** one of the rules of an institution; *the University Statutes*.

**statutory** (stat-yoo-ter-i) *adjective* fixed, done, or required by statute. □ **statutorily** *adverb*

**staunch**[1] *adjective* firm in attitude, opinion, or loyalty. □ **staunchly** *adverb*

**staunch**[2] alternative spelling of STANCH.

**stave** *noun* **1** one of the curved strips of wood forming the side of a cask or tub. **2** (also **staff**) a set of five parallel horizontal lines on which music is written. ●*verb* (**stove** or **staved, staving**) dent or break a hole in; *stove it in*. □ **stave off** ward off permanently or temporarily; *we staved off disaster*.

**stay**[1] *noun* **1** a rope or wire supporting or bracing a mast, spar, pole, etc. **2** any prop or support.

**stay**[2] *verb* **1** continue to be in the same place or state; *stay here; stay awake; stay away*. **2** remain or dwell temporarily, especially as a guest or visitor. **3** satisfy temporarily; *we stayed our hunger with a sandwich*. **4** postpone; *stay judgement*. **5** pause in movement, action, or speech. **6** show endurance, e.g. in a race or task; *stay the course*. ●*noun* **1** a period of temporary dwelling or visiting; *made a short stay in Athens*. **2** a postponement, e.g. of carrying out a judgement; *was granted a stay of execution*. □ **staying power** endurance. **stay put** (*informal*) remain where it is placed; remain where one is.

**stayer** *noun* a person with great staying power.

**stays** *plural noun* (*old use*) a corset.

**staysail** *noun* a sail extended on a stay.

**STD** *abbreviation* subscriber trunk dialling.

**stead** (*pronounced* sted) *noun* □ **in a person's** or **thing's stead** instead of this person or thing. **stand a person in good stead** be of great advantage or service to him or her.

**steadfast** (sted-fahst) *adjective* firm and not changing or yielding; *a steadfast refusal*. □ **steadfastly** *adverb*, **steadfastness** *noun*

**steady** *adjective* (**steadier, steadiest**) **1** firmly supported or balanced. **2** uniform and regular; *a steady pace*. **3** behaving in a serious and dependable manner, not frivolous or excitable. ●*noun* (*informal*) a regular boyfriend or girlfriend. ●*adverb* steadily. ●*verb* (**steadied, steadying**) make or become steady. □ **go steady** (*informal*) go out with a person as a regular boyfriend or girlfriend. **steady on!** slow!; stop! □ **steadily** *adverb*, **steadiness** *noun*

**steak** *noun* **1** a thick slice of meat or fish, cut for grilling or frying etc. **2** beef from the front of an animal, cut for stewing or braising.

**steakhouse** *noun* a restaurant that specializes in serving steaks.

**steal** *verb* (**stole, stolen, stealing**) **1** take another person's property without right or permission. **2** obtain by surprise or a trick or surreptitiously; *stole a kiss; stole a look at her*. **3** move secretly or without being noticed; *stole out of the room*. ●*noun* (*Amer. informal*) **1** stealing, theft. **2** an easy task; a good bargain. □ **steal a march on** gain an advantage over (a person). **steal the show** outshine other performers.

**stealth** (*pronounced* stelth) *noun* stealthiness.

**stealthy** (stel-thi) *adjective* (**stealthier, stealthiest**) acting or done in a quiet or secret way. □ **stealthily** *adverb*, **stealthiness** *noun*

**steam** *noun* **1** invisible gas into which water is changed by boiling, used as motive power. **2** the mist that forms when steam condenses in the air. **3** energy or power; *run out of steam*. ●*verb* **1** give out steam or vapour. **2** cook or treat by steam. **3** move by the power of steam; *the ship steamed down the river*. □ **steamed up** (*informal*) excited or angry. **steam engine** an engine or locomotive driven by steam. **steam iron** an electric iron that emits jets of steam.

**steamboat** *noun* a steam-driven boat, especially a paddle-wheel craft.

**steamer** *noun* **1** a steamboat. **2** a container in which things are cooked or treated by steam.

**steamroller** *noun* a heavy slow-moving engine with a large roller, used in road-making. ●*verb* crush or force by weighty influence.

**steamship** *noun* a steam-driven ship.

**steamy** *adjective* (**steamier, steamiest**) **1** like steam; full of steam. **2** (*informal*) erotic; sexually explicit. □ **steaminess** *noun*

**steatite** (stee-ă-tyt) *noun* a greyish talc that feels smooth and soapy.

**steed** *noun* (*poetic*) a horse.

**steel** *noun* **1** a very strong alloy of iron and carbon. **2** a tapered steel rod for sharpening knives. ●*verb* make hard or resolute; *steel oneself; steel one's heart*. □ **steel band** a band playing West Indian style music on percussion instruments made from oil drums. **steel wool** a mass of fine steel shavings used as an abrasive.

**steely** *adjective* (**steelier, steeliest**) like steel in colour or hardness; severe, determined.

**steelyard** *noun* a weighing-apparatus with a graduated arm along which a weight slides.

**steep**[1] *verb* **1** soak or be soaked in liquid. **2** permeate thoroughly; *the story is steeped in mystery*.

**steep²** *adjective* **1** sloping sharply. **2** (*informal*) (of a price) unreasonably high. □ **steeply** *adverb*, **steepness** *noun*

**steepen** *verb* make or become steeper.

**steeple** *noun* a tall tower with a spire on top, rising above the roof of a church.

**steeplechase** *noun* **1** a horse race across country or on a course with hedges and ditches to jump. **2** a cross-country race for runners. □ **steeplechasing** *noun*

**steeplejack** *noun* a person who climbs tall chimneys or steeples to do repairs.

**steer¹** *verb* **1** direct the course of. **2** guide (a vehicle or boat etc.) with its wheel, rudder, etc. □ **steer clear of** take care to avoid.

**steer²** *noun* a young male of domestic cattle, castrated and raised for beef; a bullock.

**steerage** *noun* **1** steering. **2** (*old use*) the cheapest passenger accommodation in a ship, situated below decks.

**steering** *noun* the mechanism by which a vehicle or boat etc. is steered. □ **steering committee** a committee deciding the order of business, the general course of operations, etc. **steering wheel** a wheel for controlling the steering mechanism of a vehicle.

**steersman** *noun* (*plural* **steersmen**) a person who steers a ship.

**stegosaurus** (steg-ă-**sor**-ŭs) *noun* (*plural* **stegasauruses**) a plant-eating dinosaur with a double row of pointed bony plates along its back.

**Stein** (*rhymes with* mine), Gertrude (1874–1946), American writer who settled in Paris.

**stein** (*rhymes with* mine) *noun* a large earthenware mug, especially for beer.

**Steinbeck** (styn-bek), John Ernst (1902–68), American writer, author of *The Grapes of Wrath*.

**stela** (stee-lă) *noun* (*plural* **stelae**) (also **stele**, *pronounced* stee-li *or* steel) (*Archaeol.*) an upright slab or pillar, usually shaped and inscribed as a gravestone.

**stellar** *adjective* of a star or stars.

**stem** *noun* **1** the main central part (usually above the ground) of a tree, shrub, or plant. **2** a slender part supporting a fruit, flower, or leaf. **3** any slender upright part, e.g. that of a wineglass between bowl and foot. **4** the main part of a noun or verb, from which other parts or words are made e.g. by altering the endings. **5** the curved piece at the fore end of a ship; a ship's bows. ●*verb* (**stemmed**, **stemming**) stop the flow of; check. □ **stem from** arise from, have as its source.

**stench** *noun* a foul smell.

**stencil** *noun* **1** a sheet of metal or card etc. with a design cut out, which can be painted or inked over to produce a design on the surface below. **2** a waxed sheet from which a stencil is made by a typewriter. **3** the decoration or lettering etc. produced by a stencil. ●*verb* (**stencilled**, **stencilling**; *Amer.* **stenciled**, **stenciling**) produce or ornament by means of a stencil.

**Sten gun** a lightweight sub-machine-gun.

**stenographer** (sten-og-ră-fer) *noun* (especially *Amer.*) a person who can write shorthand.

**stenography** (sten-og-răfi) *noun* shorthand.

**stentorian** (sten-**tor**-iăn) *adjective* (of a voice) extremely loud.

**step** *verb* (**stepped**, **stepping**) **1** lift and set down the foot as in walking. **2** move a short distance in this way. **3** (often foll. by *into*) achieve something easily; *step into a job*. ●*noun* **1** a complete movement of one foot in stepping. **2** the distance covered by this. **3** a short distance. **4** a series of steps forming a pattern in dancing. **5** the sound of a step; *I recognized your step*. **6** each of a series of things done in some process. **7** a level surface for placing the foot on in climbing up or down. **8** (**steps**) a stepladder. □ **in step 1** stepping in time with other people in marching or dancing. **2** conforming to what others are doing. **out of step** not in step. **step in** intervene. **step on it** (*informal*) hurry. **step out** walk briskly, stride. **step up** increase. **watch your step** be careful.

**step-** *combining form* related by remarriage of one parent. □ **stepchild** (*plural* **stepchildren**), **stepdaughter**, **stepson** *noun* the child of one's wife or husband, by an earlier marriage. **stepbrother**, **stepsister** *noun* the child of one's stepfather or stepmother. **stepfather**, **stepmother**, **step-parent** *noun* the husband or wife of one's parent, by a later marriage.

**stephanotis** (stef-ăn-oh-tiss) *noun* a tropical climbing plant with fragrant white waxy flowers.

**Stephen¹** king of England 1135–54.

**Stephen²**, St (died *c.* AD 35), the first Christian martyr. Feast day, (in the West) 26 December, (in the East) 27 December.

**Stephen³**, St (*c.* 997–1038), the first king and patron saint of Hungary. Feast day, 2 September; principal festival in Hungary 20 August.

**Stephenson**, George (1781–1848), English engineer, pioneer of railways.

**stepladder** *noun* a short folding ladder with flat steps.

**steppe** (*pronounced* step) *noun* a huge grassy plain with few trees, in Russia and elsewhere.

**stepping-stone** *noun* **1** a raised stone providing a place to step on in crossing a stream etc. **2** a means or stage of progress towards achieving something.

**stereo** (ste-ri-oh *or* steer-i-oh) *noun* (plural **stereos**) **1** stereophonic sound or recording. **2** a stereophonic hi-fi system. **3** a stereoscope. ● *adjective* **1** = STEREOPHONIC. **2** = STEREOSCOPIC.

**stereophonic** (ste-ri-ŏ-**fon**-ik *or* steer-) *adjective* (of sound reproduction) using two transmission channels to give the effect of naturally-distributed sound. □ **stereophonically** *adverb*, **stereophony** (-**off**-ŏni) *noun*

**stereoscope** (ste-ri-ŏ-skohp *or* steer-) *noun* a device for giving a stereoscopic effect.

**stereoscopic** (ste-ri-ŏ-**skop**-ik *or* steer-) *adjective* giving a three-dimensional effect, e.g. in photographs. □ **stereoscopically** *adverb*

**stereotype** (ste-ri-ŏ-typ *or* steer-) *noun* **1** a person or thing regarded as a conventional type rather than an individual; a preconceived and over-simplified idea of the characteristics which typify a person, situation, etc. **2** a printing-plate cast from a mould. ● *verb* standardize as a stereotype.

**sterile** (ste-ryl) *adjective* **1** unable to produce fruit or young. **2** free from living micro-organisms; absolutely clean. **3** unproductive; *a sterile discussion.* □ **sterility** (ster-il-iti) *noun*

**sterilize** (ste-ri-lyz) *verb* (also **sterilise**) **1** make sterile or free from micro-organisms. **2** make unable to produce offspring, especially by removal or obstruction of reproductive organs. □ **sterilization** *noun*

**sterling** *noun* British money. ● *adjective* **1** (of precious metal) genuine, of standard purity. **2** excellent, of solid worth; *her sterling qualities.*

**stern**[1] *adjective* strict and severe, not lenient or cheerful or kindly. □ **sternly** *adverb*, **sternness** *noun*

**stern**[2] *noun* the rear end of a boat or ship.

**Sterne**, Laurence (1713–68), Irish-born British novelist, author of *Tristram Shandy*.

**sternum** *noun* (plural **sterna** *or* **sternums**) the breastbone.

**steroid** (steer-oid *or* ste-roid) *noun* any of a group of organic compounds that includes certain hormones and other bodily secretions.

**sterol** (ste-rol) *noun* a naturally occurring steroid alcohol.

**stertorous** (ster-ter-ŭs) *adjective* making a snoring or rasping sound.

**stet** *verb* (placed beside a word that has been crossed out or altered by mistake) ignore the alteration. (¶ Latin, = let it stand.)

**stethoscope** (steth-ŏ-skohp) *noun* an instrument for listening to sounds within the body, e.g. breathing and heartbeats.

**stetson** *noun* a slouch hat with a very wide brim and a high crown.

**stevedore** (stee-vě-dor) *noun* a person employed in loading and unloading ships.

**Stevenson**, Robert Louis (1850–94), Scottish-born writer, whose novels include *Treasure Island* and *Kidnapped*.

**stew** *verb* **1** cook by simmering for a long time in a closed vessel. **2** fret; be anxious. **3** (*informal*) swelter. **4** (of tea) become bitter and strong from infusing for too long. **5** (as **stewed** *adjective*) (*informal*) drunk. ● *noun* a dish (especially of meat) made by stewing. □ **in a stew** (*informal*) in a state of great agitation. **stew in one's own juice** suffer the consequences of one's own actions.

**steward** *noun* **1** a person employed to manage another's property, especially a great house or estate. **2** one whose job is to arrange for the supply of food to a college or club etc. **3** a passengers' attendant and waiter on a ship, aircraft, or train. **4** any of the officials managing a race meeting or show etc.

**stewardess** *noun* a woman attendant and waitress on a ship or aircraft.

**Stewart**, Jackie (John Young) (born 1939), British world champion racing driver.

**stick** *noun* **1** a short relatively slender piece of wood. **2** a walking stick. **3** the implement used to hit the ball in hockey, polo, etc. **4** punishment by caning or beating. **5** a slender more or less cylindrical piece of a substance, e.g. sealing wax, rhubarb, dynamite. **6** (*informal*) criticism; teasing. **7** (*informal*) a person; *he's not a bad old stick.* ● *verb* (**stuck**, **sticking**) **1** thrust (a thing or its point) into something, stab. **2** fix by means of a pointed object. **3** (*informal*) put; *stick the parcel on the table.* **4** fix or be fixed by glue or suction etc. or as if by these. **5** fix or be fixed in one place and unable to move. **6** (*informal*) remain in the same place; *they stuck indoors all day.* **7** (*informal*) (of an accusation) be established as valid; *we couldn't make the charges stick.* **8** (*slang*) endure, tolerate. **9** (*informal*) impose a difficult or unpleasant task upon; *we were stuck with the job of clearing up.* □ **stick at it** (*informal*) continue one's efforts. **sticking plaster** a strip of adhesive material for covering small wounds. **stick in one's throat** be against one's principles. **stick insect** an insect with a twiglike body. **stick-in-the-mud** *noun* an old-fashioned or unadventurous person. **stick it out** endure in spite of difficulty or unpleasantness. **stick one's neck out** be rashly bold. **stick out 1** stand above the surrounding

surface; be conspicuous. **2** (*informal*) persist in one's demands; *stick out for a pay rise.*
**stick to** remain faithful to (a friend or promise etc.); abide by and not alter; *he stuck to his story.* **stick to one's guns** hold one's position against attack or argument.
**stick-up** *noun* (*slang*) a robbery using a gun.
**stick up for** (*informal*) defend, stand up for. **stick with** remain with or faithful to.
**up sticks** (*slang*) go and live somewhere else; leave.

**sticker** *noun* **1** an adhesive label or sign. **2** a person who persists in his or her efforts.

**stickleback** *noun* a small fish with sharp spines on its back.

**stickler** *noun* a person who insists on something; *a stickler for punctuality.*

**sticky** *adjective* (**stickier, stickiest**) **1** sticking or tending to stick to what is touched. **2** (of weather) hot and humid. **3** (*informal*) awkward, unhelpful; *he was very sticky about giving me leave.* **4** (*slang*) very unpleasant; *he'll come to a sticky end.* □ **sticky wicket** (*informal*) difficult circumstances. □ **stickily** *adverb*, **stickiness** *noun*

**stiff** *adjective* **1** not bending, moving, or changing shape easily. **2** not fluid, thick and hard to stir; *a stiff dough.* **3** difficult; *a stiff examination.* **4** formal in manner, not sociable or friendly. **5** (of a price or penalty) high, severe. **6** (of a breeze) blowing briskly. **7** (of a drink or dose) strong. ● *adverb* (*informal*) to an extreme degree; *bored stiff.* ● *noun* (*slang*) **1** a corpse. **2** a hopeless or foolish person. □ **stiff-necked** *adjective* obstinate; haughty. **stiff upper lip** fortitude in enduring grief etc. **stiff with** (*informal*) full of; packed with. □ **stiffly** *adverb*, **stiffness** *noun*

**stiffen** *verb* make or become stiff. □ **stiffener** *noun*

**stifle** *verb* **1** suffocate; feel unable to breathe for lack of air. **2** restrain or suppress; *stifled a yawn.* □ **stifling** *adjective*

**stigma** *noun* **1** a mark of shame, a stain on a person's good reputation. **2** the part of a pistil that receives the pollen in pollination.

**stigmata** (stig-mă-tă *or* stig-**mah**-tă) *plural noun* marks corresponding to those left on Christ's body by the nails and spear at his Crucifixion.

**stigmatize** (stig-mă-tyz) *verb* (also **stigmatise**) brand as something disgraceful.

**stile** *noun* **1** an arrangement of steps to help walkers climb over a fence or wall. **2** a vertical piece in the frame of a panelled door etc.

**stiletto** *noun* (*plural* **stilettos**) **1** (in full **stiletto heel**) a high pointed heel on a shoe; a shoe with such a heel. **2** a dagger with a

narrow blade. **3** a pointed device for making eyelet-holes etc.

**still** *adjective* **1** without moving, without or almost without motion or sound. **2** (of drinks) not sparkling or fizzy. **3** distilling apparatus for making spirits. ● *noun* **1** silence and calm; *in the still of the night.* **2** a photograph as distinct from a motion picture. ● *verb* make or become still; *to still the waves.* ● *adverb* **1** without or almost without moving. **2** then or now or for the future as before; *the Pyramids are still standing.* **3** nevertheless. **4** in a greater amount or degree; *that would be still better, better still.* □ **still life** a painting of lifeless things such as cut flowers or fruit. **still-room** *noun* a housekeeper's storeroom in a large house. □ **stillness** *noun*

**stillbirth** *noun* the birth of a dead child.

**stillborn** *adjective* **1** born dead. **2** (of an idea or plan) not developing.

**stilt** *noun* **1** either of a pair of poles with a rest for the foot, enabling the user to walk above the ground. **2** each of a set of piles or posts supporting a building etc.

**stilted** *adjective* stiffly or artificially formal; *written in stilted language.*

**Stilton** *noun* (*trade mark*) a cheese, often strong-tasting, with blue veins.

**stimulant** *adjective* stimulating. ● *noun* a stimulant drug or drink; a stimulating event etc.

**stimulate** *verb* **1** make more vigorous or active. **2** apply a stimulus to. □ **stimulation** *noun*, **stimulator** *noun*

**stimulative** (stim-yoo-lă-tiv) *adjective* stimulating.

**stimulus** *noun* (*plural* **stimuli**, *pronounced* stim-yool-I) something that rouses a person or thing to activity or that produces a reaction in the body.

**stimy** alternative spelling of STYMIE.

**sting 1** a sharp-pointed part or organ of an insect etc., used for wounding and often injecting poison; a similar sharp-pointed hair on certain plants. **2** infliction of a wound by a sting; the wound itself. **3** any sharp bodily or mental pain; *the sting of remorse.* **4** (*slang*) a swindle. ● *verb* (**stung, stinging**) **1** wound or affect with a sting; be able to do this. **2** feel sharp pain; stimulate sharply as if by a sting; *I was stung into answering rudely.* **3** (*slang*) cheat (a person) by over-charging; extort money from. □ **stinging-nettle** *noun* a nettle that stings.

**stinger** *noun* a thing that stings; a sharp painful blow.

**stingray** *noun* a broad flatfish with a poisonous spine at the base of its tail.

**stingy** (stin-ji) *adjective* (**stingier, stingiest**) grudging, mean. □ **stingily** *adverb*, **stinginess** *noun*

**stink** *noun* **1** an offensive smell. **2** (*informal*) a row or fuss; *kicked up a stink about it.* ●*verb* (**stank** *or* **stunk, stunk, stinking**) **1** give off an offensive smell. **2** seem very unpleasant or unsavoury or dishonest; *the whole business stinks.* □ **stink bomb** a device letting off an unpleasant smell when opened.

**stinker** *noun* (*slang*) a very unpleasant or difficult person or thing.

**stinking** *adjective* **1** that stinks. **2** (*slang*) very unpleasant. ●*adverb* (*slang*) extremely; *stinking rich.*

**stint** *verb* restrict to a small allowance, be niggardly; *don't stint on food.* ●*noun* **1** a limitation of supply or effort; *gave help without stint.* **2** a fixed or allotted amount of work; *did her stint.* **3** a small sandpiper.

**stipend** (sty-pend) *noun* a salary; the official income of a member of the clergy.

**stipendiary** (sty-**pend**-i-er-i) *adjective* receiving a stipend. □ **stipendiary magistrate** a paid professional magistrate.

**stipple** *verb* **1** paint, draw, or engrave in small dots (not in lines or strokes). **2** roughen the surface of (cement etc.). ●*noun* stippling; this effect.

**stipulate** *verb* demand or insist on as part of an agreement. □ **stipulation** *noun*

**stir** *verb* (**stirred, stirring**) **1** move or cause to move; *not a leaf stirred.* **2** mix or move (a substance) by moving a spoon etc. round and round in it. **3** arouse, excite, or stimulate; *the story stirred their interest.* ●*noun* **1** the act or process of stirring; *give the soup a stir.* **2** a commotion or excitement; *the news caused a stir.* **3** (*slang*) prison. □ **stir-fry** *verb* fry rapidly while stirring. ●*noun* a stir-fried dish. **stir up** stimulate; cause; rouse; *stir up trouble.*

**stirring** *adjective* exciting, stimulating.

**stirrup** *noun* a support for a rider's foot, hanging from the saddle. □ **stirrup-cup** *noun* a drink handed to a person about to leave, originally a rider. **stirrup-pump** *noun* a small portable water pump with a stirrup-shaped foot rest, used for extinguishing small fires.

**stitch** *noun* **1** (in sewing, knitting, etc.) a single complete movement of a needle or hook. **2** the loop of thread made in this way. **3** a particular method of arranging the thread; *cross stitch; purl stitch.* **4** the least bit of clothing; *without a stitch on.* **5** a sudden sharp pain in the muscles at the side of the body, often caused by running. ●*verb* sew, join, or close with stitches. □ **in stitches** (*informal*) laughing uncontrollably. **stitch up** (*slang*) trick, betray.

**stoat** *noun* the ermine, especially when its fur is brown.

**stock** *noun* **1** an amount of something available for use. **2** the total of goods kept by a trader. **3** livestock. **4** a line of ancestry; *a woman of Irish stock.* **5** money lent to a government in return for fixed interest. **6** the capital of a business company; a portion of this held by an investor (differing from *shares* in that it is not issued in fixed amounts). **7** a person's standing in the opinion of others; *his stock is high.* **8** liquid made by stewing bones, meat, fish, or vegetables, used as a basis for making soup, sauce, etc. **9** a garden plant with fragrant flowers. **10** the lower and thicker part of a tree trunk. **11** a growing plant into which a graft is inserted. **12** a part serving as the base, holder, or handle for the working parts of an implement or machine; *the stock of a rifle.* **13** a band of material worn round the neck. **14** a piece of black or purple fabric worn over the shirt front by a member of the clergy, hanging from a clerical collar. ●*adjective* **1** kept in stock and regularly available. **2** commonly used; *a stock argument.* ●*verb* **1** keep (goods) in stock. **2** provide with goods, livestock, or a supply of something; *stocked his farm with Jersey cows; a well-stocked library.* □ **in stock** available in a shop etc. without needing to be obtained specially. **out of stock** sold out. **stock-car** *noun* an ordinary car strengthened for use in racing where deliberate bumping is allowed. **Stock Exchange** a place where stocks and shares are publicly bought and sold; an association of dealers conducting such business according to fixed rules. **stock-in-trade** *noun* **1** all the stock and other requisites for carrying on a trade or business. **2** a person's characteristic behaviour or qualities. **stock market** the Stock Exchange; transactions there. **stock-still** *adjective* motionless. **stock up** assemble a stock of goods etc. **take stock** review a situation etc.

**stockade** *noun* a protective fence of upright stakes.

**stockbreeder** *noun* a farmer who raises livestock. □ **stockbreeding** *noun*

**stockbroker** *noun* = BROKER (sense 2). □ **stockbroking** *noun*

**Stockhausen** (stok-how-zěn), Karlheinz (born 1928), German composer, pioneer of electronic music.

**stockholder** *noun* a person who holds financial stock or shares.

**Stockholm** the capital of Sweden.

**stockinet** *noun* (also **stockinette**) fine stretchable machine-knitted fabric.

**stocking** noun a close-fitting covering for the foot and part or all of the leg. □ **in one's stockinged feet** wearing socks or stockings but no shoes. **stocking stitch** alternate rows of plain and purl in knitting, giving a plain smooth surface on one side.

**stockist** noun a business firm that stocks certain goods for sale.

**stockpile** noun an accumulated stock of goods or materials etc. kept in reserve. ●verb accumulate a stockpile of.

**stocks** plural noun 1 (hist.) a wooden framework with holes for the legs of a seated person, used like the pillory. 2 a framework on which a ship rests during construction.

**stocktaking** noun 1 making an inventory of stock in a shop. 2 reviewing of one's position and resources.

**stocky** adjective (**stockier, stockiest**) short and solidly built. □ **stockily** adverb, **stockiness** noun

**stockyard** noun an enclosure with pens etc. for the sorting or temporary keeping of livestock.

**stodge** noun (informal) stodgy food.

**stodgy** adjective (**stodgier, stodgiest**) 1 (of food) heavy and filling; indigestible. 2 dull, uninteresting; heavy-going. □ **stodgily** adverb, **stodginess** noun

**stoep** (pronounced stoop) noun (in South Africa) a veranda at the front of a house.

**stoic** (**stoh**-ik) noun a stoical person. (¶ Named after the Stoics, Greek and Roman philosophers of the 3rd century BC onwards, who taught that goodness is based on knowledge and that the truly wise man is indifferent to changes of fortune.)

**stoical** (**stoh**-ikăl) adjective calm and not excitable; bearing difficulties or discomfort without complaining. □ **stoically** adverb

**stoicism** (**stoh**-i-sizm) noun being stoical.

**stoke** verb (often foll. by up) 1 put fuel on (a furnace or fire etc.). 2 (informal) eat large quantities of food.

**stokehold** noun a compartment in which a steamship's fires are tended.

**stokehole** noun a space for stokers in front of a furnace.

**Stoker**, Bram (Abraham) (1847–1912), Irish novelist, author of Dracula.

**stoker** noun 1 a person who stokes a furnace etc. 2 a mechanical device for doing this.

**Stokowski** (stŏ-**kof**-ski), Leopold (1882–1977), British-born American conductor.

**STOL** abbreviation short take-off and landing; a system in which an aircraft needs only a short run for taking off and landing.

**stole**[1] noun 1 a clerical vestment consisting of a long strip of material worn round the neck with the ends hanging down in front.

2 a woman's wide scarf-like garment worn round the shoulders.

**stole**[2], **stolen** see STEAL.

**stolid** adjective not feeling or showing emotion; not excitable. □ **stolidly** adverb, **stolidity** (stŏ-**lid**-iti) noun

**stoma** noun (plural **stomas** or **stomata**) 1 a minute pore in the epidermis of a leaf. 2 a small mouthlike hole made in the stomach.

**stomach** noun 1 the internal organ in which the first part of digestion occurs. 2 the abdomen. 3 appetite for food. 4 appetite or spirit for danger or an undertaking etc.; had no stomach for the fight. ●verb endure or tolerate; can't stomach all that violence. □ **stomach-pump** noun a syringe for emptying the stomach or forcing liquid into it.

**stomacher** noun (hist.) a decorative pointed panel at the front of a dress of the 15th–17th centuries (originally worn by both men and women).

**stomp** verb tread heavily. ●noun a lively jazz dance with heavy stomping.

**stone** noun 1 a small piece of rock. 2 stones or rock as a substance or material, e.g. for building. 3 a piece of stone shaped for a particular purpose, e.g. a tombstone or millstone. 4 a precious stone (see PRECIOUS). 5 a small piece of hard substance formed in the bladder, kidney, or gall bladder. 6 the hard case round the kernel of certain fruits. 7 (plural **stone**) a unit of weight, = 14lb. ●adjective made of stone. ●verb 1 pelt with stones. 2 remove the stones from (fruit). □ **leave no stone unturned** try every possible means. **Stone Age** the very early period of civilization when weapons and tools were made of stone not metal. **stone-fruit** noun a fruit (e.g. plum, peach, cherry) containing a single stone. **stone's throw** a short distance.

**stone-** combining form completely; stone-cold, stone-deaf.

**stonechat** noun a small brown songbird with black and white markings.

**stonecrop** noun a sedum with yellow flowers, growing on rocks and walls.

**stoned** adjective (slang) drunk; under the influence of drugs.

**stoneground** adjective (of flour) ground with millstones.

**Stonehenge** a megalithic monument in Wiltshire in southern England, dating from the Bronze Age.

**stonemason** noun a person who cuts and dresses stone or builds in stone.

**stonewall** verb obstruct by stonewalling.

**stonewalling** noun 1 obstructing a discussion etc. by noncommittal replies. 2 batting in cricket without attempting to score runs.

**stoneware** *noun* items of pottery made from a mixture of clay and stone that will withstand heat.

**stonewashed** *adjective* (especially of denim) washed with abrasives to give a worn, faded look.

**stonework** *noun* stone(s) forming a building or other structure.

**stonker** *noun* (*slang*) a very large or impressive thing.

**stony** *adjective* (**stonier, stoniest**) **1** full of stones. **2** hard as stone, unfeeling; not responsive; *a stony gaze.* □ **stony-broke** *adjective* (*slang*) having no money at all. □ **stonily** *adverb*

**stood** *see* STAND.

**stooge** *noun* (*informal*) **1** a comedian's assistant, used as a target for jokes. **2** a subordinate who does routine work. **3** a person whose actions are entirely controlled by another. ● *verb* (*informal*) **1** act as a stooge. **2** wander about aimlessly.

**stook** *noun & verb* = SHOCK³.

**stool** *noun* **1** a movable seat without arms or a back. **2** a footstool. **3** the base of a plant from which new stems or foliage shoot up. **4** (**stools**) faeces. □ **stool-pigeon** *noun* **1** a person acting as a decoy, especially to trap a criminal. **2** a police informer.

**stoop** *verb* **1** bend forwards and down. **2** condescend, lower oneself morally; *he wouldn't stoop to cheating.* ● *noun* a posture of the body with shoulders bent forwards; *he walks with a stoop.*

**stop** *verb* (**stopped, stopping**) **1** put an end to (movement, progress, operation, etc.). **2** cease motion or working. **3** (*informal*) stay; *will you stop for tea?* **4** keep back, refuse to give or allow; *the cost will be stopped out of your wages.* **5** (in full **stop payment of** *or* **on**) order the bank not to honour (a cheque) when it is presented for payment. **6** close by plugging or obstructing; *stop the holes; stop them up.* **7** fill a cavity in (a tooth). **8** press down a string or block a hole in a musical instrument to obtain the desired pitch. ● *noun* **1** stopping; being stopped, a pause or check; *ran without a stop; put a stop to it.* **2** a place where a train or bus etc. stops regularly. **3** a punctuation mark, especially a full stop. **4** an obstruction or device that stops or regulates movement or operation. **5** a row of organ pipes providing tones of one quality; the knob or lever controlling these. **6** a key or lever regulating pitch in a wind instrument. **7** any of the standard sizes of aperture in an adjustable lens. □ **pull out all the stops** make all possible efforts. **stop down** reduce the aperture of a lens in photography. **stop-go** *noun* alternate stopping and progressing. **stop off** *or* **over** break

one's journey. **stop press** late news inserted in a newspaper after printing has begun.

**stopcock** *noun* a valve in a pipe to regulate the flow of liquid or gas.

**Stopes** (*rhymes with* hopes), Marie Charlotte Carmichael (1880–1958), Scottishborn pioneer of birth control.

**stopgap** *noun* a temporary substitute.

**stopoff** *noun* a stopover.

**stopover** *noun* a break in one's journey, especially for a night.

**stoppage** *noun* **1** stopping; being stopped. **2** an obstruction.

**Stoppard**, Tom (born 1937), Czech-born British playwright.

**stopper** *noun* a plug for closing a bottle etc. ● *verb* close with a stopper.

**stopwatch** *noun* a watch that can be stopped and started, used to time races etc.

**storage** *noun* **1** storing of goods etc. or of information. **2** space available for this. **3** the charge for it. □ **storage heater** an electric radiator accumulating heat in off-peak periods.

**store** *noun* **1** a stock or supply of something available for use. **2** a large shop. **3** a warehouse where things are stored. **4** a device in a computer or calculator for storing and retrieving information. ● *verb* **1** collect and keep for future use. **2** put into a store. **3** put (furniture etc.) into a warehouse for temporary keeping. **4** stock with something useful. □ **in store 1** being stored; kept available for use. **2** destined to happen, imminent; *there's a surprise in store for you.* **set store by** value greatly.

**storehouse** *noun* a place where things are stored.

**storekeeper** *noun* **1** a person in charge of a store or stores. **2** (*Amer.*) a shopkeeper.

**storeroom** *noun* a storage room.

**storey** *noun* (*plural* **storeys**) one horizontal section of a building, all the rooms at the same level. □ **storeyed** *adjective*

**stork** *noun* a large long-legged wading bird with a long straight bill, humorously pretended to be the bringer of babies.

**storm** *noun* **1** a violent disturbance of the atmosphere with strong winds and usually rain, snow, or thunder etc. **2** a violent shower of missiles or blows. **3** a great outbreak of applause, anger, or criticism etc. **4** a violent military attack. ● *verb* **1** (of wind or rain) rage, be violent. **2** behave very angrily; rage; *stormed out of the room; stormed at us for being late.* **3** attack or capture by storm; *they stormed the citadel.* □ **storm centre** the area at the centre of a storm; the centre of a disturbance or trouble. **storm-door** *noun* an additional outer door for extra protection against storms. **storm in a teacup** great agitation over a trivial matter. **storm petrel** (also **stormy petrel**) **1** a small black and white N. Atlantic petrel, said to be active before storms. **2** a person who causes unrest. **take by storm** capture by a violent attack; captivate rapidly.

**Stormont** a suburb of Belfast, seat of the parliament of Northern Ireland (suspended since 1972, when direct rule from London was imposed).

**stormy** *adjective* (**stormier**, **stormiest**) **1** affected by storms; *a stormy night*; *stormy coasts*. **2** (of wind etc.) violent as in a storm. **3** full of violent anger or outbursts; *a stormy interview*. □ **stormy petrel** = STORM PETREL. □ **stormily** *adverb*, **storminess** *noun*

**story** *noun* **1** an account of an incident either true or invented. **2** (in full **storyline**) the plot of a novel or play etc. **3** a report of an item of news; material for this. **4** (*informal*) a lie.

**stoup** (*pronounced* stoop) *noun* a stone basin for holy water, especially in the wall of a church.

**stout** *adjective* **1** of considerable thickness or strength; *a stout stick*. **2** (of a person) solidly built and rather fat. **3** brave and resolute; *a stout heart*. ●*noun* a strong dark beer brewed with roasted malt or barley. □ **stoutly** *adverb*, **stoutness** *noun*

**stove**[1] *noun* **1** a closed apparatus burning fuel or using electricity for heating or cooking. **2** a hothouse. □ **stove-pipe** *noun* a pipe carrying smoke and gases from a stove to a chimney.

**stove**[2] *see* STAVE.

**stow** *verb* place in a receptacle for storage. □ **stow away 1** put away in storage or in reserve. **2** conceal oneself as a stowaway.

**stowage** *noun* **1** stowing; being stowed. **2** space available for this. **3** the charge for it.

**stowaway** *noun* a person who hides on a ship or aircraft etc. so as to travel free.

**Stowe**, Mrs Harriet Beecher (1811–96), American novelist, author of *Uncle Tom's Cabin*.

**strabismus** (strǎ-**biz**-mǔs) *noun* *Med.* a squint.

**Strachey** (**stray**-chi), (Giles) Lytton (1880–1932), English biographer and critic.

**straddle** *verb* **1** sit or stand across (a thing) with the legs or supports wide apart. **2** stand with the legs wide apart. **3** drop shots or bombs short of and beyond (a certain point).

**Stradivarius** (strad-i-**vair**-iǔs) *noun* a violin or other stringed instrument made by

Antonio Stradivari (*c.*1644–1737), Italian violin-maker, or his followers.

**strafe** (*pronounced* strahf *or* strayf) *verb* bombard, attack with gunfire.

**straggle** *verb* **1** grow or spread in an irregular or untidy manner. **2** go or wander separately; drop behind others. □ **straggler** *noun*

**straggly** *adjective* straggling.

**straight** *adjective* **1** extending or moving continuously in one direction, not curved or bent. **2** correctly arranged; tidy. **3** in unbroken succession; *ten straight wins*. **4** candid, not evasive; honest. **5** (*slang*) heterosexual. **6** not modified or elaborate; without additions; (of alcoholic drinks) not diluted. ●*adverb* **1** in a straight line. **2** direct, without delay; *went straight home*. **3** straightforwardly; *told him straight*. ●*noun* **1** the straight part of something, e.g. the last section of a racecourse. **2** (*slang*) a heterosexual person. **3** a sequence of five cards in poker. □ **go straight** live an honest life after being a criminal. **straight away** without delay. **straight face** one without a smile even though amused. **straight fight** a contest between only two candidates. **straight flush** a hand of cards of a single suit in numerical order. **straight man** a comedian's stooge. **straight off** (*informal*) without hesitation or deliberation etc. □ **straightness** *noun*

**straighten** *verb* make or become straight.

▪**Usage** Do not confuse *straightened* with *straitened*.

**straightforward** *adjective* **1** honest, frank. **2** (of a task etc.) without complications. □ **straightforwardly** *adverb*, **straightforwardness** *noun*

**strain**[1] *verb* **1** stretch tightly; make taut. **2** injure by excessive stretching or exertion. **3** make an intense effort. **4** apply (a meaning or rule etc.) beyond its true application. **5** pass through a sieve or similar device to separate solids from a liquid; (of liquid) filter. ●*noun* **1** straining; being strained; the force exerted. **2** an injury caused by straining a muscle etc. **3** a severe demand on one's mental or physical strength or on one's resources; exhaustion caused by this. **4** a passage from a tune. **5** the tone or style of something written or spoken; *continued in a more cheerful strain*. □ **straining at the leash** eager to begin.

**strain**[2] *noun* **1** a line of descent of animals, plants, or micro-organisms; a variety or breed of these; *a new strain of flu virus*. **2** a slight or inherited tendency in character; *there's a strain of insanity in the family*.

**strained** *adjective* (of behaviour or manner) tense, distrustful; awkward, artificial.

**strainer** noun **1** a device for keeping something taut. **2** a utensil for straining liquids.

**strait** noun **1** (also **straits**) a narrow stretch of water connecting two seas; *the Strait of Gibraltar*. **2** (**straits**) a difficult state of affairs; *in dire straits*.

**straitened** adjective **1** poverty-stricken. **2** (*old use*) made narrow, not spacious enough.

∎**Usage** Do not confuse with *straightened*.

**strait-jacket** noun **1** a strong jacket-like garment with long sleeves for restraining a violent prisoner or mental patient. **2** a situation or measure that severely restricts one's actions. ●verb **1** restrain by a strait-jacket. **2** restrict severely.

**strait-laced** adjective very prim and proper.

**strand** noun **1** one of the threads or wires etc. twisted together to form a rope, yarn, or cable. **2** a single thread or strip of fibre. **3** a lock of hair. **4** a shore. ●verb run or cause to run aground.

**stranded** adjective left in difficulties, e.g. without funds or means of transport.

**strange** adjective **1** not familiar or well known; not one's own, alien; *in a strange land*. **2** unusual, surprising; *it's strange that you haven't heard*. **3** (foll. by *to*) unaccustomed; *she is strange to the work.* □ **strangely** adverb, **strangeness** noun

**stranger** noun **1** a person in a place or company etc. to which he or she does not belong; a person one does not know. **2** one who is unaccustomed to a certain experience or task; *a stranger to poverty*.

**strangle** verb **1** kill or be killed by squeezing the throat. **2** restrict or prevent the proper growth, operation, or utterance of. □ **strangler** noun

**stranglehold** noun a strangling grip.

**strangulate** verb compress (a vein or intestine etc.) so that nothing can pass through it.

**strangulation** noun **1** strangling; being strangled. **2** strangulating; being strangulated.

**strap** noun **1** a strip of leather, fabric, etc., often with a buckle, for holding things in place. **2** a shoulder strap. **3** a loop for grasping to steady oneself in a moving vehicle. ●verb (**strapped, strapping**) **1** secure with a strap or straps. **2** bind (an injury); *strap it up*. **3** beat with a strap.

**straphanger** noun (*slang*) a standing passenger in a bus, train, etc.

**strapless** adjective without shoulder straps.

**strapped** adjective (*slang*) short of something; *strapped for cash*.

**strapping** adjective tall, sturdy, and healthy-looking.

**Strasbourg** a city in NE France, where sessions of the European Parliament are held.

**strata** see STRATUM.

**stratagem** (strat-ă-jěm) noun a cunning plan or scheme; a piece of trickery.

**strategic** (stră-tee-jik) adjective **1** of strategy. **2** giving an advantage; *a strategic position*. □ **Strategic Defense Initiative** a former US defence proposal (popularly known as 'Star Wars') in which enemy weapons would be destroyed in space by lasers, missiles, etc. directed from satellites. **strategic materials** those essential for war. **strategic weapons** missiles etc. that can reach an enemy's home territory (as distinct from *tactical weapons* which are for use in a battle or at close quarters). □ **strategically** adverb

**strategist** (strat-i-jist) noun an expert in strategy.

**strategy** (strat-i-ji) noun **1** the planning and directing of a campaign or war. **2** a plan or policy to achieve something; *our economic strategy*.

**Strathclyde** a local government region of Scotland.

**strathspey** (strath-**spay**) noun a slow Scottish dance; music for this.

**stratified** adjective arranged in strata, grades, layers, etc. □ **stratification** noun

**stratigraphy** (stră-**tig**-răfi) noun Geol. & Archaeol. **1** the order and relative proportions of strata. **2** the scientific study of these. □ **stratigraphic** adjective (also **stratigraphical**).

**stratosphere** (strat-ŏ-sfeer) noun a layer of the earth's atmosphere between about 10 and 60 km above the earth's surface.

**stratum** (strah-tŭm) noun (*plural* **strata**) **1** one of a series of layers, especially of rock in the earth's crust. **2** a social level or class; *the various strata of society*.

∎**Usage** The word *strata* is a plural; it is incorrect to speak of a *strata* or *this strata*, or of *stratas*.

**Strauss**[1] (*rhymes with* house), Johann (II) (1825–99), Austrian composer (son of Johann I (1804–49), composer of dance music), famous for his waltzes.

**Strauss**[2] (*rhymes with* house), Richard (1864–1949), German composer.

**Stravinsky** (stră-**vin**-ski), Igor (1882–1971), Russian-born composer.

**straw** noun **1** dry cut stalks of grain used as material for bedding, thatching, fodder, etc. **2** a single stalk or piece of this. **3** a narrow tube of paper or plastic for sucking up liquid in drinking. **4** a pale yellow colour. □ **a straw in the wind** a slight indication of how things may develop. **straw**

**poll** *or* **vote** an unofficial poll as a test of general feeling.

**strawberry** *noun* a soft juicy edible red fruit with seeds on the surface; the plant that bears it. □ **strawberry mark** a reddish birthmark.

**stray** *verb* **1** leave one's group or proper place with no settled destination or purpose; roam. **2** go aside from a direct course; depart from a subject. ● *adjective* **1** having strayed. **2** isolated, occurring here and there not as one of a group. ● *noun* a person or domestic animal that has strayed; a stray thing.

**streak** *noun* **1** a thin line or band of a different colour or substance from its surroundings. **2** an element in a person's character; *has a jealous streak*. **3** a spell or series; *had a long winning streak*. ● *verb* **1** mark with streaks. **2** move very rapidly. **3** run naked through a public place as a humorous or defiant act. □ **streaker** *noun*

**streaky** *adjective* full of streaks; (of bacon etc.) with alternate layers or streaks of fat and lean. □ **streakily** *adverb*, **streakiness** *noun*

**stream** *noun* **1** a flowing body of water; a brook or small river. **2** a flow of any liquid or of a mass of things or people. **3** (in certain schools) a section into which children with the same level of ability are placed. **4** the current or direction of something moving; *against the stream*. ● *verb* **1** flow or move as a stream. **2** emit a stream of; run with liquid; *the wound streamed blood*; *with streaming eyes*. **3** (of hair, ribbons, etc.) be blown at full length in the wind. **4** arrange (schoolchildren) in streams. □ **on stream** in operation or production.

**streamer** *noun* **1** a long narrow flag. **2** a long narrow ribbon or strip of paper attached at one or both ends.

**streamline** *verb* **1** give a streamlined form to. **2** make more efficient by simplifying, removing superfluities, etc.

**streamlined** *adjective* having a smooth even shape that offers the least resistance to movement through air or water.

**Streep**, Meryl (original name: Mary Louise) (born 1949), American film actress.

**street** *noun* a public road in a town or village with houses along one or both sides. □ **on the streets** **1** living by prostitution. **2** homeless. **street credibility** (also **street cred**) a personal image of being fashionable, confident, and successful in modern city life. **streets ahead of** (*informal*) much superior to. **up one's street** (*informal*) within one's field of knowledge or interests.

**streetcar** *noun* (*Amer.*) a tram.

**streetwalker** *noun* a prostitute looking for customers in the street.

**streetwise** *adjective* knowing how to survive in modern city life.

**Streisand**, Barbra (original name: Barbara Joan) (born 1942), American singer and film actress.

**strength** *noun* **1** the quality of being strong; the intensity of this. **2** a source of strength; the particular respect in which a person or thing is strong. **3** the number of people present or available; the full complement; *the department is below strength*. □ **in strength** in large numbers; *supporters were present in strength*. **on the strength of** on the basis of, using (a fact etc.) as one's support.

**strengthen** *verb* make or become stronger.

**strenuous** *adjective* **1** energetic, making great efforts. **2** requiring great effort; *a strenuous task*. □ **strenuously** *adverb*, **strenuousness** *noun*

**streptococcus** *noun* (*plural* **streptococci**, *pronounced* strep-tŏ-**kok**-I) any of a group of bacteria that cause serious infections. □ **streptococcal** *adjective*

**streptomycin** (strep-tŏ-**my**-sin) *noun* an antibiotic drug.

**stress** *noun* **1** a force acting on or within a thing and tending to distort it, e.g. by pressing, pulling, or twisting. **2** mental or physical distress caused by difficult circumstances. **3** = EMPHASIS (senses 1 and 3). ● *verb* **1** lay emphasis on. **2** cause stress to.

**stressful** *adjective* causing stress. □ **stressfully** *adverb*

**stretch** *verb* **1** pull out tightly or into a greater length or size. **2** be able to be stretched without breaking; tend to become stretched; *knitted fabrics stretch*. **3** be continuous from a point or between points; *the wall stretches right round the estate*. **4** thrust out one's limbs and tighten the muscles. **5** make great demands on the abilities of (a person). **6** strain to the utmost or beyond a reasonable limit; *stretch the truth*. ● *noun* **1** stretching; being stretched. **2** a continuous expanse or tract; a continuous period of time. **3** (*slang*) a period of service or imprisonment. ● *adjective* able to be stretched; *stretch fabrics*. □ **at a stretch** without interruption. **at full stretch** *or* **fully stretched** working to the utmost of one's powers. **stretch a point** agree to something beyond the limit of what is normally allowed. **stretch one's legs** go for a walk.

**stretcher** *noun* **1** a framework of poles, canvas, etc. for carrying a sick or injured person in a lying position. **2** any of various devices for stretching things or holding things taut. **3** a board against which a rower braces his or her feet. **4** a brick in a wall laid horizontally with its long side showing.

**stretchy** *adjective* (*informal*) able to be stretched.

**strew** *verb* (**strewed, strewn** *or* **strewed, strewing**) scatter over a surface; cover with scattered things.

**'strewth** alternative spelling of 'STRUTH.

**stria** (stry-ă) *noun* (*plural* **striae**) *Geol.* a slight ridge or furrow.

**striated** (stry-ay-tid) *adjective* marked with slight ridges.

**striation** (stry-ay-shŏn) *noun* a pattern or series of ridges or furrows.

**stricken** *adjective* affected or overcome by an illness, shock, or grief.

**strict** *adjective* **1** precisely limited or defined, without exception or deviation. **2** requiring complete obedience or exact performance; not lenient or indulgent. □ **strictly speaking** if one uses words in their exact sense. □ **strictly** *adverb*, **strictness** *noun*

**stricture** *noun* **1** severe criticism or condemnation. **2** abnormal constriction of a tube-like part of the body.

**stride** *verb* (**strode, stridden, striding**) **1** walk with long steps. **2** stand astride. ●*noun* **1** a single long step, the length of this. **2** a person's manner of striding. **3** progress; *has made great strides towards independence.* □ **get into one's stride** settle into a fast and steady pace of work. **take in one's stride** do without needing a special effort.

**strident** (stry-dĕnt) *adjective* loud and harsh. □ **stridently** *adverb*, **stridency** *noun*

**strife** *noun* quarrelling, conflict.

**strike** *verb* (**struck, striking**) **1** bring or come into sudden hard contact with; knock with a blow or stroke. **2** attack suddenly; (of a disease) afflict. **3** (of lightning) descend upon and blast. **4** produce (sparks or a sound etc.) by striking something; produce (a musical note) by pressing a key; make (a coin or medal) by stamping metal etc.; ignite (a match) by friction. **5** bring into a specified state by or as if by striking; *he was struck blind.* **6** indicate (the hour) or be indicated by a sound; *the clock struck two.* **7** reach (gold or mineral oil etc.) by digging or drilling. **8** occur to the mind of; produce a mental impression on; *an idea struck me*; *she strikes me as being efficient.* **9** lower or take down (a flag or tent etc.). **10** stop work in protest about a grievance. **11** penetrate or cause to penetrate; fill with sudden fear etc. **12** proceed in a certain direction; *strike north-west through the forest.* **13** reach or achieve; *strike a balance*; *strike a bargain.* **14** assume (an attitude) suddenly

and dramatically. ●*noun* **1** an act or instance of striking. **2** an attack. **3** a workers' refusal to work, in protest about a grievance. **4** a sudden discovery of gold or oil etc. □ **on strike** (of workers) striking. **strike it rich** find a source of prosperity. **strike off** cross off; remove (a person) from a professional register because of misconduct. **strike out** *or* **through** cross out. **strike pay** an allowance made by a trade union to members on strike. **strike up 1** begin playing or singing. **2** start (a friendship etc.). **strike while the iron is hot** take action promptly while the opportunity is available.

**strikebound** *adjective* immobilized by a workers' strike.

**strikebreaker** *noun* a person who works while fellow employees are on strike or who is employed in place of strikers.

**striker** *noun* **1** a person or thing that strikes. **2** a worker who is on strike. **3** a footballer whose main function is to score goals.

**striking** *adjective* sure to be noticed, attractive and impressive. □ **strikingly** *adverb*

**Strindberg**, (Johan) August (1849–1912), Swedish dramatist and novelist.

**Strine** *noun* **1** a comic transliteration of Australian pronunciation. **2** Australian speech, especially of an uneducated type. (¶ The alleged pronunciation of 'Australian' in Australian speech.)

**string** *noun* **1** narrow cord. **2** a length of this used to fasten or lace something, or interwoven in a frame to form the head of a racket. **3** a piece of catgut, wire, etc. stretched on a musical instrument, producing a note by vibration. **4** a strip of tough fibre on a bean etc. **5** a set of objects strung together or of people or events coming after one another; a series or line. **6** *computers* a one dimensional array of characters. **7** the racehorses trained at one stable. **8** a condition that is insisted upon; *the offer has no strings attached.* **9** (**strings**) stringed instruments; their players. ●*verb* (**strung, stringing**) **1** fit or fasten with string(s). **2** thread (beads etc.) on a string. **3** trim the tough fibre from (beans). □ **pull strings** *see* PULL. **string along** (*informal*) deceive. **string along with** (*informal*) accompany. **string-course** *noun* a projecting horizontal line of bricks etc. round a building. **string out** spread out in a line; cause to last a long time. **string quartet** a quartet for stringed instruments. **string up** kill by hanging. **string vest** a vest made of large mesh.

**stringed** *adjective* (of musical instruments) having strings.

**stringent** (strin-jĕnt) *adjective* (of a rule) strict, precise. □ **stringently** *adverb*, **stringency** *noun*

**stringer** *noun* **1** a lengthwise structural part in a framework, especially in a ship or aircraft; one of the side pieces of a staircase. **2** a newspaper correspondent who is not on the regular staff.

**stringy** *adjective* **1** like string. **2** (of beans etc.) having a strip of tough fibre.

**strip** *verb* (**stripped**, **stripping**) **1** take off (clothes, coverings, etc.). **2** undress oneself. **3** deprive, e.g. of property or titles. **4** damage the thread of (a screw) or the teeth of (a gear wheel). **5** (often foll. by *down*) take apart (a machine, engine, etc.) in order to overhaul it. ●*noun* a long narrow piece or area. □ **strip cartoon** = COMIC STRIP. **strip club** a club where striptease is performed. **strip light** a long tubular fluorescent light. **strip-search** *noun* a search involving the removal of all a person's clothes.

**stripe** *noun* **1** a long narrow band on a surface, differing in colour or texture from its surroundings. **2** a chevron on a sleeve, indicating the wearer's rank.

**striped** *adjective* marked with stripes.

**stripling** *noun* a youth.

**stripper** *noun* **1** a person or thing that strips something. **2** a device or solvent for removing paint etc. **3** a striptease performer.

**striptease** *noun* entertainment in which the performer undresses slowly and erotically.

**stripy** *adjective* striped.

**strive** *verb* (**strove**, **striven**, **striving**) **1** make great efforts. **2** carry on a conflict.

**strobe** *noun* (*informal*) a stroboscope.

**stroboscope** (stroh-bŏ-skohp) *noun* an apparatus for producing a rapidly flashing bright light. □ **stroboscopic** (-skop-ik) *adjective*

**strode** *see* STRIDE.

**Stroganoff** (strog-ăn-off) *noun* a dish of strips of beef cooked in a sauce containing sour cream.

**stroke** *noun* **1** the act or process of striking something. **2** a single movement or action or effort, a successful or skilful effort; *he hasn't done a stroke of work; a stroke of genius; a stroke of luck.* **3** each of a series of repeated movements; a particular sequence of these (e.g. in swimming). **4** one hit at the ball in various games; (in golf) this used as a unit of scoring. **5** (in full **stroke oar**) the oarsman nearest the stern of a racing boat, setting the time of the stroke. **6** a mark made by a movement of a pen or paintbrush. **7** the sound made by a clock striking; *on the stroke of ten.* **8** an attack of apoplexy or paralysis. **9** an act or spell of stroking. ●*verb* **1** pass one's hand

gently along the surface of (hair, skin, etc.). **2** act as stroke to (a boat or crew).

**stroll** *verb* walk in a leisurely way. ●*noun* a leisurely walk.

**stroller** *noun* **1** a person who strolls. **2** a pushchair.

**Stromboli** (strom-**boh**-li) an active volcano forming one of the Lipari Islands off the SW coast of Italy.

**strong** *adjective* **1** having power of resistance to being broken, damaged, captured etc. **2** capable of exerting great power, physically powerful; powerful through numbers, resources, or quality. **3** concentrated, having a large proportion of flavouring or colouring; (of a drink) containing much alcohol. **4** having a considerable effect on one of the senses; *a strong smell.* **5** having a specified number of members; *an army 5000 strong.* **6** *Grammar* (of verbs) changing the vowel in the past tense (as *ring/rang, strike/struck*), not adding a suffix (as *float/floated*). ●*adverb* strongly, vigorously; *going strong.* □ **strong-arm tactics** use of force or sheer strength. **strong language** forcible language; oaths or swearing. **strong suit** a suit (in a hand of cards) in which one can take tricks; a thing at which one excels. □ **strongly** *adverb*

**strongbox** *noun* a small strongly made chest for valuables.

**stronghold** *noun* **1** a fortified place. **2** a centre of support for a cause etc.

**strongroom** *noun* a room, especially in a bank, for keeping valuables safe from fire and theft.

**strontium** (stron-ti-ŭm) *noun* a chemical element (symbol Sr), a soft silver-white metal. □ **strontium-90** *noun* a radioactive isotope of strontium that is found in nuclear fallout and concentrates in bones and teeth when taken into the body.

**strop** *noun* a strip of leather on which a razor is sharpened. ●*verb* (**stropped**, **stropping**) sharpen on or with a strop.

**stroppy** *adjective* (*slang*) bad-tempered, awkward to deal with.

**strove** *see* STRIVE.

**struck** *see* STRIKE. □ **struck on** (*slang*) impressed with, liking.

**structural** *adjective* of a structure or framework. □ **structurally** *adverb*

**structuralism** *noun* the theory that societies, languages, works of literature, etc. can be understood only by analysis of their structure (rather than their function). □ **structuralist** *noun* & *adjective*

**structure** *noun* **1** the way in which something is constructed or organized. **2** a supporting framework or the essential parts of a thing. **3** a constructed thing; a complex whole; a building. ●verb construct; organize.

**strudel** (stroo-děl) noun thin pastry filled especially with apple.

**struggle** verb **1** move one's limbs or body in a vigorous effort to get free. **2** make a vigorous effort under difficulties. **3** try to overcome an opponent or problem etc. ●noun a spell of struggling; a vigorous effort; a hard contest.

**strum** verb (**strummed, strumming**) play on a guitar, piano, etc., especially casually or unskilfully. ●noun the sound made by strumming.

**strumpet** noun (old use) a prostitute.

**strung** see STRING.

**strut** noun **1** a bar of wood or metal inserted into a framework to strengthen and brace it. **2** a strutting walk. ●verb (**strutted, strutting**) walk in a pompous self-satisfied way.

**'struth** interjection (also **'strewth**) (informal) an exclamation of surprise. (¶ = God's truth.)

**strychnine** (strik-neen) noun a bitter highly poisonous substance, used in very small doses as a stimulant.

**Stuart** the name of the royal house of Scotland from the accession (1371) of Robert II, and of Britain from the accession of James VI of Scotland to the English throne as James I (1603) until the death of Queen Anne (1714).

**stub** noun **1** a short stump. **2** the counterfoil of a cheque, receipt, etc. ●verb (**stubbed, stubbing**) **1** strike against a hard object; stub one's toe. **2** (foll. by out) extinguish (a cigarette) by pressing the end against something hard.

**stubble** noun **1** the lower ends of the stalks of cereal plants left in the ground after the harvest. **2** a short stiff growth of hair or beard. □ **stubbly** adjective

**stubborn** adjective obstinate, not easy to control or deal with. □ **stubbornly** adverb, **stubbornness** noun

**stubby** adjective (**stubbier, stubbiest**) short and thick.

**Stubbs**, George (1724–1806), English animal painter and engraver.

**stucco** noun plaster or cement used for coating walls or moulding to form architectural decorations. □ **stuccoed** adjective

**stuck** see STICK. ●adjective **1** unable to move or make progress. **2** (of an animal) that has been stabbed or had its throat cut. □ **get stuck in** (slang) begin working seriously (at a job etc.). **stuck on** (slang) infatuated with (a person or thing). **stuck-up** adjective (informal) conceited; snobbish. **stuck with** (informal) unable to get rid of.

**stud¹** noun **1** a short large-headed nail; a rivet; a small knob projecting from a surface. **2** a device like a button on a shank, used e.g. to fasten a detachable shirt-collar. ●verb (**studded, studding**) decorate with studs or precious stones set into a surface; strengthen with studs.

**stud²** noun **1** a number of horses kept for breeding. **2** (in full **stud-farm**) a place where horses are bred. □ **at stud** (of a male horse) available for breeding on payment of a fee. **stud-book** noun a book containing the pedigrees of horses.

**studding-sail** (stun-săl) noun an extra sail set at the side of a square sail in light winds.

**student** noun a person engaged in studying something, a pupil at a university, college, etc.

**studied** adjective carefully and intentionally contrived; she answered with studied indifference.

**studio** noun (plural **studios**) **1** the workroom of a painter, sculptor, photographer, etc. **2** a place where cinema films are made. **3** a room from which radio or television programmes are regularly broadcast or in which recordings are made. □ **studio couch** a divan-like couch that can be converted into a bed. **studio flat** a flat consisting of a bed-sitting-room with a kitchen and bathroom.

**studious** adjective **1** involving study; habitually spending much time in studying. **2** deliberate, painstaking; studious politeness. □ **studiously** adverb, **studiousness** noun

**study** noun **1** the process of studying. **2** its subject; a thing that is investigated. **3** a musical composition designed to develop a player's skill. **4** a preliminary drawing; a study of a head. **5** a room in a house used for work that involves writing, reading, etc. ●verb (**studied, studying**) **1** give one's attention to acquiring knowledge of (a subject). **2** look at carefully; we studied the map. **3** give care and consideration to.

**stuff** noun **1** material. **2** (slang) unnamed things, belongings, subject-matter, activities, etc.; leave your stuff in the hall; westerns are kids' stuff. **3** (slang) valueless matter, trash; stuff and nonsense! ●verb **1** pack or cram; fill tightly. **2** fill the empty skin etc. of (a bird or animal) with material to restore its original shape, e.g. for exhibition in a museum. **3** fill with savoury stuffing. **4** fill (a person or oneself) with food; eat greedily. **5** (vulgar, offensive) have sexual intercourse with (a woman). **6** (slang) dispose of as unwanted; you can stuff the job. □ **get stuffed!** (slang) go away, stop annoying me. **stuffed shirt** (informal) a pompous person.

**stuffing** *noun* **1** padding used to stuff cushions etc. **2** a savoury mixture put as a filling into poultry, vegetables, etc. before cooking. □ **knock the stuffing out of** (*informal*) make feeble or weak; defeat utterly.

**stuffy** *adjective* (**stuffier, stuffiest**) **1** lacking fresh air or sufficient ventilation. **2** dull, uninteresting. **3** (of the nose) blocked so that breathing is difficult. **4** (*informal*) old-fashioned and narrow-minded. □ **stuffily** *adverb*, **stuffiness** *noun*

**stultify** *verb* (**stultified, stultifying**) impair or make ineffective; *a boring job that stultifies the brain.* □ **stultification** *noun*

**stum** *noun* unfermented grape juice, must.

**stumble** *verb* **1** strike one's foot on something and lose one's balance. **2** walk with frequent stumbles. **3** make a blunder or frequent blunders in speaking or playing music etc. ●*noun* an act of stumbling. □ **stumble across** *or* **on** discover accidentally. **stumbling block** an obstacle; a difficulty.

**stumm** (*pronounced* shtuum) *adjective* (*slang*) silent; *keep stumm.*

**stump** *noun* **1** the base of a tree remaining in the ground when the rest has been cut down. **2** a corresponding remnant e.g. of a broken tooth or an amputated limb. **3** one of the three uprights of a wicket in cricket. ●*verb* **1** walk stiffly or noisily. **2** (of a wicket-keeper) put out (a batsman) by dislodging the bails while he is out of the crease. **3** (*informal*) be too difficult for, baffle; *the question stumped him.* **4** (*Amer.*) travel round (an area) making political speeches. □ **stump up** (*slang*) pay or produce (the money required).

**stumpy** *adjective* (**stumpier, stumpiest**) short and thick. □ **stumpiness** *noun*

**stun** *verb* (**stunned, stunning**) **1** knock senseless. **2** daze or shock.

**stung** *see* STING.

**stunk** *see* STINK.

**stunning** *adjective* (*informal*) extremely attractive. □ **stunningly** *adverb*

**stunt**¹ *verb* hinder the growth or development of.

**stunt**² *noun* (*informal*) something unusual or difficult done as a performance or to attract attention. □ **stunt man** a person employed to take an actor's place in performing stunts.

**stupa** (stew-pă) *noun* a round usually domed Buddhist monument, usually containing a sacred relic.

**stupefy** *verb* (**stupefied, stupefying**) **1** dull the wits or senses of. **2** stun with astonishment. □ **stupefaction** *noun*

**stupendous** (stew-pend-ŭs) *adjective* amazing, exceedingly great. □ **stupendously** *adverb*

**stupid** *adjective* **1** not intelligent or clever, slow at learning or understanding. **2** in a state of stupor; *he was knocked stupid.* □ **stupidly** *adverb*, **stupidity** *noun*

**stupor** (stew-per) *noun* a dazed or almost unconscious condition brought on by shock, drugs, drink, etc.

**sturdy** *adjective* (**sturdier, sturdiest**) strongly built, hardy, vigorous. □ **sturdily** *adverb*, **sturdiness** *noun*

**sturgeon** *noun* (*plural* **sturgeon** *or* **sturgeons**) a large shark-like fish with flesh that is valued as food and roe that is made into caviare.

**stutter** *verb* stammer, especially by repeating the first consonants of words. ●*noun* stuttering speech; a tendency to stutter.

**sty**¹ *noun* (*plural* **sties**) a pigsty.

**sty**² *noun* (also **stye**) (*plural* **sties** *or* **styes**) an inflamed swelling on the edge of the eyelid.

**Stygian** (stij-iăn) *adjective* (*literary*) of or like the Styx or Hades; gloomy, murky.

**style** *noun* **1** the manner of writing, speaking, or doing something (contrasted with the subject-matter or the thing done). **2** shape or design; *a new style of coat.* **3** elegance, distinction. **4** a narrow extension of the ovary in a plant, supporting the stigma. ●*verb* design, shape, or arrange, especially in a fashionable style. □ **in style** elegantly; luxuriously.

**stylish** *adjective* in fashionable style, elegant. □ **stylishly** *adverb*, **stylishness** *noun*

**stylist** *noun* **1** a person who achieves or aims at a good style in what he or she does. **2** a hairdresser or designer.

**stylistic** *adjective* of literary or artistic style. □ **stylistically** *adverb*

**stylized** *adjective* (also **stylised**) made to conform to a conventional style.

**stylus** *noun* (*plural* **styluses**) **1** a needle-like device following a groove in a gramophone record to reproduce the sound. **2** a pointed writing tool.

**stymie** (sty-mi) (also **stimy**) *noun* **1** the situation in golf where an opponent's ball is between a player's ball and the hole. **2** something that blocks or thwarts one's activities. ●*verb* (**stymied, stymieing**) **1** subject to a stymie in golf. **2** block or thwart the activities of.

**styptic** (stip-tik) *adjective* checking the flow of blood by causing blood vessels to contract.

**styrene** *noun* a liquid hydrocarbon used in plastics.

**Styx** (*pronounced* stiks) (*Gk. myth.*) one of the rivers of the Underworld, over which Charon ferried the souls of the dead.

**suasion** (sway-zhŏn) *noun* (*formal*) persuasion.

**suave** (*pronounced* swahv) *adjective* smooth-mannered; sophisticated. □ **suavely** *adverb*, **suavity** *noun*

**sub** *noun* (*informal*) **1** a submarine. **2** a subscription. **3** a substitute. **4** a sub-editor. ●*verb* **1** (usually foll. by *for*) act as a substitute. **2** sub-edit.

**sub-** *combining form* **1** under (as in *substructure*). **2** subordinate, secondary (as in *subsection*).

**subaltern** (**sub-ăl-**tern) *noun* a second lieutenant.

**sub-aqua** *adjective* (of sport etc.) taking place under water.

**subaquatic** *adjective* underwater.

**subarctic** *adjective* of regions bordering on the Arctic Circle.

**subatomic** *adjective* (of a particle of matter) occurring in an atom; smaller than an atom.

**subcommittee** *noun* a committee formed for a special purpose from some members of the main committee.

**subconscious** *adjective* of the part of the mind that influences our attitudes, behaviour, etc. without us being aware of it. ●*noun* this part of the mind. □ **subconsciously** *adverb*

**subcontinent** *noun* a large land mass that forms part of a continent.

**subcontract** (sub-kŏn-**trakt**) *verb* give or accept a contract to carry out all or part of another contract. □ **subcontractor** *noun*

**subculture** *noun* a social culture within a larger culture.

**subcutaneous** (sub-kew-**tay**-niŭs) *adjective* under the skin.

**subdivide** *verb* divide into smaller parts after a first division. □ **subdivision** *noun*

**subdue** *verb* **1** overcome, bring under control. **2** make quieter or less intense; *subdued lighting*.

**sub-edit** *verb* (**sub-edited**, **sub-editing**) prepare (material) as a sub-editor.

**sub-editor** *noun* **1** an assistant editor. **2** a person who prepares material for printing in a book or newspaper etc.

**subgroup** *noun* a subset of a group; a group within a larger group.

**subheading** *noun* a subordinate heading.

**subhuman** *adjective* less than human; not fully human.

**subject** *adjective* (*pronounced* **sub-**jikt) **1** not politically independent; *subject peoples*. **2** owing obedience to, under the authority of; *we are all subject to the laws of the land*. ●*noun* (*pronounced* **sub-**jikt) **1** a person subject to a particular political rule, any member of a State except the supreme ruler; *British subjects*. **2** the person or thing that is being discussed, described, represented, or studied. **3** *Grammar* the word or words in a sentence that name who or what does the action or undergoes what is stated by the verb, e.g. *'the book'* in *the book fell off the table*. **4** the theme or chief phrase in a sonata etc. ●*verb* (*pronounced* sŭb-**jekt**) **1** bring (a country) under one's control. **2** cause to undergo or experience; *subjecting the metal to severe tests*. □ **subject-matter** *noun* the matter treated in a book or speech etc. **subject to 1** liable to; *trains are subject to delay during fog*. **2** depending upon as a condition; *subject to your approval*; *subject to contract*. □ **subjection** *noun*

**subjective** (sŭb-**jek**-tiv) *adjective* **1** existing in a person's mind and not produced by things outside it, not objective. **2** depending on personal taste or views etc. □ **subjectively** *adverb*

**subjoin** *verb* add at the end.

***sub judice*** (sub joo-dis-i) under judicial consideration, not yet decided (and, in the UK, for this reason not to be commented upon). (¶ Latin, = under a judge.)

**subjugate** (**sub**-jŭ-gayt) *verb* subdue or bring (a country etc.) into subjection. □ **subjugation** *noun*, **subjugator** *noun*

**subjunctive** *adjective* *Grammar* of the form of a verb used in expressing what is imagined or wished or possible, e.g. *'were'* in *if I were you*. ●*noun* a subjunctive form.

**sublease** *noun* a lease granted to a subtenant. ●*verb* lease by a sublease.

**sublet** *verb* (**sublet**, **subletting**) let (accommodation etc. that one holds by lease) to a subtenant.

**sub-lieutenant** *noun* an officer ranking immediately below a lieutenant.

**sublimate** (sub-lim-ayt) *verb* **1** divert the energy of (an emotion or impulse arising from a primitive instinct) into a culturally higher activity. **2** sublime (a substance); purify. □ **sublimation** *noun*

**sublime** *adjective* **1** of the most exalted, noble, or impressive kind. **2** extreme, lofty, like that of a person who does not fear the consequences; *with sublime indifference*. ●*verb* **1** convert (a solid substance) into a vapour by heat (and usually allow it to solidify again). **2** undergo this process. **3** purify; make sublime. □ **sublimely** *adverb*, **sublimity** (sŭb-**lim**-iti) *noun*

**subliminal** (sub-**lim**-inăl) *adjective* below the threshold of consciousness; (of advertising, messages, etc.) containing a hidden picture, message, etc. that influences people without them being consciously aware of it. □ **subliminally** *adverb*

**sub-machine-gun** *noun* a lightweight machine-gun held in the hands for firing.

**submarine** *adjective* under the surface of the sea; *submarine cables*. ●*noun* a ship that can operate under water.

**submerge** *verb* **1** place below water or other liquid; flood. **2** (of a submarine) dive, go below the surface. □ **submergence** *noun*, **submersion** *noun*

**submersible** *adjective* able to be submerged. ●*noun* a ship or other craft that can operate under water.

**submicroscopic** *adjective* too small to be seen by an ordinary microscope.

**submission** *noun* **1** submitting; being submitted. **2** something submitted; a theory etc. submitted by counsel to a judge or jury. **3** being submissive, obedience.

**submissive** *adjective* submitting to power or authority, willing to obey. □ **submissively** *adverb*, **submissiveness** *noun*

**submit** *verb* (**submitted**, **submitting**) **1** yield (oneself) to the authority or control of another, surrender. **2** subject (a person or thing) to a process. **3** present for consideration or decision.

**subnormal** *adjective* **1** less than normal. **2** below the normal standard of intelligence.

**subordinate** *adjective* (*pronounced* sŭb-**or**-din-ăt) **1** of lesser importance or rank. **2** working under the control or authority of another person. ●*noun* (*pronounced* sŭb-**or**-din-ăt) a person in a subordinate position. ●*verb* (*pronounced* sŭb-**or**-din-ayt) make subordinate, treat as of lesser importance than something else. □ **subordinate clause** a clause acting as an adjective, adverb, or noun in a main sentence. □ **subordination** *noun*

**suborn** (sŭb-**orn**) *verb* induce (a person) by bribery or other means to commit perjury or some other unlawful act.

**sub-plot** *noun* a secondary plot in a play.

**subpoena** (sŭ-**pee**-nă) *noun* a writ commanding a person to appear in a lawcourt. ●*verb* (**subpoenaed** or **subpoena'd**, **subpoenaing**) summon with a subpoena.

***sub rosa*** in confidence, in secrecy. (¶ Latin, = under the rose, which was an emblem of secrecy.)

**subroutine** *noun* a self-contained section of a computer program, for performing a specific task but not itself a complete program.

**subscribe** *verb* (usually foll. by *to*) **1** pay a sum of money) especially regularly for membership of an organization, receipt of a magazine, etc.; arrange to receive a magazine etc. regularly. **2** express one's agreement; *we cannot subscribe to this theory*.

**subscriber** *noun* **1** a person who subscribes. **2** one who rents a telephone. □ **subscriber trunk dialling** a system of dialling numbers for trunk calls instead of asking an operator to obtain these.

**subscript** *adjective* written below the line. ●*noun* a subscript number or character.

**subscription** *noun* **1** subscribing. **2** money subscribed. **3** a fee for membership of a society etc. □ **subscription concert** one of a series of concerts arranged by a private organization, for which the costs are subscribed by sale of tickets in advance.

**subsection** *noun* a division of a section.

**subsequent** *adjective* following in time or succession; coming after. □ **subsequently** *adverb*

**subservient** *adjective* **1** subordinate. **2** servile, obsequious. □ **subserviently** *adverb*, **subservience** *noun*

**subset** *noun Maths* a set of which all the elements are contained in another set.

**subside** *verb* **1** sink to a lower or to the normal level. **2** (of land) sink, e.g. because of mining operations underneath. **3** become less active or intense; *the excitement subsided.* □ **subsidence** (sŭb-sy-dĕns *or* sub-sid-ĕns) *noun*

**subsidiary** *adjective* **1** of secondary importance. **2** (of a business company) controlled by another. ●*noun* a subsidiary thing.

**subsidiarity** *noun* **1** the state of being subsidiary. **2** *Politics* the principle that a central authority should perform only tasks which cannot be performed effectively at a local level.

**subsidize** *verb* (also **subsidise**) pay a subsidy to or for; support by subsidies.

**subsidy** *noun* a grant paid to an industry or cause needing help, or to keep down the price at which commodities are sold.

**subsist** *verb* exist or continue to exist; keep oneself alive; *they managed to subsist on a diet of nuts and berries.*

**subsistence** *noun* subsisting; a means of doing this. □ **subsistence farming** farming in which almost all the crops etc. are consumed by the farmer's household. **subsistence level** merely enough to supply the bare necessities of life.

**subsoil** *noun* soil lying immediately beneath the surface layer.

**subsonic** *adjective* (of speed) less than the speed of sound; (of aircraft) flying at subsonic speeds, not supersonic. □ **subsonically** *adverb*

**substance** *noun* **1** matter with more or less uniform properties; the material of which something consists. **2** the essence of something spoken or written; *we agree with the substance of this argument.* **3** reality, solidity. **4** (*old use*) wealth and possessions; *a woman of substance.*

**substandard** *adjective* below the usual or required standard.

**substantial** *adjective* **1** of solid material or structure. **2** of considerable amount, intensity, or validity; *a substantial fee*; *substantial reasons*. **3** possessing much property or wealth; *substantial farmers*. **4** in essentials, virtual; *we are in substantial agreement*. □ **substantially** *adverb*

**substantiate** (sŭb-**stan**-shi-ayt) *verb* support (a statement or claim etc.) with evidence; prove. □ **substantiation** *noun*

**substantive** *adjective* (*pronounced* sŭb-**stan**-tiv) **1** genuine, actual, real. **2** not slight; substantial. **3** (of military rank) permanent, not temporary. ● *noun* (*pronounced* **sub**-stăn-tiv) *Grammar* a noun.

**substation** *noun* a subordinate station, e.g. for the distribution of electric current.

**substitute** *noun* a person or thing that acts or serves in place of another. ● *verb* (often foll. by *for*) **1** put or use as a substitute. **2** (*informal*) serve as a substitute. □ **substitution** *noun*

**substratum** (sub-**strah**-tŭm) *noun* (*plural* **substrata**) an underlying layer or substance.

**substructure** *noun* an underlying or supporting structure.

**subsume** *verb* (usually foll. by *under*) include (an instance, idea, category, etc.) in a particular rule or classification etc.

**subtenant** *noun* a person who rents accommodation etc. from its tenant. □ **subtenancy** *noun*

**subterfuge** (**sub**-ter-fewj) *noun* a trick or excuse used to avoid blame or defeat; trickery.

**subterranean** (sub-ter-**ayn**-iăn) *adjective* underground.

**subtext** *noun* an underlying theme.

**subtitle** *noun* **1** a subordinate title. **2** a caption on a cinema film, television programme, etc. giving a translation of foreign dialogue or a summary of speech for people with hearing difficulties. ● *verb* provide with a subtitle.

**subtle** (sut'l) *adjective* **1** slight and difficult to detect or analyse. **2** (of colour, scent, etc.) faint, delicate. **3** making or able to make fine distinctions, having acute perception; *a subtle mind*. **4** ingenious, crafty. □ **subtly** *adverb*, **subtlety** (sut'l-ti) *noun*

**subtotal** *noun* the total of part of a group of figures.

**subtract** *verb* deduct, remove (a part, quantity, or number) from a greater one. □ **subtraction** *noun*

**subtropical** *adjective* of regions bordering on the tropics.

**suburb** *noun* a residential district lying outside the central part of a town.

**suburban** *adjective* **1** of a suburb or suburbs. **2** having only limited interests and narrow-minded views.

**suburbanite** *noun* a person who lives in a suburb.

**suburbia** *noun* suburbs and their inhabitants.

**subvention** (sŭb-**ven**-shŏn) *noun* a subsidy.

**subversion** *noun* subverting.

**subversive** *adjective* tending to subvert (especially a government). □ **subversively** *adverb*, **subversiveness** *noun*

**subvert** (sŭb-**vert**) *verb* overthrow the authority of (a religion or government etc.) by weakening people's trust or belief.

**subway** *noun* **1** an underground passage, e.g. for pedestrians to cross below a road. **2** (*Amer.*) an underground railway.

**subzero** *adjective* (of temperatures) below zero.

**succeed** *verb* **1** be successful. **2** come next to in time or order; follow; take the place previously filled by; *Edward the Seventh succeeded Queen Victoria*; *he succeeded to the throne*.

**success** *noun* **1** a favourable outcome; doing what was desired or attempted; the attainment of wealth, fame, or position. **2** a person or thing that is successful.

**successful** *adjective* having success. □ **successfully** *adverb*

**succession** *noun* **1** following in order; a series of people or things following each other. **2** succeeding to the throne or to an inheritance or position; the right of doing this; the sequence of people with this right. □ **in succession** one after another.

**successive** *adjective* following one after another, in an unbroken series. □ **successively** *adverb*

**successor** *noun* a person or thing that succeeds another.

**succinct** (sŭk-**sinkt**) *adjective* concise; expressed briefly and clearly. □ **succinctly** *adverb*, **succinctness** *noun*

**succour** (**suk**-er) (*Amer.* **succor**) (*literary*) *noun* help given in time of need. ● *verb* give such help.

**succulent** (**suk**-yoo-lĕnt) *adjective* **1** juicy. **2** (of plants) having thick fleshy leaves or stems. ● *noun* a succulent plant. □ **succulence** *noun*

**succumb** (sŭ-**kum**) *verb* (often foll. by *to*) give way to something overpowering; die (from).

**such** *adjective* **1** of the same kind or degree; *people such as these*. **2** of the kind or degree described; *there's no such person*. **3** so great or intense; *it gave her such a fright*. ● *pronoun* that, the action or thing referred to; *such being the case, we can do nothing*. □ **as such** as what has been specified, in itself; *interested in getting a good photograph, not in the castle as such*. **such-and-such** *adjective* particular but not now specified; *says he will* *arrive at such-and-such a time but is always late.* **such as** for example.

**suchlike** *adjective* (*informal*) of the same kind. □ **and suchlike** and things of this kind.

**suck** *verb* **1** draw (liquid or air etc.) into the mouth; draw liquid etc. from (a thing) in this way. **2** squeeze in the mouth using the tongue; *sucking a toffee.* **3** draw in; *plants suck moisture from the soil; the canoe was sucked into the whirlpool.* ●*noun* the act or process of sucking. □ **suck up to** (*informal*) behave in a flattering, servile way towards (a person) to gain advantage.

**sucker** *noun* **1** a person or thing that sucks. **2** an organ of certain animals, or a device of rubber etc., that can adhere to a surface by suction. **3** a shoot coming up from the roots or underground stem of a tree or shrub. **4** (*slang*) a person who is easily deceived. □ **be a sucker for** (*slang*) be always unable to resist the attractions of.

**suckle** *verb* **1** feed (young) at the breast or udder. **2** (of young) take milk in this way.

**suckling** *noun* a child or animal that is not yet weaned.

**Sucre** (soo-kray) the legal capital and seat of the judiciary of Bolivia.

**sucrose** (sook-rohz) *noun* sugar obtained from plants such as sugar cane or sugar beet.

**suction** *noun* **1** sucking. **2** production of a partial or complete vacuum so that external atmospheric pressure forces fluid or other substance into the vacant space or causes adhesion of surfaces; *vacuum cleaners work by suction.*

**Sudan** (sŭ-dahn) a country in north-east Africa. □ **Sudanese** (soo-dă-neez) *adjective & noun* (*plural* **Sudanese**).

**sudden** *adjective* happening or done quickly, unexpectedly, or without warning. □ **all of a sudden** suddenly. **sudden death** (*informal*) decision of a drawn or tied contest by the result of the next game or point. **sudden infant death syndrome** = COT-DEATH. □ **suddenly** *adverb*, **suddenness** *noun*

**sudorific** (soo-dŏ-rif-ik) *adjective* causing sweating. ●*noun* a sudorific drug.

**Sudra** (soo-dră) *noun* a member of the lowest of the four great Hindu classes (the labourer class).

**suds** *plural noun* soapsuds.

**sue** *verb* (**sued**, **suing**) **1** begin legal proceedings against. **2** make an application; *sue for peace.*

**suede** (*pronounced* swayd) *noun* leather with the flesh side rubbed so that it has a velvety nap.

**suet** *noun* hard fat from round the kidneys of cattle and sheep, used in cooking. □ **suet**

**pudding** a pudding made with flour and suet. □ **suety** *adjective*

**Suez** an isthmus connecting Egypt to the Sinai peninsula, site of the **Suez Canal**, a canal connecting the Mediterranean with the Red Sea.

**suffer** *verb* **1** undergo or be subjected to (pain, grief, damage, etc.). **2** feel pain or grief; be subjected to damage or a disadvantage. **3** permit. **4** tolerate; *she does not suffer fools gladly.* □ **sufferer** *noun*, **suffering** *noun*

**sufferance** *noun* □ **on sufferance** tolerated but only grudgingly or because there is no positive objection.

**suffice** (sŭ-fys) *verb* be enough; meet the needs of.

**sufficient** *adjective* enough. □ **sufficiently** *adverb*, **sufficiency** *noun*

**suffix** *noun* (*plural* **suffixes**) a letter or combination of letters added at the end of a word to make another word (e.g. *y* added to *rust* to make *rusty*) or as an inflexion (e.g. *ing* added to *suck* to make *sucking*).

**suffocate** *verb* **1** kill by stopping the breathing. **2** cause discomfort to (a person) by making breathing difficult. **3** be suffocated. □ **suffocation** *noun*

**Suffolk** a county of eastern England.

**suffragan** (suf-ră-găn) *noun* a bishop consecrated to help the bishop of a diocese with administration; a bishop in relation to an archbishop.

**suffrage** (suf-rij) *noun* the right to vote in political elections.

**suffragette** (suf-ră-jet) *noun* a woman who, in the early 20th century, campaigned for women to have the right to vote in political elections.

**suffuse** (sŭ-fewz) *verb* (of colour or moisture) spread throughout or over. □ **suffusion** *noun*

**Sufi** (soo-fi) *noun* a Muslim ascetic mystic. □ **Sufic** *adjective*, **Sufism** *noun*

**sugar** *noun* **1** a sweet crystalline substance obtained from the juices of various plants. **2** *Chem.* a soluble crystalline carbohydrate, e.g. glucose. **3** (especially *Amer.* as a term of address) darling. ●*verb* sweeten or coat with sugar. □ **sugar beet** beet from which sugar is extracted. **sugar cane** a tropical grass with tall jointed stems from which sugar is obtained. **sugar-daddy** *noun* (*slang*) an elderly man who lavishes gifts on a young woman. **sugar loaf** a solid cone-shaped mass of sugar, as sold in former times. **sugar soap** an abrasive compound for cleaning or removing paint.

**sugary** *adjective* **1** containing or resembling sugar. **2** sweet; excessively sweet or sentimental in style or manner. □ **sugariness** *noun*

**suggest** verb **1** cause (an idea or possibility) to be present in the mind. **2** propose (a plan or theory).

**suggestible** adjective **1** easily influenced by people's suggestions. **2** that may be suggested. □ **suggestibility** noun

**suggestion** noun **1** suggesting; being suggested. **2** something suggested. **3** a slight trace; *he speaks with a suggestion of a French accent.*

**suggestive** adjective **1** conveying a suggestion. **2** tending to convey an indecent or improper meaning. □ **suggestively** adverb, **suggestiveness** noun

**suicidal** adjective **1** of suicide. **2** (of a person) liable to commit suicide. **3** destructive to one's own interests. □ **suicidally** adverb

**suicide** noun **1** the intentional killing of oneself; an instance of this. **2** a person who commits suicide. **3** an act that is destructive to one's own interests; *political suicide.* □ **commit suicide** kill oneself intentionally. **suicide pact** an agreement between people to commit suicide together.

*sui generis* (sew-y **jen**-ĕ-ris *or* soo-ee **gen**-ĕ-ris) (the only one) of its own kind; unique. (¶ Latin.)

**suit** noun **1** a set of clothing to be worn together, especially a jacket and trousers or skirt. **2** clothing for use in a particular activity; *a diving suit.* **3** any of the four sets (spades, hearts, diamonds, clubs) into which a pack of cards is divided. **4** a lawsuit. **5** (*informal*) a request or appeal; *press one's suit.* ●verb **1** satisfy, meet the requirements of. **2** be convenient or right for. **3** give a pleasing appearance or effect upon; *red doesn't suit her.* **4** adapt, make suitable; *suit your style to your audience.* □ **suit oneself** do as one pleases.

**suitable** adjective right for the purpose or occasion. □ **suitably** adverb, **suitability** noun

**suitcase** noun a rectangular case for carrying clothes, usually with a hinged lid and a handle.

**suite** noun **1** a set of rooms or furniture. **2** a set of attendants, a retinue. **3** a set of musical pieces or extracts.

**suitor** noun **1** a man who is courting a woman. **2** a person bringing a lawsuit.

**Sulawesi** (suul-ă-**way**-si) a large island of Indonesia, east of Borneo, formerly called Celebes.

**Suleiman I** (suul-i-**mahn**) 'the Magnificent', sultan of Turkey 1520–66.

**sulfa, sulfate, sulfur,** etc. Amer. spelling of SULPHA, SULPHATE, SULPHUR, etc.

**sulk** verb be sulky. ●noun (also **the sulks**) a fit of sulkiness.

**sulky** adjective (**sulkier, sulkiest**) sullen or silent because of resentment or bad temper. □ **sulkily** adverb, **sulkiness** noun

**sullen** adjective **1** gloomy and unresponsive from resentment or bad temper. **2** dark and dismal; *sullen skies.* □ **sullenly** adverb, **sullenness** noun

**Sullivan**, Sir Arthur (1842–1900), English composer, noted for the comic operas produced with W. S. Gilbert.

**sully** verb (**sullied, sullying**) stain or blemish; spoil; *sullied his reputation.*

**sulpha** adjective (*Amer.* **sulfa**) sulphonamide; *sulpha drugs.*

**sulphate** noun (*Amer.* **sulfate**) a salt of sulphuric acid.

**sulphide** noun (*Amer.* **sulfide**) a binary compound of sulphur.

**sulphite** noun (*Amer.* **sulfite**) a salt or ester of sulphurous acid.

**sulphonamide** (sul-fon-ă-myd) noun (*Amer.* **sulfonamide**) any of a class of antibiotic drugs containing sulphur.

**sulphur** noun (*Amer.* **sulfur**) a chemical element (symbol S), a pale yellow substance that burns with a blue flame and a stifling smell, used in industry and medicine.

**sulphureous** (sul-**fewr**-iŭs) adjective (*Amer.* **sulfureous**) of or like sulphur.

**sulphuric** (sul-**fewr**-ik) adjective (*Amer.* **sulfuric**) containing a proportion of sulphur. □ **sulphuric acid** a strong corrosive acid.

**sulphurous** (**sul**-fer-ŭs) adjective (*Amer.* **sulfurous**) **1** of or like sulphur. **2** containing a proportion of sulphur. □ **sulphurous acid** a weak acid used as a reducing and bleaching acid.

**sultan** noun the ruler of certain Muslim countries.

**sultana** noun **1** a seedless raisin. **2** the wife, mother, sister, or daughter of a sultan.

**sultanate** noun the territory of a sultan.

**sultry** adjective (**sultrier, sultriest**) **1** hot and humid. **2** (of a person) passionate and sensual. □ **sultriness** noun

**sum** noun **1** a total. **2** an amount of money. **3** a problem in arithmetic. ●verb (**summed, summing**) find the sum of. □ **in sum** briefly, in summary. **sum total** a total. **sum up 1** give the total of. **2** summarize. **3** (of a judge) summarize the evidence or argument. **4** form an opinion of; *sum a person up.*

**sumac** (**soo**-mak *or* **shoo**-mak) noun **1** a shrub whose leaves are dried and ground for use in tanning and dyeing. **2** these leaves.

**Sumatra** (sŭ-**mah**-tră) a large island of Indonesia, separated from the Malay Peninsula by the Strait of Malacca.

**Sumerian** (soo-**meer**-iăn) noun a member of an ancient people of southern

Mesopotamia (Sumer) in the 4th millennium BC.

**summarize** *verb* (also **summarise**) make or be a summary of.

**summary** *noun* a statement giving the main points of something briefly. ● *adjective* **1** brief, giving the main points only; *a summary account.* **2** done or given without delay or attention to detail or formal procedure. □ **summary offence** an offence that can be tried in a magistrates' court. □ **summarily** *adverb*

**summation** (sum-ay-shŏn) *noun* finding of a total or sum; summing up.

**summer** *noun* the warmest season of the year, from June to August in the northern hemisphere. □ **summer house** a light building in a garden or park, providing shade in summer. **Summer Palace** a palace (now in ruins) of the Chinese emperors, near Peking. **summer pudding** a pudding of soft fruit pressed in a bread or sponge-cake case. **summer school** a course of lectures etc. held during the summer vacation. **summer solstice** the solstice occurring about 21 June. **summer time** the time shown by clocks that are put forward in some countries in summer to give longer light evenings during the summer months.

**summertime** *noun* the season of summer.

**summery** *adjective* like summer; suitable for summer.

**summit** *noun* **1** the highest point of something; the top of a mountain. **2** (in full **summit meeting, talks,** etc.) a meeting between heads of governments.

**summon** *verb* **1** send for (a person); order to appear in a lawcourt. **2** call together; order to assemble; *summon a meeting.* **3** gather together (one's strength or courage). **4** call upon (a person etc.) to do something; *summon the fort to surrender.*

**summons** *noun* (*plural* **summonses**) a command to do something or appear somewhere; an order to appear in a lawcourt. ● *verb* serve with a summons.

■**Usage** It is equally correct to use *summon* as a verb with this meaning.

**sumo** (soo-moh) *noun* Japanese wrestling in which a person is considered defeated if he touches the ground except with his feet or fails to keep within a marked area.

**sump** *noun* **1** an inner casing holding lubricating-oil in a petrol engine. **2** a hole or low area into which waste liquid drains.

**sumptuary** *adjective Law* regulating (especially private) expenditure.

**sumptuous** *adjective* splendid and costly-looking. □ **sumptuously** *adverb*, **sumptuousness** *noun*

**Sun.** *abbreviation* Sunday.

**sun** *noun* **1** the star round which the earth travels and from which it receives light and warmth. **2** this light or warmth; *let the sun in.* **3** any fixed star with or without planets. ● *verb* (**sunned, sunning**) expose to the sun; *sun oneself.* □ **sun-god** *noun* the sun worshipped as a god. **Sun King** Louis XIV of France. **sun-roof** *noun* a sliding panel in the roof of a car. **sun-up** *noun* (*Amer.*) sunrise.

**sunbathe** *verb* expose one's body to the sun.

**sunbeam** *noun* a ray of sun.

**sunbed** *noun* a bed for artificial sunbathing under a sunlamp.

**sunblock** *noun* a cream that protects the skin from the sun.

**sunburn** *noun* tanning or inflammation of the skin caused by exposure to sun. □ **sunburnt** *adjective* (also **sunburned**)

**sundae** (sun-day) *noun* a dish of ice cream and crushed fruit, nuts, syrup, etc.

**Sunday** *noun* **1** the first day of the week, observed by Christians as a day of rest and worship. **2** a newspaper published on Sundays. □ **Sunday best** best clothes, kept for Sunday use. **Sunday school** a school for religious instruction of children, held on Sundays.

**sunder** *verb* break or tear apart, sever.

**sundew** *noun* a small bog-plant with hairs secreting moisture that traps insects.

**sundial** *noun* a device that shows the time by the shadow of a pointer on a dial.

**sundown** *noun* sunset.

**sundry** *adjective* various, several. ● *plural noun* (**sundries**) various small items not named individually. □ **all and sundry** everyone.

**sunfish** *noun* a large ocean fish with an almost spherical body.

**sunflower** *noun* a tall plant bearing very large flowers with golden petals and a dark centre, producing seeds that yield an edible oil.

**sung** *see* SING.

**sunglasses** *plural noun* glasses with tinted lenses to protect the eyes from sunlight.

**sunk** *see* SINK.

**sunken** *adjective* **1** lying below the level of the surrounding area. **2** (of cheeks etc.) hollow.

**sunlamp** *noun* a lamp producing ultraviolet rays, with effects like those of the sun.

**sunlight** *noun* light from the sun.

**sunlit** *adjective* lit by sunlight.

**Sunna** *noun* the traditional portion of Islamic law, based on Muhammad's words or acts but not written by him.

**Sunni** (suu-ni) **1** one of the two major groups in Islam (the other is Shiite), comprising the main community in most Muslim countries other than Iran. **2** (also **Sunnite**) a member of this group.

**sunny** *adjective* (**sunnier, sunniest**) **1** bright with sunlight, full of sunshine. **2** (of a person or mood) cheerful. □ **the sunny side** the more cheerful aspect of circumstances. □ **sunnily** *adverb*

**sunrise** *noun* the rising of the sun; the time of this.

**sunset** *noun* **1** the setting of the sun; the time of this. **2** the western sky full of colour at sunset.

**sunshade** *noun* **1** a parasol. **2** an awning.

**sunshine** *noun* **1** direct sunlight uninterrupted by cloud. **2** (*informal*) a form of address.

**sunspot** *noun* **1** one of the dark patches sometimes observed on the sun's surface. **2** (*informal*) a place with a sunny climate.

**sunstroke** *noun* illness caused by too much exposure to sun.

**suntan** *noun* a brownish skin colour caused by exposure to the sun. □ **suntanned** *adjective*

**suntrap** *noun* a sunny sheltered place.

**Sun Yat-sen** (1866–1925), Chinese statesman, who played a crucial part in the revolution which established a republic in China, organized the Kuomintang (1911-12), and was briefly president of the new republic.

**sup** *verb* (**supped, supping**) **1** take (liquid) by sips or spoonfuls. **2** (*old use*) eat supper. **3** (*informal*) drink (alcohol). ●*noun* a mouthful of liquid.

**super** *noun* (*informal*) **1** a superintendent, especially in the police force. **2** a supernumerary. ●*adjective* (*informal*) excellent, superb.

**super-** *combining form* **1** over, beyond (as in *superimpose, superhuman*). **2** extremely (as in *superabundant*).

**superabundant** *adjective* very abundant, more than enough. □ **superabundance** *noun*

**superannuate** *verb* **1** discharge (an employee) into retirement with a pension. **2** discard as too old for use.

**superannuation** *noun* **1** superannuating. **2** a pension granted to an employee on retirement; payment(s) contributed towards this during employment.

**superb** *adjective* of the most impressive or splendid kind, excellent. □ **superbly** *adverb*

**supercargo** *noun* (*plural* **supercargoes**) an officer on a merchant ship who manages sales etc. of cargo.

**supercharge** *verb* increase the power of (an engine) by using a device that supplies air or fuel at above the normal pressure. □ **supercharger** *noun*

**supercilious** (soo-per-**sil**-iŭs) *adjective* with an air of superiority, haughty and scornful. □ **superciliously** *adverb*, **superciliousness** *noun*

**supercomputer** *noun* a powerful computer capable of dealing with complex mathematical problems.

**superconductivity** *noun* the property of certain metals, at temperatures near absolute zero, of having no electrical resistance, so that once a current is started it flows without a voltage to keep it going. □ **superconductive** *adjective*, **superconductor** *noun*

**superego** (soo-per-**eeg**-oh) *noun Psychol.* the part of a person's mind that acts like a conscience in directing his or her behaviour.

**supererogation** (soo-per-e-rŏ-**gay**-shŏn) *noun* the doing of more than is required by duty; *works of supererogation*.

**superficial** *adjective* **1** of or on the surface, not deep or penetrating; *a superficial wound*; *superficial knowledge*. **2** (of a person) having no depth of character or feeling. □ **superficially** *adverb*, **superficiality** (soo-per-fish-i-**al**-iti) *noun*

**superfine** *adjective* of extra-high quality.

**superfluity** (soo-per-**floo**-iti) *noun* a superfluous amount.

**superfluous** (soo-**per**-floo-ŭs) *adjective* more than is required. □ **superfluously** *adverb*

**superglue** *noun* very strong glue that sets instantly.

**supergrass** *noun* (*slang*) a person who informs against a large number of people.

**superhuman** *adjective* **1** beyond ordinary human capacity or power. **2** higher than humanity, divine.

**superimpose** *verb* lay or place (a thing) on top of something else. □ **superimposition** *noun*

**superintend** *verb* supervise. □ **superintendence** *noun*

**superintendent** *noun* **1** a person who superintends. **2** a police officer next above the rank of chief inspector.

**Superior, Lake** one of the five Great Lakes of North America.

**superior** *adjective* **1** higher in position or rank. **2** better or greater in some way; of higher quality. **3** showing that one feels oneself to be better or wiser etc. than others; conceited, supercilious. ●*noun* **1** a person or thing of higher rank, ability, or quality. **2** the head of a monastery or other religious community. □ **superiority** *noun*

**superlative** (soo-per-**lă**-tiv) *adjective* **1** of the highest degree or quality; *a man of superlative wisdom*. **2** of a grammatical form that expresses the highest or a very high degree of quality, e.g. *dearest, shyest, best*. ●*noun* a superlative form of a word. □ **super-latively** adverb

**superman** noun (plural **supermen**) a man of superhuman powers.

**supermarket** noun a large self-service shop selling groceries and household goods.

**supermodel** noun a very successful internationally famous professional fashion model.

**supernatural** adjective of or caused by power above the forces of nature. □ **supernaturally** adverb

**supernova** noun (plural **supernovae** or **supernovas**) a star that suddenly increases greatly in brightness because of an explosion disrupting its structure.

**supernumerary** (soo-per-**new**-mer-er-i) adjective **1** in excess of the normal number, extra. **2** engaged for extra work. **3** (of an actor) appearing on stage but not speaking. ● noun a supernumerary person or thing.

**superphosphate** noun a fertilizer containing soluble phosphates.

**superpower** noun one of the most powerful nations of the world.

**superscript** adjective written or printed just above and to the right of a word, figure, or symbol. ● noun a superscript number or symbol.

**supersede** (soo-per-**seed**) verb **1** take the place of; *cars have superseded horse-drawn carriages*. **2** put or use in place of (another person or thing).

**supersession** noun superseding.

**supersonic** adjective of or having a speed greater than that of sound. □ **supersonically** adverb

**superstar** noun a great star in entertainment etc.

**superstition** noun **1** belief that events can be influenced by supernatural forces; an idea or practice based on this. **2** a belief that is held by a number of people but without foundation.

**superstitious** adjective based on or influenced by superstition. □ **superstitiously** adverb, **superstitiousness** noun

**superstore** noun a large supermarket.

**superstructure** noun a structure that rests on top of something else; a building as distinct from its foundations.

**supertanker** noun a very large tanker.

**supertax** noun an additional tax on incomes above a certain level.

**supervene** (soo-per-**veen**) verb occur as an interruption or a change from some condition or process. □ **supervention** (soo-per-ven-shŏn) noun

**supervise** verb direct and inspect (work or workers or the operation of an organization). □ **supervision** noun, **supervisor** noun

**supervisory** (soo-per-vy-zer-i) adjective supervising; *supervisory duties*.

**superwoman** noun a woman of exceptional strength or ability.

**supine** (soo-**pyn**) adjective **1** lying face upwards. **2** not inclined to take action, indolent. □ **supinely** adverb

**supper** noun an evening meal or snack; the last meal of the day.

**supplant** verb oust and take the place of.

**supple** adjective bending easily, flexible, not stiff. □ **supplely** adverb, **suppleness** noun

**supplement** noun (pronounced sup-li-měnt) **1** a thing added as an extra or to make up for a deficiency. **2** a part added to a book etc. to give further information or to treat a particular subject; a set of special pages issued with a newspaper. ● verb (pronounced sup-li-ment) provide or be a supplement to. □ **supplemental** adjective, **supplementation** noun

**supplementary** adjective serving as a supplement.

**suppliant** (sup-li-ănt) noun a person asking humbly for something.

**supplicate** verb ask humbly for, beseech. □ **supplication** noun

**supplier** noun one who supplies something.

**supply** verb (**supplied**, **supplying**) **1** give or provide with (something needed or useful); make available for use. **2** make up for, satisfy; *supply a need*. ● noun **1** provision of what is needed. **2** a stock or store; an amount of something provided or available; *the water supply*; *an inexhaustible supply of fish*. □ **supply-side** adjective Economics describing a policy of low taxation etc. to encourage production and investment.
**supply teacher** a teacher employed as a temporary substitute for one who is away from school.

**support** verb **1** keep from falling or sinking, hold in position, bear the weight of. **2** give strength to, enable to last or continue; *too little food to support life*. **3** supply with necessaries; *he has a family to support*. **4** assist by one's approval or presence or by subscription to funds; be a fan of (a particular sports team). **5** take a secondary part; *the play has a strong supporting cast*. **6** corroborate, bring facts to confirm (a statement etc.). **7** endure or tolerate; *we cannot support such insolence*. ● noun **1** supporting, being supported; *we need your support*. **2** a person or thing that supports. □ **support price** the minimum price guaranteed to farmers etc. and made up (if necessary) by government subsidy. □ **supporter** noun

**supportive** adjective providing support and encouragement.

**suppose** verb **1** be inclined to think, accept as true or probable; *I don't suppose they will* *come.* **2** assume as true for the purpose of argument; *suppose the world were flat.* **3** consider as a proposal; *suppose we try another.* **4** require as a condition, presuppose; *that supposes a mechanism without flaws.* □ **be supposed to** be expected or intended to; have as a duty.

**supposed** *adjective* believed to exist or to have a certain character or identity; *his supposed brother.*

**supposedly** (sŭ-**poh**-zidli) *adverb* according to supposition.

**supposition** *noun* supposing, what is supposed; *the article is based on supposition not on fact.*

**suppositious** (sup-ŏ-**zish**-ŭs) *adjective* hypothetical, based on supposition.

**supposititious** (sŭ-poz-i-**tish**-ŭs) *adjective* substituted for the real person or thing; spurious; hypothetical.

**suppository** (sŭ-**poz**-it-er-i) *noun* a solid piece of medicinal substance placed in the rectum or vagina and left to melt.

**suppress** *verb* **1** put an end to the activity or existence of; *suppress the rebellion.* **2** keep from being known or seen; *suppress the truth.* □ **suppression** *noun*, **suppressible** *adjective*

**suppressor** *noun* a person or thing that suppresses; a device to suppress electrical interference.

**suppurate** (**sup**-yoor-ayt) *verb* form pus; fester. □ **suppuration** *noun*

**supra** (**soo**-pră) *adverb* above or further back in the book etc. (¶ Latin, = above.)

**supra-** *combining form* above, over.

**supranational** *adjective* transcending national limits.

**supremacy** (soo-**prem**-ăsi) *noun* being supreme; the position of supreme authority or power.

**supreme** *adjective* **1** highest in authority or rank; *the supreme commander.* **2** highest in importance, intensity, or quality; *supreme courage.* **3** (of a penalty, sacrifice, etc.) involving death. **4** (of food) served in a rich cream sauce; *chicken supreme.* □ **Supreme Court** the highest judicial court. □ **supremely** *adverb*

**supremo** *noun* (*plural* **supremos**) a person in overall charge.

**surcharge** *noun* **1** payment demanded in addition to the usual charge. **2** an additional or excessive load. **3** a mark printed over a postage stamp, changing its value. ● *verb* **1** make a surcharge on; charge extra. **2** overload. **3** print a surcharge on (a stamp).

**surd** *noun* a mathematical quantity (especially a root) that cannot be expressed in finite terms of whole numbers or quantities; an irrational number.

**sure** *adjective* **1** having sufficient reason for one's beliefs; free from doubts. **2** certain to do something or to happen; *the book is sure to be a success.* **3** undoubtedly true; *one thing is sure.* **4** reliable, secure, unfailing; *there's only one sure way.* ● *adverb* (*Amer. informal*) certainly; *it sure was cold.* □ **as sure as** as certainly as. **for sure** for certain. **make sure** ensure, make certain. **sure enough** certainly, in fact. **sure-fire** *adjective* (*informal*) certain to succeed. **sure-footed** *adjective* never slipping or stumbling. **to be sure** it is admitted, certainly; *he's not perfect, to be sure.* □ **sureness** *noun*

**surely** *adverb* **1** in a sure manner, without doubt; securely. **2** used for emphasis; *surely you won't desert us?* **3** (as an answer) certainly; *'Will you help?' 'Surely.'*

**surety** (**shoor**-iti) *noun* **1** a guarantee. **2** (especially in **stand surety for**) a person who makes himself or herself responsible for another person's debts, promises, etc.

**surf** *noun* the white foam of waves breaking on a rock or shore.

**surface** *noun* **1** the outside of an object. **2** any of the sides of an object. **3** the uppermost area, the top of a table or desk etc. **4** the top of a body of water. **5** the outward appearance of something; the qualities etc. perceived by casual observation (as distinct from deeper or hidden ones). ● *adjective* of or on the surface only; of the surface of the earth or sea (as distinct from in the air or underground, or under water). ● *verb* **1** put a particular surface on; *road surfacing.* **2** come or bring to the surface. **3** (*informal*) wake after sleep or unconsciousness. □ **surface mail** mail carried by sea not by air. **surface tension** the tension of the surface-film of a liquid.

**surfboard** *noun* a long narrow board used in surfing.

**surfeit** (**ser**-fit) *noun* too much of something (especially food and drink); a feeling of discomfort arising from this. ● *verb* cause to take too much of something, satiate, cloy.

**surfer** *noun* a person who goes surfing.

**surfing** *noun* the sport of balancing on a board carried on waves to the shore.

**surge** *verb* move forward in or like waves; increase in volume or intensity. ● *noun* a wave; a surging movement or increase, an onrush.

**surgeon** *noun* a medical practitioner who performs surgical operations.

**surgery** *noun* **1** the treatment of injuries and disorders and disease by cutting or manipulation of the affected parts. **2** the place where a doctor or dentist etc. gives advice and treatment to patients. **3** the place where an MP or lawyer etc. is regularly available for consultation. **4** the hours during which a doctor etc. is available to patients at a surgery.

**surgical** *adjective* **1** of surgery or surgeons; used in surgery. **2** worn to correct an injury, deformity, etc. □ **surgical spirit** methylated spirits used for cleansing etc. □ **surgically** *adverb*

**Suriname** (soor-i-**nam**) (also **Surinam**) a country on the north coast of South America. □ **Surinamer** *noun*, **Surinamese** *adjective & noun* (*plural* **Surinamese**).

**surly** *adjective* (**surlier**, **surliest**) bad-tempered and unfriendly. □ **surliness** *noun*

**surmise** (ser-**myz**) *noun* a guess; a supposition. ● *verb* guess; suppose; infer.

**surmount** *verb* overcome (a difficulty); get over (an obstacle). □ **be surmounted by** have on or over the top; *the spire is surmounted by a weather vane.* □ **surmountable** *adjective*

**surname** *noun* the name held by all members of a family. ● *verb* give as a surname.

**surpass** *verb* do or be better than; excel.

**surpassing** *adjective* greatly excelling or exceeding others. □ **surpassingly** *adverb*

**surplice** (ser-plis) *noun* a loose white vestment with full sleeves, worn over the cassock by clergy and choir at a religious service.

**surplus** (ser-plŭs) *noun* an amount left over after what is required has been used, especially an excess of revenue over expenditure. ● *adjective* extra; additional; spare.

**surprise** *noun* **1** the emotion aroused by something sudden or unexpected. **2** an event or thing that arouses this emotion. **3** the process of catching a person etc. unprepared. **4** (usually used as *adjective*) unexpected; *a surprise visit.* ● *verb* **1** cause to feel surprise. **2** come upon or attack suddenly and without warning. **3** (foll. by *into*) startle (a person) into action by catching him or her unprepared.

**surprised** *adjective* experiencing surprise. □ **be surprised at** be shocked or scandalized by; *we are surprised at your behaviour.*

**surprising** *adjective* causing surprise. □ **surprisingly** *adverb*

**surreal** *adjective* unreal; dreamlike; bizarre.

**surrealism** (sŭ-ree-ăl-izm) *noun* a 20th-century movement in art and literature attempting to express what is in the unconscious mind by depicting dreamlike images and unusual combinations of things. □ **surrealist** *noun & adjective*, **surrealistic** *adjective*

**surrender** *verb* **1** hand over, give into another person's power or control, especially on demand or under compulsion. **2** give oneself up, accept an enemy's demand for submission. **3** give way to an emotion; *surrendered herself to grief.* **4** give up one's rights under (an insurance policy) in return for a smaller sum payable immediately. ● *noun* surrendering; being surrendered. □ **surrender to bail** appear duly in a lawcourt after being released on bail.

**surreptitious** (su-rĕp-**tish**-ŭs) *adjective* acting or done stealthily. □ **surreptitiously** *adverb*

**Surrey** a county of SE England.

**surrogate** (**su**-rŏ-găt) *noun* a deputy; a substitute. □ **surrogate mother** a woman who bears a child on behalf of another. □ **surrogacy** *noun*

**surround** *verb* **1** come or lie or be all round. **2** place all round; encircle with enemy forces. ● *noun* a border or edging.

**surroundings** *plural noun* the things or conditions around and liable to affect a person or place.

**surtax** *noun* an additional tax, especially on income over a certain amount. ● *verb* impose a surtax on.

**surtitle** *noun* a caption above the stage during an opera, providing a translation of the words being sung.

**surveillance** (ser-**vayl**-ăns) *noun* supervision or close observation, especially of a suspected person.

**survey** *verb* (*pronounced* ser-**vay**) **1** look at and take a general view of. **2** make a survey of; *the report surveys progress made in the past year.* **3** examine the condition of (a building etc.). **4** measure and map out the size, shape, elevation, etc. of (an area of land). ● *noun* (*pronounced* **ser**-vay) **1** a general look at something. **2** a general examination of a situation or subject; an account of this. **3** the surveying of land etc.; a map or plan.

**surveyor** *noun* a person whose job is to survey land or buildings.

**survival** *noun* **1** surviving. **2** something that has survived from an earlier time.

**survivalism** *noun* the practising of outdoor survival skills as a sport or hobby. □ **survivalist** *noun & adjective*

**survive** *verb* **1** continue to live or exist. **2** live or exist longer than; remain alive or in existence after; *few flowers survived the frost.*

**survivor** *noun* one who survives; one who survives another.

**sus** alternative spelling of SUSS.

**susceptibility** *noun* **1** being susceptible. **2** (**susceptibilities**) a person's feelings that may be hurt or offended.

**susceptible** (sŭ-**sep**-ti-bŭl) *adjective* **1** liable to be affected by something; *susceptible to colds.* **2** impressionable, falling in love easily. **3** (foll. by *of*) able to undergo something; *susceptible of proof.* □ **susceptibly** *adverb*

**sushi** *noun* a Japanese dish of balls of cold rice topped with raw fish etc.

**suspect** *verb* (*pronounced* sŭ-**spekt**) **1** have an impression of the existence or presence of; *we suspected a trap.* **2** have suspicions or doubts about; mistrust; *we suspect their motives.* **3** feel that (a person) is guilty but have little or no proof. ●*noun* (*pronounced* sus-pekt) a person who is suspected of a crime etc. ●*adjective* (*pronounced* sus-pekt) suspected, open to suspicion.

**suspend** *verb* **1** hang up. **2** keep from falling or sinking in air or liquid etc.; *particles are suspended in the fluid.* **3** postpone; *suspend judgement.* **4** put a temporary stop to. **5** deprive temporarily of a position or a right. □ **suspended animation** a temporary deathlike condition. **suspended sentence** a sentence of imprisonment that is not enforced subject to good behaviour.

**suspender** *noun* **1** an attachment to hold up a sock or stocking by its top. **2** (**suspenders**) (*Amer.*) braces. □ **suspender belt** a woman's undergarment with suspenders for holding up stockings.

**suspense** *noun* a state of anxious uncertainty while awaiting news or an event etc.

**suspension** *noun* **1** suspending; being suspended. **2** the means by which a vehicle is supported on its axles. □ **suspension bridge** a bridge suspended from cables that pass over supports at each end.

**suspicion** *noun* **1** suspecting; being suspected. **2** a partial or unconfirmed belief. **3** a slight trace.

**suspicious** *adjective* feeling or causing suspicion. □ **suspiciously** *adverb*

**suss** (also **sus**) *verb* (**sussed, sussing**) (*slang*) (often foll. by *out*) **1** investigate or reconnoitre. **2** realize, work out.

**Sussex** a former county of England, now divided into East Sussex and West Sussex.

**sustain** *verb* **1** support. **2** keep alive. **3** keep (a sound, effort, etc.) going continuously. **4** undergo; suffer; *sustained a defeat.* **5** endure without giving way; *sustained the attack.* **6** confirm or uphold the validity of; *the objection was sustained.*

**sustenance** *noun* **1** the process of sustaining life by food. **2** food, nourishment.

**Sutherland**[1], Graham (1903–80), English painter.

**Sutherland**[2], Dame Joan (born 1926), Australian operatic soprano.

**suttee** (sut-ee) *noun* **1** the act or custom (now illegal) of a Hindu widow sacrificing herself on her husband's funeral pyre. **2** a Hindu widow who did this.

**suture** (soo-cher) *noun* surgical stitching of a wound; a stitch or thread etc. used in this. ●*verb* stitch (a wound).

**Suva** (soo-vă) the capital of Fiji.

**suzerain** (soo-zer-ăn) *noun* **1** a country or ruler that has some authority over another country which is self-governing in its internal affairs. **2** an overlord in feudal times. □ **suzerainty** *noun*

**svelte** (*pronounced* svelt) *adjective* (of a person) slender and graceful.

**SW** *abbreviation* **1** south-west. **2** south-western.

**swab** (*pronounced* swob) *noun* **1** a mop or absorbent pad for cleansing, drying, or absorbing things. **2** a specimen of a secretion taken with this. ●*verb* (**swabbed, swabbing**) cleanse or wipe with a swab.

**swaddle** *verb* swathe in wraps or warm garments. □ **swaddling-clothes** strips of cloth formerly wrapped round a newborn baby to restrain its movements.

**swag** *noun* **1** (*slang*) loot. **2** a decorative festoon of flowers, drapery, etc., hung by its ends. **3** (*Austral.*) a bundle of personal belongings carried by a tramp.

**swage** *noun* **1** a die or stamp for shaping wrought iron. **2** a tool for bending metal etc. ●*verb* shape with a swage.

**swagger** *verb* walk or behave in a self-important manner; strut. ●*noun* a swaggering walk or way of behaving. □ **swagger stick** a short cane carried by a military officer.

**swagman** *noun* (*plural* **swagmen**) (*Austral.*) tramp.

**Swahili** (swah-hee-li) *noun* (*plural* **Swahili**) **1** a Bantu people of Zanzibar and the adjacent coasts. **2** their language, a Bantu language widely used in East Africa.

**swain** *noun* **1** (*old use*) a country youth. **2** (*poetic*) a young lover or suitor.

**swallow**[1] *verb* **1** cause or allow (food etc.) to go down one's throat; work the muscles of the throat as when doing this. **2** take in so as to engulf or absorb; *she was swallowed up in the crowd.* **3** accept meekly; believe readily; *he swallowed the story.* **4** repress (a sound or emotion etc.); *swallowed a sob.* ●*noun* the act of swallowing; the amount swallowed in one movement.

**swallow**[2] *noun* a small migratory insect-eating bird with a forked tail whose arrival in Britain is associated with the beginning of summer. □ **swallow-dive** *noun* a dive with arms outspread at the start. **swallowtail** **1** a deeply forked tail. **2** a butterfly with such a tail.

**swam** *see* SWIM.

**swami** (swah-mi) *noun* (*plural* **swamis**) a Hindu religious teacher.

**swamp** *noun* a marsh. ●*verb* **1** flood; drench or submerge in water. **2** overwhelm with a great mass or number of things. □ **swampy** *adjective*

**Swan**, Sir Joseph Wilson (1828–1914), English physicist and chemist, a pioneer of electric lighting.

**swan** *noun* a large usually white water-bird with a long slender neck. ●*verb* (**swanned, swanning**) (*informal*) move in a leisurely or majestic way; *swanning around*. □ **Swan of Avon** Shakespeare. **swan-upping** *noun* the annual marking (by the appropriate authorities) of swans on the Thames.

**swank** (*informal*) *noun* boastful behaviour; ostentation. ●*verb* behave with swank. □ **swanky** *adjective*, **swankily** *adverb*

**swannery** *noun* a place where swans are kept.

**swansdown** *noun* a swan's fine soft down, used for trimmings.

**swansong** *noun* a person's last work or act before death or retirement.

**swap** (also **swop**) *verb* (**swapping, swapped**) exchange. ●*noun* **1** an exchange. **2** a thing suitable for swapping.

**Swapo** (**swah**-poh) *abbreviation* (also **SWAPO**) South West Africa People's Organization, an African nationalist political organization in Namibia.

**sward** *noun* (*literary*) an expanse of short grass.

**swarm** *noun* **1** a large number of insects, birds, small animals, or people moving about in a cluster. **2** a cluster of bees leaving the hive with a queen bee to establish a new home. ●*verb* **1** move in a swarm, come together in large numbers. **2** (of bees) cluster in a swarm. **3** (of a place) be crowded or overrun; *swarming with tourists*. **4** (foll. by *up*) climb by gripping with the hands and legs.

**swarthy** (**swor**-*th*i) *adjective* (**swarthier, swarthiest**) having a dark complexion.

**swashbuckling** *adjective* swaggering aggressively. □ **swashbuckler** *noun*

**swastika** (**swos**-tik-ă) *noun* a symbol formed by a cross with the ends bent at right angles, formerly used as a Nazi emblem.

**swat** *verb* (**swatted, swatting**) hit hard with something flat; crush (a fly etc.) in this way. ●*noun* a swatting blow. □ **swatter** *noun*

**swatch** (*pronounced* swoch) *noun* **1** a sample, especially of cloth. **2** a collection of such samples.

**swath** (*pronounced* swawth) *noun* (also **swathe**) **1** the space that a scythe or mowing machine cuts in one sweep or passage. **2** a line of grass or wheat etc. lying after being cut. **3** a broad strip.

**swathe** (*pronounced* sway*th*) *verb* wrap in layers of bandage or wrappings or warm garments. ●*noun* **1** a bandage or wrapping. **2** *see* SWATH.

**sway** *verb* **1** swing or lean from side to side. **2** influence the opinions or actions of; *his speech swayed many voters*. **3** waver in one's opinion or attitude. ●*noun* **1** a swaying movement. **2** influence, power; *hold sway*.

**Swaziland** (**swah**-zi-land) a country in SE Africa. □ **Swazi** *adjective & noun* (*plural* **Swazis**).

**swear** *verb* (**swore, sworn, swearing**) **1** state or promise on oath. **2** state emphatically; *swore he hadn't touched it*. **3** cause to take an oath; *swore him to secrecy*. **4** use obscene or blasphemous language. □ **swear by** (*informal*) have great confidence in. **swear in** admit (a person) to office by making him or her take an oath. **swear off** promise to abstain from; *he's sworn off drink*. **swear word** a profane or indecent word used in anger etc. □ **swearer** *noun*

**sweat** *noun* **1** moisture that is given off by the body through the pores of the skin. **2** a state of sweating. **3** (*informal*) a state of great anxiety; *in a sweat*. **4** (*informal*) a laborious task. **5** moisture forming in drops on a surface, e.g. by condensation. ●*verb* **1** give out sweat; cause to do this. **2** be in a state of great anxiety. **3** work long and hard. □ **no sweat** (*informal*) no problem. **sweat-band** *noun* a band of absorbent material for absorbing sweat. **sweat blood** (*informal*) **1** work very hard at something. **2** be in a state of great anxiety. **sweated labour** labour of workers enduring long hours, low wages, and poor conditions. **sweat it out** (*informal*) endure it to the end. **sweat off** get rid of by sweating.

**sweater** *noun* a jumper or pullover.

**sweatshirt** *noun* a long-sleeved cotton sweater with a fleecy lining.

**sweatshop** *noun* a factory where sweated labour is used.

**sweaty** *adjective* damp with sweat.

**Swede** *noun* a native of Sweden.

**swede** *noun* a large yellow variety of turnip.

**Sweden** a country in northern Europe.

**Swedish** *adjective* of Sweden or its people or language. ●*noun* the language of Sweden.

**sweep** *verb* (**swept, sweeping**) **1** clear away with or as if with a brush. **2** clean or clear (a surface or area) by doing this. **3** move or remove swiftly or majestically; *she swept out of the room*. **4** extend in a continuous line or slope; *the mountains sweep down to the sea*. **5** pass quickly over or along; *winds sweep the hillside; a new fashion is sweeping America*. **6** touch lightly. ●*noun* **1** the act or movement of sweeping. **2** a sweeping line or slope. **3** a chimney-sweep. **4** a sweepstake. □ **make a clean sweep**

**1** get rid of everything and make a new start. **2** win all the prizes. **sweep all before one** be very successful.

**sweeper** noun **1** a person who sweeps a place. **2** a thing that sweeps; a carpet-sweeper. **3** a football player positioned just in front of the goalkeeper to tackle attacking players.

**sweeping** adjective **1** wide-ranging, comprehensive; sweeping changes. **2** (of a statement) generalized; taking no account of individual cases. ●plural noun (**sweepings**) dust or scraps collected by sweeping.

**sweepstake** noun **1** a form of gambling on horse races etc. in which the money staked is divided among those who have drawn numbered tickets for the winners. **2** a race etc. with betting of this kind.

**sweet** adjective **1** tasting as if containing sugar, not bitter. **2** fragrant. **3** melodious. **4** fresh, (of food) not stale, (of water) not salt. **5** pleasant, gratifying; pretty or charming. **6** having a pleasant nature, lovable. ●noun **1** a small shaped piece of sweet substance, usually made with sugar or chocolate. **2** a sweet dish forming one course of a meal. □ **keep a person sweet** keep him or her well-disposed towards oneself. **sweet-and-sour** adjective cooked in sauce containing sugar and either vinegar or lemon. **sweet-brier** noun a small fragrant wild rose. **sweet pea** a climbing garden plant with fragrant flowers. **sweet pepper** a mild red, green, or yellow pepper eaten as a vegetable. **sweet potato** a tropical climbing plant with sweet tuberous roots used for food. **sweet-talk** verb (informal) persuade by flattery. **sweet tooth** a liking for sweet things. **sweet william** a garden plant with clustered fragrant flowers. □ **sweetish** adjective, **sweetly** adverb, **sweetness** noun

**sweetbread** noun an animal's thymus gland or pancreas used as food.

**sweetcorn** noun maize with sweet-flavoured yellow kernels.

**sweeten** verb make or become sweet or sweeter.

**sweetener** noun **1** a substance used to sweeten food or drink. **2** (informal) a bribe.

**sweetheart** noun **1** (old use) a lover, boyfriend, girlfriend, etc. **2** a term of affection.

**sweetie** noun (informal) **1** a sweet. **2** a sweetheart.

**sweetmeal** noun sweetened wholemeal.

**sweetmeat** noun a sweet; a very small fancy cake.

**swell** verb (**swelled, swollen** or **swelled, swelling**) **1** make or become larger in size, amount, volume, numbers, or intensity.

**2** feel full of joy, pride, etc.; his heart swelled with pride. ●noun **1** the act or state of swelling. **2** the heaving of the sea with waves that do not break. **3** a gradual increase of loudness in music; a mechanism in an organ for obtaining this. **4** (informal) a person of high social position. ●adjective (informal, especially Amer.) smart; excellent. □ **have a swelled** or **swollen head** (slang) be conceited.

**swelling** noun an abnormally swollen place on the body.

**swelter** verb be uncomfortably hot.

**swept** see SWEEP. □ **swept-wing** adjective (of aircraft) with wings slanting backwards from the direction of flight.

**swerve** verb turn aside from a straight course. ●noun a swerving movement or direction.

**Swift**, Jonathan (1667–1745), Anglo-Irish poet and satirist, author of Gulliver's Travels.

**swift** adjective quick, rapid. ●noun a swift-flying insect-eating bird with long narrow wings. □ **swiftly** adverb, **swiftness** noun

**swig** (informal) verb (**swigged, swigging**) take a drink of; swigging beer. ●noun a drink or swallow.

**swill** verb **1** pour water over or through, wash or rinse. **2** drink in large quantities. ●noun **1** a rinse; give it a swill. **2** a sloppy mixture of waste food fed to pigs.

**swim** verb (**swam, swum, swimming**) **1** propel the body through water by movements of the limbs, fins, tail, etc. **2** cross by swimming; swam the Channel. **3** float. **4** be covered or flooded with liquid; eyes swimming in tears. **5** seem to be whirling or waving; have a dizzy sensation; everything swam before her eyes; my head is swimming. ●noun **1** a period of swimming. **2** a deep pool frequented by fish in a river. **3** the main current of affairs. □ **in the swim** (informal) active in or knowing what is going on. **swimming bath** a building containing a public swimming pool. **swimming costume** a garment worn for swimming. **swimming pool** an artificial pool for swimming in. □ **swimmer** noun

**swimmingly** adverb with easy unobstructed progress.

**swimsuit** noun a one-piece swimming costume for women and girls.

**Swinburne**, Algernon Charles (1837–1909), English poet and critic.

**swindle** verb cheat (a person); obtain by fraud. ●noun a piece of swindling; a fraudulent person or thing. □ **swindler** noun

**swine 1** (plural **swine**) (formal or Amer.) a pig. **2** (plural **swine** or **swines**) (informal) a hated person; a difficult or unpleasant thing. □ **swinish** adjective

**swineherd** noun (*old use*) a person taking care of pigs.

**swing** verb (**swung, swinging**) **1** move to and fro while hanging or supported; cause to do this. **2** hang by its ends. **3** move smoothly; turn to one side or in a curve; *the car swung into the drive.* **4** lift with a swinging movement. **5** change from one opinion or mood etc. to another. **6** influence (voting etc.) decisively. **7** (*informal*) succeed in arranging (something); achieve. **8** (*slang*) be executed by hanging. ●noun **1** a swinging movement, action, or rhythm. **2** a seat slung by ropes or chains for swinging in; a swing-boat; a spell of swinging in this. **3** the extent to which a thing swings; the amount by which votes, opinions, or points scored etc. change from one side to the other. **4** a kind of jazz with the time of the melody varied while the accompaniment is in strict time. □ **in full swing** with activity at its greatest. **swing-boat** noun a boat-shaped swing at fairs. **swing-bridge** noun a bridge that can be swung aside to allow boats to pass. **swing-door** noun a door that opens in either direction and closes itself when released. **swings and roundabouts** a situation involving equal gain and loss; with alternatives offering no overall advantage. **swing-wing** noun an aircraft wing that can be moved to slant backwards.

**swingeing** (**swinj**-ing) adjective **1** (of a blow) forcible. **2** huge in amount, number, or scope; *a swingeing increase in taxation.*

**swipe** verb (*informal*) **1** hit with a swinging blow. **2** steal, especially by snatching. ●noun **1** (*informal*) a swinging blow. **2** an electronic device for reading information from a card (e.g. a credit card) when the card is passed through a slot. □ **swipe card** a card which can be used in a swipe.

**swirl** verb move or carry along with a whirling movement. ●noun a swirling movement.

**swish** verb strike or move with a hissing sound. ●noun a hissing sound. ●adjective (*informal*) smart, fashionable.

**Swiss** adjective of Switzerland or its people. ●noun (*plural* **Swiss**) a native of Switzerland. □ **Swiss guards** Swiss mercenary troops employed formerly by sovereigns of France etc. and still at the Vatican. **Swiss roll** a rolled sponge cake with a jam or cream filling.

**switch** noun **1** a device for completing and breaking an electric circuit. **2** (*Amer.*) a device for diverting trains from one track to another. **3** a flexible shoot cut from a tree; a tapering rod or whip. **4** a tress of real or false hair tied at one end. **5** a shift or change in opinion, methods, policy etc. ●verb **1** turn (an electrical or other appliance) on or off by means of a switch. **2** transfer (a train) to another track. **3** divert (thoughts or talk) to another subject. **4** change or exchange (positions, methods, or policy etc.). **5** whip with a switch. □ **switched-on** adjective (*informal*) alert to what is going on, up to date. **switch off** (*informal*) stop paying attention.

**switchback** noun **1** a railway ride at a funfair with a series of steep descents and ascents. **2** a road with alternate ascents and descents.

**switchboard** noun a panel with a set of switches for making telephone connections or operating electric circuits.

**Swithin**, St (died 862), bishop of Winchester (*see* ST SWITHIN'S DAY).

**Switzerland** a country in central Europe.

**swivel** noun a link or pivot between two parts enabling one of them to revolve without turning the other. ●verb (**swivelled, swivelling;** *Amer.* **swiveled, swiveling**) turn on or as if on a swivel. □ **swivel chair** a chair with a seat that can turn horizontally on a pivot.

**swizz** noun (also **swiz**) (*informal*) a swindle, a disappointment.

**swizzle** noun **1** (*informal*) a frothy mixed alcoholic drink. **2** (*slang*) = SWIZZ. □ **swizzle-stick** noun a stick used for stirring a drink to make it frothy or flat.

**swollen** *see* SWELL.

**swoon** verb faint. ●noun a faint.

**swoop** verb come down with a rushing movement like a bird upon its prey; make a sudden attack. ●noun a swooping movement or attack.

**swop** alternative spelling of SWAP.

**sword** (*pronounced* sord) noun a weapon with a long blade and a hilt. □ **sword dance** a dance in which swords are brandished or a performer dances around swords placed on the ground.

**swordfish** noun a sea fish with a long swordlike upper jaw.

**swordsman** noun (*plural* **swordsmen**) a person of skill with a sword. □ **swordsmanship** noun

**swordstick** noun a hollow walking stick containing a blade that can be used as a sword.

**swore, sworn** *see* SWEAR.

**sworn** adjective open and determined in devotion or enmity; *sworn friends; sworn foes.*

**swot** (*informal*) verb (**swotted, swotting**) study hard. ●noun a person who studies hard.

**swum** *see* SWIM.

**swung** *see* SWING.

**sybarite** (**sib**-er-ryt) noun a person who is excessively fond of comfort and luxury. □ **sybaritic** (sib-er-**it**-ik) adjective

**sycamore** (sik-ă-mor) *noun* **1** a large tree of the maple family. **2** (*Amer.*) a plane tree.

**sycophant** (sik-ŏ-fant) *noun* a person who tries to win favour by flattering people. □ **sycophancy** *noun*, **sycophantic** (sik-ŏ-fan-tik) *adjective*, **sycophantically** *adverb*

**Sydney** the capital of New South Wales.

**syllabary** (sil-ă-ber-i) *noun* a list of characters representing syllables and serving the purpose, in some languages or stages of writing, of an alphabet.

**syllabic** (sil-ab-ik) *adjective* of or in syllables. □ **syllabically** *adverb*

**syllabify** *verb* divide into syllables. □ **syllabification** *noun*

**syllable** (sil-ă-bŭl) *noun* one of the units of sound into which a word can be divided; *there are two syllables in 'unit', three in 'divided', and one in 'can'.* □ **in words of one syllable** expressed very plainly or bluntly.

**syllabub** (sil-ă-bub) *noun* (also **sillabub**) a dish made of sweetened whipped cream flavoured with wine etc.

**syllabus** (sil-ă-bŭs) *noun* (*plural* **syllabuses** or **syllabi**) an outline of the subjects that are included in a course of study.

**syllepsis** (sil-ep-sis) *noun* a figure of speech in which a word is applied to two others in different senses (e.g. *he took the oath and his seat*) or to two others of which it grammatically suits only one (e.g. *neither you nor he knows*).

**syllogism** (sil-ŏ-jizm) *noun* a form of reasoning in which a conclusion is reached from two statements, as in *'All men must die; I am a man; therefore I must die'.* □ **syllogistic** (sil-ŏ-jis-tik) *adjective*

**sylph** (*pronounced* silf) *noun* **1** a slender girl or woman. **2** a spirit of the air.

**sylvan** *adjective* (also **silvan**) **1** of the woods. **2** having woods; rural.

**sylviculture** alternative spelling of SILVICULTURE.

**symbiosis** (sim-by-oh-sis) *noun* **1** an association of two different organisms living attached to each other or one within the other, usually to the advantage of both. **2** a similar relationship between people or groups. □ **symbiotic** (sim-by-ot-ik) *adjective*

**symbol** *noun* **1** a thing regarded as suggesting something or embodying certain characteristics; *the cross is the symbol of Christianity.* **2** a mark or sign with a special meaning, for example a mathematical sign, a punctuation mark, or a printed note in music.

**symbolic** *adjective* of, using, or used as a symbol. □ **symbolically** *adverb*

**symbolism** *noun* use of symbols to express things; an artistic movement using symbols to express ideas. □ **symbolist** *noun*

**symbolize** *verb* (also **symbolise**) **1** be a symbol of. **2** represent by means of a symbol. □ **symbolization** *noun*

**symmetrical** (sim-et-rik-ăl) *adjective* able to be divided into parts that are the same in size and shape and similar in position on either side of a dividing line or round a centre. □ **symmetrically** *adverb*

**symmetry** (sim-it-ri) *noun* **1** being symmetrical. **2** pleasing proportion between parts of a whole.

**sympathetic** *adjective* **1** feeling, expressing, or resulting from sympathy. **2** likeable; *he's not a sympathetic character.* **3** (often foll. by *to*) showing approval or support; *he is sympathetic to our plan.* □ **sympathetically** *adverb*

**sympathize** *verb* (also **sympathise**) **1** feel or express sympathy. **2** agree. □ **sympathizer** *noun*

**sympathy** *noun* **1** sharing another person's emotions or sensations. **2** a feeling of pity or tenderness towards one suffering pain, grief, or trouble. **3** liking for each other produced in people who have similar opinions or tastes. □ **be in sympathy with** feel approval of (an opinion or desire).

**symphonic** (sim-fon-ik) *adjective* of or like a symphony. □ **symphonic poem** an orchestral piece, usually descriptive or rhapsodic. □ **symphonically** *adverb*

**symphony** (sim-fŏn-i) *noun* a long musical composition (usually in several movements) for a full orchestra. □ **symphony orchestra** a large orchestra playing symphonies etc.

**symposium** (sim-poh-ziŭm) *noun* (*plural* **symposia**) a meeting for discussion of a particular subject; a conference.

**symptom** *noun* a sign of the existence of a condition, especially a perceptible change in the body, indicating disease or injury.

**symptomatic** (simp-tŏm-at-ik) *adjective* serving as a symptom.

**synagogue** (sin-ă-gog) *noun* a building for public Jewish worship.

**synapse** *noun* a junction of two nerve cells in the body.

**sync** (*pronounced* sink) (also **synch**) (*informal*) *noun* synchronization. ● *verb* synchronize.

**synchromesh** (sink-roh-mesh) *noun* a device that makes parts of a gear revolve at the same speed while they are being brought into contact.

**synchronic** (sink-ron-ik) *adjective* concerned with a subject as it exists at a particular time, not with its historical antecedents. □ **synchronically** *adverb*

**synchronism** (sink-rŏn-izm) *noun* **1** being or treated as synchronous or synchronic. **2** synchronizing.

**synchronize** (**sink**-rŏ-nyz) *verb* (also **synchronise**) **1** occur or exist at the same time. **2** operate at the same rate and simultaneously. **3** cause to occur or operate at the same time; cause (clocks etc.) to show the same time. □ **synchronization** *noun*, **synchronizer** *noun*

**synchronous** (**sink**-rŏn-ŭs) *adjective* **1** existing or occurring at the same time. **2** operating at the same rate and simultaneously.

**syncopate** (**sink**-ŏ-payt) *verb* change the beats or accents in (a passage of music) by putting a strong stress instead of a weak one (and vice versa). □ **syncopation** *noun*

**syncope** (**sink**-ŏ-pi) *noun* **1** a faint; fainting. **2** the omission of sounds or letters in the middle of a word (e.g. in the pronunciation of *Gloucester*).

**syncretic** (sink-**ret**-ik) *adjective* combining different beliefs or principles.

**syncretize** (**sink**-ri-tyz) *verb* (also **syncretise**) combine (different beliefs or principles).

**syndic** (**sin**-dik) *noun* any of various university or government officials.

**syndicalism** *noun* (*hist.*) a movement for transferring industrial ownership and control to workers' unions. □ **syndicalist** *noun*

**syndicate** *noun* (*pronounced* **sin**-dik-ăt) an association of people or firms combining to carry out a business or commercial undertaking. ●*verb* (*pronounced* **sin**-dik-ayt) **1** combine into a syndicate. **2** publish through an association that acquires stories, articles, cartoons, etc. for simultaneous publication in numerous newspapers and periodicals. □ **syndication** *noun*

**syndrome** (**sin**-drohm) *noun* **1** a set of symptoms that together indicate the presence of a disease or abnormal condition. **2** a combination of opinions, behaviour, etc. that are characteristic of a particular condition.

**synecdoche** (sin-**ek**-dŏ-ki) *noun* a figure of speech in which a part is made to represent the whole or vice versa (e.g. *new faces at the club*; *England lost to Holland*).

**Synge** (*pronounced* sing), (Edmund) John Millington (1871–1909), Irish playwright.

**synod** (**sin**-ŏd) *noun* a council attended by clergy, church officials, and sometimes lay people to discuss questions of policy, teaching, etc.

**synonym** (**sin**-ŏ-nim) *noun* a word or phrase with a meaning similar to that of another in the same language (e.g. *shut* and *close*).

**synonymous** (sin-**on**-im-ŭs) *adjective* (often foll. by *with*) **1** equivalent in meaning. **2** associated with, suggestive of; *his name was synonymous with terror.*

**synopsis** (sin-**op**-sis) *noun* (*plural* **synopses**) a summary; a brief general survey.

**synoptic** (sin-**op**-tik) *adjective* of or forming a synopsis. □ **Synoptic Gospels** those of Matthew, Mark, and Luke.

**synovia** (sy-**noh**-viă) *noun* a thick sticky fluid lubricating joints etc. in the body. □ **synovial** *adjective*

**syntax** (**sin**-taks) *noun* the way in which words are arranged to form phrases and sentences; the rules governing this. □ **syntactic** (sin-**tak**-tik) *adjective*, **syntactically** *adverb*

**synth** *noun* (*informal*) a synthesizer.

**synthesis** (**sin**-thi-sis) *noun* (*plural* **syntheses**) **1** the combining of separate parts or elements to form a complex whole. **2** the combining of substances to form a compound; artificial production of a substance that occurs naturally in plants or animals.

**synthesize** (**sin**-thi-syz) *verb* (also **synthesise**) make by synthesis.

**synthesizer** *noun* an electronic (usually keyboard) instrument that can produce a variety of sounds imitating musical instruments, speech, etc.

**synthetic** *adjective* **1** made by synthesis; manufactured as opposed to produced naturally; *synthetic rubber.* **2** (*informal*) artificial, affected; *decorated in synthetic Tudor style.* ●*noun* a synthetic substance or fabric (e.g. nylon). □ **synthetically** *adverb*

**syphilis** (**sif**-i-lis) *noun* a contagious venereal disease causing sores on the body. □ **syphilitic** *adjective*

**Syria** a country in the Middle East. □ **Syrian** *adjective & noun*

**Syriac** (**si**-ri-ak) *noun* an ancient language based on a form of Aramaic and still used as the liturgical language of certain Eastern Churches.

**syringa** (si-**ring**-ă) *noun* **1** the mock orange. **2** the botanical name for lilac.

**syringe** (si-**rinj**) *noun* a device for drawing in liquid and forcing it out again in a fine stream. ●*verb* wash out or spray with a syringe.

**syrinx** (**si**-rinks) *noun* the part of a bird's throat where its song is produced.

**syrup** *noun* (*Amer.* **sirup**) **1** a thick sweet liquid; water in which sugar is dissolved. **2** excessive sentimentality. □ **syrupy** *adjective*

**system** *noun* **1** a set of connected things or parts that form a whole or work together; *a railway system*; *the nervous system*; *the solar system.* **2** an animal body as a whole; *too much alcohol poisons the system.* **3** a set of rules, principles, or practices forming a particular philosophy or form of government etc. **4** a method of classification, notation, or measurement; *the metric system*. **5** orderliness, being systematic. □ **systems analysis** analysis of an operation in order to decide how a computer may be used to perform it. **systems analyst** an expert in systems analysis.

**systematic** *adjective* methodical, according to a plan and not casually or at random. □ **systematically** *adverb*

**systematize** (**sis**-těm-ă-tyz) *verb* (also **systematise**) arrange according to a system. □ **systematization** *noun*

**systemic** (sis-**tem**-ik) *adjective* **1** of or affecting the body as a whole. **2** (of a fungicide etc.) entering a plant and passing into the tissues. □ **systemically** *adverb*

**systemize** *verb* (also **systemise**) = SYSTEMATIZE. □ **systemization** *noun*

**systole** (**sis**-tŏl-i) *noun* the rhythmical contraction of chambers of the heart, alternating with diastole to form the pulse. □ **systolic** (sis-**tol**-ik) *adjective*

# Tt

**T** *symbol* tritium. □ **to a T** exactly; perfectly; in every respect.

**t.** *abbreviation* (also **t**) **1** ton(s). **2** tonne(s).

**TA** *abbreviation* Territorial Army.

**Ta** *symbol* tantalum.

**ta** *interjection* (*informal*) thank you.

**tab** *noun* a small projecting flap or strip by which something can be grasped, hung, fastened, or identified. ●*verb* (**tabbed**, **tabbing**) provide with tabs. □ **keep a tab** *or* **tabs on** (*informal*) keep account of; keep under observation. **pick up the tab** (*Amer. informal*) pay the bill.

**tabard** (**tab**-ard) *noun* **1** a short tunic open at the sides, worn by a herald, emblazoned with the arms of the sovereign. **2** a woman's garment shaped like this.

**tabasco** *noun* **1** a hot-tasting pepper. **2** (**Tabasco**) (*trade mark*) a sauce made from this.

**tabby** *noun* a cat with grey or brownish fur and dark stripes.

**tabernacle** *noun* **1** (in the Bible) the portable shrine used by the Israelites during their wanderings in the wilderness. **2** (in the RC Church) a receptacle containing consecrated elements of the Eucharist. **3** a meeting-place for worship used by Nonconformists (e.g. Baptists) or Mormons.

**tabla** *noun* a pair of small Indian drums played with the hands.

**table** *noun* **1** a piece of furniture consisting of a flat top supported on one or more legs. **2** food provided in a household; *she keeps a good table*. **3** the flat part of a machine tool on which material is put to be worked. **4** a list of facts or figures arranged in columns. **5** a multiplication table. ●*verb* submit (a motion or report in Parliament etc.) for discussion. □ **on the table** offered for consideration or discussion. **table licence** a licence to serve alcoholic drinks with meals only. **table linen** tablecloths, napkins, etc. **table manners** ability to behave properly while eating. **table tennis** a game played with bats and a light hollow ball on a table with a net across it. **table wine** wine of ordinary quality.

**tableau** (**tab**-loh) *noun* (*plural* **tableaux**, *pronounced* **tab**-lohz) **1** a silent motionless group of people etc. arranged to represent a scene. **2** a dramatic or picturesque scene.

**table d'hôte** (tahbl **doht**) (of a restaurant meal) served at a fixed inclusive price. (¶ French, = host's table.)

**tablecloth** *noun* a cloth spread over a table, especially for meals.

**tableland** *noun* a plateau of land.

**Table Mountain** a flat-topped mountain overlooking Cape Town in South Africa.

**tablespoon** *noun* **1** a large spoon especially for serving food. **2** the amount held by this. □ **tablespoonful** *noun* (*plural* **tablespoonfuls**).

**tablet** *noun* **1** a panel bearing an inscription, especially one fixed to a wall as a memorial. **2** a small flattish piece of a solid substance (e.g. soap). **3** a small amount of medicine in solid form; a pill.

**tabloid** *noun* a newspaper (usually popular in style) with pages that are half the size of those of larger newspapers.

**taboo** *noun* (also **tabu**) a ban or prohibition on something that is regarded by religion or custom as not to be done, touched, or used. ●*adjective* prohibited by a taboo; *taboo words*. ●*verb* place under a taboo.

**tabor** (**tay**-ber) *noun* a small drum formerly used to accompany a pipe.

**tabu** alternative spelling of TABOO.

**tabular** (**tab**-yoo-ler) *adjective* arranged or displayed in a table or list.

**tabulate** (**tab**-yoo-layt) *verb* arrange (facts or figures) in a table or list. □ **tabulation** *noun*

**tabulator** *noun* **1** a person or thing that tabulates facts or figures. **2** a device on a typewriter for advancing to a series of set positions in tabular work.

**tacho** *noun* (*plural* **tachos**) (*informal*) = TACHOMETER.

**tachograph** (**tak**-ŏ-grahf) *noun* a device that automatically records the speed and travel time of a motor vehicle in which it is fitted.

**tachometer** (tă-**kom**-it-er) *noun* an instrument for measuring the speed of a vehicle etc. or of the rotation of its engine.

**tacit** (**tas**-it) *adjective* implied or understood without being put into words. □ **tacitly** *adverb*

**taciturn** (**tas**-i-tern) *adjective* habitually saying very little, uncommunicative. □ **taciturnity** (tas-i-tern-iti) *noun*

**tack** *noun* **1** a small nail with a broad head. **2** a long stitch used to hold fabric in position temporarily. **3** a rope for securing the corner of some sails; the corner to which this is fastened. **4** the direction of a ship's course as determined by the position of its sails; a temporary oblique course to take advantage of a wind. **5** a course of action or policy; *he's on the wrong tack.* **6** riding saddles, bridles, etc. **7** (*informal*) cheap, shoddy things; tat, kitsch. ●*verb* **1** nail with a tack or tacks. **2** stitch with tacks. **3** (foll. by *on*) add as an extra thing; *a service charge was tacked on to the bill.* **4** sail a zigzag course to take advantage of a wind; make a tack or tacks.

**tackle** *noun* **1** a set of ropes and pulleys for lifting weights or working a ship's sails. **2** equipment for a task or sport; *fishing tackle.* **3** the act of tackling in football. ●*verb* **1** try to deal with or overcome (an awkward thing, opponent, or problem); *tackle a person about something.* **2** (in hockey, football, etc.) intercept (an opponent running with the ball). □ **tackler** *noun*

**tacky** *adjective* (**tackier, tackiest**) **1** (of paint or varnish etc.) slightly sticky, not quite dry. **2** (*informal*) in poor taste, cheap; shabby. □ **tackiness** *noun*

**taco** *noun* (*plural* **tacos**) a Mexican dish of a folded tortilla with a savoury filling.

**tact** *noun* skill in avoiding giving offence or in winning goodwill by saying or doing the right thing.

**tactful** *adjective* having or showing tact. □ **tactfully** *adverb*

**tactic** *noun* **1** a piece of tactics. **2** (**tactics**) (treated as *singular* or *plural*) the art of placing or manoeuvring forces skilfully in a battle. **3** (**tactics**) manoeuvring; procedure adopted in order to achieve something.

**tactical** *adjective* **1** of tactics (distinguished from *strategic*). **2** (of bombing etc.) done in immediate support of armed forces. **3** planning or planned skilfully. □ **tactical voting** voting for the candidate most likely to defeat the leading candidate; used when one's first choice has no chance of winning and one does not want the favourite to win. **tactical weapons** *see strategic weapons.* □ **tactically** *adverb*

**tactician** (tak-**tish**-ăn) *noun* an expert in tactics.

**tactile** (**tak**-tyl) *adjective* of or using the sense of touch; *tactile organs.* □ **tactility** *noun*

**tactless** *adjective* lacking in tact. □ **tactlessly** *adjective*, **tactlessness** *noun*

**Tadjikistan** (taj-ik-i-**stahn**) a mountainous country in central Asia (formerly part of the USSR).

**tadpole** *noun* the larva of a frog or toad etc. at the stage when it lives in water and has gills and a tail.

**taffeta** *noun* a shiny silklike fabric.

**taffrail** (**taf**-rayl) *noun* a rail round the stern of a ship.

**Taffy** *noun* (*informal*, often *offensive*) a Welshman.

**tag**[1] *noun* **1** a metal or plastic point at the end of a shoelace etc. **2** a label tied to something. **3** a loop or flap; a loose or ragged end. **4** a stock phrase or much-used quotation. **5** a children's game in which one chases the rest until he or she touches another. ●*verb* (**tagged, tagging**) **1** label with a tag. **2** (often foll. by *on*) add as an extra thing; *a postscript was tagged on to her letter.* □ **tag along** (*informal*) go along with another or others. **tag end** (especially *Amer.*) the last remaining bit; the last part.

**Tagalog** *noun* **1** a member of the principal people of the Philippines. **2** their language.

**tagliatelle** (tal-yă-**tel**-i) *noun* pasta in ribbon-shaped strips.

**Tagore** (tă-**gor**), Sir Rabindranath (1861–1941), Bengali poet and philosopher.

**Tagus** (**tay**-gŭs) a river of Spain and Portugal, flowing into the Atlantic near Lisbon.

**Tahiti** (tă-**hee**-ti) one of the Society Islands in the South Pacific, administered by France. □ **Tahitian** (tă-**hee**-shăn) *adjective & noun*

**t'ai chi** (ty chee) *noun* (in full **t'ai chi ch'uan**) a Chinese martial art and system of exercises with slow controlled movements.

**tail**[1] *noun* **1** the hindmost part of an animal, especially when extending beyond the rest of the body. **2** something resembling this in its shape or position; the rear part; an inferior part. **3** (*informal*) a person following or shadowing another. **4** (**tails**) a tailcoat; evening dress with this. **5** (**tails**) the reverse of a coin as a choice when tossing; the side that does not bear the head. ●*verb* **1** remove the stalks of; *top and tail gooseberries.* **2** (*informal*) follow closely, shadow. □ **on a person's tail** following closely. **tail away** = TAIL OFF (*see below*). **tail-end** *noun* the hindmost or very last part. **tail-lamp**, **tail-light** *noun* a light at the back of a vehicle, train, or bicycle. **tail off** become fewer, smaller, or slighter; (of remarks etc.) end inconclusively. **tail-spin** *noun* an aircraft's spiral dive with the tail making wider circles than the front. **tail wind** a following wind.

**tail**[2] *noun* limitation of ownership, especially of an estate limited to a person and his or her heirs. □ **in tail** under such a limitation.

**tailback** *noun* a long line of traffic extending back from an obstruction.

**tailboard** *noun* a hinged or removable flap at the back of a lorry etc.

**tailcoat** *noun* a man's coat with a long divided flap at the back, worn as part of formal dress.

**tailgate** noun **1** = TAILBOARD. **2** the rear door of an estate car or hatchback.

**tailless** adjective having no tail.

**tailor** noun a maker of men's clothes, especially to order. ● verb **1** make (clothes) as a tailor; make in a simple smoothly-fitting design. **2** make or adapt for a special purpose; *the new factory is tailored to our needs*. □ **tailormade** adjective **1** made by a tailor. **2** perfectly suited for the purpose.

**tailpiece** noun a decoration printed in the blank space at the end of a chapter or book.

**tailpipe** noun the rear section of an exhaust pipe.

**tailplane** noun the horizontal surface of the tail of an aeroplane.

**taint** noun a trace of some bad quality, decay, or infection. ● verb affect with a taint.

**Taipei** (ty-**pay**) the capital of Taiwan.

**Taiwan** (ty-**wann**) an island off the SE coast of China, regarded by China as one of its provinces. □ **Taiwanese** adjective & noun

**Taj Mahal** (tahj mă-**hahl**) a mausoleum at Agra in northern India, completed *c.*1648 by the Mogul emperor Shah Jahan in memory of his favourite wife.

**take** verb (**took, taken, taking**) **1** lay hold of, get into one's hands. **2** get possession of, capture, win; *took many prisoners*; *took first prize*. **3** be successful or effective; *the inoculation did not take*. **4** remove from its place; *someone has taken my bicycle*. **5** subtract. **6** make use of, indulge in; *take this opportunity*; *take a holiday*; *take the train*. **7** occupy (a position), especially as one's right. **8** obtain after fulfilling necessary conditions; *take a degree*; *take lodgings*. **9** require; *it takes a strong man to lift that*; *these things take time*. **10** cause to come or go with one; carry or remove; *take the letters to the post*. **11** be affected by; catch; *the sticks took fire*. **12** experience or exert (a feeling or effort); *took pity on him*; *take care*. **13** find out and record; *take his name*. **14** interpret in a certain way; understand; accept; *we take it that you are satisfied*; *I take your point*. **15** perform, deal with; *take a decision*; *take an examination*. ● take (a person or thing). ● noun **1** an amount of game or fish etc. caught. **2** an instance of photographing a scene for a cinema film. □ **be taken by** or **with** find attractive. **take after** resemble (a parent etc.). **take against** develop a dislike of. **take-away** adjective (of food) bought at a restaurant for eating elsewhere; ● noun **1** this food. **2** a restaurant selling this. **take back 1** withdraw (a statement). **2** carry (a person) back in thought to a past time. **take down** write down (spoken words). **take-home pay** the amount remaining after tax etc. has been deducted from wages. **take in 1** accept into one's house etc. **2** include. **3** make (a garment etc.) smaller. **4** understand. **5** deceive or cheat (a person). **6** (*informal*) visit (a place) en route. **take it into one's head** decide suddenly. **take it out of** exhaust the strength of. **take it out on** work off one's frustration by attacking or maltreating (a person etc.). **take it upon oneself** undertake, assume a responsibility. **take life** kill. **take off 1** mimic humorously. **2** leave the ground and become airborne. **take-off** noun **1** a piece of humorous mimicry. **2** the process of taking off in flying. **take on 1** acquire; undertake (work or responsibility); engage (an employee). **2** agree to play against (a person in a game). **3** (*informal*) show great emotion, make a fuss. **take one's time** be slow and careful; not hurry. **take out 1** escort on an outing. **2** obtain or get (an insurance policy etc.) issued. **3** (*slang*) destroy, kill. **take over** take control of (a business etc.). **take part** share in an activity. **take sides** support one side or another. **take stock** make an inventory of the stock in a shop etc.; examine one's position and resources. **take to 1** adopt as a habit or course. **2** develop a liking or ability for. **take up 1** start doing as a hobby or business. **2** occupy (time or space). **3** resume the point where something was left; investigate (a matter) further. **4** shorten (a garment). **5** accept (an offer etc.). **take up with** begin to associate with.

**takeover** noun assumption of control (especially of a business).

**taker** noun a person who takes a bet, accepts an offer, etc.

**taking** adjective attractive, captivating. ● plural noun (**takings**) the amount of money taken in a shop, at a show, etc.

**talc** noun **1** talcum powder. **2** a form of magnesium silicate used as a lubricator.

**talcum** noun **1** = TALC (sense 2). **2** (in full **talcum powder**) talc powdered and usually perfumed, applied to the skin to make it feel smooth and dry.

**tale** noun **1** a narrative or story. **2** a report spread by gossip.

**talent** noun **1** special or very great ability; people who have this. **2** a unit of money used in certain ancient countries. **3** (*informal*) attractive members of the opposite sex; *eyeing up the local talent*. □ **talent-scout, talent-spotter** noun a person whose job is to find talented people, especially in sport or entertainment.

**talented** adjective having talent.

**talisman** (tal-iz-măn) noun (plural **talismans**) an object supposed to bring good luck. □ **talismanic** adjective

**talk** *verb* **1** convey or exchange ideas by spoken words. **2** have the power of speech. **3** influence by talking; *talked him into going to Spain*. **4** give away information; *we have ways of making you talk*. ●*noun* **1** talking, conversation, discussion. **2** an informal lecture. **3** rumour, gossip; its theme; *there is talk of a general election*. **4** talking or promises etc. without action or results. □ **money talks** it has influence. **now you're talking** (*informal*) I welcome that offer or suggestion. **talk down 1** silence (a person) by talking loudly or persistently. **2** bring (a pilot or aircraft) to a landing by radio instructions from the ground. **talk down to** speak to in condescendingly simple language. **talking book** a recorded reading of a book. **talking-shop** *noun* a place for empty talk; an institution without power, only able to discuss things. **talk over** discuss. **talk through one's hat** talk nonsense. **talk to** (*informal*) reprove. **talking-to** *noun* a reproof.

**talkative** *adjective* talking very much.

**talkie** *noun* (*informal*) an early film with a soundtrack.

**tall** *adjective* **1** of more than average height. **2** having a certain height; *six feet tall*. □ **tall order** (*informal*) a difficult task. **tall story** (*informal*) one that is difficult to believe (and probably untrue). □ **tallish** *adjective*, **tallness** *noun*

**tallboy** *noun* a tall chest of drawers.

**Tallinn** the capital of Estonia.

**Tallis**, Thomas (*c.*1505–85), English composer and organist.

**tallow** *noun* animal fat used to make candles, soap, lubricants, etc.

**tally** *noun* the reckoning of a debt or score. ●*verb* (**tallied**, **tallying**) correspond; *see that the goods tally with what we ordered*; *the two witnesses' stories tallied*.

**tally-ho** *interjection* a huntsman's cry on sighting the fox.

**Talmud** (**tal-**mŭd) *noun* a collection of ancient writings on Jewish civil and ceremonial law and tradition. □ **Talmudic** (tal-**muud**-ik) *adjective*

**talon** (**tal-**ŏn) *noun* a claw, especially of a bird of prey.

**talus** (**tay-**lŭs) *noun* (*plural* **tali**) the anklebone supporting the tibia (the shin-bone).

**tamarind** (**tam-**er-ind) *noun* **1** a tropical tree bearing fruit with acid pulp. **2** its fruit.

**tamarisk** (**tam-**er-isk) *noun* an evergreen shrub with feathery branches and spikes of pink or white flowers.

**tambour** (**tam-**boor) *noun* **1** a drum. **2** a circular frame for holding fabric taut while it is being embroidered.

**tambourine** (tam-ber-**een**) *noun* a percussion instrument consisting of a small hoop fitted with jingling metal discs and often a drum-like skin.

**tame** *adjective* **1** (of animals) gentle and not afraid of human beings. **2** docile. **3** not exciting or interesting. ●*verb* make tame or manageable. □ **tamely** *adverb*, **tameness** *noun*, **tameable** *adjective*

**tamer** *noun* a person who tames and trains wild animals; *lion-tamer*.

**Tamil** (**tam-**il) *noun* **1** a member of a people of southern India and Sri Lanka. **2** their language.

**Tamil Nadu** (tam-il na-**doo**) a State in SE India.

**tam-o'-shanter** *noun* a beret with a soft full top.

**tamp** *verb* pack or ram down tightly.

**tamper** *verb* (foll. by *with*) **1** meddle or interfere with, alter without authority. **2** influence illegally, bribe; *tamper with a jury*.

**tampon** *noun* a plug of absorbent material inserted into the body, especially used by women to absorb menstrual blood.

**tan** *verb* (**tanned**, **tanning**) **1** convert (animal hide) into leather by treating it with tannic acid or mineral salts etc. **2** make or become brown by exposure to sun. **3** (*slang*) thrash. ●*noun* **1** yellowish brown. **2** brown colour in skin exposed to sun. **3** tree-bark used in tanning hides. ●*adjective* yellowish-brown. ●*abbreviation* Maths tangent.

**tandem** *noun* **1** a bicycle with seats and pedals for two or more people one behind another. **2** an arrangement of people or things one behind another. ●*adverb* one behind another. □ **in tandem 1** arranged in this way. **2** together; alongside each other; *the issues have to be dealt with in tandem*.

**tandoor** *noun* a clay oven.

**tandoori** *noun* food cooked over charcoal in a clay oven.

**tang** *noun* **1** a strong flavour or smell. **2** a projection on the blade of a knife or chisel etc. by which it is held firm in its handle.

**T'ang** the name of a dynasty which ruled in China from 618 to *c.*906.

**Tanganyika** (tang-ăn-**eek**-ă) see TANZANIA. □ **Lake Tanganyika** a large lake in central Africa between Tanzania and Zaïre.

**tangent** (**tan-**jĕnt) *noun* **1** a straight line that touches the outside of a curve but does not intersect it. **2** the ratio of the two sides (other than the hypotenuse) opposite and adjacent to an acute angle in a right-angled triangle. □ **go off at a tangent** diverge suddenly from a line of thought etc. or from the matter in hand.

**tangential** (tan-**jen**-shăl) *adjective* **1** of or along a tangent. **2** divergent. **3** peripheral. □ **tangentially** *adverb*

**tangerine** (tan-jer-een) *noun* **1** a small orange similar to a mandarin. **2** a deep orange-yellow colour.

**tangible** (tan-ji-bŭl) *adjective* **1** able to be perceived by touch. **2** clear and definite, real; *tangible advantages*. □ **tangibly** *adverb*, **tangibility** *noun*

**Tangier** (tan-jeer) a seaport of Morocco, almost opposite Gibraltar.

**tangle** *verb* **1** twist or become twisted into a confused mass. **2** entangle. **3** (foll. by *with*) become involved in conflict with. ● *noun* a tangled mass or condition. □ **tangly** *adjective*

**tango** *noun* (*plural* **tangos**) a slow South American ballroom dance with gliding steps; music for this. ● *verb* dance the tango.

**tangram** *noun* a Chinese puzzle consisting of a square cut into seven pieces to be combined into various figures.

**tangy** (tang-i) *adjective* (**tangier**, **tangiest**) having a strong sharp flavour or smell.

**tank** *noun* **1** a large container for liquid or gas. **2** a heavily armoured tracked vehicle carrying guns. ● *verb* (usually foll. by *up*) fill the tank of a vehicle etc. □ **tanked up** (*slang*) drunk.

**tankard** *noun* a large one-handled drinking vessel, usually of silver or pewter and often with a lid.

**tanker** *noun* a ship, aircraft, or vehicle for carrying oil or other liquid in bulk.

**tanner** *noun* a person who tans animal hides.

**tannery** *noun* a place where hides are tanned.

**tannic** *adjective* of tannin. □ **tannic acid** tannin.

**tannin** *noun* any of several compounds obtained from oak-galls and various treebarks (also found in tea), used chiefly in tanning and dyeing.

**Tannoy** *noun* (*trade mark*) a public-address system.

**tansy** *noun* a plant with yellow flowers in clusters and feathery leaves.

**tantalize** *verb* (also **tantalise**) tease or torment by the sight of something that is desired but kept out of reach or withheld. (¶ From the name of Tantalus.)

**tantalum** (tan-tă-lŭm) *noun* a hard white metallic element (symbol Ta). □ **tantalic** *adjective*

**Tantalus** (tan-tă-lŭs) (*Gk. myth.*) a king condemned to stand in Hades surrounded by water and fruit that receded when he tried to reach them.

**tantalus** *noun* a stand in which decanters of spirits are locked up but visible.

**tantamount** (tant-ă-mownt) *adjective* (foll. by *to*) equivalent; *the Queen's request was tantamount to a command.*

**tantra** *noun* each of a class of Hindu, Buddhist, or Jain sacred texts that deal with mystical and magical practices.

**tantrum** *noun* an outburst of bad temper, especially in a child.

**Tanzania** (tan-ză-nee-ă) a country in East Africa (formerly called Tanganyika). □ **Tanzanian** *adjective* & *noun*

**Taoiseach** (tee-shăk) the prime minister of the Republic of Ireland. (¶ Irish, = chief, leader.)

**Taoism** (tow-izm) *noun* a Chinese religious and philosophical system whose central concept and goal is the Tao, the code of behaviour in harmony with the natural order. □ **Taoist** *noun*

**tap**[1] *noun* **1** a device for drawing liquid or gas from a cask or pipe in a controllable flow. **2** a device for cutting a screw-thread inside a cavity. **3** a connection for tapping a telephone. ● *verb* (**tapped**, **tapping**) **1** fit a tap into (a cask) to draw out its contents. **2** draw off (liquid) by means of a tap or through an incision. **3** extract or obtain supplies or information from. **4** cut a screw-thread inside (a cavity). **5** make a connection in (a circuit etc.) so as to divert electricity or fit a listening device for overhearing telephone calls. □ **on tap** (of liquid or gas) ready to be drawn off by a tap; (*informal*) freely available. **tap root** the chief root of a plant, growing straight downwards.

**tap**[2] *verb* (**tapped**, **tapping**) **1** strike with a quick light blow; knock gently on (a door etc.). **2** strike (an object) lightly against something. ● *noun* **1** a quick light blow; the sound of this. **2** a metal attachment on a tap-dancer's shoe. □ **tap-dance** *noun* a dance in which an elaborate rhythm is tapped with the feet wearing shoes with metal taps.

**tapas** *plural noun* small savoury (especially Spanish) dishes.

**tape** *noun* **1** a narrow strip of woven cotton etc. used for tying, fastening, or labelling things; a piece of this stretched across a racetrack at the finishing line. **2** a narrow continuous strip of paper or other flexible material; adhesive tape; insulating tape; magnetic tape. **3** a tape-measure. **4** a tape recording. ● *verb* **1** tie or fasten with tape. **2** record on magnetic tape. □ **have a person** *or* **thing taped** (*informal*) understand fully; have an effective method of dealing with it. **tape deck** a machine for playing and recording audiotapes. **tape-measure** *noun* a strip of tape or flexible metal marked in inches or centimetres etc. for measuring length. **tape recorder** an apparatus for recording sounds or computer data on magnetic tape and playing back the recording or reproducing the data. **tape recording** a recording made on magnetic tape.

**taper** noun a slender candle, burnt to give a light or to light other candles etc. ● verb make or become gradually narrower. □ **taper off** make or become gradually less.

**tapestry** (tap-i-stri) noun a piece of strong material with a picture or design woven into it or embroidered on it, used for hanging on walls or as an upholstery fabric.

**tapeworm** noun a flat worm with a segmented body that can live as a parasite in the intestines of humans and other animals.

**tapioca** (tap-i-oh-kă) noun a starchy substance in hard white grains obtained from cassava and used for making puddings.

**tapir** (tay-per) noun a pig-like animal of Central and South America and Malaysia with a flexible snout.

**tappet** noun a projection in a piece of machinery that causes a certain movement by tapping against something, used e.g. to open and close a valve.

**taproom** noun a room in a pub where alcoholic drinks are on tap.

**tar** noun 1 a thick dark inflammable liquid obtained by distilling wood, coal, or peat etc. 2 a similar substance formed by burning tobacco. 3 (informal) a sailor. ● verb (**tarred**, **tarring**) coat with tar. □ **be tarred with the same brush** have the same faults as someone else.

**Tara** (tar-ă) a hill in County Meath, Ireland, site in early times of the residence of high kings of Ireland.

**taramasalata** (ta-ră-mă-să-lah-tă) noun pâté made from the roe of mullet or smoked cod.

**tarantella** (ta-răn-tel-ă) noun a rapid whirling South Italian dance.

**tarantula** (tă-ran-tew-lă) noun 1 a large black spider of southern Europe. 2 a large hairy tropical spider.

**tarboosh** (tar-boosh) noun a cap like a fez, worn alone or as part of a turban.

**tardy** adjective (**tardier**, **tardiest**) 1 slow to act or move or happen. 2 behind time. □ **tardily** adverb, **tardiness** noun

**tare** (pronounced tair) noun 1 a vetch, especially as a cornfield weed or fodder. 2 an allowance made to the purchaser for the weight of the container in which goods are packed, or for the vehicle transporting them.

**target** noun 1 the object or mark that a person tries to hit in shooting etc.; a disc painted with concentric circles for this purpose. 2 a person or thing against which criticism or scorn etc. is directed. 3 an objective, a minimum result aimed at; export targets. ● verb (**targeted**, **targeting**) 1 aim (a weapon etc.) at a target. 2 plan or schedule (a thing) so as to attain an objective.

**tariff** noun 1 a list of fixed charges, especially for rooms and meals etc. at a hotel. 2 duty to be paid on imports or exports.

**tarlatan** (tar-lă-tăn) noun a thin stiff open kind of muslin.

**Tarmac** noun (trade mark) 1 tarmacadam. 2 (**tarmac**) an area surfaced with tarmacadam. ● verb (**tarmac**) (**tarmacked**, **tarmacking**) surface with tarmacadam.

**tarmacadam** noun stone or slag bound with bitumen, used in surfacing roads etc.

**tarn** noun a small mountain lake.

**tarnish** verb 1 lose or cause (metal) to lose its lustre by exposure to air or damp. 2 stain or blemish (a reputation etc.). ● noun loss of lustre; a stain or blemish.

**taro** (tah-roh) noun (plural **taros**) a tropical plant with edible tuberous roots.

**tarot** (ta-roh) noun a game played with a pack of 78 cards which are also used for fortune-telling.

**tarpaulin** (tar-paw-lin) noun 1 canvas made waterproof, especially by being tarred. 2 a sheet of this used as a covering.

**tarragon** (ta-ră-gŏn) noun a bushy herb with narrow fragrant leaves used in cooking.

**tarry**[1] (tar-i) adjective of or like tar.

**tarry**[2] (ta-ri) verb (**tarried**, **tarrying**) (old use) delay in coming or going.

**tarsal** adjective of the tarsus. ● noun one of the tarsal bones.

**tarsus** noun (plural **tarsi**) the group of bones that make up the ankle and upper foot.

**tart**[1] adjective 1 sharp-tasting, acid. 2 sharp in manner, biting; a tart reply. □ **tartly** adverb, **tartness** noun

**tart**[2] noun 1 a pie containing fruit or sweet filling. 2 an open pastry case containing jam etc. 3 (slang, offensive) a girl or woman (especially of immoral character); a prostitute. □ **tart up** (informal) dress or decorate gaudily or with cheap smartness; smarten up.

**tartan** noun 1 the distinctive pattern of a Highland clan, with coloured stripes crossing at right angles. 2 fabric woven in such a pattern.

**Tartar** noun 1 a member of an Asiatic people of Siberia and eastern Europe. 2 (**tartar**) a person who is violent-tempered or difficult to deal with.

**tartar** noun 1 a hard chalky deposit that forms on the teeth. 2 a reddish deposit that forms on the side of a cask in which wine is fermented. □ **cream of tartar** see CREAM.

**tartar sauce** a cold sauce of mayonnaise, chopped gherkins, capers, etc.

**tartaric** (tar-ta-rik) adjective of or derived from tartar; tartaric acid.

**tartlet** *noun* a small pastry tart.

**tartrazine** (tar-tră-zeen) *noun* bright yellow dye from tartaric acid, used as a food colouring.

**Tarzan** the hero of novels by the American author Edgar Rice Burroughs (1875-1950) and subsequent films. He is a man of powerful physique reared by apes in the jungle.

**Tas.** *abbreviation* Tasmania.

**tash** *noun* (*informal*) a moustache.

**task** *noun* a piece of work to be done. ●*verb* make great demands upon (a person's powers). □ **take to task** rebuke. **task force** a group and resources specially organized for a particular task.

**taskmaster** *noun* a person who makes others work hard.

**Tasman**, Abel Janszoon (1603-59), Dutch explorer, after whom Tasmania (which he named Van Diemen's Land) is named.

**Tasmania** (taz-**mayn**-iä) an island State off the south-east coast of Australia. □ **Tasmanian** *adjective & noun*

**Tasman Sea** the sea (part of the South Pacific) between Australia and New Zealand.

**Tass** the official news agency of the former Soviet Union.

**tassel** *noun* **1** a bunch of threads tied at one end and hanging loosely, used as an ornament. **2** the tassel-like head of certain plants (e.g. maize).

**tasselled** *adjective* (*Amer.* **tasseled**) ornamented with a tassel or tassels.

**taste** *noun* **1** the sensation caused in the mouth by things placed in it. **2** the faculty of perceiving this. **3** a small quantity of food or drink taken as a sample; a slight experience of something; *a taste of fame.* **4** a liking; *she has always had a taste for foreign travel; add sugar to taste.* **5** ability to perceive and enjoy what is beautiful or harmonious or to know what is fitting for an occasion etc.; choice made according to this; *the remark was in bad taste.* ●*verb* **1** discover or test the flavour of (a thing) by taking it into the mouth. **2** be able to perceive flavours. **3** have a certain flavour; *it tastes sour.* **4** experience; *taste the joys of freedom.* □ **taste bud** one of the small projections on the tongue by which flavours are perceived.

**tasteful** *adjective* showing good taste. □ **tastefully** *adverb*, **tastefulness** *noun*

**tasteless** *adjective* **1** having no flavour. **2** showing poor taste; *tasteless decorations.* □ **tastelessly** *adverb*, **tastelessness** *noun*

**taster** *noun* **1** a person employed to judge teas or wines etc. by tasting them. **2** a small sample.

**tasty** *adjective* (**tastier, tastiest**) having a strong pleasant flavour; appetizing. □ **tastily** *adverb*, **tastiness** *noun*

**tat** *noun* tattiness; tatty, tasteless, or fussily ornate things.

**ta-ta** *interjection* (*informal*) goodbye.

**Tate Gallery** a national gallery of British art in London, founded by (Sir) Henry Tate (1819-99), sugar manufacturer.

**tattered** *adjective* ragged, torn into tatters.

**tatters** *plural noun* rags; irregularly torn pieces.

**Tattersalls** (tat-er-sawlz) an English firm of horse auctioneers founded in 1776 by Richard Tattersall.

**tatting** *noun* **1** a kind of lace made by hand with a small shuttle. **2** the process of making this.

**tattle** *verb* chatter or gossip idly; reveal information in this way. ●*noun* idle chatter or gossip.

**tattoo**[1] *noun* **1** an evening drum or bugle signal calling soldiers back to their quarters. **2** an elaboration of this with music and marching, as an entertainment. **3** a drumming or tapping sound.

**tattoo**[2] *verb* mark (skin) with indelible patterns by puncturing it and inserting a dye; make (a pattern) in this way. ●*noun* a tattooed pattern.

**tatty** *adjective* (**tattier, tattiest**) (*informal*) **1** ragged; shabby and untidy. **2** tawdry, fussily ornate. □ **tattily** *adverb*, **tattiness** *noun*

**taught** *see* TEACH.

**taunt** *verb* jeer at, try to provoke with scornful remarks or criticism. ●*noun* a taunting remark.

**taupe** (*rhymes with* hope) *noun* grey with a tinge of another colour, usually brown.

**Taurus** (tor-ŭs) *noun* the second sign of the zodiac, the Bull. □ **Taurean** *adjective & noun*

**Taurus Mountains** (tor-ŭs) a range of mountains in SW Turkey.

**taut** *adverb* stretched firmly, not slack. □ **tautly** *adverb*

**tauten** *verb* make or become taut.

**tautology** (taw-**tol**-ŏji) *noun* saying of the same thing again in different words, especially as a fault of style, as in 'free, gratis, and for nothing'. □ **tautological** (taw-tŏ-loj-ikäl) *adjective*, **tautologous** (taw-tol-ŏ-gŭs) *adjective*

**tavern** *noun* (*old use*) an inn or public house.

**taverna** *noun* a Greek restaurant.

**tawdry** (taw-dri) *adjective* (**tawdrier, tawdriest**) showy or gaudy but without real value. □ **tawdrily** *adverb*, **tawdriness** *noun*

**tawny** *adjective* brownish-yellow or brownish-orange.

**taws** (*pronounced* tawz) *noun* (also **tawse**) (*Scottish*) a leather strap with a slit end, formerly used for punishing children.

**tax** *noun* **1** a sum of money to be paid by people or businesses to a government, used for public purposes. **2** something that makes a heavy demand; *a tax on one's strength.* ● *verb* **1** impose a tax on; require (a person) to pay tax. **2** make heavy demands on. **3** pay the tax on; *the car is taxed until June.* **4** accuse in a challenging or reproving way; *taxed him with having left the door unlocked.* □ **tax avoidance** reducing the amount of tax payable by careful financial management. **tax-deductible** *adjective* (of expenses) legally deductible from income before tax assessment. **tax disc** a circle of paper displayed on a windscreen as proof that road tax has been paid. **tax evasion** illegal non-payment or underpayment of tax. **tax-free** *adjective* exempt from taxes. **tax haven** a country where income tax etc. is low. **tax return** a form to complete giving a declaration of income and expenditure for a particular year so that tax can be assessed.

**taxable** *adjective* able or liable to be taxed.

**taxation** *noun* the imposition or payment of tax.

**taxi** *noun* (*plural* **taxis**) (in full **taxi-cab**) a car that plies for hire, usually with a meter to record the fare payable. ● *verb* (**taxied**, **taxiing**) **1** go or convey in a taxi. **2** (of aircraft) move along ground or water under its own power, especially before or after flying. □ **taxi rank** (*Amer.* **taxi stand**) a place where taxis wait to be hired.

**taxidermy** (tak-si-derm-i) *noun* the art of preparing, stuffing, and mounting the skins of animals in lifelike form. □ **taxidermist** *noun*

**taximeter** (taks-i-meet-er) *noun* an automatic device indicating the fare payable, fitted to a taxi.

**taxman** *noun* (*plural* **taxmen**) an inspector or collector of taxes.

**taxonomy** (taks-on-ŏmi) *noun* the scientific process of classifying living things. □ **taxonomic** *adjective*, **taxonomically** *adverb*, **taxonomist** *noun*

**taxpayer** *noun* a person who pays tax (especially income tax).

**Tay** a river of Scotland, flowing into the North Sea.

**Taylor**, Elizabeth (born 1932), American film actress.

**Tayside** a local government region of eastern Scotland.

**TB** *abbreviation* (*informal*) tuberculosis.

**Tb** *symbol* terbium.

**t.b.a.** *abbreviation* to be announced.

**T-bone** *noun* a T-shaped bone, especially in a steak from the thin end of the loin.

**tbsp.** *abbreviation* tablespoonful.

**Tc** *symbol* technetium.

**Tchaikovsky** (chy-kof-ski), Pyotr Ilyich (1840–93), Russian composer.

**TCP** *abbreviation* (*trade mark*) a disinfectant and antiseptic.

**Te** *symbol* tellurium.

**te** *noun* (also **ti**) the seventh note of a major scale in music.

**tea** *noun* **1** the dried leaves of the tea plant. **2** the hot drink that is made by steeping these in boiling water. **3** a meal at which tea is served, especially a light meal in the afternoon or evening. **4** a drink made by steeping the leaves of other plants in water; *camomile tea*; *beef tea.* □ **tea bag** a small porous bag holding about a teaspoonful of tea for infusion. **tea break** an interruption of work allowed for drinking tea. **tea chest** a light cubical chest lined with thin sheets of lead or tin, in which tea is exported. **tea cloth** a tea towel. **tea cosy** a cover placed over a teapot to keep the tea hot. **tea leaf** a leaf of tea, especially after infusion. **tea plant** an evergreen shrub grown in China, India, etc. **tea rose** a rose with a delicate tealike scent. **tea towel** a towel for drying washed dishes.

**teacake** *noun* a flat sweet bread-bun usually served toasted and buttered.

**teach** *verb* (**taught**, **teaching**) **1** impart information or skill to (a person) or about (a subject etc.). **2** do this for a living. **3** put forward as a fact or principle; *Christ taught forgiveness.* **4** cause to adopt (a practice etc.) by example or experience; (*informal*) deter by punishment etc.; *that will teach you not to meddle.*

**teachable** *adjective* **1** able to learn by being taught. **2** (of a subject) able to be taught.

**teacher** *noun* a person who teaches others, especially in a school.

**teaching** *noun* what is taught; *the teachings of the Church.*

**teacup** *noun* a cup from which tea or other hot liquids are drunk.

**teak** *noun* the strong heavy wood of a tall evergreen Asian tree, used for making furniture and in shipbuilding.

**teal** *noun* (*plural* **teal**) a small freshwater duck.

**team** *noun* **1** a set of players forming one side in certain games and sports. **2** a set of people working together. **3** two or more animals harnessed together to draw a vehicle or farm implement. ● *verb* combine into a team or set or for a common purpose. □ **team spirit** willingness to act for the good of one's group rather than oneself.

**teamster** *noun* **1** a driver of a team of animals. **2** (*Amer.*) a lorry-driver.

**teamwork** *noun* organized cooperation.

**teapot** *noun* a pot with a handle, lid, and spout, in which tea is made and from which it is poured.

**tear¹** (*pronounced* tair) *verb* (**tore**, **torn**, **tearing**) **1** pull forcibly apart or away or to pieces. **2** make (a hole or a split) in this way. **3** become torn, be able to be torn; *paper tears easily.* **4** subject (a person etc.) to conflicting desires or demands; *torn between love and duty.* **5** run, walk, or travel hurriedly. ●*noun* a hole or split caused by tearing. □ **tear into** (*informal*) criticize severely. **tear oneself away** leave in spite of a strong desire to stay. **that's torn it** (*informal*) that has spoilt our plans or efforts.

**tear²** (*pronounced* teer) *noun* a drop of the salty water that appears in or flows from the eye as the result of grief or irritation by fumes etc. □ **in tears** crying. **tear-drop** *noun* a single tear. **tear-duct** *noun* a drain for carrying tears to the eye or from the eye to the nose. **tear gas** a gas that causes severe irritation of the eyes. **tear-jerker** *noun* (*informal*) a sentimental story etc. calculated to make people cry.

**tearaway** *noun* an impetuous or unruly young person.

**tearful** *adjective* crying or about to cry; sad. □ **tearfully** *adverb*

**tearing** (**tair**-ing) *adjective* extreme; violent, overwhelming; *in a tearing hurry.*

**tearoom** *noun* = TEASHOP.

**tease** *verb* **1** try to provoke in a playful or unkind way by jokes or questions or petty annoyances. **2** pick (wool etc.) into separate strands. **3** brush up the nap on (cloth). ●*noun* a person who is fond of teasing others.

**teasel** (**tee**-zĕl) *noun* **1** a plant with bristly heads formerly used to brush up nap on cloth. **2** a device used for this purpose.

**teaser** *noun* (*informal*) a problem that is difficult to solve.

**teaset** *noun* a set of crockery for serving tea.

**teashop** *noun* a small restaurant serving tea, cakes, and perhaps light meals.

**teaspoon** *noun* **1** a small spoon for stirring tea. **2** the amount held by this. □ **teaspoonful** *noun* (*plural* **teaspoonfuls**).

**teat** *noun* **1** a nipple on an animal's milk-secreting organ. **2** a device of rubber etc. on a feeding-bottle, through which the contents are sucked.

**teatime** *noun* the time towards the end of the afternoon when tea is served.

**tech** (*pronounced* **tek**) *noun* (also **tec**) (*informal*) a technical college.

**technetium** (tek-**nee**-shŭm) *noun* an artificially produced radioactive element (symbol Tc).

**technical** *adjective* **1** of the mechanical arts and applied sciences; *a technical education*; *technical college.* **2** of a particular subject or craft etc. or its techniques; *the technical terms of chemistry*; *technical skill.* **3** (of a book etc.) requiring specialized knowledge, using technical terms. **4** in a strict legal sense; *technical assault.* □ **technical knockout** a ruling by a referee that a boxer is unfit to continue and has lost the fight. □ **technically** *adverb*

**technicality** (tek-ni-**kal**-iti) *noun* **1** being technical. **2** a technical word, phrase, or point; *he was acquitted on a technicality.*

**technician** (tek-**nish**-ăn) *noun* an expert in the techniques of a particular subject or craft.

**Technicolor** *noun* **1** (*trade mark*) a process of producing cinema films in colour. **2** vivid or artificially brilliant colour.

**technique** (tek-**neek**) *noun* the method of doing or performing something (especially in an art or science); skill in this.

**technocracy** (tek-**nok**-răsi) *noun* management by technocrats.

**technocrat** (**tek**-nŏ-krat) *noun* a technical expert who manages a country's resources. □ **technocratic** *adjective*

**technology** *noun* **1** the scientific study of mechanical arts and applied sciences (e.g. engineering). **2** these subjects, their practical application in industry etc. □ **technological** *adjective*, **technologically** *adverb*, **technologist** *noun*

**tectonics** (tek-**tonn**-iks) *noun* the scientific study of the earth's structural features.

**teddy** *noun* (also **Teddy**) (in full **teddy bear**) a soft toy bear.

**Teddy boy** (*informal*) a youth, especially of the 1950s, wearing Edwardian-style clothes.

**Te Deum** (tee **dee**-ŭm) a Latin hymn beginning 'Te Deum laudamus' (= we praise thee O God).

**tedious** (**tee**-di-ŭs) *adjective* tiresome because of its length or slowness or dullness, boring. □ **tediously** *adverb*, **tediousness** *noun*

**tedium** (**tee**-di-ŭm) *noun* tediousness.

**tee** *noun* **1** the cleared space from which a player strikes the ball in golf at the beginning of play for each hole. **2** a small pile of sand or piece of wood etc. on which the ball is placed for being struck. **3** the mark aimed at in quoits, bowls, and curling. ●*verb* (**teed**, **teeing**) place (a ball) on a tee in golf. □ **tee off** play the ball from the tee.

**teem** *verb* **1** (foll. by *with*) be full of; *the river was teeming with fish.* **2** be present in large numbers. **3** (of water or rain etc.) flow in large quantities, pour.

**teenage** *adjective* of teenagers.

**teenaged** *adjective* in one's teens.

**teenager** *noun* a person in his or her teens.

**teens** *plural noun* the period when one is between 13 and 19 years old.

**teeny** *adjective* (**teenier, teeniest**) (*informal*) tiny. □ **teeny-bopper** *noun* a young teenager following the latest fashions in clothes, music, etc.

**teepee** alternative spelling of TEPEE.

**tee shirt** alternative spelling of T-SHIRT.

**teeter** *verb* stand or move unsteadily.

**teeth** *see* TOOTH.

**teethe** *verb* (of a baby) have its first teeth beginning to grow through the gums. □ **teething troubles** problems arising in the early stages of an enterprise.

**teetotal** *adjective* abstaining completely from alcoholic drinks. □ **teetotaller** *noun*

**TEFL** *abbreviation* teaching of English as a foreign language.

**Teflon** *noun* (*trade mark*) a non-stick coating for cooking pots and pans.

**Tegucigalpa** (teg-yoo-si-**gal**-pă) the capital of Honduras.

**Tehran** (tay-**rahn**) the capital of Iran.

**Te Kanawa** (te **kah**-nă-wă), Dame Kiri (born 1947), New Zealand operatic soprano.

**Tel.** *abbreviation* (also **tel.**) telephone.

**tele-** *combining form* **1** at or to a distance. **2** television. **3** by telephone.

**tele-ad** *noun* an advertisement placed in a newspaper etc. by telephone.

**telecast** *noun* a television broadcast. ●*verb* transmit by television. □ **telecaster** *noun*

**telecommunications** *plural noun* the means of communication over long distances, as by cable, telegraph, telephone, radio, or television.

**telecottage** *noun* a centre equipped with office machinery, shared by people who are self-employed or who work freelance or at a distance from their employer.

**telegram** *noun* a message sent by telegraph.

■**Usage** Not in UK official use since 1981 except for international messages.

**telegraph** *noun* a system or apparatus for sending messages to a distance, especially by transmission of electrical impulses along wires. ●*verb* send (a message) or communicate with (a person) by telegraph. □ **telegraph pole** a pole supporting overhead telephone wires.

**telegraphic** *adjective* **1** of or by telegraphs or telegrams. **2** using few words; concise. □ **telegraphically** *adverb*

**telegraphist** (til-eg-ră-fist) *noun* a person whose job is to send and receive messages by telegraph.

**telegraphy** (til-eg-ră-fi) *noun* communication by telegraph.

**telekinesis** (tel-i-ky-**nee**-sis) *noun* the supposed process of moving things without touching them and without using ordinary physical means.

**Telemann** (**tayl**-ĕ-man), Georg Philipp (1681–1767), German composer.

**telemarketing** *noun* attempting to sell goods or services by unsolicited telephone calls.

**telemessage** *noun* a message sent by telephone or telex and delivered in printed form.

■**Usage** In UK official use since 1981 for inland messages, replacing *telegram*.

**telemetry** (til-**em**-it-ri) *noun* the process of recording the readings of an instrument at a distance, usually by means of radio.

**teleology** (teel-i-**ol**-ŏji) *noun* the doctrine that there is evidence of design or purpose in nature. □ **teleological** (tel-i-ŏ-**loj**-ikăl) *adjective*

**telepathic** (tel-i-**path**-ik) *adjective* of or using telepathy; able to communicate by telepathy. □ **telepathically** *adverb*

**telepathy** (til-**ep**-ă-thi) *noun* communication from one mind to another without the use of speech, writing, or gestures etc.

**telephone** *noun* **1** a system of transmitting sound (especially speech) to a distance by wire, cord, or radio. **2** an instrument used in this, with a receiver and mouthpiece. ●*verb* send (a message) or speak to (a person) by telephone. □ **telephone directory** or **book** a book listing the names and numbers of people who have a telephone. **telephone number** a number assigned to a particular telephone and used in making connections to it. □ **telephonic** (teli-**fon**-ik) *adjective*, **telephonically** *adverb*

**telephonist** (til-**ef**-ŏn-ist) *noun* an operator in a telephone exchange or at a switchboard.

**telephony** (til-**ef**-ŏni) *noun* the process of transmitting sound by telephone.

**telephotography** *noun* photographing distant objects using a telephoto lens.

**telephoto lens** a lens producing a large image of a distant object that is photographed.

**teleprinter** (**tel**-i-print-er) *noun* a device for transmitting, receiving, and printing telegraph messages.

**teleprompter** *noun* a device beside a television camera that unrolls a speaker's script out of sight of the viewers.

**telesales** *plural noun* selling by telephone.

**telescope** noun an optical instrument using lenses or mirrors or both to make distant objects appear larger when viewed through it. ●verb 1 make or become shorter by sliding overlapping sections one inside another. 2 compress or become compressed forcibly. 3 condense so as to occupy less space or time.

**telescopic** adjective 1 of a telescope; magnifying like a telescope. 2 visible only through a telescope; telescopic stars. 3 capable of being telescoped; telescopic umbrella. □ **telescopic sight** a telescope fitted to a rifle for magnifying the image of the target. □ **telescopically** adverb

**teletext** noun a system in which news and information can be selected and produced on a television screen.

**telethon** noun a very long television programme broadcast to raise money for charity.

**televise** verb transmit by or broadcast on television.

**television** noun 1 a system for reproducing on a screen visual images transmitted with sound by radio signals or cable. 2 (also **television set**) an apparatus with a screen for receiving these signals. 3 televised programmes; television as a medium of communication. □ **televisual** adjective

**telex** (also **Telex**) noun a system of telegraphy in which printed messages are transmitted and received by teleprinters using public transmission lines. ●verb send (a message) or communicate with (a person) by telex.

**Telford**, Thomas (1757–1834), Scottish civil engineer, builder of many great roads, bridges, and canals.

**Tell**, William, a legendary hero (traditionally placed in the 14th century) of the liberation of Switzerland, who was required to hit with an arrow an apple placed on the head of his son.

**tell** verb (**told, telling**) 1 make known, especially in spoken or written words. 2 give information to. 3 utter; tell the truth. 4 reveal a secret; promise you won't tell. 5 direct or order; tell them to wait. 6 decide or determine; how do you tell which button to press? 7 distinguish; I can't tell him from his brother. 8 produce a noticeable effect; the strain began to tell on him. 9 count (especially votes). □ **tell off** (informal) scold. **tell tales** report what is meant to be secret. **tell the time** read the time from a clock. **you're telling me** (slang) I am fully aware of that.

**teller** noun 1 a person who tells or gives an account of something. 2 a person appointed to count votes. 3 a bank cashier.

**telling** adjective having a noticeable effect, striking; a telling argument.

**tell-tale** noun 1 a person who tells tales. 2 a mechanical device that serves as an indicator. ●adjective revealing or indicating something; a tell-tale blush.

**tellurium** (tel-yoor-iŭm) noun an element (symbol Te) chemically related to sulphur and selenium, used in semiconductors.

**telly** noun (informal) television; a television set.

**Telugu** (tel-ŭ-goo) noun 1 a member of a Dravidian people in SE India. 2 their language.

**temerity** (tim-e-riti) noun audacity, rashness.

**temp** (informal) noun a temporary employee. ●verb work as a temp.

**temper** noun 1 the state of the mind as regards calmness or anger; in a good temper. 2 a fit of anger; in a temper. 3 calmness under provocation; keep one's temper. 4 a tendency to have fits of anger; have a temper. 5 the condition of a tempered metal as regards hardness and elasticity. ●verb 1 bring (metal) to the required degree of hardness and elasticity by heating and then cooling. 2 bring (clay etc.) to the required consistency by moistening and mixing. 3 moderate or soften the effects of; temper justice with mercy.

**tempera** noun a method of painting with powdered colours mixed with egg yolk or size, used in Europe chiefly in the 12th–15th centuries.

**temperament** noun a person's or animal's nature and character; a nervous temperament.

**temperamental** adjective 1 of temperament. 2 not having a calm temperament, having fits of excitable or moody behaviour. □ **temperamentally** adverb

**temperance** noun 1 self-restraint in one's behaviour or in eating and drinking. 2 total abstinence from alcoholic drinks.

**temperate** adjective 1 self-restrained in one's behaviour, moderate. 2 (of climate) having a mild temperature without extremes of heat and cold. □ **temperate zone** the regions of the earth lying south of the Arctic Circle to the tropic of Cancer and north of the Antarctic Circle to the tropic of Capricorn. □ **temperately** adverb

**temperature** noun 1 the intensity of heat or cold in a body or room or country etc. 2 a measure of this shown by a thermometer. 3 an abnormally high temperature of the body; have a temperature.

**tempest** noun a violent storm.

**tempestuous** (tem-pest-yoo-ŭs) adjective stormy, full of commotion. □ **tempestuously** adverb

**tempi** *see* TEMPO.

**template** *noun* a piece of thin board or metal used as a pattern or guide in cutting, drilling, or shaping.

**Temple**, Shirley (born 1928), American child film star who later (as Mrs Shirley Black) represented the USA at the United Nations and served as an ambassador in several countries.

**temple¹** *noun* a building dedicated to the presence or service of a god or gods. □ **Inner Temple, Middle Temple** two Inns of Court in London (*see* INN).

**temple²** *noun* the flat part at each side of the head between forehead and ear.

**tempo** *noun* (*plural* **tempos** *or* **tempi**) **1** the speed or rhythm of a piece of music; *in waltz tempo*. **2** the pace of any movement or activity; *the tempo of the war is quickening*.

**temporal** (temp-er-ăl) *adjective* **1** secular, of worldly affairs as opposed to spiritual. **2** of or denoting time. **3** of the temples of the head; *the temporal artery*. □ **Lords temporal** *see* LORD.

**temporary** *adjective* lasting or meant to last for a limited time only, not permanent. ●*noun* a person employed temporarily. □ **temporarily** *adverb*

**temporize** *verb* (also **temporise**) compromise temporarily, or avoid giving a definite answer or decision, in order to gain time.

**tempt** *verb* **1** persuade or try to persuade (especially into doing something wrong or unwise) by the prospect of pleasure or advantage. **2** arouse a desire in, attract. **3** risk provoking (fate or Providence) by deliberate rashness. □ **tempter** *noun*, **temptress** *noun*

**temptation** *noun* **1** tempting; being tempted. **2** something that tempts or attracts.

**tempting** *adjective* attractive, inviting; *a tempting offer*. □ **temptingly** *adverb*

**tempura** *noun* a Japanese dish of fish, vegetables, etc. fried in batter.

**ten** *adjective & noun* one more than nine (10, X). □ **the Ten Commandments** (in the Bible) the ten rules of correct behaviour given by God to Moses. **ten-gallon hat** a cowboy's large wide-brimmed hat.

**tenable** (ten-ăbŭl) *adjective* **1** able to be defended against attack or objection; *a tenable position*. **2** (of an office) able to be held for a certain time or by a certain class of person etc. □ **tenability** *noun*

**tenacious** (tin-ay-shŭs) *adjective* **1** holding or clinging firmly to something (e.g. rights or principles). **2** (of memory) retentive. **3** sticking firmly together or to an object or surface. □ **tenaciously** *adverb*, **tenacity** (tin-**ass**-iti) *noun*

**tenancy** *noun* **1** the use of land or buildings as a tenant. **2** the period of this.

**tenant** *noun* **1** a person who rents land or buildings from a landlord. **2** (in law) an occupant or owner of land or a building.

**tenantry** *noun* the tenants of land or buildings on one estate.

**tench** *noun* (*plural* **tench**) a freshwater fish of the carp family.

**tend** *verb* **1** take care of or look after (a person or thing). **2** be likely to behave in a certain way or to have a certain characteristic. **3** have a certain influence; *recent laws tend to increase customers' rights*. **4** take a certain direction; *the track tends upwards*.

**tendency** *noun* **1** the way a person or thing tends to be or behave; *a tendency towards fatness*; *homicidal tendencies*. **2** the direction in which something moves or changes; a trend; *an upward tendency*.

**tendentious** (ten-den-shŭs) *adjective* (of a speech or piece of writing etc.) aimed at helping a cause, not impartial. □ **tendentiously** *adverb*

**tender¹** *adjective* **1** not tough or hard; easy to chew; *tender meat*. **2** easily damaged, delicate; *tender plants*; *of tender age*. **3** sensitive, painful when touched. **4** easily moved to pity or sympathy; *a tender heart*. **5** loving, gentle. □ **tender mercies** (*ironic*) bad treatment. □ **tenderly** *adverb*, **tenderness** *noun*

**tender²** *verb* **1** offer formally; *tender one's resignation*. **2** make a tender (for goods or work). ●*noun* a formal offer to supply goods or carry out work at a stated price. □ **legal tender** currency that must, by law, be accepted in payment. **put out to tender** ask for competitive tenders for (work).

**tender³** *noun* **1** a person who tends or looks after something. **2** a vessel or vehicle travelling to and from a larger one to convey stores or passengers etc. **3** a truck attached to a steam locomotive, carrying fuel and water etc.

**tenderfoot** *noun* (*plural* **tenderfoots** or **tenderfeet**) a newcomer; an inexperienced person.

**tenderize** *verb* (also **tenderise**) make more tender. □ **tenderizer** *noun*

**tenderloin** *noun* the middle part of pork loin.

**tendon** *noun* a strong band or cord of tissue connecting a muscle to some other part.

**tendril** *noun* **1** a thread-like part by which a climbing plant clings to a support. **2** a slender curl of hair etc.

**tenebrous** *adjective* (*literary*) dark, gloomy.

**tenement** (ten-i-mĕnt) *noun* **1** (in law) land or other permanent property held by a tenant; *lands and tenements*. **2** a flat or room rented for living in. **3** a large block of flats.

**Tenerife** (ten-ĕ-reef) a volcanic island which is the largest of the Canary Islands.

**tenet** (ten-it) *noun* a firm belief, principle, or doctrine.

**tenfold** *adjective & adverb* ten times as much or as many.

**Tenn.** *abbreviation* Tennessee.

**tenner** *noun* (*informal*) **1** £10; a ten-pound note. **2** a ten-dollar note.

**Tennessee** (ten-i-see) a State of the central south-eastern USA.

**tennis** *noun* either of two ball games for 2 or 4 players, played with rackets over a net with a soft ball on an open court (**lawn tennis**) or with a hard ball in a walled court (**real tennis**, in the USA called **court tennis**). □ **tennis elbow** a sprain caused by overuse of the forearm muscles.

**Tennyson**, Alfred, 1st Baron (1809–92), English poet, Poet Laureate from 1850.

**tenon** (ten-ŏn) *noun* a projection shaped to fit into a mortise.

**tenor** (ten-er) *noun* **1** the general routine or course of something; *disrupting the even tenor of his life.* **2** the general meaning or drift; *the tenor of his lecture.* **3** the highest ordinary adult male singing-voice; a singer with this; a part written for it. **4** a musical instrument with approximately the range of a tenor voice; *tenor saxophone.*

**tenosynovitis** (tenŏ-synŏ-vy-tĭs) *noun* an injury especially of a wrist tendon resulting from repetitive strain.

**tenpin bowling** a game similar to ninepins.

**tense**[1] *noun* any of the forms of a verb that indicate the time of action etc. as past, present, or future; *'came' is the past tense of 'come'.*

**tense**[2] *adjective* **1** stretched tightly. **2** with muscles tight in attentiveness for what may happen. **3** unable to relax, edgy. **4** causing tenseness; *a tense moment.* ●*verb* make or become tense. □ **tensely** *adverb*, **tenseness** *noun*

**tensile** (ten-syl) *adjective* **1** of tension; *tensile strength.* **2** capable of being stretched. □ **tensility** (ten-sil-iti) *noun*

**tension** *noun* **1** stretching; being stretched. **2** tenseness, the condition when feelings are tense. **3** the effect produced by forces pulling against each other. **4** electromotive force, voltage; *high-tension cables.* **5** (in knitting) the number of stitches and rows to a unit of measurement (e.g. 10 cm or 1 inch); the tightness of the stitches.

**tent** *noun* a portable shelter or dwelling made of canvas etc.

**tentacle** *noun* a slender flexible part extending from the body of certain animals (e.g. snails, octopuses), used for feeling, grasping, or moving. □ **tentacled** *adjective*

**tentative** (tent-ă-tiv) *adjective* hesitant, not definite, done as a trial; *a tentative suggestion.* □ **tentatively** *adverb*

**tenter** *noun* a machine for stretching cloth to dry during manufacture.

**tenterhook** *noun* each of the hooks that hold cloth stretched for drying during its manufacture. □ **on tenterhooks** in a state of suspense or strain because of uncertainty.

**tenth** *adjective & noun* **1** next after ninth. **2** one of ten equal parts of a thing. □ **tenthly** *adverb*

**tenuous** (ten-yoo-ŭs) *adjective* **1** very thin in form or consistency; *tenuous threads.* **2** having little substance or validity, very slight; *tenuous distinctions.* □ **tenuously** *adverb*, **tenuity** (tin-yoo-iti) *noun*

**tenure** (ten-yer) *noun* the holding of office or of land, property, or accommodation; the period or manner of this; *freehold tenure; she was granted security of tenure.*

**Tenzing Norgay** (1914–86), Sherpa mountaineer who, with Sir Edmund Hillary, was the first to reach the summit of Mount Everest (1953).

**tepee** (tee-pee) *noun* (also **teepee**) a N. American Indian's conical tent.

**tepid** *adjective* slightly warm, lukewarm. □ **tepidly** *adverb*, **tepidity** (ti-pid-iti) *noun*

**tequila** (tek-ee-lă) *noun* a Mexican liquor made from agave.

**terbium** *noun* a metallic element (symbol Tb).

**tercel** (ter-sĕl) *noun* (also **tiercel**) a male hawk.

**tercentenary** (ter-sen-teen-er-i) *noun* a 300th anniversary.

**terebinth** (te-ri-binth) *noun* a tree of southern Europe, yielding turpentine.

**teredo** (ter-ee-doh) *noun* (*plural* **teredos**) a mollusc that bores into submerged timber.

**Teresa** (ter-ee-ză), Mother (born 1910), Roman Catholic nun, born of Albanian parents in the former Yugoslavia, founder of the Missionaries of Charity, an order noted for its work among the poor and the dying in Calcutta, India, and throughout the world.

**tergiversate** (ter-ji-ver-sayt) *verb* **1** change one's party or principles. **2** make conflicting or evasive statements. □ **tergiversation** *noun*, **tergiversator** *noun*

**teriyaki** *noun* a Japanese dish of grilled marinated meat or fish.

**term** *noun* **1** the time for which something lasts; a fixed or limited time; *during his term of office; a term of imprisonment.* **2** completion of this; *a pregnancy approaching term.* **3** one of the periods during which instruction is given in a school, college, or university or in which a lawcourt holds sessions, alternating with holidays or vacations. **4** each of the quantities or expressions in a mathematical series or ratio etc. **5** a word or phrase considered as the name or symbol of something; *'the nick' is a slang term for 'prison'*. **6** (**terms**) language or the manner of its use; *we protested in strong terms*. **7** (**terms**) stipulations made, conditions offered or accepted; *peace terms*. **8** (**terms**) payment offered or asked; *hire purchase on easy terms*. **9** (**terms**) a relation between people; *on friendly terms*. ● *verb* call by a certain term or expression; *this music is termed plainsong*. □ **come to terms** reconcile oneself to a difficulty etc.; *came to terms with his handicap*. **in terms of** referring to, regarding.

**termagant** (ter-mă-gănt) *noun* a shrewish bullying woman.

**terminable** *adjective* able to be terminated.

**terminal** *adjective* **1** of, forming, or situated at the end or boundary of something. **2** forming or undergoing the last stage of a fatal disease; *terminal cancer*. **3** of or done each term; *terminal examinations*. ● *noun* **1** a terminating point or part. **2** a terminus for railway trains or long-distance buses; a building (at an airport or in a town) where air passengers arrive and depart. **3** a point of connection in an electric circuit or device. **4** an apparatus with a VDU and keyboard for transmitting messages to and from a computer or communications system etc. □ **terminal velocity** a velocity of a falling body such that the resistance of the air etc. prevents any further increase of speed under gravity. □ **terminally** *adverb*

**terminate** *verb* end. □ **terminator** *noun*

**termination** *noun* **1** terminating or being terminated. **2** an induced abortion. **3** an ending or result.

**terminology** *noun* **1** the technical terms of a particular subject. **2** the proper use of words as names or symbols. □ **terminological** *adjective*, **terminologist** *noun*

**terminus** *noun* (*plural* **termini**, *pronounced* ter-min-I, *or* **terminuses**) the end of something; the last station or stop at the end of a railway or bus route.

**termite** *noun* a small antlike insect that is very destructive to timber, especially in tropical areas.

**tern** *noun* a seabird with long pointed wings and a forked tail.

**ternary** *adjective* composed of three parts.

**Terpsichore** (terp-sik-ŏ-ri) (*Gk. & Rom. myth.*) the Muse of lyric poetry and dance.

**Terpsichorean** *adjective* of or relating to dancing.

**terrace** *noun* **1** a raised level place; one of a series of these into which a hillside is shaped for cultivation. **2** a flight of wide shallow steps, e.g. for spectators at a sports ground. **3** a paved area beside a house. **4** a row of houses joined to each other by party walls. ● *verb* form into a terrace or terraces. □ **terrace house** (also **terraced house**) a house forming one of a terrace.

**terracotta** *noun* **1** brownish-red unglazed pottery. **2** its colour.

**terra firma** dry land; the ground. (¶ Latin.)

**terrain** (te-rayn) *noun* a stretch of land with regard to its natural features.

**terra incognita** (in-kog-ni-tă) an unexplored region. (¶ Latin, = unknown land.)

**terrapin** (te-ră-pin) *noun* **1** an edible North American freshwater tortoise. **2** (**Terrapin**) (*trade mark*) a prefabricated one-storey building.

**terrarium** (te-rair-iŭm) *noun* (*plural* **terrariums** *or* **terraria**) **1** a place for keeping small land animals. **2** a sealed transparent globe etc. containing growing plants.

**terrazzo** (ti-rats-oh) *noun* (*plural* **terrazzos**) a flooring material of stone chips set in concrete and given a smooth surface.

**terrene** (te-reen) *adjective* of the earth, earthly; terrestrial.

**terrestrial** (tĕ-rest-riăl) *adjective* **1** of the earth. **2** of or living on land.

**terrible** *adjective* **1** appalling, distressing. **2** extreme, hard to bear; *the heat was terrible*. **3** (*informal*) very bad; *I'm terrible at tennis*. □ **terribly** *adverb*

**terrier** *noun* a small hardy active dog.

**terrific** *adjective* (*informal*) **1** of great size or intensity; *a terrific storm*. **2** excellent; *you did a terrific job*. □ **terrifically** *adjective*

**terrified** *adjective* feeling terror.

**terrify** *verb* (**terrified**, **terrifying**) fill with terror. □ **terrifying** *adjective*, **terrifyingly** *adverb*

**terrine** (tĕ-reen) *noun* **1** pâté or a similar food. **2** an earthenware dish holding this.

**territorial** *adjective* **1** of territory or a district; *territorial rights*. **2** tending to defend one's territory. ● *noun* (**Territorial**) a member of the Territorial Army. □ **Territorial Army** a local volunteer reserve force. **territorial waters** the sea within a certain distance of a country's coast and subject to its control. □ **territorially** *adverb*

**territory** *noun* **1** land under the control of a ruler, State, city, etc. **2** (**Territory**) a country or area forming part of the USA, Australia, or Canada but not ranking as a State or Province. **3** an area for which a person has responsibility. **4** a sphere of action or thought, a province. **5** an area claimed or dominated by one person, group, or animal and defended against others.

**terror** *noun* **1** extreme fear. **2** a terrifying person or thing. **3** (*informal*) a formidable

person; a troublesome person or thing.
□ **the Terror** or **Reign of Terror** the period of the French Revolution during 1793–4 when Robespierre and his supporters ruthlessly executed opponents to their regime.

**terrorism** noun use of violence and intimidation, especially for political purposes. □ **terrorist** noun

**terrorize** verb (also **terrorise**) fill with terror; coerce by terrorism. □ **terrorization** noun

**terry** noun a cotton fabric used for towels and nappies, with raised loops left uncut.

**terse** adjective concise; curt. □ **tersely** adverb, **terseness** noun

**tertiary** (ter-sher-i) adjective **1** coming after secondary, of the third rank or stage etc. **2** (of education) above secondary level. **3** (**Tertiary**) Geol. of the first period of the Cainozoic era. ●noun (**Tertiary**) the Tertiary period.

**Terylene** noun (trade mark) a synthetic textile fibre.

**TESL** abbreviation teaching of English as a second language.

**tesla** (tes-lă) noun the SI unit of magnetic induction. (¶ Named after the American scientist N. Tesla (1856–1943).)

**TESSA** abbreviation (Brit.) tax exempt special savings account; an account providing tax-free interest after five years on a limited amount of savings.

**tessellated** (tess-il-ayt-id) adjective (of a pavement) made from small flat pieces of stone in various colours arranged in a pattern.

**tessellation** noun an arrangement of shapes fitting together, especially in a repeated pattern.

**tessera** noun (plural **tesserae**) a small square block used in mosaics.

**test** noun **1** an examination or evaluation of the qualities or abilities of a person or thing. **2** a means or procedure for making this. **3** an examination (especially in a school). **4** (informal) a test match. **5** the shell of some invertebrates. ●verb subject to a test. □ **test case** a lawsuit providing a decision which is taken as applying to similar cases in the future. **test drive** a drive taken in order to judge the performance of a car. **test-drive** verb take a test drive in (a car). **test match** a cricket or Rugby match between teams of certain countries, usually one of a series in a tour. **test pilot** a pilot employed to fly new aircraft to test their performance. **test-tube** noun a tube of thin glass with one end closed, used in laboratories. **test-tube baby** (informal) one conceived by in vitro fertilization.

**testa** noun (plural **testae**) the protective outer covering of a seed.

**testaceous** adjective having a hard continuous shell.

**testacy** (test-ă-si) noun the state of being testate.

**testament** noun **1** (usually in **last will and testament**) a will. **2** (informal) a written statement of one's beliefs. **3** a covenant. □ **Old Testament** the books of the Bible telling of the history of the Jews and their beliefs. **New Testament** the books of the Bible telling of the life and teaching of Christ and his earliest followers.

**testamentary** adjective of or given in a person's will.

**testate** (tes-tayt) adjective having left a valid will at death.

**testator** (tes-tay-ter) noun a person who has made a will.

**testatrix** noun a woman who has made a will.

**tester** noun **1** a person or thing that tests. **2** a bottle etc. containing a cosmetic or perfume for trial in a shop. **3** a canopy, especially over a four-poster bed.

**testes** see TESTIS.

**testicle** noun a male reproductive organ in which sperm-bearing fluid is produced, (in man) each of the two enclosed in the scrotum.

**testify** verb (**testified**, **testifying**) **1** bear witness to (a fact etc.); give evidence. **2** be evidence of.

**testimonial** noun **1** a formal statement testifying to a person's character, abilities, or qualifications. **2** something given to a person to show appreciation of his or her services or achievements.

**testimony** noun **1** a declaration or statement (especially one made under oath). **2** evidence in support of something.

**testis** noun (plural **testes**, pronounced tes-teez) a testicle.

**testosterone** (test-ost-er-ohn) noun a male sex hormone.

**testy** adjective easily annoyed, irritable. □ **testily** adverb, **testiness** noun

**tetanus** (tet-ăn-ŭs) noun a disease in which the muscles contract and stiffen (as in lockjaw), caused by bacteria that enter the body.

**tetchy** adjective peevish, irritable. □ **tetchily** adverb, **tetchiness** noun

**tête-à-tête** (tayt-ah-tayt) noun a private conversation between two people. ●adverb & adjective together in private. (¶ French, = head to head.)

**tether** noun a rope or chain by which an animal is fastened. ●verb fasten (an animal) with a tether. □ **at the end of one's**

**tether** having reached the limit of one's endurance.

**tetrad** noun a group of four.

**tetragon** noun a plane figure with four angles and sides.

**tetrahedron** (tet-ră-hee-drŏn) noun (plural **tetrahedra** or **tetrahedrons**) a solid with four faces, a pyramid with three triangular faces and a triangular base.

**tetralogy** noun a group of four related novels, plays, etc.

**Teutonic** (tew-tonn-ik) adjective **1** of the Germanic peoples (Teutons) or their languages. **2** German.

**Tex.** abbreviation Texas.

**Texas** a State of the southern USA. □ **Texan** adjective & noun

**text** noun **1** the wording of something written or printed. **2** the main body of a book or page etc. as distinct from illustrations or notes. **3** a sentence from Scripture used as the subject of a sermon or discussion. **4** a book or play etc. prescribed for study. □ **text editor** Computing a system or program allowing the user to enter and edit text. **text processing** Computing the manipulation of text, especially converting it from one form into another.

**textbook** noun a book of information for use in studying a subject.

**textile** noun a woven or machine-knitted fabric. ● adjective of weaving or cloth.

**textual** adjective of or in a text. □ **textually** adverb

**texture** noun the way a fabric or other substance feels to the touch; its thickness, firmness, or solidity. □ **textural** adjective, **texturally** adverb

**textured** adjective **1** having a certain texture; coarse-textured. **2** (of yarn or fabric) crimped, curled, or looped.

**Th** symbol thorium.

**Thackeray**, William Makepeace (1811–63), English satirical novelist.

**Thai** (pronounced as tie) adjective of Thailand or its people or language. ● noun **1** (plural **Thai** or **Thais**) a native or inhabitant of Thailand. **2** the language of Thailand.

**Thailand** (ty-land) a country in SE Asia.

**thalidomide** (thă-lid-ŏ-myd) noun a sedative drug found (in 1961) to have caused malformation of the limbs of babies whose mothers took it during pregnancy.

**thallium** (thal-iŭm) noun a chemical element (symbol Tl), a soft white poisonous metallic substance.

**Thames** a river of southern England, flowing through London to the North Sea.

**than** conjunction used to introduce the second element in a comparison; his brother is taller than he is; I am taller than him.

■**Usage** With reference to the last example, it is also legitimate to say I am taller than he, but this is much more formal.

**thank** verb **1** express gratitude to. **2** hold (a person) responsible; he has only himself to thank. ● plural noun (**thanks**) expressions of gratitude; (informal) thank you. □ **thank God** (or **thank goodness** etc.) an exclamation of relief. **thanks to** on account of, as the result of. **thank you** a polite expression of thanks.

**thankful** adjective feeling or expressing gratitude.

**thankfully** adverb **1** in a thankful way. **2** we are thankful; thankfully it has stopped raining.

■**Usage** The use in sense 2 is similar to that of hopefully which some people regard as unacceptable.

**thankless** adjective **1** not likely to win thanks; unappreciated; a thankless task. **2** ungrateful. □ **thanklessly** adverb, **thanklessness** noun

**thanksgiving** noun **1** an expression of gratitude, especially to God. **2** (**Thanksgiving** or **Thanksgiving Day**) a holiday for giving thanks to God, in the USA on the fourth Thursday in November, in Canada on the second Monday in October.

**that** adjective & pronoun (plural **those**) the, the person or thing referred to or pointed to or understood; the further or less obvious one of two. ● adverb so, to such an extent; I'll go that far. ● relative pronoun used to introduce a clause that is essential in order to define or identify something; the book that I sent you; the man that she married. ● conjunction introducing a dependent clause; we hope that all will go well. □ **that's that** that is settled or finished.

■**Usage** As a relative pronoun that usually specifies or identifies something referred to, whereas who or which need not: compare the book that you sent me is lost with the book, which you sent me, is lost.

**thatch** noun **1** a roof or roof-covering made of straw, reeds, etc. **2** (informal) a thick growth of hair on the head. ● verb roof or cover with thatch; make (a roof) of thatch. □ **thatcher**

**Thatcher**, Margaret Hilda, Baroness (born 1925), British Conservative stateswoman, first woman Prime Minister of the UK 1979–1990.

**thaw** verb **1** pass into a liquid or unfrozen state after being frozen. **2** become warm enough to melt ice etc. or to lose numbness. **3** become less cool or less formal in manner. **4** cause to thaw. ●*noun* thawing; weather that thaws ice etc.

**the** *adjective* (called the *definite article*) **1** applied to a noun standing for a specific person or a thing (*the Queen*; *the man in grey*), or representative or all of a kind (*diseases of the eye*; *the rich*), or an occupation or pursuit etc. (*too fond of the bottle*). **2** (*pronounced thee*) used to emphasize excellence or importance; *he's the Sir Lawrence*. **3** (*informal*) my, our, your, etc.; *the wife*. **4** (of prices) per; *oysters at £5 the dozen*. ●*adverb* in that degree, by that amount; *all the better*; *the more the merrier*.

**theatre** *noun* (*Amer.* **theater**) **1** a building or outdoor structure for the performance of plays and similar entertainments. **2** a room or hall for lectures etc. with seats in tiers. **3** an operating theatre. **4** a scene of important events; *Belgium was the theatre of war*. **5** the writing, acting, and producing of plays. □ **theatre weapons** those that are of intermediate range, between tactical and strategic.

**theatrical** *adjective* **1** of or for the theatre. **2** (of behaviour) exaggerated and designed to make a showy effect. ●*plural noun* **theatricals** theatrical performances; *amateur theatricals*. □ **theatrically** *adverb*, **theatricality** *noun*

**Thebes** (*pronounced* theebz) **1** an ancient city of Upper Egypt that was the capital *c.*1550–1290 BC. **2** a city of Greece, northwest of Athens, leader of the whole of Greece for a short period in the 4th century BC. □ **Theban** *adjective & noun*

**thee** *pronoun* the objective case of **thou**.

**theft** *noun* stealing.

**their** *adjective* of or belonging to them.

**theirs** *possessive pronoun* of or belonging to them, the thing(s) belonging to them.

■**Usage** It is incorrect to write *their's* (see the note under ITS).

**theism** (th'ee-izm) *noun* belief in the existence of gods or a god, especially a God supernaturally revealed to man. □ **theist** *noun*, **theistic** *adjective*

**them** *pronoun* **1** the objective case of **they**; *we saw them*. **2** (*informal*) = they; *it's them all right*.

**thematic** (th'ee-mat-ik) *adjective* of or according to a theme or themes. □ **thematically** *adverb*

**theme** (*pronounced* theem) *noun* **1** the subject about which a person speaks, writes, or thinks. **2** a melody which is repeated or on which variations are constructed. □ **theme park** an amusement park in which all the activities etc. are related to a particular subject.

**themselves** *pronoun* corresponding to *they* and *them*, used in the same ways as **himself** and **herself**.

**then** *adverb* **1** at that time. **2** next, after that; and also. **3** in that case, therefore; *if that's yours, then this must be mine*. ●*adjective* of that time; *the then duke*. ●*noun* that time; *from then on*.

**thence** *adverb* from that place or source.

**thenceforth**, **thenceforward** *adverb* (*informal*) from then on.

**theocracy** (thi-ok-ră-si) *noun* **1** government by God or a god directly or through priests. **2** a country governed in this way.

**theodolite** (thi-od-ŏ-lyt) *noun* a surveying-instrument with a rotating telescope used for measuring horizontal and vertical angles.

**Theodosius** (thi-ŏ-**doh**-siŭs) 'the Great' (*c.* 346–95), emperor of the Eastern Roman Empire from 379 and of the Western Empire from 392.

**theologian** (thi-ŏ-**loh**-jiăn) *noun* an expert in theology.

**theology** (thi-ol-ŏji) *noun* the study of religion; a system of religion. □ **theological** *adjective*, **theologically** *adverb*

**theorem** *noun* **1** a mathematical statement to be proved by a chain of reasoning. **2** a rule in algebra etc., especially one expressed as a formula.

**theoretical** *adjective* based on theory not on practice or experience. □ **theoretically** *adverb*

**theoretician** (th'ee-ŏ-ri-tish-ăn) *noun* a person who deals with the theoretical (not practical) parts of a subject.

**theorist** *noun* a person who theorizes.

**theorize** *verb* (also **theorise**) form a theory or theories.

**theory** *noun* **1** a set of ideas formulated (by reasoning from known facts) to explain something; *Darwin's theory of evolution*. **2** an opinion or supposition. **3** ideas or suppositions in general (contrasted with *practice*). **4** a statement of the principles on which a subject is based; *theory of music*.

**theosophy** (thi-oss-ŏfi) *noun* any of several systems of philosophy that aim at a direct knowledge of God by means of spiritual ecstasy and contemplation. □ **theosophical** *adjective*, **theosophist** *noun*

**therapeutic** (th'e-ră-pew-tik) *adjective* of the relief or healing of disease etc., curative. ●*noun* (**therapeutics**) (usually treated as *singular*) medical treatment of disease. □ **therapeutically** *adverb*

**therapist** *noun* a specialist in a certain kind of therapy.

**therapy** *noun* **1** any treatment designed to relieve or cure a disease or disability etc. **2** physiotherapy; psychotherapy.

**Theravada** (th'e-ră-vah-dă) *noun* a form of Buddhism practised in Sri Lanka and parts of SE Asia.

**there** *adverb* **1** in, at, or to that place. **2** at that point in a process or series of events. **3** in that matter; *I can't agree with you there.* **4** used for emphasis in calling attention; *hey, you there!* **5** used to introduce a sentence where the verb comes before its subject; *there was plenty to eat.* ● *noun* that place; *we live near there.* ● *interjection* an exclamation of satisfaction or dismay (*there! what did I tell you!*) or used to soothe a child etc. (*there, there!*).

**thereabouts** *adverb* (also **thereabout**) **1** somewhere near there. **2** somewhere near that number or quantity or time etc.

**thereafter** *adverb* after that.

**thereby** *adverb* by that means. □ **thereby hangs a tale** there is much that could be told about that.

**therefore** *adverb* for that reason.

**therein** *adverb* (*formal*) in that place; in that respect.

**thereof** *adverb* (*formal*) of that, of it.

**thereto** *adverb* (*formal*) to that, to it.

**thereupon** *adverb* in consequence of that; immediately after that.

**therm** *noun* a unit of heat, used especially in measuring a gas supply (= 100,000 thermal units).

**thermal** *adjective* **1** of heat; using or operated by heat. **2** warm or hot; *thermal springs.* ● *noun* a rising current of hot air. □ **thermal unit** a unit for measuring heat.

**thermionic valve** (thermi-on-ik) a vacuum tube in which a flow of electrons is emitted by heated electrodes, used in radio etc.

**thermocouple** *noun* a device for measuring temperatures by means of the thermoelectric voltage developing between two pieces of wire of different metals joined to each other at each end.

**thermodynamics** *noun* a branch of physics dealing with the relation between heat and other forms of energy. □ **thermodynamic** *adjective*, **thermodynamically** *adverb*

**thermoelectric** *adjective* producing electricity by difference of temperature.

**thermometer** *noun* an instrument for measuring temperature, especially a graduated glass tube containing mercury or alcohol which expands when heated.

**thermonuclear** *adjective* **1** of nuclear reactions that occur only at very high temperatures. **2** (of weapons) using such reactions.

**thermoplastic** *adjective* becoming soft and plastic when heated and hardening when cooled. ● *noun* a thermoplastic substance.

**Thermos** *noun* (in full **Thermos flask**) (*trade mark*) a vacuum flask.

**thermosetting** *adjective* (of plastics) setting permanently when heated.

**thermosphere** *noun* the region of the atmosphere beyond the mesosphere.

**thermostat** *noun* a device that automatically regulates temperature by cutting off and restoring the supply of heat to a piece of equipment or a room etc. □ **thermostatic** *adjective*, **thermostatically** *adverb*

**thesaurus** (thi-sor-ŭs) *noun* (plural **thesauri**, *pronounced* thi-sor-I, or **thesauruses**) a book that lists words in groups of synonyms and related concepts.

**these** *see* THIS.

**Theseus** (th'ee-si-ŭs) (*Gk. legend*) the national hero of Athens, whose exploits include the slaying of the Minotaur in Crete.

**thesis** (th'ee-sis) *noun* (plural **theses**, *pronounced* -seez) **1** a statement or theory put forward and supported by arguments. **2** a lengthy written essay submitted by a candidate for a university degree.

**Thespian** (thess-pi-ăn) *adjective* of drama or the theatre. ● *noun* an actor or actress. (¶ Named after Thespis, Greek tragic dramatist of the 6th century BC.)

**Thessalonian** (thess-ă-loh-niăn) *adjective* of ancient Thessalonia (modern Salonica), a city in NE Greece. ● *noun* a native of Thessalonia. □ **Epistle to the Thessalonians** either of two books of the New Testament, letters of St Paul to the Church at Thessalonia.

**Thessaly** (thess-ă-li) a district of NE Greece. □ **Thessalian** (thess-ay-liăn) *adjective & noun*

**theta** (thee-tă) *noun* the eighth letter of the Greek alphabet (Θ, θ).

**they** *pronoun* **1** the people or things mentioned. **2** people in general; *they say the play is a success.* **3** those in authority; *they are increasing income tax.* **4** used informally instead of 'he or she'; *I am never angry with anyone unless they deserve it.*

**they'd** (*informal*) = they had; they would.

**they'll** (*informal*) = they will.

**they're** (*informal*) = they are.

**they've** (*informal*) = they have.

**thiamine** (thy-ă-min *or* thy-ă-meen) *noun* (also **thiamin**) vitamin B₁, important in energy production and for healthy muscles and nerves, found in unrefined cereals, yeast extract, and beans.

**thick** *adjective* **1** of great or specified distance between opposite surfaces. **2** (of a line etc.) broad not fine. **3** made of thick material; *a thick coat.* **4** crowded or numerous; dense; *a thick forest; thick fog.* **5** densely covered or filled; *her roses were thick with greenfly.* **6** (of a liquid or paste) relatively stiff in consistency, not flowing easily. **7** (of the voice) not sounding clear. **8** (of an accent) very noticeable. **9** (*informal*) stupid. **10** (*informal*) on terms of close association or friendliness; *her parents are very thick with mine.* ●*adverb* thickly; *blows came thick and fast.* ●*noun* the busiest part of a crowd, fight, or activity; *in the thick of it.* □ **a bit thick** (*slang*) unreasonable, unfair. **thick ear** (*slang*) an ear that is swollen as the result of a blow. **thick head** a feeling of muzziness. **thick-skinned** *adjective* not sensitive to criticism or snubs. **through thick and thin** in spite of all difficulties. □ **thickish** *adjective*, **thickly** *adverb*

**thicken** *verb* **1** make or become thicker or of a stiffer consistency. **2** become more complicated; *the plot thickens.* □ **thickener** *noun*

**thicket** *noun* a number of shrubs and small trees etc. growing close together.

**thickhead** *noun* (*informal*) a stupid person. □ **thickheaded** *adjective*

**thickness** *noun* **1** the quality of being thick; the extent to which something is thick. **2** a layer; *use three thicknesses of cardboard.* **3** the part between opposite surfaces; *steps cut in the thickness of the wall.*

**thickset** *adjective* **1** with parts set or growing close together; *a thickset hedge.* **2** having a stocky or burly body.

**thief** *noun* (*plural* **thieves**) one who steals, especially secretly. □ **thievish** *adjective*, **thievery** *noun*

**thieve** *verb* be a thief; steal.

**thigh** *noun* the part of the human leg between hip and knee; the corresponding part in other animals. □ **thigh-bone** *noun* = FEMUR.

**thimble** *noun* a small metal or plastic cap worn on the end of the finger to protect it and push the needle in sewing.

**thimbleful** *noun* (*plural* **thimblefuls**) a very small quantity of liquid to drink.

**Thimphu** (tim-poo) the capital of Bhutan.

**thin** *adjective* (**thinner**, **thinnest**) **1** of small thickness or diameter. **2** (of a line etc.) narrow, not broad. **3** made of thin material; *a thin dress.* **4** lean, not plump. **5** not dense; not plentiful. **6** having units that are not crowded or numerous. **7** (of a liquid or paste) flowing easily, not thick. **8** lacking strength or substance or an important ingredient, feeble; *a thin excuse.* ●*adverb* thinly; *cut the bread thin.* ●*verb* (**thinned**, **thinning**) make or become thinner. □ **thin end of the wedge** a change that will open the way to further similar ones. **thin on top** balding. **thin out** make or become fewer or less crowded; *thin out seedlings.* □ **thinly** *adverb*, **thinness** *noun*

**thine** *possessive pronoun* (*old use*) of or belonging to thee; the thing(s) belonging to thee. ●*adjective* (before a vowel) = THY; *thine eyes.*

**thing** *noun* **1** whatever is or may be an object of perception or knowledge or thought. **2** an unnamed object or item; *there are 6 things on my list.* **3** an inanimate object as distinct from a living creature. **4** (in pity or contempt) a creature; *poor thing!* **5** an act, fact, idea, or task etc.; *a difficult thing to do.* **6** (**the thing**) what is conventionally proper or is fashionable; what is important or suitable; *the latest thing in computers; just the thing.* **7** (**things**) personal belongings, clothing; *pack your things.* **8** (**things**) implements or utensils; *my painting things.* **9** (**things**) circumstances or conditions; *things began to improve.* □ **do one's own thing** (*informal*) follow one's own interests or urges. **have a thing about** (*informal*) have an obsession or prejudice about. **make a thing of it** get excited about it; insist that it is important.

**thingummy** *noun* (also **thingumabob**, **thingumajig**) (*informal*) a person or thing whose name one has forgotten or does not know.

**thingy** *noun* (*informal*) a thing.

**think** *verb* (**thought**, **thinking**) **1** exercise the mind in an active way, form connected ideas. **2** have as an idea or opinion; *we think we shall win.* **3** form as an intention or plan; *can't think what to do next; she's thinking of emigrating.* **4** take into consideration; *think how nice it would be.* **5** call to mind, remember; *can't think where I put it.* **6** be of the opinion, judge; *it is thought to be a fake.* ●*noun* (*informal*) an act of thinking; *must have a think about that.* □ **put on one's thinking-cap** (*informal*) try to find a solution to a problem by thought. **think better of it** change one's mind after reconsideration. **think nothing of** consider unremarkable. **think-tank** *noun* (*informal*) a group of experts providing advice and ideas, especially on national and commercial problems. **think twice** consider very carefully before doing something. **think up** (*informal*) invent or produce by thought.

**thinker** *noun* a person who thinks deeply or in a specified way; *an original thinker.*

**thinking** *adjective* using thought or rational judgement about things; *all thinking people.*

**thinner** *noun* a substance for thinning paint.

**thinnish** *adjective* rather thin.

**third** *adjective* next after second. ●*noun* **1** something that is third. **2** third-class honours in a university degree. **3** third gear. **4** one of three equal parts of a thing. □ **third degree** long and severe questioning by police to get information or a confession. **third-degree burn** a burn of the most severe kind, affecting lower layers of tissue. **third man** (in cricket) a fielder positioned near the boundary behind the slips. **third party** another person etc. besides the two principal ones involved. **third-party insurance** that in which the insurer gives protection to the insured against liability for damage or injury to any other person. **third person** see PERSON. **third-rate** adjective very inferior in quality. **Third Reich** the Nazi regime in Germany, 1933–45. **Third World** the developing countries of Asia, Africa, and Latin America. □ **thirdly** adverb

**thirst** noun **1** the feeling caused by a desire or need to drink. **2** a strong desire; *a thirst for adventure.* ● verb feel a thirst.

**thirsty** adjective (**thirstier, thirstiest**) **1** feeling thirst. **2** (of land) in need of water. **3** (informal) causing thirst; *thirsty work.* □ **thirstily** adverb

**thirteen** adjective & noun one more than twelve (13, XIII). □ **thirteenth** adjective & noun

**thirty** adjective & noun **1** three times ten (30, XXX). **2** (**thirties**) the numbers or years or degrees of temperature from 30 to 39. □ **Thirty-nine Articles** the set of statements adopted by the Church of England in 1571 as a definition of the doctrines it upheld. **Thirty Years War** the religious wars of 1618–48, fought chiefly on German soil. □ **thirtieth** adjective & noun

**this** adjective & pronoun (plural **these**) the person or thing close at hand or touched, or just mentioned or about to be mentioned; the nearer or more obvious one of two. ● adverb to such an extent; *we're surprised he got this far.* □ **this and that** various things.

**thistle** noun a prickly plant with purple, white, or yellow flowers.

**thistledown** noun the very light fluff on thistle seeds by which they are carried by the wind.

**thistly** adjective overgrown with thistles.

**thither** adverb (old use) to or towards that place.

**thole** noun (in full **thole-pin**) a peg set in the gunwale of a boat to serve as a rowlock.

**Thomas**[1], Dylan Marlais (1914–53), Welsh-born poet, author of the radio drama *Under Milk Wood.*

**Thomas**[2], St (1st century AD), an Apostle, who refused to believe that Christ had risen from the dead unless he could see and touch his wounds. Feast day, 21 December. □ **doubting Thomas** a sceptical person.

**Thomas Aquinas** see AQUINAS.

**Thompson**, Daley (born 1958), English athlete, Olympic decathlon champion in 1980 and 1984.

**Thomson**, Sir John Joseph (1856–1940), English physicist, who discovered the electron.

**thong** noun a narrow strip of hide or leather used as a fastening or lash etc.

**Thor** (*Scand. myth.*) the god of thunder and the weather. Thursday is named after him.

**thorax** (**thor-aks**) noun (plural **thoraces**, pronounced **thor-ă-seez**, or **thoraxes**) the part of the body between the head or neck and the abdomen. □ **thoracic** (thor-**ass**-ik) adjective

**thorium** (**thor-iŭm**) noun a radioactive metallic element (symbol Th), with a variety of industrial uses and important also as a nuclear fuel.

**thorn** noun **1** a sharp pointed projection on a plant. **2** a thorny tree or shrub. □ **a thorn in one's flesh** (or **side**) a constant source of annoyance. □ **thornless** adjective

**Thorndike**, Dame (Agnes) Sibyl (1882–1976), English actress.

**thornproof** adjective unable to be penetrated by thorns.

**thorny** adjective (**thornier, thorniest**) **1** having many thorns. **2** like a thorn. **3** troublesome, difficult; *a thorny problem.*

**thorough** adjective complete in every way; doing things or done with great attention to detail. □ **thoroughly** adverb, **thoroughness** noun

**thoroughbred** adjective (especially of a horse) bred of pure or pedigree stock. ● noun a thoroughbred animal.

**thoroughfare** noun a public way open at both ends. □ **no thoroughfare** (as a notice) this road is private or is obstructed.

**thoroughgoing** adjective thorough.

**those** see THAT.

**thou**[1] pronoun (old use) (in speaking to one person) you.

**thou**[2] (pronounced thow) noun (plural **thou** or **thous**) (informal) **1** thousand. **2** one thousandth.

**though** conjunction in spite of the fact that, even supposing; *it's true, though hard to believe.* ● adverb (informal) however; *she's right, though.*

**thought** see THINK. ● noun **1** the process or power of thinking. **2** a way of thinking that is characteristic of a particular class, nation, or period; *in modern thought.* **3** meditation; consideration; *deep in thought.* **4** an idea or chain of reasoning produced by thinking. **5** an intention; *we had no thought of giving offence.*

**thoughtful** adjective **1** thinking deeply; often absorbed in thought. **2** (of a book, writer, or remark etc.) showing signs of careful thought. **3** showing thought for the needs of others, considerate. □ **thoughtfully** adverb, **thoughtfulness** noun

**thoughtless** *adjective* **1** not alert to possible effects or consequences. **2** inconsiderate. □ **thoughtlessly** *adverb*, **thoughtlessness** *noun*

**thousand** *adjective & noun* ten hundred (1000, M); *a few thousand.* □ **thousandth** *adjective & noun*

**thousandfold** *adjective & adverb* one thousand times as much or as many.

**Thrace** an ancient country in the east of the Balkan Peninsula, west of modern Istanbul. □ **Thracian** *adjective & noun*

**thrall** (*pronounced* thrawl) □ **in thrall** in bondage; enslaved.

**thrash** *verb* **1** beat with a stick or whip. **2** defeat thoroughly in a contest. **3** thresh. **4** (foll. by *about* or *around*) make violent movements. □ **thrash out** discuss thoroughly.

**thread** *noun* **1** a thin length of any substance, especially a length of spun cotton or wool etc. **2** a continuous link or aspect of a thing; *lose the thread of an argument*; *pick up the threads of one's life.* **3** the spiral ridge of a screw. ● *verb* **1** pass a thread through the eye of (a needle). **2** pass (a strip of film etc.) through or round something into the proper position for use. **3** put (beads) on a thread. **4** cut a thread on (a screw). □ **thread one's way** make one's way through a crowd or streets etc.

**threadbare** *adjective* **1** (of cloth) with the nap worn off and threads visible. **2** (of a person) wearing threadbare or shabby clothes.

**threadworm** *noun* a small threadlike worm, especially one sometimes found in the rectum of children.

**threat** *noun* **1** an expression of one's intention to punish or harm a person or thing. **2** an indication of something undesirable; *there's a threat of rain.* **3** a person or thing regarded as liable to bring danger or catastrophe; *machinery was seen as a threat to people's jobs.*

**threaten** *verb* **1** make a threat or threats against (a person etc.); try to influence by threats. **2** be a warning of; *the clouds threatened rain.* **3** (foll. by *to*) seem likely to be or do something undesirable; *the scheme threatens to be expensive.* **4** be a threat to; *the dangers that threaten us.*

**three** *adjective & noun* one more than two (3, III). □ **three-cornered** *adjective* triangular; (of a contest) between three parties. **three-dimensional** *adjective* having three dimensions (length, breadth, depth). **three-legged race** a race between pairs of runners with the right leg of one tied to the left leg of the other. **three-line whip** a written notice to MPs from their leader insisting that they attend a particular de-

bate and vote as stated. **three-piece suite** a matching suite consisting of a settee and two easy chairs. **three-ply** *adjective* made of three strands or layers. **three-point turn** a method of turning a vehicle in a narrow space by driving forwards, backwards, and forwards. **three-quarter** (*adjective*) consisting of three-quarters of a whole; (*noun*) a player with a position just behind the half-backs in Rugby football. **three-quarters** *noun* three parts out of four. **the three Rs** reading, writing, and arithmetic, as the basis of elementary education.

**threefold** *adjective & adverb* **1** three times as much or as many. **2** consisting of three parts.

**threepence** (threp-ĕns or thrup-ĕns) *noun* the sum of three pence. □ **threepenny** *adjective*

**threescore** *noun* (*old use*) sixty.

**threesome** *noun* three people together, a trio.

**threnody** (**thren**-ŏdi) *noun* a song of lamentation, especially on a person's death.

**thresh** *verb* **1** beat out or separate (grain) from husks of corn. **2** make violent movements; *threshing about.*

**threshold** *noun* **1** a piece of wood or stone forming the bottom of a doorway. **2** the entrance of a house etc. **3** the point of entry or beginning of something; *on the threshold of a new era.* **4** the lowest limit at which a stimulus becomes perceptible. **5** the highest limit at which pain etc. is bearable.

**threw** *see* THROW.

**thrice** *adverb* (*old use*) three times.

**thrift** *noun* **1** economical management of money or resources. **2** the sea pink.

**thriftless** *adjective* not thrifty, wasteful.

**thrifty** *adjective* (**thriftier, thriftiest**) practising thrift, economical. □ **thriftily** *adverb*

**thrill** *noun* a nervous tremor caused by emotion or sensation; a wave of feeling or excitement. ● *verb* feel or cause to feel a thrill.

**thriller** *noun* an exciting story, play, or film, especially one involving crime.

**thrips** *noun* (*plural* **thrips**) a very small insect that is harmful to plants.

**thrive** *verb* (**throve** *or* **thrived, thrived** *or* **thriven, thriving**) **1** grow or develop well and vigorously. **2** prosper, be successful; *a thriving industry.*

**throat** *noun* **1** the front of the neck. **2** the passage in the neck through which food passes to the oesophagus and air passes to the lungs. **3** a narrow passage or funnel.

**throaty** *adjective* **1** uttered deep in the throat. **2** hoarse. □ **throatily** *adverb*, **throatiness** *noun*

**throb** *verb* (**throbbed, throbbing**) **1** (of the heart or pulse etc.) beat with more than usual force or rapidity. **2** vibrate or sound with a persistent rhythm; hurt in this way; *a throbbing wound.* ●*noun* throbbing.

**throes** *plural noun* severe pangs of pain. □ **in the throes of** struggling with the task of; *in the throes of spring-cleaning.*

**thrombosis** (throm-**boh**-sis) *noun* (*plural* **thromboses**) formation of a clot of blood in a blood vessel or organ of the body.

**throne** *noun* **1** the special ceremonial chair or seat used by a king, queen, or bishop etc. **2** sovereign power; *came to the throne.* ●*verb* enthrone.

**throng** *noun* a crowded mass of people. ●*verb* **1** come or go or press in a throng. **2** fill (a place) with a throng.

**throstle** *noun* a song thrush.

**throttle** *noun* a valve controlling the flow of fuel or steam etc. to an engine; the lever or pedal operating this. ●*verb* strangle. □ **throttle back** *or* **down** obstruct the flow of fuel or steam and reduce the speed of (an engine).

**through** *preposition* **1** from end to end or side to side of; entering at one side and coming out at the other. **2** between or among; *scuffling through fallen leaves.* **3** from beginning to end of; so as to have finished or completed. **4** (*Amer.*) up to and including; *Friday through Tuesday.* **5** by reason of; by the means or fault of; *lost it through carelessness.* ●*adverb* **1** through something. **2** with a connection made to a desired telephone etc.; *you're through.* **3** finished; *wait till I'm through with these papers.* **4** having no further dealings; *I'm through with that bastard!* ●*adjective* going through something; (of traffic) passing through a place without stopping; (of travel or passengers etc.) going to the end of a journey without a change of line or vehicle etc. □ **through and through** through again and again; thoroughly, completely.

**throughout** *preposition & adverb* right through, from beginning to end of (a place, course, or period).

**throughput** *noun* the amount of material processed.

**throve** *see* THRIVE.

**throw** *verb* (**threw, thrown, throwing**) **1** send with some force through the air or in a certain direction. **2** hurl to the ground; *the horse threw its rider.* **3** (*informal*) disconcert; *the question threw me.* **4** put (clothes etc.) on or off hastily or casually. **5** cause (dice) to fall to the table; obtain (a number) by this. **6** shape (rounded pottery) on a potter's wheel. **7** turn, direct, or move (a part of the body) quickly; *threw his head back.* **8** cause to be in a certain state; *they were thrown out of work; thrown into confusion.* **9** move (a switch or lever) so as to

operate it. **10** have (a fit or tantrum). **11** give (a party). ●*noun* **1** the act of throwing. **2** the distance something is or may be thrown. □ **throw away** part with as useless or unwanted; fail to make use of; *throw away an opportunity.* **throw-away** *adjective* to be thrown away after one use. **throw in 1** include (a thing) without additional charge. **2** put in (a remark) casually or as an addition. **throw-in** *noun* the throwing in of a ball at football after it has gone out of play over the touchline. **throw in the towel** (*or* **sponge**) admit defeat or failure. (¶ From the practice of admitting defeat in a boxing match by throwing into the air the sponge used between rounds.) **throw off** manage to get rid of or become free from; *throw off a cold.* **throw out 1** throw away. **2** put out suddenly or forcibly; expel (a trouble-maker etc.). **3** reject (a proposed plan etc.). **throw over** desert or abandon. **throw the book at** (*informal*) make all possible charges against (a person). **throw up 1** bring to notice; *his researches threw up some interesting facts.* **2** give up; *throw up one's job.* **3** vomit.

**throwback** *noun* an animal etc. showing characteristics of an ancestor that is earlier than its parents.

**thru** (especially *Amer.*) = THROUGH.

**thrum**[1] *verb* (**thrummed, thrumming**) strum; sound monotonously. ●*noun* a thrumming sound.

**thrum**[2] *noun* the uneven end of a warp-thread left when the finished web is cut away.

**thrush**[1] *noun* any of several songbirds, especially one with a brownish back and speckled breast.

**thrush**[2] *noun* **1** an infection in which a minute fungus produces white patches in the mouth and throat, especially in children. **2** a similar disease of the vagina.

**thrust** *verb* (**thrust, thrusting**) **1** push forcibly. **2** make a forward stroke with a sword etc. **3** put forcibly into a position or condition, force the acceptance of; *some have greatness thrust upon them.* ●*noun* **1** a thrusting movement or force. **2** a hostile remark aimed at a person.

**thud** *noun* a low dull sound like that of a blow or something that does not resound. ●*verb* (**thudded, thudding**) make a thud; fall with a thud.

**thug** *noun* a vicious or brutal ruffian. □ **thuggery** *noun*

**thulium** (**thew**-li-ŭm) *noun* a metallic element (symbol Tm).

**thumb** *noun* **1** the short thick finger set apart from the other four. **2** the part of a glove covering this. ●*verb* wear or soil, or turn pages etc., with the thumbs; *a well-thumbed* *book*. □ **be all thumbs** be very clumsy at handling things. **thumb a lift** obtain a lift by signalling with one's thumb, hitchhike. **thumb index** a set of notches on the edges of a book's leaves, marked with letters etc. to enable the user to open the book directly at a particular section. **thumb one's nose** cock a snook (*see* SNOOK). **thumbs down** an indication of rejection. **thumbs up** an indication of satisfaction or approval. **under a person's thumb** completely under his or her influence.

**thumbnail** *noun* **1** the nail of the thumb. **2** (used as *adjective*) concise, brief; *a thumbnail sketch*.

**thumbscrew** *noun* a former instrument of torture for squeezing the thumb.

**thump** *verb* beat, strike, or knock heavily (especially with the fist); thud. ●*noun* a heavy blow; a dull sound made by this.

**thumping** *adjective* (*informal*) very big; *a thumping lie; a thumping great bill*.

**thunder** *noun* **1** the loud noise accompanying lightning. **2** any similar noise; *thunders of applause*. ●*verb* **1** sound with thunder; *it thundered*. **2** make a noise like thunder, sound loudly; *the train thundered past*. **3** utter loudly; make a forceful attack in words; *reformers thundered against gambling*. □ **steal a person's thunder** use his or her ideas or words etc. before he or she is able to do so. (¶ From the remark of a dramatist (*c.*1710) when the stage thunder intended for his play was taken and used for another.)

**thunderbolt** *noun* **1** a flash of lightning accompanying thunder. **2** an imaginary destructive missile thought of as sent to earth with a lightning flash. **3** a very startling event or statement.

**thunderclap** *noun* a clap of thunder.

**thundercloud** *noun* a cloud charged with electricity and producing thunder and lightning.

**thundering** *adjective* (*informal*) very big; *a thundering nuisance*.

**thunderous** *adjective* like thunder.

**thunderstorm** *noun* a storm accompanied by thunder.

**thunderstruck** *adjective* amazed.

**Thur.** *abbreviation* (also **Thurs.**) Thursday.

**Thurber**, James (Grove) (1894–1961), American humorist, writer, and cartoonist.

**thurible** (**thewr**-i-bŭl) *noun* a censer.

**Thuringia** (thewr-**in**-jiă) a region of central Germany.

**Thursday** the day of the week following Wednesday.

**thus** *adverb* (*formal*) **1** in this way, like this; *hold the wheel thus*. **2** as a result of this; *he was the eldest son and thus heir to the title*. **3** to this extent; *thus far*.

**thwack** *verb* strike with a heavy blow. ●*noun* a heavy blow; the sound of this.

**thwart** *verb* prevent (a person) from doing what he or she intends; prevent (a plan etc.) from being accomplished. ●*noun* a rower's bench across a boat.

**thy** *adjective* (*old use*) of or belonging to thee.

**thyme** (*pronounced as* time) *noun* any of several herbs with fragrant leaves.

**thymol** *noun* a substance obtained from oil of thyme, used as an antiseptic.

**thymus** *noun* (*plural* **thymi**) a gland near the base of the neck.

**thyristor** (th'y-**rist**-er) *noun* a switch in the form of a semiconductor device in which a small electric current is used to start the flow of a large current.

**thyroid** *noun* (in full **thyroid gland**) a large ductless gland at the front of the neck, secreting a hormone which regulates the body's growth and development. □ **thyroid cartilage** the large cartilage of the larynx forming the Adam's apple.

**thyself** *pronoun* corresponding to *thee* and *thou*, used in the same ways as **himself** and **herself**.

**Ti** *symbol* titanium.

**ti** alternative spelling of TE.

**tiara** (ti-**ar**-ă) *noun* **1** a woman's jewelled ornamental crescent-shaped headdress. **2** the pope's diadem, pointed at the top and surrounded by three crowns.

**Tiber** (**ty**-ber) a river of central Italy, on which Rome stands, flowing west.

**Tiberias, Lake** *see* GALILEE.

**Tiberius** (ty-**beer**-iŭs) Roman emperor AD 14–37.

**Tibet** (tib-**et**) a former country north of India; a self-governing region of China since 1965.

**Tibetan** *noun* **1** a native of Tibet. **2** the language of Tibet. ●*adjective* of Tibet or its people or language.

**tibia** *noun* (*plural* **tibiae**) the inner of the two bones extending from the knee to the ankle; the shin-bone. □ **tibial** *adjective*

**tic** *noun* an involuntary spasmodic twitching of the muscles, especially of the face.

**tick**¹ *noun* **1** a regularly repeated clicking sound, especially that of a watch or clock. **2** (*informal*) a moment. **3** a mark (often √) placed against an item in a list etc. to show that it has been checked or is correct. ●*verb* **1** (of a clock etc.) make a series of ticks. **2** put a tick against (an item). □ **tick off** (*informal*) reprimand. **tick over 1** (of an engine) idle. **2** (of activities) continue in a routine way. **what makes a person tick** (*informal*) his or her basic motivation.

**tick**² *noun* any of several blood-sucking mites or parasitic insects.

**tick**³ *noun* the case of a mattress or pillow, holding the filling.

**tick**⁴ *noun* (*informal*) credit; *buying on tick*.

**ticker** *noun* (*informal*) **1** a watch. **2** a teleprinter. **3** the heart. □ **ticker-tape** *noun* paper tape from a teleprinter etc.; this or similar material thrown in long strips from windows to greet a celebrity.

**ticket** *noun* **1** a written or printed piece of card or paper that entitles the holder to a certain right (e.g. to travel by train or bus etc. or to a seat in a cinema) or serves as a receipt. **2** a certificate of qualification as a ship's master or pilot etc. **3** a label attached to a thing and giving its price or other particulars. **4** an official notification of a traffic offence; *parking ticket*. **5** (*Amer.*) a list of the candidates put forward by one party in an election. **6** (**the ticket**) (*informal*) the correct or desirable thing. ● *verb* (**ticketed, ticketing**) put a ticket on (an article for sale etc.).

**ticking** *noun* strong fabric (often striped) used for covering mattresses, pillows, etc.

**tickle** *verb* **1** touch or stroke lightly so as to cause a slight tingling sensation, usually with involuntary movement and laughter. **2** feel this sensation; *my foot tickles*. **3** amuse, please (a person's vanity or sense of humour etc.). ● *noun* the act or sensation of tickling. □ **tickled pink** *or* **to death** (*informal*) extremely amused or pleased.

**ticklish** *adjective* **1** sensitive to tickling. **2** (of a problem or person) requiring careful handling. □ **ticklishness** *noun*

**tick-tack** *noun* a kind of semaphore signalling used by bookmakers on a racecourse.

**tidal** *adjective* of or affected by a tide or tides. □ **tidal wave 1** a great ocean wave, e.g. one caused by an earthquake. **2** a great wave of enthusiasm or indignation etc. □ **tidally** *adverb*

**tidbit** *noun* (*Amer.*) a titbit.

**tiddler** *noun* (*informal*) **1** a stickleback or other small fish that children try to catch. **2** an unusually small thing.

**tiddly** *adjective* (*informal*) **1** very small. **2** slightly drunk. □ **tiddly-wink** *noun* one of the small counters flicked into a cup in the game of **tiddly-winks**.

**tide** *noun* **1** the regular rise and fall in the level of the sea, caused by the attraction of the moon and the sun. **2** water as moved by this. **3** a trend of opinion, fortune, or events; *the rising tide of discontent*. **4** (*old use*) a season; *yule-tide*. ● *verb* float with the tide. □ **tide over** help (a person) through a difficult period by providing what is needed.

**tidemark** *noun* **1** a mark made by the tide at high water. **2** a line left around a bath by dirty water; a line between washed and unwashed parts of a person's body.

**tideway** *noun* the tidal part of a river.

**tidings** *plural noun* (*literary*) news.

**tidy** *adjective* (**tidier, tidiest**) **1** neat and orderly in arrangement or in one's ways. **2** (*informal*) fairly large, considerable; *left a tidy fortune when he died*. ● *noun* a receptacle for odds and ends. ● *verb* (**tidied, tidying**) make tidy. □ **tidily** *adverb*, **tidiness** *noun*

**tie** *verb* (**tied, tying**) **1** attach, fasten, or bind with a cord or something similar. **2** arrange (string or ribbon or a necktie etc.) to form a knot or bow; form (a knot or bow) in this way. **3** unite (notes in music) with a tie. **4** achieve the same score as another competitor; *they tied for second place*. **5** restrict or limit to certain conditions or to an occupation or place etc. ● *noun* **1** a cord etc. used for fastening or by which something is tied. **2** a strip of material worn round the neck, passing under the collar and knotted at the front. **3** something that unites things or people, a bond. **4** something that restricts a person's freedom of action. **5** a curved line (in a musical score) over two notes of the same pitch, indicating that the second is not sounded separately. **6** equality of score between two or more competitors. **7** a sports match between two of a set of competing teams or players. □ **tie-beam** *noun* a horizontal beam connecting rafters. **tie-break** *noun* (also **tie-breaker**) a means of deciding the winner when competitors have tied. **tie-dyeing** *noun* a method of producing dyed patterns by tying parts of a fabric so that they are protected from the dye. **tie in** link or (of information or facts) agree or be connected with something else. **tie-pin** *noun* an ornamental pin for holding a tie in place. **tie up 1** fasten with a cord etc. **2** invest or reserve (capital etc.) so that it is not readily available for use; make restrictive conditions about (a bequest etc.). **3** occupy (a person) so that he or she has no time for other things. **tie-up** *noun* a connection, a link.

**tied** *see* TIE. ● *adjective* **1** (of a pub) bound to supply a particular brewer's beer. **2** (of a house) for occupation only by a person who works for its owner.

**tier** (*pronounced* teer) *noun* any of a series of rows, ranks, or units of a structure placed one above the other.

**tiercel** *noun* = TERCEL.

**tiered** *adjective* (*pronounced* teerd) arranged in tiers.

**Tierra del Fuego** (ti-e-ră del **fway**-goh) an archipelago off the southern tip of South America, of which the west and south belong to Chile, the east to Argentina.

**tiff** *noun* a petty quarrel.

**tiffin** *noun* (in India) a light midday meal.

**tiger** *noun* **1** a large Asian animal of the cat family, with yellowish and black stripes. **2** (**Tigers**) a Tamil military organization in Sri Lanka seeking independence for their community. □ **tiger-cat** *noun* **1** any of several animals resembling the tiger (e.g. the ocelot). **2** the largest of the Australian marsupial cats. **tiger lily** a tall garden lily with dark-spotted orange flowers. **tiger moth** a moth with wings that are streaked like a tiger's skin.

**tight** *adjective* **1** fixed or fastened or drawn together firmly and hard to move or undo. **2** fitting closely; made so that a specified thing cannot penetrate; *a tight joint; watertight*. **3** with things or people arranged closely together; *a tight little group*. **4** tense, stretched so as to leave no slack. **5** (*informal*) drunk. **6** with no time, resources, etc. to spare; *a tight schedule*. **7** (of money or materials) not easily obtainable; (of the money market) in which money and credit are severely restricted; (of a programme, regulation, etc.) strictly enforced, stringent. **8** stingy; *tight with his money*. ● *adverb* tightly; *hold tight*. □ **in a tight corner** or **spot** in a difficult situation. **tight-fisted** *adjective* stingy. **tight-lipped** *adjective* keeping the lips compressed firmly together to restrain one's emotion or comments; grim-looking. □ **tightly** *adverb*, **tightness** *noun*

**tighten** *verb* make or become tighter. □ **tighten one's belt** live more frugally.

**tightrope** *noun* a rope stretched tightly high above the ground, on which acrobats perform.

**tights** *plural noun* a thin close-fitting garment covering the feet, legs, and lower part of the body, worn by women and also dancers, acrobats, etc.

**tigress** *noun* a female tiger.

**Tigris** (**ty**-gris) a river of SW Asia, flowing from Turkey through Iraq east of the Euphrates, which it joins.

**tike** alternative spelling of TYKE.

**tilbury** *noun* a light open two-wheeled carriage fashionable in the first half of the 19th century.

**tilde** (**til**-dĕ) *noun* a mark (˜) put over a letter, e.g. over a spanish *n* when pronounced *ny* as in *señor*.

**tile** *noun* **1** a thin slab of baked clay or other material used in rows for covering roofs, walls, or floors. **2** any of the small flat pieces used in mah-jong. ● *verb* cover with tiles. □ **on the tiles** (*informal*) out having a good time, especially drinking a lot.

**tiling** *noun* a surface made of tiles.

**till¹** *verb* prepare and use (land) for growing crops.

**till²** *preposition & conjunction* = until.

■**Usage** See the note on **until**.

**till³** *noun* a drawer for holding money in a shop, bank, etc., usually with a device for recording transactions.

**tillage** *noun* **1** the tilling of land. **2** tilled land.

**tiller** *noun* a horizontal bar by which the rudder of a small boat is turned in steering.

**tilt** *verb* **1** move or cause to move into a sloping position. **2** run or thrust with a lance in jousting. ● *noun* tilting; a sloping position. □ **at full tilt** at full speed; with full force. **tilt at windmills** battle with enemies who are only imaginary. (¶ From the story of Don Quixote who attacked some windmills, thinking they were giants.)

**tilth** *noun* **1** tillage, cultivation. **2** tilled soil.

**timber** *noun* **1** wood prepared for use in building or carpentry. **2** trees suitable for this. **3** a piece of wood or a wooden beam used in constructing a house or ship.

**timbered** *adjective* **1** (of a building) constructed of timber or with a timber framework. **2** (of land) wooded.

**timberline** *noun* the level of land above which no trees grow.

**timbre** (*pronounced* tambr) *noun* the characteristic quality of the sound produced by a particular voice or instrument.

**timbrel** *noun* (*old use*) a tambourine.

**Timbuktu** **1** a town of Mali in Africa. **2** a very remote place.

**time** *noun* **1** all the years of the past, present, and future. **2** the passing of these taken as a whole; *time will show who is right*. **3** a portion of time associated with certain events, conditions, or experiences; *in Tudor times; in times of hardship; have a good time*. **4** a portion of time between two points; the point or period allotted, available, or suitable for something; *the time it takes to do this; now is the time to buy; lunch time*. **5** the point of time when something must occur or end. **6** an occasion or instance; *the first time we saw him; I told you three times*. **7** a point of time stated in hours and minutes of the day; *the time is exactly two o'clock*. **8** any of the standard systems by which time is reckoned; *Greenwich Mean Time*. **9** measured time spent in work etc.; the rate paid for this period; *on short time; paid time and a half*. **10** tempo in music, rhythm depending on the number and accentuation of beats in a bar. **11** (**times**) expressing multiplication; *five times six is thirty; three times as old*. ● *verb* **1** choose the time or moment for, arrange the time of. **2** measure the time taken by (a race or runner or a process etc.). **3** (**times**) (*informal*) multiply; *what do you get if you times 3 by 2?* □ **at the same time** in spite of this, however. **at times** sometimes. **do time** (*informal*) serve a prison sentence. **for the time being** until some other arrangement is made. **from time to time** at intervals. **half the time** (*informal*) as often as not. **have no time for** be unable or unwilling to spend time on; despise. **in no time** in an instant, very rapidly. **in one's own time 1** outside working hours. **2** when one chooses to do something, at one's own rate. **in time 1** not late. **2** eventually, sooner or later. **on time** punctually. **time after time** on many occasions; in many instances. **time and again** *or* **time and time again** time after time. **time-and-motion** *adjective* concerned with measuring the efficiency of industrial or other operations. **time bomb** a bomb that can be set to explode after a certain interval. **time capsule** a container holding objects typical of the present time, buried for future discovery. **time clock** a clock with a device for recording workers' hours of work. **time-consuming** *adjective* occupying much time. **time exposure** a photographic exposure in which the shutter is left open for more than a second or two and not operated at an automatically-controlled speed. **time-honoured** *adjective* honoured because of long tradition or custom. **time-lag** *noun* an interval of time between two connected events. **time limit** a limit of time within which something must be done. **the time of one's life** a period of exceptional enjoyment. **time-served** *adjective* having completed a period of training. **time-server** *noun* (*scornful*) a person who changes his or her opinion to suit the current fashion, circumstances, etc. **time-sharing** *noun* **1** operation of a computer by two or more users simultaneously. **2** (also **time-share**) the joint ownership and right to use a holiday home for a limited time each year. **time sheet** a record of hours worked. **time signal** an audible indication of the exact time of day. **time signature** an indication of the speed and rhythm of a piece of music following the clef. **time switch** a switch that can be set to act automatically at a certain time. **time zone** a region (between two lines of longitude) where a common standard time is used.

**timekeeper** *noun* **1** a person who times something; one who records workers' hours of work. **2** a person in respect of punctuality; a watch or clock in respect of its accuracy of operation; *a good timekeeper*.

**timeless** *adjective* **1** not to be thought of as having duration. **2** not affected by the passage of time.

**timely** *adjective* occurring at just the right time; *a timely warning.* □ **timeliness** *noun*

**timepiece** *noun* a clock or watch.

**timer** *noun* a person who times something; a timing device.

**timetable** *noun* a list showing the time at which certain events will take place.

**timid** *adjective* easily alarmed, not bold, shy. □ **timidly** *adverb*, **timidity** (tim-id-iti) *noun*

**timing** *noun* **1** the way something is timed. **2** the control of the opening and closing of valves in an internal-combustion engine.

**Timor** (tee-mor) an Indonesian island in the southern Malay Archipelago. □ **Timor Sea** the part of the Indian Ocean between Timor and NW Australia.

**timorous** (tim-er-ŭs) *adjective* timid. □ **timorously** *adverb*, **timorousness** *noun*

**Timothy**, St (1st century AD), a convert and colleague of St Paul, to whom two of the epistles in the New Testament are addressed.

**timpani** (timp-ăn-ee) *plural noun* (also **tympani**) kettledrums. □ **timpanist** *noun*

**tin** *noun* **1** a chemical element (symbol Sn), a silvery-white metal. **2** iron or steel sheets coated with tin. **3** a container made of tin plate; one in which food is sealed for preservation. ●*verb* (**tinned**, **tinning**) **1** coat with tin. **2** seal in a tin for preservation. □ **tin can** a tin for preserving food. **tin foil** a thin sheet of tin, aluminium, or tin alloy, used for wrapping food. **tin god** a person who is unjustifiably given great veneration. **tin-opener** *noun* a tool for opening tins. **tin-pan alley** the world of composers and publishers of popular music. (¶ Originally the name given to a district in New York where many songwriters and music publishers were based.) **tin plate** sheet iron or steel coated thinly with tin. **tin-tack** *noun* a tin-coated iron tack. **tin whistle** = PENNY WHISTLE.

**tincture** *noun* **1** a solution consisting of a medicinal substance dissolved in alcohol; *tincture of quinine.* **2** a slight tinge or trace of some element or quality. ●*verb* tinge.

**tinder** *noun* any dry substance that catches fire easily. □ **tinder-box** *noun* a metal box formerly used in kindling a fire, containing dry material that caught fire from a spark produced by flint and steel.

**tine** *noun* any of the points or prongs of a fork, antler, or comb.

**ting** *noun* a sharp ringing sound. ●*verb* make a ting.

**tinge** (*pronounced* tinj) *verb* (**tinged**, **tingeing**) **1** colour slightly; *tinged with pink.* **2** give a slight trace of some element or quality to; *their admiration was tinged with envy.* ●*noun* a slight colouring or trace.

**tingle** *verb* have a slight pricking or stinging sensation. ●*noun* this sensation.

**tinker** noun **1** a travelling mender of pots and pans. **2** (*Scottish & Irish*) a Gypsy. **3** (*informal*) a mischievous person or animal. ●verb work at something casually, trying to repair or improve it.

**tinkle** noun a series of short light ringing sounds. ●verb make or cause to make a tinkle.

**tinnitus** (ti-**ny**-tŭs) noun a condition causing repeated ringing or other sounds in the ears.

**tinny** adjective **1** of or like tin; (of metal objects) not looking strong or solid. **2** having a metallic taste or a thin metallic sound.

**tinpot** adjective (*scornful*) worthless, inferior.

**tinsel** noun a glittering metallic substance used in strips or threads to give an inexpensive sparkling effect. □ **tinselled** adjective, **tinselly** adjective

**tint** noun **1** a variety of a particular colour. **2** a slight trace of a different colour; *red with a bluish tint.* ●verb apply or give a tint to, colour slightly.

**tintinnabulation** noun a ringing or tinkling of bells.

**Tintoretto**, Jacopo Robusti (1518–94), Venetian painter.

**tiny** adjective (**tinier**, **tiniest**) very small. □ **tinily** adverb, **tininess** noun

**tip¹** noun **1** the very end of a thing, especially of something small or tapering. **2** a small part or piece fitted to the end of something; *cigarettes with filter tips.* ●verb (**tipped**, **tipping**) provide with a tip; *filter-tipped.* □ **on the tip of one's tongue** just about to be spoken or remembered.

**tip²** verb (**tipped**, **tipping**) **1** tilt or topple; cause to do this. **2** discharge (the contents of a truck or jug etc.) by doing this. **3** strike or touch lightly. **4** name as a likely winner of a contest etc. **5** make a small present of money to (a person), especially in acknowledgement of his or her services. ●noun **1** a small money present. **2** private or special information (e.g. about horse races or the stock market) likely to profit the receiver. **3** a small but useful piece of advice. **4** a slight tilt or push. **5** a place where rubbish etc. is tipped. □ **tip off** give an advance warning or hint or inside information to (a person). **tip-off** noun advance or inside information etc. **tip a person the wink** give him or her a private signal or piece of information. **tip the balance** or **scale** be the deciding factor for or against something. **tip-up** adjective (of seats) able to be tipped up so as to allow people to pass easily, e.g. in a theatre. □ **tipper** noun

**tippet** noun a small cape or collar of fur etc. with ends hanging down in front.

**Tippett**, Sir Michael Kemp (born 1905), English composer.

**tipple** verb drink (wine or spirits etc.); be in the habit of drinking. ●noun (*informal*) alcoholic drink.

**tipstaff** noun **1** a sheriff's officer. **2** a metal-tipped staff carried as a symbol of office.

**tipster** noun a person who gives tips about horse races etc.

**tipsy** adjective slightly drunk. □ **tipsily** adverb, **tipsiness** noun

**tiptoe** verb (**tiptoed**, **tiptoeing**) walk very quietly with heels not touching the ground. □ **on tiptoe** walking or standing in this way.

**tiptop** adjective (*informal*) excellent, very best; *tiptop quality.*

**TIR** abbreviation Transport International Routier, = international road transport. (¶ French.)

**tirade** (ty-**rayd**) noun a long angry or violent piece of criticism or denunciation.

**Tiranë** (ti-**rah**-në) the capital of Albania.

**tire¹** verb **1** make or become tired. **2** (foll. by *of*) become bored with; lose interest in; *he soon tired of looking after his pets.*

**tire²** noun Amer. spelling of TYRE.

**tired** adjective **1** feeling that one would like to sleep or rest. **2** (of a joke, idea, etc.) used or suggested so often that it has become dull and uninteresting. □ **tired of** having had enough of (a thing or activity) and feeling impatient or bored. □ **tiredly** adverb, **tiredness** noun

**tireless** adjective not tiring easily, having inexhaustible energy. □ **tirelessly** adverb

**tiresome** adjective annoying.

**tiro** (**ty**-roh) noun (*plural* **tiros**) (also **tyro**) a beginner, a novice.

**Tirol** alternative spelling of TYROL.

**'tis** (*old use*) = it is.

**tissue** (**tiss**-yoo or **tish**-oo) noun **1** the substance forming an animal or plant body; a particular kind of this; *muscular tissue.* **2** tissue-paper. **3** a disposable piece of soft absorbent paper used as a handkerchief etc. **4** fine gauzy fabric. **5** something thought of as an interwoven series; *a tissue of lies.* □ **tissue-paper** noun very thin soft paper used for wrapping and packing things.

**tit** noun **1** any of several small birds, often with a dark top to the head. **2** (*informal*) a nipple or teat. **3** (*vulgar*) a woman's breast. □ **tit for tat** an equivalent given in retaliation for an injury etc.

**Titan** (**ty**-tǎn) noun **1** (*Gk. myth.*) any of the older gods who preceded the Olympians. **2** (often **titan**) a person of great size, strength, or importance.

**Titanic** (ty-**tan**-ik) a British passenger liner that struck an iceberg in the Atlantic on her maiden voyage in 1912 and sank with the loss of 1490 lives.

**titanic** (ty-**tan**-ik) *adjective* gigantic, immense.

**titanium** (ty-**tay**-nium *or* ti-) *noun* a grey metallic element (symbol Ti), used in alloys for parts of aircraft, space vehicles, etc.

**titbit** *noun* (*Amer.* **tidbit**) a choice bit of something, e.g. of food or of gossip or information.

**titfer** *noun* (*slang*) a hat. (¶ Short for *tit for tat*, rhyming slang = hat.)

**tithe** (*pronounced* ty*th*) one tenth of the annual produce of agriculture etc., formerly paid as tax to support clergy and church. □ **tithe barn** a barn built to store tithes.

**Titian** (**tish**-ăn) (Tiziano Vecellio) (*c.*1488–1576), Italian painter. ● *adjective & noun* bright golden auburn, red (as a colour of hair, favoured by Titian in his pictures).

**Titicaca** (tit-i-**kah**-kă), **Lake** a lake in the Andes, between Peru and Bolivia, the highest large lake in the world.

**titillate** (**tit**-i-layt) *verb* excite or stimulate pleasantly. □ **titillation** *noun*

**titivate** (**tit**-i-vayt) *verb* (*informal*) smarten up; put the finishing touches to. □ **titivation** *noun*

**title** *noun* **1** the name of a book, poem, or picture etc. **2** a word used to show a person's rank or office (e.g. *king, mayor, captain*) or used in speaking of or to a person (e.g. *Lord, Mrs, Doctor*). **3** the legal right to ownership of property; a document conferring this. **4** a championship in sport; *the world heavyweight title.* ● *verb* give a title to (a book etc.). □ **title-deed** *noun* a legal document proving a person's title to a property. **title-page** *noun* a page at the beginning of a book giving the title, author's name, and other particulars. **title role** *noun* the part in a play etc. from which the title is taken, e.g. the part of Hamlet in the play of that name.

**titled** *adjective* having a title of nobility; *titled ladies.*

**titmouse** *noun* (*plural* **titmice**) a small active tit.

**Tito** (**tee**-toh) (Josip Broz) (1892–1980), statesman of the former Yugoslavia, leader of the Communist resistance movement during the Second World War, afterwards head of the new government and President from 1953.

**titrate** (ty-**trayt**) *verb* calculate the amount of a constituent in (a substance) by using a standard reagent. □ **titration** *noun*

**titter** *noun* a high-pitched giggle. ● *verb* give a titter.

**tittle-tattle** *verb* tattle. ● *noun* tattle.

**titular** (**tit**-yoo-ler) *adjective* **1** of or belonging to a title. **2** having the title of ruler etc. but without real authority; *the titular head of the State.*

**Titus**[1] (ty-tŭs) Roman emperor 79–81.

**Titus**[2] (ty-tŭs), St (1st century AD), a convert and helper of St Paul.

**tizzy** *noun* (*informal*) a state of agitation or confusion; *in a tizzy.*

**T-junction** *noun* a junction where one road or pipe etc. meets another but does not cross it, forming the shape of a T.

**Tl** *symbol* thallium.

**Tm** *symbol* thulium.

**TNT** *abbreviation* trinitrotoluene, a powerful explosive.

**to** *preposition* **1** in the direction of, so as to approach or reach (a place, position, or state etc.); *walked to the station; rose to power; was sent to prison; back to back.* **2** as far as, not falling short of; *patriotic to the core; from noon to 2 o'clock; goods to the value of £10; cooked to perfection.* **3** as compared with, in respect of; *won by 3 goals to 2; made to measure; his remarks were not to the point.* **4** for (a person or thing) to hold, possess, or be affected etc. by; *give it to me; spoke to her; kind to animals; accustomed to it.* **5** (with a verb) forming an infinitive, or expressing purpose or consequence etc.; *he wants to go; does it to annoy; I meant to call but forgot to.* ● *adverb* **1** to or in the normal or required position; to a closed or almost closed position; *push the door to.* **2** into a state of consciousness; *when she came to.* **3** into a state of activity; *set to.* □ **to and fro** backwards and forwards. **toing and froing** going to and fro.

**toad** *noun* **1** a froglike animal, an amphibian living chiefly on land. **2** a repulsive person. □ **toad-in-the-hole** *noun* sausages baked in batter.

**toadflax** *noun* a wild plant with spurred yellow or purple flowers.

**toadstool** *noun* a fungus (especially a poisonous one) with a round top and a slender stalk.

**toady** *noun* a person who flatters and behaves obsequiously to another in the hope of gain or advantage. ● *verb* (**toadied**, **toadying**) behave as a toady.

**toast** *noun* **1** a slice of toasted bread. **2** the person or thing in whose honour a company is requested to drink; an instance of drinking in this way. ● *verb* **1** brown the surface of (bread etc.) by placing it close to heat. **2** warm (one's feet etc.) in this way. **3** honour or pledge good wishes to by drinking. □ **toast rack** a rack for holding slices of toast at the table.

**toaster** *noun* an electrical device for toasting bread.

**toastmaster** *noun* a person responsible for announcing toasts at a reception, ceremonial dinner, etc.

**tobacco** *noun* **1** a plant grown for its leaves, which are used for smoking or for making snuff. **2** its leaves, prepared for smoking.

**tobacconist** *noun* a shopkeeper who sells cigarettes, cigars, and pipe-tobacco.

**Tobago** (tŏ-**bay**-goh) an island in the West Indies (*see* TRINIDAD). □ **Tobagan** *adjective & noun*, **Tobagonian** (toh-bă-**goh**-niăn) *adjective & noun*

**-to-be** soon to become; *the bride-to-be*.

**toboggan** *noun* a long light narrow sledge curved upwards at the front, used for sliding downhill. □ **tobogganing** *noun*

**toby jug** a mug or jug in the form of an old man with a three-cornered hat.

**toccata** (tŏ-**kah**-tă) *noun* a musical composition for a piano or organ etc., in a free style with rapid running passages.

**tocsin** *noun* an alarm bell or signal.

**tod** □ **on one's tod** (*slang*) on one's own.

**today** *noun* this present day or age. ● *adverb* **1** on this present day. **2** at the present time.

**toddle** *verb* **1** (of a young child) walk with short unsteady steps. **2** (*informal*) walk.

**toddler** *noun* a child who has only recently learnt to walk.

**toddy** *noun* a sweetened drink of spirits and hot water.

**to-do** *noun* a fuss or commotion.

**toe** *noun* **1** one of the divisions (five in man) of the front part of the foot. **2** the part of a shoe or stocking that covers the toes. **3** the lower end or tip of a tool etc. ● *verb* (**toed**, **toeing**) touch or reach with the toes. □ **on one's toes** alert. **toe-hold** *noun* **1** a slight foothold. **2** a small beginning or advantage. **toe the line** conform (especially under compulsion).

**toecap** *noun* the outer covering (usually strengthened) of the toe of a boot or shoe.

**toenail** *noun* the nail on each toe.

**toff** *noun* (*slang*) a well-dressed or upper-class person.

**toffee** *noun* a sweet made with heated butter and sugar. □ **can't do it for toffee** (*slang*) is very bad at doing it. **toffee-apple** *noun* a toffee-coated apple on a stick. **toffee-nosed** *adjective* (*slang*) snobbish, pretentious.

**tofu** (**toh**-foo) *noun* soft white soya bean curd used in cooking.

**tog** *verb* (**togged**, **togging**) (*informal*) (foll. by *up* or *out*) dress. ● *noun* **1** a unit used in measuring the power of clothing or bedding to keep the user warm by preventing body heat from escaping. **2** (**togs**) (*informal*) clothes.

**toga** (**toh**-gă) *noun* a loose flowing outer garment worn by men in ancient Rome.

**together** *adverb* **1** in or into company or conjunction, towards each other, so as to unite. **2** one with another; *talking together*. **3** simultaneously; *both shouted together*. **4** in an unbroken succession; *he is away for weeks together*. □ **together with** as well as, and also.

**togetherness** *noun* being together; feeling or belonging together.

**toggle** *noun* **1** a fastening device consisting of a short piece of wood or metal etc. secured by its centre and passed through a loop or hole. **2** *Computing* a switch action that is operated the same way but has the opposite effect on successive occasions. □ **toggle switch** an electric switch operated by a projecting lever.

**Togo** (**toh**-goh) a country in West Africa. □ **Togolese** *adjective & noun* (*plural* **Togolese**).

**toil** *verb* **1** work long hours or laboriously. **2** move laboriously; *we toiled up the hill*. ● *noun* hard or laborious work.

**toilet** *noun* **1** the process of dressing and grooming oneself. **2** a lavatory; the room containing this. □ **toilet paper** paper for cleaning oneself after going to the toilet. **toilet roll** a roll of toilet paper. **toilet soap** soap for washing oneself. **toilet-training** *noun* the training of a young child to use a lavatory. **toilet water** diluted perfume for use on the skin.

**toiletries** *plural noun* articles or preparations used in washing and grooming.

**toilette** (twa-**let**) *noun* = TOILET (sense 1).

**toils** *plural noun* a snare; a net.

**toilsome** *adjective* involving toil.

**Tokay** (tŏ-**kay**) *noun* a sweet Hungarian wine.

**token** *noun* **1** a sign, symbol, or evidence of something; *a token of our esteem*. **2** a keepsake or memorial of friendship etc. **3** a voucher or coupon that can be exchanged for goods; *book token*. **4** a device like a coin bought for use in machines or for making certain payments; *milk tokens*. ● *adjective* **1** serving as a token or pledge but often on a small scale; *token resistance; a token effort*. **2** chosen by tokenism to represent a group; *the token woman on the committee*. □ **by the same token** similarly; moreover.

**tokenism** *noun* making only a token effort or granting only small concessions, especially to minority or suppressed groups.

**Tokyo** (**toh**-ki-oh) the capital of Japan.

**told** *see* TELL[1]. □ **all told** counting everything or everyone; *we were 16 all told*.

**Toledo** (tŏ-**lay**-doh) a city of Spain, famous for the manufacture of sword blades.

**tolerable** *adjective* **1** able to be tolerated, endurable. **2** fairly good, passable. □ **tolerably** *adverb*, **tolerableness** *noun*

**tolerance** *noun* **1** willingness or ability to tolerate a person or thing. **2** the permitted variation in the measurement or weight etc. of an object.

**tolerant** *adjective* having or showing tolerance. □ **tolerantly** *adverb*

**tolerate** *verb* **1** permit without protest or interference. **2** bear (pain etc.); be able to take (a medicine) or undergo (radiation etc.) without harm. □ **toleration** *noun*

**Tolkien** (**tol**-keen), J(ohn) R(onald) R(euel) (1892–1973), British philologist, Professor of English at Oxford, and author of *The Hobbit* and *The Lord of the Rings*.

**toll**[1] (*rhymes with* hole) *noun* **1** a tax or duty paid for the use of a public road or harbour etc. or for service rendered. **2** the loss or damage caused by a disaster or incurred in achieving something; *the death toll in the earthquake*. □ **take its toll** be accompanied by loss or injury etc. **toll-bridge** *noun* a bridge at which a toll is charged. **toll-gate** *noun* a gate across a road to prevent anyone passing until the toll has been paid. **toll-road** *noun* a road maintained by the tolls collected on it.

**toll**[2] (*rhymes with* hole) *verb* **1** ring (a bell) with slow strokes, especially for a death or funeral. **2** (of a bell) sound in this way; indicate by tolling. ●*noun* the stroke of a tolling bell.

**Tolstoy** (tol-**stoi** *or* tol-stoi), Count Leo Nikolaevich (1828–1910), Russian writer, author of *War and Peace* and *Anna Karenina*.

**toluene** (**tol**-yoo-een) *noun* a liquid hydrocarbon derivative of benzene, used in explosives etc.

**tom** *noun* (in full **tom-cat**) a male cat.

**tomahawk** *noun* a light axe used as a tool or weapon by North American Indians.

**tomato** *noun* (*plural* **tomatoes**) **1** a glossy red or yellow fruit eaten as a vegetable. **2** the plant bearing this.

**tomb** (*pronounced* toom) *noun* **1** a grave or other place of burial. **2** a vault or stone monument in which one or more people are buried.

**tombola** (tom-**boh**-lă) *noun* a lottery with tickets drawn from a drum for immediate prizes.

**tomboy** *noun* a girl who enjoys activities traditionally associated with boys. □ **tomboyish** *adjective*

**tombstone** *noun* a memorial stone over a grave.

**Tom, Dick, and Harry** ordinary people, people taken at random.

**tome** (*rhymes with* home) *noun* a book or volume, especially a large heavy one.

**tomfool** *adjective* extremely foolish. ●*noun* an extremely foolish person.

**tomfoolery** *noun* foolish behaviour.

**Tommy** *noun* (*informal*) a British private soldier.

**tommy-gun** *noun* a sub-machine-gun.

**tommy-rot** *noun* (*slang*) nonsense, rubbish.

**tomography** (tŏ-**mog**-răfi) *noun* radiography producing an image of a selected plane in the body or other object. □ **tomographic** *adjective*

**tomorrow** *noun* **1** the day after today. **2** the near future. ●*adverb* on the day after today; at some future date.

**Tom Thumb** **1** the tiny hero of a nursery tale. **2** a very small person. **3** a dwarf variety of certain plants.

**tomtit** *noun* a tit, especially a blue tit.

**tom-tom** *noun* **1** an African or Asian drum beaten with the hands. **2** a deep-toned drum used in jazz bands.

**ton** (*pronounced* tun) *noun* **1** a measure of weight, either 2240 lb (**long ton**) or 2000 lb (**short ton**). **2** (in full **metric ton**) = TONNE. **3** (in full **displacement ton**) a unit of measurement of a ship's weight or volume. **4** (usually as **tons**) (*informal*) a large amount; *tons of money*. **5** (*slang*) a speed of 100 m.p.h.

**tonal** (**toh**-năl) *adjective* **1** of a tone or tones. **2** of tonality. □ **tonally** *adverb*

**tonality** (tŏ-**nal**-iti) *noun* **1** the character of a melody, depending on the scale or key in which it is composed. **2** the colour scheme of a picture.

**tone** *noun* **1** a musical or vocal sound, especially with reference to its pitch, quality, and strength. **2** the manner of expression in speaking or writing; *an apologetic tone*. **3** any one of the five intervals between one note and the next which, together with two semitones, make up an octave. **4** proper firmness of the organs and tissues of the body; *muscle tone*. **5** a tint or shade of a colour; the general effect of colour or of light and shade in a picture. **6** the general spirit or character prevailing; *set the tone with a dignified speech*. ●*verb* **1** give a particular tone of sound or colour to. **2** (often foll. by *in, with*) harmonize in colour; *the curtains tone in with the wallpaper*. **3** give proper firmness to (muscles, organs, or skin etc.). □ **tone-deaf** *adjective* unable to perceive accurately differences of musical pitch. **tone down** make or become softer in tone of sound or colour; make (a statement) less strong or harsh. **tone language** a language that uses variations in pitch to distinguish words that would otherwise sound the same. **tone poem** an orchestral composition illustrating a poetic idea.

**toneless** *adjective* without positive tone, not expressive. □ **tonelessly** *adverb*

**toner** *noun* a substance similar to ink used in a photocopier, laser printer, etc.

**Tonga** a country consisting of a group of islands in the Pacific, also called the Friendly Islands. □ **Tongan** *adjective & noun*

**tongs** *plural noun* an instrument with two arms joined at one end, used for grasping and holding things.

**tongue** *noun* **1** the fleshy muscular organ in the mouth, used in tasting, licking, swallowing, and (in man) speaking. **2** the tongue of an ox etc. as food. **3** the ability to speak or manner of speaking; *a persuasive tongue; have lost one's tongue.* **4** a language; *his native tongue is German.* **5** a projecting strip or flap. **6** a tapering jet of flame. ● *verb* produce staccato or other effects in a wind instrument by use of the tongue. □ **tongue-and-groove** *noun* planking or boarding with a projecting strip down one side and a groove down the other, allowing pieces to be fitted together. **tongue-in-cheek** (*adjective*) ironic; (*adverb*) insincerely or ironically. **tongue-tied** *adjective* **1** silent because of shyness or embarrassment. **2** unable to speak normally because the ligament connecting the tongue to the base of the mouth is abnormally short. **tongue-twister** *noun* a sequence of words that is difficult to pronounce quickly and correctly, e.g. *she sells sea shells.*

**tonic** *noun* **1** a medicine with an invigorating effect, taken after illness or weakness. **2** anything that restores people's energy or good spirits. **3** a keynote in music. **4** tonic water. ● *adjective* having the effect of a tonic, toning up the muscles etc. □ **tonic sol-fa** the system of syllables *doh, ray, me, fah, soh, la, te* used (especially in teaching singing) to represent the notes of the musical scale. **tonic water** carbonated water flavoured with quinine.

**tonight** *noun* **1** the present evening or night. **2** the evening or night of today. ● *adverb* on the present evening or night or that of today.

**tonnage** (tun-ij) *noun* **1** the carrying capacity of a ship, expressed in tons. **2** the charge per ton for carrying cargo or freight.

**tonne** (*pronounced* tun) *noun* a metric ton, 1000 kg (35 lb less than a long ton).

**tonsil** *noun* either of two small organs at the sides of the throat near the root of the tongue. □ **tonsillar** *adjective*

**tonsillectomy** *noun* surgical removal of tonsils.

**tonsillitis** *noun* inflammation of the tonsils.

**tonsorial** (ton-sor-iăl) *adjective* (*humorous*) of a barber or his work.

**tonsure** (ton-sher) *noun* **1** shaving the top or all of the head of a person entering certain priesthoods or monastic orders. **2** the part of the head shaven in this way.

**too** *adverb* **1** to a greater extent than is desirable. **2** (*informal*) very; *he's not too well today.* **3** also; *take the others too.* □ **too bad** (*informal*) regrettable, a pity.

**took** *see* TAKE.

**tool** *noun* **1** a thing (usually something held in the hand) for working on something. **2** a simple machine, e.g. a lathe. **3** anything used in an occupation or pursuit; *a dictionary is a useful tool.* **4** a person used as a mere instrument by another. **5** (*vulgar slang*) a penis. ● *verb* **1** dress (stone) with a chisel. **2** cut a design on (leather). **3** (foll. by *up*) provide oneself or equip (a factory etc.) with necessary tools. **4** (*slang*) drive or ride in a casual or leisurely way; *tooling along.* □ **tool-pusher** *noun* a worker directing drilling on an oil rig.

**toolmaker** *noun* a person who makes precision tools. □ **toolmaking** *noun*

**toot** *noun* a short sound produced by a horn or whistle etc. ● *verb* make or cause to make a toot.

**tooth** *noun* (*plural* **teeth**) **1** each of the hard white bony structures rooted in the gums, used for biting and chewing things. **2** a similar structure in the mouth or alimentary canal of certain invertebrate animals. **3** a toothlike part or projection, e.g. on a gear, saw, comb, or rake. **4** a liking for a particular type of food. □ **fight tooth and nail** fight very fiercely. **in the teeth of** in spite of; in opposition to; directly against (the wind). **tooth-comb** = FINE-TOOTH COMB. **tooth powder** a powder for cleaning the teeth.

**toothache** *noun* an ache in a tooth or teeth.

**toothbrush** *noun* a brush for cleaning the teeth.

**toothed** *adjective* **1** having teeth. **2** having teeth of a certain kind; *sharp-toothed.*

**toothless** *adjective* having no teeth.

**toothpaste** *noun* paste for cleaning the teeth.

**toothpick** *noun* a small pointed piece of wood etc. for removing food from between the teeth.

**toothsome** *adjective* (of food) delicious.

**toothy** *adjective* having many or large teeth.

**tootle** *verb* **1** toot gently or repeatedly. **2** (*informal*) go in a casual or leisurely way; *tootle around.*

**top**[1] *noun* **1** the highest point or part of something; the upper surface. **2** the highest rank, degree, or position; *he is at the top of his profession.* **3** the utmost degree of intensity; *shouted at the top of his voice*. **4** a thing forming the upper part of something, e.g. the creamy part of milk; a garment covering the upper part of the body. **5** the covering or stopper of a bottle or tube. **6** top gear. ● *adjective* highest in position, rank, place, or degree; *at top speed; top prices*. ● *verb* (**topped, topping**) **1** provide or be a top for. **2** reach the top of. **3** be higher than, surpass; be at the top of. **4** add as a final thing or finishing touch. **5** remove the top of (a plant or fruit). **6** (*slang*) execute by hanging, kill. **7** (in golf) strike (the ball) above its centre. □ **on top** above; in a superior position; in addition. **on top of 1** in addition to. **2** having mastered (a thing) thoroughly. **on top of the world** very happy. **top brass** (*informal*) the highest-ranking officials. **top dog** (*informal*) the master or victor. **top drawer** the highest social position; *out of the top drawer*. **top dress** *verb* apply fertilizer on the top of soil without ploughing it in. **top dressing** this process; the substance used. **top-flight** *adjective* of the highest rank; most successful. **top gear** the highest gear, allowing parts to revolve fast. **top hat** a man's tall stiff black or grey hat worn with formal dress. **top-heavy** *adjective* overweighted at the top and therefore in danger of falling over. **top-notch** *adjective* (*informal*) first-rate. **top secret** of the highest category of secrecy. **top up** fill up (a half-empty container).

**top²** *noun* a toy that spins on its point when set in motion by hand or by a string or spring etc. □ **sleep like a top** sleep soundly.

**topaz** (toh-paz) *noun* a semiprecious stone of various colours, especially yellow.

**topcoat** *noun* **1** an overcoat. **2** an outer coat of paint etc.

**tope** *noun* a kind of small shark.

**topee** alternative spelling of TOPI.

**toper** (toh-per) *noun* a habitual drunkard.

**topi** (toh-pi) *noun* (also **topee**) a light pith sun-helmet.

**topiary** (toh-pi-er-i) *noun* the art of clipping shrubs etc. into ornamental shapes.

**topic** *noun* the subject of a discussion or written work.

**topical** *adjective* having reference to current events. □ **topically** *adverb*, **topicality** (top-i-**kal**-iti) *noun*

**topknot** *noun* a tuft, crest, or knot of ribbon etc. on top of the head.

**topless** *adjective* **1** (of a woman's garment) leaving the breasts bare. **2** (of a woman) wearing such a garment.

**topmost** *adjective* highest.

**topography** (tŏ-**pog**-răfi) *noun* the features of a place or district, the position of its

rivers, mountains, roads, buildings, etc. □ **topographical** (top-ŏ-**graf**-ikăl) *adjective*

**topology** *noun* the study of geometrical properties unaffected by changes of shape or size. □ **topological** *adjective*

**topper** *noun* (*informal*) a top hat.

**topple** *verb* **1** fall headlong or as if top-heavy, totter and fall. **2** cause to do this. **3** overthrow, cause to fall from authority; *the crisis toppled the government*.

**topsail** (top-sayl *or* top-săl) *noun* **1** a square sail next above the lowest. **2** a fore-and-aft sail on a gaff.

**topside** *noun* **1** a joint of beef cut from the upper part of the haunch. **2** the side of a ship above the waterline.

**topsoil** *noun* the top layer of soil as distinct from the subsoil.

**topspin** *noun* a spinning motion given to a ball in tennis etc. by hitting it forward and upward.

**topsy-turvy** *adverb & adjective* **1** in or into a state of great disorder. **2** upside down.

**toque** (*rhymes with* coke) *noun* a woman's close-fitting brimless hat with a high crown.

**tor** *noun* a hill or rocky peak, especially in Devon and Cornwall.

**Torah** *noun* the will of God as revealed in Mosaic law; the Pentateuch.

**torch** *noun* **1** a small hand-held electric lamp powered by a battery or electric power cell, contained in a case. **2** a burning stick of resinous wood, or of combustible material fixed on a stick and ignited, used as a light. □ **carry a torch for** be filled with unreturned love for (a person).

**torchlight** *noun* the light of a torch or torches.

**tore** *see* TEAR¹.

**toreador** (torri-ă-dor) *noun* a bullfighter, especially on horseback.

**torment** *noun* (*pronounced* **tor**-ment) **1** severe physical or mental suffering. **2** something causing this. ● *verb* (*pronounced* tor-**ment**) **1** subject to torment. **2** tease or try to provoke by annoyances etc. □ **tormentor** *noun*

**tormentil** (tor-měn-til) *noun* a low-growing herb with yellow flowers.

**torn** *see* TEAR¹.

**tornado** (tor-**nay**-doh) *noun* (*plural* **tornadoes**) a violent and destructive whirlwind advancing in a narrow path.

**Toronto** the capital of Ontario, Canada.

**torpedo** *noun* (*plural* **torpedoes**) a cigar-shaped explosive underwater missile, launched against a ship from a submarine or surface ship or from an aircraft. ● *verb* **1** destroy or attack with a torpedo. **2** ruin or wreck (a policy or conference etc.) suddenly.

**torpid** *adjective* sluggish and inactive. □ **torpidly** *adverb*, **torpidity** (tor-**pid**-iti) *noun*

**torpor** (**tor**-per) *noun* a torpid condition.

**torque** (*pronounced* tork) *noun* a force causing rotation in a mechanism.

**Torquemada** (tor-ki-**mah**-dă), Tomás de (*c.*1420–98), Spanish cleric, a Dominican monk who became Inquisitor-General.

**torr** *noun* (*plural* **torr**) a unit of pressure. (¶ Named after Torricelli.)

**torrent** *noun* **1** a rushing stream of water or lava. **2** a downpour of rain. **3** a violent flow; *a torrent of words*.

**torrential** (ter-**en**-shăl) *adjective* like a torrent.

**Torricelli** (tor-i-**chel**-i), Evangelista (1608–47), Italian scientist, inventor of the mercury barometer, the first person to produce a sustained vacuum.

**torrid** (*rhymes with* horrid) *adjective* **1** (of climate or land) very hot and dry. **2** intense, passionate; *torrid love scenes*. □ **torrid zone** the part of the earth between the tropics of Cancer and Capricorn.

**torsion** (**tor**-shŏn) *noun* **1** twisting, especially of one end of a thing while the other is held fixed. **2** the state of being spirally twisted.

**torso** (**tor**-soh) *noun* (*plural* **torsos**) **1** the trunk of the human body. **2** a statue lacking head and limbs.

**tort** *noun* (in Law) any private or civil wrong (other than breach of contract) for which the wronged person may claim damages.

**tortilla** (tor-**tee**-ă) *noun* a Mexican flat maize cake eaten hot.

**tortoise** (**tor**-tŭs) *noun* a slow-moving four-footed reptile with its body enclosed in a hard shell, living on land or in fresh water.

**tortoiseshell** (**tor**-tŭ-shel) *noun* **1** the semi-transparent mottled yellowish-brown shell of certain turtles, used for making combs etc. **2** a cat or butterfly with mottled colouring resembling this. ● *adjective* having such colouring.

**tortuous** (**tor**-tew-ŭs) *adjective* **1** full of twists and turns. **2** (of policy etc.) devious, not straightforward. □ **tortuously** *adverb*, **tortuosity** (tor-tew-**os**-iti) *noun*

**torture** *noun* **1** the infliction of severe pain as a punishment or means of coercion. **2** a method of torturing. **3** severe physical or mental pain. ● *verb* **1** inflict torture upon; subject to great pain or anxiety. **2** force out of its natural position or shape. □ **torturer** *noun*

**Torvill**, Jayne (born 1957), English skater and championship ice-dancer in partnership with Christopher Dean.

**Tory** *noun* **1** (*informal*) a member of the Conservative Party. **2** a member of the political party in the 17th–19th centuries, opposed to the Whigs, which gave rise to the Conservative Party. ● *adjective* (*informal*) Conservative. □ **Toryism** *noun*

**tosa** *noun* a dog of a breed originally kept for fighting.

**Toscanini** (tosk-ă-**nee**-ni), Arturo (1867–1957), Italian conductor.

**tosh** *noun* (*slang*) nonsense.

**toss** *verb* **1** throw lightly, carelessly, or easily. **2** send (a coin) spinning in the air to decide something according to the way it lands. **3** throw or roll about from side to side restlessly or with an uneven motion. **4** coat (food) by gently shaking it in dressing etc. ● *noun* **1** a tossing action or movement. **2** the result obtained by tossing a coin. □ **toss off 1** drink off rapidly; finish or compose rapidly or without much thought or effort. **2** (*slang*) masturbate. **toss one's head** throw it back in contempt or impatience. **toss up** toss a coin. **toss-up** *noun* **1** the tossing of a coin. **2** an even chance.

**tot**[1] *noun* **1** a small child. **2** (*informal*) a small quantity of alcoholic drink, especially spirits.

**tot**[2] *verb* (**totted**, **totting**) (foll. by *up*) (*informal*) add up; *tot this up*; *it tots up to £20*. □ **totting-up** *noun* the adding of separate items, especially of convictions for driving offences to cause disqualification.

**total** *adjective* **1** including everything or everyone, comprising the whole; *the total number of people*. **2** utter, complete; *in total darkness*. ● *noun* the total number or amount, a count of all the items. ● *verb* (**totalled**, **totalling**; *Amer.* **totaled**, **totaling**) **1** reckon the total of. **2** amount to.

**totalitarian** (toh-tal-i-**tair**-iăn) *adjective* of a dictatorial one-party government in which no rival parties or loyalties are permitted. □ **totalitarianism** *noun*

**totality** (toh-**tal**-iti) *noun* **1** the quality of being total. **2** a total number or amount.

**totalizator** *noun* (also **totalisator**) a device automatically registering the number and amount of bets staked, with a view to dividing the total amount among those betting on the winner.

**totalize** *verb* (also **totalise**) find the total of.

**totalizer** *noun* = TOTALIZATOR.

**totally** *adverb* completely; absolutely.

**tote**[1] *noun* (*slang*) a totalizator.

**tote**[2] *verb* (*informal*, especially *Amer.*) carry. □ **tote bag** a large bag for carrying shopping or other items.

**totem** (**toh**-tĕm) *noun* **1** a natural object, especially an animal, adopted among North American Indians as the emblem of a clan or family. **2** an image of this.

□ **totem-pole** *noun* a pole carved or painted with a series of totems.

**t'other** (*dialect* or *informal*) = the other.

**totter** *verb* **1** walk unsteadily. **2** rock or shake as if about to collapse. ●*noun* an unsteady or shaky walk or movement. □ **tottery** *adjective*

**toucan** (too-kăn) *noun* a tropical American fruit-eating bird with an immense beak.

**touch** *verb* **1** be or come together so that there is no space between; meet (another object) in this way. **2** put one's hand etc. on (a thing) lightly. **3** press or strike lightly. **4** draw or paint with light strokes; *touch the details in.* **5** move or meddle with; harm; *leave your things here, no one will touch them.* **6** have to do with in the slightest degree, attempt; *the firm doesn't touch business of that kind.* **7** eat or drink even a little of; *she hasn't touched her breakfast.* **8** reach; *the speedometer touched 120.* **9** equal in excellence; *no other cloth can touch it for quality.* **10** affect slightly. **11** rouse sympathy or other emotion in. **12** (*slang*) persuade to give money as a loan or gift; *touched him for a fiver.* ●*noun* **1** the act or fact of touching. **2** the faculty of perceiving things or their qualities through touching them. **3** small things done in producing a piece of work; *put the finishing touches.* **4** a manner or style of workmanship; a person's special skill; *he hasn't lost his touch.* **5** a relationship of communication or knowledge; *we've lost touch with her.* **6** a slight trace; *there's a touch of frost in the air; a touch of flu.* **7** the part of a football field outside the touchlines. **8** (*slang*) the act of obtaining money from a person. □ **in touch with 1** in communication with. **2** having interest in or information about. **out of touch** no longer in touch with a person or subject etc. **touch-and-go** *adjective* uncertain, critical, risky. **touch down 1** (in Rugby football) touch the ball on the ground behind either goal-line. **2** (of an aircraft) land. **touch-judge** *noun* a linesman in Rugby football. **touch off** cause explode; cause to start; *his arrest touched off a riot.* **touch on** deal with or mention (a subject) briefly. **touch-paper** *noun* paper impregnated with a substance that will make it burn slowly for igniting fireworks etc. **touch-typing** *noun* typing without looking at the keys. **touch up 1** improve (a thing) by making small alterations or additions. **2** (*slang*) molest; touch sexually. **touch wood** touch something made of wood in superstitious or humorous hope that this will avert bad luck.

**touchable** *adjective* able to be touched.

**touchdown** *noun* the act of touching down.

**touché** (too-**shay**) *interjection* an acknowledgment that one's opponent has made a hit in fencing or a valid accusation or criticism in a discussion. (¶ French, = touched.)

**touched** *adjective* **1** caused to feel warm sympathy or gratitude. **2** slightly mad.

**touching** *adjective* rousing kindly feelings or sympathy or pity. ●*preposition* concerning. □ **touchingly** *adverb*

**touchline** *noun* (in various sports) either of the lines marking the side boundaries of the pitch.

**touchstone** *noun* a standard or criterion by which something is judged. (¶ Alloys of gold and silver were formerly tested by being rubbed against a fine-grained stone such as black jasper.)

**touchwood** *noun* wood in a soft rotten state and easily inflammable, used as tinder.

**touchy** *adjective* (**touchier, touchiest**) easily offended. □ **touchily** *adverb*, **touchiness** *noun*

**tough** *adjective* **1** difficult to break or cut or to chew. **2** able to endure hardship, not easily hurt, damaged, or injured. **3** unyielding, stubborn, resolute. **4** difficult; *a tough job.* **5** (*informal*) (of luck etc.) hard, unpleasant. **6** vicious, rough and violent. ●*noun* a rough and violent person; *young toughs.* □ **toughly** *adverb*, **toughness** *noun*

**toughen** *verb* make or become tough.

**Toulouse-Lautrec** (too-looz loh-**trek**), Henri de (1864–1901), French painter and lithographer, noted for his depictions of theatre and café life.

**toupee** (too-pay) *noun* an artificial patch of hair worn to cover a bald spot.

**tour** *noun* a journey through a country, town, or building etc. visiting various places or things of interest, or giving performances, playing sports matches, etc. ●*verb* make a tour of. □ **Tour de France** a long-distance cycle race held annually in France.

**tour de force** (toor dĕ **forss**) (*plural* **tours de force**, *pronounced* same) an outstandingly skilful performance or achievement. (¶ French.)

**tourism** *noun* **1** visiting places as a tourist. **2** the business of providing accommodation and services etc. for tourists.

**tourist** *noun* a person who is travelling or visiting a place for recreation. □ **tourist class** the lowest class of passenger accommodation in a ship or aircraft etc. **Tourist Trophy** (also **TT**) an annual motor-cycle race held on the Isle of Man.

**touristy** *adjective* (usually *scornful*) designed to attract tourists; visited by many tourists.

**tourmaline** (toor-mă-leen) *noun* a mineral of various colours, possessing unusual electric properties and used as a gem.

**tournament** (toor-nă-měnt) *noun* a contest of skill between a number of competitors, involving a series of matches.

**tournedos** (toor-ně-doh) *noun* (*plural* **tournedos**) a small round thick cut from a fillet of beef.

**tourney** *noun* a tournament.

**tourniquet** (toor-ni-kay) *noun* a device or a strip of material drawn tightly round a limb to stop the flow of blood from an artery by compressing it.

**tousle** (tow-zěl) *verb* make (hair etc.) untidy by ruffling it.

**tout** (*rhymes with* scout) *verb* **1** try busily to obtain orders for one's goods or services; *touting for custom.* **2** pester people to buy. ●*noun* a person who touts things; a tipster touting information about racehorses etc.

**tow¹** (*rhymes with* go) *noun* short coarse fibres of flax or hemp, used for making yarn etc. □ **tow-headed** *adjective* having very light-coloured hair.

**tow²** (*rhymes with* go) *verb* pull along behind one. ●*noun* towing, being towed. □ **in tow 1** being towed. **2** (*informal*) following behind, under one's charge; *he arrived with his family in tow.* **on tow** being towed. **towbar** *noun* a bar fitted to a car for towing a caravan etc. **tow-path** *noun* a path beside a canal or river originally for use by a horse towing a boat.

**toward** *preposition* = TOWARDS.

**towards** *preposition* **1** in the direction of; *walked towards the sea.* **2** in relation to, regarding; *the way he behaved towards his children.* **3** for the purpose of achieving or promoting; *efforts towards peace.* **4** as a contribution to; *put the money towards a new bicycle.* **5** near, approaching; *towards four o'clock.*

**towel** *noun* a piece of absorbent cloth or paper for drying oneself or wiping things dry. ●*verb* (**towelled, towelling**; *Amer.* **toweled, toweling**) wipe or dry with a towel.

**towelling** *noun* fabric for making towels.

**tower** *noun* a tall usually square or circular structure, either standing alone (e.g. as a fort) or forming part of a church or castle or other large building. ●*verb* be of great height; be taller or more eminent than others; *he towered above everyone.* □ **the Tower** the Tower of London, a former fortress and palace and State prison. **tower block** a very tall block of flats or offices. **Tower of Babel** *see* BABEL. **tower of strength** a person who gives strong and reliable support.

**towering** *adjective* **1** very tall, lofty. **2** (of rage etc.) extreme, intense.

**town** *noun* **1** a collection of dwellings and other buildings, larger than a village and generally smaller than a city. **2** its inhabitants. **3** a town or city as distinct from country. **4** the central business and shopping areas of a neighbourhood. **5** London; *went up to town from Leeds.* □ **go to town** (*informal*) do something lavishly or with great enthusiasm. **on the town** out having a good time in town. **town clerk** (*Amer. & hist.*) an officer of the corporation of a town, in charge of records etc. **town crier** *see* CRIER. **town gas** manufactured gas for domestic and commercial use. **town hall** a building containing local government offices and usually a hall for public events. **town house** a residence in town as distinct from country; a terrace house or a house in a compact planned group in a town. **town planning** preparation of plans for the regulated growth and improvement of towns.

**townie** *noun* (also **townee**) (*scornful*) an inhabitant of a town.

**townscape** *noun* **1** a picture of a town. **2** the general appearance of a town.

**townsfolk** *noun* the people of a town.

**township** *noun* **1** (*old use*) a small town or village that formed part of a large parish. **2** (in South Africa) an urban area set aside for Black occupation. **3** (*Amer. & Canada*) a division of a county, a district six miles square. **4** (*Austral. & NZ*) a small town.

**townsman** *noun* (*plural* **townsmen**) an inhabitant of a town.

**townspeople** *plural noun* the people of a town.

**townswoman** *noun* (*plural* **townswomen**) a woman who lives in a town.

**toxaemia** (toks-eem-iă) *noun* (*Amer.* **toxemia**) **1** blood-poisoning. **2** a condition in pregnancy in which blood pressure is abnormally high.

**toxic** *adjective* **1** of or caused by poison. **2** poisonous. □ **toxicity** (toks-iss-iti) *noun*

**toxicology** *noun* the study of poisons. □ **toxicological** *adjective*, **toxicologist** *noun*

**toxin** *noun* a poisonous substance of animal or vegetable origin, especially one formed in the body by micro-organisms.

**toxocara** (toks-ă-kah-ră) *noun* a parasitic worm in dogs and cats.

**toxophily** (toks-off-ili) *noun* archery.

**toy** *noun* **1** a thing to play with, especially for a child. **2** a thing intended for amusement rather than for serious use. ●*adjective* **1** serving as a toy. **2** (of a dog) of a very small breed. ●*verb* (foll. by *with*) **1** handle or finger idly. **2** consider as a vague possibility; *toyed with the idea of going to Spain.* □ **toy boy** (*informal*) a woman's much younger boyfriend.

**Toynbee**, Arnold Joseph (1889–1975), English historian.

**trace¹** noun **1** a track or mark left behind. **2** a visible or other sign of what has existed or happened. **3** a very small quantity; *contains traces of soda.* ● verb **1** follow or discover by observing marks, tracks, pieces of evidence, etc. **2** mark out, sketch the outline of, form (letters etc.) laboriously. **3** copy (a map or drawing etc.) on translucent paper placed over it or by using carbon paper below. □ **trace element** a chemical element required only in minute amounts by living organisms for normal growth. □ **traceable** adjective

**trace²** noun each of the two side-straps, chains, or ropes by which a horse draws a vehicle. □ **kick over the traces** (of a person) become insubordinate or reckless.

**tracer** noun **1** a person or thing that traces. **2** a bullet that leaves a trail of smoke etc. by which its course can be observed. **3** a radioactive substance that can be traced in its course through the human body by the radiation it produces.

**tracery** noun **1** an openwork pattern in stone (e.g. in a church window). **2** a decorative pattern of lines resembling this.

**trachea** (tră-**kee**-ă) noun (plural **tracheae**) the windpipe.

**tracheotomy** (tra-ki-ot-ŏmi) noun an opening made surgically into the trachea to relieve an obstruction.

**trachoma** (tră-**koh**-mă) noun a contagious disease of the eye causing inflammation of the inner surface of the eyelids.

**tracing** noun a copy of a map or drawing etc. made by tracing it. □ **tracing-paper** noun translucent paper for making tracings.

**track** noun **1** a mark or series of marks left by a moving person, animal, or thing. **2** a course taken. **3** a course of action or procedure; *you're on the right track.* **4** a path or rough road. **5** a prepared course for racing etc. **6** a section of a CD, record, or tape containing one song, section of music, etc. **7** (in a computer etc.) the path along which information is recorded on a tape or disk. **8** a continuous line of railway. **9** a continuous band round the wheels of a tank or tractor etc. ● verb **1** follow the track of; (foll. by *down*) find by doing this. **2** (of wheels) run so that the back wheel is exactly in the front wheel's track. **3** (of electric current) leak excessively between insulated points, e.g. in damp conditions. **4** (of a film camera) follow (a moving object) while filming. □ **in one's tracks** (*informal*) where one stands; instantly. **keep** or **lose track of** keep or fail to keep oneself informed about. **make tracks** (*slang*) leave, depart. **make tracks for** (*slang*) go to or towards. **track events** running races as distinct from field events. **track record** a person's past performance. **track shoe** a

runner's spiked shoe. **track suit** a warm loose-fitting suit worn for exercising etc.

**tracker dog** a police dog tracking by scent.

**tract** noun **1** a large stretch of land. **2** a system of connected parts in an animal body along which something passes; *the digestive tract.* **3** a pamphlet containing a short essay, especially on a religious subject.

**tractable** adjective easy to manage or deal with, docile. □ **tractability** noun

**traction** noun **1** pulling or drawing a load along a surface. **2** a continuous pull on a limb etc. in medical treatment. □ **traction-engine** noun a steam or diesel engine for drawing a heavy load along a road or across a field etc.

**tractor** noun **1** a powerful motor vehicle for pulling farm machinery or other heavy equipment. **2** a device supplying traction.

**Tracy**, Spencer (1900–67), American film actor.

**trad** (*informal*) adjective traditional. ● noun traditional jazz.

**trade** noun **1** exchange of goods for money or other goods. **2** business of a particular kind; *the tourist trade.* **3** a skilled craft practised to earn a living; *he's a butcher by trade; learn a trade.* **4** the people engaged in a particular trade; *we sell cars to the trade, not to private buyers.* **5** a trade wind. ● verb **1** engage in trade, buy and sell. **2** exchange (goods etc.) in trading. □ **trade in** give (a used article) as partial payment for another article. **trade-in** noun an article given in this way. **trade mark 1** a manufacturer's or trader's registered emblem or name etc. used to identify goods. **2** a distinctive characteristic etc. **trade name** a name given by a manufacturer to a proprietary article or material; the name by which a thing is known in the trade; the name under which a person or firm trades. **trade-off** noun a balancing factor; an exchange as a compromise. **trade on** make great use of for one's own advantage; *trading on his brother's reputation.* **trade secret** a technique used in the trade but kept from being generally known. **Trades Union Congress** an association of representatives of British trade unions, meeting annually. **trade union** (also **trades union**) an organized association of employees engaged in a particular type of work, formed to protect and promote their rights and interests. **trade-unionist** noun an active member of a trade union. **trade wind** one of the winds blowing continually towards the equator over most of the tropics, from the north-east in the northern hemisphere and from the south-east in the southern hemisphere. □ **trader** noun

**tradescantia** (trad-iss-**kant**-iă) *noun* a trailing plant with striped variegated leaves and large blue, white, or pink flowers.

**tradesman** *noun* (*plural* **tradesmen**) (*old use*) = TRADESPERSON.

**tradesperson** *noun* a person engaged in trade, a shopkeeper or supplier.

**trading** *noun* buying and selling. □ **trading estate** an area designed to be occupied by a group of industrial and commercial firms. **trading post** a store in a remote or sparsely populated region.

**tradition** *noun* **1** the handing down of beliefs or customs from one generation to another, especially without writing. **2** a belief or custom handed down in this way; a long-established custom or method of procedure.

**traditional** *adjective* **1** of or based on tradition. **2** (of jazz) in the style of the early 20th century. □ **traditionally** *adverb*

**traditionalist** *noun* a person who follows or upholds traditional beliefs etc.

**traduce** (tră-**dewss**) *verb* misrepresent in an unfavourable way. □ **traducement** *noun*

**Trafalgar** (tră-**fal**-ger) a cape on the south coast of Spain, the site of Nelson's victory over the fleets of France and Spain in 1805.

**traffic** *noun* **1** vehicles, ships, or aircraft moving along a route. **2** trading, especially when illegal or morally wrong; *drug traffic.* ●*verb* (**trafficked**, **trafficking**) trade. □ **traffic island** a raised area in a road to divide traffic streams and for pedestrians to use in crossing. **traffic lights** an automatic signal of coloured lights controlling traffic at junctions etc. **traffic warden** an official employed to help control road traffic and parking. □ **trafficker** *noun*

**tragedian** (tră-**jeed**-iăn) *noun* **1** a writer of tragedies. **2** an actor in tragedy.

**tragedienne** (tră-jee-di-**en**) *noun* an actress in tragedy.

**tragedy** *noun* **1** a serious play with unhappy events or a sad ending. **2** the branch of drama that consists of such plays. **3** an event that causes great sadness, a calamity.

**tragic** *adjective* **1** of or in the style of tragedy; *he was a great tragic actor.* **2** sorrowful. **3** causing great sadness, calamitous. □ **tragically** *adverb*

**tragicomedy** (traj-i-**kom**-idi) *noun* a play with both tragic and comic elements. □ **tragicomic** *adjective*

**trail** *verb* **1** drag or be dragged along behind. **2** hang or float loosely; (of a plant) grow lengthily downwards or along the ground. **3** move wearily; lag or straggle. **4** be losing in a game or other contest. **5** diminish, become fainter; *her voice trailed away.* **6** follow the trail of, track. ●*noun* **1** some-

thing that trails or hangs trailing. **2** a line of people or things following behind something. **3** a mark left where something has passed; *a snail's slimy trail.* **4** a track or scent followed in hunting. **5** a beaten path, especially through a wild region. □ **trailblazer** *noun* **1** a person who makes a new track through wild country. **2** a person who pioneers a new idea, project, system, etc. **trailing edge** the rear edge of a moving body.

**trailer** *noun* **1** a vehicle designed to be towed by another. **2** (*Amer.*) a caravan. **3** a short extract from a film, radio programme, etc. used to advertise it. **4** a person or thing that trails.

**train** *noun* **1** a railway engine with a series of linked carriages or trucks. **2** a number of people or animals moving in a line; *a camel train.* **3** a body of followers, a retinue. **4** a series or sequence of things; *a train of events; a train of thought.* **5** part of a long dress or robe that trails on the ground behind the wearer. ●*verb* **1** bring to a desired standard of efficiency or behaviour etc. by instruction and practice. **2** undergo such a process; *she trained as a secretary.* **3** make or become physically fit for a sport by exercise and diet. **4** aim (a gun or camera etc.); *trained his gun on the doorway.* **5** cause (a plant) to grow in the required direction. □ **in train** in preparation; *put matters in train for the election.* **train-spotter** *noun* a collector of the identification-numbers of railway engines seen.

**trainee** *noun* a person being trained.

**trainer** *noun* **1** a person who trains; one who trains racehorses or athletes etc. **2** an aircraft or device simulating one, used to train pilots. **3** a soft running shoe.

**traipse** *verb* (*informal*) trudge, tramp.

**trait** (*pronounced* tray *or* trayt) *noun* a characteristic.

**traitor** *noun* a person who behaves disloyally; one who betrays his or her country. □ **traitorous** (**tray**-ter-ŭs) *adjective*

**trajectory** (tră-**jek**-ter-i) *noun* the path of a bullet or rocket etc. or of a body moving under certain forces.

**tram** *noun* a public passenger vehicle running on rails laid in the road.

**tramcar** *noun* a tram.

**tramlines** *plural noun* **1** rails for a tram. **2** (*informal*) the pair of parallel lines at each side of a doubles court in tennis etc.

**trammel** *noun* **1** a triple drag-net for catching fish. **2** (**trammels**) things that hamper one's activities. ●*verb* (**trammelled**, **trammelling**; *Amer.* **trammeled**, **trammeling**) hamper.

**tramp** *verb* **1** walk with heavy steps. **2** travel on foot across (an area); *tramping the hills.*

**3** trample; *tramp it down.* ● *noun* **1** the sound of heavy footsteps. **2** a long walk. **3** a person who goes from place to place as a vagrant. **4** (*slang, scornful*) a promiscuous woman. **5** a cargo boat that does not travel on a regular route.

**trample** *verb* tread repeatedly with heavy or crushing steps; crush or harm in this way.

**trampoline** (**tramp**-ŏ-leen) *noun* a sheet of strong canvas attached by springs to a horizontal frame, used for gymnastic jumping. □ **trampolining** *noun*

**tramway** *noun* the rails for a tram.

**trance** *noun* **1** a sleeplike state, e.g. that induced by hypnosis. **2** a dreamy state in which a person is absorbed with his or her own thoughts.

**tranny** *noun* (*informal*) a transistor radio.

**tranquil** *adjective* calm and undisturbed, not agitated. □ **tranquilly** *adverb*, **tranquillity** *noun*

**tranquillize** *verb* (also **tranquillise**, *Amer.* **tranquilize**) make tranquil, calm.

**tranquillizer** *noun* (also **tranquilliser**, *Amer.* **tranquilizer**) a drug used to relieve anxiety and make a person feel calm.

**transact** *verb* perform or carry out (business). □ **transactor** *noun*

**transaction** *noun* **1** transacting. **2** business transacted. **3** (**transactions**) published reports of discussions, papers read, etc. at meetings of a society.

**transalpine** *adjective* beyond the Alps (usually as viewed from Italy).

**transatlantic** *adjective* **1** on or from the other side of the Atlantic. **2** crossing the Atlantic; *a transatlantic flight.*

**transceiver** (tran-**seev**-er) *noun* a combined radio transmitter and receiver.

**transcend** (tran-**send**) *verb* **1** go or be beyond the range of (human experience, belief, or powers of description etc.). **2** surpass.

**transcendent** (tran-**sen**-dĕnt) *adjective* **1** going beyond the limits of ordinary experience, surpassing. **2** (of God) existing apart from the material universe. □ **transcendence** *noun*, **transcendency** *noun*

**transcendental** (tran-sen-**den**-t'l) *adjective* **1** *Philosophy* not based on experience; intuitive, innate in the mind. **2** abstract; obscure; visionary. □ **Transcendental Meditation** a method of detaching oneself from problems, anxiety, etc., by silent meditation and repetition of a mantra. □ **transcendentally** *adverb*

**transcendentalism** *noun* transcendental philosophy. □ **transcendentalist** *noun*

**transcontinental** *adjective* extending or travelling across a continent.

**transcribe** *verb* **1** copy in writing; write out (shorthand etc.) in ordinary characters.

**2** record (sound) for later reproduction or broadcasting. **3** arrange (music) for a different instrument etc. □ **transcriber** *noun*, **transcription** *noun*

**transcript** *noun* a written or recorded copy.

**transducer** *noun* a device that converts waves etc. from one system and conveys related waves to another (e.g. a radio receiver, which receives electromagnetic waves and sends out sound waves).

**transept** (**tran**-sept) *noun* the part that is at right angles to the nave in a cross-shaped church; either arm of this; *the north and south transepts.*

**transexual** alternative spelling of TRANSSEXUAL.

**transfer** *verb* (*pronounced* trans-**fer**) (**transferred**, **transferring**) **1** convey, move, or hand over (a thing) from one place or person etc. to another. **2** convey (a drawing or pattern etc.) from one surface to another. **3** change from one station, route, or form of transport to another during a journey. **4** change to another group or occupation etc.; *she has transferred to the sales department.* ● *noun* (*pronounced* trans-**fer**) **1** transferring, being transferred. **2** a document that transfers property or a right from one person to another. **3** a design that is or can be transferred from one surface to another; paper bearing such a design. □ **transfer fee** a fee paid for transfer, especially of a professional footballer to another club. **transfer list** a list of professional footballers available for transfer to other clubs.

**transferable** (trans-**fer**-ăbŭl) *adjective* able to be transferred. □ **transferable vote** a vote that can be transferred to another candidate if the first choice is eliminated. □ **transferability** *noun*

**transference** (**trans**-fer-ĕns) *noun* transferring; being transferred.

**transferral** (trans-**fer**-ăl) *noun* transferring; being transferred.

**transfiguration** *noun* **1** change of form or appearance. **2** (**the Transfiguration**) the Christian festival (6 August) commemorating Christ's transfiguration on the mountain.

**transfigure** *verb* make a great change in the appearance of, especially to something nobler or more beautiful; *her face was transfigured by happiness.*

**transfix** *verb* **1** pierce with or impale on something sharp-pointed. **2** make (a person) motionless with horror or astonishment.

**transform** *verb* **1** make a great change in the appearance or character of; *the caterpillar is transformed into a butterfly.* **2** change the voltage of (electric current). **3** become transformed. □ **transformation** noun

**transformer** noun an apparatus for reducing or increasing the voltage of alternating current.

**transfuse** verb give a transfusion of (a fluid) to a person or animal.

**transfusion** noun an injection of blood or other fluid into a blood vessel to replace lost fluid.

**transgress** verb **1** break (a rule or law etc.); go beyond (a limitation). **2** (*old use*) sin. □ **transgression** noun, **transgressor** noun

**transient** (tran-zi-ĕnt) adjective passing quickly, not lasting or permanent. ● noun a temporary visitor or worker etc. □ **transience** noun

**transistor** noun **1** a semiconductor device with three electrodes, performing the same functions as a thermionic valve but smaller and using less power. **2** (in full **transistor radio**) a portable radio set equipped with transistors.

**transistorize** verb (also **transistorise**) equip with transistors rather than valves.

**transit** noun **1** the process of going, conveying, or being conveyed; *the goods were delayed in transit*. **2** the apparent passage of a heavenly body across the disc of the sun or a planet or across the meridian of a place; *to observe the transit of Venus*. ● verb (**transited**, **transiting**) make a transit across. □ **transit camp** a camp for temporary accommodation of soldiers or refugees etc. **transit visa** a visa allowing the holder to pass through a country but not to stay there.

**transition** (tran-zi-shŏn) noun the process of changing from one state or style etc. to another; *the transition from childhood to adult life*. □ **transitional** adjective, **transitionally** adverb

**transitive** adjective (of a verb) used with a direct object, e.g. *ride* in *ride a bike*. □ **transitively** adverb

**transitory** adjective existing only for a short time, not lasting. □ **transitorily** adverb, **transitoriness** noun

**translate** verb **1** express in another language or in simpler words, or in code for use in a computer. **2** be able to be translated; *the poems don't translate well*. **3** interpret; *we translated his silence as disapproval*. **4** move or change, especially from one person, place, or condition to another. □ **translatable** adjective, **translation** noun, **translator** noun

**transliterate** verb represent (letters or words) in the letters of a different alphabet. □ **transliteration** noun

**translucent** (tranz-**loo**-sĕnt) adjective allowing light to pass through but not

transparent. □ **translucence** noun, **translucency** noun

**transmigration** noun migration. □ **transmigration of the soul** the passing of a person's soul into another body after death. □ **transmigrate** verb

**transmissible** adjective able to be transmitted.

**transmission** noun **1** transmitting; being transmitted. **2** a broadcast. **3** the gear by which power is transmitted from engine to axle in a motor vehicle.

**transmit** verb (**transmitted**, **transmitting**) **1** send or pass on from one person, place, or thing to another; *transmit the message*; *the disease is transmitted by mosquitoes*. **2** allow to pass through or along, be a medium for; *iron transmits heat*. **3** send out (a signal or programme etc.) by telegraph wire or radio waves.

**transmittable** adjective able to be transmitted.

**transmitter** noun a person or thing that transmits; a device or equipment for transmitting electric or radio signals.

**transmogrify** verb (**transmogrified**, **transmogrifying**) (*humorous*) transform, especially in a magical or surprising way. □ **transmogrification** noun

**transmute** verb cause (a thing) to change in form, nature, or substance. □ **transmutation** noun

**transoceanic** adjective **1** on or from the other side of the ocean. **2** crossing the ocean.

**transom** noun **1** a horizontal bar of wood or stone across the top of a door or window. **2** (in full **transom window**) a window above the transom of a door or larger window.

**transparency** (trans-**pa**-rĕn-si) noun **1** being transparent. **2** a photographic slide.

**transparent** (trans-**pa**-rĕnt) adjective **1** allowing light to pass through so that objects behind can be seen clearly. **2** easily understood; (of an excuse or motive etc.) of such a kind that the truth behind it is easily perceived. **3** clear and unmistakable; *a man of transparent honesty*. □ **transparently** adverb

**transpire** verb **1** (of information etc.) leak out, become known; *no details of the contract were allowed to transpire*. **2** (*informal*) happen; *these events transpired a hundred years ago*. **3** (of plants) give off watery vapour from the surface of leaves etc. □ **transpiration** noun

■**Usage** The use in sense 2 is considered incorrect by some people.

**transplant** verb (*pronounced* trans-**plahnt**) **1** remove and replant or establish elsewhere. **2** transfer (living tissue or an organ) from one part of the body or one person or animal to another. **3** be able to be transplanted. ●*noun* (*pronounced* **trans-**plahnt) **1** transplanting of tissue or an organ. **2** something transplanted. □ **transplantation** *noun*

**transponder** *noun* a device for receiving a radio signal and automatically transmitting a different signal.

**transport** *verb* (*pronounced* trans-**port**) **1** convey from one place to another. **2** (*old use*) deport (a criminal) to a penal settlement. **3** carry away by strong emotion; *she was transported with joy.* ●*noun* (*pronounced* **trans**-port) **1** the act or process of transporting something. **2** means of conveyance; *have you got transport?* **3** the condition of being carried away by strong emotion; *in transports of rage.* □ **transport café** a roadside café catering chiefly for long-distance lorry drivers. □ **transportation** *noun*

**transportable** *adjective* able to be transported.

**transporter** *noun* a vehicle used to transport other vehicles, heavy machinery, etc. □ **transporter bridge** a bridge carrying vehicles on a suspended moving platform.

**transpose** *verb* **1** cause (two or more things) to change places; change the position of (a thing) in a series. **2** put (a piece of music) into a different key. □ **transposition** *noun*

**transputer** *noun* a microprocessor with integral memory designed for parallel processing.

**transsexual** *noun* (also **transexual**) **1** a person who emotionally feels himself or herself to be a member of the opposite sex. **2** a person who has had a sex change.

**transship** *verb* (**transshipped**, **transshipping**) transfer (cargo) from one ship or conveyance to another. □ **transshipment** *noun*

**transubstantiation** *noun* the Roman Catholic doctrine that the bread and wine in the Eucharist are converted by consecration into the body and blood of Christ.

**transuranic** (trans-yoor-**an**-ik) *adjective* belonging to a group of radioactive elements whose atoms are heavier than those of uranium.

**Transvaal** (tranz-**vahl**) a province of the Republic of South Africa, lying north of the Orange Free State and separated from it by the River Vaal.

**transverse** *adjective* lying or acting in a crosswise direction. □ **transversely** *adverb*

**transvestite** *noun* a man who gets pleasure from dressing in women's clothes. □ **transvestism** *noun*

**Transylvania** (tran-sil-**vay**-niă) a large tableland region in Romania.

**trap**[1] *noun* **1** a device for catching and holding animals. **2** an arrangement for capturing or detecting a person unawares; anything deceptive. **3** a golf bunker. **4** a device for sending something into the air to be shot at. **5** a compartment from which a greyhound is released at the start of a race. **6** a device for preventing the passage of water or steam or silt etc.; a U-shaped or S-shaped section of a pipe that holds liquid and so prevents foul gases from coming up from a drain. **7** a two-wheeled carriage drawn by a horse. **8** a trapdoor. **9** (*slang*) the mouth; *shut your trap.* ●*verb* (**trapped**, **trapping**) catch or hold in a trap.

**trap**[2] *noun* (in full **trap-rock**) dark volcanic rock.

**trapdoor** *noun* a door in a floor, ceiling, or roof.

**trapeze** *noun* a horizontal bar hung by ropes as a swing for acrobatics.

**trapezium** (tră-**pee**-ziŭm) *noun* (*plural* **trapeziums** *or* **trapezia**) **1** a quadrilateral in which two opposite sides are parallel and the other two are not. **2** (*Amer.*) a trapezoid.

**trapezoid** (**trap**-i-zoid) *noun* **1** a quadrilateral in which no sides are parallel. **2** (*Amer.*) a trapezium.

**trapper** *noun* a person who traps animals, especially for furs.

**trappings** *plural noun* **1** ornamental accessories, symbols of status, etc.; *he had all the trappings of high office but very little power.* **2** the harness of a horse, especially when ornamental.

**Trappist** *noun* a member of a Cistercian order founded at La Trappe in France, noted for silence and other austere rules.

**trash** *noun* **1** worthless stuff, rubbish. **2** worthless people. □ **trash can** (*Amer.*) a dustbin. □ **trashy** *adjective*

**trattoria** (trat-ŏ-**ree**-ă) *noun* an Italian restaurant.

**trauma** (**traw**-mă) *noun* **1** a wound or injury. **2** emotional shock producing a lasting effect upon a person.

**traumatic** (traw-**mat**-ik) *adjective* **1** of or causing trauma. **2** (*informal*) (of an experience) very unpleasant. □ **traumatically** *adverb*

**traumatize** *verb* (also **traumatise**) cause (a person) to suffer trauma or distress.

**travail** (**trav**-ayl) *noun* **1** (*literary*) painful or laborious effort. **2** (*old use*) the pains of childbirth. ●*verb* **1** (*literary*) make a painful or laborious effort. **2** (*old use*) undergo the pains of childbirth.

**travel** *verb* (**travelled**, **travelling**; *Amer.* **traveled**, **traveling**) **1** go from one place

or point to another, make a journey.
**2** journey along or through; cover (a distance) in travelling. **3** go from place to place as a salesperson. **4** (*informal*) withstand a long journey; *some wines travel badly*. **5** (*informal*) move at high speed; *the car was certainly travelling*. ●*noun* **1** travelling, especially in foreign countries. **2** the range, rate, or method of movement of a machine part. □ **travel agency**, **travel agent** one making arrangements for travellers. **travelling clock** a small clock in a case. **travel-sickness** *noun* a feeling of nausea caused by motion when travelling.

**travelled** *adjective* (*Amer.* **traveled**) experienced in travelling.

**traveller** *noun* (*Amer.* **traveler**) **1** a person who travels or is travelling. **2** a person living the life of a Gypsy. **3** a travelling salesperson. □ **traveller's cheque** a cheque for a fixed amount, sold by a bank etc. and usually able to be cashed in various countries. **traveller's joy** wild clematis.

**travelogue** (trav-ĕl-og) *noun* a film or illustrated lecture about travel.

**traverse** *noun* (*pronounced* trav-ers) **1** a thing (especially part of a structure) that lies across another. **2** a zigzag course or road; each leg of this. **3** a lateral movement across something. **4** a steep slope that has to be crossed from side to side in mountaineering. ●*verb* (*pronounced* tră-vers) travel across; lie or extend across. □ **traversal** *noun*

**travesty** (trav-iss-ti) *noun* an absurd or inferior imitation; *his trial was a travesty of justice*. ●*verb* (**travestied**, **travestying**) make or be a travesty of.

**trawl** *noun* a large wide-mouthed fishing-net dragged along the bottom of the sea etc. by a boat. ●*verb* **1** fish with a trawl or seine. **2** catch by trawling.

**trawler** *noun* a boat used in trawling.

**tray** *noun* **1** a flat utensil, usually with a raised edge, on which articles are carried. **2** a tray of food; *have a tray in one's room*. **3** a shallow lidless box for papers or small articles, sometimes as a drawer in a cabinet etc.

**treacherous** *adjective* **1** behaving with or showing treachery. **2** not to be relied on, not giving a firm support; *the roads were icy and treacherous*. □ **treacherously** *adverb*, **treacherousness** *noun*

**treachery** *noun* betrayal of a person or cause; an act of disloyalty.

**treacle** *noun* a thick sticky dark liquid produced when sugar is refined.

**treacly** *adjective* **1** like treacle. **2** excessively sweet or sentimental.

**tread** *verb* (**trod**, **trodden**, **treading**) **1** set one's foot down; walk or step. **2** press or crush with the feet; make (a path or trail or mark etc.) by walking. ●*noun* **1** the manner or sound of walking; *a heavy tread*. **2** the top surface of a stair. **3** the part of a wheel or tyre etc. that touches the ground. □ **tread on air** feel very happy. **tread on a person's toes** (*informal*) offend him or her. **tread the boards** be an actor. **tread water** keep oneself upright in water by making treading movements with the legs.

**treadle** (tred'l) *noun* a lever worked by the foot to drive a wheel, e.g. in a lathe or sewing machine.

**treadmill** *noun* **1** a wide mill-wheel turned by the weight of people treading on steps fixed round its edge, formerly worked by prisoners as a punishment. **2** a device worked by treading an endless belt, used for testing reactions to exertion. **3** monotonous routine work.

**treason** *noun* treachery towards one's country or its ruler (e.g. by plotting the sovereign's death).

**treasonable** *adjective* involving the crime of treason.

**treasure** *noun* **1** precious metals or gems; a hoard of these; *buried treasure*. **2** a highly valued object; *art treasures*. **3** a beloved or highly valued person. ●*verb* value highly, keep or store as precious; *a treasured possession*. □ **treasure hunt** a search for treasure; a game in which players try to find a hidden object from a series of clues. **treasure trove** treasure found hidden and of unknown ownership.

**treasurer** *noun* a person in charge of the funds of an institution or club etc.

**treasury** *noun* a place where treasure is stored; something regarded as containing things of great value or interest; *the book is a treasury of useful information*. □ **the Treasury** the department managing the public revenue of a country. **Treasury bench** the front bench in the House of Commons occupied by Cabinet ministers. **treasury bill** a bill of exchange issued by the government in return for sums of money lent by bankers, brokers, etc.

**treat** *verb* **1** act or behave towards (a person or thing) in a certain way; *treated him roughly*; *treat it as a joke*. **2** present or deal with (a subject); *recent events are treated in detail*. **3** give medical or surgical treatment to; *treated him for sunstroke*. **4** subject (a substance or thing) to a chemical or other process. **5** entertain (a person) at one's own expense; buy, give, or allow to have as a treat; *treated myself to a taxi*. **6** (foll. by *with*) negotiate terms; *treating with their enemies to secure a cease-fire*. ●*noun* **1** something that gives great pleasure, especially something special or unexpected. **2** an entertainment etc. designed to do this. **3** the treating of others to something at one's own expense; *it's my treat.*

**treatise** (tree-tiz) *noun* a written work dealing systematically with one subject.

**treatment** *noun* **1** the process or manner of dealing with a person or thing. **2** something done in order to relieve or cure an illness or abnormality etc.

**treaty** *noun* **1** a formal agreement between two or more countries. **2** a formal agreement between people, especially for the purchase of property.

**treble** *adjective* **1** three times as much or as many. **2** (of a boy's voice, musical instrument, etc.) high-pitched, soprano. ●*noun* **1** a treble quantity or thing. **2** a hit in the narrow ring between the two middle circles of a dartboard, scoring treble. **3** a bet where winnings and stakes from a race are restaked on a second and then a third race. **4** a high-pitched or soprano voice, instrument, etc. ●*verb* make or become three times as much or as many; *costs had trebled.* □ **treble chance** a type of football pool in which matches are selected and points are awarded according to whether the result is a home win, an away win, or a draw. **treble clef** *Music* a clef placing the G above middle C on the second lowest line of the stave. □ **trebly** *adverb*

**Treblinka** (treb-link-ă) a Nazi concentration camp in Poland in the Second World War.

**tree** *noun* **1** a perennial plant with a single stem or trunk without branches for some distance above the ground. **2** a framework of wood for various purposes; *shoe-tree.* **3** = FAMILY TREE. □ **tree-fern** *noun* a large fern with an upright woody stem. **tree-house** *noun* a structure built in a tree, for children to play in. **tree line** = TIMBERLINE. **tree surgeon** a person who prunes trees, treats damaged trees to preserve them, etc. **up a tree** (*slang*) in great difficulties. □ **treeless** *adjective*

**treecreeper** *noun* a small creeping bird feeding on insects in tree-bark.

**treetop** *noun* the topmost branches of a tree.

**trefoil** (tref-oil) *noun* **1** a plant with three leaflets, e.g. clover. **2** an ornament or design shaped like this.

**trek** *noun* a long arduous journey. ●*verb* (**trekked, trekking**) make a trek.

**trellis** *noun* (in full **trellis-work**) a light framework of bars, used to support climbing plants.

**trematode** (trem-ă-tohd) *noun* a parasitic flatworm.

**tremble** *verb* shake involuntarily from fear or cold etc.; quiver. ●*noun* a trembling or quivering movement, a tremor.

**trembler** *noun* a spring that makes an electrical contact when shaken.

**trembly** *adjective* (*informal*) trembling.

**tremendous** *adjective* **1** immense. **2** (*informal*) excellent; *gave a tremendous performance.* □ **tremendously** *adverb*, **tremendousness** *noun*

**tremolo** (trem-ŏ-loh) *noun* (*plural* **tremolos**) a trembling or vibrating effect in music.

**tremor** (trem-er) *noun* **1** a slight shaking or trembling movement, a vibration; (in full **earth tremor**) a slight earthquake. **2** a thrill of fear or other emotion.

**tremulous** (trem-yoo-lŭs) *adjective* **1** trembling from nervousness or weakness. **2** easily made to quiver. □ **tremulously** *adverb*

**trench** *noun* a long narrow hole cut in the ground, e.g. for drainage or to give troops shelter from enemy fire. ●*verb* dig trenches in (ground). □ **trench coat** a belted coat or raincoat with pockets and flaps like those of a military uniform coat.

**trenchant** (tren-chănt) *adjective* (of comments or policies etc.) penetrating, strong and effective; *made some trenchant criticisms.* □ **trenchantly** *adverb*, **trenchancy** *noun*

**trencher** *noun* (*old use*) a wooden platter for serving food.

**trencherman** *noun* (*plural* **trenchermen**) a person who eats well, or in a specified way.

**trend** *noun* the general direction that something takes, a continuing tendency; *the trend of prices is upwards.* □ **trend-setter** *noun* a person who leads the way in fashion etc.

**trendy** *adjective* (**trendier, trendiest**) (*informal*) up to date, following the latest trends of fashion. □ **trendily** *adverb*, **trendiness** *noun*

**trepan** (tri-pan) *noun* a cylindrical saw formerly used by surgeons for removing part of the skull.

**trepidation** (trep-i-day-shŏn) *noun* a state of fear and anxiety, nervous agitation.

**trespass** *verb* **1** enter a person's land or property unlawfully. **2** intrude or make use of unreasonably; *I don't want to trespass on your time.* **3** (*old use*) sin or do wrong; *as we forgive them that trespass against us.* ●*noun* **1** the act of trespassing. **2** (*old use*) sin, wrongdoing. □ **trespasser** *noun*

**tress** *noun* **1** a long lock of hair. **2** (**tresses**) the hair of the head, especially of a woman or girl.

**trestle** *noun* **1** each of a pair or set of supports on which a board is rested to form a table; (in full **trestle-table**) the table itself. **2** (in full **trestle-work**) an open braced framework for supporting a bridge.

**trews** *plural noun* close-fitting trousers.

**TRH** *abbreviation* Their Royal Highnesses.

**tri-** *combining form* three, three times, triple.

**triad** (try-ad) *noun* **1** a group or set of three. **2** a Chinese secret organization.

**trial** *noun* **1** an examination in a lawcourt by a judge to decide on the guilt or innocence of an accused person. **2** the process of testing qualities or performance by use and experience. **3** a sports match to test the ability of players who may be selected for a team. **4** a test of individual ability on a motor cycle over rough ground or on a road. **5** a person or thing that tries one's patience or endurance; a hardship. □ **on trial** undergoing a trial; on approval. **trial and error** the process of trying repeatedly and learning from one's failures.

**triangle** *noun* **1** a geometric figure with three sides and three angles. **2** something shaped like this; a percussion instrument consisting of a steel rod bent into this shape and struck with another steel rod.

**triangular** *adjective* **1** shaped like a triangle. **2** involving three people; *a triangular contest.*

**triangulate** *verb* **1** divide into triangles. **2** measure or map out (an area) in surveying by means of calculations based on a network of triangles. □ **triangulation** *noun*

**Trianon** (tree-ă-nawn) either of two small palaces in the park at Versailles, built by Louis XIV (1687) and XV (1762–8).

**Triassic** (try-ass-ik) *Geol. adjective* of the first period of the Mesozoic era. ● *noun* this period.

**triathlon** (try-ath-lon) *noun* an athletic contest in which competitors take part in three events.

**tribal** *adjective* of a tribe or tribes.

**tribalism** *noun* tribal organization.

**tribe** *noun* **1** a racial group (especially in a primitive or nomadic culture) living as a community under one or more chiefs. **2** a set or class of people; *he despises the whole tribe of politicians.*

**tribesman** *noun* (*plural* **tribesmen**) a member of a racial tribe.

**tribulation** (trib-yoo-lay-shŏn) *noun* great affliction; a cause of this.

**tribunal** (try-bew-năl) *noun* a board of officials appointed to make a judgement or act as arbitrators on a particular problem.

**tribune** (trib-yoon) *noun* **1** (in ancient Rome) an official chosen by the people to protect their liberties; an officer in periodic command of a legion. **2** a leader of the people.

**tributary** *noun* a river or stream that flows into a larger river or lake. ● *adjective* flowing in this way.

**tribute** *noun* **1** something said, done, or given as a mark of respect or admiration. **2** (foll. by *to*) an indication of the effectiveness of; *his recovery is a tribute to the doctor's skill.* **3** payment that one country or ruler was formerly obliged to pay to a more powerful one.

**trice** *noun* □ **in a trice** in an instant.

**triceps** (try-seps) *noun* the large muscle at the back of the upper arm, which straightens the elbow.

**triceratops** *noun* (try-se-ră-tops) a dinosaur with three horns on the forehead and a wavy-edged collar round the neck.

**trichology** (trik-ol-ŏji) *noun* the study of hair and its diseases. □ **trichologist** *noun*

**trick** *noun* **1** something done in order to deceive or outwit someone. **2** a deception or illusion; *a trick of the light.* **3** a particular technique, the exact or best way of doing something. **4** a feat of skill done for entertainment; *conjuring tricks.* **5** a mannerism; *he has a trick of repeating himself.* **6** a mischievous, foolish, or discreditable act; a practical joke. **7** the cards played in one round of a card game; the round itself; a point gained as a result of this. ● *verb* **1** deceive or persuade by a trick, mislead. **2** (foll. by *out* or *up*) deck or decorate. □ **do the trick** (*informal*) achieve what is required. **how's tricks?** (*slang*) how are things? **trick or treat** (especially *Amer.*) a phrase said by children who call at houses at Hallowe'en asking to be given sweets etc. and threatening to do mischief if these are not provided.

**trickery** *noun* use of tricks, deception.

**trickle** *verb* **1** flow or cause to flow in a thin stream. **2** come or go slowly or gradually; *people trickled into the hall.* ● *noun* a small amount coming or going slowly; *a trickle of information.* □ **trickle charger** a device for slow continuous charging of an accumulator.

**trickster** *noun* a person who tricks or cheats people.

**tricksy** *adjective* full of tricks, playful.

**tricky** *adjective* (**trickier**, **trickiest**) **1** crafty, deceitful. **2** requiring skilful handling; *a tricky task.* □ **trickily** *adverb*, **trickiness** *noun*

**tricolour** (trik-ŏl-er) *noun* (*Amer.* **tricolor**) a flag with three colours in stripes, especially those of France and Ireland.

**tricot** (trik-oh) *noun* fine jersey fabric.

**tricycle** *noun* a three-wheeled pedal-driven vehicle.

**trident** (try-děnt) *noun* **1** a three-pronged spear, carried by Neptune and Britannia as a symbol of power over the sea. **2** (**Tri-**

dent) a submarine-launched ballistic missile.

**tried** see TRY.

**triennial** (try-en-iăl) *adjective* **1** lasting for three years. **2** happening every third year. □ **triennially** *adverb*

**trier** *noun* **1** a person who tries hard, one who always does his or her best. **2** a tester.

**trifle** *noun* **1** something of only slight value or importance. **2** a very small amount, especially of money; *it cost a mere trifle.* **3** (**a trifle**) somewhat, rather; *he seems a trifle angry.* **4** a dish made of sponge cake soaked in wine or jelly etc. and topped with custard and cream. ●*verb* behave or talk frivolously.

**trifling** *adjective* trivial.

**triforium** (try-for-iŭm) *noun* (*plural* **triforia**) an arcade or gallery above the arches of the nave and choir in a church.

**trig** *noun* (*informal*) trigonometry. □ **trig point** a reference point on high ground, used in triangulation.

**trigger** *noun* a lever or catch for releasing a spring, especially so as to fire a gun. ●*verb* (often foll. by *off*) start; set (an action or process) in motion; *the announcement triggered off riots.* □ **trigger-happy** *adjective* apt to shoot on slight provocation.

**trigonometry** (trig-ŏn-om-itri) *noun* the branch of mathematics dealing with the relationship of sides and angles of triangles etc. □ **trigonometric** *adjective*, **trigonometrical** *adjective*

**trike** *noun* (*informal*) a tricycle.

**trilateral** (try-lat-er-ăl) *adjective* having three sides or three participants.

**trilby** *noun* a man's soft felt hat with a lengthwise dent in the crown and a narrow brim.

**trilingual** (try-ling-wăl) *adjective* speaking or using three languages.

**trill** *noun* **1** a vibrating sound made by the voice (pronouncing *r* with the tongue vibrating) or in birdsong. **2** quick alternation of two notes in music that are a tone or semitone apart. ●*verb* sound or sing with a trill.

**trillion** *noun* **1** a million million ($10^{12}$). **2** (*formerly, esp. Brit.*) a million million million ($10^{18}$).

**trilobite** (try-lŏ-byt) *noun* a marine creature, an invertebrate with a segmented body and jointed limbs, now only found as a fossil.

**trilogy** (tril-ŏji) *noun* a group of three related literary or operatic works.

**trim** *adjective* (**trimmer, trimmest**) neat and orderly; having a smooth outline or compact structure. ●*verb* (**trimmed, trimming**) **1** make neat or smooth by cutting away irregular parts. **2** remove or reduce by cutting. **3** ornament. **4** make (a boat or air-

craft) evenly balanced by arranging the position of its cargo or passengers etc. **5** arrange (sails) to suit the wind. **6** (*informal*) get the better of (a person) in a bargain etc. ●*noun* **1** condition as regards readiness or fitness; *in good trim.* **2** the trimming on a dress or furniture etc.; the colour or type of upholstery and other fittings in a car. **3** the trimming of hair etc. **4** the balance or the even horizontal position of a boat in the water or an aircraft in the air. □ **trimly** *adverb*, **trimness** *noun*, **trimmer** *noun*

**trimaran** (try-mă-ran) *noun* a vessel like a catamaran, with three hulls side by side.

**trimming** *noun* **1** something added as an ornament or decoration on a dress or furniture etc. **2** (**trimmings**) pieces cut off when something is trimmed. **3** (**trimmings**) the usual accompaniments of something; extras; *roast turkey and all the trimmings.*

**Trinidad** an island in the West Indies, forming part of the country of **Trinidad and Tobago.** □ **Trinidadian** (trin-i-day-diăn) *adjective & noun*

**trinitrotoluene** *noun* (also **trinitrotoluol**) = TNT.

**trinity** *noun* **1** being three. **2** a group of three. **3** (**the Trinity**) the three persons of the Christian Godhead (Father, Son, Holy Spirit) as constituting one God. □ **Trinity Sunday** the Sunday after Whit Sunday.

**Trinity House** the British institution that licenses ships' pilots and maintains lighthouses etc.

**trinket** *noun* a small fancy article or piece of jewellery.

**trio** (tree-oh) *noun* (*plural* **trios**) **1** a group or set of three. **2** a group of three singers or players; a musical composition for these.

**trip** *verb* (**tripped, tripping**) **1** walk, run, or dance with quick light steps; (of rhythm) run lightly. **2** (*informal*) have a long visionary experience caused by a drug. **3** (often foll. by *up*) stumble, catch one's foot on something and fall; cause to do this. **4** (often foll. by *up*) make a slip or blunder; cause to do this. **5** release (a switch or catch) so as to operate a mechanism. ●*noun* **1** a journey or excursion, especially for pleasure. **2** (*informal*) a long visionary experience caused by a drug. **3** a stumble. **4** a device for tripping a mechanism. □ **trip-wire** *noun* a wire stretched close to the ground, actuating a trap or warning device etc. when disturbed.

**tripartite** (try-par-tyt) *adjective* consisting of three parts.

**tripe** *noun* **1** the stomach of an ox etc. as food. **2** (*informal*) nonsense; something worthless.

**Tripitaka** (trip-i-**tah**-kă) *noun* the sacred canon of Theravada Buddhism, written in the Pali language.

**triple** *adjective* **1** consisting of three parts; involving three people or groups. **2** three times as much or as many. ●*verb* make or become three times as much or as many. □ **triple crown** winning of all three of a group of important events in horse racing, Rugby football, etc. **triple jump** an athletic contest comprising a hop, a step, and a long jump. **triple time** (in music) rhythm with three beats to the bar. □ **triply** *adjective*

**triplet** *noun* **1** one of three children or animals born at one birth. **2** a set of three things, especially three equal musical notes.

**triplex** *adjective* triple, threefold.

**triplicate** *adjective* (*pronounced* **trip**-li-kăt) existing in three parts, copies, or examples; tripled. ●*noun* (*pronounced* **trip**-li-kăt) each of a set of three copies or corresponding parts. ●*verb* (*pronounced* **trip**-li-kayt) **1** make in three copies. **2** multiply by three; triple. □ **in triplicate** in three copies.

**tripod** (**try**-pod) *noun* a three-legged stand for a camera or surveying instrument etc.

**Tripoli** the capital of Libya.

**tripos** (**try**-poss) *noun* the final examination for the degree of BA at Cambridge University.

**tripper** *noun* a person who goes on a pleasure trip.

**triptych** (**trip**-tik) *noun* a picture or carving on three panels fixed or hinged side by side, especially as an altarpiece.

**Tripura** (**trip**-oor-ă) a State in NE India.

**trireme** (**try**-reem) *noun* an ancient Greek warship with three banks of oars.

**trisect** (try-**sekt**) *verb* divide into three equal parts. □ **trisection** *noun*

**trite** (*rhymes with* kite) *adjective* (of a phrase or opinion) commonplace, hackneyed. □ **tritely** *adverb*

**tritium** *noun* a radioactive isotope of hydrogen (symbol T).

**Triton** (**try**-tŏn) (*Gk. myth.*) **1** the son of Poseidon. **2** a minor seagod, usually represented as a man with a fish's tail carrying a trident and a shell-trumpet.

**triumph** *noun* **1** the fact of being successful or victorious; joy at this. **2** a great success or achievement. ●*verb* be successful or victorious; rejoice at one's success etc.

**triumphal** *adjective* of or celebrating a triumph. □ **triumphal arch** one built to commemorate a victory.

**triumphant** *adjective* **1** victorious, successful. **2** rejoicing at success etc. □ **triumphantly** *adverb*

**triumvirate** (try-**um**-ver-ăt) *noun* a ruling group of three persons.

**trivalent** (try-**vay**-lĕnt) *adjective* having a valence of three.

**trivet** (**triv**-it) *noun* an iron stand, especially a tripod, for a kettle or pot etc.

**trivia** *plural noun* trivial things.

**trivial** *adjective* of only small value or importance. □ **trivially** *adjective*, **triviality** (triv-i-**al**-iti) *noun*

**trivialize** *verb* (also **trivialise**) treat (something) as being trivial.

**trochee** (**troh**-kee) *noun* a metrical foot consisting of one long or stressed syllable followed by one short or unstressed syllable. □ **trochaic** (trŏ-**kay**-ik) *adjective*

**trod, trodden** *see* TREAD.

**troglodyte** (**trog**-lŏ-dyt) *noun* a cave-dweller in ancient times.

**troika** (**troi**-kă) *noun* **1** a Russian vehicle with a team of three horses abreast. **2** this team. **3** a group of three people, especially as an administrative council.

**Troilus** (in medieval legend) the forsaken lover of Cressida.

**Trojan** *adjective* of Troy or its people. ●*noun* a native or inhabitant of Troy. □ **Trojan Horse** (*Gk. legend*) the hollow wooden horse used by the Greeks (who concealed warriors inside it) to enter Troy. **Trojan War** (*Gk. legend*) the ten-year siege of Troy by the Greeks, ending in its capture after the trick of the wooden horse. **work like a Trojan** work with great energy and endurance.

**troll** (*rhymes with* hole) *verb* fish by drawing bait along in the water. ●*noun* (*Scand. myth.*) a member of a race of supernatural beings formerly thought of as giants but now as friendly but mischievous dwarfs.

**trolley** *noun* (*plural* **trolleys**) **1** a platform on wheels for transporting goods; a small cart or truck. **2** a small table on wheels or castors for transporting food or small articles. □ **trolley bus** a bus powered by electricity from an overhead wire to which it is linked by a pole and contact-wheel.

**trollop** *noun* a disreputable woman; a prostitute.

**Trollope**, Anthony (1815–82), English novelist.

**trombone** *noun* a large brass wind instrument with a sliding tube. □ **trombonist** *noun*

**trompe-l'oeil** (tromp lĕ-ee) *noun* a painting on a wall etc. designed to give an illusion of reality. (¶ French, = deceives the eye.)

**troop** *noun* **1** a company of people or animals, especially when moving. **2** a cavalry unit commanded by a captain; a unit of artillery. **3** a unit of three or more Scout patrols. **4** (**troops**) soldiers, armed forces.

●*verb* assemble or go as a troop or in great numbers. □ **trooping the colour** the ceremony of carrying the regimental flag along ranks of soldiers.

**trooper** *noun* **1** a soldier in a cavalry or armoured unit. **2** (*Amer.* & *Austral.*) a member of a State police force. □ **swear like a trooper** swear forcibly.

■**Usage** Do not confuse with **trouper**.

**trophy** *noun* **1** something taken in war or hunting etc. as a souvenir of success. **2** an object awarded as a prize or token of victory. □ **trophy wife** a wife regarded as a status symbol for a (usually older) man.

**tropic** *noun* **1** a line of latitude 23°27' north of the equator (**tropic of Cancer**) or the same latitude south of it (**tropic of Capricorn**). **2** (**the Tropics**) the region between these, with a hot climate.

**tropical** *adjective* of, found in, or like the Tropics.

**troposphere** (trop-ŏ-sfeer) *noun* the layer of atmospheric air extending about 6–10 km upwards from the earth's surface.

**trot** *noun* **1** the running action of a horse etc. with legs moving as in a walk. **2** a slowish run. ●*verb* (**trotted, trotting**) **1** go or cause to go at a trot. **2** (*informal*) walk or go; *trot round to the chemist.* □ **on the trot** (*informal*) **1** continually busy; *kept him on the trot.* **2** in succession; *for five weeks on the trot.* **trot out** (*informal*) produce, bring out for inspection or approval etc.; *trotted out the same old excuse.* **trotting race** a horse race in which the horses pull small vehicles.

**troth** *see* PLIGHT.

**Trotsky**, Leon (original name: Lev Davidovich Bronstein) (1879–1940), Russian leader and revolutionary urging worldwide socialist revolution.

**Trotskyist** *noun* a supporter of Trotsky; a radical left-wing Communist. □ **Trotskyism** *noun*, **Trotskyite** *noun*

**trotter** *noun* **1** a horse of a special breed trained for trotting races. **2** an animal's foot as food; *pigs' trotters.*

**troubadour** (troo-băd-oor) *noun* a lyric poet in southern France etc. in the 11th–13th centuries, singing mainly of chivalry and courtly love.

**trouble** *noun* **1** difficulty, inconvenience; distress, vexation; misfortune. **2** a cause of any of these. **3** conflict, public unrest; (**the Troubles**) rebellions and unrest in Ireland in 1919–23 and in Northern Ireland from 1968. **4** unpleasantness involving punishment or rebuke. **5** faulty functioning of a mechanism or of the body or mind; *engine trouble*; *stomach trouble.* ●*verb* **1** cause trouble, distress, pain, or inconvenience to. **2** be disturbed or worried, be subjected to

inconvenience or unpleasant exertion; *don't trouble about it.* □ **in trouble 1** involved in something liable to bring punishment or rebuke. **2** (*informal*) pregnant while unmarried. **take trouble** use much care and effort in doing something. **trouble spot** a place where trouble frequently occurs.

**troublemaker** *noun* a person who habitually stirs up trouble. □ **troublemaking** *noun*

**troubleshooter** *noun* **1** a person who acts as a mediator in disputes. **2** a person who traces and corrects faults in machinery or in an organization. □ **troubleshooting** *noun*

**troublesome** *adjective* giving trouble; causing annoyance.

**trough** (*pronounced* trof) *noun* **1** a long narrow open receptacle, especially for holding water or food for animals. **2** a channel for conveying liquid. **3** a depression between two waves or ridges. **4** an elongated region of low atmospheric pressure.

**trounce** *verb* **1** thrash. **2** defeat heavily.

**troupe** (*pronounced* troop) *noun* a company of actors or acrobats etc.

**trouper** (troop-er) *noun* **1** a member of a theatrical troupe. **2** a loyal and supportive friend, helper, etc.; *a good trouper.*

■**Usage** Do not confuse with **trooper**.

**trousers** *plural noun* a two-legged outer garment reaching from the waist usually to the ankles. □ **trouser suit** a woman's suit of jacket and trousers.

**trousseau** (**troo-soh**) *noun* (*plural* **trousseaus** *or* **trousseaux**, *pronounced* **troo-sohz**) a bride's collection of clothing etc. to begin married life.

**trout** *noun* (*plural* **trout** *or* **trouts**) any of several chiefly freshwater fish valued as food and game.

**trowel** *noun* **1** a small tool with a flat blade for spreading mortar etc. **2** a small garden tool with a curved blade for lifting plants or scooping things.

**Troy** (*Gk. legend*) a city in Asia Minor, besieged for ten years by Greek forces in their attempt to recover Helen, wife of Menelaus, who had been abducted by the Trojan prince Paris.

**troy weight** a system of weights used for precious metals and gems, in which 1 pound = 12 ounces or 5760 grains.

**truant** *noun* a child who stays away from school without leave. ●*verb* play truant. □ **play truant** stay away as a truant. □ **truancy** *noun*

**truce** *noun* an agreement to stop fighting or arguing temporarily.

**truck** *noun* **1** an open container on wheels for transporting loads; an open railway wagon. **2** a lorry. □ **have no truck with** have no dealings with.

**trucker** *noun* a long-distance lorry driver.

**trucking** *noun* driving a lorry.

**truckle** *verb* submit obsequiously; *refusing to truckle to bullies.* □ **truckle-bed** *noun* a low bed on wheels so that it can be pushed under another.

**truculent** (truk-yoo-lĕnt) *adjective* defiant and aggressive. □ **truculently** *adverb*, **truculence** *noun*

**Trudeau** (troo-doh), Pierre Elliott (born 1919), Canadian Liberal statesman, Prime Minister 1968–79 and 1980–4.

**trudge** *verb* walk laboriously. ●*noun* a trudging walk.

**true** *adjective* **1** in accordance with fact. **2** in accordance with correct principles or an accepted standard; genuine and not false; *he was the true heir.* **3** exact, accurate; (of the voice etc.) in good tune. **4** accurately placed, balanced, or shaped. **5** loyal, faithful. ●*adverb* truly, accurately. □ **true-blue** *adjective* completely true to one's principles, firmly loyal. **true north** north according to the earth's axis, not magnetic north.

**truffle** *noun* **1** a rich-flavoured edible fungus that grows underground. **2** a soft sweet made of a chocolate mixture.

**trug** *noun* a shallow wooden basket used by gardeners.

**truism** (troo-izm) *noun* a statement that is obviously true, especially one that is hackneyed, e.g. *nothing lasts for ever.*

**truly** *adverb* **1** truthfully. **2** sincerely, genuinely; *we are truly grateful.* **3** faithfully, loyally.

**Truman**, Harry S (1884–1972), 33rd President of the USA 1945–53.

**trump** *noun* **1** a playing card of a suit temporarily ranking above others. **2** (*informal*) a very helpful or loyal person. **3** (*old use*) the sound of a trumpet. ●*verb* take (a card or trick) with a trump; play a trump. □ **trump card 1** a card of the trump suit. **2** a valuable resource, a means of getting what one wants. **trump up** invent (an excuse or accusation etc.). **turn up trumps** (*informal*) **1** turn out successfully. **2** behave with great kindness or generosity.

**trumpery** *adjective* showy but worthless. ●*noun* worthless things; rubbish.

**trumpet** *noun* **1** a brass wind instrument with a penetrating tone, consisting of a narrow straight or curved tube flared at the end. **2** something shaped like this. ●*verb* (**trumpeted**, **trumpeting**) **1** blow a trumpet; proclaim by or as if by the sound of a trumpet. **2** (of an elephant) make a loud resounding sound with its trunk. □ **trumpeter** *noun*

**truncate** (trunk-ayt) *verb* shorten by cutting off the top or end. □ **truncation** *noun*

**truncheon** (trun-chŏn) *noun* a short thick stick carried as a weapon by police.

**trundle** *verb* roll or move along, especially heavily on wheels; *trundling a wheelbarrow*; *a bus trundled up.*

**trunk** *noun* **1** the main stem of a tree. **2** the body apart from head and limbs. **3** a large box with a hinged lid for transporting or storing clothes etc. **4** (*Amer.*) the boot of a car. **5** the long flexible nose of an elephant. **6** (**trunks**) shorts worn by men or boys for swimming, boxing, etc. □ **trunk call** a long-distance inland telephone call. **trunk line** a main line or route of a railway, telephone system, etc. **trunk road** an important main road.

**truss** *noun* **1** a bundle of hay or straw. **2** a compact cluster of flowers or fruit. **3** a framework of beams or bars supporting a roof or bridge etc. **4** a padded belt or other device worn to support a hernia. ●*verb* **1** tie or bind securely; *truss him up*; *truss a chicken.* **2** support (a roof or bridge etc.) with trusses.

**trust** *noun* **1** firm belief in the reliability, truth, or strength etc. of a person or thing. **2** confident expectation. **3** responsibility arising from trust placed in the person given authority; *a position of trust.* **4** property legally entrusted to a person with instructions to use it for another's benefit or for a specified purpose. **5** an organization founded to promote or preserve something; *Slimbridge Wildfowl Trust.* **6** an association of business firms, formed to reduce or defeat competition; *anti-trust legislation.* ●*verb* **1** have or place trust in, treat as reliable. **2** entrust. **3** hope earnestly; *I trust he is not hurt.* □ **in trust** held as a trust (*see* sense 4). **on trust** accepted without investigation; *don't take the statement on trust.* **trust to** place reliance on; *trusting to luck.*

**trustee** *noun* **1** a person who holds and administers property in trust for another. **2** a member of a group of people managing the business affairs of an institution.

**trustful** *adjective* full of trust or confidence. □ **trustfully** *adverb*

**trusting** *adjective* having trust, trustful. □ **trustingly** *adverb*

**trustworthy** *adjective* worthy of trust, reliable. □ **trustworthiness** *noun*

**trusty** *adjective* (*old use*) trustworthy; *his trusty sword.* ●*noun* a prisoner who is granted special privileges because of good behaviour.

**truth** *noun* **1** the quality of being true. **2** something that is true.

**truthful** *adjective* **1** habitually telling the truth. **2** true; *a truthful account of what happened.* □ **truthfully** *adverb*, **truthfulness** *noun*

**try** *verb* (**tried, trying**) **1** attempt, make an effort to do something. **2** use, do, or test the possibilities of something to discover whether it is satisfactory or useful; *try your strength*; *try soap and water*; *try shaking it*. **3** try to open (a door or window) to discover whether it will be locked. **4** be a strain on; *you are trying my patience*. **5** examine and decide (a case or issue) in a lawcourt; hold a trial of (a person); *he was tried for murder*. ●*noun* **1** an attempt. **2** a touch-down by a player in Rugby football, scoring points and entitling the scoring side to a kick at goal. □ **try it on** (*informal*) do something to discover whether it will be tolerated. **try-on** *noun* (*informal*) an experimental action of this kind. **try on** put (a garment) on to see whether it fits and looks good. **try one's hand** attempt something for the first time. **try one's luck** attempt something to see if one can be successful. **try-out** *noun* an experimental test.

**trying** *adjective* putting a strain on one's temper or patience; annoying.

**tryst** *noun* (*old use*) a meeting, especially of lovers in secret.

**tsar** (*pronounced* zar) *noun* (also **czar**) the title of the former emperors of Russia.

**tsetse fly** (**tset**-si *or* **tet**-si) a tropical African fly that transmits disease (especially sleeping-sickness) by its bite.

**T-shirt** *noun* (also **tee shirt**) a casual short-sleeved cotton top with no collar.

**tsp.** *abbreviation* (*plural* **tsps.**) teaspoonful.

**T-square** *noun* a T-shaped instrument for measuring or obtaining right angles.

**tsunami** (tsoo-**nah**-mi) *noun* **1** a series of long high sea waves caused by earth-movement. **2** an exceptionally large tidal wave. (¶ Japanese.)

**TT** *abbreviation* **1** tuberculin-tested. **2** Tourist Trophy. **3** teetotal.

**Tuareg** (**twah**-reg) *noun* (*plural* **Tuareg** *or* **Tuaregs**) **1** a member of a Berber group of nomadic pastoral people in North Africa. **2** their language.

**tub** *noun* **1** an open flat-bottomed container used for washing or for holding liquids, plants, etc. **2** (*informal*) a bath. □ **tub-thumper** *noun* (*informal*) a ranting preacher or orator.

**tuba** (**tew**-bă) *noun* a large low-pitched brass wind instrument.

**tubby** *adjective* (**tubbier, tubbiest**) short and fat. □ **tubbiness** *noun*

**tube** *noun* **1** a long hollow cylinder. **2** anything shaped like this. **3** a cylinder of flexible material with a screw-cap, holding pastes etc. **4** (**the tube**) (*informal*) the underground railway system in London. **5** (**the tube**) (*Amer. informal*) television. **6** a cathode-ray tube in a television set. **7** a thermionic valve. **8** (*Austral. slang*) a can of beer.

**tuber** *noun* a short thick rounded root (e.g. of a dahlia) or underground stem (e.g. of a potato), producing buds from which new plants will grow.

**tubercle** (**tew**-ber-kŭl) *noun* a small rounded projection or swelling, especially as characteristic of tuberculosis.

**tubercular** (tew-**ber**-kew-ler) *adjective* of or affected with tuberculosis.

**tuberculin-tested** (tew-**ber**-kew-lin) *adjective* (of milk) from cows tested for and free from tuberculosis.

**tuberculosis** (tew-ber-kew-**loh**-sis) *noun* an infectious wasting disease in which tubercles appear on body tissue, especially in the lungs.

**tuberose** (**tew**-ber-ohz) *noun* a tropical plant with fragrant white funnel-shaped flowers.

**tuberous** *adjective* of or like a tuber; bearing tubers.

**tubing** *noun* tubes; a length of tube.

**tubular** *adjective* tube-shaped; (of furniture) made of tube-shaped pieces. □ **tubular bells** an orchestral instrument of hanging brass tubes struck with a hammer.

**tubule** (**tew**-bewl) *noun* a small tube or tube-shaped part.

**TUC** *abbreviation* Trades Union Congress.

**tuck** *noun* **1** a flat fold stitched in a garment etc. to make it smaller or as an ornament. **2** (*slang*) food, especially sweets and cakes. ●*verb* **1** put a tuck or tucks in (a garment etc.). **2** turn (ends or edges etc.) or fold (a part) in, into, or under something so as to be concealed or held in place. **3** cover snugly and compactly; *tucked him up in bed*. **4** put away compactly; *tucked it in a drawer*. □ **tuck in** (*informal*) eat food heartily. **tuck shop** a shop selling sweets etc. to school-children.

**tucker** *noun* (*Austral. informal*) food.

**Tudor** *noun* a member of the royal family of England from Henry VII to Elizabeth I. ●*adjective* of the Tudors; or of imitating the style of houses etc. of that period.

**Tues.** *abbreviation* (also **Tue.**) Tuesday.

**Tuesday** the day of the week following Monday.

**tufa** (**tew**-fă) *noun* **1** porous rock formed round springs of mineral water. **2** tuff.

**tuff** *noun* rock formed from volcanic ashes.

**tuft** *noun* a bunch of threads, grass, feathers, hair, etc. held or growing together at the base. □ **tufty** *adjective*

**tufted** *adjective* having a tuft or tufts; (of a bird) having a tuft of projecting feathers on its head.

**tug** *verb* (**tugged, tugging**) **1** pull vigorously or with great effort. **2** tow by means of a tug. ●*noun* **1** a vigorous pull. **2** a small powerful boat for towing others. □ **tug of love** (*informal*) a situation in which custody of a child is in dispute, e.g. between its parents who are separated. **tug of war** a contest in which two teams hold a rope at opposite ends and pull until one hauls the other over a central point.

**tugboat** *noun* a tug ( = TUG *noun* sense 2).

**tuition** (tew-**ish**-ŏn) *noun* teaching, instruction.

**tulip** *noun* a garden plant growing from a bulb, with a large cup-shaped flower on a tall stem. □ **tulip tree** any of various trees with large tulip-like flowers.

**tulle** (*pronounced* tewl) *noun* a fine silky net used for veils and dresses.

**tum** *noun* (*informal*) the stomach.

**tumble** *verb* **1** fall helplessly or headlong. **2** fall in value or amount. **3** roll over and over in a disorderly way. **4** move or rush in a hasty careless way; *tumbled into bed.* **5** (of a pigeon) throw itself over backwards in flight. **6** throw or push carelessly in a confused mass. **7** rumple or disarrange. **8** (often foll. by *to*) (*informal*) realize or grasp the meaning of something; *I eventually tumbled to their plan.* ●*noun* **1** a tumbling fall. **2** an untidy state. □ **tumble-drier** *noun* (also **tumble-dryer**) a machine for drying washing in a heated drum that rotates.

**tumbledown** *adjective* falling or fallen into ruin, dilapidated.

**tumbler** *noun* **1** a drinking glass with no handle or foot. **2** an acrobat. **3** a pivoted piece in a lock that holds the bolt until lifted by a key. **4** a pigeon that tumbles in flight.

**tumbrel** *noun* (also **tumbril**) (*old use*) an open cart, especially used to carry condemned people to the guillotine during the French Revolution.

**tumescent** (tew-**mess**-ĕnt) *adjective* swelling. □ **tumescence** *noun*

**tumid** (tew-mid) *adjective* **1** swollen, inflated. **2** (of style) pompous. □ **tumidity** *noun*

**tummy** *noun* (*informal*) the stomach. □ **tummy-button** *noun* the navel.

**tumour** (tew-mer) *noun* (*Amer.* **tumor**) an abnormal mass of new tissue growing on or in the body.

**tumult** (tew-mult) *noun* **1** an uproar. **2** a state of confusion and agitation; *her mind was in a tumult.*

**tumultuous** (tew-**mul**-tew-ŭs) *adjective* noisy; crowded, confused, and disorderly. □ **tumultuously** *adverb*

**tumulus** *noun* (*plural* **tumuli**) an ancient burial mound.

**tun** *noun* a large cask for wine or beer etc.

**tuna** (tew-nă) *noun* (*plural* **tuna** or **tunas**) **1** a large edible sea fish. **2** (in full **tuna-fish**) its flesh as food.

**tundra** *noun* the vast level treeless Arctic regions where the subsoil is frozen.

**tune** *noun* a melody. ●*verb* **1** put (a musical instrument) in tune. **2** tune in (a radio receiver etc.). **3** adjust (an engine) to run smoothly. □ **in tune 1** playing or singing at the correct musical pitch. **2** (usually foll. by *with*) harmonizing or in sympathy with one's company, surroundings, etc. **out of tune** not in tune. **to the tune of** (*informal*) to the considerable sum of; *received compensation to the tune of £5000.* **tune in** set a radio receiver to the right wavelength. **tune up** (of an orchestra) bring instruments to the correct pitch.

**tuneful** *adjective* melodious, having a pleasing tune. □ **tunefully** *adverb*

**tuneless** *adjective* not melodious, without a tune. □ **tunelessly** *adverb*

**tuner** *noun* **1** a person who tunes pianos etc. **2** a radio receiver, especially as part of a hi-fi system.

**tungsten** (tung-stĕn) *noun* a chemical element (symbol W), a heavy grey metallic substance used for the filaments of electric lamps and in making steel.

**tunic** *noun* **1** a close-fitting jacket worn as part of a uniform. **2** a woman's light hip-length garment. **3** a loose garment reaching to the hips or knees.

**tuning fork** a steel device like a two-pronged fork, which produces a note of fixed pitch when struck.

**Tunis** (tew-nis) the capital of Tunisia.

**Tunisia** (tew-**niz**-iă) a country in North Africa. □ **Tunisian** *adjective & noun*

**tunnel** *noun* an underground passage; a passage for a road or railway through a hill or under a river etc. ●*verb* (**tunnelled, tunnelling**; *Amer.* **tunneled, tunneling**) dig a tunnel; make a tunnel through. □ **tunnel vision 1** vision which is poor outside the centre of the normal field of vision. **2** (*informal*) an inability to grasp the wider implications of a situation.

**tunny** *noun* (*plural* **tunny** or **tunnies**) = TUNA.

**tup** *noun* a male sheep, a ram.

**tuppence** *noun* = TWOPENCE.

**tuppenny** *adjective* = TWOPENNY.

**Tupperware** *noun* (*trade mark*) a range of plastic containers for storing food.

**turban** *noun* **1** a man's headdress of a scarf wound round a cap, worn especially by Muslims and Sikhs. **2** a woman's hat resembling this.

**turbid** *adjective* **1** (of liquids) muddy, not clear. **2** confused, disordered; *a turbid imagination.* □ **turbidity** (ter-**bid**-iti) *noun*

**turbine** (ter-byn) *noun* a machine or motor driven by a wheel that is turned by a flow of water or gas; *gas turbines*.

**turbocharger** *noun* a supercharger driven by a turbine powered by the engine's exhaust gases.

**turbofan** *noun* a jet engine in which a turbine-driven fan provides additional thrust.

**turbojet** *noun* **1** a turbine engine that delivers its power in the form of a jet of hot gases. **2** an aircraft driven by this instead of by propellers.

**turboprop** *noun* **1** a jet engine in which a turbine is used as a turbojet and also to drive a propeller. **2** an aircraft driven by this.

**turbot** *noun* (*plural* **turbot** or **turbots**) a large flat edible sea fish.

**turbulent** (ter-bew-lĕnt) *adjective* **1** in a state of commotion or unrest; (of air or water) moving violently and unevenly. **2** unruly, riotous. □ **turbulently** *adverb*, **turbulence** *noun*

**turd** *noun* (*vulgar*) **1** a ball or lump of excrement; *dog turds*. **2** a contemptible person.

**tureen** (tewr-een) *noun* a deep covered dish from which soup is served.

**turf** *noun* (*plural* **turfs** or **turves**) **1** short grass and the surface layer of earth bound together by its roots. **2** a piece of this cut from the ground. **3** a slab of peat for fuel. **4** (**the turf**) horse racing; a racecourse. ●*verb* lay (ground) with turf. □ **turf accountant** a bookmaker. **turf out** (*informal*) throw out.

**turgid** (ter-jid) *adjective* **1** swollen or distended and not flexible. **2** (of language or style) pompous, not flowing easily. □ **turgidly** *adverb*, **turgidity** (ter-jid-iti) *noun*

**Turk** *noun* a native or inhabitant of Turkey.

**Turkey** a country in SW Asia and SE Europe.

**turkey** *noun* (*plural* **turkeys**) **1** a large bird reared for its flesh. **2** its flesh as food. **3** (*Amer. slang*) a theatrical failure; a flop. □ **talk turkey** (*Amer. informal*) talk in a frank and businesslike way.

**turkeycock** *noun* a male turkey.

**Turkish** *adjective* of Turkey or its people or language. ●*noun* the language of Turkey. □ **Turkish bath** a hot-air or steam bath followed by washing or massage. **Turkish coffee** strong black coffee. **Turkish delight** a sweet consisting of lumps of flavoured gelatin coated in powdered sugar. **Turkish towel** a towel made in terry towelling.

**Turkistan** a region of central Asia east of the Caspian Sea.

**Turkmenistan** a republic of western central Asia, lying between the Caspian Sea and Afghanistan.

**Turks and Caicos Islands** (kay-koss) a British dependency in the Caribbean, a group of islands south-east of the Bahamas.

**turmeric** (ter-mer-ik) *noun* **1** a plant of the ginger family. **2** its root powdered for use as a dye, stimulant, or spicy flavouring.

**turmoil** (ter-moil) *noun* a state of great disturbance or confusion.

**turn** *verb* **1** move or cause to move round a point or axis. **2** change or cause to change in position so that a different side becomes uppermost or outermost. **3** give a new direction to, take a new direction; *the river turns north at this point*; *turn the hose on them*; *our thoughts turned to Christmas*. **4** go or move or travel round, go to the other side of; *turn the corner*. **5** pass (a certain hour or age); *it's turned midnight*. **6** cause to go, send or put; *turn the horse into the field*. **7** change or become changed in nature, form, or appearance etc.; *the caterpillar turned into a chrysalis*; *the leaves turned brown*. **8** make or become sour; *the milk has turned*. **9** make or become nauseated; *it turns my stomach*. **10** shape in a lathe. **11** give an elegant form to. ●*noun* **1** turning; being turned; a turning movement. **2** a change of direction or condition etc.; the point at which this occurs. **3** an angle; a bend or corner in a road. **4** character or tendency; *he's of a mechanical turn of mind*. **5** service of a specified kind; *did me a good turn*. **6** an opportunity or obligation etc. that comes to each of a number of people or things in succession; *wait your turn*. **7** a short performance in an entertainment. **8** (*informal*) an attack of illness; a momentary nervous shock. □ **at every turn** in every place; continually. **in turn** in succession. **not turn a hair** show no agitation. **out of turn 1** before or after one's turn. **2** indiscreetly, inappropriately; *speak out of turn*. **to a turn** so as to be cooked perfectly. **turn down 1** fold down. **2** reduce the volume or flow of (sound, gas, or heat etc.) by turning a knob or tap. **3** reject. **turn in 1** hand in. **2** achieve as a score etc. **3** (*informal*) go to bed. **4** (*informal*) abandon as a plan or work. **turn off 1** enter a side-road. **2** stop the flow or operation of by turning a tap or switch. **3** (*informal*) cause to lose interest. **turn-off** *noun* **1** a turning off a road. **2** (*informal*) something that causes disgust or loss of interest. **turn of speed** ability to go fast. **turn on 1** start the flow or operation of by turning a tap or switch. **2** (*informal*) excite (a person) sexually or with drugs etc. **3** (of events etc.) depend on. **turn-on** *noun* (*informal*) a person or thing that causes sexual excitement. **turn one's back on** abandon. **turn out 1** expel. **2** turn off (an electric light etc.). **3** equip or dress; *well turned out.* **4** produce by work. **5** empty and search or clean; *turn out the attic.* **6** (*informal*) come out. **7** prove to be, be eventually; *we'll see how things turn out.* **turn over 1** hand over; transfer. **2** consider carefully; *turn it over in your mind.* **turn over a new leaf** abandon one's previous bad ways. **turn round** unload and reload (a ship, aircraft, etc.) so that it is ready to leave again. **turn tail** run away. **turn the corner** pass a critical point safely, e.g. in an illness. **turn the tables** reverse a situation and put oneself in a superior position. **turn turtle** capsize. **turn up 1** discover or reveal; be found; make one's appearance; happen or present itself. **2** increase the volume or flow of (sound, gas, or heat etc.) by turning a knob or tap. **turn-up** *noun* **1** a turned-up part, especially at the lower end of trouser legs. **2** (*informal*) an unexpected event.

**turncoat** *noun* a person who changes his or her principles.

**Turner**, Joseph Mallord William (1775–1851), English landscape painter.

**turner** *noun* a person who works with a lathe.

**turnery** *noun* **1** work on a lathe. **2** its products.

**turning** *noun* a place where one road meets another, forming a corner. □ **turning-circle** *noun* the smallest circle in which a vehicle can turn without reversing. **turning point** a point at which a decisive change takes place.

**turnip** *noun* **1** a plant with a round white root used as a vegetable and for feeding cattle etc. **2** its root.

**turnkey** *noun* (*old use*) a jailer.

**turnout** *noun* **1** the number of people who come to a public or social function. **2** something arrayed, an outfit.

**turnover** *noun* **1** turning over. **2** a small pie of pastry folded over a filling. **3** the amount of money turned over in a business. **4** the rate at which goods are sold. **5** the rate at which workers leave and are replaced; *a rapid turnover of staff.*

**turnpike** *noun* (*old use & Amer.*) a toll-gate; a road with toll-gates.

**turnstile** *noun* a device for admitting people to a building etc. one at a time, with barriers that revolve as each person passes through.

**turntable** *noun* a circular revolving platform or support, e.g. for the record in a record player.

**turpentine** (ter-pěn-tyn) *noun* an oil distilled from the resin of certain trees, used

for thinning paint and as a solvent. □ **turpentine substitute** = WHITE SPIRIT.

**Turpin**, Dick (1706–39), English highwayman.

**turpitude** (ter-pi-tewd) *noun* wickedness.

**turps** *noun* (*informal*) turpentine.

**turquoise** (ter-kwoiz) *noun* **1** a greenish-blue semiprecious stone. **2** a greenish-blue colour. ● *adjective* of this colour.

**turret** *noun* **1** a small tower-like projection on a building or defensive wall. **2** a low revolving structure protecting a gun and gunners in a ship, aircraft, fort, or tank. **3** a rotating holder for various dies and cutting tools in a lathe or drill etc. □ **turreted** *adjective*

**turtle** *noun* a sea-creature resembling a tortoise, with flippers used in swimming. □ **turn turtle** *see* TURN. **turtle-dove** *noun* a wild dove noted for its soft cooing and for its affection towards its mate and young. **turtle-neck** *noun* a high round close-fitting neck on a knitted garment.

**Tuscany** a region of west central Italy. □ **Tuscan** *adjective & noun*

**tusk** *noun* one of the pair of long pointed teeth that project outside the mouth in the elephant, walrus, etc.

**Tussaud** (too-soh), Marie (1760–1850), Swiss founder of 'Madame Tussaud's', a permanent exhibition in London of waxworks of eminent or notorious people.

**tussle** *noun* a struggle, a conflict. ● *verb* take part in a tussle.

**tussock** *noun* a tuft or clump of grass.

**tut** = TUT-TUT.

**Tutankhamun** (too-tăn-kah-**moon**) (*c.*1370–1352 BC), an Egyptian pharaoh who came to the throne while still a boy, whose tomb and its rich contents were found virtually intact in 1922.

**tutelage** (tew-til-ij) *noun* **1** guardianship. **2** instruction.

**tutelary** (tew-til-er-i) *adjective* serving as a guardian, giving protection.

**tutor** *noun* **1** a private teacher. **2** a university teacher directing the studies of undergraduates. ● *verb* act as tutor to, teach.

**tutorial** (tew-**tor**-iǎl) *adjective* of or as a tutor. ● *noun* a period of tuition given by a college or university tutor.

**tutti** *adverb & adjective Music* with all voices or instruments together.

**tutti-frutti** (too-ti-**froo**-ti) *noun* ice cream containing or flavoured with mixed fruits.

**tut-tut** *interjection* (also **tu**•) an exclamation of impatience, annoyance, or rebuke. ● *verb* express disapproval with this exclamation.

**Tutu**, Desmond Mpilo (born 1931), South African Anglican clergyman and anti-apartheid activist.

**tutu** (too-too) a ballet dancer's short skirt made of layers of stiffened frills.

**Tuvalu** (too-vah-loo) a country consisting of a group of islands in the western Pacific. □ **Tuvaluan** adjective & noun

**tu-whit, tu-whoo** an owl's cry.

**tuxedo** (tuks-ee-doh) noun (plural **tuxedos** or **tuxedoes**) (Amer.) a dinner jacket; evening dress including this.

**TV** abbreviation television.

**TVEI** abbreviation (Brit.) Technical and Vocational Educational Initiative.

**twaddle** noun nonsense.

**Twain**, Mark (pseudonym of Samuel Langhorne Clemens) (1835–1910), American writer, author of The Adventures of Tom Sawyer and The Adventures of Huckleberry Finn.

**twain** adjective & noun (old use) two.

**twang** noun 1 a sharp ringing sound like that made by a tense wire when plucked. 2 a nasal intonation in speech. ●verb make or cause to make a twang.

**'twas** (old use) = it was.

**twat** noun (vulgar slang) 1 a contemptible person; an idiot. 2 the female genitals.

**tweak** verb 1 pinch and twist sharply; pull with a sharp jerk. 2 make fine adjustments to (a mechanism). ●noun a sharp pinch, twist, or pull.

**twee** adjective affectedly dainty or quaint.

**tweed** noun 1 a twilled usually woollen material, often woven of mixed colours. 2 (**tweeds**) clothes made of tweed.

**Tweedledum and Tweedledee** two people or things differing only or chiefly in name.

**tweedy** adjective 1 of or dressed in tweed. 2 (Brit.) characteristic of upper-class country people.

**tweet** noun the chirp of a small bird. ●verb make a tweet.

**tweeter** noun a small loudspeaker for accurately reproducing high-frequency signals.

**tweezers** plural noun small pincers for picking up or pulling very small things.

**twelfth** adjective & noun 1 next after eleventh. 2 any of twelve equal parts of a thing. □ **twelfth man** a reserve member of a cricket team. **Twelfth Night** 5 January, the Eve of Epiphany. □ **twelfthly** adverb

**twelve** adjective & noun 1 one more than eleven (12, XII). 2 (**12**) (of films) for people of 12 and over. □ **twelve-note** adjective (also **twelve-tone**) (of music) using the twelve chromatic notes of the octave arranged in a chosen order without a conventional key.

**twenty** adjective & noun 1 twice ten (20, XX). 2 (**twenties**) the numbers or years or degrees of temperature from 20 to 29. □ **twenty-twenty vision 1** normal good vision. 2 (informal) clear perception, understanding, or hindsight. **twenty-two** noun a line across the ground 22 metres from either goal in hockey and Rugby football; the space enclosed by this. □ **twentieth** adjective & noun

**'twere** (old use) = it were.

**twerp** noun (also **twirp**) (slang) a stupid or objectionable person.

**Twi** (pronounced twee) noun 1 the chief language spoken in Ghana. 2 its speakers.

**twice** adverb 1 two times, on two occasions. 2 in a double amount or degree; twice as strong.

**twiddle** verb twirl or handle aimlessly; twist (a thing) quickly to and fro. ●noun 1 a slight twirl. 2 a twirled mark or sign. □ **twiddle one's thumbs 1** twist them round each other idly. 2 have nothing to do. □ **twiddly** adjective

**twig** noun a small shoot issuing from a branch or stem. ●verb (**twigged, twigging**) (informal) realize or grasp (the meaning of something). □ **twiggy** adjective

**twilight** noun 1 light from the sky when the sun is below the horizon (especially after sunset); the period of this. 2 a faint light. 3 a period of decline or destruction. □ **twilight of the gods** (Scand. myth.) the destruction of the gods and of the world in conflict with the powers of evil. **twilight zone 1** a run-down urban area. 2 an area or concept which is undefined or halfway between two other areas or concepts.

**twilit** adjective dimly lit by twilight.

**twill** noun textile fabric woven so that parallel diagonal lines are produced.

**'twill** (old use) = it will.

**twin** noun 1 either of two children or animals born at one birth. 2 either of two people or things that are exactly alike. 3 (**the Twins**) a sign of the zodiac, Gemini. ●adjective being a twin or twins; twin sisters. ●verb (**twinned, twinning**) 1 combine as a pair. 2 (often foll. by with) link (a town) with another in a different country, for social and cultural exchange. □ **twin beds** a pair of single beds. **twin-engined** adjective having two engines. **twin set** a woman's matching jumper and cardigan. **twin towns** two towns (usually in different countries) that establish special cultural and social links.

**twine** noun strong thread or string made of strands twisted together. ●verb twist, wind or coil.

**twinge** (pronounced twinj) noun a slight or brief pang.

**twinkle** verb 1 shine with a light that flickers rapidly, sparkle. 2 (of the eyes) be bright or sparkling with amusement. 3 (of the feet in dancing etc.) move with short rapid movements. ●*noun* a twinkling light, look, or movement. □ **in a twinkle**, **in the twinkling of an eye** in an instant.

**twirl** *verb* twist lightly or rapidly. ●*noun* **1** a twirling movement. **2** a twirled mark or sign.

**twirp** alternative spelling of TWERP.

**twist** *verb* **1** wind (strands etc.) round each other so as to form a single cord; interweave. **2** make by doing this. **3** pass or coil round something. **4** give a spiral form to, e.g. by turning the ends in opposite directions. **5** take a spiral or winding form or course; turn or bend round; *the road twisted and turned*; *he twisted round in his seat*. **6** rotate or revolve; cause to do this. **7** wrench out of its normal shape. **8** distort the meaning of; *tried to twist his words into an admission of guilt*. **9** (as **twisted** *adjective*) (of a person's mind) emotionally unbalanced. **10** (*informal*) swindle. ●*noun* **1** twisting; being twisted. **2** something formed by twisting, a turn in a twisting course. **3** a dance with vigorous twisting of the body. **4** a peculiar tendency of mind or character. **5** (*informal*) a swindle. □ **round the twist** (*slang*) crazy. **twist a person's arm** (*informal*) persuade or coerce him or her, especially using moral pressure. □ **twisty** *adjective*

**twister** *noun* (*informal*) an untrustworthy person, a swindler.

**twit** *verb* (**twitted, twitting**) taunt. ●*noun* (*slang*) a foolish person.

**twitch** *verb* **1** pull with a light jerk. **2** quiver or contract spasmodically. ●*noun* a twitching movement.

**twitcher** *noun* (*informal*) a bird-watcher who tries to see as many species as possible.

**twitchy** *adjective* (*informal*) nervous. □ **twitchiness** *noun*

**twitter** *verb* **1** make a series of light chirping sounds. **2** talk rapidly in an anxious or nervous way. ●*noun* twittering.

**'twixt** *preposition* (*old use*) = BETWIXT.

**two** *adjective & noun* one more than one (2, II). □ **be in two minds** be undecided. **be two a penny** be readily obtainable and so almost worthless. **two-bit** *adjective* (*Amer. informal*) cheap; petty. **two-dimensional** *adjective* having two dimensions (length, breadth). **two-edged** *adjective* **1** having two cutting edges. **2** cutting both ways, having two interpretations. **two-faced** *adjective* insincere, deceitful. **two-piece** *noun* a suit of clothes or a swimsuit consisting of two separate parts. **two-ply** *adjective* made of two strands or layers. **two-step** *noun* a dance in march or polka time. **two-stroke** *adjective* (of an engine) having its power cycle completed in one up-and-down movement of the piston. **two-time** *verb*

(*informal*) be unfaithful to (a lover); double-cross. **two-way** *adjective* involving two ways or participants. **two-way mirror** a panel of glass that can be seen through on one side but appears as a mirror on the other. **two-way switch** a switch that allows electric current to be turned on or off from either of two points.

**twofold** *adjective & adverb* **1** twice as much or as many. **2** consisting of two parts.

**twopence** (**tup-ĕns**) *noun* (also **tuppence**) the sum of two pence. □ **not care twopence** care hardly at all.

**twopenny** (**tup-ĕni**) *adjective* (also **tuppenny**) **1** costing or worth twopence. **2** cheap, worthless. □ **twopenny-halfpenny** *adjective* insignificant, almost worthless.

**twosome** *noun* two people together, a couple or pair.

**'twould** (*old use*) = it would.

**TX** *abbreviation* Texas.

**tycoon** *noun* a wealthy and influential businessman or industrialist, a magnate.

**tying** *see* TIE.

**tyke** *noun* (also **tike**) **1** a coarse or unpleasant person. **2** a small child.

**Tyler**, Wat (died 1381), the leader of the Peasants' Revolt in England.

**tympani** alternative spelling of TIMPANI.

**tympanum** (**tim-pă-nŭm**) *noun* (*plural* **tympanums** *or* **tympana**) **1** the middle ear. **2** the eardrum. **3** *Archit.* a recessed triangular area, especially over a doorway.

**Tyndale** (**tin-dăl**), William (*c.*1494–1536), English translator of the Bible, a leading figure of the Reformation in England.

**Tyne and Wear** (*pronounced* weer) a metropolitan county of NE England.

**Tynwald** (**tin-wolld**) *noun* the governing assembly of the Isle of Man.

**type** *noun* **1** a class of people or things that have characteristics in common, a kind. **2** a typical example or instance. **3** (*informal*) a person of specified character; *brainy types*. **4** a letter or figure etc. used in printing; a set, supply, kind, or size of these; *printed in large type*. ●*verb* **1** classify according to type. **2** write using a typewriter or keyboard.

**typecast** *verb* (**typecast, typecasting**) cast (an actor or actress) repeatedly in the kind of part which he or she has the reputation of playing or which seems to fit his or her personality.

**typeface** *noun* a set of printing types in one design.

**typescript** *noun* a typewritten document.

**typesetter** *noun* **1** a person who sets type for printing. **2** a machine for doing this. □ **typesetting** *noun*

**typewriter** *noun* a machine for producing characters similar to those of print by pressing keys which cause raised metal letters etc. to strike the paper, usually through an inked ribbon.

**typewritten** *adjective* written with a typewriter.

**typhoid** *noun* (in full **typhoid fever**) a serious infectious feverish disease that attacks the intestines, caused by bacteria taken into the body in food or drink.

**typhoon** (ty-foon) *noun* a violent hurricane in the western Pacific or East Asian seas.

**typhus** *noun* an infectious disease with fever, great weakness, and a purple rash.

**typical** *adjective* **1** having the distinctive qualities of a particular type of person or thing, serving as a representative specimen; *a typical Scotsman.* **2** characteristic; *he answered with typical curtness.* □ **typically** *adverb*

**typify** (tip-i-fy) *verb* (**typified**, **typifying**) be a representative specimen of.

**typist** *noun* a person who types, especially one employed to do so.

**typo** *noun* (*plural* **typos**) (*informal*) a printing error.

**typography** (ty-**pog**-răfi) *noun* **1** the art or practice of printing. **2** the style or appearance of printed matter. □ **typographical** (ty-pŏ-**graf**-ikăl) *adjective*

**tyrannical** (ti-**ran**-ikăl) *adjective* as or like a tyrant, obtaining obedience by force or threats. □ **tyrannically** *adverb*

**tyrannize** (**ti**-ră-nyz) *verb* (also **tyrannise**) rule as or like a tyrant.

**tyrannosaurus** (ti-ran-ŏ-**sor**-ŭs) *noun* (*plural* **tyrannosauruses**) (also **tyrannosaur**) a very large dinosaur that walked on its hind legs.

**tyrannous** (ti-ră-nŭs) *adjective* tyrannical.

**tyranny** (**ti**-ră-ni) *noun* **1** government by a tyrannical ruler. **2** oppressive or tyrannical use of power.

**tyrant** (**ty**-rănt) *noun* a ruler or other person who uses power in a harsh or oppressive way, insisting on absolute obedience.

**tyre** *noun* (*Amer.* **tire**) a rubber covering fitted round the rim of a wheel to absorb shocks, usually filled with air.

**tyro** alternative spelling of TIRO.

**Tyrol** (**ti**-rŏl *or* ti-**rol**) (also **Tirol**) an Alpine district of Austria and Italy. □ **Tyrolean** (ti-rŏ-**lee**-ăn) *adjective*, **Tyrolese** (ti-rŏl-**eez**) *adjective & noun* (*plural* **Tyrolese**).

**Tyrone** (ty-**rohn**) a district and former county of Northern Ireland.

**tzatziki** (tsa-**tsee**-kee) *noun* a Greek side dish of yoghurt and cucumber.

# Uu

**U** *symbol* uranium. ●*abbreviation* (also **U.**) universal; a film classification indicating that it is suitable for all ages. ●*adjective* (*pronounced* yoo) (*informal*) upper-class, supposedly characteristic of upper-class speech or behaviour.

**UAE** *abbreviation* United Arab Emirates.

**UB40** *abbreviation* (in Britain) **1** a card issued to people claiming unemployment benefit. **2** (*informal*) a person registered as unemployed.

**ubiquitous** (yoo-**bik**-wit-ŭs) *adjective* being everywhere; widespread. □ **ubiquity** *noun*

**U-boat** *noun* a German submarine, especially in the war of 1939–45.

**UCCA** *abbreviation* (in Britain) Universities Central Council on Admissions.

**UDA** *abbreviation* Ulster Defence Association; a loyalist Protestant paramilitary organization in Northern Ireland.

**udder** *noun* a baglike milk-secreting organ of a cow, ewe, or female goat, with two or more teats.

**UDI** *abbreviation* Unilateral declaration of independence.

**UDR** *abbreviation* Ulster Defence Regiment.

**UEFA** *abbreviation* Union of European Football Associations.

**Uffizi** (oo-**feets**-i) the chief public art gallery in Florence, containing Italian paintings chiefly from the 13th to the 18th century.

**UFO** (also **ufo**) *abbreviation & noun* (*plural* **ufos**) unidentified flying object, a term often applied to supposed vehicles ('flying saucers') piloted by beings from outer space.

**Uganda** (yoo-**gan**-dǎ) a country in East Africa. □ **Ugandan** *adjective & noun*

**ugh** (*pronounced* uh *or* ug) *interjection* an exclamation of disgust or horror.

**Ugli** *noun* (*plural* **Uglis** *or* **Uglies**) (*trade mark*) a citrus fruit that is a hybrid of grapefruit and tangerine.

**ugly** *adjective* (**uglier, ugliest**) **1** unpleasant to look at or to hear. **2** unpleasant in any way; hostile and threatening; *the crowd was in an ugly mood*. □ **ugly customer** an unpleasantly formidable person. **ugly duckling** a person who at first seems unpromising but later becomes much admired or very able (¶ like the cygnet in the brood of ducks in Hans Andersen's story). □ **ugliness** *noun*

**UHF** *abbreviation* ultrahigh frequency.

**uh-huh** *interjection* (*informal*) yes.

**UHT** *abbreviation* ultra heat treated (of milk, for long keeping).

**UK** *abbreviation* United Kingdom.

**Ukraine** (yoo-**krayn**) a country of SW Asia bordering the Black Sea, formerly a republic of the USSR. □ **Ukrainian** *adjective & noun*

**ukulele** (yoo-kǔ-**lay**-li) *noun* a small four-stringed guitar.

**Ulan Bator** (oo-**lahn bah**-tor) the capital of Mongolia.

**ulcer** *noun* an open sore on the surface of the body or one of its organs. □ **ulcerous** *adjective*

**ulcerate** *verb* cause an ulcer in or on; become affected with an ulcer. □ **ulceration** *noun*

**ulna** (**ul**-nǎ) *noun* the thinner and longer of the two long bones in the forearm; the corresponding bone in an animal. □ **ulnar** *adjective*

**Ulster 1** a former province of Ireland comprising the present Northern Ireland and the counties of Cavan, Donegal, and Monaghan (which are now in the Republic of Ireland). **2** (used loosely) = NORTHERN IRELAND. □ **Ulster Unionist, Ulster Democratic Unionist** a member of one or other of the political parties in Northern Ireland seeking to maintain the union of Northern Ireland with Britain. □ **Ulsterman** *noun* (*plural* **Ulstermen**), **Ulsterwoman** *noun* (*plural* **Ulsterwomen**).

**ulster** *noun* a long loose overcoat of rough cloth.

**ult.** *abbreviation* ultimo.

**ulterior** *adjective* not obvious or admitted; hidden, secret; *ulterior motives*.

**ultimate** *adjective* **1** last or last possible, final; *the ultimate deterrent*. **2** basic, fundamental; *the ultimate cause*. ●*noun* **1** (**the ultimate**) the best; *the ultimate in sports cars*. **2** a final or basic fact or principle. □ **ultimately** *adverb*

**ultimatum** (ulti-**may**-tǔm) *noun* (*plural* **ultimatums**) a final demand or statement of terms, rejection of which may lead to hostility or conflict.

**ultimo** *adjective* (in commerce) of last month; *the 3rd ultimo*. (¶ Latin, = in the last.)

**ultra-** *combining form* beyond, extremely, excessively; *ultra-conservative, ultra-modern*.

**ultrahigh** *adjective* (of frequency) in the range of 300 to 3000 MHz.

**ultramarine** (ultrǎ-mǎ-**reen**) *adjective & noun* bright deep blue.

**ultramicroscope** *noun* a kind of optical microscope used to detect particles smaller than a wavelength of light.

**ultramicroscopic** *adjective* **1** too small to be seen with an ordinary microscope. **2** of or involving the use of the ultramicroscope.

**ultramontane** *adjective* **1** situated beyond the Alps. **2** supporting the supreme authority of the Pope. ●*noun* **1** a person from the other side of the Alps. **2** a supporter of the supreme authority of the Pope.

**ultrasonic** (ultră-**sonn**-ik) *adjective* (of sound waves) with a pitch above the upper limit of normal human hearing. ●*noun* (**ultrasonics**) the science and application of ultrasonic waves. □ **ultrasonically** *adverb*

**ultrasound** *noun* ultrasonic waves.

**ultraviolet** *adjective* **1** (of radiation) having a wavelength that is slightly shorter than that of visible light rays at the violet end of the spectrum. **2** of or using this radiation; *an ultraviolet lamp.*

**ululate** (**yoo**-loo-layt) *verb* howl, wail. □ **ululation** *noun*

**Ulysses** the Roman name for Odysseus.

**umbel** (**um**-běl) *noun* a flower cluster like that of cow-parsley with stalks springing from a common centre to form a flat or curved surface. □ **umbellate** *adjective*

**umbelliferous** (um-běl-**if**-er-ŭs) *adjective* bearing umbels.

**um** *interjection* expressing hesitation or a pause in speech.

**umber** *noun* a natural colouring matter like ochre but darker and browner. □ **burnt umber** reddish-brown.

**umbilical** (um-**bil**-ikăl) *adjective* of the navel. □ **umbilical cord 1** the long cordlike structure connecting the placenta to the navel of a foetus. **2** an essential connecting-line or cable.

**umbilicus** *noun* (*plural* **umbilici** *or* **umbilicuses**) the navel.

**umbra** *noun* (*plural* **umbrae**, *pronounced* um-bree, *or* **umbras**) the dark central part of the shadow cast by the earth or the moon in an eclipse, or of a sunspot.

**umbrage** (**um**-brij) *noun* a feeling of being offended. □ **take umbrage** take offence.

**umbrella** *noun* **1** a collapsible ribbed canopy mounted on a central pole or stick, used as protection against rain, strong sun, etc. **2** protection or support. **3** (usually used as *adjective*) coordinating or supervising; *an umbrella organization.*

**Umbria** a region of central Italy. □ **Umbrian** *adjective & noun*

**umlaut** (**uum**-lowt) *noun* **1** a mark (¨) used over a vowel, especially in German, to indicate a change in its pronunciation. **2** such a vowel change.

**Umm al Qaiwain** (kay-**wayn**) an emirate belonging to the federation of United Arab Emirates.

**umpire** *noun* a person appointed to see that the rules of a game or contest are observed and to settle disputes (e.g. in a game of cricket or baseball), or to give a decision on any disputed question. ●*verb* act as umpire in (a game).

**umpteen** *adjective* (*informal*) very many. □ **umpteenth** *adjective*

**UN** *abbreviation* United Nations.

**un-** *combining form* **1** not (as in *uncertain, uncertainty*). **2** reversing the action indicated by the simple verb (as in *unlock* = release from being locked).

---

■**Usage** The number of words with this prefix is almost unlimited, and many of those whose meaning is obvious are not listed below.

---

**unable** *adjective* not able.

**unabridged** *adjective* not abridged, complete.

**unaccompanied** *adjective* **1** not accompanied. **2** without musical accompaniment.

**unaccountable** *adjective* **1** unable to be explained or accounted for. **2** not accountable for one's actions etc. □ **unaccountably** *adverb*

**unaccustomed** *adjective* not accustomed.

**unadopted** *adjective* (of a road) not taken over for maintenance by a local authority.

**unadulterated** *adjective* pure.

**unalloyed** (un-ă-**loid**) *adjective* not alloyed; pure; *unalloyed joy.*

**un-American** *adjective* **1** not in accordance with American characteristics. **2** contrary to the interests of the USA.

**unanimous** (yoo-**nan**-im-ŭs) *adjective* all agreeing in an opinion or decision; (of an opinion or decision etc.) held or given by everyone. □ **unanimously** *adverb*, **unanimity** (yoo-năn-**im**-iti) *noun*

**unanswerable** *adjective* **1** unable to be disputed or disproved; *an unanswerable case.* **2** unable to be answered; *unanswerable questions.* □ **unanswerably** *adverb*

**unarmed** *adjective* not armed, without weapons.

**unashamed** *adjective* **1** feeling no guilt. **2** bold, blatant. □ **unashamedly** *adverb*

**unasked** *adjective & adverb* not asked, without being requested.

**unassailable** *adjective* unable to be attacked or challenged. □ **unassailably** *adverb*

**unassuming** *adjective* modest, unpretentious.

**unattached** *adjective* **1** not attached to another thing, person, or organization. **2** not engaged, married, or involved in a relationship.

**unattended** *adjective* **1** (of a vehicle etc.) having no person in charge of it. **2** (foll. by *to*) not being attended to or dealt with.

**unavailing** *adjective* ineffectual.

**unavoidable** adjective unable to be avoided. □ **unavoidably** adverb

**unaware** adjective not aware.

**unawares** adverb unexpectedly; without noticing.

**unbacked** adjective 1 having no back or no backing. 2 (in betting) having no backers.

**unbalanced** adjective 1 not balanced. 2 mentally unsound.

**unbearable** adjective not bearable, unable to be endured. □ **unbearably** adverb

**unbeatable** adjective impossible to defeat or surpass.

**unbeaten** adjective not defeated; (of a record etc.) not surpassed.

**unbecoming** adjective 1 not suited to the wearer; *an unbecoming hat.* 2 not suitable; *behaviour unbecoming to a gentleman.*

**unbeknown** adjective (also **unbeknownst**) (foll. by *to*) without the knowledge of; *they did it unbeknown to us.*

**unbelief** noun lack of belief, especially religious belief. □ **unbeliever** noun, **unbelieving** adjective

**unbelievable** adjective not believable. □ **unbelievably** adverb

**unbend** verb (**unbent, unbending**) 1 change or become changed from a bent position. 2 become relaxed or affable.

**unbending** adjective inflexible, refusing to alter one's demands.

**unbiased** adjective (also **unbiassed**) not biased.

**unbidden** adjective not commanded or invited.

**unblock** verb remove an obstruction from.

**unbolt** verb release (a door etc.) by drawing back the bolt.

**unborn** adjective not yet born.

**unbosom** verb □ **unbosom oneself** reveal one's thoughts or feelings.

**unbounded** adjective boundless, without limits.

**unbreakable** adjective not breakable.

**unbridled** adjective unrestrained; *unbridled insolence.*

**unbroken** adjective 1 not broken. 2 untamed; *an unbroken horse.* 3 uninterrupted; *unbroken sleep; unbroken sunshine.* 4 not beaten; *an unbroken record.*

**unbuckle** verb release the buckle of (a strap, shoe, etc.).

**unburden** verb remove a burden from. □ **unburden oneself** relieve oneself or one's conscience, especially by confessing or disclosing something.

**unbusinesslike** adjective not businesslike.

**unbutton** verb unfasten the buttons of.

**uncalled-for** adjective (of a remark, action, etc.) rude, unnecessary.

**uncanny** adjective 1 strange or frightening. 2 extraordinary, beyond what is normal; *they predicted the results with uncanny accuracy.* □ **uncannily** adverb, **uncanniness** noun

**uncared-for** adjective neglected.

**unceasing** adjective not ceasing. □ **unceasingly** adverb

**unceremonious** adjective without proper formality or dignity. □ **unceremoniously** adverb

**uncertain** adjective 1 not known or knowing certainly; *uncertain what it means; the result is uncertain.* 2 not to be depended on; *his aim is uncertain.* 3 changeable; *an uncertain temper.* □ **in no uncertain terms** clearly and forcefully. □ **uncertainly** adverb, **uncertainty** noun

**unchangeable** adjective unable to be changed.

**uncharitable** adjective making severe or unsympathetic judgements about people or acts.

**unchristian** adjective contrary to Christian principles, uncharitable.

**uncial** (un-si-ăl) adjective of or written in a script with rounded unjoined letters resembling modern capitals, found in manuscripts of the 4th–8th centuries. ●noun an uncial letter, style, or manuscript.

**uncivil** adjective ill-mannered, impolite.

**uncle** noun 1 a brother or brother-in-law of one's father or mother. 2 (*children's informal*) an unrelated man friend. 3 (*slang*) a pawnbroker. □ **Uncle Sam** (*informal*) the government or people of the USA.

**unclean** adjective 1 not clean. 2 unchaste. 3 religiously impure; forbidden.

**unclothe** verb 1 remove the clothes from. 2 uncover. □ **unclothed** adjective

**uncoil** verb unwind from being coiled.

**uncomfortable** adjective 1 not comfortable. 2 uneasy, disquieting; *an uncomfortable silence.*

**uncommon** adjective not common, unusual.

**uncommunicative** adjective not inclined to give information or an opinion etc., silent.

**uncompromising** (un-kom-prŏ-my-zing) adjective not allowing or seeking compromise, inflexible.

**unconcern** noun lack of concern, indifference. □ **unconcerned** adjective, **unconcernedly** adverb

**unconditional** adjective not subject to conditions or limitations; *unconditional surrender.* □ **unconditionally** adverb

**unconscionable** (un-kon-shŏn-abŭl) adjective 1 having no conscience. 2 against one's conscience. 3 excessive or unreasonable. □ **unconscionably** adverb

**unconscious** adjective 1 not conscious, not aware. 2 done or spoken etc. without conscious intention; *unconscious humour.* ●noun the unconscious mind, that part of the mind whose content is not normally accessible but which is found to affect behaviour. □ **unconsciously** adverb, **unconsciousness** noun

**unconstitutional** adjective not in accordance with the constitution of a country etc. □ **unconstitutionally** adverb

**unconventional** adjective unusual, unorthodox. □ **unconventionality** noun

**uncouth** (un-**kooth**) adjective awkward or clumsy in manner, boorish.

**uncover** verb **1** remove the covering from. **2** reveal or expose; *their deceit was uncovered.*

**uncrowned** adjective not crowned. □ **uncrowned king** or **queen** a person who has widespread status or respect without official recognition.

**unction** (**unk**-shŏn) noun **1** anointing with oil, especially as a religious rite. **2** pretended earnestness; excessive politeness.

**unctuous** (**unk**-tew-ŭs) adjective having an oily manner, smugly earnest or virtuous. □ **unctuously** adverb, **unctuousness** noun

**uncut** adjective not cut; (of a film) complete, uncensored; (of a gem) not shaped by cutting; (of fabric) with the loops of the pile not cut.

**undeceive** verb free (a person) from a mistaken belief, deception, or error.

**undecided** adjective **1** not yet settled or certain; *the point is still undecided.* **2** not yet having made up one's mind.

**undeniable** adjective impossible to deny, undoubtedly true. □ **undeniably** adverb

**under** preposition **1** in or to a position lower than, below. **2** less than; *it's under a mile from here.* **3** inferior to, of lower rank than; *no one under a bishop.* **4** governed or controlled by; *the country prospered under his rule; under oath.* **5** undergoing; *the road is under repair.* **6** in accordance with; *it is permissible under our agreement.* **7** designated or indicated by; *writes under an assumed name.* **8** in the category of; *file it under 'Estimates'.* **9** (of land) planted with; *50 acres under wheat.* **10** powered by (sail, steam, etc.). ● adverb **1** in or to a lower position or subordinate condition. **2** in or into a state of unconsciousness. **3** below a certain quantity, rank, or age etc.; *children of five and under.* ● adjective lower, situated underneath; *the under layers.* □ **under age** not old enough, especially for some legal right; not yet of adult status. **under the sun** anywhere in the world; existing. **under way** in motion; in progress.

**under-** combining form **1** below, beneath; *underseal.* **2** lower, subordinate; *undermanager.* **3** insufficient, incompletely; *undercooked.*

**underachieve** verb do less well than was expected, especially in school-work. □ **underachiever** noun

**underarm** adjective & adverb **1** in the armpit. **2** (in cricket etc.) bowling or bowled with the hand brought forward and upwards and not raised above shoulder level. **3** (in tennis) with the racket moved similarly.

**underbelly** noun the undersurface of an animal etc., especially as being vulnerable to attack.

**underbid** verb (**underbid, underbidding**) **1** make a lower bid than (another person). **2** bid less than is justified in the game of bridge.

**undercarriage** noun an aircraft's landing-wheels and their supports.

**undercharge** verb charge too low a price.

**underclass** noun the lowest social group in a community, consisting of its least privileged members (e.g. the poor and the unemployed).

**underclothes** plural noun underwear.

**underclothing** noun underclothes.

**undercoat** noun **1** a layer of paint under a finishing coat; the paint used for this. **2** (in animals) a coat of hair under another.

**undercover** adjective **1** doing things secretly, done secretly. **2** engaged in spying by working among those to be spied on; *undercover agents.*

**undercurrent** noun **1** a current that is below a surface or below another current. **2** an underlying feeling, influence, or trend.

**undercut** verb (**undercut, undercutting**) **1** cut away the part below. **2** sell or work for a lower price than (another person).

**underdeveloped** adjective **1** not fully developed. **2** (of a country) not having reached its full economic potential.

**underdog** noun a person or country etc. in an inferior or subordinate position.

**underdone** adjective not thoroughly done; (of meat) not completely cooked throughout.

**underemployed** adjective not fully employed.

**underestimate** verb (pronounced un-der-est-i-mayt) make too low an estimate of. ● noun (pronounced un-der-est-i-măt) an estimate that is too low. □ **underestimation** noun

**underexpose** verb expose (film etc.) for too short a time. □ **underexposure** noun

**underfed** adjective not sufficiently fed.

**underfelt** noun felt for laying under a carpet.

**underfloor** adjective situated beneath the floor.

**underfoot** adverb on the ground, under one's feet.

**undergarment** noun a piece of underwear.

**undergo** verb (**underwent, undergone, undergoing**) experience, endure, be subjected to; *the new aircraft underwent intensive trials*.

**undergraduate** *noun* a university student who has not yet taken a degree.

**underground**[1] *adverb* (*pronounced* un-der-**grownd**) **1** under the ground. **2** in secret; into secrecy or hiding. ● *adjective* (*pronounced* **un**-der-grownd) **1** under the surface of the ground. **2** secret, subversive. **3** artistically or morally unconventional; *underground literature*. ● *noun* (*pronounced* **un**-der-grownd) **1** an underground railway. **2** an underground organization.

**undergrowth** *noun* shrubs and bushes etc. growing closely, especially when beneath trees.

**underhand** *adjective* (*pronounced* un-der-hand) **1** done or doing things in a sly or secret way. **2** (in cricket etc.) underarm. ● *adverb* (*pronounced* un-der-**hand**) in an underhand manner. □ **underhanded** *adjective*

**underlay**[1] *verb* (*pronounced* un-der-**lay**) (**underlaid**, **underlaying**) lay something under (a thing) as a support or in order to raise it. ● *noun* (*pronounced* **un**-der-lay) a layer of material (e.g. felt, rubber, etc.) laid under another as a protection or support.

**underlay**[2] (un-der-**lay**) *see* UNDERLIE.

**underlie** *verb* (**underlay**, **underlain**, **underlying**) **1** lie or exist beneath. **2** be the basis of (a theory etc.), be the facts that account for; *the underlying reasons for her behaviour*.

**underline** *verb* **1** draw a line under. **2** emphasize.

**underling** *noun* a subordinate.

**undermentioned** *adjective* mentioned below, or later.

**undermine** *verb* **1** make a mine or tunnel beneath, especially one causing weakness at the base. **2** weaken gradually; *his confidence was undermined*.

**undermost** *adjective & adverb* furthest underneath.

**underneath** *preposition* beneath, below; on the inside of (a thing). ● *adverb* at, in, or to a position underneath something.

**underpants** *plural noun* a man's undergarment covering the lower part of the body from the waist or hips to the thighs.

**underpart** *noun* the part underneath.

**underpass** *noun* a road that passes under another; a crossing of this kind.

**underpay** *verb* (**underpaid**, **underpaying**) pay too little to (a person) or in discharge of (a debt).

**underpin** *verb* (**underpinned**, **underpinning**) **1** support (a building) from beneath, with masonry etc. **2** support or strengthen (a theory, relationship, etc.).

**underprivileged** *adjective* less privileged than others, not enjoying the normal standard of living or rights in a community.

**underrate** *verb* have too low an opinion of. □ **underrated** *adjective*

**underscore** *verb* underline.

**undersea** *adjective* below the surface of the sea.

**underseal** *verb* coat the lower surface of (a motor vehicle etc.) with a protective sealing layer. ● *noun* a substance used for this.

**under-secretary** *noun* a subordinate official, especially a junior minister or senior civil servant.

**undersell** *verb* (**undersold**, **underselling**) **1** sell at a lower price than (another person). **2** fail to communicate forcefully enough the virtues of (a thing or person).

**undersexed** *adjective* having less than the normal degree of sexual desires.

**undershoot** *verb* (**undershot**, **undershooting**) (of an aircraft) land short of; *the plane undershot the runway*.

**underside** *adjective* the side or surface underneath.

**undersigned** *adjective* who has or have signed at the bottom of this document; *we, the undersigned*.

**undersized** *adjective* of less than the usual size.

**underskirt** *noun* a garment for wearing beneath a skirt or dress, a petticoat.

**underslung** *adjective* **1** supported from above. **2** (of a vehicle chassis) hanging lower than the axles.

**underspend** *verb* (**underspent**, **underspending**) spend too little.

**understaffed** *adjective* having less than the necessary number of staff.

**understand** *verb* (**understood**, **understanding**) **1** perceive the meaning, importance, or nature of. **2** know the significance or cause of; *don't understand why he came*. **3** sympathize with, know how to deal with; *I understand your difficulty*. **4** become aware from information received, draw as a conclusion; *I understand she is in Paris*. **5** supply (a missing word or words) mentally; *before 'ready?' the words 'are you' are understood*.

**understandable** *adjective* able to be understood. □ **understandably** *adverb*

**understanding** *noun* **1** the ability to understand or think; intelligence. **2** an individual's perception of a situation. **3** tolerance or sympathy. **4** an informal or preliminary agreement; *reached an understanding*. ● *adjective* having or showing insight, good judgement, or sympathy.

**understate** *verb* **1** express (an idea) in very restrained terms. **2** represent (an amount) as being less than it really is.

□ **understated** adjective, **understatement** noun

**understeer** verb (of a car etc.) have a tendency to turn less sharply than was intended. ●noun this tendency.

**understudy** noun a person who studies the part in a play or the duties etc. of another in order to be able to take his or her place at short notice. ●verb (**understudied, understudying**) act as understudy to; learn (a part etc.) as understudy.

**undertake** verb (**undertook, undertaken, undertaking**) 1 agree or promise to do something, make oneself responsible for; *undertook the cooking.* 2 guarantee; *we cannot undertake that you will make a profit.*

**undertaker** verb one whose business is to prepare the dead for burial or cremation and make arrangements for funerals.

**undertaking** noun 1 work etc. undertaken. 2 a promise or guarantee. 3 the business of an undertaker.

**undertone** noun 1 a low or subdued tone; *they spoke in undertones.* 2 a colour that modifies another; *pink with mauve undertones.* 3 an underlying quality or feeling; *a threatening undertone.*

**undertow** (un-der-toh) noun a current below the surface of the sea, moving in an opposite direction to the surface current.

**undervalue** verb put too low a value on.

**underwater** adjective situated, used, or done beneath the surface of water. ●adverb beneath the surface of water.

**underwear** noun garments worn under indoor clothing; underclothes.

**underweight** adjective weighing less than is normal, required, or permissible.

**underwent** see UNDERGO.

**underworld** noun 1 professional criminals and their associates. 2 (in mythology) the abode of the dead under the earth.

**underwrite** verb (**underwrote, underwritten, underwriting**) 1 sign and accept liability under (an insurance policy, especially for ships), guaranteeing payment in the event of loss or damage. 2 undertake to finance (an enterprise). 3 undertake to buy all the unsold stock in (a company etc.). □ **underwriter** noun

**undeserved** adjective not deserved as reward or punishment. □ **undeservedly** (un-di-zerv-idli) adverb

**undeserving** adjective not deserving reward, praise, sympathy, etc.

**undesirable** adjective not desirable, objectionable. ●noun a person who is undesirable to a community. □ **undesirably** adverb, **undesirability** noun

**undetermined** adjective 1 not yet decided. 2 undiscovered.

**undies** plural noun (*informal*) women's underwear.

**undine** (un-deen) noun a female water-spirit.

**undo** verb (**undid, undone, undoing**) 1 unfasten, untie; unwrap. 2 annul, cancel the effect of; *cannot undo the past.* 3 cause the ruin of.

**undoing** noun bringing or being brought to ruin; a cause of this; *drink was his undoing.*

**undone** adjective 1 unfastened. 2 not done; *left the work undone.* 3 (*old use*) brought to ruin or destruction; *we are undone!*

**undoubted** adjective certain, beyond doubt or dispute. □ **undoubtedly** adverb

**undreamed** adjective (also **undreamt**) (often foll. by *of*) not imagined, not thought to be possible.

**undress** verb take off one's clothes or the clothes of (another person). ●noun 1 the state of being not clothed or not fully clothed. 2 clothes or a uniform for non-ceremonial occasions.

**undue** adjective excessive, disproportionate. □ **unduly** adverb

**undulate** (un-dew-layt) verb have or cause to have a wavy movement or appearance. □ **undulation** noun

**undying** adjective everlasting, never-ending; *undying fame.*

**unearned** adjective not earned. □ **unearned income** income from interest on investments or rent from property rather than from working.

**unearth** verb 1 uncover or obtain from the ground by digging. 2 bring to light, find by searching.

**unearthly** adjective 1 not earthly. 2 supernatural, mysterious and frightening. 3 (*informal*) absurdly early or inconvenient; *getting up at this unearthly hour.* □ **unearthliness** noun

**uneasy** adjective 1 not comfortable; *passed an uneasy night.* 2 not confident, worried. 3 worrying; *an uneasy suspicion that all was not well.* □ **uneasily** adverb, **unease** noun, **uneasiness** noun

**uneatable** adjective not fit to be eaten (because of its rotten or unattractive condition).

**uneconomic** adjective not profitable.

**uneconomical** adjective not economical; wasteful.

**uneducated** adjective not educated; ignorant.

**unemployable** adjective unfit for paid employment, e.g. because of lack of abilities or qualifications.

**unemployed** adjective 1 having no employment, temporarily without a paid job. 2 not in use.

**unemployment** noun 1 the condition of being unemployed. 2 the lack of employment in a country, region, etc. □ **unemployment benefit** a regular State payment made to an unemployed person.

**unencumbered** adjective **1** not encumbered with a burden etc. **2** (of an estate) having no liabilities (e.g. a mortgage).

**unending** adjective endless.

**unequal** adjective **1** not equal. **2** (of work or achievements etc.) not of the same quality throughout. **3** not with equal advantage to both sides, not well matched; *an unequal contest.* **4** (foll. by *to*) unable to deal with the demands of a particular job or task. □ **unequally** adverb

**unequalled** adjective (*Amer.* **unequaled**) without an equal; supreme.

**unequivocal** (un-i-**kwiv**-ŏkăl) adjective clear and unmistakable, not ambiguous. □ **unequivocally** adverb

**unerring** adjective making no mistake; *with unerring accuracy.* □ **unerringly** adverb

**UNESCO** (yoo-**ness**-koh) abbreviation (also **Unesco**) United Nations Educational, Scientific, & Cultural Organization.

**unethical** adjective not ethical, unscrupulous in business or professional conduct. □ **unethically** adverb

**uneven** adjective **1** not level or smooth. **2** varying, not uniform. **3** unequal; *an uneven contest.* □ **unevenly** adverb, **unevenness** noun

**unexampled** adjective having no precedent; *an unexampled opportunity.*

**unexceptionable** adjective with which no fault can be found; entirely satisfactory. □ **unexceptionably** adverb

---

■**Usage** Do not confuse with **unexceptional**.

---

**unexceptional** adjective not exceptional, quite ordinary.

---

■**Usage** Do not confuse with **unexceptionable**.

---

**unexpected** adjective not expected, surprising. □ **unexpectedly** adverb

**unfailing** adjective never-ending, constant, reliable; *his unfailing good humour.*

**unfair** adjective not impartial, not in accordance with justice. □ **unfairly** adverb, **unfairness** noun

**unfaithful** adjective **1** not loyal; not keeping to one's promise. **2** having committed adultery. □ **unfaithfully** adverb, **unfaithfulness** noun

**unfamiliar** adjective **1** strange, unknown; *unfamiliar territory.* **2** (foll. by *with*) not used to or acquainted with; *unfamiliar with your way of doing things.* □ **unfamiliarity** noun

**unfasten** verb make or become loose, open the fastening(s) of.

**unfeeling** adjective **1** lacking the power of sensation or sensitivity. **2** unsympathetic, not caring about others' feelings. □ **unfeelingly** adverb, **unfeelingness** noun

**unfettered** adjective **1** released from fetters. **2** not subject to the usual controls or limitations; *unfettered corporate greed.*

**unfit** adjective **1** unsuitable. **2** not in perfect health or physical condition.

**unfix** verb detach.

**unflappable** adjective (*informal*) remaining calm in a crisis, not getting into a flap. □ **unflappability** noun

**unfledged** adjective **1** (of a person) inexperienced. **2** (of a young bird) not yet fledged.

**unfold** verb **1** open, spread (a thing) or become spread out. **2** become visible or known; *as the story unfolds.*

**unforeseen** adjective not foreseen.

**unforgettable** adjective not able to be forgotten.

**unfortunate** adjective **1** having bad luck. **2** unsuitable, regrettable; *a most unfortunate choice of words.* **3** miserable, unhappy. ●noun an unfortunate person. □ **unfortunately** adverb

**unfounded** adjective (of beliefs, fears, etc.) without good reasons or evidence.

**unfreeze** verb (**unfroze**, **unfrozen**, **unfreezing**) **1** thaw, cause to thaw. **2** remove restrictions on (financial assets etc.).

**unfrock** verb dismiss (a priest) from office.

**unfurl** verb unroll, spread out.

**ungainly** adjective awkward-looking, clumsy, ungraceful. □ **ungainliness** noun

**unget-at-able** adjective (*informal*) difficult or impossible to reach, inaccessible.

**ungodly** adjective **1** impious, wicked. **2** (*informal*) outrageous, very inconvenient; *phoning at this ungodly hour.* □ **ungodliness** noun

**ungovernable** adjective uncontrollable; *an ungovernable temper.*

**ungracious** adjective not courteous; grudging. □ **ungraciously** adverb

**ungreen** adjective not concerned with the protection of the environment; harmful to the environment.

**unguarded** adjective **1** not guarded. **2** thoughtless, incautious; *in an unguarded moment.*

**unguent** (ung-**wěnt**) noun an ointment or lubricant.

**ungulate** (ung-yoo-**lăt**) adjective having hooves. ●noun a mammal that has hooves.

**unhallowed** adjective **1** not consecrated. **2** wicked.

**unhand** verb (*literary*) take one's hands off (a person), let go of.

**unhappy** adjective (**unhappier**, **unhappiest**) **1** not happy, sad. **2** unfortunate. **3** un-

**suitable.** □ **unhappily** adverb, **unhappiness** noun

**unharness** verb remove the harness from.

**unhealthy** adjective (**unhealthier, unhealthiest**) **1** not having good health. **2** harmful to health. **3** (informal) unwise, dangerous. □ **unhealthily** adverb, **unhealthiness** noun

**unheard** adjective not heard. □ **unheard-of** adjective not previously known of or done.

**unhinge** verb cause to become mentally unbalanced; the shock unhinged his mind.

**unholy** adjective (**unholier, unholiest**) **1** wicked; irreverent. **2** (informal) very great, outrageous; making an unholy row. **3** unnatural; an unholy alliance. □ **unholiness** noun

**unhook** verb **1** detach from a hook or hooks. **2** unfasten by releasing the hook(s).

**unhoped-for** adjective not hoped for or expected.

**unhorse** verb throw or drag (a rider) from a horse.

**uni** (yoo-ni) noun (informal) university.

**Uniat** (yoo-ni-ăt) adjective (also **Uniate**) of the Churches in eastern Europe and the Middle East that acknowledge the pope's supremacy but retain their own liturgy etc. ●noun a member of such a Church.

**unicameral** (yoo-ni-**kam**-er-ăl) adjective having only one legislative chamber.

**UNICEF** (yoo-ni-sef) abbreviation United Nations Children's (originally International Children's Emergency) Fund, established to help governments to meet the long-term needs of the welfare of mothers and children.

**unicellular** (yoo-ni-**sel**-yoo-ler) adjective (of an organism) consisting of one cell.

**unicorn** noun a mythical animal resembling a horse with a single horn projecting from its forehead.

**unicycle** noun a single-wheeled cycle, used especially by acrobats. □ **unicyclist** noun

**unidentified** adjective not identified.

**unification** noun unifying; being unified. □ **Unification Church** a religious order founded in Korea by Sun Myung Moon; its members are sometimes known as Moonies.

**uniform** noun distinctive clothing intended to identify the wearer as a member of a certain organization or group. ●adjective always the same, not varying; planks of uniform thickness. □ **uniformly** adverb, **uniformity** (yoo-ni-**form**-iti) noun

**uniformed** adjective wearing a uniform.

**unify** verb (**unified, unifying**) form into a single unit, unite.

**unilateral** (yoo-ni-**lat**-erăl) adjective one-sided, done by or affecting one person or group or country etc. and not another. □ **unilaterally** adverb, **unilateralism** noun

**unimpeachable** adjective completely trustworthy, not open to doubt or question; unimpeachable honesty. □ **unimpeachably** adverb

**uninhabitable** adjective not suitable for habitation.

**uninhabited** adjective not inhabited.

**uninhibited** adjective not inhibited, having no inhibitions.

**uninspired** adjective not inspired; commonplace, not outstanding.

**unintelligible** adjective not intelligible, impossible to understand. □ **unintelligibly** adverb

**uninterested** adjective not interested; showing or feeling no concern (compare DISINTERESTED).

**union** noun **1** uniting; being united. **2** a whole formed by uniting parts; an association formed by the uniting of people or groups. **3** a trade union. **4** marriage. **5** a fabric with mixed materials, e.g. cotton with linen or jute. **6** (**Union**) a university social club. **7** Maths the totality of the members of two or more sets. □ **Union Jack** (also **Union Flag**) the national flag of the United Kingdom.

**unionist** noun **1** a member of a trade union; a supporter of trade unions. **2** (usually **Unionist**) one who favours union between Britain and Northern Ireland. □ **unionism** noun

**unionize** verb (also **unionise**) organize into or cause to join a trade union. □ **unionization** noun

**Union of Soviet Socialist Republics** a former country extending from eastern Europe to the Pacific, consisting of 15 republics.

**Union Territory** any of the six administrative areas that are not States within the Republic of India.

**unique** (yoo-**neek**) adjective **1** being the only one of its kind; this vase is unique. **2** unusual, remarkable; a unique opportunity; this makes it even more unique. □ **uniquely** adverb

■**Usage** Many people regard the use in sense 2 as illogical and incorrect.

**unisex** (yoo-ni-seks) adjective (of clothing, hairstyles, etc.) suitable for people of either sex.

**unison** noun □ **in unison 1** sounding or singing together at the same pitch or a corresponding one. **2** in agreement or concord; acted in unison.

**unit** noun **1** an individual thing, person, or group regarded as single and complete, or as the smallest part of a complex whole; the family unit. **2** a quantity chosen as a standard in terms of which other quantities may be expressed, or for which a stated charge is made. **3** a part or group with a specified function within a complex machine or organization. **4** a piece of furniture, especially one designed to be fitted with others like it. □ **unit cost** the cost of producing one item. **unit price** the price charged for each unit of goods supplied. **unit trust** a company investing contributions from many people in various securities and paying them all a dividend in proportion to their holdings.

**Unitarian** (yoo-ni-**tair**-iăn) *noun* a member of a Christian sect maintaining that God is one person, not a Trinity. □ **Unitarianism** *noun*

**unitary** *adjective* **1** of a unit or units. **2** marked by unity.

**unite** *verb* **1** join together, make or become one. **2** agree or combine or cooperate; *they all united in condemning the action.*

**United Arab Emirates** a State formed from sheikhdoms lying along the Persian Gulf.

**United Kingdom** Great Britain and Northern Ireland.

**United Nations** an organization of about 150 countries set up in 1945 to promote international peace, security, and cooperation.

**United Reformed Church** that formed in 1972 from the English Presbyterian Church and the majority of the Congregational Church.

**United States (of America)** a country in North America consisting of 50 States and the Federal District of Columbia.

**unity** *noun* **1** the state of being one or a unit. **2** a thing forming a complex whole. **3** the number one in mathematics. **4** harmony, agreement in feelings, ideas, or aims etc.; *dwell together in unity.*

**univalent** (yoo-ni-**vay**-lĕnt) *adjective* having a valency of one.

**univalve** (**yoo**-ni-valv) *noun* a shellfish with a shell consisting of only one part (valve).

**universal** *adjective* of, for, or done by all. □ **universal coupling** or **joint** one that connects two shafts in such a way that they can be at any angle to each other. **universal time** that used for astronomical reckoning at all places. □ **universally** *adverb*, **universality** *noun*

**universe** *noun* all existing things, including the earth and its creatures and all the heavenly bodies.

**university** *noun* an educational institution of advanced learning and research which awards degrees.

**unjust** *adjective* not just or fair. □ **unjustly** *adverb*

**unkempt** *adjective* looking untidy or neglected.

**unkind** *adjective* not kind, harsh. □ **unkindly** *adverb*, **unkindness** *noun*

**unknown** *adjective* not known, not identified. ● *noun* an unknown person or thing. □ **unknown to** without the knowledge of. **unknown quantity** a mysterious or unfamiliar person or thing. **Unknown Soldier** an unidentified soldier ceremonially buried to symbolize all of a nation's armed forces killed in war.

**unladen** *adjective* not laden. □ **unladen weight** the weight of a vehicle etc. when not loaded with goods.

**unleaded** *adjective* (of petrol) containing no added lead compounds.

**unlearn** *verb* discard and forget (habits, knowledge, etc.) deliberately.

**unleash** *verb* **1** set free from a leash or restraint. **2** set (a thing) free so that it can attack or pursue something.

**unleavened** (un-**lev**-ĕnd) *adjective* not leavened; (of bread) made without yeast or other raising agent.

**unless** *conjunction* if not, except when; *we shall not move unless we are obliged to.*

**unlike** *adjective* **1** not like, different. **2** not characteristic of; *such behaviour is quite unlike him.* ● *preposition* differently from; *behaves quite unlike anyone else.*

**unlikely** *adjective* **1** not likely to happen or be true; *an unlikely tale.* **2** not likely to be successful; *the most unlikely candidate.*

**unlimited** *adjective* not limited; very great in number or quantity.

**unlined** *adjective* **1** without a lining. **2** not marked with lines.

**unlisted** *adjective* not included in a list; not in a published list of telephone numbers or Stock Exchange prices.

**unload** *verb* **1** remove (a load) from (a ship etc.); remove cargo. **2** get rid of. **3** remove the charge from (a gun etc.).

**unlock** *verb* **1** release the lock of (a door etc.). **2** release by or as if by unlocking.

**unlooked-for** *adjective* unexpected.

**unloose** *verb* (also **unloosen**) loose; set free.

**unlucky** *adjective* not lucky, wretched, having or bringing bad luck. □ **unluckily** *adverb*

**unmade** *adjective* not made; (of a bed) not yet arranged ready for use.

**unman** *verb* (**unmanned**, **unmanning**) **1** weaken the self-control or courage of. **2** make effeminate.

**unmanned** *adjective* **1** operated without a crew. **2** without staff or personnel, empty; *left the office unmanned.*

**unmarked** *adjective* **1** not marked; with no mark of identification. **2** not noticed.

**unmask** *verb* **1** remove the mask from; remove one's mask. **2** expose the true character of.

**unmentionable** *adjective* so bad, embarrassing, or shocking that it may not be spoken of.

**unmistakable** *adjective* clear and obvious, not able to be mistaken for another. □ **unmistakably** *adverb*

**unmitigated** (un-**mit**-i-gayt-id) *adjective* not modified, absolute; *an unmitigated success*.

**unmoved** *adjective* not moved; not changed in one's purpose; not affected by emotion.

**unnatural** *adjective* **1** not natural or normal. **2** lacking natural feelings of affection. **3** artificial. □ **unnaturally** *adverb*

**unnecessary** *adjective* **1** not necessary. **2** more than is necessary; *with unnecessary care*. □ **unnecessarily** *adverb*

**unnerve** *verb* cause to lose courage or determination.

**unnumbered** *adjective* **1** not marked with a number. **2** countless.

**UNO** *abbreviation* United Nations Organization.

**unobtrusive** (un-ŏb-**troo**-siv) *adjective* not obtrusive, not making oneself or itself noticed. □ **unobtrusively** *adverb*

**unofficial** *adjective* not officially authorized or confirmed. □ **unofficial strike** one not formally approved by the strikers' trade union. □ **unofficially** *adverb*

**unpack** *verb* **1** open and remove the contents of (luggage etc.). **2** take out from its packaging or from a suitcase etc.

**unpaid** *adjective* **1** (of a debt) not yet paid. **2** not receiving payment for work etc.

**unparalleled** *adjective* not equalled; supreme; *unparalleled enthusiasm*.

**unparliamentary** *adjective* contrary to parliamentary custom. □ **unparliamentary language** oaths or abuse.

**unperson** *noun* a person whose name or existence is ignored or denied.

**unpick** *verb* undo the stitching of.

**unplaced** *adjective* not placed as one of the first three in a race etc.

**unplayable** *adjective* (of a ball in games) unable to be played or returned etc.

**unpleasant** *adjective* not pleasant, disagreeable. □ **unpleasantly** *adverb*, **unpleasantness** *noun*

**unplug** *verb* (**unplugged**, **unplugging**) **1** disconnect (an electrical device) by removing its plug from the socket. **2** unstop.

**unplumbed** *adjective* **1** not plumbed. **2** not fully investigated or understood.

**unpopular** *adjective* not popular, not liked or enjoyed by people in general. □ **unpopularly** *adverb*, **unpopularity** *noun*

**unprecedented** (un-**press**-i-dent-id) *adjective* for which there is no precedent; unparalleled.

**unprepared** *adjective* **1** not prepared beforehand. **2** not ready or equipped to do something.

**unprepossessing** (un-pree-pŏ-**zess**-ing) *adjective* unattractive, not making a good impression.

**unpretentious** (un-pri-**ten**-shŭs) *adjective* not pretentious, not showy or pompous.

**unprincipled** *adjective* without good moral principles, unscrupulous.

**unprintable** *adjective* too rude or indecent to be printed.

**unprofessional** *adjective* **1** contrary to professional standards of behaviour. **2** unskilled, amateurish. **3** not belonging to a profession. □ **unprofessionally** *adverb*

**unprompted** *adjective* not prompted, spontaneous.

**unputdownable** *adjective* (*informal*) (of a book) gripping, compulsively readable.

**unqualified** *adjective* **1** (of a person) not legally or officially qualified to do something. **2** not restricted or modified; *gave it our unqualified approval*.

**unquestionable** *adjective* not questionable, too clear to be doubted. □ **unquestionably** *adverb*

**unquestioned** *adverb* not disputed or doubted.

**unquote** *verb* (in dictation etc.) end the quotation, close the inverted commas (compare QUOTE sense 4); *Churchill said (quote) 'We shall never surrender' (unquote)*.

**unravel** *verb* (**unravelled**, **unravelling**; *Amer.* **unraveled**, **unraveling**) **1** disentangle. **2** undo (knitted fabrics). **3** probe and solve (a mystery etc.). **4** become unravelled.

**unreadable** *adjective* too bad, dull, or difficult to read.

**unready** *adjective* **1** not ready. **2** not prompt in action. **3** (*old use*) rash, lacking good advice; *Ethelred the Unready*.

**unreal** *adjective* **1** not real, existing in the imagination only. **2** (*slang*) incredible, amazing. □ **unreality** (un-ri-al-iti) *noun*

**unreason** *noun* lack of reasonable thought or action.

**unreasonable** *adjective* **1** not reasonable in one's attitude etc. **2** excessive, going beyond the limits of what is reasonable or just. □ **unreasonably** *adverb*

**unrelenting** *adjective* not becoming less in intensity or severity.

**unrelieved** *adjective* not relieved, without anything to give variation; *unrelieved gloom; a plain black dress unrelieved by any touches of colour*.

**unremitting** (un-ri-**mit**-ing) *adjective* not relaxing or ceasing, persistent.

**unrepeatable** *adjective* **1** that cannot be done or offered etc. again; *unrepeatable bargains*. **2** too obscene to be said again.

**unrequited** (un-ri-**kwy**-tid) *adjective* (of love) not returned or rewarded.

**unreserved** *adjective* **1** not reserved. **2** without reservation or restriction, complete. □ **unreservedly** (un-ri-**zerv**-idli) *adverb*

**unrest** *noun* disturbance or dissatisfaction; *industrial unrest*.

**unrighteous** *adjective* not righteous, wicked.

**unripe** *adjective* not yet ripe.

**unrivalled** (un-**ry**-văld) *adjective* (*Amer.* **unrivaled**) having no equal, incomparable.

**unroll** *verb* open or become opened after being rolled.

**unruly** (un-**roo**-li) *adjective* not easy to control or discipline, disorderly. □ **unruliness** *noun*

**unsaddle** *verb* **1** remove the saddle from (a horse). **2** unseat (a rider).

**unsaid** (un-**sed**) *see* UNSAY. ● *adjective* not spoken or expressed; *many things were left unsaid*.

**unsalted** *adjective* not seasoned with salt.

**unsaturated** *adjective Chem.* (of a fat or oil) capable of further reaction by combining with hydrogen.

**unsavoury** *adjective* (*Amer.* **unsavory**) **1** disagreeable to the taste or smell. **2** morally unpleasant or disgusting; *an unsavoury reputation*.

**unsay** *verb* (**unsaid, unsaying**) take back or retract; *what's said can't be unsaid*.

**unscathed** (un-**skay**thd) *adjective* without suffering any injury.

**unscientific** *adjective* not in accordance with scientific principles. □ **unscientifically** *adverb*

**unscramble** *verb* **1** sort out from a disordered or confused state. **2** make (a scrambled transmission) intelligible.

**unscrew** *verb* loosen (a screw or nut etc.) by turning it; unfasten by turning or removing screws, or by twisting.

**unscripted** *adjective* without a prepared script.

**unscrupulous** (un-**skroo**-pew-lŭs) *adjective* without moral scruples, unprincipled. □ **unscrupulously** *adverb*, **unscrupulousness** *noun*

**unseasonable** *adjective* **1** not seasonable. **2** untimely. □ **unseasonably** *adverb*

**unseat** *verb* **1** dislodge (a rider) from horseback or from a bicycle etc. **2** remove from a parliamentary seat; *was unseated at the last election*.

**unseeded** *adjective* (of a tennis player etc.) not seeded.

**unseeing** *adjective* not seeing anything.

**unseemly** *adjective* not seemly, improper. □ **unseemliness** *noun*

**unseen** *adjective* **1** not seen, invisible. **2** (of translation) done without previous preparation.

**unselfish** *adjective* not selfish, considering the needs of others before one's own. □ **unselfishly** *adverb*, **unselfishness** *noun*

**unsettle** *verb* make uneasy; disturb the calm or stability of.

**unsettled** *adjective* not settled, liable to change.

**unshackle** *verb* release from shackles, set free.

**unshakeable** *adjective* not able to be shaken, firm, unwavering.

**unsheathe** *verb* remove (a knife etc.) from a sheath.

**unshockable** *adjective* not able to be shocked.

**unsightly** *adjective* not pleasant to look at, ugly. □ **unsightliness** *noun*

**unskilled** *adjective* not having or needing skill or special training.

**unsociable** *adjective* not sociable, disliking company. □ **unsociably** *adverb*

**unsocial** *adjective* **1** not suitable for society. **2** outside the normal working day; *unsocial hours*. **3** not conforming to standard social practices; antisocial. □ **unsocially** *adverb*

**unsolicited** (un-sŏ-**liss**-it-id) *adjective* not asked for; given or done voluntarily.

**unsophisticated** *adjective* not sophisticated; simple and natural or naïve.

**unsound** *adjective* not sound or strong; not free from defects or mistakes. □ **of unsound mind** insane.

**unsparing** (un-**spair**-ing) *adjective* giving freely and lavishly; *unsparing in one's efforts*.

**unspeakable** *adjective* **1** unable to be described in words. **2** indescribably bad or evil.

**unstable** *adjective* **1** not stable, tending to change suddenly. **2** mentally or emotionally unbalanced. □ **unstably** *adverb*

**unsteady** *adjective* not steady; unstable. □ **unsteadily** *adverb*, **unsteadiness** *noun*

**unstick** *verb* (**unstuck, unsticking**) separate (a thing stuck to another).

**unstinting** *adjective* given freely and lavishly.

**unstitch** *verb* undo the stitches of (something sewn).

**unstop** *verb* (**unstopped, unstopping**) **1** free from an obstruction. **2** remove the stopper from.

**unstoppable** *adjective* unable to be stopped or prevented.

**unstressed** *adjective* (of a syllable) not pronounced with a stress.

**unstructured** *adjective* without a formal structure.

**unstuck** *adjective* detached after being stuck on or together. □ **come unstuck** (*informal*) suffer disaster, fail.

**unstudied** *adjective* natural in manner, not affected; *with unstudied elegance*.

**unsubstantial** *adjective* not substantial, flimsy; having little or no factual basis.

**unsuited** *adjective* **1** not fit (for a purpose). **2** not adapted (to a specified thing).

**unsung** *adjective* not acknowledged or honoured; *unsung heroes*.

**unsuspecting** *adjective* feeling no suspicion. □ **unsuspected** *adjective*

**unswerving** *adjective* not turning aside, unchanging; *unswerving loyalty*.

**untangle** *verb* free from a tangle, disentangle.

**untapped** *adjective* not tapped, not yet made use of; *the country's untapped resources*.

**untaught** *adjective* **1** not instructed by teaching. **2** not acquired by teaching.

**untenable** (un-ten-ăbŭl) *adjective* (of a theory or position) not tenable, not able to be held, because strong arguments can be produced against it.

**unthinkable** *adjective* incredible, too unlikely or undesirable to be considered.

**unthinking** *adjective* thoughtless, done or said etc. without consideration. □ **unthinkingly** *adverb*

**untidy** *adjective* (**untidier**, **untidiest**) not tidy. □ **untidily** *adverb*, **untidiness** *noun*

**untie** *verb* (**untied**, **untying**) unfasten; release from being tied up.

**until** *preposition & conjunction* up to (a specified time or event); *until last year we had never been abroad*; *leave it until she gets back*.

───────────

■**Usage** Used in preference to *till* when it stands first or in formal contexts.

───────────

**untimely** *adjective* **1** happening at an unsuitable time. **2** (of death) premature. □ **untimeliness** *noun*

**unto** *preposition* (*old use*) to.

**untold** *adjective* **1** not told. **2** not counted; too much or too many to be counted; *untold wealth*.

**untouchable** *adjective* not able to be touched, not allowed to be touched. ●*noun* a member of the lowest Hindu group (noncaste) in India, held to defile members of a higher caste on contact.

───────────

■**Usage** Use of the term, and the social restrictions which accompany it, were declared illegal in India in 1949 and in Pakistan in 1953.

───────────

**untoward** (un-tŏ-wor'd) *adjective* inconvenient, awkward; *if nothing untoward happens*.

**untrammelled** *adjective* not hampered.

**untried** *adjective* not yet tried or tested.

**untrue** *adjective* **1** not true, contrary to facts. **2** not faithful or loyal.

**untruth** *noun* **1** an untrue statement, a lie. **2** lack of truth. □ **untruthful** *adjective*, **untruthfully** *adverb*

**untwist** *verb* open from being twisted or spiralled.

**unused** *adjective* **1** (*pronounced* un-yoozd) not yet used. **2** (*pronounced* un-yoost) (foll. by *to*) not accustomed.

**unusual** *adjective* **1** not usual. **2** exceptional, remarkable. □ **unusually** *adverb*

**unutterable** *adjective* too great or too intense to be expressed in words; *unutterable joy*. □ **unutterably** *adverb*

**unvarnished** *adjective* **1** not varnished. **2** (of a statement etc.) plain and straightforward; *the unvarnished truth*.

**unveil** *verb* **1** remove a veil from; remove one's veil. **2** remove concealing drapery from, as part of a ceremony; *unveiled the portrait*. **3** disclose, make publicly known.

**unversed** *adjective* (usually foll. by *in*) not experienced or skilled; *unversed in court etiquette*.

**unvoiced** *adjective* **1** not spoken. **2** (of a consonant) not voiced.

**unwaged** *adjective* (of a person) not receiving a wage, unemployed.

**unwarranted** *adjective* unauthorized; unjustified.

**unwary** (un-wair-i) *adjective* not cautious. □ **unwarily** *adverb*, **unwariness** *noun*

**unwell** *adjective* not in good health.

**unwholesome** *adjective* **1** harmful to health or to moral well-being. **2** unhealthy-looking. □ **unwholesomeness** *noun*

**unwieldy** (un-weel-di) *adjective* awkward to move or control because of its size, shape, or weight. □ **unwieldiness** *noun*

**unwilling** *adjective* not willing, reluctant, hesitating to do something. □ **unwillingly** *adverb*

**unwind** *verb* (**unwound**, **unwinding**) **1** draw out or become drawn out from being wound. **2** (*informal*) relax after a period of work or tension.

**unwinking** *adjective* **1** not winking; gazing or (of a light) shining steadily. **2** watchful.

**unwise** *adjective* not wise, foolish. □ **unwisely** *adverb*

**unwitting** *adjective* **1** unaware. **2** unintentional. □ **unwittingly** *adverb*

**unwonted** (un-wohn-tid) *adjective* not customary or usual; *spoke with unwonted rudeness*. □ **unwontedly** *adverb*

**unworldly** *adjective* **1** spiritual, not materialistic. **2** unsophisticated, naïve. □ **unworldliness** *noun*

**unworthy** *adjective* **1** not worthy, lacking worth or excellence. **2** not deserving; *he is unworthy of this honour*. **3** unsuitable to the character of a person or thing; *such conduct is unworthy of a king.* □ **unworthily** *adverb*, **unworthiness** *noun*

**unwrap** *verb* (**unwrapped**, **unwrapping**) open or become opened from being wrapped.

**unwritten** *adjective* **1** not written. **2** (of a law, agreement etc.) based on custom rather than being officially established.

**unyielding** *adjective* **1** firm in texture, not yielding. **2** firm in resisting persuasion, threats, etc.

**unzip** *verb* (**unzipped**, **unzipping**) open or become opened by the undoing of a zip.

**up** *adverb* **1** to an erect or vertical position; *stand up.* **2** to, in, or at a higher place, level, value or condition; to a larger size; further north. **3** in a stronger or leading position; *they are two goals up; I am £5 up on the transaction.* **4** so as to be inflated; *pump up the tyres.* **5** at or towards a central place or a university. **6** to the place, time, or amount etc. in question; *up till now; can take up to four passengers.* **7** out of bed; (of a stage curtain) raised at the start of a performance; (of a jockey) in the saddle. **8** into a condition of activity or efficiency; *getting up steam; stirred up trouble; house is up for sale.* **9** apart, into pieces; *tore it up.* **10** into a compact state, securely; *pack it up; tie it up.* **11** finished; *your time is up.* **12** (*informal*) happening (especially of something unusual or undesirable); *something is up.* ●*preposition* **1** upwards along, through, or into; from bottom to top of. **2** at a higher part of; *fix it further up the wall.* ●*adjective* **1** directed upwards; *an up stroke.* **2** travelling towards a central place; *an up train.* ●*verb* (**upped**, **upping**) (*informal*) **1** begin to do something suddenly or unexpectedly; *he upped and went.* **2** increase; *they promptly upped the price.* □ **on the up** (or **up and up**) (*informal*) steadily improving. **up against 1** close to. **2** in or into contact with. **3** (*informal*) confronted with (a problem, challenge, etc.). **up-and-coming** *adjective* (*informal*) promising; progressing. **up and down** to and fro. **up-and-over** *adjective* (of a door) opened by being raised and pushed back into a horizontal position. **up front** (*informal*) **1** in front; in a prominent position. **2** in advance. **3** straightforward, uninhibited. **ups and downs** alternate good and bad fortune. **up to 1** until; *busy up to 7 o'clock.* **2** below or equal to; *caused up to seven deaths.* **3** occupied with, doing; *what is he up to?* **4** required as a duty or obligation from; *it's up to us to help her.* **5** capable of; *I don't feel up to a long walk.* **up to date** (as *adjective* **up-to-date**) **1** in current fashion. **2** in accordance with what is now known or required; *bring the files up to date.*

**upbeat** *noun* an unaccented beat in music. ●*adjective* (*informal*) cheerful, encouraging.

**upbraid** *verb* reproach.

**upbringing** *noun* a person's rearing and education during childhood.

**up-country** *adverb* & *adjective* inland.

**update** *verb* (*pronounced* up-**dayt**) bring up to date. ●*noun* (*pronounced* **up**-dayt) updating; updated information.

**Updike**, John Hoyer (born 1932), American novelist and short-story writer.

**up-end** *verb* set or rise up on end.

**upfield** *adverb* in or to a position nearer to the opponents' end of a field.

**upgrade** *verb* **1** raise to a higher grade or rank. **2** improve (equipment etc.).

**upheaval** *noun* a violent change or disturbance.

**uphill** *adverb* in an upward direction; further up a slope. ●*adjective* **1** going or sloping upwards. **2** difficult; *it was uphill work.*

**uphold** *verb* (**upheld**, **upholding**) **1** support, keep from falling. **2** support a decision, statement, or belief.

**upholster** *verb* put a fabric covering, padding, springs, etc. on (furniture). □ **upholsterer** *noun*

**upholstery** *noun* **1** the work of upholstering furniture. **2** the material used for this.

**upkeep** *noun* **1** keeping something in good condition and repair. **2** the cost of this.

**upland** *noun* higher or inland parts of a country. ●*adjective* of uplands.

**uplift** *verb* (*pronounced* up-**lift**) **1** raise. **2** elevate emotionally or morally. ●*noun* (*pronounced* **up**-lift) **1** being raised. **2** a mentally or morally elevating influence. **3** support for the bust (from a bra).

**up-market** *adjective* & *adverb* of or towards the more expensive end of the market.

**upon** *preposition* on; *Stratford-upon-Avon; Christmas is almost upon us.* □ **once upon a time** *see* ONCE. **upon my word!** an exclamation of shock or surprise.

**upper** *adjective* **1** higher in place or position. **2** situated on higher ground or to the north; *Upper Egypt.* **3** ranking above others; *the upper class.* ●*noun* **1** the part of a boot or shoe above the sole. **2** (*slang*) an amphetamine or other stimulant. □ **on one's uppers** (*informal*) very short of money. **upper case** capital letters. **Upper Chamber** or **House** the House of Lords as an assembly. **upper crust** (*informal*) the aristocracy. **upper-cut** *noun* a blow in boxing, delivered upwards with the arm bent. **the upper hand** mastery, dominance; *gained the upper hand.*

**uppermost** *adjective* highest in place or rank. ●*adverb* on or to the top or most prominent position.

**uppish** *adjective* (*informal*) uppity.

**uppity** adjective (*informal*) presumptuous, arrogant.

**upright** adjective **1** in a vertical position. **2** (of a piano) with the strings mounted vertically. **3** strictly honest or honourable. ●noun **1** a post or rod placed upright, especially as a support. **2** an upright piano. □ **uprightness** noun

**uprising** noun a rebellion or revolt.

**uproar** noun a violent outburst of noise and excitement or anger.

**uproarious** adjective very noisy; with loud laughter. □ **uproariously** adverb

**uproot** verb **1** pull out of the ground together with its roots. **2** force to leave a native or established place. **3** remove or destroy completely.

**upset** verb (*pronounced* up-**set**) (**upset**, **upsetting**) **1** overturn; become overturned. **2** disrupt; *fog upset the timetable*. **3** distress mentally or emotionally. **4** make physically ill; *an upset stomach*. ●noun (*pronounced* **up**-set) noun upsetting, being upset; *a stomach upset*.

**upshot** noun an outcome.

**upside down** adverb & adjective **1** with the upper part underneath instead of on top. **2** in or into total disorder.

**upstage** adjective & adverb nearer the back of a theatre stage. ●verb **1** move upstage to make (another actor) face away from the audience. **2** divert attention from or outshine (a person).

**upstairs** adverb up the stairs, to or on an upper floor. ●adjective situated upstairs.

**upstanding** adjective **1** standing up. **2** strong and healthy. **3** law-abiding, honest.

**upstart** noun a person who has risen suddenly to a high position, especially one who behaves arrogantly.

**upstate** (*Amer.*) adjective of the part of a State remote from large cities, especially the northern part. ●noun this part.

**upstream** adjective & adverb in the direction from which a stream flows, against the current.

**upsurge** noun an upward surge, a rise.

**upswept** adjective (of the hair) combed to the top of the head.

**upswing** noun an upward movement or trend.

**upsy-daisy** interjection (also **ups-a-daisy**) an expression of encouragement to a child who is being lifted or has fallen.

**uptake** noun ability to understand what is meant; *quick on the uptake*.

**uptight** adjective (*informal*) **1** nervously tense. **2** annoyed. **3** (*Amer.*) rigidly conventional.

**upturn** noun (*pronounced* up-**tern**) **1** an upheaval. **2** an upward trend in business or fortune etc., an improvement. ●verb (*pronounced* up-**tern**) turn upwards; turn upside down.

**upward** adjective moving, leading, or pointing towards what is higher or more important or earlier. ●adverb (also **upwards**) towards what is higher etc.

**upwind** adjective & adverb in the direction from which the wind is blowing.

**Ur** an ancient city in what is now southern Iraq, where rich royal tombs of *c.*2600–2000 BC were discovered.

**Ural Mountains** (yoor-ăl) (also **Urals**) a mountain range in the former USSR forming a natural boundary between Europe and Asia.

**uranium** (yoor-ay-niŭm) noun a chemical element (symbol U), a heavy grey metal used as a source of nuclear energy.

**Uranus** (yoor-ăn-ŭs *or* yoor-ay-nŭs) **1** (*Gk. myth.*) the most ancient of the gods, ruler of the universe, overthrown by his son Cronus. **2** one of the major planets.

**urban** adjective of or situated in a city or town. □ **urban guerrilla** a terrorist operating in an urban area.

**urbane** (er-bayn) adjective elegant, sophisticated. □ **urbanity** (er-ban-iti) noun

**urbanize** verb (also **urbanise**) change (a place) into a townlike area. □ **urbanization** noun

**urchin** noun **1** a mischievous or ragged child. **2** a sea urchin.

**Urdu** (oor-doo) noun a language related to Hindi, one of the official languages of Pakistan.

**urea** (yoor-ee-ă) noun a soluble colourless compound contained especially in urine.

**ureter** (yoor-ee-ter) noun either of the two ducts by which urine passes from the kidneys to the bladder.

**urethra** (yoor-ee-thră) noun the duct by which urine is discharged from the body.

**urge** verb **1** drive onward, encourage to proceed; *urging them on*. **2** try hard or persistently to persuade; *urged him to accept the job*. **3** (often foll. by *on*) recommend strongly; *urged on them the importance of keeping to the schedule*. ●noun a feeling or desire that urges a person to do something.

**urgent** adjective **1** needing immediate attention, action, or decision. **2** showing that something is urgent; *spoke in an urgent whisper*. □ **urgently** adverb, **urgency** noun

**uric** (yoor-ik) adjective of urine. □ **uric acid** a liquid present in urine.

**urinal** (yoor-I-năl) noun a place or receptacle for men to urinate in.

**urinary** (yoor-in-er-i) adjective of urine or its excretion; *urinary organs*.

**urinate** (yoor-in-ayt) verb discharge urine from the body. □ **urination** noun

**urine** (**yoor**-in) *noun* waste liquid which collects in the bladder and is discharged from the body.

**urn** *noun* **1** a vase, usually with a stem and base, especially one used for holding the ashes of a cremated person. **2** a large metal container with a tap, in which tea or coffee is made or from which it is served.

**urogenital** (yoor-ŏ-**jen**-i-t'l) *adjective* of the urinary and reproductive systems.

**urology** (yoor-**ol**-ŏji) *noun* the scientific study of the urinary system.

**Ursa Major** the constellation known as the Great Bear or the Plough.

**Ursa Minor** the constellation known as the Little Bear, containing the pole star.

**ursine** (**er**-syn) *adjective* of or like a bear.

**Uruguay** (**yoor**-ŭ-gwy) a country in South America, south of Brazil. □ **Uruguayan** *adjective* & *noun*

**US** *abbreviation* United States (of America).

**us** *pronoun* **1** the objective case of **we**. **2** (*informal*) = we; *it's us*. **3** (*informal*) me; *give us your hand*.

**USA** *abbreviation* United States of America.

**usable** *adjective* able to be used; fit for use.

**USAF** *abbreviation* United States Air Force.

**usage** (**yoo**-sij) *noun* **1** the manner of using or treating something; *it was damaged by rough usage*. **2** a habitual or customary practice, especially in the way words are used; *modern English usage*.

**use** *verb* (*pronounced* yooz) **1** cause to act or serve for a purpose. **2** cause oneself to be known or addressed by (a name or title). **3** treat in a specified way, behave towards; *they used her shamefully*. **4** exploit selfishly. ● *noun* (*pronounced* yooss) **1** using; being used. **2** the right or power of using something; *lost the use of his arm*. **3** the purpose for which something is used; *work that a person or thing is able to do*. **4** benefit, advantage; *be of use*; *it's no use talking to him*. □ **have no use for 1** not need. **2** dislike, be contemptuous of. **make use of** use, exploit. **use up 1** use the whole of (material etc.). **2** find a use for (remaining material or time). □ **user** *noun*

**used**[1] (*pronounced* yoozd) *adjective* (of clothes or vehicles) second-hand.

**used**[2] (*pronounced* yoost) *verb* was or were accustomed in the past; *we used to go by train*; *they used not to do this*. ● *adjective* having become familiar with (a thing) by practice or habit; *he is used to getting up early*.

**useful** *adjective* **1** able to produce good results, able to be used for some practical purpose. **2** (*informal*) good or skilful; *a useful snooker player*. □ **make oneself useful** help. □ **usefully** *adverb*, **usefulness** *noun*

**useless** *adjective* **1** serving no useful purpose. **2** (*informal*) extremely poor or bad; *useless at football*. □ **uselessly** *adverb*, **uselessness** *noun*

**usher** *noun* **1** a person who shows people to their seats in a public hall etc. or into someone's presence, or who walks before a person of rank. **2** an official acting as doorkeeper in a lawcourt. ● *verb* lead in or out; escort as an usher.

**usherette** *noun* a woman who ushers people to their seats in a cinema or theatre.

**USSR** *abbreviation* Union of Soviet Socialist Republics.

**Ustinov** (**yoo**-stin-off), Sir Peter Alexander (born 1921), British stage and film actor, director, and playwright.

**usual** *adjective* such as happens or is done or used in most instances; customary, habitual. □ **as usual** as happens normally. □ **usually** *adverb*

**usurer** (**yoo**-*zh*er-er) *noun* a person who lends money at excessively high interest.

**usurp** (yoo-**zerp**) *verb* take (power or a position or right) wrongfully. □ **usurpation** *noun*, **usurper** *noun*

**usury** (**yoo**-*zh*er-i) *noun* **1** the lending of money at excessively high interest. **2** an excessively high rate of interest. □ **usurious** (yooz-**yoor**-iŭs) *adjective*

**UT** *abbreviation* **1** universal time. **2** Utah.

**Utah** (**yoo**-tah) a State of the western USA.

**UTC** *abbreviation* coordinated universal time, an international reference time-scale for civil use based on atomic clocks and adjusted to keep it close to mean solar time on the Greenwich meridian (= GREENWICH MEAN TIME).

**utensil** (yoo-**ten**-sĭl) *noun* an instrument or container, especially for kitchen use.

**uterine** (**yoo**-teryn) *adjective* of the uterus.

**uterus** (**yoo**-ter-ŭs) *noun* (*plural* **uteri**) the womb.

**utilitarian** (yoo-tili-**tair**-iăn) *adjective* **1** designed to be useful rather than decorative or luxurious, severely practical. **2** of utilitarianism. ● *noun* an advocate of utilitarianism.

**utilitarianism** *noun* the doctrine that actions are right if they benefit or are useful to most people.

**utility** *noun* **1** usefulness. **2** a useful thing. **3** (also **public utility**) a company supplying water, gas, or electricity etc. to the community. ● *adjective* basic and standardized; *utility furniture*. □ **utility room** a room containing large fixed domestic appliances (e.g. a washing machine). **utility vehicle** a vehicle serving various purposes.

**utilize** *verb* (also **utilise**) use, find a use for. □ **utilization** *noun*

**utmost** *adjective* furthest, greatest, extreme;

*with the utmost care.* ● *noun* the furthest point or degree etc. □ **do one's utmost** do as much as possible.

**Utopia** (yoo-**toh**-piă) *noun* an imaginary place or state of things where everything is perfect. □ **Utopian** *adjective* (also **utopian**). (¶ The title of a book by Sir Thomas More (1516), meaning 'Nowhere'.)

**Utrillo** (oo-**tril**-oh), Maurice (1883–1955), French painter.

**Uttar Pradesh** (**uut**-ar pră-**desh**) a State in northern India.

**utter**[1] *adjective* complete, absolute; *utter bliss.* □ **utterly** *adverb*

**utter**[2] *verb* **1** make (a sound or words) with the mouth or voice; express; *uttered a sigh.* **2** *Law* put (forged money etc.) into circulation.

**utterance** *noun* **1** the act or power of uttering. **2** something spoken.

**uttermost** *adjective & noun* = UTMOST.

**U-turn** *noun* **1** the driving of a vehicle in a U-shaped course so as to proceed in an opposite direction. **2** a reversal of policy.

**UV** *abbreviation* ultraviolet.

**uvula** (**yoov**-yoo-lă) *noun* (*plural* **uvulae**) the small fleshy projection hanging from the back of the roof of the mouth above the throat. □ **uvular** *adjective*

**uxorious** (uks-**or**-iŭs) *adjective* obsessively fond of one's wife.

**Uzbek** (**uuz**-bek) *noun* **1** a native of Uzbekistan. **2** the language of Uzbekistan.

**Uzbekistan** (uuz-bek-i-**stahn**) a country (formerly a republic of the USSR) lying south and south-east of the Aral Sea.

# Vv

**V** *noun* (as a Roman numeral) 5. ● *abbreviation* volt(s). ● *symbol* vanadium.

**v.** *abbreviation* **1** versus. **2** very. **3** (as an instruction in a reference to a passage in a book etc.) see, consult. (¶ Latin *vide*).

**VA, Va.** *abbreviation* Virginia.

**vac** *noun* (*informal*) **1** a vacation. **2** a vacuum cleaner.

**vacancy** *noun* **1** the condition of being vacant, emptiness. **2** an unoccupied position of employment; *we have a vacancy for a typist.* **3** unoccupied accommodation; *this hotel has no vacancies.*

**vacant** *adjective* **1** empty, not filled or occupied; *a vacant seat; applied for a vacant post.* **2** showing no sign of thought or intelligence, having a blank expression. □ **vacant possession** (of a house etc.) the state of being empty of occupants and available for the purchaser to occupy immediately. □ **vacantly** *adverb*

**vacate** (vă-**kayt**) *verb* cease to occupy (a place or position).

**vacation** (vă-**kay**-shŏn) *noun* **1** any of the intervals between terms in universities and lawcourts. **2** (*Amer.*) a holiday. **3** vacating; *immediate vacation of the house is essential.* ● *verb* (*Amer.*) spend a holiday.

**vaccinate** (**vak**-sin-ayt) *verb* inoculate with a vaccine to immunize against a disease. □ **vaccination** *noun*

**vaccine** (**vak**-seen) *noun* a preparation injected or administered orally to give immunity against an infection.

**vacillate** (**vass**-il-ayt) *verb* **1** waver, keep changing one's mind. **2** swing or sway unsteadily. □ **vacillation** *noun*, **vacillator** *noun*

**vacuity** (vă-**kew**-iti) *noun* **1** emptiness. **2** vacuousness.

**vacuous** (**vak**-yoo-ŭs) *adjective* emptyheaded, inane, expressionless; *a vacuous stare.* □ **vacuously** *adverb*, **vacuousness** *noun*

**vacuum** *noun* (*plural* **vacuums** or, *in science,* **vacua**) **1** space completely empty of matter; space in a container from which the air has been pumped out. **2** absence of normal or previous contents. **3** (*informal*) a vacuum cleaner. ● *verb* (*informal*) clean with a vacuum cleaner. □ **vacuum cleaner** an electrical appliance that takes up dust, dirt, etc. by suction. **vacuum flask** a flask with a double wall that encloses a vacuum, used for keeping liquids hot or cold. **vacuum-packed** *adjective* sealed in a pack from which most of the air has been removed.

**vacuum tube** a sealed tube with an almost perfect vacuum, allowing free passage of electric current.

**vade-mecum** (vah-di-**may**-kŭm) *noun* a handbook or other small useful work of reference. (¶ Latin, = go with me.)

**Vaduz** (va-**doots**) the capital of Liechtenstein.

**vagabond** *noun* a wanderer, a vagrant, especially an idle or dishonest one. ● *adjective* wandering, roving.

**vagary** (**vayg**-er-i) *noun* a capricious act or idea; a fluctuation; *vagaries of fashion.*

**vagina** (vă-**jy**-nă) *noun* the passage leading from the vulva to the womb in women and female animals. □ **vaginal** *adjective*

**vagrant** (**vay**-grănt) *noun* a person without a settled home or regular work. □ **vagrancy** *noun*

**vague** *adjective* **1** not clearly expressed, perceived, or identified. **2** not expressing one's thoughts clearly or precisely. □ **vaguely** *adverb*, **vagueness** *noun*

**vain** *adjective* **1** conceited, especially about one's appearance. **2** having no value or significance; *vain triumphs.* **3** useless, futile; *in the vain hope of persuading him.* □ **in vain** with no result, uselessly; *we tried, but in vain.* **take God's name in vain** use it irreverently. □ **vainly** *adverb*

**vainglory** *noun* extreme vanity; boastfulness. □ **vainglorious** *adjective*

**Vaisya** (vys-yă) *noun* a member of the third of the four great Hindu classes (the farmer or merchant class).

**valance** (**val**-ăns) *noun* (also **valence**) a short curtain round the base or canopy of a bed, above a window, or under a shelf.

**vale** *noun* a valley; *the Vale of Evesham.*

**valediction** (vali-**dik**-shŏn) *noun* saying farewell; the words used in this.

**valedictory** (vali-**dik**-ter-i) *adjective* saying farewell; *a valedictory speech.*

**valence** (**vay**-lĕns) *noun* **1** = VALENCY. **2** alternative spelling of VALANCE.

**Valencia** (vă-**len**-siă) **1** a city and port of eastern Spain. **2** a region of eastern Spain, on the Mediterranean Sea.

**valency** (**vay**-lĕn-si) *noun* the capacity of an atom to combine with others, measured by the number of hydrogen atoms it can displace or combine with.

**Valentine**, St, an early Italian saint (possibly a Roman priest martyred *c.*269), regarded as the patron of lovers. Feast day, 14 February.

**valentine** noun **1** a lover chosen on St Valentine's day (14 February). **2** a card sent on this day (often anonymously) to one's valentine.

**Valentino** (val-ĕn-**teen**-oh), Rudolph (original name: Rodolfo Guglielmi di Valentino) (1895–1926), Italian-born American film actor, famous for his romantic roles.

**valerian** (vă-**leer**-iăn) noun a strong-smelling herb with pink or white flowers.

**valet** (**val**-it or val-**ay**) noun **1** a man's personal attendant who takes care of clothes etc. **2** a hotel employee with similar duties. ● verb (**valeted**, **valeting**) **1** act as valet to. **2** clean or clean out (a car).

**valetudinarian** (vali-tew-din-**air**-iăn) noun a person of poor health or who pays excessive attention to preserving health. □ **valetudinarianism** noun

**Valhalla** (val-**hal**-ă) (*Scand. myth.*) the hall in which the souls of slain heroes feasted with Odin.

**valiant** adjective brave, courageous. □ **valiantly** adverb

**valid** (**val**-id) adjective **1** having legal force, legally acceptable or usable; *a valid passport*. **2** (of reasoning etc.) sound and to the point, logical. □ **validly** adverb, **validity** (vă-**lid**-iti) noun

**validate** (**val**-id-ayt) verb make valid, confirm. □ **validation** noun

**valise** (vă-**leez**) noun (*Amer.*) a small suitcase.

**Valium** noun (*trade mark*) a drug used as a tranquillizer and relaxant.

**Valkyrie** (**val**-ki-ri) noun (*Scand. myth.*) any of Odin's twelve handmaidens who hovered over battlefields and carried chosen slain warriors to Valhalla.

**Valletta** (vă-**let**-ă) the capital of Malta.

**valley** noun (*plural* **valleys**) **1** a long low area between hills. **2** a region drained by a river; *the Nile valley*.

**valour** (**val**-er) noun (*Amer.* **valor**) bravery, especially in fighting. □ **valorous** adjective

**valse** (*pronounced* vahls) noun a waltz. (¶ French.)

**valuable** adjective of great value or price or worth. ● *plural noun* (**valuables**) valuable things, especially small personal possessions. □ **valuably** adverb

**valuation** noun estimation of a thing's value (especially by a professional valuer) or of a person's merit.

**value** noun **1** the amount of money or other commodity or service etc. considered to be equivalent to something else or for which a thing can be exchanged. **2** desirability, usefulness, importance; *he learnt the value of regular exercise*. **3** the ability of a thing to serve a purpose or cause an effect; *the food value of milk*; *news value*. **4** the amount or quantity denoted by a figure etc., the duration of a musical sound indicated by a note, the relative importance of each playing card etc. in a game. **5** (in full **value for money**) a good bargain. **6** (**values**) standards or principles considered valuable or important in life; *moral values*. ● verb **1** estimate the value of. **2** consider to be of great worth or importance. □ **value added tax** tax on the amount by which the value of an article has been increased at each stage of its production.

**valueless** adjective having no value.

**valuer** noun a person who estimates values professionally.

**valve** noun **1** a device for controlling the flow of gas or liquid through a pipe. **2** a structure in the heart or in a blood vessel allowing blood to flow in one direction only. **3** a device for varying the length of the tube in a brass wind instrument. **4** each piece of the shell of molluscs such as oysters. **5** a thermionic valve.

**valvular** (**val**-vew-ler) adjective of the valves of the heart or blood vessels.

**vamoose** verb (*Amer. slang*) go away hurriedly.

**vamp**[1] noun the upper front part of a boot or shoe. ● verb **1** (foll. by *up*) make from odds and ends; *we'll vamp something up*. **2** improvise a musical accompaniment to a song or dance.

**vamp**[2] (*informal*) noun a seductive woman who uses her attraction to exploit men, an unscrupulous flirt. ● verb exploit or flirt with (a man) unscrupulously.

**vampire** noun **1** a ghost or reanimated body supposed to leave a grave at night and suck the blood of living people. **2** a person who preys on others. □ **vampire bat** a tropical bat that bites or is said to bite animals and suck their blood.

**van** noun **1** a small covered vehicle for transporting goods etc. **2** a railway carriage for luggage or goods, or for the use of the guard. **3** the vanguard, the forefront.

**vanadium** (vă-**nay**-diŭm) noun a hard grey metallic element (symbol V) used in certain steels.

**Van Allen belt** each of two regions of intense radiation partly surrounding the earth at heights of several thousand kilometres. (¶ Named after the American physicist J. Van Allen (born 1914) who discovered them.)

**Vanbrugh** (**van**-brŭ), Sir John (1664–1726), English baroque architect, who collaborated with Hawksmoor in producing Castle Howard in Yorkshire and Blenheim Palace in Oxfordshire.

**Vancouver** (van-**koo**-ver) a city and sea-port of British Columbia, Canada. □ **Vancouver Island** a large island off the Pacific coast of Canada, opposite Vancouver. (¶ Named after the English explorer George Vancouver (1757–98), who charted the west coast of America in 1792–4.)

**vandal** *noun* a person who wilfully or maliciously damages property or natural features. □ **vandalism** *noun* (¶ Named after the **Vandals**, a Germanic people who ravaged Gaul, Spain, North Africa, and Rome in the 4th–5th centuries, destroying many books and works of art.)

**vandalize** *verb* (also **vandalise**) damage (property etc.) as a vandal.

**van de Graaff generator** a machine which generates electrostatic charge by means of a vertical endless belt collecting charge from a voltage source and transferring it to a large insulated metal dome.

**van de Velde** *see* VELDE.

**Van Dyck** (*rhymes with* like), Sir Anthony (1599–1641), Flemish painter, noted for his portraits of the court of Charles I.

**Vandyke** *adjective* in the style of dress etc. common in portraits by Van Dyck. □ **Vandyke beard** a neat pointed beard. **Vandyke brown** deep rich brown.

**vane** *noun* **1** a weather vane. **2** the blade of a propeller, sail of a windmill, or similar device acting on or moved by wind or water.

**Van Eyck** (*rhymes with* like), Jan (died 1441), Flemish painter, noted for his oil paintings.

**Van Gogh** (*pronounced* gof), Vincent Willem (1853–90), Dutch post-impressionist painter, who used colours for their expressive or symbolic values and vigorous swirling brushstrokes.

**vanguard** *noun* **1** the foremost part of an advancing army or fleet. **2** the leaders of a movement or fashion etc.

**vanilla** *noun* **1** a flavouring obtained from the pods of a tropical climbing orchid, or made synthetically. **2** this orchid.

**vanish** *verb* disappear completely. □ **vanishing-point** *noun* the point at which receding parallel lines viewed in perspective appear to meet.

**vanity** *noun* **1** conceit, especially about one's appearance. **2** futility, worthlessness, something vain; *the vanity of human achievement*. □ **vanity bag** *or* **case** a small bag or case used by a woman for carrying cosmetics etc. **vanity unit** a washbasin set into a flat top with cupboards beneath.

**vanquish** *verb* conquer.

**vantage** *noun* (in tennis) an advantage. □ **vantage point** a place from which one has a good view of something.

**Vanuatu** (van-wah-**too**) an island country in the SW Pacific.

**vapid** (**vap**-id) *adjective* insipid, uninteresting. □ **vapidity** (vă-**pid**-iti) *noun*

**vaporize** *verb* (also **vaporise**) change into vapour. □ **vaporization** *noun*, **vaporizer** *noun*

**vapour** *noun* (*Amer.* **vapor**) **1** moisture or other substance diffused or suspended in air. **2** the air-like substance into which certain liquid or solid substances can be converted by heating (*see* GAS). □ **vapour trail** a trail of condensed water from an aircraft etc. □ **vaporous** *adjective*, **vapoury** *adjective*

**Varanasi** (vă-**rah**-nă-si) a Hindu holy city on the Ganges in the State of Uttar Pradesh, India.

**variable** *adjective* varying, changeable; (of a star) periodically varying in brightness. ●*noun* something that varies or can vary, a variable quantity. □ **variably** *adverb*, **variability** *noun*

**variance** *noun* □ **at variance** disagreeing, conflicting; (of people) in a state of discord.

**variant** *adjective* differing from something or from a standard; *'gipsy' is a variant spelling of 'gypsy'.* ●*noun* a variant form or spelling etc.

**variation** *noun* **1** varying; the extent to which something varies. **2** a variant. **3** a repetition of a melody in a different (usually more elaborate) form.

**varicoloured** (vair-i-kul-erd) *adjective* (*Amer.* **varicolored**) **1** variegated in colour. **2** of various or different colours.

**varicose** (va-ri-kohs) *adjective* (of a vein) permanently swollen or enlarged. □ **varicosity** (va-ri-**koss**-iti) *noun*

**varied** *see* VARY. ●*adjective* of different sorts, full of variety.

**variegated** (vair-i-**gayt**-id) *adjective* **1** marked with irregular patches of different colours. **2** having leaves of two or more colours. □ **variegation** *noun*

**variety** *noun* **1** the quality of not being the same or of not being the same at all times. **2** a quantity or range of different things; *for a variety of reasons.* **3** a class of things that differ from others in the same general group, a member of such a class; *several varieties of spaniel.* **4** entertainment consisting of a series of short performances of different kinds (e.g. singing, dancing, acrobatics).

**various** *adjective* **1** of several kinds, unlike one another. **2** more than one, individual and separate; *we met various people.* □ **variously** *adverb*

**varlet** *noun* (*old use*) **1** a menial servant. **2** a rascal.

**varmint** *noun* (*dialect* or *Amer.*) a mischievous or discreditable person or animal.

**varna** *noun* any of the four great Hindu classes (Brahmin, Kshatriya, Vaisya, Sudra).

**varnish** *noun* **1** a liquid that dries to form a hard shiny transparent coating, used on wood or metal etc. **2** nail varnish. **3** a deceptive outward appearance or show. ● *verb* coat with varnish.

**Varuna** (vă-**roo**-nă) (in Hinduism) the ancient ruler of the universe, later the god of the waters.

**vary** *verb* (**varied, varying**) **1** make or become different; *you can vary the pressure; his temper varies from day to day.* **2** be different or of different kinds; *opinions vary on this point.*

**Vasari** (vă-**sar**-i), Giorgio (1511–74), Italian painter and biographer, whose writings are important for the study of Renaissance art.

**Vasco da Gama** *see* GAMA.

**vascular** (vas-**kew**-ler) *adjective* consisting of vessels or ducts for conveying blood or sap within an organism; *vascular system.*

**vas deferens** (vas de-**fĕ**-renz) (*plural* **vasa deferentia**) each of the ducts through which semen passes from the testicle to the urethra.

**vase** (*pronounced* vahz) *noun* an open usually tall vessel of glass, pottery, etc. used for holding cut flowers or as an ornament.

**vasectomy** (vă-**sekt**-ŏmi) *noun* surgical removal of part of each vas deferens, especially as a method of birth control.

**Vaseline** (vas-i-leen) *noun* (*trade mark*) petroleum jelly used as an ointment or lubricant.

**vassal** *noun* a humble servant or subordinate. □ **vassalage** *noun*

**vast** *adjective* immense, huge; *a vast expanse of water; it makes a vast difference.* □ **vastly** *adverb*, **vastness** *noun*

**VAT** *abbreviation* value added tax.

**vat** *noun* a tank or other great vessel for holding liquids.

**Vatican** *noun* **1** the Pope's official residence in Rome. **2** the papal government. □ **Vatican City** an independent papal State in Rome, including the Vatican and St Peter's.

**vaudeville** (vaw-dĕ-vil) *noun* variety entertainment, popular from about 1880 to 1932.

**Vaughan Williams** (*pronounced* vawn), Ralph (1872–1958), English composer.

**vault** *noun* **1** an arched roof. **2** a vault-like covering; *the vault of heaven.* **3** a cellar or underground room used as a place of storage. **4** a burial chamber; *the family vault.* **5** an act of vaulting. ● *verb* **1** jump or leap, especially using the hands or with the help of a pole; *vaulted over the gate.* **2** make in the form of a vault; provide with a vault or vaults. □ **vaulter** *noun*

**vaulting** *noun* arched work in a roof or ceiling. □ **vaulting horse** a padded structure for vaulting over in a gymnasium.

**vaunt** *verb* boast. ● *noun* a boast.

**VC** *abbreviation* Victoria Cross.

**VCR** *abbreviation* video cassette recorder.

**VD** *abbreviation* venereal disease.

**VDU** *abbreviation* visual display unit.

**'ve** (*informal*) (especially after pronouns) have; *they've finished.*

**veal** *noun* calf's flesh as food.

**vector** *noun* **1** (in mathematics) a quantity that has both magnitude and direction (e.g. velocity, = speed in a given direction). **2** the carrier of a disease or infection.

**Veda** (vay-dă) *noun* (also **Vedas**) the most ancient and sacred literature of the Hindus.

**Vedic** (vay-dik *or* vee-dik) *adjective* of the Vedas. ● *noun* the language of the Vedas, an old form of Sanskrit.

**veer** *verb* change direction or course; (of wind) to change gradually in a clockwise direction.

**veg** (*pronounced* vej) *noun* (*informal*) vegetable(s).

**vegan** (vee-găn) *noun* a strict vegetarian who eats no animal products (e.g. eggs or milk).

**vegeburger** alternative spelling of VEGGIE BURGER.

**vegetable** *noun* **1** a plant of which some part is used (raw or cooked) as food, especially as an accompaniment to meat. **2** a person leading a dull monotonous life. **3** (*informal*) a person who is without mental faculties because of brain damage. ● *adjective* of, from, or relating to plant life.

**vegetal** (vej-i-t'l) *adjective* of or like plants.

**vegetarian** *noun* a person who eats no meat. ● *adjective* excluding food from animals, especially meat; *a vegetarian diet.* □ **vegetarianism** *noun*

**vegetate** (vej-i-tayt) *verb* live an uneventful or monotonous life.

**vegetation** *noun* **1** plants collectively. **2** vegetating.

**vegetative** (vej-i-tă-tiv) *adjective* **1** concerned with the growth and development of living organisms. **2** of vegetation.

**veggie** *noun* & *adjective* (also **vegie**) (*informal*) = VEGETARIAN. □ **veggie burger** (also **vegeburger**) a flat savoury cake like a hamburger but containing vegetables or soya protein instead of meat.

**vehement** (vee-i-mĕnt) *adjective* showing strong feeling, intense; *a vehement denial.* □ **vehemently** *adverb*, **vehemence** *noun*

**vehicle** (vee-i-kŭl) *noun* **1** a conveyance for transporting passengers or goods on land or in space. **2** a means by which something is expressed or displayed; *art can be a vehicle for propaganda; the play was an excellent vehicle for this actress's talents.*

**vehicular** (vi-**hik**-yoo-ler) *adjective* of vehicles; *vehicular access.*

**veil** *noun* a piece of fine net or other fabric worn as part of a headdress or to protect or conceal the face. ●*verb* **1** cover with a veil. **2** partly conceal; *a veiled threat.* □ **beyond the veil** in the unknown state of life after death. **draw a veil over** avoid discussing or calling attention to. **take the veil** become a nun.

**vein** *noun* **1** any of the tubes carrying blood from all parts of the body to the heart. **2** any of the threadlike structures forming the framework of a leaf or of an insect's wing. **3** a narrow strip or streak of a different colour, e.g. in marble. **4** a long continuous or branching deposit of mineral or ore, especially in a fissure. **5** a mood or manner; *she spoke in a humorous vein.* □ **veined** *adjective*

**Velázquez** (vi-**las**-kwiz), Diego Rodriguez de Silva y (1599–1660), Spanish painter.

**Velcro** *noun* (*trade mark*) a fastener for clothes etc. consisting of two strips of fabric which cling together when pressed.

**veld** (*pronounced* velt) *noun* (also **veldt**) open grassland in South Africa.

**Velde** (*pronounced* velt), **van de** the name of a Dutch family of painters, Willem I (1611–93) being noted for his portraits of ships, Adriaen (1636–72) for landscapes, biblical scenes, and portraits, and Willem II (1633–1707) for paintings of ships at sea.

**veleta** (vĕl-ee-tă) *noun* a ballroom dance in triple time.

**vellum** *noun* **1** a kind of fine parchment. **2** smooth writing paper.

**velocity** *noun* speed, especially in a given direction.

**velour** (vil-**oor**) *noun* (also **velours**, *pronounced* same) a plushlike fabric.

**velvet** *noun* **1** a woven fabric (especially of silk or cotton) with thick short pile on one side. **2** a furry skin covering a growing antler. □ **on velvet** in an advantageous or prosperous position. **velvet glove** outward gentleness of treatment. □ **velvety** *adjective*

**velveteen** *noun* cotton velvet.

**Ven.** *abbreviation* Venerable (as the title of an archdeacon).

**venal** (veen-ăl) *adjective* **1** able to be bribed. **2** (of conduct) influenced by bribery. □ **venally** *adverb*, **venality** (veen-al-iti) *noun*

■**Usage** Do not confuse with *venial.*

**vend** *verb* sell or offer for sale. □ **vending machine** a slot machine where small articles can be obtained.

**vendetta** (ven-**det**-ă) *noun* a feud.

**vendor** *noun Law* a person who sells something, especially property.

**veneer** *noun* **1** a thin layer of fine wood covering the surface of a cheaper wood in furniture etc. **2** a superficial show of some good quality; *a veneer of politeness.* ●*verb* cover with a veneer.

**venerable** (**ven**-er-ăbŭl) *adjective* **1** worthy of deep respect because of age or associations etc.; *these venerable ruins.* **2** the title of an archdeacon in the Church of England. □ **venerably** *adverb*, **venerability** *noun*

**venerate** *verb* regard with deep respect. □ **veneration** *noun*, **venerator** *noun*

**venereal** (vin-**eer**-iăl) *adjective* **1** (of disease or infection) contracted chiefly by sexual intercourse with a person who is already infected. **2** of sexual desire or intercourse. □ **venereally** *adverb*

**Venetian** (vin-ee-shăn) *adjective* of Venice. ●*noun* a native or inhabitant of Venice. □ **venetian blind** a window blind consisting of horizontal slats that can be adjusted to let in or exclude light.

**Venezuela** (ven-iz-**way**-lă) a country on the north coast of South America. □ **Venezuelan** *adjective & noun*

**vengeance** *noun* retaliation for hurt or harm done to oneself or to a person etc. whom one supports. □ **with a vengeance** in an extreme degree.

**vengeful** *adjective* seeking vengeance. □ **vengefully** *adverb*, **vengefulness** *noun*

**venial** (veen-iăl) *adjective* (of a sin or fault) pardonable, not serious. □ **venially** *adverb*, **veniality** *noun*

■**Usage** Do not confuse with *venal.*

**Venice** a city of NE Italy built on numerous islands on a lagoon of the Adriatic Sea.

**venison** (ven-i-sŏn) *noun* deer's flesh as food.

**Venn diagram** a diagram using overlapping and intersecting circles etc. to show the relationships between mathematical sets. (¶ Named after J. Venn (died 1923), British logician.)

**venom** (ven-ŏm) *noun* **1** poisonous fluid secreted by certain snakes, scorpions, etc. and injected into a victim by a bite or sting. **2** strong bitter feeling or language; hatred. □ **venomous** (ven-ŏm-ŭs) *adjective*, **venomously** *adverb*

**venous** (vee-nŭs) *adjective* **1** of veins. **2** contained in veins; *venous blood.* **3** full of veins.

**vent** noun **1** an opening allowing air, gas, or liquid to pass out of or into a confined space; *a smoke vent.* **2** a slit in a garment (especially a coat or jacket) at the bottom of a back or side seam. ●verb **1** make a vent in. **2** give vent to; *vented his anger on the boy.* ☐ **give vent to** give an outlet to (feelings etc.), express freely; *gave vent to his anger.* **vent light** a small window hinged at the top edge.

**ventilate** verb **1** cause air to enter or circulate freely in (a room etc.). **2** express (an opinion etc.) publicly so that others may consider and discuss it. **3** *Med.* admit or force air into (the lungs). ☐ **ventilation** noun

**ventilator** noun **1** a device for ventilating a room etc. **2** *Med.* = RESPIRATOR (sense 2).

**ventral** adjective of or on the abdomen; *this fish has a ventral fin.* ☐ **ventrally** adverb

**ventricle** (ven-trik-ŭl) noun a cavity or chamber in an organ of the body, especially one of the two in the heart that pump blood into the arteries by contracting. ☐ **ventricular** adjective

**ventriloquist** (ven-tril-ŏ-kwist) noun an entertainer who produces voice-sounds without moving the lips so that they seem to come from another source. ☐ **ventriloquism** noun, **ventriloquize** verb, **ventriloquy** noun

**venture** noun an undertaking that involves risk. ●verb **1** dare; *did not venture to stop him.* **2** dare to go, do, or utter; *did not venture forth; ventured an opinion.* **3** expose to risk; take risks. ☐ **Venture Scout** a member of the senior section of the Scout Association.

**venturesome** adjective ready to take risks, daring.

**venue** (ven-yoo) noun an appointed place of meeting; a place fixed for a sports match, concert, etc.

**Venus 1** (*Rom. myth.*) the goddess of love, identified with Aphrodite. **2** one of the planets, also known as the morning and evening star. ☐ **Venus fly-trap** a plant which traps and consumes insects. **Venus of Milo** a sculpture of Aphrodite made *c.*100 BC, discovered on the Greek island of Melos in 1820 and now in the Louvre.

**veracious** (ver-ay-shŭs) adjective **1** truthful. **2** true. ☐ **veracity** (ver-ass-iti) noun

**veranda** noun a roofed terrace along the side of a house.

**verb** noun a word indicating action, occurrence, or being, e.g. *bring, came, exists.*

**verbal** adjective **1** of or in words; *verbal accuracy.* **2** spoken, not written; *a verbal statement.* **3** of a verb; *verbal inflexions.* ●noun (*informal*) a verbal statement, especially one made to the police. ☐ **verbal**

**noun** a noun (such as *singing, drinking*) derived from a verb. ☐ **verbally** adverb

**verbalize** verb (also **verbalise**) put into words. ☐ **verbalization** noun

**verbatim** (ver-bay-tim) adverb & adjective in exactly the same words, word for word; *copied it verbatim.*

**verbena** (ver-been-ă) noun the plant vervain or a cultivated variety of this, with clusters of fragrant flowers.

**verbiage** (verb-i-ij) noun an excessive number of words used to express an idea.

**verbose** (ver-bohs) adjective using more words than are needed. ☐ **verbosity** (ver-boss-iti) noun

**verdant** adjective (of grass or fields) green. ☐ **verdancy** noun

**Verdi** (vair-di), Giuseppe (1813–1901), Italian composer, whose most famous operas include *Rigoletto, La Traviata,* and *Aida.*

**verdict** noun **1** the decision reached by a jury. **2** a decision or opinion given after examining, testing, or experiencing something.

**verdigris** (verd-i-grees) noun green rust on copper or brass.

**verdure** noun green vegetation; its greenness.

**verge** noun **1** the extreme edge or brink of something. **2** the point beyond which something new begins or occurs; *on the verge of ruin.* **3** the grass edging of a road or flower-bed etc. ●verb (foll. by *on*) border on, approach closely.

**verger** (ver-jer) noun **1** a caretaker and attendant in a church. **2** an official who carries the mace etc. in front of a bishop or other dignitary.

**verify** verb (**verified, verifying**) check the truth or correctness of; *please verify these figures.* ☐ **verifiable** adjective, **verification** noun, **verifier** noun

**verily** adverb (*old use*) in truth.

**verisimilitude** (ve-ri-sim-il-i-tewd) noun an appearance of being true or real.

**veritable** adjective real, rightly named; *a veritable villain.* ☐ **veritably** adverb

**verity** noun (*old use*) the truth of something.

**Vermeer** (ver-meer), Jan (Johannes) (1632–75), Dutch painter.

**vermicelli** (verm-i-chel-i) noun pasta made in long slender threads. ☐ **chocolate vermicelli** very small rod-shaped pieces of chocolate used for decorating cakes etc.

**vermicide** noun a substance that kills worms.

**vermiform** (verm-i-form) adjective worm-like in shape; *the vermiform appendix.*

**vermilion** noun **1** bright red pigment. **2** cinnabar. ●adjective bright red.

**vermin** plural noun **1** common animals and birds (such as foxes, rats, mice) that harm crops, food, or game. **2** unpleasant or parasitic insects (e.g. lice). **3** people who are unpleasant or harmful to society. □ **verminous** *adjective*

**Vermont** (ver-**mont**) a State of the northeastern USA.

**vermouth** (ver-**mŭth**) *noun* white wine flavoured with aromatic herbs.

**vernacular** (ver-**nak**-yoo-ler) *noun* **1** the language of a country, district, or group of people. **2** homely speech. ●*adjective* (of language) native; not foreign or formal.

**vernal** *adjective* of or occurring in spring. □ **vernally** *adverb*

**Verne** (*pronounced* vairn), Jules (1828–1905), French writer of science fiction, whose novels include *Journey from the Earth to the Moon* and *Twenty Thousand Leagues under the Sea.*

**vernier** (**ver**-ni-er) *noun* a small movable graduated scale for indicating fractions of the main scale on a measuring device.

**Veronese** (ve-rŏ-**nay**-zi) (Paolo Caliari) (*c.*1528–88), Italian painter, born at Verona, noted for his frescoes and scenes of splendour such as *The Marriage Feast of Cana.*

**Veronica**, St, a woman of Jerusalem said to have offered her headcloth to Christ on the way to his Crucifixion to wipe blood and sweat from his face. The cloth is said to have retained the image of his features.

**veronica** *noun* a herb often with blue flowers, speedwell.

**verruca** (ver-**oo**-kă) *noun* (*plural* **verrucas** or **verrucae**, *pronounced* ver-**oo**-see) a wart or wart-like swelling, especially on the foot.

**Versailles** (vair-**sy**) a town south-west of Paris, noted for its royal palace built in the 17th century by Louis XIII and XIV.

**versatile** (**ver**-să-tyl) *adjective* able to do, or be used for, many different things. □ **versatility** (ver-să-**til**-iti) *noun*

**verse** *noun* **1** poetry. **2** a poem. **3** a group of lines forming a unit in a poem or hymn. **4** each of the short numbered divisions of a chapter of the Bible.

**versed** *adjective* □ **versed in** experienced or skilled in; having a knowledge of.

**versicle** (**ver**-si-kŭl) *noun* each of the short sentences in the liturgy, said or sung by the clergyman and alternating with the 'responses' of the congregation.

**versify** *verb* (**versified**, **versifying**) express in verse; write verse. □ **versification** *noun*

**version** *noun* **1** a particular person's account of a matter. **2** a particular edition or translation of a book etc.; *the Revised Version of the Bible.* **3** a special or variant form of a thing; *the de luxe version of this car.*

**vers libre** (*pronounced* vair **leebr**) verse with no regular metrical pattern. (¶ French, = free verse.)

**verso** *noun* (*plural* **versos**) **1** the left-hand page of an open book. **2** the back of a leaf of a manuscript etc. (compare RECTO).

**versus** *preposition* against; *Stoke versus Scarborough.*

**vertebra** (ver-**tib**-ră) *noun* (*plural* **vertebrae**, *pronounced* ver-**tib**-ree) any of the individual bones or segments that form the backbone. □ **vertebral** *adjective*

**vertebrate** (**vert**-i-brăt) *noun* an animal that has a backbone.

**vertex** *noun* (*plural* **vertexes** or **vertices**, *pronounced* **ver**-ti-seez) the highest point of a hill or structure; the apex of a cone or triangle.

**vertical** *adjective* **1** perpendicular to the horizontal; moving or placed in this way; upright. **2** in the direction from top to bottom of a picture etc. ●*noun* a vertical line, part, or position. □ **vertically** *adverb*

**vertiginous** (ver-**tij**-in-ŭs) *adjective* causing vertigo.

**vertigo** (**vert**-i-goh) *noun* a sensation of dizziness, especially caused by heights.

**vervain** (**ver**-vayn) *noun* a tall wild plant with hairy leaves and small blue, white, or purple flowers.

**verve** (*pronounced* verv) *noun* enthusiasm, liveliness, vigour.

**very** *adverb* **1** in a high degree, extremely; *very good.* **2** in the fullest sense; *drink it to the very last drop.* **3** exactly; *sat in the very same seat.* ●*adjective* **1** itself or himself etc. and no other, actual, truly such; *it's the very thing we need!* **2** extreme, utter; *at the very end.* □ **very high frequency** (in radio) 30–300 megahertz. **very well** an expression of consent.

**Very light** (**veer**-i) a flare projected by a pistol for signalling or to give temporary light on a battlefield etc.

**vesicle** (**vess**-i-kŭl) *noun* **1** a small hollow structure in a plant or animal body. **2** a blister.

**vespers** *plural noun* a church service held in the evening; evensong.

**vessel** *noun* **1** a hollow structure designed to travel on water and carry people or goods, a ship or boat. **2** a hollow receptacle, especially for liquid. **3** a tube-like structure in the body of an animal or plant, conveying or holding blood or other fluid.

**vest** *noun* **1** a knitted or woven undergarment covering the trunk of the body. **2** (*Amer.* & *Austral.*) a waistcoat. ●*verb* **1** confer as a firm or legal right; *the power of making laws is vested in Parliament; Parliament is vested with this power.* **2** (*old use*) clothe. □ **vested interest 1** personal interest in something, usually with an expectation of gain. **2** *Law* an interest in land or money recognized as belonging to a person.

**Vesta** (*Rom. myth.*) the goddess of the hearth and household.

**Vestal** *adjective* of Vesta. □ **vestal virgin** (in ancient Rome) a virgin consecrated to Vesta and vowed to chastity.

**vestibule** (vest-i-bewl) *noun* an entrance hall or lobby of a building.

**vestige** *noun* **1** a trace, a small remaining bit of what once existed; *not a vestige of the abbey remains*. **2** a very small amount; *not a vestige of truth in it*. **3** a functionless part or organ of a plant or animal that was well developed in ancestors. □ **vestigial** (ves-tij-iăl) *adjective*

**vestment** *noun* a ceremonial robe or other garment, especially one worn by clergy or choir at a religious service.

**vestry** *noun* a room or building attached to a church, where vestments are kept and where clergy and choir robe themselves.

**Vesuvius** (vi-soo-viŭs) an active volcano near Naples in Italy.

**vet** *noun* **1** a veterinary surgeon. **2** (*Amer.*) a veteran. ●*verb* (**vetted, vetting**) examine carefully and critically for faults or errors etc.

**vetch** *noun* a plant of the pea family, used as fodder for cattle.

**veteran** *noun* **1** a person with long experience, especially in the armed forces. **2** (*Amer.*) an ex-serviceman or servicewoman. □ **veteran car** a car made before 1916, or (strictly) before 1905.

**veterinarian** (vet-er-in-**air**-iăn) *noun* a veterinary surgeon.

**veterinary** (vet-rin-ri) *adjective* of or for the treatment of diseases and injuries of farm and domestic animals. □ **veterinary surgeon** a person who is qualified in such treatment.

**veto** (**veet**-oh) *noun* (*plural* **vetoes**) **1** an authoritative rejection or prohibition of something that is proposed. **2** the right to make such a rejection or prohibition. ●*verb* (**vetoed, vetoing**) reject or prohibit authoritatively.

**vex** *verb* annoy, irritate, cause worry to (a person). □ **vexed question** a problem that is difficult and much discussed.

**vexation** *noun* **1** vexing; being vexed, a state of irritation or worry. **2** something that causes this.

**vexatious** (veks-**ay**-shŭs) *adjective* causing vexation, annoying.

**VHF** *abbreviation* very high frequency.

**via** (**vy**-ă) *preposition* by way of, through; *from Exeter to York via London*.

**viable** (**vy**-ăbŭl) *adjective* **1** practicable, able to exist successfully; *a viable plan*; *is the newly-created State viable?* **2** (especially of a

foetus) sufficiently developed to be able to survive independently. □ **viably** *adverb*, **viability** *noun*

**viaduct** (**vy**-ă-dukt) *noun* a long bridge-like structure (usually with a series of arches) for carrying a road or railway over a valley or dip in the ground.

**vial** (**vy**-ăl) *noun* a small bottle, especially for liquid medicine.

**viands** (**vy**-ăndz) *plural noun* (*formal*) articles of food.

**viaticum** (vy-at-ik-ŭm) *noun* (*plural* **viatica**) the Eucharist given to a dying person.

**vibes** (*pronounced* vybz) *plural noun* (*informal*) **1** a vibraphone. **2** mental or emotional vibrations; a feeling or atmosphere communicated.

**vibrant** (**vy**-brănt) *adjective* vibrating; resonant; lively; (of colours) bright.

**vibraphone** (**vy**-bră-fohn) *noun* a percussion instrument like a xylophone but with electronic resonators underneath the bars, giving a vibrating effect.

**vibrate** *verb* **1** move rapidly and continuously to and fro. **2** resonate; sound with a rapid slight variation of pitch.

**vibration** *noun* **1** a vibrating movement, sensation, or sound. **2** (**vibrations**) mental stimuli thought to be given out by a person or place etc.; the emotional sensations these produce.

**vibrato** (vi-**brah**-toh) *noun* a vibrating effect in music, with rapid slight variation of pitch.

**vibrator** (vy-**bray**-ter) *noun* a device that vibrates or causes vibration, especially an instrument for massage or sexual stimulation. □ **vibratory** (vy-bră-ter-i) *adjective*

**viburnum** (vy-**ber**-nŭm) *noun* a kind of shrub, usually with white flowers.

**Vic.** *abbreviation* Victoria (Australia).

**vicar** *noun* (in the Church of England) a member of the clergy in charge of a parish, who formerly was paid by stipend rather than tithes (compare RECTOR). □ **Vicar of Christ** the Pope.

**vicarage** *noun* the house of a vicar.

**vicarious** (vik-**air**-iŭs) *adjective* **1** (of feelings or emotions) experienced indirectly, through other people; *vicarious pleasure*. **2** acting or done for another. **3** delegated; *vicarious authority*. □ **vicariously** *adverb*

**vice**[1] *noun* **1** immoral conduct, great wickedness; a particular form of this. **2** a fault or bad habit; *smoking isn't one of my vices*. □ **vice ring** a group of criminals organizing prostitution. **vice squad** a police department concerned with prostitution etc.

**vice**[2] *noun* (*Amer.* **vise**) an instrument with two jaws that grip a thing securely so as to leave the hands free for working on it, used especially in carpentry and metalworking.

**vice³** (vy-si) *preposition* in place of; *Mr Smith has been appointed as chief accountant vice Mr Brown, who has retired.* (¶ Latin, = by change.)

**vice-** *combining form* **1** acting as substitute or deputy for; *vice-president.* **2** next in rank to; *vice admiral.*

**vice-chancellor** *noun* a deputy chancellor (especially of a university, performing most of the chancellor's administrative duties).

**vice-president** *noun* an official ranking below and deputizing for a president.

**viceregal** (vys-**ree**-găl) *adjective* of a viceroy.

**viceroy** *noun* a person governing a colony or province etc. as the sovereign's representative.

**vice versa** (vy-si **ver**-să) the other way round; *we gossip about them and vice versa.* (¶ Latin, = the position being reversed.)

**Vichy** (**vee**-shee) a town in central France, famous for its mineral water and as the headquarters of the French government administering southern France during the German occupation in the Second World War.

**vichyssoise** (vee-shee-**swahz**) *noun* a creamy soup of leeks and potatoes, often served chilled.

**vicinity** (vis-**in**-iti) *noun* the surrounding district; *there is no good school in the vicinity.*

**vicious** (**vish**-ŭs) *adjective* **1** acting or done with evil intentions, brutal, strongly spiteful. **2** (of animals) savage and dangerous, bad-tempered. **3** severe; *a vicious wind.* □ **vicious circle** a state of affairs in which a cause produces an effect which itself produces or intensifies the original cause. **vicious spiral** a similar continual interaction, especially one causing inflation. □ **viciously** *adverb,* **viciousness** *noun*

**vicissitude** (viss-**iss**-i-tewd) *noun* a change of circumstances affecting one's life.

**victim** *noun* **1** a person who is injured or killed by another or as the result of an occurrence; *victims of the earthquake.* **2** a person who suffers because of a trick. **3** a living creature killed and offered as a religious sacrifice.

**victimize** *verb* (also **victimise**) make a victim of, single out (a person) to suffer ill-treatment. □ **victimization** *noun*

**victor** *noun* the winner in a battle or contest.

**Victoria¹** queen of the United Kingdom 1837–1901. □ **Victoria and Albert Museum** a national museum of fine and applied art in London, containing pictures, textiles, ceramics, and furniture. **Victoria Cross** a military decoration awarded for conspicuous bravery. **victoria plum** a large red juicy variety of plum. **Victoria sand-**wich *or* **sponge** a cake having two layers of sponge with a jam filling.

**Victoria²** a State of SE Australia.

**Victoria³, Lake** (also **Victoria Nyanza**) the largest lake in Africa, in Uganda, Tanzania, and Kenya.

**Victoria Falls** a spectacular waterfall on the River Zambezi at the border of Zimbabwe and Zambia.

**Victorian** *adjective* **1** belonging to or characteristic of the reign of Queen Victoria (1837–1901). **2** prudish, strict. ●*noun* a person living at this time.

**Victoriana** (vik-tor-i-**ah**-nă) *plural noun* objects from Victorian times.

**victorious** *adjective* having gained the victory; triumphant.

**Victory** the flagship of Lord Nelson at the battle of Trafalgar, now restored and on display at dry dock in Portsmouth.

**victory** *noun* success in a battle, contest, or game etc. achieved by gaining mastery over one's opponent or achieving the highest score.

**victualler** (**vit**-ler) *noun* (*Amer.* **victualer**) a person who supplies victuals. □ **licensed victualler** the licensee of a public house.

**victuals** (**vit**-lz) *plural noun* food, provisions.

**vicuña** (vik-**yoo**-nă) *noun* **1** a South American animal related to the llama, with fine silky wool. **2** cloth made from its wool; an imitation of this.

**vid** *noun* (*informal*) a video recording, especially of a film.

**video** (**vid**-i-oh) *noun* **1** recorded or broadcast pictures as distinct from sound. **2** a video recorder or recording. □ **video cassette** a cassette of videotape. **video game** a game in which points of light are moved on a television screen by means of an electronic control. **video nasty** (*informal*) a horror or pornographic video film. **video recorder** (also **video cassette recorder**) a device for recording a television programme etc. on magnetic tape for playing back later.

**videotape** *noun* magnetic tape for recording television pictures and sound. ●*verb* record on this.

**videotex** *noun* (also **videotext**) viewdata and/or teletext.

**vie** *verb* (**vied, vying**) carry on a rivalry, compete; *vying with each other.*

**Vienna** the capital of Austria. □ **Viennese** *adjective & noun* (*plural* **Viennese**).

**Vientiane** (vi-en-ti-**ahn**) the capital of Laos.

**Vietcong** (vi-et-**kong**) *noun* (*plural* **Vietcong**) a member of the Communist guerrilla forces active in Vietnam 1954–76.

**Vietminh** (vi-et-**min**) *noun* (*plural* **Vietminh**) **1** a nationalist independence movement

(1941–50) in French Indo-China; the movement succeeding this. **2** a member of either of these movements.

**Vietnam** a country in SE Asia.

**Vietnamese** noun **1** (plural **Vietnamese**) a person from Vietnam. **2** the language of Vietnam. ● adjective of Vietnam or its people or language.

**view** noun **1** what can be seen from a specified point, fine natural scenery; the view from the summit. **2** range of vision; the ship sailed into view. **3** visual inspection of something; we had a private view of the exhibition before it was opened. **4** a mental survey of a subject etc. **5** a mental attitude, an opinion; they have strong views about tax reform. ● verb **1** survey with the eyes or mind. **2** inspect; look over (a house etc.) with the idea of buying it. **3** watch television. **4** regard or consider; we view the matter seriously. □ **in view of** having regard to, considering; in view of the excellence of the work, we do not grudge the cost. **on view** displayed for inspection. **with a view to** with the hope or intention of.

**viewdata** noun a system in which a television set is connected to a central computer by means of a telephone link, so that information can be selected and produced on the television screen.

**viewer** noun **1** a person who views something. **2** a device used in inspecting photographic slides etc.

**viewfinder** noun a device on a camera by which the user can see the area that will be photographed through the lens.

**viewpoint** noun a point of view, a standpoint.

**vigil** (**vij**-il) noun **1** staying awake to keep watch or to pray; a period of this; keep vigil; a long vigil. **2** the eve of a religious festival.

**vigilant** (**vij**-i-lănt) adjective watchful, on the lookout for possible danger etc. □ **vigilantly** adverb, **vigilance** noun

**vigilante** (vij-il-**an**-ti) noun a member of a self-appointed group of people who try to prevent crime and disorder in a community.

**vignette** (veen-**yet**) noun **1** a short description or character sketch. **2** a photograph or portrait with the edges of the background gradually shaded off. ● verb shade off in the style of a vignette.

**vigorous** adjective full of vigour. □ **vigorously** adverb, **vigorousness** noun

**vigour** noun (Amer. **vigor**) **1** active physical or mental strength, energy; flourishing physical condition. **2** forcefulness of language or composition etc.

**Viking** (**vy**-king) noun a Scandinavian trader and pirate of the 8th–11th centuries.

**Vila** (**vee**-lă) the capital of Vanuatu.

**vile** adjective **1** extremely disgusting; a vile smell. **2** despicable on moral grounds. **3** (informal) bad; this vile weather. □ **vilely** adverb, **vileness** noun

**vilify** (**vil**-i-fy) verb (**vilified**, **vilifying**) say evil things about. □ **vilification** noun

**villa** noun **1** a country house, especially in Italy or southern France. **2** a rented holiday home, especially abroad. **3** a detached or semi-detached house in a suburban or residential district.

**village** noun a collection of houses etc. in a country district, smaller than a town and usually having a church.

**villager** noun an inhabitant of a village.

**villain** (**vil**-ăn) noun **1** a person who is guilty or capable of great wickedness; a wrongdoer, a criminal. **2** a character in a story or play whose evil actions or motives are important in the plot. **3** (informal) a rascal. □ **villainy** noun, **villainous** (**vil**-ăn-ŭs) adjective

**villein** (**vil**-in) noun (hist.) a feudal tenant entirely subject to a lord or attached to a manor. □ **villeinage** noun

**Vilnius** the capital of Lithuania.

**vim** noun (informal) vigour, energy.

**vina** (**vee**-nă) noun an Indian musical instrument with four strings and a half-gourd at each end.

**vinaigrette** (vin-i-**gret**) noun **1** salad dressing made of oil, wine, vinegar, and seasoning. **2** a small ornamental bottle for holding smelling salts.

**vindicate** (**vin**-dik-ayt) verb **1** clear of blame or suspicion. **2** establish the existence, merits, or justice of (something disputed etc.). **3** justify by evidence or argument. □ **vindication** noun, **vindicator** noun

**vindictive** (vin-**dik**-tiv) adjective having or showing a desire for revenge. □ **vindictively** adverb, **vindictiveness** noun

**vine** noun **1** a climbing or trailing woody-stemmed plant whose fruit is the grape. **2** a slender climbing or trailing stem.

**vinegar** noun a sour liquid made from wine, cider, malt, etc. by fermentation, used in flavouring food and for pickling. □ **vinegary** adjective

**vineyard** (**vin**-yard) noun a plantation of vines producing grapes for wine-making.

**vino** (**vee**-noh) noun (informal) wine.

**vinous** (**vy**-nŭs) adjective **1** of or like wine. **2** addicted to wine.

**vintage** (**vint**-ij) noun **1** the gathering of grapes for wine-making, the season of this. **2** wine made from a particular season's grapes; the date of this as an indication of the wine's quality. **3** the date or period when something was produced or existed. ● adjective of high quality, especially from a past period. □ **vintage car** a car made between 1917 and 1930.

**vintner** (vint-ner) *noun* a wine-merchant.

**vinyl** (vy-nil) *noun* a kind of plastic, especially polyvinyl chloride.

**viol** (vy-ŏl) *noun* a medieval stringed musical instrument similar to a violin but held vertically.

**viola¹** (vee-oh-lă) *noun* a stringed musical instrument slightly larger than a violin and of lower pitch.

**viola²** (vy-ŏ-lă) *noun* a plant of the genus to which pansies and violets belong, especially a hybrid cultivated variety.

**violable** *adjective* able to be violated.

**violate** *verb* **1** break or act contrary to (an oath or treaty etc.). **2** treat (a sacred place) with irreverence or disrespect. **3** disturb (a person's privacy). **4** rape. □ **violation** *noun*, **violator** *noun*

**violence** *noun* being violent; violent acts or conduct etc. □ **do violence to** act contrary to, be a breach of.

**violent** *adjective* **1** involving great force, strength, or intensity. **2** involving the unlawful use of force; *violent crime*. **3** (of death) caused by physical violence, not natural. □ **violently** *adverb*

**violet** *noun* **1** a small wild or garden plant, often with purple flowers. **2** the colour at the opposite end of the spectrum from red, bluish purple. ● *adjective* bluish-purple.

**violin** *noun* a musical instrument with four strings of treble pitch, played with a bow. □ **violinist** *noun*

**violist** (vi-oh-list) *noun* a person who plays the viola.

**violoncello** (vy-ŏ-lŏn-**chel**-oh) *noun* (*plural* **violoncellos**) a cello.

**VIP** *abbreviation* very important person.

**viper** *noun* **1** a small poisonous snake. **2** a malicious or treacherous person.

**virago** (vi-**rah**-goh) *noun* (*plural* **viragos**) a fierce or abusive woman.

**viral** (vy-răl) *adjective* of or caused by a virus.

**Virchow** (**ver**-koh), Rudolf Karl (1821–1902), German physician and pathologist, founder of the modern study of the pathology of cells.

**Virgil** (**ver**-jil) (Publius Vergilius Maro) (70–19 BC), Roman poet, whose most famous work was the *Aeneid*.

**virgin** *noun* **1** a person who has never had sexual intercourse. **2** (**the Virgin**) the Virgin Mary, mother of Christ. **3** (**the Virgin**) a sign of the zodiac, Virgo. ● *adjective* **1** virginal. **2** spotless, undefiled. **3** untouched, in its original state, not yet used; *virgin soil*; *virgin wool*. □ **virgin birth** (in Christian teaching) the birth of Christ without a human father. **Virgin Queen** Queen Elizabeth I of England. □ **virginity** *noun*

**virginal** *adjective* of, being, or suitable for a virgin. ● *plural noun* (**virginals**) a keyboard instrument of the 16th–17th centuries, the earliest form of harpsichord.

**Virginia** a State on the Atlantic coast of the USA. □ **Virginia creeper** an ornamental climbing plant with leaves that turn red in autumn.

**Virgin Islands** a group of islands in the Caribbean Sea divided between British and US administration.

**Virgo** (**ver**-goh) the sixth sign of the zodiac, the Virgin. □ **Virgoan** *adjective & noun*

**virile** (vi-ryl) *adjective* **1** having masculine strength or vigour. **2** (of a man) sexually potent. **3** of a man as distinct from a woman or child. □ **virility** (vi-**ril**-iti) *noun*

**virology** (vyr-ol-ŏji) *noun* the study of viruses. □ **virological** *adjective*, **virologist** *noun*

**virtual** *adjective* being so in effect though not in name or according to strict definition; *he is the virtual head of the firm; gave what was a virtual promise.* □ **virtual reality** a computer-generated simulation of reality. □ **virtually** *adverb*

**virtue** *noun* **1** moral excellence, goodness; a particular form of this; *patience is a virtue.* **2** chastity, especially of a woman. **3** a good quality, an advantage; *the seat has the virtue of being adjustable.* □ **by** *or* **in virtue of** by reason of, because of; *he is entitled to a pension by virtue of his long service.*

**virtuoso** (ver-tew-**oh**-soh) *noun* (*plural* **virtuosos** *or* **virtuosi**) a person who excels in the technique of doing something, especially singing or playing music. □ **virtuosity** (ver-tew-**oss**-iti) *noun*

**virtuous** *adjective* having or showing moral virtue. □ **virtuously** *adverb*, **virtuousness** *noun*

**virulent** (vi-rew-lĕnt) *adjective* **1** (of poison or disease) extremely strong or violent. **2** strongly and bitterly hostile; *virulent abuse.* □ **virulence** *noun*

**virus** (vy-rŭs) *noun* (*plural* **viruses**) **1** a very simple organism (smaller than bacteria) capable of causing disease. **2** a hidden destructive code in a computer program.

**visa** (vee-ză) *noun* an official stamp or mark put on a passport by officials of a foreign country to show that the holder may enter their country.

**visage** (viz-ij) *noun* (*literary*) a person's face.

**vis-à-vis** (veez-ah-vee) *preposition* **1** in a position facing, opposite to. **2** in relation to, as compared with. ● *adverb* opposite.

**viscera** (vis-er-ă) *plural noun* the internal organs of the body, especially the intestines.

**visceral** (vis-er-ăl) *adjective* **1** of the viscera. **2** of feelings rather than reason.

**viscid** (**vis**-id) *adjective* (of liquid) thick and gluey.

**viscose** (**vis**-kohz) *noun* **1** cellulose in a viscous state, used in the manufacture of rayon etc. **2** fabric made of this.

**viscount** (**vy**-kownt) *noun* **1** a nobleman ranking between earl and baron. **2** the courtesy title of an earl's eldest son; *Viscount Linley*. □ **viscountcy** *noun*

**viscountess** (**vy**-kownt-ess) *noun* **1** a viscount's wife or widow. **2** a woman holding the rank of viscount.

**viscous** (**vis**-kŭs) *adjective* thick and gluey, not pouring easily. □ **viscosity** (vis-**kos**-iti) *noun*

**vise** Amer. spelling of VICE².

**Vishnu** (**vish**-noo) one of the major gods of modern Hinduism, the supreme being.

**visibility** *noun* **1** being visible. **2** the range or possibility of vision as determined by conditions of light and atmosphere; *the aircraft turned back because of poor visibility*.

**visible** *adjective* able to be seen or noticed. □ **visibly** *adverb*

**Visigoth** *noun* a member of the western branch of the Goths, who invaded the Roman Empire in the 3rd–5th centuries.

**vision** *noun* **1** the faculty of seeing, sight. **2** something seen in the imagination or in a dream etc. **3** imaginative insight into a subject or problem etc., foresight and wisdom in planning; *a statesman with vision*. **4** a person or sight of unusual beauty. **5** a television or cinema picture, especially of a specified quality; *poor vision*.

**visionary** *adjective* **1** existing only in the imagination, fanciful, not practical; *visionary schemes*. **2** indulging in fanciful ideas or theories. ●*noun* a person with visionary ideas.

**visit** *verb* **1** go or come to see (a person or place etc.), socially, on business, or for some other purpose. **2** stay temporarily with (a person) or at (a place). **3** (of a disease, calamity, etc.) attack. **4** (in the Bible) inflict punishment for; *visiting the sins of the fathers upon the children*. ●*noun* an act of visiting; a temporary stay.

**visitant** *noun* **1** a visitor, especially a supernatural one; a ghost. **2** a migratory bird that is staying temporarily in an area.

**visitation** *noun* **1** an official visit, especially of inspection. **2** trouble or disaster looked upon as punishment from God. **3** (**the Visitation**) a Christian festival on 2 July, commemorating the visit of the Virgin Mary to her kinswoman Elizabeth.

**visitor** *noun* **1** one who visits a person or place. **2** a migratory bird that lives in an area temporarily or at a certain season.

**visor** (**vy**-zer) *noun* (also **vizor**) **1** the movable front part of a helmet, covering the face. **2** a shield for the eyes, especially one at the top of a vehicle windscreen.

**vista** *noun* **1** a view, especially one seen through a long narrow opening such as an avenue of trees. **2** a mental view of an extensive period or series of past or future events.

**Vistula** (**vis**-tew-lǎ) a river of Poland flowing into the Baltic Sea.

**visual** *adjective* of or used in seeing, received through sight. □ **visual aids** pictures or film-strips etc. as an aid to teaching. **visual display unit** (*or* **terminal**) *Computing* a device resembling a television screen on which data can be displayed. □ **visually** *adverb*

**visualize** *verb* (also **visualise**) form a mental picture of. □ **visualization** *noun*

**vital** *adjective* **1** connected with life, essential to life; *vital functions*. **2** essential to the existence, success, or operation of something; extremely important. **3** full of vitality; *she's a very vital sort of person*. ●*plural noun* (**vitals**) the vital parts of the body (e.g. heart, lungs, brain). □ **vital statistics 1** statistics relating to population figures or births and deaths. **2** (*informal*) the measurement of a woman's bust, waist, and hips. □ **vitally** *adverb*

**vitality** (vy-**tal**-iti) *noun* liveliness, vigour, persistent energy.

**vitalize** *verb* (also **vitalise**) put life or vitality into. □ **vitalization** *noun*

**vitamin** (**vit**-ǎ-min) *noun* any of a number of organic substances present in many foods and essential to the nutrition of man and other animals.

**vitaminize** *verb* (also **vitaminise**) add vitamins to (a food).

**vitiate** (**vish**-i-ayt) *verb* **1** make imperfect, spoil. **2** weaken the force of, make ineffective; *this admission vitiates your claim*. □ **vitiation** *noun*

**viticulture** (**vit**-i-kul-cher) *noun* the process of growing grapes.

**vitreous** (**vit**-ri-ŭs) *adjective* having a glasslike texture or finish; *vitreous enamel*. □ **vitreous humour** clear fluid in the eye between the lens and the retina.

**vitrify** (**vit**-ri-fy) *verb* (**vitrified**, **vitrifying**) change into glass or a glasslike substance, especially by heat. □ **vitrifaction** *noun*, **vitrification** *noun*

**vitriol** (**vit**-ri-ŏl) *noun* **1** sulphuric acid or one of its salts. **2** savagely hostile comments or criticism.

**vitriolic** (vit-ri-**ol**-ik) *adjective* (of speech or criticism) bitter or hostile.

**vituperate** (vy-**tew**-per-ayt) *verb* use abusive language. □ **vituperation** *noun*, **vituperative** *adjective*

**Vitus** (vy-tŭs), St (*c.*300), a martyr of the persecution in the reign of Diocletian, invoked against epilepsy, chorea (= St Vitus's dance), and rabies. Feast day, 15 June.

**viva¹** (vy-va) (*informal*) noun a viva voce examination. ● verb (**vivaed**, **vivaing**) examine in a viva.

**viva²** (vee-vă) *interjection* long live (a person or thing).

**vivace** (vi-vah-chi) *adverb Music* in a lively manner.

**vivacious** (viv-ay-shŭs) *adjective* lively, high-spirited. □ **vivaciously** *adverb*, **vivacity** (viv-**ass**-iti) *noun*

**Vivaldi** (vi-**val**-di), Antonio (1678–1741), Italian composer and violinist, whose best-known work is *The Four Seasons*.

**vivarium** (vy-**vair**-iŭm) *noun* (*plural* **vivaria** or **vivariums**) a place prepared for keeping animals in conditions as similar as possible to their natural environment, for purposes of study etc.

**viva voce** (vy-vă voh-chi) *adjective* (of an examination in universities) oral. ● *adverb* orally. ● *noun* an oral examination.

**vivid** *adjective* **1** (of light or colour) bright and strong, intense. **2** producing strong and clear mental pictures; *a vivid description*. **3** (of the imagination) creating ideas etc. in an active and lively way. □ **vividly** *adverb*, **vividness** *noun*

**viviparous** (vi-**vip**-er-ŭs) *adjective* producing young in a developed state from the mother's body, not hatching by means of an egg (compare OVIPAROUS).

**vivisect** *verb* perform vivisection on.

**vivisection** *noun* performance of surgical experiments on living animals. □ **vivisectionist** *noun*

**vixen** *noun* **1** a female fox. **2** a spiteful woman.

**viz.** *adverb* namely; *the case is made in three sizes, viz. large, medium, and small.*

■**Usage** In reading aloud, the word 'namely' is usually spoken where 'viz.' (short for Latin *videlicet*) is written.

**vizier** (viz-**eer**) *noun* an official of high rank in certain Muslim countries.

**vizor** alternative spelling of VISOR.

**Vladivostok** a seaport of far eastern Russia, on the Pacific coast.

**V-neck** *noun* a V-shaped neckline on a pullover etc.

**vocable** (voh-kă-b'l) *noun* a word, especially with reference to its form rather than its meaning.

**vocabulary** *noun* **1** a list of words with their meanings, especially one given in a reading-book etc. of a foreign language. **2** the words known to a person or used in a particular book or subject etc.

**vocal** (voh-kăl) *adjective* **1** of, for, or uttered by the voice. **2** expressing one's feelings freely in speech; *he was very vocal about his rights.* ● *noun* a piece of sung music. □ **vocal cords** the voice-producing part of the larynx. □ **vocally** *adverb*

**vocalic** (vŏ-**kal**-ik) *adjective* of or consisting of a vowel or vowels.

**vocalist** (voh-kăl-ist) *noun* a singer, especially in a pop group.

**vocalize** (voh-kă-lyz) *verb* (also **vocalise**) utter; express.

**vocation** (voh-**kay**-shŏn) *noun* **1** a strong feeling of suitability for a particular career. **2** this regarded as a divine call to a career in the Church. **3** a person's trade or profession. □ **vocational** *adjective*

**vocative** *noun* the grammatical case of a noun used in addressing a person or thing.

**vociferate** (vŏ-**sif**-er-ayt) *verb* say loudly or noisily, shout. □ **vociferation** *noun*

**vociferous** (vŏ-**sif**-er-ŭs) *adjective* making a great outcry, expressing one's views forcibly and insistently. □ **vociferously** *adverb*, **vociferousness** *noun*

**vodka** *noun* alcoholic spirit distilled chiefly from rye, especially in Russia.

**vogue** *noun* **1** current fashion; *large hats are the vogue.* **2** popular favour or acceptance; *his novels had a great vogue ten years ago.* □ **in vogue** in fashion.

**voice** *noun* **1** sounds formed in the larynx and uttered by the mouth, especially human utterance in speaking, singing, etc. **2** ability to produce such sounds; *she has a cold and has lost her voice.* **3** expression of one's opinion etc. in spoken or written words, the opinion itself, the right to express opinion; *gave voice to his indignation; I have no voice in the matter.* **4** *Grammar* any of the sets of forms of a verb that show whether it is active or passive. ● *verb* **1** put into words, express; *she voiced her opinion.* **2** (usually as **voiced** *adjective*) uttered with resonance of the vocal cords, not only with the breath (e.g. *b*, *d*). □ **in good voice** singing or speaking well or easily. **voice-box** *noun* the larynx. **voice-over** *noun* narration (e.g. in a film) by a voice not accompanied by a picture of the speaker. **with one voice** unanimously.

**voiceless** *adjective* **1** dumb, speechless. **2** uttered without vibration of the vocal cords (e.g. *f*, *p*).

**void** *adjective* **1** empty, vacant. **2** not legally valid. ● *noun* empty space, emptiness. ● *verb* **1** make legally void; *the contract was voided by his death.* **2** excrete (urine or faeces).

**voile** (*pronounced* voil) *noun* a very thin light dress-material.

**volatile** (vol-ă-tyl) *adjective* **1** (of a liquid) evaporating rapidly. **2** (of a person) lively, changing quickly or easily from one mood or interest to another. **3** (of trading conditions) unstable. **4** (of a political situation etc.) liable to erupt into violence. □ **volatility** (vol-ă-**til**-iti) *noun*

**volatilize** (vŏ-**lat**-i-lyz) *verb* (also **volatilise**) turn or become turned into vapour. □ **volatilization** *noun*

**vol-au-vent** (vol-oh-vahn) *noun* a small circular puff pastry case filled with a sauce containing meat, fish, etc. (¶ French, = flight in the wind.)

**volcanic** *adjective* of or from a volcano. □ **volcanically** *adverb*

**volcano** *noun* (*plural* **volcanoes**) a mountain or hill with openings through which lava, gases, etc. from below the earth's crust are or have been expelled.

**vole** (*rhymes with* hole) *noun* a small plant-eating rodent.

**Volga** the longest river in Europe, flowing from the north-west of the former USSR to the Caspian Sea.

**volition** (vŏ-**ish**-ŏn) *noun* use of one's own will in choosing or making a decision; *she did it of her own volition.* □ **volitional** *adjective*

**volley** *noun* (*plural* **volleys**) **1** simultaneous discharge of a number of missiles; the missiles themselves. **2** a number of questions or curses etc. directed in quick succession at someone. **3** return of the ball in tennis, football, etc. before it touches the ground. ●*verb* **1** discharge or fly in a volley. **2** return (a ball) by a volley.

**volleyball** *noun* a game for two teams of six players who volley a large ball by hand over a net.

**volt** (*rhymes with* bolt) *noun* a unit of electromotive force, force sufficient to carry one ampere of current against one ohm resistance. (¶ Named after the Italian physicist Count Alessandro Volta (1745–1824).)

**voltage** (vohl-tij) *noun* electromotive force expressed in volts.

**Voltaire** (vol-tair) (pseudonym of François-Marie Arouet) (1694–1778), author of plays, poetry, and histories, an outspoken critic of the civil and ecclesiastical establishments.

**voltameter** *noun* an instrument for measuring an electric charge.

**volte-face** (volt-**fahs**) *noun* a complete change of one's attitude towards something.

**voltmeter** *noun* an instrument measuring electric potential in volts.

**voluble** (vol-yoo-bŭl) *adjective* talking very much; speaking or spoken with great fluency. □ **volubly** *adverb*, **volubility** (vol-yoo-**bil**-iti) *noun*

**volume** *noun* **1** a book, especially one of a set. **2** the amount of space (often expressed in cubic units) that a three-dimensional thing occupies or contains. **3** the size or amount of something, a quantity; *the great volume of water pouring over the weir; the volume of business has increased.* **4** the strength or power of sound; *the noise had doubled in volume.*

**volumetric** (vol-yoo-**met**-rik) *adjective* of or using measurement by volume; *volumetric analysis.* □ **volumetrically** *adverb*

**voluminous** (vŏl-oo-min-ŭs) *adjective* **1** (of drapery etc.) large and full; *voluminous skirts.* **2** (of writings) great in quantity; (of a writer) producing many works.

**voluntary** *adjective* **1** acting, done, or given etc. of one's own free will and not under compulsion. **2** working or done without payment; *voluntary work.* **3** (of an organization) maintained by voluntary contributions or voluntary workers. **4** (of bodily movements) controlled by the will. ●*noun* an organ solo played before, during, or after a church service. □ **voluntarily** *adverb*, **voluntariness** *noun*

**volunteer** *noun* **1** a person who offers to do something. **2** a person who enrols for military or other service voluntarily, not as a conscript. ●*verb* undertake or offer voluntarily, be a volunteer.

**voluptuary** (vŏl-**up**-tew-er-i) *noun* a person who indulges in luxury and sensual pleasure.

**voluptuous** (vŏl-**up**-tew-ŭs) *adjective* **1** fond of luxury or sumptuous living. **2** giving a sensation of luxury and pleasure. **3** (of a woman) having a full and attractive figure. □ **voluptuously** *adverb*, **voluptuousness** *noun*

**volute** (vŏl-**oot**) *noun* a spiral scroll in stonework.

**vomit** *verb* (**vomited**, **vomiting**) **1** eject (matter) from the stomach through the mouth, be sick. **2** (of a volcano, chimney, etc.) eject violently, belch forth. ●*noun* matter vomited from the stomach.

**Vonnegut** (**von**-i-gut), Kurt (born 1922), American writer of novels and short stories.

**voodoo** *noun* a form of religion based on belief in witchcraft and magical rites, as practised especially in the West Indies. □ **voodooism** *noun*, **voodooist** *noun*

**voracious** (ver-**ay**-shŭs) *adjective* **1** greedy in eating, ravenous. **2** very eager; *a voracious reader.* □ **voraciously** *adverb*, **voracity** (ver-**ass**-iti) *noun*

**vortex** *noun* (*plural* **vortexes** *or* **vortices**, *pronounced* **vor**-ti-seez) **1** a whirling mass of water or air, a whirlpool or whirlwind. **2** a thing viewed as swallowing things which approach it. □ **vortical** *adjective*

**Vosges** (*pronounced* vohzh) a mountain system of eastern France.

**vote** *noun* **1** a formal expression of one's opinion or choice on a matter under discussion, e.g. by ballot or show of hands. **2** the total number of votes given by a certain group; *that policy will lose us the Labour vote.* **3** (**the vote**) the right to vote. ●*verb* **1** express an opinion or choice by a vote. **2** decide by a majority of votes. **3** (*informal*) declare by general consent; *the meal was voted excellent.* **4** (*informal*) suggest; *I vote that we avoid him in future.* □ **vote down** reject (a proposal etc.) by votes. **vote with one's feet** (*informal*) indicate an opinion by one's presence or absence. □ **voter** *noun*

**votive** (voh-tiv) *adjective* given in fulfilment of a vow; *votive offerings at the shrine.*

**vouch** *verb* (foll. by *for*) guarantee the certainty, accuracy, reliability, etc. of; *I will vouch for his honesty.*

**voucher** *noun* **1** a document (issued in token of payment made or promised) that can be exchanged for certain goods or services. **2** a receipt.

**vouchsafe** *verb* give or grant, often in a gracious or condescending manner; *they did not vouchsafe a reply.*

**vow** *noun* a solemn promise or undertaking, especially in the form of a religious oath. ●*verb* promise solemnly; *they vowed vengeance against their oppressor.*

**vowel** *noun* **1** a speech sound made without audible stopping of the breath (opposed to a CONSONANT). **2** a letter or letters representing such a sound, as *a, e, i, o, u, ee.*

**vox pop** (*informal*) (in broadcasting) popular opinion as represented by informal comments from members of the public. (¶ Abbreviation of Latin *vox populi* = voice of the people.)

**voyage** *noun* a journey by water or in space, especially a long one. ●*verb* make a voyage. □ **voyager** *noun*

**Voyager** each of two US space probes launched in 1977 to Jupiter, Saturn, Uranus, and Neptune.

**voyeur** (vwah-yer) *noun* **1** a person who obtains sexual gratification from looking at the sexual actions or organs of others. **2** a spectator, especially in secret. □ **voyeurism** *noun*, **voyeuristic** *adjective*

**vs.** *abbreviation* versus.

**V-sign** *noun* **1** a sign of the letter V made with the first two fingers pointing up and the back of the hand facing outwards, as a gesture of abuse. **2** a similar sign made with the palm of the hand facing outwards, as a symbol of victory.

**VSO** *abbreviation* Voluntary Service Overseas.

**VT, Vt.** *abbreviation* Vermont.

**VTO** *abbreviation* vertical take-off.

**VTOL** *abbreviation* vertical take-off and landing.

**VTR** *abbreviation* videotape recorder.

**Vulcan** (*Rom. myth.*) the god of fire and metalworking, identified with Hephaestus.

**vulcanite** *noun* hard black vulcanized rubber.

**vulcanize** *verb* (also **vulcanise**) treat (rubber or similar material) with sulphur at a high temperature in order to increase its elasticity and strength. □ **vulcanization** *noun*

**vulcanology** *noun* the scientific study of volcanoes. □ **vulcanologist** *noun*

**vulgar** *adjective* **1** lacking in refinement or good taste, coarse. **2** commonly used and incorrect (but not coarse). □ **vulgar fraction** a fraction represented by numbers above and below a line (e.g. $\frac{2}{3}$, $\frac{5}{8}$), not decimally. **vulgar tongue** the national or vernacular language. □ **vulgarly** *adverb*, **vulgarity** *noun*

**vulgarian** (vul-gair-iǎn) *noun* a vulgar person, especially a rich one.

**vulgarism** *noun* **1** a word or expression in coarse or uneducated use; *'he is learning her to drive' is a vulgarism for 'he is teaching her'.* **2** a coarse action or habit.

**vulgarize** *verb* (also **vulgarise**) **1** cause (a person or manners etc.) to become vulgar. **2** reduce to the level of being usual or ordinary, spoil by making ordinary or too well known. □ **vulgarization** *noun*

**Vulgate** (vul-gayt) *noun* the 4th-century Latin version of the Bible.

**vulnerable** (vul-ner-ǎbǔl) *adjective* **1** able to be hurt or wounded. **2** unprotected, exposed to danger or attack. □ **vulnerably** *adverb*, **vulnerability** *noun*

**vulpine** (vul-pyn) *adjective* **1** of or like a fox. **2** crafty, cunning.

**vulture** *noun* **1** a large bird of prey that lives on the flesh of dead animals. **2** a greedy person seeking to profit from the misfortunes of others.

**vulva** *noun* the external parts of the female genital organs.

**vying** *see* VIE.

# Ww

**W** *abbreviation* (also **W.**) **1** watt(s). **2** West; Western. ● *symbol* tungsten.

**w.** *abbreviation* **1** wicket(s). **2** wide(s). **3** with.

**WA** *abbreviation* **1** Washington. **2** Western Australia.

**wacky** *adjective* (**wackier, wackiest**) (*slang*) crazy.

**wad** (*pronounced* wod) *noun* **1** a lump or bundle of soft material used to keep things apart or in place, stop up a hole, etc. **2** a bundle of documents or banknotes. ● *verb* (**wadded, wadding**) line, stuff, or protect with wadding.

**wadding** *noun* soft fibrous material used for padding, packing, or lining things.

**waddle** *verb* walk with short steps and a swaying movement. ● *noun* a waddling walk.

**wade** *verb* **1** walk through water, mud, etc., especially with difficulty. **2** (foll. by *through*) progress slowly and with difficulty; *wade through a book.* □ **wade in** (*informal*) intervene; make a vigorous attack. **wade into** (*informal*) attack (a person or task) vigorously. **wading bird** = WADER.

**wader** *noun* **1** a long-legged waterbird that wades in shallow water. **2** (**waders**) high waterproof boots worn in fishing etc.

**wadi** *noun* a rocky watercourse in N. Africa etc., dry except in the rainy season.

**wafer** *noun* **1** a thin light biscuit. **2** a thin disc of unleavened bread used in the Eucharist. □ **wafer-thin** *adjective* very thin.

**waffle¹** (**wof-ŭl**) (*informal*) *noun* vague wordy talk or writing. ● *verb* talk or write waffle.

**waffle²** (**wof-ĕl**) *noun* a small cake made of batter and eaten hot. □ **waffle-iron** *noun* a utensil with two hinged metal plates used for cooking waffles.

**waft** (*pronounced* woft) *verb* carry or travel lightly and easily through the air or over water. ● *noun* (usually foll. by *of*) a whiff or smell.

**wag¹** *verb* (**wagged, wagging**) shake or move briskly to and fro. ● *noun* a single wagging movement.

**wag²** *noun* a person who is fond of making jokes or playing tricks.

**wage¹** *verb* engage in; *wage war.*

**wage²** *noun* (also **wages**) regular payment to an employee in return for work or services. □ **wage-earner** *noun* a person who works for wages.

**waged** *adjective* employed; working.

**wager** (**way-jer**) *noun* a bet. ● *verb* bet.

**waggish** *adjective* of or like a wag; said or done in a joking way. □ **waggishly** *adverb*, **waggishness** *noun*

**waggle** *verb* wag. ● *noun* a wagging movement. □ **waggly** *adjective*

**waggon, waggoner** alternative spelling of WAGON, WAGONER.

**Wagner** (**vahg**-ner), Richard (1813–83), German composer of operas and music dramas, often based on Germanic myths and legends.

**Wagnerian** (vahg-**neer**-iǎn) *adjective* of or characteristic of the works of Wagner, especially with regard to their large dramatic scale.

**wagon** *noun* (also **waggon**) **1** a four-wheeled vehicle for heavy loads. **2** an open railway truck, e.g. for coal. **3** a tea trolley. □ **on the wagon** *or* **water-wagon** (*slang*) abstaining from alcohol.

**wagoner** *noun* (also **waggoner**) the driver of a wagon.

**wagtail** *noun* any of several small birds with a long tail that moves up and down constantly when the bird is standing.

**Wahabi** (wǎ-**hah**-bi) *noun* a member of a sect of Muslims following strictly the original words of the Koran, named after Muhammad ibn Abd al-Wahab (1703–92).

**waif** *noun* a homeless and helpless person; an unowned or abandoned child.

**wail** *verb* **1** utter a long sad cry; lament or complain persistently. **2** (of wind etc.) make a sound like a person wailing. ● *noun* a wailing cry, sound, or utterance.

**wain** *noun* (*old use*) a farm wagon.

**wainscot** *noun* wooden panelling on the lower part of the wall of a room.

**wainscoting** *noun* wainscot; material for this.

**waist** *noun* **1** the part of the human body below the ribs and above the hips. **2** the part of a garment covering this. **3** a narrow part in the middle of a long object.

**waistband** *noun* a band (e.g. at the top of a skirt) that fits round the waist.

**waistcoat** *noun* a close-fitting waist-length sleeveless collarless garment, worn usually over a shirt and under a jacket.

**waisted** *adjective* **1** having a waist; narrowed in the middle. **2** having a waist of a specified kind; *thick-waisted.*

**waistline** *noun* **1** the circumference of the body at the waist. **2** the part of a garment fitting at or near the waist.

**wait** *verb* **1** postpone an action or departure for a specified time or until some expected event occurs; *we waited until evening.* **2** be postponed; *this question will have to wait until our next meeting.* **3** wait on people at a meal. **4** stop a motor vehicle for a time at the side of a road; *No Waiting.* ●*noun* an act or period of waiting; *we had a long wait for the train.* □ **waiting game** deliberate delay in taking action so as to act more effectively later. **waiting-list** *noun* a list of people waiting for a chance to obtain something when it becomes available. **waiting-room** *noun* a room provided for people to wait in, e.g. at a doctor's surgery. **wait on** hand food and drink to (a person) at a meal; fetch and carry for (a person) as an attendant.

**Waitangi** (wy-**tang**-i) a settlement in New Zealand at which in 1840 the treaty forming the basis of British annexation was negotiated. □ **Waitangi Day** 6 February, celebrated in New Zealand as a public holiday.

**waiter** *noun* a man who serves at table in a hotel or restaurant.

**waitress** *noun* a woman who serves at table in a hotel or restaurant.

**waive** *verb* refrain from using or insisting on (one's right, claim, or privilege etc.); forgo or dispense with.

■**Usage** Do not confuse with **wave**.

**waiver** *noun* the waiving of a legal right; a document recording this.

■**Usage** Do not confuse with **waver**.

**wake**[1] *verb* (**woke, woken, waking**) **1** = WAKE UP (see below). **2** disturb with noise; cause to re-echo; evoke. ●*noun* **1** a watch by a corpse before burial; lamentations and merrymaking in connection with this. **2** (**wakes**) (formerly) an annual holiday in industrial areas of northern England; *wakes week.* □ **wake up 1** cease to sleep; arouse (a person) from sleep. **2** become alert; cease or cause to cease from inactivity or inattention etc.; *he needs something to wake him up.* **wake up to** realize; *he woke up to the fact that she meant it.*

**wake**[2] *noun* **1** the track left on water's surface by a ship etc. **2** air currents left behind an aircraft etc. moving through air. □ **in the wake of** behind; following after.

**wakeful** *adjective* **1** (of a person) unable to sleep. **2** (of a night etc.) with little sleep.

**waken** *verb* wake.

**waking** *adjective* being awake; *in his waking hours.*

**Waldheim** (valt-hym), Kurt (born 1918), Austrian statesman, secretary-general of the United Nations 1972–81, President of Austria from 1986.

**wale** *noun* **1** = WEAL (sense 1). **2** a ridge on corduroy etc. **3** a broad thick timber along a ship's side.

**Wales** the country in the west of Great Britain.

**Walesa** (va-**wen**-să), Lech (born 1943), Polish trade unionist, leader of Solidarity, President of Poland from 1990.

**walk** *verb* **1** progress by lifting and setting down each foot in turn, never having both or all feet off the ground at once. **2** travel or go on foot; take exercise in this way. **3** go over on foot; *walked the fields.* **4** cause to walk with one; accompany in walking. **5** ride or lead (a horse or dog etc.) at a walking pace. ●*noun* **1** a journey on foot, especially for pleasure or exercise; *went for a walk.* **2** the manner or style of walking; a walking pace. **3** a place for walking; a route followed in walking. □ **walk away with** (*informal*) win easily. **walking frame** a metal frame used as a support by people who have difficulty walking. **walking stick** a stick used for support when walking. **walk off with** (*informal*) **1** win easily. **2** steal. **walk of life** social rank; profession or occupation. **walk on air** feel elated. **walk-on part** a non-speaking role in a play or film. **walk out** leave suddenly and angrily; go on strike suddenly. **walk-out** *noun* a sudden angry departure, especially as a protest or strike. **walk tall** feel justifiable pride.

**walkabout** *noun* **1** an informal stroll among a crowd by a visiting royal person etc. **2** a period of wandering by an Australian Aboriginal.

**Walker**, Alice Malsenior (born 1944), American novelist.

**walker** *noun* **1** a person who walks. **2** a framework for a person (e.g. a baby or a disabled person) who is unable to walk without support.

**Walker Cup** a golf tournament played in alternate years between teams of male amateurs representing the USA and Great Britain and Ireland.

**walkie-talkie** *noun* a small portable radio transmitter and receiver.

**Walkman** *noun* (*plural* **Walkmans**) (*trade mark*) a personal stereo.

**walkover** *noun* an easy victory.

**walkway** *noun* a passage for walking along (especially one connecting different sections of a building).

**wall** *noun* **1** a continuous upright structure forming one of the sides of a building or room, or serving to enclose, protect, or divide an area. **2** something thought of as resembling this in form or function; the outermost part of a hollow structure; tissue surrounding an organ of the body etc. ●*verb*

**1** surround or enclose with a wall; *a walled garden.* **2** (often foll. by *up*) block (a space) by building a wall. □ **drive** *or* **send up the wall** (*informal*) make crazy or furious. **go to the wall** suffer defeat, failure, or ruin; *the weakest goes to the wall.* **wall bars** a set of parallel bars on the wall of a gymnasium. **wall-eye** *noun* **1** an eye with a streaked or opaque white iris. **2** an eye squinting outwards. **wall-to-wall** *adjective* **1** (of a carpet) fitted to cover the whole room. **2** (*informal, scornful*) found everywhere, ever-present; *wall-to-wall pop music.*

**wallaby** (wol-ă-bi) *noun* **1** a marsupial similar to but smaller than a kangaroo. **2** (**the Wallabies**) an Australian international Rugby Union team.

**Wallace¹**, Alfred Russel (1823–1913), British naturalist, who independently formulated a theory of the origin of species that was identical with that of Darwin. □ **Wallace's line** an imaginary line, proposed by Wallace, marking the boundary between countries with Australasian fauna and those with Asian fauna.

**Wallace²**, (Richard Horatio) Edgar (1875–1932), English novelist and playwright, noted for his prolific output of thrillers.

**Wallace³**, Sir William (*c.*1270–1305), a national hero of Scotland, leader of the Scottish resistance to Edward I.

**wallah** *noun* (*slang*) a person concerned with or in charge of a specified occupation or task; *the maintenance wallahs.*

**Waller**, Fats (Thomas Wright Waller) (1904–43), American jazz pianist and singer.

**wallet** *noun* a small flat folding case for banknotes or small documents etc.

**wallflower** *noun* **1** a garden plant blooming in spring, with clusters of fragrant flowers. **2** (*informal*) a woman sitting out dances for lack of partners.

**Wallis**, Sir Barnes Neville (1887–1979), English inventor, who designed aircraft, radio telescopes, and bombs.

**Walloon** (wol-oon) *noun* **1** a member of a people living in southern Belgium and neighbouring parts of France. **2** their language, a French dialect.

**wallop** (*informal*) *verb* (**walloped, walloping**) thrash, hit hard. ●*noun* **1** a heavy resounding blow. **2** beer or other drink.

**walloping** (*informal*) *adjective* big, thumping; *a walloping lie.* ●*noun* a beating; a defeat.

**wallow** *verb* **1** roll about in water or mud etc. **2** take unrestrained pleasure in something; *wallowing in luxury.* ●*noun* the act of wallowing.

**wallpaper** *noun* paper for pasting on the interior walls of rooms.

**Wall Street** a street in New York City, in or near which the chief American financial institutions are concentrated; the American money market.

**wally** *noun* (*slang*) a stupid person.

**walnut** *noun* **1** a nut containing an edible kernel with a wrinkled surface. **2** the tree that bears it. **3** the wood of this tree.

**Walpole¹**, Horace, 4th Earl of Orford (1717–97), English writer and connoisseur.

**Walpole²**, Sir Hugh (1884–1941), British novelist, born in New Zealand.

**Walpole³**, Sir Robert, 1st Earl of Orford (1676–1745), British statesman, generally recognized as the first Prime Minister of Britain.

**Walpurgis Night** (val-**poor**-gis) the eve of 1 May, on which (according to German legend) a witches' sabbath took place on the Brocken in the Harz mountains. (¶ Named after St Walburga, an 8th-century nun in Germany.)

**walrus** *noun* (*plural* **walrus** *or* **walruses**) a large amphibious animal of Arctic regions, related to the seal and sea lion and having a pair of long tusks. □ **walrus moustache** a long thick moustache that hangs down at the sides.

**Walton¹**, Izaak (1593–1683), English writer.

**Walton²**, Sir William Turner (1902–83), English composer.

**waltz** *noun* **1** a ballroom dance for couples, with a flowing melody in triple time. **2** music for this. ●*verb* **1** dance a waltz. **2** (*informal*) move in a casual, confident manner; *came waltzing in.* □ **waltz off with** (*informal*) win easily.

**Waltzing Matilda** an Australian song with words by A. B. Paterson (1895). A 'Matilda' is a tramp's pack of belongings; to 'waltz Matilda' is to travel with this.

**wampum** (**wom**-pŭm) *noun* strings of shell beads formerly used by North American Indians as money or for ornament.

**wan** (*pronounced* wonn) *adjective* (**wanner, wannest**) pale; looking exhausted or unhappy. □ **wanly** *adverb*, **wanness** *noun*

**wand** *noun* **1** a slender rod for carrying in the hand, especially one associated with the working of magic. **2** a staff as a symbol of office.

**wander** *verb* **1** go from place to place without a settled route, destination, or purpose. **2** (of a road or river) wind, meander. **3** leave the right path or direction; stray from one's group or from a place. **4** digress from a subject; be inattentive or speak disconnectedly through illness or weakness. ●*noun* an act of wandering. □ **Wandering Jew 1** a legendary person said to have been condemned by Christ (as punishment for an insult) to wander the earth until Christ's second coming. **2** a type of trailing plant. □ **wanderer** noun

**wanderlust** noun strong desire to travel.

**wane** verb **1** (of the moon) show a gradually decreasing area of brightness after being full. **2** decrease in vigour, strength, or importance; *his influence was waning.* ● noun **1** the process of waning. **2** a defect in a plank etc. when the corners are not square. □ **on the wane** waning.

**wangle** (*slang*) verb obtain or arrange by using trickery, improper influence, persuasion, etc. ● noun an act of wangling.

**wank** (*vulgar slang*) verb masturbate. ● noun an act of masturbating.

**Wankel engine** (**wank**-ĕl) an internal-combustion engine with a rotary piston. (¶ Named after the German engineer F. Wankel (1902–88) who invented it.)

**wanker** noun (*vulgar slang*) an unpleasant or useless person.

**want** verb **1** desire, wish for. **2** require or need; *your hair wants cutting*; *you want to be more careful.* **3** lack, have an insufficient supply of. **4** be without the necessities of life; *waste not, want not*; *want for nothing.* **5** fall short of. ● noun **1** a desire for something, a requirement; *a man of few wants.* **2** lack or need of something, deficiency; *the plants died from want of water.* **3** lack of the necessities of life; *living in great want.*

**wanted** adjective (of a suspected criminal) being sought by the police.

**wanting** adjective lacking; deficient; not equal to requirements.

**wanton** (**wonn**-tŏn) adjective irresponsible, lacking proper restraint or motives. □ **wantonly** adverb, **wantonness** noun

**wapiti** (**wop**-it-i) noun a large North American deer.

**war** noun **1** armed conflict between countries, ethnic groups, etc. **2** open hostility between people. **3** a strong effort to combat crime, disease, poverty, etc. □ **at war** engaged in a war. **have been in the wars** (*informal*) show signs of injury or rough usage. **war crime** a crime violating the international laws of war. **war cry** a word or cry shouted in attacking or in rallying one's side; the slogan of a political or other party. **war dance** a dance performed by certain primitive peoples before battle or after a victory. **war game** a game in which models representing troops etc. are moved about on maps; a training exercise in which sets of armed forces participate in mock opposition to each other. **war memorial** a memorial erected to those who died in a war. **war of nerves** an effort to wear down one's opponent by gradually destroying

morale. **Wars of the Roses** the civil wars of the 15th century between Yorkists with the white rose and Lancastrians with the red rose as their emblem. **war widow** a woman whose husband has been killed in a war.

**War.** abbreviation Warwickshire.

**warble** verb sing, especially with a gentle trilling note as certain birds do. ● noun a warbling sound.

**warbler** noun any of several small songbirds.

**ward** (*rhymes with* ford) noun **1** a room with beds for patients in a hospital. **2** an area (e.g. of a city) electing a councillor to represent it. **3** a person, especially a child, under the care of a guardian or the protection of a lawcourt. **4** each of the notches and projections in a key (or the corresponding parts in a lock). □ **ward off** keep at a distance (a person or thing that threatens danger), fend off.

**warden** noun **1** an official with supervisory duties. **2** a churchwarden. **3** the title of certain governors or presidents of colleges etc.

**warder** noun an official in charge of prisoners in a prison.

**wardrobe** noun **1** a large cupboard where clothes are stored, with pegs or rails from which they hang. **2** a stock of clothes. **3** a theatrical company's stock of costumes.

**wardroom** noun the mess-room for commissioned officers in a warship.

**wardship** noun the state of being a ward; a guardian's care.

**ware** noun **1** manufactured goods (especially pottery) of the kind specified; *delftware.* **2** (**wares**) articles offered for sale; *traders displayed their wares.*

**warehouse** noun a building for storing goods.

**warfare** noun making war, fighting; a particular form of this; *guerrilla warfare.*

**warhead** noun the explosive head of a missile, torpedo, or similar weapon.

**Warhol** (**wor**-hohl), Andy (1930–87), American painter, graphic artist, and film-maker, prominent in the New York pop art of the 1960s.

**warlike** adjective **1** hostile, aggressive; *a warlike people.* **2** of or for war; *warlike preparations.*

**warlock** noun (*old use*) a sorcerer.

**warm** adjective **1** moderately hot, not cold or cool. **2** (of clothes etc.) keeping the body warm. **3** enthusiastic, hearty; *a warm supporter*; *the speaker got a warm reception.* **4** kindly and affectionate; *she has a warm heart.* **5** (of colours) suggesting warmth, containing reddish shades. **6** (of the scent in hunting) still fairly fresh and strong. **7** (in children's games etc.) near the object sought, on the verge of guessing. ●*verb* make or become warm or warmer. □ **warm-blooded** *adjective* having blood that remains warm (ranging from 36° to 42°C) permanently. **warm front** an advancing mass of warm air. **warm-hearted** *adjective* having a kindly and affectionate disposition. **warming-pan** *noun* a covered metal pan with a long handle, formerly filled with hot coals and used for warming beds. **warm to** become cordial or well-disposed to (a person); become more animated about (a task). **warm up 1** make or become warm; reheat (food etc.). **2** prepare for athletic exercise by practice beforehand. **3** make or become more lively. **4** put (an audience) into a receptive mood before a performance. **warm-up** *noun* a period of preparatory exercise. □ **warmish** *adjective*, **warmly** *adverb*, **warmness** *noun*

**warmonger** (wor-mung-er) *noun* a person who seeks to bring about war.

**warmth** *noun* warmness; the state of being warm.

**warn** *verb* inform (a person) about a danger or about something that must be reckoned with; advise about action in such circumstances; *we warned them to take waterproof clothing.* □ **warn off** tell (a person) to keep away or to avoid (a thing).

**warning** *noun* something that serves to warn.

**warp** (*pronounced* worp) *verb* **1** cause (timber etc.) to become bent by uneven shrinkage or expansion; become bent in this way. **2** distort (a person's judgement or principles). **3** haul (a ship) along by pulling on a rope fixed to an external point. ●*noun* **1** a warped condition. **2** threads stretched lengthwise in a loom, to be crossed by the weft. **3** a rope used in warping a ship.

**warpaint** *noun* **1** paint used to decorate the body before battle. **2** (*informal*) make-up.

**warpath** *noun* □ **on the warpath** (*informal*) angry about something.

**warrant** (wo-rănt) *noun* **1** written authorization to do something; *the police have a warrant for his arrest.* **2** a voucher entitling the holder to receive certain goods or services; *a travel warrant.* **3** a proof or guarantee. ●*verb* **1** serve as a warrant for, justify; *nothing can warrant such rudeness.* **2** prove or guarantee; assure; *he'll be back, I'll warrant you.* □ **warrant officer** a member of the armed services ranking between commissioned officers and NCOs.

**warranty** (wo-răn-ti) *noun* **1** a guarantee, especially one given to the buyer of an article. **2** authority or justification for doing something.

**warren** *noun* **1** a network of rabbit burrows. **2** a building or district with many narrow winding passages.

**warring** *adjective* engaged in a war.

**warrior** *noun* a person who is experienced in battle.

**Warsaw** the capital of Poland. □ **Warsaw Pact** a treaty of mutual defence and military aid signed at Warsaw in 1955 by the Communist countries of Europe under Russian leadership.

**warship** *noun* a ship for use in war.

**wart** *noun* **1** a small hard roundish abnormal growth on the skin, caused by a virus. **2** a similar growth on a plant. □ **warts and all** without concealment of blemishes, defects, or unattractive features.

**warthog** *noun* an African wild pig with two large tusks and wart-like growths on its face.

**wartime** *noun* the period when a war is being waged.

**Warwickshire** (wo-rik-sher) a midland county of England.

**wary** (**wair**-i) *adjective* (**warier**, **wariest**) cautious, in the habit of looking out for possible danger or difficulty. □ **warily** *adverb*, **wariness** *noun*

**was** *see* BE.

**Wash, the** a short broad inlet of the North Sea on the east coast of England, between Lincolnshire and Norfolk.

**wash** *verb* **1** cleanse with water or other liquid. **2** wash oneself; wash clothes etc. **3** be washable. **4** flow past or against, go splashing or flowing; *the sea washes the base of the cliffs; waves washed over the deck.* **5** (of moving liquid) carry in a specified direction; *a wave washed him overboard.* **6** sift (ore) by the action of water. **7** coat with a wash of paint or wall-colouring etc. **8** (*informal*) (of reasoning) be valid; *that argument won't wash.* ●*noun* **1** washing, being washed; *give it a good wash.* **2** the process of laundering. **3** a quantity of clothes etc. that are being washed or to be washed or have just been washed. **4** disturbed water or air behind a moving ship or aircraft etc. **5** liquid food or swill for pigs etc. **6** a thin coating of colour painted over a surface. □ **come out in the wash** be revealed and resolved or eliminated in the course of time. **wash dirty linen in public** discuss one's private scandals or quarrels publicly. **wash down 1** wash completely. **2** (usually foll. by *with*) accompany or follow (food) with a drink; *a sandwich washed down with a pint of beer.* **washed out** faded by washing; faded-looking; pallid. **washed up** (*slang*) defeated, having failed. **wash one's hands of** refuse to take responsibility for. **wash out 1** wash (clothes etc.). **2** make (a game etc.) impossible by heavy rainfall. **wash-out** *noun* (*informal*) a complete failure. **wash up 1** wash (crockery etc.) after use.

**2** cast up on the shore. **3** (*Amer.*) wash oneself.

**Wash.** *abbreviation* Washington (State).

**washable** *adjective* able to be washed without suffering damage.

**washbasin** *noun* a basin (usually fixed to a wall) for washing one's hands and face in.

**washboard** *noun* a ribbed board for scrubbing clothes on when washing; this used as a percussion instrument.

**washer** *noun* **1** a machine for washing things. **2** a ring of rubber or metal etc. placed between two surfaces (e.g. under a nut) to give tightness or prevent leakage. □ **washer-up** *noun* (*plural* **washers-up**) (also **washer-upper**) a person who washes dishes.

**washerwoman** *noun* (*plural* **washerwomen**) a woman whose occupation is washing clothes etc.

**washing** *noun* clothes etc. that are being washed or to be washed or have just been washed. □ **washing machine** a machine for washing clothes. **washing-powder** *noun* powder of soap or detergent for washing clothes. **washing soda** sodium carbonate, used (dissolved in water) for washing and cleaning things. **washing-up** *noun* the process of washing dishes etc. after use; the dishes etc. for washing.

**Washington**[1] **1** a State in the northwest of the USA, bordering on the Pacific. **2** the administrative capital of the USA, covering the same area as the District of Columbia.

**Washington**[2], George (1732–99), American military commander and statesman, 1st President of the USA 1789–96.

**washroom** *noun* (*Amer.*) a toilet.

**washstand** *noun* a piece of furniture to hold a basin, jug, soap, etc.

**washy** *adjective* **1** (of liquids) thin, watery. **2** (of colours) washed-out.

**wasn't** (*informal*) = was not.

**wasp** *noun* (also **WASP**) (*Amer.*, usually *scornful*) a middle-class American White Protestant. (¶ From the initials of White Anglo-Saxon Protestant.)

**wasp** *noun* a stinging insect with a black and yellow striped body. □ **wasp-waist** *noun* a very slender waist.

**waspish** *adjective* making sharp or irritable comments. □ **waspishness** *noun*

**wassail** (woss-ayl *or* woss-ăl) (*old use*) *noun* making merry (especially at Christmas) with much drinking. ●*verb* (**wassailed**, **wassailing**) make merry in this way.

**Wassermann** (vass-er-man), August Paul von (1866–1925), German bacteriologist, inventor of a test for diagnosing syphilis.

**wast** (*old use*) the past tense of **be**, used with *thou*.

**wastage** *noun* **1** loss by waste. **2** (also **natural wastage**) loss of employees through retirement or resignation, not through declaring them redundant.

**waste** *verb* **1** use extravagantly or needlessly or without an adequate result; *he is wasted as a schoolmaster*. **2** fail to use (an opportunity). **3** make or become gradually weaker; *wasting away for lack of food*; *a wasting disease*. ●*adjective* **1** left over or thrown away because not wanted; *waste products*. **2** (of land) not used or cultivated or built on. ●*noun* **1** an act of wasting or using something ineffectively; *a waste of time*. **2** waste material or food; waste products. **3** a stretch of waste land. □ **go** (*or* **run**) **to waste** be wasted. **waste breath** *or* **words** talk uselessly or in vain. **waste paper** paper regarded as spoilt or valueless and thrown away. **waste-paper basket** an open container in which waste paper is placed for removal. **waste pipe** a pipe that carries off water etc. that has been used or is not required.

**wasteful** *adjective* using more than is needed, showing waste. □ **wastefully** *adverb*, **wastefulness** *noun*

**wasteland** *noun* **1** an expanse of barren or useless land. **2** a place or time considered spiritually or intellectually barren.

**waster** (wayst-er) *noun* **1** a wasteful person. **2** (*informal*) a wastrel.

**wastrel** (wayst-rĕl) *noun* a good-for-nothing person.

**watch** *verb* **1** look at, keep under observation. **2** be on the alert, take heed; *watch for an opportunity*. **3** be careful about. **4** (often foll. by *over*) safeguard, exercise protective care. ●*noun* **1** the act of watching, especially to see that all is well; constant observation or attention; *keep watch*. **2** a small portable device indicating the time. **3** a period (usually 4 hours) for which a division of a ship's company remains on duty; a turn of duty; the part (usually half) of a ship's company on duty during a watch. □ **on the watch** alert for something. **watching brief** the brief of a barrister who is present during a lawsuit to advise a client who is not directly concerned in it. **watch-night service** a religious service on the last night of the year. **watch one's step** be careful not to stumble or do something wrong. **watch out** be on one's guard. **watchtower** *noun* a tower from which soldiers etc. can keep watch. □ **watcher** *noun*

**watchdog** *noun* **1** a guard dog. **2** a person or organization acting as a guardian of people's rights.

**watchful** *adjective* watching or observing closely. □ **watchfully** *adverb*, **watchfulness** *noun*

**watchmaker** *noun* a person who makes or repairs watches.

**watchman** *noun* (*plural* **watchmen**) a person employed to look after a building etc. at night.

**watchword** *noun* a word or phrase expressing briefly the principles of a party or group.

**water** *noun* **1** a colourless odourless tasteless liquid that is a compound of oxygen and hydrogen. **2** a body of water, e.g. a lake or sea. **3** water as supplied for domestic use. **4** a watery secretion (e.g. sweat or saliva); urine. **5** a watery infusion or other preparation; *lavender water; soda water.* **6** the level of the tide; *at high water.* **7** the transparency and lustre of a gem; *a diamond of the first water.* **8** (**waters**) amniotic fluid, released during labour. ●*verb* **1** sprinkle with water. **2** supply with water; give drinking water to (an animal). **3** dilute with water. **4** (of a ship etc.) take in a supply of water. **5** secrete tears or saliva; *make one's mouth water.* □ **the Water-bearer** = THE WATER-CARRIER (see below). **water-bed** *noun* a mattress filled with water. **water-biscuit** *noun* a thin crisp unsweetened biscuit. **water buffalo** the common domestic buffalo of India and Indonesia etc. **water bus** a boat carrying passengers on a regular route. **water-butt** *noun* a barrel used to catch rainwater. **water-cannon** *noun* a device for shooting a powerful jet of water to disperse a crowd etc. **the Water-carrier** *noun* a sign of the zodiac, Aquarius. **water chestnut** the corm from a sedge, used in Chinese cookery. **water-closet** *noun* a lavatory that is flushed by water. **water colour** artists' paint in which the pigment is diluted with water (not oil); a picture painted with paints of this kind. **water down** dilute; make less forceful or vivid. **water-glass** *noun* a thick liquid used for coating eggs to preserve them. **water-hammer** *noun* a knocking noise in a water pipe when a tap is turned off. **water-ice** *noun* frozen flavoured water. **watering-can** *noun* a portable container with a long spout, for watering plants. **watering hole 1** a pool from which animals drink. **2** (*informal*) a pub. **watering place 1** a pool from which animals drink. **2** a spa or seaside resort. **water jump** a place where a horse in a steeplechase etc. must jump over water. **water level 1** the surface of water in a reservoir etc.; the height of this. **2** = WATER TABLE (see below). **water lily** a plant that grows in water, with broad floating leaves and showy flowers. **water main** a main pipe in a water-supply system. **water-meadow** *noun* a meadow that is kept fertile by being flooded periodically by a stream. **water melon** a melon with a

smooth green skin, red pulp, and watery juice. **water-mill** *noun* a mill worked by a waterwheel. **water-pistol** *noun* a toy pistol that shoots a jet of water. **water polo** a game played by teams of swimmers with a large ball. **water-power** *noun* power obtained from flowing or falling water, used to drive machinery or generate electric current. **water-rat** *noun* = WATER-VOLE. **water-rate** *noun* the charge made for use of a public water supply. **water-ski** *noun* either of a pair of skis on which a person stands for **water-skiing**, the sport of skimming over the surface of water, holding a towline from a motor boat. **water-softener** *noun* a substance or apparatus for softening hard water. **water table** the level below which the ground is saturated with water. **water-tower** *noun* a tower that holds a water-tank at a height to secure pressure for distributing water. **water-vole** *noun* a rodent, a vole found in and near freshwater streams and rivers. **water-wings** *plural noun* inflated floats worn on the arms by a person learning to swim.

**waterbird** *noun* a bird that swims on or wades in water.

**watercourse** *noun* a stream, brook, or artificial waterway; its channel.

**watercress** *noun* a cress that grows in streams or ponds, with sharp-tasting leaves, used in salads.

**watered** *adjective* (of fabric, especially silk) having an irregular wavy marking.

**waterfall** *noun* a stream that falls from a height.

**waterfowl** *plural noun* waterbirds, especially game birds that swim.

**waterfront** *noun* the part of a town that borders on a river, lake, or sea.

**Watergate** an incident during the US election campaign of 1972, when the Republican Party supporting President Nixon attempted to bug the offices of the Democratic Party at the Watergate building in Washington, DC. The attempted cover-up and subsequent inquiry caused a major political scandal and forced the resignation of President Nixon.

**waterhole** *noun* a shallow dip in the ground where water collects.

**waterline** *noun* the line along which the surface of water touches a ship's side.

**waterlogged** *adjective* saturated or filled with water.

**Waterloo** a village in Belgium where in 1815 Napoleon's army was defeated by the British and Prussians. □ **meet one's Waterloo** lose a decisive contest.

**waterman** *noun* (*plural* **watermen**) a boatman.

**watermark** *noun* **1** a mark showing how high a river or tide rises or how low it falls. **2** a manufacturer's design in some paper, visible when the paper is held against light.

**waterproof** *adjective* unable to be penetrated by water. ●*noun* a waterproof coat or cape. ●*verb* make waterproof.

**watershed** *noun* **1** a line of high land where streams on one side flow into one river or sea and streams on the other side flow into another. **2** a turning-point in the course of events. **3** a catchment area.

**waterside** *noun* the edge of a river, lake, or sea.

**waterspout** *noun* a funnel-shaped column of water between sea and cloud, formed when a whirlwind draws up a whirling mass of water.

**watertight** *adjective* **1** made or fastened so that water cannot get in or out. **2** (of an excuse or alibi) impossible to set aside or disprove; (of an agreement) leaving no possibility of escape from its provisions.

**waterway** *noun* **1** a route for travel by water; a canal. **2** a navigable channel.

**waterwheel** *noun* a wheel turned by a flow of water, used to work machinery.

**waterworks** *noun* **1** an establishment with pumping machinery etc. for supplying water to a district. **2** (*informal*) crying; tears. **3** (*informal*) the urinary system in the body.

**watery** *adjective* **1** of or like water. **2** made weak or thin by too much water. **3** full of water or moisture; *watery eyes.* **4** (of colours) pale. □ **watery grave** death by drowning.

**Watson¹, Dr** a doctor who is the companion and assistant of Sherlock Holmes in stories by Sir Arthur Conan Doyle.

**Watson²**, James Dewey (born 1928), American biologist, who together with F. H. C. Crick proposed a structure for the DNA molecule.

**Watson³**, John Broadus (1878–1958), American psychologist.

**Watt** (*pronounced* wot), James (1736–1819), Scottish engineer, who greatly improved the steam engine.

**watt** (*pronounced* wot) *noun* a unit of electric power. □ **watt-hour** *noun* the energy used when one watt is applied for one hour. (¶ Named after James Watt.)

**wattage** (wot-ij) *noun* an amount of electric power, expressed in watts.

**wattle¹** (wot'l) *noun* **1** a structure of interwoven sticks and twigs used as material for fences, walls, etc. **2** an Australian acacia with long flexible branches and golden flowers, adopted as the national emblem. □ **wattle and daub** a network of rods and twigs plastered with clay or mud as a building material.

**wattle²** (wot'l) *noun* a red fleshy fold of skin hanging from the head or throat of certain birds, e.g. the turkey.

**Watts**, George Frederick (1817–1904), English painter and sculptor.

**Waugh** (*pronounced* waw), Evelyn Arthur St John (1903–66), English novelist, author of *Brideshead Revisited*.

**wave** *noun* **1** a ridge of water moving along the surface of the sea etc. **2** something compared to this, e.g. an advancing group of attackers, a temporary increase of an influence or condition (*a wave of anger*), a spell of hot or cold weather (*a heat wave*). **3** a wave-like curve or arrangement of curves, e.g. in a line or in hair. **4** an act of waving. **5** the wave-like motion by which heat, light, sound, or electricity etc. is spread or carried; a single curve in the course of this, plotted (in a graph) against time. ●*verb* **1** move loosely to and fro or up and down. **2** move (one's hand or something held) to and fro as a signal or greeting. **3** signal or express in this way; *waved him away; waved goodbye.* **4** give a wavy course or appearance to. **5** be wavy. □ **make waves** be a disturbing influence. **wave aside** dismiss (an objection etc.) as unimportant. **wave down** signal (a vehicle or its driver) to stop, by waving one's hand. **wave-form** *noun Physics* a curve showing the shape of a wave at a given time.

▪**Usage** Do not confuse with **waive**.

**waveband** *noun* a range of wavelengths between certain limits.

**wavelength** *noun* the distance between corresponding points in a sound wave or an electromagnetic wave.

**wavelet** *noun* a small wave.

**waver** *verb* **1** be or become unsteady; begin to give way; *his courage wavered.* **2** (of light) flicker. **3** show hesitation or uncertainty; *he wavered between two opinions.* □ **waverer** *noun*

▪**Usage** Do not confuse with **waiver**.

**wavy** *adjective* (**wavier, waviest**) full of waves or wave-like curves. □ **waviness** *noun*

**wax¹** *noun* **1** beeswax. **2** any of various soft sticky substances that melt easily (e.g. obtained from petroleum), used for various purposes such as making candles or polishes. **3** a yellow wax-like substance secreted in the ears. ●*verb* **1** coat, polish, or treat with wax. **2** remove unwanted hair from (the legs etc.) using wax. □ **waxy** *adjective*, **waxiness** *noun*

**wax²** *verb* **1** (of the moon) show a bright area that is becoming gradually larger until it becomes full. **2** increase in vigour, strength, or importance; *kingdoms waxed and waned.* **3** become; *wax lyrical.*

**waxen** *adjective* **1** made of wax. **2** like wax in its paleness or smoothness.

**waxwing** *noun* any of several small birds with small red tips (like sealing wax) on some wing-feathers.

**waxwork** *noun* an object modelled in wax, especially a lifelike model of a person.

**way** *noun* **1** a line of communication between places, e.g. a path or road. **2** the best route, the route taken or intended; *asked the way to Norwich.* **3** a method or style, a person's chosen or desired course of action; *do it my way.* **4** travelling distance; *it's a long way to Tipperary.* **5** the amount of difference between two states or conditions; *his work is a long way from being perfect.* **6** space free of obstacles so that people can pass; *make way.* **7** the route over which a person or thing is moving or would naturally move; *don't get in the way of the trucks.* **8** a specified direction; *which way is she looking?* **9** a manner; *she spoke in a kindly way.* **10** a habitual manner or course of action or events; *you'll soon get into our ways.* **11** a talent or skill; *she has a way with flowers.* **12** an advance in some direction, progress; *we made our way to the front.* **13** a respect, a particular aspect of something; *it's a good plan in some ways.* **14** a condition or state; *things are in a bad way.* ●*adverb* (*informal*) far; *the shot was way off the target.* □ **by the way 1** by the roadside during a journey. **2** incidentally, as a more or less irrelevant comment. **by way of** as a substitute for or a form of; *smiled by way of greeting.* **come one's way** fall to one's lot; become available. **in a way** to a limited extent; in some respects. **in no way** not at all. **in the way** forming an obstacle or hindrance. **on the way 1** in the course of a journey. **2** coming, but not yet arrived. **under way** see UNDER. **way back** (*informal*) a long way back; long ago. **way-leave** *noun* a right of way that is rented to a mine-owner, electricity company, etc. **way-out** *adjective* (*informal*) exaggeratedly unusual in style; exotic. **ways and means** methods of achieving something; (in Parliament) a means of providing money.

**waybill** *noun* a list of passengers or goods on a vehicle.

**wayfarer** *noun* a traveller, especially on foot.

**waylay** *verb* (**waylaid, waylaying**) lie in wait for, especially so as to talk to or rob.

**Wayne,** John (original name: Marion Michael Morrison) (1907–79), American film actor, noted for his many performances as the hero of westerns.

**wayside** *noun* the side of a road or path; land bordering this.

**wayward** *adjective* childishly self-willed, not obedient or easily controlled. □ **waywardness** *noun*

**Wb** *abbreviation* weber(s).

**WC** *abbreviation* **1** water-closet. **2** West Central.

**we** *pronoun* **1** used by a person referring to himself or herself and another or others, or speaking on behalf of a nation, group, or organization. **2** used instead of 'I' by a royal person in formal proclamations and by the writer of an editorial article in a newspaper etc. **3** (used humorously or condescendingly) you; *and how are we today?*

**w/e** *abbreviation* week ending.

**WEA** *abbreviation* (*Brit.*) Workers' Educational Association.

**weak** *adjective* **1** lacking strength, power, or numbers; easily broken, bent, or defeated. **2** lacking vigour, not acting strongly. **3** not convincing or forceful; *the evidence is weak.* **4** dilute, having little of a substance in proportion to the amount of water; *weak tea.* **5** *Grammar* (of verbs) forming the past tense etc. by adding a suffix (as *walk/walked, waste/wasted*), not by changing the vowel (as *ring/rang*). □ **weak-kneed** *adjective* (*informal*) giving way weakly, especially when intimidated. **weak-minded** *adjective* lacking determination.

**weaken** *verb* make or become weaker.

**weakling** *noun* a feeble person or animal.

**weakly** *adverb* in a weak manner. ●*adjective* sickly, not robust.

**weakness** *noun* **1** the state of being weak. **2** a weak point; a defect or fault. **3** inability to resist something, a particular fondness; *she has a weakness for coffee creams.*

**weal** *noun* **1** a ridge raised on the flesh by a stroke of a rod or whip. **2** (*literary*) welfare, prosperity; *for the public weal.*

**weald** *noun* the formerly wooded district of south-east England, including large parts of Kent, Surrey, and East Sussex.

**wealth** *noun* **1** riches; possession of these. **2** a great quantity; *a book with a wealth of illustrations.* □ **wealth tax** tax levied on a person's capital.

**wealthy** *adjective* (**wealthier, wealthiest**) having wealth, rich. □ **wealthiness** *noun*

**wean** *verb* **1** accustom (a baby) to take food other than milk. **2** cause (a person) to give up a habit or interest etc. gradually.

**weapon** *noun* **1** a thing used as a means of inflicting bodily harm, e.g. a gun, bomb, or hammer. **2** a means of getting the better of someone in a conflict; *use the weapon of a general strike.*

**weaponry** *noun* weapons collectively.

**wear** *verb* (**wore, worn, wearing**) **1** have on the body, e.g. as clothing, ornaments, or make-up. **2** have (a certain look) on one's face; *wearing a frown.* **3** (*informal*) accept or tolerate; *the boss wouldn't wear it.* **4** injure the surface of or become injured by rubbing, stress, or use; make (a hole etc.) in this way. **5** (foll. by *down*) exhaust or overcome by persistence; *wore down the opposition.* **6** endure continued use; *this fabric wears well.* **7** (of time) pass gradually; *the night wore on.* ●*noun* **1** wearing or being worn as clothing; *choose cotton for summer wear.* **2** clothing; *men's wear is on the ground floor.* **3** (also **wear and tear**) damage resulting from ordinary use. **4** capacity to endure being used; *there's a lot of wear left in that coat.* □ **wear off 1** remove or be removed by wear. **2** become gradually less intense. **wear one's heart on one's sleeve** show one's affections quite openly. **wear out** use or be used until no longer usable. **wear the trousers** be the dominant partner in a relationship. □ **wearer** *noun*

**wearisome** *adjective* causing weariness.

**weary** *adjective* (**wearier, weariest**) **1** very tired, especially from exertion or endurance. **2** (foll. by *of*) tired of something; *weary of war.* **3** tiring; tedious. ●*verb* (**wearied, wearying**) make or become weary. □ **wearily** *adverb*, **weariness** *noun*

**weasel** *noun* a small fierce animal with a slender body and reddish-brown fur, living on small animals, birds' eggs, etc. □ **weasel words** words that are intentionally ambiguous or misleading. (¶ Said to allude to the weasel's alleged habit of sucking out the contents of an egg and leaving only the shell.)

**weather** *noun* the condition of the atmosphere with reference to the presence or absence of sunshine, rain, wind, etc. ●*adjective* windward; *on the weather side.* ●*verb* **1** dry or season by exposure to the action of the weather. **2** become dried, discoloured, worn, etc. in this way. **3** sail to windward of; *the ship weathered the Cape.* **4** come safely through; *weathered the storm.* □ **keep a weather eye open** be watchful. **make heavy weather of** exaggerate (a difficulty or problem). **under the weather** feeling unwell or depressed. **weatherbeaten** *adjective* bronzed or worn by exposure to weather. **weather vane** a weathercock.

**weatherboard** *noun* a sloping board for keeping out rain and wind, especially one attached at the bottom of a door.

**weatherboarding** *noun* a series of weatherboards with each overlapping the one below, fixed to the outside wall of buildings.

**weathercock** *noun* **1** a revolving pointer, often in the shape of a cockerel, turning easily in the wind to show from which direction the wind is blowing. **2** an inconstant person.

**weatherman** *noun* (*plural* **weathermen**) a meteorologist, especially one who broadcasts a weather forecast.

**weatherproof** *adjective* unable to be penetrated by rain or wind.

**weave**[1] *verb* (**wove, woven, weaving**) **1** make (fabric etc.) by passing crosswise threads or strips under and over lengthwise ones. **2** form (thread etc.) into fabric in this way. **3** put together into a connected whole; compose (a story etc.). ●*noun* a style or pattern of weaving; *a loose weave.* □ **weaver-bird** *noun* a tropical bird that builds a nest of elaborately interwoven twigs etc. □ **weaver** *noun*

**weave**[2] *verb* (**weaved, weaving**) move from side to side in an intricate course; *weaved his way through the crowd.* □ **get weaving** (*slang*) begin energetically; hurry.

**web** *noun* **1** the network of fine strands made by a spider etc. **2** a network; *a web of deceit.* **3** skin filling the spaces between the toes of birds such as ducks and animals such as frogs. **3** a large roll of paper used in printing. □ **web-footed** *adjective* having the toes joined by webs. □ **webbed** *adjective*

**Webb**, Sidney James (1859–1947) and his wife Beatrice (1858–1943), English socialists and social reformers.

**webbing** *noun* strong bands of woven fabric used in upholstery, belts, etc.

**Weber** (vay-ber), Carl Maria von (1786–1826), German composer.

**weber** (vay-ber) *noun Physics* the SI unit of magnetic flux. (¶ Named after the German physicist W. E. Weber (died 1891).)

**Webern** (vay-bern), Anton von (1883–1945), Austrian composer, pupil of Schoenberg whose technique of serial composition he adopted.

**Webster**, John (*c.*1578–*c.*1632), English dramatist, who wrote the tragedies *The White Devil* and *The Duchess of Malfi.*

**Wed** *abbreviation* (also **Weds.**) Wednesday.

**wed** *verb* (**wedded, wedding**) **1** marry. **2** unite; *if we can wed efficiency to economy.* □ **wedded to** devoted to and unable to abandon (an occupation or opinion etc.).

**we'd** (*informal*) **1** we had. **2** we should. **3** we would.

**wedding** *noun* a marriage ceremony and festivities. □ **wedding breakfast** a meal between a wedding and the departure for the honeymoon. **wedding cake** a rich iced cake eaten at a wedding. **wedding ring** a ring worn by a married person.

**wedge** *noun* **1** a piece of wood or metal etc. thick at one end and tapered to a thin edge at the other, thrust between things to force them apart or prevent free movement etc. **2** a wedge-shaped thing; *a wedge of cake.* ●*verb* **1** force apart or fix firmly by using a wedge. **2** thrust or pack tightly between other things or people or in a limited space; be immovable because of this.

**Wedgwood** *noun* (*trade mark*) china and ceramic ware named after Josiah Wedgwood, its original 18th-century manufacturer. □ **Wedgwood blue** the blue colour characteristic of this.

**wedlock** *noun* the married state.

**Wednesday** the day of the week following Tuesday.

**Weds.** *see* WED.

**wee**[1] *adjective* **1** (*Scottish*) little; *wee Georgie.* **2** (*informal*) tiny; *it's a wee bit too long.*

**wee**[2] *noun & verb* (*informal*) = WEE-WEE.

**weed** *noun* **1** a wild plant growing where it is not wanted. **2** (**the weed**) (*slang*) marijuana; tobacco. **3** a thin weak-looking person. **4** (**weeds**) (in full **widow's weeds**) deep mourning formerly worn by widows. ●*verb* remove weeds from; uproot weeds. □ **weed out** remove as inferior or undesirable.

**weedkiller** *noun* a chemical used to destroy weeds.

**weedy** *adjective* **1** full of weeds. **2** thin and weak-looking.

**week** *noun* **1** a period of seven successive days, especially one reckoned from midnight at the end of Saturday. **2** the six days other than Sunday; the five days other than Saturday and Sunday; *never go there during the week.* **3** the period for which one regularly works during a week; *a 40-hour week.*

**weekday** *noun* a day other than Sunday or Saturday and Sunday.

**weekend** *noun* Sunday and all or part of Saturday (or occasionally slightly longer, especially as a time for a holiday or visit).

**weekly** *adjective* happening, published, or payable etc. once a week. ●*adverb* once a week. ●*noun* a weekly newspaper or magazine.

**weeny** *adjective* (*informal*) tiny.

**weep** *verb* (**wept, weeping**) **1** cry, shed tears. **2** shed or ooze moisture in drops. ●*noun* a spell of weeping.

**weepie** *noun* (*informal*) a sentimental or emotional play, film, etc.

**weeping** *adjective* (of a tree) having drooping branches; *weeping willow.*

**weepy** *adjective* (*informal*) inclined to weep, tearful.

**weevil** *noun* a small beetle that feeds on grain, nuts, tree-bark, etc.

**wee-wee** (*informal*) *verb* urinate. ●*noun* urine; an act of urinating.

**weft** *noun* crosswise threads woven under and over the warp to make fabric.

**weigh** *verb* **1** measure the weight of. **2** have a certain weight. **3** consider the relative importance or value of; *weigh the pros and cons.* **4** have importance or influence; *this evidence weighed with the jury.* **5** be burdensome; *the responsibility weighed heavily upon him.* □ **weigh anchor** raise the anchor and start a voyage. **weigh down 1** bring or keep down by its weight. **2** depress or make troubled; *weighed down with cares.* **weigh in** be weighed, (of a boxer) before a contest, (of a jockey) after a race. **weigh-in** *noun* the official weighing of a boxer before a fight. **weigh in with** (*informal*) contribute (a comment) to a discussion. **weigh one's words** select carefully those words that convey exactly what one means. **weigh out** (of a jockey) be weighed before a race. **weigh up** (*informal*) assess, form an estimate of.

**weighbridge** *noun* a weighing machine with a plate set in a road etc. onto which vehicles can be driven to be weighed.

**weight** *noun* **1** an object's mass numerically expressed according to a recognized scale of units. **2** the property of heaviness. **3** a unit or system of units by which weight is measured; *tables of weights and measures; troy weight.* **4** a piece of metal of known weight used with scales for weighing things. **5** a heavy object, especially one used to bring or keep something down; *the clock is worked by weights.* **6** a load to be supported; *the pillars carry a great weight.* **7** a heavy burden of responsibility or worry. **8** importance, influence, a convincing effect; *the weight of the evidence is against you.* ●*verb* **1** attach a weight to; hold down with a weight or weights. **2** burden with a load. **3** bias or arrange the balance of; *the test was weighted in favour of candidates with scientific knowledge.* □ **throw one's weight about** (*informal*) use one's influence aggressively. **weight training** physical training using weights.

**weighting** *noun* extra pay or allowances given in special cases, e.g. to allow for the higher cost of living in a capital city.

**weightless** *adjective* having no weight, or with no weight relative to its surroundings; of objects in a spacecraft, apparently unaffected by gravity. □ **weightlessness** *noun*

**weightlifting** *noun* the sport of lifting heavy weights. □ **weightlifter** *noun*

**weighty** *adjective* (**weightier, weightiest**) **1** having great weight, heavy. **2** burdensome. **3** showing or deserving earnest thought. **4** important, influential. □ **weightily** *adverb*, **weightiness** *noun*

**Weill** (*pronounced as* vile), Kurt (1900–50), German composer, noted for satirical operas written in collaboration with Bertolt Brecht.

**Weimar** (vy-mar) a town in eastern Germany, seat of the National Assembly of Germany 1919–33. □ **Weimar Republic** the German republic of this period.

**weir** (*pronounced* weer) *noun* **1** a small dam built across a river or canal so that water flows over it, serving to regulate the flow or to raise the level of water upstream. **2** the water flowing over it in a waterfall.

**weird** *adjective* strange and uncanny or bizarre. □ **weirdly** *adjective*, **weirdness** *noun*

**weirdo** *noun* (*plural* **weirdos**) (*informal*) an odd or eccentric person.

**Weismann** (vy-smăn), August Friedrich Leopold (1834–1914), German biologist, one of the founders of the modern study of genetics.

**Weizmann** (vyt-sman), Chaim Azriel (1874–1952), Israeli statesman, a leading Zionist, the first President of Israel 1949–52.

**welch** alternative spelling of WELSH.

**welcome** *adjective* **1** received with pleasure; *a welcome guest; welcome news.* **2** ungrudgingly permitted; *anyone is welcome to try it.* ● *interjection* a greeting expressing pleasure at a person's coming. ● *verb* **1** greet with pleasure or ceremony. **2** be glad to receive; *we welcome this opportunity.* ● *noun* a greeting or reception, especially a glad and kindly one.

**weld** *verb* **1** unite or fuse (pieces of metal or plastic) by hammering or pressure, usually after softening by heat. **2** make by welding. **3** unite into a whole. ● *noun* a joint made by welding. □ **welder** *noun*

**welfare** *noun* **1** well-being. **2** welfare work. □ **welfare state** a system whereby a country tries to ensure the welfare of all its citizens by means of social services operated by the State. **welfare work** organized efforts to secure the welfare of the poor, disabled, etc.

**welkin** *noun* (*poetic*) the sky.

**well**[1] *noun* **1** a shaft dug in the ground to obtain water or oil etc. from below the earth's surface. **2** a spring serving as a source of water. **3** an enclosed space resembling the shaft of a well; a deep enclosed space containing a staircase or lift in a building. **4** a railed-off space for solicitors etc. in a lawcourt. ● *verb* (usually foll. by *up*) rise or spring; *tears welled up in her eyes.* □ **well-head** *noun* (also **well-spring**) a source.

**well**[2] *adverb* (**better, best**) **1** in a good or suitable way, satisfactorily, rightly. **2** thoroughly, carefully; *polish it well.* **3** by a

considerable margin; *she is well over forty.* **4** favourably, kindly; *they think well of him.* **5** with good reason, easily, probably; *you may well ask; it may well be our last chance.* ● *adjective* **1** in good health. **2** in a satisfactory state or position; *all's well.* ● *interjection* expressing surprise, resignation, etc., or used to introduce a remark when one is hesitating. □ **as well, as well as** *see* AS. **be well away** have started and made considerable progress. **let well alone** leave things as they are and not meddle unnecessarily. **well-adjusted** *adjective* **1** mentally and emotionally stable. **2** in a good state of adjustment. **well-advised** *adjective* showing good sense. **well-appointed** *adjective* having all the necessary equipment. **well-being** *noun* good health, happiness, and prosperity. **well-born** *adjective* born of good family. **well-bred** *adjective* showing good breeding, well-mannered; (of a horse etc.) of good breed or stock. **well-built** *adjective* of good construction; (of a person) big, strong, and well-proportioned. **well-connected** *adjective* related to good families. **well-disposed** *adjective* having kindly or favourable feelings (towards a person or plan etc.). **well-heeled** *adjective* (*informal*) wealthy. **well-known** *adjective* known to many; known thoroughly. **well-mannered** *adjective* having good manners. **well-meaning, well-meant** *adjective* acting or done with good intentions but not having a good effect. **well-nigh** *adverb* almost. **well off** in a satisfactory or good situation; fairly rich. **well-oiled** *adjective* (*informal*) drunk. **well-preserved** *adjective* (of an old person) showing little sign of age. **well-read** *adjective* having read much literature. **well-spoken** *adjective* speaking in a polite and correct way. **well-to-do** *adjective* fairly rich. **well-tried** *adjective* often tested with good results. **well-trodden** *adjective* much frequented. **well-wisher** *noun* a person who wishes another well. **well-worn** *adjective* much worn by use; (of a phrase) much used, hackneyed.

**we'll** (*informal*) = we shall; we will.

**Welles**, (George) Orson (1915–85), American film director and actor.

**wellies** *plural noun* (*informal*) wellingtons.

**Wellington**[1] the capital of New Zealand.

**Wellington**[2], Arthur Wellesley, 1st Duke of (1769–1852), British soldier and statesman, known as the 'Iron Duke', victor over Napoleon at the battle of Waterloo (1815).

**wellington** *noun* (in full **wellington boot**) a boot of rubber or similar waterproof material, usually reaching almost to the knee.

**Wells**, H(erbert) G(eorge) (1866–1946), English novelist.

**Welsh** *adjective* of Wales or its people or language. ● *noun* **1** the Welsh language.

**2** (**the Welsh**) Welsh people. □ **Welsh rabbit** or **rarebit** melted or toasted cheese on toast. (¶ *Welsh rabbit* is the original name for this dish. The humorous use of *rabbit* was misunderstood and the word was altered to *rarebit* in an attempt to make it sound more understandable, but there is no independent evidence for the word *rarebit*.) □ **Welshman** noun (plural **Welshmen**), **Welshwoman** noun (plural **Welshwomen**).

**welsh** verb (also **welch**) **1** (of a bookmaker at a racecourse) swindle by decamping without paying out winnings. **2** avoid paying one's just debts, break an agreement; *they welshed on us.* □ **welsher** noun

**welt** noun **1** a strip of leather etc. sewn round the edge of the upper of a boot or shoe for attaching it to the sole. **2** a ribbed or strengthened border of a knitted garment, e.g. at the waist. **3** a weal, the mark of a heavy blow.

**welter** verb **1** (of a ship etc.) be tossed to and fro on the waves. **2** (foll. by *in*) wallow, lie soaked in blood etc. ● noun **1** a state of turmoil. **2** a disorderly mixture.

**welterweight** noun a boxing-weight (67 kg) between lightweight and middleweight.

**wen** noun a benign tumour on the skin, especially on the head.

**Wenceslas**, St (907–29), prince of Bohemia and patron saint of the Czech Republic. Feast day, 28 September.

**wench** noun (*old use*) a girl or young woman.

**wend** verb □ **wend one's way** go.

**Wendy house** a children's small house-like structure for playing in. (¶ Named after a character in J. M. Barrie's *Peter Pan*.)

**Wensleydale** noun a cheese made originally in Wensleydale in North Yorkshire.

**went** see GO¹.

**wept** see WEEP.

**were** see BE.

**we're** (*informal*) = we are.

**weren't** (*informal*) = were not.

**werewolf** (**wair**-wuulf) noun (plural **werewolves**) (in myths) a person who at times turns into a wolf.

**Werner** (**ver**-ner), Alfred (1866–1919), Swiss chemist, noted for his work on the structure of chemical compounds.

**wert** (*old use*) the past subjunctive of **be**, used with *thou*.

**Wesley**, John (1703–91), English preacher, the founder of Methodism. His brother Charles (1707–88) was also a preacher and the composer of many well-known hymns. □ **Wesleyan** adjective & noun

**Wessex** the kingdom of the West Saxons, which by the 10th century covered much of southern England.

**West**, Dame Rebecca (real name: Cicily Isabel Fairfield) (1892–1983), English novelist, journalist, and feminist.

**west** noun **1** the point of the horizon where the sun sets, opposite east; the direction in which this lies. **2** the western part of something. **3** (**the West**) Europe in contrast to Oriental countries; the States of western Europe and N. America. ● adjective **1** towards or in the west. **2** (of a wind) blowing from the west. ● adverb **1** towards or in the west. □ **go west** (*slang*) be destroyed, lost, or killed. **West Bank** the area on the west side of the River Jordan occupied by Israel from 1967. **West Country** the SW region of England. **West End** the part of London near Piccadilly, containing famous theatres, restaurants, shops, etc. **West Side** (*Amer.*) the western part of Manhattan.

**West Bengal** a State in eastern India.

**westbound** adjective travelling or leading westwards.

**westering** adjective (of the sun, etc.) moving towards the west.

**westerly** adjective **1** in or towards the west. **2** (of a wind) blowing from the west. ● noun a westerly wind.

**western** adjective **1** of or in the west. **2** of westerns. ● noun a film or story dealing with life in western North America during the wars with the American Indians, or with cowboys etc. □ **Western Church** the Churches of western Christendom as distinct from the Eastern or Orthodox Church. **Western hemisphere** the half of the earth containing the Americas.

**Western Australia** a State comprising the western part of Australia.

**westerner** noun a native or inhabitant of the west.

**Western Isles 1** the Hebrides. **2** an island area of Scotland consisting of the Outer Hebrides.

**westernize** verb (also **westernise**) make (a person or country) more like the West in ideas and institutions etc. □ **westernization** noun

**westernmost** adjective furthest west.

**Western Samoa** a country consisting of a group of nine islands in the SW Pacific.

**West Glamorgan** a county of South Wales.

**West Indies** a chain of islands in the Atlantic Ocean off Central America, enclosing the Caribbean Sea. □ **West Indian** adjective & noun

**West Midlands** a metropolitan county of central England.

**Westminster** Parliament or the Houses of Parliament in London. (¶ From the name of the district of London where the Houses of Parliament (**Palace of Westminster**) are situated.)

**Westminster Abbey** a church in London, originally the abbey church of a Benedictine monastery, where most of the kings and queens of England and of the UK have been crowned.

**Westphalia** (west-fay-liă) a former province of NW Germany.

**West Sussex** a county of SE England.

**West Virginia** a State of the USA, to the west of Virginia.

**westward** *adjective & adverb* (also **westwards**) in or towards the west.

**West Yorkshire** a metropolitan county of northern England.

**wet** *adjective* (**wetter, wettest**) **1** soaked, covered, or moistened with water or other liquid. **2** rainy; *wet weather*. **3** (of paint or ink etc.) recently applied and not yet dry. **4** allowing the sale of alcohol. **5** (*slang*, of a person) lacking good sense or mental vitality, dull. ● *verb* (**wetted, wetting**) **1** make wet. **2** urinate on. ● *noun* **1** moisture, liquid that wets something. **2** wet weather. **3** (*informal*) a drink. **4** (*informal*) a dull or unenterprising person. **5** (*informal*) a conservative politician with liberal tendencies. □ **wet behind the ears** immature, inexperienced. **wet blanket** (*informal*) a gloomy person who prevents others from enjoying themselves. **wet dream** a sexual dream in which semen is emitted involuntarily. **wet-nurse** (*noun*) a woman employed to suckle another's child; (*verb*) act as wet-nurse to; look after or coddle as if helpless. **wet one's whistle** (*informal*) have a drink. □ **wetly** *adverb*, **wetness** *noun*

**wether** *noun* a castrated ram.

**wetlands** *plural noun* swamps and marshes.

**wetsuit** *noun* a rubber garment worn by divers, windsurfers, etc. to keep warm.

**WEU** *abbreviation* Western European Union; an association of European countries formed to coordinate defence policies etc.

**we've** (*informal*) = we have.

**Weyden** (vy-děn), Rogier van der (*c.*1400–64), Flemish painter.

**whack** *noun* **1** a heavy resounding blow. **2** (*slang*) a share; *do one's whack*. ● *verb* strike or beat vigorously.

**whacked** *adjective* (*informal*) tired out.

**whacking** (*informal*) *adjective* very large. ● *adverb* very; *a whacking great house*.

**whale** *noun* (*plural* **whales** or **whale**) a very large sea mammal with a horizontal tail and a blowhole on the top of the head for breathing. □ **a whale of a** (*informal*) an exceedingly good; *had a whale of a time.*

**whalebone** *noun* a horny springy substance from the upper jaw of some kinds of whale, formerly used as stiffening.

**whaler** *noun* a person or ship engaged in hunting whales.

**whaling** *noun* hunting whales.

**wham** *interjection & noun* (*informal*) the sound of a forcible impact.

**wharf** (*pronounced* worf) *noun* (*plural* **wharves** *or* **wharfs**) a landing-stage where ships may be moored to load and unload.

**wharfage** (**wor**-fij) *noun* accommodation at a wharf; the charge for this.

**what** *adjective* **1** asking for a statement of amount, number, or kind; *what stores have we got?* **2** which; *what languages does he speak?* **3** how great or strange or remarkable; *what a fool you are!* **4** the or any that; *lend me what money you can spare.* ● *pronoun* **1** what thing or things; *what did you say?; this is what I mean.* **2** a request for something to be repeated because one has not heard or understood. ● *adverb* to what extent or degree; *what does it matter?* ● *interjection* an exclamation of surprise. □ **give a person what for** (*slang*) punish or scold him or her. **what-d'you-call-it, what's-his-** (*or* **her-** *or* **its-**) **name** (*informal*) substitutes for a name that one cannot remember. **what have you** (*informal*) other similar things. **what is more** as an additional point, moreover. **what not** other similar things. **what's what** (*informal*) what things are useful or important etc.; *she knows what's what.* **what with** on account of (various causes); *what with overwork and undernourishment he fell ill.*

**whatever** *adjective* **1** of any kind or number; *take whatever books you need.* **2** of any kind at all; *there is no doubt whatever.* ● *pronoun* anything or everything that; no matter what; *do whatever you like; keep calm, whatever happens.* □ **or whatever** or anything similar.

**whatnot** *noun* **1** something trivial or indefinite. **2** a stand with shelves for small objects.

**whatsoever** *adjective & pronoun* = WHATEVER.

**wheat** *noun* **1** grain from which flour is made. **2** the plant that produces this. □ **wheat germ** the embryo of the wheat grain, extracted as a source of vitamins.

**wheatear** *noun* a small migratory bird.

**wheaten** *adjective* made from wheat.

**wheatmeal** *noun* wholemeal flour made from wheat.

**Wheatstone**, Sir Charles (1802–75), English physicist, inventor of the kaleidoscope, stereoscope, concertina, and various electrical devices. □ **Wheatstone bridge** a device for measuring electrical resistance.

**wheedle** *verb* coax; persuade or obtain by coaxing.

**wheel** *noun* **1** a disc or circular frame arranged to revolve on a shaft that passes through its centre. **2** something resembling this. **3** a machine etc. of which a wheel is an essential part. **4** motion like that of a wheel or of a line of persons that pivots on one end. **5** (**wheels**) (*slang*) a car. ●*verb* **1** push or pull (a bicycle or cart etc. with wheels) along. **2** turn or cause to turn like a wheel; change direction and face another way; *he wheeled round in astonishment.* **3** move in circles or curves. □ **at the wheel 1** driving a vehicle or directing a ship's course. **2** in control of affairs. **wheel and deal** scheme so as to exert influence. **wheel clamp** a clamp for locking the wheel of an illegally parked vehicle to immobilize it until the driver pays a fine. **wheels within wheels** secret or indirect motives and influences interacting with one another.

**wheelbarrow** *noun* an open container for moving small loads, with a wheel beneath one end and two handles and legs at the other.

**wheelbase** *noun* the distance between the front and rear axles of a vehicle.

**wheelchair** *noun* a chair on wheels, for use by a person who cannot walk.

**wheeler-dealer** *noun* a scheming person who negotiates political or commercial deals.

**wheelhouse** *noun* a steersman's shelter.

**wheelie** *noun* the stunt of riding a bicycle or motor cycle with the front wheel off the ground.

**wheelwright** *noun* a maker or repairer of wooden wheels.

**wheeze** *verb* breathe with an audible hoarse whistling sound. ●*noun* **1** the sound of wheezing. **2** (*slang*) a clever scheme or plan. □ **wheezy** *adjective*, **wheeziness** *noun*

**whelk** *noun* any of several sea snails, especially one used as food.

**whelp** *noun* a young dog, a pup. ●*verb* give birth to (puppies).

**when** *adverb* **1** at what time?; on what occasion? **2** at which time; *there are times when joking is out of place.* ●*conjunction* **1** at the time that, on the occasion that; whenever; as soon as. **2** although; considering that, since; *why risk it when you know it's dangerous?* ●*pronoun* what or which time; *from when does the agreement date?*

**whence** *adverb & conjunction* (*formal or old use*) from where, from what place or source; from which.

■**Usage** In questions, *whence* is now replaced by *where…from.* The phrase *from whence* is found frequently in translations of the Bible and occurs also in Shakespeare and Dickens, but strictly the word *from* is unnecessary and should be omitted.

**whenever** *conjunction & adverb* at whatever time; on whatever occasion; every time that.

**whensoever** *conjunction & adverb* (*formal*) whenever.

**where** *adverb & conjunction* **1** at or in what or which place, position, or circumstances. **2** in what respect; from what place, source, or origin. **3** to what place. **4** in or at or to the place in which; *leave it where it is.* ●*pronoun* what place; *where does it fit?*

**whereabouts** *adverb* in or near what place. ●*noun* (treated as *singular* or *plural*) a person's or thing's approximate location; *his whereabouts are uncertain.*

**whereas** *conjunction* **1** since it is the fact that. **2** but in contrast; *he is English, whereas his wife is French.*

**whereby** *adverb* by which.

**wherefore** *adverb* (*old use*) for what reason; for this reason.

**wherein** *adverb* in what; in which.

**whereof** *adverb & conjunction* of what or which.

**wheresoever** *adverb & conjunction* (*formal*) wherever.

**whereupon** *conjunction* after which, and then.

**wherever** *adverb* at or to whatever place. ●*conjunction* in every place that.

**wherewithal** *noun* (*informal*) the things (especially money) needed for a purpose.

**wherry** *noun* a light rowing-boat or barge.

**whet** *verb* (**whetted**, **whetting**) **1** sharpen by rubbing against a stone etc. **2** stimulate; *whet one's appetite.*

**whether** *conjunction* introducing an alternative possibility; *we don't know whether she will come or not.*

**whetstone** *noun* a shaped stone used for sharpening tools.

**whew** *interjection* an exclamation of astonishment, dismay, or relief.

**whey** (*pronounced* way) *noun* watery liquid left when milk forms curds, e.g. in cheese-making.

**which** *adjective & pronoun* **1** what particular one or ones of a set of things or people; *which Bob do you mean?* **2** and that; *we invited him to come, which he did very willingly.* ●*relative pronoun* the thing or animal referred to; *the house, which is large, is left to his son.*

■**Usage** As a relative pronoun *which* is used especially of an incidental description rather than one which defines or identifies something; see note at THAT.

**whichever** *adjective & pronoun* any which; that or those which; *take whichever one you like.*

**whiff** *noun* a puff of air, smoke, or odour.

**Whig** *noun* (*hist.*) a member of the political party in the 17th–19th centuries opposed to the Tories, succeeded in the 19th century by the Liberal Party.

**while** noun a period of time, the time spent in doing something; *a long while ago; we've waited all this while.* ● conjunction **1** during the time that, as long as; *make hay while the sun shines.* **2** although; *while I admit that he is sincere, I think he is mistaken.* **3** on the other hand; *she is dark, while her sister is fair.* ● verb (foll. by *away*) pass (time) in a leisurely or interesting manner.

**whilst** adverb & conjunction while.

**whim** noun a sudden fancy or impulse.

**whimper** verb whine softly, make feeble frightened or complaining sounds. ● noun a whimpering sound.

**whimsical** (wim-zik-ăl) adjective **1** impulsive and playful. **2** fanciful, quaint. □ **whimsically** adverb, **whimsicality** (wim-zi-kal-iti) noun

**whimsy** noun a whim.

**whin** noun (also **whins**) gorse.

**whinchat** noun a small brownish songbird.

**whine** verb **1** make a long high complaining cry like that of a dog. **2** make a long high shrill sound resembling this. **3** complain in a petty or feeble way; utter complainingly. ● noun a whining cry or sound or complaint. □ **whiner** noun, **whiny** adjective

**whinge** (informal) verb (**whinged**, **whingeing** or **whinging**) whine, grumble persistently. ● noun a whine or grumble.

**whinny** noun a gentle or joyful neigh. ● verb (**whinnied**, **whinnying**) utter a whinny.

**whip** noun **1** a cord fastened to a handle, used for urging animals on or for punishment. **2** a hunt official in charge of hounds. **3** an official of a political party in parliament with authority to maintain discipline among members of the party; party discipline and instructions given by such officials; *asked for the Labour whip.* **4** a written notice (underlined with a number of lines indicating the degree of urgency) issued by party whips, requesting members to attend on a particular occasion; *a three-line whip.* **5** a dessert made by whipping a mixture of cream etc. with fruit or flavouring. ● verb (**whipped**, **whipping**) **1** strike or urge on with a whip. **2** beat (cream or eggs etc.) into a froth. **3** move or take suddenly; *whipped out a knife.* **4** sew (an edge) with overcast stitches; bind (the end of a rope etc.) with a spiral of cord. □ **have the whip hand** be in a controlling position. **whipping boy** noun a person who is blamed regularly for someone else's mistakes. **whip-round** noun (informal) a collection of money from a group of people. **whip up** incite, stir up; *whip up support for the proposal.*

**whipcord** noun **1** cord made of tightly twisted strands. **2** twilled fabric with prominent ridges.

**whiplash** noun the lash of a whip. □ **whiplash injury** injury to the neck caused by a sudden jerk of the head (e.g. when travelling in a vehicle that collides with something and stops suddenly).

**whipper-in** noun (plural **whippers-in**) a person who is the whip of a pack of hounds.

**whippersnapper** noun a young and insignificant person who behaves in a presumptuous way.

**whippet** noun a small dog resembling a greyhound, used for racing.

**whippoorwill** noun the American nightjar.

**whippy** adjective flexible, springy.

**whipstock** noun the handle of a whip.

**whirl** verb **1** swing or spin round and round; cause to have this motion. **2** travel swiftly in a curved course. **3** convey or go rapidly; *the car whirled them away.* ● noun **1** a whirling movement. **2** a confused state; *her thoughts were in a whirl.* **3** a bustling activity; *the social whirl.* **4** (informal) a try; *give it a whirl.*

**whirligig** noun **1** a spinning or whirling toy. **2** a merry-go-round.

**whirlpool** noun a current of water whirling in a circle, drawing objects towards its centre.

**whirlwind** noun **1** a mass of air whirling rapidly about a central point. **2** (used as adjective) very rapid; *a whirlwind courtship.*

**whirr** verb make a continuous buzzing or vibrating sound like that of a wheel etc. turning rapidly. ● noun this sound.

**whisk** verb **1** move with a quick light sweeping movement. **2** convey or go rapidly; *he was whisked off to London.* **3** brush or sweep lightly from a surface; *whisk away the crumbs.* **4** beat (eggs etc.) into a froth. ● noun **1** a whisking movement. **2** an instrument for beating eggs etc. **3** a bunch of strips of straw etc. tied to a handle, used for flicking flies or dust away.

**whisker** noun **1** each of the long hair-like bristles growing near the mouth of a cat and certain other animals. **2** (**whiskers**) hair growing on a man's face, especially on the cheek. **3** (informal) a very small distance; *within a whisker of it.* □ **whiskered** adjective, **whiskery** adjective

**whisky** noun (Irish & Amer. **whiskey**) spirit distilled from malted grain (especially barley).

**whisper** verb **1** speak or utter softly, using the breath but not the vocal cords. **2** converse privately or secretly; plot or spread (a tale) as a rumour in this way. **3** (of leaves or fabrics etc.) rustle. ● noun **1** a whispering sound or remark; whispering speech; *spoke in a whisper.* **2** a rumour.

**whist** noun a card game usually for two pairs of players. □ **whist drive** a series of games of whist in which a number of people take part.

**whistle** noun **1** a shrill sound made by forcing breath through narrowed lips. **2** a similar sound made by a bird or by something thrown, or produced by a pipe etc. **3** an instrument that produces a shrill sound when air or steam is forced through it. ●verb make this sound; summon or signal or produce a tune in this way. □ **blow the whistle on** reveal and so bring to an end (an underhand deal, unacceptable practice, etc.); inform on. **whistle-blower** noun a person who blows the whistle on an underhand activity. **whistle for** (informal) expect in vain, wish for but have to go without. **whistle-stop** noun a brief stop (during a tour made by a politician etc.) e.g. for electioneering. □ **whistler** noun

**Whistler**, James Abbott McNeill (1843–1903), American-born painter and etcher.

**Whit** adjective of, including, or close to **Whit Sunday**, the seventh Sunday after Easter, commemorating the descent of the Holy Spirit upon the Apostles at Pentecost.

**whit** noun the least possible amount; not a whit better.

**White**, Patrick Victor Martindale (1912–90), Australian novelist.

**white** adjective **1** of the very lightest colour, like snow or common salt. **2** (**White**) of the human group with light-coloured skin. **3** pale in the face from illness or fear etc. ●noun **1** white colour. **2** a white substance or material; white clothes. **3** (**White**) a white person. **4** the white part of something (e.g. of the eyeball, round the iris). **5** the transparent substance round the yolk of an egg, turning white when cooked. **6** the white pieces in chess etc.; the player using these. □ **white ant** a termite. **white cell, white corpuscle** a leucocyte, a white blood cell. **white Christmas** one with snow. **white-collar worker** an office worker; one who is not engaged in manual labour. **white dwarf** a small very dense star. **white elephant** a useless possession. **white feather** a symbol of cowardice. **white flag** a symbol of surrender. **White Friars** Carmelites (so called from their white cloaks). **white gold** gold mixed with platinum to give a silver-coloured alloy. **white goods** large domestic electrical equipment. **white heat** the temperature at which heated metal looks white. **white hope** a person who is expected to attain fame. **white horses** white-crested waves on the sea. **white-hot** adjective at white heat, hotter than red-hot. **White House** the official residence (in Washington) of the President of the USA. **white lie** a harmless lie (e.g. one told for the sake of politeness).

**white magic** magic used for beneficial purposes. **white meat** poultry, veal, rabbit, and pork. **white noise** noise containing many frequencies with equal intensities; a harsh hissing sound. **white-out** noun a dense snowstorm with almost no visibility. **White Paper** (Brit.) a report issued by the government to give information on a subject. **white rose** the emblem of Yorkshire. **White Russian** Belorussian. **white slave** a woman who is tricked and sent (usually abroad) into prostitution. **white spirit** light petroleum used as a solvent. **white tie** a man's white bow-tie worn with full evening dress. **white wine** golden or pale yellow wine. □ **whiteness** noun, **whitish** adjective

**whitebait** noun (plural **whitebait**) a small silvery-white fish, the young of herrings and sprats.

**Whitehall** noun the British Government. (¶ From the name of a London street where there are many Government offices.)

**whiten** verb make or become white or whiter. □ **whitener** noun

**whitewash** noun **1** a liquid containing quicklime or powdered chalk used for painting walls, ceilings, etc. **2** a means of glossing over mistakes or faults. ●verb **1** paint with whitewash. **2** clear the reputation of (a person etc.) by glossing over mistakes or faults.

**whitewood** noun a light-coloured wood, especially one prepared for staining etc.

**whither** (old use) adverb to what place. ●conjunction to the or any place which.

**whiting** noun **1** (plural **whiting**) a small sea fish with white flesh, used as food. **2** ground chalk used in white-washing, plate-cleaning, etc.

**Whitlam**, (Edward) Gough (born 1916), Australian Labour statesman, Prime Minister 1972–5.

**whitlow** (wit-loh) noun a small abscess under or near a nail.

**Whitman**, Walt (1819–92), American poet.

**Whitney**, Eli (1765–1825), American inventor, remembered for his mechanical cotton-gin, pioneer of the manufacture of interchangeable parts, enabling weapons to be repaired instead of wholly replaced.

**Whitsun** noun (also **Whitsuntide**) Whit Sunday and the days close to it.

**Whittington**, Sir Richard (Dick) (died 1423), a medieval mayor of London, the subject of a popular folk tale.

**Whittle**, Sir Frank (born 1907), English engineer, inventor of the turbojet engine.

**whittle** verb **1** trim or shape (wood) by cutting thin slices from the surface. **2** (foll. by down or away) reduce by removing various amounts; whittled down the cost.

**Whitworth**, Sir Joseph (1803–87), English engineer, who in 1841 introduced standard screw-threads.

**whiz** (also **whizz**) *verb* (**whizzed**, **whizzing**) **1** make a sound like that of something moving at great speed through air. **2** move very quickly. ●*noun* a whizzing sound. □ **whizkid** *noun* (*informal*) an exceptionally brilliant or successful young person.

**WHO** *abbreviation* World Health Organization.

**who** *pronoun* **1** what or which person or persons? **2** the particular person or persons; *this is the man who wanted to see you.*

**whoa** *interjection* a command to a horse etc. to stop or stand still.

**who'd** (*informal*) **1** who had. **2** who would.

**whodunit** *noun* (also **whodunnit**) (*informal*) a detective story, play, etc. (¶ Humorous representation of the incorrect phrase 'who done it?')

**whoever** *pronoun* any or every person who, no matter who.

**whole** *adjective* **1** with no part removed or left out; *told them the whole story.* **2** not injured or broken; *there's not a plate left whole.* ●*noun* **1** the full or complete amount, all the parts or members. **2** a complete system made up of parts; *the universe is a whole and the earth is part of this.* □ **on the whole** considering everything; in respect of the whole though some details form exceptions. **a whole lot** (*informal*) a great amount. **whole number** a number consisting of one or more units with no fractions.

**wholefood** *noun* food which has not been unnecessarily processed or refined.

**wholegrain** *adjective* containing or consisting of whole grains.

**wholehearted** *adjective* with all possible effort or sincerity; total. □ **wholeheartedly** *adverb*

**wholemeal** *adjective* made from the whole grain of wheat etc.

**wholesale** *noun* the selling of goods in large quantities to be retailed by others. ●*adjective & adverb* **1** in the wholesale trade. **2** on a large scale; *wholesale destruction.* ●*verb* sell in the wholesale trade. □ **wholesaler** *noun*

**wholesome** *adjective* good for physical or mental health or moral condition; showing a healthy condition. □ **wholesomeness** *noun*

**wholewheat** *noun* wheat with none of the bran or germ removed.

**wholism** alternative spelling of HOLISM.

**who'll** (*informal*) = who will.

**wholly** *adverb* entirely, with nothing excepted or removed.

**whom** *pronoun* the objective case of WHO.

■**Usage** *who* is commonly used instead of *whom* in less formal contexts.

**whomever** *pronoun* the objective case of WHOEVER.

**whomsoever** *pronoun* the objective case of WHOSOEVER.

**whoop** (*pronounced* woop) *verb* utter a loud cry of excitement. ●*noun* this cry. □ **whoop it up** (*informal*) engage in noisy revelry.

**whoopee** *interjection* an exclamation of exuberant joy. □ **make whoopee** (*informal*) **1** have fun; live it up. **2** make love.

**whooping cough** (**hoop**-ing) an infectious disease especially of children, with a cough that is followed by a long rasping indrawn breath.

**whoops** (*pronounced* woops) *interjection* (*informal*) an exclamation of surprise or apology.

**whop** *verb* (**whopped**, **whopping**) (*slang*) thrash; defeat.

**whopper** *noun* (*slang*) **1** something very large. **2** a big lie.

**whopping** *adjective* (*slang*) very large or remarkable; *a whopping lie.*

**whore** (*pronounced* hor) *noun* a prostitute; a sexually immoral woman.

**whorehouse** *noun* a brothel.

**whorl** *noun* **1** a coiled form; one turn of a spiral. **2** a complete circle formed by ridges in a fingerprint. **3** a ring of leaves or petals round a stem or central point.

**whortleberry** *noun* a bilberry.

**who's** (*informal*) **1** who is. **2** who has. □ **Who's Who** a reference book containing a list of notable people and facts concerning them.

■**Usage** Do not confuse with WHOSE.

**whose** *pronoun & adjective* of whom, of which; *the people whose house we admired; the house whose owner takes pride in it; whose book is this?*

■**Usage** Do not confuse with WHO'S.

**whosoever** *pronoun* = WHOEVER.

**why** *adverb* **1** for what reason or purpose? **2** on account of which; *the reasons why it happened are not clear.* ●*interjection* an exclamation of surprised discovery or recognition. □ **whys and wherefores** reasons.

**Whymper**, Edward (1840–1911), English pioneer mountaineer.

**WI** *abbreviation* **1** West Indies. **2** Wisconsin. **3** Women's Institute.

**wick** *noun* a length of thread in the centre of a candle, oil-lamp, etc., by which the flame is kept supplied with fuel. □ **get on a person's wick** (*slang*) annoy or irritate him or her.

**wicked** *adjective* **1** morally bad, offending against what is right. **2** very bad or formidable, severe. **3** mischievous; *a wicked grin.* **4** (*slang*) excellent. □ **wickedly** *adverb*, **wickedness** *noun*

**wicker** *noun* thin canes or osiers woven together as material for making furniture or baskets etc.

**wickerwork** *noun* **1** wicker. **2** things made of wicker.

**wicket** *noun* **1** a wicket-door or wicket-gate. **2** a set of three stumps and two bails used in cricket, defended by the batsman. **3** the part of a cricket ground between or near the wickets. □ **wicket-door, wicket-gate** *noun* a small door or gate usually beside or within a larger one for use when this is not open. **wicket-keeper** *noun* a fielder in cricket stationed close behind the batsman's wicket.

**widdershins** *adverb* (also **withershins**) (especially *Scottish*) in a direction contrary to the apparent course of the sun (considered unlucky); anticlockwise.

**wide** *adjective* **1** measuring much from side to side, not narrow; *a wide river.* **2** in width; *one metre wide.* **3** extending far, having great range; *a wide knowledge of art.* **4** open to the full extent; *staring with wide eyes.* **5** at a considerable distance from the point or mark aimed at; *his guess was wide of the mark.* ● *adverb* widely; to the full extent; far from the target. ● *noun* (in full **wide ball**) a bowled ball in cricket that passes the wicket beyond the batsman's reach and counts one point to the batsman's team. □ **give a wide berth to** *see* BERTH. **wide-angle** *adjective* (of a lens) able to include a wider field of vision than a standard lens does. **wide awake** completely awake; (*informal*) fully alert. **wide boy** (*slang*) a person who is skilled in sharp practice. **wide-eyed** *adjective* surprised; innocent or naïve. **wide open** (of a place) exposed to attack; (of a contest) with no contestant who can be predicted as a certain winner. **wide-ranging** *adjective* covering an extensive range. **wide world** the whole world, great as it is. □ **widely** *adverb*, **wideness** *noun*

**widen** *verb* make or become wider.

**widespread** *adjective* found or distributed over a wide area.

**widgeon** (wij-ŏn) *noun* (also **wigeon**) any of several kinds of wild duck.

**widow** *noun* a woman whose husband has died. □ **widow's peak** a V-shaped growth of hair towards the centre of the forehead. □ **widowhood** *noun*

**widowed** *adjective* made a widow or widower.

**widower** *noun* a man whose wife has died.

**width** *noun* **1** wideness. **2** distance or measurement from side to side. **3** a piece of material of full width as woven; *use two widths to make this curtain.*

**widthways** *adverb* in the direction of the width of something.

**wield** (*pronounced* weeld) *verb* **1** hold and use (a weapon or tool etc.) with the hands. **2** have and use (power).

**Wiener schnitzel** (vee-ner **shnits**-ĕl) a veal cutlet covered in breadcrumbs and fried.

**wife** *noun* (*plural* **wives**) a married woman in relation to her husband. □ **wifely** *adjective*

**wig** *noun* a covering made of real or artificial hair, worn on the head.

**wigeon** alternative spelling of WIDGEON.

**wigging** *noun* (*informal*) a rebuke, a scolding.

**wiggle** *verb* move or cause to move repeatedly from side to side, wriggle. ● *noun* a wiggling movement.

**Wight** *see* ISLE OF WIGHT.

**wight** *noun* (*old use*) a person.

**Wightman Cup** an annual lawn tennis contest between women players of the USA and Britain, named after the American player Mrs H. H. Wightman.

**wigwam** (wig-wam) *noun* a hut or tent made by fastening skins or mats over a framework of poles, as formerly used by American Indians.

**Wilberforce**, William (1759–1833), English philanthropist, best known for his work for the abolition of the slave trade.

**wilco** *interjection* = 'will comply', used in signalling etc. to indicate that directions received will be carried out.

**wild** *adjective* **1** living or growing in its original natural state, not domesticated or tame or cultivated. **2** not civilized, barbarous. **3** (of scenery) looking very desolate; not cultivated. **4** lacking restraint or discipline or control, disorderly. **5** tempestuous, stormy; *a wild night.* **6** full of strong unrestrained feeling; very eager, excited, enthusiastic, or angry etc. **7** extremely foolish or unreasonable; *these wild ideas.* **8** random; *a wild guess.* ● *adverb* in a wild manner; *shooting wild.* □ **the wilds** districts far from civilization. **run wild** grow or behave without being checked or restrained. **wild card 1** a card having any value chosen by the player holding it. **2** *Computing* a character that will match any character or combination of characters. **wild-goose chase** a useless search, a hopeless quest. **wild rice** a tall grass (not of the rice family) yielding slender edible grains with a black husk. **Wild West** the western States of the USA during the period when they were lawless frontier districts. □ **wildly** *adverb*, **wildness** *noun*

**wildcat** *adjective* **1** reckless or impracticable, especially in business and finance; *wildcat schemes*. **2** (of strikes) sudden and unofficial.

**Wilde**, Oscar Fingal O'Flahertie Wills (1854–1900), Irish-born playwright and poet.

**wildebeest** (**wil-di-beest**) *noun* (*plural* **wildebeest** *or* **wildebeests**) a gnu.

**wilderness** *noun* a wild uncultivated area.

**wildfire** *noun* □ **spread like wildfire** (of rumours etc.) spread very fast.

**wildfowl** *noun* birds that are hunted as game (e.g. ducks and geese, quail, pheasants).

**wildlife** *noun* wild animals collectively.

**wile** *noun* a piece of trickery intended to deceive or attract someone.

**wilful** *adjective* (*Amer.* **willful**) **1** done with deliberate intention and not as an accident; *wilful murder*. **2** self-willed, obstinate; *a wilful child*. □ **wilfully** *adverb*, **wilfulness** *noun*

**will**[1] *auxiliary verb* (**wilt** is used with *thou*), see SHALL.

**will**[2] *noun* **1** the mental faculty by which a person decides on and controls his or her own actions or those of others. **2** will-power. **3** determination; *they set to work with a will*. **4** that which is desired or determined; *may God's will be done*. **5** a person's attitude in wishing good or bad to others; *with the best will in the world*. **6** written directions made by a person for the disposal of his or her property after death. ●*verb* **1** exercise one's will-power; influence or compel by doing this. **2** intend unconditionally; *God has willed it*. **3** bequeath by a will; *she willed her money to a hospital*. □ **at will** whenever one pleases; *he comes and goes at will*. **will-power** *noun* control exercised by one's will, especially over one's own actions and impulses.

**willful** Amer. spelling of WILFUL.

**William**[1] the name of two kings of England, one of Great Britain, and one of the United Kingdom, reigning as William I 'the Conqueror' (1066–87), William II 'Rufus' (1087–1100), William III 'of Orange' (1689–1702), William IV (1830–7).

**William**[2], Prince (other names: Arthur Philip Louis) (born 1982), eldest son of Charles, Prince of Wales.

**Williams**, Tennessee (real name: Thomas Lanier Williams) (1911–83), American playwright.

**willie** *noun* **1** alternative spelling of WILLY. **2** (**the willies**) (*slang*) nervous discomfort.

**willing** *adjective* **1** doing readily what is required, having no objection. **2** given or performed willingly; *we received willing help*. ●*noun* willingness; *to show willing*. □ **willingly** *adverb*, **willingness** *noun*

**will-o'-the-wisp** *noun* **1** a phosphorescent light sometimes seen on marshy ground. **2** an elusive person. **3** a hope or aim that lures a person on but can never be fulfilled.

**willow** *noun* a tree or shrub with very flexible branches, usually growing near water. □ **willow-pattern** *noun* a conventional Chinese design including a willow tree and a river, done in blue on a white background, especially on china. **willow-warbler** *noun* a small woodland bird with a tuneful song.

**willowherb** *noun* a plant with leaves like a willow and pale purple flowers.

**willowy** *adjective* **1** slender and supple. **2** having willow trees.

**willy** *noun* (also **willie**) (*informal*) a penis.

**willy-nilly** *adverb* whether one desires it or not.

**Wilson**, (James) Harold, Baron Wilson (born 1916), British Labour statesman, Prime Minister 1964–70 and 1974–6.

**wilt**[1] *see* WILL[1].

**wilt**[2] *verb* **1** (of plants or flowers) lose freshness and droop. **2** (of a person) become limp from exhaustion. ●*noun* a plant-disease that causes wilting.

**Wilton** *noun* a carpet with loops cut into thick pile, first made at Wilton in Wiltshire.

**Wilts.** *abbreviation* Wiltshire.

**Wiltshire** a county of SW England.

**wily** (**wy-li**) *adjective* (**wilier**, **wiliest**) full of wiles, crafty, cunning. □ **wiliness** *noun*

**Wimbledon** a suburb of London containing the headquarters of the All England Lawn Tennis and Croquet Club, and scene of an annual lawn tennis tournament.

**wimp** *noun* (*informal*) a feeble or ineffective person. □ **wimpish** *adjective*

**wimple** *noun* a medieval headdress of linen or silk folded round the head and neck, covering all but the front of the face.

**win** *verb* (**won**, **winning**) **1** be victorious in (a battle, game, race, etc.). **2** obtain or achieve as the result of a battle or contest or bet etc. **3** obtain as a result of effort or perseverance; *he won their confidence*. ●*noun* victory in a game or contest. □ **win over** persuade, gain the support of. **win through** achieve success eventually. **you can't win** (*informal*) there is no way of achieving success or of pleasing people.

**wince** *verb* make a slight involuntary movement from pain, distress, embarrassment, etc. ●*noun* a wincing movement.

**winceyette** *noun* a soft fabric woven of cotton and wool, used for nightclothes etc.

**winch** *noun* a machine for hoisting or pulling things by means of a cable which winds round a revolving drum or wheel. ●*verb* hoist or pull with a winch.

**wind¹** (*rhymes with* tinned) *noun* **1** a moving current of air, especially occurring naturally in the atmosphere. **2** a smell carried by the wind; *the deer we were stalking had got our wind.* **3** gas forming in the stomach or intestines and causing discomfort. **4** breath as needed in exertion, speech, or playing a musical instrument. **5** the wind instruments of an orchestra. **6** useless or boastful talk. ● *verb* **1** detect by the presence of a smell; *the hounds had winded the fox.* **2** cause to be out of breath; *we were quite winded by the climb.* **3** make (a baby) bring up wind after feeding. □ **get** *or* **have the wind up** (*informal*) feel frightened. **get wind of** hear a hint or rumour of. **in the wind** happening or about to happen. **like the wind** very swiftly. **put the wind up** (*informal*) alarm or frighten. **take the wind out of a person's sails** take away his or her advantage suddenly; frustrate him or her by anticipating arguments etc. **wind-break** *noun* a screen or row of trees etc. shielding something from the full force of the wind. **wind-cone** = WIND-SOCK. **wind instrument** a musical instrument in which sound is produced by a current of air, especially by the player's breath (e.g. a clarinet or flute). **wind-jammer** *noun* a merchant sailing-ship. **wind-sock** *noun* a tube-shaped piece of canvas open at both ends, flown at an airfield to show the direction of the wind. **wind-tunnel** *noun* a tunnel-like device in which an air-stream can be produced to move past models of aircraft etc. for studying the effects of wind. □ **windless** *adjective*

**wind²** (*rhymes with* find) *verb* (**wound** (*rhymes with* found), **winding**) **1** go or cause to go in a curving, spiral, or twisting course; *the road winds through the hills.* **2** twist or wrap closely round and round upon itself so as to form a ball. **3** wrap, encircle; *wound a bandage round his finger.* **4** haul, hoist, or move by turning a handle or windlass etc.; *wind the car window down.* **5** wind up (a clock etc.). ● *noun* **1** a bend or turn in a course. **2** a single turn in winding a clock or string etc. □ **winding-sheet** *noun* a sheet in which a corpse is wrapped for burial. **wind up 1** set or keep (a clock etc.) going by tightening its spring. **2** bring or come to an end. **3** settle and finally close the business and financial transactions of (a company going into liquidation). **4** (*informal*) arrive finally, end up; *he'll wind up in jail.* **5** (*informal*) provoke or tease (a person). □ **winder** *noun*

**windbag** *noun* (*informal*) a person who talks lengthily.

**windburn** *noun* inflammation of the skin caused by exposure to the wind.

**windcheater** *noun* a casual wind-resistant jacket.

**windfall** *noun* **1** an apple or pear etc. blown off a tree by the wind. **2** a piece of unexpected good fortune, especially a sum of money acquired.

**Windhoek** (vint-huuk) the capital of Namibia.

**windlass** (wind-lăs) *noun* a device for pulling or hoisting things by means of a rope or chain that winds round an axle.

**windmill** *noun* a mill worked by the action of wind on projecting parts (sails) that radiate from a central shaft.

**window** *noun* **1** an opening in the wall of a building or in a car etc., usually of glass in a frame. **2** this glass; *broke the window.* **3** a space for the display of goods behind the window of a shop etc. **4** an opening resembling a window. **5** an interval during which the positions of planets etc. allow a specified journey by a spacecraft; an opportunity. □ **window-box** *noun* a trough outside a window, for growing plants and flowers. **window-dressing** *noun* the displaying of goods attractively in a shop window; presentation of facts so as to create a favourable impression. **window-pane** *noun* a pane of glass in a window. **window-seat** *noun* a seat fixed under a recessed window; a seat next to a window in a train, plane, etc. **window-shopping** *noun* looking at goods displayed in shop windows etc. without necessarily intending to buy. **window sill** a sill below a window.

**windpipe** *noun* the principal passage by which air reaches the lungs, leading from the throat to the bronchial tubes.

**Windscale** *see* SELLAFIELD.

**windscreen** *noun* the glass in the window at the front of a motor vehicle.

**windshield** *noun* (*Amer.*) a windscreen.

**Windsor** the name assumed by the British royal house in 1917. □ **Duke of Windsor** the title conferred on Edward VIII on his abdication in 1936—an event precipitated by his decision to marry a divorced American woman, Mrs Wallis Simpson.

**Windsor Castle** a royal residence in Berkshire.

**windsurfing** *noun* the sport of surfing on a board to which a sail is fixed. □ **windsurfer** *noun*

**windswept** *adjective* exposed to or made untidy by the wind.

**windward** *adjective* situated in the direction from which the wind blows. ● *noun* the windward side or region.

**Windward Islands** a group of islands in the eastern Caribbean Sea, including Dominica, Martinique, St Lucia, and Barbados.

**windy** *adjective* (**windier**, **windiest**) **1** with much wind; *a windy night.* **2** exposed to high winds. **3** wordy, full of useless talk. □ **windiness** *noun*

**wine** *noun* **1** fermented grape juice as an alcoholic drink. **2** a fermented drink made from other fruits or plants; *ginger wine.* **3** dark purplish red. ● *verb* drink wine; entertain with wine; *they wined and dined us.* □ **wine bar** a bar or small restaurant where wine is the main drink available.

**wineglass** *noun* a glass for wine, usually with a stem and foot.

**winepress** *noun* a press in which grapes are squeezed in making wine.

**wing** *noun* **1** each of a pair of projecting parts by which a bird, bat, or insect etc. is able to fly. **2** a corresponding part in a non-flying bird or insect. **3** each of the parts projecting from the sides of an aircraft. **4** something resembling a wing in appearance or position (e.g. a projection on maple and sycamore seeds). **5** a projecting part extending from one end of a building; *the north wing was added in the 17th century.* **6** the part of the bodywork above the wheel of a motor vehicle. **7** either end of an army lined up for battle. **8** either of the players (*left wing, right wing*) in football or hockey etc. whose place is at the extreme end of the forward line; the side part of the playing area in these games. **9** an air-force unit of several squadrons. **10** a section of a political party or other group, with more extreme views than those of the majority. **11** (**wings**) the sides of a theatre stage out of sight of the audience; *waiting in the wings.* **12** (**wings**) a pilot's badge in the RAF etc. ● *verb* **1** fly; travel; *a bird winging its way home.* **2** enable to fly; send in flight. **3** wound slightly in the wing or arm. □ **on the wing** flying. **take wing** fly away. **under one's wing** under one's protection.

**wing-case** *noun* the horny cover of an insect's wing. **wing-chair** *noun* an armchair with projecting side-pieces at the top of a high back. **wing-collar** *noun* a high stand-up collar with turned-down corners. **wing commander** an officer of the RAF, next below group captain. **wing-nut** *noun* a nut with projections so that it can be turned by thumb and finger. □ **wingless** *adjective*

**winged** *adjective* having wings.

**winger** *noun* a wing forward in football etc.

**wingspan** *noun* (also **wing-spread**) the measurement across wings from one tip to the other.

**wink** *verb* **1** close and open one eye deliberately, especially as a private signal to someone. **2** (of a light or star etc.) shine with a light that flashes quickly on and off or twinkles. ● *noun* **1** an act of winking. **2** a brief period of sleep; *didn't sleep a wink.* □ **tip a person the wink** see TIP². **wink at** pretend not to notice something that should be stopped or condemned.

**winker** *noun* a signal-light on a motor vehicle, flashing to indicate a change of direction.

**winkle** *noun* an edible sea snail. ● *verb* (foll. by *out*) extract, prise out. □ **winkle-pickers** *plural noun* shoes with long pointed toes.

**winner** *noun* **1** a person who wins. **2** something successful; *her latest novel is a winner.*

**winning** see WIN. ● *adjective* charming, persuasive; *a winning smile.* ● *plural noun* (**winnings**) money won in betting or at cards etc. □ **winning post** a post marking the end of a race.

**Winnipeg** the capital of Manitoba, Canada. □ **Lake Winnipeg** a large lake north of the city.

**winnow** *verb* **1** expose (grain) to a current of air so that the loose dry outer part is blown away; separate (chaff) in this way. **2** sift or separate from worthless or inferior elements; *winnow out the truth from the falsehoods.*

**wino** (wy-noh) *noun* (*plural* **winos**) (*slang*) an alcoholic.

**winsome** *adjective* having an engagingly attractive appearance or manner. □ **winsomely** *adverb*

**winter** *noun* the coldest season of the year, from December to February in the northern hemisphere. ● *verb* spend the winter; *decided to winter in Egypt.* □ **winter garden** a garden or conservatory of plants kept flourishing in winter. **winter solstice** the solstice occurring about 22 December. **winter sports** open-air sports on snow or ice (e.g. skiing, skating).

**wintergreen** *noun* any of various creeping or low shrubby plants with leaves that remain green in winter, especially a North American plant yielding an oil used in medicine and for flavouring.

**Winterhalter** (vint-er-hal-ter), Franz Xavier (1806–73), German artist and international court painter.

**Winter Palace** the former Russian imperial palace in St Petersburg, later used as a museum and art gallery.

**wintertime** *noun* the season of winter.

**wintry** *adjective* **1** of or like winter, cold; *wintry weather.* **2** (of a smile etc.) chilly, lacking warmth or vivacity. □ **wintriness** *noun*

**winy** *adjective* like wine; *a winy taste.*

**wipe** *verb* **1** clean or dry the surface of by rubbing something over it. **2** remove by wiping; *wipe your tears away.* **3** spread (a substance) thinly over a surface. ● *noun* the act of wiping; *give this plate a wipe.* □ **wipe the floor with** (*informal*) inflict a humiliating defeat on. **wipe off** cancel or annul (a debt etc.). **wipe out** cancel; destroy completely; *the whole army was wiped out.*

**wiper** *noun* **1** something that wipes or is used for wiping. **2** (in full **windscreen wiper**) a rubber strip moving to and fro across a windscreen to remove rain etc.

**wire** *noun* **1** a strand or slender flexible rod of metal. **2** a barrier or framework etc. made from this. **3** a piece of wire used to carry electric current. ●*verb* **1** provide, fasten, or strengthen with wire. **2** install wiring in (a house). □ **get one's wires crossed** become confused and misunderstood. **wire-haired** *adjective* (of a dog) having stiff wiry hair. **wire-tapping** *noun* the tapping of telephone lines to eavesdrop. **wire wool** a mass of fine wire used for cleaning kitchen utensils etc.

**wireless** *noun* **1** radio, radio communications. **2** a radio receiver or transmitter.

**wireworm** *noun* the destructive worm-like larva of a kind of beetle.

**wiring** *noun* a system of wires for conducting electricity in a building.

**wiry** *adjective* (**wirier, wiriest**) **1** like wire. **2** (of a person) lean but strong. □ **wiriness** *noun*

**Wis.** *abbreviation* Wisconsin.

**Wisconsin** (wis-**kon**-sin) a State in the northern USA.

**wisdom** *noun* **1** being wise, soundness of judgement. **2** wise sayings. □ **wisdom tooth** the hindmost molar tooth on each side of the upper and lower jaws, usually cut (if at all) after the age of 20.

**wise**[1] *adjective* **1** having or showing soundness of judgement. **2** having knowledge. **3** (*slang*) aware, informed; *wise to something.* □ **be none the wiser** know no more than before; be unaware of what has happened. **wise guy** (*informal*) a know-all. **wise man** a wizard; one of the Magi. **wise up** (*informal*) become aware; learn (about); inform. **wise woman** a woman who is a witch; a fortune-teller. □ **wisely** *adverb*

**wise**[2] *noun* (*old use*) way, manner; *in no wise.*

**-wise** *combining form* **1** indicating direction or manner; *clockwise; lengthwise.* **2** with respect to; *businesswise.*

**wiseacre** (**wy**-zay-ker) *noun* a person who pretends to have great wisdom, a know-all.

**wisecrack** (*informal*) *noun* a witty or clever remark. ●*verb* make a wisecrack.

**wish** *noun* **1** a desire or mental aim. **2** an expression of desire about another person's welfare; *with best wishes.* ●*verb* **1** have or express as a wish. **2** formulate a wish; *wish when you see a shooting star.* **3** hope or express hope about another person's welfare; *wish me luck*; *wish him 'good day'.* **4** (*informal*) foist; *the dog was wished on us while its owners were on holiday.* □ **wish for** desire to have; express a wish that one may have (a thing).

**wishbone** *noun* a forked bone between the neck and breast of a bird (pulled by two people, the one who gets the longer part having the supposed right to magic fulfilment of any wish).

**wishful** *adjective* desiring. □ **wishful thinking** a belief that is founded on what one wishes to be true rather than on fact.

**wishy-washy** *adjective* weak or feeble in colour, character, etc.

**wisp** *noun* **1** a small separate bunch or bundle of something; *wisps of hair.* **2** a small streak of smoke or cloud etc. **3** a small thin person. □ **wispy** *adjective*

**wisteria** (wis-**teer**-iă) *noun* (also **wistaria**, *pronounced* wis-**tair**-iă) a climbing plant with hanging clusters of blue, purple, or white flowers.

**wistful** *adjective* full of sad or vague longing. □ **wistfully** *adverb*, **wistfulness** *noun*

**wit** *noun* **1** the ability to combine words or ideas etc. ingeniously so as to produce clever humour. **2** a witty person. **3** intelligence, understanding; *hadn't the wit to see what was needed; use your wits.* □ **at one's wits' end** at the end of one's mental resources, not knowing what to do. **have** or **keep one's wits about one** be or remain mentally alert. **to wit** that is to say, namely.

**witch** *noun* **1** a person (especially a woman) who practises witchcraft. **2** a bewitching woman. **3** an ugly old woman. □ **witch-doctor** *noun* the tribal magician of a primitive people. **witch hazel** (also **wych hazel**) an astringent lotion obtained from the bark of an American shrub; the shrub itself. **witch-hunt** *noun* a search to find and destroy or persecute people suspected of holding unorthodox or unpopular views.

**witchcraft** *noun* **1** the practice of magic. **2** bewitching charm.

**witchery** *noun* = WITCHCRAFT.

**with** *preposition* **1** in the company of, among. **2** having, characterized by; *a man with a sinister expression.* **3** using as an instrument or means; *hit it with a hammer.* **4** on the side of, of the same opinion as; *we're all with you on this matter.* **5** in the care or charge of; *leave a message with the receptionist.* **6** in the employment etc. of; *he is with Shell.* **7** at the same time as, in the same way or direction or degree as; *rise with the sun; swimming with the tide.* **8** because of; *shaking with laughter.* **9** feeling or showing; *heard it with calmness.* **10** under the conditions of; *sleeps with the window open.* **11** by addition or possession of; *fill it with water; laden with baggage.* **12** in regard to, towards; *lost my temper with him.* **13** in opposition to; *he argued with me.* **14** in spite of; *with all his roughness, he's very good-natured.* **15** so as to be separated from; *we parted with our luggage reluctantly.* □ **be with child** (*old use*) be pregnant. **I'm not with you** (*informal*) I cannot follow your meaning. **with it** (*informal*) **1** up to date, fashionable. **2** alert and clear-headed.

**withdraw** *verb* (**withdrew, withdrawn, withdrawing**) **1** take back or away; *withdrew troops from the frontier.* **2** remove (money deposited) from a bank etc. **3** cancel (a promise or statement etc.). **4** go away from company or from a place.

**withdrawal** *noun* **1** withdrawing. **2** the process of ceasing to take drugs to which one is addicted, often with unpleasant reactions; *withdrawal symptoms.*

**withdrawn** *adjective* (of a person) unresponsive, unsociable.

**withe** (*pronounced* with *or* wyth) *noun* (also **withy**) a tough flexible shoot, especially of willow, used for basketry, binding, etc.

**wither** *verb* **1** make or become shrivelled; lose or cause to lose freshness and vitality. **2** subdue or overwhelm by scorn; *withered him with a glance.*

**withers** (with-erz) *plural noun* the ridge between a horse's shoulder blades.

**withershins** = WIDDERSHINS.

**withhold** *verb* (**withheld, withholding**) **1** refuse to give, grant, or allow; *withhold permission.* **2** hold back, restrain; *we could not withhold our laughter.*

**within** *preposition* **1** inside, enclosed by. **2** not beyond the limit or scope of; *success was within our grasp; he acted within his rights.* **3** in a time no longer than; *we shall finish within an hour.* ●*adverb* inside; *seen from within.*

**without** *preposition* **1** not having or feeling or showing; free from; *without food; they are without fear.* **2** in the absence of; *no smoke without fire.* **3** with no action of; *we can't leave without thanking them.* **4** (*old use*) outside; *without a city wall.* ●*adverb* (*formal*) outside; *the house as seen from without.*

**withstand** *verb* (**withstood, withstanding**) endure successfully, resist.

**withy** = WITHE.

**witless** *adjective* foolish, unintelligent.

**witness** *noun* **1** a person who sees or hears something; *there were no witnesses to their quarrel.* **2** a person who gives evidence in a lawcourt. **3** a person who is present at an event in order to testify to the fact that it took place; one who confirms that a signature is genuine by adding his or her own

signature. **4** something that serves as evidence; *his tattered clothes were a witness to his poverty.* ●*verb* be a witness at or of; sign (a document) as a witness. □ **witness-box** *noun* (*Amer.* **witness-stand**) an enclosure from which witnesses give evidence in a lawcourt.

**witter** *verb* (*informal*) speak at annoying length about trivial matters.

**Wittgenstein** (vit-gĕn-styn), Ludwig Josef Johann (1889–1951), Austrian-born philosopher.

**witticism** (wit-i-sizm) *noun* a witty remark.

**wittingly** *adverb* knowing what one does, intentionally.

**witty** *adjective* (**wittier, wittiest**) full of wit. □ **wittily** *adverb*, **wittiness** *noun*

**wives** *see* WIFE.

**wizard** *noun* **1** a male witch, a magician. **2** a person with amazing abilities; *a financial wizard.* ●*adjective* (*slang*) wonderful, excellent. □ **wizardry** *noun*

**wizened** (wiz-ĕnd) *adjective* full of wrinkles, shrivelled with age; *a wizened face.*

**woad** *noun* **1** a blue dye formerly obtained from a plant of the mustard family. **2** this plant.

**wobble** *verb* **1** stand or move unsteadily; rock from side to side. **2** (of the voice) quiver. ●*noun* a wobbling movement, a quiver.

**wobbly** *adjective* wobbling, unsteady. □ **throw a wobbly** (*informal*) have a fit of annoyance or panic.

**Wodehouse** (wuud-howss), Sir P(elham) G(renville) (1881–1975), English humorous writer, whose best-known characters include Bertie Wooster and Jeeves.

**wodge** *noun* (*informal*) a chunk, a lump.

**woe** *noun* **1** sorrow, distress. **2** trouble causing this, misfortune. □ **woe betide** an expression of warning; *woe betide you if you get it wrong.*

**woebegone** (woh-big-on) *adjective* looking unhappy.

**woeful** *adjective* **1** full of woe, sad. **2** deplorable; *woeful ignorance.* □ **woefully** *adverb*

**wog** *noun* (*slang, offensive*) a foreigner, especially one who is non-white.

**wok** *noun* a large bowl-shaped frying pan, used especially in Chinese cookery.

**woke, woken** *see* WAKE[1].

**wold** *noun* an area of open upland country.

**wolf** *noun* (*plural* **wolves**) **1** a fierce wild animal of the dog family, feeding on the flesh of other animals and often hunting in packs. **2** a greedy or grasping person. **3** (*slang*) a man who seduces women. ●*verb* (often foll. by *down*) eat (food) quickly and greedily. □ **cry wolf** raise false alarms (¶ like the shepherd-boy in the fable, so that eventually a genuine alarm is ignored).

**keep the wolf from the door** ward off hunger or starvation. **wolf in sheep's clothing** a person who appears friendly but is really an enemy. **wolf-whistle** noun a whistle uttered by a man in admiration of a woman's appearance.

**Wolfe**, James (1727–59), British general, who captured Quebec in the struggle to end French rule in Canada.

**wolfhound** noun any of several large dogs of a kind originally used for hunting wolves.

**wolfram** (wuul-främ) noun tungsten (ore).

**wolfsbane** noun aconite, a poisonous plant with tall spikes of yellow flowers.

**Wolfson** (wuulf-sŏn), Sir Isaac (born 1897), British businessman and philanthropist.

**Wolsey** (wuul-zi), Thomas (c.1474–1530), English cardinal and leading statesman in the time of Henry VIII.

**wolverine** (wuul-ver-een) noun a N. American animal, the largest of the weasel family.

**wolves** see WOLF.

**woman** noun (plural **women**) **1** an adult female person. **2** women in general. **3** (informal) a charwoman. □ **women's lib** (in full **women's liberation**) a movement urging the liberation of women from domestic duties and from a subordinate role in society and business etc. **women's rights** the right of women to have a position of legal and social equality with men.

**womanhood** noun the state of being a woman.

**womanish** adjective **1** (scornful) effeminate, unmanly. **2** suitable for women but not for men.

**womanize** verb (also **womanise**) chase after women. □ **womanizer** noun

**womankind** noun (also **womenkind**) women in general.

**womanly** adjective having or showing qualities that are characteristic of or suitable for a woman. □ **womanliness** noun

**womb** (pronounced woom) noun the hollow organ (in woman and other female mammals) in which a child or the young may develop before birth; the uterus.

**wombat** noun an Australian animal resembling a small bear.

**women** see WOMAN.

**womenfolk** noun women in general; the women of one's family.

**womenkind** = WOMANKIND.

**Women's Institute** a worldwide organization of women, founded to enable those in rural areas to meet and engage in crafts, cultural activities, social work, etc.

**won** see WIN.

**wonder** noun **1** a feeling of surprise mingled with admiration, curiosity, or bewilderment. **2** something that arouses this; a remarkable thing. ●verb **1** feel wonder or surprise; I wonder that he wasn't killed. **2** feel curiosity about; try to form an opinion or decision about; we're still wondering what to do next. □ **do** or **work wonders** produce remarkably successful results. **I shouldn't wonder** (informal) I should not be surprised. **no** (or **small**) **wonder** it is not surprising.

**wonderful** adjective marvellous, surprisingly fine or excellent. □ **wonderfully** adverb

**wonderland** noun **1** a land or place full of wonderful things. **2** fairyland.

**wonderment** noun a feeling of wonder, surprise.

**wondrous** adjective (poetic) wonderful. □ **wondrously** adverb

**wonky** adjective (slang) shaky, unsteady; crooked.

**wont** (pronounced wohnt) adjective (old use) accustomed; he was wont to go to bed early. ●noun a habit or custom; he went to bed early, as was his wont.

**won't** (informal) = will not.

**woo** verb (**wooed, wooing**) **1** (old use) court (a woman). **2** try to achieve or obtain; woo success. **3** seek the favour of; try to coax or persuade; wooing customers into the shop.

**Wood**, Sir Henry (1869–1944), English conductor, noted for his association with the Promenade Concerts.

**wood** noun **1** the tough fibrous substance of a tree and its branches, enclosed by the bark. **2** this cut for use as timber or fuel etc. **3** (also **woods**) trees growing fairly densely over an area of ground. **4** a ball of wood or other material used in the game of bowls. **5** a golf club with a wooden head. □ **can't see the wood for the trees** cannot get a clear view of the whole because of too many details. **out of the wood** (or **woods**) clear of danger or difficulty.

**woodbine** noun wild honeysuckle.

**woodchuck** noun a reddish-brown and grey North American marmot.

**woodcock** noun a game bird related to the snipe.

**woodcraft** noun knowledge of woodland conditions, especially that used in hunting.

**woodcut** noun **1** an engraving made on wood. **2** a print made from this, especially as an illustration in a book.

**wooded** adjective covered with growing trees.

**wooden** adjective **1** made of wood. **2** stiff and unnatural in manner, showing no expression or animation. □ **wooden spoon** a spoon made of wood, used in cookery or given as a prize to the competitor with the lowest score. □ **woodenly** adverb

**woodland** noun wooded country.

**woodlouse** *noun* (*plural* **woodlice**) a small wingless creature with seven pairs of legs, living in decaying wood, damp soil, etc.

**woodman** *noun* (*plural* **woodmen**) a forester.

**woodpecker** *noun* a bird that clings to tree trunks and taps them with its beak to find insects.

**woodpigeon** *noun* a large grey pigeon with white patches on its neck and across its wings.

**woodwind** *noun* **1** any of the wind instruments of an orchestra that are (or were originally) made of wood, e.g. clarinet, oboe. **2** these collectively.

**woodwork** *noun* **1** the art or practice of making things from wood. **2** things made from wood, especially the wooden fittings of a house.

**woodworm** *noun* the larva of a beetle that bores into wooden furniture and fittings.

**woody** *adjective* **1** like wood, consisting of wood; *the woody parts of a plant.* **2** full of woods; *a woody area.* □ **woodiness** *noun*

**woof**[1] *noun* the gruff bark of a dog. ● *verb* bark gruffly.

**woof**[2] *noun* = WEFT.

**woofer** (**woo**-fer) *noun* a loudspeaker for reproducing low-frequency signals.

**wool** *noun* **1** the fine soft hair that forms the fleece of sheep and goats etc. **2** yarn or fabric made from this. **3** something resembling sheep's wool in texture. □ **pull the wool over someone's eyes** deceive him or her. **wool-gathering** *noun* being in a dreamy or absent-minded state.

**Woolf**, (Adeline) Virginia (1882–1941), English novelist.

**woollen** (*Amer.* **woolen**) *adjective* made of wool. ● *plural noun* (**woollens**) woollen cloth or clothing.

**woolly** *adjective* (**woollier**, **woolliest**) **1** covered with wool or wool-like hair. **2** like wool, woollen; *a woolly hat.* **3** not thinking clearly, not clearly expressed or thought out. ● *noun* (*informal*) a knitted woollen garment, a jumper or cardigan. □ **woolliness** *noun*

**Woolsack** *noun* the large wool-stuffed cushion on which the Lord Chancellor sits in the House of Lords.

**Woolworth**, Frank Winfield (1852–1919), American businessman, who opened a chain of shops, in the USA and elsewhere, selling low-priced goods.

**woozy** *adjective* (*informal*) dizzy; dazed. □ **wooziness** *noun*

**wop** *noun* (*slang*, *offensive*) a person from southern Europe, especially an Italian.

**Worcester** (**wuus**-ter) *see* HEREFORD AND WORCESTER. ● **Worcester sauce** a sauce containing soy, vinegar, and spices, first made in the city of Worcester.

**word** *noun* **1** a sound or sounds expressing a meaning and forming one of the basic elements of speech. **2** this represented by letters or symbols. **3** something said, a remark or statement; *he didn't utter a word.* **4** a message, information; *we sent word of our safe arrival.* **5** a promise or assurance; *take my word for it.* **6** a command or spoken signal; *don't fire till I give you the word.* ● *verb* phrase, select words to express; *word it tactfully.* □ **by word of mouth** in spoken (not written) words. **have a word** converse briefly. **have words** quarrel. **word-blindness** *noun* = DYSLEXIA. **word for word** in exactly the same or corresponding words; *translate it word for word.* **the Word of God** (*or* **the Word**) the Bible. **word-perfect** *adjective* having memorized every word perfectly. **word processing** the use of a word processor to produce text. **word processor** a computer program designed for producing and altering text and documents; a computer and printer designed specifically for this purpose.

**wording** *noun* the way something is worded.

**wordless** *adjective* without words, not expressed in words; *wordless sympathy.*

**wordplay** *noun* witty use of words, especially punning.

**Wordsworth**, William (1770–1850), English poet, living chiefly in the Lake District.

**wordy** *adjective* using too many words. □ **wordily** *adverb*, **wordiness** *noun*

**wore** *see* WEAR.

**work** *noun* **1** physical or mental activity, especially as contrasted with play or recreation. **2** something to be undertaken; the materials for this. **3** a thing done or produced by work; the result of action. **4** a piece of literary or musical composition; *one of Mozart's later works.* **5** what a person does to earn a living; employment. **6** doings or experiences of a certain kind; *nice work!* **7** ornamentation of a specified kind; articles having this; things or parts made of certain materials or with certain tools; *fine filigree work.* **8** (**works**) (treated as *singular* or *plural*) a factory. **9** (**works**) the working parts of a machine, clock, etc. **10** (**works**) building operations, road repairs, etc. ● *verb* **1** perform work, be engaged in bodily or mental activity. **2** make efforts; *work for peace.* **3** be employed, have a job; *she works in a bank.* **4** operate, do this effectively; *it works by electricity; a tin-opener that really works; that method won't work.* **5** operate (a thing) so as to obtain material or benefit from it; *the mine is still being worked.* **6** purchase with one's labour; *work one's passage.* **7** cause to work or function; *he works his staff very hard; can you work the lift?* **8** bring about, accomplish; *work miracles.* **9** shape, knead, or hammer etc. into a desired form or consistency; *work the mixture into a paste.* **10** do or make by needlework or fretwork etc.; *work your initials on it.* **11** excite progressively; *worked them into a frenzy.* **12** make (a way) or pass or cause to pass slowly or by effort; *the grub works its way into timber; work the stick into the hole.* **13** become through repeated stress or pressure; *the screw had worked loose.* **14** be in motion; *his face worked violently.* **15** ferment; *the yeast began to work.* □ **the works** (*slang*) **1** everything. **2** complete or drastic treatment. **work-basket** *noun* a basket holding sewing materials. **work camp** a camp at which community work is done, especially by young volunteers. **work experience** temporary experience of employment offered to young people. **work in** find a place for, insert. **work-in** *noun* a takeover by workers of a factory etc. threatened with closure. **work of art** a fine picture, building, composition, etc. **work on** use one's influence on (a person). **work out 1** find or solve by calculation; be calculated; *it works out at £5 each.* **2** plan the details etc. of; *work out a plan.* **3** have a specified result; *it worked out very well.* **4** engage in physical exercise or training. **work over 1** examine thoroughly. **2** treat with violence. **work-shy** *adjective* disinclined to work. **work study** study of people's work and methods, with a view to making them more efficient. **work to rule** follow the rules of one's occupation with excessive strictness in order to cause delay, as a form of industrial protest. **work-to-rule** *noun* this practice. **work up** bring gradually to a more developed state; excite progressively; advance gradually to a climax.

**workable** *adjective* able to be worked, used, or acted upon successfully.

**workaday** *adjective* ordinary, everyday.

**workaholic** *noun* (*informal*) a person who is addicted to working.

**workbench** *noun* a bench for woodwork, metalwork, etc.

**workbook** *noun* a student's book with exercises.

**workday** *noun* a day on which work is regularly done.

**worker** *noun* **1** a person who works; one who works hard or in a specified way; *a slow worker.* **2** a neuter or undeveloped female bee or ant etc. that does the work of the hive or colony but cannot reproduce. **3** a member of the working class.

**workforce** *noun* the total number of workers employed or available.

**workhouse** *noun* a former public institution where people unable to support themselves

were housed and (if able-bodied) made to work.

**working** *adjective* engaged in work, especially manual labour; working-class; *a working man.* ●*noun* a mine or quarry etc.; a part of this in which work is or has been carried on; *disused mine-workings.* □ **working capital** capital used in the carrying on of business, not invested in its buildings and equipment etc. **working class** the class of people who are employed for wages, especially in manual or industrial work. **working-class** *adjective* of the working class. **working day** a day on which work is regularly done; the portion of the day spent in working. **working hypothesis** a hypothesis used as a basis for action. **working knowledge** knowledge adequate for dealing with something. **working order** a condition in which a machine etc. works satisfactorily. **working party** a group of people appointed to investigate and report or advise on something.

**workload** *noun* the amount of work to be done.

**workman** *noun* (*plural* **workmen**) **1** a man employed to do manual labour. **2** a person who works in a certain way; *a conscientious workman.*

**workmanlike** *adjective* characteristic of a good workman, practical.

**workmanship** *noun* a person's skill in working; the quality of this as seen in something produced.

**workmate** *noun* a person working with another.

**workout** *noun* a session of physical exercise.

**workpiece** *noun* a thing for working on with a tool or machine.

**workplace** *noun* the place where a person works.

**worksheet** *noun* **1** a paper on which work done is recorded. **2** a paper listing questions or activities etc. for students to work through.

**workshop** *noun* a room or building in which manual work or manufacture is carried on.

**workstation** *noun* **1** a computer terminal and keyboard; a desk or table with this. **2** the location of an individual worker or stage in manufacturing etc.

**worktop** *noun* a flat surface for working on, especially in a kitchen.

**world** *noun* **1** the universe, all that exists. **2** the earth with all its countries and peoples. **3** a heavenly body like it. **4** a section of the earth; *the western world.* **5** a time, state, or scene of human existence. **6** the people or things belonging to a certain class or sphere of activity; *the sporting world; the insect world.* **7** everything, all people; *felt that the world was against him.*

**8** material things and occupations (contrasted with spiritual); *renounced the world and became a nun.* **9** a very great amount; *it will do him a world of good.* □ **for all the world like** precisely like. **man** *or* **woman of the world** a person who is experienced in the ways of human society. **world-beater** *noun* a person or thing surpassing all others. **world-famous** *adjective* famous throughout the world. **world music** rock music incorporating elements of traditional music, especially from the developing world. **world war** a war involving many important nations; **First World War** that of 1914–18; **Second World War** that of 1939–45. **world-weary** *adjective* bored with human affairs.

**World Bank** the popular name of the International Bank for Reconstruction and Development, set up by the UN to promote the economic development of member countries.

**World Cup 1** any of various international sports competitions or the trophies awarded for these. **2** an international competition in Association football, held every fourth year between teams who are winners from regional competitions.

**World Health Organization** a UN agency whose aim is the attainment by all peoples of the world of the highest possible level of health.

**worldly** *adjective* **1** of or belonging to life on earth, not spiritual. **2** devoted to the pursuit of pleasure or material gains or advantages. □ **worldly goods** property. **worldly wisdom** wisdom and shrewdness in dealing with worldly affairs. **worldly-wise** *adjective* prudent or shrewd. □ **worldliness** *noun*

**World Meteorological Organization** a UN agency whose aim is to facilitate worldwide cooperation in meteorological research and services etc.

**worldwide** *adjective* occurring or known in all parts of the world. ●*adverb* throughout the world.

**worm** *noun* **1** any of several types of animal with a soft rounded or flattened body and no backbone or limbs. **2** the worm-like larva of certain insects, especially those that damage fruit or wood. **3** an insignificant or contemptible person. **4** the spiral part of a screw. ●*verb* **1** move with a twisting movement like a worm; make one's way by wriggling or with slow or patient progress. **2** obtain by crafty persistence; *wormed the secret out of him.* **3** rid of parasitic worms. □ **worm-cast** *noun* a tubular pile of earth sent up by an earthworm on to the surface of the ground. **worm's-eye view** (*humorous*) a view as seen from below or from a humble position.

**wormeaten** *adjective* **1** full of worm-holes; decayed. **2** old and dilapidated.

**wormwood** *noun* **1** a woody plant with a bitter flavour. **2** bitter mortification.

**wormy** *adjective* full of worms; wormeaten.

**worn** *see* WEAR. ●*adjective* **1** damaged by use or wear. **2** looking tired and exhausted.

**worried** *adjective* feeling or showing worry.

**worrisome** *adjective* causing worry.

**worry** *verb* (**worried, worrying**) **1** be troublesome to, disturb the peace of mind of. **2** give way to anxiety. **3** (often foll. by *at*) seize with the teeth and shake or pull about; *like a dog worrying at an old rag.* ●*noun* **1** a state of worrying, mental uneasiness. **2** something that causes this. □ **worry beads** a string of beads for fiddling with to occupy or calm oneself. **worry out** obtain (a solution to a problem etc.) by persistent effort. □ **worrier** *noun*

**worse** *adjective & adverb* **1** more bad, more badly; more evil or ill. **2** less good, in or into less good health or condition or circumstances. ●*noun* something worse; *there's worse to come.* □ **the worse for wear** damaged by use; injured or exhausted. **worse luck!** such is my bad fortune. **worse off** in a worse (especially financial) position.

**worsen** *verb* make or become worse.

**worship** *noun* **1** reverence and respect paid to a god. **2** acts or ceremonies displaying this. **3** adoration of or devotion to a person or thing. ●*verb* (**worshipped, worshipping**) **1** honour as a deity, pay worship to. **2** take part in an act of worship. **3** idolize, treat with adoration. □ **Your** (*or* **His** *or* **Her**) **Worship** a title of respect used to or of a mayor or certain magistrates. □ **worshipper** *noun*

**worshipful** *adjective* (also **Worshipful**) (in certain titles of respect) honourable; *the Worshipful Company of Goldsmiths.*

**worst** *adjective & adverb* most bad, most badly; most evil or ill, least good. ●*noun* the worst part, feature, state, event, etc.; *we are prepared for the worst.* ●*verb* get the better of, defeat or outdo. □ **if the worst comes to the worst** if the worst happens.

**worsted** (**wuu-stid**) *noun* fine smooth yarn spun from long strands of wool; fabric made from this.

**wort** (*pronounced* wert) *noun* **1** (*old use except in names of plants*) plant, herb; *St John's wort.* **2** an infusion of malt before it is fermented into beer.

**worth** *adjective* **1** having a specified value; *a book worth £10.* **2** giving or likely to give a satisfactory or rewarding return for, deserving; *the book is worth reading.* **3** possessing as wealth, having property to the value of; *he was worth a million pounds when he died.*

●*noun* **1** value, merit, usefulness; *people of great worth to the community.* **2** the amount of something that a specified sum will buy; *give me a pound's worth of stamps.* □ **worth while** *or* **worth one's while** worth the time or effort needed; *the scheme isn't worth while.*

■**Usage** *Worth while* is often written as *worthwhile*, and always when preceding the noun that it qualifies.

**worthless** *adjective* having no value or usefulness. □ **worthlessness** *noun*

**worthwhile** *adjective* worth the time or effort needed; *a worthwhile undertaking.*

■**Usage** See the note at WORTH.

**worthy** *adjective* (**worthier, worthiest**) having great merit; deserving respect or support; *a worthy cause; the cause is worthy of support; worthy citizens.* ●*noun* a worthy person. □ **worthily** *adverb*, **worthiness** *noun*

**would** *auxiliary verb* used **1** in senses corresponding to WILL[1] in the past tense (*we said we would do it*), conditional statements (*you could do it if you would only try*), questions (*would they like it?*), and polite requests (*would you come in please?*). **2** expressing something to be expected (*that's just what he would do!*) or something that happens from time to time (*occasionally the machine would go wrong*). **3** expressing probability; *she would be about 60 when she died.* □ **would-be** *adjective* desiring or pretending to be; *a would-be humorist.*

■**Usage** With the verbs *like, prefer, be glad,* etc., 'I would' and 'we would' are often used informally, but 'I should' and 'we should' are required in formal written English.

**wouldn't** (*informal*) = would not.

**wound**[1] (*pronounced* woond) *noun* **1** an injury done by a cut, stab, blow, or tear. **2** an injury to a person's reputation or feelings etc. ●*verb* inflict a wound on.

**wound**[2] (*pronounced* wownd) *see* WIND[2].

**wove, woven** *see* WEAVE[1].

**wow**[1] *interjection* an exclamation of astonishment or admiration. ●*noun* (*slang*) a sensational success. ●*verb* (*slang*) impress or excite greatly.

**wow**[2] *noun* a slow fluctuation of pitch in sound-reproduction, perceptible in long notes.

**WP** *abbreviation* word processor.

**WPC** *abbreviation* woman police constable.

**w.p.m.** *abbreviation* words per minute.

**WRAC** *abbreviation* Women's Royal Army Corps.

**wrack** *noun* **1** seaweed thrown up on the shore or growing there. **2** destruction; a wreck or wreckage.

**WRAF** *abbreviation* Women's Royal Air Force.

**wraith** (*pronounced* rayth) *noun* a ghost; a spectral apparition of a living person supposed to be a sign that he or she will die soon.

**wrangle** *verb* have a noisy angry argument or quarrel. ●*noun* an argument or quarrel of this kind.

**wrap** *verb* (**wrapped, wrapping**) **1** enclose in soft or flexible material used as a covering. **2** arrange (a flexible covering or a garment etc.) round a person or thing; *wrap a scarf round your neck.* **3** (foll. by round) *Computing* (of a line of text) continue on the next visible line when the edge of the screen is reached; (of a block of text) flow round a diagram, picture, etc. inserted in a document. **4** (foll. by round) (*slang*) crash (a vehicle); *he wrapped the car round a tree.* ●*noun* a shawl, scarf, cloak, etc. □ **under wraps** in concealment or secrecy. **wrap over** (of a garment) overlap at the edges when worn. **wrapped up in 1** with one's attention deeply occupied by; *she is completely wrapped up in her children.* **2** deeply involved in; *the country's prosperity is wrapped up in its mineral trade.* **wrap up 1** enclose in wrappings; put on warm clothing. **2** (*informal*) finish; cease talking.

**wraparound** *adjective* (also **wrapround**) (especially of clothing) designed to wrap round; curving or extending round at the edges.

**wrapper** *noun* **1** a cover of paper etc. wrapped round something. **2** a loose dressing gown.

**wrapping** *noun* material used to wrap something.

**wrasse** (*pronounced* rass) *noun* a brightly-coloured sea fish with thick lips and strong teeth.

**wrath** (*pronounced* roth) *noun* anger, indignation.

**wrathful** *adjective*, full of anger or indignation. □ **wrathfully** *adverb*

**wreak** (*pronounced* reek) *verb* inflict, cause; *wreak vengeance on a person; fog wreaked havoc with the train schedules.*

**wreath** (*pronounced* reeth) *noun* (*plural* **wreaths**, *pronounced* reethz) **1** flowers or leaves etc. fastened into a ring and used as a decoration or placed on a grave etc. as a mark of respect. **2** a curving line of mist or smoke.

**wreathe** (*pronounced* reeth) *verb* **1** encircle or cover with or as if with a wreath. **2** wind; *the snake wreathed itself round the branch.* **3** move in a curving line; *smoke wreathed upwards.*

**wreck** *noun* **1** the disabling or destruction of something, especially of a ship by storms or accidental damage. **2** a ship that has suffered a wreck. **3** the remains of a greatly damaged building, vehicle, etc. **4** a person whose physical or mental health has been damaged or destroyed; *a nervous wreck.* ●*verb* cause the wreck of, involve in shipwreck.

**wreckage** *noun* **1** the remains of something wrecked. **2** wrecking.

**wrecker** *noun* **1** a person who wrecks something. **2** a person employed in demolition work.

**Wren**[1] *noun* a member of the WRNS.

**Wren**[2], Sir Christopher (1632–1723), English architect and scientist, foundermember of the Royal Society, and designer of St Paul's Cathedral.

**wren** *noun* a small brown songbird with a short erect tail.

**wrench** *verb* twist or pull violently round; damage or pull by twisting; *wrenched it off.* ●*noun* **1** a violent twist or twisting pull. **2** pain caused by parting; *leaving home was a great wrench.* **3** an adjustable tool like a spanner.

**wrest** (*pronounced* rest) *verb* **1** wrench away; *wrested his sword from him.* **2** obtain by effort or with difficulty; *wrested a confession from him.*

**wrestle** *verb* **1** fight (especially as a sport) by grappling with a person and trying to throw him or her to the ground. **2** fight with (a person) in this way; *police wrestled him to the ground.* **3** (foll. by *with* or *against*) struggle to deal with or overcome; *wrestled with the problem.* ●*noun* **1** a wrestling match. **2** a hard struggle. □ **wrestler** *noun*

**wretch** *noun* **1** a very unfortunate or miserable person. **2** a despicable person. **3** (in playful use) a rascal.

**wretched** (**rech**-id) *adjective* **1** miserable, unhappy. **2** of poor quality, unsatisfactory. **3** causing discomfort or nuisance; displeasing; *this wretched car won't start.* □ **wretchedly** *adverb*, **wretchedness** *noun*

**wrick** alternative spelling of RICK[2].

**wriggle** *verb* move with short twisting movements. ●*noun* a wriggling movement. □ **wriggle out of** avoid (a task etc.) on some pretext; escape from (a difficulty) cunningly.

**Wright**[1], Frank Lloyd (1869–1959), American architect, who advocated a close relationship between building and landscape and the nature of the materials used.

**Wright**[2], Orville (1871–1948) and Wilbur (1867–1912), American brothers, pioneers of powered aeroplane flight.

**wring** *verb* (**wrung**, **wringing**) **1** twist and squeeze to remove liquid. **2** remove (liquid) in this way. **3** squeeze and twist firmly or forcibly; *wrung his hand; wrung the bird's neck.* **4** extract or obtain with effort or difficulty; *wrung a promise from him.* ●*noun* a wringing movement, a squeeze or twist. □ **wringing wet** very wet indeed.

**wringer** *noun* a device with a pair of rollers for wringing water out of washed clothes etc.

**wrinkle** *noun* **1** a small crease; a small furrow or ridge in the skin (especially the kind produced by age). **2** (*informal*) a useful hint about how to do something. ●*verb* make wrinkles in; form wrinkles. □ **wrinkly** *adjective*

**wrist** *noun* **1** the joint connecting hand and forearm. **2** the part of a garment covering this. □ **wrist-watch** *noun* a watch worn on a strap or band etc. round the wrist.

**writ**[1] (*pronounced* rit) *noun* a formal written command issued by a lawcourt or ruling authority directing a person to act in a certain way.

**writ**[2] *adjective* (*old use*) written. □ **writ large** in an emphasized form, clearly recognizable.

**write** *verb* (**wrote**, **written**, **writing**) **1** make letters or other symbols on a surface, especially with a pen or pencil on paper. **2** form (letters or words or a message etc.) in this way. **3** compose in written form for publication, be an author; *write music; he makes a living by writing.* **4** write and send a letter; *write to me often.* **5** (*Amer.*) write to; *I will write you soon.* **6** indicate clearly; *guilt was written all over her face.* **7** enter (data) in or on any computer storage device or medium; transfer from one storage device or medium to another; output. □ **write off** cancel; recognize as lost. **write-off** *noun* something written off as lost; a vehicle too badly damaged to be worth repairing. **write out** write (a thing) in full or in a finished form. **write up 1** write an account of; write entries in (a diary etc.). **2** praise in writing. **write-up** *noun* a published account of something; a review.

**writer** *noun* **1** a person who writes or has written something; one who writes in a specified way. **2** a person who writes books etc., an author. □ **writer's cramp** cramp in the muscles of the hand. **Writer to the Signet** a Scottish solicitor who conducts cases in the Court of Session.

**writhe** (*pronounced* ryth) *verb* **1** twist one's body about, as in pain. **2** suffer because of great shame or embarrassment; *writhing under the insult.*

**writing** *noun* **1** handwriting. **2** literary work, a piece of this; *in the writings of Charles Dickens.* □ **the writing on the wall** an event signifying that something is doomed (¶ after the Biblical story of the writing that appeared on the wall of Belshazzar's palace, foretelling his doom). **writing paper** paper for writing on, especially for writing letters.

**written** *see* WRITE.

**WRNS** *abbreviation* Women's Royal Naval Service.

**wrong** *adjective* **1** (of conduct or actions) contrary to justice or to what is right. **2** incorrect, not true. **3** not what is required or suitable; *backed the wrong horse.* **4** not in a normal condition, not functioning normally; *there's something wrong with the gearbox.* ●*adverb* in a wrong manner or direction, mistakenly; *you guessed wrong.* ●*noun* **1** what is morally wrong; *a wrong action.* **2** injustice, an unjust action or treatment; *they did us a great wrong.* ●*verb* **1** do wrong to, treat unjustly; *a wronged wife.* **2** attribute bad motives to (a person) mistakenly. □ **get a person wrong** misunderstand him or her. **in the wrong** guilty or mistaken. **on the wrong side of 1** in disfavour with or not liked by (a person). **2** over (a certain age); *on the wrong side of forty.* **wrong-foot** *verb* catch (a person) off balance or unprepared. **wrongheaded** *adjective* perverse and obstinate. □ **wrongly** *adverb*, **wrongness** *noun*

**wrongdoer** *noun* a person who acts illegally or immorally. □ **wrongdoing** *noun*

**wrongful** *adjective* contrary to what is fair, just, or legal. □ **wrongfully** *adverb*

**wrote** *see* WRITE.

**wroth** (*rhymes with* both) *adjective* (*literary*) angry.

**wrought** (*pronounced* rawt) (*old use*) = worked. ●*adjective* (of metals) beaten out or shaped by hammering. □ **wrought iron** iron made by forging or rolling, not cast.

**wrung** *see* WRING.

**WRVS** *abbreviation* Women's Royal Voluntary Service.

**wry** (*pronounced as* rye) *adjective* (**wryer**, **wryest**) **1** twisted or bent out of shape. **2** twisted into an expression of disgust or disappointment or mockery; *a wry face.* **3** (of humour) dry and mocking. □ **wryly** *adverb*, **wryness** *noun*

**wryneck** *noun* a small bird related to the woodpecker, able to twist its head over its shoulder.

**wt** *abbreviation* weight.

**WV, W.Va.** *abbreviation* West Virginia.

**WY** *abbreviation* Wyoming.

**wych elm** an elm with broader leaves and more spreading branches than the common elm.

**wych hazel** alternative spelling of WITCH HAZEL.

**Wyclif** (wik-lif), John (*c.* 1330–84), English theologian, a precursor of the Reformation.

**Wyo.** *abbreviation* Wyoming.

**Wyoming** (wy-**oh**-ming) a State of the western central USA.

**WYSIWYG** (**wi**-zi-wig) *adjective* (also **wysiwyg**) *Computing* indicating that text etc. is displayed on the screen in exactly the same way as it will appear when printed. (¶ From the initial letters of *what you see is what you get.*)

**wyvern** *noun* (in heraldry) a dragon with wings, two legs, and a barbed tail.

# Xx

**X** *noun* (also **x**) (*plural* **Xs** *or* **X's**) **1** (as a Roman numeral) ten. **2** an unknown or unspecified quantity (in maths usually **x**), person, etc. **3** a cross-shaped symbol used to mark a position on a chart, diagram, etc., to indicate that an answer etc. is wrong, to mark one's vote in an election, to symbolize a kiss, or used as a signature by a person who cannot write. ●*symbol* (of films) classified as suitable for adults only (in the UK superseded by *18*). □ **X chromosome** a sex chromosome, of which female cells have twice as many as male cells.

**Xavier** (**zay**-vi-er *or* **zav**-), St Francis (1506–52), Spanish missionary, one of the original seven Jesuits.

**Xe** *symbol* xenon.

**xenon** (**zen**-on) *noun* a chemical element (symbol Xe), a colourless odourless gas.

**xenophobia** (zen-ŏ-**foh**-biă) *noun* hatred or distrust of foreigners. □ **xenophobic** *adjective*

**Xenophon** (**zen**-ŏ-fŏn) (*c.*428/7–*c.*354 BC), Greek general and historian.

**xerography** (zeer-**og**-răfi) *noun* a dry copying process in which powder adheres to areas remaining electrically charged after exposure of the surface to light from the image of the document to be copied. □ **xerographic** *adjective*

**Xerox** (**zeer**-oks) *noun* (*trade mark*) **1** a xerographic process for producing photocopies. **2** a photocopy made in this way. ●*verb* (**xerox**) photocopy by a process of this kind.

**Xerxes** (**zerks**-eez) king of Persia 486–465 BC.

**Xhosa** (**koh**-să *or* **kaw**-să) *noun* **1** (*plural* **Xhosa** *or* **Xhosas**) a member of a Bantu people of Cape Province, South Africa. **2** their language.

**Xmas** *noun* (*informal*) = CHRISTMAS. (¶ The *X* represents the Greek letter chi (= ch), the first letter of *Christos* (the Greek word for *Christ*).)

**X-ray** *noun* a photograph or examination made by means of a kind of electromagnetic radiation (**X-rays**) that can penetrate solids and make it possible to see into or through them. ●*verb* photograph, examine, or treat by this radiation.

**xylophone** (**zy**-lŏ-fohn) *noun* a musical instrument consisting of flat wooden bars, graduated in length, which produce different notes when struck with small hammers. □ **xylophonist** *noun*

**Y** *noun* (usually **y**) (in maths) a second unknown quantity. ●*symbol* yttrium. □ **Y-chromosome** a sex chromosome occurring only in males. **Y-fronts** *plural noun* (*trade mark*) men's briefs with a Y-shaped seam at the front.

**yacht** (*pronounced* yot) *noun* **1** a light sailing vessel for racing. **2** a larger power-driven vessel for cruising. □ **yachtsman** *noun* (*plural* **yachtsmen**), **yachtswoman** *noun* (*plural* **yachtswomen**).

**yack** *verb* (*slang*) chatter persistently.

**yackety-yack** *noun* (*slang*) persistent chatter.

**yah** *interjection* (also **yah boo**) an exclamation of scorn or defiance.

**yahoo** (yă-**hoo**) *noun* a rough coarse person.

**Yahweh** (yah-way) (also **Yahveh**) the Hebrew name of God in the Old Testament (compare JEHOVAH).

**yak** *noun* a long-haired ox of central Asia.

**Yale lock** (*trade mark*) a type of lock for doors, with a revolving barrel.

**Yale University** an American university of New Haven, Connecticut, named after a notable 18th-century benefactor.

**yam** *noun* **1** the edible starchy tuber of a tropical climbing plant; the plant itself. **2** the sweet potato.

**Yama** (yam-ă) (*Hindu myth.*) the first man to die, who became the guardian, judge, and ruler of the dead.

**yammer** (*informal*) *verb* **1** complain peevishly or persistently. **2** jabber. ●*noun* yammering talk.

**Yamoussoukro** the capital of the Ivory Coast.

**yang** *noun* (in Chinese philosophy) the active male principle of the universe (complemented by *yin*).

**Yangon** (yang-awn) *see* RANGOON.

**Yangtze Kiang** (yang-tsi ki-ang) the principal river of China, flowing from Tibet to the East China Sea.

**Yank** *noun* (*informal*, often *scornful*) an American.

**yank** (*informal*) *verb* pull with a sudden sharp tug. ●*noun* a sudden sharp tug.

**Yankee** *noun* **1** = YANK. **2** (*Amer.*) an inhabitant of the northern States of the USA. □ **Yankee Doodle** a national song of the USA, originally used by British troops in the War of American Independence to deride the colonial revolutionaries.

**Yaoundé** (ya-uun-day) the capital of Cameroon.

**yap** *noun* a shrill bark. ●*verb* (**yapped, yapping**) **1** bark shrilly. **2** (*informal*) chatter.

**yarborough** (yar-ber-ŏ) *noun* a hand of cards in whist or bridge with no card above a 9. (¶ Named after the Earl of Yarborough (19th century) who is said to have betted against its occurrence.)

**yard¹** *noun* **1** a measure of length, = 3 feet or 0.9144 metre. **2** a long pole-like piece of wood stretched horizontally or crosswise from a mast to support a sail. □ **yard-arm** *noun* either end of a yard supporting a sail.

**yard²** *noun* **1** a piece of enclosed ground, especially one attached to a building, surrounded by buildings, or used for a particular kind of work etc.; *a timber yard*. **2** (*Amer.*) the garden of a house. **3** (**the Yard**) (*informal*) Scotland Yard.

**yardage** *noun* a length measured in yards.

**Yardie** *noun* (*slang*) a member of a Jamaican criminal gang, involved especially in drug-trafficking.

**yardstick** *noun* a standard of comparison.

**yarmulke** (yar-mul-kă) *noun* (also **yarmulka**) a skullcap worn by Jewish men.

**yarn** *noun* **1** any spun thread, especially for knitting or weaving. **2** (*informal*) a tale, especially one that is exaggerated or invented. ●*verb* (*informal*) tell yarns.

**yarrow** (ya-roh) *noun* a plant with feathery leaves and clusters of strong-smelling white or pinkish flowers.

**yashmak** *noun* a veil concealing the face except for the eyes, worn in public by Muslim women in certain countries.

**yaw** *verb* (of a ship or aircraft etc.) fail to hold a straight course, turn from side to side. ●*noun* a yawing movement or course.

**yawl** *noun* **1** a sailing boat with two masts. **2** a fishing boat.

**yawn** *verb* **1** open the mouth wide and draw in breath (often involuntarily), as when sleepy or bored. **2** have a wide opening, form a chasm. ●*noun* **1** the act of yawning. **2** (*informal*) something boring.

**yaws** *noun* a tropical skin-disease causing raspberry-like swellings.

**Yb** *symbol* ytterbium.

**yd** *abbreviation* (*plural* **yds**) yard.

**ye¹** *pronoun* (*old use*) you (more than one person).

**ye²** *adjective* (*supposed old use*) the; *ye olde teashoppe*.

**yea** (*pronounced* yay) *adverb & noun* (*old use*) yes.

**yeah** (*pronounced* yair) *adverb* (*informal*) yes.

**year** *noun* **1** the time taken by the earth to make one complete orbit of the sun, about 365¼ days. **2** (also **calendar year**) the period from 1 January to 31 December inclusive. **3** any period of twelve consecutive months. **4** (**years**) age, time of life; *he looks younger than his years.*

**yearbook** *noun* an annual publication dealing with events or aspects of the previous year.

**yearling** (yer-ling) *noun* an animal between 1 and 2 years old.

**yearly** *adjective* happening, published, or payable etc. once a year; annual. ● *adverb* annually.

**yearn** *verb* be filled with great longing. □ **yearning** *noun*

**yeast** *noun* a fungus that produces alcohol and carbon dioxide while it is developing, used to cause fermentation in making beer and wines and as a raising agent in baking.

**yeasty** *adjective* frothy like yeast when it is developing. □ **yeastiness** *noun*

**Yeats** (*pronounced* yayts), W(illiam) B(utler) (1865–1939), Irish poet and dramatist.

**yell** *verb* give a loud cry, shout. ● *noun* a loud cry, a shout.

**yellow** *adjective* **1** of the colour of buttercups and ripe lemons. **2** (*informal*) cowardly. ● *noun* **1** yellow colour. **2** a yellow substance or material, yellow clothes. ● *verb* make or become yellow. □ **yellow card** such a card shown by the referee to a football-player being cautioned. **yellow fever** a tropical disease with fever and jaundice. **yellow flag** a flag displayed by a ship in quarantine. **yellow line(s)** line(s) painted on the road beside a pavement to indicate that there are parking restrictions. **Yellow Pages** (*trade mark*) a telephone directory printed on yellow pages and grouping entries for businesses under the type of goods or services that they offer. **yellow streak** (*informal*) cowardice. □ **yellowish** *adjective*, **yellowness** *noun*

**yellowhammer** *noun* a small European bird, a bunting with a yellow head and yellow streaks on its body.

**Yellowstone** a National Park of the USA in Wyoming and Montana.

**yelp** *noun* a sharp shrill cry or bark. ● *verb* utter a yelp.

**Yeltsin,** Boris (Nikolayevich) (born 1931), Russian statesman, President of Russia from 1991.

**Yemen** (yem-ĕn) a country in the south and south-west of the Arabian peninsula. (North Yemen and South Yemen united in 1990.) □ **Yemeni** (yem-ĕni) *adjective & noun*

**yen**[1] *noun* (*plural* **yen**) the unit of money in Japan.

**yen**[2] *noun* a longing, a yearning. ● *verb* (**yenned, yenning**) feel a yen.

**yeoman** (yoh-măn) *noun* (*plural* **yeomen**) (especially *hist.*) a man who owns and farms a small estate. □ **Yeoman of the Guard** a member of the British sovereign's bodyguard, wearing Tudor dress as uniform. **Yeoman Warder** the official term for a 'beefeater' at the Tower of London.

**yeomanry** (yoh-măn-ri) *noun* a body of yeomen.

**Yerevan** the capital of Armenia.

**yes** *adverb* **1** it is so, the statement is correct. **2** what you request or command will be done. **3** (as a question) what do you want? **4** (in answer to a summons etc.) I am here. ● *noun* the word or answer 'yes'. □ **yes-man** *noun* a person who always agrees with a superior in a weak or sycophantic way.

**yesterday** *noun* **1** the day before today. **2** the recent past. ● *adverb* on the day before today; in the recent past.

**yesteryear** *noun* (*literary*) last year; the recent past.

**yet** *adverb* **1** up to this or that time and continuing; still; *there's life in the old dog yet.* **2** by this or that time; so far; *it hasn't happened yet.* **3** besides, in addition; *heard it yet again.* **4** before the matter is done with; eventually; *I'll be even with you yet.* **5** even; *she became yet more excited.* **6** nevertheless; *strange yet true.* ● *conjunction* nevertheless, but in spite of that; *he worked hard, yet he failed.*

**yeti** (yet-i) *noun* (*plural* **yetis**) = ABOMINABLE SNOWMAN.

**yew** *noun* **1** an evergreen tree with narrow dark green leaves and red berries. **2** its wood.

**Yggdrasil** (ig-dră-sil) (*Scand. myth.*) an ash tree whose roots and branches connect earth, heaven, and hell.

**YHA** *abbreviation* Youth Hostels Association.

**Yid** *noun* (*offensive slang*) a Jew.

**Yiddish** *noun* a language used by Jews of central and eastern Europe, based on a German dialect and with words from Hebrew and various modern languages.

**yield** *verb* **1** give or return as fruit, gain, or result; *the land yields good crops; the investment yields 15%.* **2** surrender, do what is requested or ordered; *the town yielded; he yielded to persuasion.* **3** be inferior or confess inferiority; *I yield to none in appreciation of his merits.* **4** (of traffic) allow other traffic to have right of way. **5** be able to be forced out of the natural or usual shape, e.g. under pressure. ● *noun* the amount yielded or produced; the quantity obtained.

**yin** *noun* (in Chinese philosophy) the passive female principle of the universe (complemented by *yang*).

**yippee** *interjection* an exclamation of excitement.

**YMCA** *abbreviation* Young Men's Christian Association.

**yob** *noun* (*slang*) a lout, a hooligan.
□ **yobbish** *adjective*

**yobbo** *noun* (*plural* **yobbos**) (*slang*) = YOB.

**yodel** (yoh-d'l) *verb* (**yodelled, yodelling;** *Amer.* **yodeled, yodeling**) sing so that the voice alternates continually between falsetto and its normal pitch, in the manner of Swiss mountain-dwellers. ●*noun* a yodelling cry. □ **yodeller** *noun*

**yoga** (yoh-gă) *noun* a Hindu system of meditation and self-control designed to produce mystical experience and spiritual insight; a system of physical exercises and breathing control used in yoga.

**yoghurt** (yog-ert) *noun* (also **yogurt**) a food prepared from milk that has been thickened by the action of certain bacteria.

**yogi** (yoh-gi) *noun* a person who is highly skilled in yoga.

**yoicks** *interjection* a cry used by fox-hunters to urge on hounds.

**yoke** *noun* **1** a wooden crosspiece fastened over the necks of animals pulling a cart or plough etc. **2** a piece of timber shaped to fit a person's shoulders to hold a pail or other load slung from each end. **3** a part of a garment fitting round the shoulders or hips and from which the rest hangs. **4** oppression, burdensome restraint; *throw off the yoke of servitude.* ●*verb* **1** harness by means of a yoke; *yoke oxen to the plough.* **2** link, unite; *yoked to an unwilling partner.*

**yokel** (yoh-kěl) *noun* a simple country person, a country bumpkin.

**yolk** (*rhymes with* coke) *noun* the round yellow internal part of an egg.

**Yom Kippur** (yom kip-**oor**) the most solemn religious fast day of the Jewish year, the Day of Atonement.

**yomp** *verb* (*slang*) march across country, humping heavy equipment and weapons. ●*noun* (*slang*) a march of this kind.

**yon** *adjective & adverb* (*dialect*) yonder.

**yonder** *adverb* over there. ●*adjective* situated or able to be seen over there.

**yonks** *plural noun* (*slang*) a long time, ages; *I haven't seen him for yonks.*

**yore** *noun* □ **of yore** formerly; of long ago.

**York 1** a city in North Yorkshire, seat of the archbishop, Primate of England. **2** the name of the English royal house (descended from the 1st Duke of York) from 1461 (Edward IV) until the death of Richard III (1485).

**yorker** *noun* a ball bowled in cricket so that it pitches immediately under the bat.

**Yorkist** *adjective* of the family descended from the 1st Duke of York (died 1402) or of the White Rose party supporting it in the Wars of the Roses. ●*noun* a member or adherent of the Yorkist family.

**Yorks.** *abbreviation* Yorkshire.

**Yorkshire** a former county of England, now divided among Humberside, North Yorkshire, and the metropolitan counties of South Yorkshire and West Yorkshire. □ **Yorkshire pudding** a baked batter pudding eaten with roast beef. **Yorkshire terrier** a small long-haired terrier.

**Yoruba** (yo-ruu-bă) *noun* (*plural* **Yoruba** or **Yorubas**) **1** a member of a Black people on the coast of West Africa, especially in Nigeria. **2** their language.

**Yosemite** (yoh-sem-iti) a National Park in eastern California in the USA.

**you** *pronoun* **1** the person(s) addressed. **2** one; anyone; everyone; *you can never tell.*

**you'd** (*informal*) **1** you had. **2** you would.

**you'll** (*informal*) = you will.

**young** *adjective* **1** having lived or existed for only a short time; not the eldest. **2** not far advanced in time; *the night is young.* **3** youthful, having little experience. **4** used in speaking of or to a young person; *young Smith.* ●*noun* the offspring of animals, before or soon after birth. □ **young person** *Law* a person between 14 and 17 years of age.

**youngish** *adjective* fairly young.

**youngster** *noun* a young person, a child.

**your** *adjective* of or belonging to you.

**you're** (*informal*) = you are.

**yours** *possessive pronoun* **1** belonging to you; the thing(s) belonging to you. **2** used in phrases for ending letters: **Yours** *or* **Yours ever** used casually to friends. **Yours faithfully** used for ending business or formal letters beginning 'Dear Sir' or 'Dear Madam'. **Yours sincerely** used in letters to acquaintances and to friends (other than close friends), and often also in business letters addressing a person by name (e.g. beginning 'Dear Mr Brown'), where it is now more frequently used than *Yours truly.* **Yours truly 1** used to slight acquaintances and in business letters (less formal than *yours faithfully* but more formal than *yours sincerely*). **2** (*informal*) = me; *the awkward jobs are always left for yours truly.*

━━━━━━━━━━━━━━━━━━━━━━

■**Usage** It is incorrect to write *your's* (see the note under ITS).

━━━━━━━━━━━━━━━━━━━━━━

**yourself** *pronoun* (*plural* **yourselves**) corresponding to *you*, used in the same ways as HIMSELF, HERSELF, etc.

**youth** *noun* (*plural* **youths**, *pronounced* yoothz) **1** being young. **2** the period between childhood and maturity; the vigour or lack of experience etc. characteristic of this. **3** a young man; *a youth of 16.* **4** young people

collectively; *the youth of the country.*
□ **youth club** a club where leisure activities
are provided for young people. **youth
hostel** a hostel providing cheap accommodation where people who are hiking or
on holiday etc. may stay overnight. **youth
hostelling** staying in youth hostels.

**youthful** *adjective* **1** young; looking or seeming young. **2** characteristic of young
people; *youthful impatience.* □ **youthfully**
*adverb,* **youthfulness** *noun*

**you've** (*informal*) = you have.

**yowl** *noun* a loud wailing cry, a howl. ● *verb*
utter a yowl.

**yo-yo** *noun* (*plural* **yo-yos**) **1** a toy consisting
of two circular parts with a deep grove
between, which can be made to rise and
fall on a string. **2** a thing that repeatedly
falls and rises.

**Ypres** (**ee-prĕ** *or humorously* **wy-perz**) a
town in Belgium, scene of some of the
bitterest fighting during the First World
War.

**yr.** *abbreviation* **1** year(s). **2** younger. **3** your.

**yrs.** *abbreviation* **1** years. **2** yours.

**YT** *abbreviation* Yukon Territory.

**YTS** *abbreviation* Youth Training Scheme.

**ytterbium** (**it-er-biŭm**) *noun* a metallic
element (symbol Yb).

**yttrium** (**it-ri-ŭm**) *noun* a metallic element
(symbol Y), compounds of which are used
to make red phosphors for colour-
television tubes.

**yuan** (**yoo-ahn**) *noun* (*plural* **yuan**) the chief
unit of money in China.

**Yucatan** (**yoo-kă-tahn**) a peninsula in SE
Mexico.

**yucca** (**yuk-ă**) *noun* a tall plant with white
bell-like flowers and stiff spiky leaves.

**yuck** *interjection* (also **yuk**) (*slang*) an expression of strong dislike, disgust, etc.

**yucky** *adjective* (also **yukky**) (*slang*) **1** messy,
disgusting. **2** sickly, sentimental.

**Yugoslavia** (**yoo-gŏ-slah-viă**) a former
country in the Balkans, bordering on the
Adriatic Sea. □ **Yugoslav** (**yoo-gŏ-slahv**),
**Yugoslavian** *adjective & noun*

**yuk, yukky** alternative spellings of YUCK,
YUCKY.

**Yukon** (**yoo-kon**) a river of North America,
rising in Canada and flowing through
Alaska to the Bering Sea.

**Yukon Territory** (**yoo-kon**) a Territory of
NW Canada.

**yule** (*pronounced* **yool**) *noun* (in full **yule-
tide**) (*old use*) the Christmas festival.
□ **yule log 1** a large log traditionally burnt
in the hearth on Christmas Eve. **2** a log-
shaped chocolate cake eaten at Christmas.

**yummy** *adjective* (*informal*) tasty, delicious.

**yum-yum** *interjection* an exclamation of
pleasure at eating or at the thought of
eating.

**yuppie** *noun* (also **yuppy**) (*informal, often
scornful*) a young urban professional person.

**YWCA** *abbreviation* Young Women's Christian
Association.

**z** *noun* (in maths) a third unknown quantity.

**zabaglione** (za-bă-**lyoh**-ni) *noun* an Italian dessert of whipped egg yolks, sugar, and wine.

**Zagreb** (zag-reb) the capital of Croatia.

**Zaïre** (zah-eer) **1** a major river in central Africa, largely within the republic of Zaïre, flowing into the Atlantic Ocean. **2** a country in central Africa with a short coastline on the Atlantic Ocean. □ **Zaïrean** *adjective & noun*

**Zambezi** (zam-bee-zi) a river of Africa forming the border between Zambia and Zimbabwe, flowing into the Indian Ocean.

**Zambia** a landlocked country in central Africa. □ **Zambian** *adjective & noun*

**zany** *adjective* (**zanier, zaniest**) crazily funny.

**Zanzibar** an island off the coast of East Africa, united with Tanganyika to form the republic of Tanzania.

**zap** *verb* (**zapped, zapping**) (*slang*) hit; attack; knock out, kill.

**zappy** *adjective* (*informal*) lively; striking and forceful.

**Zarathustra** (za-rǎ-**thuss**-trǎ) the Old Persian name for Zoroaster.

**Zátopek** (zah-tǒ-pek), Emil (born 1922), Czech long-distance runner, Olympic gold medallist.

**zeal** (*pronounced* zeel) *noun* enthusiasm; hearty and persistent effort.

**zealot** (zel-ǒt) *noun* a zealous person, a fanatic. □ **zealotry** *noun*

**zealous** (zel-ǔs) *adjective* full of zeal. □ **zealously** *adverb*

**zebra** (zeb-rǎ or zee-brǎ) *noun* (*plural* **zebra** or **zebras**) an African animal of the horse family with a body covered by black and white stripes. □ **zebra crossing** a pedestrian crossing where the road is marked with broad white stripes.

**zebu** (zee-boo) *noun* (*plural* **zebu** or **zebus**) a humped ox found in India, East Asia, and Africa.

**Zechariah** (zek-ǎ-ry-ǎ) **1** a Hebrew minor prophet of the 6th century BC. **2** a book of the Old Testament containing his prophecies.

**zed** *noun* the letter Z.

**zee** *noun* (*Amer.*) the letter Z.

**Zeeman**, Pieter (1865–1943), Dutch physicist, who discovered what is now known as the 'Zeeman effect', the splitting of the spectral lines of a substance by a magnetic field.

**Zeitgeist** (tsyt-gyst) *noun* the spirit of the times. (¶ German.)

**Zen** *noun* a form of Buddhism emphasizing the value of meditation and intuition.

**zenana** (zin-ah-nǎ) *noun* the part of the house where women of high-caste families in India and Iran are secluded.

**Zend** *noun* an interpretation of the Avesta, each Zend being part of the **Zend-Avesta**, Zoroastrian scriptures consisting of Avesta (=text) and Zend (= commentary).

**zenith** (zen-ith) *noun* **1** the part of the sky that is directly above an observer. **2** the highest point; *his power was at its zenith.*

**Zephaniah** (zef-ǎn-I-ǎ) **1** a Hebrew minor prophet of the 7th century BC. **2** a book of the Old Testament containing his prophecies.

**zephyr** (zef-er) *noun* (*literary*) a soft gentle wind.

**Zeppelin**, Ferdinand, Count von (1838–1917), German airship pioneer, whose airships (known as Zeppelins) were used during the First World War.

**zero** *noun* (*plural* **zeros**) **1** nought, the figure 0. **2** nothing, nil. ● *verb* (**zeroed, zeroing**) adjust (an instrument etc.) to zero. □ **zero hour** the hour at which something is timed to begin. **zero in on** focus one's aim on; go purposefully towards. **zero option** a disarmament proposal for the total removal of certain types of weapons. **zero-rated** *adjective* (of goods or services) on which the purchaser pays no VAT.

**zest** *noun* **1** keen enjoyment or interest. **2** a pleasantly stimulating quality; *the risk added zest to the adventure.* **3** the coloured part of the peel of an orange or lemon, used as flavouring. □ **zestful** *adjective*, **zestfully** *adverb*

**zeugma** (zewg-mǎ) *noun* a figure of speech using a verb or adjective with two nouns where it is appropriate to only one of these, e.g. *with weeping eyes and hearts.*

**Zeus** (*pronounced* zewss) (*Gk. myth.*) the supreme god, identified with Jupiter.

**Ziegfeld** (zeeg-feld), Florenz (1867–1932), American theatre manager, creator of the revues known as the *Ziegfeld Follies*, based on the productions of the Folies Bergère.

**ziggurat** (zig-er-at) *noun* a pyramid-shaped tower in ancient Mesopotamia surmounted by a temple, built in tiers which become smaller in size towards the summit.

**zigzag** *noun* a line or course that turns right and left alternately at sharp angles. ● *adject-*

*ive & adverb* forming or in a zigzag. ●*verb* (**zigzagged, zigzagging**) move in a zigzag course.

**zilch** *noun* (*slang*) nothing.

**zillion** *noun* (*informal*) an indefinite large number.

**Zimbabwe** (zim-**bahb**-wi) a country in SE Africa. □ **Zimbabwean** *adjective & noun*

**Zimmer frame** (*trade mark*) a walking frame.

**zinc** *noun* a white metallic element (symbol Zn), used in alloys and to coat iron and steel as a protection against corrosion.

**zing** (*informal*) *noun* vigour, energy. ●*verb* move swiftly or with a shrill sound.

**zinnia** (**zin**-iă) *noun* a daisy-like garden plant with brightly coloured flowers.

**Zion** (**zy**-ŏn) *noun* **1** ancient Jerusalem; its holy hill. **2** the Jewish religion. **3** the Christian Church. **4** a Nonconformist chapel. **5** the kingdom of heaven.

**Zionism** (**zy**-ŏn-izm) *noun* a movement founded in 1897 that has sought and achieved the founding of a Jewish homeland in Palestine. □ **Zionist** *noun & adjective*

**zip** *noun* **1** a short sharp sound like that of a bullet going through the air. **2** energy, vigour, liveliness. **3** a zip-fastener. ●*verb* (**zipped, zipping**) **1** open or close with a zip-fastener. **2** move with a zip or at high speed. □ **zip-fastener** *noun* a fastening device consisting of two flexible strips of material with projections that interlock when brought together by a sliding tab.

**Zip code** (*Amer.*) a postal code.

**zipper** *noun* (especially *Amer.*) a zip-fastener.

**zippy** *adjective* (**zippier, zippiest**) (*informal*) lively, speedy.

**zircon** (**zer**-kon) *noun* a bluish-white gem cut from a translucent mineral.

**zirconium** (zer-**koh**-niŭm) *noun* a grey metallic element (symbol Zr), with a variety of uses in industry.

**zit** *noun* (*slang*) a pimple.

**zither** (**zi**th-er) *noun* a musical instrument with many strings stretched over a shallow boxlike body, played by plucking with the fingers of both hands.

**zloty** (**zwot**-i) *noun* (*plural* **zloty** or **zlotys**) the unit of money in Poland.

**Zn** *symbol* zinc.

**zodiac** (**zoh**-di-ak) *noun* (in astrology) **1** a band of the sky containing the paths of the sun, moon, and principal planets, divided into twelve equal parts (called **signs of the zodiac**) each named from a constellation that was formerly situated in it. **2** a diagram of these signs. □ **zodiacal** (zŏ-**dy**-ăkăl) *adjective*

**Zola** (**zoh**-lă), Émile (1840–1902), French novelist, the leading exponent of naturalism.

**zombie** *noun* **1** (*informal*) a person who acts mechanically or lifelessly. **2** a corpse said to have been revived by witchcraft.

**zone** *noun* an area that has particular characteristics or a particular purpose or use; a defined region or area. ●*verb* **1** divide into zones. **2** arrange or distribute by zones; assign to a particular area. □ **zonal** *adjective*

**zonked** *adjective* (*slang*) exhausted; intoxicated.

**zoo** *verb* a zoological garden.

**zoological** (zoh-ŏ-**loj**-ikăl *or* zoo-ŏ-**loj**-ikăl) *adjective* of zoology. □ **zoological garden** (*or* **gardens**) a public garden or park with a collection of animals for exhibition, conservation, and study.

**zoology** (zoh-**ol**-ŏji *or* zoo-**ol**-ŏji) *noun* the scientific study of animals. □ **zoologist** *noun*

**zoom** *verb* **1** move quickly, especially with a buzzing sound. **2** rise quickly; *prices had zoomed.* **3** (often foll. by *in* or *in on*) (in photography) alter the size of the image by means of a zoom lens. □ **zoom lens** a camera lens that can be adjusted from a long shot to a close-up (and vice versa), giving an effect of going steadily closer to (or further from) the subject.

**zoophyte** (**zoh**-ŏ-fyt) *noun* a plantlike animal, especially a coral, sea anemone, or sponge.

**Zoroaster** (zo-roh-**ast**-er) the Greek name for the Persian prophet Zarathustra (6th century BC or earlier), founder of Zoroastrianism.

**Zoroastrian** (zo-roh-**ast**-ri-ăn) *noun* a person who believes in **Zoroastrianism**, the ancient Persian religion taught by Zoroaster (or Zarathustra) and his followers, based on the conflict between a spirit of light and good and one of darkness and evil. ●*adjective* of Zoroaster or Zoroastrianism.

**Zr** (*symbol*) zirconium.

**zucchini** (zuuk-ee-ni) *noun* (*plural* **zucchini** or **zucchinis**) (especially *Amer. & Austral.*) a courgette.

**Zulu** *noun* (*plural* **Zulus**) **1** a member of a Bantu people of South Africa. **2** their language.

**Zululand** a region of South Africa, in Natal.

**Zurbarán** (thoor-ber-**ahn**), Francisco (1598–1664), Spanish painter, especially of religious pictures.

**Zurich** (**zewr**-ik) the largest city in Switzerland, situated on Lake Zurich.

**zygote** (**zy**-goht) *noun* a cell formed by the union of two gametes.

**OXFORD**

# MORE OXFORD PAPERBACKS

This book is just one of nearly 1000 Oxford Paperbacks currently in print. If you would like details of other Oxford Paperbacks, including titles in the World's Classics, Oxford Reference, Oxford Books, OPUS, Past Masters, Oxford Authors, and Oxford Shakespeare series, please write to:

**UK and Europe:** Oxford Paperbacks Publicity Manager, Arts and Reference Publicity Department, Oxford University Press, Walton Street, Oxford OX2 6DP.

Customers in UK and Europe will find Oxford Paperbacks available in all good bookshops. But in case of difficulty please send orders to the Cash-with-Order Department, Oxford University Press Distribution Services, Saxon Way West, Corby, Northants NN18 9ES. Tel: 0536 741519; Fax: 0536 746337. Please send a cheque for the total cost of the books, plus £1.75 postage and packing for orders under £20; £2.75 for orders over £20. Customers outside the UK should add 10% of the cost of the books for postage and packing.

**USA:** Oxford Paperbacks Marketing Manager, Oxford University Press, Inc., 200 Madison Avenue, New York, N.Y. 10016.

**Canada:** Trade Department, Oxford University Press, 70 Wynford Drive, Don Mills, Ontario M3C 1J9.

**Australia:** Trade Marketing Manager, Oxford University Press, G.P.O. Box 2784Y, Melbourne 3001, Victoria.

**South Africa:** Oxford University Press, P.O. Box 1141, Cape Town 8000.

# Oxford Reference

The Oxford Reference series offers authoritative and up-to-date reference books in paperback across a wide range of topics.

Abbreviations
Art and Artists
Ballet
Biology
Botany
Business
Card Games
Chemistry
Christian Church
Classical Literature
Computing
Dates
Earth Sciences
Ecology
English Christian
  Names
English Etymology
English Language
English Literature
English Place-Names
Eponyms
Finance
Fly-Fishing
Fowler's Modern
  English Usage
Geography
Irish Mythology
King's English
Law
Literary Guide to Great
  Britain and Ireland
Literary Terms

Mathematics
Medical Dictionary
Modern Quotations
Modern Slang
Music
Nursing
Opera
Oxford English
Physics
Popes
Popular Music
Proverbs
Quotations
Sailing Terms
Saints
Science
Ships and the Sea
Sociology
Spelling
Superstitions
Theatre
Twentieth-Century Art
Twentieth-Century
  History
Twentieth-Century
  World Biography
Weather Facts
Word Games
World Mythology
Writer's Dictionary
Zoology

# OXFORD REFERENCE

## THE CONCISE OXFORD COMPANION TO ENGLISH LITERATURE

### Edited by Margaret Drabble and Jenny Stringer

Based on the immensely popular fifth edition of the *Oxford Companion to English Literature* this is an indispensable, compact guide to the central matter of English literature.

There are more than 5,000 entries on the lives and works of authors, poets, playwrights, essayists, philosophers, and historians; plot summaries of novels and plays; literary movements; fictional characters; legends; theatres; periodicals; and much more.

The book's sharpened focus on the English literature of the British Isles makes it especially convenient to use, but there is still generous coverage of the literature of other countries and of other disciplines which have influenced or been influenced by English literature.

From reviews of *The Oxford Companion to English Literature*:

'a book which one turns to with constant pleasure . . . a book with much style and little prejudice' Iain Gilchrist, *TLS*

'it is quite difficult to imagine, in this genre, a more useful publication' Frank Kermode, *London Review of Books*

'incarnates a living sense of tradition . . . sensitive not to fashion merely but to the spirit of the age' Christopher Ricks, *Sunday Times*